EXPLORE THE WORLD *Your Way*

with

World History: Continuity and Change's

- *Global History Resource Center CD-ROM*
- *World History and Cultures Videodiscs*
- *Course Customizer Software*
- *Global Skill Builder CD-ROM*

You know that teaching a world history course is one of the toughest challenges a teacher can face. You've got thousands of years to cover, overwhelming amounts of material to wade through, and not enough planning time. We know all these things, too. As such, we designed a variety of integrated technology components for *World History: Continuity and Change* with you in mind. Now you'll be able to bring the world right into your classroom with the simple touch of a button or click of a mouse.

WORLD HISTORY
CONTINUITY & CHANGE

Your Curriculum, Your Way

We listened to what you had to say—you asked for technology products that are user-friendly, educationally beneficial, instructionally sound, and completely flexible. Our *Global History Resource Center CD-ROM*, *World History and Cultures Videodiscs*, *Course Customizer Software*, and *Global Skill Builder CD-ROM* give you the utmost in control and performance while letting you structure your course the way you want. Ignite your students' imaginations and keep them coming back for more!

- Our *Global History Resource Center CD-ROM* was designed for both you and your students to use. It contains:

    Global History Explorer, a comprehensive, full-color database of audio and video clips, maps, photos, artwork, charts, and readings accessible for further in-depth study.

    Presentation Maker, enabling you to create lectures or your students to create exciting presentations using a collection of rich images and information from the Global History Explorer. Documents and/or images from compatible programs can be brought in and used as well, making each presentation unique and individual.

    Teacher's Planning Center, developed just for you! The Course Planner supports various curriculum approaches and allows for customized lesson planning. A Professional Library includes essays on teaching world history, daily quotations, trivia challenges, and other teaching tools.

- The lively *World History and Cultures Videodiscs* consist of 30 segments—one per chapter—blending historical and contemporary culture. An Image Bank plus point-of-use bar codes in the *Annotated Teacher's Edition* and Core Lesson Plans make it easy for you to incorporate the information whenever and wherever you wish. Closed-captioning and English and Spanish soundtracks are also provided.

- You asked us for a way to combine your resources the way you want without spending too much time doing it. Our *Course Customizer Software* gives you a way to quickly and easily reorganize program lessons and resources according to a variety of curriculum approaches or to create your own lessons. Curriculum approaches include:

    World History: Beginnings to the Present

    Ancient World History: Beginnings to 1650

    Modern World History: The Renaissance to the Present

    Western Civilization

    Eastern Civilization

    World Regions and Civilizations

    The Modern World: The Rise of Democratic Ideas to the Present

- Our *Global Skill Builder CD-ROM*—developed for your world history and world geography classrooms—includes both English and Spanish instruction, and delivers 13 important skill lessons requiring students to engage in a variety of interactive responses. Those lessons include:

    1. Navigating the Internet
    2. Mapping the Earth
    3. Understanding Map Projections
    4. Determining Absolute and Relative Location
    5. Understanding Time Zones
    6. Using Map Legends and Symbols
    7. Identifying Types of Maps
    8. Comparing Maps
    9. Using Time Lines
    10. Reading Graphs
    11. Presenting Data Graphically
    12. Creating Graphic Organizers
    13. Interpreting Diagrams

Now's your chance to see and hear exactly what we mean! Just fill out the attached postage-paid reply card and return it to us either by mail or by fax (512/314-6787). We'll take care of the rest!

EXPLORE THE WORLD YOUR WAY . . . NOW.

WORLD HISTORY

WORLD HISTORY

CONTINUITY & CHANGE

GENERAL EDITOR

William Travis Hanes III
University of Texas at Austin

CONTRIBUTORS

Toyin Falola
University of
Texas at Austin

H. W. Brands
Texas A & M
University

Alida C. Metcalf
Trinity University

Elton Daniel
University of
Hawaii at Manoa

Pierre F. Cagniart
Southwest Texas
State University

Peter John Brobst
University of
Texas at Austin

EDITORIAL ADVISORY BOARD

Theodore K. Rabb
Princeton University
Early modern Europe

Philip D. Curtin
Johns Hopkins
University
*Africa and Caribbean,
economic and political*

Akira Iriye
Harvard University
*American diplomatic,
American-Asian
relations, international*

Ainslie T. Embree
Columbia University
Indian civilization

Bernard Lewis
Princeton University
*History of the
Middle East*

HOLT, RINEHART AND WINSTON
Harcourt Brace & Company
Austin • New York • Orlando • Atlanta • San Francisco • Boston • Dallas • Toronto • London

Cover: *Silver coin*, Larry Stevens/Nawrocki Stock Photo; *Greek column*, Kathleen Campbell/Gamma-Liaison; *Quetzacoatl*, John Neubauer/PhotoEdit; *Mercator's map*, The British Library/HRW Photo by Lance Shriner; *Maria Theresa*, Minamikawa/Sipa Press; *African mask*, The Metropolitan Museum of Art, the Michael C. Rockefeller Memorial Collection, Gift of Nelson A. Rockefeller, 1972. (1978.412.323) Photograph by Schecter Lee. Photo © 1985 The Metropolitan Museum of Art; *Beware the Dog*, Scala/Art Resource, NY; *Shapur II mask*, The Metropolitan Museum of Art, Fletcher Fund, 1965. (65. 126) Photo © 1982 The Metropolitan Museum of Art; *Indian maiden*, Ancient Art & Architecture Collection; *Temple of Ramses II*, Ancient Art & Architecture Collection; *Chinese Immortal Army soldier*, Dennis Cox/ChinaStock; *Asian horse*, The Tokyo Museum; *Lenin statue*, Reuters/Bettmann; *Guidoricco da Fogliano* (detail) by Simone Martini, Scala/Art Resource, NY; *gold coin*, Larry Stevens/Nawrocki Stock Photo; *NASA Challenger*, courtesy of NASA; *background woodcut*, Boston Athenaeum.

Back Cover: Ancient Art & Architecture Collection

Spine: The Metropolitan Museum of Art, the Michael C. Rockefeller Memorial Collection, Gift of Nelson A. Rockefeller, 1972. (1978.412.323) Photograph by Schecter Lee Photo © 1986 The Metropolitan Museum of Art

End Pages: *An Account of an Embassy to the Kingdom of Ava* © 1800

Half Title Page: The Metropolitan Museum of Art, the Michael C. Rockefeller Memorial Collection, Gift of Nelson A. Rockefeller, 1972. (1978.412.323) Photograph by Schecter Lee

Title Page: Boston Athenaeum

You Asked For It

WORLD HISTORY
CONTINUITY & CHANGE

HOLT, RINEHART AND WINSTON

You asked for a world history program that would let you structure your course the way you want, that allows you to teach from either print- or technology-based resources, and that provides you an incredible array of materials to use as you see fit.

v

We Listened!

HOLT, RINEHART AND WINSTON IS PROUD TO OFFER THE SOLUTION YOU'VE BEEN LOOKING FOR—*WORLD HISTORY: CONTINUITY AND CHANGE*. IT'S THE FIRST WORLD HISTORY PROGRAM THAT'S TRULY WHAT YOU MAKE IT. BECAUSE WE LISTENED TO YOU AND DEVELOPED

a program that lets you emphasize the history you want to teach...

You've never seen instruction like this before! Using both **print- and technology-based resources,** *World History: Continuity and Change* lets you tailor your course in a variety of ways that best suit you and your students. You pick and choose the content you want to teach and how you want to teach it—so you end up with a customized curriculum that meets your classroom needs exactly. Whether you want to focus on Western civilization or take a more comprehensive approach to world cultures, this exciting program lets you make your course your own. You get complete and balanced world coverage, with the opportunity for an even more in-depth study of world history.

World History: Continuity and Change provides you with a full array of support material available in a wide variety of forms and formats. Whether print-based, delivered on CD–ROM, or online materials via the Internet, these resources provide the support you need to make planning easy.

"Wow! *I never knew history was so cool!"*

All history teachers long to hear these words from their students. But getting and keeping students involved can be a daunting task. *World History: Continuity and Change* is special, taking into account your students' perspectives and how world history relates to their lives.

IGNITE your students' imaginations with the *Pupil's Edition*, which features manageable sections, a lively narrative, primary sources and in-text biographies, and an integrated map and graphics program. And there's so much more! *Teenagers in History* stories depict the lives of young people through time. *Then and Now* features form connections between past events and present-day issues.

The program incorporates a wide array of INTEGRATED TECHNOLOGY resources that help you illustrate key topics more effectively—keeping your students interested and enthusiastic about learning!

Chapter 14
Renaissance and Reformation 1300–1650

Understanding the Main Idea

The European civilization that emerged between 1000 and 1300 was rocked by famine, plague, and warfare after 1300. As Europe recovered, the growth of trade, a rediscovery of classical learning, and new ideas about art and religion led to a new worldview—one that no longer had the church at its center, but human beings. As Christian unity declined, however, war and violence once again erupted.

Themes

• **Cross-cultural Interaction** How might trade influence the spread of ideas between cultures?

• **The Arts** What sources influence the works of artists and writers?

• **War and Diplomacy** Why might differing views on religion lead to conflict?

In 1498 the Dominican monk Girolamo Savonarola (sah-voh-nah-roh-lah) and two of his disciples were burned at the stake in Florence, Italy. An observer described the scene:

"In a few hours they were burnt, their legs and arms gradually dropping off . . . a quantity of stones were thrown to make them fall, . . . and then the hangman and those whose business it was, hacked down the post and burnt it on the ground, bringing a lot of brushwood, and stirring the fire up over the dead bodies, so that the very least piece was consumed."

Savonarola had angered the pope and the leaders of Florence by preaching against the vice and corruption he believed were destroying the church, the government, and society. At the heart of this decay, he argued, was the revival of the teachings of ancient Greece and Rome. These teachings, which sought to glorify the grace and creativity of humankind, ran counter to the medieval worldview that people could achieve little in a universe dominated by God. But Savonarola and others could not stop this medieval worldview from being challenged as Europeans rediscovered the ancient past and questioned the authority of the church.

School of Athens, a Renaissance fresco by Raphael, 1509–1511

1309	1337	1347	1378	c. 1450	1508	1517	1545–1563	1588	1648
Babylonian Captivity begins.	Hundred Years' War begins.	Black Death strikes Europe.	Great Schism begins.	Johannes Gutenberg begins using movable metal type to print books.	Michelangelo begins painting Sistine Chapel.	Martin Luther posts 95 theses.	Council of Trent codifies Catholic doctrines.	English defeat Spanish Armada.	Treaty of Westphalia ends Thirty Years' War.

360   CHAPTER 14

RENAISSANCE AND REFORMATION   361

We're making history with a

Most print components are found on the Teaching Resources CD-ROM, while components marked with this icon offer additional support and are only found on the Teaching Resources CD-ROM.

TEACHING RESOURCES

From block scheduling guides to chapter investigations and video viewing guides, we give you everything you need to help your students succeed. Resources such as Explorations in Daily Life Enrichment Activities and People in World History Enrichment Activities allow you and your students to approach learning in a variety of exciting ways.

Furthermore, *the Annotated Teacher's Edition* includes extensive core lesson plans at the beginning of each chapter, as well as page-by-page sidebars that provide the teacher with extended student activities, informational annotations, and much more as the lesson progresses. On-page bar codes provide a handy way to quickly integrate videodisc segments into your lesson.

Teaching Resources CD-ROM

Chapter Investigations: Simulations and Other Creative Strategies for Teaching World History

Vocabulary Activities

Readings in World History

Explorations in Daily Life Enrichment Activities

People in World History Enrichment Activities

Writing Projects

Themes Reviews

World History & Cultures Video Viewing Guides

Block Scheduling Handbook

World and Regional Outline Maps

Geography Activities

The Complete School Atlas

The World Today Gazetteer with Regional Location Maps

World Beat Newsletter

Skills Activities

Visual Resources

SHELTERED ENGLISH RESOURCES

World History: Continuity and Change helps students with limited English proficiency excel by providing them with material on a level that they can more easily understand. From specially designed quizzes and study guides to a

Spanish-language glossary and activities in the *Annotated Teacher's Edition*, *World History: Continuity and Change* helps students of all languages have a real opportunity for success.

Main Idea Activities for Reteaching and Sheltered English

Reading Strategies for Social Studies

Audio Program in English and Spanish

Spanish Glossary

Sheltered English Chapter and Unit Tests

VARIETY of integrated resources.

HRW These components can be accessed through the HRW Web site.

POWERFUL TEACHING TECHNOLOGY!

World History: Continuity and Change gives you and your students access to a wealth of information and resources—for easier lesson planning and more engaging learning activities. The *Global History Resource Center CD-ROM* features a comprehensive, full-color database of audio and video clips, maps, photos, readings, and much more that your class can integrate with the text for in-depth study. It also includes a Presentation Maker for your lectures or for exciting student multimedia presentations, as well as a Course Planner that supports a range of curricula and allows you to customize and edit lesson plans. The Course Planner is also found in our Course Customizer Software. Plus, the integrated videodiscs feature 30 segments— one per chapter—as well as a bank of still images that blend historical and contemporary culture.

- Global History Resource Center CD-ROM
- World History and Cultures Videodiscs
- Religions of the World Video Series
- Test Generator
- Test Generator Test Item Listing
- Course Customizer Software
- Global Skill Builder CD-ROM
- Audio Program
- Internet Resources for Social Studies
- World History Teaching Toolkit

ASSESSMENT RESOURCES

Every student is different—and one standardized method of assessment may not accurately reflect each student's abilities. That's why *World History: Continuity and Change* goes beyond the traditional chapter-and-test philosophy and provides a range of subjective and objective assessment options. From familiar unit tests and section quizzes to alternative assessment and portfolio assessment forms, you'll have all the tools and rubrics you need to adequately and thoroughly assess each student's performance. What's more, you'll be able to let your students know exactly what is expected of them, whether they are writing an essay or making a classroom presentation.

TEACHING RESOURCES

- Section Study Guides
- Daily Quizzes
- Chapter Reviews
- Unit Syntheses
- Chapter and Unit Tests
- Main Idea Activities for Reteaching and Sheltered English
- Portfolio and Performance Assessment for Social Studies
- Test Item Listing
- Alternative Assessment Forms

INTRODUCTION TO THE PROGRAM

The study of world history can be approached from many directions. Some people emphasize Western Civilization; others prefer a regional or a global approach. **World History: Continuity and Change** is designed to accommodate this diversity. The keys to the success of this program are flexibility, ease of use, and student accessibility:

FLEXIBILITY

World History: Continuity and Change is organized in a way that allows teachers to focus on Western Civilization, teach a basically simultaneous history of the world, or adopt a regional approach. Support for the latter two approaches is possible because of the unit and chapter organization—many units and chapters trace similar developmental themes occurring in different regions of the world at roughly the same time. Chapter 1, "The Rise of Civilization," for example, examines on a regional basis the traits common to emerging civilizations.

EASE OF USE

This flexibility in curriculum approach is made manageable by software that allows teachers to sort program lessons by various curriculum approaches and to edit existing lessons or create new ones. (See the descriptions of the **Course Customizer Software** and the **Global History Resource Center CD-ROM**.)

STUDENT ACCESSIBILITY

Flexibility and ease of use are of little consequence if students' imaginations are not captured by the study of world history. **World History: Continuity and Change** sparks student interest through the lively and clear narrative of the **Pupil's Edition**, the rich array of activities and readings in the textbook and ancillaries, and the exciting video, graphic, and text resources of the **World History and Cultures Videodiscs** and the **Global History Resource Center CD-ROM**.

PROGRAM COMPONENTS

The Pupil's Edition

The **Pupil's Edition** of **World History: Continuity and Change** provides comprehensive coverage of world history from prehistory to the present. The text consists of 7 units divided thematically and chronologically into 30 chapters. Each chapter is divided into 3–5 sections, which focus on particular periods of time, regions, or themes in world history. The story of the important people and events that shaped world history is enhanced with details about daily life and culture in the civilization under study. The narrative is also enhanced by a wide variety of maps, charts, graphs, and images.

BALANCE

The book combines a solid core of Western Civilization coverage with balanced coverage of other regions of the world. Balance is achieved by adopting both a micro and a macro view of world history—each civilization's history is explored from the perspective of that civilization's internal development and from the perspective of how cross-cultural interaction and historical legacies affected its development and the development of other civilizations. Thus, for example, the development of Chinese civilization is explored from two perspectives—(1) the inner dynamics of China and (2) how China influenced and was influenced by Western and other cultures.

THEMES

World History: Continuity and Change traces eight themes through history: Geography; Economic Organization; Politics and Law; War and Diplomacy; Technology; Religion, Philosophy, Science, and the Arts; Social Relations; and Cross-cultural Interaction. These themes are introduced in the **Themes in World History** section of the *Pupil's Edition* front matter and are reinforced in the chapter introductions, running text, and Section Reviews.

STUDENT INTEREST

The lively narrative captures students' attention and draws them into the story. But an exciting story is not enough—students must also grasp the cause-and-effect relationships that are at the heart of historical inquiry. *World History: Continuity and Change*'s success rests in part on the book's extensive use of primary sources and its comprehensive map, graph, and illustration program.

FEATURES

A rich assortment of in-text and boxed features help spark student interest:

Biographies, which are woven into the running text, place important people in their historical context and offer engaging details.

History Through the Arts explores topics in painting, sculpture, architecture, and the graphic arts.

Through Others' Eyes presents an outsider's viewpoint on specific events or issues.

Sacred Traditions provides excerpts from great religious works.

Literature Through Time provides excerpts from great works of literature from many different cultures across time.

Geography and History explores the links between historical events and geographical factors.

Teenagers in History explores the roles played by young people in history.

Then and Now makes connections between past events and today's world.

History in the Making examines issues of historical debate, comparative historical traditions, and how historians practice their craft.

SKILL DEVELOPMENT

Careful attention is paid to skills instruction throughout *World History: Continuity and Change*. **Critical Thinking and the Study of History** (see Pupil's page xviii) presents an overview of the critical thinking skills students will be asked to apply throughout their study of world history and the **World History Skills Handbook** (see Pupil's page xxiii) provides instruction and practice in important social studies skills. Students are given additional opportunities to practice skills in the Section and Chapter Reviews, the mapping program, the Lesson Plans and Chapter Investigations, the *Core Resource Booklets,* and the *Global Skill Builder CD-ROM.* Extended skills activities in the *Annotated Teacher's Edition* offer teachers opportunities to reinforce important skills.

STUDENT APPARATUS

The chapter organization in *World History: Continuity and Change* is designed to maximize student understanding. Each numbered section is divided into manageable subsections for easier understanding. Students can use the headings in the section to outline the section's content. In addition, the following chapter elements help guide student reading and measure understanding. The first three elements are found on the opening spread of the chapter. The remaining elements are part of the section structure:

Understanding the Main Idea provides a concise statement of the chapter's main topics.

Themes questions provide a prereading context for the chapter's content. The questions focus on the main themes covered in the chapter.

A **Time Line** provides students with a chronological framework for major events.

Focus questions at the beginning of each numbered section alert students to main ideas.

Essential Points, set off by colored type in the text, provide a running summary of the section's main ideas. Each essential point ties back to a specific focus question.

Section Reviews ask students to first identify and explain the significance of important people, terms, and events. Next students use textbook maps to locate important places. Then students answer five questions. The questions include fact-recall questions, theme-based questions with a strong emphasis on geography, writing activities, and critical thinking questions. Section Review questions work together with the Focus questions and the Essential Points to provide students with a framework for grasping section content. Each chapter ends with a one-page **Chapter Review** that includes fact-recall exercises, critical thinking questions, and portfolio activities. Additional opportunities for review are provided by *Chapter Reviews*, *Section Study Guides*, *Main Idea Activities for Reteaching and Sheltered English,* and *Audio CDs* in English and Spanish.

The Teacher Management System

The *World History: Continuity and Change* teacher management system is divided into two parts: the *Annotated Teacher's Edition* and the *Course Customizer Software*. The system is designed to reduce teacher preparation time while increasing flexibility and providing full instructional support.

ANNOTATED TEACHER'S EDITION

The *Annotated Teacher's Edition* includes interleaf pages and side-column annotations. Because the main teaching strategies are located in the interleaf, rather than in a top or bottom wrap, it has been possible to retain the *Pupil's Edition* pages at near full size.

Each chapter interleaf begins with a two-page introduction that includes a **Chapter Planning Guide** on the left-hand page and strategies for introducing the chapter by using the themes and the *World History and Cultures Videodiscs* on the right-hand page. The right-hand page also includes a chapter overview and a list of additional resources.

The introduction is followed by the **Lesson Plans**, which provide a combination of active-learning and lecture-based teaching strategies and activities. Each two-page section Lesson is built around a seven-step instructional model:

1 Hook
2 Develop
3 Probe
4 Conclude
5 Extend
6 Meet Individual Needs
7 Assess

In addition to focusing on traditional assessment, the Lessons contain imbedded assessment throughout.

The Lessons are designed to accommodate a wide range of learning styles. The learning styles addressed in *World History: Continuity and Change* are based on seven of the multiple intelligences outlined by Howard Gardner of Harvard University: linguistic, visual-spatial, logical-mathematical, kinesthetic, musical-rhythmic, interpersonal, and intrapersonal. For a fuller explanation of Gardner's multiple intelligences, see the essay on page xv of the *Annotated Teacher's Edition.*

The **side columns** of the *Annotated Teacher's Edition* provide a wealth of supplemental information plus the answers to all map, chart, feature, and section and chapter review questions. The **informational annotations** include topics related to daily life, biography, current events, cross-curricular connections, and the program's eight themes. Each informational annotation includes a critical thinking question designed to help students analyze and synthesize material. A suggested answer is included for each question.

The side columns also offer additional classroom activities. **Resource Activities** suggest ways to use materials from the *Core Resource Booklets* and the *Global History Resource Center CD-ROM*. **Internet Activities** help teachers guide students in using the HRW Website and other sites on the World Wide Web to locate and apply information about world history. **Multimedia Presentation Strategies** provide suggestions for using the *Global History Resource Center CD-ROM* and the *Visual Resources Binder* to engage students, provide interdisciplinary connections, and reinforce map skills. All of the Resource Activities, Internet Activities, and Multimedia Presentation Strategies are categorized by ability level to help teachers further customize their instruction to meet individual student needs. These side-column strategies provide hundreds of point-of-use activities that can be used to enrich instruction.

COURSE CUSTOMIZER SOFTWARE

The *Course Customizer Software* helps ensure maximum program flexibility and ease of use. The software makes it possible to reorganize Lessons and resources according to seven curriculum approaches:

- World History: Beginnings to the Present
- Ancient World History: Beginnings to 1650
- Modern World History: The Renaissance to the Present
- Western Civilizations
- Eastern Civilizations
- World Regions and Civilizations
- The Modern World: The Rise of Democratic Ideas to the Present

In addition, the *Course Customizer Software* includes **Lesson Plan Submission Forms** and a **Custom Lesson Template** that can be used to create new lessons. All Lessons and Lesson Plan Submission Forms are editable.

Program Resources

A wide variety of print and multimedia resources have been fully integrated into the instructional design of *World History: Continuity and Change.*

CORE RESOURCE BOOKLETS

The *Core Resource Booklets* include a wide range of activities and readings to support *World History: Continuity and Change.* Each of the booklets contains an answer key, where applicable, and reproducible blackline masters:

Vocabulary Activities review the key terms and concepts covered in the chapter.

Writing Projects develop students' skills in research and writing.

Geography Activities explore the links between geography and important chapter themes and ideas.

Skills Activities provide students with the opportunity to practice important skills.

Readings in World History reinforce chapter themes and main ideas through a combination of literature and poetry, primary source documents, and secondary sources.

Chapter Reviews revisit each chapter's content, providing students with another chance to assess their progress.

Themes Reviews explore chapter content through the eight themes.

People in World History Enrichment Activities guide students through research activities focused on important individuals.

Explorations in Daily Life Enrichment Activities offer research opportunities designed to enhance students' understanding of daily life in different historical periods.

Block Scheduling Handbook provides expanded instructional options to meet block scheduling needs.

Chapter Investigations: Simulations and Other Creative Strategies for Teaching World History allow students to explore topics from throughout the chapter in order to create a group product. The investigations, which are on the *Course Customizer Software* in an editable format, can be used in combination with the Lessons or as an alternative strategy for teaching chapter content.

Unit Syntheses provide a summary of each chapter in a unit, with accompanying questions. The syntheses can be used as a unit review or as a synopsis of material that you wish to exclude from your course outline.

TEACHING RESOURCES CD-ROM

The *Teaching Resources CD-ROM* boosts flexibility and ease of use by offering the program's print resources in noneditable Acrobat files. The CD-ROM also includes the following additional resources: *Section Study Guides*, which provide section summaries and review questions to assist students in mastering content, *Daily Quizzes*, which offer a quick assessment tool on a section-by-section basis, *Main Idea Activities for Reteaching and Sheltered English*, which present content and activities for Limited English Proficiency students, *Sheltered English Chapter and Unit Tests*, which offer assessment tools for Limited English Proficiency students, and a *Spanish Glossary*, which presents the *Pupil's Edition* glossary in a Spanish-language format.

VISUAL RESOURCES

The *Visual Resources Binder* delivers three complete transparency packages—**Geography and History Transparencies, Everyday Life Transparencies**, and **Art and History**

Transparencies. Each set of transparencies includes fact sheets and student worksheets.

TESTING PROGRAM

The Testing Program provides ready-made assessment tools.

Chapter and Unit Tests offer three-page Chapter Tests and four-page Unit Tests in a blackline master format.

Test Generator delivers 2,250 objective and enhanced questions. The *Test Generator* has a simple *User's Guide*, a write-it-yourself question option, graphic capabilities, and revision and scrambling options. A print *Test-Item Listing* is included with the program.

Daily Quizzes and *Sheltered English Chapter and Unit Tests*, which are located on the *Teaching Resources CD-ROM*, round out the Testing Program.

AUDIO CDS

The **Audio CDs** provide easy-to-use chapter summaries appropriate for use by special-needs and Limited English Proficiency students. The **Audio CDs** are available in English and Spanish.

WORLD HISTORY AND CULTURES VIDEODISCS

The lively, two-disc *World History and Cultures Videodiscs* set includes 30 segments—one per chapter—blending historical and contemporary culture. English and Spanish soundtracks are available on all segments. The videodisc set also includes an Image Bank of maps, charts, and still images, with point-of-use barcodes in the *Annotated Teacher's Edition.* The program includes the *World History and Cultures Video Viewing Guides* and a manual with a barcode directory.

GLOBAL HISTORY RESOURCE CENTER CD-ROM

The *Global History Resource Center* brings a wide array of hard-to-find resources and tools to the world history classroom. The CD-ROM is divided into three sections: the **Global History Explorer,** which provides teachers and students with an interactive database that includes audio and video clips, images, maps, charts, and readings, the **Presentation Maker,** which enables teachers and students to create presentations using the multimedia material contained in the Global History Explorer, and the **Teacher's Planning Center,** which contains a Course Planner and a Professional Library.

GLOBAL SKILL BUILDER CD-ROM

The *Global Skill Builder CD-ROM* contains 13 important skill lessons requiring students to engage in a variety of interactive responses. The 13 lessons, which are provided in both English and Spanish, focus on developing map, graph, and computer skills. The CD-ROM is accompanied by a *User's Manual and Teacher's Guide* that contains student project sheets for each of the lessons.

HRW WEB SITE

The HRW Web site provides a wealth of teacher and student resources, including our *Internet Resources for Social Studies*, an impressive collection of links to world history-related Internet sites. Other HRW Internet resources include *Reading Strategies for Social Studies*, designed to improve students' reading skills, and *Portfolio and Performance Assessment for Social Studies*, a collection of rubrics and models for evaluating student projects and presentations.

Teaching to Multiple Intelligences

by Diane Hart and Elizabeth F. Russell

Howard Gardner, a neuropsychologist at Harvard University, has urged educators to rethink how they view intelligence. He argues that the term *intelligence* should encompass a far wider set of human competencies than have traditionally been addressed by IQ tests.

Gardner uses neurological research to argue that people display seven relatively distinct and autonomous "intelligences." He defines an intelligence as "the ability to solve problems, or to create products, that are valued within one or more cultural settings."[1] These intelligences are linguistic, visual-spatial, logical-mathematical, kinesthetic, musical-rhythmic, interpersonal, and intrapersonal. In the past, schools have valued the products of only two or three of these seven intelligences. Now, with the knowledge of multiple intelligences, the challenge for teachers is to create tasks that require students to think and to learn in a much broader range of modes.

No one has just one kind of intelligence; each person is a blend of intelligences, with some stronger than others. The individual mix of intelligences helps to create each person's learning style. The implications for instruction are powerful: teach to a variety of learning styles to reach more students more effectively. Here are descriptions of the seven intelligences and suggested classroom strategies that will engage these competencies in the learning process.

Linguistic Intelligence

Linguistic intelligence deals with the production and use of language in all its many forms including reading, writing, speaking, debating, and conceptual thinking. Linguistic learners love language-based activities, are expressive and fluent in their use of language, and have well-developed vocabularies. Strategies that work well with these students include:

- reading books, poetry, primary sources, etc.
- participating in plays and choral readings
- notetaking, dictation
- lectures
- formal writing activities (essays, reviews)
- informal writing activities (journals, letters)
- speaking
- storytelling
- interviews
- simulations, role playing, mock trials, etc.
- debates

Visual-Spatial Intelligence

Visual-spatial intelligence is linked to the ability to use space and to form images. This intelligence is essential in the visual arts, navigation, cartography, and games such as chess and architecture. Visual-spatial learners prefer learning with images, pictures, charts, diagrams, art, videos, maps, and models. Strategies that work well with these students include:

- games
- puzzles
- mindmapping, clustering
- working with all artistic media
- mapping
- cartooning
- illustrating
- using time lines, charts, graphs, and graphic organizers
- making models
- designing displays, presentations

Logical-Mathematical Intelligence

Logical-mathematical intelligence is usually associated with scientific thinking and deductive reasoning. It includes the ability to observe and understand patterns, draw conclusions, make judgments, and formulate hypotheses. Logical-mathematical learners enjoy asking questions, forming concepts, looking for patterns and relationships, and proceeding step-by-step in a logical sequence through activities. Strategies that work well with these students include:

- working with numbers, statistics, and probability

- experiments and research projects
- looking for patterns
- classifying information
- charts, graphs
- brainteasers, puzzles
- diagrams, flow charts
- sequencing, time lines
- conducting surveys and analyzing results

Kinesthetic Intelligence

Kinesthetic intelligence is the ability to use the body to express ideas and emotions, to play games and sports, and to create and invent new products. Kinesthetic learners prefer learning by moving, touching, and doing, not by hearing or seeing. Strategies that work well with these students include:

- movement activities
- role playing
- simulations
- field trips
- making things (dioramas, exhibits, models, books, collages)
- storyboarding
- art activities
- teaching others
- working with manipulatives
- puppet shows
- mini-dramas

Musical-Rhythmic Intelligence

Musical-rhythmic intelligence relates to sensitivity to sound, music, and other rhythmic and tonal patterns. Musical-rhythmic learners enjoy rhythm and melody; learn easily when information is sung, tapped, or clapped out; and like listening to, playing, or creating music. Strategies that work well with these students include:

- drawing, moving, and writing to music
- making up rhythms
- reading or writing music
- relating history or culture to music
- creating lyrics using facts
- studying music history
- clapping out ideas, facts
- rapping, singing
- exploring musical traditions

Interpersonal Intelligence

Interpersonal intelligence involves the ability to work and communicate well with other people. Interpersonal learners enjoy learning by interaction or working in cooperative groups, respond to discussions, are interested and sensitive to the feelings of others, display empathy, and like all kinds of social activities. Strategies that work well with these students include:

- personalizing events
- cooperative learning
- coaching, mentoring, or teaching others
- role playing
- conflict resolution
- interviewing
- simulations
- problem solving activities
- letter writing
- storyboarding

Intrapersonal Intelligence

Intrapersonal intelligence is linked to self-knowledge—knowing one's own feelings, emotional responses, thinking processes, sense of self, and spiritual connection to the universe. Intrapersonal learners are independent, self-directed, thoughtful, and look for personal relevance and connections. They need quiet time to process feelings, to dream and imagine, and to problem-solve. Strategies that work well with these students include:

- independent projects, research reports
- journal writing
- diary and letter writing
- creative writing
- interior monologues
- poetry
- identifying, comparing values
- personal portfolios
- conversations
- self-assessment activities

[1] Bert Bower et. al., *History Alive*, Menlo Park, CA, Addison-Wesley, 1994.

WORLD HISTORY
CONTINUITY & CHANGE

CONTENTS

UNIT 1

The Beginnings Of Civilization

1

BEGINNINGS–200 B.C.

Egyptian carved wooden
model from the Middle Kingdom

Bronze statue of Siva as the
Nataraja, "Lord of the Dance"

Black-on-white Mimbres pottery bowls

UNIT 3
The World in Transition
220–1707   **218**

UNIT 4

Beginnings of the Modern World
358

1300–1815

UNIT 5

Expansion of the Modern World
1700–1914

480

Irish women march for independence.

Louis "Satchmo" Armstrong

REFERENCE SECTION

FEATURES

The Discus Thrower

Gold Ottoman Jug

U.S. Apollo astronaut on the moon

MAPS

Ruins of the Inca city of Machu Picchu

Muslim women reading the Qur'an

CHARTS AND GRAPHS

African carved mask

*W*orld History: Continuity and Change presents historical information from the perspective of three key ideas fundamental to human history throughout the world. These ideas provide a basis for analyzing and evaluating past events.

The first key idea is that civilization resulted from individual and group efforts to survive by adapting to the physical environment, adopting new behaviors if necessary as the environment itself changed. In the process of adapting, people have established patterns for ensuring the basic physical requirements for survival—food and shelter. From these adaptations people have established various economic, political, and social systems.

The second key idea is that as self-aware beings, humans try to ensure not only their physical well-being but also their emotional and spiritual well-being. As a means of understanding themselves, the nature of the world, and their place in it, people have developed many different worldviews.

The third key idea is that the more flexible human beings are in responding to changing circumstances, the more likely they are to survive. The growth and development of individuals or groups depends primarily on how much contact and interaction they have with other individuals and groups from whom they may gain new knowledge and awareness.

From these basic ideas come a series of themes. *World History: Continuity and Change* begins every chapter with a set of theme questions. These questions are drawn from and develop eight broad themes central to world history: geography; economic organization; politics and law; war and diplomacy; technology; religion, philosophy, science, and the arts; social relations; and cross-cultural interaction. These themes provide a framework for the historical events in each chapter. This framework will help you understand the connections between historical events and see how past events are relevant to the world today.

As you begin each chapter, examine the theme questions and answer them based on your own experiences or prior knowledge. At the end of each chapter, you will be asked to answer another set of questions, this time using specific facts learned from studying the chapter. This process will help you develop critical thinking skills and encourage you to synthesize the information you have learned. In addition, by tracing the themes throughout the book, you will be able to see how each theme has developed over time.

The **Chapter Opener** theme questions raise broad issues relevant to the chapter.

Geography

This theme underlies the most fundamental aspects of our existence in the world. Geography shapes the nature of the world, which we depend on for our physical survival. Different geographical factors will produce different types or styles of human society. These ideas are included in the five themes of geography: location, place, region, movement, and human-environment interaction.

Economic Organization

As we adapt to our environment, we have to guarantee the basic necessities of life. Through hunting and gathering, livestock-herding, agriculture, trade, and manufacturing we establish economic organizations to obtain these necessities. The methods we develop influence the kinds of civilizations we build.

Politics and Law

As we live together in groups, we have to learn how to get along with one another. In order to better coordinate the activities of many individuals and to provide security for everyone, we have developed governments and institutions that regulate our interaction with one another. Such political and legal structures have provided the framework on which we have built our civilizations.

War and Diplomacy

The search for security in a hostile environment has been a major problem for people since the earliest civilizations developed. Many groups have tried to ensure their own security at the expense of others. Such efforts have often led to warfare among competing groups or societies. Yet warfare is another area in which we have learned new techniques of survival. Sometimes we have learned by developing more destructive weapons and tactics; sometimes we have learned to make peace and avoid warfare altogether. In all cases, however, warfare has had a tremendous effect on our development.

Technology

As we pursue the basic tasks of living and providing food, shelter, and security, we have always tried to make our job of survival easier by using tools. The development and use of tools—in other words, technology—has been one of our principal means of adapting to our environment. In the process, the technologies we have adopted have both shaped and been shaped by the societies and civilizations in which we live.

Religion, Philosophy, Science, and the Arts

As human beings, we have all had to ask ourselves basic questions about who and what we are and why we are here. How we answer these questions depends primarily on how we see ourselves in relationship to the world around us. We have sought answers to these questions in religion, philosophy, and science, and have expressed the answers through the arts.

Social Relations

In answering our basic questions about who and what we are, we form our sense of identity in relationship to those around us. We identify ourselves as members of families, as men or women, as children or adults, as members of a particular social or economic group. We may also see ourselves as members of religious, cultural, or other groups. These identities are influenced by many other factors, including politics, economics, geography, warfare, and technology.

Cross-cultural Interaction

The story of humanity has in many ways been the story of increasing contact among different groups of people. Such interaction has led to further exchanges and contacts of people and of ideas. Through exploration, trade, warfare, conquest, migration, and new methods of communication, people have carried a wealth of information around the world. The constant challenges of taking in new experiences and ideas have contributed to the ability of human beings to grow and change.

Throughout *World History: Continuity and Change*, you are asked to think critically about the events and issues that have shaped the history of the world. Critical thinking is the reasoned judgment of information and ideas. People who think critically study information to determine its accuracy. They evaluate arguments and analyze conclusions before accepting them. Critical thinkers are able to recognize and define problems and develop strategies for resolving them.

The development of critical thinking skills is essential to effective citizenship. Such skills empower you to exercise your civic rights and responsibilities. For example, critical thinking skills equip you to judge the messages of candidates for political office and to evaluate news reports.

Helping you develop critical thinking skills is an important tool of *World History: Continuity and Change*. Using the following 14 critical thinking skills throughout your study of world history will help you better understand the forces that create global events. Additional skills strategies can be found in the World History Skills Handbook, which begins on p. xxiii.

The following 14 critical thinking skills, along with specific theme questions, appear in the **Section Reviews** and the **Chapter Reviews**.

1 **Using Historical Imagination** is mentally stepping into the past to consider an event or situation as people at the time would have considered it. By putting yourself in their place, you might note whether they lived *before* or *after* historical turning points. Ask yourself: Did these people live before or after major medical advances such as penicillin? before or after technological advances such as the automobile? before or after World War II? Keep in mind what the people of the time knew and did not know. For example, to grasp the experience of a soldier wounded in the Crimean War, you need to understand that little was known then about the causes of disease and infection.

2 **Gaining a Cultural Perspective** means viewing historical events and situations in ways that are fair and sensitive to all cultural groups affected. A broad cultural perspective widens your understanding of cultures while deepening your appreciation of the variety of beliefs and traditions around the world. For example, studying American Indian cultures before the arrival of Christopher Columbus helps you understand that Europeans did not "discover" the Americas. They encountered a land already settled by peoples with rich cultures.

Bronze lion from the 400s B.C.

3 **Recognizing Point of View** involves identifying the factors that color the outlook of an individual or group. A person's point of view includes beliefs and attitudes that are shaped by factors such as age, gender, religion, race, and economic status. This thinking skill helps us examine why people see things as they do and reinforces the realization that people's views may change over time, or with a change in circumstances. When a point of view is highly personal or based on unreasoned judgment, it is considered *bias*.

4 **Comparing and Contrasting** is examining events, situations, or points of view for their similarities and differences. *Comparing* focuses on both the similarities and the differences. *Contrasting* focuses only on the differences. For example, a comparison of the Umayyad and Abbasid dynasties might point out that both sought to establish governments that were grounded in Islam. In contrast, the Abbasids relied more on Persian influences in government than did the Umayyads, who followed Arab traditions.

English women working in a munitions factory during World War I.

For further practice in the skills on this page, have students study the picture of the World War I munitions workers on page xix and imagine these women's attitudes toward their work. Next have students discuss historical factors, such as the war or the women's rights movement, that might have affected the women's attitudes. Then have students assume the perspective of a woman working during the war and write newspaper editorials about either the war or female workers. Have students annotate their editorials with explanations of how they reveal point of view or bias. Finally, have students compare and contrast their own views on the subject in a group discussion.

SKILLS ACTIVITY

Identifying Cause and Effect

Analyzing

Assessing Consequences

For further practice in the skills on this page, have students analyze the process by which a person learns how to drive. Have them break the learning process down into steps. Next have students consider how learning to drive might affect a person's life. Have them create a cause-and-effect chart on the subject. Also have students consider the short-term and long-term consequences of learning how to drive.

Spread of the Black Death

| Trade route |
| Areas affected: |
| 1347 |
| 1348 |
| 1349 |
| 1350 |
| After 1350 |
| Unaffected areas |

In its deadly march across Europe, the Black Death spared a few small areas. Experts are not sure why.

NORTH SEA · BALTIC SEA · ATLANTIC OCEAN · BLACK SEA · MEDITERRANEAN SEA

London · Warsaw · Kiev · Paris · Prague · Vienna · Venice · Florence · Genoa · Marseilles · Siena · Rome · Lisbon · Barcelona · CORSICA · SARDINIA · KINGDOM OF SICILY · Constantinople

0   250   500 Miles
0   500   500 Kilometers
Azimuthal Equal-Area Projection

5 **Identifying Cause and Effect** is part of interpreting the relationships between historical events. A *cause* is any action that leads to an event; the outcome of that action is an *effect*. To explain historical developments, historians may point out multiple causes and effects. For instance, population decreases during the Black Death combined with new farming techniques to produce a surplus of agricultural products, which in turn led to lower prices, a higher standard of living in Europe, and increased demand for trade goods. (For a more detailed discussion of Identifying Cause and Effect, see pp. xxiv–xxv.)

Waves of Death The bustling trade routes of the 1300s carried more than a wealth of goods. They were also the main routes by which the Black Death entered Europe's cities and spread across the continent.

Movement Why did the Black Death reach Marseilles so quickly?

6 **Analyzing** is the process of breaking something down into its parts and examining the relationships between them. Analysis enables you to better understand the whole. For example, to analyze how Roman law developed, you might study the conflicts between plebeians and patricians in Rome, as well as how those conflicts were resolved.

7 **Assessing Consequences** means studying an action, an event, or a trend to predict its long-term effects and to judge the desirability of those effects. *Consequences* are effects that are indirect and unintended. They may appear long after the event that led to them. An example of assessing consequences is an analysis of the decision to impose war reparations on Germany after World War I. Consequences included economic instability that contributed to the Great Depression and led many Germans to seek a leader who would restore their country to power and prosperity.

Statue of a Roman merchant ship

8 **Distinguishing Fact from Opinion** means separating the facts about something from what people say about it. A fact can be proved or observed; an opinion, on the other hand, is a personal belief or conclusion. We often hear facts and opinions mixed in everyday conversation—in advertising, in political debate, and in historical sources. Although some opinions can be supported by facts, in an argument they do not carry as much weight as facts. (For a more detailed discussion of Distinguishing Fact from Opinion, see p. xxv.)

Siege of Baghdad

9 **Identifying Values** involves recognizing the core beliefs held by a person or group. Values are more deeply held than opinions and are less likely to change. Values commonly concern matters of right and wrong and may be viewed as desirable in and of themselves. In Hinduism, for example, the fulfillment of moral duties is highly valued, and Hindus believe that each person will encounter consequences for his or her actions.

10 **Hypothesizing** is forming a possible explanation for an event, a situation, or a problem. A hypothesis is not a proven fact. Rather it is an "educated guess" based on available evidence and tested against new evidence. A historian, for instance, might hypothesize that Galileo argued that the earth revolved around the sun in order to weaken the authority of the Roman Catholic Church. The historian would then organize the evidence to support this hypothesis and challenge other explanations of Galileo's actions.

Mohandas Gandhi leads marchers in protest.

SKILLS ACTIVITY

Distinguishing Fact from Opinion

Identifying Values

Hypothesizing

For further practice in the skills on this page, copy and distribute a newspaper article and an editorial on the United States's relations with a foreign country. Ask students to find at least one opinion and one fact in the editorial and ask them to describe how they identified the example of bias and distinguished fact from opinion. Then have them use the information in the article to identify the values each country considers most important. Next have students hypothesize about what might happen in the future between these two countries, using evidence from the article to support their hypothesis. Finally, have students evaluate both sources. They should consider factors such as language, corroboration with other sources, and information about the author.

SKILLS ACTIVITY

Synthesizing

Problem Solving and Decision Making

Evaluating

Taking a Stand

For further practice in the skills on this page, have students select and discuss a current event that poses many problems. Then have students work in groups to write short articles that synthesize the range of different opinions toward the issue.

Next have students work on problem-solving and decision-making processes. Students should follow the processes outlined below in this activity and in the other problem-solving and decision-making exercises throughout the textbook.

Problem Solving

1. Identify a problem.
2. Gather information.
3. List and consider options.
4. Consider advantages and disadvantages.
5. Choose and implement a solution.
6. Evaluate the solution.

Decision Making

1. Identify a situation that requires a decision.
2. Gather information.
3. Identify options.
4. Predict consequences.
5. Implement a decision.

11 **Synthesizing** involves combining information and ideas from several sources or points in time to gain a new understanding of a topic or event. Much of the narrative writing in *World History: Continuity and Change* is a synthesis. It pulls together historical data from many sources into a chronological story of the world. Synthesizing the history of the Great Depression, for example, might involve studying photographs and economic statistics from the 1930s, together with interviews of people from all parts of the world who lived through the period.

Indo-Iranian figurine

12 **Problem Solving and Decision Making** is a process of reviewing a situation and making recommendations for improving or correcting it. Before beginning, however, the problem must be identified and stated. You then need to gather information on the issue. For instance, in seeking a solution to the problems caused by the international drug trade, you might state the issue in terms of the relationship of drug addiction to violent crime. You would then list and evaluate possible solutions or courses of action, selecting the one you think is best and giving the reasons for your choice.

If possible, you would evaluate your solution.

13 **Evaluating** is assessing the significance or overall importance of something, such as the success of a reform movement or the impact of a president on society. You should base your judgment on standards that others will understand and are likely to consider valid. An evaluation of international relations after World War II, for example, would assess the political and economic tensions between the United States and the Soviet Union, and the ways those tensions affected other countries around the world.

14 **Taking a Stand** is identifying an issue, deciding what you think about it, and persuasively expressing your position. Your stand should be based on specific information. In taking a stand, even on a controversial issue such as international terrorism, state your position clearly and give reasons to support it.

Renaissance artist Raphael painted *School of Athens* in 1509–1511.

History is more than a series of events to be memorized. In order to understand the forces that shape history, you will need to use a variety of skills. The skills listed in this section will enable you to analyze events and developments in the past. Historical information can be found in many sources and can be presented in many forms. Your understanding and appreciation of the past will grow as your study skills improve. The lessons in this section will help you learn to identify and analyze historical information, as well as sharpen your research, writing, and test-taking abilities.

1 Identifying the Main Idea

In the study of history, the truly significant events and issues may sometimes get lost among endless details. The ability to identify what is central is a key to understanding any complex issue. *World History: Continuity and Change* is designed to help you focus on the main ideas in world history. The paragraph titled Understanding the Main Idea that introduces each chapter and the Focus Questions that begin each section are intended to guide your reading. The Essential Points placed throughout the text highlight and reinforce the main ideas presented. But not everything you read is structured this way. Applying these general guidelines will help you identify the main ideas in what you read.

How to Identify the Main Idea

1. **Read introductory material.** Read the title and the introduction, if there is one, which may point to the main ideas to be covered.
2. **Have questions in mind.** Formulate questions about the subject that you think might be answered by the material. Having such questions in mind will focus your reading.

3. **Note the outline of ideas.** Pay attention to any headings or subheadings, which may provide a basic outline of the major ideas.
4. **Distinguish supporting details.** As you read, distinguish sentences providing additional details from the general statements they support. A trail of facts, for instance, may lead to a conclusion that expresses a main idea.

Applying Your Skill

Read the paragraph below, from the subsection in Chapter 14 titled "Environmental Challenges of the 1300s," to identify its main idea.

By the end of the 1200s, Europe had reached its natural limits of expansion. Despite their new farming technology, Europeans knew little about fertilizers and the importance of replenishing nutrients in the soil. They fed the growing population by simply bringing more land under cultivation. But by 1300, however, the majority of available farmland was in use. Pushed beyond its capacity, the land began to lose its fertility, and food production leveled off. Farmers could no longer grow enough food to feed Europe's people.

Hindu god Ganesha

Identifying the Main Idea

For further practice identifying the main idea, have students find magazine articles on other countries. Ask them to identify the introductory material and formulate a question based on that material. Then have them read the article and outline it. Finally, have students separate the main idea of the article from the supporting details. Students will receive additional reinforcement in this skill in **Skills Activity 7:** *Identifying the Main Idea.*

**Practicing
Your Skill**

1. colder and wetter climate resulted in famine; details about agricultural problems
2. The second paragraph supports the information of the first one by providing more details about the situation described in the first paragraph. By the end of the 1200s, food supplies in Europe were no longer sufficient to feed its growing population, and destructive climate changes made the problem even worse.

**SKILLS
ACTIVITY**

**Identifying Cause
and Effect**

For further practice identifying cause and effect, have students use the clue words and phrases on page xxiv to write a short paragraph describing the causes and effects of something they do everyday. They may choose to write about brushing their teeth, traveling to school, eating lunch, or talking on the phone. Ask them to make their descriptions as detailed and complex as possible. Students will receive additional reinforcement in this skill in **Skills Activity 5:** *Understanding Sequence.*

As the lead sentence indicates, the paragraph focuses on changes in European society. Details about agricultural production—such as the fact that the Europeans knew little about fertilizers or how to replenish the soil's nutrients and that farmers increased production by simply bringing more land under cultivation—are included to provide a background to the problem. The main idea—Europe's population had exceeded the land's capacity for production, and food supplies were no longer sufficient—is best captured in the concluding sentence.

Practicing Your Skill

Now read the second paragraph of the subsection on environmental challenges (p. 362) and answer the following questions.

1. What is the paragraph's main idea? How does the writer support that idea?
2. What is the relationship of these two paragraphs' main ideas? Combine them into one statement that summarizes both paragraphs.

2 Identifying Cause and Effect

Identifying and understanding cause-and-effect relationships is crucial to the study of history. To investigate why an event took place and what else happened as a result of that event, historians ask such questions as, What is the immediate activity that triggered the event? What is the background leading up to the event? Who were the people involved? Your task is simpler than the historian's: to trace what he or she has already determined about the web of actions and outcomes.

How to Identify Cause and Effect

1. **Look for clues.** Certain words and phrases are immediate clues to the existence of a cause-and-effect relationship.

CLUE WORDS AND PHRASES	
Cause	**Effect**
as a result of	aftermath
because	as a consequence
brought about	depended on
inspired	gave rise to
led to	originating from
produced	outcome
provoked	outgrowth
spurred	proceeded from
the reason	resulting in

2. **Identify the relationship.** Read carefully to identify how events are related. Writers do not always state the link between cause and effect. Sometimes a reader of history has to *infer* the cause or the effect from the clues given in the text.
3. **Check for complex connections.** Beyond the immediate, or superficial, cause and effect, check for other, more complex relationships among various events. Note, for example, whether (1) there were additional causes of a given effect; (2) a cause had multiple effects; and (3) these effects themselves caused further events.

Applying Your Skill

The chart below presents an important cause-and-effect relationship in the conflicts surrounding the Russian Revolution. Poverty and wartime defeat led many Russians to protest government actions during the early 1900s. A diagram of one of the conflicts follows.

Cause	**Effect**
Many Russians experienced poor living conditions, hunger, mistreatment from the government, and losses during World War I.	The Russian people grew increasingly dissatisfied with the harsh rule of the czar's government.

The diagram below describes how Lenin encountered opposition in Russia after the treaty of Brest-Litovsk. Note how an effect may in turn become a cause.

Cause		Effect/Cause		Effect
Lenin signs treaty of Brest-Litovsk.	→	Former army officers feel betrayed by treaty.	→	Officers form White Army to fight Lenin.

Practicing Your Skill

From your knowledge of recent world history, choose a sequence of events shaped by cause-and-effect relationships. Draw a chart showing the relationships between the actions and the outcomes. Then write a paragraph that explains the cause-and-effect connections.

Practicing Your Skill

Students should chart and describe a recent historical development in terms of cause and effect.

---

3 Distinguishing Fact from Opinion

Historical sources may contain facts and opinions. Sources such as letters, diaries, and speeches usually express personal views. The ability to distinguish facts from opinions is essential in judging the soundness of an argument or the reliability of a historical account.

How to Distinguish Fact from Opinion

1. **Identify the facts.** Ask yourself: Can it be proven? Determine whether the idea can be checked for accuracy in a source such as an almanac or encyclopedia. If so, it is probably factual. If not, it probably contains an opinion.
2. **Identify the opinions.** Look for clues that signal a statement of opinion: phrases such as *I think* or *I believe*. Comparative words like *greatest* or *more important* and value-laden words like *extremely* or *ridiculous* imply a judgment, and thus an opinion.

Applying Your Skill

Assessments of a person's character often mix fact and opinion. Read the Greek philosopher Isocrates' description of Artaxerxes II, a Persian king who gained control over Greek city-states in A.D. 387:

"He is a despot [cruel and harsh leader] to whose court we sail to accuse each other. We call him the Great King, as though we were subject prisoners of war, and if we engage in war with each other, it is on him that our hopes are set, though he would destroy both sides without compunction [remorse]."

Isocrates' assessment—that Artaxerxes was a tyrant—is clearly an opinion. Note the value-laden words and phrasing: *despot, subject prisoners, without compunction.*

Practicing Your Skill

Read the excerpt below, in which Isocrates advises Philip of Macedon on how a king should rule Greece:

"I maintain that you should be the benefactor of Greece, and gain to the greatest possible extent the empire of the non-Greek world. If you accomplish this, you will win universal gratitude: from the Greeks for the benefits they gain, from Macedonia if your rule of them is kingly and not tyrannical, and from the rest of the world if it is through you that they are liberated from Persian despotism and exchange it for Greek protection."

1. Is this excerpt a statement of fact or a statement of opinion?
2. What words does Isocrates use to describe the kind of king he thinks Greece needs?
3. Which words provide clues to Isocrates' view on Persian rule in Greece?

Delegates sign the Versailles peace settlement.

S SKILLS ACTIVITY

Distinguishing Fact from Opinion

For further practice distinguishing fact from opinion, bring in an editorial or letter to the editor. Have students identify the statements that are verifiable and those that are not. Then ask students to list key words and phrases from the editorial that reveal bias. Finally, ask students to make an overall assessment of the source's validity. Students will receive additional reinforcement in this skill in **Skills Activity 3:** *Distinguishing Fact from Opinion.*

Practicing Your Skill

1. Statement of opinion: Isocrates is describing what he believes Philip should do.
2. benefactor, kingly, not tyrannical, protection
3. liberated from, despotism

4 Reading a Time Line

Knowing the chronological order of historical events—that is, the sequence in which they occurred—is essential to understanding them. Chronology has been called "the skeleton of history." A time line is a visual framework representing the chronology of a particular historical period. It enables you to see at a glance what happened when. Studying a time line involves seeing relationships between events as well as remembering important dates. Time lines provide a source of information about people, places, and events associated with a particular historical period. Time lines sometimes cover a great number of years, such as decades or centuries. Other time lines cover individual years within a decade (1941, 1942, 1945, and so on).

How to Read a Time Line

1. **Determine its framework.** Note the years covered and the intervals of time into which the time line is divided.
2. **Study the sequence of events.** Study the order in which the events appear on the time line, particularly noting the length of time between events.
3. **Supply missing information.** Think about the people, places, and other events associated with each item on the time line. In this way you can expand and develop the framework.
4. **Note relationships.** Ask how an event relates to earlier or later events. Look for cause-and-effect relationships and long-term developments.

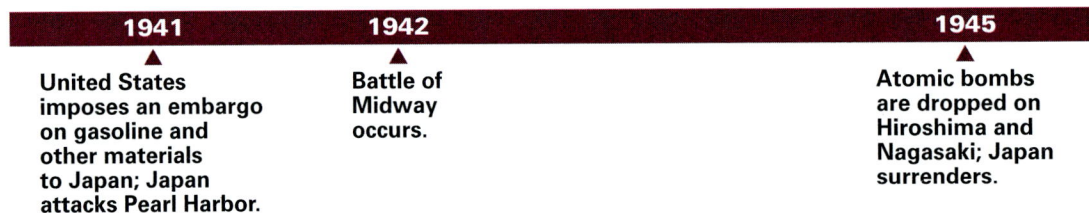

1941	1942	1945
United States imposes an embargo on gasoline and other materials to Japan; Japan attacks Pearl Harbor.	Battle of Midway occurs.	Atomic bombs are dropped on Hiroshima and Nagasaki; Japan surrenders.

Applying Your Skill

Study the time line above, which covers the years 1941 to 1945. It lists important events in the history of World War II in the Pacific.

When more than one event is listed for the same year, the events are stacked with the earliest on top. The entries for 1941 illustrate the background to the surprise attack on Pearl Harbor: Japanese aggression in Southeast Asia and a mounting trade war with the United States.

Practicing Your Skill

From the information in the time line above, answer the following questions.

1. Based on the framework provided here, what other events might belong on this time line for the years between Pearl Harbor and the dropping of the atomic bombs?
2. What cause-and-effect relationship is suggested by the sequence of entries for 1945?

Marcel Duchamp's 1918 painting *Tú m'*

5 Reading Charts and Graphs

Charts and graphs are means of organizing and presenting information visually. They categorize and display data in a variety of ways, depending on their subject. Several different types of charts and graphs are used in this textbook.

Charts

You are already familiar with the time line, which is a chart that lists historical events in their chronological order. Other charts include flow charts, organization charts, and tables. A *flow chart* shows a sequence of events or the steps in a process. Cause-and-effect relationships are often shown by flow charts. An *organization chart* displays the structure of an organization, indicating the ranking or function of its internal parts and the relationships between them. For example, see the chart titled "Government of the Ottoman Empire." A *table* generally is a multicolumn chart that presents data in categories that are easy to

understand and compare. Tables, such as the one titled "Emperors of the Pax Romana," are effective in displaying statistics.

How to Read a Chart

1. **Read the title.** Read the title to identify the focus or purpose of the chart.
2. **Study the chart's parts.** Read the chart's headings, subheadings, and labels to identify the categories used and the specific data given for each category.
3. **Analyze the details.** When reading quantities, note increases or decreases in amounts. When reading dates, note intervals of time. When viewing an organization chart, use directional arrows or lines to help you understand the relationship between the items.
4. **Put the data to use.** Form generalizations or draw conclusions based on the data.

SKILLS ACTIVITY

Reading a Chart

For further practice reading a chart, have students work in groups to create a chart of the administration of their school based on the chart of the Ottoman Empire on page xxvii. Have students provide a title and at least one analytical question that the information in their chart could answer. Students will receive additional reinforcement in this skill in **Skills Activity 4:** *Creating a Table* and **Skills Activity 26:** *Interpreting a Diagram.*

Government of the Ottoman Empire

A Complex Government The members of the divan were handpicked by the sultan and reported directly to him.

❖ **Analyzing** Why do you think the Ottomans found it necessary to have the divan between the sultan and the other three branches of government?

Emperors of the Pax Romana
27 B.C.–A.D. 180

Period	Title	Emperors
27 B.C.–A.D 14		Augustus
A.D. 14–68	Julio-Claudian Emperors	Tiberius (14–37)* Caligula (37–41) Claudius (41–54) Nero (54–68)
A.D. 68–69	Army Emperors	Galba, Otho, Vitellius *(Chosen by various legions during a succession crisis)*
A.D. 69–96	Flavian Emperors	Vespasian (69–79) Titus (79–81) Domitian (81–96)
A.D. 96–180	The Good Emperors	Nerva (96–98) Trajan (98–117) Hadrian (117–138) Antoninus Pius (138–161) Marcus Aurelius (161–180)

* Indicates dates of reign

Graphs

There are several types of graphs; each has certain advantages in displaying data for a particular emphasis. A *line graph* plots information by dots connected by a line. A line graph such as the one titled "Output of Manufactured Products" shows changes or trends over time. A *bar graph* displays amounts or quantities in a way that makes comparisons easy. For example, see the bar graph titled "Execution Rates in Witchcraft Trials." A *pie graph*, or *circle graph*, such as the one titled "World Religions by Type" and the one titled "Distribution of Islam Worldwide," displays proportions by showing sections of a whole like slices of a pie.

Execution Rates in Witchcraft Trials

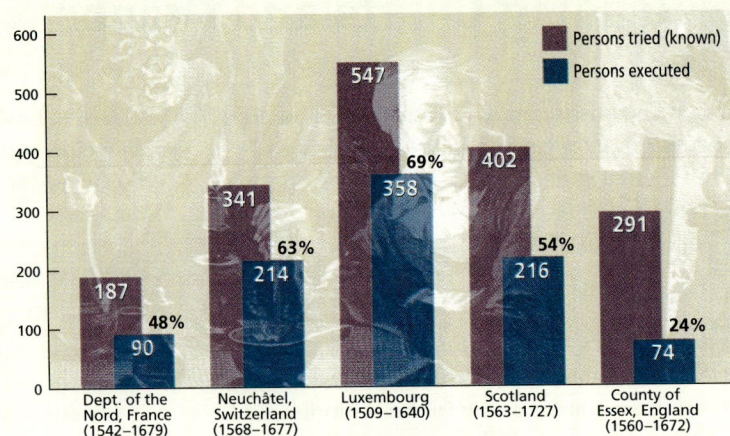

Witch-hunts During the 1500s and 1600s, thousands of Europeans were tried and many were executed as suspected witches.

◆ **Analyzing** Where was the number of witchcraft trials and executions the highest? What political events might explain the higher number of witchcraft trials and executions on the European continent than in England at this time?

How to Read a Graph

1. **Read the title.** Read the title to identify the subject and purpose of the graph. Note the kind of graph you are viewing, remembering the types of relationships each kind is designed to emphasize.
2. **Study the labels.** To identify the type of information presented in the graph, read the labels that define each axis. The *horizontal* axis runs from left to right generally at the bottom of the graph, while the *vertical* axis runs up and down generally along the left side. If the axes include dates or amounts, note the intervals. Be aware that intervals may not always be even.
3. **Analyze the data.** Note increases or decreases in quantities. Look for trends, relationships, and changes in the data.
4. **Put the data to use.** Use the results of your analysis to form generalizations and to draw conclusions.

Output of Manufactured Products: 1750–1913

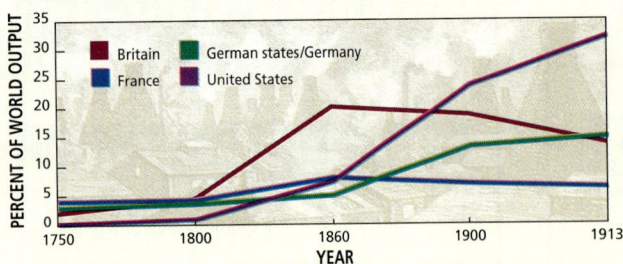

Production Industrialization had an enormous impact on the amount of manufactured goods that nations produced.

◆ **Analyzing** Which country had the most dramatic rise in output of manufactured goods between 1750 and 1913? What factors allowed this country to produce so many manufactured goods?

Applying Your Skill

Study the pie graphs shown on the next page, which illustrate religious involvement around the world. From the first graph you can see that there are five major world religions: Buddhism, Hinduism, Judaism, Christianity, and Islam. In addition, you can see that 28.5 percent of the world's population does not belong to any of these religions. The second graph shows the percentages of people who practice Islam in different parts of the world. This graph indicates that nearly two thirds of the world's Muslims live in Asia.

Practicing Your Skill

Use the line graph "Output of Manufactured Products" on the previous page to answer the following:

1. Describe the type of data illustrated and the intervals used for **(a)** the horizontal axis and **(b)** the vertical axis.

2. What happened to the production of manufactured goods in Britain during the period of 1860–1913? What happened to the production of German manufactured goods during the same period?

3. What generalizations or conclusions can you draw from the information in this graph?

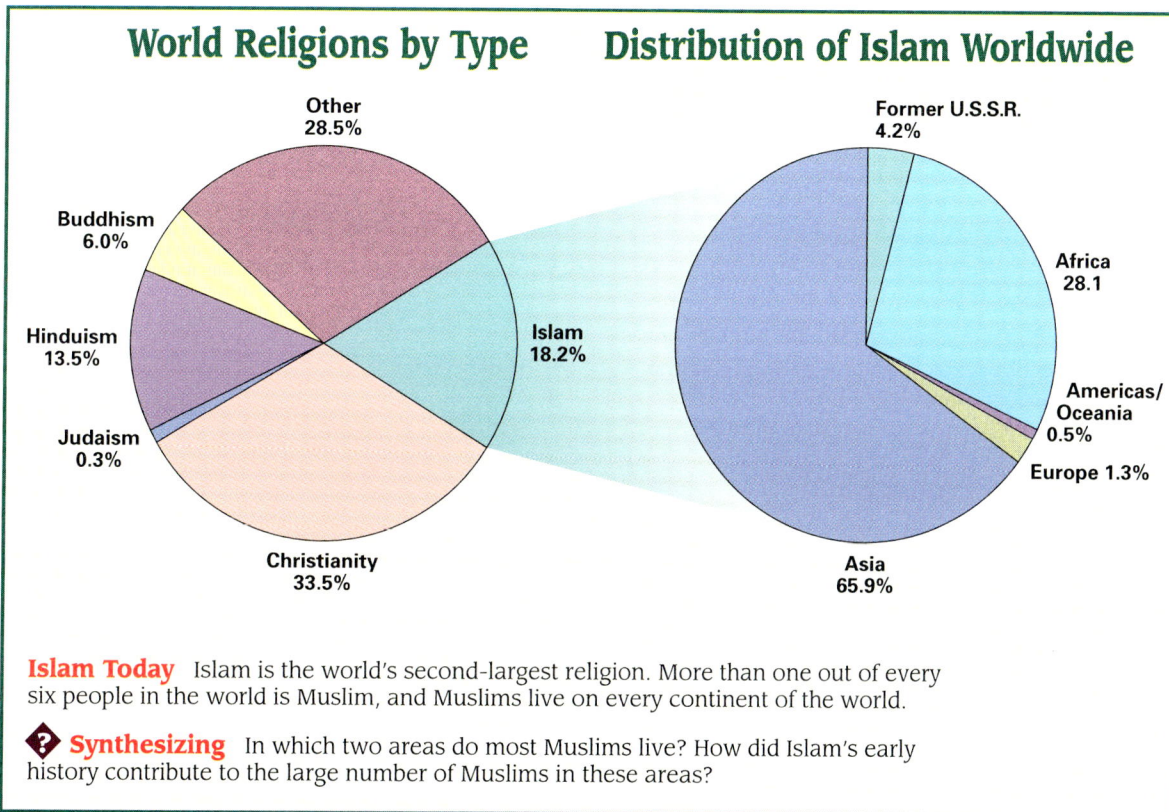

World Religions by Type

Other 28.5%
Buddhism 6.0%
Hinduism 13.5%
Judaism 0.3%
Christianity 33.5%
Islam 18.2%

Distribution of Islam Worldwide

Former U.S.S.R. 4.2%
Africa 28.1
Americas/Oceania 0.5%
Europe 1.3%
Asia 65.9%

Islam Today   Islam is the world's second-largest religion. More than one out of every six people in the world is Muslim, and Muslims live on every continent of the world.

Synthesizing   In which two areas do most Muslims live? How did Islam's early history contribute to the large number of Muslims in these areas?

6 Studying Primary and Secondary Sources

There are many sources of firsthand historical information, including diaries, letters, editorials, and legal documents such as wills and titles. All of these are *primary sources*. Newspaper reports also are considered to be primary sources, although they are generally written after the fact, as are personal memoirs and autobiographies, which are usually written late in a person's life. The paintings, photographs, and political cartoons that make up history's visual record also are primary sources. Because they permit a close-up look at the past—a chance to get inside people's minds—primary sources are valuable historical tools.

Secondary sources are descriptions or interpretations of events written after the events have occurred by persons who did not participate in the events they describe. History books such as *World History: Continuity and Change,* biographies, encyclopedias, and other reference works are examples of secondary sources. Writers of secondary sources have the

Practicing Your Skill

1. primary—firsthand historical information; secondary—interpretations written after an event occurred
2. objectivity and wider perspective
3. Doing so might help put the source in its historical context.
4. primary—newspaper, private journal, cartoon, tapestry, deed, snapshot, autobiography
secondary—biography, magazine article
   Some primary sources may be written long after events occurred—for example, autobiographies. But they also have the secondary source's characteristic of the wider perspective than a source that was written as the event was occurring.

SKILLS ACTIVITY

Building Vocabulary

For further practice building vocabulary, have students find and define key words in this handbook. Then ask them to use these words in a paragraph about the study of history.
   Remind students to apply the tips for building vocabulary throughout their study of world history. They can apply and expand their skill in section and chapter reviews and in the **Vocabulary Activities**.

The Zimmermann Note angered many people in the United States.

advantage of seeing what happened beyond the historical moment that is being studied. They can provide a perspective wider than that available to one person at a specific time.

How to Study Primary and Secondary Sources

1. **Study the material carefully.** Consider the nature of the material. Is it verbal or visual? Is it based on firsthand information or on the accounts of others? Note the major ideas and supporting details.

2. **Consider the audience.** Ask yourself: For whom was this message originally meant? Whether a message was intended, for instance, for the general public or for a specific, private audience may have shaped its style or content.

3. **Check for bias.** Watch for words or phrases that present a one-sided view of a person or situation.

4. **When possible, compare sources.** Study more than one source on a topic. Comparing sources gives you a more complete, balanced account of historical events and their relationships.

Practicing Your Skill

1. What distinguishes secondary sources from primary sources?
2. What advantage do secondary sources have over primary sources?
3. Why should you consider the original audience of a historical source?
4. Of the following, identify which are primary and which are secondary sources: a newspaper, a private journal, a biography, an editorial cartoon, a medieval tapestry, a deed to property, a snapshot of a family vacation, a magazine article about the history of Thailand, an autobiography. How might some of these sources prove to be both primary and secondary sources?

7 Building Vocabulary

The study of history may challenge your reading comprehension. You will probably encounter many new and unfamiliar words. But with regular effort you can master them and turn history reading into an opportunity to enlarge your vocabulary. Following the steps outlined below will assist you in building your vocabulary.

How to Build Vocabulary

1. **Identify unusual words.** As you read, be aware of words that you cannot pronounce or define. Make a list of these words. Words that are somewhat familiar are the easiest to learn.

Isabel Allende's *La Casa de los Espiritus* (House of the Spirits) has been made into a feature film.

2. **Study context clues.** Study the sentence and paragraph where you find the new term. This setting, or *context*, may give you clues to the word's meaning. The word may be defined either by another, more familiar word that means the same thing or by an example of what the term means.
3. **Use the dictionary.** Use a dictionary to help you pronounce and define the words on your list.
4. **Review new vocabulary.** Look for ways to use the new words and social studies terms—in homework assignments, conversation, or classroom

discussions. The best way to master a new word is to use it.

Practicing Your Skill

1. What is context? How can it provide clues to a word's meaning?
2. As you read a chapter, list any unusual words that you find. Write down what you think each word means; then check your definitions against those in a dictionary.

8 Creating an Outline

An outline is a tool for organizing information. It is a logical summary that presents the main points of what you have read or plan to communicate. An outline is an important part of preparing to write a paper. An essay outline, for example, would highlight the main ideas that you intend to express and sketch the details that you want to include for support. An outline is only a skeletal structure. It must be fleshed out in use. But if an outline is thorough and well thought-out, it makes writing the final product much easier.

How to Create an Outline

1. **Order your material.** Decide what you want to emphasize or focus on. Order or classify your material with that in mind. Determine what information belongs in an introduction, what should make up the body of your paper, and what to leave for the conclusion.
2. **Identify main ideas.** Identify the main ideas to be highlighted in each section. Make these your outline's main headings.
3. **List supporting details.** Determine the important details or facts that support each main idea. Rank and list them as subheadings, using additional levels of subheadings as necessary.

The French Revolution

I. Grievances against French monarchy
   A. Political and economic inequality in structure of Three Estates
   B. Heavy taxes and large national debt
II. Increased turmoil
   A. Formation of National Assembly
      1. Conflict at Meeting of Estates General
      2. Tennis Court Oath
   B. Storming of the Bastille
   C. The Great Fear
III. End of the Old Regime
   A. Abolition of privileges for First and Second Estates
   B. Adoption of Declaration of Rights of Man
   C. Adoption of first national constitution
      1. Reduced royal power
      2. Established elected Legislative Assembly
      3. Did not include all of ideals of Declaration of Rights of Man
         a. Excluded women from vote and Jews from public office
         b. Voting eligibility requirements returned power to wealthy
   D. Royal family arrested
   E. Louis XVI executed
IV. From the Republic to Napoleon Bonaparte
   A. Reign of Terror
      1. Directed against people of all classes
      2. Ended with execution of Robespierre
   B. Directory
   C. Power assumed by Napoleon Bonaparte

Subheadings must come in pairs, at the least: no A's without B's, no 1's without 2's.

4. **Put your outline to use.** Structure your essay or report according to your outline. Each main heading, for instance, might form the basis for a topic sentence to begin a paragraph. Subheadings would then make up the content of the paragraph. In a more lengthy paper, each subheading might be the main idea of a paragraph.

The sample outline shown on the previous page could have been used in preparation for writing about the French Revolution. Note the several levels of headings that make up the various parts of the outline.

Practicing Your Skill

Read the subsection in Chapter 5 titled "The Roman Republic" (pp. 116–17). Then create an outline that you could use in writing about this subject. Use the supporting details in the text.

9 Doing Research

Research is at the heart of all historical inquiry. To complete papers or special projects, you may need to use resources beyond this textbook. For example, you may want to research specific subjects or people not discussed here, or to learn additional information about a certain topic.

How to Find Information

To find a particular book, you need to know how libraries organize their materials. To classify books, libraries assign each book a *call number* that tells you its location.

To find the call number, look in the library's *card catalog.* The catalog lists books by author, by title, and by subject. If you know the author or title of the book, finding it is simple. If you do not know this information, or if you just want to find any book about a particular subject, look up that subject heading. Many libraries have computerized card catalogs. These catalogs generally contain the same information as a traditional card catalog, but take up less space and are easier to update and to access. You may also want to find information on the World Wide Web, the part of the Internet where people put files called Web sites for other people to access. To search the World Wide Web, you may use a search engine, which will provide you with a list of Web sites that contain keywords relating to your topic, or a Web directory, which

will allow you to browse by subject. Once you have found a site relating to your topic, you will probably be able to find links to other sites that also relate to your topic. The Web contains a wealth of information; however, most of it is unregulated. Use the skills you have developed for evaluating sources, such as detecting bias and distinguishing fact from opinion, to judge the validity of any Web site you access.

How to Use Resources

In a library's reference section, you will find encyclopedias, specialized dictionaries, atlases, almanacs, and indexes to recent material in magazines and newspapers. *Encyclopedias* often will be your best resource. Encyclopedias include biographical sketches of important historical figures; geographic, economic, and political data on individual nations, states, and cities; and

Author

Call number
(Library of Congress
Catalog number)

Title

Publisher

Other headings
under which book
is listed

```
355.0943
C844
P71
```

```
The Politics of the Prussian Army,
1640-1945

Craig, Gordon A.
    The Politics of the Prussian Army,
    1640-1945/Gordon A. Craig—New York:
    Oxford University Press, 1973 (c1955)
    xx, 538 pp. 22cm.

Includes Bibliography and Index.

    I. Germany, Prussia, Germany—
politics and government. II. Title:
The Politics of the Prussian Army,
1640-1945.
```

discussions of historical events and religion, social and cultural issues, and much more.

Specialized dictionaries exist for almost every field. A biographical dictionary has entries about far more people than an encyclopedia has. A *gazetteer* is a geographical dictionary that lists significant natural physical features and place-names. An *atlas* contains maps and visual representations of geographic data.

To find up-to-date facts, you can use almanacs, yearbooks, and periodical indexes. References like *The World Almanac and Book of Facts* include historical information and a variety of statistics.

Periodical indexes, particularly *The Readers' Guide to Periodical Literature*, can help you locate informative, current articles published in magazines.

The New York Times Index catalogs the news stories published in the *Times*.

When conducting research, you should keep track of the materials you use. You should then compile your sources into a bibliography and turn it in with papers and other kinds of written assignments.

Practicing Your Skill

1. What types of information can you get from the card catalog, whether traditional or electronic?
2. What kinds of references contain information about geography?
3. Where would you look to find the most recent coverage of a political or social issue?

Practicing Your Skill

1. a book's call number, title, author, subjects, and publication information
2. encyclopedias, specialized dictionaries, gazetteers, and atlases
3. almanacs, yearbooks, and periodical indexes

---

10 Writing About History

World History: Continuity and Change provides you with numerous writing opportunities. Section Reviews have writing exercises (labeled Writing to Explain, Writing to Persuade, and so on) that give you the chance to write about a historical subject with a particular focus in mind. Chapter Reviews contain additional opportunities to write.

How to Write with a Purpose

Always keep your purpose for writing in mind. That purpose might be to analyze, to evaluate, to synthesize, to inform, to persuade, to hypothesize, or to take a stand. As you begin, your purpose will determine the most appropriate approach to take and when you are done, it will help you evaluate your success.

Each different purpose for writing requires its own form, tone, and content. The point of view you are adopting will shape what you write, as will your intended audience: whoever will be reading what you write.

Historical Imagination

Many writing opportunities in *World History: Continuity and Change* ask you to create a specific

The French philosophe Voltaire was one of the great writers and thinkers of the Enlightenment.

type of writing—a diary entry, a letter, a newspaper editorial, a poem, or an advertisement. Often such writing about history involves using historical imagination—that is, writing from the perspective of a person living *then* rather than *now*. An assignment may require, for instance, that you address a particular historical figure, such as a former president, or that you write as if living through a specific historical crisis. When writing such an assignment, try to imagine what people at the time would have thought or said about a particular event.

S SKILLS ACTIVITY

Writing with a Purpose

For further practice writing with a purpose, list the different purposes that students may have for writing—to evaluate, to inform, and so on. Have students suggest a current issue on which they might write with different purposes. Encourage them to list and explain their different purposes.

S SKILLS ACTIVITY

Using Historical Imagination

For further practice using historical imagination, have students select a historical period and list the kinds of things they might need to know to write a diary entry from the perspective of a person who lived during that period.

The guidelines that follow pertain to particular kinds of writing.

- A *diary* is an informal, personal log of your experiences and recollections (or those of someone else). Entries are dated and consist of brief accounts of the day's happenings and your reactions as they occur.
- A *letter* is a personal communication meant for a specific individual.
- A newspaper *editorial* is a public statement of an opinion or viewpoint. It takes a stand on an issue and gives reasons for that stand.
- An *advertisement* is an announcement to promote a product or event. Effective ads are direct and to the point and use memorable language, such as jingles and slogans, to highlight important features.

How to Write a Paper or Essay

Each writing opportunity will have specific directions about what and how to write. But whether you are writing a diary entry describing your experiences as a soldier on the western front during World War I or an essay about changes in military technology, you should follow certain basic steps.

There are four major stages to writing a paper or essay: prewriting, writing a first draft, evaluating and revising your draft to eliminate any awkward passages, and proofreading and producing a final draft of your paper for publication. Each of these stages can be further divided into more specific steps and tasks. The guidelines for each of these four steps outlined below can help you improve your writing abilities and produce more accurate and interesting writing assignments.

Prewriting

1. **Choose a topic.** Select a topic for your paper. Whenever possible, choose a topic that interests you. Take care to narrow your subject so that you will be able to develop and support a clear argument.

Jakob and Wilhelm Grimm

2. **Identify your purpose for writing the essay or paper.** Read the directions carefully to identify the purpose for your writing. Keep the purpose of the assignment in mind as you plan and write your paper.

3. **Determine your audience.** When writing for a specific audience, choose the tone and style that will best communicate your message.

4. **Collect information.** Write down your ideas and the information you already know about your topic, and do additional research if necessary. Your writing will be more effective if you first know what information you need to look for and then have many details at hand.

5. **Create an outline.** Think and plan before you begin writing your first draft. Organize themes, main ideas, and supporting details into an outline. Your outline will help you stay on track as you write so you do not forget to cover important information or get bogged down in endless details.

Writing the Draft

6. **Write a first draft and evaluate it.** In your first draft, remember to use your outline as a guide. Each paragraph should express a single main idea or set of related ideas, with details for support. Be careful to show the relationships between ideas and to use proper *transitions*—sentences that build connections between paragraphs.

Evaluating and Revising the Draft

7. **Review and edit.** Revise and reorganize your draft as needed to make your points. Improve sentences by adding appropriate adjectives and adverbs. Omit words, sentences, or paragraphs that are unnecessary or unrelated to a main idea or that stray too far from the main point.

8. **Evaluate your writing style.** Make your writing clearer by changing the length or structure of awkward sentences. Replace inexact wording with more precise word choices.

Proofreading and Publishing

9. **Proofread your paper carefully.** Check for proper spelling, punctuation, and grammar.
10. **Write your final version.** Prepare a neat final version. Appearance is important; it may not affect the quality of your writing itself, but it can affect the way your writing is perceived.

Practicing Your Skill

1. What factor—more than any other—should affect how and what you write? Why?
2. Why is it important to consider the audience for your writing?
3. What is involved in the editing of a first draft of a writing assignment?

11 Taking a Test

When it comes to taking a test, for history or any other subject, nothing can take the place of preparation. A good night's sleep and consistent study habits give you a much better chance for success than hours of late-night, last-minute cramming. By preparing well, you will be better able to ignore distractions during the test.

But keeping your mind focused on the test and free from distractions is not all you can do to improve your test scores. Mastering some basic test-taking skills can also help. Keeping up with daily reading assignments and taking careful notes as you read can turn taking a test into a mere matter of review. Reviewing material that you already know takes less time—and causes less stress—than trying to learn something new under pressure.

You will face several basic types of questions on history tests, such as fill-in-the-blank, short answer, multiple choice, matching, and essay. In answering multiple-choice questions, eliminate any answers that you know are wrong, in order to narrow your field of choice. When doing a matching exercise, first go through the entire list, matching those that you know for sure. Then study any that remain.

School children in Astoria, Oregon

Read essay questions carefully so that you know exactly what you are being asked to write. Make an outline of the main ideas and supporting details that you plan to include in your essay. Keep your answer clear and brief, but cover all necessary points.

How to Take a Test

1. **Prepare beforehand.** This all-important step involves more than studying and reviewing the material prior to the test. It also means being rested and mentally focused on the day of the test.
2. **Follow directions.** Read all instructions carefully. Listen closely if the directions are oral rather than written.
3. **Preview the test.** Skim through the entire test to determine how much time you have for each section. Try to anticipate which areas will be the most difficult for you.
4. **Concentrate on the test.** Do not "watch the clock," but stay aware of the time. If you do not know an answer, move on to the next question. It is best to answer as many questions as you can within the time limit.
5. **Review your answers.** If you have time, return to questions that you skipped or were unsure of and work on them. Review your essays to catch and correct any mistakes in spelling, punctuation, or grammar.

Practicing Your Skill

1. How can you improve your chances on multiple-choice questions?
2. Why is it important to skim through the entire test before you begin?
3. Name three things that can help you in taking a test.

Practicing Your Skill

1. the writer's purpose for writing; different purposes require different forms, tones, and contents
2. Writing will be shaped by the intended audience.
3. revising; reorganizing; improving sentences; omitting words, sentences, or paragraphs

S SKILLS ACTIVITY

Taking a Test

For further practice taking a test, have students look at a few pages of the first chapter of the textbook. Have students devise two fill-in-the-blank questions, two short-answer questions, and one essay question that they might see on a test covering the pages in that chapter.

Practicing Your Skill

1. by eliminating any answers you know are wrong
2. to determine how much time will be required for each section of the test and to anticipate difficult areas
3. preparing in advance, getting a good night's sleep the night before the exam, and keeping focused on the test and free from distractions

12 Reading Maps

History and geography share many common elements. History describes the events that have taken place from ancient times until the present day. Geography, particularly the field of cultural geography, describes how physical environments affect human events and how people influence the environment around them. To describe a series of events without placing them in their physical settings is to tell only part of the story. Geographers have developed five themes—location, place, region, movement, and human-environment interaction—to organize information.

Location describes a site's position and can be expressed in two ways: absolute location and relative location. *Absolute location* describes the exact spot on the earth that a site occupies. It is most often presented in terms of latitude and longitude. For example, Seoul, the capital of South Korea, is located at 37° north latitude and 127° east longitude. *Relative location*, on the other hand, describes the position of a site in relation to other sites. Seoul's relative location might be described as the northwestern area of South Korea, near the mouth of the Han River.

Place refers to the physical features and human influences that define a site and make it different from other sites. Physical features include landscape, climate, and vegetation. Human influences include land use, architecture, and population size.

To better understand the earth, geographers divide it into *regions*. One region may be distinguished from another on the basis of physical characteristics, such as landforms or climate, or on the basis of cultural features, such as dominant languages or religions.

Movement describes the way people interact as they travel, communicate, and trade goods and services. Movement includes human migration as well as the exchange of goods and ideas.

Human-environment interaction deals with all the ways in which people interact with their natural environments, like clearing forests, irrigating the land, and building cities. This theme is particularly important to the study of history in that it shows how people shape and are shaped by their surroundings.

The Silk Road, c. A.D. 100s

Linking East and West Stretching from the Wei He valley in China to the shores of the Mediterranean, the Silk Road passed through rugged mountain ranges, harsh deserts, and the territory of strong empires.

? Movement Which major mountain ranges did traders on the Silk Road pass through?

New Nations in South America by 1828

CARIBBEAN SEA
CENTRAL AMERICA
TRINIDAD (British)
Caracas
GRAN COLOMBIA 1819
GUIANAS (Br.) (Neth.) (Fr.)
Isthmus of Panama
Bogotá
Quito
0° Equator
Amazon River
PERU, 1821
EMPIRE OF BRAZIL, 1822
Lima
15°S
Salvador
La Paz
BOLIVIA, 1825
Chuquisaca
São Paulo
PACIFIC OCEAN
PARAGUAY 1811
Asunción
Rio de Janeiro
Paraná River
N
URUGUAY 1828
30°S
W E
S
Santiago CHILE 1818
Buenos Aires
Montevideo
Río de la Plata
ATLANTIC OCEAN
UNITED PROVINCES OF LA PLATA, 1816 (ARGENTINA)

| 1819 | Date of independence |

45°S
0   750   1,500 Miles
0   750   1,500 Kilometers
Miller Cylindrical Projection
Strait of Magellan
FALKLAND ISLANDS (ISLAS MALVINAS)
Cape Horn
75°W   60°W   45°W   30°W

Liberty and Union After gaining independence, the former Spanish viceroyalties struggled to unite, while Portugal's former colony of Brazil remained intact.

? Location Which South American country was the last to gain independence?

These themes—and the information they organize—can be described in written passages or represented visually in maps. Maps convey a wealth of varied information through colors, lines, symbols, and labels. To read and interpret maps, you must be able to understand their language and symbols.

Types of Maps

A map is an illustration drawn to scale of all or part of the earth's surface. Types of maps include physical maps, political maps, and special-purpose maps. *Physical maps* illustrate the natural landscape of an area—the landforms that mark the earth's surface. Physical maps often use shading to show relief—the existence of mountains, hills, and valleys—and colors to show elevation or the height above sea level.

The map of the world on pp. 852–53 is strictly a physical map.

Political maps illustrate political units such as states and nations, and use color variations and lines to mark boundaries, dots for major cities, and stars or stars within circles for capitals. Political maps show information such as territorial changes or military alliances. "New Nations in South America" is a political map.

Special-purpose maps present specific information such as the routes of explorers, the outcome of an election, regional economic activity, or population density. The "Silk Road" and "Oil Deposits in the Middle East and North Africa" maps shown here are special-purpose maps.

Many maps combine different features of the types listed above. For example, a map may combine information from a political map with that found on a special-purpose map by showing national boundaries as well as trade routes.

Map Features

Most maps have a number of features in common. Familiarity with these basic elements makes reading any map easier.

Titles, legends, and labels. A map's *title* tells you what the map is about, what area is shown, and usually what time period is being represented. The *legend*, or key, explains any special symbols, colors, or shadings used on the map. *Labels* designate political and geographic place-names, as well as physical features like mountain ranges, oceans, and rivers.

The global grid. The *absolute location* of any place on the earth is given in terms of *latitude* (degrees north or south of the equator) and *longitude* (degrees east or west of the prime meridian). The symbol for a degree is °. Degrees are divided into 60 equal parts called minutes, which are represented by the symbol '. The *global grid* is created by the intersecting lines of latitude (*parallels*) and lines of longitude (*meridians*). Lines of latitude and longitude may sometimes be indicated by tick marks near the edge of the map, or by lines across an entire map. Many maps also have *locator maps*, which place the area of focus in a larger context, showing it in relation to a continent or the entire world.

Directions and distances. Most maps in this textbook have a *compass rose*, or *directional indicator*. The compass rose indicates the four cardinal points—*N* for north, *S* for south, *E* for east, and *W* for west.

You can also find intermediate directions—northeast, southeast, southwest, and northwest—using the compass rose. This helps in describing the relative location of a place. (If a map has no compass rose, assume that north is at the top, east is to the right, and so on.)

Many maps in this textbook include a *scale*, showing both miles and kilometers, to help you relate distances on the map to actual distances on the earth's surface. You can use a scale to find the true distance between any two points on the map.

Map projections. Because the earth is a sphere, it is best represented by a three-dimensional globe. Although a flat map is an imperfect representation of the earth's surface, mapmakers have devised various ways of showing the earth two-dimensionally. These different flat views of the earth's surface are called *projections*.

Every map projection, and therefore every map, distorts to some extent at least one of the following aspects: (1) the shape of land areas, (2) their relative sizes, (3) directions, or (4) distances. Mapmakers choose the projection that least distorts what they wish to show. For example, an *equal-area projection* shows the relative sizes of different countries or continents quite accurately but distorts shapes somewhat.

Conformal projections preserve the shape and scale of small areas around a point or a line. They cannot, however, preserve the shape of large countries or continents because scale varies from point to point. For example, in a world map using a Mercator conformal projection, sizes and shapes are accurate along the equator but are distorted toward the poles. As a result, Greenland and South America appear to be the same size, even though South America is actually nine times as large as Greenland.

In *World History: Continuity and Change* the locator maps are *orthographic projections*, which provide a view of a particular region from space. This projection provides an accurate view of size and shape, but does not show the surface of the entire world.

Oil Deposits in the Middle East and Africa, 1990

The Oil Region   The desert sands of the Middle East and parts of Africa yield rich and easily attainable supplies of oil. These regions contain the majority of the world's oil reserves.

❖ Location   Why has access to the Strait of Hormuz been so important for oil-producing nations?

How to Read a Map

1. **Determine the focus of the map.** Read the map's title and labels to determine the map's focus—its subject and the geographic area it covers.
2. **Study the map legend.** Read the legend and become familiar with any special symbols, lines, colors, and shadings used in the map.
3. **Check directions and distances.** Use the directional indicator and scale as needed to determine direction, location, and distance between various points on the map.
4. **Check the grid lines.** Refer to lines of longitude and latitude, or to a locator map, to fix the area on the map in its larger context.

Navigational chart from 1625

5. **Study the map.** Study the map's basic features and details, keeping its purpose in mind. If it is a special-purpose map, study the specific information being presented.

Practicing Your Skill

For each of the special-purpose maps in this lesson—"The Silk Road," "Oil Deposits in the Middle East and Africa," and "Peoples of Europe"—answer the following questions.

1. What is the special focus of the map?
2. How is a map helpful in presenting this information?
3. What special symbols, if any, are used in the map?
4. What do the color variations and different lines indicate?

Practicing Your Skill

1. "The Silk Road": the route known as the Silk Road that traders followed from Asia to Europe and back and the geography of the land through which the route went; "Oil Deposits in the Middle East and Africa": the oil reserves in Iraq, Iran, Kuwait, Saudi Arabia, and northern Africa; "Peoples of Europe": invasions of Vikings, Magyars, and Muslims into Europe
2. all three provide titles, labels, identifying colors, legends, scales, and compass roses
3. "The Silk Road": red line for Silk Road, notched line for Great Wall; "Oil Deposits in the Middle East and Africa": oil barrels, numbers representing oil reserves; "Peoples of Europe": arrows to show invasions
4. "The Silk Road": different colors indicate different political regions; lines indicate the Silk Road, the Great Wall, and rivers; "Oil Deposits in the Middle East and Africa": color indicates nations that are OPEC members; lines indicate national boundaries; "Peoples of Europe": different colored arrows indicate different groups of people

Peoples of Europe, 600–1000

Renewed Invasions Viking, Magyar, and Muslim invaders raided towns across Europe and northern Africa. In this chaotic period, the balance of power shifted from east to west.

? Location What body of water separated the Viking homeland from the Western Slavs? from the Celts?

Chapter 1
The Rise of Civilization

Civilizations develop where water is available, the climate is somewhat mild, and the soil is fertile and easily tilled. Technological advances such as the development of the plow and irrigation techniques allow civilizations to grow more food and support more people.

Unit 1
The Beginnings of Civilization
Beginnings–200 B.C.

Chapter 1

The Rise of Civilization Beginnings–200 B.C.

When early humans began to live in villages and practice agriculture, civilization developed. The first civilizations arose in fertile river valleys. The peoples of the river valleys built great cities, produced beautiful works of art, and developed systems of writing. How might geographic features and technological developments affect the rise of civilizations?

In the earliest era of human existence, people lived on a very basic level, gathering just enough plants and hunting just enough animals to survive. Eventually, they settled in villages and learned how to cultivate plants. At this point, civilized societies began to develop. Neighboring nomadic peoples recognized the advantages of civilization and soon established a pattern that would recur time and time again. The nomadic peoples used their superior fighting skills to conquer existing civilizations. As they became civilized and began building empires, these peoples spread civilization even farther. As time went on, however, other nomadic peoples wanted the benefits of civilization for themselves, and they began the process of conquest and civilization all over again.

Chapter 2
The First Empires
2400 B.C.–500 B.C.

As civilization spread, hardy nomadic peoples conquered existing civilizations and expanded their territory. They built the first empires in world history and spread civilization even farther. As new peoples moved into a region, they often adapted elements of the existing culture to their own ways of life. The result was a rich blending of cultural ideas. In an era before mass communications, how might a ruler keep an empire unified?

A ruler might develop a complex bureaucratic structure, in which individual officials have specific tasks and responsibilities. The ruler might offer those officials incentives to keep them loyal to the empire. In that way, the ruler could maintain authority over a larger area without physically being present.

✓ REVIEW & ASSESSMENT RESOURCES

- Unit Synthesis 1
- Unit Test 1
- Sheltered English Unit Test 1

All Levels

Chapter 1

The Rise of Civilization Beginnings–200 B.C.

Chapter Planning Guide

	TEXTBOOK	CORE RESOURCES	VISUAL RESOURCES	MULTIMEDIA
Introduction	pp. 2–3	Block Scheduling Handbook: Ch. 1		Videodisc Segment 1 and Viewing Guide: *The Rise of Civilization*
Lesson 1.1 Before Civilization	pp. 4–7 Through Others' Eyes: *Discovering Lucy*, p. 6	Reading 1.1: *The First Painters* Skills Activity 1: *Reading a Time Line* Geography Activity 1: *Anthropology and Geology*	Art and History 1: *Hall of Bulls, Lascaux Cave* Geography and History 1: *World Domestication*	GHRC 1 Readings: *Women and the Neolithic Revolution; The First Painters of Prehistory* GHRC 1/Videodiscs: Images— *A Paleolithic Grave; Neolithic God with Sickle*
Lesson 1.2 In the Land of Sumer	pp. 8–12 Literature Through Time: *The Epic of Gilgamesh*, p. 9 Map: *The Fertile Crescent*, p. 10 Teenagers in History: *School Days*, p. 11	Reading 1.2: *The Development of Literacy*	Geography and History 35: *Southwest Asia*	GHRC 1 Readings: *A Murder Trial in Sumer; Schooling in Sumer* GHRC 1/Videodiscs: Image— *Sculpture from Ancient Sumer*; Chart—*Development of Cuneiform*
Lesson 1.3 On the Banks of the Nile	pp. 13–16 Map: *Ancient Egypt*, p. 14	Reading 1.3: *Advice for Egyptian Students*	Everyday Life 1: *Irrigation in Ancient Egypt* Geography and History 35: *Southwest Asia*	GHRC 1 Readings: *Egyptian Papermaking and Medical Science; Herodotus on the Egyptian Art of Embalming* GHRC 1/Videodiscs: Images— *Old Kingdom Sculpture; Mummy from Ancient Egypt*
Lesson 1.4 Civilization in India and China	pp. 17–22 Map: *Harappan Civilization*, p. 18 Map: *Early Chinese Civilizations*, p. 19 Geography and History: *Life in the River Valleys*, pp. 20–21	Reading 1.4: *The Indus Valley and Sumer* Writing Project 1: *Determining Relevance*	Geography and History 38: *South Asia*	GHRC 1/Readings: *Harappan Civilization; Yangshao Culture; The Pottery People of Ancient China* GHRC 1/Videodiscs: Images— *Painted Earthenware; Tripod Pitcher*; Maps—*Harappan Civilization; Mohenjo-Daro; Agriculture in Asia*; Video Clip—*Archeology in Action: Mohenjo-Daro*
Lesson 1.5 The Americas	pp. 23–26 Map: *Early Civilizations in the Americas*, p. 24 History in the Making: *Reconstructing the Past*, pp. 28–29	Reading 1.5: *Olmec Civilization at La Venta*		GHRC 1 Readings: *The Olmec; The Chavín Culture* GHRC 1/Videodiscs: Images— *Olmec Stone Carving; Chavín Owl Vessel*; Map— *Bering Land Bridge*
Chapter Investigation and Enrichment	pp. 2–27	Chapter 1 Investigation: *Living History Park of Ancient Cultures* People in World History 1 Explorations in Daily Life 1		GHRC 1/Videodiscs
Review and Assessment	Section 1 Review, p. 7 Section 2 Review, p. 12 Section 3 Review, p. 16 Section 4 Review, p. 22 Section 5 Review, p. 26 Chapter 1 Review, p. 27	Chapter Review Activity 1 Vocabulary Activity 1 Themes Review 1 Section Study Guides 1.1–1.5 Main Idea Activities 1.1–1.5 Daily Quizzes 1.1–1.5 Chapter 1 Test Sheltered English Ch. 1 Test Ch. 1 Test Generator		Audio CDs: Ch. 1 Summary (English and Spanish)

INTRODUCING THE CHAPTER

Textbook pp. 2–3

CHAPTER OVERVIEW

The history of human life on Earth began long before civilizations arose. The first civilizations developed in the world's great river basins, where fertile soil and abundant water made agriculture possible. The Sumerian city-states appeared in Mesopotamia, the Nile gave birth to Egyptian cultures, and the Indus River in modern India and the Huang He in China supported civilizations. Hunters and gatherers migrating from Asia to the Americas also developed sophisticated societies.

PRESENTING THEMES

On the chalkboard or on an overhead transparency, write the following open-ended theme questions.

- **GEOGRAPHY** What environmental features might affect the emergence of civilization?
- **TECHNOLOGY** What technologies might be important in the development of civilization and why?
- **RELIGION** How might religious beliefs show the influence of the natural environment in which they developed?

Have students suggest responses to the questions. For the geography question, students might suggest that the environment must have enough water and fertile soils to support agriculture. For the technology question, students might suggest that the development of tools and techniques needed to build and live in cities are necessary for civilization. For the religion question, students might suggest that people might attach religious significance to natural forces such as the sun and rain, and try to control them through religious ritual. Save the responses. Once students have studied the chapter, you may wish to have them complete the Themes Review, then compare the two sets of answers.

USING THE VIDEO

Segment 1: *The Rise of Civilization*

ENGLISH

Search Chapter 1
Videodisc 1, Side A

SPANISH

Search Chapter 1
Videodisc 1, Side A

Tell students that in this chapter they will examine the factors that led to the emergence of civilization in different parts of the world. Then show Segment 1 of the *World History and Cultures Videodiscs*. This segment looks at the first civilization that emerged in the land between the Tigris and Euphrates Rivers and at the Marsh Arabs, who follow a way of life rooted in ancient traditions developed more than 3,000 years ago.

Before showing the video, ask students to pay attention to the natural environment, particularly the availability of water. To help students grasp the significant points of the segment, have them complete Video Viewing Guide 1.

Key to Ability Levels

All strategies and activities are coded to the following ability levels:

LEVEL 1   **Basic** activities suitable for all students

LEVEL 2   **Average** activities suitable for average to above-average students

LEVEL 3   **Challenging** activities suitable for above-average students

SHELTERED ENGLISH   Activities suitable for students with **Limited English Proficiency**

Additional Resources

BOOKS FOR TEACHERS

Robbins, Lawrence H. *Stones, Bones, and Ancient Cities.* St. Martin's Press, 1990. Looks at ancient humans from Lucy to the advent of writing.

Starr, Clifford. *A History of the Ancient World,* 4th ed. Oxford, 1991. Begins with the origins of civilization.

Wood, Michael. *Legacy: The Search for Ancient Cultures.* Sterling, 1995. Looks at Mesopotamia, China, and India.

BOOKS FOR STUDENTS

Gowlett, John A. J. *Ascent to Civilization: The Archaeology of Early Humans.* McGraw Hill, 1993. Details developments of agriculture, metalwork, the wheel, and writing.

Scarre, Chris. *Smithsonian Timelines of the Ancient World.* Dorling Kindersley, 1993. Discusses art, technology, shelter, and food up to A.D. 1500.

Whitehouse, Ruth, and John Wilkins. *The Making of a Civilization.* Knopf, 1986. Offers an archaeological perspective.

MULTIMEDIA MATERIALS

The Ancient River Civilizations. New York Times. Video, 41 min. Discusses the links between rivers and societies.

Archaeological Dating: Retracing Time. Encyclopaedia Britannica. Video, 17 min. Explains how scientists date artifacts.

In Search of Human Origins: Nova. WGBH Boston. 3 videos, 60 min. each. Looks at human ancestry.

Lesson 1.1 *Before Civilization*

Textbook pp. 4–7

RESOURCES

Pupil's Edition
Through Others' Eyes, p. 6: *Discovering Lucy*

Core Resources
Reading 1.1: *The First Painters*
Skills Activity 1: *Reading a Time Line*
Geography Activity 1: *Anthropology and Geology*

Visual Resources
Art and History 1: *Hall of Bulls, Lascaux Cave*
Geography and History 1: *World Domestication*

Global History Resource Center
Reading: *Women and the Neolithic Revolution*
Reading: *The First Painters of Prehistory*

Videodiscs or Global History Resource Center

Image: *A Paleolithic Grave*

Search Frame 676

Image: *Neolithic God with Sickle*

Search Frame 677

LESSON FOCUS
How did prehistoric peoples live, and how can we learn about them?

OBJECTIVES

After completing this lesson, students will be able to:
- describe how archaeologists study prehistoric peoples;
- identify ways that early humans differed from the humanlike creatures that preceded them;
- explain the impact of the Agricultural Revolution.

HOOK: Link to Today

Discuss the roots of civilization in Paleolithic times.
Ask students what they think are enjoyable camping experiences. Then ask them if they would like living like that on a daily basis. Point out that early humans did live like that—only without the benefit of modern camping equipment.

Ask students to place the Paleolithic period in time. *[about 2.5 million years ago to about 12,000 years ago]* Have students speculate on what might have given pleasure to early humans. *[perhaps children, relationships with others, a favorite food]* Return to the camping concept, pointing out that campsites can reveal interesting things about the people who camped there. Draw a parallel between campsites and archaeological sites. Then display the electronic media image of a Paleolithic grave. **Ask: How do archaeologists study prehistoric times?**
[They uncover the remnants of prehistoric living sites and try to interpret what life was like based on the artifacts that remain.]

Have students read the Through Others' Eyes feature on the discovery of Lucy. Johanson's account should help students appreciate the element of luck involved in finding early hominid remains and help explain why future discoveries may alter our understanding of early hominids. Then help students name some of the methods used by archaeologists to date and to interpret what they find. *[analyzing artifacts, stratigraphy, radiocarbon dating]*

Link to Today. Tell students that some archaeologists have investigated modern American landfills to see what they reveal about American life. Then have students work in small groups to brainstorm significant aspects of modern American culture and to identify representative items they would like anthropologists to uncover 50,000 years from now. Discuss what these items would tell future people about our culture.

DEVELOP

Discuss how Paleolithic and Neolithic cultures met their needs. Ask students to identify basic human needs. *[food, clothing, shelter, possibly need to communicate and to find meaning in life]* Make a chart on the board, with *Basic Needs, Social Groups, Technology,* and *Other Characteristics* listed across the top of the chart, and *Paleolithic, Mesolithic,* and *Neolithic* in the left-hand column. Have students work in small groups to complete the chart. *[**Paleolithic:** People were hunter-gatherers, using stone tools to get food and clothing. They probably lived in small bands. Later in the Paleolithic period, graves show that they placed importance on death. Paintings show ability to think abstractly.*
***Mesolithic:** People developed more specialized stone tools, bow and arrow, fishhooks, fish spears, harpoons, and dugout canoes.*
***Neolithic:** People developed more advanced tools. They settled in villages, which eventually grew more complex.]*
Ask: ***What changes set modern people apart from their hominid ancestors?***
[Students should understand that the development of culture set Homo sapiens *apart from earlier hominids.]*

PROBE

Examine art as an expression of a culture. Have students complete the Global History Resource Center reading on prehistoric painters. Then show students Art and History Transparency 1, and have them complete the accompanying worksheet. Also show students the electronic media image of a Neolithic god. Conclude by discussing what these artworks might have meant to the peoples who created them.

CONCLUDE

Discuss the significance of the change from hunting and gathering to agriculture. Display the Geography and History transparency on domestication, and have students complete the accompanying worksheet. Ask students to discuss what the transparency tells them. They should understand that between about 8000 and 5000 B.C., peoples began to shift from hunting and gathering to domestication and pastoralism as their primary means of obtaining food. They should also understand that most scholars think that the Agricultural Revolution occurred independently in several places.

Tell students that archaeologist William Howells has written that the greatest change in human history from its beginnings to the present has been the change from hunting and gathering to settled agriculture. He goes on to explain that while the change was not dramatic to those who were participating in it, the change was a crucial one because everything else that humans have achieved since that time comes out of the Agricultural Revolution. Discuss Howells's opinion, and then have students write a brief paragraph explaining why Howells called the change to an agricultural way of life the most important change in human history.

EXTEND

Cross-Curricular Connection: *Language Arts*

Have students read *The Caves of the Great Hunters* by Hans Baumann (Pantheon, 1962), about the discovery of the caves at Lascaux, France, in 1940, and report to the class on what they learned.

Cross-Curricular Connection: *Physics*

Have interested students investigate radiocarbon-dating techniques in detail and report to the class. They may also wish to investigate and explain to the class other dating techniques such as obsidian hydration, thermoluminescence, archaeomagnetism, and potassium-argon dating.

MEET INDIVIDUAL NEEDS

Students Having Difficulty/Students Acquiring English

Assign Skills Activity 1 to students needing extra help. They may also benefit from making flash cards of the new terms introduced in the chapter and practicing with a partner until they have learned them.

Linguistic Learners

People in prehistoric times communicated with each other although they had no writing. Have students imagine they are storytellers in a Neolithic village, explaining their group's history to the children of the group. Have them create a brief "story" and relate it to the class.

ASSESS

Review

Have students complete the Section 1 Review. Use answers in the Teacher's Edition, page 7, to assess student mastery of this section.

Lesson 1.2   *In the Land of Sumer*

Textbook pp. 8–12

RESOURCES

Pupil's Edition

Literature Through Time, p. 9: *The* Epic
  of Gilgamesh
Map, p. 10: *The Fertile Crescent,
  c. 2900 B.C.*
Teenagers in History, p. 11: *School Days*

Core Resources

Reading 1.2: *The Development of
  Literacy*

Visual Resources

Geography and History 35:
  Southwest Asia

Global History Resource Center

Reading: *A Murder Trial in Sumer*
Reading: *Schooling in Sumer*

Videodiscs or Global History Resource Center

Image: *Sculpture from Ancient Sumer*

Search Frame 678

Chart: *Development of Cuneiform,
  3000 B.C.–600 B.C.*

Search Frame 687

LESSON FOCUS

*What was life like in Sumer, the earliest
civilization?*

OBJECTIVES

After completing this lesson, students will be able to:
- explain how the environment influenced the development of Sumer;
- identify why cities might have developed in Mesopotamia;
- list the key features of civilization;
- describe how writing first developed.

HOOK

Discuss the geography of the Fertile Crescent. Discuss people's need for water and the methods we have devised to provide a reliable supply. Ask students if American farmers depend on the weather to keep their crops watered. Then ask them how they think life would change if Americans could not turn on a tap to get water.

Next link the need for a reliable water supply to settlement in the Fertile Crescent. Display Geography and History Transparency 35, and ask a volunteer to locate the Fertile Crescent. Direct students' attention to the map on textbook

page 10. Ask students to find the Tigris and Euphrates Rivers on their maps. Have students describe the region's climate. *[Students should note that it is harsh and rivers unpredictably flood the land, enriching it with silt.]*

Ask: What effect did flooding have on the lives of the Sumerians?
[Students should recognize that flooding enriched the soil, making it good for agriculture, but the flooding was also destructive. Building canals and dikes to control the floods required intense cooperation.]

DEVELOP

Discuss the rise of civilization in Sumer. Discuss how the complex irrigation systems, which depended on the cooperation of many people, could have led to the development of towns.

Ask: Why might cities have developed in Sumer?
[Students should recognize that a division of labor probably evolved as farmers grew surplus food under the direction of the priests. Surplus food supported priests, artisans, and merchants. Cities offered protection from other groups.]

Then have students form small groups and develop a chart (web or organizational) focusing on life in Sumer. Major categories should include Economics, Religion, Architecture, Government, and Social Organization. **[Economics:** *economy* based on farming and trade; **Government:** independent city-states ruled by kings or governors; king protected large walled cities; **Religion:** Sumerians were polytheistic, gods represented forces of nature, more often cruel than kindly, each city guarded by a different god; **Architecture:** Ziggurats or great temples honored gods, served as religious and administrative centers; **Social Organization:** strict hierarchy with kings, priests, nobles, and government officials at top; merchants, artisans, and farmers in the middle; and slaves at the bottom] Have groups share their charts with the class.

To increase students' understanding of Sumer, show them the electronic media image of a Sumerian sculpture and have them read about a murder case in Sumer in the Global History Resource Center. Then discuss with students what impression they get of Sumerian life from the image and reading.

PROBE

Explore the innovation of writing in Sumer. Have students describe how writing developed. *[Students should recognize that Sumerians used reeds to make marks on clay tablets. Eventually pictograms came to represent syllables.]* If available, show students the electronic media chart of the development of cuneiform writing so that they can see the changes that took place. Note that writing changed from a way to keep accounts to a way to record activities and ideas. Then have students discuss the feature Teenagers in History on textbook page 11 and the Global History Resource Center reading on Sumer, which provide good examples of how early written records have enriched our knowledge of ancient peoples.

Ask: *How has writing affected the study of history?*
   [Students should note that writing is an essential component of studying history, which depends upon written documents. The kind of detail provided in the practice tablet could not be gained from strictly archaeological evidence.]

Direct students' attention to the feature on the *Epic of Gilgamesh* on textbook page 9.

Ask: *How did the purpose of writing change in Sumer, from initial record keeping to the epic about Gilgamesh?*
   [By the time of the Epic of Gilgamesh, *people began using writing to express emotions, convey abstract thought, and create literature.]*

CONCLUDE

Evaluate Sumer as a civilization. Have students identify key features of civilizations. *[Students should mention development of urban centers, organized system of government, different social classes, large-scale public works, nonagricultural specialists, and artistic and intellectual achievements, particularly writing.]* Create a checklist on the board and ask volunteers to contribute information evaluating how Sumer "measures up" as a civilization. Then perform the same activity, using a Neolithic village as the subject. Conclude by having students write a statement explaining why many historians think of Sumer as the earliest civilization.

EXTEND

Cross-Curricular Connection: *Language Arts*

Have interested students read more of the *Epic of Gilgamesh* and then write a short essay comparing *Gilgamesh* to myths from another culture.

Other Media

Have students search the Internet for electronic sources of information on Sumer. Have students either prepare a list of information sources or communicate with a particular source and report on its offerings.

MEET INDIVIDUAL NEEDS

Students Acquiring English

Pair new speakers of English with fluent speakers to help them learn key vocabulary such as *civilization, specialists, domesticate, irrigation, artisans, canals, polytheism, pessimism, documents, scribes,* and *cylinder.*

Visual-Spatial Learners

Have students research the development of cuneiform writing. Then ask them to present a demonstration to the class, showing the evolution from pictographs to syllables. Have students supply translations of several words.

ASSESS

Review

Have students complete the Section 2 Review. Use answers in the Teacher's Edition, page 12, to assess student mastery of this section.

On the Banks of the Nile

RESOURCES

Pupil's Edition

Map, p. 14: *Ancient Egypt, c. 3000 B.C.*

Core Resources

Reading 1.3: *Advice For Egyptian Students*

Visual Resources

Everyday Life 1: *Irrigation in Ancient Egypt*

Geography and History 35: *Southwest Asia*

Global History Resource Center

Reading: *Egyptian Papermaking and Medical Science*

Reading: *Herodotus on the Egyptian Art of Embalming*

Videodiscs or Global History Resource Center

Image: *Old Kingdom Sculpture of Egyptian Woman*

Search Frame 679

Image: *Mummy from Ancient Egypt*

Search Frame 680

LESSON FOCUS

How did Egyptian civilization develop, and what records did the ancient Egyptians leave?

OBJECTIVES

After completing this lesson, students will be able to:

- explain why peoples first settled in the Nile Valley;
- examine how Egyptian civilization changed after it united under King Menes;
- explain why scribes and schools were important in ancient Egypt;
- describe the accomplishments that Egyptians made during the Old and Middle Kingdoms;
- compare Egyptian and Sumerian civilization.

HOOK: Link to Today

Compare ancient Egypt to the present-day United States. Ask students why ancient peoples first settled along the Nile. *[Students should realize that the marshes around the Nile were attractive to hunter-gatherers and regular flooding of the Nile made the land fertile and suitable for agriculture.]* Display the electronic media image of the Egyptian woman.

Ask: When did the first written records appear in Egypt?

[at least as early as 3000 B.C.]

Ask students how old our country is, and contrast the brief span of American history to the some 5,000 years of Egyptian history. Illustrate this difference on a time line on the board. Tell students that even with great differences between Americans and ancient Egyptians, they will be surprised at the similarities.

DEVELOP

Identify political, social, and educational conditions during the Old and Middle Kingdoms. Remind students that before Menes united Egypt there had been two kingdoms—Lower Egypt and Upper Egypt. Menes, by uniting the two kingdoms, put in place a system that could sustain a larger kingdom.

Ask: What characterized the long period after Lower and Upper Egypt were united?

[stability with only a few periods of disorder]

Next ask students to form small groups and list details highlighting the political, social, and educational conditions during the two kingdoms. *[Political: Menes founded a dynasty; some 30 dynasties rose and fell in ancient Egypt; pharaoh was considered divine. Social: Below the pharaoh were the royal family, the priests, and government officials; below them were the peasants. Educational: People in upper* classes were literate; scribes served an important function; schools appeared during the Middle Kingdom.]

Explore the accomplishments of Egyptians during the Old and Middle Kingdoms.

Link to Today. Have students complete Core Resources Reading 1.3 and ask them what they think of the advice that is given and how it compares to advice a parent would give today. Then discuss the importance of education in Egyptian society. If available, have students complete the Global History Resource Center reading on papermaking and medicine to give students an idea of the sophistication of Egyptian learning.

Ask: *What function did schools serve in Egyptian society?*
[Students should recognize that in the Middle Kingdom, schools trained administrators to run the country.]

Discuss other examples of Egyptian learning. Students should realize that building the Great Sphinx and the pyramids required skillful engineering. Egyptians were also good ship builders and sailors, allowing merchants to trade around the Mediterranean, Red, and Aegean Seas.

PROBE

Explore the role of religion in ancient Egypt. Students should note that Egyptian religion was polytheistic and that Egyptians looked at death as the beginning of a new life in the next world. They mummified bodies and filled tombs with goods so that people could be assured of an afterlife of well-being.

Ask: *What are the important features of Egyptian faith?*
[belief that physical world is an extension of a spiritual world that has many gods; strong belief in an afterlife]

Ask: *How do you think the focus on death has helped archaeologists to learn about ancient Egypt?*
[Egyptians left objects in tombs; inscriptions, biographies, and monuments reveal much about Egyptian life. Mummified bodies yield information about health and disease.]

CONCLUDE

Compare Egyptian civilization to Sumerian civilization.
Show students Geography and History Transparency 35 and have a volunteer identify the site in Iraq of Sumerian civilization. Ask volunteers to briefly review the geography, religion, and writing system of Sumer. [Sumer emerged along the Tigris

and Euphrates Rivers, a site of devastating floods. Religion was polytheistic, emphasizing the gods' cruelty. Pictographs developed into the cuneiform system.]

Then direct students' attention to the map of ancient Egypt on textbook page 14.
Ask: *How did ancient Egyptian civilization compare to Sumerian civilization in the categories of geography, religion, and system of writing?*
[**Geography:** Both were river valley civilizations, but flooding of Nile was more predictable. **Religion:** Gods and goddesses of Egypt reflected the relatively stable and gentle nature of the physical environment; both were polytheistic. **Writing:** The Egyptians developed system of hieroglyphics; used papyrus instead of clay tablets.]

Bring closure to the lesson by having students work in small groups to develop a response to this evaluative question: Which was most important to the development of Egyptian and Sumerian civilization—geography, religion, or writing? Have groups share answers and discuss reasons for their choices.

EXTEND

Cross-Curricular Connection: *Art*
Have students create a display of Egyptian art, using a variety of mediums. Have them be prepared to discuss materials, forms, and meanings of the art.

MEET INDIVIDUAL NEEDS

Visual-Spatial Learners
Have students make a poster illustrating the Egyptian gods and what they symbolize. Have students explain how they did their research.

Logical-Mathematical Learners
Have students construct a time line of ancient Egyptian history through the Middle Kingdom. They may annotate their time line if they wish. Remind them to use B.C. correctly.

ASSESS

Review
Have students complete the Section 3 Review. Use answers in the Teacher's Edition, page 16, to assess student mastery of this section.

Lesson 1.4   Civilization in India and China

Textbook pp. 17–22

RESOURCES

Pupil's Edition
Map, p. 18: *Harappan Civilization,*
  c. 1700 B.C.
Map, p. 19: *Early Chinese Civilizations*
Geography and History, pp. 20–21: *Life
  in the River Valleys*

Core Resources
Reading 1.4: *The Indus Valley and Sumer*
Writing Project 1: *Determining Relevance*

Visual Resources
Geography and History 38: *South Asia*

Global History Resource Center
Reading: *The Harappan Civilization of
  India*
Reading: *The Yangshao Culture of China*
Reading: *The Pottery People of Ancient
  China*

Videodiscs or Global History Resource Center

Image: *Painted Earthenware from
  Yangshao China*

Search Frame 684

Image: *Tripod Pitcher from
  Longshan China*

Search Frame 685

Map: *Sites of Harappan Civilization*

Search Frame 688

Map: *Mohenjo-Daro*

Search Frame 689

Map: *Early Agriculture in Asia*

Search Frame 690

Video Clip: *Archeology in Action:
  Mohenjo-Daro*

Search 1121, Play to 1696
Videodisc 1, Side A
Video Clip 1

LESSON FOCUS
**What features characterized Indus and
Huang He river valley civilizations?**

OBJECTIVES
After completing this lesson, students will be able to:
- explain the conditions that favored the emergence of
  civilization along the Indus River valley;
- analyze the importance of cities to Harappan civilization;
- describe how Neolithic peoples contributed to the cultural
  continuity of China;
- compare development along these rivers to that along the
  Nile and the Tigris and Euphrates.

HOOK
**Discuss the location and importance of cities in the
development of Indus Valley civilization.** Show students the
video clip of the archaeological dig in Mohenjo-Daro. Then, on a

transparency map of South Asia, point out the Indus River and its
tributaries. Then display the electronic media map of Harappan
civilization and refer students to the map on textbook page 18.
**Ask: What was it about the Indus River valley that favored
  the development of civilization?**
  *[Land was easy to clear; the river flooded periodically,
  providing a rich, loose soil.]*

Have students form small groups and list how Harappans met
basic needs of food, clothing, and shelter. **[Food: wheat, barley,
dates, sesame, mustard, some meat; Clothing: cotton; Shelter:
made of bricks]** Have groups share information as you create
a master list on the board. Then display the electronic media
map of Mohenjo-Daro and discuss what it reveals about
Harappan civilization.
**Ask: What characteristics of Harappan culture provide
  evidence that it was a civilization?**
  *[Students should mention that civilization centered
  around great brick cities; urban areas followed same
  layout; water system was well developed; bricks were*

standardized; uniform writing (not yet deciphered) over large territory suggests a centralized government; manufactured goods were produced by specialists; trade existed between cities.]

Have students complete Core Resources Reading 1.4 and the Global History Resource Center reading on Harappan civilization, then discuss how these readings aid in their understanding of Harappan life.

DEVELOP

Discuss life in prehistoric China. Direct students' attention to the map of the Huang He civilization on textbook page 19. Have them locate the Yellow River.

Ask: How did the Yellow River affect the development of civilization?
[Students should recognize that the yellow dust on the plain was washed into the river and deposited as fertile silt when the river flooded. Neolithic peoples settled near hills to escape flooding.]

Then ask students to work in small groups to gather information from the textbook about the Huang He cultures. If available, also display the electronic media images of Yangshao and Longshan pottery. Have students list the information in these categories: social grouping of Yangshao and Longshan cultures, food resources, and pottery. [They lived in groups of related families; grew millet and wheat, hunted, and fished; Yangshao culture made painted pottery, and the Longshan people made black, shiny pottery.]

Ask: What characteristics of Chinese culture can be seen in these Neolithic cultures?
[A reliance on intensive agriculture and possibly strong, clan-based society can be seen.]

PROBE

Examine the effect of geography on the rise of civilization. Have students locate Sumer, Egypt, the Indus Valley, and the Huang He valley on the map on textbook pages 20–21. Have them use a finger to draw a line from one civilization to another on the map. If available, also show students the electronic media maps of Harappan civilization and early agriculture in Asia. [Students should note that all are in similar latitude along great river systems—environments favorable to agriculture.]

Ask: Why did these civilizations develop in river valleys?
[Students should recognize that rivers provided fertile soil, water, transportation—they were a natural place to settle.]

CONCLUDE

Describe technological achievements of these civilizations. Bring closure to the lesson by returning to the focus question: What features distinguished ancient civilizations in the Indus and Huang He river valleys? Create two columns on the board, one for each culture. Ask students to list technological developments for each culture. [**Indus River valley:** weights and measures, copper and bronze tools, careful city planning, elaborate water system, bricks for building; **Huang He valley:** pottery, hoes, grinding stones, potters' wheels]

EXTEND

Cross-Curricular Connection: *Government*
Some scholars believe that uniformity in Harappan culture is evidence of a single political authority. Have students do more research on the details that suggest a uniform culture, such as weights and measures. They will find information on this subject in the Global History Resource Center article on Harappan civilization. Have students present this evidence as a case for or against a single political authority.

MEET INDIVIDUAL NEEDS

Kinesthetic Learners
Have students try to duplicate pottery of the Yangshao or Longshan cultures, with or without the aid of a potter's wheel. Have them display their completed projects.

Intrapersonal Learners
Have students compare the social groupings and dwellings of the Indus Valley civilization and the Huang He civilization. Have them develop a dialogue that two people (one from each culture) might have had regarding the subject of housing.

ASSESS

Review
Have students complete the Section 4 Review. Use answers in the Teacher's Edition, page 22, to assess student mastery of this section.

Lesson 1.5 *The Americas*

Textbook pp. 23–26

RESOURCES

Pupil's Edition
Map, p. 24: *Early Civilizations in the Americas*

History in the Making, pp. 28–29: *Reconstructing the Past*

Core Resources
Reading 1.5: *Olmec Civilization at La Venta*

Global History Resource Center
Reading: *The Olmec of Mesoamerica*

Reading: *The Chavín Culture of the Andes*

Videodiscs or Global History Resource Center
Image: *Olmec Stone Carving of a Jaguar Spirit*

Search Frame 682

Image: *Chavín Owl Vessel from the Andes*

Search Frame 683

Map: *Bering Land Bridge*

Search Frame 686

LESSON FOCUS
How did civilizations in the Americas differ from those of Africa and Asia?

OBJECTIVES
After completing this lesson, students will be able to:
- explain how the Americas became populated;
- describe the Olmec civilization's best-known achievement;
- explain some of the characteristics of civilization in South America.

HOOK
Discuss the Paleo-Indians' journey to the Americas.
Explain that during the Ice Age great sheets of ice covered the Northern Hemisphere. The water level of oceans became lower as the ice formed, and new land was exposed. Show the electronic media map of the Bering land bridge. Discuss how the environment influenced the arrival of humans in the Americas. *[Because land was exposed during the Ice Age, migrating herds and the peoples who hunted them were able to come to the Americas.]*

Then on the map on textbook page 24, have students identify the Olmec and the early Peruvian civilizations. Discuss the extent to which the Americas had been settled by 2000 B.C.

DEVELOP
Identify distinctive features of the Olmec civilization.
Have students describe the environment where the Olmec thrived. *[Climate around Veracruz, Mexico, is warm and wet. Land yields two crops annually.]*

Ask: **What evidence exists that identifies the Olmec as great artists and architects?**
[Ruins of pyramids, temples, plazas, and huge basalt sculptures show that the Olmec produced work of high artistic quality.]

Then display the electronic media image of the jaguar spirit.
Ask: **What does Olmec art suggest about their religious beliefs?**
[a prominent religious role for a creature that was part jaguar and part human; may have been a rain god—many other Indian societies associated the jaguar with rain and fertile soil]

Assign Core Resources Reading 1.5 and the Global History Resource Center reading on the Olmec. Then have students compare the Olmec to other groups of the time.

PROBE
Examine the attributes of ancient Peruvian civilization.
Have students explain how the environment in which ancient Peruvian civilizations arose differed from those of the Olmec.

[*Peruvian civilization developed on a narrow coastal plain subject to droughts and unpredictable rainfall and with few fertile river valleys. Irrigation agriculture had to be supplemented by other food sources.*]

Ask: *What role did trade play in Peru?*
[*established links between coastal villages and inland villages; fish, shellfish, and salt traded for highland crops*]

If available, have students read the Global History Resource Center article on the Chavín culture, and show students the electronic media image of the owl vessel.

Conclude by having students summarize what we know about religion in ancient Peru. [*Peruvians built religious centers that differed significantly from each other—which suggests that each had its own system of beliefs. Chavín de Huantar became a major religious center; the jaguar was an important religious symbol.*]

CONCLUDE

Compare the civilizations of the Americas to those of Africa and Asia. Return to the focus question at the beginning of the lesson: How did civilization in the Americas differ from those in Africa and Asia? Make a two-column chart on the board, listing Africa and Asia at the top of one column and the Americas at the top of the other. Have students organize into small groups to fill in the chart; then call on each group to contribute to the master chart on the board. [*African and Asian civilizations had wheels, draft animals, and iron tools; those in the Americas did not. Civilizations in the Americas had high-yielding plant foods and different foods from those in Africa and Asia.*]

Next ask students to choose a civilization in Asia or Africa that they consider most like the Olmec. Have them write a brief paragraph explaining their choice. Their paragraph should include a description of the cultures' similarities and differences. Once they have finished writing their paragraphs, have volunteers read their paragraphs aloud to the class.

EXTEND

Cross-Curricular Connection: *Art*

Have interested students select a piece of Olmec or Chavín art that they find interesting. Then have them imagine that it was made by a contemporary artist who is holding an exhibit in your community. Have them write a critique of the piece for the arts section of their local newspaper.

Community Resources

Have students find out if any centers for Hispanic culture are located in your area. If so, have them contact a center and find out if it has access to information about the Olmec and Chavín cultures. If not, have students check with a nearby university or library. Have them report their findings to the class.

MEET INDIVIDUAL NEEDS

Gifted Students

Point out that the jaguar was a sacred symbol in both the Olmec and the Chavín cultures. Have students do research to find out if this interest in the jaguar extended to other ancient cultures in the Americas and if the jaguar appears in the folktales of later cultures. Have them note what other animals serve as focal points in religion and myth.

Logical-Mathematical Learners

Have students make a two-column chart to show what is known about one of the ancient cultures in the Americas and what questions are still unanswered. Have them suggest how they might try to investigate questions that they find particularly interesting.

ASSESS

Review

Have students complete the Section 5 Review. Use answers in the Teacher's Edition, page 26, to assess student mastery of this section.

In preparation for the chapter test, you may wish to have students complete all or part of the Chapter 1 Review on textbook page 27, the Chapter 1 Review Activity, and, the Chapter 1 Themes Review.

Understanding the Main Idea

Call on a volunteer to read aloud the *Understanding the Main Idea* paragraph. Then tell students that by studying the tools, art, and other evidence that ancient cultures have left behind, scientists understand those early societies better. The change from hunting and gathering as a means of survival to the development of agriculture led to the creation of complex civilizations. Some of these civilizations developed writing, leaving records for today's scholars.

Presenting Themes

See p. 1B for suggestions on introducing themes.

Using the Time Line

Have students list the time line events in their notebooks. After they have read about each event in the chapter, have students write a paragraph explaining its significance.

Chapter 1
The Rise of Civilization

Beginnings–200 B.C.

Understanding the Main Idea

For most of human existence, human beings lived a precivilized life, gathering plants and hunting to survive. Only when early humans began to live in villages and cultivate plants did it become possible for civilized societies to develop. One sign of the beginning of civilization was the development of writing—and the beginning of recorded human history.

Themes

- *Geography* What environmental features might affect the emergence of civilization?

- *Technology* What technologies might be important in the development of civilization and why?

- *Religion* How might religious beliefs show the influence of the natural environment in which they develop?

On a late fall day about 5,000 years ago, a man lay down to rest in a little hollow on a mountain pass 10,500 feet up in the Alps. He was dressed in animal skins stitched together with tendons. Putting down the wooden backpack he carried, he propped his copper-bladed ax against a rock. Then, exhausted and in pain from several broken ribs, he stretched himself across a flat rock to sleep.

He never awoke. Instead, he froze to death and his resting place filled up with snow, preserving his body through the centuries. During an unusually warm summer in 1991, the snows began to melt. The body of the Iceman, as he has come to be known, emerged once again into the light of day and was discovered by two hikers who had wandered off their path.

The Iceman lived and died before recorded history began. Scholars must build their knowledge of the Iceman's world based on whatever objects of that period have survived to the present. The clothes the Iceman wore, the items he carried with him, and even his body tell scientists a great deal about the time in which he lived. Civilization had not yet begun in the Iceman's Europe. Thousands of miles away, however, along the Nile River and in the

c. 2,500,000 B.C.	c. 8000 B.C.	c. 5000–3000 B.C.	c. 3500 B.C.
▲	▲	▲	▲
Paleolithic Age begins.	Neolithic period begins.	Yangshao culture grows in China.	City-states emerge in Sumer.

Mesopotamian plains, civilized life was taking shape and humanity was beginning to emerge from the shadows of the prehistoric age.

Cave paintings, estimated to be at least 30,000 years old, from the Ardèche region of France

c. 3200 B.C.	c. 2600 B.C.	c. 2500 B.C.	c. 1500 B.C.	c. 850–200 B.C.
▲	▲	▲	▲	▲
Menes unites all of Egypt into one kingdom.	Great Pyramid is built as the tomb for the pharaoh Cheops.	Harappan civilization arises.	Olmec civilization emerges in Mesoamerica.	Chavín de Huantar flourishes.

CORE LESSON PLAN
See pages 1C and
1D for Lesson Plan
1.1.

History and Current Events

Scientists working on the excavation of the Indus River civilizations (see p. 17) had to cope with the fact that much of the critical information about early Harappan civilization lies more than 32 feet under the Indus floodplain, which is far beneath the water table. Archaeologists worked in the mud, while pumps were used to remove some of the underground water.

Critical Thinking Ask students to suggest some of the other factors that might make archaeological excavations difficult or impossible.

ANSWER: Students might list the problem of finding the archaeological site, buildings on top of the site, bad weather, lack of funding, or many other obstacles.

SECTION 1
Before Civilization

FOCUS

- How do archaeologists study prehistoric peoples?
- How did early humans differ from the humanlike creatures that preceded them?
- What was the impact of the Agricultural Revolution?

Although humanlike creatures have lived on Earth for hundreds of thousands of years, written records have only been kept for about the last 5,000 years. The period of human existence before written records were kept is called prehistory. On the basis of a few incomplete remains, scholars try to piece together a picture of what life was like during prehistoric times. New discoveries, however, can greatly alter our understanding of the prehistoric past.

Olduvai Gorge in Tanzania, Africa, is the site where Mary Leakey found Australopithecine remains.

Early Hominids

According to anthropologists, the first hominids, or humanlike creatures, appeared in Africa millions of years ago. In 1974 anthropologist Donald Johanson of the United States and geologist Maurice Taieb of France discovered the remains of a young female hominid in Ethiopia that may be 3 million years old. Calling her "Lucy," Johanson declared her to be a member of the species known as Australopithecus, or "southern ape." In 1978 anthropologist Mary Leakey unearthed even older Australopithecine remains in Tanzania, dating to about 3.7 million years ago.

Although most experts believe there is a relationship between Australopithecines and modern humans, they are not sure what it is. After examining fragments of Lucy's leg and foot, Johanson concluded that she had walked upright. Many scientists believe that an upright posture, which left the hands free to use tools, was a major step in early human development.

This search for the human past relies not only on the work of anthropologists but also on the work of **archaeologists**—scientists who study past cultures by analyzing human remains and **artifacts**, objects made or altered by human beings. Archaeologists have developed special techniques and methods for studying the lives of prehistoric humans. For example, archaeologists try to determine the sequence of past events through **stratigraphy**. Stratigraphy is based on the idea that artifacts found in deeper layers of earth are usually older than those found above them.

Stratigraphy, however, is not always reliable, since the layers may have shifted. Stratigraphy cannot tell archaeologists how old an individual artifact is. To determine the approximate age of artifacts made of organic materials, such as wood or animal bone, archaeologists use **radiocarbon dating**. All living things absorb radioactive carbon 14 from the atmosphere, but after they die the carbon begins to decay and give off radioactive particles. By measuring the amounts of carbon remaining in the object, scientists can roughly determine the age of any plant or animal remains up to 50,000 years old. Other, similar forms of dating also allow scientists to estimate the age of objects that are several million years old.

> *Because prehistoric peoples left no written records, archaeologists must interpret human remains and artifacts in order to understand how people lived.*

The First People

Despite the many findings of scholars, knowledge of early humans and the hominids that preceded them is based on partial remains. Scientists often disagree on the significance of such remains, and future discoveries may lead to theories different from those commonly held today.

Homo sapiens. At present, most scholars believe that by about 200,000 B.C. modern humans, known as *Homo sapiens*, or "thinking man," had begun to appear in Africa. Over the next 60,000 years or so, according to this theory, they spread out of Africa into all the areas previously occupied by early hominid populations. Sometime after 40,000 B.C. they even moved into northern Eurasia and Australia. The earliest evidence of *Homo sapiens* in North America also dates from about 40,000 B.C. According to this picture of the past, once the early humans left Africa they began adapting to their new environments. In the process of adaptation they began to develop the great variety of genetic traits that are present in humans today.

Other scientists, however, hold the view that the first *Homo sapiens* emerged much earlier—several hundred thousand years ago. These scientists believe that *Homo sapiens* arose in several places at different times, thus developing different genetic traits almost from the beginning.

Scholars currently believe that there were two principal types of *Homo sapiens*: Neanderthal (nee-AN-duhr-tawl), which emerged earlier; and Cro-Magnon, which emerged later. Cro-Magnon represents the first truly modern human population, known as *Homo sapiens sapiens*, or "thinking thinking man." Whether Cro-Magnon competed with the earlier Neanderthal, or even hunted them out of existence, is unclear. Evidence from Southwest Asia and Europe suggests that communities of both sometimes lived near each other,

▲ A scientist carefully cleans the well-preserved body of the Iceman.

apparently in harmony. Cro-Magnon was seemingly the more environmentally adaptive, however, for by 30,000 B.C. the Neanderthal record disappears.

Hunters and gatherers. For most of their existence, early humans lived in small bands as hunters and gatherers—eating wild plants, seeds, fruits, and nuts, and obtaining meat from dead animals. Entirely dependent on the environment, early humans were **nomads**. They moved constantly in search of food and water and took shelter where they could, often in caves. Eventually, they learned to hunt animals—an activity that required cooperation. Many experts believe this led them to develop language. They also mastered fire and began to use tools.

Scholars usually divide the era in which humans relied primarily on stone tools into three great stages. The Paleolithic, or Old Stone Age, lasted from roughly 2.5 million years ago to about 12,000 years ago. The Mesolithic, or Middle Stone Age, lasted from about 12,000 to about 10,000 years ago. The Neolithic, or New

THROUGH OTHERS' EYES

Discovering Lucy

In 1974 Donald Johanson and Maurice Taieb led a team of French and American scientists searching for evidence of human origins in northern Ethiopia. In November, at a place called Hadar, where they had already found some early humanlike bone fragments, they found what they were looking for. Johanson later described the experience:

❝I spent the morning of November 30 scanning the ground for fossils with my associate Tom Gray. . . . At midday, under a murderous sun and in temperatures topping 100 degrees, we reluctantly headed back toward camp. Along the way I glanced over my right shoulder. Light glinted off a bone. I knelt down for a closer look. This time I knew at once I was looking at a hominid elbow. . . . Everywhere we looked on the slope around us we saw more bones lying on the surface. Here was the hominid skeleton. . . . The find launched a celebration in camp. . . . We must have been a curious sight to the nomads in the desert, our work tent aglow with butane lamps and the music of 'Lucy in the Sky with Diamonds' blasting from a cassette player. Inspired by the song, we affectionately named the partial skeleton Lucy.❞

Stone Age, lasted roughly from 10,000 to about 5,500 years ago. These terms refer not to ages of time, however, but to the development and use of particular kinds of stone tools.

Paleolithic culture. Scholars agree that one of the factors that sets humans apart from earlier hominids is the development of **culture**—including their customs, art, religious beliefs, and sense of identity. Cave paintings and bone carvings show that early humans were able to think about the world in which they lived. The earliest known examples of paintings are about 40,000 years old. Found on cave walls in Australia, France, and northern Spain, these paintings usually depict animals that were hunted.

Early humans also carved figures out of stone, ivory, and bone. Some of the more famous carvings are those of female figures, known as "Venus" figurines. The purpose of these carved figures is unknown, but scholars have suggested that they involved religious rituals.

The development of culture helped set modern humans apart from earlier hominids.

The Later Stone Age

In the Mesolithic Age, people in parts of Asia and Africa began to develop new methods of adapting to their environment. In particular, they developed more specialized kinds of chipped stone tools. They also invented the bow and arrow, as well as fishhooks, fish spears, and harpoons made from bone and antlers. Some Mesolithic peoples learned to make dugout canoes by hollowing out logs. They used these canoes to travel on rivers or to fish in deeper water.

Technological developments during the Neolithic Age allowed for even more highly specialized tools. People began not only to chip stone tools but also to polish them. This allowed people to produce tools with much sharper edges. Among the new tools they created were awls, wedges, saws, drills, chisels, and needles.

Early human settlement. Meanwhile, in some places people began to give up their nomadic ways and settle down. Climatic changes around 12,000 B.C. in the region of present-day Israel and Jordan, for example, apparently allowed the rapid spread of wild varieties of barley and wheat plants. The people who settled in the area eventually came to depend upon gathering these wild grains, supplementing them with the meat of animals, as well as nuts and other foodstuffs.

So rich was the region that between about 10,500 and 8000 B.C. a new type of human adaptation, the Natufian culture, emerged in parts of the Middle East. The people of the Natufian culture lived in large permanent settlements of rounded mud-brick huts. They stored the wild grain they gathered and, using large stone slabs, they ground it up in order to prepare it as food, perhaps making it into bread or some kind of porridge.

The Agricultural Revolution. As the climate began to grow drier, and the herds of large game animals shifted their migration patterns, between 8000 and 5000 B.C. people began to practice **domestication**—the purposeful adaptation of plants and animals for the benefit of humans. Domestication of plants led to the development of agriculture. Domestication of animals like goats, sheep, pigs, and cattle led to the development of **pastoralism**. Pastoralists, or herders, came to depend on their animals for milk and meat as their primary food source. This shift from food gathering to food producing is called the **Agricultural Revolution**. Most scholars agree that the Agricultural Revolution occurred independently in several places around the world.

From the Neolithic to the Bronze Age. By the late Neolithic period, people in Southwest Asia were creating many new objects to make their lives easier. For example, the art of making pottery allowed them to create vessels to hold food. The ox yoke and the plow made it easier to till the soil. These people also learned to use metal—first copper and then bronze, which is a combination of copper and tin. When people began to make tools from these metals, they left the Stone Age and entered the Bronze Age.

The movement toward civilization. As a result of the developments of the Neolithic period, populations increased. Many of the old hunting-and-gathering settlements turned to farming and grew larger and more complex. By about 9,000 years ago, agricultural villages of up

▲ Reconstruction of a shrine found in Catal Hüyuk, dating from around 6800 B.C.

to several hundred people dotted the hills and valleys of many parts of the world. Some of these villages soon grew into towns. In present-day Turkey, for example, archaeologists have excavated Catal Hüyuk (chah-TUHL hoo-YOOHK), a town that had nearly 3,000 residents more than 8,500 years ago. As such communities grew and became more highly developed, their cultures stood on the brink of becoming what historians term a **civilization**. For most historians, the term *civilization* refers to people living together in complex societies. These societies have several basic elements—production of surplus food, large towns or cities, and divisions of labor in which many workers are specialists. According to these definitions, civilized people are those who have given up nomadic ways in favor of settled community life.

The development of agriculture and the domestication of animals allowed many Neolithic peoples to establish village communities.

SECTION 1 REVIEW

IDENTIFY and explain the significance of the following:

- archaeologists
- artifacts
- stratigraphy
- radiocarbon dating
- *Homo sapiens*
- nomads
- culture
- domestication
- pastoralism
- Agricultural Revolution
- civilization

1. **Main Idea** How can archaeologists study prehistoric peoples who left behind no written records describing their lives?
2. **Main Idea** What set early humans apart from earlier hominids?
3. **Technology** What changes in the Neolithic period transformed people's lives?
4. **Writing to Explain** Write a short essay explaining the greatest consequence of the Agricultural Revolution.
5. **Hypothesizing** Why do you think the development of metalworking was an important step for early humans?

SECTION 2

In the Land of Sumer

FOCUS

- Where did Sumerian civilization develop?
- What were the roles of rulers in Sumerian society?
- What were the consequences of the development of writing?

The first civilizations that we know of apparently developed out of the need to control water supplies for large-scale settled agriculture. The transition to such large-scale farming occurred first on the banks of the Tigris (TY-gruhs) and the Euphrates (yooh-FRAYT-eez) Rivers in Southwest Asia. There, between 5000 and 4000 B.C., Neolithic farmers began to build the first identifiable civilization.

Carved figure from Ur, probably the evil bird-shaped god, Anzu; c. 2000 B.C.

The Geography of Mesopotamia

The first known civilization arose in the Fertile Crescent, a rich area of land between the Tigris and the Euphrates Rivers in present-day Iraq (see map p. 10). These rivers, which both originate in present-day Turkey, flow southeast, and today unite just north of the Persian Gulf to become the Shatt al Arab. This region is also known as Mesopotamia, which is Greek for "land between the rivers."

Conditions in the deserts and hills surrounding the Fertile Crescent were harsh, but the grasses and other plants that grew there were able to sustain tribes of nomadic herders and some agricultural communities. Eventually, however, these peoples migrated into the river valleys, where life was easier than in the surrounding area.

The Tigris and Euphrates supplied the water that was essential to farming, but the yearly floods brought great destruction. The floods were seldom predictable, either in their timing or in their extent. They could quickly turn farm fields into lakes, but they also left behind **silt**—deposits of mud and sand that made the soil rich.

The deposits of silt along the river banks made Mesopotamia an extremely advantageous location for the development of agriculture. But in the southern region of Mesopotamia, known as Sumer, the silt built up. This accumulation frequently caused the river to overflow its banks, sending floodwaters swirling destructively across the land. As rich as the soil was, it could only be used effectively by farmers after they had dug canals and dikes to control the floodwaters, channeling them to the fields. Such projects required intense coordinated labor. This cooperation gave rise to Sumerian civilization.

Sumerian civilization emerged in Mesopotamia, in the fertile land between the Tigris and Euphrates Rivers.

The Sumerian City-States

The first settlers in Mesopotamia lived in small villages along the banks of the rivers. As people banded together to control the floodwaters,

Literature THROUGH TIME

The *Epic of Gilgamesh*

Across cultures and across time, literature often reflects a society's beliefs. The Mesopotamians' live-for-the-day attitude toward daily life was reflected in the Epic of Gilgamesh, *perhaps their greatest literary work. Gilgamesh, who was part human and part god, was the mythical king of the city of Uruk. Gilgamesh traveled to the Land of the Dead to discover the mysteries of life and death, but he never found the immortality he sought.*

Gilgamesh is told several times that it is no use trying to avoid death—everyone must die sooner or later. He is advised to live his life to the fullest instead of searching for immortality. This view, that there was no life after death, was understandable in ancient Mesopotamia. The harshness of the environment and the dependence upon the flooding of the rivers made life very uncertain. Mesopotamians believed that they had to make the most of their life because it could end suddenly the very next day.

Gilgamesh's first advice about life and death came from a wine maiden in the Land of the Dead. Gilgamesh told her:

"Enkidu [Gilgamesh's friend] my brother, whom I loved, the end of mortality has overtaken him. I wept for him seven days and nights till the worm fastened on him. Because of my brother I am afraid of death. Because of my brother I stray through the wilderness and cannot rest. But now young woman, maker of wine, since I have seen your face do not let me see the face of death which I dread so much."

She answered, "Gilgamesh, where are you hurrying to? You will never find that life for which you are looking. When the gods created man they allotted [assigned] to him death, but life they retained in their own keeping. As for you, Gilgamesh, fill your belly with good things; day and night, night and day, dance and be merry, feast and rejoice. Let your cloths be fresh, bathe yourself . . . , and make your wife happy in your embrace; for this too is the lot of man."

Gilgamesh later questions his ancestor Utnapishtim about how to obtain immortality:

"I wish to question you concerning the living and the dead, how shall I find the life for which I am searching?"

Utnapishtim said, "There is no permanence. Do we build a house to stand for ever, do we seal a contract to hold for all time? Do brothers divide an inheritance to keep for ever, does the flood-time of rivers endure? It is only the nymph of the dragon-fly who sheds her larva and sees the sun in his glory. From the days of old there is no permanence. The sleeping and the dead, how alike they are, they are like a painted death. What is there between the master and the servant when both have fulfilled their doom? When the Annunaki, the judges, come together, and Mammetun the mother of destinies, together they decree the fates of men. Life and death they allot but the day of death they do not disclose."

Understanding Literature

Why do you think the Mesopotamians developed a myth like the *Epic of Gilgamesh?*

Gilgamesh wrestling with a lion, c. 1200 B.C.

Understanding Literature

The Mesopotamians' environment was harsh and their lives were uncertain. The myth points this out and tells them to try and enjoy life when they can.

R RESOURCE ACTIVITY

READINGS IN WORLD HISTORY
Reading 1.2
The Development of Literacy

Have students read the information about Sumerian culture and the invention of writing. Then have them complete the questions.

Level 2

R RESOURCE ACTIVITY

WRITING PROJECTS
Writing Project 1
Determining Relevance

Have students complete the activity on deciding what information is relevant to a topic.

Level 2

The Fertile Crescent, c. 2900 B.C.

Center of Civilization The rich lands of the Fertile Crescent arched from the southeastern Mediterranean coast to the Persian Gulf.

Location Along which river were the Sumerian cities of Uruk and Ur located?

critical to knowing how to control the rivers as well as how and when to plant. As the primary organizers of Sumerian society, the priests naturally ruled the city-states in the name of the gods.

Sumerians constructed large buildings to honor the gods. The most important buildings were the great temples, known as **ziggurats**. These ziggurats were both religious and administrative centers. The ziggurats were often enormous, built upon raised platforms and visible from miles away in the flat plains.

From the ziggurats the priests oversaw a complex society, in which people performed specialized tasks. This specialization was possible because, under the direction of the priests, Sumerian farmers raised a surplus of food. The surplus food not only sustained the temples but also freed other people to specialize as merchants and artisans.

As the cities grew wealthy under the priests' leadership, however, they became targets for nomadic raiders. The cities also fought among themselves over water rights. Gradually, war leaders emerged and took control of the cities. These leaders ruled in the name of the city gods, and often acted as the gods' high priests. The rulers were therefore not only war leaders but also the ones responsible for conducting the most important sacrifices to the gods. The Sumerians began to see the war leaders as the representatives of the gods.

As the rulers of the Sumerian city-states came to be seen as kings who ruled with the support of the gods, Sumerian society became a strict **hierarchy**, or graded social order. The king, priests, nobles, and government officials were at the top of society; merchants, artisans, and farmers were in the middle; and slaves were at the lowest level.

Trade. In addition to agriculture, the Sumerian city-states also came to depend on long-distance trade. Perhaps as early as 3000 B.C., Sumerians began trading with other peoples of Southwest Asia for the raw materials that were not available in Mesopotamia—wood, stone, and metals. Trade in these items was financed by the king or the priests, coordinated by merchants, and regulated by laws. One of the most successful merchants was Gudea, a priest who was also the governor of the city of Lagash around 2150 B.C. As a clay tablet revealed:

eventually some of the villages grew into towns. By about 3500 B.C. the first true cities had appeared in Sumer. As the cities grew larger, however, they soon began to compete with one another for water and the other precious resources of the region. Consequently, throughout most of its history, Sumer never developed into a single unified country. It remained instead a land of **city-states**, independent cities with their own governments, orchards, and fields. The major city-states, such as Ur, Uruk, and Kish, had thousands of residents.

Social organization. The early leaders of the cities were priests. Like most Neolithic peoples, the ancient Sumerians saw natural forces—such as lightning, rain, wind, and thunder—as spirits. They believed everything was inhabited by a spirit or god that gave it its shape and function—even the rivers, canals, reeds, and water. The Sumerians believed that priests had specialized knowledge about these natural spirits. Such knowledge was

Teenagers IN HISTORY

School Days

A clay tablet dating from sometime around 2000 B.C. includes the writings of a schoolteacher about the daily activities of a Sumerian schoolboy of that time. The simple, straightforward account sounds familiar even today. In this ancient essay the youth fears being tardy for school because the punishment for being late was to be struck with a cane. In the morning before school, he urges his mother to speed up her lunch preparations so that he will not be late. The composition begins with a dialogue:

66 'Schoolboy, where did you go from earliest days?'
'I went to school.
"What did you do in school?'
'I recited my tablet, ate my lunch, prepared my [new] tablet, wrote it, finished it; then they assigned me my oral work, and in the afternoon they assigned me my written work. When school was dismissed, I went home, entered the house, and found my father sitting there. I told my father of my written work, then recited my tablet to him, and my father was delighted. . . . When I awoke early in the morning, I faced my mother and said to her: "Give me my lunch, I want to go to school." My mother gave me two "rolls" and I set out. . . . In school the monitor in charge said to me: "Why are you late?" Afraid and with pounding heart, I entered before my teacher and made a respectful curtsy.' 99

Cuneiform on Sumerian clay tablet, c. 2400 B.C.

---

66 In the quarries which nobody had entered before, Gudea . . . made a path and thus their stones were delivered in large blocks. . . . Like giant snakes, cedar rafts were floating down the water of the river from Cedar Mountain. 99

Over time Sumerian rulers came to be seen as military and religious leaders; they also financed trade, allowing the city-states to prosper.

Sumerian Culture

Sumerian cities had a rich culture. The Sumerians produced beautiful works of art, made developments in mathematics and music, and created toys for their children and sophisticated board games for adults. They also developed a complex religious structure and a writing system.

Religion. Sumerian religion was **polytheistic**, meaning that Sumerians worshipped many gods and goddesses. The Sumerians saw their gods as sometimes kind, but more often they were cruel. These gods and goddesses ruled the natural elements on which the Sumerians depended. Enlil was god of the air and of life on Earth, Enki was the god of water and of wisdom, and Ki was the Earth goddess, while her brother Utu was the sun god. These gods also guarded individual cities. The city of Nippur, for example, was overseen by the god Enlil, while his son Nanna, who was the god of the moon, guarded the city of Ur.

In addition to these public gods, each Sumerian worshipped a personal god. The personal gods supposedly knew their way around the world of the great gods and could negotiate with

RESOURCE ACTIVITY

GLOBAL HISTORY RESOURCE CENTER
Reading: *A Murder Trial in Sumer*

Print out and distribute the reading. Have students read about this ancient trial. Then have each student create lists of similarities and differences between the system of justice in ancient Sumer and the system of justice in the present-day United States. Finally, ask students to read selected items from their lists, and lead them in a discussion of those points.

Level 3

REVIEW & ASSESSMENT RESOURCES

- Study Guide 1.2
- Daily Quiz 1.2
- Main Idea Activity 1.2

All Levels

the great gods on behalf of their worshippers. To keep the support of the great gods, Sumerians believed they had to obey their own personal gods.

Development of writing. Perhaps the most important Sumerian development was writing. For centuries human memory and verbal instructions had served society well, but as trade expanded Sumerians needed a method of keeping records.

Eventually people began to convey messages using small pictures, called **pictographs**, on clay tablets. The difficulty of using pictographs, however, was that they were complicated to create. Gradually, the Sumerians began simplifying the pictographs until they no longer looked like the objects they represented, and many began to stand for ideas. In addition, some

▲ This Sumerian pictograph from around 3000 B.C. is one of the oldest carved in stone.

of these simplified pictographs began to represent sounds instead of objects. This new script is known as **cuneiform** (kyooh-NEE-uh-fawrm).

While writing was first used to keep accounts, it soon became a way to record the activities and ideas of daily life. Because of its usefulness, traders may have spread the use of writing to other areas. It eventually enabled ideas and literature to develop. By 2450 B.C. writing was well established in Sumer.

Writing was the work of highly trained specialists called scribes. Speed, accuracy, and clarity were prized among scribes, whose competitive nature sometimes led to arguments, such as this one recorded on a clay tablet:

66 *You dolt, numskull, school pest, you illiterate, you Sumerian ignoramus, your hand is terrible; it cannot even hold the stylus [pen-shaped instrument] properly; it is unfit for writing and cannot take dictation. And yet you say you are a scribe like me.* 99

When writing progressed from simple record keeping to a way of recording events, myths, and stories, human beings moved from prehistory into the historical era. Written documents are some of the most important sources that historians use to understand the past.

By developing a written language, Sumerians created a record of their culture and society and entered the historical era.

SECTION 2 REVIEW

IDENTIFY and explain the significance of the following:
   silt
   city-states
   ziggurats
   hierarchy
   polytheistic
   pictographs
   cuneiform

LOCATE and explain the importance of the following:

Tigris River
Euphrates River
Mesopotamia
Sumer

1. **Main Idea** Why did people settle in Mesopotamia?
2. **Main Idea** What advances did the development of writing make possible?
3. **Social Relations** What were the functions and

responsibilities of the rulers of the city-states in Sumerian society?

4. **Writing to Explain** In a short essay explain how trade contributed to the development of writing.
5. **Analyzing** Why did the Sumerians think of their natural surroundings as hostile forces controlled by angry gods and goddesses?

On the Banks of the Nile

Along the lush, life-giving Nile River, Egyptian civilization developed and prospered. The early Egyptians left behind a rich history of monumental pyramids, statues, inscriptions, and documents. Ancient Egypt was a united and powerful kingdom, driven by a complex bureaucracy and supported by a sophisticated culture.

The Great Sphinx, Giza, Egypt

Early Steps Toward Civilization

From the air, the Nile Valley looks like a thin green ribbon snaking across an enormous expanse of barren desert. It is only a few miles wide at any point. In prehistoric times, however, the Nile Valley was wetter and marshier than it is today, and the region was attractive to early hunter-gatherers. There is evidence of human life in the Nile Valley by at least 12,000 B.C. Eventually, they built settlements and turned to farming the rich soil along the Nile.

Life in Egypt depended on the Nile, which flooded at the same time every year—quite unlike the unpredictable and destructive floods in Mesopotamia. As the Nile flooded it watered the fields, and as it receded it left behind a rich deposit of silt that renewed the soil.

Hieroglyphic writing. As early as 3000 B.C. peoples in the Nile Valley began to write using a system of **hieroglyphics** (hy-ruh-GLI-fiks). Hieroglyphic writing used more than 600 signs, pictures, or symbols to indicate words or sounds. At first, Egyptians carved hieroglyphics primarily on monuments and tombs. Later they began to use **papyrus**, a paperlike material made from the papyrus plant, which grew abundantly along the Nile. It was easy to make, lightweight, and could be stored and transported easily.

Solving the hieroglyphic puzzle. Modern scholars learned to read the language of the ancient Egyptians through some clever detective work. In A.D. 1798 a French army invaded Egypt. The next year a French officer discovered a stone with inscriptions in Greek, hieroglyphics, and an Egyptian writing called demotic. This stone, called the Rosetta Stone, provided the key to understanding Egyptian writing.

Scholars guessed that the three inscriptions had the same meaning. In the 1820s a French language expert named Jean François Champollion (sham-pawl-yawn) solved the mystery. Beginning with the Greek, which he could read, he deciphered the hieroglyphics and established the principles by which all other hieroglyphics could be read.

The regular flooding of the Nile River made the Nile Valley fertile, which attracted early peoples.

Theme: Geography

The climate around the Nile provided early Egyptians with an excellent system for farming. The two main tributaries of the Nile, the Blue Nile and the White Nile, received heavy rainfall during the summer. When the Nile overflowed its banks, it flooded the Nile Valley and Delta. In October and November the water receded and the remaining moisture in the soil sustained the crops until harvest, in March or April.

Critical Thinking Ask students why the seasonal cycle of the Nile was ideal for farming.

ANSWER: Students should answer that the Nile floods came at a convenient time, after crops had been harvested.

Egyptian Civilization

Over the centuries strong leaders united early Egyptian settlements to form two kingdoms—Lower Egypt, in the Nile Delta near the Mediterranean Sea, and Upper Egypt, farther south along the Nile Valley. City-states briefly emerged, but Egypt developed a system of government that could sustain larger kingdoms.

A united kingdom. Sometime after 3200 B.C. the king of Upper Egypt, Menes (MEE-neez), united all of Egypt into one kingdom. Menes founded a **dynasty**, or a family of rulers in which the right to rule passes on within the family, usually from father to son or daughter. In ancient Egypt about 30 dynasties rose and fell. Historians have divided this span of time into four periods—the Old Kingdom, the Middle Kingdom, the New Kingdom, and the Late Period. (The New Kingdom and the Late Period will be discussed in Chapter 2.)

The Old Kingdom. Scholars generally date the Old Kingdom from about 2650 B.C. to 2180 B.C. At the top of Old Kingdom society was the **pharaoh**, whom Egyptians believed to be a divine ruler—a god on Earth. Below the pharoah were the royal family, the priests, and the government officials. Beneath them was a lower class of peasants. Gradually, government officials in the upper class became a hereditary group of nobles.

Toward the end of the Old Kingdom, the pharaohs grew weaker and the nobles grew stronger. After about 2160 B.C., a period of civil war brought the collapse of the central authority. Local nobles began to fight each other for power and Egypt went into a period of decline.

The Middle Kingdom. In about 2040 B.C. a strong new line of pharaohs from the city of Thebes united Egypt again. The Middle Kingdom, as this period is called, lasted about three centuries. During this time, Egypt was strong, well organized, and at peace. It was a time of great achievement in art and architecture, as well as a time of literary sophistication. By the 1780s B.C., however, the Middle Kingdom had begun to fall into disorder. The pharaohs' power had weakened, while the nobles and the priests fought to gain more power for themselves. Beginning in the 1760s B.C., Egypt endured increasing attacks by foreign invaders.

After Lower and Upper Egypt united, Egypt entered a long era of stability, broken only by a few periods of disorder.

Ancient Egypt, c. 3000 B.C.

The River's Gift The rich silt deposited by the flooding Nile River provided soil for the thriving farms of ancient Egypt.

? Region What type of land lay to the east and west of Egypt?

Egyptian Society and Culture

Although dynasties rose and fell, Egyptian culture remained stable for many centuries. This stability allowed agriculture, trade, the arts, education, and religion to flourish.

Farming and trade. At the heart of Egyptian civilization was the Nile River. Egyptians

◀ This 4,000-year-old wooden model was carved during the Middle Kingdom to accompany an Egyptian after death.

worshipped the Nile as a life-giving god—as the "Hymn to the Nile" proclaimed:

66 *Hail to thee, O Nile, that issues from the earth and comes to keep Egypt alive! . . . When the Nile floods, offering is made to thee, oxen are sacrificed to thee . . . birds are fattened for thee, lions are hunted for thee in the desert, fire is provided for thee. And offering is made to every other god, as is done for the Nile. . . . So it is 'Verdant [green] art thou!' So it is 'Verdant art thou!' So it is 'O Nile, verdant art thou, who makest man and cattle to live!'* 99

Farmland in Egypt was divided into large estates. Peasants did most of the farming, using crude hoes or wooden plows. The peasants, however, kept only part of the crop. The rest went to the pharaoh for rents and taxes.

Wheat and barley ranked as the chief grain crops. Farmers grew flax to be spun and woven into linen. Ancient Egypt usually produced more food than its people required, and the surplus was traded for other products. Egyptians built sea-going ships that sailed the Mediterranean, Red, and Aegean Seas, as well as along the African coast. On land, merchants joined caravans east into Asia and south into Africa.

Architecture and the arts. Among the most famous ancient Egyptian monuments are the Great Sphinx and the pyramids. Believed by most scholars to be about 4,500 years old, the huge stone figure of the Sphinx, with the body of a lion and the head of a man, may represent the ancient Egyptian sun god. The Egyptian pyramids were built as tombs for the pharaohs. Most of the 80 or so pyramids that still stand are clustered in groups

along the west bank of the Nile. The best known are at Giza, including the Great Pyramid, built about 2600 B.C. as the tomb of the pharaoh Cheops.

The building of these pyramids obviously required skillful engineering. Egyptian architects and engineers were among the best in the ancient world. They built ramps, along which enormous stones were pushed or pulled to raise them above the ground.

BIOGRAPHY The most famous pyramid architect was Imhotep, who designed the famous step pyramid of King Djoser, a ruler of the Old Kingdom. Imhotep not only was a brilliant architect but also became known as a great healer and author. An inscription on the pyramid indicates that Imhotep was "Chancellor of the king of Lower Egypt, . . . hereditary prince, controller of the palace, great seer, . . . builder and sculptor." So great was Imhotep's reputation that long after his death, he came to be worshipped as a god, particularly by scribes.

Imhotep
B I O G R A P H Y

Education. Over time Egypt developed a **bureaucracy**, a complex governmental structure in which civil servants carried out many specialized tasks. The Egyptian bureaucracy required many scribes to keep records. The scribes were all men, and they enjoyed positions of honor. Although women were not permitted to be scribes, some women among the upper classes were probably literate.

During the Old Kingdom, boys were usually trained by their fathers to read and write. After the Old Kingdom fell, many of the skills needed to run a state were lost, and the old system of fathers teaching sons was no longer adequate. By the time of the Middle Kingdom, actual schools began to appear.

Around the time of the first dynasties, Egyptians began building tombs for the burying of their dead. Called by the Arabic word *mastaba*, these tombs had flat tops and sloped sides and were made of mud bricks. Within the tomb, which was usually below the ground, was a chamber for the body and other chambers for burial goods. Over time, people began to build larger tombs, some with as many as 30 chambers.

Critical Thinking Ask students to compare American monuments to dead leaders, such as the Washington Monument, to Egyptian pyramids. Do these reflect similar concepts of death and leaders?

ANSWER: Students might point out that, although American monuments are built to honor leaders, they are not tombs and have no religious significance.

Religion. In Egypt, as in Mesopotamia, people saw life primarily in religious terms, with the physical world as an extension of the spiritual world. While the gods and goddesses of Mesopotamia reflected the unpredictable and violent nature of the local environment, in Egypt the gods and goddesses reflected the relatively predictable gentle nature of life along the Nile River.

The Nile itself was a primary god. Equally important was the sun, which Egyptians saw as a guardian spirit. Each village and district also had its own local gods and goddesses, usually associated with a sacred animal symbol—such as the cat, the bull, the crocodile, or the scarab (a type of beetle). As Egypt became united under the pharaohs, however, these local gods and goddesses were also united.

During the Old Kingdom, for example, local gods associated with guardianship were generally combined into the single great sun god called Re. Under the dynasties of the Middle Kingdom, Re became known as Amon Re, after the chief sun god of the capital city of Thebes. In the same way, all local gods or goddesses associated with vegetation and the fertility of the Nile were gathered into the god Osiris.

During the dynastic era, people believed that the pharaoh was either Osiris or Amon Re, or both, in human form.

Reflecting the constant ebb and flow of the Nile, life for Egyptians was a never-ending cycle of birth, life, death, and regeneration, or rebirth. The Egyptians believed that death was simply the beginning of a new life in the next world. Because they believed the body would be needed in the afterlife, Egyptians developed the process of **mummification**, which involved treating the body with chemicals so that it would dry and remain preserved for centuries. The mummy was placed in a tomb and provided with clothing, food, jewelry, tools, weapons, and servants in the form of sculptured or painted figures.

During the Old and Middle Kingdoms, Egyptians developed an overseas trade, built monuments, created a bureaucracy, and developed complex religious beliefs.

◄ **The Egyptian goddess Bastet had a cat's head with a woman's body. Statues similar to this bronze from around 800 B.C. were worshipped in homes.**

SECTION 3 REVIEW

IDENTIFY and explain the significance of the following:
hieroglyphics
papyrus
dynasty
pharaoh
Imhotep
bureaucracy
mummification

LOCATE and explain the importance of the following:

Nile River
Lower Egypt
Upper Egypt

1. **Main Idea** How did unification change Egypt?
2. **Main Idea** What were some characteristics of Egyptian society and culture during the Old and Middle Kingdoms?
3. **Geography: Location** What drew early peoples to settle in the region of the Nile Valley?
4. **Writing to Create** Imagine that you are an Egyptian pharaoh. In several paragraphs, write the autobiography that will appear in your tomb.
5. **Comparing and Contrasting** How was civilization in Egypt similar to and different from civilization in Sumer?

Civilization in India and China

- What conditions favored the emergence of a civilization in the Indus River valley?
- Why were cities important to Harappan civilization?
- How did Neolithic peoples contribute to the cultural continuity of China?

Uncovering information about life in early India and China has been more difficult than learning about ancient Mesopotamia or Egypt. Scholars are still unable, for example, to read the written records of the Indus River valley civilization. Like Mesopotamia and Egypt, the first cultures in India and China developed in the basins of great rivers. While the first Indian civilization developed into a complex urban culture early on, the first Chinese cultures did not develop cities until much later.

Yangshao pottery bowl

Geography of the Indus Valley

The first civilization to arise on the Indian subcontinent was in the Indus River valley of present-day Pakistan. The Indus Valley is a broad plain hemmed in by desert to the east and mountains to the west. Geographically, it is much like the valleys of the Nile, the Tigris, and the Euphrates. The land was dry, and people could easily clear it for settlement without the use of iron tools.

The flooding of the river provided both the water essential for agriculture and the enriching silt that replenished the soil. With its source in the Himalayas, the Indus River flooded when the melting mountain snows rushed into the river. It also flooded when the **monsoons**, seasonal rain-bearing winds, brought heavy rains to the western Himalayas.

By about 3000 B.C. people were living along the Indus River in small, widely scattered villages, which consisted primarily of mud-brick houses. Although these people mainly used stone tools, they were also beginning to use metals, such as copper. As farmers began to produce surplus food, cities began to develop, and by about 2500 B.C. civilization had arisen in India.

*D*ry land, periodic flooding, and a rich, loose soil made conditions favorable for the development of a civilization in India.

Indus Valley Cities

The two most important cities in the Indus Valley civilization were Mohenjo-Daro on the lower Indus, and Harappa, 400 miles to the northeast. Harappa has provided archaeologists and historians with so much evidence of early Indus Valley life that they have named the civilization in this area **Harappan civilization**.

From about 2300 to 1750 B.C. Harappan civilization developed in an area larger than all of Sumer. Over this vast expanse of territory existed a civilization that was remarkably uniform. Weights and linear measures were the same throughout the region. The people living in the Harappan area also used the same types of copper and bronze tools. Some scholars believe that this suggests there may have been some sort of political unity in the region.

Daily Life

Scientists have discovered some of the early village sites along the Indus River. One such village was Amri, located a little less than a mile from the Indus, just beyond the flood line. The oldest artifacts found were handmade pottery. During a later phase of development, people began using a pottery wheel to make pottery. They also made copper and bronze objects. During the final phase of development in Amri, people built mud-brick buildings and made painted pottery that depicted domesticated animals.

Critical Thinking Ask students why Amri was located beyond the flood plain of the Indus river.

ANSWER: Students should suggest that the village was located beyond the flood line so that it would not be flooded.

Harappan Civilization, c. 1700 B.C.

HINDU KUSH
Khyber Pass
HIMALAYAS
Jhelum River
Ravi River
Chenab River
Indus River
Sutlej River
Harappa
Kalibangan
INDIA
Mohenjo-Daro
THAR DESERT
Lothal
Narmada River
ARABIAN SEA

0 100 200 Miles
0 100 200 Kilometers
Lambert Conformal Conic Projection

Farming and Trade Harappan farmers and artisans provided produce and merchandise for trade.

? Movement What geographical feature allowed merchants to cross the Hindu Kush mountains?

The cities of Harappa and Mohenjo-Daro were well planned and had a sophisticated design. Each city had a population of about 35,000—all of whom lived in an area roughly a mile square. The cities each had a strong central fortress, or **citadel**, to the west, while to the east lay the houses and public buildings. Each city was laid out in a grid pattern, so that streets intersected at right angles.

Harappan houses faced inward, on open interior courtyards, to ensure privacy. The walls along the main street were solid brick, broken only by openings for drainage chutes. Almost every house had its own bathroom, with brick floors and covered drains that carried wastewater to the main street drains of the city's water-removal system. Some homes had their own wells, while others used public water sources.

The buildings of Harappa and Mohenjo-Daro were designed for practical use. Many of these buildings were constructed with durable burnt bricks. These bricks were baked in kilns, or ovens, which made them far stronger than the sun-dried bricks commonly used in Mesopotamia.

Harappan Culture

Although Harappan civilization was quite urbanized, farming was still essential to the survival of city residents. Wheat was the most important crop, but farmers also grew barley, peas, dates, and mustard seeds. Harappan people also kept many animals, including cattle, pigs, goats, and sheep.

City-dwellers worked primarily in industry or trade. Indus Valley artisans produced fine articles, including excellent cotton cloth, painted pottery, artistic bronze sculpture, copper and bronze weapons and tools, and gold and silver jewelry. As early as 2500 B.C. they may have traded these goods with Mesopotamian merchants.

People of the Harappan civilization also developed a written form of language. Pictographs dating from about 2300 B.C. have been found, but scholars have not yet deciphered the language. Although additional writing has been found on clay pots and fragments, no connection with any other language has been established.

No Harappan temples, shrines, or religious writings have been found, but scholars believe that the people of the Indus Valley worshipped a great god and used images of certain animals, such as the bull, the buffalo, and the tiger, in religious rituals. Other evidence indicates that a mother goddess symbolized fertility.

The Harappans buried their dead with personal possessions, such as pottery or jewels. Some were buried in large brick chambers, but most were buried outstretched on their backs with their heads pointing north. At the city of

▶ **This small clay figure represents the mother goddess of Harappa.**

▶ The Huang He transports about 1.5 billion tons of silt to the Yellow Sea each year.

Lothal, about 400 miles southeast of Mohenjo-Daro, archaeologists have found several double graves, each containing a male and female skeleton.

Despite this rich and thriving culture, the unity of Harappan civilization shattered sometime around 1500 B.C. Scholars today are still not exactly sure why this occurred. For many years scholars believed that the civilization had been destroyed by invaders. More recently some have suggested that changes in the course of the Indus River disrupted agriculture. Other scholars believe that major earthquakes and flooding struck the region about 1700 B.C. The discovery of several unburied skeletons, together with homes and personal belongings hastily abandoned, seems to indicate some disastrous event at Mohenjo-Daro. The evidence needed to verify this theory, however, remains incomplete.

Harappan civilization centered around great brick cities, where artisans crafted tools and jewelry and wove fine cloth for trade.

Civilization in China

During the Neolithic period, one of the first settlements in China was along the Huang He, or Yellow River, which flows through the great plain of northern China. Nomadic peoples settled in areas between wooded hills and swampy lowlands, where enough plants and animals existed to keep them alive whether or not their farming was successful.

The climate of the Huang He valley. Like the other ancient civilizations, Chinese civilization originated in regions with fertile soil and plentiful water supplies. Over many centuries the winds had deposited a fine yellow dust along the North China Plain. This dust formed into a very rich soil called **loess** (LES), which in some places formed a layer 350 feet thick.

This fine yellow dust was also carried along in great quantities by the Huang He, which got its name from the yellow silt created by the dust.

Much of the silt was deposited on the riverbed, which made the Huang He too shallow for navigation, though still useful for irrigation, and created new lowland.

Every few years, after heavy rains the Huang He would overflow its banks in destructive floods.

Text continues on page 22.

Early Chinese Civilizations

Cradle of Civilization Major archaeological finds along the Huang He have shown evidence of settled villages existing as early as 6000 B.C.

❓ **Location** In what mountain range does the Huang He originate?

Map Answer
Amne Machin Shan

Theme:
Geography

In early Neolithic China, two patterns of agricultural development emerged as early as 5000 B.C. In northern China, people relied on drought-resistant crops like millet, and supplemented their diets with green vegetables and fruits, such as the apricot and pear. In southern China, people grew rice and ate fish and native water plants. The difference between the agriculture in these two areas still exists today.

Critical Thinking Ask students to make educated guesses about how the climates of northern and southern China might be different.

ANSWER: Based on the crops, students might suggest that southern China has a wetter climate, while northern China is drier and subject to droughts.

Theme: Geography

Living along the Nile, the Egyptians were some of the earliest developers of water transportation. An image on a pot dated from around 3200 B.C. shows that Egyptians were already using the sail to travel on the Nile. Early boats floated downriver, and then their captains could raise a sail and be carried back upstream by the wind, which blows most often from the north. Rafts and barges carried goods up and down, and ferries traveled across the river and along the canals. Boats on the Nile were also used by the pharaohs as a quick way to send messages to other parts of their domain.

Critical Thinking Ask students to consider how the geography of the Nile Valley and the development of water transportation might have contributed to the rise of a unified government in Egypt.

ANSWER: Students should note that the use of boats for transportation would have made it easier for a leader to impose his or her authority on points along the river. This would probably have helped a leader to dominate the entire population of Egypt.

Geography AND HISTORY

Life in the River Valleys

Although the first four civilizations all flourished in relation to rivers, the different characteristics of the rivers affected the peoples along their shores in various ways.

The Nile, for example, is a rather slow-moving river that floods with great regularity. The climate in Egypt is sunny and dry, and in ancient times the area was also protected from outsiders' raids by the deserts surrounding the river valley. The lushness and relative safety of this area led to the development of a culture with a basically positive outlook. The early Egyptians' religion indicated that they had a strong belief in an afterlife, and the monumental tombs they built for the dead indicated that their leaders had the confidence to undertake projects that would require decades to complete. Overall, the stability of the climate and the river's flooding was strongly reflected in Egyptian culture.

The geography of the river valleys was also reflected in Sumerian culture, but in a quite different manner. In the land between the rivers, the people were at the mercy of raging floods, drought, starvation, and bandits. From these harsh conditions a culture arose that reflected the uncertainty of life. The inhabitants of the Tigris and Euphrates River valley believed that they had been

River Valley Civilizations, c. 2500 B.C.

The Birth of Civilizations The earliest civilizations arose in similar latitudes and along rivers that nourished agriculture.

Sumerians built this giant ziggurat in the 1100s B.C.

created to serve the gods, but that the gods could not necessarily be trusted to protect them. Sumerian ziggurats were not luxurious preparations for a trip to the afterlife but were built as houses and shrines for the angry gods of Sumerian culture in an effort to appease them.

Scholars have much less information about the other two major river valley civilizations. We do know that the waters of the Indus River played a great role in the cities of Mohenjo-Daro and Harappa. Both cities had highly advanced methods of plumbing with a complex system of cov-

ered drains and sewers. Houses were serviced by wells and had bathrooms and latrines. The drainage system that served these facilities in the Indus towns was an engineering feat unrivaled anywhere in the ancient world until the time of the Roman Empire, nearly 2,000 years later.

Civilization along the Huang He faced droughts, cold, and destructive flooding. Perhaps it was the power of the river that required the method of building structures using stamped earth. Pounding thin layers of earth within a movable wooden frame made a product as hard as cement. This building technique, which was first found in Longshan sites, has been used throughout China's history.

? **Location** Between which degrees of latitude did all the early river civilizations lie?

Linking Geography and History

1. What characteristics did the early river valley civilizations have in common?

2. How did geography influence the cultures of Egypt and Sumer?

3. What role did geography play in architecture along the Huang He and Indus River?

Linking Geography and History

1. complex civilizations that relied upon the rivers

2. The overall stability of the environment in Egypt led to a culture with a generally positive outlook, while the harsh conditions in which the Sumerians lived led them to have a more negative outlook.

3. Waters from the Indus were used to form the basis of the advanced plumbing systems of the early Harappan civilizations. Along the Huang He, people created stamped-earth structures that could survive the flooding of the river.

Map Answer
between 40° and 20° north

✓ **REVIEW & ASSESSMENT RESOURCES**

- Study Guide 1.4
- Daily Quiz 1.4
- Main Idea Activity 1.4

All Levels

For significance, see the
following pages:
monsoons (p. 17)
Harappan civilization
(p. 17)
citadel (p. 18)
loess (p. 19)

For locations, see the
maps on pp. 18 and 19.

1. The land was dry and
easily cleared, and mon-
soons and melting snow
flooded the river, leaving
silt that made land rich
for farming.
2. Harappan cities were
well planned and had
sophisticated wastewater
drains. Each city had a
citadel and a population
of around 35,000.
3. Their development of
stamped earth construc-
tion, a writing system,
religious practices, intensive agriculture, and
strong family ties would
be features of later
Chinese civilizations.
4. Articles should explain
that archaeologists have
discovered artifacts that
show what types of
buildings were con-
structed, what tools were
used, and that a written
language existed.
5. The river's floods were
devastating; the climate
was severe, with long,
cold winters and short,
hot summers; and dust
storms and unpredictable
rains further discouraged
settled civilizations.

Raging floodwaters destroyed everything in their path and turned once usable farmland into waterlogged swamps. Such destructive floods led the ancient Chinese to nickname the Huang He "China's Sorrow."

The climate in the valley of the Huang He was severe. Winters were long and cold, summers short and hot. Dust storms swept across the valley in the spring. Rainfall was also very unpredictable, and heavy rains alternated with periods of drought and famine.

Yangshao and Longshan cultures. One of the earliest prehistoric cultures in China is called the Yangshao, after the northern village where its artifacts were first discovered. The Yangshao culture lasted from about 5000 to 3000 B.C. and is recognized mainly for its painted pottery. This pottery is decorated with pictures of fish, animals, and plants.

People in the Yangshao culture were farmers, although they also hunted and fished. Yangshao farmers relied solely on human labor, tilling the soil with hoes since they did not yet have the plow. They grew a type of grain called millet and raised pigs and sheep. In addition, farmers grew hemp to make into fabric, and some evidence suggests that Yangshao farmers even raised silkworms.

◀ This animal-shaped pot was made out of clay by a Yangshao artist in the Neolithic Age.

Yangshao peoples built their houses in clusters, which some archaeologists believe suggests that people lived in groups of related families. If this interpretation is correct, it would be the earliest example of the strong, clan-based type of society that was a feature of later Chinese civilization.

The Yangshao culture was followed by the Longshan culture, which lasted from about 3000 to 2000 B.C. The highly polished, delicate black pottery of the Longshan culture has been found throughout the North China Plain, the Yangzi River valley, and the southeastern coast of China.

The cultures of China developed in relative isolation. Many scholars believe that some contact with other cultures may have filtered across the mountains and deserts that separated China from the Middle East, but it seems that by the end of the Neolithic period, the peoples of China had already begun to develop a writing system and complex religious practices that would form the basis for a distinct Chinese culture.

Chinese Neolithic cultures established the patterns of strong families and intensive agriculture that would be part of Chinese civilization for centuries.

SECTION 4 REVIEW

IDENTIFY and explain the significance of the following:
  monsoons
  Harappan civilization
  citadel
  loess

LOCATE and explain the importance of the following:
  Indus River
  Mohenjo-Daro
  Harappa
  Huang He

1. *Main Idea* Why did civilization emerge in the Indus Valley?
2. *Main Idea* How would you characterize Harappan cities?
3. *Geography: Human-Environment Interaction* How did Neolithic peoples influence later patterns of Chinese civilization?
4. *Writing to Explain* Imagine that you are an archaeologist. Write a short

article for an archaeological journal explaining how you are able to put together a picture of what life was like in the Indus Valley when you cannot decipher the Harappan system of writing.
5. *Hypothesizing* Why do you think early Chinese peoples did not build great cities along the Huang He like the cities of Harappan civilization?

The Americas

- How did the Americas become populated?
- For what is Olmec civilization best known?
- What were some characteristics of civilization in South America?

In the coastal areas of Peru and in Mesoamerica, civilization emerged between 1800 and 1500 B.C. Although civilization developed a few centuries later in the Americas than it did in Eurasia, these early American societies left behind sophisticated ceremonial centers and stunning works of art.

Giant carved head, created by the Olmec of central Mexico

The Earliest Americans

The first humans probably migrated to the Americas from Asia between 50,000 and 14,000 years ago, during the time of the last **Ice Age**—an era when ice covered more of the earth's surface than it does today. At that time there was a land bridge between Alaska and Siberia. Early hunting peoples may have been following the large game animals—woolly mammoths, steppe bison, wild horses, and caribou—that they depended on for meat. In addition to hunting, these nomadic peoples, who some archaeologists call Paleo-Indians, lived by fishing and gathering wild plants.

Paleo-Indians. Perhaps to escape the harshness of the cold arctic climate, many groups of Paleo-Indians kept moving south. By 9000 B.C. and possibly much earlier, humans had spread throughout the Americas. According to an American Indian creation myth:

> **"**For a long time everyone spoke the same language, but suddenly people began to speak in different tongues. Kulsu [the Creator], however, could speak all languages, so he called his people together and told them the names of the animals in their own language, taught them to get food, and gave them their laws and rituals. Then he sent each tribe to a different place to live.**"**

When the last Ice Age ended around 7000 B.C., the climate became warmer and caused great environmental changes. Some scholars believe that these changes led to the rapid extinction of many of the animals on which Ice Age hunters had depended. To survive, Paleo-Indians gathered more plants, caught more fish, and hunted smaller animals.

Farming in the Americas. Paleo-Indians learned to farm sometime around 7000 B.C. Although Mesoamerica (present-day Central America and central and southern Mexico) was rich in wild edible vegetation, people also grew beans, pumpkin, squash, and chili peppers. The most important domesticated plant in Mesoamerica was **maize**, or corn, which may have been grown as early as 6600 B.C. Farther south, the agriculture of Andean peoples was based primarily on the potato.

Early Civilizations in the Americas

The Olmec Lowlands

Bay of Campeche
Acula R.
Tres Zapotes
San Lorenzo
La Venta
Tonalá River
Coatzacoalcos R.
Uspanapa River
Gulf of Tehuantepec
Azimuthal Equal-Area Projection

Gulf of Mexico
Yucatán Peninsula
Mesoamerica
CARIBBEAN SEA
PACIFIC OCEAN
0° Equator
ATLANTIC OCEAN
Marañón R.
Amazon River
ANDES MTS.
SOUTH AMERICA
Santa River
Chavín de Huantar
Casma
Kotosh
El Paraíso (c. 1800 B.C.)

Olmec, c. 1200 B.C.–400 B.C.
Chavín, c. 900 B.C.–200 B.C.

0   500   1,000 Miles
0   500   1,000 Kilometers
Azimuthal Equal-Area Projection

Cradle of Rivers Like the early civilizations of Asia and Africa, the Olmec and Chavín cultures in the Americas arose near lands watered by abundant rivers.

❓ Location Along which rivers did Chavín de Huantar develop?

Maize, in particular, was more productive than the rice, wheat, or millet that had sustained the civilizations of Asia and Africa. Even though the plow, the wheel, and iron tools were unknown in the Americas, farmers in Mesoamerica and the Andean region produced the large food surpluses that allowed civilizations to develop.

After crossing a land bridge from Asia, Paleo-Indian peoples gradually migrated southward until they had spread throughout the Americas.

The Olmec

Many scholars believe that the first civilization to arise on the North American continent was in Mesoamerica. This civilization, which archaeologists call the Olmec, developed sometime around 1500 B.C. from small settlements that dotted the swampy lowlands of what is now the Mexican state of Veracruz.

In Mesoamerica there was abundant rainfall and the warm climate allowed crops to be grown year-round. During the rainy season, the rivers flooded and deposited silt along their banks, much the same way as on the Nile. The Olmec heartland was therefore one of great agricultural potential.

San Lorenzo and La Venta. Two Olmec archaeological sites, San Lorenzo and La Venta, provide most of the knowledge that scholars have about the Olmec. Settlers first built small villages in the area of San Lorenzo around 1700 B.C. By about 1500 B.C. the Olmec had built a huge gravel platform, upon which they constructed San Lorenzo itself. The site consisted of small pyramids, a grouping of earthen mounds, and a rectangular courtyard, which archaeologists believe may have been the earliest ball court in Mesoamerica.

At this site, which flourished between 1200 and 900 B.C., the Olmec placed ten huge heads carved of basalt, a type of rock. These heads may have been portraits of Olmec rulers. Scholars believe that San Lorenzo was a ritual center to which people came from miles around.

▶ This Olmec carving is thought to represent a ruler.

At La Venta, the other major Olmec site, archaeologists have discovered ruins of an extensive complex, including a pyramid, temples, and plazas, as well as the remains of monumental stone sculptures. Radiocarbon dating has established that La Venta reached its height between 1100 and 600 B.C.

Olmec society and culture.

Olmec society was divided into at least two classes of people. Most people were farmers, who tilled the poorer soil of higher elevations to raise two crops of maize per year. The elites of Olmec society were a small minority that had power over governmental, military, and religious matters. These elites controlled the richer lands along the rivers, which produced a much larger harvest than the highlands.

The artwork that the Olmec created suggests that they had a strong religious belief in a creature that was part jaguar and part human. Some scholars believe that the Olmec worshipped this animal as a rain god, since many other ancient American Indian societies associated the jaguar with the notions of rain and the fertility of the soil. The Olmec may have worshipped this rain god in order to persuade him to control precipitation in this rainy part of Mexico.

Whatever the purpose of their art, Olmec civilization was one of great artistic achievement. As scholar Miguel Covarrubias has noted, the region is still rich in artifacts:

▲ This Olmec baby figurine is carved of jade.

66Everywhere there are archaeological treasures that lie hidden in the jungles . . . , burial mounds and pyramids, masterfully carved colossal monuments of basalt, splendid statuettes of precious jade, and sensitively modeled figures of clay, all of an unprecedented [never before seen], high artistic quality.**99**

The end of Olmec society.

Scholars disagree about how the Olmec civilization came to an end. Some scholars believe that Olmec civilization ended in violence. They suggest that San Lorenzo was destroyed around 900 B.C. and La Venta was crushed around 400 B.C. These scholars have not been able to determine who the destroyers were, however.

Other scholars believe that Olmec society came to a more gradual end. They suggest that San Lorenzo declined slowly from about 900 to 700 B.C., and that La Venta faced a similar fate between 450 and 325 B.C.

Olmec civilization is best known for its great ceremonial centers with their massive sculptures.

🔶 South America

In Peru a great prehistoric civilization arose in a harsh and difficult environment. There were few fertile river valleys similar to those in other regions where civilization developed. The narrow coastal plain of Peru was subject to severe droughts and unpredictable rainfall. In this environment, crops from irrigation agriculture had to be supplemented with other food sources.

Early Andean communities. Scholars believe that by around 8500 B.C., hunter-gatherers lived in small settlements on this coastal plain of Peru. They also fished and farmed to supplement their diets. Over time villagers developed links to others farther inland, exchanging fish, shellfish, and salt for highland crops, such as cotton, and bird feathers.

Early Andean people did not build vast cities, but they did construct numerous religious centers 1,000 years before the flowering of Olmec culture in Mexico. Their sites include pyramids, sunken

**Theme:
The Arts**
The Olmec created art in a variety of forms. In addition to the colossal sculptures like those found at San Lorenzo, they created stone altars, axes, small sculptures, figurines, and pendants. Made of blue-green jade, basalt, and other stones, the sculptures were usually three-dimensional, with curving lines. Olmec artisans made the sculptures by carving, cutting, and drilling, using wet sand and a reed. Occasionally, pottery and wood objects were made.

Critical Thinking Ask students why scholars might know less about Olmec wood objects than Olmec stone objects.

ANSWER: Students should suggest that wood does not preserve well in the wet climate of Central America.

SECTION 5 REVIEW ANSWERS
(p. 26)

IDENTIFY
For significance, see the following pages:
Ice Age (p. 23)
maize (p. 23)

LOCATE
For locations, see the map on p. 24.

plazas, residences, and storage areas. Their purpose may have been to show the wealth and status of the people who built them.

By 1800 B.C. a new style of temple architecture had appeared at El Paraíso, near the present-day city of Lima, Peru. There the temple-builders constructed at least six temple buildings laid out in a U-shape around a giant plaza. Although scholars know very little about the religious beliefs of the people who used these temples, the differences in architectural styles suggest that the people of each area may have had their own system of beliefs.

Chavín de Huantar. One of the best-known sites of prehistoric Andean civilization was discovered in A.D. 1919 near the small village of Chavín de Huantar. Located in the foothills of the Andes Mountains, Chavín stood at the crossroads of several trade routes linking the mountains with the coast. This strategic location may have been why the site developed into a ceremonial center of some importance. Its distinctive culture spread over a wide area along the northern coast and the northern highland region of Peru.

Chavín de Huantar flourished between about 850 and 200 B.C. In its early years, Chavín was a small village and shrine, but by the 300s B.C. the village had become a rapidly growing town,

◄ A Chavín artist decorated this ceramic vessel with carved images of snarling cats.

probably famous over a large area for its religious shrine and its production of religious objects. Artisans in Chavín decorated seashells with feline patterns and made ceramic objects used for religious purposes.

Some scholars believe that the Andean people had two major gods. The first was a "smiling god," a half-human, half-feline creature with the body of a man and head, hands, and feet like a jaguar. The other was a "staff god," a snarling manlike figure wearing a serpent headdress and holding two staffs with feline heads and jaguar mouths at their ends. Like the Olmec, the Andean people also considered the jaguar to be an important religious symbol.

Chavín represents a significant achievement in art, technology, and culture. For unknown reasons, however, it disappeared rather abruptly from the archaeological record around 300 B.C.

*A*long the narrow coastal plain at the base of the Andes Mountains, the Chavín made great achievements in arts, technology, and culture.

SECTION 5 REVIEW

IDENTIFY and explain the significance of the following:
  Ice Age
  maize

LOCATE and explain the importance of the following:
  Mesoamerica
  San Lorenzo
  La Venta
  Andes Mountains

Chavín de Huantar

1. *Main Idea* How did humans first come to the Americas?
2. *Main Idea* What were the greatest accomplishments of Olmec civilization?
3. *Geography: Location* What factors made the conditions right for the rise of civilization in Mesoamerica?

4. *Writing to Describe* Imagine that you are an archaeologist working in Peru. Write a journal article describing the achievements of the Chavín civilization you are uncovering.
5. *Hypothesizing* What factors might have hindered the development of civilization in areas north of Mesoamerica?

Review

On a separate sheet of paper, complete the following exercises:

WRITING A SUMMARY
Using the essential points in the text, write a brief summary of the chapter.

REVIEWING TERMS
From the following list, choose the term that correctly matches the definition.

civilization
cuneiform
dynasty
loess
maize
pastoralism

1. family of rulers in which the right to rule passes on within the family, usually from father to son or daughter
2. Sumerian form of writing in which simplified pictographs represent sounds or ideas instead of just objects
3. corn; was the most important agricultural crop in Mesoamerica
4. highly organized society with complex institutions and ideas that link many people together
5. very rich soil that was formed as the wind deposited a fine yellow dust across the North China Plain, then carried by floodwaters down the Huang He

REVIEWING CHRONOLOGY
List the following events in their correct chronological order.

1. Harappan civilization prospers in India.
2. Menes unites Upper and Lower Egypt into a single kingdom.
3. Olmec civilization arises in Mesoamerica.
4. Cities develop in Sumer.
5. The Yangshao culture emerges in China.

UNDERSTANDING THE MAIN IDEA
1. What was the Agricultural Revolution, and why was it important?
2. Where and how did Sumerian civilization develop?
3. What achievements did the Egyptians make during the Old and Middle Kingdoms?
4. How did Neolithic cultures contribute to the cultural continuity of China?
5. Where and how did civilization arise in Mesoamerica and South America?

THINKING CRITICALLY
1. *Comparing* What geographical factors allowed for the development of civilization in the river valleys of Mesopotamia, Egypt, India, and China?
2. *Synthesizing* What was the significance of the development of writing for ancient civilizations?

Building Your Portfolio

Complete the following activities individually or in groups.

1. *Pyramid-Builders* Imagine that you (and your coworkers) are a team of archaeologists excavating an ancient Egyptian pyramid. Create a presentation for a museum describing what you have uncovered in your excavations. You could include drawings of the inside and outside of the pyramid and the things you discovered inside. In your presentation be sure to include some details about life along the Nile and the civilization that built the pyramids. Your presentation should also be accompanied by the descriptive journal you have kept while working at the site.
2. *City Planning* Imagine that you (and your coworkers) are Harappan city planners. You have been asked by the ruler of a Harappan city to plan a new community. The ruler has been greatly impressed with Mohenjo-Daro and Harappa and has asked you to plan the new community with that in mind. You may choose to present your plan in the form of drawings, or you may choose to build a model of the new city in clay or some other medium. With your presentation also prepare a written report describing the features of your proposed city and their functions.

UNDERSTANDING THE MAIN IDEA
1. The Agricultural Revolution is the period when people began to practice domestication and shifted from food gathering to food producing. Populations increased, settlements grew larger and more complex, and eventually civilizations developed.
2. Sumerian civilization emerged in Mesopotamia, between the Tigris and Euphrates Rivers. People were able to use the fertile land and the water from the rivers for farming.
3. During the Old and Middle Kingdoms, Egyptians developed overseas trade, created schools, formed a bureaucracy, and developed complex religious beliefs.
4. The Neolithic cultures' development of intensive agriculture and strong family ties would be features of later Chinese civilizations.
5. Mesoamerica—settlers built small villages in what is now the Mexican state of Veracruz; South America—original settlements were made up of hunter-gatherers on the coastal plain of Peru

THINKING CRITICALLY
1. These ancient civilizations developed near rivers that flooded and provided rich silt for farming.
2. Not only were people able to communicate better with each other for trade and other purposes, but they also left a historical record of their civilizations.

It is thought that some of the earliest archaeological excavations were undertaken in Italy during the 1400s, when an interest in ancient Greek culture led to the digging up of Greek sculpture for study. During the 1700s excavations at Pompeii and Herculaneum—ancient Italian cities buried by an eruption of Mount Vesuvius in A.D. 79—revealed much about the cities that had existed there. Herculaneum, which was located on the Bay of Naples at the foot of Vesuvius, was a popular Roman resort and residential town. Archaeological finds include fine villas—one with a library and bronze and marble statues—as well as a basilica decorated with murals, and a theater. Pompeii was a thriving port and resort city. Finds there include streets and footpaths, beautiful examples of Roman art, villas, and public buildings decorated with statues.

Critical Thinking Ask students to suggest why a city buried in a volcanic eruption would differ from most archaeological sites.

ANSWER: Students should suggest that a city buried in an eruption would probably leave a relatively complete archaeological record of the specific time of the eruption.

HISTORY IN THE Making

Reconstructing the Past

Many historians have defined history as the period of time in which written records have been kept. The story of peoples before the development of writing is called prehistory. Although the study of prehistory is carried out by anthropologists and archaeologists, many other scientists are lending their knowledge and techniques to the study of the prehistoric past.

Archaeological Digs

The purpose of an archaeological excavation, or dig, is to determine the chronology of human occupation in a particular site. Archaeologists begin by making a survey of the general terrain. Next, the archaeological team digs several trial holes and long trenches across the site. This type of digging allows archaeologists to estimate what kinds of artifacts they may find, how deep those artifacts may be located, and how large the archaeological site may be. Most of the digging is done slowly and carefully by hand, using trowels, shovels, and even brushes to preserve the artifacts in their original positions. This positioning, called stratification, is essential to determining the sequence of events at the site.

As workers uncover the site, every discovery—whether pottery, other artifacts, buildings, or human or animal remains—is carefully photographed and cataloged. In the records that are kept, the precise position of each find is marked according to a careful grid pattern of the site

▲ A team of archaeologists works among ruins in Athens, Greece. By this stage, most of the work is done with trowels and small brushes.

laid out by the archaeologists. The archaeologists also record the depth of each find. In addition, everything is recorded on scale drawings of the site.

Dating Techniques

For many years, archaeologists had little means of determining dates for their finds. In the 1800s the science of geology helped establish a sequence of geologic periods, in which certain rock formations were recognized to have been created before others. By associating archaeological finds within a particular level of rock, or strata, archaeologists tried to determine the relative age of their finds—in other words, which artifacts or remains came first in the historical record. This relative dating method, known as stratigraphy, could not determine the actual age of the remains, however.

The discovery of radioactivity in the late 1800s provided a new means of establishing the age of rocks and minerals. This new method involved measuring the rate of decay of radioactive elements within the rocks and minerals—a technique known as radiometric dating. Although radiometric dating revolutionized scientists' knowledge of the age of the earth, it did not help them determine the dates for the cultural and social development of early humans. Finally, in 1947 an American chemist, Willard F. Libby, developed a technique for determining these dates—the carbon 14 dating technique.

Carbon 14 is a radioactive carbon found in living organisms. The level of carbon 14 in a living thing—whether human, animal, or plant—remains constant as long as the organism is alive. Once death occurs, the carbon 14 begins to decay. By determining how much of the carbon 14 remains in the organism, scientists are able to date the remains of living things. Carbon 14 dating methods are only useful for dating remains up to about 50,000 years old. In recent years, however, other methods, such as potassium-argon dating, have been used to date remains up to 3 million years old.

Interdisciplinary Controversies

Archaeologists rely heavily on other fields of study, including anthropology, geology, climatology, chemistry, and astronomy. As more scientific fields become involved in the study of both the prehistoric and the historic past, however, the results can sometimes be controversial.

One recent controversy concerns the chronology of Egyptian history—particularly the dating of the Sphinx, a large monument carved in the shape of a lion with the head of a man, on the Giza Plateau. New analysis of the Sphinx's date of origin has caused disagreement among geologists and Egyptologists—historians of ancient Egypt.

Most Egyptologists believe that the Sphinx was built around 2500 B.C., at the same time that the pyramids were built. Drawing heavily on geological evidence, however, an Egyptologist named John Anthony West began to argue in the 1980s that the Sphinx was built much earlier. West sought support for his ideas from Robert M. Schoch, a professor of geology and geophysics at Boston University.

After carefully analyzing the pattern of weathering on the Sphinx, Schoch concluded that the pattern was primarily from rainwater erosion, not from wind and sand. This conclusion suggested that the Sphinx must have been built during a period when the Giza Plateau experienced frequent rainfall. The most recent such period occurred between 9000 and 7000 B.C.

Although the Geological Society of America later endorsed Schoch's conclusions, most Egyptologists remain skeptical. If the Sphinx were so much older, many argue, evidence would exist to suggest a well-developed civilization from the earlier period that could have organized the construction of such a massive monument. Such evidence seems entirely lacking. In response to this argument, West suggested that evidence might exist, buried beneath the sands of Egypt.

Undoubtedly, the argument over the Sphinx will continue until further evidence is found to support or contradict the new theory. This controversy, however, illustrates a growing desire among historians to utilize all the tools available in their search for the past.

◄ **This scientist is using a mass spectrometer to radiocarbon-date an artifact.**

Chapter 2

The First Empires 2400 B.C.–500 B.C.

Chapter Planning Guide

	TEXTBOOK	CORE RESOURCES	VISUAL RESOURCES	MULTIMEDIA
Introduction	pp. 30–31	Block Scheduling Handbook: Ch. 2		Videodisc Segment 2 and Viewing Guide: *The First Empires*
Lesson 2.1 Empires in Mesopotamia	pp. 32–36 Map: *Akkadian Empire,* p. 33	Reading 2.1: *The Code of Hammurabi*	Geography and History 2: *The Eastern Mediterranean*	GHRC 2 Readings: *The Code of Hammurabi; The War Chariot* GHRC 2/Videodiscs: Images— *Babylonian Goddess of Fertility; Hittite Warrior*
Lesson 2.2 Invasion and Empire in Egypt	pp. 37–41 Map: *The World: Physical,* pp. 852–53 Map: *Egypt: The New Kingdom,* p. 38 Teenagers in History: *Tutankhamen,* p. 40	Reading 2.2: *Egyptian Temples* Skills Activity 2: *Identifying Sources of Evidence*	Geography and History 36: *Africa* Everyday Life 2: *Egyptian Tomb Painting*	GHRC 2 Reading: *Looking Good in Ancient Egypt* GHRC 2/Videodiscs: Image— *Nubians Bringing Gifts to Egypt*
Lesson 2.3 Kingdoms in the Aegean	pp. 42–45 Map: *Aegean Civilization,* p. 43	Reading 2.3: *Theseus and the Slaying of the Minotaur* Geography Activity 2: *The End of an Island Civilization*		GHRC 2 Reading: *Mycenaeans Speak from the Grave* GHRC 2/Videodiscs: Images— *Painted Sarcophagus; Mycenaean Death Mask;* Map—*Aegean Lands*
Lesson 2.4 Kingdoms and Empires in the Levant	pp. 46–51 Map: *The Eastern Mediterranean,* p. 47 Sacred Traditions: *The Torah,* p. 49 Map: *Assyrian Empire,* p. 50	Reading 2.4: *The Babylonian Captivity* Writing Project 2: *Writing a Comparison Essay*	Art and History 2: *Ashurnasirpal II Killing Lions*	GHRC 2 Readings: *The Hebrews Build a Temple in Jerusalem; The Assyrians in Victory and Defeat; The Jewish Captivity in Babylon* GHRC 2/Videodiscs: Images— *Phoenician Beads; Assyrian Warriors;* Map—*Phoenician Sea Routes*
Lesson 2.5 Invasion and Empire in Asia	pp. 52–56 Map: *Shang and Zhou Dynasties,* p. 55	Reading 2.5: The Book of Songs	Geography and History 38: *South Asia*	GHRC 2 Readings: *The Oracle Bones of Shang China; The Origins of Silk; The Indian Vedas* GHRC 2/Videodiscs: Image— *Shang Bronze Ritual Vessel;* Map—*Indo-Aryan Migration*
Chapter Investigation and Enrichment	pp. 30–57	Chapter 2 Investigation: *Time Capsules from the Ancient World* People in World History 2 Explorations in Daily Life 2		GHRC 2/Videodiscs
Review and Assessment	Section 1 Review, p. 36 Section 2 Review, p. 41 Section 3 Review, p. 45 Section 4 Review, p. 51 Section 5 Review, p. 56 Chapter 2 Review, p. 57	Chapter Review Activity 2 Vocabulary Activity 2 Themes Review 2 Section Study Guides 2.1–2.5 Main Idea Activities 2.1–2.5 Daily Quizzes 2.1–2.5 Chapter 2 Test Sheltered English Ch. 2 Test Ch. 2 Test Generator		Audio CDs: Ch. 2 Summary (English and Spanish)

INTRODUCING THE CHAPTER

Textbook pp. 30–31

CHAPTER OVERVIEW

The success of the first civilizations attracted migrating peoples and invaders. In Mesopotamia the Akkadian ruler Sargon conquered his neighbors and created the first empire. Egypt also created a strong empire. Aegean societies thrived by trading, and the Phoenicians and Assyrians prospered in the Levant. Distance and natural obstacles allowed Asian empires to grow in relative isolation.

PRESENTING THEMES

On the chalkboard or on an overhead transparency, write the following open-ended theme questions.

- **POLITICS AND LAW** What techniques might a ruler use to keep an empire unified?
- **RELIGION** What qualities in a religion are necessary for it to endure and spread beyond the time and place of its origin?
- **SOCIAL RELATIONS** How might a social hierarchy develop out of a political system?

Have students, either individually or in groups, suggest responses to the questions. For the politics and law question, students might suggest that a ruler could develop an army. The ruler might also reinforce religious and cultural values. For the religion question, students might suggest that a religion must provide explanations for the occurrence of natural events and provide meaning to people's lives. For the social relations question, students might suggest that the political system could create a small elite that becomes an aristocracy. Different social classes would then develop. Save the responses. Once students have studied the chapter, you may wish to have them complete the Themes Review.

USING THE VIDEO

Segment 2: *The First Empires*

ENGLISH

Search Chapter 2
Videodisc 1, Side A

SPANISH

Search Chapter 2
Videodisc 1, Side A

Tell students that in this chapter they will examine the factors that led to the empires and kingdoms that arose as civilization began to spread beyond its river valley origins. Then show Segment 2 of the *World History and Cultures Videodiscs*, which focuses on the enduring legacies of the cultures and religions that arose during this time period. The importance of Judaism, for example, is expressed through the comments of several boys who have been studying the Torah in preparation for their bar mitzvahs.

Before showing the segment, ask students to pay attention not only to what the students in this piece have to say about their religion but also to the feelings that underlie their words. To help students grasp the significant points of the segment, have them complete Video Viewing Guide 2.

Key to Ability Levels

All strategies and activities are coded to the following ability levels:

LEVEL 1	**Basic** activities suitable for all students
LEVEL 2	**Average** activities suitable for average to above-average students
LEVEL 3	**Challenging** activities suitable for above-average students
SHELTERED ENGLISH	Activities suitable for students with **Limited English Proficiency**

Additional Resources

BOOKS FOR TEACHERS

Bottero, Jean. *Mesopotamia: Writing, Reasoning, and the Gods.* University of Chicago Press, 1992. Appraises the development of writing.

Dickinson, Oliver. *The Aegean Bronze Age.* Cambridge University Press, 1994. Examines Minoan and Mycenaean civilizations.

Ruby, Robert. *Jericho: Dreams, Ruins, Phantoms.* Henry Holt and Co., 1995. Presents the city's history.

BOOKS FOR STUDENTS

James, T. G. H. *Ancient Egypt: The Land and Its Legacy.* University of Texas Press, 1988. Focuses on cities and monuments.

Starr, Chester G. *A History of the Ancient World.* Oxford University Press, 1991. Surveys Greek, Mesopotamian, Indian, and Chinese cultures.

Time-Life, eds. *The Age of God-Kings: TimeFrame 3000–1500 B.C.* Time-Life, 1987. Presents an overview of the period.

MULTIMEDIA MATERIALS

Early Civilizations. BFA Educational Media. Video, 20 min. Includes Greece, Egypt, and Phoenicia.

The Interactive Archeologist. E.M.M.E. CD-ROM, MAC, MPC formats. Takes users to actual sites to investigate ancient life.

The Pyramids and Cities of the Pharaohs: Great Cities of the Ancient World. Questar. Video, 75 min. Uses computer-generated images to portray ancient sites.

Lesson 2.1   *Empires in Mesopotamia*

Textbook pp. 32–36

LESSON FOCUS

What influenced the rise and fall of ancient empires in Southwest Asia?

OBJECTIVES

After completing this lesson, students will be able to:

- describe how the Akkadians were able to build the world's first empire;
- explain how the Akkadian example affected Sumerian and Babylonian empire-builders;
- identify the advantages that Indo-European-speaking peoples had over others in Southwest Asia;
- demonstrate how the Hittites built their empire.

HOOK: Link to Today

Note how the Akkadians were able to build the world's first-known empire. Have students imagine they are watching two young children playing in a sandbox. One child has a new dump truck; the other, a battered bucket and shovel. Ask students how they think the second child feels and what they think he or she might do. Point out that this situation is similar to that of Sumer and its neighbors. Jealous of the riches of the Mesopotamians, the Akkadians tried to conquer them. Point out that these efforts at conquest led to the first great empire. Make sure students understand the significance of this by asking them to

distinguish between the terms *kingdom* and *empire*. *[A kingdom is a territorial unit governed by a ruler; an empire is a group of kingdoms, states, or territories under one ruler or government.]*

Refer students to the map on textbook page 33 and have them note the extent of the Akkadian Empire.

Ask: How were the Akkadians able to establish the world's first great empire?
[military prowess, seizing control of valuable resources, adopting Sumerian ways]

Conclude by pointing out that trade links extended Akkadian influence far beyond the empire.

DEVELOP

Outline the succession of ancient empires in and around Mesopotamia, and discuss the influence of the Akkadian example on later empires. Have students create a chart with vertical lines to mark the centuries from 2400 B.C. to 1200 B.C. Then have students draw horizontal bands, starting and stopping at the appropriate century, to represent the Akkadian, Sumerian, Babylonian, and Hittite empires. Suggest that students color-code the bands to differentiate between empires and add annotations marking each empire's major events and achievements. Encourage students to keep the chart, adding to it as they learn about other empires.

Once again, refer students to the map of the Akkadian Empire on textbook page 33. Point out that the Sumerian and Babylonian empires occupied much the same territory as the Akkadian Empire. Then display History and Geography Transparency 2 and have students note that the Hittites were centered in a different geographic location but came to control much of Mesopotamia. Encourage students to look for the relationships among these empires.

Ask: *In what ways were the Sumerian and the Babylonian empires similar to the Akkadian Empire?*
[**All:** *occupied much the same territory;* **Sumerians and Akkadians:** *centralized government and economy;* **Babylonians and Akkadians:** *built on Sumerian culture]*

Ask: *Why did the Hittite Empire differ from other Mesopotamian empires?*
[The Hittites were a different culture group from a different geographic area.]

If time permits, you may wish to have students examine the two readings on Hammurabi's Code and the electronic media image of the Babylonian goddess. Students can discuss what they can infer about Babylonian society and culture from the resource materials.

PROBE
Explore the advantages Indo-European-speaking peoples had over other peoples of Southwest Asia. Remind students that by about 1600 B.C. the Indo-European peoples had begun to encroach upon Mesopotamian territory. Write *Indo-Europeans* on the chalkboard as a heading.

Ask: *What innovations gave the Indo-Europeans an advantage?*
[horses, war chariots, and compound bows]

List student responses on the chalkboard.

Ask: *How did these innovations help?*
*[***Horses:*** mobility; ***Chariots:*** speed in battle; ***Compound bow:*** more power]*

Note student responses opposite the appropriate innovation. Connect innovations and their corresponding effects with arrows to help students see cause-effect relationships.

CONCLUDE
Explain how the Hittites built their empire. Display the electronic media image of the Hittite warrior and read the following Hittite prayer:

Strength and vigor to the King, the Queen, the Princes, and their troops, and may their land be bounded on the left by the sea and by the sea on the right.

Have students infer what kind of people the Hittites were. *[war-like, intent on conquest]* Refer students to the Global History Resource Center reading on Hittite war chariots and have students consider what role the Hittites' warlike nature played in empire-building.

Ask: *How did the Hittites build an empire?*
[They combined iron weapons, military prowess, and Indo-European war technology and social structure to establish an empire.]

Point out that the Hittite Empire was relatively short-lived. Conclude by asking students to identify the patterns in the rise and fall of empires in the region. *[Nomads invaded settled agricultural lands and adopted the conquered people's ways; great leaders built the empires; empires fell to new waves of invaders.]*

EXTEND
Cross-Curricular Connection: *Language Arts*
Have students conduct research on Babylon during the time of Hammurabi. Then have students write a descriptive paragraph on what Hittite raiders would have seen upon first entering Babylon.

MEET INDIVIDUAL NEEDS
Gifted Students
Link to Today. Have students write a short paper or give a presentation comparing the United States's concept of justice with that in Hammurabi's Code.

Kinesthetic Learners
Have students explore the significance of ancient military technology. For example, scratch tests could show why certain metals were better, or toys could be used to show the advantages of two-wheeled chariots.

ASSESS
Review
Have students complete the Section 1 Review. Use answers in the Teacher's Edition, page 151, to assess student mastery.

Lesson 2.2　　*Invasion and Empire in Egypt*

Textbook pp. 37–41

RESOURCES

Pupil's Edition
Map, pp. 852–53: *The World: Physical*
Map, p. 38: *Egypt: The New Kingdom,
c. 1450 B.C.*
Teenagers in History, p. 40:
Tutankhamen: The Life of a Boy King

Core Resources
Reading 2.2: *Egyptian Temples*
Skills Activity 2: *Identifying Sources of
Evidence*

Visual Resources
Geography and History 36: *Africa*
Everyday Life 2: *Egyptian Tomb Painting*

Global History Resource Center
Reading: *Looking Good in Ancient Egypt*

Videodiscs or Global History Resource Center
Image: *Nubians Bringing Gifts to Egypt*

Search Frame 694

LESSON FOCUS

*Why and how did Egypt flourish in the era of
the New Kingdom?*

OBJECTIVES

After completing this lesson, students will be able to:
- discuss the consequences of the Hyksos' conquest of Egypt;
- explain why the New Kingdom pharaohs expanded Egypt's borders;
- explore how the exposure to new cultures and ideas during the New Kingdom affected religious developments in Egypt;
- examine the consequences of Kush's intervention in Egypt.

HOOK

Examine the geography of ancient Egypt. Have students imagine they are defense advisors to the government of ancient Egypt. Their task is to advise the government on the areas of the country that are vulnerable to attack. Have students brainstorm in small groups, using the map on textbook page 38 and the atlas map as references. Call on group representatives to volunteer their ideas. Display the map transparency of Africa and critique group plans in terms of geographic factors. Help students appreciate that the vast expanses of the Sahara,

the Red Sea, and the Mediterranean Sea protected ancient Egypt against invasion from the west, the east, and the north. No geographic barriers, however, protected the south and northeast. Conclude by pointing out that the period of Egyptian history discussed in this section began with an invasion from the northeast and ended with an invasion from the south.

DEVELOP

Discuss the consequences of the Hyksos' conquest of Egypt. Have students consider how they would feel if they lived in a country that invaders had conquered and occupied. Focus on students' responses that mention the desire for freedom and the need to drive out the invaders. Then point out to students that this is how the Egyptians reacted. They fought a long war of liberation that eventually expelled the Hyksos.

Continue by asking students to discuss how Egyptian experiences during the Hyksos' occupation might have motivated their subsequent expansion. Have students refer to the map on textbook page 38 and identify areas conquered during the New Kingdom.
Ask: Why did Egypt conquer these areas?
　　[The pharaohs hoped to plug the "openings" into Egypt

from the south and northeast—the conquered territories were to act as buffers against future invasions.]

Mention that expansion brought the Egyptians into contact with the outside world. As a result, new ideas and new wealth flowed into Egypt.

Ask: *How did contact with the outside world affect Egypt's economic and cultural life?*

[It brought great prosperity and cultural diversity to Egypt.]

Use the electronic media image showing Nubians bringing gifts and the Global History Resource Center reading on looking good in ancient Egypt to illustrate Egypt's economic strength and cultural diversity. Also, use Hatshepsut's biography and the Teenagers in History feature to underscore the vivid characters of this period of Egyptian history. Conclude by asking students to use the information they have gathered to create a flowchart or cause-effect chain titled "Egypt—From Occupation to Glory."

PROBE

Discuss the effect of exposure to outside cultures on religion in the New Kingdom. Have students consider how Egyptian expansion helped inspire Akhenaton's religious ideas.

Ask: *What made Akhenaton abandon the old gods for the sun god Aton?*

[Contact with other cultures revealed that outside peoples had different gods. This realization may have led Akhenaton to abandon the old gods in favor of Aton.]

Then have students discuss how Akhenaton's introduction of new religious ideas affected life in Egypt.

Ask: *Why did Akhenaton's religious changes fail?*

[Changes threatened the power of the priests; the common people and the aristocracy never gave up their old religious beliefs; priests pressured the new pharaoh to renounce Aton.]

To provide students with a better understanding of the role of religion in Egyptian life, assign Core Resources Reading 2.2.

CONCLUDE

Examine the consequences of Kush's intervention in Egypt. Point out that the struggle between Akhenaton and the followers of Amon-Re weakened Egypt. During this religious conflict, the empire's defenses were neglected. Invasions, especially by peoples from the west and northeast, forced the empire to give up outlying lands. Display the electronic media image showing Nubians bringing gifts to Egypt. Then point out that the kingdom of Kush had long been under Egyptian control, and the Kushites were expected to pay tribute to their rulers. As the New Kingdom declined, however, Kush began to flourish and expand. In time, the Kushites overran Egypt.

Ask: *What were the consequences of the Kushite conquest of Egypt in the mid-700s B.C.?*

[Student responses should indicate that the Kushites were able to reunite Egypt but could not halt its decline. Eventually, Egypt fell to the Assyrians in 671 B.C.]

If students are keeping an ongoing chart on empires in Southwest Asia and North Africa, have them add information from this section.

EXTEND

Cross-Curricular Connection: *Environmental Science*
Have interested students prepare a display poster or give a presentation on the environment of ancient Egypt. In addition to describing the environment, students should address how it influenced Egyptian ways of life, ways of making a living, and ideas and attitudes.

MEET INDIVIDUAL NEEDS

Students Acquiring English
Pair students acquiring English with fluent speakers. Then display Everyday Life Transparency 2 and have pairs complete the accompanying worksheet. Encourage nonfluent partners to briefly explain what they have learned about life in Egypt from studying the transparency.

Interpersonal Learners
Suggest that students work in small groups to create a class presentation about the Egyptians from the viewpoint of the Hyksos or the Kushites.

ASSESS

Review
Have students complete the Section 2 Review. Use answers in the Teacher's Edition, page 41, to assess student mastery of this section.

Lesson 2.3   *Kingdoms in the Aegean*

Textbook pp. 42–45

RESOURCES

Pupil's Edition

Map, p. 43: *Aegean Civilization, c. 1450 B.C.*

Core Resources

Reading 2.3: *Theseus and the Slaying of the Minotaur*

Geography Activity 2: *The End of an Island Civilization*

Global History Resource Center

Reading: *The Mycenaeans Speak from the Grave*

Videodiscs or Global History Resource Center

Image: *Minoan Painted Sarcophagus*

Search Frame 695

Image: *Mycenaean Death Mask*

Search Frame 696

Map: *Turmoil in Aegean Lands, 1250–1100 B.C.*

Search Frame 702

LESSON FOCUS
How did Aegean civilizations rise to power, and why did their power fade?

OBJECTIVES

After completing this lesson, students will be able to:
- explain how the Minoans prospered despite having few natural resources;
- analyze the causes of the collapse of Mycenaean civilization;
- illustrate how Greece changed after the collapse of Mycenaean civilization.

HOOK

Understand the basis of Minoan prosperity. Ask students to imagine that a time machine has whisked them back to a village in ancient Crete. They walk the streets, watching artisans making gold and copper jewelry and shopkeepers bargaining with customers over the price of olive oil and wine. They can see, out in the harbor, a ship taking on a cargo. Then encourage students to offer their own speculations about the ship. Have them suggest where it might be going and what it might be carrying. Ensure that students understand that Cretan ships carried on trade throughout the Mediterranean. Illustrate this point by locating sites of Cretan trading posts—Greece, Sardinia, Syria, and the Aegean Islands, for example—on a

large wall map of the Mediterranean region. Continue by mentioning that Crete's chief exports were wine and olive oil, and that the island imported an array of goods including the raw materials—gold, copper, and precious stones—used by artisans. Point to the numerous destinations and the diversity of goods to dramatize the importance of trade to Minoan prosperity.

DEVELOP

Compare Minoan and Mycenaean civilizations. Call on volunteers to graph on the chalkboard the rise and fall of the Minoan and Mycenaean civilizations. Suggest that they use wave-shaped lines to show the rise, peak, and decline of each civilization. The wave for Minoan civilization should show a long peak—from about 2000 B.C. to 1630 B.C.—and a sharp decline; Mycenaean civilization should have a shorter peak—from about 1450 B.C. to 1300 B.C.—and a longer decline, to 1100 B.C.

Next have students consider the major features of these two civilizations. A review of the Global History Resource Center readings on Minoan and Mycenaean discoveries and the electronic media images showing the painted sarcophagus and the death mask of Agamemnon might help students identify these features. Note student responses under the appropriate wave on the chalkboard. Have students use the information on the chalkboard to compare and contrast these two civilizations in a Venn diagram. [Points that the diagram should show include: Both were seafaring civilizations that prospered through trade. Both had environments with limited natural resources. Both used linear-B script. Minoan civilization was based on great palace complexes, while Mycenaean civilization was based on fortified citadels. Minoans were not warlike, while the Mycenaeans were. Minoan social order consisted of absolute rulers, nobles, artisans, merchants, farmers and herders, and scribes. Mycenaean social order consisted of warrior kings, warrior nobles, artisans and merchants, and peasants and slaves.]

PROBE

Account for the decline of Minoan civilization. Point out that the physical geography of the region contributed to the rise of Minoan civilization. Crete's situation as a large island surrounded by smaller island neighbors made it a center of trade. Then have students consider how physical geography might have contributed to Minoan decline.

Ask: What brought about the collapse of Minoan civilization?

[Crete lies near an active fault line, and it is prone to earthquake and volcanic activity. A huge volcanic explosion around the 1620s B.C. destroyed many Minoan cities. While the Minoans rebuilt, their civilization was weakened and probably was overrun by invaders around 1500 B.C.]

Have students review the reasons for Minoan decline by completing the Geography Activity.

CONCLUDE

Analyze the causes of the collapse of Mycenaean civilization. Refer students to the map on textbook page 43, and have them note the extent of Mycenaean influence in the Mediterranean. Then display the electronic media map of the Aegean, and have students note how invaders from the north drove the Mycenaeans out of Greece. Call on volunteers to identify the factors that might have helped to end Mycenaean power. List student responses on the chalkboard. [Student responses should include earthquakes, wars among Mycenaean cities, and the war against Troy.]

Ask: How might these factors have led to the downfall of Mycenaean civilization?

[Earthquakes and warfare would weaken the civilization, leaving it vulnerable to outside attack.]

EXTEND

Cross-Curricular Connection: *Language Arts*
Have students study the Global History Resource Center reading about Mycenaean grave goods. Then ask them to write a diary entry that an archaeologist might have written on the day the graves were first discovered.

MEET INDIVIDUAL NEEDS

Gifted Students
Assign Core Resources Reading 2.3, which is a retelling of the myth of Theseus and the Minotaur by British author Robert Graves. Then, based on the known facts of Minoan/Mycenaean interactions, have students hypothesize historical events that might have given rise to the legend. To complete this activity, you may wish to hold a class discussion or have students write a short essay that they could include in their portfolios.

Visual Learners
Have students draw up an itinerary of ports to visit and a list of goods to trade for a Cretan ship. Suggest that students present their itinerary and list of goods as an annotated map.

ASSESS

Review
Have students complete the Section 3 Review. Use answers in the Teacher's Edition, page 45, to assess student mastery of this section.

Lesson 2.4   *Kingdoms and Empires in the Levant*

Textbook pp. 46–51

RESOURCES

Pupil's Edition

Map, p. 47: *The Eastern Mediterranean*
Sacred Traditions, p. 49: *The Torah*
Map, p. 50: *Assyrian Empire, c. 650 B.C.*

Core Resources

Reading 2.4: *The Babylonian Captivity*

Visual Resources

Art and History 2: *Ashurnasirpal II Killing Lions*

Global History Resource Center

Reading: *The Hebrews Build a Temple in Jerusalem*

Reading: *The Assyrians in Victory and Defeat*

Reading: *The Jewish Captivity in Babylon*

Videodiscs or Global History Resource Center

Map: *Phoenician Sea Routes*

Search Frame 701

Image: *Phoenician Glass Trading Beads*

Search Frame 697

Image: *Assyrian Warriors with Severed Heads*

Search Frame 691

LESSON FOCUS

How did ancient peoples in the Levant build new kingdoms and empires?

OBJECTIVES

After completing this lesson, students will be able to:

- explain how the Phoenicians contributed to the spread of civilization in the Mediterranean;
- describe how and why the Hebrews were able to establish their own kingdoms;
- outline the methods used by the Assyrians and Chaldeans to build their empires and discuss the impact of the Assyrian and Chaldean conquests in Southwest Asia.

HOOK

Illustrate the value of the Phoenician alphabet and discuss how the Phoenicians contributed to the spread of civilization in the Mediterranean. Organize students into pairs. Have half the pairs act as traders and the rest of the pairs act as people living in port towns. Have pairs brainstorm lists of items they might want to sell and items they might want to buy. Have "trader" pairs visit "port" pairs and bargain for goods. Pairs should record their business transactions *without using written*

words. Then have them post their "accounts" around the room, and encourage them to discuss the difficulties they faced in recording precise information by using only pictures. Use the discussion to highlight the power and efficiency of a writing system based on a phonetic alphabet.

Ask: *Why did the Phoenician alphabet come into such wide use?*

> *[Phoenician traders traveled widely in the Mediterranean, introducing their culture wherever they set up trading posts.]*

If available, use the electronic media map of Phoenician sea routes to dramatize the range of the Phoenician trade network. To increase students' understanding of the Phoenicians and trade, have them review the electronic media image of the glass beads the Phoenicians used for trade.

DEVELOP

Explore how and why the Hebrews were able to establish their own kingdoms. Draw on the chalkboard a time line, marking the beginning date as mid-1200s B.C. and the end date as c. 926 B.C. Call on volunteers to enter on the time line the major events in the history of the Hebrews. *[Entries might include **mid-1200s:** Moses leads the Hebrews out of Egypt, receives the Ten Commandments; leads Hebrews to*

Palestine; **c. 1010:** *Hebrews unite under Saul, establish kingdom of Israel;* **early 900s:** *David strengthens kingdom;* **mid-900s:** *Israel reaches peak of its power;* **c. 926:** *kingdom divides into Israel and Judah.]* Encourage students to copy and retain the time line for review purposes.

Next have students consider the themes in the time line.
Ask: What enabled the Hebrews to build a kingdom?
> *[united by covenant with God; the need to maintain a central shrine for the Ark of the Covenant; their religion]*

Use the Sacred Traditions feature on textbook page 49 to highlight the importance of written scriptures in Judaism. Then, if available, have students review the Global History Resource Center reading on building the temple.

PROBE

Discuss the methods used by the Assyrians and Chaldeans to build their empires. Make students aware of the size of the Assyrian Empire by referring them to the textbook map. Have students note the present-day countries located in the area occupied by the Assyrian Empire. Then ask students to consider the Assyrians' methods. Guide student discussion by writing the following categories on the chalkboard: Military Strategy and Technology, Internal Organization, Terror Tactics.
Ask: How did the Assyrians build their empire?
> *[**Military Strategy and Technology:** army organized into regular units, iron weapons, wheeled iron battering rams, cavalry, massed archers; **Internal Organization:** standardized law and government, good communications and transportation system, a nearly universal language; **Terror Tactics:** harsh punishments, settlement of soldiers in areas of potential revolt, mass deportations]*

To illustrate Assyrian military strategy and use of terror, students review the Global History Resource Center reading on the Assyrians and the electronic media image of Assyrian warriors.

Conclude by pointing out that the Chaldeans used similar methods, particularly terror and deportation, to build their empire.

CONCLUDE

Examine the impact of the Assyrians and Chaldeans on Southwest Asia. Have students consider how the Assyrians and Chaldeans affected life in Southwest Asia. Suggest that

they give particular note to conquest and deportation policies.
Ask: What effect did the Assyrian and Chaldean empires have on the peoples of Southwest Asia?
> *[They resulted in a mixing of peoples and cultures and the Hebrew Diaspora; the deportation of the people of Judah ultimately contributed to the further development of Judaism.]*

Draw students' attention to the Babylonian Captivity, a major event of the Chaldean Empire. Assign Core Resources Reading 2.4, which gives the biblical account of the Babylonian Captivity. Then have students read the Global History Resource Center selection on the Babylonian Captivity, which argues that the Jews benefited from their time in exile. Have them compare the two readings.

If students are keeping an ongoing chart on empires in Southwest Asia and North Africa, have them add information from this section.

EXTEND
Other Media
Have students view the video on Judaism in the Holt, Rinehart and Winston series *Religions of the World.* Then ask students to present a brief synopsis of the early development of this religion.

MEET INDIVIDUAL NEEDS
Visual Learners
Display Art and History Transparency 2 and have students complete the worksheet. Then invite students to explain what the transparency and accompanying information tell them about the Assyrians.

Linguistic Learners
Suggest that students try developing a new nonphonetic writing system, teach it to a friend, and then write letters in it. Have them tell the class what they learned about the value of a phonetic alphabet.

ASSESS
Review
Have students complete the Section 4 Review. Use answers in the Teacher's Edition, page 51, to assess student mastery of this section.

Lesson 2.5   *Invasion and Empire in Asia*

Textbook pp. 52–56

RESOURCES

Pupil's Edition

Map, p. 55: *Shang and Zhou Dynasties*

Core Resources

Reading 2.5: *The Book of Songs*

Visual Resources

Geography and History 38: *South Asia*

Global History Resource Center

Reading: *The Oracle Bones of Shang China*

Reading: *The Origins of Silk*

Reading: *The Indian Vedas*

Videodiscs or Global History Resource Center

Map: *Indo-Aryan Migration Into India, c. 1750 B.C.*

Search Frame 703

Image: *Shang Bronze Ritual Vessel*

Search Frame 700

LESSON FOCUS

How did Indian and Chinese civilizations begin to form in the second millennium B.C.?

OBJECTIVES

After completing this lesson, students will be able to:

- discuss how geography influenced the development of civilization in India;
- describe the advantages the Shang enjoyed over previous civilizations in the Huang He valley;
- explain how the Zhou were able to overthrow the Shang dynasty.

HOOK

Examine how geography influenced the development of Indian civilization. Have students view the electronic media map on Indo-Aryan migrations and have them indicate the route by which the Indo-Aryans entered the Indian subcontinent. If the map is not available, use Geography and History Transparency 38 or a wall map of South Asia to point out the routes. *[southeast through the Hindu Kush Mountains, then flowing east and west into the Ganges Plain]* While students are looking at the map, read aloud the following description of India: The Ganges Plain, so called because it is drained by the Ganges River, lies in the north. To the south, the Vindhya

Mountains separate the Ganges Plain from the peninsula of India. The peninsula is dominated by the Deccan, a hilly area with many river valleys.

Ask: *How did the geography of the Indian subcontinent influence the development of civilization there? [Civilization came to be centered in the Ganges Valley, which supported rice cultivation, rapid population growth, and ultimately the development of many kingdoms; the Vindhya Mountains and the difficult terrain in the south slowed the spread of Sanskrit and Indo-European ideas. Small, isolated kingdoms developed, many of which turned to the sea to survive.]*

DEVELOP

Describe the advantages the Shang enjoyed over previous civilizations in China. Direct students' attention to the map of the Shang and Zhou dynasties in the textbook. Then write on the chalkboard *Shang China*. Draw four lines radiating from the title. At the end of each, draw a large circle. Label the circles *Government, Economy, Religion,* and *Culture*. Organize students into four groups and assign each group one of the circle subjects. Have groups brainstorm information that might be entered in their circles. Call on group representatives to enter their information in the appropriate circles. *[Entries might include **Government:** first verifiable Chinese dynasty, centralized empire, complex bureaucracy; **Economy:** agriculture, royal* ownership of land, specialized artisans in towns; **Religion:** animism, ancestor worship, oracle bones; **Culture:** pictograms, ideographs, calligraphy, artistic bronze casting]

Encourage students to copy and retain the diagram of Shang society for review purposes.

Use the Global History Resource Center reading on oracle bones and the electronic media image of the Shang ritual vessel to assist students in learning more about Shang religious beliefs.

PROBE

Explain how the Zhou were able to overthrow the Shang. Have students consider the problem of keeping a society unified in ancient times, and challenge them to relate this problem to the fall of the Shang. Guide discussion by pointing out that the Shang Empire was surrounded by hostile neighbors and defending the whole border eventually became impossible. Defending one part of the border, then, might open the Shang to attack elsewhere.

Ask: *How were the Zhou able to defeat the Shang?*

[The Zhou formed alliances with neighboring tribes and attacked from the west when the Shang were weakened after fighting nomadic invaders in the north and east.]

CONCLUDE

Discuss how Zhou political order led to stability but eventually brought about the fall of the Zhou dynasty. Write the word *Feudalism* on the chalkboard. Beneath it, write *Rights—Obligations* and explain that feudal relationships involved a system of rights and obligations. For instance, in return for the right of controlling the land, nobles were obliged to show allegiance to the king. Encourage students to construct a pyramid-style diagram to show the feudal relations that existed between classes in Zhou China. Call on volunteers to display and discuss their diagrams.

Next point out that this political and social system brought China about two centuries of relative peace. Have students study the map on textbook page 55 to note how the Zhou extended the boundaries of the old Shang Empire. Then have students consider how this expansion might have led to the fall of the Zhou.

Ask: *What brought about the decline of the Zhou dynasty?*

[Under the feudal system nobles gained great power, and in time their loyalty to the king weakened, and the king found it difficult to raise armies. The Zhou could not mount an adequate defense of border lands when attacked by nomadic invaders, and in time the border lands fell to the invaders, beginning the Zhou's decline.]

EXTEND

Cross-Curricular Connection: *Science*

Have students research and report on bronze casting and silk production, two important technological breakthroughs that took place in Shang China. Students who select silk as their subject might begin their research by reviewing the Global History Resource Center reading on the origins of silk.

MEET INDIVIDUAL NEEDS

Auditory Learners

Encourage students to make dramatic readings from the Vedas and *The Book of Songs*. After the readings have been completed, have students discuss what the Vedas and *The Book of Songs* tell about life in ancient India and China. Students might prepare for this activity by reviewing Core Resources Reading 2.5 and the Global History Resource Center reading on the Vedas.

Intrapersonal Learners

Have students explore the caste system by imagining themselves a member of each caste. Encourage them to write a diary entry about how the world looks to them from each caste position.

ASSESS

Review

Have students complete the Section 5 Review. Use answers in the Teacher's Edition, page 56, to assess student mastery of this section.

In preparation for the chapter test, you may wish to have students complete all or part of the Chapter 2 Review on textbook page 57, the Chapter 2 Review Activity, and the Chapter 2 Themes Review.

Chapter 2
The First Empires

2400 B.C.–500 B.C.

Understanding the Main Idea

As civilization spread beyond the river valleys, surrounding peoples began to want its advantages for themselves. Soon a pattern arose in which hardy nomadic peoples used their greater fighting skills to conquer existing civilizations. Drawing on the resources provided by their conquests, these nomadic peoples expanded their territory and built the first empires—in the process spreading civilization even further.

Themes

- **Politics and Law** What techniques might a ruler use to keep an empire unified?

- **Religion** What qualities in a religion are necessary for it to endure and spread beyond the place and time of its origin?

- **Social Relations** How might a social hierarchy develop out of a political system?

In November 1922 archaeologist Howard Carter made a remarkable discovery. After five years of intensive digging in the hot, dusty Egyptian desert, Carter had finally found the tomb of Tutankhamen, a king who had died more than 3,000 years before. Carter wrote, "A sealed doorway—it was actually true, then! Our years of patient labour were to be rewarded after all. . . . Anything, literally anything, might lie beyond that passage. . . ."

After two more weeks of preparations, Carter and his crew were ready to open the tomb:

66*The decisive moment had arrived. . . . At first I could see nothing, the hot air escaping from the chamber causing the candle flame to flicker, but presently, as my eyes grew accustomed to the light, details of the room within emerged slowly from the mist, strange animals, statues, and gold— everywhere the glint of gold.*99

Nearly untouched by the hands of ancient tomb-robbers, Tutankhamen's tomb revealed treasures almost beyond comprehension—golden jewelry, alabaster lamps and vases, gold-inlaid furniture, and gilded chariots. Carter had made one of the greatest archaeological discoveries of the early 1900s, a discovery that focused the world's attention on ancient Egypt.

c. 2330 B.C.
▲
Sargon I seizes control of Sumer; Akkadian Empire begins.

1792 B.C.
▲
Hammurabi becomes king of Babylon.

c. 1750 B.C.
▲
Indo-Aryans begin migrating into India.

c. 1380 B.C.
▲
Akhenaton begins reign as pharaoh of Egypt.

Tomb of King Tutankhamen

Because Tutankhamen died unexpectedly, his royal tomb had not been completed at the time of his death. Therefore, his body was placed in a smaller tomb, which remained undetected until Howard Carter and Lord Carnarvon discovered it in 1922. When they opened the doorway, they found a room filled with gold treasures, things used by the king during his lifetime as well as those for his use in the afterlife. The funeral mask of Tutankhamen shown here is made of solid gold inlaid with semiprecious stones. It weighs over 24 pounds.

Critical Thinking Ask students to suggest why very few Egyptian royal tombs have been discovered intact and undisturbed.

ANSWER: Students should suggest that robbers would try to break into the royal tombs, and therefore most royal tombs have either been looted or are so well-hidden that archaeologists cannot find them.

1200s B.C.	1122 B.C.	c. 1000 B.C.	722 B.C.
Moses leads Hebrews from Egypt to Palestine.	Zhou dynasty begins in China.	Hymns of the Rig-Veda are collected.	Assyria conquers the kingdom of Israel.

Theme: Geography

Geographically, Mesopotamia is readily accessible from almost all directions. The mountains to the north and east have many valleys and natural passes. The desert to the west and south also provides easy access. While the area is crisscrossed by many rivers, they are easy to ford. Thus, the Sumerians had few natural barriers to protect their cities and farmland from invasion by nomadic peoples.

Critical Thinking

Ask students to suggest how Mesopotamia's lack of natural boundaries might also have been an advantage.

ANSWER: Although Mesopotamia was vulnerable to invasion, it was also able to reach the areas around it to engage in trade, exchange ideas, or invade its neighbors.

SECTION 1
Empires in Mesopotamia

FOCUS

- How were the Akkadians able to build the world's first empire?

- How did the Akkadian example affect Sumerian and Babylonian empire-builders?

- What advantages did Indo-European-speaking peoples have over others in Southwest Asia?

- How did the Hittites build their empire?

The wealth of Mesopotamian civilization was irresistible to nomadic peoples living in the surrounding hills and deserts. By about 2300 B.C. these peoples had begun to attack the Mesopotamians in order to get some of the benefits of civilization for themselves. A pattern emerged in the region in which invaders seized control of a civilization, built an empire, and eventually became a civilized people—only to fall to new invaders later.

Sandstone carving depicting an Akkadian king's victory

Migration and Empire

Between 3000 B.C. and 2000 B.C., a great many peoples began to move around in western Asia in larger numbers than ever before. They came from two major linguistic groups and two different areas—peoples speaking related Semitic languages from the Arabian and Syrian Deserts, and peoples speaking related Indo-European languages from north of the Black Sea.

Semitic migrations. The first to move into the region of Mesopotamia were various groups of Semitic-speaking peoples from the desert grasslands of Arabia and Syria. Although probably not members of a single ethnic group, the Semitic-speaking peoples shared a common culture. That culture was reflected in the similar structure, vocabulary, and ideas of their related languages. Even today, Semitic languages such as Arabic and Hebrew are closely related linguistically.

The Semitic-speaking peoples were originally nomadic or seminomadic pastoralists who survived by herding their flocks of sheep. As early as the 3000s B.C., some of these peoples began to filter from the Syrian deserts into the northern cities of Sumer. There they settled down and adopted the Sumerian style of civilization. Some lived among the local people and served Sumerian kings. Others established towns and cities of their own along the middle and upper Euphrates and Tigris Rivers. From the harsh desert environment, they brought with them their own drive for survival and their military skill.

The Akkadians. In about 2330 B.C., one of these Semitic-speaking individuals emerged in northern Sumer to establish his own city and to lead his people in conquering all the surrounding cities. We do not know his real name, but he is known to history by his title—Sargon I of Akkad.

BIOGRAPHY Sargon was the leader of a Semitic-speaking people who had settled near the Sumerian city of Kish. There they had absorbed many Sumerian customs, including the use of cuneiform script—a script using wedge-shaped characters—that they adapted for their own Akkadian language. Sargon achieved a high position under the king of Kish. Sometime in the

Akkadian Empire, c. 2330 B.C.

Sargon's Domain Sargon's empire had its capital at the magnificent city of Akkad.

❓ **Location** What was the southernmost city in the Akkadian Empire?

adopted Akkadian as the language of administration throughout the empire, Sumerian continued to be the primary religious and literary language. Sargon's successors also left many aspects of Sumerian civilization, such as the powerful Sumerian priesthoods, intact. The priests' continuing influence in Akkadian society ensured the continuity of Sumerian culture.

Sargon's empire lasted only about a century before it was overthrown by revolt from within and an invasion by raiders from the Zagros Mountains. By that time, however, the Akkadians had adopted and spread the cultural heritage of the Sumerians far beyond the original river valleys. They also had established the standard for future empires in the region.

Combining the techniques of Sumerian civilization with military skills they had learned as nomads, Akkadians built the first empire.

mid-2300s B.C., however, Sargon left Kish and established his own city of Agade, or Akkad.

Sargon was the first empire-builder known to history. From Akkad he conquered all of Sumer. Sargon also conquered territories to the north and west to gain control over valuable cedar forests and silver mines. He eventually ruled a territory that stretched from the Mediterranean Sea to the Persian Gulf. Sargon was so victorious that he became known as "the Great." A legend created after his death stated that Sargon's mother was a high priestess, and hinted that his father was a god. Such legends helped Sargon's successors justify their hold over the empire.

Although the dynasty that Sargon founded

Sargon
BIOGRAPHY

Sumerian Revival and Decline

Sometime around 2100 B.C., the southern Sumerian city-states began a period of renewal that lasted more than 100 years under the authority of the kings of the Third Dynasty of Ur. These kings brought much of the old Akkadian Empire under their rule.

The rulers of Ur gradually created a centralized government and economy. Economic records from the period show a wide variety of work activities for the people of the empire. Men dug canals, harvested crops, and towed canal boats, while women wove fabrics, drained fields, and also helped with the harvests. Workers were paid with bread, oil, and beer. Many traders worked for the kings, importing wood, herbs, and metal ores, which they paid for with wool, barley, or uncoined silver.

However, the kings of Ur were not strong enough to keep the empire unified. Confronted by raids from unruly nomads, cities gradually became isolated from each other, and people abandoned their farms as they sought protection

BIOGRAPHY
Sargon
When Sargon and his forces conquered a region, he appointed a governor to oversee the interests of the expanding Akkadian Empire. He supported these administrators by establishing a military garrison in the area. A large bureaucracy developed to control the expanding trade, the payment of tribute to the king, and the maintenance of military forces. Sargon's administration grew so large that he once claimed to feed 5,400 men at his table every day.

Critical Thinking Ask students to try to imagine what motivated Sargon to establish the world's first empire.

ANSWER: Students might mention pride in himself or in his culture, or a feeling that he could make his territory more secure or prosperous by conquering neighboring territories.

within city walls. Some cities rebelled against Ur's authority. In about 2000 B.C. Ur fell to invaders from the east. The Sumerians interpreted the event as an act of the gods:

> *The utter destruction of my city they [the gods] directed. . . . The righteous house they break up with the pickaxe. . . . In the rivers of my city dust has gathered, into fox-dens they have been made.*

At about the same time, new Semitic-speaking invaders appeared from the northwest.

Having learned the lessons of empire from the Akkadians, the kings of Ur led a brief revival of Sumerian power before being overwhelmed by new invaders.

The Babylonians

Sometime before 1800 B.C., one group from the northwest settled the city of Babylon, on the middle reaches of the Euphrates River. The Amorites, as they called themselves, were part of the new movement of peoples into the region. In 1792 B.C. the Amorite king Hammurabi (ham-uh-RAHB-ee) assumed the throne in Babylon. Hammurabi reunited Mesopotamia in what scholars call the Old Babylonian Empire.

Hammurabi is perhaps best remembered for the collection of legal rulings known as the Code of Hammurabi, which became the basis for later Mesopotamian legal codes as well as a model of literary style. The code included regulations covering everything from divorce, contracts, and physicians' fees to agriculture and commerce.

In general, the Code of Hammurabi put forward the principle of "an eye for an eye":

▶ **This ferocious looking clay lion was carved in Mesopotamia about 2000 B.C.**

> *If a builder constructed a house for a seignior [gentleman], but . . . the house which he built collapsed and so has caused the death of the owner of the house, that builder shall be put to death.*

Equal treatment did not exist between members of different social classes, however. For example, if one gentleman struck another, he was fined a small amount of silver. If a slave struck a gentleman, he had his ear cut off.

Like the Akkadians before him, Hammurabi absorbed and built upon the civilization that had begun in Sumer. Hammurabi honored the old Sumerian gods and allowed the Sumerian priests to retain their power and influence in society. Although Akkadian became the common language of the empire, Sumerian continued to be studied in Babylonian schools. The Babylonians thus maintained relative peace in Mesopotamia for about 400 years. They too, however, eventually fell to raiders from the north. These new invaders were not Semitic-speaking peoples but peoples speaking a group of languages that scholars have called Indo-European.

The Semitic-speaking Babylonians restored the imperial tradition of the Akkadians and preserved the cultural heritage of the Sumerians.

Indo-European Migrations

Although scholars still debate their origins, the Indo-European-speaking peoples probably originated somewhere north of the Black Sea in what is now southwestern Russia. Like Semitic-speaking peoples, Indo-European-speakers probably did not represent a single ethnic group, but rather many groups who shared common cultural traits.

The Indo-Europeans were the first to domesticate the horse, which made them extremely mobile and also gave them an advantage in raiding other more settled peoples. Cattle were also very important economically to many Indo-European peoples. Ritual sacrifices of cattle to the gods was a significant aspect of Indo-European religion.

Indo-Europeans organized themselves according to kinship ties into clans and tribes. Their society was **patriarchal**—that is, fathers exercised strong control over their families. The Indo-Europeans also had a strong warrior tradition—apparently an outgrowth of raiding one another for horses, cattle, and women.

From their homeland, the Indo-Europeans began to spread out in all directions sometime between 4000 and 3000 B.C. Many small groups gradually migrated south into Asia Minor (present-day Turkey) and into the mountains north and east of Mesopotamia. The movement of Indo-European speakers increased into what seems to have been two large-scale waves of migration—the first around 2000 B.C. and the second around 1200 B.C. Eventually, Indo-European languages spread by these movements were being spoken from Ireland in the west to India in the east.

After about 2000 B.C. the Indo-Europeans became masters in battle by combining their skill with horses with the Sumerian four-wheeled cart. Adapting the cart for battle, the Indo-Europeans developed a light two-wheeled **war chariot**. Improved breeds of horses pulled the war chariots more effectively and more rapidly—a tremendous advantage on an open battlefield. The Indo-Europeans also armed themselves with short **compound bows**—wooden bows reinforced with pieces of bone for added power.

With the use of the horse and new war technology, the migrating Indo-European peoples had an advantage over settled peoples.

▲ **This war chariot shows the style developed by the Indo-Europeans. It gave them a tremendous advantage over their enemies.**

The Hittites

One of the most successful groups of the Indo-Europeans in Southwest Asia was the Hittites. The Hittites had originally filtered into Asia Minor sometime before 2000 B.C. There they settled down and assimilated into the local population, sometimes even adopting local gods. As the migration of more Indo-Europeans from the north led to instability and increasing warfare in the region, however, sometime in the 1600s B.C. the Hittites came together under a powerful king named Hattusilis (hat-uh-SIL-uhs) I. From his hilltop fortress Hattusilis began to conquer the surrounding region. Eventually, the Hittites built a strong kingdom in Southwest Asia Minor.

Hittite technological advantages. Like other conquerors, the Hittites had a technological advantage—in addition to mastering the art of chariot warfare they were the first to use iron weapons on a large scale. Although we do not know whether the Hittites were the first to learn the technique for making iron, they did control rich iron ore deposits in their territory. With iron, they produced stronger weapons than their enemies' bronze ones. Iron plows also allowed the Hittites to farm more productively.

Hittite society. Hittite society reflected its Indo-European background. At the top, the king functioned primarily as a war chief. He was the supreme commander, and he generally took part in the battles himself. As the chief priest the king also fulfilled an important religious role in preserving society's relationship with the gods. The king was aided by his queen, who had a much more important role than most queens had in Mesopotamian society. The queen was an important religious figure and conducted special religious ceremonies.

Beneath the monarchs were the Hittite nobles, including the rest of the royal family. The king gave Hittite nobles land in exchange for a regular tribute in horses and soldiers. The ordinary soldiers provided the base on which Hittite society rested.

Expansion and decline. As the Hittites expanded their territory, they soon came into conflict with other powers, notably a growing Egyptian Empire. In the 1200s B.C., however, both the Egyptians and the Hittites fell victim to the second great wave of Semitic and Indo-European migrations. While Egypt survived the attacks, the Hittites were so weakened that they soon fell to yet more Indo-European invaders from the north. In the Hittites' place, smaller kingdoms eventually emerged to dominate Southwest Asia.

The Hittites combined the use of iron weapons and tools with Indo-European war technology to create a great empire.

▲ In this stone stela from Marash, Syria, carved around 1000 B.C., Hittites feast at a banquet.

SECTION 1 REVIEW

IDENTIFY and explain the significance of the following:
Sargon I of Akkad
Hammurabi
patriarchal
war chariot
compound bows
Hattusilis I

LOCATE and explain the importance of the following:
Akkad
Ur
Babylon

1. **Main Idea** Why were the Indo-European-speaking invaders able to conquer other peoples of Southwest Asia?
2. **Main Idea** What military advantages did the Hittites have over other peoples?
3. **Politics and Law** What techniques did the Akkadians use to build the first empire?
4. **Writing to Explain** Write a short essay explaining how Sargon and the Akkadians' foundation of the first empire served as an example for later empire-builders in Mesopotamia.
5. **Synthesizing** How and why did empires rise and fall in Mesopotamia between 2330 B.C. and the 1200s B.C.? In answering this question, consider the role played by (a) the geography of Southwest Asia; (b) military skill and equipment; and (c) the power of individual leaders.

Invasion and Empire in Egypt

SECTION 2

CORE LESSON PLAN
See pages 29E and 29F for Lesson Plan 2.2.

FOCUS

- What were the consequences of the Hyksos' conquest of Egypt?

- Why did the New Kingdom pharaohs expand Egypt's borders?

- How did exposure to new cultures and ideas during the New Kingdom affect religious developments in Egypt?

- What were the consequences of Kush's intervention in Egypt?

*B*y the 1700s B.C. Egypt had built a strong and glorious civilization. The Egyptians took such great pride in their culture that they ignored foreign ideas and practices. In the 1600s B.C., however, foreign invaders moved in and conquered Egypt. This opened Egypt's eyes to the outside world and later inspired the Egyptians to build an empire.

Pyramids at Giza, Egypt

The Hyksos' Invasion and Conquest

Like Mesopotamia, Egypt also experienced the effects of great migrations. As elsewhere, the initial stages of the migrations were probably relatively peaceful. From the northeast, Semitic-speaking peoples known collectively as the Hyksos began to move into the region of the Nile Delta and to settle among the Egyptians. By about 1650 B.C., however, the Hyksos, perhaps together with a new group arriving from the east, had overthrown the ruling Egyptian dynasty.

The Hyksos had an advantage over the Egyptians because of their superior war technology—particularly the horse-drawn war chariot. In addition, the Hyksos knew how to cast bronze—a much harder substance than the copper that the Egyptians used—to make both weapons and tools. Despite these advantages, the Hyksos' rule in Egypt was rather fragile.

Although they eventually adopted Egyptian styles of civilization and tried to rule as traditional pharaohs, the Hyksos remained outsiders in Egypt. In addition, they never ruled directly over the entire Nile Valley, but only its northernmost regions known as Lower Egypt. The middle portion of the Nile Valley was ruled by an Egyptian prince from the city of Thebes who had to pay tribute to the Hyksos. Upper Egypt became an independent kingdom ruled by Nubian princes. Although Nubian princes supported the Hyksos pharaohs, some Nubian mercenaries fought with the Egyptians to expel the Hyksos.

By the 1500s B.C. the Theban rulers had mastered Hyksos war technology and tactics. They launched a war of liberation that lasted several generations to drive the foreign Hyksos out of Egypt. After one defeat in battle, the Theban ruler Kamose denounced Egyptians who collaborated with the Hyksos against him. He threatened to "reduce their homes to red mounds because of the damage that they did to Egypt when they put themselves at the service of the Asiatics [Hyksos], forsaking Egypt." Eventually, in about 1570 B.C., Kamose's brother and successor, Ahmose, drove the Hyksos out of Egypt once and for all.

*A*fter conquering Egypt, the Hyksos adopted the Egyptian way of life, but they were eventually driven out.

Theme: Social Relations

After the Hyskos were driven from Egypt, a new warrior tradition arose. It became the duty of Egyptian kings to lead their armies into battle. The most famous of these warrior-kings was Thutmose III, who has been called the Napoleon of Egypt. Through Thutmose's military expertise and courage, Egypt conquered land in Southwest Asia and established it as a part of the New Kingdom.

Critical Thinking Ask students if they think the concept of a "warrior-king" applies to present-day national leaders.

ANSWER: Students might say no, because modern national leaders do not usually lead battles, or they might say yes, since some modern leaders have used war to gain personal glory.

The New Kingdom in Egypt

The two centuries of Hyksos rule showed the Egyptians the danger of ignoring the outside world. After the expulsion of the Hyksos, Ahmose became the first ruler of the Eighteenth dynasty in the mid-1500s B.C., and established what became known variously as the **New Kingdom**, or the empire. The New Kingdom was characterized by imperial expansion and a rich culture.

Imperial expansion. The pharaohs of the New Kingdom believed that building an empire was the best way to prevent Egypt from ever being invaded again. Consequently, they established a standing army. To keep the south secure, the pharaohs kept the capital at Thebes. With little danger from the desert to the west, Egyptian armies and chariots crossed into Palestine and Syria, conquering territory as far as Asia Minor. The Egyptian Empire grew so great that Pharaoh Thutmose I claimed that Egypt stretched "as far as the circuit of the sun."

As the empire expanded, Egypt came into greater contact with foreign ideas and peoples. In addition, foreigners brought their customs as well as their wealth to Egypt, helping to create both great prosperity and cultural diversity. With this new wealth, Egyptian rulers adopted a more imperial style of art—depicting Egypt's glory and conquest of other peoples. The extent of Egyptian peace and prosperity under the empire was perhaps best illustrated in the reign of one of the few women to rule Egypt in her own right—Queen Hatshepsut (hat-SHEP-soot).

The daughter of a pharaoh, Hatshepsut married her half-brother, Thutmose II, who became pharaoh when their father died around 1512 B.C. When Thutmose II died, his son, Thutmose III, was too young to rule, so Hatshepsut ruled Egypt until he became an adult.

Hatshepsut had the support of her father's court officials and the priests of the god Amon-Re, but her greatest power came from her will to rule. Taking all the rightful titles of a pharaoh, she called on the gods to justify her rule:

Hatshepsut
BIOGRAPHY

> 66 *Came forth the king of the gods, Amon-Re, from his temple saying, 'Welcome my sweet daughter, my favorite, the King of Upper and Lower Egypt, . . . Hatshepsut. Thou art the king, taking possession of the Two Lands [of Egypt].'* 99

Hatshepsut ruled Egypt for 20 years. Her reign was generally peaceful and prosperous. She sent commercial expeditions from Egypt down the Red Sea, and refurbished temples and undertook other public works projects. After her death in 1482 B.C., Thutmose III had Hatshepsut's images removed from her monuments, and replaced them with those of himself and his father.

Egypt: The New Kingdom, c. 1450 B.C.

Pyramid — Trade route

Asia Minor
25°E · CRETE · 30°E · 35°E · Euphrates River
SYRIA · CYPRUS
35°N
Kadesh
MEDITERRANEAN SEA · ASIA
DEAD SEA
PALESTINE
LIBYAN DESERT · LOWER EGYPT · Giza · Memphis
Sinai Peninsula
Tell el-'Amârna (Akhetaton)
ARABIAN DESERT
AFRICA · UPPER EGYPT · Thebes · 25°N
Nile River
RED SEA
SAHARA · NUBIA · 20°N
Kerma
KUSH
Napata
0   100   200 Miles
0   100   200 Kilometers
Lambert Conformal Conic Projection
Meroe

Reign of the Pharaohs The pharaohs of the New Kingdom revitalized Egypt's empire.

? Movement Why did the New Kingdom expand to the northeast rather than to the west?

38 CHAPTER 2

Akhenaton's religious revolution. The increased contact with foreign cultures resulting from Egyptian expansion had a great impact on religion in Egypt. Around 1380 B.C. the young pharaoh Amenhotep (ahm-uhn-HOH-tep) IV came to power. Amenhotep came to believe that the supreme god was the sun, which he called Aton. Defying the priests of Amon-Re, Amenhotep renamed himself Akhenaton (ahk-NAHT-uhn), which means "pleasing to Aton." Confronted by continuing priestly resistance, he soon proclaimed that Aton was the only god and suppressed the worship of all others. He also removed the name of Amon-Re from all public inscriptions. Finally, Akhenaton built a magnificent new capital city at Tell el-'Amârna dedicated to Aton, which he called Akhetaton.

The priests of Amon-Re reacted strongly against these changes. Not only did Akhenaton challenge their religious beliefs, he challenged their power as well. Most of the priests were closely linked with noble families, who held the majority of the state offices. Moving the government to Tell el-'Amârna weakened their power. The priests also feared that Aton's followers, who had few links with the aristocracy, would grow stronger at their expense. The conflict over religion thus became a struggle for power.

The priests of Amon-Re eventually won the power struggle. Neither the common people nor the aristocracy had given up their traditional religion for the pharaoh's Aton worship. Under priestly pressure, Akhenaton's successor, the young Tutankhaten (too-tang-KAHT-uhn),

▲ In this carving Akhenaton is a sphinx basking in Aton's rays.

> *The New Kingdom in Egypt aggressively expanded its borders to prevent further invasion.*

THROUGH OTHERS' EYES

An Egyptian View of Syria

When the pharaoh Amenemhet I was assassinated around 1960 B.C., an Egyptian court official named Sinuhe fled Egypt either from fear or because he was involved. In "Upper Retenu," the highlands of northern Palestine and southern Syria, the local Amorite ruler took Sinuhe into his service. Sinuhe returned to Egypt in his old age and later wrote of the Amorite chief's hospitality and the land to which he had fled:

❝He set me at the head of his children. He married me to his eldest daughter. He let me choose [land] for myself of his country, of the choicest of that which was with him on his frontier with another country. It was a good land, named Yaa. Figs were in it, and grapes. It had more wine than water. Plentiful was its honey, abundant its olives. Every (kind of) fruit was on its trees. Barley was there, and emmer [wheat]. There was no limit to any (kind of) cattle. Moreover, great was that which accrued [came] to me as a result of the love of me.❞

rejected Aton and took the new name Tutankhamen. Soon thereafter Aton's name was replaced by that of Amon-Re on all public inscriptions. Tutankhamen abandoned Tell el-'Amârna, which was swallowed up by the desert.

> *Exposure to new cultures and ideas contributed to a religious revolution under Akhenaton, but traditional Egyptian religious ideas eventually triumphed.*

Egyptian Decline

Akhenaton's religious reforms contributed to the decline of Egyptian power in the 1300s B.C. In his struggle with the priests of Amon-Re, the pharaoh had neglected Egypt's defenses, particularly its territory in Palestine and Syria. Rival powers soon took advantage of the situation.

**Theme:
Religion**
Akhenaton is considered one of the first monotheists in history because he promoted the worship of only one god—Aton. In his effort to eradicate all of the old gods, he commanded his servants to climb to the top of towering structures to erase images that were not even visible from the ground. Akhenaton's reforms failed, however, partly because of his religion's focus on the afterlife, instead of life on Earth, and its lack of traditional lavish ceremonies.

Critical Thinking Ask students to consider why Akhenaton's religion did not gain popularity among Egyptians.

ANSWER: Students should suggest that the ancient Egyptian people probably expected their religion to promise benefits to life on Earth, not only in the afterlife, and that they felt that lavish ceremonies were a necessary part of a legitimate religion.

Teenagers IN HISTORY

Tutankhamen: The Life of a Boy King

In comparison to other rulers of ancient Egypt, Tutankhamen was a relatively minor king. He came to the throne when he was only nine years old and died in his late teens. The few accomplishments of his brief reign were erased from official records by later rulers, probably because of Tutankhamen's relationship with Akhenaton. In time, Tutankhamen was completely forgotten. So too was his tomb, buried under the debris from the construction of other tombs. This uncelebrated status almost certainly protected Tutankhamen's burial place from robbers.

Since pharaohs were buried with all the things they might need in the afterlife, the discovery of the tomb provided a detailed picture of this "boy king."

For example, Tutankhamen seems to have taken great care of his personal appearance. The contents of his tomb included mirror holders, elaborate shaving tools, and an array of boxes that had once contained various oils and ointments. A linen bag in the tomb held malachite and galena, the makings for eye-paint. (In ancient Egypt both women and men wore makeup.) Although much of the clothing in the tomb had decayed over time, it was obvious that Tutankhamen had an extensive wardrobe. Some of the clothes were highly colored and decorated with gold and precious stones. Many pieces of jewelry were also found in the tomb.

Tutankhamen probably was fond of playing board games, for one of the rooms in the tomb—the Annex—contained a variety of game pieces. Also, Tutankhamen almost certainly liked hunting and chariot racing. He was buried with chariots and hunting weapons, and other items found in the tomb show scenes of him hunting.

The personal items buried with the young king suggest that he remained attached to the things of his childhood. Many of the clothes stored in the tomb were child-sized. The jewelry included several pairs of earrings and ear studs, which only young children wore. One of the chairs was so small that Tutankhamen probably used it when he was an infant. Among the most interesting personal items was a tiny coffin containing a lock of hair. Some scholars believe this was a keepsake given to Tutankhamen by one of his favorite relatives—perhaps his grandmother.

One piece of information the tomb did not provide was exactly how Tutankhamen died. Many have theorized that he was murdered by one of the advisors who governed the country for him. Whatever the truth may be, the artifacts of Tutankhamen's tomb present an intriguing picture of the life of the boy king.

Tutankhamen

The Hittites, for example, encouraged local people in the northern Egyptian provinces to rebel. The Hittites themselves attacked the Egyptian Empire throughout the next century.

Around 1288 B.C. Pharaoh Ramses II engaged in a great battle against the Hittites at Kadesh. Hittite records state that the Egyptians lost. Egyptian sources, on the other hand, claim that Ramses himself single-handedly took on 2,500 Hittite chariots and, with the help of newly arrived troops, drove back the Hittite forces, thus achieving victory. Whatever the truth, the outcome of the battle seems to have been a draw. Before long, however, both the Hittites and Egyptians experienced far worse blows from beyond their borders.

Renewed invasions. Beginning in the middle of the 1200s B.C., Egypt, like the other states of the region, came under almost constant attack from new invaders. The Egyptians called these invaders the "Sea Peoples." Their attacks essentially put an end to the Egyptian Empire, forcing the Egyptians to abandon the outlying provinces and to retreat to the Nile Delta and Nile Valley. Over the next two centuries, the shattered empire became simply a kingdom once again. Around 1200 B.C. new invaders from the west—the Libyans—began to appear in the Nile Delta. There they set up independent kingdoms under their own dynasties. In the mid-900s B.C. one of these dynasties claimed the throne of Egypt and ruled for over 200 years.

Throughout these centuries of growing insecurity, Egyptian culture began to change. Religion gradually became less concerned with morality and more concerned with magic rituals. Egyptians began to believe that they could pass into paradise with the right charms in their coffins instead of having led a good life to achieve immortality in the hereafter. As the state became less a source of protection, loyalty to the state also declined.

The Nubian dynasty. Meanwhile, to the south the rulers of the kingdom of Kush began to advance down the Nile River. Kush, with its capital city, Kerma, had first emerged about 2000 B.C. around the trade routes that connected northeastern Africa with both Egypt and the Red Sea trade. The Kushites were heavily influenced by Egyptian civilization, having been under Egyptian control for many years. Eventually, the Kushites created a new vibrant culture that blended Egyptian gods, hieroglyphics, and techniques for building temples and pyramids with the cultural traditions of African peoples.

By 730 B.C. a new Kushite kingdom, with its capital at Napata, had grown powerful enough to sweep north and conquer the kingdom of Thebes. Within the next 20 years, Kushite princes conquered all of Egypt and reunited the country for the first time since the fall of the New Kingdom. Known as the **Nubian dynasty**, the Kushite pharaohs governed Egypt for some 50 years. However, even the Kushite kings were not strong enough to reverse Egypt's decline, and under the pressure of a new invasion in 671 B.C. the Nubian dynasty also fell. The Kushites abandoned Egypt and withdrew to Nubia.

Although the kingdom of Kush reunited Egypt, it could not reverse Egyptian decline and had to retreat.

SECTION 2 REVIEW

IDENTIFY and explain the significance of the following:
   Ahmose
   New Kingdom
   Hatshepsut
   Akhenaton
   Ramses II
   Nubian dynasty

LOCATE and explain the importance of the following:
   Lower Egypt
   Thebes
   Upper Egypt
   Palestine

Syria
Tell el-'Amârna
Kush

1. **Main Idea** What were the results of the Hyksos' invasion and conquest of Egypt?
2. **Main Idea** What were the consequences of the Kushite invasion of Egypt in the late 700s B.C.?
3. **Geography: Human-Environment Interaction** How was geography a factor

in the pharaohs' desire to expand the New Kingdom?
4. **Writing to Explain** Imagine that you are a priest of Amon-Re. Explain why you are resisting participation in Akhenaton's religious revolution. Consider both your personal and professional reasons for opposing the revolution.
5. **Analyzing** Why did Egyptian rulers often try to erase all traces of previous rulers?

SECTION 3
Kingdoms in the Aegean

FOCUS

- How did the Minoans prosper with few natural resources?
- What caused the collapse of Mycenaean civilization?
- How did Greece change after the collapse of Mycenaean civilization?

Around the Aegean Sea, the land often could not support the abundant crops that grew in Mesopotamia or the Nile Valley. The hot, dry climate and the rocky soil were too harsh in some regions for grains or vegetables, but were ideal conditions for growing grapes and olives. Wine and olive oil were highly prized in the ancient world, and Aegean societies built a lively sea trade around these products. They built powerful civilizations, but as in Mesopotamia, nomadic migrations took their toll.

This dolphin fresco decorated the queen's room in a Minoan palace.

Minoan Civilization

As new technology, such as the plow, made it possible to grow more crops in rain-watered regions, civilization was able to spread beyond the river valleys. In addition, people living along the shores of the seas and oceans could supplement agriculture with fishing. In the eastern Mediterranean, these factors contributed to the rise of civilization on the island of Crete sometime around 3000 B.C.

Although scholars still debate the origins of the first inhabitants of Crete, it is clear that by about 2000 B.C. the Cretans had established a strong and prosperous Bronze Age civilization. This civilization was based on great palace complexes, the most famous of which was at Knossos (NAHS-uhs). Historians have named the civilization Minoan, after the legendary King Minos of later Greek mythology.

Writing. Knowledge of early Minoan history depends primarily on archaeological discoveries. For instance, the early Minoans' written language, today known as **linear A**, has been preserved on clay tablets, but scholars do not yet know how to decipher it. Later, after the Minoans came into contact with Indo-European-speaking groups migrating into the Greek Peninsula, a new form of writing, called **linear B**, came into use in Minoan palaces. In this new writing—an early form of Greek—scribes recorded details of the palaces' administration in Crete's later period.

Minoan society. At the top of Minoan society stood the rulers of the various palaces. Apparently they were absolute rulers and governed all aspects of Minoan society. Below them were nobles, followed by a class of artisans, merchants, farmers, and herders, and a specially trained class of scribes who served as the ruler's bureaucracy. Judging from the lack of weapons displayed in Minoan art or found in their tombs, the Minoans were not warlike and did not fortify their cities against invaders.

The Minoans built—and, because Crete lies on an active fault zone and suffers many earthquakes, often rebuilt—structures that were technologically and architecturally advanced. Most families had timber and stucco houses. The royal and noble families also had indoor running water and lavatories. Homes were often decorated with magnificent and remarkably modern-looking **frescoes**, paintings made directly on the plaster walls. Many frescoes depicted animals and plants from Mesopotamia and the Nile Valley, suggesting trade contacts with these other regions.

Minoan men and women probably had equal status. Frescoes show women as well as men participating in such activities as boxing and leaping over bulls in special bullrings. Minoan religion also reflected women's status. Its main figure was the Mother Goddess, whose ritual worship was performed by priestesses. Minoan religion seems to have been concerned mostly with fertility and the natural cycle of life.

The Minoans lived primarily by taking to the sea. Excellent sailors, they traveled widely, bringing Crete into closer contact with other civilizations. They grew rich trading olive oil and wine. The Minoans established trading posts in Greece, Sardinia, Syria, and the Aegean islands.

Minoan decline. The decline of Minoan civilization probably began with a major natural disaster. Sometime before 1500 B.C., a massive volcanic eruption occurred on the nearby island of Thera, about 70 miles north of the Cretan coast. The eruption was so powerful that it created a tidal wave that flooded much of Crete. The cloud of ash that spewed from the volcano ruined crops and buried many Minoan cities.

Although the Minoans rebuilt after this disaster, it must have weakened their civilization. At any rate, by about 1500 B.C. all the Minoan palaces except Knossos had been destroyed. Knossos was also burned about 1400 B.C.—possibly by the Indo-European-speaking peoples who earlier had migrated into Greece and established their own civilization.

> *With few natural resources, the Minoan civilization built a lively sea trade that allowed their culture to flourish for centuries.*

Early Civilization in Greece

As early as the mid-6000s B.C., small Neolithic farming communities had appeared in Greece. After about 3000 B.C. people in the region had

Aegean Civilization, c. 1450 B.C.

Sea of Civilization The Minoans and Mycenaeans drew on the riches of the Aegean to create their vibrant cultures.

Location How many miles separated the cities of Pylos and Knossos?

learned to make and use bronze. Small towns, some fortified with walls, appeared on the mainland and in the islands. Scholars still dispute who the inhabitants of these towns were, but they agree that around 2000 B.C. a new wave of Indo-European-speaking migrants from Asia Minor or the Balkans arrived in Greece. Whether the arrival of these people affected the emergence of Minoan civilization is unknown. Their culture, however, soon showed signs of Minoan influence.

The Mycenaeans. By about 1700 B.C. these early Greeks had begun to build strong fortresses at places like Athens, Pylos, and Tiryns. From these fortresses, the Greeks commanded the surrounding countryside. Their most important city was Mycenae, which was built on an easily defensible rocky hill at the intersection of two important trade routes. It is because of this city that scholars have named these Greeks the Mycenaeans.

The Mycenaeans interacted with the Minoans for a considerable length of time and

Theme:
Religion
Ancient artifacts found on Crete suggest that women played prominent roles in Minoan religion. In fact, there is evidence that a woman may have sat on the throne at Knossos as chief priestess or ruler.

Critical Thinking Ask students to suggest possible reasons why scholars might not be sure whether the woman was chief priestess or ruler.

ANSWER: Students should suggest that scholars are probably basing their knowledge on very limited written records or archaeological evidence.

Map Answer
approximately 225 miles

R **RESOURCE ACTIVITY**

READINGS IN WORLD HISTORY
Reading 2.3
Theseus and the Slaying of the Minotaur

Have students read the legend of Theseus and the Minotaur. Then have them complete the questions.

Level 2

Perhaps our best picture of Mycenaean life is preserved in the great epic poems—the *Iliad* and the *Odyssey*—attributed to the later Greek poet Homer. From Homer we know that the Mycenaeans worshipped Indo-European gods, headed by Zeus, the sky god. The Mycenaeans often sacrificed burnt offerings of animals to please the gods.

From both Homer and the archaeological record, scholars also know that warfare was an important element in Mycenaean society. Royalty and nobles were buried with bows and arrows, swords, daggers, and shields. Scenes of battle decorated the walls of the palaces. In the mountainous terrain of Greece, the various Mycenaean cities remained largely independent and often declared war on one another.

▲ This doorway led to the so-called Treasury of Atreus. Atreus was a legendary king of Mycenae.

eventually adopted some Minoan culture. Many scholars believe that Mycenaean invaders destroyed the Minoan cities and took over the palace at Knossos. Thereafter, Mycenaean kings began to run their own economies in much the same way as the Minoans—highly centralized and overseen by a specialized administration—and to keep their own palace records in the linear B script. Mycenaean traders also replaced Minoans in the eastern Mediterranean and the Aegean. Their goods traveled as far as Spain and southern Russia.

Mycenaean society. Warrior-kings, supported by nobles who exchanged their military service for lands and favors, dominated Mycenaean society. Below this warrior aristocracy, artisans and craftsmen produced pottery and other luxury items such as jewelry and inlaid metalwork. Mycenaean architects built impressive palaces and other works, such as bridges and a fine network of roads. Merchants handled overseas trade, often on the king's behalf. At the bottom of society, peasants and slaves kept the herds and tilled the soil. Everything was overseen by the palace officials, who maintained detailed records.

Mycenaean decline. Sometime around 1200 B.C. Mycenaean civilization began to collapse. Many of the cities were destroyed, possibly by earthquakes. Warfare among the cities further weakened the Mycenaeans. At about the same time, the Mycenaeans managed to band together for an attack on the city of Troy, which lay across the Aegean on the coast of Asia Minor. This war became the basis for the *Iliad* and the *Odyssey*.

The Trojan War was the last great enterprise of the Mycenaeans. As they went back to fighting among themselves, the Mycenaeans also fell prey to the second great wave of Indo-European migrants around 1100 B.C. Centuries later, a Greek historian wrote:

66 *After the Trojan War Greece was still subject to migrations and settlements, so that it could not enjoy the tranquillity needed for growth. Thus the Greek return from Troy was long drawn-out and caused many revolutions.* 99

Natural disasters and warfare led to the collapse of the Mycenaean civilization.

The Dorians

The migrations of Indo-European-speaking peoples into the Greek Peninsula following the destruction of Mycenaean civilization set up a chain reaction. Other groups were also pushed into new territories. As an ancient historian wrote:

66 *The country . . . had no settled population . . . ; instead there was a series of migrations, as the various tribes, being under the constant pressure of invaders who were stronger than they were, were always prepared to abandon their own territory.* 99

One of the most important of these tribes was the Dorians. Like other Indo-European-speaking groups, the Dorians were pastoralists, or livestock herders. Even in the Greek Peninsula they continued their traditional way of life. They scorned city life, and lived instead in open encampments, moving when necessary to find grazing lands for their herds. The Dorians also did not build military fortifications; in fact,

▶ **Lions and men struggle fiercely in the hunting scene on this bronze Mycenaean sword.**

they allowed Mycenaean fortifications to fall into decay. Instead, they relied on their own weapons and skill in battle—as a fragment of a Dorian song explained:

66 *My riches are spear, sword, and stout protective shield; with them I plough, with them I reap, with them I tread the sweet wine from the grape, with them I am entitled master of the serfs.* 99

The Dorians looked down on farming and often turned conquered peoples into servants to grow crops for them.

As other Indo-European tribes followed the Dorians, they also displaced the earlier inhabitants of Greece. One of the most lasting effects of these invasions was the disruption of trade. In the chaos that followed the mass migrations, Mycenaean civilization practically disappeared. Greece entered what modern scholars call the **Dark Age**.

Internal warfare and renewed Indo-European migrations followed the fall of the Mycenaean civilization.

SECTION 3 REVIEW

IDENTIFY and explain the significance of the following:
King Minos
linear A
linear B
frescoes
Dark Age

LOCATE and explain the importance of the following:
Aegean Sea
Crete
Knossos
Thera
Greece
Mycenae

1. **Main Idea** Why do scholars refer to the time after the fall of Mycenaean civilization as Greece's Dark Age?
2. **Main Idea** Why did Mycenaean civilization finally collapse?
3. **Geography: Place** With so few natural resources, how were the Minoans able to survive and build a prosperous society?
4. **Writing to Persuade** Write a short essay giving evidence to support the following statement:

Geographical factors allowed the Minoans to deemphasize the military, and forced the Mycenaeans to remain a warlike people.

5. **Synthesizing** Why were the Dorians able to displace the Mycenaeans? In your answer, consider (a) the Mycenaean political situation; (b) the Mycenaeans' geographical situation and the force of natural disasters; (c) the difference between Dorian and Mycenaean lifestyles; and (d) weaponry.

**GLOBAL HISTORY
RESOURCE CENTER**
Map: *Phoenician Sea
Routes*
Image: *Phoenician Glass
Trading Beads*

Print out and distribute
the image and map. Tell
students to write a
description of the
necklace, which will
appear in a Phoenician
mail-order catalog.
Show the image and
map as you discuss
Phoenicia and the
Hebrews. The captions
that accompany each
CD-ROM map and image
offer additional details.

**Level 1/
Sheltered English**

SECTION 4
Kingdoms and Empires in the Levant

FOCUS

- How did the Phoenicians and the Philistines contribute to the spread of civilization in the Mediterranean?

- How and why were the Hebrews able to establish their own kingdoms?

- What methods did the Assyrians use to build their empires, and what were the effects of the Assyrian and Chaldean conquests in Southwest Asia?

While great empires rose and fell in Egypt and Mesopotamia, smaller kingdoms began to grow in power in the Levant, the region along the eastern Mediterranean Sea. These small kingdoms, with their few resources and hostile neighbors, left legacies to the modern world that are felt even today. The modern alphabet and one of the world's major religions originated in the small kingdoms of the Levant.

Phoenician ivory carving

The Phoenicians and the Philistines

As the great waves of nomadic invaders battered and brought down empires in Southwest Asia, new, smaller states began to emerge in their place in the Levant. After the collapse of Minoan and Mycenaean trade, for example, the Phoenicians emerged to fill the void. The Phoenicians were a Semitic-speaking people who had settled in small city-states in present-day Lebanon. With few natural resources, the Phoenicians turned to the sea for survival. They developed fast and seaworthy ships, rowed by two tiers of oarsmen. By 1500 B.C. they had established a lively trade with Egypt. By about 900 B.C. the Phoenicians dominated trade in the Mediterranean, and carried goods as far away as Cornwall in England. They traded their own dyes and textiles, as well as goods from all over the ancient world.

The Phoenicians established many trading colonies on the islands and coasts of the western Mediterranean and North Africa. The most famous was Carthage. They took with them their 22-character script, used primarily for keeping trade records. Unlike the writing systems of Mesopotamia and Egypt, the Phoenician script was a true alphabet—each symbol represented a particular sound rather than a word or an idea. The Greeks adopted this alphabet, which later developed into our modern alphabet.

While the Phoenicians emerged during the great age of migrations and took to the sea, farther south in the Levant another migrant people, the Philistines, began to settle the land. In the 1200s and 1100s B.C., the Philistines were part of a larger group of peoples who terrorized the civilizations of Southwest Asia and the eastern Mediterranean. They were not simply raiders, however. As they invaded they brought their families with them. By the 1100s B.C. many Philistines had settled on the coast of Canaan, in present-day Israel.

With the advantage of iron weapons, they finally pushed out the Egyptians and established their own rule over the local Canaanites. The whole region soon became known as Philistia, or Palestine. The Philistines built substantial, well-planned cities. They became famous for their remarkable ceramic ware, and over time they grew prosperous by trading with Egypt, Phoenicia, and Cyprus. In addition, they tried to control other surrounding peoples, many of whom had also recently migrated into the region.

The Phoenicians and Philistines traded with other peoples of the Mediterranean, increasing cross-cultural contacts.

The Hebrews

Like other Semitic-speaking peoples, the Hebrews were originally nomadic pastoralists living in the desert grasslands around the Fertile Crescent. Much of what we know about them comes from their own later writings, which contained not only the laws and requirements of their religion but also much of their early history. These writings later formed the foundation for the Bible.

According to these accounts, the founder of the Hebrews was a shepherd named Abraham, who originally lived in Sumer. From there, he migrated with his family to Palestine. Later generations of Hebrews believed they were descended from Abraham through his grandson Jacob, whose own 12 sons had each established a tribe. They called themselves the **Twelve Tribes of Israel**. From Palestine some Hebrews apparently went to Egypt, perhaps during a time of famine. There they eventually became slaves of the pharaohs.

The origins of Judaism. Sometime in the mid-1200s B.C., a leader named Moses led the Hebrews out of Egypt and into the desert of the Sinai Peninsula in search of the "promised land." Their flight, called the **Exodus**, is commemorated in the Jewish festival of Passover. Following the Exodus, according to the Bible, Moses climbed Mount Sinai and returned bearing stone tablets inscribed with the **Ten Commandments**—the moral laws revealed to him by the Hebrew god Yahweh (YAH-way).

The commandments emphasized the importance of the family, the worship of God, human life, self-restraint, and justice. They also taught a moral system of behavior, in which people should deal fairly and honestly with one another—neither lying nor stealing, for example. When the Hebrew people agreed to follow the Ten

The Eastern Mediterranean, c. 1200 B.C.–1000 B.C.

Hittite Empire c. 1200 B.C.

Kingdom of Israel c. 1000 B.C.

Phoenicia c. 1200 B.C.

The Levant and Asia Minor To the east of the Mediterranean Sea, the empires and kingdoms of the Levant and Asia Minor flourished through trade and conquest.

? Region Which region had the most coastal trading cities?

Commandments, they entered into a **covenant**, or solemn agreement, with God, whom they now accepted as their guardian and supreme authority.

The Hebrews' basic conceptions about God changed over time. Originally, they seem to have thought of Yahweh as a tribal god, one god among others. Gradually, however, they came to see him as the only God—Lord and Creator of the universe. We call this idea **monotheism**. Its adoption by the Hebrews marks the beginning of the religion we know today as Judaism.

Establishing a homeland. Moses eventually led his people back to Palestine, although he died without setting foot in the promised land.

After a decisive defeat at the battle of Aphek in 1050 B.C., the tribes of Israel realized they were fighting a losing battle against the Philistines. In order to develop a united front, they chose Saul as king of all the tribes. Though Saul had successfully defended his own tribe, he was unable to win a decisive victory over the Philistines. This task fell to his successor, David. A true warrior-king, David used military strength to consolidate the kingdom of Israel and establish a capital at Jerusalem. David's son Solomon succeeded him and used diplomacy and political alliances to advance the economic development of Israel and to strengthen the power of the king.

Critical Thinking Ask students to review the actions taken by David and Solomon, and ask them if they think Solomon would have been as successful if David had not come before him.

ANSWER: Students might answer that David's military skills set the stage for Solomon's diplomatic and economic successes.

The Hebrews remained a loose confederation of tribes bound together in part by the need to maintain a strong central shrine for the Ark of the Covenant—the container of Moses' stone tablets. Tribal leaders known as Judges ruled in these years, enforcing God's laws and settling disputes among the tribes. The Hebrews also sometimes acknowledged the authority of holy men known as prophets, who appeared from time to time to warn people that they were incurring God's anger by straying from the terms of the covenant.

The kingdom of Israel. As the Hebrew tribes had to fight the earlier inhabitants of Palestine, they eventually came closer together for purposes of defense. Around 1020 B.C. the tribes united under a king named Saul, who established the kingdom of Israel. The dynasty established by Saul's successor, David—who ruled from the great fortified capital city, Jerusalem—established the new kingdom as a strong, independent state. Even then, religion remained the binding force among these new Israelites. Beginning with David, the kings of Israel established a tradition of making a covenant with their people similar to the covenant with God. According to a Bible account of a later coronation,

> 66 Jehoida [the priest] solemnized the covenant between the Lord, on the one hand, and the king and the people, on the other—as well as between the king and the people—that they should be the people of the Lord. 99

Under David's successor, Solomon, Israel reached the height of its wealth and influence. Solomon established relations with all the other leading powers of the region. One of his wives, for example, was a daughter of the Egyptian pharaoh. Through trade with Arabia, Solomon became enormously rich. With this wealth he built a magnificent temple to God in Jerusalem. The temple became the center of religious life and a symbol of the Israelite state.

After Solomon's death, however, internal struggles over succession and the growth of foreign influences, especially in religion, caused the kingdom to divide in about 926 B.C. Israel, the northern kingdom, was composed of the ten northern tribes, with its capital ultimately at Samaria. The remaining two tribes constituted the kingdom of Judah, with Jerusalem as its capital. Although the two kingdoms survived for several hundred years, eventually both fell to rising new imperial powers from Mesopotamia—the Assyrians and the Chaldeans. Meanwhile, under the relative peace and prosperity provided by the early kings, the Hebrew religion began to take on a more definite character, largely in the form of an extended set of religious laws.

The Torah and Mosaic law. The teachings of Moses were written down in five books, known as the **Torah**. The law of Moses, or Mosaic law, included the Ten Commandments as well as laws developed during later periods. It reflected the influence of Mesopotamian legal codes. Like the Code of Hammurabi, Mosaic law demanded "an eye for an eye"—though, unlike Hammurabi's code, it did not allow for the substitution of a money payment for those who could afford it. In fact, Mosaic law set a much higher value on human life. For example, although slavery was acceptable under Mosaic law, the law demanded kindness for slaves.

In the confusion created by nomadic migrations, the Hebrews were able to establish their own states bound together by their religious views.

▲ This menorah (a candleholder used in Jewish worship) pattern is found in the floor tiles of an ancient synagogue in Israel.

Sacred TRADITIONS

The Torah

The word Torah, in a literal sense, means "teaching" or "instruction." Used in this way, Torah includes all Jewish religious writings, consisting of the 39 books of the Hebrew Bible, as well as the oral Torah, the commentaries and discussions on the Scriptures written by rabbis over the years. Technically, however, the Torah is made up of the first five books of the Bible—Genesis, Exodus, Leviticus, Numbers, and Deuteronomy.

The Torah includes a description of the creation of the universe and a narrative history of the Hebrews up to the death of Moses. One of the most momentous events in this history was the Hebrews' covenant with God. This covenant included the Ten Commandments, as well as more than 600 laws that detailed how the Jews were to conduct themselves in their everyday lives.

You shall not ill-treat any widow or orphan. If you do mistreat them, I will heed their outcry as soon as they cry out to Me.

You shall not oppress a stranger, for you know the feelings of the stranger, having yourselves been strangers in the land of Egypt.

You shall not defraud your fellow [countryman]. You shall not commit robbery. The wages of a laborer shall not remain with you until morning.

You shall not insult the deaf, or place a stumbling block before the blind. You shall fear your God: I am the LORD.

Ancient Torah

Do not deal basely [dishonestly] with your countrymen. Do not profit by the blood of your fellow [countryman]: I am the LORD.

. . . You shall not take vengeance or bear a grudge against your countrymen. Love your fellow as yourself: I am the LORD.

For the LORD your God . . . shows no favor and takes no bribe, but upholds the cause of the fatherless and the widow, and befriends the stranger, providing him with food and clothing. You too must befriend the stranger, for you were strangers in the land of Egypt.

If . . . there is a needy person among you . . . do not harden your heart and shut your hand against your needy kinsman. Rather, you must open your hand and lend him sufficient for whatever he needs.

Understanding Sacred Traditions

1. What is the technical definition of the Torah?
2. Why do you think the Torah became the basis for early Jewish society and law?

The Assyrians and the Chaldeans

The Assyrians who conquered the kingdom of Israel were a Semitic-speaking people from northern Mesopotamia. As early as the 2000s B.C. they had settled the city of Assur on the upper Tigris River and adopted Sumerian civilization. This relatively open and accessible homeland, however, made the Assyrians an easy target for invaders.

For centuries the Assyrians had been dominated by others. They had briefly established an empire of their own in the 1300s B.C., only to have it broken apart in the nomadic migrations of about 1200 B.C. Unlike the Hittites, however, the Assyrians eventually recovered their strength and began to rebuild their empire. Determined not to be dominated again, they set out to become the foremost military power in Southwest Asia.

The Assyrian army. The Assyrians were the first to organize their army into regular units of a uniform size. All adult Assyrian men served in the army, which was commanded by officers who were promoted or demoted according to their ability in battle. Since they controlled iron mines in the mountains to the north, the Assyrians were able to arm their warriors with the latest military technology—iron weapons and iron battering rams on wheels. These rams were highly effective in breaking through city walls. The Assyrians also added cavalry to their infantry and chariots. The most important part of the army was probably the

massed archers, who fought on foot and were protected by shield bearers. With this powerful force, the Assyrians brought most of Southwest Asia under their control.

Techniques of imperial control. At its height, the Assyrian Empire included all of Mesopotamia, Syria, Palestine, and the Nile Valley of Egypt. The Assyrians established a standardized system of law and government over their empire. They kept the provinces in close communication through the use of a messenger system of relay riders. To speed these messengers and to make troop movements easier, the Assyrians built a road network throughout their empire. The new roads also had the advantage of making trade easier. Soon merchants from all over the empire were bustling along the new imperial highways. The imperial language, Aramaic, became almost universally used throughout the region.

The Assyrians ruled their empire through terror, inflicting enormously cruel punishments on any who defied or opposed them. To counter opposition, they settled large groups of soldiers as colonists in areas of potential revolt. They also resorted to the mass deportation of peoples from their homelands, resettling them in other parts of the empire. As part of their sweep across Southwest Asia, for example, the Assyrians conquered the kingdom of Israel about 722 B.C. They deported most of the Israelites to Assyria and settled Babylonians and others in Samaria, where they eventually became known as Samaritans. The remaining Israelites soon lost their own identity as they mixed with the Samaritans and so became known as the Ten Lost Tribes of Israel.

Such brutal techniques allowed the Assyrians to control their vast empire for a time, but they probably fueled more rebellions than they prevented. Soon the empire was also plagued by assaults from beyond its borders. In 612 B.C. the Medes, an Indo-European-speaking people from northwestern Iran, joined the Chaldeans of Babylon to destroy the Assyrian capital of Nineveh.

Assyrian Empire, c. 650 B.C.

Warrior Empire The powerful Assyrian military conquered the Mesopotamian heartland and much of the Levant.

? **Region** What major cities in the Nile Valley did the Assyrians control?

*U*sing superior military force and terror, the Assyrians established a vast empire that contributed to the mixing of peoples and cultures in Southwest Asia.

▲ A king and queen feast in the Hanging Gardens of Babylon. According to legend these gardens were created by King Nebuchadnezzar for his wife, a Medean princess who missed the hills of her homeland.

The Chaldeans. As the Assyrian Empire crumbled, the Chaldeans took their place. The Chaldeans were originally a Semitic-speaking nomadic people. In addition to preserving much of the ancient Sumerian civilization, they also made considerable advances in astronomy, astrology, and mathematics.

Like the Assyrians, the Chaldeans could be hard masters. In 587 B.C., for example, the Chaldean king Nebuchadnezzar conquered the kingdom of Judah and destroyed Jerusalem, including Solomon's great temple. The Chaldeans deported Judah's entire population to Babylon, in what became known as the **Babylonian Captivity**. This marked the beginning of the Jewish **Diaspora**, or scattering. The people of Judah—or Jews as they became known—maintained their religion and identity. Nevertheless, while in Babylon the Jews were exposed to new ideas coming from the east, where the Indo-European-speaking peoples of the Plateau of Iran were beginning to create strong states of their own. These influences contributed to the continuing development of Judaism.

The Chaldeans did not last long. In 539 B.C. they too were overthrown, this time by yet another group of Indo-European-speaking invaders, the Persians.

> *Like the Assyrians, the Chaldeans contributed to the mixing of peoples and cultures in Southwest Asia.*

SECTION 4 REVIEW

IDENTIFY and explain the significance of the following:
   Abraham
   Twelve Tribes of Israel
   Exodus
   Ten Commandments
   covenant
   monotheism
   Torah
   Babylonian Captivity
   Diaspora

LOCATE and explain the importance of the following:
   Canaan
   Phoenicia
   kingdom of Israel
   kingdom of Judah
   Samaria

1. **Main Idea** How were the Assyrians able to conquer and maintain their empires, and what effects did the Assyrian and Chaldean conquests have on Southwest Asia?
2. **Main Idea** Why was religion important to the establishment of Hebrew states?
3. **Economic Organization** How did the Phoenicians and the Philistines survive and prosper?

4. **Writing to Explain** You are a merchant in Phoenicia. Write a letter to your ruler explaining why maintaining peace with the Assyrians would benefit your business and the Phoenician economy.
5. **Synthesizing** How and why did Judaism endure in the face of opposition? In answering this question, consider the role played by (a) monotheism; (b) the covenant with Yahweh; and (c) conflicts with other peoples.

SECTION 4 REVIEW ANSWERS

IDENTIFY
For significance, see the following pages:
Abraham (p. 47)
Twelve Tribes of Israel (p. 47)
Exodus (p. 47)
Ten Commandments (p. 47)
covenant (p. 47)
monotheism (p. 47)
Torah (p. 48)
Babylonian Captivity (p. 51)
Diaspora (p. 51)

LOCATE
For locations, see the maps on pp. 47 and 50.

1. They used superior military force, terror, mass deportation, and resettlement. Subjects were mixed and many lost their cultural identities.
2. Religion bound the nomadic Hebrew tribes together, giving them a strong sense of identity.
3. The Phoenicians and Philistines survived and prospered by trading with other Mediterranean peoples.
4. Letters could include the ideas that peace would be profitable because of the size of the Assyrian Empire, their standardized system of law and government, and their system of highways.
5. The unique concept of covenant with one God bound the 12 tribes; tribes united and formed a kingdom to defend themselves.

CORE LESSON PLAN
See pages 29K and 29L for Lesson Plan 2.5.

Theme: Religion

The Vedas were initially passed on orally by early Indo-Aryans but were later recorded in Sanskrit. These sacred texts provide both the basis for the religion that became known as Hinduism and many details about life of the period. These details include the arrival of the first Indo-Europeans in India, their conquest of the indigenous peoples, and the creation of their society.

Critical Thinking Ask students why scholars might not take the "historical" accounts in the Vedas to be literally true.

ANSWER: Students might suggest that the Vedas are ancient and might have been altered through time, or that the accounts might contain biases.

SECTION 5
Invasion and Empire in Asia

FOCUS

- How did Indo-Aryan migrations affect northeast India?
- How did geography influence the development of civilization in India?
- What advantages did the Shang have over previous civilizations in the Huang He Valley?
- How were the Zhou able to overthrow the Shang?

While the civilizations of the Mediterranean, Southwest Asia, and northeastern Africa developed in contact with each other, Indian and Chinese civilizations grew up quite independently. Great geographical barriers separated them from other civilizations, allowing India and China to develop their own rich, unique cultures and traditions. Many of the cultural contributions made by these civilizations have endured for centuries.

Clay ox cart from the Indus Valley

Indo-Aryan Migrations in India

As Harappan civilization declined in the Indus Valley, around 1750 B.C. bands of nomadic warriors began to migrate into India through the Hindu Kush Mountains from the Plateau of Iran. These warriors, who called themselves "Aryans," were a branch of the Indo-European-speaking peoples who were also migrating into Southwest Asia and Europe about the same time. Modern scholars usually refer to them as "Indo-Aryans" to distinguish them from those Aryans who remained in Iran.

Indo-Aryan religion. Most of what we know about these early Indo-Aryans comes through their religious texts, the **Vedas**. The Vedas were hymns to the gods in which the people expressed their ideal conceptions of religion and society. The Vedas were originally an oral tradition. The oldest, the **Rig-Veda** (rig VAY-duh), or "Verses of Knowledge," is a collection of more than 1,000 ancient hymns used in rituals and sacrifices. Although it had probably been compiled by 1000 B.C., the Rig-Veda was not written down until about A.D. 1300.

The Indo-Aryans worshipped many gods, whom they associated with the forces of nature. Two of the most important were Indra, god of storm and war, and Varuna, who was associated with the sky. The Indo-Aryans worshipped the gods in a complex ritual based on the sacrifice of food items and animals. As they intermingled with the earlier Indian peoples, the Indo-Aryans also began to blend older Indian gods and traditions with their own.

Indo-Aryan society. As the Indo-Aryans established their rule over the earlier inhabitants of India, their language, an early form of **Sanskrit**, soon spread over much of India. Preserved as a sacred language, Sanskrit is the oldest version of an Indo-European language remaining today. Indo-Aryan social structure also spread. According to the Vedas, the Indo-Aryans at first recognized three great classes, or **varnas**. Initially, the Kshatriyas, or warrior nobles, were the highest class. Over time they were overshadowed by the Brahmins, priests who performed the sacred rituals. The Vaisyas—merchants, traders, and farmers—were the third and largest class. A fourth varna, the Sudras, made up of artisans and servants, was apparently added later to incorporate non-Aryan Indians into the Indo-Aryan scheme of society and religion. The first three classes considered the Sudras unclean, and forbade them to study or hear the sacred hymns of the Vedas.

According to the Rig-Veda, the varnas had been created along with all other forms of life when Purusha, the universal spirit, was sacrificed to himself:

66 *The Brahmin was his mouth, of both his arms was the [Kshatriya] made. His thighs became the Vaisya, from his feet the Sudra was produced. . . . Indra [the chief god] and Agni [god of fire] from his mouth were born, and Vayu [the wind] from his breath.* 99

Political structure of northern India. By the 600s B.C. the Ganges Valley had become the center of Indian civilization. The Indo-Aryans had learned to cultivate rice, allowing increased food production and thus a rapidly expanding population. With growing numbers to support larger armies, many kingdoms gradually developed on the flat plains.

At the head of each state was a **raja**, or king, usually a member of the Kshatriya. According to the Rig-Veda, "the king abides prosperous in his own abode. The earth bears fruit for him at all seasons. His subjects willingly pay homage to him." The kings lived in palaces and wore brilliant clothes that set them apart from others. In addition, the Rig-Veda also indicates that the kings had councils composed of noblemen, who were also Kshatriyas.

The Indo-Aryans established their own religion and social structure in the conquered territories of northern India.

Southern India. Far less is known about developments in southern India. Archaeological evidence suggests that development in the southern regions was much slower than in the Indus and Ganges Valleys. People in the south learned metalworking later, and while the north united into large kingdoms, the south remained fragmented. Nevertheless, the south was also affected by the spread of Sanskrit and Indo-European ideas. Thus, the peoples of the south also eventually identified themselves as Brahmins, Kshatriyas, Vaisyas, and Sudras.

One reason that the south developed later was its difficult geography. The southern peninsula of India, called the Deccan, was cut off from the technological advances of the north by the jungle-clad Vindhya Mountains. In addition, much of the terrain in the Deccan is hilly, which made consolidating territory more difficult than in the flat plains of the north. A major consequence of this comparative isolation by land, however, was that many peoples of the south turned to the sea. Through coastal ports, they eventually established important trade contacts with other regions around the Indian Ocean and in Southeast Asia.

Southern India developed along different lines than northern India, largely because of different geography.

Daily Life

Life in Aryan clans and families was somewhat freer and more open than in other societies. Although the Aryans were a patriarchal society, tribal chiefs did not have absolute authority over the affairs of the group. Aryan customs and laws governed the chief's actions. When the Aryans first came to India, women were also freer to choose their own husbands, rather than being told whom they must marry. This practice, however, changed over time.

Critical Thinking Ask students to suggest possible reasons why this freedom for women might have been taken away over time.

ANSWER: Answers will vary, but students might suggest that cultural attitudes toward women might have changed, or that families might have begun arranging women's marriages as a way of gaining power, for example, through family alliances.

▲ The rough terrain of the Deccan slowed the flow of ideas and goods between northern and southern India.

The belief system of the Shang religion legitimized the power of the ruling king. According to this religion, the god Ti could bestow bountiful harvests and victory in battle on the Shang people, and Ti supposedly could be influenced in these matters by the king's ancestors. Through prayer and sacrifice, the king was believed to be able to communicate with his ancestors and ask them to intercede with Ti on behalf of the Shang people. Therefore, it was the king himself who could produce abundant crops and ensure military triumphs, and consequently, religious and political power were concentrated in his hands.

Critical Thinking Ask students how the Shang beliefs about their kings could turn out to be a disadvantage for a ruler.

ANSWER: Students might suggest that a random event such as a drought could discredit a ruler.

R RESOURCE ACTIVITY

READINGS IN WORLD HISTORY
Reading 2.5
The Book of Songs

Have students read the song dating from the Zhou dynasty. Then have them complete the questions.

| Level 1 |

54

Shang China

Like Europe and the rest of Asia, China felt the impact of the new war technologies developed first by Indo-European peoples farther west. Sometime around 1700 B.C. chariot-driving invaders came to dominate the farming populations of the Huang He Valley. These invaders belonged to a tribal people called the Shang.

Shang government. Sometime between 1750 and 1500 B.C., the Shang established their rule over the Huang He region. They established the first historically verifiable dynasty in China. Under the Shang, China developed a complex bureaucracy to rule its expanding empire. At the center of this bureaucracy was the king, a member of the Tsu clan. The king, who was believed to be a descendant of the gods, was the supreme military leader. At its height, the Shang Empire stretched over 40,000 square miles, about the size of Kentucky.

The Chinese believed that kings should rule fairly. The Shang king Tsu Chia was praised for his sense of justice:

&6 *Tsu Chia . . . refused to be king unrighteously, and was at first one of the lower people. When he came to the throne, he . . . was able to exercise a protecting kindness toward their masses. He did not dare to treat with contempt [scorn] wifeless men and widows. Thus it was that he enjoyed the throne thirty and three years.* 99

Shang economy and handicrafts. Like earlier civilizations, the Shang economy was built on agriculture. Farmers grew a grain called millet, wheat, vegetables, and fruits, and they raised cattle, chickens, and pigs for meat. However, farmers did not own their land. The king owned all territory within the empire.

Many people lived in walled towns that gave them

protection during war. A Shang poem celebrated the building of a house in town:

&6 *To give continuance to foremothers and forefathers*
We build a house, many hundred cubits of wall; . . .
Here we shall live, here rest,
Here laugh, here talk. 99

In these towns lived specialized workers, such as woodcarvers, leatherworkers, and stonecutters. Under the Shang dynasty, skilled artisans learned to raise silkworms, to spin thread from their cocoons, and to weave silk cloth.

The bronze castings of Shang artisans are widely regarded as outstanding works of art. Although the technique of casting was also known in Sumer at this time, bronze casting developed independently in China. The forms of the vessels and the designs of the decorations were uniquely Chinese. Shang artisans cast small figures as well as large ceremonial vessels with surfaces that featured delicate decorations.

Shang religion. The religion that developed during the Shang dynasty combined ancestor worship and **animism**, the belief that all things in nature have a spirit. The Chinese worshipped the gods of the wind, earth, sun, moon, and clouds. However, the most important god was Ti, who they believed had the power to provide abundant harvests or victories in battle.

The Chinese also believed that the way to influence Ti was through the king's ancestors. The king supposedly communicated with his ancestors through diviners, or priests. The diviners made incisions on tortoise shells or cattle bones, called **oracle bones**, which they heated over a fire. They used the pattern of cracks that formed to interpret divine messages. Diviners consulted the oracle bones during sacrifices, requests for good weather, or for interpretation of events such as dreams, illness, or death.

▲ **Two bronze owls back-to-back formed a Shang dynasty wine vessel around 1500 B.C.**

Shang and Zhou Dynasties

Legend:
- Shang dynasty, c. 1750 B.C.–1122 B.C.
- Western Zhou dynasty, 1122 B.C.–771 B.C.

GOBI (DESERT)

Huang He (Yellow R.)

Anyang

North China Plain

Huang He

Zhengzhou
Luoyang

Wei He

YELLOW SEA

EAST CHINA SEA

Chang Jiang (Yangzi River)

Changsha

Xi Jiang

SOUTH CHINA SEA

0   200   400 Miles
0   200   400 Kilometers
Azimuthal Equal-Area Projection

40°N
30°N
20°N
110°E   120°E

China's Early Dynasties The Shang dynasty arose on the fertile plain around the Huang He. The Zhou dynasty grew out of the valley of the Wei He.

? Movement What physical feature may have limited the northern expansion of the Shang and Zhou dynasties?

Development of writing. The Chinese also began to develop a writing system under the Shang that is remarkably similar to Chinese writing today. Instead of using a phonetic system of writing, the Chinese assigned a special symbol, or character, to every word in their language. At first these characters were pictographs, or drawings of objects. As the language became more complex, the Chinese developed ideographs, which conveyed ideas rather than objects.

The early Chinese soon used writing to compose and preserve literary works. Writing became a highly beautiful art form, called **calligraphy**. Characters were written with a brush in lines that ran from the top to the bottom of a page, beginning on the right side.

Fall of the Shang dynasty. The Shang kingdom collapsed in the early 1100s B.C., apparently because the last Shang king, Ti Hsin, exhausted his kingdom's strength in wars against nomads to the north and east. Ti Hsin failed to guard the frontier against a people called the Zhou (JOH). Led by Wu Wang, the Zhou formed an alliance with nearby tribes and invaded the Shang kingdom. When King Ti Hsin set fire to his palace and died in the blaze, Wu Wang seized control of the Shang capital.

Through military superiority and a bureaucracy, the Shang dominated the Huang He region and created the first major Chinese empire.

The Western Zhou Dynasty

The Zhou believed that the gods determined who should rule China, a right known as the **Mandate of Heaven**. When the Zhou conquered the Shang in 1122 B.C., they called themselves the Sons of Heaven, claiming that the Mandate of Heaven had passed from the Shang to the Zhou.

The Zhou political order. After the last Shang king was overthrown, the Zhou campaigned for years to expand their power. Rebellions by the remaining Shang and their allies drove the Zhou to create a new system to preserve order, which many scholars call **feudalism**.

In the feudal system of Zhou China, the king owned all of the land. The king gave the right to control land in strategic locations to his kinsmen, who became feudal lords. The lords built fortified cities to use as bases from which to conquer the outlying lands in the name of the king. Because the king and his lords were related, the bonds between them were strong. Over time, however, these lords became quite powerful, and local people looked to them as their protectors. As the lords grew stronger, the king's power diminished.

Zhou society was divided into classes. At the top was the king and the royal family, which included most of the hereditary feudal lords.

Theme: Politics and Law

Initially, the Zhou were merely a minor satellite state of the powerful Shang dynasty. Around 1100 B.C., however, the Zhou began to form alliances with several smaller states to the south and the west of the Shang. In 1122 B.C. the Zhou and their allies decisively defeated the demoralized Shang at Mu-yeh. The former subjects had triumphed over the most dominant empire in ancient China.

Critical Thinking Ask students to list the ways the Zhou, a minor power, were able to defeat the Shang.

ANSWER: Students should note that the Zhou formed alliances with other states and waited until the military power of the Shang was weakened.

REVIEW & ASSESSMENT RESOURCES

- Study Guide 2.5
- Daily Quiz 2.5
- Main Idea Activity 2.5

All Levels

For significance, see
the following pages:
Vedas (p. 52)
Rig-Veda (p. 52)
Sanskrit (p. 52)
varnas (p. 52)
raja (p. 53)
animism (p. 54)
oracle bones (p. 54)
calligraphy (p. 55)
Wu Wang (p.55)
Mandate of Heaven
   (p. 55)
feudalism (p. 55)

1. The Indo-Aryans
brought the Vedic reli-
gion and Sanskrit and
established the social
structure based on the
varnas.
2. Military superiority
and centralized bureau-
cracy allowed the Shang
to build their empire.
3. It was cut off from
north by a mountain
range, and hilly terrain
made building kingdoms
more difficult.
4. Accounts should
include the idea that the
Zhou used their superior
military skills to take
advantage of the later
Shang. The feudal sys-
tem also provided a sta-
ble form of government.
5. Powerful kings were
believed to be descended
from gods, a hierarchy of
rulers included the king's
family, the government
was centralized, the
economy was based on
agriculture, and the
empires declined at the
hands of invaders.

The lords were sup-ported by aristocratic warriors, and together they ruled over the masses of peasants and slaves that made up the majority of the Chinese population.

The feudal system provided a stability that kept Zhou China rela-tively at peace for about two centuries. The Zhou expanded their borders both northward and southward and eventu-ally controlled an area much larger than the territory that had for-merly been ruled by the Shang kingdom.

Decline of the Zhou dynasty. By the 800s B.C., however, Zhou power had begun to diminish. The feudal lords grew less loyal to the king, and invading nomads chipped away at Zhou strong points. An uprising of the nobility drove out the tenth Zhou king in 841 B.C., and a period of disorder began.

The greatest threat to the Zhou kingdom, how-ever, came in 771 B.C. According to legend, King Yu wanted to impress the princess Pao-Ssu. To make her laugh, he raised an alarm by lighting

西 周 23

斗，见到它就退走了。"后人用
"木鸡养到"称赞人的修养到家
（见《庄子·达生》）。
周幽王姬宫涅（？—前771年）
宣王之子。即位第二年（前780
年），周王室心腹地带三川（渭、
泾、洛）地区发生大地震，同时
旱情严重，农业生产受到严重破
坏，民众流亡。西北诸牧游部族又
侵扰不止，蚕食周王朝的土地。前
779年，幽王纳褒姒，有宠。故废
申后及太子宜臼，以褒姒为后，立
其子伯服为太子。又任用"善谀好
利"的虢石父，政治混乱。申侯因
而与缯侯勾结犬戎，攻杀幽王于骊
山下。西周遂亡。
褒姒 周幽王后。据说夏王朝末

年，褒人的两个神化为龙，降于夏
王宫庭中。夏王占卜如何处置，结
果是杀掉与赶走都不吉利，只有把
龙涎水藏起来才吉利。于是夏王将
龙涎藏在匣中，二龙才离去。周
厉王末年，打开匣子来看，龙涎流
淌地上，又化为黑色大鼋而入王
府。一个很小的宫女，碰上了大鼋
而怀孕。周宣王时，宫女生下褒
姒。因无婚不孕，故弃之于路。恰
好此时有童谣说：。"山桑做弓，箕
木做箭筒，灭亡周国。"周宣王派
人捕杀卖山桑弓、箕木箭筒的人。
有夫妇二人闻此令而逃，于路边见
被弃大婴正在啼哭，遂携而逃往褒
国。女婴长大，花容月貌。褒人因
得罪周幽王，遂献褒姒。幽王宠爱
褒姒，故废申后而立褒姒为王后。
引起申后娘家申侯的不满，于是联
合缯和犬戎，灭亡了西周。
烽火戏诸侯 传说褒姒一笑百媚
生，然不常笑。幽王为博得褒姒欢
心，于是令人燃烽火，召诸侯。诸
侯见烽火报警，以为王室有难，纷
纷率兵而至。幽王说："没有敌人
侵犯，不过想让褒姒笑一笑罢
了。"而褒姒见诸侯如临大敌而
至，愤慨不平而去，竟喜笑颜开。
如此数次，失信于诸侯。后，申侯勾
结犬戎攻打周王室，幽王令燃烽火
召诸侯而救兵不至。犬戎遂杀幽
王。西周灭亡。

signal fires and sounding a big drum. When the feudal lords hurried to defend the king, they found no enemy, merely Pao-Ssu and King Yu laughing. Later, when nomadic invaders really attacked the royal capi-tal, the feudal lords did not respond to King Yu's alarm. Yu was killed, Pao-Ssu was captured, and the Zhou dynasty in the west came to an end.

King Yu's son fled eastward to establish what became known as the Eastern Zhou dynasty. The period before 771 B.C. thus is known as the Western Zhou dynasty. The kings of the Eastern Zhou, however, were never able to attain any real political or military power.

◀ **This reproduced Chinese document shows King Yu and princess Pao-Ssu.**

The Zhou, a frontier people familiar with Shang civilization, used their military skills and the weakness of the Shang dynasty to establish a new dynasty.

SECTION 5 REVIEW

IDENTIFY and explain the significance of the following:
   Vedas
   Rig-Veda
   Sanskrit
   varnas
   raja
   animism
   oracle bones
   calligraphy
   Wu Wang
   Mandate of Heaven
   feudalism

1. **Main Idea** How did the Indo-Aryans affect civilization in northern India?
2. **Main Idea** What advan-tages did the Shang have that enabled them to build an empire in China?
3. **Geography: Place** What influence did geography have on the development of southern India?
4. **Writing to Describe** Imagine that you are an official of the Zhou court. Write a brief account describ-ing how the Zhou were able to defeat the Shang and establish their own empire. In your account also describe the importance of feudalism to the Zhou Empire.
5. **Comparing** How were the first empires in China similar to the first empires in Southwest Asia and northern Africa?

Review

On a separate sheet of paper, complete the following exercises:

WRITING A SUMMARY

Using the essential points in the text, write a brief summary of the chapter.

REVIEWING TERMS

From the following list, choose the term that correctly matches the definition.

Rig-Veda
Diaspora
frescoes
monotheism
covenant
Mandate of Heaven

1. painting made directly on plaster walls
2. belief that Chinese rulers received the right to rule from the gods
3. solemn agreement between the Hebrews and Yahweh, made when the Hebrews accepted the Ten Commandments
4. scattering of Jewish people outside Israel, beginning with the Babylonian Captivity
5. sacred collection of more than 1,000 ancient Indian hymns that were collected about 1000 B.C.

REVIEWING CHRONOLOGY

List the following events in their correct chronological order.

1. The nomadic Zhou destroy the Shang and found their own dynasty.
2. Chaldean Empire collapses at the hands of the Persians.
3. Sargon seizes control of Sumer and establishes the Akkadian Empire.
4. The Code of Hammurabi establishes the idea of "an eye for an eye."
5. Assyrians conquer Israel and deport the Ten Tribes.

UNDERSTANDING THE MAIN IDEA

1. How did the Assyrians build and maintain their vast empire in Southwest Asia?
2. Why did the pharaohs want to expand the New Kingdom?
3. With few natural resources, how did the Minoans build a prosperous society?
4. How did the Phoenicians influence other peoples of the Mediterranean?
5. What enduring religious and social effects did the Indo-Aryans have?

THINKING CRITICALLY

1. **Contrasting** What role did geography play in the different ways that Indian and Mesopotamian civilizations developed?
2. **Comparing** How did oppression by foreign peoples affect the development of Egyptian and Hebrew civilizations?

Building Your Portfolio

Complete the following activities individually or in groups.

1. **Cross-cultural Interaction** Imagine that you are a Mesopotamian traveler in the year 1500 B.C. You and your fellow adventurers will travel from Mesopotamia through the Levant to Egypt. Write a travel journal that describes the geography of the lands you visit, the people you meet, the difficulties you face, and the souvenirs and ideas that you will take back with you to Mesopotamia. You should also include a map of your route, showing the major geographical features and civilizations you encounter. You may also wish to illustrate your journal.
2. **Art and Culture** Imagine that you are an artist living in Minoan Crete. You (and your fellow artists) have been asked to plan a fresco that expresses your culture. Consider the location of your fresco, and plan to include depictions of the geography of your country, your relationship to the sea, your knowledge of other peoples, your agriculture, and your way of life. Either create a large and detailed sketch of your planned fresco, or produce an actual model of it.

58

Unit 2
The Growth of Civilization

1800 B.C.–A.D. 1532

Chapter 3

The Persian and Greek World 1000 B.C.–404 B.C.

The Persians built a multiethnic empire that ultimately stretched from India to Egypt, while the people of Greece founded their own great civilization based on the city-state. What kinds of threats might nomadic peoples pose to more settled populations?

Chapter 5

The Roman World 509 B.C.–A.D. 476

The Roman Republic gradually transformed into an empire, which ultimately collapsed because of invasions and internal disorder. How might the establishment of a universal set of laws help to unify a society?

Chapter 4

The Hellenistic World and the Rise of Rome 1000 B.C.–133 B.C.

The Macedonians conquered the Greek city-states and expanded their empire, carrying Greek civilization with them, while a new power, Rome, emerged in central Italy. How might warfare and conquest influence the exchange of culture?

In southern Europe and western Asia, a series of great civilizations rose and fell. The Persians built a multiethnic empire that stretched from Egypt to India, while the Greeks built a remarkable civilization in the eastern Mediterranean. The Macedonians later conquered both the Greeks and the Persians and carried Greek culture across their empire to India. In the western Mediterranean, the city-state of Rome emerged and transformed from a small republic to a vast empire. Civilizations also arose in India and China, where the vibrant religions of Hinduism and Buddhism developed. In addition, civilizations arose in Africa, where trade-based kingdoms and empires flourished, and in the Americas, where cities sprang up in Mesoamerica and the Andes Mountains.

Chapter 6
The Growth of Asian Civilizations
700 B.C.–A.D. 550

As Greek and Roman civilizations grew in the Mediterranean, civilizations also flourished in China and India. India was the birthplace of two of the world's great religions—Hinduism and Buddhism—while Confucian ideas shaped the development of Chinese culture and society. How might a society's religion influence the relations between different groups of people?

Chapter 7
Early African Civilizations c. 1800 B.C.–c. A.D. 1235

As Africa entered the Iron Age, powerful states and empires emerged, sustained by vigorous trade. How might geography influence the development of trade?

Chapter 8
Civilizations in the Americas 500 B.C.–A.D. 1532

In isolation from much of the world, civilization, and later empires, developed in the Americas as agriculture replaced gathering as the means of sustaining human communities. How might geography affect the location and development of cities?

Chapter 6
The Growth of Asian Civilizations

Religious beliefs may include the idea of social hierarchy. This may result in conflict among various social groups.

Chapter 7
Early African Civilizations

Trade might develop in areas located near cross-roads, navigable rivers, or good harbors. Trade might also increase in places that are near the sources of raw materials, such as gold or iron, or near the places where manufactured goods are produced.

Chapter 8
Civilizations in the Americas

Cities may emerge where a reliable water supply exists and where the land is fertile and easily tilled. Easy access to transportation, trade, and religious sites might also encourage the development of cities.

Chapter 3

The Persian and Greek World 1000 B.C.–404 B.C.

Chapter Planning Guide

	TEXTBOOK	CORE RESOURCES	VISUAL RESOURCES	MULTIMEDIA
Introduction	pp. 60–61	Block Scheduling Handbook: Ch. 3		Videodisc Segment 3 and Viewing Guide: *How Do We Decide?*
Lesson 3.1 The Persian Empire	pp. 62–68 Map: *Persian Empire*, p. 64 Through Others' Eyes: *Noble Children in the Persian Court*, p. 67	Reading 3.1: *A Debate on Government*		GHRC 3/Videodiscs: Image— *Portrait of Zoroaster*
Lesson 3.2 The City-States of Greece	pp. 69–75 Map: *Ancient Greece*, p. 71	Reading 3.2: *The Making of Spartan Soldiers*		GHRC 3 Readings: *Euripides on the Unhappy Lot of Greek Women; Homer Defines the Ideal Greek Hero* GHRC 3/Videodiscs: Image— *Greek Vase with the Goddess Athena*
Lesson 3.3 War and Empire in the Aegean	pp. 76–80 Map: *The Persian Wars*, p. 77	Reading 3.3: *The Greatness of Athens* Geography Activity 3: *Greek Alliances*	Geography and History 3: *The Peloponnesian War*	GHRC 3 Readings: *Xerxes Decides on War Against the Greeks; How the Persians Crossed the Hellespont; Thucydides on the Fall of the Delian League; Spartans Versus Persians at Thermopylae* GHRC 3/Videodiscs: Images— *The Acropolis as It Was in Ancient Times; A Greek Warship;* Maps—*The Battle of Thermopylae; The Long Walls of Athens; The Battle of Salamis*
Lesson 3.4 The Golden Age of Greek Culture	pp. 81–86 Literature Through Time: *The Odyssey*, p. 84	Reading 3.4: *Athenian Values and Antigone* Skills Activity 3: *Distinguishing Fact from Opinion* Writing Project 3: *Creating an Outline*	Art and History 3: *Dipylon Vase* Everyday Life 3: *Greek Architecture*	GHRC 3 Readings: *Greek Drama in the 400s B.C.; The Olympic Games* GHRC 3/Videodiscs: Image— *Greek Sculpture of the God of Medicine*
Chapter Investigation and Enrichment	pp. 60–86	Chapter 3 Investigation: *Athens Today!* People in World History 3 Explorations in Daily Life 3		GHRC 3/Videodiscs
Review and Assessment	Section 1 Review, p. 68 Section 2 Review, p. 75 Section 3 Review, p. 80 Section 4 Review, p. 86 Chapter 3 Review, p. 87	Chapter Review Activity 3 Vocabulary Activity 3 Themes Review 3 Section Study Guides 3.1–3.4 Main Idea Activities 3.1–3.4 Daily Quizzes 3.1–3.4 Chapter 3 Test Sheltered English Ch. 3 Test Ch. 3 Test Generator		Audio CDs: Ch. 3 Summary (English and Spanish)

INTRODUCING THE CHAPTER

Textbook pp. 60–61

CHAPTER OVERVIEW

On the Plateau of Iran, the Persians forged a great empire that stretched thousand of miles. In the west a new civilization, which Persia tried to control, developed around city-states in Greece. Once the Greeks defeated the Persians, however, the city-states began warring with each other. In spite of these conflicts, Greek civilization came to dominate the Mediterranean.

PRESENTING THEMES

On the chalkboard or on an overhead transparency, write the following open-ended theme questions.

- **CROSS-CULTURAL INTERACTION** Why might the members of a well-established society fear nomadic peoples living on their borders?
- **GEOGRAPHY** How might armies and navies use geography to their advantage?
- **POLITICS AND LAW** What conditions might make it difficult for a small group of individuals to exercise political power over a larger majority?

Have students, either individually or in groups, suggest responses to the questions. For the cross-cultural interaction question, students might suggest that nomadic peoples might import new political or religious ideas. For the geography question, students might suggest that the armies might use geographic features as natural defenses. A navy's knowledge of bays and tides might influence the outcome of a battle. For the politics and law question, students might suggest that if a small ruling group's policies become too unpopular, the majority might revolt. Save the responses. Once students have studied the chapter, you may wish to have them complete the Themes Review, then compare the two sets of answers.

USING THE VIDEO

Segment 3: *How Do We Decide?*

ENGLISH

Search Chapter 3
Videodisc 1, Side A

SPANISH

Search Chapter 3
Videodisc 1, Side A

Tell students that in this chapter they will examine the factors that led to the new and very different civilizations that emerged in Persia and Greece 2,500 years ago. Conclude by showing Segment 3 of the *World History and Cultures Videodiscs*. This segment explores what many consider to be the most important legacy left to us by the ancient Greeks: the idea of democracy. In the video students see the process of "direct democracy" at work today in a New England town meeting. Before showing the video, ask students to think about the distinction between "direct democracy" and "representative democracy" as they watch this segment. To help students grasp the significant points of the segment, have them complete Video Viewing Guide 3.

Key to Ability Levels

All strategies and activities are coded to the following ability levels:

LEVEL 1	**Basic** activities suitable for all students
LEVEL 2	**Average** activities suitable for average to above-average students
LEVEL 3	**Challenging** activities suitable for above-average students
SHELTERED ENGLISH	Activities suitable for students with **Limited English Proficiency**

Additional Resources

BOOKS FOR TEACHERS

Blundell, Sue. *Women in Ancient Greece*. Harvard University Press, 1995. Looks at social roles.

Drews, Robert. *The Coming of the Greeks: Indo-European Contacts in the Aegean and Near East*. Princeton University Press, 1988. Looks at the early history of Greek civilization.

Grant, Michael. *The Rise of the Greeks*. Collier, 1987. Offers a general introduction.

BOOKS FOR STUDENTS

Hamilton, Edith. *The Echo of Greece*. Norton, 1987. Provides an introduction to Greece, with emphasis on literature.

Martin, Thomas R. *Ancient Greece from Prehistoric to Hellenistic Times*. Yale University Press, 1996. Presents an overview of Greek history.

Stewart, Gail. *The Trojan War*. Greenhaven, 1989. Attempts to separate the myths about Troy from the reality.

MULTIMEDIA MATERIALS

Ancient Persia. Coronet. Video, 11 min. Provides examples of the achievements of Cyrus and Darius.

Our Heritage from Ancient Greece. Guidance Associates. Video with guide, 27 min. Examines art, philosophy, and drama.

Perseus. Annenberg/CPB Project. Videodisc, CD-ROM, MAC format. Includes a wealth of materials on Greece.

The Persian Empire

RESOURCES

Pupil's Edition

Map, p. 64: *Persian Empire, c. 500 B.C.*

Core Resources

Reading 3.1: *A Debate on Government*

Videodiscs or Global History Resource Center

Image: *Portrait of Zoroaster*

Search Frame 704

LESSON FOCUS

What were the achievements of the Persian Empire that flourished around 500 B.C.?

OBJECTIVES

After completing this lesson, students will be able to:

- identify the Medes and Persians and locate where they came from;
- explain Zoroaster's religious message;
- describe how the Persians built their empire and explain how Darius organized it;
- note how the Persians generally treated the peoples they conquered.

HOOK

Identify the Medes and Persians and examine their migration from the Eurasian plain. Remind students of the waves of migration from Eurasia that began around 2000 B.C. Point out that the Medes and the Persians were among the many Indo-European-speaking tribes that took part in this great movement. Then draw students' attention to the map on textbook page 64 and have students locate the area that the Medes and the Persians left.

Ask: Where did the Medes and Persians live before migrating to the Plateau of Iran?

[Eurasian plain of southern Russia]

Then ask students to use their fingers to trace on the map the route the Medes and Persians took on their journey to the Plateau of Iran. Encourage students to write a sentence describing the route. *[The route went south across the Caucasus Mountains or around the Caspian Sea to the Plateau of Iran.]*

DEVELOP

Discuss how the Persians established their empire and examine Darius's system of imperial government.

Remind students that between the late 600s and the mid-500s B.C., the Medes built a large kingdom. In 550 B.C., however, the Persian ruler Cyrus II conquered the Medes, taking the title "king of the Medes and Persians." Cyrus and his successors continued their conquests, and by about 500 B.C. the Persians controlled the largest empire the world had yet seen. You might direct students to the map on textbook page 64 to help them appreciate the extent of the Persian Empire.

Next point out that Darius I, who came to power in 522 B.C., established an efficient system to govern this vast empire. Ask students to use the information on textbook pages 65–67 to create a graphic organizer on Darius's system of administration. Suggest that they focus on such topics as type of government, organization of the provinces, the role of the army, the legal system, and the economy. Encourage students to share and discuss their graphic organizers.

Then assign Core Resources Reading 3.1 and have students evaluate Darius's arguments in support of monarchy.

PROBE

Identify the major tenets of Zoroastrianism. To prepare students for this activity, display the electronic media image of Zoroaster. Call on a student to read aloud the discussion of Zoroastrianism on textbook pages 63–64. While the student is reading, note the following key features of Zoroastrianism on the chalkboard: belief in one god, Ahura Mazda; life is a struggle between good and evil; those who choose to follow good will receive eternal blessings, while those who follow evil will suffer punishment in hell; the basic principle of religion is to lead a moral life devoted to the truth, for lying is the greatest sin. After the reading has been completed, have students use the chalkboard notes to write a brief paragraph that answers the question *What was Zoroastrianism?*

Conclude by asking students to note which of Zoroaster's beliefs are reflected in today's world religions.

CONCLUDE

Discuss how the Persians generally treated the peoples they conquered. Have students consider the Persians as conquerors.

Ask: *How did the Persians generally treat the peoples they conquered?*
[Generally, Persians allowed conquered peoples a degree of self-rule; also, they allowed conquered peoples to follow their own customs, religions, and legal practices.]

Conclude by encouraging students to consider the impact of these actions on the Persian Empire.
Ask: *In what sense was the Persian Empire multicultural?*

[Persians conquered peoples of many different ethnic and cultural backgrounds. For the most part, however, they allowed conquered peoples to retain their cultural identity. And Persians adopted some aspects of the cultures of peoples they conquered.]

EXTEND

Cross-Curricular Connection: *Language Arts*
Encourage students to imagine they lived in one of the areas conquered by Darius I. Have them write a letter to a friend discussing the advantages and disadvantages of living under Persian rule.

MEET INDIVIDUAL NEEDS

Visual-Spatial Learners
Have students use library resources or the Internet to discover more information about Persian art and architecture of the period discussed in this section. Call on volunteers to share their findings in oral presentations supported by visuals.

Linguistic Learners
Have students close their eyes as you read aloud the description of the Persian landscape on textbook pages 62–63. When you have completed the reading, ask students to jot down key words or phrases in the description. Then have students use these words and phrases to write a poem that presents a "word picture" of the Persian landscape.

ASSESS

Review
Have students complete the Section 1 Review. Use answers in the Teacher's Edition, page 68, to assess student mastery of this section.

Lesson 3.2   The City-States of Greece

Textbook pp. 69–75

RESOURCES

Pupil's Edition

Map, p. 71: *Ancient Greece,*
750 B.C.–450 B.C.

Core Resources

Reading 3.2: *The Making of Spartan*
Soldiers

Videodiscs or Global History Resource Center

Image: *Greek Vase with the Goddess*
Athena

Search Frame 709

Global History Resource Center

Reading: *Euripides on the Unhappy Lot*
of Greek Women
Reading: *Homer Defines the Ideal Greek*
Hero

LESSON FOCUS

What kind of society emerged in Greece around 700 B.C.?

OBJECTIVES

After completing this lesson, students will be able to:
- explain how the Greeks viewed the polis;
- investigate why the Greek city-states established colonies;
- examine how Athens eventually became a democracy;
- compare and contrast Athens and Sparta.

HOOK: Link to Today

Discuss the role that the polis played in Greek identity.
Poll the class to find which students are members of particular groups, such as the scouts, sports teams, or the chess or drama club. Call on volunteers to explain why they joined these groups. Prompt students to give such answers as feeling pride in what the group does, support for the group's principles, and feeling of belonging to a special group. Then point out that the groups a person belongs to provide clues to his or her identity. Help students recognize that a similar situation existed between the Greeks and their city-states.
Ask: How was Greek identity related to the polis?
[The polis was the center of Greek identity and loyalty. No

individual identity, as such, existed. Rather, all citizens were part of the extended community of the polis.]

DEVELOP

Examine the reasons why the Greek city-states founded colonies. Write on the chalkboard the following incomplete cause-effect chain: *peace and prosperity—population growth—food shortages—[establishment of colonies].* Inform students that the chain describes the situation of the Greek city-states after the Dark Age. Then have them complete the cause-effect chain.

Next call on volunteers to identify other reasons why the Greek city-states established colonies. Note their responses below the "food shortages" entry in the cause-effect chain. *[hunger for land, commercial opportunities, political problems]* Then give students an idea of the extent of Greek city-states' colonization by drawing their attention to the map on textbook page 71.

Have students use this information to write a brief paragraph explaining why the Greek city-states needed to establish colonies.

PROBE

Trace the development of democracy in Athens. Work with students to create a pyramid-shaped diagram of the social

---

structure of Athens under the aristocratic order. *[The pyramid should show adult male citizens with political rights at the top; below that, citizens with no political rights, such as women and children; and finally, at the bottom, noncitizens, such as slaves and resident foreigners.]*

Make a large copy of the pyramid on the chalkboard or on a piece of butcher paper. Then point out that, as a result of the decline of the Greek aristocracy after the 700s B.C., changes occurred in the social structure of Athens.

Ask: What led to the decline of the Athenian aristocracy?

> *[As commoners began to play a greater part in commerce and in defending Athens, they started to demand a greater voice in government.]*

Assist students in understanding how different Athenian law-makers tried to adjust to the breakdown of the aristocratic order. Create a chart on the chalkboard with *Solon*, *Peisistratus*, and *Cleisthenes* as column headings. Then ask students what changes each leader made. Call on volunteers to enter changes in the appropriate column. *[**Solon:** canceled debts, abolished enslavement for debt; divided citizenry into four groups based on wealth; made public offices available to upper three classes; allowed all classes to vote; advocated expansion of trade; **Peisistratus:** beautified the city; increased sense of citizenship with festivals; **Cleisthenes:** created tribes that crossed areas, destroying the aristocracy's regional power; created a Council of Five Hundred to prepare matters for the assembly made up of all voting citizens]*

Direct students to copy the chart into their notebooks. Then refer them back to the pyramid diagram. Have them draw a new diagram that incorporates the changes introduced by Solon, Peisistratus, and Cleisthenes.

You may wish to point out that women benefited little from this move toward democracy. To illustrate the status of women in Greek society, assign the Global History Resource Center reading on women.

CONCLUDE

Compare life in Sparta to life in Athens. Ask students what kind of society developed in Sparta. *[militarist]* You may wish to assign Core Resources Reading 3.2 to give students an insight into the militarist nature of Spartan life.

Encourage students to compare and contrast Athens and Sparta. Begin with similarities—for example, both were confined to relatively small geographic areas, and both had forms of democracy. Then focus on differences—for example, Sparta had a small number of citizens ruling over a large group of slaves; Spartans concentrated on the arts of war; Athenians were interested in the fine arts. Record students' responses in chart form on the chalkboard.

Next organize students into two groups—Athenians and Spartans. Have group members use the chart information to discuss what they think about the other group. Then call on group representatives to present their group's ideas. Ensure that students recognize that Athens and Sparta represented very different ideas and values.

EXTEND

Cross-Curricular Connection: *Language Arts*

Students might want to read the selection from the *Iliad* in the Global History Resource Center. Then they might work in pairs to practice dramatic readings of this excerpt or other excerpts from the *Iliad* or the *Odyssey* for presentation to the class.

MEET INDIVIDUAL NEEDS

Visual-Spatial Learners

Link to Today. Display the Art and History transparency and the electronic media image. Explore with students what can be learned about Greek life from the designs on vases. Then have students imitate the Greek style in designing a vase illustration that conveys something about American life today.

Students Acquiring English

Point out that many English words have their origins in the Greek language. Pair new speakers of English with fluent speakers. Have pairs research the meanings and etymologies of the following words and report their findings to the class: *agoraphobia, aristocrat, democracy, Spartan, tyrant*.

ASSESS

Review

Have students complete the Section 2 Review. Use answers in the Teacher's Edition, page 75, to assess student mastery of this section.

Lesson 3.3   *War and Empire in the Aegean*

Textbook pp. 76–80

RESOURCES

Pupil's Edition

Map, p. 77: *The Persian Wars,*
500 B.C.–479 B.C.

Core Resources

Reading 3.3: *The Greatness of Athens*

Visual Resources

Geography and History 3: *The*
Peloponnesian War

Global History Resource Center

Reading: *Xerxes Decides on War*
Against the Greeks

Reading: *How the Persians Crossed the*
Hellespont

Reading: *Thucydides on the Fall of the*
Delian League

Reading: *Spartans Versus Persians at*
Thermopylae

Videodiscs or Global History Resource Center

Image: *The Acropolis as It Was in*
Ancient Times

Search Frame 708

Image: *A Greek Warship*

Search Frame 711

Map: *The Battle of Thermopylae*

Search Frame 714

Map: *The Battle of Salamis*

Search Frame 715

Map: *The Long Walls of Athens*

Search Frame 716

LESSON FOCUS

What were the causes and results of the conflict between the Greek city-states and Persia and later among the Greek city-states themselves?

OBJECTIVES

After completing this lesson, students will be able to:

- explain how Greece was saved from Persian invasion;
- describe Athens during its Golden Age;
- examine the causes of the Peloponnesian War.

HOOK

Examine how Greece saved itself from Persian domination. Work with students to create a flowchart of key events in the Persian Wars, beginning with Persia's crushing of the Asiatic Greeks and including the battles of Marathon,

Thermopylae, Salamis, and Plataea. To reinforce the role played by geography in key battles, draw students' attention to the map on textbook page 77. You might also use the electronic media maps of the Battle of Thermopylae and the Battle of Salamis for this purpose. If time permits and the items are available, assign the Global History Resource Center readings on Xerxes and the Persians crossing the Hellespont. These readings give the historian Herodotus's view of key events in the Persian Wars.

DEVELOP: Link to Today

Discuss the achievements of Athens during its Golden Age. Point out that during the 400s B.C. Athenian society reached new heights. Then write the word *government* on the chalkboard. Call on volunteers to describe developments in government during Athens's Golden Age. Note their responses on the chalkboard. *[Students should understand that direct democracy reached its height during the Golden Age.]* Students might better understand the nature of Athenian democracy by comparing the government of Athens to the U.S. government.

Next write the word *empire* on the chalkboard and invite volunteers to discuss how Athens became a great power in the Mediterranean. Students should understand that the various Greek city-states established a mutual-defense alliance called the Delian League. At first, all city-states had equal say in league matters. Later, however, Athens dominated the league, treating other members as its subjects. Encourage students to use the information on the chalkboard to create a graphic organizer entitled "Athens's Golden Age." You may wish to have volunteers share their organizers with the class.

PROBE

Examine the part that Pericles played in Athens's rise to greatness. Display the electronic media image of the Acropolis and assign Core Resources Reading 3.3, which gives Pericles' view of Athens during the Golden Age. Have students use information from the image, the reading, and their textbooks to write a brief paragraph supporting or opposing the following statement: *Without Pericles, Athens would not have enjoyed a Golden Age.* Have students place their paragraphs in their portfolios.

CONCLUDE

Examine the reasons why war broke out among the Greek city-states. Write this statement on the chalkboard: *Athens's greatness was the major cause of its downfall.* Ask students to respond to this statement. *[Students should recognize that as Athens grew in power, its actions became arrogant. Instead of treating other members of the Delian League as partners, Athens treated them as subjects, generating incredible resentment. In addition, turning the Delian League into an empire hurt the Athenians, because it undermined the concept of the polis.]*

Next display the Geography and History transparency of the Peloponnesian War and assign the accompanying worksheet. In addition, have students complete the Global History Resource Center reading on Thucydides, if it is available. Then encourage students to focus on the causes of the Peloponnesian War. *Ask: Why did Sparta attack Athens?*

> *[Students should understand that the two had long-standing differences. The Athenians saw the Spartans as crude and ignorant; the Spartans saw the Athenians as weak and overly concerned with commerce.]*

EXTEND

Cross-Curricular Connection: *Journalism*

Have students review the Global History Resource Center reading on the Battle of Thermopylae. Then encourage students to imagine they are war correspondents for contemporary newspapers. Ask them to write a news story on the Spartans' stand against the Persians. Suggest that some write the story from a Greek point of view and others write it from a Persian point of view. Others might wish to write a story on the unique challenges of covering a war in that time and place. Invite the correspondents from both sides to read their stories to the class, and have them include the stories in their portfolios.

Other Media

Link to Today. Have students view the video *Athenian Democracy* (Encyclopedia Britannica, color, 15 min.). Then lead them in a class discussion comparing ancient Greek democracy to modern-day democracy.

MEET INDIVIDUAL NEEDS

Gifted Students

Point out that battle plans from this period of Greek history have been studied through the ages. American Civil War general Robert E. Lee, for example, was an avid student of the battles of ancient Greece. Encourage students to research the battles discussed in the section. Students might work individually or in small groups to map the strategy of one particular battle and present it to the class. Students may consult the electronic media image of a Greek warship and the electronic media maps of the battles of Thermopylae and Salamis and the electronic media map of the long walls of Athens.

Students Having Difficulty

Jill Paton Walsh's novel *Children of the Fox* (Farrar, Straus and Giroux, 1978) consists of three stories featuring a young person's encounter with Themistocles. It offers insights into the society of the time—particularly the role of women. Those students having trouble understanding Greece in the 400s B.C. may benefit from reading this novel.

ASSESS

Review

Have students complete the Section 3 Review. Use answers in the Teacher's Edition, page 80, to assess student mastery of this section.

Lesson 3.4   *The Golden Age of Greek Culture*

Textbook pp. 81–86

RESOURCES

Pupil's Edition
Literature Through Time,
  p. 84: *The* Odyssey

Core Resources
Reading 3.4: *Athenian Values and
Antigone*

Visual Resources
Art and History 3: *Dipylon Vase*
Everyday Life 3: *Greek Architecture*

Global History Resource Center
Reading: *Greek Drama in the 400s B.C.*
Reading: *The Olympic Games*

Videodiscs or Global History Resource Center
Image: *Greek Sculpture of the God of
Medicine*

Search Frame 710

LESSON FOCUS

What important developments took place in Greek culture between 1000 B.C. and the 400s B.C.?

[Students should recognize that the early Greeks believed their gods set events in motion and also that the gods shared many human qualities and demanded the attention of humans.]

OBJECTIVES

After completing this lesson, students will be able to:
- explain how the Greek conception of religion changed over time;
- identify the subjects that concerned early Greek philosophers;
- describe how Greek authors and artists depicted humanity.

HOOK

Examine early Greek religion by looking at Greek myths.
Call on volunteers to briefly retell any Greek myths they know. Myths with which they may be familiar include the stories of King Midas, Icarus and Daedalus, Pandora, and Narcissus. Alternatively, read aloud one or two myths. (Good sources include collections by Sally Benson, Bernard Evslin, and Roger Lancelyn Green.) Then discuss the major points of the myths, specifically the part played by the gods.
Ask: **What were the Greek gods like? What role did they play in Greek life?**

DEVELOP

Discuss the decline of early religious ideas and the rise of the ideas of early Greek philosophers.
Remind students that Greek religious ideas expressed in the myths started to change in the 600s B.C.
Ask: **What caused the Greeks to turn away from a mythological view of the world?**
[People came into contact with other civilizations; they began to see institutions as created by people, not gods.]

List the names of the key Greek thinkers, such as Thales, Pythagoras, Parmenides, and Democritus, on the chalkboard. For each, ask students to identify the ideas the individual put forward. Select students to come to the chalkboard and note the ideas under the appropriate philosopher. *[**Thales:** argued that water was the basic substance of the world; **Pythagoras:** believed everything in the universe could be understood through numerical relationships; **Parmenides:** established formal logic; **Democritus:** believed the universe was made up of atoms]*

Next have students use the information on the chalkboard to contrast the way of thinking of these four philosophers with the earlier ways of thinking about the universe.

Ask: *How do the ideas of the early Greek philosophers differ from ideas about the gods?*

[They brought logical thinking to ideas about the universe. They sought reasons for the order of the universe, rather than looking upon it as the work of the gods.]

PROBE

Examine Greek achievements in literature and history.
Have students read and discuss the Literature Through Time feature on textbook page 84. Then take eight index cards and write one of the following names on each: *Homer, Pindar, Aeschylus, Sophocles, Euripides, Aristophanes, Herodotus, Thucydides*. Organize students into eight groups and hand each group one of the cards. Tell each group that it will act as the writer named on its card. Allow groups 5 to 10 minutes to develop an oral "autobiography." Suggest that they focus on the contributions their writer made to literature or history. Have groups base their autobiographies on information in the textbook. The Global History Resource Center selections of Euripides, Herodotus, Homer, and Thucydides will also provide students with further information. Ask group representatives to share their autobiographies with the class.

CONCLUDE

Discuss the chief qualities of Greek art and architecture.
Display Art and History Transparency 3 and ask students to study it. Point out that this is an example of early Greek art.

Ask: *What aspects of the vase suggest that it is by an early Greek artist?*

[decorations include animal and human figures; human form abstract, rather than perfect]

Next display the electronic media images of the Greek sculpture and vase, if available. Point out that they show a major development in art during the Golden Age of Greek culture—artists began to represent the human body in its ideal, perfect form.

Continue by showing Everyday Life Transparency 3. Have students consider what message Greek architects were trying to convey with their designs.

Ask: *What did the architecture of buildings such as the Parthenon proclaim?*

[the power and achievements of the city-states]

You might conclude by having students discuss their impressions of these works of art and architecture.

EXTEND

Cross-Curricular Connection: *Sociology*
Link to Today. Ask students to write an essay comparing the role of the Olympic Games in ancient Greek society with the role they play today. The Global History Resource Center reading on the games provides information on their role in ancient times.

Other Media
Have interested students watch the video *Great Cities of the Ancient World: Athens and Ancient Greece* (Questar, color, 60 min.). Have students describe the buildings shown in the video.

MEET INDIVIDUAL NEEDS

Visual-Spatial Learners
Have students research and report on the Greek mathematical formula known as "the golden section," which was used to achieve aesthetically pleasing proportions. Students could then use Everyday Life Transparency 3, which shows the Parthenon, to explain the formula to the rest of the class.

Kinesthetic Learners
Students might perform scenes from a play by one of the dramatists mentioned in this section. Suggest that they make masks to use in their performances. Display the electronic media image of Greek drama to show an example of a mask.

ASSESS

Review
Have students complete the Section 4 Review. Use answers in the Teacher's Edition, pages 85–86, to assess student mastery.

In preparation for the chapter test, you may wish to have students complete all or part of the Chapter 3 Review on textbook page 87, the Chapter 3 Review Activity, and the Chapter 3 Themes Review.

Understanding the Main Idea

Call on a volunteer to read aloud the *Understanding the Main Idea* paragraph. Explain that the Persian Empire controlled a number of Greek cities along the coast of Asia Minor. As time passed, Greece and Persia came into increasing conflict. While Persia relied on an imperial system of control, Greece was made up of individual city-states. These city-states developed different systems of government and emphasized different political and social values.

Presenting Themes

See p. 59B for suggestions on introducing themes.

Using the Time Line

Have students list the time line events in their notebooks. After they have read about each event in the chapter, have students write a paragraph explaining its significance.

Chapter 3
The Persian and Greek World
1000 B.C.–404 B.C.

Understanding the Main Idea

In the 500s B.C. the Persians began to create a multicultural empire that ultimately stretched from India to Egypt. At about the same time the people of Greece were founding their own great civilization based on the idea of the city-state. By 450 B.C. Greek civilization had reached a high point of artistic creation and dominance in the eastern Mediterranean.

Themes

- **Cross-cultural Interaction** Why might the members of a well-established society fear nomadic peoples living on their borders?

- **Geography** How might armies and navies use geography to their advantage?

- **Politics and Law** What conditions might make it difficult for a small group of individuals to exercise political power over a larger majority?

By 480 B.C. the Persian king, Xerxes (ZURK-seez), had determined to punish a handful of Greek city-states in the Balkan Peninsula. The Greeks had dared to interfere with Persia's subject cities along the western coast of Asia Minor. In 490 B.C. the Greeks had even defeated the forces of Xerxes' father, Darius, outside the city of Athens. Summoning troops from all the provinces of the empire, Xerxes assembled a massive army. A Greek historian recounted the awesome scene as the Persian army crossed the Hellespont, the straits between Europe and Asia:

66 *The infantry and cavalry went over by the upper bridge—the one nearer the Black Sea; the pack-animals and underlings [servants] by the lower one towards the Aegean. The first to cross were the Ten Thousand, all with wreaths on their heads, and these were followed by the mass of troops of all the nations. Their crossing occupied the whole of the first day. On the next day the first over were the thousand horsemen, and the contingent [group] which marched with spears reversed—these, too, all wearing wreaths. Then came the sacred horses and sacred chariot, and after them Xerxes himself with his spearmen and his thousand horsemen.* 99

776 B.C.	594–93 B.C.	550 B.C.	522 B.C.	508 B.C.
Greeks hold first Olympic Games.	Athenians elect Solon to run the government.	Cyrus overthrows the Medes.	Darius gains the Persian throne.	Cleisthenes comes to power in Athens, restoring democracy.

Despite this massive army the Greeks once again defeated the Persians. Even after the Greeks defeated Xerxes, Greece and Persia continued to interact and to influence each other's political affairs for many years.

The Erechtheion, temple of the goddess Athena, built 421 B.C.–405 B.C. on the Acropolis of Athens

500 B.C.	490 B.C.	478 B.C.		431 B.C.	404 B.C.
Ionian city-states revolt against Persian rule.	Greeks defeat Persians at Marathon.	Greek city-states form Delian League.		Sparta and its allies wage war on Athens.	Sparta defeats Athens, ending the Athenian Empire.

Theme:
Geography

Today, Iran extends south beyond the Plateau of Iran to the Persian Gulf. The region's numerous oilfields provide great wealth. Oil and natural gas are among Iran's chief exports, while textiles, carpets, and food processing form the basis of the economy's manufacturing sector.

Critical Thinking Ask students what might be important about the fact that Iran now extends to the Persian Gulf.

ANSWER: Students should suggest that ports on the Persian Gulf allow shipping and trade.

SECTION 1
The Persian Empire

FOCUS

- Who were the Medes and the Persians, and where did they come from?
- What was Zoroaster's religious message?
- How did the Persians build their empire, and how did Darius organize the empire?
- How did the Persians generally treat the peoples they conquered?

In 550 B.C. an Indo-European-speaking tribe known as the Persians overthrew their rulers, the Medes. In a matter of years, the Persians forged one of the greatest multicultural empires in history. At its height the Persian Empire encompassed tens of millions of people in a territory that stretched from northern India to Egypt and from the Black Sea to the Indian Ocean. Under its broad umbrella, ideas and cultures mingled as never before, stimulating developments within the empire and along its borders.

Indo-Iranian sacrificial horse figurine, c. 2000 B.C.

The Indo-Iranians

Sometime before 1500 B.C. numerous Indo-European-speaking tribes migrated from the Eurasian plain of southern Russia across the Caucasus Mountains and around the Caspian Sea to settle on the Plateau of Iran. While many tribes moved farther southeast to settle in northern India, others settled in the valleys of the Elburz and Zagros Mountains. Among the latter groups of settlers were the Medes and the Persians, related peoples who would soon establish the foundations for the largest empire the world had yet seen. Calling themselves Aryans, they named their new homeland Iran, which meant "land of the Aryans." Historians often refer to these peoples as Indo-Iranians.

Geography. The Plateau of Iran was a forbidding area. With little rainfall except in the mountains, the plateau presented a stark landscape with extremes of heat and cold. To the north, the Elburz Mountains rose sharply from the plain to the snowcapped peak of Mount Demavend, over 18,000 feet above sea level. To the west lay the great Zagros mountain range, rising to some 14,000 feet in places. This range, with its narrow passes that often clogged with ice and snow in winter months, descended steeply into the steamy plains of Mesopotamia below.

In the center of the plateau, just south of the Elburz range, the Dasht-e-Kavīr Desert stretched out into the plateau. Southeastward the plateau ran through the great desert of the Dasht-e-Lūt, then down into the Helmand River basin, before coming up against the jagged peaks of the Hindu Kush Mountains. In some places of this arid interior plateau, the soil remained dry for months at a time, and the heavy winds turned the sand and dry, gravelly soil into dangerous dust storms.

Only in the northeast, the direction from which the tribes had come, was the landscape open and relatively fertile. In this region people could grow crops and graze herds. These northeastern grasslands became perhaps the richest part of Iran, providing many rulers with wealth and power.

Agriculture. Most of the Plateau of Iran was arid, lacking open sources of water. Scattered throughout the plateau, however, were areas of vegetation called **oases**, where water filtered up from underground. Such a landscape did not lend itself to settled agriculture except in a few locations, such as the oases and the narrow valleys of the western mountains. Nevertheless, the inhabitants of the plateau learned to make the most of their resources.

Melted snow from the mountains, for example, normally ran off in spring and summer. Water reaching the lower slopes evaporated in the intense summer heat. To supply water to their villages and fields on the plains, people dug long, horizontal underground tunnels called *qanats*. These tunnels channeled water from aquifers, natural underground reservoirs of water contained in layers of gravel and rock. Some *qanats* extended several miles and provided the ancient Iranians with reliable water sources for the development of irrigation agriculture. While some of the early Iranian tribes were utilizing such techniques to make agriculture possible, most continued to lead a seminomadic existence, herding their horses, cattle, and sheep.

Early culture and society. Like many other nomadic peoples, the Indo-Iranians were patriarchal. By the time they had settled in the plateau, both the Medes and the Persians were ruled by tribal chieftains who had become local kings. The leading men of the clans and tribes advised these kings. Historians know little of the role of women in society, but they do know that it was common for men to have more than one wife.

Living on the fringes of Mesopotamian civilization, the Medes and the Persians were exposed to new ways of life. Still primarily pastoral, however, the tribes spent much of their time raiding and being raided for cattle, horses, and women. War and raiding were a natural part of life.

Early religious practices. The early tribes of Iran believed the whole world was alive with spirits. They worshipped these spirits, especially the sun and the moon. Their most important gods were Mithra, the god of the sun, and Anahita (ah-nah-HEE-tah), the goddess of fertility and vegetation. In western Iran, Median tribes developed a religious system much like that of the Indo-Aryans in northern India.

Fire played an important role in religious rites. Many of the early temples were constructed around the naturally occurring gas fires and

▲ The Ka'aba Zadocht fire temple from c. 400 B.C. in Naksh-i-Rustam, Iran, is one of the ancient temples built around natural gas fires.

became known as fire temples. Although the Iranians did not worship fire itself, they believed it represented the forces of nature.

The Medes and the Persians were Indo-European-speaking tribes who migrated to the Plateau of Iran from the plains of southern Russia.

Zoroaster

Sometime before 600 B.C. a prophet-reformer named Zoroaster (ZOHR-uh-was-tuhr)–Zarathushtra (zah-rah-THOOSH-truh) in Persian–launched a major religious reform movement in Iran. Zoroaster preached against the widespread practice of polytheism and called on people to worship one god, Ahura Mazda. Zoroaster taught that the earthly world was a battleground between the good forces of Ahura Mazda and the evil forces of Ahriman, "the Enemy." People were free to choose between the two, but their actions were to be judged after

Theme:
Cross-cultural Interaction

Elements of Zoroastrianism were incorporated into traditional Iranian religions, which continued to follow polytheistic practices. Some of Zoroaster's beliefs also are reflected in today's world religions. Like Zoroastrians, Christians and Jews believe in the idea of a supreme god who created the universe and will judge the just and the wicked. Zoroaster's devotion to truth is also shared by Christians and Jews alike.

Critical Thinking Ask students what made it possible for elements of Zoroastrianism to be incorporated into Jewish and Christian beliefs.

ANSWER: Students should note that the homeland of the Jews was part of the Persian Empire, allowing for cultural interaction.

Persian Empire, c. 500 B.C.

The Lands of Persia Persian emperors controlled a vast territory of towering mountains, inhospitable deserts, and mighty rivers.

? Movement Which cities did the Royal Road link?

their death. The just person supposedly would be rewarded by a life of eternal blessings, while the wicked would suffer punishment in hell.

Zoroastrianism was based on the principle of leading a moral life devoted to truth. Lying was the greatest sin, for it was believed to be the primary tool of Ahriman, who was also called the Great Liar. Zoroaster probably conceived of Ahura Mazda as the only true god, the supreme creator and judge of the universe. But Zoroaster's concept of Ahura Mazda was relatively impersonal and abstract. Many people wanted a sense of closer contact with the divine. Consequently, in spite of its influence and success, Zoroastrianism never fully took the place of the worship of the traditional Iranian gods, such as Mithra and Anahita. In later years these figures were incorporated into Persian religion, sometimes as children of Ahura Mazda who continued the struggle against the forces of evil on Earth.

Zoroaster founded a religion based on truth and belief in one god, Ahura Mazda.

From Kingdom to Empire

Sometime in the late 600s B.C., from their capital at Ecbatana (probably modern-day Hamadan) in the northern Zagros Mountains, the Medes set about conquering the other Iranian tribes, forging them into a confederation. In alliance with the Chaldeans, in 610 B.C. the Median kings also finally conquered the declining Assyrian Empire, to which they had long owed tribute. In the early 500s B.C. they further extended their influence westward to the Halys River in Asia Minor. As they grew in power, however, the Medes imposed greater controls and increasingly higher taxes on their subjects.

Among the Medes' subjects were the Persians. The Persians lived in the southern Zagros Mountains and had their capital at Susa. In 550 B.C. Cyrus II, king of the Persians, overthrew the Median king and proclaimed himself "king of the Medes and Persians." In so doing, Cyrus established the **Achaemenid dynasty**. Cyrus was a great conqueror. He brought Lydia, the kingdom of the famous king Croesus (KREE-suhs), and the Greek cities of Asia Minor under his control. To the east, Cyrus pushed the frontiers of the empire into northern India, and in the northeast, he extended them to the Jaxartes (jak-SAHRT-eez) River (today known as the Syr Darya River). In 539 B.C. he conquered Babylon and was proclaimed king of Babylonia. Cyrus's son and successor, Cambyses (KAM-bi-suhs) II, added Egypt to the empire in 525 B.C. Cambyses died in Egypt under mysterious circumstances.

In 522 B.C. Cambyses's cousin Darius became King Darius I during a period of internal turmoil. After putting down numerous rebellions, he too pursued an expansionist policy, particularly in the east, where he consolidated the conquests of Cyrus. In the west, Darius campaigned into Europe, conquering Thrace and even crossing the Danube River.

After a series of stunning military victories, the Persians established a vast empire in western Asia.

🏛 Imperial Administration

Darius was in many ways the real founder of the Persian imperial system. He is best known for instituting administrative reforms that enabled him to turn the empire into a prosperous, stable, and well-organized system. The Persian Empire was an absolute monarchy. Taking the title *shah-in-shah*, "king of kings," or "great king," Darius and his successors ruled in the name of Ahura Mazda:

66*Ahuramazda, when he saw this earth in commotion, thereafter . . . made me king. . . . By the favor of Ahuramazda I put it down in its place.*99

The provinces. Darius divided the empire into provinces, each ruled by a governor, whom Darius himself appointed. The governors were extremely powerful officers much like kings in their own right. Over time, the governors' functions tended to become hereditary. They were in charge of the provinces' civil administration, finances, and justice, as well as the recruitment of troops for the imperial army.

The great king feared that the powerful governors might plot his overthrow. Thus, he used imperial agents, "The King's Eyes and Ears," as inspectors to keep a careful eye on the governors and to control his possessions. On a regular basis, these imperial inspectors traveled throughout the provinces checking tax and judicial records, and investigating citizens' complaints about the governors' administrations.

What made Darius's system work was the excellent road system he built to connect the far-flung domains of the empire. The roads allowed Persian armies to move quickly to wherever they were needed. The famous "Royal Road" from Sardis to Susa also made it possible for royal couriers traveling on horseback through a system of relay stations to cover some 1,700 miles in a week. Most people, however, traveled at a more

▲ In his autobiography Darius I claimed to have fought 19 battles and taken 9 kings prisoner in 522 B.C., the first year of his reign. This is his tomb in Iran.

R **RESOURCE ACTIVITY**

READINGS IN WORLD HISTORY Reading 3.1 *A Debate on Government*

Have students read the arguments for and against different types of government. Then have them complete the questions.

Level 1

🏛 *Theme:* **Technology**

To keep wagons from sinking into mud, the wheel ruts of Persian roads were paved in stone. The roads were marked off in *parasangs*, which measured how far a traveler could move in an hour. The distance varied, therefore, based on the terrain in a particular area.

Critical Thinking Ask students if they think the benefits of the Persian "Royal Road" were worth the great effort and expense such a road would have taken to build.

ANSWER: Students' answers will vary but should note the benefits of the road in governing such a large empire.

Reliefs at the Persian palace of Persepolis show the impressive attire worn by the Persian army. The most lavishly dressed soldiers were the "10,000 Immortals," who served as the king's body-guards. Wearing long purple or yellow robes and leather shoes, their hair was tied back with green cord. Their beards were curled, and they wore gold ornaments. In addition, each Immortal carried a bow and a quiver of arrows. The rest of the army wore tradi-tional clothing based on regional dress.

Critical Thinking Ask students to suggest pos-sible reasons why the Immortals were so lav-ishly equipped.

ANSWER: Students might suggest that the dress and equipment of the Immortals was a demon-stration of the power and wealth of the Persian Empire.

leisurely pace on foot. The Greek historian Herodotus (hee-RAHD-uh-tuhs) described the great imperial highway:

66 *At intervals all along the road are recognized sta-tions, with excellent inns, and the road itself is safe to travel by, as it never leaves inhabited country. . . . The total num-ber of stations, or post-houses, on the road from Sardis to Susa is 111. . . . Traveling, then, at the rate of 150 furlongs [19 miles] a day, a man will take just ninety days to make the journey.* 99

Darius maintained a general policy of tolerating the local customs, religions, languages, and even legal systems of his diverse subjects. In fact, the subject populations retained a great deal of self-government. As long as they paid their trib-ute and furnished troops to the royal army when requested, the king interfered little in their domestic affairs. This was a par-ticularly effective policy for ruling a multiethnic and multi-cultural empire.

The Persian army. Although the policy of tol-eration was important, what ultimately allowed the Persians to maintain control over their vast domains and to expand them even farther was the army. The core of the Persian army was made up of professional soldiers. The elite unit was the famous battalion of the "10,000 Immortals." The name came from the fact that casualties were immediately replaced to maintain the numbers. This army was reinforced with local recruits as needed. The Persians were also famed for their archers and their war chariots with iron sickles attached to the axles.

The army had some weaknesses, however. The regiments that were recruited from the

▲ **This frieze of glazed tiles, made around 500 B.C., is from the Palace of Darius at Susa; the archer represents one of the "10,000 Immortals" of the Persian army.**

imperial provinces, for exam-ple, fought according to their own customs, using their own weapons and tactics. This mixture contributed to the Persian army's being some-what disorganized. Against forces that had a high degree of training and coordinated discipline, even the Persians might have been at a disad-vantage. In addition, the Persians had to rely on non-Persians within the empire for naval strength. Their navy was made up of Greek, Phoenician, Egyptian, and Cypriot sailors.

Law. Heirs of the Babylonians in legal matters, the Persians attached a great importance to the organizing of society based on the rule of law. The king was the source of law and the final judge. Although the Persians respected the legal customs of the diverse peoples inside their empire, they also set up a uni-form imperial law, the "Laws of the Medes and the Persians," that covered everyone.

Royal judges throughout the provinces implemented the legal system. The judges were kept under strict observation to ensure fairness and to discour-age corruption. The ideal of justice and fairness was very much a part of Persian civilization, as emphasized in the following inscription:

66 *Within these countries [those under Persian rule], the man who was loyal, him I rewarded well, [but he] who was evil, him I punished well; by the favor of Ahuramazda these countries showed respect toward my law.* 99

Darius's administrative and military reforms, as well as the construction of roads, helped establish a prosperous and stable empire.

The Imperial Economy

As in most large empires, agriculture was the major economic activity in the Persian Empire. The Persian kings and the aristocracy owned many large estates, but many independent landowners also farmed their own plots. The kings used land to reward and reinforce political loyalty. They distributed large amounts of land to friends and relatives. They also rewarded civil servants and soldiers with hereditary estates.

The imperial government encouraged trade and commerce by maintaining the excellent road system and a climate of peace and security. Furthermore, the government established a standardized system of weights and measures, as well as a sound currency. The currency was based on the silver *shekel* and the gold *daric*. The *daric* became the chief gold currency in the world of trade. On land, roads crossed the empire without regard to internal barriers. On the sea, a prosperous international trade was carried on by Persian subjects, particularly Greeks and Phoenicians.

Imperial taxes were generally heavy, for the Persians insisted that all conquered lands were actually the property of the king. The Persians themselves paid little in taxes; the bulk of the empire's revenue was drawn solely from the provinces. Each province was required to pay a fixed amount in gold or silver, and each subject state paid a fixed tribute in goods. A huge amount of money flowed into the treasury every year. The Persian Empire thus became one of the wealthiest empires in the ancient world. Taxes served to finance the army, the administration, and the royal court. Despite the

▶ This Persian *daric* was made around 500 B.C. Because of standardized currency, merchants could have used coins like this one across the entire empire from India to Egypt to Thrace.

THROUGH OTHERS' EYES

Noble Children in the Persian Court

Because there are so few surviving written materials from the Achaemenid dynasty, most of the information about the empire comes from observations of the Greeks. Xenophon (ZEN-uh-fuhn), an Athenian soldier, traveled to Persia and wrote about his experiences there. Scholars disagree over how he viewed the Persians; some of his writings seem to indicate that he admired them, while others present a negative view. The following passage, at least, seems to record Xenophon's admiration for the education of noble Persian youths at the royal court, where they learned proper behavior. Here Xenophon describes the upbringing of Cyrus the Younger, younger son of the king of Persia:

❝All the sons of the noblest Persians are educated at the King's court. There one may learn discretion [good judgment] and self-control in full measure, and nothing that is base can be either heard or seen. The boys have before their eyes the spectacle of men honoured by the King and of others dishonoured; . . . and so from earliest boyhood they are learning how to rule and how to submit to rule. Here, then, Cyrus was reputed to be . . . the most modest of his fellows, and even more obedient to his elders than were his inferiors.❞

importance of having a solid currency, however, after Darius's reign Persia's rulers began to hoard their tribute in the royal treasury, rather than keeping it in circulation for trading purposes.

Using a standard currency, the Persian kings maintained the army and the imperial administration through high taxes on the provinces.

Theme: Economic Organization

Before weights and measures were standardized, different methods were used across the Persian Empire. This made trade difficult. To determine volume, Darius established the king's measure, which was similar to the modern bushel. The unit of length was the royal cubit, measuring 18 inches, and the standard for weight was the *karsha*, which equaled about one fifth of a pound.

Critical Thinking Ask students to imagine why standardized measures would have made trade easier.

ANSWER: Students should suggest that standardized measures would have allowed people to easily know the cost of a product, without having to convert units of measure.

REVIEW & ASSESSMENT RESOURCES

• Study Guide 3.1
• Daily Quiz 3.1
• Main Idea Activity 3.1

All Levels

SECTION 1
REVIEW ANSWERS

IDENTIFY

For significance, see the following pages:
oases (p. 63)
qanats (p. 63)
Zoroaster (p. 63)
Cyrus II (p. 64)
Achaemenid dynasty
   (p. 65)
Cambyses II (p. 65)
Darius I (p. 65)
shekel (p. 67)
daric (p. 67)

LOCATE

For locations, see the map on p. 64.

1. The Persians generally allowed conquered subjects to maintain some self-rule. They also allowed people to speak their own languages and to continue traditional religions and legal practices.
2. Darius instituted many administrative and military reforms, and constructed roads linking the empire.
3. The Persians and the Medes were Indo-European tribes from southern Russia that settled in northwestern Iran.
4. Letters should include an explanation of monotheism and a description of the importance of truth.
5. Cyrus II—overthrew Median king, defeated Lydia, expanded territory; Cambyses II—conquered Egypt; Darius I—developed administrative reforms, built roads, established large army, maintained sound currency; answers should compare the contributions of rulers listed

🏛 Society and Culture in the Empire

The social structure of the empire was like a pyramid with the king on top and slaves at the bottom. Nobles and ordinary people were in between. Slavery took many different forms according to the different regional traditions within the empire. Yet much of the imperial economy did not depend upon slave labor. Most Persians preferred to use free workers rather than slaves.

The status of women also depended on cultural traditions. Women had little independence in Persia, for example, but some upper-class Babylonian women enjoyed a degree of freedom. Babylonian women could own property and dispose of it as they liked. They could write contracts and could manage their own businesses.

Like so many other invaders from the fringes of civilizations, once they established their empire the Persians found themselves in charge of many peoples whose cultural development was more advanced than their own. Learning from their subjects, the Persians employed artists from all parts of their empire. They borrowed many distinctive art forms. Nevertheless, they succeeded in creating a specific "Persian art." Persian artists specialized in sculptures, metalwork, and jewelry, particularly gold. Persian art usually carried political meaning. It symbolized the might of the empire and the greatness of royal power.

▲ This bronze lion from the 400s B.C. appears to have been a standard weight for measuring taxes paid in gold and silver at the royal treasury at Susa.

The Persians established a multicultural empire, usually respecting local government, laws, and religious customs.

SECTION 1 REVIEW

IDENTIFY and explain the significance of the following:
   oases
   qanats
   Zoroaster
   Cyrus II
   Achaemenid dynasty
   Cambyses II
   Darius I
   shekel
   daric

LOCATE and explain the importance of the following:
   Plateau of Iran
   Elburz Mountains
   Zagros Mountains

   Susa
   Lydia
   Egypt
   Sardis

1. **Main Idea** What was the Persian attitude toward their conquered subjects?
2. **Main Idea** Why is Darius I often called the "true" founder of the Persian Empire?
3. **Geography: Movement** Who were the Persians and the Medes? Where did they come from and where did they settle?

4. **Writing to Explain** Imagine that you have just attended a lecture by Zoroaster. Write a letter to a friend explaining Zoroaster's religious message.
5. **Evaluating** Make a chart like the one below, listing the contributions of each of these great kings of Persia. Which leader made the greatest contributions? Why do you think so?

GREAT KING	CONTRIBUTIONS
Cyrus II	
Cambyses II	
Darius I	

The City-States of Greece

While the Persians were founding their vast imperial domains, another branch of the Indo-European-speaking peoples developed a very different kind of civilization to the west, along the rocky coast and islands of Greece. In the 700s B.C. the Greeks began to emerge from the isolation of the Dark Age. This century marked the beginning of the Archaic Age in Greek history. Greek civilization developed around hundreds of independent city-states, which became the centers of Greek identity.

Now known as the "Elgin Marbles" after having been removed and taken to the British Museum by Lord Elgin, this frieze was once part of the Parthenon.

The Rise of the Polis

As the isolation of the so-called Dark Age began to decline during the 700s B.C., Greeks once again looked out to the larger world. At the core of the emerging Greek worldview lay the conception of the **polis**, the Greeks' primary form of political and social organization. During the insecure and violent days of the Dark Age, the Greek tribes had banded together in many small groups, each centered around a hill or strong point for protection. Although today we translate *polis* as "city-state," for the Greeks it was much more. The polis involved three interlocking ideas: geographical territory, community, and political and economic independence. The word *polis* is also the origin of many modern English words, such as *policy* and *politician*.

Independent city-states. Physically, the polis consisted of a city built around a defensible fortification called an **acropolis** and the surrounding countryside, from which the city drew all its food. Generally small, the average polis covered between 30 and 500 square miles. Athens, perhaps the most famous polis, was an exception. It covered over 1,000 square miles. Ideally, all the citizens of the polis knew one another. Most poleis (plural of polis) seem to have had fewer than 1,000 adult male citizens, with perhaps 10 times as many noncitizens. Here again, Athens was an exception. In 431 B.C., for example, Athens had about 40,000 adult male citizens and a total population of about 200,000.

Whatever its size, the polis became the center of Greek identity and commanded intense loyalties among its inhabitants. One later Greek philosopher actually defined a human being as "an animal whose nature is to live in a polis." The Greeks also identified the polis as an absolutely independent and self-sufficient entity. It is for this reason that scholars call it a city-state.

Political identity. One of the most important ideas of the polis was that a citizen was not an individual but rather belonged to the state. The Greeks made little distinction between public and private sectors. Relying on its citizens for everything, the polis had no professional bureaucracy, no professional army, and no professional politicians.

Periods of Ancient Greek History

	c. 1250 B.C.–700 B.C. DARK AGE		c. 700 B.C.–500 B.C. ARCHAIC AGE	c. 500 B.C.–336 B.C. CLASSICAL AGE

1300 B.C. 1200 1100 1000 900 800 700 600 500 400 300 B.C.

By the same token, the polis allowed for no sense of individualism as we now understand it. All Greeks were members of an extended community that included a family, a clan, a brotherhood, a tribe, and the polis, in that order. Thus, in a polis any citizen could take up a legal case in a matter of public concern. Moreover, anyone who avoided participation in political life could lose the privilege altogether. As one Athenian statesman put it:

> 66 *Here [Athens] each individual is interested not only in his own affairs but in the affairs of the state as well: even those who are mostly occupied with their own business are extremely well-informed on general politics. . . . We do not say that a man who takes no interest in politics is a man who minds his own business; we say that he has no business here at all.* 99

🏛 Life in the Polis

Within the city walls, life centered around the *agora*, or marketplace. Here the food supplies from the countryside were bought and sold in exchange for the goods made by artisans in the city or brought from outside the polis by traders. The inhabitants of the polis were divided into three groups: adult men, who were citizens with political rights; free people with no political rights, such as women, children, and resident foreigners; and slaves.

The polis was a male-dominated society. Women were supposed to stay in the home and take care of household responsibilities. One ancient fragment of text stated that sons were always brought up somehow, even by the poorest families. The text went on to say that female infants were often left, even by the wealthiest families, out in the open to die. Part of the problem was that girls were considered economic liabilities, since they had to be provided with

dowries (money or goods) before they could get married.

Slavery was widespread in Greece as in much of the ancient world. Although some early sources suggest that the Greeks once lived without slavery, over time it became an important institution in Greek society. In addition to enslaving prisoners of war, Greeks themselves could be enslaved for debt. Sometimes whole populations were enslaved to work as laborers for their conquerors. Slaves not only worked in households but also in workshops, fields, and in the mines. The worst life for a slave was probably in the mines, where conditions were extremely harsh.

The Greeks viewed the politically and economically independent polis as the center of their loyalty.

🏛 Colonization

Following the Dark Age, increasing security and returning prosperity were accompanied by a rise in population. With such growth, many cities soon found it difficult to feed all of their inhabitants. In at least one instance, some people had to leave the city to prevent the starvation of the entire polis.

Many Greek cities solved their population problems by establishing colonies. It was the beginning of a colonization movement that spread Greek settlers and Greek culture all over the Mediterranean region. For three centuries, Greeks from the mainland left their cities to establish colonies elsewhere. From Spain to southern France, all over the southern shores of Italy and Sicily, even as far away as the Black Sea, they went, "like frogs around a pond," as one Greek observer would later put it.

Colonization was motivated primarily by hunger for land and the need to find new agricultural bases. The colonists who settled around the Black Sea, for example, generally became great

Ancient Greece, 750 B.C.–450 B.C.

The Greek Heartland

BLACK SEA
Byzantium
Asia Minor
AEGEAN SEA
Thebes
Phocaea
Chios
ATTICA
Corinth
Athens
Miletus
Peloponnesus
Sparta
Rhodes
IONIAN SEA
MEDITERRANEAN SEA
Azimuthal Equal-Area Projection

EUROPE

Tanais
Olbia
Grain, Timber, Slaves
Tyras
Grain Iron
Gold Copper
BLACK SEA
Trapezus
Asia Minor

Timber

Massilia
Nicaea

ADRIATIC SEA

Silver Timber

Copper, Iron

Pots, Oil, Wine, Silver

AEGEAN SEA

Gold, Metal, Slaves

Iron, Copper

Grain

Pots, Oil, Wine

Iberian Peninsula
40°N

ATLANTIC OCEAN

0°
10°E

Grain

Grain, Perfume

MEDITERRANEAN SEA

| Colony | • City-state | → Trade route |

20°E
30°E
Naucratis
Grain

AFRICA

Grain

EGYPT

0   250   500 Miles
0   250   500 Kilometers
Azimuthal Equal-Area Projection

Trade and Colonization   The ancient Greek city-states along the Aegean Sea colonized and traded at Mediterranean, Aegean, Adriatic, and Black Sea ports.

❖ **Region**   What regions exported slaves?

agricultural producers, shipping grain back to the home cities. Trading opportunities and politics also often played a role in the decision to go overseas. Some colonies, for example, were established by the losing factions of an internal political struggle. The result of colonization was an explosion in commercial activities, benefiting the colonies and the Greek mainland.

Greek city-states established overseas colonies to ease overcrowding in mainland Greece.

Decline of the Aristocratic Order

The city-states of Greece had originated as small kingdoms ruled by warrior chieftains from their hilltop fortresses. These chieftains had in turn relied on wealthy landowners in battle. The

wealthy landowners could afford the expensive horses, chariots, and bronze weapons necessary to discourage raiders and maintain security. By the 700s B.C. these landowning *aristocrats*, or "best men" in Greek, had generally overthrown the chieftains and made themselves masters of the city-states.

Aristocrats controlled every aspect of Greek society. They had a monopoly over the military, and as major landowners they controlled the economy. They acted as judges and determined the laws. They even held control over religion, since the gods supposedly would not listen to commoners. Before the 600s B.C. aristocrats were the only people who participated in politics.

▲ **Greek aristocrats enjoying music around 450 B.C.**

Theme: Economic Organization

Colonization stemmed in large part from the need for more agricultural development. In Greece crop yields were so low that on average, six farmers were needed to produce enough for one non-farmer. By the 700s B.C., Greek agriculture focused so extensively on olive and grape cultivation that olive oil and wine were the region's primary exports. Colonies along the Black Sea, on the other hand, produced grain that could be shipped back to Greece.

Critical Thinking   Ask students how a nation's dependency on imported vital products could be a potential risk.

ANSWER: Students might suggest that an enemy could try to cut off the imports.

▲ This marble relief, carved around 500 B.C., shows Athenian hoplites marching to battle.

Migration and technological innovation. This aristocratic order began to break down, however, as the impact of population, emigration, and new military technological developments began to be felt. As colonization spread, wealth was no longer entirely concentrated in the hands of a few aristocratic families. Trading and commercial opportunities had made it possible for commoners to acquire wealth. Soon they were able to buy land.

By the 600s B.C. iron weaponry, which had been introduced much earlier by the Dorians, was costing the aristocrats their military monopoly. Bronze weapons had been expensive and in short supply because of the scarcity of the ingredients for bronze itself. Iron, however, came from an ore that was much more plentiful, easier to work with, and therefore cheaper. As nonaristocrats began to be able to afford land, they could also afford both weapons and farming tools of iron.

Iron was also harder than bronze. A single soldier armed with a long iron-tipped spear could easily challenge even a charioteer armed only with bronze weapons. Soon, Greek armies consisted of **hoplites**, heavily armed infantrymen who fought in the porcupine-like **phalanx** formation—a large body of closely packed hoplites each extending a long spear outward. Even cavalry was nearly helpless against the phalanx. The phalanx formation required far more soldiers than the small aristocratic class could provide. The use of the phalanx thus meant that

commoners became more important to the defense of the polis. As more commoners served in the army, they claimed that they deserved a greater voice in the government.

Law codes and lyric poetry. As such demands grew, in the second half of the 600s B.C., the commoners helped force the aristocrats to codify, or write down, the customary laws and procedures governing the cities. Up to this point, aristocratic judges had enforced the laws, many of which were extremely harsh, as they saw fit. Under the direction of the politician Draco, the death penalty could be given for even the most trivial offenses. Commoners often did not know precisely what the laws were, and therefore could not challenge the judges' rulings. As the laws were made public for all to see, however, the rule of aristocrats was brought to an end.

The decline of aristocratic control over Greek society was perhaps best illustrated by cultural developments. For example, a new form of literature—**lyric poetry**—emerged. It focused on personal feelings and emotions, subjects with which everyone, not just the aristocracy, could identify. Everyone could relate to feelings of love, friendship, or longing, which poets like Archilochus (ahr-KIL-uh-kuhs), Terpander, and Sappho (SAF-oh) began to write about during this "Lyric Age" of Greek literature.

BIOGRAPHY In her time Sappho was considered one of the greatest lyric poets—male or female. The philosopher Plato called her "the tenth Muse," placing her among the mythical goddesses of poetry and song. Born sometime around 600 B.C., Sappho is believed to have been a member of the aristocracy on the Greek island of Lesbos. It is believed that she was married and had a daughter, Cleis (KLAY-uhs). The ancient Greeks had as many as nine volumes of her poetry, but most have been lost over the centuries. All that remain today are one complete poem and fragments of her work.

In spite of this, Sappho has had an enormous influence on the development of poetry. One of the meters, or rhythms, she used is still known today as the Sapphic meter. Equally as important, her deeply personal poems touched people in her own time and inspired later poets. The ideal of deep personal love, for example, comes through in Sappho's poem, "Sleep, Darling," in which she describes her feelings for her daughter:

"Sleep, darling

I have a small daughter called Cleis, who is

like a golden flower
I wouldn't take all Croesus' kingdom with love thrown in, for her"

Athenian Political Development

Athens offers the best example of the evolution of Greek political institutions and culture—largely because the sources that have survived from this period of Greek history are overwhelmingly Athenian. By the beginning of the 500s B.C., Attica, the region that Athens controlled and from which the city drew its basic food supply, was at the point of revolution. At the center of the problem was the aristocrats' continuing control of most of the land. Many small farmers had to sell or mortgage their farms, borrowing from the wealthier aristocrats. Many even had to sell themselves into slavery to pay their debts. Social tensions mounted. The situation was so critical that the aristocrats, in fear of losing everything, decided to give one man complete power to find a solution to the growing social tensions. In 594–93 B.C. they chose Solon, an Athenian noble.

Solon the lawgiver. Solon canceled debts and abolished enslavement for debt. Solon also realized that if Athens wanted to grow it needed to open itself further to trade and industry. Above all, he tried to eliminate the social pressures by transforming Athens's political structure, from citizenship based on aristocratic birth to citizenship based entirely on wealth. Solon

▲ As a politician, Solon was known as one of the Seven Wise Men of Greece. He was also known as one of Athens's great poets.

divided the whole citizenry into four groups according to people's incomes.

Public offices were available to the upper three classes. The members of the fourth class, while ineligible for office, were nevertheless members of the assembly that elected the officials. The genius of Solon's plan was that it opened the door for the rising nonaristocratic class. In time the nonaristocrats would have access to all public offices.

But Solon was not a revolutionary. He refused to follow the wish of commoners to redistribute the land. Instead he called for the expansion of Athenian trade and manufacturing to provide new opportunities for people and to make the city less dependent on agriculture for its survival. As part of this plan, Solon encouraged olive growers to turn their produce into oil, which was easier to ship and was in greater demand overseas. Thus, while Solon set the future of Athens both economically and politically, problems for poor farmers continued.

Peisistratus the tyrant. As the old aristocratic order broke down, aristocrats also adjusted to the new political situation. Taking advantage of the instability in Athens, for example, around 546 B.C. the aristocrat Peisistratus (py-SIS-truht-uhs) appealed to the masses for political support. By manipulating public opinion, he soon became a **tyrant**, wielding sole political power in violation of the established law, but with the support of the people.

Only later did the word *tyrant* take on the meaning of an oppressive and cruel leader. Peisistratus and his sons who succeeded him actually brought Athens peace, stability, and commercial prosperity for a time. They used public funds to beautify the city with a major building program and to increase Athenians' sense of citizenship by instituting major civic festivals. As Athens prospered, however, and political tensions between aristocrats and nonaristocrats died down, the people soon tired of the tyrants. In 514 B.C. Hipparchus (huh-PAHR-kuhs), one of the sons of Peisistratus, was murdered and his brother

According to Spartan tradition, the polis's laws had been developed by Lycurgus. Legend held that Lycurgus was descended from Hercules, a mythical hero of incredible strength. Lycurgus passed laws that eliminated inequalities and luxuries from Spartan life. He did not permit the laws to be written down. Instead, he required the laws to be taught in schools so that every citizen of Sparta would learn and memorize the laws through discipline.

Critical Thinking Ask students to suggest reasons why scholars know more about the government and society of Athens than they do about Sparta.

ANSWER: Students should suggest that because Spartans were focused on the military, they did not leave the large body of political, philosophical, and historical writings that the Athenians did.

Hippias became afraid for his own life. In 510 B.C. a popular rising forced Hippias into exile, and Athens recovered its freedom.

Cleisthenes and democracy. As they considered how best to reestablish order, in 508 B.C. the Athenians turned to Cleisthenes (KLYS-thuh-neez). While keeping the four social classes established by Solon, Cleisthenes also divided the Athenian population into ten new tribes based on residency. By mixing the population of each tribe with people from the city, the countryside, and the coastal regions, Cleisthenes hoped to destroy the regional power of the aristocracy.

He also created a Council of Five Hundred, which was to prepare all matters for presentation to the popular assembly. Each month, a different tribe was in charge of this council, which was chosen by lot, or random ballot. Nobody could serve on the council more than twice. This gave as many people as possible a chance to serve. But all legislative and electoral power remained with the popular assembly, made up of all voting citizens. We call this system **direct democracy**.

As commoners began to play a larger role in defending Athens, they demanded more voice in their government.

Sparta

The city-state of Sparta developed very differently from Athens. A look at the physical map (see p. 71) of the Peloponnesus (pel-uh-puh-NEE-suhs), the southern peninsula of Greece, explains part of the history of Sparta: it was an isolated country, nearly an island. Sparta was covered by hills and mountains. Perhaps this geographical isolation contributed to the Spartans' desire to be left alone.

▶ This bronze figure of a Spartan soldier from the 500s B.C. captures the focus of most Spartans' lives—the military.

Sparta's later history was also greatly influenced by the Spartans' conquest of neighboring peoples, beginning around 800 B.C. These conquests made Sparta one of the largest poleis in Greece. After the conquests, the victors divided the population of Sparta into three categories: the Spartan citizens, known as "equals"; half-citizens; and helots. Half-citizens were members of the surrounding communities that were dependent on Sparta. They paid taxes and could serve in the army but had no political rights. They were in charge of all commercial activities of the state. The helots were state slaves who were given to each citizen to work the land. They farmed the land for Spartan masters. Consequently, the citizens of Sparta were relieved of the need to perform economic activities and could concentrate on only one task—military training. The Spartans saw their militaristic way of life as a vital necessity. Citizens were outnumbered seven to one by noncitizens. Furthermore, the helots were always ready to revolt against their masters. In effect, the Spartans lived in a continuous state of emergency. Thus, they decided that the only way for such a small minority to control the majority was by keeping the helots in constant terror by ensuring that the Spartans themselves were always ready for battle.

The militaristic nature of the Spartans' method of adaptation to their circumstances affected all aspects of their society and culture.

▼ In this stone relief carved in Sparta around 400 B.C., Artemis pours an offering to Apollo.

▶ These crumbling remains are almost all that is left of the once-thriving city-state of Sparta.

The Spartan system of education, for example, focused entirely on physical fitness and military training. At birth, both male and female children were examined by a council of elders. If considered weak, a baby was left in the mountains until it died. Spartans believed that they could not afford unfit citizens.

From ages 7 to 18, boys trained intensively in what might be called early "boot camps." From ages 18 to 20, they trained specifically for war. From ages 20 to 30, all Spartan men were full-time soldiers, living with their fellow soldiers in barracks. Only after the age of 30 could a Spartan go home at night. Even then Spartans remained in the military, and, until age 60, had to eat at least one meal every day with their fellow soldiers. Although a Spartan man could marry earlier, he could not live with his wife and family before age 30. Women also underwent intensive physical training. Although their primary role in Spartan society was to bear children, Spartan women were known for their wealth and independence.

As might be expected, Spartan military training produced the best soldiers the world had known. Military might was achieved at the expense of other activities, however. Spartans had almost no interest in the arts, philosophy, or any other form of civilized culture. Only in sports, of which the primary purpose was to provide conditioning for war, did Spartans, both men and women, excel.

The Spartans created a state based solely on military force to rule their vast number of noncitizens.

SECTION 2 REVIEW

IDENTIFY and explain the significance of the following:
polis
acropolis
agora
hoplites
phalanx
lyric poetry
Sappho
Solon
Peisistratus
tyrant
Cleisthenes
direct democracy

LOCATE and explain the importance of the following:
Athens
Mediterranean Sea
Black Sea
Attica
Sparta
Peloponnesus

1. *Main Idea* How did the Greeks define the polis?
2. *Main Idea* What factors contributed to the rise of democracy in Athens?

3. *Social Relations* What factors made Athenian society different from Spartan society?
4. *Writing to Explain* Write a paragraph explaining how colonization was beneficial to the Greek city-states.
5. *Evaluating* In a short essay, evaluate the following statement: *The Athenians developed a form of government that was truly democratic.*

SECTION 2 REVIEW ANSWERS

IDENTIFY
For significance, see the following pages:
polis (p. 69)
acropolis (p. 69)
agora (p. 70)
hoplites (p. 72)
phalanx (p.72)
lyric poetry (p. 72)
Sappho (p. 72)
Solon (p. 73)
Peisistratus (p. 73)
tyrant (p. 73)
Cleisthenes (p. 74)
direct democracy (p. 74)

LOCATE
For locations, see the map on p. 71.

1. geographical territory, community, economic and political independence, center of their loyalties
2. high numbers of commoners in military, codified laws, citizenship based on wealth, assignment of legislative and electoral power to all voting citizens
3. Athenian—emphasis on law, development of lyric poetry, expansion of political rights and citizenship; Spartan—emphasis on military strength and physical fitness, citizenship based on residency, women known for their wealth and independence
4. Colonization allowed Greek city-states to expand their populations as well as their economic bases.
5. Essays should reflect an understanding of the Athenian limitations of democracy, such as its exclusion of the majority of society.

Theme: **War and Diplomacy**

In Greece alliances traditionally were formed between individual poleis; the basic principle was "to have the same friends and the same enemies." As alliances grew and overlapped, this concept became more difficult to define. As the idea of a league of states developed, Sparta emerged as a military leader. Conflicts arose among the poleis forming the Peleponnesian League, as members disagreed about the manner in which military operations should be carried out. Eventually the League acted only after debate and vote.

Critical Thinking Ask students why they think the poleis had trouble creating large systems of alliances.

ANSWER: Students might suggest that the poleis placed great value on their independence.

SECTION 3
War and Empire in the Aegean

FOCUS

- How was Greece saved from Persian invasion?
- What new heights did Athens reach during its Golden Age?
- What were the causes of the Peloponnesian War?

Despite the advances they made during the Archaic period, residents of the city-states of Greece long remained merely a less civilized people on the border of the more sophisticated and powerful Persian Empire. As the Greeks developed their own sense of identity and civilization, however, they soon reacted to Persian efforts to control them. As the Persians tried to extend their control and influence across the Aegean Sea, growing friction led to years of war between the great empire and the unruly city-states. After the defeat of the Persians, the city-states once again began to fight among themselves.

Mausoleum of Cyrus the Great (585 B.C.–529 B.C.) in present-day Pasargadae, Iran

The Persian Wars

The great king Cyrus's conquest of the kingdom of Lydia in Asia Minor in 546 B.C. also gave him the Greek city-states of the western coast, an area known as Ionia. The submission of the Asiatic Greeks to Persian rule, however, was not an event of major consequence. The Greeks had long been subjects of Lydia and had little desire to break free of imperial rule, since they had been mostly left alone. Similarly, as long as the Greeks paid their taxes and contributed to the royal army, the Persians did not interfere with the Greek cities' local governments and customs.

The death of King Cambyses II in 522 B.C. and the rise of Darius I to the Persian throne, however, brought important changes. Darius faced internal rebellions and opposition. He was able to assert his authority only after years of fighting. When secure, Darius began the reorganization of the empire, focusing on improving imperial finances. A substantial rise in taxes angered the Greeks in Asia Minor.

Beginning in 500 B.C. under the leadership of the city of Miletus, the Ionian Greeks revolted. They appealed to the cities of mainland Greece for help, but only Athens and Eretria (e-REE-tree-uh) responded. The Greeks had misjudged the will and resources of the Persian Empire. By 494 B.C. the revolt was crushed, the city of Miletus destroyed, and its population deported or sold into slavery.

Even before the revolt of Ionia, Darius had conquered parts of the European continent. Now he had a motive to interfere in the Greek Peninsula as well—to punish Athens and Eretria for their intervention on the side of the Ionian rebels. In 490 B.C. a Persian army crossed the Aegean Sea. After destroying Eretria, the Persians landed on the coast of Attica, at Marathon near Athens. There, to the surprise of all, the Athenians and their allies pushed the Persians back to the sea. Herodotus, the great historian of the Persian Wars, described the battle:

❝The struggle at Marathon was long drawn out. . . . The Athenians on one wing and the Plataeans on the other were both victorious . . . chasing the routed enemy, and cutting them down until they came to the sea, and men were calling for fire and taking hold of the ships.❞

The Persian Wars, 500 B.C.–479 B.C.

Map showing the Persian Wars with legend:
- Persian Empire
- Rebellious Ionian city-states
- Greek city-states allied against the Persians
- Neutral and pro-Persian city-states
- ✦ Greek victory
- ✦ Persian victory

Failed Conquest The independent city-states of Greece repelled the powerful Persian army and navy in the Persian Wars.

? Location What battle marked the final victory for the Greeks?

Map Answer
Plataea

According to legend, after the battle a messenger ran more than 20 miles back to Athens to carry the news of the victory before dying of exhaustion.

Marathon became a legendary battle. The victory of the small, democratic city of Athens against the huge, autocratic Persian Empire was a turning point in Western history. As Herodotus described it, the Athenians had preserved the freedom of the Greek world. Yet while the Battle of Marathon seemed to be a humiliating defeat for the Persians, in reality it was only a minor setback. Plans for a massive combined naval and land invasion of Greece were prepared. The plans could not be carried out, however, until 480 B.C. The death of Darius and the succession

of Xerxes to the throne had led to another series of domestic disorders and provincial revolts that needed to be settled before any overseas campaigns could begin.

In 480 B.C. the Persian army crossed the Hellespont on its way to invade Greece. Flanking it by sea was the Persian navy. As Xerxes' forces moved south into the Greek Peninsula, however, they were stopped suddenly in the narrow mountain pass of Thermopylae (thuhr-MAHP-uh-lee). A small force of 300 Spartans led by their king, Leonidas (lee-AHN-uhd-uhs), and several Spartan allies had hurried north to hold the pass. For several days the gallant band held the Persian army at bay. In the end, a fellow Greek betrayed them by showing the Persians a way around the pass. Surrounded, the Spartans fought to the death.

In spite of the heroic sacrifice of the Spartans at Thermopylae, the Greeks were unable to stop the Persian advance from northern Greece or to save Athens from destruction. Leonidas and his men had gained valuable time, however. Taking advantage of the delay, Athens engineered an alliance of Greek states under Spartan command to meet the invaders. The Athenian general Themistocles (thuh-MIS-tuh-kleez) was able to organize his naval forces and to lure the Persian fleet into a trap in the Salamis strait. The narrow waters of the strait made the Persian ships easy targets for the Greeks. Xerxes returned home but left a powerful army in Greece. The next year a combined Greek army defeated the Persians at Plataea and won the war.

The century after the Persian Wars was the greatest period of Greek civilization. Persia, however, was little affected by the failure of the war. The empire remained powerful and its rulers continued to interfere in Greek affairs for another 150 years.

The victories at Marathon, Salamis, and Plataea ensured the independence of the Greek city-states.

▲ Some 2,500 years after the battle, this memorial honors the Spartan soldiers who held the pass at Thermopylae against Xerxes' army.

The Golden Age of Athens

In 478 B.C., after the Persians were defeated at Plataea, the Greek city-states joined together under the leadership of Athens in an alliance known as the **Delian League**. The League included most of the Greek city-states and islands of Asia Minor, the Aegean, and the Black Sea. It was formed for mutual defense against the Persians and to protect grain shipments from the Black Sea. At its peak, the League included more than 140 cities.

From Delian League to Athenian Empire. At first each member of the alliance was independent and on equal terms with the other members, Athens included. But soon, Athens transformed this alliance into its own empire, changing allies into subjects, forbidding any city to withdraw from the League, forcing neutral cities to join the alliance, and using the annual tributes from the League treasury at Delos for its own advantage. Athens used the alliance to keep the Persians out of the Aegean, to clear the eastern Mediterranean of piracy, and to ensure stability and economic prosperity in this part of the world. The members of the League received these advantages at the cost of independence.

The Delian League made Athens rich and powerful. Between 447 B.C. and 438 B.C. the contributions of the members of the League financed the building of the Parthenon, a symbol of the Golden Age of Athenian culture. Even some Athenians were shocked by such a policy and criticized it bitterly. Unmoved, Pericles, the architect of Athens's Golden Age, answered his critics proudly:

66 The Athenians are not obliged to give the allies any account of how their money was spent provided that they carried on the war for them and kept the Persians away. They do not give us a single horse, nor a soldier, nor a ship. All they supply is money and this belongs not to the people who give it, but to those who receive it, provided they provide the services they are paid for. 99

Athenian democracy. The 400s B.C. saw the completion of Athenian democracy. Direct democracy reached its height under the leadership of Pericles. One of the greatest Athenian

▲ Built as a sacred temple to the goddess Athena, the Parthenon has gone through several transformations, including periods as a Christian church and a Turkish mosque.

orators and politicians, Pericles dominated the city and its empire for more than 30 years—from around 460 to 429 B.C. The height of this period is known as the Age of Pericles. The assembly of the citizens was the sovereign organ of the state; all legislative and electoral matters were controlled by the citizens. Domestic and foreign matters were decided by the assembly without intervention from professional politicians. The principle of one citizen, one vote was absolute.

In the assembly any citizen could take the floor to propose a bill or to give an opinion on a bill that had been proposed. But no proposal could be presented without the Council of Five Hundred's prior approval. The council prevented the submission of inappropriate proposals and put legitimate proposals in the proper form to be presented to the voters. The people could then veto, change, or return the proposal for further considerations.

With few exceptions (notably in military matters), all public administrative functions were also assigned to citizens by lot. For the Athenians the lot was the only truly fair way to let the people participate in the management of public affairs. Elections, they believed, depended too much on influence, reputation, the mastery of oratory, and even bribery. Consequently, every year about 1,000 public officials were chosen from among the people and no one could repeat the same office. In earlier days officials had served without pay—a policy that had barred many poorer citizens from public office. To make the system truly democratic and allow everyone to participate, the Athenians began to pay all public officials from public funds.

Thus, citizens controlled both the legislative and the executive functions of government.

Even the judicial system rested totally in the hands of the citizens. Each year 6,000 jurors were chosen by lot from a list left open to anybody who might be interested. To avoid financial burdens, jurors, like other public officials, were paid at public expense. In court cases the plaintiff and the defendant both presented their arguments to a jury panel that decided the outcome.

Under Pericles, Athens built a prosperous empire and all adult male Athenian citizens gained an equal voice in government.

The Peloponnesian War

Although Pericles rejected the criticism of Athens's use of the Delian League's treasury for its own ends, he was playing a dangerous game. The central element in Greek political and social life since the rise of the city-states had been the polis. Yet the concept of the polis involved its absolute independence and self-reliance. By turning the Delian League into Athens's own empire, Athenian statesmen were undermining the concept of the polis. Even Athens itself could no longer be considered independent, since the city increasingly relied on the subjects of the empire to sustain it. In addition, while government within Athens remained democratic, the Athenians did not rule their empire in similar fashion. As the historian Thucydides (thoo-SID-uh-deez) recorded, one Athenian statesman reminded his fellow citizens:

❝ *Your empire is a tyranny . . . over subjects who do not like it and who are always plotting against you; you will not make them obey you by injuring your own interests . . . ; your leadership depends on superior strength and not on any goodwill of theirs.* ❞

As discontent grew within the Athenian Empire, the other cities of Greece began to resent and to fear Athens's growing arrogance. As rivalries increased between Athens and other city-states, particularly Corinth, many Greek city-states looked to Sparta for protection.

Sparta and Athens had long-standing differences. In part this stemmed from their very different kinds of society and culture. Athenians saw Sparta's system as a challenge to their democratic government. Many in Sparta feared that Athenian power would continue to grow if not stopped. As Athens continued to flaunt its power, in 431 B.C. Sparta and its allies launched the Peloponnesian War. The devastating conflict soon involved most of the Greek city-states. A spirit of anticipation on both sides largely contributed to the outbreak of fighting. "The Peloponnesus and Athens were both full of young men whose inexperience made them eager to take up arms," Thucydides recorded.

The Spartans made the first move, invading Attica and laying waste to its farms and villages. The entire Athenian population of the region withdrew for safety behind Athens's walls. With great foresight, the Athenians had built a major defensive wall that protected their access and control of their harbor at Piraeus (py-REE-uhs). From there they continued to control the sea, so the Spartans were unable to starve them out. As

◀ A plate found at the Sanctuary of the Nymph shows Athenian warriors fighting a battle.

the siege of Athens continued for years, however, disease swept through the overcrowded population. A terrible plague killed enormous numbers of Athenians, including Pericles. Although Spartan forces could not break through the Athenian walls, the war went on for a full generation, punctuated by truces and periods of armed peace.

The struggle even spilled into the rest of the Greek world. During one truce, for example, the Athenians launched a major attack against the Greek city-state of Syracuse in Sicily. When the Athenians were driven off with enormous losses, the democratic government of Athens was discredited. A group of aristocrats took control of Athens for a time and abolished democracy. The aristocrats were soon overthrown and democracy restored, but the internal strife only further weakened the Athenians. After more bloodshed and constant sieges by Sparta and its allies, in 404 B.C. Athens surrendered. Stripped not only of its empire but also of its powerful fleet, Athens was reduced for a time to a second-rate power in Greece.

Athens's dominance of many Greek city-states and its long-standing rivalry with Sparta brought on the Peloponnesian War.

SECTION 3 REVIEW

IDENTIFY and explain the significance of the following:
    Xerxes
    Leonidas
    Delian League
    Pericles

LOCATE and explain the importance of the following:
    Ionia
    Marathon
    Hellespont
    Salamis

1. **Main Idea** How did society in Athens change in the Age of Pericles?
2. **Main Idea** What factors led to the outbreak of the Peloponnesian War?
3. **Geography: Human-Environment Interaction** How did the Greeks save their cities from the Persians? How did geography aid the Greeks in their victories, both on land and at sea?
4. **Writing to Persuade** Imagine that you are an Athenian citizen. Write an essay explaining why Athens should or should not be allowed to use the funds from the Delian League as it pleases.
5. **Synthesizing** How were the changes in Athenian society during the Age of Pericles beneficial to the city? How were they harmful?

The Golden Age of Greek Culture

*L*ike other peoples, the Greeks displayed both their values and their conception of reality in their arts, their literature, and their religious and philosophical ideals. Above all, this meant expressing their sense of excellence. In the arts the Greeks sought a sense of balance and proportion. In religion they sought to understand the divine order of the universe. Eventually, through philosophy, they pursued a clearer understanding of nature—both the world around them and the nature of humanity itself.

Slaves carrying the Greek jars or vases known as amphorae

Religion

In its origin, the polis had been both a religious and a civic institution. In addition to acting as a community of tribes, the polis was a means by which the people kept faith with their gods, the same gods that other Indo-European-speaking peoples worshipped. Each city-state saw itself under the special protection of one particular god or goddess. Athens, for example, was the city of Athena. All the Greek tribes worshipped the ruler of the gods, Zeus, and his son Apollo, the god of sunlight and prophecy. Mount Olympus in northeastern Greece was believed to be the home of the gods.

Through religious sacrifices, which were usually burnt offerings, the early Greeks called on the gods' help and protection for the polis. In return, the Greeks offered them praise. When necessary, the Greeks would send delegations to special shrines where the oracles (priests or priestesses) of certain gods would give advice and answers to questions. The oracle at Delphi (DEL-fi), sacred to Apollo, was probably the most famous.

Athletic competitions, such as the Olympic games held every four years at Olympia, were also a common way of honoring the gods. The Olympic games honoring Zeus first began in 776 B.C. Initially there was only one event, a footrace. Other events, such as wrestling and horse races, were added over time. Winning was everything to the Greeks. Winners were treated as heroes when they returned home, while losers were disgraced.

As they came into contact with the other civilizations of the eastern Mediterranean, over time a few Greeks became less concerned with the religious views of their society. Particularly as they moved away from government based on kingship, these few Greek thinkers began to see laws and government as institutions created by ordinary human beings, not by the gods. Gradually they turned away from a mythological view of the world toward a more rational one. The first steps in this direction began in Ionia.

*A*s the Greeks came into contact with other civilizations, a few Greek thinkers began to see their world as controlled less by gods and more by humans.

Although Greek gods and goddesses were supposedly very powerful, they exhibited human traits and characteristics. Hera, for example, was believed to be extremely jealous. Hephaestus, although a god, was said to limp as the result of a childhood injury. As the god of thievery, Hermes frequently played tricks on those around him.

Critical Thinking Ask students if they think the Greek gods and goddesses represented a state of perfection or resembled humans in their behavior.

ANSWER: Students should answer that the Greek gods and goddesses reflected the behavior and faults of humans, rather than representing perfect beings.

Chart Answer

These events were caused by immense forces beyond the control of humans, and ancient Greeks had little knowledge of the scientific causes of natural phenomena.

Greek Gods and Goddesses of Olympus

God or Goddess	Functions
ZEUS	Leader of the gods; god of lightning, law, and morality
HERA	Wife of Zeus; goddess of marriage and childbirth
POSEIDON	God of the sea and earthquakes
DEMETER	Goddess of cultivation and the earth
HESTIA	Goddess of the home and the hearth
APOLLO	God of the sun, archery, music, prophecy, and medicine
ARTEMIS	Goddess of wild animals and nature
ATHENA	Goddess of wisdom and protector of heroes
HEPHAESTUS	God of crafts and artisanship
ARES	God of war
APHRODITE	Goddess of love
HERMES	Messenger of the gods; god of business, speech, and thievery; guide to travelers

Religion Most ancient Greeks believed in numerous gods and goddesses. These gods and goddesses represented all natural events in the Greeks' world.

? Hypothesizing Why do you think many ancient Greeks explained natural phenomena, such as earthquakes or lightning, as the work of gods and goddesses?

The Origins of Greek Philosophy

According to tradition, Thales (THAY-leez) of Miletus in Ionia was the first Greek philosopher. Thales and others like him were particularly interested in the nature of the universe, or cosmos, as they called it. Thales sought reasonable explanations for how the world had developed. After careful consideration, he concluded that water was the basic substance of the world, from which all else was composed. In reaching this view, however, Thales refused to accept any explanation that depended on the gods, insisting that all things in nature must be explainable by natural processes.

As Thales and other Ionian philosophers searched for answers that would explain the nature of the universe, their ideas spread across the trade routes to others in the Greek world. The Greek colonies in southern Italy proved to be fertile ground for new speculation and thought.

Pythagoras (puh-THAG-uh-ruhs), perhaps the most famous of these Italian Greek philosophers,

concluded that everything in the universe was made up of numerical relationships and could therefore be understood, described, and manipulated mathematically. Pythagoras is probably best remembered for the Pythagorean theorem of geometry, which states that the square of the length of the hypotenuse of a right triangle equals the sum of the squares of the lengths of the other two sides.

As Pythagoras and his students developed their mathematical ideas, Parmenides (pahr-MEN-uh-deez) of Elea applied the same kinds of mathematical rules to philosophy itself. He suggested that a philosophical argument must be internally consistent—meaning without self-contradictions—in order to be true. Parmenides established what we now call **formal logic**. According to formal logic, all assertions must be based on reasoned proof.

Democritus (di-MAHK-ruht-uhs), a Thracian philosopher, tried to build on Parmenides' use of logic. He proposed a description of the universe that would be both logical and mathematical. Democritus also combined the major elements of the earlier philosophers' models by suggesting that the universe consisted of an infinite number of atoms—basic units of matter—that floated endlessly in empty space. According to Democritus's atomic theory, all things were formed by the constant collision and combination of these atoms.

Early Greek philosophers were concerned with the composition and workings of the universe.

Literature

The earliest examples of Greek literature are the two long epic poems, the *Iliad* and the *Odyssey*, supposedly composed by a blind poet named Homer in the 700s B.C. The poems were recited or sung by traveling poets throughout the Greek world. The epics became the basis for Greek education. Schoolboys were required to memorize the poems, and young men were encouraged to imitate the deeds of heroism and bravery described in the epics. The images of brave heroes and human emotion in Homer's epics had a lasting impact on Greek writers and artists.

Poetry. Poetry continued to be an important literary form in Classical Greece. Possibly the greatest poet of the 400s B.C. was the professional wandering poet, Pindar. Pindar is best known for his "victory odes," poems celebrating individual victories of athletes. Pindar found excellence in athletic achievements. About a boxer, for example, Pindar wrote:

66 *Zeus, honor the successful boxer,*
  And give him the respect and gratitude
  Of citizen and stranger alike.
  For he has walked the straight road which
    hates violence
  And has learned well the lessons taught
  By the wisdom of his fathers. 99

Greek theater. One of the most popular means by which the Greeks explored the nature of their world was through theater. The Greeks were the first to write dramas, or plays, usually performed at the religious festivals honoring Dionysus (dy-uh-NY-suhs), the god of wine. By the 400s B.C. Greek drama consisted of several actors and a chorus of singers. Focusing on the meaning of human existence and on human responsibilities, Greek theater became an educational experience for the public.

In Athens, audiences assembled in the theater of Dionysus, which could accommodate between 14,000 and 17,000 spectators. Everybody could attend the plays, including women, foreigners, and slaves. The plays were organized and financed by rich citizens, and the poor were given free tickets. Every spring, three of the greatest playwrights from throughout the Greek world were invited to compete in the Festival of Dionysus. At the end of the festival, 10 judges ranked the performances and awarded prizes.

Tragedies. The three greatest Athenian playwrights of the 400s B.C.—Aeschylus (ES-ke-luhs), Sophocles (SAHF-uh-kleez), and Euripides (yoo-RIP-uh-deez)—frequently competed in the Festival of Dionysus. In the plays of Aeschylus, people's actions

◀ This clay pot depicts a scene from Sophocles' tragedy *Oedipus Rex*, in which Oedipus solves the riddle of the Sphinx before continuing on his journey to Thebes.

▲ Greek plays were performed in amphitheaters like this one at the acropolis in Athens.

The *Odyssey* is both an exciting adventure story and a literary portrait of Greek values. Odysseus undertakes a 10-year voyage from Troy to his home in Ithaca, encountering exotic characters and extreme dangers throughout the Mediterranean. He is able to survive because of his cunning, as shown in his encounter with the Kyklops. Odysseus's continuing efforts to return to his family as well as to his kingdom reflect the importance of family connections in ancient Greece.

Critical Thinking Ask students if they think Odysseus demonstrates ancient Greek values and religious beliefs in this selection.

ANSWER: Students might answer that Odysseus appeals to the Kyklops for hospitality, an important Greek custom, and that he justifies blinding the Kyklops as proper punishment for hubris. They might also mention that Odysseus is shown to be courageous, a virtue for a war leader.

Understanding Literature
He is blinded by Odysseus.

Literature THROUGH TIME

The *Odyssey*

The Odyssey is a long epic poem filled with the legends, values, and religious beliefs of the ancient Greeks. It is believed that the Odyssey and its companion poem, the Iliad, were composed sometime in the 700s B.C. by a poet named Homer, who lived in Asia Minor. Both the Iliad and the Odyssey were oral poems. They were carried all over the Greek world by traveling minstrels who sang or recited the epics as entertainment. The Odyssey is the story of the hardships that befall the hero Odysseus on his way home from fighting the Trojan War. A main theme of the Odyssey is the value Greeks placed on hospitality. One of the greatest virtues a Greek could possess was to be a good host. Those who showed their hubris, or pride, and refused to be hospitable could expect to be punished—an idea illustrated when Odysseus and his men enter the cave of the one-eyed monster, the Kyklops.

It was our luck to come here;
    here we stand,
beholden for your help, or any
    gifts
you give—as custom is to
honor strangers.
We would entreat you, great Sir,
    have a care
for the gods' courtesy; Zeus will
    avenge
the unoffending guest. . . .

Neither reply nor pity came
    from him,
but in one stride he clenched at
    my companions
and caught two in his hands like
    squirming puppies
to beat their brains out, spatter-
    ing the floor.
Then he dismembered them
    and made his meal,
gaping and crunching like a
    mountain lion—
everything; innards, flesh, and
    marrow bones.
We cried aloud, lifting our hands
    to Zeus,
powerless, looking on at this,
    appalled.

The next day, while the Kyklops was gone, Odysseus and his men took a long pole, sharpened the end and stuck it in the fire to heat it. That evening, the Kyklops returned, and Odysseus offered him wine.

Three bowls I brought him, and
    he poured them
    down.
I saw the fuddle
    and flush come
    over him. . . .

Even as he spoke,
    he reeled and
    tumbled back-
    ward,
his great head
    lolling to one
    side, and sleep
    took him like any
creature. Drunk, hiccuping,
he dribbled streams of liquor
    and bits of men.

Now, by the gods, I drove my
    big hand spike
deep in the embers, charring it
    again,
and cheered my men along with
    battle talk
to keep their courage up: no
    quitting now.
The pike of olive, green though
    it had been,
reddened and glowed as if
    about to catch.
I drew it from the coals and my
    four fellows
gave me a hand, lugging it near
    the Kyklops
as more than natural force
    nerved them; straight
forward they sprinted, lifted it,
    and rammed it
deep in his crater eye, and I
    leaned on it
turning it as a shipwright turns a
    drill. . . .

The Kyklops bellowed and the
    rock roared round him,
and we fell back in fear. Clawing
    his face
he tugged the bloody spike out
    of his eye.

Understanding Literature
How is the Kyklops punished for his hubris?

Odysseus and his men drive the spike into the Kyklops's eye after he has become befuddled with wine.

◀ **Medea, contemplating her destiny of revenge. After killing her husband's new queen, she sacrificed her own children to punish him**.

were controlled entirely by the gods, while in Sophocles' works political and social issues were more important. Both Aeschylus and Sophocles were greatly concerned with the idea of **hubris**, or pride. For Aeschylus, this meant defying the will of the gods. Sophocles, on the other hand, believed that hubris involved choosing to go against the natural order of the universe, of which the gods were a part:

❝*The man who goes his way overbearing in word and deed, who fears no justice, honors no temples of the gods—may an evil destiny seize him. And punish his ill-starred pride.*❞

Euripides portrayed humans in control of their own destinies. For instance, in Euripides' masterpiece *Medea*, the main character, Medea, must choose between her obligation to seek revenge against her husband for abandoning her and the murder of her own children to fulfill this revenge. In the play, the gods remain neutral. Medea's destiny lies in her own hands.

Comedies. Greek comedies mocked ideas and people. No social and political institutions escaped the wit of the great comic playwright Aristophanes (ar-uh-STAHF-uh-neez). In his plays, Aristophanes made fun of education, women, politicians, and legal institutions. Even in comedies, Greek spectators were forced to confront serious matters. For example, Aristophanes often used the Peloponnesian War for the background of his plays, and though many scenes are extremely funny, the lesson he most tried to convey was the absurdity of the war.

🏛 History

The Greeks' interest in human nature and conduct also led them to an interest in history. Herodotus, often called the Father of History, wrote a detailed account of the Persian Wars "to preserve the memory of the past by putting on record the astonishing achievements both of our own [the Greek] and of other peoples." Herodotus, a Greek from Asia Minor, was a wonderful storyteller and a man of great curiosity who had traveled extensively in the eastern Mediterranean. He is one of the best literary sources for the history of the Persian Empire and of Greece in the 400s B.C.

Thucydides, another great Greek historian of the 400s B.C., was fascinated by the human aspects of history. Thucydides was born around 460 B.C. into an Athenian family with estates in Thrace. He served as a general in the Athenian army in the great war against Sparta. After failing to stop the Spartans from taking the city of Amphipolis in 424 B.C., however, Thucydides was exiled from Athens.

Thucydides drew on his military experiences to write his *History of the Peloponnesian War*. Unlike most writers before him, however, Thucydides did not try to explain events as having been caused by the intervention of the gods. Instead he focused on how human choices affected the course of the war. In his introduction, Thucydides explained his reasons for writing about the war:

Thucydides
BIOGRAPHY

❝*[I] Thucydides the Athenian wrote the history of the war, . . . in the belief that it was going to be a great war and more worth writing about than any of those which had taken place in the past. . . . This was the greatest disturbance in the history of the Hellenes [the Greeks], affecting also a large part of the non-Hellenic world, and indeed, I might almost say, the whole of mankind.*❞

Through careful analysis, and the use of evidence to support his interpretation, Thucydides hoped to explain how the actions of the Greeks themselves brought about the terrible catastrophe.

REVIEW & ASSESSMENT RESOURCES

- Study Guide 3.4
- Daily Quiz 3.4
- Main Idea Activity 3.4

All Levels

SECTION 4 REVIEW ANSWERS
(p. 86)

IDENTIFY
For significance, see the following pages:
Thales (p. 82)
Pythagoras (p. 82)
Parmenides (p. 82)
formal logic (p. 82)
Democritus (p. 82)
Pindar (p. 83)
Aeschylus (p. 83)
Sophocles (p. 83)
Euripides (p. 83)
hubris (p. 85)
Herodotus (p. 85)
Thucydides (p. 85)

1. the nature of the universe, numerical relationships, formal logic, and atomic construction of matter

2. Greek authors, historians, and artists were interested in the role of humans in the universe. Over time, more and more Greeks came to glorify humans and downplay the role of the gods.
3. The move away from kingship caused people to search for rational rather than mythological explanations of the world.
4. Responses should include the drama's focus on human existence and moral and educational purpose.
5. Greek culture reflected the importance of humanity by discussing human characteristics such as hubris and by depicting the human form in visual arts.

CHAPTER 3 REVIEW ANSWERS
(p. 87)

WRITING A SUMMARY
See essential points in the text.

REVIEWING TERMS
1. polis
2. phalanx
3. Delian League
4. hubris
5. direct democracy

REVIEWING CHRONOLOGY
3, 1, 5, 2, 4

UNDERSTANDING THE MAIN IDEA
1. by allowing conquered peoples to maintain their religions, legal systems, and languages
2. a belief in independence and self-sufficiency, as well as a sense of community and a strong geographical identity

Painting, Sculpture, and Architecture

Just as the human condition provided the main subject for Greek writers, the human form deeply fascinated Greek artists. Although the Greeks borrowed and improved upon many styles and techniques from other cultures around the Mediterranean, they eventually developed an artistic culture that was entirely their own.

Painting on vases and drinking vessels was one of the most common forms of Greek art. After the Dark Age, Greek traders were impressed with the animal images they found painted on pottery in places such as Egypt. Greek artists adopted this style, but within a few centuries began replacing animals with human figures. Early Greek sculptures of people also show Egyptian influence, with statues of men and women standing straight with their arms by their sides. Sculptors used mathematical proportions to ensure that their works looked as realistic as possible.

By the 500s B.C. Greek artists were even more interested in depicting the ideal human form. Greek vase painters had learned to outline an image, allowing the orange clay to show through, and then paint the rest of the background and the details in black. In this way, they were able to create very detailed and realistic images. Inspired by the accomplishments of their civilization, Greek sculptors began to create detailed statues of athletes, warriors, and even ordinary citizens. *The Discus Thrower*, a statue by the great sculptor Myron, for example, represented excellence in human competition.

In Classical Greece, art was meant for public enjoyment. Public buildings in Athens contained massive stone statues from the greatest sculptors of the day. The architecture of the buildings was meant to be a monument to the power and glory of the polis. Possibly the greatest architectural achievement of ancient Greece was the reconstruction of the acropolis under the direction of Pericles. The buildings of the acropolis, including the Parthenon, used ordered columns and ornate carvings on their exteriors to fill visitors to the city with awe and wonder.

▲ The power of Myron's *The Discus Thrower*, c. 450 B.C., is its "Myronic movement"—the capture of motion in a still figure.

Greek artists tried to represent the perfect human form, while authors praised human achievements and explored human flaws.

SECTION 4 REVIEW

IDENTIFY and explain the significance of the following:
    Thales
    Pythagoras
    Parmenides
    formal logic
    Democritus
    Pindar
    Aeschylus
    Sophocles
    Euripides
    hubris
    Herodotus
    Thucydides

1. **Main Idea** What subjects did early Greek philosophers explore?
2. **Main Idea** What subjects interested Greek authors, historians, and artists?
3. **Religion** Why might political changes in the city-states have helped change some Greeks' view of the role of the gods?
4. **Writing to Explain** Imagine that you are an Athenian and have just attended one of the Greek dramas discussed in this chapter. Write a response to the play.
5. **Synthesizing** In what ways did Greek culture reflect the Greeks' view of the importance of humanity?

Chapter 3

Review

On a separate sheet of paper, complete the following exercises:

WRITING A SUMMARY

Using the essential points in the text, write a brief summary of the chapter.

REVIEWING TERMS

From the following list, choose the term that correctly matches the definition.

phalanx   *shekel*
Delian League   polis
direct democracy   hubris

1. Greek city-state, considered by the Greeks to be politically independent and economically self-sufficient
2. Greek military formation
3. alliance among several Greek city-states around the Aegean Sea, headed by Athens, that later became the Athenian Empire
4. human pride; going against the natural order of things
5. political system in which every citizen has a direct and equal voice in decisions

REVIEWING CHRONOLOGY

List the following events in their correct chronological order.

1. The Persians are defeated at the Battle of Marathon.
2. Pericles uses funds from the Delian League to rebuild the acropolis.
3. Darius becomes king of the Persian Empire.

4. Sparta and its allies declare war against Athens.
5. The Spartans and their allies hold out against the Persians at Thermopylae.

UNDERSTANDING THE MAIN IDEA

1. How were the Persians able to govern such a large and multicultural empire?
2. What ideas made up the Greeks' concept of the polis?
3. What were the results of the Persian Wars?
4. What were some of the causes of the Peloponnesian War?
5. Who were some of the early Greek philosophers and what topics did they study?

THINKING CRITICALLY

1. **Synthesizing** What did the Greeks' view of the importance of human achievement have to do with their conception of the polis?
2. **Hypothesizing** How might the Greeks' loyalty to a particular polis have caused problems when their civilization was threatened from outside invaders?
3. **Evaluating** What made Athenian democracy a fair form of political representation? What were some of its limitations? Under what circumstances might such a system of government be ineffective?

Building Your Portfolio

Complete the following activities individually or in groups.

1. **Religion** Imagine that you are an architect in ancient Greece. You (and your coworkers) have been asked by the leaders of the polis to design a new temple for the acropolis. You must first present your proposal to the city leaders for approval. For your proposal you will create either a detailed diagram or a three-dimensional model of the temple you are proposing. Be sure to include all statues and carvings that will go in and on the building. You will also need to prepare a written report describing the importance of the temple to the polis.

2. **Warfare** The famous historians of ancient Greece, Herodotus and Thucydides, both recorded the great wars of their time. Imagine that you are a participant or a spectator in either the Persian Wars or the Peloponnesian War. Write a historical account of either war, also explaining the war's causes and consequences. Be sure to give details on one or more battles you have observed, including how each side is organized. Give your opinion as to why the war you are describing is important to the Greek or Persian world. You may wish to enhance your account with illustrations or maps.

3. Greek independence from Persia, development of Delian League, rise of Athens as major power of League
4. conflict between Athens and Sparta, objections to Athenian domination of Delian League, rivalries among poleis
5. Thales—natural processes of nature; Pythagoras—numerical relationships; Parmenides—internal consistency of arguments, formal logic; Democritus—atomic basis of matter

THINKING CRITICALLY

1. Independence and individual achievement meant that each person could play a role in government. This led to the development of democracy.
2. Poleis might have had trouble establishing common goals and working together rather than for their own benefit.
3. The fairness of Athenian democracy stemmed from the idea of "one person, one vote" and from the inclusion of many people in the electoral process. It was limited by its definition of citizenship and by reliance on a leader who was willing to maintain a democratic system. Such a government might be ineffective if members were unwilling to compromise or if quick action was necessary.

Chapter 4

The Hellenistic World and the Rise of Rome 1000 B.C.–133 B.C.

Chapter Planning Guide

	TEXTBOOK	CORE RESOURCES	VISUAL RESOURCES	MULTIMEDIA
Introduction	pp. 88–89	Block Scheduling Handbook: Ch. 4		Videodisc Segment 4 and Viewing Guide: *A Socratic Education*
Lesson 4.1 The Crisis of Greek Civilization	pp. 90–95	Reading 4.1: *Aristotle's Views on Education* Writing Project 4: *Formulating a Thesis Statement*		GHRC 4 Readings: *The Sophists of Athens; Plato: The Philosopher as King; The Trial and Death of Socrates*
Lesson 4.2 The Rise of Macedonia and Alexander the Great	pp. 96–99 Map: *Alexander the Great's Empire*, p. 97 Teenagers in History: *Alexander and Bucephalus*, p. 98	Reading 4.2: *Alexander's Deification at the Temple of Zeus-Ammon* Geography Activity 4: *The Hellenistic World and the Rise of Rome*		GHRC 4 Reading: *Plutarch on Alexander's Accomplishments* GHRC 4/Videodiscs: Image— *Alexander's Legacy: The Library of Alexandria*
Lesson 4.3 Hellenistic Civilization	pp. 100–107 Map: *Hellenistic Kingdoms*, p. 101 History Through the Arts: *The Foundations of Hellenistic Sculpture*, p. 104	Reading 4.3: *The Medical Aphorisms of Hippocrates* Skills Activity 4: *Creating a Table*	Art and History 4: *Veiled and Masked Dancer*	GHRC 4 Readings: *Epicurus on Achieving Peace of Mind; The Jews' Long Struggle with Hellenization; Plutarch on the Genius of Archimedes; Aristarchus and Hellenistic Astronomy* GHRC 4/Videodiscs: Images— *Winged Victory of Samothrace; Hellenistic Science Goes to War; Maps—Division of Alexander's Empire; The Economy of the Hellenistic Era; The Hellenization of Asia*
Lesson 4.4 The Rise of Rome	pp. 108–112 Map: *The Growth of the Roman Republic*, p. 110 Through Others' Eyes: *A Warning Against Roman Expansion*, p. 111	Reading 4.4: *Rome's Perfect Location*	Everyday Life 4: *Etruscan Musicians* Geography and History 4: *The Spread of Etruscan Culture*	GHRC 4 Readings: *Polybius on the Roman Army; The Romans Take Revenge on Carthage; Rome's Growing Empire* GHRC 4/Videodiscs: Image— *Roman Soldiers' Triumphal Procession*
Chapter Investigation and Enrichment	pp. 88–112	Chapter 4 Investigation: *A Debate About Power* People in World History 4 Explorations in Daily Life 4		GHRC 4/Videodiscs
Review and Assessment	Section 1 Review, p. 95 Section 2 Review, p. 99 Section 3 Review, p. 107 Section 4 Review, p. 112 Chapter 4 Review, p. 113	Chapter Review Activity 4 Vocabulary Activity 4 Themes Review 4 Section Study Guides 4.1–4.4 Main Idea Activities 4.1–4.4 Daily Quizzes 4.1–4.4 Chapter 4 Test Sheltered English Ch. 4 Test Ch. 4 Test Generator		Audio CDs: Ch. 4 Summary (English and Spanish)

INTRODUCING THE CHAPTER

Textbook pp. 88–89

CHAPTER OVERVIEW

While Greek philosophers such as Plato and Aristotle changed Western thought, the failure of the Greek city-states to unite after the Peloponnesian War opened the way for the Macedonian conqueror Philip II. His son Alexander expanded his empire and spread Greek civilization from the Mediterranean world to the borders of India. As a result, a new Hellenistic civilization combining elements of Greek and Persian culture emerged. Meanwhile, the city of Rome was becoming the center of a new civilization.

PRESENTING THEMES

On the chalkboard or on an overhead transparency, write the following open-ended theme questions.

- **RELIGION** Why might people adopt a new religion?
- **POLITICS AND LAW** What problems could be involved in governing a vast and multiethnic empire?
- **CROSS-CULTURAL INTERACTION** How might warfare and conquest influence the exchange of culture?

Have students, either individually or in groups, suggest responses to the questions. For the religion question, students might suggest that a defeated people might believe that their conqueror's religion is more powerful. For the politics and law question, students might suggest that the government of a large, varied empire would have difficulty devising policies that pleased most of the empire's population. For the cross-cultural interaction question, students might suggest that conquest often forces people to accept new cultural values. Save the responses. Once students have studied the chapter, you may wish to have them complete the Themes Review, then compare the two sets of answers.

USING THE VIDEO

Segment 4: *A Socratic Education*

ENGLISH

Search Chapter 4
Videodisc 1, Side A

SPANISH

Search Chapter 4
Videodisc 1, Side A

Tell students that in this chapter they will examine the factors that led to the vast and diverse Hellenistic Empire created by Alexander the Great in the 300s B.C. Conclude by showing Segment 4 of the *World History and Cultures Videodiscs*. This segment demonstrates the Socratic method of teaching. The segment also looks at the contributions of other Greek philosophers and the School of Athens in the areas of politics, science, and philosophy. To help students grasp the significant points of the segment, have them complete Video Viewing Guide 4.

Key to Ability Levels

All strategies and activities are coded to the following ability levels:

LEVEL 1	**Basic** activities suitable for all students
LEVEL 2	**Average** activities suitable for average to above-average students
LEVEL 3	**Challenging** activities suitable for above-average students
SHELTERED ENGLISH	Activities suitable for students with **Limited English Proficiency**

Additional Resources

BOOKS FOR TEACHERS

Boardman, John, Griffin, Jasper, and Murray, Oswyn, eds. *The Oxford History of Greece and the Hellenistic World.* Oxford University Press, 1986. Provides a collection of essays.

Bosworth, A. B. *Conquest and Empire: The Reign of Alexander the Great.* Cambridge University Press, 1988. Examines issues of empire.

Green, Peter. *Alexander of Macedon, 356–323 B.C.* University of California Press, 1991. Considers Alexander's personality.

BOOKS FOR STUDENTS

Arrian. *Alexander the Great, 356–323 B.C.* Cambridge University Press, 1981. Presents a biography written only 400 years after Alexander's death.

Briant, Pierre. *Alexander the Great: Man of Action, Man of Spirit.* Harry N. Abrams, Inc., 1996. A well-illustrated introduction to Alexander.

Stone, I. F. *The Trial of Socrates.* Little, Brown, 1988. Inquiries into the death of the philosopher.

MULTIMEDIA MATERIALS

Greece and Rome: 1200 B.C.–A.D. 200. Network Television Production. Video, 26 min. Includes material on Alexander.

Greeks: In Search of Meaning. Learning Corporation of America. Video, 25 min. Looks at Greek thought.

History Through Art: Ancient Greece. ZCI. CD-ROM, MAC, DOS, WIN, MPC formats. Explores changes in art and ideas from 800–146 B.C.

Lesson 4.1　　*The Crisis of Greek Civilization*

Textbook pp. 90–95

RESOURCES

Core Resources

Reading 4.1: *Aristotle's Views on Education*

Global History Resource Center

Reading: *The Sophists of Athens*

Reading: *Plato: The Philosopher as King*

Reading: *The Trial and Death of Socrates*

LESSON FOCUS

What new ideas emerged during the period of crisis that followed the Peloponnesian War?

OBJECTIVES

After completing this lesson, students will be able to:

- describe the political situation in Greece after the Peloponnesian War;
- explain why many people rejected the ideas of the Sophists;
- outline Plato's and Aristotle's philosophies concerning the existence of all things.

HOOK: Link to Today

Describe the political situation in Greece after the Peloponnesian War. Have students imagine that their state has just been the scene of terrible warfare. The invading army has gone, leaving their state defeated. Encourage students to share their reactions.

Ask: *How would you feel? What actions would you take?*

[*Some students may suggest that they would be demoralized; others may say they would be ready to pick up the pieces and start over.*]

Focus on student responses that use such terms as *strife*, *unrest*, *uncertainty*, *instability*, and *insecurity*. Then point out that a period of unrest and instability in Greece followed the Peloponnesian War.

Lead students to recognize that living in the shadow of the Persian Empire created continuous uncertainty in Greek life. Then prompt students to discuss the impact of this uncertainty.

Ask: *What happened to Greek unity?*

[*Sparta failed to replace Athens as the leading power in Greece; the Persians, through diplomacy, were able to keep the Greeks warring among themselves; attempts by Thebes and Athens to unite Greece failed.*]

Ask: *What happened to the polis as a result of this continuing political crisis?*

[*The idea of the polis was greatly undermined; since it formed the basis of Greek life, many certainties about life began to be questioned.*]

DEVELOP

Describe the ideas of the Sophists and explain why many people rejected such thinking. Point out that this new questioning attitude led to transformations in thinking in Greece. Then write the words *Traditional Ideas* and *Sophists' New Ideas* on the chalkboard. Draw an imaginary line down the center of the classroom. Have students to the left of the line act as people who held traditional ideas; students to the right of the line should play the role of Sophists. Allow the two groups five minutes to list their key ideas. Then have the traditionalists state their ideas one at a time; the Sophists should then counter with their own views on each issue. Enter responses under the appropriate heading on the chalkboard. Encourage students to copy the chart into their notebooks and to retain it for review purposes.

Next focus students' attention on Protagoras's most famous statement.

Ask: *How does Protagoras's statement "Man is the measure of all things" sum up the ideas of the Sophists?*

[*Answers should recognize that the statement demonstrates the Sophists' shift away from the idea that there could be an absolute truth and toward the idea that everything is relative.]*

Conclude by encouraging students to consider the impact of the Sophists' ideas.

Ask: *Why might people find the ideas of the Sophists dangerous?*
[Many people felt their ideas would undermine stability.]

To provide students with more information about Protagoras and the Sophists, assign the Global History Resource Center reading on the Sophists.

PROBE

Explore the philosophies of Socrates, Plato, and Aristotle.

Organize students into three groups and assign each group to study the ideas of either Socrates, Plato, or Aristotle. The group studying the ideas of Aristotle might find Core Resources Reading 4.1 useful, while the groups studying Socrates and Plato might find valuable information in the appropriate Global History Resource Center readings. Allow groups 10 minutes for research. Then call on group representatives to play their assigned philosopher, explaining his ideas.

Next have students compare the philosophers' ideas.

Ask: *What did each philosopher believe about the importance of relativism?*
[Students should recognize that Socrates, Plato, and Aristotle, unlike the Sophists, believed there was an absolute truth.]

Ask: *How did Plato and Aristotle differ in their ideas of ideal Forms and reality?*
[Plato believed there are ideal Forms behind the physical, while Aristotle believed that the ideal Form and the matter itself exist together.]

Ask: *How did Plato and Aristotle differ about how government should be organized?*
[Plato believed in government by philosopher-rulers, while Aristotle believed in government by society's middle level.]

CONCLUDE

Evaluate keys ideas of Protagoras, Socrates, Plato, and Aristotle.
Have students examine the information in the textbook about the ideas of Protagoras, Socrates, Plato, and Aristotle. Have them choose one of these philosophers and write a paragraph supporting or refuting his ideas. Have students share their paragraphs.

Then ask students to consider all they know of the ideas of the four named philosophers and answer the following question: If you lived in a time of crisis, as the Greeks did, to which philosopher's ideas would you turn? Have students cast votes for each philosopher; then call on volunteers to explain their choices.

EXTEND

Cross-Curricular Connection: *Language Arts*
Have students find and react to examples of well-known sayings from the four philosophers discussed in this section. Suggest that they use *Bartlett's Familiar Quotations*, *The Oxford Dictionary of Quotations*, or another reference source for quotations.

MEET INDIVIDUAL NEEDS

Gifted Students
Have students read the Global History Resource Center reading on Plato and discuss Plato's ideas about who is best equipped to rule. Then have them write a brief essay comparing Plato's views with those of such founders of the United States as Thomas Jefferson, James Madison, Alexander Hamilton, and John Adams.

Students Having Difficulty
Have students who need help with some of the abstract philosophical concepts work in small groups to discuss a major Greek philosopher and his ideas.

ASSESS

Review
Have students complete the Section 1 Review. Use answers in the Teacher's Edition, page 95, to assess student mastery of this section.

The Rise of Macedonia and Alexander the Great

Textbook pp. 96–99

RESOURCES

Pupil's Edition

Map, p. 97: *Alexander the Great's Empire, 323 B.C.*

Teenagers in History, p. 98: *Alexander and Bucephalus*

Core Resources

Reading 4.2: *Alexander's Deification at the Temple of Zeus-Ammon*

Geography Activity 4: *The Hellenistic World and the Rise of Rome*

Global History Resource Center

Reading: *Plutarch on Alexander's Accomplishments*

Videodiscs or Global History Resource Center

Image: *Alexander's Legacy: The Library of Alexandria*

Search Frame 718

LESSON FOCUS

How did Macedonia build a vast empire far beyond its Mediterranean homeland?

OBJECTIVES

After completing this lesson, students will be able to:

• explain how Macedonia was easily able to conquer the Greek city-states;

• identify the qualities that made Alexander a great conqueror;

• explain how Alexander the Great established a multicultural empire.

HOOK: Link to Today

Explore why Macedonia was easily able to conquer the Greek city-states. To emphasize the factors that enabled Macedonia to conquer an empire, have a student read aloud the information on Philip II on textbook page 96. Then have students read about the development of cavalry in the Global History Resource Center. Have students suggest elements of Macedonia's strength. List responses on the chalkboard as they are offered. *[The list should include a professional army and the use of phalanx formations, archers, and cavalry in battle.]*

Ask: *From where did Philip II gain his knowledge to improve Macedonian warfare? Why is this ironic?*

[As a hostage in Thebes, Philip II studied Greek military strategy under the brilliant Greek strategist Epaminondas.

It is ironic because he later used the knowledge to conquer the Greek city-states.]

Next draw students' attention to some of the first peoples who the Macedonians sought to conquer—the Greeks.

Ask: *In the face of a Macedonian invasion, what kind of front did the Greek city-states present?*

[Failure of the Greek city-states to unite made Greece a relatively easy target for the well-organized, efficient Macedonian army.]

DEVELOP

Discuss factors that made Alexander a great conqueror. To give students a sense of the scale of Alexander the Great's conquests, have them study the map on textbook page 97. Then ask students to trace with their finger the routes followed by Alexander and his armies. Tell them that in 10 years of conquest, Alexander's armies covered around 22,000 miles in their marching and fighting.

Next point out that Alexander was able to become a great conqueror in part because of certain qualities he possessed. Have students note some of these qualities. In addition to the text, have them read the Teenagers in History feature on textbook page 98. Provide students with information on another aspect of Alexander's character by assigning Core Resources Reading 4.2.

Ask: *What qualities make someone a great military leader?*

Which of these qualities did Alexander possess?
[Qualities students might mention include a powerful personality, military skills, aggressiveness, ambition, decisiveness, persistence, and courage. Students might suggest that Alexander possessed all these qualities. Most importantly, however, Alexander was a brilliant military tactician who possessed natural charisma.]

To underscore Alexander's standing as a great military leader, mention that only natural obstacles seemed to be able to halt his conquests. Illustrate this point by assigning Geography Activity 4.

Conclude by asking students to write a short biography of Alexander, focusing on his leadership qualities.

PROBE
Discuss the problems Alexander faced in ruling his vast empire. Have students consult the map on textbook page 97. Direct them to note the various areas Alexander conquered and the location of the new cities he established. Then have them consider the difficulties he faced in maintaining control over a vast empire populated by diverse peoples.
Ask: *What problems might ruling peoples of so many different cultures create?*
[Conquered peoples might refuse to accept the customs and traditions of outsiders. Such cultural conflicts might lead to unrest and conflict.]

CONCLUDE
Examine the policies that Alexander adopted to hold together his vast multicultural empire. Return to the subject of Alexander's leadership qualities by pointing out that he seemed to know how to balance ruthlessness with magnanimity and good sense. Encourage students to explore this aspect of Alexander's leadership. You might prepare the students for this discussion by assigning the Global History Resource Center reading on Plutarch's view of Alexander.
Ask: *What steps did Alexander take to integrate new territories and peoples with those he already had conquered?*
[Alexander spread Greek culture wherever he went, tried to integrate conquered peoples into his army, and

encouraged intermarriage among the various peoples he conquered.]

Conclude by asking students to evaluate the wisdom of Alexander's policies toward conquered peoples. Help students recognize that treating conquered peoples with respect made them less likely to resist new rule.

EXTEND
Cross-Curricular Connection: *Art*
Have students study the electronic media image that shows an artist's depiction of the library of Alexandria. Then ask them to explain how the image illustrates Alexander's legacy.

Cross-Curricular Connection: *Geography*
Have students compare the map on textbook page 97 with a modern map of the same area. Have them identify the countries that lie—partially or completely—within the area that formed Alexander's empire. *[present-day Greece, India, Turkey, Egypt, Israel, Lebanon, Syria, Iran, Iraq, Pakistan, Afghanistan, Libya, and Cyprus]*

MEET INDIVIDUAL NEEDS
Gifted Students
Have students report on the speeches that Demosthenes made in defense of Athens, with specific reference to the arguments that he advanced against Philip II. Suggest that students consult Lewis Copeland and Lawrence Lamm's *The World's Great Speeches* (Dover) or Houston Peterson's *Treasury of the World's Great Speeches* (Simon and Schuster) to locate these orations.

Intrapersonal Learners
Have students imagine that they live in an area conquered by Alexander. Have them write diary entries describing their reactions. Point out the textbook subsection on "Alexander's Legacy" for ideas.

ASSESS
Review
Have students complete the Section 2 Review. Use answers in the Teacher's Edition, page 99, to assess student mastery of this section.

Lesson 4.3   *Hellenistic Civilization*

Textbook pp. 100–107

RESOURCES

Pupil's Edition

Map, p. 101: *Hellenistic Kingdoms, 185 B.C.*

History Through the Arts, p. 104: *The Foundations of Hellenistic Sculpture*

Core Resources

Reading 4.3: *The Medical Aphorisms of Hippocrates*

Skills Activity 4: *Creating a Table*

Visual Resources

Art and History 4: *Veiled and Masked Dancer*

Global History Resource Center

Reading: *Epicurus on Achieving Peace of Mind*

Reading: *The Jews' Long Struggle with Hellenization*

Reading: *Plutarch on the Genius of Archimedes*

Reading: *Aristarchus and Hellenistic Astronomy*

Videodiscs or Global History Resource Center

Map: *Division of Alexander's Empire, 303 B.C.*

Search Frame 728

Image: *Winged Victory of Samothrace*

Search Frame 719

Image: *Hellenistic Science Goes to War*

Search Frame 722

Map: *The Hellenization of Asia*

Search Frame 729

Map: *The Economy of the Hellenistic Era*

Search Frame 730

LESSON FOCUS

How was Hellenistic civilization different from Hellenic civilization?

OBJECTIVES

After completing this lesson, students will be able to:

- explain what happened to Alexander's empire after his death;
- describe how traditional Greek society changed during the Hellenistic era;
- describe the impact of the growth of Hellenistic cities on people's views of philosophy and religion;
- identify scientific and technological advances in the Hellenistic era.

HOOK

Explain what happened to Alexander's empire after his death. Point out to students that after Alexander's death, his empire split into three major kingdoms, each ruled by one of his generals or their descendants. Choose three students to represent the rulers Ptolemy, Seleucus, and Antigonus. Assign each ruler a "retinue" of five assistants. Give each group about five minutes to help their leader prepare a description of the area he ruled. Have groups refer to the map on textbook page 101 or the electronic media maps to write their descriptions.

DEVELOP

List the changes in traditional Greek life and culture that took place in the Hellenistic era. Write on the chalkboard Isocrates' statement about what it meant to be a Greek—"The people we call Greeks are those who have the same culture as us, not the same blood." Ask students to consider the social impact on the Hellenistic world of this new view of "Greekness."

Ask: What do Isocrates' words tell us about Hellenistic society?
    [Hellenistic society was open enough to allow anyone to

rise in society; however, only those who adopted Greek culture actually advanced.]

Next draw a chart on the chalkboard using the following headings: 1) Social Structure; 2) Status of Women; 3) Art; 4) Literature; 5) Philosophy; 6) Religion; 7) Science and Technology. Have students copy the chart into their notebooks. Then ask them to list in their charts the changes in society and culture during the Hellenistic era. To assist students in listing new ideas in the arts, point out the feature on textbook page 104. You might also display and discuss the Art and History transparency and the electronic media image *Winged Victory of Samothrace*.

PROBE

Relate the growth of Hellenistic cities to new ideas in philosophy and religion. Remind students that during the Hellenistic period many people had the new experience of living in urban settings. Tell them that many people felt lost and alone in this new setting.

Ask: *Why might feelings of being lost and alone lead people to seek new philosophies or religions?*
[These feelings often make people search for sources of stability and support. Greeks who had once been secure in their communal role were now seeking new answers.]

Next organize the class into four groups and assign each group one of the following philosophies—Cynicism, Skepticism, Epicureanism, and Stoicism. Have each group give a presentation on its assigned philosophy. The group that is assigned Epicureanism might study the Global History Resource Center reading on Epicurus. Encourage groups to explain what their philosophies offer to people who feel lost and alone. Finally, have the class as a whole debate the merits of each philosophy.

Conclude by writing *Ruler-worship*, *Mystery religions*, and *Judaism* on the chalkboard. Assign the Global History Resource Center reading on Judaism.

Ask: *What did each of these religions offer people in a period of uncertainty?*
[Ruler-worship: offered people authority figures to follow and filled them with a new sense of civic duty; Mystery religions: offered security, a sense of personal worth, and a promise of immortality; Judaism: attempted to blend with Hellenistic culture and eventually embraced new ideas about resurrection and the coming of a Messiah to save Jewish people from their enemies]

CONCLUDE

Discuss advances in science and technology in the Hellenistic era. Remind students that Hellenistic scientists were less concerned with the ideal and more concerned with how things actually worked. Call on volunteers to play the roles of Archimedes, Euclid, Aristarchus, and Herophilus. Then ask students to describe these scientists' contributions to society in a brief presentation. The rest of the class should prepare questions for the scientists. After the scientists have finished their presentations, have the audience quiz them about their general ideas.

For more information, assign Core Resources Reading 4.3 and the Global History Resource Center readings on Archimedes and Aristarchus, and display the electronic media image on Hellenistic science.

EXTEND
Other Media

Have interested students watch the video *Hanukkah: Let There Be Lights* (PBS Video, color, 30 min.). Then call on volunteers to explain how this Jewish holiday celebrates the victory of the Maccabees over the Seleucids.

MEET INDIVIDUAL NEEDS
Gifted Students

Have students prepare oral reports on the Hellenistic philosopher whose ideas they find most appealing. Encourage them to describe the philosopher's ideas, as well as the impact these ideas had during the Hellenistic era. Encourage students to explain why they find this particular philosopher interesting.

Students Having Difficulty

Encourage students who might be having difficulty organizing information to work on creating a table by using Skills Activity 4. Review students' work to assure they have mastered the skill.

ASSESS
Review

Have students complete the Section 3 Review. Use answers in the Teacher's Edition, page 107, to assess student mastery of this section.

Lesson 4.4   *The Rise of Rome*

Textbook pp. 108–112

RESOURCES

Pupil's Edition

Map, p. 110: *The Growth of the Roman Republic, 509 B.C.–133 B.C.*

Core Resources

Reading 4.4: *Rome's Perfect Location*

Global History Resource Center

Reading: *Polybius on the Roman Army*

Reading: *The Romans Take Revenge on Carthage*

Reading: *Rome's Growing Empire*

Videodiscs or Global History Resource Center

Image: *Roman Soldiers' Triumphal Procession*

Search Frame 725

LESSON FOCUS

How did Rome come to dominate the entire Mediterranean region?

OBJECTIVES

After completing this lesson, students will be able to:

- explain why Rome's location was advantageous;
- describe how Rome was able to conquer Italy;
- identify the eventual consequences of Rome's initial expansion in Italy.

HOOK

Discuss the advantageous location of Rome. Write on the chalkboard the heading *The Perfect Location.* Ask students to identify the various elements that they think would make the perfect location for a city. *[fertile land, water for irrigation and transportation, location on important trade routes, ease of defense, and so on]* Note their responses on the chalkboard.

Have students discuss how Rome's location measures up to their description of the perfect location. You might assign Core Resources Reading 4.4 on the subject.

Ask: *Why was Rome's location advantageous?*

[Rome's location on the Tiber River gave it control of trade routes and easy sea access.]

DEVELOP

Explain how Rome was able to bring Italy under its rule. Continue to focus on location. Point out that the Romans used their central location on the Italian peninsula to bring Italy under their control. Ask students to consider how the Romans were able to dominate the peninsula. Prompt students by displaying the electronic media image that shows a victory parade of Roman soldiers. As soon as a student responds correctly, write on the chalkboard the word ARMY and circle it. List the following underneath: *citizens, property, 17, 46, maniples, cohorts, legion, centurions, 10, 600.* Direct students to use the listed words and numbers to write a brief paragraph describing how the Roman army was organized.

Ask: *What made the Roman army effective?*

[The Roman army was highly disciplined and well trained.]

To illustrate how the Romans maintained discipline in the army, you might assign the Global History Resource Center reading on the Roman army.

Conclude by pointing out that one of the most important aspects of the army was that it was made up of citizens.

Ask: *Why did the Romans want property-owning citizens as soldiers?*

[They believed that people with something to protect at home would fight bravely.]

PROBE

Explain how Rome defeated Carthage in the First and Second Punic Wars. Have students locate Carthage and Rome on the map on textbook page 110. Ask them to discuss why these two Mediterranean powers might have come into conflict. Then create a chart on the chalkboard with Rome and Carthage as vertical column headings and Advantages and Disadvantages as horizontal column headings. Have students complete the chart in reference to advantages and disadvantages the two powers had in warfare. **[Rome's advantage:** *citizen army;* **Carthage's advantage:** *its navy;* **Rome's disadvantage:** *its initial lack of a navy;* **Carthage's disadvantage:** *army made up of mercenaries]*

When students have completed the chart, lead them to see that, in terms of fighting capabilities, Rome and Carthage were well balanced.

Ask: *What development broke this balance and led to Rome's victory in the First Punic War?*
[Rome eventually mastered the art of naval warfare.]

Continue by mentioning that in the Second Punic War, Hannibal of Carthage had the superior fighting force, yet the Romans finally won.

Ask: *Why was Rome victorious in the Second Punic War?*
[Rome was persistent and refused to yield, despite heavy losses. In addition, the Romans changed their strategy, using hit-and-run tactics and attacking Hannibal's supply routes and bases in Spain.]

CONCLUDE

Examine the eventual consequences of Rome's initial expansion in Italy. Have students return to the map on textbook page 110. Inform them that one outcome of the Second Punic War was that Carthage lost its Spanish possessions to Rome. Have students locate on the map the territory that Rome gained. Point out that a little more than 50 years later Rome and Carthage went to war again. This time, however, Rome completely destroyed Carthage. To give students a firsthand view of this act, you might assign the Global History Resource Center reading about Roman revenge on Carthage.

Next mention that the Punic Wars had brought Rome into the affairs of the eastern Mediterranean, for Macedonia had allied itself with Carthage. After the Second Punic War, the Romans attacked and conquered Macedonia and eventually controlled the entire region. Direct students to locate on the map the territories Rome gained after these victories.

Ask: *After taking control of Italy, where did Rome expand?*
[Spain, Carthage, Greece, Asia Minor, Balearic Islands, Sardinia, Corsica, Sicily]

Ask: *What was Rome's standing in the Mediterranean region by 133 B.C.?*
[It was the greatest power in the region.]

You might conclude by assigning the Global History Resource Center reading of a modern historian's view of the relationship between Rome and its growing empire.

EXTEND

Cross-Curricular Connection: *Literature*

Have interested students present a dramatic reading from Thomas Babington Macaulay's poetic work the *Lays of Ancient Rome,* which celebrates the major events in Roman history. After the reading, some students might want to research the accuracy of Macaulay's work.

MEET INDIVIDUAL NEEDS

Visual-Spatial Learners

Have students create two parallel time lines, one for Rome's development and one for events in the Mediterranean world, using the Roman defeat of Carthage in 146 B.C. as the culminating point for both. Encourage students to illustrate their time lines.

Students Acquiring English

Pair new speakers of English with native speakers. Have pairs write a summary of the content of this section by answering the Focus questions on page 108.

ASSESS

Review

Have students complete the Section 4 Review. Use answers in the Teacher's Edition, pages 111–12, to assess student mastery of this section.

In preparation for the chapter test, you may wish to have students complete all or part of the Chapter 4 Review on textbook page 113, the Chapter 4 Review Activity, and the

Understanding the Main Idea

Call on a volunteer to read aloud the *Understanding the Main Idea* paragraph. Then tell students that many great changes occurred in the Greek world after the end of the Peloponnesian War. Because the city-states could not unite to protect themselves, they fell under the domination of the conquering powers of Persia and Macedonia. Under the Macedonians, a new Hellenistic, or Greeklike, culture developed. The conquering Macedonians carried Greek culture with them as they expanded their empire. Meanwhile, Rome, a new power, began to rise in Italy.

Presenting Themes

See p. 87B for suggestions on introducing themes.

Using the Time Line

Have students list the time line events in their notebooks. After they have read about each event in the chapter, have students write a paragraph explaining its significance.

Chapter 4
The Hellenistic World and the Rise of Rome
1000 B.C.–133 B.C.

Understanding the Main Idea

The quarreling among the Greek city-states following the end of the Peloponnesian War in 404 B.C. ultimately led to their conquest by the powerful Macedonians to the north. As the Macedonians expanded their empire all the way to the Indus River, they carried Greek culture with them. At roughly the same time, Rome, a new power in central Italy, was emerging to create a dynamic civilization in the western Mediterranean.

Themes

- *Religion* Why might people adopt a new religion?
- *Politics and Law* What problems could be involved in governing a vast and multiethnic empire?
- *Cross-cultural Interaction* How might warfare and conquest influence the exchange of culture?

In a series of stunning victories, Alexander, the young king of Macedonia, led his small army to a crushing defeat of the vast armies of the mighty Persian Empire. Because of his brilliant military tactics and vast conquests, he has been known forever since as Alexander "the Great." By the time of his death at age 32, Alexander had conquered a territory stretching all the way from the Mediterranean to the Indus River valley. Although Alexander loved Greek art and literature and spread Greek culture across his empire, he also appealed to the loyalty of his new subjects by adopting many of their customs. An ancient historian wrote about Alexander's wearing of Persian clothing:

> **“**During a pause in the campaign . . . he [Alexander] first began to wear barbarian [non-Greek] dress. He may have done this from a desire to adapt himself to local habits, because he understood that the sharing of race and of customs is a great step towards softening men's hearts.**”**

Alexander's great experiment in cultural adaptation was short-lived, however. As quickly as he had conquered his empire, it began to break apart.

753 B.C.	c. 509 B.C.	399 B.C.	338 B.C.
▲ Italians found the city of Rome on the Tiber River.	▲ Roman aristocrats overthrow Tarquinius Superbus, the last Etruscan king.	▲ Socrates is put on trial in Athens for his teachings.	▲ Philip II of Macedonia defeats the Greeks, ending the independence of the Greek city-states.

Bronze statue of Alexander the Great

323 B.C.
Alexander the Great dies in Babylonia.

c. 310 B.C.
Zeno of Citium begins teaching his philosophy of Stoicism in Athens.

216 B.C.
Hannibal's army defeats the Romans at the Battle of Cannae.

133 B.C.
The Roman Republic controls the entire Mediterranean region.

SECTION 1
The Crisis of Greek Civilization

FOCUS

- What was the political situation of Greece after the Peloponnesian War?

- Why did many people reject the ideas of the Sophists?

- What were Plato's and Aristotle's philosophies concerning the existence of all things?

n the 300s B.C. Greek civilization underwent a series of challenges from which it was unable to recover. After the disaster of the Peloponnesian War, the city-states of Greece never succeeded in uniting under strong leadership. Confronted by a growing insecurity, many Greeks began to lose their loyalty to the polis, which had once been the heart of their sense of identity. As they struggled to understand the changes occurring around them, Greek philosophers developed new ideas about human nature and the role of the individual in society.

Gold Greek coins with Philip of Macedonia on upper right

The Crisis of Greek Politics

Sparta's crushing defeat of Athens during the Peloponnesian War destroyed the balance of power in the Greek world. Sparta tried to replace Athens as the leading power in Greece but it was never able to do so successfully. In addition to wrecking the Athenian Empire, the Spartans had also agreed to allow the Persian Empire to take control once more of the Ionian Greek cities in exchange for its support against Athens. The Spartans then decided to intervene in the internal affairs of the Persian Empire on behalf of Prince Cyrus the Younger, possible successor to the Persian throne, who may have promised autonomy for the Ionian cities in return for Sparta's support of his claims.

Continuing warfare. In 401 B.C., 10,000 Greek mercenaries largely under Spartan leader-ship achieved a stunning victory over the Persian army at the battle of Cunaxa (kyoo-NAK-suh) in Mesopotamia north of Babylon. Prince Cyrus, however, died during the fighting. Although the Greeks had won the battle, with Cyrus's death they had effectively lost the war. While the Spartans continued for many years to harass Persia in an effort to regain control of the Greek cities of Ionia, their efforts were all in vain. In 394 B.C. Sparta's hopes were dashed at the battle of Cnidus (NYD-uhs), when a Persian fleet utterly destroyed the Spartan fleet.

For the next several decades, the Greek city-states fought among themselves for power. This continuous squabbling was caused in part by a skillful Persian diplomacy designed to keep the Greeks divided. In 387 B.C. the Persian king con-cluded a settlement among the warring Greek city-states. Under the terms of the so-called King's Peace, the mainland Greeks finally recognized the Persian king Artaxerxes (ahrt-uh-ZUHRK-seez) II's rule over the Ionian city-states. They also agreed that war in Greece would cease, and that the city-states would remain separate and independent, without forming alliances or empires.

Pan-Hellenism. In Athens the orator Isocrates (eye-SAHK-ruh-teez) grasped the significance of the Persian threat. He warned his fellow Greeks of Artaxerxes' intentions:

> *He is a despot [tyrant] to whose court we sail to accuse each other. We call him the Great King, as though we were subject prisoners of war, and if we engage in war with each other, it is on him that our hopes are set, though he would destroy both sides without compunction [care].*

Isocrates called for the Greeks to settle their own differences and band together against Persia, a position known as **Pan-Hellenism**.

The Greek city-state of Thebes, which finally destroyed Spartan power by liberating the helots, tried to unite the Greeks. After Thebes failed in its attempt, Athens also tried to establish Greek unity. By 357 B.C., however, Athens's second attempt to turn an alliance into an empire backfired as the allies once again revolted. Greek independence began to draw rapidly to a close.

After the Peloponnesian War, the city-states of Greece continued to fight among themselves and failed to establish any political unity.

▲ **This water jug from Greece is decorated with images of women carrying water jugs on their heads.**

The Crisis in Greek Society and Culture

The continuing political crisis in the Greek world both reflected and contributed to the erosion of the central element in Greek society—the polis. From the time of the Persian Wars and the creation of the Delian League, the old concept of the polis as absolutely independent and self-sufficient had gradually broken down. As the concept of the polis broke down, the basic certainties of Greek civilization also eroded.

The Sophists. Perhaps nowhere was the trend of change clearer than in the transformations occurring in Greek philosophy. Beginning in the 400s B.C. a new group of philosophers, the **Sophists**, emerged in the cities of Sicily and Asia Minor. The Sophists reflected the growing conviction in Greek society that there was no absolute truth to be discovered. The Sophists

argued that all truths were relative—in other words, truth depended on a particular time and place.

The Sophists claimed to have the answer to how people could get along in a world that had grown uncertain. Unlike earlier Greek philosophers, the Sophists believed it was useless to try to understand the nature of the universe. Instead, they taught that people should simply try to improve both themselves and their cities by applying reason to solve their everyday problems. Drawing on the old Greek idea of human excellence, the Sophists claimed that they could teach people political excellence, by showing them how to formulate laws and how to persuade people through the use of **rhetoric**, or making public speeches.

Protagoras. One of the most famous and important of the Sophists, Protagoras (proh-TAG-uh-ruhs) of Abdera, spent his life traveling around the Greek world teaching. He became extremely popular and wealthy from his

Theme: War and Diplomacy

After the King's Peace was declared by Persia, Thebes and Athens became allies for a short period and engaged in a sporadic war with Sparta. In 371 B.C. the three attempted to sign a treaty. Negotiations fell through when the leaders of Thebes tried to sign the treaty representing all cities in the region of Boeotia. They hoped to establish a sort of land empire, which would be headed by Thebes. Sparta then invaded Boeotia, only to be defeated by Thebes at Leuctra in 371 B.C.

With the victory at Leuctra, Thebes completely destroyed Sparta's hold over Greece and thus had the opportunity to unite all of the Greek city-states. Thebes was eventually confronted by a coalition of Sparta, Athens, Elis, Achaea, and Mantinea at the battle of Mantinea. Thebes's leading general, Epaminondas, was killed, and Thebes retreated into isolationism again.

Critical Thinking Ask students what might be concluded from the fact that Athens and Sparta, recently enemies, joined together against Athens's former ally, Thebes.

ANSWER: Students might conclude that the leaders of the city-states placed less value on old attachments and rivalries than they did on defeating any city-state that looked too powerful.

Possibly because Sparta had been isolationist before the Peloponnesian War, its leaders had trouble controlling a vast empire. The Thirty Tyrants, who took over Athens with the backing of the Spartan leader Lysander, were known for their brutality and their corruption. After their successful coup in 404 B.C., they decided to purge the city of "unreliable elements" by killing hundreds of people. Not only were these purges a way for the Spartan leaders to rid the city of political opposition, they also used them to kill many of Athens's richest inhabitants and appropriate the wealth of the executed men for themselves.

Critical Thinking Ask students why isolationism might have left Spartan leaders unprepared for the responsibilities of governing an empire.

ANSWER: Students may answer that Spartan leaders had no experience with other cultures and had difficulty controlling different people. In addition, after leading such austere lives in Sparta, they may have been particularly susceptible to Athenian luxuries.

▲ This image of a young Greek woman with a hand mirror decorates a vase made about 430 B.C.

lecturing. In his most famous work, titled *Truth*, Protagoras summed up the Sophists' view of the world:

> 66 Man is the measure of all things, of being in so far as it exists and of non-being in so far as it does not exist. . . . About the gods I can say nothing, neither that they exist nor that they do not; many things prevent one from knowing, such as the obscurity [hidden nature] of the problem and the shortness of human life. 99

With this kind of reasoning, the Sophists questioned many traditional Greek values.

As such ideas filtered through the Greek world they broke down people's faith in the polis even further. For some citizens politics became less important as a civic duty, for example, than as a field for personal ambition and the pursuit of individual power. **Demagogues**—people who use their skills of oratory, or speech-making, to sway crowds—became alarmed at the moral views of the Sophists. If people believed all traditions, laws, and social conventions were purely human in origin, rather than divine, demagogues feared that they would feel free to disregard the laws, and chaos would result. A conservative reaction against the Sophists soon occurred.

Reaction to the Sophists. The reaction was perhaps most severe in Athens in the aftermath of its defeat by Sparta during the Peloponnesian War. The Spartans not only had destroyed Athenian naval and military power but also had tampered with Athenian democratic institutions. They had encouraged the establishment of an **oligarchy**—the rule of a few powerful individuals—to take control of the city. Although the Athenians quickly overthrew the new tyranny and reestablished democracy, they remained suspicious of all who had known or helped the oligarchs. Many Athenians came to blame their defeat on the teachings of the Sophists, which had seemed to inspire the oligarchs. In 399 B.C. Athenians took their anger out on the philosopher Socrates (SAHK-ruh-teez). Although not a Sophist, Socrates had taught many of those who supported the oligarchy.

BIOGRAPHY Born in 470 B.C., Socrates was the son of a sculptor and a midwife. Although he had little education as a child, Socrates was driven by an inner voice. He believed that this voice was

Socrates
B I O G R A P H Y

calling him to discover what was truly good in life, and to teach the good to others. Eventually Socrates developed a reputation as a great teacher who was willing to discuss any matter with anyone. He taught by engaging his students in logical discussions. This involved asking questions that forced people to think very deeply about a particular problem.

As they came up with answers, Socrates posed further questions based on these answers. Today we call this the **Socratic method** of teaching.

Socrates' new method of logical discussion reflected his own belief that "the unexamined life is not worth living." Like the Sophists, Socrates was a champion of the intellect, but he rejected the Sophists' concept of truth being relative. Socrates argued that knowledge and truth were the only things that mattered. Although the truth might be difficult or impossible to find, he insisted that the true philosopher must never stop looking for it. Socrates submitted even the traditional values and beliefs of Athens to his method of investigation. As a result, many conservative Athenians also began to fear that, like the Sophists, he was challenging the stability and safety of their way of life.

In 399 B.C. Socrates was officially accused of corrupting the youth of Athens and of refusing to believe in the traditional gods of the city. Both crimes were punishable by death. During the trial that followed, Socrates refused to compromise his own beliefs. He denied the charges and refused to seek forgiveness from the court:

66 Men of Athens, I honor and love you; but I shall obey God rather than you, and while I have life and strength I shall never cease from the practice and teaching of philosophy. . . . Wherefore, O men of Athens . . . do as my accuser bids or not as he bids, and either acquit me or not; but . . . understand that I shall never alter my ways, not if I have to die many times. 99

Faced with his refusal to compromise, the court ordered Socrates to drink poison. Despite the pleas of his friends and admirers, Socrates refused to escape his punishment and live in exile. Demonstrating his complete obedience to the laws of the city, Socrates willingly drank the poison as prescribed by the law, and so died as he had lived, faithful to his sense of truth and duty.

Many people blamed the Sophists for Athens's defeat in the war with Sparta and felt that their views would lead to social and moral chaos.

Toward a New Greek Identity

Even in death, Socrates contributed, as had the Sophists, to the final downfall of the concept of the polis. Above all, Socrates represented a new type of person in the Greek world. Although Socrates had loved his city, it ceased to be the center of his sense of identity. In its place he had put his own conscience and his own conception of what was good and true. Soon, others in the Greek world also emphasized individualism, and many of the earlier values of Greek culture and society began to change.

Plato. Socrates' death came as a profound shock to many of his students. Among them was an Athenian named Plato. In fact, Plato is responsible for most of our knowledge of Socrates, as Socrates himself never left any writings. Plato, however, wrote extensively, and many of his writings have survived. His most famous works are in the form of dialogues, or conversations of questions and answers between Socrates and other people.

Theme: Social Relations

According to Plato, when Socrates was convicted, the offense he was charged with had no penalty. Greek law mandated that on such an occasion the prosecutor and the convicted person each had to propose a penalty. The prosecutor proposed death, while Socrates proposed that he be given free meals at the public's expense for the rest of his life, which was a common civic honor. Socrates felt that he had done nothing wrong. Maintaining his innocence, Socrates refused to curtail his teachings. His friends finally convinced him to change his proposal to a fine, but this still did not save him.

Critical Thinking Ask students if they feel Socrates made a wise choice in maintaining his innocence.

ANSWER: Students might answer that Socrates acted wisely, because he felt he had not committed any crime, or they may answer that he acted unwisely, since he increased his chance of being executed.

◄ Over the centuries, many artists have illustrated the events surrounding the death of Socrates. This painting was done by Jacques-Louis David in 1787.

The Metropolitan Museum of Art, Catharine Lorillard Wolfe Collection, Wolfe Fund, 1931 © 1995 by The Metropolitan Museum of Art.

While Socrates was from the mid-levels of Athenian society, Plato was an aristocrat. He had little use for democracy. In part, Plato was simply a product of his times. He grew up during the disastrous Peloponnesian War and his youth was capped by Socrates' death. Disillusioned, Plato later devoted himself to philosophy and established a school called the Academy.

Like Socrates, Plato rejected many of the Sophists' views. He came to believe not only in absolute truth and goodness but also that every visible thing was simply a particular example of a universal "Form," or idea. Because the senses could be fooled, Plato argued, a true philosopher pursued knowledge of the perfect Form that lay beyond the senses. Just as an ideal geometrical figure, like a square, could be expressed perfectly as a mathematical formula—even though in practical terms it was almost impossible to make a perfect physical square—Plato believed that every thing and concept could be expressed perfectly as a Form.

For Plato, the realm of perfect Forms had been conceived by the "divine worker," or God. This realm, he believed, existed apart from the particular physical examples of the Forms. Influenced by the Pythagoreans, and perhaps by similar ideas from India, Plato saw human beings as consisting of two parts—the soul and the body. The soul, he taught, was the creation of God. Plato believed that through reincarnation the soul would eventually be united with the Forms.

Applying his **theory of Forms**, as it is often called, to politics, Plato proposed an ideal alternative to Athenian democracy. Plato's conception of political perfection rejected individualism in favor of a more traditional emphasis on the polis as the center of a person's identity. In his book, the *Republic,* Plato outlined his ideal society, in which everyone would be placed according to his or her own natural skills. Most people would be workers, fulfilling the necessary functions of farming, craftsmanship, or other types of labor. Above the workers would be the Guardians, those with above average strength, both physically and mentally. Most of this Guardian class would be trained as warriors to protect the state. Those who showed the greatest intelligence and strongest sense of discipline would be trained as philosophers. These people would become the rulers of the state.

Plato's ideas on politics, as on many other topics, were never put into practice. Although he became interested for a time in the politics of Syracuse, in Sicily, where he worked as a tutor to the son of the tyrant Dionysius I, his efforts at political influence failed. Eventually Plato returned to Athens, where he taught until his death. Plato's best pupil, the philosopher Aristotle, developed his own political ideas. He, too, became a tutor to the son of a ruler, Philip II of Macedonia.

▲ This mosaic, titled *The School of Plato,* shows Plato surrounded by his students.

*P*lato believed that ideal Forms existed apart from observable reality.

Aristotle. While Plato had become increasingly interested in the theory of Forms, Aristotle tried to bring philosophy back down to earth. His own early training had been in medicine, since his father was court physician to the king of Macedonia. After going to Athens, Aristotle remained interested in natural science. At first he accepted Plato's conception of the ideal behind all things, but eventually he rejected the notion that the realm of Forms existed apart from the physical world. Instead, according to Aristotle, every living thing consisted of two parts—the matter that made up its physical existence and the ideal "blueprint," or structure, from which the matter was molded. In short, the actual matter and the ideal Form existed together, not separately—just as a pot only exists once the potter imposes its ideal structure on a lump of clay.

Aristotle saw the world as divided between inorganic, or strictly material, beings and organisms, which not only were matter but also had souls. Only human beings had intellect or the ability to reason. Since humans were the most highly developed creatures, Aristotle thought they should rule the other creatures and not be subject to them. Aristotle believed that the ultimate goal human beings sought was happiness. Happiness, he taught, could be reached only through virtue or wisdom. Virtue was achieved by keeping a balance in all areas of life—an idea known as the "golden mean."

Throughout his life, Aristotle investigated and wrote many works on all kinds of subjects. His interests spanned not only philosophy but also

▶ Aristotle was 13 when he went to Plato's Academy; he studied there for 20 years.

many other areas, such as politics, medicine, and the natural sciences. Above all, Aristotle was a great cataloger and organizer of knowledge. He tried to fit the things he investigated into what he considered their proper categories.

In politics, as in so many areas, Aristotle believed in the idea of "moderation in all things, and all things in moderation." Aristotle distrusted tyranny of any kind. He defined tyranny as rule designed to serve the interests only of the rulers rather than the whole of society. Aristotle concluded that the best form of government was probably one run by the mid-levels of society, who were neither rich enough nor poor enough to want to tyrannize others. Ironically, perhaps, Aristotle's own most famous pupil, Alexander of Macedonia, would eventually overthrow democracy in Greece and lead the Greek world once again into an age of absolute monarchy.

Aristotle believed that matter and an ideal structure were both necessary for the existence of all things.

SECTION 1 REVIEW

IDENTIFY and explain the significance of the following:
Isocrates
Pan-Hellenism
Sophists
rhetoric
Protagoras
demagogues
oligarchy
Socrates
Socratic method
Plato

theory of Forms
Aristotle

1. *Main Idea* How did the Peloponnesian War mark an important turning point in Greek politics?
2. *Main Idea* How would you describe Plato's and Aristotle's philosophies concerning the existence of all things?

3. *Philosophy* What did the Sophists believe, and why did people react against them?
4. *Writing to Explain* Write a paragraph explaining the events that led to the death of Socrates.
5. *Analyzing* What was Plato's ideal political organization? Do you think his plan would have worked? Why or why not?

SECTION 2

CORE LESSON PLAN
See pages 87E and
87F for Lesson Plan
4.2.

![icon] *Theme:* **War and Diplomacy**

Philip II's most characteristic strategy was an echeloned, or slant-wise, attack, which involved holding back the left and center parts of the formation of soldiers while the right side fought. The purpose of this maneuver was to stretch and thin the enemy's front line. As the enemy forces rushed to meet the attackers on one part of the line, they left other parts of the line exposed. The cavalry then charged into the gap from the right, followed by the infantry.

Critical Thinking Ask students to suggest reasons why this tactic would work best against a disorganized army.

ANSWER: Students might suggest that a disorganized army would fall into the trap and leave one side open to attack.

SECTION 2
The Rise of Macedonia and Alexander the Great

FOCUS

- Why was Macedonia easily able to conquer the Greek city-states?
- What factors made Alexander a great conqueror?
- How did Alexander the Great establish a multiethnic empire?

The growing disunity of the Greek city-states during the 300s B.C. opened the door to new invaders—the Macedonians. As with so many civilizations, however, the less civilized invaders soon absorbed the more sophisticated culture of their new subjects. As the Macedonians expanded their empire, they spread Greek civilization to much of North Africa and western Asia.

Greek orator
Demosthenes

The Rise of Macedonia

Macedonia was strategically located on the land route between the Balkans and Asia. The Greeks considered the Macedonians semibarbaric, however, since they did not live in cities but in villages. In order to survive constant raids, the Macedonians became excellent horsemen and perfected the use of cavalry. The Macedonians also learned from their Greek neighbors. Greek influence became particularly important after 359 B.C., when a new king, Philip II, came to the throne of Macedonia.

Philip II. As a youth, Philip II had spent several years as a hostage in the Greek city of Thebes. There he had studied Greek military techniques under the brilliant Greek strategist, Epaminondas (i-pam-uh-NAHN-duhs). Philip learned the discipline and uses of the Greek phalanx. After he became king, Philip drew on this knowledge to improve Macedonian methods of warfare. Philip also established a permanent professional army. By combining three elements—cavalry, the phalanx, and archers—Philip made the Macedonian army one of the strongest armies in the world.

Philip's obsession with these military reforms reflected his growing ambitions. His first conquests were in Thrace. Moving farther east, he threatened to dominate the flow of trade between the Athenian colonies of the Black Sea and the Aegean. Since Athens relied on these colonies for its grain supplies, Philip's expansion directly threatened Athens's interests. His ultimate target, however, was the Persian Empire.

In the 300s B.C. some Greeks began to feel that Macedonia was a natural ally against the Persians. Isocrates, for example, saw Philip as the potential leader of Pan-Hellenism: "I maintain that you should be the benefactor of Greece, and King of Macedon," he wrote to Philip:

> **66** and gain to the greatest possible extent the empire of the non-Greek world. If you accomplish this, you will win universal gratitude: from the Greeks . . . , from the Macedonians . . . , and from the rest of the world. **99**

Macedonia and the Greeks. With such encouragement Philip began to consider expanding into mainland Greece. Realizing Philip's intent, many Greeks who had rejected Isocrates' Pan-Hellenism called for a united front against the Macedonians. The great Athenian orator, Demosthenes (di-MAHS-thuh-neez), begged his fellow citizens:

❝Consider the facts, gentlemen, consider the outrageous lengths to which Philip has gone. He does not offer us a choice between action and inaction. He utters threats . . . in overbearing terms. He is not content to rest on his laurels but is continually adding to the haul he collects in the net in which he ensnares [traps] our hesitant, inactive country.❞

Eventually only Athens and Thebes stood against the Macedonian invaders. At the battle of Chaeronea (ker-uh-NEE-uh) in 338 B.C., Philip defeated the Greeks, thus ending the political independence of the Greek city-states.

With no further opposition, Philip forced all the Greek city-states, except Sparta, into a new League of Corinth, with himself in charge. The following year, Philip began to plan for a new war against Persia. Before he could carry out his plans, however, the ambitious king was murdered by an unhappy Macedonian noble.

Unable to unite, the city-states of Greece lost their independence to the rising power of Macedonia.

Alexander the Great

Philip II was succeeded by his son Alexander. Although only 20 years old, Alexander proved even more ambitious than his father. Philip had trained his son as a youth in the arts of war. He had also insisted that his son receive a Greek education. As news of Philip's death spread, however, Alexander faced many rebellions among the Greek city-states. Over the next year, he

Alexander the Great's Empire, 323 B.C.

The March of Empire Alexander's ambition drove his army from Macedonia to North Africa and the slopes of the Himalayas.

❓ **Movement** How many of the cities Alexander founded were named after him?

RESOURCE ACTIVITY

READINGS IN WORLD HISTORY
Reading 4.2
Alexander's Deification at the Temple of Zeus-Ammon

Have students read the selection by a Greek historian. Then have them complete the questions.

Level 2

RESOURCE ACTIVITY

(p. 99)
GEOGRAPHY ACTIVITIES
Geography Activity 4
Stopping Alexander the Great

Have students study the map and text, and complete the questions on Alexander's invasion of India.

Level 2

REVIEW & ASSESSMENT RESOURCES

- Study Guide 4.2
- Daily Quiz 4.2
- Main Idea Activity 4.2

All Levels

Teenagers IN HISTORY

Alexander and Bucephalus

Not a great deal is known about Alexander the Great's upbringing. Some stories about his youth and childhood have survived, however. One of the best-known stories involves Alexander's first horse, Bucephalus.

The story is that a close friend of Alexander's father, Philip II, had bought a fine stallion from Thessalian horse traders to present to Philip. When anyone approached and tried to mount the horse, however, he shied and reared. Most of the people watching thought that the horse was wild and untrained, and that no one would be able to ride him. Alexander observed Bucephalus bolting about and realized that the animal was shying away from his own shadow. Alexander took Bucephalus by the bridle and turned him

Bucephalus

so that he faced into the sun. With his shadow behind him, the stallion quieted and was gentle.

Although it is questionable whether the horse was truly so frightened of his shadow, the story does illustrate that the young Alexander was thoughtful. Bucephalus was given to Alexander and he rode the horse for many years until the animal died on one of Alexander's campaigns. In honor of his favorite horse, Alexander founded the ancient city of Alexandria Bucephala at the place where Bucephalus died.

campaigned from Thrace to Illyria to mainland Greece, restoring his control. After forcing the Greeks back into submission, Alexander felt free to carry on his father's dream, the conquest of Persia.

Alexander's conquest of Persia. In the spring of 334 B.C., Alexander crossed the Hellespont with an army of about 35,000 infantry and 5,000 cavalry. Alexander's force looked tiny but his men were well disciplined and fiercely loyal to Alexander. On the other hand, the Persian army of King Darius III was enormous but it was disorganized. When they engaged Alexander at the Granicus River, the Persians concentrated their generals in the left center of their line. Because of this reckless strategy and Alexander's control over his own men, Alexander was able to charge the Persians where they appeared to be strongest, killing two of Darius's brothers himself and routing Persian forces.

The following winter, Alexander visited Gordium in central Asia Minor. In Gordium an ancient prophecy had foretold that whoever untied the knot left by King Gordius in the harness of his royal chariot would become king of all Asia. According to tradition Alexander solved the puzzle by cutting the Gordian knot in two with his sword. With this good omen, he continued on to the key strategic pass of Issus. There, in 333 B.C., the Greeks once again defeated Darius's armies.

The victory at Issus opened the road to Egypt. After taking control of Syria and Phoenicia along the way, Alexander arrived on the Nile in 332 B.C. After founding a new city, which he called Alexandria, he turned northeast toward the heart of the Persian Empire. In 331 B.C. at Gaugamela in Assyria, Alexander's forces destroyed the Persian army. Darius fled the field, only to be murdered for his incompetence and cowardice in 330 B.C. by one of his nobles.

Alexander's vast empire. After this final victory, Alexander took control of the Persian Empire. When news came of Darius's death, Alexander took the title "king of kings." Still not satisfied, however, the world conqueror undertook more campaigns. Between 330 B.C. and 327 B.C. Alexander conquered Central Asia. From there he pushed his tired men on to the Indus River. There at last, after 22,000 miles of marching and fighting, his soldiers finally had had enough. As they rose in rebellion, Alexander reluctantly agreed to halt. After the long march home, in which much of his army died while crossing the desert in southern Iran, Alexander returned to Susa. In 10 years he had conquered the largest empire yet seen in world history.

Because of his brilliant military tactics and natural charisma, Alexander established the largest empire the world had yet seen.

Alexander's Legacy

Alexander of Macedonia, who became known as Alexander the Great, died of a fever in Babylon in June 323 B.C. He was not yet 33 years old. Although we know little about Alexander's policies as a ruler, there are some indications of how he thought the empire should be run. First, Alexander deliberately spread Greek culture wherever he went. Second, he established many new cities, many of which he named Alexandria. Third, he did his best to integrate the newly conquered peoples, especially the Persians, into his armies. Alexander realized that he needed the old Persian imperial administration to help rule his empire. Consequently, he encouraged his Greek and Macedonian followers to intermarry with his new Persian subjects. In 324 B.C., for example, Alexander married over 10,000 of his troops to Persian women. He himself married the daughter of Darius.

Alexander's conquests opened cultural interaction, as ideas and peoples flowed from the Mediterranean to Central Asia and even to the borders of India. The combination of Greek civilization with elements from the civilizations of the Persian Empire produced a new culture among the ruling elite. No longer purely Hellenic, or Greek, this new culture would later become known as **Hellenistic**, or "Greeklike."

In his pursuit of a world empire, Alexander stimulated a blending of Greek and Persian cultural ideas.

▶ **Alexander the Great had himself proclaimed a god in some of the cities he conquered or founded.**

SECTION 2 REVIEW

IDENTIFY and explain the significance of the following:
  Philip II
  Demosthenes
  Alexander
  Darius III
  Hellenistic

LOCATE and explain the importance of the following:
  Macedonia
  Chaeronea
  Granicus
  Gaugamela

1. **Main Idea** Why were the Greeks unable to withstand Philip's invasion?
2. **Main Idea** How was Alexander able to control his vast empire?
3. **War and Diplomacy** Why was Alexander considered a great leader?
4. **Writing to Persuade** Write a paragraph defending or refuting the following statement: *The conquest of Greece by Macedonia was the best thing that ever happened to Greek civilization.*
5. **Hypothesizing** What do you think might have happened to Alexander's empire if he had lived a long life? Why do you think so?

Daily Life

Leagues of cities were common in mainland Greece during the Hellenistic period. These leagues were an attempt to avoid domination by a royal power. For example, seven small cities grouped together to form the Achaean League. The goals of the league were "the expulsion of the Macedonians from the Peloponnese, the overthrow of tyrannies, and the guarantee for each city of their common, ancestral freedom."

Critical Thinking Ask students what these goals tell us about the attitudes of the Greeks toward the Macedonians during the Hellenistic period.

ANSWER: Students should suggest that some Greeks felt the Macedonians were oppressive and tyrannical rulers.

SECTION 3
Hellenistic Civilization

FOCUS

- What happened to Alexander's empire after his death?

- How did traditional Greek society change in the Hellenistic era?

- How did the growth of Hellenistic cities affect people's views of philosophy and religion?

- How did science and technology advance in the Hellenistic era?

Beginning in the 300s B.C., Greek civilization underwent a tremendous period of transformation. United through the conquests of Alexander the Great, Hellenistic civilization spread from the eastern Mediterranean to the borders of India. From the adaptation of Persian political theory to Greek civilization, a new Hellenistic society emerged, ruled by a Greek-speaking elite. This elite group lived in relative isolation from the masses who supported it.

Turkish disk showing the victory of Seleucus I at the battle of Ipsus, 301 B.C.

The Hellenistic Kingdoms

Alexander's death caused a crisis. The conqueror had established no plan for choosing a successor. Almost immediately his generals began to fight among themselves for possession of the empire, but none were powerful enough to defeat the others. By 275 B.C. three major kingdoms had emerged, each ruled by one of Alexander's generals or their descendants. Ptolemy (TAHL-uh-mee) took possession of Egypt. The vast Asia territories, which stretched from the eastern Mediterranean to the Indus River, became the prize of Seleucus (suh-LOO-kuhs). Macedonia, Thrace, and mainland Greece eventually came under the rule of Antigonus (an-TIG-uh-nuhs).

Of the three Hellenistic kingdoms, Egypt was by far the most secure and the wealthiest. Following Alexander's example, Ptolemy and his descendants adapted to Egyptian styles of rule. These Ptolemaic pharaohs, however, used their power to patronize the arts according to Greek tastes. Also, realizing their fragile position as a foreign dynasty, they relied almost exclusively on Greek and Macedonian immigrants as administrators for the kingdom.

Egypt's stability under the Ptolemies contrasted sharply with Hellenistic Asia under the Seleucids. The Seleucids (named after Seleucus) established a new, vibrant urban style of rule. Throughout Asia they built new Greek-style cities and populated them with immigrants from Greece and Macedonia. The new cities became islands of Greek culture and civilization. Even so, the empire proved too diverse and vast to remain intact. After Seleucus I died in 281 B.C., large areas, such as Bactria and Parthia, seceded.

The least successful of the great Hellenistic kingdoms was Macedonia. The Antigonids (named after Antigonus) were plagued by constant warfare. They also suffered from a loss of population as large numbers of emigrants moved into the new cities being established in Asia and North Africa. The Antigonids' efforts to control the cities of Greece proved a heavy drain on finances and soldiers. Two new organizations—the Aetolian League and the Achaean League—allowed the Greek cities to establish new constitutions under which they were able to challenge Macedonian authority.

Hellenistic Kingdoms, 185 B.C.

The Spread of Greek Culture   After his death, Alexander the Great's empire eventually disintegrated into many smaller kingdoms. However, Greek culture continued to influence these kingdoms.

? Region   Which important rivers did the two largest Hellenistic kingdoms control?

In general, rising prosperity contributed to the strong growth of the new Hellenistic civilization. Alexander's conquests had opened up trade and communications from Gibraltar in the western Mediterranean to the Indus River. These conquests had also provided the money necessary for a burst of economic development when Alexander opened the Persians' treasure house. While the Persians had hoarded gold and silver as a sign of royal wealth and power, the Greeks preferred to spend it. More people used currency for transactions, and trade expanded.

The Hellenistic rulers generally pursued careful policies to encourage economic growth. For example, they maintained and repaired roads to make travel and trade easier. Both manufacturing and trade increased dramatically. This increase, however, was also accompanied by a general rise in prices, which eventually weakened less productive areas like Macedonia and Greece. A new merchant and artisan class began to emerge in the Hellenistic cities, which further increased trade in goods such as pottery, glass, and perfume. Agriculture also flourished, particularly as the Hellenistic monarchs in Egypt and Asia took great care to improve and maintain irrigation systems.

After Alexander's death, his empire was divided among his generals into three parts, but many regions soon began to break away.

Hellenistic Society and Culture

Although Hellenistic society remained purely Greek in language and culture, it was no longer as exclusive as the society of the polis had been. The Hellenistic monarchs who ruled over the many diverse peoples allowed anyone of non-Greek descent to rise to the upper levels of society, as long as they adopted Greek culture. Isocrates had

After her flight to Egypt, Arsinoë II accused Ptolemy II's wife of plotting against him. Ptolemy in turn exiled his wife and married Arsinoë, who was his full-blooded sister. While this was an accepted custom in Egypt, it was considered an outrage in Macedonia and Greece. Most scholars agree that the marriage between the two was based upon the political advantages that each could provide the other.

To ensure her power, Arsinoë had all other possible heirs killed on charges of plotting against the king. Despite her ruthless dealings, Arsinoë was much revered by Greeks and Egyptians during her reign. She was eventually given goddess status by her husband.

Critical Thinking Ask students how Arsinoë's goddess status reflected a change from earlier Greek religious practice.

ANSWER: Students might note that proclaiming rulers to be gods and goddesses was not practiced by the Greeks until the Hellenistic period, when it became common.

an even broader idea of what it meant to be Greek: "The people we call Greeks are those who have the same culture as us, not the same blood." On the other hand, Hellenistic culture had little influence on the farmers and herders of the countryside, but remained primarily an elite culture.

Changes in society. The collapse of the ideal of the polis not only meant an end to democracy as practiced in Greece but also a transformation of society in general. At the top of Hellenistic society stood the monarchs and their courts. Next came the urban populations, largely Greek and Macedonian immigrants, led by oligarchies of the wealthiest merchants and landowners. Catering to the elites was a large class of artisans, lower-level administrators, local merchants, small landowners, teachers, and other professionals. At the bottom of society, supporting it through their labor in the fields, were the local peasants. Slavery was widespread and was an important part of trade.

Family life also began to change. In the Hellenistic cities, husbands and wives began to work more closely together than had been the case in the old Greek city-states. In general the position of women improved during the Hellenistic period. Some women could now pursue an education and engage in commerce and business. They also had more property rights. Legally, however, women often were disadvantaged. Although in practice women could run their own affairs, they usually had to have a male guardian to oversee their activities outside the home. Among the royal families, however, several powerful queens emerged who ruled in their own right. Their success did much to improve perceptions of women's capacities in general.

BIOGRAPHY One of the most powerful of the Hellenistic queens was Arsinoë (ahr-SIN-oh-ee) II of Egypt. Born around 316 B.C., Arsinoë led a dangerous and adventurous

▶ This clay figurine from around 200 B.C. represents the Hellenistic ideal of female beauty.

early life. At the age of only 15 or 16, she was married to Lysimachus, ruler of Thrace. When war broke out between Lysimachus and Seleucus of Asia, Arsinoë traveled to Asia Minor with her husband. The death of Lysimachus and the defeat of his army, however, left her in a very unsafe position. To escape, she dressed in a maid's clothes and fled in the middle of the night. Safe in Macedonia, Arsinoë then hoped to make her eldest son king. To accomplish this, she agreed to marry Ceraunus, who had been crowned king of Thrace and Macedonia after Lysimachus's death. As soon as they were married, Ceraunus ordered Arsinoë's two youngest children murdered as they lay in her arms. She and her eldest son fled to Egypt.

Soon after her arrival, around 277 B.C., Arsinoë married her brother Ptolemy II and began her rule as queen of Egypt. Ptolemy was content to spend much of his time leading a life of pleasure. Many scholars agree that until her death in 270 B.C. the real power in Egypt rested with Arsinoë. In what began as a disastrous war with Antiochus I of Asia, Egypt achieved a spectacular victory thanks to Arsinoë's leadership. She personally toured frontier defenses to ensure their quality. During her short reign, Egypt rose once again to a position of power and glory in the Mediterranean world.

As Hellenistic civilization moved away from the old idea of the polis, society became organized as a hierarchy, and the position of women improved.

The arts and literature. New attitudes toward women and relations between men and women were also reflected in Hellenistic art and literature. Hellenistic sculptors such as Praxiteles (prak-SIT-uhl-uhs), for example, emphasized the beauty of the female form. In Classical Greece, women had been portrayed primarily in their roles as mothers, while the male form had represented the ideal of human beauty. In the Hellenistic period

Arsinoë II

BIOGRAPHY

women were also portrayed as beings of physical beauty. Sculptors became interested less in portraying the ideal human form than in showing people as they truly were.

In literature, love between men and women became a major theme of Hellenistic writers. Apollonius of Rhodes, for example, in his *Argonautica*, centered his version of an old mythological story around the love between Medea, daughter of the king of Colchis, and Jason, who had come to Colchis to steal the magical Golden Fleece.

In theater, playwrights no longer concerned themselves with the kind of civic and political themes that had inspired the Greeks. Menander, for example, one of the most famous Athenian playwrights of the late 300s B.C., was noted for his comedies focusing on domestic and private matters. Aristophanes, chief librarian at Alexandria, pointed out the realism of the new style when he asked: "O Menander and Life, which of you imitated the other?"

Perhaps the most enduring element of Hellenistic art was architecture. The new cities that sprang up all over the Hellenistic world created a boom in urban architecture and building. Although the basic styles and types of building were drawn from Greek models, they also began to reflect the needs of a relatively small elite to impress the masses beneath them. Consequently, Hellenistic architecture tended to be larger and more spectacular than earlier

Greek architecture. Most scholars refer to it as a **colossal style**. The style is named after its best example, the famous Colossus—a gigantic statue that stood beside the harbor entrance on the island of Rhodes.

Hellenistic artists and writers focused on themes of love and ordinary life, while architects created larger and more spectacular structures.

Hellenistic Philosophy

In the new large-scale urban civilization of the Hellenistic kingdoms many people began to feel lost and alone. In their efforts to adapt to their changing society many turned to new religions and philosophies. Four great philosophical schools developed during this period: Cynicism, Skepticism, Epicureanism, and Stoicism.

Cynicism. Founded by Diogenes (dy-AHJ-uh-neez) in the 300s B.C., cynicism was based on the belief that human beings should live according to nature. Cynics scorned pleasure, wealth, and social responsibilities. They also rejected all social customs, particularly those dealing with morality. Happiness, the Cynics taught, was for each individual to fulfill his or her "natural needs." The wild behavior of some individual Cynics gave the group its name: in Greek, the term *cynic* meant people who behaved "like dogs."

Skepticism. Skepticism— the conviction that sure knowledge was impossible and that beliefs are merely opinions—had always been a popular idea in Greek philosophy. At the beginning of the Hellenistic period, this philosophical attitude was formally developed in Athens by Pyrrho (PIR-oh). Happiness, Pyrrho taught, was to resign oneself to the idea that one could never know how things really are, and to live "with

▲ This painting shows one artist's perspective of the giant statue of the Colossus at Rhodes, one of the Seven Wonders of the World.

In addition to sculpture, several other art forms were popular during the Hellenistic period. Although few works survive today, painting was very popular, as were mosaics, in which artists used carefully arranged stones to make designs. Because precious metals were more readily available after Alexander's conquests, there was a great abundance of gold jewelry, such as necklaces, bracelets, and earrings. Vases, candelabra, and other objects were made in bronze and silver. Blown glass developed during the Hellenistic period and was used for vases and goblets. Much of Greek art during this period affected later Roman artistic development.

Critical Thinking Ask students if they know of other places and periods in which Greek influence on art and architecture were felt.

ANSWER: Answers will vary, but students might suggest the many artists of the Renaissance who were inspired by the Classical Greeks, or famous American structures such as the White House and the Jefferson Memorial.

History THROUGH THE ARTS

The Foundations of Hellenistic Sculpture

Hermes and the Infant Dionysus, by Praxiteles

Few original works of Greek sculpture still exist today. Much of what is known about this artwork comes from literary descriptions and copies made in Roman times. These copies show that sculptors of the Classical Period—between the 400s and 300s B.C.—had mastered the rendering of the human form. Most Classical sculptors created huge statues of gods or athletes, emphasizing the strength, nobility, and dignity of their subjects. During the 300s B.C., however, great artists, such as Praxiteles and Lysippus, introduced new styles to Greek sculpture.

Praxiteles, whose work flourished from about 370 B.C. to 330 B.C., hoped to show gracefulness in his sculptures. Creating delicate, lifelike figures, Praxiteles celebrated the beauty of the human body, illustrated by his *Hermes and the Infant Dionysus*. These gods do not appear formal and severe, but very human. Hermes seems to smile as he teases the child with a bunch of grapes (part of the original statue).

Lysippus, who lived in the early 300s B.C., was reportedly Alexander the Great's favorite sculptor. He was very productive, creating more than 1,500 bronzes of gods, heroes, and athletes. Lysippus took a realistic approach to portraying his subjects, showing muscles in great detail. He also revolutionized the representation of the human form by changing the proportions of the body to make the head smaller and the limbs and trunk longer and more slender. In addition, Lysippus gave his statues a feeling of movement in space by extending the arms in various directions.

Thinking About Art

What new styles did Praxiteles and Lysippus introduce to Greek sculpture?

Apoxyomenos, by Lysippus

ever a smile and never a passion." In accepting this idea as a fact, the Skeptics hoped to achieve "peace of the mind."

Epicureanism. Epicurus, who taught in Athens, was likewise concerned with achieving human happiness. His approach was to eliminate the fears that made people unhappy—death and the gods' meddling in human affairs. In their lives, he taught, people should avoid pain and pursue pleasure—but not excessive pleasure, since that would become painful. The Epicureans also called for withdrawal from public life to achieve happiness.

Stoicism. Perhaps the most influential school of Hellenistic philosophy was founded in Athens around 310 B.C. by Zeno of Citium. Zeno's teachings became known as Stoicism, so named because he lectured and talked with his students in a *stoa*, or covered porch. Zeno taught that the universe was guided by an organizing principle, variously called divine reason, the divine fire, or God, which the Greeks called *Logos*, "the word" or "reason."

According to the Stoics, all human beings had a spark of divine reason within their souls. Since everyone had this spark, the Stoics believed, they must all be considered equal. Unlike the Skeptics and the Cynics, Stoics did not encourage people to withdraw from society but to engage in it, as one ancient student of Stoicism explained:

❝ *They [the Stoic philosophers] hold that the universe is governed by divine will; it is a city or state of which both men and gods are members, and each one of us is a part of this universe; from which it is a natural consequence that we should prefer the common advantage to our own. For just as the laws set the safety of all above the safety of individuals, so a good, wise and law-abiding man, conscious of his duty to the state, studies the advantage of all more than that of himself or of any single individual.* ❞

For the Stoics, human happiness could be achieved only by figuring out how best to fulfill the role assigned by the divine fire within. They taught the importance of self-discipline, control of the emotions, and a calm attitude toward death.

Hellenistic Religions

While the new philosophical ideas of the Hellenistic period appealed to people's intellects, developments in religion appealed to many people's need for a more emotional approach to life. Although worship of the Olympian gods did not disappear, other forms of worship became more popular. All focused on satisfying people's growing need for a sense of belonging.

Ruler-worship. The Hellenistic kings in Egypt and in Asia established the practice of ruler-worship. Ruler-worship provided a useful means to fill people with a new sense of civic duty. This became particularly true as the central role of the polis was replaced by that of the monarch. As one Athenian playwright put it: "To transfer to men the honor due to the gods is to dissolve the democracy." Confronted by an increasingly complex civilization, many people looked to authority figures for guidance.

The Mystery religions. As people sought spiritual and emotional comfort in a world that was increasingly difficult to control, many turned to the so-called **Mystery religions**—cults that introduced worshippers to secret teachings or mysteries. These teachings usually had to do with the secrets of life after death and immortality. By going through a ritual of purification, the believers supposedly entered into oneness with a particular god or goddess and with other members of the religion. The shared experience provided a feeling of unity, security, and personal worth, as well as a promise of immortality.

Judaism in the Hellenistic era. One of the most important areas in which Greek and Eastern conceptions of religion and philosophy came together was in Judaea. Here the Jews had returned to Jerusalem under Persian rule and rebuilt the Temple of Solomon. Like other elites in the Hellenistic world, the Jewish elite soon became fascinated by the Greek culture of the Hellenistic ruling classes and adopted aspects of the culture. Celebration of the Sabbath and other traditional Jewish religious ceremonies were prohibited. For a time even the Temple of Solomon was turned into a shrine to Zeus. As they began to accept Greek culture, Hellenized Jews also tried to transform the ancient Jewish religion.

▲ Antiochus IV is best remembered for his efforts to expand Greek culture and institutions.

R **RESOURCE ACTIVITY**

GLOBAL HISTORY RESOURCE CENTER
Reading: *The Jews' Long Struggle with Hellenization*

Print out and distribute the reading. Have students read about the Jewish resistance to Hellenization. Have students imagine they are recruiters for the Jewish forces fighting against King Antiochus Epiphanes. Then have each student create a recruiting poster giving reasons why people should join this cause.

Level 2

Thinking About Art

(p. 104)
Praxiteles tried to show gracefulness in his works. He created delicate, lifelike figures that celebrated the beauty of the human body. Lysippus used a realistic approach in portraying his subjects' human form, emphasizing muscles, reducing the size of the head, and elongating the limbs and trunk. He also gave his statues a feeling of movement.

RESOURCE ACTIVITY

READINGS IN WORLD HISTORY
Reading 4.3
The Medical Aphorisms of Hippocrates

Have students read Hippocrates' statements about medicine and health. Then have them complete the questions.

Level 1

RESOURCE ACTIVITY

SKILLS ACTIVITIES
Skills Activity 4
Creating a Table

Have students complete the activity on creating a table, using information about Greek scientists.

Level 1

REVIEW & ASSESSMENT RESOURCES

- Study Guide 4.3
- Daily Quiz 4.3
- Main Idea Activity 4.3

All Levels

Under King Antiochus IV, for example, they obtained the status of a Greek polis for Jerusalem and tried to rename it Antioch. According to an ancient book of Jewish writings:

> Lawless men arose in Israel and seduced many with their plea, 'Come, let us make a covenant with the gentiles around us, because ever since we have kept ourselves separated from them we have suffered many evils. . . .' Thereupon they built a gymnasium [Greek school] in Jerusalem according to the customs of the gentiles. . . . They joined themselves to the gentiles and became willing slaves to evil-doing.

Such actions soon brought a reaction from more conservative Jews. Eventually, the Jewish people rose in revolt and established a conservative Jewish kingdom under the Hasmonean (Maccabees) dynasty. As the Hasmonean kings expanded their rule, they forcefully converted surrounding peoples to Judaism. As Judaic traditions mingled with influences from other religious traditions of the region, however, new doctrines became a part of the increasingly diverse teachings of Judaism. These included new beliefs concerning a final Judgment Day and the coming of a Messiah to save the Jewish people from their enemies.

In the large cities of the Hellenistic world, people began to turn to new philosophies and religions for a sense of personal belonging.

Hellenistic Technology and Science

While many people sought the comfort of philosophy and religion, others turned to more concrete investigations of the world around them. Among the Classical Greeks, science had been primarily abstract—with no sense of the need for experimentation, for example, to prove how a natural process might work. As long as Greek philosophy remained solely concerned with abstract principles, science had little chance of developing.

During the Hellenistic period, however, a split occurred between science and philosophy. Hellenistic scientists were somewhat less concerned with discovering the ideal nature of the world, and more interested in discovering how the world worked and what laws governed it. Such a shift in attitude also led to the practical application of scientific knowledge. Hellenistic scientists also often became inventors.

Probably during a stay in Egypt, Archimedes (ahr-kuh-MEED-eez) of Syracuse invented his famous water screw, a device that raised water from one level to another for irrigation purposes. The most extensive use of new engineering techniques came in war. Archimedes, for example, became famous for his battering rams and other engines of war. Working with levers and fulcrums, he managed to raise a fully loaded ship out of the water by means of a crane. This accomplishment was preceded by his famous boast: "Give me a place to stand on and I can move the earth."

Hellenistic scientists and inventors developed a wide variety of remarkable devices, including a working model of a steam engine, which was used to power mechanical toys. They showed little interest, however, in using such devices to improve the quality of life by turning them into labor-saving machines. Archimedes himself, for example, preferred to be known for his reputation as a mathematician rather than an inventor. Although he wrote many books, none dealt with his mechanical inventions. According to the historian Plutarch:

▼ The water screw that Archimedes invented is still used today for irrigation in Egypt.

> *[Archimedes rejected] as sordid and ignoble [dishonorable] the whole trade of engineering, and every sort of art that lends itself to mere use and profit, [and] placed his whole affection and ambition in those purer speculations where there can be no reference to the vulgar needs of life.*

Sometime around 300 B.C., another mathematician, Euclid (YOO-kluhd), formalized the fundamental truths of geometry. The ideas of his *Elements* textbook are the basis of geometry today. Using principles of geometry, Hellenistic scientists made significant advances in astronomy as they came into contact with the knowledge of the Egyptians and the Babylonians. Aristarchus (ar-uh-STAHR-kuhs) of Samos, for example, developed the first **heliocentric**, or sun-centered, description of the universe arguing that the earth revolved around the sun. In geography, too, Eratosthenes (er-uh-TAHS-thuh-neez) of Cyrene applied his mathematical knowledge to figure the circumference of the globe with remarkable accuracy.

Perhaps the most practical applications of Hellenistic science came in medicine. When Greek and Egyptian traditions came together in the city of Alexandria, for example, Hellenistic doctors learned from the Egyptian art of embalming to examine and catalog the parts of the human body. Some scientists dissected the corpses of executed criminals, provided to them by the kings, in their effort to understand how the body works. The practice, which many people found offensive, was soon halted, but significant discoveries were made in the process. Herophilus (huh-RAHF-uh-luhs), for example, concluded that the brain was the center of the human nervous system.

Hellenistic scientists applied scientific knowledge and mathematics to practical new inventions and discoveries in geography, astronomy, medicine, and engineering.

SECTION 3 REVIEW

IDENTIFY and explain the significance of the following:

Arsinoë II
Praxiteles
Apollonius
Menander
colossal style
Diogenes
Pyrrho
Epicurus
Zeno
Mystery religions
Archimedes
Euclid
Aristarchus
heliocentric
Eratosthenes
Herophilus

1. **Main Idea** How did Alexander's empire change after his death?
2. **Main Idea** Why did people during the Hellenistic period turn to new philosophies and religions?
3. **Science** How did science during the Hellenistic period differ from earlier Greek science?
4. **Writing to Explain** In a short essay explain how Hellenistic society and culture differed from earlier Greek society and culture.
5. **Comparing and Contrasting** What did the philosophies of Cynicism, Skepticism, Epicureanism, and Stoicism have in common? How were they different? How might the large size of Hellenistic cities have encouraged people to embrace these new philosophies?

SECTION 4
The Rise of Rome

FOCUS

- Why was Rome's location advantageous?
- How was Rome able to conquer Italy?
- What were the eventual consequences of Rome's initial expansion in Italy?

While Alexander laid the foundations for Hellenistic civilization in the east, the interaction of different cultures also gave rise to a new civilization to the west. Phoenician cities had flourished in northern Africa and Spain for many centuries, while Greek cities dotted southern Italy and eastern Sicily. In northern Italy the mysterious Etruscans had established their own highly structured and sophisticated kingdoms. As all of these groups came into contact with one another, a new civilization began to emerge. The center of this civilization was a group of Latin villages along the Tiber River near the western coast of Italy, from which grew the great imperial capital—Rome.

Carved relief of
Romulus and Remus

Italy's Geography

At even a first glance, the Italian Peninsula seems a logical place for the emergence of an empire that would dominate the Mediterranean region. (See map on p. 110.) The boot-shaped peninsula juts south from Europe into the Mediterranean Sea nearly halfway to Africa. It also lies almost halfway between the eastern and western boundaries of the Mediterranean world. From north to south, Italy stretches some 750 miles, with an average width of about 120 miles.

To the north, the peninsula was protected, though not isolated, by the high mountain range of the Alps. To the south, east, and west, the sea provided both protection and a means of rapid transportation. Much of the peninsula contained relatively rich soil and had a pleasant climate, able to feed a large population. Compared to Greece, for example, the western part of Italy provided much better soil and trees, and a better balance between agriculture and fishing. On the other hand, Italy's rivers were short and swift, providing little means of internal navigation.

In the middle of the peninsula, the city of Rome grew up from several small villages grouped together around a central market, or **Forum**. According to legend, Romulus and Remus, twin brothers who were raised by a she-wolf, founded the city of Rome in 753 B.C. The city prospered at least partly from its strategic location on the banks of the Tiber River just 16 miles from the western coast. In addition, Rome was a bridge-city, controlling access across the river. Thus, Rome not only lay across valuable trade routes between northern and southern Italy but also had convenient access to the sea. Early Romans appreciated the location of the city, as the Roman statesman Cicero (SIS-uh-roh) explained:

❝ *It seems to me that Romulus must at the very beginning have [had] a divine intimation [idea] that the city would one day be the site and hearthstone of a mighty empire; for scarcely could a city placed upon any other site in Italy have more easily maintained our present widespread dominion.* ❞

Rome's strategically important location in central Italy commanded trade routes and provided easy access to the sea.

The Conquest of Italy

Whether or not Romulus and Remus actually existed, the people who established Rome were members of an Indo-European-speaking group, known as Latins, who had migrated to the Italian Peninsula from the northeast sometime before the mid-700s B.C. In Italy the Latins came under the influence of the Greek city-states, as well as the Etruscan civilization in northern Italy.

The early Italians. At first Rome was ruled by Latin kings, much like many Greek cities which had begun as small kingdoms. Sometime around 600 B.C., however, Rome came under the rule of Etruscan kings. From evidence mainly gathered at Etruscan cemeteries, scholars believe that the Etruscans were great metalworkers and jewelers and that they enjoyed dancing and banquets. In contrast to the societies of Greece, women in Etruscan society enjoyed considerably greater freedom.

As part of a regionwide revolt against Etruscan rule, around 509 B.C. the Roman aristocracy threw out Tarquinius Superbus, the last of the Etruscan monarchs. The Roman aristocrats established a **republic**—in which elected officials governed the state. In the early days of the Republic, the heads of a limited number of aristocratic families, known as **patricians**, elected officials from among themselves. Eventually the nonaristocrats, known as **plebeians**, also took part in republican government. Like the Greek cities, Rome suffered from internal conflict between aristocrats and commoners, but in times of danger they could unite to confront their common foes.

Like the early Greeks, the Romans were a tribal people who had learned how to organize themselves for city life. After the establishment of the Roman Republic, they prided themselves on their connection with the soil. In one story of the early Republic, for example, the people

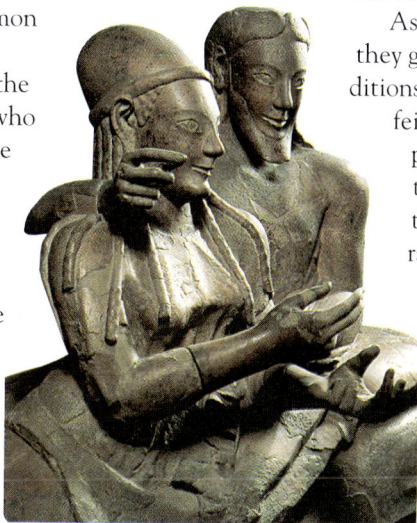

▶ This Etruscan married couple had their portrait carved about 500 B.C.

turned to their greatest general, Cincinnatus, who was plowing his fields at the time, to save them from attacking enemies. Cincinnatus defeated the enemies—and then promptly returned to his plow.

As the Roman population continued to grow, so too did the need for more land. Soon Rome began to settle its own surplus population on the land it had acquired by conquering its neighbors.

The Roman army. The heart of Rome's successful expansion lay in its military organization. The Romans believed that only those citizens who had some property to protect would fight bravely. Therefore, all Roman citizens between the ages of 17 and 46 with a minimum amount of property were required to serve in the military.

At first the Romans used the Greek phalanx formation. Sometime in the 300s B.C., the Romans replaced it with smaller, more elastic formations called **maniples**, which were well suited to fighting in rough terrain. Maniples were combined into larger groups called cohorts. Eventually, 10 cohorts of about 600 men each made up a **legion**. The backbone of the legions were centurions, noncommissioned officers who each commanded a century of about 100 men. Above all, the Roman army was a highly disciplined and well-trained infantry force.

Further expansion. Roman expansion suffered a setback in 390 B.C., when a band of Gaulic warriors swept down from the north, sacking and burning the city. Recovery was rapid, however, and Roman expansion increased after the raid. By about 265 B.C. the Romans had defeated the Etruscans and the Greek cities in southern Italy.

As the Romans conquered Italy they generally imposed two strict conditions on their subject peoples: to forfeit any independent foreign policy and to provide troops to the Roman army. Apart from these two conditions, Rome rarely interfered with the domestic affairs, customs, or religions of its subject peoples.

Using both their central location and a highly disciplined military, the Romans brought all of Italy under their rule.

Theme: War and Diplomacy

Rome began building its fleet of warships to compete with the Carthaginian navy in 260 B.C. Roman shipbuilders modeled their ships on ones that had been captured from the Carthaginians. The vessels carried a crew of 300 sailors, which was divided into groups of five to an oar. During the majority of the 23-year war, the Romans maintained a fleet of more than 200 warships.

Critical Thinking Ask students to suggest reasons why Rome had to build a navy, since its army was probably superior to that of Carthage.

ANSWER: Students might suggest that the war was being fought for supremacy in the Mediterranean Sea, so Rome had to challenge the Carthaginian navy. They might also suggest that the city of Carthage was separated from Roman territory by water, so Rome would need a navy to attack Carthage.

The Growth of the Roman Republic, 509 B.C.–133 B.C.

Legend:
- Roman territory, 509 B.C.
- Territory added, 508 B.C.–265 B.C.
- Territory added, 264 B.C.–133 B.C.
- Hannibal's route, 218 B.C.–203 B.C.
- Battle site
- City

A Mediterranean Power The destruction of Carthage made Rome the greatest power in the Mediterranean.

? Region What territories did Rome acquire after 265 B.C.?

Rome and Carthage

Once in control of southern Italy, Rome soon intervened in Sicily, to the south of the peninsula. In agreeing to help the Greek city of Messina against its enemy Syracuse, Rome came into conflict with Carthage—a city on the North African coast that had been established by the Phoenicians in the 700s B.C.

Carthage. At first Carthage was only a small anchorage for ships from Tyre trading in the central and western Mediterranean. When Tyre was conquered by Nebuchadnezzar II in the 500s B.C., however, Carthage became independent. The city soon became a major trading center. By the 200s B.C. Carthaginian outposts and colonies dotted the coasts of North Africa and southern Spain. In addition, the Carthaginians had taken control of Sardinia, western Sicily, and the island of Corsica.

The heart of the Carthaginians' strength was their powerful navy. As a great trading empire, Carthage had little interest in dominating large areas of land. However, as Rome extended its control southward, over the coastal regions of Italy fronting on the Strait of Messina that separated the mainland from Sicily, Carthage feared that its commerce would be threatened. Soon the two great powers of the western Mediterranean—the land power, Rome, and the sea power, Carthage—found themselves engaged in a struggle for supremacy.

The First Punic War. The first war between Rome and Carthage began in 264 B.C. Although Carthage had a magnificent navy, the city was at a disadvantage because the mercenaries who the city depended on for land defenses were less loyal than the citizen-soldiers of Greece and Rome. Fortunately for Carthage, the First Punic (the Latin word for "Phoenician") War depended less on land power than on sea power. Only when the Romans decided to build a navy of their own were they finally able to challenge Carthage.

Since they had to learn a new form of fighting, the Romans initially had difficulty waging war at sea against the Carthaginians. They lost hundreds of ships—along with their crews and soldiers—mostly in storms or because of inexperienced admirals. In an effort to transform sea battles into land battles, the Romans at first developed bridges that could be used to board enemy ships. These bridges made ships too unstable at sea, however, and had to be abandoned. In the meantime, the Romans mastered more conventional methods of naval warfare and finally defeated the Carthaginians.

The results of the first war were important for Rome. In the peace treaty the Romans demanded a huge monetary settlement. The Carthaginians were also forced to abandon Sicily, where the Romans created their first overseas imperial province. Instead of treating Sicily as they had the Italian cities, the Romans appointed a governor and established a military occupation to collect a regular tribute.

▲ **This Carthaginian ship is carved in stone.**

The victory gave the Romans a taste of the potential benefits of imperial expansion. A few years later, in the 230s B.C., the Romans took advantage of a revolt among Carthage's mercenaries in North Africa and seized the islands of Sardinia and Corsica.

Hannibal's invasion. As relations between Rome and Carthage became worse, the great Carthaginian general Hannibal hoped to use Spain's manpower to create a land force to challenge Rome. After the outbreak of the Second Punic War, in 218 B.C. Hannibal led a well-trained army and a force of war elephants across the Pyrenees and the Alps to invade Italy. For many years Hannibal dominated the Italian countryside, defeating one Roman army after another. At the Battle of Cannae (KAN-ee) in 216 B.C., Hannibal's troops killed or wounded as many as 50,000 Romans, the worst defeat

THROUGH OTHERS' EYES

A Warning Against Roman Expansion

In 73 B.C. Roman armies attacked King Mithradates VI of Pontus. Defeated, Mithradates fled Pontus and took refuge with his son-in-law King Tigranes of Armenia. According to the contemporary Roman historian Sallust, Mithradates wrote the following letter to King Arsaces of Parthia in 69 B.C. proposing an alliance against Rome:

❝King Mithradates to King Arsaces, greeting. . . . The Romans have never had but a single reason for making war on all nations, all peoples, and all kings, their insatiable [uncontrollable] desire for power and wealth. . . . I know well that you have great resources of men, arms, and gold; it is for that reason that we seek an alliance, while the Romans seek your spoils. . . . What can you expect from them except deception in the present and war in the future? The Romans have weapons against all men, the sharpest ones for those whose defeat will bring the greatest spoils; by audacity [boldness] and treachery and pursuing war after war they have grown great. In this manner they will annihilate [destroy] all or perish.❞

ever suffered by Rome. Still, the Romans refused to surrender or to ask for peace. The historian Polybius wrote that after Cannae the Romans:

❝established the rule for their own men that they must either conquer or die on the field. . . . [Thus] Hannibal experienced less joy from his victory than disappointment, when he saw with amazement the unshaken resolve and the lofty spirit which the Romans showed.❞

By 215 B.C. Rome seemed on the verge of destruction. The Romans had lost some 100,000 soldiers, either killed or captured. Rome's southern Italian allies had defected to Hannibal,

REVIEW & ASSESSMENT RESOURCES

- Study Guide 4.4
- Daily Quiz 4.4
- Main Idea Activity 4.4

All Levels

SECTION 4 REVIEW ANSWERS
(p. 112)

IDENTIFY
For significance, see the following pages:
Forum (p. 108)
republic (p. 109)
patricians (p. 109)
plebeians (p. 109)
maniples (p. 109)
legion (p. 109)
Hannibal (p. 111)
Fabius Maximus (p. 112)
Publius Cornelius Scipio (p. 112)

LOCATE
For locations, see the map on p. 110.

1. Rome had a larger population, it was centrally located, and it had a better-trained army.
2. Rome entered the Punic Wars with Carthage and eventually defeated Carthage. Then Rome conquered Macedonia and the Hellenistic kingdoms.
3. Rome was located in central Italy on the Tiber River, close to trade routes, with convenient access to the sea.

and Sicily was no longer on Rome's side. To make matters worse, the powerful king of Macedonia, Philip V, had made a military alliance with Hannibal. Despite their desperate situation, however, the Roman population stood firmly behind its leaders.

In Italy, command was given to Fabius Maximus, whose tactics were to strike the Carthaginian forces with hit-and-run attacks while avoiding a major battle. In the end, by transporting a strong Roman army across the Mediterranean to attack Hannibal's supply routes and bases in Spain, the Roman general Publius Cornelius Scipio (SIP-ee-oh) was able to wear down his opponent. Eventually, Scipio besieged Carthage itself and forced Hannibal to withdraw his forces from Italy in order to defend the city. In 202 B.C. Scipio routed Hannibal's forces on the plain of Zama outside Carthage and took the city, thus ending the Second Punic War.

The Conquest of the Mediterranean World

The Romans imposed a harsh peace. Carthage lost the bulk of its navy, its Spanish possessions, and its independence in foreign policy. The victory made Rome the leading power in the west-ern Mediterranean. The dramatic losses of the Second Punic War, however, remained in the memories of Romans. Outraged by the decision not to destroy Carthage utterly, for example, one Roman statesman ended every speech with the phrase "Carthage must be destroyed."

In 149 B.C. Rome decided to destroy its old enemy once and for all and declared war for the third time. After a siege of three years Carthage fell. The Romans enslaved the entire population and completely destroyed the city. Finally, they sowed the ground with salt, dedicating the city to the gods of the underworld.

Meanwhile, the Punic Wars had also involved Rome in the politics of the eastern Mediterranean and the Hellenistic kingdoms. During the Second Punic War, Macedonia had allied itself with Carthage. Once the war with Carthage was over, Romans were eager to punish this new enemy and declared war on Macedonia. In 197 B.C. they defeated Philip V. As the Romans became involved in the politics of Greece and Syria, Rome eventually became master of the entire region. By 133 B.C. the powerful Republic of Rome stretched from one end of the Mediterranean to the other, and beyond.

Roman expansion in Italy led first to the conquest of Carthage, then Macedonia, and eventually the Hellenistic kingdoms to the east.

SECTION 4 REVIEW

IDENTIFY and explain the significance of the following:
  Forum
  republic
  patricians
  plebeians
  maniples
  legion
  Hannibal
  Fabius Maximus
  Publius Cornelius Scipio

LOCATE and explain the importance of the following:
  Italian Peninsula
  Alps
  Rome
  Tiber River
  Carthage
  Messina
  Sardinia
  Sicily
  Cannae

1. **Main Idea** What factors allowed the Romans to conquer all of Italy?

2. **Main Idea** What were the consequences of Rome's expansion in Italy?

3. **Geography: Location** How did Rome's unique location in the Italian peninsula help it to become the center of a new civilization?

4. **Writing to Explain** Write a short essay explaining how Rome was able to triumph over Carthage.

5. **Analyzing** Why might Romans have prided themselves on being at heart a rural people? How might this belief have strengthened the empire?

Review

On a separate sheet of paper, complete the following exercises:

WRITING A SUMMARY

Using the essential points in the text, write a brief summary of the chapter.

REVIEWING TERMS

From the following list, choose the term that correctly matches the definition.

Pan-Hellenism   rhetoric
colossal style   plebeians
Socratic method   Forum

1. way of teaching, using a series of questions to lead learners to discover answers on their own
2. art of public speaking
3. central marketplace of Rome; originally it was the area between several Latin villages
4. idea of Greek unity and cooperation against Persia put forward by Isocrates
5. members of the lower class of Roman citizens

REVIEWING CHRONOLOGY

List the following events in their correct chronological order.

1. The First Punic War breaks out.
2. Philip II becomes king of Macedonia.
3. Alexander establishes the largest empire the world had ever seen.
4. The Romans drive the Etruscans out of Rome.
5. The Greek mainland falls to Macedonia.

UNDERSTANDING THE MAIN IDEA

1. How was Philip II of Macedonia able to conquer the Greek city-states?
2. Why did people's religious and philosophical views change during the Hellenistic period?
3. What were the causes and consequences of the Punic Wars?
4. How did Hellenistic art and literature differ from earlier Greek art and literature?
5. How were the Romans able to conquer Italy?
6. What new advances were made in science and technology during the Hellenistic period?

THINKING CRITICALLY

1. **Synthesizing** What role did strong leadership play in the successes of Roman and Macedonian expansion? What characteristics did the powerful leaders of these two civilizations have in common?
2. **Analyzing** In what ways did Greek identity change during the Hellenistic period? How were the new philosophies, religions, and scientific and technological advances of the time a reflection of this changing identity?

Building Your Portfolio

Complete the following activities individually or in groups.

1. **Journal** Imagine that you (and your coworkers) are the official historian(s) of either Macedonia or Carthage. You have been ordered to accompany either Alexander or Hannibal on his military campaigns. Choose one of the great leaders and write a journal with entries describing your experiences. Where have you traveled? What are the people like? How would you describe your leader? With your description also include a map showing the progress of your campaign. You may also include illustrations of your leader and the things you have seen on your travels.

2. **Drama** Create a play depicting the life of one of the famous people you have read about in the chapter, such as Socrates, Philip II, Alexander the Great, Arsinoë II, Hannibal, or Scipio. You may need to do research to include other characters who were important to the main character's life. Your play could cover the entire span of the main character's life, or could focus on an important event or time period. You may also wish to design scenery and some simple costumes and props to make the performance more realistic.

3. Both Rome and Carthage were trying to expand. Their initial conflict was over intervention in Messina. Consequences: first war—Rome built navy; second war—leaders attacked Hannibal's supply routes and bases in Spain, and eventually Carthage itself; third war—Rome destroyed Carthage completely, enslaved population, and sowed the ground with salt
4. New attitudes toward women and changed relations between men and women caused changes in art and literature. In art, women were portrayed as being physically beautiful. Love between men and women became a major theme in literature. Realism was also popular.
5. Rome's central location and its disciplined army allowed it to conquer Italy.
6. New scientific and technological advances were made during the Hellenistic period in geography, astronomy, medicine, and engineering.

THINKING CRITICALLY
1. Strong military leadership played a major role in the successes of Rome and Macedonia. Leaders of both were able to defeat their opponents because of excellent military strategies.
2. The concept of the polis had died out, and society was changing and growing. New philosophies, religions, and technological innovations were a result of a society that was coping with the problems and changes that a large and diverse society will bring.

Chapter 5

The Roman World 509 B.C.–A.D. 476

Chapter Planning Guide

	TEXTBOOK	CORE RESOURCES	VISUAL RESOURCES	MULTIMEDIA
Introduction	pp. 114–115	Block Scheduling Handbook: Ch. 5		Videodisc Segment 5 and Viewing Guide: *What Made Rome Great?*
Lesson 5.1 Roman Society and the Crises of the Republic	pp. 116–122 Through Others' Eyes: *The Fiery Queen, Boudicca,* p. 120	Reading 5.1: *Caesar's Funeral* Skills Activity 5: *Understanding Sequence* Writing Project 5: *Writing a Speech*		GHRC 5 Readings: *Spartacus and the Slave Revolt; The Roman Legion* GHRC 5/Videodiscs: Image—*Roman House and Family*
Lesson 5.2 The Pax Romana	pp. 123–129 History Through the Arts: *Roman Portrait Sculpture,* p. 124 Map: *The Height of the Roman Empire,* p. 127	Reading 5.2: *Roman Law* Geography Activity 5: *Rome During the Reign of Augustus*	Art and History 5: *Head of a Roman*	GHRC 5 Readings: *A Barbarian Denounces the Pax Romana; A Greek Praises the Pax Romana; Life in the City of Rome; Rome at Its Height* GHRC 5/Videodiscs: Images—*Roman Religion; The Pantheon; Rome in Its Glory Days;* Map—*Roman Roads in A.D. 14*
Lesson 5.3 Imperial Crises and the Rise of Christianity	pp. 130–135 Map: *The Spread of Christianity,* p. 133 Sacred Traditions: *Paul's Letter to the Romans,* p. 134	Reading 5.3: *Christians in the Roman Empire*	Everyday Life 5: *The Catacombs of Saint Calixtus* Geography and History 5: *The Spread of Christianity*	GHRC 5 Readings: *Persecution of Christians in Gaul; The Teachings of Jesus; The Appeal of Christianity to Rome* GHRC 5/Videodiscs: Images—*Cavalry Battle Between Romans and Barbarians; Catacomb Used by Early Christians*
Lesson 5.4 The Later Roman Empire	pp. 136–142 Map: *Invasions into the Roman Empire,* p. 140 Then and Now: *The Many Legacies of Rome,* p. 141	Reading 5.4: *A Description of the Barbarians*		GHRC 5 Reading: *An Eyewitness to the End of Roman Rule* GHRC 5/Videodiscs: Image—*Vandals March on Rome;* Map—*Division of the Roman Empire*
Chapter Investigation and Enrichment	pp. 114–142	Chapter 5 Investigation: *Documentary Newscast on the Fall of Rome* People in World History 5 Explorations in Daily Life 5		GHRC 5/Videodiscs
Review and Assessment	Section 1 Review, p. 122 Section 2 Review, p. 129 Section 3 Review, p. 135 Section 4 Review, p. 142 Chapter 5 Review, p. 143	Chapter Review Activity 5 Vocabulary Activity 5 Themes Review 5 Section Study Guides 5.1–5.4 Main Idea Activities 5.1–5.4 Daily Quizzes 5.1–5.4 Chapter 5 Test Sheltered English Ch. 5 Test Ch. 5 Test Generator		Audio CDs: Ch. 5 Summary (English and Spanish)

INTRODUCING THE CHAPTER

Textbook pp. 114–115

CHAPTER OVERVIEW

Protests against aristocratic rule led to the creation of a constitution and the founding of the Roman Republic. As Rome grew in size, republicanism gave way to monarchy, and the reign of emperors such as Augustus marked the empire's height. Threats from the Germanic tribes and economic and social woes, however, weakened Rome. Christianity became the state religion and lengthened the empire's life, but could not prevent its ultimate collapse.

PRESENTING THEMES

On the chalkboard or on an overhead transparency, write the following open-ended theme questions.

- **POLITICS AND LAW** How might establishing universal laws help to unify a society?
- **RELIGION** Why might people follow new religious leaders?
- **WAR AND DIPLOMACY** How can the maintenance of a large army strain a society?

Have students, either individually or in groups, suggest responses to the questions. For the politics and law question, students might suggest that a universal system of laws creates common standards and expectations between people. For the religion question, students might suggest that new religious leaders can offer more meaningful explanations for changes in society and one's place in the world. For the war and diplomacy question, students might suggest that maintaining a large army is expensive. The cost could cause hardships among the people. Save the responses. Once students have studied the chapter, you may wish to have them complete the Themes Review, then compare the two sets of answers.

USING THE VIDEO

Segment 5: *What Made Rome Great?*

ENGLISH

Search Chapter 5
Videodisc 1, Side B

SPANISH

Search Chapter 5
Videodisc 1, Side B

Tell students that in this chapter they will apply these theme questions to the most powerful ancient empire—Rome. Then show Segment 5 of the *World History and Cultures Videodiscs*. This segment looks at the different kinds of "cement"—such as written law—that helped Rome expand from a small city to a vast empire stretching from northern Europe into Africa and Southwest Asia.

Before showing the segment, ask students to listen carefully to the description of the rights of a Roman citizen. To help students grasp the significant points of the segment, have them complete Video Viewing Guide 5.

Key to Ability Levels

All strategies and activities are coded to the following ability levels:

LEVEL 1	**Basic** activities suitable for all students
LEVEL 2	**Average** activities suitable for average to above-average students
LEVEL 3	**Challenging** activities suitable for above-average students
SHELTERED ENGLISH	Activities suitable for students with **Limited English Proficiency**

Additional Resources

BOOKS FOR TEACHERS

Casson, Lionel. *Travel in the Ancient World.* Johns Hopkins, 1994. Includes accounts of travel in Rome.

Dudley, Donald R. *The Civilization of Rome.* Meridian, 1993. Presents a general introduction to Roman history.

Giardina, Andrea, ed. *The Romans.* University of Chicago, 1993. Offers a series of portraits of typical Roman lives.

BOOKS FOR STUDENTS

Adkins, Lesley and Roy A. Adkins. *Handbook to Life in Ancient Rome.* Facts on File, 1994. Contains material on many facets of life.

Corbishley, Michael. *The Roman World.* Watts, 1986. Features brief chapters on food, art, religion, and other topics.

Windrow, Michael. *The Roman Legionary.* Watts, 1985. Presents an illustrated look at the Roman military and its soldiers.

MULTIMEDIA MATERIALS

Our Heritage from Ancient Rome. Guidance Associates. Video with guide, 32 min. Offers an overview of the empire.

The Rise and Decline of the Roman Empire. Coronet. Video, 19 min. Looks at law, architecture, and literature.

Rome and Pompeii: Great Cities of the Ancient World. Questar. Video, 75 min. Uses computer images to show ancient sites.

Roman Society and the Crises of the Republic

Textbook pp. 116–122

RESOURCES

Pupil's Edition
Through Others' Eyes, p. 120: *The Fiery Queen, Boudicca*

Videodiscs or Global History Resource Center
Image: *Roman House and Family*

Search Frame 731

Core Resources
Reading 5.1: *Caesar's Funeral*

Global History Resource Center
Reading: *Spartacus and the Slave Revolt*
Reading: *The Roman Legion*

LESSON FOCUS

How did the Roman Republic evolve, and why did it unravel?

OBJECTIVES

After completing this lesson, students will be able to:

- describe how Roman government was organized;
- sketch a broad picture of the foundations of Roman society;
- analyze the consequences of Roman conquests;
- identify factors that led to the breakup of the Republic.

HOOK: Link to Today

Describe the structure of Roman government and compare it to that of the Unites States. Refer students to the quotation by a Roman statesman on page 117 of the textbook. Ask them if they think this statement would also apply to the Constitution of the United States. Then create a chart comparing the government structure of Rome to that of the United States. Ask students to name the institutions and positions that were part of the governing process under the Roman constitution. List students' responses on the chalkboard. *[senate, popular assemblies, and magistrates (consuls, censors, and praetors)]* Next ask students to name the nearest American equivalent for each item on the chalkboard. Write responses in a second column next to their equivalents. *[the Senate (executive branch); popular assemblies (legislative branch); consuls (executive branch); tribunes (no direct equivalent, right to veto unjust laws could be compared to Supreme Court's right to overturn*

unconstitutional laws or to president's veto power); censors (executive branch—Census Bureau); and praetors (judicial branch)] Students should understand that, like that of the United States, Rome's government contained checks and balances that prevented any one person or office from ruling Rome.

Ask: *How did the Romans go about establishing this threefold system of government?*

[Responses should include descriptions of the Conflict of the Orders, the Plebeian Council, and election of tribunes.]

DEVELOP

Sketch a broad picture of the foundations of Roman society. To begin the discussion, you may wish to show students the image of a Roman house and family from the Global History Resource Center. Then organize students into two groups: family and religion. Have the first group create and present a diagram of the Roman family. *[The diagram should show that a paterfamilias with absolute authority headed the family; families with a common ancestor were members of a clan.]*

Ask: *How did the Conflict of the Orders influence this basic structure of society?*

[reinforced the importance of the family as the primary unit of society; led to emergence of new class—the nobilitas, which was open to plebeians with money and patronage]

Have the second group create and present a diagram of Roman religious life. *[The diagram should sketch the relationship between the Pontifex Maximus, augurs, and paterfamilias; it* should also include important deities such as the Lares and Penates.]

Display each diagram on the bulletin board and discuss similarities and differences between them.

Ask: *What values did both the family and religious structure promote?*

[importance of family, civic duty, and devotion to gods]

PROBE

Analyze the consequences of Roman conquests. Direct students' attention to the Through Others' Eyes feature. Remind students that by the middle of the 100s B.C., Rome was becoming a vast empire in spite of fierce opposition from conquered peoples. You may wish to assign the Global History Resource Center reading on the Roman legion to help students understand the basis of Roman military strength.

Remind students that while conquests increased Roman power, they created problems. Have students imagine that they are legionnaires returning from battle.

Ask: *How would legionnaires feel if they returned to find their farms ruined or sold?*

[angry, disillusioned, rebellious]

Ask: *What were some negative effects of the conquests?*

[Administrative structure became inadequate; ex-soldiers often joined urban unemployed; slaves revolted; Hellenistic influences undermined Roman values.]

Have students complete the Global History Resource Center reading on Spartacus and lead them in a discussion about why the slave revolt began and why it was so successful.

CONCLUDE

Identify some factors that led to the breakup of the Republic. First call on students to identify some of the warning signs that the Republic was growing weak and troubled. Ask students to pretend they are Roman citizens during the 100s and early first century B.C. In small groups, have students list the major newspaper headlines that might have ocurred during this period. *[For example: Mobs Lynch Gracchi, Blood Spills on Forum!*

Volunteers Flood Army, Allies Grow Restless, Sulla Seizes Power] List headlines on the chalkboard. Emphasize that by the time Caesar was murdered most Romans knew something had gone wrong.

Have students read Core Resources Reading 5.1, Seutonius's account of Caesar's funeral, and discuss the events surrounding Caesar's murder.

Ask: *Who murdered Caesar and why?*

[a group of senators who wanted to save the Republic from devolving into a monarchy]

Have students write short speeches to be delivered in the Senate the day after Caesar's death, recounting the Republic's glories and mourning its shortcomings. Ask student volunteers to share their speeches with the class.

EXTEND
Other Media
Suggest that students view a videotape of the movie *Spartacus*, which is set in the age of Sulla, and compare Hollywood's version of these events with the historical account in the Global History Resource Center. Discuss the picture both accounts give of Roman society.

MEET INDIVIDUAL NEEDS
Visual-Spatial Learners
Have students diagram the government of the Roman Republic just before the advent of the Gracchi.

Interpersonal Learners
Have students stage a trial for the assassins of Julius Caesar. Advocates for each side should explore arguments dealing with democracy, tyranny, social disorder, and Roman law. To make their arguments, students might draw on the Seutonius reading.

ASSESS
Review
Have students complete the Section 1 Review. Use answers in the Teacher's Edition, page 122, to assess student mastery of this section.

RESOURCES

Pupil's Edition

History Through the Arts, p. 124: *Roman Portrait Sculpture*

Map, p. 127: *The Height of the Roman Empire*, A.D. 117

Core Resources

Reading 5.2: *Roman Law*

Geography Activity 5: *Rome During the Reign of Augustus*

Visual Resources

Art and History 5: *Head of a Roman*

Global History Resource Center

Reading: *A Barbarian Denounces the Pax Romana*

Reading: *A Greek Praises the Pax Romana*

Reading: *Life in the City of Rome*

Reading: *Rome at Its Height*

Videodiscs or Global History Resource Center

Image: *Roman Religion: The Pantheon*

Search Frame 734

Image: *Rome in Its Glory Days*

Search Frame 735

Map: *Roman Roads in* A.D. 14

Search Frame 742

LESSON FOCUS

How did the Pax Romana contribute to peace and prosperity throughout the Roman Empire?

OBJECTIVES

After completing this lesson, students will be able to:

- explore how Augustus restored order to the Roman Empire;
- identify ways in which the Good Emperors hoped to strengthen the empire;
- describe Roman civilization during the Pax Romana;
- analyze how Romans applied advances in science and technology.

HOOK

Explore how Augustus restored order to Rome. Share with students the following excerpt from Tacitus's summary of how Augustus acquired his power (from *The Annals of Imperial Rome*):

He seduced the army with bonuses, and his cheap food policy was successful bait for civilians. Indeed, he attracted everybody's goodwill by the enjoyable gift of peace. Then he gradually pushed ahead and absorbed the functions of the senate, the officials, and even the law. Opposition did not exist. War or judicial murder had disposed of all men of spirit. Upper-class survivors found that slavish obedience was the way to succeed, both politically and financially.

Have students discuss whether, based on Tacitus's statement, they would have been for or against Augustus. Then ask students to think about how Augustus might have responded to Tacitus, and have them draft notes for a speech Augustus might have given listing his achievements. You may wish to assign students Geography Activity 5 as background information for the speech. *[Students should mention pacifying the empire's western border, rebuilding Rome "in marble," organizing municipal services, building temples, supporting moral and religious reforms, and supporting the arts.]*

Next direct students' attention to the History Through the Arts feature on Roman portraiture and discuss how Augustus promoted literature, art, and technology. *[The emperor and the urban rich patronized artists; the state financed massive public works.]* You may then wish to display Art and History Transparency 5 and assign the accompanying worksheet. If available, you may also wish to show the electronic media image of the Pantheon, which was built in Hadrian's time, to illustrate how Augustan architecture—and religious policies—survived his death.

DEVELOP

Discuss the ways in which the Good Emperors worked to strengthen the empire. Have students examine the map of the

Roman Empire on textbook page 127. Emphasize the vast size of the empire. Then discuss the problems plaguing the empire during the periods of the Julio-Claudians and Army Emperors. *[raging civil wars, unclear succession, government scandals]*

Ask: How did the Good Emperors try to restore stability to the empire?

[They expanded governmental administration to include provincial elites, reformed government to prevent corruption and increase efficiency, and improved frontier defenses.]

PROBE

Analyze changes in Roman civilization during the Pax Romana. Display the map of Roman roads from the Global History Resource Center. Point out that older people who remembered the Republic must have spoken of those times to the younger generation. Ask students to think about how they might have compared "then" to "now." Next create a two-column chart on the chalkboard. Have students brainstorm differences between the Republic and the early empire in categories such as government, provincial life, law, farming, trade, and transportation. *[Governmental anarchy gave way to order as a central authority replaced competing power centers; Roman-style towns proliferated in the provinces; Roman law moved toward one universal system controlled by professionals; tenant farmers replaced slave labor on farms; trade boomed; roads improved.]* To increase students' understanding of legal changes during the Pax Romana, assign Core Resources Reading 5.2. You may also wish to assign the two Global History Resource Center readings on the Pax Romana to help students understand the consequences of the Pax Romana from both "barbarian" and Greek points of view. If time permits, you may also wish to have students work in pairs to debate the merits of the Pax Romana from these two perspectives.

To further explore Roman life during this period, have students view the electronic media image of Rome. Ask them to compare this image to the description in the Global History Resource Center reading on urban life. Then make two columns on the blackboard and have students brainstorm to create lists of adjectives describing the "two sides" of Roman life. *[Possible responses include beautiful, modern, and entertaining versus violent, harsh, and decaying.]*

Ask: What signs of trouble were evident even during the Pax Romana?

[Students may cite such factors as a burgeoning underclass, urban decay paired with apathy, overextended borders, and hostile barbarians across most borders.]

CONCLUDE

Discuss how Romans applied advances in science and technology to everyday life. Point out that the Romans are known for their practical applications of scientific knowledge.

Ask: What contributions did Romans make to engineering?

[concrete, arch and vaulted domes to build larger buildings than the Greeks, improved water and sewage systems]

Ask: How did the Romans differ from the Greeks in their approach to knowledge?

[The Greeks appreciated scientific research for its own sake, whereas the Romans were known as organizers and engineers.]

EXTEND

Cross-Curricular Connection: *Language Arts*

Suggest that students select and prepare an oral reading of an excerpt from Latin literature. Possible sources include an ode by Horace, a love poem by Catullus, or a story from Ovid's *Metamorphosis*.

MEET INDIVIDUAL NEEDS

Linguistic Learners

Suggest that students write a character sketch about a fictional Roman. They should portray a day in his or her life, seasoned with vivid descriptions and realistic, historically accurate dialogue. The Global History Resource Center reading on Rome at its height provides excellent background information on daily life.

Logical-Mathematical Learners

Have students research and then explain to classmates why Roman roads, bridges, and aqueducts were much-admired engineering achievements. Students should explain the kinds of problems the Romans faced and how they were solved.

ASSESS

Review

Have students complete the Section 2 Review. Use answers in the Teacher's Edition, page 129, to assess student mastery of this section.

RESOURCES

Pupil's Edition
Map, p. 133: *The Spread of Christianity,* A.D. *300–600*
Sacred Traditions, p.134: *Paul's Letter to the Romans*

Core Resources
Reading 5.3: *Christians in the Roman Empire*

Visual Resources
Geography and History 5: *The Spread of Christianity*
Everyday Life 5: *The Catacombs of Saint Calixtus*

Global History Resource Center
Reading: *Persecution of Christians in Gaul*
Reading: *The Teachings of Jesus*
Reading: *The Appeal of Christianity to Rome*

Videodiscs or Global History Resource Center
Image: *Cavalry Battle Between Romans and Barbarians*

Search Frame 737

Image: *Catacomb Used by Early Christians*

Search Frame 739

LESSON FOCUS
How did the crumbling structure of the Roman Empire contribute to the rise of Christianity?

OBJECTIVES
After completing this lesson, students will be able to:
- identify the problems confronting the empire in the A.D. 200s and one of the consequences;
- analyze the rise of Christianity;
- explain how Christianity spread.

HOOK
Discuss the problems facing the empire in the A.D. **200s.**
Tell students that as the Roman Empire grew more complex, the emperors must have felt like cooks with too many pots to stir. Display the electronic media image of the cavalry battle and liken each border attack to a pot that must be stirred.
Ask: Who had the military advantage, Rome or its barbarian enemies? Why?
[While each barbarian group could attack a single point, Rome had to defend its whole border. For Rome, winning 9 battles out of 10 was a loss: it meant that barbarians had invaded.]

DEVELOP
Explore the internal consequences for Rome of its external problems. In a circle on the chalkboard, write EMPIRE UNDER ATTACK. Then ask students to consider how border troubles affected life at the heart of the Roman world. Have students brainstorm all the consequences they can think of. Use their ideas to diagram a web of interconnected consequences around the phrase on the chalkboard. *[Examples might include even more money spent on the military, increasingly independent military, constant violent change of emperors, declining trade, falling revenues, shrinking government services, rising crime, higher taxes, bad business climate, inflation, growing poverty, and widening gap between rich and poor.]*

PROBE: Link to Today
Discuss the rise of Christianity. Ask students why they think some people in the industrialized nations today join cults or new religious groups. Then remind students that new philosophies, cults, and creeds also sprouted throughout the Roman world in the A.D. 200s. Use the web diagram on the chalkboard to suggest a reason for the appeal of new religions to Romans: the widespread anxiety generated by a troubled world created an environment of spiritual longing. Have students list

some of the religions that became popular during this time. [*Mystery religions, Mithraism, the goddess cults of Isis and Cybele, various sects of Judaism, and finally Christianity*]

Next have students read the biography of Jesus and, if available, his teachings in the Global History Resource Center.

Ask: **What are the core elements of Jesus' teachings?**
[*love of God, the golden rule, humility, charity*]

Ask: **Why did these teachings initially attract the poor and dispossessed of the empire?**
[*Students should mention that Christianity's vision of an afterlife gave meaning to hardship; its reverence for the meek gave dignity to poverty; its emphasis on love and charity promoted communal solidarity and mutual aid—immediate and practical benefits to the poor.*]

To aid students in their understanding of Christianity's appeal in Roman times, you may wish to have them complete the Global History Resource Center reading. Then have them read the Sacred Traditions feature on page 134 of their textbook.

Ask: **What were St. Paul's distinctive contributions to Christianity?**
[*St. Paul formalized the distinction between Christianity and Judaism by dropping culturally specific Mosaic regulations, made central the doctrine of original sin and redemption through Jesus, and established churches throughout the Eastern Empire and Rome.*]

CONCLUDE

Explore how and why Christianity spread around the Mediterranean world. Discuss how the Pax Romana helped to spread Christianity. Students should realize that the same factors that facilitated trade favored the movement of ideas. Have students view the Geography and History transparency showing the spread of Christianity and complete the accompanying worksheet. You may wish to assign Core Resources Reading 5.3 and discuss how attitudes toward Christianity changed in the Roman Empire. [*Christianity grew from an outlaw cult into an accepted religion.*] Discuss the reasons for the rapid spread of Christianity during the 200s. Note that in a time when people felt insecure and institutions seemed to be eroding, Christianity was gaining stability—and thus drew converts from all walks of life. Help students relate the growth of Christianity to the internal consequences of Rome's external problems. Students may diagram the development of Christianity by drawing three concentric circles with Jesus at the center, Paul in the second

ring, and Hellenized Christianity in the outermost ring. In each ring, students should list the traits that the new religion acquired as it developed. [*Jesus: emphasized love, humility, and charity, teaching that all people would be rewarded in heaven; Paul: expanded Christianity's appeal to non-Jews; Hellenized Christianity: developed a theology by trying to combine Christian ethical creed with Greek philosophy*]

EXTEND

Cross-Curricular Connection: *Language Arts*

Have interested students create a short dialogue between a Christian missionary and a student of Plato's philosophy. You may wish to suggest that the dialogue be written in the form of a play.

OTHER MEDIA

The movies *Ben Hur* and *Quo Vadis* portray the early Christian era. Have students view these movies and compare them in a written review that focuses on historical insights and accuracy.

MEET INDIVIDUAL NEEDS

Interpersonal Learners

Have students view Everyday Life Transparency 5 and complete the accompanying worksheet. You may wish to have students read about the persecution of Christians in the Global History Resource Center and view the electronic media image of the catacombs. Ask students to imagine that they are about to die because of their religion. Have them write a letter to a friend, explaining why they chose this fate over renouncing their faith.

Musical-Rhythmic Learners

Have students write and perform a political song about Roman times in the A.D. 200s as if they were rap artists.

Students Acquiring English

Pair new speakers of English with fluent speakers. Have each pair make flash cards of every name and term in the Section Review. Then have each pair use the cards to quiz each other.

ASSESS

Review

Have students complete the Section 3 Review. Use answers in the Teacher's Edition, page 135, to assess student mastery of this section.

Lesson 5.4   *The Later Roman Empire*

Textbook pp. 136–142

RESOURCES

Pupil's Edition

Map, p. 140: *Invasions into the Roman Empire, A.D. 340–481*

Then and Now, p. 141: *The Many Legacies of Rome*

Core Resources

Reading 5.4: *A Description of the Barbarians*

Global History Resource Center

Reading: *An Eyewitness to the End of Roman Rule*

Videodiscs or Global History Resource Center

Map: *Division of the Roman Empire*

Search Frame 743

Image: *Vandals March on Rome*

Search Frame 738

LESSON FOCUS

How did the Roman Empire change in its declining centuries?

OBJECTIVES

After completing this lesson, students will be able to:

• outline steps taken by Diocletian to save the Roman Empire;
• analyze how Christianity changed after becoming the state religion of Rome;
• identify factors that led to the collapse of the Roman Empire.

HOOK: Link to Today

Examine how the atmosphere of Roman society changed under Diocletian. On the chalkboard write two titles—*First Citizen* and *Master and Living God*—and ask students which feels more natural to use for the president of the United States.

Then ask students to imagine a United States in which Master and Living God would seem more natural, and have them discuss how such a society would differ from the one in which we live today. Point out that under Diocletian just such a change took place in Rome when Diocletian went from being known as Princeps ("First Citizen") to Dominus et Deus ("Master and God"). Emphasize that this change in title reflected a change in the texture of Roman life.

DEVELOP

Outline Diocletian's efforts to save the empire. Challenge students to draft a proclamation announcing Diocletian's main "reforms" in a few simple sentences. The document should include major aspects of Diocletian's social, economic, and political policy. Break the class into three groups to draft the sentences. Then have students combine their efforts into a single poster. [*Students' posters should mention that every person's occupation and social status were fixed by law, that all economic decisions were made by the state and regulated by bureaucrats, that the economy was regulated to meet the empire's defense needs, that the empire was divided in two— with two emperors—to improve efficiency.*] Ask students if their sentences remind them of any twentieth-century states. [*Possible responses include any of the Communist, Nazi, or Fascist states.*] You may wish to display the Global History Resource Center map of the division of the Roman Empire to help students with this activity.

PROBE

Examine the changing character of Christianity in the late empire. First discuss Constantine's historic conversion to Christianity. Have students update their poster with key measures promulgated by Constantine [*"Christianity shall be legal"*] and Theodosius. [*"All religions other than Christianity shall be outlawed"*] Then discuss how the church changed after gaining official status. Students should recognize that a priestly class headed by patriarchs, metropolitans, and bishops developed and that the church and state became intertwined once Christianity gained official status. The emperor decreed that all bishops should acknowledge the authority of the pope. Discuss how the state took a role in shaping Christian doctrine when disputes threatened to destroy the unity of the church. You may wish to display the electronic media image of the First Church Council of Nicaea in order to dramatize the change in status of Christians from that of persecuted minority to partners in power.

Ask: How did Christians respond to these changes?

> *[Students should recognize that monasticism was a reaction to these developments.]*

CONCLUDE

Survey factors that contributed to the fall of the Roman Empire. Remind students that maintaining Christian unity did not solve the problems of the empire and that many explanations have been given for the decline and fall of the Roman Empire. Organize the class into small groups and have each one brainstorm possible answers to the question *What caused the decline and fall of the Roman Empire?* Take suggestions from each group in turn to create a master list on the chalkboard. *[Factors might include sheer size; too much bureaucracy; too large a gap between rich and poor; financial mismanagement; decline of spiritual values; weak emperors; imperial mistakes; inadequate procedures for finding and promoting talented people; plots by ambitious people in the military; and barbarian attacks.]*

Next turn students' attention to the textbook map showing barbarian invasions, and discuss the effects of these onslaughts on an already weakened empire. Assign Core Resources Reading 5.4. If available, refer students to the electronic media image of the Vandals marching on Rome and the Global History Resource Center reading on the end of Roman rule. Then ask students to draft a short speech that could have been made by Romulus Augustulus, the last Roman emperor, in which he outlines the reasons for the empire's demise and surrenders to the Ostrogoth commander Odoacer.

EXTEND

Community Resources

Link to Today. Assign the Then and Now feature and discuss how the legacy of ancient Rome touches our lives today. Then have students go on a scavenger hunt for reflections of Roman civilization in their own community. Have students report their findings to the class.

Cross-Curricular Connection: *Law*

Have interested students research the influence of Roman law on the legal heritage of the United States. Students might choose to focus on a particular area of influence, such as the Constitution, the legal heritage of states that were once part of New Spain, or Louisiana, which was once part of France's colonial holdings.

MEET INDIVIDUAL NEEDS

Visual-Spatial Learners

Use the textbook map of barbarian invasions and, if available, the electronic media images of the cavalry battle and the Vandals' march on Rome to reinforce how Germanic invasions led to the disintegration of the Western Roman Empire.

Gifted Students

Suggest that students do some research and create parallel diagrams of church and state hierarchies in the late empire to illustrate their similarities and differences. After students have finished their diagrams, encourage them to share their work with the class.

ASSESS

Review

Have students complete the Section 4 Review. Use answers in the Teacher's Edition, page 142, to assess student mastery of this section.

In preparation for the chapter test, you may wish to have students complete all or part of the Chapter 5 Review on textbook page 143, the Chapter 5 Review Activity, and the Chapter 5 Themes Review.

Chapter 5
The Roman World

509 B.C.–A.D. 476

Understanding the Main Idea

As the Roman Republic expanded to include new territories, it was transformed into an empire. Power rested in the hands of emperors, who gained increasing control over society. Under the rule of the early emperors, a long period of relative peace descended over the empire. This peace allowed trade and culture to flourish. Ultimately, however, the empire collapsed under the weight of invasions and internal disorder. Part of Rome's legacy was the birth of Christianity—a new and dynamic religion that would long outlive the empire.

Themes

- **Politics and Law** How might establishing universal laws help to unify a society?
- **Religion** Why might people follow new religious leaders?
- **War and Diplomacy** How can the maintenance of a large army strain a society?

A great turning point in the history of Rome came shortly after the assassination of the dictator Julius Caesar in 44 B.C. Civil war had broken out between Caesar's heir, Octavian, and one of Caesar's most loyal supporters, Marc Antony—each of whom had taken command of half of the empire after avenging Caesar's death. In 31 B.C. Octavian forced Antony and his ally, Queen Cleopatra of Egypt, into a naval battle at Actium in Greece. The Roman historian Plutarch described the scene:

66 *[Octavian's ships] . . . deliberately avoided a head-on collision with their enemies' bows, which were armored with massive plates and spikes of bronze. . . . And so the fighting took on much of the character of a land battle, or, to be more exact, of an attack upon a fortified town. Three or four of Octavius's ships clustered round each one of Antony's, and the fighting was carried on with wicker shields, spears, poles, and flaming missiles, while Antony's soldiers also shot with catapults from wooden towers.* 99

The fighting continued for several hours. In the end, Octavian's forces soundly defeated Antony's fleet. Octavian became undisputed master of the Roman world.

494 B.C.	c. 450 B.C.	73 B.C.	44 B.C.	27 B.C.
Plebeians refuse to defend Rome unless they are granted more equality.	The laws of the Republic are written down as the Law of the Twelve Tables.	Slaves led by the ex-gladiator Spartacus rebel in southern Italy.	The Roman Senate declares Julius Caesar dictator for life.	The Senate gives Octavian the title of Augustus, beginning the Pax Romana.

His victory at Actium marked the end of the old Roman Republic and the birth of something new—the Roman Empire.

Octavian's victory at the Battle of Actium; 31 B.C.

c. 6 B.C.	A.D. 66–70	A.D. 180	A.D. 313	A.D. 476
Jesus of Nazareth is born.	Romans sack Jerusalem, killing thousands.	The Pax Romana comes to an end with the death of Marcus Aurelius.	Emperor Constantine issues the Edict of Milan, legalizing Christianity in the empire.	The Western Roman Empire falls to Germanic invaders.

Roman Society and the Crises of the Republic

FOCUS

- How was Roman government organized?
- What were the foundations of Roman society?
- What were the consequences of Roman conquests?
- What factors led to the breakup of the Republic?

As in Greece, the early Roman city-states underwent a period of political and social evolution as ordinary citizens challenged the dominance of the landowning aristocracy. Eventually, the Roman Republic emerged from this struggle with a constitution that accommodated all levels of society. This early Republic reflected the basic unit of Roman society—the patriarchal family. As the empire expanded, however, Romans began to turn away from the traditional foundations of their society and consequently brought the Republic to an end.

A gold necklace from a Roman grave

The Roman Republic

The expulsion of the last king in 509 B.C. left Roman society divided between patricians and plebeians. Organized in clans, patrician families controlled every aspect of society—politics, religion, the economy, and the military. Patricians maintained their power through a patronage system, in which they provided financial, social, or legal support for their client families in return for political backing and loyalty. From the beginning of the Republic, however, plebeians challenged the patricians over a period of several hundred years in what became known as the Conflict of the Orders.

Conflict of the Orders. Plebeian participation in the army was critical to Rome's ability both to defend itself and to expand. As in Greece, however, in the late 500s B.C. and early 400s B.C., problems of debt and land hunger worsened the plight of small landowners and the poor, and drove many into debt slavery. This threatened not only the people's well-being but that of the state as well. Believing that only people with property to defend would fight well, patricians had established property qualifications for military service. However, plebeians were increasingly disqualified from service because they lacked property, and army recruitment began to decline.

When foreign invaders threatened the city in 494 B.C., the plebeians staged a walkout, leaving Rome and refusing to fight until changes were made. Patricians grudgingly accepted a decree abolishing debt slavery, and the plebeians returned to defend the city. They soon formed their own assembly, the *concilium plebis*, or "Plebeian Council," through which they began to regulate their own affairs.

To further guarantee their rights, the plebeians also gained the right to elect their own officials, known as **tribunes** of the people, to protect the plebeians against unjust treatment by patrician officials. Eventually, these tribunes even had the right to veto laws that seemed harmful or unjust. Meanwhile, wealthier plebeians continued to demand greater access to administrative and religious positions in the state. Then, around 450 B.C., the plebeians forced the patricians to have all laws written down in what became known as the Law of the Twelve Tables. Henceforth, patrician judges could not make decisions based merely on their own opinions. On the other hand, one of the laws was a new ban on intermarriage between patricians and plebeians—an attempt by the patricians to preserve their special status.

Although the Conflict of the Orders changed the nature of the Roman political system, it was a long, drawn-out process. With both sides committed to the preservation of the state, the Romans hammered out a practical and flexible **constitution**, or political structure. In later years they were extremely proud of this system—as one statesman explained:

66 *The reason for the superiority of the constitution of our city to that of other states is that the latter almost always had their laws and institutions from one legislator. But our republic was not made by the genius of one man, but of many, nor in the life of one, but through many centuries and generations.* 99

The Conflict of the Orders did not end until the 200s B.C., when laws passed by the Plebeian Council finally applied to all citizens.

Roman republican government. In addition to developing new offices and institutions of government, the Romans also retained older elements from the days of the monarchy. Ultimately, the government consisted of three parts: (1) the **Senate**, a senior body of former state officials who acted as advisors, controlled public finances, and handled all foreign relations; (2) various popular assemblies, in which all citizens voted on laws and elected officials; and (3) the officials themselves, called magistrates, who put the laws into practice and governed in the name of the Roman Senate and the people. Though initially dominated by patricians, eventually all state offices, including the Senate, were open to both patricians and plebeians.

After the end of the monarchy, the king's place was taken by two **consuls**. Both elected for one year, the consuls became the dual chief executives of the state. Next to the consuls, the most important magistrates were the **censors**, who were elected every 5 years for 18-month terms. Censors recorded the wealth and residence of the entire population. They also maintained the normal Senate membership of 300 by appointing candidates when necessary. In addition they oversaw the moral conduct of all citizens and conducted the bidding and awarding process for government contracts.

In the 300s B.C. Romans also began to elect magistrates called **praetors**. Primarily judges, praetors could also act for the consuls when they were away. As Rome expanded, both consuls and praetors were usually given military commands or were appointed as provincial governors after finishing their terms of office. Such appointments brought a chance for glory as well as wealth through plunder and the collection of taxes. Many other officials were also elected to handle various aspects of administration.

*T*he Romans eventually developed a threefold system of government based on the Senate, popular assemblies, and the magistrates.

▲ **This marble frieze shows a gathering of Roman senators.**

Theme: Politics and Law

In addition to the original city praetorship established in 366 B.C., a new praetorship was established in 242 B.C. Called the *praetor peregrinus,* or "peregrine praetor," the new praetor judged on all legal matters involving non-Roman citizens. This development was significant because in the past, under the law of the Twelve Tables, noncitizens had no rights.

Critical Thinking Ask students to suggest reasons why the peregrine praetor's role would have grown more important over time.

ANSWER: Students should suggest that Rome came into contact with more noncitizens as it expanded and increased its commercial, political, and social relations with other states.

Republican Society

The Conflict of the Orders shaped not only Roman constitutional institutions but also the structure of Roman society. Only wealthy plebeians could really afford to participate equally in public life with the patricians. Since public officials were not paid, only the wealthy could afford to hold office.

Like the patricians, wealthy plebeians also practiced the patronage system. Consequently, Roman politics often reflected the influence of wealthy political groups in which members owed their loyalty to even wealthier public officials. Ties of marriage, friendship, and family alliances were as important as common class interests. In addition, Roman politicians often relied on their public-speaking skills to sway the popular assemblies.

The nobility. After 445 B.C., when intermarriage between patricians and plebeians again became legal, political groups began to develop across class boundaries. As wealthy plebeians and patricians began to cooperate politically, a new class—the *nobilitas*, or "nobility"—emerged. The *nobilitas* included both patrician and wealthy plebeian families with at least one ancestor who had been a consul. Thus, while restricted in numbers and access, the nobility was not completely closed. Under this system, all it took to get into politics was patronage and money.

The ultimate goal of a political career in Rome was the consulship, an office that elevated the successful candidate and his entire family to the highest social class. To achieve this goal, bribery and efforts to gain public favor were common. In a letter one Roman advised his brother on how to win in his campaign for the consulship:

❝The people like to be called by name . . . courted, receive favors, hear about you, feel that you are working for the public good. . . . You must flatter endlessly; this is wrong and shameful in ordinary life, but necessary in running for office. . . . Let the voters . . . think that you know them well . . . that you are generous and open-handed. . . . If possible accuse your competitors of having a bad reputation for crime, vice or bribery. . . . Remember that this is Rome, a city made up of many peoples, in which plots, lies and all kinds of vices abound. You must suffer much arrogance, many insults, much ill-will and the pride and hatred of many people.❞

The Roman republican system was neither a democracy nor a tyranny. Romans respected authority and did not generally challenge the position of the ruling elite. The patronage system reinforced elite control of society, particularly after the rise of the nobility. Above all, the patronage system safeguarded the primary unit of society—the family.

The Roman family. Like many other tribal peoples, Romans were patriarchal. The head of the family—the **paterfamilias** (pah-tuhr-fuh-MI-lee-uhs), or family father—was the oldest living male and had extensive powers over other members of the extended family. This included his wife, his sons with their wives and children, his unmarried daughters, and his family slaves. Within this basic family structure, Romans emphasized the virtues of the farmer-soldier—above all, simplicity, religious devotion, and obedience.

Families were grouped into clans, whose members claimed descent from a common, though often mythical, ancestor. Children were considered part of the family only if the paterfamilias

◀ **Roman sculptors often created statues of famous public officials, such as this consul of the Republic.**

▲ **Many wealthy Romans were drawn to the mild, sunny climate of Pompeii, where they built luxurious villas like this one.**

accepted them. As in Greece, the early Romans often left unwanted children to die. Adoption was an important aspect of Roman society. Some families that had no sons would adopt a teenage boy or young man to serve as the heir to the paterfamilias. Adoption was one way of ensuring that the family name was carried on to the next generation.

In theory, Roman women could do little without the intervention of a male guardian. When a woman married, guardianship usually passed from her father to her husband. In practice, however, women were probably much freer and in greater control of their own lives than the Roman ideal would suggest. Unlike upper-class Athenian women, for example, upper-class Roman women were not segregated from males in the home. They could also leave the home without an escort.

Religion. In their religious views, the Romans displayed strong elements of animism—the belief that spirits dwelled in all objects of the natural world. One of the most important duties of the paterfamilias was to ensure the proper worship of the *Lares*, the ancestral spirits on whom the family's prosperity depended. Other household spirits included the *Penates*, or "Guardians of the storeroom." Private worship also focused on Vesta, guardian of fire and the hearth.

Public worship became the responsibility of state priests led by the *Pontifex Maximus*, or "High Priest." Like the Greeks, Romans had a relationship with the gods based less on morality than on ritual. In exchange for exact performance of the proper ceremonies, the gods would sustain Roman prosperity. Sharing a common Indo-European religious tradition, Romans also believed in Greek mythology and eventually identified their gods with those of Olympus. "We have overcome all the nations of the world," observed the statesman Cicero, "because we have realized that the world is directed and governed by the gods."

The Romans also believed that the gods sent signs and warnings to human beings in the form of natural phenomena, such as the flight of birds, or the color and arrangement of entrails in sacrificial animals. They paid particular respect to the priests known as *augurs*, who specialized in interpreting these signs. Nothing important, in either family or public life, was undertaken without first consulting the *augurs*.

Organized around patriarchal families and dominated by a wealthy elite, Roman society was based on civic duty and devotion to the gods.

Consequences of the Conquests

In the mid-100s B.C. Rome had no rival in the Mediterranean world. Nevertheless, the republic's possessions were still ruled by the institutions of a small Italian city. The responsibilities of running such vast territories soon stretched the system to its limits.

Ordinary citizens serving in the legions found the overseas conquests increasingly burdensome.

Spartacus hoped that after revolting his men would return to their homelands. However, once they began to win, Spartacus's men remained in Italy and looted the countryside. The government finally organized a force against Spartacus, under an ex-praetor named Crassus. Crassus assembled and trained an army of 40,000, eventually cornered Spartacus, and killed him and 6,000 of his followers.

Critical Thinking Ask students what aspect of Spartacus's revolt was the most dangerous to the Roman state.

ANSWER: Students might suggest that the example of a successful slave revolt might cause slaves throughout the empire to revolt.

RESOURCE ACTIVITY

GLOBAL HISTORY RESOURCE CENTER
Reading: *The Roman Legion*

Read aloud the article on the organization of the Roman army. Have students create charts showing the organization and structure of a Roman legion, including these units: cohorts, centuries, and contubernia.

Level 1/ Sheltered English

After long years of service, many legionnaires returned to find that their farms had been sold or were in such bad shape that they had to be abandoned. Ex-soldiers often joined a growing mass of urban unemployed in Rome.

Adding to the strains on the system was a series of slave revolts, beginning in 135 B.C. in

THROUGH OTHERS' EYES

The Fiery Queen, Boudicca

Boudicca, queen of the Icenian kingdom, is remembered as Britain's first heroine. Known as the "Fiery Queen" because of her temper and her red hair that fell to her knees, Boudicca led her people against the Roman troops that occupied her country.

For many years Boudicca's husband, King Prasutagus, had managed to prevent his people from rising against the Romans, whom they were forced to support with crippling taxes, food, livestock, and labor. But peaceful relations ended after Prasutagus's death in A.D. 60. In addition to being a queen, Boudicca was a warrior, trained from childhood to fight with weapons against both men and women. Her outrage over the wrongs her people had suffered led her to stage an uprising against the Roman troops who came to collect the Icenian wealth. She rallied hundreds of thousands of Celts against the Romans, often fighting in the front lines herself. The following speech to her people showed the passion with which she led them:

66 We British are used to women commanders in war. I am fighting as an ordinary person for my lost freedom, my bruised body, and my outraged daughters. The gods will give us the vengeance we deserve! The Roman division that dared to fight is annihilated. The others cower in their camps. They will never face even the din and roar of all our thousands, much less the shock of our onslaught [fierce attack]. Look and see how many of you are fighting—and what you are fighting for— and why! Then you will win this battle, or perish. 99

southern Italy and Sicily. The most serious revolt began in 73 B.C. under a slave-gladiator, or professionally trained fighter, named Spartacus. It took the Romans eight legions and about two years to defeat Spartacus and crush the revolt.

The continuing conquests of more territories also brought foreign philosophies and religions to Rome. By the 300s B.C. Greek influences had started to make Rome a Hellenistic city. Traditional Roman ideals of faithfulness, honor, and civic duty no longer satisfied many citizens, who began to question the selfishness of the ruling elite. As Hellenistic influences grew, individualism began to conflict with the old Roman emphasis on duty to the state.

*R**oman conquests strained Roman society and challenged traditional Roman values.***

The Roman Revolution

As the pressures of world empire grew, a revolution began in Roman political and social institutions during the 100s and early first century B.C. Similar to what had happened in Athens, the source of this revolution was the growing tension between the plebeians and the Roman elite.

The Gracchi. In 133 B.C. the tribune Tiberius Gracchus (GRAK-uhs) began to complain about the treatment of the farmer-soldiers, who were being reduced to poverty:

66 The savage beasts in Italy have their particular dens, they have their places of repose [rest] and refuge; but the men who bear arms, and expose their lives for the safety of their country, enjoy in the meantime nothing more in it but the air and light; and having no houses or settlements of their own, are constrained [forced] to wander from place to place with their wives and children. 99

Tiberius and his younger brother Gaius tried to eliminate the plight of the poor by redistributing public land to small farmers. The Gracchus brothers (the Gracchi) had public support, but the Roman elite reacted violently. Fearing that the Gracchi were planning to reduce its power,

▲ This illustration shows Tiberius Gracchus locking the treasury. His opposition to the aristocracy led to his murder by clubbing.

the Senate urged mobs to kill first Tiberius and later his brother, along with hundreds of their supporters. For the first time in Roman history the blood of citizens was shed in the Forum. By questioning the ruling elite's control of the Republic, the Gracchi had in effect begun the Roman Revolution.

Marius. In 107 B.C. the revolution was carried further when a general named Marius was elected to the consulship. Marius had become popular because of his military talents. Anxious to improve recruitment for the army, he eliminated the property qualifications for military service and began to accept anyone into the army who wanted to join. Poor people began to join the army, attaching themselves to a general in hopes of sharing the plunder and land at the end of a war. To a large extent, armies became private forces devoted to the general, who held the economic future of soldiers in his hands. Marius's successors soon realized the political potential of such armies.

The Social War. Meanwhile, events were brewing among Rome's Italian allies that would force a dramatic transformation of the nature of the Roman state and the Roman identity. For decades the allies had been trying to obtain Roman citizenship, but the Senate, wanting to maintain its monopoly on power, had stubbornly refused. Although the allies had shared somewhat in the benefits of Roman expansion, such benefits had only raised their expectations. The local oligarchies in the Italian cities wanted access to public offices in Rome. Finally, in 90 B.C., the Italian allies of Rome rebelled.

The conflict that broke out (known as the Social War, from the Latin *socius*, meaning "ally") was one of the bloodiest in Roman history. Italians had served with the legions and were as well trained and disciplined as the Romans. In the end, the rebels were defeated militarily—but the Senate also finally agreed to grant them citizenship. With this decision, the Roman state grew to include all of Italy.

Sulla. The Social War had revealed the talent of one general in particular, Lucius Cornelius Sulla. As a result of his military success, Sulla rose to the consulship in 88 B.C. After Sulla's consulship, Marius and his supporters defied Roman custom by trying to prevent him from taking a military command. Sulla responded by marching on Rome with his legions—an act that was considered offensive to the gods.

In the civil war that followed, Sulla emerged victorious and became dictator. In a bloody purge he executed those who had opposed him or whom he believed to be a danger to the state. He then carried out a program of reforms aimed at restoring the power of the Senate and the oligarchy. Eventually, believing he had restored the traditional government of the old Republic, Sulla voluntarily retired. He died peacefully on his farm. By

R RESOURCE ACTIVITY

(p. 122)
READINGS IN WORLD HISTORY Reading 5.1
Caesar's Funeral

Have students read the excerpt from the Roman historian Suetonius. Then have them complete the questions.

Level 1

R RESOURCE ACTIVITY

WRITING PROJECTS Writing Project 5
Writing a Speech

Have students complete the activity on writing a speech, using information on Julius Caesar.

Level 2

✓ REVIEW & ASSESSMENT RESOURCES

• Study Guide 5.1
• Daily Quiz 5.1
• Main Idea Activity 5.1

All Levels

SECTION 1
REVIEW ANSWERS

IDENTIFY
For significance, see the following pages:
tribunes (p. 116)
constitution (p. 117)
Senate (p. 117)
consuls (p. 117)
censors (p. 117)
praetors (p. 117)
paterfamilias (p. 118)
Spartacus (p. 120)
the Gracchi (p. 120)
Marius (p. 121)
Sulla (p. 121)
Julius Caesar (p. 122)
Marc Antony (p. 122)
Cleopatra (p. 122)

1. The government consisted of the Senate, various popular assemblies, and the officials, or magistrates.
2. Expansion was putting strains on Roman society and people became more individualistic. Growing tensions between the plebeians and the elite, internal warfare, and the restructuring of the army for personal gain led to the decline of the Republic.
3. Roman politics and society were dominated by the wealthy. Roman families were patriarchal and emphasized civic duty and devotion to the gods.
4. Essays should explain that conquests made the elite rich, while ordinary people, such as the legionnaires, often lost their land or became part of the masses of urban unemployed.
5. The army became an instrument for personal gain. Both Marius and the Gracchi took steps to eliminate a form of control by the elite.

establishing the example of dictatorship, however, Sulla had unintentionally carried the Roman Revolution one step further.

Caesar and Octavian.
Within a generation of Sulla's death, the old Republic was practically gone. The end of the Republic came with the ambitions of three men: Gnaeus Pompey (PAHM-pee), Julius Caesar, and Licinius Crassus. Combining themselves in a private alliance, these three men followed in Sulla's footsteps by using the personal loyalty of their legions to achieve their own ambitions. In 60 B.C. they dominated the Roman state through what became known as the First Triumvirate, or rule of three men. Eventually, after Crassus's death, Caesar defeated Pompey in a civil war and took full control of the state. In 44 B.C. the Senate declared Caesar dictator for life. In a last attempt to save the Republic, however, a group of senators soon murdered Caesar in the Senate chamber on the Ides of March—March 15.

Caesar's murder did not solve anything. In 43 B.C. the assembly empowered the Second Triumvirate—composed of Caesar's heir and adopted son, Octavian, a loyal officer named Marc Antony, and the high priest Lepidus—to

▲ **In this 1867 painting by Jean-Léon Gérome, Caesar's assassins wave the daggers with which they murdered the dictator.**

take control of the affairs of the Republic. Soon Lepidus was pushed aside as Antony and Octavian agreed to govern half the empire each—Octavian in the west and Antony in the east. When civil war between the two eventually broke out, Octavian defeated Antony and his ally, Queen Cleopatra of Egypt, at the naval battle of Actium in 31 B.C. The double suicide of Antony and Cleopatra the following year marked the end of an era. Octavian alone now controlled Rome. The Republic was effectively dead and a new period in Roman history was now beginning.

Internal warfare and a reorganized army based on personal gain led to the downfall of the Republic.

SECTION 1 REVIEW

IDENTIFY and explain the significance of the following:
tribunes
constitution
Senate
consuls
censors
praetors
paterfamilias
Spartacus
the Gracchi
Marius
Sulla

Julius Caesar
Marc Antony
Cleopatra

1. *Main Idea* How was the Roman government organized during the Republic?
2. *Main Idea* What factors led to the fall of the Roman Republic?
3. *Social Relations* What were some characteristics of Roman society?

4. *Writing to Explain* Write a short essay explaining how some people prospered and others suffered as a result of Roman expansion.
5. *Determining Cause and Effect* What were the ultimate consequences of Marius's reorganization of the army? Why are the reforms supported by the Gracchi and Marius referred to as the Roman Revolution?

The Pax Romana

- How did Augustus restore order to the Roman Empire?
- How did the Good Emperors hope to strengthen the empire?
- What was Roman civilization like during the Pax Romana?
- How did the Romans apply advances in science and technology?

With the fall of the Republic, a new phase of Roman development began. The Republic was transformed from a city-state to an empire. Under a series of emperors, republicanism was swept away and replaced with a centralized imperial administration. Through this central government, Rome established a period of stability and prosperity throughout the Mediterranean world that would be remembered as the Pax Romana—the Roman Peace.

Octavian, Caesar's heir

Augustus and the Principate

By 29 B.C. Octavian faced the task of restoring order in the empire. He had no intention of establishing a dictatorship, but he had also decided that it was impossible to return to the old republican system. Claiming that he was "restoring the republic," Octavian succeeded in establishing a new political order. Today it is known as the empire, but Octavian was very careful to avoid the title of king or emperor. Instead, he presented himself as *princeps*, or "first citizen." The government he established is known as the Principate. Octavian insisted that he had no powers greater than those of other magistrates—his leadership came from his higher moral authority:

❝May I be privileged to build firm and lasting foundations for the government of the state. May I also achieve the reward to which I aspire: that of being known as the author of the best possible constitution, and of carrying with me, when I die, the hope that these foundations which I have established for the State will abide secure.❞

In 27 B.C. the Senate gave Octavian a title of honor—Augustus, "the revered one." Largely in control of the army, Augustus brought to the Roman people what they desired most—internal peace. For more than 40 years, Augustus remained at the head of the state. This very long reign made possible a smooth transition toward the new imperial government. Augustus divided the power to rule Rome and its empire between himself and the Senate. His own appointees, drawn from his personal household and a few carefully chosen senators, proved more efficient than those appointed by the Senate. Soon most financial and administrative matters came under Augustus's control.

In foreign affairs Augustus at first started a vast program to bring peace to the west, particularly to Gaul and Spain. He also embarked upon a series of conquests that pushed the border of the empire eastward to the Danube River. His ultimate goal was to push the border to the Elbe River. When German tribes under their leader, Arminius, wiped out three Roman legions in A.D. 9, however, Augustus decided to retreat to the Rhine.

History THROUGH THE ARTS

Roman Portrait Sculpture

Portrait sculptures of both famous and ordinary people were a favorite theme of Roman artists. Thousands of portrait sculptures have survived from the Republic and the empire. Roman artists showed great talent and skill in representing realistic characteristics. Reality was an important theme in making portraits, although sometimes artists were also inspired by idealistic images of Greek gods and goddesses. The portrait bust of the emperor Vespasian shows a very realistic interpretation of the emperor's personality. His portrait reflects his honesty and simple origins, as well as his good-humored nature. The portrait of Livia, the wife of Augustus, on the other hand, shows both realistic and idealistic qualities. Livia's grace and devotion to her husband, Augustus, are portrayed in her strong features, but the overwhelming beauty of the portrait is similar to the depictions of Greek goddesses. The idealism in Livia's portrait is largely a reflection of her times. Under the reign of Augustus, Rome was at the height of its glory and power. Many artists hoped to capture the spirit of the times by portraying leading citizens with divine characteristics.

Livia

Thinking About Art

1. What makes the portrait pictured here look realistic?
2. What do you think the sculptor was trying to convey?

In the east Rome's primary opponent was the Parthian Empire. The Parthians were a local Persian family that had emerged from the chaos of the Hellenistic Seleucid Empire and gradually gained control of the Plateau of Iran. Eventually, the Parthians also began to expand westward into territory claimed by Rome, and the border regions between the two great empires were often ablaze with fighting.

In Rome the legacy of what became known as the Augustan Age was even more impressive. Augustus took special care of Rome itself, organizing a police force, fire brigades, and food and water supplies. Augustus also initiated a vast building program, boasting, "I found Rome built of bricks; I leave her clothed in marble." Augustus presided over moral and religious reforms, arguing that since the gods had made the empire possible, it was wise to respect them. He restored old temples, built new ones, and reorganized many neglected cults.

Culturally, the Augustan Age was a great period of creativity in Latin literature, which included many late-republican writers such as the poet Catullus, and the great orator Cicero. Realizing that literature and the arts could enhance his fame, Augustus supported development in these areas. Great writers flourished, such as the poets Horace and Ovid, the historian Livy, and above all, the poet Virgil, who in his epic poem the *Aeneid* tried to imitate Homer by offering Rome a national epic.

In the *Aeneid*, Virgil's hero was the Trojan prince Aeneas, who had supposedly become the founder of the Roman people. In an exchange between the prince and his dead father's ghost, Virgil conveyed the Romans' own conception of their growing responsibilities:

66 *Roman, remember by your strength to rule*
Earth's peoples—for your arts are to be these:
To pacify, to impose the rule of law,

> *To spare the conquered, battle down the proud.* 99

To restore order to the empire, Augustus undertook new military campaigns, revitalized the city of Rome, and encouraged renewed religious devotion.

The Julio-Claudians and Flavians

Augustus died in A.D. 14. For the next 54 years, relatives of Julius Caesar, called the Julio-Claudian Emperors, ruled the empire. Tiberius, Augustus's adopted son, was a good soldier and a competent administrator, despite his difficult situation as the direct successor of the great Augustus. His brutal and mentally unstable successor, Caligula, however, once supposedly demonstrated his power to the Roman Senate by appointing his favorite horse as consul.

Claudius, an intelligent and scholarly man, followed Caligula. Claudius improved the imperial administration and extended citizenship rights to many people in the provinces. This helped to strengthen and stabilize the empire. But like many other emperors, Claudius met with a violent end—according to reports, his wife, Agrippina, poisoned him with tainted mushrooms.

During the reign of Nero, Claudius's successor, a disastrous fire swept through Rome. Many Romans believed that Nero started the fire. (He tried to deflect such criticism by instead blaming it on Christians, a growing religious group in the city.) Eventually, coming to realize that he faced certain assassination, Nero committed suicide in A.D. 68—a scene described by a Roman historian:

66 *In terror he [Nero] snatched up the two daggers . . . but threw them down again, protesting that the fatal hour had not yet come. . . . He kept moaning about his cowardice, and muttering: 'How ugly and vulgar my life has become!'* 99

After Nero's death, civil wars raged in the Roman world, and four provincial leaders with military backing claimed the throne in turn. Fortunately, the last one, Vespasian, reestablished order. During his reign and those of his sons Titus

Emperors of the Pax Romana 27 B.C.–A.D. 180

Period	Emperors
27 B.C.–A.D 14	Augustus
A.D. 14–68	**Julio-Claudian Emperors** Tiberius (14–37)* Caligula (37–41) Claudius (41–54) Nero (54–68)
A.D. 68–69	**Army Emperors** Galba, Otho, Vitellius *(Chosen by various legions during a succession crisis)*
A.D. 69–96	**Flavian Emperors** Vespasian (69–79) Titus (79–81) Domitian (81–96)
A.D. 96–180	**The Good Emperors** Nerva (96–98) Trajan (98–117) Hadrian (117–138) Antoninus Pius (138–161) Marcus Aurelius (161–180)

* Indicates dates of reign

and Domitian, order, peace, and prosperity returned to the empire. These Flavians, as they are known, were not from the old Roman aristocracy like their predecessors, but from other parts of Italy.

The Good Emperors

In A.D. 96 a new dynasty established itself on the Roman throne. Five emperors presided over the empire for nearly a century: Nerva, Trajan, Hadrian, Antoninus Pius, and Marcus Aurelius. They are known as the **Good Emperors**. With the exception of Nerva, the Good Emperors all were from the provinces rather than from Rome. Consequently, they continued opening up Roman imperial society by admitting more members of the provincial elites into the Senate and the imperial administration.

The Good Emperors were especially interested in providing their subjects with an honest and efficient administration, as well as a sound imperial financial policy. Hadrian in particular spent most of his time touring the provinces and

Nero was accused of starting the Great Fire of Rome to build his Domus Aurea, or "Golden House." The residence consisted of numerous pavilions set among formally designed landscapes. Most of the land used for the Golden House was heavily populated before it was destroyed by the fire in A.D. **64**. The Golden House required the largest amount of land that any monarch has ever taken to create a personal residence. The Golden House was subsequently abandoned by Nero's successors.

Critical Thinking Ask students to suggest reasons why Nero (if he did start the Great Fire of Rome) would have found it convenient to blame it on Christians.

ANSWER: Students might suggest that the Christians were a growing minority that was unpopular with some Romans, and blaming the fire on them would have given Nero justification for persecuting them further.

inspecting their administrations. The Good Emperors managed to get along reasonably well with the Senate, but they also progressively increased the scope of the emperor's control.

Under the Good Emperors the empire reached the limits of its territorial expansion. Trajan added Dacia (present-day Romania), Armenia, Mesopotamia, and the Sinai Peninsula to the empire. His successor, Hadrian, withdrew from all these additions except Dacia and the Sinai. Hadrian also followed a policy of building defensive fortifications along the empire's frontiers to guard against invasions of the provinces by tribal peoples. In northern Britain, for example, Hadrian built a wall some 73 miles long.

The Good Emperors improved frontier defenses and governmental administration, thus strengthening the empire.

Roman Imperial Civilization

The period from the beginning of Augustus's reign in 27 B.C. until the death of Marcus Aurelius in A.D. 180 is often called the **Pax Romana**—the Roman Peace. Several essential characteristics, such as stable government, law, military organization, and widespread trade and transportation helped the Romans build their empire and maintain its peace. During the Pax Romana only two short periods of civil war disrupted the imperial government.

Government. The Roman government provided the strongest unifying force in the empire. The government maintained order, enforced the laws, and defended the frontiers. By the A.D. 100s the supreme position of the emperor had been well established. Both in the central administration and in the provinces, members of the aristocracy participated in government, but the emperors made all the important decisions.

The Roman Empire was divided into provinces under governors appointed from Rome. Provincial administration was both more efficient and fairer than it had been under the Republic, largely because the government in Rome kept a closer check on the governors than before. Moreover,

▲ The Arch of Caracalla and a forum were built in Algeria by Roman subjects.

any citizen could appeal a governor's decision directly to the emperor.

Through this provincial organization, the empire brought a certain uniformity to the cities of the Mediterranean world. Cities were governed in imitation of Rome, complete with their own local senates and magistrates. Theaters, amphitheaters, public baths, and temples could be seen all over the empire from Britain to Asia Minor. Wealth was concentrated in the hands of the urban elites.

On the other hand, the vast majority of the population in the countryside saw little improvement in their living conditions. Although Roman authorities maintained a level of peace rarely before known, they were unable to eliminate robbery and thievery in the countryside. Traveling outside the main centers of the Roman world remained dangerous and expensive. The only way for most Romans to get away from their villages was to join the army.

Law. Roman law also unified the empire. The Romans distinguished between two legal systems: *ius civilis*, or "civil law," which applied to all citizens, and *ius gentium*, the "law of peoples," which applied to disputes between citizens and noncitizens. Over time, however, these two approaches blended. Eventually, Roman law became a single, universal system—though local customs generally did not disappear. Roman law spread as more people became Roman citizens. In later years the Roman system of law became the foundation for the laws of most of the European countries that had once been part of the empire.

Stability in the Roman legal system was achieved by laws, or statutes, passed by popular assemblies, the Senate, or the emperor. These laws specified exactly what could or could not be done and what the penalties were for breaking the law. In addition, Roman law changed over time. When hearing some cases, magistrates, including provincial governors, took into account new social and economic circumstances that might require a change in the law.

Trade and transportation. Throughout the Pax Romana, agriculture remained the primary occupation of people in the empire. A new type of agricultural worker—the tenant farmer, known as the **colonus**—began to replace slaves on the large estates. Each of these farmers received a small plot of land from the owner. In return the colonus had to remain on the land for a certain period of time and pay the owner with a certain amount of the harvest. Most agricultural activities, however, continued to be performed by independent farmers who first had to feed their families and seldom had surplus to sell.

Meanwhile, manufacturing increased considerably in the empire's cities. In Italy, Gaul, and Spain, artisans made inexpensive pottery and textiles by hand in small shops. The most important manufacturing centers, however, were in the east, where cities such as Damascus and Alexandria manufactured products such as steel and fine glassware.

The Roman Empire also provided enormous opportunities for commerce. The exchange of goods was easy, taxes on trade remained low, and people everywhere used Roman currency. From the provinces, Italy imported grain, meat, and raw

The Height of the Roman Empire, A.D. 117

Trade Across a Vast Empire   When the Roman emperor Trajan died in A.D. 117, the Roman Empire stretched from Britain in the north to Mesopotamia in the east and included all of the lands bordering the Mediterranean Sea.

Linking Geography and History   Which products did the Romans import from Africa? from Britain?

materials such as wool and hides. From Asia, merchants brought silks, linens, glassware, jewelry, and furniture to satisfy the tastes of the wealthy. Rome and Alexandria became the empire's greatest commercial centers. Alexandria was particularly important, since Egypt, along with the rest of North Africa, produced the grain surpluses with which the emperors fed Rome's urban population.

All this commercial activity was possible largely because of two factors: the empire's geographical location around the Mediterranean, and its elaborate and extensive road network. Ultimately there were about 50,000 miles of roads binding the empire together. Most roads, however, were built and maintained for military purposes. Local roads were not paved, and bad weather conditions often made overland travel impossible. It was actually cheaper to transport grain by ship from one end of the Mediterranean to the other than to send it 75 miles overland. Consequently, most goods went by sea.

In the Pax Romana, emperors made all important decisions, Roman law became more universal, and trade and transportation became easier.

Life in the Empire

The Pax Romana provided prosperity to many people, but citizens did not share equally in this wealth. Rich citizens usually had both a city home and a country home that included conveniences such as running water and baths. On the other hand, many of the nearly 1 million residents of Rome lived in crowded three- and four-story apartment buildings. Fire posed a constant threat because of the torches used for light and the charcoal used for cooking. In part to keep poorer citizens from rebelling against such conditions, free food and public entertainment became a major feature of city life in Rome. Juvenal, the Roman satirical poet, once noted that only two things interested the Roman masses—"bread and circuses."

Romans enjoyed the theater, particularly light comedies and satires. Performers such as mimes, jugglers, dancers, acrobats, and clowns also became quite popular. Nothing was more popular, however, than chariot racing. In Rome the races were held in the Circus Maximus, a racetrack that could

▲ This street in Ostia, Italy, would have been bustling with inhabitants during the time of the Pax Romana.

accommodate 250,000 spectators. Roman audiences particularly enjoyed the spectacular crashes that frequently occurred.

Romans also enjoyed bloody spectacles in the amphitheater, where wild animals were brought to battle each other or professional fighters. Often, condemned criminals were thrown into the arena to be torn to pieces by beasts. The most popular entertainment offered in the amphitheaters, however, were gladiatorial combats. Such shows often ended with the death of one or both of the fighters, who were usually slaves. In Rome such spectacles were performed in the Colosseum, which seated some 50,000 people. While the games were in progress the city could seem deserted—leading the Stoic philosopher Seneca to reflect: "Who respects a philosopher or any liberal study except when the games are called off for a time or there is some rainy day which he is willing to waste?"

In Rome people were provided with public entertainment and free food to keep the peace during the Pax Romana.

Science, Engineering, and Architecture

The Romans were less interested in scientific research to increase knowledge than in collecting and organizing information. For example, Galen, a physician who lived in Rome during the A.D. 100s, wrote several volumes that summarized all the medical knowledge of his day. For centuries people regarded him as the greatest authority in medicine. Similarly, people accepted Ptolemy's theory in astronomy—that the earth was the center of the universe—partly because he brought the knowledge and opinions of others together into a single system.

Unlike the Greeks, who were primarily interested in knowledge for its own sake and preferred abstract reasoning to practical scientific research, the Romans were very practical. They tried to apply the knowledge they gained from the Greeks, for example, in planning their cities, building water and sewage systems, and improving farming methods. Roman engineers surpassed all other ancient peoples in their ability to construct roads, bridges, amphitheaters, public buildings, and **aqueducts**—man-made channels used to bring water to the cities. Perhaps the most important engineering contribution by the Romans was the development of concrete, which made such large public structures possible.

Roman architects also designed other great public structures, such as law courts, palaces,

▲ **The top of these Roman aqueducts served as a bridge across the valley.**

temples, amphitheaters, and triumphal arches. Although they often based their buildings on Greek models, the Romans learned to use the arch and the vaulted dome—features that allowed them to construct much larger buildings than the Greeks had done. With such tools and techniques, the Romans emphasized size as well as pleasing proportions in their architecture.

During the Pax Romana, the Romans made new advances in science and engineering, allowing them to build new types of architectural structures.

SECTION 2 REVIEW

IDENTIFY and explain the significance of the following:
 Augustus
 Virgil
 Hadrian
 Good Emperors
 Pax Romana
 colonus
 Galen
 aqueducts

LOCATE and explain the importance of the following:
 Danube River
 Elbe River
 Dacia
 Sinai Peninsula
 Britain

1. **Main Idea** How was the Roman Republic transformed under Augustus and the Good Emperors?
2. **Main Idea** How did government, law, and commerce develop during the Pax Romana?
3. **Science** How did the Romans apply scientific knowledge?
4. **Writing to Describe** Imagine that you are an ordinary citizen living in Rome during the Pax Romana. Write

a description of what a typical day in your life might be like. Also describe the benefits of living in the Roman Empire.
5. **Synthesizing** Create a chart like the one below, showing how the Romans were able to hold their empire together. For each of the following categories, note what improvements were made over time and what impact they had on the empire: imperial power, administration, law, literature, and transportation.

CATEGORY	IMPROVEMENTS OVER TIME	IMPACT ON THE EMPIRE
imperial power		

SECTION 3

CORE LESSON PLAN
See pages 113G and
113H for Lesson Plan
5.3.

SECTION 3
Imperial Crises and the Rise of Christianity

FOCUS

- What problems confronted the empire in the A.D. 200s, and what was one consequence of these problems?
- How did Christianity arise?
- How did Christianity spread around the Mediterranean?

he end of the reign of the Good Emperors showed signs of the troubles to come. Military difficulties began on the Danube frontier, as Germanic tribes pressed against the empire's borders. Plague brought back by the army from the East ravaged the empire. Soon the empire was confronted not only by challenges from outside but also by growing problems within.

Marcus Aurelius

The Crises of the A.D. 200s

When Marcus Aurelius decided on his successor in A.D. 180, he failed to show his usual wisdom and foresight. He chose his weak, spoiled son Commodus (KAHM-uh-duhs). Commodus proved to be a disaster for the empire and was eventually assassinated, plunging the empire into a series of civil wars. During this time, the legions installed and dethroned emperors. According to one historian, after Marcus Aurelius's death the Roman Empire declined from "a kingdom of gold into one of iron and rust."

Threats of invasion. Part of the problem was that Rome found itself under increasing threat of invasion by tribal peoples along both the eastern and western frontiers. To meet this growing threat, emperors increased the size of Rome's army. Soon the growing demands on both the empire's financial resources and its military caused a serious and prolonged economic crisis. This crisis in turn weakened the stability and prosperity of the Pax Romana. In the west, migrating Germanic tribes constantly tested the empire's defenses. After A.D. 226 the eastern borders of the empire were also threatened by a renewed Persian Empire.

As the military crisis continued, eventually the empire became a kind of military dictatorship. The legions had become the center of power in the empire, as they deposed unpopular emperors and elevated their own commanders to the throne. On his deathbed in A.D. 211, the emperor Septimius Severus advised his successor: "Enrich the soldiers and scorn all other men." The advice proved devastating for the stability of imperial government—between A.D. 235 and 284, 20 emperors reigned. All but one died violently.

Economic troubles. The growing insecurity of civil wars and invasions affected many aspects of Roman life. Robbery and piracy increased and travel even within the bounds of the empire became hazardous. Merchants hesitated to send goods by land or by sea. Military needs required ever-increasing amounts of money. In an effort to collect more taxes, the emperor Caracalla granted Roman citizenship to all free people of the empire in A.D. 212. As taxes rose, however, the value of money declined.

◀ **This stone carving shows a Roman merchant ship transporting barrels of wine**.

Since Rome was no longer expanding in territory, military conquests no longer brought in new sources of gold. Instead, gold was actually disappearing from the empire as Romans used it to pay foreign merchants for luxury goods from China and India. To maintain the money supply, emperors minted new coins containing copper and lead as well as silver. When people realized their coins contained less silver, they refused to accept the currency at its face value. The result was growing **inflation**, or a dramatic rise in prices, in the empire.

These economic conditions caused important changes in the social order. The senatorial elite, for example, lost some of its privileges and influence. Emperors filled the Senate with their own followers, particularly men from the army.

Changing beliefs. The destruction of the old imperial order and prosperity generated an important psychological crisis in the Roman Empire. The old civic religion of the empire offered little comfort, however, and in an increasingly hostile world many people took refuge in mysticism or more personal forms of religion.

The A.D. 200s witnessed an increase in belief in Mystery religions. Mithraism, for example, a cult that developed out of Zoroastrianism in Persia, became particularly popular among soldiers in the Roman Empire. It stressed the virtues of fellowship and bravery. Other popular cults were those of Isis, from Egypt, and Cybele, from Asia Minor, which both worshipped mother goddesses. The most important movement that benefited from this environment of spiritual longing, however, was a new religion that had developed out of late Hellenistic Judaism—Christianity.

Invasions and economic problems during the A.D. 200s led many people in the empire to turn to new religions.

🔺 The Rise of Christianity

Unlike most conquered peoples of the Roman Empire, the people living in the kingdom of Judaea had always resisted the mixing of their monotheistic religion with the polytheistic state religion of the empire. In general, Roman emperors were content to allow Jews a great deal of religious freedom as long as they maintained civic order. Judaism, however, had many different branches, with varying ideas of whether they should cooperate with the Roman conquerors. For example, one group—the Zealots (ZE-luhts)—were particularly vocal about overthrowing Roman rule. Others preferred to wait for the coming of the Messiah, a spiritual leader who, according to prophecy, would restore the ancient Kingdom of David.

In A.D. 6, Zealots began to form pockets of armed resistance against the Roman occupation forces. In response to a mass uprising in A.D. 66–70, the Romans sacked Jerusalem and killed thousands of Jews. They also destroyed the Second Temple, leaving only the western wall intact. A Jewish historian recorded the disaster:

❝One of the soldiers . . . snatched up a blazing piece of wood and climbing on another soldier's back hurled the brand through a golden aperture [opening] giving access on the north side to the chambers. . . . As the flames shot into the air the Jews sent up a cry that matched the calamity and dashed to the rescue, with no thought now of saving their lives . . . ; for that which hitherto they had guarded so devotedly was disappearing before their eyes.❞

After the destruction of the Temple, Jewish priests were replaced by **rabbis**, scholars who specialized in interpreting the Scriptures and were learned in religious law. Finally, in A.D. 135 the Romans brutally crushed a revolt led by Simon Bar Kokhba (KAWK-bah), and all Jews were banned from Jerusalem.

Theme:
Religion

From the first century B.C. to the decline of paganism several hundred years later, the cult of Isis had the largest following in Rome. The cult was extremely popular among women, who believed that Isis's power as a woman helped give them greater equality with men. According to the Egyptians, Isis was the daughter of the sky. The cow was Isis's sacred symbol. Legend held that Isis had discovered wheat and barley and showed men how to cultivate it. She eventually came to be regarded as the queen of the whole universe, and her followers believed that she would watch over them in their earthly lives, as well as give them a blessed eternal life.

Critical Thinking Ask students to suggest characteristics the cult of Isis had in common with Christianity that might have given both religions their appeal.

ANSWER: Both religions promised rewards in the afterlife and appealed to people's need for spiritual comfort.

The abbreviations B.C. and A.D. stand for "before Christ" and "Anno Domini," or "in the year of our Lord." The year of Jesus' birth, now determined to be around 6 B.C., was miscalculated by a monk living during the A.D. 500s, and therefore the year A.D. 1 is not considered the actual date of Jesus' birth. The use of the abbreviations became common during the Middle Ages.

Muslims number years from the date that the prophet Muhammad left Mecca (A.D. 622 in the Christian calendar), an event known as the *hijrah*. They use the abbreviation A.H. with dates to stand for "Anno Hegirae," or "in the year of the *hijrah*."

Critical Thinking Ask students why cultures would use the founding date of their religion as the basis for their system of chronology.

ANSWER: Students might suggest that people often see the founding event of their religion as the start of a new era in world history.

Jesus of Nazareth. Against this turbulent background in Judaea, a spiritual leader named Jesus emerged. The message he taught was not one of armed revolt but of the need for people to seek forgiveness for their sins in preparation for the coming of God's Judgment Day.

Our knowledge of Jesus comes almost exclusively from the first four books of the New Testament of the Christian Bible—the Gospels of Matthew, Mark, Luke, and John. According to these Gospels, Jesus was born in Bethlehem, near Jerusalem around 6 B.C., and grew up in the town of Nazareth. Although he apparently learned the carpentry trade, he was also a student of the writings of the Jewish prophets.

In time, Jesus began to preach a message of religious renewal and warning. As he traveled through the villages of Judaea, he gathered a small group of **disciples**, or followers. According to the biblical account, Jesus created a great deal of excitement by performing miracles of healing and by defending the poor and the oppressed in Jewish society. Above all, however, he warned that God was about to judge humanity—people must repent of their sins and seek God's forgiveness.

Jesus laid down two primary rules for his followers: they must love God above all else, and they must love others as they loved themselves. In addition, he emphasized the values of humility and charity. These ideals were perhaps best expressed in the Sermon on the Mount:

> 66 *Blessed are the poor in spirit: for theirs is the kingdom of heaven.*
> *Blessed are those who mourn: for they will be comforted.*
> *Blessed are the meek: for they will inherit the earth.*
> *Blessed are those who hunger and thirst for righteousness: for they will be filled.*
> *Blessed are the merciful: for they will be shown mercy.* 99

Such teachings, and the crowds Jesus apparently drew, alarmed Jewish religious authorities. In addition, Jesus began to attack many Jewish practices openly. Eventually, the leading priests of the Temple decided he was a threat to their authority.

Jesus
BIOGRAPHY

After hearing that he claimed to be the son of God, they condemned him and convinced the Roman authorities in Judaea to put him to death.

According to the Gospels, after being crucified, or nailed to a wooden cross—a common form of Roman execution—and buried, Jesus rose from the dead, spent another 40 days teaching his disciples on Earth, and then ascended into heaven. His followers believed that the Resurrection and Ascension revealed that Jesus was the promised Messiah and the Son of God. They believed that Jesus was God himself come to redeem the sins of humanity before the final Day of Judgment. His followers called him Jesus Christ—after *Christos*, the Greek word for Messiah.

Early Christian doctrine. The Resurrection became the central message of Christianity. The disciples of Jesus began teaching that through Christ's redeeming death, all people could receive salvation—the forgiveness of sins and the promise of everlasting life. Believing that God's judgment was close at hand, the disciples urgently set out to spread this message of salvation.

At first the disciples worked mainly in the Jewish communities of Palestine. They were also

▲ In this painting from the A.D. 200s, Jesus is represented as the Good Shepherd, who watched over his flock, or followers.

The Spread of Christianity, A.D. 300–600

Christianity in the Roman Empire From its beginnings in Judaea, in some 300 years Christianity spread across all of the lands of the Roman Empire and beyond.

❖ **Linking Geography and History** Which Roman cities shown on the map were converted to Christianity after 300?

Map Answer
Athens, Antioch, Tarsus, and Damascus

persecuted by the Jewish authorities, and some were actually killed. With the promise of everlasting life, however, those killed were seen by the early Christians as **martyrs**, people who voluntarily suffer death for the sake of their faith and thus inspire others to believe. As martyrs calmly accepted death, even many nonbelievers were impressed by their faith. Still, had it not been for the work of a Hellenized Jew named Saul, Christianity might have remained a branch of Judaism.

Saul of Tarsus. Saul, who later became known as Paul, was born in the town of Tarsus in Asia Minor. As a young man, he actually worked for the Jewish leadership persecuting Christians. During a trip to Damascus, however, he supposedly had a conversion experience and became a Christian. He convinced the original disciples of Jesus in

Jerusalem that Christ had given him a special mission to convert non-Jews, or **Gentiles**. With this mission in mind, Paul soon transformed Christianity into a universal religion, attracting many new followers. Paul helped establish Christian churches throughout the eastern Mediterranean, and even in Rome itself. His Epistles, or Letters, to these churches later became an important part of the sacred Christian writings of the New Testament. The New Testament together with the Torah and other Jewish Scriptures make up the present-day Christian Bible.

Finding that some regulations of Moses, such as food prohibitions, were hindering missionary work among non-Jews, Paul eventually dispensed with them as requirements for Christians. In place of these regulations, Paul emphasized certain new doctrines that

Sacred TRADITIONS

Paul's Letter to the Romans

The most extensive record of the history of early Christian congregations comes to us from the apostle Paul. Born in the city of Tarsus in Asia Minor, Paul traveled widely throughout the Mediterranean. After he converted to Christianity, Paul visited many cities, spreading the ideas of the new religion. While he was in the city of Corinth in Greece, Paul wrote an open letter to the people of Rome announcing his plans to travel to the city and preach the Word of God. One of his main goals was to deliver the message that all Christians—whether Gentiles or Jews newly converted to Christianity—should live together in harmony. Paul's Letter to the Romans describes some of the most basic principles of the Christian faith:

Let love be genuine; hate what is evil, hold fast to what is good. Love one another with brotherly affection; outdo one another in showing honor. Never flag [grow tired] in zeal, be aglow with the Spirit, serve the Lord. Rejoice in your hope, be patient in tribulation [great trouble], be constant in prayer. Contribute to the needs of saints, practice hospitality.

Bless those who persecute you; bless and do not curse them. Rejoice with those who rejoice, weep with those who weep. Live in harmony with one another; do not be haughty, but associate with the lowly; never be conceited. Repay no one evil for evil, but take thought for what is noble in the sight of all. If possible, so far as it depend upon you, live peaceably with all. Beloved, never avenge yourselves, but leave it to the wrath of God, for it is written, "Vengeance is mine, I will repay, says the Lord." No, "if your enemy is hungry, feed him; if he is thirsty; give him drink; for by so doing you will heap burning coals upon his head." Do not be overcome by evil, but overcome evil with good. . . .

Owe no one anything, except to love one another; for he who loves his neighbor has fulfilled the law. The commandments, "You shall not commit adultery, You shall not kill, You shall not steal, You shall not covet," and any other commandments are summed up in this sentence, "You shall love your neighbor as yourself."

Understanding Sacred Traditions

What is Paul's message to the Christians of Rome?

Saint Paul the Apostle and a fragment of his Letter to the Romans

distinguished Christianity from Judaism. Above all, perhaps, Paul established the doctrine of original sin—the idea that since Adam and Eve had first disobeyed God in the Garden of Eden, all human beings were born sinful. Paul emphasized the uselessness of human beings' attempts to achieve salvation alone; their only hope, he taught, was faith in Jesus.

Through the teachings of Jesus and the work of his disciples, the religion of Christianity emerged.

The Spread of Christianity

The spread of Christianity was partly served by a progressive decline in the appeal of Hellenism. Stressing the intellect and self-reliance, Greco-Roman thought did not provide for the emotional needs of the people. The Christian message of love on Earth and eternal life after death, regardless of social position or wealth, appealed to the poor, the oppressed, and the enslaved. Many were attracted by the sense of community the new religion offered.

The Roman tradition of religious toleration and the climate of peace and stability in the early years of the empire also contributed to the spread of Christianity. Missionaries, for example, benefited from easy communications within the empire. Moreover, during the first two centuries after Jesus' life, official persecution by the Romans was rare, although Christians often were treated with great hostility on the local level. Most emperors were indifferent to the new religion. Christians might become the objects of scapegoating, such as when Nero tried to blame them for burning Rome, but more common was the attitude displayed by the emperor Trajan in a letter to Pliny, the governor of Bithynia and Pontus:

66 They [the Christians] are not to be sought out; or if they are denounced and proved guilty [of refusing to offer sacrifices to the state gods], they are to be punished. . . . But anonymously posted accusations ought to have no place in any prosecution. For this is both a dangerous kind of precedent and out of keeping with [the spirit of] our age. **99**

Some early Christians wanted to keep their religion entirely separate from the ideas of Greek philosophy. Others, however, tried to reconcile the Christian ethical creed with Greek philosophy. In doing so, they developed Jesus' teachings into a **theology**—a formulation of knowledge about the nature of God, God's laws, and God's requirements of human beings. This transformation is often called the Hellenization of Christianity.

The Hellenization of Christianity had two great advantages that contributed to the new faith's ability to spread and adapt to changing circumstances. First, this development made it easier for people believing in the Greek philosophies of Plato and the Stoics to accept Christianity. Second, it allowed Christians to combine the strengths of religious faith and spiritual comfort with the Greek tradition of rational thought. With both strands embedded in it, the new faith could appeal to a vast range of people under many diverse circumstances.

The spread of Christianity was aided by the work of missionaries, a lack of vigorous persecution by the Romans, and a declining belief in Hellenistic philosophy.

SECTION 3 REVIEW

IDENTIFY and explain the significance of the following:
   inflation
   rabbis
   Simon Bar Kokhba
   Jesus of Nazareth
   disciples
   martyrs
   Saul of Tarsus
   Gentiles
   theology

LOCATE and explain the importance of the following:

Kingdom of Judaea
Jerusalem
Nazareth

1. **Main Idea** What crises faced the empire following the reign of the Good Emperors? What was the result?
2. **Main Idea** What factors contributed to the successful spread of Christianity?
3. **Religion** Why were people in the empire looking to different religions for comfort during the A.D. 200s?
4. **Writing to Explain** Imagine that you have been sent to Judaea by the emperor to find out information about Jesus. Write a report explaining Jesus' message and why it is so popular.
5. **Analyzing** What effect might the political situation in Judaea have had on the early growth of Christianity?

CORE LESSON PLAN
See pages 113I and 113J for Lesson Plan 5.4.

The Later Roman Empire

Theme:
Economic Organization

To support his military, Diocletian had to ensure that he received the maximum in taxes that his subjects could pay. He tried, however, to divide the financial responsibility fairly. For example, he fixed prices on goods to prevent price hikes. He also determined a maximum wage for all workers. His efforts to achieve a stable economy ultimately failed because he had no means of enforcing these decisions.

Critical Thinking Ask students what advantages the U.S. government today has over Diocletian in efforts to control the economy.

ANSWER: Students might suggest that the U.S. government has a much more efficient structure for enforcing policy, such as collecting taxes and controlling prices.

FOCUS

- In what ways did Diocletian try to save the empire?
- How did Christianity change after it became the state religion of Rome?
- Why did the Roman Empire finally collapse?

The crises of the A.D. 200s shattered the Roman world. Drastic reforms had to be made if the empire were to survive. This was the goal of the emperor Diocletian, who assumed the imperial throne in A.D. 284. Diocletian succeeded in giving the empire another two centuries of life, but in the process he completely transformed it. However, by the late A.D. 400s the western part of the empire collapsed under the pressure of foreign invasions.

Diocletian's palace

The Diocletian Reforms

In an effort to stem the flood that was steadily weakening the empire's foundations, in the late A.D. 200s and early 300s the emperor Diocletian changed the Principate into an absolute monarchy. Diocletian placed himself far above his subjects and ruled with no accountability to anyone.

Social and economic changes. Diocletian's reforms transformed Roman imperial society into a bureaucratic and rigid order. Almost every aspect of life was regulated by the imperial administration. Individual freedom became a privilege of the past. Under Diocletian's decrees, sons had to follow the trades and social positions of their fathers. Peasants were permanently tied to the land they farmed. Diocletian also made provinces smaller for better administrative control, and grouped them together under the control of four governors called **prefects**. He increased the army to 500,000 soldiers, and gave the defense of the empire his full attention.

The imperial economy also came under state direction. Everywhere, commercial and manufacturing activities were geared toward the needs of imperial defense. A new tax system raised more money for the new administration and for the army. Initially these drastic reforms were successful. Diocletian did save the empire from collapse, but the price was enormous, particularly in the loss of individual freedom.

Political reforms. As part of his efforts to improve the efficiency of imperial administration, Diocletian divided the empire in two. Ruling the eastern half himself, he appointed a co-emperor to rule the western provinces. Both emperors named assistants, called caesars, who were supposed to help administer the empire and eventually succeed peacefully to the throne in their turn. As long as Diocletian remained emperor, these arrangements worked reasonably well. However, in A.D. 305 Diocletian decided to retire. His co-emperor also retired so that the two caesars could rise to become co-emperors at the same time. It was not long before the two new emperors quarreled, and the empire plunged into civil war. Not until A.D. 312 did Constantine, the son of one of the original caesars, emerge victorious and restore peace.

◄ According to his testimony, as he charged into battle, Constantine saw a vision of a cross in the sky.

Constantine continued Diocletian's policies of rigid state control over society. At the same time, he also made two decisions that would profoundly affect the direction of the future empire. First, he converted to Christianity. Second, he established a second capital, Constantinople, or "the city of Constantine," on the site of the tiny village of Byzantium on the western shore of the Bosporus, the strait separating Europe from Asia.

Attempting to save the empire, Diocletian reformed Roman society and government and concentrated on defense.

The Triumph of Christianity

The conversion of Constantine to Christianity was apparently triggered by a vision that he claimed to have experienced just before the last battle of the civil wars in A.D. 312. Before the battle the emperor saw a cross of light in the sky inscribed with the words "In this sign, conquer." After winning the battle, Constantine decided to become a Christian. In A.D. 313 he issued the **Edict of Milan**, making Christianity legal within the empire. Although he did not go so far as to make Christianity the official state religion, with Constantine's support the new religion began to flourish throughout the empire.

From a tiny religious minority, Christians soon grew to constitute a majority of the population. In A.D. 391 the emperor Theodosius the Great outlawed all religious worship in the empire except Christianity. Paganism (as Christians called all polytheistic religions), which had once held sway

throughout the Greco-Roman world, eventually disappeared from the empire.

Development of the church. Early Christian congregations not only had been spiritual organizations but also had acted as close-knit families. These congregations provided all kinds of support for their members, from nursing and burial services to food and shelter for the poor. Part of the church's early success came from the development of special ceremonies and rituals designed to inspire people's faith and make them feel closer to Christ.

Those who organized and performed the special ceremonies gradually became a special class within Christianity. Called priests, they derived their authority from the apostles, or disciples of Jesus, who had passed on the authority given them by Christ himself to their own followers. Those Christians who were part of this **apostolic succession** were soon distinguished from the laity, or general congregation of the church. To maintain this distinction, many believed that priests should devote themselves solely to God and remain unmarried.

Over time, distinctions also appeared within the priesthood. As the church expanded, it too began to develop an administrative structure. Soon a single priestly official, called a **bishop**, emerged to oversee church affairs in most cities. Bishops had authority over all other priests within the region. In the empire's large cities, bishops called themselves metropolitans and claimed jurisdiction over the clergy in entire provinces. By the A.D. 300s the heads of the oldest and largest Christian congregations in Rome, Jerusalem, Antioch, Alexandria, and Constantinople were called **patriarchs**, and

Theme: **Politics and Law**

The Christian Church prospered under Roman law after Constantine's conversion. The clergy began to receive benefits and exemptions, and the government provided funding for new churches.

Later, the Roman government became even more involved with the Christian Church. In an imperial edict issued under Theodosius, Gratian, and Valentinian II, the teachings of Christianity were officially defined in Roman law: "It is our will that all the peoples whom the government of our Clemency rules shall follow the religion [Christianity] . . . [Those who do not follow it] we require, since they are insane and raving, to bear the infamy of heretical teaching; their gatherings shall not receive the name of churches; they are to be smitten first with the divine punishment, and after with the vengeance of our indignation, which has the divine approval."

Critical Thinking Ask students what this imperial edict might have meant for citizens of the Roman Empire who practiced religions other than Christianity.

ANSWER: Students should note that other religions were in effect outlawed and were persecuted until they eventually disappeared from the empire.

Saint Peter came to Rome around A.D. 55. He was head of the local church and was later crucified under Nero as a martyr. The Vatican hill, the location of the pope's residence, is considered the site of Peter's martyrdom. The emperor Constantine erected a church at Peter's supposed burial site, and when this church fell into disrepair, Saint Peter's Church, the main shrine of Europe, was built on the same spot. One of the divisive questions of Christianity is that of the Petrine supremacy. The Eastern Orthodox Church supports the belief that the position of the pope in Rome is a position of honor, rather than one of authority over all Catholic churches. Roman Catholics, however, believe in the Petrine supremacy.

Critical Thinking Ask students to suggest reasons why Christians in the Western Roman Empire might have accepted the pope's authority, while Christians in the Eastern Roman Empire did not.

ANSWER: Students might suggest that Christians in the Western Roman Empire might have been more likely to look to Rome as their center of authority since it was still their political capital, while Rome was no longer the capital of the Eastern Roman Empire.

claimed authority over the metropolitans. Primarily administrators, these bishops, metropolitans, and patriarchs also led in the development of Christian doctrine.

At first, questions concerning correct doctrine and church organization were handled by general councils, with representatives from all the major churches in attendance. Councils continued to be an important part of the church government, but the position of the bishops of Rome and of Constantinople, as the leading churchmen in the imperial capitals, also became increasingly influential.

Most Christians accepted the idea that Saint Peter the Apostle had founded the Roman Church and acted as its first bishop. As a result, later bishops of Rome were seen as Peter's spiritual heirs. The bishops of Rome interpreted a verse from the Gospel of Matthew, in which Christ apparently gave Peter "the keys of the kingdom of heaven," to mean that all future Roman bishops would also inherit the keys—a doctrine known as the Petrine theory. In A.D. 444 the emperor Valentinian III decreed that all bishops should acknowledge the authority of the bishop of Rome, or **pope**, as he was now being called, after the Latin word for father.

The problem of heresy. Heresy—or beliefs that did not agree with those of the majority of Christians—seriously threatened to destroy the unity of Christianity in its early years of imperial support. In A.D. 325 Emperor Constantine summoned the first Council of Nicaea to settle the so-called Arian heresy, in which a priest named Arius believed that Jesus and God could not be the same being, since Jesus was God's son. After condemning Arius and his followers for this belief, the council was to establish a uniform doctrine for all of Christianity. The council affirmed the concept of the Holy Trinity—that God the Father, God the Son, and God the Holy Spirit were three separate persons and at the same time one God.

Saint Augustine. One of the greatest opponents of heresy and paganism was Saint Augustine. Born in A.D. 354 in the Carthaginian village of Tagaste, Augustine was well educated in his youth. He showed a natural talent in rhetoric and soon put his talent to work, ultimately traveling to Milan in Italy to teach

▲ Saint Augustine's studies and writings have influenced church leaders for centuries.

political oratory. Until his arrival in Milan, Augustine had been a pagan, but contact with Christians in Italy convinced him to convert. In his *Confessions*, Augustine thanked God for showing him the error of his pagan ways:

❝*But you, O Lord, abide forever, and you are not angry with us forever since you are merciful to dust and ashes, and it was pleasing in your sight to reform my deformity. And you kept stirring me with your secret good to make me restless until you should become clear to the gaze of my soul. Through the secret hand of your healing . . . the troubled and darkened sight of my mind gained strength by the stinging ointment of wholesome sorrow.*❞

Returning to North Africa, Augustine settled in the town of Hippo to study the Holy Scripture. There he quickly developed a reputation as a devout Christian and was soon elected bishop.

Augustine devoted much of his time to defending the doctrines of Christianity. He argued that no one group of Christians was more important than any other. Only through faith, he taught, could Christians gain salvation. He also taught that Christians belonged to a much more important community than that of imperial Rome—the community of Christ and his church.

Shortly after Rome fell to invaders in the early A.D. 400s, Augustine published his beliefs in a book called *The City of God*. Rome might fall, he argued, but this mattered little since the Kingdom of Heaven was eternal.

Monasticism

As the church became increasingly involved in the daily affairs of people's lives, many worried that it was losing sight of Christ's original message. To recapture the humble spirit they believed Jesus had wanted, individuals sometimes turned to **monasticism**, becoming monks and living solitary lives of religious devotion and self-denial.

During the A.D. 300s monasticism spread rapidly throughout the church, especially in the east, where the idea first emerged. Monks became known for their religious devotion and faith. Many experienced a direct and personal sense of communication with God. One monk left the following account:

❝ *Often He [God] showed me the hosts of angels that stand before Him; often I have beheld the glorious company of the righteous, the martyrs, and the monks—such as had no purpose but to honor and praise God in singleness of heart.* ❞

Some monks went to extreme lengths to practice their devotion to God. Saint Simeon Stylites, for example, lived on a platform atop a tall pole for 30 years, while people gathered below to worship in the presence of such a religious man. As monasticism reached new heights of self-torture, however, some church leaders, such as Saint Basil, decided that a community approach to devotion would be more productive. Basil developed plans and rules for monastic communities that would replace the individualism of the early monks. Instead of self-denial, Basil

▲ **In this early Christian artwork found in Rome, Christ appears to be the source of sunlight.**

suggested that hard work, prayer, and contemplation would better serve the needs of both the individual and the Lord.

After Christianity became the official religion of Rome, the church developed a hierarchy of authority and faced internal disputes over doctrine and methods of worship.

The End of the Roman Empire

The institution of Christianity as the state religion did not solve the overwhelming problems of the empire. During the A.D. 300s and 400s, these problems were primarily caused by increasing pressures on the frontiers from invading tribal peoples. For centuries Germanic-speaking tribes had lived along the frontiers, occasionally raiding the wealthier civilization of Rome. As new peoples began to move west from Central Asia, however, they pushed these Germanic tribes into the empire.

The Huns. In the late A.D. 300s a new nomadic Central Asian people, the Huns, stormed out of the east and sent the Germanic tribes fleeing. Imperial defenses in the east managed to hold, but those in the west were soon overwhelmed. A fierce nomadic people, the Huns lived by looting and plundering. They struck terror in the people they attacked. A Germanic historian later described the Huns' appearance:

❝ *By the terror of their features they inspired great fear. . . . They had . . . a sort of shapeless lump, not a head, with pin-holes rather than eyes. . . . They are beings who are cruel to their children on the very day they are born. For they cut the cheeks of the males with a sword, so that . . . they must learn to endure wounds.* ❞

Invasions into the Roman Empire, A.D. 340–481

The Chaos of Invasion Invaders' attacks from every direction struck the final blow in the collapse of the Roman Empire.

❓ **Linking Geography and History** Which tribe originated in the northern Black Sea region?

Under strong leadership, the Huns formed a vast empire among the nomadic steppe peoples of Eurasia. Around A.D. 370 they attacked the Ostrogoths, a Germanic people living north of the Black Sea. This assault frightened the Visigoths, kinsmen of the Ostrogoths, and sent them fleeing into the territories of the Roman Empire. It was not just fear of the Huns that drove peoples into the empire, however—like the Huns, the Germans found Roman wealth inviting. In A.D. 402 the Visigoths moved into Italy. Thus, in A.D. 410 the Visigothic king Alaric captured and sacked Rome itself.

Eventually, the Huns made their headquarters in the plains of Hungary. From there they demanded that Rome pay tribute to prevent the Huns from attacking and sacking the empire's cities.

In the face of such challenges, rulers in both Rome and Constantinople tried desperately to hold the crumbling Roman Empire together. One such ruler was the empress Galla Placidia of Rome. Galla Placidia was born around A.D. 388, the daughter of the emperor Theodosius.

At the age of 15, she began to rule as regent for her brother, Honorius, in the Western Empire. Her life, however, was not to be an easy one. In A.D. 410 Alaric swept into Italy and captured Rome. He took Placidia prisoner and carried her back to Gaul. In A.D. 414 she was forced to marry Ataulf, Alaric's successor. After Ataulf

▲ **The burial place of Galla Placidia in Ravenna, Italy, built in A.D. 426**

Then & NOW

The Many Legacies of Rome

After the Western Roman Empire fell in A.D. 476, much of what was Rome continued to exist. We can still see many of the legacies of the great empire today.

Language

One example is in the Romance (from *Roman*) languages, all of which developed from Latin. Every person speaking French, Italian, Spanish, Romanian, or Portuguese is speaking a language that has its roots in the language of Rome. Although English developed from Germanic languages, it owes much of its vocabulary to borrowings from Latin—a result of England's close contact with the French during the Norman period, beginning in 1066. Examples of words of direct Latin origin in English are *et cetera*, *veto*, and *curriculum*. Many words show the influence of Latin when the prefixes *pri-* and *pro-* or the suffixes *-tion* and *-ment* are added to them.

Art and Architecture

Roman legacies in art and architecture are also strong. Many examples of Roman architecture can still be seen throughout the countrysides of southern Europe, North Africa, and Southwest Asia. The dominant Roman architectural advances, the round arch and the vault, have been used for many centuries and are still seen in the architecture of many countries. Roman bridges still span French, German, and Spanish rivers, and roads that connected Rome with its provinces still survive today. In each city they conquered, the Romans added their own urban plan—a grid system of roads, temples, baths, theaters, and a central forum. Many cities developed by the Romans owe their layouts to Roman engineers.

The ruins of Roman buildings, often based on Greek models, inspired generations of architects. Michelangelo used Roman models to design Saint Peter's Basilica in Rome in 1547. Thomas Jefferson studied Roman architecture when he built his home, Monticello, in 1770. Many other examples of Roman architecture abound throughout modern Europe and North America.

Literature and Drama

Modern literature and drama also owe a great debt to Roman traditions. In drama both comedy and tragedy have come through Roman theater, and in literature the technique of satire was derived from Roman authors. *Satura*, the word from which we get "satire," means mocking and witty criticism.

Law

Roman law left its imprint on the world, too. Roman laws were adopted by many countries in Europe after the empire fell. Centuries later, those nations carried their systems of law to their colonies in Asia, Africa, and the Americas. Thus, although it has been greatly modified through time, the Roman influence can be seen in the legal systems of most countries of the world. For example, the English system became the model for the English-speaking part of North America, as well as most former British colonies in Africa, southern Asia, Australia, and New Zealand. France's Napoleonic Code, also based on Roman law, governed the French province of Louisiana, along with many French colonies in Africa and Asia.

This Roman bridge in Córdoba, Spain, is still used today.

REVIEW & ASSESSMENT RESOURCES

- Study Guide 5.4
- Daily Quiz 5.4
- Main Idea Activity 5.4

All Levels

SECTION 4 REVIEW ANSWERS
(p. 142)

IDENTIFY

For significance, see the following pages:
Diocletian (p. 136)
prefects (p. 136)
Constantine (p. 136)
Edict of Milan (p. 137)
Theodosius the Great (p. 137)
apostolic succession (p. 137)
bishop (p. 137)
patriarchs (p. 137)
pope (p. 138)
Saint Augustine (p. 138)
monasticism (p. 139)
Galla Placidia (p. 140)
Attila (p. 142)

LOCATE

For locations, see the map on p. 140.

1. He reformed the government, regulated people's personal lives, increased the army, and divided the empire in two.
2. The church developed an administrative hierarchy and had to answer questions about uniform doctrine and methods of worship.
3. Their attacks on the Ostrogoths frightened the Visigoths, who fled into the Roman Empire. Also attracted to Rome's wealth, the Visigoths moved into Italy and eventually sacked Rome.
4. While Rome may have lost control over the region, its civilization still existed. Legacies of Roman art, architecture, language, and law remain and influence much of modern society.
5. During the A.D. 300s and 400s Christianity spread and became the official religion. Rigid reforms limiting personal freedom restructured society. The empire itself was divided and was racked by invasion and internal strife.

CHAPTER 5 REVIEW ANSWERS
(p. 143)

WRITING A SUMMARY
See essential points in the text.

REVIEWING TERMS
1. monasticism
2. tribunes
3. colonus
4. bishop
5. consuls

REVIEWING CHRONOLOGY
4, 2, 5, 1, 3

was murdered, the Visigoths treated Placidia harshly. Finally, in A.D. 416 they allowed her to return to her brother in Rome.

The next year Placidia married Constantius, a prominent general, who became co-emperor with Honorius in A.D. 421. When Constantius died shortly thereafter, Placidia began to quarrel with her brother and eventually fled to the court of Theodosius II in Constantinople. After Honorius's death, Theodosius placed Placidia's young son, Valentinian, on the throne, and Placidia governed as regent. Placidia exercised enormous influence over the affairs of the empire until her death in A.D. 450. She is often remembered as a great patron of the arts. But Placidia, like her predecessors, was unable to stop the waves of invasion.

Final invasions in the west. Pushed by the Huns, other migrating tribes also soon attacked the Roman Empire. The Vandals crossed into North Africa, from which they attacked Rome in the A.D. 450s. The Vandals were so infamous for destroying everything in their path, that the term *vandal* came to mean one who causes senseless destruction.

In the mid-A.D. 400s Attila (AT-uhl-uh), the leader of the Huns, led an attack on Gaul. The Roman army could not repel him alone, so they allied with the Visigoths and defeated the Huns in a great battle at Châlons (shah-LOHN) in A.D. 451. Withdrawing from Gaul, Attila turned on Rome itself. Just as the Huns marched on the city, however, Rome was struck with an outbreak

▲ The Roman cavalry struggles against an attack by an invading tribe in the first century A.D.

of disease. Meeting Attila before the city gates, Pope Leo I warned the Hun leader of the epidemic and persuaded him not to sack the city. Since Attila's own forces were also tired and suffering from sickness, he withdrew. The event was later used to enhance the influence of the popes.

Despite the Huns' withdrawal, in their wake the Western Empire lay in a shambles. Germanic tribes controlled most of the western provinces, including Italy itself. Finally, in A.D. 476 the Ostrogothic commander Odoacer (oh-doh-AY-suhr) overthrew Romulus Augustulus, the last emperor in the west. Although Odoacer obtained recognition from the remaining emperor in Constantinople, he had effectively put an end to the Western Roman Empire.

Constant pressure from Germanic tribes ultimately led to the fall of Rome.

SECTION 4 REVIEW

IDENTIFY and explain the significance of the following:
  Diocletian
  prefects
  Constantine
  Edict of Milan
  Theodosius the Great
  apostolic succession
  bishop
  patriarchs
  pope
  Saint Augustine
  monasticism

Galla Placidia
Attila

LOCATE and explain the importance of the following:
  Constantinople
  Bosporus

1. **Main Idea** What reforms did Diocletian make?
2. **Main Idea** How did Christianity change in the later Roman Empire?

3. **Geography: Movement** How did the westward expansion of the Huns affect events in Italy?
4. **Writing to Explain** Write a paragraph explaining the limitations of the following statement: *Roman civilization came to an end in A.D. 476.*
5. **Synthesizing** How was the Roman Empire of the A.D. 300s and 400s different from the earlier empire?

Review

On a separate sheet of paper, complete the following exercises:

WRITING A SUMMARY

Using the essential points in the text, write a brief summary of the chapter.

REVIEWING TERMS

From the following list, choose the term that correctly matches the definition.

tribunes   colonus
monasticism   bishop
disciples   consuls

1. pursuit of a life of religious devotion and contemplation
2. Roman public officials elected to protect the interests of the plebeians
3. Roman farmer who worked the land and paid rent to a wealthy landowner
4. church official who oversaw the members of the clergy in a particular city in the empire
5. two top Roman republican officials who ran the government

REVIEWING CHRONOLOGY

List the following events in their correct chronological order.

1. The Council of Nicaea establishes the idea of the Holy Trinity as part of official Christian doctrine.
2. Octavian defeats Marc Antony and Cleopatra at the Battle of Actium.
3. Tribal peoples overthrow the last Roman emperor in the West.
4. Tiberius Gracchus is killed in Rome by a mob.
5. Roman soldiers destroy the Second Temple in Jerusalem, crushing the Jewish revolt.

UNDERSTANDING THE MAIN IDEA

1. How did Christianity change in the A.D. 300s and 400s?
2. What crises did the Roman Empire face in the A.D. 200s and what was the result?
3. How did Augustus transform the Roman Republic into the empire?
4. How did the conquests affect the Roman Empire?
5. What factors contributed to the spread of Christianity in the Mediterranean world?

THINKING CRITICALLY

1. *Identifying Cause and Effect* Why might a person argue that most of the problems of the Roman Empire stemmed from the continuing need to defend its borders?
2. *Analyzing* Why might Roman emperors have been eager to stamp out heresy after Christianity became the state religion?

Building Your Portfolio

Complete the following activities individually or in groups.

1. *Culture* As you have read, Roman civilization has had an enormous influence on the cultural development of the West. Create a poster showing some of the many legacies of Rome that still exist today, such as buildings, institutions, language, art, or literature. Look at the special feature "The Many Legacies of Rome," on p. 141 for some ideas. On your poster or on a separate sheet of paper, write brief descriptions of the items you have pictured and describe their importance.
2. *Religion* Imagine that you (and your coworkers) are early organizers of the Christian faith. Create a flyer to attract people to hear a Christian sermon, perhaps given by Saul of Tarsus. You should try to convey Jesus' message as well as give some reasons why people might want to convert to Christianity. In doing so you should consider the current situation in the empire. You will also need to make your flyer as eye-catching as possible, since you will need to attract people's attention before they will read the information.

UNDERSTANDING THE MAIN IDEA

1. The church developed an administrative hierarchy and had to answer questions about doctrine and methods of worship.
2. Civil wars and the threat of invasion led many to turn to new religions.
3. He established himself as first citizen, or princeps, in charge of his government, the Principate. He divided the power to rule between himself and the Senate. He eventually controlled all financial and administrative matters.
4. The empire was putting strains on Roman society and traditional values. Growing tensions between the plebeians and the elite, internal warfare, and the restructuring of the army for personal gain led to the decline of the Republic.
5. Factors included the decline of Hellenistic thought, toleration by Roman officials, the early empire's stability, the work of missionaries, and the Hellenization of Christianity.

THINKING CRITICALLY

1. In the A.D. 200s Rome's borders were threatened, and leaders bulked up the army, creating a military dictatorship that weakened the government and led to further problems. In the A.D. 300s, further invasions eventually destroyed the empire in the west.
2. The leaders had imposed a very rigid system of control during this period in an attempt to salvage the empire. They did not want anything, such as religious dissension, to threaten stability.

The Growth of Asian Civilizations 700 B.C.–A.D. 550

Chapter Planning Guide

	TEXTBOOK	CORE RESOURCES	VISUAL RESOURCES	MULTIMEDIA
Introduction	pp. 144–145	Block Scheduling Handbook: Ch. 6		Videodisc Segment 6 and Viewing Guide: *Confucius, Laozi, and the Buddha*
Lesson 6.1 Indian Society and Religion	pp. 146–151 Sacred Traditions: *The Bhagavad Gita,* p. 148 History Through the Arts: *Siva,* p. 150	Reading 6.1: *Nobility and Virtue in the* Ramayana Writing Project 6: *Determining Relevance*	Everyday Life 6: *Ganesha, Hindu Deity*	GHRC 6 Readings: *The Five Great Vows of Jainism; The Life of Mahavira; Buddha on the Equality of All People; Buddha's First Sermon* GHRC 6/Videodisc: Images—*Hindu Gods at War; Hindu Temple; Map—Centers of Jainism Today; Audio Clip—Tibetan Buddhist Chanting*
Lesson 6.2 The Beginnings of Imperial India	pp. 152–157 Map: *Mauryan Empire,* p. 153 Map: *Gupta Empire,* p. 156	Reading 6.2: *Asoka's Edicts*		GHRC 6 Readings: *A Hindu View of Life and Death; Hindu Religious Beliefs; The Hindu Law of Karma* GHRC 6/Videodisc Images—*Hindu Gods at War; Hindu Temple*
Lesson 6.3 The Beginnings of Classical China	pp. 158–161	Reading 6.3: *The Wisdom of Confucius* Geography Activity 6: *Political Turmoil in China* Skills Activity 6: *Analyzing a Primary Source*	Geography and History 6: *The Rise of Buddhism and Daoism*	GHRC 6 Readings: *The Moral Teachings of Confucius; The Five Great Relationships of Confucianism; Wisdom of the Dao Da Jing; Daoism Versus Confucianism* GHRC 6/Videodisc: Images—*Confucius; Laozi; Laozi Meets Confucius; Map—Early Confucianism*
Lesson 6.4 Imperial China	pp. 162–170 Map: *Qin and Han Dynasties,* p. 164 Geography and History: *The Silk Road,* pp. 166–167 Then and Now: *Acupuncture,* p. 169	Reading 6.4: *Pan Ku's History*	Art and History 6: *Han Dynasty Court Scene* Geography and History 6: *The Rise of Buddhism and Daoism*	GHRC 6/Videodisc: Image—*Daoist Art:* Map—*The Spread of Buddhism;* Video Clip—*The Amazing Tomb of China's "First Emperor"*
Chapter Investigation and Enrichment	pp. 144–170	Chapter 6 Investigation: *The All-Asian Conference on Religion and Philosophy* People in World History Explorations in Daily Life		Global History Resource Center 6/Videodisc
Review and Assessment	Section 1 Review, p. 151 Section 2 Review, p. 157 Section 3 Review, p. 161 Section 4 Review, p. 170 Chapter 6 Review, p. 171	Chapter Review Activity 6 Vocabulary Activity 6 Themes Review 6 Section Study Guides 6.1–6.4 Main Idea Activities 6.1–6.4 Daily Quizzes 6.1–6.4 Ch. 6 Test Sheltered English Ch. 6 Test Ch. 6 Test Generator		Audio CDs: Ch. 6 Summary (English and Spanish)

INTRODUCING THE CHAPTER

Textbook pp. 144–145

CHAPTER OVERVIEW

Important civilizations developed in India and in China. In India religion exerted a profound influence on society, and a strict class structure developed. However, India did not have a strong centralized government until the rise of the Mauryan Empire. While competing warlords engulfed China in conflict, philosophers such as Confucius developed new ideas concerning society and government. The triumph of the Qin dynasty marked the beginning of imperial China.

PRESENTING THEMES

On the chalkboard or on an overhead transparency, write the following open-ended theme questions.

- **SOCIAL RELATIONS** How might a society's religion influence the relations between different groups of people?
- **POLITICS AND LAW** What factors might help hold a large empire together?
- **RELIGION** How do religious beliefs develop to satisfy the spiritual needs of a culturally diverse people?

Have students, either individually or in groups, suggest responses to the questions. For the social relations question, students might suggest that religion can determine how people of different social classes treat one another. For the politics and law question, students might suggest that universal laws and shared religious practices might unify the people of a large empire. For the religion question, students might suggest that the religious beliefs of a culturally diverse people might draw on features of each group's values and thus serve to unify the groups. Save the responses. Once students have studied the chapter, you may wish to have them complete the Themes Review, then compare the two sets of answers.

USING THE VIDEO

Segment 6: *Confucius, Laozi, and the Buddha*

ENGLISH

Search Chapter 6
Videodisc 1, Side A

SPANISH

Search Chapter 6
Videodisc 1, Side A

Tell students that in this chapter they will examine the civilizations and religious traditions that grew up in India and China more than 2,000 years ago. Then show Segment 6 of the *World History and Cultures Videodiscs*. This segment suggests that Chinese culture is rooted in the ideas of three great religious teachers—Confucius, Laozi, and the Buddha.

Before showing the video, ask students to look for familiar symbols that reveal the continuing vitality of ancient Asian religious traditions. To help students grasp the significant points of the video, have them complete Video Viewing Guide 6.

Key to Ability Levels

All strategies and activities are coded to the following ability levels:

LEVEL 1	**Basic** activities suitable for all students
LEVEL 2	**Average** activities suitable for average to above-average students
LEVEL 3	**Challenging** activities suitable for above-average students
SHELTERED ENGLISH	Activities suitable for students with **Limited English Proficiency**.

Additional Resources

BOOKS FOR TEACHERS

Craven, Roy C. *Indian Art: A Concise History*. Thames and Hudson, 1991. Surveys Indian art.

Franck, Irene M. and David M. Brownstone. *The Silk Road: A History*. Facts On File, 1986. Presents a complete history of the Silk Road.

Murowchick, Robert E., ed. *China: Ancient Culture, Modern Land*. University of Oklahoma Press, 1994. Presents a well-illustrated survey.

BOOKS FOR STUDENTS

Bhargava, D.C. *Founders of India's Civilization*. Asian Humanities Press, 1992. Presents short profiles.

Cotterell, Arthur. *China: A Cultural History*. New American Library, 1990. Offers a survey.

Sheng-Hen. *China's Buried Kingdoms*. Time-Life, 1992. Looks at the ancient cultures of China.

MULTIMEDIA MATERIALS

China: The Mandate of Heaven. Ambrose. Video, 57 min. Looks at the religion and arts of China.

India: The Empire of Spirit. Ambrose. Video, 57 min. Examines over 5,000 years of tradition.

The World Religions: 600 B.C.–A.D. 500. Network Television Productions. Video, 26 min. Includes Hinduism and Buddhism.

143B

Lesson 6.1   *Indian Society and Religion*

Textbook pp. 146–151

RESOURCES

Pupil's Edition

Sacred Traditions, p. 148: *The Bhagavad Gita*

History Through the Arts, p. 150: *Siva*

Core Resources

Reading 6.1: *Nobility and Virtue in the Ramayana*

Visual Resources

Everyday Life 6: *Ganesha, Hindu Deity*

Global History Resource Center

Reading: *The Five Great Vows of Jainism*

Reading: *The Life of Mahavira, Founder of Jainism*

Reading: *Buddha on the Equality of All People*

Reading: *Buddha's First Sermon*

Videodiscs or Global History Resource Center

Image: *Hindu Gods at War*

Search Frame 744

Image: *Hindu Temple*

Search Frame 746

Map: *Centers of Jainism Today*

Search Frame 754

Audio Clip: *Tibetan Buddhist Chanting*

Search 5034, Play to 5543
Videodisc 1, Side A
Audio Clip 6

LESSON FOCUS

What are the religious and philosophical foundations of Indian life?

OBJECTIVES

After completing this lesson, students will be able to:
- explain the purpose of the epics;
- identify the basic beliefs of Hinduism;
- describe how and why Jainism and Buddhism developed.

HOOK: Link to Today

Discuss caste. Ask students about social divisions in American society today. Then ask how they compare with the caste system of India. Students should understand that the caste system is more structured and rigid than the class system in the

United States and allows for less social mobility.

Ask: **What were the four main groupings in early Indian society?**
[Brahmans, Kshatriyas, Vaisyas, and Sudras were the four main groupings.]

Ask: **How did the caste system evolve?**
[Students should note that the Brahmans replaced the Kshatriyas as the leading group; development of a new group, the untouchables; the subdivision of castes into jati.]

DEVELOP

Examine Hinduism. Point out to students that the Brahmins—who were both the priests and at the top of the caste system—became the most influential group but that some began to question their authority.

Ask: How did this questioning influence Vedic religion?

> [It gave rise to the Vedanta school of thought that sought a more personal religion; Vedanta ideas—including the idea of people's oneness with a single universal being, or Brahma—were expressed in the Upanishads.]

If available, display the electronic media image of the Hindu gods at war, which shows Khrisna in combat.

Ask: What role did the epics play in the development of Hinduism?

> [Ordinary Indians found spiritual comfort in the epics, especially the Mahabharata and the Ramayana; the Bhagavad Gita, part of the Ramayana, taught that salvation was available to all.]

To add to students' understanding of Hinduism, have them read and discuss the Sacred Traditions feature, the History Through the Arts feature, the Core Resources reading, and the three Global History Resource Center readings on Hinduism.

Next create a chart on the board with two columns. Label one *Origins* and one *Concepts*. Add a row labeled *Hinduism*. Have students fill out the chart using information from the textbook. [Students should note that the origins of Hinduism lay in Aryan and pre-Aryan religion and in written materials such as the Vedas, the Upanishads, and the epics. Concepts included the idea of many gods that are—along with living beings— representations of a single universal being, Brahma, and belief in reincarnation, karma, and dharma.]

Ask: How are reincarnation, dharma, and karma related?

> [Dharma—one's moral duty—depends on the position in life one is born into; each cycle of reincarnation is determined by karma—the moral consequences of actions during one's lifetime.]

PROBE

Describe Jainism and Buddhism. Ask students why some Indians objected to Vedic religion. [Many Indians wanted a more personal connection with the gods. Some were unhappy with the religious power of the Brahmins.] Mention that rituals were very important in Vedic practice and that only Brahmins were allowed to perform them. Then ask students why Jainism and Buddhism developed. [They should understand that both religions were a reaction to Vedic religion and the power of the Brahmins.] For more information have students read the Global History Resource Center selection on Buddhism and equality.

Link to Today. Display the electronic media map to show where Jainism is practiced today. Then add row labels for Jainism and Buddhism to the chart on the chalkboard, and have students fill out the chart. [**Jainism:** origins—founded by Mahavira; concepts—everything in nature has a soul, nonviolence, self-denial; **Buddhism:** origins—Gautama's search for the reasons for suffering; concepts—Four Noble Truths, Eightfold Path; nirvana] For additional background, have students read the Global History Resource Center selections on Jainism and Buddhism.

CONCLUDE

Analyze Indian religions. Display the Everyday Life transparency and have students complete the accompanying worksheet. Then show the electronic media image of the Hindu temple and discuss with students the role of religion in people's lives. Then ask how Indian religions served people's needs. Students should note that these religions provided a sense of community and common culture and provided answers to universal questions about the meaning of life. Conclude by reviewing the similarities and differences of these religions.

EXTEND
Other Media

Have students listen to the audio selection of the Tibetan Buddhist chant. Then have them do a quick-writing exercise in which they note their immediate impressions of the chanting and their responses to it.

MEET INDIVIDUAL NEEDS
Gifted Students

Have interested students examine the Everyday Life transparency. Then have them research and report on another Hindu god, illustrating their talk with drawings.

Kinesthetic Learners

Have pairs or small groups of students read the Global History Resource Center reading A *Hindu View of Life and Death*, which tells the story of Nachiketa's journey to the house of Death, and prepare and perform a short skit based on the reading.

ASSESS
Review

Have students complete the Section 1 Review. Use answers in the Teacher's Edition, page 151, to assess student mastery.

Textbook pp. 152–157

RESOURCES

Pupil's Edition

Map, p. 153: *Mauryan Empire, c. 320 B.C.–232 B.C.*

Map, p. 156: *Gupta Empire, c. A.D. 400*

Core Resources

Reading 6.2: *Asoka's Edicts*

Global History Resource Center

Reading: *A Hindu View of Life and Death*

Reading: *Hindu Religious Beliefs*

Reading: *The Hindu Law of Karma*

Videodiscs or Global History Resource Center

Image: *Hindu Gods at War*

Search Frame 744

Image: *Hindu Temple*

Search Frame 746

LESSON FOCUS

What were the main features of imperial India?

OBJECTIVES

After completing this lesson, students will be able to:

- explain why northern India was disunited before Alexander left the region;
- explain why Hinduism became more popular in the period after the fall of the Mauryan Empire;
- analyze the contributions of the Gupta Empire to Indian unity;
- explain why the Gupta period is called India's classical age.

HOOK: Link to Today

Discuss the rise of Magadha. Ask students to consider the leaders at their school and identify the qualities that make them leaders. Then ask what qualities it would take to lead a kingdom. [*strength of purpose, vision, and organizational skills*] Remind students that there were many warring kingdoms in India in the 500s B.C., led by many different rulers.

Ask: Which kingdom eventually triumphed over the others and why?

[*Magadha eventually emerged victorious largely because of access to resources and the strength and talents of its first rulers, Bimbisara and his son Ajatasatru. (Have students discuss what these kings did to rule successfully.)*]

DEVELOP

Describe the origins of imperial India. Point out that although Magadha was able to expand, it did not unite all of northern India.

Ask: What prevented the unification of northern India?

[*Persia—which was more powerful—conquered northwestern India in the late 500s B.C. and ruled the area until Alexander the Great ended Persian control in 326 B.C.*]

Ask students to explain the consequences for Indian history of Persian control and of Alexander's conquest. [*Students might note that Persia became an educational center for young men and the Greek withdrawal from India paved the way for the creation of an Indian empire.*]

Ask: What empire was the first to unify India, and what were its origins?

[*Mauryan Empire, founded by Chandragupta Maurya, with origins in Magadha kingdom*]

Ask: Why did this empire fall apart?

[*Asoka's sons fought each other for the throne, and the empire faced invaders in the north.*]

Ask: What was the second empire of India, and how and when was it created?

[Gupta Empire, created five centuries after Maurya, in 320 A.D.; origins in Magadha]

Then have students look at the maps on textbook pages 153 and 156 and compare the size and extent of the two empires. You might also have students complete Reading 6.2, *Asoka's Edicts*.

PROBE

Examine the reasons for the increase in popularity of Hinduism after the fall of the Mauryan Empire. Remind students that after the collapse of the Mauryan Empire, India entered a long period of political unrest and disunity, and it was during this period that the Vedic religion was transformed into Hinduism. Ask students what religious changes contributed to the rise of Hinduism and list their responses on the chalkboard. [emphasis on worship of one of the major gods—particularly Vishnu as the savior of humanity—and their female counterparts; emergence of popular tales—the Puranas; compilation of Hindu legal codes; popularity of concept of bhakti that gave people a more personal connection with the gods] You may wish to refer students back to the images and readings on Hinduism in the Global History Resource Center.

Ask: What was the Law Code of Manu?

[Students should understand that the Law Code of Manu stated the sacred laws of dharma and outlined caste laws and duties.]

Ask: Why were the laws significant?

[They were codified by the Brahmins after the fall of Maurya and were significant because they provided a framework of customs and rules that held Indian society together during the period of instability and unrest between Mauryan and Gupta rule.]

CONCLUDE

Analyze Gupta contributions to Indian unity and explain why the Gupta period is called the classical age. Review the development of the Gupta Empire with students. [They should note that Chandra Gupta came to power in A.D. 320 in Magadha, the capital of the Mauryans, and expanded his kingdom; his successors eventually brought all of northern India under Gupta control. Guptas promoted Hinduism.]

Next explore why this period is referred to as India's classical age. Organize the class into three groups, one for the arts, one for the sciences, and one for medicine. Have each group make a list of the advances in its assigned area. If time permits, you may want to have the groups do library research to find additional information on the advances mentioned in the textbook. Have the groups report their findings to the class.

Ask: What other developments characterized Gupta society during this period?

[expansion of the jati system; Brahmins established a scheme of conduct by dividing life into four periods]

EXTEND

Cross-Curricular Connection: *Language Arts*

Have interested students read some of the fables in the *Panchatantra* and compare them to Aesop's fables.

MEET INDIVIDUAL NEEDS

Musical-Rhythmic Learners

Have interested students research classical Indian music and report on their findings. Encourage them to bring recordings of this music to play in class.

Gifted Students

Help students see the factors behind the rise and fall of Indian empires. [**Rise:** wealth and resources of the Ganges plain, resentment of invaders and foreign rule, powerful rulers who used taxes and trade to ensure prosperity, official patronage of religion; **Collapse:** death of great rulers and the onset of feuding among political rivals, which opened the door to foreign invasion] Then have students imagine that they have been appointed policy advisors to an ancient Indian kingdom. Have them compile a master list of policies and goals they would recommend to their ruler in order to establish a strong, stable government.

ASSESS

Review

Have students complete the Section 2 Review. Use answers in the Teacher's Edition, page 157, to assess student mastery.

Lesson 6.3   *The Beginnings of Classical China*

Textbook pp. 158–161

RESOURCES

Core Resources

Reading 6.3: *The Wisdom of Confucius*

Geography Activity 6: *Political Turmoil in China*

Skills Activity 6: *Analyzing a Primary Source*

Visual Resources

Geography and History 6: *The Rise of Buddhism and Daoism*

Global History Resource Center

Reading: *The Moral Teachings of Confucius*

Reading: *The Five Great Relationships of Confucianism*

Reading: *Wisdom of the Dao Da Jing*

Reading: *Daoism Versus Confucianism*

Videodiscs or Global History Resource Center

Image: *Confucius: The Chinese Philosopher*

Search Frame 750

Image: *Laozi Meets Confucius*

Search Frame 752

Map: *Early Confucianism, c. 200 B.C.*

Search Frame 756

Image: *Laozi: The Chinese Sage*

Search Frame 751

LESSON FOCUS

What ideas emerged during the beginnings of China's classical age that helped shape the future of Chinese civilization?

OBJECTIVES

After completing this lesson, students will be able to:

- explain how the Zhou dynasty ended;
- describe the teachings of Confucius;
- explain the appeal of Daoism;
- contrast Legalism with Confucianism and Daoism.

HOOK

Discuss conditions during the end of the Zhou dynasty. Read, or have a student read, the quotation on textbook page 161. Have students discuss what it reveals about China during this period.

Ask: What were conditions like during this period in China? *[Students should understand that the end of the Zhou dynasty was marked by frequent warfare among feuding warlords, which caused great anxiety among the Chinese people.]*

Next have students complete Geography Activity 6 and identify the warring states. Then discuss responses to the turmoil that plagued China.

Ask: What was the Era of the Hundred Schools, and how was it a response to life during the Era of Warring States? *[It was a period in which scholars proposed ideas to help return stability and order to China.]*

DEVELOP

Describe the ideas of Confucius. Have students complete Reading 6.3, *The Wisdom of Confucius*. Then remind students that at the heart of many of the philosophies that emerged during the Era of the Hundred Schools was the concept of yin and yang—balancing complementary opposites.

Ask: How did the concept of yin and yang apply to politics?

[People believed that when these forces were in balance, peace and prosperity resulted; if rulers were "in balance" dynasties prospered.]

Remind students that Confucius embodied this quest for balance and harmony.

Ask: What ideas did Confucius stress and how did he apply them to politics?

[importance of the family, respect for one's elders, reverence for the past; acceptance and fulfillment of one's roles; if these ideas were applied to politics, order would return]

Next have students consider Daoism, another philosophy that emerged during the Era of a Hundred Schools.

Ask: Why did Daoism appeal to many Chinese?

[It emphasized the independence of the individual and the individual's relationship to nature; artists found inspiration in the contemplation of nature that Daoism advocated; and it counterbalanced the rigid ethics of Confucianism.]

To show the spread of these traditions in China, you may wish to show and discuss the electronic media map of Confucianism and display the Geography and History transparency and have students complete the accompanying worksheet.

Next discuss how Legalism differed from Daoism and Confucianism. [Students should realize that Legalism advocated rule by force to ensure order.]

PROBE

Apply the philosophies. You may wish to show the three electronic media images of Confucius and Laozi, asking students what the images reveal about the two philosophers. You may also wish to have students read the selections in the Global History Resource Center on Confucius, on the *Dao Da Jing,* and on Daoism and Confucianism before beginning this activity. Then organize the class into groups of three students each and have students pick the roles of Confucius, Laozi, or a Legalist scholar. Have each group debate the following open-ended questions, with each student assuming a different philosophical perspective:

- What should the main goal in life be?
- Are people basically good or bad?
- What is the best kind of government?

After students have discussed these issues, bring the class back together and ask students to describe the positions they took in representing the various philosophers. Write their answers on the chalkboard and have students arrive at a consensus on how the issues would be viewed by each philosopher.

CONCLUDE

Analyze ideas and policies. To help students clarify their understanding of the three philosophies, present the following scenario: A ruler has been governing China for some time, but he is corrupt and inefficient, and his control over government and society is weak. Crime and disorder are rampant, and rebellion threatens. Then ask students what policy or set of policies a Confucian, a Daoist, and a Legalist would offer as a response to this situation. Have students consider the problem individually and write down their answers. Then invite students to share their answers in class, and write the responses on the chalkboard. Have students discuss the various answers and decide which positions most accurately represent the Confucian, Daoist, and Legalist viewpoints.

EXTEND

Cross-Curricular Connection: *Government*
Link to Today. Have interested students pick one of the three Chinese philosophical traditions and devise a plan of government for their community based on that tradition.

MEET INDIVIDUAL NEEDS

Students Having Difficulty
Students who are having difficulty understanding the concepts of Daoism may benefit from completing Skills Activity 6.

Interpersonal Learners
Have interested students read the selection in the Global History Resource Center on Confucius's teachings. Then, working in pairs or in small groups, have them create a short skit or drama in which they role-play Confucian values expressed in the selection.

ASSESS

Review
Have students complete the Section 3 Review. Use answers in the Teacher's Edition, page 161, to assess student mastery.

Lesson 6.4   *Imperial China*

Textbook pp. 162–170

RESOURCES

Pupil's Edition

Map, p. 164: *Qin and Han Dynasties, 221 B.C.–A.D. 220*

Geography and History, pp. 166–167: *The Silk Road*

Then and Now, p. 169: *Acupuncture*

Core Resources

Reading 6.4: *Pan Ku's History*

Visual Resources

Art and History 6: *Han Dynasty Court Scene*

Geography and History 6: *The Rise of Buddhism and Daoism*

Videodiscs or Global History Resource Center

Image: *Daoist Art:* Clear Weather *by Tung Yuan*

Search Frame 753

Map: *The Spread of Buddhism, 500s B.C. to A.D. 600s*

Search Frame 755

Video Clip: *The Amazing Tomb of China's "First Emperor"*

Search 4555, Play to 5032
Videodisc 1, Side A
Video Clip 6

LESSON FOCUS

How did Chinese rulers unify China and forge an empire?

OBJECTIVES

After completing this lesson, students will be able to:

- explain how the Qin maintained their brief empire;
- explain how Han rule differed from that of the Qin;
- describe how Chinese civilization developed during the Qin and Han periods;
- analyze what happened to Chinese civilization after the fall of the Han.

HOOK

Discuss the rise of Qin. Read, or have a student read, the quotation on textbook page 163. Have students discuss this passage and ask what it reveals about the origins and nature of the Qin. You may also want to show the Global History Resource Center video clip of the "First Emperor's" tomb.

Ask: *Based on your textbook reading, what other features of the Qin state contributed to its success?*

[Students should understand that Qin's creation of a strong, centralized state with standardized weights, measures, and coinage, a legal code, a tax system, and public works all contributed to its success. The emperor also abolished feudal landholding and forced aristocratic families to move to the capital.]

DEVELOP

Contrast the Qin and Han empires. Have students complete the Core Resources reading, which discusses Qin and Han ways of ruling. Next have students look at the map on page 164 of their textbook and compare the size of the Qin and Han states. Then have them name important features of each empire, including dates, type of government, and major achievements.

Ask: *How did the ruling style of the Qin and Han empires differ?*

[Students should understand that the Qin were harsh Legalists and aroused great opposition, while the Han ruled under a system of Confucian ethics, which allowed them to stay in power much longer.]

PROBE

Discuss the features of Chinese civilization that developed during the Qin and Han periods. Begin by having students read and discuss the Geography and History feature. Then to provide additional background display the electronic media image of the Daoist painting and the Art and History transparency and have students complete the accompanying worksheet.

Next organize students into eight groups. On the chalkboard, write the headings *Family, Economy, Education and Literature,* and *Science and Technology.* Assign each topic to two groups. Have the groups make a list of features of Chinese civilization that relate to their topic. When they have finished, have the two groups with the same topic meet to compile a master list and write their points on the chalkboard under their topic heading. **[Family:** *primary social unit, ruled by father;* **Economy:** *family primary economic unit, based on peasant farmers, policy of leveling, state controlled trade, standardized currency, weights, and measures aided trade;* **Education and Literature:** *development of civil service system elevated the study of Confucian Five Classics, established a university;* **Science and Technology:** *observed sunspots, invented instruments to observe planetary movements, a primitive seismograph, paper, wood-block printing, acupuncture]* Then have students discuss how the different features of Chinese civilization were interrelated. For example, an emphasis on family could be linked to the importance of farming as an economic activity, since in most peasant families everyone would help run the farm. You might have students draw lines between items on the board that have some relation to each other, explaining the reasoning behind each connection.

CONCLUDE

Analyze the enduring foundations of Chinese civilization.
Write the following questions on the chalkboard:
- How did a strong state contribute to the development of Chinese civilization?
- How did the growth of Chinese civilization contribute to the development of government in China?

Organize the class into small groups. Assign the first question to half of the groups, the second to the other half. Have groups work out answers to the questions. Then bring students back together to compare their findings. *[Strong state provided the stability and prosperity that encouraged the development of civilization. Enduring traditions of Chinese civilization— including development of bureaucracy guided by Confucian ethics and the importance of the group over the individual— shaped government.]* Encourage students to consider how the growth of the state and of civilization reinforced each other in China during this period.

You may wish to display Geography and History Transparency 6 or the electronic media map again to show the spread of Buddhism in China during this period. Discuss how a new period of instability promoted the spread of Buddhism.
Ask: What happened to Chinese civilization after the fall of the Han dynasty?
> [political and economic organization fell apart; nomadic tribes sacked cities but eventually settled and adopted Chinese ways; Buddhism spread]

EXTEND
Cross-Curricular Connection: *Science*
Encourage interested students to find out more about ancient Chinese achievements in the area of science and technology. Students could prepare a short report to the class on a subject of interest.

Cross-Curricular Connection: *Health*
Link to Today. Have students read and discuss the Then and Now feature. Have them comment on why they think acupuncture is gaining the interest of some health practitioners in the West.

MEET INDIVIDUAL NEEDS
Intrapersonal Learners
Have students think about the Chinese family, considering how it affected and reflected Chinese society or how it compares with Western family life. Students might respond in writing or through a drawing or other art form.

Students Acquiring English/Students Having Difficulty
Have students who need extra practice work in pairs to quiz each other about the Qin and Han dynasties and the features of Chinese civilization, asking questions based on the journalistic "Ws": Who? What? When? Where? Why?

ASSESS
Review
Have students complete the Section 4 Review. Use answers in the Teacher's Edition, pages 169-170, to assess student mastery.

In preparation for the chapter test, you may wish to have students complete all or part of the Chapter 6 Review on textbook page 171 or the Chapter 6 Review Activity and Themes Review.

Understanding
the Main Idea

Call on a volunteer to read aloud the *Understanding the Main Idea* paragraph. Then tell students that before the first century A.D. major civilizations had already developed in China and India. India developed a complicated social hierarchy and a diverse set of religions, including Hinduism, Buddhism, and Jainism. In China, the insecurities caused by war among the states promoted the development of the philosophies of Confucianism, Daoism, and Legalism.

Presenting Themes

See p. 143B for suggestions on introducing themes.

Using the Time Line

Have students list the time line events in their notebooks. After they have read about each event in the chapter, have students write a paragraph explaining its significance.

Chapter 6
The Growth of Asian Civilizations
700 B.C.–A.D. 550

Understanding the Main Idea

Long before the first century A.D., major civilizations flourished in both India and China. Relatively isolated and dependent on intensive agriculture, China developed a highly centralized state based on Confucianism. In contrast, India's civilization was rooted in cultural diversity and developed Hinduism, a religious and social system that was capable of adjusting to other cultures.

Themes

- **Social Relations** How might a society's religion influence the relations between different groups of people?

- **Politics and Law** What factors might help hold a large empire together?

- **Religion** How do religious beliefs develop to satisfy the spiritual needs of culturally diverse people?

In the late A.D. 300s a Chinese monk named Fa Xian (FAH-shee-EN) traveled to India to visit the holy Buddhist shrines and to collect manuscripts. Leaving China in A.D. 399, Fa Xian traveled throughout India for 15 years. After returning to China in A.D. 414, Fa Xian wrote an account, in which he described the lives of both monks and common people:

66 *The inhabitants are rich and prosperous, and vie [struggle] with one another in the practice of benevolence [goodwill] and righteousness. Every year on the eighth day of the second month they celebrate a procession of images. They make a four-wheeled car[t], and on it erect a structure of five stories by means of bamboos tied together. . . . White and silk-like cloth of hair is wrapped all round it, which is then painted in various colors. They make figures of devas [gods and goddesses]. . . . On the four sides are niches [openings], with a Buddha seated in each. . . . The monks and laity [non-clergy] within the borders all come together; they have singers and skillful musicians; they pay their devotions with flowers and incense.* 99

Although Fa Xian's purpose in traveling to India was to record Buddhist holy books, he also provided a unique outsider's view of Indian society in the A.D. 400s.

c. 563 B.C.	551 B.C.	403 B.C.	305 B.C.
Siddhartha Gautama (the Buddha) is born.	Confucius is born.	The Era of Warring States begins in China.	Chandragupta Maurya signs a treaty to establish the borders of the Mauryan Empire.

A monk prays before the figure of the Buddha in Sri Lanka.

221 B.C.
Qin dynasty unites China into an empire.

214 B.C.
Shi Huangdi begins building the Great Wall of China.

202 B.C.
The peasant general Liu Bang founds the Han dynasty.

A.D. 220
Ts'ao P'ei overthrows the Han dynasty.

C. A.D. 550
Gupta Empire ends.

SECTION 1

CORE LESSON PLAN
See pages 143C and
143D for Lesson Plan
6.1.

History and Current Events

Only recently has the system of *jati* begun to change. In 1950 the Indian government adopted a new constitution outlawing untouchability. It took several more years, however, before punishment for discrimination against the untouchables was enforced. Since the 1950s the Indian government has tried to broaden opportunities for former untouchables. Today, the children of former untouchables also receive benefits, such as special scholarships to Indian universities.

Critical Thinking Ask students how a society might benefit from a system of *jati*.

ANSWER: Students might suggest that a system of *jati* would likely add stability to a society.

SECTION 1
Indian Society and Religion

FOCUS

- What purpose did the epics serve?
- What are the basic beliefs of Hinduism?
- How and why did Jainism and Buddhism develop?

By 500 B.C. the Ganges Valley had become the center of northern Indian civilization. The Indo-Aryans had developed a complex religion based on ritual offerings to the gods, and the ancient hymns of the Rig-Veda had become the source of knowledge and power for the Brahmins, or priests. As society grew more complex, this traditional Vedic religion faced challenges. Some people sought more opportunities to participate in religious practices, while others traveled new pathways in their search for truth.

The Vedic figures of a nature spirit and a serpent god

A Changing Society

By 500 B.C. the basic social structure of India, based on the varnas, or social classes of the Indo-Aryans, had begun to take shape. As time went on, the varna system grew more complex. The Brahmins, who performed the sacred rituals, rose to the top, displacing the Kshatriyas, or warriors. The Vaisyas (merchants, traders, and farmers) and the Sudras (artisans and servants) remained in their earlier positions. A new group developed outside the system, however. The "untouchables" performed jobs that other Indians considered unclean, such as tanning animal skins, which involved working with animal carcasses, or sweeping among the ashes of the cremation grounds.

For all people, certain interactions with people of a different varna, such as marriage or eating together, were prohibited. For the untouchables, these restrictions were even more severe:

> **"** Not only does one not take water from them [the untouchables], they may not even take water from the same well. . . . Not only does one not marry them, they may not even enter the temple or the house or stroll on the main village streets. Even their cattle may often not drink from the same pool as [others]. **"**

The system became even more complex during the Vedic period, when the varna began to divide into *jati*, or subgroups. Each *jati* had its own customs, including different diets, marriage and funeral traditions, and worship practices. This system later became known to westerners as the caste system.

The Vedanta and the *Upanishads*. As early as the 700s B.C. the Brahmins had become the most influential group in the social structure. Some Indian thinkers, however, began to raise questions about the authority of the Brahmins. Many of these thinkers, both women and men, became wanderers who taught their new spiritual message to worthy disciples in the forests of the Ganges Plain. This new school of thought was known as the Vedanta, or "end of the Veda," and was most powerfully expressed in a series of written philosophical dialogues called the *Upanishads*.

Although these thinkers did not reject the Vedas, they sought a more personal and direct connection with spiritual matters than was offered through Vedic ritual. As a verse from the *Upanishads* stated:

> **"** *From the unreal lead me to the real!*
> *From darkness lead me to light!*
> *From death lead me to immortality!* **"**

The *Upanishads* taught that the world and all things in it, including human beings, are part of a single universal being, or Brahma, which never changes. Everything that humans see or feel through their senses is illusion, and the purpose of life is to see through this illusion and to experience the oneness of Brahma.

The epics. The intellectual and philosophical nature of the Vedanta had little appeal for many ordinary Indians, however. Most Indians found more spiritual comfort in another source—epic poetry based on historical and religious themes. The two greatest epics of this tradition were the *Mahabharata* (mah-HAH-bahr-UH-tuh) and the *Ramayana*.

The *Mahabharata* tells the story of a great civil war among royal cousins battling over the king's domain. Perhaps the most famous part of this epic, known as the *Bhagavad Gita*, or "song of the lord," stresses that fulfillment comes through *bhakti*, or complete love and devotion to god. The *Bhagavad Gita* taught that salvation was available to everyone. People did not have to perform the sacrifices required by the Rig-Veda, or to live the difficult life of self-denial prescribed by the *Upanishads* in order to achieve salvation.

The *Ramayana*, or "story of Rama," was the tale of Rama, an exiled prince, and his faithful wife, Sita. Rama was exiled, then Sita was kidnapped and taken to Ceylon (present-day Sri Lanka) by a demon. Rama defeated the demon and became king. Because of their devotion to each other and to their people, Rama and Sita began to symbolize the ideals of Indian manhood and womanhood.

> *B* *ased on historical and religious themes, the* **Mahabharata** *and the* **Ramayana** *brought India's various strains of religion together in a way that appealed to Indians of all backgrounds.*

▶ **A three-headed, six-armed god representing Vishnu, Brahma, and Siva sits under a tree.**

Hinduism

From the literary works of the Vedic texts and the popular epics arose the predominant Indian religion of Hinduism. Combining elements of both Aryan and pre-Aryan religion, Hinduism represents a synthesis of Indian religious cultures. It is a religion that recognizes many gods—most notably Brahma the Creator, Vishnu the Preserver, and Siva the Destroyer. Nevertheless, Hinduism teaches that all gods and living beings are representations of a single universal spirit, Brahma.

The three most important concepts of Hindu belief are reincarnation, dharma, and karma. According to Hinduism, when people die their souls are reborn in new bodies, a process called **reincarnation**. During each cycle of reincarnation, people must fulfill a moral duty, called **dharma**, which depends upon the position into which they are born. Hindus believe that the actions that people take during their lifetimes have moral consequences, called **karma**, which determine the next cycle of reincarnation.

RESOURCE ACTIVITY

READINGS IN WORLD HISTORY
Reading 6.1
Nobility and Virtue in the Ramayana

Have students read the excerpt from the *Ramayana*. Then have them complete the questions.

Level 1

MULTIMEDIA PRESENTATION STRATEGY

VISUAL RESOURCES
Everyday Life 6
Ganesha, Hindu Deity

Show the transparency and share the information from Everyday Life Fact Sheet 6. Then have students complete the accompanying worksheet.

Level 2

Understanding Sacred Traditions

1. He was upset that he had to fight his own cousins.
2. He must be a courageous warrior.
3. Their dharmas depend upon the class into which they are born. Their fulfillment of their dharma might mean being the best at whatever job they have.

MULTIMEDIA PRESENTATION STRATEGY

WORLD HISTORY AND CULTURES VIDEODISCS
(p. 149)

Image: *The Buddha as Portrayed in Sri Lanka*

Search Frame 749

Image: *Buddhist Stupa in India*

Search Frame 748

Image: *Buddha in the Earliest Surviving Printed Book*

Search Frame 747

Show the images as you discuss Buddhism. The captions that accompany each CD-ROM image offer additional details.

All Levels

Sacred TRADITIONS

The *Bhagavad Gita*

One of the best-known Hindu texts involves the story of Prince Arjuna and his dialogue with the god Krishna (another name for Vishnu) on the field of battle. Arjuna is deeply troubled with the thought of having to fight a battle against his own cousins, who have wronged his family. As the time of battle draws closer, Arjuna asks his chariot driver Krishna (the god in disguise) what to do. Krishna's answer and their continuing conversation make up the text known as the Bhagavad Gita, or "song of the lord." Krishna tells Arjuna that he can only fulfill his duty in life by being completely devoted to Krishna. Krishna also tells Arjuna that he must follow his sacred duty in life, or dharma, by living up to the expectations of his social class. For Arjuna that means being the most courageous warrior he can be.

"Krishna, I see my kinsmen gathered here, wanting war.

My limbs sink,
my mouth is parched,
my body trembles,
the hair bristles on my flesh.

The magic bow slips
from my hand, my skin burns,
I cannot stand still,
my mind reels.

I see omens of chaos,
Krishna; I see no good
in killing my kinsmen
in battle. . . ."

Arjuna, sad and tearful, seeks council. Krishna replies:

"Why this cowardice
in time of crisis, Arjuna?
The coward is ignoble [lowly],
    shameful,
foreign to the ways of heaven.

Don't yield to impotence
    [powerlessness]!
It is unnatural in you!
Banish this petty weakness
    from your heart.
Rise to the fight, Arjuna! . . .

Look to your own duty;
do not tremble before it;
nothing is better for a warrior
than a battle of sacred duty.

The doors of heaven open
for warriors who rejoice
to have a battle like this
thrust on them by chance.

If you fail to wage this war
of sacred duty,
you will abandon your own duty
and fame only to gain evil.

People will tell
of your undying shame,
and for a man of honor
shame is worse than death."

Understanding Sacred Traditions

1. What is the cause of Arjuna's unhappiness?
2. According to Krishna, what is Arjuna's dharma?
3. How might Hindus transfer the idea of dharma expressed in the *Bhagavad Gita* to their daily lives?

These rock carvings from the A.D. 600s illustrate part of Arjuna's tale from the *Bhagavad Gita*.

People who fulfill their dharma are rewarded with good karma. They are reborn into a higher social group. Those who do not fulfill their dharma are reborn into a lower group or even as an animal or insect. According to Hinduism, people who consistently fulfill their dharma may eventually break the cycle of birth and rebirth, and realize their true oneness with Brahma.

According to Hinduism, in the cycle of reincarnation people who fulfill their duty in life may eventually achieve a realization of their oneness with Brahma.

▲ A modern-day Jain temple in Bombay, India. The altar attendant wears a face cloth.

Reactions Against Vedic Religion

As Hinduism incorporated various beliefs, many religious subgroups developed. The two most important were Jainism and Buddhism. These two movements arose in reaction to the religious beliefs and authority of the Brahmins. Not surprisingly, these movements developed in the warrior class, which stood beneath the Brahmins in Indian society and sometimes resented their power.

Jainism. Jainism was founded during the 500s B.C. by Mahavira, a member of the warrior class whose name means "Great Hero." When Mahavira was around 30 years old, he abandoned the pleasures of the world to become a wandering teacher. He denied the special holiness of the Vedas and taught that humans were not the only creatures to possess a soul. He believed that everything in nature—animals, plants, even stones—possessed a soul. Although Mahavira was a member of the warrior class, he rejected violence:

66 *All breathing, existing, living, sentient [conscious] creatures should not be slain, nor treated with violence, nor abused, nor tormented, nor driven away.* 99

This belief in nonviolence is called **ahimsa**.

Mahavira also believed in living a life of deliberate self-denial for religious purposes. He had such remarkable powers of self-control that

his followers called him *jina*, or conqueror. Mahavira and his followers turned away from Vedic religion, in part because of the Brahmins' use of animal sacrifice, and established a religious sect that later became known as Jainism.

The Jains' belief that everything had a spirit went against the Hindu belief in a universal oneness. Applying the law of ahimsa toward life at every level, Jains were vegetarians and often covered their noses with cloth to avoid breathing in insects and killing them. They avoided occupations such as farming in which they might harm living things.

Buddhism. As Jainism began to develop, Buddhism, another spiritual philosophy of even greater impact, was also emerging in India. The founder of Buddhism, Siddhartha Gautama (sid-DAHR-tuh GOW-tuh-muh), became known to his followers as the Buddha, the "Enlightened One."

BIOGRAPHY About 563 B.C. Gautama was born the son of a prince in northern India. Gautama lived a luxurious life, shielded from the world's suffering. At age 29, however, he ventured out of his palace and learned about hunger, disease, and death. Vowing to discover the reasons for this suffering, Gautama gave up his family and possessions and set out in search of the truth.

Like many teachers of the *Upanishads*, Gautama wandered for years through the woods of Kosala and Magadha. He lived as a hermit, meditated, and fasted. None of these practices produced the

The Buddha
BIOGRAPHY

Thinking
About Art

Art can use symbolism to reflect religious ideas and concepts.

History THROUGH THE **ARTS**

Siva

Religion has always played an important part in the creation of Indian art. Paintings and sculptures of the three main gods of the Hindu faith—Brahma, Vishnu, and Siva—fill numerous temples across India. Among the most spectacular works of Hindu art are the many representations of Siva the Destroyer. Sculpture of Siva reached its height in India around the A.D. 900s. One of the most common images of Siva is as the *Nataraja,* "Lord of the Dance."

Like most works of Hindu art, the bronze statue pictured here is meant to symbolize religious teachings. The circle of flame surrounding the god represents the continuous creation and destruction of the universe, as well as the cycle of death and rebirth. Likewise, the drum held in one of Siva's hands is a symbol for the creation of the universe, and the fire in another of his hands stands for its destruction. The sculpture also conveys Siva's power over death, represented by his standing on the body of a demon. Siva's guidance in life is represented by the hand pointing downward, telling worshippers that they should have no fear.

Through its symbolism, the statue of Siva the *Nataraja* represents a basic idea of Hinduism: things that seem contradictory—birth and death, creation and destruction—are merely part of one ongoing universe.

Thinking About Art
Why might works of art be important tools in teaching religious ideas?

Bronze statue of Siva as the *Nataraja,* "Lord of the Dance"

answers he sought. After six years of searching, however, Gautama was meditating under a tree when he suddenly achieved enlightenment—a state of inner calm and understanding. He became known as the Buddha and spread his philosophy far and wide until his death around 483 B.C.

The Buddha accepted the Hindu belief in reincarnation, but his teachings centered on the **Four Noble Truths**: (1) all human life contains suffering and sorrow; (2) desire causes suffering; (3) by rejecting desire, people can attain **nirvana**, or perfect peace, which frees the soul from reincarnation; and (4) following the Eightfold Path leads to renunciation, or the rejection of desire, and the attainment of nirvana. The Eightfold Path requires right faith, intentions, speech, action, living, effort, mindfulness, and meditation. In one of his sermons, the Buddha explained this cycle:

❝*A learned, noble hearer of the word becomes weary of body, weary of sensation, weary of perception . . . weary of consciousness. Becoming weary of all that, he divests himself of [gets rid of] passion; by absence of passion he is made free; when he is free, he becomes aware that he is free; and he realizes that re-birth is exhausted; that holiness is completed; that duty is fulfilled; and that there is no further return to this world.*❞

▲ **Buddhist worshippers gather at a richly decorated shrine in Barcelona, Spain. Buddhism is a growing faith in Western countries.**

Some of the Buddha's beliefs were new and revolutionary to Indian society. He believed that the Vedas were not sacred works of literature. The Buddha believed that virtue could not be inherited, and that priests should practice virtuous conduct, nonviolence, and poverty. These ideas directly opposed the beliefs of the Brahmins. In addition, Buddhism rejected the rigid nature of the varna system. This made Buddhism very appealing to the Sudras, the lowest varna, and the untouchables.

As Buddhism spread, it divided into two main branches. The first, called Theraveda, or "way of the elders," recognized the Buddha as a great spiritual leader and followed the Buddha's original teachings. The second branch, called Mahayana, or "greater vehicle," turned the teachings of the Buddha into an organized religion, with priests, temples, and rituals. Eventually, Buddhism spread to many other parts of Asia.

*B*eginning as reactions to the teachings of the Brahmins, Jainism and Buddhism eventually developed into separate religions.

SECTION 1 REVIEW

IDENTIFY and explain the significance of the following:
- jati
- Upanishads
- bhakti
- reincarnation
- dharma
- karma
- Mahavira
- ahimsa
- Siddhartha Gautama
- Four Noble Truths
- nirvana

1. **Main Idea** Why were the *Mahabharata* and the *Ramayana* important to ordinary Indians?
2. **Main Idea** What concepts are central to the teachings of Hinduism?
3. **Religion** How did Jainism and Buddhism grow out of Hinduism?
4. **Writing to Explain** Imagine that you are an Indian living shortly after the death of the Buddha. In a short essay, explain why you are drawn to follow the teachings of Hinduism, Jainism, or Buddhism.
5. **Assessing Consequences** How did the great influence of the Brahmins lead to the transformation of Hinduism through the epics? Why do you think many Indians resisted the power of the Brahmins?

CORE LESSON PLAN
See pages 143E and 143F for Lesson Plan 6.1.

Theme:
Cross-cultural Interaction

Arrian, a Greek historian, recorded what happened when Alexander the Great reached India and his men refused to go farther. According to Arrian, Alexander made a long speech asking the men to go on. After Alexander finished, Coenus, son of Polemocrates, spoke for the men. He finished his speech, "Sir, if there is one thing above all others a successful man like you should know, it is *when to stop.*"

Critical Thinking Ask students why Alexander's men had lost their desire to go forward.

ANSWER: Students might suggest that the army had already marched thousands of miles, risked their lives in many battles, and spent years away from home.

The Beginnings of Imperial India

FOCUS

- Why was northern India disunited before Alexander left the region?
- Why did Hinduism become more popular in the period after the fall of the Mauryan Empire?
- How did the Gupta Empire contribute to Indian unity?
- Why is the Gupta period called India's classical age?

In the 500s B.C. the kingdom of Magadha rose above the other Indian states. A true empire did not arise in India, however, until invasions by the Persians and Greeks inspired Chandragupta Maurya to unite most of India. After the decline of this Mauryan Empire and centuries of disunity, the Gupta Empire arose and India enjoyed a classical age of great cultural development.

The crown of one of Asoka's stone pillars, c. 240 B.C.

Powerful Kings and Outside Invasions

By the early 500s B.C., 16 kingdoms had arisen in northern India. In 540 B.C. the kingdom of Magadha was the most powerful under its king Bimbisara, who became a supporter of Buddhism. Bimbisara annexed the state of Anga on the Ganges Delta, which gave him access to the valuable trade on the Bay of Bengal. His son Ajatasatru (ah-JAHT-uh-SAH-troo) continued these expansionist policies and, although a series of ineffective rulers succeeded Ajatasatru, Magadha remained dominant in the east until the 300s B.C.

Meanwhile, northwestern India faced conquest and occupation. In the late 500s B.C. Darius the Great of Persia exerted power over the northwest Indian region of Gandhara. For nearly 200 years the Persians ruled the region with an iron hand, collecting tributes or taxes of gold dust that helped support the rest of the Persian Empire. At the same time, the Persian state became an educational center for young men from other parts of India, including Magadha.

In 326 B.C. Alexander the Great ended Persian control over the Gandhara region when he invaded with more than 25,000 soldiers. At one point, Alexander encountered a powerful Indian army, equipped with 200 war elephants and thousands of infantry. Moving swiftly, Alexander's cavalry outflanked the Indian forces, terrorizing the war elephants with flaming arrows, which caused them to stampede over the Indian soldiers. After that, opposition melted. Eventually, however, Alexander's march stalled. Unable to sustain the morale of his troops so far from home, he had to turn back. Alexander withdrew from India, leaving little trace of his presence.

Beginning in the 500s B.C. Magadha ruled northeastern India, while the Persians and later Alexander invaded the northwest.

The Mauryan Empire

While Alexander was in northwestern India he met a man called Sandrocottos, later known as Chandragupta Maurya, the founder of the first Indian empire. Chandragupta Maurya may have been inspired by Alexander's example. A few years after Alexander withdrew from India, Chandragupta Maurya seized the throne of Magadha.

Chandragupta Maurya. The Mauryan Empire brought strong centralized rule to northern India for the first time. Chandragupta Maurya was an efficient ruler who established a rigid bureaucracy to carry out his commands. Fearful of potential assassins, Chandragupta Maurya also set up a spy network that kept close watch over his suspected enemies.

Chandragupta Maurya spent the latter part of his life building his empire. In 305 B.C. he signed a treaty with Seleucus Nicator, Alexander's Greek heir to western Asia. The treaty fixed the borders between the two empires and established diplomatic relations. Under Chandragupta Maurya the government also cleared forest land for cultivation, operated mines and weapon-making centers, established quality standards for physicians, and set standards for weights and measures.

In 301 B.C. Chandragupta Maurya gave up power to lead the life of a Jainist monk. He passed the throne to his son, Bindusara, who expanded the empire farther south.

Asoka. Bindusara's successor, Asoka, was one of India's most powerful and enlightened emperors. Initially, Asoka continued the expansionist policies of his grandfather, Chandragupta Maurya, conquering all of India except the southern tip of the subcontinent. The campaign against the kingdom of Kalinga, southeast of the Mauryan Empire, was exceedingly brutal. This brutality caused Asoka to abandon his policy of conquest.

Asoka became a Buddhist, in part because of Buddhism's emphasis on nonviolence. He publicized the fact of his conversion on engraved stone pillars scattered throughout his territory: "But after the conquest of Kalinga, the Beloved of the Gods [Asoka] began to follow Righteousness, to love Righteousness, and to give instruction in Righteousness."

In an effort to unite his diverse empire, Asoka improved living conditions for his people. He explained, "On the roads I have had banyan trees planted which will give shade to beasts and men." He also ordered wells to be dug and had rest houses built along trade routes. In addition, Asoka pledged to spread Buddhism by sending missionaries to Ceylon and Burma.

Mauryan Empire, c. 320 B.C.–232 B.C.

Chandragupta Maurya's Empire Chandragupta Maurya, the founder of the Mauryan dynasty, first took control of Magadha and then extended his empire north to the Indus and south to the Narmada River.

Location On which river were major cities of the Mauryan empire located?

Asoka urged religious toleration and nonviolence. On another pillar he had inscribed his attitude toward other religions:

> The Beloved of the Gods . . . honors members of all sects. . . . Whoever honors his own sect and disparages [speaks ill of] another man's . . . does his own sect the greatest possible harm. Concord [harmony] is best, with each hearing and respecting the other's teachings.

In 232 B.C. Asoka died, and the strength of the Mauryan Empire began to decline. Asoka's sons fought each other for the throne, and invaders attacked the northern provinces. Finally, in 184 B.C., the last Mauryan emperor was killed by one of his Brahmin generals, who

THROUGH OTHERS' EYES

A Report by the Greek Ambassador

In 302 B.C. the Hellenistic monarch Seleucus Nicator sent the Greek historian Megasthenes as his ambassador to the court of Chandragupta Maurya. An observant man, Megasthenes wrote a famous work, *Indika,* describing the people, customs, and geography of India. Megasthenes described the precautions Chandragupta Maurya took against potential assassins:

❝Attendance on the king's person is the duty of women. . . . Outside the gates of the palace stand the bodyguards and the rest of the soldiers. . . . Nor does the king sleep during the day, and at night he is forced at various hours to change his bed because of those plotting against him. Of his nonmilitary departures from the palace one is to the courts, in which he passes the day hearing cases to the end. . . . When he leaves to hunt, he is thickly surrounded by a circle of women, and on the outside by spear-carrying bodyguards. The road is fenced off with ropes, and to anyone who passes within the ropes as far as the women, death is the penalty.❞

Apparently the security measures worked well— Chandragupta Maurya died peacefully in 298 B.C. after having retired from the throne.

began his own dynasty. The Mauryan Empire, which had lasted some 140 years, collapsed.

Invasions and Cultural Development

As the Mauryan Empire collapsed, it was replaced by many regional kingdoms. These kingdoms often fought among themselves, while successive waves of invaders from Central Asia imposed their own rule over northwestern India. The most important of these invaders were the Kushans, who established a vast empire controlling the overland trade routes between China, India, and the Mediterranean. Even as the imperial traditions of the Mauryans became a distant memory, however, India continued to experience great cultural creativity and economic development.

Overseas trade blossomed, as the demand for Indian goods grew in both the Roman and the Chinese Empires. Merchant sailors discovered the patterns of the monsoon winds in the Indian Ocean, which aided them in making regular trading voyages between the Red Sea, the Persian Gulf, Africa, and India. New cities bustling with activity sprang up along the trade routes. As the use of money for exchange became more commonplace, a new class of Indian bankers and moneylenders emerged in the cities. India's growing wealth and increased trade contacts also stimulated dynamic religious and social developments. In particular, important changes occurred in both Buddhism and Hinduism in the centuries after Mauryan collapse.

Changes in Buddhism. As cultural interactions grew between India and Central Asia, particularly under the Kushan Empire, Mahayana Buddhism developed and spread. Mahayana Buddhism was able to incorporate elements of other religions by arguing that their gods were *Bodhisattvas*—those who had attained enlightenment like Buddha, but had turned back from nirvana in order to help the rest of humanity achieve salvation.

Yet while Buddhism remained an important feature of Indian life, by the A.D. 300s it had begun to decline in influence. It became a monastic religion, with priests and nuns living in monasteries and dependent on the support of rulers and wealthy contributors.

The development of Hinduism. In part, Buddhism declined because of the rise of Hinduism. It was during this period of political unrest and disunity that the old Vedic religion of the Brahmins was transformed into what is known as Hinduism. The emphasis on ritual fire sacrifices gave way to a new emphasis on the worship of one of the major gods—generally either Vishnu or Siva. Many people also worshipped some form of a Mother Goddess—each of the Hindu gods had a female counterpart.

A new popular literature emerged, known as the Puranas, or "Ancient Tales"—myths and fables about the gods. Hindus began to worship Vishnu in particular as the great savior of humanity. He supposedly would appear on Earth in various forms to fight the forces of darkness and evil. The most popular of Vishnu's forms were described in the two great epics: Krishna in the *Mahabharata*, and Rama in the *Ramayana*.

Perhaps in an effort to cope with the growing insecurity that followed the collapse of the Mauryan Empire, Brahmins also began to compile Hindu legal codes describing the gods and the requirements expected of people. For example, the sacred laws of dharma were written in the Law Code of Manu. The laws in this code differed according to a person's station in life. For example, the code states that the untouchables:

66 *shall not walk about in villages and towns [at night]. . . . By day . . . they shall carry out the corpses of persons who have no relatives. . . . They shall take for themselves the clothes, the beds, and the ornaments of [executed] criminals.* 99

The Law Code of Manu also described the duties of women. They could not study the Vedas, nor could they own property. Women were supposed to be obedient to the men in their families: to their fathers during childhood, to their husbands during marriage, and to their sons after their husbands died. However, men were expected to treat their female relatives with respect. As the Law Code of Manu noted: "Where the female relations live in grief, the family soon wholly perishes; but that family where they are not unhappy ever prospers." Despite the influence of the law code, these regulations primarily represented the views of Brahmins and were not widely observed by the masses of ordinary people.

In addition to law codes, people also began to seek security through a closer, more personal connection with the gods. The concept of *bhakti*, which had appeared in the *Bhagavad Gita*, grew in popularity. The intensity of this devoted worship is revealed in one passage of

▲ Two-faced Agni, the Hindu fire god, is seen here with his companion, the ram.

the *Bhagavad Gita*, in which Krishna appeals for devotion: "Give me thy heart! adore me! serve me! cling in faith and love and reverence to me!"

*W*hile the influence of Buddhism began to decline in India after the fall of the Mauryan Empire, developments in the old Vedic religion gave new rise to Hinduism.

The Gupta Empire

The rise of a new dynasty also contributed to the relative decline of Buddhism and the growth of Hinduism in India. In the A.D. 300s the Gupta family came to power in Magadha, the old capital of the Mauryans. Chandra Gupta I, the founder of the Gupta Empire, took power in A.D. 320 and soon began to expand his kingdom. Expansion continued under his successors, and by around A.D. 400 the Gupta Empire stretched from the Bay of Bengal to the Arabian Sea. Like the Mauryans, the Guptas eventually united all of northern India under their rule. Unlike the Buddhist Mauryans, however, the Guptas favored Hinduism. Although they continued to support Buddhism, building some of the most spectacular Buddhist temples ever constructed in India, they were more active in promoting and spreading Hindu culture.

During Chandra Gupta II's reign, from A.D. 375–415, Indian arts flourished and Indian society prospered. Under his successors, however, the Gupta Empire weakened. The Gupta political system, which was less centralized than the Mauryan government had been, gave considerable power to local leaders.

▶ This gold coin from Chandra Gupta II's reign bears his image.

Theme:
The Arts

The *Panchatantra* is an anonymous collection of Buddhistic tales most likely compiled sometime before A.D. 500. The framework of the *Panchatantra* consists of one narrative thread that holds together several different stories. The characters of the tales tell the stories themselves, creating a narrative with many different levels. The stories, which combine both prose and verse, were originally intended for the instruction of the sons of royalty.

Critical Thinking Ask students why the author of Panchatantra might have used multiple narrators.

ANSWER: Students might suggest that the author used multiple narrators to tell a broad, realistic story from different perspectives.

Gupta Empire, c. A.D. 400

Hindu Empire The Gupta rulers united northern India, where they built ornate temples to the Hindu gods.

? Location What bodies of water bordered the Gupta Empire?

In addition, invading nomads from Central Asia forced Skanda Gupta, the last great Gupta king, to drain his treasury in an attempt to defend the empire. Soon after Skanda Gupta's death, the invaders gained control over the Punjab and by around A.D. 550 they had destroyed the Gupta Empire.

The Gupta Empire brought all of northern India under one rule and gave new life to Indian culture.

The Flowering of Hindu Culture

The Guptas' support for Hinduism stimulated a flowering of religious art and culture. The Gupta period was India's classical age, a time of great advances in art, literature, and science.

Art and literature. The Gupta era produced extraordinary works of art and literature that combined religious images with scenes of everyday life. Sculptors produced beautiful stone and bronze statues, and painters created elaborate murals, such as the Buddhist cave paintings at Ajanta. Architects began to construct beautiful and symbolic Hindu temples, which were meant to represent the universe in stone. The centers of these temples were square, the imagined shape of the universe. Above was a tall spire meant to connect heaven and Earth. Covering the temples were detailed carvings of spiritual and earthly subjects. Through this architecture, the builders tried to convey the mythology of Hinduism. Many Indians also believed that the creation of religious art, combined with proper rituals, was itself an act of worship.

In addition to great architectural works, the Gupta age also produced lasting literary works. One work to appear at this time was a book of fables called the *Panchatantra*. In these fables, animals speak and act like human beings.

Gupta writers also produced sophisticated, emotional poetry and drama. Plays were never tragic, but always ended on a happy note. The greatest writer of the era was Kalidasa, often called the "Shakespeare of India." His plays and poems captured the beauty and refinement of Gupta culture.

Mathematics and science. Indians also made great advances in mathematics and science. Indian mathematicians developed numerals, which were later introduced to the West as the Arabic numeral system, and the decimal system. Astronomers calculated π (pi) to 3.1416 and determined that the earth was spherical and rotated on an axis.

Many of these advances took place at universities such as Nalanda, a Buddhist center of learning in northeastern India that drew students from all parts of Asia. In medicine, Gupta physicians made important discoveries about human anatomy and disease. They set broken bones and pioneered the practice of sterilization in surgery. They also used vaccinations to prevent disease.

Gupta Society

Along with the growth of Hindu culture came an expansion of the *jati* system. There were now hundreds of *jati* in Indian society, each with its own rules and customs. There were also many fixed relationships among *jati*. For example, within the villages every craftsman, such as a blacksmith or a barber, owed annual service to some peasant, who in turn provided the craftsman's family with enough rice to survive.

At the top level of society, the Brahmins established an idealized scheme of conduct for themselves to follow. They divided life into four stages—student, householder, hermit, and wanderer. After a period of study and learning about life in general, a man was expected to settle down and raise a family. Thereafter, he would gradually withdraw from the world in an effort to purify himself and attain *moksha*, or liberation from the wheel of reincarnation. Few people, however, observed this scheme strictly.

Life for women was far more restricted than for men. A Gupta legal document recommended that a woman worship her husband as a god. It became common for men to have more than one

◀ **A Hindu widow discusses her husband's funeral with the local prince.**

wife. Also common was **suttee**, the practice in which a wife committed suicide after the death of her husband by throwing herself on his cremation fire.

For Indians in lower social groups, life under Gupta rule varied little from previous centuries. Most people worked as farmers or artisans, but even for the poor, the vitality of Hindu culture provided welcome diversions, as this account shows:

> 66 *It is a day of festival. . . . The streets are broad rivers of people, folk of every race, buying and selling in the marketplace or singing to the music of wandering minstrels. A drum beats, and a royal procession passes down the street, with elephants leading. . . . Chariots follow, with prancing horses and fierce footmen.* 99

During the Gupta period, India enjoyed a classical age in which art, literature, mathematics, and science made great advances while the empire enjoyed great prosperity.

SECTION 2 REVIEW

IDENTIFY and explain the significance of the following:
- Bimbisara
- Chandragupta Maurya
- Asoka
- Chandra Gupta I
- Chandra Gupta II
- Skanda Gupta
- suttee

LOCATE and explain the importance of the following:
- Magadha
- Bay of Bengal
- Gandhara

1. ***Main Idea*** What did the Gupta rulers accomplish politically?
2. ***Main Idea*** Which period is considered to be India's classical age? How would you describe this period?
3. ***Geography: Place*** Why was northern India politically divided before the rise of the Mauryan Empire?
4. ***Writing to Explain*** Imagine that you are an ordinary Indian living after the fall of the Mauryan Empire. Write a letter to a friend explaining why Hinduism is becoming so popular.
5. ***Analyzing*** Why did the ancient Indian empires collapse after a few centuries?

SECTION 2 REVIEW ANSWERS

IDENTIFY
For significance, see the following pages:
Bimbisara (p. 152)
Chandragupta Maurya (p. 152)
Asoka (p. 153)
Chandra Gupta I (p. 155)
Chandra Gupta II (p. 155)
Skanda Gupta (p. 156)
suttee (p. 157)

LOCATE
For locations, see the maps on pp. 153 and 156.

1. The Gupta rulers united all of northern India and rejuvenated Indian culture.
2. The Gupta period is India's classical age. Society was prosperous and developments were made in the arts, literature, mathematics, and science.
3. The kingdom of Magadha ruled the northeastern part of India, while the northwestern part was conquered by Persia and invaded by Alexander the Great.
4. Students' letters should indicate that Hinduism was popular because of the decline of old ritual sacrifices and the emergence of a new popular literature—the Puranas. People wanted a greater sense of security through connection to the gods. The Gupta Empire adopted Hinduism.
5. A decline in strong central leadership along with invasions caused the empires to collapse.

R RESOURCE ACTIVITY

GEOGRAPHY ACTIVITIES

Geography Activity 6
Political Turmoil in China

Have students study the map and complete the questions on the Era of Warring States.

Level 2

R RESOURCE ACTIVITY

READINGS IN WORLD HISTORY
(p. 159)

Reading 6.3
The Wisdom of Confucius

Have students read about the Confucian concepts of family and government. Then have them complete the questions.

Level 2

158

SECTION 3

The Beginnings of Classical China

FOCUS

- How did the Zhou dynasty end?
- What did Confucius teach?
- What was the appeal of Daoism?
- How was Legalism different from Confucianism and Daoism?

When nomadic invaders stormed the capital of the Zhou dynasty in 771 B.C., the power of the kings came to an end. Although the Zhou kings moved the capital eastward to Luoyang, real power passed into the hands of mighty feudal lords. For the next 500 years, China entered a period of great turbulence, as hundreds of warlords fought each other for territorial control. During this time of turmoil, major political and social ideas developed that would serve as a firm foundation for classical Chinese civilization.

Bronze bells from the Era of Warring States

Political Turmoil

As the power of the Zhou rulers steadily declined, feudal lords who had once been loyal to the kings began building their own power in the walled cities of their estates. The kings became little more than figureheads with religious functions, but no political or military power.

The Spring and Autumn period. After the fall of the Western Zhou dynasty, China entered what later became known as the **Spring and Autumn period**, named after official state records of the same name. At the beginning of this period, around 722 B.C., about 200 independent states competed against each other for territory. As the intensity of warfare gradually increased, some states sought diplomatic solutions to their conflicts. They held frequent negotiations and conferences, signed treaties, and formed alliances. Gradually, however, the fighting became more ruthless and diplomacy failed, as feuding states expanded and came into closer contact with each other. Strong lords conquered weaker ones, thereby growing ever more powerful. As chariot warfare died out, the Chinese developed new, deadlier techniques of warfare. Armies swelled with large numbers of peasant soldiers armed with iron weapons. Eventually cavalry and mounted archers were introduced, adding to the destructiveness of war.

The Era of Warring States. In 403 B.C., as Chinese leaders abandoned diplomacy and turned to brute conquest, the **Era of Warring States** began. Over the next several hundred years, powerful states destroyed or absorbed weaker ones, and the number of states in China declined sharply. At the beginning of the 400s B.C., seven important states had emerged as the leading powers in China, battling each other for dominance. By the end of this period, the state of Qin (CHIN) triumphed over the others.

As the Chinese states grew stronger, they became more centralized—largely to support bigger, more powerful armies. Bureaucracies staffed by appointed officials replaced the old system of government by hereditary nobles. The need to support larger, centralized states also brought economic changes. New crops, tools, and irrigation techniques helped expand agricultural production. Trade increased, and cities grew larger and more prosperous.

The Era of a Hundred Schools. This period of turmoil was one of the most creative periods for Chinese philosophy. In response to the insecurity generated by near-constant warfare, Chinese thinkers looked for ways to restore harmony in society. This period of philosophical development is also known as the **Era of a Hundred Schools**, because so many different approaches to philosophy arose.

At the root of many of these philosophies was an ancient Chinese idea that everything in the world results from a balancing of complementary forces, called **yin and yang**. Yin was associated with darkness, weakness, and inactivity, while yang was characterized by brightness, strength, and activity. Many Chinese believed that when yin and yang were in balance, peace and prosperity would reign. For example, when opposing forces in nature, such as rain and drought, were in balance, crops would grow and the people would prosper; when they were out of balance, floods or drought would cause people to suffer.

▲ **Pangu, a legendary Chinese figure, holds the yin-yang symbol.**

The late Zhou dynasty ended in political turmoil, as warlords battled for power.

Confucianism

Kongzi, better known as Confucius, was the most influential philosopher in Chinese history and the one who best represented the search for balance and harmony in Chinese life. Confucius promoted a code of conduct that he believed would bring order to Chinese society.

BIOGRAPHY Born around 551 B.C. to an aristocratic family that had fallen on hard times, Confucius was raised in humble circumstances. He dreamed of holding government office, and as a young man he wandered from state to state in search of an official post. Unable to find work in government, Confucius became a teacher. He soon gained many followers among the sons of families hoping to get jobs in the growing bureaucracies of the Chinese kingdoms.

In his teachings, Confucius emphasized the need for a system of ethics and values that would restore social harmony and political stability in China. Confucius believed that in an earlier age, all people had known their proper places in society and fulfilled their duties accordingly. He saw the structure of the family as the best model for society. Convinced that the best way to solve China's current problems was to return to that imagined golden age, Confucius called for respect of traditional culture and strict observance of the principle of order.

In time, Confucius's teachings were written down in *The Analects,* a work that formed the basis for Confucianism, a philosophy that continues to influence Chinese thought today. Generally conservative, Confucianism stressed the importance of the family, respect for one's elders, and reverence for the past.

Confucius believed that if his ideas were applied to politics, order would return to China. In his view, this could be accomplished in two ways. First, people should accept and carry out their given roles. "Let the ruler rule as he should and the minister be a minister as he should," he stated. "Let the father act as a father should and the son act as a son should." In this way, society and government would function smoothly. Confucius's second point was that people, particularly rulers, should act virtuously. As he put it:

66 *When a prince's personal conduct is correct, his government is effective without the issuing of orders. If his personal conduct is not correct, he may issue orders but they will not be followed.* 99

Confucius

B I O G R A P H Y

R **RESOURCE ACTIVITY**

SKILLS ACTIVITIES (p. 160)
Skills Activity 6
Analyzing a Primary Source

Have students complete the questions about Laozi's passage on government.

Level 2

MULTIMEDIA PRESENTATION STRATEGY

WORLD HISTORY AND CULTURES VIDEODISCS

Image: *Confucius: The Chinese Philosopher*

Search Frame 750

Image: *Laozi: The Chinese Sage*

Search Frame 751

Image: *Laozi Meets Confucius*

Search Frame 752

Show the images as you discuss Confucianism and Daoism. The captions that accompany each CD-ROM image offer additional details.

All Levels

▲ This Confucian ceremony in Seoul, Korea, honoring the shrine of royalty, demonstrates the continuing influence of Confucianism today.

Confucius's emphasis on ethics in government, however, did not appeal to most Chinese rulers, who were mainly interested in gaining and holding on to power. As a result, Confucius never received the official support he desired. During his lifetime his efforts to influence the functioning of government had little impact.

After Confucius's death, however, others carried on his teachings, and his reputation grew. Eventually, his ideas would have an enormous impact on Chinese life. He was even raised to the status of a god by some followers.

Confucius emphasized moral codes designed to restore order and stability to Chinese society.

Daoism

Next to Confucianism, the most important Chinese philosophy that emerged during the Era of a Hundred Schools was Daoism (DOW-ih-zuhm). In part, Daoism was a reaction against the social and moral conformist teachings of Confucianism as well as against the bitter power struggles of the Era of Warring States. Daoists emphasized the independence of each individual, whose sole task and importance was to fit into the great pattern of nature. The road, or the way, to fit into nature was the Dao.

Laozi (LOWD-ZOO), the founder of Daoism, is thought to have lived sometime around the 500s B.C. and is credited with writing the principal Daoist work, the *Dao Da Jing*. Daoists believed that the Dao could not be defined or explained, but only experienced: "The one who knows does not speak, and the one who speaks does not know."

At the heart of Daoism is the effort to balance opposites. For Daoists, life is basically a paradox, or a combination of contradictory ideas. The principle of **wuwei** (WOO-WAY), or "nonaction," is central to Daoist thought: "Do by not doing, act by non-action, taste the taste-less, regard small as great, much as little." By nonaction, Daoists did not mean complete inaction, but doing what comes naturally. Daoists believed that if left to itself, the universe would proceed along its own harmonious course.

The Daoists also believed that the desire for power or material wealth clouded people's minds to truth. Real knowledge and contentment, Daoists said, came from self-contemplation:

❝To understand others is to be wise,
But to understand one's self is to be illumined [enlightened].
One who overcomes others is strong,
But he who overcomes himself is mighty.❞

▲ Daoists consider Laozi to be a great saint.

Eventually, Daoism was turned into a religion, with its own temples and rituals, and became quite popular. Even as a philosophy, however, it appealed to many Chinese. Artists in particular found inspiration in its emphasis on the contemplation of nature. Many Confucians found Daoism appealing as a kind of release from the restrictiveness of Confucian moral codes. In that sense, Daoism and Confucianism complemented each other, much like yin and yang.

Daoism appealed to many Chinese who favored a more mystical approach to life and found Confucian ethics too restrictive.

▲ Han Feizi was the greatest Chinese Legalist philosopher. This is a copy of the first page of one of his essays.

Legalism

The third major philosophical school that developed during the Era of a Hundred Schools was Legalism. The Legalists did not favor the calm, balanced approach to human conduct of the Confucians or Daoists. Instead, they believed that strictly enforced laws, not ritual observances or mysticism, would resolve the problems of political disunity and insecurity.

In the Legalist view, people were by nature selfish and untrustworthy. One Legalist philosopher noted:

66 *Men have likes and dislikes; thus they can be controlled by means of rewards and punishments. . . . The ruler need only hold these handles [rewards and punishments] firmly, in order to maintain his supremacy. . . . These handles are the power of life and death. Force is the stuff that keeps the masses in subjection [under control].* 99

Legalists believed that the state would be best served by putting the king's interests first and that kings should vigorously enforce laws to preserve order in society. Legalism, with its principle of rule by force, would become the official philosophy during the next Chinese dynasty, the Qin. Under this dynasty China would be controlled by its first truly centralized, imperial state.

Legalism differed from both Confucianism and Daoism in its view of human nature as selfish and its promotion of force to ensure order.

SECTION 3 REVIEW

IDENTIFY and explain the significance of the following:
Spring and Autumn period
Era of Warring States
Era of a Hundred Schools
yin and yang
Confucius
Laozi
wuwei

1. **Main Idea** What was the main teaching of Confucianism?
2. **Main Idea** In what way was Daoism a reaction against Confucianism?
3. **War and Diplomacy** How did the Zhou dynasty come to an end?

4. **Writing to Explain** In a short essay, compare the basic beliefs of Confucianism, Daoism, and Legalism.
5. **Synthesizing** How did the political situation during the Era of Warring States contribute to the development of philosophy?

IDENTIFY
For significance, see the following pages:
Spring and Autumn period (p. 158)
Era of Warring States (p. 158)
Era of a Hundred Schools (p. 159)
yin and yang (p. 159)
Confucius (p. 159)
Laozi (p. 160)
wuwei (p. 160)

1. Confucianism taught that China needed a system of ethics and values to restore order to society.
2. Daoism was a reaction against the social and moral conformity of Confucianism.
3. Beginning in 403 B.C. Chinese state leaders began fighting each other for power. Out of the seven important states that emerged, the Qin dynasty eventually gained control.
4. Confucianism—emphasized system of ethics and values, importance of family, reverence for the past; Daoism—emphasized independence of the individual and relationship to nature; Legalism—emphasized strictly enforced laws to solve problems of political disunity, kings should rule by force, people are selfish and untrustworthy
5. People were reacting against the insecurity and destruction of constant warfare.

Theme: **War and Diplomacy**

Shi Huangdi ruled his state on the Legalist principles of reward and punishment. As Shang Yang, his advisor, put it: "To club together and keep your mouth shut is to be good; to be alienated from and spy on each other is to be a scoundrel. If you glorify the good, errors will be hidden; if you put scoundrels in charge, crime will be punished."

Critical Thinking Ask students to describe what it might be like to live in a society based on Legalist principles.

ANSWER: Students' answers will vary, but they might include a concentration of power in the government, laws enforced by the threat of violence, and rewards given to encourage cooperation.

SECTION 4
Imperial China

FOCUS

- How did the Qin maintain their brief empire?
- How did Han rule differ from that of the Qin?
- How did Chinese civilization develop during the Qin and Han periods?
- What happened to Chinese civilization after the fall of the Han?

By the 200s B.C. the Chinese people had endured 500 years of warfare and instability. Centuries of fierce fighting among local warlords resulted in the rise of one noble family, the Qin, to rule over all others. The Qin dynasty began a pattern of strong centralized government that influenced China for centuries afterward. The complex bureaucracy put in place during the Qin dynasty allowed a remarkable degree of continuity in Chinese civilization despite the rise and fall of later dynasties.

Kneeling Qin warrior made of terra-cotta

The Qin Dynasty

By the early 300s B.C., the Qin state on China's western border had become one of China's dominant powers. Adopting Legalist ideas, the rulers of Qin created a strong state with a centralized bureaucracy financed by a direct tax on the peasantry. The Qin defeated other Chinese kingdoms one by one, and by 221 B.C. they had unified the country under their rule. According to the Chinese historian Sima Qian, the Qin swallowed up the other kingdoms "as a silkworm devours a mulberry leaf."

The first emperor. The ruler of this new, unified China took the name Shi Huangdi, which means "first emperor." From his capital at Changan in western China, Shi Huangdi ruled a larger area than either of the preceding dynasties and controlled it more firmly. Although the Qin Empire lasted only 15 years, it produced many lasting changes in Chinese life. The Qin dynasty, from which the Western name for China comes, standardized weights, measures, and coinage. In addition, the Qin established a uniform system of writing.

Shi Huangdi applied Legalist concepts to government. To control his nobles, he abolished all feudal landholdings and forced the aristocratic families to move to the capital. He divided China into military districts ruled by governors who exercised stern authority. The Code of Qin replaced conflicting local laws with a uniform legal system. Shi Huangdi also enacted a single tax system throughout the country, ending chaos in tax collection.

Not content with ruling northwestern China, Shi Huangdi sent his armies far to the south. His armies conquered large parts of southern China, penetrating as far as the Xi Jiang River Delta on the South China Sea. The armies also pushed back the peoples living on the northwestern borders.

To strengthen the empire, Shi Huangdi undertook massive public works. He built roads, bridges, and canals to move troops and supplies more easily. To guard against nomadic invasions from the north and west, Shi Huangdi built a long defensive wall in 214 B.C. to separate Chinese civilization from other peoples. Later rulers would extend this wall, until by the

▲ The Great Wall of China was built in stages and took centuries to complete. Its purpose was to keep out foreign invaders.

A.D. 1500s it stretched nearly 2,000 miles and became known as the Great Wall of China.

Qin autocracy. The Qin maintained order in the empire by establishing an **autocracy** in which the emperor held total power. Believing that it was dangerous to allow scholars to investigate and discuss problems freely, Shi Huangdi decided to eliminate all opposition. He burned books that deviated from official Legalist doctrine, including classics of Chinese Confucian literature. This policy was supported by Shi Huangdi's grand councillor, Li Si:

66 *There are those who unofficially propagate [spread] teachings directed against imperial decrees and orders. . . . All persons possessing works of literature and discussions of the philosophers should destroy them. Those who have not destroyed them . . . are to be branded and work as convicts.* 99

When some scholars did not heed this warning, Shi Huangdi had 460 of them executed.

The Qin believed in harshly punishing groups of people for an individual's wrongdoing. When a person broke the law, his or her entire family and several other families were held accountable for that individual's misdeeds. To avoid punishment, people had to inform on all wrongdoers immediately. Because citizens were required to inform on their relatives and neighbors, many people grew to resent Qin authority.

Discontent spread quickly under the harsh rule of the Qin dynasty. The aristocrats had lost their land and power, and the peasantry had suffered heavy taxation and excessive burdens of forced labor. Many people found the Qin rule intolerable. Shortly after the death of Shi Huangdi in 210 B.C., many communities exploded in open rebellion against the Qin, bringing the short-lived Qin dynasty to an end.

*B*y putting Legalist principles into practice, the Qin dynasty established a strong centralized Chinese empire.*

The Han Dynasty

In 202 B.C., four years after the fall of the Qin dynasty, a peasant general named Liu Bang seized power and founded the Han dynasty. While the Qin dynasty had collapsed soon after the death of its first emperor, the Han dynasty stayed in power for 400 years, ruling over a prosperous domain that was larger than its contemporary, the Roman Empire.

The civil-service system. When Liu Bang seized power, he wanted to maintain the authority of the Qin state without bringing on the hostility of the Chinese people that Qin autocracy had raised. He believed that it was important to achieve a balance of yin and yang in imperial government. Liu Bang kept the administrative structure that the Qin had built, but softened it by bringing Confucian ethics into government. Liu Bang was not well educated, so he invited scholars to advise him. Thus began the strong Confucian influence over the Chinese government that persisted for centuries afterward.

During the reign (140–87 B.C.) of the strongest Han emperor, Wudi, this informal collection of wise advisors became an organized **civil service**. The efficiency of the civil service was improved by the introduction of an examination system.

Theme: Religion

The establishment of the ruler as a divine power— the Son of Heaven—was extremely important to the Han dynasty. Using an earlier theory of divine authority that had been created by the Zhou dynasty—the Mandate of Heaven—the Han emperors legitimized their claims to divine authority by saying that the Mandate of Heaven had been reborn in their new ruler. The Han religion established that the ruler should be responsible for the well-being of his subjects and for being an example of moral virtue. The emperor showed his moral virtue by performing daily rituals and ceremonies.

Critical Thinking Ask students if they think the Han emperors' rule was an example of a pure autocracy, or an arrangement that placed obligations on both rulers and people.

ANSWER: Students may say that the emperors held total power because there were no real checks on their rule, or that the rulers were required to consider the welfare of their subjects and show moral virtue in exchange for the people's obedience.

Qin and Han Dynasties, 221 B.C.–A.D. 220

The Administration of Empire The Qin and Han dynasties dramatically expanded Chinese territory. The Qin built the Great Wall to defend themselves from northern nomads and a system of roads and canals to administer their new territories.

Linking Geography and History What may have inspired the Han conquest of the territory around the Takla Makan desert?

Although government officials were still recommended on the basis of family connections, they also had to pass competitive examinations before being appointed to government posts.

The highest government officials prepared for these exams at the imperial university, established in Changan in 124 B.C. Students learned the Confucian **Five Classics**: the *Book of Poetry*, the *Book of History*, the *Book of Divination*, the *Spring and Autumn Annals*, and the *Book of Rites*. The exams tested candidates on their knowledge of the Five Classics, which the Han believed offered great insights into the art of government.

As a result of these competitive examinations, many of the best scholars became government officials. Known as **mandarins**, these officials controlled the government bureaucracy. In theory, anyone could take the examinations, and it was possible for a poor boy to rise to great heights in the civil service. In general, however, few peasants could afford the expensive education needed to pass the exams, so it was mainly the sons of wealthy families who became civil servants.

Imperial expansion. During Wudi's energetic reign, the Han Empire expanded at a rapid rate. Chinese armies marched north into Manchuria and what is now Korea, and south into what is now Vietnam. Wudi's greatest challenge, however, was the Xiongnu (shee-UNG-noo), a confederation of nomads who lived in the steppe to the northwest. The Xiongnu, who may have been related to the Huns who later invaded the Roman Empire, periodically raided northern China and made it impossible for the Chinese to control the profitable trade with western Asia.

▲ The powerful Han emperor Wudi's interest in Confucianism led him to make it China's state religion.

Wudi used three tactics to conquer the Xiongnu: military force, diplomacy, and bribery. In a drawn-out war, Wudi's huge army finally destroyed Xiongnu power south of the Gobi Desert. Afterward, Wudi attempted to build alliances with the Xiongnu's enemies to protect China's frontier. Finally, Wudi resorted to a policy of "peace and kinship" by which Han emperors entertained nomadic chieftains and gave them lavish gifts. The nomadic Xiongnu soon learned that if they appeared to accept the authority of the Han emperor, they would profit enormously.

However, conflict between the Xiongnu and the Han continued after Wudi's death. Chinese armies moved beyond the empire's borders to conquer the nomads. They gradually extended Han military strength more than 2,000 miles— farther from their capital than the Roman legions had been from Rome.

To maintain this vast empire, the Han government taxed the peasants in northern China heavily. Many peasants fled from this heavy tax burden by migrating south or moving to the estates of great landowners, whose rental fees were lower than the taxes. To make up for the shortfall, those peasants who stayed behind in northern China had to pay even higher taxes. This inspired a revolt against the Han government.

In the A.D. 100s aristocratic families, university students, and Daoist religious leaders also rebelled, seriously weakening the empire. Gradually, the empire began to divide into three parts. In the north the last Han emperor was overthrown in A.D. 220 by Ts'ao P'ei, who founded a new dynasty called the Wei. New kingdoms also emerged in the west and south, and China entered a turbulent and disunited era.

Building upon the foundations laid by the Qin, the Han rulers made Confucian principles their official doctrine and created the largest empire China had ever seen.

The Growth of Chinese Civilization

Under the centralized rule of the Qin and Han dynasties, Chinese culture flourished. Traditional elements of Chinese society, such as an emphasis on family life, combined with new economic and technological developments to produce a civilization of great sophistication and brilliance.

Family and social life. Chinese society rested on the Confucian principle that the family was central to the welfare of the state. The values that governed family life—reverence for one's family, respect for age as a source of wisdom, and acceptance of the decisions made by one's social superiors—governed most aspects of Chinese life.

The family, not the individual, was the most important unit in Chinese society. The father ruled the family. His most important duties included arranging his children's and his grandchildren's marriages, deciding how his sons would be educated, and even choosing his sons' careers. Women were supposed to be obedient to men. According to Confucian doctrine, any attempt to achieve equality between men and women would result in social disharmony. Therefore, women generally did not own property or receive a Confucian education. Women could achieve a certain amount of power within the family, however, because of the reverence that traditional Chinese society held for mothers and mothers-in-law.

Text continues on page 168.

Daily Life

Vegetable fibers, hemp, and silk were the most common fabrics in use during the Han dynasty. While few examples of hemp cloth exist today, historians assume that the majority of the population used hemp or other fibers for their clothes. Silk was very expensive and is known to have been used for imperial robes and servicemen's uniforms.

Because so few pieces still exist today, it is thought that people wore their silk garments until they disintegrated. The high price of silk led people to try and get as much use as possible out of their garments—often, patchwork garments were created out of remaining pieces of fabric that were not threadbare.

Critical Thinking Ask students to suggest reasons why soldiers' uniforms might have been made from a luxury fabric like silk.

ANSWER: Students might suggest that soldiers can be considered representatives of the government, and silk uniforms would emphasize the wealth and power of the state.

Geography AND HISTORY

The Silk Road

In 1933 Swedish explorer Sven Hedin set out on an expedition traveling along the ancient route of the Silk Road through Central Asia. Hedin related the beauty and the danger of his trip as he described one evening's travel:

66 *The valley became wilder and wilder, with steep cliffs and delightful views. The evening light on the mountains was magnificent; the peaks shone out a brilliant orange as we serpentined [snaked] sharply along that extraordinary road, which was certainly not made for cars. . . . We crossed a side valley by a bridge and climbed again on a narrow, dangerous winding cliff road, sloping steeply towards the precipice [cliff]. We wondered all the time how long we should be able to keep the cars on an even keel. One error, and we should have dashed down the slope and been crushed to a pulp.* 99

The trip along the paths of the 9,000-mile caravan route known as the Silk Road was no less dangerous for merchants and travelers in ancient times. People moving along the Silk Road had to fear freezing to death in sudden blizzards in the mountains, dying of thirst, becoming delirious in the desert, or falling victim to roving bands of robbers. So why were people willing to risk their lives and possessions to travel the Silk Road? The story begins many centuries ago, in the legends of ancient China.

Chinese texts relate the legend of Leizu, a woman in the court of the emperor Shi Huangdi. Legend has it that one day Leizu was sitting quietly watching a worm in a mulberry tree spin its cocoon when she came up with the idea that the thread produced by the worm could be spun into cloth. By the first century A.D., under the reign of the Han, silk had become the most important product in Chinese society.

The traditional process for making

Workers learn to use silkworms.

Checking a bolt of finished silk

raw silk has changed little since ancient times. Young silkworms must be kept at a warm temperature and must be fed fresh mulberry leaves every half hour. When the worms are ready to form their cocoons, they are placed on trays made of straw. Once the cocoons are almost completed, they are thrown into boiling water, which kills the worms and removes the gum from the thread. The boiled cocoons are carefully unraveled and the threads of several cocoons joined together. Then the thread is ready to be spun into silk cloth.

The process of making silk was a secret carefully guarded by the Chinese. People smuggling the eggs of silkworms out of the empire could face the death penalty. Since silk was only available in China, people in far-off kingdoms were willing to pay high prices to obtain the precious material. Silk was probably first seen in Rome around 40 B.C., when it was used for the tents of the rulers. Within only a few years, silk clothing became so popular in Rome that the Senate had to ban men from wearing it, because so much gold was flowing out of the empire to pay for silk.

In order for silk to reach Rome, it had to travel across Asia and pass through many

The Silk Road, c. A.D. 100s

Linking East and West Stretching from the Wei He valley in China to the shores of the Mediterranean, the Silk Road passed through rugged mountain ranges, harsh deserts, and the territory of strong empires.

❖ Movement Which major mountain ranges did traders on the Silk Road pass through?

hands. The Silk Road began at Changan in western China. Silk cloth was brought to the city from Shandong and Hangzhou, major silk-producing regions. From Changan the silk—and other goods such as precious stones, furs, and cinnamon—began the overland trek in large camel caravans. In the first century A.D. one large caravan left Changan every month. The goods then passed through a series of middlemen, from the Kushans to the Persians, to the Parthians, to the Greek and Jewish merchants in the eastern Mediterranean. There the goods were often traded for gold and silver headed ultimately for China.

In addition to goods, ideas also traveled along the Silk

Road. Buddhism came to China in the first century A.D. through missionaries traveling over the Silk Road. Within the next few hundred years, Buddhist pilgrims from China traveled the Silk Road to India, bringing Chinese artistic influence with them. In the A.D. 600s and 700s a new religion, Islam, also was carried by merchants along the Silk Road to western China, where it was adopted by many people.

Ambassadors regularly traveled among the various kingdoms of Central Asia along the Silk Road. In A.D. 166 the Romans sent an ambassador to the Han court to discuss trade. Chinese ambassadors also traveled west to visit the royal courts of the Asian empires.

Today ships, trains, trucks, and airplanes have made international trade and contacts a common part of everyday life. There was a time, however, when the dangerous camel paths known as the Silk Road provided the most important link between the great civilizations of the ancient world.

Linking Geography and History

1. Traders traveling along the Silk Road passed through what four empires?
2. What geographical features made traveling along the Silk Road difficult?
3. How might trade along the Silk Road help increase people's knowledge of other cultures?

Theme: Cross-cultural Interaction

While the penalty for smuggling silkworm eggs out of China was death, it is said that in the early A.D. 550s two former missionaries to China smuggled out, in a hollow staff, both the eggs of the silkworm and the seeds of the mulberry tree to Constantinople, under the urging of Emperor Justinian. Byzantium subsequently became famous for its beautiful silk material and embroidery, which was used for royal and religious costumes. Over the centuries, the art of silk culture and weaving continued to spread throughout Europe.

Critical Thinking Ask students why they think the penalty for smuggling silkworm eggs out of China was so harsh.

ANSWER: Students might suggest that the Chinese authorities wanted to keep a monopoly on the supply of silk.

Linking Geography and History

1. Chinese, Kushan, Parthian, Roman
2. mountain ranges and deserts
3. Traders encountered many different cultures, and ideas were exchanged.

▲ Han mandarins enjoyed great power and privileges. Here, an official travels in a personal, slave-drawn carriage.

As in every age, there were some women who achieved positions of authority despite social restrictions. In Han China, an educated woman named Ban Zhao served as the imperial historian in the first century A.D. In *Lessons for Women*, Ban Zhao described the complementary nature of the ideal relationship between Chinese men and women:

> As Yin and Yang are not of the same nature, so man and woman have different characteristics. . . . Man is honored for strength; a woman is beautiful on account of her gentleness. . . . The correct relationship between husband and wife is based upon harmony and . . . love is grounded in proper union.

The economy. During the Qin and Han periods, the family remained the primary economic unit. Despite the growth of towns and cities, most Chinese families continued to live as peasant farmers in small villages. Not only did they face the challenge of raising enough food to survive, but they also had to fulfill the government's demands for taxes and labor. For part of each year, they left their farms and worked on roads, canals, or other local construction projects.

Under the Han dynasty, the government enacted a policy that helped peasant farmers by stabilizing the price of farm products. Called **leveling**, the policy had the government buy and store surplus crops in years of good harvests. In years of poor harvests the government would sell the stored crops to prevent scarcity and high prices.

Although trade was less important to China than farming, its role in the economy gradually increased. The Qin policy of standardizing the currency and weights and measures stimulated commerce. Much of the trade was controlled by the state with the profits going into the imperial treasury. As one Chinese official remarked:

> The furs of sables, marmots, foxes and badgers, colored rugs and decorated carpets fill the imperial treasury, while jade and auspicious [wonderful] stones, corals and crystals, become national treasures. That is to say, foreign products keep flowing in, while our wealth is not dissipated [taken away]. . . . National wealth not being dispersed [distributed] abroad, the people enjoy abundance.

In addition, once the Han dynasty gained control over much of Central Asia, trade prospered along a number of routes that together became known as the **Silk Road**.

Science and technology. Although education was available only to a privileged few in China, the Qin and Han periods saw dramatic developments in the fields of science and technology. In astronomy, for example, Han scientists calculated the length of the year with great accuracy. In 28 B.C. Chinese astronomers first observed sunspots, which Europeans did not discover until the A.D. 1600s. Sometime before A.D. 100, the Chinese also built special instruments to observe the movement of planets. Other scientific achievements included the invention of a primitive seismograph that registered even faint earthquakes.

One of the most important Chinese inventions was paper. First created in A.D. 105, by A.D. 700 the use of paper had spread to other parts of Asia and to Europe, where it became the main writing material. The Chinese also invented woodblock printing, as well as a sundial and a water clock.

By the 400s B.C., the Chinese were using **acupuncture** to treat illnesses. The development of acupuncture stemmed from the Daoist belief that good health depends on the movement of a life-force energy through the body and that illness or pain results when something interferes with that movement. Doctors using acupuncture insert needles into certain points on the body,

Then & NOW

Acupuncture

Some scholars believe that the use of acupuncture—treatment of health problems with needles—extends as far back as 7,000 years to Neolithic times. The first written evidence of its use is found in *The Yellow Emperor's Classic of Internal Medicine,* believed to have been written down in the 200s or 300s B.C. It wasn't until about the A.D. 900s that traditional Chinese medicine began to find its way into foreign lands. It was much later, in 1929, that a French consul in China translated a Chinese text and introduced the practice of acupuncture to France. During the mid-1800s Chinese immigrants brought the medical practices to the United States. Slowly but surely, knowledge of an ancient form of treating ailments spread across the world.

The practice of acupuncture is based on belief in the influence on the body of two opposing but complementary principles—yin and yang—whose balance affects everything in the universe. The two forces create an energy known as *qi* (CHEE)—which is associated with the thought of vitality or life-force energy. Traditional Chinese medicine teaches that many disorders of the body are the result of an imbalance of *qi.* As the life-force energy, *qi* affects the entire body. When a person has an ailment, Chinese medicine considers the entire body to be out of balance, rather than locating a specific problem and isolating it for treatment. The treatment is applied by inserting extremely slender, sterile, stainless-steel needles into certain points on the body. The pressure of the needles is believed to affect the flows of *qi,* resulting in healing. Frequently herbs are also administered as part of the treatment.

Today in the United States and other Western countries, many people use acupuncture for the

Acupuncture chart showing treatment points

treatment of such medical problems as allergies, chronic pain, drug and alcohol addictions, and migraine headaches. In addition acupuncture has also been used for thousands of years in China as an anesthetic during surgery. While there is much skepticism regarding this treatment because it seems so foreign to physicians and patients of Western medicine, there are also many true believers.

Currently, in the United States there are about 3,000 medical doctors and osteopaths (practitioners who believe that ailments can be treated by the adjustment of various parts of the body and therapeutic measures) and 7,000 nonphysicians who treat health problems with some sort of traditional Eastern techniques. In addition, animals receive acupuncture treatments from the approximately 200 veterinarians who are members of the International Veterinary Acupuncture Society. As the debate continues over the benefits of this ancient medical practice, several Western research groups are attempting to prove the many claims of success with acupuncture. Studies are being performed that may someday confirm acupuncture as an established form of treatment in the West for many health problems.

Acupuncture treatment at a Chinese medical university

SECTION 4 REVIEW ANSWERS
(p. 170)

IDENTIFY
For significance, see the following pages:
Shi Huangdi (p. 162)
autocracy (p. 163)
Wudi (p. 163)
civil service (p. 163)
Five Classics (p. 164)
mandarins (p. 164)
leveling (p. 168)
Silk Road (p. 168)
acupuncture (p. 168)

LOCATE
For locations, see the maps on pp. 164 and 167.

1. Using Legalist principles of control by force, the Qin dynasty established a strong state with a centralized bureaucracy and an all-powerful emperor.

◀ This device, invented by scholar Chang Heng in A.D. 132, warned of earthquakes when balls from the dragons' mouths dropped into the frogs' mouths.

which are believed to be connected to internal organs through a network of channels.

Many elements of later Chinese civilization developed during the Qin and Han dynasties. For example, government developed into a complex bureaucracy guided by Confucian ethics, while among the people, the belief of the importance of groups over individuals became firmly entrenched. Chinese technology became quite advanced, while China's armies built a vast empire. During the Qin and Han dynasties, the Chinese achieved a brilliant civilization and established many traditions that would influence China for centuries.

Chinese civilization flourished under the stable, prosperous conditions of imperial rule.

Political Disunion and the Rise of Buddhism

After the fall of the Han dynasty in A.D. 220, China's political and economic organization began to fall apart. The nomadic tribes living along the frontier swarmed into northern China, sacking cities and killing people, at about the same time Germanic nomads were attacking the Roman Empire. By the A.D. 300s competition between Chinese kingdoms became fierce. In the north, 16 kingdoms fought for control, while in the south, a series of weak Chinese kingdoms rose and fell along the Yangzi River.

Eventually, the northern nomads settled down, established kingdoms, and adopted the Chinese way of life. They also encouraged the growth of Buddhism, which first entered China from India during Han times. Buddhism's promise of spiritual salvation gave comfort to many Chinese during a time of chaos and instability. Consequently, Buddhism soon spread throughout China.

Even after the fall of the Han dynasty, Chinese civilization continued to grow as Buddhism spread across China.

SECTION 4 REVIEW

IDENTIFY and explain the significance of the following:
Shi Huangdi
autocracy
Wudi
civil service
Five Classics
mandarins
leveling
Silk Road
acupuncture

LOCATE and explain the importance of the following:

Changan
Xi Jiang River
Gobi Desert

1. Main Idea How did Legalism influence the Qin Empire?
2. Main Idea In what ways was the rule of the Han dynasty different from the rule of the Qin?
3. Religion What role did Buddhism play in China after the fall of the Han dynasty?

4. Writing to Describe Imagine that you are a Chinese student during the Han dynasty studying for the civil-service examinations. Write a brief report describing the achievements of civilization under the rule of the Han.
5. Evaluating Why do you think that groups were more important than individuals during the Qin and Han dynasties?

Review

On a separate sheet of paper, complete the following exercises:

WRITING A SUMMARY

Using the essential points in the text, write a brief summary of the chapter.

REVIEWING TERMS

From the following list, choose the term that correctly matches the definition.

ahimsa
dharma
Five Classics
Four Noble Truths
Upanishads
yin and yang

1. according to ancient Chinese belief, complementary forces that must be kept in balance to achieve peace and prosperity
2. the major Confucian texts that persons taking the civil-service exam were required to know
3. the moral duty that people, according to their social position, must fulfill during their lifetime
4. the belief in nonviolence that is of utmost importance to Jains
5. teachings of the Buddha, which proclaim that all sorrow in life is caused by desire, and that if people reject desire and follow the Eightfold Path, they may achieve nirvana

REVIEWING CHRONOLOGY

List the following events in their correct chronological order.

1. Siddhartha Gautama achieves enlightenment.
2. The Han dynasty is founded.
3. The Zhou capital is destroyed.
4. The Qin dynasty rules northern China.
5. Chandragupta Maurya founds first Indian empire.

UNDERSTANDING THE MAIN IDEA

1. What are the central beliefs of Hinduism?
2. Which period is considered to be India's classical age? Why?
3. What are the main teachings of Confucianism?
4. Why did Daoism appeal to many Chinese people?
5. How did Legalist philosophy influence the government of the Qin Empire?

THINKING CRITICALLY

1. **Comparing and Contrasting** In what ways were Hinduism and Buddhism similar? How were they different?
2. **Analyzing** Why was the Han dynasty able to maintain power for 400 years, while the Qin dynasty endured little longer than the reign of its first emperor?

Building Your Portfolio

Complete the following activities individually or in groups.

1. **Social Classes** Write a short story that takes place during the Gupta age. Create five or more characters, including at least one Brahmin, Kshatriya, Vaisya, Sudra, and untouchable. In your story, be sure to relate what the characters do for a living, how and where they live, and how they interact with the rest of society. For added interest, you may include information about the religious beliefs of your characters, particularly those who follow Buddhism or Jainism. You may want to provide illustrations with your story.
2. **Science** Prepare a report about the development and use of acupuncture. Address the following questions in your report: What are the underlying beliefs that support the use of acupuncture? How did Chinese doctors discover its use? When and where did the practice of acupuncture spread? How has the modern Western medical community viewed acupuncture? How popular is the use of acupuncture today? To accompany your report, create a diagram showing the points of the body in which the acupuncture needles are used to treat certain ailments.

REVIEWING CHRONOLOGY

3, 1, 5, 4, 2

UNDERSTANDING THE MAIN IDEA

1. Hindus believe that if you live a good life and fulfill your dharma, then through reincarnation you will be born into a higher class, eventually becoming one with Brahma.
2. The Gupta period is India's classical age because the society was prosperous and great developments were made in the arts, literature, mathematics, and science.
3. Confucius emphasized a system of ethics and values and stressed the importance of family, respect for one's elders, and reverence for the past.
4. Daoism appealed to many Chinese because it did not support the social and moral conformity of Confucianism.
5. Using Legalist principles of control by force, the Qin dynasty established a strong state with a centralized bureaucracy and an all-powerful emperor.

THINKING CRITICALLY

1. similar—both believe in reincarnation; different—Buddhism rejected the varna system, emphasized the Four Noble Truths instead of the belief in karma and dharma
2. While keeping the structure of Qin government, the Han dynasty softened its rigid social control by applying the principles of Confucianism.

Herodotus is considered by most scholars to be the first historian. He traveled from his native Greece to faraway lands and recorded the customs of the peoples he encountered. His work is considered significant not only because of its age but also because Herodotus was extremely conscientious in recording all of the significant circumstances of an event, as well as the factors motivating the people involved. He also recorded myths and customs and speculated about the people he encountered. His speculations led, in many cases, to a greater understanding of ancient peoples. Not all of Herodotus's works can be considered reliable, however, because he occasionally used unverified information and did not always distinguish between fact and myth in his writings.

Critical Thinking Ask students how scholars might make use of Herodotus's writings given knowledge of their weaknesses.

ANSWER: Students may answer that scholars try to corroborate Herodotus's writings with writings of other ancient historians, compare his descriptions with archeological evidence, and use what they know about Herodotus's point of view and biases to sort out fact from speculation.

HISTORY IN THE Making

Comparative Historical Traditions

History is the accumulated record of the past. Yet it would be an impossible task to preserve the endless mass of details that constitute our daily lives. As people pick and choose the facts and events they want to remember, in a sense they become the creators of their own history. At the same time, what information people choose to preserve and how they do so may change over time. Such changes in a society's historical tradition, or historiography, often reflect shifts in the society's self-image and worldview.

Origins of the Western Historical Tradition

The foundation of modern Western historical tradition lies in the traditions of the ancient Hebrews and the ancient Greeks and Romans. From the Hebrews we have taken the idea that history has a definite beginning and a definite end, and that human events move in a relatively straight line from one event to the other. Scholars call this a "linear view" of history. From the Greeks and Romans we have taken the view that human beings, rather than some supernatural or divine force, are the primary makers of history. Both traditions reflect the basic worldview of the societies that created them.

The Torah and other writings of the ancient Hebrews constitute some of the earliest attempts to present the narrative history of a group of people. At the same time, the Hebrews thought of history as God's will being worked out in the world. History had begun, they believed, with the creation of Adam and Eve, the first man and woman, in the Garden of Eden. History would eventually end with a Day of Judgment, when God would determine who would receive everlasting life. In this view, history was not just a catalog of events, but a tale, in which God instructed his people.

Both Greek and Roman historians were heavily influenced by a more secular, or worldly, view. Greek and Roman historians did not see history as an expression of divine actions in people's lives, but rather as a record of purely human affairs. They also saw history as a political tool that could be used to give citizens a sense of civic identity and duty to the state. Consequently, Greek and Roman history generally

▲ The painted scene on this Greek vase illustrates a historic battle.

focused on stories of politics and war in an effort to draw lessons from the past that would help people make better decisions in the present.

In order to ensure the accuracy of their facts and conclusions about these historical lessons, both the Greek historian Thucydides and the Roman historian Polybius (puh-LIB-ee-uhs) laid down rules they believed historians should follow. These rules emphasized the importance of examining written and oral sources critically in order to determine their reliability and accuracy. At the same time, the Greeks and Romans saw history as part of a larger field of literature and rhetoric. Good history, they believed, should provide a narrative or story that would engage the reader's interest.

The rise of Christianity as the dominant religion of western Eurasia at first led to the decline of the Greco-Roman historical tradition. Like the ancient Hebrews, Christian writers such as Saint Augustine emphasized the importance of studying God's plan for humanity rather than what they saw as the otherwise disconnected stories of human events. Stories of miracles and the lives of Christian saints tended to replace the narrative histories of the Greeks and Romans. Eventually, however, the Greco-Roman tradition reemerged and blended with the Judaeo-Christian historical tradition. As a result, modern Western historical tradition not only emphasizes the importance of accurate factual information but also generally

▶ Ssu-ma Ch'ien was the grand historian of the Han emperor Wudi and is sometimes called the "Father of Chinese History."

accepts the linear view of history found in the Bible.

The Chinese Historical Tradition

Not all peoples have such a linear view of history, however. In China, for example, historians traditionally viewed history as a basic pattern that repeated itself over and over again. Drawing on the teachings of Daoism, Chinese historians saw history as a constant process of balance as the ever-changing actions of human beings interacted with the reality and moral order of the Dao.

Like the Hebrews, Chinese historians saw history as a source of lessons for human behavior. Where the Hebrews interpreted these moral lessons as acts of God, however, the Chinese saw them as natural consequences of the unchanging reality of the impersonal Dao. In this view, history was not so much the story of God's will being played out on Earth, but rather a record of the collected wisdom and knowledge of humanity.

Consequently, Chinese historians regarded history not simply as the story of politics and war, as the Greeks and Romans did, but as an integrated tale of political, economic, social, and natural events. While the vari-

ous elements of this tale might change through time, they believed the basic pattern remained the same. Thus, they tried to explain both historical change and what they believed to be the orderly natural cycle of human existence.

China's historical tradition also reflected the increasingly bureaucratic nature of imperial Chinese society. Early Chinese historians like Ssu-ma Ch'ien (sooh-MAH-chee-EN) and Pan Ku, for example, explained Chinese history in terms of the passing of the Mandate of Heaven from one dynasty to another. The history of imperial dynasties thus followed a path much like that found in nature—an endless cycle of the rise, flowering, decline, and fall. Later Chinese historians added refinements, noting the attempted renewal that often came midway through a dynastic cycle, as a weakening dynasty tried to regain its strength. Yet such refinements in historical tradition only reinforced the Chinese cyclical view of history.

One of the most famous of the early Jewish historians was Josephus. Included among his works are *Jewish Antiquities*, a history of the Jews from Creation to the war with Rome; *The History of the Jewish War*, which details the Jewish-Roman conflict; and *Against Apion*, a defense of the Jewish race.

Josephus took part in the Jewish rebellion against the Romans that began in A.D. 66. He was sent to command the army in Galilee, but when he decided he could not defeat the Romans, he withdrew to the town of Jotapata. The Romans besieged the town for seven weeks, and finally Josephus went over to the Roman side. Josephus accompanied Titus on his siege of Jerusalem. He then went to Rome, where he was given a pension and Roman citizenship and began his writing.

Critical Thinking Ask students what sorts of biases scholars might be watchful for when studying the works of Josephus.

ANSWER: Students might say that Josephus may not have presented all the faults in Jewish history, since he had been a patriotic Jewish leader. He might also have tried to avoid criticizing Rome, since he was a Roman citizen receiving a pension.

Chapter 7

Early African Civilizations c. 1800 B.C.– c. A.D. 1235

Chapter Planning Guide

	TEXTBOOK	CORE RESOURCES	VISUAL RESOURCES	MULTIMEDIA
Introduction	pp. 174–175	Block Scheduling Handbook: Ch. 7		Videodisc Segment 7 and Viewing Guide: *Early African Traditions*
Lesson 7.1 Patterns of African History	pp. 176–180 Map: *Africa*, p. 177 Geography and History: *Africa's Geography and Peoples*, p. 177 Literature Through Time: *Africa's Oral Literature Tradition*, p. 179	Reading 7.1: *Oral History and Folktales* Skills Activity 7: *Identifying the Main Idea* Writing Project 7: *Writing a Descriptive Essay*		GHRC 7 Reading: *How Africans Viewed Their Land* GHRC 7/Videodiscs: Audio Clip—*African "Talking Drums"*
Lesson 7.2 Kingdoms in the Sudan: Kush and Aksum	pp. 181–184 Map: *The Kingdoms of Kush and Aksum*, p. 182 History Through the Arts: *Stonemasons of Aksum*, p. 183	Reading 7.2: *The Fall of Meroe*		GHRC 7 Readings: *Daily Life in Kush; The Silent Trade of the Aksumites* GHRC 7/Videodiscs: Image—*Nubians Bringing Gifts to Egypt*
Lesson 7.3 North Africa and the Sahara	pp. 185–189 Then and Now: *Crossing the Sahara*, p. 186 Map: *North Africa and the Sahara*, p. 187 Through Others' Eyes: *Herodotus's Travels in Africa*, p. 188	Reading 7.3: *Trade and Civilization in Carthage* Geography Activity 7: *The Spread of Ironworking*	Geography and History 7: *North Africa and the Sahara*	GHRC 7 Readings: *Carthage at the Peak of Its Prosperity; The Romans Take Revenge; Roman North Africa* GHRC 7/Videodiscs: Images—*Gold Jewelry from Ancient Carthage; Ruins of a Roman Marketplace in North Africa; Map—African Caravan Routes*
Lesson 7.4 Iron-Age Developments in Sub-Saharan Africa	pp. 190–194 Map: *The Iron-Age Kingdoms of Africa*, p.192	Reading 7.4: *The Land of Zanj*	Art and History 7: *Terracotta Portrait Head* Everyday Life 7: *Coptic Crosses*	GHRC 7 Readings: *An East African King; The Markets of West Africa; Bantu Law Courts; Bantu System of Kingship; The Meaning of Cattle to African Herders* GHRC 7/Videodiscs: Images—*Ethiopia's Ancient Christian Tradition; Masai Cattle Herders*
Chapter Investigation and Enrichment	pp. 174–194	Chapter 7 Investigation: *Museum of Early African History* People in World History 7 Explorations in Daily Life 7		GHRC 7/Videodiscs
Review and Assessment	Section 1 Review, p. 180 Section 2 Review, p. 184 Section 3 Review, p. 189 Section 4 Review, p. 194 Chapter 7 Review, p. 195	Chapter Review Activity 7 Vocabulary Activity 7 Themes Review 7 Section Study Guides 7.1–7.4 Main Idea Activities 7.1–7.4 Daily Quizzes 7.1–7.4 Chapter 7 Test Sheltered English Ch. 7 Test Ch. 7 Test Generator		Audio CDs: Ch. 7 Summary (English and Spanish)

INTRODUCING THE CHAPTER

Textbook pp. 174–175

CHAPTER OVERVIEW

Africans developed diverse societies, from subsistence farming communities to wealthy kingdoms built on trade. The kingdom of Kush was a major source of gold, while Aksum grew rich on the ivory trade. The trade routes along the rim of the Sahara enriched Ghana and other small city-states. Trade also allowed Christianity to exert powerful influences on some north African societies. In central and southern Africa, migrating Bantu-speaking peoples came to dominate the area.

PRESENTING THEMES

On the chalkboard or on an overhead transparency, write the following open-ended theme questions.

- **GEOGRAPHY** In what ways might geography influence the development of trade?
- **TECHNOLOGY** How might the use of improved weapons affect the development of a society?
- **ECONOMIC ORGANIZATION** What makes certain items valuable trading goods?

Have students, either individually or in groups, suggest responses to the questions. For the geography question, students might suggest that natural obstacles could make trade between two areas difficult. For the technology question, students might suggest that improved weapons could allow society to use warfare to meet its needs. For the economic organization question, students might suggest that items that are attractive and rare, such as gold, or necessary for human survival, such as salt, often become valuable trading items. Save the responses. Once students have studied the chapter, you may wish to have them complete the Themes Review, then compare the two sets of answers.

USING THE VIDEO

Segment 7: *Early African Traditions*

ENGLISH

Search Chapter 7
Videodisc 1, Side B

SPANISH

Search Chapter 7
Videodisc 1, Side B

Tell students that in this chapter they will examine the factors that led to the development of powerful empires, wealthy kingdoms, and enduring patterns of life across Africa many hundreds of years ago. Then show Segment 7 of the *World History and Cultures Videodiscs*. This segment explores the importance of music, especially drumming, in traditional African life and culture through the eyes of Kwaku Daddy, a folklorist and master drummer from Ghana.

Before showing the segment, ask students to pay particular attention to the ways Africans have traditionally used music. To help students grasp the significant points of the segment, have them complete Video Viewing Guide 7.

Key to Ability Levels

All strategies and activities are coded to the following ability levels:

LEVEL 1	**Basic** activities suitable for all students
LEVEL 2	**Average** activities suitable for average to above-average students
LEVEL 3	**Challenging** activities suitable for above-average students
SHELTERED ENGLISH	Activities suitable for students with **Limited English Proficiency**

Additional Resources

BOOKS FOR TEACHERS

Davidson, Basil. *The Lost Cities of Africa,* rev. ed. Back Bay Books, 1970. Offers a well-written discussion of ancient kingdoms.

Gurney, Gene. *Kingdoms of Asia, the Middle East, and Africa.* Crown Publishers, 1986. Offers an encyclopedic discussion.

Monro-Hay, Stuart. *Aksum: An African Civilization of Late Antiquity.* Edinburgh University Press, 1991. Presents a scholarly discussion of Aksum.

BOOKS FOR STUDENTS

Connah, Graham. *African Civilizations: Precolonial Cities and States in Tropical Africa.* Cambridge University Press, 1987. Offers an accessible overview of early African kingdoms.

Koslow, Philip. *The Kingdoms of Africa.* Chelsea House, 1995. Discusses Ghana, Mali, and others.

Oliver, Ronald Anthony. *A Short History of Africa.* Facts On File, 1989. Includes early Africa.

MULTIMEDIA MATERIALS

Africa. WorldView Software. Apple II, PC, WIN formats. Includes a wide variety of resources.

Africa: Caravans of Gold/Kings and Cities. RM Arts. Video, 17 minutes. Presents noted scholar Basil Davidson discussing ancient kingdoms.

North Africa: The Great Sahara. Coronet. Video, 16 min. Looks at how the desert affected the region.

Lesson 7.1   *Patterns of African History*

Textbook pp. 176–180

RESOURCES

Pupil's Edition

Map, p. 177: *Africa, c. 3000 B.C.–A.D. 1200*
Geography and History, p. 177: *Africa's Geography and Peoples*

Literature Through Time, p. 179: *Africa's Oral Literature Tradition*

Core Resources

Reading 7.1: *Oral History and Folktales*
Writing Project 7: *Writing a Descriptive Essay*

Global History Resource Center

Reading: *How Africans Viewed Their Land*

Videodiscs or Global History Resource Center

Audio Clip: African *"Talking Drums"*

Search 2272, Play to 2723
Videodisc 1, Side B
Audio Clip 7

LESSON FOCUS

What characterizes the geography and peoples of Africa?

OBJECTIVES

After completing this lesson, students will be able to:

- name the main features of the African environment;
- describe how African peoples adapted to their various environments;
- identify the characteristics that many African peoples have in common.

HOOK

Describe geographical regions of Africa. Have students examine the map on textbook page 177, and ask a volunteer to draw on the chalkboard a rough outline of the continent, as large as possible. Have the volunteer draw and label the equator on the map, and ask students what this tells them about the climate of Africa. *[The equator's location in mid-continent suggests that much of Africa is tropical.]*

Then have students locate, label, and describe (with books closed) the following geographical regions: (1) the northern coastal region *[Mediterranean climate; enough rainfall for agriculture]*; (2) the Sahara *[harsh desert]*; (3) the Sahel *[dry grasslands south of the Sahara]*; (4) tropical rainforests *[rainy, hot, and humid forested regions in west and central Africa]*; (5) southern savannas *[grasslands]*; (6) the Kalahari *[dry, hot desert in the south]*; (7) the southern coastal plain *[temperate]*. Have students compare the map on the chalkboard with the textbook map and make any corrections or helpful additions, such as rivers and mountains.

Ask: What effects can a continent's geography have on its history?

[Possible effects: Deserts can be barriers to trade, travel, and invasion; adequate rainfall—or a nearby river—encourages agriculture; people migrate out of regions with harsh climates.]

For more information, refer students to the Geography and History feature on textbook page 177, and assign the reading in the Global History Resource Center on how Africans viewed their land.

DEVELOP

Identify elements that demonstrate Africa's diversity.
Begin a chart on the chalkboard titled *Africa's Diversity.* Use the following column headings: Geography, Peoples, Patterns of

173C

Life. Have students list elements under each heading that reveal the diversity of Africa. [**Geography:** *chart might include geographical zones and major features;* **Peoples:** *chart might include a description of the different language groups;* **Patterns of Life:** *chart might include the development of sedentary farming and nomadic herding societies, as well as descriptions of social structures]*

Ask: *How did African peoples adapt to their environment?*

[*African peoples adapted in a variety of ways—farming, herding, fishing, or hunting and gathering. Some lived in stateless societies, while others developed strong states.]*

PROBE

Discuss the characteristics that many African peoples had in common. Tell students that despite the many different lifestyles that African peoples developed according to their environments, many shared common characteristics. Point out that many African societies maintained their links to the past through oral traditions. Have students examine the Literature Through Time feature on textbook page 179, as well as Core Resources Reading 7.1.

Ask: *What are oral traditions and how are they important to the African past?*

[*Oral traditions include stories, songs, poems, and proverbs. Much of African literature and history has been passed down through oral traditions, allowing Africans to maintain their sense of identity and ties to the past.]*

Then ask students to list other characteristics that many African peoples share. [*Lists should include the importance of family ties, religion, and children. Also, men usually had many wives and traditionally hunted, fished, and tended livestock, while women raised children and farmed and gardened.]*

You might want to lead a brief discussion of the importance of religion to many African peoples, pointing out the significance of the spirit world and magic. You could accompany this discussion with the audio clip of the "Talking Drums."

CONCLUDE

Write an encyclopedia entry about early Africa. Organize the class into groups and have them develop encyclopedia entries that might be written about the geography and history of early Africa. Students within each group could write brief paragraphs about these topics: 1) Geography (major geographic regions and features); 2) The People and their Politics (social and political structures and patterns of life); 3) Shared characteristics of many African peoples.

Encourage groups to compare their encyclopedia entries. Have them save their entries in their notebooks for review purposes.

EXTEND

Cross-Curricular Connection: *Language Arts*

Have students research the oral traditions of Africa, and ask them to write a brief essay about the subject. You may want to have them refer to Writing Project 7 for guidance on writing a descriptive essay, and have them read Core Resources Reading 7.1, as well as the Literature Through Time feature.

OTHER MEDIA

You might wish to show and discuss the video *Life on the Edge* (Coronet/MTI, color, 20 min.), which examines the people, plants, and animals of the Sahel and the struggle to prevent desertification.

MEET INDIVIDUAL NEEDS

Intrapersonal Learners

Invite students to imagine they are Africans who regularly hear tales told by a griot. Have students write a journal entry to describe how they feel when they hear legends about the past of their culture, community, family, or school. They should also tell why they value these stories.

Visual-Spatial Learners

Have students work together to create a three-dimensional map of Africa, showing geographical features, climatic regions, language groups, or other facets of the continent.

Gifted Students

Link to Today. Have students research and write a report on the history of the San up to the present day. Students might focus on their social structure, their language, and how they have been affected by other groups in their territories.

ASSESS

Review

Have students complete the Section 1 Review. Use answers in the Teacher's Edition, page 180, to assess student mastery of this section.

Kingdoms in the Sudan: Kush and Aksum

Textbook pp. 181–184

RESOURCES

Pupil's Edition

Map, p. 182: *The Kingdoms of Kush and Aksum*

History Through the Arts, p. 183: *Stonemasons of Aksum*

Core Resources

Reading 7.2: *The Fall of Meroe*

Global History Resource Center

Reading: *Daily Life in Kush*

Reading: *The Silent Trade of the Aksumites*

Videodiscs or Global History Resource Center

Image: *Nubians Bringing Gifts to Egypt*

Search Frame 759

LESSON FOCUS

What were the keys to success for the kingdoms of Kush and Aksum?

OBJECTIVES

After completing this lesson, students will be able to:
- explain how Nubia interacted with Egypt;
- identify the factors that contributed to the development of the distinctive Meroitic culture;
- describe the accomplishments of Aksum.

HOOK

Examine how Nubia interacted with Egypt. Tell students that Nubia, a region south of Egypt, became very important to ancient Egyptians as Egypt obtained gold, ivory, ebony, and ostrich feathers through trade with the Nubian kingdom of Kerma. Then point out that Egypt profited greatly from this trade with Nubia and twice imposed control over the region. While under Egyptian control, Nubians adopted many aspects of Egyptian culture. Illustrate the discussion with the electronic media image of Nubians bringing gifts to Egypt. As the New Kingdom of Egypt declined, however, a new kingdom—Kush—was established in Nubia that would eventually have serious consequences for Egypt.

Link to Today. Pose this question to students: Could you imagine Canada taking control of the United States?

Accept only a few responses. Then briefly review Egyptian history, reminding students that Egypt's New Kingdom controlled Nubia for about 500 years. Invite students to consider whether Egyptians, at the height of their power, could have imagined being conquered by Kush. *[probably not]* Help students relate this attitude to their own responses to the question about Canada.

Ask: Why was Kush able to conquer Egypt? What was unique about the creation of the Nubian dynasty?
[Students might say that Kush was able to conquer Egypt because of the New Kingdom's decline, Kush's wealth and power, or Kush's adoption of elements of Egyptian civilization. The Nubian dynasty reunited Egypt for the first time since the fall of the New Kingdom.]

Have students read the Global History Resource Center selection on daily life in Kush to supplement their knowledge of the kingdom.

DEVELOP

Discuss what conditions contributed to an early society's growth as a cultural center. Remind students that the

Kushite dynasty fell to the Assyrians in 671 B.C. Kush's rulers then abandoned Napata and established a new capital at Meroe. Assign Core Resources Reading 7.2.

Ask: *What led to Meroe's success as a cultural center?*
> [It was a major center of ironworking because of great amounts of iron ore; it was better situated for trade and agriculture.]

Have students read the History Through the Arts feature on textbook page 183 as an example of what other cultural developments were taking place at this time.

Next have students pretend that they are "architects" of a new civilization. Invite them to build, in their minds, the ideal civilization in the Sudan, using the successful features of Meroe as a starting point. Have students read King Ezana's biography on textbook page 184 to give them an idea of how his rule affected his kingdom. Then have students consider the successes of Aksum, including the Red Sea trade with India. Each student should write a list of factors that would attract settlers to a new civilization. Have students share and discuss their ideas.

PROBE

Create a time line of events of the kingdoms of the Sudan. Organize the story of the rise and development of the kingdoms of Kush and Aksum by drawing a time line on the chalkboard. Have students provide the events, beginning with the establishment of the kingdom of Kush and ending with the decline of Aksum. You might write events related to Kush above the line and events related to Aksum below the line. *[1500 B.C.: New Kingdom takes control of Nubia; 1300s B.C.: decline of New Kingdom; 800s B.C.: establishment of Kush; 730–710 B.C.: Kush conquers Egypt; 600s B.C.: Kushite dynasty falls to Assyrians; Meroe established; 250 B.C.–A.D. 150: Kush civilization reaches its peak; after A.D. 200: Kush's vitality ends; around A.D. 330: Kush falls to Aksum; A.D. 1–100: independent kingdom of Aksum has been established; A.D. 330: Aksum conquers Kush; A.D. 300s–700s: Aksum dominates Red Sea trade; after A.D. 600s: Aksum's prosperity declines]*

When students have completed the time line, have them circle each event that represents a coming to power or an event that represents a falling from power. For each circled event, have students note the reasons for that shift of power.

CONCLUDE: Link to Today

Analyze the declines of Kush and Aksum. Refer students to the map of Kush and Aksum on textbook page 182 and the map of Africa on page 177. Ask students what factors—including geographic ones—led to the decline of the kingdoms of Kush and Aksum. *[Both kingdoms suffered from a loss of trade, over-exploitation of the environment, and a loss of land productivity.]* Invite students to take a closer look at these factors. Write the first factor—*trade*—on the chalkboard.

Ask: *Why might kingdoms such as Kush and Aksum experience a decline in trade?*
> [Trade could have declined when warring groups cut off supply lines or trade routes, or when competitors entered the trade market.]

Have students analyze each of the other factors in a similar way. *[They might note that the location of Kush and Aksum in the desert and savanna climate zones would make them susceptible to environmental damage from over-exploitation.]*

EXTEND

Cross-Curricular Connection: *Art*

Have students design a flag for the kingdom of Kush or Aksum. Each flag should contain one or more symbols that represent the kingdom.

MEET INDIVIDUAL NEEDS

Kinesthetic Learners

Have students read and discuss the Global History Resource Center reading on the silent trade. Then invite small groups of students to role-play silent traders from early Africa to show how two cultures with different languages communicated. Each group should create props and discuss its bargaining strategies before beginning the exchange.

Gifted Students

Have students research some aspect of trade in the kingdoms of Kush or Aksum, such as ironworking, the making of luxury goods, or the minting of coins. Have them report to the class on their findings.

ASSESS

Review

Have students complete the Section 2 Review. Use answers in the Teacher's Edition, page 184, to assess student mastery of this section.

RESOURCES

Pupil's Edition

Then and Now, p. 186: *Crossing the Sahara*

Through Others' Eyes, p. 188: *Herodotus's Travels in Africa*

Map, p.187: *North Africa and the Sahara*

Core Resources

Reading 7.3: *Trade and Civilization in Carthage*

Visual Resources

Geography and History 7: *North Africa and the Sahara*

Global History Resource Center

Reading: *Carthage at the Peak of Its Prosperity*

Reading: *The Romans Take Revenge on Carthage*

Reading: *Roman North Africa*

Videodiscs or Global History Resource Center

Map: *African Caravan Routes*

Search Frame 768

Image: *Gold Jewelry from Ancient Carthage*

Search Frame 760

Image: *Ruins of a Roman Marketplace in North Africa*

Search Frame 761

LESSON FOCUS

How did civilization develop in North Africa?

OBJECTIVES

After completing this lesson, students will be able to:

- identify factors that contributed to the development of civilization in North Africa;
- explain the benefits of the trans-Saharan trade;
- identify how Carthage grew to become a leading city in North Africa;
- explain how North Africa changed under Roman rule.

HOOK: Link to Today

Explain the impact of new developments on North African civilization. Ask students why most teenagers look forward to getting their driver's license. Lead them to see that a car is not just a mode of transportation—it is also a catalyst for change, often resulting in a new self-image and a sense of greater independence. Then use Core Resources Reading 7.3 to help students see that certain developments in North Africa had similarly significant effects.

Ask: **What developments took place in North Africa that compare with the arrival of the automobile? What were the effects of these developments?**

[Students should note that the introduction of horses, war chariots, and camels improved transportation and communication, led to the use of cavalry, and greatly stimulated trade.]

DEVELOP

Chart causes and effects related to the development of civilization in North Africa. Have students create cause-and-effect flowcharts on the chalkboard to organize the factors that promoted change in North Africa. Each chart might take the form of boxed entries connected with arrows. The first entry might be the spread of iron technology.

Ask: **What changes were prompted by the development of iron technology?**

[Arrows from the first box might lead to two entries— improved tools and better weapons.]

Remind students that effects can also become causes. Have students convert the tools and weapons entries into causes and then provide effects, such as better houses and control of the weak by people with iron weapons.

Continue in this manner with other causes, including the introduction of horses and camels, the trans-Saharan trade, and contacts with non-African peoples. Students should copy the finished chart into their notebooks. You may wish to have students read Herodotus's description of Africa in the Through Others' Eyes feature to illlustrate North Africa's contacts with non-African peoples.

PROBE

Analyze the risks and benefits of the trans-Saharan trade. Display Geography and History Transparency 7, have students complete the accompanying worksheet, and then have them read the Then and Now feature. Next have them describe the rigors of the journey across the Sahara. *[Descriptions should suggest that the journey was difficult, risky, and long.]*

Ask: **What skills did these traders need in order to make a living from the trans-Saharan trade?**
[Students' answers will vary, but skills could include handling horses or camels, organizing complex journeys, managing workers, and negotiating with West Africans as well as various foreign traders.]

List student responses on the chalkboard. Then lead a class discussion on the benefits of trans-Saharan trade. *[It brought the goods of West Africa to the north and vice versa, and connected North African traders to Southwest Asia and Europe. It was extremely profitable.]*

CONCLUDE

Assess the effects of outside contacts on North Africa.
Have students examine Geography and History Transparency 7 again, and invite them to read the Global History Resource Center selections on Carthage, the Romans and Carthage, and on Roman North Africa. Then show the electronic media images of the jewelry and the marketplace ruins to set the scene for a discussion on how contact with the Phoenicians and later the Romans changed North Africa. Students might refer to their cause-and-effect flowcharts for help.

Ask: **How did Carthage grow to become a powerful empire on the North African coast?**
[The Phoenicians originally established it as a colony; Carthage later became an independent empire that drew its wealth and power from an extensive seaborne trade network.]

Ask: **What changes occurred in North Africa under Carthaginian rule?**
[The use of iron spread rapidly, the population expanded, and trade and agriculture expanded.]

Then ask students what happened to the Carthaginian Empire and why. *[It was destroyed by the Romans. Conflict occurred when Carthaginian interest revived in Sicily and Spain, leading to a long series of wars with Rome, until Carthage was destroyed in 146 B.C.]*

Conclude with a discussion of North Africa under the Romans.
Ask: **How did North Africa change under Roman rule?**
[Under the Romans, North Africa became a source of raw materials; taxation was high; the region was divided along class lines; a road network connected major ports; and Christianity spread through the region.]

Invite students to imagine they live in North Africa under Carthaginian or Roman rule. Have them write a letter to a friend describing one of the changes and how it has affected them, their family, and their community. Students should express either positive or negative feelings about the changes and about the outsiders who made them.

EXTEND

Other Media
You might wish to show and discuss the video *Morocco: Berber Profile* (Films for the Humanities & Sciences, color, 30 min.), which looks at the history, traditions, and popular life of Morocco.

MEET INDIVIDUAL NEEDS

Students Having Difficulty/Students Acquiring English
Have students play "20 Questions" in order to review the information in the section. One student should pick a person, place, thing, or an idea from the chapter. The student then answers only yes or no as other students ask up to 20 questions to try to determine the answer.

Visual-Spatial Learners
Invite students to illustrate one of the advances in civilization that took place during this period—for example, iron technology or the introduction of the horse. Students could illustrate conditions before the development and afterward to show how life changed.

ASSESS

Review
Have students complete the Section 3 Review. Use answers in the Teacher's Edition, page 189, to assess student mastery of this section.

173H

Lesson 7.4   *Iron-Age Developments in Sub-Saharan Africa*

Textbook pp. 190–194

RESOURCES

Pupil's Edition

Map, p. 192: *The Iron-Age Kingdoms of Africa, c. 300 B.C.–A.D. 1200*

Core Resources

Reading 7.4: *The Land of Zanj*

Visual Resources

Art and History 7: *Terracotta Portrait Head*
Everyday Life 7: *Coptic Crosses*

Global History Resource Center

Reading: *The Amazing Story of an East African King*

Reading: *The Markets of West Africa*

Reading: *The Traditional Bantu Law Courts*

Reading: *A Bantu People's System of Kingship*

Reading: *The Meaning of Cattle to African Herders*

Videodiscs or Global History Resource Center

Image: *Ethiopia's Ancient Christian Tradition*

[barcode]

Search Frame 764

Image: *Masai Cattle Herders*

[barcode]

Search Frame 763

LESSON FOCUS

How did the early civilizations of sub-Saharan Africa develop?

OBJECTIVES

After completing this lesson, students will be able to:

- describe how Ghana became a major power in West Africa;
- identify the kind of civilizations that emerged along the East African coast;
- explain what the Zagwe dynasty contributed to the kingdom of Ethiopia;
- explain how Bantu society was organized.

HOOK

Analyze the development of the kingdom of Ghana. Ask students to name the key to Ghana's wealth and power. *[trade]* Write *trade* on the chalkboard. Then ask students why Ghana was able to profit so much from trade. *[possible answers: geographical position midway between the salt-producing region and the gold fields; strong armies to maintain control of the trade]* Tell students that geographical position was a matter of luck, but managing an army and profiting from trade took skill.

Draw a triangle around the word *trade*. Write the following factors at each angle of the triangle: (1) warrior-kings; (2) strong armies; (3) control of kingdom and enforcement of laws. Challenge students to connect each factor with trade and with other factors. *[Possible answers: warrior-kings controlled the strong armies and negotiated with merchant-traders. Strong armies were able to enforce the laws, control the kingdom, and conquer new territories. Control of kingdom and territory gave the kings more power.]*

Ask: Why did war leaders make natural kings?

> *[Possible answers: They had courage, leadership skills, and power; they were respected by their people.]*

To give students more information on everyday life in West Africa, have them read the Global History Resource Center reading on markets in West Africa.

DEVELOP

Describe East African civilization. If available, read aloud the story from the Global History Resource Center of the East African king who was kidnapped by Arab traders. Then have students make a quick drawing or sketch that captures, for them, the essence of the civilization that emerged along the

East African coast. Encourage students to show their sketches and summarize them in a single word, phrase, or sentence. Write their answers on the chalkboard. *[possible sketches and answers: raiders, sailors, fishermen; a land of market towns; reliance on sailing ships; the export of raw materials]*

Have students complete Core Resources Reading 7.4. Ask how their pictures of this civilization match those of the reading and the description in the text.

PROBE

Describe the revitalization of the Ethiopian kingdom under the Zagwe dynasty. Remind students that the kingdom of Aksum went into decline after the A.D. 600s.

Ask: Why did Ethiopia experience a revitalization after A.D. 1100?
[A burst of economic activity, credited to the Zagwe dynasty, took place, and Ethiopia began to export trade goods again.]

Ask: How did the Zagwe kings improve Ethiopia?
[built a powerful army and expanded kingdom]

Remind students that the rulers of Aksum were Christians and that this Christian legacy survived the decline of the kingdom.

Ask: How did the Zagwe kings view their religion? How did Christianity change in Ethiopia?
[The Zagwe kings considered themselves defenders of the faith. They set up monasteries and built churches. Ethiopian Christianity developed its own unique characteristics.]

Show students the electronic media image illustrating Ethiopia's Christian tradition and point out the church in the photograph on page 193 to show the importance of Christianity as a unifying element in the Ethiopian kingdom.

CONCLUDE

Examine the Bantu social structure. Tell students that the use of iron and agriculture spread to parts of central and southern Africa as new peoples moved into the region from the west and north. Most scholars attribute this development to a group of peoples who spoke varieties of the Bantu languages.

Ask: How did scholars develop this theory?
[They traced the migration through the family of Bantu languages, linked to Proto-Bantu and believed to have developed in modern-day Cameroon and Nigeria.]

Then tell students that by the A.D. 900s the Bantu-speaking peoples had developed complex social structures. Ask students to write a short paragraph describing the characteristics of these societies, and then have a volunteer read his or her paragraph aloud. *[Paragraphs should mention that they built large dwellings of various types; lived in chiefdoms, with a ruler from a hereditary royal clan; grew crops; and tended cattle, which were considered a form of wealth.]*

Conclude by having students read the Global History Resource Center readings on Bantu kingship and Bantu court systems.

EXTEND

Cross-Curricular Connection: *Government*
Link to Today. Have students read the selections from the Global History Resource Center on traditional Bantu law courts and the kingship system. Ask how these Bantu institutions differ from those we are familiar with today in the United States. What advantages and disadvantages do students see in the Bantu approach to maintaining an orderly society?

MEET INDIVIDUAL NEEDS

Gifted Students
Invite students to do research and write an essay exploring one of the cultures mentioned in this section. Have them give an oral report to the class on what they have learned. Encourage them to accompany their presentation with visuals.

Visual-Spatial Learners
Have students read the selection about herders in the Global History Resource Center, and have them view the electronic media image of the Masai. Then ask them to use art, such as drawings or sculptures, to show how important cattle and products from cattle were to many African peoples.

ASSESS

Review
Have students complete the Section 4 Review. Use answers in the Teacher's Edition, pages 193–194, to assess student mastery of this section.

In preparation for the chapter test, you may wish to have students complete all or part of the Chapter 7 Review on textbook page 195, the Chapter 7 Review Activity, and the Chapter 7 Themes Review.

Understanding the Main Idea

Call on a volunteer to read aloud the *Understanding the Main Idea* paragraph. Then tell students that the geography of the African continent is extremely diverse. Because of this diversity, early African peoples developed a variety of means of adapting to their surroundings. As early as 650 B.C. North African peoples began to enter the Iron Age, which led to increased populations and the emergence of states. Many of these states achieved great wealth and power as a result of trade.

Presenting Themes

See p. 173B for suggestions on introducing themes.

Using the Time Line

Have students list the time line events in their notebooks. After they have read about each event in the chapter, have students write a paragraph explaining its significance.

Chapter 7
Early African Civilizations
C. 1800 B.C.– C. A.D. 1235

Understanding the Main Idea

Throughout their early history, African peoples adapted to their environments in unique ways, creating a variety of social structures that reflected the resources around them. Beginning in about 1800 B.C. great changes occurred in Africa. As early as 650 B.C. North Africans began to enter the Iron Age. Societies grew and states emerged to govern them. Trade played a role in the development of major kingdoms and empires, as people used their resources to gain more wealth and power.

Themes

- **Geography** In what ways might geography influence the development of trade?

- **Technology** How might the use of improved weapons affect the development of a society?

- **Economic Organization** What makes certain items valuable trading goods?

The routes that led to Ghana were paved with gold— or so it might have seemed to visitors to the ancient African kingdom, which reached the height of its power during the A.D. 1000s. Ghana long had controlled the gold and salt trade along the trans-Saharan trade routes. A traveler to the region described Ghana's fabulous wealth:

❝*The king of Ghana [is] a great king. In his territory are mines of gold, and under him a number of kingdoms, among them the kingdom of Sugham and the kingdom of Sama. In all this country there is gold.*❞

A later Arab geographer left this account:

❝*The best gold in the country comes from Ghiaru, a town situated eighteen days' journey from the capital [Kumbi Saleh] in a country that is densely populated. . . . All pieces of native gold found in the mines of the empire belong to the sovereign, although he lets the public have the gold dust that everybody knows about; without this precaution, gold would become so abundant as practically to lose its value. . . . The . . . traders . . . carry gold dust from Iresni all over the place.*❞

c. 800 B.C.	c. 730 B.C.	c. 650 B.C.	146 B.C.	C. A.D. 330
▲	▲	▲	▲	▲
Carthage is established.	Kushite armies sweep north and begin the conquest of Egypt.	The Iron Age begins in much of North Africa.	Carthage falls to Rome.	The kingdom of Kush falls to Aksum.

This trade, as in so many other regions of Africa, was of great importance to the development of Ghanaian society. Trade contributed to the development of many of the great early societies of Africa.

A village in Mali, West Africa, built in the Bandiagara cliffs

c. A.D. 900
Development of Bantu-speaking social systems.

c. A.D. 1065
The kingdom of Ghana reaches the height of its power under Tunka Manin.

A.D. 1076
Ghana's capital falls to invaders.

c. A.D. 1100
Zagwe dynasty revives Ethiopia.

SECTION 1

CORE LESSON PLAN
See pages 173C and
173D for Lesson Plan
7.1.

Theme: Geography

Ancient volcanic action helped diversify Africa's original flat surface. Mount Kilimanjaro and Mount Cameroon are both Volcanic cones. Volcanic action has produced steep-sided calderas—deep depressions in the earth's surface caused by violent explosions. Some of these depressions filled with water and formed part of Africa's lake system.

Critical Thinking Ask students how this volcanic activity might have affected developing civilizations in Africa.

ANSWER: Students should note that the presence of such high mountains and deep depressions would make transportation and communication difficult. In addition, the lakes which formed from the calderas might provide water for developing cities.

SECTION 1
Patterns of African History

- What are some of Africa's major geographical features?
- How did African peoples adapt to their various environments?
- What characteristics did many African peoples have in common?

As in Asia and Europe, people in Africa built unique societies as they adapted to their environment. Across the vast continent, hundreds of different peoples emerged with their own languages and their own methods of adaptation. Some became farmers and developed towns, cities, and large states based on surplus agriculture. Others pursued a nomadic existence herding camels, goats, or cattle. Still others remained hunters and gatherers.

Mount Kilimanjaro, located in Tanzania, is the tallest mountain in Africa.

Geographic Diversity

Africa is a vast continent with a very diverse landscape—its geographical features include mountains, deserts, grasslands, and rain forests. The equator cuts across Africa, and much of the continent lies in the tropics. Along the western coast northeasterly winds and steady ocean currents made it difficult for early sailing vessels to travel below Cape Verde and return. This limited contacts between the western coast and the outside world for many centuries.

Below the Mediterranean coastal region lies the vast Sahara Desert, which covers more than one fourth of the continent's surface. Once fertile and well watered, the Sahara has been getting increasingly dry for thousands of years. The edge of the Sahara is a region known as the Sahel, from the Arabic word for "shore." Below the Sahel lie **savannas**, vast grasslands dotted with trees, into which the desert advances yearly. Even farther south are forested regions, which in places give way to tropical rain forests. Africa has few real jungles—places where sunlight penetrates the canopy of the rain forest and permits thick, dense vegetation to grow on the forest floor. South of the rain forests, the savannas resume only to be broken in the far south by the Namib and Kalahari Deserts. Higher rainfall patterns give the southern tip of Africa a climate similar to that of the Mediterranean coast.

The major feature of Africa's central and southern interior is a great plateau that straddles the equator and drops off sharply to the coastal plains. The Great Rift Valley, a natural fault zone with high, steep sides, slices through the eastern edge of the plateau from its origins in Syria. Along the Rift's length lie many narrow lakes. Other important highland regions are the Ethiopian highlands in the northeast, the Fouta Djallon (FOOT-uh juh-LOHN) Mountains in the west, the Atlas Mountains in the northwest, and the jagged Drakensberg Mountains in the southeast. Some parts of Africa, such as Gabon and eastern Central Africa, also have active volcanoes.

Fed by annual rains and melting snows, many rivers rise in the highland regions and make their way to the coasts. The largest and most important—the Nile, Niger, Congo, and Zambezi Rivers, with their various tributaries—drain great portions of the interior before reaching the sea.

Geography AND HISTORY

Africa's Geography and Peoples

Historically, the diets of African peoples have varied according to where they lived. The variety of food staples in African diets is a reflection of the enormous geographic diversity of the African continent.

At its widest points, Africa is 4,970 miles from north to south and 4,600 miles from east to west, with a land area more than three times that of the continental United States. Most of Africa is a giant plateau, broken up by rolling hills, deep lakes, and wide rivers. In the east and south, the plateau rises over 3,300 feet, but in other areas it is only between 500 and 2,000 feet. Along the coasts, the plateau drops to sea level in very steep cliffs. Rivers often plunge over the cliffs in spectacular waterfalls, usually making navigation from the sea impossible.

The continent can be divided into five major climate zones: Mediterranean, desert, savanna, forest, and highland. These climate zones determined what foods people could produce. As farming techniques began to spread south in Africa around 3000 B.C., farmers in the savannas grew grains, such as sorghum, millet, and African rice. Farmers in the forested regions grew root crops, such as yams and sweet potatoes.

The areas where savannas met the deserts proved better suited for herding cattle than growing crops. Herders often had to lead their animals many miles over the course of a year to follow the rains.

Whether in the desert, grasslands, or forests, the survival and prosperity of a society depended upon its ability to adapt to the surrounding environment.

Linking Geography and History

1. Using the map legend, estimate the greatest north to south distance and the greatest east to west distance in the kingdoms of Kush and Mali.
2. How might the sizes of these kingdoms and the types of land they contained have affected their development?

Africa, c. 3000 B.C.–A.D. 1200

Climate zones:
- Desert
- Savanna
- Forest
- Mediterranean
- Highland

Mapping the Kingdoms The diverse geography of Africa gave birth to a host of wealthy trading kingdoms.

❖ **Region** In what types of regions did most of the early African kingdoms arise?

Linking Geography And History

1. Mali—approximately 400 miles north to south and 1200 miles east to west; Kush—approximately 600 miles north to south and 500 miles east to west
2. The large size of Mali and its location in the savanna would have made it a good place for herding societies. Relatively small Kush might have been easier to defend and could have developed trade because of its location.

Map Answer
desert and savanna

R **RESOURCE ACTIVITY**

READINGS IN WORLD HISTORY
Reading 7.1
Oral History and Folktales

Have students read the folktale about the downfall of Ghana. Then have them complete the questions.

Level 2

R **RESOURCE ACTIVITY**

WRITING PROJECTS
Writing Project
Writing a Descriptive Essay

Have students follow the steps for writing an essay on the purposes and techniques of oral history. Encourage students to use information from their own research to complete this assignment.

Level 2

Because of rapids and waterfalls, traveling along the rivers is difficult. Nevertheless, people have been able to use the rivers for short-distance transportation and communications. Rich silt from some of these rivers contributed to the growth of agriculture.

Africa's geographical features include mountains, deserts, grasslands, rain forests, and great rivers.

▲ Distinctive styles of African architecture, like this in Cameroon, have existed for centuries.

Adaptation to the Environment

African peoples are as diverse as the landscape. Most scholars prefer to classify African peoples according to four major African language groups: Niger-Kordofanian, Khoisan, Afroasiatic, and Nilo-Saharan. Each of these major groups has many different subgroups. Perhaps the best-known African languages are the Niger-Kordofanian subfamily called **Bantu languages**, which are spoken over most of the southern third of the continent.

African peoples have developed a wide variety of adaptations to their different environments. A few African peoples, notably the San of southern Africa, remained organized in small bands as hunter-gatherers. Most, however, became farmers, herders, or fishermen, depending on local conditions.

In West Africa, for example, many peoples, particularly in forested regions, became farmers because they had access to adaptable food crops. In addition, the **tsetse fly**, which is common in that area of Africa, carried a disease that would have killed any domestic animals they might have herded. Settling first in small villages, many West African peoples eventually developed cities. As trade grew, states emerged, usually along major trade routes or around market towns. Similar developments occurred in other parts of the continent where land was suitable for farming.

In many areas, such as the dry grasslands of the Sahel and the savannas of eastern and southern Africa, the climate was more suited to grazing than to agriculture. In these regions, peoples like the Masai of modern-day Kenya and Tanzania learned to live by herding animals, particularly cattle. As in other parts of the world, nomadic herding peoples in Africa sometimes clashed with farming peoples.

Still other Africans adapted to life along Africa's rivers and lakes. For example, the Nuer and Dinka peoples survived by fishing and by growing some crops in the swamps of the upper Nile River. Preferring to live in isolated family groups, the Nuer and Dinka maintained what scholars often call "stateless societies"—remaining bound to one another by family ties and shared culture, but without developing a state structure. On the other hand, states did emerge among the fishing peoples of Lake Victoria in present-day Uganda and Tanzania.

African peoples adapted to their environment in a variety of ways— farming, herding, fishing, or hunting and gathering. Many developed strong states.

Family, Religion, and Oral Traditions

Despite their diversity, most African peoples shared some common characteristics. Family ties, for example, were important in all African communities because people identified themselves as part of larger kinship groups, or clans. In most early African societies, men usually had many wives. Children were particularly important, since they cared for their parents in old age. Throughout much of Africa, in addition to their responsibilities for bearing and raising children, women were the primary farmers and gardeners, while men traditionally hunted or fished and looked after livestock.

Religion also played an important role in the lives of Africans, and many shared similar

Literature THROUGH TIME

Africa's Oral Literature Tradition

When people think of literature, they usually think of something written in a book, such as a poem, short story, or novel. Much of the literature of Africa, however, has been passed down orally through many generations. Storytellers repeat stories and poems they have heard in the past. Oral literature is very different from written literature. An important aspect of oral literature is that it is performed, not read. In a sense, oral literature is more like drama, dance, or music. The way the storyteller uses different tones, gestures, and facial expressions in the performance contributes to the richness of the literary experience for the audience.

Although there are many types of oral literature, among the most popular are entertaining stories about animals who play tricks on one another. These stories about trick-sters are common all over Africa and often are meant to teach a lesson to the audience. Sometimes these lessons are tacked on to the end of a story to make the meaning clearer. The following is an example of a popular animal story, called "The Trapper Trapped."

Goat and Fox were quarreling and Goat told Fox that he intended to get him into trouble so bad he would never be able to get out. Fox said, "All right; you do that, and I will return the favor to you."

Goat went for a walk and saw Leopard; being frightened, he asked, "Auntie, what are you doing here?" "My little one is sick," said Leopard. Then Goat, thinking quietly, said, "Fox has medicine that will make your little one well." Leopard said to call him, so Goat went to Fox and said, "They are calling you."

"Who is calling me?" replied Fox. "I don't know," said Goat; "I think it is your friend. Go this way and you will run into him." Fox went down the path and at length came upon Leopard. Fox was frightened, and inquired: "Did you call me?" "Yes, my son; your brother is sick. Goat came just a while ago and told me you had medicine that would make my little one well." "Yes," said Fox, "I have medicine that will cure your little one, but I must have a little goat horn to put it in. If you get me a goat horn I will let you have the medicine." "Which way did Goat go?" asked Leopard. "I left him up there," replied Fox. "You wait here with my little one, and I will bring you the horn," said Leopard, and away she ran. Soon after, Leopard killed Goat and returned with his horns to Fox. Beware, lest you fall into the trap you set for someone else.

Understanding Literature
How do Goat's and Fox's actions prove the moral of the story?

In a village in Côte d'Ivoire, a storyteller passes a legend on to the next generation.

religious ideas. For example, most early African peoples believed that the world was alive with spirits. These included the spirits of their own ancestors, who remained an important part of the ongoing life of the clan. Most early Africans also believed in a supreme creator god, usually associated with the sky or heaven. Many worshipped other gods associated with some aspect of nature or a type of human activity, such as farming. Most early Africans also believed that magic was a natural means through which the physical world interacted with the spirit world.

Although most early African societies never developed their own systems of writing, they maintained their sense of identity and continuity with the past through **oral traditions**. Oral traditions include stories, songs, poems, and proverbs. Often, they held some moral lesson or were tales recounting the deeds of past heroes. Some societies had oral historians, like the **griots** (GREE-ohz) of West Africa. The Mandingo griot Djeli Mamoudou Kouyaté explained the importance of the griot in African culture:

▲ An African artist of the lower Niger region created this bronze figure of a hunter.

66 *I am a griot. It is I, Djeli Mamoudou Kouyaté, son of Bintou Kouyaté and Djeli Kedian Kouyaté, master in the art of eloquence [fine speaking]. . . . We [Kouyatés] are vessels of speech, we are the repositories [storage places] which harbor secrets many centuries old. The art of eloquence has no secrets for us; without us the names of kings would vanish . . . ; by the spoken word we bring to life the deeds and exploits of kings for younger generations.* 99

Through their oral traditions, preliterate African peoples—peoples without written languages—passed on their sense of identity and their values from generation to generation. Yet not all African societies remained preliterate. Some African peoples eventually created highly literate civilizations that interacted with other civilizations of the ancient world.

Despite their diversity, many African peoples shared common ideas on religion and the importance of family, and preserved these ideas through a rich oral tradition.

SECTION 1 REVIEW

IDENTIFY and explain the significance of the following:
  savannas
  Bantu languages
  tsetse fly
  oral traditions
  griots

LOCATE and explain the significance of the following:
  Sahara Desert
  Kalahari Desert
  Great Rift Valley
  Nile River

1. *Main Idea* How did geography and climate affect the development of early African societies?
2. *Main Idea* What characteristics were shared by many early African societies?
3. *Geography: Place* How would you describe the major geographical features of Africa?
4. *Writing to Explain* Imagine you are a historian trying to recreate the history of a

certain African region. How might knowledge of oral traditions help you? What difficulties might these sources also present?

5. *Hypothesizing* Since the particular environment of a region played such an important role in the development of African societies, what sorts of changes in environment might cause problems for these societies? What might these problems be?

Kingdoms in the Sudan: Kush and Aksum

FOCUS

- How did Nubia interact with Egypt?
- What factors contributed to the development of Kush's unique culture at Meroe?
- What were some of the accomplishments of the kingdom of Aksum?

While ancient Egypt flourished in the lower Nile Valley, other important states were developing along the upper reaches of the river to the south in the area known as the Sudan. Kush and Aksum were two powerful kingdoms that emerged in the upper Nile Valley and Ethiopia. Both kingdoms relied on trade to create societies that thrived and left rich cultural histories.

Funeral stela from ancient Kush

The Kingdom of Kush

Along the middle reaches of the Nile, south of the centers of ancient Egypt, lay the region of Nubia. Here, sometime during the Egyptian Middle Kingdom, the Nubian kingdom of Kerma arose to take advantage of trade with Egypt. From trade with Nubia, Egypt obtained gold, ivory, ebony, and ostrich feathers. In order to dominate trade in the region, the Egyptians imposed their own control over the kingdom. Nubia became not only a trading center but also a buffer zone for Egypt against raids by African peoples farther south. When Egypt fell under Hyksos rule in 1650 B.C., however, the rulers of Nubia fought with the invaders against the Theban dynasty in Middle Egypt. As a result, Nubia remained independent of Egyptian control for a time.

Then in about 1500 B.C., after the rise of the New Kingdom, the Egyptians once again imposed their control over the region and ruled Nubia for about the next 500 years. Along the narrow valley of the Nile, Egyptians built new cities and temples and the local Nubian rulers adopted Egyptian religious practices, writing, language, and culture. Meanwhile, regular shipments of gold from Nubia contributed to the New Kingdom's great wealth. Beginning in the 1300s B.C., however, the decline of the New Kingdom in Egypt gradually cut Nubia off from the Mediterranean world.

As Egyptian control declined, sometime in the 800s B.C. a new city-state emerged at Napata a short distance from Kerma. With Napata as their capital, local Nubian rulers established the kingdom of Kush. For nearly 300 years Kush remained rather isolated from Mediterranean cultures. The kingdom continued to flourish, however, and remained heavily influenced by Egyptian culture.

By 730 B.C. Kush had grown powerful enough to conquer Thebes. Within 20 years, Kushite princes had conquered all of Egypt. The Kushite ruler Piankhi (PAYNG-kee) completed the conquest and recorded his great victory at Memphis on a granite **stela**, or carved stone pillar, which he ordered built near Napata:

66 *When day broke . . . his majesty reached Memphis. . . . There was found no way of attacking it. . . . Then his majesty was enraged against it like a panther; he said: 'I swear as Re loves me, as my father, Amon . . . favors*

SECTION 2

CORE LESSON PLAN
See pages 173E and 173F for Lesson Plan 7.2.

R RESOURCE ACTIVITY

GLOBAL HISTORY RESOURCE CENTER
Reading: *Daily Life in Kush*

Print out and distribute the reading. Have students read about Kush. Ask students to design a floor plan for *Better Homes and Gardens of Kush,* a magazine that ordinary citizens of Kush might read for home decorating tips. Their floor plans should show the latest home fashions for ordinary householders.

Level 1

me, this shall befall [happen to] it, according to the command of Amon . . . I will take it like a flood of water.' **"**

Piankhi thus reunited Egypt for the first time since the New Kingdom. He and his successors of the Nubian dynasty ruled Egypt for nearly a century.

After the decline of the New Kingdom of Egypt, the kingdom of Kush in Nubia eventually became strong enough to take control of the Nile Valley.

Meroe

Kushite control of Egypt ended in 671 B.C., when the Kushite dynasty fell to invading Assyrian armies. Forced to retreat home, the

▲ A blend of African and Hellenistic architectural features is seen in this Meroitic temple, dating from about 300 B.C.

rulers of Kush abandoned their former capital at Napata and eventually reorganized their kingdom around a new capital at Meroe, on the Nile River. There they began a new period of growth and cultural achievement. So well known was Meroe that the famous Greek historian Herodotus left an account gathered from other travelers:

" *In twelve days [one] reaches a big city named Meroe, said to be the capital city of the Ethiopians [the inhabitants of the kingdom of Kush]. The inhabitants worship Zeus and Dionysus alone of the gods, holding them in great honor. There is an oracle of Zeus there, and they make war according to its pronouncements [declarations].* **"**

Meroe offered tremendous economic opportunities. The area was rich in iron ore and it was one of the earliest centers of ironworking in Africa. Fertile soil and the use of iron tools made Meroe an ideal location for agriculture. Meroe not only controlled areas with a high level of annual rainfall but also possessed abundant land for growing crops and grazing cattle.

Meroe was also in an excellent location for trade. Its rulers maintained trade links with Egypt in a shorter, overland route that avoided the dangers of the cataracts, or rapids, on the Nile. In addition, the capital controlled a caravan route from the Nile River to the Red Sea coast. Caravans from the coast brought back Hellenistic, Persian, and Indian influences

The Kingdoms of Kush and Aksum

MEDITERRANEAN SEA

EGYPT
Memphis

Thebes

Nile River

RED SEA

NUBIAN DESERT

Kerma
NUBIA
Napata

Meroe

Atbara River

Adulis

Blue Nile

Aksum

SUDAN

Arabian Peninsula

Gulf of Aden

ETHIOPIA

ETHIOPIAN HIGHLANDS

| | Kush, c. 500 B.C. |
| | Aksum, c. A.D. 400 |

0   300   600 Miles
0   300   600 Kilometers
Azimuthal Equal-Area Projection

Kingdoms of the Nile The traders of Kush and Aksum brought great wealth to their kingdoms.

? Human-Environment Interaction How did the locations of Kush and Aksum help them dominate trade?

History THROUGH THE ARTS

The Stonemasons of Aksum

The kingdom of Aksum in the Ethiopian highlands was a center of considerable artistic creativity. Aksumite artisans produced fine glassware and brass and copper ornaments for export. Aksumite builders and architects were particularly famous for erecting magnificent stone temples, tombs, and palaces of monumental proportions. In 1906 an expedition of German archaeologists uncovered three enormous buildings which they believed to be palaces.

Some of the most impressive architectural remains of Aksum are its carved stone pillars, or stelae, which were apparently raised to mark the graves of dead monarchs. One of the largest stelae is found in Aksum itself. Carved from a single block of granite, it stands about 70 feet high. Skilled masons carved it in the likeness of a 10-story house, complete with a life-sized false door at the base. Several other larger stelae have also been found lying in pieces on the ground. The largest was about 108 feet high, and carved to represent 13 stories. One scholar has called it "probably the largest single block of stone ever quarried, carved and set up in the ancient world."

Thinking About Art

What does the architecture of Aksum have in common with the architecture of other ancient societies, particularly Egypt?

Several stelae remain standing in Ethiopia as impressive monuments to the ancient kingdom of Aksum.

Thinking About Art

Architects in Aksum created magnificent stone temples and tombs.

INTERNET ACTIVITY

ETHIOPIAN LANGUAGES
Ge'ez is just one of many Ethiopian languages and is connected to many different language systems.

Activity: Have students search the Internet for more information on Ge'ez, its use in present-day Ethiopia, and its connection to other languages. Compare the shape of the letters in the Ge'ez alphabet to the alphabet we use today. Then have students present some of the information they have found in the form of a chart which links Ge'ez to other languages.

All Levels

REVIEW & ASSESSMENT RESOURCES

- Study Guide 7.2
- Daily Quiz 7.2
- Main Idea Activity 7.2

All Levels

---

that the people of Meroe adapted to their own culture.

Kush civilization reached its peak during the period from 250 B.C. to A.D. 150. The people of Meroe created new shrines for the worship of new gods and developed a written form of their language. In addition, the people erected great pyramids and temples and crafted beautiful pottery and ornaments. Kushite art depicted animals such as lions and elephants, which were rarely seen in Egyptian works.

After A.D. 200, as Meroe began to lose control over the trade routes, this great vitality ended. In addition, the land lost its fertility from overuse. Sometime around A.D. 330, the powerful neighboring kingdom of Aksum invaded Kush and brought its independence to an end.

Trade, ironworking, and fertile lands contributed to Meroe's growth as a cultural center in Kush.

Aksum

Situated in the Ethiopian highlands south and east of Kush, Aksum drew much of its wealth from the Red Sea trade with India. Its people had lived in the region for many centuries and had developed their own written language, called Ge'ez. By the first century A.D., the people of Aksum had developed an independent kingdom and established a thriving seaport at Adulis, which became the leading ivory market in northeastern Africa. Prosperity followed, and by A.D. 300 Aksum was already a strong military power. In A.D. 330 King Ezana of Aksum inflicted a crushing defeat on Kush, which gave Aksum greater control over trade in the region.

BIOGRAPHY Ezana was a powerful king. Like other kings of Aksum, he held direct power in the capital. Outside of the kingdom's center, the king collected tribute from neighboring rulers. Ezana gained additional wealth from the control of foreign trade. At Adulis his officials collected taxes on imports and exports.

During his reign Ezana also converted to Christianity and made it the official religion of Aksum. Ezana's conversion may have been intended to strengthen his rule over the kingdom. It may also have been a matter of conscience, as indicated by the granite inscriptions Ezana made on monuments built after his conversion:

> **I will rule the people with righteousness and justice, and will not oppress them [keep them down], and may they preserve this Throne which I have set up for the Lord of Heaven.**

Ezana laid the foundations of the Ethiopian Church. Under his rule Aksum launched an era of great prosperity.

Aksum became a major center of long-distance trade. Between the A.D. 300s and 700s, for example, it dominated the African side of the Red Sea trade. The kingdom sent war elephants, rhinoceros horn, tortoiseshell, incense, and spices to the Mediterranean world by way of the Red Sea. The Aksumites imported glass, brass, and copper luxury items, as well as wine and olive oil. Aksum also minted its own coins.

Aksum's prosperity began to decline after the A.D. 600s for several reasons. Environmental problems such as erosion—caused by excessive land use and the long-term practice of cutting down trees—made the land less productive. By A.D. 600 the Persians, a trading rival, had gained control over much of the Red Sea trade. Beginning in the early A.D. 700s, Arab forces controlled both the Arabian and the African sides of the Red Sea. As a result Aksum lost most of its external trade. The people retained their Christian heritage, however, which continues to the present day.

The people of Aksum developed an international trade, adopted Christianity, created a written language, and built impressive stone structures.

◄ **This stela still stands where it was built in Ethiopia. Carved out of granite, it was built around A.D. 200.**

SECTION 2 REVIEW

IDENTIFY and explain the significance of the following:
  Piankhi
  stela
  Ezana

LOCATE and explain the importance of the following:
  Nubia
  Napata
  Meroe

Red Sea
Ethiopian highlands
Adulis

1. **Main Idea** How did the relationship between Nubia and Egypt change from 1800 B.C. to 700 B.C.?
2. **Main Idea** What are some of the things for which Aksum is famous?

3. **Geography: Location** What factors contributed to the growth of Meroe as a cultural center?
4. **Writing to Explain** In a short essay explain what common factors led to the decline of Kush and Aksum.
5. **Analyzing** How did trade spur the development of Kush and Aksum?

North Africa and the Sahara

FOCUS

- What factors contributed to the development of civilization in North Africa?

- What were some of the benefits of the trans-Saharan trade?

- How did Carthage grow to become a leading city in North Africa?

- How did North Africa change under Roman rule?

With its long coastline on the Mediterranean, North Africa was part of a wider world that connected peoples in both Europe and Asia. As many peoples traveled the Mediterranean and settled or traded along North Africa's shores, they carried with them new ideas and technologies, which mingled with those of local inhabitants. The spread of iron technology, and the introduction first of the horse and later the camel, allowed North African peoples to improve their agriculture and trade. With better weapons they also built stronger armies and developed large empires.

Berber cave paintings of horses, Algeria

New Developments in Technology

By 1800 B.C. urbanization, knowledge of agriculture, and centralized political authority had spread to many parts of North Africa. In the centuries that followed, new technologies brought the expansion of cities and trade. Perhaps the most important development was the spread of iron technology.

The Iron Age in the north. North Africa entered the Iron Age sometime around 650 B.C. As elsewhere, iron tools soon replaced those made of bronze or copper. Iron was more plentiful and could be used to make harder weapons and tools that were better for farming, hunting, and clearing land. Iron also became a source of military power, as people with iron-tipped spears and arrows had an advantage over enemies still using softer metals. Iron farm tools also helped increase food production, and soon people started to settle in larger communities. States and organized governments developed, partly to meet the challenges of a growing population and urbanization.

Among the Berber people of North Africa, settled farmers grew crops and built towns, while nomadic herders wandered and hunted in the countryside, where they developed better fighting techniques. The herders often provided farmers with milk and meat in exchange for grain and oil.

Horses and camels. The introduction of the horse to North Africa sometime after 1700 B.C., along with the new war chariot first pioneered by Indo-European-speaking peoples, caused significant changes in North Africa. Before then, people relied on donkeys for transportation and fought wars on foot. By 1235 B.C., however, the Berbers were using war chariots. After about 900 B.C. chariots gave way to cavalry, which provided increased mobility.

Perhaps even more important than the use of the horse was the introduction of the domesticated camel from the Arabian Peninsula. Camels could carry heavier loads than donkeys and go long periods without water. In addition, camels also withstood the heat of the desert better than horses and donkeys. Before the A.D. 100s, camels were being used for trade and travel in North Africa.

SECTION 3

CORE LESSON PLAN
See pages 173G and 173H for Lesson Plan 7.3.

Daily Life

Archaeologists' discoveries have shown that many of the early settled Berbers grew a number of crops, including chick peas, wheat, and beans.

The nomadic groups often carried ornamental weapons and wore beads, pendants, and bracelets. Other findings indicate that they may have dressed in hooded cloaks and clothes made of striped cloth. The nomads' lives depended on hunting and raising sheep, goats, and cattle.

Critical Thinking Ask students what kinds of evidence might help archaeologists know about a culture that left no written records.

ANSWER: Students might answer that archaeologists could use evidence from decorations on pottery, materials buried with the dead, and remains found at once-inhabited sites.

In 1922 Captain Angus Buchanan traveled across the Sahara with a salt-trade caravan. During this time, Buchanan endured many hardships, including being trampled in a camel stampede.

Each day the group traveled around 40 miles, often for 18 hours straight. Buchanan noted that toward the end "Men and animals weakened perceptibly . . . nearly everyone limped . . . suffering from numerous dry cracks that had opened cruelly in toes and soles of sandalled feet. . . ."

Critical Thinking Ask students what other hardships people encountered crossing the Sahara.

ANSWER: Students might list hunger, thirst, heat exhaustion, and sand storms.

MULTIMEDIA PRESENTATION STRATEGY

VISUAL RESOURCES
Geography and History 7
North Africa and the Sahara

Show the transparency and share the information from Geography and History Fact Sheet 7. Then have students complete the accompanying worksheet.

Level 2

Then & Now

Crossing the Sahara

The Sahara Desert is 3,000 miles wide from near the Atlantic coast to the Red Sea and extends 1,000 miles southward from the North African coast. The world's largest desert, the Sahara covers about 3.5 million square miles—about one sixteenth of the earth's total land area. Less than one quarter of the great desert is actually sand. The Ahaggar mountain chain, with peaks of about 9,000 feet, lies in the center of the area and is surrounded by smaller mountain ranges. Around these mountains are huge gravel plains, which cover over half of the Sahara. Beyond these are the oceans of sand.

The first military or commercial routes were opened across the Sahara probably as early as 1000 B.C. At this time travelers rode or led donkeys, carrying as much water as possible with them and following a trail from one watering hole to the next. Horses, like cattle before them, had been driven out of the area by the harsh conditions of the once lush land. The native camels, which had existed there much earlier but had become extinct, were reintroduced at the time of the Roman occupation of North Africa before the A.D. 100s. For many hundreds of years afterward, camels, which could travel long distances without water, were the main form of transportation across the desert.

Modern transportation came to the Sahara in 1922, when André Citroën, the French car maker, drove six of his 'caterpillar' cars across the desert. Based on the British tank, Citroën's cars traveled only 15 miles per hour and crossed the desert in almost exactly one month. Since even fast camel caravans took at least six months, the introduction of the automobile opened many new parts of the desert to exploration, changing travel in the Sahara forever. Today, four-wheel drive vehicles—with much of the air let out of the tires to increase traction and prevent sinking—provide a dependable means of travel. Roads now also crisscross the Sahara, providing even greater access.

However, much of the travel across the desert still takes place on camels, often in caravans. There are many areas where the sand is too soft or the terrain too rough for vehicles.

Even with modern forms of transportation, there is still danger involved in desert travel. Large supplies of water, fuel, repair gear, and a compass are all necessary, regardless of the length of the trip. Only a few miles into the sand, a traveler can become isolated, out of sight of humanity or landmarks. With the frequent sandstorms, which can block out even the sun, travelers may become completely disoriented, wandering lost in the sand until their supplies run out.

Camel caravan crossing sand dunes

The introduction of iron, horses, and camels stimulated trade and urban development in North Africa.

The trans-Saharan trade. Between about A.D. 100 and 400, the use of camels led to the development of major trade routes across the Sahara Desert. These routes for the new **trans-Saharan trade** connected North and West Africa. The Berbers in the Atlas Mountains and the northern Sahara served as middlemen to carry goods across the desert. The trade brought

North Africa and the Sahara, 600 B.C.–A.D. 395

North African Colonies The many colonies along Africa's northern coast were bridges of commerce and culture between the continents.

? Linking Geography and History Which cultures were probably linked by the colonies in North Africa?

the many goods of West Africa to the north to be exchanged for salt, cloth, beads, and metal. The Saharan Berbers also sold West African goods to traders from the north, who in turn traded them with merchants from across Southwest Asia and Europe. These merchants in return traded goods from their own homelands.

Although trade was profitable, crossing the Sahara was difficult, risky, and time-consuming. One famous Arab traveler of the A.D. 1300s, Ibn Battuta, left a firsthand account of its difficulties:

66 [At first] we used to go ahead of the caravan, and when we found a place suitable for pasturage we would graze our beasts. We went on doing this until one of our party was lost in the desert; after that I neither went ahead nor lagged behind. 99

Trans-Saharan trade provided valued goods to West and North Africa and connected Africa with Southwest Asia and Europe.

The Carthaginian Empire

North Africa was in many ways the crossroads of the continent. As peoples from beyond Africa's shores, such as Phoenicians, Greeks, and Romans, settled or traded there, they contributed to the spread of technology and ideas. As they occupied the coastal regions and interacted with the local Berber populations, trade increased and cities began to develop.

Beginnings of an empire. Sometime around 1000 B.C. seafaring Phoenicians began establishing trading stations along the North African coast. By 800 B.C. these stations had grown into colonies. With the fall of Phoenicia to the Assyrians, the colonies became largely independent. The colony of Carthage, in what is now Tunisia, was established among the Berbers of North Africa. Along the coastal strip, Carthage grew into a powerful empire.

Under the Carthaginians, the use of iron spread rapidly. The population grew and changed as Phoenicians intermingled with Berbers. Trade expanded to the Atlantic coast of North Africa and agriculture developed further, with the countryside supplying the cities with food. According to contemporary Greek and Roman accounts, Carthage had become the wealthiest city in the western Mediterranean by 600 B.C. This great power was built upon an extensive seaborne trade network, in which Carthage exchanged inexpensive manufactured goods for metals and other raw materials.

Carthaginian merchants even sailed out into the Atlantic Ocean and down the western coast of Africa in search of trade. Although many modern historians now question the authenticity of the story, the Greek historian Herodotus left an account of how the Carthaginians conducted trade with peoples along the West African coast:

> **On reaching this country, they unload their goods, arrange them tidily along the beach, and then, returning to their boats, raise a smoke. Seeing the smoke, the natives come down to the beach, place on the ground a certain quantity of gold in exchange for the goods, and go off again to a distance. The Carthaginians then come ashore and take a look at the gold; and if they think it represents a fair price for their wares, they collect it and go away; if, on the other hand, it seems too little, they go back aboard and wait, and the natives come and add to the gold until they are satisfied.**

In search of further wealth, the Carthaginians established colonies in Spain and Sicily and on other islands in the western Mediterranean.

Carthaginian society. In Sicily, however, the Carthaginians clashed with colonists from the Greek city-states. After suffering a major defeat by the Greeks of Sicily in the early 400s B.C., Carthage was isolated for a time. During this period, Carthage's political system changed from a kingship to an oligarchy. Although Carthage, like Rome, had an assembly of the people and a senate, the real rulers were the wealthiest merchant families. These families controlled elections and determined who would be the magistrates and generals of the empire.

Carthage became a great urban culture. Like other cities in the Mediterranean, it was largely influenced by Greek culture during the Hellenistic period. Despite the Greek influence, however, the Carthaginians did not give up their original religion. According to ancient sources, which are supported by modern archaeological finds, in times of trouble the Carthaginians appealed for help to their most important deities—the god Baal Hammon and the goddess Tanit—by sacrificing male children.

The fall of Carthage. As Carthage rose to power in North Africa, surrounding Berbers began to develop states of their own in self-defense—

THROUGH OTHERS' EYES

Herodotus's Travels in Africa

Herodotus, born about 484 B.C., was one of the most famous historians of ancient Greece. He traveled extensively in North Africa and Asia, gathering the stories and legends of many peoples. Herodotus took many of these stories, which were sometimes exaggerated, as historical fact. The following excerpt recounts the experience of a group of young men traveling in northern Africa.

> **The story then was that [several Nasamonian] young men, sent off by their companions on their travels with a good supply of food and water, passed through the inhabited parts of the country to the region of wild beasts and then came to the desert, which they proceeded to cross in a westerly direction. After traveling for many days over the sand they saw some trees growing on a level spot; they approached and began to pick the fruit which the trees bore, and while they were doing so were attacked by some little men—of less than middle height—who seized them and carried them off. The speech of these dwarfs was unintelligible, nor could they understand the Nasamonians. They took their captives through a vast tract of marshy country, and beyond it came to a town, all the inhabitants of which were of the same small stature, and all black. A great river with crocodiles in it flowed past the town from west to east.**

notably the kingdoms of Numidia and Mauretania. Meanwhile, Carthaginian interest in both Sicily and Spain revived, bringing Carthage into a long struggle with the Romans. After Rome finally destroyed Carthage in 146 B.C., much of North Africa eventually fell under Roman domination.

Through its reliance on trade, Carthage grew to become a wealthy empire.

Roman North Africa

By the first century A.D., under Roman control, North Africa soon became an important contributor to the economy of the empire, producing olive oil and grain. Taxation was high, however, and many of the local people took to banditry and rebellion.

Roman civilization in Africa became even more urban and sophisticated than earlier Carthaginian civilization had been. No fewer than 500 cities developed in North Africa, with perhaps as many as 2 million people living in them. The Romans constructed great buildings in the cities, and a network of roads connected the cities and the major ports along the coast. A ruling class, as well as wealthy merchants, lived in the coastal cities or on large estates worked

▲ This stela was used as a place to make offerings to the Carthaginian goddess Tanit.

by slaves. Outside the cities and large estates lived nomadic Berbers, who maintained their language and culture and often resented Roman rule. In some places, such as Numidia, local kings were allowed for a time to remain semi-independent as Roman allies.

One of the many developments during Roman rule was the spread of Christianity to many parts of North Africa. Alexandria, the commercial capital of Egypt, was one of the most important Christian centers during the first century A.D. The city was home to many early Christian scholars.

In Egypt the **Coptic Church** arose, which eventually split from the Roman Catholic Church. By A.D. 600 Coptic Christians had carried their religion southward into Nubia, where they converted many people and contributed to the long-lasting Christian history also left by the Aksumites.

From Egypt, Christianity spread west to the Berbers, among whom it gained a mass following. Many priests and bishops were appointed among the Berbers. Perhaps the most important was Aurelius Augustinus—later known as Saint Augustine of Hippo—considered one of the fathers of Christian doctrine.

During the period of Roman rule, major cities grew and Christianity spread throughout parts of North Africa.

SECTION 3 REVIEW

IDENTIFY and explain the significance of the following:
   trans-Saharan trade
   Baal Hammon
   Tanit
   Coptic Church
   Aurelius Augustinus

LOCATE and explain the importance of the following:
   Carthage

Sicily
Alexandria

1. ***Main Idea*** How did the trans-Saharan trade benefit different parts of Africa?
2. ***Main Idea*** How did Carthage rise to become a powerful empire?
3. ***Economic Organization*** What factors contributed

to the expansion of trade and urbanization in North Africa?
4. ***Writing to Explain*** In a short essay explain what effects, both good and bad, Roman rule had on North Africa.
5. ***Synthesizing*** How did North Africa's location on the Mediterranean affect its development?

SECTION 3 REVIEW ANSWERS

IDENTIFY
For significance, see the following pages:
trans-Saharan trade
  (p. 186)
Baal Hammon (p. 188)
Tanit (p. 188)
Coptic Church (p. 189)
Aurelius Augustinus
  (p. 189)

LOCATE
For locations, see the map on p. 187.

1. The trans-Saharan trade brought the goods of West Africa to the north for exchange and also connected Africa with Southwest Asia and Europe.
2. By exchanging inexpensive manufactured goods for metals and raw materials in an extensive overseas trade network, Carthage grew to become a powerful empire.
3. The spread of iron technology and the introduction of the horse and camel contributed to the expansion of trade and urban development in North Africa.
4. Essays should mention the great buildings and the network of roads that were constructed, and that Christianity spread to parts of North Africa. However, taxation was high and local peoples were sometimes enslaved.
5. North Africa's location on the Mediterranean affected its development because people from other civilizations traveled, traded, and settled there, spreading new ideas and technology.

SECTION 4

CORE LESSON PLAN
See pages 173I and
173J for Lesson Plan
7.4.

SECTION 4
Iron Age Developments in Sub-Saharan Africa

FOCUS

- How did Ghana become a major power in West Africa?

- What kind of civilizations emerged along the East African coast?

- What did the Zagwe dynasty contribute to the kingdom of Ethiopia?

- How was Bantu society organized?

As in the north, African society south of the Sahara changed as people began to use iron technology. Populations grew, and trade and religion became important factors in the emergence of African states in East and West Africa. Along the desert fringe in West Africa, strong states such as the kingdom of Ghana arose and became wealthy on the trans-Saharan trade. City-states sprang up along the eastern coast to take advantage of the Indian Ocean trade. Christianity became an important influence in Ethiopian civilization. Meanwhile, Bantu-speaking peoples spread their languages and culture into central and southern Africa, absorbing older hunter-gatherer peoples.

Clay head sculpted in the Nok style

West Africa

Just as iron transformed civilization in North Africa, the spread of ironworking south into the interior also had dramatic effects on many West African peoples. The beginning of the Iron Age in West Africa dates to a period before 500 B.C. As the use of iron tools improved food produc-tion, towns and even states began to form. These growing settlements soon engaged in trade and became even more prosperous.

Nok culture. The best-known of the early iron cultures is Nok, named after a site in central Nigeria. Archaeological evidence indicates that these peoples established themselves in the region sometime between 500 and 200 B.C. Unfortunately, scholars know little about the nature of Nok society. Nok artisans crafted remarkable terra-cotta figurines in the shape of animals and human heads. Some of the tech-niques used to produce these figurines suggest that the Nok people may also have produced wood carvings, but wooden artifacts do not last long in the West African climate.

The rise of Ghana. As long-range trade net-works grew, they stimulated higher levels of political organization. The kingdom of Ghana, one of the early large-scale states in West Africa, was established by the Soninke people sometime after the A.D. 300s. The Soninke lived in the western Sahel, northwest of the present-day nation of Ghana. Midway between the salt-producing region of the Sahara and the gold fields south of the Senegal River, they became intermediaries between North and West Africa, exchanging gold for salt. The Soninke also used iron tools to farm and to clear more land for farming and grazing. They also probably bene-fited from the development of agriculture along the upper Niger River.

As the Soninke settled in larger communi-ties, kings arose to act as war leaders and to negotiate with foreign merchants. Ghanaian kings were powerful, wealthy, and able to build large armies to conquer new territories and to control the kingdom. Most of their wealth came from the gold trade. Around A.D. 773, for exam-ple, the Arab geographer Al-Fazari described Ghana as "the land of gold."

Tunka Manin. One of the most powerful Ghanaian rulers was Tunka Manin, who ruled around A.D. 1065. Tunka Manin governed a strong, secure, and prosperous empire. Al-Bakri, an Arab geographer from Spain, described him as "the master of a large empire and a formidable power," who could mobilize an army of 200,000 warriors, well equipped with bows, arrows, and iron-pointed spears. Al-Bakri explained:

66 *When [the king] gives audience to his people, to listen to their complaints and set them to rights, he sits in a pavilion around which stand ten pages holding shields and gold-mounted swords: and on his right hand are the sons of the princes of his empire, splendidly clad and with gold plaited [braided] into their hair.* 99

▲ Ghanaian kings carried this double-bladed ceremonial sword as a symbol of their authority.

Ghana's decline. In the late A.D. 1000s, however, the great power that Ghana had achieved began to decline. After A.D. 1076, in particular, when invaders destroyed the capital of Kumbi Saleh, the empire began to fall apart. Gradually losing control of the salt trade to neighboring peoples, the people around Kumbi Saleh began to migrate to the south and east in search of more fertile farming lands. Finally, sometime around A.D. 1235, the neighboring Malinke people overthrew Ghana and established the empire of Mali.

As the use of iron led to increased food production and population growth in West Africa, states like Ghana grew strong by controlling trade routes.

The East African Coast

While the Sahara Desert had long acted as a barrier between West African peoples and the larger world, in East Africa the story was very different. Perhaps the most important feature of life along the eastern coast was the influence of the Indian Ocean and its monsoon winds.

Between November and March the monsoons blew southwest, from the coast of India toward Africa. From May to September they reversed and blew northeast, toward India and the Persian Gulf. As sailors learned to take advantage of the winds to get around the Indian Ocean, eastern Africa came into contact with a larger world that included the peoples of Arabia, India, and Southeast Asia. The island of Madagascar off the southeastern coast, for example, was settled early by peoples from Indonesia.

Many important food crops, such as bananas and certain types of rice, also came across the Indian Ocean from Southeast Asia. The use of these foods gradually spread throughout Africa. Meanwhile, towns eventually sprang up along the coast to take advantage of trade with peoples overseas and in the interior.

The East African coast was well known to ancient Greek traders, who called it "Azania." A sailors' handbook, *The Periplus of the Erythraean Sea*, by an Egyptian-Greek merchant, mentions a number of market towns along the Azanian coast that supplied ivory, rhinoceros horn, coconut oil, and tortoiseshell in exchange for iron tools, weapons, cotton cloth, and wheat. Azanians were also great fishermen, skilled in using small boats

▲ These Tanzanians are sailing a boat that is similar to ones that Arab people have used for centuries.

Theme:
Geography
Early West African cities and states were primarily inland, and the coast remained relatively unsettled. The prevailing northerly winds made sailing off the West African coast difficult.

The East African coast, on the other hand, promoted maritime activities and settlement. The monsoon winds and Indian Ocean currents aided traders in sailing there.

Critical Thinking Ask students how these geographical differences might affect technological development.

ANSWER: Students might answer that technological advances in the west might focus on herding and farming; advances in the east might focus on boats and sailing.

R RESOURCE ACTIVITY

GLOBAL HISTORY RESOURCE CENTER
Reading: *The Amazing Story of an East African King*

Print out and distribute the reading. Have students read the selection out loud. Ask the students to create a map of the king of Zanj's travels, illustrating the other kingdoms and peoples that he might have encountered.

Sheltered English

191

made of wood knotted together with coconut fiber. Azanian chiefs governed the market towns and conducted trade with their neighbors.

By A.D. 1000 the coastal towns of East Africa had grown in wealth and had interacted with the peoples of Arabia, Persia, and even India. Arab traders called East Africa the land of Zanj and used the monsoon winds to visit such ports as Mogadishu (mahg-uh-DISH-oo) and Lamu. One traveler, al-Masudi, left this firsthand account of a visit to Zanj:

      ❝ The sea of Zanj reaches down to the country of Sofala . . . which produces gold in abundance and other marvels; its climate is warm and its soil fertile. . . . The Zanj speak elegantly, and they have orators in their own language. . . . These peoples have no code of religion; their kings follow custom and . . . a few political rules. . . . Each [of the Zanj] worships what he pleases, a plant, an animal, a mineral. They possess a great number of islands where the coconut grows, a fruit that is eaten by all the peoples of the Zanj. ❞

East African towns imported items such as glassware, East Asian pottery, and Indian silk and cotton in exchange for raw materials. Included among East African exports were ivory, which was highly prized in many countries; wooden mangrove poles, used for building houses in the areas around the Persian Gulf; and small quantities of gold, copper, shells, leopard skins, and coconut oil. They also exported slaves captured in the interior.

A long the East African coast, market towns sprang up to take advantage of the Indian Ocean trade.

Iron-Age Kingdoms of Africa
c. 300 B.C.–A.D. 1200

Trade route

Bantu migration route from c. 300 B.C.

Iron-working area before A.D. 400

0   500   1,000 Miles
0   500   1,000 Kilometers
Azimuthal Equal-Area Projection

Empires of Iron   The use of iron first gave rise to strong trading empires in East and West Africa and then spread steadily southward with the Bantu-speaking peoples.

❓ **Location**   Between which latitudes did most of the Bantu migrations originate?

Ethiopia

While the towns of East Africa prospered from Indian Ocean trade, a strong kingdom emerged in the highlands of northeastern Africa from the remnants of Aksum. Following years of relative isolation, after about A.D. 1100, Ethiopia once again began to export gold and ivory to Egypt, and myrrh, frankincense, and African slaves to the Arab world. This burst of economic activity has been credited to the Zagwe dynasty.

Taking over from the old Aksumite rulers, the Zagwe kings built a large, powerful army and expanded Ethiopia. Like the Aksumite rulers, the Zagwe were also Christians and regarded themselves as defenders of the Christian faith. The Zagwe kings helped missionaries set up monasteries that became centers of Christian culture and education. Ethiopian Christianity soon developed its own unique characteristics. For example, Ethiopians saw themselves as a "chosen tribe of God" and developed many of their rituals and beliefs from the Old Testament. Most Ethiopian people believed themselves to be descendants of the ancient Israelites.

During the reign of King Lalibela in the first half of the A.D. 1200s, Christian monks built many churches named after holy sites in Jerusalem. Carved from solid rock, the churches still stand as monuments that mark the strength and devotion of Ethiopian Christianity. Christianity served as a symbol of identity and unity for the entire Ethiopian kingdom.

▲ **African Christians in Ethiopia carved this church in the 1100s directly from stone in the ground.**

Under the Zagwe dynasty, the kingdom of Aksum was revived through increased trade and expanded into an Ethiopian kingdom with its own unique version of Christianity.

Central and Southern Africa

While trading centers were developing in the north, the west, and along the eastern coast, the majority of central and southern Africa continued to be occupied by various hunting-and-gathering peoples. In the Congo basin lived communities of pygmies—peoples who were much smaller than other human populations. Scattered throughout the rest of the region were two other groups: the Khoikhoi and the San, or "bushmen." Both groups spoke related languages that used distinctive "click" sounds. Scholars refer to these peoples collectively as the Khoisan.

By the A.D. 400s the use of agriculture and iron had spread to parts of central and southern Africa, as new peoples moved into the region from the west and north. Some of the Khoisan peoples adopted these new technologies and intermarried with the new groups. The Khoikhoi, for example, began herding cattle. Others, however, particularly among the San, were pushed out of their normal hunting areas and into the dry, inhospitable regions of the great Kalahari Desert. There they adapted their hunter-gatherer lifestyle to the harsher environment.

Bantu migrations. Scholars still dispute exactly how and when both agriculture and iron-working technology spread in central and southern Africa. Most scholars, however, accept that it had something to do with the spread of peoples who spoke varieties of the Bantu language group. Linguists trace this migration through a family of more than 2,000 Bantu languages, all linked to a common origin. **Proto-Bantu**—the "parent" of all the Bantu languages—probably developed in a region in modern-day Cameroon and Nigeria. From there, Bantu languages began to spread to the east and south.

For many years, scholars believed that Bantu-speaking peoples had carried ironworking with them. More recent evidence, however, suggests that the earliest phase of the spread of Bantu-speaking peoples occurred before the spread of iron technology in central and southern Africa. Only after Bantu-speakers had reached the great central African lakes did the

RESOURCE ACTIVITY

GLOBAL HISTORY RESOURCE CENTER
Reading: *The Traditional Bantu Law Courts*
Reading: *A Bantu People's System of Kingship*

Print out and distribute the readings. Have students read both documents. Have some students pantomime how they think the law courts appeared and others pantomime how they think the Incwala ceremony appeared.

Level 1

REVIEW & ASSESSMENT RESOURCES

• Study Guide 7.4
• Daily Quiz 7.4
• Main Idea Activity 7.4

All Levels

SECTION 4 REVIEW ANSWERS
(p. 194)

IDENTIFY
For significance, see the following pages:
Tunka Manin (p. 191)
Proto-Bantu (p. 193)
lobola (p. 194)

LOCATE
For locations, see the map on p. 192.

spread of Bantu languages begin to coincide with the spread of iron technology. Bantu-speaking peoples with a knowledge of ironmaking absorbed the earlier Khoisan peoples and established themselves as the dominant population throughout central and southern Africa.

Bantu societies. By the A.D. 900s Bantu-speaking peoples had established complex social systems. They built large dwellings, which varied from region to region. Among the Nguni of southern Africa, for example, dwellings were dome-shaped houses made of grass. The nearby Sotho-Tswana peoples built thatched, round huts of mud. The Bantu-speaking peoples generally lived in chiefdoms, or kingdoms, made up of many clans. Rulers came from hereditary royal families. For food, Bantu-speaking peoples grew such crops as millet and sorghum and kept cattle. Women farmed, while men spent most of their time tending cattle.

Cattle was the most important resource in most Bantu-speaking societies. Cattle were used for food and ritual sacrifices, and were a major form of wealth. Among many southern Bantu-speaking peoples, for example, a man could only obtain a wife by offering a payment of cattle, known as **lobola**, or "bridewealth," to her family. Thus, a man with a large supply of cattle could marry many wives and have many children. This would expand his household and provide labor to create yet more wealth.

▶ This Bantu-speaking warrior carries a hunting spear and wears traditional body decorations.

Bantu societies were organized in clans, led by a ruler who was a member of a royal family.

◀ Villages of many Bantu-speaking peoples consisted of thatched mud huts built in traditional styles.

SECTION 4 REVIEW

IDENTIFY and explain the significance of the following:
Tunka Manin
Proto-Bantu
lobola

LOCATE and explain the importance of the following:
Ghana
Kumbi Saleh
Mogadishu

Ethiopia

1. **Main Idea** How did the Zagwe dynasty affect the development of civilization in Ethiopia?
2. **Main Idea** What factors contributed to Ghana's power in West Africa?
3. **Geography: Location** How did geography affect the

kind of civilizations that developed in East Africa?

4. **Writing to Explain** In a short essay explain how Bantu society was structured.
5. **Analyzing** How might East Africa's location as a center for international trade and cross-cultural interaction affect the overall makeup of its population?

Review

On a separate sheet of paper, complete the following exercises:

WRITING A SUMMARY

Using the essential points in the text, write a brief summary of the chapter.

REVIEWING TERMS

From the following list, choose the term that correctly matches the definition.

griots
savannas
stela
Bantu languages
Coptic Church
Proto-Bantu

1. tall, thin stone monument built by the people of Aksum
2. emerged in Egypt and split from the Roman Catholic Church because of a difference in beliefs
3. the "parent" of all languages of a certain group, which evolved in modern-day Cameroon and Nigeria
4. African oral historians
5. open grasslands dotted with trees

REVIEWING CHRONOLOGY

List the following events in their correct chronological order.

1. Kushite dynasty falls to invading Assyrian armies.
2. Ethiopia is revived by the Zagwe kings.
3. Aksum declines because of environmental problems and loss of trade.
4. Horses are introduced in North Africa.
5. The city of Napata is established to take advantage of trade with Egypt.

UNDERSTANDING THE MAIN IDEA

1. What are some of the major geographical features in Africa?
2. What features did many African societies have in common?
3. What were some of the accomplishments of Kush and Aksum?
4. What developments occurred in North Africa during the periods of Carthaginian and Roman rule?
5. How did location affect the development of societies in East and West Africa?

THINKING CRITICALLY

1. **Synthesizing** The development of major kingdoms and empires occurred throughout Africa. What were some of the common problems that caused the downfall of these large societies?
2. **Hypothesizing** How did control by foreign empires affect the local populations of North Africa? What effects might this have for later history?

Building Your Portfolio

Complete the following activities individually or in groups.

1. **Kingdom-building** Imagine that you (and your friends) live in early Africa. You have decided to relocate and create a kingdom of your own. You must decide what part of Africa you will go to and how you will get there. Write a detailed description answering the following questions: Why did you choose this location? What regions did you cross to get there? Provide a map that shows the route to your new location. What kinds of people are living there already? What hardships might your kingdom face in the new location? To build a successful kingdom, you must have a source of wealth. What kinds of resources are available? Create a map of your new kingdom to accompany your description. You may want to provide illustrations of things you will see along the way.
2. **Oral history** Imagine that you (and your friends) are oral historians like the griots of West Africa. Consider the important events that have happened in your life, family, community, or culture. How would you relate these events to others? Write a script of your oral history and present it to the class.

mountain ranges and river systems make up Africa's main geographical features.
2. In many African societies, family ties and religion were important; having more than one wife was acceptable; women concentrated on farming and gardening while men traditionally hunted, fished, and tended to livestock.
3. Kushites built pyramids and shrines for the worship of new gods, established a thriving trade, and crafted pottery and ornaments. Aksumites created their own written language, developed a thriving international trade, created fine luxury items, minted their own coinage, and adopted Christianity.
4. Technology and new ideas spread, the population grew and changed, agriculture developed further, buildings and roads were constructed, and Christianity spread throughout North Africa.
5. East African societies, located along the coast, were reliant on the monsoon winds and Indian Ocean trade. West African societies, such as Ghana, profited as a result of the trade that crossed the Sahara.

THINKING CRITICALLY

1. invasions by other peoples, loss of trade, and environmental deterioration
2. The local population was enslaved or forced to pay major taxes. Eventually, these societies might become so resentful that they would rise in rebellion.

Civilizations in the Americas 500 B.C.–A.D.1532

Chapter Planning Guide

	TEXTBOOK	CORE RESOURCES	VISUAL RESOURCES	MULTIMEDIA
Introduction	pp. 196–197	Block Scheduling Handbook: Ch. 8		Videodisc Segment 8 and Viewing Guide: *Tools and Transformations*
Lesson 8.1 Mesoamerica	pp. 198–203 Map: *Civilizations in Mesoamerica*, p. 199 History Through the Arts: *Chichén Itzá*, p. 200 Through Others' Eyes: *The Aztec Empire*, p. 203	Reading 8.1: *Maya Technology* Geography Activity 8: *The Maya Empire* Skills Activity 8: *Paraphrasing Information*	Art and History 8: *The Castillo and Temple of Kukulcán* Everyday Life 8: *The Maya Number System*	GHRC 8 Reading: *Maya Farmers; A Tour of the Marketplace at Tenochtitlán; An Aztec Lecture on Table Manners; Maya Creation Myth from the Popol Vuh* GHRC 8/Videodiscs: Images—*Maya Statues from the Ruins of Copán; Aztec Floating Gardens at Tenochtitlán*
Lesson 8.2 South America	pp. 204–209 Map: *Civilizations in South America*, p. 205	Reading 8.2: *The Inca: Worshippers of the Sun* Writing Project 8: *Creating an Outline*		GHRC 8 Reading: *The Agricultural Achievements of the Inca* GHRC 8/Videodiscs: Image—*Inca Terraces at Machu Picchu*
Lesson 8.3 North America	pp. 210–216 Map: *Peoples of North America*, p. 211 Sacred Traditions: *Iroquois Creation Myth*, p. 213	Reading 8.3: *Women Leaders in North American Indian Societies*	Geography and History 8: *Native American Culture Areas*	GHRC 8 Readings: *The Inuit: Life Beside the Arctic Ocean; An Inuit Shaman Fights Off Famine; How the Iroquois Shaped Their Environment; The Great Peace of the Iroquois; The Tlingit Potlatch Tradition* GHRC 8/Videodiscs: Images—*Inuit Hunters' Dance; Iroquois Longhouses; Pueblo Ceremonial Dance; Cliff Dwelling at Mesa Verde; Tlingit Salmon Rattle; Northwest Coast Salmon Fishing Camp*
Chapter Investigation and Enrichment	pp. 196–216	Chapter 8 Investigation: *A Food Fair of the Americas* People in World History 8 Explorations in Daily Life 8		GHRC 8/Videodiscs
Review and Assessment	Section 1 Review, p. 203 Section 2 Review, p. 209 Section 3 Review, p. 216 Chapter 8 Review, p. 217	Chapter Review Activity 8 Vocabulary Activity 8 Themes Review 8 Section Study Guides 8.1–8.3 Main Idea Activities 8.1–8.3 Daily Quizzes 8.1–8.3 Chapter 8 Test Sheltered English Ch. 8 Test Ch. 8 Test Generator		Audio CDs: Ch. 8 Summary (English and Spanish)

INTRODUCING THE CHAPTER

Textbook pp. 196–197

CHAPTER OVERVIEW

Civilizations developed in the Americas in isolation from the rest of the world. In Mesoamerica the Maya devised a sophisticated calendar. The Aztec possessed a complex social organization and oversaw a powerful empire, and their cities rivaled the urban centers of Europe in size and beauty. Far to the south the Inca created a great empire in the Andes. In North America hundreds of tribes from the Arctic to the temperate south developed a variety of cultures and religious beliefs.

PRESENTING THEMES

On the chalkboard or on an overhead transparency, write the following open-ended theme questions.

- **GEOGRAPHY** How does geography affect the locations of cities?
- **SCIENCE** Why might societies based on agriculture place particular importance on the calendar?
- **SOCIAL RELATIONS** How might the conquest of a region affect the society of the peoples conquered and of the conquerors?

Have students, either individually or in groups, suggest responses to the questions. For the geography question, students might suggest that cities must develop in environments that can sustain large populations. For the science question, students might suggest that a calendar allows agricultural societies to know when to plant and harvest crops. For the social relations question, students might suggest that both the conquered peoples and the conquerors might share ideas that influence social development. Save the responses. Once students have studied the chapter, you may wish to have them complete the Themes Review, then compare the two sets of answers.

USING THE VIDEO

Segment 8: *Tools and Transformations*

ENGLISH

Search Chapter 8
Videodisc 1, Side A

SPANISH

Search Chapter 8
Videodisc 1, Side A

Tell students that in this chapter they will examine the new civilizations and changing patterns of life that appeared in the Americas as knowledge of agriculture spread throughout this part of the world. Conclude by showing Segment 8 of the *World History and Cultures Videodiscs*. This segment illustrates how American Indians first adapted to and then began to shape different environments to meet their basic needs. Before showing the segment, ask students to pay particular attention to the types of natural materials they see, and to the uses made of these materials. To help students grasp the significant points of the segment, have them complete Video Viewing Guide 8.

Key to Ability Levels

All strategies and activities are coded to the following ability levels:

LEVEL 1   **Basic** activities suitable for all students

LEVEL 2   **Average** activities suitable for average to above-average students

LEVEL 3   **Challenging** activities suitable for above-average students

SHELTERED ENGLISH   Activities suitable for students with **Limited English Proficiency**

Additional Resources

BOOKS FOR TEACHERS

Fagan, Mark. *Kingdoms of Gold, Kingdoms of Jade: The Americas Before Columbus.* Thames and Hudson, 1991. Includes excellent illustrations.

Josephy, Alvin J., Jr. *America in 1492.* Vintage, 1991. Includes essays on precontact North America.

Porskouriakoff, Tatiana. *Maya History.* University of Texas Press, 1993. Interprets Maya history through glyphs.

BOOKS FOR STUDENTS

Acatos, Sylvia. *Pueblos: Prehistorical Indian Cultures of the Southwest.* Facts On File, 1990. Offers an overview of the American Southwest.

Bingham, Hiram. *Lost City of the Incas: The Story of Machu Picchu and Its Builders.* Duell, 1948. Written by the ancient city's modern discoverer.

Reader's Digest. *America's Fascinating Indian Heritage.* Reader's Digest Association, 1990. Discusses American Indian life.

MULTIMEDIA MATERIALS

The Americas Before the Europeans. Network Television Production. Video, 26 min. Discusses pre-Columbian societies.

Lost Kingdoms of the Maya. National Geographic Society. Video, 60 min. Visits several ruins with archaeologists.

North American Indians. Quanta Press. CD-ROM, MAC, DOS, MPC formats. Provides a database and photo archive.

Lesson 8.1   *Mesoamerica*

Textbook pp. 198–203

RESOURCES

Pupil's Edition

Map, p. 199: *Civilizations in Mesoamerica, c. 500 B.C.– A.D. 1521*

History Through the Arts, p. 200: *Chichén Itzá*

Through Others' Eyes, p. 203: *The Aztec Empire*

Core Resources

Reading 8.1: *Maya Technology*
Geography Activity 8: *The Maya Empire*

Visual Resources

Everyday Life 8: *The Maya Number System*
Art and History 8: *The Castillo and Temple of Kukulcán*

Global History Resource Center

Reading: *Maya Farmers*
Reading: *A Tour of the Marketplace at Tenochtitlán*
Reading: *An Aztec Lecture on Table Manners*
Reading: *Maya Creation Myth from the Popol Vuh*

Videodiscs or Global History Resource Center

Image: *Maya Statues from the Ruins of Copán*

Search Frame 771

Image: *Aztec Floating Gardens at Tenochtitlán*

Search Frame 772

LESSON FOCUS

How did advanced civilizations develop in Mesoamerica?

OBJECTIVES

After completing this lesson, students will be able to:

- find the locations of the first American cities;
- identify accomplishments of the Classic Maya;
- explain why archaeologists think the Toltec were at the center of a great trading network;
- explain how the Aztec were able to build a powerful empire.

HOOK

Discuss the location of the first American cities.
Encourage students to consider the civilizations they studied in earlier chapters. Have them pay close to attention to the locations of the major cities of these civilizations.

Ask: What factors determined the location of early cities?
[Answers might include proximity to fertile land for agriculture, proximity to water for irrigation and transportation, nearness of important trade routes, and ease of defense.]

Point out that generally these were the reasons for the establishment of early cities in Mesoamerica. Then have students consult the map on textbook page 199 to determine where the first cities in Mesoamerica were located. Have students note the locations of Monte Albán, Teotihuacán, Tikal, Palenque, Copán, Tula, and Chichén Itzá. You may wish to assign Geography Activity 8 for additional information on the Maya Empire.

DEVELOP

Review the major achievements of Maya and Toltec cultures. Remind students that the Classic Maya civilization is noted for several achievements. Help students appreciate the level of Maya technology by assigning Core Resources Reading 8.1. Mention that among the most important of these achievements were the development of a writing system and the refinement of the Mesoamerican calendar.

Ask: What was notable about Maya writing?
[Maya hieroglyphs, or glyphs, formed the first complete writing system in the Americas.]

Ask: What purposes did the Maya calendars serve?
[Sacred and agricultural calendars helped the Maya plan

for rituals and agricultural tasks; the Long Count helped them record history.]

Assist students in understanding Maya mathematical achievements by showing Everyday Life Transparency 8 and assigning the accompanying worksheet. Also display the electronic media image of Maya statues and assign the Global History Resource Center reading on Maya farming.

Remind students that as the Maya declined, the Toltec rose to power. Encourage students to read the History Through the Arts feature on textbook page 200. You might also display the Art and History transparency and have students complete the accompanying worksheet.

Finally, focus on why scholars have arrived at the conclusion that the Toltec were at the center of a great trading network. **Ask: *What evidence have archaeologists found to support this conclusion?***

[Pottery from distant places has been found at Toltec sites; Toltec architectural styles are seen in Maya cities; late Maya and Toltec religions have similarities; some Maya royalty claimed descent from the Toltec.]

Have students summarize the information by creating a graphic organizer titled "Achievements of the Maya and Toltec."

PROBE

Investigate the rise of the Aztec and their way of life.
Organize students into five groups and assign each group one of the following questions:
- Where did the Aztec come from and when did they arrive in the Valley of Mexico?
- What was the Triple Alliance and why was it important?
- What did Tenochtitlán look like?
- What was the social organization of Tenochtitlán?
- What were the main features of Aztec religion?

Allow groups about five minutes to develop an answer to their questions. Call on group representatives to present their answers. Then have students write a brief essay describing Aztec civilization.

CONCLUDE

Discuss how the Aztec brought Mesoamerican culture to its culmination. Point out that scholars consider Aztec culture

the culmination of preconquest Mesoamerican civilization. Have students explore the reasons for the development of Aztec culture by asking them to explain how:
- the Aztec gained power after they settled in the Valley of Mexico;
- conquest and expansion affected the Aztec;
- wealth from conquests changed Aztec society.

Guide students to recognize that Aztec culture evolved into greatness by drawing on previous cultures, through wealth acquired by conquest, and through a clear, coherent social organization. Display the electronic media image of the Aztec gardens and assign the Global History Resource Center readings on Tenochtitlán and the lecture on table manners.

EXTEND

Cross-Curricular Connection: *Mathematics*
Link to Today. Invite students to research the Maya number system. Ask them to evaluate ways in which the Maya system is different from the Arabic system they use today.

Other Media
Have interested students view the video *Lost Kingdoms of the Maya* (National Geographic Society, color, 60 min.). Then have them identify what they think is the most remarkable aspect of Maya culture.

MEET INDIVIDUAL NEEDS

Visual-Spatial Learners
Have students research the pyramids built by the Maya and those built by the Egyptians, comparing them in size, function, and methods of construction. They might also create labeled cardboard or papier-mâché models of the pyramids.

Linguistic Learners
Have students read the Maya creation myth in the Global History Resource Center. Have them compare it with the story of creation in other religions and then write a brief report.

ASSESS

Review
Have students complete the Section 1 Review. Use answers in the Teacher's Edition, page 203, to assess student mastery of this section.

Lesson 8.2 *South America*

Textbook pp. 204–209

RESOURCES

Pupil's Edition

Map, p. 205: *Civilizations in South America*

Core Resources

Reading 8.2: *The Inca: Worshippers of the Sun*

Global History Resource Center

Reading: *The Agricultural Achievements of the Inca*

Videodiscs or Global History Resource Center

Image: *Inca Terraces at Machu Picchu*

Search Frame 773

LESSON FOCUS

How did civilizations flourish in the varied geographical zones in and around the Andes?

OBJECTIVES

After completing this lesson, students will be able to:
- describe how Andean peoples adapted to their environment;
- explain how the Nazca, Moche, and Chimú were able to create civilizations along the Andean coast;
- identify the factors that allowed the Inca to control their empire.

HOOK

Examine how the Andean peoples adapted to their environment. Write the following statement on the chalkboard: *Environment influences way of life.* Then call on volunteers to recall what they learned from previous chapters on how environment influenced the way peoples in early civilizations structured their societies. Note responses under the statement on the chalkboard.

Next direct students' attention to the map on textbook page 205. Have them locate on the map the areas occupied by the Nazca, Moche, Chimú, and Inca civilizations. Encourage students to consider the geography of the areas these civilizations occupied. Then have them suggest how environment might have influenced life in these civilizations.

Ask: *How did the Andean peoples adjust to their environment?* [Coastal peoples fished the waters of the Pacific and farmed the river-fed valleys. In the mountains, peoples built irrigation systems and terraced fields to allow them to farm. In higher elevations, peoples herded animals. Trade and the desire to control rivers contributed to the empire-building and conquest characteristic of early Andean civilizations.]

Link to Today. Now that students have learned how environment affected early civilizations' patterns of life, have them think of modern examples of how people adjust their lives to their environment. Have them compare people's lives in the country to lifestyles in huge cities, such as New York City.

DEVELOP

Note the major features of the Nazca, Moche, and Chimú civilizations. Divide the chalkboard into three sections with the headings *Nazca*, *Moche*, and *Chimú*. Organize students into three groups, assigning one of these civilizations to each group. Direct groups to use their textbooks to develop a list of the major features of their assigned civilization. Suggest that they list such points as location, social organization, religious beliefs, and technology. Call on group representatives to write their lists under the appropriate heading on the chalkboard. After group representatives have finished writing their lists on the chalkboard, encourage all students to compare these three civilizations.

Ask: **What features did the Nazca, Moche, and Chimú civilizations have in common?**

[They lived in coastal desert areas, constructed buildings with sun-dried adobe bricks, and constructed elaborate irrigation systems to allow them to farm.]

Suggest that students copy and retain the chart.

PROBE

Examine how the Inca established a vast empire. Have students turn again to the map on textbook page 205, and ask them to note the extent of the Inca Empire. Point out that this vast empire was made up of hundreds of villages that the Inca had conquered. Further, the population of the empire consisted of many different groups of people who spoke different languages. Have students consider how the Inca were able to forge this diverse population into a single empire.

Ask: **How were the Inca able to keep the conquered lands within the empire?**

[The Inca often left local customs and chieftains in place in conquered areas. However, chieftains had to send a sacred object to Cuzco. Nobles also had to send their sons to Cuzco to learn Quechua, the Inca language. Such measures, the Inca hoped, would prevent village rebellions.]

CONCLUDE

Discuss the measures the Inca took to control their empire. Organize students into several small groups. Have groups develop a list of the major features of Inca civilization. Suggest that groups include such features as government, social organization, religion, communications, and military organization in their lists. Direct groups to draw their lists from the text on pages 207–209. To provide students with further information on Inca civilization, you might assign Core Resources Reading 8.2 and the Global History Resource Center reading on the agricultural achievements of the Inca. Call on group representatives to present their lists to the class.

Conclude by having students discuss which of the listed features might have helped the Inca maintain control of their empire.

Ask: **What factors allowed the Inca to control their empire?**

[A system of taxes, which took the form of goods and labor, supported imperial government. A strong army and an elaborate system of roads held the empire together.]

EXTEND

Cross-Curricular Connection: *Drama*

Have students work in small groups to prepare a brief one-act play about Andean villagers and their feelings about being part of the Inca Empire. They might, for example, write a dramatic play about bringing a sacred object to the temple in Cuzco, or about paying taxes to the local imperial officer. Encourage students to perform their plays for the class.

Cross-Curricular Connection: *Architecture*

Have students view the electronic media image of the terraces of Machu Picchu. Also point out the photograph of the city on textbook page 207. Then direct them to the description of the Inca capital, Cuzco, on textbook page 208. Ask students to research ancient Inca cities and provide information on their architectural designs and settings.

MEET INDIVIDUAL NEEDS

Students Acquiring English

Have pairs of students write statements on strips of paper defining key names and terms from the section. For example, a statement might read *Pachacutec rebuilt Cuzco and declared himself the earthly son of the Sun*. Students should then cut apart the strips between subject and predicate, mix up the subjects and predicates, and then play a matching game with the strips. Have partners review each other's matches.

Linguistic Learners

Have students work individually or in small groups to develop a dramatic reading of one of the events discussed in this section. One event that students might consider is the civil war that weakened the Inca Empire. Encourage students to present their readings to the class.

ASSESS

Review

Have students complete the Section 2 Review. Use answers in the Teacher's Edition, page 209, to assess student mastery of this section.

RESOURCES

Pupil's Edition

Map, p. 211: *Peoples of North America, 2500 B.C.–A.D. 1500*

Sacred Traditions, p. 213: *Iroquois Creation Myth*

Core Resources

Reading 8.3: *Women Leaders in North American Indian Societies*

Visual Resources

Geography and History 8: *Native American Culture Areas*

Global History Resource Center

Reading: *The Inuit: Life Beside the Arctic Ocean*

Reading: *An Inuit Shaman Fights Off Famine*

Reading: *How the Iroquois Shaped Their Environment*

Reading: *The Great Peace of the Iroquois*

Reading: *The Tlingit Potlatch Tradition*

Videodiscs or Global History Resource Center

Image: *Inuit Hunters' Dance*

Search Frame 774

Image: *Pueblo Ceremonial Dance*

Search Frame 780

Image: *Tlingit Salmon Rattle*

Search Frame 776

Image: *Iroquois Longhouses*

Search Frame 778

Image: *Cliff Dwelling at Mesa Verde*

Search Frame 779

Image: *Northwest Coast Salmon Fishing Camp*

Search Frame 777

LESSON FOCUS

How did native peoples adapt to the different environments of North America?

OBJECTIVES

After completing this lesson, students will be able to:

- explain how peoples of the Arctic and Subarctic adapted to their environment;
- describe cultural traits of Eastern Woodlands peoples;
- discuss how peoples of the Great Plains adapted to their environment;
- compare and contrast life in the West, the Southwest, and the Pacific Coast.

HOOK

Discuss how northern hunting peoples viewed the land *and animals.* Begin by asking students to discuss the environmental challenges the peoples of the northern regions faced. *[long, cold winters; little arable land for farming; lack of trees for building and fuel]* Continue by having students consider how the peoples of the northern regions met these challenges. To provide students with more information, you might have them review the Global History Resource Center reading on Inuit life.

Ask: How did the peoples of the Arctic and Subarctic regions adapt to their environment?

[by relying on hunting and fishing]

Mention that the peoples of the Arctic and Subarctic regions revered the animals they hunted. To illustrate this point, display the electronic media image of the Inuit dance. To further illustrate the spiritual nature of hunting among these peoples, you might also assign the Global History Resource Center reading on the Inuit shaman.

DEVELOP

Discuss the cultures of the Eastern Woodlands and the Great Plains. Tell students that they will be charting information about the Eastern Woodlands peoples. Display Geography and History Transparency 8 and draw students' attention to the map on textbook page 211. Call on a volunteer to point out the Eastern Woodlands area on the transparency and have students locate the region on their maps.

Then write the following headings on the chalkboard: *Adena, Hopewell, Mississippian,* and *Iroquois.* On the left side of the chart, add the following categories: *Time Period, Food, Shelter, Burial Practices,* and *Other Information.* Have students copy and complete the chart. You might assign the Sacred Traditions feature and the Global History Resource Center readings on the Iroquois, and display the electronic media image of Iroquois longhouses. Then lead a discussion comparing the Eastern Woodlands cultures.

Next call on a volunteer to point out the Great Plains on the Geography and History transparency, and have students locate the region on their textbook maps. Have them make another chart for the peoples of the Great Plains. Suggest that they use *Peoples of the Eastern Great Plains* and *Peoples of the Western Great Plains* as headings. Ask students to compare the two.

PROBE

Compare and contrast life in the West, the Southwest, and the Pacific Coast. Ask students to describe the soil conditions and climates of these areas. *[Students should be aware that the West and the Southwest are dry areas, while the Pacific Coast has good soil and ample water.]*

Discuss reasons why different cultures would develop in these areas. Then conclude by displaying the electronic media images of the Pueblo dance, Mesa Verde, the rattle, and the fishing camp. Have students discuss how these images illustrate the different ways of life of the peoples of the Southwest and of the Northwest Coast. You might also have them read the Global History Resource Center selection on the potlatch tradition.

CONCLUDE

Analyze the impact of environment on the ways of life followed by North American peoples. Help students recall which cultures were migratory and which cultures developed settlements. Students should recognize the peoples of the Arctic and Subarctic, the western Great Plains, and the Desert West as migratory, and the peoples of the Eastern Woodlands, the eastern Great Plains, the Southwest, and the Pacific Coast as settled. Then discuss why the ways of life of these groups differed. *[Some areas were not suitable for agriculture, and people had to migrate to search for food. In other areas, agriculture enabled people to develop a secure food supply and thus settle in one place. In still other areas, resources were abundant and there was no need to move or to develop agriculture.]*

Assign Core Resources Reading 8.3. Discuss whether or not environment influenced the roles played by American Indian women.

EXTEND

Cross-Curricular Connection: *Language Arts*
Organize students into small groups. Direct each group to find a story, myth, or poem from an American Indian culture. Have each group present its selection and lead a discussion.

Other Media
Encourage students to use the CD-ROM *The American Indian: A Multimedia Encyclopedia* to find information on how environment influenced American Indian ways of life.

MEET INDIVIDUAL NEEDS

Gifted Students
Have students research one of the California tribes, such as the Yurok or the Yokuts, and report on their way of life.

Visual-Spatial Learners
Have students research Northwest American Indian art. Have them create and present a work in a style they admire.

ASSESS

Review
Have students complete the Section 3 Review. Use answers in the Teacher's Edition, page 216, to assess student mastery of this section.

In preparation for the chapter test, you may wish to have students complete all or part of the Chapter 8 Review on textbook page 217, the Chapter Review Activity, and the Chapter 8 Themes Review.

Understanding the Main Idea

Call on a volunteer to read aloud the *Understanding the Main Idea* paragraph. Then tell students that many civilizations existed in the Americas before the arrival of Europeans. These civilizations arose in widely divergent environments, developing social and economic systems, methods of government, and religious beliefs that drew on the challenges and opportunities provided by their physical surroundings.

Presenting Themes

See p. 195B for suggestions on introducing themes.

Using the Time Line

Have students list the time line events in their notebooks. After they have read about each event in the chapter, have students write a paragraph explaining its significance.

Chapter 8
Civilizations in the Americas

500 B.C. – A.D. 1532

Understanding the Main Idea

The civilizations of the Americas developed in near isolation from Europe, Africa, and Asia. Around 500 B.C., as agricultural improvements dramatically increased harvests, cities began to appear in Mesoamerica and the Andes, the cradles of American civilization. Some civilizations established vast and powerful empires, conquering their weaker neighbors.

Themes

- *Geography* How does geography affect the locations of cities?

- *Science* Why might societies based on agriculture place particular importance on the calendar?

- *Social Relations* How might the conquest of a region affect the society of the peoples conquered and of the conquerors?

Sometime during the A.D. 1300s, the Aztec founded a vast empire in central Mexico. They built their capital, Tenochtitlán (tay-NAWCH-tee-TLAHN), on a network of islands in a shallow lake. According to legend, the Aztec discovered the site while fleeing from their enemies following a defeat. A god is said to have spoken to the people, telling them of their destiny:

> 66 *Here we will make ourselves lords of all these people, of their possessions, their sons and daughters; here they must serve us and pay us tribute; in this place shall the famous city be built that is destined to be the queen and lady of all the others—where we will one day receive all the kings and lords, and where they will have to come in homage, as to the supreme capital.* 99

The city was a marvel of architectural and strategic planning. The Aztec built temples, palaces, houses, and market squares. Canals and causeways aided transportation and communication among the various islands. Causeways to the mainland made the city easily defensible. The construction of the Aztec capital is only one example of the thriving civilizations of the early Americas. From the Andes in South America to the frozen reaches of North America, people built complex societies before the arrival of Europeans.

c. 500 B.C.	c. 200 B.C.	c. 200 B.C.–A.D. 900	A.D. 200s
Monte Albán is built in Mesoamerica.	Nazca culture emerges in South America.	Maya culture flourishes in Mesoamerica.	The Mogollon culture combines farming with hunting and gathering.

The Temple of the Magician at Uxmal, an ancient Maya city in the Yucatán Peninsula, Mexico

About the Image

The Temple of the Magician towers over Uxmal, one of the Maya city-states. The pyramid was constructed in five stages, its elliptical base making it unique among Maya structures. Uxmal is believed to have been built around A.D. 909, based on archaeological evidence including a date appearing on a capstone. Although many of the large buildings at Uxmal have been restored, much of the surrounding area has not yet been mapped in any detail.

Critical Thinking Ask students what geographic feature makes it difficult to locate and map some Mesoamerican sites such as Uxmal.

ANSWER: Students should note that many Mesoamerican sites are overgrown with dense rain forests.

A.D. 800	A.D. 1050	A.D. 1420s	c. A.D. 1462–1470	A.D. 1530–1532
Maize agriculture appears in Eastern Woodlands.	Mississippians establish Cahokia.	Aztec form Triple Alliance.	Inca Empire conquers the Chimú.	Civil war divides the Inca.

CORE LESSON PLAN
See pages 195C and 195D for Lesson Plan 8.1.

Theme:
Technology

Archaeologists have found that large-scale irrigation projects allowed agricultural production in the valley below Monte Albán and provided an economic base for population growth.

The residents of Monte Albán chose the site for its strategic location. The settlement was enclosed on two sides by the mountain, offering protection from attack. The inhabitants built walls along the other two sides of the mountain.

Critical Thinking Ask students what drawbacks these fortifications might have presented to the residents of Monte Albán.

ANSWER: Students might suggest that Monte Albán would have been cut off from its food sources in the valley in case of war.

SECTION 1
Mesoamerica

FOCUS

- Where did the peoples of central Mexico build the first American cities?

- What were some of the accomplishments of the Classic Maya?

- Why do archaeologists believe that the Toltec were at the center of a great trading network?

- How were the Aztec able to build such a powerful empire?

*I*n Mesoamerica—the area that includes present-day Central America and central and southern Mexico—great cities and empires rose and fell between A.D. 1 and 1500. In the competition for trade and territory, some of these cities disappeared, leaving archaeologists few clues to explain their downfall. Others, however, prospered and grew into great empires. In the valley of central Mexico and the steamy rain forests of the Yucatán Peninsula, for example, empires with complex religious and scientific beliefs arose.

Head of Xipe Totec, Aztec god, dressed in the skin of a sacrificial victim

---

The First Cities

Complex cultures existed in Mesoamerica long before the founding of the first cities. The Olmec culture on the western coast of the Gulf of Mexico, for example, spread its influence south and east between 1200 and 400 B.C. Much of the region was home to small farming villages. As irrigation and other farming techniques increased food production, these settlements eventually grew into cities.

Monte Albán. The Zapotec people of the Classic Monte Albán period were among the earliest Mesoamericans to develop an urban civilization. The historical period is named after Monte Albán, one of the most important Zapotec sites. The Zapotec people built Monte Albán sometime around 500 B.C. atop a mountain at the point where the three arms of the Valley of Oaxaca (wuh-HAHK-uh) intersect. From this easily defensible site, the powerful Zapotec lords were able to rule the valley for over 1,000 years.

Archaeologists disagree over whether Monte Albán was a true city or simply a ceremonial center. There is evidence, however, that by the Classic Period the mountain had been terraced to support residences.

Teotihuacán. Beginning about 200 B.C. Teotihuacán (tay-uh-tee-wah-KAHN), located far north of Monte Albán on a well-watered plain in the Valley of Mexico, became Monte Albán's rival. Scholars believe that by A.D. 500 as many as 200,000 people may have lived in Teotihuacán, making it among the world's largest cities at the time. One reason for the city's rapid growth was its strategic location on a major trade route. The city's inhabitants prospered from trade. As they grew wealthier, they were able to increase their control over the surrounding region and eventually over the entire Valley of Oaxaca.

Teotihuacán contained numerous plazas, a great marketplace, hundreds of pyramids, apartment blocks, and residential neighborhoods. Everything at Teotihuacán was carefully laid out according to a planned grid. An enormous pyramid, painted in bright red and white, dominated the city. The pyramid was built over a natural cave that the Teotihuacanos enlarged into a cloverleaf chamber. Scholars believe that the people of Teotihuacán may have viewed this

Civilizations in Mesoamerica, c. 500 B.C.–A.D. 1521

Gulf of Mexico

Tula
Teotihuacán
Tlacopán
Tenochtitlán
Lake Texcoco
Valley of Mexico

Uxmal
Chichén Itzá

YUCATÁN PENINSULA

20°N

Monte Albán
Valley of Oaxaca
ZAPOTEC

Palenque

Tikal

CARIBBEAN SEA

PACIFIC OCEAN

Copán

15°N

100°W   95°W

N
W   E
S

Legend:
- Monte Albán c. 500 B.C.–A.D. 700
- Teotihuacán c. 200 B.C.–A.D. 700
- Classic Maya c. 200 B.C.–A.D. 900
- Toltec c. A.D. 900–1100
- Aztec c. A.D. 1400–1521
- • City

0   100   200   300 Miles
0   100   200   300 Kilometers
Azimuthal Equal-Area Projection

90°W

City Builders With wealth gained from agriculture and trade, the Mesoamerican civilizations built bustling cities.

? Region Which Mesoamerican civilization controlled the most territory at any time between 500 B.C. and A.D. 1521?

cave as the location from which their ancestors emerged from the earth.

Both Teotihuacán and Monte Albán rapidly declined after A.D. 700. The people abandoned the cities, and the central areas of Teotihuacán were burned. Archaeologists believe that since these cities depended on the surrounding lands to supply them with food, intensive farming may have damaged the environment. This, combined with drought or other natural disasters, may have caused the cities to lose their stable food supply.

Mesoamericans built the first American cities in easily defensible locations near land suitable for farming.

The Maya

At about the same time that Teotihuacán was extending its influence across central Mexico, the Maya people were growing in power farther to the

south, in the area around the Yucatán Peninsula. There, from about 200 B.C. to A.D. 900, Maya civilization flourished. Archaeologists call the period of greatest achievement, from A.D. 300 to A.D. 900, the **Classic Maya.**

By the time of the Classic Maya, trade was an important part of the Mesoamerican economy. Archaeologists believe, for example, that the Maya traded highland quetzal feathers, which were associated with royalty, for black obsidian from Teotihuacán. Teotihuacán's obsidian was highly prized by the many skilled artisans who appear to have lived in Maya cities. Most Maya, however, farmed the land, constructed the roads and reservoirs, and built and maintained the great cities that were home to the majority of the population.

The Maya developed the only complete writing system in the Americas. The system—based on a complex series of hieroglyphs, or **glyphs** for short—enabled the Maya to express all of their language in writing. Archaeologists can now translate some of the glyphs and thus have begun to uncover the history of the Maya. For instance,

History THROUGH THE ARTS

Chichén Itzá

At a site in the northern Yucatán, the steamy Central American rain forest opens to an ancient plaza surrounded by massive limestone buildings that were constructed almost 1,000 years ago. The place is Chichén Itzá, an ancient civic, political, and cultural center of the Maya. After the arrival of Toltec invaders in the A.D. 900s, the northern Maya began construction of the central plaza.

On the western side of the central plaza lies a large I-shaped ball court complex, similar to those found throughout Mesoamerica. The court itself is about 272×99 feet long with a temple at each end. Scholars believe that two opposing teams faced off on the court, trying to score points by putting the ball through one of the two rings on the walls of the court. Images on the walls indicate that the losers paid a heavy price—they became human sacrifices.

Chichén Itzá contains an astronomical observatory and several important temples, such as the Temple of the Warriors and the Castillo (castle). The temples were dedicated to the feathered serpent god Kukulcán, or Quetzalcóatl. On two days each year, in the fall and the spring, the afternoon sun and the shifting shadows cast shimmering light on the serpent carvings that line the exterior walls of the Castillo, making them appear to wiggle as if they were alive.

The name *Chichén Itzá* means "mouth of the well of Itzá." The name refers to the site's huge natural sinkhole, or well. The well was an important religious place to the ancient Maya. Pilgrims came from all over the region to offer human sacrifices in an effort to please the gods and ward off disaster. Archaeologists have dredged up a vast assortment of ornaments, masks, jewelry, and other artifacts from the bottom of the great well.

Thinking About Art

1. What are some of the features of Chichén Itzá that indicate that the Maya were deeply religious?
2. What does Chichén Itzá mean? Where does the name come from?

The astronomical observatory at Chichén Itzá

they now know that Tikal in present-day Guatemala, Palenque (puh-LENG-kay) in what is now Mexico, and Copán in present-day Honduras were three principal Maya cities.

The Maya also refined the Mesoamerican calendar so that they could track various cycles of time. Their sacred calendar, for example, was based on 260 days, while their agricultural calendar was based on 365 days. The Maya also kept time through the **Long Count**, which allowed them to record more than 5,000 years of history by combining five cycles of time.

◀ In this wall carving, the Maya ruler "Shield Jaguar" watches as his wife, Lady Xoc, pulls a thorned rope through her tongue in a bloodletting ceremony.

glyphs, and a jade mask of his face lay on the lid. The king also was buried with an image of the sun, reflecting the Maya belief that he would one day rise again.

The Classic Maya developed the only complete writing system in the Americas and refined the Mesoamerican calendar.

The Toltec

For reasons not yet known, Maya civilization began to decline during the A.D. 900s. During this period the Maya came into contact with a newly developing civilization to the north—the Toltec. It is believed that the Toltec were the descendants of nomadic tribes that migrated to central Mexico from the deserts to the north. After establishing their capital at Tula, about 40 miles northwest of present-day Mexico City, the Toltec conquered neighboring regions and created an empire.

Archaeologists believe that the Toltec were at the center of a great trading network. Pottery from as far away as present-day Costa Rica has been found at Toltec sites. Evidence of Toltec cultural influence is even more apparent. Several Maya cities, including Chichén Itzá (chee-CHEN eet-SAH), show examples of Toltec architecture. The late Maya and the Toltec also shared some common religious beliefs, and some Maya royalty claimed descent from the Toltec.

The Toltec Empire did not last long. Tula was somehow destroyed in the late A.D. 1100s. A later poet described the downfall of the city:

❝ *Everywhere there met the eye, everywhere can be seen the remains of clay vessels. . . everywhere are their ruins, truly the Toltecs once lived there.* **❞**

Foreign pottery found at Toltec sites and the widespread influence of Toltec culture lead scholars to believe that the Toltec were at the center of a great trading network.

Among the historical events recorded by the Long Count were the reigns of the rulers. Most Maya rulers were males, although glyphs indicate that there were a few female rulers. Maya kings and queens became wealthy through conquest and tribute payments. They also served as ritual leaders. These monarchs interpreted the wishes of the gods, and offered human and other sacrifices to the gods on behalf of the people.

One of the greatest Maya leaders was Pacal, king of Palenque, who ruled for 68 years. Pacal ascended the throne of the city of Palenque in A.D. 615. Only 12 years old, he inherited the throne from his mother, Lady Zac-Kuk. Possibly his greatest accomplishment was the construction of the Temple of the Inscriptions, the corridors of which display the lists of the past kings of Palenque. The detailed documentation of royal ancestry adorning the temple demonstrates the importance of history to the Maya.

In 1952 archaeologists discovered Pacal's tomb within the Temple of the Inscriptions. The sides of the king's coffin were carved with his ancestors'

Pacal
BIOGRAPHY

R **RESOURCE ACTIVITY**

READINGS IN WORLD HISTORY Reading 8.1 *Maya Technology*

Have students read the description of Maya intellectual achievement. Then have them complete the questions.

Level 2

BIOGRAPHY
Lady Zac-Kuk
When Pacal claimed the throne of Palenque, his mother was still alive. Lady Zac-Kuk lived for another 25 years. Some scholars think that she may have held actual power during that period, because Pacal did not commission inscriptions relating to his rule until after her death.

Critical Thinking Ask students to suggest other reasons why Pacal might have waited until after his mother's death to commission inscriptions relating to his rule.

ANSWER: Students might suggest that Pacal's culture emphasized parents' status in relation to that of their children, even if a child was a ruler.

The Aztec

After the fall of Tula, tribes from northern Mexico migrated south and settled in the Valley of Mexico around Lake Texcoco, a shallow lake ringed with volcanoes. In the early 1200s the Aztec arrived in the area of the lake. They were poor and humble, but still extremely warlike. The Aztec spoke **Nahuatl**, the language of central Mexico, which helped them adopt aspects of their neighbors' culture. They established their capital, Tenochtitlán (tay-NAWCH-tee-TLAHN), on a swampy island in the lake, and quickly emerged as an important political power.

In the A.D. 1420s the Aztec secretly struck an alliance with Texcoco and Tlacopán, two other lake cities. Known as the **Triple Alliance**, the allies defeated the lake's other towns and cities and forced them to pay tribute. Since most of the tribute went to the Aztec, Tenochtitlán soon grew into a wealthy and powerful city.

The Aztec constructed three wide causeways to connect the city to the lake's shores. They drained swamps and built dikes to create more usable land. An aqueduct brought in fresh water. The great pyramid with its twin temples dominated the city. From the top of the pyramid, priests could look down and see the city of 250,000 people, the busy marketplace, the blue lake dotted with canoes, and the shimmering pyramids of the cities around the lake.

In Tenochtitlán ordinary citizens lived in clans. Each clan had its own school and temple. Families grew maize (corn) and beans on raised gardens called *chinampas*. Mothers

▲ This copy of an original Aztec tax record shows feathered headgear, cotton tunics, shields, and other items that were to be collected as tribute.

taught their daughters to weave, to grind maize, and to make round maize tortillas. Fathers taught their sons to fish in Lake Texcoco and to farm. All children attended school. Male clan members fought together as squadrons in battle.

Over time an Aztec nobility emerged. Wealthy from conquered lands, they set themselves apart from the simple, ordinary citizens of Tenochtitlán. Government officials and the men and women who served as priests usually came from the nobility. At the bottom of Aztec society were farm laborers, servants, porters, and slaves. Many people worked as porters and haulers, as there were no beasts of burden in Mesoamerica. If people fell deeply in debt, they had to sell themselves into slavery. However, such servitude lasted only until the debts were paid.

▲ This Aztec stone "chacmool" was used as a receptacle for the hearts of sacrificial victims.

Aztec Religion

The Aztec saw life as fragile and temporary. To the eternal human question "Why do we live on earth?" they replied in haunting verses:

> *Truly do we live on earth?*
> *Not forever on earth; only a little while here.*
> *Although it be jade, it will be broken,*
> *Although it be gold, it is crushed,*
> *Although it be quetzal feather,*
>   *it is torn asunder [apart].*
> *Not forever on earth; only a little*
>   *while here.*

Like earlier Mesoamericans the Aztec believed that their safety and good fortune depended on pleasing the gods. They tried to help the gods in order to gain their favor. The Aztec believed, for instance, that Huitzilopochtli (wee-tsee-loh-POHCH-tlee), the sun god, had to battle the forces of darkness each night in order for a new day to dawn. To give Huitzilopochtli the strength to fight the moon and stars, the Aztec offered the god human sacrifices.

The Aztec did not invent the use of human sacrifice in Mesoamerica, but they greatly increased its frequency. They believed that human sacrifice was necessary to keep the gods happy and the world safe from destruction. As a result, they viewed warfare as a sacred duty, since it was through battle that warriors captured the victims who would be sacrificed atop the Aztec pyramids.

Through alliances and conquests, the Aztec created a wealthy and powerful empire in central Mexico.

THROUGH OTHERS' EYES

The Aztec Empire

The Aztec often used the occasion of the crowning of a new king to remind the leaders of their conquered territories just who the true masters were. Such ceremonies included fiery speeches and religious rituals to scare the conquered peoples into obedience. But the Aztec also showered local leaders with gifts to convince them of the wealth of the empire. An observer in Tenochtitlán recalled one such event:

> The intentions of these Mexicans [Aztec], in preparing a festival . . . was to make known their king, and to ensure that their enemies . . . should be terrorized and filled with fear; and that they should know, by the . . . wealth of jewels and other presents, given away at the ceremonies, how great was the abundance of Mexico, its valor and its excellence. Finally, all was based on ostentation [extravagance] and vain glory, with the object of being feared, as the owners of all the riches of the earth and of its finest provinces. To this end they ordered these feasts and ceremonies so splendidly.

SECTION 1 REVIEW

IDENTIFY and explain the significance of the following:
Classic Maya
glyphs
Long Count
Pacal
Nahuatl
Triple Alliance
chinampas

LOCATE and explain the importance of the following:
Monte Albán
Valley of Oaxaca
Valley of Mexico
Teotihuacán
Yucatán Peninsula
Palenque
Chichén Itzá
Lake Texcoco
Tenochtitlán

1. *Main Idea* What are some of the things for which the Classic Maya are noted?
2. *Main Idea* Why do scholars believe that the Toltec were long-distance traders?
3. *Geography: Location* How did geography influence where the first cities and empires developed in Mesoamerica?
4. *Writing to Explain* Write a brief essay explaining how the Aztec were able to create their empire.
5. *Analyzing* Provide evidence to support the following statement: *History and ancestry were important to the Maya.*

SECTION 2

CORE LESSON PLAN
See pages 195E and
195F for Lesson Plan
8.2.

Across the Curriculum: Biology

Llamas and alpacas, along with guanacos and vicuñas, are members of the camel family, called lamoids. Unlike camels, however, lamoids do not have humps. All four species are natives of South America. Llamas and alpacas do not live in the wild; they have been domesticated by the South American Indians for centuries.

Critical Thinking Ask students what economic value llamas and alpacas offer, besides their use as pack animals.

ANSWER: Students might note that llamas and alpacas are used as sources of wool.

SECTION 2
South America

FOCUS

- How did Andean peoples adapt to their environment?

- How were the Nazca, Moche, and Chimú able to create civilizations along the Andean coast?

- What factors allowed the Inca to control their vast empire?

During the same period that the Aztec ruled central Mexico, the Inca dominated the central Andes region of South America, in what is now Peru, Bolivia, and Ecuador. Like the Aztec, the Inca did not build their civilization from scratch. They inherited much from earlier South American civilizations such as the Nazca, Moche, and Chimú. These cultures had all mastered the strategies needed to build complex civilizations in the arid and mountainous regions of the Andes.

Inca knife used for sacrifices

Geography and Culture

South America is a study in physical contrasts. The towering Andes Mountains run almost the entire length of the continent's Pacific Coast. To the west of the northern and central Andes, a narrow coastal desert skirts the rich fishing grounds of the Pacific. To the east is Amazonia, the hot, wet, river-crossed rain forest. To the north of the rain forest is a mixture of wet lowlands, river floodplains, and dry coastal regions. To the south are highlands, woodlands, steppes, prairies, and—at the continent's narrow, southern tip—the barren and windswept plains of Tierra del Fuego. Rainfall and temperature can vary dramatically over short distances, due in large part to changes in elevation and to differences in wind and ocean currents. In many areas of the continent, intensive agriculture depends on irrigation.

Archaeologists believe that geographic factors can help explain why the central Andes gave rise to South America's most highly developed civilizations. In earlier times, as today, the region's people faced a varied environment. On the coast, people fished the waters of the Pacific and raised cotton and other crops in the river-fed valleys. In the mountains they constructed irrigation systems and terraced fields that allowed them to grow maize, beans, squash, and peppers at lower elevations and potatoes at higher elevations. At the very top of the mountains, where few crops would grow, they grazed their llamas (LAH-mas) and alpacas. Not surprisingly, people were eager to trade with one another for the region's varied goods.

Scholars believe that this desire for trade goods contributed to the patterns of conquest and empire-building that were characteristic of the central Andes. An even greater push, however, may have come from the desire to control the rivers that provided the irrigation that was essential for the intensive farming needed to feed the large population. Lending support to this view is the fact that each of the central Andean civilizations that emerged between 370 B.C. and the A.D. mid-1400s controlled more land and rivers than the last.

Andean peoples adapted to their environment by establishing empires to control access to irrigation and trade.

The Nazca

Sometime around 200 B.C. the Nazca culture emerged along the coastal desert plain in present-day Peru. Very little is known about the culture, which flourished until about A.D. 450. From the evidence that exists, however, archaeologists believe that the Nazca civilization expanded over time as the result of either military campaigns or religious influence. In Nazca cities most public buildings were made of sun-dried adobe brick, while private homes were constructed of cane. Archaeologists have also discovered rich tapestries and ceramic pottery decorated with religious images common to the Nazca and earlier civilizations. Among these images are severed heads. The Nazca, like many other South American cultures, believed that their agricultural gods demanded sacrifices of human heads and blood.

Possibly the most interesting legacy of the Nazca is the complex system of interlocking lines that they drew on the desert floor. Some of these lines, or **geoglyphs**, run straight for several miles while others form huge animal and plant shapes that can be properly viewed only from the air. No one knows for sure why the Nazca constructed the geoglyphs, but some scholars believe that the lines are sacred paths that the people followed during religious ceremonies.

The Moche

Around A.D. 100 the Moche, another coastal desert civilization, emerged to the north of the Nazca. The Moche settled the valleys cut by the rivers that flow west across the desert. They constructed irrigation canals to transform the desert into fields of maize, peanuts, cotton, peppers, and potatoes.

The Moche lived in hierarchical communities presided over by wealthy lords. These lords organized work groups to build canals and adobe pyramids. The largest of these pyramids—the Pyramid of the Sun—was a sacred temple where human sacrifices and other religious ceremonies were performed. Moche artisans produced intricate textiles and gold and ceramic vessels for the nobility. Moche potters portrayed scenes from myths and daily life on plates, jugs, and cups.

▶ **This highly sophisticated Moche pottery depicts the "Captive Deer Man."**

Civilizations in South America

Nazca
c. 300 B.C.–A.D. 450

Moche
c. A.D. 100–700

Chimú
c. A.D. 1000–1470

Inca
c. A.D. 1438–1535

Inca roads

A Diverse Continent Among South America's towering Andes, vast deserts, and teeming rain forests arose a variety of American Indian cultures. Nomadic groups, settled farmers, and complex civilizations adapted to these diverse environments.

? **Movement** What geographical features did the Inca roads span to link the empire?

The Moche abandoned the area around A.D. 700, possibly because a prolonged drought or other natural disaster disrupted their agriculture. Their culture may have influenced the Chimú civilization that emerged a few centuries later.

The Chimú

Archaeologists have determined that after the fall of the Moche, a new civilization, called the Chimú, began to grow in power along the coastal desert of central Peru. The Chimú constructed the buildings of their capital, Chan Chan, out of sun-dried adobe and built an extensive irrigation system. The enormous city stretched over 2.3 square miles and consisted of 10 massive adobe compounds. The Chimú used the city as a base on which to found their empire. The empire was well organized and kept under careful government administration.

Like the Nazca and Moche before them, the Chimú worshipped their ancestors. When a Chimú king died, one son inherited his office, and the rest of the children inherited responsibility for preparing his body for burial. After turning the body into a mummy, they buried it in a tomb with the king's most lavish possessions. They sacrificed his wives and servants and placed them in the tomb, too. The tomb was not sealed, but kept open so that the mummy could be brought out during important ceremonies.

▲ The elaborate architecture of the Chimú can still be seen in the walls of Chan Chan, the capital of their powerful empire.

The powerful Chimú ruled almost the entire northern coast of present-day Peru until sometime between A.D. 1462 and 1470. During that period the great empire fell to a new imperial force to the south—the Inca.

The Nazca, Moche, and Chimú relied on irrigation to build great civilizations along the coastal desert of the central Andes.

The Foundation of the Inca Empire

The Inca, the builders of the most powerful South American empire, came from the region around Cuzco, high in the Andes Mountains. When they recited their history they gave themselves a glorious past, but in fact they had started out as a small highland chiefdom. Then, in the A.D. 1400s, particularly ambitious leaders began to conquer the surrounding lands. With each generation the Inca Empire grew larger until it extended north to present-day Colombia and south to present-day Chile.

BIOGRAPHY Most historians believe that the Inca Empire began around A.D. 1438, when Pachacutec (pah-chah-KOO-tek), the prince of Cuzco, defeated invaders who had besieged and destroyed the town. After his great victory Pachacutec rebuilt Cuzco and sent his armies to gain control of the farmland around Lake Titicaca. A later historian described Pachacutec's transformation of Cuzco from a wood-and-thatch town to a city of stone:

❝ He [Pachacutec] ordered twenty thousand men in from the provinces, and that the villages supply them with food. . . . Four thousand of them quarried and cut the stones; six thousand hauled them with great cables of leather and hemp; the others dug the ditch and laid the foundations, while still others cut poles and beams for the timbers. ❞

◀ The ruins of the Inca city of Machu Picchu show its complex structures, its varied stonework, and its dramatic setting.

Each village had its own sacred place and its own sacred objects. When the Inca kings added new regions to their empire, they often allowed local rulers to stay in power. But in return, they required that each village bring a sacred object to the great temple in Cuzco. The Inca believed that fear of losing the sacred object would prevent a village from rebelling. Nobles also had to send their sons to school in Cuzco, so that they would learn the empire's laws and its official language, **Quechua** (KE-chuh-wuh).

Pachacutec also replaced the Inca chiefdom with a centralized state, with Cuzco as its capital. The state was guided by a religion based on worship of the sun and royal ancestors. Pachacutec ruled over all of this as the Inca, the earthly son of the Sun. (Over time *Inca* has come to refer to both the kings and their people.)

Pachacutec and the Inca kings who followed him conquered villages that were scattered throughout the Andes. Inhabited by people who descended from a common ancestor, each village had its own land, chief, and customs. The families of the village worked together to manage the land and dig the irrigation canals that they depended on for their survival. Families helped each other plant and harvest the fields. The village chief resolved conflicts, distributed land and water to each family, made sure that planting and harvesting began at the proper times, and negotiated for the village with the gods. In return, village families worked for the chief.

Pachacutec

B I O G R A P H Y

Inca Civilization

Quechua had no written form, yet the Inca ruled a vast empire composed of hundreds of groups who spoke different languages. This was possible in part because the Inca kings quickly saw the need for effective communication. They built roads throughout their empire. These roads, paved in stone, allowed armies to move from one end of the empire to the other. Messengers swiftly communicated news and orders from the capital at Cuzco to the provinces. A group of relay runners could carry a message as far as 150 miles per day. Engineers suspended woven rope bridges across the steep canyons of the Andes, and way stations allowed travelers to rest on long journeys. Royal officials maintained each stretch of road, each bridge, and each way station in good repair.

Government. The Inca organized the conquered peoples into groups of 10, 50, 100, 500, 1,000, 5,000, and 10,000 families. They appointed an officer to head each group. Each family in the

Theme: War and Diplomacy

On a steep hill near Cuzco, Pachacutec began construction of a fortified refuge known as Sacsahuaman. This site was supposed to be able to shelter 10,000 people behind stone walls that stood more than 50 feet tall. Sacsahuaman was also considered to be sacred to the sun, and religious rituals may have been performed there.

Critical Thinking Ask students what advantages stone would have over wood in constructing Sacsahuaman.

ANSWER: Students might suggest that stone is stronger and more resistant to the elements than wood. In addition, stone is probably more available than wood in the high mountain environment around Cuzco.

✓ REVIEW & ASSESSMENT RESOURCES

- Study Guide 8.2
- Daily Quiz 8.2
- Main Idea Activity 8.2

All Levels

---

empire had to pay taxes to the local imperial officer. These taxes usually took the form of goods and labor. Women paid with cloth that they wove out of cotton and llama wool. Men paid by laboring in work gangs. The Inca also took over some of the farm lands in the conquered territories. Whatever was produced on these lands was used to support the Inca king, the nobility, the imperial officials, and the priests who oversaw the worship of the sun and moon.

The Inca recorded numbers by using the *quipu* (KEE-poo), a series of knots on parallel strings. On these *quipus* officials stored important numerical information, such as records of harvests, population numbers, and important dates.

Women in the Inca Empire. The Inca believed in Viracocha, a supreme god who created the sun and the moon. They believed that men were descended from the sun and women from the moon. The Inca king—the Son of the Sun—led the worship of the sun, and the Inca queen—the Daughter of the Moon—led the worship of the moon. The Inca queen ruled in Cuzco when the king was away at war. She had her own palace with shrines, gardens, and baths. Many ladies-in-waiting dressed her in beautifully woven garments and met her every need.

As the Inca armies defeated villages, officials collected young girls as tribute. Chosen for their beauty or their nobility, these girls went to a school in Cuzco where they learned to spin, weave, and cook for the gods or the king. When they reached the age of 14 or 15, the king told them that they were chosen women and sent them to their new duties. Some became attendants in the temples of the sun and moon, some became servants to the king and queen, some became wives of nobles, and some were set aside for sacrifice in religious ceremonies.

▶ **The Inca spanned Andean canyons with braided rope bridges. Peruvians still cross rivers on bridges originally built by the Inca.**

The capital, Cuzco. Cuzco was built in the shape of a puma, a jungle cat, high in the cold Andes. It contained palaces, temples, and fortresses constructed of stone and decorated with gold and silver. Inca stonemasons fit together huge stones to create the smooth stone foundations of the city. The palaces had gardens, running water piped into bathrooms, and bathtubs made out of silver. A later explorer vividly described the gold-encrusted city:

66 *The temples of the Sun and the royal apartments, wherever they existed, were lined with plates of gold, and many gold and silver figures copied from life— of men and women, birds of the air and waterfowl, and wild animals . . . —were placed round the walls in spaces and niches.* 99

Civil war. Around A.D. 1500 the Inca Empire began to suffer serious problems. When Inca armies pushed into the deep forests of Amazonia, they met stiff resistance from the local inhabitants. Eventually, they were forced to retreat from the area, having lost thousands of troops in battle and to fever. The problems of the Inca continued with the death of the king Huayna Capac, grandson of Pachacutec, in A.D. 1525. Two of the king's sons, Huáscar (WAHS-kahr) and Atahualpa (ah-tah-WAHL-pah), began to quarrel over who would assume the empire's throne. Since Huáscar was the elder son, he became the new king.

Huáscar soon proposed that lands belonging to the nobility be taken over by the royal family. Greatly angered, the Inca nobles turned to Atahualpa to lead a rebellion against Huáscar. Around A.D. 1530 a bitter civil war divided the empire as the two Inca armies clashed in fierce fighting. In A.D. 1532 Atahualpa's army captured Cuzco and Huáscar, ending the conflict. But the civil war left the Inca army too weak to control the far-flung empire, and, more importantly, left the empire vulnerable to outside invaders.

The Inca built a vast empire in the Andes, supported by taxes and held together by a strong army and good roads.

LA NOVENA COIA MAMA ANAVAR QVE

▲ A Spanish explorer made this sketch of the Inca queen Mama Anauarque Coya. She is believed to have been Pachacutec's wife.

SECTION 2 REVIEW

IDENTIFY and explain the significance of the following:
geoglyphs
Pachacutec
Quechua
quipu
Viracocha
Huayna Capac
Huáscar
Atahualpa

LOCATE and explain the importance of the following:
Andes
Amazonia
Chan Chan
Cuzco

1. **Main Idea** What role did irrigation play in the rise of the Nazca, Moche, and Chimú civilizations?
2. **Main Idea** How did the Inca conquer and maintain their vast empire in the central Andes?
3. **Geography: Human-Environment Interaction** How did geographic diversity contribute to the rise of complex civilizations in South America?
4. **Writing to Persuade** Write a paragraph defending or refuting the following statement: *People in Andean villages were better off after having been conquered by the Inca.*
5. **Comparing** Make a chart like the one below of the religious beliefs and ceremonies of the Nazca, Moche, Chimú, and Inca. Which beliefs or ceremonies did they have in common?

CULTURE	RELIGIOUS BELIEFS/CEREMONIES
Nazca	

CORE LESSON PLAN
See pages 195G and 195H for Lesson Plan 8.3.

R RESOURCE ACTIVITY

GLOBAL HISTORY RESOURCE CENTER
Image: *Inuit Scratchers for Luring Seals*
Reading: *The Inuit: Life Beside the Arctic Ocean*

Display the image and read aloud about how the Inuit depended on animals for much more than food. Have students work in small groups to create diagrams showing how the Inuit used different parts of animals.

Sheltered English

SECTION 3
North America

FOCUS

- How did the peoples of the Arctic and Subarctic adapt to their environment?
- What were some of the common cultural traits of the peoples of the Eastern Woodlands?
- How did the peoples of the Great Plains adapt to their environment?
- How did life in the West, the Southwest, and the Pacific Coast differ?

W hile South American peoples were adapting to the unique environments of the Andes, North American tribes were also developing distinct cultures. Most of the peoples of the North originally lived as hunters and gatherers. As agriculture spread north from Mesoamerica, larger and more complex societies began to form.

This American corn, or maize, shows a mix of red, blue, and yellow corn types.

The Arctic and Subarctic

Like the peoples of South America, the peoples of North America faced varied environments. Nowhere was the North American environment more extreme than in the areas bordering the Arctic Circle. Since the cold weather of the North made agriculture impossible, these people relied on hunting for survival. Hunting groups had intimate knowledge of their environment and the habits of the animals they pursued. Most hunting communities moved their homes frequently, to take advantage of the movements of game. Hunting communities valued cooperation, for only through carefully planned hunts could the members of the community trap and kill the animals needed for survival.

The Inuit and the Aleut occupied the lands north of the Arctic Circle. Their vast territory covered an area from present-day Alaska to Greenland. They lived by hunting seal, whale, walrus, and caribou, which they stockpiled for the long, dark winters. These tribes invented different kinds of canoes, such as **kayaks**, to pursue game, and they sewed intricate garments to keep warm during the winter.

South of the Arctic, in the region known as the Subarctic, the Athabascan family of tribes made their homes on the plains of present-day Canada. During the long, snowy winters and short, warm summers, they tracked caribou and moose across the tundra, hunted rabbit and otter in the pine forests, and fished the large freshwater lakes. A mobile people, they packed up their skin tents and moved frequently to follow game.

The Arctic and Subarctic hunters worshipped the animals that they relied on for survival. They believed that humans shared a special relationship with animals. In a hunt, humans either had to trick animals or convince them to let themselves be taken. Hunters believed that animals often let themselves be killed, out of pity for humans. But if an animal were offended, it might not allow itself to be caught, and humans would starve.

The peoples of the Arctic and Subarctic adapted to their environments by relying on hunting and fishing.

Peoples of North America, 2500 B.C.–A.D. 1500

Culture areas:
- Arctic
- Subarctic
- Pacific Coast
- Plateau
- Great Plains
- Eastern Woodlands
- Great Basin
- California
- Southwest
- Southeast

Native Cultures From the frozen Arctic to the desert Southwest, more than 100 American Indian cultures thrived in the diverse geographic areas of North America.

Region According to the map, which culture area surrounded the Great Lakes region of North America?

Map Answer
Eastern Woodlands

History and Current Events

Some of the most important archaeological sites for the study of North American Indians are Indian burial grounds. Scientists maintain that excavations at these sites provide invaluable information about early American Indian cultures. American Indians, however, regard these sites as sacred resting places for their ancestors. In recent years, American Indian groups have filed lawsuits to regain possession of sacred items taken from Indian burial sites over the years. In 1990 Congress passed the Native American Graves Protection and Repatriation Act, which has allowed American Indians to request the return of sacred objects from museums.

Critical Thinking Ask students if they agree with American Indians' efforts to restrict archaeological excavation of burial sites.

ANSWER: Students' answers will vary. Some students might argue that Indians have a right to protect their ancestors' graves, while other students might argue that gathering and preserving national historical information should take precedence.

Daily Life

Developments in agriculture led to dramatic changes in settlement patterns. The Adena and Hopewell lived in fairly small villages, but the Mississippians developed great population centers walled with palisades. The introduction of beans and resistant strains of maize provided an increased food supply, which was able to support larger, more concentrated populations in centers like Cahokia.

Critical Thinking Ask students to identify other parts of the world and other eras in which increased food supplies led to larger population centers.

ANSWER: Students may identify any of several instances of this pattern, going as far back as the Sumerian city-states around 3500 B.C. (See Chapter 1 for more information).

The Eastern Woodlands

In what is today the eastern United States, society developed along different lines than in the Arctic and Subarctic. Between about 2500 B.C. and A.D. 400, most of the peoples of the Eastern Woodlands developed ways of life that combined hunting and gathering with the cultivation of squash, sunflowers, and other plants. By about A.D. 800 many areas had advanced to maize agriculture.

The Adena and the Hopewell. The Adena, who established themselves in the Ohio Valley region by at least 700 B.C., were among the early Eastern Woodlands cultures to develop an economy based on both hunting and gathering and plant cultivation. The Adena grew squash, sunflowers, and other crops; collected nuts and wild plants; and hunted and fished. They lived in small settlements of circular houses made of wood. The Adena produced fine pottery and copper bracelets and ornaments. They also built elaborate burial mounds that consisted of clay or log tombs covered by huge piles of earth.

Sometime around 300 to 200 B.C., a new culture—the Hopewell—appeared in the Ohio Valley. By the time their culture declined around A.D. 400, Hopewell influences had spread as far away as present-day Illinois, Wisconsin, Iowa, Minnesota, New York, Mississippi, and Louisiana.

▲ This serpent-shaped mound in present-day Ohio is over 400 yards long. Its builders, perhaps the Adena or the Hopewell, never saw the entire structure from above.

Like the Adena, the Hopewell were mound-builders. The design of their mounds varied, depending on location. The Illinois Hopewell, for instance, constructed log tombs and then covered them with earth. A common size for the burial mounds was around 40 feet high and 100 feet across. From the many objects discovered in the mounds, archaeologists believe that the Hopewell traded over long distances for exotic materials to use in making items for their burial chambers, and other objects. Grizzly-bear teeth and obsidian from present-day Wyoming, mica from the Appalachian Mountains, and shark teeth and turtle shells from the Gulf Coast have all been found in Hopewell graves.

The Mississippian. The next major Eastern Woodlands culture did not appear until around A.D. 800. This new tradition became known as the Mississippian culture. The Mississippian expanded their cultivation of plants beyond crops such as squash and sunflowers to include maize and beans. The introduction of these new crops allowed the Mississippian populations to increase in size. The desire for land, in turn, led to expansion—particularly into the Southeast.

Like earlier Eastern Woodlands societies, the Mississippian were great mound-builders. Many large settlements centered around mound constructions. In these settlements, mounds usually marked a central plaza, in the middle of which stood a temple built on a much larger mound. Outside the ceremonial centers were villages where people farmed, hunted, and fished. Cahokia, located near present-day East St. Louis, was the largest of the ceremonial centers of North America. Between A.D. 1050 and 1250 Cahokia was home to 10,000 people. The chiefs of Cahokia traded far and wide for copper, shells, and mica, and they collected tribute from the nearby villages.

The Iroquois. Like the Adena, Hopewell, and Mississippian peoples, the Iroquois, who lived in what is today New York State, also practiced a combination of hunting, gathering, and plant cultivation. After about A.D. 1000, this cultivation increasingly focused on growing maize, beans, and squash.

The Iroquois used controlled fires to clear the forest for village sites and farmland. In the clearings, women tended the fields. Women held a

Sacred TRADITIONS

Iroquois Creation Myth

Archaeologists believe that the ancestors of the Iroquois arrived in the Northeast sometime between 1700 and 700 B.C. By about A.D. 1000 the Seneca, Cayuga, Onondaga, Oneida, and Mohawk—the five tribes that would eventually form the Iroquois League—were becoming established throughout the region.

Like most American Indian cultures, the Iroquois created a myth describing how the earth and their people came to be. Following are several excerpts from that myth.

The Council Tree

In the faraway days of this floating island there grew one stately tree that branched beyond the range of vision. Perpetually laden with fruits and blossoms, the air was fragrant with its perfume, and the people gathered to its shade where councils were held.

One day the Great Ruler said to his people: "We will make a new place where another people may grow. Under our council tree is a great cloud sea which calls for our help. It is lonesome. It knows no rest and calls for light. We will talk to it. The roots of our council tree point to it and will show the way."

Having commanded that the tree be uprooted, the Great Ruler peered into the depths where the roots had guided, and summoning Ata-en-sic, who was with child, bade her look down. Ata-en-sic saw nothing, but the Great Ruler knew that the sea voice was calling, and bidding her carry its life, wrapped around her a great ray of light and sent her down to the cloud sea.

Hah-nu-nah, the Turtle

Dazzled by the descending light enveloping Ata-en-sic, there was a great consternation [confusion] among the animals and birds inhabiting the cloud sea, and they counciled in alarm.

"If it falls, it may destroy us," they cried.

"Where can it rest?" asked the Duck.

"Only the oeh-da (earth) can hold it," said the Beaver, "the oeh-da which lies at the bottom of our waters, and I will bring it." The Beaver went down but never returned. Then the Duck ventured, but soon its dead body floated to the surface.

Many of the divers had tried and failed when the Muskrat, knowing the way, volunteered to obtain it and soon returned bearing a small portion in his paw. "But it is heavy," said he, "and will grow fast. Who will bear it?"

The Turtle was willing, and the oeh-da was placed on his hard shell.

And Hah-nu-nah, the Turtle, became the Earth Bearer. When he stirs, the seas rise in great waves, and when restless and violent, earthquakes yawn and devour.

The Iroquois called this carved wooden mask a "False Face."

Understanding Sacred Traditions

What does the myth describe?

special place in Iroquois society. Iroquois families traced their ancestry through women, and Iroquois women had a voice in village government. Beyond the village clearings, Iroquois men hunted deer, trapped beaver, and fished the rivers and lakes. Villages often moved in the winter to take advantage of better hunting grounds.

Competition over hunting grounds often led to war in this region. The Iroquois frequently fought with the Huron, who lived north of the Great Lakes along the St. Lawrence River in what is today Canada. They also warred among themselves and with the Algonquian, a group that lived farther west. By the A.D. 1500s warfare threatened to destroy the lives of the northeastern tribes. The Iroquois decided to seek peace among themselves and formed the **Iroquois League**. According to Iroquois legend the Great Spirit gave the idea of the league to the mystic Dekanawidah and Hiawatha, his Mohawk disciple. Together they convinced the five principal Iroquois tribes—the Seneca, Cayuga, Onondaga, Oneida, and Mohawk—to live in peace. Hiawatha supposedly explained:

❝We must unite ourselves into one common band of brothers. We must have but one voice. Many voices makes confusion. We must have one fire, one pipe, and one war club. This will give us strength.❞

In the league a council, composed of 50 representatives, discussed group matters. Each decision had to be unanimous. The league brought to an end hostilities among the Iroquois, although wars still erupted between the Iroquois and other groups.

Eastern Woodlands cultures practiced a combination of hunting, gathering, and plant cultivation, including maize and beans after about A.D. 800.

The Great Plains

Probably the most common image people associate with American Indians is of the Great Plains warrior mounted on horseback chasing after a herd of buffalo. But this idea is misleading prior to the A.D. 1500s. Until the time the Spanish reintroduced the horse to North America in the A.D. 1500s, the peoples of the eastern Great Plains led a mostly agricultural life, while those who lived in the western Great Plains hunted and gathered on foot.

Beginning in about 250 B.C., farmers from the Hopewell culture of the East began to migrate west onto the vast open plains. They brought their techniques of tilling the soil with them, establishing small agricultural villages. Later Great Plains tribes continued to exhibit aspects of Hopewell culture, such as building mounds. By around A.D. 900, villages in the eastern plains began to grow much larger, as farmers planted maize.

▲ Mandan tribes of the northern Plains lived in lodges built of sod and wooden beams. Even the smaller lodges could house several families.

Tribes of the western plains, such as the Dakota, lived as nomadic hunters and gatherers. To make it easier to move quickly, people lived in **tepees**—shelters made of animal skins stretched over poles tied together. A later observer described a typical migration on the Great Plains:

❝They travel . . . with their tents and troops of dogs loaded with poles. . . . When the load gets disarranged, the dogs howl, calling someone to fix them right. . . . They are a people who wander around here and there, wherever seems to them best.❞

The peoples of the eastern Great Plains established small farming villages, while those on the western Great Plains survived by hunting and gathering on foot.

The West and Southwest

The civilizations of the West and Southwest faced the endless challenge of trying to support a population in a harsh climate with limited amounts of water. In the deserts of what is today the western United States, this problem was particularly serious.

The Desert West. The Desert West may be divided into two distinct regions: the Great Basin and the Plateau. Life in the Great Basin saw little change from around 2500 B.C. to the A.D. 1800s. During the warmer months the peoples of the Basin lived off the small game and birds that inhabited the lakes and rivers on the Basin floor. In the colder months they migrated to the mountains, where they gathered nuts to sustain them through the winter. Life on the Plateau revolved primarily around salmon fishing along the Columbia and Fraser Rivers. Decreases in the salmon population, however, often threatened the existence of the Plateau peoples.

The Southwest. The peoples of the deserts of the Southwest also faced the challenges of life in a harsh environment. They reacted to the challenges by becoming masters of the art of irrigation, which allowed them to grow maize and a variety of other crops in the desert sands. Among the early Southwestern peoples were those who created the Hohokam, Mogollon, and Anasazi cultures.

Archaeologists do not know for sure when the Hohokam peoples settled the Southwest. The principal Hohokam site of Snaketown, located along the banks of the now dry Gila River in present-day southern Arizona, has been dated anywhere from 300 B.C. to A.D. 500. Archaeologists have discovered some striking parallels with Mesoamerican cultures at Snaketown and other Hohokam sites. For example, they have found a ball court and a few mounds shaped like low, flat pyramids. Copper bells, probably made in Mexico, have also surfaced in excavations. These clues have led archaeologists to hypothesize that the Hohokam traded in central Mexico.

The Mogollon lived in the mountains of what is today southwestern Arizona, northern Mexico, and southern New Mexico. Beginning in the A.D. 200s the Mogollon successfully adapted to the arid climate by combining the cultivation of such crops as maize, beans, and squash with hunting and the gathering of wild plants. The early Mogollon lived in circular pit houses, partially dug into the ground. They constructed adjoining rectangular rooms out of logs and mud. Later they built above-ground adobe villages, known as **pueblos**. An artistic people, the Mogollon crafted beautiful ceramics. The potters of the Mimbres Valley, for example, depicted animal spirits and sacred symbols using black and white paint.

The Anasazi, or "ancient ones," lived in the San Juan River basin, which extends over the four adjoining corners of the present-day states of Utah, Arizona, Colorado, and New Mexico. In the A.D. 900s, beneath the rocky cliffs of the Chaco Canyon, the Anasazi began to cultivate the desert. They built dams, canals, and ditches to capture the precious rainfall from the top of the mesa and channel it to carefully planned gardens. The Anasazi constructed pueblos, where extended families lived in apartments built around plazas. Each extended family had its own **kiva**, a round, sacred, ceremonial room. From the pueblos extended long, straight roads, with stairs and ramps to descend the cliffs. Along these roads, trade grew between the Chaco pueblos and outlying areas.

Eventually, the Hohokam, Mogollon, and Anasazi abandoned their large settlements and returned to a simpler way of life in smaller villages. Scholars believe that around A.D. 1100 a prolonged drought toppled the delicate balance between the Mogollon and their environment. The Anasazi began to abandon their pueblos around A.D. 1300, and crop failures forced the Hohokam to abandon Snaketown sometime around the middle of the A.D. 1400s.

▲ Black-on-white Mimbres pottery bowls were often called "story bowls"; these were made in the A.D. 1100s or 1200s.

Peoples of the Desert West relied on hunting, gathering, and fishing for survival, while those of the Southwest relied on agriculture.

The Pacific Coast

The peoples of what are today Washington, Oregon, British Columbia, and southern Alaska developed cultures based on the rich resources of the land and sea. The Haida, Tlingit, and Tsimshian fished for whale, salmon, and herring and hunted deer and bear in the forests. Unlike

The people of the Mimbres Valley in what is now southwestern New Mexico were part of the Mogollon culture. Although they disappeared before the arrival of the Spanish in the 1500s, the people are remembered for their beautiful black-on-white pottery. The holes in the bases of the bowls at the left indicate that they were burial offerings. The people of the valley ritually "killed" burial-offering bowls by punching holes in their bases.

Critical Thinking Ask students to suggest what advantage the custom of burial offerings gives to modern archaeologists.

ANSWER: Students might suggest that this custom might provide archaeologists with well-preserved artifacts.

other hunting regions, larger and more complex societies formed here because an abundant food supply allowed people to build permanent villages along the coast.

The wealthiest people in these villages formed a nobility. They organized work gangs to construct huge communal houses out of wood and commissioned tall wooden totem poles to be erected in front of the houses. The poles, which symbolized the nobility's wealth and status, extended as high as 80 feet. Artisans also carved boxes, bowls, spoons, and combs for daily life. They carved masks in the likenesses of animal spirits for ceremonies. Tools, large canoes, paddles, spears, harpoons, and other weapons, except for the sharp stone points, were all made from wood.

Farther south in what is today California, many hunting and gathering groups lived along the coast and in the coastal valleys. California differed from other culture areas of North America in its extraordinary geographic diversity—from the Pacific seacoast, to fertile river valleys, to high mountain elevations. The plentiful and varied natural resources of the California area

meant that the peoples who lived there did not need to develop agriculture to survive. Society centered around small tribes, each hunting or gathering items particular to the local area. Some fished and gathered shells; some hunted small game, such as rabbits; and others gathered nuts and wild plants.

By A.D. 500 at least 500 small tribes populated the region. A complex system of trade developed among the tribes. The leader of a tribe would trade surplus goods to neighboring tribes in exchange for their surpluses. In this way people could enjoy a variety of items and could grow wealthy from skillful trading. The system of barter allowed people to remain relatively stationary. Consequently, California was the most densely populated region north of Mesoamerica.

The people of the Pacific Coast developed a complex system of trade based on local abundance.

◄ The Pomo tribe created elaborate coiled baskets with bird feathers worked into the exterior designs.

SECTION 3 REVIEW

IDENTIFY and explain the significance of the following:
  kayaks
  Iroquois League
  Hiawatha
  tepees
  pueblos
  kiva

LOCATE and explain the importance of the following:
  Arctic and Subarctic
  Eastern Woodlands
  Cahokia
  Great Plains
  Snaketown
  Chaco Canyon

1. **Main Idea** What was the primary means of support for the peoples of the Arctic and Subarctic? How did this means of support affect their religious beliefs?
2. **Main Idea** How did the peoples of the Southwest use new technologies to adapt to their hostile environment?
3. **Geography: Place** How did variation in climate affect the development of the different cultures of early North America?
4. **Writing to Classify** Write a paragraph listing the

primary means of support for each culture region: Arctic/Subarctic, Eastern Woodlands, eastern Great Plains, western Great Plains, West, Southwest, Northwest, California. Then describe some of the similarities and differences among the agricultural societies and the hunter-gatherer societies.
5. **Synthesizing** In what ways did some American Indian cultures influence others? How do archaeologists know this?

Review

On a separate sheet of paper, complete the following exercises:

WRITING A SUMMARY

Using the essential points in the text, write a brief summary of the chapter.

REVIEWING TERMS

From the following list, choose the term that correctly matches the definition.

pueblos
Triple Alliance
geoglyphs
chinampas
kayaks
quipu

1. canoes used by the Inuit and Aleut to hunt game at sea
2. device consisting of a series of knotted strings used by the Inca to keep track of numerical information
3. agreement among Tenochtitlán, Texcoco, and Tlacopán for military cooperation
4. raised gardens used by the Aztec
5. villages of adobe buildings, often constructed in canyon walls of the present-day southwestern United States

REVIEWING CHRONOLOGY

List the following events in their correct chronological order.
1. Monte Albán and Teotihuacán rapidly decline.

2. The Aztec found Tenochtitlán on Lake Texcoco.
3. The Inca establish their empire.
4. Northeastern Indian tribes form the Iroquis League.
5. Mississippian culture emerges.

UNDERSTANDING THE MAIN IDEA

1. What are some of the effects that plant cultivation had on the peoples of the Eastern Woodlands and the Southwest?
2. How did trade influence early American societies?
3. What were some of the common religious beliefs of early American societies?
4. How did geography affect the location of cities in the Americas?
5. In what ways did some American Indian civilizations draw on earlier traditions?

THINKING CRITICALLY

1. **Hypothesizing** Why might leaders, such as Pachacutec, have encouraged their people to worship royal ancestors?
2. **Comparing** How did the conquest of other regions affect the Aztec and Inca Empires? Was the expansion of the empires always beneficial? Why or why not? How did it affect the lives of the conquered peoples?

Building Your Portfolio

Complete the following activities individually or in groups.

1. **Early Cities** Imagine that you are an archaeologist working for a large museum. You (or your team) have been given the task of making a replica of one of the great cities of the early Americas. You may either create a three-dimensional model of the city you choose or draw a large and detailed sketch of the city. To accompany the model or sketch, you or someone on your team will need to prepare a short report indicating why people chose to build the city on its particular site, and describing some of the interesting features of the city. You or someone else should also prepare a short report on what daily life was like for the city's inhabitants.
2. **Religion** Choose one of the cultures from the chapter and investigate its religious practices and ceremonies. Make a poster illustrating one of these religious rituals. Either on the poster or in a separate report describe the ritual, explain its significance to the culture, and try to give some ideas about its origins. You may also wish to investigate contemporary cultures that still carry on these rituals and describe how the rituals have changed or remained the same over time.

CHAPTER 8 REVIEW ANSWERS

WRITING A SUMMARY
See essential points in the text.

REVIEWING TERMS
1. kayaks
2. *quipu*
3. Triple Alliance
4. *chinampas*
5. pueblos

REVIEWING CHRONOLOGY
1, 5, 2, 3, 4

UNDERSTANDING THE MAIN IDEA
1. encouraged settlement of villages, concentrated populations
2. brought them into contact with distant cultures
3. ancestor worship, human sacrifices, sun worship
4. often near arable land, easily defensible
5. adopting architectural techniques, religious beliefs, methods of agriculture

THINKING CRITICALLY
1. The leaders might have felt that worshipping royal ancestors would have encouraged people to show more respect for the current leader.
2. Conquering powers, such as the Aztec and the Inca, absorbed elements of other cultures, providing the conquerors with new populations as well as expanded territories. Sometimes expansion provided benefits, such as improved communications through the Inca road systems. But expansion also deprived conquered peoples of their political autonomy. They became part of a more unified political body.

Unit 3
The World in Transition 220–1707

Chapter 9

Persia, Byzantium, and the Rise of Russia 226–1240

As other empires crumbled, civilization flourished in Persia and Byzantium. These civilizations transmitted their values and cultural heritage to other peoples. Why might a society adopt elements of a nearby culture?

Chapter 10

The Islamic World 570–1258

The new religion of Islam united the nomadic tribes of Arabia and inspired a rich culture that spread to much of Southwest Asia, North Africa, and parts of Europe. What impact might religious values have on a country's culture, politics, and law?

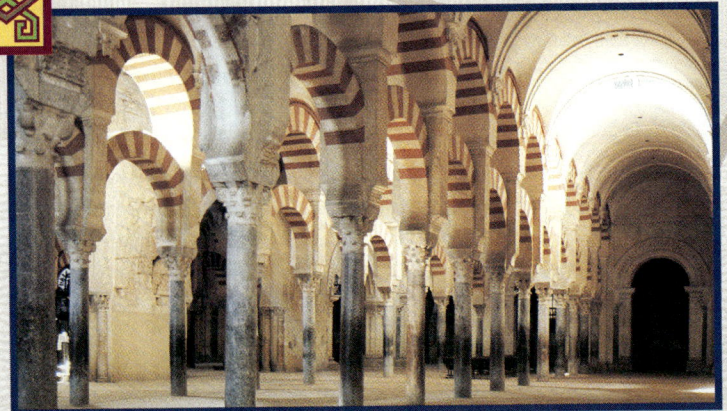

Following the fall of Rome, the Persians and Byzantines maintained the concept of imperial organization, while Europeans looked to local leaders for protection. Eventually, Europeans developed a new culture that blended Roman, Germanic, and Christian traditions. Meanwhile, a vibrant new religion, Islam, emerged and spread rapidly throughout much of Southwest Asia, Africa, and parts of southern Europe.

Muslim invaders united the kingdoms of India and spread their culture to parts of Southeast Asia. At the same time, China enjoyed a golden age of prosperity.

Soon Eurasia was shaken by the Mongols, who built a huge empire from China to eastern Europe. As the Mongol threat retreated, new and enormously powerful empires arose in Southwest Asia, Persia, and India.

Chapter 11

A New Civilization in Western Europe 476–1350

After the fall of Rome and the invasions by Germanic peoples, Europeans created a new culture that blended Roman, Germanic, and Christian traditions. What factors might prevent a society from becoming united?

Chapter 13

New Empires in Asia and Africa 1200–1707

While emperors in the Ottoman Empire, Safavid Persia, and Mughal India ruled over their large empires, Chinese emperors sought to revive the traditional rule neglected during the Mongol period. Meanwhile, smaller states rose and fell in Africa. How might trade spread languages, cultures, and religious ideas?

Chapter 12

Transformations in Asia 220–1350

While China enjoyed a golden age, Muslim invaders united much of India. In the 1200s the nomadic Mongols united Eurasia in their own vast empire. Why might steppe nomads like the Mongols have a military advantage over settled civilizations?

Chapter 9

Persia, Byzantium, and the Rise of Russia 226–1240

Chapter Planning Guide

	TEXTBOOK	CORE RESOURCES	VISUAL RESOURCES	MULTIMEDIA
Introduction	pp. 220–221	Block Scheduling Handbook: Ch. 9		Videodisc Segment 9 and Viewing Guide: *The Russian Orthodox Church*
Lesson 9.1 Sassanid Persia	pp. 222–228 Map: *Sassanid Persia*, p. 224 Sacred Traditions: *The Avesta*, p. 227	Reading 9.1: *Book of Countries*	Geography and History 35: *Southwest Asia*	GHRC 9 Readings: *A Chinese Envoy's View of Sassanid Persia; The Army of Sassanid Persia; Zoroastrianism on the Judgment of Souls* GHRC 9/Videodiscs: Images—*Sassanid Gold and Silver Plate; Sassanid King Battles Roman Emperor;* Map—*Sassanid Empire*
Lesson 9.2 The Byzantine Empire	pp. 229–236 Through Others' Eyes: *Two Faces of Constantinople*, p. 230 Map: *The Byzantine Empire*, p. 231 History Through the Arts: *The Church of Hagia Sophia*, p. 234	Reading 9.2: *Justinian's Code* Geography Activity 9: *Constantinople—Crossroads of Europe and Asia* Writing Project 9: *Writing a Diary*	Art and History 9: *San Apollinaire in Classe Apse Mosaic* Everyday Life 9: *The Role of the Byzantine Emperor* Geography and History 9: *Roman Catholicism and Orthodoxy*	GHRC 9 Readings: *Byzantine Military Strategy; Icons Divide Byzantium* GHRC 9/Videodiscs: Images—*Constantinople's Defensive Walls; Byzantine Gold and Jewels;* Map—Series of three on *Growth of Byzantine Empire*
Lesson 9.3 The Rise of Russia	pp. 237–240 Map: *Kievan Russia*, p. 238	Reading 9.3: *The Pravda Russkaia* Skills Activity 9: *Analyzing a Primary Source*		GHRC 9 Readings: *A Russian Attack on Byzantium; Prince Vladimir's Conversion to Christianity; Prince Yaroslav Dooms Kievan Russia* GHRC 9/Videodiscs: Images—*Conversion of Kievans to Christianity; Olga of Kiev Burns Diplomats in Their Bath;* Map—*Kiev as Strategic Trading City*
Chapter Investigation and Enrichment	pp. 220–240	Chapter 9 Investigation: *Barbarian Information Agency* People in World History 9 Explorations in Daily Life 9		GHRC 9/Videodiscs
Review and Assessment	Section 1 Review, p. 228 Section 2 Review, p. 236 Section 3 Review, p. 240 Chapter 9 Review, p. 241	Chapter Review Activity 9 Vocabulary Activity 9 Themes Review 9 Section Study Guides 9.1–9.3 Main Idea Activities 9.1–9.3 Daily Quizzes 9.1–9.3 Chapter 9 Test Sheltered English Ch. 9 Test Ch. 9 Test Generator		Audio CDs: Ch. 9 Summary (English and Spanish)

INTRODUCING THE CHAPTER

Textbook pp. 220–221

CHAPTER OVERVIEW

In Persia the Sassanids replaced the Parthian Empire, initiating a prosperous era in which the Sassanids revived old Persian culture, including the Zoroastrian religion. The eastern remnants of the Roman Empire became the Byzantine Empire, which preserved aspects of Greek and Roman culture and classical learning. Byzantine culture and Christianity, in turn, heavily influenced the leaders of Kiev in the Ukraine. The growth of this Kievan state marked the beginnings of Russia.

PRESENTING THEMES

On the chalkboard or on an overhead transparency, write the following open-ended theme questions.

- **POLITICS AND LAW** Why might a monarchy and an aristocracy be essential features of a particular society?
- **RELIGION** Why might an empire try to promote certain religions?
- **CROSS-CULTURAL INTERACTION** Why might a society adopt elements of a nearby culture?

Have students, either individually or in groups, suggest responses to the questions. For the politics and law question, students might suggest that a society might rely upon an elite to make decisions for an uneducated public. For the religion question, students might suggest that a religion could reinforce the ruler's right to govern. For the cross-cultural interaction question, students might suggest that elements of a nearby culture might be useful for solving a society's problems. Save the responses. Once students have studied the chapter, you may wish to have them complete the Themes Review, then compare the two sets of answers.

USING THE VIDEO

Segment 9: *The Russian Orthodox Church*

ENGLISH

Search Chapter 9
Videodisc 1, Side A

SPANISH

Search Chapter 9
Videodisc 1, Side A

Tell students that in this chapter they will examine how these theme questions apply to the empires of Byzantium and Persia as well as to the new center of civilization that arose in Kievan Russia more than a thousand years ago. Conclude by showing Segment 9 of the *World History and Cultures Videodiscs*. This segment shows a service in an Orthodox church in Russia today and stresses the power of religious belief as a unifying force.

Before showing the segment, ask students to pay particular attention to the expressions on the faces of the people and what these expressions reveal about their faith. To help students grasp the significant points of the segment, have them complete Video Viewing Guide 9.

Key to Ability Levels

All strategies and activities are coded to the following ability levels:

LEVEL 1	**Basic** activities suitable for all students
LEVEL 2	**Average** activities suitable for average to above-average students
LEVEL 3	**Challenging** activities suitable for above-average students
SHELTERED ENGLISH	Activities suitable for students with **Limited English Proficiency**

Additional Resources

BOOKS FOR TEACHERS

Norwich, John Julius. *Byzantium: The Early Centuries.* Alfred A. Knopf, 1994. Offers a survey.

Obolensky, Dimitri. *Byzantium and the Slavs.* St. Vladimir's Seminary Press, 1994. Discusses Byzantine influences on early Russian culture.

Vasiliev, A. A. *A History of the Byzantine Empire,* 2 vols. University of Wisconsin Press, 1961. Serves as a standard reference text.

BOOKS FOR STUDENTS

Browning, Robert. *The Byzantine Empire.* Scribner, 1980. Presents a general survey.

Dmytryshn, Basil. *Medieval Russia: A Source Book, 850–1700.* 3rd ed. Holt, Rinehart and Winston, 1991. Offers a wealth of primary sources.

Mango, Cyril. *Byzantine Architecture.* Rizzoli, 1985. Offers a discussion of architecture and includes illustrations.

MULTIMEDIA MATERIALS

Byzantium: From Splendor to Ruin. Films for the Humanities & Sciences. Video, 43 min. Describes the history and influence of Byzantium on the West.

Early Russia. New York Times. Video, 22 min. Presents Russia from early Byzantine influence to the 1600s.

The Russian Revolution. ZCI. CD-ROM, MAC, WIN, MPC formats. Reviews early Russian history from the Mongol invasions.

Lesson 9.1 *Sassanid Persia*

Textbook pp. 222–228

RESOURCES

Pupil's Edition

Map, p. 224: *Sassanid Persia, 531–579*

Sacred Traditions, p. 227: *The Avesta*

Core Resources

Reading 9.1: *Book of Countries*

Visual Resources

Geography and History 35: *Southwest Asia*

Global History Resource Center

Reading: *A Chinese Envoy's View of Sassanid Persia*

Reading: *The Army of Sassanid Persia*

Reading: *Zoroastrianism on the Judgment of Souls*

Videodiscs or Global History Resource Center

Image: *Sassanid Gold and Silver Plate*

Search Frame 783

Image: *Sassanid King Battles Roman Emperor*

Search Frame 782

Map: *Sassanid Empire, 500s and 600s*

Search Frame 791

LESSON FOCUS

How did the Sassanid Empire represent a revival of Persia, and what was the nature of Sassanid society?

OBJECTIVES

After completing this lesson, students will be able to:

- explain how the Sassanid rulers built and maintained their empire;
- describe the structure of Sassanid society;
- identify causes of the decline of the Sassanid Empire.

HOOK: Link to Today

Examine the origin and spread of the Sassanid Empire.
Ask students to bring in current news clippings about events involving present-day Iran, Iraq, Syria, Turkey, Turkmenistan, Afghanistan, or Pakistan. Show Geography and History Transparency 35 of Southwest Asia and help students find locations mentioned in the stories. At the same time, correlate the present-day geography of the Middle East with the electronic media map of the Sassanid Empire or the map on textbook page 224.

Ask: What were the origins of the Sassanid Empire?
[Ardashir, a former military commander for the Parthian king, made himself the first Sassanid ruler around 226. He began to expand his kingdom, forming the Sassanid Empire.]

Ask: What important modern city stands on the approximate site of the old Sassanid capital city of Ctesiphon?
[Baghdad, capital of Iraq]

To give students a background on the Sassanid dynasty as a period of great Persian wealth and prosperity, you may wish to have the class view and discuss the electronic media image showing a gold and silver plate. Also have students read about and discuss details of Sassanid life in the Global History Resource Center selection by the Chinese envoy to the Sassanid Empire. For more information on Baghdad, have students complete Core Resources Reading 9.1.

DEVELOP

Discuss how the Sassanid rulers maintained their empire despite challenges. Again using the Sassanid Empire maps, ask students to locate main areas of military conflict between the Sassanids and their neighbors. To show the advanced state of Sassanid military capability, assign the Global History Resource Center reading on the Sassanid army. To illustrate the long-standing conflict with Rome, have students view and discuss the electronic media image showing a Sassanid king and a Roman emperor.

*Ask: **What outside military threats did the Sassanids have to confront?***

[Central Asian nomads and raiders from the Arab Peninsula attacked; Sassanids clashed with Romans in the west; Hephthalites tried to invade in the east.]

*Ask: **What internal challenge did Sassanid kings confront?***

[The most serious internal challenge came from Mazdak, a priest who led a movement to improve conditions for the rural poor. By initially supporting this movement, Kavadh outraged powerful aristocratic families and Zoroastrian clergy, throwing the empire into chaos.]

*Ask: **Who was Khosrow I and how was he important as a Sassanid emperor?***

[Khosrow I gained power by killing many of his own relatives, then executed Mazdak and his followers. Khosrow expanded the empire to the west and northeast. Internally, he made taxation more efficient, financed public works, particularly irrigation projects, and reorganized government to gain control over the nobility.]

PROBE

Examine Sassanid social structure. Remind students that Mazdak's reform movement horrified the wealthy because it threatened to upset the strict class system. Point out that in Sassanid society there was strict separation between the wealthy aristocrats and the masses of ordinary people. The classes were not supposed to associate with each other, share entertainment with each other, or intermarry.

*Ask: **How did this class system shape the role that Sassanid kings were expected to play?***

[People expected a strong king who could keep the class system stable.]

*Ask: **How did the Sassanid rulers control the powerful aristocracy?***

[They separated them from the ordinary people, granted them special privileges, and tried to make them dependent on the royal court.]

Next lead the class in a discussion of how Sassanid rulers used religion in imposing royal authority. Have students gain background on Zoroastrianism by reading the feature on the Avesta on textbook page 227; you may also wish to assign the

Global History Resource Center reading on Zoroastrianism.

*Ask: **How did Sassanid rulers use religion?***

[Rulers glorified themselves as descendants of god-kings and emphasized their own semi-divine status as rulers. Sassanid rulers made Zoroastrianism the state religion and abolished others.]

CONCLUDE

Discuss why the Sassanid Empire declined. Show the transparency of Southwest Asia again, and point out that most countries today in the area of the old Sassanid Empire are predominantly Muslim, rather than Zoroastrian.

*Ask: **What caused the Sassanids to decline and lose their empire to newer powers?***

[Discontent among the military nobility, later attacks by Arabs and eastern Romans, and other internal disputes left the Sassanids unable to resist invading Arab armies in the 630s.]

EXTEND

Cross-Curricular Connection: *Anthropology*

Have a group of students research and report on the Parsis or Parsees of India, a present-day religious group descending from Zoroastrians who fled Persia at about the time Arabs conquered the Sassanids. Have students focus on the Parsis' Zoroastrian traditions—such as the fire temples and funeral customs—that are said to be carried on today much as in Sassanid times.

MEET INDIVIDUAL NEEDS

Visual-Spatial Learners

Have students view the image showing a Sassanid plate and then re-create the scene depicted on the plate in the form of a political cartoon showing Sassanid Persia riding among its enemies.

Students Acquiring English

Pair students acquiring English with students who are proficient in English. Have the pairs work together to answer the focus questions on page 222 of their textbook.

ASSESS

Review

Have students complete the Section 1 Review. Use answers in the Teacher's Edition, page 228, to assess student mastery.

Lesson 9.2   The Byzantine Empire

Textbook pp. 229–236

RESOURCES

Pupil's Edition
Through Others' Eyes, p. 230: *Two Faces of Constantinople*
Map, p. 231: *The Byzantine Empire, 526–565*
History Through the Arts, p. 234: *The Church of Hagia Sophia*

Core Resources
Reading 9.2: *Justinian's Code*
Geography Activity 9: *Constantinople—Crossroads of Europe and Asia*
Writing Project 9: *Writing a Diary*

Visual Resources
Art and History 9: *San Apollinaire in Classe Apse Mosaic*

Everyday Life 9: *Role of the Byzantine Emperor*
Geography and History 9: *Roman Catholicism and Orthodoxy*

Global History Resource Center
Reading: *Byzantine Military Strategy*
Reading: *Icons Divide Byzantium*

Videodiscs or Global History Resource Center

Map: Series of three on *Growth of Byzantine Empire*

Search Frames 792–94

Image: *Constantinople's Defensive Walls*

Search Frame 786

Image: *Byzantine Gold and Jewels*

Search Frame 787

LESSON FOCUS
How did the power of the former Roman Empire shift east to the Byzantine Empire after the fall of Rome, and what were the contributions of Byzantine culture?

OBJECTIVES
After completing this lesson, students will be able to:
- explain why Byzantine rulers gave up efforts to reunite the Roman world;
- describe the nature of Byzantine society;
- discuss changes in Byzantine society after the 700s.

HOOK: Link to Today
Discuss Constantinople's strategic role in enabling the eastern empire to survive the fall of Rome. Have students examine the map of the Byzantine Empire on textbook page 231 and the series of electronic media maps showing the extent of the Byzantine Empire in 526, 565, and 1050 to see Constantinople's geographic importance. Assign Geography Activity 9 to highlight the military and economic importance of the Byzantine capital. You may also wish to show the electronic media image of Constantinople's defensive walls.

Ask: *Since the Roman Empire is said to have fallen in the 400s, how did the eastern part of the empire stay powerful for another 1,000 years?*
[In the 400s Germanic tribes overran the western but not the eastern Roman Empire, which remained strong partly because of its strategically located capital, Constantinople.]

To help students see the importance of Byzantine military ability, assign the Global History Resource Center Reading on military strategy. On the map on textbook page 231, have students trace the boundaries of the empire, locating areas of the old empire that were never brought within the Byzantine Empire. *[western and northern Europe, including present-day Spain, France, Germany, and Britain]*

Ask: *Why did Byzantine emperors stop trying to restore the Roman Empire?*
[The Byzantine Empire was vulnerable on three fronts and faced almost constant threats of invasion.]

DEVELOP
Examine Byzantine political and social structure. Display and discuss Everyday Life Transparency 9 and have students

complete the accompanying worksheet. Then have students break into groups and use dictionaries to look up meanings of *autocracy, theocracy,* and *aristocracy*. Next ask groups to create a graphic organizer that will convey the nature of Byzantine society. Have groups share their solutions with the class. [*Charts should show that the two pillars of society were the monarchy and the church. The emperors' authority was both autocratic and theocratic because their power was both personal and absolute and because they claimed to rule by divine authority and used elaborate ceremonies to portray themselves as lofty and godlike. Civil society was hierarchical and dominated by the aristocracy; people were not equal under the law; nobles received favored treatment, had great wealth and power, and married only within their class. Women were under the authority of men; aristocratic women were sheltered and could travel outside only if accompanied; upper-class women often were educated, and a few played major roles in public and intellectual life. The church was hierarchical with the patriarch at the head; the emperor oversaw church law but did not govern the church.*]

After students have presented their graphic organizers, discuss the Byzantine Empire's lasting contributions. You may wish to provide students with additional background by assigning Core Resources Reading 9.2 and by displaying and discussing the electronic media image of Byzantine gold and jewels.

Ask: What were Byzantine contributions in law, art, and architecture?
  [*Justinian's* Corpus juris civilis *formed a basis of western European laws. Art and architecture featured mosaic masterpieces and domed churches.*]

PROBE

Examine the importance of the church in Byzantine society. To emphasize church architecture as an expression of Byzantine Christianity, have students examine the History Through the Arts feature on page 234, and show Art and History Transparency 9 and assign the accompanying worksheet.

Ask: How was the Orthodox Church governed?
  [*Its leaders were patriarchs of Constantinople, Alexandria, Antioch, Jerusalem, and the pope in Rome. The patriarch of Constantinople became head of the church.*]

CONCLUDE

Discuss changes in Byzantine society after about 700.

To give students additional background on the iconoclast movement, assign the Global History Resource Center Reading on icons. Then display Geography and History Transparency 9 and have students complete the accompanying worksheet.

Ask: How did the iconoclast movement help split the Orthodox Church and the Roman Catholic Church?
  [*It was opposed by many people and many church leaders. The Council of Orthodoxy had ended the controversy in 843, but it added to tensions with Rome. In 1054 the church split into the Roman Catholic and the Orthodox churches.*]

Remind students that the schism with Rome helped make Byzantium more Greek and for a time increased the emperor's authority. Have students identify achievements during the Macedonian "golden age." [*Macedonian emperors improved conditions for peasants, strengthened the monarchy, promoted education to improve government, recaptured lands from Arabs, and won the Bulgarian kingdom in the north.*]

EXTEND

Cross-Curricular Connection: *Music*
Interested students may wish to research Eastern Orthodox liturgical music to see how it has changed since Byzantine times. Have students report their findings to the class and play examples of the music.

MEET INDIVIDUAL NEEDS

Logical-Mathematical Learners
Have students create a geometrical model out of posterboard to show the principle of a circle or dome supported by pendentives—the central architectural feature of the Hagia Sophia and similar churches.

Intrapersonal Learners
Refer students to Writing Project 9 for guidance in writing a diary entry. Then have them write a diary entry from the point of view of a Byzantine ruler in which he or she reflects on the empire and his or her rule.

ASSESS

Review
Have students complete the Section 2 Review. Use answers in the Teacher's Edition, page 236, to assess student mastery.

Lesson 9.3   *The Rise of Russia*

Textbook pp. 237–240

RESOURCES

Pupil's Edition
Map, p. 238: *Kievan Russia, 860–1240*

Core Resources
Reading 9.3: *The Pravda Russkaia*

Global History Resource Center
Reading: *A Russian Attack on Byzantium*
Reading: *Prince Vladimir's Conversion to Christianity*
Reading: *Prince Yaroslav Dooms Kievan Russia*

Videodiscs or Global History Resource Center

Map: *Kiev as Strategic Trading City, 1000s*

Search Frame 795

Image: *Conversion of Kievans to Christianity*

Search Frame 789

Image: *Olga of Kiev Burns Diplomats in Their Bath*

Search Frame 788

LESSON FOCUS
How did Kievan Russia develop, and how did ties with the Byzantine Empire influence this development?

OBJECTIVES
After completing this lesson, students will be able to:
- explain who the Rus were;
- describe how Byzantium influenced Kievan Russia;
- trace causes of the decline and fall of the Kievan state.

HOOK
Examine Kievan Russia's early development. First ask students to consider why countries typically engage in war. On the chalkboard, write the heading *Typical Objectives of War*, and have students contribute to the list. *[Students might suggest: to seize land or wealth, to defend against invasion, or to secure independence.]* Next have students read the chapter introduction on textbook page 220 and the Global History Resource Center selection about the Russian attack on Byzantium.
Ask: What were objectives of the Rus and the Byzantines in early warfare with each other?
[The Rus were trying to expand; Byzantine forces tried primarily to defend their capital.]

Have students view the map on textbook page 238 for perspective on the Rus homelands and display the electronic media map to show the importance of Kiev's location to trade.
Ask: Who were the Rus?
[The Rus were either a Scandinavian or a Slavic tribe who became dominant along the Dnieper River. They united Slavic tribes.]

To illustrate the stormy rivalry between the early Kievan Russians and neighboring tribes, have students view the image of Olga and the diplomats and discuss the incident described in the image caption.

Next trace the reasons a Rus-Byzantine alliance developed. On the chalkboard, write the heading *Objectives of a Peaceful Alliance*.
Ask: What could Kievan Russia and the Byzantine Empire gain from a peaceful alliance?
[mutually profitable trade, defeat common enemies]

DEVELOP
Discuss how religion became the main area of Byzantine influence on Kievan Russia. Have students complete the Global History Resource Center reading about Prince Vladimir's conversion and view the electronic media image on the conversion of Kievans. Students should see, especially from

the reading, that the Russians' acceptance of Christianity involved practical considerations.

Ask: **What advantage did the Byzantines see in establishing Christianity among the Rus?**

[Byzantines believed Kievan Russia would be a less hostile neighbor if it shared Christianity.]

Point out that the account of Vladimir's conversion suggests that the Russian prince carefully "shopped" for an appropriate religion.

Ask: **What were the long-term consequences of Vladimir's adoption of the Orthodox Christianity of the Byzantines?**

[It strengthened ties to the Byzantine Empire, which brought a strong Byzantine influence to Kievan Russian culture.]

PROBE

Examine the main ways Kievan Russia was influenced by Byzantine religion and culture. On the chalkboard, draw a diagram showing an arc bridging blocks labeled *Kievan Russia* and *Byzantine Culture*. Then label the arc or bridge *Eastern Orthodox Christianity*.

Ask: **During the reign of Vladimir, how did the "bridge" of religion help carry Byzantine influences into Russian culture?**

[Vladimir and his wife built many churches. These Orthodox churches used local languages in the services, unlike Roman Catholic churches, which used Latin. As a result, Russian churches were closer to the people and helped build Russian national culture.]

Then have students form small groups to develop a list of the ways in which Byzantine culture continued to influence Kievan Russian during the reign of Yaroslav the Wise. [Yaroslav built churches and monasteries, promoted scholarship and the use of the Cyrillic alphabet, which Byzantine missionaries had introduced, and encouraged the spread of Byzantine art, architecture, and learning in Russia. Because of Byzantine influence, Russian culture developed its own identity distinct from that of western Europe.]

After groups report their findings, point out that one of Yaroslav's major contributions was his establishment of a legal code. Have students read Core Resources Reading 9.3 and work in groups to answer the questions.

CONCLUDE

Trace the main causes of the decline of Kievan Russia.
To help students understand how internal disputes weakened Kievan Russia after Yaroslav's death, assign the Global History Resource Center reading on Yaroslav's effect on Kievan Russia.

Ask: **What additional factors led to the decline and fall of the Kievan state?**

[Polovtsian attacks, new trade routes that bypassed Russia, regional political disputes, and a shift of power away from Kiev toward Novgorod and Moscow led to the decline and fall of the Kievan state.]

EXTEND

Cross-Curricular Connection: *Computer Literacy*
Assign students to reorganize the information in Core Resources Reading 9.3 to show the relative values the Kiev Russian legal code assigned to offenses. Have students enter the grievances and corresponding compensation amounts into a computer and then sort or graph the data by size of payment.

MEET INDIVIDUAL NEEDS

Linguistic Learners
Have students research and prepare a class report on the Cyrillic alphabet. Students might also report on Cyril and Methodius and their reason for devising the Cyrillic writing system.

Visual-Spatial Learners
Have interested students study illustrations or slides of Russian art of the period to look for examples of Byzantine influence. Students should then make a chart of elements that are common to both artistic traditions.

ASSESS

Review
Have students complete the Section 3 Review. Use answers in the Teacher's Edition, page 240, to assess student mastery of this section.

In preparation for the chapter test, you may wish to have students complete all or part of the Chapter 9 Review on textbook page 241, the Chapter 9 Review Activity and the Chapter 9 Themes Review.

Chapter 9

Persia, Byzantium, and the Rise of Russia

Understanding the Main Idea

Call on a volunteer to read aloud the *Understanding the Main Idea* paragraph. Explain to students that after the fall of the Roman Empire, the ideal of imperial civilization continued to influence the Byzantines. They dreamed of reuniting the empire. However, near-constant invasions made the recovery of the western provinces impossible. In addition, the Byzantine world had evolved into a brilliant culture in its own right.

Presenting Themes

See p. 219B for suggestions on introducing themes.

Using the Time Line

Have students list the time line events in their notebooks. After they have read about each event in the chapter, have students write a paragraph explaining its significance.

220

Persia, Byzantium, and the Rise of Russia 226–1240

Understanding the Main Idea

In an age when many empires shattered and fell apart, Persia and Byzantium transformed and maintained the concept of imperial civilization. They eventually transmitted their values and cultural heritage to new peoples. The Persian and Byzantine empires declined slowly as the result of religious rivalry, territorial warfare, and nomadic migrations.

Themes

- **Politics and Law** Why might a monarchy and an aristocracy be essential features of a particular society?
- **Religion** Why might an empire try to promote certain religions?
- **Cross-cultural Interaction** Why might a society adopt elements of a nearby culture?

In the early 900s a group of adventurous warriors swiftly sailed down the Dnieper (NEE-puhr) River to attack Constantinople, the dazzling capital of the mighty Byzantine Empire. These warriors, known as the Rus, terrified the Byzantines. As the Rus were poised to attack the city, the Byzantines proposed a peaceful solution. An account in a Russian chronicle explained:

> **66** *The Russes who come hither shall receive as much grain as they require. Whosoever come as merchants shall receive supplies for six months, including bread, wine, meat, fish, and fruit. . . . When the Russes return homeward, they shall receive from your Emperor food, anchors, cordage [ropes], and sails, and whatever else is needful for the journey.* **99**

The Byzantine emperor bound himself to this treaty by uttering a solemn oath and kissing a cross. Then, according to the account, the Rus leader and his men "swore by their weapons and by their god Perun, as well as by Volos, the god of cattle" to uphold the treaty.

Although the Byzantines had proven unable to halt the Rus militarily, through diplomacy and sometimes even bribery they managed to keep their empire intact. As the two peoples interacted, over time the older and more sophisticated civilization of Byzantium triumphed, placing a lasting mark on Russian culture and religion.

226	330	528	630s
▲	▲	▲	▲
Ardashir founds the Sassanid dynasty in Persia.	City of Constantinople is formally dedicated.	Justinianic Code is prepared.	Sassanid Empire is left weak and divided by invasions.

This image of Saint Michael dates from the 1000s. Made of gold and enamel, it was used as a cover for a book containing the four gospels.

Icons, or devotional images of divine figures or saints, were essential to religious worship in the Orthodox Church. Used to decorate churches or devotional books, icons conveyed a message through the use of images rather than words.

The use of icons flourished for centuries. Developed first in the Byzantine Empire, icons spread to Russia, where they were incorporated into the Russian Orthodox Church.

Icons were painted in intense colors, with strong lines and shapes. In Orthodox churches, flickering candlelight and clouds of incense could obscure visibility, so the icons had to be clear and visually distinctive.

Critical Thinking Ask students the advantages of using icons to convey religious messages.

ANSWER: Students might suggest that icons can be easily understood by illiterate people and sometimes inspire people by their great beauty.

862
Rurik seizes Novgorod.

980s
Orthodox Christianity becomes the official religion of Kievan Russia.

1054
Schism develops between the Roman Catholic Church and the Eastern Orthodox Church.

1240
Mongols demolish Kiev.

SECTION 1
Sassanid Persia

FOCUS

- How did the Sassanids build and maintain their empire?
- What was the structure of Sassanid society?
- Why did the Sassanid Empire eventually decline?

In the early A.D. 200s, the Sassanid dynasty replaced the Parthian rulers of Persia. In many ways, the Sassanids revived the traditions of the old Achaemenid Persian Empire. They emphasized sacred kingship, centralized the empire, and resisted foreign enemies. Agriculture and commerce grew so much that the Sassanid era was to be remembered as one of the most prosperous in the history of Mesopotamia and Iran.

King Ardashir receives his crown.

The Rise of the Sassanid Empire

By the beginning of the A.D. 200s, the Parthian dynasty, which had ruled the Plateau of Iran and adjacent territories for over 400 years, was under great strain. Although the last of the periodic wars with Rome had ended with a peace treaty, the years of harsh fighting had sapped Parthia's strength. Parthian territory in the east had been taken over by the Kushans, a Central Asian people who had established an empire based in northern India. The most important weakness of the Parthian Empire, however, lay in its structure—a confederation of powerful noble families and regional rulers held together in a delicate balance by the Parthian kings. These weak kings could easily be challenged for power by strong nobles.

Ardashir. In the early A.D. 200s, such a challenge came from a local military commander named Ardashir. After 20 years of subduing local leaders and seizing control of huge territories in the province of Persia, Ardashir was powerful enough to confront the Parthian king. In a decisive battle around 226, Ardashir defeated and killed the Parthian ruler.

Ardashir quickly defeated the other noble families and local rulers and established his control over the entire Parthian Empire. By 226 he had captured the capital city of Ctesiphon and was crowned as *shah-an-shah eran*, or "king of kings of Iran."

To emphasize his right to rule, Ardashir proclaimed that he descended from the ancient rulers of Iran through an ancestor named Sasan. Thus, the dynasty that Ardashir founded became known as the **Sassanid dynasty**, which would rule Persia for more than 400 years.

Imperial expansion. Ardashir immediately began expanding his territory. He pushed as far east as the Indus River and probably conquered the territories along the Oxus River (now known as the Amu Darya) in west-central Asia. Although Ardashir did not conquer the Kushan rulers in Bactria and the Punjab, he did force them to acknowledge Sassanid superiority. In effect, this restored the boundaries of the old Achaemenid Persian Empire in the east.

As the frontier with India became peaceful, however, the Sassanid Empire faced assaults by

Central Asian nomads and raiders from the Arabian Peninsula. Ardashir's successors dealt with the Central Asian threat by incorporating some of the warriors into the Persian system of defense. They solved the problem with the Arabs by establishing a buffer state to protect the border. Ruled by the Lakhmids, a friendly and loyal Arab dynasty, this buffer state helped protect the agricultural heart of the empire in Mesopotamia.

Threats to the Empire

Although the Sassanids built a stable and lasting empire, they faced a number of serious problems. Threats to the empire came from both external enemies and from internal challenges.

External enemies. In the west the greatest external enemy of the Sassanid Empire remained the Eastern Roman Empire. The Sassanids thought of themselves as the rulers not only of Iran but also of territories beyond Iran as far as the Aegean Sea. The Romans feared that the Sassanids intended to re-create a strong empire in the east. Thus any Sassanid movement to the west produced conflict, as did any Roman attempt to move eastward into Armenia or Mesopotamia. This situation led to years of skirmishes and warfare with neither side ever achieving a decisive victory.

During the 400s the Sassanids' struggle with the Romans subsided as the Sassanid Empire suffered other severe challenges. The most serious was the appearance of the Hephthalites (HEP-thuh-lyts)—a group of nomads also known as the White Huns—on the empire's eastern frontier. The Hephthalites defeated Persian armies and forced the king of kings to pay tribute. The Hephthalites even began to interfere in Sassanid politics. For example, they twice assisted Kavadh, a member of the Sassanid royal family, in his efforts to become king.

Internal challenges. Meanwhile, the Sassanids also faced internal problems. During Kavadh's reign, for example, a revolt led by a priest named Mazdak surged through the empire. Mazdak supported **egalitarianism**, the removal of inequalities among people. His basic goal seems to have been to improve the conditions of the rural poor and to protect them from oppression by the powerful aristocratic families, which had amassed huge estates. Exactly how Mazdak proposed to do this is unclear. Most likely it involved breaking up estates and distributing land to peasants, giving handouts of food, freeing slaves, and liberating women from the harems so that they could marry lower-class men.

Kavadh initially supported Mazdak in his reforms, probably in order to break the power of the aristocratic families. However, the aristocrats and the orthodox Zoroastrian clergy were horrified by Mazdak's ideas and resisted them with all their power. Eventually, they forced Kavadh to turn against Mazdak, but in the meantime, the empire was thrown into chaos.

Imperial reconstruction. The task of restoring order to the Sassanid Empire fell to Kavadh's son, Khosrow I, also known as Anushirvan, which means "immortal soul."

Although Kavadh had named Khosrow as his successor, other members of the family contested his choice. To remove any challenges to his authority, Khosrow killed all but one of his brothers and their male children. He then turned with a vengeance upon the Mazdakites, executing Mazdak and thousands of his followers.

▲ The Roman emperor Valerian is captured by Sassanid king Shapur I in A.D. 260.

Theme: Religion

According to legend, a series of foreboding events occurred around 570, the forty-second year of Khosrow I's reign. It was around this time that the prophet Muhammad was born. Muslim legend holds that on the night of Muhammad's birth, the Persian royal palace was shaken by earthquakes so powerful that 14 of its battlements fell to the ground. At the same time, the Sacred Fire, which had burned continuously for 1,000 years, was extinguished, and the Lake of Sáwa suddenly dried up. The chief Zoroastrian priest also had a vision in which he foresaw the invasion of western Persia. The Persian Empire fell to the Muslims in the 630s.

Critical Thinking Ask students to imagine why these legends might be important to Muslim invaders.

ANSWER: Students might comment that such legends suggest that their religion is approved by a higher power and that their territorial advances are destined to happen.

While in the process of securing his throne, Khosrow had agreed to a peace with Rome, but he soon became concerned about what appeared to be the revival of the Eastern Roman Empire. In 540 Khosrow launched a surprise attack against the Eastern Romans and raided as far as Antioch. He even hoped to establish a Persian colony on the Black Sea in order to build up a navy and attack Constantinople by sea. The war with the Romans dragged on until 562, when the two sides negotiated another peace.

Khosrow then turned his attention eastward. With the help of the Turks, another rising power in Central Asia, he crushed the Hephthalites and reestablished the Oxus River as the northern border of the Sassanid Empire.

In addition to his military successes, Khosrow also managed internal affairs with great skill. He

Khosrow I
BIOGRAPHY

completed a land survey and census and reformed and standardized the collection of taxes. Instead of paying taxes with part of their crops, for example, peasants paid a fixed rate in cash after the harvest. With these new, predictable revenues, Khosrow financed beneficial public works, particularly irrigation projects to open up more land for farming.

Khosrow also completely reorganized both the imperial administration and the army. His goal was to reduce the power of the nobility and increase the power of the central government. Khosrow encouraged the use of **dihqans** (di-kahnz), soldier-peasants who were in charge of a village, as the backbone of the army and the main line of defense in frontier areas. In addition to these reforms, Khosrow also took steps to promote learning, establish justice, and protect religious minorities.

Sassanid Persia, 531–579

Expanding Frontiers Khosrow I's mighty armies stormed the territories surrounding the Plateau of Iran. But these military conquests sapped the Persian treasury and eventually brought about the downfall of the empire.

◆ **Linking Geography and History** What empire's territory would Persia have gained if it had continued to expand to the northwest?

Sassanid Society

To the Sassanids, the ideal society was one that could maintain stability and order. According to the *Letter of Tansar*, supposedly written by the chief Zoroastrian priest under Ardashir, Sassanid people were theoretically divided into four classes—priests, soldiers, scholars, and artisans. In reality, society was divided in two: a small group of privileged aristocrats and the masses of ordinary people.

Membership in a class was generally determined by birth, although it was possible for an exceptional individual to move to another class on the basis of merit. Most Persians believed that all people should remain within their class and engage only in the activities appropriate to it. The necessary instrument to maintain this system, people believed, was a strong monarchy.

◀ **This gilded silver cover was used on a Persian monastery Gospel around A.D. 500.**

Sacred kingship. The function of the king was to be above all the classes and to ensure that each class remained within its proper boundaries. This was so that the strong did not oppress the weak and the weak did not rise up against the strong. Maintenance of this social balance depended on royal authority, which came from the glorification of the monarchy above the rest of society. Kingship was regarded as sacred. The Persians believed that the king was chosen by God, who gave him the authority to rule.

Persian kings impressed their subjects with the glory of their status in many ways. For example, rulers emphasized their great ancestors—ancient kings and gods—and took godlike titles. Shapur I, Ardashir's successor, referred to himself in the following terms:

❝ *I, the Mazda worshipper, the god Shapur, King of Kings of Iranians and Non-Iranians, of the race of gods, son of the Mazda worshipper, of the god Ardashir, King of Kings of the Iranians, of the race of gods, grandson of Papak, king of the Empire of Iran, I am the sovereign.* ❞

Sassanid kings proclaimed these same ideas in monumental rock carvings that depicted the kings with their ancestors. In these scenes the kings received the emblem of royalty from the supreme god, Ahura Mazda.

The Sassanids also strengthened their royal authority by linking it to both religious and national beliefs. Special fire temples in honor of the Sassanid dynasty were established, and kings were worshipped as gods after their death. Tansar reportedly even linked what it meant to be Aryan, or Iranian, with humbleness in service to the kings by playing on the fact that the Persian word for Aryan also meant "humble."

❝ *We are called 'the Iranian people,' and there is no quality or trait of excellence or nobility which we hold dearer than this, that we have ever showed humility and lowliness and humbleness in the service of kings, and have chosen obedience and loyalty, devotion and fidelity [loyalty].* ❞

◀ **These ancient Iranian altars were probably used for the worship of the god of fire, Atar. It was Atar who carried sacrifices to the gods.**

Theme: Politics and Law

The Sassanids maintained that even the humblest subject could appeal directly to the monarch to right a wrong. In practice, however, administration of the law was largely in the hands of the Zoroastrian clergy. The law itself was based heavily on the principles of Zoroastrianism, royal decrees, and precedents set in earlier cases. A manual of the law, known as the *Book of a Thousand Legal Decisions,* was compiled during the reign of Khosrow II.

Critical Thinking Ask students how the king's supposed judicial power might have bolstered his image.

ANSWER: Students should note that by seeming approachable the king appeared more interested in his subjects.

RESOURCE ACTIVITY

GLOBAL HISTORY RESOURCE CENTER
Reading: *A Chinese Envoy's View of Sassanid Persia*

Print out and distribute the reading. Have students read the Chinese description of Persia. Have the students write a letter from the Chinese emperor to his envoy, giving him further instructions.

Level 3

Through military strength and internal reforms, the Sassanids were able to build and maintain a strong empire that resisted Roman armies and nomadic warriors.

Mani believed that Light and Darkness symbolized the realms of God and Satan. These two realms were in constant conflict with each other.

Mani considered human beings to be a product of this struggle. People were made of matter, which belonged to Satan, but they were also given some of God's light.

Mani's followers were divided into two groups. The elect would be summoned to heaven after death because of the high level of spiritual enlightenment that they attained. They gained this enlightenment by living austere lives. They never married, and they spent their time teaching and preaching.

The auditors, or hearers, supported the elect. They could marry, but they could not have children. The auditors hoped to be reborn as the elect. The Manichaeans believed that all other people were sinners whose ultimate and unchangeable fate was to spend eternity in hell.

Critical Thinking
Ask students why Manichaeism might have demanded that its elect lead such strict lives.

ANSWER: Students might suggest that Manichaeism demanded that the elect sacrifice worldly pleasures to enjoy the rewards of heaven after death.

The aristocracy. Below the king in the Sassanid social hierarchy were the aristocrats, who were clearly separate from the masses of ordinary people. The aristocracy had many special rights and privileges. According to one ancient text:

> 66 [The king] has established a visible and general distinction between men of noble birth and common people with regard to horses and clothes, houses and gardens, women and servants. . . . So no commoner may share sources of enjoyment of life with the nobles, and alliance and marriage between the two groups is forbidden. 99

Since the aristocracy was so powerful, the kings sought to bring the aristocratic families and local rulers under their control. The kings granted aristocrats titles and privileges, hoping to attach them to the royal court and make them dependent on the king.

The state religion. Sassanid rulers also used religion to impose royal authority over their subjects. The Sassanids were Zoroastrians, as were the Parthians who had ruled before them. However, the Sassanids did not practice tolerance of other religions, as the earlier Parthians had done.

As early as the A.D. 200s, Ardashir apparently began the process of destroying the regional religious cults and temples that had arisen under Parthian rule. He was particularly concerned with getting rid of the sacred fires that had been established by local authorities in Parthian times. Ardashir permitted only the maintenance of fires associated with his own dynasty.

Tansar, the chief Zoroastrian priest, defended Ardashir's actions on the grounds that Ardashir was restoring the only true religion. The priest emphasized the harmony between the monarchy and the official Zoroastrian religion. The monarchy and the temple, he wrote, "were born of the one womb, joined together and never to be sundered [separated]."

◀ **Zoroastrian priests carried rods like this bull-headed one as a symbol of the war they constantly fought against evil.**

One important consequence of Sassanid rule was their policy of maintaining written records of their culture. The hymns and teachings of Zoroastrianism were collected in an official written version. This collection, called the **Avesta**, contains the oldest, most basic scriptures of Zoroastrianism. The Sassanids also extended their encouragement of literary scholarship to nonreligious learning. Works of history, such as the *Shah-nameh*, or *Book of Kings*, were prepared under the supervision of royal officials and priests.

Manichaeism. Ardashir's successor, Shapur I, completed the process of religious consolidation by proclaiming Zoroastrianism to be the sole official state religion. At the same time, however, he also began to favor the ideas of a reforming prophet named Mani. The prophet Mani believed that Zoroaster, Jesus, Buddha, and other divine beings had all tried to reveal the same religious truth. He maintained that these leaders had been misunderstood by their followers. Mani proclaimed that he could bring people back to that original truth through Manichaeism (MA-nuh-kee-i-zuhm), a religion based on a combination of aspects of Zoroastrianism, Buddhism, Christianity, and other beliefs.

Mani saw the world as a struggle between Light and Darkness. He believed that this struggle would end in the collapse of the universe, the triumph of Light, and the imprisonment of Darkness. Mani also believed in reincarnation and in the role of Buddha and Jesus as special agents of Light.

After Shapur I died in 272, Mani lost his royal protector, and the powerful Zoroastrian priesthood fought to end the influence of the Manichaeans. Shapur I's son executed Mani and persecuted many of his followers, thus destroying the practice of Manichaeism in the Sassanid Empire. However, some of Mani's followers migrated into the Roman Empire and Central Asia, spreading their beliefs. Although

Sacred TRADITIONS

The Avesta

In the 500s B.C., under the protection of the emperor Cyrus, the religious leader Zoroaster (Zarathustra) began to spread his spiritual message across Persia. Under the Sassanids the prayers, hymns, and stories of Zoroaster's religion were gathered into a collection known as the Avesta. Over the centuries many more texts were added to the original Avesta. Since the A.D. 800s, however, many of the texts of the Avesta have been lost. All that remains today of the collection is a group of prayers, called the Yasna (Worship), which includes some of Zoroaster's original teachings. One of Zoroaster's most important teachings was his belief that the world has always been a place of conflict between the forces of good and evil, two forces created by the supreme god Ahura Mazda. By using an ancient Persian myth about two divine twins, Zoroaster demonstrated that people must willingly choose between the paths of good and evil in life. According to Zoroaster, people have the power to determine their own destiny. As the Avesta states:

Yasna 30.3–6

3 Now, these are the two original Spirits who, as Twins, have been perceived through a vision. In both thought and speech, these two are what is good and evil. Between these two, the pious, not the impious, will choose rightly.

4 Furthermore, the two Spirits confronted each other; in the beginning each created for himself life and nonlife, so that in the end there will be the worst existence for the rugwants [evil ones], but the best Mind for the Righteous.

5 Of these two spirits, the deceitful chose the worst course of action, the most beneficent [kind] Spirit who is clothed in the hardest stones chose Truth, as also do those who believingly appease Ahura Mazdā.

6 Between these two Spirits the daewas [demons] did not choose rightly at all since, while they were taking council among themselves, delusion came upon them, so that they chose the worst Mind. Then, all together they ran to Wrath with which they infect the life of man.

Understanding Sacred Traditions

1. What does Zoroaster say is the correct choice for the pious?
2. Why do you think Zoroaster used an ancient myth to illustrate his point about choosing between good and evil?

Zoroaster was the founder of the religion that became the single faith of the Sassanids.

Manichaeism was eventually eclipsed by other religious beliefs and vanished by the 1400s, it had a great influence on other religions, such as Christianity.

Although primarily an aristocratic society, the Sassanid Empire revolved around sacred kingship, which was supposed to provide justice and prosperity.

Decline and Fall of Sassanid Persia

The Sassanid Empire reached its peak in the early 600s under Khosrow II, also known as Parviz, or "the victorious." Despite his accomplishments, the empire had begun a rapid decline by the end of his reign in 628. One factor contributing to this decline was widespread discontent among the military nobility. A revolt led by Bahram Chubin, a general descended from an old Parthian family, came close to overthrowing the Sassanid dynasty.

Khosrow II defeated Bahram and retained his throne largely because of assistance from the Eastern Roman emperor Maurice. When Maurice was overthrown in a similar revolt led by his own discontented soldiers in 602, Khosrow II launched another war against the Eastern Romans. The Persian forces were able to take Jerusalem and Alexandria, and these successes apparently convinced Khosrow II that he was destined to be the ruler of the world from the Mediterranean to China.

In fact, Khosrow II's wars and the extravagant luxury of his court severely overextended his resources. He also made a serious mistake when, for personal reasons, he deposed the king of the Lakhmid Arab buffer state in 602. This ultimately produced an Arab revolt that defeated a Sassanid army in 611. By 627 the Persians were also being badly beaten by the Eastern Romans. A new revolt broke out, in which some of Khosrow II's own sons were involved, and Khosrow II was deposed and murdered.

The remaining years of the dynasty were marked by internal strife and frequent changes of rulers. These disturbances often led to the neglect and disruption of the crucial irrigation systems in Mesopotamia. This in turn contributed to serious outbreaks of disease and famine. Weakened and bitterly divided, the empire was unable to resist new, swift, and devastating attacks by united Arab armies in the 630s.

By the end of Khosrow II's reign, the Sassanid Empire was rapidly declining due to internal power struggles and external invasion.

◄ **The scene on this Sassanid plate shows a hunter and his attendant, astride a camel, pursuing deer.**

SECTION 1 REVIEW

IDENTIFY and explain the significance of the following:
  Sassanid dynasty
  Mazdak
  egalitarianism
  Khosrow I
  dihqans
  Shapur I
  Avesta
  Mani
  Khosrow II

LOCATE and explain the importance of the following:
  Indus River
  Oxus River
  Bactria

1. **Main Idea** How did the Sassanids come to power and how did they control their empire?
2. **Main Idea** How was Sassanid society structured?
3. **Geography: Location** What impact did the location of the Eastern Roman Empire and of the Hephthalites have on Sassanid Persia?
4. **Writing to Explain** Imagine that you are a Sassanid court historian. Write a short account explaining why the empire is declining.
5. **Synthesizing** Create a chart like the one below that demonstrates the major accomplishments of Ardashir, Shapur I, and Khosrow I.

RULER	INTERNAL REFORMS	FOREIGN POLICY	RELIGIOUS DEVELOPMENTS
Ardashir			

The Byzantine Empire

FOCUS

- Why did Byzantine emperors give up efforts to reunite the Roman world?

- What was the nature of Byzantine society?

- How did Byzantine society change after the 700s?

The Byzantine Empire developed gradually out of what had been the eastern portions of the Roman Empire and survived for nearly a thousand years after the fall of Rome. The Byzantines successfully blended the traditions of imperial Rome with Christian and Greek culture into a distinct and influential civilization. They kept alive Roman law, contributed to the development of Christianity, protected the eastern borders of Europe from nomadic invasions, and preserved much of classical Greek learning.

Constantinople, c. 950

The Eastern Roman Empire

Since the reign of Diocletian, the Roman Empire had been officially divided in two. As the western half declined in the 400s, the power and glory of Rome shifted to the eastern half of the empire. Although the people who lived in the east continued to call themselves Romans, later historians refer to this new civilization as the Byzantine Empire.

Constantinople. The capital of the Byzantine Empire was Constantinople, the city that Emperor Constantine had built on the site of the Greek colony of Byzantium. It was dedicated in 330 and named New Rome. The city was built on a peninsula overlooking the Bosporus, a narrow strait that connects the Black Sea to the Aegean through the Sea of Marmara. In this strategic location the city was protected from attack on two sides by the sea, and on the landward sides by a great wall. This location also allowed the city to control shipping through the Bosporus. Ships, goods, sailors, and merchants poured into Constantinople. Even before the fall of Rome, the eastern capital was the richest city of the Roman Empire.

Justinian. After the fall of Rome in 476, the eastern emperors did not give up their claim to rule the western provinces of the empire. Many longed to recover the lost provinces and restore the unity of the old Roman Empire. The Byzantine emperor Justinian began this recovery during his reign, which lasted from 527 to 565. Funneling the wealth of the Byzantine Empire into his battles against the Germanic invaders, by the end of his reign Justinian had reconquered most of the territory around the Mediterranean.

Justinian owed much of his success to his wife, Theodora, who served as co-ruler of the empire. Scorned by many for her early career as an actress, Theodora was a strong, intelligent woman who was exceptionally influential in governmental affairs. Her advice during a critical rebellion perhaps even saved Justinian's throne.

Early in his reign, Justinian faced strong opposition from the people, many of whom resented government officials. Some people also did not consider Justinian to be a legitimate ruler, since he was not a member of the family of Anastasius, an

SECTION 2

CORE LESSON PLAN
See pages 219E and 219F for Lesson Plan 9.2.

R RESOURCE ACTIVITY

GLOBAL HISTORY RESOURCE CENTER
Reading: *Byzantine Millitary Strategy*
Image: *Constantinople's Defensive Walls*

Print out and distribute the reading and the image. Have students act as military analysts and write short reports describing the Byzantines' military strengths and weaknesses.

Level 3

THROUGH OTHERS' EYES

Two Faces of Constantinople

There are many stories about the grandeur of Constantinople and the beauty of the art and architecture there. However, Constantinople was a large city, and like almost all big cities, ancient or modern, it had a seamy side. A European traveler, Odo of Deuil, went to Constantinople in the mid-1100s. When he first arrived in the city, Odo was struck by the wonder of the outer walls and the beauty of the interior. The underground tunnels that provided fresh water also impressed Odo. Upon entering the city proper, however, he learned that this dazzling metropolis also had a grimy, less attractive side:

66 The city itself is squalid and fetid [filthy] and in many places harmed by permanent darkness, for the wealthy overshadow the streets with buildings and leave these dirty, dark places to the poor and to travelers; there murders and robberies and other crimes which love the darkness are committed. Moreover, since people live lawlessly in this city, which has as many lords as rich men and almost as many thieves as poor men, a criminal knows neither fear nor shame, because crime is not punished by law and never entirely comes to light. In every respect she exceeds moderation; for, just as she surpasses other cities in wealth, so, too, does she surpass them in vice. 99

earlier emperor. In 532 a popular rebellion known as the Nika Revolt erupted in Constantinople. With the city in flames and the people rioting, Justinian prepared to flee. Theodora convinced him to stay, saying: "It is impossible for a man, when he has come into the world, not to die; but for one who has reigned, it is intolerable to be an exile." Justinian and his generals eventually suppressed the revolt.

Ultimately, however, Justinian's attempt to reunite the old Roman Empire proved too expensive. His treasury had a small surplus left by his predecessor, but for the most part, Justinian paid for his wars by levying heavy taxes on the Byzantine people. When he died in 565, Justinian left the Byzantine treasury nearly bankrupt.

New invasions. Justinian had pushed the empire beyond its limits. Over the next several decades, anarchy, poverty, and plagues ravaged the empire. Byzantine efforts to bypass Persia in trading with China led to renewed conflict with the Sassanids that lasted for decades. Meanwhile, the migrating Avars and Slavs invaded the Balkans, while the Lombards sacked Italy. Since the empire could not fight wars on three fronts, the western provinces once more slipped away.

These pressures continued until the reign of Heraclius, who became emperor in 610. Heraclius drove back the Persians. Through shrewd diplomacy, he also held off the Avars and Slavs. Imitating an old Roman tactic, he settled other migrating peoples, the Croats and Serbs, within the Balkan frontiers of the empire to act as buffers against the new invaders. He also tried to use Christianity to prevent his new subjects from turning on the empire. As one historian at the time explained:

66 After their baptism the Croats made a covenant, confirmed with their own hands and by oaths sure and binding in the name of St. Peter the Apostle, that never would they go upon a foreign country and make war on it, but rather would live at peace with all who were willing to do so. 99

The extension of Christianity into the Balkans established a Byzantine influence that would last for centuries. Under Heraclius, the Byzantine Empire seemed to be at the height of its power.

Then a new, unexpected, and more formidable threat appeared—the Arabs. Assisted by disgruntled Egyptians and Syrians, Arab forces defeated the Byzantines at the battle of Yarmuk in 636, then drove the Byzantines out of much Arab territory. In a few years, the empire was reduced to a core of territory stretching from the Adriatic to Armenia.

Leo III. Even this reduced Byzantine Empire was still in danger from outside raids. In 712 the Bulgars, another tribal people, reached the walls of Constantinople. In 717, however, a powerful general named Leo the Isaurian rose to become emperor. In addition to founding a new dynasty,

Leo III drove back a major Arab assault on Constantinople and defeated the Bulgars. To provide for the defense of the empire, Leo also perfected a system of administration and defense known as the **theme system**.

The theme system organized the empire into a number of provinces, each under the command of a military governor. In exchange for military service, military officers were given farmland. Both the land and its associated military duty could be inherited. The object of the system was to provide a militia that could respond quickly to an invasion. However, it also meant that the civilian administration surrendered its authority in the provinces to military commanders.

The near-constant threat of invasion caused the Byzantine emperors in Constantinople to abandon efforts to restore the old Roman Empire.

Byzantine State, Society, and Culture

At the heart of the Byzantine state and society was the emperor, who was regarded as a sacred priest-king, a notion reinforced by Christian doctrine. For example, early Christians had taught obedience to the rule of emperors:

66 *For the sake of the Lord, accept the authority of every social institution: the emperor, as the supreme authority, and the governors as commissioned by him to punish criminals and praise good citizenship.* 99

The Byzantine emperor was considered both the deputy of Christ on Earth and his co-ruler.

Emperors indicated their elevated status in many ways. They emphasized the greatness of

Theme: Politics and Law

Leo the Isaurian's decisive victory over the Arabs brought an end to the Arab threat to the empire for nearly two centuries. Afterward, Leo embarked upon a program of reform, and had a code of civil law compiled.

Leo had this code written in Greek, not Latin. This signaled a growing distance between the eastern and western parts of the old Roman Empire.

Critical Thinking Ask students why written legal codes would have been advantageous to the Byzantine Empire.

ANSWER: Students may respond that written laws ensured fairness and helped unify the large territory of the empire.

Map Answer
about 2,000 miles

R RESOURCE ACTIVITY

GLOBAL HISTORY RESOURCE CENTER
Reading: *Power Struggles in Byzantium*

Print out and distribute the reading. Have students read about land reform efforts. Ask students to imagine they are peasants during the reign of Basil II and write a diary entry about their response to his land reforms.

Level 2

The Byzantine Empire, 526–565

The Reign of Justinian In the 500s, Emperor Justinian's armies battled the Germanic invaders and regained the tattered remnants of the Roman Empire.

❓ **Movement** About how many miles of African coastline did Justinian's armies recapture?

▲ This 1028 image of Constantine and Zoe shows their imperial status. Seated with Christ, on only slightly smaller thrones, each has a halo.

their office, for example, through *prokypsis*—a ceremony in which the emperor sat on a raised platform behind a curtain, which was then drawn back to reveal him bathed in a brilliant light. Portraits of the emperor not only showed him in magnificent imperial attire holding the symbols of office, but also depicted him with a halo as if he were a saint or apostle. For example, the image of Justinian in the Church of San Vitale in Ravenna, Italy, depicts him as a holy priest-king. He and Theodora are the only figures in the image with halos.

Byzantine law. In Byzantium the emperor was responsible for establishing justice and order in society. Although technically above the law and free to change it at will, many emperors displayed great restraint. Justinian wrote:

66 *[The emperor] must be not only glorified with arms, but also armed with laws, so that alike the time of war and the time of peace may be rightly guided; he must be the strong protector of law as well as the triumpher over vanquished enemies.* 99

Some emperors preserved earlier Roman law by preparing written codes that compiled the laws of the empire, which had evolved over centuries.

Justinian was the greatest compiler of these laws. In 528 he ordered the preparation of the Justinianic Code, a collection of 10 books containing the constitutions that had been used since the reign of Emperor Hadrian. In later years Justinian ordered the creation of other law books. Along with the Justinianic Code, these books formed the **Corpus juris civilis**, or "body of civil law." The books of the *Corpus juris civilis* were updated and amended by later emperors, and translated from Latin into Greek. They remained the basic framework of Byzantine law. By the 1100s Justinian's code was being rediscovered and used as the basis of legal systems across western Europe.

An aristocratic society. In general, Byzantine society was hierarchical in nature and dominated by the aristocracy. Although law codes were meant to apply to everyone, great inequality still existed among the different levels of Byzantine society. For example, an ordinary person would be hanged for committing a particular crime, but a nobleman would simply be sent into exile.

The Byzantine social structure was not completely closed. Generally, "nobility" was defined primarily by the political office an individual held. These positions were not hereditary, but instead based largely on merit. Many aristocrats, including emperors, rose from lower classes to the highest levels of society.

At other times, noble status was acquired by birth into one of the powerful aristocratic families. These families possessed huge amounts of land and monopolized military commands on a hereditary basis. They also emphasized the importance of ancestry and protected their property holdings by marrying only within their own class. By late in the empire, a relatively permanent hereditary aristocracy composed of wealthy landowning families transformed the Byzantine imperial system, which earlier had been based on merit.

Women in Byzantine society. Byzantine society reflected both the Roman idea that women should be subject to the authority of men and the Christian notion that women, as daughters of Eve, were a source of temptation and trouble and should be strictly supervised. In Byzantine society some women protected their virtue by entering convents. Most women, however, married and devoted their time to raising children, managing the household, and engaging in spinning, weaving, sewing, and embroidering.

Among the aristocracy, women and girls were kept apart from the outside world—in part to protect them. In the royal palace, for example, noble women and girls lived in a section of the palace called the **gynaeceum**, or women's apartments. Women might travel outside the palace, however, as long as servants accompanied them. In addition, aristocratic women were usually well educated, although in general they were not allowed to study classical literature. A few educated women, such as Anna Comnena, daughter of Emperor Alexius I, who wrote a history of her father's reign, played prominent roles in politics, religious life, and intellectual life.

Art and architecture. Religious themes dominated Byzantine art and architecture. In churches, cathedrals, and burial chambers, rich **mosaics**—intricate pictures or designs formed by inlaid pieces of stone—illustrated stories from the Bible using commonly understood symbols. For example, in several mosaics in the cathedral of San Apollinaire in Italy, Jesus was represented by his spiritual symbol—the cross. Twelve lambs symbolized the Lord's flock on Earth, while a hand above the cross symbolized the hand of God. The artist did not try to make the mosaics resemble the physical reality; instead, their flatness tells a spiritual story without making reference to the earthly world.

▲ This mosaic from the church of San Apollinaire in Italy was created in the 500s. It shows Apollinaris, the patron saint of the church.

Religion was also the force behind Byzantium's remarkable architectural advances. Early in the Byzantine period, architects learned to build churches by placing a round dome over a square foundation. They did this by resting the dome on corner supports, instead of walls. The most spectacular example of this style is the Church of Hagia Sophia. Byzantine architecture would later influence architects across Europe and Asia.

Byzantine Christianity

Together with the monarchy, Christianity was the other great pillar of Byzantine society. The church was as hierarchical as the state. Seen as Christ's representative on Earth, the emperor had special responsibility for both civil and religious law. As Justinian wrote in the *Corpus juris civilis*: "If we make every effort to enforce civil laws, how much more should we not try to enforce the . . . divine laws designed for the salvation of our souls?"

The Orthodox Church. Although the emperor oversaw church law, he did not govern the church. The leaders of the church were the bishops of the great cities—the pope in Rome and the patriarchs of Constantinople, Alexandria, Antioch, and Jerusalem. These five church leaders were known as the **pentarchy**. In the 600s, however, Arab expansion left only the Roman pope and the patriarch of Constantinople free to govern the church.

While the Byzantines generally acknowledged that the pope had special importance, they did not accept that he had supreme authority over religious matters. Instead, they placed such authority in councils where church officials from the pentarchy would meet and settle major issues. Since there was less contact between Rome and Byzantium after 476, the patriarch of Constantinople became the sole leader of the Orthodox Church—the official Christian church of the Byzantine Empire.

History THROUGH THE ARTS

The Church of Hagia Sophia

Nothing displays the splendor of Constantinople during the reign of Justinian and Theodora more than the spectacular Church of Hagia Sophia. The church was built for the emperor between 532 and 537 by the architects Anthemius of Tralles and Isidorus of Miletus. The main part of the building is 270 feet long and 240 feet wide. From a great distance, the towering dome in the center of the church is clearly visible. Four minarets, tall towers from which people were called to prayer, were added to the structure after Constantinople fell to the Turks in 1453. As one nears the church, the outside seems somewhat plain and undecorated, but upon entering the central cathedral, the true beauty of the building becomes obvious. Over the centuries, visitors to the church have remarked on how it is flooded with light. The 40 windows around the central dome make it appear that the dome is floating on a cushion of light. A historian in Justinian's time described the scene: "One would declare that the place were not illuminated from the outside by the sun, but that the radiance originated from within, such is the abundance of light which is shed about the shrine."

The greatest contribution of Hagia Sophia to the development of architecture is through its use of giant stone supports, called pendentives, four of which hold up the entire great dome. The pendentives support all the weight of the dome; no columns or extra walls are needed. This means that the interior of the church can remain much more open than in earlier churches. This new architectural design was a great advance in church-building by the architects. In its own time and still today, the Church of Hagia Sophia remains one of the world's greatest architectural masterpieces.

The Church of Hagia Sophia

Thinking About Art

What was new and different about the design of the Church of Hagia Sophia?

The iconoclast movement. In the 700s a major religious controversy threatened the strength of both church and state. For many years in the eastern provinces, a strong movement against the worship of icons, or sacred images, had been growing. Some Christians objected to the practice because they believed that worshipping icons was idolatry and too close to paganism. This reaction against the use of icons was called the **iconoclast movement**.

Leo III believed that as emperor, he had the duty to prevent all Byzantines from harmful beliefs and practices. He also believed that icon-worship was a relic of paganism. He ordered the destruction of icons, beginning with the icon of Christ at the entrance to the imperial palace. This sparked a riot because many people opposed the iconoclast movement.

The iconoclast movement was also unpopular within the church hierarchy. Church officials found images useful for teaching people about Christianity. In response to an earlier controversy over icons, Pope Gregory I had written, "To adore a picture is one thing, but to learn through the story of the picture what is to be adored, is another." Saint John of Damascus believed that to reject Christ's icons was to reject the core Christian concept of Jesus as the physical form of God: "If you do not worship the image neither do you cherish the Son of God who is the living image of the invisible God."

The iconoclast movement raged on and off for a century, until the meeting of the Council of Orthodoxy ended the controversy by accepting icons in 843. However, the years of conflict had heightened tensions between Constantinople and Rome.

As time went on the churches in Rome and Constantinople grew farther apart. The language, culture, and doctrine of the western and eastern churches differed, and in 1054 the church divided in two—the Roman Catholic Church in the west, and the Orthodox Church in the east. This break was called a **schism** (SI-zuhm) and resulted at first in the increased authority of the Byzantine emperor in the east. In later years, however, this schism would prove dangerous to the Byzantine Empire, which could never again rely on western help against invaders.

With the emperor and the church as the two pillars of the Byzantine state, society was strongly hierarchical in nature.

The Macedonian Era

By the 800s the Byzantine Empire had endured a century of devastating wars, religious upheavals, and great territorial losses. The iconoclast controversy increasingly became a fierce struggle between the western, Latin-speaking and eastern, Greek-speaking parts of the old Roman Empire. In the process the high culture of Byzantium became more uniformly Greek. In addition, anxious to regain the security of the past, Byzantine scholars started to emphasize the collection of traditional knowledge rather than the creation of new works.

▶ **This golden Byzantine goblet was made in the 700s. The figure is a symbol of Rome.**

The Metropolitan Museum of Art, Gift of J. Pierpont Morgan, 1917.

Changes in society. In many cities, the style of classical urban life was also increasingly difficult to maintain against a background of war and insecurity. From the late 500s on, towns declined in size or were abandoned as people sought refuge on fortified hills and turned from trade to agriculture for their survival. This only increased the importance of Constantinople, the remaining great city, as the center of the empire. Struggling to maintain control, the emperor and the court aristocracy became even more hierarchical.

These changes coincided with the reign of the Macedonian dynasty of emperors, who ruled from 867 to 1056. The Macedonian period was in some ways the golden age of Byzantine history. The Macedonian emperors gradually improved the conditions of the peasantry. The emperors also increased imperial authority over the church and enhanced the importance of the monarchy through even more elaborate court rituals and etiquette. They established a law school to train officials in the art of government. They also recovered parts of Syria from the Arabs and annexed the Bulgarian kingdom to the north.

Instability in the empire. In the 1000s, however, the Macedonian dynasty began to decline. A series of incompetent emperors came and went, while invaders pressed against the weakening defenses of the diminished Byzantine Empire. Military leaders and aristocrats, who had been struggling against the power of the central government, gained the upper hand. They forced emperors to abdicate, demanded that empresses marry certain men, and often dictated policy.

BIOGRAPHY This era of instability created an opportunity for one woman to achieve a measure of political power. The empress Zoe gained access to power by placing three husbands on the throne. Born in 980, Zoe was the talented and strong-willed daughter of Emperor Constantine VIII. She married the nobleman Romanus Argyrus at her father's insistence. After her father's death, Romanus, who had no talent for leadership, became emperor. His legitimacy as emperor

PERSIA, BYZANTIUM, AND THE RISE OF RUSSIA **235**

was based only on his marriage to Zoe. Their marriage continued until 1034, when Romanus was found murdered in his bath, probably the victim of a plot by Zoe and a handsome young courtier named Michael, whom she married that same evening.

Michael then became Emperor Michael IV, but he tried to keep Zoe out of state affairs. He had her watched by spies so that he would not wind up meeting the same fate as Romanus. Michael soon became fatally ill, however, so he forced Zoe to adopt his nephew and make him Emperor Michael V. After Michael IV's death, Zoe and Michael V were to rule jointly.

However, Michael V wanted to control the empire alone and attempted to banish Zoe to a convent. The people of Constantinople refused to accept such actions and rose in rebellion and deposed Michael V. With Michael V no longer in control of state affairs, Zoe and her sister Theodora became joint empresses. Byzantine historian Michael Constantine Psellus praised the general success of the empresses:

Empress Zoe

BIOGRAPHY

66 *Both the civilian population and the military caste were working in harmony under empresses, and more obedient to them than to any proud overlord issuing arrogant commands. In fact, I doubt if any other family was ever so favoured by God as theirs was— a surprising thing, when one reflects on the unlawful manner in which the family fortune was, so to speak, rooted and planted in the ground with murder and bloodshed.* 99

Eventually, Zoe married a third time. Until her death in 1050, Zoe continued to rule with her husband, Constantine IX, and Theodora. Their court was one of intellectual brilliance, but neither they nor their successors could save the empire from decline.

Continuing strife between the military aristocracy and the central government weakened the empire, making it vulnerable to challengers from the outside. In 1071 Turkish warriors defeated the Byzantine army at Manzikert in Armenia, permanently destroying the strength of the Byzantines in Asia Minor.

After the challenges of the 700s, under the Macedonian dynasty Greek cultural elements fully overtook Latin elements in the Byzantine Empire.

SECTION 2 REVIEW

IDENTIFY and explain the significance of the following:
Justinian
Theodora
theme system
Corpus juris civilis
gynaeceum
mosaics
pentarchy
iconoclast movement
schism
Zoe

LOCATE and explain the importance of the following:
Constantinople
Bosporus

1. **Main Idea** Why did Byzantine emperors abandon their dream of restoring the old Roman Empire?
2. **Main Idea** How did Byzantine society and culture change under the rule of the Macedonian dynasty?
3. **Social Relations** What were the most important elements of Byzantine society, and what was the result of their influence?
4. **Writing to Explain** In a short essay, explain the role of aristocratic women in Byzantine society. Be

sure to include their access to education, their role in the government of the empire, and their access to power.
5. **Synthesizing** Was the dream of Byzantine emperors to restore the Roman Empire a reasonable dream? In your answer, consider the following: (a) the regional political climate; (b) the development of Byzantine and Roman Christianity; and (c) the cost of reconquering territory lost to invaders.

The Rise of Russia

After Sassanid Persia had fallen and Byzantium had entered the golden age of the Macedonian era, a people known as the Rus began building a powerful new state based in the city of Kiev in the Ukraine. Heavily influenced by Byzantium—particularly in religious matters—Kievan leaders established cultural and political patterns that would have an enormous effect on later Russian history.

Use of Greek Fire to repel a Rus attack on Constantinople in the 900s

Origins of the Rus

The Rus (RUHS) were one of the most important peoples that the Byzantines encountered. The Rus first appear in the historical record in 860, when they launched a fierce naval attack against Constantinople. The Rus attackers appeared suddenly from the north with a fleet of 200 vessels, striking Constantinople when the Byzantine army and fleet were away on another campaign. Photius, the patriarch of Constantinople at the time, described the ferocity of the attack:

> 66 [T]he unexpectedness of the incursion [attack] and its extraordinary speed, the mercilessness of the barbarous race and the harshness of their temper and the savagery of their habits, prove that this blow has been sent from heaven like a thunderbolt. 99

However, the Rus were unable to pierce the city's walls and eventually withdrew.

Who were these Rus, after whom the Russian nation would eventually be named? Some historians believe the Rus were Scandinavian and that their attack on Constantinople was yet another example of the Viking raids that devastated much of Europe and the Mediterranean world during the 800s. Other scholars have rejected this theory, believing that the Rus were a Slavic people.

The *Russian Primary Chronicle*, a historical record, described how the Rus came to rule Russia. The peoples living along the Dnieper (NEE-puhr) River supposedly told the Rus:

> 66 'Our whole land is great and rich, but there is no order in it. Come to rule and reign over us!' They thus selected three brothers, with their kinsfolk, who took with them all the Russes and migrated. 99

In 862 the oldest of the three brothers, Rurik, seized control of Novgorod, an important trading center. A few years later, Rurik's successor, Oleg, took command of the Rus, seized Kiev, and began uniting Slavic tribes into a confederation.

During the 800s the Rus established themselves as rulers of the peoples along the Dnieper River and a confederation of Slavic tribes.

⬚ Kievan Russia

The Rus confederation grew rapidly in size and power. Oleg forced or persuaded a number of Slavic tribes to recognize the authority of the Rus, and he gathered enough support from them to successfully battle the Byzantines. Legend claims that Oleg nailed his shield to the gates of Constantinople as a sign of victory. While Russian claims of Oleg's victories may be exaggerated, he was successful enough against the Byzantines to secure a very advantageous trade treaty in 911.

Oleg's successor, Igor, campaigned against nomadic steppe-peoples, whose persistent raids continually threatened the young Kievan state. Igor died in battle in 945, and his wife, Olga, ruled Kievan Russia for 17 years until their son Svyatoslav (SVYAH-tuh-sluhf) was old enough to rule. Olga was the first female ruler of Russia and after her death became the first Russian saint of the Orthodox Church.

Russian-Byzantine relations. Svyatoslav was Kievan Russia's first great empire-builder, extending Russian control from the Volga River to the Danube by defeating the Volga Bulgars and the ferocious Khazars to the east. Then, after forming an alliance with the Byzantines, he attacked the Danubian Bulgars to the west.

The alliance went sour, however, when Svyatoslav turned his armies against the Byzantine Empire. The Byzantine emperor John Tzimisces crushed the Russian invasion in 969 and extracted a peace treaty from Svyatoslav

Kievan Russia, 860–1240

Kievan Russia at the death of Yaroslav, 1054
Byzantine Empire, c. 1045
Trade route

Trade in Russia Trade routes spanned the length of Kievan Russia, from the icy Baltic Sea to the shores of the Black Sea. Thriving cities grew up along these busy routes.

? Movement What geographic features did the Kievan trade routes follow?

in 971. Svyatoslav was forced to give up the Balkans and the Crimea. On his way back to Kiev, Svyatoslav died at the hands of the Pechenegs.

Conflicts between Kievan Russia and the Byzantine Empire proved that Byzantium was by far the superior power. At the same time, the Byzantines wisely perceived that there was much to be gained from trying to cooperate with the Russians. Trade was beneficial to both peoples, and they had common enemies, such as the Bulgars and Pechenegs. By forming alliances, they could build trade and defeat their enemies. The Byzantines permitted Russians to serve in the Byzantine army. Some Russians even joined the elite Varangian [Scandinavian] Guard, the Byzantine emperor's bodyguard corps.

Religion. The most critical factor drawing Kievan Russia and Byzantium together was religion. The Byzantines believed that if Kievan Russia joined the Christian "family of kings," Russia would be a less hostile neighbor. Although Christian traders had brought their faith to Kievan Russia by the 800s, little Christian activity took place until the next century, when Olga, Svyatoslav's mother, converted to Christianity in a ceremony in Constantinople.

However, Christianity did not become the state religion of Kievan Russia until the reign of Vladimir I. Vladimir accepted Orthodox Christianity prior to his marriage to the Byzantine princess, Anna, in the late 980s. Vladimir supposedly had considered converting to Judaism or Roman Catholic Christianity but found the rituals and ideas of Orthodox Christianity more appealing. With Vladimir's conversion, the Kievan state was firmly connected to the Orthodox Church under the guidance of the patriarch of Constantinople. For this decision, the church viewed Vladimir as a saint and "the equal of the Apostles." Vladimir and his wife Anna devoted

the rest of their lives to building churches, including the beautiful Cathedral of the Tithes.

Vladimir's acceptance of the Orthodox Church rather than the Roman Catholic Church would greatly affect later Russian history. Unlike the Roman Catholic Church, the Orthodox Church in Russia used local languages, which helped bring religion closer to the common people. It also began building a national culture and strengthened Russian ties with the Byzantine Empire.

Byzantine influence. Orthodox Christianity brought a strong Byzantine influence to the culture of Kievan Russia, particularly during the reign of Yaroslav the Wise in the early 1000s. Yaroslav built the Kievan state to its greatest size, stretching from the Baltic to the Black Sea and from the Carpathian Mountains to the mouth of the Oka River. Yaroslav arranged diplomatic marriages between his daughters and kings of France, Hungary, and Norway, and he welcomed exiled rulers and princes from all over Europe.

However, Yaroslav is best known for his work inside Kievan Russia. He ordered the construction of spectacular new churches, notably the Cathedral of Saint Sophia in Kiev, which was inspired by the example of Hagia Sophia. He also founded monasteries, including the famous Cave Monastery near Kiev.

Two Byzantine missionaries, Cyril and Methodius, had vastly improved scholarship among the Slavs by devising a written language based on the Cyrillic script in the 800s. The church provided scholars with their education and most literature was religious, so scholars, with Yaroslav's support, focused on translating religious texts from Greek into the Slavonic language used by the church.

Yaroslav's support of Kievan culture made his reign the cultural high point of Kievan Russia. Drawing from Byzantine culture, Yaroslav promoted art, architecture, and learning. Russian culture, however, began to develop separately from that of western

▲ Before his death Yaroslav the Wise divided his kingdom among his sons and told them how to rule it. They ignored his advice, however, and civil war resulted.

WRITING A SUMMARY
See essential points in
the text.

REVIEWING TERMS
1. theme system
2. egalitarianism
3. *Corpus juris civilis*
4. pentarchy
5. schism

**REVIEWING
CHRONOLOGY**
2, 5, 4, 1, 3

**UNDERSTANDING
THE MAIN IDEA**
1. The Persians defeated
local rulers and seized
control of huge territories
before conquering the
Parthians. Later, they
enacted many reforms,
which strengthened the
empire.
2. The emperor and the
Orthodox Christian
Church were the pillars
of Byzantine society.
3. The cost of fighting
against near-constant
invasions in the western
part of the old Roman
Empire made it too
expensive for the
Byzantines to hold onto
their dream of reuniting
the old empire.
4. Changing trade routes,
internal rivalries, and
external invasions con-
tributed to the decline
of Kievan Russia.
5. At the top of Sassanid
society was the semi-
divine king. Beneath him
was the aristocracy, while
the ordinary people were
beneath the aristocracy.
6. The Sassanid Empire
declined because of prob-
lems in the army and aristocracy, financial strains,
internal strife, and fre-
quent changes in rulers.

Europe, largely because of the cultural split between Byzantium and the West.

Influenced by Byzantium, the Kievan state adopted Orthodox Christianity and many elements of Byzantine culture.

Decline of Kievan Russia

After Yaroslav died in 1054, Kievan Russia began a slow decline. For several years after his death, Yaroslav's sons battled for control. Exhausted by this civil war, Russian resources were further drained by a group of Turkic invaders known as Polovtsians, who attacked Kievan Russia from the southeast.

Changes in international trade also contributed to the decline of Kievan Russia. Trade between western Europe and Byzantium began to bypass Kiev, as Italian merchants built closer connections between Europe and Asia Minor. In addition, the Russians were unable to protect their trade routes through the steppe to the Black Sea from nomadic raiders.

Regional political instability was another major factor in the decline. Kievan Russia was not an organized bureaucratic state; rather, it was a loose confederation of princely states held together by the skills of talented rulers. This loose political structure led to frequent disputes, which were further complicated by regional rivalries, particularly between the cities of Kiev and Novgorod. Novgorod tended to follow a more independent course since it had its own prince, nobility, and political assembly. Gradually, the political and economic center of Russia began shifting northward from Kiev in the south to Novgorod and eventually the city of Moscow.

However, Kievan Russia had a brief revival during the reign of Vladimir Monomakh, who had played a major role in protecting the state from the raiding Polovtsians before becoming grand prince of Kiev in 1113. Vladimir Monomakh waged relentless military campaigns against the Polovtsians, killing some 200 Polovtsian princes. According to legend, speaking Vladimir's name aloud to Polovtsian children was enough to strike terror in their hearts.

Despite his ruthless reputation among his enemies, at home Vladimir interested himself in social reform, creating legislation to ease the conditions of the poor. He also built the town of Vladimir, which would later become the seat of the grand prince.

Vladimir Monomakh's successors could not maintain the strength of Kievan Russia, and the state fell again into civil war. Its greatest test, however, was against the invading Mongols, a people from central Asia. By 1240 the Mongol armies had swept into Russia and demolished the city of Kiev.

Plagued by changing trade routes, internal rivalries, and external invasions, the Kievan state slowly declined and fell.

SECTION 3 REVIEW

IDENTIFY and explain the significance of the following:
Rurik
Oleg
Olga
Svyatoslav
Vladimir I
Yaroslav the Wise
Vladimir Monomakh

LOCATE and explain the importance of the following:

Dnieper River
Kiev
Volga River
Novgorod
Moscow

1. *Main Idea* Who were the Rus and how did they first establish the Kievan state?
2. *Main Idea* What factors led to the decline and fall of Kievan Russia?

3. *Cross-cultural Interaction* How did Byzantium play an important role in the development of Kievan Russia?
4. *Writing to Explain* In a short essay, explain how and why Kievan Russia converted to Orthodox Christianity.
5. *Synthesizing* Why was Kievan Russia unable to become a stable, long-lasting empire?

Chapter 9

Review

On a separate sheet of paper, complete the following exercises:

WRITING A SUMMARY

Using the essential points in the text, write a brief summary of the chapter.

REVIEWING TERMS

From the following list, choose the term that correctly matches the definition.

pentarchy
iconoclast movement
schism
egalitarianism
theme system
Corpus juris civilis

1. method of organizing the Byzantine Empire into provinces under the command of a military governor
2. the removal of inequalities among people supported by Mazdak
3. the "body of civil law," composed of the Justinianic Code and other law books
4. the pope and the patriarchs of Constantinople, Antioch, Alexandria, and Jerusalem
5. the split between the Roman Catholic Church and the Orthodox Church in 1054

REVIEWING CHRONOLOGY

List the following events in their correct chronological order.

1. Olga rules Kievan Russia until Svyatoslav becomes an adult.
2. Ardashir defeats the Parthian ruler.
3. The Mongols attack Kiev.
4. Emperor Justinian orders compilation of the Justinianic Code.
5. Constantinople is formally dedicated.

UNDERSTANDING THE MAIN IDEA

1. How did the Sassanids build their empire?
2. What were the main foundations of Byzantine society?
3. Why did rulers of the Byzantine Empire ultimately abandon their efforts to restore the old Roman Empire?
4. What factors led to the decline of the Kievan state?
5. How was Sassanid society structured?
6. What were some reasons for the decline of the Sassanid Empire?

THINKING CRITICALLY

1. **Analyzing** Looking at the geography of the Byzantine Empire, why do you think the Byzantines were plagued with the constant threat of invasion?
2. **Comparing** How was the concept of kingship in Kievan Russia comparable to the kingships in Sassanid Persia and in the Byzantine Empire?

Building Your Portfolio

Complete the following activities individually or in groups.

1. **Religion** Imagine that you are a member of the Council of Orthodoxy, which is trying to reach a solution to the iconoclastic controversy that has been raging for nearly a century. You have very strong reasons either to support or oppose the use of icons in the Christian church. Prepare for a debate. You should not only prepare arguments that support your particular point of view but also anticipate the arguments that may arise from the opposing group.

2. **Legends and History** Legends serve a useful purpose in giving people a sense of their own history. Although the details of legends cannot be relied upon as historical fact, they often reflect different interpretations of actual historical events.

   You have been hired to create a legend about Vladimir Monomakh, based on your knowledge of his life. While Russians might have considered Vladimir Monomakh a hero, the Polovtsians would have viewed him quite differently. Your legend should be told from either the Russian or the Polovtsian point of view. You may also wish to illustrate your legend.

THINKING CRITICALLY

1. The Byzantine Empire lay at the intersection of three continents—Europe, Asia, and Africa. Thus, the Byzantines had to guard every frontier at once. In addition, Constantinople was a great trading center. Byzantine enemies hoped to control this important city.
2. Kievan Russia was not an organized bureaucratic state with a monarch at its head. Instead, it was a confederation of princely states, which required cooperation among the regional leaders in order to keep the Kievan state together. In contrast, the rulers of both Sassanid Persia and the Byzantine Empire were emperors who controlled highly organized states. The Sassanid emperors proclaimed their descent from the gods, so their authority was both religious and secular. The Byzantine emperor served as a priest-king. He did not claim descent from the gods, but he was considered to be the deputy of Christ on Earth and his co-ruler. Kievan Russians, on the other hand, linked their religious belief and practice not with their own rulers, but with the Orthodox Christian Church in Constantinople.

Chapter 10

The Islamic World C. A.D. 570–1258

Chapter Planning Guide

	TEXTBOOK	CORE RESOURCES	VISUAL RESOURCES	MULTIMEDIA
Introduction	pp. 242–243	Block Scheduling Handbook: Ch. 10		Videodisc Segment 10 and Viewing Guide: *At the Crossroads*
Lesson 10.1 The Development of Islam	pp. 244–249 Through Others' Eyes: *Sailing to Yemen*, p. 245 Sacred Traditions: *The Qur'an*, p. 248	Reading 10.1: *Religious Conflict in Medina* Writing Project 10: *Writing an Introductory Paragraph*	Geography and History 35: *Southwest Asia* Everyday Life 10: *Nomadic Encampment*	GHRC 10 Reading: *An Introduction to the Qur'an* GHRC 10/Videodiscs: Images—*A Bedouin Encampment; Muslim Traders and Their Camels*
Lesson 10.2 The Expansion of Islam	pp. 250–255 Map: *Expansion of Islam*, p. 251 Then and Now: *The Martyrdom of Husayn*, p. 253	Reading 10.2: *The Role of the Imam in Sunni Islam* Skills Activity 10: *Interpreting a Map*	Geography and History 35: *Southwest Asia*	GHRC 10 Readings: *Jihad and the Expansion of Islam; The Rise of Muslim Civilization* GHRC 10/Videodiscs: Image— *A Muslim Battle Scene;* Map—*Outline Map: Southwest Asia*
Lesson 10.3 The Development of Islamic Civilization	pp. 256–263 Map: *Expansion of Islam*, p. 251 Geography and History: *The World of Arab Geographers*, p. 260	Reading 10.3: *Sufi Storytelling* Geography Activity 10: *The Spread of Islam*	Geography and History 10: *Islam in Spain* Art and History 10: *Stoneware Bowl*	GHRC 10 Readings: *Islamic Law; The Five Pillars of Islam; The Muslim Trading Empire; Ibn Khaldun's Advice to Merchants* GHRC 10/Videodiscs: Images—*Page from an Early Qur'an; A Muslim Illustrated Manuscript; Inside the Mosque at El Azhar University;* Maps—*Major Religions of the World; Muslim Lands in the 1100s; Muslim Trade Routes*
Lesson 10.4 The Coming of the Turks	pp. 264–268 Author's Commentary: *A Dynamic Civilization*, p. 268	Reading 10.4: *Organization of the Saljuq Armies*	Geography and History 34: *Russia and Northern Eurasia*	GHRC 10 Reading: *Muslim Poems from the Golden Age* GHRC 10/Videodiscs: Image— *A Singing Poet from* The Book of Songs
Chapter Investigation and Enrichment	pp. 242–268	Chapter 10 Investigation: *The Islamic Heritage Museum* People in World History 10 Explorations in Daily Life 10		GHRC 10/Videodiscs
Review and Assessment	Section 1 Review, p. 249 Section 2 Review, p. 255 Section 3 Review, p. 263 Section 4 Review, p. 268 Chapter 10 Review, p. 269	Chapter Review Activity 10 Vocabulary Activity 10 Themes Review 10 Section Study Guides 10.1–10.4 Main Idea Activities 10.1–10.4 Daily Quizzes 10.1–10.4 Chapter 10 Test Sheltered English Ch. 10 Test Ch. 10 Test Generator		Audio CDs: Ch. 10 Summary (English and Spanish)

INTRODUCING THE CHAPTER

Textbook pp. 242–243

CHAPTER OVERVIEW

In the 600s Muhammad, a dynamic prophet, proclaimed the tenets of a new religion—Islam. His followers quickly spread their faith across the Arabian peninsula and into Africa and Central Asia. Although the creation of the Abbasid dynasty marked a peak of Muslim power and culture, the large empire became difficult to control. The invasion of Turkish peoples contributed to the empire's decline. The Turks, however, soon adopted Persian culture and carried it with them to new areas.

PRESENTING THEMES

On the chalkboard or on an overhead transparency, write the following open-ended theme questions.

- **GEOGRAPHY** Why might a region with vast geographic diversity and a reliance on trade develop great cultural diversity?
- **RELIGION** What impact might religious values have on a country's culture, politics, and law?
- **CROSS-CULTURAL INTERACTION** What are some ways that a people might spread its beliefs and customs to other regions?

Have students, either individually or in groups, suggest responses to the questions. For the geography question, students might suggest that while geographic features might serve to isolate people from others in a region, an economy based on trade could expose them to distant peoples and their customs. For the religion question, students might suggest that religious values shape ethical codes, which are reflected in law. For the cross-cultural interaction question, students might suggest that missionary activity, trade, and warfare can all spread religious beliefs. Save the responses. Once students have studied the chapter, you may wish to have them complete the Themes Review, then compare the two sets of answers.

USING THE VIDEO

Segment 10: *At the Crossroads*

ENGLISH

Search Chapter 10
Videodisc 1, Side B

SPANISH

Search Chapter 10
Videodisc 1, Side B

Tell students that in this chapter they will examine the rise and spread of Islam. Conclude by showing Segment 10 of the *World History and Cultures Videodiscs*. This segment explores some of the reasons for the rapid expansion of the Islamic faith and empire during this period.

Before showing the segment, ask students to pay attention to the types of things that people exchange at commercial crossroads—trade goods, information, and ideas. To help students grasp the significant points of the segment, have them complete Video Viewing Guide 10.

Key to Ability Levels

All strategies and activities are coded to the following ability levels:

LEVEL 1	**Basic** activities suitable for all students
LEVEL 2	**Average** activities suitable for average to above-average students
LEVEL 3	**Challenging** activities suitable for above-average students
SHELTERED ENGLISH	Activities suitable for students with **Limited English Proficiency**

Additional Resources

BOOKS FOR TEACHERS

Harvey, L. D. *Islamic Spain: 1250 to 1500*. University of Chicago Press, 1990. Details the last centuries of Muslim control.

Lewis, Bernard. *The Arabs in History,* rev. ed. Oxford University Press, 1992. Includes several chapters on Islam.

Watt, Montgomery W. *Early Islam: Collected Articles.* Edinburgh University Press, 1990. Collects the work of a noted scholar on Islamic religion.

BOOKS FOR STUDENTS

Cook, Michael. *Muhammed*. Oxford University Press, 1983. Offers a biography of the founder of Islam.

Hitti, Philip Khuri. *History of the Arabs from the Earliest Times to the Present*. St. Martin's Press, 1970. Provides a comprehensive survey.

Holt, P. M., Ann K. S. Lambton, and Bernard Lewis, eds. *The Cambridge History of Islam.* Cambridge University Press, 1978. Offers a survey.

MULTIMEDIA MATERIALS

Christians, Jews, and Moslems in Medieval Spain. Films for the Humanities. Video, 52 min. Looks at Spain from the 700s to the 1400s.

Islam and the Sciences. Phoenix. Video, 23 min. Examines science in the Islamic world.

The Story of Islam: Faith and Nations. PSA. Video, 120 min. Looks at Islamic history from its beginnings to the modern era.

241B

Lesson 10.1 The Development of Islam

Textbook pp. 244–249

RESOURCES

Pupil's Edition

Through Others' Eyes, p. 245: *Sailing to Yemen*

Sacred Traditions, p. 248: *The Qur'an*

Core Resources

Reading 10.1: *Religious Conflict in Medina*

Visual Resources

Geography and History 35: *Southwest Asia*

Everyday Life 10: *Nomadic Encampment*

Global History Resource Center

Reading: *An Introduction to the Qur'an*

Videodiscs or Global History Resource Center

Image: *A Bedouin Encampment*

Search Frame 796

Image: *Muslim Traders and Their Camels*

Search Frame 804

LESSON FOCUS

How and why did Islam emerge in Arabia during the 600s?

OBJECTIVES

After completing this lesson, students will be able to:

- explain how geographic diversity contributed to cultural diversity in Arabia;
- describe how the growth of towns changed Arab cultural values;
- identify the two earliest messages Muhammad preached;
- describe how Muhammad unified the Arabian Peninsula.

HOOK

Discuss the geography of the Arabian Peninsula. Display Geography and History Transparency 35 and read, or have a student read, the Through Others' Eyes description of Yemen on textbook page 245. Then point out Yemen and Mecca on the map transparency. Remind students that although Mecca and Yemen are both near the coast, their environments are very different. Mecca is in a rocky valley and had to depend on trade—it lies along the intersection of two ancient trade routes. Yemen had fertile soil and water and grew wealthy through agriculture and trade.

Ask: How did geography contribute to the development of a variety of economic and social patterns in Arabia? [Yemen's location and fertile soil led to the growth of agriculture and trade. Because of a good water source, Mecca became an important town along the caravan routes. Most of Arabia was desert and best suited to the bedouins' nomadic life. Relations were uneasy between the bedouins and the townspeople—mostly artisans, merchants, and farming and herding families.]

DEVELOP

Outline the social, political, and economic conditions in Arabia in Muhammad's time. Display Everyday Life Transparency 10 and have students complete the accompanying worksheet. Then ask students to describe details of bedouin life and list them on the chalkboard. [nomadic lifestyle, clan structure, emphasis on loyalty and generosity]

If available, display the electronic media images of bedouins and of the traders. Then ask how these images support what students have read about life in Arabia around the 600s.

Ask: How did Arabian life change as more people moved into towns?

[Students should note that the emphasis on tribal loyalty broke down under economic and political competition.]

Conclude by having students create a Venn diagram showing the similarities and differences between nomadic and town life. You may wish to have students place their diagrams in their portfolios.

PROBE

Examine Muhammad's life and main ideas. Have students read the Sacred Traditions feature on textbook page 248 and discuss the central message of these verses *[that God (Allah) is all-knowing and all-powerful and that he must be revered]*. To provide additional background for this discussion, have students read the Global History Resource Center selection on the Qur'an, which discusses how Muhammad's revelations were recorded for his followers.

Ask: *What were the main cultural and religious influences that shaped Muhammad's ideas about religion? [Students should understand that Muhammad was influenced by the Jewish and Christian ideas of one God.]*

Ask: *What were Muhammad's most important teachings? [that there is only one God and that believers formed a special community of equals]*

CONCLUDE

Identify reasons why Muhammad was successful in spreading his teachings. Ask students general questions about why people might be open to new religious ideas or why they might resist new religious ideas. Note their answers on the chalkboard. Then have students answer these same questions for people in Muhammad's time. *[Students should understand that people who had once counted on tribal loyalties and generosity were now feeling insecure amidst conflicts over wealth and property. Muhammad's teachings offered them a community to belong to in which all members were equals and took care of each other.]*

You may wish to have students complete Core Resources Reading 10.1, then discuss the religious conflict in Medina. Tell students that Muhammad's earliest followers were drawn primarily from Mecca's middle and lower classes. Then ask students why, given Muhammad's message, this is not surprising. *[When discussing the resistance to Muhammad's message of Mecca's merchant rulers, students should understand that many Meccans made their living serving pilgrims who were polytheistic. Thus, they saw Muhammad's teachings as a threat.]*

Next refer students to the Chapter 10 time line on textbook pages 242–243 to find out how long it took Muhammad to gain control of Arabia. Then discuss how he could be so successful in so little time. *[He converted many of the bedouins, who helped him unify Mecca and Arabia.]*

EXTEND

Cross-Curricular Connection: *Language Arts*

Have students develop a list of questions they would ask Muhammad in a half-hour interview if they were either a bedouin or a Meccan.

MEET INDIVIDUAL NEEDS

Interpersonal Learners

Have students work in pairs to review the information in the chapter. Have one student rephrase a chapter subheading as a question and the other student answer it in several sentences. Then have students switch roles, and continue in this manner until they have mastered the content of this section.

Students Acquiring English

Pair new speakers of English with fluent speakers to help them learn unfamiliar vocabulary terms such as *peninsula, irrigation, resin, incense, diversity, merciless, oasis, clan, paternalistic,* and *polytheists.*

ASSESS

Review

Have students complete the Section 1 Review. Use answers in the Teacher's Edition, page 249, to assess student mastery of this section.

Lesson 10.2 The Expansion of Islam

Textbook pp. 250–255

RESOURCES

Pupil's Edition

Map, p. 251: *Expansion of Islam, 632–750*

Then and Now, p. 253: *The Martyrdom of Husayn*

Core Resources

Reading 10.2: *The Role of the Imam in Sunni Islam*

Visual Resources

Geography and History 35: *Southwest Asia*

Global History Resource Center

Reading: *Jihad and the Expansion of Islam*

Reading: *The Rise of Muslim Civilization*

Videodiscs or Global History Resource Center

Image: *A Muslim Battle Scene*

Search Frame 805

Map: *Outline Map: Southwest Asia*

Search Frame 1099

LESSON FOCUS

How and why did Islam expand beyond the borders of Arabia following the death of Muhammad?

OBJECTIVES

After completing this lesson, students will be able to:

- explain how the leaders of the Muslim community resolved the problems they faced after Muhammad's death;
- explain the causes and consequences of Islamic expansion;
- outline the reasons for and effects of divisions within Islam;
- describe why the Abbasid Empire can be considered less "Arab" and more "Muslim" than the Umayyad Empire.

HOOK: Link to Today

Discuss the problems Muhammad's followers faced after his death. Ask students who would take over if the president of the United States died suddenly. Then ask why this provision is spelled out in the U.S. Constitution. Have students contrast this established procedure for succession with what happened after Muhammad died.

Ask: *Why did Muhammad's death lead to a crisis among his followers?*

[Muhammad governed as both a spiritual and political

leader. Because he did not name a successor, his followers had to choose a successor based on political as well as religious considerations. For this reason, factions emerged, each supporting its own candidate.]

Ask: *What were the religious issues at stake? the political issues?*

[Muhammad's religious leadership was based on his stature as a prophet of God; his political leadership depended in part on the personal loyalty of bedouin tribes. Without another prophet and without the desert tribes, the new Islamic state faced the danger of collapse. These religious and political issues set the stage for both expansion of and divisions within Islam for centuries to come.]

DEVELOP

Identify the causes and consequences of Islamic expansion. Ask students who succeeded Muhammad and how the new leader resolved Arabia's religious and political problems. *[Abu Bakr became caliph or "deputy" of the Prophet. He conquered bedouin tribes and in so doing built up the armies of Islam.]*

If available, show and discuss the electronic media image of the Muslim battle scene.

241E

Ask: Why did Abu Bakr follow a course of military expansion? [Help students see how conquering neighboring lands not only expanded Arab territory but also kept tribes from fighting each other and from contesting Abu Bakr's rule.]

For additional background information, students might also complete the readings on the expansion of Islam and on Muslim civilization in the Global History Resource Center.

You may wish to have the class work individually or in small groups to create annotated time lines of Islamic expansion from Muhammad through the Umayyad dynasty. When students have finished making their time lines, call on volunteers to contribute to a master time line on the chalkboard. As you review each leader, have students locate this period of expansion on the map on page 251 of their textbook. After discussing the time lines, students may wish to save them for their portfolios.

PROBE

Examine the development of divisions within Islam.

Using the textbook discussion as a reference, have students outline the issues and events that led to the split between Sunnis and Shi'ahs. You may also wish to have students complete Core Resources Reading 10.2 at this time. [Sunnis supported Mu'awiya to succeed Muhammad, while Shi'ahs supported 'Ali as the only true heir of the Prophet because he was a blood relation.]

Tell students that this split in the Islamic world continues to affect international relations. Shi'ahs, led by the Ayatollah Khomeini, overthrew the Shah of Iran in 1979, set up a government based on Shi'ah principles, then entered into a long war with Sunni-led Iraq. The Then and Now feature on textbook page 253 will help students understand the connection between Khomeini and the followers of 'Ali.

CONCLUDE

Contrast the Umayyad and Abbasid Empires.
Have students consider why the Abbasids can be considered less "Arab" and more "Islamic" than the Umayyads. To help students formulate an answer, discuss why non-Arab converts to Islam were unhappy with their second-class status and why Shi'ahs did not like Umayyad rule. Point out how these dissatisfactions helped Arab opponents of the Umayyads build support to overthrow the dynasty.

Draw a two-column chart on the chalkboard with the headings *Umayyads* and *Abbasids*. Have students suggest traits that define the Umayyads as Arab and the Abbasids as Muslim and list these under the appropriate headings. [Students should note the Umayyads' efforts to keep their Arab identity and the Abbasids' efforts to gain support from all members of the community, turning the religion into a universal faith that attracted people of many cultures.]

Conclude by asking the Lesson Focus question at the beginning of this lesson. Students may use the map on textbook page 251 to help them answer this question. Then ask them to compare and contrast the Islamic community at the time of Muhammad's death and at the rise of the Abbasids.

EXTEND

Other Media
You may wish to show and discuss the video on Islam from the Holt, Rinehart and Winston *Religions of the World* series.

MEET INDIVIDUAL NEEDS

Students Having Difficulty
Students needing extra help may benefit from creating a flowchart showing the succession of Islamic leaders. Students should annotate their flowcharts with major accomplishments of each leader.

Visual-Spatial Learners
Have students print the Global History Resource Center outline map or project Geography and History Transparency 35 on a large piece of butcher paper and trace the outline of Southwest Asia. Then have students label Mecca, Medina, and the areas and dates of conquest described in this section.

ASSESS

Review
Have students complete the Section 2 Review. Use answers in the Teacher's Edition, page 255, to assess student mastery of this section.

The Development of Islamic Civilization

Textbook pp. 256–263

RESOURCES

Pupil's Edition

Map, p. 251: *Expansion of Islam, 632–750*

Geography and History, p. 260: *The World of Arab Geographers*

Core Resources

Reading 10.3: *Sufi Storytelling*

Geography Activity 10: *The Spread of Islam*

Visual Resources

Art and History 10: *Stoneware Bowl*

Geography and History 10: *Islam in Spain*

Global History Resource Center

Reading: *Islamic Law*

Reading: *The Five Pillars of Islam*

Reading: *The Muslim Trading Empire*

Reading: *Ibn Khaldun's Advice to Merchants*

Videodiscs or Global History Resource Center

Map: *Major Religions of the World*

Search Frame 808

Map: *Muslim Lands in the 1100s*

Search Frame 806

Image: *Page from an Early Qur'an*

Search Frame 797

Image: *A Muslim Illustrated Manuscript*

Search Frame 798

Image: *Inside the Mosque at El Azhar University*

Search Frame 801

Map: *Muslim Trade Routes*

Search Frame 807

LESSON FOCUS

How and why did Islamic civilization flourish between the 700s and 1200s?

OBJECTIVES

After completing this lesson, students will be able to:

- explain how Islamic religion and law changed after Muhammad's death;
- describe the influence of cross-cultural contacts in Islamic culture;
- explain what role trade played in the expansion of Islam under the Abbasids.

HOOK: Link to Today

Discuss Islam's place in the world today. Display the electronic media map showing world religions and have students contrast the areas of Islamic dominance today with the areas of expansion shown on the textbook map on page 251 and with the electronic media map of Muslim lands in the 1100s. Students should see that Islam's early expansion has continued into Africa, Asia, and Southeast Asia today. Tell students that Muslims number more than 971 million worldwide, almost four times the population of the United States. To emphasize this point, you may also wish to have students complete Geography Activity 10 on Islam in Southeast Asia.

DEVELOP

Examine changes in Islamic law and religion that occurred after Muhammad's death. Begin by having students read the Global History Resource Center selection on Islamic law and the selection on the Five Pillars of Islam. **Ask: What were the most important duties expected of Muslims?**

[those that Muhammad practiced, which were specified in the Qur'an and became known as the Five Pillars of Islam,

along with the so-called sixth pillar, the struggle for the faith, or jihad]

Ask: **What concerns led to the development of the shari'ah?**
[Students should understand that concern for salvation led to the creation of the shari'ah, *or the Muslim legal system, to guide personal conduct.]*

Ask: **What other questions concerned Muslim scholars?**
[the status of the Qur'an—it came to be accepted as the literal, divine word of God; the place of free will and how much weight should be given to human reason to solve problems not covered by the Qur'an and the sayings and deeds of Muhammad, which in turn led to the emergence of four major schools of Islamic legal interpretation]

PROBE

Examine the flowering of Muslim culture under the Abbasids and Spanish Umayyads. To help orient students you may wish to show Geography and History Transparency 10 of Islam in Spain and Art and History Transparency 10 and have students complete the accompanying worksheets. Next have students complete Core Resources Reading 10.3 on Sufi stories, and display the electronic media images of the Qur'an page, the illustrated manuscript, and the mosque. Then discuss the reasons why the arts and learning flourished in the Muslim world under Abbasid and Spanish Umayyad rule, and also discuss the influence of Greek and Indian learning on Muslim thinkers.

Have students, either individually or in groups, create graphic organizers on chart paper to identify Abbasid and Spanish Umayyad achievements in science, geography, literature, art, and architecture, and their cross-cultural influences. For example, the graphic organizer for science should include mathematical advances such as the adoption of the Indian number system, the development of algebra, and the publication of al-Khwarizmi's textbook, as well as advances in astronomy and medicine. Have students share graphic organizers with the class.

CONCLUDE

Explore the role of trade in Islamic expansion. To provide additional background you may wish to have students complete the Global History Resource Center readings on the trading empire and on advice to merchants. Discuss with students how Abbasids used trade to extend their influence, in contrast to Umayyad military expansion. Next display the electronic media map and ask students to use this map of Islamic trade routes and the information in their textbook to explain how the Muslim empire became the heart of a trade network linking three continents. List key responses on the chalkboard and have students copy them in their notebooks for later review. *[Students should note such evidence as the importance of Baghdad as a trading center, the establishment of trading colonies as far away as China, the role of merchants in spreading Islam, the development of Swahili, the use of Abbasid currency as the standard for other currencies, the development of banks and lending policies, and the various trade goods exchanged.]*

EXTEND

Cross-Curricular Connection: *Science and Learning*
Have interested students research the work of Muslim scholars. They may report on Ibn Sina's (also known as Avicenna) contributions to medical science, geology, and zoology; al-Khwarizmi's mathematics textbook; or al-Razi's smallpox treatments.

MEET INDIVIDUAL NEEDS

Gifted Students
Travelers' reports contributed to the knowledge of geography. Have interested students research and report to the class on one of the geographers mentioned in the Geography and History feature. Other students might report on the description of Baghdad given by the traveler Ibn Jubayr.

Musical-Rhythmic Learners
Have interested students research Arabic music and bring in selections to play for the class. Students should explain the significance of each musical selection and describe the instruments used.

ASSESS

Review
Have students complete the Section 3 Review. Use answers in the Teacher's Edition, page 263, to assess student mastery of this section.

Lesson 10.4   *The Coming of the Turks*

Textbook pp. 264–268

RESOURCES

Pupil's Edition

Author's Commentary, p. 268: *A Dynamic Civilization*

Core Resources

Reading 10.4: *Organization of the Saljuq Armies*

Videodiscs or Global History Resource Center

Image: *A Singing Poet from* The Book of Songs

Search Frame 803

Visual Resources

Geography and History 34: *Russia and Northern Eurasia*

Global History Resource Center

Reading: *Muslim Poems from the Golden Age*

LESSON FOCUS

How did the rise of the Turks affect the Islamic world?

OBJECTIVES

After completing this lesson, students will be able to:

- identify the factors that led to the decline of the Abbasids;
- describe the effects of Turkish rule on Muslim political and religious institutions;
- analyze how the Turks affected Muslim cultural development.

HOOK

Identify the Turks and their origins. Project Geography and History Transparency 34 and help students locate the Central Asian steppes. Explain, if necessary, that steppes are flat, cold, arid grasslands. Make and distribute copies of the electronic media outline map of Russia and Northern Eurasia. Have students color in their idea of the Turkish homelands, based on the extent of the steppes and factors that would have checked the spread of pastoral nomads—mountains (Himalayas, Caucasus); water (Oxus, or Amu Darya, River, Caspian Sea); and "civilized" powers (China, Muslim Empire). Finished maps should show a band of Turkish power running east/west along

the borders of the Muslim world, north of Persia and Afghanistan, between the Caspian Sea and China.

Tell students that while the Turks were ultimately to preside over a new flowering of Muslim civilization, they first entered the Muslim world as mamluks, or military slaves. Either captured or purchased while young, they were brought back from Central Asia to be converted to Islam, educated, and trained for the armies. Later, independent Turkish tribes moved into the empire.

DEVELOP

Describe the consequences of the Turkish encounter with the Islamic world. Divide the class into Turks and non-Turks. Then divide the Turks into two groups, Ghaznavids and Saljuqs. Split the non-Turks into Samanids and Abbasids. Let each group prepare a brief description of who they are and how they lost and gained power around the 900s. [The four statements combined should reveal that the Persian Samanids, while declaring their allegiance to the Abbasids, ruled independently; they came to depend on Turkish mamluks and were supplanted by them under the Ghaznavids. The Arab Abbasids faced internal divisions and external challenges; the viziers used their positions to their own advantage and *provincial governors became virtually independent; they used mamluks to combat Shi'ah rebels, but ended up being dominated by the mamluks, then dominated by the Buyids; the Turkish Saljuqs who offered military assistance to the Ghaznavids and Samanids eventually came to dominate both of them and rule a vast territory. Saljuq expansion was ended by outside forces—European Christians and Central Asian nomads, who captured Baghdad in 1258 and ended the caliphate.]* Students may find it helpful to diagram this chain of events on the chalkboard.

You may wish to have students complete Core Resources Reading 10.4 to add to their understanding of Saljuq army organization, and then have them add the Ghaznavid and Saljuq empires in new colors to their maps.

PROBE

Analyze how Turkish rule affected Muslim political and religious institutions. Reconstitute the two larger groups—Turks and non-Turks—but reverse the arrangement: the Turks are now rulers, the non-Turks subservient subjects. Have the non-Turks present their candid view of their new Turkish rulers: Do the latter have a right to rule? *[Possible answer: "No, only the might to rule—they were recently pagans and our mamluks."]*

Challenge the Turkish group to devise a strategy for winning their subjects over by championing the people's religion. *[Tactics cited should include: labeling oneself deputy of the caliph; campaigning against infidels and rebel sects; supporting religious institutions and popular religious movements.]*

Discuss how Ghaznavid and Saljuq policies reflected these strategies. *[The Ghaznavids raided India; the Saljuqs campaigned against the Byzantines; both built mosques and schools for the study of Sunni law; both promoted the concept of a sultan as a secular partner of the caliph, who remained the spiritual head of Islam; the Saljuqs patronized the Sufi movement.]*

CONCLUDE

Explain cultural developments in the Muslim world in light of militaristic Turkish rule. Assign the Author's Commentary on textbook page 268. You may wish to show the electronic media image from *The Book of Songs* and assign the Muslim poetry from the Global History Resource Center to give students a flavor of the period's literary achievements.

Ask: What were some of the cultural contributions made to the Islamic world under the rule of the Turks? *[Achievements include elegant poetry, such as Firdausi's* Shah-nameh, *written at the Ghaznavid court; Rumi's works, including the* Mathnawi, *written in Saljuq times; al-Ghazali's theological works, through which Sufism was absorbed into the Sunni mainstream of Islam; and Saljuq architectural styles.]*

Ask: How can you explain such cultural developments under the leadership of the warrior Turks? *[Students should recognize that the Turks shed their image of barbarism by patronizing the artistic and cultural traditions of their subjects, and that they particularly encouraged the revival of Persian culture.]*

EXTEND

Cross-Curricular Connection: *Language Arts*
Have students find other works by Muslim writers of this period. Encourage them to "translate the translations" into contemporary language and share the results with the class.

MEET INDIVIDUAL NEEDS

Logical-Mathematical Learners
Have these students diagram the structure of the Muslim world in two eras—800 and 1100—by illustrating graphically the relationships among the following figures: caliph, vizier, sultan, *ulama*, Sunnis, Shi'ahs, and Sufis.

Interpersonal Learners
Suggest that students create and perform a dialogue between a Sufi and a member of the *ulama*, illustrating how they find common ground.

ASSESS

Have students complete the Section 4 Review. Use answers in the Teacher's Edition, pages 267–268, to assess student mastery of this section.

In preparation for the chapter test, you may wish to have students complete all or part of the Chapter 10 Review on textbook page 269, the Chapter 10 Review Activity, and the Chapter 10 Themes Review.

Understanding the Main Idea

Call on a volunteer to read aloud the *Understanding the Main Idea* paragraph. Then tell students that during the 600s Islam unified the Arabian Peninsula. Although Muhammad was originally persecuted, gradually he converted the Arab peoples to Islam. His revelations, along with Islamic law developed by later religious scholars, govern Islamic culture today. Following his death, Muhammad's successors developed a massive Islamic empire. The Islamic religion and the Arabic language spread to parts of Asia, Africa, and Europe by the 700s.

Presenting Themes

See p. 241B for suggestions on introducing themes.

Using the Time Line

Have students list the time line events in their notebooks. After they have read about each event in the chapter, have students write a paragraph explaining its significance.

Chapter 10

The Islamic World
c. 570–1258

Understanding the Main Idea

In the early 600s Islam, a vital new religion, burst out of the Arabian Peninsula and onto the stage of world history. Islam united the nomadic tribes of Arabia and inspired the development of a rich culture. By the 700s the followers of Islam had spread their religion and culture to much of Southwest Asia, North Africa, and parts of Europe.

Themes

- *Geography* Why might a region with vast geographic diversity and a reliance on trade develop great cultural diversity?

- *Religion* What impact might religious values have on a country's culture, politics, and law?

- *Cross-cultural Interaction* What are some ways that a people might spread its beliefs and customs to other regions?

"God is Greatest! I bear witness that there is no deity but the One God! I bear witness that Muhammad (moo-HAHM-muhd) is the Messenger of God! Come to worship! Come to success! God is Greatest! There is no deity but the One God!" Five times a day in countries throughout the world, these words ring out, each line repeated twice, summoning the faithful to pray. Over 1 billion Muslims answer the call worldwide. Muslims are the followers of the prophet Muhammad, an Arab merchant who began to preach a message of religious renewal to the peoples of the Arabian Peninsula in the early 600s. He called his message Islam, which means submission to God. Muhammad taught his followers to worship the One God—*Allah* in Arabic—and to live in harmony as brothers and sisters.

Muhammad converted many Arabs to Islam before he died in 632. After his death, loyal followers spread the Prophet's message of unity and devotion to God beyond Arabia as they created a new empire. In less than 200 years, the Islamic empire stretched from the Atlantic Ocean to the borders of India and China, and from southern Europe to North Africa. Throughout this vast expanse

c. 570	622	632	661
▲ The prophet Muhammad is born.	▲ The *hijrah*—migration to Medina—marks the beginning of the Muslim era.	▲ Muhammad dies and the caliphate begins.	▲ The Umayyad dynasty begins with a new capital at Damascus.

of territory, the unifying force of Islam brought together the cultural achievements of many diverse peoples to create a brilliant new civilization.

Arches in the courtyard of a mosque in Córdoba, Spain

About the Image

The mosque in this photograph is located in Córdoba, Spain. Early Muslims worshipped in Muhammad's house and courtyard in Medina. After his death, Muslims used almost any type of structure as a place to pray, creating the first mosques. The main requirements were that the structure be clean and large enough for a congregation and that it enable the congregation to face in the direction of Mecca to pray. This direction is called the *qiblah*.

Critical Thinking Ask students to look at a map and decide what directions Muslims in Baghdad, Córdoba, Constantinople, Jerusalem, and Cairo would face during prayers.

ANSWER: Students should answer that to face Mecca from Baghdad they would turn southwest, from Córdoba and Cairo they would turn southeast, and from Constantinople and Jerusalem they would turn south.

711 Muslim Arabs and Berbers begin the conquest of Spain.

732 Defeat in the Battle of Tours marks the end of the Arab advance into northern Europe.

750 Revolution ushers in the Abbasid dynasty.

786–809 Under the reign of Caliph Harun al-Rashid, the Abbasid Empire reaches its height.

1258 A nomadic invasion destroys Baghdad and puts an end to the caliphate.

Daily Life

Bedouins camped in tents in groups of related families. The scarcity of rainfall in the desert prevented the nomadic bedouins from staying in one place for more than a few days. By that time, the animals had exhausted the grass supply in the area. In years when rainfall was scarce, tribes often had to travel hundreds of miles to find water and grazing land. Incursions on another tribe's land inevitably led to clashes, which normally took the form of raiding the rival's herds.

Critical Thinking Ask students to suggest how this lifestyle of scarce resources and frequent conflict might affect a culture.

ANSWER: Students might suggest that a culture would probably come to emphasize virtues such as bravery and skill in battle.

The Development of Islam

FOCUS

- How did geographic diversity contribute to cultural diversity in Arabia?
- How did the growth of towns change many Arabs' ways of life?
- What were the two earliest messages that Muhammad preached?
- How did Muhammad unify the cities and tribes of the Arabian Peninsula?

In 610 the prophet Muhammad described receiving a series of revelations that would become the foundation of the Islamic faith. Well known for his holiness and wisdom, Muhammad spread his message throughout Arabia for the remainder of his life. By the time of his death in 632, almost every tribe in the Arabian Peninsula had pledged allegiance to Islam and its Prophet.

Richly ornamented
copper pitcher

Arabia's Geography

The Arabian Peninsula—a vast plain of deserts and small mountains in Southwest Asia—lies across the Red Sea from the northeastern coast of Africa. North to south, it stretches about 1,400 miles—from the Syrian Desert to the Arabian Sea. West to east, it spans about 1,200 miles—from the Red Sea to the Persian Gulf. While the majority of the peninsula is desert, the southwestern corner, known as Yemen, has fertile mountain lands and good ports.

Agriculture and trade in the Southwest. As early as 1400 B.C. people in Yemen created wealthy kingdoms based on agriculture and trade. They built great dams and irrigation networks to grow wheat and other crops. They also extracted tree sap to get frankincense and myrrh (MUHR), resins used for incense. Traders grew rich exporting frankincense, myrrh, cinnamon, and other spices to Africa, Europe, and the rest of Southwest Asia.

Over time the merchants and rulers of Yemen gained control of the sea routes for the profitable spice and silk trade between Asia, India, and the Mediterranean. Yemen's wealth attracted the attention of other kingdoms. At various times Ethiopians, Romans, Persians, and Byzantines invaded Yemen. Through these invasions and trade, the people of Yemen came in contact with new ideas and cultures. From Yemen new ideas spread along the trade routes to the rest of Arabia.

Yemen's agricultural wealth and its location on major trade routes made it a center of cultural diversity.

Oases, towns, and deserts. In much of the rest of the peninsula, the merciless glare of the desert sun and the lack of water prevented people from growing crops. In this harsh environment, most Arabs survived by herding animals. Called **bedouins** (BE-duh-wuhnz), the herders lived in tents and moved from place to place with their sheep, goats, and camels. Since struggles over water rights and livestock were a way of life in the desert, bedouins were mobile, armed, and used to fighting.

Some bedouins settled in oases, shady areas with water sources, where they could grow grain, dates, and other crops. In some oases, particularly along the trade routes, towns sprang up. The

▲ This bedouin farmer tills the soil of an oasis with a camel-drawn plow.

town of Yathrib (YATH-ruhb) in western Arabia, for example, was located in an oasis with fertile soil ideal for growing dates. Farming and herding families lived within the oasis. The merchants and craftsmen who serviced the caravan trade between Yemen and the Mediterranean lived in town with their families.

Eventually, some bedouins came to depend entirely on the caravan trade for their living. South of Yathrib, in a rocky valley about 50 miles from the Red Sea, local bedouins and immigrants from Yemen turned the town of Mecca, or Makkah in Arabic, into a major caravan center. Although Mecca was not in a fertile oasis, it was located near the intersection of two trade routes and controlled the fabled well of Zamzam. It was also the site of an area that many people believed to be sacred. Meccans made a living by supplying the caravan trade and the pilgrims who came to pray at the sacred site. Other important oases and caravan communities developed along the northern borders with Syria and Mesopotamia.

Fear of bedouin raids made relations between the nomadic bedouins and the people of the towns and oases uneasy. Often, however, merchants could guarantee their safety by reaching an agreement with the bedouins. Merchants would pay to travel along bedouin-controlled trade routes and then market their goods in the cities of the Arabian Peninsula.

Bedouins traveled the harsh desert with their herds, while other Arabs built settled communities in fertile oases and along trade routes.

Arab Society and Culture

Bedouin culture deeply influenced the political and social organization of Arabia. Arab society was organized in clans and tribes. The Arabs cherished extended family relationships because people depended on families for survival. "Take for thy brother whom thou wilt in the days of peace," went one Arab verse, "but know that when fighting comes thy kinsman alone is near." Fathers made important decisions within the family and took part in politics. Male clan leaders advised the **sheikh** (SHAYK), the leader of the tribe. But all the men of the tribe regularly came together to make major decisions.

Although men had most of the power in Arab society, women had some freedom. For example, many women could own and inherit property. Women contributed to the group through such

THROUGH OTHERS' EYES

Sailing to Yemen

Greek traders sailed the Red Sea and became familiar with the Arabian Peninsula. The anonymous author of *The Circumnavigation of the Red Sea*, written in the first century A.D., gave the following account of the region:

❝Different tribes inhabit [Arabia]. . . . The land next [to] the sea is . . . dotted here and there with caves of the Fish-Eaters, but the country inland is peopled by rascally men speaking two languages, who live in villages and nomadic camps, by whom those sailing off the middle course are plundered, and those surviving shipwreck are taken for slaves. . . . Navigation is dangerous along this whole coast of Arabia, which is without harbors . . . and terrible in every way. Therefore we hold our course down the middle of the gulf and pass on as fast as possible. . . .

Beyond these places, . . . there is a . . . market town. . . . And the whole place is crowded with ship owners and seafaring men, and is busy with the affairs of commerce.❞

Theme: **Politics and Law**
Because the bedouins had no central government to enforce regulations, their conduct was regulated by unwritten customs. One of these was that when a person committed a murder, he or she began a fight called a blood feud, in which the victim's family had the right to kill the murderer or a member of the murderer's family in retaliation. Blood feuds had no rules, and sometimes innocent bystanders were killed, beginning new feuds. Blood feuds could continue for many years, with a great deal of violence.

Critical Thinking Ask students why a tradition like the blood feud might become part of a society.

ANSWER: Students might suggest that in a society without central authority, people may see no other way to punish murderers.

▲ These Arab women are weaving fabric for rugs, blankets, and other uses. Textiles were traditionally woven of goats' hair.

activities as spinning and weaving. A woman's primary role, however, was that of mother.

Arab values reflected the struggle for survival in a harsh environment. Above all, Arabs prized loyalty, honor, courage, generosity, and hospitality. Leaders displayed loyalty and generosity by holding feasts and giving presents to their followers. For poorer members of society, such generosity in times of want could mean the difference between life and death. Hospitality to guests also was a matter of honor and sacred obligation.

As Arabs settled down in the relative security of towns and oases, they found tightly knit tribal organization less essential for survival. Tribal loyalties began to give way to those of immediate family and clan. The growing wealth and the accumulation of private property that were part of merchant life also caused changes. For instance, families sometimes experienced conflicts over inheritance.

In Mecca, conflict among the different clans of the ruling tribe became particularly intense in the last half of the 500s, as each clan sought to control trade and town government. Such rivalry increased people's sense of insecurity. As they struggled to deal with this insecurity, new ideas began to circulate.

As some Arabs exchanged the harsh environment of the desert for the relative security of towns, their cultural values also began to change.

The Prophet Muhammad

In 613 Muhammad, a member of a relatively poor clan of Mecca's ruling tribe, began to preach a particularly powerful set of new ideas. Muhammad was born in Mecca around 570. His early life was not easy. His merchant father died before he was born, and his mother died when he was six. He was raised by his grandfather and his uncle, Abu Talib (uh-boo tah-LEEB). As a young man, Muhammad became the manager of a caravan business owned by Khadijah (ka-DEE-jah), a wealthy widow. When Muhammad was 25, he married Khadijah, who was 15 years older. They had three sons and four daughters, but they experienced tragedy, as all except one daughter, Fatimah, died young.

Early influences. In his early years Muhammad must have been familiar with the religious traditions of his city. Although some wandering Arab holy men had already begun to preach the existence of only one god, most people in Arabia were polytheists. They worshipped their gods and goddesses at special shrines. One of the most important shrines, the **Ka'bah** (KAH-buh), was in Mecca. Many people journeyed there every year.

As a caravan manager traveling the trade routes, Muhammad probably became familiar with Jewish and Christian ideas. Perhaps around the campfires at night, with the stars shining brilliantly above in the desert sky, Muhammad heard Jewish and Christian merchants telling stories from the Torah and the Gospels. Such experiences may have contributed to his own belief in the existence of only one god.

From the time he was young, Muhammad often escaped the crowded life of Mecca by going to the nearby hills to pray and meditate. One day, when he was about 40 years old, Muhammad went alone

◄ **Many Muslims believe that it is wrong to show images of the prophet Muhammad. This calligraphy, which means "Muhammad is the Prophet of God," is often used in place of a picture.**

▲ The Ka'bah in the Great Mosque of Mecca is a sanctuary for Muslims. It inspires their faith and the worship of God.

To Arabs who worshipped many gods, Muhammad's message was radical. Although called Allah—the name of the most important Arab god—Muhammad's God was the God of Christians and Jews. Muhammad believed that just as God had sent his divine message to humanity through prophets such as Abraham, Moses, and Jesus, he was now sending new revelations through Muhammad.

Muhammad's earliest messages centered on the oneness of God and the special nature of the community of believers who obeyed God's will.

to meditate in a cave among the hills. Suddenly in the silence of the cave, the angel Jibreel (Gabriel in English) spoke to Muhammad. According to Islamic belief, Jibreel the angel commanded him to "Recite! Recite!" When Muhammad asked what he was to recite, Jibreel answered:

66 *Recite: In the name of thy Lord who created, created Man of a blood-clot. Recite: And thy Lord is the Most Generous, who taught by the Pen, taught Man that he knew not.* 99

Muhammad believed that God had spoken to him through the angel Jibreel. Over the next 22 years, Muhammad reported receiving many more revelations. These revelations became the **Qur'an** (kuh-RAN), the holy book of Islam.

Muhammad's message. Muhammad's earliest revelations contained two simple messages. First, there was only one God: "Say God is One; God the Eternal: He did not beget [have children] and is not begotten, and no one is equal to Him." Second, those who accepted God's message had to obey his will. In doing so they formed a special community in which all believers were equal in the sight of God. As equals they were responsible for looking out for each other, particularly for the weak or needy.

The flight from Mecca. As Muhammad preached these revolutionary ideas of social equality and monotheism, the merchant rulers of Mecca became alarmed. Muhammad's claim that all the faithful belonged to a single Islamic community seemed to threaten tribal and clan authority. His rejection of polytheism also seemed a threat to those who profited from the annual pilgrimages to the Ka'bah. The rulers of Mecca soon began to harass the Prophet and his small band of followers.

Meanwhile, however, Muhammad's reputation for both piety (religious devotion) and justice spread beyond Mecca. Nearly 10 years after he had begun preaching in Mecca, a delegation of tribesmen from Yathrib asked him to settle in their city and serve as a kind of arbitrator, or referee, among the feuding tribes of the oasis. With the Meccan leaders growing increasingly hostile, Muhammad accepted the offer in 622. He and many of his followers left Mecca and traveled north to Yathrib. This journey became known in Islamic history as the *hijrah* (hi-JY-ruh)—the flight, or migration.

Muhammad's arrival in Yathrib marked an important milestone in Islamic history. In Yathrib, he governed as both a spiritual and a political leader. Yathrib itself became known as Medina (muh-DEE-nuh), or Al-Madīnah in Arabic,—short for *Madinat al-Nabi*, or "City of the Prophet." Later, Muslims marked the year of the

READINGS IN WORLD HISTORY
(p. 247)
Reading 10.1
Religious Conflict in Medina

Have students read the description of a battle during Muhammad's lifetime. Then have them complete the questions.

Level 1

Understanding Sacred Traditions

God (Allah) is all-knowing and all-powerful, and people must revere him.

REVIEW & ASSESSMENT RESOURCES

- Study Guide 10.1
- Daily Quiz 10.1
- Main Idea Activity 10.1

All Levels

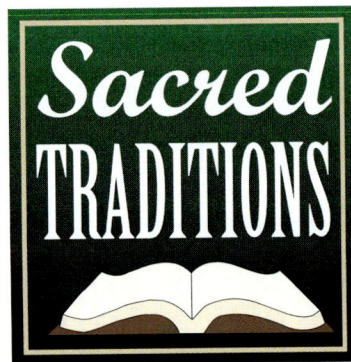

Sacred TRADITIONS

The Qur'an

The Qur'an has a tremendous literary as well as religious significance for the Arabs. It is the first book to be written in Arabic, since none of the earlier Arabic oral literature was collected in written form until the 600s. Muhammad's revelations were originally written down on "smooth stones, leather bits, camel's shoulder [bones], [and] palm leaves" and memorized by his early followers. After Muhammad's death his followers collected these revelations into one book. Muslims consider every word and sura, or chapter, of the Qur'an to be inspired by God.

The Opening

In the Name of God, the
    Merciful, the
    Compassionate
Praise belongs to God, the
    Lord of all Being,
the All-merciful, the All-
    compassionate,
the Master of the Day of Doom.
Thee only we serve; to Thee
    alone we pray for succor
    [aid].
Guide us in the straight path,
the path of those whom Thou

hast blessed,
not of those against whom
    Thou art wrathful,
nor of those who are astray.

Power

In the Name of God, the
    Merciful, the Compassionate
Behold, We sent it down on the
    Night of Power;
And what shall teach thee what
    is the Night of Power?
The Night of Power is better
    than a thousand months;
in it the angels and the spirits
    descend,
by the leave of their Lord, upon
    every command.
Peace it is, till the rising of
    dawn.

The Throne Verse

Allah: There is no deity save
    Him, the Living, the Eternal,
Neither slumber nor sleep
    overtakes him.
To Him belongs whatever is in
    the heavens and whatever is
    on the earth.
Who can intercede with Him
    but by

His leave?
He knows what is in front of
    them and what is behind
    them,
while they encompass of His
    knowledge only what He
    wills.
His throne comprises the
    heavens and the earth,
and He is never weary of
    preserving them.
He is the Sublime [Great], the
    Mighty.

The Light Verse

Allah is the light of the heavens
    and the earth.
The likeness of His light is like
    a niche in which
there is a lamp.
The lamp is in a glass.
The glass is as if it were a
    shining constellation kindled
    from a blessed tree,
an olive tree that is neither
    eastern nor western.
Its oil nearly spends its light
    though no fire has touched it.
Light upon light.
Allah guides to His light
    whomever He wills.
And Allah speaks to mankind in
    parables, for Allah is the
    knower of all things.

Understanding Sacred Traditions

What is the most important message of these verses from the Qur'an?

◀ This copy of the Qur'an from 704 is rich with decorative gold. The elaborate decoration is intended to express the holiness of this text.

▲ **Five times a day around the world, Muslims kneel on their prayer rugs and face the Ka'bah in Mecca to recite the prayers of the Qur'an.**

hijrah as the first year in the Islamic calendar. The move also led to a shift in the character of Muhammad's teaching.

In Medina, Muhammad's revelations began to include rules and principles governing the social, political, and economic organization of the community. In addition, some practices that had seemed similar to Christian and Jewish practices became uniquely Islamic. For example, a new revelation changed the direction Muslims face in prayer from Jerusalem to the Ka'bah in Mecca.

The conversion of Mecca.
As the community at Medina grew stronger, tribes from the desert began to accept Islam. With their help, Muslims raided Meccan caravans. In 630, after several years of warfare, the people of Mecca gave in. They opened the gates of the city to the Prophet and accepted Islam. Muhammad destroyed the pagan idols in the Ka'bah so that Muslims could make the pilgrimage to worship God there as commanded by the revelations. After this victory most of the Arabian tribes acknowledged Muhammad's leadership and the power of Islam. By the time the Prophet died in 632 at his home in Medina, he had laid the groundwork for a new religion that would soon spread far beyond the borders of Arabia.

From his base in Medina, Muhammad converted many bedouins and with their help unified Mecca and the rest of Arabia under Islam.

SECTION 1 REVIEW

IDENTIFY and explain the significance of the following:
  bedouins
  sheikh
  Muhammad
  Ka'bah
  Qur'an
  hijrah

LOCATE and explain the importance of the following (see map on p. 251):
  Arabian Peninsula
  Mecca
  Medina

1. ***Main Idea*** What were the two main messages of Muhammad's earliest revelations?
2. ***Main Idea*** How did Muhammad unify most of the Arabian Peninsula under Islam?
3. ***Geography: Location*** How did Yemen's location contribute to its cultural diversity? How did geographic factors affect where people chose to live in the rest of Arabia?
4. ***Writing to Explain*** Imagine you are a resident of Mecca around A.D. 600. Write a letter to a friend explaining how the growth of towns has affected traditional Arab values.
5. ***Synthesizing*** How and why did Islam emerge in Arabia during the 600s? In answering this question, consider the role played by (a) Arabia's geographic and cultural diversity; (b) trade; (c) the message of Islam; and (d) Muhammad.

Theme: War and Diplomacy

The period of rebellion after the death of Muhammad is known to Arabs as the *Ridda*, which means "apostasy," or the renunciation of religious faith. The *Ridda* began when the majority of the Arabian tribes announed that they were no longer Muslims and would no longer pay the poor tax to Medina. The tribes were brought back to the faith through military force.

Critical Thinking Ask students how the victories of the Islamic forces over the rebelling Arabian tribes marked a defeat for the old bedouin system of social organization.

ANSWER: Students might answer that the rebelling groups were adhering to an older system of loyalty to clans and tribes, while the Islamic forces were unifying Arabia in the name of religion.

SECTION 2
The Expansion of Islam

FOCUS

- How did the leaders of the Muslim community resolve the problems they faced after Muhammad's death?

- What were the causes and consequences of Muslim expansion?

- How and why did divisions occur in Islam?

- Why might the Abbasid Empire be considered less "Arab" and more "Muslim" than the Umayyad Empire?

United under the banner of the Prophet, Muslims spread out from their Arabian homeland after Muhammad's death. Over the next hundred years they carried the Prophet's message of religious renewal into Byzantium, Persia, and parts of Africa, Europe, and India. By the early 700s the Islamic empire stretched from the Atlantic Ocean to the Indus River and from Central Asia to the Arabian Sea.

Engraved eagle from around 1000

The Caliphate

The prophet Muhammad's death created a crisis in the new Muslim community. Many desert tribes had converted to Islam only out of loyalty to Muhammad. His death, they believed, released them from their allegiance. Faced with the potential collapse of the young Muslim state, Muhammad's followers moved quickly to choose the Prophet's successor.

The search for a successor, however, caused rifts among Muhammad's followers. Some preferred Muhammad's cousin 'Ali, who was also married to Muhammad's daughter Fatimah. But the leaders chose Abu Bakr (uh-BOO BAK-uhr), Muhammad's oldest friend and one of his first converts.

The Qur'an stated that Muhammad would be the last prophet. Thus, Abu Bakr and all later leaders of the community were not prophets, but **caliphs** (KAY-luhfs)—"deputies" or "successors"— of the Prophet. The caliphs, or Khalifahs (kah-LEE-fahs), ruled according to the Qur'an and Muhammad's example. Under their rule, religious and political authority were no longer identical. According to a Muslim saying, however, they remained close:

❛*Islam, the government, and the people are like the tent, the pole, the ropes, and the pegs. The tent is Islam; the pole is the government; the ropes and pegs are the people. None will do without the others.*❜

As caliph, Abu Bakr moved quickly to reconvert the bedouin tribes that had broken with Islam. In a series of campaigns over the next year, Abu Bakr brought all of Arabia back under the Prophet's banner. In the process he forged strong new armies under experienced military leaders.

Abu Bakr now needed to discourage the tribes from fighting one another, and to demonstrate the advantage of accepting Islam. As the rebellions in Arabia came to an end, the caliph directed his armies, which included many reconverted bedouins, in campaigns into Iraq and Syria against the Persians and Byzantines.

Muslim leaders settled the crisis over Muhammad's succession by choosing Abu Bakr as caliph. He reunified Arabia under the Prophet's banner.

Islamic Expansion

Weakness in the Persian and Byzantine empires aided Muslim expansion. Both empires were exhausted from years of fighting. By 637, Muslim armies had conquered most of Syria, Iraq, and southern Persia.

Expansion under 'Umar. On his deathbed in 634 Abu Bakr chose 'Umar (oo-mahr), another of Muhammad's closest companions, to succeed him. Under 'Umar, the new Muslim state continued to expand. To build the military strength of the state, 'Umar established a kind of national registry. People on the registry qualified for a share in the wealth of the community when they or members of their families enlisted in the armies. Many Arabs joined the armies to qualify for these new allowances. As a result, Arab armies grew even stronger.

'Umar's policies led to the rapid expansion of the Muslim empire. In 637 an Arab army defeated Persian forces at Kadisiya in southern Iraq. Shortly thereafter the Arabs captured the winter capital of the Persian Empire and with it all of Iraq. Finally, in 642, they delivered a devastating blow—which the Arabs called the Victory of Victories—to the Persians at the Battle of Nehaward.

To the west the great Byzantine armies also proved no match for the highly mobile bedouins. Between 635 and 636 the Byzantine Empire lost Damascus, the capital of Syria, to Arab forces. In 638 Arab forces took Jerusalem. In 639 another Arab army invaded the Byzantine province of Egypt and by 642 Islam had conquered the Nile Valley. In little more than a decade, the Arabs had carved out a vast new empire.

People of the Book. This Muslim expansion represented a movement of the newly united

Map Answer
Tours

Theme: War and Diplomacy
The period of expansion begun under Abu Bakr and continued under 'Umar was not originally intended as an organized series of military campaigns designed to create an empire. The conflicts did not become strategically organized campaigns until the first battles had been successful.

Critical Thinking Ask students what the goals of the early fighting might have been.

ANSWER: Students might answer that the goals of the early battles were to obtain wealth and to keep the tribes from fighting each other.

Expansion of Islam, 632–750

Map Legend:
- Islamic lands at Muhammad's death, 632
- Territory added, 633–661
- Territory added, 662–750
- ☀ Battle site

Robinson Projection

The Muslim Empire Muslim warriors suffered few defeats as they expanded the Muslim empire. Charles Martel, the ruler of the Franks, was one of the few to win a victory over the Muslims.

Location Where did Charles Martel defeat the Muslims in 732?

While 'Uthman was thought by many to be a well-meaning man, he enraged many Arabs by appointing his relatives to important positions. In addition, 'Uthman accepted gifts that his governors and their representatives sent him.

The rebellion against 'Uthman began in al-Kufah among 'Ali's followers and grew in strength in Egypt. Five hundred rebels went to Medina in 656. They stormed 'Uthman's home. Muhammad, the son of Abu Bakr, was the first to break into the residence and attack 'Uthman. 'Uthman was then killed by the rebels.

Critical Thinking Ask students what factor might have compounded the tension caused by 'Uthman appointing his relatives to power.

ANSWER: Students might answer that Uthman's clan, the Umayyads, had once been enemies of Muhammad.

R RESOURCE ACTIVITY

READINGS IN WORLD HISTORY
Reading 10.2
The Role of the Imam in Sunni Islam

Have students read the analysis of Islamic rule. Then have them complete the questions.

Level 2

252

Arabs out of the poverty of Arabia into wealthier civilizations nearby. In these early years Arab armies were more concerned with filling the Islamic treasury than with converting non-Arabs to Islam. In fact, the conversion of conquered peoples was discouraged in some ways.

The Qur'an had given special recognition to Jews, Christians, and other peoples with a written scripture, calling them "People of the Book." Once conquered, they were to be "protected peoples." Thus, although Muslims would accept converts, they generally did not practice forced conversion. Protected peoples paid for the right to retain their religious freedom, however. Whereas Muslims paid the alms for the poor, protected peoples paid a larger tax. However, taxes under the Muslims were in general lighter than they had been under the Persians and Byzantines.

United by Islam, Arab armies swept out of Arabia and threatened the Persian and Byzantine empires.

Divisions Within Islam

In 644 a Persian slave stabbed 'Umar. As he lay dying, the caliph appointed a small group of men to choose his successor. Bypassing 'Ali once again, they decided on 'Uthman (ooth-MAHN), another of Muhammad's earliest converts.

'Uthman was a member of the powerful Umayyad (oom-Y-yuhd) clan. The Umayyads had been among the Prophet's worst enemies in Mecca. They had converted to Islam, but only under pressure. 'Uthman became a tool in the hands of his more ambitious clan members. Soon the old ruling elite of Mecca had reasserted themselves in the new Muslim empire.

Rising tensions. After 'Uthman's election, tensions began to build among the Muslims. Many accused 'Uthman of favoring members of his own clan. As discontent grew, rebellious forces from Egypt marched against Medina and killed 'Uthman in 656. In reaction against the Umayyads, 'Ali was chosen caliph at last.

The Umayyads did not give up power easily, however. Upon 'Uthman's death, his cousin Mu'awiya (mooh-AH-wee-ya), the governor of Syria, became head of the clan. As kinsman and avenger of the murdered caliph, Mu'awiya demanded that 'Ali punish the assassins. He then accused 'Ali of sheltering them. Supported by Syrian Arabs, Mu'awiya openly challenged 'Ali's fitness as caliph and claimed the caliphate for himself. A period of conflict followed. By 657 the tide of battle had turned in 'Ali's favor. Mu'awiya called for a truce. When 'Ali agreed, however, some of his own followers turned against him. The war dragged on until 661, when 'Ali was assassinated by one of his own former supporters. Mu'awiya assumed sole power.

The split. Most Muslims reluctantly accepted Mu'awiya as caliph and remained **Sunnis** (SOOH-nees), meaning "followers of the Sunna," or "way of the Prophet." 'Ali's supporters did not. They became known as the **Shi'ah** (SHEE-ah), from the term *Shi'at Ali*, or "Party of 'Ali." The Shi'ah believed that 'Ali's descendants were specially blessed by God because they were the true heirs of Muhammad. The Shi'ah called 'Ali's successors **imam** (i-MAHM), a general term that Muslims use for any prayer leader. For the Shi'ah, only the imams could interpret the Qur'an.

Conflict between the new Islamic order and older Arab traditions resulted in the division of Islam into two main branches: Shi'ah and Sunni.

▲ The calligraphy in these ceramic tiles from 1226 lists the names of the twelve imams of the Shi'ah.

Then & Now

The Martyrdom of Husayn

The clash between 'Ali and Mu'awiya resulted in the splintering of Islam into the Shi'ah and Sunnis. The later battle between Yazid—Mu'awiya's son and successor—and Husayn—'Ali's son—deepened the division.

Many devout Muslims protested when Yazid became caliph after Mu'awiya's death in 680. They criticized Yazid for not being a faithful Muslim and for having illegitimately taken the caliphate. As opposition to Yazid grew, the Shi'ah in Kufa, Iraq, turned to Husayn to lead them.

Although Husayn was aware that Yazid had ordered the suppression of the growing rebellion, he gathered more than 70 followers, including his wives and children, and marched from Mecca toward Kufa to oppose Yazid. Husayn's group reached the plain of Karbala, where Yazid's commander tried to force Husayn to pledge his support to Yazid. Husayn refused, and Yazid's army attacked Husayn's small force on October 10, 680. During the bloody battle of Karbala, Yazid's army rained arrows on Husayn's camp and gradually thinned the rebel's ranks. Husayn, with his infant son in his arms, was shot down. Yazid's soldiers then looted the tents, decapitated many of the dead, and took the surviving women and children prisoner.

Husayn's martyrdom, mourned by Sunni and Shi'ah alike, deepened the split between the Shi'ah and the state. Today, the Shi'ah intensely revere Husayn. They annually mourn him during Muharram, the month in which he was killed. On the anniversary of Ashura, the day of the battle of Karbala, many Shi'ah gather to hear recited the sufferings of Husayn. They may also take part in funeral processions for Husayn and, in some areas, reenact the battle.

For the Shi'ah, Husayn's martyrdom served an important purpose. The Shi'ah believe that on judgment day:

> 66 [Fatimah, Husayn's mother] will take the Imam Husayn's blood-stained shirt to the throne of God and say, 'Oh God, you have given me and my son a promise. For the sake of his sacrifice, have mercy upon the people of the Last Prophet!' Then, for the sake of Husayn, the son of 'Ali, God will forgive them, there will be peace, and the fire of hell will turn into a rose garden. 99

Some 10 percent of Muslims today are Shi'ah. In Iran and Azerbaijan they constitute a large majority. They are also a large, perhaps even majority, element in Iraq, as well as being the largest single minority in Lebanon. Shi'ah minorities also live in India and Pakistan. Shi'ah minorities sometimes oppose ruling Sunni governments. For the Shi'ah, Husayn serves as a model of brave opposition in the face of overwhelming odds.

Husayn is particularly important in Iran. In 1979—almost 1300 years after Husayn's martyrdom—the Ayatollah Ruhollah Khomeini, a Shi'ah religious leader, led a revolution against the reigning Shah of Iran. The Shi'ah likened Khomeini's efforts to Husayn's struggles at the battle of Karbala. A popular slogan during the revolution was "Everywhere is Karbala and every day is Ashura." Khomeini and his supporters won their battle and established a government based on Shi'ah principles.

A symbol of the 1979 Iranian Revolution, Ayatollah Ruhollah Khomeini was both a political and religious leader.

History and Current Events

In 1990 Iraqi ruler Saddam Hussein openly defied Western interests in the region when he seized Kuwait, provoking the Gulf War. Hussein appealed to some Arabs' anti-Western views when he gave as a reason for the invasion the fact that the boundaries between Iraq and Kuwait had been drawn by Western nations—Britain and France—after World War I, and that they had created these boundaries to protect their own interests. His seizure of Kuwait appealed to some Arabs who hoped that boundaries would be redrawn and wealth redistributed.

Critical Thinking Ask students why Saddam Hussein depicted Kuwait, an Arab country, as a tool of Western interests.

ANSWER: Students might answer that Kuwait had grown rich by selling oil to the Western countries, and by claiming that Kuwait had historically been a part of Iraq before Britain and France created the modern borders in the region.

▲ The *mueddhin* (mooh-ed-DIN) **calls Muslims to prayer from the minaret (tower) of a mosque. The first *mueddhin* was chosen by Muhammad.**

The Umayyad Dynasty

Early Umayyad caliphs ruled more like desert chieftains than religious leaders. To help secure their power, in 661 the Umayyads moved their capital from Medina to Damascus, which was closer to their supporters among the Arab tribes of Syria.

Many Umayyads in Damascus at first longed for the freedom of desert life in Arabia. One of Mu'awiya's wives, a bedouin named Maysun, used verse to complain about the change:

❝*A tent with rustling breezes cool*
Delights me more than palaces high,
And more the cloak of simple wool
Than robes in which I learned to sigh.

The crust I ate beside my tent
Was more than this fine bread to me;
The wind's voice where the hill-path went
Was more than tambourine can be.❞

Over time, however, the Umayyads could not escape being influenced by Byzantine civilization in Syria, particularly as they adopted the old Byzantine bureaucracy to rule their empire.

Umayyad expansion. With a desire for power and wealth, and eager to take more territory for Islam, the Umayyads continued to expand the empire. In the east their armies reached deep into Central Asia. They conquered many Turkish tribes, came into contact with the Tang Empire of China, and conquered the kingdoms of northwestern India. From Syria the Umayyads took to the sea and soon controlled the eastern Mediterranean trade routes. Umayyad forces even tried to conquer the Byzantine capital of Constantinople, though without success. They also sent armies west, conquering the Byzantine provinces in North Africa.

Beyond Tunisia the Umayyads were temporarily halted by the Berbers, a North African people much like the pre-Islamic Arabs. By 700, however, Muslim forces had reached the Atlantic Ocean. The Berbers eventually converted to Islam, and in 711 a combined Arab and Berber army began the rapid conquest of Spain. By 732 they had swept across the Pyrenees into France, where a Muslim raiding force was stopped by Frankish forces near the city of Tours. Although later European accounts marked this as a major Muslim defeat, Muslims regarded it as only a minor engagement.

Islamic forces remained in southern France for many years. However, the Arabs and Berbers were used to the deserts and high plains of Southwest Asia, Africa, and Spain. They found the landscape did not favor their methods of warfare, which depended on light cavalry, or their farming techniques and crops. Their camels suffered from the humidity and died from the cold, and their light, wiry horses were not bred for the muddy fields or forests of France. Eventually, the Muslims withdrew to the friendlier sunlit plains of Spain.

The fall of the Umayyads. As Umayyad power grew, many of the newly conquered peoples began to see advantages in converting to Islam. Following ancient practice, the Umayyads insisted that non-Arab converts become clients of Arab tribes. Soon Islamic society consisted of two classes: Arab conquerors and second-class clients. Below both Arabs and clients were Christians, Jews, Hindus, and Zoroastrians, who had chosen not to convert.

As they became more numerous, the clients began to resent their second-class status. Arab opponents of the Umayyads used this discontent and that of the Shi'ah to encourage a revolution. In 750 a new dynasty came to power: the Abbasids (AB-buh-sidz), who claimed descent from the Prophet's uncle 'Abbas.

The Abbasid Caliphate

On the banks of the Tigris River the Abbasids built a great new imperial capital at Baghdad. The move to Baghdad marked the beginning of the decline of Arab dominance of the Muslim empire and the rise of Persian influence. The caliphs adopted the Persian style of government and ruled as semidivine leaders. They were majestically enthroned, generally behind a magnificently carved screen or embroidered curtain so that their subjects could not see them. A new official title proclaimed the caliph as the "Shadow of God on Earth."

Distrusting the Arab tribes, the Abbasids recruited most of their fighting men from the old Persian province of Khorasan. They also used the old Persian bureaucracy to run the empire and relied increasingly on non-Arabs and even non-Muslims. Specialized government departments were headed by a **vizier** (vuh-ZIR), or "deputy," who oversaw affairs of state.

Under the Abbasid Empire, the Arab nature of Islam gradually began to give way. The Abbasids appealed to all members of the community for support. Over the course of their rule, they turned Islam, originally a religion that appealed mostly to Arabs, into a truly universal religion that attracted peoples of many diverse cultures.

The Abbasid Empire reached its height under Caliph Harun al-Rashid, who reigned from 786 to 809. Harun had come to the throne after the mysterious death of his brother, who had ruled but one year. As caliph, Harun followed a policy of trying to unite the Arab and Persian peoples, as well as others within the empire, into a single Islamic identity.

When Harun died, however, two of his sons, one supported by the Persian side and the other the Arab side, plunged the empire into civil war. The Persian side triumphed, but the conflict signaled the beginning of Abbasid decline.

Unlike the Umayyads, who remained bound by their Arab identity, under Persian influence the Abbasids tried to create a multicultural Muslim empire.

SECTION 2 REVIEW

IDENTIFY and explain the significance of the following:
 Abu Bakr
 caliphs
 Umayyads
 Sunnis
 Shi'ah
 imam
 Abbasids
 vizier

LOCATE and explain the importance of the following:
 Syria
 Kadisiya
 Damascus
 Tigris River
 Baghdad

1. ***Main Idea*** What role did Abu Bakr play in solving the problems faced by the Muslim community after Muhammad died?
2. ***Main Idea*** What factors led to a split within Islam in the early years following Muhammad's death?
3. ***Geography: Movement*** Why did Muslims begin to expand their empire? What were the results of this expansion?
4. ***Writing to Persuade*** Write a short essay defending or refuting the following statement: *The Umayyads considered themselves Arabs first and Muslims second, while the Abbasids considered themselves Muslims first and Arabs second.*
5. ***Determining Cause and Effect*** Develop a chart like the one below to explore how and why Arabs expanded far beyond the borders of Arabia to create a Muslim empire after the death of the Prophet.

Muslim Expansion

	Social Forces	Military Actions	Consequences
Abu Bakr	*need to reunify Islam need to control bedouins*	*against bedouins against Persians and Byzantines*	*reconversion of bedouins control of most of Syria, Iraq, and southern Persia*
'Umar			
Umayyads			
Abbasids			

SECTION 2 REVIEW ANSWERS

IDENTIFY
For significance, see the following pages:
Abu Bakr (p. 250)
caliphs (p. 250)
Umayyads (p. 252)
Sunnis (p. 252)
Shi'ah (p. 252)
imam (p. 252)
Abbasids (p. 254)
vizier (p. 255)

LOCATE
For locations, see the map on p. 251.

1. Abu Bakr was chosen as caliph. He reconverted the bedouin tribes and brought all of Arabia back under Muslim rule.
2. Conflict between supporters of 'Ali and supporters of Mu'awiya led to a split in Islam between Sunni and Shi'ah.
3. The nearby civilizations were wealthier, and Arabs profited from this wealth.
4. The Umayyads were part of the clan system that existed in Arabia before Islam. The Abbasids based their power on their descent from Muhammad's uncle.
5. 'Umar—army grew as people joined registry; against Persians and Byzantines; Arabia gained wealth; Umayyads—desire for power and wealth; against Turkish tribes, Indian kingdoms, Constantinople, Byzantines, Berbers, Franks; Islam spread, converts resented second-class status and revolted; Abbasids—discontent of Shi'ah and non-Arab converts; revolution against Umayyads; decline of Arab dominance and rise of Persian influence

SECTION 3

CORE LESSON PLAN
See pages 241G and
241H for Lesson Plan
10.3.

SECTION 3
The Development of Islamic Civilization

FOCUS

- What changes occurred in Islamic religion and law after Muhammad's death?

- How did cross-cultural contacts influence the development of Muslim culture under the Abbasids and Spanish Umayyads?

- What role did trade play in the expansion of Islam under the Abbasids?

The rule of the Abbasids marked a high point of Muslim learning and culture. The achievements of earlier Hellenistic, Persian, and Roman civilizations, and new ideas from neighboring civilizations in India, China, and Byzantium, influenced the development of Muslim philosophy, science, and mathematics. Architecture, the arts, and literature reached new heights, inspired by Islam and funded by the wealth of the empire. Although the Abbasids were unable to maintain the political unity of the Muslim world, Muslim culture continued to flourish and to expand.

Abbasid horseman on a coin
from around 920

Developments in Islam

Muhammad did not develop a systematic code of Islamic practices during his lifetime. Many of his revelations and teachings existed only in oral form and addressed specific problems faced by the community. After his death Muslims faced the task of codifying their religious duties.

Five Pillars of Islam. The most important duties expected of Muslims—those practiced by the Prophet himself—were laid down in the Qur'an. They became known as the **Five Pillars of Islam**. They commanded Muslims: (1) to say the confession of faith, "I bear witness that there is no deity except Allah (God) and that Muhammad is His Servant and Messenger"; (2) to pray five times a day; (3) to support the poor members of the community through payment of alms; (4) to fast during the holy month of Ramadan (RAH-muh-dahn); and (5) to make the **hajj** (HAJ), or "pilgrimage," to Mecca at least once if possible.

There were other requirements as well. For example, Muslims were forbidden to eat certain food, like pork. They could not drink alcoholic beverages. They were encouraged to free their slaves, particularly those that converted to Islam. If they chose not to free them, they were required to treat their slaves humanely. No free Muslim could be enslaved, and the children of a female slave and her master were free.

Islam also established new standards for relations between men and women. Men could have no more than four wives and had to treat each equally. Women were restricted to one husband. To reinforce the stability of the extended family, the Qur'an laid down specific rules for inheritance and for ownership of property by women.

One important requirement was **jihad** (ji-HAHD). Europeans, threatened by Muslim armies, later translated this term as "holy war," but a more accurate translation would be "struggle for the faith." In the early years of Muslim expansion, however, jihad did mean primarily fighting and dying for the faith. Muslims believed that a warrior who died in battle for the faith would immediately be admitted to paradise. The term also means the constant inner struggle people experienced in their effort to obey God's will or any effort in the cause of faith.

Muhammad and the Qur'an taught that the reward for obeying God's will was eternal salvation. Like Judaism and Christianity, Islam saw the history of the world as having a definite beginning and end. Muhammad had preached that on the final day God would judge all human beings. Those who had faithfully tried to obey his commandments would be granted eternal life in paradise. The Qur'an described paradise as a beautiful garden full of earthly delights such as fine food and drink. Those who did not obey God, however, would suffer in a place of eternal fire.

Islamic law. With eternal salvation at stake, it was extremely important for Muslims to understand exactly what God wanted them to do. People found that neither the Qur'an nor Muhammad's own actions and sayings covered every specific situation. After Muhammad's death, Muslims naturally looked to the caliphs to uphold and expand the faith; but under the Umayyads many devout Muslims came to distrust the caliphs' motives and religious sincerity.

As distrust of the spiritual authority of the caliphs grew, a body of experts gradually emerged to whom people looked for religious guidance. These men, known as the *ulama*, were not priests but religious scholars. They specialized in studying and interpreting the Qur'an and the Traditions, the sayings and deeds of the Prophet. Drawing on these sources, the *ulama* developed a fully Islamic legal system, called *shari'ah* (shuh-REE-uh). The *shari'ah* guided the personal conduct of all Muslims, including religious observances, marriage, divorce, business affairs, and inheritance. It also outlined the appropriate practices of Islamic government. Adherence to the *shari'ah* soon became one of the most important elements of the Muslims' sense of identity.

The Islamic worldview. While developing the legal system, Muslim scholars explored many of the same types of religious questions that Christian scholars faced. For example, they debated the nature of the Qur'an. Eventually, they accepted it as being the literal, divine word of God, and therefore beyond dispute.

One of the greatest controversies concerned free will. If God were all-knowing and all-powerful, some scholars asked, then how could human beings do anything he had not already determined? Like Christian scholars, Muslim

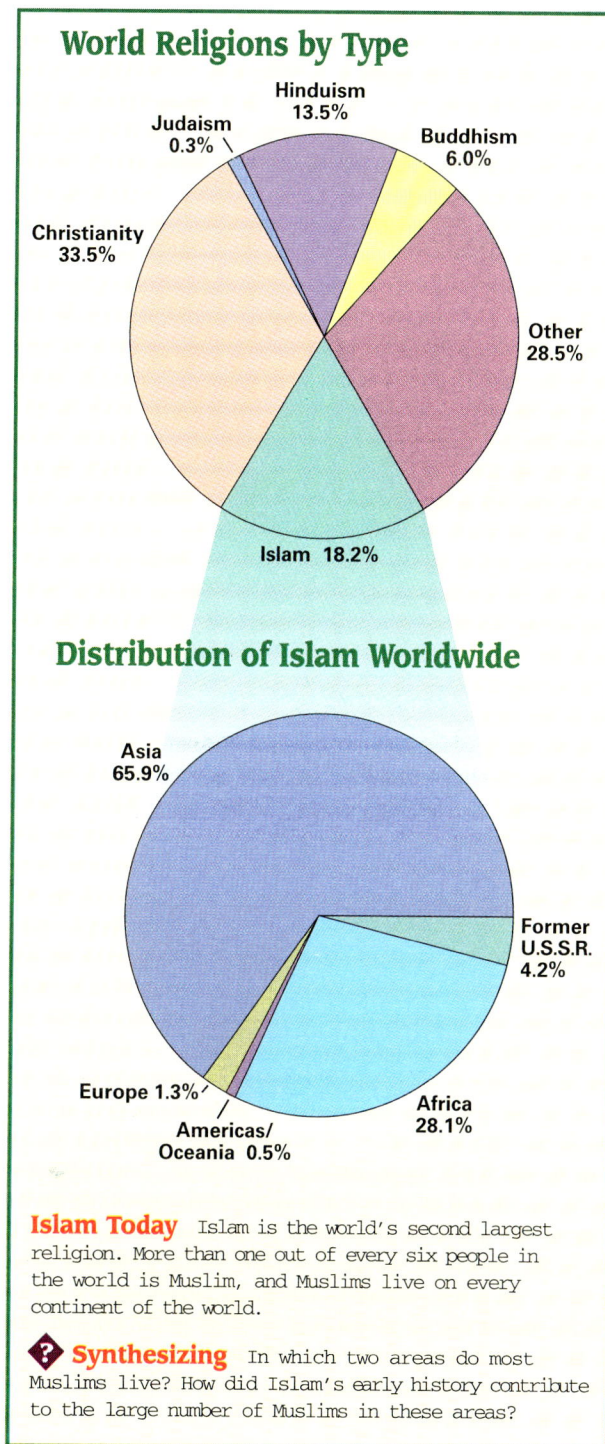

World Religions by Type

Judaism 0.3%
Hinduism 13.5%
Buddhism 6.0%
Christianity 33.5%
Other 28.5%
Islam 18.2%

Distribution of Islam Worldwide

Asia 65.9%
Former U.S.S.R. 4.2%
Europe 1.3%
Americas/Oceania 0.5%
Africa 28.1%

Islam Today   Islam is the world's second largest religion. More than one out of every six people in the world is Muslim, and Muslims live on every continent of the world.

Synthesizing   In which two areas do most Muslims live? How did Islam's early history contribute to the large number of Muslims in these areas?

scholars examined the teachings of the Greek philosophers Plato and Aristotle for answers. The major question that arose out of these efforts was how much weight Muslims should give to human reason to solve problems that the Qur'an and the Traditions did not cover directly.

Scholars were deeply divided over the issue. Some believed that human reason should be the

Chart Answer
Asia and Africa—the Muslim empire expanded extensively in these areas

Theme: Religion
Many devout Muslims felt that Umayyad authority had become corrupt with the power and wealth of conquest. The *ulama* developed in reaction to these problems.

One major complaint of the *ulama* was the Umayyad practice of retaining the existing system of rule in conquered lands, rather than instituting a system ruled by the traditions of Islam. In addition, the *ulama* believed that relying on a system ruled by the caliphs' and their judges' decisions often resulted in contradictory laws. They felt that all conquered regions and cities should be ruled under one system—God's law.

Critical Thinking   Ask students to suggest reasons why the Umayyad might have left the legal systems of areas they had conquered in place.

ANSWER: Students might suggest that leaving local legal systems in place might have eased acceptance of Umayyad rule in conquered areas. It might also have been easier than creating a new structure of law and courts.

BIOGRAPHY

Rabi ʻa al-ʻAdawiyya

Rabi ʻa al-ʻAdawiyya's beliefs permanently influenced the development of Sufism. Early Sufists had rejected worldly pleasures and emotions. Rabi ʻa expressed her intense love of God. She declined offers of marriage, not wanting anything to detract her from her religious commitment. Rabi ʻa's intense devotion attracted a group of followers, and Sufism eventually grew into a much larger movement that spread through Arabia, Egypt, Iraq, and Syria.

Critical Thinking Ask students how Rabi ʻa's popularity signaled a shift in Sufism.

ANSWER: Students should respond that early Sufists rejected all pleasures—even those connected to the expression of emotion. Rabi ʻa's popularity suggests that many Sufists were attracted to her open expression of love for God.

guiding force. Others held that guidance should come from the Prophet's Traditions. A scholar named al-Shafiʻi attempted to resolve the debate in the late 700s. Al-Shafiʻi emphasized the importance of modeling human activity on Muhammad's example. The examples set by Muhammad and the rules established by the Qur'an thus came to dominate Islamic thought.

Al-Shafiʻi also described the elements on which Islamic law must be founded and interpreted. The Qur'an and the sayings and deeds of the Prophet were the most important sources of the *shariʻah*. In cases not covered by these sources, people were to draw a parallel with some case that was covered. The next important source of legal authority was the consensus of the community. Human reason as a means of interpreting the law was to be used only through this highly disciplined process.

Al-Shafiʻi was not the only Muslim scholar dealing with these issues. Eventually, four major schools of Islamic legal interpretation emerged—Hanafi, Maliki, Shafiʻi, and Hanbali—each named for its founder. In later years, these schools of interpretation became associated with particular geographic regions in the Islamic world.

Following Muhammad's death, scholars struggled to establish a set of laws that would guide Muslim beliefs and practices.

Sufism. While al-Shafiʻi had been influenced by Greek philosophy, some Muslims were more heavily influenced by Indian philosophy. These Muslims worried about the growing materialism of Muslim civilization. Many of them sought refuge in a life of simplicity and devotion to God. Greek and Judeo-Christian mystical traditions that emphasized spiritual rather than earthly attainment also appealed to them. These traditions contributed to a new movement in Islam called **Sufism**.

Many Sufis declared that their goal was union with God. They emphasized loving God, calling him their Beloved. Some wrote beautiful poems of devotion.

One of the most famous of the early Sufis was Rabiʻa al-ʻAdawiyya. Rabiʻa was born in Basra sometime around 713. She was kidnapped from her parents while she was still an infant and sold into slavery. According to tradition she was so saintly and devout even as a child that her master soon freed her. She then retired to a life of seclusion and contemplation, but her reputation caused many disciples to seek her out. She died in Basra in 801. Rabiʻa expressed her love for God in magnificent devotional verses.

> *In two ways have I loved Thee, selfishly,*
> *And with a love that is worthy of Thee.*
> *In selfish love my joy in Thee I find,*
> *While to all else, and others, I am blind.*
> *But in that love which seeks Thee worthily,*
> *The veil is raised that I may look on Thee. Yet*
> *is the praise in that or this not mine. In this*
> *and that the praise is wholly Thine.*

Like other Sufis, Rabiʻa sought union with God: "My hope is for union with Thee, for that is the goal of my desire. . . . I have ceased to exist and have passed out of self. I have become one with God and am altogether His."

◀ **In this illustration from a Persian manuscript, men, women, and children eagerly gather to listen to a famous Sufi teacher visiting their community.**

More traditional Muslims often distrusted and sometimes abused Sufis. As time went on, however, Muslim society became more diversified and consequently less hostile to the personal emphasis that Sufism placed on religion. Sufism itself also underwent changes. By the 1000s many Sunni Muslims felt free to practice Sufism as a private and personal expression of their religious faith.

As Islamic civilization became more complex and worldly, Sufi Muslims sought a more spiritual life.

Science and Learning

Greek and Indian teachings also influenced Muslim science and learning. In the 800s Muslim scholars introduced the Indian number system, including the use of zero, into the Greek science of mathematics. Later, Muslims also imported the decimal system from India. A Muslim mathematician named al-Khwarizmi used these new tools to write a textbook on arithmetic and what he called *al-jabr*, or "algebra." This book circulated in Europe in the 1500s, where it was very influential. Europeans called the new numbers introduced in the book "Arabic" numerals.

Muslim scientists also made great advances in astronomy. They rediscovered the **astrolabe**, an instrument invented by the Greeks that allowed observers to chart the positions of the stars and thereby calculate their own position on earth. As they learned to navigate by the stars, Muslim merchants and explorers traveled more widely than ever. To aid them, Muslim geographers developed new maps and more accurate ways of calculating distances.

Perhaps the greatest Muslim scientific achievements came in the area of medicine. As early as the

▶ **After Arab astronomers improved the astrolabe, sailors in the 1100s could calculate latitude and time of day.**

800s, Muslim doctors in Baghdad were required to pass rigorous examinations in order to practice medicine. They established the first school of pharmacy and the first list and descriptions of known drugs and their effects. Caliph Harun al-Rashid founded the first Muslim public hospital in Baghdad. Al-Razi, who became head of the hospital, discovered how to diagnose and treat smallpox. Another doctor, Ibn-Sina, wrote a medical encyclopedia that became the standard reference throughout Europe until the 1600s.

Literature and the Arts

As the Islamic world grew wealthier, Muslim rulers became great patrons of literature and the arts. Each court tried to outdo its rivals. Poets composed elegant verses in both Arabic and Persian. Short stories were also a favorite. For example, the folktales told by the fabled Scheherazade

▲ **Calligraphy as a form of high art is captured in carved stone and tile in Morocco.**

(shuh-HEHR-uh-zahd) about Sinbad the Sailor, Aladdin, and Ali Baba and the Forty Thieves were brought together under the title *The Thousand and One Nights*. Many of these tales had originated in India, Egypt, and other lands that were in contact with the Muslim world. The introduction of paper manufacturing from China allowed such literary masterpieces to be published for a growing audience.

Meanwhile, the Qur'an itself provided a major inspiration for Muslim artists. To prevent idol worship, Islam discouraged the creation of animal images and prohibited human images. Instead, artists turned calligraphy, or decorative writing, into a high art form. Verses from the Qur'an were transformed into magnificent works of art. Muslim artists created special scripts to decorate mosques—or *masjids* (mus-jids), Islamic places of worship—and other

**GEOGRAPHY
ACTIVITIES**
Geography Activity 10
The Spread of Islam

Have students study the
map and complete the
questions on the spread
of Islam.

Level 2

**Linking Geography
and History**
They traveled to distant
lands and made
observations.

🔶 **Theme:
Geography**

One of the greatest
Muslim geographers was
Yaqut ibn-'Abdullah al-
Hamawi, who lived from
1179 to 1229. As a young
man, Yaqut was enslaved
by a merchant, who edu-
cated him and used him
as a traveling clerk. When
the merchant freed him,
Yaqut traveled from place
to place, copying and selling manuscripts to sup-
port himself. He wrote a
geographical dictionary,
which contained not only
geographical information
but also historical, cul-
tural, and scientific information.

Critical Thinking Ask
students why scholars
consider Yaqut to be
such a good geographer.

ANSWER: Students might
suggest that Yaqut based
his information on obser-
vation and experience.

Geography AND HISTORY

The World of Arab Geographers

Geography became one of the greatest of Muslim sciences during the Abbasid period. Arab geographers published the geographic knowledge of Muslim merchants and travelers. One of these, Ibn Hawqal, an early Arab traveler, explored Muslim lands in the mid-900s. In his *Book of the Image of the Earth*, Ibn Hawqal gave information about old trade routes:

❝ *The oases [in Upper Egypt] were in the past a region irrigated by watercourses, with trees and villages. . . . This region was crossed in the past in order to travel west to the Bilad al-Sudan, along the route which used to be followed between Egypt and Ghana. This route is not used any longer, although it is not without oases or ruins of human dwellings.* ❞

On one of his voyages along the east coast of Africa, Ibn Hawqal reached a point just 20° north latitude from the equator. He noted that thousands of people lived in those latitudes. This finding disproved Aristotle's theory that areas near the equator would be too hot for people to survive.

Other Arab geographers made important discoveries about climate. The world's first climatic atlas, published in the 900s, included observations about temperature patterns from places south of the equator and proved that Aristotle's uninhabitable zone did not exist. In 985 a geographer named al-Muqaddasi completed a geographic encyclopedia with a map showing 14 world climatic regions in place of the 3 identified by Aristotle.

Al-Muqaddasi also described the cultural geography of Muslim lands in his book. His description of al-Fustat (Cairo) in the 900s gives a vivid impression of the daily lives of its residents:

❝ *No town is more densely populated than al-Fustat, with its numerous sheiks and notables, its wonderful specialties and merchandise, its good souks [markets] and its good crafts, its [public] baths which are the height of excellence, its enclosed markets. . . . Houses have four floors and even five . . . ; they draw sunlight from an inner courtyard. I have been told that a single building can house as many as two hundred souls.* ❞

During the mid-1100s, al-Idrisi, a Muslim who lived in Palermo, Sicily, began to compile the huge volume of data accumulated by Arab travelers. When al-Idrisi doubted the accuracy of the location of a mountain, river, or coastline, he sent out trained geographers to make careful observations.

With this fund of accurate information, al-Idrisi wrote what he called a "new geography." Completed in 1154, al-Idrisi's *Amusement for Him Who Desires to Travel Around the World* corrected a number of mistaken notions. For example, he disproved the idea that land completely encircled the Indian Ocean. Al-Idrisi's work, along with that of other Arab geographers, mapped much of the world and laid the basis for later explorations.

**Linking Geography
and History**
How did Arab geographers
dispel myths about the
earth's geography?

**The maps that
al-Idrisi created
in the 1100s were
an important
progression in
the development
of geography.**

▲ Muslims built the Dome of the Rock in 691 in Jerusalem as a shrine over the place where they believed Muhammad had ascended to God.

buildings. Qur'anic verses appeared in stunning calligraphy painted on glazed tiles that shone like jewels, woven into intricately designed carpets, or hammered into finely decorated steel blades.

Most other Muslim art avoided depicting animals or people by using only geometric shapes or complex floral patterns. Apart from some early Umayyad art, which reflected Byzantine influences, the primary exceptions appeared in Persia. There the pre-Islamic tradition of miniature paintings remained strong. Persian artists painted legendary beasts, hunters, warriors, and historical figures in such delicate detail that often the rich colors could only be applied with a single hair.

Architecture was one of the most important Muslim art forms. From the days of the Umayyads, Muslim rulers began to express their power and devotion to Islam in stone. The most important buildings at first were mosques. The first mosques resembled the courtyard of Muhammad's house in Medina, where he had led the community in prayer. Eventually, the mosques became more elaborate. One of the most famous and most beautiful is the Dome of the Rock, a shrine that the Umayyads built on the site of Solomon's Temple in Jerusalem.

Soon Umayyad architects were building palaces, marketplaces, libraries, and a host of other buildings. The Abbasids adopted their own style, even more elaborate than the Umayyads'.

▶ The design of this mosque in Seville, Spain, is an architectural example of the mixture of Islamic and Spanish elements.

They also built great mosques, palaces, hospitals, and libraries, often setting them in elaborate Persian-style gardens.

Andalusia: Umayyad Spain

While the Abbasids were creating a great Islamic civilization from Syria to the east on a Persian model, another pattern emerged in the west. Umayyad Spain, or al-Andalus as Muslims called it, only briefly acknowledged Baghdad's rule. Under a survivor of the Umayyad family, a new empire developed rivaling that of the Abbasids. From their capital at Córdoba, the Spanish Umayyads ruled an elegant and courtly domain. Córdoba had piped water, and at night the city was lit with a public lighting system.

Umayyad Spain reached its height under 'Abd al-Rahman (uhb doohl-rah-MAHN) III in the 900s. In the first 20 years of his reign 'Abd al-Rahman established a unified and centralized government. Religious toleration was his focus. Christians, Jews, and Muslims lived together in relative peace under his rule, as did peoples of various ethnic backgrounds from Arabia, Africa, and Europe. With Spain largely unified and at peace, 'Abd al-Rahman presided over a flowering of Muslim culture.

A strong economy supported Muslim civilization in Spain. The Arabs had brought with them many of the techniques and skills they had learned in Persia. In southern Spain, for example, they built irrigation systems using underground canals like those they had seen in Persia. They also introduced new crops, such as oranges, rice, sugarcane, and cotton, all of which had been brought from India, China, and Southeast Asia. Spain once again produced fine steel, as well as magnificent textiles of silk, cotton, and wool.

Umayyad Spain became a great center of learning. Scholars from throughout the Muslim world and Europe came to study at the university in Córdoba. Muslim, Christian, and Jewish scholars translated the Greek classics. They also studied, debated, and translated the new works on mathematics, medicine, astronomy, geography, and history that were produced in the Muslim world. From Spain these works reached the rest of Europe.

Under the Abbasids and Spanish Umayyads, Muslim traditions blended with other cultural traditions to achieve new heights of beauty and knowledge.

Expansion Through Trade

The basis for Muslim cultural development was the growing wealth of the Muslim world. While the Umayyads had expanded the Islamic empire by military conquest, during the Abbasid period expansion by trade and commerce became more common. To a considerable extent this development was the result of geography. Islam had arisen in the heart of a great world trade network that linked three continents.

Baghdad itself set the pace. Located at the hub of both overland and water routes, it became a major meeting place for trade from China, India, Africa, and Europe. While Arab ships set sail for eastern ports, Chinese ships docked at wharves along the Tigris River, unloading shimmering silk, spices, and jeweled treasures from India and Asia.

China and India. Muslim merchants established trading colonies as far away as China. They brought ivory, slaves, rhinoceros horn, tortoiseshell, and gold from Africa and southern Arabia. They also carried silks and porcelains back to Baghdad, Damascus, Cairo, and the Mediterranean world. Drawn by the message of Islam carried by these merchants, in some places, like Malaya, local rulers adopted the new faith.

In India, Muslim traders were the primary means of spreading Islamic religion and culture. Although the interior Indian kingdoms remained Hindu, coastal cities and trading centers soon had large Muslim communities. From these bases and the Islamic lands of southern Arabia, Muslim merchants dominated the Indian Ocean trade.

Africa. In East Africa, Muslim trading communities set up business next to African market towns. Muslim merchants sought gold, ivory, cloves, and slaves. In return they brought porcelain from China, cloth goods from India, and iron from Southwest Asia and Europe. Soon a society emerged that displayed both African and Muslim influences. Arabic influenced local African languages to produce Swahili, a new language that gave its name to the new culture of the East African coast.

In West Africa as well merchants were the most effective transmitters of Muslim culture and civilization. Muslim merchants traveled south across the Sahara in search of gold

▲ In this 1306 illustration from Rashid al-Din's *Universal History*, a Muslim delegation visits at the court of an Abyssinian ruler.

▲ Muslim merchants transported goods across the seas in dhows—ships designed by Arab shipbuilders.

African grasslands near the Sahara became Muslims.

Money and banking. The Islamic economy expanded tremendously because of trade. The Abbasids minted their own gold and silver coins. These coins allowed for the development of an economy based on money rather than barter and trade. The Abbasid currency became a standard for other currencies around the Muslim world.

As Muslim merchants traveled to distant lands, they needed a way to exchange the different kinds of money they received for their goods. Muslims began to set up money exchanges. These exchanges soon became banks, which issued letters of credit to those who deposited their cash. The letters of credit could be exchanged almost anywhere in the Muslim world, even across political boundaries like those between the Abbasids and the Spanish Umayyads. Thus, the first checking system was born.

from the African empire of Ghana. In exchange, they carried salt, which was scarce south of the desert. Along with the salt Muslim merchants also spread the word of Islam. Many rulers of the

*U*nder the Abbasids, traders carried Islam with them as they traveled to distant lands.

SECTION 3 REVIEW

IDENTIFY and explain the significance of the following:
  Five Pillars of Islam
  hajj
  jihad
  ulama
  shari'ah
  al-Shafi'i
  Sufism
  Rabi'a al-'Adawiyya
  astrolabe

1. **Main Idea** How did the Islamic legal system and Sufism develop under the Abbasids?

2. **Main Idea** How did cross-cultural contacts play an important role in the development of Muslim civilization under the Abbasids and the Spanish Umayyads?

3. **Geography: Movement** In what ways did trade assist in the expansion of Islam under the Abbasids? What role did geography play in the development of this trade?

4. **Writing to Explain** Imagine you are a scholar studying the Abbasid Empire. Write a short essay summarizing the reasons for the Abbasids' growing prosperity.

5. **Analyzing** Describe three ways in which trade and cross-cultural exchanges had an effect on the development and spread of Islamic civilization between the 700s and 1200s.

SECTION 4

CORE LESSON PLAN
See pages 241I and
241J for Lesson Plan
10.4.

Theme: Politics and Law

The Ismailis were a revolutionary group of Shi'ah who attacked and killed Sunni political and religious leaders in attempts to seize power. The Ismailis were made up of several subgroups, one of which was the Fatimid dynasty. From the 900s to the 1100s the Fatimid dynasty challenged Abbasid rule and spread its control over North Africa, Sicily, Egypt, Syria, Palestine, and Western Arabia.

Critical Thinking Ask students what justification the Ismailis might have given for their violent actions against Sunni leaders.

ANSWER: Students might answer that the Ismailis believed that their interpretation of Islam was the correct one, and force was a necessary means to win power.

SECTION 4
The Coming of the Turks

FOCUS

- What led to the decline of the Abbasids?
- What effects did Turkish rule have on Muslim political and religious institutions?
- How did the Turks affect Muslim cultural development?

As Arab power declined in the Abbasid Empire, Persian culture revived and briefly flowered before being overrun by Turkish peoples from Central Asia. Although the movement of Turkish-speaking tribes from Central Asia contributed to the decline of the Abbasid Empire, the conversion of the Turks to Islam led to a renewed energy in Muslim civilization. The migrating Turks moved west and south from their homelands, spreading as far as Egypt, Asia Minor, and northern India. They soon adopted the more sophisticated culture of the Persians, carrying it with them in their further expansion.

Muslim vase from Syria, created in the late 1100s

Decline of the Abbasids

By the late 800s the Abbasid caliphs had begun to lose control of their empire. Corruption grew as viziers began to use their positions for their own advantage. The enormous size of the empire also created problems as governors of distant provinces became practically independent.

In Khorasan, the former seat of Abbasid power, a local Persian family called the Samanids took control. The Samanids also extended their rule farther east, where they tapped into the profitable trade of the Silk Road from China. A contemporary historian described the wealthy Samanid court at Bukhara:

> *Bukhara was . . . the focus of splendor, the shrine of empire, the meeting place of the most unique intellects of the age, the horizon of the literary stars of the world, and the fair of the greatest scholars of the period.*

Although the Samanids proclaimed allegiance to the Abbasid caliphate, the loss of control over Khorasan was a major blow to the caliphs' power. Khorasan had been the main source of troops for Abbasid armies. The caliphs turned to Turkish **mamluks**, or military slaves, to fill their armies. The Turkish mamluks, however, soon held the real power in Baghdad.

The most serious threat to the Abbasids came from Shi'ism. In the early 900s a new dynasty emerged that claimed descent from 'Ali and Fatimah. The Fatimids, as they became known, eventually captured Egypt. Ruling from their new capital of Cairo, they challenged the Abbasids by proclaiming themselves the true caliphs. In addition to attacking Syria, they also secretly sent missionaries into the Abbasid territories to win converts for their claim to the caliphate.

Meanwhile, Shi'ah groups also launched rebellions against Abbasid rule in Persia. In 945 the Buyids, a Shi'ah dynasty from Persia, took control of Baghdad and "rescued" the caliph from his Turkish mamluks. Although Sunni control was eventually restored in Baghdad, the Abbasids never fully regained their former power—instead, it passed to new independent Turkish tribes that had begun to move into the empire.

Internal divisions and external challenges from the Shi'ah and other invaders led to the decline of Abbasid power and influence.

The Turks and Islam

As early as the first century A.D., Turkish-speaking groups had appeared all across Eurasia. Turkish social customs, like those of other nomadic tribal peoples, were geared toward survival in a harsh environment. The Turks had adapted to life on horseback in the great grasslands of Asia. They also herded sheep and goats, and used the two-humped Bactrian camel as a beast of burden. They lived as much by fighting and raiding as by herding their animals, and they valued physical endurance and skill in battle.

Around 550 a group known as the Gök Turks emerged from their homeland in western Mongolia to establish a great steppe empire that stretched from the Oxus River to Manchuria. The empire soon fell into civil war, and by the time Muslim Arab armies first encountered the Turks in Central Asia, the Turkish Empire had disintegrated. Impressed by their fighting abilities, however, Muslim leaders began to enslave the Turks for use as mamluks. Particularly under Samanid influence, many Turks began to absorb elements of Persian as well as Muslim culture.

The Ghaznavids. Like the Abbasids, the Samanids also used Turkish slave soldiers in their court and army, with equally severe consequences. In 977 the Samanids' Turkish garrison commander in Ghazna founded his own dynasty, called the Ghaznavids. Soon the Ghaznavids and other Turkish peoples overthrew the Samanids and divided up their lands. The Ghaznavids eventually controlled Khorasan, Afghanistan, and part of northern India.

Mahmud of Ghazna was particularly infamous for his wars in India. Raiding into the Punjab and the Ganges Plain, his troops demolished many Buddhist and Hindu temples and carried off vast amounts of jewels, gold, silver, and slaves. Despite such destruction, however, the Ghaznavids played a major role in carrying Islam further into India.

The Saljuqs. Not long after the rise of the Ghaznavids, another Turkish dynasty, the Saljuqs, established themselves north of the Caspian Sea. Having converted to Islam, the Saljuqs fought against still-pagan Turks and offered military assistance to other Muslim rulers such as the Ghaznavids and Samanids. However, as their numbers grew, the Saljuqs began to move west and south. They seized control of Khorasan from the Ghaznavids and other local rulers. In 1055 the Saljuqs conquered the Buyids and took control of Baghdad. Eventually, they ruled a territory that stretched from Syria to Central Asia.

In 1071 the Saljuqs won a major victory against the Byzantines at the Battle of Manzikert. After the battle a junior branch of the dynasty, known as the Saljuqs of Rum (ROOM), established themselves in Asia Minor, where they continued to fight against Byzantium.

◀ **Ismail Samanid's burial place in Bukhara is made of clay bricks held together with egg yolk and camel's milk.**

Partly as a means of gaining popularity among the population, the Saljuqs were great patrons of the arts and higher learning. For this reason they promoted the establishment of religious colleges, called *madrasas*. The Nizamiyah was the first academy of this type and served as a model for all future *madrasas*. The Nizamiyah was a theological seminary, where the basis of study in the humanities was the Qur'an and ancient poetry.

These *madrasas* spread to other Muslim towns, until there were many throughout the empire. One later traveler, Ibn-Jubayr, reported that he counted around 30 schools in Baghdad. Some scholars believe that the organization of early European universities was based on the *madrasas*.

Critical Thinking Ask students why colleges of law were not separate from theological schools in the Muslim empire.

ANSWER: Students might answer that Islamic law was derived from religious sources, so the study of law was not separate from the study of the Qur'an.

▲ This 1237 illustration from Baghdad shows a caliph's standard, or flag, bearers.

The end of Saljuq expansion. Outside forces put an end to this period of Muslim expansion. By 1113 Christian armies from Western Europe had captured Antioch, Edessa, and Jerusalem. Although the Christian states occupied only a small portion of the Muslim world for a relatively short time, they contributed to the collapse of the Fatimid caliphate in Egypt. At the same time that European Christians were invading from the west, nomads from Mongolia were invading from the east. The invaders captured Baghdad in 1258, killing the Abbasid caliph and bringing the caliphate to an end.

The Nature of Turkish Rule

As it had done for the Arabs, Islam seems to have provided a powerful inspiration for Turkish groups like the Ghaznavids and Saljuqs. Many saw themselves as *ghazis*, or "warriors for the faith." The *ghazi* ideal appealed to many newly converted Turks who continued to flow into the Muslim heartland from Central Asia. After taking control of Baghdad, the Saljuqs encouraged such tribesmen to settle along the Byzantine frontier to control Anatolia and to lead raids against Christians.

The sultanate. Most Turkish rulers saw themselves as champions of the Abbasid caliphate and Sunni Islam. Mahmud of Ghazna, for example, put the caliph's name on his coinage and fought Shi'ism. In return, the caliph confirmed Mahmud as his "deputy," the "right arm of the state," and "protector of God's religion." Mahmud used the title of **sultan**, meaning one to whom authority is granted.

Like the Ghaznavids, the Saljuqs claimed to be servants of the caliph. The Saljuqs also made the defeat of the Fatimids and the suppression of Shi'ism one of their prime objectives. As the Saljuqs first began to use the title of sultan officially, however, they finally abandoned the idea that the caliph should be the spiritual and political ruler of the Muslim world.

The Saljuqs insisted that while the caliph was the spiritual head of Islam, the sultan controlled the military power and secular affairs. The Saljuq sultan's official title proclaimed this new status: "Emperor of Emperors, King of the East and the West, Reviver of Islam, Lieutenant of the Imam, and Right Hand of the Caliph of God." The Saljuqs realized that this idea of the sultanate did not conform to Islamic tradition. Like the Abbasids, they tried to reinforce their role as Muslim rulers by building mosques and establishing schools for advanced study in Sunni law.

Developments in Sufism. In addition to supporting the Sunni caliphate, the Turks were also patrons of Sufism. Sufism had attracted the Turks since the early days of their exposure to Islam.

▶ This minaret was built in Turkey by the Saljuqs in the 1200s. Its pointed top seems to reach toward heaven.

Although early Sufism had often aroused the hostility of many conservative Muslims, by Saljuq times, divisions between Sufis and more conservative Muslims were already breaking down. Perhaps the most important scholar to reconcile Sufism with Sunni Islam was Muhammad al-Ghazali, a well-respected legal scholar from Khorasan. As a young man, al-Ghazali was consumed by an overwhelming desire to understand religion, as he described in his book *Savior from Error*:

66 *[Before] I was yet twenty years of age . . . until now, when my age approaches fifty, I ceased not to dare the depths of this deep sea . . . investigating the creed of every sect, and discovering the secrets of every creed, that I might distinguish between the holders of true and false doctrine, and between the orthodox and the heretical.* 99

Al-Ghazali ultimately rejected Shi'ism, philosophy, and theology. Instead, he favored a Sufism that would remain within Islamic law. This synthesis soon became characteristic of Sunni Islam. Al-Ghazali became so revered that he was called "The Proof of Islam."

Under Turkish rule, the sultanate emerged as a legitimate institution of government, and Sufism was integrated into Sunni Islam.

Revival of Persian culture.
The Turks enthusiastically supported Muslim-Persian culture and eventually carried it with them as far as India. Arts, literature, and the sciences flourished under Turkish support. Turkish rulers encouraged the revival of Persian as a literary language, particularly for use in poetry. The Ghaznavids, for example, were also patrons of poets like Firdausi, who gave the magnificent ancient epic poem of Iran, the *Shah-nameh*, or "*Book of Kings*," its final form.

Perhaps the greatest poet under the Saljuqs was Jalal al-Din Rumi. In Konya, the capital of the Saljuqs of Rum, Rumi founded the Mevlevi Dervishes, a Sufi group sometimes called the "whirling dervishes" because of their ritual dance. His poetic masterpiece, the *Mathnawi*, expressed his conviction that all life moves toward God:

66 *I died from mineral, and plant became;*
Died from the plant and took a sentient [conscious] frame;
Died from the beast, and donned a human dress;
When by my dying did I e'er grow less:
Another time from manhood I must die
To soar with angel-pinions [wings] through the sky.
'Midst Angels I must also lose my place
Since 'Everything shall perish save His Face.'
Let me be Naught! The harp-strings tell me plain
That unto Him do we return again. 99

Rumi thus combined elements of the cultural and religious flowering that occurred under both Persian and Turkish rulers in the Muslim world.

Many Turkish rulers encouraged the revival of Persian culture, particularly in literature and poetry.

▶ **These modern dervishes continue the tradition of the whirling Sufi dance. This dancer has spun himself into a trance.**

SECTION 4 REVIEW ANSWERS
(p. 268)

IDENTIFY
For significance, see the following pages:
mamluks (p. 264)
Fatimids (p. 264)
Mahmud of Ghazna (p. 265)
Saljuqs (p. 265)
ghazis (p. 266)
sultan (p. 266)
Muhammad al-Ghazali (p. 267)

1. Divisions within the Abbasid empire, along with invasions by the Shi'ah and other groups, led to the decline of the power of the Abbasid caliphate.

▲ This illustration from 1237 shows a Muslim traveler meeting merchants with their camel caravan.

Author's Commentary

A DYNAMIC CIVILIZATION

It used to be fashionable among Western historians to describe the early Abbasid caliphate as the Golden Age of Islam—after which Muslim civilization went into a permanent decline. Such views reflected their sources, Muslim historians and political theorists of the 700s to 1000s. These Muslim scholars worried about the decline of the caliphs' power and the rise of independent rulers in their own times. The separation of political and spiritual authority seemed to them to contradict Muhammad's example. They feared that political disunity meant spiritual and cultural decline.

Modern scholars, however, have begun to broaden their perspective. No longer studying just the political sphere, modern scholars now rely on more varied sources. By examining non-Muslim accounts, tax rolls, census data, and other information from the period, they have concluded that Muslim civilization after the Abbasids was more fruitful and creative than ever. The patronage of the Samanids, the Ghaznavids, and the Saljuqs led to an even greater flowering of culture as dynasties competed with each other to prove themselves civilized and enlightened Muslim rulers. Such competition spread Muslim civilization and culture more widely than ever.

As Muslim civilization spread, it brought all the regions of Eurasia, as well as parts of Africa, into direct contact with each other for the first time ever. Moreover, Islam acted as a kind of translator between cultures. The English language bears testimony to this. Words like *algebra*, *alchemy*, *sofa*, and many others were derived from Arabic, Persian, or Turkish. In short, the decline of political unity in Islam apparently released an even greater vitality and creativity in Muslim civilization. This vitality, in turn, stimulated developments in other civilizations. In the process, the world became smaller than ever.

SECTION 4 REVIEW

IDENTIFY and explain the significance of the following:
  mamluks
  Fatimids
  Mahmud of Ghazna
  Saljuqs
  ghazis
  sultan
  Muhammad al-Ghazali

1. **Main Idea** Why did the Abbasid caliphate decline in power?
2. **Main Idea** How did Turkish rule affect Muslim politics and religion?
3. **Religion** What role did Sufism play in the Turkish sultanate?

4. **Writing to Explain** In a short essay, explain how and why the Turkish rulers encouraged the revival of Persian culture.
5. **Hypothesizing** What might have happened to Muslim civilization if the Turks had not converted to Islam?

Review

On a separate sheet of paper, complete the following exercises:

WRITING A SUMMARY

Using the essential points in the text, write a brief summary of the chapter.

REVIEWING TERMS

From the following list, choose the term that correctly matches the definition.

hajj   caliph
vizier   Qur'an
Shi'ah   *hijrah*

1. deputy to the caliph; oversaw Abbasid affairs of state
2. followers of 'Ali and his descendants
3. Muhammad's migration to Medina; marks the first year of the Muslim calendar
4. presents God's laws and teachings as revealed to Muhammad
5. successor to the Prophet

REVIEWING CHRONOLOGY

List the following events in their correct chronological order.

1. Muslim leaders choose Abu Bakr as the first caliph.
2. Islam divides into two main branches: Sunni and Shi'ah.
3. Muhammad flees Mecca and settles in Medina.
4. Saljuq Turks "liberate" the Abbasid caliph in Baghdad.
5. Nomadic Arabs begin to settle in towns such as Mecca.

UNDERSTANDING THE MAIN IDEA

1. What were the two earliest messages that Muhammad preached?
2. Why did Islam spread? What effects did Islamic expansion have on neighboring empires?
3. Why did a division occur within Islam? What consequence did this division have?
4. What role did trade play in the expansion of Islam under the Abbasids?
5. How did Turkish rule affect the political and religious institutions of the Muslim territories?

THINKING CRITICALLY

1. **Analyzing** How did geography, trade, and military efforts contribute to the expansion of Islam and Muslim culture between the 600s and 1200s? Provide examples.
2. **Synthesizing** How did the personal characteristics of the caliphs affect the growth or decline of their empires?
3. **Hypothesizing** Think about the division between Sunnis and the Shi'ah and the conflicts that have arisen as a result. How might the history of Muslim civilization have been different if leaders had chosen 'Ali instead of Abu Bakr as Muhammad's immediate successor?

Building Your Portfolio

Complete the following activities individually or in groups.

1. **Trade** Imagine that you are a Muslim trader sometime between 570 and 1000. You may choose to be a sea captain or the leader of an overland caravan. Write a journal of an expedition you might be leading to some far-off places. In your journal, describe the people you meet along the way, the difficulties of the journey, and the goods and ideas you take to a distant culture and bring back with you. To accompany your journal, create a map showing your journey. You may also wish to illustrate your journal.
2. **World Religions** Since you began studying world history, you have learned about several major world religions, such as Judaism, Christianity, Hinduism, Buddhism, Confucianism, and Islam. Write a script for a representative of each of these religions to be used in a panel discussion. Each representative should describe his or her religion and how it is different from other religions. At the end of the discussion, the representatives should look for things that their religions have in common. Be sure to add the part of a moderator to your script.

2. Islam expanded as a result of military conquests under 'Umar. Neighboring empires were defeated, and Arabs profited from their wealth.
3. Conflict between supporters of 'Ali and supporters of Mu'awiya led to a split in Islam into Sunni and Shi'ah. This division created future conflicts between the two branches and helped lead to the downfall of the Abbasids.
4. Muslim merchants established trading colonies in distant lands and spread Muslim religion and culture.
5. The Turkish rulers went against Muslim tradition and said that while the caliph would rule in spiritual matters, the sultan would control military and secular affairs.

THINKING CRITICALLY

1. Arabia was well situated for overland and overseas trade. Trade helped promote the spread of Islam as merchants traveled to different areas. Conquests helped expand and enrich Muslim civilization.
2. The Umayyad caliphs expanded the Muslim world through military conquest, while the Abbasid caliphs expanded through increased trade and commerce. The result was that increased wealth from trade allowed greater cultural development and further expansion of Islamic ideas.
3. Muslim society would not have been divided and would probably have been better able to defend itself against outside invasions.

Chapter 11

A New Civilization in Western Europe 476–1350

Chapter Planning Guide

	TEXTBOOK	CORE RESOURCES	VISUAL RESOURCES	MULTIMEDIA
Introduction	pp. 270–271	Block Scheduling Handbook: Ch. 11		Videodisc Segment 11 and Viewing Guide: *Cathedrals and Castles*
Lesson 11.1 The Emergence of the Franks	pp. 272–279 Map: *Germanic Kingdoms,* p. 273 Map: *Charlemagne's Empire,* p. 276 Map: *Peoples of Europe,* p. 278	Reading 11.1: *Peasant Life During the Time of Charlemagne*		GHRC 11 Reading: *How Charlemagne Ruled His Empire* GHRC 11/Videodiscs: Map—*A Medieval Manor;* Chart—*A Monk's Day*
Lesson 11.2 Feudalism, Manorialism, and the Church	pp. 280–284 Author's Commentary: *Feudalism,* pp. 281–82	Reading 11.2: *The Table of a Thirteenth-Century English Lord* Skills Activity 11: *Analyzing a Primary Source*		GHRC 11 Readings: *Lord of the Manor; Francis of Assisi* GHRC 11/Videodiscs: Images—*King and Queen; Peasant Life; Ladies of the Manor; A Priest;* Map—*A Medieval Manor*
Lesson 11.3 Kings, Nobles, Popes, and Emperors	pp. 285–289 Map: *The Growth of France,* p. 287 History Through the Arts: *Gothic Architecture,* p. 288	Reading 11.3: *A Saxon View of William the Conqueror* Geography Activity 11: *England Under the Normans* Writing Project 11: *Formulating a Thesis Statement*	Art and History 11: *Bayeux Tapestry*	GHRC 11 Readings: *The Rules of the Pope; The Norman Conquest of England; Chaucer's Portraits of Medieval Pilgrims*
Lesson 11.4 The Crusades	pp. 290–293 Map: *The Major Crusades,* p. 291 Through Others' Eyes: *Islamic View of the Crusades,* p. 292	Reading 11.4: *Salah al-Din's Courage and Steadfastness*		GHRC 11 Readings: *Francis of Assisi; A Knight's Poem; The "People's Crusade"* GHRC 11/Videodiscs: Image—*Crusaders in Battle*
Lesson 11.5 Beginnings of European Transformation	pp. 294–298 Literature Through Time: *The Nibelungenlied,* p. 296	Reading 11.5: *On the Government of Cities*	Everyday Life 11: *A University Classroom in the Middle Ages* Geography and History 11: *Trade Routes in the Middle Ages*	GHRC 11 Readings: *A Medieval Merchant's Advice; Troubadour Ballads* GHRC 11/Videodiscs: Images—*Nobleman Visits a Baker; Queen Blanche;* Map—*European Trade*
Chapter Investigation and Enrichment	pp. 270–298	Chapter 11 Investigation: *How-to Book for the Middle Ages* People in World History 11 Explorations in Daily Life 11		GHRC 11/Videodiscs
Review and Assessment	Section 1 Review, p. 279 Section 2 Review, p. 284 Section 3 Review, p. 289 Section 4 Review, p. 293 Section 5 Review, p. 298 Chapter 11 Review, p. 299	Chapter Review Activity 11 Vocabulary Activity 11 Themes Review 11 Section Study Guides 11.1–11.5 Main Idea Activities 11.1–11.5 Daily Quizzes 11.1–11.5 Chapter 11 Test Sheltered English Ch. 11 Test Ch. 11 Test Generator		Audio CDs: Ch. 11 Summary (English and Spanish)

INTRODUCING THE CHAPTER

Textbook pp. 270–271

CHAPTER OVERVIEW

In western Europe a new civilization arose from the ruins of the Roman Empire. The Germanic kings accepted Christianity and longed to re-create the glories of empire. These kings were generally weak and required the support of the more powerful nobles and the Christian Church to retain their positions. However, as the threat of barbarian invasions ended, successful kingdoms prospered. People once again looked eastward and willingly heeded the pope's call to recover the Holy Land.

PRESENTING THEMES

On the chalkboard or on an overhead transparency, write the following open-ended theme questions.

- **RELIGION** How might religion unite peoples of different cultures and customs?
- **POLITICS AND LAW** What factors influence the development of governmental institutions?
- **CROSS-CULTURAL INTERACTION** How might cross-cultural exchanges enrich a society?

Have students, either individually or in groups, suggest responses to the questions. For the religion question, students might suggest that shared religious beliefs can overcome cultural and social differences. For the politics and law question, students might suggest that the economy of a society, conflict with other kingdoms, and technological changes can all affect the development of governmental institutions. For the cross-cultural interaction question, students might suggest that such exchanges can introduce new artistic techniques or technological innovations. Save the responses. Once students have studied the chapter, you may wish to have them complete the Themes Review, then compare the two sets of answers.

USING THE VIDEO

Segment 11: *Cathedrals and Castles*

ENGLISH

Search Chapter 11
Videodisc 1, Side A

SPANISH

Search Chapter 11
Videodisc 1, Side A

Tell students that in this chapter they will apply these theme questions to the new civilization that emerged out of the ashes of the Roman Empire. Then show Segment 11 of the *World History and Cultures Videodiscs*. This segment looks at the architecture of modern and medieval cities and draws a parallel between the size and grandeur of buildings and the importance of the institutions they represent.

Before showing the segment, ask students to think about the most prominent buildings in their own community and the kinds of activities that take place in those buildings. To help students grasp the significant points of the segment, have them complete Video Viewing Guide 11.

Key to Ability Levels

All strategies and activities are coded to the following ability levels:

LEVEL 1	**Basic** activities suitable for all students
LEVEL 2	**Average** activities suitable for average to above-average students
LEVEL 3	**Challenging** activities suitable for above-average students
SHELTERED ENGLISH	Activities suitable for students with **Limited English Proficiency**

Additional Resources

BOOKS FOR TEACHERS

Bayard, Tania, ed. *The Medieval Home Companion: Housekeeping in the Fourteenth Century.* HarperPerennial, 1991. Looks at everyday life during the period.

Cantor, Norman F. *The Medieval Reader.* HarperPerennial, 1994. Offers a collection of nearly 100 primary sources.

BOOKS FOR STUDENTS

Barber, Richard and Juliet Barber. *Tournaments: Jousts, Chivalry, and Pageants in the Middle Ages.* Weidenfeld & Nicholson, 1989. Looks at the more colorful aspects of medieval history.

Graham-Campbell, James, ed. *Cultural Atlas of the Viking World.* Facts on File, 1994. Offers an atlas with text, time lines, illustrations, and photos.

MULTIMEDIA MATERIALS

The Anglo-Saxons. Learning Resources. CD-ROM, MPC format. Looks at Anglo-Saxon culture.

Charlemagne: Holy Barbarian. Learning Corporation of America. Video, 23 min. Dramatizes his life.

Crusades. BBC/A&E. 4 videos, 200 min. total. Offers a thorough look at the Crusades.

Lesson 11.1   The Emergence of the Franks

Textbook pp. 272–279

RESOURCES

Pupil's Edition
Map, p. 273: *Germanic Kingdoms, 526*
Map, p. 276: *Charlemagne's Empire, 768–814*
Map, p. 278: *Peoples of Europe, 600–1000*

Core Resources
Reading 11.1: *Peasant Life During the Time of Charlemagne*

Global History Resource Center
Reading: *How Charlemagne Ruled His Empire*

Videodiscs or Global History Resource Center
Map: *A Medieval Manor*

Search Frame 821

Chart: *A Monk's Day*

Search Frame 820

LESSON FOCUS
How did the Roman Catholic Church and the Frankish rulers help reunify Europe after the spread of Germanic groups over the former Roman Empire?

OBJECTIVES
After completing this lesson, students will be able to:
- outline the main features of Germanic society;
- describe how the church provided unity in Europe after the decline of Roman authority;
- explain how the Franks helped reunify Europe;
- identify the main causes of the decline of Charlemagne's empire.

HOOK
Clarify the role of the Germanic people in their new territories, and discuss the main features of Germanic society. Have students work in small groups to study the map on Germanic kingdoms on textbook page 273 and compare this map with the map of invasions into the Roman Empire on page 140. Have groups outline areas of the Roman Empire that Germanic tribes successfully settled and discuss which peoples already lived in the invaded areas.

Ask students to speculate about some of the problems these Germanic invaders might have faced when they conquered formerly Roman areas. *[Students might suggest that invaders would have trouble governing local peoples and they would face the threat of invasions from other tribes.]*

Ask: In what ways were the Germanic groups alike?
[They were migratory; they hunted and fished; they were warlike; they were organized into kinship groups and were patriarchal but believed women to have special wisdom; they prized generosity, hospitality, and friendship.]

Ask: How did the Germans' warlike culture help shape their methods of government?
[Once settled, war chiefs became kings and gave lands to warriors who became landed nobles; kings and nobles came to exercise power in peacetime but allowed conquered peoples to keep Roman laws; gradually Germanic customs blended with Roman law.]

DEVELOP
Discuss how the church helped unify the Germanic kingdoms into Latin Christendom. Remind students that the Catholic Church was the most important social institution to

survive the collapse of the Roman state. On the chalkboard, write *Main Survival Skills (Qualities) of the Church*. Then ask students to help you list the main survival skills of the medieval church. *[strong organization, appealing message, monasticism and missionary successes, ability to provide education and service, ability to adapt to features of Germanic culture]*

PROBE

Trace the rise and later disintegration of Frankish empires from 400 to 1000. Point out that as the Franks rose to power under Clovis, the church and the Franks formed a mutually beneficial relationship.

Ask: What did each side get from this relationship?

> *[Clovis needed the administrative organization of the church to help him run his empire. The church, in turn, needed Frankish military power to help spread and solidify the church's influence.]*

Trace Frankish rule from the reign of Clovis and the Merovingians to the rise of Carolingian power under Charlemagne. Have students view the map of Charlemagne's empire on textbook page 276 and see that it covered most of western Europe.

Ask: Why was the crowning of Charlemagne by Pope Leo III on Christmas Day in the year 800 seen as such a significant event in Europe's history?

> *[The crowning of Charlemagne as emperor of the Holy Roman Empire created a combined universal church and universal empire over most of western Europe.]*

Discuss the main causes of the decline of Charlemagne's empire. Point out that Charlemagne's empire, though vast, did not last long after his death.

Ask: What two main things helped bring about this decline?

> *[1. internal disputes, partly from Frankish customs requiring a king to divide his kingdom among his sons at death; 2. new waves of invaders coming into the empire]*

Have students study the map on textbook page 278 of Viking, Magyar, and Muslim invasions and trace the origins of these invading groups. *[Vikings raided by sea from what is now Norway and Sweden; Magyars came across the Danube into what is now Hungary; Muslims came from north Africa and the eastern Mediterranean.]*

CONCLUDE

Examine ordinary peasant life on a typical manor during Charlemagne's era. Have students complete Core Resources Reading 11.1; use the Reading Review questions to guide discussion. Show the electronic media map to acquaint students with a typical manor and a peasant family's place within it.

EXTEND

Cross-Curricular Connection: *Computer Literacy*

Have students analyze the electronic media chart of a monk's day and then use a computer with a database program or spreadsheet program to convert the chart information into a pie graph showing the extent of a monk's daily time at each activity.

Cross-Curricular Connection: *Government*

Link to Today. Assign students to prepare a political speech for a present-day candidate for state governor who wants to model his policies after Charlemagne. Have students base their candidate's goals on information from textbook p. 277 and from the Global History Resource Center reading on Charlemagne. Have students present the speech in class, then ask *Which of Charlemagne's policies would make good government policies today? Which policies might not be, and why?*

MEET INDIVIDUAL NEEDS

Visual-Spatial Learners

Assign students to research the histories of holidays such as Christmas and Easter and to find information about Christian elements or symbols and older Germanic or pagan elements associated with these holidays. Have students prepare a chart divided into sections for holidays, with illustrations of "Christian Elements" and "Pagan Elements." Ask the students to show and explain their chart in class. Remind students that the blending of Christian and pagan customs was encouraged by early church leaders.

ASSESS

Review

Have students complete the Section 1 Review. Use answers in the Teacher's Edition, page 279, to assess student mastery of this section.

RESOURCES

Pupil's Edition
Author's Commentary, p. 281–82: *Feudalism*

Core Resources
Reading 11.2: *The Table of a Thirteenth-Century English Lord*

Skills Activity 11: *Analyzing a Primary Source*

Global History Resource Center
Reading: *The Ideal Lord of the Manor*

Reading: *Francis of Assisi's Advice to Monks*

Videodiscs or Global History Resource Center

Image: *King and Queen with Their Lords*

Search Frame 814

Image: *Ladies of the Manor at Leisure*

Search Frame 812

Map: *A Medieval Manor*

Search Frame 821

Image: *Peasant Life in Winter*

Search Frame 811

Image: *A Priest Celebrating Mass*

Search Frame 815

LESSON FOCUS

How was society during the Middle Ages structured by feudalism, the manorial system, and the church?

OBJECTIVES

After completing this lesson, students will be able to:
- describe feudalism;
- describe the manorial system;
- outline the church's role in feudal society.

HOOK

Discuss feudalism and how it shaped medieval society.

Have students work in groups to prepare monologues representing a medieval king, noble, and knight. Ask groups to elect a member to role-play each character and present the monologue to the class. Tell groups that each character—king, noble, or knight—receives benefits via the feudal system and in turn provides benefits to others; these trade-offs are to be clearly stated in each character's monologue. At this time, you may want to have students complete Skills Activity 11, which discusses the relationship between free peasants and the lord of the manor. For additional background, have students view the electronic media image of a king and queen and read the Global History Resource Center selection about an ideal lord.

Ask each role-player: Speaking in the voice of your character, explain what you get through the feudal system and what you must give in return.

*[**King:** to get income and military forces to protect kingdom, he gives fiefs to nobles, who become his vassals; **Noble:** to get lands, he must pledge to give the king military support; to get knights and foot soldiers for armies, he must subdivide lands to give fiefs to knights in exchange for service; **Knight:** in exchange for fief, he becomes noble's vassal, fights for the lord, and helps train foot soldiers.]*

Next turn students' attention to the Author's Commentary.

Ask: What factors led to the spread of feudalism?

[The constant need for land to give to potential vassals led to the spread of feudalism; feudalism was adopted by some to counter the threat posed by feudal neighbors.]

DEVELOP

Examine the relationship between nobles and peasants in the primary economic system—the manorial system.

For background on the two extremes of manor life, have students complete Core Resources Reading 11.2 about the English lord's table, then view the electronic media image showing peasant life in winter. Next ask groups to prepare monologues representing a medieval noble and a peasant and have one member of each group present the monologue to the class. Emphasize again that each character—noble and peasant—has *needs* to be met through the manorial system, and in return must *give* certain things; instruct groups to state these trade-offs clearly in their monologues. *[Lord: needs workers to farm the land, maintain the manor; to get help, he gives peasants a place to live and grow food; he also provides protection; Peasant: needs a place to live and land for growing food; also needs protection and religious participation; to get these, the peasant farms the lord's land, gives the lord part of his crop, and pays feudal taxes.]*

Ask: *Since the feudal and manorial systems met the needs of people in medieval society, why did these systems tend to fragment society?*
[Students' responses should indicate that because each manor was largely self-sufficient, people saw themselves as part of a manor or small community, not as part of a larger state.]

PROBE

Explore the roles of women in manorial society. Ask
students to develop monologues explaining the roles of a noblewoman and a peasant woman and present them in class. Students may wish to consult the electronic media image of ladies of the manor and Core Resources Reading 11.1 for information. *[Peasant woman: makes clothing, cooks, tends garden, gathers wild food and firewood; helps harvest the fields; Noblewoman: lord's wife supervises all aspects of the household and governs the manor in lord's absence.]*

CONCLUDE

Examine the role of the church in unifying feudal society.

Have students complete the Global History Resource Center reading on Francis of Assisi and view the electronic media image of the priest conducting mass. Help students identify

features in both of these sources that emphasize humility and service. Point out that in medieval society the church helped unify people by providing a larger social structure that offered them a sense of connection.

Ask: **What were some ways in which the church provided this unifying structure?**
[Religious ceremonies and festivals created a sense of community.]

Discuss the relationship between the church and the noble class, again examining the mutual benefits.

Ask: **What did the church and the nobility receive from each other, and what did they provide each other?**
[Nobles provided money and land for the church. The church provided assurance of heavenly rewards and monastic careers for members of noble families.]

Ask: **As the church was drawn into the feudal system, what reforms were needed?**
[Monks and church officials needed freedom from feudal obligations, and people needed a unified system of worship.]

EXTEND

Cross-Curricular Connection: *Science*

The mutual-dependency relationships basic to manorialism may remind students of a term from science class: *symbiosis.* Ask a group of students to research symbiotic relationships in nature and report on some of these to the class. Have them point out parallels with feudal-manorial society.

MEET INDIVIDUAL NEEDS

Visual-Spatial Learners

Have students use the electronic media map of a manor to construct a tabletop model of a manor.

ASSESS

Review

Have students complete the Section 2 Review. Use answers in the Teacher's Edition, page 284, to assess student mastery of this section.

Lesson 11.3   *Kings, Nobles, Popes, and Emperors*

Textbook pp. 285–289

RESOURCES

Pupil's Edition
History Through the Arts, p. 288: *Gothic Architecture*

Map, p. 287: *The Growth of France*

Core Resources
Reading 11.3: *A Saxon View of William the Conqueror*

Geography Activity 11: *England Under the Normans*

Visual Resources
Art and History 11: *Bayeux Tapestry*

Global History Resource Center
Reading: *The Rules of the Pope*

Reading: *The Norman Conquest of England*

Reading: *Chaucer's Portraits of Medieval Pilgrims*

LESSON FOCUS
How did rulers compete for power with nobles and church officials in medieval Europe, and what resulted from these conflicts?

OBJECTIVES

After completing this lesson, students will be able to:

- describe effects of the power struggle in England between kings and nobles;
- trace how French kings strengthened their power;
- discuss consequences of the rivalry between popes and the Holy Roman Empire.

HOOK: Link to Today

Examine goals and strategies of typical "power struggles." On the chalkboard write the heading *Power Struggles Today*. Ask students to give examples. *[Students may cite examples at the school, community, or national level.]* Write the heading *What Each Side Usually Wants*. Continue by asking the class to list typical goals of those engaged in power struggles. When students name power as a goal, agree, but ask them to break it down. *[Students should see that each side typically struggles to gain economic advantage, to win public support, or to control the other side.]*

DEVELOP

Explore how these principles apply to the power struggles in England and France among kings, nobles, and the church. Form students into six strategy groups. Ask each group to list how-to-win-power strategies for one of three factions—kings, nobles, or clergy (for example, How to Win Power as an English King After 1066). Have three groups list strategies for these factions in England; the other three for France. Each group's strategies should reflect the real actions and events described in pages 285–87 of the textbook. As groups work, circulate around the room to help students translate the historical events into imaginary how-to advice. Then ask each group to report.

Have the "English" groups identify main strategies for kings, nobles, and clergy. *[**Kings:** disperse nobles throughout kingdom to prevent alliances; carry out Domesday survey to assess taxes; create central treasury to collect taxes; create national court system so people will look to common law rather than nobles' local laws; **Nobles:** rebel against king; force him to sign agreement (Magna Carta) not to raise taxes without consent and not to imprison anyone illegally or confiscate land; **Clergy:** try to remain outside king's control by asserting that clergy should answer to pope, not king; if the king acts against a church official, declare the official a saint (Thomas Becket) and force king to admit wrongdoing]*

Have the "French" groups identify main strategies for kings, nobles, and clergy. [**Kings:** *strengthen central power of monarchy; appoint strong officials to run central government; extend court system by creating a supreme court (Parlement of Paris) for the entire realm; gain public support by creating an assembly (Estates General) representing clergy, nobles, and commoners but in fact giving these groups no real power;* **Nobles:** *while king tries to unite kingdom, maintain feudal government imposed by lords; wait for the Capetian kings to die out (by 1328), leading to monarchy's decline;* **Clergy:** *try to retain power despite the king's use of Estates General to gain public support for policies that opposed the clergy*]

Ask: *What were the outcomes of these struggles in England? in France?*

[**England:** *a limited monarchy with power shared between king and Parliament, creating national unity and a spirit of community of the realm; church kept power to rule itself in spiritual matters;* **France:** *Capetian kings built centralized government that bypassed the nobility and gained control over the clergy; however, most of France was still ruled by feudal nobles; monarchy declined after last Capetian king died in 1328.*]

PROBE

Examine the power struggles between popes and rulers in the Holy Roman Empire. Have students read the Global History Resource Center reading on the rules of the Pope.

Ask: *How did emperors and popes try to dominate each other in Germany and Italy, and what effects did the struggle have on governments there?*

[*Emperors claimed power to appoint popes and bishops; popes in turn claimed power to control the church and to depose kings and emperors. Although the Concordat of Worms was a compromise effort, it was unsatisfactory; the struggle between popes and emperors kept the Holy Roman Empire from developing a strong central monarchy.*]

CONCLUDE

Further examine the Norman Conquest as a pivotal event in English history. Display Art and History

Transparency 11 and have students complete the accompanying worksheet. Then have students complete Core Resources Reading 11.3, the Global History Resource Center reading on the Norman Conquest, and Geography Activity 11 to further their understanding of the importance of early Norman rule in English history.

EXTEND

Cross-Curricular Connection: *Literature*

Point out that after his murder, Archbishop Thomas Becket was declared a saint and memorialized by a shrine at Canterbury, England. This shrine is the destination of the pilgrims in Geoffrey Chaucer's *The Canterbury Tales*. To give students more insight into the lives and personalities of medieval people, have the class complete the Global History Resource Center reading from Chaucer. You may wish to read additional portraits from *The Canterbury Tales* to the class and to play an audio recording of *The Canterbury Tales* as spoken in authentic Middle English. The class may be surprised to hear what English speakers of the 1300s sounded like.

Cross-Curricular Connection: *Architecture*

Refer students to the History Through the Arts feature on the elements of Gothic architecture. Have interested students research and report to the class on the construction of Gothic cathedrals.

MEET INDIVIDUAL NEEDS

Interpersonal Learners

Have students work in a group to create and perform brief "eyewitness" accounts bringing some aspects of the Norman Conquest and the rule of William the Conqueror to life. For example, two students might enact an argument between two peasants about the accomplishments or misdeeds of King William.

ASSESS

Review

Have students complete the Section 3 Review. Use answers in the Teacher's Edition, page 289, to assess student mastery of this section.

Lesson 11.4   *The Crusades*

Textbook pp. 290–293

RESOURCES

Pupil's Edition

Map, p. 291: *The Major Crusades, 1096–1204*

Through Others' Eyes, p. 292: *Islamic View of the Crusades*

Core Resources

Reading 11.4: *Salah al-Din's Courage and Steadfastness*

Global History Resource Center

Reading: *Francis of Assisi's Advice to Monks*

Reading: *A Knight's Poem in Praise of Combat*

Reading: *The Tragic Fate of the "People's Crusade"*

Videodiscs or Global History Resource Center

Image: *Crusaders in Battle*

Search Frame 816

LESSON FOCUS

What motivated Europeans to undertake the Crusades, and what effects did the Crusades and their aftermath have on Europe?

OBJECTIVES

After completing this lesson, students will be able to:

- describe the causes and consequences of the early Crusades;
- identify how the crusading spirit was used in Europe;
- discuss effects of later Crusades in northern and eastern Europe.

HOOK: Link to Today

Discuss European motivations for undertaking the Crusades. Have students identify modern cases in which people have considered violence justifiable to achieve goals related to strong religious beliefs. From students' answers, focus discussion on the Crusades as an example of a "holy war," a war waged by followers of a religion to promote or defend their faith. You may wish to have students discuss whether the means used by the crusaders [*warfare*] seem consistent with Christian teachings such as those in the Global History Resource Center reading about Francis of Assisi's advice to monks.

Explain that most Europeans who joined the Crusades believed their cause was sacred; they believed it was God's will for them to destroy infidels (people not of the faith) to gain access to the Holy Land for Christians. But point out that "holy" causes may be promoted by some for political or economic advantage.

Ask: Although many crusaders considered their cause holy, to what extent did the Crusades serve political or economic aims?

[The Crusades were originally undertaken because the Byzantine emperor wanted to get back parts of his land taken by Turks; he appealed for help to Pope Urban II, who called for the First Crusade. Others had different motives: plunder, adventure, or profits from expanded eastern trade.]

DEVELOP

Examine early Crusades as military campaigns and discuss their outcomes. Have students review the map of the four Crusades on textbook page 291 and break into four groups. Ask each group to study and report to the class on one of the first four Crusades—its leadership or makeup, its efforts to seize its objectives, and the eventual outcome of its efforts. *[Students should gather from this series of reports that the Crusades were in the long run unsuccessful at wresting the Holy Land from Turks and Muslims.]*

Examine how these campaigns were seen by forces opposing the crusaders. For more insight into the leadership of armies facing the crusaders, have the class complete Core Resources Reading 11.4. Have students also review the Through Others' Eyes feature and study the electronic media image of the crusaders. Point out that in the image the two armies appear equally resolute and well armed.

Ask: Why were the Crusades not more successful?

[*Crusaders were met by forces who were dedicated and able and who were in some cases better organized and better led than were the crusaders.*]

Ask: What effect might Richard the Lion Heart's execution of the captured Muslim soldiers and their families have had on Muslims who met the crusaders in future battles?

[*Students might suggest that it probably strengthened the Muslims' desires for revenge; also, if soldiers knew that they and their families faced certain death upon surrendering, they were more likely to fight fiercely and not surrender.*]

PROBE

Examine how the crusading spirit later took other forms within Europe. Have students point out examples of the results of later Crusades. [*The Fourth Crusade resulted in Christians fighting Christians; the Children's Crusade resulted in many children being sold into slavery.*] Then ask students to identify the forms that the crusading spirit took within Europe itself. [*It was directed against Spanish Muslims and heretic Christians such as the French Albigensians, and it gave rise to the Inquisition.*]

CONCLUDE

Discuss directions the crusading spirit took in northern and eastern Europe. Point out that in northeastern Europe, the crusading spirit led Christians to colonize areas inhabited by pagan tribes.

Ask: Who were the Teutonic Knights, and how did their conquests affect Europe?

[*They were soldier monks who fought in Hungary and Prussia to conquer the pagan inhabitants and to spread Christianity; they came to rule most of the present-day Baltic States and introduced feudalism; they promoted trade and growth of towns.*]

EXTEND

Community Resources

Link to Today. The word *crusade* has come to mean something more general than a medieval war against heresy. Ask an interested group of students to survey others in the school and in the community to see what answers people give to this question: When you think of the word *crusade*, what is the first example that comes to mind? Have students record their findings and present them to the class. Then invite students to discuss these questions: What aspects of these present-day examples seem similar to the original Crusades? What aspects seem to reflect a difference between older and newer meanings of *crusade*? If people have come to develop negative associations with the word *crusade*, why might this be?

MEET INDIVIDUAL NEEDS

Linguistic Learners

The two Global History Resource readings reveal great contrast between two types of early crusaders. Have students read the knight's poem and then the description of the People's Crusade. Ask them to write a "reply poem" to the knight from the point of view of a disillusioned peasant who survived the People's Crusade.

ASSESS

Review

Have students complete the Section 4 Review. Use answers in the Teacher's Edition, page 293, to assess student mastery of this section.

RESOURCES

Pupil's Edition
Literature Through Time, p. 296: *The Nibelungenlied*

Core Resources
Reading 11.5: *On the Government of Cities*

Visual Resources
Geography and History 11: *Trade Routes in the Middle Ages*
Everyday Life 11: *A University Classroom in the Middle Ages*

Global History Resource Center
Reading: *A Medieval Merchant's Advice*
Reading: *Maimonides on Jewish Education and Charity*
Reading: *Troubadour Ballads*

Videodiscs or Global History Resource Center

Map: *European Trade in the 1200s*

Search Frame 822

Image: *Nobleman Visits a Baker and His Wife*

Search Frame 817

Image: *Queen Blanche and the King of the Troubadours*

Search Frame 818

LESSON FOCUS
How did technological advances, growing prosperity, and revival of intellectual life change European society?

OBJECTIVES

After completing this lesson, students will be able to:
- describe effects of new technology that helped change European society after 1000;
- explain how prosperity and security affected feudal culture;
- identify the subjects that interested educated Europeans as intellectual life revived.

HOOK: Link to Today

Discuss new technology that came into use around 1000 and how it affected European society. Have the class identify modern examples of technological developments that have caused social change.
Ask: *What are some technological developments that have affected our own society?*
[Cars and freeways have promoted commuting and suburban culture; TV has changed family interaction in homes; computers and the Internet have promoted awareness of a "global village."]

Ask: *What main technological advances occurred in Europe around 1000, and how did these help change society?*
[Three-field cultivation system and wheeled plows increased food supply and population growth. Windmills and watermills with interlocking gears helped process increased yields.]

DEVELOP

Examine new trade structures resulting from increasing prosperity and the growth of towns. Have the class view Geography and History Transparency 11 and the electronic media map depicting trade. Remind students that trade means exporting products produced locally in exchange for needed products that are imported from elsewhere. Assign groups of students to imagine that they live in some of the locations on the map and then have them prepare group lists of what was shipped from and to their "home" locality.

Have students gain insight into the life of a medieval tradesman by reading the advice of a medieval merchant on the Global History Resource Center; ask what parallels they see to modern business. Also remind students of the strong role of Jewish merchants in medieval trade.
Ask: *What gave Jewish merchants an important role in European trade?*

[Many had ties to Mediterranean Jewish communities and thus had access to necessary services, and they were not forbidden to borrow or lend money at interest.] If you assign the Maimonides reading, remind students of its key point: As merchants prosper, they should be ethical and charitable.

PROBE

Explore key causes/effects of increased growth of towns and cities. Point out to students that increased food, products, and trade spurred growth and independence of towns and cities. Also note the importance of the charter of incorporation as a means of freeing towns from their feudal overlords. Then have students complete Core Resources Reading 11.5.

Ask: In what ways did incorporated cities offer people more freedom?

[Serfs who stayed in a town for a year and a day could claim freedom. Merchants could govern towns under the king's protection; merchants paid taxes to the king but set taxes so as not to hinder trade.]

Discuss how this growth of cities helped break down feudal social order. Have students view the electronic media image of the nobleman and the baker. Discuss what social changes the details of the picture suggest. [The discussion should point out that the nobleman will pay the baker to buy the bread. On the manor, the baker was required to give the lord bread for no payment except a livelihood on the manor.]

CONCLUDE

Discuss how the decline of feudalism led to an intellectual revival and a change in interests among the nobility. Point out that although we associate the word *chivalry* with knighthood, it actually reflected a change in the knight's function.

Ask: How did "chivalry" reflect a change in the role of feudal knights?

[As the king began to rely less on knights, the knights began fighting each other. Chivalry began as a code of conduct to stop Christian knights from killing each other; it required knights to be brave, fight fairly, and protect women, children, and the clergy.]

Display the electronic media image of Queen Blanche and have students read the Literature Through Time feature and the

Global History Resource Center reading on troubadour ballads.

Ask: How did changes in feudalism relate to poets or troubadours and courtly love?

[With their military role diminished, nobles' interests turned to music and poetry. Poets entertained nobility with narratives glorifying romances between noblewomen and knights.]

Discuss two other significant features of this intellectual revival: a renewed interest in science, and the beginnings of European universities.

Ask: Roger Bacon and Thomas Aquinas were examples of a new class of Europeans—what background did such people share?

[Both were products of new liberal arts curriculum taught in the universities that grew out of the cathedral schools. The new educated class used Latin and shared a common culture.]

EXTEND

Cross-Curricular Connection: *Art*

Show students Everyday Life Transparency 11 to offer students an example of how art can provide information about the life of its period. Have students complete the worksheet, or use the questions for discussion.

MEET INDIVIDUAL NEEDS

Gifted Students

Have students form two groups to conduct a debate outlining the conflict between Aristotelian and traditional Christian views on how truth is best determined. Have another group of students then summarize the attempts of Thomas Aquinas and the Scholastics to reconcile the two views.

ASSESS

Review

Have students complete the Section 5 Review. Use answers in the Teacher's Edition, page 297, to assess student mastery of this section.

In preparation for the chapter test, have students complete the Chapter 11 Review on textbook page 299, the Chapter 11 Review Activity, and the Chapter 11 Themes Review.

Chapter 11

A New Civilization in Western Europe

Understanding the Main Idea

Call on a volunteer to read aloud the *Understanding the Main Idea* paragraph. Then tell students that one of the most important aspects of the Middle Ages was the search for the security and stability that characterized the Roman Empire. In this search, people developed new institutions, such as feudalism, and strengthened existing institutions, such as the Roman Catholic Church.

Presenting Themes

See p. 269B for suggestions for introducing themes.

Using the Time Line

Have students list the time line events in their notebooks. After they have read about each event in the chapter, have students write a paragraph explaining its significance.

A New Civilization in Western Europe 476–1350

Understanding the Main Idea

The Germanic invasions into the Roman Empire transformed European society. People no longer looked to the Roman emperor for protection, but instead to local Germanic kings. This transfer of power resulted in a less stable and less unified society in western Europe. However, western Europeans were able to create a new culture that blended Roman, German, and Christian traditions.

Themes

- **Religion** How might religion unite people of different cultures and customs?
- **Politics and Law** What factors influence the development of governmental institutions?
- **Cross-cultural Interaction** How might cross-cultural exchanges enrich a society?

On Christmas Day in the year of the Lord 800 by the Christian calendar, a great crowd gathered for mass in Saint Peter's Church in Rome. They came to rejoice and pray in honor of the birth of their savior, Jesus Christ. At the high altar, Pope Leo III was to sing the mass and preside over Holy Communion. Among the congregation were bishops, nobles, Roman senators, and Charles, king of the Franks.

Moved by being in the place of Saint Peter's martyrdom, Charles knelt to pray. Behind him the congregation was hushed and expectant. As the king rose from praying, the pope suddenly moved to his side. Before the entire congregation, the head of the most Holy Roman Catholic and Apostolic Church lifted a golden crown. Placing the crown upon the Frankish king's brow, the pope proclaimed:

❝*To Charles Augustus, crowned by God, great and pacific emperor of the Romans, life and victory!*❞

Three times the pope and all those assembled shouted these words in homage. After more than 300 years, Rome had another emperor at last. Yet despite the rejoicing, the empire that Charles ruled was not that of ancient Rome, but rather a new civilization rising from its ashes.

476	496	c. 529	732	800
▲ Roman Empire in the West collapses.	▲ King Clovis converts to Christianity.	▲ Saint Benedict establishes Benedictine order.	▲ Charles Martel defeats Muslims near Tours.	▲ Pope Leo III crowns Charlemagne "emperor of the Romans."

In A.D. 800 Pope Leo III crowned the Frankish king Charlemagne emperor of the Romans.

1066	1095	1187	1215	1302
William of Normandy conquers England.	Pope Urban II promotes First Crusade.	Jerusalem falls to Muslims under Salah al-Din.	English barons force King John to sign Magna Carta.	Philip the Fair of France convenes the Estates General.

Theme:
Cross-cultural Interaction

In the 500s a Goth named Jordanes wrote *On the Origin and History of the Goths*, in which he claimed that the Amazons, a group of female warriors from Roman myths, were in fact Goths. According to Jordanes, when the men of the Gothic army were away, "a neighboring tribe attempted to carry off women of the Goths as booty. But they made a brave resistance, . . . and routed in disgrace the enemy who had come upon them." Inspired by this victory, the Goths chose two women to lead them in the conquest of new territories.

Critical Thinking Ask students why Jordanes might have used a Roman myth in his history.

ANSWER: Students may answer that Jordanes hoped to integrate Roman traditions into Gothic stories.

SECTION 1
The Emergence of the Franks

FOCUS

- What was Germanic society like?
- How did the church provide unity in Europe after the decline of Roman authority?
- How did the Franks help reunify the West?
- What factors contributed to the decline of Charlemagne's empire?

Rome had fallen. Grass grew between the broken paving stones of the great forum. Where once the caesars had ruled, Germanic kings now feasted on the remains of the empire. Yet people still held the Roman Empire in awe. Many of the new Germanic kings sought recognition from the remaining emperor in Constantinople as a sign of their legitimacy. Such efforts, however, could not hide the fact that Roman civilization had collapsed in western Europe. In its place a new civilization was about to emerge. This civilization drew on Germanic traditions for its strength, Roman traditions for its vision of the universal state, and Christian traditions for the unity to hold everything together. Later historians have referred to this time in European history as the "Middle Ages" or the "medieval" period.

Viking lion's head, 800s

The Germanic Invaders

The Ostrogoths and Visigoths who overthrew the western provinces of the Roman Empire had long lived in the shadow of the Roman world. After they took power, the kings of these Germanic peoples retained their respect for the empire's laws and traditions. Theodoric the Great, for example, an Ostrogothic king who ruled Italy from 493 to 526, maintained the senate and the old Roman imperial administration. As the great Germanic migrations continued, however, many other peoples continued to flood into the western provinces behind the Ostrogoths and Visigoths. Largely untouched by Roman ways, these Franks, Angles, Saxons, and others who established kingdoms in the old Roman provinces of northern Gaul and Britain in the 400s retained their pagan beliefs and Germanic customs.

German origins. Scholars know little of the Germans' origins, since they did not develop a written language of their own until after contact with the Roman world. Culturally and linguistically, they were part of the enormous group of Indo-European-speaking peoples. Archaeological evidence indicates that the Germans settled in Scandinavia and along the southern shores of the Baltic Sea between the Oder and Elbe Rivers as early as 750 B.C. From this southern region, some Germanic peoples, including the Saxons and Franks, moved west, reaching the Rhine River about 250 B.C. Also in the 200s a third group, including the Visigoths, Ostrogoths, and Vandals, crossed over the Baltic Sea from Scandinavia, settling between the Oder and Vistula Rivers in northeastern Europe. These eastern Germans gradually spread south to the shores of the Black Sea and the banks of the lower Danube River.

Family and cultural values. The Germans who invaded northern Europe were migratory, moving when necessary to guarantee food supplies or to flee from invaders. They were not nomadic, however, and often settled in an area for generations. They survived by hunting and fishing in the region's great forests and rivers and by herding cattle, sheep, and pigs. They lived in crude huts grouped together in small villages carved out of the forests. Warlike, they often raided their neighbors.

The Germans organized themselves into kinship groups. Primary loyalties were to the family, the clan, and sometimes to a larger tribal grouping. Tribes, however, seem to have developed primarily during times of warfare or other emergencies, and could easily dissolve or be re-formed by a different set of clans. The heads of the wealthiest families, including chiefs whose families claimed descent from the gods, ruled the villages through councils. These leading families also often acted as patrons to less wealthy families, helping them with money or support against their enemies in exchange for political and military loyalty.

The Germans were patriarchal, and fathers ruled over their families with complete authority. Those men who could afford to provide for them often had several wives. German women were primarily responsible for raising the children, preparing food, brewing beer, spinning thread, and weaving cloth. They were held in high esteem and often had a voice in tribal affairs. Around A.D. 100, the Roman historian Tacitus wrote that Germans believed women had "a certain uncanny and prophetic sense: they [the Germans] neither scorn to consult them [women] nor slight their answers." Tacitus also reported that German women supported their men on the battlefield, bringing food and encouraging warriors to be brave.

As with the pre-Islamic Arabs, the Germans developed values that reflected their struggle for survival in a harsh environment. They prized generosity and friendship. According to Tacitus:

66 *No race indulges more lavishly in hospitality and entertainment. To close the door against any human being is a crime. Everyone according to his means welcomes guests generously. Should there not be enough, he who is your host goes with you next door, without an invitation, but it makes no difference; you are received with the same courtesy.* 99

▲ Early 700s Frankish casket made of carved whalebone

Germanic Kingdoms, 526

The Migrant Tribes Germanic migrations swept across Europe and as far south as northern Africa.

❓ **Region** What group controlled northern Italy?

Despite this emphasis on generosity and friendship, Germanic society recognized different levels of status. For example, individuals gained status according to the number of cattle they owned or their leadership abilities in war.

War and social structure. Since the early Germans were migratory raiders, they were organized for fighting. This organization continued even after they began to settle down. In times of crisis, tribal assemblies chose leaders from powerful families. These chiefs organized bands of warriors who took solemn oaths of personal loyalty and obedience. In return the chief promised to provide them with food and drink and a share in the plunder.

Once the Germanic tribes moved into the Roman Empire, many of the war chiefs established themselves as kings. They distributed much of the land they conquered to their warriors, who thus became landed **nobles**. Below the king and nobles in social status were **freemen**, who could own land and had some political rights. Beneath freemen were groups of semi-free peasants, who generally had to work the land. Under all these groups were slaves—captives taken in war raids or people who had sold themselves to pay off their debts.

Germanic law. As Germanic society became increasingly hierarchical, kings and nobles began to exercise power even in times of peace. Although they eventually established kingdoms, the Germans had no concept of a state that enforced the same laws on everyone. Each Germanic tribe established its own list of offenses and appropriate penalties. When people committed offenses, the injured parties and their families handled the matter, generally by seeking revenge on the offenders and their kin. Thus, the threat of blood feuds was always present. Since such feuds were destructive, the Germans eventually devised the same alternative used by many tribal peoples—the substitution of blood money as compensation for the injury.

Since the majority of the population in the territories they invaded was non-German, the Germans did not try to impose their own legal system after conquest. Instead, former Roman citizens were allowed to continue using Roman laws. Gradually Roman law and Germanic custom began to blend, so that the flexible Roman legal traditions became a part of European society even under Germanic rule.

Although their societies remained largely tribal, the Germans established kingdoms and adopted many Roman laws and traditions after invading the Roman Empire.

The Rise of Latin Christendom

To a large degree, German acceptance of Roman influences was made possible by the one great imperial institution to survive intact—the Catholic Church. The church was organized along the lines of the Roman imperial administrative system: every district, or diocese, was headed by a bishop, and every province, made up of many dioceses, was headed by an archbishop. The bishop of Rome, who was called the pope, from the Latin word for "father,"

was generally acknowledged as the head of the church. When the Roman imperial system failed, the church took over. Soon, the church exercised secular as well as spiritual authority in many cities of the old empire.

The influence of monasticism. The church had been sustained amid the collapse of the Roman state by the faith of its members. Its message seemed particularly appropriate in the years following the fall of Rome. As people's lives became less and less secure, the church taught that earthly existence was only a step toward a better life to come. Not only did this message comfort the Romans, but in the 400s and 500s, it even began to move beyond the old Roman world. This expansion was greatly aided by monasticism.

Christian monasticism, which began in the Eastern Empire and spread to the Western Empire in the 300s and 400s, was centered around monasteries. Most monasteries in western Europe were ruled by male abbots, although some communities were under the direction of female abbesses. From these monasteries, nuns and monks often undertook missionary work in an effort to spread the word of God. Among these was the Roman-British monk Saint Patrick of Ireland. According to tradition, in the early 400s Saint Patrick converted the Irish to Christianity and established a series of monasteries.

From these communities, Irish monks and nuns carried the gospel message. They had great success, particularly in northern Britain, and established many new monasteries, such as the so-called double monastery established at Whitby. This monastery included both monks and nuns under the rule of an abbess. Saint Hilda, the founder and perhaps the most famous

◄ **When the growth of towns increased the need for agriculture, monks cleared the forests to increase the size of fields for farming. They taught this important skill to peasants.**

◀ **The brilliant decoration on the first page of the *Book of Kells*, a manuscript containing the four Gospels, was typical for ancient works transcribed by monks.**

abbess of Whitby, was praised by an early chronicler for her learning and administrative skills:

66 *So great was her prudence that not only ordinary folk, but kings and princes used to come and ask her advice in their difficulties and take it. Those under her direction were required to make a thorough study of the Scriptures and occupy themselves in good works, to such good effect that many were found fitted for Holy Orders and the service of God's altar.* 99

In addition to spreading Christianity, the monasteries kept alive the knowledge of the past. Monks lovingly copied the Gospels and other writings by hand on great sheets of scraped and cured sheepskin. They decorated the treasured writings with magnificent calligraphy in blue and red and thin layers of gold.

Although some Irish missionaries carried their message to the European mainland, Benedict of Nursia, a wealthy Roman, was primarily responsible for spreading monasticism, and thus Christianity, in Europe. Around 529 Benedict established a monastery at Monte Cassino near Naples. Although influenced by earlier models, he wrote his own set of rules to govern monastic life. The **Benedictine Rule** eventually became a fundamental pattern for Catholic monasteries.

Benedict regulated almost every aspect of monastic life, from what the monks should wear, to how much they could eat:

66 *Let one pound of bread suffice for a day, whether there be one principal meal, or both dinner and supper. . . . All must abstain from the flesh of four-footed beasts, except the delicate and the sick.* 99

The Rule described the virtues that monks should develop, including humility and obedience to God, pope, and abbot. It also offered detailed instructions about the monks' daily rounds of prayers, readings, and songs that began long before daybreak. It even regulated their hours of sleep, manual work, and meals. In their local communities, many monks held such positions as librarians, estate managers, and secretaries to kings. Some began schools to keep education and learning alive. They also undertook missionary efforts. As the Benedictines spread throughout western Europe, they preached Catholicism and reinforced the pope's authority.

Pope Gregory the Great. One of the most effective advocates of both papal authority and expansion of the church was Pope Gregory I, later called Gregory the Great. Gregory, who had been a Benedictine monk, fully supported the monastic missionary movement. To assist the movement, he adopted a policy of encouraging conversion by absorbing some pagan customs into Christianity. In 601 he sent a message advising Bishop Augustine in England of the policy:

66 *We have been giving careful thought to the affairs of the English, and have come to the conclusion that the temples of the idols among that people should on no account be destroyed. The idols are to be destroyed, but the temples themselves are to be aspersed [sprinkled] with holy water, altars set up in them, and relics deposited there. . . . In this way, we hope that the people, seeing that their temples are not destroyed, may abandon their*

error and, flocking more readily to their accustomed resorts, may come to know and adore the true God. . . . For it is certainly impossible to eradicate all errors from obstinate minds at one stroke, and whoever wishes to climb to a mountain top climbs gradually step by step, and not in one leap. "

Under the influence of leaders like Gregory, Roman and Christian traditions and institutions interacted with Germanic culture to produce a new civilization—**Latin Christendom**.

As monastics spread Christianity, the Roman Catholic Church became the primary unifying force that gave rise to Latin Christendom.

The Franks

One of the church's great hopes for Latin Christendom was the establishment of a universal Catholic church allied with a revived universal state. Toward this end, church leaders tried their best to convert the Germanic invaders. Initially they had little success, since the first wave of Germanic tribes had converted to Arian Christianity rather than Catholicism before entering the empire. As pagan tribes followed in the wake of the Ostrogoths and Visigoths, however, church authorities saw fresh opportunities to achieve their goals.

The Merovingians. By the end of the 400s, the pagan Franks of northern Gaul had emerged as the most powerful of the Germanic kingdoms and the best potential allies for the church. Under their leader Clovis and his descendants, they conquered the neighboring Visigoths and Burgundians, creating a great empire that covered much of Gaul.

Clovis was the first king of the Merovingian dynasty, which took its name from Merovech, one of his ancestors. According to tradition,

Charlemagne's Empire, 768–814

Conqueror of Europe Charlemagne's goal to renew the Roman Empire required him to conquer most of Europe. However, the empire did not survive long after his death in 814.

? Location Where did Charlemagne establish his imperial capital?

Clovis converted from paganism to Catholic Christianity in 496. It was a shrewd move that gained him the support of the church and of the old Roman aristocracy. Clovis hoped to use the church to help him run his new empire. Germanic tribal society had never developed the administrative institutions necessary to run a realm the size of the Merovingian domain. For its part, the church was more than willing to supply administrators and advice to the new Germanic king.

Clovis's empire did not last long, however, partly due to his allegiance to Germanic inheritance customs. On his deathbed in 511, Clovis divided his kingdom among his four sons as custom decreed. Plagued by civil war, the growing power of the Frankish nobility, and challenges from Byzantine and Germanic forces invading from the east, Clovis's heirs could not maintain control of the realm. By the 700s real power in the Frankish empire rested with the most important official of the king's household, the mayor of the palace. The Merovingian kings, like the Abbasids in Baghdad, had become mere figureheads.

The Carolingians. In 732 Charles Martel, the mayor of Austrasia and Neustria, gained the church's favor when he defeated a Muslim raiding party near the French town of Tours. Many hailed it as a great Christian victory, and Charles achieved enormous fame. However, when the pope called for his aid against the Lombards in Italy, Charles refused. His son, Pepin, later answered a similar call only after the pope had agreed that Pepin should depose the last Merovingian king and assume the throne himself. In 751 the pope traveled to France to proclaim Pepin "king by the grace of God." Pepin's crowning launched what came to be called the Carolingian dynasty.

In 754 and 756 Pepin achieved victories against the Lombards. He turned the lands he captured in central Italy over to the pope. This gift, called the **Donation of Pepin**, created the Papal States. The gift made the papacy a secular as well as a spiritual power and further strengthened the alliance between the Carolingian kings and the church.

The Carolingian dynasty took its name from Pepin's son Carolus Magnus, or Charlemagne (Charles the Great). Charlemagne was born in 742. Both a deeply religious and highly intelligent man, he became an outstanding ruler although he had little formal education. Charlemagne wanted to establish an empire with the power and glory of the old Roman Empire. On his father's death in 768, however, the kingdom was divided between Charlemagne and his brother Carloman. Not until his brother died in 771 was Charlemagne able to assume sole power as king of the Franks and pursue his ambition. He soon took as his motto the Latin phrase, *Renovatio imperii romani,* "Renewal of the Roman Empire."

Charlemagne
BIOGRAPHY

Like many kings of his day, Charlemagne spent much of his life at war. He defeated the Lombards in Italy, as well as the Saxons in northern Germany and the Avars in central Europe. Although unable to evict the Muslims from Spain, he drove them across the Pyrenees Mountains, establishing a Spanish buffer zone. Eventually, Charlemagne controlled most of western Europe.

Charlemagne divided his realm into counties, ruled by counts. The border regions, known as marches, were ruled by dukes. Each of these nobles was directly responsible to Charlemagne and carried out the king's commands in their territories. To show his support of this system, on Christmas Day in the year 800, Pope Leo III crowned Charlemagne "emperor of the Romans." The ideal of a universal empire allied with the universal church seemed close at hand.

The Carolingian renaissance. Charlemagne did his best to live up to the image of a Roman emperor. He was admired for his skills as a warrior as well his devotion to Christianity. His secretary Einhard has left a glimpse of the man:

❝ *Charles was large and strong, and of lofty stature . . . ; the upper part of his head was round, his eyes very large and animated, nose a little long, hair fair, and face laughing and merry. Thus his appearance was always stately and dignified . . . although his neck was thick and somewhat short, and his belly rather prominent. . . . His gait [stride] was firm, his whole carriage manly, and his voice clear, but not so strong as his size led one to expect.* ❞

Charlemagne was particularly interested in education. He established a palace school for young nobles, where scholars from throughout western Europe came to teach. He also encouraged the establishment of schools at monasteries and cathedrals across Europe to give priests a basic education. This revival of learning is sometimes called the **Carolingian renaissance**, or rebirth.

Despite Charlemagne's efforts, his empire did not last long after his death in 814. During the reign of his one surviving son, Louis the Pious, civil war wracked the kingdom as Louis's sons fought among themselves for their father's

Charlemagne
Charlemagne's interest in education extended foremost to his children. When his sons and daughters were young, Charlemagne educated them in math, science, and other subjects. As the boys grew up, he taught them horsemanship and war skills, while the girls learned how to spin thread and make cloth.

Critical Thinking Ask students what political reasons Charlemagne might have had for spending so much time on his children's education.

ANSWER: Students might suggest that Charlemagne hoped to leave the empire in capable hands.

R **RESOURCE ACTIVITY**

GLOBAL HISTORY RESOURCE CENTER
Reading: *How Charlemagne Ruled His Empire*

Print out and distribute the reading. Ask students to imagine they live in medieval village that has just been visited by Charlemagne's missionaries. Have each student write a newspaper account of the visit.

Level 3

REVIEW &
ASSESSMENT
RESOURCES

- Study Guide 11.1
- Daily Quiz 11.1
- Main Idea Activity
  11.1

All Levels

Map Answer
Baltic Sea, North Sea

R RESOURCE ACTIVITY

**READINGS IN
WORLD HISTORY
Reading 11.1**
*Peasant Life During the
Time of Charlemagne*

Have students read the
account a peasant fam-
ily living during the time
of Charlemagne. Then
have them complete the
questions.

Level 2

R RESOURCE ACTIVITY

**GLOBAL HISTORY
RESOURCE CENTER
Image:** *Viking Warrior*

Print out and distribute
the image of the Viking
warrior. Have students
pick two elements of the
Viking's costume—hel-
met, breastplate, sword,
and so on. Then have stu-
dents write a brief explanation of the purpose of
each item.

Sheltered English

throne. The civil wars continued even after Louis's death in 840. In 843 his sons finally signed the Treaty of Verdun, which divided the empire into a western, a middle, and an eastern kingdom. The empire had begun to crumble.

Although short-lived, the Frankish empires kept alive the idea of a universal state allied with a universal church.

✠ Renewed Invasions

Charlemagne's empire splintered not only because of internal feuds and divisions but also because of invaders, who once again swarmed into the empire from every direction. Among the most feared of the invaders were the Vikings, Magyars, and Muslims.

Vikings. In the late 700s and early 800s—for reasons that scholars still dispute—the peoples of Scandinavia burst onto the stage of history. While the Germans had begun gradually to give in to Christianity and the civilizing influence of the old Roman world, the Vikings remained both pagan and warlike. In long shallow-draft ships, driven by oars and a single large square sail, the Vikings swept into Europe. For nearly 200 years wave after wave of raiders sailed out of Scandinavia every spring, returning to their northern homes before the icy gales of winter had set in, or when their ships had been filled with plunder and slaves.

To the east, they sailed down the rivers of Russia as far as the Black Sea. To the west, they attacked not only the British Isles and northern France, but also Ireland and Spain, and they even sailed as far as North America. In the south, some raided the Mediterranean.

Peoples of Europe, 600–1000

Renewed Invasions Viking, Magyar, and Muslim invaders raided towns across Europe and northern Africa. In this chaotic period, the balance of power shifted from east to west.

? Location What body of water separated the Viking homeland from the Western Slavs? from the Celts?

Everywhere, Viking raiders struck terror in the hearts of their victims, for their attacks were swift and savage. Monks were favorite targets. To protect themselves, Irish monks built tall stone towers with doors high off the ground. At the first sign of Viking ships, the monks would flee to the towers and draw up the ladders. Even in times of relative peace, their prayers often ended with the heartfelt plea: "and from the wrath of the Vikings, dear Lord, deliver us." In other parts of Europe, too, local lords built stone castles into which villagers might flee for safety.

Over time Vikings began to settle many of the lands they had formerly raided. For example, large Viking settlements known as the Danelaw were established in northeast England, while across the Channel the Viking chief Rollo claimed what became known as Normandy in northern France. As the Vikings began to settle, they turned from raiding to long-distance commerce and trade.

Magyars. At the end of the 800s, a new wave of invasions from the east once again terrorized Europe. Magyar tribes crossed the Danube and moved westward through Europe, attacking villages and taking peasants to sell in eastern slave markets. In many early attacks on isolated settlements, the Magyars killed or carried off everyone in the villages. Convinced that such brutal raiders must be returning Huns, people began to call them Hungarians. Eventually the Magyars settled in the area known today as Hungary. North of the Magyars, Slavic tribes also migrated from the east to settle in Europe.

Muslims. The most serious and longterm challenge to Christian Europe, however, continued to come from across the Mediterranean. Muslim forces attacked from North Africa and Spain in the 800s and 900s. Since Europe offered little in the way of other valuable commodities, Muslim raiders invaded Europe largely in search of slaves. In addition, Muslims saw Christians as their most serious religious rivals. In 846 Muslim forces captured and sacked Rome before retreating.

Around the same time, Muslim fleets blocked Byzantine trade in the Mediterranean, cutting Italy off from the Eastern Empire. Deprived of eastern support, the popes had little choice but to turn to the Franks for protection. As a result, the balance of power in Latin Christendom shifted to the Frankish homeland in northwestern Europe.

In the face of internal divisions and renewed invasions, Charlemagne's empire fell apart.

▶ Scholars believe that this ship, found in a burial site at Gokstad, Norway, probably belonged to a Viking chieftain in the 800s.

SECTION 1 REVIEW

IDENTIFY and explain the significance of the following:
nobles
freemen
Benedictine Rule
Gregory the Great
Latin Christendom
Charles Martel
Donation of Pepin
Charlemagne
Carolingian renaissance

LOCATE and explain the importance of the following:
Tours
Pyrenees

1. *Main Idea* How did the church provide Europe with a sense of unity?
2. *Main Idea* How did Charlemagne's empire change western Europe?

3. *Geography: Place* How did geography help raiders invade Europe?
4. *Writing to Explain* Explain how life in the Germanic tribes changed after the fall of Rome.
5. *Analyzing* Why might people in Europe after the fall of Rome have wanted to establish European unity?

CORE LESSON PLAN
See pages 269E and 269F for Lesson Plan 11.2.

Theme: Politics and Law

The most important nobles held large fiefs received directly from the king, and they in turn divided their land and granted fiefs to lesser nobles. This division continued down to the level of the lowest noble, who held a single manor. Originally, the granting of fiefs was repeated whenever a lord or vassal died, but eventually control of the fief became hereditary.

Critical Thinking Ask students what advantages hereditary control of fiefs would have held compared to redistributing the fiefs whenever a lord or vassal died.

ANSWER: Students might suggest that hereditary control gave nobles further incentives to take care of their lands and protect them so their children could inherit them.

SECTION 2
Feudalism, Manorialism, and the Church

FOCUS

- What was feudalism?
- What was the manorial system?
- What role did the church play in society?

In its weakened state, the Carolingian Empire could no longer guarantee the safety of its people against invaders. Soon, smaller kingdoms emerged in Europe. Real power in these kingdoms, which were generally headed by weak kings, rested in the hands of the nobles. In return for land, these nobles pledged military service to the kings and provided protection to the local people. As civilization retreated to the local level, new political and economic systems emerged that emphasized personal loyalty, mutual responsibilities, and local self-sufficiency. Yet despite these challenges to European unity, the church continued to bind people together through a larger sense of Christian identity.

Communion plate, 800s

The Emergence of Feudal Society

The Carolingian government—like earlier Germanic kingdoms—had long granted nobles land in exchange for military service. When the land passed to new generations, the obligation of service passed with it. After the dynasty's collapse, this exchange of land for service took on new importance. Although rich in land, the rulers of the kingdoms that emerged after the end of the Carolingian Empire were generally too weak to protect their people from invasion. The burden of protection fell increasingly on local nobles, some of whom were as powerful as the kings they served.

Providing protection meant supporting large numbers of foot soldiers as well as mounted warriors called **knights**. Both foot soldiers and knights, with their horses and equipment, were expensive to maintain. Thus, nobles demanded land from the new kings in exchange for providing these troops. In return, the kings demanded pledges of loyalty and faithfulness from the nobles, and promises of support in times of war. Nobles then granted portions of their land to their own knights in exchange for similar pledges of loyalty and service. The person who granted the land—or **fief** (FEEF), as it was called—became a **lord**. The person who received the land became a **vassal**. Because fiefs could be subdivided, one might be both a lord and a vassal. For each fief, vassals were expected to pledge their military service, often including a set number of knights and foot soldiers. This practice later came to be called **feudalism.**

Feudalism was above all a personal set of mutual obligations between lord and vassal. At the heart of feudalism was the oath of loyalty. In front of witnesses, a vassal placed his clasped hands between those of the lord and pledged to become "his man." The new relationship was usually sealed by a ceremonial kiss between the two men. The vassal then took an oath of faithfulness. For his part, the lord also promised to "do justice" for the vassal and his family. If he failed to ensure such justice, the vassal might rightfully conclude that the bonds of the relationship had been broken, and that he no longer owed the lord his loyalty. Galbert of Bruges, a Flemish chronicler, offered the following account of the

▶ Knights were able to attack more forcefully after the introduction of the stirrup and changes in saddle design that gave riders more body support in the front and back. These innovations allowed knights to wear heavier armor and to stand in their saddles as they galloped forward to engage the enemy.

oath-taking ceremony between Count William of Flanders and his new vassals in 1127:

" *He who had done homage [acknowledged himself a vassal] gave his fealty [oath] to the representative of the count in these words, 'I promise on my faith that I will in future be faithful to Count William, and will observe my homage to him completely against all persons in good faith and without deceit,' and . . . took his oath to this upon the relics of the saints. Afterward, with a little rod which the count held in his hand, he gave investitures [land grants] to all who by this agreement had given their security and homage and accompanying oath.* "

Author's Commentary

FEUDALISM

Although the basic elements of what we now call feudalism were eventually used throughout much of Europe, it is important to understand that feudalism was not a single, unified, and universal system from the beginning. Instead, it developed over time. Even the term *feudalism* was not coined until the early 1800s.

Feudalism can best be understood as part of a larger and more diverse social system in which aristocratic patrons established various kinds of relationships with "clients." Some clients, for example, might simply have acted as a lord's household retainers or servants. In exchange for food and shelter, they provided military service when necessary and perhaps acted as household guards or even farm managers.

The exchange of land for service was the highest form of such a patronage system, and the least common. For one thing, there were far more potential clients around than there was land to give them. One consequence of this shortage of land and the abundance of potential vassals was an expansion of feudalism from the old Frankish kingdoms. Lords sought more land in order to give it to more vassals, who could then provide more soldiers with which to take more land.

Under this kind of pressure, feudalism spread from northern Europe into regions unfamiliar with it. The Normans, for example, after extending the practice to England, also carried it into Wales and Ireland, where Celtic people at the time lived under very different ideas of land ownership. Other Norman and northern Frankish knights also carved out fiefs for themselves by conquering Sicily and parts of southern Italy. In eastern Europe, too, German knights began to spread into lands still held by pagan Slavic tribes in order to obtain landed fiefs.

Sometimes, local people themselves saw the advantages of feudalism, particularly when threatened by neighbors who practiced it. Scottish kings, for example, fearful of the growing strength of feudal knights and especially the building of castles across their borders, deliberately invited some Anglo-Norman nobles to settle in southern Scotland as their own vassals. Thus, the lowlands of Scotland became a feudal region. Where such expansion was unsuccessful, however—as, for example, in the Scottish highlands and in most of central and northern Italy—feudalism did not take hold and older forms of patronage survived. Europe thus continued to be a region of enormous social diversity.

Feudalism was a system by which lords granted their vassals land in exchange for military service and personal loyalty.

The Manorial System

Feudalism was essentially a political and military system. The primary economic system during the Middle Ages was the **manorial system**. Under the manorial system, nobles gave peasants the right to work the land on their estates—or manors—in return for a fixed payment. While a small fief might have only one manor, large fiefs had several.

The manor generally consisted of the manor house or castle, pastures, fields, woods, and a village. The lord kept about one third of the manor land, called the **domain**, for himself. Peasants farmed the remaining two thirds of the land. In exchange they gave the lord part of their crops, worked his land, paid feudal taxes, and did various other jobs on the manor. A typical manor village might be located on a pond or stream that furnished water power for a mill. Houses were usually clustered together for safety a short distance away from the manor house or castle. The manor's land surrounded the village and included

▲ In this illustration from the 1400s, men and women are seen working in the fields to gather crops during the busy harvest time.

vegetable plots, cultivated fields, open pastureland, and forests. As town life dwindled and trade diminished, most manors became nearly self-sufficient. Only a few items, such as iron, salt, and tar, may have needed to be imported.

Peasant life. Most peasants on a manor were **serfs** who could not leave the land without their lord's permission. Serfs were not slaves, since they could not be sold away from the land. If the land passed to a new lord, the serfs became the new lord's tenants. In addition, manors often had some free people who rented land from the lord. Free people might have included skilled workers necessary to the village economy, such as millers and blacksmiths. Most villages also had a priest to provide for spiritual needs.

Peasants usually lived in small, single-room wooden houses with earthen floors, which the family shared with their animals. Food was simple—coarse brown bread, cheese, vegetables, and, on occasion, pork or bacon. In northern Europe people usually drank beer with their meals; in southern Europe they drank wine. The family worked as a unit. Men tended to do most of the heavy farming, including labor on the lord's lands. Women made the family's clothing, cooked, tended the vegetable garden, and foraged through the woods for nuts, berries, and firewood. Children helped herd sheep, tend poultry, and care for younger brothers and sisters. At harvest time, the whole family helped bring in the crops. Life expectancy was short due to hunger, disease, accidents, and chronic warfare.

Life of the nobility. Although the nobility had more wealth and power than serfs, they did not necessarily lead luxurious or easy lives. Disease and accidents affected them also, and they were responsible for the welfare of their vassals and serfs during times of famine and warfare. Many noble families lived in castles that served as a base for protecting the lord's domain and enforcing his authority. The lord might spend much of his day administering his land and dispensing justice to vassals and serfs. Sometimes he might carry out inspection tours of his domain to ensure that he received the services and rents he was due. He might have to spend some time each year fighting, either for his own lord or for himself.

Women in a noble household had their own important duties. They supervised the running of the household, helped prepare men's clothing and equipment for battle, and governed the estate when their husbands or fathers were away. They also cared for the sick and injured, provided religious instruction to the household, and cared for the children. Mothers in the nobility were also responsible for securing their children's education. Daughters often went to the home of a respected lady to learn how to manage a large household in preparation for marriage. There they learned the manners and

▶ When the men of the home were absent, women of noble families exercised authority, often running the manor.

skills expected in noble society. Sons went to live in knightly households as early as the age of eight. There they learned to ride, to handle the sword, lance, and heavy shield, to swing an ax, and to do their duties with knightly manners.

Under the manorial system, a lord allowed peasants to work his manor, or estate, in exchange for set payments. The self-sufficient manor was the period's basic economic unit.

The Church

While feudalism and the manorial system served to fragment European society, common Christian beliefs pulled people back together. For most people, life centered on the parish church. Religious ceremonies marked every major event in a person's life, from birth to death. Frequent religious festivals offered everyone an opportunity to celebrate and socialize.

Many nobles gave large amounts of money and land to monasteries and convents in an effort to safeguard their souls and the souls of their relatives. They believed that having religious men and women praying for them would help erase some of their own sins and make it easier for them and their families to enter heaven. Nobles also found monastic careers useful for widows, daughters who did not marry, and younger sons who would not inherit their fathers' lands. With such benefactors, many religious orders became extremely wealthy.

As monasteries and the church in general became more and more involved in the feudal system, problems arose. Many churches and monastic communities

Theme:
Technology
Although castles were the homes of the aristocracy, their main purpose was to defend against attack. The strongest part of the castle was the keep, where the lord and his family lived. The keep was surrounded by a wall or a series of walls, which were flanked by towers. The outermost walls were often protected by moats or by the sheer drop of cliffs. Castles proved to be effective defensive fortifications until the use of gunpowder allowed artillery to penetrate castle walls.

Critical Thinking Ask students to speculate on how the invention of gunpowder might have affected the manorial system.

ANSWER: Students may suggest that once castles could not protect local people, laborers would feel little obligation to work the land in return for safety. Peasants might leave the land or demand more in return for their labor.

REVIEW & ASSESSMENT RESOURCES

• Study Guide 11.2
• Daily Quiz 11.2
• Main Idea Activity 11.2

All Levels

284

IDENTIFY

For significance, see the following pages:
knights (p. 280)
fief (p. 280)
lord (p. 280)
vassal (p. 280)
feudalism (p. 280)
manorial system (p. 282)
domain (p. 282)
serfs (p. 282)
William of Aquitaine (p. 284)
sacraments (p. 284)

1. The king or a noble granted land to a lesser noble in exchange for military service and loyalty.

2. Serfs farmed and were bound to the land; free peasants worked as artisans or tenant farmers. Noblemen oversaw their domains and fought wars; noblewomen ran the household and governed estates when the men were absent.

3. People believed that the church and the system of sacraments provided them with a definite way to attain salvation.

4. Feudalism distributed power among many lords, each of whom controlled his own domain and the people who lived on it; people viewed themselves as belonging to a local community rather than to a larger state or empire.

5. Monasteries grew larger and wealthier; kings and nobles appointed church leaders; reformers sought change to free the church from interference by secular authorities.

received their land from nobles in return for payments or armed knights. Consequently, before about 1000, many nobles actually appointed abbots, frequently from their own families. Kings even appointed bishops and archbishops.

By the 900s some people were calling for reforms. Among these was Duke William of Aquitaine. When he founded the abbey of Cluny in the early 900s, the duke required that the monastery answer only to the pope. Freed from feudal obligations, the monks could focus all of their attention on their spiritual work. The monks of Cluny became well known for their discipline and for their close ties to the pope. Reformers flocked to Cluny to learn how to transform their own monasteries, and nobles richly endowed the reformed institutions.

In an effort to extend the discipline of the monastery to all Christendom, the monks of Cluny encouraged the development of a uniform set of **sacraments**, the most important ceremonies of the church, through which Christians believed they could achieve salvation. In 1215 church leaders recognized seven sacraments—baptism (admission to the Christian community); Holy Eucharist (Holy Communion); confirmation (admission to church membership); penance (acts showing repentance for sins); the taking of Holy Orders (admission to the priesthood); matrimony (marriage); and extreme unction (anointing the sick and dying). All sacraments, except

This jeweled silver chalice and communion plate were crafted in Germany in the 1200s.

confirmation and ordination, which had to be performed by the bishops, could be administered by the parish priest.

The centerpiece of Christian worship became the Eucharist. The church taught that in celebrating the Eucharist those who sought forgiveness for their sins could share in the body and blood of Christ. Although bread and wine were used in the ceremony, the doctrine of transubstantiation taught that God's power transformed them into the elements of Christ's body and blood. By sharing in this sacred meal, people hoped to be reunited with God.

The church and the sacraments provided people with a common path by which they believed they could achieve salvation.

SECTION 2 REVIEW

IDENTIFY and explain the significance of the following:
knights
fief
lord
vassal
feudalism
manorial system
domain
serfs
William of Aquitaine
sacraments

1. *Main Idea* How was the feudal system in medieval Europe organized?

2. *Main Idea* What was daily life like for the peasantry and nobility on the medieval European manor?

3. *Religion* What role did the Roman Catholic Church and the system of sacraments play in European society during the Middle Ages?

4. *Writing to Explain* Imagine that you are a medieval king or queen. Write a paragraph explaining how the feudal system caused the fragmentation of European society.

5. *Synthesizing* How did the Roman Catholic Church begin to change by the 900s? Why did reformers seek to change the church and what were the results of reform?

Kings, Nobles, Popes, and Emperors

FOCUS

- What were the consequences of the struggle for power between kings and nobles in England?
- How did the French kings strengthen their power?
- What were the consequences of the rivalry between the popes and the Holy Roman Empire?

As the descendants of Charlemagne died out in the early 900s, strong local lords elected new kings from among themselves to act as regional war leaders. As the invasions ended, these new kings began to consolidate and expand their power. In the process, they often had to fight both their own nobles and the church, which now began to claim authority over all secular rulers. The most effective of these new kingdoms emerged in England, France, and Germany.

The Metropolitan Museum of Art. Gift of George Blumenthal, 1941.
©1986/94 Metropolitan Museum of Art.

Otto I offers Christ the Magdeburg cathedral in this carved ivory piece from about 970.

England

The process of establishing royal power in England was greatly extended by the **Norman Conquest**. In 1066 Duke William of Normandy invaded England, claiming the English throne. William's conquest took a long time, however, since the Saxon nobles bitterly resisted the Norman advance. Because William was able to grant lands to his Norman nobles only as he conquered new territory, most of them ended up with holdings scattered throughout the country. Thus, it was difficult for any single lord to gather enough power to challenge the king's authority.

William strengthened his power by ordering a survey of the entire realm. The result was the enormous **Domesday Book**, whose title refers to the Day of Judgment. A chronicler recorded the process:

> **❝**He sent his men over all England into every shire and had them find out how many hundred hides [one hide supported one family] there were in the shire, or what land and cattle the king himself had, or what dues he ought to have in twelve months from the shire. . . . So very narrowly did he have it investigated, that there was no single hide nor yard of land, nor . . . one ox nor one cow nor one pig was there left out, and not put down in his record.**❞**

In this way William and his agents knew exactly who owned what and what it was worth. This was an invaluable tool for levying taxes, distributing land fairly, and figuring out exactly how many knights and foot soldiers each lord owed in military service. It also made it easier for the king to administer the kingdom as a single entity.

William's son Henry I took advantage of the Domesday record by creating a central treasury department, which collected taxes from the entire realm for the king. Henry II further strengthened royal power by creating the most efficient government bureaucracy in Europe. He also moved toward establishing a uniform system of justice. Instead of local feudal courts handling all cases but the most important ones, Henry appointed traveling judges who enforced the king's law throughout the kingdom. Thus, he laid the foundations for what would become the

SECTION 3

CORE LESSON PLAN
See pages 269G and 269H for Lesson Plan 11.3.

MULTIMEDIA PRESENTATION STRATEGY

VISUAL RESOURCES
Art and History 11
Bayeux Tapestry

Show the transparency and share the information from Art and History Fact Sheet 11. Then have students complete the accompanying worksheet.

Level 2

RESOURCE ACTIVITY

GLOBAL HISTORY RESOURCE CENTER
Reading: *The Norman Conquest of England*

Print out and distribute the reading and have students read this description of the Battle of Hastings aloud. Have students create an illustrated map of England based on this information, outlining events before, during, and after the Norman victory.

Sheltered English

▲ This inventory for the Domesday Book listed all property in Bedfordshire and helped settle boundary disputes among small tenants.

common law—the laws common to all England. Justice in the king's courts was uniform and applied equally to all. As the king's justice replaced that of the feudal lords, people began to identify with the central authority.

Only the church remained outside the king's authority. The church claimed that the clergy owed their allegiance not to kings but to the pope, and therefore that they could be tried only in church courts. As Henry clashed with the church over the issue, Thomas Becket, the archbishop of Canterbury, was murdered in his own church by some of Henry's men. Within three years Becket was proclaimed a saint by the church. King Henry had to undergo a humiliating public confession of fault and a symbolic lashing by the monks of Canterbury. He also had to give up his efforts to make the clergy in England subject to the king's law.

During the reign of Henry's son John, the nobility rebelled against the growth of royal power. In 1215 they forced John to sign **Magna Carta,** the Great Charter, in which he agreed to obtain their consent before raising new taxes. In addition, the charter made it clear that even the king must observe the law. He could not imprison anyone or confiscate their property without following legal procedures. Nor could he take property without paying for it. The charter laid the foundation for a limited monarchy in England, in which the king shared power with his most important subjects.

By the mid-1200s a group of nobles called the Great Council regularly advised the king. In the 1260s, during another rebellion, the council was expanded to include some townspeople and knights. The new body provided an early model for what eventually became **Parliament,** a representative assembly that gradually evolved over the next several centuries into a two-chamber body—the House of Lords and the House of Commons. As both kings and their subjects became used to these institutions, they began consciously to identify with what they called "the community of the realm."

As English kings and their nobles struggled for power after the Norman Conquest, they developed a limited monarchy and a new sense of unity.

France

While the English kings struggled for power with their nobles, a similar scene was being played out in France, but with a different outcome. Under the last of the Carolingians, France had been divided into large provinces, each ruled by a count or duke. These French nobles ruled their lands as they liked. In 987 they elected Hugh Capet—the first of the Capetian dynasty—as king.

At first the French kings were no more powerful than their great nobles—indeed, they were less powerful than some. Despite this handicap, the Capetians ruled for more than 300 years and gradually extended the power of the French monarchy.

Where the nobles of England eventually came to identify with the entire kingdom, in France only the kings thought of the kingdom as a whole. As French monarchs sought to assert their authority over their vassals, they increased the power of the central government. Unable to rely on their lords, they looked for loyal, well-trained officials to maintain a strong central government. They also extended the jurisdiction of their courts. Between 1285 and 1314, for example, Philip the Fair tried to gain royal control over the entire legal system. He designated the **Parlement of Paris** as the supreme court for the entire realm and expanded its functions. Philip also succeeded, where Henry II of England had failed, in controlling the clergy. To gain the support of his people for this challenge to the church, in 1302 Philip convened the **Estates General**, a representative body drawn from the three great classes, or estates, of French society: the clergy, the nobility, and the commoners.

Through the Estates General, later French kings were also able to rally support for their policies. Although kings consulted the Three Estates, they never granted them any real power like that exercised by the English Parliament. In England, Parliament had been used by the nobility to check the power of the king, while in France the Estates General had been created by the king in order to control the clergy and bypass the nobility.

Despite these reforms, France remained largely feudal. While French kings might have had a vision of the kingdom as a united nation, at the local level such an idea was still almost nonexistent. When the last Capetian king died in 1328, the power of the monarchy began to decline.

The French kings tried to create a strong centralized government through legal reforms and by establishing their authority over the clergy.

The Holy Roman Empire

Not all of Charlemagne's old territories produced strong monarchies like those in France and England. In Germany and Italy, where once the popes and emperors had stood united, the two soon became bitter rivals for power.

The Growth of France, 1035–1328

Legend: French royal domain | Fiefs of French kings | English possessions in France

The Capetian King   The Capetian king Philip II, who ruled from 1179 to 1223, seized lands that the English had gained through marriages with French nobles.

◆ **Linking Geography and History**   What were the English possessions remaining in France in 1328?

History THROUGH THE ARTS

Gothic Architecture

By the 1100s Europe's Romanesque-style architecture —which, as the name implies, was heavily influenced by Roman traditions—was beginning to give way to Gothic architecture. The great churches built during this period provide some of the best examples of this new and innovative style.

Light was a central element in Gothic archi-

Notre Dame of Paris

tecture. As one of the leading supporters of the new style put it, "It was most cunningly provided that . . . the whole [church] would shine with the wonderful and uninterrupted light of most sacred windows, pervading the interior beauty." Ceilings that soared heavenward were also characteristic of Gothic churches.

To achieve these effects, architects and builders developed a whole new set of engineering skills. For example, to free up the interior and carry the roof as high as possible, the wall supports were redesigned and moved to the outside. These new flying buttresses,

Interior of Sainte-Chapelle

as they were called, pressed in upon the walls to keep them from collapsing. The architects and builders also designed elaborate vaulted ceilings that used the interior arches to sustain the roof. As a result, Gothic churches could rise higher and have more windows than Romanesque churches.

Thinking About Art

1. What are some of the central design elements of Gothic architecture?
2. How do the churches pictured on this page reflect the ideas of Gothic architecture?

Otto the Great. In 936 the German feudal lords elected Otto I, known as Otto the Great, as king. When Otto defended Pope John XII against unruly Roman nobles, the pope crowned him "emperor of the Romans" in 962. Otto's title was the same as Charlemagne's, but his empire was much smaller—just Germany and northern Italy. This new Holy Roman Empire established a unique relationship between Germany and Italy that continued for more than 800 years.

The power of the Holy Roman emperors reached a high point under Henry III, who was crowned emperor in 1046. During his reign

three different men claimed to be pope. He deposed them and selected his own candidate. He then reformed the papacy, until, as one person put it:

❝ *The kingdom and the priesthood . . . shall be so closely united by the grace of mutual charity, that it will be possible to find the king in the Roman pontiff [pope], and the Roman pontiff in the king.* ❞

Henry also chose the next three popes, but his successors were unable to maintain such power.

Pope Gregory VII. Henry III's son, Henry IV, was only six years old when his father died. While Henry was a child, the popes tried to regain their independence. In 1059 the pope declared that only the **college of cardinals** in Rome, a body of bishops chosen for the purpose, would appoint future popes. Soon a major struggle between the Holy Roman Empire and the papacy broke out. The struggle intensified when Gregory VII became pope.

Gregory and Henry clashed over the appointment of church officials by kings or emperors. Henry insisted that he had the right to appoint bishops within the empire just as Charlemagne and other German kings had done. Gregory, however, insisted that because spiritual matters were more important than worldly ones, the pope not only controlled the church but also had the power to depose kings and emperors.

Henry convinced the German bishops to call for Gregory's removal. Gregory responded by excommunicating the emperor and declaring him deposed. Cleverly, the pope played on the rivalries of the German lords, who disliked the idea of a strong emperor who might limit their own power. The lords rose in rebellion.

Henry proved just as clever, however. In the winter of 1077 he traveled to northern Italy.

Standing barefoot in the snow before the pope, Henry begged for forgiveness and readmission to the church. He knew that as a priest Gregory could not refuse. Gregory reluctantly lifted the excommunication. The feud continued, however. When Gregory again excommunicated him, Henry marched on Rome—forcing Gregory to flee to Salerno, where he died in 1085.

Finally, in 1122, Emperor Henry V and the church reached a compromise in the **Concordat of Worms**. The emperor agreed that the pope should invest the bishops of Germany with spiritual authority, but he retained the right to grant them symbols of earthly power and to insist that they remain obligated to him as feudal vassals. Although England and France made similar deals, no one was really happy with the compromise. More importantly, the ongoing struggle between popes and emperors prevented the development of a strong, centralized government in the Holy Roman Empire, as well as the establishment of the pope's supreme authority over earthly rulers.

Rivalry between popes and emperors weakened the power of the church and prevented the establishment of a strong central government in the Holy Roman Empire.

SECTION 3 REVIEW

IDENTIFY and explain the significance of the following:
Norman Conquest
Domesday Book
common law
Magna Carta
Parliament
Parlement of Paris
Estates General
college of cardinals
Concordat of Worms

LOCATE and explain the importance of the following:
Normandy
Paris
Holy Roman Empire

1. *Main Idea* What problems did kings in England, France, and Germany face in trying to consolidate their power?
2. *Main Idea* What were the consequences of the rivalry between the church and the Holy Roman emperors?
3. *Religion* In what ways did the Catholic Church become a political power in Europe?
4. *Writing to Explain* Explain some of the tactics Pope Gregory VII used in his struggle against the Holy Roman emperor Henry IV.

5. *Contrasting* Make a chart in two columns like the one below. List the ways in which England and France differed in their political development. How did the establishment of Parliament and the signing of Magna Carta set England apart from other kingdoms in Europe?

ENGLAND	FRANCE

A NEW CIVILIZATION IN WESTERN EUROPE **289**

SECTION 4
The Crusades

FOCUS

- What were the causes and consequences of the early Crusades?
- How was the crusading spirit used in Europe?
- How did the crusading spirit affect northern and eastern Europe?

As Europeans began to recover from the era of barbarian invasions, they once again looked eastward. The rise of the Saljuq Turks seriously threatened the Byzantine Empire. When the Byzantine emperor appealed to Pope Urban II for help in recovering his lost provinces from the Turks in the 1090s, Urban urged men of all ranks to wage a great war, or Crusade, to recover the Holy Land for Christ. Throughout Europe people heeded the call. Some were inspired by faith and the hope of being cleansed of sin. Many knights sought more earthly rewards like land or plundered wealth. Merchants saw a chance to improve their profitable trade with Byzantium. Some simply wanted the adventure.

Christian pilgrims visit the Church of the Holy Sepulchre at Jerusalem.

✠ The Early Crusades

On November 27, 1095, Pope Urban II assembled a group at Clermont, France. In an impassioned speech he described how the Turks had seized Christian lands and "killed or captured many people, . . . destroyed churches, and devastated the kingdom of God." Urban's words fired his listeners with enthusiasm, and they spread the news throughout France. Those who joined the movement sewed a cross on their clothes and became **crusaders**, from the Latin word *cruciata*, "marked with a cross."

The first crusaders—bands of undisciplined and untrained peasants—left for the Holy Land in 1096. As they traveled, they attacked all whom they considered enemies of Christ. Solomon Bar Simson, a Jewish chronicler, described an attack on a Jewish community:

❝ *The steppe-wolves [crusaders]. . . pillaged men, women, and infants, children and old people. They pulled down the stairways and destroyed the houses, looting and plundering; and they took the Torah Scroll, trampled it in the mud, and tore and burned it.* ❞

As destructive as the peasants were, however, they were no match for trained warriors. Most died quickly in battle against the Turks.

The forces led by French and Norman nobles encountered other difficulties. The journey was strenuous. Wearing wool, leather, and heavy armor, the crusaders suffered severely from the heat. Food and water ran short. As Fulcher of Chartres, an eyewitness, recorded:

❝ *The people for the love of God endured cold, heat, and torrents of rain. Their tents became old and torn and rotten from the continuous rains. . . . Many people had no cover but the sky. . . .*

The elect were tried by the Lord and by such suffering were cleansed of their sins. . . . When they struggled against the pagans they labored for God. . . .

I feel that at the cost of suffering to the Christians He wills that the pagans shall be destroyed, they who have so many times foully trod underfoot all which belongs to God. ❞

The Major Crusades, 1096–1204

Holy Wars European crusaders traveled over land and sea to wrest control of the Holy Land from the Turks.

? Location From which towns did the Europeans launch the First Crusade?

Despite the crusaders' suffering, they took the city of Antioch in 1098, then marched on Jerusalem, which they quickly captured in 1099. Crusaders slaughtered inhabitants of both towns. One Muslim chronicler recorded that the crusaders killed more than 70,000 men, women, and children.

The victorious crusaders set up four small states in the newly captured Holy Land: the county of Edessa, the principality of Antioch, the county of Tripoli, and the kingdom of Jerusalem. They subdivided the land into fiefs controlled by lords and vassals.

The Europeans' First Crusade had succeeded only because the Muslims were disunited. They soon organized their forces and counterattacked, recapturing the city of Edessa in 1144. A new call for troops went out in Christendom. In 1147 the first wave of eager crusaders set off for the Holy Land on the Second Crusade. The crusade, however, was a miserable failure, ending after only two years.

Then word reached Europe that the Muslims had recaptured Jerusalem in 1187. Crusaders once again sharpened their swords and spearpoints, and polished their chain-mail shirts. Richard the Lion Heart of England, Philip Augustus of France, and the Holy Roman emperor Frederick Barbarossa each led an army on the Third Crusade. Once again the crusaders failed. Barbarossa drowned on his way to the Holy Land. Philip and Richard quarreled, and Philip took his army home to seize English lands in France. Richard and his army fought on, but were unable to capture Jerusalem. In the end, Richard had to settle for a truce that gave him control of a few coastal towns and guaranteed Europeans the right to travel to Jerusalem.

Inspired by faith and a desire for wealth and glory, the crusaders conquered the Holy Land and established their own kingdoms. However, Muslim forces soon recaptured the land.

R RESOURCE ACTIVITY

READINGS IN WORLD HISTORY
Reading 11.4
Salah al-Din's Courage and Steadfastness

Have students read the selection about Salah al-Din. Then have them complete the questions.

Level 2

MULTIMEDIA PRESENTATION STRATEGY

WORLD HISTORY AND CULTURES VIDEODISCS

Image: *Crusaders in Battle*

Search Frame 816

Show the image as you discuss the Crusades. In particular, use the image as a way to discuss typical Christian attitudes toward Muslims. The caption that accompanies the CD-ROM image offers additional details.

All Levels

Initially, inquisitors allowed the accused a month's grace period to renounce their heresy. If they did, they received only a light penance. After the grace period, the inquisitors put all other accused heretics on trial. The inquisitors commonly tortured the accused to elicit information. Most people accused of heresy were eventually found guilty. While some were burned at the stake, the most common punishments were fines, penance, imprisonment, and the confiscation of property.

Critical Thinking Ask students what might be the consequences of enforcing religious doctrine in this way.

ANSWER: Students might answer that the Inquisition could have unified medieval society by forcing people to believe the same things. However, it also stifled free thought.

THROUGH OTHERS' EYES

Islamic View of the Crusades

Christians viewed the Crusades as holy wars to regain the lands in which Christ had lived. However, Muslims also considered Jerusalem a holy city. They saw the Crusades as "Frankish invasions."

In the late 1100s the Muslim sultan Salah al-Din reconquered most of the Holy Land. During the Third Crusade, in the summer of 1191, Philip Augustus of France and Richard the Lion Heart of England recaptured the city of Acre from Salah al-Din's forces. A Muslim witness, Baha' al-Din, recorded the reactions to Acre's fall:

❝The Franj [Franks] let out an immense cry of joy, while in our camp everyone was stunned. The soldiers wept and lamented. As for the sultan, he was like a mother who has just lost her child. I went to see him to do my best to console him. I told him that now we had to think of the future of Jerusalem and the coastal cities, and to do something about the fate of the Muslims captured in Acre.❞

Despite Salah al-Din's efforts to negotiate their release, Richard ordered the execution of the 2,700 captive soldiers from the Acre garrison, along with their families, including some 300 women and children.

Later Crusades

Despite these failures, the crusading spirit died slowly. In 1202, for example, Pope Innocent III persuaded a group of French knights to embark on the Fourth Crusade to reestablish the Kingdom of Jerusalem. The crusaders did not have the money to pay for their travel, however. When merchants from Venice persuaded them to attack the Christian city of Zara, a commercial rival, as partial payment for their transportation, the outraged pope excommunicated the entire army for attacking a Christian city. The pope soon lifted the ban, however, and the Venetians and the crusaders turned their attention to Constantinople. The Venetians hoped to take control of the entire eastern Mediterranean, which the Byzantines still dominated. In 1204 the crusaders breached the great walls of Constantinople and looted gold and treasure from the city.

Later crusades in the Holy Land were also ineffective. The Children's Crusade of 1212 resulted only in many children being sold into slavery. By 1291 Muslims had captured the last Christian stronghold at Acre.

Although the major thrust of the crusading spirit had been directed against Muslims in the Holy Land, the overflow of Christian zeal (and the desire for plunder) also found other targets. Spain became a major battleground, as Christian knights fought to reconquer the peninsula from Spanish Muslims, or Moors, the name Christian Europeans gave them. By 1212, Christian armies had driven the Moors from all but the southern coast and the city of Granada.

The Crusade Against Heresy

As the popes unleashed and directed the pent-up violence of European knighthood against the Muslim "infidels," they also used it against European infidels—Christians accused of heresy. Among those who the church attacked were the Albigensians, or Cathars, a group of Christians in southern France. The Albigensians believed that spirit was good and matter was evil. If matter was evil, they argued, Jesus could not be the incarnation of God, as the Roman Catholic Church taught.

Such beliefs not only clashed with more orthodox interpretations of Christianity but also undermined the authority of church and state. In 1208 Pope Innocent III mobilized an army of crusaders to kill the heretics. The Albigensians, however, had the support of many nobles and local townspeople. As a result, the fighting continued for nearly 20 years, destroying the population and the prosperity of one of France's richest regions. It also gave rise to the **Inquisition**, an official department of the church created to investigate and prosecute charges of heresy.

In Europe the crusading spirit was turned against heretic Christians and Spanish Muslims.

The Crusade in the North

The end of the Albigensian crusade coincided with the beginning of a new eastward movement in northern Europe. This new movement brought together the passion of the Crusades with the economic colonization of eastern Germany and Poland.

As German lords began to colonize northeastern Europe, they ran into tribes that were untouched by Christianity. The Teutonic Knights, an order of soldier monks, accepted the call of Andrew II, the king of Hungary, to fight against the pagans. After the pagans had been defeated, however, Andrew, fearing the knights' power, expelled them from his kingdom.

In 1226 the order agreed to conquer the pagan inhabitants of Prussia and bring them into the fold of Christendom. They established a fortified base at Torún, north of the Vistula River. Over the next 50 years, the Teutonic Knights almost completely wiped out the pagan peoples of Prussia and established the whole region firmly within the Christian sphere. Eventually the order came to rule most of the present-day Baltic States, with the exception of Lithuania.

By the 1500s the order had turned their territories into secular dukedoms under either the Polish Crown or the Holy Roman Empire. During their rule, however, the Teutonic Knights brought feudalism to eastern Europe and the Baltic, fostered the growth of towns, and gave rise to trade. Under their protection the cities of northern Germany banded together in what became known as the **Hanseatic League**. The league eventually controlled most of the trade between Europe, the Baltic, and Russia, with its important links to civilizations of the East.

The Teutonic Knights brought the pagan regions of eastern Europe into Christendom and imposed feudalism in their domains.

◀ In 1204 Christian crusaders sacked Constantinople, leaving the city in ruins and plundering its wealth.

SECTION 4 REVIEW

IDENTIFY and explain the significance of the following:
Urban II
crusaders
Richard the Lion Heart
Inquisition
Hanseatic League

LOCATE and explain the importance of the following:

Holy Land
Venice
Vistula River

1. **Main Idea** Why did Europeans undertake the Crusades?
2. **Main Idea** How was the spirit of the Crusades used against Europeans?

3. **Geography: Place** How did the climate of the Holy Land affect the crusaders?
4. **Writing to Explain** Explain how some Europeans used the crusading spirit for economic gain.
5. **Synthesizing** What did the crusaders in the Middle Ages ultimately accomplish?

Beginnings of European Transformation

FOCUS

- How did improvements in technology affect European society after 1000?
- How did growing prosperity and security affect feudal culture?
- As intellectual life revived in Europe, what subjects interested educated Europeans?

As the last wave of invasions came to an end, Europe began to thrive once again. New technological developments helped spur a revival of trade. Growing prosperity soon transformed feudal culture, as the nobility began to develop less warlike pastimes. With less need to worry about security and survival, learning and creativity blossomed once more. No longer concerned with simply holding on to an ideal Roman past, Europeans began to forge a new civilization with a character and identity of its own.

Illuminated French manuscript, c. 1316, showing Arthur, Lancelot, and Guinevere

A Technological Explosion

The last wave of invasions came to an end in the 900s. With returning security came a new prosperity. Underlying this prosperity was an explosion of new technological developments.

Perhaps the most important new development was the heavy-wheeled plow. European farmers had long used the Roman plow, designed for the dry, shallow soil of the Mediterranean. The soil of northern Europe was deep and rocky, and the heavy-wheeled plow allowed farmers to cut deep into the soil, pulling rich nutrients to the surface. With richer soil, farmers could grow more crops. They further increased their yields by using horses, which were faster than oxen, to pull their plows.

Farmers also began to adopt the **three-field system** to bring more land under cultivation. Since the days of the Romans, European farmers had typically planted only half their land at a time. The other half was allowed to "rest." Under the three-field system, farmers planted two thirds of their land, leaving a different third unplanted each season.

To help process the new, bigger crop yields, Europeans began to use interlocking gears to build watermills and windmills. Mills were used to grind grain and to aid in such activities as manufacturing paper, processing wool, and pressing grapes or olives for wine and oil. By the 1100s increased food production spurred population growth.

Revival of Trade

With increasing prosperity and population growth, trade also began to pick up. In the Mediterranean, the cities of northern Italy, particularly Venice, took advantage of their locations to dominate international trade between the rest of Europe and eastern civilizations.

Jewish merchants were particularly active in international trade. Many Jewish merchants living in northern Europe maintained close ties with Jewish communities in the Mediterranean region. This gave them safe places to store their wares in distant towns and helped them learn local business customs. They also benefited from the church's view that Christians should not practice usury, the charging of interest on loans. Jewish bankers and merchants became the primary moneylenders of Europe.

Europe's internal trade also expanded in the 1100s and 1200s. Great trade fairs sprang up in the French county of Champagne, drawing people from all over Europe. Elsewhere, traders and merchants bustled along the trade routes of the Baltic, the North Sea, the Rhine and Rhone river valleys, and across the Alpine passes between Germany and Italy carrying grains, metals, wood products, oils, dates, slaves, and exotic eastern wares.

Revival of Urban Life

With trade and surplus food came the growth—and independence—of towns and cities. Under feudalism, towns were controlled by feudal lords. A lord could charge merchants for using his roads and for setting up a market. This made trade difficult and expensive. Around the 1000s, however, merchants began to realize that the king could free them from the lords' control. To free towns from their feudal overlords, kings and merchants devised the **charter of incorporation**. Such a royal charter allowed merchants to govern a town under the king's protection. The town paid taxes to the king, but merchants could set taxes in ways that did not hurt trade. Serfs who stayed in an incorporated town for a year and a day could claim freedom from all feudal obligations. Consequently, the growth of towns not only spurred trade but also contributed to the breakdown of feudalism.

Merchants controlled town politics, electing the mayor and a town council. Below the merchants were artisans, such as shoemakers, brewers, smiths, tanners, and weavers. Beneath artisans were manual laborers. By the 1100s artisans had begun to organize themselves into **guilds**, or trade associations. The guilds set quality standards, restricted competition, and regulated the training of new artisans. They also helped set prices. Not least, guilds acted as

▶ Stained glass in France in the 1200s often represented secular patrons, such as the cloth merchants in this window in Chartres.

mutual aid societies. Some guilds admitted both men and women, others were exclusively male or female. Women dominated many crafts, especially in the cloth industry.

Growing security and improved technology led to a revival of trade and the growth of towns.

The Rise of Chivalry

By the 1200s feudal culture also was changing. Instead of relying on their nobles for troops, kings collected taxes from them and used the money to hire mercenary soldiers. As kings made fewer military demands, knights had more time to quarrel with their neighbors and to fight one another. The church tried to stop Christians from killing Christians by forbidding combat on certain days. Although such rules were often ignored, by the late 1100s they had led to a code of conduct called **chivalry**. Chivalry required a knight to be brave, to fight fairly, and to protect women, children, and the clergy.

As the nobility's military role changed, so did the culture of the aristocracy. Nobles became interested in new forms of music and poetry. Traveling poets entertained noble courts with

1. Siegfried laments the cowardice and dishonor of his murderers; Siegfried is saddened that Gunther's and Hagen's actions will bring dishonor upon the family; as he lies dying, Siegfried is greatly concerned about the welfare of his wife.
2. Hagen wanted to end Siegfried's power and to rule without opposition.

REVIEW & ASSESSMENT RESOURCES

- Study Guide 11.5
- Daily Quiz 11.5
- Main Idea Activity 11.5

All Levels

Literature THROUGH TIME

The *Nibelungenlied*

The Germanic peoples had a long-standing oral tradition of epic poems, which told stories of the adventures of brave warriors. Around the 1100s, epics such as the German Nibelungenlied *(nee-buh-LOONG-uhn-LEET) and the French Song of Roland had begun to be written down in vernacular languages, the languages that ordinary peoples spoke.*

As vernacular literature grew more popular, many epics reappeared as romances in the new tradition of courtly love. The Nibelungenlied, *for instance, blended elements of courtly love, adventure, and Christian ideals into a tale of love, revenge, and murder. The following passage relates the death of the hero Siegfried (ZEEG-freed) at the hands of his brother-in-law, King Gunther (GOON-tuhr) of Burgundy, and Gunther's vassal Hagen (HAH-guhn). The men are acting on behalf of the king's wife, Brunhild (BROON-hilt), who is seeking revenge on Siegfried. Years earlier Siegfried had helped Gunther trick Brunhild into marrying him.*

When lord Siegfried felt the great wound, maddened with rage he bounded back from the stream with the long shaft jutting from his heart. . . .

The hero's face had lost its color and he was no longer able to stand. His strength had ebbed away, for in the field of his bright countenance he now displayed Death's token. Soon many fair ladies would be weeping for him.

The lady Kriemhild's lord [Siegfried] fell among the flowers, where you could see the blood surging from his wound. . . . "You vile cowards," he said as he lay dying. "What good has my service done me now that you have slain me? I was always loyal to you, but now I have paid for it. Alas, you have wronged your kinsmen so that all who are born in days to come will be dishonored by your deed. You have cooled your anger on me beyond all measure. You will be held in contempt and stand apart from all good warriors."

The knights all ran to where he lay wounded to death. It was a sad day for many of them. Those who were at all loyal-hearted mourned for him, and this, as a gay and valiant knight, he had well deserved.

The King of Burgundy too lamented Siegfried's death.

"There is no need for the doer of the deed to weep when the damage is done," said the dying man. "He should be held up to scorn. It would have been better left undone."

"I do not know what you are grieving for," said Hagen fiercely. "All our cares and sorrows are over and done with. We shall not find many who will dare oppose us now. I am glad that I have put an end to his supremacy."

"You may well exult," said Siegfried. "But had I known your murderous bent I should have easily guarded my life from you. I am sorry for none so much as my wife, the lady Kriemhild. May God have mercy on me for ever having got a son who in years to come will suffer the reproach that his kinsmen were murderers. If I had the strength I would have good reason to complain. But if you feel at all inclined to do a loyal deed for anyone, noble King," continued the mortally wounded man, "let me commend [entrust] my dear sweetheart to your mercy. Let her profit from being your sister. By the virtue of all princes, stand by her loyally! . . ."

Understanding Literature

1. What elements of courtly love and the code of chivalry are expressed in this passage?
2. What justification does Hagen give for killing Siegfried?

Following the code of chivalry, a lady arms her knight as other noblewomen watch.

narrative poems called romances, which told of the adventures knights undertook for love. The poems were part of a growing tradition of **courtly love** that glorified noble women and praised heroic and gentle virtues in knights. **Chrétien de Troyes** [KRAY-tyan duh trwah] of France reflected the new tradition in his romance, *Perceval, or The Story of the Grail*:

> **66** *The squires were followed by a maiden who bore a grail, with both hands laden. The bearer was of noble mien [appearance], well-dressed, and lovely, and serene, and when she entered with the grail, the candles suddenly grew pale, the grail cast such a brilliant light, as stars grow dimmer in the night when sun or moonrise makes them fade.* **99**

Poets like Chrétien often had royal patrons who provided them with a livelihood. One such patron was Eleanor of Aquitaine, the most powerful woman of her time.

BIOGRAPHY Born about 1122, Eleanor of Aquitaine inherited the provinces of Aquitaine, Poitou, and Gascony, almost one third of present-day France. She married Louis VII of France but the couple grew apart and their marriage was annulled in 1152. She soon married the heir to the English throne, Henry II. This marriage united the couple's vast landholdings, and together they ruled all of England and almost half of France.

In the early years of their marriage, they ruled as partners, with Eleanor governing the French territories. In 1173, however, Eleanor helped her sons rebel against Henry. The revolt failed, and Henry imprisoned his wife for 15 years. When he died, Eleanor was freed. She ensured that her favorite son, Richard the Lion Heart, succeeded Henry as king, and she governed while Richard was away on the Third Crusade. When Richard was imprisoned in Germany on his way home, she helped to raise the ransom that freed him. Before she died in France in 1204, she was still active enough to raise an army to help her son John, Richard's heir, against the French.

Eleanor of Aquitaine had access to power and influence that few women of her time had.

Eleanor of Aquitaine
BIOGRAPHY

Few women inherited land or managed estates. Marriages were arranged in order to build family alliances; the most valuable function of women was still considered to be bearing children.

As feudalism lost its military purpose, chivalry and courtly love replaced warfare as noble pastimes.

Revival of European Intellectual Life

While feudal life was changing, so too was intellectual life. Toward the end of the 1000s, the church led the way in a cultural revival that soon spread throughout Europe. Conflicts with kings had encouraged the clergy to study church history in search of support for the pope's authority. As they looked backward for knowledge, they rediscovered Roman law and began to read classical Greek and Latin authors once again—especially the works of Aristotle.

Scholasticism. Contact with Muslim Spain revived interest in Aristotle and Greek philosophy. These ideas sparked a major controversy in the church over how human beings could learn about the world around them. Aristotle believed that truth could be discovered only through human reason. Christians, on the other hand, believed that truth was revealed by God, and depended solely on faith. In the 1200s Thomas Aquinas, a Dominican monk, tried to reconcile the two approaches.

Influenced by Muslim philosopher Ibn Rushd, Aquinas argued that both reason and faith were necessary for a complete understanding of truth. His approach, known as **Scholasticism**, tried to demonstrate that what Christian revelation taught was also knowable and provable through the use of logic and reason. By using human reason, the Scholastics thought, one could make logical deductions from the revelations found in the Bible and the knowledge discovered through observation. Thus, reason and faith together would reveal truth. Aquinas's

IDENTIFY
For significance, see the following pages:
three-field system (p. 294)
charter of incorporation (p. 295)
guilds (p. 295)
chivalry (p. 295)
courtly love (p. 297)
Eleanor of Aquitaine (p. 297)
Thomas Aquinas (p. 297)
Scholasticism (p. 297)
Roger Bacon (p. 298)
curriculum (p. 298)
liberal arts (p. 298)

1. Technological innovations increased crop yields, which led to a growth in population; increased trade and surplus food led to the growth of towns and cities.
2. Clergy studied church history to support the pope's authority in conflicts with kings; revival of interest in classical Greek and Roman authors led to the development of Scholasticism; renewed interest in learning led to the founding of universities.
3. It dug deeper into the soil, bringing nutrients to the surface, which increased crop yields.
4. Fictional sources could be useful for describing major battles and expressing ideals and values of the time. However, they might over-idealize situations and could contain exaggerations.
5. The expansion of trade and contact with other cultures brought new ideas and traditions to the attention of Europeans.

▲ Universities played an important role in the intellectual, political, and social life of Europe. This Notre Dame facade shows student life.

writings ensured that in Latin Christendom human reason would remain a primary element in determining truth.

Science. While Aquinas and others tried to reconcile Greek philosophy with Christian theology, other scholars studied the scientific works of the ancients. In the 1200s the English monk Roger Bacon became a pioneer of science in Europe by advocating detailed observation and controlled experimentation to understand things in the natural world. He predicted technological innovations in the future:

❝ Machines may be made by which the largest ships, with only one man steering them, will move faster than if they were filled with rowers; wagons may be built which will move with unbelievable speed and without the aid of beasts. ❞

Universities. Both Bacon and Aquinas were products of a new system of education. In the 1100s cathedral schools taught Latin grammar, rhetoric, and logic. Eventually, universities sprang up and developed a regular **curriculum**, or course of studies. The first universities were in Italy, but the concept quickly spread to Paris, and then to England and Germany. Paid lecturers, usually members of the clergy, taught not only Latin grammar, rhetoric, and logic but also geometry, arithmetic, astronomy, and music. The courses were collectively called the **liberal arts**. As they spread throughout western Europe, the universities helped revive a tradition of learning. They also created a new educated class, who spoke and wrote in Latin and shared a common culture.

As intellectual life revived in Europe, some Christian scholastics tried to reconcile faith and reason, while others began to explore the workings of the world around them.

SECTION 5 REVIEW

IDENTIFY and explain the significance of the following:
three-field system
charter of incorporation
guilds
chivalry
courtly love
Eleanor of Aquitaine
Thomas Aquinas
Scholasticism
Roger Bacon
curriculum
liberal arts

1. **Main Idea** How did the growth of trade and new technologies change life in Europe after 1000?

2. **Main Idea** In what ways did intellectual life revive in Europe by the 1100s?

3. **Geography: Human-Environment Interaction** Why was the invention of a new type of plow beneficial to the farmers of northern Europe?

4. **Writing to Explain** Imagine you are a historian trying to recreate the history of the Middle Ages. How might knowledge of romances and epic poems help you? What difficulties might you have in using these works?

5. **Synthesizing** How did the expansion of trade and the rediscovery of past cultures help revive intellectual life in Europe?

Review

On a separate sheet of paper, complete the following exercises:

WRITING A SUMMARY

Using the essential points in the text, write a brief summary of the chapter.

REVIEWING TERMS

From the following list, choose the term that correctly matches the definition.

guilds   vassal
fief   Parliament
Hanseatic   chivalry
  League

1. governmental body in England, later composed of the House of Lords and the House of Commons
2. land given to a noble by a king for military service
3. noble who served a higher noble or a king by providing knights and soldiers
4. system of labor organization in towns, under which apprentices learned trades from master craftsmen
5. group of northern European cities that banded together for protection and to increase trade

REVIEWING CHRONOLOGY

List the following events in their correct chronological order.

1. Pope Urban II calls on Christians to begin the First Crusade.
2. King John of England signs Magna Carta.
3. Charlemagne is crowned as "emperor of the Romans."
4. England is conquered by William the Norman.
5. Pope Gregory I expands power of the papacy and the church.

UNDERSTANDING THE MAIN IDEA

1. What motivated Europeans to go on Crusades?
2. How did the rulers of European states try to consolidate their power?
3. How did the growth of trade affect life in Europe around 1100?
4. How did Charlemagne's empire unify western Europe?
5. How was feudal society organized?

THINKING CRITICALLY

1. **Hypothesizing** What dangers might have faced the Roman church as a result of the conflict between popes and monarchs? How might these conflicts have affected the church's ability to establish Christian unity?
2. **Analyzing** How did literary romances reflect the reality of everyday life? Why might these romances have been so popular at the time?
3. **Assessing Consequences** Why might the continued growth of towns have threatened the existence of the feudal system?

Building Your Portfolio

Complete the following activities individually or in groups.

1. **Towns** Imagine what life must have been like in a town in medieval Europe. Choose a particular type of person from an early European town, such as an apprentice, laborer, or farmer coming to town to sell produce. Write a detailed description of one or several days in your life (or lives if you are doing the activity in groups). Include descriptions of the other people you encounter and of your surroundings. Where do you live? What is your work like? You may also wish to add a drawing of your town with your description.
2. **The Arts** Imagine that you are a poet or storyteller in the court of an important noble. You (and your fellow poets) are supposed to come up with a new romance to be recited at a feast tonight in the castle. You hope to impress the noble and his guests with your performance. Your story or poem should include examples of courtly love and chivalry. If you are working with others, you may wish to write your romance in the form of a play to be performed. The most important thing is to be creative—the last court poets who failed to entertain the lord's guests lost their jobs, and their heads!

4. People sought security in their faith and in the church during the unstable Middle Ages; by building a strong alliance between the empire and the church, Charlemagne ensured that people would identify the empire with the same strength and stability as the church.
5. The king or a noble granted land to a lesser noble in exchange for military service. Nobles offered protection to peasants, who became serfs and farmed the land for their lord.

THINKING CRITICALLY

1. If people had felt more loyalty to their kings than to the pope, they could have pulled away from Christianity and weakened the power and the wealth of the church. States would no longer have offered to protect church property, which would have left the papal states at the mercy of invaders.
2. Romances told tales of adventures that knights undertook for love. The tradition of courtly love expressed the ideals of medieval society—beautiful, serene, noblewomen and gentle, yet courageous, knights.
3. Serfs could free themselves by escaping to the towns; lords collected no taxes from towns.

Chapter 12

Transformations in Asia 220–1350

Chapter Planning Guide

	TEXTBOOK	CORE RESOURCES	VISUAL RESOURCES	MULTIMEDIA
Introduction	pp. 300–301	Block Scheduling Handbook: Ch. 12		Videodisc Segment 12 and Viewing Guide: *The Golden Age of Asian Civilization*
Lesson 12.1 Imperial Reunification in China	pp. 302–308 Map: *The Tang Dynasty,* p. 303 Sacred Traditions: *Religions of East Asia,* p. 305 Map: *The Song and Jin Empires,* p. 306 History Through the Arts: *Two Tang Painters,* p. 307	Reading 12.1: *Trade and International Relations* Skills Activity 12: *Analyzing Poetry*	Art and History 12: *Seated Buddha Preaching the First Sermon* Everyday Life 12: *Chinese Tea Processing*	GHRC 12 Readings: *Preparing for China's Civil Service Exams; Poetry from Tang China* GHRC 12/Videodiscs: Images—*Women Silk Workers; The Cottage of Du Fu, the Great Tang Poet;* Maps—*Changan; Population Shifts in China*
Lesson 12.2 Korea, Japan, and Vietnam	pp. 309–316 Map: *New Cultures in Asia,* p. 310	Reading 12.2: *The Tale of Genji* Geography Activity 12: *The Wind that Saved Japan*	Geography and History 12: *New Cultures in Asia, c. 670–1392*	GHRC 12 Readings: *The Li Dynasty; Court Life of Heian Japan; Buddhist Devotional Poems* GHRC 12/Videodiscs: Images—*Buddhism Comes to Korea; Literary Men in Heian Japan; Korean Celadon Vase; Covered Jar from Vietnam;* Audio Clip—*"Kei Myon";* Video Clip—*Heian Shrine*
Lesson 12.3 India and Southeast Asia	pp. 317–320 Map: *Religions in Asia,* p. 319	Reading 12.3: *Construction at Angkor Wat*		GHRC 12 Readings: *A New Sultan Takes Control of Delhi; Daily Life in a Khmer King's Court* GHRC 12/Videodiscs: Images—*Khmer Warriors; Entrance Gate at Angkor Thom*
Lesson 12.4 The Mongol Empire	pp. 321–326 Teenagers in History: *Temujin,* p. 322 Through Others' Eyes: *From Venice to Beijing,* p. 324 Geography and History: *The Mongol Horsemen,* p. 325 Map: *The Mongol Empire,* p. 325	Reading 12.4: *Diplomacy and the Golden Horde* Writing Project 12: *Writing a Rough Draft*		GHRC 12 Readings: *How the Mongols Lived; The Mongols Sack Baghdad; Marco Polo Visits Mongol China* GHRC 12/Videodiscs: Images—*Mongol Empire; Mongols on the Move; Mongol Arms and Armor*
Chapter Investigation and Enrichment	pp. 300–326	Chapter 12 Investigation: *Asian Travelogues* People in World History 12 Explorations in Daily Life 12		GHRC 12/Videodiscs
Review and Assessment	Section 1 Review, p. 308 Section 2 Review, p. 316 Section 3 Review, p. 320 Section 4 Review, p. 326 Chapter 12 Review, p. 327	Chapter Review Activity 12 Vocabulary Activity 12 Themes Review 12 Section Study Guides 12.1–12.4 Main Idea Activities 12.1–12.4 Daily Quizzes 12.1–12.4 Chapter 12 Test Sheltered English Ch. 12 Test Ch. 12 Test Generator		Audio CDs: Ch. 12 Summary (English and Spanish)

INTRODUCING THE CHAPTER

Textbook pp. 300–301

CHAPTER OVERVIEW

After centuries of division, China was reunited by a series of powerful dynasties. An era of prosperity and learning followed. The neighboring societies in Korea, Japan, and Vietnam borrowed many elements from Chinese civilization, which they blended with their own traditions. Indian culture also spread throughout Southeast Asia, even though the Gupta Empire in India collapsed. Then, in the thirteenth century, Genghis Khan transformed the nomadic Mongols into a dynamic, conquering people.

PRESENTING THEMES

On the chalkboard or on an overhead transparency, write the following open-ended theme questions.

- **WAR AND DIPLOMACY** Why might nomadic peoples have a military advantage over settled civilizations?
- **CROSS-CULTURAL INTERACTION** How could one culture influence another without war or conquest?
- **POLITICS AND LAW** How might a ruler unite many kingdoms into an empire?

Have students, either individually or in groups, suggest responses to the questions. For the war and diplomacy question, students might suggest that nomads can avoid attacking armies while settled civilizations are forced to defend cities and towns. For the cross-cultural interaction question, students might suggest that trade and travel are ways to bring new ideas to societies without conflict. For the politics and law question, students might suggest that a ruler might use common religious and cultural traditions as a way to unite an empire. Save the responses. Once students have studied the chapter, you may wish to have them complete the Themes Review, then compare the two sets of answers.

USING THE VIDEO

Segment 12: *The Golden Age of Asian Civilization*

ENGLISH

Search Chapter 12
Videodisc 1, Side B

SPANISH

Search Chapter 12
Videodisc 1, Side B

Tell students that in this chapter they will examine the struggles that engaged Asian rulers from the 500s to the 1200s as they sought to create strong and stable kingdoms. Conclude by showing Segment 12 of the *World History and Cultures Videodiscs*. This segment looks at the development of government and the arts—including the ancient martial art of kung fu—during the rule of the Tang dynasty in China.

Before showing the segment, ask students to pay particular attention to the connections being made between religion, government, the arts, and the martial art of kung fu. To help students grasp the significant points of the segment, have them complete Video Viewing Guide 12.

Key to Ability Levels

All strategies and activities are coded to the following ability levels:

LEVEL 1	**Basic** activities suitable for all students
LEVEL 2	**Average** activities suitable for average to above-average students
LEVEL 3	**Challenging** activities suitable for above-average students
SHELTERED ENGLISH	Activities suitable for students with **Limited English Proficiency**

Additional Resources

BOOKS FOR TEACHERS

Marshall, Robert. *Storm from the East: From Genghis Khan to Kublai Khan.* Univ. of California Press, 1993. Offers an overview.

Morgan, David. *The Mongols.* Blackwell, 1986. Offers a general survey.

Tillman, Hoyt C. and Stephen H. West. *China Under Jurchen Rule.* State Univ. of New York Press, 1995. Offers essays on the Ch'in emperors.

BOOKS FOR STUDENTS

Dramer, Kim. *Kublai Khan: Mongol Emperor.* Chelsea, 1989. Presents a general biography.

Hartog, Leode. *Genghis Khan, Conqueror of the World.* St. Martin's Press, 1989. Looks at the military aspects of the Mongol leader's rule.

Polo, Marco. *The Travels of Marco Polo.* Penguin, 1958. Presents Polo's account of his travels.

MULTIMEDIA MATERIALS

China's Cosmopolitan Age: The Tang. The Annenberg/CPB Project, 1993. Video, 60 min. Examines the lasting influence of the Tang.

Cosmology of Kyoto: A Visual Mindscape of Old Japan. Yano Electric Co. CD-ROM, MAC format. Offers interactive role-playing and database.

The Mongol Empire: November 18, 1247. Maryland Public Television. Video, 30 min. Re-creates a day in Mongol history.

Lesson 12.1 *Imperial Reunification in China*

Textbook pp. 302–308

RESOURCES

Pupil's Edition

Map, p. 303: *The Tang Dynasty, 814*

Sacred Traditions, p. 305: *Religions of East Asia*

Map, p. 306: *The Song and Jin Empires, 1141*

History Through the Arts, p. 307: *Two Tang Painters*

Core Resources

Reading 12.1: *Trade and International Relations*

Skills Activity 12: *Analyzing Poetry*

Visual Resources

Art and History 12: *Seated Buddha Preaching the First Sermon*

Everyday Life 12: *Chinese Tea Processing*

Global History Resource Center

Reading: *Preparing for China's Civil Service Exams*

Reading: *Poetry from Tang China*

Videodiscs or Global History Resource Center

Map: *Changan, 750*

Search Frame 835

Image: *The Cottage of Du Fu, the Great Tang Poet*

Search Frame 823

Image: *Women Silk Workers in Song China*

Search Frame 826

Map: *Population Shifts in China, 750–1250*

Search Frame 836

LESSON FOCUS
How was China transformed under the Sui, Tang, and Song dynasties?

OBJECTIVES

After completing this lesson, students will be able to:

- explain the main significance of the Sui dynasty;
- describe the accomplishments of the Tang rulers;
- analyze the problems that nomadic invaders caused the Song dynasty;
- outline the major social and economic changes that occurred under the Tang and Song dynasties.

HOOK

Discuss the revival of the Chinese empire. Ask students to describe what they think might be needed to establish an empire. *[Answers will vary but might include: a strong state and military, a well-organized government.]* Then ask them to describe China's situation after the fall of the Han dynasty. *[It was in ruins.]*

Ask: How did Wendi create an empire?
[He defeated the states of southern China and created a strong, centralized state with a new legal code, a reformed bureaucracy, a strengthened northern border, and an established practice of leveling.]

Point out to students that while the Sui dynasty was short-lived, it left an important legacy.

DEVELOP

Discuss the rise and fall of the Tang and Song dynasties.
Point out to students that the Tang dynasty, established on the foundations of the Sui, lasted for almost 300 years. When emphasizing the empire's vast size, refer students to the map on textbook page 303. You may also wish to display the electronic media map of Changan when discussing the city's importance.

Ask: How did expansion of China's borders under the Tang affect Chinese culture?

[*Changan became a center of world culture, with many different peoples living there. Expansion also affected religion, as Buddhism spread across China.*]

To understand Buddhism, have students read the Sacred Traditions feature on textbook page 305; then display Art and History Transparency 12 and assign the worksheet.

Next tell students that the Tang dynasty came to an end after a decline in power. After a period of disorder, a new dynasty came to power—the Song. Have students name the characteristics of the Song dynasty's government under Zhao Kuangyin. [*He replaced military officials with civilian ones, established a strong centralized bureaucracy that tightly controlled tax collection, and restored the civil service exams. Emperors had tighter control.*] For more information, have students review the selection on China's civil service exams in the Global History Resource Center.

Tell students that eventually the power of the Song came to an end. Have them explain the significance of the Liao Empire and the Ruzhen. [*The Liao clashed with the Song and forced them to pay tribute; the Ruzhen were a Manchurian people who conquered the Liao Empire and renamed it the Jin Empire.*]

To conclude, refer students to the map of the Song and Jin empires on textbook page 306, and have them consider how the existence of the Jin Empire affected the Song. [*The Jin invaded and captured the Song capital, forcing the Song court to flee and establish a new capital at Hangzhou.*]

PROBE

Analyze changes under the Tang and Song. Tell students that many economic and social changes occurred under the Tang and Song dynasties. Have students make a web chart on the chalkboard, filling in circles for *Economy, Society, Technology,* and *Arts.* [**Economy:** *increased trade on the Silk Road and overseas, introduction of a money and banking system;* **Society:** *growth of cities, growing power of the gentry through trade, contrast between wealthy and poor in the cities, decline of women's status, concentration of land in hands of landlords after abandonment of policies to redistribute land;* **Technology:** *new irrigation techniques, new quick-ripening varieties of rice, cultivation of tea and cotton, gunpowder, printed books, nautical compass, suspension bridge, abacus;* **Arts:** *sculptures, textiles, jade-carving, porcelain, painting, literature*]

To provide more information about life during this period, display Everyday Life Transparency 12 and have students complete the worksheet. Then have them read Core Resources Reading 12.1 and the History Through the Arts feature. You might also have them read the Global History Resource Center selection on Tang poetry and view the electronic media images of Du Fu's cottage and of silk workers.

CONCLUDE

Draw conclusions about the development of Chinese civilization. Have students look at the web of ways in which China changed under the Tang and Song. Then have them form small groups and rank those changes based on their importance for the development of Chinese civilization. Have students come to a consensus on which changes were most and least important. Ask students why they ranked the factors as they did.

EXTEND

Cross-Curricular Connection: *Literature*
Students may read and complete the Skills Activity 12 on the poet Du Fu. Then have them read and discuss the other examples of Tang poetry from the Global History Resource Center.

MEET INDIVIDUAL NEEDS

Visual-Spatial Learners
Have students examine the History Through the Arts feature. Then have them discuss their impressions of Tang art. Interested students might create their own work of art in a style reminiscent of a Tang painting.

Logical-Mathematical Learners
Refer students to the electronic media map of population shifts in China. Have students locate information on China's population between 750 and 1250. Have them calculate China's total population in 750 and 1250 and the percentage of Chinese living in the north and in the center-south during the period.

ASSESS

Review
Have students complete the Section 1 Review. Use answers in the Teacher's Edition, page 308, to assess student mastery of this section.

Lesson 12.2 *Korea, Japan, and Vietnam*

Textbook pp. 309–316

RESOURCES

Pupil's Edition
Map, p. 310: *New Cultures in Asia, c. 670–1392*

Core Resources
Reading 12.2: *The* Tale of Genji

Visual Resources
Geography and History 12: *New Cultures in Asia, c. 670–1392*

Global History Resource Center
Reading: *The Li Dynasty Brings Stability to Vietnam*
Reading: *The Elegant Court Life of Heian Japan*
Reading: *Buddhist Devotional Poems from Korea*

Videodiscs or Global History Resource Center

Image: *Buddhism Comes to Korea*

Search Frame 828

Image: *Korean Celadon Vase*

Search Frame 827

Image: *Literary Men in Heian Japan*

Search Frame 829

Image: *Covered Jar from Vietnam*

Search Frame 830

Audio: *"Kei Myon": Korean Buddhist Religious Music*

Search 4288, Play to 4808
Videodisc 1, Side B, Audio Clip 12

Video: *Heian Shrine in Kyoto, Japan*

Search 3916, Play to 4286
Videodisc 1, Side B, Video Clip 12

LESSON FOCUS
How did Korea, Japan, and Vietnam create unique cultures by blending Chinese influences with their own traditions?

OBJECTIVES
After completing this lesson, students will be able to:
- describe how China influenced Korea;
- analyze the factors that influenced the development of early Japanese culture;
- explain how Japan developed its government;
- describe the effects of Chinese rule on Vietnam.

HOOK
Analyze relations between nations. Have students imagine that they are the rulers of small kingdoms that border on a large empire. What might their attitudes be toward their powerful neighbor? List their ideas on the chalkboard. Then have students look at Geography and History Transparency 12 and complete the worksheet, or refer them to the map on textbook page 310. Then discuss the location of Korea, Japan, and Vietnam relative to China.

Ask: *What were the historical responses of Korea, Japan, and Vietnam to China?*
[a mixture of envy, fear, resentment, admiration, imitation, and defiant nationalism]

Have students discuss how these responses compare with the responses listed previously on the board.

DEVELOP
Identify how China influenced Korea. Tell students that geography was a significant influence on Korea's development. Ask them to explain why this is true. *[The proximity of China had a major impact, along with the fact that Korea is very*

mountainous and close to the sea. Its location between China and Japan also made it a bridge between the two.]

Ask: What happened to Chosŏn?

[Han China turned it into a Chinese colony.]

Ask: How did Korea become independent?

[China and Silla conquered Paekche and Koguryo. Then Silla drove the Chinese from Korea, but agreed to pay tribute to China.]

Create a chart on the board with headings across the top reading *Similarities* and *Differences*. Help students fill out the chart, summarizing the similarities and differences between China and Korea. To give students information about life in Korea, have them read the Global History Resource Center selection on Buddhist poems and view the electronic media images of the celadon vase and of Buddhism in Korea.

PROBE

Discuss Japanese culture and government. Tell students that, like Korea, Japan's geography greatly influenced its development. Its proximity to China, its rugged and mountainous terrain, and its dependence on the sea all influenced its culture. Then have students consider China's influence on Japan. [*Chinese writing; Buddhism; Chinese Buddhist styles of literature, architecture, sculpture, and painting; laws reflecting Confucian thought; growth of strong central government; Chinese knowledge of engineering, medicine, weights and measures, and agriculture; Taika reforms (although never fully enacted)]* To give students an idea of imperial Japanese culture, have them read Core Resources Reading 12.2. You might also have them examine the Global History Resource Center selection on court life in Japan and view the electronic media image of literary men and the video of the shrine.

Next have students discuss Japanese government.

Ask: Why did the power of the government decline, and what were the results?

[The Fujiwara family came to dominate the emperor, but could not maintain strong central rule. Armed conflict grew, and local lords developed their own armies.]

Ask: How did the shoguns affect imperial power?

[The Kamakura and Ashikaga shogunates took power away from the central imperial government and contributed to the development of feudal society in Japan.]

CONCLUDE

Identify how Chinese rule affected Vietnam. Have students reconsider Chinese influences on Korean and Japanese society and culture. Then ask them to list similarities of Chinese influence in the three countries. [*writing system, Confucian thought, government, Buddhist religion, learning, art, and architecture]*

Then have students consider how rule by Han China affected Vietnam. [*Han rulers eventually began to take advantage of Vietnamese resources and people, who were taxed and put to work for China.]*

Ask: How did the Vietnamese people react to China's heavy-handed rule?

[They rebelled, and eventually gained independence.]

Conclude by pointing out that independence was important to the Vietnamese people; while they adopted aspects of Chinese culture, they continued to maintain their own culture. To illustrate Vietnamese culture, have students read the selection on the Li dynasty in the Global History Resource Center and view the electronic media image of the covered jar.

EXTEND

Cross-Curricular Connection: *Literature*

Have students read and analyze Core Resources Reading 12.2, an excerpt from the *Tale of Genji.*

MEET INDIVIDUAL NEEDS

Gifted Students

Have students read the Buddhist devotional poems from Korea in the Global History Resource Center. Then have them give examples of how the poems convey Buddhist thought.

Musical-Rhythmic Learners

Have students listen to the audio clip of Korean music. Then ask them to discuss their impressions of the music and describe ways in which it differs from or is similar to other forms of music.

ASSESS

Review

Have students complete the Section 2 Review. Use answers in the Teacher's Edition, page 316, to assess student mastery of this section.

RESOURCES

Pupil's Edition

Map, p. 319: *Religions in Asia, c. 750–1450*

Core Resources

Reading 12.3: *Construction at Angkor Wat*

Global History Resource Center

Reading: *A New Sultan Takes Control of Delhi*

Reading: *Daily Life in a Khmer King's Court*

Videodiscs or Global History Resource Center

Image: *Khmer Warriors from Relief at Angkor Wat*

Search Frame 831

Image: *Entrance Gate at Angkor Thom*

Search Frame 832

LESSON FOCUS

How did India and Southeast Asia develop after the 600s?

OBJECTIVES

After completing this lesson, students will be able to:

- describe the consequences of the fall of Harsha's empire;
- explain how Muslim invasions affected India;
- identify India's influence on Southeast Asia.

HOOK

Discuss the consequences of the fall of Harsha's empire.
Ask students to imagine that they have just become the rulers of a powerful state. They are planning on conquering nearby lands and forming an empire. Then point out that Harsha Vardhana—who was 16 years old at the time—experienced such a rise to power when he became king of Thanesar, a Indian state north of Delhi.

Ask: What did Harsha achieve?
[He controlled most of northern India.]

Then tell students that the unity achieved during Harsha's rule did not last.

Ask: What happened to India's unity after Harsha's death?
[India once again split into competing kingdoms.]

Conclude by pointing out to students that India's lack of unity had serious consequences as it faced invasions by outside forces.

DEVELOP

Examine the effects of Muslim invasions on India. Tell students that the Muslim invasions greatly affected life in northern India.

Ask: Why were Muslims and Hindus hostile toward each other in northern India?
[Mahmud of Ghazna raided the area, sacking cities, smashing temples, looting, and taking prisoners. He brought much of northern India into the Ghaznavid Empire.]

Then tell students that a subsequent Turkish dynasty, the Ghurids, swept into India, defeating the Ghaznavids and bringing most of northern India under their control.

Ask: What happened to Buddhism?
[The Ghurids destroyed Buddhist temples and suppressed Buddhist religious practices, and Buddhism almost disappeared from India for hundreds of years.]

Ask: Why was the establishment of the Delhi sultanate a critical event in the history of India?
[Students should understand that the Delhi sultanate imposed Muslim rule over most of northern India and established Muslim religious and cultural values as a

major element in the life of the Delhi sultanate. As a result, many elements of Islamic and Indian life were combined.]

To give students an example of life during the Delhi sultanate, have them read the Global History Resource Center reading on the new sultan.

To conclude, have students discuss the differences between Islam and Hinduism and how the arrival of Islam affected Indian society and culture.

PROBE

Discuss India's influence on Southeast Asia. Remind students how China influenced developments in neighboring countries. Ask if India had a similar effect on neighboring countries, and where its influence was felt. *[Students should understand that elements of Indian culture, most notably Hinduism and Buddhism, had a great impact on Southeast Asia.]* Have students look at the textbook map and discuss the spread of Hinduism and Buddhism.

Ask: How did elements of Indian culture and religion spread?
[through trade and through Brahmins and Buddhist monks; local rulers adopted elements of Indian culture to enhance their standing]

Next have students read Core Resources Reading 12.3 on the construction of Angkor Wat. Then point out that the architecture of Angkor Wat showed strong Indian influences.

Ask: Who built Angkor Wat?
[the Khmer Empire]

Have students describe the Khmer Empire. *[Students should mention that the Khmer Empire was the most powerful Indian-influenced empire in Southeast Asia. Its rulers adopted Hindu and Buddhist beliefs. They constructed irrigation systems for rice production, which led to a large population and increased tax revenue, which was used for public works, the building of the capital at Angkor, and the building of Angkor Wat and other temples.]*

To give students more information on the Khmer Empire, have them read the Global History Resource Center reading on the Khmer king's court and view the electronic media images of the relief from Angkor Wat and the gate at Angkor Thom. Conclude by asking students to summarize other Indian contacts with Southeast Asia. *[Students should mention the*

Srivijaya Empire on the island of Sumatra, as well as the contribution of Muslim merchants from India to Islamic states in Sumatra, the Malay Peninsula, Borneo, and the Philippines.]

CONCLUDE

Analyze the transformation of India and Southeast Asia.
To summarize information in the section, organize the class into small groups and have them answer the question: What kinds of important transformations did India and the countries of Southeast Asia undergo during the period from 600 to 1400? Have students work within their groups to answer the question. *[the emergence of competing kingdoms in India after Harsha's death; the Muslim invasions of India; the spread of Hindu, Buddhist, and Islamic cultures from India throughout Southeast Asia]* Then have the various groups discuss their answers. List their points on the board and work with the class to write a statement that expresses the most significant ideas.

EXTEND

Cross-Curricular Connection: *Art*
Have students read Core Resources Reading 12.3 and view the electronic media image of the relief from Angkor Wat. Then ask students to write a brief report on the construction of Angkor Wat, in which they provide additional information on the temple from research they have done outside of class.

MEET INDIVIDUAL NEEDS

Gifted Students
Have students find articles in periodicals that show the ongoing conflicts between Hindu and Muslim traditions in India and Southeast Asia. Have students report their findings in class.

Students Having Difficulty/Students Acquiring English
Have students who are having difficulty retaining the information in this section work in pairs to quiz each other on the main points. Instruct them to ask each other questions based on the section subheads.

ASSESS

Review
Have students complete the Section 3 Review. Use answers in the Teacher's Edition, page 320, to assess student mastery of this section.

Lesson 12.4   The Mongol Empire

Textbook pp. 321–326

RESOURCES

Pupil's Edition

Teenagers in History, p. 322: *Temujin*
Through Others' Eyes, p. 324: *From Venice to Beijing*
Geography and History, p. 325: *The Mongol Horsemen*
Map, p. 325: *The Mongol Empire, 1294*

Core Resources

Reading 12.4: *Diplomacy and the Golden Horde*

Global History Resource Center

Reading: *How the Mongols Lived*
Reading: *The Mongols Sack Baghdad*
Reading: *Marco Polo Visits Mongol China*

Videodiscs or Global History Resource Center

Map: *Mongol Empire, 1200s*

Search Frame 837

Image: *Mongols on the Move*

Search Frame 834

Image: *Mongol Arms and Armor*

Search Frame 833

LESSON FOCUS

How was Eurasia transformed by the Mongol Empire?

[Students should understand that Genghis Khan founded the empire in the early 1200s by uniting the Mongols under a system of laws and then leading them in an aggressive campaign of conquest.]

OBJECTIVES

After completing this lesson, students will be able to:
- describe the early successes achieved by Genghis Khan and the Mongols;
- identify the main goal of China's Yuan dynasty;
- describe the consequences of Il-khanid rule in Persia;
- explain the effect of the Golden Horde on developments in Russia.

Have students discuss Genghis Khan's political and military methods and the effectiveness of his strategy. Have them read the Geography and History feature to give them an idea of Mongol strategies.

Next tell students that using his strategies, the Mongols were able to establish a large empire.

Ask: What happened to the Mongol Empire after Genghis Khan's death?

[Several successors followed Genghis Khan as great khan, and these leaders continued the campaign of Mongol expansion. The Mongols expanded into northern China, Persia, Russia, Poland, Hungary, and Korea.]

HOOK

Describe the creation of the Mongol Empire. Ask students to recall what their goals were when they were small children. After they have responded, tell students that as a child, Temujin was determined to be the ruler of his people. Have them read the Teenagers in History feature and the biography.

Ask: How did Temujin achieve his goal?

[After years of struggle, he was named Genghis Khan, and he built the Mongol state by combining the strength of his cavalry with a feudal system.]

Ask: How did he build an empire?

DEVELOP

Discuss the Yuan dynasty in China. Tell students that under Kublai Khan, the Mongols continued their conquest in China, where it took them nearly 20 years to conquer the Song dynasty.

Ask: What did Kublai Khan establish in China?

[his own dynasty—the Yuan dynasty]

Ask: How did this affect the Chinese people?

[The Mongols were very destructive, but they tried to preserve China's ability to provide them with wealth.]

Ask students to imagine that they are living in China under the new Mongol rulers. Have them write a journal entry in which they describe everyday life under Mongol rule. You might wish to have them read the Global History Resource Center selections on Mongol life and view the electronic media images on the Mongols and their arms and armor.

PROBE

Examine the evolution of the empire. On the chalkboard, write the names of the three parts of the Mongol Empire covered in the textbook: *Yuan dynasty, the Il-khans,* and *Golden Horde.* Have students cite features of each and write these on the board under the appropriate heading. Ask them to consider 1) what characterized the Yuan dynasty's rule; 2) how the Il-khans differed from the Yuan rulers in their approach to government; 3) the Golden Horde's effect on Russia. *[In addition to other information from the text, students should point out:* **Yuan dynasty:** *their main goal was to make sure China continued to supply wealth to the Mongols;* **Il-khans:** *they adopted Islam and relied on local Persian officials of the old bureaucracy to rule, in contrast to the Yuan rulers who filled higher posts with non-Chinese;* **Golden Horde:** *in Russia they converted to Islam and allowed the Russians to rule over their own affairs; however, the Mongols' continuing requirements of obedience eventually led to struggles against Mongol domination.]* Next have students look for similarities and differences between the various parts of the empire.

For more information on Mongol expansion, have students read Core Resources Reading 12.4. If available, have students read the Global History Resource Center selection on the sack of Baghdad and show them the electronic media map of the Mongol Empire.

CONCLUDE

Analyze the impact of Mongol rule. Organize students into small groups and have them look again at the list of points on the board. Then ask them to consider the impact of Mongol rule on the territories they governed.

Have each group make a list of the consequences of Mongol rule for China, Persia, and Russia and Eastern Europe. While they make their lists, sketch a large map of the Eurasian land mass on the chalkboard.

Next bring students back together and discuss their various points, helping them draw conclusions about the effects of Mongol rule. Then have them list these points in the appropriate areas of the map. Finally, ask students whether they think the overall impact of the Mongol Empire was significant or minimal, and have them explain their answers. For more insight into the effects of Yuan rule on China, you might have students reread the Through Others' Eyes feature, and then have them read the Global History Resource Center selection on Marco Polo's visit.

EXTEND

Cross-Curricular Connection: *Geography*

Have students reread the Geography and History feature and discuss the importance of horses to the Mongol conquests. Then have them examine the map on textbook page 325 and consider the types of terrain the Mongols crossed during their conquests.

MEET INDIVIDUAL NEEDS

Kinesthetic Learners

Have students reread the biography and Teenagers in History feature on Genghis Khan. Then have them work individually or in small groups to prepare a short drama portraying the life of Genghis Khan. Have them present their performance in class.

Interpersonal Learners

Have pairs of students work together using the available visual resources to create a comic book or storyboard portraying the creation of the Mongol Empire. Have them share their work in class.

ASSESS

Review

Have students complete the Section 4 Review. Use answers in the Teacher's Edition, page 326, to assess student mastery of this section.

In preparation for the chapter test, you may wish to have students complete all or part of the Chapter 12 Review on textbook page 327, the Chapter 12 Review Activity, and the Chapter 12 Themes Review.

Chapter 12

Transformations in Asia

220–1350

Understanding the Main Idea

Call on a volunteer to read aloud the *Understanding the Main Idea* paragraph. Then tell students that the expansion of the Chinese economy and the flowering of the arts during the Tang and Song dynasties greatly influenced Korea, Japan, and Vietnam. Indian civilization too was influencing the Southeast Asian peoples. Then, in the 1200s, the Mongols swept across Eurasia, uniting most of the region into a vast empire.

Presenting Themes

See p. 299B for suggestions on introducing themes.

Using the Time Line

Have students list the time line events in their notebooks. After they have read about each event in the chapter, have students write a paragraph explaining its significance.

Understanding the Main Idea

Under the rule of the Tang and Song dynasties, China enjoyed a golden age of prosperity. China's cultural brilliance heavily influenced Korea, Japan, and Vietnam, all of which blended Chinese customs and institutions with their own native cultures. Meanwhile, Muslim invaders united the kingdoms of India into an Islamic empire, while Indian culture spread into Southeast Asia. By the mid-1200s, however, Eurasia was shaken by the Mongols, who rapidly built an empire that extended from China to eastern Europe.

Themes

- *War and Diplomacy* Why might nomadic peoples have a military advantage over settled civilizations?
- *Cross-cultural Interaction* How could one culture influence another without war or conquest?
- *Politics and Law* How might a ruler unite many kingdoms into an empire?

As kings, nobles, popes, and emperors struggled for power in Europe, mighty empires rose and fell in Asia. By the 1100s, after centuries of rule under the Tang and Song dynasties, China had developed one of the world's most advanced civilizations. Even after nomadic invaders forced the Song rulers to flee from northern China in 1126, the Song soon established a new capital at Hangzhou (HANG-CHOW) in the south. Hangzhou rapidly became one of the world's largest and most prosperous cities. With a population of at least 1 million, Hangzhou covered an area of seven or eight square miles. An anonymous observer recorded the following impressions of Hangzhou:

66 *During the morning hours, markets extend from Tranquility Gate of the palace all the way to the north and south sides of the New Boulevard. Here we find pearl, jade, talismans, [charms] exotic plants and fruits, seasonal catches from the sea, wild game—all the rarities of the world seem to be gathered here. . . .*

Some of the most famous specialties of the capital are the sweet-bean soup at the Miscellaneous Market, the pickled dates of the Ko family, . . . Sister Sung's fish broth . . . , [and] the sticky rice pastry of the Chang family. 99

The great city of Hangzhou is only one example of the thriving civilizations that prospered in China, Japan, Korea, India, and Southeast Asia by the 1200s.

589	c. 670	794	868	939
Wendi creates a unified Chinese empire.	Kingdom of Silla unites Korea for the first time.	Heian period begins in Japan.	Chinese produce the world's first printed book.	Vietnam achieves independence from China under Ngo Quyen.

A Chinese river festival in the 1100s

About the Image

River festivals were common in many Chinese cities, including Hangzhou. The Venetian Marco Polo praised Hangzhou as "without doubt the finest and most splendid city in the world." The city had a wide variety of diversions, including bookstores, pet shops, restaurants, wine shops, tea houses, popular entertainment, and boating. The city also tried to take care of its citizens through state hospitals, orphanages, and homes for the elderly. Charity was available for the poor, and everyone, including paupers, received a proper burial.

Critical Thinking Ask students if they would have agreed with Marco Polo that Hangzhou was the most splendid city in the world.

ANSWER: Students' answers will vary, but in size and sophistication Hangzhou was one of the leading cities of the world.

960	1192	1206	1271
Zhao Kuangyin proclaims the Song dynasty.	The Kamakura shogunate begins in Japan.	The Delhi sultanate begins.	Kublai Khan proclaims the Yuan dynasty in China.

History and Current Events

When the Sui reorganized the state bureaucracy, they stipulated that local government officials serve no more than three years in the same locality. At the end of that time, however, the official could be reassigned to another region. Term limits for elected officials continue to be an issue today. Some states and cities in the United States have passed legislation that restricts the time that elected officials can serve, and many people want term limits for members of Congress.

Critical Thinking Ask students what objections people might make to term limits for members of Congress.

ANSWER: Students might suggest that some people consider term limits an unconstitutional restriction of the voters' right to choose a candidate.

Imperial Reunification in China

FOCUS

- What was the main significance of the Sui dynasty?
- What did the Tang rulers accomplish?
- What problems did nomadic invaders cause for the Song dynasty?
- What social and economic changes occurred under the Tang and Song dynasties?

After the fall of the Han dynasty in A.D. 220, China was divided for more than three centuries. Finally a new dynasty, the Sui, united the country once again. Although this dynasty lasted only a short time, it paved the way for two longer-lived dynasties, the Tang and Song. Under these rulers, China enjoyed another golden age of prosperity and cultural brilliance.

The Grand Canal, still an important waterway today

From Division to Reunification

The collapse of the Han dynasty brought an end to stability in China. Nomadic invaders sacked Han cities and left them in ruins. As one writer noted in the early 300s, "At this time in the city . . . there were not more than one hundred families. Weeds and thorns grew thickly as if in a forest." Eventually, however, the nomadic invaders settled down, established kingdoms, and adopted Chinese customs.

Wendi, the leader of one of these invading tribes, founded the Sui dynasty in 581. By 589 he had defeated the states of southern China, creating a new, unified Chinese empire.

Learning from the Han example, Wendi set out to build a powerful centralized state. He created a new legal code, reformed the bureaucracy, and strengthened the northern border against invasion. He also established a system—similar to the Han practice of leveling—of "ever-ready granaries." These state-owned deposits of grain could be dispensed in times of famine.

After Wendi's death in 604, his son Yangdi continued his father's policies. Yangdi's greatest achievement was the completion of the largest sections of the **Grand Canal**, a 1,000-mile-long series of rivers and canals that connected northern and southern China. However, Yangdi's many schemes strained the state's resources. Discontent grew into rebellion, and in 617 Yangdi was assassinated. The short-lived Sui dynasty came to an abrupt end.

Despite its short reign, the Sui dynasty reunited much of China.

The Tang Dynasty

Although short-lived, the Sui dynasty had reestablished the principle of strong imperial rule. On this foundation the Sui's successors, the Tang, another dynasty of nomadic origins, built an empire that lasted for nearly three centuries.

Tang expansion and foreign relations. Under the Tang dynasty, China expanded rapidly. Chinese armies defeated Turkish nomads

The Tang Dynasty, 814

Chinese Expansion The powerful Tang rulers controlled a vast empire covering the northern and southern Chinese heartland and extending west to Central Asia and south into Indochina.

? Location Which cities were linked by the Grand Canal?

in Central Asia and extended China's frontiers far to the west, making contact with India and the Islamic world. China also turned parts of Korea, Manchuria, and Vietnam into subject states, and Chinese culture influenced Japan.

This contact with other lands and peoples also affected China. From 618 to 907 the Tang capital of Changan became a center of world culture. With a population of around 1 million, Changan was the largest city in the world at the time and was home to many peoples, including Persians, Arabs, Jews, and Greeks.

Buddhism under the Tang. Foreign contact also affected China's religion. Buddhism had first entered China from India during Han times, and its growth had been greatly encouraged by the northern nomadic tribes who preceded the Sui dynasty. By the time of the Tang dynasty, Buddhism had spread across China.

BIOGRAPHY For the first two centuries of their rule, the Tang made Buddhism the state religion in China. One Tang ruler who gave great support to Buddhism was the Empress Wu. During the reign of her husband, Gao Zong, Empress Wu greatly influenced politics, but after his death she grew even more powerful. In 690 Empress Wu claimed the Mandate of Heaven and became the only woman to hold the Chinese throne in her own right.

A tough, authoritarian ruler, Wu ordered her rivals executed and began a reign of terror that led many to oppose her rule. Nevertheless, she was also a gifted leader who filled her government with talented administrators.

Empress Wu embraced Buddhism partly because, unlike Confucianism, Buddhism did not

Empress Wu
BIOGRAPHY

Theme: Cross-cultural Interaction

During the Tang dynasty Chinese inventions flourished and spread to the outside world through China's increased contact with other states. China improved the manufacture of paper and porcelain and invented the wheelbarrow and gunpowder during this period. In addition, the use of coal as a fuel originated in northern China sometime around the 300s.

Critical Thinking Ask students how Chinese inventions reached foreign countries.

ANSWER: Students should answer that trade spread new Chinese inventions throughout the world.

Map Answer
Tianjin and Hangzhou

MULTIMEDIA PRESENTATION STRATEGY

VISUAL RESOURCES
Art and History 12
Seated Buddha Preaching the First Sermon

Show the transparency and share the information from Art and History Fact Sheet 12. Then have students complete the accompanying worksheet.

Level 2

The most compelling problem that Zhao Kuangyin—himself a former general—faced was the almost absolute power held by local military leaders. In order to assert his authority, Zhao Kuangyin transferred generals to other posts, coaxed them into retirement, and limited their scope of operations. As these military leaders retired or died, Zhao Kuangyin replaced them with civilian administrators from the central government.

Though successful in consolidating his power, Zhao Kuangyin's military reform had an unanticipated effect: it weakened the competence and effectiveness of the fighting forces. Thus, the Song were never able to reconquer northern Vietnam, any of Central Asia, or the northern steppe. The Song were also challenged on their northwestern borders by Tibetan tribes.

Critical Thinking Ask students what factors in Zhao Kuangyin's background might have led him to consider military leaders a threat to his rule.

ANSWER: Students might answer that Zhao Kuangyin had himself been a general and had seized power to establish the Song dynasty.

disapprove of female rulers. As a young woman, she had been a Buddhist nun, and during her reign she built many temples. Buddhism reached new heights in China during the reign of Empress Wu, but eventually it lost official favor. The growing power of the monasteries was seen as a threat to the state. In the mid-800s, officials launched a crackdown, destroying temples and forcing monks and nuns to live secular lives.

Decline of the Tang dynasty. The Tang dynasty reached its height around 750 and then gradually declined under weak emperors. In 755 General An Lu-shan rose in rebellion and forced the Tang to flee their capital. Although the rebellion eventually failed, it permanently damaged the public image and influence of the Tang dynasty. By the end of the 800s tax revenues had diminished, nomadic peoples had invaded from the north, and bands of brutal thugs roamed the countryside. Chaos became commonplace in the empire. In 907 a powerful general killed the emperor and seized the throne, ending the Tang dynasty.

At the height of the Tang dynasty, China expanded its borders and became a center of international trade and culture.

▲ Chinese artisans created this detailed silver pagoda during the Song dynasty.

The Song Dynasty

Fifty years of political upheaval followed the fall of the Tang dynasty. Finally, in 960 a leading general named Zhao Kuangyin (JOW KWAHNG-yin) seized power and declared a new dynasty, the Song. During the three centuries of Song rule, China would lead the world in technological, political, and governmental development.

Song reforms. Once Zhao Kuangyin established the dynasty, he rapidly reformed the government. He took power away from the military by forcing generals to retire and by replacing

military governors in the provinces with civilian officials. Unlike the Tang, whose government had relied on the aristocracy, the Song reestablished a centralized bureaucracy. Zhao Kuangyin strengthened the civil service by restoring the examination system. He also centralized tax collection.

The Song established their capital at Kaifeng, a vibrant city about three times the size of ancient Rome. At Kaifeng the Song emperors brought the government more directly under their personal control than the Tang had. The Song tightly controlled the tax income of the empire, and by the 1000s Chinese revenues were three times greater than they were at the height of the Tang dynasty.

The Liao Empire. Despite their economic strength, however, the Song were unable to regain control over the northern steppe. From about 916 until 1125, the northern part of China was ruled by the Qidan (CHI-DAHN), a seminomadic tribal people who established a dynasty known as the Liao.

The Liao often clashed with the Song, who eventually agreed to pay tribute to the nomadic raiders. Over time, this tribute became a crushing burden that caused resentment, and eventually rebellion, within China. One rebel leader complained:

❝Our enemies have become richer each day, and not showing gratitude, they have become more aggressive and more insulting instead. . . . Though we work hard all year round, we have never had a full stomach, and our wives and children suffer constantly from cold and hunger.❞

The Jin Empire. In 1125 the Ruzhen, a Manchurian people, conquered the Liao Empire and renamed it the Jin ("Golden") Empire. The following year, the Jin invaded and captured the Song capital of Kaifeng. The Song court fled to southern China, where it established a new capital at Hangzhou. Though their domain was reduced in size, this "Southern Song Dynasty" continued to rule in southern China for another 150 years.

Sacred TRADITIONS

Religions of East Asia

Buddhism

The sacred writings of Buddhism are so numerous that no one individual could know them all. The core beliefs of Buddhism are contained in a collection of writings called Sutta, *or "Discourses." In this selection the Buddha offers an explanation of life from the Four Noble Truths.*

And this is the Noble Truth of Sorrow. Birth is sorrow, age is sorrow, disease is sorrow, death is sorrow; contact with the unpleasant is sorrow, separation from the pleasant is sorrow, every wish unfulfilled is sorrow—in short all the . . . components of individuality are sorrow.

And this is the Noble Truth of the Way which Leads to the Stopping of Sorrow. It is the Noble Eightfold Path—Right Views, Right Resolve, Right Speech, Right Conduct, Right Livelihood, Right Effort, Right Mindfulness, and Right Concentration.

Daoism

The most important text of Daoism is the Dao Da Jing, *or "The Book of the Way and Its Power." It was supposedly written in the 500s B.C. by philosopher Laozi in response to a request for an explanation of his teachings. The following selection illustrates a central idea of Daoism, that life is guided by a set of opposite yet complementary forces.*

When everyone knows beauty is beauty, this is bad.
When everyone knows good is good, this is not good.
So being and nonbeing produce each other:
difficulty and ease complement each other,
long and short shape each other,
high and low contrast with each other,
voice and echoes conform to each other,
before and after go along with each other.

Confucianism

Confucianism is actually more of an ethical philosophy than a religion. Confucius was concerned with establishing an orderly system of government for China. To accomplish this, he taught that people should be loyal and dutiful, particularly to their families. In the Analects, a collection of Confucius's sayings, he explained:

Great Man applies himself to the fundamentals, for once the fundamentals are there System comes into being. It is filial duty and fraternal duty [duty to one's parents and siblings] that are fundamental to Manhood-at-its-best. . . .

While his father lives, observe a man's purposes; when the father dies, observe his actions. If for the three years [of mourning] a man does not change from the ways of his father, he may be called filial.

Understanding Sacred Traditions

1. In your opinion, how are Buddhism and Daoism similar?
2. How is Confucianism different from Buddhism and Daoism?

This page is from the earliest known copy of *Dao Da Jing,* the sacred text of Daoism.

Understanding Sacred Traditions

1. Each of these religions offers an explanation of life based on a set of guiding beliefs.
2. Confucianism is more a philosophy dealing with establishing an orderly society than a religion.

MULTIMEDIA PRESENTATION STRATEGY

WORLD HISTORY AND CULTURES VIDEODISCS

Map: *Changan, 750*

Search Frame 835

Image: *Women Silk Workers in Song China*

Search Frame 826

Map: *Population Shifts in China, 750–1250*

Search Frame 836

Show the maps and image as you discuss the Song dynasty. The captions that accompany each CD-ROM map and image offer additional details.

All Levels

The Song and Jin Empires, 1141

Map legend:
- Jin Empire
- Song Empire
- Capital city
- Grand Canal

0 200 400 Miles
0 200 400 Kilometers
Modified Conic Projection

Warring Empires After capturing the Song capital at Kaifeng, the Jin's Ruzhen warriors expanded southward beyond the Huang He.

? Location How far apart were the new Song and Jin capitals?

The Ruzhen adopted the Chinese bureaucracy. In addition, they collected taxes from the Chinese peasants, which they used to buy the allegiance of other nomadic groups. The Ruzhen accepted Chinese civilization more wholeheartedly than had the Liao. They also swept much farther south than the earlier Liao. Eventually, the Jin Empire stretched from Manchuria to the Yangzi River.

Invaders forced the Song to pay tribute and ultimately drove them from their capital.

Tang and Song Economy and Society

The move of the great Song dynasty to southern China highlighted a shift in Chinese civilization that had been occurring for some time. The creation of the Grand Canal, for example, had signaled the growing importance of the south in national development. By the 600s increasing numbers of Chinese were migrating south to settle on the rich, rice-growing lands of the Yangzi Valley. By the 1000s the south had surpassed the north in population and economic power.

Economic expansion. The migration southward under the Tang and Song dynasties occurred during a period of great economic prosperity. Tang expansion into Central Asia increased trade on the Silk Road, while China's extensive canal and river system promoted the growth of a large internal market. China also became an important overseas trading nation. By the late Song period, China had also become a major naval power.

Growing commerce led to the beginnings of a money and banking system. Ever since the Zhou dynasty, the Chinese had used strings of copper coins as cash, but these were very cumbersome for trading across great distances. In the early 800s the Tang issued "flying cash"—paper money drafts that were redeemable for copper coins in the capital city. By the early 1000s, however, the first true paper currency developed when private bankers began issuing notes to depositors. People found these notes so convenient that they began exchanging them instead of coins. Soon the government took over the printing of these notes, and China had the world's first paper money.

Urban life. As trade expanded, regional trading centers became thriving cities, bustling with activity. City streets were filled with traffic and lined with shops selling everything from noodles and candles to silk and pearls. Amusement districts featured restaurants, tea shops, puppet shows, and plays.

Leading landowning families, known as the gentry, grew quite powerful in the cities. Earlier the gentry had made their money through agriculture, but as the cities grew, they began to depend more on trade for their wealth.

In the Song capital of Hangzhou the wealthy lived in sturdy, well-decorated houses. In contrast, ordinary residents lived in crowded apartments, while many of the poor were homeless. The state set up hospitals and orphanages to help the poor, but poverty remained a serious urban problem.

History THROUGH THE ARTS

Two Tang Painters

The Tang dynasty was "the greatest period of creative art in China," according to one critic. The work of the painters Wu Daozi and Wang Wei provide ample evidence to back up this claim.

Wu Daozi, who lived from about 689 to 760, revolutionized Tang painting styles. Other Tang painters used a style known as the iron wire line. Their wirelike brush strokes were precise and controlled, but somewhat stiff.

Wu Daozi, however, adopted a style called the orchid petal line. His brush strokes were bold, free flowing, and of varying thicknesses, giving his paintings an almost three-dimensional appearance. Wu Daozi's brushwork also seemed to give the subjects of his paintings life and vigor. To some people, this suggested that he possessed magical powers. At any rate, Wu Daozi certainly worked quickly. He once painted a massive mural at the imperial palace in one day. He has been described as having a "whirlwind brush."

Wang Wei, Wu Daozi's contemporary, was a poet and

▲ Painting of Confucius by Wu Daozi

◀ Snowy winter landscape, painted by Wang Wei

scholar as well as a painter. Using bold, flowing brush strokes, he painted landscapes of great beauty. Bringing nature to life with a brush was, Wang Wei said, "the joy of painting." His work also had an almost lyrical quality. "In his paintings are his poems," one scholar once commented.

The influence of these two artists continued long after the fall of the Tang dynasty. Later generations recognized Wu Daozi as one of the greatest Chinese painters. So many artists adopted Wang Wei's methods that he is credited with the founding of a particular style of landscape painting.

Thinking About Art

How were the styles of the painters Wu Daozi and Wang Wei similar?

Thinking About Art

Their work is similarly flowing. Wu Daozi's bold, flowing brushwork appeared to give the subjects of his paintings life and vigor. Wang Wei is also said to have brought nature to life with bold, flowing brush strokes.

R RESOURCE ACTIVITY

GLOBAL HISTORY RESOURCE CENTER
Reading: *Poetry from Tang China*

Print out and distribute the reading. Call on different students to read the poems out loud. Then have students pick their favorite poem and illustrate it. Encourage students to incorporate the text into their illustrations.

Sheltered English

✓ REVIEW & ASSESSMENT RESOURCES

- Study Guide 12.1
- Daily Quiz 12.1
- Main Idea Activity 12.1

All Levels

During this period the status of women began to change. Women's work became less essential in the cities than it had been on farms. One of the clearest examples of women's lesser status was the growing custom of footbinding among the upper classes. From the age of five, upper-class girls had their feet bound tightly with all of their toes, except for the big toe, turned under the feet. Over time, their feet would grow into a deformed shape, half the size of normal feet. Footbinding crippled girls for life but was an accepted custom because it showed that men could afford to support these women who could not work.

Rural life. Despite the growing size of China's cities, most Chinese still lived in the countryside. To promote rural progress, the Tang rulers tried to break up large estates and give every farmer a piece of land. The later Tang rulers, however, abandoned this policy, and land became increasingly concentrated in the hands of large landlords.

Meanwhile, technological improvements in agriculture—including new irrigation techniques and new quick-ripening varieties of rice from Southeast Asia—allowed farmers to produce more food. The cultivation of tea, a new Southeast Asian crop, and cotton also became more common.

SECTION 1
REVIEW ANSWERS

IDENTIFY
For significance, see the following pages:
Wendi (p 302)
Yangdi (p. 302)
Grand Canal (p. 302)
Empress Wu (p. 303)
Zhao Kuangyin (p. 304)
abacus (p. 308)

LOCATE
For locations, see the maps on pp. 303 and 306.

1. The Sui reunited most of China.
2. Under both dynasties the economy expanded, cities grew, and many new technological and artistic improvements took place.
3. The invaders forced the Song to pay tribute and drove them from their capital.
4. Accounts should mention the Tang's geographic expansion through military conquest, economic expansion at home and abroad, and the distribution of land to all farmers.
5. Responses will vary, but may include the idea that regardless of an empire's stability, it remained vulnerable to attack by outside invaders desiring its wealth.

These new crops contributed to a revolution in the economy. Instead of simply growing their own food, people began to produce goods for market.

Technology. Spurred on by social and economic trends, Chinese inventors helped make China a world leader in technology. One of the most significant Chinese inventions was gunpowder. Developed sometime around the A.D. 200s, gunpowder was being used in hand grenades and mines by the early 1100s.

In 868 the Chinese, the pioneers of printing techniques, used carved blocks to produce the world's first printed book—a Buddhist text called the *Diamond Sutra*. Other notable technological advances included the magnetic compass and the suspension bridge. The Chinese also made use of the **abacus**—a device for doing mathematical calculations by moving beads along rods. Chinese products were so advanced that the word for "Chinese" became a synonym for "superior" in many Asian languages.

▲ This tray held the carved blocks of Chinese type used in creating early printed books.

in creating sculptures, weaving textiles, and carving jade. The fine Chinese pottery known as porcelain became famous around the world. However, the genius of Chinese artists was perhaps most evident in painting. Inspired by the Daoist and Buddhist love of nature, painters created some of the finest landscape paintings of the period.

Like painting, the literature of this era was also highly developed and reflected the Daoist and Confucian roots of Chinese culture. The greatest literature of the time was produced by Tang poets. Chinese literary volumes contain nearly 50,000 poems written by more than 2,000 poets.

Two of the most famous Tang poets reflected the contrasting tendencies in Chinese thought. Li Bai (Li Po), a Daoist, spent much of his life seeking pleasure. His writings—happy, light, and elegant—described the delights of life. Du Fu, on the other hand, possessed a more serious nature and devoutly followed Confucian teachings. His carefully written verses showed his deep concern for the suffering and tragedy of human life.

✚ Literature and the Arts

The period of Tang and Song rule also produced a flowering of Chinese arts. The Chinese excelled

Under Tang and Song rule, China's economy expanded, its cities grew, its inventors pioneered new technologies, and its artists and writers produced great masterpieces.

SECTION 1 REVIEW

IDENTIFY and explain the significance of the following:
  Wendi
  Yangdi
  Grand Canal
  Empress Wu
  Zhao Kuangyin
  abacus

LOCATE and explain the importance of the following:

Kaifeng
Hangzhou

1. **Main Idea** What was the most significant accomplishment of the Sui dynasty?
2. **Main Idea** How did Chinese civilization change under the Tang and Song dynasties?
3. **War and Diplomacy** What were the results of conflict

between the Song and invaders from the north?
4. **Writing to Explain** Imagine that you are a historian under the Tang. Write a brief account explaining what Tang rulers have accomplished.
5. **Synthesizing** What generalizations can you make about the rise and fall of Chinese dynasties?

Korea, Japan, and Vietnam

SECTION 2

CORE LESSON PLAN
See pages 299E and 299F for Lesson Plan 12.2.

FOCUS

- How did China influence Korea?
- What factors influenced the development of early Japanese culture?
- How did Japan develop a decentralized government?
- What effect did Chinese rule have on Vietnam?

The growth of Chinese civilization under the Tang and Song dynasties had a significant effect on neighboring Korea, Japan, and Vietnam. Exposed to the richness of Chinese culture, these countries adopted many Chinese ways. Yet each country also retained elements of its own culture, which blended with Chinese customs to create unique cultural traditions.

Koreans learned to use movable type from the Chinese.

The Emergence of Civilization in Korea

Korea is a rugged, mountainous peninsula that juts south from Manchuria into the sea between China and Japan. Because of its location, Korea has long served as a bridge, allowing the passage of people and ideas from the mainland to the islands.

Korea was first settled by nomadic peoples from northeastern Asia, who entered the peninsula in prehistoric times. As early as 300 B.C., Chinese migrants began to arrive, bringing with them a knowledge of metalworking and agriculture. Not long afterward, the first strong Korean kingdom, **Chosŏn**, emerged in the northern part of the country. By the early 100s B.C., Chosŏn was strong enough to exert some control over much of the Korean Peninsula.

The growth of Korean kingdoms. In about 108 B.C. troops from Han China conquered Chosŏn and turned it into a Chinese colony. For the next 400 years the Chinese imposed tight control over northwestern Korea, looking down on native Koreans and allowing them little voice in their government.

Elsewhere on the peninsula, however, three Korean kingdoms—Koguryo, Paekche, and Silla—developed in opposition to Chinese rule. Because these kingdoms also fought amongst themselves, they were unable to challenge China's dominant position in Korea until after the fall of the Han dynasty. Finally, in A.D. 313 Koguryo invaded and took over the Chinese colony.

For the next several centuries, Korea's three kingdoms continued to fight among themselves. During the early 600s China, under Sui rule, tried to conquer Korea but failed. Later, however, the rulers of Silla made a strategic alliance with the Tang emperor of China. Working together, the armies of Silla and China conquered Paekche and Koguryo. Silla then turned on the Chinese forces and drove them from Korea. By about 670 the kingdom of Silla had united Korea for the first time.

Although Silla was independent, its leaders agreed to pay tribute to China to ensure the harmony and goodwill of their powerful neighbor. They also embraced many aspects of Chinese civilization, such as a centralized government, in effect

As the ancient tribal systems broke down, Silla's government and culture were heavily influenced by China. Silla sent tribute missions to the Tang capital regularly. In addition, many students and monks from Silla pursued their education and training in China. Thus, a flow of new ideas and philosophies arose. Eventually, the people of Silla embraced Buddhism and duplicated the Tang political system.

Critical Thinking Ask students why Silla accepted Tang systems.

ANSWER: Students should suggest that Silla wanted to replace older tribal customs.

MULTIMEDIA PRESENTATION STRATEGY

VISUAL RESOURCES
Geography and History 12
New Cultures in Asia, c. 670–1392

Show the transparency and share the information from Geography and History Fact Sheet 12. Then have students complete the accompanying worksheet.

| Level 2 |

310

creating their own version of Tang China. The age of Silla, which roughly matched the era of Tang rule, was peaceful and prosperous.

As with the Chinese dynasties, however, Silla eventually grew weak and was shaken by internal rebellions. In the early 900s a new kingdom, Koryo (from which the name Korea comes), rose to challenge Silla's power. By 935 Koryo had taken control of the Korean Peninsula, which it ruled until 1392.

Korean culture and society. The influence of Chinese culture and civilization on Korea is deep-rooted. Chosŏn, the first Korean kingdom, was founded in part by immigrants from China and bore the imprint of Chinese culture. Korean rulers adopted Chinese as their written language. They also embraced the Chinese tradition of Confucianism.

Korean rulers also looked to China for their model of government. They established dynasties controlled by hereditary kings. The rulers of Koryo established a Confucian examination system to train their officials and built Kaesong, an elaborate capital city much like Changan, the Tang imperial city. Korean kings embraced Chinese Buddhism, building enormous temples that became major centers of learning.

New Cultures in Asia, c. 670–1392

| Kingdom of Silla, c. 670–935 | Khmer Empire, 850–1250 |
| Kingdom of Koryo, 935–1392 | Annam (Vietnam), 1010–1225 |

Chinese Influence The kingdoms bordering China to the northeast and to the southeast fought to gain their independence from Chinese control. However, Chinese culture continued to influence these small kingdoms.

Human-Environment Interaction What physical feature linked the Khmer Empire from north to south and helped it prosper?

▲ This Korean gold and bronze dragon's head was originally placed at the top of a flagstaff.

Despite these similarities, however, ancient Korea was not an identical copy of China. As one ruler of Koryo proclaimed in 982: "Let us follow China in poetry, history, music, ceremony, and the five relationships [of Confucius], but in riding and dressing let us be Koreans." Moreover, Korean Buddhism also included elements of Korea's traditional animism.

Another important difference was the presence of a powerful nobility in Korea. Unlike Chinese nobles, the Korean aristocracy continued to influence politics and was able to limit the power of Korea's Confucian bureaucracy. As a result, a significant scholar-gentry class never developed in Korea. Unlike Chinese society, in which the gentry formed a kind of middle class between the traditional noble families and the peasantry, Korean society was more sharply divided between a small upper class and a very large lower class.

The age of Silla and Koryo was a time of great artistic achievement. Korean artists produced beautiful landscapes in the Tang and Song styles, and Korean writers produced great works of literature and historical scholarship. Korean artisans of this period created fine pottery that rivaled Song porcelain in beauty. Korean and Chinese traditions also blended in this period, resulting in a unique new culture.

Because of its nearness to China, Korea adopted many features of Chinese culture, blending them with native Korean traditions.

The Rise of Japanese Civilization

Japan's early history is similar to that of Korea, and culturally Japan shared much with both China and Korea. Over time, however, Japan developed a very different social and political structure. Like Korea, Japan has been strongly influenced by its geography and location. A chain of several thousand islands stretching over a distance of nearly 1,400 miles, Japan has always been wedded to the sea. Even on the largest islands—Honshu, Hokkaido, Kyushu, and Shikoku—no one is more than 100 miles from the ocean. Because Japan is very mountainous—less than one fifth of the land is good for farming—the sea has always served as a vital source of food and means of transportation.

Japan was settled thousands of years ago by Stone Age peoples who migrated from the Asian mainland, pushing the Ainu, the first inhabitants of the islands, into the far north. By the first century B.C. these early migrants were crafting tools and weapons from bronze and iron and practicing early forms of agriculture. These cultural developments probably came from China and were reinforced by continued migration from the mainland.

Early Japanese society and religion. By the first centuries A.D. the Japanese people were organized in clans, the most powerful of which were located on the island of Honshu. An early Chinese account described Japanese society:

❝ *The land of [Japan] is warm and mild. In winter as in summer, the people live on raw vegetables and go about barefooted. . . . When a person dies, they prepare a single coffin, without an outer one. . . . When the funeral is over, all members of the family go into the water to cleanse themselves in a bath of purification.* ❞

Ritual purification was a feature of Japanese religion, known as **Shinto**, meaning "way of the gods." The gods of Shinto were nature spirits called *kami,* and the purpose of Shinto rituals was to win their favor. Many clans also traced their origins to a particular *kami,* which they honored as their special spirit.

Theme: Politics and Law

In 702 the Taiho Code expanded the Taika reforms. This code was based on the Chinese bureaucratic model and divided Japan into three levels of governmental administration: provinces, districts, and villages. Taxes were collected in goods, such as grain or cloth, or in labor. Furthermore, all males were liable for conscription into the military. However, a Chinese-style civil-service examination system was not adopted by the Japanese. Thus, despite much borrowing from the mainland—religion, written language, government, laws, tax systems, and land reform—the aristocratic families retained ultimate authority.

Critical Thinking Ask students to name the primary factor in obtaining government positions in Japan, in the absence of civil-service examinations.

ANSWER: Students might answer that birth into one of the powerful families or clans was the most important factor.

▲ Mountain priests, called *yamabushi*, participate in a traditional Japanese Shinto ritual.

Shinto also helped give rise to Japan's imperial family. According to legend, the founder of the Yamato, a powerful clan, was the grandson of the Shinto sun goddess, Amaterasu. By A.D. 400, other clans, accepting the Yamato claim of divine ancestry, made the Yamato leader the emperor of Japan. Since then, all Japanese emperors have come from the Yamato line. Until recently, the Japanese claimed that these rulers were gods.

China and Japanese civilization. Like Korea, Japan had long been influenced by Chinese civilization. Much of that influence first came through Korea. For example, it was Koreans who introduced Chinese writing into Japan. Because Japan had no written language, the Chinese script soon came into wide use by the Japanese nobility, although the Japanese eventually developed their own script. Also, in A.D. 552 a Korean ruler sent Buddhist texts as a gift to the Japanese emperor. Buddhism took hold in Japan, and along with it came styles of literature, architecture, sculpture, and painting associated with Chinese Buddhism.

The greatest supporter of Chinese civilization in Japan was Prince Shotoku, who ruled from 593 to 622. Shotoku introduced laws modeled on Confucian thought and encouraged the growth of a strong central government led by the emperor. Under Shotoku's leadership, Buddhism also gained strength, and impressive temples sprang up across Japan. Japanese missions to China brought back knowledge about engineering, medicine, weights and measures, and agriculture. The Japanese absorbed these influences and eventually transformed them into a culture that was uniquely their own.

The Taika reforms. Prince Shotoku died before he was able to carry out many of his planned reforms. In 645, however, other reformers put forth a plan calling for more changes based on the Chinese model. This plan, the **Taika reforms**, was designed to transplant the centralizing ideas of the Tang government to Japan. The Taika reforms declared all land to be the property of the state and established a census to allow fair distribution of land to peasants. As the emperor announced:

❝Let men of solid capacity and intelligence who are skilled in writing and arithmetic be appointed assistants and clerks. . . . Let there now be provided for the first time registers of population, books of account and a system of the receipt and regranting of distribution-land.**❞**

The ambitious Taika reforms were never completely enacted, however. This was in large part because of the Japanese nobility's strong opposition to the transfer of land from private hands to the state.

Unlike the situation in China, noble families continued to hold great power and influence in Japan. Eventually, the Japanese developed a tradition of indirect government in which the emperor was honored as a figurehead but real power was exercised by others.

Nevertheless, the Taika reforms did establish the idea of imperial rule in Japan and introduced many important principles of government. The reforms also led to the creation of new capital cities, first at Nara and then at Heian (HAY-ahn), today known as Kyoto.

Imperial Japanese society and culture. Heian was a beautiful city, modeled on Changan and filled with magnificent temples, palaces, and gardens. During the Heian period, a golden age that lasted from 794 to 1185, Japanese culture flourished. This cultural awakening centered around the the royal court. There, members of noble families encouraged the refined tastes and love of beauty that have remained important elements of Japanese culture.

Life at court was marked by great elegance and style. Men and women lavished attention on their appearances and turned even gift wrapping into an art. The ability to write poetry was deemed essential to a well-bred person. Sei Shonagon, a lady-in-waiting to the empress, conveyed the atmosphere of court life:

❝ Early one morning, when a pale moon still hung in the sky, we went out into the garden, which was thick with mist. . . . Her Majesty got up herself, and all the ladies in attendance joined us in the garden. As we strolled about happily, dawn gradually appeared on the horizon. . . . 'So you have been out moon-viewing,' said [a gentleman] admiringly and composed a poem in praise of the moon. ❞

Much of early Japanese literature was written by women. They composed five-line poems called *tanka*, which were about love and nature, and they wrote the first Japanese prose. The most famous of these prose works is the *Tale of Genji*, by Lady Murasaki Shikibu, which describes life at the Heian court.

Japan's geography, the Shinto religion, and ideas from China influenced the development of Japanese culture.

The Emergence of Feudal Japan

By the mid-1100s the Fujiwara family, which had served as regents for Japan's emperors, had come to dominate the imperial court through a string of marriages between their daughters and the young men of the imperial family. Although the Fujiwara had weakened the emperor's power, they did

▲ This painting from the 1100s shows the glory of a Japanese samurai in battle.

not have the strength to maintain a centralized government themselves. As central authority declined, armed conflict became more common, and people began to seek protection from the growing chaos.

Feudal order. To protect themselves and their property, owners of large estates hired bands of warriors. These warriors, called **samurai**, were like European knights. They wore armor, fought with swords, and often rode on horseback. As the samurai developed into a fighting class, they also developed a strict set of rules governing their behavior. In later centuries these rules became known as **Bushido**, or "the way of the warrior." Both men and women from samurai families were expected to follow the code of behavior.

The main elements of Bushido were courage, honor, unflinching acceptance of hardship, instant obedience to a superior's orders, and—above all—loyalty to one's overlord. In exchange for loyalty, the lord had an obligation to provide for the samurai and reward them appropriately for services rendered. Any samurai who disobeyed a lord might be ordered to commit seppuku, suicide by means of ritual disembowelment. If the lord did not order seppuku, often a samurai would request the privilege of committing suicide rather than live with the shame of dishonor or failure.

Like European knights, samurai warriors were expensive to support because they required

R RESOURCE ACTIVITY

READINGS IN WORLD HISTORY
Reading 12.2
The *Tale of Genji*

Have students read about the elegance of life in the Japanese imperial court. Then have them complete the questions.

Level 2

R RESOURCE ACTIVITY

GLOBAL HISTORY RESOURCE CENTER
Reading: *The Elegant Court Life of Heian Japan*

Print out and distribute the reading. Have students read Sei Shonagon's description of court life. Then ask students to write short five-line poems, called *tanka*, describing the scenes that Sei Shonagon recorded.

Level 3

When the Kamakura shogunate was unable to reward the samurai with the usual plunder after they defeated the Mongol invaders, the warriors began to lose faith in the regents and shifted their loyalty to local lords. As the shogunate and centralized authority began to break down, the samurai became more influential, until they were the dominant class in Japan under the Ashikaga shogunate. Though the samurai code was not formalized until the 1600s, its fundamental practices—virility, altruism, integrity, honesty, and fearlessness, even in the face of death—were already in place during the Kamakura and Ashikaga shogunates.

Critical Thinking Ask students what the samurai might have been able to get from the local lords as opposed to the shoguns.

ANSWER: Students might suggest that the samurai might have received land, food, or prestigious social contacts from the shoguns.

costly armor, weapons, and horses. Samurai were financed primarily through a land distribution system based on the *shoen*, or "estate." Unlike the medieval European manor, the *shoen* was not a single piece of land with a manor house surrounded by grazing land. Instead, a *shoen* was made up of scattered farmland that was governed as a single unit.

Those who held a *shoen* did not necessarily live on it; they simply had a right to its income or its harvests, usually in rice. Often many people would have a share in a single *shoen*, and most would also have shares in other *shoen*. Although many samurai had once held interests in the productivity of certain lands, by the late 1400s many were paid in goods.

The Kamakura shogunate. In 1156, as the power of both the imperial family and the Fujiwara declined, civil war broke out between the Taira and Minamoto clans. In 1192, after considerable intrigue and fighting, Minamoto Yoritomo forced the emperor to grant him the title of **shogun**, or "general." Although the imperial court remained the spiritual heart of Japanese society, the real power lay with the shoguns. Yoritomo created a military government with its capital at Kamakura, which lasted until 1333. Historians have named this government the Kamakura shogunate.

The Kamakura shogunate was remarkable in that it survived after the Minamoto clan fell from power. Yoritomo killed all of his rivals except for his two sons. When Yoritomo died, his eldest son became the shogun, but the rival Hojo clan forced him to abdicate in 1203. Sixteen years later the Hojo assassinated Yoritomo's second son. Although the Hojo never claimed the title of shogun, they ruled the shogunate as regents until the end of the Kamakura period.

In the late 1200s the Hojo faced an external threat—an invasion from the Mongols of Asia. In several great battles the regents were able to turn the Mongols back, and in the

end the Mongol fleet was destroyed by a great storm, which the Japanese thereafter called kamikaze, or "divine wind." With little plunder from the struggle, however, the Hojo could not reward their samurai. Over the next century, amidst increasing dissatisfaction on all sides, the entire feudal system began to break down.

By the early 1300s Japanese society had reached a crisis. The samurai class had grown considerably, but its landholdings and income had dropped sharply. Discontented samurai warriors began to offer their loyalty to anyone who could afford to maintain them. As more local lords gained samurai warriors, the potential for violence also grew. When Emperor Go-Daigo tried to revive imperial power, Japan exploded into full civil war.

The Ashikaga shogunate. In 1331 Go-Daigo launched a revolt against the Hojo in an attempt to restore the power of the imperial court. Enlisting the support of local military leaders and powerful Buddhist monasteries, Go-Daigo finally succeeded in destroying the Kamakura shogunate. However, he was unable to regain real power. One of Go-Daigo's generals, Ashikaga Takauji (ah-shee-KAH-gah tah-KOW-jee), forced him to restore the shogunate—but this time under the Ashikaga clan. The Ashikaga shogunate lasted nearly two and a half centuries, from 1338 to 1573.

Although the Ashikaga claimed the shogunate, they did not in fact restore any sort of central authority. Instead, they allowed local lords to run their own affairs. Gradually, with little central control, stronger lords began to overcome weaker ones, forcing them to become vassals. Soon only strong lords remained, supported by many subject families and their own personal samurai. Under the Ashikaga shoguns, the samurai became the most important class in Japanese society.

► **Japanese samurai are helped in their fight against the Mongols by the kamikaze, the "divine wind."**

Under the Kamakura and Ashikaga shoguns, Japan gradually became a politically decentralized feudal society.

Civilization in Vietnam

Like Japan and Korea, Vietnam (called Annam at the time) was strongly influenced by Chinese civilization. In fact, China ruled Vietnam for more than 1,000 years. The Vietnamese maintained many of their customs, however, and eventually threw off Chinese domination.

Geography and the people.

Located just south of China, Vietnam is a long, curved strip of land that runs along the South China Sea. It is the easternmost country of Indochina, a peninsula of Southeast Asia that includes the areas of present-day Laos, Burma, Cambodia, Thailand, and the Malay Peninsula. Much of Vietnam is mountainous, except for a narrow coastal plain and two large river deltas: the Red River Delta in the north and the Mekong Delta in the south.

Vietnam's geography, like that of Burma, Siam, and Malaya, gave rise to two distinct types of peoples: lowland-dwellers,

▲ This Vietnamese statue of Ganesha, son of Siva, from the 600s shows the importance of Indian religions in Southeast Asia.

who occupied the coastal plain and river deltas, and mountain people, who inhabited the more remote highland areas. Historically, it was the lowland peoples who were most open to outside influence and who dominated national life.

The early history of Vietnam.
The origins of the Vietnamese are surrounded in myth. One legend claims that the Dragon Lord of the Lac and a mountain princess of Vietnam produced the first people in Vietnam. Historians believe that a people known as the Lac did form an early kingdom in the Red River Delta, where they practiced rice farming and developed simple stone and bronze tools.

In 208 B.C. the Lac kingdom was taken over by Trien Da (TREEN-DAH), the governor of a southern Chinese province. Trien Da broke with China and formed the new kingdom of Nam Viet, which included parts of northern Vietnam and southern China. He adopted the customs of the local people and consulted with the Lac rulers in running the kingdom.

A century later, in 111 B.C., the armies of Han China overran Nam Viet and turned it into a Chinese colony. Thus began more than 1,000 years of Chinese rule in Vietnam. At first the Chinese ruled with a light hand. Although they brought in Chinese ideas of government, arts, and culture, they allowed the Lac rulers to control their villages. In this way the Chinese confirmed an old Vietnamese saying: "The King's laws bow before village customs."

Eventually, though, the Chinese began to tighten their control over Vietnam. Vietnam had agricultural resources and a sizable population that could be taxed and put to work for the Chinese Empire. Under heavy-handed domination by the Chinese, the Vietnamese people began to rebel. Around A.D. 40 two women, the Trung sisters, organized a revolt and overthrew the Chinese overlords. The Trung sisters briefly ruled Vietnam before China regained control. Over the next several centuries other Vietnamese uprisings occurred, though with little success.

Vietnamese independence.
The fall of the Tang dynasty in China in the early 900s provided the Vietnamese with another chance for independence, and this time they succeeded. In 939 a Vietnamese leader named Ngo Quyen (en-GOH ky-EN) rose up and defeated the Chinese forces. He ruled for only a short time, however, before the country fell into chaos. For the next two decades local warlords fought each other for

power. Finally, strong rulers established a series of dynasties that brought some stability to Vietnam and allowed the nation to develop.

The Li dynasty, which ruled from 1010 until 1225, built and stabilized the Vietnamese state. The Li constructed canals and roads and developed agriculture. They also established a civil service patterned after the Chinese system.

Under succeeding dynasties Vietnam began to expand southward. Attacking the kingdoms of Champa and Khmer (kuh-MER), Vietnam added new territory. Eventually, the Li captured the Mekong Delta area and established borders similar to those of modern Vietnam.

Vietnamese culture and society. Because of its long occupation by China, Vietnam absorbed many traits of Chinese civilization. The Vietnamese adopted the Chinese writing system and incorporated many features of Chinese government, including a Confucian-style bureaucracy. Vietnam embraced Mahayana Buddhism from China and with government support Buddhist learning, art, and architecture became the most important features of Vietnamese culture. Under government

▶ **Modern Vietnamese women work in rice fields in much the same way that their ancestors worked.**

sponsorship, Confucianism and Daoism also heavily influenced the development of Vietnamese culture and society.

Yet, as in Korea and Japan, Vietnam's admiration for Chinese culture did not lead to integration with China. The Vietnamese maintained many of their traditional customs, such as the worship of nature spirits, which they practiced alongside Chinese customs. While Chinese rule left a strong cultural imprint, it actually made the Vietnamese more determined to preserve their own culture and identity as a people.

Chinese rule had a great impact on the culture of Vietnam but also reinforced the Vietnamese desire for independence.

SECTION 2 REVIEW

IDENTIFY and explain the significance of the following:
    Chosŏn
    Shinto
    Taika reforms
    samurai
    Bushido
    shoen
    Minamoto Yoritomo
    shogun
    Go-Daigo
    Ngo Quyen

LOCATE and explain the importance of the following:

Korea
Japan
Honshu
Heian
Vietnam
Red River
Mekong River

1. *Main Idea* How and why did Japan develop a decentralized government?
2. *Main Idea* What effect did invasion and conquest by China have on the development of Vietnam?

3. *Geography: Location* How did China's proximity to Korea affect the development of Korean culture?
4. *Writing to Explain* In a short essay, explain how various factors influenced early Japanese culture.
5. *Comparing and Contrasting* China greatly influenced Korea, Japan, and Vietnam. How was that influence similar in all three countries? In what ways was it different?

India and Southeast Asia

SECTION 3

CORE LESSON PLAN
See pages 299G and 299H for Lesson Plan 12.3.

FOCUS

- What were the consequences of the fall of Harsha's empire?
- How did Muslim invasions affect India?
- What influence did India have on Southeast Asia?

As the Gupta Empire dissolved around A.D. 550, local kingdoms once again emerged throughout northern India. After a brief reunification during the reign of Harsha, northern India fell into disunity once more. Eventually, Islamic invaders—first Arabs, then Turks and other Central Asians—seized northern India and established their own states. They brought new and very different cultural traditions to India. Meanwhile, Indian civilization had also been spreading overseas along the trade routes to Southeast Asia. Hindu, Buddhist, and Islamic cultures heavily influenced Southeast Asian peoples—much as Chinese culture did in Korea, Japan, and Vietnam.

Indian-influenced sculpture and architecture in Java

The Aftermath of the Gupta Empire

For about 50 years after the collapse of the Gupta Empire, northern India once again saw the rise of many competing kingdoms. In 606 a 16-year-old named Harsha Vardhana became the king of Thanesar, a state north of Delhi. Harsha set out to conquer all of northern India. During his reign Harsha gradually expanded his control over most of northern India and shifted his capital to the eastern city of Kanauj to better administer his state.

After Harsha's death, however, India was once again divided among many local dynasties. In the south the most powerful dynasties to emerge were the Chalukya of the Deccan and the Pallava and the Chola of far southern India.

By the early 800s three important kingdoms fought for control of northern India. The Pratihara, a dynasty from the western state of Rajasthan, started to expand eastward in the mid-800s. In the east the Pala, a Buddhist dynasty from Bengal, began pushing westward and seized Kanauj. Meanwhile, the Rashtrakuta from the south expanded northward. These kingdoms clashed as their territories overlapped, but eventually the Pratihara kingdom won control over Kanauj and emerged as the strongest state in northern India. Despite this strength, however, the Pratihara were unable to establish a strong central government.

*A*fter Harsha Vardhana's death, India splintered into competing kingdoms.

The Coming of Islam

In the early 900s, as Pratihara rule weakened, strong local rulers emerged once again in northern India. Many of these rulers were the heads of Rajput clans, which had established kingdoms in northern India where they practiced Hindu cultural and religious traditions. The Rajput emphasized warfare and valued heroism in battle. As the kings fought among themselves and against outsiders, however, northern India remained divided. Eventually, the region fell to new groups of invaders.

Theme: **Politics and Law**

The reign of Harsha Vardhana is well documented in two sources: the *Life of Harsha*, written by a member of the royal court named Bana, and a chronicle written by the renowned Chinese Buddhist, Xuan Zang. An able warrior as well as a gifted monarch, Harsha reunited almost all of northern India during his 41-year reign. Harsha was also a devoted brother. He rescued his sister from ritual death by preventing her from leaping onto her husband's funeral pyre.

Critical Thinking Ask students the scholarly advantages of having two written sources on Harsha Vardhana instead of only one.

ANSWER: Students might answer that having two sources could help scholars identify inaccuracies and biases in either source.

Early Muslim invasions. In 711, Arab forces anxious to extend their new faith, Islam, invaded and conquered Sind, a region of western India. However, Islam did not spread much beyond Sind for nearly 300 years. In 997 the Turkish sultan Mahmud of Ghazna launched the first of his 17 devastating raids on India, sacking cities and smashing temples. Each time, according to one account, Mahmud returned home "with so much booty, prisoners and wealth, that the fingers of those who counted them would have been tired." This destruction brought down the Pratihara dynasty and brought much of northern India into the Ghaznavid Empire. It also bred a deep-seated hostility between Hindus and Muslims in the region.

After Mahmud's death in 1030, the Ghaznavids were content to rule the territory they had already gained. For more than a century, northern India was relatively peaceful. In the late 1100s, however, yet another Turkish dynasty, the Ghurids, swept into India.

With large numbers of mercenaries, better horses, and stronger weapons, the Ghurids crushed the Ghaznavids in Sind. Then they moved against an alliance of Rajput kings. Meanwhile, the Ghurids turned against the Buddhist monasteries, crushing Buddhist religious practices so severely that Buddhism nearly disappeared from India. Ultimately, the Muslim armies overran the Rajput defenders, and by the early 1200s Muslims had taken control of most of northern India.

▲ This Muslim monument, the Qutb Minar, was built by the Delhi sultanate to celebrate a military victory.

The Delhi sultanate. The new Muslim government, founded in 1206 with its capital at Delhi, became known as the **Delhi sultanate**. Brutal in conquest, the sultans of Delhi were less harsh as rulers. They generally allowed Indians to continue their traditional way of life. At the same time, however, they ended the power of local rulers and established a strong central administration.

The sultans opened their courts to artists and intellectuals from other parts of the Islamic world. As a result, the Delhi sultanate became a center of Islamic culture. A distinctive Indo-Muslim architecture emerged, combining elements of Indian and Islamic styles. Islamic literature and customs became common at the royal court in Delhi. In addition, a new language, Urdu, was created, combining Arabic words with Sanskrit grammar.

Islam and Hinduism. Islam had a powerful effect on Indian life. Great differences separated Hindus from Muslims. Hindus worshipped many gods and goddesses, while Muslims worshipped only Allah. The Hindu varna system seemed to contradict the Islamic belief that all people were equal before God. Hindus and Muslims even had different rules about the kind of food and drink they could consume. At times, religious differences led to violent conflict between Muslims and Hindus. Such differences remain a troubling issue in modern India and a strong reminder of India's past.

The Muslim invasions of India led to Muslim rule and the spread of Islamic culture in India.

Indian Influence in Southeast Asia

The growth of Indian civilization had a great impact on Southeast Asia. As early as the A.D. 100s, Indian traders had begun a prosperous sea trade with Southeast Asia. By the Gupta age, Brahmins and Buddhist monks were spreading Hinduism and Buddhism in the region.

Local rulers, seeking to enhance their standing, embraced many of these new ideas. The Sanskrit language came into wide use, which in turn led to the introduction of Indian literary classics, such as the *Ramayana*. Some rulers adopted Indian names and built temples in the Indian style, such as the massive Buddhist complex at Borobudur, in Java. From the Malay Peninsula to southern Vietnam, many Southeast Asian kingdoms showed strong Indian influences.

The Khmer Empire. The most powerful Indian-influenced empire in Southeast Asia was that of the Khmer, in present-day Cambodia. Beginning in the early 800s, the first great Khmer ruler, Jayavarman II, began to expand his kingdom. At the height of its power, from around 850 to 1250, the Khmer Empire controlled much of Southeast Asia. Khmer rulers adopted Hindu and Buddhist beliefs.

The Khmer constructed large irrigation systems to ensure year-round rice production, which in turn allowed for a growing population and for increased tax revenues. The Khmer channeled this wealth into public works, including roads, reservoirs, and hospitals. They also built a magnificent capital at Angkor and many Hindu and Buddhist temples.

The most famous Khmer temple is **Angkor Wat**, built in the 1100s. Angkor Wat, which stands in ruins today, covers nearly one square mile and is surrounded by a three-mile-long moat. Its towers, monuments, and walls are covered with intricate carvings representing Indian religious beliefs. The enormous expense required to build Angkor Wat weakened

Religions in Asia, c. 750–1450

Religions:
- Spread of Buddhism, c. 750–1450
- Hindu in 750
- Muslim in 750
- Mixed faiths
- Spread of Islam, c. 750–1450

Competing Religions Traders and missionaries spread the faiths of Buddhism, Hinduism, and Islam throughout Asia.

Linking Geography and History Which areas of Buddhism could be reached only by sea?

Map Answer
Japan, Java, Sumatra, and Ceylon

SECTION 3
REVIEW ANSWERS

IDENTIFY

For significance, see the following pages:
Harsha Vardhana (p. 317)
Mahmud of Ghazna (p. 318)
Delhi sultanate (p. 318)
Jayavarman II (p. 319)
Angkor Wat (p. 319)

LOCATE

For locations, see the map on p. 319.

1. India broke into opposing kingdoms.
2. Muslim rule was established in northern India, and Islamic culture spread to many parts of India. The brutality of conquest provoked Hindu/Muslim conflict.
3. Sea trade spread Islam, Hinduism, and Buddhism as well as Sanskrit and Indian literature.
4. Essays should mention the vast differences between the two religions, including the Hindus' worship of many gods and goddesses and the Muslims' monotheism. Essays should also include the Hindu varna system's conflict with the Islamic belief that all people were equal before God and the different beliefs about rules regarding the consumption of food and drink.
5. Answers could include the idea that the sultans wanted to create a lasting Islamic base in India from which Muslim culture could continue to spread.

the Khmer Empire, however, and attacks from outside, notably by the Mongols, eventually led to the empire's fall. By the 1400s the Thai people from the region south of China had conquered the Khmer Empire.

Srivijaya. Indian culture also influenced the islands of Southeast Asia, particularly the Srivijaya (sree-wi-JAW-yuh) Empire on the island of Sumatra. Srivijaya was primarily a seafaring empire. Its prosperity depended on control of the overseas trade that passed through the Sunda and Malacca Straits. From its capital at Palembang, the empire also ruled over the Philippines, Borneo, western Java, Ceylon, and the Malay Peninsula.

In the early 1000s, as a result of the earlier collapse of the Tang dynasty, shipping through the straits began to diminish. As revenues dropped, the Srivijaya rulers began to raise taxes and duties on all shipping. Eventually, in an attempt to retaliate for these high duties, the navy of the Chola Empire in eastern India attacked the empire. The Srivijaya Empire finally disintegrated altogether in the 1300s.

Islamic influences. Indian contacts with Southeast Asia continued even after the forces of Islam had begun to conquer India. As India's

▲ Even in ruins, Angkor Wat is a spectacular architectural treasure.

thriving overseas trade continued to grow, Muslim merchants from India contributed to the already growing presence of Muslim merchants from Arabia and Persia throughout much of Southeast Asia. The result was the establishment of Islamic states in Sumatra, the Malay Peninsula, Borneo, and the Philippines—areas where Muslim rule enhanced trade and Muslim culture remains vibrant today.

Islam particularly appealed to the rulers of port cities and kingdoms that depended primarily on overseas trade for their prosperity. Perhaps the most important Islamic state was Malacca, which emerged on the Malay Peninsula in the early 1400s.

With the wealth they obtained from trade, the Malaccan sultans became not only rich but also extremely powerful. Malacca became the major clearinghouse for the goods of Asia, India, Africa, and even Europe. Silks from China; cotton goods from India; pepper, cloves, and nutmeg from East Africa and southern Arabia; and pearls from Japan and the islands of Southeast Asia, all passed through the warehouses of Malacca.

Hindu, Buddhist, and later Islamic cultures spread from India throughout Southeast Asia.

SECTION 3 REVIEW

IDENTIFY and explain the significance of the following:
Harsha Vardhana
Mahmud of Ghazna
Delhi sultanate
Jayavarman II
Angkor Wat

LOCATE and explain the importance of the following:
Delhi
Malacca

1. **Main Idea** What was the long-term effect of the fall of Harsha's empire?
2. **Main Idea** What impact did the Muslim invasions have on India?
3. **Geography: Location** How did the relatively short distance between India and Southeast Asia affect the development of culture in Southeast Asia?

4. **Writing to Explain** In a short essay, explain why there was conflict between Muslims and Hindus after the Muslim conquest of India. Be sure to consider both political developments and the beliefs of each religion.
5. **Hypothesizing** Why do you think that it was important to the sultans to make Delhi a center of Islamic culture?

The Mongol Empire

- What early successes did Ghenghis Khan and the Mongols achieve?

- What was the main goal of the Yuan dynasty in China?

- What were the consequences of Il-khanid rule in Persia?

- How did the Golden Horde affect developments in Russia?

In the mid-1200s the Mongols, a new group of nomadic invaders from Central Asia, swept across Eurasia. Eventually, the Mongols spread from China to eastern Europe. Under the authority of the great khan, the Mongols united Eurasia as no empire had ever done before. Travelers and merchants could move freely from one end of the vast empire to the other.

A Mongol leads his horse in this painting from 1347.

Genghis Khan

Like the Turks, the Mongols were a pastoral and nomadic people who emerged in Central Asia, in present-day Mongolia. There they made seasonal migrations as they searched for pastures for their herds of sheep and goats. They became master horsemen, accustomed to fighting and raiding as they competed for survival on the scarce grazing lands. In the 1200s, however, this pattern of life changed dramatically under a new leader, Temujin—better known as Genghis Khan.

BIOGRAPHY Temujin was born the son of a petty Mongol chieftain sometime around 1162. Even as a child he was determined to one day rule the Mongols. After years of struggle and bloodshed, several Mongol leaders gave Temujin the new title of Genghis Khan, or "Universal Ruler," in 1206.

Genghis Khan established the Mongol state by overcoming the limitations of the traditional Mongol clan system. He established a type of feudal system by giving land and the people who lived on it to his generals in exchange for their loyalty. By combining the military superiority of his nomadic cavalry with a feudal system, Genghis Khan gave the Mongols the strength to conquer most of Asia.

Genghis Khan
BIOGRAPHY

The Mongols used the battle tactics of the steppe nomads. Mongol armies stalked their enemies like prey. "In daylight," Genghis Khan reportedly told his men, "watch with the vigilance [careful observation] of an old wolf, at night with the eyes of the raven. In battle, fall upon the enemy like a falcon."

In 1206 Genghis Khan summoned all the chiefs of the peoples of Mongolia to a great gathering, or **quriltai** (KUHR-uhl-ty). There he laid down the **yasa**, or "laws," that were to regulate all Mongols—even after his death. Although these regulations have not survived intact, we know that they imposed a strict discipline on both civilians and warriors. As Giovanni da Pian del Carpini, a Franciscan friar who was traveling in Asia, observed in the 1240s:

❝ The Tartars—that is, the Mongols—are the most obedient people in the world in

SECTION 4

CORE LESSON PLAN
See pages 299I and 299J for Lesson Plan 12.4.

MULTIMEDIA PRESENTATION STRATEGY

WORLD HISTORY AND CULTURES VIDEODISCS

Image: *Mongol Arms and Armor*

Search Frame 833

Image: *Mongols on the Move*

Search Frame 834

Map: *Mongol Empire, 1200s*

Search Frame 837

Show the images and map as you discuss the Mongols. The captions that accompany each CD-ROM image and map offer additional details.

All Levels

Teenagers IN HISTORY

Temujin

Sometime around 1162 a son was born to Yesugei, the chieftain of a Mongol clan. The baby was called Temujin—though in later years he would be known to the world as Genghis Khan.

As a child Temujin suffered greatly. When he was about 12 years old, neighboring Tatars, another nomadic people of the steppe, poisoned his father Yesugei as he ate with them. Although Temujin should have inherited his father's flocks and herds, as well as the chieftainship, his people refused to obey a boy of 12. Instead, they took the herds themselves and deserted Temujin and his immediate family—his mother, three brothers, and two half-brothers.

In the Kentei Mountains, Temujin and his family struggled to survive by hunting and fishing. Even as a youth Temujin displayed the ruthlessness for which he would later be famous. One day while hunting, for example, his half-brother Bekter stole a fish and a lark from Temujin. Without a word, the young Mongol grabbed his younger brother Qasar's bow and arrows and shot Bekter dead.

The young Temujin learned all the tricks of survival. He also became a cunning warrior, highly skilled with the bow. The new leader of Temujin's clan grew fearful of the boy's stubborn survival. One day he captured Temujin. Placing a wooden collar around the young man's neck, he kept Temujin prisoner. As the people feasted one night, however, Temujin used the wooden collar to knock out his guard, and then he escaped.

As he grew, Temujin set out to recover his father's power. Gradually, with his skill as both warrior and hunter, he began to gather his own herds of horses and sheep. According to the *Secret History of the Mongols*, written sometime in the 1200s, "He had now nine horses!" With this growing wealth, Temujin also began to gather followers—the first step toward retrieving his rightful place as chieftain, and his place in history as one of the greatest of the world's conquerors.

This Persian book illustration from around 1300 shows Genghis Khan presiding from his throne.

regard to their leaders, more so even than our own clergy to their superiors. They hold them in the greatest reverence and never tell them a lie.**"**

After many years of hardship and bitter fighting Genghis Khan united the nomadic Mongol tribes under one system of governmental laws.

The Rise of the Mongol Empire

Having united all the Mongols under his command, Genghis Khan next set out to create an empire. In 1209, after laying siege to the capital of the Tangut state in northwest China, Genghis Khan forced the Tangut to pay tribute to the

Mongols. In 1211 Genghis Khan began a long campaign against the Jin dynasty. This campaign ended in 1234, years after his death, with the total conquest of the Jin Empire. By 1222 the Mongols had taken all of Turkistan and Afghanistan, and Genghis Khan had raided into northern India, while other Mongol forces operated in Persia and farther north in Russia.

Genghis Khan died in 1227. The location of his burial site is unknown—Mongol tradition required the burial places of rulers to be hidden and all burial participants to be executed to hide the tomb forever.

Two years after Genghis Khan's death, a *quriltai* gathered and named his third son, Ogodei, as great khan. Ruling from the city of Karakorum, Ogodei continued the transition of the Mongol Empire from a military state into a centralized bureaucratic state. He relied on Chinese-trained officials, and accepted the advice of one, Yelu Chucai, who told him: "The empire was created on horseback, but it cannot be governed on horseback."

Ogodei also resumed the expansion of the empire. To the east he completed the conquest of northern China. To the west he sent 30,000 troops to Persia, killing the sultan and crushing all resistance.

The Mongols then headed toward Europe. Relentlessly attacking Russia, even during the bitter winter of 1237–38, the Mongols conquered Moscow and other Russian cities. Then with lightning speed they moved into eastern Europe. They sped through Poland, leaving death and destruction in their wake and in 1241 they stormed through Hungary, adding it to the huge Mongol Empire. Only Ogodei's death stopped the Mongols from pushing farther into Europe. As the Mongol leaders hurried back to Karakorum for the election of a new great khan, their armies returned to southern Russia.

In 1251 Mangu, one of Genghis Khan's grandsons, succeeded as great khan. Like his grandfather, Mangu Khan was a remarkably

▲ The rich colors of this earthenware bowl have been protected since the 1200s by a clear glaze.

strong leader. He restored the strong central control over the empire that had been lost since Genghis's death. Heavily influenced by his mother's faith, Nestorian Christianity, Mangu Khan practiced religious toleration throughout his domains. He appointed both Buddhists and Daoists to high positions in the imperial government, and he also received a Christian ambassador from Louis IX of France—a monk named William of Rubruck. To William, Mangu Khan observed, "All religions are like the five fingers of one hand."

Mangu Khan also continued Mongol expansion. Under his rule, his brother Hulegu completed the conquest of Persia, while Mongol armies also conquered and occupied Korea. Mangu Khan and another brother, Kublai (KOO-bluh), were preparing a final assault on the Song Empire, when the great khan died in 1259.

Within only a few years, the Mongols expanded their empire from Central Asia to eastern Europe.

The Yuan Dynasty in China

After a brief struggle Kublai succeeded Mangu as great khan and, hoping to gain the wealth China could pay in tribute, began a campaign to conquer the Song dynasty. Southern China was more difficult for the Mongols to conquer than northern China had been. In the north, broad plains of wheat and millet had made ideal conditions for the Mongol army, with plenty of food for their horses. In the south, however, the major crops were rice and tea, which made the Mongols' traditional tactic of living off the land much less effective.

It took nearly 20 years for Kublai Khan to conquer the southern Song dynasty. Before the final defeat of the Song, Kublai Khan proclaimed

Theme: Politics and Law
Genghis Khan divided the Mongol Empire into four khanates, each ruled by one of his sons or his grandsons. The chart below shows the khanates, the rulers of the khanates, and the dates during which they ruled.

GREAT KHAN (East Asia including China)	
Ogodei third son of Genghis	1229–1241
Mangu grandson of Genghis	1251–1259
Kublai grandson of Genghis	1260–1294

KHANATE OF CHAGHADAI (Turkistan)	
Chaghadai second son of Genghis	1227–1242

KHANATE OF PERSIA	
Hulegu grandson of Genghis	1217–1265

KHANATE OF KIPCHAK (Lower Volga, Russia)	
Batu grandson of Genghis	1227–1255

Critical Thinking Ask students to calculate which of these Khans ruled the longest amount of time, and which ruled the shortest amount of time.

ANSWER: Students should answer that Hulegu ruled the longest (48 years) and Mangu ruled the shortest (8 years).

THROUGH OTHERS' EYES

From Venice to Beijing

Between 1271 and 1295, a young Venetian merchant named Marco Polo supposedly traveled overland from Europe to China and back again. Although some modern scholars have begun to question whether his visit was authentic, Marco Polo's *Description of the World* was in its day one of the most widely read books in Europe. In the following passage the author accurately describes the Chinese use of paper money:

❝The Emperor's mint, then, is in this same city of Cambaluc [Beijing]. . . . He makes them take of the bark of . . . the mulberry tree, the leaves of which are the food of the silkworms . . . and this they make into something resembling sheets of paper, but black. . . . And when all is prepared duly, the chief officer deputed [assigned] by the Khan smears the seal entrusted to him with vermilion [red], and impresses it on the paper, . . . the money is then authentic. Anyone forging it would be punished with death. . . . And, indeed, everybody takes them [the bills] readily, for wherever a person may go throughout the Great khan's dominions he shall find these pieces of paper current, and shall be able to transact all sales and purchases of goods by means of them just as well as if they were coins of pure gold.❞

his own dynasty, the Yuan dynasty, in 1271. After defeating the Song in 1279, Kublai Khan moved the capital from Karakorum to Beijing. Ruling as the Yuan, the Mongols continued to expand their empire. Kublai, for example, sent armies south into Vietnam and east into Korea.

Distrusting the Chinese bureaucracy, the Yuan rulers suspended the Confucian civil-service examination system. Although they had to rely on Chinese officials in the lower levels of the bureaucracy, they limited their advancement and filled higher posts with many non-Chinese.

While the initial conquest and early phases of Mongol rule were extremely destructive in China, the Mongols' interest in tribute led them to preserve China's ability to provide them with wealth. For example, they repaired the canal system on which Chinese agricultural prosperity depended. The Yuan rulers also encouraged overseas trade. In addition, the Mongols built and improved roads to Central Asia and Persia. Foreign traders and merchants were often granted special trading privileges in the empire.

In China the Mongol Yuan dynasty ruled as overlords whose primary interest was tribute.

The Il-khans of Persia

While Kublai Khan established the Yuan dynasty in China, Hulegu Khan and his Mongol successors, the Il-khans, ruthlessly conquered Persia. The Il-khans built a large empire in Southwest Asia. The extent of the Mongol terror was vividly described by a Muslim historian of the day:

❝*The luck-forsaken land lay desolate . . .*
In heaps on every side the corpses lay,
Alike on lonely path and broad high-way.
Uncounted bodies cumbered [blocked]
*   every street:*
Scarce might one find a place to set
*   one's feet.*❞

In 1258 Hulegu Khan's forces sacked Baghdad, killing the last Abbasid caliph and thousands of citizens. They looted Baghdad, the richest city of Southwest Asia, then moved into Syria. In 1260 the Mongols also sacked Damascus; then they advanced south as far as Gaza. Hulegu threatened the Mamluk ruler of Egypt with invasion, but the Mamluks, who were descendants of steppe peoples themselves, sent a vast army to meet the Mongols. At the **Battle of 'Ayn Jalut**, the Mamluks defeated the Mongols.

Although Hulegu tried to destroy Islamic culture in his domains, eventually his successors converted to Islam. In addition, the Mongols relied on local Persian officials of the old bureaucracy to rule their new domains. Many such officials, however, met a violent death at the hands of their suspicious masters. For a time in the late

Geography AND HISTORY

The Mongol Horsemen

Like earlier nomadic conquerors, the Mongols were able to build a vast steppe empire because of their development and mastery of "horsepower." They bred small, wiry, tough horses, perfectly suited to the Eurasian steppes. On these hardy beasts, they could go wherever they liked.

The Mongols took great care of their horses and honored them as fighting companions. Sometimes horses even guaranteed the survival of the Mongols, because mares could provide milk on long trips when food was scarce.

Members of the cavalry had several mounts, and these were changed regularly to prevent any one horse from becoming exhausted. By alternating them, the mounted troops could ride 60 to 90 miles in a day and still have fresh horses.

Linking Geography and History

How did the Mongols' ability to adapt to their environment help them to expand their empire?

The Mongol Empire, 1294

The Triumph of the Horse The Mongols' sturdy horses galloped across rough terrain and covered long distances to help the Central Asian nomads create a vast empire.

? Movement What physical features surrounding Mongolia made expansion of the empire particularly challenging?

Linking Geography and History

The Mongols' skills with horses and their ability to live off the land allowed them the ability to travel long distances rapidly and conquer their less mobile foes.

R RESOURCE ACTIVITY

GLOBAL HISTORY RESOURCE CENTER (p. 324)
Reading: *The Mongols Sack Baghdad*

Print out and distribute the reading. Have students read about Hulegu's attack on Baghdad. Ask students to write diary entries as if they were an ordinary soldier in Hulegu's army. Encourage them to use the text and the reading to describe a few days in the life of a Mongol horseman.

Level 1

Map Answer
the Gobi Desert and the Tian Shan

✓ REVIEW & ASSESSMENT RESOURCES

- Study Guide 12.4
- Daily Quiz 12.4
- Main Idea Activity 12.4

All Levels

SECTION 4 REVIEW ANSWERS

IDENTIFY

For significance, see the following pages:
Genghis Khan (p. 321)
quriltai (p. 321)
yasa (p. 321)
Ogodei (p. 323)
Mangu Khan (p. 323)
Kublai Khan (p. 323)
Battle of 'Ayn Jalut (p. 324)

LOCATE

For locations, see the map on p. 325.

1. He established a feudal government with one system of laws and a highly effective nomadic cavalry. Once united, the Mongols began to build a vast empire.
2. The Mongols' primary interest was tribute.
3. The Il-khans converted to Islam and established it as the official state religion. Internal struggles weakened Il-khanid rule and led to its collapse.
4. Essays should mention that the Golden Horde demanded tribute from the Russians, setting up Moscow as its agent. Russian rulers, including those in Moscow, began a struggle against the Mongols but were unable to throw off Mongol rule until the late 1400s, when Moscow emerged as a powerful Russian state.
5. They encouraged overseas trade, built and improved roads and canal systems, established centralized government, and provided stability.

▲ **This Persian book illustration shows the siege of Baghdad by the Mongols.**

1200s, the Il-khan Arghun relied heavily on Jewish advisors and officials. When Arghun fell ill in 1291, however, his enemies began a major massacre of Jews throughout the empire.

In 1295 the Il-khan Ghazan assumed the throne. A convert to Islam, Ghazan established Islam as the official religion of the Il-khanid state and did his best to become an Islamic ruler. By the 1340s, however, internal struggles among Mongol princes had so weakened Il-khanid rule that it finally collapsed, and the empire fell into the hands of local dynasties.

After an initial period of destructive rule, the Mongol Il-khans of Persia became more stable Muslim rulers.

The Golden Horde

Like the Il-khans of Persia, the Mongols who settled in southern Russia after Ogodei's death also soon converted to Islam. In a terrain that was similar to their homeland, the Mongols continued their nomadic way of life. They demanded tribute from the more settled peoples of the region. As long as local Russian princes paid the tribute, the Mongols of the Golden Horde, as they were soon called, allowed the Russians to run their own affairs.

By the 1300s the Golden Horde had come to rely on the strongest of the Russian principalities, Moscow, to act as its primary agent for regulating the affairs and collecting the tribute of the other Russian states. They granted the ruler of Moscow the title of grand duke. To symbolize the Mongols' continuing dominance, however, once a year the khan of the Golden Horde came to Moscow and required that the grand duke publicly feed the khan's horse.

Such marks of obedience soon wearied the Russian rulers, and Moscow became the leader in a struggle against Mongol domination. In 1380 the Muscovites defeated a Mongol army, only to have the Mongols burn Moscow to the ground two years later. Not until the late 1400s were the Muscovites able to throw off Mongol rule.

The Golden Horde's control over Russia contributed to the emergence of Moscow as a powerful Russian state.

SECTION 4 REVIEW

IDENTIFY and explain the significance of the following:
Genghis Khan
quriltai
yasa
Ogodei
Mangu Khan
Kublai Khan
Battle of 'Ayn Jalut

LOCATE and explain the importance of the following:
Karakorum
Beijing

1. *Main Idea* How did Genghis Khan unite the Mongols, and what was the result?
2. *Main Idea* What was the main reason the Mongols maintained the Yuan dynasty in China?
3. *Cross-cultural Interaction* How did the Mongols influence developments in Persia?
4. *Writing to Explain* In a short essay, explain how the Golden Horde affected political developments in Russia.
5. *Evaluating* What long-term contributions did the Mongol invaders make to the territories and peoples they conquered?

Review

On a separate sheet of paper, complete the following exercises:

WRITING A SUMMARY
Using the essential points in the text, write a brief summary of the chapter.

REVIEWING TERMS
From the following list, choose the term that correctly matches the definition.

Angkor Wat
abacus
quriltai
samurai
shoen
yasa

1. great Mongol gathering in which major issues affecting all Mongols were discussed
2. Khmer temple built in the 1100s that is covered with detailed carvings representing Indian religious beliefs
3. estate in Japan owned by a feudal lord and made up of scattered landholdings that were administered as a single unit
4. Japanese warriors hired by landowners to protect their property—later became a significant fighting class that offered its services to the highest bidder
5. device invented by the Chinese to do mathematical calculations

REVIEWING CHRONOLOGY
List the following events in their correct chronological order:

1. Zhao Kuangyin establishes the Song dynasty.
2. Minamoto Yoritomo becomes shogun in Japan.
3. After years of fighting, the Mongols founded the Yuan dynasty in China under Kublai Khan.
4. Wendi establishes the Sui dynasty.
5. Silla Empire unites Korea.

UNDERSTANDING THE MAIN IDEA

1. Why was the Sui dynasty in China important, despite its short duration?
2. How did Chinese civilization influence Korea and Vietnam?
3. How was the Japanese feudal system structured?
4. What long-term effects did the Muslim conquest have on India?
5. How were the Mongols able to build their huge empire that stretched across Asia and Europe?

THINKING CRITICALLY
1. **Contrasting** How was the influence of Chinese culture different in Japan than in Korea and Vietnam?
2. **Assessing Consequences** How did the fall of the Gupta Empire eventually lead to India's conquest by Muslims?

Building Your Portfolio

Complete the following activities individually or in groups.

1. **Cross-cultural Interaction** Imagine that you (and your friends) are Mongols living in Persia. You were in the service of Hulegu, the Il-khan of Persia, when the Mongols sacked Baghdad. Years later you have settled among the Muslims in Persia. You have not seen your family in Central Asia for many years, and you have decided to write them a letter to tell them about your experiences. Since most of your family has never seen Persia, you will need to compare Persian culture to what they know in Central Asia. You may also want to describe differences in customs, food, clothing, and religion.

2. **Architecture** You (and your co-workers) are architects living in the Khmer Empire in the 1100s. The Khmer ruler wants to build an exquisite temple. Prepare a presentation that will convince him to hire you. You will need to provide a floor plan of the building and a sketch of the exterior to show him. You may also want to add color to your sketch. You will also need to prepare a script of the oral presentation that you will make to the king, which will clearly describe the appearance and functions of your temple's features.

People in some cultures believe that magic and rituals can control the forces of the universe. Fetishism—the belief that an inanimate object holds some kind of power—is often part of rituals. A fetish can take many forms, including a claw, bone, or feather.

Anthropologists note that the use of magic can also take different forms. Aboriginal peoples in Australia who practice magic, for example, believe that they can cripple their enemies by placing sharp objects, such as glass or bone, in their footsteps. Similarly, the Ojibwa Indians of North America traditionally stuck pins into wooden dolls made to resemble their enemy, so that the enemy would be afflicted.

Critical Thinking Ask students if they feel that beliefs in magic fulfill a role similar to that of other religions.

ANSWER: Students' answers will vary, but might include the common human desire to explain and control the unseen forces of the universe.

HISTORY
IN THE
Making

Religions and Worldviews

Since the earliest times when human beings began to reflect on the nature of the world around them, people have often stood in awe, even fear, of the vast forces of the universe beyond their control. Particularly in the face of death, people have tried to find some larger order in the universe that might help them understand the meaning of their lives. Who are we? Where do we come from? Where are we going? Why are we here? By exploring these questions, human beings try to discover their place in the world.

The Nature of Religion

Different peoples have found various answers to these questions in many different times and places. At one time or another, all societies have found the answers in religion. By studying a people's religious ideas and practices, historians may gain valuable insights into how and why people act as they do.

Scholars disagree over precise definitions of religion. But one definition views religion as any system of beliefs that uses ceremonies, rituals, or other practices to worship either one or many gods. The word *religion* comes from the Latin verb *religare*, meaning "to bind back," or "re-tie." The implication is

that human beings, having somehow become separated from the overarching order of the universe, must reestablish their connection with it through religion. Along these lines, the scholar Peter L. Berger describes religion as "the establishment, through human activity, of an all-embracing sacred order, that is, of a sacred cosmos that will be capable of maintaining itself in the ever-present face of chaos." For believers, of course, religion is established not by human beings, but by divine forces. Whether established by a human or a divine being, however, religion is a fundamental part of the search for certainty in an uncertain universe.

Types of Religions

Although all religious systems involve some sort of ceremony or ritual through which people can feel part of a larger group, not all religions are the same. In general, scholars identify two categories of religion—ethnic and universal. Ethnic religious systems are usually confined to a small group of people sharing a common culture, kinship, or a particular place. Most often, the people are strongly influenced

▶ These two rocks in Ise Bay, Japan, are called the "Wedded Rocks." In Japanese legend, they are believed to have sheltered mythical figures.

by their immediate physical environment. Shintoism in Japan, for example, revolves around the worship of ancestral spirits or nature spirits. Outsiders are not usually allowed to participate in ethnic religions.

Universal religions, on the other hand, are belief systems that are open to anyone, regardless of their ethnic or geographic identity. Such religions teach that there are answers to the most basic questions of life and death. These beliefs are generally based on the idea that people can achieve some sort of salvation or immortality after physical death, and that the key to salvation lies in following the correct religious system or true god.

Despite their similarities, however, even universal religions have many differences. Some of the most important involve both ideas about the nature of divine forces and the nature of the human spirit or soul. Judaism, Christianity, and Islam, for example, view God as a kind of supernatural person—the Creator of the world who ultimately judges the affairs of human beings. Buddhism, on the other hand, like Hinduism, generally sees the ultimate divine force as an impersonal state of being that underlies everything. Although both Buddhists and Hindus may worship many gods and goddesses, most see these beings as particular aspects of the one underlying, impersonal force.

Such differences have significant consequences for the aims of each religious system. For example, Christians and Muslims hope to achieve individual salvation and eternal life in heaven, or paradise, after physical death. Buddhists, on the other hand, hope for release from the wheel of reincarnation and the suffering that they associate with the living world.

Religious Practices

In addition to other similarities, most religious traditions also have both a public practice and a private tradition. Public devotional practices include worship, prayers, rites of initiation, and any other effort to establish group contact with the divine. Private practices are those that allow a person to communicate directly with the divine being.

For example, Christians often express their sense of having achieved oneness with God through intense love and devotion, by means of prayer and meditation. Similar practices are common in Sufism, the highly personal tradition of Islam. In Buddhism, the Zen branch teaches the limitations of reason in understanding the divine and emphasizes instead efforts to stop the flow of thoughts in order to achieve nirvana, or oneness with the universal being.

Religious Systems and Worldviews

As people pursue their own religious beliefs, they also formulate the basic values that underlie their societies. As they do so, they construct the broader framework of

▶ **This 1600s statue of Saint Teresa tries to capture the sense of spiritual devotion she felt for God.**

belief that we call a "worldview." In its broadest sense, a worldview may actually be more than simply a people's religious system. It includes their whole conception of the nature of the universe and how it works, as well as the nature of human beings, the divine, and how people fit into the overall scheme of life. In the 1600s and 1700s, for example, Europeans began to develop a new worldview that was rooted less in the religious ideas of their past than in their growing scientific knowledge.

Yet even as the so-called scientific worldview took hold in Western societies, religious traditions and values remained strong. So long as the ultimate secrets of the universe—such as whether there is indeed life after physical death—remain unknown, religious beliefs will continue to play an important role in people's lives.

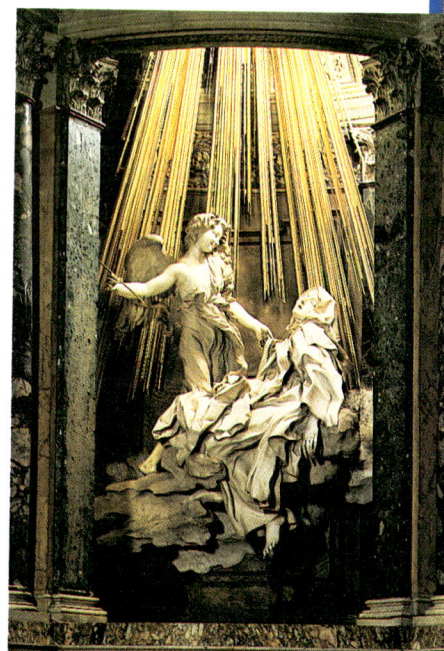

Theme: Religion

Religious scholars sometimes use the additional classifications of "revealed" or "nonrevealed" to group the world's religions. These classifications are based on the origins of the knowledge on which the religion is founded. For example, Judaism and Christianity are revealed religions—in Judaism, God revealed the Commandments to Moses, while in Christianity, Jesus revealed the Word of God to the people. Nonrevealed religions, which include Daoism, and variations of Buddhism, are the result of human inquiry alone and are sometimes reliant on an enlightened leader, rather than on a god.

Critical Thinking Ask students how they would classify Islam.

ANSWER: Students should answer that Islam is a revealed religion, since in Islam the angel Jibreel (Gabriel) relayed God's will to Muhammad.

Chapter 13

New Empires in Asia and Africa 1200–1707

Chapter Planning Guide

	TEXTBOOK	CORE RESOURCES	VISUAL RESOURCES	MULTIMEDIA
Introduction	pp. 330–331	Block Scheduling Handbook: Ch. 13		Videodisc Segment 13 and Viewing Guide: *The Mughals in India*
Lesson 13.1 The Ottoman Empire	pp. 332–338 Map: *The Ottoman Empire*, p. 333 Map: *Europe: Political*, p. 858 Map: *Asia: Political*, p. 859	Reading 13.1: *Süleyman the Magnificent Captures Belgrade* Writing Project 13: *Making Revisions*		GHRC 13 Readings: *Mehmet the Conqueror's Monster Cannon; A European Admires Ottoman Government* GHRC 13/Videodiscs: Images—*Ottoman Architecture; Ottoman Design: The Süleyman Mosque*
Lesson 13.2 Safavid Persia	pp. 339–343 Map: *Safavid Persia*, p. 340 Literature Through Time: *Shah-nameh*, p. 342	Reading 13.2: *The Character of Shah 'Abbas*		GHRC 13/Videodiscs: Images—*Safavid Tilework from the Royal Mosque; Safavid Persian Tapestry*
Lesson 13.3 Mughal India	pp. 344–348 Map: *The Mughal Empire*, p. 345	Reading 13.3: *A Day in the Life of a Mughal Emperor* Skills Activity 13: *Recognizing Fallacies in Reasoning*		GHRC 13 Readings: *The Story of the Taj Mahal; Poetry from Mughal India* GHRC 13/Videodiscs: Images—*The Taj Mahal; Mughal Painting*; Audio Clip—*Music of Mughal India*
Lesson 13.4 Neo-Confucian China	pp. 349–352 Map: *The Ming Empire*, p. 350 Through Others' Eyes: *A Chinese View of Mecca*, p. 351	Reading 13.4: *Chinese Naval Expeditions*	Art and History 13: *Landscape on a Fan*	GHRC 13 Readings: *The First Ming Emperor's First Year; A European Looks at Ming China's Government; Famine in China* GHRC 13/Videodiscs: Images—*Ming China; Ming Landscape*; Maps—Series of three on *Expansion of the Manchu*
Lesson 13.5 State-Building in Africa	pp. 353–356 Map: *Trading Kingdoms of Africa*, p. 354 History Through the Arts: *Royal West African Figure*, p. 355	Reading 13.5: *Mansa Musa's Pilgrimage* Geography Activity 13: *Natural Resources and State-Building*	Geography and History 13: *African Trading Kingdoms* Everyday Life 13: *Great Zimbabwe*	GHRC 13 Readings: *Sundiata's War for Mali; Mansa Musa's Pilgrimage to Mecca; Ibn Battuta's Travels in Mali* GHRC 13/Videodiscs: Image—*Bronze Portrait of an African Ruler*; Map—*African Trade*
Chapter Investigation and Enrichment	pp. 330–356	Chapter 13 Investigation: *Training Seminar—How to Run an Empire* People in World History 13 Explorations in Daily Life 13		GHRC 13/Videodiscs
Review and Assessment	Section 1 Review, p. 338 Section 2 Review, p. 343 Section 3 Review, p. 348 Section 4 Review, p. 352 Section 5 Review, p. 356 Chapter 13 Review, p. 357	Chapter Review Activity 13 Vocabulary Activity 13 Themes Review 13 Section Study Guides 13.1–13.5 Main Idea Activities 13.1–13.5 Daily Quizzes 13.1–13.5 Chapter 13 Test Sheltered English Ch. 13 Test Ch. 13 Test Generator		Audio CDs: Ch. 13 Summary (English and Spanish)

INTRODUCING THE CHAPTER

Textbook pp. 330–331

CHAPTER OVERVIEW

Asia and Africa saw the appearance of several new empires. In Asia Minor, a small Islamic state grew into the Ottoman Empire. On the Plateau of Iran, the Safavid Empire preserved and enriched Persian culture. The Turkish invader Babur created a new civilization in India, while in China the expulsion of the Mongols led to the founding of the Ming dynasty. In Africa, several wealthy trading empires appeared.

PRESENTING THEMES

On the chalkboard or on an overhead transparency, write the following open-ended theme questions.

- **TECHNOLOGY** How might a monopoly over military technology affect the building of empires?
- **POLITICS AND LAW** Why might rulers try to revive past traditions after a time of political disunity?
- **CROSS-CULTURAL INTERACTION** How might trade spread languages, cultures, and religious ideas?

Have students, either individually or in groups, suggest responses to the questions. For the technology question, students might suggest that a monopoly on military technology might allow an empire to expand through force. For the politics and law question, students might suggest that old traditions could reassure people facing rapid political and social change. For the cross-cultural interaction question, students might suggest that traders from distant lands might bring new ideas and values to cultures and that learning their languages would facilitate trade. Save the responses. Once students have studied the chapter, you may wish to have them complete the Themes Review, then compare the two sets of answers.

USING THE VIDEO

Segment 13: *The Mughals in India*

ENGLISH

Search Chapter 13
Videodisc 1, Side B

SPANISH

Search Chapter 13
Videodisc 1, Side B

Tell students that in this chapter they will apply the theme questions to African and Asian empires from the 1200s to the 1700s. Then show Segment 13 of the *World History and Cultures Videodiscs*. This segment looks at how the Mughal ruler Akbar used tolerance and pluralism to rule a religiously diverse empire.

Before showing the segment, ask students to note the number of religions mentioned in the segment. To help students grasp the significant points of the segment, have them complete Video Viewing Guide 13.

Key to Ability Levels

All strategies and activities are coded to the following ability levels:

LEVEL 1	**Basic** activities suitable for all students
LEVEL 2	**Average** activities suitable for average to above-average students
LEVEL 3	**Challenging** activities suitable for above-average students
SHELTERED ENGLISH	Activities suitable for students with **Limited English Proficiency**

Additional Resources

BOOKS FOR TEACHERS

Koprulu, M. Faud. *The Origins of the Ottoman Empire.* State University of New York Press, 1992. Examines the early years of the empire.

Waldron, Arthur. *The Great Wall of China.* Cambridge University Press, 1990. Discusses agriculture and isolationism as well as the Great Wall.

BOOKS FOR STUDENTS

Duran, Tulay. *The Ottoman Empire in the Reign of Suleyman the Magnificent.* Istanbul Research Center, 1988. Offers a Turkish perspective.

Jones, Constance. *Africa 1500–1900.* Facts On File, 1993. Presents a survey and a list of suggested readings.

MULTIMEDIA MATERIALS

China and Japan: 1279–1600. Network Television Production, 26 min. Examines the Shoguns' foreign rule in China.

The Ottoman Empire: 1280–1683. Network Television Production. Video, 26 min. Profiles the ruling sultans.

Lesson 13.1   The Ottoman Empire

Textbook pp. 332–338

RESOURCES

Pupil's Edition

Map, p. 333: *The Ottoman Empire, 1453–1566*

Map, p. 858: *Europe: Political*

Map, p. 859: *Asia: Political*

Core Resources

Reading 13.1: *Süleyman the Magnificent Captures Belgrade*

Global History Resource Center

Reading: *Mehmet the Conqueror's Monster Cannon*

Reading: *A European Admires Ottoman Government*

Videodiscs or Global History Resource Center

Image: *Ottoman Architecture: The Blue Mosque*

Search Frame 838

Image: *Ottoman Design: The Süleyman Mosque*

Search Frame 839

LESSON FOCUS

What were the keys to the success of the Ottoman Empire?

OBJECTIVES

After completing this lesson, students will be able to:
- explain how the Ottomans built a world empire;
- identify what kept the Ottoman Empire united;
- discuss Ottoman cultural advances.

HOOK

Appreciate the power and size of the Ottoman Empire.
Direct students' attention to the map of the Ottoman Empire on textbook page 333. Explain to them that in a relatively short time the Ottoman Empire had grown from a small area in Anatolia to include most of Anatolia and much of the Balkans and the eastern Mediterranean. Have students speculate, based on information shown on the map, why the Italians might have been concerned about the Ottomans. *[Students should understand that the Ottomans were building their empire rapidly through conquest. Italians would be concerned because the northwestern border of the Ottoman Empire was just a short sea voyage from Italy's Adriatic coast.]* Conclude by informing students that in the 1500s many Europeans shared the Italians' concern over the growing power of the Ottomans.

This concern was well founded, for the Ottomans developed tough, disciplined fighting forces, and they were determined to build an Islamic empire to match that of the Byzantine Empire.

DEVELOP

Outline the rise of the Ottoman Empire. Ask students to imagine that they have been asked to write the outline for a movie script on the rise of the Ottoman Empire. Point out that the outline should include a list of the major characters, with brief biographical details; a list of the major events, with dates, of the Ottomans' rise to power; and a synopsis of the Ottomans' rise from the reign of Osman to the end of Süleyman the Lawgiver's reign. Interested students might like to expand on this synopsis by scripting a scene involving one of the major events in the rise of the Ottomans—the capture of Constantinople, the capture of Belgrade, or the siege of Vienna, for example. Provide students with additional information by assigning Core Resources Reading 13.1 on Süleyman's capture of Belgrade and the Global History Resource Center readings on Mehmet the Conqueror and on the Ottoman government.

Call on volunteers to present their outline materials to the rest of the class. Use these presentations to initiate a discussion on the factors that contributed to the rise of the Ottomans.
Ask: What factors enabled the Ottomans to build a great empire?

[superior leadership and the use of advanced military technology]

PROBE

Identify the methods by which the Ottomans kept their empire united. Encourage students to consider how great empire-builders they studied in earlier chapters attempted to keep order among the diverse peoples under their rule. Guide the discussion by asking students to compare the methods of the Assyrians and Chaldeans with those of the Persians. (If necessary, have students review information on the Assyrians, Chaldeans, and Persians in Chapters 2 and 3.) *[Students should note that the Assyrians kept order among their subjects by use of fear and terror tactics. The Persians, in contrast, generally allowed their subjects a degree of self-rule and allowed them to follow their own customs and religions.]*

Ask: ***Whom did the Ottomans most resemble in the methods they used—the Assyrians and Chaldeans or the Persians? What were these methods?***
[They most resembled the Persians. They used the millet system, which guaranteed each religious community within the empire religious freedom and a degree of autonomy in internal affairs.]

Ask: ***What were the pros and cons of the millet system?***
[The millet system minimized conflict between different groups and maintained peace, but it also led to a lack of unity that would hurt the empire later.]

Conclude by pointing out that the Ottomans' recognition of the diversity within their empire lessened internal unrest and helped hold the empire together.

CONCLUDE

Discuss the development of Ottoman culture. Display the electronic media image of the Blue Mosque. You might also direct students' attention to the photograph of Süleyman's mosque on textbook page 338. Have students study the image and the photograph and ask them to note the features of the buildings that are reminiscent of Byzantine architecture. *[Students should recognize that the use of the dome reflected Byzantine architecture.]* Then point out that in the fields of architecture and the arts the Ottomans borrowed from other civilizations. Point to their use of Arabic calligraphy to design

the interiors of mosques as an example. To illustrate this, display the electronic media image showing the Süleyman mosque.

Conclude by asking students to consider the areas of scholarship in which the Ottomans were interested.
Ask: ***In what fields of scholarship did the Ottomans make advances?***
[The Ottomans made advances in philosophy, theology, mathematics, astronomy, astrology, history, and geography. They were most interested in history and geography.]

EXTEND

Cross-Curricular Connection: *Geography*
Have students study the map of the Ottoman Empire on textbook page 333. Have them describe the extent of the empire, using the names of continents, bodies of water, rivers, present-day countries, or other geographical terms. Suggest that they consult the maps on textbook pages 858–859 for assistance.

Cross-Curricular Connection: *Art*
Have students study the electronic media images of the mosques. Have them draw the exterior of a mosque of their own design, reflecting the Ottomans' style. Display the drawings, and have students describe the ideas behind their drawings.

MEET INDIVIDUAL NEEDS

Gifted Students
Point out that Süleyman was not only a great ruler and military leader, but also an accomplished poet and goldsmith and a supporter of the arts. Encourage students to write a biographical sketch of Süleyman that focuses on his artistic accomplishments.

Interpersonal Learners
Organize students into small groups. Have groups role-play to develop a dialogue between two non-Muslims on their feelings about life in the Ottoman Empire. Have groups select representatives to present their dialogues to the class.

ASSESS

Review
Have students complete the Section 1 Review. Use answers in the Teacher's Edition, page 338, to assess student mastery of this section.

Lesson 13.2 — *Safavid Persia*

Textbook pp. 339–343

RESOURCES

Pupil's Edition

Map, p. 340: *Safavid Persia, 1500–1636*
Literature Through Time, p. 342: *Shah-nameh*

Core Resources

Reading 13.2: *The Character of Shah 'Abbas*

Videodiscs or Global History Resource Center

Image: *Safavid Tilework from the Royal Mosque*

Search Frame 841

Image: *Safavid Persian Tapestry*

Search Frame 840

LESSON FOCUS

How did the Safavids build a successful empire in Persia?

OBJECTIVES

After completing this lesson, students will be able to:

- describe how the Safavids began their rise to power;
- analyze the consequences of the Safavids' adoption of Shi'ism as the state religion;
- explain how 'Abbas brought Safavid Persia to its height of power and culture.

HOOK

Recognize the events that led to the founding of the Safavid Dynasty. Direct students to turn to Chapter 12 and read the paragraphs on the Mongol invasions on textbook pages 324–326. Encourage them to imagine that they have lived through a Mongol invasion of their community. Have them describe the feelings they have about this experience. *[Most students will use such words as terrified, fearful, distraught, or confused in their descriptions. They might also express fears about loss of home or family.]* Then have them compare their feelings to the way Safi al-Din reacted.

Ask: *What was Safi al-Din's response to the Mongol invasion? [Disillusioned, Safi al-Din withdrew from the world and turned to Sufism to try to find spiritual truth.]*

Next call on a student to read the dictionary definition of the word *irony* *[a situation where the actual results of an event are quite different from the expected results]*. Have students consider the irony in the outcome of Safi al-Din's actions. *[Students should note that Safi al-Din had turned to Sufism as a means of withdrawing from the world. His successors, however, saw religion as a reason to involve themselves in the world, and their actions resulted in the establishment of a powerful dynasty.]*

DEVELOP

Graph the history of the Safavid dynasty. Write the title *The Rise of the Safavids* at the top of the chalkboard. Draw the vertical axis and horizontal axis for a standard line graph. Label the horizontal axis *Years* and mark off dates in 50-year increments, from 1250 to 1650. Label the vertical axis *Major Events*. Tell students that their task is to identify important events in Safavid history in chronological order and then to mark and label the events on the graph. Point out that the position of each event on the vertical axis should suggest how much that event contributed to the rise of the Safavids. Assist students by marking the first event, *Safi al-Din turns to Sufism*, between 1200 and 1300 and about one fifth of the way up the vertical axis. Have volunteers identify and mark succeeding events. Remind students that events should be placed relative to other events. For example, an entry for *Defeat by the Ottomans* should be placed below other events.

When students have finished entering events, connect the dots marking the events to form a line. Have students note when the Safavids were at their most powerful.

Ask: When did the Safavids reach the height of their power?
   [During the reign of 'Abbas]

Conclude by asking students to copy and retain the finished graph for review purposes.

PROBE

Explore the consequences of the Safavid adoption of Shi'ism as the state religion. Remind students that the first step Isma'il took toward becoming king was to make Shi'ism the official state religion. Have them consider the benefits and costs of Isma'il's action.

Ask: What were the consequences of the establishment of Shi'ism as the Safavid state religion?
   [It appealed to the sizable Shi'ah minority in Safavid Persia, gave the Safavid state a unique identity and laid the foundations of modern Persian culture, and sharply distinguished the Safavid state from the surrounding Sunni Muslim states. In addition, it helped to gain support from the enemies of the Sunni Muslim states. However, it embittered relations between the two branches of Islam and led to recurring conflict between Safavid Persia and its Sunni neighbors.]

CONCLUDE

Assess the accomplishments of Shah 'Abbas. Direct students' attention to the map of Safavid Persia on textbook page 340. Have them note the greatest extent of the Safavid Empire and point out that this was achieved during the reign of 'Abbas. Draw a four-column chart on the chalkboard, using *Military Reforms, Conquests, Economic Developments,* and *Art and Architecture* as column headings. Call on students to identify actions taken by 'Abbas in these four areas that helped bring the Safavid Empire to the height of its power. *[military reforms: limited power of kizilbash, reorganized and expanded army, introduced modern weapons; conquests: defeated Uzbeks, recovered territory lost to Ottomans; economic developments: encouraged manufacturing and trade; art and architecture: transformation of the Safavid capital of Isfahan into one of the world's most magnificent cities]*

Conclude by inviting students to use the information to write one or two paragraphs in support of the following statement: *'Abbas brought Safavid Persia to the height of its power and culture.* Before students complete this activity, you might have them read the Core Resources Reading 13.2 and view the electronic media images of Safavid tiles and tapestries as an illustration of the art that was encouraged during the reign of 'Abbas.

EXTEND

Cross-Curricular Connection: *Literature*
Have students read the Literature Through Time feature on textbook page 342. Then ask them to consider how the events and people discussed in *Shah-nameh* might have influenced Safavid leaders in their drive to create a great empire.

Cross-Curricular Connection: *Art*
Have students examine the electronic media images that show the Safavid tapestry and tiles. Ask them what appeals to them about the designs. Then have them design their own tapestry or tiles reflecting influences of Persian style.

MEET INDIVIDUAL NEEDS

Gifted Students
Link to Today. Have students research present-day Iran to find examples of how the national culture reflects the blending of Persian tradition and Shi'ism. Encourage them to share their findings with the class

Visual-Spatial Learners
Have students use library resources to discover how storyboards are employed in the making of movies or television shows. Then have them work in small groups to draw four or five storyboards showing the various stages in the rise of the Safavid Empire.

ASSESS

Review
Have students complete the Section 2 Review. Use answers in the Teacher's Edition, page 343, to assess student mastery of this section.

Lesson 13.3   *Mughal India*

Textbook pp. 344–348

RESOURCES

Pupil's Edition

Map, p. 345: *The Mughal Empire, 1526–1707*

Core Resources

Reading 13.3: *A Day in the Life of a Mughal Emperor*

Global History Resource Center

Reading: *The Story of the Taj Mahal*
Reading: *Poetry from Mughal India*

Videodiscs or Global History Resource Center

Image: *The Taj Mahal*

Search Frame 843

Image: *Mughal Painting of Shah Jahan*

Search Frame 842

Audio Clip: *Music of Mughal India*

Search 5267, Play to 5744
Videodisc 1, Side B, Audio Clip 13

LESSON FOCUS

How did the Mughals establish and maintain an empire in India?

OBJECTIVES

After completing this lesson, students will be able to:

- explain why Babur built an empire in India rather than in Central Asia;
- examine how Akbar tried to unify the empire;
- discuss how the Mughal emperors of the 1600s improved the empire.

HOOK

Investigate why Babur built his empire in India rather than in Central Asia. Point out to students that Babur built a vast empire in India. Then direct them to read the information on Babur on textbook pages 344–345. Ask them why Babur originally dreamed of building an empire in Central Asia. *[Students should respond that Central Asia was Babur's homeland, which he loved. Also, his ancestors, Genghis Khan and Timur, came from that region and began their empire-building there, and he may have dreamed of emulating their accomplishments.]* Then have them consider why Babur gave up this dream.
Ask: *Why did Babur turn his attention from Central Asia to India?*
[Babur suffered repeated defeats by the Uzbeks in Central

Asia. As a result, he gave up his plan to build an empire there and turned his attention to India, attacking the weak and crumbling Sultanate of Delhi.]*

Conclude by having a student read aloud Babur's description of the battle at Panipat on textbook page 344.
Ask: *What factors contributed to Babur's success at Panipat?*
[He had new gunpowder weapons and effective mounted warriors.]

DEVELOP

Note the steps that Akbar took to unify the Mughal Empire. Direct students' attention to the map on textbook page 345 and have them note how the Mughal Empire expanded during the reign of Akbar. Then have them identify the efforts that Akbar made to bring unity to his growing empire. Guide students by writing the following clues on the chalkboard: *marriage, cadets, tax reform, military reform, religious policy.* Note student responses under the appropriate clue on the chalkboard.

Next encourage students to imagine they are journalists working on an *Empires in the News* page for a world news magazine. Ask them to write a 250- to 300-word article for the page detailing the way in which Akbar unified the Mughal Empire. Remind them to include an attention-grabbing headline and ideas for illustrations. Call on volunteers to read their articles to the class.

Conclude by assigning Core Resources Reading 13.3, which describes a typical day in Akbar's court.

PROBE

Examine cultural diversity in the Mughal Empire. Lead students in an examination of the sources of Mughal culture. First, have students note the cultural mix created by the Mughal invasion of India. Students should recall that before the arrival of the Mughals, Islam had been established in India by the Delhi sultans. Even so, India remained overwhelmingly Hindu. The Mughals reintroduced Islam to the area, but for the most part did not impose their beliefs on the Indian people. Persian culture greatly influenced life in Mughal India, and Akbar established Persian as the official language of the Mughal court. At the same time, however, he encouraged the development of literature in native languages.

To illustrate how different elements blended together to create Mughal culture, you might point to the Taj Mahal. Show the electronic media image of the Taj Mahal and have students review the Global History Resource Center reading on the Taj Mahal. You might also direct students' attention to the photograph of the Taj Mahal on textbook page 347. Point out that the dome and the geometric design of the decoration show strong Islamic and Persian influences. Then have students view the electronic media image of Persian-influenced Mughal art and review the Mughal poetry in the Global History Resource Center reading. Ask students to discuss how the blending of different cultural elements is reflected in this art and poetry.

CONCLUDE

Review the achievements of the later leaders of the Mughal Empire. Draw a three-column chart on the chalkboard with the following column-headings: *Leader, Major Events of Reign, Rating.* Enter these leaders' names in the first column: *Jahangir, Nur Jahan, Shah Jahan, Aurangzeb.* Call on volunteers to identify and discuss the major events of each of these leaders' reigns. Note responses in the appropriate cell on the chart. Then organize students into several groups. Tell groups it is their task to rate each leader on a scale of 1 to 5—1 being the lowest and 5 the highest— based on the leader's contribution to the Mughal Empire. Allow groups to deliberate and call on group representatives to present and justify their ratings. Conclude by asking students to note and explain similarities and differences among the ratings for each leader.

EXTEND

Cross-Curricular Connection: *Language Arts*
Have students view the electronic media image of the Taj Mahal or the photograph on textbook page 347. Invite students to "paint" a one-paragraph word-picture of the Taj Mahal for someone who has never seen the structure.

Cross-Curricular Connection: *Music*
Play the audio clip of music of Mughal India. Then ask students to research the music of Mughal India, concentrating on such questions as the instruments used, whether the music is still listened to today, and who composed it. Then have them write brief reports.

Link to Today. Have interested students research what kinds of music are popular in India today and how traditional kinds of music have changed.

MEET INDIVIDUAL NEEDS

Intrapersonal Learners
Have students study the electronic media image of Shah Jahan holding court. Have them write an account of the scene shown in the image, as if they are one of the people meeting with Shah Jahan, including their impressions of the emperor and the surroundings. Students might review Core Resources Reading 13.3 about life at Akbar's court.

Visual-Spatial Learners
Ask students to make a time line of the development of the Mughal Empire from Babur's to Aurangzeb's reign. Encourage students to also include events in the reigns of Ottoman and Safavid emperors from the same time period. Display time lines and have students compare developments in these empires.

ASSESS

Review
Have students complete the Section 3 Review. Use answers in the Teacher's Edition, page 348, to assess student mastery of this section.

Lesson 13.4   *Neo-Confucian China*

Textbook pp. 349–352

RESOURCES

Pupil's Edition

Map, p. 350: *The Ming Empire, 1424*

Through Others' Eyes, p. 351: *A Chinese View of Mecca*

Core Resources

Reading 13.4: *Chinese Naval Expeditions*

Visual Resources

Art and History 13: *Landscape on a Fan*

Global History Resource Center

Reading: *The First Ming Emperor's First Year*

Reading: *A European Looks at Ming China's Government*

Reading: *A Ming Official Reports on Famine in China*

Videodiscs or Global History Resource Center

Maps: Series of three on *Expansion of the Manchu*

Search Frames 848–850

Image: *Ming China: The Forbidden City*

Search Frame 844

Image: *Ming Landscape of the Four Seasons*

Search Frame 845

LESSON FOCUS

What accounted for the rise and fall of the Ming dynasty?

OBJECTIVES

After completing this lesson, students will be able to:

- discuss the accomplishments of Hongwu;
- explain why the Ming withdrew from sea trade;
- describe how the Ming affected China's economy and society;
- establish how the Ming dynasty collapsed.

HOOK

Identify and examine the accomplishments of Hongwu.
Tell students that in 1368 Zhu Yuanzhang overthrew the Yuan dynasty and established the Ming, or "Brilliant," dynasty. As Hongwu emperor, he accomplished many things, but he was extremely overbearing.

Then ask students what Hongwu accomplished during his reign. *[Hongwu consolidated his power. He also rebuilt the provinces; reintroduced the use of civil-service examinations, which brought scholars back into government service; and established neo-Confucian doctrines in the government.]*

Conclude by asking students to speculate on how some of these achievements might have weakened the government. *[Students should note that the emphasis placed on neo-Confucian doctrines discouraged innovation and change, which ultimately was disastrous for the Ming dynasty.]*

To provide students with more information on Hongwu's accomplishments, assign the Global History Resource Center readings on Ming government and on Hongwu's first year as emperor.

DEVELOP

Analyze why the Ming withdrew from sea trade and turned inward. Display a large wall map of the world. Then call on a volunteer to read aloud the paragraphs about early Ming sea power on textbook pages 350–351 and the Through Others' Eyes feature on textbook page 351. As the reader mentions locations visited by Zheng He, have another student locate them on the wall map. After the reading has been completed, have students work in small groups to create annotated maps of Zheng He's voyages. You may wish to suggest that they accompany their maps with captions that explain the purpose of these voyages.

Next have students consider why the Ming abandoned these voyages.

Ask: Why did the Ming withdraw from the sea trade and turn inward?

[They wanted to save money and to satisfy the demands of the scholar-gentry, who felt that the voyages had increased the prestige of the court eunuchs. Also, the Ming turned their attention to the northern frontier, which was under threat of invasion by the Mongols.]

To provide students with further information on Zheng He's voyages, assign Core Resources Reading 13.4.

PROBE

Evaluate the impact of Ming policies on the Chinese economy and society. Point out that Ming policies designed to rebuild regions damaged by the Mongol conquest spurred population growth. The growing population, in turn, helped to drive urban growth and trade. To illustrate this, direct students' attention to the map of the Ming Empire on textbook page 350. Have them locate the canal system, which facilitated the transportation of goods. Continue by noting that trade and urban growth encouraged the production of luxury goods.

Ask: Based on this information, what impact did Ming policies have on the Chinese economy?

[The economy expanded under Ming policies.]

Then have students consider the impact of this economic growth on Chinese society.

Ask: How did economic expansion affect the lives of the vast majority of the Chinese population?

[Despite economic growth, the vast majority of Chinese continued to live in rural villages, working the land as farmers. The expansion of the Chinese economy had little impact on their living conditions.]

CONCLUDE

Discuss the collapse of the Ming dynasty. Have students review how earlier Chinese dynasties fell. *[Students should note that most dynasties fell when weakened imperial governments failed to put down revolts, often led by peoples from China's borderlands.]* Then ask students to explain the collapse of the Ming dynasty and the rise of the Qing dynasty. *[Students should note that the Ming dynasty was weakened by emperors' inattention, the growing power of the Manchu, famine, epidemics, and rebellions.]* Conclude by having students discuss how closely the fall of the Ming followed the

usual pattern of dynastic collapse in China. You may wish to have them read the Ming official's report in the Global History Resource Center. You might also have students track the rise of the Manchus and the establishment of the Qing dynasty on the electronic media maps of Manchu expansion.

EXTEND

Cross-Curricular Connection: *Sociology*

Have students view the electronic media image of the Forbidden City. Then lead a class discussion on how the isolation of Ming emperors within the walls of the Forbidden City might have affected the way in which they governed.

Cross-Curricular Connection: *Art*

Display Art and History Transparency 13 and have students complete the worksheet. Then display the electronic media image of the Ming landscape painting. Have students discuss the painting in terms such as subject, styles, features, and use of color.

MEET INDIVIDUAL NEEDS

Visual-Spatial Learners

Have students draw a political cartoon concerning some aspect of Ming China. Possible subjects include the bandit who became emperor, Hongwu's establishing neo-Confucianism doctrines in Ming government, the turning inward of the Ming, or the fall of the Ming. Ask students to display and explain their cartoons.

Students Acquiring English

Pair new speakers of English with fluent speakers and have them analyze the term *neo-Confucian*. They should start by reviewing the place of Confucius in Chinese thought, and then they should define and apply the prefix *neo-*. Pairs might then examine events in the section in light of the results of their analysis.

Gifted Students

Have students write a paper on the role of the civil service in Ming government. Have students begin by reviewing the material on the Ming civil-service system on textbook page 349.

ASSESS

Review

Have students complete the Section 4 Review. Use answers in the Teacher's Edition, page 352, to assess student mastery of this section.

State-Building in Africa

RESOURCES

Pupil's Edition

Map, p. 354: *Trading Kingdoms of Africa, c. 1230–1591*

History Through the Arts, p. 355: *Royal West African Figure*

Core Resources

Reading 13.5: *Mansa Musa's Pilgrimage*

Geography Worksheet 13: *Natural Resources and State-Building*

Visual Resources

Geography and History 13: *African Trading Kingdoms*

Global History Resource Center

Reading: *A Griot History of Sundiata's War for Mali*

Reading: *Mansa Musa's Pilgrimage to Mecca*

Reading: *Ibn Battuta's Travels in Mali*

Videodiscs or Global History Resource Center

Map: *African Trade, c. 1450–1600*

Search Frame 851

Image: *Bronze Portrait of an African Ruler*

Search Frame 847

LESSON FOCUS

On what did the city-states and empires of East and West Africa base their success?

OBJECTIVES

After completing this lesson, students will be able to:

- investigate why the East African city-states developed a mixed culture;
- identify characteristics of the Mutapa and Mali empires;
- explain why the Songhay Empire declined in the late 1500s.

HOOK

Investigate why the coastal areas of East Africa developed a mixed culture. On a large classroom map, point out the locations of Arabia, Persia, and Indonesia. Mention that for hundreds of years, traders from these areas had been traveling to the East African coast. Ask a student to point out the routes the Arabs and the Persians might have taken to the East African coast. In addition, have the student mark the Indonesians' likely sea route to Madagascar. Continue by mentioning that these traders freely intermingled and intermarried with East African coastal peoples, and by the 1100s they had established a thriving society along the coast.

Ask: What kind of culture emerged on the East African coast as a result?
[Islamic, African, and Asian elements combined to form the distinct Swahili culture.]

Tell students that over time the Swahili communities on the East African coast became the focal point of trade on the Indian Ocean. Direct students' attention to the map on textbook page 354 and ask them to locate and name the major East African coastal trading cities. Alternatively, project Geography and History Transparency 13 and call on a volunteer to point out the trade centers on the East African coast. Conclude by asking students to complete the worksheet that accompanies the transparency.

DEVELOP

Classify the major characteristics of the Mutapa and Mali empires. Have students continue to view the map on textbook page 354 or the transparency. Ask them to locate on the map the kingdoms of Great Zimbabwe and Mali. Then write the headings *Mutapa* and *Mali* on the chalkboard. Direct students to identify the major characteristics of these two empires. Guide students by offering the following categories: geographical extent, time period, economic activities, religious practices, important leaders. Note students' responses under the appropriate heading on the chalkboard. Then ask students to use the information on the chalkboard to create a graphic organizer on these two empires. Encourage students to display and discuss their graphic organizers.

Ask: *What were the major characteristics of the Mutapa and Mali empires?*

[Mutapa and Mali were powerful empires whose wealth was based on trade. In addition, Mali was a center for the spread of Islam in West Africa.]

Have students learn more about Mali by assigning the Global History Resource Center readings on Sundiata, Mansa Musa, and Ibn Battuta. You might also have them read Core Resources Reading 13.5 on Mansa Musa's pilgrimage.

PROBE

Evaluate the importance of salt and gold in West African trade. Have students view the electronic media map showing African trade. Ask students to focus on West Africa and list the major goods involved in the trade between North Africa and West Africa. *[Students should recognize that West Africa's major export to North Africa was gold, while its major import from North Africa was salt.]*

Continue by pointing out that salt was scarce in West Africa and highly prized. Gold, however, was found in plentiful supply, and West Africans readily traded gold for the much-needed salt. Conclude by stressing that gaining control of the gold-for-salt trade enabled kingdoms like Ghana, Mali, and Songhay to become wealthy and powerful. Reinforce this point by assigning Geography Worksheet 13.

CONCLUDE

Account for the decline of the Songhay Empire in the late 1500s. Remind students of the list of characteristics of the Mutapa and Mali empires that they made for the Develop activity. Have them suggest a similar list for the Songhay Empire. Note suggestions on the chalkboard. Next ask students to identify the internal and external challenges the empire faced. Add responses to the list on the chalkboard. Then encourage students to use the information on the chalkboard to write a newspaper article on the empire's collapse. Call on volunteers to read their articles to the class and then lead the class in a discussion of the reasons for the collapse of the Songhay Empire.

EXTEND

Cross-Curricular Connection: *Geography/Fine Arts*
Have students read the History Through the Arts feature on textbook page 355. Then display the electronic media image of the African ruler. Ask students to explore the geography of West Africa to suggest the materials available to West African sculptors and other artists.

Cross-Curricular Connection: *Language Arts*
Link to Today. Have students read the griot history in the Global History Resource Center. Ask students to research the role of griots in West African life. Then ask them to develop a story in the style of the griots concerning an event recently in the news. Call on volunteers to tell their stories to the class.

MEET INDIVIDUAL NEEDS

Interpersonal Learners
Point out that transactions between North African and West African merchants were referred to as the "silent trade" because the merchants never met each other. Have interested students research the silent trade.

Visual-Spatial Learners
Some students might like to conduct research on Mansa Musa's pilgrimage to Mecca. Students might begin their research by reviewing the Global History Resource Center reading on the pilgrimage. Suggest that they present their findings in visual form, such as in an annotated map or an illustrated time line.

Students Having Difficulty
Have students convert the boldfaced headings and subheadings in the section into a question about material in the section. Students should note their answers on a separate sheet of paper. Then have students use their questions to quiz each other.

ASSESS

Review
Have students complete the Section 5 Review. Use answers in the Teacher's Edition, page 356, to assess student mastery of this section.

In preparation for the chapter test, you may wish to have students complete all or part of the Chapter 13 Review on textbook page 357, the Chapter 13 Review Worksheet, and the Chapter 13 Themes Review.

Understanding the Main Idea

Call on a volunteer to read aloud the *Understanding the Main Idea* paragraph. Then tell students that powerful leaders conquered and ruled enormous states during this period, through the effectiveness of their fighting forces and the efficiency of their governments. The resulting cultures blended the traditions of the conquerors and the conquered peoples.

Presenting Themes

See p. 329B for suggestions on introducing themes.

Using the Time Line

Have students list the time line events in their notebooks. After they have read about each event in the chapter, have students write a paragraph explaining its significance.

Chapter 13
New Empires in Asia and Africa 1200–1707

Understanding The Main Idea

In the Ottoman Empire, Safavid Persia, and Mughal India, powerful emperors ruled over large territories with culturally diverse populations. Meanwhile, in China the Ming dynasty sought to revive the traditions and policies that had been neglected during the Mongol period. In Africa smaller states rose and fell as Africans expanded their trade.

Themes

- **Technology** How might a monopoly over military technology affect the building of empires?

- **Politics and Law** Why might rulers try to revive past traditions after a time of political disunity?

- **Cross-cultural Interaction** How might trade spread languages, cultures, and religious ideas?

In 1605 the Mughal Empire was at the height of its brilliance and splendor. Akbar, the great sultan, had spent a lifetime conquering vast territories to build the empire. When he died, Jahangir, Akbar's son and successor, inherited his father's empire. Jahangir's coronation ceremony reflected the greatness of the imperial throne:

> 66 *Having thus seated myself on the throne of my expectation and wishes, I caused also the imperial crown . . . to be brought before me, and then, in the presence of the whole assembled Emirs [high government officials], . . . placed it on my brows. . . . For forty days and forty nights I caused the . . . great imperial state drum, to strike up, without ceasing, the strains of joy and triumph; and . . . around my throne, the ground was spread by my directions with the most costly brocades [silks] and gold embroidered carpets. . . . Numbers of blooming youth, . . . clad in dresses of the most costly materials, woven in silk and gold . . . awaited my commands . . . in attitude most respectful. And finally, the Emirs of the empire, . . . covered from head to foot in gold and jewels . . . stood round in brilliant array.* 99

Jahangir inherited tremendous wealth and power when he became emperor of India, but like many other imperial rulers of his day, he faced frequent challenges to his authority.

c. 1240	c. 1326	1368	1421	1453
Sundiata establishes a new capital at Niani.	Ottomans conquer much of Anatolia.	Zhu Yuanzhang establishes the Ming dynasty.	Yongle moves the capital of China from Nanjing to Beijing.	Ottomans seize Constantinople.

بالغه بذلك لعصًا أحواج الناس وقال عطآء لان يرانى
الرحل سنين فيكتب جا ما لعيش فيه مومن انتم

Emperor Jahangir, surrounded by his courtiers

About the Image

During Jahangir's reign, Persian culture and customs held sway not only in the Mughal court but throughout the upper levels of Indian society. One of the ways the Persian influence made its presence felt was in the arts. The mingling of the Persian Muslim styles with the Indian Hindu styles produced some of the world's most beautiful paintings. In fact, Hindu painters, borrowing Persian techniques, became masters at miniatures, portraits, and paintings of the heroes from the great Hindu epics.

Critical Thinking Ask students to suggest the ways in which the image demonstrates Jahangir's interest in the arts.

ANSWER: Students might answer that the image represents Jahangir's support of the arts by showing him examining a book in a room decorated with beautiful carpets and paintings.

1556	1587	1591	1636	1658
Akbar becomes emperor in India.	'Abbas becomes king of Safavid Persia.	Songhay troops defeated in battle of Tendibi.	Nurhachi proclaims the beginning of the Qing dynasty.	Aurangzeb kills his brother to become Mughal emperor.

Theme: Cross-cultural Interaction

Many Orthodox Christians in captured territories eventually chose to convert to Islam for various reasons. Whether or not these peoples converted, they became integrated into Ottoman society. Intermarriage was not unusual; Asians and Europeans, along with Christians and Muslims, came together to form a new multicultural society.

Critical Thinking Ask students why assimilating different religions and peoples might have benefited Ottoman society.

ANSWER: Students may answer that by assimilating these different religions and peoples, the Ottoman Empire could more easily control its subjects and that by combining many traditions it would make its own culture more diverse.

SECTION 1
The Ottoman Empire

FOCUS

- How did the Ottomans build a world empire?
- What kept the Ottoman Empire united?
- What cultural advances did the Ottomans make?

*F*rom a tiny kingdom in Asia Minor, the Ottomans built a vast empire that rivaled even the Abbasid caliphate in power and brilliance. The Ottoman Empire thrived on expansion, and Ottoman sultans built an efficient imperial system for conquering territories and incorporating new peoples. For most of its early history the Ottoman Empire provided a framework for allowing a great variety of ethnic groups, religions, and languages to coexist with a remarkable degree of harmony and prosperity.

An Ottoman sultan dining, c. 1500

The Rise of the Ottomans

After the Mongol conquests and the destruction of the Saljuq sultanate of Rum in the mid-1200s, growing numbers of Turkomans—Turkish *ghazi* warriors—began to establish small independent states along the frontiers of Christian Byzantium. One of the most successful of these warriors was a chieftain named Osman. Osman's success as a *ghazi* leader brought him many new followers, including other Turkomans, Sufis, and even ex-Byzantine frontier soldiers who had converted to Islam. These soldiers became known as Osmanlis, or Ottomans.

In the late 1200s, the Ottomans started to expand from their base in northwestern Anatolia (earlier known as Asia Minor). By 1326 they controlled much of Anatolia. Unable to take Constantinople, they nevertheless crossed into Europe. In 1361 the Ottomans captured Adrianople, the second most important Byzantine city, which they renamed Edirne and made their capital. Within a few decades the Ottomans had established their rule over much of the Balkans.

From principality to empire. With the dramatic victories in the Balkans, the Ottoman state became a true empire. Not only was its territory larger and wealthier, but its population was more diverse. Many of these new subjects soon came to support Ottoman rule, and the Ottoman policy of religious freedom reassured the Greek Orthodox population of the Balkans. Ottoman land and taxation policies actually improved conditions for many peasants. In addition, the Ottomans usually left cities and castles intact, allowing local economies to recover from conquest.

Military success in the Balkans also led to improvements in the Ottoman army. The sultans began to use war captives and other enslaved Christians from the Balkans to create a superbly trained elite force of slave soldiers called **Janissaries**. The Janissaries became the heart of the imperial army, owing their allegiance solely to the particular sultan on whom they depended for survival. In addition, many Christian feudal lords on the sultan's borders chose to become Ottoman vassals or allies, and even served in the military.

Setback and recovery. As their empire grew in southwestern Europe, Ottoman rulers also decided to expand the Islamic territory that owed them allegiance. In the late 1300s, they began to conquer many of the *ghazi* states in eastern Anatolia. As the rulers of these states fled east, however, they sought revenge against the Ottomans. The powerful Turko-Mongol ruler Timur, better known in Europe as Tamerlane, responded to his fellow Muslims' pleas for help. Timur invaded Anatolia and defeated the Ottomans in 1402. Although he allowed the Ottomans to keep the lands they had taken from Christians, he made them restore the lands of the Muslim rulers. Defeat by Timur threw the Ottoman state into a crisis. A struggle for the throne led to civil war, and the empire held together only after bloody fighting.

The Ottomans survived these challenges partly because war was their way of life. In addition to the strength they drew from their slave troops, for example, the Ottomans had a genius for adapting to new weapons—particularly gunpowder, artillery, and muskets. As they mastered these new inventions from China and Europe, the Ottomans developed one of the toughest, most disciplined fighting forces in the world. Soon, the Ottomans resumed their imperial expansion. In 1444 Sultan Murad II crushed the forces of the last important European crusading effort at the Battle of Varna.

Mehmet the Conqueror. The most spectacular phase of Ottoman expansion began in 1444 with the reign of the ambitious sultan Mehmet II,

The Ottoman Empire, 1453–1566

Ottoman Empire, 1453

Territory added, 1454–1519

Territory added, 1520–1566

Battle site

0   250   500 Miles
0   250   500 Kilometers
Robinson Projection

A Diverse Empire At its height, the Ottoman Empire under Süleyman ranged over three continents. The "magnificent" Muslim emperor's diverse subjects included Catholics, Orthodox Christians, Jews, and Muslims.

Movement How far did Ottoman troops have to march home to Constantinople after unsuccessfully besieging Vienna in 1529?

Theme: War and Diplomacy

Only Muslims were eligible for military service in the Ottoman Empire. This was important because land in conquered territories was distributed as a reward to the victorious soldiers. The soldiers knew that those who faced the greatest risks in battle would receive the richest grants of land. Bertrand de Broquière, a traveler of the times, wrote of the Ottoman forces: "They can start suddenly, and a hundred Christian soldiers would make more noise than ten thousand Osmanlis [Ottomans]. When the drum sounded they put themselves immediately in march, never breaking step, never stopping till the word is given. Lightly armed, in one night they travel as far as their Christian adversaries in three days."

Critical Thinking Ask students what effect the Ottoman spoils system might have had on soldiers.

ANSWER: Students might suggest that soldiers who knew they would receive land for their efforts would be more likely to fight fiercely. In addition, this system would assure that at least some of the peoples in conquered territory would become Muslims.

Mehmet hired Urban, a Hungarian engineer, to manufacture large and small cannons for the assault on Constantinople. The largest cannon Urban made was 26 feet in length and 8 inches in diameter. It required 15 pair of oxen to move the cannon; 700 soldiers were assigned to transport it. Mehmet's forces had to level roads and reinforce bridges to transport the cannon to a position outside Constantinople's walls.

Urban's modern weapons were used effectively during the siege of Constantinople. A direct hit by the 26-foot cannon created a breach in the walls that allowed the Ottoman troops to enter the city.

Critical Thinking Ask students why Mehmet was willing to expend so many resources on the cannon.

ANSWER: Students may answer that he wanted to gain more territory, and that the cannon gave him a decisive military advantage.

---

also known as "the Conqueror." A Venetian visitor to his court described Mehmet's goals:

> 66 *He burns with the desire to rule. . . . The Empire of the world, he says, must be one, one faith and one kingdom. To make this unity there is no place in the world more worthy than Constantinople.* 99

In early 1453 Mehmet attacked the fortified city of Constantinople by land and sea. Using artillery, the Ottoman forces battered down the powerful walls that had protected the city for centuries. After a long siege the Ottomans broke through the Byzantine defenses on May 29, 1453. Mehmet went straight to Hagia Sophia, the heart of Orthodox Christianity, to set up his throne. He made Hagia Sophia a mosque, and the Ottomans triumphantly claimed the center of eastern Christianity for Islam.

Mehmet made Constantinople his new capital, which was known also by its Turkish name, Istanbul. He repaired the war damage and built

new palaces, mosques, and a huge central marketplace—the covered bazaar. To repopulate the city, he encouraged people from all over the empire—and even some from outside it, such as Jews who were being persecuted in Christian Spain—to settle in Constantinople. By the end of Mehmet's reign, the city once more thrived as the center of an extensive trade network and the magnificent capital of a vast empire.

Selim the Grim. Mehmet's rapid conquest of Constantinople renewed the momentum of Ottoman expansion. Ottoman armies pushed up through the Balkans, conquering Serbia, Bosnia, Herzegovina, and Albania with little trouble. These victories established the Ottomans' position as major Islamic rulers. Increasingly, sultans measured their greatness in Islamic terms. Above all, they saw themselves as the defenders of Sunni Islam.

Meanwhile, in Iran a new Shi'ah dynasty, the Safavids (sah-FAH-vidz), emerged to challenge Ottoman leadership in the Islamic world. The Safavids had also learned to use the new gunpowder weapons and were therefore a considerable military as well as religious threat to the Ottoman state. With thousands of Shi'ah living in the eastern parts of the Ottoman Empire, the Safavids threatened to stir up internal rebellion against the sultan.

For Sultan Selim I in particular, the new Persian threat seemed to overshadow all others. Selim, known as "the Grim," became sultan by deposing his father and killing all potential rivals—his brothers, their sons, and four of his own five sons.

Selim believed that the Shi'ah were the greatest danger to the Ottoman Empire. Making peace with his European enemies, Selim led the Ottoman army into Anatolia. In 1514 he crushed the Safavids at the battle of Chaldiran. He then annexed eastern Anatolia and temporarily occupied the Safavid capital of Tabriz (tuh-BREEZ).

Selim then turned south to attack the Mamluks in Syria and Egypt. By 1517 he had defeated them, thus bringing Syria and Egypt into the Ottoman Empire. The Hijaz region of the Arabian Peninsula, with the holy cities of

◀ **This illustration from a 1455 book shows the conquest of Constantinople by the Ottomans in 1453.**

Mecca and Medina, then submitted to Ottoman rule. These triumphs made the Ottoman Empire the greatest Islamic state of its time and a major world power. Ottoman rulers now assumed, and jealously guarded, the title of Guardian of the Holy Cities. Before long they also assumed the ultimate Islamic title—caliph.

Süleyman the Lawgiver

The empire reached its peak under Selim's son, Süleyman, who reigned from 1520 to 1566. Westerners called him "the Magnificent," but Ottomans called him "the Lawgiver." Süleyman inherited a vast empire from his father. Enriched by new sources of revenue and the control of international trade routes, the empire under Süleyman experienced few internal disputes and faced no foreign enemy capable of seriously threatening its security.

Süleyman the Lawgiver
BIOGRAPHY

Süleyman proved to be an energetic and talented ruler. Early in his reign, Süleyman's primary interest was in Europe, where his great enemy was the powerful Holy Roman Empire of the Habsburgs. In his wars with the Habsburgs, Süleyman dealt the Hungarians, the Austrians' allies, a crushing blow at Mohács on the Danube River in 1526. Three years later he unsuccessfully besieged the Habsburg capital of Vienna. The siege of Vienna marked the northernmost point of the Ottoman advance.

Süleyman also understood the importance of sea power. He expanded the Ottoman navy and made the pirate captain Khayr ad-Din (ky-roohd-DEEN), better known in the West as Barbarossa, or Red Beard, his grand admiral. Barbarossa terrorized Habsburg territories in southern Europe and won a great victory in 1538 in the battle of Préveza, giving the Ottomans control of the eastern Mediterranean.

Ogier Ghiselin de Busbecq, the Holy Roman ambassador to Süleyman's court, described the sultan in his later years:

▲ The Ottoman navy, commanded by the former pirate Barbarossa, secured control of Tunisia in 1534.

66 *His majestic bearing and indeed his whole demeanor [behavior] are such as beseem [suit] the lord of so vast an empire. He has always had the character of being a careful and temperate [calm] man; even in his early days . . . his life was blameless. . . . As an upholder of his religion and its rites he is most strict, being quite as anxious to extend his faith as to extend his empire.* 99

Süleyman's accomplishments at home were just as impressive as his expansion of the empire. He reformed the tax system and overhauled the government bureaucracy. He commissioned the construction of many mosques, schools, hospitals, bridges, baths, and other public works. He was particularly concerned with the establishment of justice in his empire. His improvement of the court system and issuing of new laws and law codes earned him the name of Süleyman the Lawgiver.

With strong leadership and advanced military technology, the Ottomans created a great Islamic world empire that stretched from the Balkans to the Indian Ocean by the 1500s.

✴ Ottoman Institutions and Society

Süleyman presided over a society that was clearly divided into two groups—the military ruling class, called *askeri*, and the masses of ordinary subjects, known as the *reaya*, or "protected flock." The *reaya* was extremely diverse. It included nomads, farmers, city-dwellers, peasants, herders, merchants, and artisans. These groups spoke many languages, practiced many different religions, and included many ethnic cultures. Despite these social differences, the Ottoman government successfully provided a framework within which these different groups could coexist peacefully.

The sultanate. In the Ottoman Empire the most important institution was the sultanate. Originally, the Ottoman ruler had been a simple tribal chief, the leader of a band of *ghazi* warriors. As the Ottomans began to build a complex state, their leader became a sultan, based on the traditional model used by the Saljuqs.

After the conquest of the Balkans, Constantinople, and most of the Arab world, however, the Ottoman sultan became something quite new. The sultan became *padishah*, or "emperor"—a world-ruler, a lawgiver, the "Shadow of the Provider." It was his responsibility to guarantee harmony and prosperity by establishing justice according to Islamic law.

The first 10 Ottoman sultans were all capable and successful. Only after the death of Süleyman did the quality of the rulers decline. One reason for this was the manner of succession to the throne. In some cases, when the old sultan died, the throne went to whichever son was closest to the capital and able to seize the throne. This helped guarantee the ability of the new ruler but also led to bitter and bloody struggles between rival brothers.

To prevent such disputes, the Ottomans began to deal more harshly with the losers in the succession struggles. Mehmet II, for example, decreed that the new sultan could execute his brothers in the interest of political stability: "For the welfare of the state, the one of my sons to whom God grants the Sultanate may lawfully put his brothers to death. This has the approval of a majority of jurists." When Mehmet III ascended the throne in 1595, the court executioner strangled all 19 of the new sultan's brothers, many of whom were mere children. When Mehmet III's successor, Ahmed, came to the throne, however, he did not kill his only brother, who was thought to be insane. He believed that the prophet Muhammad did not wish his brother to die.

From this point on the Ottoman sultans stopped the practice of killing their brothers. Instead, to prevent the old struggles for power they kept all Ottoman princes in the "cage," a special place within the palace, along with their mothers, nurses, wives, and their slaves. From the cage, a prince emerged only once—either to reign or to die—and the oldest usually became sultan. Having not learned how to govern by holding political offices, however, few sultans raised in the cage system proved capable rulers when they finally ascended the throne.

▲ **This gold Ottoman jug from the 1500s is studded with diamonds and rubies.**

Government and administration. Below the sultan and his court, the Ottoman Empire was a large centralized state, and its government was complex. It was basically composed of three subdivisions—the leaders of the military, the bureaucrats, and the men in charge of the religious and judicial institutions. Above these three branches were the heads of the major government departments, who made up the **divan**, or imperial council. Among the members of the divan were the grand vizier, ministers and governors of key provinces, the admiral of the navy, the commander of the Janissaries, the head of the treasury, and the chief judges. The council advised the sultan on important government decisions, carried out his orders, and supervised government administration.

At the heart of the Ottoman system of government was the **devshirme**, a tribute levied every few years on the sultan's Christian subjects.

Government of the Ottoman Empire

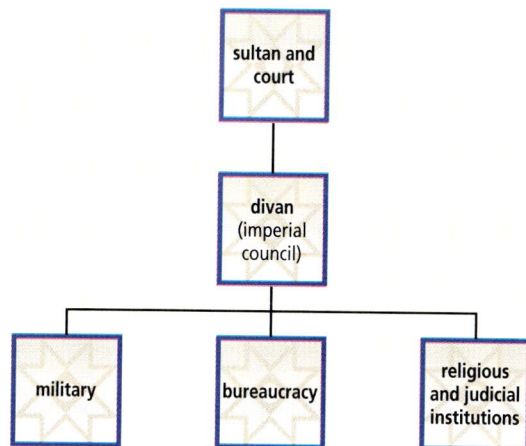

```
        ┌──────────────┐
        │ sultan and   │
        │ court        │
        └──────┬───────┘
               │
        ┌──────┴───────┐
        │ divan        │
        │ (imperial    │
        │ council)     │
        └──────┬───────┘
               │
     ┌─────────┼──────────┐
┌─────────┐ ┌─────────┐ ┌───────────┐
│military │ │bureau-  │ │religious  │
│         │ │cracy    │ │and judicial│
│         │ │         │ │institutions│
└─────────┘ └─────────┘ └───────────┘
```

A Complex Government The members of the divan were handpicked by the sultan and reported directly to him.

Analyzing Why do you think the Ottomans found it necessary to have the divan between the sultan and the other three branches of government?

The tribute consisted of the strongest and brightest Christian boys who became the sultan's personal slaves. These boys learned Turkish, converted to Islam, and received training to prepare them for government service. Most entered the Janissary corps, but the best were given special education in the palace schools. According to their ability, they then became Janissary officers, slave cavalry, or government officials. These "slaves" really constituted one of the most elite groups in the Ottoman Empire. For a time nearly all of the grand viziers were of slave origin.

The *millet* system. Although officially the champions of Sunni Islam, the Ottomans ruled over an extremely diverse empire with little internal unrest. In the early years there was much integration of the Muslim and non-Muslim populations, but after the acquisition of extensive Muslim territories, rigid distinctions developed between Muslims and non-Muslims. However, the Ottomans gave non-Muslims certain rights and considerable independence through the *millet* (muh-LET) system.

Four *millets*, or religious communities, were recognized in the Ottoman Empire: Muslim, Orthodox Christian, Armenian Christian, and Jewish. Each had its own religious hierarchy, with the top leader responsible to the sultan. Each followed its own religious law and regulated its own internal affairs.

Keeping various groups separated in this way minimized conflicts and maintained internal peace. At the same time, however, by reinforcing people's sense of religious identity, this approach prevented them from feeling a unified Ottoman identity. In later years this lack of unity would leave the Ottoman Empire open to challenges and influences from western Europe.

The military state. The Ottoman Empire suffered from one major flaw—it depended on continuing conquest. The entire Ottoman state was essentially a means of support for the army, through which the sultan continued to bring more territory under Ottoman rule. As long as the army brought in new lands and new wealth, the state remained stable. When expansion ended, however, the expense of maintaining the military gradually became unbearable.

Perhaps more importantly, the justification for the sultan's rule as a *ghazi* warrior was called into question. This challenged both the Ottomans' sense of identity and their right to govern other Muslims. Thus, the end of Ottoman expansion during Süleyman's reign can also be seen as the beginning of Ottoman decline.

The Ottomans maintained their empire through strong government, religious toleration, and continuing conquest.

Ottoman Culture

Like its political institutions, the high culture of the Ottoman Empire tended to copy styles from previous civilizations. Nonetheless, the Ottomans achieved considerable brilliance and beauty in many cultural fields, particularly architecture and the arts.

Architecture and the arts. From Budapest to Basra, the Ottomans left behind a rich array of mosques, palaces, baths, schools, hospitals, bridges, and other public monuments. Byzantine

IDENTIFY
For significance, see the following pages:
Osman (p. 332)
Janissaries (p. 332)
Mehmet the
    Conqueror (p. 333)
Selim the Grim (p. 334)
Süleyman the
    Lawgiver (p. 335)
padishah (p. 336)
divan (p. 336)
devshirme (p. 336)
millet (p. 337)

LOCATE
For locations, see the map on p. 333.

1. The Ottomans were warriors at heart and resourceful in war. Slave troops added strength, and the Ottomans quickly adopted new weapons, including gunpowder, artillery, and muskets.
2. The Ottomans maintained their empire through well-organized and centralized government and continuing military conquest.
3. Constantinople renewed the momentum of expansion by allowing armies access to territory in the Balkans and gave the Ottomans control of trade between the Black and Mediterranean Seas.
4. Ottomans excelled in the fields of architecture, the arts, astronomy, history, and geography.
5. beneficial—kept own religious and cultural practices; ran own internal affairs; harmful—slaves forced to serve in army; rigid distinctions between Muslims and non-Muslims

influence on the Ottoman architectural style was very strong, most notably in the use of domes. One of the masters of dome design and construction was Sultan Süleyman's court architect, Sinan.

During his career Sinan designed more than 300 buildings. One of the greatest of all Islamic builders, he found graceful solutions to the classic architectural problem of combining a round dome with a rectangular building. The mosque of Süleyman in present-day Istanbul and the mosque of Selim in Edirne are considered his masterpieces.

Perhaps the finest Ottoman art was calligraphy. Ottoman artists refined older styles and created new ones. Among the most impressive examples of Ottoman calligraphy were the official documents produced by the Ottoman government and the royal emblems created for the Ottoman sultans' signatures.

Scholarship. The Ottomans also produced outstanding scholars of philosophy, theology, mathematics, and the sciences. Several sultans encouraged the study of astronomy and astrology. For example, even though it was later torn down, in 1579 the Ottomans constructed a great astronomical observatory in Constantinople.

▲ The mosque of Süleyman, built from 1550 to 1557, was inspired by Hagia Sophia in Constantinople.

The Ottomans had a particular interest in history and geography. In history they recorded the origins and development of the Ottoman Empire and compared their history to those of earlier peoples. As the Ottomans became a leading naval power, they also expanded geographical knowledge about the rest of the world. The *Book of the Sea* by the Ottoman admiral Piri Reis is particularly famous for its accurate maps and charts of the known world.

*O*ttoman culture made great advances in the fields of architecture and scholarship.

SECTION 1 REVIEW

IDENTIFY and explain the significance of the following:
    Osman
    Janissaries
    Mehmet the Conqueror
    Selim the Grim
    Süleyman the Lawgiver
    padishah
    divan
    devshirme
    millet

LOCATE and explain the importance of the following:

Anatolia
Constantinople
Edirne
Balkans
Vienna

1. *Main Idea* Why was the Ottoman military so successful in expanding the empire?
2. *Main Idea* How did the Ottomans maintain their empire?
3. *Geography: Location* Why was control of

Constantinople important to the Ottomans?
4. *Writing to Explain* Write a short essay explaining the many cultural achievements made under the rule of the Ottoman sultans.
5. *Evaluating* Why might it be said that Ottoman imperial expansion was both beneficial and harmful to the peoples who were incorporated into the empire? Be sure to give specific examples.

Safavid Persia

- How did the Safavids begin their rise to power?
- What were the consequences of the Safavids' adoption of Shi'ism as the state religion?
- How did 'Abbas bring Safavid Persia to its height of power and culture?

While the Ottomans were building their empire, a new dynasty of rulers known as the Safavids gained power over the Plateau of Iran. This dynasty did not last as long or control as much territory as its Ottoman rival. The Safavids did succeed, however, in blending together Persian cultural traditions and Shi'ah Islam in ways that would lay the foundation for the later emergence of Iran as a nation-state. At its peak Safavid Persia was a significant world power with a brilliant civilization much admired by its neighbors.

Safavid tilework on a mosque in Isfahan, Persia

Origins of the Safavids

The Safavids began their rise to power in Persia during the 1200s. The head of the family, Safi al-Din, lived near the town of Ardabil in northwestern Persia. In the turmoil that resulted from the Mongol invasion, Safi al-Din became disillusioned with the world and turned to religion. In search of spiritual truth, he became a student of Sufism and eventually became the leader of a Sufi order. Thereafter, every head of the Safavid family was also recognized as the *murshid*, or "perfect spiritual guide," of the Sufi order.

Although Safi al-Din had turned to Sufism to withdraw from the world, his successors soon saw religion as a reason to involve themselves in the world. The Safavid *murshids* began to direct a secret organization of missionaries who spread Safavid doctrines as far as Syria and Afghanistan. Also, the Safavids began to shift from Sunni Islam to Shi'ism.

The Safavids began their rise to power as spiritual leaders of a Sufi order in northwestern Persia.

The Rise of the Safavid Empire

In the last half of the 1400s, the Safavid movement began to change from a purely religious organization into a political state. This transformation was made possible by the military power of the Safavids' loyal Turkoman tribal followers, known as *kizilbash*, or "Red Heads," because of their distinctive red hats.

Even with the support of the *kizilbash*, the first Safavid leaders to attempt the creation of a state were unsuccessful. Other Persians killed or imprisoned as many of the Safavids as they could, but one of the youngest, Isma'il (is-mah-EEL), escaped to a more distant part of Persia in 1494.

Isma'il. Despite this persecution, the core of the *kizilbash* supporters had come to view the Safavid leader as a divine figure. They remained eager to fight on his behalf.

In 1500 Isma'il came out of hiding. Almost immediately an army of *kizilbash* rallied around

Theme: **Politics and Law**

According to legend, Isma'il was not merely a tribal chieftain but a descendant of a Shi'ah-imam. His status as saint and ruler was solidified when he established the Safavid Empire in Persia and Shi'ism as the Empire's state religion. Isma'il was described as "fair, handsome, and very pleasing; not very tall, but of a light and well-framed figure; rather stout than slight, with broad shoulders. His hair is reddish. He only wears mustachios, and uses his left hand instead of his right."

Critical Thinking Ask students why rulers of many cultures have claimed divine status.

ANSWER: Students might suggest that people who consider a ruler divine are more likely to follow him or her without question.

Safavid Persia, 1500–1636

Embattled Frontiers   Through religious faith and military might, the Safavid rulers revived the former glory of the Persian empire. In doing so, they clashed with the Ottomans and the Uzbeks for control of key territory.

Linking Geography and History   The Safavids relocated their capital from Tabriz to Qazvin and later to Isfahan. What do you think motivated the first move?

him. As a contemporary Venetian traveler in Persia observed:

> *[Isma'il] is loved and revered by his people as a god, and especially by his soldiers, many of whom enter into battle without armour, expecting their master Ismael [Isma'il] to watch over them in the fight. . . . The name of God is forgotten throughout Persia and only that of Ismael remembered.*

Isma'il's forces won victory after victory. In 1501 they occupied Tabriz, the most important city in northwestern Persia. Tabriz became the Safavid capital, and Isma'il took the ancient Persian title of "king of kings" and firmly established the Safavid dynasty in Persia.

Safavid religious policy. Isma'il's first act as king was to proclaim Shi'ism as the official state religion. Since most of his subjects were Sunnis, Isma'il's advisors urged him to be cautious about this policy. Isma'il ignored them, however, and ordered the forcible conversion of the population. He proclaimed:

> *I am committed to this action; God and the Immaculate [pure] Imams are with me, and I fear no one; by God's help, if the people utter one word of protest, I will draw the sword and leave not one of them alive.*

Isma'il's policy was not as unwise as it appeared to his advisors. There was a sizable Shi'ah minority in Safavid Persia. Moreover, by championing Shi'ism, Isma'il attracted support from the enemies of neighboring Sunni Muslim states.

The Safavids claimed descent from 'Ali and from the ancient Persian monarchy, which gave the Safavid rulers both worldly and religious authority. This blending of Persian tradition and Shi'ah religion gave the Safavid state a unique identity and laid the foundation for a national culture in modern Iran. At the same time, Shi'ism sharply distinguished the Safavid state from its Sunni rivals, notably the Ottomans to the west and the Uzbeks, a Sunni Muslim people who lived east of Safavid territory. The combination of religious and political rivalry between Sunni and Shi'ah states embittered relations and led to bloody persecutions on both sides.

Foreign affairs. While Isma'il dreamed of converting the entire Muslim world to Shi'ism through conquest, the Ottomans and the Uzbeks attempted to keep Isma'il in check. Although Isma'il initially defeated the Uzbeks, eventually the Uzbek army regrouped and routed the Safavid forces in Central Asia, beginning a long struggle for control of the region.

Although the Uzbeks remained a problem for the Safavids, Isma'il faced a far more serious problem after the Ottomans defeated his army at the Battle of Chaldiran in 1514. The enthusiasm and fearlessness of the *kizilbash* cavalry was no match for the massed firepower of the Ottomans. The Safavid army was severely weakened and lost many of its top officers. Many people also began to lose faith in Isma'il's supposedly divine powers.

After the Ottoman defeat, Isma'il became depressed and lost interest in state affairs. He died in 1524 and was succeeded by his son, Tahmasp, who was too young to rule on his own. Tahmasp's advisors found themselves confronting foreign enemies on most borders, in addition to internal competition between the *kizilbash* soldiers and Persian bureaucrats.

Safavid recovery. Despite these challenges the Safavid state survived. Eventually, Tahmasp asserted his own authority and began dealing with these difficulties. Although Tahmasp could not defeat either the Ottomans or the Uzbeks, he did continue to resist them effectively. In 1548 he made his capital more secure by moving it from Tabriz to Qazvin (kaz-VEEN).

Tahmasp also expanded Persian authority into the Caucasus region. For the first time, the Safavids controlled a non-Persian, non-Muslim population—mostly Armenians and Georgians. Some non-Persians entered the service of the Safavids as vassals, and large numbers were deported to Persia as state slaves. The Safavids used these slaves alongside the *kizilbash* to support their rule.

The Safavids' adoption of Shi'ism as their state religion threatened their Sunni neighbors and led to conflict along Persian borders.

✶ 'Abbas the Great

After the death of Tahmasp in 1576, the Safavid state experienced over a decade of instability before 'Abbas, the greatest Safavid ruler, became shah in 1587. An English ambassador to the Persian court described 'Abbas as "infinitely royall, wise, valiant, liberall, temperate [calm], mercifull, and an exceeding lover of Justice."

'Abbas's reforms. When 'Abbas became king he realized that the *kizilbash* warriors who had brought the dynasty to power were becoming disloyal. To limit their power he formed a new group of Turkoman supporters, known as "friends of the king," who were loyal to him personally. Now the king did not have to rely solely on the *kizilbash* for military support.

To strengthen the military even further, 'Abbas completely reorganized the army. Copying the Ottomans, he trained foreign slave boys to be elite warriors, forming a standing army that was loyal only to the king. He also armed his soldiers with modern gunpowder weapons. As an English writer commented at the time:

▲ Although they were fierce warriors, the Safavid Persians were frequently outmatched in battle by the superior Ottoman army.

Understanding Literature

Dara responds "in a strong voice" despite the fact that he is dying and both men speak in highly elevated language.

✦ Across the Curriculum: Literature

Firdausi was the pen name of Abu ol-Qasem, a Persian landowner, who wrote the *Shah-nameh* to provide his daughter with a dowry. After 35 years of work, he presented his epic poem to sultan Mahmud of Ghazna. Unfortunately, Mahmud gave Firdausi only a pittance for his work.

Critical Thinking Ask students how they think Firdausi's need for money might have affected his work.

ANSWER: Students may suggest that he might have glorified characters related to his patrons.

Literature THROUGH TIME

Shah-nameh

*Shah-nameh, the epic of Persian history, was compiled by Firdausi, perhaps the greatest of the Iranian poets. Firdausi was born around 935 in the province of Khorasan in present-day eastern Iran. He began compiling Shah-nameh when he was in his forties, completing the massive work of close to 60,000 rhyming couplets 35 years later in 1010. Shah-nameh, or "Book of Kings," tells the story of Persia's monarchs—both mythical and historical—from the beginning of humankind to the Arab invasion in the 600s. Firdausi drew heavily on written histories, oral tales, and legends as sources. His main goal, however, was to tell a story in poetic form, not necessarily to be historically accurate. Even so, Shah-nameh remains a major source of infor-*mation *on early Persian history. The following selection tells how Sekander (Alexander the Great) took the throne of Persia from the dying Dara (Darius).*

He [Sekander] looked to see if the wounded man could still speak, and he rubbed his face with his hand. From the royal head he lifted the diadem [crown] and he eased the Pahlavi armor on his breast. Shedding tears as he gazed on the wounded body so far from a physician's help, he said to him,

"This pain shall be alleviated [eased] for you, and the hearts of your enemies shall be smitten [struck] with fear. Arise and seat yourself in this golden litter, or mount your horse if you have the strength. I will have physi-cians brought for you from India and Rum and I will cause tears of blood to flow for the pain you have suffered. I will surrender the kingship and the throne to you and when you recover I will depart from hence [here]. The men who have outraged you I will at once hang [their] head[s] downwards on the gallows. My heart bled and a cry issued from my lips when yesterday I heard from my elders that we two are of one stock and share a single shirt. Why should we extirpate [wipe out] our seed in rivalry?"

On hearing this, Dara said in a strong voice,

"See to my children and my kinsfolk and my loved ones whose faces are veiled. Marry my pure-bodied daughter and maintain her in security in your palace. Her mother named her Rowshanak [Roxana] and with her provided the world with joy and adornment."

Understanding Literature

How does this passage illustrate that Firdausi was more interested in telling a story than in historical accuracy?

Sekander and the dying Dara

> ❝The [Safavids] . . . hath now five hundred pieces of brasse, and sixty thousand musketiers: so that they, which at hand with the sword were before dreadful to the Turkes [Ottomans], now also, in remoter blows and sulfurian arts [the use of gunpowder], are growne terrible.❞

Once 'Abbas was firmly in control of the empire, he turned to his foreign problems, beginning with the Uzbeks. In 1598 he defeated the Uzbeks outside Herat and pacified the region. This freed him to deal with the Ottomans. Distinguishing himself by his personal bravery and leadership qualities, 'Abbas reconquered territory in Iraq that had been lost to the Ottomans since 1534. He restored the sacred Shi'ah cities to Safavid Persia, thereby reinforcing his power as a Shi'ah ruler.

Economic developments. 'Abbas also began a series of major economic developments in the empire. In particular, he encouraged trade and manufacturing. To improve the production of glazed tilework and ceramics, for example, he brought skilled Chinese potters to Persia. In addition to passing on their skills to Persian artisans, these craftsmen also provided the tiles with which many Safavid buildings were decorated.

'Abbas was also responsible for transforming the production of carpets in Persia from a home industry into a major national industry. In one city, for example, thousands of weavers worked in factories that produced carpets and many other fine woven goods, such as silks and velvets. These goods were used for overseas trade.

Imperial Isfahan. By 1599 'Abbas had moved his capital from Qazvin to Isfahan, near the center of the Plateau of Iran. Under 'Abbas, Isfahan, an ancient city, which had been the capital of the Saljuq Empire, was transformed into one of the most magnificent cities in the world, the supreme expression of Safavid art and architecture.

In an impressive example of city planning, 'Abbas constructed a long, straight avenue to link his gardens and palace in the north to the suburbs beyond the Zayandeh Rūd, a river in the south. The center of his city was an enormous rectangular park large enough for polo games. This park was surrounded by an arcade of shops. A monumental gateway at the south gave access to the Shah's Mosque. The soaring mosque, with its huge dimensions, colorful tiles, and imposing dome, was widely regarded as the most impressive mosque in Persia. Isfahan was one of the great cities of the world in the 1600s. The city was so magnificent that, according to a Persian saying of the times, "Isfahan is half the world."

'Abbas brought Safavid Persia to its height by reforming the military, improving the economy, and establishing a new imperial capital.

◀ **The Shah's Mosque, completed after 'Abbas died, was carefully restored in the 1900s.**

SECTION 2 REVIEW

IDENTIFY and explain the significance of the following:
  Safi al-Din
  murshid
  kizilbash
  Isma'il
  Tahmasp
  'Abbas

LOCATE and explain the importance of the following:
  Ardabil
  Tabriz
  Qazvin
  Isfahan

1. **Main Idea** How did the Safavids first come to power?
2. **Main Idea** What were some characteristics of Safavid Persia under 'Abbas?
3. **Geography: Location** How did Safavid Persia's location in relation to other Muslim states affect the strength of its empire?

4. **Writing to Persuade** Imagine that you are Isma'il, and you have decided to make Shi'ism the official state religion. Write a short speech to your advisors explaining why you think they are wrong to oppose you.
5. **Synthesizing** How did people's perceptions of the abilities of the Safavid kings affect the successes and failures of the empire?

SECTION 3
Mughal India

FOCUS

- Why did Babur build an empire in India instead of Central Asia?

- How did Akbar try to unify the empire?

- How did the Mughal emperors of the 1600s improve the empire?

With a blend of Turkish, Persian, Islamic, and Hindu cultural elements, the Mughals built a successful and brilliant dynasty in India. Like the Ottomans, the Mughals acquired and united a vast and ethnically diverse empire. They left a dazzling cultural heritage, particularly in poetry and architecture.

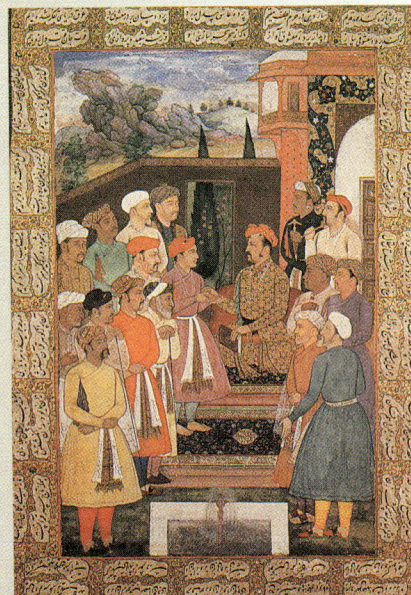

Emperor Jahangir holding court in the early 1600s

The Establishment of the Mughal Dynasty

BIOGRAPHY   The founder of the Mughal dynasty was Zahir ud-Din Muhammad, known as Babur (BAH-boohr), "the Tiger." Born in 1483, Babur descended on his father's side from Timur and on his mother's side from Genghis Khan. Despite this Mongol parentage, Babur consid- ered himself Turkish, not Mongol.

Babur
BIOGRAPHY

Babur always dreamed of building a powerful empire in Central Asia. First, he conquered the region of Samarkand, the ancient homeland of his people, only to be quickly driven out by the Uzbeks in 1500. After the Persian ruler Isma'il soundly defeated the Uzbeks, he granted Babur Samarkand in exchange for Babur's acceptance of Shi'ism. When the Uzbeks returned in 1512, however, Babur was driven out once again.

Giving up hope of establishing an empire in Central Asia, Babur turned his attention to India, where he decided to attack the crumbling Sultanate of Delhi, which was led by Ibrahim Lodi. A great battle took place at Panipat, a town north of Delhi, in April 1526. As Babur described it in his autobiography:

❝ *I placed my foot in the stirrup of resolution and my hands on the reins of confidence in God, and marched against Sultan Ibrahim . . . whose army in the field was said to amount to a hundred thousand men and who . . . had nearly a thousand elephants.* ❞

Although greatly outnumbered, Babur was victo- rious. Babur's gunpowder weapons and mounted warriors made up for the difference in numbers.

The following year Babur defeated a much larger army, commanded by the Rajput noble- man Rana Sanga, at the battle of Khanua. These two battles won Babur a vast empire in northern India, but for the rest of his life he longed for his home in Central Asia. He believed that India could never compare to his homeland.

Fittingly, after Babur died in 1530 his body was moved from Agra, the Mughal capital, to Kabul in Afghanistan, in the Central Asian landscape that he loved.

After suffering repeated defeats against the Uzbeks in Central Asia, Babur turned to India, where he defeated the Sultan of Delhi and founded the Mughal Empire.

The Growth of the Mughal Empire

The task of strengthening Babur's conquests fell to his descendants. His son Humayun did not have Babur's ambition—he was more interested in entertainment than in expanding his empire. Humayun even lost the throne temporarily to an Afghan general and his descendants, but regained it in 1555. The following year Humayun died and was succeeded by his 13-year-old son, Akbar.

Akbar's consolidation of power. Until Akbar was 20 years old, the government was run by his loyal guardian, Bayram Khan, and then by his nurse, Maham Anaga. In 1562 Akbar took control of the government. Although he experienced strong mood swings and lived with epilepsy, he proved to be a ruler of the highest quality.

Akbar recognized that Indian society was diverse, and used every means possible to keep control of the empire. For example, he married a Rajput princess in an effort to gain the loyalty of her father, the ruler of a small Indian state. He also took the sons of some Indian rulers as "cadets" in his service—in effect as hostages. At the same time, Akbar abolished taxes on Hindu pilgrims traveling to holy shrines and the poll tax, which all non-Muslims had to pay.

Akbar not only won support through diplomacy and generosity, but also through force. By 1570 he had crushed all remaining resistance in the Rajput kingdoms, and by the end of his reign in 1605, Akbar had conquered all of northern India and much of the central region. In fact, his control over northern India was stronger than the Mauryans' had been.

In part, this strength came from Akbar's improvement of the tax system. Akbar introduced

The Mughal Empire, 1526–1707

Jeweled Empire From Central Asia, the Turkish Mughals blazed south across the Hindu Kush to build a wealthy empire in India.

? Region What mountain chains bordered the Mughal Empire to the north?

a standard tax assessment system based on the average a village might produce over a 10-year period. In times of bad harvest his central government did not try to collect taxes, while in times of good harvest, the villages got to keep whatever they produced above the designated tax level.

To oversee this new tax system, Akbar also established the ***mansabdari* system**—a hierarchy of salaried imperial military officials. Most were foreigners, but about one third were Indian Muslims and Hindus. While this system relied on foreigners, it also brought many talented Indians into Akbar's service. Thus, the *mansabdari* system performed the same function for the Mughals that the *devshirme* system did for the Ottomans.

Religious policy. Akbar hoped to unify his people through a tolerant religious policy. Although illiterate, Akbar had an inquisitive

In his final years as Mughal emperor, Akbar was embroiled in a struggle for power with his eldest son, Jahangir. While Akbar was on a military campaign in 1601, Jahangir claimed the throne for himself. In response, Akbar dispatched an agent to dispose of his rebellious son, but Jahangir had the agent murdered before he could fulfill his mission. Akbar regained power briefly before he died in 1605, apparently poisoned by his son. Jahangir then assumed complete rule of the empire.

Critical Thinking Ask students what effect a power struggle between father and son might have on a country.

ANSWER: Students might suggest that these power struggles could confuse people about who was leading the country, cause instability, and also might lead to civil war.

R **RESOURCE ACTIVITY**

READINGS IN WORLD HISTORY
Reading 13.3
A Day in the Life of a Mughal Emperor

Have students read the excerpt from the British writer Laurence Binyon. Then have them complete the questions.

Level 1

mind, and he turned to the *ulama*, or religious scholars, for answers to his questions about life and death. He established a religious assembly hall to hold discussions about Islam. Dissatisfied with the answers he received from the *ulama*, Akbar consulted other religious leaders. After much consideration, he began to believe that no single religion, including Islam, held all of the answers.

Gradually, Akbar began to see himself as a divine ruler. First, he issued a decree declaring himself the final judge of Islamic law. Next, he asserted that he was God's representative on Earth; therefore he ruled over all people, regardless of religion. Thus, he was above Islamic law and the laws of all other religions.

In 1581 Akbar established a creed called the "**Divine Faith**," with the motto *Allahu Akbar*, which meant either "God is great" or "Akbar is God," depending on whether the person using it was a devout Muslim or an imperial Mughal. The Divine Faith blended ideas and practices from Islam, Hinduism, Jainism, Christianity, and other religions, while many of its rituals were Sufi in origin. It attracted few followers beyond the imperial court, however, and brought growing opposition from conservative Muslims. In 1581 Muslim leaders backed a revolt against Akbar but he easily crushed it.

Cultural achievements. During Akbar's reign, Persian culture greatly influenced life at the Mughal court. Persian was the language of the court, and Persian styles of dress, decor, and manners were adopted by the aristocracy. Akbar also encouraged the development of literature in the Hindi and Urdu languages. By appointing Raja Birbal as the court poet for Hindi, Akbar encouraged educated men to study this language, which would eventually become one of the national languages of India. Akbar also encouraged the translation of popular classics, such as the *Ramayana*.

▲ The Gate of Victory, the southern entrance to the mosque in Fatehpur Sikri, is one of India's greatest architectural works.

Architecture during Akbar's reign demonstrated a blending of Persian, Islamic, and Hindu styles. A good example of this is the city of Fatehpur Sikri, which Akbar built in 1571. Its huge mosque and beautiful gateway are ranked among the best of Mughal creations. The city was abandoned in 1585, perhaps because of an inadequate water supply, or because it was not easily defensible, but it remains today as a symbol of Akbar's energetic spirit.

While expanding his empire through military force, Akbar tried to establish unity within the empire through tax reforms and religious tolerance.

The Height of Mughal Power

In the 1600s Mughal emperors expanded the empire to its greatest extent and focused on building lavish monuments in the capital and other major cities. The height of this productive period, which was by no means peaceful, began with the accession of Akbar's rebellious son Jahangir to the Mughal throne.

Jahangir. Almost immediately after gaining the throne, Jahangir faced a revolt by his own son, Khusrau. After putting down the revolt, Jahangir blinded Khusrau and executed the Sikh (SEEK) guru, or religious leader, who had supported Khusrau in the rebellion. (The Sikhs were a religious group that believed in a combination of Islamic and Hindu ideas.) This execution greatly angered the Sikh community and created hostilities between Sikhs and Muslims.

Throughout his reign Jahangir presided over a culture in which the blending of Persian and Indian traditions led to a burst of artistic creativity. Jahangir's interest in gardens and natural beauty inspired artists to favor a naturalistic style of painting. Persian artists such as Aqa Rida and Mansur, and Indian artists such as Govardhan and Manohar painted for the emperor. Jahangir also encouraged development of literature and historical writing and wrote an autobiography.

As his reign progressed, Jahangir's health weakened because of asthma and other illnesses. His wife, Nur Jahan, ruled in his place. An educated, charming, and politically outspoken woman, Nur Jahan skillfully managed the state for more than a decade. At the height of her power, she minted coins bearing her name, demonstrating that she was the true ruler of India. Nur Jahan ruled until Jahangir's death in 1627. Upon hearing of Jahangir's death, his son Shah Jahan rushed back to Agra from northern battlefields and seized the throne from Nur Jahan.

Shah Jahan. During his 30-year reign Shah Jahan was consumed with building enormous monuments, but most of all, he was devoted to his wife, Mumtaz Mahal. When she died in 1631 while giving birth to their fourteenth child, Shah Jahan was

▲ Shah Jahan and one of his sons ride horses in a 1615 painting by Manohar.

deeply depressed. He is said to have wailed, "Empire has no sweetness, life itself has no relish left for me now." Mumtaz Mahal was buried in Agra, where Shah Jahan built the great **Taj Mahal** to hold her tomb. Designed by Persian architects, the Taj Mahal took 20,000 workers more than 20 years to complete.

Shah Jahan was an extremely vigorous ruler. He put down rebellions, built a monumental new capital at Delhi, and conquered new territories in the Deccan. He also launched an unsuccessful attempt to recapture the old Mughal homeland in Central Asia.

Shah Jahan's great Peacock Throne was the greatest symbol of Mughal splendor. The throne was heavily encrusted with gold and the largest diamonds, emeralds, and other precious gems to be had in the empire. The beauty of the dazzling gardens, shimmering marble monuments, and glittering gems of Shah Jahan's capital was

▲ Shah Jahan brought workers and materials from all over India and Central Asia to build the Taj Mahal.

IDENTIFY

For significance, see the following pages:

Babur (p. 344)
Akbar (p. 345)
mansabdari system
(p. 345)
Divine Faith (p. 346)
Jahangir (p. 346)
Nur Jahan (p. 347)
Shah Jahan (p. 347)
Taj Mahal (p. 347)
Aurangzeb (p. 348)

LOCATE

For locations, see the map on p. 345.

1. Akbar's methods included military force, intermarriage, an improved tax system, religious tolerance, and a blending of Persian, Islamic, and Hindu traditions.
2. Jahangir—encouraged painting, literature, and historical writing; Shah Jahan—built monuments and capital at Delhi, conquered territory; Aurangzeb—expanded empire, compiled Islamic law
3. The Uzbeks kept Babur out of Central Asia, but the Sultanate of Delhi was in decline and was defeated by Babur's military advance.
4. Essays should focus on the ideas that the *mansabdari* system relied on Indian Muslims and Hindus and that architecture and art sprang from this blend of culture.
5. He persecuted, taxed, and placed restrictions on religious minorities, provoking rebellion. Enemies could join these persecuted groups to gain support and win territory.

348

captured by a Persian verse carved on the walls of Shah Jahan's palace in Delhi. The verse read: "If there be Paradise on earth, It is Here, It is Here, It is Here!"

The cost of this luxurious lifestyle and of Shah Jahan's military misadventures were paid for by the backbreaking labor of India's peasantry. Shah Jahan demanded half of all crops grown in his empire and many people suffered under this burden.

Aurangzeb. When Shah Jahan fell ill, his sons fought each other to succeed him. His son Aurangzeb triumphed in 1658. He ruthlessly killed his rival older brother, then delivered his head in a box to the ill Shah Jahan, whom Aurangzeb had imprisoned in the Agra fortress. Three years later Aurangzeb executed his younger brother as well, to eliminate competition for the throne. Aurangzeb then came to the Mughal throne as Alamgir, or "World Conqueror."

A devout Sunni Muslim, Aurangzeb reversed the tolerant religious policies of Akbar. Hoping to win the favor of the *ulama*, he appointed a censor of public morals and insisted on strict observance of the *shari'ah*, the holy law of Islam. He restored the poll tax on Hindus, and refused to grant permission to build new Hindu temples. He persecuted the Shi'ah and Sufis, and when crowds gathered to protest his policies, Aurangzeb sent imperial elephants to crush them.

These religious restrictions and increased taxes led many peasants to rebel. One subject wrote to the emperor:

66 *Your subjects are trampled underfoot; every province of your Empire is impoverished. . . . If Your Majesty places any faith in those books by distinction called divine, you will be there instructed that God is the God of all mankind, not the God of Mussalmans [Muslims] alone.* 99

In the last half of the 1600s, violent revolt occurred throughout much of the empire as a result of Aurangzeb's harsh measures.

Aurangzeb had expanded the Mughal Empire to its largest extent. He also followed Islamic morals in his personal life, compiled a digest of Islamic law, and promoted Islamic scholarship. Even on his deathbed, however, he remained uncertain whether his actions would please his God. As he lay dying in 1707, Aurangzeb confessed to one of his sons, "I have sinned terribly, and I do not know what punishment awaits me."

Although challenged by rebellious relatives, the Mughal emperors of the 1600s built beautiful monuments in many cities and expanded the empire to its greatest power.

SECTION 3 REVIEW

IDENTIFY and explain the significance of the following:
Babur
Akbar
mansabdari system
Divine Faith
Jahangir
Nur Jahan
Shah Jahan
Taj Mahal
Aurangzeb

LOCATE and explain the importance of the following:
Samarkand

Panipat
Delhi
Agra

1. **Main Idea** What methods did Akbar use to unify his empire?
2. **Main Idea** How did Jahangir, Shah Jahan, and Aurangzeb improve the Mughal Empire during the 1600s?
3. **War and Diplomacy** What conditions made it easier for Babur to build an empire

in India rather than in Central Asia?
4. **Writing to Explain** Write a short essay explaining why the Mughal Empire's success depended so heavily on the blending of Islamic and Hindu cultures.
5. **Hypothesizing** How did Aurangzeb's policies harm the Mughal Empire? What problems might Aurangzeb's policies have caused for the empire with respect to outside enemies?

Neo-Confucian China

- What did Hongwu accomplish?
- Why did the Ming withdraw from sea trade?
- How did the Ming affect China's economy and society?
- How did the Ming dynasty collapse?

After 89 years of Mongol rule, the new Ming dynasty restored peace and stability to China by reimposing what it considered the country's traditional values and policies. Although at first this included expanding China's sea power and overseas trade, the Ming emperors eventually withdrew from the sea and focused their attention inward. The Ming created a stable political and social order that remained the foundation of Chinese life for nearly 300 years after the fall of their dynasty.

Enamel water sprinkler from the Ming dynasty

Foundation of the Ming Dynasty

In 1368 a new Chinese leader, Zhu Yuanzhang (JOO YOO-en-JAHNG), emerged to overthrow the Yuan dynasty of the Mongols. A former beggar, Buddhist monk, and bandit, Zhu Yuanzhang brought huge numbers of people together to drive out the Mongols. He ascended the imperial throne in Nanjing as the Hongwu, or "Vastly Martial" emperor, and named his dynasty the Ming, or "Brilliant," dynasty.

China under the Hongwu emperor. The Hongwu emperor spent the next 15 years reuniting China. Eventually, he firmly secured his rule in all of China. States around China's borders were once again forced to acknowledge the authority of the emperor and their own status as subjects of China.

By the time that he had driven out the Mongols, Hongwu had gained tremendous personal power, which he used freely. When, for example, he discovered in 1380 that his prime minister was plotting against him, the emperor ordered the man beheaded—along with his family and everyone associated with them, which over time amounted to thousands of people.

Hongwu used the treachery of his prime minister as an excuse to abolish many senior government positions, including that of prime minister. This made the emperor's power personal and direct. Under an energetic leader like Hongwu, this expansion of power worked efficiently.

Hongwu also eventually revived the civil-service examination system, bringing scholars back into government. Officials could obtain jobs in two ways: by passing the rigorous Imperial University exams, or by passing the civil-service exams. While only the sons of officials could attend the Imperial University, anyone could take the civil-service examinations. By training his new officials to conform in their thinking, Hongwu ensured that his will would not be questioned.

Warfare with the Mongols had severely damaged both the land and the economies of the provinces. Hongwu understood that what the provinces needed most was reconstruction and more money. He planted trees for erosion control

Across the Curriculum: Literature

Some men who did not advance through the university or civil-service examination system turned to writing popular dramas and stories. Feng Meng-lung was one such author. His literary works, which were popular among the educated elite and the working classes, covered a broad range of subjects. According to one critic: "Their range includes: quasi-historical tales of kings and generals, faithful friends and filial sons; romantic yarns of strange lands and people's supernatural stories of marvels and prodigies, spirits and ghosts, Buddhist monks and Daoist immortals: realistic stories of scandals in monastic establishments; daring exploits of brigands and thieves; murders, lawsuits, and court trials; domestic tragedies and bloody revenges; social comedies and family reunions."

Critical Thinking Ask students to name contemporary works which contain a similar range of elements.

ANSWER: Answers will vary. Students might mention soap operas, television mini-series, and popular novels.

The Ming Empire, 1424

The Brilliant Dynasty At its height, the Ming dynasty created an elegant new capital city and sent treasure-laden ships to foreign lands.

? **Place** What waterway linked Nanjing to Beijing?

and cut land taxes. He repaired water control projects, such as dams and dikes. In 1395, for example, workers completed more than 40,000 such projects.

Government weakness. Without experienced, upper-level government officials, later emperors were often overwhelmed with the work of government. They began to rely more heavily on **eunuchs**, special male servants of the emperor's personal household. Eventually, there were 70,000 eunuchs carrying out government business.

With the eunuchs managing the upper levels of government, inefficiency and corruption became commonplace. This paralysis at the top allowed the traditional Confucian scholar-gentry to return to power in the lower levels of government. Matteo Ricci, an Italian missionary to China in the late 1500s, described the role of the scholar-gentry:

> "[T]he entire kingdom is administered by the Order of the Learned, commonly known as The Philosophers. . . . The army, both officers and soldiers, hold them in high respect and show them the promptest obedience and deference [respect], and not infrequently the military are disciplined by them as a schoolboy might be punished by his master."

Allowing the scholar-gentry so much power, however, was ultimately disastrous for China. The philosophy of the Chinese scholar-officials focused on the past and discouraged change. This emphasis revived interest in ancient texts, but it stalled improvements.

After overthrowing the Mongols, Hongwu expanded his power while rebuilding the provinces and firmly establishing neo-Confucian doctrine in Ming government.

Building and Expanding the Ming Empire

Ming China continued to grow and prosper after Hongwu's death in 1398. Yongle, the third Ming emperor, fostered the growth of the navy, and Chinese voyagers conducted diplomatic and trade missions with Southeast Asia and India.

Early Ming sea power. Between 1405 and 1433 the Chinese admiral Zheng He, a Muslim eunuch of the imperial court, undertook seven naval expeditions. The first involved a fleet of 317 ships, 62 of which were huge "treasure-ships" that could carry as many as 500 men. These ships carried a combined staff of 70 eunuchs, 180 physicians, 300 military officers, and about 27,000 men. There were even 5 official astrologers.

On his first three voyages, Zheng He visited Southeast Asia and India. On the fourth visit he went as far as Hormuz, and on the last three the fleets sailed along the East African coast. These were diplomatic and trade missions, not voyages of discovery.

Zheng He established relations with many countries, convincing some of them to become tributaries of the Ming emperor. "Those who refused submission," wrote a historian, "they [the

Chinese] over-awed by a show of armed might." Zheng He's voyages opened up official trade, exchanging beautiful silks and porcelain for other luxury items for the emperor and his court. Zheng He also gathered considerable geographical information and brought back items of curiosity, such as a giraffe, for the emperor's amusement.

The new capital. In 1421 Emperor Yongle moved the capital city from Nanjing to Beijing. Yongle's new capital was built according to the grid pattern of the classical Chinese city, in which the city was divided into distinct quarters.

At the center of the city was the imperial palace, called the **Forbidden City**, which was enclosed by a moat and a high wall. The entryway to the Forbidden City was the Meridian Gate, which faced Tiananmen Square. Monumental in size and painted in vivid red, the Meridian Gate is considered by many to be among the finest works of Chinese architecture.

Near the Forbidden City were beautiful fields, temples, and pavilions for the enjoyment of the emperor. Sacrificial altars were also nearby for the emperor to perform important sacred rituals. The construction of this impressive new capital and the extensive sea voyages showed the prosperity that Ming China had achieved after the devastation left behind by the Mongols.

Turning inward. After the death of Zheng He in 1433, China gradually turned away from the sea. These voyages had been enormously expensive, and the scholar-gentry opposed them because they had greatly increased the importance of Zheng He and the eunuchs. Confucian officials even burned the records of Zheng He's expeditions to prevent them from being repeated.

In addition, a revival of Mongol power forced the emperors to focus their attention on the northern frontier, rather than on diplomacy and trade. To protect against Mongol invasion, emperors continued to build the network of walls with watchtowers that had been started under the Qin. These walls, however, which together are now known as the Great Wall of China, proved to be utterly futile in keeping out invaders.

After sponsoring many sea voyages, Ming emperors pulled away from the sea to save money, satisfy the scholar-gentry, and focus on preventing Mongol attacks.

THROUGH OTHERS' EYES

A Chinese View of Mecca

In 1432 Zheng He, the grand eunuch of the imperial Chinese court, sailed with a vast fleet of "treasure-ships" under orders to "go to the various foreign countries in the Western Ocean [the Indian Ocean] to read out the imperial commands and to bestow [give] rewards." Touching shore at Jidda, a port on the Red Sea, Zheng He, himself a Muslim, traveled to Mecca. The expedition's historian, Ma Huan, described the scene:

❝From Jidda you go west, and after traveling for one day you reach the city where the king resides; it is named the capital city of Mecca. . . . The people of this country are stalwart [strong] and fine-looking, and their limbs and faces are of a very dark purple colour. The menfolk bind up their heads; they wear long garments; and on their feet they put leather shoes. The women all wear a covering over their heads, and you cannot see their faces. They speak the A-la-pi [Arabic] language. The law of the country prohibits wine-drinking. The customs of the people are pacific [peaceful] and admirable.❞

✺ Ming Society and Economy

Under the early Ming emperors, China flourished. Ming emperors helped the areas that had suffered under the Mongol conquest by providing free seeds, oxen, and land. Soon the population began to grow again—from about 80 million people in the mid-1300s to about 160 million in the 1600s.

As the Chinese population increased, so did cities and trade. Rice had to be transported from the fields to Beijing and other growing cities. The government expanded the internal canal system, particularly since Japanese pirates made sea transportation difficult. Urban growth also encouraged the production of luxury goods, such

352

as silks and porcelain. Enormous quantities of porcelain were produced for the imperial court.

Despite the growth of cities, however, most Chinese people continued to live in villages, working as farmers. Although emperors tried to improve the conditions of the peasantry, the aristocracy began expanding their landholdings at the expense of the peasants, turning much of the peasantry into tenant farmers.

Although the Chinese economy expanded under the Ming dynasty, conditions improved little for most peasants.

The Fall of the Ming Dynasty

By about the early 1600s the Ming dynasty was showing signs of weakness. Emperors began to ignore government affairs, and without their attention many important tasks, such as maintaining the Grand Canal, remained undone. At the same time, the power of the Manchu, a forest-dwelling people from Manchuria, north of China's border, also began to grow.

▲ Ivory statue of a Daoist figure carved during the Ming dynasty

While some Ming emperors bought peace with large payments of tribute, soon the Manchu wanted more.

Under their leader, Nurhachi, the warriors of Manchuria united and established a powerful empire on China's northern frontier. After taking all of the Ming's lands northeast of the Great Wall and making Korea a vassal state, Abahai (AH-BAH-HY), Nurhachi's son and successor, proclaimed the Qing (CHING), or "Pure," dynasty in 1636.

Meanwhile, famine, epidemics, and rebellions further weakened Ming control. In 1644 the Qing took advantage of this disorder and swept into Beijing, establishing their seven-year-old king as the first Qing emperor. It took many years for the Manchu to completely subdue China, however. Resistance long remained active in southern China, where secret societies soon emerged, dedicated to restoring the rightful Ming heir. Nevertheless, the new Qing dynasty soon consolidated its control and ruled China until 1911 as the last of the imperial dynasties.

The Manchu took advantage of the weakness of the Ming central government, captured Beijing, and began their takeover of China.

SECTION 4 REVIEW

IDENTIFY and explain the significance of the following:
   Hongwu
   eunuchs
   Yongle
   Zheng He
   Forbidden City
   Nurhachi

LOCATE and explain the importance of the following:
   Nanjing

Beijing
Manchuria

1. *Main Idea* How did Hongwu transform China after he became emperor?
2. *Main Idea* How did the Ming dynasty improve China's economy? What was the effect on Chinese society?
3. *Cross-cultural Interaction* Why did the Ming pull away

from contact with other Asian cultures?
4. *Writing to Explain* Imagine that you are an official in the Ming court. Write a letter to your family explaining why the dynasty is collapsing.
5. *Identify Cause and Effect* Why were the Ming emperors unable to sustain their empire once the Manchu united?

State-Building in Africa

FOCUS

- Why did the East African city-states develop a mixed culture?
- What were some characteristics of the Mutapa and Mali empires?
- Why did the Songhay Empire decline in the late 1500s?

While Muslim rulers in Southwest Asia were building and expanding empires, similar activities were taking place in Africa. The small Swahili city-states of East Africa gained great cultural diversity through trade, while farther south the Shona established a magnificent capital whose ruins still awe many visitors. The Mali Empire grew so wealthy that it dazzled the Muslim world, while the Songhay Empire struggled to surpass Mali. Cross-cultural contacts increased as Africans traded and built their empires.

Ruins at Great Zimbabwe

The Swahili States

By the late 1100s a new society that combined elements of African, Asian, and Islamic cultures had begun to emerge along the East African coast. Many Arabian and Persian Muslims settled along the coast, while Indonesians settled on the island of Madagascar. As these groups began to intermingle with the African population, they formed a new society that became known as **Swahili**.

Trade across the Indian Ocean dominated the communities that the Swahili formed along the coast. The cities of Mogadishu, Mombasa, Kilwa, and Sofala all enjoyed a thriving trade, which reached its peak in the 1300s and 1400s. Many of the cities produced specialized goods for export. For example, Sofala produced cotton goods for the African interior trade, as described by a traveler:

> **❝** In this same Sofala now of late they make great store of cotton and weave it, and from it they make much white cloth, and as they know not how to dye it, or have not the needful dyes, they take the Cambay cloths [from northwest India], blue or otherwise colored, and unravel them and make them up again, so that it becomes a new thing. With this thread and their own white [cloth] they make much colored cloth, and from it they gain much gold. **❞**

*A*s part of the great Indian Ocean trading network, the Swahili city-states of the East African coast became the center of a dynamic cross-cultural exchange.

The Mutapa Empire

The growing wealth of the overseas trade in African goods also stimulated developments in the Central African interior. There, around the end of the 900s, numerous Bantu-speaking, pastoral peoples had begun to develop small kingdoms. By the 1300s the Shona people had arrived in the region north of the Limpopo

SECTION 5

CORE LESSON PLAN
See pages 329K and 329L for Lesson Plan 13.5.

MULTIMEDIA PRESENTATION STRATEGY

VISUAL RESOURCES
Everyday Life 13
Great Zimbabwe

Show the transparency and share the information from Everyday Life Fact Sheet 13. Then have students complete the accompanying worksheet.

Level 2

R RESOURCE ACTIVITY

GLOBAL HISTORY RESOURCE CENTER
Image: *Bronze Portrait of an African Ruler*

Show students the bronze and ask them to think about what the artist was trying to say about this ruler through his art. Then have students synthesize this information and write an imaginary biography of this ruler.

Level 2

River, where they began to build their kingdom of Great Zimbabwe.

In the 1400s King Mutota brought much of the territory surrounding the Kingdom of Great Zimbabwe under his control, which earned him the title **Mwene Mutapa**, or "master soldier." His successors took the same title, and by the end of the 1400s, the Mwene Mutapa controlled the entire region between the Zambezi and Limpopo Rivers, from the coast to the edges of the Kalahari Desert.

The Shona believed that the Mwene Mutapa was the only one who could communicate with the spirits who brought rain to their dry country. Therefore, the Mwene Mutapa held complete religious authority. His reign was symbolized by a royal fire, which burned continuously. When a king died, his fire was extinguished, and another was lit for the new king.

The Empire of Mali

Meanwhile, in West Africa, the collapse of Ghana had left several small kingdoms constantly at war with one another. Around 1200 the Malinke people of the kingdom of Kangaba, who had long been part of the Ghanaian Empire, began to reunite the region. Kangaba had a large population and a thriving agricultural economy. The Malinke soon developed the Mali Empire, which was even more powerful than Ghana.

After 1240 a Malinke ruler named Sundiata established his capital at Niani, on the upper reaches of the Niger River. He gained control of the gold-producing regions once controlled by Ghana. This made Mali immensely important to traders and increased the power of the Mali Empire.

Mansa Musa. Mali reached the height of its power under Mansa ("Emperor") Musa in the early 1300s. Organizing a powerful army, Mansa Musa set out to conquer the old Ghanaian territories and more. After conquering a territory nearly twice the size of Ghana and gaining control of the north-south trans-Saharan trade, Mansa Musa became fabulously wealthy.

Like Ghana before it, the Mali Empire was ruled by a warrior elite, which was sustained by local farmers and traders. The emperor ruled the center of the empire personally, appointing governors to rule the provinces. To prevent potential rivals among the governors, Mansa Musa appointed his own family members as provincial governors.

Unlike his predecessors, Mansa Musa became a devout Muslim. Although most of the Malinke remained true to their traditional religion, Islamic practices became more influential in the empire after the emperor and the court converted to Islam. In 1324 Mansa Musa displayed the wealth and power of his empire when he made a pilgrimage

Trading Kingdoms of Africa, c. 1230–1591

Rise and Fall of Empires Traders brought great wealth to the cities along the east coast of Africa and to the trans-Saharan trading empires of Mali and Songhay.

? **Location** What was the closest port city to Great Zimbabwe?

History THROUGH THE ARTS

Royal West African Figure

Many people consider sculpture to be the most beautiful of Africa's arts. Some of the greatest masterpieces of African sculpture come from the city of Ife (EE-fay) in Nigeria. Archaeologists have not had an easy time finding the lost treasures of Ife because the site is now a bustling metropolis. Ancient religious sites are still used for worship by people in Ife today, also making excavations there difficult.

The various sculptures recovered have led archaeologists to believe that between the 1000s and the 1100s, the people of Ife began making bronze sculptures from wax molds. Before, sculpture had primarily been in wood. The new technique in sculpture production meant that artists could now make very accurate figures with highly detailed features.

The figure shown here is of a legendary divine king of Ife. The figure reflects the style called naturalism, because it tries to

This bronze statue shows the great skill of the artists of Ife.

show the king with natural human features, rather than imaginary characteristics of ideal human beauty. This early style of African sculpture became an important influence for other African peoples. For example, the kingdom of Benin in the 1400s and 1500s improved on the techniques of casting sculptures and produced still more detailed works. Even today, realistic human figures continue to be a popular theme of African sculpture.

Thinking About Art
What features of the figure indicate that it is a work of the naturalistic style?

to Mecca. Arriving in Cairo with some 80,000 attendants carrying gold bars and sacks of gold dust, he dazzled the people of Egypt. He brought so much gold with him that the value of gold in Cairo fell sharply after his visit. Twelve years later an Egyptian historian wrote that he believed the economy still suffered from the effects of Mansa Musa's visit.

The spread of Islam. When Mansa Musa returned to Mali, he brought with him Islamic scholars, architects, and legal experts to transform Mali's cities into centers of learning. He built a university at Timbuktu that attracted students from throughout the Muslim world. He also built mosques in the larger cities, from which Islam spread extensively throughout the empire.

As Islam spread through the support of the Malian rulers, Muslim traders and merchants began to travel more widely in the empire. Many of these Muslims married African women and thus carried Islam even farther among the local African populations. Such cross-cultural intermingling soon gave Mali a reputation for both tolerance and justice. In the mid-1300s a Muslim traveler named Ibn Battuta noted:

> 66 *[The Malians] are seldom unjust, and have a greater horror of injustice than other people. Their sultan shows no mercy to anyone who is guilty of the least act of it. There is complete security in their country. Neither traveler nor inhabitant in it has anything to fear from robbers or men of violence.* 99

The fall of Mali. Although Mansa Musa proved to be an impressive empire-builder, he also sowed the seeds of his empire's destruction by not

SECTION 5 REVIEW ANSWERS

IDENTIFY
For significance, see the following pages:
Swahili (p. 353)
Mwene Mutapa (p. 354)
Mansa Musa (p. 354)
Askia the Great (p. 356)

LOCATE
For locations, see the map on p. 354.

1. similar—wealthy and powerful; different—Mutapans maintained indigenous religion, Mali leaders eventually converted to Islam and spread the religion
2. Fighting among subject peoples and powerful neighboring enemies led to the Songhay decline.
3. Trade and resulting settlement of Arabian and Persian Muslims and Indonesians produced a blend of African, Asian, and Islamic cultures.
4. Accounts should include the ideas that the Mwene Mutapa was a master soldier who conquered and held a large empire and was the only person who supposedly could speak with spirits.
5. The Mutapa Empire developed because of trade. The Mali Empire became wealthy after conquering gold-producing territory and territory that controlled north-south trade. Mali also became a great Islamic cultural center. The Songhay Empire grew because it controlled major trade routes and fertile land.

providing a plan for succession to the throne. After his death, members of the royal court fought one another for control of the empire, weakening central authority. By the late 1400s the empire of Mali broke apart, and the city of Gao became the center of a new empire called the Songhay.

Mutapa and Mali were wealthy and powerful African empires, and Mali became a center for the spread of Islam in West Africa.

✴ The Songhay Empire

Founded in 1464 by Sunni Ali, the kingdom of Songhay grew to be a larger empire than Mali. It controlled major trade routes and the fertile lands along the Niger River.

The most prominent king of the Songhay Empire was Muhammed Touré, also known as Askia the Great. After making a pilgrimage to Mecca in 1495, he turned his attention to empire-building. He conquered all of the land that had belonged to Mali and extended Songhay's borders eastward to Hausaland.

Askia the Great fostered an Islamic culture in his empire. Like Mansa Musa, he hired Islamic scholars and encouraged a cultural revival. Under Askia's rule Timbuktu became a great commercial center. European goods were in much demand, as were goods from as far away as India and China. Such items were brought by a growing number of merchants—not only Arabs, but also Jews, Italians, and many others.

The slave trade was also an important factor in the economy. Askia the Great increased the slave supply with his constant wars of expansion. Slaves were bought and sold in the market at Gao, with traders buying slaves to sell in Egypt, Turkey, and other areas of Southwest Asia.

Timbuktu was also a thriving cultural center, particularly because of its university. Leo Africanus, a Muslim traveler around 1500, was greatly impressed with this center of learning. He wrote:

❝ *Here are great numbers of religious teachers, judges, scholars and other learned persons, who are bountifully maintained at the king's expense. Here too are brought various manuscripts or written books from Barbary, which are sold for more money than any other merchandise.* ❞

Despite this prosperity, however, problems existed. As the Tuareg, Fulani, Malinke, and other subject peoples often fought among themselves, the Songhay Empire began to experience a steady decline after the reign of Askia the Great. The empire also had many powerful neighbors. In 1591 an army from Morocco, armed with firearms, crushed the Songhay troops in the battle of Tondibi, spelling the end of the empire.

Despite its wealth, the Songhay Empire finally declined due to internal conflict and external enemies.

SECTION 5 REVIEW

IDENTIFY and explain the significance of the following:
Swahili
Mwene Mutapa
Mansa Musa
Askia the Great

LOCATE and explain the importance of the following:
Sofala
Limpopo River
Zambezi River
Niger River

1. **Main Idea** How were the Mutapa and Mali empires similar? How were they different?
2. **Main Idea** What led to the decline of the Songhay Empire in the 1500s?
3. **Cross-cultural Interaction** How did the East African Swahili states represent a blend of several cultures?
4. **Writing to Explain** Imagine that you are a foreign traveler in Africa during the time of the Mutapa Empire. Write a brief account explaining the importance of the Mwene Mutapa to the empire.
5. **Synthesizing** What role did the spread of ideas and trade play in the development of empires in Africa from the 1300s to the 1500s?

Review

On a separate sheet of paper, complete the following exercises:

WRITING A SUMMARY

Using the essential points in the text, write a brief summary of the chapter.

REVIEWING TERMS

From the following list, choose the term that correctly matches the definition:

devshirme   kizilbash
Divine Faith   millet
Forbidden City   Swahili

1. new society formed from a blending of African, Asian, and Islamic cultures
2. Ottoman administrative system that allowed subjects to follow their own religious law and regulate their own internal affairs
3. creed established by Akbar that blended ideas and practices from different religions
4. imperial palace in the heart of Beijing, built during the reign of Yongle
5. Ottoman system in which the strongest Christian boys were taken from their families, converted to Islam, and trained for life service to the sultan

REVIEWING CHRONOLOGY

List the following events in their correct chronological order.

1. Akbar becomes ruler of the Mughal Empire in India.
2. Mehmet II leads the Ottomans in the conquest of Constantinople.
3. Zhu Yuanzhang overthrows the Mongols in China.
4. The Ottoman navy defeats the Habsburgs at the battle of Préveza.
5. Sundiata founds the Mali Empire.

UNDERSTANDING THE MAIN IDEA

1. How were the Ottomans able to maintain their vast and multiethnic empire?
2. What were the consequences of the Safavids' adoption of Shi'ism as the state religion of Persia?
3. How did Akbar try to unify the Mughal Empire?
4. What did Hongwu accomplish as ruler of the Ming dynasty?
5. How did the Swahili states of East Africa help spread goods and ideas?

THINKING CRITICALLY

1. **Comparing** In what ways were the methods used by the Ottomans, Safavids, and Mughals to consolidate power in multiethnic empires similar?
2. **Analyzing** What benefits did the Safavids gain by championing the cause of Shi'ah Islam? What were the drawbacks of this policy?

Building Your Portfolio

Complete the following activities individually or in groups.

1. **Architecture** Imagine that you (and your coworkers) are architects hired by the rulers of either the Ottoman, Safavid Mughal, Ming, Mutapa, or Malian empires to plan the construction of a great city or monument. You could choose any number of structures to plan, such as the Taj Mahal or the Forbidden City. Your plan should include sketches and illustrations of the structure along with a map showing where the site is located. You should also create a narrative presentation describing the details of your structure. You may also wish to create a scale model of all or part of the structure you are planning.
2. **Politics and Social Relations** Imagine that you are a boy who has been selected for training in the devshirme system in the Ottoman Empire. Keep a journal describing your experiences. Be sure to include journal entries about the culture from which you came, your first moments in the system, your training, your job responsibilities, and your lifestyle once your training has been completed.

CHAPTER 13 REVIEW ANSWERS

WRITING A SUMMARY
See essential points in the text.

REVIEWING TERMS
1. Swahili
2. millet
3. Divine Faith
4. Forbidden City
5. devshirme

REVIEWING CHRONOLOGY
5, 3, 2, 4, 1

UNDERSTANDING THE MAIN IDEA
1. The Ottomans relied on continuing conquests and a strong central government.
2. Safavids gained support from enemies of Sunni Muslim states and made enemies of Sunni rivals.
3. Akbar used force, intermarriage, religious tolerance, and a blending of Persian, Islamic, and Hindu traditions to unify the Mughal Empire.
4. Hongwu revived traditional values, expanded the empire, and protected it from the Mongols.
5. The Swahili spread goods and ideas by being at the center of a great Indian Ocean trading network.

THINKING CRITICALLY
1. All three empires had strong leaders and centralized states. They also used new military technology and slave troops. In addition, the empires blended various cultural traditions.
2. benefits—led to unique identity and national culture and distinguished them from Sunni rivals; drawbacks—led to rivalry and persecution between the two branches of Islam

Beginnings of the Modern World

Chapter 14
Renaissance and Reformation

Religious beliefs might change as people are exposed to new ideas from outside cultures, or religious leaders may put forward new interpretations of religious texts.

Chapter 15
A New Worldview in Europe

As people begin to seek answers about the world around them, they might begin to question their long-standing beliefs. They might come up with new ideas about the role of individuals and the ideal forms of society. After forming these new ideas, they might try to rebuild their society and government to reflect their newfound beliefs.

Unit 4
Beginnings of the Modern World 1300–1815

Chapter 14
Renaissance and Reformation 1300–1650

After facing famine, plague, and warfare, European civilization changed tremendously. As trade increased, Europeans rediscovered classical learning and developed new ideas about religion. Why might people change their religious beliefs over time?

Chapter 15
A New Worldview in Europe 1450–1715

As Europeans began to investigate the world around them—exploring the natural world and the territories beyond their borders—they began to seek new authorities on which to rebuild their sense of purpose, identity, and security. How might changes in people's view of the world affect the development of their systems of government?

Between 1300 and 1815 European civilization made the great transformation from the medieval period to the modern world. Trade increased contact between peoples, which led Europeans to question their long-standing beliefs. Eventually, human beings, not the church, became the center of people's worldview. This new worldview weakened the power and unity of the church, and the power of European states grew. The application of new scientific knowledge allowed Europeans to explore lands beyond their borders, where they began to establish colonies and profoundly change the cultures with which they made contact. In addition, new ideas about society and government led to an unsettled period of revolution.

Chapter 16
The World in the Age of European Expansion 1400–1763

In the process of tapping the rich spice trade of the East Indies, the Portuguese and other Europeans influenced Asian civilizations, founded empires in the Americas, and devastated African cultures through the slave trade. How might trade lead to conflict and cooperation between peoples?

Chapter 17
Revolutions of Society and State 1714–1815

During the 1700s new ideas about the workings of the universe and the structure of society arose in Europe. These ideas influenced American colonists to break free of Great Britain and inspired revolution in France, which ultimately resulted in the dictator Napoleon ruling much of Europe. How might revolutionary ideas translate into new political structures?

Chapter 16
The World in the Age of European Expansion

Trade might lead to conflict between peoples when one group is stronger than the other. The stronger group might try to trade unfairly to its own advantage by imposing trade restrictions or using forced labor. Peoples might cooperate, however, when trade is mutually beneficial.

Chapter 17
Revolutions of Society and State

Revolutionary ideas might lead to the overthrow of an old, corrupt system. If the revolutionaries have thought about long-term goals, they may have come up with ideas for new political structures that might embrace their revolutionary ideals. They might, for example, give the vote to all adults, or allow anyone of age to be a representative in the government.

REVIEW & ASSESSMENT RESOURCES

- Unit Synthesis 4
- Unit Test 4
- Sheltered English Unit Test 4

All Levels

Chapter 14

Renaissance and Reformation 1300–1650

Chapter Planning Guide

	TEXTBOOK	CORE RESOURCES	VISUAL RESOURCES	MULTIMEDIA
Introduction	pp. 360–361	Block Scheduling Handbook: Ch. 14		Videodisc Segment 14 and Viewing Guide: *The Renaissance Perspective*
Lesson 14.1 The Transformation of European Civilization	pp. 362–366 Map: *Spread of the Black Death,* p. 363	Reading 14.1: *The Black Death in Paris*	Everyday Life 14: *The Triumph of Death* Geography and History 14: *The Great Schism*	GHRC 14 Readings: *The Economic Impact of the Black Death; Gunpowder and the New Warfare in Europe* GHRC 14/Videodiscs: Image—*The New Weapons of Renaissance Warfare;* Maps—Series of four on *The Hundred Years' War*
Lesson 14.2 The Italian Renaissance	pp. 367–374 Map: *Renaissance Italy,* p. 370	Reading 14.2: *Advice to Princes* Skills Activity 14: *Analyzing Art*		GHRC 14 Readings: *Humanists' Fascination with Greece and Rome; Da Vinci's Job Application; The Genius of Michelangelo; Europe's Economic Revolution* GHRC 14/Videodiscs: Images—*Leonardo da Vinci's Anatomical Studies; Renaissance Prince; Moses by Michelangelo; Painting by a Renaissance Woman Artist;* Map—*European Finance and Trade*
Lesson 14.3 The Northern Renaissance	pp. 375–379 History Through the Arts: *Renaissance Painting: Realism and Perspective,* p. 378	Reading 14.3: *On the Education of Women*	Art and History 14: *Knight, Death, and Devil*	GHRC 14 Readings: *The Power of the Printing Press; Renaissance Women as Wives and Workers* GHRC 14/Videodiscs: Images—*The Chateau de Chambord; Massacre of the Innocents by Brueghel;* Chart—*Printing Centers in Europe;* Audio Clip—"Greensleeves"
Lesson 14.4 The Reformation	pp. 380–386 Through Others' Eyes: *Violence in the Reformation,* p. 384 Map: *European Religions,* p. 385	Reading 14.4: *Luther's Refusal at the Diet of Worms* Geography Activity 14: *The Thirty Years' War* Writing Project 14: *Writing a Comparison Essay*		GHRC 14 Readings: *Luther Criticizes the Catholic Church; Calvin and Calvinism; Loyola's Rules; The Inquisition* GHRC 14/Videodiscs: Map—*European Religions*
Chapter Investigation and Enrichment	pp. 360–386	Chapter 14 Investigation: *TV Documentary on the Renaissance and Reformation* People in World History 14 Explorations in Daily Life 14		GHRC 14/Videodiscs
Review and Assessment	Section 1 Review, p. 366 Section 2 Review, p. 374 Section 3 Review, p. 379 Section 4 Review, p. 386 Chapter 14 Review, p. 387	Chapter Review Activity 14 Vocabulary Activity 14 Themes Review 14 Section Study Guides 14.1–14.4 Main Idea Activities 14.1–14.4 Daily Quizzes 14.1–14.4 Chapter 14 Test Sheltered English Ch. 14 Test Ch. 14 Test Generator		Audio CDs: Ch. 14 Summary (English and Spanish)

INTRODUCING THE CHAPTER

Textbook pp. 360–361

CHAPTER OVERVIEW

In the 1300s the plague, the building of national monarchies, and the Commercial Revolution initiated profound change in Europe. Italy became a center of trade with the East, and it was there that the ancient learning of Greece and Rome was first reintroduced. Inspired, humanist scholars created a Renaissance of learning and the arts. Humanists in northern Europe often focused on religious and social reform. Luther's call for reform in the church led to the Protestant Reformation and the wars of religion.

PRESENTING THEMES

On the chalkboard or on an overhead transparency, write the following open-ended theme questions.

- **CROSS-CULTURAL INTERACTION** How might trade influence the spread of ideas between cultures?
- **THE ARTS** What sources influence the works of artists and writers?
- **WAR AND DIPLOMACY** Why might differing views on religion lead to conflict?

Have students suggest responses to the questions. For the cross-cultural interaction question, students might suggest that traders would be exposed to the cultures of the peoples with whom they traded. For the arts question, students might suggest that new ideas, elements of everyday life, and religious feeling encourage artistic creativity. For the war and diplomacy question, students might suggest that people might find other religions threatening and believe that they should be suppressed. Save the responses. Once students have studied the chapter, you may wish to have them complete the Themes Review, then compare the two sets of answers.

USING THE VIDEO

Segment 14: *The Renaissance Perspective*

ENGLISH

Search Chapter 14
Videodisc 1, Side B

SPANISH

Search Chapter 14
Videodisc 1, Side B

Tell students that in this chapter they will apply these theme questions to a time of cultural rebirth and religious revolution—the Renaissance and Reformation. Conclude by showing Segment 14 of the *World History and Cultures Videodiscs*. This segment introduces students to the spirit of discovery that characterized the Renaissance by examining the development of linear perspective in art during this period.

Before showing the video, remind students that the television screen they are watching is flat, and ask them to keep this fact in mind as they watch the segment. To help students grasp the significant points of the video, have them complete Video Viewing Guide 14.

Key to Ability Levels

All strategies and activities are coded to the following ability levels:

LEVEL 1	**Basic** activities suitable for all students
LEVEL 2	**Average** activities suitable for average to above-average students
LEVEL 3	**Challenging** activities suitable for above-average students
SHELTERED ENGLISH	Activities suitable for students with **Limited English Proficiency**

Additional Resources

BOOKS FOR TEACHERS

Hibbert, Christopher. *The House of Medici: Its Rise and Fall.* Morrow Quill Paperbacks, 1980. A history of the Medici family.

Manchester, William. *A World Lit Only by Fire: The Medieval Mind and the Renaissance.* Little, Brown and Company, 1992. Presents a portrait of the 1500s.

Ozment, Steven. *Protestants: The Birth of a Revolution.* Doubleday, 1992. Examines the Reformation.

BOOKS FOR STUDENTS

Hale, J. R., ed. *The Thames and Hudson Encyclopaedia of the Italian Renaissance.* Thames and Hudson, 1981. A useful reference work on the Renaissance.

Plumb, J. H. *The Italian Renaissance.* American Heritage, 1985. Provides an illustrated overview of the history of the Italian Renaissance.

Virgoe, Roger, ed. *Private Life in the Fifteenth Century: Illustrated Letters of the Paston Family.* Weidenfeld & Nicolson, 1989. Provides a glimpse into English life in the 1400s.

MULTIMEDIA MATERIALS

Art and Music: The Renaissance. ZCI. CD-ROM, MAC, DOS, WIN, MPC formats. Highlights the period's artistic accomplishments.

Newscast from the Past: September 19, 1356. Agency for Instructional Technology. Video, 15 min. Examines events around the world and covers history, politics, and daily life.

Renaissance and Reformation. Queue. CD-ROM, MAC, and DOS formats. Covers the period's main events; includes an art gallery and the complete text of several literary works.

Lesson 14.1   *The Transformation of European Civilization*

Textbook pp. 362–366

RESOURCES

Pupil's Edition

Map, p. 363: *Spread of the Black Death*

Core Resources

Reading 14.1: *Black Death in Paris*

Visual Resources

Everyday Life 14: *The Triumph of Death*
Geography and History 14: *The Great Schism*

Global History Resource Center

Reading: *The Economic Impact of the Black Death*
Reading: *Gunpowder and the New Warfare in Europe*

Videodiscs or Global History Resource Center

Image: *The New Weapons of Renaissance Warfare*

Search Frame 852

Map: Series of four on *The Hundred Years' War*

Search Frames 862–65

LESSON FOCUS

How did events of the 1300s and 1400s weaken the structures of feudalism and the Catholic Church in Europe?

OBJECTIVES

After completing this lesson, students will be able to:

- explain how a changing climate and the Black Death affected Europe;
- describe how warfare affected Europeans in the 1300s;
- explain how the rise of national monarchies affected the church;
- compare challenges faced in the 1300s and the 1900s.

HOOK

Discuss the effects of climate and the Black Death on Europe's population. Tell the class that they represent Europe's population in 1300. Then tap the heads of half of the students. Ask those tapped to put their heads down. Explain that those who remain represent the estimated population by the mid-1400s.
Ask: What explains this drastic decline in population?
[famine from crop failures; the Black Death]

Link to Today. Then ask students to predict the general reaction today if a similar catastrophe hit the United States. As a real-world example, you might want to remind students that when cases of pneumonic plague were reported in western India in September 1994, some 300,000 people fled the city of Surat. Many of the fleeing Suratians headed for Bombay—a city of over 12 million people.
Ask: How did people of the 1300s react to the plague?
[Students should mention Flagellants, physical attacks on and charges of witchcraft against Jews, and strained social relations caused by labor shortages and wage issues.]

Next direct students' attention to the textbook map.
Ask: How and in what direction did the plague travel?
[spread from Asia through Europe along trade routes]

To assist students in understanding the effects of the Black Death on European social life, you may wish to assign Core Resources Reading 14.1 and the Global History Resource Center reading on the plague. You may also wish to show Everyday Life Transparency 14 and assign the accompanying worksheet. Then ask students to write a short journal entry from the perspective of a plague survivor.

DEVELOP

Summarize events of the 1300s and 1400s that changed Europeans' political loyalties and their views of the feudal system. In groups of two or three, have students develop a chart with three columns: 1) Major Events of the 1300s and 1400s; 2) Causes; and 3) Effects on Feudalism. *[Charts should include the Black Death, new weapons, the Hundred Years' War, the War of the Roses, and struggles in the Holy Roman Empire.]* Students should list factors that precipitated each major event and indicate how each event changed people's attitudes toward feudalism and political leaders. In addition to their textbook, students may draw on the Global History Resource Center readings and electronic media images of weapons to complete their charts.

Next have students examine the electronic media maps of the Hundred Years' War.
Ask: **What were the effects of the Hundred Years' War?**
[French monarchy strengthened; English monarchy discredited, leading to the War of the Roses; England lost claim to French territory; new weapons revolutionized warfare and allowed kings to control nobles.]

Conclude by asking students to review the information they have gathered in their charts and identify reasons for the decline of feudalism and the rise of national monarchies. *[The period's natural disasters undermined feudalism, while wars strengthened monarchies and contributed to the nobles' loss of power; technological developments in warfare led to the decline in the knight's importance.]*

PROBE

Examine how the rise of national monarchies affected the church. Remind students that the power of national monarchies increased during the late Middle Ages.

Next have students examine the map transparency and complete the accompanying worksheet.
Ask: **How did the increasing power of the national monarchies affect the church?**
[Power of the monarchies increased, church's power decreased; clash between Philip IV of France and Pope Boniface VIII led to the Babylonian Captivity and the Great Schism and ultimately to a loss of the church's political power and some of its spiritual and moral authority.]

CONCLUDE: Link to Today

Compare the 1300s to the 1900s. Tell students that historian Barbara Tuchman says in her book *A Distant Mirror: The Calamitous 14th Century* (Alfred A. Knopf, 1978) that historians have tended to avoid dealing with the 1300s because the violence and disorder associated with that time run counter to our belief in human progress. She feels, however, that people who have lived through the 1900s should have a certain sympathy and understanding for those who lived during the 1300s.
Ask: **Why might Tuchman find these two centuries similar?**
[Both of these centuries have been characterized by violent conflict and attacks on long-standing institutions.]

EXTEND

Cross-Curricular Connection: *Language Arts*
Have students imagine they are living in France or England during the last half of the 1300s. Have them write a letter to a young relative, describing the many events they have experienced over the course of the past 60 or so years.

Other Media
Have interested students view Ingmar Bergman's movie *The Seventh Seal*, in which a knight during the time of the Black Death plays chess with Death. Then have students discuss the film's relationship to what they have learned.

MEET INDIVIDUAL NEEDS

Students Acquiring English
Pair new speakers of English with fluent speakers. Have them make flash cards with the chapter's boldfaced terms on one side and their definitions on the other side. Then have each pair use the cards to quiz each other until they have mastered the vocabulary terms.

Visual-Spatial Learners
Have students create a time line of important events discussed in the section. If they wish, they may illustrate the time line.

ASSESS

Review
Have students complete the Section 1 Review. Use answers in the Teacher's Edition, page 366, to assess student mastery of this section.

Lesson 14.2   The Italian Renaissance

Textbook pp. 367–374

LESSON FOCUS

Why did the Renaissance develop in Italy, and what forms did it take?

OBJECTIVES

After completing this lesson, students will be able to:

- describe causes of the Commercial Revolution in Italy;
- identify influences that inspired Italian humanists;
- explain how struggles for power in Renaissance Italy affected people's views of politics;
- explain how humanist ideas were reflected in art.

HOOK

Compare Renaissance and medieval art. Show students examples of medieval and Renaissance art, such as the electronic media images of the medieval painting of monks delivering a book to their abbot or the Renaissance statue of Moses by Michelangelo. Have students identify the historical period of each image.

Ask: What elements serve as clues to each image's time period?
[Medieval pieces often hide the human form, portray ideal types, not individuals, and are static. Renaissance pieces focus on the human form, depict individuals, and convey emotion.]

Explain that instead of using ideal types, Renaissance artists wanted to portray the world as they saw it. Tell students that they are going to explore the reasons behind this remarkable change in perception.

DEVELOP

Discuss the Commercial Revolution and how trade and other factors influenced humanists. Have the class identify sources of the Commercial Revolution. *[Population loss from the plague led to a higher standard of living; increased demand led to specialized production and increased trade.]* Then direct students' attention to the textbook map on page 370. You might also display the electronic media map on

European finance and trade and assign the Global History Resource Center reading on Europe's Economic Revolution.

Ask: Why did the Commercial Revolution begin in Italy?
[Italian cities became centers of specialized production and trade with the East; wealth led to efforts to raise capital, new ways of thinking about property, development of banking facilities, and new business methods.]

Point out that the Commercial Revolution helped lay the foundation for the Renaissance by creating wealth.

Ask: What other factors besides wealth influenced Italian humanists?
[arrival of Greek scholars and the reintroduction of ancient literature; Roman ruins]

Ask: How did Italian scholars respond to the rediscovery of ancient learning?
[developed a worldview that valued human reason, creativity, and the virtuous life; promoted classical education]

To assist students in understanding the importance of ancient works to Renaissance scholars, you may wish to assign the Global History Resource Center reading on humanists' interest in Greece and Rome.

Conclude by asking students to create a visual metaphor comparing medieval and Renaissance views of humanity's place in the universe. [possible response: a wheel with God/the church as the hub (medieval); humanity as the hub (Renaissance)]

PROBE

Focus on the political developments of city-states and diplomacy. Begin by discussing how the political situation in Italy led to the formation of city-states. Explain that cities stayed independent by taking advantage of power struggles between the Guelphs and the Ghibellines. Point out that this led to chaos as well as to the emergence of strong leaders. Have students cite examples of those who seized power when the opportunity arose. [the Medici, the Este, the Visconti, Sforza] Remind students that by about 1453, Florence, Milan, Venice, Naples, and the Papal States had emerged as major powers.

Ask: Why did the Italian city-states turn to diplomacy and a balance of power system?
[Rulers—tired of war—wanted to keep peace.]

Link to Today. You may wish to assign Core Resources Reading 14.2, then discuss how Machiavelli's theories were exemplified by Italian rulers. [use of intrigue, fear, and force to keep power] Have students consider whether Machiavelli's political judgments would apply today.

Finally, ask students to differentiate between humanism and civic humanism. Conclude by assigning the Global History Resource Center reading on da Vinci. Then discuss how the concept of the Renaissance man evolved from civic humanism.

CONCLUDE

Identify the effects of humanist ideas on Italian art and artists. Focus on the artistic expression of the time. Have students read the History Through the Arts feature. Then show the electronic media images, pointing out the realism and richness of detail. You may also wish to assign the Global History Resource Center reading on Michelangelo and the Skills Activity on analyzing art.

Ask: Could this flowering of art have happened without the changes that reshaped Italy?
[All of these changes produced a freedom that encouraged artistic expression; political leaders also supported the arts.]

EXTEND

Cross-Curricular Connection: *Art*
Have students create a photo essay of the 10 pieces of Renaissance art that they think have been most influential. Remind them to defend their choices.

MEET INDIVIDUAL NEEDS

Gifted Students
Both Castiglione and Machiavelli are considered civic humanists. Ask students to write a paragraph comparing the two thinkers.

Logical-Mathematical Learners
Have students research how innovations in banking and accounting aided the growth of capitalism.

ASSESS

Review
Have students complete the Section 2 Review. Use answers in the Teacher's Edition, page 374, to assess student mastery of this section.

Lesson 14.3   *The Northern Renaissance*

Textbook pp. 375–379

RESOURCES

Pupil's Edition

History Through the Arts, p. 378: *Renaissance Painting: Realism and Perspective*

Core Resources

Reading 14.3: *On the Education of Women*

Visual Resources

Art and History 14: *Knight, Death, and Devil*

Global History Resource Center

Reading: *The Power of the Printing Press*

Reading: *Renaissance Women as Wives and Workers*

Videodiscs or Global History Resource Center

Image: *The Chateau de Chambord of Francis I*

Search Frame 859

Chart: *Printing Centers in Europe Before 1500*

Search Frame 869

Image: *Massacre of the Innocents by Brueghel*

Search Frame 860

Audio Clip: *"Greensleeves" Played on a Lute*

Search 6425, Play to 6855
Videodisc 1 Side B
Audio Clip 14

LESSON FOCUS

How did Renaissance ideas spread throughout Europe, and in what ways were the Northern and English Renaissances different from the Italian Renaissance?

OBJECTIVES

After completing this lesson, students will be able to:

- explain how Renaissance ideas spread across northern Europe;
- describe the form humanism took in northern Europe;
- compare the Renaissance in England to the Renaissance in other parts of Europe;
- describe how Northern Renaissance art was similar to and different from Renaissance art in Italy.

HOOK: Link to Today

Discuss how ideas spread. Ask students how fads, clothing trends, slang, and music spread among teenagers from place to place. Then discuss how styles evolve as they travel. Ask for examples. Explain that serious ideas spread in similar ways. You may wish to display the electronic media image of the Chateau de Chambord to show the Italian Renaissance's influence on French architecture.

DEVELOP

Discuss the spread of Renaissance ideas from Italy to the rest of Europe. Begin by discussing the contributions of diplomacy, education, and printing to the spread of humanist ideas across northern Europe. To increase students' understanding, you may wish to have them examine the chart on the spread of printing and the reading on the printing press from the electronic media.

Ask: *How did each of these factors help the Renaissance spread?*

[Ambassadors provided communication links between countries; students studying in Italy returned home with new ideas; the wealth generated by the Commercial

Revolution made it possible for more people to seek higher education and thus led to the establishment of new universities; printing allowed books to be produced in quantity, cheaply, and quickly.]

Discuss the education of women during the Renaissance and point out that not only were noblewomen better educated than in earlier periods, they also played an active role in spreading humanist ideas. To help students better understand the effect of the Renaissance on women, assign Core Resources Reading 14.3. You may also wish to assign the Global History Resource Center reading on Renaissance women as wives and workers.

PROBE

Identify forms that humanism and the Renaissance assumed in northern Europe and England. Discuss the northern humanists' focus on social and religious reform.

Ask: How did humanism change as it moved north? What was this form of humanism called? Who were among the notable Christian humanists?
[Northern humanists tended to be more interested in applying humanist principles to religion than to secular topics, hence the term Christian humanism. Notable Christian humanists included Desiderius Erasmus, who wanted to reform the church, and Thomas More, who wanted to reform society.]

Next explore the Renaissance in England. Tell students that the English Renaissance occurred during the reign of the well-educated Elizabeth I. Thus the period is also called the Elizabethan Age. Then have students scan textbook pages 376–377.

Ask: What was unique about the Renaissance in England?
[It occurred later in time; it was expressed primarily in poetry and drama and emphasized national pride and unlimited human possibilities.]

To further students' understanding of the English Renaissance, have them choose and read a scene from a Shakespearean play to the class. This could be done as a group or as individual monologues. Then ask students to discuss the Renaissance ideas and values reflected in the scene.

CONCLUDE

Compare and contrast Renaissance art in Italy and in northern Europe. Refer students to the History Through the Arts feature on page 378 of their textbook.

Ask: How did the styles of Italian and Northern Renaissance painting differ?
[Italian painters often depicted people as Greek gods; northern painters tended to depict real people and to paint darker landscapes.]

Next display Art and History Transparency 14 and assign the accompanying worksheet. You may also wish to display the Brueghel painting from the electronic media.

Conclude by having students form small groups and create simple charts describing the differences between the forms the Renaissance took in Italy and in northern Europe. [Charts should include differences between humanism in Italy and Christian humanism in northern Europe, the late date of the English Renaissance and its emphasis on drama, and differences in artistic styles.]

EXTEND

Cross-Curricular Connection: Literature/Drama
Link to Today. In Shakespeare's play Hamlet, Polonius advised "to thine own self be true." Have students think about this statement and about the consequences of following it. Then, individually or in groups, have students write a short one-act play with this theme as its basis. You may wish to have one or more of the groups perform or read their plays.

MEET INDIVIDUAL NEEDS

Musical-Rhythmic Learners
Have interested students listen to the Global History Resource Center audio selection of "Greensleeves," which is played on a lute. Then ask them either to research the history of the lute or to compose a short piece in the Elizabethan style.

Students Acquiring English
Pair students acquiring English with students who are proficient in English. Have pairs of students work together to answer the focus questions on page 375 of their textbook.

ASSESS

Review
Have students complete the Section 3 Review. Use answers in the Teacher's Edition, page 379, to assess student mastery of this section.

RESOURCES

Pupil's Edition

Through Others' Eyes, p. 384: *Violence in the Reformation*

Map, p. 385: *European Religions, 1600*

Core Resources

Reading 14.4: *Luther's Refusal at the Diet of Worms*

Geography Activity 14: *The Thirty Years' War*

Writing Project 14: *Writing a Comparison Essay*

Global History Resource Center

Reading: *Martin Luther Criticizes the Catholic Church*

Reading: *John Calvin and Calvinism*

Reading: *Loyola's Rules for Thinking with the Church*

Reading: *The Inquisition in Spain*

Videodiscs or Global History Resource Center

Image: Massacre of the Innocents *by Brueghel*

Search Frame 860

Map: *European Religions, 1600*

Search Frame 870

LESSON FOCUS

What were the causes and effects of the Protestant Reformation?

OBJECTIVES

After completing this lesson, students will be able to:

- identify issues leading to the Protestant Reformation in Germany;
- explain how Protestant ideas spread to other parts of Europe;
- describe how the Catholic Church tried to counter the Protestant Reformation;
- outline the causes of the wars of religion.

HOOK

Discuss the causes of the Protestant Reformation. Ask students how they would feel if they had worked hard for an A or B in a class, then were told that because their school needed money, they could get that grade only if they paid for it—say, $100 for an A, $75 for a B. Discuss the effects of such a system. Then have students relate this system to the church's selling of indulgences in the 1500s. Discuss how people who were concerned about their spiritual welfare must have felt about such a system.

Ask: What issues sparked the Protestant Reformation?
[Many people were offended by the sale of indulgences, misconduct among priests and monks, and the church's political power.]

Have students complete Core Resources Reading 14.4: *Luther's Refusal at the Diet of Worms.*

Ask: Why did Luther escape the fate of earlier dissenters?
[He had political support—German princes resented the church's property and lack of taxes.]

DEVELOP

Develop a flow chart illustrating the spread of the Protestant Reformation and the Catholic Church's response to it. Have students read textbook pages 380–384 and the Global History Resource Center readings on Luther, Calvin, Loyola, and the Inquisition. Next create a flow chart for the Reformation by writing class responses on the chalkboard or on transparencies. List the events for each denomination on parallel branches, each of which feeds into the Catholic Reformation. *[Students should cover at least these events/ideas—***Lutheranism:*** Luther's 95 theses; Diet of Worms; doctrine of predestination; Calvinist control of priesthood of all believers;* **Calvinism:** *Zwingli; Geneva;* **Church of England:**

Henry VIII's motives; sale of Catholic lands; nobles' commitment to the new church; **Catholic Reformation: (list as parallel events)** Loyola and the Jesuits, new religious orders, Council of Trent, Inquisition.*] To further students' understanding of the Protestant and Catholic Reformations, have them complete Writing Project 14 on composing a comparison essay.

PROBE

Explore the reasons people went to war for the sake of religion. Have students discuss the Through Others' Eyes on page 384 of their textbook. Note that while some had hoped the Reformation would lead to more tolerance, the opposite occurred. Then discuss the reasons for the wars between Protestants and Catholics that began in Germany in 1531. Students should understand that Protestants and Catholics both believed their faith was the only true one and that rulers used religious conflict to further political ambitions.

Ask: ***What was the result of the conflict between the German Protestant princes and Charles V?***
[The conflict ended with the Peace of Augsburg, which allowed each German prince to determine the religion in his territory.]

Ask: ***What other conflicts occurred between Protestants and Catholics?***
*[**Northern Netherlands:** Calvinists successfully revolted from Catholic Spain; **Spain:** unsuccessfully tried to invade Protestant England; **France:** civil war ended with the Edict of Nantes, which allowed Protestant Huguenots to retain their cities; **Germany:** the Thirty Years' War ended with the Treaty of Westphalia and reaffirmed the Peace of Augsburg]*

You may also wish to show the electronic media image of Brueghel's *Massacre of the Innocents*, which depicts the horrors of the Thirty Years' War.

Next direct students' attention to the map of European religions on page 385 of their textbook or in the electronic media. Have students summarize the information shown. *[Years of fighting failed to impose religious uniformity in either predominately Catholic or Protestant countries.]* You may then wish to have students complete Geography Activity 14.

CONCLUDE: Link to Today

Examine long-term effects of the Reformation. Bring a telephone book to class, and use an overhead projector to illustrate

to students the number of Protestant denominations that exist in your community. Explain that among the denominations tracing their origins to Calvinism are Reformed, Presbyterian, and Church of Christ; among those tracing their origins to the Church of England are Episcopal and Methodist.

Ask: ***How does the way we think of religious commitment today compare to the time of the Reformation?***
[We tend to think of religion as a personal choice; in Luther's time many people believed that the state should make everyone conform to one faith.]

Have students suggest reasons for this change. *[Students might suggest that religious wars did not make everyone conform and may have made the need for tolerance more apparent.]*

EXTEND

Cross-Curricular Connection: *Journalism*
Link to Today. Have students list the articles, editorials, and letters to the editor in the local newspaper that deal with the separation of church and state. Have them bring in an example and then ask them to describe the issues involved.

MEET INDIVIDUAL NEEDS

Students Having Difficulty/Students Acquiring English
Students having difficulty or those acquiring English may enjoy a work of historical fiction dealing with the Reformation. *The Hawk That Dare Not Hunt by Day* by Scott O'Dell (Boston: Houghton Mifflin, 1975) has a fourth- through sixth-grade reading level.

Gifted Students
Have students imagine they are living in Germany at the time of the Thirty Years' War. Then have them write a sonnet addressed to a childhood friend who has been lost because of the religious conflict.

ASSESS

Review
Have students complete the Section 4 Review. Use answers in the Teacher's Edition, page 385, to assess student mastery of this section.

In preparation for the chapter test, you may wish to have students complete all or part of the Chapter 14 Review on textbook page 387, the Chapter 14 Review Activity, and the Themes Review.

Understanding the Main Idea

Call on a volunteer to read aloud the *Understanding the Main Idea* paragraph. Then tell students that during the late Middle Ages Europeans rediscovered the teachings of the ancient Greeks and Romans. The excitement generated by these teachings helped spark the Renaissance and the Reformation. The result was a transformation of European intellectual, political, artistic, and religious life between the 1300s and the 1600s.

Presenting Themes

See p. 359B for suggestions on introducing themes.

Using the Time Line

Have students list the time line events in their notebooks. After they have read about each event in the chapter, have students write a paragraph explaining its significance.

Chapter 14
Renaissance and Reformation 1300–1650

Understanding the Main Idea

European civilization was rocked by famine, plague, and warfare after 1300. As Europe recovered, the growth of trade, a rediscovery of classical learning, and new ideas about art and religion led to a new worldview—one that placed human beings, rather than the church, at its center. As Christian unity declined, however, war and violence once again erupted.

Themes

- **Cross-cultural Interaction** How might trade influence the spread of ideas between cultures?

- **The Arts** What sources influence the works of artists and writers?

- **War and Diplomacy** Why might differing views on religion lead to conflict?

In 1498 the Dominican monk Girolamo Savonarola (SAH-voh-nah-roh-lah) and two of his disciples were burned at the stake in Florence, Italy. An observer described the scene:

> *In a few hours they were burnt, their legs and arms gradually dropping off . . . a quantity of stones were thrown to make them fall, . . . and then the hangman and those whose business it was, hacked down the post and burnt it on the ground, bringing a lot of brushwood, and stirring the fire up over the dead bodies, so that the very least piece was consumed.*

Savonarola had angered the pope and the leaders of Florence by preaching against the vice and corruption he believed were destroying the church, the government, and society. At the heart of this decay, he argued, lay the revival of the teachings of ancient Greece and Rome. These teachings, which sought to glorify the grace and creativity of humankind, ran counter

1309	1337	1347	1378	c. 1450
▲ Babylonian Captivity begins.	▲ Hundred Years' War begins.	▲ Black Death strikes Europe.	▲ Great Schism begins.	▲ Johannes Gutenberg begins using movable metal type to print books.

to the medieval worldview that people could achieve little in a universe dominated by God. But Savonarola and others could not stop this medieval worldview from being challenged as Europeans rediscovered the ancient past and questioned the authority of the church.

School of Athens, a Renaissance fresco by Raphael, 1509–1511

About the Image

In 1508 the Renaissance artist Raphael received a commission from Pope Julius II to paint the papal apartments in the Vatican in Rome. In one room of the apartments, Raphael designated each wall with the heading of a different branch of human knowledge: Theology, Law, Poetry, and Philosophy. Raphael filled the walls with images depicting the glory of human learning. One of these was the *School of Athens*. The painting shows the great philosophers of ancient Greece, such as Plato and Aristotle. Around them stand the great classical scientists and mathematicians, such as Pythagoras.

Critical Thinking Ask students to suggest why Raphael chose to focus on ancient Greek scholars in this painting.

ANSWER: Students should mention that the Renaissance was sparked in part by new interest in classical learning.

1508	1517	1545–1563	1588	1648
Michelangelo begins painting Sistine Chapel.	Martin Luther posts 95 theses.	Council of Trent codifies Catholic doctrines.	English defeat Spanish Armada.	Treaty of Westphalia ends Thirty Years' War.

SECTION 1

Theme:
Geography

From the mid-700s to the mid-1100s, Europe experienced a period of relatively mild winters and dry summers. Scholars suggest that this moderate weather not only allowed European farmers to produce more food but also made land and sea travel easier, thereby helping to expand trade and urbanization. When colder, wetter weather returned to Europe in the 1200s, it had devastating effects. Crops failed and famine spread. Some scholars believe that Europe's weather was the coldest it had been since the prehistoric Ice Age.

Critical Thinking Ask students what connection there might have been between this period of frequent famine and the Black Death.

ANSWER: Students might suggest that Europeans weakened by malnutrition were less able to resist disease.

SECTION 1
The Transformation of European Civilization

FOCUS

- How did a changing climate and the Black Death affect Europe?
- What were the consequences of warfare in the 1300s?
- What effect did the rise of national monarchies have on the church?

By the 1200s the new civilization that had emerged in Europe after 1000 had achieved maturity. After 1300, however, Europeans confronted a series of dramatic challenges. Changes in the environment, increasing warfare, and a reduction in the authority of the church forced European civilization to make rapid adaptations or face another collapse. Where the Roman Empire had been unable to transform itself quickly enough to avoid disintegration, the diversity of the new European civilization gave it flexibility, which allowed Europeans to survive these challenges and to emerge stronger than ever.

Detail from *February,* by the Limbourg brothers

Environmental Challenges of the 1300s

By the end of the 1200s, Europe had reached its natural limits of expansion. Despite their new farming technology, Europeans knew little about fertilizers and the importance of replenishing nutrients in the soil. They fed the growing population by simply bringing more land under cultivation. By 1300, however, the majority of available farmland was in use. Pushed beyond its capacity, the land began to lose its fertility, and food production leveled off. Farmers could no longer grow enough food to feed Europe's people.

The problem was made worse by the weather. In the late 1200s Europe grew noticeably colder and wetter. The change in climate had disastrous effects on agriculture. Increased rain washed away the topsoil and rotted seedlings in the fields. Early winter storms destroyed crops before the harvest. Harvests began to fail on a regular basis. Between 1315 and 1317 famine spread across Europe.

The Black Death. The most serious challenge, however, came in 1347 when the **Black Death** arrived from Asia. The Black Death, or bubonic plague, first broke out in China in 1331. The plague was carried by black rats but transmitted by fleas. When infected rats died, their fleas began biting people, thus spreading the disease. An infected person suffered from painfully swollen lymph glands, high fever, large purple blotches on the skin, and black spots at the point of the flea bite. Death usually came within days. Victims lucky enough to survive the illness developed an immunity against further infection. Pneumonic plague, a more serious and almost always fatal form of the disease, attacked the lungs and was spread through the air as victims coughed or sneezed.

From China the disease traveled along the trade routes of the Mongol Empire. By 1346 it had reached Crimean ports along the Black Sea. Merchant ships carried it to Sicily and Italy and from there to northern Europe. The disease swept through the European population, especially in crowded towns and cities. People died so rapidly that survivors could not always keep up with burying the dead. Agnolo di Tura, a survivor of the plague in Siena, Italy, wrote:

> *Members of a household brought their dead to a ditch as best they could, without priest, without divine offices. . . . They died by the hundreds, both day and night, and all were thrown in those ditches and covered with earth. And as soon as those ditches were filled, more were dug. And I buried my five children with my own hands.*

Scholarly estimates of plague mortality in Europe range from 25 to 45 percent. Most estimates say that about a third of Europe's people died between 1347 and 1351. China's population, which had peaked around 125 million in the late 1200s, had dropped to about 90 million in the late 1300s. Central Asia, North Africa, and the Byzantine Empire were all ravaged. Ibn Khaldun, a Muslim observer, wrote: "Cities and buildings were laid waste, . . . settlements and mansions became empty, and dynasties and tribes grew weak. The entire inhabited world changed." By the mid-1400s the worst of the plague had run its course, although the disease established itself among the rodent population. Consequently, epidemics periodically broke out over the next 500 years.

Consequences of the Black Death. The Black Death not only attacked people's physical health, it also undermined their sense of self-confidence. Some regarded the disease as a punishment from God. Many of these people became **flagellants**. They beat themselves with sticks and whips and adopted other forms of self-abuse as punishment for their supposed sins. Still other people blamed witchcraft and sorcery for the plague, or turned to

such practices themselves, hoping to escape illness. Often, frightened mobs accused the Jews of causing the plague by poisoning wells. Despite church protests, brutal massacres were not uncommon.

The Black Death also strained social relationships in Europe to the breaking point. Troubled that labor shortages were driving up prices, nobles and kings, for example, tried to lower prices and wages to their pre-plague levels. In 1351 the English Parliament passed the Statute of Laborers:

> *Whereas, to curb the malice of servants who after the pestilence were idle and unwilling to serve without securing excessive wages . . . such servants, both men and women, shall be bound to serve in return for the salaries and wages that were customary . . . five or six years earlier.*

Spread of the Black Death

In its deadly march across Europe, the Black Death spared a few small areas. Experts are not sure why.

Trade route
Areas affected:
1347
1348
1349
1350
After 1350
Unaffected areas

0   250   500 Miles
0   500   500 Kilometers
Azimuthal Equal-Area Projection

Waves of Death   The bustling trade routes of the 1300s carried more than a wealth of goods. They were also the main routes by which the Black Death entered Europe's cities and spread across the continent.

? **Movement**   Why did the Black Death reach Marseilles so quickly?

▲ This engraving from the *Nuremburg Chronicles,* published in 1493, depicts the burning of Jews during the Black Death.

The law was never effectively enforced, and when further efforts were made to raise taxes on adult males, peasants revolted. Thus, scholars argue that the plague may have contributed to the final decline of feudalism in western Europe. This was not the case in eastern Europe, where many rulers were able to reimpose serfdom by the 1400s.

The changing climate and the Black Death led to population decline, social unrest, and growing insecurity in Europe.

The Challenge of War and National Unity

As the feudal order began to break down in western Europe, people had to look beyond local lords for protection and a sense of security. Many found both in the strong kings who began to limit the power of the nobles and to claim **sovereign power**, or sole authority, throughout their realms. Through allegiance to these kings, many Europeans began to feel a new sense of national identity.

The Hundred Years' War. England and France were the first countries in which kings established strong governments and a new sense of nationhood. From 1337 until 1453, however, a series of conflicts, known collectively as the **Hundred Years' War**, disrupted both kingdoms. There were many reasons for the war, but chief among them was the fact that the English king Edward III held territories in southern France, which made him a vassal of the French king. When the last male member of France's Capetian dynasty died, Edward claimed the French throne, despite French opposition.

During the first half of the war it seemed as if the English would win. In 1429, however, an illiterate French peasant girl, Joan of Arc, emerged from obscurity to save France. Joan believed she had received a revelation from God commanding her to locate the dauphin, the heir to the French throne, and see that he was crowned king. Then she was to help him drive the English out of France.

After the dauphin was crowned as Charles VII, Joan dictated a letter to the English, calling on them to withdraw:

❝ *Surrender to The Maid sent hither by God, the King of Heaven, the keys of all the towns you have taken and laid waste in France. . . . If you do not, expect to hear tidings from The Maid who will shortly come upon you to your very great hurt.* ❞

Inspired by Joan's leadership, the French troops began to defeat the English. When Joan was captured by Burgundian allies of the English and burned at the stake as a heretic, her martyrdom only inspired the French even more. By 1453 they had driven the English out of all French territory except the port of Calais, on the English Channel.

While France's victory strengthened the French monarchy, it discredited the monarchy in England. In 1455 civil war broke out as two English noble houses competed for the throne. One, York, was represented by a white rose; and the other, Lancaster, was represented by a red rose. The **Wars of the Roses**, as the civil wars became known, lasted until 1485, when Henry Tudor, the Lancastrian heir, emerged victorious as Henry VII. The new Tudor dynasty established a strong central monarchy. The Tudors limited the power of the nobility and gained the support of the growing merchant and artisan classes, who had grown tired of the bloodshed and destruction of the civil wars.

The Hundred Years' War also had other effects. It revolutionized warfare in Europe and contributed to the downfall of feudalism. At the battles of Crécy and Poitiers, English bowmen proved that a new weapon, the Welsh longbow, could pierce a knight's armor. As the flower of French nobility withered under the deadly hail of English arrows, the knightly era came to an end.

Even more significantly, both the French and English began to use gunpowder and cannons. Cannons changed power relationships between nobles and kings in Europe. Cannons could blast apart castle defenses. Consequently, kings, who had the wealth to pay for the expensive new weapons, could at last control rebellious nobles.

The Holy Roman Empire. While France and England emerged stronger and more unified after the Hundred Years' War and the Wars of the Roses, in eastern Europe a different pattern developed. The Holy Roman emperors had gradually given up most of their power to the German princes and knights in exchange for military support. In 1356 Charles IV tried to rebuild his authority by removing the popes from the process of electing the emperor. In a decree known as the **Golden Bull**, he designated seven hereditary electors: three archbishops and four German princes.

For the first time since the coronation of Charlemagne in 800, the pope would play no formal role in electing the emperor. Ironically, Charles's action only further weakened the emperors' real power. The new electors became almost completely independent rulers in their own territories. For the next hundred years, the imperial title was little more than honorary.

In 1438, however, the Habsburg family, which had held the title in the 1200s, once again assumed the imperial crown. From their hereditary bases in Austria and Bohemia they set out to increase their wealth and power. Through conquest and marriage, the Habsburgs became the most powerful dynasty in Europe. Although unable to unify the empire, they controlled enough resources to dominate Germany and Italy.

Increasing warfare helped strong national monarchies to emerge in western Europe. The Holy Roman Empire remained splintered.

Divisions in the Church

While the national monarchies of Europe responded to the challenges of the 1300s by becoming even more firmly established, the authority of the church steadily declined. In 1294, for example, Philip IV of France demanded that the French clergy pay taxes to his treasury; Pope Boniface VIII rejected these demands. In a decree entitled *Unam Sanctam*, Boniface reasserted the pope's authority over all earthly kings.

This declaration proved to be the beginning of the end of papal authority. Infuriated, Philip

▲ With 200-yard precision aim, the six-foot longbow with its three-foot arrows dramatically altered the outcome of the Hundred Years' War.

RESOURCE ACTIVITY

GLOBAL HISTORY RESOURCE CENTER
Image: *The New Weapons of Renaissance Warfare*
Reading: *Gunpowder and the New Warfare in Europe*

Print out and distribute the reading. Then show students the image. Ask students to imagine that they are film directors filming a movie about the Renaissance. Have them outline a battle scene for their movie, accurately depicting the changing technology of the age.

Level 1

MULTIMEDIA PRESENTATION STRATEGY

VISUAL RESOURCES Geography and History 14
The Great Schism

Show the transparency and share the information from Geography and History Fact Sheet 14. Then have students complete the accompanying worksheet.

Level 2

REVIEW & ASSESSMENT RESOURCES

• Study Guide 14.1
• Daily Quiz 14.1
• Main Idea Activity 14.1

All Levels

SECTION 1
REVIEW ANSWERS

IDENTIFY

For significance, see the following pages:
Black Death (p. 362)
flagellants (p. 363)
sovereign power (p. 364)
Hundred Years' War
(p. 364)
Joan of Arc (p. 364)
Wars of the Roses
(p. 364)
Golden Bull (p. 365)
Unam Sanctam (p. 365)
Babylonian Captivity
(p. 366)
Great Schism (p. 366)

1. death, illness, population decline, fear, growing insecurity
2. Following the Babylonian Captivity, French cardinals in Avignon continued to elect popes, as did the cardinals in Rome.
3. The weather grew colder, destroying crops; heavy rains washed away seedlings; famine became widespread.
4. French troops drove English forces out of France, except for the port of Calais; French victory strengthened the French monarchy; English defeat discredited the English monarchy; use of the Welsh longbow made knights ineffective, and cannons and gunpowder could destroy castle defenses.
5. With little medical knowledge, many people thought that if they changed their behavior or their religion, they might be spared from the disease.

▲ Jan Hus, shown here being led to his death for preaching reform, was burned alive on July 6, 1415.

accused the pope of heresy and selling positions in the church, then kidnapped and imprisoned him. Boniface was quickly released, but the political power of the papacy had been damaged beyond repair. After Boniface's death, Philip had one of his French advisors elected pope as Clement V. In 1309 Clement moved the papacy from Rome to Avignon in France. The French kings controlled the papacy for nearly 70 years. This troubled period of papal history is called the **Babylonian Captivity**, after the period of Hebrew exile in Babylon in the 500s B.C.

Pope Gregory XI returned to Rome in 1377, and died shortly thereafter. The cardinals in Rome then elected an Italian pope. Meanwhile, the cardinals in Avignon elected a French pope. From 1378 until 1417 this **Great Schism** (SI-zuhm), or division, split Latin Christendom in two.

The disunity caused by the Babylonian Captivity and the Great Schism increased criticism of the church, even from within its own ranks. In England in the late 1300s, for example, John Wycliffe, a scholar at Oxford University, attacked the wealth of the church, immorality among the clergy, and the pope's claim to absolute authority. Wycliffe argued that the only true guide to faith and salvation was the Bible. The English royal court, which was quarreling with the papacy at the time, defended him against charges of heresy. Jan Hus, a teacher at the University of Prague, who took up Wycliffe's ideas, was not so lucky. He lost royal support, and in 1415 was burned at the stake as a heretic.

Hus and Wycliffe's ideas, however, could not be so easily destroyed. Both had attracted the support of thousands of people who believed in the importance of individual faith. With this powerful idea as inspiration, Christians came to believe that they could achieve salvation through personal faith without having to rely on the clergy. By the mid-1400s the church had lost much of its political power, and even more seriously, some of its spiritual and moral authority as well.

As national monarchies grew in power, church authority declined.

SECTION 1 REVIEW

IDENTIFY and explain the significance of the following:
Black Death
flagellants
sovereign power
Hundred Years' War
Joan of Arc
Wars of the Roses
Golden Bull
Unam Sanctam
Babylonian Captivity
Great Schism

1. ***Main Idea*** What problems did the Black Death cause for European societies?
2. ***Main Idea*** What events led to the Great Schism?
3. ***Geography: Place*** How did changes in climate affect food production in Europe around 1300?
4. ***Writing to Describe*** Imagine that you are the court historian for either France or England during the Hundred Years' War. Write a brief account explaining some of the consequences of the war for both countries, including technological advances.
5. ***Hypothesizing*** Why might the Black Death have caused many Europeans to react in such extreme ways as becoming flagellants or rejecting their religious faith?

The Italian Renaissance

Between the 1300s and the 1500s, a new movement swept through Italy that would eventually transform the nature of European civilization. At the heart of this movement was a "rediscovery" by Europeans of the literature and philosophy of classical Greece and Rome. As they rediscovered the works of the ancients, and were exposed to the learning of Islamic civilization, a new curiosity moved many Italians to investigate the world around them. Soon, a whole new conception of the world emerged, which placed human beings at its center.

Donatello's *Mary Magdalene,* c. 1454–1455

The Commercial Revolution

By the middle of the 1400s, European civilization had begun to bounce back from the challenges of the Black Death, starvation, and warfare that had overtaken it around 1300. Ironically, perhaps, the enormous loss of population Europe experienced during this period may actually have stimulated its economic recovery.

Specialization. New farming techniques introduced during the Middle Ages had led to such a rapid growth of population that eventually, even with the new techniques, farmers could not produce enough to feed everyone. The Black Death had greatly reduced the population, however. Farmers could once again produce more food than was needed. As the prices of basic commodities like grain went down, the **standard of living** rose as people had more money with which to buy goods.

As people had more money for basic and luxury goods, the various regions of Europe began to produce only those products for which their terrain or climate were specially suited. In France, for example, farmers in many regions devoted their lands to growing grapes for wine. In England, farmers focused on raising sheep for wool. As farm production became more specialized, each region had to trade for the products that it did not produce. Through this trade in basic commodities, a more integrated economy emerged.

Urban areas also began to specialize, particularly in Italy. Venice, for example, became a center of glass manufacturing. Milan was known throughout Europe for its production of armaments. Many northern Italian cities specialized in producing finished silk and other textiles. Port cities like Venice and Genoa became the primary importers of spices and other luxury items from the East. In northern Europe the Hanseatic League controlled and expanded trade in the Baltic and North Seas. All this economic development led to improvements in business methods and practices, sparking what many scholars call the **Commercial Revolution**.

New business practices. At the heart of the Commercial Revolution were new attitudes toward property and money. In earlier

days Europeans had thought of property as
something solid and concrete—land, gold,
jewels, or other valuable items. With more
and more surplus wealth available, European
merchants and landowners began to think of
property in more general and abstract terms—
as a source of income, a means to produce
money with which to buy other things—what
we call **capital**.

As merchants began to accumulate large
amounts of money, they needed a way to keep
track of it efficiently. They also needed a safe way
to transfer the money from place to place in
order to pay for goods and services. Drawing on
their experiences with similar practices in the
Muslim world, Italian merchants established
banking facilities.

By 1400 the great Italian banking families,
like the Medici (MED-ee-chee) in Florence, were
creating business methods that made possible
international transactions on a scale never
before possible. For example, bankers began to
use a double-entry bookkeeping system that
allowed them to keep better track of their
profits and losses throughout Europe. Banking
expanded and became more stable. Credit transfers between banks became common, which lessened the need to move money around. Anxious
to minimize their risk of losses, merchants also
began to develop methods of insuring their goods
and expeditions. These new methods soon
spread north, where banking families like the
Fuggers in Germany financed not only the
Hanseatic merchants but also
princes and emperors.

The growth of banking had a
profound effect on European economic development. Merchants
began to devise new ways to raise
capital through partnerships.
Eventually, they developed **joint-
stock companies**, in which people bought shares of an enterprise
in exchange for an equal share of
the profits. Such arrangements
helped spread the risk involved
in investment.

▶ **Early banks became more than
money-changers when they began
holding deposits of money for
international transactions.**

With growing prosperity, Europeans' expectations rose. After the gloom and depression of the
Black Death, by the early 1400s many Europeans
had begun to concentrate their thoughts less on
the inevitability of death and more on the
promise of living. The Commercial Revolution
laid the foundations on which Europeans would
soon transform their civilization into the first
modern society in the world.

*Rising standards of living, economic
specialization, new attitudes toward
property, and the growth of a money economy led to a Commercial Revolution.*

Rediscovering the Past

By the middle of the 1300s, Italy had become the
gateway for European trade with the peoples of the
Mediterranean and Asia. Italian merchants traveled along the shores of the eastern Mediterranean
and North Africa, bringing back to Europe silk and
spices from Byzantium, China, and India.

Italy's growing wealth, combined with its
location between the rest of Europe and the
Islamic world, set the stage for a great burst of
cultural development. In the 1300s, as the
Ottomans advanced against the last remnants of
Byzantium, the ships of Venice began to carry a
new cargo: scholars seeking refuge in Italy from
the advancing Turkish warriors. These Greek

scholars brought works by Plato, Aeschylus, Herodotus, Thucydides, and many other ancient writers—literature that their Italian colleagues had thought to be lost.

Suddenly the gates to a whole new world opened for Italians who could read. Inspired, scholars began to search old libraries in Europe, locating many forgotten manuscripts. In the pages of these texts, scholars rediscovered the splendors of ancient Greece and Rome. They hoped for the rebirth, or **Renaissance**, as we call it, of a civilization more spectacular than any they had known.

Humanism

It was no accident that the Renaissance began first in Italy. Surrounded by the relics of a glorious past—the broken remains of marble statues, the empty, overgrown forums where cattle grazed—no one could forget that Italy had been the heartland of imperial Rome. Even after Rome's decline, the imperial past remained alive, a fact symbolized by the pope's almost continuous residence in Rome itself.

As they rediscovered the literature of the classical world, Italian scholars became intrigued by the nature of Greek and Roman knowledge and by the beauty of the classical Latin and Greek languages. In the mid-1300s, contrasting ancient achievements with those of his own age, Francesco Petrarch (PEE-trahrk) complained:

▲ Humanist Francesco Petrarch inspired fundamental changes in scholastic education.

66 O inglorious age! that scorns antiquity, its mother, to whom it owes every noble art—that dares to declare itself not only equal but superior to the glorious past. . . . What can be said in defense of men of education who ought not to be ignorant of antiquity and yet are plunged in . . . darkness and delusion? 99

Petrarch was inspired by the classical commitment to leading a virtuous life, not only in private matters but also in public affairs. The ancient writers seemed to provide a guide to morality he wished for in the church of his own day.

Petrarch inspired a generation of scholars. Under their influence, the church's scholastic education began to give way to one based on the classics: rhetoric, grammar, poetry, history, and above all, Latin and Greek. Thus, the new approach became known as a **classical education**. These subjects came to be known as humanities, and the new movement started by this changing attitude toward learning came to be called **humanism**. The scholars involved in this movement, or humanists, felt that style was as important as knowledge. "Information . . . which lacks all grace of expression," wrote one scholar, Leonardo Bruni (BROO-nee), "would seem to be put under a bushel or partly thrown away."

Humanism introduced a whole new conception of the nature of human beings. In his *Oration on the Dignity of Man*, Giovanni Pico della Mirandola (PEE-koh DAYL-lah mee-RAHN-doh-lah) of Florence expressed this new view of human nature. Quoting a Muslim scholar, he wrote, "There is nothing to be seen more wonderful than man." Pico went on:

66 On Man . . . the Father conferred the seeds of . . . every way of life. Whatever seeds each man cultivates will grow to maturity and bear in him their own fruit. If they be vegetative, he will be like a plant. If sensitive, he will become brutish. If rational, he will grow into a heavenly being. If intellectual, he will be an angel and the son of God. 99

This was a very different idea from the church's teaching that human beings were by nature sinful.

The revival of Greek and Roman learning inspired Italian humanists to emphasize the worth and creativity of individual human beings.

Across the Curriculum: Foreign Language

According to historian John Hale, the Renaissance was the first great age of translations. For example, by the early 1500s the works of Caesar, Xenophon, Thucydides, Livy, Sallust, and Suetonius had been translated into French. Many titles also had been translated into Italian, Dutch, and Spanish. The English were slower to begin translations. In his 1570 translation of Euclid, Englishman Henry Billingsley lamented that the translation efforts of the French, Dutch, Italians, and Spanish were "the chiefest cause that among them do florishe so many cunning and skilful men in the inventions of straunge and wonderfull thinges."

Critical Thinking Ask students which they believe was more significant, the rediscovery of classical Greek and Latin literature, or the translation of those works into French, English, and other modern languages.

ANSWER: Students' answers will vary but might mention that works in Latin and Greek could be read by influential scholars, whereas works in modern languages were accessible to many more people.

Renaissance Italy, c. 1500

Transfer Point Classical learning from the East first flowed through Italy's wealthy trading cities. As a result, the Renaissance first took root in Italy.

? Location Which powerful city-state controlled several islands in the Adriatic Sea?

Renaissance Politics

Italy had remained the most urbanized and culturally sophisticated part of Europe throughout the Middle Ages. City life never really died out, even under the pressure of constant invasion. Italian nobles and aristocrats lived in great villas and palaces in the towns and cities. There they mingled with bankers, merchants, and other professionals. Soon, intermarriage between aristocratic, merchant, and banking families blurred such class distinctions. The result was a growing, wealthy, literate urban population ripe for cultural development.

Italy's political situation contributed to the emergence of a new urban elite. Ongoing warfare between the papacy and the Holy Roman Empire had split Italy into two great factions: the Guelphs (GWELFS) supporting the church and the Ghibellines (GI-buh-leens) supporting the empire. Families and even whole cities were forced to choose sides. Though fierce and bloody, the struggle allowed the cities to remain relatively independent by playing off popes and emperors against each other. Like the ancient Greek poleis, the Italian city-states became the center of most people's sense of identity and security.

By 1300 most city-states had achieved the status of independent republics. As a consequence of the struggle between popes and emperors, however, rival family groups often competed for power within the cities. Plagued by constant riots, family feuds, and bloodshed, city politics descended into near chaos. Eventually, strong rulers, such as the Medici in Florence, the Este (ES-tay) in Ferrara, and the Visconti (vees-KOHN-tee) in Milan, began to emerge in an effort to restore stability.

Many of the new rulers did not come from an aristocratic background. In Florence, for example, the Medici, originally a family of doctors, made a vast fortune in banking. By 1434 Cosimo de' Medici had emerged as the strongman of Florence. The Medici family controlled the city almost uninterrupted until the early 1700s. Although Florence theoretically remained a republic, the Medici ruled the city much like the tyrants of ancient Greece.

Only Venice remained free of dictatorship. Venice was situated at the head of the Adriatic Sea and built upon a series of islands protected from the mainland by lagoons. Looking mainly to the sea, where Venetian merchant vessels came to dominate the trade of the Mediterranean world, Venice carved out an empire of mainland ports and islands that stretched as far east as Crete. By the 1400s it was not simply an Italian power but a major international power. Even in Venice, however, government remained in the hands of a small group of wealthy citizens.

By the 1400s the ongoing struggle between popes and emperors had resulted in a rough division of the Italian Peninsula into three major areas: Sicily and the Kingdom of Naples in the south, the Papal States in central Italy, and independent city-states in the north. Between 1395 and about 1453, the largest and most prosperous of the northern city-states began to gobble up their neighbors. Florence, Milan, and Venice emerged from this struggle as the dominant powers. Genoa remained independent, but without expanding its influence. Thus, by mid-century, the Italian Peninsula came to be divided among five major powers: Florence, Milan, Venice, Naples, and the Papal States.

In the struggle for power, many of the rising Italian families and city-states hired professional soldiers, known as *condottieri,* to fight for them. Even the popes used *condottieri* in their constant struggle to maintain control of the Papal States. Waging war with mercenaries, however, proved very expensive. Moreover, the mercenaries were not always trustworthy. They might easily change sides for more money, or go into business for themselves. In 1450, for example, Francesco Sforza (SFAWRT-sah), one of the most successful of the *condottieri,* conquered Milan and made himself duke.

As Italians became increasingly sick of war, rival city-states began to use new diplomatic methods to achieve their goals. Instead of the church, once the main institution regulating peace among all Christian countries, rulers began to use professional diplomats and resident

▲ Although his power originally came from his role as a *condottieri,* Francesco Sforza became a respected prince from 1450 to 1466.

ambassadors to settle disputes. In 1454 the leading states signed a general peace treaty. For the next 50 years they did their best to keep the peace. If any state threatened its neighbors, others would join together to oppose it. This system became known as a **balance of power**.

The warfare and almost continuous struggles for power in Renaissance Italy convinced many leaders to look to diplomacy to settle their differences.

Civic Humanism and Politics

In 1494 the fitful peace of Italy was shattered when Charles VIII of France, drawn by Italy's wealth, began the first of a series of invasions designed to take control of the entire Italian Peninsula. After more than 30 years of fighting, the French were finally driven out of Italy by the forces of Charles V, king of Spain and Holy Roman emperor. Although ultimately a failure, the French invasions had ravaged the peninsula. They had also stimulated once again the rivalry between the pope and the Holy Roman emperor, as each side sought to play the French off against the other. In 1527, for example, troops of Charles V sacked and pillaged Rome, forcing the pope to flee for his life.

The ravages of warfare made life in Italy extremely insecure. The church no longer served as a source of stability and peace. To seek comfort and guidance amidst the destruction of foreign invasions, some people turned to a form of humanism developed from Petrarch's ideas.

Where Petrarch emphasized the importance of individual achievement and worth, later humanists emphasized aspects of his message that came to be known as **civic humanism**. The civic humanists argued that individual achievement and education could be fully expressed only if people used their talents and abilities in the service of their cities. Under the influence of civic humanists, the ideal Renaissance man came to be the "universal man," well versed in the classics, but also a man of action—one who could respond to all situations.

In his book *The Courtier,* the Italian diplomat Baldassare Castiglione (kahs-teel-YOH-nay)

▲ The main principle of Castiglione's instructions for the nobility of Italian courts was *sprezzatura*, an effortless superiority.

Theme: **Politics and Law**

After being dismissed from his post in 1512, Niccolò Machiavelli was suspected of supporting an anti-Medici plot and had no hope of ever returning to government service. While in this forced retirement, he wrote *The Prince* and other works that would make him famous. However, most of these works were not published until after his death.

Critical Thinking Ask students why Machiavelli would not have wanted his works published while he was alive.

ANSWER: Students might suggest that he would not want people to judge him for his work's emphasis on ruthlessness.

described how the perfect Renaissance gentle-man—and gentlewoman—should act:

❝ *I would have him speak not always of serious subjects but also of amusing things, such as games and jests and jokes. . . . He should always, of course, speak out fully and frankly, and avoid talking nonsense. . . .*

He should have a knowledge of Greek as well as Latin [and] he should be very well acquainted with the poets, and no less with the orators and historians, and also skilled at writing both verse and prose, especially in our own language. . . .

[The lady must have] those virtues of the mind . . . in common with the courtier, such as prudence, magnanimity [generosity] . . . , and also the qualities that are common to all kinds of women, such as goodness and discretion, the ability to take good care . . . of her husband's belongings and house and children, and the virtues belonging to a good mother. . . . Her serene and modest behavior . . . should be accompanied by a quick and vivacious spirit. ❞

As nobles lost their military role, Castiglione gave them a new idea of refined behavior.

Perhaps the most famous and influential of the civic humanists was Niccolò Machiavelli (mahk-yah-VEL-lee), a citizen of Florence and an official in its government until 1512. Serving his city as a diplomat, Machiavelli was acutely interested in the actual workings of government and the nature of relations between states. Like many humanists, Machiavelli insisted that people should not try to live up to impossibly high ideals of human behavior, but instead should face life as it was and deal with it accordingly.

In 1513 he wrote *The Prince*, an essay to serve as a sort of handbook for rulers. Observing the realities of Italian power politics in his own day, he argued that power and ruthlessness were more important to a leader than idealism. "If you have to make a choice," he wrote, "to be feared is much safer than to be loved." His advice to princes was purely practical; if they wanted to succeed, then they would have to use any means necessary.

Under the influence of men like Machiavelli, many European rulers began to practice politics and diplomacy with less emphasis on the ideal of preserving Christian unity and peace, and more emphasis on enhancing their own power and prestige. With this new approach to affairs of state, first Italy and then the rest of Europe finally gave up any remaining hope that Christendom would become a single political as well as spiritual entity.

The political situation in Italy caused many civic humanists to call for a more realistic and secular attitude toward politics.

The Arts

Even more than politics, the arts reflected the new humanist spirit. Giotto (JAWT-oh), one of the earliest Renaissance painters, revived the Roman belief that observation was the key to artistic creativity. Whereas medieval artists had used idealized and symbolic representation to try to achieve a closeness with God, Giotto believed that artists should depict the things they observed in nature. Above all, the human form took primary importance in Giotto's paintings. He tried to show human figures as if they were sculptures, just as he observed them. Because of his departure from earlier medieval traditions, many scholars consider him the founder of Western pictorial art.

Renaissance Florence. The humanist revival of Classical Greco-Roman culture expanded these artistic developments, particularly in the city of Florence in the 1400s. Under the Medici family, the city was the scene of an intensive artistic awakening. Great competitions were often held to find the most talented artists to paint and sculpt decorations for public buildings.

Out of this frenzy of artistic creativity came one of the greatest sculptors of the Italian Renaissance, Donatello (doh-nah-TEL-loh). Unlike many artists who specialized in one type of person, Donatello was able to sculpt young children, warriors, church fathers, women, and many others with equal detail and convincing realism. Donatello also was greatly concerned with showing the human body in motion, just as ancient Greek and Roman sculptors had done. Above all, he wanted to convey the beauty of the human form.

▼ Like many female Renaissance artists, Sofonisba Anguissola's success was accepted only as a pursuit of "womanly virtue." She painted this self-portrait in 1561.

Patrons of the arts. Like the Medici of Florence, many noble Italian families and wealthy merchants supported the efforts of Renaissance artists. Artists depended on wealthy patrons for their living. Ruling families became the greatest patrons, using the arts to proclaim their own fame and as political statements of their power and wealth. Isabella d'Este, for example, who ruled the northern city-state of Mantua as regent for her husband and son, filled her palace with paintings and sculptures by the finest contemporary artists.

BIOGRAPHY   Isabella was born in 1474 to the powerful and well-educated Este family, the rulers of the Italian city-state of Ferrara. At age 16 she married Francesco Gonzaga (gohn-DZAH-gah), the ruler of Mantua. As she grew older, she exercised her keen intellect by engaging in the intricacies of politics among the city-states of Italy. Through careful negotiations she increased the wealth and power of her possessions. One of Isabella's subjects once said of her: "She trusts no one and will know the motive of everyone."

Long a patron of humanist scholars and artists, in later life Isabella concentrated on filling her palace

Isabella d'Este

BIOGRAPHY

with the greatest works of art and literature of her time. Her court was home to writers, sculptors, and painters, and she had various rooms in the palace designed by leading architects of the day. Even after her death in 1539, her legacy as a great patron lived on in the portraits of her by two of the greatest Renaissance artists, Titian (TISH-uhn) and Leonardo da Vinci (lay-oh-NAHR-doh dah VEEN-chee).

Leonardo da Vinci. Da Vinci himself represented the ideal of the Renaissance man. In addition to being a painter, he was also a sculptor, an architect, and an engineer. He was fascinated by nature and technology. He made sketches of plants and animals, as well as detailed drawings of a flying machine and a submarine. To make his paintings more realistic, he studied anatomy, dissecting human and animal corpses to find out

374

▲ In this detail from the ceiling of the Sistine Chapel Michelangelo expressed his vision of a new and grander humanity. He captured a fleeting moment of action as God extends his finger to touch Adam's with the spark of life.

how they worked. Yet da Vinci's paintings were not simply anatomically correct. They also tried to capture the complexity of the human spirit, as his famous portrait, the *Mona Lisa*, illustrates with its mysterious smile.

Michelangelo and Raphael. Even the art commissioned by the church displayed the humanist influence. Pope Julius II, for example, patronized perhaps the two greatest and most famous artists of the Renaissance, Michelangelo (mee-kay-LAHN-jay-loh) and Raphael (RAF-ee-uhl). One of Michelangelo's most famous works is the painting he completed between 1508 and 1512 on the ceiling of the Sistine Chapel in the Vatican, the pope's residence in Rome. Strongly inspired by Michelangelo, the artist Raphael painted contemporary, Biblical, and classical scenes with a fluidity that made each figure that he portrayed individual and unique. In particular, his portraits captured the realistic form of his subjects, their mood, and their personality.

Like ancient Roman and Greek artists, artists of the Italian Renaissance placed people at the center of their art.

SECTION 2 REVIEW

IDENTIFY and explain the significance of the following:
   standard of living
   Commercial Revolution
   capital
   joint-stock companies
   Renaissance
   Francesco Petrarch
   classical education
   humanism
   balance of power
   civic humanism
   Niccolò Machiavelli
   Isabella d'Este
   Leonardo da Vinci
   Michelangelo

LOCATE and explain the importance of the following:
   Venice
   Milan
   Florence

1. *Main Idea* How did trade influence life in Italy?
2. *Main Idea* What was the focus of Italian Renaissance art and literature?

3. *Geography: Location* How did geography make Italy a logical place for the Renaissance to begin?
4. *Writing to Explain* Explain why, by the 1400s, many Italians felt that they could no longer rely on the church as a means of security and stability.
5. *Synthesizing* What did humanism and politics have to do with one another in Renaissance Italy?

The Northern Renaissance

The new ideas of the humanists in Italy began to spread north to other parts of Europe at the end of the 1400s. As northern writers and artists studied the humanities, many of them took the Renaissance in a new direction. Northern European writers applied humanist principles to Christianity, calling for reform of the church. Artists used Italian techniques to render more down-to-earth interpretations of human figures.

Latin version of the Gutenberg Bible, Mainz, 1456

The Spread of the Renaissance

Around 1500, humanist ideas began to spread across the Alps from Italy to the countries of northern Europe. Diplomacy played a role in this expansion. As rulers sought to escape from constant warfare, states across Europe began to establish resident ambassadors in other royal courts to increase international communication. These ambassadors provided an important link through which new humanist ideas could be shared. But two other factors—the growth of education and new printing methods—played even greater roles.

Education. Students from northern Europe had been traveling to Italy for centuries to study law and medicine at the highly respected Italian universities. By the end of the 1400s, they also had begun to study with Italian humanists. When these students returned to their homes, they brought new humanist ideas with them. As the Commercial Revolution in Europe created new wealth and more people could afford higher education, many new universities were established in France, the Netherlands, and Germany.

Noble families encouraged daughters as well as sons to study the classics, learn languages, and engage in religious and philosophical discussions. One woman described her opportunity to study the humanities as "one of the greatest benefits that God ever gave me." Noblewomen were often influential in spreading humanism. For example, Queen Marguerite of Navarre encouraged the study of Petrarch in France.

Printing. The growing emphasis on education and the spread of humanist ideas were greatly aided by new printing technology. Around 1450 a German printer named Johannes Gutenberg (GOO-tuhn-berk) began to use movable metal type to print books. Centuries earlier, Chinese artisans had learned to use wooden blocks smeared with ink to make many copies of an image or words on paper. Muslim traders had picked up the technique, and by 1400, Spanish Muslims had introduced printed works to Europe. But Gutenberg's new technique allowed multiple copies of books to be produced more

Across the Curriculum: Literature

In *Utopia*, Sir Thomas More called for rulers to tend to the affairs of their own nations rather than make war against other Europeans. However, More did not hold out much hope that things would change. His imaginary traveler from Utopia explains: "Suppose I were at the court of the French king [and I could prove] that all this warmongering [would] . . . end in naught . . . what reception from my listeners . . . do you think this speech of mine would find?" More's reply was, "not a very favorable one."

Critical Thinking Ask students why More might be interested in promoting peace.

ANSWER: Students may answer that after so much war in Europe, More, like many others, hoped for some stability.

▲ Gutenberg invented the printing press with movable metal type, which allowed quick and economical multiple printings of books.

quickly and cheaply. As the technique spread, new ideas reached a growing audience.

As diplomats and students brought humanist ideas from Italy, the growth of universities and the development of printing helped spread the new ideas across northern Europe.

Northern Humanism

As the Renaissance moved north, its character changed. Northern humanists, for example, were often more interested in applying humanist principles and the lessons of the classics to religion than to secular topics. This form of humanism came to be known as **Christian humanism**. The Dutch scholar Desiderius Erasmus (i-RAZ-muhs) was the most influential northern humanist. In 1509 he published *The Praise of Folly*, in which he called for church reform. He was especially critical of ignorance and vice on the part of the clergy. About monks he wrote:

66 *Among them are some who make a great thing out of their squalor and beggary, who stand at the door bawling out their demands for bread— . . . depriving other beggars of no small share of their income. And in this manner these most [dis]agreeable fellows,*

with their filth, ignorance, coarseness, impudence, [are supposed to] re-create for us, as they say, an image of the apostles. 99

In addition to reforming the clergy, Erasmus wanted to eliminate what he considered meaningless rituals such as fasting and the worshipping of holy relics. He emphasized instead personal devotion to God and the moral lessons of Christ's Sermon on the Mount.

Another influential humanist was Erasmus's close friend Sir Thomas More of England. In his most famous work, *Utopia*, published in 1516, More wrote about an ideal society, where citizens could live together in harmony. In this society all citizens were equal and everyone worked to support the group. *Utopia* reflected More's belief in the humanist idea that people were capable of managing their own affairs—they did not need the church to tell them what to do.

Unlike humanism in Italy, humanism in the North led to calls for social and religious reform.

The Renaissance in England

The writings of More and Erasmus were enormously popular in England. But the Renaissance in England did not reach its height until the late 1500s, when it was already dying out in Italy and other parts of Europe. Since England received Renaissance ideas later, it developed them independently. When the well-educated Queen Elizabeth I ascended the throne in 1558, she encouraged the patronage of court poets, playwrights, and actors. In part because of her patronage of the arts, the Renaissance in England has often been called the **Elizabethan Age**.

For their spark of inspiration, writers of the Elizabethan Age looked to Petrarch and other Italian humanists. Like their Italian predecessors, English writers glorified human endeavors and the beauty of human love. From Petrarch the English adapted the type of poetry known as the sonnet. Sonnets, like the following verse by William Shakespeare, possibly the greatest of the Elizabethan writers, often praised the beauty of a woman or explored the nature of love:

> *Shall I compare thee*
> *to a summer day?*
> *Thou art more lovely and*
> *more temperate.*
> *Rough winds do shake*
> *the darling buds of May.*
> *And summer's lease hath*
> *all too short a date.*

Many writers of the English Renaissance combined the glorification of humankind with a strong sense of national pride. For many people in England, the Renaissance seemed a time of unlimited possibilities for the nation and the individual. National histories became popular reading for members of the upper classes. In England as in other countries, authors began to write in their own languages, rather than in Latin as earlier humanist scholars had done.

The unique spirit of the Elizabethan Age was captured in drama. Plays had been a popular form of entertainment for many centuries. Religious "morality" plays were performed in or near churches, and servants at the courts of nobles performed comic plays. In the Elizabethan Age, however, groups of professional actors roamed the countryside performing for the public.

The first public theaters were not built in London until the end of the 1500s, but by the time of Shakespeare's death in 1616, London was the scene of a thriving theater district, with some theaters able to hold up to 2,000 spectators. The great English theaters allowed the ideas of the Renaissance to reach a mass audience, not merely the literate upper classes. Shakespeare, for example, wrote comedies and tragedies that appealed to ordinary people. Through themes as diverse as history, romantic love, murder, magic, and witchcraft, he explored the depths of human nature.

The main character in *The Tragicall History of Dr. Faustus*, a play published in 1604 by Christopher Marlowe, summed up the spirit of the English Renaissance by saying:

> *O what a world of profit and delight,*
> *Of power, of honor, of omnipotence,*
> *Is promised to the studious artisan!*
> *All things that move between the quiet poles*
> *Shall be at my command.*

▲ Elizabeth's support of the arts allowed the Renaissance to flourish in England even as it faded in Italy.

Renaissance thinkers believed that with creativity human beings could control their own destinies and the world around them.

> **W**riters of the English Renaissance combined the humanist celebration of human potential with a belief that the English nation possessed unlimited possibilities in the world.

Northern Renaissance Art

Like their literary counterparts, the artists of northern Europe were also influenced by the Italian Renaissance. Not only did northern artists travel to Italy to study the techniques of Italian painters, but Italian works of art were commonly bought by the nobility and wealthy merchants of northern Europe.

Although northern Renaissance artists adopted Italian techniques, their works reflected a more down-to-earth view of humanity. Whereas Italian artists tried to capture the classical beauty of Greek and Roman gods in their paintings, northern artists often tried to depict people as they really were.

One of the most influential artists of the northern Renaissance was the German painter and engraver Albrecht Dürer (DYUR-uhr). Dürer was the first northern artist to study in Italy.

People in the Renaissance paintings look more realistic; the Renaissance artists use perspective to depict depth.

History THROUGH THE ARTS

Renaissance Painting: Realism and Perspective

The story goes that as an admirer stood gazing at an early Renaissance painting, he reached up to brush a fly away from the canvas. He was pleasantly shocked, however, to find that the fly was in fact part of the painting! The artist, Giotto, had succeeded in painting a scene so lifelike that it gave viewers the impression that they were looking at a panorama of reality. Painting during the Renaissance marked a dramatic change in the way artists perceived their subjects. In the medieval period, the dominant theme of art was the glory of God and his authority over humanity. As humanists reestablished human beings as the central figures in life on Earth, artists placed humanity at the center of Renaissance painting.

The technique artists used to achieve realism in Renaissance painting is known as perspective. Perspective involves the placement of objects and figures in a painting to appear as they would be seen if they were real—some close, some farther away, some bathed in light, others hidden in shadow. Artists often made detailed mathematical calculations of the exact proportions of different parts of the human body in order to make more realistic figures.

Although Renaissance painting in northern Europe resembles Italian painting, the two styles also illustrate the differences between northern and southern artists and their societies. Many Italian paintings, such as Michelangelo's *The Last Judgment,* depict human figures based on the models of Greek and Roman art. Athletic figures with rippling muscles demonstrate the artist's admiration of the human form. In Dürer's *The Four Apostles,*

Albrecht Dürer, *Four Apostles*, 1526

however, the figures seem more like Europeans of the 1500s, bald, frail, and imperfect, than Greek gods. By depicting the early fathers of the Christian Church and by emphasizing the importance of the Bible as the basis for Christianity, *The Four Apostles* also reflects the ideas of Christian humanism.

Michelangelo, *The Last Judgment*, 1534–1541

Thinking About Art

How do the two Renaissance paintings above differ from the medieval painting on the left?

Anon., *The Annunciation to the Shepherds*, 1002–1014

He learned the Italian sense of achieving accurate proportions in the human form but, unlike his teachers, Dürer often chose ordinary subjects for his work. Even in his religious works, he modeled many figures after ordinary Europeans. He also found a mass market for his art through cheap woodcuts and engravings, which his wife sold at fairs and markets.

Another artist, Hans Holbein (HAWL-byn) the Younger, a contemporary of Dürer, was most famous for his portraits. He painted many of the well-known Europeans of his day, including Erasmus, Thomas More, and King Henry VIII of England. He often tried to capture the spirit of his subjects' Renaissance outlook. In *The French Ambassadors*, for example, he posed his two subjects standing by a table filled with books, globes, and astronomical devices.

In the area of the Netherlands known as Flanders, a group of Renaissance painters developed their own distinct style. Known as the **Flemish School**, these painters were noted for the exquisite detail of their work and for their landscapes. These landscapes were much darker and colder than those of Italian painters, due to the difference in climate between northern Europe and Italy. Pieter Brueghel (BROO-guhl), one of the most famous of the Flemish painters, often depicted scenes of local landscapes, featur-

▲ *The French Ambassadors* is an example of Holbein's style of reserve and total control of surface and design.

ing common peasants performing everyday tasks. By showing the peasants, Brueghel hoped to demonstrate the often cruel treatment they received from the upper classes.

Although northern European artists were inspired by the techniques of Italian artists, their figures generally resemble ordinary Europeans, rather than ancient gods and goddesses.

SECTION 3 REVIEW

IDENTIFY and explain the significance of the following:
  Marguerite of Navarre
  Christian humanism
  Erasmus
  Sir Thomas More
  Elizabethan Age
  Albrecht Dürer
  Hans Holbein
  Flemish School

1. **Main Idea** What factors contributed to the spread of humanist ideas across Europe?

2. **Main Idea** What form did humanism take as it spread from Italy to northern Europe?
3. **The Arts** How was northern Renaissance art similar to and different from the art of the Italian Renaissance?
4. **Writing to Explain** Explain why a person could argue

that the Renaissance in England was more "democratic" than in other places in Europe.
5. **Analyzing** How is the painting below an example of Renaissance art in general and of northern Renaissance art in particular?

Detail from
The Isenheim Altarpiece

Theme: Religion

Angela de Merici was at the center of the group of 12 women who founded the Ursuline order. Merici's interest in educating women in the Christian faith began when she was about 20. She turned her home in Desenzano, Italy into a school, which was later relocated to Brescia. Merici recruited other women to help with her work, and in 1535 the group formed the Ursulines.

Critical Thinking Ask students why religious reformers focused on education.

ANSWER: Students could suggest that it might be easier to train a new generation in the principles of reform than to change the minds of people who had already learned something different.

SECTION 4
The Reformation

FOCUS

- What issues led to the Protestant Reformation in Germany?
- How and why did the Protestant Reformation spread to other parts of Europe?
- How did the Catholic Church counter the Protestant Reformation?
- What were the causes of the wars of religion?

The questioning spirit of the Renaissance also affected the church. Some Christians began to seek a more personal, inward faith as a means of achieving salvation, while others continued to rely on the guidance of the church and the priesthood. As the church became mired in the struggle for earthly power and wealth, many Christians demanded reform. In the 1500s and 1600s, calls for reform broke apart the unity of western Christendom. As those who left the Catholic Church clashed with those who remained, the old medieval world was swept away. In its place a new, increasingly secular sense of European identity emerged.

Saint Bartholomew's Day Massacre, 1572; German woodcut from the late 1500s

The Protestant Reformation

Erasmus and other humanists who openly complained about corruption in the church were not alone in their views. Many Europeans were troubled by the low level of morality and education among many of the clergy. They also increasingly feared and resented the power of the popes, who raised armies, conquered territory, and ruled the church more like territorial princes than priests. Above all, perhaps, people wanted reassurance that they had the means to achieve salvation and eternal life after death.

Indulgences. People also resented church efforts to raise money. Among the most despised practices was the selling of **indulgences**. Since the days of Pope Gregory the Great, Catholics had believed that after dying people went to a place halfway to heaven called purgatory, where their souls worked off the sins they had committed while alive. Indulgences were pardons issued by the pope that people could buy in order to reduce their time in purgatory. In the early 1500s Pope Leo X approved the sale of indulgences in Germany to raise money for the construction of Saint Peter's Basilica in Rome. For Martin Luther, a monk in the German town of Wittenberg, this was the last straw.

Luther's revolt. On October 31, 1517, Luther posted a list of 95 theses, or statements, on the door of the church at Wittenberg Castle. In these statements he challenged the sale of indulgences and other papal practices and stated his own views on doctrine. Although the action was not unusual—this was the way church scholars generally put forward ideas for debate—Luther's attack struck a chord throughout Germany. His action began what is known as the **Protestant Reformation**, because its supporters protested against the Catholic Church.

BIOGRAPHY   Martin Luther was born in 1483 in Eisleben, a mining town in Saxony. His parents were fairly prosperous and saw to it that their son received a good education. Following his father's wishes, Luther entered the university at Erfurt to study law. On a trip back to Erfurt from visiting his family, he was caught in a violent thunderstorm. When a blinding bolt of lightning struck

Martin Luther
BIOGRAPHY

close to him Luther cried out: "Saint Anne, help! I will become a monk!" Surviving the storm, he kept his promise and entered an Augustinian monastery.

Luther had always been troubled by the question of how he could overcome his sins and enter heaven. One evening as he studied the Bible, the answer came to him: salvation could be achieved through faith in God alone—no acts or works that people performed would assure them salvation. He also came to believe that Christian practices must come from the Bible alone. All other practices should be abolished.

Luther had not initially intended to break away from the Roman Catholic Church. All he wanted was reform. His actions at Wittenberg, however, came at a sensitive time. Many German princes resented the church's power and wealth. The church owned vast tracts of the best land throughout the German states, land that could not be taxed by the rulers. When Luther's defiance became public, therefore, people all over Germany gathered to support him, including many of the princes.

The Diet of Worms. Pope Leo X responded to Luther's claims by branding him a heretic and ordering him excommunicated. To enforce the ruling, the Holy Roman emperor Charles V ordered Luther to the city of Worms (VOHRMS) in 1521 to appear before the Imperial Diet, a council of rulers in the empire. Luther was shown a pile of his writings. When asked if he would take back what he had written he replied:

❝ *My conscience is captive to the Word of God. I cannot and I will not recant anything, for to go against conscience is neither right nor safe. Here I stand. I cannot do otherwise. God help me. Amen.* ❞

The full Diet refused to take action, since many of the princes supported Luther. However, the emperor, supported by the remaining members of the Diet, condemned Luther as an outlaw. Quickly, Luther's patron, Elector Frederick the Wise of Saxony, whisked him out of town and hid him in the Wartburg, a castle in southeastern Germany.

Luther's message. In the Wartburg, Luther began to translate the New Testament from Greek into German. Translation of the Bible into the language of ordinary people meant that the scriptures could be heard and easily understood by even the simplest peasants, not just by those who knew Latin or Greek. Luther also soon began to develop a whole new doctrine based on the idea that no individual needed the help of a priest or anyone else to have a direct relationship with God. This doctrine became known as the "priesthood of all believers."

The implications of this idea were profound. Without the need for a priesthood, there was really no need for a church hierarchy supported by huge landed estates. This appealed to many German princes, who resented the taxes and property the church enjoyed. They were also delighted to have an issue on which they could assert their independence from the emperor. Soon Lutheranism had become the new state religion of most of northern Germany.

In 1525 Luther married a former nun, Katharina von Bora, illustrating his belief that the clergy should be free to marry. Through the rest of his life he continued to write essays, pamphlets, and hymns. As the results of his protest became clear, however, he complained that it had resulted in the destruction of the unity of Christendom. In his old age Luther actually became more conservative than many younger followers. Nevertheless, when asked on his deathbed in 1546 whether he still believed in his ideas about Christianity, he answered simply, "Yes."

◀ **Katharina von Bora, Martin Luther's wife**

The printing press played an important role in spreading Reformation ideas. By 1550, Protestant authors had produced perhaps as many as 10,000 different titles. Many of these titles took the form of pamphlets. In the early years these pamphlets were often fewer than 20 pages long and were meant to be read aloud to audiences as sermons. In addition, Protestant reformers published many one-page woodcuts aimed at influencing the nonreading public.

Critical Thinking Ask students what forms a "mass media" campaign might take today.

ANSWER: Student answers should include television, radio, and movies, as well as printed material.

Dissatisfaction with the Roman Catholic Church, combined with economic and political grievances in Germany, led to the Protestant Reformation.

The Spread of Protestantism

The Reformation spread rapidly throughout northern Europe, but not all reformers agreed with Luther's doctrine. Many humanists, for example, believed that people had some degree of free will to make choices in life. They rejected Luther's view that people could not change the pattern God had created for them. As this and other issues were debated, many Protestants founded their own small religious groups, or **sects**, across northern Europe. Each of these small groups had its own ideas about salvation. Some relied on the believer's direct communication with God and put little emphasis on the Bible. Others abolished private property and lived with everything owned in common.

Calvinism. In Switzerland a new Protestant movement attempted to inject strict discipline into the Reformation. The pioneer in this movement was a reformer named Huldrych Zwingli (TSVING-lee). Zwingli was killed in battle in 1531, defending his faith, but his ideas were carried on by John Calvin, a French Protestant. Inspired by Saint Augustine, Calvin preached the doctrine of **predestination**—the idea that God knew who would be saved even before people were born, and therefore guided the lives of those destined for salvation.

In 1536 Calvin settled in Geneva, where he and his followers, called **Calvinists**, soon came to control the local city government. Convinced that people were by nature sinful, Calvinists passed laws regulating many aspects of the daily lives of citizens. Laws prohibited dancing, card playing, showy dress, and profane language. Violators were often severely punished. Rather than being seen as a burden, however, this strictness was the heart of Calvinism's appeal. It gave its followers a sense of mission and discipline. Calvinists felt they were setting an example and making the world fit for the "elect," those who had been chosen for salvation.

Offering a new sense of discipline based on their belief that they were predestined for salvation from birth, the Calvinists encouraged the spread of the Protestant Reformation.

The Church of England. Meanwhile, in England a protest was developing against the Roman Catholic Church for very different reasons. King Henry VIII had defended the church against Luther, calling his ideas "false and wicked." For this the pope granted Henry the title "Defender of the Faith." But in 1529 Henry asked the church to grant him a divorce from his wife, Catherine of Aragon. Catherine had borne Henry a daughter, Mary, but the couple had been unable to have a son to secure the royal succession. Pope Clement VII refused the divorce. Infuriated, Henry rejected the pope's authority, proclaimed himself head of the church in England, and forced the English bishops to accept his authority. The church in England quickly granted the divorce.

Henry soon grew dissatisfied with his new wife, Anne Boleyn. With her, too, he had a daughter—Elizabeth—rather than a son. After three years of marriage, Henry had Boleyn executed for treason on trumped-up charges. Still hoping for a male heir who could prevent a recurrence of the

▲ Geneva was about this size when Calvin arrived there in 1536; he and his followers soon controlled the city government.

previous century's civil wars, Henry eventually married six times in all. Only his third wife, Jane Seymour, had a son, Edward.

Since Henry's break with Rome was more for personal reasons than religious ones, he made little attempt to rid the Church of England of Catholic rituals. He took other steps, however, that made a reconciliation with Rome unlikely. An extravagant king, he was usually in need of funds. To raise money Henry closed the Catholic monasteries and convents across England and sold most of the vast estates to the nobles. This action committed not only the king but most of his nobles to maintaining the break with Rome, since a reconciliation might force them to return their new lands.

Henry VIII and Catherine of Aragon were married in 1509. He divorced her 24 years later.

*W*hen the Catholic Church refused him a divorce from his wife, King Henry VIII made England a Protestant nation.

The Catholic Reformation

By 1560 England, Scotland, Sweden, Denmark, and parts of Germany, France, Poland, Switzerland, and the Netherlands all had large Protestant populations. Realizing the need for reform, Catholic leaders had launched a major reform movement known as the **Catholic Reformation**, or Counter-Reformation. Between 1545 and 1563 church leaders met in the Italian city of Trent to redefine the doctrines of the Catholic faith. Among the reforms introduced by the **Council of Trent** were a ban on the sale of indulgences and church offices and new rules for the conduct of the clergy.

Above all, the Council of Trent rejected the Protestants' emphasis on self-discipline and individual faith. The council argued that the church could help believers achieve salvation by using rich display, mystery, and magnificent ceremonies to inspire faith. Millions of people, indeed the majority of Europeans, agreed and remained Catholic.

Catholics also founded several new religious orders to help win back support for the church. In Italy in 1535, for example, a group of devoted women founded the Ursulines, a religious order focused on religious education for women. Perhaps the most successful and influential of the new orders, however, was the Society of Jesus, or **Jesuits**. The Jesuit order was founded in 1534 by Ignatius de Loyola, a Basque nobleman and ex-soldier. The order was approved by the pope in 1539. Loyola, the Father General, ran the Jesuits like a military organization, emphasizing, above all, obedience to the church:

66 *Putting aside all private judgement, we should keep our minds prepared and ready to obey promptly and in all things the true spouse of Christ our Lord, our Holy Mother, the hierarchical Church.* 99

The Jesuits, like the Ursulines, concentrated on education as a means of combating the Protestant Reformation. They established missions, schools, and universities. With such effective organizations, the Catholic Church began to regain ground against Protestantism. Between 1570 and 1650, for example, Protestant control over Europe fell from about 40 percent to about 20 percent.

RESOURCE ACTIVITY

GLOBAL HISTORY RESOURCE CENTER
Reading: *Loyola's Rules for Thinking with the Church*

Print out and distribute the reading. Have students read Loyola's suggestions for Catholics. Then have each student imagine he or she is a Protestant and write a response to one of Loyola's rules, including specific reasons why they object to it or agree with it.

Level 2

RESOURCE ACTIVITY

WRITING PROJECTS
Writing Project 14
Writing a Comparison Essay

Have students study the chapter and follow the steps for completing a paper comparing the Protestant and Catholic Reformations.

All Levels

To help in the struggle against Protestant doctrines, the Catholic Church also revived the Inquisition and the *Index Expurgatorius*, a list of books that the church warned people not to read on peril of losing their souls. Similar measures were also enacted by Protestants, as they too tried to enforce conformity to their new theology. As each side sought to reestablish certainty in the means necessary for salvation, intolerance grew and dissenters on both sides suffered torture and death.

The Catholic Church countered the Protestant Reformation by enacting internal reforms, restating its official doctrines, and establishing new religious orders to spread the faith.

THROUGH OTHERS' EYES

Violence in the Reformation

The religious warfare following the Reformation shocked the people of Europe, Christians and non-Christians alike. Many Jews hoped that the Reformation would bring about a new spirit of tolerance among religious groups, but the brutality shown by Protestants and Catholics toward one another dashed those hopes. A Jewish observer in Poland described the waves of violence and offered his own explanation:

66 We have both heard and seen accounts printed in Christian books of the great acts of vengeance perpetrated in England in these times. For even to this very day the priests of the Papist faith of Rome and all who believe in it and are drawn to it are subjected to a cruel death. The reverse is the case in Spain and France, where a brutal death is meted out to those who believe in and follow the instructions of Martin Luther. The reports received make one's hair stand on end. All this has come to pass on account of their sins. For in the three kingdoms mentioned, much Jewish blood was spilled through libellous accusations, oppressive measures and forced conversions, until they expelled the Jews from their lands and none of them remained. 99

The Wars of Religion

As people and nations divided along religious lines, Europe entered a period of more than 100 years of almost continuous warfare. The wars left much of northern Europe, particularly Germany, in ruins and took a heavy toll in human lives.

Germany. In 1531 Protestant princes and free cities in Germany joined together for mutual protection against attack from the forces of the leading Catholic ruler, the emperor Charles V. In 1547 Charles defeated the Protestant princes in battle, but was unable to break their power. With their treasuries emptied by the years of warfare, in 1555 Charles and the princes signed the **Peace of Augsburg**. Under the terms of the treaty, each prince would choose the religion of his own territory. The agreement settled the issue of religion for the moment, but created a patchwork of Protestant and Catholic states across Germany, where neighbors kept an uneasy peace.

Spain. Elsewhere in Europe, tensions between Protestants and Catholics also erupted into warfare. For example, Calvinists in the northern provinces of the Netherlands revolted against Spanish rule. After many years of bloody fighting, the Protestants finally gained a truce with Spain in 1609. The seven northern provinces formed the independent nation of the Netherlands, while the southern provinces remained Spanish possessions.

Perhaps more serious was the conflict between Spain and England. In 1588 King Philip II of Spain attempted to invade England. He hoped to depose the Protestant Queen Elizabeth and reclaim England for the Roman Catholic Church. The Spanish sent a huge fleet of about 130 ships, known as the "Invincible Armada," against England. As the Armada lay at anchor in Calais, the English set ships on fire and sent them drifting toward the Spanish fleet. This caused the Spanish ships to scatter, making them easier targets. The Armada fled, only to be struck by heavy storms in the North Sea. Less than half the fleet returned to Spain. The defeat of the Armada ensured England's future as a Protestant nation.

European Religions, 1600

Map legend:
- Lutheran
- Calvinist
- Anglican
- Roman Catholic with Protestant minorities
- Roman Catholic
- Orthodox
- Muslim
- Boundary of Holy Roman Empire

A Conflict of Faiths From 1517 to 1600, the Reformation gained many converts in northern Europe. However, southern Europe remained largely Catholic.

Linking Geography and History What religion was dominant in England? Sweden? Italy?

France. Meanwhile, France also descended into religious civil war. At one point, Calvinists controlled nearly one third of the country. But the French kings of the Valois dynasty opposed having Protestants, or **Huguenots** as they were called, within the country. Religious warfare during the late 1500s split France apart. The Huguenots continued to resist even after the Saint Bartholomew's Day massacre in 1572, when rioters in Paris and other cities killed about 20,000 Protestants around the country.

When Henry III, the last Valois king, died without a male heir, the religious warfare became a dynastic struggle as well. Eventually, the fighting ended in 1598, when Henry IV, the first king of the new Bourbon dynasty, signed the **Edict of Nantes**. The edict called a truce between Roman Catholics and Protestants. It allowed the Huguenots to retain control of the cities they occupied at the time. Henry himself had once been a Calvinist leader but had converted to Catholicism in order to assume the throne, reportedly observing, "Paris is well worth a mass!" He spent the rest of his reign trying to heal the wounds of civil war and to reestablish the unity of France.

SECTION 4 REVIEW ANSWERS
(p. 386)

IDENTIFY
For significance, see the following pages:
indulgences (p. 380)
Martin Luther (p. 380)
Protestant Reformation (p. 380)
Charles V (p. 381)
sects (p. 382)
predestination (p. 382)
Calvinists (p. 382)
Catholic Reformation (p. 383)
Council of Trent (p. 383)
Jesuits (p. 383)
Peace of Augsburg (p. 384)
Huguenots (p. 385)
Edict of Nantes (p. 385)
Treaty of Westphalia (p. 386)

LOCATE
For locations, see the map on p. 385.

1. indulgences, church corruption, church control of land, doctrinal issues
2. Council of Trent, establishment of the Jesuits and the Ursulines
3. German princes supported Luther's attempt to break free from the Holy Roman emperor; rulers used religion as an excuse to seize territory.

385

The Thirty Years' War. The most brutal and destructive of the religious wars in Europe was the Thirty Years' War. The war began in 1618 in the city of Prague when Protestant rebels tossed two representatives of the Holy Roman emperor out of a castle window. News of the event quickly spread and the province erupted in general rebellion. The Holy Roman emperor called on Catholic allies in Germany and Spain to help put down the revolt. The war rapidly spread throughout Germany.

The Thirty Years' War turned much of Germany into a wasteland. Soldiers plundered towns and killed anyone suspected of supporting the enemy. An eyewitness reported the brutality of the sack of the city of Magdeburg in 1631:

66 *Then there was naught but beating and burning, plundering, torture, and murder. . . . In this frenzied rage, the great and splendid city that had stood like a fair princess in the land was now, in its hour of direst need and unutterable distress and woe, given over to the flames, and thousands of innocent men, women, and children . . . were tortured and put to death.* 99

◀ The burning of the city of Baussen was typical of the destruction caused in the Thirty Years' War.

As the war progressed, other factors besides religion sparked hostilities. German princes who wanted to remain independent of the emperor's authority often became Protestants. National and dynastic rivalries also played a role. Catholic France, for example, which feared the power of the Habsburg emperors, usually sided with Protestants. Gustavus Adolphus, the ambitious king of Sweden, saw a chance to carve out an empire, and tried to make himself leader of the Protestant cause.

The war finally came to an end in 1648 when, out of sheer exhaustion, the warring parties signed the **Treaty of Westphalia**. After three decades of bloodshed in which an estimated one third of the German population died, the settlement of Westphalia did little more than reaffirm the right of rulers to choose the religion of their territories.

The Reformation and political rivalries unleashed the most bitter and destructive internal wars European civilization had ever experienced.

SECTION 4 REVIEW

IDENTIFY and explain the significance of the following:
 indulgences
 Martin Luther
 Protestant Reformation
 Charles V
 sects
 predestination
 Calvinists
 Catholic Reformation
 Council of Trent
 Jesuits
 Peace of Augsburg
 Huguenots
 Edict of Nantes
 Treaty of Westphalia

LOCATE and explain the importance of the following:
 Wittenberg
 Worms
 Geneva
 Prague

1. *Main Idea* What factors led to the Protestant Reformation?
2. *Main Idea* In what ways did Catholics respond to the Protestant Reformation?
3. *Religion* How did religion become a political issue in the 1500s and 1600s?

4. *Writing to Explain* Explain the consequences of Henry VIII's decision to break away from the Roman Catholic Church and form the Protestant Church of England.
5. *Synthesizing* In what ways did the division of Christianity into Protestantism and Catholicism lead to violence? Why do you think religion played a role in warfare? What other similar examples of violence over religious issues can you think of in history or from the present?

Review

On a separate sheet of paper, complete the following exercises:

WRITING A SUMMARY
Using the essential points in the text, write a brief summary of the chapter.

REVIEWING TERMS
From the following list, choose the term that correctly matches the definition.

Peace of Augsburg
standard of living
Treaty of Westphalia
indulgences
Great Schism
humanism

1. intellectual movement focusing on the celebration of human potential and emphasizing classical learning
2. pardons from the pope to cut down on the time a person spends in purgatory
3. agreement of 1555 between the Holy Roman emperor and the Protestant princes stating that each ruler would have the power to determine the religion in his or her own territory
4. the level at which people exist in society based on their ability to obtain needed and desired goods and services
5. division in the Catholic Church, caused by the French king's establishment of the papacy at Avignon

REVIEWING CHRONOLOGY
List the following events in their correct chronological order.

1. Martin Luther posts his 95 theses.
2. The Hundred Years' War breaks out.
3. The Treaty of Westphalia is signed.
4. The Spanish Armada is defeated by the English.

UNDERSTANDING THE MAIN IDEA
1. What were the causes of the Protestant Reformation?
2. How did the Renaissance spread from Italy to other parts of Europe?
3. How did humanism change as it spread to northern Europe?
4. What were some of the consequences of the Thirty Years' War?
5. How did new technology affect the fighting during the Hundred Years' War?

THINKING CRITICALLY
1. **Assessing Consequences** Why might a person argue that the Peace of Augsburg only set the stage for the bloody Thirty Years' War?
2. **Analyzing** In what ways did religion become very much a political issue in Europe between 1350 and 1648?

Building Your Portfolio

Complete the following activities individually or in groups.

1. **Religion** During the time of the Reformation, both Protestant and Catholic leaders created posters, called "broadsides," to persuade people to either become Protestant or remain Catholic. The posters were usually composed only of images, because most people could not read. Imagine that you are an artist in Europe in the 1500s and have been given the task of creating a broadside for either the Protestant or Catholic cause. Your poster should include positive images to attract people to your side. Your poster should also contain positive slogans, aimed at persuading the more educated members of society to become Protestant or remain loyal to the Roman Catholic Church.
2. **The Arts** Imagine that you are a Renaissance author or artist. If you are an author, write a poem or short play reflecting the ideas of humanism. If you choose to be an artist, create an original painting, drawing, or sculpture based on Renaissance ideas. Write a short presentation for your work, explaining how it reflects the ideas of the Renaissance. Also, explain why you chose the subject you did.

3. Many northern scholars used humanism to call for social and religious reform.
4. spread great destruction across central Europe; many people were killed, particularly in Germany; Treaty of Westphalia did little more than reaffirm agreement of the Peace of Augsburg of 1555 that rulers could choose the religion of their territories
5. The Welsh longbow allowed English archers to pierce knights' armor, putting an end to feudal military tactics; both sides began to use gunpowder and cannons to destroy castle defenses.

THINKING CRITICALLY
1. The Peace of Augsburg set up a patchwork of Protestant and Catholic territories across central and northern Europe. Small local disputes could easily turn into wars of religious intolerance.
2. French kings hoped to dominate the papacy by keeping the popes in France; in Italy popes became involved in political disputes over territory; Protestant princes supported Martin Luther in an attempt to break free from control by the Holy Roman emperor; Catholic Spain tried to defeat Protestant England and restore the country to Catholicism; during the Thirty Years' War, rulers used religion as an excuse to conquer new territories.

Chapter 15

A New Worldview in Europe 1450–1715

Chapter Planning Guide

	TEXTBOOK	CORE RESOURCES	VISUAL RESOURCES	MULTIMEDIA
Introduction	pp. 388–389	Block Scheduling Handbook: Ch. 15		Videodisc Segment 15 and Viewing Guide: *A Different Way of Thinking*
Lesson 15.1 The Era of Absolutism	pp. 390–397 Biography: *Louis XIV*, p. 392 Map: *Europe by 1714*, p. 393	Reading 15.1: *Charles I's Speech on the Scaffold*	Art and History 15: *Peter I at the Founding of St. Petersburg*	GHRC 15 Readings: *Thomas Hobbes: Pessimist or Realist?; Jacques Bossuet on Royal Authority; The Gilded Life at Louis XIV's Court* GHRC 15/Videodiscs: Images— *Queen Elizabeth I at Prayer; The Palace of Versailles*
Lesson 15.2 Early Modern European Society	pp. 398–401	Reading 15.2: *Witch Trials in Europe*	Everyday Life 15: *The Frost Fair*	
Lesson 15.3 The Scientific Revolution	pp. 402–409 Literature Through Time: *Don Quixote de la Mancha*, p. 405 Through Others' Eyes: *News Spread Fast About Western Science*, p. 408	Reading 15.3: *On the Motion of the Heart and Blood*		GHRC 15 Readings: *Nicolaus Copernicus Revolutionizes Astronomy; René Descartes on Doubt and Truth; Isaac Newton and the Apple* GHRC 15/Videodiscs: Images— *The Copernican View of the Universe; Louis XIV Founds an Observatory*
Lesson 15.4 A New Spirit of Exploration	pp. 410–416 Geography and History: *Sailing into the Unknown*, pp. 414–415	Reading 15.4: *Marco Polo in China* Geography Activity 15: *Crossing the Atlantic* Writing Project 15: *Writing a Diary* Skills Activity 15: *Analyzing Secondary Sources*	Geography and History 15: *The World Atlas Circa 1500*	GHRC 15 Readings: *Christopher Columbus Finds a New World; Ferdinand Magellan Prepares to Sail* GHRC 15/Videodiscs: Images— *Mercator and Hondius Map the World; Two Worlds Meet in 1492;* Map—*European Idea of the Atlantic Before Columbus*
Chapter Investigation and Enrichment	pp. 388–416	Chapter 15 Investigation: *Talk Show: Changing Europe's Worldview* People in World History 15 Explorations in Daily Life 15		GHRC 15/Videodiscs
Review and Assessment	Section 1 Review, p. 397 Section 2 Review, p. 401 Section 3 Review, p. 409 Section 4 Review, p. 416 Chapter 15 Review, p. 417	Chapter Review Activity 15 Vocabulary Activity 15 Themes Review 15 Section Study Guides 15.1–15.4 Main Idea Activities 15.1–15.4 Daily Quizzes 15.1–15.4 Chapter 15 Test Sheltered English Ch. 15 Test Ch. 15 Test Generator		Audio CDs: Ch. 15 Summary (English and Spanish)

INTRODUCING THE CHAPTER

Textbook pp. 388–389

CHAPTER OVERVIEW

Europe's monarchs sought to strengthen their hold over their people's lives but found themselves challenged by political thinkers who argued that it was the people who were the source of political authority. The spirit of challenge also extended to scientific thought, as scholars sought to apply new techniques of reasoning to the study of the natural world. Europeans also used new scientific and technological developments to extend their explorations to a search for new trade routes.

PRESENTING THEMES

On the chalkboard or on an overhead transparency, write the following open-ended theme questions.

- **POLITICS AND LAW** How might changes in people's worldview affect the development of their systems of government?
- **SCIENCE AND PHILOSOPHY** How might new methods of investigation change people's worldview?
- **CROSS-CULTURAL INTERACTION** Why might cross-cultural contacts lead people to explore the unknown?

Have students, either individually or in groups, suggest responses to the questions. For the politics and law question, students might suggest that changes in worldview could destroy assumptions about political organization. For the science and philosophy question, students might suggest that if new methods find new knowledge that contradicts accepted ways of looking at the world, many people would be challenged to change their worldview. For the cross-cultural interaction question, students might suggest that cross-cultural contacts could expose people to knowledge that might inspire some people to explore new areas. Save the responses. Once students have studied the chapter, you may wish to have students complete the Themes Review, then compare the two sets of answers.

USING THE VIDEO

Segment 15: *A Different Way of Thinking*

ENGLISH

Search Chapter 15
Videodisc 1, Side B

SPANISH

Search Chapter 15
Videodisc 1, Side B

Tell students that in this chapter they will apply these theme questions to Europe at a time when new discoveries were challenging old assumptions. Then show Segment 15 of the *World History and Cultures Videodiscs*. In this segment students are introduced to a "pre-Newtonian" auto mechanic whose—to us—rather strange, even humorous, ideas about how things work predate the Scientific Revolution. To help students grasp the significant points of the video, have them complete Video Viewing Guide 15.

Key to Ability Levels

All strategies and activities are coded to the following ability levels:

LEVEL 1	**Basic** activities suitable for all students
LEVEL 2	**Average** activities suitable for average to above-average students
LEVEL 3	**Challenging** activities suitable for above-average students
SHELTERED ENGLISH	Activities suitable for students with **Limited English Proficiency**

Additional Resources

BOOKS FOR TEACHERS

Birn, Raymond. *Crisis, Absolutism, Revolution: Europe 1648–1789.* Harcourt Brace Jovanovich College Publishers, 1992. Deals with the social history and political culture of early modern Europe.

Huff, Toby E. *The Rise of Early Modern Science: Islam, China, and the West.* Cambridge University Press, 1993. Explains why modern science developed in the West rather than elsewhere.

BOOKS FOR STUDENTS

Boorstin, Daniel J. *The Discoverers: A History of Man's Search to Know His World and Himself.* Vintage Books, 1985. Discusses several important inventions, exploration, and other intellectual breakthroughs.

Spangenburg, Ray and Diane K. Moser. *The History of Science from the Ancient Greeks to the Scientific Revolution.* New York: Facts on File, 1993. Looks at the development of scientific thought.

MULTIMEDIA MATERIALS

The English Civil War. Encyclopaedia Britannica Educational Corp. Video, 38 min. Examines the many factors that led to the English Civil War.

History Through Art: The Baroque. ZCI. CD-ROM, MAC, DOS, WIN, MPC formats. Illustrates the history and art of Baroque Europe from 1545 to 1715 and has information about the artists, and the ideas and conflicts that inspired them.

RESOURCES

Pupil's Edition

Biography, p. 392: *Louis XIV*
Map, p. 393: *Europe by 1714*

Core Resources

Reading 15.1: *Charles I's Speech on the Scaffold*

Visual Resources

Art and History Transparency 15: *Peter I at the Founding of St. Petersburg*

Global History Resource Center

Reading: *Thomas Hobbes: Pessimist or Realist?*
Reading: *Jacques Bossuet on Royal Authority*

Reading: *An Englishman's View of Czar Peter's Reforms*
Reading: *Louis XIV's Instructions on How to Rule*
Reading: *The Gilded Life at Louis XIV's Court*
Reading: *Three Views of Elizabeth I*

Videodiscs or Global History Resource Center

Image: *Queen Elizabeth I at Prayer*

Image: *The Palace of Versailles*

Search Frame 874

Search Frame 871

LESSON FOCUS

How did absolute rule change European perspectives on government?

OBJECTIVES

After completing this lesson, students will be able to:

- explain how some Europeans justified absolutism;
- discuss how French and Russian rulers used absolutism;
- describe the effect that absolutism had in Germany and eastern Europe;
- explain why absolutism failed in England.

HOOK: Link to Today

Explain how some Europeans justified absolute rule.
Have students predict what might happen in their community if there were no government. Focus their thinking by reminding them of government services such as garbage collection and law enforcement. Then ask students if they think people would exchange some personal rights for peace and security.

Encourage students to compare this hypothetical situation with the actual disorder, uncertainty, and insecurity in Europe during the 1500s and 1600s. Remind students that lawlessness was a problem throughout Europe following the decline of feudalism. Also, the political chaos of the Reformation caused further destabilization. Then inform students that philosophers, such as Thomas Hobbes, stressed that the only way to end this chaos was through absolute rule. To underscore this point, assign the Global History Resource Center reading on Hobbes.

Continue by mentioning that some people defended absolute rule with religious arguments. Absolute monarchs, they stated, ruled by divine right. To help students understand religious justifications for absolutism, assign the Global History Resource Center reading from the works of Bishop Jacques Bossuet. To provide an example of the link between absolute monarchs and the church, you may wish to display the image of Elizabeth I from the frontispiece of a sixteenth-century prayer book.

Conclude by inviting students to summarize the justifications for absolutism.

Ask: How did people defend absolute rule?
[They thought monarchs ruled through divine right—it was God's will. Also, it was necessary to control the violent nature of people.]

DEVELOP

Compare the effects of absolutism in France and Russia with its effect in Germany and eastern Europe. Have students work individually or in small groups to create a time line showing the development of absolute rule in France and Russia. Encourage them to pay close attention to the biography of Louis XIV. To provide students with additional information, show students Art and History Transparency 15 and assign the accompanying worksheet. You may also wish to assign the Global History Resource Center readings on the czar's reforms, Louis XIV's ideas about ruling, and life at his court, and show the image of Versailles.

When students have completed this activity, call on volunteers to discuss their time lines. Then lead students in a discussion to develop a class generalization of how absolutism affected the two countries. *[Possible response: Absolutism led to the establishment of centralized, sovereign states at the expense of the nobility and some religious groups.]*

Next have students compare absolutism in France and Russia with absolutism in Germany and eastern Europe. Students should recognize that there were many small and medium-sized states in this area of Europe. To illustrate this point, draw students' attention to the map on page 393, noting the number of states in eastern Europe. The rulers of these states did practice absolute rule. This bolstered their power and prevented the rise of a strong central state. Ask students to suggest a generalization about absolutism in Germany and eastern Europe.

PROBE

Discuss absolutism in England. Have students list on the chalkboard England's rulers and major events that occurred during the period discussed in the section. *[Students should mention Henry VIII, Elizabeth I, James I, Charles I, Oliver Cromwell, Charles II, James II, William and Mary; Civil War, Glorious Revolution, Bill of Rights.]* For each leader and event, have students comment on the relationship that existed between the monarchy and Parliament.

Next encourage students to rank each leader and event on a scale of 1 to 10, where 1 represents absolute rule and 10, a powerful Parliament. To help students develop their rankings, assign the Global History Resource Center reading on

Elizabeth I and Core Resources Reading 15.1. Call on volunteers to discuss their rankings. Conclude by asking students to consider the success of absolutism in England. ***Ask: Why did absolutism fail in England?***
> *[The power of Parliament as a representative body prevented the monarchy from establishing absolute rule.]*

CONCLUDE

Evaluate the effects of absolute rule in Europe. Invite students to imagine they are English travelers touring France, Russia, or Germany and eastern Europe in the 1600s. Direct students to write a travel journal entry on observations on the effects of absolute rule on life in their selected area. Suggest that in writing their entries, students make comparisons with life back home. When students have completed this activity, encourage them to compare observations with students who "toured" another area.

EXTEND

Other Media
You may wish to show and discuss the video *The Age of Absolute Monarchs in Europe* (Coronet, color, 13 min.), which focuses on the court of Louis XIV to explain absolute rule.

MEET INDIVIDUAL NEEDS

Gifted Students
Have interested students investigate the St. Bartholomew's Day massacre of Huguenots in France. Have them write a report showing how this action represents absolute rule.

Kinesthetic Learners
Have students create a T-shirt design for one of Europe's absolute monarchs. Use symbols and/or slogans to represent the monarch's ideas about government. (See the Teaching Toolkit in the Global History Resource Center for hints on T-shirt design.)

ASSESS

Review
Have students complete the Section 1 Review. Use answers in the Teacher's Edition, page 397, to assess student mastery of this section.

387D

Textbook pp. 398–401

RESOURCES

Core Resources

Reading 15.2: *Witch Trials in Europe*

Visual Resources

Everyday Life 15: *Frost Fair on the Thames, 1683*

LESSON FOCUS

How did European society change in the 1500s and 1600s?

OBJECTIVES

After completing this lesson, students will be able to:

- identify the social and economic changes that affected life in early modern Europe;
- describe the consequences of higher standards of living in European towns;
- explain why many people in early modern Europe were accused of being witches.

HOOK: Link to Today

Identify a major social problem of the 1500s and 1600s. Call on students to identify what they think are the major social problems confronting the United States today. Note their responses on the chalkboard.

Then tell students that Pope Sixtus V noted a very different social problem in 1587. He observed that starving people could be found everywhere, not only in private houses and in public places, but even in the churches. The pope went on to note that many of the starving were so desperate to find food that they were roaming the countryside like "brute beasts."

Ask: Based on the pope's observations, what do you think was a major social problem of the late 1500s?
[hunger]

Point out that the problem of hunger was related to the social and economic changes that took place in early modern Europe.

DEVELOP

Examine how the period's social and economic changes were related. Create a cause-effect chain diagram on the chalkboard by drawing a series of boxes, each one connected to the next with an arrow. Help students recognize the relations among the period's various economic and social changes by

```
                    Population Increase
                    /                 \
            Higher prices          Food shortages
                 |                       |
         Lower incomes           Migration from rural
         for landlords              to urban areas
                 |                       |
            Enclosure                Wages fall
                  \                   /
                     Insecurity
                    /           \
         Quarrels among       Witch hunts
           neighbors
```

having them complete the diagram. Begin this exercise by writing "Population Increase" in the first box. Then call on volunteers to come to the chalkboard and fill in other boxes, encouraging them to include as many facts and events as they are able to link together.

Have students copy the completed diagram into their notebooks for review purposes.

PROBE

Examine the growing power of the urban middle class.
Remind students that the class of merchants and guild people that had developed during the Middle Ages grew wealthier and more powerful during the 1500s and 1600s.

Ask: *What were the consequences of higher standards of living in European urban areas?*

[Higher standards of living gave rise to a new middle class. Over time, monarchs came to rely on this wealthy group for financing and political support.]

To assist students in understanding the importance of commerce in urban life in the 1500s and 1600s, you may wish to show the Everyday Life 15 transparency and assign the accompanying worksheet.

CONCLUDE

Investigate the great witch-hunts of Europe.
Assign Core Resources Reading 15.2. When students have completed the reading, ask them to imagine that they are preparing to write a magazine article on the witch-hunts that took place in early modern Europe. Have students work in small groups to draw up an outline for the article. Suggest that they begin their outlines by mentioning specific subject areas, such as causes of the witch-hunts, who were accused, how the accused were interrogated, and what punishments they received. Each subject area in the outline should include a synopsis of information to be included and ideas for visuals. Call on group representatives to present and discuss their outlines. Conclude by encouraging students to discuss why they think these witch-hunts took place.

Ask: *Why was there a wave of witch-hunts in early modern Europe?*

[Insecurity, jealousy, and continuing belief in supernatural powers led many people to accuse unpopular neighbors of witchcraft.]

EXTEND

Cross-Curricular Connection: *Government*
Tell students that some towns and cities in early modern Europe passed laws to keep out people who had migrated from rural areas in search of work. Invite students to imagine they are local government officials. Ask them to write a preamble to such a law, explaining the reasons for barring strangers from entering their town or city.

MEET INDIVIDUAL NEEDS

Musical-Rhythmic Learners
Have students research and record music of the period to present to the class. They should relate the music to European society, perhaps by identifying who listened to this type of music and where it might have been performed. Students should also provide lyrics, if any, and be ready to describe instruments of the period.

Linguistic Learners
Present students with the following statement from a letter written by an English official in 1576:

> *The people are increased and ground for ploughs doth want, corn and all other victual is scant . . . and dear.*

Have students "translate" this statement and explain why it is a good summary of the economic problems that affected early modern Europe.

Students Acquiring English
Pair students acquiring English with students who are proficient in English. Have pairs of students work together to answer the focus questions on page 398 of their textbook.

ASSESS

Review
Have students complete the Section 2 Review. Use answers in the Teacher's Edition, page 401, to assess student mastery of this

Lesson 15.3   *The Scientific Revolution*

Textbook pp. 402–409

RESOURCES

Pupil's Edition

Literature Through Time, p. 405: *Don Quixote de la Mancha*

Core Resources

Reading 15.3: *On the Motion of the Heart and Blood*

Global History Resource Center

Reading: *Nicolaus Copernicus Revolutionizes Astronomy*

Reading: *René Descartes on Doubt and Truth*

Reading: *Isaac Newton and the Apple*

Videodiscs or Global History Resource Center

Image: *Copernican View of the Universe*

Search Frame 876

Image: *Galileo Faces the Inquisition*

Search Frame 877

Image: *Robert Hooke's Microscope*

Search Frame 878

LESSON FOCUS

How did the European worldview change in the 1500s and 1600s?

OBJECTIVES

After completing this lesson, students will be able to:

- explain why some Europeans began to question the traditional Christian worldview and describe how they finally shattered it;
- describe the scientific method and how it affected the European worldview;
- detail Sir Isaac Newton's contribution to the Scientific Revolution.

HOOK: Link to Today

Discuss the traditional Christian worldview and how some Europeans began to challenge it. Ask students to describe the path of the sun from morning to night. *[The sun rises in the east and sets in the west.]* Point out that this observation makes it appear true that the sun revolves around the earth. Scientific study, however, shows us that it is the revolution of the earth on its axis that creates this illusion of the sun moving across the sky.

Inform students that the idea of the sun moving around the earth was the basis of the geocentric model of the universe.

Continue by mentioning that the geocentric model is similar to the way a young child looks at the world. Sketch an earth-centered solar system on the chalkboard, labeling the earth "Me" and the various planets as family members and friends. Lead students to see how natural it was for humans to think of their planet as the center of the universe. Then point out that the geocentric model of the universe was the traditional Christian worldview.

Ask: Why did some Europeans begin to question the traditional Christian worldview?

[These people found that the ideas of Plato, the Neoplatonists, and Pythagoras, rediscovered during the Renaissance, contradicted the Christian worldview. Further, these Europeans' interest in magic, astrology, and alchemy encouraged them to question traditional views of how the world around them worked.]

Conclude by informing students that one of the first Europeans to challenge these traditional views was Polish astronomer Nicolaus Copernicus. He suggested that the universe was heliocentric, not geocentric. To illustrate Copernicus's ideas, show the electronic media image of the Copernican universe.

DEVELOP

Discuss the scientists who shattered the traditional Christian worldview. Organize students into small groups and instruct each group to design a "Wanted" poster describing a "scientific revolutionary." Assign each group one of the following: Copernicus, Kepler, Galileo, Vesalius, Harvey, van Leeuwenhoek, or Hooke. Posters should include biographical information and a description of how the scientist's work challenged traditional thinking. In addition to textbook pages 404–406, you might also assign Core Resources Reading 15.3 and the Global History Resource Center reading on Copernicus to provide further details. In addition, you might show the electronic media images of Galileo and of Hooke's microscope as examples of "scientific revolutionaries" and their works.

Display the finished posters. Have students use the information to create a graphic organizer entitled "Scientists Who Shattered the Traditional Worldview."

PROBE

Describe the scientific method and show how it affected the European worldview.

Place unbreakable objects of different sizes on the edge of a table. Present students with the following problem: If I knock all these objects off the table at the same time, which one will land first? Why?

Ask: *How might Francis Bacon approach this problem?*
[by using experimental data to produce a general explanation—inductive reasoning]

Ask: *How might René Descartes try to solve the problem?*
[by working from an unquestionable general truth to the specific—deductive reasoning]

At this point you might assign the Global History Resource Center reading on Descartes. Then have students consider the impact of Bacon's and Descartes's ideas on modern scientific study.

Ask: *Which of these two approaches does the scientific method employ?*
[It combines the two methodologies.]

Conclude by having students discuss why the scientific method was revolutionary. Students should appreciate that it provided the basis for radical changes in the way people thought about their world.

CONCLUDE

Evaluate the contributions to the Scientific Revolution.

Invite students to review the contributions of Copernicus and Galileo. Then have them consider Sir Isaac Newton's contributions.

Ask: *How did Newton add to the Scientific Revolution?*
[He developed laws that described the universe as a well-ordered system.]

Next have students discuss which of these people made the greatest contribution to the Scientific Revolution. Encourage students to offer reasons for their choices. *[Possible responses that students could give include: Copernicus's theory started the revolution; Galileo's observations and measurements solidified it; Newton's laws secured it.]* Conclude by assigning the Global History Resource Center reading on Newton, which provides further information on his work.

EXTEND

Other Media

Have students view the video *Galileo and the Universe: You Are There* (CBS News, color, 22 min.). Then have students discuss why church leaders were so upset by Galileo's ideas.

Cross-Curricular Connection: *Language Arts*

Link to Today. Direct students' attention to the Literature Through Time feature. Then ask them to write a short paragraph on what they think Cervantes would satirize were he living today.

MEET INDIVIDUAL NEEDS

Students Having Difficulty

Assign each student one or more of the scientists discussed in the section. Tell students to devise a statement summarizing their scientist's beliefs or contributions. Students might use their statements to create flash cards and then quiz each other.

Intrapersonal Learners

Have students consider Descartes's single truth: "I think, therefore I am." Invite them to write a poem or an interior monologue based on this statement. For more information on Descartes, have them read the Global History Resource Center selection.

ASSESS

Review

Have students complete the Section 3 Review. Use answers in the Teacher's Edition, page 409, to assess student mastery of this

Lesson 15.4   *A New Spirit of Exploration*

Textbook pp. 410–416

RESOURCES

Pupil's Edition

Geography and History, pp. 414–415: *Sailing into the Unknown*

Core Resources

Reading 15.4: *Marco Polo in China*
Geography Activity 15: *Crossing the Atlantic*

Visual Resources

Geography and History 15: *The World Atlas Circa 1500*

Global History Resource Center

Reading: *Ferdinand Magellan Prepares to Sail*

Videodiscs or Global History Resource Center

Image: *Two Worlds Meet in 1492*

Search Frame 880

Map: *European Idea of the Atlantic Before Columbus*

Search Frame 884

Map: *Treaty of Tordesillas, 1494*

Search Frame 885

LESSON FOCUS

How did Europeans' ideas about geography change as a result of exploration?

OBJECTIVES

After completing this lesson, students will be able to:

- explain why Europeans began exploring other parts of the world;
- identify the technological developments that made European exploration possible;
- contrast the initial phases of Portuguese and Spanish exploration and explain the consequences of the differences between them.

HOOK: Link to Today

Discuss reasons for exploration. Ask students where exploration is taking place today. *[possible responses: outer space, under the seas, Antarctica]* Then ask volunteers to suggest what forces motivate modern exploration. Responses may include curiosity, adventure, economics, and defense.

Next you may wish to have students complete Core Resources Reading 15.4 to acquaint students with the earliest European exploration. Then display a large wall map of the world. Have students identify on the map the areas Europeans began to explore in the 1400s and 1500s. *[Africa, Asia, the Americas]* Encourage students to consider why Europeans undertook voyages of exploration.

Ask: Were the reasons for exploration in the 1400s the same as they are today? Explain your answer.

[Curiosity and adventure drove Europeans to explore. Economics played a part, as many voyages were undertaken to establish trade routes. Exploration also had defensive purposes, for many countries were in search of allies against the Ottoman Turks. Religious zeal, which drove some Europeans to explore, does not play a role in modern exploration.]

DEVELOP

Describe the technological advances that helped make exploration possible. Review with students the technological advances that made ocean travel feasible. Students probably will identify the astrolabe, the compass, *portalanos*, deep-draft ships, lateen sails, caravels, and smaller cannons. As students identify them, list the advances and information about them on the chalkboard.

Next have students use the information listed on the chalkboard to create a three-column table titled "Technology and

Exploration." The first column should contain illustrations that depict the technological advances. The second column should describe each advance. In the third column, students should briefly explain how each advance aided exploration.

Conclude by pointing out that to be successful, explorers needed good maps and an understanding of winds and currents. To underscore this point, have students examine the map transparency and complete the accompanying worksheet. Also, have them complete Geography Activity 15.

PROBE

Investigate Magellan's voyage of circumnavigation.

Direct students to turn to the Geography and History feature on textbook pages 414–415. Work through the text with students. Suggest that they follow the progress of Magellan's circumnavigation by using their fingers to trace the route on the map. You might also assign the Global History Resource Center reading on Magellan.

Then encourage students to imagine they are members of Magellan's crew. Have them write journal entries on major points in the voyage. These points might include leaving Spain, entering the Pacific Ocean, the long and arduous journey across the Pacific, the death of Magellan, arriving in the Moluccas, returning to Spain. Call on volunteers to read their journal entries to the class.

Conclude by having students identify how Magellan's journey was typical of Spanish voyages of exploration.
Ask: What did Magellan's voyage have in common with other Spanish voyages of exploration?
[He sailed west to reach Asia.]

CONCLUDE

Compare Portuguese and Spanish voyages of exploration.

Display the electronic media map of the European idea of the Atlantic and a large wall map of the world. Invite volunteers to use a pointer to trace the routes followed by Portuguese and Spanish ships in their quest to reach Asia. Call on students to describe the routes traced.
Ask: What general direction did Portuguese ships take in their journey to Asia? In what direction did Spanish ships sail?
[Portuguese—south and east around Africa; Spanish—west]

Ask: What happened as a result of Portugal's and Spain's voyages of exploration?
[The Portuguese established an ocean route to Asia; the Spanish accidentally reached the Americas.]

To illustrate the second part of this answer, you might display the electronic media image depicting Columbus's landing and the electronic media map of the Treaty of Tordesillas to show how the pope divided the newly discovered territories between Spain and Portugal. Conclude by informing students that the impact of these voyages will be more fully discussed in Chapter 16.

EXTEND

Other Media

You might wish to show and discuss *An Idea Takes Shape* (Films for the Humanities and Sciences, 58 min.), in the *Columbus and the Age of Discovery* series. This program focuses on technological advances that made Columbus's voyages possible.

Cross-Curricular Connection: *Journalism*

Have students write an article for an imaginary Portuguese or Spanish newspaper of the 1500s. The article should be titled "Intrepid Sailors Reach the Indies."

MEET INDIVIDUAL NEEDS

Visual-Spatial Learners

Have students draw two maps: one entitled "The World as Columbus Saw It," the other, "The World After Magellan's Voyage." Then have students discuss how the voyages aided map makers.

Logical-Mathematical Learners

Have interested students create a simple astrolabe, demonstrate how it works, and explain why it—along with the compass—was so helpful to overseas exploration.

ASSESS

Review

Have students complete the Section 4 Review. Use answers in the Teacher's Edition, pages 415–416, to assess student mastery of this section. In preparation for the chapter test, you may wish to have students complete all or part of the Chapter 15 Review on textbook page 417, the Chapter 15 Review Activity, and the Chapter 15 Themes Review.

Understanding the Main Idea

Call on a volunteer to read aloud the *Understanding the Main Idea* paragraph. Then tell students that Europe experienced profound changes in government, religion, and philosophy between 1450 and 1715. The centralization of government, the spread of Protestantism, and the growth of trade networks shifted sources of power on the continent. At the same time, scientific advances and exploratory voyages caused many to question the nature of the universe.

Presenting Themes

See p. 387B for suggestions on introducing themes.

Using the Time Line

Have students list the time line events in their notebooks. After they have read about each event in the chapter, have students write a paragraph explaining its significance.

Chapter 15
A New Worldview in Europe 1450–1715

Understanding the Main Idea

The Renaissance and the Reformation challenged the assumptions of the Middle Ages about the nature of the universe and humanity. By 1500, with new technology and a renewed interest in economic expansion, Europeans had begun to explore new territories. At the same time, philosophers and scholars began to investigate the nature of the universe itself.

Themes

- **Politics and Law** How might changes in people's worldview affect the development of their systems of government?

- **Science and Philosophy** How might new methods of investigation change people's worldview?

- **Cross-cultural Interaction** Why might cross-cultural contacts lead people to explore the unknown?

In the spring of 1633, a frail, elderly man was ordered to appear before the Inquisition in Rome. So ill that he had to be carried in on a cot, Galileo Galilei answered the summons to defend himself against charges of heresy. It was not his first encounter with the Inquisitors. In 1616 they had ordered him to "forsake the opinion . . . that the sun is the center of the sphere and immovable, and that the earth moves." Galileo had accepted the order, but protested:

❝I do not . . . believe that . . . God who has endowed us with senses, reason, and intellect has intended to forgo their use. . . . He would not require us to deny sense and reason in physical matters which are set before our eyes and minds. ❞

This time, however, the Inquisitors convicted Galileo of heresy for declaring that the earth moved around the sun. Under threat of torture, Galileo publicly admitted the error of his views. Many people in Europe knew that he did so only to save his life. The story soon spread that as the old man rose from his knees before the Inquisition, he muttered, "Yet the earth does

1488	1492	1522	1543	1558
Bartholomeu Dias sails around the Cape of Good Hope.	Christopher Columbus reaches the Americas.	The Spanish complete first voyage around the world.	Nicolaus Copernicus publishes *On the Revolutions of the Celestial Spheres,* expressing his sun-centered view of the universe.	Elizabeth I becomes queen of England.

move!" Galileo spent the rest of his life under house arrest, but the church could not stop the spread of new ideas. A new worldview had begun to unfold that would shake the foundations of Europe's conception of reality.

As astronomers were probing the mysteries of the universe, navigators were using the same instruments to calculate their location.

1628	1633		1682	1688		1713
▲	▲		▲	▲		▲
William Harvey accurately describes the working of the human circulatory system.	Galileo appears before the Inquisition in Rome and recants his views on astronomy under force.		Peter the Great becomes czar of Russia.	Glorious Revolution takes place in England.		Louis XIV accepts the Treaty of Utrecht.

SECTION 1

CORE LESSON PLAN
See pages 387C and
387D for Lesson Plan
15.1.

Theme: War and Diplomacy

New weapons allowed kings to increase their control over the nobility. Castles defended by archers proved to be no defense against cannons. Steel crossbows, while expensive, were more accurate than traditional crossbows or longbows. These new weapons became increasingly expensive, and frequently kings were the only people able to raise enough funds to buy the new instruments of war.

Critical Thinking Ask students how such weapons would fuel the rise of absolutism.

ANSWER: Students may answer that they would give monarchs enough force to maintain their power and to defeat local nobles.

SECTION 1
The Era of Absolutism

- How did some Europeans justify absolutism?
- To what effect did French and Russian rulers use absolutism?
- What effect did absolutism have in Germany and eastern Europe?
- Why did absolutism fail in England?

As the political structures of feudalism finally began to dissolve in the 1400s and 1500s, the Roman Catholic Church, weakened by the Reformation, was unable to provide unity as it had in the Middle Ages. Europeans began to look for another source of legitimate political authority to restore their sense of order and security. Many turned to the increasingly powerful monarchs, and some suggested that monarchs should have absolute authority. Other Europeans rejected this view and argued instead that the true source of political authority lay with the people themselves.

James I of England and his wife, Anne of Denmark

Doctrines of Political Absolutism

As the unity of Christendom collapsed under the weight of Reformation-era warfare, a new form of political organization—national monarchies—emerged in Europe. Although they had their roots in the old medieval monarchies, national monarchies were something new. Medieval monarchies had been basically feudal. Monarchs had the direct allegiance only of important nobles. These nobles in turn had the direct allegiance of their vassals. In national monarchies, monarchs and their governments were the central authority and commanded the loyalties of all of their citizens.

The rise of political absolutism. The growth of national monarchies changed ideas about the proper role of the state. Eager for order and security in the wake of the religious wars of the 1500s and early 1600s, many political thinkers supported the centralization of political authority in the hands of national monarchs. This form of government has been called **absolutism** because monarchs had complete, or absolute, political power over their subjects.

Jean Bodin (boh-DAN), a French lawyer, was the first European political thinker to clearly describe the **sovereignty**, or supreme power, of national monarchs. In *Six Books on the Commonwealth*, first published in 1576, Bodin wrote:

> ❝A prince is bound by no law of his predecessor, and much less by his own laws. . . . He may repeal, modify, or replace a law made by himself and without the consent of his subjects.❞

Justifications for absolutism. By the late 1500s national monarchs began to seek a way to justify their absolute political authority. They found that justification in God. Most Europeans had long believed that all authority came from God. Before the Renaissance and Reformation, however, many people believed that God limited the power of rulers by placing overall authority in the hands of the universal church. National monarchs now asserted that their supreme political authority came directly from God. Since all that happened was God's will, they argued, God must want monarchs to have absolute power.

This idea came to be called the **divine right of kings**. "The state of monarchy is the supremest thing upon earth," declared King James I of England, "for kings are not only God's lieutenants upon earth, and sit on God's throne, but even by God himself they are called gods." In France, Bishop Jacques-Bénigne Bossuet (BO-soo-e) carried such arguments even further. His work *Politics Drawn from Holy Scripture* was published in 1709. The book was a manual of instruction for the heir to the throne. "Princes thus act as ministers of God," Bossuet wrote, "and as His lieutenants on earth. It is through them that He acts on His empire."

Not all supporters of absolutism appealed to religious authority, however. The Englishman Thomas Hobbes supported absolutism for more practical reasons. In his work *Leviathan*, Hobbes asserted that originally people had lived like animals in a ruthless "state of nature," with no laws. Such an existence, he argued, was a constant "war . . . of every man against every man—solitary, poor, nasty, brutish, and short." Since people could not be counted on to cooperate as a society of equals, they had developed civilization as a kind of contract in which everyone agreed to give up their own power to a higher authority:

66 *As if every man should say to every man, 'I authorize and give up my right of governing myself to this man, or to this assembly of men, on this condition, that you give up your right to him and authorize all his actions in like manner.' This done, the multitude so united in one person is called a COMMONWEALTH. . . . This is the generation of that great LEVIATHAN . . . that mortal god, to which we owe under the immortal God, our peace and defense.* 99

Like the Legalists of China, Hobbes insisted that people had to obey the ruler no matter what, or else their natural selfishness would result in disaster for everyone.

While some Europeans justified the absolute rule of monarchs on religious grounds, others saw it as necessary to control the violent nature of humanity.

Absolutism in France

By the end of the 1600s, France was the most powerful absolute state in Europe and a model for others to follow. The French kings of the Bourbon dynasty and their advisors had achieved this position since the end of the civil wars in the 1500s by centralizing government and using force. Only by establishing a royal monopoly on power throughout the land could the state become truly sovereign.

Cardinal Richelieu. Henry IV's efforts to control the nobility and restore the power of the central government in France were cut short by an assassin in 1610. The next most important architect of absolutism in France was Cardinal Richelieu (RISH-uhl-oo), chief advisor to Henry's son, Louis XIII. Richelieu desired nothing more than to make France a strong power. Determined to bring the nobility under control, he destroyed their castles and replaced nobles in the royal government with well-educated, often loyal professionals. Richelieu also attempted to break the power of the Huguenots, not because they were Protestants but because they formed a "state within

◀ Symbols of secular and spiritual power surround the central illustration of the title page of Thomas Hobbes's *Leviathan*. The towering figure indicates a sovereign's power over the people.

the states" which he saw as dangerous to French unity. In 1627 he sent an army to attack Huguenot cities, greatly reducing their power.

Louis XIV. Richelieu's policies strengthened the state's power, but his successor, Cardinal Mazarin, faced a major rebellion because of them between 1648 and 1653. The rebellion, known as the Fronde, swept through Paris, forcing Louis XIII's terrified son to flee for his life. The revolt was crushed, but it made a lasting impression on the young Louis XIV.

Born in 1638, Louis XIV became king at age five, on the death of his father in 1643. From that day on, the boy was prepared by his mother and instructors for his role as king. He learned to be a soldier, a statesman, and a judge. In addition to geography, mathematics, French, Spanish, and Italian, he also learned to fence, dance, ride, and hunt. Most importantly, Louis was taught how to rule. As an adolescent he learned to read state papers, participate in council meetings, and interview foreign ambassadors. Anne of Austria, his mother the queen regent, taught him religion and courtly manners. Although Louis was declared able to rule when he turned 13 in 1651, his mother and Cardinal Mazarin continued to rule according to Richelieu's centralizing policies. Louis too maintained these policies after taking over the reins of government in 1661. He ruled until 1715.

Perhaps still remembering the turmoil of the Fronde, Louis reduced the power of his nobles. To counteract the power of the old nobility, he created a whole new set of nobles from the merchant class to serve the government. He also built a new capital at Versailles (ver-SY), a few miles outside of Paris, and required that his nobles regularly visit the huge new palace-city. Instead of fighting, nobles now gained prestige by becoming servants in the king's court. As one minister described, they even helped the king dress:

❝ Then all [the nobles] passed into the cabinet of the council. . . . [An] officer gave him his dressing-gown; immediately after, other privileged courtiers entered, and then everybody, in time to find the King putting on his shoes and stockings. . . . Every other

day we saw him shave himself; and he had a little short wig in which he always appeared. ❞

Louis chose the sun as his personal symbol, signifying that the world revolved around him. He thus became known as the Sun King. So absolute was Louis's power that he could say with complete accuracy, *"L'état c'est moi,"*—"I am the state."

France under Louis XIV. One of the ways Louis established absolute authority was by destroying the power of the Huguenots once and for all. Since the reign of Henry IV, the Huguenots had been protected under the Edict of Nantes. Even Richelieu had been unable to do away with this protection. In 1685, however, Louis revoked the edict and outlawed Protestantism. Over 200,000 Huguenots fled France, taking their wealth and skills with them.

To strengthen the French treasury, Louis decided to reform the old feudal tax structure. Accepting the recommendation of Cardinal Mazarin, Louis appointed Jean-Baptiste Colbert

Louis XIV
BIOGRAPHY

▼ The stunning beauty of the Hall of Mirrors at Versailles captures the wealth and splendor of Louis XIV's absolute rule.

(kawl-BAIR) as finance minister. Colbert, a businessman and member of the merchant class, managed to reduce the government's debt, and even to simplify the tax system. He also tried, though with limited success, to abolish internal tariffs that made it expensive to move goods from one region of France to another.

Louis's wars. Louis's greatest ambition was to expand French territory to France's "natural boundaries": the Rhine River and the Alps in the east, the sea in the north and west, and the Pyrenees in the south. Louis's minister of war rebuilt the army, expanding it from some 70,000 troops to over 200,000 disciplined and well-equipped soldiers. With this army Louis became the most powerful ruler in Europe. He plunged France into four wars between 1667 and 1714.

By the end of the third war in 1697, France was under tremendous financial strain. Louis even melted down the royal silver to help pay for army supplies. His most costly war, however, came after 1700, when he tried to place his grandson Philip of Anjou on the Spanish throne. In this War of the Spanish Succession, the other nations of Europe fought the French all over the world on land and sea. After many defeats Louis accepted the **Treaty of Utrecht** in 1713. Although Louis's grandson Philip got the Spanish throne, Louis had to agree that France and Spain would never be ruled by the same monarch. Louis also had to give up most of the territory he had taken. Despite these setbacks, Louis XIV remained a model for absolute monarchs all over Europe.

In addition to unifying France, absolutism allowed Louis XIV to increase his power through internal reforms and war, thus making France the most powerful nation in Europe.

Europe by 1714

Territory gained by:
- Austria
- Great Britain
- Savoy
- Prussia
- Boundary of the Holy Roman Empire

A Balance of Power The settlements following the War of the Spanish Succession reshuffled territory in Europe.

Linking Geography and History Which European country received the most territory after the war?

Absolutism in Russia

While France moved steadily toward absolutism under the Bourbon dynasty, on the other side of Europe, Russian rulers had been strengthening their right to absolute rule since the mid-1400s. After being dominated by the Mongols for over 100 years, Russia finally gained its independence in 1480 under the leadership of the grand dukes of Moscow. As they recovered their independence, these Muscovite princes took the title of czar, Russian for "caesar."

Map Answer
Austria

Theme: Economic Organization
Louis XIV was troubled by the royal family's lack of financial capital and was determined to increase his personal wealth. During his reign he acquired many precious stones, including the Hope Diamond—the largest blue diamond in the world.

Critical Thinking Ask students why Louis XIV would have been so troubled by his lack of financial capital.

ANSWER: Students may answer that financial capital would allow Louis XIV to remain financially independent, letting him complete expensive projects or increase his arsenal without needing to borrow money or levy new taxes. Financial capital also ensured that he could maintain, or even increase, his and his family's power.

The rule of Ivan IV began in 1533, but his mother served as regent until 1538. A powerful group of boyars—nobles who ranked just below royal princes in Russia—then controlled the country until 1546, when Ivan began to rule in his own right. He had himself crowned czar in 1547, becoming the first Russian ruler to use the title officially. In Russian, *czar* meant "caesar."

Critical Thinking Ask students what associations Ivan IV may have called to mind when he took a title that meant "caesar."

ANSWER: Students may answer that Ivan hoped to associate himself with Julius Caesar's military power and with Caesar's leadership of the Roman Empire.

MULTIMEDIA PRESENTATION STRATEGY

VISUAL RESOURCES
Art and History 15
Peter I at the Founding of St. Petersburg

Show the transparency and share the information from Art and History Fact Sheet 15. Then have students complete the accompanying worksheet.

Level 2

Ivan the Terrible. The power and absolute authority of the czars was consolidated in the 1500s under Ivan IV. A strange, moody, even mystical man, Ivan was also emotionally unstable. Trusting no one, he decided early in his reign to check the power of the nobles once and for all. He ordered the execution of many of the more powerful nobles and redistributed their estates to the lower nobility.

Ivan was also determined to extend his domains. His first campaigns were against the last remnants of the Mongols to the south and east. He was able to incorporate these areas into the Russian Empire. When he turned west and attacked Poland, Lithuania, and Sweden, however, the costly wars gained him little.

In his later years Ivan, who justly became known as "the Terrible," was a tormented man. In a fit of anger, he even ordered the death of his oldest son. Ivan's death in 1584 began a period of turmoil called the Time of Troubles. He left a weak, younger son to inherit the throne and civil war wracked the empire as various groups struggled for power. Finally, in 1613, the

▲ To discourage his noblemen from traditional Russian ways, Peter I ordered them to shave their beards. Here a Russian barber is shown cutting off a nobleman's beard.

exhausted nobles agreed to elect Michael Romanov, Ivan IV's grandnephew, as czar. Michael and his successors continued the absolutist rule of Ivan the Terrible in Russia for the next 300 years.

Peter the Great. In 1682 Peter I, also known as Peter the Great, ascended the Russian throne. Peter was determined to make Russia more powerful by introducing new techniques and ideas from western Europe. Believing that the best way to learn was by doing, Peter traveled to the West, where, for example, he worked in a Dutch shipyard to learn shipbuilding. In England he talked to ordinary people to find out how their tax system worked. There too he impressed his hosts with his willingness to work with his hands, as one English bishop recorded:

> ❝He is mechanically turned, and seems designed by nature rather to be a ship carpenter than a great prince; this was his chief study and exercise while he stayed here; he wrought much with his own hands, and made all about him work at the models of ships.❞

Returning home with many western European artisans and experts, Peter began a program of **westernization**, deliberately copying western European methods and culture.

Peter strengthened his army by adopting many new military reforms from the West. With these newly trained forces, he defeated Sweden in 1709. By 1721 he had gained access to the Baltic Sea. On the Baltic he built a new capital city. He named the city St. Petersburg and called it his "window to the West." Meanwhile, in the south he fought the Turks and for a time gained limited access to the Black Sea.

Peter's reforms alienated many of his people. The Russian Orthodox Church objected to his interference in traditional church practices. The nobility resented Peter's restructuring of the government. Peter elevated the army to the most powerful position in the government. Like Ivan IV, he also tried to reduce the nobility to state servants by tying their official status to the government post they held rather than to their titles. Like Louis XIV, he also required that they build homes in St. Petersburg and spend much of their time in attendance at court. Despite opposition, however,

▲ Schönbrunn Palace near Vienna was the summer residence of the Habsburg rulers. It is actually much smaller than the structure the architect had originally planned to build.

Peter's reforms continued, particularly under his daughter, the empress Elizabeth, and her German-born daughter-in-law, Catherine the Great.

Russian czars used absolutism to control their nobles, expand their empire, and, under Peter the Great and his successors, westernize Russia.

Absolutism in Germany and Central Europe

Absolutism had a different outcome in central Europe than in other parts of the continent. Since the Holy Roman emperor had no real authority over the German territorial princes, instead of a large centralized government in Germany, dozens of small and medium-sized states emerged. The rulers of these states began to use the same techniques of absolutism as Louis XIV used to maintain control, such as collecting high taxes and ruthlessly suppressing revolts. Thus, absolutism in Germany did not lead to the emergence of a centralized state, but instead reinforced the power of the many small states.

As the vision of a strong Holy Roman Empire faded, the Habsburgs also concentrated on building up their power in their own domains. In Austria and Bohemia they ruled as absolute

monarchs. By the end of the century they also had extended their territories to the east into Hungary and the territories of the Ottoman sultan.

Despite their growing power, however, the Habsburgs were never able to restore centralized government in the empire. New powers, such as Prussia, began to emerge and to challenge Habsburg influence in the northern and central German states.

In Germany and eastern Europe absolutism bolstered the power of small states and prevented the rise of a strong centralized empire.

The English Challenge to Absolutism

Not all nations of Europe developed absolute forms of government. England, in particular, took a different course. England had moved toward absolutism under Henry VIII, who had proclaimed himself head of the Church of England as well as king. Henry's successors, however, especially his daughter Elizabeth I, were less heavy-handed.

Elizabethan England. After she became Queen in 1558, Elizabeth was able to enact most of her policies by skillfully managing Parliament.

As the daughter of Henry VIII by his second wife, Anne Boleyn, Elizabeth was considered illegitimate by Catholics, and therefore ineligible for the throne. Consequently, she could rule only as a Protestant queen. Yet Elizabeth had seen the consequences of instability in the state. She had barely escaped the executioner's ax during the reign of her half sister, Mary I, who had briefly returned England to Catholicism. After she became queen, Elizabeth adopted a policy of national reconciliation, or healing.

Elizabeth gave the appearance of obeying the wishes of Parliament. She summoned Parliament into session often during her reign. Although she rarely allowed its members to influence her decisions, she gave many the impression that she did. When Elizabeth died without children, however, the throne passed to a new dynasty, the Stuarts of Scotland. Her successors, James I and Charles I, were not as clever at keeping the power of Parliament in check.

The Stuarts and the English Civil War. James strongly believed in the divine right of kings. He not only wrote books defending the doctrine but also lectured Parliament on it. His plan was to limit Parliament's power and run England as he saw fit. When Parliament refused to grant him the taxes he wanted to run the government, James began selling titles of nobility for cash and raising customs duties. These actions greatly angered Parliament.

Tension grew between the Crown and Parliament after James died in 1625 and his second son Charles I, came to the throne. When Charles was unable to persuade Parliament to give him money, he began imposing taxes and fines on the English people on his own. Parliament protested, and he disbanded the body, hoping never to call it into session again. However, Charles's religious policy soon caused trouble. He tried to enforce a uniform religious practice on all his subjects. He particularly feared that the Puritans, extreme Protestants who had very strict moral beliefs, would threaten the unity of the nation. He also tried to extend his control over religion to Scotland, where John Knox, one of Calvin's disciples, had established Presbyterianism as the state religion. Outraged by Charles's interference, the Scots raised an army and defied the king. Needing money to fight, Charles had to summon Parliament in 1640.

Parliament was in no mood to satisfy the king's demands without major concessions. When Charles tried to arrest six of his opponents, England erupted into civil war. Eventually, parliamentary forces led by the Puritan Oliver Cromwell overwhelmed the royalists, and in 1646 Charles surrendered. In 1649 King Charles was condemned to death and publicly beheaded. Cromwell abolished the monarchy and ran England as a "commonwealth." By the time he died in 1658, however, people had grown tired of Puritan control. Parliament restored the monarchy under Charles II, Charles I's son, who returned from exile to rule.

▲ Charles I opens a session of Parliament in 1625 and its members present him with their Speaker.

The Glorious Revolution.

Charles II learned the lesson that his father never did; he had to work with Parliament rather than oppose it. His brother James II, however, who succeeded him, learned nothing. James had little use for Parliament. He was also Catholic and married to a Catholic. Many English Protestants feared he would be the first of a long line of Catholic rulers. The danger became real in 1688, when the queen gave birth to a son who would have inherited the English throne.

Fearful of a Catholic dynasty, a group of nobles and parliamentary leaders deposed James in the **Glorious Revolution** of 1688. They offered the crown jointly to his daughter Mary and her husband William of Orange, the Protestant Dutch prince. Before ascending the throne, William and Mary had to accept the **English Bill of Rights**, which guaranteed certain fundamental freedoms, such as the right to complain to the king without fear of punishment. The Bill of Rights was a major step toward **constitutional monarchy**. Its acceptance established the principle of parliamentary supremacy, meaning that Parliament could overrule the monarch.

◀ **King William and Queen Mary of Orange are shown on a 1691 commemorative plate celebrating their ascension to the throne.**
Ashmolean Museum

When parliamentary leaders 17 years later tried to legitimize their overthrow of James II, they turned to the ideas of one of their supporters, John Locke. In his *Two Treatises of Government*, mostly written before the revolution, Locke had argued that human beings had certain natural rights that could not be taken away, even by a king:

> 66 *The state of nature has a law of nature to govern it, which obliges every one: and reason, which is that law, teaches all mankind, who will but consult it, that being all equal and independent, no one ought to harm another in his life, health, liberty, or possessions.* 99

Such arguments would soon have powerful effects, in England and around the world.

In England, the power of Parliament as a representative body prevented the establishment of absolute rule.

SECTION 1 REVIEW

IDENTIFY and explain the significance of the following:

absolutism
sovereignty
divine right of kings
Thomas Hobbes
Louis XIV
Treaty of Utrecht
Ivan the Terrible
Peter the Great
westernization
Charles I of England
Oliver Cromwell
Glorious Revolution
English Bill of Rights
constitutional monarchy
Two Treatises of Government

1. **Main Idea** What effects did absolutism have on France, Russia, and the Holy Roman Empire?
2. **Main Idea** Why did England follow a different political course than much of the rest of Europe?
3. **Politics and Law** How did the actions of Charles I cause the English Civil War?
4. **Writing to Explain** Explain how Louis XIV was a model of an absolute monarch.
5. **Comparing and Contrasting** Make a chart like the example below for the following monarchs: Louis XIV, Ivan the Terrible, Peter the Great, James I, Charles I. List the things these monarchs were able to accomplish during their reign and some obstacles to their power. What similarities and differences do you observe?

MONARCH	ACCOMPLISHMENTS	OBSTACLES
Louis XIV		

English Bill of Rights
(p. 397)
constitutional monarchy
(p. 397)
Two Treatises of Governmen
(p. 397)

1. France—centralized government, simplified tax system, made France most powerful nation in Europe; Russia—controlled nobles, expanded territory, began westernization; Holy Roman Empire—reinforced power of small states, led to growth of Habsburg state
2. Absolute rule was not possible because of the power of Parliament.
3. He tried to limit the power of Parliament and religious freedom.
4. He worked to reduce the power of French nobles, simplified the tax system, and raised a large army.
5. Louis XIV—a: built new palace, raised army, reformed taxes; o: insufficient funds, conflict with other rulers; Ivan the Terrible—a: expanded territory to south and west; o: failed to conquer Poland, Lithuania, and Sweden; Peter—a: began westernization, gained access to the Baltic and Black Seas; o: met opposition from nobles and church leaders; James I—a: sold titles; o: Parliament limited power; Charles I—a: imposed taxes, disbanded Parliament; o: civil war, execution; many rulers shared lack of financial stability, but only England had representative political body to check the power of the monarch

SECTION 2

CORE LESSON PLAN
See pages 387E and
387F for Lesson Plan
15.2.

Theme:
Economic Organization

Urban areas expanded at a much faster rate than the total population of Europe. Between 1500 and 1600 the general population increased by 25 percent, while the urban population grew by 75 percent. In 1500 there were 158 towns in Europe with more than 10,000 inhabitants. By 1600 the number of towns this size reached 220.

Critical Thinking Ask students how the agricultural movement of enclosure contributed to urban growth during the 1600s.

ANSWER: Students should answer that the enclosure movement decreased the amount of land available to farmers. Some of these displaced farmers moved to cities in search of work.

SECTION 2
Early Modern European Society

FOCUS

- What social and economic changes affected life in early modern Europe?
- What were the consequences of higher standards of living in European towns?
- Why were many people in early modern Europe accused of being witches?

*D*espite the long-term impact of the Renaissance and the early Reformation, daily life changed little for ordinary Europeans in the 1400s and early 1500s. For all its creativity, the Renaissance was largely an upper-class movement. By the 1600s and 1700s, however, the upheaval of the Reformation was calling into question many of the church's teachings. As a result, many ordinary Europeans began to question the old certainties and seek new ways to explain the chaos in the world around them.

In this painting by Pieter Brueghel the Younger, peasants of the 1500s share a meal as they rest from mowing the fields.

Breakdown of the Medieval Social Order

Most medieval Europeans believed that all of God's creations in the universe existed in a hierarchical relationship with one another. All things and all people had been assigned their places in what many scholars and theologians called the **Great Chain of Being**. At the top of the chain was God, whose will was revealed through the vast hierarchy of nature. God's will passed from angels through the clergy, and down to ordinary believers. Europeans believed that society, too, reflected the natural order through its relation to a body—an idea they borrowed from the ancient Greeks. Monarchs functioned as the head of this "Body Politic"; military forces, like nobles and knights, were the arms of society; merchants and artisans were the hands; and the peasants and serfs acted as the feet.

Economic changes. By the 1500s, however, this medieval view of society had begun to break down under the pressures of economic and social change. In the late Middle Ages, the devastating outbreaks of the Black Death had ended, causing the European population to rise sharply from a low point. At first, this increase in population had been beneficial, providing more children who could work and earn money for their families. Soon, however, farmers could not produce enough food to feed all the extra mouths. People in rural villages began to migrate to towns and cities to work as laborers. With so many laborers available, wages began to fall, even while food prices rose due to the lack of food surpluses.

European landlords also felt the rise in prices and looked for ways to raise their income to keep pace. Many began to fence in their land, since larger parcels could be farmed more efficiently and provide greater profits for landowners than small ones. This process, called **enclosure**, allowed landowners to close off land that had previously been left as common fields or open pastures, converting lands used freely by villagers to their own private property. In addition, farmers who had once farmed as they liked now found themselves reduced to the status of tenants or wage laborers for the landowners.

Growing population and rising prices led many landowners to enclose their lands and contributed to migration from the countryside to towns and cities.

Town life. While peasants in the countryside struggled against changing circumstances, town and city dwellers also experienced considerable transformations in early modern Europe. During the 1500s the class of merchants and guild people that had developed in the Middle Ages became increasingly important. They had a higher standard of living than other commoners and brought a great deal of new wealth and trade to towns. They had better houses, more money, and more luxury items.

Both men and women were an important part of this new prosperity. Women helped their husbands run family businesses and looked after the apprentices. An English merchant noted that Dutch women often played a major role in business when their husbands were away:

66 *[They are] well versed in all sorts of languages. . . . Nor are the Men only expert therein but the Women and Maids also . . . in Holland the Wives are so well versed in Bargaining, Cyphering [calculating] & Writing, that in the Absence of their Husbands in long sea voyages they beat the trade at home and their Words will pass in equal Credit.* 99

◀ **A moneychanger and his wife work together at their banking business in the 1500s.**

Over time monarchs and nobles became more dependent on the wealth of this growing **middle class** to finance armies and conduct trade. Often, monarchs formed alliances with merchants and artisans of the towns to overcome the opposition of their nobles. As kings used the money provided by such townspeople to assert their authority over the nobility, the middle class became more influential in the decisions of local government.

Higher standards of living led to the growth of a new middle class, which gave kings potential allies against their nobles.

Family and Community

Despite the changes occurring in European society, some things remained essentially the same. The basic unit of society remained the family. People usually lived in small families, consisting of a father, a mother, and several children.

The father was the head of the family. Servants and apprentices reported to the wife. Although women often helped run family businesses and worked in the fields, their main responsibility was to bear and raise children. Primitive medical conditions often made this a dangerous and painful responsibility, as the wife of one Jewish merchant of the day made clear:

66 *The next time I came with child I suffered terribly. I came down with a fever, God save us! in my seventh month. . . . If it began in the morning I suffered chills for four whole hours, then I burned for four hours, and finally, for four hours again, I sweat, and that was worse than either the chills or the burning. You may imagine my torments.* 99

Daily Life

People in the 1600s often believed that witches had a strange, powerful effect on animals. People blamed witches for causing fits in animals and preventing hens from laying eggs.

Critical Thinking Ask students why people might have blamed witches for disturbing animals.

ANSWER: Students might suggest that people did not know much about animal behavior during the 1600s.

Graph Answer

Luxembourg; the Reformation, the Thirty Years' War, religious warfare in France

Although people in early modern Europe identified primarily with their family, they also saw themselves as part of a local community. People in towns felt strong ties to others of their profession. People in rural villages, which contained a few dozen families, felt connected to their entire community. In both towns and rural areas, small groups allowed for close relationships as members of the community worked and made decisions together.

Quarrels and arguments between neighbors were also common, however, and although local communities were usually tightly knit, the bonds of friendship and mutual reliance that held them together could loosen in times of stress. As people lost the general sense of security in their lives, they often looked for someone to blame for their growing problems. In the 1500s and 1600s this search for scapegoats led to one of the tragedies in European history, the witch-hunts.

Witchcraft and Witch-Hunts

Since the days before the Roman Empire and Christianity, most people in Europe had believed in magic and the existence of witches as the best means of explaining both good and bad fortune in their lives. For advice and assistance many villagers relied on local "wise" people, usually older women with special knowledge of the healing property of herbs. Yet just as they believed these special powers might be used to help people, most Europeans also believed they could be used to harm. Such beliefs became particularly powerful during difficult times, when misfortunes seemed to multiply for no apparent reason.

In the later Middle Ages, European conceptions of supernatural powers became increasingly complex. Eventually, people came to believe that witches had made a pact with the devil, through which they gained the power to fly and to change themselves into animals. Witches also were thought to gather at night in the woods, where they would dance and perform rituals to worship the devil.

Most people believed that witches practiced "black" magic, designed to do harm. If crops failed, livestock died, or people became sick, a community member might be accused of having used witchcraft to cause these misfortunes. Older women and widows were especially vulnerable to accusations of witchcraft, since they often lived alone with no one to argue on their behalf. Men also might be accused of witchcraft, particularly if they had become rich enough to inspire jealousy. Jews and other minority groups also were easy targets.

Those accused of being witches were tried as criminals. The accused were relentlessly questioned, and witnesses "testified" to the supposed acts of witchcraft they had seen. If the accused did not quickly admit their guilt, they were often tortured until they did. The consequences were often gruesome, as the following description by

Execution Rates in Witchcraft Trials

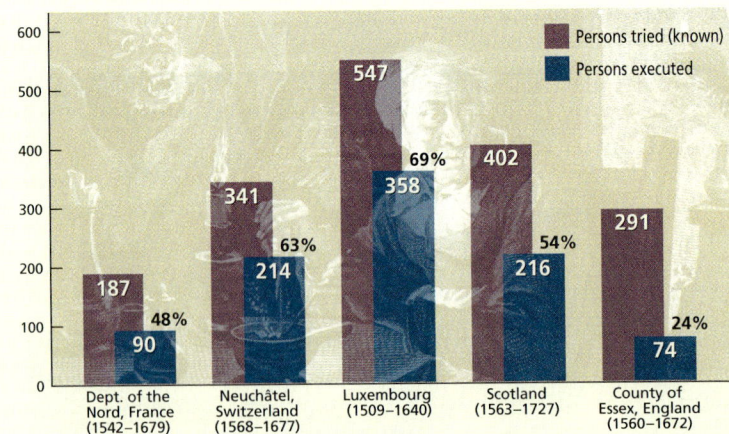

Legend: Persons tried (known); Persons executed

- Dept. of the Nord, France (1542–1679): 187 tried, 90 executed (48%)
- Neuchâtel, Switzerland (1568–1677): 341 tried, 214 executed (63%)
- Luxembourg (1509–1640): 547 tried, 358 executed (69%)
- Scotland (1563–1727): 402 tried, 216 executed (54%)
- County of Essex, England (1560–1672): 291 tried, 74 executed (24%)

Witch-hunts During the 1500s and 1600s, thousands of Europeans were tried and many were executed as suspected witches.

❓ **Analyzing** Where was the number of witchcraft trials and executions the highest? What political events might explain the higher number of witchcraft trials and executions on the European continent than in England at this time?

▶Accused of raising a storm to destroy a ship, these supposed witches were beaten.

an observer of a Scottish witch trial interrogation in 1591 illustrates:

66*His nailes upon all his fingers were riven and pulled off. . . . Then was hee . . . convaied againe to the torment of the bootes, wherein hee continued a long time, and did abide so many blowes in them, that his legges were crusht and beaten together as small as might be; and the bones and flesh so brused, that the bloud . . . spouted forth in great abundance.*99

After suffering such torment, admitting guilt must almost have been a relief to the accused. In England the punishment for witchcraft was death by hanging. In the rest of Europe, the association of witches with devil-worship led religious leaders to brand them as heretics. The punishment for heresy—and therefore witchcraft—was burning at the stake.

The number of witch trials increased during the 1500s and 1600s as Europe was shaken by religious warfare. Town and church leaders, as well as country nobles, saw the existence of witches as a reasonable explanation for the problems in the world around them. The witch-hunts of early modern Europe thus reflected people's growing sense of insecurity and a loss of control over their lives.

As the religious wars came to an end, however, and security returned to most people's lives, fewer cases of witchcraft were reported. In addition, as Europeans began to question the old doctrines of the church and to learn more about the nature of the world around them, they developed a new worldview rooted in science. This new worldview led many to doubt even the existence of witches, and to demand more concrete legal proofs of guilt than those obtained by torture.

Rising levels of insecurity and continuing beliefs in supernatural forces led many Europeans to accuse their unpopular neighbors of witchcraft.

SECTION 2 REVIEW

IDENTIFY and explain the significance of the following:
Great Chain of Being
enclosure
middle class

1. **Main Idea** How did daily life change in Europe after the 1500s?

2. **Main Idea** What factors led to the European witch-hunts?

3. **Social Relations** How did new prosperity affect town life in early modern Europe?

4. **Writing to Describe** Imagine that you are a resident of an early modern European town. Write an account of what a typical day in your life might be like.

5. **Synthesizing** What responsibilities did family members have in early modern European society? In your answer consider the responsibilities of both women and men.

CORE LESSON PLAN
See pages 387G and 387H for Lesson Plan 15.3.

Theme: **Science**

Chemist Robert Boyle worked to disprove Aristotle's scientific theories. Boyle developed Boyle's Law—the theory that the volume of a gas is inversely proportional to the pressure at a constant temperature.

Critical Thinking Ask students how Boyle's Law might have affected science.

ANSWER: Students might suggest that it contributed to knowledge of chemistry.

SECTION 3
The Scientific Revolution

FOCUS

- Why did some Europeans begin to question the medieval Christian worldview, and how did they finally shatter it?

- What is the scientific method, and how did it affect the European worldview?

- How did Sir Isaac Newton contribute to the Scientific Revolution?

y the end of the 1500s, Europeans had begun to cut themselves loose from many of the old certainties of the medieval past. Some even began to question the church's vision of nature and the Creation. As their investigations cast doubt on long-held theories about nature, and their mathematics became more complex, European scholars and philosophers began to interpret the world through observation and new kinds of reasoning.

Sir Isaac Newton's *The Mathematical Principles of Natural Philosophy,* 1687

The Beginnings of Modern Science

Before the Renaissance, European scholars and philosophers looked for answers to their problems primarily in writings from the past. Latin Christians turned to the Bible and to ancient Greek and Roman philosophers for answers. Scholastics believed that the teachings of these ancient authorities should not be questioned but simply accepted as truth. They believed that such general truths could be used to reach solutions to specific problems. This process of reasoning from the general to the specific, known as deductive logic, was the basis of European learning until the Renaissance.

The Christian worldview. The major authority to whom Scholastics looked for their view of the universe was Aristotle. Aristotle believed that knowledge could be acquired through observation using the five senses. He believed that everything had its own natural qualities, such as heaviness or lightness. Things that were heavy naturally fell down, while things that were light rose. Since his senses told him that the earth moved neither up nor down, he concluded that it was both the heaviest part of the universe and its center. He concluded that the planets and stars revolved around the earth because they were lighter. They were kept from floating off, he decided, because they were held in what he called "crystalline spheres."

In the A.D. 100s Ptolemy, a Greek astronomer living in Egypt, provided support for Aristotle's common-sense model of the universe. Rejecting earlier ideas that the earth rotated on its axis as it moved around the sun, Ptolemy put forward a complex mathematical explanation for the movements of the stars and planets based on Aristotle's earth-centered, or **geocentric**, model. According to Ptolemy, the planets and stars all moved in perfect circles within their own spheres as the spheres moved in perfect circles around the earth.

The geocentric model of the universe fit nicely with the basic doctrines of the Christian church. Accepting the "authority" of Aristotle and Ptolemy, church leaders added their own Christian dimension to the geocentric model.

The spheres beyond the moon, priests and church scholars believed, were the heavens, including Paradise. Angels worked to keep them in motion. Within the orbit of the moon, all things were earthly and tainted with the sin that humanity had brought into the world at the time of Adam and Eve. Perfection in the heavens and sin on Earth, with each sphere governed by its own set of basic laws, became the official Christian view of the universe.

Plato and Pythagoras.

The rediscovery of Plato during the Renaissance, however, challenged the church's Aristotelian conceptions. Unlike Aristotle, Plato had not accepted the authority of the five senses in determining the nature of the universe. Plato looked beyond the appearances and insisted that behind all physical things lay an invisible reality—a perfect idea that was unchanging, rational, and simple. Even when this reality could not be detected with the senses, it could be described mathematically.

In addition, Renaissance Europeans rediscovered the work of the Neoplatonists and Pythagoras. Beginning in the A.D. 200s, the Neoplatonists had argued that the entire universe was

▲ The bands around this geocentric globe, made in 1543, represent planets and stars orbiting the earth.

alive and interconnected—everything and everyone had a soul that was part of the great World Soul of Creation itself. There was no difference between the heavenly sphere and the earthly sphere; therefore, a single, universal set of rules must govern both. The Pythagoreans added the idea that everything in the universe was made up of numbers and the relationships, or ratios, between them. By understanding and manipulating these ratios, they believed, people could learn the rules of the universe and use them to control and change the world around them.

Magical background.

The first Europeans to begin looking for these universal rules were probably magicians, astrologers, and alchemists. Unlike the Scholastics, who usually wanted to understand the nature of the universe without trying to change it, practitioners of the magical "sciences" hoped to use their knowledge in practical ways.

Astrologers used complex mathematical calculations to determine the location of the heavenly bodies, whose positions and movements, they believed, affected the course of events on Earth. Alchemists used mixtures of chemicals and elements to find the mythical "philosopher's stone," a mysterious substance that could change worthless materials such as lead into precious materials such as gold. As they mixed and distilled chemicals, alchemists laid the foundations for modern chemistry. Paracelsus, the most famous alchemist, discovered many basic chemical processes.

Magicians and astrologers also contributed to mathematics, physics, astronomy, and medicine. John Dee, for example, an English magician and astrologer in Queen Elizabeth I's court, lectured on mathematics and used his skills to help English sailors develop new methods of navigation, even as he tried to make himself rich by commanding angels to lead him to buried treasure. For, like all his colleagues in the magical arts, Dee believed that the universe was controlled by supernatural forces.

Inspired by Plato and a long-standing interest in magic, Europeans began to question traditional explanations of the nature of the world around them.

Traditionally, scientific reports were written in Latin, limiting their circulation to people with classical educations. Galileo, however, chose to write his work in Italian, which made the Roman Catholic Church perceive him as a serious threat.

Critical Thinking Ask students why Galileo chose to write in Italian rather than Latin.

ANSWER: Students may answer that writing in Italian gave Galileo a larger audience and allowed ordinary people to understand him.

Looking Outward

As Europeans began to question the accepted authorities of the past, they also began to demolish the basic explanations those authorities had provided about how the world worked. In the early 1500s, for example, a Polish astronomer named Nicolaus Copernicus challenged the established Ptolemaic view by claiming that the earth and other planets revolved around the sun. It was the opening to what we today call the **Scientific Revolution**.

Copernicus had studied under Neoplatonists in Italy, where he had come across ancient Greek references that suggested the earth rotated on its axis and revolved around the sun. Finding Ptolemy's system too complex and influenced by the mystical Pythagorean idea of numbers, Copernicus began to suspect that there was a simpler explanation for the movements in the heavens. After considerable study, he concluded that a **heliocentric**, or sun-centered, model of the universe would be both more accurate and less complicated than the geocentric model. Copernicus published his ideas in 1543 in a book called *On the Revolutions of the Celestial Spheres*.

▲ This 1708 illustration shows the Copernican system of the universe with the sun at the center and the planets orbiting it.

Kepler. In 1609 a brilliant mathematician in Germany named Johannes Kepler, who was also an astrologer and a mystic, used new mathematical formulas to prove Copernicus's heliocentric theory. Kepler had been the assistant of Tycho Brahe, a great Danish scholar who had used his wealth to build the finest observatory in Europe. Over many years Brahe made thousands of observations concerning the position and motion of the heavenly bodies. When he died, he left this information to Kepler.

Drawing on Brahe's observations as well as his own, Kepler eventually discovered that planetary orbits disproved ancient theories even more completely. Copernicus had been on the right track, but he had accepted the idea that the planets moved in perfect circles around the sun. Kepler found that they moved in ellipses, or ovals. From this basic insight, Kepler developed his famous laws of planetary motion. Because Kepler's proof could not be seen, however, the only people who could understand his work were other mathematicians. It took an Italian professor of mathematics, Galileo Galilei, to prove both Kepler and Copernicus correct.

Galileo. Galileo was born in Pisa in 1564. Although his family had expected him to pursue a medical career, Galileo was more interested in studying the world outside the body. After teaching in Pisa, he became a professor of mathematics at the university in Padua, where he became fascinated with astronomy.

Already a firm believer in the theories of Copernicus, Galileo wanted to observe the planetary bodies for himself. When he heard that a Dutch lens maker had made a device known as a **telescope** for observing faraway objects, Galileo quickly constructed his own. He used it first to investigate the surface of the moon, which he found very different from the way most people had described it. According to Aristotle and the teachings of the church, heavenly objects must by nature be round and smooth; Galileo saw something different:

Literature THROUGH TIME

Don Quixote de la Mancha

Don Quixote de la Mancha was written as a satire—a type of writing that criticizes human vice or weakness—of the outdated ideas of chivalry that had arisen in Europe during the Middle Ages. The novel was written by Miguel de Cervantes, and the first part was published in 1605. The novel tells the story of an aging man who calls himself Don Quixote and who sets out to prove his courage as a knight. Quixote had read the many popular stories of his time about chivalry and wanted to put what he had learned into practice. By poking fun at the past, Cervantes also expressed the new worldview that was sweeping Europe in the 1500s and 1600s. Just as scientists began to reject traditional teachings about the workings of the universe, Cervantes used Don Quixote to reject outdated ideas about human behavior and literary ideals. In one passage from the novel, Cervantes describes what happens when Don Quixote comes upon a field of windmills:

At this point they came in sight of thirty or forty windmills that there are on that plain, and as soon as Don Quixote saw them he said to his squire, "Fortune is arranging matters for us better than we could have shaped our desires ourselves, for look there, friend Sancho Panza, where thirty or more monstrous giants present themselves, all of whom I mean to engage in battle and slay, and with whose spoils we shall begin to make our fortunes; for this is righteous warfare, and it is God's good service to sweep so evil a breed from off the face of the earth."

"What giants?" said Sancho Panza.

"Those thou seest there," answered his master, "with the long arms, and some have them nearly two leagues long. . . ."

So saying, he gave the spur to his steed Rocinante, heedless of the cries his squire Sancho sent after him, warning him that most certainly they were windmills and not giants he was going to attack. . . .

[H]e charged at Rocinante's fullest gallop and fell upon the first mill that stood in front of him; but as he drove his lance-point into the sail the wind whirled it round with such force that it shivered [broke] the lance to pieces, sweeping with it horse and rider, who went rolling over on the plain, in a sorry condition.

Don Quixote attacks a windmill.

Understanding Literature

How does Cervantes make fun of outdated ideas?

66 *The surface of the moon is not smooth, uniform, and precisely spherical as a great number of philosophers believe it (and the other heavenly bodies) to be, but is uneven, rough, and full of cavities and prominences . . . not unlike the face of the earth, relieved by chains of mountains and deep valleys.* 99

Galileo also observed the true shape of Saturn, the moons of Jupiter, sun spots, and a comet. He recorded his findings in two great works, *The Starry Messenger,* published in 1610, and *Dialogue on the Two Great Systems of the World,* published in 1632. The church eventually condemned Galileo for his beliefs, but his observations made it impossible for any true astronomer to accept a geocentric theory of the universe.

Eventually, Galileo shattered the rest of Aristotle's explanation of the universe. Aristotle had argued that the natural state of all things in the universe was rest. Things moved only if some outside force were applied to them. A new set of experiments convinced Galileo this was not true. Experimenting with balls rolling down inclined planes, Galileo showed how the speed of falling objects naturally accelerated. In addition to calculating a mathematical explanation for acceleration, Galileo found that things remained in whatever state they were, either rest or motion, unless acted upon by some outside force. With the discovery of this law of inertia, Aristotle's universe was now a shambles.

Through more accurate observation and description of the universe, scholars like Copernicus, Kepler, and Galileo shattered the traditional Christian worldview.

Looking Inward

While scholars like Copernicus and Galileo looked outward to discover the mysteries of the stars and planets, others were looking inward, trying to understand the workings of the human body. There, too, challenging ancient authorities proved crucial to achieving a more accurate understanding of how things worked. In medicine, Europeans had traditionally looked to the ancient Greek physician Galen, whose descriptions of human anatomy formed the basis of accepted medical knowledge. In the mid-1500s, however, the Flemish physician Andreas Vesalius challenged Galen's work.

▶ In 1632 these men gathered to observe a lecture on anatomy. The instructor indicates how the muscles of the arm work.

Vesalius, a professor of medicine in Italy, conducted his own dissections of bodies for his classes. His experience convinced him that Galen had not always been correct. Vesalius concluded that all descriptions of anatomy must be based on observation and experimentation, not philosophy. In 1543 he published *On the Fabric of the Human Body,* which revolutionized the European understanding of human anatomy. Following Vesalius's example, in 1628 an English doctor named William Harvey discovered how the blood circulated through veins and arteries and described a beating heart as being like a mechanical pump.

Meanwhile, a tool based on the same principles of optics as the telescope began to change ideas about the world within. A Dutch scientist named Antoni van Leeuwenhoek (LAY-ven-huk) used a new invention called the **microscope**, developed in the late 1500s, to study bacteria. Just as the telescope allowed Galileo to see objects far away, the microscope permitted people to see tiny forms of life never seen before. Using the new instrument, an English scientist named Robert Hooke discovered cells, the basic structural units of living tissues.

Just as closer observation changed European views of the universe, it also led to a better understanding of the body.

Toward a New Worldview

Galileo had overturned the Aristotelian conception of the universe primarily through simple observations and measurements that anyone could repeat. The work of Vesalius, Harvey, and others interested in the human body also rested on direct experimentation and observation. In England this new process of experimentation and demonstration intrigued another thinker, Sir Francis Bacon.

Bacon. Like many others, Bacon found constant references to the authority of the ancients by scholars of his own day irritating. It was not the conclusions such scholars reached, however, but the means by which they arrived at them—in other words, their methodology—that troubled him. In his book *Novum Organum*, Bacon rejected deductive reasoning and argued that with repeated experiments and observation one should develop a mass of experimental data, or information, from which one could develop a general explanation. This process of reasoning from the specific to the general, known as inductive logic, would produce an explanation that could be tested through other experiments. Relying on proof that could be physically demonstrated, Bacon's approach later became known as empiricism. Bacon himself eloquently defined the object of the "new science": "The real and legitimate goal of the sciences is endowment of human life with new inventions and riches."

Descartes. Not all new thinkers in Europe shared Bacon's contempt for deductive logic. In 1637 René Descartes, a Frenchman, published his own *Discourse on Method*. Like Bacon, Descartes disapproved of the blind acceptance of ancient authorities as a sound foundation for

▲ René Descartes believed in questioning all ideas before accepting them as knowledge.

◀ Francis Bacon rejected deductive reasoning and believed that only experimental data could be the foundation of true knowledge.

knowledge. For Descartes, however, there was nothing wrong with deducing knowledge from a basic idea—so long as the idea was true beyond any reasonable doubt. For this certainty, Descartes turned to algebra and geometry, which provided ideas that were clear, simple, and unquestionably true. Even then, he believed, one should question all assumptions before accepting them. As Descartes stated:

> 66 [I] was never to accept anything as true that I did not know to be evidently so: that is to say carefully to avoid precipitancy [hasty decisions] and prejudice, and to include in my judgements nothing more than what presented itself so clearly and so distinctly to my mind that I might have no occasion to place it in doubt. 99

Across the Curriculum: Mathematics

Many technological advances in the 1600s were made possible by an increased understanding of mathematics. The development of logarithms and calculus allowed more accurate timekeeping. Logarithms and calculus also aided in the improvement of optical tools such as the telescope and the microscope.

Critical Thinking Ask students how these technological advances might have affected the lives of middle class people.

ANSWER: Students might suggest that middle class people used clocks to chart their business hours. Students might also suggest that the microscope improved health care for middle class people.

Theme: Religion

Although Descartes worked to develop a scientific worldview that would not conflict with his belief in Christianity, the Catholic Church did not share his assessment. Descartes's works were placed on the church's *Index,* a list of prohibited books. Louis XIV refused to allow Descartes to be buried in France with a religious ceremony because of the dangers of skepticism as advocated in Descartes's beliefs.

Critical Thinking Ask students why the church would object to Descartes's ideas although he felt that belief in God was an incontrovertible fact.

ANSWER: Students might answer that the church feared that by claiming all ideas could be doubted, Descartes might encourage others to doubt ideas he himself believed.

THROUGH OTHERS' EYES

News Spread Fast About Western Science

For centuries before the time of Galileo, Chinese astronomers had been looking at the stars and recording their observations. When Jesuit missionaries came to China around 1600, however, they brought with them new devices, which the Chinese recognized as beneficial to their study of astronomy. Missionaries were anxious to gain influence in the Chinese court by using their knowledge of astronomy: "These globes, clocks, spheres, astrolabes, and so forth, which I have made and the use of which I teach, have gained for me the reputation of being the greatest mathematician in the world," wrote one priest. When the telescope was introduced by Europeans, the Chinese quickly realized its value—both as an astronomical device and as a military weapon. One Chinese scholar in the emperor's court explained:

❝If there should break out unexpectedly a military revolution, . . . one can look at, from a distance, the place of the enemy, the encampments, the men, the horses, whether armed more or less, and to know thus whether one is ready or not, whether it is fitting to attack or to defend oneself, and also whether it is fitting to discharge the cannon. Nothing is more useful than this instrument.❞

Within a short time, use of the telescope began to spread to other parts of East Asia, even as far away as Japan.

Descartes tried to develop a complete description of the universe on the basis of a single truth that he could personally accept as beyond doubt: "I think, therefore I am." Descartes saw the world divided into two distinct substances—physical matter and something he called mind, which included thought and spirit. This division marked a fundamental shift in the European worldview that separated it from other worldviews.

Instead of a living universe in which every physical object had a spiritual counterpart, Descartes had proposed a physical universe composed of matter that was essentially dead, without any spiritual essence at all. Only mind, which allowed a being to think about and know itself, could be considered alive. The natural universe could be explained as something that operated not with consciousness but as a machine operates according to the basic laws of physics. This mechanistic philosophy became the foundation of the modern European view of the universe.

Descartes, a devout Christian, never questioned the basic Christian idea that spirit, which he associated with mind, was the essence of God and was therefore more important than matter. At the same time, he believed that through their capacity for thought and reason, human beings shared in both God's nature and his creativity. The material with which humans created objects was physical matter. This idea soon set western European science apart from science in India and China, which made little distinction between mind and matter. Accepting Descartes's view, many Europeans came to believe that they could manipulate their physical environment to suit themselves.

Although Bacon and Descartes seemed to have taken opposite approaches to the pursuit of knowledge, most European scholars soon realized that combining the two methods provided the most powerful means of investigation. The combination of logical deductive reasoning from self-evident principles, and inductive reasoning from the collection and observation of data through repeatable experiments, is what we now call the **scientific method**.

The scientific method, a combination of inductive and deductive reasoning, changed the way Europeans looked at the world and their role in it.

Newton. Sir Isaac Newton, the man most responsible for the general acceptance of both the method and the worldview of the emerging new science, was born in England in 1642. Newton replaced the old Aristotelian and Ptolemaic worldview that Galileo and others had demolished. Even as a student young Newton had been puzzled by a nagging question: If Copernicus and Galileo were right, then what held the heavenly bodies in their places and caused them to move? Fully aware of both Kepler's laws of planetary motion and Galileo's observations on the movement of objects on Earth, Newton became convinced that the two seemingly different types of motion were somehow connected. After many years of research, in 1687 he published his conclusions in *The Mathematical Principles of Natural Philosophy.*

Newton realized that the force that held the planets in their orbits and the force that caused objects to fall to the earth were one and the same. Galileo's laws of falling bodies and Kepler's laws of planetary motion were both examples of the law of universal gravitation. In the course of reaching this discovery, Newton also explained the laws of motion and developed calculus, a mathematical means to describe and measure motion. (A German scientist named Gottfried Leibniz independently developed calculus at about the same time.) In one sweeping system Newton tied together the movement of all things in the heavens and on Earth.

Equally important, Newton's work reinforced Descartes's idea of a physical universe made up

◄ **Sir Isaac Newton's publication of *Mathematical Principles* led to a seat in Parliament, knighthood, directorship of the royal mint, and presidency of the Royal Society.**

of matter that simply responded to mechanical laws of motion. No longer would most well-educated Europeans see the universe as a place in which everything moved according to the constant attention of God and his angels, or because of some underlying spiritual force. Although most still accepted God as the creator, they now began to think of the Creation as a kind of giant clock: once wound up by the divine clockmaker, it moved according to the natural universal laws of motion. So great was Newton's influence on scientific thought that the English poet Alexander Pope wrote:

66 *Nature and Nature's laws lay hid in night; God said, 'Let Newton be!' and all was light.* 99

Using the scientific method, Newton discovered a unified set of laws that transformed the European worldview by describing the universe as a well-ordered system.

SECTION 3 REVIEW

IDENTIFY and explain the significance of the following:
- geocentric
- Nicolaus Copernicus
- Scientific Revolution
- heliocentric
- Johannes Kepler
- Galileo Galilei
- telescope
- Andreas Vesalius
- William Harvey
- microscope
- Sir Francis Bacon

- René Descartes
- scientific method
- Sir Isaac Newton

1. ***Main Idea*** How did new astronomical observations shatter the existing view of the universe?
2. ***Main Idea*** What new advances were made in the study of human anatomy?
3. ***Technology*** How did technological innovations

help scientists make new discoveries?

4. ***Writing to Explain*** Write a brief essay explaining how the discoveries of the Scientific Revolution affected other thinkers.
5. ***Synthesizing*** Why might the new discoveries of the 1500s and 1600s in astronomy, physics, and anatomy be called a "Scientific Revolution"?

Theme:
The Arts

Marco Polo's immensely popular book was written while he was a prisoner of war in Genoa. Also imprisoned was a writer named Rusticiano or Rustichello, who transcribed Polo's stories of his trip. The style of Polo's narrative reflects one of Rustichello's earlier works, an Arthurian romance. For example, in the narrative the description of Polo's arrival at Kublai Khan's court is modeled on an earlier description of Sir Tristan's arrival at Camelot.

Critical Thinking Ask students how Rusticiano may have improved the popularity of Polo's book.

ANSWER: Students may answer that Rusticiano gave Polo's true life adventures a romantic tone and put his story into a form the readers would have recognized.

SECTION 4
A New Spirit of Exploration

FOCUS

- Why did Europeans begin exploring other parts of the world?
- What technological developments made European exploration possible?
- How did the initial phases of Portuguese and Spanish exploration differ? What were the consequences?

Both the Renaissance and the Reformation were heavily influenced by growing contacts between Europe and the wider world. Since the time of the Crusades, Europeans had grown used to having access to the riches and luxuries of China, India, and the Spice Islands of Southeast Asia. Europeans became determined to find direct access to the commodities of the East without having to go through the Islamic world that dominated all overland trade routes. By the end of the 1400s, new developments in technology made such a search possible, not by land, but by sea. A new era of exploration had begun.

Marco Polo departs from Venice in 1271; his travels would influence thinkers and explorers hundreds of years later.

Looking Toward the East

As Europeans rediscovered the classical world, they also began to learn more about the world around them. In many ways the Renaissance represented an internal reflection of a new spirit of discovery and exploration that began to emerge in Europe in the 1300s. The causes of this spirit of discovery were complex, but they seem to have been partially stimulated by the rise and fall of the Mongol Empire.

During its heyday, the Mongol Empire provided safe, direct contact between Europe and East Asia. In the mid-1300s its collapse disrupted this contact and freed the Turks to resume their expansion of Islam in Southwest Asia and Europe. The revival of Ottoman power in particular threatened European access to eastern trade, which had been monopolized during the 1200s and early 1300s by merchants from Genoa and Venice. Although some trade continued along the eastern Mediterranean coast, the Ottomans restricted the flow of goods.

Religious zeal, fears of invasion, and simple curiosity also played major roles in the new spirit of exploration. In the early 1300s hardy and daring merchants, like Marco Polo of Venice, had traveled directly to China and India. Their travel accounts generated intense curiosity about the fabulous sights they described. Polo's account was one of the most widely read books in Christendom.

Papal envoys went east hoping to convert the Mongols and to obtain their help against Islam. In the late 1280s Arghûn, the Mongol ruler of Persia, was also anxious for allies against the Mamluks and sent representatives to Europe with plans for a joint campaign. He died, however, before they could be carried out.

Still, rumors of other potential allies continued to draw people eastward. For example, tales circulated in Europe about a great Christian kingdom beyond the Islamic world, ruled by Prester [Priest] John, probably a reference to the Christian rulers of Ethiopia.

Anxious both for trade goods and allies against Islam, after the collapse of the Mongol Empire, Europeans sought new routes to the East.

Advances in Technology

Whatever their reasons for exploring, without new developments in technology Europeans would not have gotten very far. During the later Middle Ages and Renaissance, they proved particularly good at combining different ideas and tools in new ways to produce new technologies and new uses for old technologies. These skills were particularly important in developing the ships and navigational techniques suitable for sailing the open oceans of the world.

During the Renaissance, European navigators learned from Muslims how to use the astrolabe to calculate their latitude by measuring the distance of the sun and stars above the horizon. As they figured out the latitudes of many well-known places, such as major ports or islands, they compiled the information in tables. Since the 1200s Europeans had begun using the **compass**, a magnetized needle that pointed north-south, which had probably been developed in China. The compass, together with the astrolabe and accurate navigational tables, allowed sailors to calculate the courses they should follow to reach faraway destinations and return safely home. Another navigational tool was a *portolano*, a chart showing ports and places to anchor. Sailors used *portolanos* to help plot their course across the open sea.

Equally important advances came in shipbuilding. Both in the Mediterranean, where Italian shipbuilders were anxious to increase the cargo capacity for their oar-driven galleys, and in the rougher seas of northern Europe, European shipbuilders learned to build deep-draft vessels. These ships could better withstand the heavy seas of the Atlantic Ocean. As early as 800, Europeans had already begun using the **lateen sail**, an innovation that may have come from seafarers in the Persian Gulf and Indian Ocean.

Lateen sails were rigged to the mast as large triangles that could be trimmed, or adjusted, to take advantage of the wind no matter what its direction. Such sails gave ships much greater maneuverability. To combine the new sails with their own square sails, which were still better for sailing before the wind, shipbuilders added extra masts. This in turn meant widening and deepening the hulls. Such ships could carry much more cargo than the old galleys. In addition, they were more suitable for sailing on the open sea. Steering was improved by replacing steering oars on the ship's sides with rudders, which were attached directly to the stern, or rear, of the ship.

Then, in the 1400s, Portuguese shipbuilders developed ships that were almost perfectly suited to exploration. Called **caravels**, these new vessels were also equipped with lateen sails and stern-post rudders, but they were smaller and more maneuverable than the cargo ships. Soon, the Portuguese also armed their caravels with weapons. With deeper and wider hulls than the old Mediterranean galleys, caravels were capable of withstanding the recoil from cannon fire. When European gun manufacturers began to cast smaller, lighter cannons that could still deliver tremendous firepower, European shipbuilders were quick to mount the new guns on the new ships. In the mid-1400s the combination of new ship designs and the use of cannons gave the Portuguese technological superiority over their rivals at sea.

▲ This 1626 *portolano* shows a network of geometric lines that lie across the chart; mariners used the lines to plot a sailing course across the Mediterranean Sea.

Development and adaptation of new shipbuilding and navigational technologies made it possible for Europe to explore overseas.

Portuguese Explorations

Located on the western edge of the Iberian Peninsula, Portugal was uniquely situated to begin the great age of European overseas exploration. Like the Christian kingdoms of Spain, Portugal developed an independent crusading spirit by having to struggle with Muslim forces in the south. After defeating the Moors, the Portuguese began to look outward.

Prince Henry, the third son of King John I of Portugal, opened a new era of exploration. In 1419 he retired from the court and founded a small court of his own devoted to encouraging voyages of discovery through improved ship-building, cartography, and navigational instruments. Later historians have called him Henry the Navigator, although he never actually embarked on the voyages he sponsored.

Under Prince Henry's guidance and inspiration, Portuguese explorers began to make short voyages westward into the Atlantic and southward along the coast of Africa. To the west they settled the islands of the Azores and Madeira, where they grew olives and sugarcane. Southward, they advanced along the West African coast in search of gold and allies against the Muslims.

Despite the new technology, travel on the open sea remained dangerous and often terrifying, as this firsthand account testified:

> 66 *[Four galleys] were provisioned for several years, and were away three years, but only one galley returned and even on that galley most of the crew had died. And those which survived could hardly be recognized as human. They had lost flesh and hair, the nails had gone from hands and feet. . . . They spoke of heat so incredible that it was a marvel that ships and crews were not burnt.* 99

Nevertheless, the Portuguese pushed ever farther down the African coast, establishing bases from which to trade with local peoples. By the 1460s they had reached the Guinea coast from which they sent back shipments of gold and enslaved Africans. Still they pushed on, hoping now to find a route to the Indies.

In 1488 Bartholomeu Dias, a Portuguese captain, and his men sailed around the Cape of Good Hope at the southern tip of Africa after being caught in a violent storm. Although the weary crew forced Dias to turn back, they had found a way into the Indian Ocean. Efforts to find the route to India and China took on a new urgency when the Portuguese learned that Spain had sent a fleet west across the Atlantic to find China. Finally, in 1498, Vasco da Gama made landfall at Calicut on the west coast of India. A sea route to the East had been discovered at last.

▲ Known as Henry the Navigator, Prince Henry of Portugal is shown here as an inspiration guiding overseas exploration.

Spanish Exploration

Spain also became eager to establish new trade routes to Asia and to carry the Christian crusade to new lands. In 1486 Christopher Columbus, a Genoese sailor, appeared at the glittering court of Ferdinand and Isabella, the Spanish monarchs. Columbus presented a daring plan: to reach the riches of the Indies not by sailing east around Africa, but by sailing directly west. He begged the Spanish monarchs to finance an expedition, promising them great riches, new territory, and Catholic converts for Spain. After six years, Isabella granted his request.

BIOGRAPHY Isabella was born in 1451 in the town of Madrigal, Spain. She was only a small child when her father, the king of Castile, died and her stepbrother Enrique succeeded to the throne. For most of her childhood, Isabella lived a lonely life of near exile. As she grew older, however, the childless Enrique accepted her as his heir, and brought her to his court to be taught proper values. In 1469 Isabella married Ferdinand, heir to the throne of Aragon, and in 1474 she became queen of Castile. In 1479 Ferdinand and Isabella united the two most powerful kingdoms in Spain.

As a queen in her own right, Isabella ruled equally with her husband. She had to agree before Ferdinand could declare war, and all official documents had to be signed by both rulers. Immediately after gaining the throne, the new king and queen were challenged by a war with Portugal and a rebellion among their own nobles. After successfully defeating both, they turned their attention to conquering Granada, the last Muslim kingdom in Spain. They completed their task in 1492. Confident that war would no longer drain their treasury, they decided to fund Columbus's risky venture.

Columbus's voyage. In August 1492, Columbus set sail from Palos, Spain, with three small ships, the *Niña*, the *Pinta*, and the *Santa María*. On October 12, 1492, he and his exhausted crew landed on a small island in the Bahamas called Guanahani (gwahn-uh-HAHN-ee) by its inhabitants, the Taino (TY-noh). Believing he had reached islands near Japan, Columbus marveled at

Isabella

BIOGRAPHY

▲ With Isabella and Ferdinand's support, Columbus was able to outfit his small fleet of caravels that would carry him and his crew to the Americas.

the blend of familiar and new in what seemed to him a paradise: "In all the island, the trees are green and the plants and grasses as well, as in the month of April in Andalusia." Columbus praised the islanders, whom he called Indians, thinking they lived in the Indies. "They willingly traded everything they owned," he later explained, and could be easily conquered since they lacked metal weapons. Columbus and his men claimed the island for Spain, naming it San Salvador.

In 1493 Columbus returned to Spain convinced that he had found the Indies. In his report to the royal court, he called for more expeditions and suggested a policy for dealing with the Indians:

> ❝I shall give [their Highnesses] all the gold they require, if they will give me but a little assistance; spices also, and cotton, as much as their Highnesses shall command to be shipped; and . . . slaves, as many of those idolators [idol worshippers] as their Highnesses shall command be shipped.❞

Text continues on page 416.

Geography AND HISTORY

Sailing into the Unknown

In November 1520 three small Spanish ships emerged from the strait at the tip of South America that now bears the name of the fleet's commander, Ferdinand Magellan. For the first time, Europeans were sailing into the unknown waters of the vast Pacific Ocean. Antonio Pigafetta (pee-gah-FAYT-tah), a member of Magellan's crew, recalled the difficult crossing of the Pacific:

" *We were three months and twenty days without getting any kind of fresh food. We ate biscuit, which was no longer biscuit, but powder of biscuits swarming with worms, for they had eaten the good. . . . We drank yellow water that had been putrid [spoiled] for many days. We also ate some*

European Exploration, 1487–1682

Sailing the Globe After Bartholomeu Dias rounded Africa's Cape of Good Hope in 1488, and Columbus reached the Americas in 1492, Europeans raced to discover new lands and new routes to the riches of the East.

ox hides that covered the top of the mainyard . . . and often we ate sawdust from boards. Rats were sold for one-half ducado [gold coin] apiece. "

Magellan had set sail from Spain on September 20, 1519, with a total of five ships and 237 men. The goal of his ambitious voyage was to reach the rich Moluccas (Spice Islands). Portuguese traders had been bringing cargoes of cinnamon, cloves, and pepper from the islands back to Europe for years. Spain was eager to cash in on the wealth of the growing spice trade. After consulting maps based on Ptolemy's view of the world, Magellan was convinced that the Americas were a part of Asia, separated from the East Indies only by the small body of water known as the *Magnus Sinus*.

Magellan would never complete his voyage, however. After sailing around South America and across the Pacific, he was killed in a battle with natives of the Philippine Islands. After Magellan's death, Juan Sebastián de Elcano took command of the fleet. On November 8, 1521, with only two ships remaining, Elcano finally reached Magellan's goal, the Moluccas. On September 6, 1522, Elcano returned to Spain, with just one leaky ship and 18 tired and hungry men.

By successfully circumnavigating the globe, however, Magellan and Elcano had given Europeans their first glimpse of the true geography of the world. Within only 200 years, explorers and traders from Portugal, Spain, France, England, and the Netherlands sailed east and west, establishing trading posts and colonies overseas.

Linking Geography and History

1. Which other voyages reached the East Indies after Magellan?
2. How long did it take the ships to return to Spain from the tip of South America?
3. What hardships did the sailors encounter on the voyage? How might these hardships have affected the attitudes of the sailors?
4. How do you think the voyages of the Spanish, Portuguese, and later explorers changed the way most Europeans thought about the earth's geography?

? Movement Which wide-ranging explorer ventured to the most continents on his voyage? What continents were they? For which country did he sail?

Before long, new expeditions set out to trade and to convert the Indians. By the time of Isabella's death in 1504, Spain had begun to build a huge overseas empire.

Other explorers. As explorers prepared to sail west after Columbus, Spain and Portugal began to quarrel over overseas territory. To settle the dispute, in 1493 Pope Alexander VI drew an imaginary line on the globe dividing the world into two parts. In the Treaty of Tordesillas signed one year later, all new territories east of the line were to belong to Portugal; all territories west of the line would belong to Spain. The treaty also moved the line farther west of the pope's line, allowing Portugal to claim Brazil.

Columbus went to his grave believing that he had discovered the Indies. Other explorers, however, were not so sure. Amerigo Vespucci, for whom the Americas were later named, claimed that the land Columbus had found

◀ Pigafetta, one of Magellan's crew members, sketched this scene in his diary of the 1520 voyage; in it two crew members try sailing a native boat near the island of present-day Guam.

was not India, but a "New World." In 1513 the Spanish explorer Vasco Núñez de Balboa strengthened Vespucci's claim by crossing the Isthmus of Panama and discovering an enormous body of water, later called the Pacific, or "peaceful," Ocean. In 1520 Ferdinand Magellan, a Portuguese navigator who was sailing for Spain, finally proved that the Americas were separate from Asia by leading the first voyage to **circumnavigate**, or travel a full circle around, the globe.

While the Portuguese went south and east to reach the Indies, Spanish explorers sailed west, accidentally encountering the Americas.

SECTION 4 REVIEW

IDENTIFY and explain the significance of the following:
  compass
  lateen sail
  caravels
  Prince Henry
  Bartholomeu Dias
  Vasco da Gama
  Christopher Columbus
  Ferdinand and Isabella
  Amerigo Vespucci
  Vasco Núñez de Balboa
  Ferdinand Magellan
  circumnavigate

LOCATE and explain the importance of the following:
  Portugal
  Azores
  Cape of Good Hope
  Indian Ocean
  Spain
  Pacific Ocean

1. Main Idea What did explorers from Spain and Portugal hope to gain from their explorations?

2. Main Idea How did technology contribute to European exploration?

3. Geography: Movement Why would transporting goods by sea have been preferable to transporting them over land?

4. Writing to Create Imagine that you are a sailor on a Spanish or Portuguese ship. Write a brief account of your experiences on a long voyage. What hardships do you face?

5. Synthesizing How did the fall of the Mongol Empire affect European trade? Why do you think Spain and Portugal chose to seek new trade routes to Asia instead of dealing with the Turks and Italians?

Chapter 15

Review

On a separate sheet of paper, complete the following exercises:

WRITING A SUMMARY

Using the essential points in the text, write a brief summary of the chapter.

REVIEWING TERMS

From the following list, choose the term that correctly matches the definition.

Treaty of Utrecht
heliocentric
middle class
absolutism
scientific method
circumnavigate

1. political organization under which a ruler has complete political power
2. to travel around the world
3. agreement in 1713 ending the War of the Spanish Succession; under the agreement, France was forced to make territorial concessions
4. theory of astronomy stating that the planets revolve around the sun
5. way of approaching inquiry into the unknown, using a combination of deductive and inductive logic

REVIEWING CHRONOLOGY

List the following events in their correct chronological order.
1. The pope negotiates the Treaty of Tordesillas between Spain and Portugal.
2. Ivan the Terrible gains power in Russia.
3. Oliver Cromwell wins the English civil war and takes control of the country.
4. As an old man, Galileo is taken before the Inquisition in Rome to answer for his astronomical writings.
5. Christopher Columbus reaches the Americas the first time.

UNDERSTANDING THE MAIN IDEA

1. How did new technologies contribute to the growth of overseas exploration and of scientific investigation?
2. How was absolutism in England different than in other countries in Europe?
3. Why did the Spanish and Portuguese begin searching for new overseas trade routes?
4. How did the Scientific Revolution change people's conception of the universe?
5. How was France under Louis XIV the model of absolutism for the rest of Europe?
6. How did daily life change for many Europeans in the 1500s and 1600s?

THINKING CRITICALLY

1. **Synthesizing** How might a person argue that events in Asia led to voyages of exploration in the Americas?
2. **Analyzing** Why was absolutism able to arise and thrive in Europe in the 1600s?

Building Your Portfolio

Complete the following activities individually or in groups.

1. **Exploration** Imagine that you (and your coworkers) are European cartographers (mapmakers) around 1500. You have been hired to create a map of the new territories that have been discovered by either the Spanish or the Portuguese. The monarchs who have hired you want your map not only to reflect geography but also to be illustrated with important trade goods, scenery, and/or people from the new regions. Your map could also reflect some things that explorers thought they would encounter in the new territories. For example, when Columbus reached the Americas, he thought he was in the Indies. Be prepared to present your map to the class.

2. **Science** If you were a member of the scientific community in Europe during the 1500s or 1600s, you would probably want to share some of the great new discoveries of your colleagues with society. Choose one of the great discoveries of this time and write a description of the event, including who made the new discovery, and how you think it will affect the future. You may also wish to provide illustrations of the discovery to help convey your news.

UNDERSTANDING THE MAIN IDEA

1. New shipbuilding techniques made longer voyages possible; navigation tools, such as the astrolabe and the compass, allowed navigators to create more accurate charts and records; the microscope allowed examination of tiny forms of life; the telescope allowed observation of planets and stars.
2. England's Parliament provided representation and worked against the development of absolutism.
3. desire to avoid Venetian and Ottoman control of trade
4. challenged view of Catholic Church as supreme authority and encouraged inquiry into nature of world and universe
5. most powerful state due to centralized government and use of force
6. higher standard of living for middle class, growing insecurity for laborers led to social tension

THINKING CRITICALLY

1. As trade and travel in Asia and the Middle East grew more difficult after the fall of the Mongol Empire, the need for new avenues for commerce encouraged voyages of exploration.
2. Absolutism thrived in Europe as the feudal order became increasingly less efficient. In addition, religious upheaval reduced the Catholic Church's authority, much of which was appropriated by monarchs.

Chapter 16

The World in the Age of European Expansion 1400–1763

Chapter Planning Guide

	TEXTBOOK	CORE RESOURCES	VISUAL RESOURCES	MULTIMEDIA
Introduction	pp. 418–419	Block Scheduling Handbook: Ch. 16		Videodisc Segment 16 and Viewing Guide: *Linking Two Worlds*
Lesson 16.1 European Trading Empires in Asia	pp. 420–427 Map: *The Ottoman Empire*, p. 333 Map: *European Empires in Asia and Africa*, p. 422 Map: *World: Physical*, pp. 852–853 History Through the Arts: *Japanese Popular Culture Under the Tokugawa*, p. 426	Reading 16.1: *A Chinese View of Europe* Skills Activity 16: *Analyzing Consequences*	Art and History 16: *Cicada on a Palm Leaf*	GHRC 16 Readings: *Friar Gaspar da Cruz on the Lure of China; Prince Henry's Motives for Exploration; The Portuguese Arrive in India* GHRC 16/Videodiscs: Images—*Chinese Ceramic Tea Pot; Portuguese Traders in Japan*
Lesson 16.2 The Spanish and Portuguese in the Americas	pp. 428–434 Through Others' Eyes: *First Impressions*, p. 429 Map: *European Empires in the Americas*, p. 432	Reading 16.2: *First Impression of the New World*		GHRC 16 Readings: *An Aztec Account of the Spanish in Mexico; Pizarro Conquers the Inca Empire; European Conquest and Disease* GHRC 16/Videodiscs: Image—*The Fall of Tenochtitlán;* Map—*The Aztec and Inca*
Lesson 16.3 The Dutch, French, and English in the Americas	pp. 435–440 Map: *European Empires in the Americas*, p. 432	Reading 16.3: *France and the New World* Geography Activity 16: *The English Colonies* Writing Project 16: *Writing an Advertisement*	Everyday Life 16: *Gravestone Styles in the Early English Colonies*	GHRC 16 Reading: *Richard Hakluyt* GHRC 16/Videodiscs: Image—*The Fur Traders;* Maps—Series of four on *European Imports*
Lesson 16.4 Trade and Empire in Africa	pp. 441–446 Map: *Trade Across the Atlantic*, p. 442	Reading 16.4: *The Atlantic Slave Trade*	Geography and History 16: *The Slave Trade, 1451–1870*	GHRC 16 Reading: *Venture Smith* GHRC 16/Videodiscs: Image—*Captive Africans to Be Sold as Slaves;* Map—*Africa in 1750;* Audio Clip—*Music from Costa Rica*
Chapter Investigation and Enrichment	pp. 418–446	Chapter 16 Investigation: *Historians' Conference on European Expansion* People in World History 16 Explorations in Daily Life 16		GHRC 16/Videodiscs
Review and Assessment	Section 1 Review, p. 427 Section 2 Review, p. 434 Section 3 Review, p. 440 Section 4 Review, p. 446 Chapter 16 Review, p. 447	Chapter Review Activity 16 Vocabulary Activity 16 Themes Review 16 Section Study Guides 16.1–16.4 Main Idea Activities 16.1–16.4 Daily Quizzes 16.1–16.4 Chapter 16 Test Sheltered English Ch. 16 Test Ch. 16 Test Generator		Audio CDs: Ch. 16 Summary (English and Spanish)

INTRODUCING THE CHAPTER

Textbook pp. 418–419

CHAPTER OVERVIEW

The expansion of Europe and the founding of colonies led to changes throughout the world. The Spanish conquest of Mexico brought the Aztec Empire to an end and devastated the native population. Desire for trade led the French and Dutch to North America, while the British established colonies along the continent's eastern coast. The relentless demand for labor in the new European colonies fueled the slave trade, causing warfare and untold hardship among the peoples of Africa.

PRESENTING THEMES

On the chalkboard or on an overhead transparency, write the following open-ended theme questions.

- **ECONOMIC ORGANIZATION** How might trade lead to both conflict and cooperation between nations?
- **CROSS-CULTURAL INTERACTION** What difficulties might arise when one culture conquers another and the two combine to form a new culture?
- **GEOGRAPHY** How might geographic factors influence colonization patterns?

Have students suggest responses to the questions. For the economic organization question, students might suggest that a nation's need for markets might lead to friendly relations or to conflict if nations compete for markets. For the cross-cultural interaction question, students might suggest that the beliefs of the conquering nation might conflict with those of the conquered peoples. For the geography question, students might suggest that obstacles such as oceans might prevent colonization. Save the responses. Once students have studied the chapter, you may wish to have them complete the Themes Review, then compare the two sets of answers.

USING THE VIDEO

Segment 16: *Linking Two Worlds*

ENGLISH

Search Chapter 16
Videodisc 2, Side A

SPANISH

Search Chapter 16
Videodisc 2, Side A

Tell students that in this chapter they will examine how these theme questions apply to the expansion of European power and influence in Africa, Asia, and the Americas as a result of exploration and colonization. Conclude by showing Segment 16 of the *World History and Cultures Videodiscs*. This segment explores how Columbus's voyages set off a movement of peoples, plants, animals, and disease referred to as the Columbian Exchange. Before showing the segment, ask students to pay particular attention to the kinds of things that Europeans brought to the Americas and what they carried back across the Atlantic. To help students grasp the significant points of the segment, have them complete Video Viewing Guide 16.

Key to Ability Levels

All strategies and activities are coded to the following ability levels:

LEVEL 1   **Basic** activities suitable for all students

LEVEL 2   **Average** activities suitable for average to above-average students

LEVEL 3   **Challenging** activities suitable for above-average students

SHELTERED ENGLISH   Activities suitable for students with **Limited English Proficiency**

Additional Resources

BOOKS FOR TEACHERS

Bodmer, Beatriz Pastor. *The Armature of Conquest: Spanish Accounts of the Discovery of America, 1492–1589.* Stanford University Press, 1992. Translated from the original Spanish.

Dussel, Enrique. *The Invention of the Americas.* Continuum Publishing Company, 1995. Discusses the discovery of the Americas and the beginnings of modernism.

Karttunen, Frances. *Between Worlds: Interpreters, Guides, and Survivors.* Rutgers University Press, 1994. Looks at the lives of 16 guides in the Americas.

BOOKS FOR STUDENTS

Dunn, Charles James. *Everyday Life in Traditional Japan.* Putnam, 1969. Daily life during the Tokugawa era.

Eccles, W. J. *France in America,* rev. ed. Michigan State University Press, 1990. Discusses French trade in America and suggests additional readings.

Marks, Richard Lee. *Cortes: The Great Adventurer and the Fate of Mexico.* Knopf, 1983. Uses biography to focus on sixteenth-century Mexico.

MULTIMEDIA MATERIALS

Age of Discovery: English, French and Dutch Explorations. Coronet. Video, 12 min. Looks at Cartier, Drake, and other explorers.

Age of Discovery: Spanish and Portuguese Explorations. Coronet. 12 min. Looks at Spanish explorer Balboa and others.

The Discoverers. Random House. CD-ROM, DOS, WIN formats. Links the past and the present by comparing historic discoveries to current research.

417B

RESOURCES

Pupil's Edition

Map, p. 333: *The Ottoman Empire, 1453–1566*

Map, p. 422: *European Empires in Asia and Africa, 1700*

Map, pp. 852–853: *World: Physical History Through the Arts, p. 426: Japanese Popular Culture Under the Tokugawa*

Core Resources

Reading 16.1: *A Chinese View of Europe*

Visual Resources

Art and History 16: *Cicada on a Palm Leaf*

Global History Resource Center

Reading: *Friar Gaspar da Cruz on the Lure of China*

Reading: *Prince Henry's Motives for Exploration*

Reading: *The Portuguese Arrive in India*

Videodiscs or Global History Resource Center

Image: *Chinese Ceramic Tea Pot*

Image: *Portuguese Traders in Japan*

Search Frame 887   Search Frame 888

LESSON FOCUS

How did European traders interact with Asian societies in the 1500s and 1600s?

OBJECTIVES

After completing this lesson, students will be able to:

- explain how relations between Europe and the Ottoman Empire changed in the 1600s;
- describe the methods Europeans used to establish trading empires in Asia;
- outline how China and Japan initially responded to European contact.

HOOK: Link to Today

Examine factors that shaped the European expansion into Asia. Distribute current editions of such magazines as *Newsweek* and *Time* among students. Ask them to scan the magazines for advertisements showing imported luxury items, such as high-performance cars, electronic goods, and fine watches. Identify these items as modern trade goods. Then point out that imported luxuries for Europeans in the 1500s would have included silk, spices, fine china, and other items produced in Asia. You may wish to assign the Global History Resource Center reading on the lure of China to illustrate why Europeans were interested in trade with Asia. You might also display the electronic media image of the Chinese teapot to provide an example of Asian luxury trade goods.

DEVELOP

On the world physical map in the Atlas, have students use their fingers to trace a possible overland route from western Europe to China and India. Then have students turn to the map of the Ottoman Empire.

Ask: What made overland trade with China and India difficult for Europeans in the 1500s?
[*Ottomans controlled much of the land around the eastern Mediterranean.*]

Ask: How might Europeans have overcome these difficulties?
[*Students might suggest that Europeans might have negotiated treaties with the Ottomans or sought to bypass them and looked for new routes to Asia.*]

Point out to students that during the 1500s, Europe's power increased while the strength of the Ottoman Empire declined.

Ask: *What brought about this change in the balance of power between Europe and the Ottoman Empire?*
[capitulations, which led to economic weakness; military losses to Europeans]

Finally, mention that the decline in Ottoman power coincided with European expansion into Asia.

PROBE

Analyze how and where Europeans built trade empires in Asia. Students should note that Europeans had many motives for undertaking their expansion into Asia. To illustrate this you may wish to assign the Global History Resource Center readings on Prince Henry and on the Portuguese in India. If these readings are not available, have students turn to the map of European overseas empires. Ask them to note which European countries were involved in expansion into Asia and where these countries established trading empires. Point out that European trade empires developed in India and the East Indies because naval strength gave Europeans control of the Indian Ocean.

Next have students work in small groups to develop a chart with three columns—1) Country; 2) How Country Established Trading Empire; and 3) Asian Holdings. Have students use their textbooks and the map to complete the charts. Have students use their charts to note similarities and differences among the European trading powers. [All were major naval powers; the Portuguese, English, French established trading posts, whereas the Dutch attempted to conquer territory.]

CONCLUDE

Investigate how China and Japan reacted to the arrival of European traders. Lead students in a discussion of why a country might want to limit trade with other nations. Students should recognize that some nations may limit trade to protect domestic businesses while others may limit trade to avoid contact with cultures different from their own.
Ask: *How did China and Japan generally respond to traders from Europe?*
[China restricted trade with Europeans; Japan forced foreign traders to leave.]

Point out that the Europeans had little that the Japanese and Chinese wanted. Further, the Europeans brought with them

unwelcome cultural influences. Display the electronic media image of the Portuguese traders and have students work in small groups to script an exchange that might have taken place between these Japanese officials and Portuguese traders. You might then assign Core Resources Reading 16.1 to give students a fuller view of how the Chinese viewed the Europeans.

Students should recognize that Qing China and Tokugawa Japan were able to respond in this way because they had powerful, unified governments. Also, both had cultures that rulers wished to protect. To highlight the vigor of Japanese and Chinese cultures at this time, direct students' attention to the History Through the Arts feature and have them view Art and History Transparency 16 and complete the accompanying worksheet.

EXTEND
Other Media
Students might check their library for the videotape *A Day on the Grand Canal*, a "tour" of a 72-foot scroll depicting life in China at the time of Qing emperor Kangxi.

MEET INDIVIDUAL NEEDS
Visual-Spatial Learners
To give students a hands-on understanding of the development of European trading empires in Asia, display a large wall map of the world. Have students use colored pushpins—a different color for each European country—to track the spread of European trading posts in Asia.

Gifted Students
Have students imagine that they are Portuguese traders who have just arrived in India. Direct them to write a letter to friends in Portugal, describing the wealth that can be found in India. Suggest that they include details from the chapter to support their descriptions. After they have finished their letters, have volunteers read their letters aloud to the class.

ASSESS
Review
Have students complete the Section 1 Review. Use answers in the Teacher's Edition, page 427, to assess student mastery of this section.

417D

Lesson 16.2   The Spanish and Portuguese in the Americas

Textbook pp. 428–434

LESSON FOCUS

How did the Spanish and Portuguese change life in the Americas?

OBJECTIVES

After completing this lesson, students will be able to:

- describe the effects that Spanish exploration and colonization had in the Caribbean;
- identify factors that helped the Spanish conquer the powerful Aztec and Inca empires;
- describe the societies that emerged in the Americas after the Spanish and Portuguese conquests;
- outline the policies pursued by the Spanish and Portuguese to control their colonial economies.

HOOK

Examine the initial impact of Spanish exploration and colonization in the Caribbean region. Assign Core Resources Reading 16.2, encouraging students to note how American Indians and Columbus responded to each other. Then tell students that in 1542 Spanish priest Bartolomé de Las Casas wrote *Brief Report on the Destruction of the Indians*. In this report Las Casas tells how the Spanish attacked the Indians who came out to meet them. He said that some 3,000 Indians—including women and children—were killed in his presence and that this had happened even though the Indians had cheerfully greeted the Spanish and brought them food.

Again, encourage students to note the attitudes of the Spanish and the American Indians toward each other.

Ask: Based on the reading and the observations of Las Casas, what was the impact of the Spanish arrival in the Caribbean?

[It was a disaster for the native peoples of the region, for it led to their near extinction.]

DEVELOP

Summarize the Spanish and Portuguese conquests in the Americas. Encourage students to imagine the Spanish and Portuguese conquests in the Americas as news events and ask them to think of newspaper headlines that might have accompanied these events. Elicit suggestions covering the discovery and conquest of the Caribbean islands, Mexico, Peru, and Brazil. [*Example: Cortés Overruns Aztec Capital!*] Write the headlines on the chalkboard as they are suggested. Then have students reduce the list to the six most crucial entries, using the textbook as a reference. The final list should tell the story of the Spanish and Portuguese conquests in outline form.

Next refer students to the Through Others' Eyes feature. Ask them to consider their list of headlines from the point of view of

American Indians. Then ask them how these headlines would be worded if Indians had written them. Have students work in small groups to rewrite the headlines. Have groups share their revisions.

PROBE

Analyze how the Spanish conquered the powerful Aztec and Inca empires. Make students aware of the size and power of the Aztec Empire by displaying the electronic media map. Point out that the Aztec Empire had an estimated population of more than 10 million. Have students consider how a small Spanish force could have conquered such an empire. To guide student discussion, display the electronic media image of Tenochtitlán and assign the Global History Resource Center readings about the Spanish in Mexico and conquest and disease.

Ask: *What accounted for Cortés's conquest of the Aztec Empire?*

[Cortés forged alliances with local leaders who opposed the Aztec; he had more advanced weaponry; European diseases weakened the Aztec; legends led the Aztec to believe that the Spanish were gods.]

Conduct a similar discussion on the conquest of the Inca Empire. To provide students with additional background information, you may also wish to have them complete the Global History Resource Center reading on Pizarro's conquest of the Inca.

Ask: *How large was the Inca Empire?*

[It extended along the Andes from present-day Ecuador to Chile.]

Ask: *How were Pizarro and his small band able to defeat the Inca?*

[The Inca Empire was torn by civil war and devastated by smallpox; the Spanish had superior weapons.]

To conclude, have students make a Venn diagram comparing the conquest of the Aztec and the Inca.

CONCLUDE

Describe the legacy of the Spanish and Portuguese conquests in the Americas. Point out that a distinct colonial society developed under Spanish and Portuguese rule. Have students diagram the structure of this society. *[Diagrams should resemble a layered pyramid.]* Direct students to add annotations that identify the underlying principles of social rank in this society—race, wealth, and connection to Europe.

Continue the review of the consequences of Spanish and Portuguese conquests by mentioning that these countries adopted the economic policy of mercantilism. Call on a student to define mercantilism. Ask others to explain how Spain and Portugal implemented this policy in their colonies. Then encourage students to imagine they are Spanish politicians who realize the consequences of these policies. Direct them to write a speech pointing out the ultimate effects of the policies on the Spanish economy and on the colonial economies. *[The economic policies will harm manufacturing and agriculture in Spain, spur inflation, prevent colonies from trading in the open market, and harm colonial industries.]* Call on volunteers to make their speeches to the class.

EXTEND

Cross-Curricular Connection: *Fine Arts*
Assign the Global History Resource Center reading on the European conquest, which deals with one aspect of the Columbian Exchange. Have students create a poster illustrating other aspects of the Columbian Exchange.

Other Media
Suggest that students view *1492: The Conquest* and *Columbus*. Both of these films were released to coincide with the quincentennial of Columbus's transatlantic voyage. Invite them to report on the films' historical accuracy.

MEET INDIVIDUAL NEEDS

Visual-Spatial Learners
Have small groups of students use the map on page 432 to create a map transparency showing Spanish and Portuguese holdings in the Americas by 1750.

Students Acquiring English
Pair students who are learning English with fluent speakers. Have them work through the class's headline outline of the Spanish and Portuguese conquests, reading aloud and discussing each item.

ASSESS

Review
Have students complete the Section 2 Review. Use answers in the Teacher's Edition, page 434, to assess student mastery of this section.

The Dutch, French, and English in the Americas

Textbook pp. 435–440

RESOURCES

Pupil's Edition
Map, p. 432: *European Empires in the Americas, 1700s*

Core Resources
Reading 16.3: *France and the New World*

Global History Resource Center
Reading: *Richard Hakluyt: Why England Should Expand*

Videodiscs or Global History Resource Center

Image: *The Fur Traders*

Search Frame 893

Map: Series of four on *European Imports, 1770s*

Search Frame 898–901

LESSON FOCUS

What features distinguished French, Dutch, and English colonization in the Americas?

OBJECTIVES

After completing this lesson, students will be able to:
- identify what northern European explorers hoped to find, and discuss the consequences of their failure;
- identify the primary goals of French and Dutch colonization;
- relate how and why English colonies were established in North America;
- describe the consequences of cultural interaction between Europeans and American Indians.

HOOK

Discuss why northern European seafarers explored the Americas and note the results of their explorations. Ask students to turn to page 432 of the textbook and have them study the map of European empires in the Americas. Then direct their attention to the voyages undertaken by such explorers as Cabot, Cartier, and Hudson. Point out that these explorers, like Columbus, sailed west to try to reach Asia.

Ask: What were these explorers looking for?

[a route—referred to as the Northwest Passage—through the Americas to Asia]

Mention that although these explorers failed to find a westward route to Asia, their explorations established the claims of such countries as England, France, and the Netherlands to territory in the Americas.

Ask: How did the failure to find the Northwest Passage affect northern European countries' goals in the Americas?

[They turned to colonization.]

DEVELOP

Discuss the primary goals of French and Dutch colonization in the Americas. Note that North America was one prize in a global competition for territory among European powers. Have students focus on the numbers of settlers who came from different European nations at various times. To give students more insight into French exploration and colonization, you may wish to have them complete Core Resources Reading 16.3.

Next examine differences in the kinds of colonies established by European nations. Remind students that the Spanish conquered and absorbed the native peoples as laborers in a system of near-feudal estates. The Spanish also focused on the extraction of precious metals. Point out that French and Dutch approaches to colonization were different. Display the electronic media image, mentioning that it illustrates the primary goal of French and Dutch colonization. You may also wish to display the electronic media maps showing the trade goods that the French and Dutch, the Spanish, and the Portuguese were importing from their colonies by the 1770s.

Ask: *What was the goal of French and Dutch colonization?*

[trade, focusing on furs]

Ask: *What approaches to colonization did the French and Dutch take?*

[The French Crown controlled colonization, limiting it to Catholics; encouraged settlers to live among the Indians and convert them to Catholicism and French ways of life. The Dutch encouraged private companies to establish colonies by awarding them a monopoly on trade.]

Encourage students to use their answers to create a graphic organizer on French and Dutch colonization.

PROBE

Examine why English colonies were established in North America. Help students review the reasons for the development of English colonies in North America by assigning the Global History Resource Center reading. To show the importance of trade between Britain and its colonies, display the electronic media map of British imports in the 1770s.

Ask: *What were the most important reasons for the establishment of England's North American colonies?*

[search for wealth, freedom to practice religious beliefs]

As a study aid, suggest that students create a table showing the reasons for the establishment of the English colonies discussed in the text.

CONCLUDE

Discuss the consequences of the cultural interaction between Europeans and American Indians. Have students turn to page 439 and read again the exchange between the American Indian leader and Samuel de Champlain. Then tell students that Ted Morgan in his book *Wilderness at Dawn* (Simon & Schuster, 1993) discusses another exchange between Champlain and an American Indian leader. According to this account, Champlain tells the Indian leader that he envisions a united French-Indian nation in North America. Morgan comments, however, that when two groups with such different values are forced together, one of them generally loses out to the other.

Ask: *Do you think that the results of the cultural interaction between Europeans and American Indians supports Morgan's opinion?*

[Most students will answer yes, noting that the fur trade caused overhunting, which upset local balances of power among Indian tribes; that European diseases decimated Indian populations; and that land disputes often resulted in American Indians being driven from their territories.]

Then tell students to illustrate their answer with information from the text.

EXTEND

Cross-Curricular Connection: *Language Arts*

Nathaniel Hawthorne's classic *The Scarlet Letter* offers great insights into life in colonial New England. Encourage students to read the novel, and have them follow up by writing an essay relating the novel's events to what they have learned about the role of religion in New England colonial life.

Cross-Curricular Connection: *Anthropology*

To help students appreciate the ways in which material culture can aid in understanding the past, have students view the Everyday Life Transparency 16, on gravestone styles. Students interested in learning more about colonial artifacts may enjoy reporting to the class on James Deetz's *In Small Things Forgotten: The Archaeology of Early American Life* (Anchor Press/Doubleday, 1977).

MEET INDIVIDUAL NEEDS

Logical-Mathematical Learners

Point out that the European powers were simultaneously colonizing the Americas and building trade empires in Asia. Have students create parallel time lines identifying key events of European empire-building in Asia and in the Americas. Encourage students to share their time lines with other members of the class.

ASSESS

Review

Have students complete the Section 3 Review. Use answers in the Teacher's Edition, page 440, to assess student mastery of this section.

Lesson 16.4   *Trade and Empire in Africa*

Textbook pp. 441–446

RESOURCES

Pupil's Edition
Map, p. 442: *Trade Across the Atlantic, 1451–1870*

Core Resources
Reading 16.4: *The Atlantic Slave Trade*

Visual Resources
Geography and History 16: *The Slave Trade, 1451–1870*

Global History Resource Center
Reading: *Venture Smith: How I Became a Slave*

Videodiscs or Global History Resource Center

Image: *Captive Africans to Be Sold as Slaves*

Search Frame 895

Map: *Africa in 1750*

Search Frame 902

Audio Clip: *Afro-Limonese Music from Costa Rica*

Search 1493, Play to 1964
Videodisc 2, Side A
Audio Clip 16

LESSON FOCUS

How did the Atlantic slave trade affect Africa and the Americas?

OBJECTIVES

After completing this lesson, students will be able to:

- describe how the arrival of the Europeans changed the African slave trade;
- describe how the expansion of the slave trade affected Africa;
- identify the consequences of the Atlantic slave trade in the Americas.

HOOK

Compare African slavery before and after European involvement. Ask students what they understand about the word *slavery*. Note responses on the chalkboard. Then tell students that the definition of slavery has varied depending on the time and place. For example, Basil Davidson's *The African Slave Trade* (Little, Brown and Company, 1961) paints a somewhat-surprising picture of slavery in Asante society. There, slaves could own property—including other slaves—and marry. They often married their slaveholder's relatives and inherited their slaveholder's property.

Ask students to compare this description to the responses listed on the chalkboard. Most will note that the Asante attitude toward slavery was relatively enlightened. Continue by reminding students that slavery in Africa took different forms. A good number of African societies, however, held views similar to those of the Asante.

Next ask students to discuss how the arrival of Europeans changed the nature of slavery in Africa. You might encourage discussion by showing the electronic media image of captured slaves.

Ask: How did the presence of Europeans change slavery and the slave trade in Africa?

[The European demand for slaves greatly increased the slave trade; in time, slavery and the slave trade became the major economic activity of some African societies.]

DEVELOP

Explain the impact of the expansion of the slave trade on Africa. Have students examine the map transparency, or have them view the electronic media map of African kingdoms. Direct students to identify and locate the main West African and Central African kingdoms mentioned in the text—Oyo, Dahomey, Akan, Kongo. As students locate each kingdom, have them discuss how and why each one was involved in the slave trade.

Restate that one result of the arrival of Europeans in Africa was that the slave trade became the main economic activity for such African kingdoms as Oyo, Dahomey, Akan, and Kongo. To help students understand how this affected African economies, you may wish to assign Core Resources Reading 16.4.

Next remind students that the European interest in the North American fur trade helped to upset local balances of power among various American Indian tribes. Continue by pointing out that the slave trade had a similar social and political impact in Africa. Some states went to war or launched attacks on neighbors to obtain slaves for trading purposes. To illustrate this point, assign the Global History Resource Center reading by Venture Smith.

Conclude by asking students to organize the information on the impact of the slave trade on Africa in a three-column table, using the column-headings *Economic*, *Social*, and *Political*.

PROBE

Describe the nature of the trade among Africa, the Americas, and Europe. Set the scene by having students turn to the map on page 442 of their textbooks. Ask them to review the chain of trade binding Africa, the Americas, and Europe.

Ask: What did European merchants ship to Africa in exchange for slaves and gold?
[iron and cotton goods, weapons, liquor]

Ask: Where were the slaves transported?
[to the Americas]

Ask: What products were shipped from the Americas to Europe?
[tobacco, sugar, rum, cotton]

CONCLUDE

Identify the consequences of the Atlantic slave trade in the Americas. First, call on students to explain why slavery became an integral part of the economy of the Americas.
Ask: Why did slavery take root in the Americas?
[Colonial economies in southern North America and

Central and South America were based on labor-intensive enterprises, such as mines and plantations. Plantation and mine owners saw slaves as a way to fulfill their labor needs.]

Conclude by pointing out that the influx of African slaves created unique cultural exchanges in the Americas.
Ask: How did African peoples shape the culture of the Americas?
[Elicit the general point that slavery wove African culture into the general fabric of life in the Americas as well as the cooking, music, dance, language, and folk literature.]

If time permits have students work in groups of three or four to design a poster illustrating African influences in American culture.

EXTEND

Cross-Curricular Connection: *Music*
Have students listen to the audio clip of Afro-Limonese music. Then encourage them to compile an audiotape of examples of American music with African roots. Student tapes should, if possible, show a wide range of genres from Brazil, the Caribbean Islands, and the United States.

MEET INDIVIDUAL NEEDS

Interpersonal Learners
Suggest that students work in small groups to create an exchange among various characters involved in the slave trade, such as an Asante king, a Portuguese sea captain, an African slave trader, a captured slave, and a sailor working on a slave ship. Call on groups to present their exchanges to the class.

ASSESS

Review
Have students complete the Section 4 Review. Use answers in the Teacher's Edition, pages 445–46, to assess student mastery of this section.

In preparation for the chapter test, you may wish to have students complete all or part of the Chapter 16 Review on textbook page 447, the Chapter 16 Review Activity, and the Chapter 16 Themes Review.

Chapter 16

The World in the Age of European Expansion

Understanding the Main Idea

Call on a volunteer to read aloud the *Understanding the Main Idea* paragraph. Then tell students that Europeans searched for a sea route to the East Indies to trade in luxury items, often influencing Asian countries in the process. Europeans expanded to the Americas, where they set up empires in hopes of achieving wealth. Some of the colonies were based on agriculture, and planters wanted laborers to work the land, leading to the exportation of the African slave trade to the Americas.

Presenting Themes

See p. 417B for suggestions on introducing themes.

Using the Time Line

Have students list the time line events in their notebooks. After they have read about each event in the chapter, have students write a paragraph explaining its significance.

Chapter 16
The World in the Age of European Expansion 1400–1763

Understanding the Main Idea

In the late 1400s Europeans set out to find a sea route to the East Indies. They tapped the rich Asian spice trade and established empires in North and South America. In the process they influenced Asian civilizations and exported the African slave trade to the Americas. The expanded slave trade greatly harmed African societies.

Themes

- *Economic Organization* How might trade lead to both conflict and cooperation between nations?

- *Cross-cultural Interaction* What difficulties might arise when one culture conquers another and the two combine to form a new culture?

- *Geography* How might geographic factors influence colonization patterns?

In the early 1700s the Ottoman sultan Ahmed III ordered the construction of an ornate new summer palace in a wealthy suburb of Constantinople. Modeled after sketches of the French chateau of Marly, the palace boasted sparkling fountains and splendid statues and pavilions all done in the Western style. Its central attraction, however, was its magnificent tulip garden, where bulbs from Holland and Persia bloomed in a sea of color. Upper-class Turks copied the sultan's new palace and competed to plant the rarest tulips they could find. Tulips graced so many lavish fountains and gardens that this period in Turkish history became known as the Tulip Era. The rich also dressed in European clothes and imported European furniture for their new palaces.

The Tulip Era represented the growing attraction of Western Europe's increasingly wealthy and sophisticated culture even to older civilizations that had long possessed brilliant cultures of their own. The advances in Western culture, in turn, reflected Western Europe's growing dominance in the world's profitable trade routes, particularly in the Indian and Atlantic Oceans. By the 1500s Europeans had set up commercial empires in Asia and Africa and colonial settlements in the Americas.

1498	**1521**	**1571**	**1608**
The Portuguese arrive in India.	Cortés conquers the Aztec.	Italians and Spaniards defeat the Ottoman navy at Lepanto.	Samuel de Champlain founds Quebec.

The "Blue Mosque" of Sultan Ahmed III's summer palace

The Tulip Era was a time of great extravagance for the sultan and other upper-class Ottomans. Competition was fierce to create opulent settings. The wealthy copied the sultan's example and built their own beautiful palaces, gardens, and fountains. The sultan even distributed plots of land to relatives and high government officials, who turned the land into lavish residential areas.

The upper class also built ornate mosques, decorative fountains, and religious schools to embellish the grounds of their fabulous palaces. This photograph shows the "Blue Mosque," located on the sultan's palace grounds.

Critical Thinking Ask students what might have made Western European culture attractive, or even enviable, to the Ottomans.

ANSWER: Students might suggest that Western Europe was becoming increasingly wealthy and extending its power overseas.

1620	1652	1739	1763
English Pilgrims establish colony at Plymouth.	Dutch establish colony at the Cape of Good Hope in Africa.	Runaway slaves in Jamaica are granted land by the English government.	Rio de Janeiro is established as Brazil's capital.

SECTION 1

CORE LESSON PLAN
See pages 417C and 417D for Lesson Plan 16.1.

Theme: Politics and Law

The Ottomans hoped to strengthen their position in the region through capitulations, but the agreements had the opposite effect. Under the capitulations agreement, French merchants in the Ottoman Empire were subject to French law and rule rather than Ottoman law.

Critical Thinking Ask students why this put the Ottomans at a disadvantage to the French.

ANSWER: Students might suggest that the agreement let the French break Ottoman law without having to suffer the penalties.

European Trading Empires in Asia

FOCUS

- How did relations between Europe and the Ottoman Empire change in the 1600s?
- What methods did Europeans use to establish trading empires in Asia?
- How did China and Japan initially respond to European contact?

*T*he peoples the Europeans encountered in the Americas were less technologically advanced than the Europeans, and thus easier to dominate. In Asia, however, Europeans came across civilizations that were both more populous and more technologically equal. Consequently, although the Europeans were gradually able to establish trading empires, they generally were not able to conquer vast territories as they were doing across the Atlantic Ocean.

Islamic ceramic dish from around 1540 decorated with flowers, leaves, and pomegranates

Europe and the Ottoman Empire

During the 1500s and much of the 1600s, the Islamic Ottoman Empire remained the primary threat to Christian civilization in Europe. Nevertheless, the period also marked the beginning of a relative decline in Ottoman strength just as Europe became stronger.

The Ottoman decline can be traced in part to European economic expansion into Turkish territory. In the early 1500s, in his wars against the Safavids and the Habsburgs, Süleyman I pursued an alliance with France. As part of this alliance, in 1535 Süleyman granted France tax exemptions and other special trade privileges. These privileges, or **capitulations**, had the effect of giving the French a stronger position than intended in the competition for the internal trade of the empire. Later sultans established similar agreements with other Western nations, further weakening the Ottoman economy.

The Turks nevertheless remained a major military power in the 1500s and 1600s. When a combined Spanish and Italian fleet defeated the Ottomans in 1571 at the **Battle of Lepanto**, it was only a minor setback. After the battle the Ottoman grand vizier assured the sultan, Selim II, that "the might of the empire is such that if it were desired to equip the entire fleet with silver anchors, silken rigging and satin sails, we could do it." Within a year, the sultan had a new fleet that once again dominated the Mediterranean.

The Ottomans remained extremely powerful on land as well. In 1683 the Ottoman army marched to Vienna, the glittering Habsburg capital. Seeing the huge dust cloud stirred up by the advancing Turks, wealthy Viennese citizens "fled their houses, courtyards and beautifully tapestried rooms, leaving wine in the cellars and rugs on the floors." At least 200,000 Ottoman soldiers under the command of Grand Vizier Kara Mustafa (kah-RAH moohs-tah-FAH) set up camp in a great tent city outside the gates and settled in for a long siege.

The siege was not the first time the Ottomans had attacked Vienna. Süleyman had besieged the city in 1529. It was, however, the last time. After nearly two months, the city had not fallen. Then, responding to the desperate pleas of the Habsburg emperor, Polish and German troops led by

◄ **The rout of the Turks in 1683 outside of Vienna's gates marked the beginning of the Ottoman Empire's decline.**

the Polish king John Sobieski (sohb-YAY-skee) arrived and routed the Turks. An Ottoman historian of the time described this defeat:

66 *The accursed infidels [non-Muslims] . . . succeeded in capturing such quantities of money and supplies as cannot be described. They therefore did not even think of pursuing the soldiers of Islam and had they done so it would have gone hard. May God preserve us. This was a calamitous [disastrous] defeat of such magnitude that there has never been its like since the first appearance of the Ottoman state.* 99

The defeat at Vienna marked the beginning of a more rapid decline in Ottoman power. Further defeats led to the 1699 **Treaty of Karlowitz**, in which the Turks lost control over much of their European territory. Although they were able to retake some European territory in the 1700s, the Ottomans never regained their former power.

The balance of power between the Ottoman Empire and Europe began to shift in Europe's favor in the late 1600s.

The Portuguese in Asia

The balance of power in the Mediterranean took many years to shift from the Ottoman Empire to the European powers. In the meantime, first the Portuguese, followed by the Dutch, French, and English, sailed their deep-water vessels armed with heavy cannons around Africa in search of the spices, silks, and other luxuries of the East. From trading posts and forts scattered throughout the Indian Ocean and southern Asia, European merchants tried to impose their own control over the Indies trade.

As the first Europeans to discover the way into the Indian Ocean, the Portuguese were also the first Europeans to challenge the Islamic dominance of eastern trade and to establish their own commercial empire in Asia. When Vasco da Gama's crew landed at Calicut, India, in 1498, for example, an astonished Muslim merchant from Tunis exclaimed, "May the devil take you! What brought you here?" "Christians and spices," replied the Portuguese crew, who returned home laden with spices, fine woods, porcelain, silk, and precious stones. Over the next several decades Portugal set up trading forts along the African coast, at the mouths of the Red Sea and Persian Gulf, and on the coasts of India and Southeast Asia.

In 1510 Afonso de Albuquerque (ahl-boo-KER-kee), the governor of Portugal's Asian possessions, attacked and drove from power the local ruler of Goa (GOH-uh), on the west coast of India. Albuquerque made Goa the administrative center of Portugal's Asian trade empire. By 1515 Albuquerque had also conquered Malacca (muh-LAK-uh), the wealthiest trading center on the Malay coast, and Hormuz, at the mouth of the Persian Gulf. In 1511 the Portuguese captured the main port in the Moluccas (mu-LUHK-uhz)—the famed Spice Islands. In the early 1500s they also began settling Ceylon (present-day Sri Lanka).

The Portuguese also gained footholds in Japan and China. They reached Japan in the 1540s and quickly profited by trading Chinese goods for Japanese silver. In 1557 the Chinese allowed the Portuguese to establish a trading station at Macao (muh-KOW). Here, however, the Portuguese were dependent on China's goodwill,

One of the causes of Portugal's decline as a trading empire was the system it set up for controlling trade. The rulers of Portugal attempted to establish a monopoly not only over Portuguese trade, but also over all trade within its entire trading sphere. Anyone trading within Asia had to pay taxes to Portugal. Traders were required to have licenses, which they purchased from Portugal, and to pay duties at the ports to Portuguese officials.

Eventually, this system broke down because Portugal did not have the strength to enforce it. Portugal could not prevent rivals from trading in the area, and native merchants began to avoid paying for licenses once they realized they could evade Portuguese ships that were attempting to block the ports.

Critical Thinking Ask students why the Portuguese system failed.

ANSWER: Students might suggest that Portugal could not prevent rivals from trading in the area, or that merchants avoided buying the licences.

Map Answer

India

---

as António Bocarro, a resident of Macao, described in 1635:

> The peace that we have with the king of China is as he likes it, for since this place is so far from India, and since he has such vastly greater numbers of men than the most that the Portuguese could possibly assemble there, never did we think of breaking with him whatever serious grievances we may have had; because the Chinese have only to stop our food-supplies to ruin our city.

The spectacular rise of Portugal's trading-post empire was followed by an equally rapid decline. A small kingdom, Portugal had neither the people nor the financial resources to maintain such a vast empire. Portuguese rulers also proved remarkably shortsighted. As early as 1496, for example, they followed Spain's example and ordered all of the Jews to leave the country. This cost Portugal not only large numbers of people but also much wealth and valuable expertise, which the country could ill afford to lose.

In addition, though revenues from the spice trade were enormous, much of the profit ended up in the hands of the Dutch merchants who distributed the spices in Europe. The Spanish Crown, which ruled Portugal from 1580 to 1640, also assisted the decline by neglecting Portugal's trade and colonies. Although Portugal continued to hold most of its trading posts, its share in the eastern spice trade declined with the entry of new rivals. In the 1600s much of the Asian trade fell into Dutch and English hands.

The Portuguese used armed force to establish a trading-post empire in Asia.

European Empires in Asia and Africa, 1700

Empires of Trade   The search for spices, gold, tea, and other luxury goods drew Europeans to Asia and Africa. Europeans came to control territory on the coasts of both continents, as well as in the Indian and Pacific Oceans.

Linking Geography and History   Which Asian country had the most European trading posts?

The Rise of the Dutch

The 1600s were in many ways a period of remarkable success for the Dutch. After winning independence from Spain, the new Dutch republic became one of the wealthiest and most progressive parts of Europe. Although Calvinists became the dominant religious group in the Netherlands, eventually the Dutch followed a policy of religious toleration. Politically, the Netherlands was a kind of federal association of the various provinces. The Netherlands was governed by the States General of the United Provinces, a parliamentary body of provincial representatives. In military matters, the princes of Orange, who had led the struggle for freedom from Spain, remained dominant.

The Dutch owed their commercial success primarily to their position on the sea. In the northern provinces deep-sea fishing had become the leading commercial activity. In addition, the Dutch dominated the coastal shipping of northern Europe by the end of the 1500s. In the 1600s nearly 10,000 Dutch vessels carried most of the trade among France, England, Spain, and the Baltic countries.

As their wealth grew, the Dutch also began to develop institutions to sustain such large-scale commercial activity. In 1609, for example, they established the Bank of Amsterdam, in part to help stabilize currency. Prior to the bank's founding, merchants had to deal with not only foreign coins but also a variety of Dutch coins from competing mints. To help simplify commercial transactions, the bank issued paper money to replace the coins. Merchants now knew that they were receiving money of the proper value. The success of the Bank of Amsterdam contributed to Amsterdam becoming the leading financial center in Europe.

The Dutch entered the Indies largely because their former rulers, the Spanish Habsburgs, tried to restrict the flow of Indies goods into Dutch ports. In 1602 a number of Dutch merchants responded by establishing the private Dutch East India Company to trade directly with Asia. The new Dutch republic granted the Company the sole right to carry on trade between the Netherlands and the East Indies and Africa. More aggressive than the Portuguese, the Dutch conquered and occupied entire islands in an effort to monopolize the spice trade at the source of production.

▲ *Portrait of a Merchant,* by Dutch painter Jan Gossaert, c. 1530

The Dutch established their first colony in Asia in 1619 at Batavia (now present-day Jakarta [juh-KAHR-tuh]) on the island of Java. From Java they expanded west to take the island of Sumatra and east to seize the valuable Spice Islands from Portugal. They also soon captured Malacca, Ceylon, and Cochin on the southwest coast of India, and established a trading post at Nagasaki, Japan. In 1652 they established a colony at the Cape of Good Hope in South Africa to supply their ships in the Asian trade.

In the 1600s the Dutch began conquering Asian territory to control the spice trade.

Other European Competitors

The Dutch were not the only ones to seek the wealth of the Asian trade. In 1600 Queen Elizabeth I granted a charter to the British East

Theme: Technology

The Dutch entered the Asian trade in part due to a work called the *Itinerario,* written by Dutchman Jan Huyghen van Linschoten. From 1583 to 1589 Linschoten had been a servant to the Portuguese archbishop of Goa. After his return to Holland, Linschoten published *Itinerario,* which gave a geographical description of the world, sailing directions for reaching India and America, and his own observations of the Eastern world. Prior to the publication of *Itinerario,* the Dutch had sailed with Portuguese crews but had not captained their own vessels to the East.

The first Dutch fleet to use Linschoten's directions sailed in 1595. Numerous voyages followed, and competition between the Dutch and Portuguese was fierce. Partly to consolidate competing Dutch companies, the Dutch established the East India Company in 1602.

Critical Thinking Ask students why Linschoten was particularly qualified to write the *Itinerario.*

ANSWER: Students should suggest that Linschoten's position in Goa would have given him unique access to information about trade and exploration.

India Company. Over the next century the Company established trading posts at Madras, Bombay, and Calcutta in India. The Company also set up a few trading posts in Malaya and the East Indies, but India remained its headquarters and chief source of wealth. By the end of the century, British ships also began trading for teas and silks in China.

Meanwhile, the French East India Company, formed in 1664, established a trading post at Pondicherry (pahn-duh-CHER-ee) on the southeast coast of India. The French soon began to involve themselves in local politics. By the 1700s the French actually controlled some Indian territory. What made this possible was the state of Indian politics and the Mughal Empire's declining grip on its subjects.

Since the death of the Mughal emperor Aurangzeb in 1707, the Mughal Empire had begun to decline in power. Aurangzeb's wars in the Deccan had drained the imperial treasury. Then, in November 1738 Nadir Shah, a powerful new Persian ruler, led his army across the Indus River. In 1739 his forces sacked Delhi, massacring some 20,000 people. Nadir Shah had effectively destroyed Mughal power,

▲ Nadir Shah returned from sacking Delhi with the fabulous Peacock Throne and the Koh-i-noor Diamond.

though weak emperors remained on the throne until 1857.

During the remainder of the 1700s, Marathas from the Deccan, Sikhs from the Punjab, and Afghan invaders fought over much of the country. In their wars with each other, many local rulers asked for support from the Europeans who had established trading posts along their coasts. In return, the Indian rulers promised increased trading privileges. Sensing great profit, the British and French allied themselves with local princes to expand their trade. By the 1740s Mughal weakness and disunity had left the door open for increasing European domination.

In India, Europeans allied themselves with local rulers to gain more access to trade.

China and Japan

Farther east, in China and Japan, a different story unfolded. Under the late Ming and early Qing dynasties, the Chinese Empire remained considerably more powerful than the new trading empires of Europe. In Japan, shoguns of the Tokugawa dynasty transformed the Japanese feudal system into a strong centralized government that dictated its own relationship with the European "barbarians."

The Qing. Under both the Ming and early Qing dynasties, China remained one of the strongest and most extensive empires in the world. As European traders and merchants appeared on China's borders, they found that China had less to gain from Europe than Europe had to gain from China. The Chinese realized this and consequently restricted European traders to certain ports along the coast. The Portuguese had been the first to arrive and had essentially become a part of the Chinese system even at their base in Macao. As other Europeans arrived, they found entry into China's trade even more difficult.

When the Manchu established the Qing dynasty in the 1640s, they continued the old Confucian dislike of merchants and trade. Having lived in China's shadow for many generations, the Manchu had learned from Chinese advisors. Once in power, they sought to increase their own power and importance by maintaining the Confucian traditions. Although they began to experience more interaction with Europeans, under their most enlightened ruler, Kangxi (KAHNG-SHEE), they remained determined to control the relationship.

BIOGRAPHY Kangxi was born in 1654, and at the age of seven he succeeded to the dragon throne of China as emperor. Like all members of the Qing dynasty, he was never allowed to forget his identity as a Manchu. As a child he learned the arts of a Manchu warrior, such as archery and hunting, in the grassy steppes of his Manchurian homeland. In that "untamed country," he later wrote, he had a "sense of freedom."

Kangxi
BIOGRAPHY

The young Manchu prince was also taught to play the role of a Chinese emperor, however. In the imperial palace, within the walls of the Forbidden City in Beijing, he learned not only to write his native Manchu but also to paint the intricate brush strokes of Chinese characters and to recite the Confucian classics from memory.

Although controlled at first by a powerful regent, at age 15 Kangxi began ruling in his own right. In his early years he fought hard and successfully to strengthen his position on the throne. In 1683 he expanded the empire by taking control of the island of Taiwan. He also firmly established China's northern and western borders. Sending an army against Russian forces in the north, in 1689 he won back territory China had lost. When Mongol warriors threatened the western borders, Kangxi personally led an army against them. He regarded his defeat of Galdan, the Mongol leader, as his finest hour. "My great task is done," he wrote to his court. "As for my . . . own life, one can say it is happy. One can say it's fulfilled."

Kangxi's later years were not as happy, however, largely due to his relationship with the Europeans. In 1704 the emperor had a serious disagreement with Catholic missionaries. For years Kangxi had allowed Jesuit priests to practice their religion in China because their scientific knowledge proved useful to him. He had appointed Jesuits

as astronomers and as advisors on geography and engineering. But when an ambassador from the pope refused to acknowledge the practice of ancestor worship, Kangxi ordered the Catholic officials to leave the country, an act that had lasting effects on China's relationship with Europe.

Kangxi's death in 1722 left China territorially strong, but facing internal and external challenges. However, China's strength allowed it to control the growing number of European merchants in its territory. In 1759 a British ambassador petitioned the imperial court for increased and more open trade. The emperor's reply was a polite but firm no. Anxious not to lose control over their trade to "foreign devils," Chinese emperors laid down strict guidelines to regulate all relations between Chinese and Europeans. For example, they allowed European ships to dock only at one port, Guangzhou, and to trade only with a small number of officially licensed Chinese merchants. The emperors also required Europeans to live in a special "foreign settlement" outside the city walls and to abide by Chinese laws. Not until the 1800s did relations begin to turn in Europeans' favor.

▲ This mounted Japanese warrior and his horse display traditional weapons and military dress.

History THROUGH THE ARTS

Japanese Popular Culture Under the Tokugawa

In the cities of Tokugawa Japan, the samurai transformed themselves from country warriors to bureaucrats schooled in the Confucian classics. Merchants, though officially the despised lowest class, obtained increasing power by selling goods throughout the country and by lending money to the samurai. The growth of cities and the increasing wealth of merchants and artisans led to the rise of a thriving popular culture.

By the early 1700s, new forms of literature, theater, and art catered to the tastes of ordinary city residents. Publishing houses flourished as literacy became widespread, even for the lower classes. Readers enjoyed illustrated how-to books, travel books, and realistic romances with commoners as heroes.

City-dwellers flocked to Kabuki plays and puppet shows. The earliest Kabuki were plays that featured women performing lively new dances. The conservative Tokugawa disliked such spectacles, agreeing with one Confucian scholar's complaints:

66 The men wear women's clothing; the women wear men's clothing, cut their hair, and wear a man's topknot, have swords at their sides, and carry purses. They sing base songs and dance vulgar dances; their lewd voices are clamorous. 99

The government banned women from performing in Kabuki plays in 1629. Thereafter male actors played women's roles in melodramatic plays about heroic samurai and tragic love affairs.

Thinking About Art
Why might the Tokugawa have disliked Kabuki plays?

In Tokyo, Japan, actors perform a Kabuki play.

Tokugawa Japan. Like the Chinese, the Japanese also controlled their relationship with the Europeans. The first contact between the two cultures took place in 1543, when a Portuguese ship wrecked on the Japanese island of Tanega-Shima. The Portuguese soon opened a trading post in Japan. Six years later, a Jesuit priest, Francis Xavier, arrived in Kyushu, hoping to convert all of Japan to Christianity, starting with its leaders, the daimyo. The Jesuits had arrived in Japan just as several strong Japanese lords had begun to restore central authority after a long period of political disunity.

One of these lords, Oda Nobunaga (noh-boo-NAH-gah), had begun the rebuilding process by creating a powerful new army. By arming peasant foot soldiers with long spears and with the firearms the Portuguese had introduced into Japan in 1543, Nobunaga defeated the more traditional cavalry forces of his enemies. From his strategic lands in central Honshu, Nobunaga expanded his control over much of Japan. Eventually, he took control of Kyoto and made himself the emperor's guardian. With the fall of the last Ashikaga shogun, Nobunaga became the undisputed master of Japan. After Nobunaga's sudden death in 1582,

Toyotomi (toh-yoh-toh-mee) Hideyoshi, a peasant who had risen to become one of Nobunaga's greatest generals, took control of the army and continued the process of unification.

In this atmosphere of intrigue and internal warfare, the Jesuits unavoidably became involved in Japanese politics. Hideyoshi at first favored Christianity and the Jesuits. At his court, Portuguese fashions and Christian religious symbols had become popular even among non-Christian Japanese. But as political intrigues grew, in 1587 Hideyoshi declared that all Portuguese traders and Christian missionaries must leave Japan. Still anxious for trade, however, the peasant general did not enforce the order.

Hideyoshi's concerns were heightened by the arrival of a Spanish ship from the Philippines in 1587. The Spanish hoped to break Portugal's monopoly on Japanese trade. With the Spanish came another Catholic order, the Franciscans, who soon challenged the Jesuits for Japanese converts. In the early 1600s the Dutch and English also found their way to the island empire. The Japanese now learned of the religious and political rivalries that divided Europeans. Many Japanese began to turn against the foreigners. When Hideyoshi's rival, Tokugawa Ieyasu, completed the process of Japanese unification and became shogun in 1603, he severely restricted European activities.

Establishing a strong, central authority, the Tokugawa shoguns brought about more than two centuries of stability in Japan. Local rulers and their samurai, headquartered in fortified castle towns, kept the peace. Confucian values of loyalty to lord and family formed the foundation of this rigid traditional social structure. To limit disruptive outside influences, the shoguns strictly controlled trade and increasingly restricted foreign travel. By 1650 they had achieved almost complete isolation. A few Dutch merchants were the only Europeans allowed to trade in Japan, from a small base at Nagasaki.

Unlike the Ottomans and Mughals, the Qing and the Tokugawa limited foreign influence by creating strong governments and controlling foreign trade.

SECTION 1 REVIEW

IDENTIFY and explain the significance of the following:
  capitulations
  Battle of Lepanto
  Treaty of Karlowitz
  Afonso de Albuquerque
  Nadir Shah
  Kangxi
  Oda Nobunaga
  Toyotomi Hideyoshi
  Tokugawa Ieyasu

LOCATE and explain the importance of the following:
  Goa
  Malacca
  Moluccas
  Ceylon
  Macao
  Batavia
  Madras
  Bombay
  Calcutta
  Pondicherry

1. **Main Idea** How did the Portuguese, the Dutch, the English, and the French establish trading empires in Asia?
2. **Main Idea** What factors helped shift the balance of power between the Ottoman Empire and Europe?
3. **Geography: Region** What parts of Asia had the Portuguese, Spanish, Dutch, British, and French conquered by 1763?
4. **Writing to Evaluate** Imagine you are a Japanese or Chinese merchant. Write a letter to the emperor explaining your view of the ban on European traders.
5. **Determining Cause and Effect** Using the information from the section, create a chart like the one below for the Ottoman Empire, India, China, Japan, and the East Indies to explain the effects of European expansion on the civilizations and empires of Asia.

Effects of European Expansion

	EUROPEAN EXPANSION	RESPONSE	EFFECT
Ottoman Empire	*trade*	*capitulations*	*Ottoman merchants driven out of business; weakened economy*

SECTION 2

The Spanish and Portuguese in the Americas

FOCUS

- What effects did Spanish exploration and colonization have in the Caribbean?

- What factors helped the Spanish conquer the powerful Aztec and Inca empires?

- What kind of societies emerged in the Americas after the Spanish and Portuguese conquests?

- What policy did the Spanish and Portuguese pursue to control their colonial economies?

In the Americas, unlike Asia, the Spanish and Portuguese who followed Christopher Columbus established huge land empires, based on plantation economies, mining, and the use of American Indian workers and slave labor brought from Africa. As American Indians, Africans, and Europeans interacted, a new multicultural civilization began to emerge.

Map of the New World by Abraham Ortelius, 1570

The Spanish in the Caribbean

As it became clear that the Americas were not the islands of Japan or the mainland of either India or China, Spanish explorers looked for other ways to make their fortunes in these new lands. In place of trade, they turned to colonization. Columbus had established the first colony to look for gold. When none was found, he soothed the discouraged colonists by introducing the *encomienda* (en-koh-mee-EN-dah) system. Under this system, the colonists, or *encomenderos*, were granted land and the labor of a certain number of American Indians who had to farm the Spaniards' land or work as servants. In return, the *encomenderos* had to teach Christianity to their Indian workers. This basic pattern became the model for all Spanish settlements that followed in the Caribbean and on the mainland.

The *encomienda* system was a disaster for American Indians. The *encomenderos* frequently overworked and mistreated the Indians and prevented them from growing their own food. American Indians rose up in revolt against the Spanish a number of times, but European diseases wiped out entire settlements and led to a massive decline in population.

Spanish settlement of the Caribbean islands resulted in the near extinction of the American Indian inhabitants.

The Conquest of the Aztec

The search for gold and other riches drew the Spanish from the Caribbean to the mainland. In 1519 an ambitious **conquistador**, or conqueror, named Hernán Cortés, landed on the Mexican coast with a force of some 600 men and 16 horses. The Spanish soon heard of a great and wealthy civilization farther inland from the local inhabitants. As the Spanish advanced to find it, word of their coming quickly reached the great city of Tenochtitlán, capital of the Aztec Empire.

Cortés and Moctezuma. The Aztec emperor Moctezuma (MAWK-tay-soo-mah) II received news of the Spaniards' arrival with some anxiety. He believed that Cortés was the great god Quetzalcoatl (kwet-suhl-koh-AH-tl) coming to reclaim his throne. Anxiously, Moctezuma sent rich gifts to Cortés. The sight of such wealth only caused the Spaniards to march on Tenochtitlán even faster. Along the way Cortés gained allies among the many enemies of the Aztec.

An Aztec tribesman described the fearsome sight of the approach of the Spanish forces. The strangers were covered with metal and rode beasts unlike any the Aztec had ever seen:

66 *They came in battle array, as conquerors, and the dust rose in whirlwinds on the roads. Their spears glinted in the sun, and their pennons [flags] fluttered like bats. They made a loud clamor as they marched, for their coats of mail and their weapons clashed and rattled. Some of them were dressed in glistening iron from head to foot; they terrified everyone who saw them.* 99

Moctezuma welcomed Cortés and gave him a palace to use inside the city. The conquistador soon took the emperor prisoner, however, and demanded gold.

The battle for Mexico. With Moctezuma imprisoned, the Spanish had seemingly taken the city without a fight, but trouble soon broke out. In May 1520 Cortés briefly left the city. While he was gone, his men attacked the Aztec, who had gathered for a religious festival. They killed many of the worshippers, including women and children. Cortés returned in late June to find the outraged Aztec besieging his men in Moctezuma's palace. Hoping to calm them, Cortés allowed the captive Moctezuma to speak to his people from the palace rooftop. This only further enraged the Aztec, who believed Moctezuma had betrayed them. Moctezuma was killed in the fight that followed, though by whose hand is uncertain.

Deciding to retreat, Cortés and his men tried to sneak out of Tenochtitlán on a dark, rainy night in late June. A woman drawing water saw them, however, and sounded the alarm: "Our enemies are escaping." The Aztec attacked the fleeing soldiers, and both sides suffered many casualties in what the Spanish later called

THROUGH OTHERS' EYES

First Impressions

When the Spanish first began arriving on the shores of Mexico, the Aztec probably observed with amazement the strange-looking creatures who bore little resemblance to any people the Mexicans had ever seen. From their ships and horses to their outward appearances, attempts were made to describe these strange visitors. An Aztec scout watched from the shore as the Spaniards fished from a small boat. The scout returned to his Aztec ruler with this report:

66 They . . . then entered a small canoe and reached the two enormous towers [the Spanish ships] and climbed inside; there must have been about fifteen of them, with a kind of coloured jackets, some blue, some brown and some green and some of a dirty colour. . . . Some had a pinkish hue, and on their heads they had coloured pieces of cloth: these were scarlet caps, some very large and round like small maize cakes, which must have served as protection against the sun. Their flesh was very white, much more than ours, except that all wore a long beard and hair to their ears. 99

La Noche Triste (lah NOH-chay TREES-tay), "the Night of Sorrows."

The Aztec celebration of driving away the Spaniards was short-lived. A smallpox epidemic swept through the battle-weary population, killing thousands of people. In May 1521 the Spaniards returned, supported by an army of Indian reinforcements, and laid siege to the city. "Nothing can compare with the horrors of that siege and the agonies of the starving," remarked an Aztec sadly. After three months of resistance, the city fell on August 13, 1521.

Consequences of the conquest. Once in control, the conquistadors systematically looted the fallen empire of its gold and silver. They also tried to abolish the Aztec religion, as the use of human sacrifice revolted them. Even before the

R **RESOURCE ACTIVITY**

GLOBAL HISTORY RESOURCE CENTER
Reading: *An Aztec Account of the Spanish in Mexico*

Print out and distribute the reading. Have students read about Cortés and his men in Mexico from the viewpoint of an Aztec writer. Then have students rewrite one of the sections of the passage, describing the same event from the viewpoint of a Spaniard.

Level 2

Daily Life

In his letters Hernán Cortés described Tenochtitlán: "This city has many squares where trading is done and markets are held continuously. There is also one square . . . where every kind of merchandise produced in these lands is found. . . . There are shops like apothecaries,' where they sell ready-made medicines as well as liquid ointments and plasters. There are shops like barbers' where they have their hair washed and shaved, and shops where they sell food and drink."

Critical Thinking Ask students how Tenochtitlán was similar to modern cities.

ANSWER: Students should suggest that it had many markets and stores that offered services.

Francisco Pizarro's navigator, Bartolomé Ruiz, was the first European to have contact with the magnificent Inca society. He described coming upon one of their rafts loaded down with goods: "They were carrying many pieces of silver and gold as personal ornaments . . . including crowns and diadems, belts and bracelets. . . . They were carrying many wool and cotton mantles and Moorish tunics . . . and many other pieces of clothing colored with cochineal, crimson, blue, yellow, and all other colors, and worked with different types of ornate embroidery. . . . They were taking all this to trade for fish shells from which they make counters, colored scarlet and white."

Critical Thinking Ask students to suggest which part of Ruiz' description might have been particularly interesting to the conquistadors.

ANSWER: Students might suggest that the presence of the silver and gold objects probably would have caught the attention of Pizarro and his men, since this suggested that the Inca civilization was wealthy.

▲ In 1521 and 1522 Cortés and his men destroyed the temples of Tenochtitlán. They then built the Catholic Metropolitan Cathedral (above) from the great twin temple pyramid of the Aztec gods of rain and war.

fall of Tenochtitlán, Cortés himself had torn down the images of the Aztec gods and replaced them with Christian statues, as he described in a report home:

❝ The most important of these idols, and the ones in whom they have most faith, I had taken from their places and thrown down the steps; and I had those chapels where they were cleaned, for they were full of the blood of sacrifices; and I had images of Our Lady and of other saints put there, which caused . . . [the] natives some sorrow. ❞

After the conquest, the Spanish destroyed much of Tenochtitlán and built their own capital—Mexico City—on its ruins. In the central square, they tore down the great pyramid and used its stones to build a Christian cathedral.

Thus, the Spanish gained most of present-day Mexico. From their new base, they explored north, claiming much of what is now the United States. To the south, they pushed into Central America. Hearing rumors of yet another fabulously wealthy civilization somewhere in the towering Andes Mountains, they also sent expeditions into South America. There the Spanish soon discovered the Inca Empire.

The Conquest of the Inca

When the Spanish arrived in the Americas, the huge empire of the Inca extended from present-day Ecuador to Chile. Though the empire looked strong, its stability was crumbling. Smallpox spread to the Andes in the late 1520s, killing one third to one half of the population in some areas. Among the dead was the Inca emperor Huayna Capac. A brutal civil war broke out between his sons—Atahualpa and Huáscar. In 1532 Atahualpa emerged victorious.

Not long after his victory Atahualpa heard reports that there was a group of foreigners in the empire. Francisco Pizarro and some 168 men had established a Spanish settlement on the empire's northern coast. Despite their strange new weapons and horses, the new Inca ruler did not fear the Spaniards. Eventually, Atahualpa agreed to meet Pizarro and his men in November 1532. At the meeting, a priest urged the emperor to convert to Catholicism and handed him a Bible. When the book did not literally speak to him as he expected, Atahualpa threw it down in disgust. On Pizarro's order, Spanish soldiers seized the emperor and killed most of his attendants.

Imprisoned by the Spanish, Atahualpa agreed to fill a room with gold and another twice over with silver artifacts as a ransom. He was as good as his word. Pizarro's share alone totaled 630 pounds of gold and more than 1,000 pounds of silver. Despite Atahualpa's show of good faith, in 1533 the Spanish executed the emperor. "With Atahualpa killed . . . and the clan of the Inca already wiped out," an Inca official explained, "the land was left without an overlord and with the tyrants in complete possession."

Pizarro and his men headed south to Cuzco, the Inca capital. There they defeated the remnants of Atahualpa's army and plundered the wealthy city. Pizarro installed Manco Inca Yupanqui, the 16-year-old son of Huayna Capac, as puppet emperor. The Spaniards' increasing demands for silver and gold turned the emperor against them, however. Manco Inca's son later recorded his father's reply to Spanish demands:

▲ In this painting from the late 1800s, Atahualpa listens to a priest named Father Valverde.

❝Ever since you entered my country, there has been nothing . . . that has been denied you, but instead any wealth I had you now possess, whether in the form of children or adults, both male and female, to serve you, or of lands, the best of which are now in your power. What in the world do you need that I have not given you?❞

Manco Inca soon raised a major rebellion against the Spaniards that spread through much of the empire. At the head of a large army, Manco Inca besieged Cuzco for 10 months. Unable to take the city, in the end he retreated with many of his people farther into the Andes Mountains, where he established an independent state beyond Spanish control. In 1572, however, the Spanish marched into the mountains, defeated Tupac Amarú, the last Inca ruler, and executed him.

The Spanish gradually extended their territory from their new capital of Lima. They conquered Chile in the 1540s. In 1536 and 1538, an expedition from Spain founded the colonies of Buenos Aires and Asunción.

Disease, superior weapons, and internal divisions among the Aztec and Inca helped the Spanish conquer both empires.

The Portuguese in Brazil

Like the Spanish, the Portuguese established a land empire in the Americas. In 1500 a Portuguese navigator, Pedro Cabral, had been blown off course while on his way to India. Sighting the coast of Brazil, he claimed the territory for Portugal under the terms of the Treaty of Tordesillas. Brazil's vast jungles and mighty rivers did not easily yield the spices, gold, or silver that the Europeans desired, however, and at first little was done about the new territory. Not until 1532, after French raids threatened Brazilian ships and settlements, did Portugal begin its colonization of Brazil.

King John III of Portugal granted huge tracts of land, called **captaincies**, that stretched westward from the coast. These captaincies were granted to **donataries**, individuals who agreed to finance colonization in exchange for political and economic control of their new territory. Because of mismanagement and vigorous resistance from Indian inhabitants, only two of the original captaincies prospered. Duarte Coelho Pereira, one of the successful donataries, complained, "We are forced to conquer by inches what Your Majesty granted by leagues."

In 1548 King John responded to such complaints by appointing Tomé de Sousa as the first governor-general of Brazil. With him, the new administrator brought colonists, bureaucrats, and Jesuit missionaries. In 1549 Sousa founded Salvador, Brazil's first capital.

Colonial Economy and Society

The conquistadors had won a vast empire for Spain that stretched from the plains of North America to the Andes Mountains of South America. To govern these geographically diverse and remote lands, the Spanish Crown sent an army of bureaucrats to transform the conquistadors

European Empires in the Americas, 1700

Territorial Empires Europeans established vast territorial empires in the Americas.

Linking Geography and History Which European colonial power did not control territory in South America in 1700?

and the conquered peoples into a settled society. Portugal controlled only part of the eastern coast of South America, but it also faced a number of challenges in governing its territory.

Colonial government. In Brazil, a governor-general appointed by the king was responsible for both civil and military administration. The power of the donataries limited his authority, however, as did the lack of effective communications among the 14 different captaincies and Portugal.

A more elaborate system emerged in Spanish America. The king appointed a **viceroy**, or governor, to oversee each viceroyalty, or large province. At first there were only two viceroyalties: New

Spain, in Mexico and Central America; and New Castile, in Peru. In the mid-1700s two more viceroyalties were added: New Granada, stretching from Panama to Ecuador and Venezuela; and La Plata in Argentina, Chile, Paraguay, Uruguay, and Bolivia.

Since all land in the New World theoretically belonged to the king, the viceroys ruled as his personal representatives. However, they ruled with the advice of a council, known as the *audiencia*, whose members reported directly and privately to the king in Spain. In addition, all senior officials were appointed from Spain, where the king's Council of the Indies oversaw the entire American empire. Thus, the Crown tried to maintain tight control over its colonial administration.

The colonial system did not always work well, however. In Spanish America the *encomenderos* exercised so much local power that they often ignored the viceroy's orders. In the 1540s, for example, Pizarro's brother Gonzalo murdered Peru's first viceroy. Later viceroys learned the practice of "I obey but I do not execute," and they simply ignored unpopular royal orders.

The colonial economy. Mines and agricultural estates provided most of the colonial wealth. Gold mining, for example, fanned the growth of Rio de Janeiro, which became the colonial capital of Brazil in 1763. Large, self-sufficient farming estates, called *haciendas* in Spanish America and *fazendas* in Brazil, introduced European crops and animals to the Americas. The Europeans largely re-created the life they had known in Europe. In areas suitable for cattle they became ranchers, producing meat and hides. Elsewhere they raised a variety of crops. For example, sugar plantations prospered in Brazil, southern Mexico, and the Caribbean. In addition to supplying local needs, the colonists exported goods to Europe.

The biggest challenge the colonists faced was finding laborers for the mines and the estates. As a result of disease and forced labor, by the mid-1500s the Indian population had declined in some areas by more than 90 percent. For example, in the viceroyalty of New Spain, covering present-day Mexico, the southwestern United States, and much of Central America, the American Indian population declined from an estimated 11 to 25 million in 1492 to 1.25 million by 1625. As growing numbers of Indians died, some conquistadors and clergymen called for the Spanish Crown to protect these potential Christian converts.

One of the most outspoken of these early reformers was Bartolomé de Las Casas. Las Casas had come to the Americas on Columbus's third voyage and had been granted an *encomienda*. After witnessing the Indians' plight, however, he gave up his *encomienda* and in 1512 became a priest. Thereafter he was tireless in his efforts to protect the American Indians. The Spanish monarchs shared Las Casas's concerns. Anxious for Catholic converts, they made laws regulating the treatment of Indians. To replace Indian labor, however, Las Casas and others suggested the use of African slaves. Soon, thousands of Africans were being imported to the Americas as slave labor. It was a fateful development that would affect four continents and the fate of millions of people.

The development of colonial society. The sometimes tense coexistence of Africans, Europeans, and American Indians shaped the

▲ **African slaves harvesting sugarcane in Brazil. Brazil had the world's first large-scale sugar plantations with African slave labor.**

social order of the Americas. Society in Spain and Portugal reflected the basic class divisions of Europe: nobles, clergy, and commoners. In the Americas, wealth rather than noble rank became the basis for high status.

As the Europeans moved into the Americas, they imposed their own social order over the local peoples, one based not only on wealth but also on race and even place of birth. A small group of *peninsulares*, Spanish or Portuguese born in Europe, and creoles, Europeans born in the colonies, ruled colonial society. The *peninsulares* looked down on the creoles. Both the *peninsulares* and the creoles looked down on the people of mixed race—the *mestizos*, those of Indian and European background, and mulattoes, those of African and European ancestry. All of these people looked down on American Indians, Africans, and those of mixed Indian and African parentage, the *zambos*.

The multicultural nature of colonial society was reflected in its religious life. Catholicism, the religion of the conquerors, spread rapidly. Catholic missionaries established schools, convents, and universities for the colonists. They also organized American Indian settlements. Within several generations, most of Spanish and Portuguese America was Catholic.

Both American Indian and African religious traditions remained important, however. In the late 1500s, for example, Father Bernardino de Sahagún wrote about his suspicion that Indian worship of the Virgin Mary disguised continuing worship of the Aztec goddess Tonantzin:

66 *At [a small mountain called Tepeyacac] they had a temple dedicated to the mother of the gods whom they called Tonantzin, which means Our Mother. There they performed many sacrifices in honor of this goddess. . . .*

And now that a church of Our Lady of Guadalupe [the Virgin Mary] is built there, they also call her Tonantzin. . . . It appears to be a Satanic invention to cloak idolatry under the confusion of this name, Tonantzin. 99

African religious practices survived in many parts of the Americas in dances, rituals, and religions such as Santeria, which mixed African and Christian beliefs.

RESOURCE ACTIVITY

GLOBAL HISTORY RESOURCE CENTER
Reading: *European Conquest and Disease*

Print out and distribute the reading. Have students read about the impact of new diseases on the peoples of the Americas. Then have students take the role of an Indian in either South America or North America and write a short personal account that describes the effects of the new European diseases on Indian communities.

Level 3

RESOURCE ACTIVITY

GLOBAL HISTORY RESOURCE CENTER
Image: *Planting Cane on a Sugar Plantation*

Pair students and then print out and distribute the image. Have student teams study the image and then imagine themselves as the African man in the center. Tell teams to work together to express the man's thoughts in two or three sentences.

Level 1

REVIEW & ASSESSMENT RESOURCES

- Study Guide 16.2
- Daily Quiz 16.2
- Main Idea Activity 16.2

All Levels

434

Spain's and Portugal's new colonies blended European, African, and American Indian cultures.

Mercantilism and Its Consequences

Both the Spanish and the Portuguese tried to regulate the economies of their colonies for their own national interests by practicing an economic policy later called **mercantilism**. Mercantilism became the dominant economic policy of Europe between 1500 and 1800. It was rooted in the belief that a country's power depended on its wealth in gold and silver. Since there was only a limited supply of such precious metals, Europeans thought that a country could only grow wealthy and powerful at the expense of other countries. Consequently, European countries used their colonies to provide raw materials and act as markets for their own goods, but closed them off to other nations.

In keeping with this theory, Spain, for example, prohibited its colonies from trading with other European countries. Every year Spanish fleets carried wine, olive oil, furniture, and textiles to the Americas, where they were exchanged for silver, gold, sugar, dyes, and other products. The Spanish Crown also allowed Mexican merchants to exchange silver for valuable Chinese silks and porcelains and Asian spices from the Spanish Philippines.

Great silver strikes in Peru and Mexico enriched the Spanish treasury for centuries. Although these riches at first made Spain the wealthiest country in Europe, they also weakened the Spanish economy. Instead of improving and expanding manufacturing and agriculture in Spain, for example, the Spanish simply purchased what they wanted or needed from other countries. The consequences of this policy of neglect became evident when the steady flow of American silver, combined with a rise in population that stimulated demand, caused inflation throughout Europe.

Both Spain and Portugal practiced mercantilism, extracting wealth from their colonies but prohibiting them from trading with other powers.

SECTION 2 REVIEW

IDENTIFY and explain the significance of the following:
encomienda
conquistador
Hernán Cortés
Moctezuma
La Noche Triste
Atahualpa
Francisco Pizarro
Manco Inca Yupanqui
Tupac Amarú
captaincies
donataries
viceroy
Bartolomé de Las Casas
mercantilism

LOCATE and explain the importance of the following:
Lima
Buenos Aires
Asunción
Rio de Janeiro

1. **Main Idea** How did the European conquest of the Caribbean affect American Indians?
2. **Main Idea** Why can it be said that Spain and Portugal created multicultural colonies? Give specific examples to support your answer.
3. **Geography: Human-Environment Interaction** What challenges did Spain and Portugal face in governing their colonies and developing their colonial economies? How did they meet these challenges, and what role did mercantilism play?
4. **Writing to Inform** Using information from the section, write a short essay indicating how the internal political problems of the Aztec and Inca, the superior weapons of the Europeans, and diseases brought by the Europeans contributed to the defeat of the Aztec and Inca empires.
5. **Analyzing** Imagine that you are a Spanish viceroy in the late 1500s. Write a letter to the king explaining why you cannot enforce laws reforming the *encomienda* system.

The Dutch, French, and English in the Americas

- What did northern European explorers hope to find in North America, and what were the consequences of their failure?
- What were the primary goals of French and Dutch colonization?
- How and why were English colonies established in North America?
- What were the consequences of cultural interaction between Europeans and American Indians?

As Spain and Portugal strengthened their empires in the Americas, the Dutch, English, and French established competing American empires of their own. The nature of their colonization reflected their different goals and priorities. While the Dutch and French were interested primarily in trade along mercantilist lines, English colonization reflected a variety of different goals. As in the Spanish and Portuguese empires, the lives of American Indians were changed by colonization.

The Bailly Globe, 1530

✴ Northern Explorations

The profitable overseas colonies of Spain and Portugal prompted other European countries to send out explorers of their own. With royal support, French and English expeditions sailed across the Atlantic in the 1500s. Like the Spanish and Portuguese, France and England were primarily interested in finding a route to the treasures of Asia. With Spain and Portugal in firm control of the southern routes, however, they sought a **Northwest Passage**—a waterway around or through North America.

In 1497 John Cabot, an Italian navigator in the pay of King Henry VII of England, sailed west to the coasts of Newfoundland and Nova Scotia. When Cabot found no passage to China, however, English seafarers spent the next half century vainly searching for a northeastern route that went through the Baltic Sea or around Scandinavia. By the 1580s they had turned back to the west.

Meanwhile, French explorers concentrated exclusively on the northwestern route. In 1534 French explorer Jacques Cartier [KAHR-tyay] set sail with a twofold mission: to search for the Northwest Passage and to discover new lands. Although he never discovered a Northwest Passage, Cartier sailed up the St. Lawrence River as far as present-day Montreal, and established France's claims to eastern Canada, or New France, as he called it.

As the Northwest Passage continued to elude them, France, England, and the Netherlands eventually turned to colonization to make a profit. During the 1600s all three countries took valuable sugar-producing islands in the Caribbean from Spain and Portugal. The major thrust of colonization, however, was aimed at North America. Early English attempts at colonization occurred in 1585 and 1587, when Sir Walter Raleigh established short-lived settlements on Roanoke Island, off the coast of what is now North Carolina. The English, French, and Dutch did not establish successful colonies in North America until the 1600s, however.

After failing to find a Northwest Passage to Asia, northern European nations eventually turned to colonization in search of wealth.

History and Current Events

Today, the city of New York has around 9 million inhabitants and is occasionally called a concrete jungle. It is hard to imagine the countryside around New York City as explorers saw it in the 1600s. The area was covered by forest, mostly made up of giant oak, poplar, hickory, and wild plum trees. Manhattan Island itself was described as having "very good woodland" and being "indented with bays, coves, and creeks." One explorer described it as having "many brooks of fresh water running through it."

Critical Thinking Ask students why many people call New York City a "concrete jungle."

ANSWER: Students might suggest that people use the term because the city has many buildings and streets. Some people also see the city as dangerous.

Dutch and French Colonization

The French and the Dutch were primarily interested in trade along mercantilist lines. The French also hoped to spread French Catholic culture to American Indians. After initial unsuccessful attempts sponsored by the French clergy to establish colonization for missionary purposes, eventually French colonization was organized by the Crown, which preferred only loyal Catholics to settle in New France. The French attempted to exclude potential troublemakers, such as the Huguenots, from the colony. The Dutch preferred to encourage private companies to establish colonies by granting them a monopoly on any trade they might develop.

Critical to both French and Dutch colonization was the fur trade. In 1603 Samuel de Champlain arrived in New France to trade for furs, specifically beaver pelts. Champlain began exploring the Great Lakes region and made agreements with local tribes to trade their furs for European goods at a string of trading posts he established. In 1608 he founded a permanent French settlement at Quebec to act as a central collection point. French colonists also settled at Montreal and in present-day Nova Scotia. From Canada, the French gradually moved south. Between 1679 and 1682 René-Robert de La Salle traveled down the Mississippi River to the Gulf of Mexico. He claimed the entire inland region of North America for France, calling it Louisiana after Louis XIV.

Meanwhile, sailing for a Dutch company in 1609, Englishman Henry Hudson sighted present-day Manhattan Island and sailed up "as fine a river as can be found, wide and deep, with good anchoring ground on both sides." In 1624 the newly chartered **Dutch West India Company** sent some 30 families to establish the colony of New Netherland in this Hudson River valley. In 1626 Peter Minuit, the first governor of New Netherland, bought Manhattan Island from the local Canarsee tribes and founded New Amsterdam, which later became New York City. By the early 1650s, the colony of New Netherland contained fewer than 4,000 settlers from all over Europe. Clashes over land with local Indian tribes, who were being squeezed out of their own territory, convinced the company to restrict further immigration and stick to fur trading.

French settlement was also relatively light. By 1750 fewer than 100,000 French people lived in North America. With trade as their first priority, French officials encouraged traders to live among the Indians, learning their ways and teaching them French ways. Many traders married Indian women.

French missionaries also did their best to spread French Catholic culture. Both priests and nuns learned American Indian languages and customs. As Father Ragueneau, a Jesuit priest, warned, "One must be very careful before condemning a thousand things among their customs, which greatly offend minds brought up and nourished in another world."

The French and the Dutch set up colonies in North America to take advantage of the fur trade, and French authorities hoped to convert the American Indians to Catholicism.

▲ This sketch of Quebec, Canada, shows the location of many important sites in the city around 1700, including the busy St. Lawrence River.

English Colonization

English colonization was more haphazard than that of the French and Dutch. Like the Dutch government, the English Crown preferred not to risk its own money on colonization ventures. Instead, it granted royal charters to private English companies to establish the first settlements. Also, unlike France, for many years the English government was happy to see political opponents leave for the colonies, often encouraging such migration to rid the country of what it viewed as disruptive elements. With such loose royal control, private companies soon established the first English colonies along the North American coast.

Settlement for profit. In 1607 the London Company established the first permanent colony at Jamestown in Virginia. The colony's leaders hoped to find gold or other precious metals. As John Smith, one of the leaders, put it, "There was no talk, no hope, no work, but dig gold, wash gold, refine gold, load gold." When no gold was found, however, the Company turned to tobacco to recover its costs. Tobacco had become popular in Europe. Although King James described smoking as "a custom loathsome to the eye, hateful to the nose, harmful to the brain, dangerous to the lungs," England imported 3 million pounds of the "noxious weed" in 1638 alone. With huge profits from tobacco, the Virginia colony began to grow.

To attract new sources of labor, Company officials offered people free passage to the colony in exchange for a set number of years of work, a system known as **indentured servitude**. The Company also encouraged women to immigrate, since "the plantation can never flourish till families be planted, and the respect of their wives and children fix [keep] the people on the soil." Free Africans were among the early indentured servants, but as labor demands rose the colonists resorted to importing enslaved Africans.

Virginia's success encouraged others. By 1732 three more English colonies—North Carolina, South Carolina, and Georgia—were organized along similar economic lines. Some of the new settlers came from the West Indies, bringing with them their knowledge of plantation farming—and their enslaved Africans. Along the coast and in the interior, colonists established large plantations and small farms. Besides tobacco, they grew export crops such as indigo, for blue dye, and rice, which they learned to cultivate from West African slaves. The forests provided wood and naval supplies such as tar and pitch.

Religious colonization. The search for wealth was not the sole motivation for European colonization. As the Reformation and Counter-Reformation continued to disrupt people's lives in Europe, many saw the Americas as a haven where they could worship as they liked. The first such religious colonists to arrive were the Pilgrims, who settled Plymouth in 1620. A larger colony was established in 1630 around present-day Boston by the Massachusetts Bay Company. The Company had been formed by English

◀ **In one of the earliest known illustrations of an American tobacco factory, African slaves work in the tobacco sheds around 1670.**

Theme: **Social Relations**

Around half the population of the new settlers in the established colonies outside New England were voluntary indentured servants. The term *indentured servant* comes from the contract, called an indenture, that the servant agreed to in order to gain passage to the colonies. While some colonizers originally hoped to establish a sort of feudal system in the new colonies in which serfs worked the land, they found that, because of the abundance of land, serfdom was not a viable option. Instead, they turned to indentured servitude.

Indentured servants were fairly expensive, but they worked the land from four to seven years. After they finished their term, they were given food, some money, clothing, and tools, and could stake a claim to land. Planters eventually discovered that importing enslaved people was more profitable, because, while initially more expensive, the slaves were tied to the planters for life.

Critical Thinking Ask students to suggest reasons why people would voluntarily become indentured servants.

ANSWER: Students might suggest that these people desired a chance to own land in the colonies, but were too poor to pay for passage across the Atlantic.

BIOGRAPHY

Anne Hutchinson
Disturbed by the religious views of many of her fellow colonists in Massachusetts, Anne Hutchinson began holding religious meetings in her home. She gathered a large following of prominent citizens, and her views eventually caused a split in Boston society that spread throughout the colony. When her male followers refused to join the other colonists in action against the Pequot Indians, Hutchinson's opposition eventually removed her supporters from office and brought her to trial.

Critical Thinking Ask students why some colonists found Hutchinson's views alarming.

ANSWER: Students might suggest that her views caused religious conflict and threatened the unity and safety of the colony.

▲ **New England colonists make their way through the snow to a town meeting.**

Puritans as part of the **Great Migration**, in which some 60,000 Puritans left England to escape the "corrupt" English society of Charles I.

Some of the Puritans of Massachusetts hoped one day to return to England. In the meantime, as John Winthrop, first governor of the colony, put it, they had come to the new world to establish a "city on a hill" as an example for all. Only church members could participate in the colony's government, and religious conformity was strictly enforced.

As more and more people migrated to the colony, land pressures and internal disagreements led some Puritans to establish new settlements of their own. In 1636 Thomas Hooker and his followers settled in what became Connecticut. Others left Massachusetts because they could not bring themselves to conform to the strict religious rule. For example, Roger Williams challenged the religious government of the colony and was banished. He and a few followers fled south, establishing the first settlement in Rhode Island. Williams was outspoken in his support of religious toleration for all. His colony soon became a haven for another critic, Anne Hutchinson.

BIOGRAPHY Born in Alford, England, in 1591, Hutchinson was raised in a strict Puritan family. Like many Puritan families, in 1634 the Hutchinsons migrated to the Massachusetts Bay Colony. Inspired by the teachings of the Puritan minister John Cotton, Hutchinson developed her own ideas about how the Bible should be interpreted. She held weekly meetings in her home to discuss his sermons and to present her own interpretations of the Bible.

Encouraged by her supporters, Hutchinson soon began to speak out against leading ministers in the colony. Many people thought Hutchinson was challenging the authority of the community's religious government by suggesting that people should follow their own consciences in matters of faith. Her attacks quickly brought the combined force of church and state against her. It was not long before Governor Winthrop ordered her to stop preaching or suffer banishment. Hutchinson replied:

> ❝You have no power over my body, neither can you do me any harm. . . . No further do I esteem of any mortal man. . . . I fear none but the great Jehovah [God], . . . and I do verily believe that he will deliver me out of your hands. . . . Therefore, take heed how you proceed against me.❞

When Hutchinson claimed to have heard God's voice directly, however, the shocked colonists denounced her for heresy. In 1638 she moved with her family to Rhode Island. After her husband died, she moved to New Netherland, where Indians killed her in 1643.

The same search for religious tolerance that had motivated Williams and Hutchinson also inspired the founding of several other colonies. In the 1630s Cecilius Calvert, second Lord Baltimore, established a haven for English Catholics in his colony of Maryland. Accepting the principle of religious toleration, Lord Baltimore eventually opened Maryland to anyone. In the 1680s the Quaker leader William Penn established Pennsylvania on a similar basis of religious toleration.

Anne Hutchinson
BIOGRAPHY

Private English companies established colonies for many reasons, including profit, religious freedom, and religious toleration.

A Clash of Cultures

Although neither the French nor the Dutch were particularly interested in conquering American Indian tribes, the foreign presence nevertheless brought enormous changes to traditional Indian ways of life. Some tribal leaders understood the implications of cultural interaction and worried about its effects. As one Indian leader told Champlain in 1633:

66 *You will build a house that is a fortress, then you will build another house . . . and then we will be nothing but dogs that sleep outdoors. . . . You will grow wheat, and we will no longer look for our sustenance in the woods; we will be no better than vagabonds. . . . You pinch our arms, and we will tremble.* 99

Changes did occur, particularly as the American Indians adapted to the fur trade.

Most of the tribes between the Hudson Bay in the north and the Great Lakes and St. Lawrence River in the south participated in the French fur trade. In the early 1600s the Huron north of Lake Ontario organized a trading empire with the Ottawa and Nipissing of Lake Huron. The Huron traded their own agricultural products for furs trapped by tribes farther north and west. They then traded the furs in Montreal or Quebec for European knives, axes, cloth, and other goods. Returning west, they exchanged some of the European goods for more furs from their Indian suppliers. Farther south, the Iroquois League became similarly involved with Dutch fur traders.

As the European demand for furs increased, some tribes overhunted the beaver in their own territories. Such occurrences often upset local balances of power. In 1640, for example, the Iroquois League decided to capture the Huron trade after trapping out their own territory. The resulting conflict nearly destroyed many tribes around Lake Erie. Such wars became even more common once the Europeans began fighting

▲ A European trader shows his selection of weapons to an American Indian who will trade furs for the goods.

each other over land and trade. Each side's Indian allies were often drawn into the fighting.

The worst conflicts, however, developed between American Indians and Europeans over land. Violent land disputes underlay the Dutch decision to restrict immigration and stick to fur trading as the basis for the New Netherland colony. Such disputes were even more common between local Indian groups and English colonists in search of free land.

As more and more European settlers arrived in North America, they soon outnumbered American Indians, whose population had been severely reduced by disease brought by settlers. English settlers often interpreted the great epidemics as signs of God's blessing on their own settlement. Edward Johnson, an early settler in New England, expressed this view when he described an epidemic that broke out among the Indians after a "quarrell" with the English:

66 *The Lord put an end to this quarrell . . . by smiting [striking] the Indians with a sore*

The fur trade eventually proved to be devastating for the American Indian population and for the Huron in particular. In 1635 the Huron population was decimated by European diseases, and by 1641 the population was cut in half.

The Huron had a long-standing rivalry with the Iroquois. In 1648 the Iroquois, armed with Dutch guns, wreaked havoc upon the Huron, who fled in many different directions. By 1649 the Iroquois, using their military strength, had driven the Huron out of all of their territory.

Critical Thinking Ask students to suggest how the outcome of this rivalry might have been different if European diseases had not caused so many deaths.

ANSWER: Students' answers will vary, but might suggest that the Huron would have been better able to resist the Iroquois and hold onto their territory.

Disease. . . . The mortality among them was very great, . . . [such] that the poor Creatures being very timourous [fearful] of death, would faine [gladly] have fled from it, but could not tell how, unless they could have gone from themselves. . . . As [the English] entered one of their [wigwams], they beheld a most sad spectacle, death having smitten them all save one poor Infant. . . . Thus did the Lord allay [calm] their quarrelsome spirits, and made room for the following part of his Army. 99

With conflicting ideas about how to use the land, English settlers and American Indians pursued ways of living that were often at odds. Eventually, the technology and greater numbers of the colonists dominated. Despite considerable resistance, American Indian peoples were driven off their lands, and they often were destroyed altogether. Even the southeastern farming tribes, who tried to adapt to European methods, were eventually driven out by European settlers.

With more land coming under cultivation, European settlers, particularly those in the southern colonies, soon found themselves in need of workers. As the Spanish and Portuguese had done under similar circumstances in Central and South America, the North American colonists turned to Africa to provide slave laborers.

▲ In 1724 a French artist made this sketch of Iroquois planting crops and harvesting sap from maple trees to make syrup.

European influences upset local balances of power among many American Indian communities and created conflict between Europeans and American Indians over land.

SECTION 3 REVIEW

IDENTIFY and explain the significance of the following:
Northwest Passage
John Cabot
Jacques Cartier
Samuel de Champlain
René-Robert de La Salle
Henry Hudson
Dutch West India Company
Peter Minuit
indentured servitude
Great Migration
John Winthrop
Anne Hutchinson

LOCATE and explain the importance of the following:

Quebec
Louisiana
Jamestown
Plymouth

1. Main Idea How did the search for the Northwest Passage contribute to the colonization of North America?

2. Main Idea How did the French, Dutch, and English differ in their reasons for establishing colonies?

3. Cross-cultural Interaction How did the settlement of Europeans in North America affect Indian populations? Be sure to consider the situation in New France, New Netherland, and English America.

4. Writing to Persuade Imagine you are a resident of the Massachusetts Bay Colony. Write a letter to an English friend explaining what you think of Anne Hutchinson's banishment.

5. Evaluating What geographic factors contributed to the exploration and settlement of New France and Louisiana?

Trade and Empire in Africa

FOCUS

- How did the arrival of the Europeans change the African slave trade?

- How did the expansion of the slave trade affect Africa?

- What were the consequences of the Atlantic slave trade in the Americas?

In Africa, as in Asia, Europeans initially encountered well-organized and powerful states with which they could establish trade relations. At first such trade centered on gold, ivory, and other luxury items. However, as Europeans began to establish plantation economies in the Americas, the slave trade in West Africa became the centerpiece of European and African interaction.

Benin bronze statue of a
Portuguese soldier with
a musket, c. 1500s

Trade and Empire in West Africa

During the great European age of overseas exploration, the Portuguese first explored the coast of Africa. As explorers advanced down the coast in search of gold and a route to Asia, they exchanged goods with African traders. In return for European goods, local traders offered gold, ivory, and slaves. At first the Portuguese were less interested in slaves than in gold and ivory. But as the demand for labor on the island plantations of the Atlantic increased, the Portuguese developed more interest in the slave trade.

With the discovery of the Americas and the establishment of additional plantations, the market for enslaved Africans grew rapidly. The slave trade eventually became more important than the gold trade. As competing Europeans from England, France, the Netherlands, and Denmark established their own coastal bases, the flow of Africans across the Atlantic dramatically increased. This **Atlantic slave trade** soon dominated all relations between Europe and western Africa.

War, technology, and the slave trade. The Atlantic slave trade was in many ways simply an extension of the internal traffic in slaves already widespread in much of Africa. The usual means of obtaining slaves in African societies was through warfare or raiding. African states rose to power by conquering their neighbors. The many wars that accompanied this process of state-building generated large numbers of slaves.

New methods of warfare in West Africa in the 1400s and 1500s contributed significantly to the formation of states and the building of empires, as well as to the development of the slave trade. The most important of these developments came first from the Islamic north. Muslims introduced cavalry into West Africa. With cavalry, many new states began to emerge in the savanna lands along the desert's edge and elsewhere where the terrain was suitable for horses. The state of Kanem-Bornu, around Lake Chad, soon imported guns and mercenaries from the Ottoman Empire to help its expansion.

To the southwest of Kanem-Bornu, Oyo imported horses from the Sudan and created a powerful cavalry that allowed it to dominate

SECTION 4

CORE LESSON PLAN
See pages 417I and 417J for Lesson Plan 16.4.

other Yoruba groups all the way south to the African coast until the mid-1800s. Farther west, Dahomey, a tributary state of Oyo, developed a strong, stable government that enabled it to extend its rule to the coast. Throughout the 1600s and 1700s, Dahomey and Oyo sent huge numbers of slaves southward to the coast for sale. During the years of nearly constant warfare between 1680 and 1730, for example, Dahomey sent about 20,000 slaves a year for sale along the so-called **Slave Coast**.

European influences. While Dahomey and Oyo largely owed their rise to developments coming from the Islamic north and east, other peoples rose to power as a consequence of the European presence on the African coast. In the 1600s, for example, the Akan people settled in the region centered on present-day Côte d'Ivoire (Ivory Coast) and Ghana. Akan merchants traded gold, textiles, slaves, and salt to peoples farther north. The arrival of Europeans caused the slave trade to become more important than the gold trade. By 1726 a confused English visitor could remark: "Why this is called the Gold Coast, I do not know."

Trade with the Europeans also strongly influenced Akan political and social organization. The introduction of many new crops from the Americas, including corn and new types of yams, led to population growth in the 1500s and 1600s. Equally important was the introduction of new weapons, such as guns. One Akan group, the Asante, purchased guns with gold and slaves and used them to conquer their neighbors all the way to the coast. Wealthy Asante kings ruled until the 1800s and long continued to provide slaves for the coastal trade.

Just as Indians in North America adapted themselves to the fur trade, many Africans took

Trade Across the Atlantic, 1451–1870

Numbers of Slaves to Various Destinations

To U.S.	0.4–0.5 million
To Caribbean	3.8–4.7 million
To Spanish America	1.6–1.7 million
To Brazil	3.6–4.2 million

Human Cargo Like sugar, cotton, and tobacco, human beings were a commodity to be traded or sold for a profit.

Place What were some of the African slave depots, or export points, where traders exchanged goods for slaves to ship to the Americas?

▶ In 1642 an African ruler called Don Alvare, King of the Kongo, receives a Dutch delegation that hopes to form a political alliance with him.

advantage of the Europeans' arrival to become intermediaries, controlling the slave trade in the African interior. This growing dependence on the slave trade had important and often devastating effects. Even when they were not at war, many African rulers organized raiding expeditions to continue supplying slaves for the trade. Olaudah Equiano (oh-LOW-duh ek-wee-AHN-oh), a West African kidnapped into slavery around 1762, described the wars caused by the slave trade:

66 They appear to have been irruptions [raids] of one little state or district on the other to obtain prisoners or booty. Perhaps they were incited to this by those [African] traders who brought the European goods . . . amongst us. Such a mode of obtaining slaves in Africa is common. . . . When a trader wants slaves he applies to a chief for them and he tempts him with his wares. It is not extraordinary if on this occasion he yields to the temptation. 99

The Kongo Empire. Along the central regions of the western coast, the initial Portuguese contacts had even more dramatic consequences. The Kongo kingdom of Central Africa, for example, at first welcomed European trade and influence. When the Portuguese first arrived in the late 1400s, Kongo was at the height of its power. As in most African states, slavery was a common practice.

In the early 1500s the Kongo ruler Nzinga Mbemba—a Catholic convert who took the name Afonso I—established Catholicism as the kingdom's official religion and encouraged missionaries from Portugal to spread Christianity. As the Portuguese became increasingly interested in the Kongo as a major source of labor for their sugar plantations, however, Afonso grew concerned

about their behavior. Afonso was particularly alarmed by the Portuguese tendency to seize people without regard to their status. In 1526 he wrote to the Portuguese monarch, urging his "royal brother" to stop the traffic in slaves:

66 We cannot reckon how great the damage is, since the . . . [slave] merchants daily seize our subjects, sons of the land and sons of our noblemen and vassals and our relatives. . . . Thieves and men of evil conscience take them . . . and cause them to be sold: and so great, Sir, is their corruption . . . that our country is being utterly depopulated. 99

The Portuguese paid little heed to the request, and the depopulation continued.

European demand for slaves contributed to the expansion of the African slave trade, causing it to be redirected to the southwestern coast.

Conflict in East and South Africa

While the slave trade increasingly shaped the relations of Europeans with Africans on the western coast, in East Africa a different pattern emerged. Once the Portuguese arrived in the Indian Ocean, they tried to establish tighter control over the region's trade. They began by taking

R RESOURCE ACTIVITY

GLOBAL HISTORY RESOURCE CENTER
Reading: *Venture Smith: How I Became a Slave*

Print out and distribute the reading. Have students read the selection and write a poem about his experience.

Level 3

Theme: **Social Relations**

The conditions of the capture and sale of Africans were terrible. Often chained by the neck, they were forced to march to the coast on journeys as long as 1,000 miles. As many as two out of five prisoners died. Once enslaved Africans reached the coast, they were kept in cages until they were sold. An observer described the conditions on the coast: "when the Europeans are to receive them [the Africans], they are brought out onto a large plain, where the ship's surgeons examine every part of every one of them."

Critical Thinking Ask students to suggest factors that led to such mortality rates among enslaved Africans.

ANSWER: Students might mention the long and difficult journey and the harsh living conditions on the coast.

---

cities along the East African coast. However, they were never strong enough to seize full control of the region. In addition, although trade in slaves flourished in East Africa, it remained minor compared to the more important trade in gold, ivory, and other goods.

The Portuguese were most successful in tapping the trade of the strong African state—in which rulers were known as the Mwene Mutapa—that had emerged in the Zambezi River Valley, north of the old empire of Great Zimbabwe. Organizing the trade from his rich agricultural lands and mines to the coast, the Mwene Mutapa commanded tribute from all traders in his lands as well as from his subjects. The arrival of Portuguese traders in the early 1500s soon weakened the empire, however.

Within a half century, the Portuguese had involved themselves in rebellions of local rulers against the Mwene Mutapa. In 1629 the Portuguese negotiated a treaty with a new emperor they had helped bring to power. The treaty gave the Portuguese a monopoly of trade in the empire, and the ruler was ordered to pay the Portuguese tribute. Soon, however, the weakened Mwene Mutapa was challenged by a rival dynasty and Portuguese influence declined.

Farther north along the coast, the Portuguese position was even weaker. In the 1640s the Muslim Ya'rubi dynasty of Oman along the south Arabian coast set out to drive their Portuguese competitors from the Indian Ocean once and for all. Around 1650 the Omani formed an alliance with the Swahili city-states in East Africa. Combining forces, they began to drive the Portuguese from their coastal forts. By the mid-1700s, although the Portuguese retained a foothold in present-day Mozambique, they were no longer a major East African power. In their place, Muslim merchants once again controlled most of the coastal trade.

Portugal's weakness soon invited other competitors to establish themselves in Africa and the Indian Ocean region. As part of their infiltration

▲ Early Dutch settlers in South Africa return home from a hunting trip. Other colonists can be seen arriving in the area with their belongings.

of the Portuguese trading empire in Asia, the Dutch also decided to obtain a foothold on the African coast. In 1652 the Dutch East India Company founded the first permanent European colony in Africa when it brought settlers to the Cape of Good Hope.

The area was sparsely populated by nomadic Khoisan peoples, who herded animals and fished. Within a decade the Dutch had settled in as landowners. Unable to force labor from the local peoples, the Dutch pushed them out and began to import slaves. Increasingly uneasy under Company control, however, eventually many Dutch settlers migrated into the interior. There they established themselves on the land just as other European settlers were doing in North America.

The slave trade strengthened some African societies and weakened others.

The Middle Passage

The Atlantic slave trade was an important link in the growing chain of trade binding Africa, the Americas, and Europe. European merchants shipped iron and cotton goods, weapons, and liquor to Africa, where they were exchanged for slaves or gold. African slaves were then transported across the Atlantic to the Americas. On American plantations and in mines, the slaves became the primary producers of goods sold throughout the world. Merchants from Brazil shipped slave-grown tobacco to Africa to buy more slaves. At the same time, other merchants shipped tobacco, sugar, rum, and cotton produced by slave labor to Europe, where they then bought manufactured goods to sell in the Americas.

Before they could be forced to labor in the Americas, enslaved Africans had to survive the long and brutal journey across the Atlantic Ocean known as the **Middle Passage**. Chained together on crude platforms between decks, many did not survive. Supplies of food and water were often inadequate and contaminated by bacteria—the resulting dysentery was a major cause of death on long voyages. Measles and smallpox epidemics also frequently broke out. One British captain warned a colleague to avoid having the slaves "sicken and die apace, as it happened aboard the *Albion* frigate, as soon as their yams were spent."

Some slaves mutinied to gain their freedom. Others voluntarily chose death. After a rumor circulated that the captives "were first to have

their Eyes put out, and then to be eaten," more than 100 slaves on the British ship *Prince of Orange* jumped overboard in 1737. According to the captain, more than 33 drowned because they "would not endeavor to save themselves, but resolved to die." Despite the death rate, at the height of the trade between 1741 and 1810, European slavers, mostly British by that time, carried an average rate of about 60,000 slaves a year, the majority of them young men. Although estimates vary, recent studies indicate that around 10 million Africans were forcibly taken across the Atlantic between 1451 and 1870.

Once ashore in the Americas, the slaves fared no better. A Jesuit priest in Cartagena, a busy port in Spanish America, described a group of slaves just off a ship:

66 They arrive looking like skeletons; they are led ashore, completely naked, and are shut up in a large court or enclosure . . . and it is a great pity to see so many sick and needy people, denied all care or assistance, for as a rule they are left to lie on the ground, naked and without shelter. 99

The slaves were next led to the auction block, where a crowd of prospective buyers could examine them, as if they were livestock.

▲ This diagram of a slave ship from the 1800s shows how the slaves were packed into the hold of a ship. About 17 percent of the slaves died on an average crossing.

2. The demand for slaves led to the violent conquest of some African peoples by others. New weapons such as guns, obtained with profits from the slave trade, facilitated this conquest.
3. New methods of warfare contributed to the building of empires in West Africa. Those conquered were often enslaved. In addition, the western coast's proximity to the Atlantic aided the transport of slaves to the colonies.
4. Paragraphs should explain that while Americans and some Africans profited from the slave trade, it had devastating effects for African peoples, not only for those enslaved, but also for the warring groups who competed against each other for the slave trade. The African diaspora, however, spread African culture to the Americas and produced multicultural societies.
5. Songs, folktales, short stories, or poems should reflect the importance of Palmares as a place where Africans could live in freedom and protect their culture and heritage.

CHAPTER 16 REVIEW ANSWERS
(p. 447)

WRITING A SUMMARY
See essential points in the text.

REVIEWING TERMS
1. Battle of Lepanto
2. captaincies
3. Northwest Passage
4. Middle Passage
5. *encomienda*

Consequences of the Slave Trade

The forced migration of millions of Africans to the Americas through the slave trade has been called the **African diaspora**. Through this diaspora, or spreading out of a people from their native land, African culture took firm root throughout the Americas as slaves and free blacks became vital members of the new American societies. Brazilian Africans, for example, joined with the Portuguese and American Indians to create a thriving culture. Food preparation, *samba* music, dances, folktales, and child-rearing practices reflected African influences. Africans also influenced politics. In the early 1600s a group of African runaways formed their own state, called Palmares, in northeastern Brazil. For almost a century, the village residents of Palmares fought off Brazilian troops and maintained their independence.

In the cities of Spanish America, Africans adapted to Spanish culture. At the same time, they kept memories of their home kingdoms alive by forming self-help organizations, including religious societies and neighborhood associations with locally elected "royal" leaders.

In the Caribbean, Africans far outnumbered European settlers. Conditions on sugar plantations were often harsh, with disease, overcrowding, brutal discipline, and poor diets leading to high death rates. Sometimes Africans were able to resist. In Jamaica, for example, Cudjoe, the leader of a group

▲ This sketch shows slaves being bought at a New Orleans auction in the 1700s.

of runaways, raided English plantations until his group was granted its own territory in 1739.

In North America, too, Africans contributed elements of their own heritage to the newly emerging colonial society. Although Africans in northern colonies tended to adapt to English culture, Africans on southern plantations maintained many of their own traditions. For example, African languages influenced the Gullah and Geechee dialects of South Carolina, Georgia, and northeastern Florida. Africans also brought with them African techniques for growing rice, indigo, and cotton. Many African cultural forms, such as the rich traditions of folktales and songs, became an important part of an emerging American culture.

Despite the tortures of the Middle Passage and forced labor, many Africans maintained their cultural traditions, which soon became a part of the new American societies.

SECTION 4 REVIEW

IDENTIFY and explain the significance of the following:
Atlantic slave trade
Slave Coast
Olaudah Equiano
Nzinga Mbemba
Middle Passage
African diaspora

LOCATE and explain the importance of the following:
Oyo
Dahomey

Cape of Good Hope

1. **Main Idea** What effect did the participation of Europeans have on the African slave trade?
2. **Main Idea** How did the slave trade intensify violence in Africa?
3. **Geography: Location** Why do you think much of the African slave trade originated in West Africa?

4. **Writing to Explain** Using the information from the section, explain the effects of the slave trade on Africa and the Americas.
5. **Assessing Consequences** Imagine you are a Brazilian slave who has escaped to Palmares. Write a song, folktale, short story, or poem that describes the importance of Palmares for enslaved Africans.

Review

On a separate sheet of paper, complete the following exercises.

WRITING A SUMMARY

Using the essential points in the text, write a brief summary of the chapter.

REVIEWING TERMS

From the following list, choose the term that correctly matches the definition.

Battle of Lepanto
captaincies
African diaspora
encomienda
Northwest Passage
Middle Passage

1. naval engagement in 1571 fought between the Ottoman Empire and the Spanish and Italians, in which the Ottoman fleet was destroyed
2. tracts of land granted by the Portuguese king to donataries in Brazil
3. supposed trade route, thought by Europeans to exist across North America to the East Indies
4. sea voyage transporting enslaved Africans from Africa to the Americas, on which the Africans suffered terribly
5. system of organization in Spain's American colonies, under which colonists were given land and a number of American Indians to use as laborers

REVIEWING CHRONOLOGY

List the following events in their correct chronological order.

1. Spanish conquistadors conquer the Aztec.
2. Pedro Cabral discovers Brazil.
3. British colonists found the settlement at Jamestown.
4. Portuguese are allowed to establish a trading station at Macao.
5. Dutch establish their first Asia colony at Batavia.

UNDERSTANDING THE MAIN IDEA

1. Why were Europeans able to increase their power in India by the 1700s?
2. How did the Spanish and Portuguese organize their colonies in the New World?
3. Why did Japan and China seek to limit contact with Europeans?
4. What were the ultimate results of Europeans' search for the Northwest Passage?
5. What pattern did Europeans follow in their trade in Asia?

THINKING CRITICALLY

1. *Hypothesizing* What possible problems might overseas trade and colonization have caused among the European nations?
2. *Synthesizing* How did trade became more global in the 1600s and 1700s?

Building Your Portfolio

Complete the following activities individually or in groups.

1. *Colonization* You (and your associates) have been granted the right by one of the European nations to found a colony overseas in the 1600s. Look at a map in order to choose a particular spot to found your colony. You should take into consideration local geographical conditions, which will determine how your colony will survive. Create a detailed map of your proposed colony, showing important buildings, defenses, and agricultural lands. Also create flyers to attract potential colonists to join you. Finally, draw up a proposal, describing how you plan to deal with some of the problems you will encounter in your venture.
2. *Point of View* Imagine that you live in some part of the world to which Europeans are first arriving. You have been sent by your village elders to observe and find out information about the new arrivals. What do they look like? What are their intentions? How should your village react to these strangers? Prepare a report for your village elders with your observations and recommendations.

REVIEWING CHRONOLOGY
2, 1, 4, 3, 5

UNDERSTANDING THE MAIN IDEA

1. They established a relationship with Indian rulers, which gained Europeans greater access to trade.
2. They established major bureaucracies to govern the colonies. They also prohibited the colonies from trading with other nations, profiting from the colonies' raw materials and creating a market for their own goods.
3. They feared control by foreign peoples, as well as outside influences on their society.
4. When they did not find the Northwest Passage, they turned to colonization in search of wealth.
5. With the exception of China and Japan, Europeans conquered parts of Asia and established trading posts along the coasts, thus controlling the trade in many areas.

THINKING CRITICALLY

1. Trying to control areas that were located so far away might become a drain on the European countries. In addition, some countries, such as Spain, came to rely so much on the wealth from the colonies that they did not develop their own industries or agriculture.
2. Europeans expanded to new regions, such as North America, and goods flowed between many different parts of the world.

When the Spanish first brought the tomato back to Europe during the 1600s, it was primarily grown as an ornamental plant called the love apple. Europeans commonly regarded it as poisonous, and it was not until the past 100 years that it became recognized as an important food. In the 1800s the tomato was reintroduced in the United States as a food crop, and it now ranks among the most valuable of fruit and vegetable crops.

Critical Thinking Ask students to suggest why the tomato is such a valuable crop.

ANSWER: Students should suggest that the tomato is valuable because it is so popular and healthful.

HISTORY IN THE *Making*

The Columbian Exchange

"In fourteen hundred and ninety-two," begins an old schoolyard verse, "Columbus sailed the ocean blue." When he did so, the world began to change in dramatic ways. Today, we are still experiencing the political, economic, and religious effects of Columbus's voyage. None of the effects of the crossing and recrossing of the major oceans that began in 1492, however, have been more important than the biological consequences.

Worlds Apart

When Columbus crossed the Atlantic, he brought into contact not only previously isolated peoples and civilizations but also plants, animals, and microorganisms. This contact has come to be known as the Columbian Exchange. The Western and Eastern Hemispheres—or the New World and Old World, as Europeans called them—had not been in contact since the retreat of the continental ice caps about 9,000 years ago. Consequently, the life-forms living in the two hemispheres had evolved separately and in different directions. By 1492, for example, there were no elephants in the Americas and no hummingbirds or rattlesnakes in Europe, Africa, or Asia.

When European explorers brought the two worlds together, an exchange of life-forms began. More species apparently have crossed westward than eastward. This is not surprising since the landmasses of Africa and Eurasia are larger than those of North and South America, and so is the number and variety of life-forms. Even so, it was a two-way exchange, and the impact on both worlds has been enormous.

Crop Exchanges

The exchange of different kinds of crops has altered landscapes and spurred population growth. For example, wheat, originally a Southwest Asian grass, now dominates farming in the low-rainfall areas in much of North America. Rice, originally an Asian grass, has also become an important crop in warmer, wetter areas of the Americas.

On the other hand, American corn (maize), first domesticated by American Indians, has become an essential crop in Romania, Egypt, South Africa, China, and other nations beyond the Americas. White potatoes, another crop originally domesticated in the Andes, feed tens of millions of people in northern Europe, Russia, and

◀ **Potatoes remain a staple crop in Ireland.**

China. In addition, without tomatoes and peppers—both imports from the Americas—modern Italian and Indian dishes would not exist.

Even weeds crossed the Atlantic with the first European migrants. Dandelions, crab grass, couch grass, sow-thistle, and Kentucky bluegrass are all immigrants to the Americas.

Animals and Insects

The Americas, which had few native species of domesticated animals, have been changed forever by the introduction of species such as Old World horses, cattle, goats, sheep, chickens, and house cats. Many of Eurasia's wild animals, such as house sparrows, starlings, mice, and rats, have now become naturalized west of the Atlantic. In exchange, American gray squirrels and muskrats have established themselves in Europe and Asia.

Insects too have crossed the oceans. The Old World honeybee is now vitally important in the Americas, not only for honey but also for its role in the pollination of crops. The Mediterranean fruit fly and Japanese beetles, on the other hand, have become infamous pests in the Western Hemisphere, while Colorado potato beetles have long ravaged European crops.

Diseases

The contrast between the disease environments of the Old and New Worlds was particularly sharp. For reasons not entirely understood, the Old World exported many more diseases than it imported—for example, smallpox, measles, malaria, and plague.

While Europeans and Africans often caught these diseases in childhood and had developed immunities to them, American Indians had no such protection. As Old World emigrants advanced into the lands occupied by American Indians, their diseases moved with them, even ahead of them.

▲ This Aztec drawing shows Europeans spreading disease among the inhabitants of the New World. The sketch shows the stages of smallpox, ending with death.

The Balance Sheet

The Columbian Exchange has had both good and bad effects for humanity. To cite one mixed example, the American white potato, amazingly productive even in poor soils if rain is plentiful, became a staple crop in Ireland. Potatoes allowed the Irish population to grow larger than ever before and seemed to be the answer to the problem of chronic famine. In the 1840s, however, an American potato fungus, *Phytophthora infestans*, destroyed Ireland's potato crop. Thousands of Irish people starved, died in epidemics caused by the famine, or emigrated to America.

The exchange continues today, with both positive and negative consequences. Perhaps the most spectacular recent negative example has been that of the so-called "killer," or Africanized, bees.

In the 1950s researchers imported African honeybees to Brazil for experimental purposes. The African bees had the advantage of being able to thrive in hot climates, but they were more easily disturbed than European bees. When irritated, they responded as a group, stinging in massive attacks. A number of swarms accidentally got loose from the laboratories. In 1976 the bees reached Venezuela. In 1982 they passed over the Panama Canal. They arrived in California and Texas in the early 1990s.

Whether the effects are positive or negative, as international trade continues to expand, the world becomes increasingly smaller. There is little doubt that the exchange of goods, organisms, and ideas between the Old World and the New World will continue well into the future.

Theme:
Cross-cultural Interaction
Another example of cross-mingling of species occurred during the 1800s, when the phylloxera, an American root louse, arrived in Europe and nearly devastated the continent's vineyards. In desperation, European farmers imported American grapevine roots, which were resistant to phylloxera. By grafting their own plants onto the new pest-resistant American roots, Europeans saved their ancient industry.

Critical Thinking Ask students how the case of the phylloxera root louse was similar to the Irish potato famine.

ANSWER: In both cases an American pest reached Europe and caused massive damage to a crop that was unable to resist it.

Chapter 17

Revolutions of Society and State 1714–1815

Chapter Planning Guide

	TEXTBOOK	CORE RESOURCES	VISUAL RESOURCES	MULTIMEDIA
Introduction	pp. 450–451	Block Scheduling Handbook: Ch. 17		Videodisc Segment 17 and Viewing Guide: *The Enlightenment*
Lesson 17.1 An Era of Global Warfare	pp. 452–456 Map: *European Possessions in 1763,* p. 455 Map: *The Partitions of Poland,* p. 456	Reading 17.1: *The Outbreak of War*		GHRC 17 Reading: *Frederick II of Prussia on Monarchy* GHRC 17/Videodiscs: Images—*Frederick II of Prussia; Catherine II in Costume*
Lesson 17.2 The Enlightenment	pp. 457–463 Biography: *Mary Wollstonecraft,* p. 461	Reading 17.2: *Voltaire's Vision of Universal Tolerance*	Everyday Life 17: *European Clothing Styles, 1700s*	GHRC 17 Readings: *Voltaire on Tolerance and Tyranny; Diderot and the Encyclopédie; Locke on the Limits of Government Power; Beccaria on Crime and Punishment; Baron de Montesquieu on Political Liberty; Joseph II on Tolerance; Catherine II of Russia* GHRC 17/Videodiscs: Image—*Enlightenment Salon*
Lesson 17.3 The American Revolution	pp. 464–468 Map: *Military Campaigns of the American Revolution,* p. 467 Map: *The United States in 1783,* p. 468	Reading 17.3: *An Edict by the King of Prussia* Writing Project 17: *Writing an Introductory Paragraph*	Geography and History 17: *The Fight for Independence, 1776–1781*	GHRC 17 Reading: *Jefferson on Life, Liberty, and Happiness* GHRC 17/Videodiscs: Image—*Drafting the Declaration of Independence*
Lesson 17.4 Revolutionary France	pp. 469–473 Through Others' Eyes: *A Lebanese Response to the French Revolution,* p. 471	Reading 17.4: *Robespierre and Saint-Just Defend the Arrest of Danton*	Art and History 17: *Marie Antoinette and Her Children*	GHRC 17/Videodiscs: Images—*Cartoon on the Oppression of the French People; The Women's March on Versailles;* Map—*Europe on the Eve of the French Revolution;* Audio Clip—"*La Marseillaise*"
Lesson 17.5 The Napoleonic Era	pp. 474–478 Map: *The Napoleonic Empire,* p. 476 Atlas: *Europe: Political,* p. 858 Literature Through Time: *Grimm's Fairy Tales,* p. 477	Reading 17.5: *A View of Napoleon's Character* Geography Activity 17: *Napoleon's Disastrous Russian Campaign* Skills Activity 17: *Distinguishing Fact from Opinion*		GHRC 17 Readings: *Napoleon's Coronation; Napoleon: For and Against* GHRC 17/Videodiscs: Image—*The French Retreat from Russia*
Chapter Investigation and Enrichment	pp. 450–478	Chapter 17 Investigation: *Enlightenment Leaders' Hall of Fame* People in World History 17 Explorations in Daily Life 17		GHRC 17/Videodiscs
Review and Assessment	Section 1 Review, p. 456 Section 2 Review, p. 463 Section 3 Review, p. 468 Section 4 Review, p. 473 Chapter 17 Review, p. 479	Chapter Review Activity 17 Vocabulary Activity 17 Themes Review 17 Section Study Guides 17.1–17.5 Main Idea Activities 17.1–17.5 Daily Quizzes 17.1–17.5 Chapter 17 Test Sheltered English Ch. 17 Test Ch. 17 Test Generator		Audio CDs: Ch. 17 Summary (English and Spanish)

INTRODUCING THE CHAPTER

Textbook pp. 450–451

CHAPTER OVERVIEW

Competition among the European nations led to war, and dissatisfaction with English rule resulted in the creation of the United States. At the same time, a revolution in thought—the Enlightenment—occurred as Europeans applied scientific methods to the study of humanity. The inspiration of Enlightenment ideals and the American Revolution led to revolution in France.

PRESENTING THEMES

On the chalkboard or on an overhead transparency, write the following open-ended theme questions.

- **WAR AND DIPLOMACY** How might a society react to a long period of warfare?
- **PHILOSOPHY** How might new ideas change the way people view themselves and the world?
- **POLITICS AND LAW** How might revolution lead to new political structures?

Have students, either individually or in groups, suggest responses to the questions. For the war and diplomacy question, students might suggest that long periods of warfare could cause shortages and suffering that would make people rebellious. For the philosophy question, students might suggest that new ideas stimulate new modes of action, bringing a new perspective on the world. For the politics and law question, students might suggest that revolutions could change the way people see society and the proper role of government. Save the responses. Once students have studied the chapter, you may wish to have them complete the Themes Activity, then compare the two sets of answers.

USING THE VIDEO

Segment 17: *The Enlightenment*

ENGLISH

Search Chapter 17
Videodisc 2, Side A

SPANISH

Search Chapter 17
Videodisc 2, Side A

Tell students that in this chapter they will apply these theme questions to Europe and North America at a time when "enlightened" thinkers were changing how people viewed the universe, society, and the individual. Then show Segment 17 of the *World History and Cultures Videodiscs*. This segment shows the impact of some of the ideas of Enlightenment thinkers on both the eighteenth and the twentieth centuries.

Before showing the segment, ask students to pay attention both to the ideas that Enlightenment thinkers put forward and to the political and social developments that sprang from those ideas. To help students grasp the significant points of the segment, have them complete Video Viewing Guide 17.

Key to Ability Levels

All strategies and activities are coded to the following ability levels:

LEVEL 1	**Basic** activities suitable for all students
LEVEL 2	**Average** activities suitable for average to above-average students
LEVEL 3	**Challenging** activities suitable for above-average students
SHELTERED ENGLISH	Activities suitable for students with **Limited English Proficiency**

Additional Resources

BOOKS FOR TEACHERS

Bailyn, Bernard. *Faces of Revolution: Personalities and Themes in the Struggle for Independence.* Vintage Books, 1990. Presents short biographies.

Maza, Sarah. *Private Lives and Public Affairs: The Causes Celebres of Prerevolutionary France.* University of California Press, 1993. Examines causes of unrest.

BOOKS FOR STUDENTS

Hibbert, Christopher. *Redcoats and Rebels: The American Revolution Through British Eyes.* Norton, 1990. Looks at colonial America through the eyes of the empire.

Kennedy, Emmet. *A Cultural History of the French Revolution.* Yale University Press, 1989. Looks at the Revolution's effects on the arts and religion.

MULTIMEDIA MATERIALS

History Through Art: The Enlightenment. ZCI. CD-ROM, MAC, DOS, WIN, MPC formats. Looks at the history and art of the Enlightenment.

Napoleon: The Making of a Dictator. Learning Corporation of America. Video, 27 min. Uses Napoleon to understand tyranny.

Lesson 17.1 — *An Era of Global Warfare*

Textbook pp. 452–456

RESOURCES

Pupil's Edition

Map, p. 455: *European Possessions in 1763*

Map, p. 456: *The Partitions of Poland, 1772–1795*

Core Resources

Reading 17.1: *The Outbreak of War*

Global History Resource Center

Reading: *Frederick II of Prussia on Monarchy*

Videodiscs or Global History Resource Center

Image: *Frederick II of Prussia*

Search Frame 904

Image: *Catherine II in Russian Costume*

Search Frame 906

LESSON FOCUS

How did the major European powers deal with their rivals during the 1700s?

OBJECTIVES

After completing this lesson, students will be able to:

- explain how European national rivalries intensified during the 1700s;
- describe how Prussia's rise to power affected the rest of Europe;
- explain the results of the Seven Years' War.

HOOK: Link to Today

Discuss the shifting balance of power in Europe during the 1700s. Tell students that rivalries escalated in Europe during the 1700s. Invite them to think of these nations as teams in a professional sports league.

Ask: Which team dominated the league at the start of the 1700s?

[France]

Ask: Which two teams had the fiercest rivalry?

[France and Great Britain]

Point out that the balance of power among sports teams is not constant. A team might become stronger—and more competitive—by spending more money to hire the best players and coaches or by adopting innovative training methods and on-field strategies. Such a team would challenge the dominance of the top teams, causing a shift in the balance of power.

Ask: Which major power in Europe began to grow stronger, causing a change in the balance of power?

[Students should name Prussia, whose emergence as a military force shook up the balance of power in Europe.]

DEVELOP

Identify the conflicts that resulted from rivalries between Britain and France during the 1700s.

Have students develop a "Hot Spots of the 1700s" historical report of British and French conflict. First direct them to sketch simple outline maps showing the major areas of conflict. Suggest that students turn to the map on textbook page 455 for assistance in locating these areas.

Next create a three-column chart on the chalkboard. For each hot spot students identify, have volunteers list the issues involved and describe the course of each conflict and its outcome. *[**Caribbean:** British resented French profits from sugar plantations; Britain tried to extend control over trade through the Navigation Acts; **North America:** British population increased, and colonists looked to French territory for expansion; French built forts to prevent expansion, causing Britain to reinforce its strength in the colonies; **India:** Great Britain and France competed for* *commercial advantages, leading to their involvement in small Indian wars.]*

Conclude by encouraging students to copy the chart into their notebooks.

PROBE

Discuss Prussia's rise to power. Invite students to work in pairs to role-play a conversation between Frederick William I and his son, Frederick II, in which the elder Frederick explains how he has built Prussia into a powerful nation; predicts Prussia's glorious future; and reproves his son for not caring about government and military affairs. The younger Frederick might counter with his ideas about philosophy and music.

Then lead students in a discussion on how Frederick II changed. Display the electronic media image of Frederick II and have students complete the Global History Resource Center reading on Frederick II. Then have students consider why Frederick later became known as "the Great."

Ask: *How did Frederick II's initiating the War of the Austrian Succession benefit Prussia?*
[Bavaria, Spain, Saxony, and France allied themselves with Prussia, forcing Austria to sign a peace treaty, and Prussia gained Silesia and became a major European power.]

Ask: *Could Prussia have grown so powerful if Frederick II had continued to show little interest in government and military matters?*
[Most students will suggest that if he had remained uninterested in government and military matters, Prussia's rise might have been slowed or even curtailed.]

CONCLUDE

Examine the balance of power after the Seven Years' War. Tell students that the European rivalries mentioned above led to the Seven Years' War, and the aftermath of this war had a major effect on the European balance of power. You may wish to show the electronic media images of Catherine II and Frederick II to illustrate major leaders of the time. Also, have students read Core Resources Reading 17.1 for more information on the conflict that sparked the Seven Years' War.

Have students evaluate the strength of nations after the Seven Years' War.

Ask: *What were the results of the Seven Years' War?*
*[**France**: lost nearly all of its North American colonial lands; **Great Britain**: major sea power that controlled Canada, Louisiana east to Mississippi, and most of India; **Prussia, Russia, and Austria**: expanded in eastern Europe]*

EXTEND

Cross-Curricular Connection: *Sociology*

Have students return to the charts of "Hot Spots of the 1700s" they developed earlier. Assign equal numbers of students to each "hot spot." Invite students to imagine it is the 1700s and they are living in their assigned areas during the time of conflict. Ask them to list ways in which the conflict might affect their lives. Call on representatives from each hot spot to share their lists with the class.

Other Media

Have interested students view the movie *The Last of the Mohicans*, which is set in North America during the French and Indian War. Then have students discuss how the rivalry between France and Great Britain is portrayed in the movie.

MEET INDIVIDUAL NEEDS

Students Acquiring English

Pair new speakers of English with fluent speakers. Have them work together to construct a statement summarizing the main ideas discussed in the section. Ensure that both partners are prepared to define and explain all terms or concepts they use in their statement.

Visual-Spatial Learners

Ask students to work in small groups to draw annotated diagrams of the various alliances forged by European powers during the 1700s. Encourage groups to be creative in their designs. Have groups present their diagrams to the class.

ASSESS

Review

Have students complete the Section 1 Review. Use answers in the Teacher's Edition, page 456, to assess student mastery of this section.

RESOURCES

Pupil's Edition

Biography, p. 461: *Mary Wollstonecraft*

Core Resources

Reading 17.2: *Voltaire's Vision of Universal Tolerance*

Global History Resource Center

Reading: *François Voltaire on Tolerance and Tyranny*

Reading: *Diderot and the Encyclopédie*

Reading: *John Locke on the Limits of Government Power*

Reading: *Cesare Beccaria on Crime and Punishment*

Reading: *Baron de Montesquieu on Political Liberty*

Reading: *Frederick II of Prussia on Monarchy*

Reading: *Joseph II of Austria on Tolerance*

Reading: *A Historian's View of Catherine II of Russia*

Videodiscs or Global History Resource Center

Image: *A French Enlightenment Salon*

Search Frame 907

LESSON FOCUS

What changes resulted from the new view of the world that arose in Europe during the 1700s?

OBJECTIVES

After completing this lesson, students will be able to:

- explain what the Enlightenment was;
- identify what many philosophes hoped to accomplish through the application of Enlightenment ideas;
- show how the ideas of the Enlightenment affected common conceptions about the roles of women;
- identify how the Enlightenment affected Europe's absolute monarchs.

HOOK

Determine the meaning of the term Enlightenment.
Write the term *Enlightenment* on the chalkboard. Then have a volunteer underline the five-letter word within the term. *[light]* Ask students if they have seen in cartoons a picture showing a light bulb turned on over a person's head. Then ask them what such a picture might mean. *[that the person has just had an idea]* Then suggest that one way to illustrate the Enlightenment

might be to picture the great thinkers of the time with light bulbs over their heads. Point out that the Enlightenment thinkers developed their ideas through an approach called rationalism, or the application of reason to observation. You might tell students that the Enlightenment is sometimes called the Age of Reason.

Conclude by working with the class to devise a definition of the Enlightenment. *[example: The period during the 1700s when great thinkers created a new view of the world by applying rationalism to society, politics, and the economy.]*

DEVELOP

Chart Enlightenment ideas and their effects and note how these ideas changed people's attitudes toward society. Organize students into three groups to gather information. Assign each group one area affected by Enlightenment ideas—society, government, or economics. Ask groups to list the new ideas that sprang up in their assigned area; the Enlightenment thinkers associated with those ideas; and the changes that resulted from the application of those ideas. Remind the group assigned to society to pay close attention to the biography of Mary Wollstonecraft on textbook page 461. To assist all groups you may wish to assign the Global History Resource Center readings on

Voltaire, Diderot, Locke, Beccaria, Montesquieu, and Rousseau, as well as Core Resources Reading 17.2.

When groups have finished gathering their information, have them display it in one chart on the chalkboard. Each group should select a representative to enter the group's findings on the chart. Then have all students copy the finished chart into their notebooks. Conclude by calling on students to summarize how people's concept of society was influenced by Enlightenment ideas.

Ask: *How did the Enlightenment change people's attitudes toward society?*

[*Enlightenment ideas encouraged people to see society as subject to natural laws; therefore, it could be improved.*]

PROBE: Link to Today

Examine the role of women in the Enlightenment.

Display the electronic media image of a French salon and ask students to discuss what the image tells them about the role of women in the Enlightenment. Review with students the controversy that developed concerning women's involvement in the Enlightenment.

Next encourage students to imagine that they are Enlightenment philosophes. Have them work in pairs to debate the issue of women's involvement in the Enlightenment, one partner taking the pro view, the other taking the con view. You might have them read the biography of Mary Wollstonecraft on textbook page 461, if they have not done so already.

Conclude by asking pairs to discuss how the philosophes might view the position of women in modern Western society.

CONCLUDE

Evaluate the effect of Enlightenment ideas on European absolute monarchs. Briefly review the major ideas of the Enlightenment. Then assign the Global History Resource Center readings on Joseph II and Frederick II and ask students to identify the Enlightenment ideas addressed in their writings.

Ask: *What were some of the Enlightenment principles that European absolute monarchs adopted?*

[*Principles included codifying laws, abolishing the use of torture, and introducing religious tolerance; Joseph II went farther and abolished serfdom and assumed responsibility for care of the sick and poor.*]

Point out that while such monarchs as Frederick II of Prussia, Joseph II of Austria, and Catherine II of Russia expressed support for the Enlightenment and adopted some of its principles, they still considered their own authority as absolute. Any Enlightenment idea that offered a threat to their power was quickly abandoned. To illustrate this, assign the Global History Resource Center reading on Catherine II of Russia.

EXTEND

Cross-Curricular Connection: *Journalism*

Link to Today. Have students create a list of questions they would ask a specific Enlightenment thinker in an interview for a television current affairs program. Pair students, and have pairs conduct the interviews, with one student playing the interviewer, the other playing the thinker. After interviews are completed, have pair members switch roles.

Cross-Curricular Connection: *Language Arts*

Have students research and then write an essay about one of the philosophers mentioned in the section. Students might want to read appropriate selections from the Global History Research Center to get started.

MEET INDIVIDUAL NEEDS

Interpersonal Learners

Invite students to imagine that they are one of the great leaders mentioned in the section. Inform them that they have just had a long talk with an Enlightenment thinker. Direct students to write a letter to an adviser describing the meeting and explaining the ideas the thinker expressed and how these ideas have affected their views on government.

Students Having Difficulty

Have students review the section by writing one question for each subsection in the section. Suggest that they note the answers on a separate sheet of paper. Encourage students to exchange their question sheets. Completed question sheets should be returned to the writer for marking.

ASSESS

Review

Have students complete the Section 2 Review. Use answers in the Teacher's Edition, page 463, to assess student mastery of this section.

Lesson 17.3   *The American Revolution*

Textbook pp. 464–468

RESOURCES

Pupil's Edition
Map, p. 467: *Military Campaigns of the American Revolution, 1775–1783*
Map, p. 468: *The United States in 1783*

Core Resources
Reading 17.3: *An Edict by the King of Prussia*

Global History Resource Center
Reading: *Jefferson on Life, Liberty, and Happiness*
Reading: *John Locke on the Limits of Government Power*

Videodiscs or Global History Resource Center
Image: *Drafting the Declaration of Independence*

Search Frame 908

LESSON FOCUS

What events and ideas contributed to the founding of the United States?

OBJECTIVES

After completing this lesson, students will be able to:

- explain how Britain's colonial policy in North America changed after the Seven Years' War and what the results were;
- explain how power struggles in Europe contributed to the founding of the United States;
- identify how the government established by the U.S. Constitution was different from other governments at the time.

HOOK: Link to Today

Discuss the response of American colonists to British efforts to tighten control over the colonies. Announce the following to students: *From this point on the class will be conducted in complete silence. Any student speaking without permission will be awarded a demerit. A student compiling five demerits will automatically fail the class.*

Ask: *Do you think this is an unfair policy? If so, how would you challenge it?*

[Steps might include making an official complaint to the principal; making an official complaint to the school council and/or the board of education; refusing to attend the class; launching a publicity campaign to gain the support of other students and teachers.]

Then point out that the American colonists felt that the British government's new imperial policy was unfair.

Ask: *To what aspects of the new British imperial policy did the colonists object?*

[mercantilist trade regulations, new taxes]

Ask: *How did they respond to the policies?*

[trade boycotts, protests, resistance]

Conclude by asking students to compare the steps they suggested taking against the new class rules with the actions of the colonists. For a satirical view of British policy, you might have students read Core Resources Reading 17.3.

DEVELOP

Explore the impact of the Seven Years' War on British colonial policy in North America. Call on students to describe Great Britain's condition after the Seven Years' War. [Great Britain was deeply in debt and began to lose control over its North American colonies.]

Next write *Seven Years' War* on the left side of the chalkboard and *United States of America* on the right side. Inform students that these are the first and last entries of a cause-effect chain on the impact of European power struggles on the creation of the United States. Ask students to complete the chain in their notebooks. As they work, have them consider these questions:

- What did the British do to relieve their debt?
- How did the American colonists respond to actions taken by the British?
- How did the struggle for power in Europe affect the fighting between the British and the Americans?

[Students' cause-effect chains should indicate that Britain exerted stronger economic control over the colonies and imposed new taxes. This led to protests and resistance by the colonists, to the Declaration of Independence, and to the War of Independence. Continuing its struggle with Britain, France offered support to the colonists, which helped the colonists win the war.] Call on volunteers to present and explain their cause-effect chains to the class.

Conclude by leading a discussion on the reasons the British lost the war. In preparation, have students examine the map on textbook page 467.

PROBE

Assess the influence of Enlightenment ideas on the Declaration of Independence. Display the electronic media image of the drafting of the Declaration of Independence and provide students with a copy of the Declaration. Ask students to describe what the image shows. Then call on volunteers to review the ideas of the Enlightenment. Organize the class into small groups. Have groups skim the first few paragraphs to note the Enlightenment ideas included in the Declaration.

Ask: Which Enlightenment principles did Thomas Jefferson incorporate in the Declaration of Independence?
[All people have certain natural rights; governments exist by the consent of the governed; when a government ceases to serve the people, they have the right to change it.]

To underscore the links between the Enlightenment and the Declaration of Independence, you may wish to assign the Global History Resource Center readings on Jefferson and Locke.

CONCLUDE

Discover how the government established by the U.S. Constitution was different from other governments.

Continue the discussion of the impact of Enlightenment ideals on the American Revolution by asking students to consider the U.S. Constitution. Write the following on the chalkboard: *Democracy, Checks and Balances, Bill of Rights.*

Ask: How do these aspects of the Constitution reflect Enlightenment thinking?
[Students' answers should indicate that democracy reflects the idea that popular government is the most acceptable form of government. A system of checks and balances among the branches of government reflects the idea that real liberty does not exist if one branch of government is more powerful than the others. The Bill of Rights reflects the idea that individuals have certain rights and that it is the task of government to protect these rights.]

Conclude by telling students that the U.S. government was different from other existing governments because it was the first to be based in part on Enlightenment principles.

EXTEND
Other Media
Have students view and discuss the video *Breaking the Colonial Ties: Declaration of Independence* (Encyclopedia Britannica, color, 20 min.), which explores the debate over independence, including the positions of women, American Indians, and slaves.

MEET INDIVIDUAL NEEDS
Gifted Students
Ask students to choose an event from the section, such as the Boston Tea Party or the Battle of Saratoga. Have them write a fictional account of the event, perhaps from the point of view of a participant the same age as themselves.

Visual-Spatial Learners
Encourage students to imagine they are cartoonists at the time of the American Revolution. Have them draw a cartoon from the colonial viewpoint of an incident or personality mentioned in the text. Display finished cartoons in the classroom.

ASSESS
Review
Have students complete the Section 3 Review. Use answers in the Teacher's Edition, page 468, to assess student mastery of this section.

Lesson 17.4   *Revolutionary France*

Textbook pp. 469–473

RESOURCES

Pupil's Edition
Through Others' Eyes, p. 471: *A Lebanese Response to the French Revolution*

Core Resources
Reading 17.4: *Robespierre and Saint-Just Defend the Arrest of Danton*

Visual Resources
Art and History 17: *Marie Antoinette and Her Children*

Videodiscs or Global History Resource Center

Image: *Cartoon on the Oppression of the French People*

Search Frame 909

Image: *The Women's March on Versailles*

Search Frame 910

Map: *Europe on the Eve of the French Revolution*

Search Frame 913

Audio Clip: *"La Marseillaise": The French National Anthem*

Search 2295, Play to 2823
Videodisc 2, Side A
Audio Clip 17

LESSON FOCUS
What were the causes of the French Revolution, and what were its consequences in France and in the rest of Europe?

OBJECTIVES

After completing this lesson, students will be able to:

- explain what the Three Estates hoped to gain from the monarchy;
- describe how Enlightenment ideas played a role in France's revolutionary government;
- detail the reactions of other European nations to the French Revolution.

HOOK

Discuss the French Revolution. Point out that during the 1700s all three Estates had grievances against the monarchy and each wanted to improve its condition by taking power away from the monarchy. Display the electronic media image of the cartoon and point out that members of the Third Estate were particularly dissatisfied, believing that they carried the rest of French society. Although they produced the goods and provided the services, members of the Third Estate—especially those at the bottom—received little for their efforts. To illustrate this point, provide the following statistics. A skilled worker in France, on average, received 15 sous for a 12-to-16-hour workday. Some workers got paid much less—even as little as four sous a day. What could they buy with these wages? A new shirt cost 30 sous; a pound of meat could be purchased for 3 sous, while 10 sous would bring a dozen eggs. In 1700 bread cost between one and two sous per pound—when harvests were good. Failed harvests resulted in soaring bread prices. But the amount of money working people had available to spend was severely limited because they also paid heavy taxes.

Contrast life for the vast majority of the Third Estate with the lifestyle of the nobility. Show the Art and History transparency and have students note the opulence of Marie Antoinette's surroundings.

Ask: What steps might members of the Third Estate take to proclaim their grievances?

[marches, demonstrations, other forms of protest]

To illustrate the response of the Third Estate, display the electronic media image of the women marching from Paris to Louis XVI's palace at Versailles. Conclude by pointing out that the protests of the Third Estate quickly turned into a revolution.

DEVELOP

Organize and chart the events of the French Revolution.

Ask students to identify who governed France, with dates, during the revolutionary period. Note responses on the chalkboard. *[Louis XVI, reign ends 1789; National Assembly, 1789–1792; National Convention, 1792–1795; Directory, 1795–1799; Napoleon Bonaparte, rule begins 1799]* Next direct students to record the information listed on the chalkboard on a time line. Have students record the main events of the revolutionary period. *[for example: the calling of the Estates-General, the storming of the Bastille, the adoption of the Declaration of the Rights of Man and Citizen, the proclamation of a republic, the Reign of Terror]* Time lines should include as many entries as are needed to summarize the revolutionary period. Suggest that students retain their time lines for review purposes.

PROBE

Note the Enlightenment ideas that inspired the French Revolution.
Ask students to consider the purpose of the Declaration of the Rights of Man and Citizen.

Ask: *What did the Declaration of the Rights of Man and Citizen represent?*
[*the principles of the French Revolution—liberty, equality, and fraternity*]

Organize students into several small groups to debate the following: *The French Revolution was the embodiment of Enlightenment principles.* Have students reread the paragraphs on textbook page 471 about the end of the Old Regime, and remind students that the new constitution did not entirely represent the ideals of the Declaration of the Rights of Man and Citizen. When the debates are completed, call on group representatives to present the pros and cons of their arguments.

CONCLUDE: Link to Today

Examine other European countries' reactions to the French Revolution.
Ask students what they would do if a mob set fire to a neighbor's house and then threatened to set their houses on fire. *[Most students will suggest various protective measures, such as*

calling the police.] Suggest to students that most European monarchs viewed the French Revolution as just such a threat—both to their countries and to themselves. Display the electronic media map of Europe on the eve of the French Revolution.

Ask: *How did Austria and Prussia respond to the French Revolution?*
[*They demanded the restoration of Louis XVI, which led to war with France.*]

Ask: *How did other European nations react to the National Convention's decision in 1793 to export the revolution?*
[*Alarmed, Great Britain, the Netherlands, Spain, and Sardinia formed an alliance with Austria and Prussia and invaded France.*]

EXTEND

Cross-Curricular Connection: *Communications*
Invite students to imagine that radio existed 200 years ago. Have them prepare a five-minute radio broadcast that describes a pivotal event in the French Revolution.

Other Media
Have interested students view the movie *Danton*. Then have students describe the Reign of Terror based on what they saw in the movie and compare it to the information in Core Resources Reading 17.4.

MEET INDIVIDUAL NEEDS

Musical-Rhythmic Learners
Provide some background information on "La Marseillaise"—the French national anthem. Then play the audio clip of "La Marseillaise" and encourage students to respond.

Intrapersonal Learners
Invite students to imagine they are teenagers in revolutionary France. Have them write diary entries that include historical information and show their reactions to the events going on around them.

ASSESS

Review
Have students complete the Section 4 Review. Use answers in the Teacher's Edition, page 473, to assess student mastery of this section.

Lesson 17.5   *The Napoleonic Era*

Textbook pp. 474–478

RESOURCES

Pupil's Edition

Map, p. 476: *The Napoleonic Empire, 1805–1815*

Atlas, p. 858: *Europe: Political*

Literature Through Time, p. 477: *Grimm's Fairy Tales*

Core Resources

Reading 17.5: *A View of Napoleon's Character*

Geography Activity 17: *Napoleon's Disastrous Russian Campaign*

Global History Resource Center

Reading: *Napoleon's Coronation*

Reading: *Napoleon: For and Against*

Videodiscs or Global History Resource Center

Image: *The French Retreat from Russia*

Search Frame 912

LESSON FOCUS

What impact did the Napoleonic Era have on Europe?

OBJECTIVES

After completing this lesson, students will be able to:
- identify how Napoleon was able to bring stability to France;
- explain why Napoleon was successful at building an empire;
- analyze the changes that Napoleon's empire created in other European nations.

HOOK: Link to Today

Review Napoleon's character and identify how he was able to bring stability to Europe. Poll the class to discover whom students think of as leaders. Then ask them what personal qualities make these people leaders. Note responses on the chalkboard. Broaden the discussion by asking students to suggest what qualities a person needs to be the leader of a country. Add any new suggestions to the list on the chalkboard. Continue the discussion by asking students to distinguish between positive and negative leadership qualities. Suggest that students make two lists—good qualities and bad qualities—in their notebooks.

Next direct students' attention to the discussion of Napoleon Bonaparte's character in the biography on textbook page 474.

To illustrate Napoleon's overwhelming ambition, assign the Global History Resource Center reading on his coronation. Also assign Core Resources Reading 17.5 to show students how one of Napoleon's contemporaries viewed him.

Refer students to the lists of leadership qualities that they recorded in their notebooks. Then have them apply their ideas about leadership to Napoleon.

Ask: *What qualities—both good and bad—did Napoleon possess that helped him to be a great leader?*
[Answers might include powerful personality, single-mindedness, military skills, aggressiveness, overwhelming ambition, disdain for the world, self-centeredness, and huge ego.]

Then point out that it was these qualities that helped Napoleon bring stability to France.

Ask: *How did Napoleon contribute to stability in France?*
[He contributed to stability through his reforms and major military victories.]

DEVELOP

Review Napoleon's success in building an empire. Direct students' attention to the map of the Napoleonic Empire on textbook page 476. Have them note the furthest extent of Napoleon's conquests. To underscore the magnitude of

Napoleon's achievement, have students turn to the political map of Europe in the Atlas and identify the modern European countries that he ruled, controlled, or influenced. Then ask students to make lists in their notebooks of the following: areas that were part of the French Empire; states controlled by Napoleon; states allied with Napoleon; neutral European states.

Ask: *How was Napoleon able to build such a vast empire?*
[*through stunning military victories*]

Next have students turn again to Core Resources Reading 17.5 and point out to students that Napoleon was once described as a good chess player who was intent on defeating his opponent—the human race.

Conclude by having students discuss whether they think this statement by Madame de Staël is an appropriate description of Napoleon's approach to empire-building.

PROBE

List the social, political, and economic reforms that Napoleon enacted in France. Write on the chalkboard the following headings: *Law, Finance, Education, Government Service.* Call on volunteers to come to the chalkboard and enter under the appropriate headings the various reforms instituted by Napoleon. **[Law:** *Napoleonic Code;* **Finance:** *Bank of France;* **Education:** *public school system;* **Government Service:** *meritocracy*] Then ask other students to provide brief details about each reform. Enter responses on the chalkboard.

Use the information on the chalkboard as a starting point for a class discussion on the following question: *In enacting his reforms, was Napoleon completing the work of the Revolution or simply strengthening his hold on power?* To help students develop arguments on this issue, assign the Global History Resource Center reading on arguments for and against *Napoleon.*

CONCLUDE

Predict the long-term effects of Napoleon's empire on Europe. Call on a volunteer to assume the role of Napoleon. Ask the student to detail to the class the changes brought about in the areas of Europe he conquered. [*Holy Roman Empire dismantled; Austro-Hungarian Empire born; Napoleonic Code established; spirit of nationalism awakened*]

Then organize students into small groups to act as editorial boards of newspapers during the early 1800s. Direct boards to draft an editorial on one of these changes, predicting the long-term consequences for Europe.

EXTEND

Cross-Curricular Connection: *Geography*

Display the electronic media image of the French retreat and explain that it shows the French retreating in disarray after Napoleon's disastrous Russian campaign. Then assign Geography Activity 17, which examines the logistics of that campaign. Have students write a brief essay supporting the following statement: *Geography,* rather than enemy armies, *defeated Napoleon in Russia.*

MEET INDIVIDUAL NEEDS

Linguistic Learners

Have students read and discuss the Literature Through Time feature on textbook page 477. The feature examines the beginnings of German nationalism as shown in Grimm's fairy tales.

Intrapersonal Learners

Invite students to imagine they are soldiers in Napoleon's army about to leave for the Russian front. They have just heard Napoleon give a rousing speech. Have them write a letter to a friend or family member in which they describe the impact of this experience.

Gifted Students

Point out that one historian has stated that Napoleon was defeated by his own conquests. Have students discuss what the historian meant by this statement and whether or not they agree.

ASSESS

Review

Have students complete the Section 5 Review. Use answers in the Teacher's Edition, page 477, to assess student mastery of this section.

In preparation for the chapter test, you may wish to have students complete all or part of the Chapter 17 Review on textbook page 479, the Chapter 17 Review Activity, and the Chapter 17 Themes Review.

Chapter 17

Revolutions of Society and State

Understanding the Main Idea

Call on a volunteer to read aloud the *Understanding the Main Idea* paragraph. Then explain to students that the 1700s and early 1800s were a time of great intellectual, social, and political development. Enlightenment thinkers challenged beliefs about society, government, and economics. Their ideas inspired the American and French revolutions.

Presenting Themes

See p. 449B for suggestions on introducing themes.

Using the Time Line

Have students list the time line events in their notebooks. After they have read about each event in the chapter, have students write a paragraph explaining its significance.

Chapter 17
Revolutions of Society and State 1714–1815

Understanding the Main Idea

As the discoveries of the Scientific Revolution were popularized during a period known as the Enlightenment, people began to adopt a more secular view of the world. These Enlightenment ideas often inspired revolution. In America, colonists declared independence from Britain, and in France, people rose in revolt against the king. In France the Revolution gave way to rule by Napoleon Bonaparte, who succeeded in conquering much of Europe.

Themes

- **War and Diplomacy** How might a society react to a long period of warfare?

- **Philosophy** How might new ideas change the way people view themselves and their world?

- **Politics and Law** How might revolution lead to new political structures?

In 1789 hunger, the burden of heavy taxes, financial crisis, and the desire for a voice in government led the French people to violently throw off the chains of the monarchy. In January 1793 the French people executed their king. A participant in the event left an account of the spectacle:

> 66 *They dragged [the king] under the axe of the guillotine, which with one stroke severed his head from his body. All this passed in a moment. The youngest of the guards, who seemed about eighteen, immediately seized the head, and showed it to the people as he walked round the scaffold. . . . At first an awful silence prevailed; at length some cries of 'Vive la République!' ['Long live the republic!'] were heard. By degrees the voices multiplied, and in less than ten minutes this cry, a thousand times repeated, became the universal shout of the multitude, and every hat was in the air.* 99

Within four years the French people had completely transformed the aristocratic government that had dominated their country for centuries. In part, they were following the example of British colonists in North America. In 1776 the colonists had also revolted against their rulers.

In addition, the uprising in France was part of a spirit of political and social revolution that was emerging

1740	1748	1763	1776
Frederick the Great becomes king of Prussia.	Montesquieu publishes *The Spirit of Laws.*	European powers agree to peace, ending the Seven Years' War.	Colonists in North America declare their independence from Britain.

throughout Europe. In the 1700s people began to put forward new philosophical ideas about the equality of humankind and new ideas on how people should be governed. Before the century was over, these "enlightened" ideas would become a powerful force in world history.

The execution of King Louis XVI, 1793

In this image vast crowds gather to witness the execution of King Louis XVI on January 21, 1793. One of the king's priests, Henry Essex Edgeworth de Firmont, recounted: "The streets were lined with citizens, all armed, some with pikes and some with guns . . . nothing was to be seen, but armed citizens—citizens, all rushing toward the commission of a crime." After arriving in the Place de Louis XV, where the guillotine was set up, Louis XVI left the carriage, walked up the steps of the scaffold, and uttered his last words: "I die innocent of all the crimes laid to my charge; I pardon those who have occasioned my death; and I pray to God that the blood you are going to shed may never be visited on France."

Critical Thinking Ask students if they think the execution of the king was a crime or if it was necessary for French independence.

ANSWER: Students' answers will vary.

1789	1793	1799	1815
French citizens storm the Bastille.	Louis XVI of France is executed by revolutionary government.	Napoleon takes control of France.	Napoleon is defeated at the Battle of Waterloo.

SECTION 1

CORE LESSON PLAN
See pages 449C and
449D for Lesson Plan
17.1.

Theme: Politics and Law

Another conflict arose between Britain and France because of a new British monarch. In 1714 Great Britain's Queen Anne died, and the crown passed to George, the elector of Hanover. King George I remained thoroughly German. He did not even trouble himself to move to Britain for a full 7 weeks after the death of Queen Anne. To the British, George I seemed unsophisticated, rude, and thoroughly unpleasant.

Critical Thinking Ask students how George I's interest in Hanover may have affected Anglo-French rivalry.

ANSWER: Students may answer that Britain would ally itself with Germany in any conflict with France.

SECTION 1

An Era of Global Warfare

FOCUS

- Why did European national rivalries intensify in the 1700s?

- How did Prussia's rise to power affect the rest of Europe?

- What were the results of the Seven Years' War?

At the end of the 1600s France dominated Europe. This domination, however, forced other nations to grow stronger and form alliances in order to balance France's influence in Europe. These alliances weakened French power during the 1700s. Other nations, particularly Great Britain and Prussia, began to challenge France's dominant position. This struggle for power and security in Europe would also change the balance of power around the world.

View of the important trading center of Calcutta, India, 1788

Anglo-French Rivalry

The succession of William of Orange, the arch-enemy of Louis XIV, to the throne of England in 1689 renewed the old rivalry between France and England. The rivalry was intensified by the political union of Scotland and England in 1707. This union had been achieved primarily because English lords feared that the Catholics in the north of Scotland, in conjunction with the French, would try to return a Catholic to the throne of England. By uniting Scotland and England, the English hoped that Scotland would cease to represent a threat. This union created the United Kingdom of Great Britain.

During the 1700s, however, French and British rivalry took on new forms. The two countries began to compete for influence among the other European states in an effort to dominate the continent. They also competed for control of overseas trade routes and colonies. By 1750 Britain and France were in direct opposition and competition in three significant regions—the Caribbean, North America, and India.

The Caribbean. In the Caribbean the French controlled Guadeloupe and Martinique, as well as a number of smaller islands. On these islands the French developed sugar plantations, creating sizable profits for French traders. British planters in the West Indies envied French profits and resented the fact that some of these profits came from trade with British colonists in North America. The British Parliament tried to extend more control over colonial trade by enforcing a series of **Navigation Acts**, which required that all goods imported to or exported from the colonies had to pass through British ports, in British ships. In this way the British could collect tariffs on all of the colonies' overseas commerce.

North America. Meanwhile, Anglo-French rivalry in North America intensified because of territorial conflicts. The population of British North America was increasing rapidly. Many colonists looked west for new lands, but this would mean moving into territory claimed by France. To prevent this expansion the French built a series of forts from the St. Lawrence River to the Mississippi. In 1711 Colonel Alexander Spotswood, the lieutenant governor of Virginia, wrote about the British settlers' fear of the French:

> **❝** The British plantations are in a manner surrounded by their [the French settlers'] commerce. . . . Should they multiply their settlements . . . so as to join their dominions of Canada to their new colony of Louisiana, they might even possess themselves of any of these [British] plantations they pleased. **❞**

In response to French fortification, Britain reinforced its strength in the colonies by sending more ships and troops and by establishing its own forts in the western territories.

India. The third region of conflict between France and Great Britain was India. As the Mughal Empire declined in the 1700s, India splintered into dozens of small states.

Both the French and the British took advantage of this chaos to increase their commercial profits. When rivals for a local Indian throne began fighting in southern India, the British and French trading interests supported opposing princes, hoping to use the future ruler's support to gain a monopoly on trade. By the 1750s this controversy had become a private war between the French and British trading companies involving local Indian rulers and focused on gaining control of the valuable Indian trade. The terms of the French surrender in 1757 left things much as they had been, with the British and French still competing for trade dominance.

In the 1700s France and Great Britain increased their competition for colonies and control over trade.

▶ **The British formed close attachments with Indian rulers in hopes of weakening French influence in the region.**

The Rise of Prussian Power

While France and Britain struggled for dominance of overseas trade and territory, a new, powerful nation began to emerge in Europe. Prussia, once a small, weak state, began to gain strength in both size and military power. In the early 1700s France still remained the single most powerful European state. Prussia's growing strength, however, forced a realignment of this balance of power in Europe.

The Prussian army. Frederick William I, who became king in 1713, spent his career building Prussia into a great European power. He established an efficient government bureaucracy and led the nation toward economic self-sufficiency. Most importantly, he built a powerful army. Frederick William loved the army; he regularly wore a uniform and spent a great deal of time with army officers. "At the table," his daughter once wrote, "nothing else was talked of but economy and soldiers."

Frederick William reorganized the army to make it more efficient and powerful. By the end of his reign in 1740, Prussia had the fourth-largest army in Europe. The man who did the most to enhance Prussian power, however, was Frederick William's son and heir, Frederick II, who became known as Frederick the Great.

Frederick the Great. Frederick II was very unlike his father. He developed a great interest in French art and philosophy and initially showed no interest in military matters. When Frederick was 10 years old, his father, hoping to create a strong sense of discipline in his son, devised a strict schedule for the young boy:

> **❝** Monday he is to be awakened at six o'clock, and he must then say a short prayer. As soon as he has done this, he

shall put on his jacket and comb out his hair. While he is combed he shall take tea and breakfast at the same time, and this must be finished before half past six o'clock. From seven to nine o'clock [his tutor] Duhan shall work at history with him; at nine o'clock [the court chaplain] Noltenius shall come, and he must instruct him in Christianity till a quarter to eleven. Duhan shall describe maps to him from two to three o'clock. From three till four o'clock he is to work at morality, from four till five o'clock Duhan shall write German letters with him. "

Although Frederick resisted, he eventually absorbed his father's dream of Prussian power.

The War of the Austrian Succession. Within a few months of inheriting the throne at age 28, Frederick II involved his country in a war with Austria. He seized the Austrian province of Silesia, which was heavily populated and rich in minerals and industry. Frederick did not want a lengthy war, so he offered the 23-year-old Austrian empress Maria Theresa an alliance with Prussia. He also promised his vote for her husband, Francis, in the upcoming election for the office of Holy Roman emperor. Maria Theresa rejected his offer, and her rejection resulted in the War of the Austrian Succession. Soon Bavaria, Spain, Saxony, and France joined Prussia in the war, each hoping to expand its territory at Austria's expense. The alliance of these nations was overwhelming, and Austria asked for peace. In 1745 Maria Theresa signed a peace treaty that gave Silesia to Frederick II. With the treaty, Prussia became a major European power, rivaling the strength of its neighbors.

▲ Maria Theresa became the first female Habsburg ruler.

The emergence of Prussia as a major military power began to change the balance of power in Europe.

The First Global War

Prussia's victory in the War of the Austrian Succession, however, intensified European rivalries. These rivalries led to the **Seven Years' War**, which began in 1756 and which was fought around the world by the European powers. The war expanded the struggle between Prussia and Austria and included all of Europe's major powers—Great Britain supported Prussia, and Austria formed alliances with France and Russia.

In 1757 Frederick II's forces defeated the French forces in Saxony and prevented Austria from reclaiming Silesia. Two years later, however, a combined Austrian and Russian army soundly defeated Frederick's army, and it appeared that Frederick might lose the war. But the alliance that opposed him began to crumble because of mistrust and financial difficulties.

Although much of the fighting took place in Europe, the war had erupted after British and French forces clashed in North America, where the Seven Years' War was called the **French and Indian War**. In North America the French had made alliances with many American Indians to prevent the British settlers from expanding their colonies. In 1759 British general James Wolfe attacked the French defenses at Quebec. In the fighting that followed, the British forces crushed the French forces, marking the end of the French Empire in North America.

The British also challenged France's position in India. In 1757 the British commander Robert Clive defeated the French-supported provincial ruler of Bengal at the Battle of Plassey. Soon after the battle began, many Bengali officers were killed, and the Bengali soldiers fled. Clive reported:

" *The whole army being visibly dispirited and thrown into some confusion, we were encouraged to storm . . . their camp. . . . On this a general rout [disorganized retreat] ensued [followed], and we pursued the enemy six miles, passing upwards of forty pieces of cannon they had abandoned.* "

Soon the victorious British had seized all of Bengal. France's hold in India had been broken, and the British became the strongest power in India.

By 1759 Britain had established itself as the greatest sea power in the world. This success was

European Possessions in 1763

A Colonial War Europeans waged the Seven Years' War over three continents. After the nations agreed to make peace in 1761, Great Britain gained the most territory, particularly in North America and India.

Linking Geography and History Which colonial power was best situated to control the spice trade of the East Indies?

largely because of the brilliant leadership of William Pitt the Elder. When Pitt joined the government as secretary of state in the first year of the Seven Years' War, he promised to do his best "in that service to which I have the glory . . . to be unalterably and totally devoted."

The Seven Years' War ended not because of any clear victories, but because neither side had the will to continue the fight. In 1761 Britain had a new king, George III, who had little desire to continue the war. The following year Russia pulled out of the alliance with France and Austria. In 1763 France and Austria finally agreed to make peace.

The Aftermath of the War in Europe

As a result of the peace treaties, Prussia held on to Silesia. France lost nearly all of its North American colonial lands. The British got control of Canada and all of Louisiana east of the

Mississippi River. They also remained the dominant European power in India.

Prussia and Russia had drained their treasuries during the war. Prussia also had lost many people. As they realized the costs of war in both lives and wealth, the European powers became reluctant to fight again, and so a period of peace descended on Europe.

Nonetheless, European monarchs remained eager to expand their national boundaries. Poland was an easy target for its stronger neighbors. In 1772 Prussia and Russia carried out the First Partition of Poland, each seizing a generous portion of their weaker neighbor's territory. To preserve the balance of power in Europe, they offered the Polish province of Galicia to Austria. In 1793, together with Prussia, Russia carried out the Second Partition of Poland, leaving Poland only a tiny strip of land wedged between Prussia, Russia, and Austria. In 1795 even that disappeared in the Third Partition of Poland.

While Poland was being divided, Russia and Austria looked to the Ottoman Empire for further possibilities of expansion. Catherine the Great

Theme: Geography

The Treaty of Paris gave the British most of France's North American territories. Hoping to gain new land, thousands of settlers from the colonies rushed westward. This brought them into conflict with American Indians living along the frontier. In 1763 Pontiac, an Ottawa chief, led thousands of American Indians in raids that resulted in the deaths of some 2,000 settlers and the destruction of British forts. To avoid further conflict, the British passed the Proclamation of 1763, barring colonists from settling west of the Appalachian Mountains.

Critical Thinking Ask students why the proclamation might have been unpopular with the British colonists.

ANSWER: Students might suggest that colonists wanted to settle the western lands and resented England for banning the activity.

REVIEW & ASSESSMENT RESOURCES

- Study Guide 17.1
- Daily Quiz 17.1
- Main Idea Activity 17.1

All Levels

The Partitions of Poland, 1772–1795

The Splintered Nation Through a series of partitions by other European countries, Poland ceased to exist.

? Linking Geography and History Which country had received the most Polish territory by 1795?

of Russia made an alliance with Joseph II of Austria, intending to divide the Turkish-held Balkans. Russia gained control of the Black Sea and the Crimea. Austria also expanded eastward at the expense of the Turks.

The Seven Years' War left Prussia as a major European power, Britain as the world's greatest sea power, and laid the foundations for Prussian, Russian, and Austrian expansion in eastern Europe.

SECTION 1 REVIEW

IDENTIFY and explain the significance of the following:
Navigation Acts
Frederick the Great
Maria Theresa
Seven Years' War
French and Indian War
William Pitt
Catherine the Great
Prussia
Silesia
Quebec
Bengal
Poland
Galicia

LOCATE and explain the importance of the following:
United Kingdom of Great Britian

1. *Main Idea* What caused rivalry between Great Britain and France to grow in the 1700s?

2. *Main Idea* What was the result of Prussia's rise to power?

3. *War and Diplomacy* How did the Seven Years' War change the international situation in Europe and around the world?

4. *Writing to Create* Imagine you are a British colonist. Explain why you support the French and Indian War.

5. *Synthesizing* Why could a person argue that territorial expansion was one of the main causes of the Seven Years' War?

The Enlightenment

- What was the Enlightenment?
- What did many philosophes hope to accomplish through the application of Enlightenment ideas?
- How did the Enlightenment affect common conceptions about the roles of women?
- How did the ideas of the Enlightenment affect Europe's absolute monarchs?

In the 1700s a revolution in intellectual activity began to change many Europeans' view of their societies. In his 1759 tale Candide, the philosopher Voltaire criticized what he saw as a pointless conflict between Great Britain and France over territory in North America: "These two nations are at war over a few acres of snow out around Canada, and . . . they are spending on that fine war much more than all of Canada is worth." As many people began to focus their attention on the secular world—rather than on the spiritual one—they began to question the traditional foundations of European politics and society. This change of ideas and attitudes was known as the Enlightenment.

Title page of Denis Diderot's *Encyclopédie*, 1751

Popularizing Enlightenment Ideas

As the Scientific Revolution progressed in the 1600s, European scholars began to accumulate a vast body of knowledge about nature through the use of systematic, scientific methods. In the 1700s the ideas and methods of the Scientific Revolution found a wider audience. Many educated people began to study the natural world around them and began to believe that for every natural phenomenon there was both a cause and an effect.

The great thinkers of the Enlightenment were called **philosophes** (fee-luh-ZAWFS), the French word for "philosophers." The philosophes popularized the application of scientific methods to the study of the human condition. They believed that truth could be arrived at solely by the application of reason, or logical thought, to observation—a belief known as **rationalism**.

A new view of the world. The philosophes based their ideas on several major assumptions. The first, rooted in the discoveries of scientific investigators like Newton, was that nature was regulated according to a uniform system of **natural law**. A second assumption was that human behavior could also be understood through the application of natural law. The last major assumption was that people should use this knowledge to work toward perfecting both themselves and society. The Enlightenment inspired a growing sense of individualism and personal freedom, and a belief in the basic equality of all individuals.

Progress. A growing faith in progress was one of the most significant outcomes of enlightened thought. Because scientists had discovered new truths, the philosophes came to believe that human life could constantly improve. Progress in individuals could be measured by their discovery and application of natural law, which would make them more aware of their role in the universe. The philosophes hoped that progress in individuals would result in progress in society.

One target of the philosophes was the Catholic Church. Some saw the church as an obstacle to progress since it taught people to focus attention on the afterlife instead of improving

▲ Voltaire (whose real name was François-Marie Arouet) wrote throughout his lifetime. Here he is shown already dictating as he gets out of bed and begins dressing.

▲ A guest reads aloud to a gathering in this French salon of the 1700s.

conditions on Earth. For example, the French writer Voltaire was a strong critic of the Catholic Church. He complained that the church taught people to believe in miracles, which contradicted the laws of nature. Instead of trusting in divine providence to improve human happiness, Voltaire believed humanity itself could create its own happiness. In his most famous work, *Candide*, he urged people to avoid excessive idealism and abstract philosophy while taking practical steps to improve human existence.

Many of the philosophes called for a new attitude toward religion, known as deism. These deists saw God as the creator of a rational, orderly universe governed by natural law. Once created, the universe proceeded to function without divine intervention. Consequently, human beings had a moral responsibility to apply the laws of nature to improve the human condition themselves.

Spreading the Enlightenment. Because the philosophes believed that knowledge was the key to human progress, they made a great effort to share their knowledge with the educated public. Philosophe Denis Diderot (dee-droh) edited the *Encyclopédie*, a multivolume collaborative work of more than 100 experts, which was intended to include the sum of human knowledge. Other philosophes published their ideas in newspapers and journals or spread their ideas through scientific or cultural clubs.

One important place for the exchange of ideas was the **salon**, a gathering of the social, political, and cultural elites. Upper-class women, who held the salons in their homes, played a crucial role in the Enlightenment by bringing about the meetings of great minds. The salons provided intelligent women with the opportunity to contribute to the intellectual debates of the day. Amid lavish entertainment and intelligent conversation, the philosophes, both men and women, could meet and exchange ideas.

The Enlightenment was a new spirit of investigation based on rationalism and natural law and aimed at improving the human condition.

Social Criticism

The philosophes used their rational arguments concerning the nature of humanity to question many established patterns of European society. The new conception of human nature put forth by John Locke in the 1600s helped shape the philosophes' attitude toward society. Locke wrote that human beings were born without pre-existing ideas or principles—in other words, the human mind was a *tabula rasa,* or clean slate. According to Locke, human beings were shaped by their environment, education, and society. The philosophes of the 1700s agreed with Locke, and they emphasized the importance of education and environment in giving people the tools needed to improve society.

Judicial reform. Many of the philosophes believed that European judicial systems were unjust and irrational. Torture was still used as a means of punishment, as it had been since the Middle Ages. During the Middle Ages, people believed that accused criminals would tell the truth when confronted with death, so that they could achieve salvation. Philosophes, however, reasoned that accused criminals would confess simply to remove the physical pain of torture, regardless of their guilt or innocence.

An Italian economist and jurist, Cesare Beccaria (bayk-kah-REE-ah), was profoundly moved by the injustice of judicial torture. He denounced torture as being useless and evil, "the sure way to acquit robust criminals and convict infirm innocents." In his book *On Crimes and Punishments,* published in 1764, Beccaria explained that punishment should be used to prevent crime, rather than as an act of vengeance, and that the severity of the punishment should fit the severity of the crime. In addition, Beccaria believed that accused criminals should not be punished until proven guilty.

▲ The publication of Cesare Beccaria's book *On Crimes and Punishments* made him an international celebrity at the age of 26.

Education. The philosophes believed that people needed education to improve their lives and society as a whole. Under the influence of the Enlightenment, many monarchs came to believe that by educating their subjects they strengthened their state.

The Austrian empress Maria Theresa made primary education available for all children in her domain in 1774. In Germany, too, basic education was made more widely available, along with professional and vocational training for civil servants, laborers, and artisans. In countries with absolute monarchies, however, education was strictly controlled. Free thought was not encouraged. Instead, students were trained to believe in the absolutist state and to become better subjects. Moreover, education was not required and literacy rates remained low.

The philosophes used their rational arguments concerning human nature to question many established patterns of European society.

Political and Economic Criticism

Philosophes of the 1700s believed that in order to achieve a society that functioned according to natural law, political and economic institutions must become more rational. Believing, as Locke had in the 1600s, that people had certain natural rights that they must never surrender, the philosophes held that a ruler who violated these rights had broken the social contract. Under such conditions, the people had the right to find another ruler.

Montesquieu. Not all philosophes reached the same conclusions from their belief in natural law. The Baron de Montesquieu (MOHN-tes-kyoo) believed that government should be suited to the needs and circumstances of a people. In 1748 he published *The Spirit of Laws,* in which he defined his idea of perfect government:

❝ *Laws should be adapted to the people for whom they are framed, in relation to the nature and principle of each government, to the climate of each country, to the quality of its soil, to the principal occupation of the natives, to the degree of liberty which the*

Theme: Philosophy

Although the Enlightenment produced ideas that could be considered revolutionary for the times, the movement did not have an immediate widespread impact. In the early years of the Enlightenment, the audiences for the philosophes' ideas were relatively small, since they had to be wealthy enough to be invited to the salons or to afford the luxury of books. Many Enlightenment beliefs would later be used to defend the ideas of democracy and social equality. During the Enlightenment itself, however, the philosophes and their wealthy, educated audience remained aloof from the common people.

Critical Thinking Ask students why it might be advantageous for the Enlightenment to initially be popular with the wealthy and educated.

ANSWER: Students might respond that rulers would be more likely to accept reforms suggested by the wealthy and educated than by common people and that the wealthy and educated would be able to spread Enlightenment ideas throughout society.

*constitution will bear, to the religion of
the inhabitants, to their inclinations,
riches, numbers, commerce, manners,
and customs.* "

After examining the great variety of governments, Montesquieu concluded that the best
form of government for Europeans included a
separation of powers—in other words, the government should be divided so that no single
branch had enough power to dominate the others. Montesquieu believed that such a balance
would prevent the development of tyranny.

Rousseau. Jean-Jacques Rousseau (roo-soh)
differed from many other philosophes in that he
believed that improving intellect at the expense
of emotion corrupted people. Rousseau wrote
that "everything is good, as it comes from the
hands of God; everything degenerates [breaks
down] in the hands of man." Rousseau believed
that all people began their lives innocent and
noble, but that the act of creating society ruined

▲ In 1756 Jean-Jacques Rousseau left the
distractions of Paris to write in seclusion
in the countryside.

their natural goodness. Rousseau also believed
that people must reform society so that conscience and emotion, instead of intellect, guided
all actions.

In *The Social Contract*, Rousseau wrote that a
perfect society would be composed of free citizens
who formed a government by meeting face-to-
face. Individuals would determine what the common good was, and the will of the people would
become law. This idea of **popular sovereignty**, a
government created by and subject to the will of
the people, would later have enormous influence
in the American Revolution.

Adam Smith. In addition to addressing the
problems of society and politics, the philosophes
also turned their attention to the economy. They
believed that the economy, like everything else in
the universe, functioned according to natural law
and that any attempt to interfere with these natural economic laws would bring certain disaster.
In 1776 Adam Smith, a Scottish economist, best
stated these ideas in *The Wealth of Nations*.

Smith reasoned that two natural laws regulated all business and economic activity—the
law of supply and demand and the law of competition. In any business, prices would be determined by the relationship of the supply of a
product to the demand for it. If an item were
scarce and in great demand, people would pay a
high price for it. Thus, profits from its sales
would rise, and more manufacturers would want
to produce the scarce item. Soon the supply of
the item would exceed the demand for it. Prices
would be driven down as manufacturers competed for people to buy their products.

Smith believed in what became known as
free enterprise, in which every person should be
free to go into any business and to operate it for
maximum profit. The result would benefit everyone—laborers would have jobs, investors and
owners would make profits, and buyers would
receive better goods at lower prices.

Many of Smith's ideas were a direct contradiction of the old economic theory of mercantilism.
Mercantilists believed that the world's nations
competed for a limited amount of wealth, which
made regulations necessary to keep other nations
from gaining an unfair amount of all the wealth.
Smith believed that the world economy was self-
regulating and should be allowed to function
with little interference. This belief was known as

▲ In the mid-1700s Adam Smith began to gain international recognition for his theories on economics.

laissez-faire (le-say FAR), meaning "let do" or leave things alone.

The philosophes used their ideas concerning human nature and natural law to question European politics and economics.

Women and the Enlightenment

Although most of the philosophes were men, women also participated in the Enlightenment. In England, for example, Mary Wollstonecraft, an author and early spokesperson for women's rights, firmly believed that Enlightenment ideals should be extended to women as well as men.

Born in 1759, Wollstonecraft became interested in intellectual pursuits at an early age. Unlike most women of her time, Wollstonecraft sought personal liberty as well as economic independence. She educated herself, and once she began earning money from outside means of employment, she became the sole supporter of her family. While a schoolteacher, she was appalled by the carefree attitude that society encouraged in young women of the elite.

She realized that women needed a sounder education to make them more serious, charitable, and moral.

She first caused controversy with the 1792 publication of *A Vindication of the Rights of Woman*. In it she expressed her belief that women and men were created equal—but that women received less education.

66 *If they [women] be really capable of acting like rational creatures, let them not be treated like slaves; . . . but cultivate their minds . . . and let them attain conscious dignity by feeling themselves only dependent on God.* 99

Although Wollstonecraft's book was warmly regarded by some philosophes in France, in Britain the conservative reaction was harsh. Horace Walpole, an aristocratic author, wrote that Wollstonecraft was a "hyena in petticoats," and Hannah More, an English religious writer, claimed that the title alone was so ridiculous that she would not read the book.

In later writings, Wollstonecraft sharply criticized the conditions in which women—particularly poor women—had to live. While traveling through Scandinavia in the 1790s she observed that "the men stand up for the dignity of man, by oppressing the women." By this time, however, many people had turned away from her ideas, in part because of her lifestyle. Defying accepted social practices, she chose not to marry the father of her first daughter. When he left her, she went into a deep depression. After recovering from her despair, in 1797 she married the writer William Godwin. She died days after giving birth to their daughter.

Unlike Wollstonecraft, some writers saw the success of women in the salons and believed that women were truly gaining in power and influence, particularly in France. The Scottish philosopher David Hume observed that in France "the females enter into all transactions and all management of church and state: and no

Mary Wollstonecraft
BIOGRAPHY

man can expect success, who takes not care to obtain their good graces." However, Hume, like many other Enlightenment thinkers, held very traditional views about the place of women. He felt that giving power to women was ultimately dangerous, since their "inferiority and infirmities are absolutely incurable."

Like Hume, most thinkers still believed that women should keep their traditional roles of wife and mother. For example, Rousseau complained that an educated woman "scorns every womanly duty, and she is always trying to make a man of herself." In the *Encyclopédie,* articles focusing on women concentrated on the common misconceptions about women's physical weakness and emotional sensitivity.

Some enlightened thinkers saw women and men as equals, while others refused to accept such ideas.

Enlightened Despotism

The philosophes believed that government could only be improved by the restructuring of European monarchies along Enlightenment principles in order to bring society, politics, and the economy in line with natural law. Many philosophes appealed directly to monarchs for change. What they wanted was **enlightened despotism**—a system of government in which absolute monarchs ruled according to Enlightenment principles.

Many European monarchs did accept some Enlightenment principles—at least those that served their own purposes. Catherine the Great of Russia, for example, read the works of Montesquieu and Beccaria, corresponded with Voltaire, and persuaded Diderot to visit her court. In 1767 she established a legislative commission to codify Russia's laws. Representatives from all classes but the serfs and practicing clergy were allowed to voice their opinions. This was the first time Russian subjects were able to advise the

▲ In spite of her knowledge of the Enlightenment and her friendship with philosophes, Catherine the Great actually increased the suffering of Russian peasants.

central government, and it would be the last time until the 1900s.

Catherine instructed the commissioners that "the Sovereign is absolute," but that the government should set "less Bounds than others to natural Liberty" and coincide "with the Views and Purposes of rational Creatures." Catherine soon became preoccupied with other issues, however, such as a war with the Turks, the Partition of Poland, and a fierce peasant revolt, which shifted her attention away from enlightened reform. The rebellion in particular convinced Catherine of the need to strengthen her authority. She imprisoned or exiled Russian Enlightenment thinkers, ordered Russian students studying abroad to return to Russia, and banned all French newspapers. Her reign, which began with the flowering of Enlightenment culture, ended in repression and fear.

Under the influence of Voltaire, Frederick II of Prussia undertook numerous reforms. His reforms, however enlightened, were intended to strengthen the state, for he believed that a strong state would benefit all of his subjects. Frederick abolished torture as a punishment and declared religious toleration, and these reforms were included in the written Common Law that was completed after Frederick's death in 1794. He wrote in 1777 that "the sovereign is attached by indissoluble [unbreakable] ties to the body of the state; hence . . . he . . . is sensible of all the ills which afflict his subjects." In spite of this view, Frederick believed strongly in the established system of class and privilege.

Perhaps the most enlightened monarch was Joseph II of Austria. He believed that the state was obligated to provide a moral example for its subjects. He abolished serfdom and assumed responsibility for caring for the poor and the sick. Joseph also proclaimed religious toleration for all Christians, Jews, and Muslims in the Austrian Empire, which meant that people of all faiths could then worship freely, hold property, become educated, and have access to all professions. In 1787 Joseph wrote:

▲ **Joseph II of Austria is shown here interacting with peasant farmers, something inconceivable for most monarchs of his time.**

66 *[Religious] fanaticism shall in future be known in my states only by the contempt I have for it; nobody shall any longer be exposed to hardships on account of his creed; no man shall be compelled in future to profess the religion of the state if it be contrary to his persuasion.* 99

Like all other enlightened despots, however, Joseph II's enlightened rule had its limits. He withdrew many of the reforms he had instituted when revolts threatened the stability of his domain. In addition, Austria's poorly paid bureaucrats were not eager to enforce the remaining reforms. Joseph complained, "Almost no one is animated by zeal for the good of the fatherland; there is no one to carry out my ideas."

*M*any European rulers accepted some Enlightenment ideals but could not reconcile them with political absolutism.

SECTION 2 REVIEW

IDENTIFY and explain the significance of the following:
  philosophes
  rationalism
  natural law
  Voltaire
  salon
  Montesquieu
  Jean-Jacques Rousseau
  popular sovereignty
  Adam Smith
  free enterprise
  laissez-faire
  Mary Wollstonecraft
  enlightened despotism

1. **Main Idea** What was the Enlightenment?
2. **Main Idea** What did the philosophes hope to change by putting Enlightenment ideas into practice?
3. **Politics** What impact did Enlightenment ideas have on absolute monarchs?
4. **Writing to Explain** Write a short essay explaining how the Enlightenment did and did not change people's views on the roles of women in society.

5. **Synthesizing** How did the Enlightenment affect European attitudes toward society and politics? In answering this question, consider the following: (a) how philosophes criticized European society and its institutions; (b) how philosophes wanted to reform the political and the economic structure; and (c) to what extent European monarchs instituted reforms based on Enlightenment ideas.

Theme: Politics and Law

Until the Seven Years' War, Britain had intervened very little in American affairs. Only governors and officials in charge of enforcing the Navigation Acts in the colonies had any control. Some colonists sat in the colonial assemblies, which not only set internal policies for the colonies but also determined the salaries of the British-appointed governors.

Critical Thinking Ask students how the colonists' experience was a factor in the revolution.

ANSWER: Students may answer that the colonists, already having political experience and structures, resented having their independence taken away and wanted to run their own government.

SECTION 3

The American Revolution

FOCUS

- How did Britain's colonial policy in North America change after the Seven Years' War and what was the result?

- How did the struggle for power in Europe contribute to the founding of the United States?

- How was the government established by the U.S. Constitution different from other governments at the time?

W hile in Europe the Enlightenment remained largely an elitist movement, British colonists in North America developed Enlightenment political ideas along more democratic lines. Strongly influenced by the political views of Locke and Rousseau, and caught up in the global struggle between Britain and France, the colonists in North America began to experience a new sense of national identity. This new sense of identity led to revolution and the establishment of a new nation.

The U.S. Declaration of Independence

Changes in British North America

The Seven Years' War had done more than redistribute the balance of power in Europe. Even as the British were taking control of a new empire in India, they began to lose control over their old empire in North America. By the 1700s the colonists had begun to see themselves as a people separate from the British.

A new American identity. There were many reasons for the emergence of a new American identity in the colonies. For one thing, the environment in which the colonists lived was very different from Britain. Land was plentiful in the colonies. By working hard on their own land, colonists could gain wealth and social standing. In Britain, wealth and social standing were determined by birth and privilege. In addition, Britain had paid little attention to the colonies in their early years, which allowed the colonists to develop self-government.

In Britain, the government was based on "virtual representation," the belief that anyone could represent the interests of a particular group without being elected by it. However, British colonists in North America, because they had been allowed a voice in their local affairs, had come to believe in "direct representation," their right to elect their own representatives.

British imperial policy. Although the differences between the Americans and the British grew over many years, it was British imperial policy that brought these differences into sharp focus. The Seven Years' War had left the British government deeply in debt. Since British troops had fought in North America to protect the colonists, the British government felt justified in requiring the colonists to help pay for their own defense. In addition, after the war Britain began to consolidate its far-flung trading interests and colonial territories into a unified imperial organization. Soon the British government tried to bring all its colonies under closer economic control by enforcing mercantilistic trade regulations, known as the Navigation Acts. Used to the old days of relative neglect, many colonists saw the imposition of these new taxes and restrictions as an unjust restriction of their liberties. As the colonists resisted new British policies, the British king, George III, became even more determined to force them into obedience.

Britain tightened colonial control after the Seven Years' War, inspiring a growing sense of American identity.

Colonial Response

One of the ways in which the British tried to gain more control over the colonies was through taxation. In 1765 Parliament passed the **Stamp Act**, which required colonists to pay a tax—in the form of special stamps—on many paper goods, including newspapers, wills, mortgages, contracts, and playing cards. The colonists united in opposition to this tax, in large part because they had not been consulted before the tax was imposed. "If Great Britain can order us to come to her for necessaries we want," complained Philadelphia lawyer John Dickinson, "and can order us to pay what taxes she pleases before we take them away, or when we land them here, we are . . . abject [lowly] slaves." After the colonists began a trade boycott of a number of British goods, Parliament repealed the Stamp Act.

Crisis seemed to follow crisis in the colonies, however. In 1770 British guards, fearing for their safety, fired into an angry mob outside a British customs house, killing several people. This incident became known as the Boston Massacre, and it fueled the growing colonial outrage against Great Britain. Tensions increased further in 1773, when the British tried to save the declining British East India Company from bankruptcy by effectively granting the Company a monopoly over the tea trade in the British

colonies. When angry colonists threw a shipment of tea into Boston Harbor—an event that became known as the **Boston Tea Party**—the British closed the port of Boston to all shipping.

In 1774 delegates from all of the colonies but Georgia met in Philadelphia in the First Continental Congress to discuss the situation. The delegates demanded that they be granted the full rights of British subjects. In April 1775, however, British troops marched from Boston to seize guns and gunpowder that colonists had stored in two nearby towns. At Lexington and Concord, the British met armed resistance from the colonists and were forced to retreat to Boston.

Colonists responded to British colonial policy with protests and resistance.

The Struggle for Independence

Even after blood had been shed, the colonists, hoping to find a peaceful solution, did not at first seek independence. Gradually, however, they began to believe that they must break free of Britain. In early 1776 a recent British immigrant, Thomas Paine, published a pamphlet called *Common Sense*:

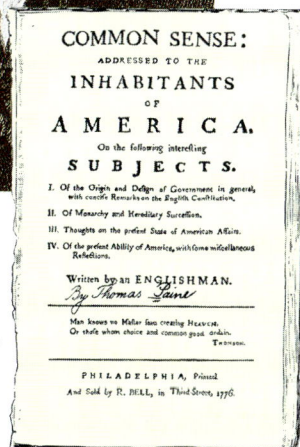

Thomas Paine's pamphlet *Common Sense* helped inspire the American colonists to revolt.

❝ *I challenge the warmest advocate for reconciliation to show a single advantage that this continent can reap, by being connected with Great Britain. . . . But the injuries and disadvantages we sustain by that connection are without number. . . . Any submission to, or dependence on, Great Britain, tends directly to involve this continent in European wars and quarrels, and sets us at variance [at odds] with nations who would otherwise seek our friendship, and against whom we have neither anger nor complaint.* ❞

466

Common Sense sold some 120,000 copies in only three months and helped transform a haphazard rebellion into a crusade for independence.

People in the colonies began to divide over the issue of independence. About one third of the delegates, called Loyalists or Tories, opposed independence. Another third, called Patriots, actively favored independence. The rest remained undecided. As enthusiasm grew, however, on July 4, 1776, the delegates to the Second Continental Congress adopted the **Declaration of Independence**, which proclaimed the United States of America as an independent nation.

The Declaration of Independence. Written by Thomas Jefferson, the U.S. Declaration of Independence clearly showed the influence of the Enlightenment. Drawing heavily on the ideas of John Locke, Jefferson asserted in the Declaration "that all men are created equal, that they are endowed by their Creator with certain unalienable Rights, that among these are Life, Liberty, and the pursuit of Happiness." No government could exist without the consent of its citizens, the Declaration insisted, because citizens created governments to protect individual rights. If a government failed to protect people's rights, then the people had the right to alter or abolish it.

In the first draft of the Declaration, Jefferson had also denounced slavery and accused King George III of violating the "sacred rights of life and liberty" of blacks by "captivating and carrying them into slavery in another hemisphere." But other slaveholders from the southern colonies objected vigorously to any attack on their rights as "property owners." Consequently, delegates removed the passage from the Declaration in order to get slaveholders' approval. Thus, the ideal of individual liberty was only applied in a limited manner. Neither women nor slaves were included in the provisions of the Declaration of Independence.

The War of Independence. The American Revolution soon became part of the ongoing rivalry between Britain and France. At the outset of the war, the Patriots were at a decided disadvantage. They had little money to finance the war, and their army at first consisted of poorly trained volunteers. British troops, on the other hand, were well trained and disciplined, and the British navy was the strongest in the world. However, the colonists were fighting for their own homes in territory they knew well. They also trusted their leader, General George Washington, a commander whose experience and judgment inspired confidence.

For Britain, supplying the war effort from across the ocean was both difficult and expensive. Because the British people had long refused to allow a large standing army, the king had to hire mercenaries. British soldiers also had to get most of their supplies from Britain. In addition, communications were difficult. Messages commonly took two months to cross the ocean. Finally, public opinion in Britain was not solidly behind the war.

Most of the fighting in the Revolution took place between 1776 and 1781. The Battle of Saratoga in 1777, in which the Patriots surrounded and defeated a British army, was a significant turning point. The outcome of the battle convinced the French to make an alliance with the colonists. After the alliance with France, Spain and the Netherlands also joined the war against the British.

France's intervention, particularly at sea, was crucial in achieving an eventual American victory in the war. In the fall of 1781, a French fleet prevented the British navy from resupplying the land forces of General Charles Cornwallis. Consequently, in October 1781 the British

▲ After many years as a military officer, George Washington was twice elected president.

suffered a disastrous defeat by the combined American and French forces at Yorktown, Virginia. By this time the British people were tired of the costly American war. In 1783 the War of Independence ended with the signing of the **Treaty of Paris**. The Americans won not only independence but also a territory much larger than the original 13 colonies, including all territory east of the Mississippi River and north of the 31st parallel to the Great Lakes.

In waging war against Britain, the colonists benefited from the ongoing rivalry between France and Great Britain.

Forging a Nation

In 1781 the American states established a government under the Articles of Confederation, a plan that the Second Continental Congress had adopted in 1777. The central government was deliberately made weak in order to avoid any abuse of centralized power and to allow the states to control most of their own affairs. This government lasted only until 1789, however.

By 1787 it was clear that the Articles of Confederation did not provide a government that was strong enough to endure. Delegates from all the

Military Campaigns of the American Revolution, 1775–1781

3 Captured by Americans, Nov. 12, 1775.

1 War begins, April 19, 1775.

Ft. Ticonderoga May 10–12, 1775

4 First great American victory, Oct. 17, 1777.

2 British defeat Americans, June 17, 1775.

6 George Rogers Clark defeats British along Ohio River, 1778–1779.

5 Campaign of Sept. 1777 to June 1778. Washington spends terrible winter at Valley Forge.

10 French blockade, Sept. 1781.

11 General Cornwallis surrenders to Washington, Oct. 19, 1781.

9 French forces join Washington's army, July 1781–Sept. 1781.

7 Controlled by British, Feb. 1781–Nov. 1781.

8 Occupied by British, May 12, 1780. Recaptured by American general Nathanael Greene, Dec. 14, 1782.

→ American campaign
→ British campaign
☼ American victory
☼ British victory
▲▲▲ Blockade

0 125 250 Miles
0 125 250 Kilometers
Albers Equal-Area Projection

Battling for Independence For six years American colonists struggled against British armies to gain independence.

? Location What city outside the colonies did the Americans capture?

The United States in 1783

Original 13 states
British territory
Territory ceded by Great Britain, 1783
Spanish territory

The New Nation   The Treaty of Paris gave the
United States territory west of the 13 colonies.

Region   What formed the western border
of the new nation?

states, except Rhode Island, met in Philadelphia to
draw up the United States Constitution, the plan
for a stronger, more effective government. They
crafted a **federal system** of government, which
divided powers between the central government
and the state governments. In addition, power
within the federal government was divided
between three separate and independent branches:
the executive, the judicial, and the legislative.

Some of the states were reluctant to ratify the
Constitution because it did not offer greater protection to individuals. In 1789 the first Congress
of the United States wrote the **Bill of Rights**,
the first 10 amendments to the Constitution.
The Bill of Rights, ratified in 1791, guaranteed
the basic rights of every citizen.

Despite the country's apparent endorsement
of Enlightenment ideals, the democracy that the
Americans achieved in 1789 was very different
from democracy as we think of it today. In their
individual constitutions, the states restricted voting to free, adult males, usually to those who
owned property. Women could not vote, and the
large slave population had no political rights at
all. Yet while many liberties still had to be won,
the American experience inspired many people
in other parts of the world.

*After the American Revolution, the
colonists established the first
government in part based on
Enlightenment principles.*

SECTION 3 REVIEW

IDENTIFY and explain the
significance of the following:
   Stamp Act
   Boston Tea Party
   Declaration of Independence
   George Washington
   Treaty of Paris
   federal system
   Bill of Rights

LOCATE and explain the
importance of the following:
   Lexington and Concord
   Saratoga

Yorktown

1. *Main Idea*   Why did the
colonists decide to declare
independence from Great
Britain?

2. *Main Idea*   How was the
government established
by the U.S. Constitution
unique?

3. *Geography: Place*   What
advantage did geography
give the American colonists
in the War of Independence?

4. *Writing to Explain*   Imagine
that you are a member of the
French government. Explain
why you would want to help
the American colonists.

5. *Synthesizing*   Consider
the following statement:
*The United States was
founded upon the principles
of the Enlightenment.*
Give three examples of why
this statement is true and
two examples showing its
limitations.

Revolutionary France

FOCUS

- What did the Three Estates hope to gain from the monarchy?
- How did Enlightenment ideas play a role in France's revolutionary government?
- How did Europe react to the French Revolution?

To many Europeans, the American Revolution showed that Enlightenment ideas could be put into practice in forming a new government. The French were particularly moved by the American example. The success of the American Revolution and the popularization of Enlightenment ideas led many to seek changes in the social and political conditions of France. These desires exploded into revolution in 1789. Rulers in other parts of Europe reacted strongly against the French Revolution, fearing that the unrest would spread to their territories.

The guillotine

The Old Regime

For more than 100 years, France had been the largest and most powerful nation in Europe. Beneath the appearance of stability, however, lay the seeds of revolution. Within a few months in 1789, King Louis XVI lost his power to make laws, and eventually the people's elected representatives voted for his execution. The new rulers of France wrote a constitution and reformed many laws. Such radical change made many feel that they were living in a new era. They referred to the political system before 1789 as the **Old Regime**.

The Three Estates. The causes of the French Revolution were complex. Since the Middle Ages, French society had been divided into three separate classes, known as the Three Estates. In the mid-1700s discontent grew among people of all three Estates, although for different reasons. The First Estate, composed of the Catholic clergy, had long been resented for its privileges and because it paid no taxes. The Second Estate, the aristocracy, was also resented because of its long-standing privileges, such as the right to collect money and services from peasants. The aristocracy also occupied the highest positions in the government and the army. Together, the First and Second Estates held most of the power and wealth in France.

The Third Estate included everybody else in France—the majority of the population. The Third Estate, however, had its own informal social divisions. At the top were the city-dwelling middle classes—merchants, manufacturers, and professional people such as doctors and lawyers. In the middle were laborers and artisans. At the bottom of French society were peasants who made a living by working the land. By acquiring large tracts of land, some peasants had become quite wealthy. Most French peasants, however, lived in inescapable poverty. Nevertheless, they were required to pay feudal dues to their lords. They paid rents for the land they worked, as well as the heaviest government tax, known as the taille. In addition, they paid one tenth of their income—the tithe—to the Catholic Church.

In the mid-1700s growing economic hardship increased the grievances of all three Estates. The already overburdened peasants suffered even more when poor harvests forced the price of bread to

SECTION 4

CORE LESSON PLAN
See pages 449I and 449J for Lesson Plan 17.4.

RESOURCE ACTIVITY

GLOBAL HISTORY RESOURCE CENTER
Image: *Cartoon on the Oppression of the French People*

Show students the cartoon images and ask them to write four short sentences expressing the attitude that each of these cartoon figures is meant to convey.

Sheltered English

RESOURCE ACTIVITY

READINGS IN WORLD HISTORY
Reading 17.4
Robespierre and Saint-Just Defend the Arrest of Danton

Have students read the selection and complete the questions.

Level 2

◀ Members of the Estates General crowd into a hall before King Louis XVI in 1789.

Theme: War and Diplomacy

By the late 1700s the Bastille had become notorious as a prison for people whose crimes had come to the attention of the king, such as conspirators against the monarchy and writers who criticized the government. While conditions in parts of the Bastille were horrifying—areas were perpetually damp, overrun with rats, open to the snow in winter and stifling heat in summer— the cells of the wealthier prisoners were reasonably comfortable. To discredit the monarchy, however, revolutionaries began to create myths about the Bastille. By the 1780s books regularly appeared that described in gruesome detail the degrading conditions of the prison.

Critical Thinking Ask students why revolutionaries might create myths about the Bastille.

ANSWER: Students might suggest that creating myths might turn the Bastille into a symbol of oppression and create a focus for people's aggression. In addition, since most people had no access to the Bastille, they had no way of disproving the myths.

skyrocket, and hunger became a serious problem. The middle classes wanted the political power to match their economic strength, and they wanted important positions in the government and the army that only nobles could obtain. The nobility and the clergy, who had struggled successfully to regain the power and influence that Louis XIV had taken from them, wanted to prevent Louis XVI from taking it away from them again.

The financial crisis. The immediate trigger of the French Revolution was a financial crisis. France had been in debt since Louis XIV's wars. Both the Seven Years' War and French support for the American Revolution had only added to the burden of debt. Louis XV borrowed heavily from bankers to keep the government running. When warned that France would soon face a real crisis, he supposedly remarked, "It will survive for my time. After me, the deluge."

By 1787 bankers refused to lend the government any more money. Financial disaster loomed. Reluctantly, Louis XVI decided to convene the **Estates General**, representatives from all three Estates, at Versailles in May 1789. The king hoped that by convening the Estates General he could gain approval for his plan to raise taxes.

Each of the three Estates wanted to improve its position by taking power away from the monarchy.

The Revolution

Expectations for the meeting of the Estates General ran high. The Count de Mirabeau (mee-rah-boh) wrote about the Estates General that "no National Assembly ever threatened to be so stormy as that which will decide the fate of the monarchy, and which is gathering in such haste and with so much mutual distrust." The Abbé Sieyès (syay-yes), a clergyman, identified the grievances of the Third Estate:

66 *What then is the Third Estate? All. But an 'all' that is fettered [chained] and oppressed. What would it be without the privileged order? It would be all; but free and flourishing. Nothing will go well without the Third Estate; everything would go considerably better without the two others.* 99

The National Assembly. Despite all hopes and expectations, the Third Estate was initially disappointed by the meeting of the Estates General. The First and Second Estates tried to outvote the Third Estate to retain their own privileges. After a period of deadlock and with the support of some members of the First Estate, the delegates of the Third Estate proclaimed themselves the **National Assembly** and vowed to write a constitution for France.

Outraged, Louis closed down the meeting. The delegates fled to a nearby tennis court. There they took the so-called **Tennis Court Oath**, pledging not to disband until they had written a constitution. Reluctantly, the king recognized the Assembly, and with the people's support it assumed power. Meanwhile, fearing that royal troops would crush the National Assembly, on July 14, 1789, the working people of Paris stormed the Bastille, a hated prison-fortress in the city, in search of weapons to defend the Assembly.

The Great Fear. The turmoil in Paris contributed to a growing crisis that spread to the countryside. During the summer of 1789, peasants throughout France became caught up in what is known as the Great Fear. As news of the uprisings in Paris and other cities spread to the country, people often exaggerated events, and many came to believe in a conspiracy by the aristocracy. Peasants also became more angry as food shortages plagued the countryside. As rumors and fear increased, peasants revolted against local lords. Angry peasants broke into manor houses, terrorized aristocrats, destroyed possessions, and burned records in hopes of eliminating their debts. All of France was now engulfed in revolution.

The end of the Old Regime. Many members of the National Assembly believed that the only way to end the violence was to remove the oppression and injustice that caused it. They abolished the special privileges of the First and Second Estates. The Assembly also adopted the Declaration of the Rights of Man and Citizen. Strongly influenced by the English Bill of Rights, the writings of Rousseau, as well as the American Declaration of Independence, this document enshrined the principles of the French Revolution: "liberty, equality, fraternity." In 1791 the National Assembly adopted France's first constitution, which greatly reduced the powers of the king and set up an elected Legislative Assembly.

The new constitution did not entirely represent the ideals of the Declaration of the Rights of Man. In 1791 the playwright and revolutionary Olympe de Gouges wrote *A Declaration of the Rights of Women and Citizenesses* in which she called on the Assembly to extend the same rights to women. The National Assembly, however, would not consider the idea of including women in the political process. They also refused to allow Jews to take public office. By limiting the vote to French men over age 25 who paid a certain amount in taxes, the Assembly placed politics back in the hands of wealthy men. The new government went into effect in October 1791, but lasted less than a year.

The National Assembly based France's new government on Enlightenment principles; however, some groups did not gain political power.

THROUGH OTHERS' EYES

A Lebanese Response to the French Revolution

While much of Europe was in turmoil from the French Revolution, the Ottoman Empire was mostly untroubled by the Christians' problems. As can be seen from historical accounts of the time, many Muslims showed little concern or even interest in what occurred in France. A Lebanese historian known as Nicola Turk wrote this brief account of the revolution in his history of Egypt:

66 We begin with the history of the appearance of the French Republic in the world after they killed their king and this at the beginning of the year 1792 of the Christian era corresponding to the year 1207 of the Islamic hijra. In this year the people of the kingdom of France rose up in their entirety against the king and the princes and the nobles, demanding a new order and a fresh dispensation [arrangement], against the existing order which had been in the time of the king. They claimed and confirmed that the exclusive power of the king had caused great destruction in this kingdom, and that the princes and the nobles were enjoying all the good things of this kingdom while the rest of its people were in misery and abasement [deep poverty]. Because of this they all rose up with one voice and said: 'We shall have no rest save by the abdication of the king and the establishment of a Republic.' And there was a great day in the city of Paris and the king and the rest of the people of his government, princes and nobles, were afraid, and the people came to the king and informed him of their purpose. 99

France at war. As news of these revolutionary events spread across Europe, many of Louis's fellow monarchs were horrified. Louis, his wife Marie Antoinette, and their children soon fled Paris, but they were quickly recognized and returned to their palace under arrest. Marie Antoinette's brother Emperor Leopold II of Austria and King Frederick William II of Prussia

▲ This painting shows one artist's interpretation of the capture and arrest of Louis XVI as he fled Paris in 1791.

issued a declaration calling for the restoration of Louis XVI to power.

In April 1792, with a nearly unanimous vote, the Legislative Assembly voted to declare war on Austria. Soon an army of Austrian and Prussian troops invaded France and headed toward Paris, touching off mass uprisings in the city. A group of radicals seized control of the city government and set up an organization called the Commune. The Commune justly accused Louis XVI of plotting with foreign monarchs. In August troops imprisoned Louis XVI and his family.

Republican France

In late 1792 a National Convention proposed a new constitution, which included **universal manhood suffrage**—the right of all adult men to vote. The National Convention governed France for three years, during which it proclaimed the end of the monarchy and the beginning of a republic. The National Convention found Louis XVI guilty of plotting against the nation. In 1793 Louis was beheaded by the guillotine (GEE-yoh-teen), a new device designed to allow for quick executions.

Meanwhile, the French army not only had stopped the Austrian and Prussian invasion but also had invaded the Austrian Netherlands. The National Convention then declared that the

French armies would spread the Revolution and liberate all the peoples of Europe. In 1793 the entire nation mobilized for war:

66 *Young men shall go forth to battle; married men shall forge weapons and transport munitions; women shall make tents and clothing, and shall serve in hospitals; children will make lint from old linen; and old men shall be brought to public places to arouse the courage of soldiers.* 99

This decision to export the Revolution alarmed all the monarchs of Europe. Great Britain, the Netherlands, Spain, and Sardinia joined with Austria and Prussia to form an alliance, called the First Coalition, against France. They drove French troops out of the Austrian Netherlands and invaded France once more.

The Reign of Terror. Not all of the Revolution's opponents were from outside. Some people still supported the Old Regime. To meet the danger of revolt from within, the National Convention declared a state of emergency and appointed a Committee of Public Safety to coordinate the defense of the new regime. The Committee soon initiated what came to be called the **Reign of Terror**, a brutal program to silence critics of the republic. The Law of Suspects, issued in 1793, defined suspected enemies of the republic:

66 *Those who have shown themselves the enemies of liberty, those who cannot justify their means of existence and the performance of their civic duties, . . . those of the former nobles who have not constantly manifested their attachment to the revolution, and those who have emigrated during the interval between July 1, 1789, to April 8, 1792.* 99

The Reign of Terror lasted for less than a year, but its effects were harsh. A Revolutionary Tribunal quickly arrested, tried, and executed many people simply on mere suspicion. Marie Antoinette was an early victim, but the Reign of

Terror was directed against people from all classes suspected of disloyalty to the Revolution. Georges-Jacques Danton and Maximilien Robespierre (roh-bes-pyer), radical members of the National Convention and the Committee of Public Safety, sent many of their political opponents to the guillotine.

Robespierre carried out a policy of suppression that aroused fear even among his supporters. After ordering the execution of some of his colleagues, however, in July 1794 Robespierre himself was arrested and guillotined. With his death, France's Reign of Terror came to an end.

The Directory. The radicalism of the Reign of Terror inspired efforts

▲ In this engraving Robespierre struggles as his head is forced into the brace of the guillotine.

to make France more politically stable. In 1795 the National Convention drafted yet another constitution. Universal manhood suffrage was eliminated, and only male property owners could vote. The new constitution established an executive branch of five directors, many of whom were corrupt. The government was known as the Directory.

Although the Directory governed France for four years, it pleased almost no one. The directors quarreled among themselves and were unable to agree on many reforms. When they did not do much to improve the overall economic situation, crowds protested. A worker in Paris summed up his feelings: "Under Robespierre blood was spilled and we had bread. Now blood is no longer spilled, and we have no bread. Perhaps we must spill some blood in order to have bread." The Directory soon became as unpopular as the Old Regime, and it too went bankrupt.

In 1799 the directors were dismissed, leaving the way open for change. Troops with bayonets surrounded the legislature and forced most of its members to leave. Those that remained turned the government over to a 30-year-old general, Napoleon Bonaparte, who later remarked, "I found the crown of France lying on the ground, and I picked it up with my sword."

As the French Revolution grew more radical, rulers across Europe tried to restore the monarchy, and the French people adopted a more conservative form of government.

SECTION 4 REVIEW

IDENTIFY and explain the significance of the following:
Louis XVI
Old Regime
Estates General
National Assembly
Tennis Court Oath
universal manhood suffrage
Reign of Terror
Georges-Jacques Danton
Maximilien Robespierre
Napoleon Bonaparte

1. **Main Idea** Why and how did the French Revolution begin?
2. **Main Idea** What were the results of the growing violence of the French Revolution?
3. **Politics and Law** How did revolutionaries in France try to reform the government?
4. **Writing to Create** Imagine that you are a member of the nobility in Europe, watching the events of the French

Revolution unfold. Explain the impact that events in France might have on your life and your outlook. How might you respond?

5. **Synthesizing** How did the revolution change society in France? In answering, consider each of the following groups: (a) the aristocracy and clergy; (b) the middle class; (c) the peasants; and (d) women.

SECTION 4 REVIEW ANSWERS

IDENTIFY
For significance, see the following pages:
Louis XVI (p. 469)
Old Regime (p. 469)
Estates General (p. 470)
National Assembly (p. 470)
Tennis Court Oath (p. 470)
universal manhood suffrage (p. 472)
Reign of Terror (p. 472)
Georges-Jacques Danton (p. 473)
Maximilien Robespierre (p. 473)
Napoleon Bonaparte (p. 473)

1. All three Estates had complaints. Louis XVI convened the Estates General, but the Third Estate proclaimed itself the National Assembly. The people of Paris stormed the Bastille in search of weapons.
2. It led to a conservative reaction. France adopted a conservative government, while European rulers fought to restore the French monarchy.
3. French revolutionaries implemented universal manhood suffrage and established a republic.
4. The nobility might fear the spread of the Revolution. They might provide refuge for fleeing French nobles, or offer funds to fight against the Revolution.
5. The aristocracy and clergy lost rights and privileges. The middle class gained power, including the vote, which they lost again during the Directory. Peasants suffered from food shortages. Women did not gain the right to vote.

The Napoleonic Era

*A*fter the radical Reign of Terror, France longed for a more stable form of government. The French turned to the young, victorious general, Napoleon Bonaparte, to lead them. Within only a few short years, Napoleon had declared France an empire with himself as emperor and had completely reformed French government and society. He used his military genius to expand the French Empire across western Europe. Although the reforms of the Revolution were carried by Napoleon throughout the continent, he failed to unify Europe politically.

The Coronation of Napoleon and Josephine by Jacques-Louis David, 1805–1807

The Napoleonic Empire

BIOGRAPHY A man of overwhelming ambition and domineering personality, Napoleon Bonaparte was one of the greatest military generals of all time. Born in 1769 on the French island of Corsica, Bonaparte trained at military schools in France. Bonaparte's genius lay in his ability to move troops rapidly and to mass forces at critical points on the battlefield. These techniques gave him a decided advantage over his opponents.

Bonaparte had gained experience and fame in the war with Austria. By 1797 he had begun to expand France by seizing territory in northern Italy from the Austrians. The next year, he launched a military expedition to Egypt. However, Horatio Nelson, the British naval leader, cut off the French general and his troops in Egypt. After a year of fierce fighting, Bonaparte finally left his army stranded and returned to France.

Napoleon Bonaparte
BIOGRAPHY

He found the country in a severe state of crisis. Britain, Austria, and Russia had formed a Second Coalition against the French republic. Internal discontent was also reaching a breaking point. When the Directory finally fell in 1799, Bonaparte restored order—then took control of the government himself. Reviving old Roman republican titles, he established the **Consulate**, with himself as First Consul.

By 1804 the First Consul's ambition had grown even more. After conducting a public referendum in which the French people "voted" to declare France an empire, Bonaparte assumed the title of Emperor Napoleon I.

Many people welcomed Napoleon's dictatorship because it promised stability. Napoleon soon reorganized and centralized the administration of France to give himself unlimited power. Under the emperor's direction, scholars revised and reorganized all French law into a system known as the **Napoleonic Code**. Napoleon established a central financial institution, the Bank of France, and his government put into place a public school system through which he hoped to strengthen the French nation by instilling young people with common ideals. In addition, Napoleon established a **meritocracy** in French government. People advanced in government service based upon their merit and abilities, not on wealth or heredity.

Napoleon also eased the strains between the French government and the Catholic Church that had developed because of the Revolution. In 1801 he reached an agreement with the pope. The **Concordat**, as it was called, acknowledged Catholicism as the religion of most French citizens, but it did not abolish the religious toleration guaranteed by the Declaration of the Rights of Man. The church also gave up claims to its property in France.

On the battlefield Napoleon destroyed the Second Coalition against France and won more territory in Italy and along the Rhine River. By the time of his coronation as emperor, Napoleon appeared to have kept his promises to win peace by military victory, achieve steady government, and create economic prosperity.

Napoleon brought stability to French society by enacting many reforms and winning military victories.

The Napoleonic Wars

Napoleon's growing power posed a threat to other European nations. When it became clear that Napoleon's ambition threatened British commerce, Great Britain became Napoleon's greatest enemy. In 1805 Britain renewed the war and, with Austria, Russia, and Sweden, formed the Third Coalition against France. Napoleon planned to crush the British by defeating their navy and invading England. His plans were ruined, however, when Admiral Nelson sank about half the combined French and Spanish fleets near Trafalgar off the Spanish coast.

The Continental System. Napoleon had one more weapon against the British—damaging their trade. Napoleon despised the British, calling them "a nation of shopkeepers." He believed that if the British lost their foreign trade, they would be willing to make peace on his terms. He declared the British Isles to be in a state of blockade. All commerce and all correspondence with Britain was forbidden. This blockade was called the **Continental System** because Napoleon controlled so much of

▲ The British won the sea battle at Trafalgar under Horatio Nelson, who died from wounds received in the fight.

the continent of Europe. The British responded with a blockade of their own. They ordered the ships of neutral nations to stop at British ports to get a license before trading with France or its allies. These policies placed neutral nations in a very awkward position. If they disregarded the British order, the British might capture their ships. If they obeyed, the French might seize their ships.

The Continental System and the British blockade hit the United States particularly hard, for it depended heavily on trade with both Britain and the continent. This conflict, in part, led to the War of 1812 between Great Britain and the United States. Although the British blockade hurt France, Napoleon continued to win battles against the Third Coalition. In December 1805 the French emperor smashed the combined forces of Russia and Austria at Austerlitz north of Vienna. The Third Coalition soon collapsed.

Military victories allowed Napoleon to build a large empire in Europe.

Napoleonic reforms in Europe. By 1806 Napoleon dominated Europe. The French Empire included Belgium, the Netherlands, and portions of Italy. He dismantled the Holy Roman Empire and replaced it with the Confederation of the Rhine, a league of German states with Napoleon as protector. The last Habsburg Holy Roman emperor responded by proclaiming himself emperor of the Austrian Empire. Wherever the French army went, it put the Napoleonic Code into effect. Without intending to do so, the French helped awaken in the people they

The Napoleonic Empire, 1805–1815

Napoleon the Conquerer Through military conquests and diplomatic alliances, Napoleon won control of most of western Europe.

Movement What country blocked Napoleon's eastward progress?

conquered a spirit of **nationalism**—a recognition that they shared a common language, culture, and history.

Although Napoleon ruled most of Europe, time worked on the side of his enemies. The coalition re-formed, and his opponents' armies grew stronger. The generals who opposed him in the field copied his methods of moving and massing troops rapidly.

Napoleon's Downfall

In 1812 Russia and France began making plans for war against each other. Using the largest army Napoleon had ever assembled, the French launched a massive invasion of Russia in 1812. The campaign was doomed from the start. Napoleon's army was immense, more than half a million men. The army was drawn largely from his "allies," however, and perhaps fewer than half the troops were French. In addition, the long distances and shortages of food and supplies weakened Napoleon's army in Russia.

Defeat at Moscow. Napoleon believed that once he had captured Moscow, the Russians would ask for peace. By the time his army arrived in the city, however, the Russians had burned Moscow. As winter approached, Napoleon began withdrawing his troops from Moscow, but the

Literature THROUGH TIME

Grimm's Fairy Tales

When the French were driven out of Germany in 1813, many Germans looked for ways to give the German people a sense of unity. Some intellectuals hoped to restore pride in the German heritage by encouraging Germans to rediscover their literary past. Even during the French occupation, two brothers, Jakob and Wilhelm Grimm, began gathering old legends and folktales from many parts of Germany. They began publishing their work, known as Grimm's Fairy Tales, in 1812 and continued to update the collection throughout their lives. The tales themselves often are versions of stories handed down through many generations. You probably recognize some, such as "Red Riding Hood," "Hansel and Grettel," and "Rapunzel." Below is one of the shorter fairy tales, "The Star-Money."

There was once upon a time a little girl whose father and mother were dead, and she was so poor that she no longer had a room to live in, or bed to sleep in, and at last she had nothing else but the clothes she was wearing and a little bit of bread in her hand which some charitable soul had given her. She was good and pious, however. And as she was thus forsaken by all the world, she went forth into the open country, trusting in the good God. Then a poor man met her, who said: "Ah, give me something to eat, I am so hungry!" She handed him the whole of her piece of bread, and said: "May God bless you," and went onwards. Then came a child who moaned and said: "My head is so cold, give me something to cover it with." So she took off her hood and gave it to him; and when she had walked a little further, she met another child who had no jacket and was frozen with cold. Then she gave it her own; and a little farther on one begged for a frock, and she gave away that also. At length she got into a forest and it had already become dark, and there came yet another child, and asked for a shirt, and the good little girl thought to herself: "It is a dark night and no one sees you, you can very well give your shirt away," and took it off, and gave away that also. And as she so stood, and had not one single thing left, suddenly some stars from heaven fell down, and they were nothing else but hard smooth pieces of money, and although she had just given her shirt away, she had a new one which was of the very finest linen. Then she put the money into it, and was rich all the days of her life.

Understanding Literature

Why might many Germans have enjoyed reading stories handed down from German folklore?

Jakob and Wilhelm Grimm

---

bitter winter weather and the pursuing Russian troops destroyed Napoleon's once proud army. Only about 100,000 men survived. One soldier described the retreat across Russia:

66 The carriages, drawn by tired and underfed horses, were traveling fourteen and fifteen hours of the twenty-four. . . . Having left Moscow with us, . . . [the carriages] had had to take up the men wounded. . . . They were put on the top-seats of the carts. . . . At the least jolt those who were most insecurely placed fell; the drivers took no care. The driver following . . . for fear of stopping and losing his place . . . would drive pitilessly on over the body of the wretch who had fallen. 99

SECTION 5 REVIEW ANSWERS (p. 478)

IDENTIFY
For significance, see the following pages:
Horatio Nelson (p. 474)
Consulate (p. 474)
Napoleonic Code (p. 474)
meritocracy (p. 475)
Concordat (p. 475)
Continental System (p. 475)
nationalism (p. 476)
Hundred Days (p. 478)
the Duke of Wellington (p. 478)

LOCATE
For locations, see the map on p. 476.

1. Napoleon enacted reforms in France and won military victories.
2. Napoleon maintained control through military conquests and diplomatic alliances.
3. Russia's distant location made obtaining supplies difficult, and troops suffered from food shortages and the bitterly cold climate.
4. Reasons in support include the crushing of European armies and the dismantling of the Holy Roman Empire. Reasons in opposition include the use of standardized law under the Napoleonic Code and the awakening of nationalism.
5. The Napoleonic Code standardized all French law. The Concordat smoothed over conflict between the Roman Catholic Church and the French government. The meritocracy brought talented people into government service.

As Napoleon once again abandoned his struggling men and returned to France to raise more troops, Prussia and Austria seized the chance to form a new coalition with Russia. The coalition attacked and defeated Napoleon at Leipzig in Germany. Meanwhile, in the southwest, British forces based in Portugal defeated Napoleon's Spanish allies and swept north over the Pyrenees. With his enemies closing in, Napoleon gathered his forces to fight one last campaign northeast of Paris in the spring of 1814. Allied armies of Britain, Austria, Russia, and Prussia soundly defeated him. In April Napoleon abdicated and went into exile on the island of Elba, off the Italian coast.

After 25 years of changing governments and near-constant warfare, France was exhausted. Napoleon's former foreign minister, Charles-Maurice de Talleyrand, took charge of restoring the Bourbon dynasty to the throne. Louis XVIII, a brother of the beheaded Louis XVI, issued a constitution to please the French people. When he soon reverted to the old authoritarian ways of his family, however, discontent in France grew.

▲ This picture captures the misery of the French army as they tried to make their way back to France after defeat at Moscow.

The Hundred Days. In early March 1815 Napoleon escaped from exile in Elba and, with a small force, marched toward Paris. Along the way he was welcomed by throngs of supporters. The French army units sent to stop him joined him instead. As Napoleon entered Paris in triumph, Louis XVIII fled into exile. So began Napoleon's final effort to restore the empire, a period known as the **Hundred Days**.

The allies who had fought to defeat the emperor the previous year rapidly massed their troops together in Belgium, north of France. Near the tiny village of Waterloo, the British commander, the Duke of Wellington, with the crucial aid of Prussian forces, soundly crushed Napoleon's army, thus bringing the Hundred Days to an end. As the Bourbons returned to power once more, the British exiled Napoleon to the South Atlantic island of St. Helena, where he lived until his death in 1821.

Before his downfall, Napoleon carried his reforms to other nations and inspired feelings of nationalism across the continent.

SECTION 5 REVIEW

IDENTIFY and explain the significance of the following:
- Horatio Nelson
- Consulate
- Napoleonic Code
- meritocracy
- Concordat
- Continental System
- nationalism
- Hundred Days
- the Duke of Wellington

LOCATE and explain the importance of the following:
- Trafalgar
- Elba
- Waterloo

1. **Main Idea** How did Napoleon strengthen France?
2. **Main Idea** How was Napoleon able to dominate Europe?
3. **Geography: Place** How did Russia's geography affect Napoleon's invasion?
4. **Writing to Persuade** Write a brief essay agreeing or disagreeing with the following statement: *Napoleon's conquest of Europe was a catastrophic event in European history.* Be sure to give examples to support your answer.
5. **Synthesizing** How did Napoleon reform French society? Consider the following in your answer: (a) the Napoleonic Code; (b) the Concordat; and (c) the establishment of the meritocracy.

Review

On a separate sheet of paper, complete the following exercises:

WRITING A SUMMARY

Using the essential points in the text, write a brief summary of the chapter.

REVIEWING TERMS

From the following list, choose the term that correctly matches the definition.

philosophes
National Assembly
Navigation Acts
Declaration of Independence
Continental System
natural law

1. Napoleon's strategy to destroy Britain's commerce
2. group composed of delegates of the Third Estate and some delegates of the First Estate
3. thinkers in the Enlightenment
4. idea that a system of laws governs the universe
5. document adopted on July 4, 1776, declaring the British colonies of North America free from British rule

REVIEWING CHRONOLOGY

List the following events in their correct chronological order.

1. Citizens of Paris storm the fortress of the Bastille.
2. The Seven Years' War breaks out.
3. The Treaty of Paris is signed, ending the American War of Independence.
4. Angry colonists throw a shipment of British tea into Boston Harbor.
5. Napoleon's army is defeated at the Battle of Waterloo.

UNDERSTANDING THE MAIN IDEA

1. How did Napoleon transform European society?
2. What was the Enlightenment?
3. Why can the Seven Years' War be called a "global war"?
4. What factors contributed to the British colonies of North America winning their independence?
5. How did the Enlightenment influence the American and the French Revolutions?
6. What were the causes of the French Revolution?

THINKING CRITICALLY

1. **Comparing and Contrasting** How was the French Revolution similar to the American Revolution? How were the outcomes of the two events different? What accounted for the difference?
2. **Distinguishing Fact from Opinion** Write a paragraph explaining why the following statement is only partially correct: *Napoleon's conquest of Europe liberated many subject peoples.*

Building Your Portfolio

Complete the following activities individually or in groups.

1. **French Revolution** Write a play about the French Revolution. You may choose to cover the entire Revolution or focus on one or more important events. In your play, be sure to cast the most important historical characters from the events you choose. You should also include narration, so that your audience will understand the background behind the scenes. If you are working in a group, you may also perform your play for the class. You might want to create some scenery, props, and simple costumes to enhance the performance.

2. **Military Campaigns** Imagine that you are a soldier or an observer traveling with either Napoleon's army in Europe or George Washington's army in North America. Create a journal describing your experiences on one or more long military campaigns. In your journal, also include some ideas of what your army is fighting for and what goals your general hopes to accomplish. With your journal also include a detailed map, showing the routes you and your army have traveled. Include the names of important cities, geographical landmarks, and battles on your map.

6. Causes include the desire of all groups to gain more power. The First and Second Estates wanted to wrest power from the king. The middle classes of the Third Estate wanted the political power to match their economic strength, while peasants wanted food and freedom from crushing taxes. The trigger of the Revolution was the calling of the Estates General, which resulted in the formation of the National Assembly and the fall of the Bastille.

THINKING CRITICALLY

1. Similarities include the desires to broaden political participation and to achieve more social equality. The American Revolution resulted in a new state, founded on Enlightenment principles, whose basic structure would remain intact for more than 200 years. The French Revolution resulted in upheaval, as France went to war, experienced the First Republic, the Reign of Terror, and the conservative reaction of the Directory before handing over power to Napoleon. In America the enemy was a distant power, while in France, elements of the Old Regime remained in place.
2. The Napoleonic Code across Europe abolished serfdom, but these peoples lived under the rule of the French, instead of their own local rulers.

Unit 5
Expansion of the Modern World 1700–1914

Chapter 18

The Industrial Revolution in the West 1700–1914

During the Industrial Revolution, mechanical power replaced muscle power as the primary energy source, which gave rise to a whole new way of life in western Europe and elsewhere. How might the shift from an agricultural society to an industrial one change the way that people interact with each other?

Chapter 19

An Era of Expansion and Reform 1765–1914

Inspired by new ideals and the French Revolution, people in Europe and the Americas began to demand political and economic changes to solve the problems arising from the Industrial Revolution. What social and political circumstances might inspire people to seek reform?

As the Industrial Revolution spread from its origin in Great Britain to western Europe and the United States, a whole new way of life began to emerge. Although industrialization brought improvements to some people's lives, it also created new problems, which only great reforms could resolve. Inspired by Enlightenment ideals and the French Revolution, reformers began to demand political and economic changes. Liberals demanded constitutions that guaranteed individual rights, while in colonized countries nationalists fought for the right to govern themselves. These ideals also made their way to Latin America, where colonists declared independence from Spain and Portugal. At the same time, European empire-building in Asia and Africa reached new heights.

Chapter 20

Nation-States and Empires in Europe
1814–1914

In the aftermath of the Napoleonic Era in Europe, conflict between monarchs and their subjects erupted as liberals demanded constitutions that guaranteed individual rights. During this same period nationalists fought for an end to imperial rule. What conflicts might arise between demands for political stability and calls for political reform?

Chapter 21

The Imperial World Order 1757–1914

The great Western industrial powers came to dominate the world as trading empires expanded into empires of occupation. How might the establishment of an overseas colonial empire affect both the colonial rulers and their subject peoples?

Chapter 20
Nation-States and Empires in Europe

Leaders who desire political stability might want to prevent any kinds of changes. These leaders might want to prevent reforms that would open up the political system to more people, regulations that would improve working conditions, or any sort of revolutionary activity designed to overthrow their rule. This might bring them into contact with people who believe that there is a great need for political, economic, or social change.

Chapter 21
The Imperial World Order

An overseas colonial empire might bring the colonial rulers great wealth and power. It might also provide them with raw materials for their industries, a cheap labor force for plantations and factories, and a market for manufactured goods. However, an overseas empire might also be quite expensive, for the colonial rulers might have to invest heavily in a strong military to defend their empire from outsiders. In addition, an overseas colonial empire might destroy or otherwise harm the culture of the subject peoples, but it might also carry with it material benefits and Western-style education.

Chapter 18

The Industrial Revolution in the West 1700–1914

Chapter Planning Guide

	TEXTBOOK	CORE RESOURCES	VISUAL RESOURCES	MULTIMEDIA
Introduction	pp. 482–483	Block Scheduling Handbook: Ch. 18		Videodisc Segment 18 and Viewing Guide: *The Industrial Revolution*
Lesson 18.1 The First Industrial Revolution	pp. 484–491 Geography and History: *Britain's First Factories,* pp. 488–489 Author's Commentary: *Old Methods, New Uses,* p. 491	Reading 18.1: *Resistance to Enclosure* Skills Activity 18: *The Industrial Revolution in the West*	Everyday Life 18: *Traditional Farming Methods* Geography and History 18: *Land Enclosures in England*	GHRC 18 Readings: *Jethro Tull Invents the Seed Drill; The Birth of the Factory System; The Development of the Steam Engine*
Lesson 18.2 Consequences of Industrialization	pp. 492–496 Map: *Population Growth in Britain,* p. 493 Literature Through Time: *Hard Times,* p. 494	Reading 18.2: *A Working Day in a Manchester Cotton Mill* Geography Activity 18: *Manchester: The Growth of an Industrial Giant*		GHRC 18 Readings: *Elizabeth Browning; The Middle Class in Rural England* GHRC 18/Videodiscs: Images— *Spindle Boys in a Cotton Mill; Women Making Cartridges;* Map—*Growth of London*
Lesson 18.3 The Second Industrial Revolution	pp. 497–500 Through Others' Eyes: *A Chinese Response to Western Technology,* p. 499 Graph: *Output of Manufactured Products,* p. 500	Reading 18.3: *The First Flight Across the English Channel* Writing Project 18: *Writing an Editorial*	Art and History 18: *The Gare Saint-Lazare, Paris*	GHRC 18 Reading: *Bigness in Business* GHRC 18/Videodiscs: Image— *An American Railway Scene by Currier and Ives;* Maps— *European Industrialization; Railroads Link British Industries*
Lesson 18.4 Changes in Western Culture and Society	pp. 501–506 History Through the Arts: *Photography,* p. 504	Reading 18.4: *Defining Women's Roles*		GHRC 18 Readings: *Charlotte Bronte; Going to the Theatre in Victorian England; Darwin on Discovering Natural Selection; Friedrich Engels on the Industrial City; The Romantics; William Wordsworth* GHRC 18/Videodiscs: Images— *Parlor of a Well-to-Do Family; The Great International Exhibition of 1851; Albert Bierstadt's Romantic View of Nature; The Greatest Show on Earth; Realism in Art; Victorian Exercise Machine*
Chapter Investigation and Enrichment	pp. 482–506	Chapter 18 Investigation: *The Great Exposition* People in World History 18 Explorations in Daily Life 18		GHRC 18/Videodiscs
Review and Assessment	Section 1 Review, p. 491 Section 2 Review, p. 496 Section 3 Review, p. 500 Section 4 Review, p. 506 Chapter 18 Review, p. 507	Chapter Review Activity 18 Vocabulary Activity 18 Themes Review 18 Section Study Guides 18.1–18.4 Main Idea Activities 18.1–18.4 Daily Quizzes 18.1–18.4 Chapter 18 Test Sheltered English Ch. 18 Test Ch. 18 Test Generator		Audio CDs: Ch. 18 Summary (English and Spanish)

INTRODUCING THE CHAPTER

Textbook pp. 482–483

CHAPTER OVERVIEW

New technologies brought economic and social changes to Western Europe. The new modes of transportation were faster and cheaper. Improved farming techniques led to more food and increased populations. The demands of industrialization also led to tremendous urban growth. The enormous wealth generated by these changes was not well distributed. The expanding middle class benefited, but the gap between the rich and poor grew. Among the responses to this rapidly changing world were romanticism and realism.

PRESENTING THEMES

On the chalkboard or on an overhead transparency, write the following open-ended theme questions.

- **SOCIAL RELATIONS** How might the shift from an agricultural society to an industrial society change the way people interact?
- **TECHNOLOGY** How might changes in technology change the way people work?
- **ECONOMIC ORGANIZATION** What effects might technological developments have on businesses?

Have students, either individually or in groups, suggest responses to the questions. For the social relations question, students might suggest that the switch to an industrialized society would lead to the loss of traditional ties. For the technology question, students might suggest that new machinery might demand workers with special training. For the economic organization question, students might suggest that technological developments might require businesses to become larger. Save the responses. Once students have studied the chapter, you may wish to have them complete the Themes Review, then compare the two sets of answers.

USING THE VIDEO

Segment 18: *The Industrial Revolution*

ENGLISH

Search Chapter 18
Videodisc 2, Side A

SPANISH

Search Chapter 18
Videodisc 2, Side A

Tell students that in this chapter they will examine the new ways of life that emerged during the Industrial Revolution. Then show Segment 18 of the *World History and Cultures Videodiscs*. This segment uses archival film footage to illustrate how the development and spread of new machine-driven technologies changed Western society.

Before showing the segment, ask students to pay particular attention to the effects of machines on the nature, location, and pace of work in the newly industrialized societies. To help students grasp the significant points of the segment, have them complete Video Viewing Guide 18.

Key to Ability Levels

All strategies and activities are coded to the following ability levels:

LEVEL 1	**Basic** activities suitable for all students
LEVEL 2	**Average** activities suitable for average to above-average students
LEVEL 3	**Challenging** activities suitable for above-average students
SHELTERED ENGLISH	Activities suitable for students with **Limited English Proficiency**

Additional Resources

BOOKS FOR TEACHERS

O'Brien, Patrick and Roland Quinalt, eds. *The Industrial Revolution and British Society.* Cambridge University Press, 1993. Discusses social changes.

Sale, Kirkpatrick. *Rebels Against the Future.* Addison-Wesley, 1995. Presents a history of the Luddites.

Stearns, Peter. *Interpreting the Industrial Revolution.* American Historical Association, 1991. Analyzes industrial growth.

BOOKS FOR STUDENTS

Graber, David. *The Industrial Revolution: Technological and Social Change in Europe and the United States.* Mark Twain Media/Carson Dellosa, 1995. Includes activities, maps, and a chronology.

Shelston, Dorothy and Alan Shelston. *The Industrial City, 1820–1870.* Humanities Press, 1990. Examines changes wrought by industrialization in urban settings.

Tilly, Louise A. and Joan W. Scott. *Women, Work and Family.* Routledge, 1987. Focuses on French and English women during the Industrial Revolution.

MULTIMEDIA MATERIALS

Art and Music: Romanticism. ZCI. CD-ROM, MAC, WIN, MPC formats. Immerses users in the romantic period.

The Industrial Revolution. New York Times. Video, 23 min. Looks at child labor and urban slums.

The Industrial Revolution. ZCI. CD-ROM, MAC, WIN, MPC formats. Examines the causes and effects of the Industrial Revolution.

Lesson 18.1   The First Industrial Revolution

Textbook pp. 484–491

RESOURCES

Pupil's Edition

Geography and History,
  pp. 488–489: *Britain's First Factories*
Author's Commentary, p. 491:
  Old Methods, New Uses

Core Resources

Reading 18.1: *Resistance to Enclosure*

Visual Resources

Everyday Life 18: *Traditional Farming
  Methods*
Geography and History 18: *Land
  Enclosures in England*

Global History Resource Center

Reading: *Jethro Tull Invents the Seed
  Drill*
Reading: *The Birth of the Factory
  System*
Reading: *The Development of the Steam
  Engine*

LESSON FOCUS

How did natural resources, new technology, and the movement of people help to bring about the first Industrial Revolution, and why did it begin in Britain?

OBJECTIVES

After completing this lesson, students will be able to:

- explain why the Industrial Revolution began in Britain;
- identify the consequences of the Agricultural Revolution;
- explain how rising demand and new technology affected the textile industry;
- identify the basic elements of the first Industrial Revolution.

HOOK

Examine the factors that made Britain an ideal location for the start of the Industrial Revolution. Begin by asking students what ideas come to mind when they hear the term *revolution*. *[Possible answers include the overthrow of govern-ments, wars, or rebellions.]* Point out that a common factor in any revolution is change. Revolutions may result in political, social, or economic changes.

Ask: **What kind of changes occurred to justify calling the Industrial Revolution a revolution?**
  [economic change from agricultural to industrial society; social change from rural to urban society]

Refer students to the Geography and History feature.
Ask: **What factors made Britain ideal for the start of the Industrial Revolution?**

[waterways, good supply of coal and iron, large overseas empire, rising population, demand for goods, stable government, property rights protected]

Next instruct students to design a cluster diagram with *Industrialization in Britain* as the center and the factors they identified above as the spokes. Next to each spoke have students write why the factor was important to industrialization. You may wish to have students place their finished charts in their portfolios.

DEVELOP

Identify causes and effects of the Agricultural Revolution in Britain. Display Everyday Life Transparency 18 and have students complete the accompanying worksheet.

Ask: **Does this picture illustrate farming before or after the Agricultural Revolution? Why?**
  [Before the Industrial Revolution—the fields are not enclosed, and the technology is basic.]

If available, have students study the Global History Resource Center reading on Jethro Tull to investigate how improvements in farm equipment influenced the Agricultural Revolution.

Ask: **What factors led to changes in farming methods?**
  [Discovery of new crops and improvements in farm methods and equipment made farming more profitable, which encouraged the enclosure of more and more land.]

To further students' understanding of how the enclosure movement affected agriculture in Britain, display Geography and History Transparency 18. Then have students complete the worksheet for Geography and History Transparency 18 and study Core Resources Reading 18.1.

Then have students discuss the enclosure movement and how it helped pave the way for industrialization in Britain. Students should recognize that enclosing common lands forced some farmers to find work in cities, thus providing labor for factories. The enclosure movement also made farming a profitable business, thus providing landowners with money to invest in industries.

PROBE

Explore how the factory system transformed the textile industry in Britain. Tell students that Marilyn Kluger's *The Joy of Spinning* (Simon & Schuster, 1971) explains that it took five people spinning for an entire workday to produce enough thread for one day's weaving. Then refer students to the description of the silk factory in the Geography and History feature on textbook page 488.

Ask: How did production of thread in a factory differ from production of thread by spinners at home?
[Factories used waterwheels to power the spinning machines. They could produce a far greater quantity of thread than a person could produce at home.]

If available, have students complete the Global History Resource Center reading about the birth of the factory system.

CONCLUDE

Identify the basic elements of the first Industrial Revolution. On the chalkboard, write the headings *Problems, Solutions,* and *Problem Solvers.* Under *Problems,* write the words *Lack of wood to supply charcoal for iron production.* Next write students' responses under the appropriate headings on the chalkboard. *[coke made from coal replaced charcoal, Abraham Darby]* Then have students fill in additional problems, solutions, and problem solvers, using material from textbook pages 490–491. *[water in mines, steam-driven pump, Thomas Savery, Thomas Newcomen; steam engine's excessive fuel demands, more efficient engine, James Watt; demand for more and better iron, steam-driven rolling mills, Henry Cort; increased demand for cotton, cotton gin, Eli Whitney]*
Ask: Why were steam power and iron essential to the first Industrial Revolution?

[Students should conclude that machines were built from iron and that steam powered the machines.]

If available, have interested students complete the Global History Resource Center reading on the development of the steam engine and report to the class on what they learned.

EXTEND

Cross-Curricular Connection: *Science*
Link to Today. Have students research and report on various agricultural methods practiced today. Possible topics include crop rotation, genetically engineered crops, or organic farming.

MEET INDIVIDUAL NEEDS

Gifted Students
Refer students to the author's commentary on textbook page 491. Ask them to research and report on the technological advances in India, France, Switzerland, China, Germany, and Italy that influenced British industrialization.

Students Having Difficulty/Students Acquiring English
Have students work in pairs to outline the lesson and then sequence it by creating flowcharts. One flowchart should sequence events leading to Britain's industrialization, while another should show the major events and effects of the Agricultural Revolution.

Kinesthetic Learners
Have students create two collages, one representing aspects of an agricultural economy, and the other, aspects of an industrial economy. For ideas, students may refer to graphics in their textbook, images from the Global History Resource Center and the *World History and Cultures Videodiscs,* and library books on the Industrial Revolution and Britain in the 1800s.

ASSESS

Review
Have students complete the Section 1 Review. Use answers in the Teacher's Edition, page 491, to assess student mastery of this section.

Lesson 18.2 Consequences of Industrialization

Textbook pp. 492–496

RESOURCES

Pupil's Edition

Map, p. 493: *Population Growth in Britain, 1751–1851*

Literature Through Time, p. 494: *Hard Times*

Core Resources

Reading 18.2: *A Working Day in a Manchester Cotton Mill*

Geography Activity 18: *Manchester: The Growth of an Industrial Giant*

Global History Resource Center

Reading: *Elizabeth Browning: "The Cry of the Children"*

Reading: *The Middle Class in Rural England*

Videodiscs or Global History Resource Center

Map: *Growth of London, 1600–1900*

Search Frame 927

Image: *Spindle Boys in a Cotton Mill*

Search Frame 916

Image: *Women Making Cartridges*

Search Frame 917

LESSON FOCUS

How did the social and political consequences of industrialization impact the lives of workers?

OBJECTIVES

After completing this lesson, students will be able to:

- identify some of the social consequences of industrialization;
- contrast the political theories that emerged in the industrial era;
- describe workers' responses to industrialization.

HOOK

Explore the social consequences of industrialization. Tell students that young children often worked long hours in coal mines during the Industrial Revolution. Then tell them about some of the tasks children working in the coal mines performed. Nicolas Bentley's *The Victorian Scene* (George Weidenfeld & Nicolson, 1968) mentions that children as young as five worked in some mines. Some of the very young children were charged with scaring the rats away from their fathers' food. Other children were used to pull the coal trucks through passages that were too small for a man to pass through. Still others had to stand in ankle-deep water for hours working the pumps. Others, sitting alone and in the dark, controlled the ventilator openings.

Work with students to identify other social consequences of industrialization. Begin by referring students to the map on textbook page 493 depicting the dramatic growth of population in industrialized areas. To further illustrate this development, display the electronic media map showing the growth of London. After discussing urbanization, ask students for other consequences and list their responses on the chalkboard. Then ask students to categorize each consequence as positive or negative. **[positive: *improved standard of living for workers and middle class; availability of goods and leisure activities;* negative: *miserable conditions in cities; unemployment in rural areas*]**

DEVELOP

Contrast political theories that emerged in the industrial era. Organize students into three groups and assign each group one of the following political theories: liberalism, utilitarianism, or socialism. Instruct groups to determine what goals their assigned theory emphasized and to whom it appealed. Each group should be ready to answer the following question based on the theory they studied: *What should be the role of government in society?*

Then have students form groups of three, consisting of one member of each original group. Members of the new groups should discuss the role of government in society from the contrasting viewpoints of liberals, utilitarians, and socialists.

[liberals: government should ensure equal treatment for all under the law; utilitarians: government should have limited power and be fully democratic; socialists: government should control the means of production and provide economic as well as political equality]

PROBE

Describe workers' responses to industrialization. Direct students' attention to the Literature Through Time feature on textbook page 494, and have them examine Core Resources Reading 18.2. If available, you may also wish to have students view the electronic media images showing spindle boys in a cotton mill and women making cartridges and read Elizabeth Browning's poem in the Global History Resource Center.

Then discuss working conditions in the early 1800s. Ask students to imagine that they are members of a trade union during that era. Have them make strike placards listing their grievances. Students might display their placards as they portray workers in a general walkout.

CONCLUDE

Categorize the effects of industrialization. Begin by asking students how industrialization affected people's lives. To elicit answers to the question, write these categories on the chalkboard: *Family Life, Work, Standard of Living, Personal Freedoms.* Have students identify and list changes for each category. [Possible answers include: **Family Life**: family members no longer worked together, children no longer learned adult jobs by watching family members work; **Work**: people worked outside their homes, machines did the work once done by people; **Standard of Living**: people had more goods, plentiful crops produced healthier people; **Personal Freedoms**: people moved from place to place and had more choices]

Then have students use the lists as a basis for writing newspaper headlines about both the negative and positive aspects of life in industrialized England. Sample headlines include: *Pollution Blackens City of London; Cholera Epidemic Erupts; Free Concert in the Park Today.*

You may wish to assign Geography Activity 18 at this time.

EXTEND

Cross-Curricular Connection: *U.S. History*
Have students research and report on the first factory in the United States—the textile mill set up in Rhode Island by Samuel Slater.

Cross-Curricular Connection: *Language Arts*
Suggest that students examine *Hard Times* and/or other works by Charles Dickens to find out how his writings reflected the consequences of industrialization. Students might role-play Dickens's characters and share excerpts of his works with the class.

MEET INDIVIDUAL NEEDS
Gifted Students
Link to Today. Have students compare the consequences of technological advances during the Industrial Revolution with the consequences of technology today. Encourage students to brainstorm technologies we have today that we did not have 20 years ago and describe the consequences. Examples include technological advances in computers and software; technologies that replace the need for human workers; and technologies that lessen dependence on certain resources.

Students Acquiring English
Pair students acquiring English with students who are proficient in English. Have the pairs of students work together to answer the focus questions on page 492 of their textbook.

ASSESS
Review
Have students complete the Section 2 Review. Use answers in the Teacher's Edition, page 496, to assess student mastery of this section.

Lesson 18.3   The Second Industrial Revolution

Textbook pp. 497–500

RESOURCES

Pupil's Edition

Through Others' Eyes, p. 499:
A Chinese Response to Western Technology

Graph, p. 500: *Output of Manufactured Products: 1750–1913*

Core Resources

Reading 18.3: *The First Flight Across the English Channel*

Visual Resources

Art and History 18: *The Gare Saint-Lazare, Paris*

Global History Resource Center

Reading: *Andrew Carnegie Defends Bigness in Business*

Videodiscs or Global History Resource Center

Image: *An American Railway Scene by Currier and Ives*

Search Frame 918

Map: *Railroads Link British Industries, c. 1850*

Search Frame 929

Map: *European Industrialization, mid-1800s*

Search Frame 928

LESSON FOCUS

What changes took place during the second Industrial Revolution, and why were these changes late in coming to France, Germany, and Russia?

OBJECTIVES

After completing this lesson, students will be able to:

- explain how the steam engine affected transportation;
- identify the foundations and consequences of the second Industrial Revolution;
- explain the results of new business practices in the late 1800s;
- analyze why industrialization was delayed in France, Germany, and Russia.

HOOK

Investigate how the steam engine improved transportation. Begin by displaying the electronic media image showing an American railway scene and Art and History Transparency 18.

Ask: Why do you think trains were popular subjects for artists in the 1800s?
[their power and novelty]

Ask: What feelings do the pictures suggest?
[Possible answers include awe and respect.]

Ask: How did railroads change people's lives?
[Railroads could quickly and cheaply move people and goods across long distances.]

Ask: What advances in technology made this revolution in transportation possible?
[steam engine, steel rails]

Have students examine Core Resources Reading 18.3 to discover how developments in transportation influenced ideas about distance. You might also wish to have students study the electronic media map showing railroads in Britain around 1850.

DEVELOP

Chart developments in industrialization and determine the impact of the second Industrial Revolution. Work with the class to make a chart showing developments that characterized the second Industrial Revolution. Write on the chalkboard the headings *Transportation, Electricity and Communications, Steel and Petroleum,* and *Other Industries*.
Ask: What kinds of engines revolutionized transportation?
[the steam engine and the internal combustion engine]

Write students' responses under the *Transportation* heading.

Ask: What impact did each development have?

> [The steam engine powered trains and steamships over long distances in less time; the internal combustion engine produced greater power, was more convenient, and powered trains, cars, and planes.]

Have students complete the chart by naming developments that characterized the second Industrial Revolution for each category. [**Electricity and Communications**: *dynamo, electric motor, electric lighting, telegraph, telephones, radio signals;* **Steel and Petroleum**: *the Bessemer, open-hearth, and Gilchrist-Thomas processes, internal combustion engine, automobiles, airplanes;* **Other Industries**: *chemical advances, civil engineering techniques]*

Ask: What were some of the effects of these developments?

> [Long-distance transportation and communication, new textile dyes, medicines, fertilizers, bridges, and canals.]

PROBE

Explain the results of new business practices in the late 1800s. Ask students why steel manufacturing and the oil business were controlled by large business organizations. *[They were very costly businesses and too expensive for individual ownership.]*

Help students understand the growth of big business by asking volunteers to define the following terms: *corporation [business owned by stockholders, who had limited liability for debts]*, *monopoly [business that controlled the sale and production of a product]*, and *trust [combination of similar businesses under the direction of one group].*

Discuss with students why businesses organized in these ways. Students should understand that consolidation made it possible to produce goods more efficiently and at lower cost. Consolidation also decreased competition, because large businesses could afford to temporarily lower prices to drive smaller businesses out of a market.

If available, have students read Andrew Carnegie's defense of big business in the Global History Resource Center. They might compare Carnegie's views with those of Wei Yuan in the Through Others' Eyes feature on textbook page 499.

CONCLUDE

Report on why Germany, France, and Russia lagged behind Britain in industrialization. Organize the class into three groups, and assign each group one of these nations: France, Germany, or Russia. Give groups about 10 minutes to prepare oral reports describing industrialization in their assigned nation, using the textbook as a resource. Students might also examine the electronic media map on European industrialization. Have groups report their findings to the class.

Next direct students' attention to the graph on textbook page 500. Ask them to draw conclusions about industrialization in the United States. *[Students should conclude that by 1900 the growth of big business enabled the United States to surpass other industrialized nations in output of manufactured goods.]*

EXTEND

Cross-Curricular Connection: *Language Arts*
Have students read a biography of Nikola Tesla, Thomas Edison, Alexander Graham Bell, or Gugliemo Marconi. Then have them prepare a report on what they learned. You may wish to share some of the most informative ones with the class.

MEET INDIVIDUAL NEEDS

Students Having Difficulty/Students Acquiring English
Have students prepare two flowcharts, one showing developments in the transportation revolution, and the other, developments in the communications revolution. Ask students to sequence the main developments, and describe the effects of each.

Kinesthetic Learners
Kinesthetic learners might enjoy constructing simple radiotelegraphs. Or they might like to learn Morse code and use it to communicate with friends (fingertaps can also convey Morse code).

ASSESS

Review
Have students complete the Section 3 Review. Use answers in the Teacher's Edition, page 500, to assess student mastery of this section.

Lesson 18.4   *Changes in Western Culture and Society*

Textbook pp. 501–506

RESOURCES

Pupil's Edition
History Through the Arts, p. 504: *Photography*

Core Resources
Reading 18.4: *Defining Women's Roles*

Global History Resource Center
Reading: *Charlotte Bronte: Inside the Crystal Palace*
Reading: *Going to the Theatre in Victorian England*
Reading: *Darwin on Discovering Natural Selection*

Reading: *Friedrich Engels on the Industrial City*
Reading: *The Romantics*
Reading: *William Wordsworth: A Romantic on Nature*

Videodiscs or Global History Resource Center

Image: *Parlor of a Well-to-Do Washington Family*

Search Frame 922

Image: *Albert Bierstadt's Romantic View of Nature*

Search Frame 925

Image: *Realism in Art:* Paris *by Caillebotte*

Search Frame 926

Image: *The Great International Exhibition of 1851*

Search Frame 919

Image: *The Greatest Show on Earth*

Search Frame 921

Image: *Ad for a Victorian Exercise Machine*

Search Frame 923

LESSON FOCUS
How did industrialization affect trends and developments in popular culture, the sciences and social sciences, and the arts?

OBJECTIVES
After completing this lesson, students will be able to:
- identify how wealth provided by the Industrial Revolution affected the middle class;
- discuss how scientific developments affected the social sciences;
- explain how romanticism and realism were reactions to industrialization.

HOOK
Discuss the new affluence of the middle class during the industrial era. If possible, have students view the electronic media image of the parlor, which shows the fussy interior design that is so characteristic of the period. Tell students that it was the height of fashion for a parlor to be crammed with knickknacks and for furniture to be decorated with ruffles and crocheted antimacassars, or protective covers.

Next have students read Bronte's description of the Crystal Palace from the Global History Resource Center. Then discuss with students how the Industrial Revolution affected the life style of middle-class families. Students should understand that not only were more goods being produced but that the rising middle class had the money to buy these goods.

DEVELOP
Discuss "the new society" created by industrialization. Have students complete Core Resources Reading 18.4. Then discuss the idea of separate spheres with them.
Ask: *What assumptions does the writer make about the proper role for women?*
[Women were solely responsible for everything that went

*into maintaining a home and family and were eager to
assume this responsibility.]*

Ask: *Within this sphere, were women expected to work just
as hard as men?*
  *[Yes, and they were expected to show just as much
  managerial ability and business acumen.]*

Ask: *What kind of work outside the home was considered to
be within women's sphere?*
  *[Nursing and teaching were acceptable because these
  jobs were seen by some as an extension of women's
  domestic roles.]*

If available, have students examine the selection on the theater
and the last three electronic media images for more information
about middle-class leisure.

PROBE

**Discuss how scientific advances influenced the social
sciences.** Write these names on the chalkboard: *Gregor Mendel,
Charles Darwin, John Dalton, Henri Becquerel, Marie Curie.*
Ask: *What contributions did these scientists make?*
  *[Mendel pioneered genetics; Darwin developed the theory
  of evolution; Dalton discovered the atomic nature of
  matter; Becquerel discovered radioactivity; Marie Curie
  applied X-rays to medical diagnosis and helped discover
  polonium and radium.]*

Ask: *How did these scientific advances influence the way
people viewed and studied society?*
  *[They reinforced people's belief that problems were
  solvable, and some people sought to apply the scientific
  method to the study of society.]*

Ask: *What were some problems associated with the new
social sciences?*
  *[Sometimes "science"—particularly the study of
  heredity—was used to reinforce racial prejudices.]*

You may wish to have students read more about Darwin and
Engels in the Global History Resource Center. Then have
students form small groups and create simple charts describing
how Galton, Spencer, and Marx and Engels applied the new
scientific ideas to the study of society. **[Galton:** *eugenics;* **Spencer:**
social Darwinism; **Marx and Engels:** *scientific socialism]*

CONCLUDE

**Use art and literature to explore reactions to indus-
trialization.** Have students read the History Through the Arts
feature about photography. If available, have them examine the
electronic media images of romanticism and realism, and the
readings on the romantics and on Wordsworth.
Ask: *How did realism differ from romanticism?*
  *[Romanticism idealized nature, reveled in emotions, and
  was a reaction against urbanization and industrialization.
  Realism focused on the everyday realities of life in the
  modern world and was a reaction to romanticism.]*

Link to Today. Ask volunteers to discuss their reactions to
what they have learned about industrialism and its effects on
society. Students should discuss the benefits and drawbacks of
life in an industrialized society.

EXTEND

Cross-Curricular Connection: *Literature and the Arts*
Have students create works showing their reaction to some
aspect of industrialization. Some ideas include writing poems,
creating story lines for novels, paintings or drawings, or music.

MEET INDIVIDUAL NEEDS
Gifted Students
Have students read a Gothic novel, such as Mary Shelley's
Frankenstein, and then report to the class, explaining how it
reflects realism or romanticism.

Visual Learners
Have students work in pairs or small groups to find reproductions
of paintings by romantic, realist, and impressionist artists. Ask
students what each painting portrays about life in the 1800s.

ASSESS
Review
Have students complete the Section 4 Review. Use answers in
the Teacher's Edition, pages 505–506, to assess student mastery
of this section.

In preparation for the chapter test, you may wish to have
students complete all or part of the Chapter 18 Review on
textbook page 507, the Chapter 18 Review Activity, and the
Chapter 18 Themes Review.

Chapter 18

The Industrial Revolution in the West

Understanding the Main Idea

Call on a volunteer to read aloud the *Understanding the Main Idea* paragraph. Then tell students that new technology led to the Industrial Revolution. The development of factories meant that machines, not people, produced goods. In the 1800s, when transportation improved and new industries developed, the second Industrial Revolution occurred. As a result, social structures changed, and new political and philosophical beliefs emerged.

Presenting Themes

See p. 481B for suggestions on introducing themes.

Using the Time Line

Have students list the time line events in their notebooks. After they have read about each event in the chapter, have students write a paragraph explaining its significance.

Chapter 18

The Industrial Revolution in the West 1700–1914

Understanding the Main Idea

In the 1700s and 1800s, the development of new technologies and methods of economic organization gradually led Europeans into what has been called the Industrial Revolution. Mechanical power replaced muscle power as the primary energy source, which gave rise to a whole new way of life in western Europe. This new way of life soon spread to other parts of the world.

Themes

- *Social Relations* How might the shift from an agricultural society to an industrial society change the way that people interact?

- *Technology* How might advances in technology change the way people work?

- *Economic Organization* What effects might technological developments have on businesses?

By the early 1800s new technological developments were beginning to have an enormous impact on the people of Great Britain. One of the most striking changes was a revolution in transportation, brought on by the invention of the railroad and the steamship. At the opening of the Liverpool to Manchester railroad in 1830, passenger Frances Kemble described the mood that accompanied the new technology: "The most intense curiosity and excitement prevailed, and . . . enormous masses of densely packed people lined the road [track], shouting and waving hats and handkerchiefs."

The joyful occasion was soon spoiled by a terrible accident. While the engine was stopped, several men were standing on another track next to the train, when suddenly they noticed a locomotive bearing down on them. Kemble continued:

66*Mr. Huskisson, . . . bewildered, too, by the frantic cries of 'Stop the engine! Clear the track!' that resounded on all sides, completely lost his head, looked helplessly to the right and left, and was instantaneously prostrated [flattened] by the fatal machine, which dashed down like a thunderbolt upon him.*99

Tragic though this event was, it could not stem the tide of technological progress. Within a short time, Britain, as well as other nations, was crisscrossed

1701	1769	1771	1807
▲ Jethro Tull invents the seed drill.	▲ James Watt patents an efficient steam engine.	▲ Richard Arkwright builds the first textile mill.	▲ Robert Fulton installs a steam engine on the *Clermont*.

482 *CHAPTER 18*

with rail lines, which moved goods and people to even the remotest areas. This revolution in technology would soon transform Western society.

Spectators in Britain gather to watch the arrival of the local train.

About the Image

This painting shows a train on the Stockton-Darlington line in Britain. On April 19, 1821, a group of businesspeople got a bill passed in Parliament for the construction of a steam rail route from Darlington to Stockton-on-Tees. The merchants were looking for a cheaper way to get coal to the sea wharves at Stockton. George Stephenson, the inventor of the first successful locomotive, convinced them that it would be better to build a track for steam locomotives that could haul both coal and people. By the time the rail opened, on September 27, 1825, more than 40,000 people were waiting to see the engine Locomotion arrive in Stockton, pulling a passenger coach and 11 coal wagons.

Critical Thinking Ask students to suggest what recent inventions in the field of transportation have caused public excitement.

ANSWER: Students' answers will vary, but might include spacecraft or bullet trains.

1829	1859	1879	1903
George Stephenson successfully tests the Rocket, a steam-powered locomotive.	Charles Darwin publishes *On the Origin of Species by Means of Natural Selection.*	Thomas Edison invents the incandescent light bulb.	Wilbur and Orville Wright fly the first motor-powered, heavier-than-air plane.

SECTION 1

CORE LESSON PLAN
See pages 481C and
481D for Lesson Plan
18.1.

Theme: Economic Organization

Before industrialization, an overseas trade was Britain's most important asset. Most manufacturing was done in the home by village artisans. Industrialization changed all this. Rural poverty would become a major problem, causing people to flock to the cities to find work. Economic emphasis would be placed on greater and faster production. Great Britain would become a major supplier of manufactured goods.

Critical Thinking Ask students if the benefits of industrialization outweighed the drawbacks.

ANSWER: Students might answer yes, industrialization improved life overall, or no, rural poverty and overcrowded cities were too great a cost.

SECTION 1
The First Industrial Revolution

FOCUS

- Why did the Industrial Revolution begin in Britain?
- What were some of the consequences of the Agricultural Revolution?
- How did rising demand and new technology affect the textile industry?
- What were the basic elements of the first Industrial Revolution?

In the 1700s Europeans experienced not only political and social revolutions but also the beginnings of an economic revolution. First Britain, then Europe, North America, and eventually other parts of the world moved from economies based primarily on agricultural production to economies based mostly on industrial production. Although the process took many years, it became known as the Industrial Revolution. It represented a combination of many developments. These included a rise in population, more efficient food production, a growing demand for manufactured goods, new attitudes toward the creation of wealth and prosperity, and new technologies.

A farming family at work

Origins of the Industrial Revolution

Before 1700 the primary energy source in societies was a combination of muscle power (both human and animal) and wind and water power. During the 1700s, however, this basic aspect of human existence began to change. When people began to use new power sources, such as steam, to run mechanical devices, they began a more intense phase of technological development known as the **Industrial Revolution**. The Industrial Revolution began in Great Britain due to a unique combination of geographical and historical features.

Geographical advantages. One of Britain's greatest assets was water. Water helped protect the island nation from invasion while wars raged on the European continent. Navigable rivers provided an efficient method of transporting raw materials and finished goods. By 1760 private developers had begun to improve on nature by building a network of canals to connect manufacturers directly with their markets. Rivers also served as power sources, turning waterwheels in gristmills and later powering machinery to produce cotton thread.

Another one of Britain's many geographical advantages was a plentiful supply of coal and iron. Britain's many abundant coal deposits were located relatively close to the surface, making the coal easier to mine. The coalfields were also near rivers, which meant that coal was easy to transport by water. As the canal system developed, coal could be moved farther inland than ever before. Large deposits of iron ore were often located near the coal mines. This iron ore could also be shipped along the same inland waterways.

Other advantages. In addition to geographical advantages, Britain also had the advantage of a stable political system. After the English Civil War of the 1640s and the Glorious Revolution of 1688, English law increasingly protected both individuals and their right to own property. **Entrepreneurs**—those who risked their wealth by investing in new technology or new business ventures—could be certain that their profits would not be unlawfully taken from them.

In addition, Britain had a global overseas commercial empire. It controlled trade routes and had important trade contacts in other countries that provided Britain with both raw materials and markets for its goods. Britain's trade was carried by its merchant fleet and protected by its navy. British merchants had long practiced **capitalism**—the use of private money or goods to produce a profit of more money or goods. Britain had also developed a banking system through which profits from trade and agriculture could be made available for investment in new ventures.

Growing market demands. While all these factors made Britain ripe for industrial development, the immediate reason for the Industrial Revolution was a growing demand for manufactured products. Since Europeans first began to expand overseas in the late 1400s and 1500s, the demand for such goods as clothing, farm tools, and weapons had risen steadily. Britain, for example, benefited from its American colonies, which needed manufactured goods. Woolen and cotton textiles were particularly in demand.

The demand for new goods in Britain itself was growing as a result of two main factors: a rising population and the production of more food at cheaper prices. More people meant a need for more goods. Lower food prices meant that people had more money to spend on clothes and other manufactured items. As demands for all these goods rose, many entrepreneurs realized that they could make enormous profits by finding more efficient means of producing them.

A combination of raw materials, internal stability, access to markets, and a growing demand for goods made Britain an ideal location for the start of the Industrial Revolution.

The Commercialization of Agriculture

An important factor that contributed to the Industrial Revolution was another revolution—this one in agriculture. Like the Industrial Revolution, the **Agricultural Revolution** that developed in Britain in the early 1700s owed a great deal to European expansion overseas. The introduction of new American crops, such as potatoes and corn, contributed to Europe's food supply and advances in farming.

New farming methods. Until the 1700s people still practiced **open-field farming**, in which land was divided into strips and worked by the villagers. About one third of the land remained unplanted so that the soil could be replenished with nutrients. Part of the land was "common" land, on which anyone in the community could graze animals.

In the 1600s, however, many farmers in the Netherlands began to alter this traditional pattern of farming. For centuries the Dutch had a relatively large population concentrated on a limited amount of land. The growth of Dutch commerce and the establishment of a far-flung commercial empire in the 1600s had caused more people to flock to the cities. Faced with a food shortage, Dutch farmers learned how to make their land produce more efficiently. They not only drained marshlands but also built dikes to reclaim more farmland from the sea. The Dutch also learned to use animal manure, as well as new crops like turnips and clover, to restore the fertility of their soil.

▶ Workers construct a dike in the Netherlands to protect farmland from the sea. Without these dikes, 27 percent of the Netherlands would be under water.

Theme: Social Relations

The enclosure movement was started in Britain around 1760 by landlords who had great power in the government. Small landholders were most affected by the movement because they relied on common holdings for firewood and pasture. The small landholders could not provide these things from their own small plots and were often reduced to becoming wage laborers dependent upon the wealthy.

Critical Thinking Ask students to suggest reasons why the enclosures had less of an effect on the lifestyle of peasants with no land than they did on small landholders.

ANSWER: Students might answer that landless peasants already had to work for wages, unlike the small landholders.

MULTIMEDIA PRESENTATION STRATEGY

VISUAL RESOURCES Geography and History 18
Land Enclosures in England

Show the transparency and share the information from Geography and History Fact Sheet 18. Then have students complete the accompanying worksheet.

Level 2

Enclosing required paying legal fees and planting extensive hedges to separate one farmer's land from another's. These costs were often too high for small farmers to bear. As a result, many of these small farmers were squeezed out and became landless laborers, while others gave up farming and moved to the cities. In their place a new class of prosperous tenant farmers emerged, leasing substantial amounts of land from the owners. Both the lease-holding farmers and the landless laborers now had to work for money rather than simply to produce enough crops to feed their families. Although the British enclosure movement concentrated more land in fewer hands, it also contributed to the increasing efficiency and productivity of British farmers. Agriculture, like trade, became a commercial enterprise. In addition, the greater availability of food meant that families could grow larger, and improved diets meant that many people lived longer. The result was an ever-increasing population.

"Turnip" Townshend. The British soon began to copy Dutch farming methods. In the early 1700s, for example, Lord Townshend, a former British statesman, began to use the Dutch technique of **crop rotation**—a method of alternating different kinds of crops to preserve soil fertility—on his own lands. He planted grains one year and root vegetables, such as potatoes and turnips, the next. The root crops also made ideal food for farm animals, which began to grow larger and healthier.

Impressed by Townshend's success, others in England also began to adopt a more scientific approach to farming. Agriculturist Jethro Tull, for example, introduced the **seed drill** in 1701. The seed drill allowed him to use seeds more efficiently by planting them in regular rows and at the proper depth, rather than scattering them by hand over a wide area. Tull also discovered that crops grew better when the area between the rows was kept clear of weeds. To eliminate the weeds from the fields, Tull developed the horse-drawn hoe.

Enclosures. The improved methods of agriculture were certainly more profitable. As more landowners adopted them, however, they found the old open-field system to be a problem. Since the 1500s some English landowners had been consolidating the narrow strips of land into larger units, which they then enclosed with hedgerows. Originally this enclosure movement had been designed to provide more grazing lands on which to raise sheep for their valuable wool. To take better advantage of the improved farming methods, landowners began to enclose even more land. By the 1830s almost the entire English countryside was enclosed by hedgerows or fences.

The Agricultural Revolution increased food production and contributed to both population growth and the commercialization of agriculture.

The Textile Industry

The textile industry was the first to feel the full impact of the Industrial Revolution. Since the Middle Ages, cloth had been produced through the **domestic system**, also sometimes called the putting-out system. Under this system people worked from their homes. Merchants bought wool from a farmer and distributed it to villagers and townspeople to clean, weave, or spin into yarn, usually during the winter months. The merchants then collected the finished cloth and sold it for a profit. This system was successful because production costs were low. Most families already owned spinning wheels, and most villages had looms. As demand for cloth began to rise, however, the domestic system was strained to the breaking point. The situation became particularly bad in the late 1700s, as demand rose for cotton goods made from the plentiful and cheap cotton grown by slave labor on American plantations.

In the 1760s James Hargreaves, a weaver from Blackburn, England, developed the **spinning jenny**, a muscle-powered wooden machine that could spin eight cotton threads at one time. The spinning jenny quickly replaced the spinning wheel. About the same time Richard Arkwright, another inventor, developed an alternative spinning method—a large water-powered spinning machine called a **water frame**.

BIOGRAPHY Born in 1732, Arkwright had been apprenticed to a barber and wigmaker during his teenage years. With money from his second wife, Arkwright was able to abandon wigmaking and start his own business. In 1768 he made a prototype of the water frame. Because the new machine required an outside source of power, it could not be set up in a worker's home, so around 1771 Arkwright built one of England's first factories in Cromford. Instead of carrying work to the spinners, Arkwright brought the spinners to the work. Within a decade this spinning mill employed 300 people.

Arkwright symbolized the spirit of enterprise. One biographer wrote about him:

Richard Arkwright
BIOGRAPHY

❝ The most marked traits in the character of Arkwright were his wonderful ardour [enthusiasm], energy, and perseverance. He commonly laboured . . . from five o'clock

▲ Workers tend the power looms in this large British textile factory in the 1800s.

in the morning till nine at night; and . . . he encroached upon [cut down on] his sleep, in order to gain an hour each day to learn English grammar, and another hour to improve his writing and orthography [spelling]! ❞

Arkwright built a fortune from his mills in Derbyshire, Lancashire, and Scotland. When he died in 1792, his mills were so profitable that his heirs received a tremendous fortune from his estate. Arkwright later became known as the "father of the factory system."

With the enormous output from the new machines, both demand and wages for cotton weavers dramatically increased. Many people who had invested in the booming new cotton industry began to look for ways to adapt machinery to weaving as well as spinning in an effort to reduce labor costs for weavers. In 1785 a preacher named Edmund Cartwright invented the first power loom. Large and expensive, power looms eventually drove the handweavers out of business. Like the powerful water frame, the new machines had to be located in large factories.

Under the pressure of rising demand, the textile industry used new technology to become the first industry to use large factories for production.

Text continues on page 490.

Geography AND HISTORY

Britain's First Factories

In the early 1700s Great Britain was a nation at the start of a new era—the age of the factory. The importance of the factory was not so much the work that was done there, but the way in which it was done. Before factories developed, artisans had provided their own power to run whatever machinery—a loom, a forge, a spinning wheel—was used in their production. In factories, the worker's job shifted from producing goods to watching over the machines that produced the goods.

One of the first real factories in England was built between 1717 and 1721 for silk production. The Lombe silk factory at Derby was a huge building, the entire concept of which amazed all who saw it. Daniel Defoe captured that amazement in his description of the factory and its machinery:

Factories in Manchester, 1885

> This engine contains 22,586 wheels and 97,746 movements, which work 73,726 yards of silk thread every time the wheel goes round, which is three times in one minute, and 318,504,960 yards in 24 hours. The waterwheel gives the motion to all the rest of the wheels and movements, of which any one may be stopped separately.

Water was the first source of power used by factories. Factory owners built giant waterwheels in the flow of a running stream, where the force of the moving water turned the wheel. The turning wheel powered the machinery within the factory. Consequently, factories were generally built over or near running water. In the 1700s a steam engine was developed that produced power

As the stream turned this waterwheel, millstones rotated inside the millhouse, grinding wheat to flour.

by burning coal. Factories then sprang up near sources of coal.

Another important consideration for the location of factories was a system of transportation. For goods to be manufactured, raw materials had to be transported to the factory. The finished products then had to be distributed to markets. The two primary means of transportation were by road and by waterway. Even though British roads and rivers were kept in good working condition, the late 1700s came to be known as the "canal era." Canals reduced the distance that goods had to be transported because they could be dug in a direct line across the land. Moving materials, such as coal, iron, and clay, on canal barges was much easier than carrying them over roads that could become impassable with mud, or down rivers that could change in course or depth. From about 1760 into the 1800s, many new canals were built across the country, creating a web of transportation routes.

By utilizing these resources of technology, labor, transportation, and power, Great Britain's factories became so successful that they served as models for the rest of the world into the industrial era.

Linking Geography and History

1. How did the factory system change the basic jobs workers did?
2. What were the first two sources of power used in factories?
3. What was a significant change in transportation that occurred in Great Britain in the late 1700s? How did this change affect the development of factories in Britain?
4. Glasgow, Scotland, was not linked to major English cities by canals. What means of transportation might Glasgow factory owners have used to reach Leeds?

The Industrial Revolution in Great Britain, 1715–1851

NORTH SEA

IRISH SEA

Glasgow

Blackburn
Leeds
Liverpool
Manchester
Derby
Birmingham
London

Seven River
Avon
Trent River
Thames

Canal

Industries:
- CI Coal
- I Iron
- CT Cotton textiles
- W Woolens
- E Engines
- Cu Cutlery

0   50   100 Miles
0   50   100 Kilometers
Lambert Conformal Conic Projection

English Channel

56°N 54°N 52°N 50°N
6°W 4°W 2°W 0° 2°E

The Geography of Industrialization The most industrialized areas in Britain grew around rich coal deposits and navigable rivers. In industrial areas without rivers, private companies dug canals to link their factories with important markets.

? **Location** Where were most of Britain's cotton textiles produced?

Linking Geography and History

1. Workers watched over the machinery that produced goods, instead of producing goods themselves.
2. steam and water power
3. system of canals to transport goods was built; factories became successful and led the way in the industrial era
4. roadways or sea

Map Answer

around Manchester, Blackburn, and Liverpool

Theme: Technology

One of the great canal-builders in Britain was Thomas Telford. He built the Ellesmere Canal in Wales, which included two great aqueducts. The canal and aqueducts have survived in their original form for almost 200 years. Telford also built the Caledonian Canal, a waterway that connects the east coast of Scotland to the west coast.

Critical Thinking Ask students to name other canals that have improved transportation for trade and travel.

ANSWER: Students might suggest the Panama Canal, noting that it allows ships to travel between the Atlantic and Pacific Oceans quickly.

The Age of Iron and Steam

Although the textile industry had already experienced tremendous technological improvement, the greatest advances in the Industrial Revolution were yet to come. While spinning and weaving machines were being developed to produce textiles, another device, the steam engine, had emerged from the mining industry. Use of the steam engine would ultimately change the world.

Iron and coal. By the 1700s British forests had been largely cut down in order to build ships and provide fuel. The demand for wood began to outstrip the country's forest supplies. The wood shortage also affected the iron-making business, which had traditionally used charcoal—a wood product—in the smelting process. Charcoal was made from young trees that were planted in groves and harvested as soon as they matured. Even though these trees were cut in yearly rotation, there was not enough wood to supply any increase in iron production. As the demand for iron rose in the 1700s, the solution to the wood shortage was found in coal. In 1709 Abraham Darby, an English ironmaker, discovered that replacing the charcoal with coke, a purified coal, made the smelting process more efficient and economical. By the 1760s coke smelting had spread throughout Britain.

The steam engine. As the demand for coal steadily increased, coal mines were dug deeper into the earth. At a certain depth, however, the mines would fill with water, which had to be removed. This required using buckets drawn to the surface by people or animals. This laborious task led to the invention of a steam-driven pump to speed up water removal. As early as 1698 an army officer, Thomas Savery, had invented a steam-powered pumping machine. Thomas Newcomen, a blacksmith, improved this machine, which became commonly available by 1720. In 1769 James Watt, a

Scottish scientist, refined Newcomen's engine, patenting a steam engine that worked efficiently and with far less fuel.

Further technological developments. The new steam engines became the primary source of power in several industries—most notably textiles, brewing, sugar refining, and even the china industry. Most important of all, perhaps, steam engines transformed the iron industry itself. With steam-driven bellows, the process of refining iron improved dramatically after 1770. In the 1780s ironmaster Henry Cort also used steam power to improve iron production further and to power rolling mills, which transformed refined iron into almost any shape.

The application of steam power to different industries stimulated technological development even further. For example, when steam power began to be used in the 1780s to drive the new power looms, the textile industry's demand for raw cotton also skyrocketed. Although the plantations of the American South were producing enormous quantities of cotton to feed the mills in Britain, picking cotton by hand and processing it by removing the seeds were very difficult and time-consuming tasks. In 1793 American inventor Eli Whitney developed the **cotton gin**,

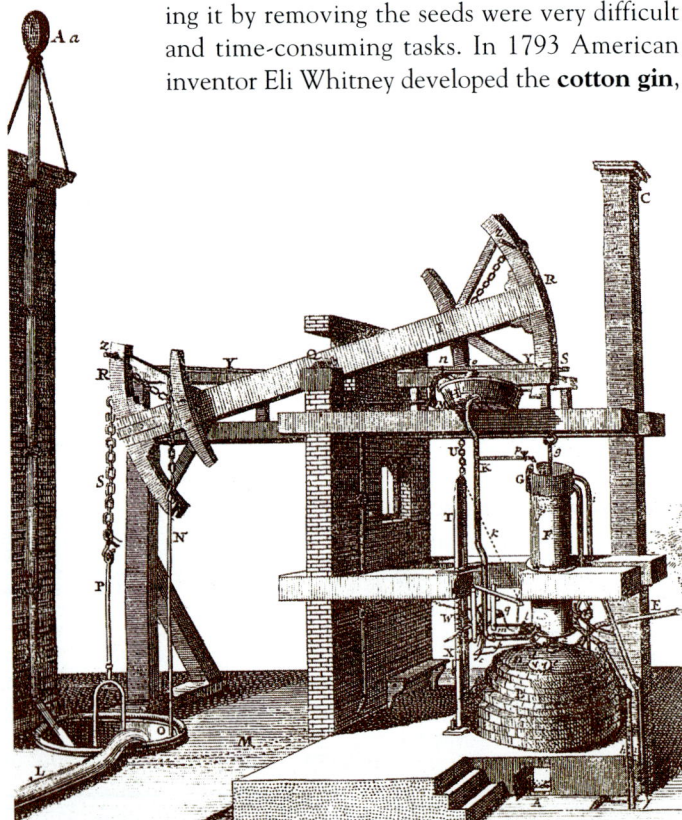

▲ This 1727 diagram shows Thomas Newcomen's improved steam engine.

◀ Growing up on a farm helped Eli Whitney become familiar with tools and aware of uses for machinery.

which separated the seeds from cotton more quickly and efficiently than doing it by hand.

The cotton gin helped make the production of cotton in the southern United States profitable. British imports of cotton from the United States and elsewhere rose from 3 million pounds in 1761 to 100 million pounds in 1815. Britain became known as the "workshop of the world" in the early 1800s because of its booming cotton textile industry and its ability to make durable and inexpensive iron goods.

Iron and steam power became the basic elements of the first Industrial Revolution.

Author's Commentary

OLD METHODS, NEW USES

In addition to Britain's other advantages, British manufacturers also displayed one important characteristic that contributed enormously to the occurrence of the Industrial Revolution in Britain. At all levels of production, merchants, spinners, weavers, dyers, and engineers actively sought out new ideas and technology from anywhere they could find them to improve their own skills and products. As cotton cloths from India became increasingly popular, for example, British clothmakers did their best to discover Indian methods of production—particularly Indian dyeing techniques. British dyers also deliberately tried to learn from the experience of their fellow producers in France and Switzerland.

Similarly, the development of new agricultural devices owed much to inventions brought initially from China, which were then improved and made suitable for use in Britain. Even the development of the steam engine in Britain drew on earlier work done in Germany, Italy, and France with which British inventors were familiar. It was this ability to absorb ideas from others and adapt them to their own needs that gave early British scientists and industrialists an added advantage in industrialization.

SECTION 1 REVIEW

IDENTIFY and explain the significance of the following:
Industrial Revolution
entrepreneurs
capitalism
Agricultural Revolution
open-field farming
crop rotation
seed drill
domestic system
spinning jenny
water frame

James Watt
cotton gin

1. **Main Idea** What materials made the Industrial Revolution possible?
2. **Main Idea** How did the Agricultural Revolution affect Britain?
3. **Geography: Place** Why was Britain an ideal location for industrialization?

4. **Writing to Explain** Imagine that you are a British textile mill owner in the early 1800s. Write a letter to a friend in another industry explaining how the textile business has changed.
5. **Hypothesizing** How do you think industrialization in Britain affected other regions of the world?

THE INDUSTRIAL REVOLUTION IN THE WEST 491

SECTION 1 REVIEW ANSWERS

IDENTIFY
For significance, see the following pages:
Industrial Revolution (p. 484)
entrepreneurs (p. 484)
capitalism (p. 485)
Agricultural Revolution (p. 485)
open-field farming (p. 485)
crop rotation (p. 486)
seed drill (p. 486)
domestic system (p. 486)
spinning jenny (p. 487)
water frame (p. 487)
James Watt (p. 490)
cotton gin (p. 490)

1. Coal, the steam engine, and improvements in iron production made the Industrial Revolution possible.
2. Food production increased, the population grew, and agriculture became commercialized as a result of the Agricultural Revolution.
3. It had access to water, a plentiful supply of coal and iron, a stable political system, access to trade markets, and a growing demand for manufactured goods.
4. Letters should explain that the technological developments of the spinning jenny, the water frame, and the large power loom increased production and created the need for large factories.
5. There was an increased demand for British goods because they were being produced at a faster and cheaper rate. Countries needed to improve their own systems of production to compete.

491

RESOURCE ACTIVITY

GEOGRAPHY ACTIVITIES
Geography Activity 18
Manchester: The Growth of an Industrial Giant

Have students study the map and complete the questions on the development of Manchester.

Level 2

RESOURCE ACTIVITY

GLOBAL HISTORY RESOURCE CENTER
Reading: *Friedrich Engels on the Industrial City*

Print out and distribute the reading. Then have students draw a political cartoon to run in a London newspaper showing the social problems Engels describes.

Level 1/ Sheltered English

SECTION 2
Consequences of Industrialization

FOCUS

- What were some of the social consequences of industrialization?
- What political theories emerged in the industrial era and how did they differ from one another?
- How did many workers respond to industrialization?

Once the Industrial Revolution had become self-sustaining in Britain in the late 1700s, it began to transform the nature of society. Although industrialization increased wealth and raised standards of living for many people, for others, particularly factory workers, life could be very harsh. Some people began to long for the seemingly simpler days of the past. Others, convinced that the new technology was here to stay, tried to soften its effects by developing new methods of social organization.

Coalbrookdale, England, at night

Social Consequences of Industrialization

The introduction of steam-powered machinery to manufacturing changed the way people worked. For the first time large numbers of people began to work in factories rather than at home. In many early factories, laborers—including men, women, and children—worked 14 hours a day, 6 days a week. The work was no longer adjusted to the seasons, as it was under the domestic system or on farms. Instead it was regulated by the time clock, since machines never needed to rest.

Industrialization also transformed the structure of society. Better farming methods and the mass production of farm tools allowed the production of more food, which in turn allowed for an increase in population. In the early 1800s, for example, the population of Britain exploded. In 1801 the population was about 10.5 million, and by 1851 it had nearly doubled. **Urbanization**—the growth of cities—also increased dramatically in the 1800s. Cities in manufacturing regions grew faster than others. In 1851 the industrial city of Leeds was 13 times larger than it had been in 1801, while the city of London merely doubled in size.

Not all workers toiled in factories, however. As the balance of economic and political power shifted from agriculture to industry, more jobs also became available for the middle class—bankers, merchants, manufacturers, lawyers, doctors, engineers, and other professionals. This in turn provided new jobs for nonindustrial workers, particularly domestic servants, both male and female.

As people streamed into the cities, conditions for workers were often miserable at first. Migrants and the urban poor crowded into shoddy buildings built so close together that there was little light or ventilation. Open sewers ran through the slums, clogged with garbage, human waste, and occasionally even dead animals. The danger of disease was so bad in London that one observer wrote:

We might lay our fingers on the . . . map, and say here is the typhoid parish, and there the ward of cholera; . . . the southern shores of the Thames [might] be christened Pestilentia. As season follows season, so does disease follow disease in the quarters that may be . . . styled the plague-spots of London.

Despite such conditions many people preferred life in the cities, where they could find jobs, to life in the countryside, where conditions could be even worse. Rural poverty was accompanied by high unemployment. If people had jobs they at least had the prospect of improving their standard of living considerably by purchasing inexpensive factory goods. Cities also provided entertainment, which some skilled workers had the time and money to enjoy. Parks, soccer matches, free concerts, and inexpensive day trips by railroad made life more interesting. Such advantages led one contemporary observer to write that city-dwellers were "in reference to health, domestic comfort, and religious culture, in a truly enviable state, compared with the average of our agricultural villages."

Life for the middle class was better and also improved more rapidly than it did for workers. With growing wealth, the middle class could afford to employ servants. Middle-class parents could also send their children to school, thus improving their children's prospects for finding middle-class jobs. As wealth increased throughout the 1800s, so did the number of people who had middle-class incomes. However, the dramatic rise in prosperity that many people experienced did not apply to everyone. Life for many industrial workers remained difficult and soon led to demands for reform.

Industrialization transformed the way people worked, led to rapid urban growth, and eventually brought greater prosperity to many people.

New Political Theories

In some ways the Industrial Revolution was an extension of the growing interest in the material world that had also led to the Scientific Revolution and the Enlightenment. Unlike these elite movements, however, the Industrial Revolution increasingly affected all levels of society. As they tried to cope with the effects of the Industrial Revolution, many people began to develop new ideas about the structure of society and the state. They hoped that industrialization would lead to greater prosperity for more of the population.

Population Growth in Great Britain, 1751–1851

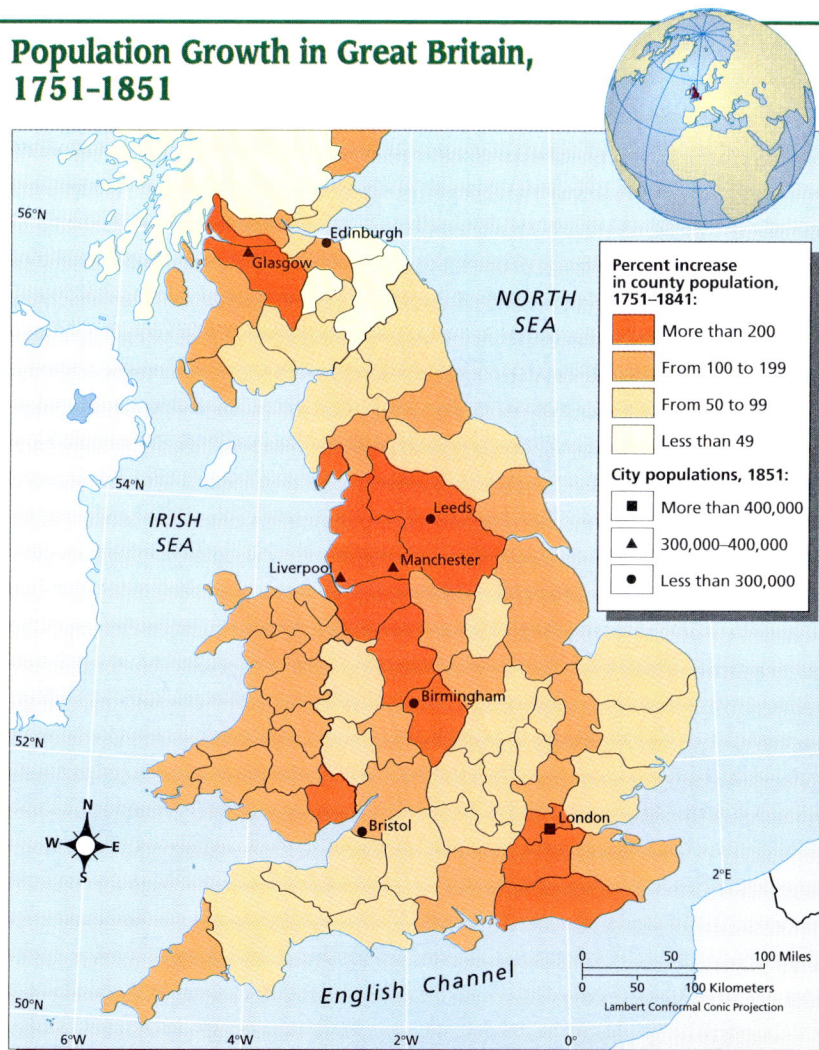

Percent increase in county population, 1751–1841:
- More than 200
- From 100 to 199
- From 50 to 99
- Less than 49

City populations, 1851:
- ■ More than 400,000
- ▲ 300,000–400,000
- ● Less than 300,000

NORTH SEA · IRISH SEA · English Channel · Edinburgh · Glasgow · Leeds · Liverpool · Manchester · Birmingham · Bristol · London

Lambert Conformal Conic Projection

Population Explosion Britain's tremendous population growth after 1751 provided laborers and consumers for the country's economic miracle.

Regions How many British counties grew more than 200 percent?

Map Answer
12

MULTIMEDIA PRESENTATION STRATEGY

WORLD HISTORY AND CULTURES VIDEODISCS

Map: *Growth of London, 1600–1900*

Search Frame 927

Image: *Women Making Cartridges*

Search 917

Show the map and image as you discuss the rapid industrialization of Britain. The captions that accompany the CD-ROM map and image offer additional details.

All Levels

Have students read the selection and complete the questions.

Level 2

Across the Curriculum: Literature

Charles Dickens appealed to the public during his lifetime as few authors have done. His novels often showed the life of the very poor in Great Britain, which his early childhood experience reflected.

Critical Thinking Ask students why they think Dickens's stories appealed to so many readers.

ANSWER: Students might suggest that many British people could relate to Dickens's experiences.

Understanding Literature

1. He thinks that it is dirty and is ruining people's individuality.
2. Workers' lives are monotonous, and the workers are like machines. Answers could either focus on the harsh conditions of working class life or on the improved quality of life.

Literature THROUGH TIME

Hard Times

Charles Dickens, the author of the novel Hard Times, *is one of the most famous critics of the problems caused by the Industrial Revolution in Britain during the 1800s. When Dickens was 12, his father was imprisoned for debt, and Charles was forced to work in a warehouse putting labels on containers of shoe polish. This childhood experience undoubtedly had a great impact on Dickens. His novels often show people, particularly children, at the mercy of factory owners, and leading poor, bleak, and unhealthy lives.*

Hard Times is the story of a cold, calculating merchant, Mr. Gradgrind, who cannot understand expressions of emotion or imagination. He believes only in facts and figures. For Dickens, Gradgrind represents the negative aspects of Britain's wealthy industrialists. The novel also contains vivid descriptions of places and people affected by the Industrial Revolution. The following are descriptions of Coketown, the fictional setting of the novel.

It was a town of red brick, or of brick that would have been red if the smoke and ashes had allowed it; but as matters stood it was a town of unnatural red and black like the painted face of a savage. It was a town of machinery and tall chimneys, out of which interminable [endless] serpents of smoke trailed themselves forever and ever, and never got uncoiled. It had a black canal in it, and a river that ran purple with ill-smelling dye, and vast piles of buildings full of windows where there was a rattling and a trembling all day long, and where the piston of the steam-engine worked monotonously up and down like the head of an elephant in a state of melancholy [depressed] madness. It contained several large streets all very like one another, and many small streets still more like one another, inhabited by people equally like one another, who all went in and out at the same hours, with the same sound upon the same pavements, to do the same work, and to whom every day was the same as yesterday and tomorrow, and every year the counterpart [duplicate] of the last and the next. . . .

The streets were hot and dusty on the summer day, and the sun was so bright that it even shone through the heavy vapour drooping over Coketown, and could not be looked at steadily. Stokers emerged from low underground doorways into factory yards, and sat on steps, and posts, and palings [fences], wiping their swarthy visages [faces], and contemplating coals. The whole town seemed to be frying in oil.

Understanding Literature

1. Judging from Dickens's description of Coketown, how would you describe his view of industrialization?
2. How does Dickens view the lives of industrial workers? Do you think his view is accurate? Why or why not?

Air pollution in Leeds, England, in 1885

Liberalism. With its foundations in both the Enlightenment and the French Revolution, **liberalism** soon became the dominant political philosophy of the new industrial middle class. Liberals emphasized the importance of individual liberty in all areas. They focused on freedom of conscience, freedom of thought and speech, and freedom to pursue their own economic interests through free trade and competition. Liberals believed that government should ensure equal treatment under the law for all people, despite wealth or social position.

To gain and protect these freedoms, liberals wanted representative, constitutional government. Most were not supporters of democracy, however. They believed that only men of property should be allowed to participate in politics. Reflecting their belief in individualism, liberals also adopted the laissez-faire economic theories of Adam Smith, which became known as the "classical political economy." As Smith explained, society would be best regulated if everyone followed their own true self-interest:

66 *Every individual is continually exerting himself to find out the most advantageous employment for whatever capital he can command. It is his own advantage, indeed, and not that of the society, which he has in view. But the study of his own advantage, naturally, or rather necessarily, leads him to prefer that employment which is most advantageous to the society.* 99

Utilitarianism. As the social problems of industrialization became increasingly clear—particularly the plight of industrial workers and the poor—many people became convinced that government action was necessary. The English political philosopher Jeremy Bentham argued that institutions and laws should be judged according to their usefulness, or utility. He defined utility as that which brought "the greatest happiness of the greatest number." Those laws that failed this test, Bentham argued, should be abandoned. This philosophy became known as **utilitarianism**.

Following Bentham's logic, John Stuart Mill eventually concluded that while government should stay out of people's lives as much as possible, it should also promote the education of the people. On the grounds of utility, Mill called for full democracy, as well as complete equality

▲ In the 1800s John Stuart Mill urged equality and representation for women.

between men and women in all aspects of life. At the same time, however, he warned against the potential tyranny of the majority and insisted that government power should be limited.

Socialism. Not everyone accepted these reformers' views, which emphasized the rights and responsibilities of individuals. Unlike liberals, those who supported **socialism** believed that individual interests must give way to the interests of society as a whole. Socialists were reacting to both the French Revolution and the Industrial Revolution. They argued that political equality was meaningless without economic equality. Consequently, socialists called for the state to take charge of the **means of production**—the capital and the equipment needed to make and exchange goods—and use them for the common good of all the people. Ironically, most early socialists were not workers but aristocrats or members of the middle class.

One of the earliest socialists was Charles Fourier (foohr-yay). Fourier wanted to create ideal communities like those described in Sir Thomas More's *Utopia*, where people could live and work together in perfect harmony. Fourier's ideas became known as **utopian socialism**. The British industrialist Robert Owen—perhaps the most famous utopian socialist—actually established several model communities. In 1825, for example, Owen founded a utopian community in New Harmony, Indiana. He explained his objective:

66 *When all shall be cordially engaged in promoting the happiness of all around them . . .*

the only contest among men then will be, who shall the most succeed in extending happiness to his fellows. **99**

Within a few years of its creation, however, New Harmony, like Owens's other communities, had run into serious financial problems, compounded by internal disagreements and bickering. The utopian community quickly fell apart. Over the next 30 years, similar communities were built both in Europe and North America, but none of these communities lasted very long. Eventually, socialists would turn to more practical methods in order to achieve their goals.

*W*hile liberals and utilitarians emphasized individual liberty and responsibility, early socialists called for new forms of community organization.*

Workers' Movements

While aristocratic and middle-class socialists theorized about working-class problems, workers themselves pursued more concrete actions. Industrialization threatened the old guilds and artisan associations that had bound craftspeople together in the preindustrial era. Early in the industrial era, some frustrated workers protested industrialization by destroying the machines that replaced skilled artisans. However, as the workers accepted the idea that industrialization was here to stay, many eventually began to organize

themselves according to their trades in groups known as **trade unions**.

Unlike the old guilds, which had generally been confined to single towns, trade unions gained members from all over the country. The most effective weapon unions used to obtain their demands for higher wages or better working conditions was the **strike**, a general walkout of all workers in the union. The more workers the union could count on to strike, the more pressure they could put on employers.

Organizing unions was difficult, however. In the early 1800s British, French, and German governments regarded workers' associations as conspiracies and made them illegal. These governments were generally in the hands of either conservatives or liberals who represented the interests of employers. For example, Britain's Combination Acts of 1799 and 1800 prohibited workers from organizing, even though employers were permitted to do so. Nevertheless, workers eventually made some progress. In 1824 the British Parliament repealed the Combination Acts, permitting workers to organize peacefully and to bargain for better wages and hours. Although the government continued to put down strikes as often as not, union strength slowly grew, providing workers with a new sense of community and security.

*M*any industrial workers eventually formed unions to improve their working conditions and to achieve a new sense of community and security.*

SECTION 2 REVIEW

IDENTIFY and explain the significance of the following:
urbanization
liberalism
utilitarianism
John Stuart Mill
socialism
means of production
utopian socialism
trade unions
strike

1. *Main Idea* How did industrialization change society?

2. *Main Idea* What different political ideas arose during the era of industrialization, and how did they differ?

3. *Geography: Movement* How did the migration of people from the countryside to the cities affect the quality of urban life?

4. *Writing to Persuade* Imagine that you are a worker in a textile mill who wants to form a union. Write an inspiring speech to convince your coworkers to join you.

5. *Assessing Consequences* Did life improve for workers who moved from rural areas into industrial cities? Explain your answer.

The Second Industrial Revolution

FOCUS

- How did the steam engine affect transportation?

- What were the foundations and the consequences of the second Industrial Revolution?

- What were the results of new business practices in the late 1800s?

- How did industrialization in France, Germany, and Russia differ from industrialization in Britain?

*B***y the mid-1800s technological changes were occurring at a staggering pace. Contributing to the pace of change was a growing collaboration among scientists, inventors, and engineers. Historians often refer to this renewed burst of technological creativity during the last half of the 1800s as the second Industrial Revolution.**

Robert Fulton's boat, the *Clermont*

The Transportation Revolution

In 1807 Robert Fulton, an American inventor and entrepreneur, installed a steam engine on his boat, the *Clermont*, which he successfully tested on the Hudson River. Fulton's invention revolutionized water-borne transportation. Ships driven by steam were not bound by the natural limitations of wind, tide, and current. Soon, steamships started to appear on the rivers of Europe and North America, and some even traveled as far as Asia. Not all were successes, however. In 1859, for example, the engine of the *Great Eastern* exploded:

> ❝*A tremendous explosion was heard. . . . Then a sweeping, rolling, swooping, rumbling sound, as of cannon balls scudding along the deck above. . . . The rumbling noise was followed by the smash of the dining saloon skylights, and the irruption [eruption] of a mass of fragments of wood and iron, followed by a thick cloud of powdered glass, and then by coaldust. . . . My next neighbour cried out, 'The boiler has burst!'*❞

Despite such occasional setbacks, by about 1870 steamships had largely replaced sailing ships on ocean voyages.

The steam engine also revolutionized land travel. In the early 1800s British inventors began experimenting with steam-powered carriages. These early versions of the automobile also stimulated improvements in road construction by two Scots, John MacAdam and Thomas Telford. In the 1820s, however, a more immediately significant technology emerged.

For many years miners had used carts pulled manually on wooden or iron rails to get coal out of the mines. In 1829 George Stephenson, an engineer who had worked with steam engines in the coalfields, built the Rocket, a steam-powered engine, or **locomotive**, which pulled a train of connected cars on iron rails at the then unheard-of speed of 30 miles per hour. Soon railways were built across Britain, the rest of Europe, and the United States to carry cargo and passengers.

*T**he steam engine offered a new source of power, which revolutionized transportation.***

A Second Revolution in Industry

In the years following 1850, a second Industrial Revolution swept over Britain and the rest of the industrializing world. Like the first revolution, this one was fueled by increasing technological developments. While the first revolution had been built on steam, coal, and iron, the second Industrial Revolution was built on electricity, steel, and oil.

Electricity. The first **dynamo**, or electric generator, was developed in 1831 and soon did for communications what steam power had done for transportation. In 1837 two Englishmen learned to send electric signals over a wire, thus inventing the telegraph. In the United States Samuel Morse improved the telegraph and developed his own Morse code, a system of short dots and long dashes, as a means of communicating over the new lines. Soon the entire world was being crisscrossed with telegraph wires and undersea cables. Further developments led to the invention of the first telephone in 1876 by the Scottish-born American Alexander Graham Bell. In 1901 Italian Guglielmo Marconi sent the first radio transmission across the Atlantic. Marconi later described the monumental event:

66 *Shortly before mid-day I placed the single earphone to my ear and started listening. . . . The answer came at 12:30 when I heard, faintly but distinctly, pip-pip-pip. . . . The result meant much more to me than the mere successful realization of an experiment. . . . I now felt for the first time absolutely certain that the day would come when mankind would be able to send messages without wires not only across the Atlantic but between the farthermost ends of the earth.* 99

The 1870s also marked the use of the electric motor to replace steam engines in industry. Because they were cleaner, smaller, and cheaper than steam engines, electric motors helped the spread of the Industrial Revolution

throughout the manufacturing sector. The new motors were used to power devices, such as sewing machines and fans—and even the new incandescent light bulbs invented by Thomas Edison in 1879.

Steel and petroleum. As electricity began to replace steam, steel started to replace iron in industrial development. Ironmasters developed new techniques—such as the Bessemer process, the open-hearth process, and the Thomas-Gilchrist process—to purify low-quality iron ore into steel. As steel production increased dramatically, prices fell. With cheap, plentiful steel, railway expansion boomed. Steel, which was much harder yet more flexible than iron, also changed the face of cities. Particularly after the invention of the elevator in the 1850s, cities began to build upward instead of outward.

Oil also began to replace coal in industry. In 1867 German inventor Nikolaus August Otto developed a practical **internal combustion engine**, which burned gasoline, a petroleum product, directly inside the engine. In 1886 Gottlieb Daimler and Carl Benz put an engine on a horse carriage to create the first automobile. In 1899 their firm began manufacturing Mercedes cars. In 1903 American aviation pioneers Wilbur and Orville Wright used a gasoline-powered engine to fly the first heavier-than-air plane.

Other industries. The second wave of industrialization also witnessed the growth and development of industries that depended heavily on science. Perhaps the most important area was the chemical

▶ **Gottlieb Daimler rides in his Mercedes.**

industry, which began with the search for new dyes and dying techniques for textiles. In the late 1800s chemists also combined their efforts with industry to develop other products, such as medicines and fertilizers.

The 1800s was also a period of enormous development in civil engineering—the techniques by which material structures, such as roads and bridges, are designed and constructed. Often these skills were pioneered by bridge builders like Thomas Telford in Britain and Gustave Eiffel in France. Major engineering projects included the construction of Telford's great suspension bridge across the Menai Strait between Britain and the Isle of Anglesey in 1826 and the construction of Eiffel's iron tower in Paris in the 1880s.

The second Industrial Revolution—built on electricity, steel, and oil—accelerated the pace and extent of industrial development.

The Growth of Big Business

All of the activity and growth during the second Industrial Revolution was expensive and contributed to the development of new business methods. The need to raise money to build expensive railroads, for example, led to the growing development of **corporations**—business organizations in which large numbers of people purchase shares of stocks, or certificates of partial ownership. Corporations were able to raise large amounts of capital for investment. As they attracted large numbers of investors, the scale of business grew enormously.

In 1901, for example, the American banker J. P. Morgan and his associates formed the United States Steel Corporation, only the first of many billion-dollar corporations. Banks and investment houses that raised capital became more important in forming and operating these large corporations. Businesspeople like Morgan were not industrialists but **financiers**, buying companies as an investment.

Competition among the companies was often fierce. Some corporations, like Standard Oil of the United States, bought so many smaller companies that they created a **monopoly**,

THROUGH OTHERS' EYES

A Chinese Response to Western Technology

It was with great reluctance that the Chinese recognized the superiority of Western technology in the 1800s. Wei Yuan was a well-known scholar who understood that China could no longer compete with the "barbarians," as he explained in the following report:

&&The materials in their shipyards are piled up like hills and craftsmen congregate there like a cloud. Within twenty or thirty days a large warship can be completed. They can instantly spread the sails and adjust the tiller with a few shouted orders. Their craftsmen compete with each other in their talents and abilities. In construction they compete for speed and in navigation also. Construction goes on all year long, the fire illuminates the sky, and the noise shakes the earth. Thus, while the British ships and guns are regarded in China as due to extraordinary skill, in the various countries of Europe they are considered as quite ordinary. . . . But in regard to their conduct of war and the effectiveness of their weapons, we are learning not a single one of their superior skills. That is, we are only willing to receive the harm and not . . . the benefit of foreign intercourse.&&

which meant that they controlled the production and sale of a product or service in order to dominate a particular market. Companies also built **trusts**—combinations of similar businesses grouped together under the direction of a single entity. Monopolies and trusts reduced competition, thus allowing companies to stabilize prices and earn high profits. In their quest for higher profits, however, large companies often ran smaller ones out of business and reduced the choices available to consumers.

New business practices in the late 1800s led to decreased competition in the marketplace.

SECTION 3 REVIEW ANSWERS

IDENTIFY

For significance, see the following pages:
Robert Fulton (p. 497)
locomotive (p. 497)
dynamo (p. 498)
Guglielmo Marconi (p. 498)
Thomas Edison (p. 498)
internal combustion engine (p. 498)
corporations (p. 499)
financiers (p. 499)
monopoly (p. 499)
trusts (p. 499)

1. The pace of industry accelerated due to new technology using electricity, oil, and steel. The chemical industry developed. New techniques in engineering led to the building of major structures.
2. Businesses hoped to reduce competition, stabilize prices, and earn steady profits.
3. The steam engine revolutionized transportation and led to the creation of the steamship and the locomotive.
4. France—slow industrialization because of political problems, an established craft industry, and low population growth; Germany—industrialized quickly, had plentiful iron deposits; Russia—industrialized slowly because of an autocratic government and serfdom
5. beneficial—were able to use technologies already developed by other countries; harmful—nonindustrialized countries could not compete in world markets

Industrialization in Europe

Before 1850 only Great Britain had industrialized significantly. The British tried to prevent their industrial techniques and knowledge from spreading. Until 1841 British industrial craftsworkers and engineers were prohibited from traveling overseas or shipping out any industrial equipment. Eventually, however, such restrictions proved impossible to maintain, and industrialization began to spread. After Britain, the next European country to industrialize was Belgium. Other countries industrialized more slowly.

In France, for example, continuing political problems, low population growth, and a conservative, well-established craft industry hindered industrialization. Nevertheless, cotton and wool production became mechanized, and coal and iron production increased between 1820 and 1870. In contrast, Germany and the United States industrialized quickly in the last half of the 1800s. Germany had plentiful iron-ore deposits. The United States, with enormous resources of coal, iron ore, and a growing population, soon outpaced all the other industrializing nations, even Britain, in industrial production.

The slowest major European country to industrialize was Russia. With an autocratic government, no entrepreneurial class had emerged in Russia, and until 1861 the majority of the Russian people were still serfs bound to the land. In the last half of the 1800s, however, the government freed the serfs, encouraged the creation of corporations, and sponsored railway development. In the 1890s Sergei Witte (VYEET-tyi), the minister of finance, pursued a deliberate policy of industrialization. The Russian railways doubled in size between 1895 and 1905.

Industrialization in France, Germany, and Russia came later and with greater government involvement than in Britain.

Output of Manufactured Products: 1750–1913

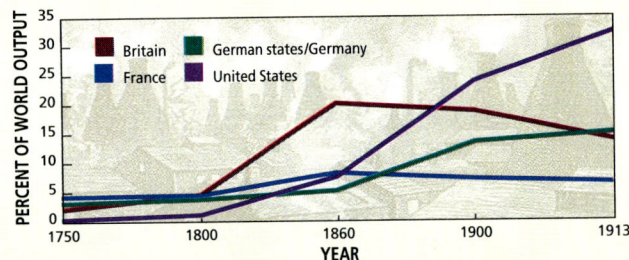

Production Industrialization had an enormous impact on the amount of manufactured goods that nations produced.

? Analyzing Which country had the most dramatic rise in output of manufactured goods between 1750 and 1913? What factors allowed this country to produce so many manufactured goods?

SECTION 3 REVIEW

IDENTIFY and explain the significance of the following:
Robert Fulton
locomotive
dynamo
Guglielmo Marconi
Thomas Edison
internal combustion engine
corporations
financiers
monopoly
trusts

1. Main Idea What factors led to the second Industrial Revolution? What were their consequences?

2. Main Idea Why did businesses form monopolies and trusts?

3. Technology How did the development and improvement of the steam engine change society in the 1800s?

4. Writing to Explain Imagine that you are a British observer in France, Germany, or Russia in the 1870s. Write a letter explaining how industrialization in one of these countries differs from Britain.

5. Hypothesizing Why might delayed industrialization have been both beneficial and harmful to French, German, and Russian industry?

Changes in Western Culture and Society

- How did the wealth provided by the Industrial Revolution affect the middle class?

- What new advances were made in science, and how did these developments affect the social sciences?

- What were romanticism and realism, and in what ways were they reactions to the industrial era?

The industrial era experienced a pace of change unrivaled by any previous age. Western society was transformed as more people had money to spend on goods and leisure. Meanwhile, developments in science improved people's lives and changed traditional outlooks. The impact of the Industrial Revolution was also reflected in art and literature, which at first rejected, then embraced, the industrial age.

Early French advertisement

Changes in Society

After 1850 more Europeans shared the prosperity of the industrial age. With a growing middle class and a more prosperous working class, a new consumer age dawned. In 1876, for example, one of the first department stores, Bon Marché, opened a new Paris shop with everything from furniture to clothing located in one building.

Toward the end of the 1800s, middle-class and working-class people also enjoyed increasing time off work, and leisure activities became more important. Theater and opera became popular among the middle class, while less sophisticated forms of entertainment generally drew working people to sporting events, such as soccer and boxing, in cities like London. Vaudeville and music halls also became increasingly popular.

Meanwhile, the Industrial Revolution had also brought changes in middle-class homes. Since the decline of the domestic system, the workplace had been separated from the home. By the mid-1800s many members of the middle class had begun to believe in the idea of **separate spheres**—that men belonged in the public world of business and government, while women ran the household. People began to see the home itself as a haven from the stresses and harshness of the outside world.

Middle-class women assumed responsibility for creating a beautiful and peaceful environment and for raising a family of healthy, well-behaved children. Women strived to be pleasant, charming, and endlessly supportive of their husbands. As one historian wrote, women were expected to "exercise constant patience and forebearance, in spite of narrow means, inconvenient houses, crying children and preoccupied husbands." When many middle-class women began to look for work outside the home in the late 1800s, they often found it in jobs like nursing or teaching, which were seen by many as extensions of their domestic role.

Perhaps the most influential symbol of this new vision of womanhood and the middle-class family was Queen Victoria of Great Britain. Devoted to her husband, Prince Albert of Saxe-Coburg-Gotha, Victoria publicly relished her role as a devoted wife and mother. For many people, not merely in Britain but throughout the Western world, she seemed a perfect example of the new middle-class values and virtues.

CORE LESSON PLAN
See pages 481I and 481J for Lesson Plan 18.4.

R RESOURCE ACTIVITY

READINGS IN WORLD HISTORY
Reading 18.4
Defining Women's Roles

Have students read the excerpt from a handbook for American women in the late 1800s. Then have them complete the questions.

Level 2

R RESOURCE ACTIVITY

GLOBAL HISTORY RESOURCE CENTER
Image: *On Our Day Off: A Watermelon Party*

Show students the image. Have students assume the role of a picnicker and write a letter to a friend describing their day off and comparing it to their usual workday.

Level 2

For the middle class the Industrial Revolution resulted in greater prosperity, new ideas about homelife, and a changing role for women.

New Scientific and Social Ideas

As they had done in industry, Europeans made quite dramatic advances in scientific knowledge in the 1800s. For many people, the success of the Industrial Revolution confirmed humanity's capacity to solve problems. At the heart of this conviction was a growing acceptance among most educated Europeans that change was the normal state of both the natural world and society.

Darwinism. One of the greatest contributors to scientific thinking in the 1800s was the English naturalist Charles Darwin. During a break from his studies at Cambridge University, in the 1830s, Darwin sailed around the world as a naturalist on the *Beagle*, gathering data on the plants, animals, and geology of the lands he encountered. He spent more than 20 years of his life studying the natural world. In 1859 he published the synthesis of his ideas in *On the Origin of Species by Means of Natural Selection*.

Darwin's book changed the way many people thought about the world around them. He argued that life-forms were involved in a perpetual struggle for survival. Those that were better adapted to their environment survived long enough to reproduce and pass those adaptations to their offspring. Darwin called this process **natural selection**, and argued that it resulted in the gradual evolution of a species into more adaptive forms. Realizing the implications of his work, Darwin did his best to reassure people that evolution did not necessarily challenge God's existence:

▲ Charles Darwin's theory of natural selection caused great controversy.

There is grandeur in this view of life, with its several powers, having been originally breathed by the Creator into a few forms or into one; and that, whilst this planet has gone cycling on according to the fixed law of gravity, from so simple a beginning endless forms most beautiful and most wonderful have been, and are being evolved.

Nevertheless, many religious leaders denounced Darwin and his ideas.

Physical sciences. The physical sciences also saw rapid advancement. In medicine, for example, the causes and cures for many diseases were being discovered. The monk Gregor Mendel discovered the laws of heredity. Physicists Michael Faraday and James Maxwell formulated the laws governing magnetism and electricity. In the early 1800s the English chemist John Dalton had discovered that all matter is composed of minute particles called atoms. French chemist Louis Pasteur discovered small micro-organisms called bacteria. He developed vaccines for deadly diseases such as anthrax and created a heat treatment method that destroyed bacteria in certain foods and drinks. In 1869 the periodic table of chemical elements was formulated, and in 1896 Antoine-Henri Becquerel discovered radioactivity.

Significant work in the field of radioactivity was conducted by Marie Curie. Born in Poland in 1867, Marie Curie moved to Paris in 1891 to study physical sciences. In 1895 she married Pierre Curie, who shared her dedication to scientific inquiry. Marie and Pierre focused their scientific investigations on radioactivity. In the process they discovered two new elements, polonium and radium. In 1903 the Curies were awarded the Nobel Prize for physics.

Marie Curie
BIOGRAPHY

Three years later Pierre died, and Marie devoted all her attention to her work. In 1906 she became the first woman to teach at the Sorbonne, and five years later she was awarded the Nobel Prize for chemistry. In later years she worked on the application of X-rays to medical diagnosis and served as the director of research for the Radium Institute from 1918 until she died in 1934.

The social sciences. The dramatic success of scientific methods in making discoveries about the physical world also led some people to apply scientific methods to the study of society. By the end of the 1800s, the fields of sociology, history, economics, anthropology, and archaeology were growing into the so-called social sciences. Scientific methods were also applied to the study of human behavior. Wilhelm Wundt (VOOHNT), a German experimental psychologist, founded the first psychological laboratory in Leipzig in 1879. From his experiments, Wundt concluded that human psychology was based on experience and reality. The Russian physiologist Ivan Pavlov demonstrated that behavior could be conditioned by outside factors in his famous experiment on the conditioned reflex in dogs.

Sometimes these new sciences, particularly the study of heredity, were used to reinforce racist and sexist attitudes. Sir Francis Galton, a cousin of Charles Darwin, promoted the "science" of eugenics, which called for the use of selective breeding techniques to "improve" the human race. Eugenics, which relied on flawed anthropological studies of less technologically advanced cultures, was used to strengthen prejudiced assumptions about racial and class inferiority. Drawing on such ideas, another English social scientist, Herbert Spencer, tried to apply Darwin's theories to society. This resulted in **social Darwinism**, which portrayed individuals and nations as part of the same struggle for survival as the species. According to this view, the wealthy were clearly fitter—and in a sense better—than the poor, and Europeans were stronger than non-Europeans because of natural selection.

Marxism. Political theorists and revolutionaries were not immune to the new "scientific" ideas. Friedrich Engels and Karl Marx, two of the most famous and influential socialists of the 1800s, developed what they called "scientific socialism." In their collaborative work *The Communist Manifesto*, Engels and Marx wrote: "The history of all hitherto existing society is the history of class struggles." Rather than viewing the social ills of the Industrial Revolution as something to be changed, Marx maintained that they were an inevitable historical development.

Marx argued that industrial capitalism naturally created a new working class, the **proletariat** (proh-luh-TAYR-ee-uht), which capitalists took advantage of to make their profits. After sufficient abuse, however, the urban proletariat would rise up and overthrow the capitalists through violent revolution. Once in power, they would establish a temporary "dictatorship of the proletariat." This dictatorship would then abolish private property,

◄ **Karl Marx joined a secret communist society in 1847. He was asked to write the political program for the league.**

▼ **Friedrich Engels joined the league with Marx, and together they wrote *The Communist Manifesto*.**

History THROUGH THE ARTS

Photography

Every time someone opens a newspaper, magazine, or book, turns on the television, or even ventures outside, he or she is likely to be bombarded with hundreds of images taken by a camera. The abundance and ease of use of cameras also means that millions of people can record the images of loved ones and important family events. Over the past 150 years, photographs have played an important role in the way people view the world around them and in the political decisions that are made to govern society.

The technique of photography was developed in the mid-1800s by two different men working independently. In 1839 Louis-Jacques-Mandé Daguerre of France developed a process of making an image on a metal plate that was coated with a solution of silver salts. Daguerre used a large wooden box with glass lenses, known as a camera obscura, to make his images. At about the same time, William Henry Fox Talbot of England discovered a way to take pictures by creating a negative image of an object, which could then be printed in many positive images. Both Daguerre's and Talbot's methods were widely used by early photographers, but after many improvements, Talbot's method grew more popular and much less expensive than Daguerre's.

Since the development of the camera in the mid-1800s, many photographers have worked to focus attention on social and political problems. Mathew Brady followed troops into battle in the American Civil War, sending pictures to be published in popular journals of the day. The photos were the first the American public had ever seen of combat, and people at home were shocked to see the brutality of warfare.

The darker side of the Industrial Revolution in Great Britain and the United States also quickly became a hot topic for photographers. In the late 1870s John Thomson and Adolphe Smith published *Street Life in London*, a collection of photos and short texts that illustrated the plight of London's poor working class. Around 1900 in the United States, Lewis W. Hine photographed immigrants in their homes and at work, making people aware of the hardships the workers faced. The hard evidence provided by photographs convinced many people that new laws were needed to improve life for the poor. From these beginnings, photography has grown to become an essential part of news reporting in every country of the world.

Talbot's photography shop, 1845

Thinking About Art

How did the use of photography influence people's attitudes about war and the problems of industrialization?

take over the means of production, and thus establish **communism**. Once this had happened, Marx concluded, the state itself would naturally wither away.

New scientific discoveries improved many aspects of life and influenced the development of philosophy and the social sciences.

Movements in Literature and Art

The dislocation and insecurities caused by the Industrial Revolution, as well as people's attempts to adjust to them, were also reflected in the arts and literature. Some artists began to reject both the rationalism of the Enlightenment and the impersonal aspects of the industrial world. By the end of the 1800s, however, many artists and writers had embraced the world around them, and they reflected its reality in their works, showing both the positive and the negative aspects.

Romanticism. Beginning in the late 1700s, many artists and writers began to react to what they saw as the cold, impersonal nature of Enlightenment rationalism and industrial society. They began to emphasize the importance of emotions and feelings rather than the intellect and reason. Their movement became known as **romanticism**.

Like the philosophes of the 1700s, the romantics were fascinated by the natural world. Unlike the philosophes, however, romantics wanted to enjoy nature's beauty and mystery, rather than try to study and understand it. Dreams and fantasy were also often common themes of romantics' works. For example, in his poem "Kubla Khan," Samuel Taylor Coleridge painted an exotic fantasy portrait of the Mongol leader's summer palace:

> ❝ *In Xanadu did Kubla Khan*
> *A stately pleasure-dome decree:*
> *Where Alph, the sacred river, ran*
> *Through caverns measureless to man*
> *Down to a sunless sea.* ❞

Above all, perhaps, romanticism emphasized the importance of the individual who dared to express "the spontaneous overflow of powerful feelings," as the English poet William Wordsworth proclaimed. Similar determination to arouse emotions also motivated painters and architects.

The novel. During the 1800s the novel became a widely popular form of literature. The Gothic novel, often set in the medieval period, deliberately tried to arouse a sense of suspense and even horror in the reader. Some romantic writers, like Scotsman Sir Walter Scott, revived an interest in the age of chivalry.

The novel was also a useful vehicle for making critical observations about society. Tales of cruel working conditions, unending poverty, and family breakdowns were common themes. In the novels *Dombey and Son* and *Hard Times*, for example, Charles Dickens chronicled the wide variety of abuses and crises that the poor faced in Britain in the 1800s. Others saw literature as a means to criticize social customs. The French writer Amandine-Aurore-Lucile Dudevant and the British author Mary Ann Evans wrote under the male pen names George Sand and George Eliot, respectively, to illustrate the constraints of male-dominated society.

Realism. As more people accepted the realities of industrialization in the last half of the 1800s, artists and writers reacted against romanticism with a movement called **realism**. While the realists also objected to the harshness and cruelty of the industrial age, they removed excessive sentimentality from their work and tried to record the daily lives of ordinary people. French novelist Gustave Flaubert (floh-ber), for example, criticized the morals and manners of the middle class. In Russia Leo Tolstoy and Fyodor Dostoyevsky (dahs-tuh-YEF-skee) both wrote novels filled

▶ In his 1849 work *Burial at Ornans*, Gustave Courbet invited the viewer to become part of the scene.

SECTION 4 REVIEW ANSWERS (p. 506)

IDENTIFY
For significance, see the following pages:
separate spheres (p. 501)
Louis Pasteur (p. 502)
natural selection (p. 502)
Marie Curie (p. 502)
social Darwinism (p. 503)
Friedrich Engels (p. 503)
Karl Marx (p. 503)
proletariat (p. 503)
communism (p. 504)
romanticism (p. 505)
realism (p. 505)

1. People enjoyed greater prosperity and more time off, and leisure activities became important. New ideas about roles of men and women led to changes in women's roles.
2. New scientific discoveries led to a better understanding of the world, improved many aspects of life, and sparked the development of the social sciences.
3. These cities were centers of development and industrialization, and the more prosperous urban society could afford to buy things from stores.
4. romanticism—emphasized emotions and feelings, enjoyed the beauty

and mystery of nature; "Kubla Khan," by Samuel Taylor Coleridge; realism—rejected romanticism and portrayed lives of everyday people; novels by Gustave Flaubert
5. They questioned the people's religious beliefs. Many people used his beliefs to justify racist and sexist arguments. Religion and science still conflict today in such matters as medical experimentation.

with violence, love, and family crises concerning people from all classes.

In the late 1800s the new medium of photography, which could represent a "real" or "true" visual image, greatly influenced art. Realist art tried to make the viewer an active participant rather than merely an observer. From the beginning French artists led the realist movement. As Jean Désiré Gustave Courbet (koor-be) wrote:

> 66 *I hold . . . that painting is an essentially con-crete art, and can consist only of the representation of things both* real *and* existing. . . . *An* abstract *object, invisible or nonexistent, does not belong to the domain of painting. . . . Show me an angel, and I'll paint one.* 99

Impressionism. In the 1860s and 1870s some painters, first in France and then elsewhere, began to abandon realism and to develop a new style called impressionism. Like the realists, the impressionists were reacting to the development of photography. Unlike the realists, however,

◀ **Claude Monet worked outside to capture nature directly on his canvas.** *Woman with Parasol,* **here, seems to glow with sunlight.**

impressionists saw photography, with its clear, precise depiction of lines, as missing the essential ingredients of real experience—color and motion. The impressionist artists sought to provide what the camera was unable to capture by working outdoors and filling their paintings with the true visual images produced by light and atmosphere. Impressionist paintings are often alive with color. As one impressionist, Paul Signac, explained: "The entire surface of the painting glows with sunlight; the air circulates; light embraces, caresses and irradiates [illuminates] forms; it penetrates everywhere, even into the shadows which it illuminates."

Reacting to the impersonal aspects of industrialization, romanticism emphasized nature and emotion while realism embraced the modern world.

SECTION 4 REVIEW

IDENTIFY and explain the significance of the following:
separate spheres
natural selection
Louis Pasteur
Marie Curie
social Darwinism
Friedrich Engels
Karl Marx
proletariat
communism
romanticism
realism

1. **Main Idea** How did life change for the middle class after the Industrial Revolution?
2. **Main Idea** What were some effects of the many new developments in science during the 1800s?
3. **Geography: Human-Environment Interaction** Why did the first department stores locate in major cities?
4. **Writing to Explain** Imagine that you are the editor of a literary journal during the 1800s. Write a short article explaining the differences between romanticism and realism. Give an example of each movement.
5. **Analyzing** Why were Charles Darwin's ideas controversial? How were his ideas used by some people to justify their own beliefs? How do scientific ideas sometimes contribute to controversy today?

Review

On a separate sheet of paper, complete the following exercises:

WRITING A SUMMARY

Using the essential points in the text, write a brief summary of the chapter.

REVIEWING TERMS

From the following list, choose the term that correctly matches the definition.

natural selection
crop rotation
separate spheres
spinning jenny
corporation
trusts

1. type of business in which investors are sold shares of stock to raise the needed capital to operate the business
2. early machine that produced thread from raw cotton
3. Darwin's theory of the survival of the fittest
4. idea held by many people during the 1800s that men belong in the world of business and government while women belong in the home
5. process of growing different crops in succession on the same land to preserve the fertility of the soil

REVIEWING CHRONOLOGY

List the following events in their correct chronological order.

1. Marie and Pierre Curie win the Nobel Prize for physics.
2. The Eiffel Tower is built in Paris.
3. George Stephenson tests the Rocket.
4. James Watt improves the steam engine.
5. Alexander Graham Bell invents the telephone.

UNDERSTANDING THE MAIN IDEA

1. How did the steam engine affect transportation in the 1800s?
2. How did the Industrial Revolution change the British textile industry?
3. What effect did the Industrial Revolution have on the working class and on the middle class?
4. What factors contributed to the second Industrial Revolution?
5. Why did the Industrial Revolution begin in Britain?
6. How did writers and artists respond to the Industrial Revolution?

THINKING CRITICALLY

1. **Evaluating** Did the Industrial Revolution improve the quality of life for people in Europe and the United States? Explain your answer.
2. **Hypothesizing** How might the growth of businesses and communities have been different if there had not been a revolution in transportation?

Building Your Portfolio

Complete the following activities individually or in groups.

1. **Technology** Imagine that you have been hired by a museum to create part of an exhibit on the lasting worldwide impact of the Industrial Revolution. Choose one of the inventions or discoveries of the Industrial Revolution, such as the steam engine or electricity, and create a poster showing how the invention or discovery has changed people's lives up to the present day. Your poster should include illustrations supported by written information about your topic. You should also include some information about the person(s) who created the new invention or made the discovery.
2. **Advertising** Imagine that you are a Parisian in charge of advertising for Bon Marché, one of the world's first department stores. Develop an ad campaign to tell the people of Paris about the benefits of shopping in this store. You will be advertising in the newspaper, on posters, and in window displays at the store. Prepare sketches or polished drawings of your ideas, including the ad copy, to entice customers to visit your store. Present your ad campaign to the class, who represents the store's management.

4. New technology using electricity, oil, and steel accelerated the pace of industry.
5. Britain's water resources, plentiful iron and coal supplies, stable political system, and access to trade markets, along with a growing demand for manufactured goods, all allowed the Industrial Revolution to begin there.
6. Some artists rejected Enlightenment ideals and the industrial world, but many others celebrated the progress and used their talents to show the good and bad aspects of industrialization. The artistic movements of romanticism and realism developed.

THINKING CRITICALLY

1. Yes—people could buy manufactured goods at lower prices, and they would enjoy greater prosperity as a result of industrialization. In Russia, too, industrialization brought the end of serfdom. No—the problems of industrialization, such as urban poverty and divisions between upper and lower classes, existed in many countries.
2. Cities would have remained very condensed, with everything that was needed accessible by walking or a carriage ride. Businesses would probably have remained small because large corporations needed better transportation to develop. In addition, companies could not rely on shipping or receiving goods by railway, which increased the size of businesses during the Industrial Revolution.

Chapter 19

An Era of Expansion and Reform 1765–1914

Chapter Planning Guide

	TEXTBOOK	CORE RESOURCES	VISUAL RESOURCES	MULTIMEDIA
Introduction	pp. 508–509	Block Scheduling Handbook: Ch. 19		Videodisc Segment 19 and Viewing Guide: *An Era of Reform*
Lesson 19.1 Reform Movements in Great Britain	pp. 510–516 Teenagers in History: *Child Labor,* p. 512 Biography: *Emmeline Goulden Pankhurst,* p. 514	Reading 19.1: *A Suffragette Goes to Prison*	Art and History 19: *Derby Day*	GHRC 19 Readings: *Chartists Demand Universal Manhood Suffrage; A Member of Parliament Warns Against Reform* GHRC 19/Videodiscs: Image—*English Children Petitioning Against Slavery;* Chart—*British Electoral Reforms;* Video Clip—*Suffragists on the March in London*
Lesson 19.2 Expansion and Reform in the British Dominions	pp. 517–521 Map: *The Growth of Canada, 1791–1912,* p. 519 Map: *The World: Political,* pp. 854–855	Reading 19.2: *A Convict Settlement in Australia* Writing Project 19: *Creating an Outline*		GHRC 19 Reading: *A Teen Convict's Prison Record in Australia* GHRC 19/Videodiscs: Image—*Maori Nobleman of New Zealand*
Lesson 19.3 Expansion and Reform in the United States	pp. 522–528 Map: *U.S. Territorial Expansion, 1785–1898,* p. 523 Through Others' Eyes: *Frances Trollope's View of American Slavery,* p. 524 History Through the Arts: *Political Cartoons,* p. 527	Reading 19.3: *A Response to the Fugitive Slave Act* Geography Activity 19: *The Slave Trade in the United States* Skills Activity 19: *Interpreting a Graph*	Everyday Life 19: *Labor Union Membership Certificate*	GHRC 19 Readings: The Liberator *Calls for Abolition Now!; From* Uncle Tom's Cabin; *The Seneca Falls Declaration of Sentiments; Susan B. Anthony on Woman's Right to Suffrage* GHRC 19/Videodiscs: Images—*Frederick Douglass; Cartoonist Thomas Nast on Money in Politics*
Lesson 19.4 Independence in Latin America	pp. 529–532 Map: *New Nations in South America by 1828,* p. 530 Map: *Mexico, Central America, and the Caribbean by 1828,* p. 531	Reading 19.4: *The Great Liberator*	Geography and History 19: *Independence in Latin America*	GHRC 19 Readings: *San Martín Fights for Independence; Latin America's Unliberated Economies* GHRC 19/Videodiscs: Images—*Bolívar and San Martín Fight for Independence; Father Hidalgo Ignites Revolution in Mexico*
Chapter Investigation and Enrichment	pp. 508–532	Chapter 19 Investigation: *An Era of Expansion and Reform: Scored Discussions* People in World History 19 Explorations in Daily Life 19		GHRC 19/Videodiscs
Review and Assessment	Section 1 Review, p. 516 Section 2 Review, p. 521 Section 3 Review, p. 528 Section 4 Review, p. 532 Chapter 19 Review, p. 533	Chapter Review Activity 19 Vocabulary Activity 19 Themes Review 19 Section Study Guides 19.1–19.4 Main Idea Activities 19.1–19.4 Daily Quizzes 19.1–19.4 Chapter 19 Test Sheltered English Ch. 19 Test Ch. 19 Test Generator		Audio CDs: Ch. 19 Summary (English and Spanish)

INTRODUCING THE CHAPTER

Textbook pp. 508–509

CHAPTER OVERVIEW

Reform movements swept much of the world as the social changes caused by industrialization led many people to reassess their societies. Great Britain peacefully abolished slavery, but the United States turned to war to resolve the issue. Both nations continued to expand, with the British turning to Canada and Australia and the United States expanding to the Pacific. Latin Americans—drawing inspiration from the earlier American and French revolutions—struggled against colonialism.

PRESENTING THEMES

On the chalkboard or on an overhead transparency, write the following open-ended theme questions.

- **ECONOMIC ORGANIZATION** How might the abolition of slavery affect a nation's economy?
- **SOCIAL RELATIONS** Why might people want to reform society?
- **POLITICS AND LAW** How might highly conservative groups be persuaded to include more people in the political process?

Have students, either individually or in groups, suggest responses to the questions. For the economic organization question, students might suggest that the loss of the slave labor force might cause economic collapse. For the social relations question, students might suggest that religious values might drive reform. For the politics and law question, students might suggest that conservative groups might realize that people might rebel if they felt excluded from the political processes. Save the responses. Once students have studied the chapter, you may wish to have them complete the Themes Review, then compare the two sets of answers.

USING THE VIDEO

Segment 19: *An Era of Reform*

ENGLISH

Search Chapter 19
Videodisc 2, Side A

SPANISH

Search Chapter 19
Videodisc 2, Side A

Tell students that in this chapter they will apply these theme questions to the powerful reform movements that reshaped society in Great Britain, North America, South America, Australia, and New Zealand in the period from 1765 to 1914. Then show Segment 19 of the *World History and Cultures Videodiscs*. This segment focuses on the expansion of voting rights that occurred between the late 1700s and the early 1900s to show how the era of reform affected democracy in the United States. To help students grasp the significant points of the segment, have them complete Video Viewing Guide 19.

Key to Ability Levels

All strategies and activities are coded to the following ability levels:

LEVEL 1	**Basic** activities suitable for all students
LEVEL 2	**Average** activities suitable for average to above-average students
LEVEL 3	**Challenging** activities suitable for above-average students
SHELTERED ENGLISH	Activities suitable for students with **Limited English Proficiency**

Additional Resources

BOOKS FOR TEACHERS

Brown, Dee. *Wondrous Times on the Frontier.* HarperPerennial, 1991. Gives an anecdotal history.

Himmelfarb, Gertrude. *Poverty and Compassion: The Moral Imagination of the Late Victorians.* Vintage Books, 1991. Analyzes responses to social problems.

Kolchin, Peter. *American Slavery, 1619–1877.* Hill and Wang, 1993. Discusses American slavery.

BOOKS FOR STUDENTS

McFeely, William S. *Frederick Douglass.* Norton, 1991. A biography that examines Douglass's writings.

Remini, Robert Vincent. *The Jacksonian Era.* Davidson, 1989. Discusses slavery and Indian Removal.

Ward, Geoffrey C. *The Civil War: An Illustrated History of the Civil War.* Knopf, 1990. A survey with photographs and illustrations.

MULTIMEDIA MATERIALS

A History of Slavery in America. Library Video, 1994. Video, 30 min. Presents an overview of slavery.

The Oregon Trail. Films for the Humanities and Sciences. Video, 113 minutes. Discusses American expansion.

The Victorian Era. ZCI. CD-ROM, MAC, WIN, MPC formats. Focuses on social, political, and economic changes in Great Britain.

Lesson 19.1   *Reform Movements in Great Britain*

Textbook pp. 510–516

RESOURCES

Pupil's Edition
Teenagers in History, p. 512: *Child Labor*
Biography, p. 514: *Emmeline Goulden Pankhurst*

Core Resources
Reading 19.1: *A Suffragette Goes to Prison*

Global History Resource Center
Reading: *Chartists Demand Universal Manhood Suffrage*
Reading: *A Member of Parliament Warns Against Reform*

Videodiscs or Global History Resource Center

Image: *English Children Petitioning Against Slavery*

Search Frame 930

Image: *Parliament Passes the Reform Bill of 1832*

Search Frame 931

Chart: *British Electoral Reforms*

Search Frame 942

Video Clip: *Suffragists on the March in London*

Search 3737, Play to 4194
Videodisc 2, Side A
Video Clip 19

LESSON FOCUS
What factors gave rise to the British reform movements of the 1800s, and what did those movements achieve?

OBJECTIVES
After completing this lesson, students will be able to:
- identify the factors that contributed to the growth of the movement to end slavery;
- explain the effect that industrialization had on political and economic reform in Britain;
- discuss how demands for social reform affected some people's view of the role of government.

HOOK
Review the factors that encouraged the growth of the antislavery movement. Write the term *Enlightenment* on the chalkboard and ask students to identify the major features of this movement. (Review the discussion in Chapter 17, if necessary.) Note responses on the chalkboard. Next read aloud this excerpt from *Candide*, by the philosopher Voltaire:

> As they drew near the town, they met a Negro [slave] lying on the ground wearing only half his clothes, that is to say, a pair of blue drawers; this poor man had no left leg and no right hand.
>
> "Good Heavens!" said Candide . . . , "what are you doing there, my friend, in this horrible state?"
>
> "I am waiting for my master, the famous merchant, Mr. Vanderdendur."
>
> "Was it Mr. Vanderdendur," said Candide, "who treated you in this way?"
>
> "Yes, sir," said the Negro, "it is the custom. We are given a pair of cotton drawers twice a year as clothing. When we work in the sugar-mills and the grindstone catches our fingers, they cut off the hand; when we try to run away, they cut off a leg. Both these things happened to me. This is the price paid for the sugar you eat in Europe."

Ask: What was Voltaire trying to convey to the reader?

[the evils of slavery and the fact that the European way of life was dependent on the suffering of slaves]

Have students discuss the impact such writings might have had in a country like Britain, which considered itself a champion of liberty.

Ask: *What other movement contributed to antislavery sentiment in Britain?*

[the evangelical movement]

To conclude, have students view the electronic media image of children petitioning against slavery.

DEVELOP

Analyze the effect that industrialization had on demands for economic and political reform in Britain. Write the following topics on the chalkboard: *Working Conditions* and *Industrial Regulation*; *Reform Bill of 1832*; *Reform Groups*. Have students discuss each topic listed above, paying particular attention to:

- how these factors affected people's lives;
- the nature of the first industrial regulations;
- the results of the early political reform movements.

In addition to the textbook, you might also want students to read the Global History Resource Center materials on Chartism and reform, and view the illustration of the passage of the 1832 Reform Bill and the chart showing the impact of electoral reform.

Encourage students to take notes on the discussion. Ask them to review their notes and identify the impact of industrialization on British reform movements. [*Responses should indicate that prosperity and the problems caused by industrialization led to calls for industrial and political reform.*]

PROBE

Discuss the tactics used by the suffragists. In addition to the text, have the students read Core Resources Reading 19.1 and view the video clip of the suffragists' march. Discuss the biography of Pankhurst on textbook page 514, and ask students to identify the suffragists' tactics discussed in the materials. [*Responses should include demonstrations and picketing, acts of civil disobedience and violence, hunger strikes, and damage to property.*]

Ask: *What was the impact of these tactics?*

[*They energized the suffrage movement but also convinced some people that women were not responsible enough to have the vote.*]

Link to Today. Were the tactics of the suffragettes justified? [*Answers will vary.*] Ask students if they can think of more recent protest movements that have sometimes resulted in violence (events prior to the abolition of apartheid in South Africa, for example). Ask students for their opinions on whether or not violence is sometimes necessary to right a wrong.

CONCLUDE

Investigate changes in people's attitudes about the role of government. Draw students' attention to the Teenagers in History feature. Then call on volunteers to identify problems of the British urban poor during the late 1800s and early 1900s. [*unsanitary living conditions and illness, for example*]

Ask: *What steps were taken to help the poor? How did this mark a change in attitude?*

[*reformed poor law; a national board of health; programs for workers' compensation, pensions, medical care, and unemployment; that social well-being could be achieved through government programs*]

EXTEND
Other Media

Have students view the video *The Changing World of Charles Dickens* (Learning Corporation of America, 5 min.). Encourage them to identify the social welfare issues addressed in these scenes from Dickens's novels.

MEET INDIVIDUAL NEEDS
Gifted Students

Have students read the pieces on Chartism and electoral reform in the Global History Resource Center. Then have small groups prepare and present a short parliamentary debate on electoral reform.

Intrapersonal Learners

Have students write one-paragraph statements that show the points of view that each of the following people in Britain might have had on the Chartists' demand for universal manhood suffrage: a wealthy member of Parliament; a poor male mill worker; and a middle-class woman suffragist.

ASSESS
Review

Have students complete the Section 1 Review. Use answers in the Teacher's Edition, page 516, to assess student mastery of this section.

Expansion and Reform in the British Dominions

Textbook pp. 517–521

RESOURCES

Pupil's Edition

Map, p. 519: *The Growth of Canada,
1791–1912*
Map, pp. 854–855: *The World: Political*

Core Resources

Reading 19.2: *A Convict Settlement in
Australia*

Global History Resource Center

Reading: *A Teen Convict's Prison Record
in Australia*

Videodiscs or Global History Resource Center

Image: *Maori Nobleman of New Zealand*

Search Frame 933

LESSON FOCUS

*How did the British colonies of Canada,
Australia, and New Zealand gain dominion
status?*

OBJECTIVES

After completing this lesson, students will be able to:

• examine what drove British colonization in the late 1700s
and 1800s;
• explain why Britain granted self-government to Canada;
• discuss the limits that the Commonwealth of Australia
placed on liberal democracy;
• describe the circumstances under which New Zealand
became a self-governing dominion.

HOOK

**Discuss the driving forces of British colonization in the
late 1700s and 1800s.** Draw students' attention to the world
political map on page 854 of the textbook. Have them trace on
the map with their fingers sea routes they might take from
Britain to such locations as Canada, South Africa, Australia,
and New Zealand. Then have students consider why Britain
chose to colonize these distant lands.

Ask: *What fueled Britain's drive to colonize in the late 1700s
and 1800s?*

[Voyages of exploration brought new areas to the
attention of the British. The industrial and agricultural
revolutions caused a population explosion. As a result,
migrants left Britain to settle in the newly discovered
lands.]

Tell students that Robert Hughes's *The Fatal Shore: The Epic of
Australia's Founding* (Alfred A. Knopf, 1987) discusses the
unique circumstances surrounding Australia's founding. Hughes
points out that although Captain James Cook had briefly stopped
on the coast of Australia, the British had not explored the
continent. Nonetheless, the British government decided to turn
Australia into a jail, thereby ridding Britain of its "criminal
class." The vast distance separating Australia from Britain would,
in effect, serve to isolate criminals from the rest of British
society. To provide students with more information on
Australia's prison colonies, assign Core Resources Reading 19.2
and the Global History Resource Center reading on the teen
convict's prison record.

DEVELOP

Examine why Britain gave Canada dominion status.
Draw a horizontal line on the chalkboard. Write *1830* at one
end of the line and *1900* at the other. Call on students to
identify the major events on Canada's path toward self-rule and
territorial expansion. Suggest that they use textbook pages
518–519, including the map on the growth of Canada, as their
information source. Note student responses on the time line.
[Time line entries might include: **1837**: *rebellions in Upper and
Lower Canada;* **1838**: *Lord Durham appointed as governor-*

general; **1839**: Upper and Lower Canada united in one province with self-government in internal affairs; **1867**: British North America Act created the Dominion of Canada; **1870**: land bought from Hudson's Bay Company]

Circle or highlight references to self-government and dominion on the time line. Then have students determine why Canada won dominion status. *[The British government wanted to keep Canada in the empire and to lessen the United States' influence.]* Ask students to copy the time line into their notebooks and to retain it for a later activity.

Link to Today. To make a connection to more modern times, ask students how the union of Canada has been affected by recent events in Quebec.

PROBE

Examine liberal democracy in Australia. Point out that throughout its history, Australia has shown a strong commitment to democracy. At times, however, Australian governments have introduced policies and taken actions that suggested this commitment was limited. Organize students into small groups. Have half the groups design posters that illustrate the actions and policies that indicate Australia's commitment to democracy. Have the rest of the groups design posters that show the limitations placed on democracy in Australia. Call on groups to display and explain their posters. *[Democratic commitment: universal manhood suffrage, the secret ballot, the separation of church and state, women's suffrage; Limitations: policies of racial exclusion, including the Immigration Restriction Act of 1901 and the Pacific Islanders' Protection Act of 1901]*

CONCLUDE

Investigate the conditions under which New Zealand became a dominion. Ask students to find in their notebooks the time line showing Canada's progress toward self-government. Then have them suggest entries for a time line for New Zealand. After students suggest entries, write their answers on the chalkboard.

Ask: What was the major feature of New Zealand's progress toward self-government?
[a long struggle with the Maori]

Encourage students to imagine that they are journalists in New Zealand in 1907. They have been asked by their editor to write a short background article about the path to dominion. Suggest that they use the notes on the chalkboard as the basis for their articles. Invite volunteers to read their articles to the class.

EXTEND

Cross-Curricular Connection: *Art*
Draw students' attention to the picture of the Maori chief on textbook page 521, or display the electronic media image of the Maori nobleman. Point out that the Maoris of New Zealand consider body tattooing an art form. Encourage students to research and report on the history and significance of body tattooing in South Pacific cultures.

MEET INDIVIDUAL NEEDS

Musical-Rhythmic Learners
Have interested students search audio and video resources in the public library to find examples of Maori or Aborigine music. Encourage them to share the examples with the rest of the class and provide some background information on the instruments used.

Visual-Spatial Learners
Encourage students to construct a large-scale map of the Canadian Pacific Railway. Suggest that they research the railroad to provide interesting points of information about its construction.

ASSESS

Review
Have students complete the Section 2 Review. Use answers in the Teacher's Edition, page 521, to assess student mastery of this section.

Lesson 19.3 — *Expansion and Reform in the United States*

Textbook pp. 522–528

RESOURCES

Pupil's Edition

Map, p. 523: *U.S. Territorial Expansion, 1785–1898*

Through Others' Eyes, p. 524: *Frances Trollope's View of American Slavery*

History Through the Arts, p. 527: *Political Cartoons*

Core Resources

Reading 19.3: *A Response to the Fugitive Slave Act*

Geography Activity 19: *The Slave Trade in the United States*

Skills Activity 19: *Interpreting a Graph*

Global History Resource Center

Reading: The Liberator *Calls for Abolition Now!*

Reading: *From* Uncle Tom's Cabin

Reading: *The Seneca Falls Declaration of Sentiments*

Reading: *Susan B. Anthony on Woman's Right to Suffrage*

Reading: *A Report Favoring Free Public Schools*

Reading: *From* How the Other Half Lives

Videodiscs or Global History Resource Center

Image: *Frederick Douglass: American Abolitionist*

Search Frame 934

Image: *Striking Workers Face Troops in Massachusetts*

Search Frame 937

Image: *Cartoonist Thomas Nast on Money in Politics*

Search Frame 936

LESSON FOCUS

What challenges did the United States encounter in its growth as a nation?

OBJECTIVES

After completing this lesson, students will be able to:

- describe how the United States tried to resolve its conflict over slavery and identify the consequences of these actions;
- discuss the role that the abolition movement played in the struggle for women's suffrage;
- identify the pressures that led to demands for social, political, and economic reform.

HOOK

Recognize that the United States was plagued by sectionalism in the mid-1800s. Refer students to the map showing U.S. expansion on textbook page 523. Ask students what typical pictures of the Northeast, the South, and the West in the mid-1800s might show. *[the Northeast—a bustling urban scene or factories; the South—a cotton plantation with slaves; the West—the wide-open spaces of the Great Plains]* Then have students speculate what differences in populations, economics, and ways of life might exist among these three sections. *[Responses should indicate that life in the North was mostly urban and industrial; life in the South was largely rural and agricultural and depended on slave labor; and the West was marked by a frontier lifestyle.]*

Conclude by pointing out that these different ways of life gave rise to different opinions on national issues, particularly on slavery. To help students understand the role of slavery in the South, assign Geography Activity 19.

DEVELOP

Discuss the struggle in the United States to resolve the conflict over slavery. Read, or have a student read, the following excerpt from Abraham Lincoln's 1858 "House Divided" speech:

A house divided against itself cannot stand. I believe this government cannot endure permanently half slave and half free. I do not expect the Union to be dissolved; I do not expect the house to fall; but I do expect it will cease to be divided. It will become all one thing, or all the other.

Call on students to explain how slavery had left the United States "divided against itself." Guide students by reminding them of the role that slavery played in southern life, and mention the abolition movement. To provide more background for discussion, you may wish to display the electronic media image of Frederick Douglass and assign Core Resources Reading 19.3 and the Global History Resource Center readings of *The Liberator* editorial and the excerpt from *Uncle Tom's Cabin*. Then ask students to explain how the United States government attempted to resolve the conflict over slavery. *[compromise]*

Point out that these efforts at compromise eventually failed, and in 1861 civil war broke out. The North emerged victorious from the war in 1865. To provide background on why the North won the war, assign Skills Activity 19.

Ask: *What impact did the North's victory in the Civil War have on slavery?*
  [It ended slavery but did not create economic and social freedom for former slaves.]

PROBE

Investigate the connection between the abolition movement and the struggle for women's suffrage. Encourage students to identify and discuss the main features of the women's suffrage movement. In addition to the text, use the Global History Resource Center readings on voting rights for women and the Seneca Falls Declaration to stimulate discussion.

Ask: *What role did the abolition movement play in the struggle for women's suffrage?*
  [Many women worked in the movement and became aware of their own inequality.]

CONCLUDE

Analyze the development of reform movements in the United States. Ask students to identify the forces that brought about a transformation in the United States during the 1800s and early 1900s. *[industrialization, immigration, and urbanization]* Point out that these forces created a number of problems, which fueled the drive for reform.

Have students study the Global History Resource Center readings of the report on free public schools, the excerpt from *How the Other Half Lives*, and the electronic media image of striking workers. Then construct a four-column chart on the chalkboard with these headings: *Educational, Social, Political,* and *Economic and Industrial*. Call on volunteers to come to the chalkboard and list reforms that were carried out in each area. [**Educational**: public schools; **Social**: settlement houses; **Political**: direct primary, secret ballot, initiative, referendum, recall; **Economic and industrial**: antitrust laws, better working conditions, labor unions]

EXTEND
Community Resources
Have students investigate the experiences of immigrants who came to their community or region in the late 1800s and early 1900s.

Link to Today. You may wish to have students investigate the experiences of contemporary immigrants. Invite them to share their findings with the class.

Cross-Curricular Connection: *Language Arts*
Ask students to read the Through Others' Eyes feature on textbook page 524. Then have them write a letter to the author responding to her comments from the viewpoint of an abolitionist.

MEET INDIVIDUAL NEEDS
Students Having Difficulty/Students Acquiring English
Have students work with partners to test each other's comprehension of the various reform movements, going over the origins and goals of each.

Visual-Spatial Learners
Have students read the History Through the Arts feature on textbook page 527 and display the electronic media image on Thomas Nast. Encourage students to create a cartoon on one of the problems that reformers confronted in the late 1800s and early 1900s.

ASSESS
Review
Have students complete the Section 3 Review. Use answers in the Teacher's Edition, page 528, to assess student mastery of this section.

Lesson 19.4   *Independence in Latin America*

RESOURCES

Pupil's Edition

Map, p. 530: *New Nations in South America by 1828*

Map, p. 531: *Mexico, Central America, and the Caribbean by 1828*

Videodiscs or Global History Resource Center

Map: *Bolívar and San Martín Fight for Independence*

Search Frame 941

Core Resources

Reading 19.4: *The Great Liberator*

Visual Resources

Geography and History 19: *Independence in Latin America*

Image: *Father Hidalgo Ignites Revolution in Mexico*

Search Frame 939

Global History Resource Center

Reading: *San Martín Fights for Independence*

Reading: *Latin America's Unliberated Economies*

Image: *Chile After Independence: Life Remains Hard*

Search Frame 938

LESSON FOCUS

What consequences did the desire for self-rule have in Latin America?

OBJECTIVES

After completing this lesson, students will be able to:

- list the results of the Haitian slave revolution;
- explain how European events affected Latin American colonies;
- discuss how other nations reacted to Latin American independence.

HOOK

Discuss the results of the slave revolution in Saint Domingue. Point out that in 1794 the French government abolished slavery in all of its colonies after a speech given in February by the French revolutionary leader Georges-Jacques Danton. In his speech Danton expressed the opinion that liberty should be universal, and if slavery were abolished and liberty established in the colonies, it would flourish and grow strong.

Ask: *How did abolition affect the French colony of Saint Domingue?*

[French settlers resisted the Declaration of the Rights of Man, which caused slaves and mulattoes to revolt. The

revolt resulted in Saint Domingue's independence as Haiti in 1804.]

DEVELOP

Examine how events in Europe influenced Latin American colonies. Ask students to imagine that they are Latin American colonists who want more control over their government. Have them discuss how they feel about the following events: Spain's introduction of the intendancy system, the French Revolution, Napoleon's invasion of Spain and Portugal, and the formation of liberal governments in Spain and Portugal. *[Responses might include: **Intendancy system**: resentment at "outsider" interference, feelings of nationalism and patriotism awakened; **French Revolution**: desire for greater freedom aroused; **Napoleon's invasions**: since legitimate governments in Europe were overthrown, control should revert to the colonies; **New liberal governments**: to protect colonial interests, colonists had to declare independence]* Have students arrange the information in a table and ask them to connect events and outcomes with arrows to show cause-effect relationships.

To provide students with more information on the revolutions in Latin America, assign Core Resources Reading 19.4 and the Global History Resource Center reading on San Martín. You might also have students view the electronic media map of Bolívar's and San Martín's major campaigns.

PROBE

Compare the revolution in Mexico to revolutions elsewhere in Spanish America.
Have students view the electronic media image of Father Hidalgo. Then ask them to compare the revolution led by Father Hidalgo in Mexico with other revolutions in Spanish America.

Ask: *How was the revolution in Mexico similar to other revolutions in Spanish America? How was it different?*
[*Similar:* it was influenced by events in Europe, particularly Napoleon's invasion of Spain; *Different:* creoles did not support revolutionaries' aims; as a result, supporters of the Mexican Revolution were mainly mestizos and Indians, not creoles]

CONCLUDE

Explore how other nations responded to independence in Latin America.
To provide students with a picture of Latin America after independence, have them study the maps on textbook pages 530 and 531. You might wish to display Geography and History Transparency 19 and ask students to complete the accompanying worksheet. Then guide students in a discussion on how other nations reacted to the new situation in Latin America. Stress that nations like Britain and the United States looked on it favorably. Call on students to explain the economic reasons for this. [*Britain:* loans, increased trade, investment; *United States:* no European control, new markets for American goods] Then have students outline the Monroe Doctrine.

Ask: *Why did Britain and the United States favor and support independence in Latin America?*
[Both Britain and the United States were afraid that Spain would attempt to reassert colonial rule there.]

You might continue by discussing difficult conditions in Latin America after independence. The struggle for independence had left many new nations unstable and heavily dependent on foreign aid. To illustrate this, ask students to review the Global History Resource Center reading on Latin American economies and to study the electronic media image of hardships in Chile after independence.

Link to Today. You might also ask students if they are familiar with the term *international debt crisis*. Mention that many Latin American countries suffered major economic problems beginning in the 1970s, when they became heavily reliant on foreign loans to keep their economies afloat during the oil crisis. The result was the international debt crisis, when people feared that if these countries missed their interest payments, U.S. and European banks would collapse (see Chapter 29 for more information).

Conclude by asking students to imagine that they are editors working on a book dealing with Latin American independence movements of the early 1800s. Have them write an outline or brief summary of the main points to be included in the book.

EXTEND

Cross-Curricular Connection: *Geography*
Have students work in pairs to match the events discussed in the lesson with the places these events occurred. Have one partner look through the text and name an important event. The other partner should find out where the event took place and locate that place on a map of Latin America. Direct partners to take turns naming events and locating places.

MEET INDIVIDUAL NEEDS

Gifted Students
Have students research and write an essay showing how Enlightenment ideals influenced such Latin American liberators as Simón Bolívar and José de San Martín.

Kinesthetic Learners
Have students work in small groups to study Bob and Jan Young's book *Liberators of Latin America* (Lothrop, Lee & Shephard Co., 1970). Then have groups write and perform a five-minute drama on an incident from the life of one of the liberators discussed in the book.

ASSESS

Review
Have students complete the Section 4 Review. Use answers in the Teacher's Edition, pages 531–532, to assess student mastery of this section.

In preparation for the chapter test, you may wish to have students complete all or part of the Chapter 19 Review on textbook page 533, the Chapter 19 Review Activity, and the Chapter 19 Themes Review.

Chapter 19

An Era of Expansion and Reform

Understanding the Main Idea

Call on a volunteer to read aloud the *Understanding the Main Idea* paragraph. Then tell students that nations experienced tremendous changes after they entered the Industrial Revolution. A growing middle class wanted more from society and rejected control by a ruling elite. Colonies of the great European empires demanded self-rule. In addition, many people questioned slavery and other institutions.

Presenting Themes

See p. 507B for suggestions on introducing themes.

Using the Time Line

Have students list the time line events in their notebooks. After they have read about each event in the chapter, have students write a paragraph explaining its significance.

Chapter 19
An Era of Expansion and Reform
1765–1914

Understanding the Main Idea

A wave of reform began to sweep through Europe, the United States, and other parts of the world in the late 1700s. Inspired by Enlightenment ideals and alarmed by social problems brought on by the Industrial Revolution, reformers demanded political and economic change. In Latin America Enlightenment ideals led colonists to declare independence from Spain and Portugal.

Themes

- **Economic Organization** How might the abolition of slavery affect a nation's economy?

- **Social Relations** Why might people want to reform society?

- **Politics and Law** How might highly conservative groups be persuaded to include more people in the political process?

When the British slave ship *Zong* sailed from Africa, it was fully laden with newly enslaved Africans. Before reaching its destination in Jamaica, the ship began to run short of water and other supplies. The ship's captain ordered 132 sick slaves to be thrown overboard to ensure that there would be enough supplies to keep the crew and remaining slaves alive. When this incident came before the court, the captain was not tried for murder. Instead, the crime was tried as an insurance case, since the ship's insurance company disputed the owner's claim for lost property.

In 1783 Lord Mansfield, the presiding judge over this case, said that "the case of slaves was the same as if horses had been thrown overboard" and awarded damages of £30 per slave to the owner of the *Zong*. The ruling angered many people and focused attention in Britain on the need to abolish the brutal slave trade. Britain's abolition of slavery was a prime example of the reforms that swept through Europe and the Americas in the late 1700s and 1800s.

1811 ▲ Simón Bolívar leads Venezuela to independence.

1819 ▲ British Parliament passes Factory Act.

1832 ▲ British Reform Bill of 1832 gives the vote to middle-class men.

1833 ▲ Slavery is abolished in the British Empire.

This photograph, taken in 1905 at a suffragist convention in Portland, Oregon, shows some of the women who participated in the struggle for women's right to vote.

Initially, the women's movement was divided. In 1869 Elizabeth Cady Stanton and Susan B. Anthony formed the National Woman Suffrage Association to fight for an amendment to the Constitution granting women's suffrage. In that same year Lucy Stone organized the American Woman Suffrage Association to fight for the vote through the state legislatures. These two groups finally merged in 1890 to become the National American Woman Suffrage Association. One of the women in the picture, Carrie Chapman Catt, served as the leader of the association from 1900 to 1904.

Critical Thinking Ask students why some men, like those pictured here, might participate in women's suffrage conventions.

ANSWER: Students might suggest that these men believed that women had the right to vote.

1863	1886	1903	1911
President Abraham Lincoln issues the Emancipation Proclamation.	American Federation of Labor is founded in the United States.	Women's Social and Political Union is founded in Britain.	National Insurance Act provides health care and benefits to unemployed workers in Britain.

SECTION 1

CORE LESSON PLAN
See pages 507C and 507D for Lesson Plan 19.1.

INTERNET ACTIVITY

ANTISLAVERY ASSOCIATIONS
Some of the antislavery organizations of the 1700s and 1800s are still in existence.

Activity: Have students search the Web for information about organizations such as the American Anti-Slavery Group. Organize students into groups and have them research continuing efforts to fight slavery. [Note: some of the photos and descriptions of modern slavery may contain graphic material.] Ask each group to report back to the class with their findings.

All Levels

SECTION 1

Reform Movements in Great Britain

FOCUS

- What factors contributed to the growth of the movement to end slavery?

- What effect did industrialization have on demands for economic and political reform in Britain?

- How did demands for social reform affect some conceptions about the role of government?

Although the Industrial Revolution brought wealth and power to Great Britain, it also created many economic and social problems. People responded by launching a host of reform movements. Influenced by Enlightenment philosophy and a new religious awakening, they sought solutions to society's problems. Just as many nations looked to Britain as a model for industrialization, they also looked to Britain as a model for reform.

"Capital and Labor," 1843 political cartoon from the magazine *Punch*

The Antislavery Movement

The first great reform movement in Britain was directed against the slave trade. By the end of the 1700s Britain had become the world's greatest slave-trading nation. British traders and planters transported as many as 2.5 million Africans into slavery and created some of the most prosperous slave colonies in the world. In the early 1800s, however, Britain turned its back on the slave trade and became a strong opponent of slavery. Great Britain led the **abolition movement** to end the trade of slaves and eventually slavery throughout the world.

The Enlightenment helped pave the way for abolition. Few people openly opposed the practice of slavery until Rousseau and other Enlightenment writers began attacking it. As Enlightenment ideas spread, discussions about liberty were often linked to slavery. American abolitionist Anthony Benezet, for example, criticized the British for being so proud of their liberties while profiting from slavery.

66 *How [can] many of those who distinguish themselves as Advocates [supporters] of Liberty remain insensible and inattentive to the treatment of thousands and tens of thousands of our fellow men, who . . . are at this very time kept in the most deplorable [terrible] state of slavery[?]* 99

British parliamentary leader Charles James Fox also appealed to Enlightenment ideals when he called for the abolition of the slave trade.

Religion was another important influence on the fight against slavery. In the late 1700s Great Britain underwent a widespread religious revival, which grew enormously in the early 1800s. The **evangelical movement**, as this revival was called, encouraged people to see their faith as a deeply personal experience and to emphasize the importance of moral conduct in their lives. Such feelings were particularly strong among **nonconformists**, or Protestants who did not belong to the Church of England. Many nonconformists believed slavery was immoral and had the time, money, and influence to campaign on behalf of slaves.

William Wilberforce, who was a devout evangelical Christian from Yorkshire, led the antislavery movement in Parliament. "The great influence of his personal connexions," wrote one admirer, "added to an amiable [friendly] and unblemished character, secure every advantage to the cause." Even with such strong leadership, however, it was not until 1807 that abolitionists persuaded Parliament to ban the slave trade in the British Empire.

In the years that followed, reformers began to press for abolition not only of the slave trade, but of slavery itself. Finally, in August 1833, the British Parliament passed a law emancipating, or freeing, all slaves held in the British Empire. Antislavery activists soon turned their attention toward freeing slaves in other countries, particularly in the United States.

Enlightenment ideals and the evangelical movement contributed to calls for the abolition of slavery.

Economic and Political Reforms

The antislavery movement was only the first of many successful reform movements in Britain during the 1700s and 1800s. As the Industrial Revolution transformed society, other groups also began to demand reforms. Among these groups were members of the growing working and urban middle classes who called for industrial regulation and political reform.

The beginnings of industrial regulation. Industrialization and urbanization increased public awareness of the conditions under which British workers and their families had to live. Growing numbers of reformers denounced the treatment of children and pregnant women in factories. Even some factory owners found the situation intolerable. In the early 1800s, for example, Robert Owen, the British socialist and factory owner, began to argue in Parliament for laws limiting the use of children in factories. In 1819 Parliament passed the Factory Act, which prohibited children under 9 years old from working in factories and set a maximum 12-hour workday for children aged 9 to 12.

Such limited measures did little to improve the system, however, and calls for further reform

▲ This picture shows young girls sifting dust to make bricks in an English brickyard in 1871. Sifting resulted in better bricks, but it meant that children constantly inhaled clay, which could hurt their lungs.

increased. In 1833 Parliament began to pass more laws regulating the uses and hours of women and children in both factories and mines. In 1842, women and children were prohibited from working underground in the mines altogether. The new regulations had a mixed effect. Although they improved working conditions, they also limited the contributions women and children made to family incomes.

To enforce the regulations, Parliament provided for government inspectors who would regularly investigate conditions in factories. With only a few inspectors and little funding for the regulatory system, abuses often continued. Nevertheless, the general standard of living for workers as well as other classes began to rise steadily after about 1850. Shorter hours and better working conditions actually increased workers' efficiency. As productivity increased, so did wages. More working-class families could afford items the previous generation had only dreamed about. Most people were eating better—more meat, fish, milk, cheese, and eggs—and the public's general health improved so much

In the early period of mill labor, the workers were almost exclusively children. In the late 1700s the Manchester Board of Health reported on the conditions in the area's cotton factories: "It appears that the children and others . . . are peculiarly disposed to be affected by the contagion of fever; . . . The large factories are generally injurious to those employed in them . . . [because of] the close confinement . . . , the debilitating effects of hot or impure air, and . . . the want of the active exercises. . . . The untimely labour of the night, and the protracted labour of the day, . . . not only tends to diminish future expectations . . . by impairing the strength, and destroying the vital stamina of the rising generation, but it too often gives encouragement to idleness, extravagance, and profligacy in the parents, who contrary to the law of nature, subsist by the oppression of their children."

Critical Thinking Ask students why mill owners might have preferred to use children as operatives.

ANSWER: Students might suggest that small children could operate machines like an adult, but would work for lower wages.

Teenagers IN HISTORY

Child Labor

Child labor was not an invention of the Industrial Revolution. From the earliest times children, as soon as they were physically able, were expected to help in the economic activities of the family. In Europe and the United States, in the years before the Industrial Revolution, children certainly worked. They often helped their parents with household chores or in domestic industries. The work was done within the family setting under the protection and guidance of parents. However, the introduction of the factory system changed everything. In the factories children were required to work long hours, often at very dangerous tasks. George Oldfield was one such child. Oldfield was born in Yorkshire, England, in the 1830s.

When he was about nine years old, he took a job in a cotton mill. In the following excerpt Oldfield describes his experiences at work:

❝We had to be up at 5 in the morning to get to the factory, ready to begin work at 6, then work while [until] 8, when we stopped 1/2 an hour for breakfast, then work to 12 noon; for dinner we had 1 hour, then work while [until] 4. We then had 1/2 an hour for [tea], . . . then commenced work again on to 8:30. If any time during the day had been lost, we had to work while [until] 9 o'clock, and so on every night till it was made up. Then we went to what was called home. Many times I have been asleep when I had taken my last spoonful of [porridge]— not even washed, we were so overworked and underfed. I used to [curse] the road we walked on. I was so [weak] and feeble I used to think it was the road [that] would not let me go along with the others. We had not always the kindest masters. I remember my master's strap, 5 or 6 feet long, about 3/4 in. broad, and 1/4 in. thick. He kept it hung on the ginney [spinning jenny] at his right hand, so we could not see when he took [hold] of it. But we could not mistake its lessons; for he got hold of it nearly in the middle, and it would be a rare thing if we did not get 2 cuts at one stroke. I have reason to believe on one occasion he was somewhat moved to compassion, for the end of his strap striped the skin of my neck about 3 in. long. When he saw the blood and cut, he actually stopped the machine, came and tied a handkerchief round my neck to cover it up.❞

A supervisor in a British cotton factory whips a young boy.

that death rates began to fall. Around 1850 many people could even afford to open savings accounts.

The Reform Bill of 1832. The increasing prosperity of the working and middle classes produced by the Industrial Revolution led to greater demands for political reform. In 1800, seats in Parliament were still primarily in the hands of landowning aristocrats. Some industrial cities, such as Birmingham and Manchester, had no representatives at all. Throughout Britain, only wealthy male property owners could vote. Catholics, Jews, and nonconformists could hold few political offices. In addition, members of the

House of Commons were not paid for their services, so public office was largely restricted to men of great wealth.

By the 1830s, however, demands for reform became too strong to ignore. In Britain, as in the rest of Europe, liberalism was challenging the old aristocratic and conservative order. Unrest increased throughout the country as ordinary people demanded greater political participation. Eventually, Parliament agreed to change the electoral laws.

The Reform Bill of 1832 gave industrial cities representation in Parliament for the first time. It also gave the vote to middle-class men, increasing the number of eligible voters by about 50 percent and significantly reducing the power of the aristocracy. However, political leaders continued to assume that only men with property and education would be responsible voters. Consequently, the bill provided that only men with a certain amount of property could vote. This requirement effectively prevented working-class men from voting. Women also continued to be excluded from voting.

Chartism. Frustrated that the working class had been left out of the new reforms, in 1836 William Lovett, a shopkeeper, drew up a reform plan called the People's Charter. The Charter called for universal manhood suffrage and equal electoral districts to provide more equal representation for everyone in the country. It also called for paying members of Parliament so that even working men could afford to enter politics. **Chartists**, as Lovett's followers became known, saw the vote as a way to improve their daily lives. As one Chartist put it:

❝ *Universal suffrage means meat and drink and clothing, good hours, and good beds, and good substantial furniture for every man and woman and child who will do a fair day's work.* ❞

Although the Chartist movement effectively died out after 1848—largely because of improving economic conditions and rising living standards for most workers—over the next several decades successive governments gradually enacted most of the Chartists' original plan.

▲ In 1844 a London hatter placed this illustration inside his hats to show his support of free trade and the Anti–Corn Law League.

Anti–Corn Law League. Chartism faded, but the desire for further reforms did not. In 1839, for example, members of the middle class formed the **Anti–Corn Law League**. The Corn Laws had been imposed in 1815 by wealthy landowners who wanted to limit the importation of cheap foreign grain in order to maintain their own profits. The Corn Laws kept the price of food high, however, causing members of the middle-class and working-class to join together to protest the laws. Eventually, the league also became a forum for other reform proposals, such as universal manhood suffrage and free trade.

Parliament resisted the league's demands at first. The failure of Ireland's potato crop in 1845, however, raised the threat of mass starvation. Food prices rose dramatically in Ireland and England. Parliament responded by finally repealing the Corn Laws in 1846. With the aid of cheap foreign grain imports, England escaped famine, although the Irish continued to suffer.

Later political reforms. The repeal of the Corn Laws had far-reaching consequences. Out of the controversy Britain's first two modern political parties emerged—the Conservatives

▲ **In May 1914 suffragettes gathered in protest outside Buckingham Palace in London. Like this woman, many were arrested.**

Women's suffrage. Throughout the 1800s women gained political experience working in various reform movements. For example, women were instrumental in the last stages of the abolition movement. It soon became clear, however, that women would have to campaign largely on their own behalf if they wanted the same rights that men had. Supported by other reformers like John Stuart Mill, women campaigned for the rights to control their own property and to have equal access to divorce, child custody, and higher education. However, as one British supporter of women's rights explained, achieving these reforms without the vote was difficult:

66 *There are women in my country who have spent long and useful lives trying to get reforms, and because of their voteless condition, they are unable even to get the ear of Members of Parliament, much less are they able to secure those reforms.* 99

Reformers signed petitions, lobbied politicians, and published journals promoting women's suffrage. By the end of the 1800s, women who owned property had gained the right to vote in some local elections. Women could even run as candidates in a few elections. Parliament itself, however, remained closed to women.

BIOGRAPHY The more aggressive wing of the women's suffrage movement was led by Emmeline Goulden Pankhurst, a dynamic activist from Manchester. Born in 1858, Pankhurst held a series of municipal offices before focusing her attention on women's suffrage. With the help of her daughters Christabel, Sylvia, and Adela, Pankhurst established the Women's Social and Political Union (WSPU) in 1903 to campaign for the universal vote.

The WSPU's early tactics included holding demonstrations and marches, some of which had nearly half a million participants. But when the government continued to ignore the issue of women's suffrage, the WSPU adopted more militant tactics: breaking windows, cutting telegraph wires, even carving the phrase "Votes for Women" in golf course greens. For these

Emmeline Goulden Pankhurst
BIOGRAPHY

and the Liberals. The Conservatives wanted to preserve the best traditions of the past while slowly accepting modern reforms. The Liberals adopted a more rapid, practical approach to solving society's problems. Both parties eventually came to embrace free trade, and both also came to accept the need to include more people in the political system.

In 1867 the Conservatives, under their leader Benjamin Disraeli, passed a second reform bill. This new reform extended the vote to most male heads of households, including most urban industrial workers. The measure roughly doubled the number of voters. Not to be outdone, under William Gladstone the Liberal party also passed major reforms. In 1872 they enacted the secret ballot, which enabled people to vote as they liked without fear of intimidation. In 1884 they also passed a third reform bill that extended the vote to most of the adult male population. Although women were still excluded from voting for Parliament, the movement toward full democracy had begun.

destructive acts, many suffragettes went to prison. Pankhurst herself was arrested and released 12 times in 1913. While in prison Pankhurst, like many other suffragettes, went on hunger strikes and was forcibly fed. Devoted to the cause, however, these women saw such hardships as martyrdom. As Pankhurst put it:

66 We know the joy of battle. When we have come out of the gates of Holloway [Prison] at the point of death, battered, starved, forcibly fed as some of our women have been, . . . their bodies bruised, they have felt when the prison bars were broken and the doors have opened, even at the point of death, they have felt the joy of battle and the exultation of victory. 99

Militant tactics energized the movement, but they also convinced many people that women were not responsible enough to have the right to vote. Meanwhile, moderate women's suffrage groups continued to use more peaceful tactics. Eventually, in 1918, Parliament granted the vote to women over the age of 30. Not until 1928, however, just a few weeks before Emmeline Pankhurst died, did women gain the right to vote on the same basis as men.

The prosperity and the problems brought on by industrialization led to labor reform and to widening political participation in Britain.

✸ Social Welfare Reforms

In addition to political reforms, Britain also moved slowly toward social reforms. The success of the antislavery movement convinced many reformers that government action could be used to improve living conditions. As new factory laws were passed to improve working conditions for women and children, reformers came to believe that government action could also resolve other social ills.

Early efforts in this direction began about the same time as the first factory acts were passed. In 1834 Parliament passed a new Poor Law to replace the one that had been in effect for more than two centuries. The Poor Law of 1834 forced able-bodied poor people to live in workhouses, ending a system that had provided financial aid to supplement low wages. However, it also provided better education for poor children and improved care for the sick and the elderly.

Increased awareness about the plight of the poor led reformers to realize the unsanitary conditions in which most of Great Britain's urban-dwellers lived. Sir Edwin Chadwick, one of the officials overseeing Britain's new poor-law system, became convinced that disease contributed to poverty since workers too sick to work did not get paid. To reduce illness, Chadwick suggested installing efficient drainage systems, modern sewers, and regular garbage collection, as well as supplying adequate clean running water in all towns and cities. In 1848 Parliament set up a national board of health to oversee such improvements.

▲ Given the conditions of most factories in the 1800s, it seems likely that these young factory workers were scrubbed clean for the inspector's visit.

The public health movement soon spread across Europe and to the United States.

The success of these early reform movements inspired increasing reform efforts in the 1880s. Some middle-class reformers established **settlement houses** in poor areas of London, in which working-class people and middle-class people could interact. They hoped that poor working-class people would thus absorb the values of the middle-class and escape their poverty. Certain middle-class reformers called for even more government action to cure Britain's social ills. One group, the socialist Fabian society, believed that "experts" should have the power to run the country.

As more people became convinced that social well-being could be achieved by government action, the Liberals enacted major government welfare programs. In 1906 one law gave workers the right to collect compensation when injured on the job, while another provided free or cheap meals for children who often went hungry. In 1909 the Liberals enacted the Old Age Pensions Bill designed to provide the elderly with a fixed income. In 1911 the National Insurance Act provided medical care and unemployment insurance to workers who made small contributions to a central fund. In a definite shift away from the earlier laissez-faire policies of the classical economists, Great Britain had moved toward the idea that the government should be responsible for the well-being of its citizens.

▲ Government reforms provided food for many poor children.

As reformers tried to solve social problems, many came to believe that government should be used to improve the well-being of citizens.

SECTION 1 REVIEW

IDENTIFY and explain the significance of the following:
abolition movement
evangelical movement
nonconformists
Robert Owen
Chartists
Anti–Corn Law League
Emmeline Pankhurst
settlement houses

1. **Main Idea** How did Great Britain transform itself from the leading slave-trading nation to the leading abolitionist nation?
2. **Main Idea** How did industrialization lead to major industrial, political, and social reforms?
3. **Social Relations** What were the results of reform movements in Britain?
4. **Writing to Persuade** Imagine that you are a middle-class British man from Manchester in 1830. You have a good job and money in the bank. However, you do not have the right to vote. Write a persuasive letter to a member of Parliament outlining why you believe the voting laws should be changed.
5. **Determining Cause and Effect** In what ways did industrialization in Britain have positive and negative consequences?

Expansion and Reform in the British Dominions

FOCUS

- What drove British colonization in the late 1700s and 1800s?

- Why did Britain grant self-government to Canada?

- What limits did the Commonwealth of Australia place on liberal democracy?

- Under what circumstances did New Zealand become a self-governing dominion?

n the 1700s and 1800s, British settlers began to colonize lands overseas. In Canada, Australia, and New Zealand, British colonists found land suitable to their style of farming and ranching with minimal competition from native inhabitants. The British soon became the majority in all three territories. As British colonists settled in, they began to demand the same kind of democratic self-government that was slowly emerging in Britain.

New Zealand jade figure called a heitiki

Christine Takata, Bishop Museum

Continuing Overseas Expansion

In the 1700s and 1800s, Europeans emerged as the most technologically advanced people in the world. At the same time, the changes in the European worldview associated with the Scientific Revolution and the Enlightenment provided Europeans with a rationale for both continuing exploration of the world and further expansion of their own civilization.

Pacific exploration. During the 1700s improved sailing methods and increased knowledge about wind and ocean currents fueled Europeans' desire to venture farther, particularly in the Pacific Ocean. Continuing exploration and expansion led Europeans to develop new technologies such as the **chronometer**. This accurate timekeeping instrument helped sailors pinpoint their exact position on the globe.

Armed with better navigational instruments and inspired by the desire for knowledge about the world, a new breed of European explorers and naturalists (scientists interested in nature) mapped more of the world. They brought plants and animals from newly discovered lands back to Europe. Perhaps the greatest explorer in the 1700s was Captain James Cook, who introduced the European world to Pacific islands such as Hawaii and Tahiti. Cook and others, like the earlier Dutch explorer Abel Tasman, also made Europeans aware of Australia and New Zealand. These discoveries laid the foundations for new European overseas colonies.

Population growth in Europe. At the same time that Europeans were learning more about the world, they were also beginning to experience the consequences of their improved technology. The agricultural and industrial revolutions, for example, not only led to improved standards of living in Europe but also contributed to an explosion in population. During the 1700s and 1800s, under the stimulus of this massive increase in population, great waves of migrants left Europe for lands overseas. In the process these emigrants carried European ways of life with them.

British colonization. In 1787 a group of about 1,100 people, including about 750 convicts,

SECTION 2

CORE LESSON PLAN
See pages 507E and 507F for Lesson Plan 19.2.

R RESOURCE ACTIVITY

WRITING PROJECTS
Writing Project 19
Creating an Outline

Have students study the chapter and fill in the outline for a paper on the expansion of British colonialism. Discuss how this outline might help them write a paper.

All Levels

R RESOURCE ACTIVITY

READINGS IN WORLD HISTORY
Reading 19.2
A Convict Settlement in Australia

Have students read about life in the Toongabby settlement. Then have them complete the questions.

Level 2

▲ In his day Captain James Cook was known for the fact that his crews survived the effects of the disease known as scurvy.

set sail from Britain. The following year they landed on the eastern coast of Australia and established a penal colony near a harbor, which they named Sydney.

From 1788 until 1868 Great Britain transported thousands of convicts to Australia. They worked many years on government farms or were assigned to private employers. At the end of their sentences, male convicts received small plots of farmland. The guards who made the journey also settled on free land provided by the new colonial government. Free colonists also founded other colonies in Australia: Van Diemen's Land (later renamed Tasmania) in 1823, Western Australia in 1829, South Australia in 1834, Victoria in 1850, and Queensland in 1859.

Colonists also settled in other territories under British control. In the early 1800s, for example, some British settlers moved into the Cape Colony at the southern tip of Africa, which Britain had obtained as a result of the wars against Napoleon. In Canada, where Britain had established its control by seizing France's remaining territories in the Seven Years' War, British colonists also began to settle on the land.

Pushed by rising population growth, British colonists began to settle around the world in territories suitable to their styles of ranching and farming.

Canada

Colonists in Canada were the first to demand political reform. By the mid-1800s many Canadian colonists had become discontented with their colonial governments, over which the popularly elected assemblies had little control. In addition, tensions were growing among the various Canadian colonies, especially between the British colonists of Upper Canada (part of present-day Ontario) and the large French-speaking population of Lower Canada (part of present-day Quebec). Within each colony, quarrels frequently broke out between the assemblies and their governors. The colonists wanted **responsible government**—government whose officials were fully responsible to the colonial voters.

Rebellions in Upper and Lower Canada in 1837 convinced the British that reform was necessary. They had learned the lesson of the American Revolution and did not want to lose more colonies the same way. They also wanted to lessen the influence of the United States in Canadian affairs. In 1838 the British government sent Lord Durham as governor-general to Canada. The following year Durham submitted a report to Parliament proposing that the colonies be given self-rule over internal affairs. Great Britain would retain control over foreign affairs, trade policy, and public lands.

Durham wanted the Canadian colonies to unite to form "a great and powerful people [who] might in some measure counterbalance the . . . increasing influence of the United States on the American continent." Accepting Durham's recommendations, the British granted the Canadian colonists self-government. By doing so, they ensured that Canada would develop along the same parliamentary lines as Britain, rather than follow the example of the United States. At the same time, Parliament united Upper and Lower Canada into one province.

Unification was not without problems. Most of the new area's good farmland was already in use, and many colonists wanted to expand westward into the land owned by the Hudson's Bay Company. By the 1850s many people had come to believe that a **confederation**, or loose union, of British North America would ensure prosperity and security for the colonies. The colonists and their politicians, however, had to put aside

The Growth of Canada, 1791–1912

Colonial Expansion In 1867 British Canada controlled areas of land on the Atlantic and Pacific Coasts. Two years later, the Dominion controlled almost all the land between the coasts from the United States northward to the Arctic Ocean.

? **Movement** How did Canada acquire most of its territory?

sectionalism, or loyalty to a particular part of the country, before a union could be formed. Creation of a confederation was further hampered by the continuing rivalry between French- and English-speakers.

As far as Great Britain was concerned, the benefits of confederation outweighed the drawbacks. In 1867 Parliament passed the British North America Act, which made Canada Britain's first **dominion**, or self-governing colony. The Dominion of Canada was created by uniting the colonies of Nova Scotia, New Brunswick, Quebec, and Ontario. To help bind the colonies together, the imperial government also authorized construction of a great transcontinental railway.

After confederation, the new dominion continued to expand westward until it eventually reached the Pacific coast. In 1896 the discovery of gold near the Klondike River in the Yukon Territory prompted a gold rush. After the gold rush ended, thousands of miners stayed in the Canadian West. Although Canada was developing its own distinct identity, it still retained close ties to Britain. Canadian politician John A. Macdonald remarked in 1891, "A British subject I was born, a British subject I will die!"

Anxious to keep Canada within the empire, Britain granted the colonies internal self-government and allowed them to unite in a confederation.

▲ **The women and men working this British Columbian mine around 1900 dreamed of finding fortunes in gold.**

Australia

Canada became a model for self-government in other British colonies. By 1850, for example, New South Wales, Victoria, South Australia, and Tasmania had all begun to call for responsible government. An intensive period of constitution-writing began, and all of the Australian colonies gained responsible governments by 1857. Reflecting the influence of the reform movements in Britain, the new constitutions were highly democratic. They included universal manhood suffrage, the secret ballot, and the separation of church and state. These political reforms were enough to satisfy the Australians. Originally they saw no need to follow Canada's example of confederation.

Australia's political reform occurred during a period of rapid economic expansion in the colonies. The discovery of rich copper and gold deposits brought great wealth to Australia and attracted thousands of immigrants. Wool became an important export, and wool production grew dramatically in the mid-1800s as Australian sheep farmers greatly expanded their landholdings.

Expansion often came at the expense of the Aborigines, the original inhabitants of Australia. In the early years of convict transportation, relations between the colonists and the Aborigines had been largely peaceful. However, when free settlers began to demand more land, the two groups often clashed. As British expansion continued, the Aborigine population declined dramatically.

In the 1880s, concerned about their national defense, Australian politicians began to call for unification. Australians feared that in the worldwide scramble for colonies, other European countries might threaten Australian territory. After drafting a new constitution, Australia officially became a dominion as the Commonwealth of Australia in 1901. One of the first acts of the new government was to give all adult women the vote.

Although the Australians extended liberal democracy for themselves, they did not extend the concept to Asians. Adopting the "White Australia" policy, they passed the Immigration Restriction Act of 1901. The act discouraged Asians from immigrating to Australia by requiring them to pass a test in the knowledge of a European language. Another law, the Pacific Islanders Protection Act of 1901, forced Polynesian agricultural workers to leave Australia.

Like Canadians, Australians developed their own distinct identity while retaining strong ties to Britain. At the same time, a growing nationalism encouraged an independent Australian self-image that emphasized strong, rugged, self-reliant individuals always ready to help their "mates."

Once Australians achieved self-government, they adopted both a liberal democracy and a policy of racial exclusion.

New Zealand

New Zealand was the third colony to achieve dominion status. The first European settlers in New Zealand were traders who sought profits from seal skins and whale oil. They encountered the Maori (MOW-ree), a Polynesian people who had lived on the islands for centuries. In the 1820s and 1830s, however, large numbers of European missionaries began to move into New Zealand. Soon other colonists also arrived, settling mostly on the South Island, where there were few Maori and plenty of rich grazing lands for cattle and sheep. Some also settled on the North Island, however, where most of the Maori lived.

After contact with the new settlers, Maori life changed dramatically. Disease killed tens of thousands, as did warfare, particularly after Europeans introduced the Maori to guns. By 1840 the Maori population may have declined by as much as 50 percent. The encounter with European culture destroyed much of the traditional Maori way of life. As one Maori chief put it: "Now this land is mixed up with the customs of the Europeans. New thoughts or habits have been imbibed [taken in] and darkness has ensued in consequence."

In 1840 Maori chiefs signed the Treaty of Waitangi, which gave the British sovereignty over the North Island—although some of the chiefs may not have realized it at the time. The treaty provided that the Maori would recognize the British monarch as their ruler and restricted the sale of their lands exclusively to the British government. In exchange, the British guaranteed the Maori's well-being and the protection of all their rights—including property rights.

The treaty did not protect the Maori, however. New settlers often seized Maori lands illegally. The Maori responded by raiding the settlers. Anxious to control their own affairs, in 1854 colonial leaders demanded responsible government. Although a measure of self-government was

▲ A New Zealand photographer captured this image of a Maori chief around 1880.

quickly granted, Britain retained the power to oversee relations with the Maori in an effort to protect them from domination by the colonists. This soon resulted in more violence.

In 1860 warfare erupted on the North Island, where a nationalist movement had united many of the tribes. By the time the war ended in 1872, thousands of Maori had died, and the British had seized 7 million acres of Maori lands as punishment for the uprising.

In the decades following the Maori uprising, New Zealanders captured the spirit of reform that was sweeping Europe. In 1893 New Zealand was the first country to give women the vote. In addition, the government provided state pensions to the elderly, enacted factory laws to protect workers, and encouraged the development of labor unions. With these reforms in place, in 1907 New Zealand became a prosperous dominion within the British Empire.

After long conflict with the Maori, New Zealand eventually became a self-governing, liberal dominion.

SECTION 2 REVIEW

IDENTIFY and explain the significance of the following:
    chronometer
    James Cook
    Abel Tasman
    responsible government
    Lord Durham
    confederation
    sectionalism
    dominion

LOCATE and explain the importance of the following:
    Upper Canada

Ontario
Lower Canada
Quebec

1. **Main Idea** What did Britain hope to gain by granting self-government to its Canadian subjects?
2. **Main Idea** How did Australia limit its practice of liberal democracy in its territories?
3. **Geography: Movement** Why did people leave

Britain to colonize new areas overseas?
4. **Writing to Describe** Imagine that you are a British official in New Zealand. Write a memo to your supervisor describing the problems surrounding New Zealand's attempt to become a self-governing dominion.
5. **Evaluating** How did the development of the dominions change the structure of the British Empire?

SECTION 3

CORE LESSON PLAN
See pages 507G and 507H for Lesson Plan 19.3.

In this image Joseph, chief of the Nez Perce tribe, is preparing to surrender to the U.S. cavalry. He and his tribe attempted to escape to Canada, but the Indians were so weakened by cold and hunger that the cavalry overtook them. At the surrender Joseph told U.S. officials: "My heart is sick and sad. From where the sun now stands, I will fight no more forever."

Critical Thinking Ask students why the United States would have wanted to move American Indians off their lands.

ANSWER: Students might suggest the history of conflict between settlers and American Indians, and that these groups had different ideas of how the land should be used.

SECTION 3
Expansion and Reform in the United States

FOCUS

- How did the United States try to resolve its conflict over slavery, and what were the consequences?

- What role did the abolition movement play in the struggle for women's suffrage?

- What pressures led to demands for social, political, and economic reform?

hen the United States ratified its Constitution in 1788, the new nation consisted of 13 states along the Atlantic coast and territories that stretched westward to the Mississippi River. The young nation was born during a time of turmoil in Europe, and most Americans wanted to stay out of European affairs and develop their nation in peace. They did this so successfully that during the next 100 years the United States grew to almost four times its original size. Although the United States tried to avoid European conflicts, the nation had its own serious problems.

Chief Joseph Rides to Surrender by Howard Terpning

✳ Territorial Expansion and Democracy

During the late 1700s and 1800s, the United States expanded rapidly, spreading both its ideals and its problems across the continent. This expansion began almost immediately after the founding of the nation. The United States acquired land from France, Spain, Mexico, Great Britain, Russia, and Hawaii. By 1898 the United States had expanded to its current borders.

This expansion created opportunities for many Americans, but it also created serious problems. To provide white settlers with land, the U.S. government forced American Indians to leave their traditional lands and move west into the Great Plains. By the 1850s the white settlers' demand for land had increased so much that the government began to confine American Indians to reservations. This provoked nearly 50 years of conflict as Indians and the U.S. army clashed over ownership of the land.

As the United States kept growing, sectionalism became a problem. During the early 1800s three major sections emerged: the urban and industrial Northeast, the agricultural South, and the frontier region of the West. People in each of these regions held very different views on national issues, reflecting their different ways of life. The most serious difference centered on the expansion of slavery.

Conflict over slavery. The controversy over slavery in the United States had existed since 1688, when Quakers protested the institution of slavery. In 1808 Congress joined Great Britain and other European powers in abolishing the foreign slave trade. However, the internal slave trade remained legal and profitable.

Soon after the American Revolution, some northern states had abolished slavery altogether, and southern states such as Virginia discussed the possibility of abolition. In the early 1800s, however, a boom in the cotton industry strengthened the South's dependence on the institution of slavery.

Slavery became a more controversial issue when Congress had to decide if slavery would be allowed in the Lousiana Purchase. To avoid direct confrontation and maintain the balance of states, Congress made many compromises, such as the **Missouri Compromise** of 1820, which only

U.S. Territorial Expansion, 1785–1898

Alaska Purchase, 1867

Azimuthal Equal-Area Projection

Louisiana Purchase, 1803	Texas Annexation, 1845
Oregon Country, 1818	Mexican Cession, 1848
Florida Cession, 1819	Gadsden Purchase, 1853
Disputed area	
Present-day boundary	

Boundary set by Oregon Treaty, 1846

Boundaries set by Webster-Ashburton Treaty, 1842

Ceded by Great Britain, 1818

CANADA

Claimed by Great Britain until 1842

ROCKY MOUNTAINS

Columbia River

Missouri River

Great Plains

Missouri Compromise Line

Arkansas River

Colorado River

Gila River

Rio Grande

Ohio River

Mississippi River

St. Lawrence River

UNITED STATES Before 1785

PACIFIC OCEAN

ATLANTIC OCEAN

Annexation of Hawaii, 1898

Albers Equal-Area Projection

Ceded by Spain, 1819

MEXICO

Gulf of Mexico

| 0 | 250 | 500 Miles |
| 0 | 250 | 500 Kilometers |

Azimuthal Equal-Area Projection

120°W 110°W 90°W 80°W 30°N 40°N 50°N 70°W

Manifest Destiny Rapid westward expansion in the United States fueled dynamic economic growth. But expansion also led to explosive conflicts with Mexico and Native American groups.

? Movement How did the United States acquire lands in the present-day Southwest?

---

allowed slavery in southern territories. By the mid-1800s Senator William H. Seward of New York remarked:

66 *Every question, political, civil, or ecclesiastical [religious]—however foreign to the subject of slavery—brings up slavery. . . . We hear of nothing but slavery, and we can talk of nothing but slavery.* 99

The American abolition movement. In the early 1800s abolitionists had begun to confront slavery head-on. One group suggested freeing the slaves and sending them to Britain's African colony of Sierra Leone. When Britain rejected

the plan, the group established its own African colony in Liberia. This colony soon ran into problems, however.

In 1833 a group of prominent abolitionists formed the **American Anti-Slavery Society**. Its supporters included Frederick Douglass, a fugitive slave whose powerful words inspired many to join the cause; William Lloyd Garrison, a journalist who helped shape public opinion; and Sojourner Truth, a former slave who campaigned both for abolition and for women's rights.

Attempts at political compromise did not solve the controversy over slavery or quiet abolitionist demands.

The Civil War was devastating to the U.S. population. However, the biggest killer in the Civil War was disease, not combat. Over 300,000 deaths were the result of disease. The leading causes of death were diarrhea, typhoid, typhus and malarial fevers, pneumonia, smallpox, and measles.

Critical Thinking Ask students why disease was such a problem during the Civil War.

ANSWER: Students might suggest that soldiers lived under cold, damp circumstances that would promote disease. They also had little food and were frequently exhausted. Finally, open wounds would provide unprotected areas in which infections could begin.

R RESOURCE ACTIVITY

SKILLS ACTIVITIES
Skills Activity 19
Interpreting a Graph

Have students study the graph on Northern and Southern resources during the Civil War. Then have students answer the questions.

| Level 2 |

✦ Secession and Civil War

The presidential election of 1860 sparked a direct confrontation over slavery. Abraham Lincoln, who campaigned against the spread of slavery to new states and territories, was elected. Lincoln's election contributed to the secession, or withdrawal, of 11 southern states from the Union, which in turn led to the Civil War. These 11 states formed the Confederate States of America

THROUGH OTHERS' EYES

Frances Trollope's View of American Slavery

In 1827 Frances Trollope, mother of the British novelist Anthony Trollope, sailed to the United States. She remained in America for nearly four years, living in various areas, traveling frequently, and writing down her observations of the inhabitants. After Trollope returned to England in 1830, her notes were published in a book titled *The Domestic Manners of the Americans.* In the book she described her views on slavery:

❝The condition of domestic slaves . . . does not generally appear to be bad; but the ugly feature is, that should it be so, they have no power to change it. I have seen much kind attention bestowed upon [given to] the health of slaves; but it is on these occasions impossible to forget, that did this attention fail, a valuable piece of property would be endangered. . . . [A friendly relationship between slave and owner] may last as long as the slave can be kept in that state of profound ignorance which precludes [shuts out] reflection. The law of Virginia has taken care of this. The State legislators . . . ensure their [own] safety by forbidding light [education] to enter among them [the slaves]. By the law of Virginia it is penal [illegal] to teach any slave to read, and it is penal to be aiding and abetting in the act of instructing them. This law speaks volumes.❞

in 1861 and engaged the United States in a bloody civil war that lasted four years.

With a larger population, more miles of railroad track, and greater resources, the North had a strong advantage over the South. However, the South had the advantage of fighting to defend its own soil. Nevertheless, the South's disadvantages proved too much to overcome, and with its troops hungry and in rags, the South surrendered in 1865.

In January 1863, before the war's end, President Lincoln had issued the **Emancipation Proclamation**, freeing slaves in those parts of the South still "in rebellion against the United States." After the Civil War, Congress passed constitutional amendments that abolished slavery, gave former slaves citizenship as well as equal protection under the law, and granted African American men the right to vote.

The Civil War did not end all problems for former slaves. Reconstruction—the period of rebuilding in the South following the Civil War—provided many African Americans with new freedoms and opportunities. However, once Southern white rule returned in 1877, many states passed so-called Jim Crow laws designed to enforce racial segregation.

The Civil War ended slavery, but it did not ensure economic and social freedom for former slaves.

✦ Women's Suffrage

After gaining experience in the abolition movement, many American women began to focus on their own struggle for equality. As in Britain, women's rights in the United States were restricted. Women had limited educational and employment opportunities. Married women could not own property, and divorced women could not get custody of their children.

Many women realized that they would have to campaign largely on their own behalf. This became clear in 1840 at the World's Anti-Slavery Convention in London, where William Lloyd Garrison asked:

❝With a young woman [Queen Victoria] placed on the throne of Great Britain, will the philanthropists [people who help others] of that country presume to object to the female delegates from the United States as members of the Convention, on the ground of their sex? **"**

The answer was yes. The convention refused to allow women to speak. This action convinced Elizabeth Cady Stanton and Lucretia Mott to lead a campaign on behalf of women's rights.

In 1848 Stanton and Mott organized the **Seneca Falls Convention**, the first women's rights convention in the United States. Delegates to the convention drew up the Declaration of Sentiments, a list of reforms needed to strengthen women's legal position. The most controversial demand was the right to vote.

As in the British women's suffrage movement, two different styles of campaigning emerged. The National American Woman Suffrage Association, headed by leaders such as Stanton and Susan B. Anthony, worked peacefully through the system, trying to persuade legislators to grant women the vote. A more radical approach was taken by the National Woman's Party, led by Alice Paul, which used the attention-getting tactics of protests, picketing, and hunger strikes. Women in the United States finally won the right to vote in 1920 with the ratification of the Nineteenth Amendment to the Constitution.

Women's experience in the abolition movement led them to campaign on behalf of their own rights.

Social and Political Reforms

The United States experienced tremendous growth from 1865 to 1900. Cities doubled and tripled in size, and a network of railroads crisscrossed the nation to link the cities together.

This growth was spurred in large part by the arrival of millions of new immigrants to the United States. Unlike earlier immigrants, who generally came from the British Isles, Germany, and the Scandinavian countries, many new

▶ **Lewis W. Hines captured this image of an immigrant family as part of his 1905 study of Ellis Island immigrants.**

arrivals in the late 1800s were from southern and eastern Europe, particularly Italy, Russia, and Austria-Hungary.

Most new immigrants lived in slums in major cities and worked at low-wage jobs. In many northern cities large ethnic communities developed as new immigrants settled near others who had also come from their homelands. In this way, immigrants could maintain their customs and culture.

Most immigrants came to the United States lured by hopes for prosperity. They often found only poverty and mistreatment, however. The plight of immigrants helped fuel a wave of social and political reform in the United States in the late 1800s and early 1900s. Eager to cure society's ills, reformers turned their attention to improving education, assisting the poor, and ending corruption in government.

Education reform. Many reformers believed that an educational system capable of teaching proper values was essential to building a strong nation. They hoped that if children learned the values of hard work and respect for authority, they would become productive citizens and workers. However, until the 1840s, most schools remained private, and many parents could not afford to send their children. The few public elementary schools that existed had little money for books, supplies, or teachers' salaries. Therefore, the quality of education in these schools was often poor.

Some reformers campaigned to open well-funded public schools that would provide a decent education for all children. The first public high school opened in Boston in 1821, and one of the first statewide systems of public elementary education was established in Massachusetts in the 1830s. These schools served as models for public education of all children.

Despite these reforms public education did not become available to all children. Few towns allowed African American children to attend public schools. Thus, free blacks had to set up private schools without the benefit of tax dollars. Women also did not have equal access to education. Reformers responded by establishing high schools and colleges that offered women the opportunity of an equal education. Not everyone favored public education, however. Some farming and working-class parents objected to public schooling because they depended on their children's labor.

The settlement-house movement. Many immigrants and other poor people lived in cramped and dirty conditions. They paid high rents for tiny tenement apartments, cramming entire families into one or two rooms. Outside, industrial pollution, raw sewage, and piles of garbage caused unhealthy conditions that led to disease and even death.

Because there was no government assistance available, some reformers established settlement houses, or community service centers, in poor neighborhoods. In 1889 Jane Addams established Hull House, one of the first American settlement houses, in Chicago. Hull House offered day care, adult education, and employment assistance to the poor. Hull House served as a model for other reformers, and by 1900 over 100 settlement houses had opened across the country.

Political reform. By the early 1900s reformers had also turned their attention to politics. In the late 1800s the American political system had grown corrupt at all levels. In New York City, for example, the Democratic party machine, called Tammany Hall, controlled city government. Political machines selected candidates for elections, pressured voters into voting for certain candidates, and often stole money from city treasuries. Many reformers on the state and local level worked hard campaigning to break the political machines.

Two ways in which reformers gave power back to the voters were through the direct primary and the secret ballot. The direct primary allowed voters to select their party's candidate for election. The secret ballot let voters cast their ballots without pressure from political machines. In some states, three other election reforms—the initiative, referendum, and recall—returned power to the voters. The initiative allows voters to initiate, or introduce, legislation, while the referendum allows voters to repeal a law passed by their legislature. The recall allows voters to remove an elected official from office by calling for a new election.

Economic and Industrial Reforms

Developments in the industrial economy of the United States also contributed to demands for reform. During the late 1800s, a few businesspeople

History THROUGH THE ARTS

Political Cartoons

The political cartoon—a humorous drawing used to sway public opinion—provides solid proof of the accuracy of the old saying, "A picture is worth a thousand words." William Marcy Tweed, boss of Tammany Hall, New York City's Democratic political machine from 1868 to 1871, certainly felt that way. Around 1870 *Harper's Weekly* cartoonist Thomas Nast targeted Tweed in a series of devastating drawings. "Stop them . . . pictures," Tweed ordered his associates. "I don't care so much what the papers write about me. My constituents [voters] can't read. But . . . they can see pictures." Tweed's fears were understandable—he was as corrupt as Nast's cartoons suggested. But even the most honest of politicians, at one time or another, have wanted to "stop them . . . pictures."

Some historians suggest that the art of political cartooning can be traced back to ancient Greek and Roman times. The political cartoon as we know it today, however, probably began with the work of the British artist William Hogarth in the 1700s. Using a style called caricature—exaggeration of a person's or object's physical features—Hogarth drew sketches that critiqued the social morals of his time. James Gillray, another British artist, took Hogarth's approach a step further, making the focus of his drawings political rather than social. Political cartooning soon spread from Britain to other parts of Europe, and to North America.

The early political cartoons were published as one-page flyers. Technological advances in printing soon brought about changes, however. By the mid-1800s illustrated humor magazines were readily available. The first such magazines were published in France in the 1830s. *Punch*, the ground-breaking British humor magazine, followed in 1841. Its staff began to develop one of political cartooning's most important features—a visual shorthand that used particular symbols for various countries, governments, and ideas. Sir John Tenniel, who worked for *Punch* from 1850 to 1901, created the symbols of the top-hatted John Bull and the lion to represent Britain. In addition, Tenniel depicted Russia as a bear in his cartoons. In the United States, Thomas Nast made important contributions to this shorthand system. For example, Nast was the first to use the symbol of the elephant for the Republican party. Cartoonists today still use these historical symbols.

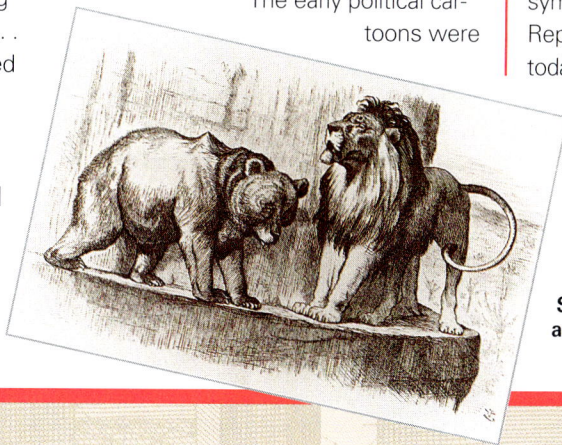

Sir John Tenniel's British lion and the Russian bear

Thinking About Art
What is a caricature and how is it used?

Theme: Politics and Law
Tammany Hall often profited at the citizens' expense. On April 4, 1900, for example, the American Ice Company was able to raise the price of a block of ice—an essential item because electric refrigeration did not exist—from 30¢ to 60¢ because it had a monopoly on the sale of ice. It maintained this monopoly because officials in Tammany were part owners of the company.

Critical Thinking Ask students how people now attempt to protect against the involvement of politicians in business.

ANSWER: The students could suggest that politicians may be held to a code of ethics and that the press also works to uncover politicians who might profit from their legislative decisions.

Thinking About Art
A caricature is an exaggerated drawing of a person's or object's physical features, often used in political cartoons.

REVIEW & ASSESSMENT RESOURCES

- Study Guide 19.3
- Daily Quiz 19.3
- Main Idea Activity 19.3

All Levels

grew extremely wealthy. Andrew Carnegie, for example, became the world's richest man through the steel industry. By controlling the companies that produced the materials and services upon which his steel company depended, Carnegie was able to make tremendous profits. He also drove smaller, less efficient companies out of business.

Economic reform. At first the government cooperated with big business. It placed high tariffs on imports, thereby making the price of domestic goods lower in comparison. In 1894, for example, tariffs made some foreign goods 40 percent more expensive than American goods. However, the government slowly began to regulate business.

▲ **Women gather at the headquarters of the Women's Trade Union League in New York in 1910.**

In 1890 Congress passed the Sherman Antitrust Act, which prohibited companies from creating monopolies to gain control over entire industries.

Industrial reform. Progressive reformers also worked to improve industrial conditions, particularly workplace safety. A tragic fire in a New York City factory in March 1911 reinforced the need for safety regulations. More than 100 people were killed or injured in the fire at the Triangle Shirtwaist Company. Many were trapped in the building because there were only two stairways, and most of the exits were blocked. This tragedy caused a public outcry over dangerous working conditions, and New York lawmakers responded by passing the nation's strictest fire code.

Labor unions. Although most reform movements were led by members of the middle class, workers also fought to improve conditions through labor unions. By the early 1900s the major labor organization was the American Federation of Labor, or AFL. Founded in 1886, the AFL was composed of many smaller unions that organized skilled workers. The AFL grew quite powerful, although most industrial workers remained outside the union movement.

The AFL opposed socialism and the use of political activism to improve workers' rights. The Industrial Workers of the World, or IWW, on the other hand, embraced socialism. The tactics of the IWW included strikes, boycotts, and industrial sabotage. Because the IWW called for the overthrow of the capitalist system, many Americans grew fearful of its power. Eventually, the IWW's strikes became less effective, and after the government cracked down on its activities, the union's power gradually faded.

Increased immigration, urbanization, corruption, and industrialization created new demands for reform.

SECTION 3 REVIEW

IDENTIFY and explain the significance of the following:
    Missouri Compromise
    American Anti-Slavery Society
    Emancipation Proclamation
    Elizabeth Cady Stanton
    Lucretia Mott
    Seneca Falls Convention

LOCATE and explain the importance of the following:
    Louisiana Purchase

1. **Main Idea** How was the issue of slavery resolved?
2. **Main Idea** What social issues helped launch reform movements in the United States? How did reformers respond to these issues?
3. **Geography: Region** What role did geography play in the slavery debate?
4. **Writing to Explain** Imagine that you are a suffragist. Write a newspaper story on how the World's Anti-Slavery Convention, Seneca Falls Convention, National American Woman Suffrage Association, and National Woman's Party have influenced the struggle for women's suffrage.
5. **Assessing Consequences** Why might it be said that the Civil War was only partially successful in resolving the issues surrounding slavery?

Independence in Latin America

FOCUS

- What were the results of the Haitian slave revolution?
- How did European events affect Latin American colonies?
- How did other nations react to Latin American independence?

By the early 1800s growing tensions among the various ethnic and social groups of Latin American society, as well as reforms imposed by colonial authorities in Europe, were leading to demands for change. The Enlightenment and the American Revolution also inspired some Latin Americans to seek greater freedom. This idea became even more widespread as the French Revolution and the Napoleonic wars contributed to the overthrow of the old order in Europe. Soon new nations began to emerge from colonial domination throughout Latin America.

Toussaint-Louverture, leader of Haiti's revolt for the freedom of slaves and mulattoes

Haiti's Slave Revolution

The first Latin American territory to break its ties with Europe was the French colony of Saint Domingue, located on the western half of the Caribbean island of Hispaniola. Sugar production had made Saint Domingue France's most prosperous overseas possession. This prosperity, however, was built on slave labor.

The French Revolution dramatically altered conditions in the colony. Under the terms of the Declaration of the Rights of Man, all free men, including mulattoes (persons of African and European ancestry), obtained the right to vote. French settlers, however, resisted the new law. As tensions rose, Toussaint-Louverture (too-san loo-ver-toor), a former slave, led a combination of mulattoes and slaves in a bloody revolt.

In 1802 Napoleon sent an army to reestablish French authority. Toussaint-Louverture was captured and died a prisoner in France, but the French were unable to restore their authority. In 1804 the revolutionaries declared Saint Domingue independent under the ancient name of Haiti. It was many years, however, before Haiti received recognition from its neighbors.

A slave revolution resulted in Saint Domingue declaring its independence as Haiti in 1804.

Spanish and Portuguese Colonies

Latin American reactions to Haitian independence varied. Some people took encouragement from Haiti's new freedom. Others, especially landowners, were horrified by the violence and bloodshed of Haiti's struggle. As events continued to unfold in Europe, however, other Latin American colonies also experienced the struggle for independence.

Growing discontent. By 1800 the social and ethnic composition of the colonies in Latin America had changed. *Peninsulares*, people of European birth, had become an even smaller minority as the number of creoles, or Europeans born in the colonies, and *mestizos*, people of mixed

SECTION 4

CORE LESSON PLAN
See pages 507I and 507J for Lesson Plan 19.4.

Theme: **War and Diplomacy**
Toussaint-Louverture rose to power after launching the slave revolt in 1791. In 1793 his forces recaptured Haiti's major cities from Britain. In 1801 Toussaint-Louverture conquered the Spanish colony on Hispaniola that Spain had ceded to France. He reorganized the government and declared only minimal allegiance to France. Fearing a loss of control, Napoleon sent a force to defeat Toussaint-Louverture.

Critical Thinking Ask students why Toussaint-Louverture might have hoped that Napoleon would support his government.

ANSWER: Students might suggest that Napoleon seemed friendly to the French Revolution, so Toussaint-Louverture felt that he might approve of the Haitian coup.

Print out and distribute the reading and show students the map. Ask students to trace the route San Martín followed as described in the reading. Then have them read the description of his fighting tactics. Ask each student to choose one incident from the reading to illustrate. Have the students find out where the incident took place. Finally, have all the students place their illustrations on a large map of South America.

Level 1/ Sheltered English

MULTIMEDIA PRESENTATION STRATEGY

VISUAL RESOURCES Geography and History 19
Independence in Latin America

Show the transparency and share the information from Geography and History Fact Sheet 19. Then have students complete the accompanying worksheet.

Level 2

Map Answer
Uruguay

American Indian and European background, rose. Mulattoes and African Americans also constituted a larger part of the population.

Creoles had not only increased in numbers, they had also increased in power. As Spain's wealth and power declined during the late 1600s and early 1700s, Spanish authorities had gradually relaxed their administration over their colonies. This relative neglect had allowed creoles to become powerful by buying land, owning mines, and running *haciendas*.

In the mid-1700s Spain tried to reassert control over its colonies. To help reestablish Spanish control, King Charles III created an **intendancy** system. The system provided for the appointment of *peninsulares* as intendants, or governors, who would be loyal to the king and not the viceroy. Charles also tightened control over the Catholic Church in Spanish territory. In addition, economic reforms were enacted in an effort to help the Spanish economy by limiting competing industries in the colonies.

As more *peninsulares* were appointed to oversee the new reforms, many creoles began to resent such "outside" interference in their affairs. A sense of nationalism and patriotism began to grow among the colonists.

Independence from Spain. While discontent among creoles grew, events in Europe also encouraged the colonists to seek independence. In 1808 Napoleon deposed and imprisoned King Ferdinand VII of Spain, placing his own brother on the Spanish throne instead. Spanish colonists believed that with no legitimate government in Spain, control over the colonies should revert to the colonists. Tensions remained, however, between *peninsulares* and creoles over who should control the colonial governments. By 1810 revolution had broken out in most of Spanish America, as creoles tried to take power.

In the viceroyalty of La Plata, José de San Martín, the son of a Spanish royal official, became the main leader against Spanish rule. By 1821 San Martín had liberated not only La Plata but also Chile and much of Peru.

As Spanish opposition continued, however, he turned for help to fellow revolutionaries from the north—particularly the Venezuelan Simón Bolívar (boh-LEE-vahr).

BIOGRAPHY Bolívar was born to a wealthy Venezuelan creole family in 1783. From his youth Bolívar envisioned an independent and united Latin America. In 1811 he led Venezuela to declare its independence from Spain. A series of startling victories earned him the nickname "the Liberator." Joining with other revolutionaries, by 1821 Bolívar had defeated the Spanish in most of northern South America. In 1822 Bolívar and other revolutionary leaders combined strength to put an end to Spanish rule throughout South America.

New Nations in South America by 1828

Liberty and Union After gaining independence, the former Spanish viceroyalties struggled to unite, while Portugal's former colony of Brazil remained intact.

? Location Which South American country was the last to gain independence?

True to his vision of a united Latin America, Bolívar established the state of Gran Colombia, which consisted of Venezuela, Colombia, Panama and Ecuador. In 1825 Bolívar tried to bring Upper Peru into the union, but leaders there had already organized Bolivia, a new state named after him.

The state of Gran Colombia proved impossible to hold together. "America is ungovernable," Bolívar complained. "Those who have served the revolution have plowed the sea." In 1830, as Venezuela and Ecuador also withdrew from the union, Bolívar died of tuberculosis.

Independence from Portugal. While Spanish America experienced violent revolution in the struggle for independence, Brazil took a rather different path. When Napoleon defeated Portugal in 1807, the Portuguese king, Dom João (zhwa-OOH) VI, and the entire royal family fled to Brazil. During Dom João's exile in Brazil, Rio de Janeiro became the center of the Portuguese Empire. After the French were driven out of Portugal in 1811, the Portuguese called for Dom João's return. The king refused—he had fallen in love with Brazil. In 1815 Dom João made Brazil equal in status to Portugal.

Meanwhile, in Portugal, liberals wanted to return Brazil to its former dependent status. Eventually, they persuaded Dom João to return to Portugal. They then stripped Brazil of power, abolishing its separate government and excluding Brazilians from political and military offices. Dom João's son Dom Pedro, however, had remained in Brazil. Refusing the liberals' demands to return to Portugal, Dom Pedro proclaimed, "The hour has come! Independence or death!" On September 22, 1822, Brazil declared independence, and Dom Pedro became the first emperor. By 1823 the Brazilians had driven out all Portuguese forces.

Napoleon's conquest of Spain and Portugal spurred colonists in Latin America to demand independence.

Mexico

As in the rest of Latin America, Napoleon's conquest of Spain in the Napoleonic wars provided the spark for revolution in Mexico. In 1810 Father Miguel Hidalgo y Costilla, a parish priest, led a movement to seize power in the name of King Ferdinand. Although most creoles and *peninsulares* found the priest's demands too radical to support, thousands of *mestizos* and Indians joined the priest as he traveled to Mexico City to seize power. Eventually, Spanish troops defeated the rebels and forced them to retreat. Spanish authorities later captured and executed Father Hidalgo.

The revolution found a new leader in Father José María Morelos y Pavón. Morelos quickly stated the rebels' demands: independence from Spain, the abolition of slavery, and land reform that would break up many large estates and

Mexico, Central America, and the Caribbean by 1828

Battling for Independence In the early 1800s patriots in Haiti, Mexico, and Central America fought fiercely for independence.

? Location Which areas remained European colonies?

LOCATE
For locations, see the maps on pp. 530 and 531.

1. The French were unable to reassert authority after Toussaint-Louverture led the slaves and mulattoes in revolt.
2. Defeat at Napoleon's hands caused disruption in Spanish and Portuguese leadership and led colonies to demand independence.
3. They benefited from trade and investment in Latin America.
4. Letters should explain Dom Pedro's love for Brazil and his desire for its independence.
5. Students might suggest class conflicts and colonial differences.

CHAPTER 19 REVIEW ANSWERS
(p. 533)

WRITING A SUMMARY
See essential points in the text.

REVIEWING TERMS
1. Monroe Doctrine
2. dominion
3. sectionalism
4. Seneca Falls Convention
5. Missouri Compromise

REVIEWING CHRONOLOGY
5, 2, 3, 4, 1

---

distribute the land among *mestizos* and Indians. He also demanded:

> 66 *a new government, by which all inhabitants, except peninsulares, would no longer be designated as Indians, mulattoes, or castas [people of mixed race], but all would be known as Americans.* 99

In 1815 the authorities captured and executed Morelos as well.

Changes in Spain, however, helped the independence movement in Mexico. When in 1820 liberals in Spain forced King Ferdinand VII to enact reforms, the conservative creole landowners in Mexico became alarmed. They soon concluded that the only way to protect themselves was to separate from Spain.

General Agustín de Iturbide (ee-toor-BEE-day) led the military campaign and declared Mexico's independence in 1821. Mexico fell into bloody civil war. Thousands of people were killed and *haciendas*, mines, and villages were destroyed. After the war, Iturbide declared himself emperor. However, his mismanagement left the nation's treasury bankrupt. In 1823 the army forced Iturbide to abdicate, and Mexico became a republic.

Conservatives in Mexico demanded independence to protect themselves against liberals in Spain.

Foreign Reactions to Independence

Many nations were pleased by Latin American independence. Britain benefited tremendously by loaning the newly independent nations great sums of money and increasing trade. Britain also invested heavily in railroads and mines. By 1913 it was the biggest investor in Latin America, controlling nearly two thirds of all foreign investment.

The United States also favored an independent Latin America because it meant the end of European control of Central and South America and thus the opening up of markets for American goods. Consequently, reports that Spain planned to retake its former colonies alarmed the United States. President James Monroe responded in 1823 by issuing a policy later known as the **Monroe Doctrine**.

The Monroe Doctrine simply stated that the United States would not tolerate European military intervention in the Western Hemisphere. While the United States did not have the power to defend against European defiance of the Monroe Doctrine, Britain's powerful navy backed up the United States to protect British trade.

Fearing Spain would reimpose colonial rule, the United States and Britain supported Latin American independence.

SECTION 4 REVIEW

IDENTIFY and explain the significance of the following:
   Toussaint-Louverture
   intendancy
   Simón Bolívar
   Dom João
   Dom Pedro
   Miguel Hidalgo y Costilla
   José María Morelos y Pavón
   Agustín de Iturbide
   Monroe Doctrine

LOCATE and explain the importance of the following:

Saint Domingue
Gran Colombia
Brazil

1. **Main Idea** How did Haiti become independent?
2. **Main Idea** How did the Napoleonic wars affect independence movements in Latin America?
3. **Cross-cultural Interaction** Why did Great Britain and the United States favor Latin American independence?

4. **Writing to Persuade** Imagine that you are Dom Pedro. You have received a letter from Portugal urging you to return now that Napoleon's forces have departed. Write a response to the Portuguese government explaining why you will stay in Brazil.
5. **Hypothesizing** Why do you think Bolívar had difficulty unifying large regions in South America?

Review

On a separate sheet of paper, complete the following exercises:

WRITING A SUMMARY

Using the essential points in the text, write a brief summary of the chapter.

REVIEWING TERMS

From the following list, choose the term that correctly matches the definition.

dominion
Missouri Compromise
Monroe Doctrine
Seneca Falls Convention
settlement houses
sectionalism

1. policy stating that the United States would not tolerate any European military intervention in the Western Hemisphere
2. colony settled by British immigrants that had been granted self-government by the British Parliament
3. loyalty to a particular part of a country
4. first women's rights convention in the United States, organized by Elizabeth Cady Stanton and Lucretia Mott
5. decision made by the U.S. Congress that allowed slavery only in southern territories

REVIEWING CHRONOLOGY

List the following events in their correct chronological order.

1. Parliament gives the vote to women over 30.
2. Britain frees all slaves in the British Empire.
3. The Confederate States of America surrender, ending the U.S. Civil War.
4. A reform bill in Parliament extends the vote to the entire male population.
5. Simón Bolívar defeats the Spanish, liberating most of northern South America.

UNDERSTANDING THE MAIN IDEA

1. What steps did Great Britain take to end slavery?
2. Why did people emigrate from Britain to overseas colonies?
3. What factors contributed to the slavery debate in the United States?
4. What effect did events in Europe have on the independence movements in Latin America?
5. What were some of the consequences of the reform movement in Britain?

THINKING CRITICALLY

1. **Hypothesizing** What might have happened if the aristocratic elite in the British Parliament had been unwilling to extend the vote to more people?
2. **Comparing** Compare the processes by which slavery was ended in the British Empire and the United States.

Building Your Portfolio

Complete the following activities individually or in groups.

1. **Labor Relations** Imagine that you are involved in a labor dispute between textile factory workers and the factory owners. The workers have gone out on strike over wages and working conditions, and they will be attempting to negotiate with the owners to settle the dispute.

   If you are completing this as a group activity, divide into teams representing the workers and the owners. Plan for these negotiations by preparing a list of grievances for your team. Conduct the negotiations by presenting both sets of grievances, and work toward a compromise that each side can agree to. If you are completing this as an individual activity, prepare both lists of grievances and write a report describing how the two sides might come to an agreement.
2. **Women's Suffrage** Using the resources of your local library, find out how women got the right to vote in national elections in your state. Use your research to write a short story, brief play, or poem about women's struggle for the vote. The central character of your work may be a leader in the women's suffrage movement.

UNDERSTANDING THE MAIN IDEA

1. Parliament banned the slave trade in 1807 and ended slavery in 1833.
2. population pressures, as punishment for crimes
3. expansion of slavery westward, adding new states, abolitionist efforts
4. Napoleon conquered Spain and Portugal, disrupting their leadership, which led Latin American colonies to demand independence.
5. Industrial reforms improved the quality of living for working class; political reforms shifted power away from the elite to other classes, created Britain's first political parties, established voting rights for the majority of the male population, and sparked the women's suffrage movement; social reforms led to a public health movement and welfare programs.

THINKING CRITICALLY

1. The protests might have become more violent as people became more dissatisfied, as occurred during the women's suffrage movement.
2. Both resulted after many years of political infighting. Britain was able to peacefully abolish slavery, while the United States went to war over the issue.

Chapter 20

Nation States and Empires in Europe 1814–1914

Chapter Planning Guide

	TEXTBOOK	CORE RESOURCES	VISUAL RESOURCES	MULTIMEDIA
Introduction	pp. 534–535	Block Scheduling Handbook: Ch. 20		Videodisc Segment 20 and Viewing Guide: *Nationalism in Europe*
Lesson 20.1 Restructuring Europe	pp. 536–540 Map: *Europe After the Congress of Vienna,* p. 537	Reading 20.1: *Talleyrand's Memoirs* Skills Activity 20: *Drawing Conclusions*	Everyday Life 20: *A Ball During the Congress of Vienna*	GHRC 20 Readings: *European Liberalism in the 1800s; Prince Metternich's Carlsbad Decrees* GHRC 20/Videodiscs: Images—*The Congress of Vienna's Balancing Act; French Women Demand Their Rights; Paris in 1848;* Audio Clip—*Fanfare from Beethoven's Fifth Symphony*
Lesson 20.2 Unification in Italy and Germany	pp. 541–545 Map: *Unification of Italy,* p. 542 Map: *Unification of Germany,* p. 544 Map: *Europe: Political,* p. 858	Reading 20.2: *A Volunteer's View of Garibaldi* Writing Project 20: *Formulating a Thesis Statement*	Art and History 20: *Departure of King William I for the Army, July 31, 1870*	GHRC 20 Readings: *Garibaldi; Mazzini Stirs up Nationalism in Italy; A French Liberal Looks at German Nationalism* GHRC 20/Videodiscs: Images—*Bismarck; Monument to Victor Emmanuel*
Lesson 20.3 Aging Empires in Eastern Europe	pp. 546–553 Map: *Ethnic Groups in Austria-Hungary,* p. 547 Map: *The Russian Empire by 1900,* p. 548 Literature Through Time: *Dead Souls,* p. 549 Through Other's Eyes: *The Great Powers and the Balkans,* p. 552 Biography: *Florence Nightingale,* p. 553	Reading 20.3: *Czar Nicholas I's Approach to Government* Geography Activity 20: *Connecting Eastern and Western Russia*	Geography and History 20: *Ethnic Groups in Austria-Hungary, 1867*	GHRC 20 Readings: *Russia's "Bloody Sunday"; Nationalism and the Ottoman Empire* GHRC 20/Videodiscs: Images—*Ottoman Empire's First Parliament; Russian Nationalism in Art; The Ottoman Empire Lies Near Death;* Maps—*War and Peace in the Crimea; The Ottoman Empire, 1800; The Ottoman Empire, 1914*
Lesson 20.4 Constitutionalism in Western Europe	pp. 554–560	Reading 20.4: *Imprisonment on Devil's Island*		GHRC 20 Reading: *The Dreyfus Affair* GHRC 20/Videodiscs: Image—*Independent Norway*
Chapter Investigation and Enrichment	pp. 534–560	Chapter 20 Investigation: *An Opinion Piece on Nationalism and Liberalism in Europe* People in World History 20 Explorations in Daily Life 20		GHRC 20/Videodiscs
Review and Assessment	Section 1 Review, p. 540 Section 2 Review, p. 545 Section 3 Review, p. 553 Section 4 Review, p. 560 Chapter 20 Review, p. 561	Chapter Review Activity 20 Vocabulary Activity 20 Themes Review 20 Section Study Guides 20.1–20.4 Main Idea Activities 20.1–20.4 Daily Quizzes 20.1–20.4 Chapter 20 Test Sheltered English Ch. 20 Test Ch. 20 Test Generator		Audio CDs: Ch. 20 Summary (English and Spanish)

INTRODUCING THE CHAPTER

Textbook pp. 534–535

CHAPTER OVERVIEW

The defeat of Napoleon brought a desire for peace to the nations of Europe. However, the return to conservative monarchies called for by the Congress of Vienna was doomed by the spirit of change and reform that swept the continent. New feelings of nationalism led to the creation of two new nations, Italy and Germany. While in Eastern Europe the struggle to preserve aging empires led to repression of liberal ideals, the nations of western Europe experienced an era of constitutional reform.

PRESENTING THEMES

On the chalkboard or on an overhead transparency, write the following open-ended theme questions.

- **POLITICS AND LAW** What conflicts might arise between supporters of political stability and supporters of political reform?
- **WAR AND DIPLOMACY** How might the end of a war give way to sweeping diplomatic agreements?
- **ECONOMIC ORGANIZATION** How might changes in an economy transform society?

Have students, either individually or in groups, suggest responses to the questions. For the politics and law question, students might suggest that those who want stability and those who want reform might come into conflict over how to promote the best interests of the society. For the war and diplomacy question, students might suggest that the victors might force sweeping changes on the losers. For the economic organization question, students might suggest that economic changes often alter the ways in which people work and live. Save the responses. Once students have studied the chapter, you may wish to have them complete the Themes Review, then compare the two sets of answers.

USING THE VIDEO

Segment 20: *Nationalism in Europe*

ENGLISH

Search Chapter 20
Videodisc 2, Side B

SPANISH

Search Chapter 20
Videodisc 2, Side B

Tell students that in this chapter they will examine the powerful new forces of liberalism and nationalism that swept across Europe during the nineteenth century. Then show Segment 20 of the *World History and Cultures Videodiscs*, which looks at the meaning of nationalism and the reasons behind its emergence in Europe in the 1800s.

Before showing the segment, ask students to think about the difference between their nationality and their ethnic heritage. To help the students grasp the signifigant points of the segment, have them complete Video Viewing Guide 20.

Key to Ability Levels

All strategies and activities are coded to the following ability levels:

LEVEL 1	**Basic** activities suitable for all students
LEVEL 2	**Average** activities suitable for average to above-average students
LEVEL 3	**Challenging** activities suitable for above-average students
SHELTERED ENGLISH	Activities suitable for students with **Limited English Proficiency**

Additional Resources

BOOKS FOR TEACHERS

Cannadine, David. *The Decline and Fall of the British Aristocracy.* Anchor, 1990. Looks at Britain in the waning days of the nineteenth century.

Palmer, Alan. *Twilight of the Habsburgs: The Life and Times of Emperor Franz Joseph.* Grove Press, 1994. Looks at a European dynasty.

Premble, John. *Venice Rediscovered.* Oxford University Press, 1995. Focuses on the city as a cultural symbol of Europe.

BOOKS FOR STUDENTS

Bredin, Jean-Denis. *The Affair: The Case of Alfred Dreyfus.* Braziller, 1986. Examines anti-Semitism in the Third Republic.

Mack Smith, Dennis. *Garibaldi.* Knopf, 1956. Gives a short biography of the Italian liberator.

Taylor, A. J. P. *Bismarck: The Man and the Statesman.* Charles, 1987. Looks at the life of the man who united Germany.

MULTIMEDIA MATERIALS

Bismarck: Germany from Blood and Iron. Learning Corporation of America. Video, 30 min. Examines Bismarck's role in unifying Germany.

La Belle Epoque, 1890–1914. Metropolitan Museum of Art. Video, 60 min. Looks at London and Paris at their heights.

Nineteenth-Century Nationalism. ZCI. CD-ROM, MAC, WIN, MPC formats. Examines nationalism in Europe between 1815 and 1914.

Lesson 20.1   *Restructuring Europe*

Textbook pp. 536–540

RESOURCES

Pupil's Edition

Map, p. 537: *Europe After the Congress of Vienna, 1815*

Core Resources

Reading 20.1: *Talleyrand's Memoirs*
Skills Activity 20: *Drawing Conclusions*

Visual Resources

Everyday Life 20: *A Ball During the Congress of Vienna*

Global History Resource Center

Reading: *European Liberalism in the 1800s*
Reading: *Prince Metternich's Carlsbad Decrees*

Videodiscs or Global History Resource Center

Image: *The Congress of Vienna's Balancing Act*

Search Frame 943

Image: *French Women Demand Their Rights in 1848*

Search Frame 945

Audio Clip: *Fanfare from Beethoven's Fifth Symphony*

Search 1603, Play to 2043
Videodisc 2, Side B
Audio Clip 20

Image: *Paris in 1848: Revolution in the Streets*

Search Frame 944

LESSON FOCUS

How did European nations search for security following the Napoleonic Wars?

OBJECTIVES

After completing this lesson, students will be able to:

- identify what the Congress of Vienna accomplished;
- describe the main aims of the Concert of Europe;
- explain how liberal revolutions affected Europe.

HOOK: Link to Today

Discuss how nations work together to avoid war. Tell students that they will be learning about the agreements made by nations to ensure peace in Europe after the Napoleonic Wars. Ask students what organizations and alliances exist for keeping peace today. *[All students should be familiar with the United Nations, some will probably mention the North Atlantic Treaty Organization, and others may identify the Southeast Asia Treaty Organization.]* Discuss the goals and methods of these organizations. *[The UN is a worldwide body designed for global peacekeeping; NATO and SEATO exist as mutual self-defense alliances for Europe and Southeast Asia.]*

Ask: Why might countries have formed alliances after Napoleon's defeat?

[Responses should indicate that those countries subject to Napoleonic imperialism might have found alliances appealing.]

DEVELOP

Identify the aims and accomplishments of the Congress of Vienna, the Holy Alliance, and the Concert of Europe. Begin by showing Everyday Life Transparency 20 to illustrate a ball during the Congress of Vienna.

Ask: What was the mood in Vienna during the Congress of Vienna?

[The mood was celebratory. The leaders gathered there hoped to restore peace in Europe forever.]

Next ask students to form small groups. Have them assume these roles: diplomats to the Congress of Vienna, rulers joining the Holy Alliance, and members of the Concert of Europe. Ask groups to discuss the goals, methods, and accomplishments of their organization or alliance. Have students refer to the map on textbook page 537 to illustrate their points. Then have a member of each group briefly summarize the group's discussion for the class. [The Congress of Vienna tried to ensure a peaceful Europe by restoring old borders, forming the German Confederation, and establishing a balance of power. Britain and Austria also formed a secret alliance with France to protect against aggression from Russia or Prussia. In keeping with its notion of legitimacy, the Congress restored the monarchs of Portugal, Spain, Sardinia, and the kingdom of the Two Sicilies to their thrones. In forming the Holy Alliance, Czar Alexander I of Russia hoped to maintain international peace. Nations pledged to assist each other against internal disturbances. The Concert of Europe, the system of diplomatic cooperation following the Congress of Vienna, aimed to combat the spread of revolutionary ideas and maintain peace.] Conclude by displaying the electronic media image of the political cartoon about the Congress of Vienna. Then assign Core Resources Reading 20.1 of Talleyrand's memoirs from the Congress of Vienna and Skills Activity 20, which deals with Metternich.

PROBE

Explain how European rebellions threatened the Concert of Europe. Remind students how the French Revolution inspired people across Europe to push for liberalism (individual rights) and nationalism (freedom from imperialist powers). Point out that even after Napoleon was defeated, these ideas did not die. Have students develop a compare/contrast chart looking at liberalism and nationalism vs. conservatism and legitimacy. Their charts should contain key elements associated with each. [Proponents of conservatism and legitimacy wanted to restore monarchies and to return to the order before the French Revolution. Liberals and nationalists wanted governments to assure people of their rights, usually through a constitution; they also wanted their countries to be free from the political influence of other countries.]
Ask: *Which set of ideas led to rebellion?*
    [The ideas of liberalism and nationalism led to rebellion.]

To assist students in understanding liberalism and nationalism, you may wish to assign the Global History Resource Center

readings on liberalism and on Prince Metternich's Carlsbad Decrees. You might also display the electronic media images of revolution in Paris and of French women demanding their rights in 1848.

CONCLUDE

Evaluate the stability of the balance of power in Europe.
Have the class review the term *balance of power.*
Ask: *How did the balance of power contribute to peace?*
    [Although there were some rebellions, there was no large-scale European war. However, the balance of power did not resolve conflicts, such as those over liberalism and conservatism.]

Ask: *What weaknesses existed that might have caused future problems?*
    [The system of alliances pledging European nations to support one another could entangle all in a war.]

EXTEND

Cross-Curricular Connection: *Language Arts*
Have students write a few paragraphs that a British romantic poet, such as Lord Byron, might have written to support Greek independence or the revolutions of 1848.

MEET INDIVIDUAL NEEDS
Gifted Students
Have students research and report on Prince Metternich, evaluating him in terms of his methods, his impact on Europe, and his ability to deal with the kind of change sweeping across Europe.

Musical-Rhythmic Learners
Have students listen to the audio clip and then research and report on how the music of Beethoven reflected the times in which he lived. Ask students to illustrate their report with Beethoven's music.

ASSESS
Review
Have students complete the Section 1 Review. Use answers in the Teacher's Edition, page 540, to assess student mastery of this section.

Lesson 20.2   Unification in Italy and Germany

Textbook pp. 541–545

LESSON FOCUS

How did Italy and Germany achieve unification in the 1800s?

OBJECTIVES

After completing this lesson, students will be able to:

- identify the goals of Italian nationalists;
- identify events and factors that led to Italian unification;
- describe the forces that inspired calls for German unity;
- describe how Bismarck's actions led to the unification of Germany.

HOOK: Link to Today

Discuss the roots of nationalism. Referring to competitive athletics and academic events, ask students to discuss what things designed to elicit school loyalty set their school apart from other schools. *[school and team colors; school songs and cheers; school traditions, and so on]* Lead students in a discussion about whether some of these same types of things could signify the independence of nations. Have a volunteer define *nationalism*. Ask students what kinds of things might heighten nationalism and have them create a list of their answers. *[Lists should touch upon these factors: outside*

threats, pride in independence or in a shared past, and desire for power over other nations. Have them save their lists as they progress through the lesson, identifying what part each factor played in the growth of nationalism in the nations discussed.]

DEVELOP

Identify the forces that led to unification in Italy and in Germany. Have a volunteer identify the goals of the Italian nationalists. *[Goals were unification of Italy and liberation from foreign rule.]*

Ask: Did Italian nationalism reflect the elements of nationalism you discussed earlier?

[yes—Italian nationalism was reflected through pride and traditions]

Refer students to the textbook map of unification, page 542, to show unification as a building process.

In groups of two or three, have students develop a chart with two columns: 1) Factors that Inspired Unity in Italy; and 2) Actual Events that Led to Italian Unity. *[Students' charts should list: **Factors:** revival of interest in country's traditions, resentfulness of foreign occupation, improvement of economy, strengthening of military, support from France; **Events:***

Sardinian troops drove the Austrians from Sardinia, annexed small kingdoms of central Italy, marched south to help Garibaldi conquer Naples]

Next, refer students to the map of German unification on textbook page 544. Then ask what impact Napoleon had on the German states. *[He united them into the Confederation of the Rhine, inspiring nationalism.]* Next ask how the Congress of Vienna contributed to the process of German unification. *[The Rhine Confederation was retained, with a new name, and Prussia was given new territory that made it a dominant power in the confederation.]*

Assign the same task as before, but with the focus on German unification. *[**Factors:** nationalism nurtured by Napoleon, economy developed, military strengthened; **Events:** liberals revolted in 1848, Bismarck headed Prussian cabinet, Prussia gained Schleswig in Danish War, Holstein in Seven Weeks' War; southern German states joined union in Franco-Prussian War; William named kaiser of German Empire]*

Conclude by asking students to review the information they have gathered and point out the similarities in the unification of Italy and Germany. You may wish to assign the Global History Resource Center readings on revolution in Germany and on German nationalism.

PROBE

Discuss the various tactics employed by the Italian and German leaders that brought about unity in their countries. Show Art and History Transparency 20. Ask a volunteer to identify the country with which King William is associated. *[Germany]* Then have students identify the leaders responsible for Italian and German unification. List them on the board. You may wish to show the electronic media images of the political cartoon of Bismarck and of the monument to Victor Emmanuel. You might also assign the Global History Resource Center readings on Garibaldi and Mazzini.

Ask: *How did the efforts of Mazzini, Cavour, and Garibaldi complement each other?*
[Students should understand that they stirred up unrest in the people, established economic stability and foreign support, and built up military strength.]

Have a student define *realpolitik*.
Ask: *How were Bismarck's actions the epitome of* realpolitik?

[He dissolved the Prussian Parliament when it disagreed with him. He used Austria as an ally to get Schleswig, then fought Austria to get Holstein. He staged war with France to bring the southern German states into a unified Germany and to expand German territory.]

CONCLUDE

Discuss how the unification of Italy and Germany affected Europe as a whole. Have students look at the map of Europe on textbook page 858, and ask them to locate Italy and Germany.
Ask: *How might the location of the new nation-states of Italy and Germany affect the balance of power in Europe?*
[Both countries were in the center of Europe, between empires in the unified nation-states. They were no longer the victims of other nations but powers in their own right.]

EXTEND

Cross-Curricular Connection: *Literature*
Have students read and report on *The Leopard*, by Giuseppe di Lampedusa (Pantheon, 1960), a novel set during Garibaldi's conquest of Sicily. The story is based on the life of the author's grandfather, a prince and feudal landowner who witnessed the changing of the old order in Italy.

MEET INDIVIDUAL NEEDS

Students Acquiring English
Pair new speakers of English with fluent speakers to help them learn unfamiliar vocabulary, such as *guarantee, dialect, resurrected, negotiating, harass, eliminated, censorship, obstacles, annexed, administer, maneuvered.*

Visual-Spatial Learners
Have students interested in drawing and cartooning view the electronic media image of the political cartoon on Bismarck and then create their own cartoon commenting on one of the events in this lesson.

ASSESS

Review
Have students complete the Section 2 Review. Use answers in the Teacher's Edition, page 545, to assess student mastery of this section.

533F

RESOURCES

Pupil's Edition
Map, p. 548: *The Russian Empire by 1900*

Biography, p. 553: *Florence Nightingale*

Map, p. 858: *Europe: Political*

Core Resources
Reading 20.3: *Czar Nicholas I's Approach to Government*

Geography Activity 20: *Connecting Eastern and Western Russia*

Visual Resources
Geography and History 20: *Ethnic Groups in Austria-Hungary, 1867*

Global History Resource Center
Reading: *Russia's "Bloody Sunday"*

Reading: *Nationalism and the Ottoman Empire*

Videodiscs or Global History Resource Center

Image: *Emancipation of a Russian Serf*

Search Frame 949

Image: *Ottoman Empire's First Parliament*

Search Frame 950

Map: *War and Peace in the Crimea, 1854–1858*

Search Frame 953

Map: *Series of two on the Ottoman Empire*

Search Frames 954–55

Image: *The Ottoman Empire Lies Near Death*

Search Frame 951

Image: *Russian Nationalism in Art*

Search Frame 948

LESSON FOCUS
How did Russia, Austria, and the Ottoman Empire respond to demands for reform?

OBJECTIVES
After completing this lesson, students will be able to:
- describe how Austria responded to demands for political reform;
- explain how reforms affected the Russian Empire;
- identify how the Ottoman Empire tried to reverse its decline;
- explain why international conflict occurred in the Balkans.

HOOK
Discuss serfdom in Russia. Show the electronic media image of the Russian serf. Then have students give reasons why liberals might have argued for the emancipation of serfs. *[humanitarian and democratic grounds; economic reasons—serfdom kept Russia's economy agricultural and prevented industrialization]*

DEVELOP
Discuss the effects of nationalism and liberalism on Austria-Hungary, Russia, and the Ottoman Empire. On the chalkboard write the question: *How did Austria-Hungary, Russia, and the Ottoman Empire respond to the growth of nationalism and liberalism?* Organize the class into groups, with each group assigned a different empire. Have each create a time line of events and developments in the empire it has been assigned. Have groups share their work with the class. *[Austria-Hungary: abolition of reforms enacted in 1848, second Hungarian rebellion, granting of constitution to Hungary and shared power in Dual Monarchy; Russia: liberal rebellion of 1825 crushed by czar, Russification in the 1830s, Emancipation Edict freeing serfs in 1861, 1905 petition to the czar resulting in Bloody Sunday and October Manifesto; Ottoman Empire: modernization of empire, including reorganization of military; defeat of Janissaries; modernization of government through Tanzimat reforms, including equal legal status for Muslims and non-Muslims, more efficient tax system, and fair system of*

military drafts; industrialization; adoption of a constitution; growth of Pan-Arabism; backlash against reform; revolution]

To assist students, show Geography and History Transparency 20 on Austria-Hungary and display the electronic media image of the Ottoman parliament. You might also assign Core Resources Reading 20.3 and the Global History Resource Center readings on Bloody Sunday and the Ottoman Empire to appropriate groups.

PROBE

Discuss why many international conflicts occurred in the Balkan Peninsula. Refer students to the map of Europe on textbook page 858 and have them locate the Balkan countries, then the former Austrian, Russian, and Ottoman empires. Point out how, although most of the Balkans belonged to the Ottoman Empire before 1878, the Russian and Austrian empires might feel that it would be geographically and politically advantageous to control the Balkans.

Refer students to the map of the Russian Empire on textbook page 548 and discuss how realistic other nations' fears of Russian expansion were. Ask students to note the three times Russia went to war over Ottoman territories in the 1800s. *[1828: Russo-Turkish War, in which Russia gained access to Danube River, control of territory in Caucasus, and self-rule for Serbia; 1853–1856: Crimean War, in which Russia invaded Ottoman territory in hopes of expanding empire; 1877: Russia supported Balkan provinces that rebelled against Ottoman Empire]* To facilitate this discussion, you may wish to show students the electronic media map of the Crimean War, and have them review the biography of Florence Nightingale on textbook page 553. Additionally, you may wish to assign Geography Activity 20, which discusses connecting Eastern and Western Russia.

Discuss the decline of the Ottoman Empire.

Ask: ***What Balkan countries became independent from the Ottoman Empire after war with Russia in 1877?***
    [Serbia, Romania, and Montenegro gained independence, while Bulgaria became a large state under Russian control.]

Ask: ***What territorial gains did other European powers make in the Balkans?***
    [Students should note that Britain gained rights to Cyprus as a naval base; Austria occupied Bosnia.]

Ask students to look at the electronic media maps of of the Ottoman Empire in 1800 and in 1914, as well as the electronic media image showing the empire as the "Sick Man of Europe." Have students read the Global History Resource Center selection explaining nationalism in the Ottoman Empire. Then ask students to work briefly in pairs to create 25-word summaries of political activity in the Balkans in the 1800s and how it affected the Ottoman Empire.

CONCLUDE

Compare the effects of liberalism and authoritarianism on the balance of power in Europe.

Ask: ***Which was more important in destroying the balance of power in Europe—liberalism, authoritarianism, or nationalism?***
    [Nationalism and liberalism put people in conflict with their authoritarian leaders and hastened the breakup of empires into smaller countries. These nations lacked the ability to offset the power of larger European rivals.]

EXTEND

Other Media
Link to Today. Have students do a search on the Internet or an on-line service to find information on this period of European history. Have students share their findings with the class.

MEET INDIVIDUAL NEEDS

Linguistic Learners
Have interested students read *The Silver Crest: My Russian Boyhood*, by Kornei Chukovsky (Holt, Rinehart and Winston, 1976), an autobiographical account of a writer's childhood in czarist Russia.

Visual-Spatial Learners
Have interested students view the electronic media image on Russian nationalism in art and look for design elements and use of symbolism.

ASSESS

Have students complete the Section 3 Review. Use answers in the Teacher's Edition, page 553, to assess student mastery of this section.

Lesson 20.4   *Constitutionalism in Western Europe*

Textbook pp. 554–560

RESOURCES

Core Resources

Reading 20.4: *Imprisonment on Devil's Island*

Global History Resource Center

Reading: *The Dreyfus Affair*

Videodiscs or Global History Resource Center

Image: *Independent Norway: Republic or Kingdom?*

Search Frame 952

LESSON FOCUS

How did western European countries respond to demands for reform in the 1800s?

OBJECTIVES

After completing this lesson, students will be able to:

- describe how French rulers responded to demands for liberal reforms;
- explain why Bismarck implemented social welfare reforms in Germany;
- identify problems faced by Spain, Portugal, and Italy in the 1800s;
- describe how industrialization affected the smaller countries of western Europe.

HOOK

Describe responses to demands for liberal reforms in France. Read this excerpt from an 1871 newspaper account, "The Paris Commune: The Finale, 29 May 1871," by Archibald Forbes. In this piece Forbes describes what he saw at Père-Lachaise, the place where the last shots in the uprising were fired during the suppression of the revolutionary government called the Commune:

Shells, however, had fallen freely, and the results were occasionally very ghastly. But the ghastliest sight in Père-Lachaise was in the south-eastern corner, where, close to the boundary wall, there had been a natural hollow. The hollow was now filled up by dead. . . . There they lay, tier above tier, each successive tier powdered over with a coating of chloride of lime—two hundred of them patent [visible] to the eye, besides those underneath hidden by the earth covering layer after layer. . . . How died these men and women? . . . Just yonder was where they were posted up against that section of pock-pitted wall . . . and were shot to death as they stood or crouched.

Ask: What was the Commune, and what happened to it? [The Commune was created by the Parisians after Paris fell to the Prussians in 1871. It was put down by the French army.]

Have students work briefly in pairs to summarize reform efforts and results under Louis Napoleon Bonaparte and the Third Republic. Then ask pairs to share results with the class. [**Louis Napoleon:** *modernized Paris, set up credit banks, built a national railway, and reduced tariffs to develop industry, but also restricted the legislature, censored the press, and banned public meetings;* **Third Republic:** *legalized trade unions, reduced working day, passed legislation to give workers one day off per week*]

DEVELOP

Explain why Bismarck implemented social welfare reforms in Germany. Have students prepare a two-column chart with the first column titled *Bismarck's Viewpoint* and the second column titled *Bismarck's Actions*. Ask volunteers to describe Bismarck's views of the Catholic Church, industrialization, and socialists, as students fill in the first column. *[He felt that the church was the enemy of the centralized state, as were socialists. Industrialization strengthened the state.]* Then have volunteers describe how Bismarck's views affected his actions. *[Students should mention Kulturkampf, which was intended to control the clergy, as well as Bismarck's efforts to reform banking and money laws, to improve communications, and to encourage trade, which furthered industrialization. His opposition to socialism led first to repression and then to limited liberal reforms intended to make socialism less attractive.]*

PROBE

Contrast conditions in southern European nations with those in the smaller, more industrialized nations of western Europe. Create a chart on the chalkboard, listing these European countries in the left-hand column: Spain, Portugal, Italy, Belgium, the Netherlands, Switzerland, Denmark, Sweden, Norway. Columns at the top of the chart should read: *Political Unrest; Constitution or Voting Rights; Church Attitude Toward Reform; Degree of Industrialization*. Have students work in small groups to copy the chart onto a piece of paper and complete it. *[Students should note that Spain, Italy, and Portugal had problems with political unrest, the Catholic Church and its efforts to fight reform, and a lack of industrialization. Belgium, Switzerland, and Norway had greater industrialization and democratic governments. The Netherlands, Denmark, and Sweden did not have political unrest, but were less industrialized than Belgium, Switzerland, and Norway.]*

Ask: *What is the relationship between industrialization and the growth of nationalism and liberalism in these countries?* *[Students should understand that industrial growth brought prosperity, which workers wanted to share. Prosperity also furthered education, and more educated middle and lower classes wanted involvement in government decisions. At the same time, industrialization weakened loyalties to local regions and often replaced them with more nationalistic feelings.]*

CONCLUDE

Compare and contrast the attitudes of conservative and liberal western European leaders. Have volunteers assume the roles of conservative and liberal leaders from France,

Germany, Spain, Italy, Belgium, and Switzerland. Tell them that they are to serve on a panel to explain and debate the policies they think should be followed in their countries. Have them include views of the importance of constitutional government, social reforms, and industrialization.

EXTEND

Cross-Curricular Connection: *Economics*
Have students select a country from the section and report on its economic structure at the end of the 1800s.

Cross-Curricular Connection: *Journalism*
Link to Today. Have students view the electronic media image on Norway's independence. Ask them to explain what they think the cartoon means. Then ask them to bring in examples of political cartoons from recent newspapers or magazines. They should accompany their examples with explanations of how the cartoons reflect current issues.

MEET INDIVIDUAL NEEDS

Interpersonal Learners
Assign Reading 20.4 and have students read more about the Dreyfus case in the Global History Resource Center. Then ask them to draw up a list of charges that prosecutors might have used against the army officers who covered up the truth. Ask them to include in their indictment a description of the damage this injustice inflicted not only on Dreyfus and his family but on France as a whole.

Students Having Difficulty
Students who need extra help may benefit from creating a time line of important events from this section. Help students notice how events in different European countries often overlapped or occurred in the same period.

ASSESS

Have students complete the Section 4 Review. Use answers in the Teacher's Edition, pages 559–560, to assess student mastery of this section.

In preparation for the chapter test, you may wish to have students complete all or part of the Chapter 20 Review on textbook page 561, the Chapter 20 Review Activity, and the Chapter 20 Themes Review.

Understanding
the Main Idea

Call on a volunteer to read aloud the *Understanding the Main Idea* paragraph. Then tell students that after the defeat of France, European leaders tried to return Europe to the way it was before the Napoleonic wars. They restored monarchies, protected empires, and re-established the ruling elite. The revolutionary ideas of France had taken hold, however, and liberal and nationalist movements sprang up across the continent as people protested the return to the old ways.

Presenting Themes

See p. 533B for suggestions on introducing themes.

Using the Time Line

Have students list the time line events in their notebooks. After they have read about each event in the chapter, have students write a paragraph explaining its significance.

Chapter 20
Nation-States and Empires in Europe 1814–1914

Understanding the Main Idea

After surviving the turmoil of the Napoleonic wars, Europeans longed for peace. Napoleon, however, had spread the republican principles of the French Revolution throughout Europe, sowing the seeds of future revolutionary conflict. In the 1800s liberalism and nationalism shook the political and social foundations of the European world.

Themes

- *Politics and Law* What conflicts might arise between supporters of political stability and supporters of political reform?
- *War and Diplomacy* How might the end of a war give way to sweeping diplomatic agreements?
- *Economic Organization* How might changes in an economy transform society?

The royalty of Europe crowded into the great hall of Vienna's royal palace on November 29, 1814. A hush fell over the audience as the composer Ludwig van Beethoven appeared on the stage. With his arms arching, Beethoven launched the musicians into the battle symphony, *Wellington's Victory*. A deep drum beat out a celebration of British general Wellington's defeat of the French at Vitoria in 1813.

Beethoven's concert was just one of the many victory celebrations held during the Congress of Vienna. This conference brought the monarchs and nobles of Europe together to celebrate Napoleon's defeat and the end of more than two decades of warfare. Every day, gold-covered carriages took kings and queens, dukes and duchesses, and princes and princesses to the many balls and banquets thrown by the noble families of the Austrian capital. "I do not see anyone without a title to his name," marveled one observer. "There is literally a royal mob here."

The "royal mob" was trying to restore the old days of royal splendor that the French Revolution had disrupted. The twin spirits of nationalism and liberalism, however, would soon make such extravagant celebrations merely fleeting echoes of the earlier days of absolute monarchy.

1814	1826	1848	1861
The Congress of Vienna begins.	Sultan Mahmud II destroys the Janissary Corps.	Revolution spreads across Europe.	Serfs in Russia are freed.

European leaders meet for the Congress of Vienna, 1814–1815.

1870
▲
Unification of Italy is complete.

1871
▲
Germany unifies under Prussian control.

1876
▲
The Ottoman Empire adopts a constitution.

1905
▲
Revolution sweeps through Russia.

About the Image

Jean-Baptiste Isabey was the official portraitist of the Congress of Vienna, and he completed as many as 50 portraits. In this painting, the official picture of the Congress, Isabey chose as his subject the Duke of Wellington's address to the Congress. Isabey complained that it was difficult to give the impression of animation and movement to a group of men sitting around a table. He also had trouble getting the statesmen to remain in place for the sittings, and he felt that it was hard to accurately portray their features without losing the noble feeling that the occasion demanded.

Critical Thinking Ask students how Isabey's job was different from that of a modern photojournalist.

ANSWER: Students might answer that a modern photojournalist would most likely be interested in recording events accurately, while Isabey tried to capture the spirit of the occasion and portray people and events.

Restructuring Europe

FOCUS

- What did the Congress of Vienna accomplish?
- What were the main goals of the Concert of Europe?
- How did liberal revolutions affect Europe?

With the final defeat of Napoleon in 1815, Europe reached an important turning point. For more than 25 years the most powerful political influence on the continent had been the French Revolution. Even though Napoleon had not always upheld the ideals of the Revolution, he had carried its influence throughout Europe and beyond. After his defeat, the major European powers tried to turn back the clock, hoping to restore peace to Europe by reinstating conservative monarchs. Once unleashed, however, the forces of revolution proved too powerful to put down.

The Treaty of Paris, ratified at the Congress of Vienna, November 12, 1815

The Congress of Vienna

Even before Napoleon's final defeat and imprisonment, representatives of the European powers gathered in Vienna to negotiate a full and definitive settlement of the peace of Europe. The **Congress of Vienna**, as the peace conference became known, met from September 1814 to June 1815. With so many statesmen and monarchs gathered together, the glittering social life of the peace conference led one witty observer to remark, "The Congress doesn't advance, it dances." As they danced, however, the diplomats were settling the fate of Europe.

The participants. Overwhelmed with the responsibility of feeding and hosting the nobility of Europe, the Austrian emperor Francis I left Austria's diplomatic decisions largely to his foreign minister, Prince Klemens von Metternich. Metternich was the dominant figure of the Congress. Charming and politically gifted, he was so convinced of his own abilities that he once confessed, "I say to myself twenty times a day how right I am and how wrong the others are." Metternich opposed the ideals of the French Revolution. Under his influence, three principles emerged to guide the decisions of the Congress: (1) compensation for the victors; (2) restoration of the balance of power in order to ensure peace; and (3) **legitimacy**—by which Metternich meant restoring the governments that had ruled Europe before Napoleon and the French Revolution.

Other leaders at the Congress generally agreed with Metternich's goals, particularly Czar Alexander I of Russia. Alexander was the most active monarch at the conference—and the most unpredictable. King Frederick William III of Prussia, grateful for Russian help against Napoleon, tended to side with Alexander in the negotiations. Perhaps the most interesting—and surprising—major participant was Charles-Maurice de Talleyrand, the representative of defeated France. A remarkably skilled diplomat and courtier, Talleyrand had first served Louis XVI. Surviving the Revolution, he then worked for both the French republic and Napoleon. Now he served the restored Bourbon dynasty, and like other leaders he supported a return to the Old Regime. Of all the powers in Vienna, the one

Europe After the Congress of Vienna, 1815

Changing Borders   The statesmen at the Congress of Vienna redrew the boundaries of Europe to achieve a peaceful balance of power.

Linking Geography and History   What countries and states were included in the German Confederation?

least interested in turning the clock back was Great Britain, represented by its foreign secretary, Viscount Castlereagh (KAS-uhl-ray).

Restoring Europe. In May 1814 the victors had stripped France of its conquests and restored its 1792 boundaries. Now they added territory to nations bordering France. The Netherlands, for example, received the former Austrian territory of Belgium. Prussia gained territory along the Rhine River to prevent French expansion there. As a further safeguard, the German states were organized in a loose German Confederation. Switzerland once again became an independent

confederation and declared itself forever neutral in all future conflicts. Meanwhile, the monarchs of Portugal, Spain, Sardinia, and the kingdom of the Two Sicilies were restored to their thrones. The principle of legitimacy was not followed everywhere, however. In exchange for giving up Belgium to the Netherlands, for example, Austria received the Italian provinces of Lombardy, Venetia, Illyria, and the Tirol—and thus became the dominant power in Italy.

Compromise. Early in the proceedings a dispute over Polish territory threatened to disrupt both the balance of power and the harmony of the

538

Alexander I, during the first years of his reign, seemed to be influenced by liberal ideas. He made several efforts at reform—he cut back on the activities of the secret police, tried to reform the educational system, and lifted the ban on books and foreign travel. After he defeated the French, Alexander's foreign policy was at first liberal as well. At the Congress of Vienna, he insisted on mild treaty terms for France and gave autonomy to Finland and a constitution to Poland. However, at about the same time he became increasingly influenced by a sort of mystical Christianity. Over time, this led to an increasing conservatism. It was this religious fervor that led to the establishment of the Holy Alliance, as well as Alexander's support of suppressing all nationalist and liberal movements.

Critical Thinking Ask students to suggest how Alexander might have used religion to justify his political conservatism.

ANSWER: Students might answer that Alexander felt that, as a legitimate Christian prince, his power had divine approval.

▲ Prince Klemens von Metternich played an important role in creating a balance of power in Europe after Napoleon's defeat.

Congress. Czar Alexander demanded the Grand Duchy of Warsaw (later called Congress Poland), which Napoleon had taken from Prussia. Prussia agreed to support Russia's claim in exchange for the German state of Saxony. Fearing both Russian expansion into central Europe as well as a more powerful Prussia, Castlereagh and Metternich opposed the plan. "I will go to war rather than surrender what is mine!" thundered Alexander. Conflict was avoided only when Talleyrand arranged a compromise. Russia received part of Poland. The rest of Poland, as well as part of Saxony, went to Prussia. To obtain British and Austrian agreement, Talleyrand proposed a secret alliance among Britain, Austria, and France. If Russia or Prussia acted aggressively, the three allies would oppose them together.

The Congress of Vienna restored monarchs to the thrones of Europe and reshuffled territory to achieve a balance of power.

The Concert of Europe

The Congress of Vienna was a success. No major power—not even defeated France—left the conference with serious grievances. In part the success was due to the arrangements the great powers established to enforce the terms of the Congress of Vienna on a continuing basis.

In September 1815, for example, Czar Alexander invited the rulers of Austria and Prussia to a grassy plateau in France. There, he held an impressive ceremony. Brilliant flags fluttered in the wind as tens of thousands of Russian troops surrounded eight altars. With this display of the symbols of his military might and religious faith, Alexander called on his fellow monarchs to join him in the **Holy Alliance**. Alexander urged all European rulers to sign the Holy Alliance, pledging to rule as Christian princes. Those who signed agreed as "fathers of families . . . to protect Religion, Peace and Justice."

Most European states—with the exception of Great Britain, the Papal States, and the Ottoman Empire—joined the Holy Alliance. Alexander hoped to use the alliance as a means of keeping international peace. The alliance would also commit European rulers to help one another put down internal rebellion and revolution. A few months later, the four major powers that had fought against France—Austria, Britain, Russia, and Prussia, known as the **Quadruple Alliance**—also agreed to meet regularly to maintain peace and discuss common interests.

The main goals of this system of diplomatic cooperation, which became known as the **Concert of Europe**, were laid down by its primary architect, Prince Metternich:

❝Liberty for every Government to watch over the well-being of its own people; a league between all Governments against factions in all States; . . . respect for the progressive development of institutions in lawful ways . . . such are happily the ideas of the great monarchs: the world will be saved if they bring them into action—it is lost if they do not.❞

Metternich's vision of "progressive development" did not mean granting the demands of liberals for greater participation in their own government, but rather a return to enlightened despotism. Not everyone, even among the great powers, accepted this vision.

The Concert of Europe hoped to combat the spread of revolutionary ideas and maintain peace through European cooperation.

The Outbreak of Revolution

As Metternich and the other continental rulers tried to turn the clock back to the days before the French Revolution, liberals began to react. They had been inspired by the ideals of the Revolution and the Declaration of the Rights of Man. In 1819, for example, German university students demanded liberal reforms and the unification of all the German states. Student Heinrich von Gagern explained:

66 We want Germany to be considered one land and the German people one people. . . . We want a constitution for the people that fits in with the spirit of the times and with the people's own level of enlightenment, rather than what each prince gives his people. 99

Similar movements swept across other parts of Europe as well. A revolt in Spain, which broke out in early 1820, forced King Ferdinand VII to restore the liberal constitution he had abolished. In July rebels in Naples forced King Ferdinand to grant a constitution, while in August a liberal revolt erupted in Portugal.

The Troppau Protocol. Metternich saw these revolts as a European emergency. In his own country Metternich clamped down on the universities, accusing them of creating "a whole generation of revolutionaries." He also called together leaders of the German Confederation at Carlsbad to adopt the **Carlsbad Decrees**, which prohibited any political reforms that conflicted with absolute monarchy. The decrees established censorship of newspapers and formed a secret police force that spied on students in an effort to detect any revolutionary activity. Metternich and leaders of the other major continental European powers convened the Congress of Troppau in 1820 to address the problem of revolution.

Although Britain remained absent in protest, the Congress of Troppau adopted the "Troppau Protocol," which promised military intervention to support governments against internal revolution. Despite British objections, Austria, Prussia, and Russia agreed to an Austrian army being sent to stop the revolt in Naples. In 1823 a French army entered Spain, crushing the revolt there. Outraged, Great Britain withdrew from the Concert of Europe.

Greek independence. The first real failure of Metternich's system occurred in Greece in 1821. Inspired by the ideals of the French Revolution and liberalism, the Greeks revolted against the rule of the Ottoman sultan. The Holy Alliance refused Greek pleas for aid, declaring that the Turkish sultan was a legitimate ruler. However, many Europeans enthusiastically supported the Greeks. Eventually, Britain, France, and even Russia intervened militarily, and by 1830 Greece had become an independent state.

Revolutions of 1830–33. Greek independence sparked yet another series of revolutions in Europe. In 1830 revolution broke out once again in Paris, where liberals overthrew the reactionary Bourbon monarch, King Charles X, and replaced him with the more moderate Louis Philippe, duke of Orléans. From Paris, revolution soon spread to the rest of Europe. In Brussels, for example, revolutionaries demanded independence from the Dutch in December 1830. After brief fighting, and considerable diplomacy, the European powers recognized Belgium's independence.

In Germany the Paris revolt caused great excitement among many intellectuals and students, but brought few changes. In southern Europe, both Spain and Portugal once again emerged as constitutional monarchies—at least in name. Liberal and

▲ The British poet Lord Byron supported Greek independence. He went to Greece in 1824 to fight the Ottomans.

SECTION 1
REVIEW ANSWERS

IDENTIFY
For significance, see the following pages:
Congress of Vienna
  (p. 536)
Klemens von Metternich
  (p. 536)
legitimacy (p. 536)
Charles-Maurice de
  Talleyrand (p. 536)
Holy Alliance (p. 538)
Quadruple Alliance
  (p. 538)
Concert of Europe
  (p. 538)
Carlsbad Decrees (p. 539)

LOCATE
For locations, see the map on p. 537.

1. It restored France's former boundaries, redivided territories among different nations, and restored former monarchs.
2. It formed an alliance between cooperating nations to maintain international as well as domestic peace.
3. While most of the revolutions ultimately failed, they threatened the unity of many European countries and reflected the strength of liberalism and nationalism in Europe.
4. Letters should explain that students are inspired by the French Revolution and think they should have a constitution. They do not want to return to the days of monarchy.
5. They attempted to restore peace by: (a) creating a balance of power and restoring old monarchies; (b) joining together to maintain peace; (c) forming a union of Christian states; and (d) using force and the threat of punishment.

nationalist revolutionaries in Italy, who had already organized in secret societies, also rose in rebellion. They were once again put down by Austrian troops, however. Perhaps the bloodiest uprising took place in Poland, where Polish nationalists and liberals had also organized secret societies to fight Russian domination. Divided between radicals and moderates, the Poles proved no match for the brutal measures imposed by Russia.

Revolutions of 1848. The revolutions of the 1830s demonstrated the growing differences between eastern and western Europe. In France, for example, the revolutions succeeded to some extent. This occurred largely because of the growing power of the middle class, which was brought on by increasing industrialization. Eastern Europe, on the other hand, remained relatively unindustrialized. There, conservative monarchies were able to put down the relatively small uprisings among liberal urban intellectuals and students.

In 1848, however, revolution once again broke out across Europe. In central and eastern Europe, nationalism was the primary cause of continuing unrest. In western Europe, continuing industrialization had led to more calls for political participation from the middle class and from workers. The growth of industrial economies had also led to periodic economic downturns, which primarily hurt industrial workers and their families. Socialists joined liberals in calling for change.

Once again, the spark for revolution came first in France. "When France sneezes, all Europe catches cold," Metternich remarked in exasperation. Rising prices and increasing unemployment fueled further liberal demands as well as the growth of socialism. Radical reformers called for the overthrow of the monarchy and the establishment of a new republic. When King Louis Philippe called out the army to keep order, violence soon followed. As Louis Philippe abdicated and France established a republic, the revolution spread to the rest of Europe. Prince Metternich himself was forced to resign when angry liberals demanded change in Austria's autocratic government.

Like the revolutions of 1830, those of 1848 also failed in the end. Liberals had little sympathy for socialist demands and often preferred to support the conservatives rather than accept more radical change. At the same time, however, conservative governments also increasingly preferred to meet some liberal demands rather than risk the more violent upheavals promised by socialist revolutionaries. Consequently, despite the failure of the 1848 revolutions, the spirit of liberal reform continued to make headway in most of Europe.

Revolutions in many countries threatened European unity and showed that nationalism and liberalism could not be destroyed.

SECTION 1 REVIEW

IDENTIFY and explain the significance of the following:
  Congress of Vienna
  Klemens von Metternich
  legitimacy
  Charles-Maurice de
    Talleyrand
  Holy Alliance
  Quadruple Alliance
  Concert of Europe
  Carlsbad Decrees

LOCATE and explain the importance of the following:
  Vienna

Congress Poland
Saxony

1. **Main Idea** What were the main accomplishments of the Congress of Vienna?
2. **Main Idea** How did the Concert of Europe attempt to keep peace in Europe?
3. **Politics and Law** What were the consequences of the revolutions of 1830 and 1848?
4. **Writing to Persuade** Imagine that you are a German student. Write a

letter to Metternich to persuade him to lift the Carlsbad Decrees. Also explain why people across Europe are turning to revolution.
5. **Synthesizing** How did Europeans attempt to restore peace and stability after the defeat of Napoleon? In answering this question, consider the role of (a) the Congress of Vienna; (b) the Concert of Europe; (c) the Holy Alliance; and (d) the Carlsbad Decrees.

Unification in Italy and Germany

*J*ust 15 years after the Congress of Vienna, a tired Metternich despaired that "the old Europe is nearing its end." Despite his efforts to stifle change, the old order had been destroyed beyond repair. Europeans of all classes were growing more nationalistic. Liberalism, which emphasized individual rights, was becoming too strong to ignore or put down. Many Europeans—particularly Italians and Germans—began to see the nation-state as the best way to guarantee individual liberties and national prosperity.

Giacomo Leopardi, an Italian nationalist poet

The Growth of Italian Nationalism

Since the fall of the Roman Empire, the Italian Peninsula had been divided into a number of competing states, each with its own government, dialect, economy, and customs. Napoleon and his invading army had united many of the Italian states into the kingdom of Italy. The Congress of Vienna, however, left Italy divided once again. After Austria took over Lombardy and Venetia, Italian nationalism grew in opposition to Austrian rule.

Early nationalist movements. Many Italian thinkers and writers revived interest in their rich cultural traditions. For example, scholars revived Dante's classic *Divine Comedy,* the first book to be written in the Italian vernacular, or common language. In his poem "To Italy," Giacomo Leopardi compared "the columns and altars, the statues/And towers our ancestors built" to Italy's present "wounded and bruised,/And bleeding" state. Leopardi and other writers called for Italians to join together and liberate Italy from foreign rule. This nationalistic movement became known as the **risorgimento**, or "resurgence." Many nationalists formed secret societies to promote their cause. The *Carbonari*, or "charcoal-burners," for example, plotted to overthrow the Austrians.

The **Young Italy movement,** launched in 1831 by the popular writer Giuseppe Mazzini, was more significant. Though exiled for his outspoken nationalism, Mazzini smuggled his patriotic pamphlets into Italy. Mazzini's Young Italy became such a threat to existing governments that the Austrians declared that the members of the movement could be sentenced to death if caught.

Revolution in Italy. Many Italian states opposed unification because they did not want to give up their power to one central government. As liberal revolution spread throughout Europe in 1848, however, Italian nationalists led rebellions of their own. After Austrian troops withdrew from Lombardy to put down a revolt in Vienna, rioting began in the Lombard city of Milan.

Other rebellions forced the rulers of Sardinia, the kingdom of the Two Sicilies, and Tuscany to grant constitutions. Revolutionaries seized Rome in 1849 and set up a republic that Mazzini and two other leaders governed. All but one of these revolutionary movements soon failed. Austrian troops recaptured Lombardy, and French troops helped the pope gain control of Rome again. The revolt succeeded only in Sardinia, which remained independent.

Anger over foreign domination led Italian nationalists to call for unity and independence.

Italian Unification

Despite the failure of the revolts of 1848 and 1849, Italian patriots continued to work for a unified nation. They could not, however, agree on how to achieve unity. Many Italians wanted a federation of states headed by the pope. Most liberals wanted a republic. Others wanted a constitutional monarchy under King Victor Emmanuel II of Sardinia.

Cavour and Sardinia. One of the main architects of Italian unification was Count Camillo Benso di Cavour (kahv-OOHR), the prime minister of Sardinia. Though initially not a supporter of unification, Cavour resented the Austrian occupation of Italy. He dreamed of a Sardinia strong enough to drive out the Austrians.

Cavour firmly believed that "the political resurrection of a nation can never be separated from its economic resurrection." Thus, he worked to improve the economy by funding railroad construction, encouraging industrialization, and negotiating free-trade agreements. Cavour also reorganized and strengthened the Sardinian army. By 1859 he had won a powerful ally, France, which agreed to aid Sardinia in its planned war against Austria. In return, Sardinia transferred control of the provinces of Savoy and Nice to France in 1860.

Garibaldi and the Red Shirts. Italians consider Cavour the "brain" of Italian unification and Mazzini its "heart." Equally important, however, was Giuseppe Garibaldi, who has been dubbed the "sword" of Italy. Garibaldi had joined Mazzini's Young Italy movement in 1833, but because of his nationalist activities, he was twice forced to flee from Italy.

In 1859, five years after Garibaldi's return to Italy, Cavour asked him to lead part of the Sardinian army in the war with Austria. Realizing that only Sardinia could lead the other Italian states to unity, Garibaldi accepted. After a few months of bitter fighting, the Austrians agreed to give up Lombardy, while keeping Venetia.

Garibaldi and his followers, known as the Red Shirts because of their colorful uniforms, next aided rebels fighting against Bourbon rule in the kingdom of the Two Sicilies. Instructing the Sicilians to "harass the enemy in any way possible," Garibaldi waged guerrilla warfare against the Bourbon troops. By July 1860 the Red Shirts controlled the island of Sicily. They then crossed to the Italian mainland. Meanwhile, Cavour had annexed the small kingdoms of central Italy. In September Sardinian troops marched south and helped Garibaldi conquer Naples. A correspondent described Garibaldi's growing popularity:

Unification of Italy, 1858–1870

Kingdom of Sardinia, 1858

Austrian territory annexed by Sardinia, 1859

Territory annexed by Sardinia to form Kingdom of Italy, 1860

Austrian territory annexed by Italy, 1866

Territory annexed by Italy, 1870

FRANCE
Vienna
SWITZERLAND
AUSTRIA-HUNGARY
Danube River
SAVOY (to France in 1860)
LOMBARDY
Milan
VENETIA
Venice
Turin
Po R.
PARMA
MODENA
NICE (to France in 1860)
Genoa
MONACO
SAN MARINO
OTTOMAN EMPIRE
Florence
TUSCANY
PAPAL STATES
Tiber R.
KINGDOM
CORSICA (French)
OF
Rome
PAPAL STATES
ADRIATIC SEA
KINGDOM OF SARDINIA
ITALY
Naples
KINGDOM OF THE TWO SICILIES
40°N
SARDINIA
TYRRHENIAN SEA
MEDITERRANEAN SEA
10°E
0   100   200 Miles
0   100   200 Kilometers
Azimuthal Equal-Area Projection
SICILY
15°E

Uniting the Kingdoms The people of Sardinia played a major role in uniting Italy.

❓ **Region** What territory did Italy annex in 1866?

▲ Giuseppe Garibaldi was known as one of the most skillful guerrilla warfare generals of all time.

❝Soon after my arrival Garibaldi made his appearance, and received his foreign visitors with that charming, quiet simplicity which characterizes him, lending himself with great complaisance [satisfaction] to the invariably recurring demands of autographs.❞

The kingdom of Italy. With the Red Shirts in control of the entire kingdom of the Two Sicilies, Garibaldi offered the territory to King Victor Emmanuel II of Sardinia. The newly united territories throughout Italy held elections in 1861, and all agreed to unification. "Our country is . . . no longer the field for every foreign ambition," rejoiced Victor Emmanuel. "It becomes, henceforth, the Italy of the Italians."

The only holdouts were Venetia, which still belonged to Austria, and the Papal States, where French troops supported the pope. When war broke out between Austria and Prussia in 1866, the Italians sided with the Prussians. Austria was defeated, and Prussia rewarded its Italian ally with Venetia. In 1870 war between France and Prussia forced the French to withdraw their troops from Rome. In September 1870 Italian troops entered Rome, thus completing the unification of Italy under King Victor Emmanuel.

As Sardinia expanded from the north and Garibaldi's Red Shirts gained ground from Sicily, Italy became united.

Calls for German Unity

Like Italy before unification, Germany in the early 1800s was a patchwork of independent states. Unlike Italy, however, Germany's nationalist spirit predated the Congress of Vienna. Napoleon had unintentionally nurtured nationalism when he united the German states into the Confederation of the Rhine. After his defeat, the Congress of Vienna retained Napoleon's confederation but renamed it the German Confederation. In addition, the Congress of Vienna gave Prussia new territory that would soon make it a dominant power in the confederation.

The *Zollverein*. The first major step toward German unity after the Congress of Vienna involved the economy. The tariffs that each state collected made movement of goods from one German state to another extremely difficult. The **Junkers** (YOOHNG-kuhrz)—the aristocratic landowners of Prussia—complained that the tariffs increased the prices of their farm goods so much that they hurt sales.

In 1818 the Junkers persuaded the king of Prussia to abolish all tariffs within his territories. Soon Prussia and other German states eliminated tariffs by setting up the **Zollverein** (TSOHL-fer-yn), or customs union. The *Zollverein* inspired businesspeople to support German unification. Friedrich von Motz, the Prussian finance minister, predicted in 1829 that "the unification of these states in a customs or commercial union will lead to one and the same political system." By 1844 the *Zollverein* included almost all of the German states.

German liberalism. Some of the strongest calls for political unification came from liberals. Though liberals differed over whether to support a republic or a constitutional monarchy, they agreed that German unity would promote individual rights and liberal reforms.

In 1848, as revolution swept through Europe, German liberals also seized the opportunity to revolt. When the people of Berlin learned that Metternich had been ousted in Vienna, they encircled the royal palace to hear the Prussian king's response. The crowd erupted when edgy soldiers fired shots. Berliners set up barricades, forcing the retreat of the royal soldiers. King Frederick William gave in to nationalist demands

Unification of Germany, 1865–1871

The German Empire Through wars and diplomacy, Bismarck created the strong German Empire out of Prussia and the smaller German states.

? Movement Into what area did Prussia extend its territory in 1866?

and proclaimed, "From now on Prussia merges with Germany!" However, the king quickly reasserted his power. German unification would be accomplished not by revolution, but by the policies of a king and his powerful chancellor.

BIOGRAPHY **Bismarck and Prussia.** The revolutions of the mid-1800s gave Otto von Bismarck, a Junker and a politician, his first taste of power. Born in 1815, Bismarck was catapulted into Prussian national politics when he gave a strongly conservative speech at the National Assembly in 1847. Bismarck soon became the leader of the conservative politicians who supported the king and opposed the liberal revolution of 1848.

In 1862 William I, the new Prussian king, appointed Bismarck as head of the Prussian cabinet. Bismarck believed it was Prussia's destiny to lead the German people to unification. Practicing what would later be called *Realpolitik* (ray-AHL-poh-li-teek), or "realistic politics,"

Bismarck pursued policies based on Prussian interests rather than on liberal ideals. As a man of action, Bismarck argued for the tremendous buildup of the Prussian military:

❝*Prussia must build up and preserve her strength for the favorable moment which has already come and gone many times. Her borders under the treaties of Vienna are not favorable for the healthy existence of the state. The great questions of the day will not be settled by speeches and majority decisions—that was the great mistake of 1848 and 1849— but by blood and iron.*❞

Otto von Bismarck
BIOGRAPHY

The Prussian Parliament refused to approve the money for military expansion, so Bismarck simply dismissed the assembly and collected the taxes anyway. Bismarck and his generals proceeded to build the Prussian army into a great war machine that would soon use "blood and iron" to forcibly unite the German states under Prussia.

The growth of liberalism, nationalism, and Prussian power led to calls for German unity.

The Unification of Germany

To increase the power and size of Prussia, Bismarck had to overcome two major obstacles. First, he had to drive Austria out of its leadership position within the German Confederation. Second, he had to overcome Austria's influence over the southern German states, which remained opposed to Prussian leadership. Bismarck accomplished these objectives in two wars: the Seven Weeks' War and the Franco-Prussian War.

Bismarck first maneuvered to drive Austria from the German Confederation. He persuaded France to remain neutral if war broke out between the German powers. Then he formed an alliance with Italy. Next, he provoked Austria into declaring war on Prussia in 1866. The superbly trained and well-equipped Prussian army defeated the Austrians in only seven weeks. The treaty ending the Seven Weeks' War dissolved the German Confederation and forced Austria to surrender the northern German state of Holstein. When several other northern states united with Prussia the next year, only three southern states remained outside Prussian control.

Bismarck decided that he could annex the southern states by provoking war with his recent ally France. When France declared war on Prussia in 1870, Bismarck persuaded the southern German states to join Prussia against the French. With the southern states' help, Bismarck secured a Prussian victory in the Franco-Prussian War. In the peace settlement, France lost Alsace and part of Lorraine and had to pay a huge indemnity, or settlement for damages. Through "blood and iron," as he put it, Bismarck had united the German states. On January 18, 1871, representatives of the allied German states met at Versailles, near Paris. With the swords of the army officers glinting off the mirrored walls, they proclaimed King William I of Prussia **kaiser**, or emperor, of the German Empire. William named Bismarck as his chancellor.

Through war and diplomacy, Bismarck united the German states into an empire under the king of Prussia.

SECTION 2 REVIEW

IDENTIFY and explain the significance of the following:
risorgimento
Carbonari
Young Italy movement
Count Camillo Benso di Cavour
Giuseppe Garibaldi
Junkers
Zollverein
Otto von Bismarck
Realpolitik
kaiser

LOCATE and explain the importance of the following:
Lombardy
Venetia

Sardinia
Papal States
Holstein
Alsace and Lorraine

1. **Main Idea** What events helped unify Italy?
2. **Main Idea** Why did many Germans call for the unification of the German states?
3. **War and Diplomacy** How did Prussia bring about German unification?

4. **Writing to Create** Imagine that you are a member of the Young Italy movement. Prepare a poster with a short paragraph describing your goals for Italy.
5. **Comparing** Create a chart like the one below. Compare the unification of the Italian Peninsula with the unification of Germany. In what other ways was the unification of the two countries similar?

	ITALY	GERMANY
Causes of Nationalism		
Nationalist Movements	*Young Italy*	
Important Figures		*Otto von Bismarck*
Date of Unification		

Theme: **Politics and Law**

Crown Prince Rudolf was a liberal who encouraged industrial and technological modernization for Austria-Hungary. In 1883, describing the International Electric Fair in Vienna, he wrote: "Here is the difference between the old fantastic fairytale and its realization in the 19th century. . . . The fairytale is an aristocratic dream. Its realization through research and invention is democratic reality." In 1889, frustrated by the conservative forces that still bound the empire, Rudolf committed suicide.

Critical Thinking Ask students how Austria-Hungary might have changed if Rudolf had become emperor.

ANSWER: Students may answer that Rudolf would have encouraged modernization and liberalization.

SECTION 3
Aging Empires in Eastern Europe

FOCUS

- How did Austria respond to demands for political change?
- What effect did liberal reforms have in the Russian Empire?
- How did the Ottoman Empire try to reverse its decline?
- Why did so many international conflicts occur in the Balkans?

While nationalism triumphed in Italy and Germany, in the east the aging Austrian, Russian, and Ottoman empires remained authoritarian. Even in these aging empires, however, demands for liberal reforms and independence were heard. Forced to control revolutionary fires, imperial rulers enacted harsh measures and initiated limited reforms aimed at modernizing and strengthening their rule. Meanwhile, international rivalries caused some European powers to support the survival of the Ottoman Empire while others sought to destroy it.

Ornamental goblets created in the style of the Wiener Werkstätten

---

The Empire of Austria-Hungary

Although ultimately unsuccessful, the revolutions that swept Europe in 1848 had a profound impact on the aging empires of central and eastern Europe, particularly on the Austrian Habsburg empire. One observer described the situation in Vienna in 1848:

> **"***A troubled, sinister mood prevails here in all circles. The Paris revolution has illuminated the obscurity of our position like a thunderbolt. The suburbs are said to be in a very irritated state. . . . Discontent is general, and I only fear it is not recognized by the authorities as it ought to be.***"**

Soon demonstrators clashed with imperial soldiers and forced Prince Metternich to resign. Emperor Ferdinand abdicated, and the throne went to his young nephew, Francis Joseph I.

Restoring order. During his long reign, Francis Joseph presided over an unstable empire. In 1848 the Hungarian Magyars rebelled against Austrian rule, and for a time it looked as though they would win their independence. However, Czar Nicholas I sent Russian troops to help Austria crush the revolt. Francis Joseph then abolished the liberal reforms enacted in 1848, but he could not stamp out nationalism in his multiethnic empire.

In 1859 Austria lost the province of Lombardy to Italy. Seven years later, in 1866, defeat in the Seven Weeks' War with Prussia provided an opening for the Hungarians to renew their demands. This time, instead of fighting the Hungarians, the Austrian emperor agreed to grant Hungary a constitution and share power in what became known as the **Dual Monarchy** of Austria-Hungary.

Vienna's cultural life. Although the Austro-Hungarian Empire declined politically, its cultural life reached lofty heights. Cosmopolitan Vienna ruled as the empire's cultural center. Artists, musicians, architects, scientists, philosophers, and writers contributed to Vienna's cultural and scientific flowering. With its many ethnic groups, Vienna offered a wealth of musical styles. Elegant, carefree Viennese waltzes by Johann Strauss became popular throughout Europe. Wealthy, aristocratic, and middle-class patrons supported the Vienna Opera, conducted by composer Gustav Mahler.

Architects transformed Vienna by laying out a grand boulevard and constructing monumental buildings in many different historical styles. Some Austrian architects, including Adolph Loos, rebelled against the old styles and designed modern, functional public buildings, train stations, and houses for the prosperous middle class. Interior designers in the Wiener Werkstätten, or "Vienna Workshops," reacted against mass-produced items and designed beautiful jewelry and finely crafted and functional furniture. In art, painter Gustav Klimt led a group of artists who adopted modern styles and themes.

Conservative Austria strengthened its monarchy to combat liberalism and nationalism.

The Russian Empire

As did the Austrian Habsburgs, the Romanov dynasty in Russia also struggled with liberal demands. By 1800 the Russian Empire was the largest and most diverse empire in Europe. Since the late 1500s Ivan the Terrible and his successors had expanded their territories west into the Baltic and south into the Caucasus Mountains. In these

Theme:
The Arts
Gustav Klimt was Vienna's foremost leader of the artistic movement called Art Nouveau, which emerged in western Europe at the end of the 1800s. Art Nouveau was richly ornamental, asymmetrical, and characterized by twining plant forms, which were adapted in architecture, painting, sculpture, and the decorative arts.

Critical Thinking Ask students why plant forms might have been such a popular motif in Vienna.

ANSWER: Students might suggest that Vienna's cultural life was flourishing, and that plants represented that growth.

Ethnic Groups in Austria-Hungary, 1867

Slavs:	Others:
Croats and Serbs	Germans
Czechs and Slovaks	Magyars
Poles	Romanians
Slovenes	Italians
Ukrainians	

MULTIMEDIA PRESENTATION STRATEGY

VISUAL RESOURCES
Geography and History 20
Ethnic Groups in Austria-Hungary, 1867

Show the transparency and share the information from Geography and History Fact Sheet 20. Then have students complete the accompanying worksheet.

Level 2

Multicultural Empire The rich mosaic of ethnic groups made Austria-Hungary a multicultural empire. But tensions between groups would one day splinter the empire.

Linking Geography and History What non-Slavic peoples lived in Austria-Hungary?

Theme: Politics and Law

When the news of Czar Alexander's death reached his family, Nicholas, Alexander's brother, declared loyalty to his other brother, Konstantin, as the new emperor. Then Alexander's mother told Nicholas that Alexander had named *him* heir apparent. But Nicholas could legally become emperor only if his brother renounced the throne. Konstantin would not formally abdicate. Nicholas eventually took the throne without formal abdication, when the threat of revolt was spreading.

Critical Thinking Ask students why the lack of an emperor might have led Russians to revolt.

ANSWER: Students might answer that Russians could seize more power and rights for themselves during the chaos.

The Russian Empire by 1900

A Continental Power Russia's imperial army marched across a continent to conquer lands to the east. But it was diplomacy that won the empire warm-water ports in Asia.

? Movement What important link connected central Russia to its new Siberian and Pacific territories?

vast lands lived a great number of ethnic groups, including Poles, Ukrainians, Finns, Jews, and Estonians. The empire had also expanded east—across the Ural Mountains and eventually all the way to Asia's Pacific Coast. Thus, the czars also came to rule the varied peoples of Central Asia and Siberia—Uzbeks, Chechens, Tadzhiks, and others.

Repression under Nicholas I. The Russian czar ruled over the empire as a supreme autocrat. As with other parts of Europe, however, Russia also experienced the influence of revolutionary ideas during the Napoleonic era. Army officers who served outside of Russia while fighting the French were particularly influenced by liberal ideals. When Czar Alexander I died in 1825, some of these officers seized their opportunity. On a chilly December day, thousands of soldiers gathered near the Czar's Winter Palace in St. Petersburg and demanded an end to autocracy.

With the sound of echoing gunshots, the new czar—Alexander's 29-year-old brother, Nicholas I—appeared on horseback in the crowded square. Loyal officers advised Nicholas to crush the revolt. "You want me to shed the blood of my subjects on the first day of my reign?" asked Nicholas. But he followed their advice and ordered soldiers to crush the rebellion. Nicholas enacted harsh measures to avoid another revolt. He imposed strict censorship and organized a secret police force to spy on suspected revolutionary groups.

Nicholas continued the expansion of the empire. In the south he tried to gain territory at the expense of the Ottomans. In the east he encouraged settlement beyond the Ural Mountains and sent Russian military forces into Central Asia. The troops forcefully incorporated many Central Asian territories into the empire. In the 1830s Nicholas began a program of **Russification** designed to force

Literature THROUGH TIME

Dead Souls

By the middle of the 1800s, things had changed little for Russian peasants since the Middle Ages. Until 1861 peasants, also known as souls, were considered the property of landowners. In his 1842 novel Dead Souls, *Nikolai Gogol criticized the practice of buying and selling peasants. Chichikov, the main character in the novel, comes up with a scheme to buy dead peasants still listed on town records as living. He is then able to use these peasants as collateral for loans. Chichikov first introduces the idea to a wealthy landowner named Manilov:*

"But allow me first to ask one question," he [Chichikov] said in a voice containing a strange, or rather strange, note. And immediately hereafter, for some unknown reason, he looked over his shoulder. Manilov also for some unknown reason did the same. "How long ago did you submit a census return for your serfs?"

"Quite a while ago. To tell you the truth, I don't remember when."

"Have many of your peasants died since then?"

"I don't know that either. We should ask the steward about this, I suppose. . . ."

"I say, my good man, how many of our peasants have died since the census was taken?"

"Why, how d'you mean, how many? Many have died since," said the steward, hiccuping and shielding his mouth with his cupped hand. . . .

"And what number, for instance?" asked Chichikov.

"Yes, what number?" Manilov chimed in.

"Why, how can I say what number? No one knows how many died, nobody counted them."

"Yes, exactly," said Manilov, turning to Chichikov. "I also supposed that the mortality [death rate] was great; there is absolutely no knowing how many have died."

"Will you kindly count them over," Chichikov said to the steward, "and make a list of their names." . . .

"And for what purpose do you need this?" asked Manilov when the steward had departed. . . .

"You ask me for what purpose? For the purpose of buying the peasants—" Here Chichikov stammered and did not finish the sentence.

"But allow me to ask you," said Manilov, "do you wish to buy peasants with land or for resettlement somewhere—without land, that is?"

"No, it's not that I mean peasants actually," said Chichikov. "I would like to have the dead ones. . . ."

Understanding Literature

How is the scheme of buying dead peasants a criticism of Russian society?

Chichikov discusses dead peasants with Manilov.

Understanding Literature

It reflects the fact that peasants were considered property, rather than human beings, and that people would still try to profit from them, even after their deaths.

R RESOURCE ACTIVITY

GLOBAL HISTORY RESOURCE CENTER

Image: *Emancipation of a Russian Serf*

Print out and distribute the image and the caption. Ask students to study both. Then ask students to create a cause and effect chart describing the emancipation of the Russian serfs and their living conditions after freedom.

Sheltered English

the empire's diverse subjects to use the Russian language, accept the Orthodox religion, and adopt Russian customs.

Reforms of Alexander II. After Nicholas's death in 1855, his son, Alexander II, came to the throne. Many people considered the new czar weak, but Alexander surprised his critics. In 1861 he issued the Emancipation Edict freeing the serfs. "It is better to abolish serfdom from above," he argued, "than to wait until the serfs begin to liberate themselves from below." In 1864 Alexander also reorganized local government. He allowed rural districts to elect *zemstvos*, local councils to oversee matters such as education, public health, and relief for the poor.

Instead of easing social tensions in Russia, however, emancipation fueled them in certain ways. For example, the government provided land to village communes, which distributed it to peasants according to their needs. However, the peasants had to pay for the land, often at inflated prices, and there was not nearly enough land to go around. One British observer remarked:

> 66 The Emancipation Law did not confer on [give] the peasants as much land as they require, and consequently the peasant who has merely his legal portion has neither enough of work nor enough of revenue. 99

Radicals and government reaction. Despite these reforms, the late 1860s witnessed a surge of radical movements against the czar. Many intellectuals of the middle and upper classes became **nihilists**—they believed that traditional social and economic institutions had to be destroyed in order to build a new Russia. Other revolutionaries, called Populists, wanted to rebuild society along the lines of communal peasant villages. Both nihilists and Populists sometimes resorted to terrorism, and in 1881 a Populist assassinated Alexander II.

▲ On March 1, 1881, a bomb planted in Alexander II's coach exploded and fatally wounded the czar.

Alexander's assassination convinced his son and successor, Alexander III, that reforms of any kind were a mistake. Both Alexander III and his own successor, Nicholas II, intensified Russification, strengthened the secret police, and persecuted non-Russians in the empire. Political opponents were often executed or exiled to Siberia. Alexander and Nicholas also persecuted Jews with **pogroms** (POH-gruhmz), officially organized massacres designed to frighten all Jews out of Russia.

The Revolution of 1905. By the early 1900s Russia was in turmoil. Peasant uprisings erupted in rural areas, and students demonstrated in the cities. In 1905 Japan defeated Russia in a war over territory in East Asia. The outcome of the Russo-Japanese War convinced many people that the government was much too corrupt, inefficient, and irresponsible. In January 1905 a huge group of unarmed workers converged upon St. Petersburg's Winter Palace to present the czar with a petition for reforms. Imperial troops fired on the crowd, killing at least 70 people. This massacre, called Bloody Sunday, triggered the Revolution of 1905. Throughout the summer there were strikes, peasant uprisings, and military revolts.

To stem the revolutionary tide, Czar Nicholas issued the **October Manifesto**, creating a constitutional monarchy. Within two years, however, Nicholas began to chip away at the rights he had granted. Discontent in Russia continued to grow.

Although the czars attempted some liberal reforms, the Russian Empire remained essentially autocratic.

The Ottoman Empire

Like the empires of Austria-Hungary and Russia, the Ottoman Empire ruled over a vast, multi-ethnic territory. Macedonians, Greeks, Bulgarians, and Romanians populated the Ottomans' European territory, while Turks, Armenians, Kurds, Syrians, Arabs, Jews, and Egyptians filled the rest of the empire. In decline since the late 1600s, the empire could barely control the fires of nationalism fanned by events in Europe.

In addition, the rising power of Western civilization, with its increasingly powerful technology, created a crisis for many Muslims.

Mahmud II's reforms. Many Ottoman leaders came to believe that only modernizing reforms along Western lines could save the empire. Until the early 1800s conservative groups in Ottoman society, such as the *ulama* (religious scholars) and the corrupt Janissary Corps, managed to prevent such modern reforms. In 1808, however, Sultan Mahmud II ascended the throne, determined to modernize the empire. He began with the army, raising new forces organized and trained along European lines. When the Janissary Corps opposed his reforms in 1826, Mahmud's new forces destroyed the corps, killing some 4,000 of its members.

Mahmud also modernized the empire's outdated government. He divided government administration into specialized ministries and departments filled with trained bureaucrats. To control the *ulama*, Mahmud took away their power to collect their own revenues. He started a government newspaper to publicize his reforms and to inform his subjects about events in other parts of the world.

The era of Tanzimat. Mahmud's reforms continued under his son, Abdülmecid (ahb-dool-mej-EED) I, who ascended the throne in 1839. "We deem it right," the new sultan's foreign minister, Mustafa Resid, announced, "to seek by new institutions to give to the Provinces composing the Ottoman Empire the benefit of a good Administration." Abdülmecid's reforms included equal legal status for Muslims and non-Muslims, a more efficient tax system, and a fair system of military service. This long era of reforms became known as the **Tanzimat**.

Along with political reforms came growing industrialization. Steamships, telegraphs, and railroads—including the first leg of the famed Orient Express—improved communications and transportation. Western influence also brought new interest in education and professional training. Attendance at secular public schools increased for both boys and girls, and new teacher-training schools were built.

▲ **Sultan Mahmud II introduced many Western reforms into Ottoman society.**

A changing sense of identity. Growing European influence and the sultans' modernizing reforms worried many Muslims in the empire. Some Muslims continued to call for a return to the simpler days of the Prophet, while others pursued a compromise path. Philosophers and teachers—such as Jamal ad-Din al-Afghani and his pupil Muhammad 'Abduh—called for reforming Islam along more modern lines. Others, who were influenced by European nationalism, called for modernization on an ethnic or cultural basis. In Syria and Lebanon, for example, many Christian Arab intellectuals began to support **Pan-Arabism**—the unity of all peoples sharing a common Arab cultural heritage.

Reform, reaction, and revolution. Perhaps the most influential of these liberal reformers was the grand vizir Midhat Pasha. In 1876 Midhat Pasha persuaded Sultan Abdülhamid II to enact a constitution. Based on the Prussian and Belgian constitutions, the Ottoman constitution created a parliament, guaranteed civil rights for all religious groups, and assured freedom of the press. However, Abdülhamid had accepted the constitution only to prevent the European powers from intervening directly in the empire's affairs. In 1877 he dismissed Midhat Pasha, suspended the constitution, and began to crack down on liberalism in the empire.

As repression grew, so too did secret societies devoted to overthrowing Abdülhamid. The most successful was the **Young Turks** movement. Mainly educated and westernized army officers and intellectuals, the Young Turks were devoted to restoring the constitution. In 1908 soldiers sympathetic to their cause revolted. Confronted by revolution, Abdülhamid gave in to demands to restore the constitution but secretly plotted to regain his absolute power. Finally, in 1909 the Young Turks deposed Abdülhamid and placed his brother, Mehmed V, on the throne.

In the 1800s Ottoman rulers tried to reverse the empire's decline through modernizing Western reforms.

The Eastern Question

Despite the Tanzimat reforms, the Ottoman Empire could not completely defend itself against internal independence movements or European invaders. In the early 1800s, for example, Egypt became practically independent, even though technically it remained in the empire, when it came under a new dynasty founded by an Albanian adventurer named Muhammad Ali. Meanwhile, in the Russo-Turkish War of 1828–29, Russia forced the Ottomans to accept Russian access to the Danube River, Russian control of territory in the Caucasus, and self-rule for Serbia.

Europeans called the Ottoman Empire "the Sick Man of Europe" because they were sure it would soon collapse from such pressures. If it did collapse, who would inherit the Sick Man's estate? This problem became known as the Eastern Question. At the heart of the controversy was Russia's long-standing desire to control Constantinople, thereby gaining access to the Mediterranean. To prevent this, Britain and France propped up the ailing empire.

The Crimean War. In the early 1850s a dispute in the Holy Land started another war. Russia objected when Roman Catholics, under French protection, were granted control of holy places in Palestine. When the Ottomans denied Orthodox Christians these same rights, the Russian czar invaded Ottoman territories in July 1853. Russia hoped to expand the empire. Great Britain, worried that Russian expansion into Ottoman territory would threaten its own position in India, joined France in an alliance against Russia. Austria, once Russia's closest ally, also feared Russian expansion on its own borders and refused to side with the czar. Most of the fighting took place in the Russian Crimea, a peninsula on the north shores of the Black Sea.

The Crimean War has been called "the most unnecessary war in history." After two years of fighting, the war reached a stalemate. The fierce battles and epidemics of cholera had taken a heavy toll on soldiers from both sides. Conditions in the crowded and filthy field hospitals were almost worse than the battlefield. As nurse Florence Nightingale explained:

THROUGH OTHERS' EYES

The Great Powers and the Balkans

When the great powers of Europe—Britain, France, Austria, and Prussia—came together in Vienna in 1853 to try to find a solution to the fighting between Russia and the Ottoman Empire, each was motivated by a desire to protect its interests in the Balkans. The ministers of the four powers looked for a way to control affairs in the region and stop the expansion of Russia. After the conference had made several unsuccessful appeals to the warring powers, the Austrian foreign minister expressed his frustration:

66 What can I tell you except that the time for [diplomatic] notes seems to me past. . . . It is precisely up to us to watch over European interests and not to allow the weaker party [the Ottoman Empire] to be unduly [unnecessarily] pressured. If only they [Russia and the Ottoman Empire] would give the conference a certain power to act! But instead of leaving the lead to it, they act without consulting it, they make it take on the role of intermediary, and they paralyze its influence by setting it in contradiction with itself. 99

66 *[Civilians] can have little idea, from reading the newspapers, of the horror & misery in a military [hospital] of operating upon these dying exhausted men. . . . We have now 4 miles of beds—& not 18 inches apart.* 99

Florence Nightingale was born in Florence, Italy, in 1820. Her aristocratic British parents at first blocked her ambition to become a nurse, but at age 31, Nightingale overcame her family's protest and went to Germany to study nursing. After she returned to England, she was named superintendent of a London hospital. Her complete reorganization of the hospital won her much praise, and she was appointed as head of a group of nurses sent to the Crimean front.

On her arrival at the war hospitals in 1854, Nightingale immediately took charge of cleaning the filthy wards to control the spread of disease. She used her own funds and donations to supply food, eating utensils, clothes, and bedding to the wounded soldiers. These supplies, and the care given by the nurses, helped improve morale. Also, Nightingale's frequent reports about the bad conditions led to reforms. By the end of her first year in the Crimea, the mortality rate had decreased from 42 percent to 22 percent. After the war, Nightingale crusaded for—and won—professional training programs for nurses and reforms in the administration of British military hospitals. Before her death in 1910, Nightingale received the British Order of Merit for her work.

Florence Nightingale
BIOGRAPHY

The Congress of Berlin. The Crimean War only put a temporary halt to Russian ambitions. In 1877 Russia once again went to war with the Ottomans, this time on behalf of the Balkan provinces that had rebelled against Ottoman rule. Though the Turks won the war's early battles, they were ultimately defeated. The terms of the peace treaty granted independence to Romania, Montenegro, and Serbia, and created a large Bulgarian state under Russian control.

With Russian troops almost at the gates of Constantinople, however, the other European powers became alarmed. Promising to be "an honest broker," Prussian chancellor Bismarck hosted the Congress of Berlin in 1878 to discuss the situation. In fact, the real purpose of the Congress was to overturn the gains Russia had made against the Ottomans.

"All questions are publicly introduced and then privately settled," noted British prime minister Benjamin Disraeli of the secret agreements that dominated the negotiations. The British agreed that Russia should have part of Bulgaria—but a much smaller and less strategically important part than the Russians had initially taken. To counterbalance Russia in Bulgaria, the British also privately agreed to the Austrian occupation of Bosnia.

To protect access to the newly built Suez Canal, Disraeli obtained control of Cyprus from the Ottomans. Although dismembered, for the time being the Ottoman Empire had been saved.

The decline of the Ottoman Empire created a power vacuum in the Balkan Peninsula that fueled international conflicts.

SECTION 3 REVIEW

IDENTIFY and explain the significance of the following:
Dual Monarchy
Russification
zemstvos
nihilists
pogroms
October Manifesto
Tanzimat
Pan-Arabism
Young Turks
Florence Nightingale

1. **Main Idea** What was the outcome of liberal reform in Russia?
2. **Main Idea** How did the Ottoman sultans try to strengthen their empire?
3. **War and Diplomacy** How did the decline of the Ottoman Empire cause problems in the Balkans?
4. **Writing to Persuade** Imagine that you are a Hungarian nationalist. Write a short speech explaining why the Dual Monarchy is or is not good for the future of Hungary.
5. **Evaluating** Write an essay comparing the Austrian, Russian, and Ottoman empires on the way they dealt with the challenges of liberalism and nationalism in their territories.

SECTION 3 REVIEW ANSWERS

IDENTIFY
For significance, see the following pages:
Dual Monarchy (p. 546)
Russification (p. 548)
zemstvos (p. 550)
nihilists (p. 550)
pogroms (p. 550)
October Manifesto (p. 550)
Tanzimat (p. 551)
Pan-Arabism (p. 551)
Young Turks (p. 551)
Florence Nightingale (p. 552)

1. Despite temporary reforms, Russian government remained autocratic and repressive.
2. Mahmud modernized the army and government. Abdülmecid gave equal legal status to Muslims and non-Muslims and reformed the tax system and military service.
3. The Balkan provinces rebelled against the Ottomans. Other European powers intervened in disputes between the Ottoman Empire and Russia.
4. good—now Hungary will have a constitution and power; not good—Hungarians want to be free from Austrian rule
5. Austrian—strengthened monarchy under Dual Monarchy; Russian—tried some reforms but went back to policy of repression; Ottoman—attempted reforms during era of Tanzimat, then returned to policy of repression

SECTION 4

CORE LESSON PLAN
See pages 533I and
533J for Lesson Plan
20.4.

Theme: Politics and Law

A liberal who was influenced by his uncle Napoleon I's ideas, Louis Napoleon was deeply involved in revolutionary activities. In 1836 he attempted a military coup at Strasbourg, but was exiled to the United States. In 1840 he attempted an uprising in France, for which he was sentenced to life in prison. He managed to escape from prison and returned to France in 1848. He gathered a following and overwhelmingly defeated his opponent in the French presidential elections in 1848.

Critical Thinking Ask students if Louis Napoleon's liberalism seems incompatible with his rise to emperor.

ANSWER: Students might note that although liberalism may seem incompatible with monarchy today, Louis Napoleon won widespread support from the people and was fairly elected.

SECTION 4
Constitutionalism in Western Europe

FOCUS

- How did French rulers respond to demands for liberal reforms?

- Why did Bismarck put social welfare reforms into place in Germany?

- What problems did Spain, Portugal, and Italy face in the 1800s?

- How did industrialization affect the smaller countries of western Europe?

*E*arly in the 1800s European diplomats had tried to impose stability on a Europe disrupted by the Napoleonic Wars. But Europeans could not escape the political implications of the rapid social and economic changes sweeping through their countries. During the 1800s the spread of the Industrial Revolution helped inspire the growth of constitutional government and social reform in much of western Europe.

Vive la République, 1848

Revolution and Reform in France

After the abdication of Louis Philippe in 1848, France adopted a new liberal constitution creating the **Second French Republic** with universal manhood suffrage. In a remarkable election, voters chose Napoleon I's nephew, Louis Napoleon Bonaparte, to head the new government. Louis Napoleon assumed power with the title of "prince-president"—a strong indication that his ambition soared higher than that of a mere elected leader.

Napoleon III. Louis Napoleon sought widespread support for his rule. To win Catholic support, he gave the church greater control over education. He also encouraged industrialization and made plans for the development of factories and railroads. After winning the approval of the middle class with such programs, Louis Napoleon soon moved to achieve his real ambition—the restoration of his uncle's empire.

The writer Victor Hugo described the fateful evening in 1851, when "Paris slumbered, like a sleeping eagle caught in a black snare." That night Louis Napoleon's troops entered Paris and arrested members of the National Assembly who opposed him. He then called for a national vote to decide whether he should be given the power to draw up a new constitution. Voters overwhelmingly approved the measure. The next year Louis Napoleon called for another vote, and the French people elected him Emperor Napoleon III. (He called himself the third because Napoleon I's son, Napoleon II, had never reigned and had died in 1832.)

The new emperor instituted many important changes. He built grand boulevards in Paris and modernized the city with parks and a new water system. Napoleon III set up credit banks to help industry and agriculture, and he built a national railway network. In addition, he reduced tariffs to develop French industry. However, Napoleon III also limited the power of the legislative assembly, censored the press, and banned public meetings. He fixed many elections so that most of the candidates directly supported his government. As his half-brother remarked, "In voting for the friends of Louis Napoleon, one will have a second chance to vote for the prince himself."

The Third Republic.

The Franco-Prussian War of 1870 brought down the strong emperor. Napoleon III surrendered and was captured by the Prussians. Vowing to fight on, the French Assembly overthrew Napoleon and proclaimed the **Third Republic**. The new republic immediately faced a crisis as the Prussians invaded France and began a siege of Paris. Food supplies became so scarce that cats, dogs, and even zoo animals were killed for their meat. An American observer noted:

▲ The menu from the "Restaurant of the Siege of Paris" included "elephant feet with German sauce" and "ragout [stew] of rat."

66 *Small portions of elephant, yak, camel, reindeer, porcupine, etc. [sold] at an average rate of four dollars a pound. . . . The charming twin elephants, Castor and Pollux, who carried children round the Garden on their backs in 1867 to 1869 . . . were . . . shot through the head. I [ate] a slice of Castor. It was tolerably good only; did very well in time of siege.* 99

In the midst of the siege, the Assembly also decided to surrender. In January 1871 Paris fell to the Prussians, and the war ended.

Only the Parisians refused to quit. Taking over the city, they proclaimed a revolutionary government called the **Commune** and tried to continue the war. The revolt was bloodily put down by the French army, however, and after several days the Commune collapsed.

Despite its troubled beginning, the Third Republic made many important reforms. Trade unions became legal in 1884, and by 1900 the working day had been reduced to 10 hours. In addition, a 1906 act required employers to give their workers one day off per week.

The Dreyfus case.

Reforms did not cure all of France's problems, however. Divisions continued to split French society. In 1894 these divisions came to a head over the controversial Dreyfus case. Captain Alfred Dreyfus, a Jewish army officer, was accused and convicted of betraying military secrets to Germany. A staff colonel discovered that another man had actually committed the crime.

Preferring to allow Dreyfus to take the blame rather than admit their own error, army officers covered up the truth and imprisoned Dreyfus. Although the colonel came forward with the real story, Dreyfus was not cleared until 1906.

The Dreyfus case revived anti-Semitism in France. Many people assumed Dreyfus was guilty because he was Jewish. Conservatives used this as an excuse to attack Jews. Others blamed the Catholic Church for framing Dreyfus. Popular sympathy swung briefly to Dreyfus's liberal supporters, who pushed through legislation separating church and state in 1905. French society, however, remained even more deeply divided than before.

Liberal demands caused French rulers to enact limited reforms, but divisions in French society led to continuing political instability.

▲ Upon being found guilty, Captain Dreyfus was publicly humiliated by having his sword broken and signs of rank removed from his uniform.

RESOURCE ACTIVITY

GLOBAL HISTORY RESOURCE CENTER

Reading: *The Dreyfus Affair*

Print out and distribute the reading. Have students write letters to the editor of a French newspaper that is covering the Dreyfus Affair. Students' letters should express their opinions on how the case has been handled so far and what should be done about the situation.

Level 2

RESOURCE ACTIVITY

GLOBAL HISTORY RESOURSE CENTER

Reading: *The Dark Side of Nationalism: Anti-Semitism*

Print out and distribute the reading. Using the reading and the textbook material on Dreyfus, students should create a pamphlet that logically refutes the claims of anti-Semites and stands up for the equality of all Europeans.

Level 3

The unification of the governments and economies of the many formerly independent German states into one cohesive unit in 1871 was no easy task. For centuries, the German states had run their own affairs. Although the new unified economy was strong, it was still susceptible to downturns. Following a period of rapid industrialization, in the mid-1870s the German economy went into recession, hurting many members of the middle and working classes. Economic problems have also plagued Germany since the reunification of East and West Germany in 1990. The union of the free-market and the command economies has led to high inflation across the country and widespread unemployment in the east.

Critical Thinking Ask students to suggest reasons why unemployment might be higher in the former territory of East Germany than in the former territory of West Germany.

ANSWER: Students might suggest that many of the industries of East Germany were not efficient enough to make a profit in a free-market economy and had to close down.

Reforms in Germany

While Napoleon III was enacting his program of economic development and industrialization in France, similar developments were taking place in Germany. As in France, one of the most important questions the new German imperial government had to face was the relationship between the state and the Catholic Church. Opposition to the church came to a head in the German Empire in the 1870s.

Liberals and the constitution. Under the terms of the 1871 constitution, each of the 25 German states had its own ruler and could handle its own domestic matters. The federal government handled all common matters, such as national defense, foreign affairs, and commerce. The legislative branch consisted of the Bundesrat, or upper house, and the Reichstag, or lower house.

Bismarck soon formed an alliance with the National Liberals, who had a majority in the Reichstag and shared his goal of centralization. To limit the power of the Catholic Church, which had been opposed to German unification, Bismarck and the National Liberals expelled the Jesuits from the empire in 1872. In the anti-Catholic *Kulturkampf* (koohl-TOOHR-kahmf), or "struggle of culture," that followed, Germany passed strict laws to control the Catholic clergy and church schools. The German Catholic Center Party, however, also had the widespread support of many Protestants who opposed the *Kulturkampf*. When a number of Center politicians were elected to the Reichstag in 1877, Bismarck began to abandon the *Kulturkampf* in an effort to maintain his influence in the lower house. By 1883 the *Kulturkampf* had come to an end.

▶ This huge steam-powered hammer, built in 1861, was nicknamed "Fritz" by workers in the Krupp cannon factory.

The economy and social welfare. In addition to his struggle against the Catholic Church, Bismarck also pursued policies designed to strengthen the empire's economic and industrial position. Germany's good transportation network and rich coal and iron deposits allowed it to develop the most powerful iron and steel industry in Europe. Bismarck's reforms greatly aided German industry. He made banking laws uniform throughout Germany and improved postal and telegraph services. In addition, the government's high-tariff policy protected German industries from foreign competition.

As in other nations, however, industrialization had its critics in Germany. German socialists protested against harsh factory conditions and called for state control of all industries. These critics united in 1875 to form the Social Democratic Party. Bismarck considered the socialists "an enemy army living in our midst." In the late 1870s he blamed socialists for two assassination attempts made on the emperor. He also persuaded the liberal government to pass antisocialist legislation that made the Social Democratic Party illegal, banned its meetings and publications, and exiled socialists from certain cities.

Even as he tried to destroy socialism, however, Bismarck also sought to reduce its appeal among the German people by enacting his own reforms. Beginning in the early 1880s, Bismarck pushed through legislation that provided benefits for health, accidents, old-age, and disability. These pioneering reforms improved conditions for the middle and working classes. But the reforms could not save Bismarck's position. When the chancellor resisted Kaiser William II's calls for more reforms, the new emperor dismissed Bismarck in 1890. William's ambitions of expanding his empire soon overshadowed such domestic concerns.

In Germany, Bismarck enacted social and economic reforms to prevent the Social Democrats from gaining power.

Unrest in the Iberian Peninsula

In Spain and Portugal, aristocratic landowners, monarchs, and the Catholic Church fought against liberalism and democracy. Political instability and violence plagued these nations, which had also industrialized little. In Italy, too, liberal politicians cared more about political infighting than promoting industrialization and democracy.

Political chaos in Spain. Although the Spanish had adopted a liberal constitution in the Napoleonic era, King Ferdinand VII, Spain's restored Bourbon monarch, overturned it. Soon the country plunged into civil war between the liberals and conservatives. After the death of Ferdinand VII in 1833, the crown passed to his infant daughter Isabella II. Ferdinand's brother Don Carlos considered himself the rightful heir to the throne and rebelled. After seven long years, the liberal generals supporting Isabella drove Carlos from his base in northern Spain.

Isabella II became queen in her own right at age 13, but the generals ran the government. To limit the power of the Catholic Church, which had supported Carlos, the liberal generals pushed through laws abolishing religious orders and forcing the sale of lands owned by the church. They also promoted public education to combat Spain's illiteracy. The generals, however, spent much of their energy and the treasury's dollars putting down conservative uprisings. With government finances in shambles and the last of the liberal generals gone, Isabella was deposed in 1868.

▲ Supporters of Don Carlos—known as Carlists—prepare to ambush a group of enemy soldiers during the civil war in Spain.

Isabella's son, Alfonso XII, became king in 1874. "I shall neither cease to be a good Spaniard, nor . . . a good Catholic, nor . . . truly liberal," he quickly assured the divided country. The king made peace with the Catholic Church and enacted a moderate constitution in 1876. Military disaster struck in 1898, however, when defeat in the Spanish-American War led to the loss of Spain's remaining major colonies.

Spaniards of all classes grew increasingly dissatisfied with both liberal and conservative politics. Peasants in the Basque lands and in Catalonia launched guerrilla raids to win their independence. Workers became increasingly militant, and support for socialism and anarchism grew. In the early 1900s a wave of assassinations and terrorism led to continued unrest.

Civil war in Portugal. Spain's Iberian neighbor, Portugal, faced similar problems. The nation was torn by civil war off and on for more than 30 years in the early 1800s. Portuguese nationalists resented the continued presence of British troops, who had helped the Portuguese drive out

After Isabella II was deposed in 1868, a search was made for a new monarch to take the throne. It was finally decided that Amadeus of Italy, the Duke of Aosta, would be offered the throne. Despite the fact that he overwhelmingly won the election of Spain's representative assembly, his coming to the throne caused a renewed outbreak of rebellion by mostly upper-class people who resented the "intrusive king." Amadeus took the throne in November 1870, and despite the fact that he tried to please all groups and made several tours throughout the kingdom, he could not please the masses. Several attempts were made on his life. He abandoned the throne in February 1873, little more than two years after his accession.

Critical Thinking Ask students why the Spanish response to the vacancy of their throne was to invite nobles from other countries to become their monarch.

ANSWER: Students might suggest that at that time many people in Europe felt that only a noble was qualified to rule a country, even if it was not the country of his or her birth.

the French. In the northern coastal city of Oporto, wealthy merchants and aristocrats took part in a coup to end British military rule in 1820. The rebels wrote a new constitution with an elected parliament, but the British remained an important influence in Portuguese politics.

The political chaos was far from over. In the early 1830s the monarchy was restored. Two princes—Pedro and Miguel—waged a civil war over control of the country. With British support and the aid of residents of Lisbon, liberal-leaning Pedro won the war in 1834. The fighting had been bitter, and liberals lashed out against the Catholic Church and the aristocracy for their support of Miguel. Pedro abolished the monasteries and sold their lands to liberal landowners. Public grammar schools and vocational schools were built to replace the church schools.

The government's attempt to privatize town lands touched off another rebellion in 1846. Peasant women from northern Portugal, who resented the government's attempt to take their land, led the revolt. The revolt brought down the government of the liberal general Costa Cabral.

The second half of the 1800s brought more stability under a constitutional monarchy. Although Portugal remained overwhelmingly agricultural, industrialization increased, particularly around Lisbon. Many peasants flocked to Lisbon to find jobs. The growth of the city's working class led to demands to extend voting rights. In 1910, revolutionaries in Lisbon overthrew the king and proclaimed a republic with separation of church and state.

Italy After Unification

After their successful fight for unification, Italians witnessed many of the same political, social, and economic tensions as the Portuguese and Spanish. Anti-Catholic feelings were particularly strong in the 1870s because the papacy had opposed Italian unification and refused to extend diplomatic relations to Italy. Liberal politicians passed laws to reduce the Catholic Church's control of education.

Though liberal in orientation, Italian politicians refused to extend voting and civil rights to women. This angered the women who had fought in Garibaldi's army and supported unification. Women's rights leader Anna Mozzoni compared women's contributions with their lack of political rights:

❝Woman, excluded by worn out customs from the councils of state, has always submitted to the law without participating in the making of it, has always contributed her resources and work to the public good and always without any reward.❞

Mozzoni organized Italy's first women's rights movement to expand women's educational, professional, and political opportunities. Change was slow in coming, however.

Liberal politicians also ignored the plight of the peasantry. It was not until the early 1880s that politicians began to worry about peasants' grievances. In 1880 Italian politician Sidney Sonnino described the poor lot of peasants, who were "ill paid, ill housed, ill nourished, and crushed by excessive labor under the most unhealthy conditions." A wave of peas-

▲ In this 1846 newspaper illustration, peasant women lead a revolt against the government that was trying to take their land.

ant revolts swept through Italy in the 1890s after high food prices and declining exports made conditions even worse.

The cities also were filled with unrest. In 1898 workers in Milan rioted to protest the high price of bread. In 1900 an anarchist assassinated King Umberto after the government violently put down the Milan riots.

Concerned about the unrest among peasants and workers, a group of liberals and socialists passed a series of reforms to prevent further disorder. They extended the vote to more males, passed factory laws, nationalized some industries, legalized trade unions, and helped set up agricultural cooperatives.

Political unrest, violence, and economic problems plagued Spain, Portugal, and Italy in the 1800s.

🛡 Industrialization in Western Europe

In stark contrast to the countries of southern Europe, the smaller nations of western Europe witnessed the triumph of liberalism and rapid industrialization. Belgium, the Netherlands, and Switzerland gradually made many important democratic reforms. Industrialization also accompanied liberal democracy in the Scandinavian countries.

Transition to democracy. European diplomatic conferences shaped the political fortunes of the Netherlands and Belgium. In 1815, diplomats at the Congress of Vienna joined the Catholic Austrian Netherlands (Belgium) with the Protestant Dutch republic under the Protestant Dutch prince William I. However, in 1830 workers in Brussels, Belgium, revolted and touched off a national crisis. Forced to call Parliament into session, William watched in horror as many Belgians spoke out against Protestant rule and called for independence.

The European powers stepped in once again. Meeting in London, diplomats from the major powers agreed that Belgium should be independent and neutral in foreign affairs. The new Belgian constitution contained several liberal ideals, such as freedom of the press, education,

L'illustration européenne

▲ **At this ice factory in Belgium in 1874, new technology allowed the production of ice in the summer—an amazing luxury at the time.**

and religion. With independence also came rapid industrialization. The iron and coal industries expanded rapidly, and a grand program of railroad-building linked Belgium's cities to the trade centers of Europe.

The Netherlands, on the other hand, remained largely agricultural and trade-oriented. Democracy developed more slowly, with Catholic politicians opposing many liberal reforms. The constitution of 1848 strengthened parliament, but it limited suffrage and still allowed the king many powers.

Switzerland. Switzerland, the most democratic European nation at the time, for the most part escaped the political chaos afflicting its neighbors in the 1800s. One Swiss nationalist writer explained that "in our common nationality we feel protected against the confusion which surrounds us on all sides." Even before the liberal revolutions that swept Europe in 1848, the Swiss **cantons**, or states, had secured liberal reforms by peaceful means.

SECTION 4 REVIEW ANSWERS (p. 560)

IDENTIFY
For significance, see the following pages:
Second French Republic (p. 554)
Napoleon III (p. 554)
Third Republic (p. 555)
Commune (p. 555)
Alfred Dreyfus (p. 555)
Kulturkampf (p. 556)
Isabella II (p. 557)
Anna Mozzoni (p. 558)
cantons (p. 559)

1. French rulers enacted some reforms, including modernizing Paris, building a railway network, setting up credit banks, legalizing trade unions, and changing some labor laws.

559

By 1848 the cantons had united in a federal republic. The Swiss approved a constitution much like that of the United States, with a two-house legislature. To protect its neutral position, the Swiss government set up a military draft to make all male citizens help protect the nation.

▲ Delegates from 16 nations gathered at the Geneva Convention in 1864 in the first meeting of the Red Cross. Today over 100 countries are members of the organization.

Switzerland's political stability encouraged industrialization, which took off after 1870. Switzerland's stability also attracted international organizations, such as the Red Cross, as well as political refugees from many countries.

Change in Scandinavia. As elsewhere, the development of liberalism and democracy in the Scandinavian countries accompanied industrial growth. In the early 1800s agricultural Denmark developed very few factories. Without pressure from workers or middle-class groups, the Danish king firmly opposed liberal reforms. As a result, liberal ideas took hold more slowly in Denmark, not being firmly established until the latter 1800s.

Sweden and Norway, to the north of Denmark, had been forcibly united by the Congress of Vienna. Sweden's aristocratic government ruled over an agricultural kingdom. In contrast, Norway already had grown more democratic and had an industrial sector.

After decades of opposition between Norway and Sweden, Norway declared its independence in 1905. It became a constitutional monarchy with extensive voting rights. Norwegian women were granted full political rights in 1913. In Sweden, although some male members of society had been allowed to vote since the 1800s, universal suffrage for men and women did not come until 1921.

In the small nations of western Europe, democratic rights and industrialization went hand in hand.

SECTION 4 REVIEW

IDENTIFY and explain the significance of the following:
  Second French Republic
  Napoleon III
  Third Republic
  Commune
  Alfred Dreyfus
  Kulturkampf
  Isabella II
  Anna Mozzoni
  cantons

1. *Main Idea* What was the result of demands for liberal reforms in France?
2. *Main Idea* What problems plagued the countries of southern Europe in the 1800s?
3. *Politics and Law* How did Bismarck hope to defeat Social Democrats?
4. *Writing to Persuade* Imagine that you are a businessperson in one of the Scandinavian countries. Write a letter to the editor of your local newspaper explaining why industrialization will be good for the country.
5. *Hypothesizing* Why do you think there were so many conflicts between liberals and the Catholic Church in Europe?

Review

On a separate sheet of paper, complete the following exercises:

WRITING A SUMMARY

Using the essential points in the text, write a brief summary of the chapter.

REVIEWING TERMS

From the following list, choose the term that correctly matches the definition.

Kulturkampf   pogroms
Realpolitik   *Zollverein*
Young Turks
Concert of Europe

1. German customs union that eliminated tariffs between the German states and encouraged German businesspeople to support unification
2. politics based on practical matters and not on liberal ideals
3. group of nationalists in the Ottoman Empire who wanted changes beyond the Tanzimat reforms
4. "struggle of culture" designed by Bismarck to limit the power of the Catholic Church
5. system of diplomatic cooperation designed to maintain peace among European nations

REVIEWING CHRONOLOGY

List the following events in their correct chronological order:

1. King William I appoints Bismarck to the Prussian cabinet.
2. Louis Napoleon becomes president of the Second French Republic.
3. Germany defeats France in the Franco-Prussian War.
4. Delegates from across Europe meet at the Congress of Vienna.
5. Sultan Mahmud II ascends the throne of the Ottoman Empire.

UNDERSTANDING THE MAIN IDEA

1. What did the Congress of Vienna try to achieve?
2. How did Prussia achieve the unification of the German states?
3. How did Ottoman rulers try to reverse the empire's decline?
4. Why did the leaders of France and Germany enact liberal reforms?
5. How did the rulers of Austria, Russia, and the Ottoman Empire respond to demands for political change?

THINKING CRITICALLY

1. **Assessing Consequences** What role did Napoleon's conquests in Europe have on German unification?
2. **Comparing** How did industrialization affect political development in western Europe and in southern Europe?

Building Your Portfolio

Complete the following activities individually or in groups.

1. **Nationalism** Imagine that you (and your friends) are elderly persons who have lived in the Balkans from the mid-1800s until the early 1900s. You experienced the growing nationalism of your ethnic group and participated in the hard-won independence of your people from the Ottoman Empire. Your grandchildren want to know what it was like to go through these experiences, so you have decided to write a short story for them. In your story, tell your grandchildren about what makes your particular ethnic group (Greeks, Serbians, Bulgarians, etc.) distinctive, and discuss the effects that foreign domination had on your life and your culture.
2. **The Congress of Vienna** In a group, stage a performance of the negotiations that took place at the Congress of Vienna. Divide your group into five subgroups representing Austria, Great Britain, Prussia, Russia, and France. For each subgroup, select one member to portray the leader of that nation. The rest of each group will be the advisors who work with the leaders. If you are doing this project individually, your work may take the form of the script for a play.

2. Otto von Bismarck provoked a war with Austria. After defeating Austria, he provoked a war with France and persuaded southern German states to join Prussia against France. In addition, Prussia defeated France and united the German states.
3. Rulers attempted modernizing reforms. Mahmud II modernized the army and government. Abdülmecid made Muslims and non-Muslims equal under the law and reformed the tax system and the military.
4. Rulers in France were responding to increasing liberal demands. Bismarck enacted reforms to keep Social Democrats from gaining power and to strengthen Germany's economic and industrial position.
5. Austria—strengthened monarchy under Dual Monarchy; Russia—imposed censorship and organized secret police; later, tried some reforms, but returned to repression; Ottoman—attempted reforms during era of Tanzimat, then returned to repression

THINKING CRITICALLY

1. Napoleon united the German states under the Confederation of the Rhine, which helped spark nationalism. When he was defeated, the Congress of Vienna retained the idea of the confederation.
2. In the west, industrialization was accompanied by important democratic reforms. In the south, where industrialization was minimal, countries were plagued with political unrest.

In very early societies, such as Egypt, Mesopotamia, and China, the historical records found by archaeologists are not narrative histories of these early cultures. Instead, many of the ancient historical writings focused on the exploits of kings, who wished to record their deeds for posterity. Other writings, such as the king lists, focused on the genealogy and glorification of royal ancestors. A third focus of early writings was religious; lessons of history were shown in the way they related to the people's religion. Historiography, or the writing of an organized history based on a critical examination of the sources, did not emerge until the time of the Greeks.

Critical Thinking Ask students why the kinds of documents left by very early societies might make it difficult for scholars to write social history and easier to write the "old" history.

ANSWER: Students should answer that the documents left by very early societies tend to focus more on elites and monarchs and less on ordinary people, giving scholars of social history less material to work with.

HISTORY IN THE Making

"Old" History versus "New" History

Until World War II, most Western historians viewed history primarily as the political story of peoples and nations. The most popular theme of history that emerged in the 1800s and 1900s in the West was the steady progression people had made to constitutional government over time.

The "Old" History

In the English-speaking world in particular, history was often seen as a kind of evolutionary progression up a political scale, with liberal democracy at the top. Historians wrote their histories on the basis of documentary material—treaties, constitutions, and laws, as well as the public speeches and letters left by the principal actors in the historical events. From these materials, historians were able to construct chronological narratives—descriptions of connected past events. Governments and the relatively few men, and sometimes women, who ruled them were considered to be the most important actors. The most important events revolved around wars, treaties, constitutions, laws, and government policies.

The "New" History

By the early 1900s, however, some historians had begun to look beyond such purely political and diplomatic subjects for topics of inquiry. In 1912 one critic of this "old" history called for the development of a "new" history that would examine not the story of ruling elites but of "the common man." This "new" history would use the findings of such fields as sociology, anthropology, economics, and psychology to reconstruct the history of ordinary people. Out of this call grew many new kinds of history as scholars began to examine the past in new ways. Perhaps the most influential of these new approaches has been what most scholars call social history—or, as the well-known British historian G. M. Trevelyan defined it, "history with the politics left out."

The rise of Marxism, which saw history as the struggle for control among various economic classes, reinforced the development

◄ **This letter from Süleyman the Lawgiver to a European ruler, written in 1528, is an example of traditional historical documentary material.**

▲ This Jewish marriage contract from 1879 is an example of material a scholar of "new" history might use.

of social history even among non-Marxist historians. Where historians had formerly emphasized the importance of individuals in history, social historians concentrated instead on the broad social forces that they believed had shaped history. Many argued that the "old" history of statesmen and warriors, of laws and constitutions, had little relevance to the daily lives of ordinary people.

The task of history, the new scholars argued, was to concentrate on people's daily existence, creating a "total" picture of what it was like. To accomplish this, they emphasized different sources of information, such as private letters and diaries, church records, birth, marriage, and death records, wills and other private legal documents, as well as editorial cartoons, music hall programs, and popular songs.

Limitations of Social History

By the 1980s social history had practically replaced political history as the mainstream of historical writing in most universities. Social historians hoped to reconstruct the history of ordinary people, particularly those groups they believed to have been left out of earlier social histories—women and racial, ethnic, and religious minorities. The new social historians used oral histories, autobiographies, workers' speeches and letters, local newspapers, and folklore to capture the daily life of the past. As they emphasized such subjects, some social historians even argued that social history had made political and diplomatic history unnecessary. Yet there were problems with such an approach.

For example, one young social historian who studied the history of a particular American town at the end of the 1700s claimed he had achieved an "in-depth" analysis of what people's lives had been like. He admitted, however, that given the kinds of questions he was investigating, and the kinds of sources he was using to write the history, he could not really get to the significance that the establishment of the United States had on the town he was studying. Yet as a critic pointed out, during the American Revolution politics had moved people to place their lives and their fortunes on the line in an effort to create a new society. Social history alone did not seem to allow for the importance of such political events even in ordinary people's lives.

Combining the Old and the New

Despite the enthusiastic claims for social history among some scholars, in recent years a few social historians have begun to re-emphasize the importance of the older historical tradition in their own work. In the early 1990s, for example, Linda Colley, a British social and cultural historian, brought the two historical traditions together in her book *Britons: Forging the Nation, 1707–1837*, a study of the formation of the British national identity.

Using many of the sources of social history—diaries, almanacs, popular songs, poetry, plays, paintings, sermons— Colley was able to explain how and why the English, Scots, Welsh, and even Irish created for themselves a new sense of British national identity. At the heart of the issue, she discovered, was the ongoing warfare between Britain and France. In the face of the French threat, the various peoples of the British Isles came together in common cause for defense. From this common cause emerged the new sense of British identity. In short, instead of downplaying politics and the importance of political history, Colley used the tools of social history to illuminate one of the most important aspects of political history—the forging of a national identity.

As Professor Colley's work suggests, perhaps the best method of understanding the past is to combine all the various approaches of history to gain a balanced picture.

Chapter 21

The Imperial World Order 1757–1914

Chapter Planning Guide

	TEXTBOOK	CORE RESOURCES	VISUAL RESOURCES	MULTIMEDIA
Introduction	pp. 564–565	Block Scheduling Handbook: Ch. 21		Videodisc Segment 21 and Viewing Guide: *Empire in Africa*
Lesson 21.1 Motives of Modern Imperialism	pp. 566–569 Literature Through Time: *Rudyard Kipling*, p. 568	Reading 21.1: *A Justification of British Colonialism in Africa*		GHRC 21 Readings: *A European Attack on Imperialism; The Tools of Empire* GHRC 21/Videodiscs: Images—*The White (?) Man's Burden; Imperialism: "The Great White Way"; A Cartoon Decrying British Imperialism;* Map—*The New Imperialism*
Lesson 21.2 Imperialism in Africa	pp. 570–578 Geography and History: *The Berlin Conference: Changing the Map of Africa*, p. 574 Map: *Resistance Movements in Africa*, p. 576 Then and Now: *Black Townships in South Africa*, p. 577	Reading 21.2: *Opportunities Abroad* Geography Activity 21: *Migration Patterns in Southern Africa*	Art and History 21: *Calendar Poster of Henry Stanley in Africa* Geography and History 36: *Africa*	GHRC 21 Readings: *Report from the Congo; Missionaries Create a "Moral Mess" in Africa* GHRC 21/Videodiscs: Image—*Imperialists Divide Up the World*
Lesson 21.3 Imperialism in India and Southeast Asia	pp. 579–584 Map: *Imperialism in India and Southeast Asia*, p. 580	Reading 21.3: *Journal of the Indian Mutiny*	Everyday Life 21: *The Indian Mutiny* Geography and History 21: *Shorter Routes Via the Canals*	GHRC 21 Readings: *The Impact of British Rule on India; Mutiny and Its Aftermath in India* GHRC 21/Videodiscs: Image—*French Troops in Vietnam*
Lesson 21.4 Imperialism in East Asia	pp. 585–590 Map: *Imperialism in East Asia*, p. 587	Reading 21.4: *Japan and the West* Skills Activity 21: *Interpreting a Cartoon* Writing Project 21: *Making Revisions*	Geography and History 37: *East and Southeast Asia*	GHRC 21 Readings: *The Boxers Attack the "Foreign Devils"; Westernization Hits Japan; Perry Introduces Japan to Western Technology* GHRC 21/Videodiscs: Images—*Boiling and Testing Opium in China; Opening the First Railway in Japan*
Chapter Investigation and Enrichment	pp. 564–590	Chapter 21 Investigation: *The "New" Imperialism* People in World History 21 Explorations in Daily Life 21		GHRC 21/Videodiscs
Review and Assessment	Section 1 Review, p. 569 Section 2 Review, p. 578 Section 3 Review, p. 584 Section 4 Review, p. 590 Chapter 21 Review, p. 591	Chapter Review Activity 21 Vocabulary Activity 21 Themes Review 21 Section Study Guides 21.1–21.4 Main Idea Activities 21.1–21.4 Daily Quizzes 21.1–21.4 Chapter 21 Test Sheltered English Ch. 21 Test Ch. 21 Test Generator		Audio CDs: Ch. 21 Summary (English and Spanish)

INTRODUCING THE CHAPTER

Textbook pp. 564–565

CHAPTER OVERVIEW

Long-standing motives—economic, political, strategic, and religious—combined with the rise of nationalism and the demands of the Industrial Revolution to inspire the new imperialism. Britain initiated the scramble, and Germany, France, and the Netherlands quickly followed; thus, they established colonies in Africa, India, and Southeast Asia. While China and Japan did not become colonies, they were forced open to European trade.

PRESENTING THEMES

On the chalkboard or on an overhead transparency, write the following open-ended theme questions.

- **CROSS-CULTURAL INTERACTION** How might an overseas colonial empire affect the development of both the colonial rulers and their subject peoples?
- **TECHNOLOGY** What role might technology play in the acquisition and development of an empire?
- **ECONOMIC ORGANIZATION** How might nations use military strength to gain an unequal trade advantage with other nations?

Have students suggest responses to the questions. List the responses on the chalkboard or the transparency. For the cross-cultural interaction question, students might suggest that both would be affected if the ruling nation used the colony's resources. For the technology question, students might suggest that technology can help a nation to conquer new areas. For the economic organization question, students might suggest that military strength can be used to control trade. Save the responses. Once students have studied the chapter, you may wish to have them complete the Themes Activity, then compare the two sets of answers.

USING THE VIDEO

Segment 21: *Empire in Africa*

ENGLISH

Search Chapter 21
Videodisc 2, Side B

SPANISH

Search Chapter 21
Videodisc 2, Side B

Tell students that in this chapter they will apply these theme questions to the scramble for colonies and empires in the late 1800s. Conclude by showing Segment 21 of the *World History and Cultures Videodiscs*. This segment examines some of the motives behind European expansion and looks at some of the legacies of empire-building in Africa.

Before showing the segment, ask students to look for changes in the physical, economic, and social landscape of Africa that resulted from European colonialism. To help students grasp the significant points of the segment, have them complete Video Viewing Guide 21.

Key to Ability Levels

All strategies and activities are coded to the following ability levels:

LEVEL 1	**Basic** activities suitable for all students
LEVEL 2	**Average** activities suitable for average to above-average students
LEVEL 3	**Challenging** activities suitable for above-average students
SHELTERED ENGLISH	Activities suitable for students with **Limited English Proficiency**

Additional Resources

BOOKS FOR TEACHERS

Pakenham, Thomas. *The Scramble for Africa.* Avon, 1995. Examines European actions in Africa.

Phillips, Anne. *The Enigma of Colonialism.* Curry, James, 1989. Looks at colonialism in West Africa.

Tidrick, Kathryn. *Empire and the English Character.* IB Taurus & Co., 1990. Includes portraits of Englishmen in the colonial service.

BOOKS FOR STUDENTS

Barthorp, Michael. *War on the Nile: Britain, Egypt and the Sudan.* Sterling Publishing Co., 1986. Looks at the military campaigns.

Bayly, C. A. *Indian Society and the Making of the British Empire.* Cambridge University Press, 1988. Asks why India failed to repulse British rule.

MULTIMEDIA MATERIALS

Africa: The Bible & the Gun/This Magnificent African Cake. RM Arts. Video, 114 min. Examines European colonialism in Africa.

Asia: 1600–1800. Network Television Production. Video, 26 min. Looks at the effects of European intrusion.

Imperialism. Clearvue. CD-ROM, MAC, DOS, MPC formats. Focuses on Spain and Britain.

Lesson 21.1   *Motives of Modern Imperialism*

Textbook pp. 566–569

RESOURCES

Pupil's Edition
Literature Through Time,
p. 568: *Rudyard Kipling*

Core Resources
Reading 21.1: *A Justification of British Colonialism in Africa*

Global History Resource Center
Reading: *A European Attack on Imperialism*
Reading: *The Tools of Empire*

Videodiscs or Global History Resource Center

Map: *The New Imperialism, 1900*

Search Frame 970

Image: *The White (?) Man's Burden*

Search Frame 957

Image: *A Cartoon Decrying British Imperialism*

Search Frame 1001

Image: *Imperialism: "The Great White Way"*

Search Frame 1000

LESSON FOCUS

How did industrial technology and nationalism encourage European imperial expansion after 1870?

OBJECTIVES

After completing this lesson, students will be able to:
- identify the factors that encouraged European imperial expansion after 1870;
- explain how technology stimulated imperialism;
- analyze the way in which westerners' attitudes about the superiority of their civilization affected imperialism.

HOOK

Identify factors that contributed to the revival of interest in imperial expansion among Western powers after 1870. Review reasons for European imperialism in the 1400s and 1500s. *[The desire for goods from Asia led to exploration and colonization.]* Remind students that motives for imperialism in that time period sometimes were characterized by the motto "God, gold, and glory," referring to the desire to spread Christianity, to acquire riches, and to gain power. Then have students identify the factors that led to the new imperialism after 1870. *[nationalism, industrialization, demand for raw materials and markets]* Challenge students to create a motto to characterize motives for European imperialism after 1870.

PROBE

Explain how modern industrial technology stimulated imperialism. Next ask students to identify the results of industrialization. *[Answers include advances in transportation, demand for raw materials, and competition for markets.]* Next have students explain how each of these factors contributed to imperialism after 1870. *[Industrial nations needed colonies to provide new markets for trade. The use of steam-powered ships created a need for coaling and supply stations.]* If available, have students examine the electronic media map on imperialism and world trade.

Ask: To European nations in the late 1800s, what economic arguments favored imperialism?

[the need for raw materials and markets to support industrial production]

Discuss how the need for raw materials to support industrial production and trade affected trading patterns. Then have students work in groups of three or four to illustrate the relationship between industrial technology and imperialism. Groups might create flow charts, diagrams, or pictorial representations. Provide time for students to share and discuss their work.

CONCLUDE

Describe how westerners' attitudes about the superiority of their civilization affected imperialism. Read the quotations on textbook pages 566 and 569 from Ferry, Livingstone, and Rhodes that express their attitudes on imperialism.

Ask: Based on these quotations, how did these Europeans feel about their civilization?
[They considered it superior to that of other peoples.]

Ask: What did they see as their duty and/or responsibility?
[to spread Western civilization]

Next have students read the Literature Through Time feature on page 568 of their textbook.

Ask: How is Kipling's attitude as expressed in this excerpt different from the attitudes expressed in the Ferry, Livingstone, and Rhodes quotations?
[While he believes in the superiority of British civilization, he affirms the ability of people to overcome cultural differences.]

After discussing Kipling, remind students that by the end of the 1800s most Europeans had some form of constitutional government.

Ask: Why might the growth of democratic institutions cause people to question imperialism?
[Democratic ideals emphasize individual human rights and freedoms.]

Next show students the electronic media images *The White (?) Man's Burden, A Cartoon Decrying British Imperialism* and *Imperialism: "The Great White Way,"* and have students complete Core Resources Reading 21.1 and the Global History

Resource Center reading on imperialism. Then ask students to consider how some people tried to reconcile imperialist motives with democratic ideals. Have students work in pairs to propose a solution to the moral conflict that European nations faced with regard to imperialism. Provide time for students to share their solutions. [Students should conclude that many Europeans justified imperialism by adopting the attitude of a moral responsibility to spread Western civilization.]

Ask: How was this attitude of cultural superiority used to justify imperialism?
[Many Europeans believed they had a moral responsibility to spread their civilization to other parts of the world.]

EXTEND

Cross-Curricular Connection: *Health*
Have students research advances in medicine that aided European colonization of tropical regions. They might use information from their text, the reading on the tools of empire in the Global History Resource Center, as well as other sources, such as encyclopedias. Then display the electronic media map showing imperialism after 1870. Have students analyze the correlation between advances in tropical medicine and imperialism in tropical regions.

MEET INDIVIDUAL NEEDS

Students Having Difficulty
Students having difficulty with this lesson may benefit from outlining major ideas and supporting details based on subheadings in the text.

Linguistic Learners
Have students read other examples of Rudyard Kipling's work. Direct students to look for words and phrases that imply British cultural superiority and contrast them with other words and phrases in the work that show an appreciation for people's ability to appreciate their common humanity.

ASSESS

Review
Have students complete the Section 1 Review. Use answers in the Teacher's Edition, page 569, to assess student mastery of this section.

Lesson 21.2 *Imperialism in Africa*

Textbook pp. 570–578

RESOURCES

Pupil's Edition
Geography and History, p. 574: *The Berlin Conference: Changing the Map of Africa*

Map, p. 576: *Resistance Movements in Africa, 1881–1914*

Then and Now, p. 577: *Black Townships in South Africa*

Core Resources
Reading 21.2: *Opportunities Abroad*

Visual Resources
Art and History 21: *Calendar Poster of Henry Stanley in Africa*

Geography and History 36: *Africa*

Global History Resource Center
Reading: *Report from the Congo*

Reading: *Missionaries Create a "Moral Mess" in Africa*

Videodiscs or Global History Resource Center
Image: *Imperialists Divide Up the World*

Search Frame 959

LESSON FOCUS

What were the consequences of European imperialism in Africa after 1870?

OBJECTIVES

After completing this lesson, students will be able to:
- describe the European presence in Africa before 1870;
- explain how Africans practiced imperialism in the 1800s;
- identify the consequences of the Berlin Conference of 1885;
- analyze African responses to European imperialism.

HOOK

Describe the state of European occupation of African territory before 1870. Project the Geography and History transparency of Africa onto a large sheet of paper. Trace the outline of the map on the paper.

Next have students use colored markers, flags, and/or labels to indicate parts of Africa occupied by Europeans before 1870. Then have students formulate a generalization about European imperialism in Africa before 1870. *[Students should recognize that except for the French occupation of Algiers in the far north and Boer and English settlement in the far south, the vast majority of African territory was not affected by European control at this time.]*

DEVELOP

Explain how and why Africans practiced imperialism in the 1800s. Remind students of the diverse cultural characteristics of African peoples. Then ask them to speculate about reasons for African imperialism. *[Possible responses include competition for resources or military conflicts.]* Have students record their answers in their notebooks.

Next divide students into three groups and assign one of the following regions to each group: southern Africa, West Africa, or northeast Africa. Instruct members of each group to study imperialism in their assigned region in the late 1700s and 1800s. Students should focus on the causes and results of imperialism in each region. *[**Southern Africa:** the Zulu used new weapons to expand militarily; **West Africa:** a Muslim revival inspired empire-building; **northeast Africa:** Egypt used European technology and organization to expand]*

Allow a few minutes for groups to complete their studies. Then create new groups of three students each, consisting of one member of each of the original groups. Have members of the new groups compare their data and draw some conclusions about how and why Africans practiced imperialism. Finally, have students compare their conclusions with the speculations they wrote in their notebooks. Discuss whether their original ideas were supported or revised.

PROBE

Identify the consequences of the Berlin Conference of 1885. Discuss with students the events that prompted the Berlin Conference.

Ask: **What prompted the Berlin Conference?**
[British occupation of Egypt and commercial and strategic rivalries triggered a European scramble for colonies.]

Ask: **What was the purpose of the conference?**
[to establish rules for partitioning the world]

Next have students examine the Geography and History feature on textbook page 574 and the electronic media cartoon image, *Imperialists Divide Up the World*, if available. Point out the disparity between tribal boundaries and those drawn by Europeans at the Berlin Conference.

Ask: **What were the territorial consequences of European imperialism in Africa after the Berlin Conference?**
[Almost the entire continent was ruled by European powers.]

Finally, have students further their understanding of the consequences of the Berlin Conference from the African point of view by having them complete the Global History Resource Center reading on the effects of imperialism in the Congo. Then read the quotation from Emperor Menelik on page 576.

Ask: **If you were African, how might you have felt toward Europeans after the Berlin Conference?**
[Responses should indicate betrayal by Europeans as a result of the Berlin Conference.]

CONCLUDE

Discuss African responses to European imperialism.
Refer students to the map on African resistance. Then write the following headings on the chalkboard: *Military, Diplomatic,* and *Religious Protest.* Ask students to cite examples of African responses to imperialism and write their responses under each heading. *[**Military:** Ethiopia obtained European weapons, defeated Italy; Asante war against British; Dahomey's struggle*

with French in West Africa; Zulu-British conflict in South Africa; ***Diplomatic:*** *the king of Daboya in Ghana signed a treaty of friendship and free trade with Britain;* ***Religious protest:*** *Shona and Ndebele uprisings in Rhodesia; Maji Maji revolt in German East Africa]*

Ask: **What was the final outcome of African resistance? Why?**
[It failed to prevent European domination; Africa was not industrialized nor was resistance unified.]

Link to Today. Have students discuss the Then and Now feature on page 577. Then have students work independently or in small groups to create a modern fable or an allegory based on the history of European imperialism in Africa. You might provide the following premise as a beginning: Once upon a time, extraterrestrials met on Asteroid G to establish ground rules for partitioning North America among themselves. . . .

EXTEND

Cross-Curricular Connection: *Language Arts*
Have students examine Core Resources Reading 21.2. Then have them do a quick-writing exercise in which they note their immediate reactions to the reading and what it tells about British colonialism in Africa.

MEET INDIVIDUAL NEEDS

Visual-Spatial Learners
Have students examine Art and History Transparency 21 showing a depiction of Henry Stanley, who worked for King Leopold to open up the Congo. Ask students how this picture reflects the beliefs and values of imperialism. Also ask students to note any biases the image contains.

Interpersonal Learners
Have interested students research the ways in which European political dominance affected the daily life of African peoples. They might wish to focus on a particular colony and investigate the influence of Western technology or education or of missionaries on traditional beliefs or ways of doing business.

ASSESS

Review
Have students complete the Section 2 Review. Use answers in the Teacher's Edition, page 578, to assess student mastery of this section.

Lesson 21.3   *Imperialism in India and Southeast Asia*

Textbook pp. 579–584

RESOURCES

Pupil's Edition

Map, p. 580: *Imperialism in India and Southeast Asia, 1857–1914*

Core Resources

Reading 21.3: *Journal of the Indian Mutiny*

Visual Resources

Everyday Life 21: *The Indian Mutiny*
Geography and History 21: *Shorter Routes Via the Canals*

Global History Resource Center

Reading: *The Impact of British Rule on India*
Reading: *Mutiny and Its Aftermath in India*

Videodiscs or Global History Resource Center

Image: *French Troops in Vietnam, 1883*

Search Frame 966

Map: *The New Imperialism, 1900*

Search Frame 970

LESSON FOCUS

What were the consequences of European imperialism in India and Southeast Asia?

OBJECTIVES

After completing this lesson, students will be able to:

- describe how the British ruled their territory in India in the early 1800s;
- explain how interaction with the British affected Indian society;
- describe how the Indian Mutiny changed the government of India;
- analyze the impact of imperialism in Southeast Asia.

HOOK

Examine British rule in India in the early 1800s. For additional background, have students complete the Global History Resource Center reading on British rule in India. Then have students list as many cultural differences as they can think of between the British and Indians. Next ask a student volunteer to review the argument Europeans used to justify imperialism. *[They had a moral obligation to spread their civilization.]*
Ask: *How did this attitude become apparent among British colonial administrators who began to train Indians to fill lower ranks of government?*

[Orientalists wanted Indian administrators to receive an essentially Indian education; Anglicists wanted them to receive a Western education.]

Ask: *How did the outcome of this debate between Orientalists and Anglicists affect British rule?*
[The British created an elite class of Western-educated Indians to help rule.]

DEVELOP

Describe the consequences of British and Indian cultural interaction. Then have students consider how efforts to spread English culture affected the rest of Indian society.
Ask: *Why did the British come to call for social and cultural reforms in India?*
[to bring India the benefits of Western civilization by ending practices they considered immoral, such as suttee and child marriages]

Review the primary responses of Indian reformers to British reform efforts and the work of Christian missionaries. Make two headings on the chalkboard: *Blend (Ram Mohun Roy)* and *Purify (Dayananda Sarasvati)*. Then call on student volunteers to outline the elements of the two Indian approaches to reform and write their responses on the board. *[**Blend**: all great religions have the same message; blended aspects of British* and Indian cultures; appealed to many Western-educated Indians; **Purify:** strengthen Hindu society by rejecting elements of religion; return to Vedic beliefs]

PROBE

Explain why the British changed their approach to governing India. Have students review the text. Then show Everyday Life Transparency 21 and have them complete the accompanying worksheet and Core Resources Reading 21.3. If available, also have them complete the Global History Resource Center reading on mutiny in India.

*Ask: **What were the causes of the Indian Mutiny?***

[Students should point out that traditional leaders resented losing power and that they played on fears that the British wanted to convert Indians to Christianity and end the caste system; rumors that cartridges were greased with beef and pork fat led to a bloody, brutal rebellion that resulted in bitterness on both sides.]

*Ask: **How did British policy change as a result of the Indian Mutiny?***

[Answers should indicate that although most of India had remained loyal, the British abandoned the Western-educated elite and sought the support of traditional leaders.]

Next refer students to the map on textbook page 580.

*Ask: **What was the primary effect of the mutiny?***

[Britain established direct control over India and extended its influence to surrounding areas.]

Next have students diagram the hierarchy of British administration in India.

*Ask: **Did the British system provide effective rule of the Indian Empire?***

[Students should recognize that the system enabled the British to collect taxes, administer justice, oversee development projects, and defend India against invasion.]

CONCLUDE

Explain how the French and Dutch extended their influence in Southeast Asia. If available, have students view and discuss the electronic media image of the French in Vietnam. Then have them view the electronic media map or the map on textbook page 580, and have them locate French Indochina, Thailand, and Indonesia. Then ask students to create map captions describing how the French and Dutch extended their influence in these regions and how Thailand remained independent.

Then present students with two opposing views of imperialism. First tell students that Sir Edward Grigg said that imperialism was the greatest force in the world because it served to spread law and keep the peace. Then counter Grigg's opinion with that of Anatole France, who equated imperialism with barbarism. Ask students which viewpoint they think applies to imperialism in India and Southeast Asia. Call on several volunteers to defend their opinions.

EXTEND

Cross-Curricular Connection: *Geography*

To familiarize students with the importance of the Suez Canal to British control of India, display Geography and History Transparency 21 and have students complete the accompanying worksheet.

MEET INDIVIDUAL NEEDS

Logical-Mathematical Learners

Have students create a time line of imperialism in India and Southeast Asia. They should include events relating to the extension of European rule.

Students Having Difficulty/
Students Acquiring English

Students may benefit from making a list of key terms from this lesson. Ask them to define each term and explain how it relates to the central question for the section.

ASSESS

Review

Have students complete the Section 3 Review. Use answers in the Teacher's Edition, page 584, to assess student mastery of this section.

Lesson 21.4 Imperialism in East Asia

Textbook pp. 585–590

RESOURCES

Pupil's Edition

Map, p. 587: *Imperialism in East Asia, 1839–1912*

Core Resources

Reading 21.4: *Japan and the West*
Skills Activity 21: *Interpreting a Cartoon*

Visual Resources

Geography and History 37: *East and Southeast Asia*

Global History Resource Center

Reading: *The Boxers Attack the "Foreign Devils"*
Reading: *Perry Introduces Japan to Western Technology*
Reading: *Westernization Hits Japan*

Videodiscs or Global History Resource Center

Image: *Boiling and Testing Opium in China*

Search Frame 968

Image: *Opening the First Railway in Japan, 1872*

Search Frame 969

LESSON FOCUS

How did Western imperialism affect China and Japan?

OBJECTIVES

After completing this lesson, students will be able to:

- explain how Western imperialism and culture influenced China;
- describe the results of westernizing reforms in the Qing Empire;
- discuss the consequences of opening Japan to foreign trade;
- explain how the Japanese responded to Western imperialism.

HOOK

Discuss Western influences on China. Divide students into four groups and provide each group with a picture of one of the following items or a card with the name of the item written on it: tea bag, poppy, silver bar, or cross. Tell students that each item symbolizes some aspect of the relationship between China and the Western powers. Challenge students to discover the significance of their item and then explain how it relates to the history of Western imperialism in China. Provide time for groups to share their findings. *[Tea bag: the English were interested in China as a source of tea; Silver bar: the Chinese*

government insisted that payment for Chinese goods must be in silver, creating a trade imbalance in China's favor; **Poppy**: a massive illegal trade in opium, which could be sold for silver, was carried out by Western merchants in China; **Cross**: the Taiping rebellion, inspired by Western cultural influences, weakened the Qing dynasty] After students have presented their findings, you may wish to display and discuss the electronic media image of opium-processing in China.

DEVELOP

Describe the results of westernizing reforms in the Qing Empire. Discuss reasons why the Chinese began a major reform movement. *[to preserve Chinese culture]* Then have students create a chart to record reforms and results.

Ask: Why did the reform efforts fail to have the results desired by the Tongzhi Restoration?
[Reforms affected only upper levels of the bureaucracy; conservatives rebelled against the use of Western methods and technology.]

If available, have students complete the Global History Resource Center reading on the Boxer Rebellion.

Ask: How did the Boxer Rebellion lead to the establishment of a Western-style Chinese Republic?
[Foreign suppression of the Boxers led to imperialist

control of China. Western-educated Chinese leaders recognized the need to overthrow the Qing and adopt Western ideas in order to restore China's independence.]

PROBE

Discuss the consequences of opening Japan to foreign trade. Display Geography and History Transparency 37 of East and Southeast Asia or refer students to the map on textbook page 587.

Ask: *Why and how was Japan important to Westerners?*
[Its location made it important as a fueling station for ships as well as a center for Far Eastern trade.]

Next have students complete Core Resources Reading 21.4 and then analyze the "opening" of Japan from different viewpoints. Before students begin working you may also wish to have them read Perry's account in the Global History Resource Center. Then ask students to create a newspaper account, an editorial, or a political cartoon about Perry's expedition expressing the viewpoint of one of the following people: Perry, the shogun, an American trader, a Japanese fisher, a member of Perry's crew, a British representative. You may want to assign roles or monitor choices to ensure adequate coverage. Call on volunteers to share their work.

Ask: *Was the opening of Japan to foreign trade a victory or a crisis?*
[Westerners considered it a victory; the Japanese viewed it as a crisis—it threatened their culture.]

CONCLUDE

Explain how the Japanese responded to the threat of Western imperialism. If possible, have students examine the electronic media image of the opening of the railway and then complete the reading on the westernization of Japan in the Global History Resource Center. Then have students list the reforms of the Meiji Restoration. *[abolished feudalism, adopted a constitution and set up a European judicial system, built up defenses, built up industrial base]*

Ask: *Why did Japan adopt Western practices?*
[to modernize, industrialize, and maintain its independence]

Ask: *What were the results of Japan's imitation of the West?*
[Japan not only maintained its independence but became an imperialist power.]

Have students contrast the results of westernizing reforms in Japan with those in China. Direct students to draw a line down the center of a sheet of paper. On the top left, they should write *China*; on the top right, *Japan*. For each nation, have students list the westernizing reforms and the results of each reform. Ask students to analyze their lists to determine how the results were alike and how they were different. Then discuss why Japan's responses to westernizing reforms changed European attitudes toward Asia. *[Students should conclude that China became a Western-style republic, and Japan became a powerful industrial power; Japan entered an alliance with Great Britain.]*

EXTEND

Cross-Curricular Connection: *Business*
Have interested students research the beginnings of the zaibatsu, which are still in existence today. Have them report their findings to the class.

MEET INDIVIDUAL NEEDS

Visual-Spatial Learners
Assign Skills Activity 21: *Interpreting a Cartoon*. Then have students compare the cartoon of China with the picture of Japan represented in the electronic media image of the opening of the railway in Japan. Discuss how these examples reflect differences in the way imperialism affected the two countries.

Gifted Students
Link to Today. Have students examine the electronic media image on opium production and the Global History Resource Center reading on the East India Company and opium. Then ask them to draw comparisons between efforts to end the drug trade in the 1800s and today's efforts.

ASSESS

Review
Have students complete the Section 4 Review. Use answers in the Teacher's Edition, pages 589–590, to assess student mastery of this section.

In preparation for the chapter test, you may wish to have students complete all or part of the Chapter 21 Review on textbook page 591, the Chapter 21 Review Activity, and the Chapter 21 Themes Review.

Chapter 21

The Imperial World Order

Understanding the Main Idea

Call on a volunteer to read aloud the *Understanding the Main Idea* paragraph. Then tell students that the demands of industrialization led nations to search for new sources of raw materials. Nationalism inspired Europeans to bring their cultures to "less civilized" nations. New technology made this expansion possible, and powerful nations occupied weaker ones. In China and Japan European nations used force to gain markets. Reactions from China and Japan had long-lasting effects.

Presenting Themes

See p. 563B for suggestions on introducing themes.

Using the Time Line

Have students list the time line events in their notebooks. After they have read about each event in the chapter, have students write a paragraph explaining its significance.

Chapter 21
The Imperial World Order
1757–1914

Understanding the Main Idea

Between the mid-1700s and the first decade of the 1900s, empire-building reached new heights throughout the world. European empires expanded from trade empires into empires of occupation. Meanwhile, Asian and African empires developed due to new technologies and renewed religious enthusiasm. By 1914 the great industrial powers dominated the world.

Themes

- **Cross-cultural Interaction** How might an overseas colonial empire affect the development of both the colonial rulers and their subject peoples?

- **Technology** What role might technology play in the acquisition and development of an empire?

- **Economic Organization** How might nations use military strength to gain an unequal trade advantage with other nations?

On January 11, 1876, *The Times of London* was delivered to the Belgian palace of Laeken in time for Leopold II's breakfast. Although Leopold read the British newspaper every day, an article in this edition caught his eye. The article described the travel notes of Lieutenant Cameron, *The Times*'s correspondent in Central Africa. Leopold, who had long dreamed of a Belgian colonial empire, became interested in Cameron's description of the wealth of the area he had explored:

66*The interior is mostly a magnificent and healthy country of unspeakable richness. I have a small specimen of good coal; other minerals such as gold, copper, iron and silver are abundant, and I am confident that with a wise and liberal (not lavish) expenditure of capital, one of the greatest systems of inland navigation in the world might be utilized . . .*99

Within a few days, Leopold had offered to pay for the expenses that Cameron had incurred on his journey and put into motion his plans for building a colony in Africa.

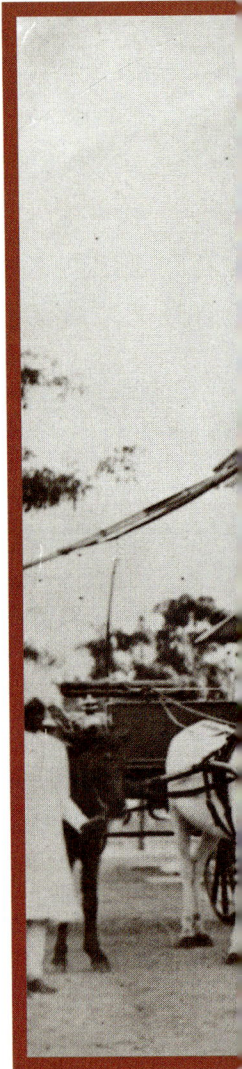

1764	1830	1835	1839	1854
Bengal falls under the rule of the British East India Company.	France occupies Algiers.	Boers begin the Great Trek into the African interior.	Britain launches the Opium War against China.	American commodore Matthew Perry forces the opening of Japan to trade negotiations.

British family in India surrounded by their Indian servants

About the Image

This photograph of members of a British family with their Indian servants reveals the grandeur in which many of the British lived during their occupation of India. Even British people of relatively modest means would have around 60 servants; the wealthy had many more. One British civil servant remarked that the British in India lived in "splendid sloth and languid debauchery. . . . Great men rode about in stagecoaches, with a dozen servants running before and behind them to bawl out their titles; and little men lounged in palanquins [litters] or drove a chariot for which they never intended to pay, drawn by horses which they bullied or cajoled out of the stables of wealthy Indians."

Critical Thinking Ask students how the lifestyle of the British in India might have affected the Indian people.

ANSWER: Students might suggest that Indians might resent the British for benefiting at the Indians' expense.

1857
Indian sepoys rebel against the British in the Indian Mutiny.

1884–1885
The Berlin Conference sets ground rules for the partitioning of Africa.

1902
The Japanese and British sign the Anglo-Japanese Alliance.

1911–1912
Revolutionaries overthrow the Qing dynasty and establish the Chinese Republic.

SECTION 1
Motives of Modern Imperialism

> **FOCUS**
>
> - What factors encouraged European imperial expansion after 1870?
> - How did technology stimulate imperialism?
> - How did westerners' attitudes about their civilization affect imperialism?

While many peoples throughout history had practiced imperialism—dominating others through the establishment of great empires—by the 1800s the industrial powers of the Western world had a clear technological advantage in this process. In addition, the rise of nationalism and the spread of the Industrial Revolution caused many European nations to commit themselves to imperial expansion. Europeans soon spread their empires over the entire globe.

The first step towards lightening
The White Man's Burden
is through teaching the virtues of cleanliness.
Pears' Soap
is a potent factor in brightening the dark corners of the earth as civilization advances, while amongst the cultured of all nations it holds the highest place—it is the ideal toilet soap.

Soap advertisement from the 1800s

Building New Empires

Between 1870 and 1914 many of the world's industrialized nations engaged in a flurry of formal empire-building. Great Britain, France, Germany, Italy, Japan, and the United States claimed large areas of the globe. By 1914 these colonial empires controlled almost the entire world.

In some places, like Australia, Algeria, and South Africa, the European powers exercised their rule through so-called **settlement colonies**, in which large numbers of Europeans occupied the land. In other parts of the world, particularly the tropics, they established what became known as **dependent colonies**, in which a few European imperial officials ruled over non-European peoples. Europeans controlled most of the rest of the world through **spheres of influence**, or territories in which the interests of a single outside nation were dominant.

The "new" imperialism. Many historians call this remarkable extension of power the **"new" imperialism**. Actually, the new imperialism differed little from the old imperialism that Europeans had been practicing since the late 1400s. Certainly, many of the motives remained the same: economic, political, strategic, religious, and humanitarian. At the same time, the rise of nationalism and the spread of the Industrial Revolution came together in the 1800s to intensify imperial expansion.

Jules Ferry, who became France's Minister of Foreign Affairs in 1883 and from that post developed France's overseas empire, gave perhaps the most complete explanation of empire-building:

> **❝** The policy of colonial expansion is a political and economic system; . . . one can relate this system to three orders of ideas: economic ideas, ideas of civilization in its highest sense, and ideas of politics and patriotism. **❞**

Underlying all these reasons were the governments' fundamental concerns for national security and people's sense of national identity and national pride. "France . . . cannot be merely a free country. . . ," Ferry insisted. "She ought to propagate [spread] [her] influence throughout the world and carry everywhere that she can her language, her customs, her flag, her arms, and her genius."

◄ Improvements in weapons and transportation played a significant role in Germany's victory in the Franco-Prussian War.

National competition and imperialism. To a considerable degree, the new imperialism sprang from the wave of nationalism that swept over Europe in the 1800s. The emergence of newly unified nations like Germany and Italy forced a realignment of the balance of power in Europe. Growing tensions among the nation-states could easily spill over into the rest of the world.

After Germany won the Franco-Prussian War of 1870–71, for example, France gave up the province of Alsace and part of Lorraine to the new German Empire. Afterward, German chancellor Otto von Bismarck encouraged the French to make up for this loss by expanding in Africa. Thus, Bismarck hoped to divert France from seeking revenge for its defeat in Europe.

The Germans' rapid victory in the Franco-Prussian War demonstrated to the world that modern industrial warfare depended not only on sheer numbers and heroism but also on railways, repeating rifles, and improved artillery. This modern technology was expensive and could be maintained only through industrialization. Therefore, in order to ensure national security, political leaders had to guarantee a growing industrial capacity and a healthy national economy. Both goals depended on access to raw materials and markets in which to sell industrial products—and access to raw materials and new markets could be obtained by building empires. After 1870 European competition for empire intensified.

The spread of the Industrial Revolution beyond Britain and Belgium had already created a new demand for raw materials. European and American businesses began to seek new materials like copper, manganese, and rubber. In South America, for example, some countries fought for control of sources of guano—bird droppings—a substance rich in the nitrate that could be used to make either fertilizer or modern explosives. Many of these new materials could only be found in Asia, Africa, or Latin America. Having found the resources, industrial nations tried to guarantee that they would have access to them.

Free trade and empire. Great Britain had developed a commitment to free trade during the 1800s. As Britain prospered, other nations lowered and even canceled their own tariffs, which gave Britain, the first nation to industrialize, a comparative advantage in economic competition with other countries.

By the 1880s, however, this situation had changed. The newly industrializing nations realized that they could not compete with Britain's well-established industrial base. To develop their own industrial capacity, these countries began to close off their markets and sources of supply—a practice called **protectionism**. The rise of protectionism and the new imperialism that followed represented a return to the old mercantilist principles of the earlier European empires.

After 1870 industrialization and nationalism gave new life to European imperial expansion.

Technology and Empire

Modern technology and weapons made the new European imperialism possible. As writer Hilaire Belloc once noted of the European ability to dominate other peoples: "Whatever happens we have got / The Maxim gun and they have not."

During the 1850s new advances in transportation technology, particularly in shipbuilding, allowed Europeans to go almost anywhere in the world safely. At the same time, advances in tropical medicine allowed Europeans to move

1. Kipling says that the differences between people in the East and West are permanent and will not change. But he says that these differences make little difference when people have recognized some essential similarity.

2. Kipling believes that when people meet each other face-to-face and find their common bonds, they can overcome their cultural differences.

Literature THROUGH TIME

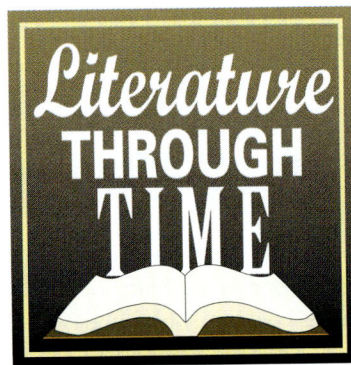

Rudyard Kipling

Few literary figures are as associated with the theme of imperialism as Rudyard Kipling. Critics of imperialism often brand him a racist. In fact, Kipling believed passionately in the potential moral worth of all human beings—though he also believed strongly that British civilization should be the model for everyone. The following passage from one of Kipling's poems illustrates the difficulties of any simple categorization of Kipling's views.

In "The Ballad of East and West," Kipling tells the story of a raid in which a Pathan chieftain steals the favorite horse of a British colonel on India's northwestern frontier. *The colonel's son follows in hot pursuit to retrieve his father's mare. Impressed by the young man's bravery, the chieftain turns to help him when his horse falls, and the two become close friends.*

They have looked each other
    between the eyes, and there
    they found no fault,
They have taken the Oath of the
    Brother-in-Blood on leavened[1]
    bread and salt:
They have taken the Oath of the
    Brother-in-Blood on fire and
    fresh-cut sod,
On the hilt and the haft[2] of the
    Khyber knife, and the
    Wondrous Names of God.
The Colonel's son he rides the
    mare and Kamal's boy the dun,[3]
And two have come back to Fort
    Bukloh where there went
    forth but one. . . .

[1]raised
[2]handle
[3]gray-brown colored horse

Rudyard Kipling was popularly known as the "poet laureate" of the British Empire.

Oh, East is East, and West is West, and never the two shall meet,
Till Earth and Sky stand presently at God's great Judgment Seat;
But there is neither East nor West, Border, nor Breed, nor Birth,
When two strong men stand face to face, tho' they come from the ends of the earth.

Understanding Literature

1. How does this poem show Kipling's feelings about the cultural differences that divide human beings?

2. How does Kipling feel these cultural differences can be overcome?

into regions that were previously unhealthy for them. For example, Europeans discovered that quinine, made from the South American cinchona bark, could be used to control malaria. After such discoveries Europeans had a better chance of surviving in the tropics.

New naval technology also supplied a motive for imperial expansion. By the 1880s steam-powered ships had largely replaced sailing ships. However, these steam-driven warships carried only a limited amount of coal. Consequently, to keep a fleet at sea, a country had to have coaling stations—bases where ships could be resupplied with coal—and ports for defense. The only way to ensure the security and availability of such stations was by annexing the surrounding territories as colonies.

Improvements in medicine and new naval technology contributed to imperial expansion and gave the industrial powers an advantage over other countries.

Humanitarian and Cultural Imperialism

Some westerners had other motives for spreading their civilization to the world. The word *civilization* itself had an almost magical appeal to them, and they associated it with the upward progress of the human race. Most westerners believed that their own civilization, the product of Christian religious values and Enlightenment rationalism, represented the highest point of human achievement and development. Many Christian missionaries carried their faith, modern medicine, and Western education to Asia and Africa. Dr. David Livingstone, perhaps the most famous missionary and explorer of the 1800s, described their sense of purpose:

66 *The stream [of missionaries] . . . is set in motion by Him who rules the nations, and is destined to overflow the world. . . . Future missionaries will see conversions following every sermon. We prepare the way for them. . . . We work for a glorious future which we are not destined to see—the golden age which has not been, but yet will be.* 99

As Europeans established their empires, they also became concerned about the moral consequences of imperialism. By the end of the 1800s, most Western nations had some form of constitutional government at home. Yet liberal democracy, with its emphasis on individual human rights and liberty, seemed at odds with imperialism.

To try to justify their actions, many imperialists adopted the moral tone of the missionaries. European imperialists spoke of their "civilizing mission." The most famous British imperialist, Cecil Rhodes, used plainer language:

66 *We happen to be the best people in the world, with the highest ideals of decency and justice and liberty and peace, and the more of the world we inhabit, the better it is for humanity.* 99

Many Western imperialists, convinced of their superiority, believed they had a moral responsibility to convey Western civilization to the rest of the world.

▲ During an expedition, a hippopotamus attacks David Livingstone and his crew.

SECTION 1 REVIEW

IDENTIFY and explain the significance of the following:
settlement colonies
dependent colonies
spheres of influence
"new" imperialism
protectionism

1. **Main Idea** Why did Western nations become interested in imperial expansion after 1870?

2. **Main Idea** How did modern technology contribute to imperialism?

3. **Cross-cultural Interaction** Why did some westerners feel a responsibility to spread their civilization through imperialism?

4. **Writing to Persuade** Imagine that you are a young British imperialist.

Write a short speech explaining why you think expanding the British Empire would benefit not only Great Britain but also the non-Western world.

5. **Hypothesizing** Why do you think Europeans were so convinced that their civilization was superior to every other civilization?

SECTION 1 REVIEW ANSWERS

IDENTIFY
For significance, see the following pages:
settlement colonies (p. 566)
dependent colonies (p. 566)
spheres of influence (p. 566)
"new" imperialism (p. 566)
protectionism (p. 567)

1. The rise of nationalism and the demand for raw materials caused by industrialization contributed to imperial expansion after 1870.
2. New advances in transportation, medicine, and naval technology contributed to imperialism by allowing quicker and safer travel with fewer medical risks.
3. They felt that their civilization was morally and intellectually superior.
4. Speeches should mention imperialist's belief that Britain was a superior society with Christian values and that foreign nations would benefit from British influence. In addition, Britain would gain raw materials from other lands.
5. In most cases, they were more industrially developed and considered themselves more advanced. Also, they often justified their superiority through Christianity.

SECTION 2

CORE LESSON PLAN
See pages 563E and
563F for Lesson Plan
21.2.

Theme:
Geography

For the most part, Africa's interior remained a mystery to early explorers. The Niger and Zambezi Rivers were swampy and full of sandbars. The hot river valleys also posed the threat of diseases. For these reasons the majority of the African interior remained unexplored by Europeans following the first expeditions to the coast.

Critical Thinking Ask students how a geographer might interpret the above information to theorize how these natural barriers might have affected European attitudes toward Africa.

ANSWER: Students might suggest that the geographer would theorize that the barriers may have made Africa and Africans seem even more alien and mysterious.

SECTION 2
Imperialism in Africa

FOCUS

- How significant was the European presence in Africa before 1870?
- How did Africans practice imperialism in the 1800s?
- What were the consequences of the Berlin Conference?
- How did Africans respond to European imperialism?

In the 1700s and 1800s, imperialism in Africa flourished. While certain African peoples were building empires in the interior, for decades Europeans remained confined to the coasts. After about 1870, however, European imperialists began to challenge the African states in the continent's interior. By 1914 almost all of Africa had come under the control of the Europeans.

THE RHODES COLOSSUS
STRIDING FROM CAPE TOWN TO CAIRO

Political cartoon showing the British imperialist Cecil Rhodes astride the continent of Africa

Early European Settlement in Africa

Except for a few missionaries and explorers, most Europeans' contacts with Africa before 1870 were largely confined to the coasts. The Portuguese had long been involved in the Congo, Angola, and along the East African coast. Portuguese contacts had greatly affected these African societies, particularly in trade, but the interior remained firmly under African control. Similarly, in West Africa, European slave-trading posts were located on the coast, while African rulers controlled the interior.

In North Africa the French occupied Algiers in 1830, partly to regain their sense of honor after the Napoleonic years and partly to put an end to the piracy and slave-raiding of the Muslim rulers of North Africa. Over the next 17 years the French waged a constant war against the Muslim Berbers and Arabs, who were led by 'Abd al-Qadir, a local chieftain.

Only in southern Africa did Europeans penetrate the interior in large numbers before 1875. The original Dutch settlers, known as Boers, had established themselves around the Cape of Good Hope beginning in 1652. Over the years other European immigrants, particularly French Huguenots seeking to escape religious persecution, also became part of the Boer population. In the 1790s British forces took control of the Cape of Good Hope as part of their struggle against revolutionary France, and in 1814 the Dutch formally surrendered the territory to Britain. Soon British settlers joined the diverse mix of peoples in Britain's new Cape Colony.

British immigration inspired a new sense of Boer ethnic identity. By the 1800s the Boers distinguished themselves from other peoples by their religion and their language. Borrowing African, French, German, and English words, their original Dutch language was transformed into a new language called **Afrikaans**. As devout Calvinist Protestants surrounded by Africans they considered pagans, the Boers came to think of themselves as a "chosen people" destined by God to rule southern Africa.

The British and the fiercely independent Boers clashed over many things, particularly the British determination to abolish slavery. Hostile to British rule, in 1835 thousands of Boers began a mass migration out of Cape Colony and into the interior. This movement is known as the **Great Trek.** There they eventually established their own independent republics, the Orange Free State and the Transvaal. As they did so, however, they discovered African imperialists—and empires.

Before 1870 the European presence in the interior of Africa was limited to the coasts, the far north, and the far south.

African Empire-Builders

In the late 1700s and early 1800s, famine and competition for resources led to a series of wars among various peoples in southern Africa. In the early 1820s the Zulu clan built a vast empire in southern Africa under their leader, Shaka.

Zulu imperialism. An effective military leader, Shaka transformed the nature of African warfare. Adopting a short stabbing spear instead of the more common throwing spear, he reorganized the Zulu warriors into military regiments and embarked on a period of imperial expansion. Combined with several other factors, such as the advance of Portuguese slave traders and ivory hunters, Zulu imperialists forced peoples all across southern Africa to relocate in what became known as the *mfecane* (em-fuh-KAH-nay), or "crushing." Eventually, the effects of the *mfecane* reached as far north as the central African lake region and south to Cape Colony.

Muslim expansion in West Africa. At the same time, a similar movement was also occurring in West Africa, stimulated by an Islamic revival. This revival began among the Fulani, a pastoral, nomadic people who had spread from the Senegal region east toward the Hausa states near Lake Chad. In 1804 a well-educated and devout Muslim named 'Uthman ibn Fudi called for a holy war against all non-Muslims. By 1811 the Fulani had emerged as the leaders of the West African region known as Hausaland.

▲ Shaka's nephew Cetshwayo fought against European imperialism.

'Uthman ibn Fudi's success inspired others. In the western Sudan, al-Hajj 'Umar, a Muslim who had married one of 'Uthman's granddaughters, established a center of Islamic learning and missionary activity in Futa Jallon. From there he inspired his followers to launch attacks against non-Muslim states in the 1850s. 'Umar established an empire that absorbed other Islamic and non-Islamic territories from upper Senegal to Timbuktu.

Egyptian imperialism. In northeastern Africa the 1800s also saw a revival of imperial ambition in Egypt. Egyptian imperialism reflected the impact of European technology and organization. In the aftermath of Napoleon's occupation of Egypt, an Albanian lieutenant in the Ottoman army named Muhammad 'Ali took control of Egypt. Modernizing the Egyptian army along European lines, Muhammad 'Ali soon expanded his control down the Red Sea coast, into western Arabia and parts of the Sudan. Eventually, Egyptian armies even marched into Palestine and Syria. Only European intervention kept Muhammad 'Ali from overthrowing the Ottoman sultan. In the settlement that followed the conflict, the Ottomans agreed to recognize the right of Muhammad 'Ali's family to be hereditary rulers of Egypt.

Muhammad 'Ali's successors were also extremely ambitious. As part of their plans for modernizing Egypt, they allowed a French company to build the Suez Canal. The Suez canal connected the Mediterranean Sea and the Red Sea, providing Europe with a direct route to East Africa, India, and China. Financing such projects, however, coupled with the rulers' extravagant lifestyles, brought Egypt to the verge of bankruptcy and made it vulnerable to European intervention.

Through new military technology and religious inspiration, many new African empires emerged in the 1800s.

THE IMPERIAL WORLD ORDER **571**

THROUGH OTHERS' EYES

An Englishman's View of Shaka

In 1818 Henry Francis Fynn, a surgeon's assistant, sailed from Great Britain to Africa. In 1824 Fynn first visited the great Zulu empire-builder Shaka. In his diary Fynn left a description of the king who united the Zulu and established a vast empire over much of southern Africa.

❝We found him sitting under a tree . . . decorating himself and surrounded by about 200 people. A servant was kneeling by his side holding a shield above him to keep off the glare of the sun. Round his forehead he wore a turban of otterskin with a feather of a crane erect in front, fully two feet long. . . . Ear ornaments made from dried sugar cane, carved round the edge, . . . were let into the lobes of the ears, which had been cut to admit them. From shoulder to shoulder, he wore bunches . . . of the skins of monkeys and genets [small mammals].

. . . Round the ring on the head . . . were a dozen bunches of the loury [a type of bird] feathers neatly tied to thorns which were stuck into the hair. Round his arms were white ox-tail tufts. . . . He had a white shield with a single black spot.❞

The Occupation of Egypt

As Egypt plunged into bankruptcy, the European powers intervened in the 1870s. They took control of Egyptian finances and established an international debt commission to pay off the country's loans. Such interference in Egypt's internal affairs, however, offended many Egyptians.

In 1881 an army leader named 'Urabi Pasha rose in Egypt, proclaiming his desire to end European domination. At first he tried to appeal to the European sense of fairness. He wrote to one sympathetic Englishman:

❝Without doubt it will please every free man to see men free . . . truthful in their sayings and doings, and determined to carry out their high projects for the benefit of mankind generally, and the advantage of their own country in particular.❞

When 'Urabi became Egypt's war minister, however, he seemed to threaten European control of the new Suez Canal. British prime minister William Gladstone, who had once characterized 'Urabi as a "nationalist struggling to be free," authorized the British invasion of Egypt. Quickly defeating 'Urabi, the British sent him into exile. Although Gladstone intended only a temporary occupation, British troops remained in Egypt for the next 70 years to ensure British access to the Suez Canal.

The Scramble for Africa

Britain's occupation of Egypt brought a reaction from the other Western powers—particularly France. Combined with commercial and strategic rivalries elsewhere in the world, the occupation helped trigger a global scramble for territory among the European powers. As the competition for colonial territory proceeded, the intensity of the rivalries increased tensions among the European nations.

The Berlin Conference. In an effort to resolve potential conflicts over the competition for colonies, the great European powers met at the **Berlin Conference** in 1884–85 to establish ground rules for partitioning the world among themselves. At the conference they agreed that no European colonies would be recognized unless they were occupied. This meant that the informal spheres of influence that had been carved out by merchants and missionaries now required the armed intervention of European governments to remain secure. On this basis, and with other provisions requiring them to discourage the slave trade, the Europeans began to extend their control over Africa.

The partition of Africa. Under the rules laid down by the Berlin Conference, the European imperial powers established their rule over all of Africa except Liberia and Ethiopia between

1885 and 1914. In central Africa King Leopold II of Belgium established the Congo Free State along the Congo River and its tributaries. Leopold initially ruled the state as a personal fief. During the early 1900s, however, stories about the brutality with which his agents were extracting wealth from the local African peoples outraged many Europeans. Eventually, the Belgian government took control of the colony, renaming it the Belgian Congo.

Germany also entered the scramble for territory. With Bismarck's approval, German colonization societies led the way, taking control of Southwest Africa (present-day Namibia), German East Africa (in present-day Tanzania), and several smaller colonies, such as Togoland and Cameroons, along the West African coast.

The Fashoda Crisis. The scramble for Africa eventually drew Europeans into local wars and conflict with each other. In 1881 Muhammed Ahmad, a Muslim leader, called for the overthrow of Egyptian rule in the Sudan. Calling himself the Mahdi, or "expected one," he had gained control of the Sudan by 1883 by inspiring his followers, the Mahdists, to crush Egyptian armies. Two years later his followers took Khartoum, the Egyptian colonial capital of the Sudan, and killed General Charles Gordon, who had been sent by the British to evacuate the Egyptians. Although Egyptian leaders wanted to retake the Sudan, the British vetoed such action, believing it was too costly.

In the 1890s, however, news reached London that the French were sending a military expedition to claim the upper Nile Valley. The possibility of a European rival establishing control over the upper Nile—which British leaders believed to be the strategic key to the control of Egypt—alarmed the British. They decided to head off the French by retaking the Sudan.

In 1898 a fierce battle took place outside the Mahdist capital of Omdurman, across the river from Khartoum. Anglo-Egyptian forces under Sir Herbert Kitchener fought not only to take the Sudan but also to avenge the death of General Gordon. Winston Churchill, a young army lieutenant working as a war correspondent, described the Mahdist attack:

▲ The architectural style of these African shops reflects lingering German colonial influences.

66 *They are advancing, and they are advancing fast. A tide is coming in. But what is this sound which we hear: a deadened roar coming up to us in waves? They are cheering for God, his Prophet [Muhammad] and his holy Khalifa [caliph]. They think they are going to win. We shall see about that presently.* 99

The British victory was complete. Kitchener destroyed the Mahdist army and lost only 48 men out of a total force of 26,000. According to British estimates, Sudanese losses were over 10,000 dead and 16,000 wounded.

Moving immediately upriver, Kitchener discovered that French captain Jean-Baptiste Marchand held the town of Fashoda and claimed the region for France. Kitchener and Marchand agreed to let their governments determine who would control Fashoda. For months Britain and France stood on the brink of war in what became known as the **Fashoda Crisis**. Eventually, the French backed down. Britain strengthened its hold over the Sudan by establishing an Anglo-Egyptian administration.

British strategic imperialism. Protection of the upper Nile also led Britain to establish a protectorate over East Africa in what is now Kenya. The British also took control of the African kingdoms that now make up Uganda. In addition, the British moved farther inland from Cape Colony. Led by the private British South Africa Company, owned by Cecil Rhodes, the British claimed central Africa.

GLOBAL HISTORY RESOURCE CENTER

Map: *The New Imperialism, 1900*

Print out and distribute the map. Use the map's caption and information from the textbook to discuss where trade goods originated and how imperialist countries used them. Then ask students to illustrate the map, using arrows to show the directions in which goods moved.

Sheltered English

Linking Geography and History

Boundaries were drawn regardless of ethnic groups or language. Africans might have found themselves living under new rulers with entirely new laws.

Map Answer

Lozi

Geography AND HISTORY

The Berlin Conference: Changing the Map of Africa

In 1880 few European statesmen would have predicted that within the next 30 years, they would partition most of sub-Saharan Africa among themselves. Growing tensions among the European powers, however, triggered a remarkable scramble for Africa.

As tensions among the imperial powers increased over competition for African territory, their representatives met in Berlin in 1884–85 at the invitation of the German chancellor Otto von Bismarck. In addition to recognizing the claims of King Leopold II of Belgium in the Congo, the delegates to the Berlin Conference agreed upon a loose set of ground rules that would guide the acquisition of imperial territory.

The most important rule was that claims to territory must be communicated to the other powers, who would then have the chance to object to them and to negotiate boundary treaties. In addition, the powers making claims to territory must have established "effective occupation" of that land—which meant that they must have established some form of government there or that their claims to annexation had been acknowledged by the local inhabitants. Finally, the annexing powers would have to pledge to end the slave trade in their territories. With these ground rules, the European powers divided almost all of Africa among themselves between 1885 and 1914, leaving only Liberia and Ethiopia free from colonial rule. In many places the establishment of geographical boundaries for the new colonies took little or no account of the African peoples and states already there.

Linking Geography and History

How might the partition of Africa have affected African states and peoples?

African Boundaries, 1883–1914

The Scramble for Africa The Berlin Conference laid the groundwork for European colonization of Africa, generally without regard for the political and cultural boundaries already established there.

? Location Which African kingdom was divided among the most colonial boundaries?

Born in England in 1853, Cecil Rhodes moved to South Africa in 1870, hoping the climate would improve his poor health. He soon moved to Kimberley, the center of diamond mining. A shrewd businessperson, by 1891 Rhodes had gained control of 90 percent of the world's diamond production. Rhodes hoped to do the same thing in the gold fields that had been discovered in the Transvaal in 1886, but was opposed by the Boer president Paul Kruger.

Rhodes's great interest in wealth was only part of his greater ambition. As a confirmed imperialist, Rhodes hoped to establish a British-controlled railway from the Cape to Cairo that would open up the African continent to British imperial control. Rhodes believed that this would bring what he saw as the benefits of British civilization to the African peoples—while people like himself would benefit from the expanded trade.

In 1890 Rhodes became the prime minister of Cape Colony. By the mid-1890s Rhodes was convinced that Britain must annex the Boer republics of Transvaal and the Orange Free State to ensure that southern Africa would remain firmly within the British Empire. In 1895 he financed an attempt to overthrow the Boer government of Transvaal in what became known as the Jameson Raid. The raid failed, however, and Rhodes was forced to resign as prime minister of Cape Colony.

In 1889 Queen Victoria had granted Rhodes a charter to colonize an area in the interior of Africa beyond the Limpopo and Zambezi Rivers. After the Cape Colony embarrassment, Rhodes focused his attention on this new British colony, which he called Rhodesia. Still drawn by the Cape-to-Cairo dream, Rhodes began building railways to connect the new colonies to southern Africa and the East African coast. In 1902, before he could see his dream fulfilled, Rhodes died. He was buried on a great hill with a spectacular view in the heart of Rhodesia (present-day Zimbabwe). In his will he specified that much of his vast fortune be used to create the fund for the Rhodes scholarships, which allow worthy students from (former) British colonies, the United States, and Germany to study at Oxford University.

▲ These Boer farmers-turned-soldiers posed for a photograph in 1900 during the Boer War.

The Boer War. Rhodes's policies at the Cape were taken up by the British colonial secretary, Joseph Chamberlain, and Cape Colony's new high commissioner, Sir Alfred Milner. By 1899 these two men had engineered another war with the Boer republics as a means of finally annexing them to the British Empire.

In spite of British expectations, the Boers resisted strongly for over two years. The Boers practiced a highly effective form of guerrilla warfare. Eventually, it took over a quarter of a million British imperial troops to defeat the Boer forces of less than 90,000 men. Although the British finally won in 1902, the bitter conflict turned many in Britain against further imperialism and led to an extremely liberal peace treaty.

At the Berlin Conference, the European powers laid the ground rules for dividing Africa and soon moved to establish full colonial rule.

African Resistance

However powerful their technology, most of the European powers could not have made their claims to African territory effective without some sort of cooperation from local African inhabitants. Many Africans sought to use the powerful Europeans for their own advantage. In 1892, for example, the king of Daboya in what is now northern Ghana signed a treaty of friendship and free trade with Britain. Afterward, he

Resistance Movements in Africa, 1881–1914

The Spark of Resistance Many Africans responded angrily to the growing presence of foreign powers. They fought to reestablish political, religious, and cultural sovereignty.

? Linking Geography and History Which African resistance movement in which country controlled the most territory?

Empress Taitu, Menelik's wife, was even more blunt: "You wish Ethiopia to be represented before the other Powers as your protectorate, but this shall never be." In 1896, using many modern weapons—rifles and cannons obtained from Russia and France—Menelik's army defeated an Italian invasion force at the battle of Adowa. Other African peoples were not so successful.

Even though they had no modern weapons, African military resistance was often strong. In West Africa both the Asante and the Dahomey fought bitter wars against European colonization. One of the most impressive examples of fierce resistance occurred in southern Africa. In 1879 the British governor of Cape Colony decided to stop the "Zulu incubus [devil]" and ordered an invasion of Zululand. Because of Zulu courage and British blundering, however, the campaign ended in a great Zulu victory at the battle of Isandhlwana. Regrouping quickly, the British invaded once again, and on July 4, 1879, they ended the Zulu Empire at the battle of Ulundi. As they mowed down the Zulu regiments with rifles and Gatling guns, an onlooking war correspondent described the Zulu resistance: "Their noble ardour [determination] could not endure in the face of the appliances of civilized warfare."

Often, African religious symbolism played an important role in rallying African resistance. Many African peoples called on their gods and ancestors for spiritual and moral guidance. Among the Shona and the Ndebele, for example,

sent a message to his new ally, in which he requested more weapons, "Let plenty [of] guns, flint, powder and cloth, and every kind of cost goods be sent here for sale. . . . Tell [the governor] also to send for sale here those short small guns firing many times." The British governor responded by taking steps to incorporate Daboya into Britain's African possessions.

When the truth about European intentions finally became known, many African peoples resisted fiercely. In Ethiopia, for example, Italy negotiated a treaty with Emperor Menelik II in 1889. When Menelik discovered that the wording of the treaty in Italian was different from his copy in Amharic, the Ethiopian language, he angrily wrote to King Umberto I of Italy:

Then & Now

Black Townships in South Africa

At the beginning of the 1900s, only about 10 percent of black South Africans lived in urban areas. The growth of industry in the first quarter of the century, however, encouraged thousands of black South Africans to head for the cities in search of work. Urban areas were generally located in lands designated for whites by the government. This led to housing problems. Some local governments established a number of townships, or segregated settlements, on the cities' outskirts. By the mid-1930s about 19 percent of black South Africans—more than 1 million in all—were living in urban areas.

Life in the townships

These townships proved terrible places to live. Most were located next to garbage dumps or sewage works. Some were surrounded by fences patrolled by armed guards. In others the living quarters were commonly known as "barracks" and the inhabitants as "inmates." Still more urban blacks squatted in shantytowns, which were largely free of government control.

The establishment of the apartheid segregation system in the late 1940s allowed the South African government to bring the townships under its authority. One set of apartheid laws gave the government the right to control the flow of labor into the cities. The government used this power to expel hundreds of thousands of African workers from the urban areas. Another law gave the government the power to resettle Africans in newly built townships. Soweto, the country's largest black township, was created as a result of this law. *Soweto* is not an African name. Rather, it is a shortened version of South-Western Township.

Living conditions in places like Soweto were much the same as in the old townships—terrible. The houses were small, boxlike buildings made of brick, wood, and corrugated iron. Few of these "matchboxes," as township-dwellers scornfully called them, had electricity, gas, or running water. In addition, few townships possessed the comforts found in a normal town, such as stores, theaters, or sports facilities. Creating conditions that met only the most basic needs was a deliberate government policy. For the government, the townships were only a temporary situation. They were merely to provide a home for migrant workers to live as long as their jobs lasted.

Protests

The grim reality of life in the black townships created resentment among the inhabitants, particu-larly the young. In 1976 this resentment exploded into violence on the streets of Soweto. The uprising lasted for months, and the government's brutal suppression of the demonstrations claimed the lives of at least 600 young Africans. In response, the South African government promised to improve living conditions. Government leaders agreed that qualified township-dwellers would be allowed to buy 99-year leases on their homes. Further, people in the townships would be able to elect their own local councils. Such changes did little to improve life in the townships, however.

Hope for the future

When South Africa's first democratically elected government took office in 1994, it faced many challenges. Not least of these was what to do about the townships. The new government proposed an ambitious policy that included encouraging homeownership, improving existing housing, and ultimately building 1 million low-cost homes. If this policy succeeds, the townships of the future will be vastly different from those of the past.

Though housing problems still remain, many South African townships now have electricity and telephone service. In this photograph, a woman from the Alexandra neighborhood makes a call on a local phone.

Africa in 1914

Carving Up Africa By 1914, the European powers had carved up Africa into their own territories.

? **Location** Which lake lies along the equator? Which European territories bordered the lake?

religious leaders led uprisings against the British who had settled in Southern Rhodesia in the 1890s. In German East Africa, during the 1905–07 Maji Maji revolt, Africans believed they had special religious magic that made them immune to bullets—until thousands died under German gunfire. African Muslims also found a strong motivation to rebel in their religion, as many did in North and West Africa.

In spite of the strong resistance put up by Africans, most could not hope to overcome the Europeans' superior military technology. In certain cases, Africans acquired European weapons themselves or made their own rifles with which to fight. Occasionally different ethnic groups formed alliances to resist colonial occupation. Often it was only after an initial defeat that Africans came to recognize the need for unified resistance.

Africans resisted the European conquests through military force and religious beliefs, but failed to prevent European domination.

SECTION 2 REVIEW

IDENTIFY and explain the significance of the following:
Afrikaans
Great Trek
Shaka
Berlin Conference
Fashoda Crisis
Cecil Rhodes

LOCATE and explain the importance of the following:
Cape Colony

Belgian Congo
Khartoum
Isandhlwana

1. **Main Idea** How extensive was European imperialism in Africa before 1870?
2. **Main Idea** How did the Berlin Conference affect Africa?
3. **Cross-cultural Interaction** In what ways did Africans respond to European imperialism?

4. **Writing to Explain** In a short essay, explain why Europeans were not the only people practicing imperialism in Africa in the 1800s.
5. **Analyzing** How might the opening of the Suez Canal have affected trade and the British attitude toward control of Egypt?

Imperialism in India and Southeast Asia

- How did the British rule their territory in India in the early 1800s?
- How did interaction with the British affect Indian society?
- How did the Indian Mutiny change the government of India?
- What was the impact of imperialism in Southeast Asia?

European imperialism followed a different pattern in Asia than in Africa. Throughout Asia, Europeans found highly organized states, powerful armies, and major cities that surpassed many European cities in size and splendor. In Asia Europeans were also surrounded by evidence of complex civilizations much older than their own, which challenged the Europeans' sense of cultural superiority.

A British magistrate's wife is attended by her servants.

British India

As in Africa and Southwest Asia, Britain set the pace of the new imperialism in Asia. The most important of the European imperial possessions was British India. The British had first entered India as traders in the early 1600s. By the mid-1700s the British, like the French, had established fortified bases along the coasts and had become involved in the internal politics of the declining Mughal Empire.

In 1764, following the end of the Seven Years' War, British victories brought the eastern province of Bengal under the rule of the British East India Company. By making alliances with Indian rulers and creating its own army of Indian soldiers known as **sepoys** (SEE-poyz), the Company became the greatest power in India.

Company rule. As the British East India Company extended its power—or **raj** (RAHZH), as it later became known—over India, the Company also became responsible for governing and maintaining order in the territories it controlled. Such stability was essential for the conduct of trade, which remained the Company's primary objective.

Initially, the Company simply maintained the administrative structure of the Mughals. The broad responsibilities of governing, however, quickly became a tremendous drain on the Company's resources. Moreover, in the early days of Company rule in India, many officials of the Company gained enormous wealth through plunder, as well as legitimate trading activities. Over time, the British government began to regulate the Company's rule. By the late 1700s a governor-general approved by the British government carried out the administration in India.

To secure the British position in India, the early governors-general gradually extended the Company's power over Indian states beyond their jurisdiction. Using Western military might, including the most up-to-date weapons, as well as superior discipline and organization, the British conquered the Marathas and brought the powerful southern Indian state of Mysore under Company rule. At other times the mere threat of war was enough to cause local Indian rulers to acknowledge the Company's authority. In exchange the governors-general usually left local Indian princes in charge of their own territories

While Thomas Babington Macaulay confessed that he had "no knowledge of either Sanskrit or Arabic," he did say this: "All the historical information which has been collected from all the books written in the Sanskrit language is less valuable than what may be found in the most paltry abridgements used at preparatory schools in England."

Critical Thinking Ask students what attitude Macaulay's comment reflects.

ANSWER: Students should answer that it reflects the new imperialists' sense of superiority over non-white peoples.

RESOURCE ACTIVITY

GLOBAL HISTORY RESOURCE CENTER
Image: *Mission Church in British Ceylon*

Show students the image and discuss the attitude of the new imperialists toward religion and morality. Have students imagine that they are residents taking part in the service. Have them write a letter to a friend about the changes the missionaries have brought to their lives.

| Level 3 |

Map Answer

Philippines

---

but subject to "advice" from a British "resident." The Company also took over full control of the princes' foreign relations.

The nature of British rule. These early governors-general also put in place an administrative system run by about 1,000 British civilians. The tremendous size of India, however, required far more civil servants than this Indian Civil Service, or ICS, could provide. By the mid-1800s colonial administrators began to train Indians to fill the lower ranks of government.

This training raised a major controversy among British colonial administrators. Some, known as Orientalists, argued that Indians should receive an essentially Indian education, using Indian texts and languages. Others, known as Anglicists, called for a Western education. Thomas Babington Macaulay, a historian and colonial administrator in India, became a leading spokesperson for the Anglicists:

> We must at present do our best to form a class who may be interpreters between us and the millions whom we govern; a class of persons, Indian in blood and colour, but English in taste, in opinions, in morals, and in intellect.

Eventually, the Anglicists won the debate. In 1835 English became the official language of higher education. The first three universities in India were founded in 1857 from which emerged an elite class of Western-educated Indians.

The British used their own civil servants and created a new class of Western-educated Indians to help rule their Indian Empire.

Women in the empire. As the British further extended their rule over India, people began to move to India from Britain. In the early days of the British East India Company, British men had

Imperialism in India and Southeast Asia, 1857–1914

Indian Mutiny 1857–1858

Territory in 1914:
- British
- French
- Dutch
- German
- Portuguese
- United States
- Area of colonial resistance

Defiance in Asia Although Great Britain and other countries claimed territory in Southern Asia, native peoples fought determinedly against foreign rule.

❓ **Region** What South Pacific territory did the United States claim?

▲ These Indian and British schoolteachers worked together at a school in India in the late 1800s.

moved to India without families, and some later married Indian women. The development of better transportation, however, allowed many British women and children to join their husbands and fathers in India.

European women, known as **memsahibs** (MEM-sah-ibz), brought British people in India greater contact with England and the comforts of traditional English life. Their presence reminded the British of their prejudices about the Indian people and reinforced the colonizers' sense that they were civilizing India. As a larger number of men and women from Britain came to India, social contact with the Indians appeared unnecessary. British rulers in India came to live apart from their subjects in small, conspicuously privileged circles. In addition, they become increasingly convinced of their own supposedly superior intellectual and moral capacities.

Cultural and social reforms. The early Company rulers had been anxious not to interfere with local customs. Their primary goal was to maintain the social stability that they needed to carry on trade. As British control increased, however, many people in Britain began to call for major social and cultural reforms in order to bring India the "benefits" of Western civilization. In the early 1800s these reformers began to prohibit Indian practices that the British considered immoral.

For example, in 1829 the British outlawed suttee (suh-TEE), the ritual burning of widows on their husbands' cremation fires, and in 1856 they made the remarriage of Hindu widows legal throughout India. The British also preached against child marriages and the practice of killing unwanted children.

Indian reformers. These measures, as well as the presence of Christian missionaries, contributed to increasing cultural reforms among the Indian people. Some Indians approved of the British reforms, believing they would revitalize Hindu culture. One of the most important of these leaders was a Bengali intellectual and reformer named Ram Mohun Roy.

Anxious to combat the missionaries' disapproval of Hindu culture, Roy studied the Vedas and particularly the *Upanishads* in an effort to find a basis for reforming Hinduism. He also read the Christian scriptures. Eventually, he became convinced that all great religions conveyed the same message. In 1828 Roy founded a society known as the Brahmo Samaj, or "Society of Brahma," that supported the blending of aspects of British and Indian cultures. Such an effort to reconcile the two cultures particularly appealed to the newly emerging Western-educated Indian elites.

As the British moved into the Punjab, other reformers also came forward to confront the challenge of Christianity and Western culture. Where Roy called for a blending of Western and Indian ideas, other Hindu reformers wanted to strengthen traditional Hindu society in order to resist rule by Europeans.

The most important of these reformers was Dayananda Sarasvati (dy-yuh-NAHN-duh sah-rahs-VAH-tee), who founded the Arya Samaj reformist society in Bombay in 1875. Sarasvati called upon Hindus to reject many aspects of their religion, including the caste system and child marriage, and to return to the purity of Vedic beliefs. The Arya Samaj became strongest in the northern province of the Punjab.

Cultural interaction between the British and Indians contributed to reforms in Indian culture and society.

The Indian Mutiny

Although many Indians accepted British rule, those who had been displaced from power,

Daily Life
While Ram Mohun Roy's philosophies appealed to the middle class, the upper class sought different answers to the problems occurring in Indian society. One such upper-class organization was the British Indian Association, formed in the 1850s. While the main goals of the association were to reestablish upper-class influence in government administration, its members occasionally represented the plight of all Indians. As a member of the association told an assembled group in Bombay in 1852: "The British Government professes to educate the Natives to an equality with Europeans, an object worthy of the age and of Britain. But if Englishmen after educating the Natives to be their equals continue to treat them as their inferiors—if they deny the stimulus of honourable ambition—are they not in effect undoing all they have done, unteaching the Native all that he has been taught, and pursuing a suicidal policy, which will inevitably array all the talent, honour, and intelligence of the country ultimately in irreconcilable hostility to the ruling power?"

Critical Thinking Ask students why the upper-class Indians would have joined with middle-class Indians on educational issues.

ANSWER: Students might suggest that both classes looked to education for advancement and equality with the British.

particularly the Indian princes and Mughal officials, did not. As the British continued to extend their rule, they lessened these traditional leaders' power. Rebellion soon broke out. Playing on the fears that the British wanted to convert Hindu and Muslim Indians to Christianity, the Indian leaders inspired a revolt in the Indian army in 1857. Fanned by the traditional Indian rulers, the revolt soon spread into the general population in parts of northern India.

While discontent with growing British power fueled the rebellion among both peasants and princes in northern India, the immediate cause of revolt in the army was the introduction of new cartridges for the Indian soldiers' rifles. The caps of the new cartridges had to be bitten off before loading. Soon, a false rumor began to spread among the troops that the cartridges were greased with beef and pork fat. This alarmed both Hindus and Muslims, since Hindus considered the cow to be sacred, while Muslims believed the pig to be unclean. Indian soldiers first rose in revolt at Meerut, and as news spread of their uprising, other sepoys took similar action.

Although confined to the Ganges plain, the rebellion was marked by brutality and considerable bloodshed on both sides. After an 18-day siege of the British garrison at Cawnpore, an Indian prince named Nana Sahib promised to release all those who would surrender. According to one account, after they surrendered, Nana Sahib had them all—men, women, and children—butchered and their bodies thrown into nearby wells. Several days later a British force,

▲ British forces recaptured the important city of Lucknow in March 1858, which gave the British the upper hand in the Indian Mutiny.

led by Sir Henry Havelock, recaptured the city and discovered the massacre. After news of the "wells of Cawnpore" spread, the British sought revenge. Sir Henry Havelock described the British counterattack against the rebels:

66 *Whenever a rebel is caught he is immediately tried, and unless he can prove a defence he is sentenced to be hanged at once. . . . My object is to inflict a fearful punishment for a revolting, cowardly, barbarous deed, and to strike terror into these rebels.* 99

The British began executing anyone even suspected of having participated in the mutiny. Such brutality left much bitterness on both sides.

The **Indian Mutiny**, as the British called the uprising, did not affect most of India. The majority of the Indian army and of Western-educated Indians remained loyal to the British. Ironically, however, the uprising convinced most British officials in India that the policy of Anglicization and reform had been a mistake. The new British government of India largely abandoned the Western-educated Indian elites and instead sought the support of more traditional Indian leaders.

The British Raj

The rebellion also convinced the British government that Company rule should be abolished once and for all. Thereafter, the governor-general, who became known as the viceroy, was appointed directly by the British government and supervised by a secretary of state for India. Administration continued to be carried out by the ICS, its members chosen by competitive examination in Britain.

The vast majority of lower-level government employees were Indian. Meanwhile, generations of young British officials in their twenties and thirties became district commissioners ruling as many as a million Indians—collecting taxes, dispensing justice, and overseeing development projects such as irrigation works and bridge-building.

As the British solidified their rule, they grew more concerned with defending India against invasion. In the northwest the British tried to establish a government in Afghanistan as a buffer state against Russian invaders. As early as the 1830s, Lord Auckland, the governor-general of India, defended Britain's extension of its influence:

66 Russia can have no legitimate ground for extending her political connections to Afghanistan, while we are necessarily interested in the peace and independence of that country by proximity [nearness] and position. 99

The British also worried about India's eastern borders. After several wars with the kingdom of Burma, by 1886 Britain had annexed all of Burmese territory. The British wanted to end Burmese raids into India and discourage the French from gaining influence in the region. Meanwhile, the British extended their control up the Malay Peninsula from Singapore, where Stamford Raffles, a British merchant and adventurer, had established a colony in 1819.

The Indian Mutiny convinced the British government that it must take control of India and rule the subcontinent as an empire.

French Indochina

As the British were establishing their rule in India in the late 1700s, a few French merchants were trading in the South China Sea off the coast of Vietnam. After a new emperor, Gia-long, established the Nguyen (NUH-WIN) dynasty in Vietnam with his capital at Hue (hoo-AY) in 1802, a group of French adventurers joined his army. At the same time, French Catholic missionaries were trying to spread Christianity in Vietnam.

The new Vietnamese dynasty did its best to remain independent from both China and France. However, in 1859 the French seized the city of Saigon, and by 1867 they were demanding control of Vietnam's southern provinces. Phan Thanh Gian (PAHN TAHN GYAHN), the governor of three provinces near Saigon, had no choice but to turn them over. He explained:

▲ The French applied their elaborate architectural style to the governor's palace in Saigon.

66 I have said: 'It would be as senseless for you to wish to defeat your enemies by force of arms as for a young fawn to attack a tiger. You attract uselessly great misfortunes upon the people whom Heaven has confided to you.' 99

From this new colony of Cochin China, the French tried to further extend their influence.

Eventually, France's expansion into Vietnam alarmed the Chinese, who considered both Vietnam and Cambodia their own tributary states. War in the mid-1880s resulted in a French victory and Chinese recognition of a French protectorate over the rest of Vietnam.

Meanwhile, during the 1860s France had also declared a protectorate over Cambodia. In the 1890s the French created another new protectorate, Laos, out of small principalities between Vietnam and Cambodia. These three protectorates—Vietnam, Cambodia, and Laos—became known as French Indochina.

Siam

The only major country in the region remaining independent of European imperial powers was Siam (present-day Thailand). In 1851 the foresighted King Mongkut ascended the throne of

SECTION 3
REVIEW ANSWERS

IDENTIFY
For significance, see the following pages:
sepoys (p. 579)
raj (p. 579)
memsahibs (p. 581)
Ram Mohun Roy (p. 581)
Indian Mutiny (p. 582)
King Mongkut (p. 583)

LOCATE
For locations, see the map on p. 580.

1. They believed that the Indians needed Western-style educations to serve as interpreters and help them run the empire.
2. Interaction with the British caused many reforms in society and culture, as well as a movement by some to return to traditional Hindu beliefs.
3. Siam was able to remain an independent state, while the rest of Southeast Asia was taken over by the French and Dutch, who established protectorates and colonies.
4. Essays should explain that the cause of the Indian Mutiny was the belief that the gun cartridges were greased with beef and pork fat. Also, ousted leaders were unhappy and incited a revolt within the army. As a result, Britain changed its imperial policy to reflect more traditional Indian beliefs.
5. The Company was responsible for the rule of India during the 1800s. This changed as a result of the Indian Mutiny.

Siam. He was fully aware of the difficult position Siam occupied between the European imperial powers.

In addition to being a devout and scholarly Buddhist, Mongkut also studied such Western subjects as English, mathematics, and Latin. Not only did this well-educated monarch play the British and French against each other in order to maintain Siam's independence, he also promoted certain Western technologies and practices, such as printing, vaccinations, and Western-style education.

Later Siamese rulers reorganized their government along Western lines. By selectively accepting Western elements, Siam achieved the internal strength and stability needed to maintain its freedom. Although Siam eventually had to give up some territory to both Britain and France, the ruling family managed to maintain Siam's independence as a buffer state between the two imperial rivals.

▶ **King Mongkut protected Siam from Western imperialism in the 1800s through diplomatic relations with Europe and the United States.**

Dutch Expansion in Indonesia

While the British and French were trying to control the Asian mainland, the Dutch were beginning to expand their 200-year-old holdings in Indonesia. Bitter resistance from the local aristocracy, however, led by the Javanese prince, Pangeran Dipanagara, sparked a war between 1825 and 1830, in which some 200,000 Javanese died. The victorious Dutch then exiled Dipanagara and extended their colonial rule.

At about the same time, the Dutch were drawn into a war with the Muslim population of western Sumatra. The Padri War, named after the town of Pedir, erupted in the early 1820s and lasted until 1837. The Dutch eventually defeated the Sumatrans, and the struggle only strengthened Dutch resolve to control the islands.

The French and the Dutch established protectorates and colonies in Southeast Asia, while Siam remained an independent buffer state.

SECTION 3 REVIEW

IDENTIFY and explain the significance of the following:
  sepoys
  raj
  memsahibs
  Ram Mohun Roy
  Indian Mutiny
  King Mongkut

LOCATE and explain the importance of the following:
  Cawnpore
  Hue
  Saigon

French Indochina
Siam
Sumatra

1. **Main Idea** Why did some British officials encourage a Western-style education for Indians?
2. **Main Idea** What effect did interaction with the British have on Indian society?
3. **Cross-cultural Interaction** How did contact with Western imperialists differ

in Siam and the rest of Southeast Asia?
4. **Writing to Explain** In a short essay, explain why the Indian Mutiny occurred and how it affected both Indian and British people living in India.
5. **Synthesizing** What role did the British East India Company play in India's government during the early 1800s? Why did this role change?

Imperialism in East Asia

While the British, French, and Dutch extended their influence in Southeast Asia, the great prize for European merchants was the China trade. By the late 1700s European and American merchants were anxious to force the Qing Empire to expand trade with the outside world. Japan was also opened to outside influences in the mid-1850s. Both China and Japan underwent enormous changes in response to Western contacts.

German advertisement for Chinese tea

The Decline of the Qing Empire

By the late 1700s the Qing dynasty was in decline. The army had fallen apart, and bandits roamed the countryside. The civil-service system had grown so corrupt that wealthy parents could buy jobs for their sons, regardless of ability. This corruption led to a neglect of the basic functions of government. The ill-maintained dikes along the Huang He allowed vast areas to flood in the late 1870s, which destroyed fields and livestock and left millions of peasants homeless.

Adding to the problem was China's population, which had grown at an alarming rate during the Qing dynasty. Between 1750 and 1850 the population more than doubled, jumping to 430 million people. The corrupt bureaucracy proved unable to cope with such rapid growth.

"Foreign devils." China also faced new challenges from outside—particularly from the Europeans. By the end of the 1700s, European merchants were eager to obtain Chinese goods. The British had become particularly interested in obtaining Chinese tea, which had become an enormously popular drink in Britain.

However, the ailing Qing dynasty feared foreign contacts. The Chinese saw the Europeans as barbarians and had little need for their products. They referred to Europeans as "foreign devils." China's foreign relations had always been conducted according to the so-called "tribute system," in which all trade from outside China was seen as tribute to the emperor. Westerners, however, now began to demand that China permit trade on an equal basis.

Under pressure from Europeans and some Chinese merchants, the Qing eventually permitted a strictly limited trade through the port city of Guangzhou. Western merchants could only trade with members of a tightly controlled Chinese merchant guild in Guangzhou, and they had to pay for their Chinese goods with silver. European trade goods held little attraction for the Chinese, however, which created a great trade imbalance in China's favor.

The Opium War. Eventually, British and American merchants discovered a product that the Chinese would pay silver to buy in increasingly

SECTION 4

CORE LESSON PLAN
See pages 563I and 563J for Lesson Plan 21.4.

Theme: Economic Organization

The spread of opium addiction can most likely be traced to increased government corruption, rapid population growth, and rebellion among the Chinese people. Importing or producing opium became illegal in 1796, and other bans were passed in the 1800s. Despite these measures, from 1800 to 1821 around 4,500 chests of opium were imported into China per year. By 1838 the number of chests had reached 40,000.

Critical Thinking Ask students why opium imports to China increased even as the government made the drug illegal.

ANSWER: Students might suggest that opium addiction caused a high demand and social disorder made enforcement difficult.

large quantities—opium. Western merchants bought opium from India, where opium poppies were legally grown, and smuggled it into China in exchange for silver. They then used the silver to buy Chinese silks, teas, and other goods in Guangzhou. By the 1830s opium sales had grown so dramatically that the imbalance of trade had been reversed.

Alarmed by the drain of silver from China's economy to pay for opium, as well as worried by the health and economic problems the drug was causing, Chinese authorities worked to stop the opium trade. In 1839 Lin Zexu, the imperial commissioner sent to Guangzhou to end the illegal trade, wrote a letter appealing to Queen Victoria:

66 *Suppose there were people from another country who carried opium for sale to England and seduced your people into buying and smoking it; certainly your honorable ruler would deeply hate it and be bitterly aroused.* **99**

Commissioner Lin's active suppression of the opium trade directly threatened the interests of foreign merchants. Under pressure from British merchants, in 1839 Britain went to war with China in an effort to force the emperor to accept equal trade relations. In what became known as the **Opium War**, the British defeated the Chinese and forced them to accept a new trade agreement. In addition, China paid a large war indemnity, or settlement, and ceded the island of Hong Kong to Great Britain.

The "unequal" treaties. Despite their defeat in the Opium War, Chinese officials continued to resist dealing with the westerners. With British gunboats threatening their coastal cities, however, over the next 20 years the Chinese signed a series of "unequal" treaties with Britain, France, the United States, and Russia. In addition to trading rights, these agreements gave westerners **extraterritoriality**, meaning that they could only be tried in Western courts under Western law. The Chinese resisted the spirit of these treaties, and in 1858 and 1860 the Europeans decided to use force to implement these agreements. British and French troops even occupied Beijing in 1860. Only then did the imper-ial court finally acknowledge the end of the old order of tributary relations.

The Taiping Rebellion. While the Chinese people suffered under direct European military intervention, Western culture also fueled the discontent that many of them felt toward their government. As the Qing continued to lose power and prestige to the Europeans, Hong Xiuquan (HOOHNG shee-oo-choo-AHN), a new leader in southern China, rebelled against the dynasty. Hong Xiuquan, who had been exposed to Christianity by missionaries, believed that he was the younger brother of Jesus Christ and that God had commanded him to save humanity.

Hong Xiuquan preached a message of social equality, including equality for women, an end to footbinding, and a call for strict moral behavior. He and his followers rebelled against the Qing emperor in 1850 and proclaimed a new dynasty, the Taiping, or "Heavenly Peace." The **Taiping Rebellion** swept through nearly half of China.

The Qing responded to the Taiping Rebellion by relying on traditional loyal Confucian supporters, as well as by adapting Western methods of warfare and technology. Eventually, imperial forces put an end to the rebellion in 1864. Millions of people died during the revolt, which left cities and countryside destroyed. The Taiping Rebellion further weakened China's position against the Europeans.

***W**hile Europeans forced China open to trade, Western cultural influences contributed to internal rebellion.*

▲ In this painting, soldiers in the Taiping Rebellion attack a Chinese town.

Reform and Reaction

Both the series of foreign interventions and the Taiping Rebellion at last convinced many Chinese scholar-officials that China could only be saved through reform. Under the Tongzhi emperor, China underwent a major reform program that became known as the **Tongzhi Restoration**.

Major reform efforts included lowering farm taxes and undertaking water-control projects, such as repairing and maintaining dikes. China tried to build a modern military to protect itself, improved its communication and transportation systems, and translated Western textbooks on technology and international law into Chinese.

Through all of these reform efforts, the Confucian officials hoped that adapting Western methods of education and technology could somehow help preserve China's traditional culture from destruction by the West. Despite efforts to eliminate corruption from the civil service, however, the reforms only affected the upper levels of the bureaucracy.

At the imperial court, reforms and foreign intervention were met by a strongly conservative reaction that was led by the Empress Dowager Cixi (TSOO-SHEE). Born in 1835, Cixi had witnessed the effects of the Opium War and the Taiping Rebellion while growing up in the imperial court. She was also present when the British and French occupied Beijing in 1860 and destroyed the emperor's

BIOGRAPHY

BIOGRAPHY

BIOGRAPHY

Empress Dowager Cixi
Empress Dowager Cixi totally dominated her young son, Emperor Tongzhi. According to Chinese legend, she even supported the life of excess that contributed to his death in January 1875 at age 19. To hold on to the power that she had enjoyed during his reign, Cixi dispensed with the laws of succession and had her four-year-old nephew selected as emperor, under the title Guangxu, which means "Glorious Succession." She continued to rule as regent until 1889, when her nephew took over his imperial duties.

Critical Thinking Ask students why Cixi may have used such ruthless methods to hold on to power.

ANSWER: Students might suggest that Cixi felt she had to fight for power or that she believed the troubled times in China demanded strong leadership.

Imperialism in East Asia, 1839–1912

Masters of the Seas The European powers and Japan claimed expansive spheres of influence for themselves in East Asia.

Location Which sphere of influence was least likely to be directly influenced by the Boxer Rebellion?

Map Answer
French

Empress Dowager Cixi

BIOGRAPHY

splendid summer palace. Thereafter, she seems to have remained a bitter opponent of westernizing reforms.

Acting as regent for the emperors, Cixi dominated China for over 40 years. Cixi remained conservative and often prevented many reforms. For example, she diverted the funds for China's new navy in the late 1880s in order to rebuild the summer palace. In place of the navy, she had a magnificent marble pavilion constructed in the shape of a boat in the lake of the new palace. Cixi, or Old Buddha, as she was often called by westerners, retired from public life in 1889, but returned in 1898 when the emperor began to enact new, more far-reaching reforms.

The Boxer Rebellion

Cixi gained the support of those who feared the effects of Western culture and technology on China. Some of those who reacted against the influence of the West were members of a secret society, the Society of the Harmonious Fists. Although initially anti-Qing, the Society was even more antiforeign. Called **Boxers** by westerners, they rose in revolt in 1900, wanting to cleanse China of foreign influences. As one Boxer poster proclaimed:

> *The Catholics . . . have conspired with foreigners, have caused China trouble, wasted our national revenue, broken up our monasteries, destroyed Buddhist images, and seized our people's graveyards. . . . Now . . . all the spirits have descended . . . to teach our young men their magic boxing so they can . . . extinguish the foreigners.*

The movement spread quickly across northern China as the Boxers called on all Chinese to "support the Qing, destroy the foreign."

For eight weeks the Boxers attacked missionaries and journalists and even laid siege to the diplomatic community in Beijing. Although suspicious of the Boxers, Cixi eventually supported their actions, declaring war on all the Western powers in China.

A German-led international army arrived to stop the violence and found thousands of Chinese Christians and foreign civilians slain by the Boxers. As the Boxers fell before the West's firepower, Cixi fled the capital and went into exile. She returned to power once more in 1902, but as the empire crumbled around her, Cixi finally accepted the need for reform and promised a constitutional government in 1906. Two years later both she and the emperor died, leaving the empire in the hands of a three-year-old child. He was to be the last emperor of China.

▲ European soldiers return to camp with flags they captured during the Boxer Rebellion in 1900.

The End of the Qing Dynasty

A new generation of Western-educated Chinese leaders concluded that the adoption of Western ideas was the only means to restore China's independence. The most influential of these leaders was Sun Yixian. He formed a revolutionary society in 1905 aimed at overthrowing the Qing and establishing a constitutional government.

That same year, the examination system for the civil service was abolished. Now Western-educated Chinese students no longer had to conform to the traditional system in order to get a government job, and they began to spread Western ideas at an even more rapid rate. The next few years were marked by rebellions against the Qing government. Eventually, between 1911 and 1912, Western-educated Chinese overthrew the dynasty and proclaimed the establishment of the Chinese Republic. The new government proved unable to maintain control of the old empire, however, and China gradually slipped into a period of chaos.

Late in the Qing Empire, Western-style reforms resulted in reaction and revolution, leaving China at the mercy of the imperial powers.

Japan and the West

While Europeans were forcing China open, the United States pursued a similar goal in Japan. Since the 1600s Japan had remained largely isolated under the Tokugawa shoguns.

Under the Tokugawa shogunate Japan kept out most foreign influences. There was some minor trade with the Dutch, but as late as 1825 an imperial decree ordered Japanese officials to drive off all foreign ships. Such regulations offended many European countries. In the 1800s whaling vessels from the Western nations also resented Japanese refusals to allow them to land and resupply or repair their ships after storms at sea. The United States in particular became determined to open Japan to the outside world.

In 1852 U.S. president Millard Fillmore commanded Commodore Matthew Perry to begin negotiations with the Japanese aimed at establishing diplomatic relations. In 1853 Perry's squadron anchored in Edo (later called Tokyo) Bay, and Perry demanded that the Japanese enter into immediate negotiations with the United States.

Unable to resist the threat of a naval bombardment, in 1854 the shogun gave in to Perry's demands and signed a treaty with the United States. Within months representatives from Great Britain, France, and Russia demanded similar recognition. Like China, Japan had to accept a series of unequal treaties with the Western powers, and the disgrace of the shogun's defeat weakened the power of the shogunate.

Japanese Responses to Imperialism

Perry's demands threw Japan into a state of crisis. Many of the Japanese aristocracy believed that unless Japan could rapidly acquire the same technology that the westerners possessed, it was only a matter of time before the country was swallowed up completely by Europeans.

The Meiji Restoration. While the Tokugawa shoguns resisted reforms, a number of leading samurai came together in the 1860s demanding Western-style reforms. In 1868 these samurai overthrew the shogunate and restored the emperor to power in what became known as the **Meiji Restoration**, named after the Meiji emperor. With the emperor's approval, they instituted wide-reaching reforms. They abolished feudalism and adopted a constitution based on the autocratic model of Prussia.

Japan also began to build up its defenses as well as its industrial base. Prince Ito Hirobumi explained Japan's method of modernization:

❝ *Being faced, from the outset, with a need for experts, we sent talented young students to Europe and America to master various fields of science and technology, and, when this task was accomplished, we established all kinds of schools in Japan. . . . We adopted the European judiciary system, enacted [necessary] laws and strengthened*

▲ **In this woodblock print, a Japanese artist recorded Commodore Perry's arrival in Edo Bay in 1853.**

THE IMPERIAL WORLD ORDER **589**

1. Europeans forced China open to trade, and Western cultural influences helped contribute to the Taiping Rebellion.
2. Westernizing reforms were met by a conservative reaction from Cixi, as well as rebellion by other groups who feared Western influence. Later rebels overthrew the government to gain Western reform.
3. Samurai overthrew the shogunate, enacted Western-style reforms and styles of government, and promoted industrialization.
4. Speeches should suggest that unless Japan enacts reforms and promotes the use of Western technology, it is in danger of being swallowed up by Western countries instead of maintaining its independence.
5. Answers should focus on the idea that China might have been better able to resist Western demands, such as the "unequal" treaties. The Qing dynasty might also have been able to remain in power.

CHAPTER 21 REVIEW ANSWERS
(p. 591)

WRITING A SUMMARY
See essential points in the text.

REVIEWING TERMS
1. Tongzhi Restoration
2. Great Trek
3. Meiji Restoration
4. extraterritoriality
5. raj

590

---

our military forces. The Europeans could have no objection."

Industrialization was carried out from the top down. The government initiated the establishment of the first major industries, building factories for producing cement, glass, textiles, and munitions, as well as such things as railways and modern shipyards. The government also sent students overseas to Western universities to study Western technology, and brought foreign experts to Japan to improve industry.

Eventually, these state enterprises were sold off to a relatively small group of well-connected samurai and others favored by the Meiji government. These entrepreneurs soon used their positions to create enormous industrial and financial organizations, known as **zaibatsu**, which came to dominate

▲ These Japanese generals, in a photograph from 1905, show the influence of Western styles of dress on Japan's military leaders.

the Japanese economy and concentrated economic power in the hands of a few families.

Japanese imperialism. By imitating the West, Japan not only remained independent but also became an imperial power in its own right. Japan defeated China in the 1894–95 Sino-Japanese War. In the peace treaty China lost Taiwan to Japan, gave Japan all privileges awarded to Western powers in China, and recognized Korea's independence.

Independent Korea soon became a target of Russian imperial expansion, however. Worried by Russian advances into the region, Japan sought an alliance with Great Britain. In the 1902 Anglo-Japanese Alliance, each nation agreed to support the other if it were attacked by two or more countries. This alliance meant that Japan had finally been accepted as an equal by a Western power.

In 1904 Japan clashed with the Russian Empire, which had expanded eastward to the Pacific Ocean during the 1800s. The Japanese soundly defeated the Russians, sinking Russia's entire fleet in the Tsushima Strait. Thus, Japan had become a great world power.

Japan responded to Western imperialism by adopting Western methods of government and industrialization to become a great power.

SECTION 4 REVIEW

IDENTIFY and explain the significance of the following:
Opium War
extraterritoriality
Taiping Rebellion
Tongzhi Restoration
Cixi
Boxers
Matthew Perry
Meiji Restoration
zaibatsu

LOCATE and explain the importance of the following:
Guangzhou

Beijing
Edo (Tokyo) Bay

1. *Main Idea* What effects did Western imperialism and cultural influences have in China?
2. *Main Idea* What were the responses to westernizing reforms within the Qing Empire?
3. *Cross-cultural Interaction* How did Japan react to the threat of Western imperialism?

4. *Writing to Persuade* Imagine that you are a Japanese samurai during the Meiji era. Write a short speech trying to convince your fellow samurai to support westernizing reform as a means of fighting off the westerners.
5. *Hypothesizing* How might China's history have been different if the Chinese had reacted to Western imperialism in a way similar to the Japanese response?

Review

On a separate sheet of paper, complete the following exercises:

WRITING A SUMMARY

Using the essential points in the text, write a brief summary of the chapter.

REVIEWING TERMS

From the following list, choose the term that correctly matches the definition.

Great Trek
extraterritoriality
Meiji Restoration
Tongzhi Restoration
raj
spheres of influence

1. period of reform in China meant to strengthen the country against the West
2. mass migration of the Boers into the African interior
3. period of Japanese history in which the shogunate was overthrown, the emperor was restored to power once more, and many Western-style reforms were enacted
4. right of Europeans to be exempt from Chinese law
5. rule of the British in India, which was first applied to the British East India Company and later to the British government

REVIEWING CHRONOLOGY

List the following events in their correct chronological order.

1. Delegates meet at the Berlin Conference to lay ground rules for imperialism in Africa.
2. Japan wins the Sino-Japanese War.
3. Chinese revolutionaries overthrow the Qing dynasty, ending imperial rule.
4. The Zulu defeat the British at the battle of Isandhlwana.
5. The Indian Mutiny breaks out.

UNDERSTANDING THE MAIN IDEA

1. What changes occurred around 1870 that renewed the interest of European nations in imperialism?
2. How did Africans respond to European imperialism?
3. Why did the Indian Mutiny occur, and what effect did it have on both the Indians and the British?
4. What impact did Western imperialism and cultural influences have on China?
5. How successful were the Japanese in their response to Western imperialism?

THINKING CRITICALLY

1. **Contrasting** How was British imperialism in China different than that in India?
2. **Evaluating** Why were the British able to build such a vast empire? Why did France and Germany lag behind in the scramble for colonies and protectorates?

Building Your Portfolio

Complete the following activities individually or in groups.

1. **Imperial Africa** Imagine that you (and your coworkers) have been hired by a museum to create an annotated map of imperialism in Africa. On posterboard or a large piece of paper, create a map showing the partition of Africa by the European imperial powers. Your map should also include important events in the division of Africa, such as battles. For at least five of the events on your map, write a brief description of the event and its significance. Place these annotations near the events' locations on the map.
2. **Cultural Change** Imagine that it is 1911 and you (and your friends) are Chinese men or women. You were born in Guangzhou 80 years ago, but as a young adult, you moved to Beijing, where you have lived ever since. You want your grandchildren to know about the changes in China that you have seen during your lifetime, so you have decided to write a passage describing how contact with Europeans changed life in China and how you saw the power of the Qing dynasty decline. Take into account that the historical context will shape your descriptions of the events taking place in 1911.

REVIEWING CHRONOLOGY

5, 4, 1, 2, 3

UNDERSTANDING THE MAIN IDEA

1. increased nationalism and demand for raw materials
2. Many Africans initially tried to use Europeans to their advantage for weapons and other goods, but resisted when Europeans' intentions became clear.
3. Ousted leaders started a revolt within the army when a rumor circulated that the gun cartridges were greased with beef and pork fat. The result was bitterness on both sides and a change in British imperial policy.
4. Although many Chinese initially opposed Western influences, a later generation of Western-educated leaders overthrew the government and proclaimed a republic, only to cause chaos in China.
5. Japan was very successful and eventually became an imperialist power in its own right.

THINKING CRITICALLY

1. Initially, British imperialism in China required the use of force because of the Chinese aversion to outside influence. In India, the political system was so disorganized that Indian rulers welcomed European allies.
2. As the first industrialized nation, Britain's political and economic power allowed it to build a vast empire. Germany and France industrialized later.

Unit 6
The Modern World in Crisis 1880–1945

Chapter 22

World War I and After
1914–1924

Between 1914 and 1918 the great powers of the world fought one of the bloodiest wars in history. The peace settlement that followed eventually became the foundation for future conflict. How might alliances among nations cause a small regional conflict to grow into a major international war?

Chapter 23

Revolution, Depression, and Totalitarianism 1917–1938

After World War I the world was rocked by uncertainty and change. Revolution swept through Russia, the Great Depression left millions of people unemployed and poverty-stricken, and dictators seized control of many national governments. What effects might massive unemployment have on governments and societies?

World War I, one of the bloodiest wars in history, left many people calling for a new world order. Across Europe, the postwar peace settlement unintentionally laid the foundation for future conflict. Europe hardly had time to recover from the war when the Great Depression hit in 1929, throwing millions of people out of work and causing many to turn to powerful dictators to restore their economies.

Soon, the totalitarian powers of Germany, Italy, and Japan began a period of rapid territorial expansion.

Meanwhile, people living in European and American colonies began to demand the same rights and privileges enjoyed by citizens of imperial nations, although the achievement of freedom would have to wait until the end of another devastating war—World War II.

Chapter 24
The Beginnings of Colonial Nationalism 1880-1939

In the age of imperialism, European colonists and non-European elites developed their own senses of identity, demanding the same rights and privileges enjoyed by citizens of imperial nations. How might imperialism contribute to the flow of ideas and worldviews from one culture to another?

Chapter 25
Growing Aggression and World War II
1922-1945

The peace settlement following World War I humiliated Germany, created unstable new states in Eastern Europe, and left two Allied powers dissatisfied. These issues ultimately contributed to the outbreak of World War II, which would prove even greater in scope and devastation than World War I. How might new technology affect the fighting of a war?

Chapter 24
The Beginnings of Colonial Nationalism

Imperialism might bring people from various cultures together through trade and colonization. As they come into contact, these people might learn about each other's cultures and ideas, and they might choose to adopt some of them as their own.

Chapter 25
Growing Aggression and World War II

Technological advances could allow for the creation of new and more powerful weapons. These weapons could give one side a great advantage over the other.

REVIEW & ASSESSMENT RESOURCES

- Unit Synthesis 6
- Unit Test 6
- Sheltered English Unit Test 6

All Levels

Chapter 22

World War I and After 1914–1924

Chapter Planning Guide

	TEXTBOOK	CORE RESOURCES	VISUAL RESOURCES	MULTIMEDIA
Introduction	pp. 594–595	Block Scheduling Handbook: Ch. 22		Videodisc Segment 22 and Viewing Guide: *The Great War*
Lesson 22.1 Origins of World War I	pp. 596–601 Map: *Europe on the Eve of World War I*, p. 598	Reading 22.1: *Leading Up to War*		GHRC 22 Readings: *Europe's Leaders Call Their Nations to War; War Fever in Vienna* GHRC 22/Videodiscs: Map— *The Schlieffen Plan, 1905*
Lesson 22.2 A New Kind of War	pp. 602–605 Then and Now: *Submarines*, p. 604	Reading 22.2: *A Soldier Remembers the Tank* Skills Activity 22: *Using an Electronic Library Catalog*		GHRC 22 Readings: *The Tank in World War I; Women and World War I; Letters from an American Nurse* GHRC 22/Videodiscs: Images— *Poison Gas; WWI Hospital for Wounded Troops; French Women in War and Peace*
Lesson 22.3 The Course of the War	pp. 606–613 Map: *The Western Front*, p. 607 Map: *The Eastern Front*, p. 608 Map: *War in the Middle East*, p. 609 Literature Through Time: *Wartime Poetry*, p. 611	Reading 22.3: *Songs of a Campaign* Geography Activity 22: *World War I*	Everyday Life 22: *American Posters from World War I*	GHRC 22 Readings: *German U-Boat 202 Attacks a Steamer; Lawrence of Arabia Destroys a Turkish Column* GHRC 22/Videodiscs: Images— *African-American Doughboy in France; "Wake Up America" Parade in WWI; Map—World War I Troop Strength and Casualties*
Lesson 22.4 The Peace Settlement	pp. 614–618 Biography: *Georges Clemenceau*, p. 615 Map: *The Mandate System*, p. 617	Reading 22.4: *The Germans are Informed of the Terms of the Treaty of Versailles* Writing Project 22: *Writing a Diary*		GHRC 22 Readings: *Georges Clemenceau at the Peace Conference; Germans Debate the Treaty of Versailles*
Lesson 22.5 Consequences of the War	pp. 619–622 Map: *Europe on the Eve of World War I*, p. 598 Map: *Europe After the Versailles Settlements*, p. 620 Graph: *World War I Battlefield Losses*, p. 622	Reading 22.5: *Charles Dawes and Reparations*	Geography and History 22: *Europe and the Middle East After World War I* Art and History 22: *In the Trenches: Battle Sketches of World War I*	GHRC 22 Readings: *A Postwar Program of Social Reconstruction; War Fever in Vienna* GHRC 22/Videodiscs: Image— *Total War in Termonde, Belgium*
Chapter Investigation and Enrichment	pp. 594–622	Chapter 22 Investigation: *Reflections on the Great War* People in World History 22 Explorations in Daily Life 22		GHRC 22/Videodiscs
Review and Assessment	Section 1 Review, p. 601 Section 2 Review, p. 605 Section 3 Review, p. 613 Section 4 Review, p. 618 Section 5 Review, p. 622 Chapter 22 Review, p. 623	Chapter Review Activity 22 Vocabulary Activity 22 Themes Review 22 Section Study Guides 22.1–22.5 Main Idea Activities 22.1–22.5 Daily Quizzes 22.1–22.5 Chapter 22 Test Sheltered English Ch. 22 Test Ch. 22 Test Generator		Audio CDs: Ch. 22 Summary (English and Spanish)

INTRODUCING THE CHAPTER

Textbook pp. 594–595

CHAPTER OVERVIEW

In 1914 the European balance of power gave way to war under the pressure of a crisis in the Balkans. Governments centralized control in an effort to command the resources needed for the war effort. Allied control of the seas and American entry into the war helped end the initial stalemate. The peace settlement failed to resolve all the issues that led to war and also created new problems, however.

PRESENTING THEMES

On the chalkboard or on an overhead transparency, write the following open-ended theme questions.

- **WAR AND DIPLOMACY** How might alliances among nations cause a small regional conflict to grow into a major international war?
- **TECHNOLOGY** How might technological developments affect the way wars are fought?
- **SOCIAL RELATIONS** How might wars affect society on the home fronts?

Have students, either individually or in groups, suggest responses to the questions. For the war and diplomacy question, students might suggest that a system of alliances could obligate nations to become involved in wars started by their allies. For the technology question, students might suggest that new technologies could make previous defensive strategies ineffective, requiring new offensive strategies. For the social relations question, students might suggest that war might lead to civilian rationing, casualties, and property losses. Save the responses. Once students have studied the chapter, you may wish to have students complete the Themes Review, then compare the two sets of answers.

USING THE VIDEO

Segment 22: *The Great War*

ENGLISH

Search Chapter 22
Videodisc 2, Side A

SPANISH

Search Chapter 22
Videodisc 2, Side A

Tell students that in this chapter they will examine World War I, the first global conflict of this century. Then show Segment 22 of the *World History and Cultures Videodiscs*. This segment uses archival film and photographs of World War I battle scenes and urban destruction. The video also illustrates trench warfare, the use of tanks and airplanes, and the extent of the devastation that resulted from the war.

Before showing the segment, ask students to watch for weapons they think were being used for the first time in World War I. To help students grasp the significant points of the segment, have them complete Video Viewing Guide 22.

Key to Ability Levels

All strategies and activities are coded to the following ability levels:

LEVEL 1	**Basic** activities suitable for all students
LEVEL 2	**Average** activities suitable for average to above-average students
LEVEL 3	**Challenging** activities suitable for above-average students
SHELTERED ENGLISH	Activities suitable for students with **Limited English Proficiency**

Additional Resources

BOOKS FOR TEACHERS

Bruce, Anthony. *An Illustrated Companion to the First World War.* Viking Penguin, 1990. Offers a documentary view of World War I.

Coffman, Edward M. *The War to End All Wars: The American Military Experience in World War I.* University of Wisconsin Press, 1986. Discusses the American military in World War I.

Schneider, Dorothy and Carl J. *Into the Breach: American Women Overseas in World War I.* Viking Penguin, 1991. Discusses the American women who took part in World War I.

BOOKS FOR STUDENTS

Bosco, Peter. *World War I.* Facts on File, 1991. Presents an overview of the war that is appropriate for students reading below grade level.

Freidel, Frank. *Over There: The Story of America's First Great Overseas Crusade.* Temple University Press, 1990. Gives an illustrated account of American involvement in the war.

Winter, J. M. *The Experience of World War I.* Oxford University Press, 1989. Makes use of dramatic photographs and text to tell the story of the war.

MULTIMEDIA MATERIALS

Causes of World War I. ZCI. CD-ROM, MAC, WIN, MPC. Focuses on the complex causes of this conflict using visuals, period music, and recent scholarship.

The Great War—1918. PBS. Video, 60 min. Depicts American involvement in the war by using letters and diaries of soldiers.

Men of Bronze. Films Incorporated. Video, 58 min. Reviews the role of African American soldiers in World War I.

Lesson 22.1 · Origins of World War I

Textbook pp. 596–601

RESOURCES

Pupil's Edition

Map, p. 598: *Europe on the Eve of World War I, 1914*

Core Resources

Reading 22.1: *Leading Up to War*

Global History Resource Center

Reading: *Europe's Leaders Call Their Nations to War*

Reading: *War Fever in Vienna*

Videodiscs or Global History Resource Center

Map: *The Schlieffen Plan, 1905*

Search Frame 981

LESSON FOCUS

How did nationalism, imperialism, militarism, and shifting alliances contribute to the outbreak of World War I?

OBJECTIVES

After completing this lesson, students will be able to:

- identify the factors that contributed to the outbreak of World War I;
- describe how the rise of a strong Germany affected the balance of power in Europe;
- explain why conflict in the Balkans spread to the rest of Europe in 1914.

HOOK: Link to Today

Analyze the effects of nationalism on attitudes and ideals in pre–World War I Europe. Poll students to discover those who are enthusiastic supporters of a sports team. Ask these fans how they show their support for their teams. *[by attending or watching games, attending pep rallies, wearing clothing with team colors or insignia, and so on]* Continue by asking students why they support sports teams. *[Possible responses include: family members or friends also support the team, supporting the team provides fans with a special identity, pride in the team's community]* Then ask students why there is rivalry among fans of different teams. *[desire for the team to win]*

Have students compare fan rivalry to national rivalries in pre–World War I Europe. Point out that many Europeans glorified their nations, which led to the scramble for empire and the drive to militarize.

Ask: Why might nationalism lead to conflict among nations?
[National rivalries, particularly when combined with militarism, might easily lead to acts of aggression by one nation against another.]

Assign Core Resources Reading 22.1. Conclude by having students discuss how nationalism can influence a government's policies.

DEVELOP

Examine how Germany's rise to power helped create the system of alliances in pre–World War I Europe. Have students carefully read the section "A New Balance of Power" on textbook pages 597–599. Encourage them to pay close attention to the map showing Europe just before the war. Ask a volunteer to explain how Germany's growing power affected relations among European nations. Ensure that students understand that European nations formed alliances to counter Germany's strength and to further their own interests.

Next ask students to identify members of the various pre–World War I alliances, and list them on the chalkboard. Organize students into small groups and have each group design a diagram or model that illustrates the European alliance system.

You may want to bring in materials (foam balls, string, pipe cleaners, paper or cardboard circles, etc.) to help groups make their diagrams or models.

Have groups display and explain their completed diagrams or models. Then display the electronic media map of the Schlieffen Plan and have students discuss the following question: Which nations would be brought into war by a German attack on France? Ask students to use their projects to demonstrate other "war scenarios."

PROBE

Explain how regional conflict in Europe touched off a world war. Write the following equation on the chalkboard:
Territorial expansion + nationalism = assassination of Archduke Francis Ferdinand

Call on a volunteer to explain the equation. *[Austria's annexation of Bosnia and Herzegovina angered Serbian nationalists, who wanted to establish a Slavic state in the Balkans. This led to a Serbian nationalist group assassinating Francis Ferdinand.]*

Next have students examine why this incident escalated into a conflict. Suggest that students refer to their diagrams or models of alliances. Illustrate the progression of events by asking these questions:

Ask: Why did Austria issue Serbia an ultimatum?
    [to punish the Serbs for the assassination]
Ask: Why did Russia order a partial mobilization against Austria?
    [to defend Serbia after Austria had declared war]
Ask: Why did Russia mobilize along the German border?
    [for fear that Germany would join forces with Austria]
Ask: Why did Germany declare war on Russia?
    [Russia refused to remove its troops from near the German border.]
Ask: Why did Germany declare war on France?
    [for fear that France would side with Russia]
Ask: Why did Great Britain enter the war?
    [Germany's violation of Belgian neutrality]

To help students understand the mood in Europe on the eve of war, you might wish to assign the Global History Resource Center readings *Europe's Leaders Call Their Nations to War* and *War Fever in Vienna.*

CONCLUDE

Evaluate the causes of World War I by debating if the conflict might have been avoided. Read aloud the following statement, which David Lloyd George, British prime minister from 1916 to 1922, made shortly after World War I:

> It was something into which they glided or rather staggered and stumbled . . . and a discussion, I have no doubt, would have averted it.

Then ask students if they agree with Lloyd George and have them give reasons for their opinion. Suggest that students review all the forces that brought about the war—imperialism, territorial expansion, nationalism, militarism, the alliance system, and so on. Allow students with opposing viewpoints to debate the question. Or organize students into discussion groups and have each group report its consensus to the class.

EXTEND

Cross-Curricular Connection: *Language Arts*
Have students work in small groups to write a script for a "You Are There" radio program on the assassination of Francis Ferdinand. Scripts should set the scene, offer eyewitness accounts, and provide a discussion on how the incident might affect relations among European nations. Ask students to "broadcast" their scripts.

Other Media
Interested students might like to view *The Guns of August*, a documentary based on Barbara Tuchman's book of the same name, on the origins of World War I. Then have students summarize Tuchman's views on the causes of the conflict.

MEET INDIVIDUAL NEEDS

Logical-Mathematical Learners
Have students construct a cause-effect chain of the events that led up to World War I. Call on volunteers to present their chains to the class.

Visual-Spatial Learners
Have students create a political cartoon illustrating one of the forces that contributed to the outbreak of World War I, such as nationalism, imperialism, or militarism.

ASSESS

Review
Have students complete the Section 1 Review. Use answers in the Teacher's Edition, page 601, to assess student mastery of this section.

Lesson 22.2   *A New Kind of War*

Textbook pp. 602–605

RESOURCES

Pupil's Edition
Then and Now, p. 604: *Submarines*

Core Resources
Reading 22.2: *A Soldier Remembers the Tank*

Skills Activity 22: *Using an Electronic Library Catalog*

Visual Resources
Everyday Life 22: *American Posters from World War I*

Global History Resource Center
Reading: *The Tank in World War I*

Reading: *"How We Zeppelined the Heart of London"*

Reading: *German U-Boat 202 Attacks a Steamer*

Reading: *Women and World War I*

Reading: *Letters from an American Nurse in World War I*

Videodiscs or Global History Resource Center

Image: *Total War in Termonde, Belgium*

Search Frame 971

Image: *Poison Gas: A Terrifying New Weapon*

Search Frame 975

Image: *French Women in War and Peace*

Search Frame 972

Image: *Anti-German Propaganda: The Iron Cross*

Search Frame 973

Image: *WWI Hospital for Wounded Troops*

Search Frame 979

LESSON FOCUS
What geographic, technological, and social factors turned World War I into a "total war"?

OBJECTIVES
After completing this lesson, students will be able to:
- illustrate why the war from 1914 to 1918 was called a "world war";
- explain the meaning of the term *total war*;
- describe the effects that the advancement of technology had on the fighting in World War I.

HOOK
Discuss the global nature of World War I. Review the alliances that existed prior to World War I, and have students name the powers in each alliance. Help students understand the geographic element of world war by telling them that besides the European powers involved in the war, the war effort recruited people from all over the world. Some of those who fought were from India, China, Canada, Australia, New Zealand, Senegal, Algeria, South Africa, Annam (today, a part of Vietnam), Japan, and the United States.

Ask students how the war affected other countries besides the major powers involved. Then ask them if they think that "world war" is an appropriate description of the 1914–1918 conflict.

DEVELOP
Describe how new technology changed the way war was fought. Ask students to read the Then and Now feature on textbook page 604, and display the electronic media images of heavy artillery bombardment in Belgium and the use of poison gas. Assign the Global History Resource Center readings on the development of the tank, on the zeppelin attack of London, and on the German U-boat. Next assign Core Resources Reading 22.2. Organize students into small groups and have them answer the question: What new technology

existed? *[Answers should include heavy artillery, submarines, tanks, poison gas, dirigibles, and airplanes.]*

Conclude by asking students to discuss how the new technology helped change the nature of warfare. *[It shifted the advantage from attacking to defending forces; increased reliance on heavy artillery bombardment; and extended fighting to the air and sea. It also required mobilization of whole societies, as labor was needed to produce the weapons for war.]*

Link to Today. You might also ask students how technological advances in weaponry affect modern conflicts, such as the Gulf War. *[Responses could include fear of the use of nuclear weapons and chemical and biological warfare.]*

PROBE

Discuss the impact of World War I on the home front.

Refer students to textbook page 603 and draw their attention to the comment by the British observer that "The whole island was an arsenal." Ask students what the observer meant by this statement. *[Total war requires nations to commit all their resources—including people—to the conflict.]* Mention that the mobilization of the home front brought great change to women's lives, as many worked outside the home for the first time. Display the electronic media image of French women at work. Have students write a caption for this image, describing changes in women's lives. Next assign the Global History Resource Center reading on women and World War I. Conclude by leading a class discussion on the impact the war had on women's lives.

CONCLUDE

Investigate the use of propaganda and its role in a total war. Call on a volunteer to define the term *propaganda*. *[ideas, facts, or rumors used—often in the form of an emotional appeal—to further a cause]* Next display Everyday Life Transparency 22. Before assigning the accompanying worksheet, lead students in a brief discussion of the posters. Explain that the word *Hun* was a derogatory term for "German," and that Liberty Bonds were notes issued by the government to raise money for the war effort.

Ask: **What kinds of emotional appeals are being made in the posters? Why?**

[Left poster plays on people's pride in accomplishment, patriotism; right poster plays on fear, painting German soldiers as ogres who prey on defenseless children. Appealing to patriotism and showing the enemy as an evil monster caused people to see supporting the war effort as their duty.]

Next display the electronic media image of anti-German propaganda.

Ask: **How does propaganda contribute to total war?**
    [mobilizes public opinion to support war effort]

Finally, have students briefly review the section to formulate a definition of *total war*. *[Definitions should mention the geographic, technological, economic, social, and psychological elements of total war.]*

EXTEND

Cross-Curricular Connection: *Health/Science*
Encourage students to research conditions in field hospitals in World War I. For example, they might investigate how technological advances in weaponry changed the nature of injuries. You may wish to assign the Global History Resource Center reading *Diary of An American Nurse in World War I* and display the electronic media image of the World War I hospital.

Other Media
Have students complete Skills Activity 22 and then use appropriate computer software to construct a database of sources they might use to compare the strengths of the armies in World War I.

MEET INDIVIDUAL NEEDS

Visual-Spatial Learners
Have students work in small groups to prepare a world map or a globe showing all the members of the Central Powers and the Allied Powers. Have groups display and discuss their projects.

ASSESS

Review
Have students complete the Section 2 Review. Use answers in the Teacher's Edition, page 605, to assess student mastery of this section.

Lesson 22.3 — *The Course of the War*

Textbook pp. 606–613

RESOURCES

Pupil's Edition

Map, p. 607: *The Western Front, 1914–1918*

Map, p. 608: *The Eastern Front, 1914–1918*

Map, p. 609: *War in the Middle East, 1914–1918*

Literature Through Time, p. 611: *Wartime Poetry*

Core Resources

Reading 22.3: *Songs of a Campaign*

Global History Resource Center

Reading: *German U-Boat 202 Attacks a Steamer*

Reading: *Lawrence of Arabia Destroys a Turkish Column*

Videodiscs or Global History Resource Center

Map: *World War I Troop Strength and Casualties*

Search Frame 982

Image: *"Wake Up America" Parade in WWI*

Search Frame 976

Image: *African-American Doughboy in France*

Search Frame 977

LESSON FOCUS

What factors influenced the course of World War I?

OBJECTIVES

After completing this lesson, students will be able to:

- contrast the war in the East and the Middle East with the war in the West;
- evaluate the importance of the war at sea;
- explain how U.S. entry affected the war.

HOOK: Link to Today

Investigate the cost of World War I in terms of human life. Display the electronic media map of troop strength and casualties, then have students skim the section to find statistics on battle casualties. List battles and casualty figures on the chalkboard. Help students grasp the magnitude of World War I battle losses by relating these figures to something familiar to them, such as the population of their city. For example, you could say, "The French losses at Verdun were comparable to half the population of this city," or "British casualties on the first day of the Somme offensive equaled a capacity crowd at our local stadium," etc. Invite students to make similar comparisons to other casualty figures.

Ask: Why was World War I the bloodiest war in history at that time?

[Technological advances produced new, deadly weapons, and strategies followed by military commanders often resulted in heavy losses.]

DEVELOP

Review the course of the war in the West, in the East and Middle East, and at sea. Organize students into three groups and assign each group one of the following topics—the war on the western front, the war on the eastern front and in the Middle East, and the war at sea. Ask group members to outline the major events of the section of the war assigned to them. Ensure that they examine the maps of the war on pages 607–609. In addition, you may wish to assign the Global History Resource Center readings on the German U-boat attack and on Lawrence of Arabia.

Call on group representatives to present and discuss their outlines. Then, invite volunteers to summarize the war in each of the three areas. *[possible responses—the western front was mostly static, and fighting resulted in stalemate; the war in the East and Middle East was primarily a war of movement, but failed to produce a decisive victory; the war at sea produced a strategic victory for the Allies because the German surface fleet stayed in port]*

[It imposed financial penalties for war damages, forced Germany to accept sole responsibility for the war, and took away Germany's overseas colonies. Most European Allied leaders wanted a harsh settlement because of feelings of hatred, bitterness, and a desire for revenge, as well as fear of a strong Germany.]

Next have students examine the Germans' response to the harsh treatment they received at the hands of the Allies. Assign Core Resources Reading 22.4 and the Global History Resource reading on the Germans' response to the treaty.

Ask: ***Why did the Germans react in a manner described as "sullen, arrogant, unrepentant"?***

[The Germans resented not only the terms of the treaty, but also that they had not been involved in negotiations. Further, they were offended by the fact that it was presented as an ultimatum.]

Conclude by asking students to consider how the peace settlement dealt with the colonies of Germany and the other Central Powers. Refer students to the map on textbook page 617. Point out how the former German and Ottoman territories were assigned to Allied powers. Then discuss the mandate system developed by the League of Nations.

Ask: ***How was a territory's right to govern itself determined under this system?***

[The League assumed responsibility for assigning the territory to a "more advanced" nation and judging when its inhabitants were ready for independence.]

CONCLUDE

Evaluate the peace settlement that ended World War I.

Refer students to the diplomat's question quoted in the section introduction on textbook page 614: "Are we making a good peace? Are we? Are we?" Point out that the answer depends on one's point of view.

Encourage students to answer the diplomat's question by writing letters to the editorial page of a contemporary newspaper expressing the viewpoint of one of the following people—an Allied leader; a German leader; a British, French, or German civilian; a soldier who fought for the Central Powers; an Allied soldier; a person in a former German colonial territory; an American supporter or opponent of President Wilson.

Interested students may want to use the letters to create a "Letters to the Editor" for classroom display. Ask the students if they think that Wilson, Clemenceau, and the other Allied leaders made a "good peace."

EXTEND

Cross-Curricular Connection: *Journalism*

Link to Today. Ask students if they recall the difficulties in the peace process for a more recent conflict—that in Bosnia. Have students research and make a time line of the efforts to reach a peace agreement in Bosnia and some of the difficulties that were encountered.

MEET INDIVIDUAL NEEDS

Interpersonal Learners

Have students reenact the Versailles Peace Conference. Ask them to play the roles of the Big Four and the German delegates. They might use quoted material from the text and/or write appropriate dialogue based on the textbook discussion.

Students Acquiring English

Pair new speakers of English with fluent speakers. Refer pairs to the Identify section in the Section 4 Review on page 618. Have them create information cards for each item listed. One side of each card should show the name or term; the other side should provide a definition or appropriate biographical, geographical, or historical information. Have pairs quiz each other.

ASSESS

Review

Have students complete the Section 4 Review. Use answers in the Teacher's Edition, page 618, to assess student mastery of this section.

Lesson 22.5   Consequences of the War

Textbook pp. 619–622

RESOURCES

Pupil's Edition

Map, p. 598: *Europe on the Eve of World War I, 1914*

Map, p. 620: *Europe After the Versailles Settlements, 1919–1920*

Graph, p. 622: *World War I Battlefield Losses*

Visual Resources

Geography and History 22: *Europe and the Middle East After World War I*

Art and History 22: *In the Trenches: Battle Sketches of World War I*

Global History Resource Center

Reading: *War Fever in Vienna*

Reading: *Women and World War I*

Reading: *A Postwar Program of Social Reconstruction*

Videodiscs or Global History Resource Center

Image: *Total War in Termonde, Belgium*

Search Frame 971

LESSON FOCUS

What were the political and social consequences of World War I?

OBJECTIVES

After completing this lesson, students will be able to:

- describe the role of the United States in international relations after World War I;
- explain how the Versailles peace settlement affected the geography of Europe and the domestic feeling in nations that had fought the war;
- discuss how the war affected people's views of society in the West.

HOOK: Link to Today

Examine the impact of World War I on postwar society.
Ask students to recall an event in their lives that has had a long-term effect. Use the metaphor of an echo to express the effects of such a significant event—just as an echo may reverberate long after the initial sound, an event may affect a person's life long after it has taken place.

Next have a student read aloud the quotation by French author Paul Valéry on textbook page 621. Ask students to apply Valéry's statement to the postwar world.

Ask: How might the echo of the Great War resound through the postwar world?
[The bloodshed, destruction of property, and political and economic upheaval would affect life in the postwar world for years to come.]

DEVELOP

Examine the political consequences of World War I. Have students compare the map on textbook page 598 with the map on textbook page 620 of Europe after the peace settlements. Have students list the changes in political boundaries. To help students focus on these changes, display Geography and History Transparency 22 and have them complete the worksheet. Then lead students in a discussion of the nature and impact of these changes.

Ask: What principle did the Allied leaders use in drawing new boundaries and creating new nations?
[Boundaries represented an attempt to apply the principle of national self-determination.]

Ask: What were the consequences of the political changes shown on the maps?
[Changes created new problems. Some national groups still lived within countries dominated by other groups;

Conclude by leading the class in a discussion of the importance of controlling the seas during wartime.

Ask: Why did ultimate victory in World War I depend on mastery of the seas?

[Control of sea lanes meant control of the flow of troops and supplies necessary to fight a war.]

PROBE

Examine soldiers' attitudes toward the war. Ask volunteers to read aloud the two quotations on pages 606 and 608 of the textbook that describe war from a soldier's viewpoint. Then ask students to identify the battles or campaigns described in the quotations and to characterize the soldiers' attitudes. [**Somme:** fear, resignation; **Gallipoli:** futility, resignation]

Next have students read and discuss the Literature Through Time selection on textbook page 611.

Ask: What similarities do you see in these two poems?

[Both remark on the horror of war. Owen likens it to winter covering the world; Frankau calls it an "outrage." Both talk of sacrifice. Owen notes the need for bloodshed to provide "seed" for the spring sowing; Frankau states that only through sacrifice can a better world be secured.]

Assign Core Resources Reading 22.3 to provide students with further examples of poetry about World War I. *Songs from a Campaign* is made up of poems about the Gallipoli campaign.

Conclude by asking students to assess the morale of Allied troops in 1917 based on what they have read. [Students should note that many began to believe their efforts in the war were futile. Allied morale was low.]

CONCLUDE

Evaluate the importance of U.S. entry into World War I. Point out that the course of history is marked by turning points—events which bring about decisive changes. Mention that the turning point in World War I came in 1917.

Ask: What events triggered this turning point?

[U.S. decision to enter the war, French soldiers' mutiny, Russia's withdrawal from the war]

Discuss the effects of each event on the course of the war. [The arrival of American troops following Congress's declaration of war on April 6 provided a morale boost and increased troop strength. The French mutiny, while devastating for morale, resulted in better officers being appointed to command positions. Russia's withdrawal from the war helped Germany by allowing it to wage war on one front rather than two.] To illustrate U.S. involvement in the war, show the electronic media images of the parade and of the African-American doughboy.

Conclude by asking students to write a subsection for an encyclopedia article on World War I titled "The Turning Point," in which they discuss the circumstances of U.S. entry into the war and substantiate the argument that it was a turning point in the conflict. Ask volunteers to read their work.

EXTEND

Cross-Curricular Connection: *Literature*

Have students work in small groups to study literary works about World War I. Students might read the poetry of Wilfred Owen, Rupert Brooke, or Siegfried Sassoon, or such novels as *All Quiet on the Western Front*, by Erich Maria Remarque, or *A Farewell to Arms*, by Ernest Hemingway. Encourage students to write brief reports on the works they read.

Other Media

Have interested students view Stanley Kubrick's film *Paths of Glory*, which deals with a mutiny among French soldiers during World War I. Then have students discuss whether they think the way the French military command settled the mutiny was justified.

MEET INDIVIDUAL NEEDS

Kinesthetic Learners

Have students create a three-dimensional map of the western front using clay, papier-maché, or some similar material. The map should show the opposing armies' trench lines and the area known as no-man's-land.

Musical-Rhythmic Learners

Encourage interested students to listen to songs from the World War I era. Ask them to learn and perform one or more for the class and give a commentary on the mood of the music and the message of the lyrics.

ASSESS

Review

Have students complete the Section 3 Review. Use answers in the Teacher's Edition, page 613, to assess student mastery of this section.

Lesson 22.4   The Peace Settlement

Textbook pp. 614–618

RESOURCES

Pupil's Edition

Biography, p. 615: *Georges Clemenceau*
Map, p. 617: *The Mandate System, 1924*

Core Resources

Reading 22.4: *The Germans Are Informed of the Terms of the Treaty of Versailles*

Global History Resource Center

Reading: *Georges Clemenceau at the Peace Conference*
Reading: *Germans Debate the Treaty of Versailles*

LESSON FOCUS

How did the new world order established by the peace settlement reflect Allied leaders' views?

OBJECTIVES

After completing this lesson, students will be able to:

- explain why the Allies were unable to agree about the formation of a postwar world order after the armistice;
- discuss the results of the peace conference at Versailles;
- explain what happened to the former territorial possessions of the defeated Central Powers.

HOOK

Address the difficulty of writing a peace settlement after a long and bitter conflict. Ask students to review the causes of the war. List their responses on the chalkboard. *[Responses should include nationalism, imperialism, militarism, and shifting alliances.]*

Next organize students into groups of five to act as advisory committees to delegates attending the Versailles Peace Conference. Ask committees to develop ideas on how to ensure that World War I would be the "war to end all wars," as it was sometimes called. Call on group representatives to briefly outline their ideas. Act as devil's advocate, challenging each idea as it is offered. Then point out that this was the problem facing the delegates to the peace conference, for Allied leaders' ideas on how to secure the peace varied greatly.

DEVELOP

Show how Allied leaders' views on the peace settlement differed. Point out that the debate over the nature of the peace settlement, by and large, became a struggle between U.S. president Woodrow Wilson and Prime Minister Georges Clemenceau of France. Direct students to create a two-column chart to compare the views of Wilson and Clemenceau on the settlement. In addition to the discussion in the text, have students draw on the biography feature on textbook page 615. To give them further information on Clemenceau's views, you might assign the Global History Resource Center reading on Clemenceau.

Next ask students to add a third column to their charts. Have them record the terms of the peace settlement that addressed the issues on which they based their comparisons.

Ask: *Did the peace settlement more closely reflect Wilson's views or Clemenceau's views?*

[The settlement reflected Clemenceau's desire to punish Germany more than Wilson's wish for "peace without victory."]

PROBE

Examine the effects of the peace settlement on the Central Powers and their territories. Point out that there was agreement among European Allied leaders that Germany alone was to blame for the war, and they wanted to impose harsh penalties on Germany.

Ask: *How did the Treaty of Versailles "punish" Germany? Why?*

some nations lost territory and resources; Japan and Italy did not achieve the territorial gains they hoped for; and Germany and Russia were treated as outcasts.]

Next discuss how the role the United States would play in postwar world affairs remained unclear.

Ask: **What action by the United States seemed to suggest it would distance itself from world affairs?**

[its refusal to join the League of Nations]

Ask: **What actions seemed to suggest the United States would play an important role in world affairs?**

[Washington Naval Conference, which limited size of major powers' navies; Dawes Plan, which eased economic pressure on Germany; actions pressuring Japan to restore Shandong Peninsula to China]

Conclude by asking students to write a paragraph of no more than 10 lines that summarizes the major political consequences of World War I. Call on volunteers to read and discuss their paragraphs.

PROBE

Investigate the social consequences of World War I.
Mention that in 1914, many Europeans looked upon war as a romantic adventure. To underscore this point, again assign the Global History Resource Center reading titled *War Fever in Vienna*. The reality of war, however, proved far different. Draw students' attention to the graph on textbook page 622, then display the electronic media image of Belgium. Inform students that four years of fighting left nearly 10 million soldiers dead, another 20 million people wounded, and much of Europe in ruins. Ask students to consider what impact this death and destruction might have had on the way people looked at life.

Ask: **How did World War I change the way many people in the West viewed life?**

[The incredible bloodshed and destruction of the war left many people in the West with a sense of disillusionment and insecurity.]

CONCLUDE

Evaluate the results of World War I. Create on the chalkboard a three-column chart with the following column headings: *Political*, *Social*, and *Economic*. Call on students to list consequences of World War I under each heading. You might assign the Global History Resource Center reading on women and World War I to explain the consequences of the war for women. [**Political:** new nations, new governments; U.S. role in

international affairs unclear; voting rights for women in Britain and the United States; **Social:** loss of life and property, feelings of disillusionment and bitterness; **Economic:** destruction of resources, debt]

Next call on students to identify positive and negative outcomes of the war, resolving differences of opinion through discussion. Make a list on the chalkboard. Continue until students have identified all outcomes of the war. Then have students write a generalization on the consequences of the war based on the lists.

EXTEND

Cross-Curricular Connection: *Art/Literature*

Have students examine Art and History Transparency 22 and complete the accompanying worksheet. Then discuss what life must have been like for an American soldier in the trenches. Ask students to find other artistic examples that reflect the violence, disillusionment, and insecurity caused by the war. Students might examine the Literature Through Time feature in Section 3 for an example of how these attitudes were reflected in literature.

MEET INDIVIDUAL NEEDS

Gifted Students

Have interested students research the effects of World War I on future leadership. Several people who served in World War I played roles in World War II. Examples include George Patton, Douglas MacArthur, Winston Churchill, and Harry Truman. Students might prepare biographic sketches of one or more of these people.

Linguistic Learners

Have students examine the Global History Resource Center reading on the National Catholic War Council's plan for reconstruction of American society after the war. Ask students to outline the main points of the program and explain the bishops' major concerns.

ASSESS

Review

Have students complete the Section 5 Review. Use answers in the Teacher's Edition, page 622, to assess student mastery of this section.

In preparation for the chapter test, you may wish to have students complete all or part of the Chapter 22 Review on textbook page 623, the Chapter 22 Review Activity, and the Chapter 22 Themes Review.

593L

Chapter 22

World War I and After

Understanding the Main Idea

Call on a volunteer to read aloud the *Understanding the Main Idea* paragraph. Then tell students that World War I was a devastating conflict that killed millions of soldiers and civilians. New weapons inspired great terror, and the huge death toll suggested that brutality lay just beneath the surface of civilization.

Presenting Themes

See p. 593B for suggestions on introducing themes.

Using the Time Line

Have students list the time line events in their notebooks. After they have read about each event in the chapter, have students write a paragraph explaining its significance.

Chapter 22
World War I and After
1914–1924

Understanding the Main Idea

The outbreak of World War I ended a long period of relative peace and stability in Europe. The great powers of the world descended into four of the bloodiest years of fighting in history. By the end of the war in 1918, many people were calling for lasting peace. The peace settlement, however, did not resolve all of the issues between the warring nations. In fact, it helped lay the foundation for future conflict.

Themes

- **War and Diplomacy** How might alliances among nations cause a small regional conflict to grow into a major international war?

- **Technology** How might technological developments affect the way wars are fought?

- **Social Relations** How might wars affect society on the home fronts?

Historians sometimes suggest that Western civilization had reached a high point by the beginning of the 1900s. Looking back on the previous century, people saw an era of progress. Reason appeared triumphant in human affairs. Science and industry had improved humanity's condition beyond what "even its most audacious [bold] optimists had dared to dream." By 1918, however, the hopeful view had turned to disillusionment. The magnificent accomplishments of the 1800s had ended in an equally stupendous disaster. In Britain a rising young politician named Winston Churchill explained what had gone so terribly wrong:

66*Far more than their vices, the virtues of nations ill-directed or mis-directed by their rulers, became the cause of their own undoing and of the general catastrophe.*99

The catastrophe of which Churchill wrote was a war of unimaginable destruction—a total war between many nations. As young men across Europe enthusiastically marched off to war in 1914, few people realized the enormous devastation that was to come. In later years, before numbering such catastrophes became necessary, people called it the Great War. Today we know it as World War I.

1914	1915	1916	1917
Nations of Europe mobilize after Austria declares war on Serbia.	German submarine sinks British passenger liner *Lusitania*.	German High Command orders an attack on strategic French city of Verdun.	United States enters the war on the side of the Allies.

594

World War I changed the face of Europe. The western front, which at some points during the war stretched for more than 450 miles, ran from Belgium to Switzerland. Armies dug massive networks of trenches and strung barbed wire as a further barrier to any troops daring enough to cross the area known as no-man's-land. Rain ran off into the trenches, which became swamps where soldiers drowned in mud. Artillery fire destroyed the landscape and the foliage, making the front a barren wasteland.

Critical Thinking Ask students if a muddy, barren battlefield like the one shown in the picture would give an advantage to the attacking side or the defending side.

ANSWER: Students should note that although these conditions caused great discomfort for the troops defending their trenches, the mud and lack of any vegetation made a successful attack extremely difficult.

Canadian troops holding "the line," a sea of mud, at Passchendaele on November 14, 1917. Many men died or lost their toes and feet from disease caused by standing for days on end in freezing mud.

1918	1919	1922	1924
German leaders agree to armistice, ending hostilities in World War I.	Conference convenes at Versailles outside Paris to write a peace treaty.	Major sea powers meet at the Washington Naval Conference, where they agree to limit the size of their navies.	American diplomat Charles Dawes presents plan to reschedule German reparations payments, easing Germany's financial problems.

SECTION 1

CORE LESSON PLAN
See pages 593C and
593D for Lesson Plan
22.1.

Theme: Social Relations

Tensions between nations were also heightened by population growth. A number of medical and agricultural advances during the 1700s and 1800s enabled more people to live to adulthood. At the same time, birth rates remained high. By 1914 the population of Europe (excluding Russia) was about 300 million, roughly double what it had been a century earlier.

Critical Thinking Ask students what effects this increase in population might have had on the governments of Europe.

ANSWER: Students might suggest that the increase in population would have increased demands on land and resources, as well as allowed for larger national armies.

SECTION 1
Origins of World War I

FOCUS

- What forces contributed to the outbreak of World War I?

- What effect did the rise of a strong Germany have on the balance of power in Europe?

- Why did conflict in the Balkans spread to the rest of Europe in 1914?

In contrast to the 1700s, the 1800s was an era of relative stability in the international relations of Europe. In the final years of the century, however, that stability began to erode as new social and political tensions emerged and the European balance of power began to shift. The stability of the 1800s finally collapsed in 1914 under the pressure of crisis in the Balkans, as national and imperial rivalries in Europe exploded in world war.

The British naval ship *Dreadnought*, c. 1906

Underlying Forces

In 1914 the nations of Europe dominated the world. The British Empire alone controlled roughly one fifth of the earth's landmass. France, Germany, and Italy also controlled vast territories with many diverse peoples. In Europe itself, however, growing social and political tensions caused many Europeans to feel uneasy. One witness recorded that a "strange temper" filled the air—despite warnings and forecasts of doom from some observers, people seemed "everywhere eager to dare."

In part this growing tension was due to the rise of new imperial and national rivalries in Europe. The emergence of new states, such as Italy and particularly Germany, had changed the European balance of power. The other nations of Europe looked for ways to contain Germany's growing ambitions. Nationalist movements in the large multiethnic empires of Russia and Austria-Hungary intensified conflict in eastern Europe, while rivalries among the large western European powers were reflected in a series of military alliances and in the competition for overseas empires.

Imperial and national rivalries also contributed to the rise of **militarism**—a glorification of military power—in Europe. Militarism was especially influential in the new German Empire, where Kaiser William II once observed, "I and the Army—we were born for each other and will cleave indissolubly [bond inseparably] to each other." William and other leaders came to believe that militarily powerful nations usually got what they wanted, while weaker nations lost out. Moreover, the side that struck first would probably win. "Attack is the best defense," declared German Field Marshal Alfred von Schlieffen (SHLEE-fuhn), describing what became known as the "cult of the offensive." By the end of the 1800s, the great powers of Europe had begun a massive military buildup.

Militarism often reflected popular sentiments. Combined with nationalism, it fostered an attitude called "jingoism," after the refrain of a popular British song of the 1870s:

> **"** We don't want to fight,
> but, by jingo, if we do,
> we've got the ships,
> we've got the men,
> we've got the money too. **"**

▲ Kaiser William II (in white cloak at right) oversees field maneuvers of the German army in 1906.

concerned Britain. In 1908 Mahan described the naval arms race between Great Britain and Germany with great accuracy as "the danger point, not only of European politics, but of world politics as well."

Growing nationalism, imperialism, and militarism led many European nations to see war as a solution to their diplomatic crises.

Many in Europe began to see war as a kind of test through which nations could demonstrate their strength and fitness to prosper.

The relationship between a nation's well-being and prosperity and its armed power was perhaps best expressed by an American naval officer named Alfred Thayer Mahan. Born in 1840, Mahan served as a U.S. naval officer during the Civil War. After the war he taught history at a special school for senior naval officers. Mahan argued that the key to world power was sea power. It had made Britain the world's richest and most powerful nation—it could do the same for the United States:

66 *The influence of the government will be felt in its most legitimate manner in maintaining an armed navy of a size commensurate with [equal to] the growth of its shipping and the importance of the interests connected with it.* 99

Translations of Mahan's writings appeared in many languages, including Japanese. Many leaders used his ideas to justify their own plans for naval expansion and modernization. Kaiser William, for example, after having "devoured" Mahan's writings, ordered a massive naval buildup in Germany. As Mahan himself had foreseen, however, the German buildup greatly

A New Balance of Power

The rise of Germany as a great power in the late 1800s had reshaped the balance of power in Europe. The older powers feared the ambition and potential aggression of a unified Germany demanding its "place in the sun." As German power grew, a system of military alliances emerged that eventually included all the major European states.

Alfred Thayer Mahan

BIOGRAPHY

Origins of the alliance system. At the root of the new alliance system were the policies of German Chancellor Otto von Bismarck. Fearing that the French would seek revenge for their defeat in the Franco-Prussian War of 1870–71, Bismarck set out to isolate France diplomatically. To help safeguard against Germany being forced to fight a war on two fronts if France and Russia ever became allies, in 1879 he concluded a defensive alliance with Austria to guard against a Russian attack. As a safeguard against France, in 1882 he persuaded Italy to join Germany and Austria in what became known as the **Triple Alliance**. Worried that Austria might drag Germany into an unwanted war, however, in 1887 Bismarck also signed the so-called Reinsurance Treaty with Russia, pledging that each country would remain

Europe on the Eve of World War I, 1914

The Alliance System   Defensive alliances polarized Europe into two armed camps before World War I actually broke out.

Linking Geography and History   What nations belonged to the Triple Entente?

neutral if the other became involved in a war, unless Germany attacked France first or Russia attacked Austria.

In 1890, however, Kaiser William dismissed Bismarck and allowed the Reinsurance Treaty to lapse. Worried by this move, in 1894 French and Russian leaders agreed to an alliance directed primarily against Germany. Bismarck had been right: France did want revenge for its defeat in the Franco-Prussian War. France also wanted the return of its province of Alsace-Lorraine. Russia, on the other hand, had ambitions in the Balkans, where local Slavic populations in the Ottoman and the Austro-Hungarian empires looked to the czar to head a nationalist, all-Slavic movement known as **Pan-Slavism**.

The Franco-Russian alliance had a dramatic effect on German officers. They now became convinced that Germany would have to fight both Russia and France in the event of war with

either nation. In 1905 Field Marshal von Schlieffen, chief of the German General Staff, worked out a plan for such a two-front war. The **Schlieffen Plan** called for delivering a knockout blow to France before taking the offensive against Russia. Thus, war with Russia automatically meant war with France as well.

Britain's new foreign policy. Germany's rise as a great military power also changed Britain's foreign policy. Throughout the 1800s Britain was the most powerful nation in the world. From this position of strength, British leaders avoided continental alliances and sought only to keep any single power from dominating Europe.

By the end of the century, however, the rise of Germany, as well as the United States and Japan, threatened Britain's dominant position. In the mid-1800s the Royal Navy, the primary instrument of British overseas power, had been almost as large as all other world navies combined. By 1900 this huge advantage had narrowed, so that the British navy could only claim to be as strong as the next two largest navies put together. Combined with the fact that British fleets had to be spread around the world, Britain's leaders could not help but feel vulnerable.

To bolster their position, British leaders set out to establish friendly relations with both the United States and Japan. They acknowledged the United States as the leading power in the Western Hemisphere, and in 1902 they concluded an alliance with Japan. The Anglo-Japanese alliance in particular freed them to concentrate their naval forces in European waters. They relied on the Japanese to keep an eye on Russian ambitions in Asia and to help safeguard the routes to British territories in Asia and the Pacific. With Germany, however, British leaders concluded there could be no compromise. They soon began to look for other European allies.

The Triple Entente. In 1904 Britain and France settled their rival territorial claims in Africa. Known as the Entente Cordiale, or "friendly understanding," this agreement laid the foundation for a closer relationship between the two countries. British differences with Russia were more difficult to resolve. Russian expansion in Asia was the major threat to British India. However, both nations mistrusted Germany, and in 1907 they agreed to define and respect each other's spheres of influence in Asia. Russia then joined Britain and France in the so-called **Triple Entente**.

Germany and the Ottoman Empire. The Anglo-Russian agreement of 1907 damaged Britain's relations with the Ottoman Empire, which had already been strained to the breaking point over the British occupation of Egypt in 1882. Now convinced that Britain and Russia had agreed to destroy and divide up the Ottoman Empire, Ottoman leaders looked to Germany for support.

The Germans had been interested in the Ottoman Empire for some time. In 1898 the German kaiser had paid a visit to the Ottoman sultan Abdülhamid in Constantinople, indicating to the Ottomans that they could look to Germany for friendship and support. German military advisors came to serve with the Ottoman army. German investors and engineers planned to build a railway from Berlin to Baghdad. By 1914 Germany's expansionist aims had heightened tension among the great powers and focused attention on the Balkan Peninsula. As national and imperial rivalries came together in the Balkans, they turned the region into a "powder keg," ready to ignite.

The rise of Germany as a great power led to shifting alliances and increased international tension.

The Balkan Powder Keg

During the 1800s local nationalism and interference from Austria and Russia had gradually caused the Ottoman Empire to lose its grip on the Balkans. This contributed to growing instability in the region. In 1878, for example, Ottoman decline had allowed the Slavic people of Serbia to declare their independence. Serbian nationalists hoped to make their country the center of a large Slavic state in alliance with Russia. In particular, the Serbs wanted control of two Ottoman provinces being administered by Austria—Bosnia and Herzegovina (hert-suh-goh-VEE-nuh). The two provinces would give the land-locked Serbian state an outlet on the Adriatic Sea.

Serbian ambitions, however, caused much concern in Austria. The Austrians feared that nationalism would spread from Serbia into their own eastern provinces. They also feared Russian expansion. Thus, in 1908 Austria annexed Bosnia and Herzegovina—a move that enraged many Serbian nationalists. A Serbian newspaper editorial, for example, urged action:

THE BOILING POINT

▲ European leaders in this British cartoon from 1912 realize that the Balkan troubles are about to reach the boiling point.

66 *Serbs, seize everything you can lay hands on   knives, rifles, bombs and dynamite. Take holy vengeance! Death to the Habsburg dynasty, eternal remembrance to the heroes who raise their hands against it!* 99

RESOURCE ACTIVITY

READINGS IN WORLD HISTORY Reading 22.1
Leading Up to War

Have students read the passages reflecting how officials of several countries viewed the rising tensions in Europe. Then have students complete the questions.

Level 2

RESOURCE ACTIVITY

GLOBAL HISTORY RESOURCE CENTER Reading: *War Fever in Vienna*

Print out and distribute the reading. Have students read about the scene in Vienna just after war was declared. Then have each student write a description of the same day from the point of view of a young Austrian army recruit.

Level 3

Tensions between Serbia and Austria increased further in 1912 when the first Balkan War broke out, pitting Serbia and its allies against the Ottoman Empire. The Ottomans lost the last of their European territory except Constantinople, while the victorious Serbs took part of the Adriatic coast. With German support, however, Austria intervened and forced Serbia to give up the coast, which became instead the independent state of Albania. Unable to aid their Serb allies during the crisis because they were unprepared for war, the Russians vowed to support Serbia fully in any future dispute with Austria.

The explosion. The spark that set off the explosion of the Balkan powder keg came on June 28, 1914. Archduke Francis Ferdinand, the heir to the Habsburg throne, and his wife had come to Sarajevo (sahr-uh-YAY-voh), the capital of Bosnia and Herzegovina, on a mission of goodwill. As they rode through the city in an open car, shots rang out, killing both the archduke and his wife. The assassin, Gavrilo Princip, belonged to the Black Hand, a secret Serbian nationalist society. Although he acted without the official authority of the Serbian government, Serbian military intelligence leaders knew of Princip's plans and furnished support.

Determined to punish the Serbs, Austria first sought assurances of German help in case Russia tried to aid Serbia. Probably influenced by senior German military officers, who were confident in their military power and anxious for war, the kaiser promised the Austrian government his full support. With this so-called "blank check," Austria gave Serbia an ultimatum—a demand which, if not agreed to, would result in military action to enforce it. Dissatisfied by Serbia's rather vague response, on July 28, 1914, Austria declared war.

Mobilization. As promised, Russia now prepared to defend Serbia against Austria. At first Czar Nicholas ordered a partial **mobilization**, the preparation of the armed forces for war, aimed only at Austria. However, his military advisors

▲ Although their army was small, Belgian men eagerly volunteered to resist Germany. Here, Belgian reservists stream out of the rail station in response to mobilization.

feared German support for the Austrians. Mobilization was a grave step. It involved taking over all available transport and support facilities and redirecting them toward the anticipated battlefront. If Germany mobilized, the military argued, and Russia had to switch in midstream from partial to complete mobilization of its forces, chaos would result. Fatefully, the czar agreed to demands for a general mobilization.

No power in the industrial era could allow a potentially hostile neighbor to mobilize along its borders without responding. The first to mobilize would have a crucial advantage. While ordering its own mobilization, Germany demanded that Russia remove its troops from near the German border or face war. Fearful that German mobilization would continue anyway, Russia ignored the ultimatum.

The German declaration of war. Germany declared war on Russia on August 1, 1914. The alliance system now took its toll. Two days later, convinced that France would support Russia, Germany also declared war on France. Following the earlier Schlieffen Plan, the German High Command hoped to defeat France quickly by attacking through the flat coastal plain of neutral Belgium. When the Germans demanded that Belgium allow German troops to cross its borders on their way into northwestern France, however, the Belgian king refused, insisting that he ruled "a country not a highway." German troops marched in anyway.

Expansion of the War

The German invasion of Belgium had serious consequences. Despite the 1904 Entente, British leaders had hesitated to go to war in defense of France. However, Britain had also guaranteed Belgian neutrality. Although some Germans did not believe they would fight over a "scrap of paper," British leaders took their obligation seriously. Consequently, on August 4, 1914, Britain declared war on Germany. In the North Sea the Royal Navy began moving into position to blockade Germany.

The Triple Entente countries of Russia, France, and Britain became known as the **Allied Powers**, or the Allies. Germany, Austria-Hungary, and the Ottoman Empire, later joined by Bulgaria, became known as the **Central Powers**. Despite its treaty obligations to Germany and Austria, Italy at first remained neutral on the grounds that Austria was the aggressor. In 1915, however, hoping to obtain Austrian territory, Italy joined the Allies.

When the war began, each side expected to win quickly. In August 1914 Kaiser William told departing German soldiers they would "be home before the leaves have fallen from the trees." Throughout Europe, men eagerly rushed to join up lest they miss out on the action. A French writer described the scene in Paris:

❝ *Thousands of men eager to fight would jostle one another outside recruiting offices, waiting to join up. Men who could have stayed home, with their wives and children. . . . But no. The word 'duty' had a meaning for them, and the word 'country' had regained its splendor.* ❞

Similar scenes occurred in all the warring nations. Fearful that Western civilization was plunging into darkness, British Foreign Secretary Sir Edward Grey was less optimistic: "The lamps are going out all over Europe; we shall not see them lit again in our lifetime."

National and imperial rivalries in the Balkans ignited World War I.

SECTION 1 REVIEW

IDENTIFY and explain the significance of the following:
militarism
Kaiser William II
Alfred Thayer Mahan
Triple Alliance
Pan-Slavism
Schlieffen Plan
Triple Entente
Archduke Francis Ferdinand
mobilization
Allied Powers
Central Powers

LOCATE and explain the importance of the following:
Serbia
Bosnia and Herzegovina

1. **Main Idea** What underlying forces led to the outbreak of World War I?
2. **Main Idea** How did events in the Balkans trigger the war?
3. **War and Diplomacy** How did other European powers try to deal with Germany's rising power?
4. **Writing to Explain**
Imagine that you are a newspaper reporter in Paris, Berlin, or Moscow on the day mobilization is announced in 1914. Write an account of what you observe

that day and explain why young men are so eager to sign up for war.
5. **Synthesizing** Create a chart like the one below, listing the participants and describing the goals of each of the following alliances: Triple Alliance, Reinsurance Treaty, Franco-Russian alliance, Anglo-Japanese alliance, and Triple Entente. Why was the alliance system in Europe by 1914 a dangerous situation?

ALLIANCE	PARTICIPANTS	GOALS
Triple Alliance		

SECTION 1 REVIEW ANSWERS

IDENTIFY
For significance, see the following pages:
militarism (p. 596)
Kaiser William II (p. 596)
Alfred Thayer Mahan (p. 597)
Triple Alliance (p. 597)
Pan-Slavism (p. 598)
Schlieffen Plan (p. 598)
Triple Entente (p. 599)
Archduke Francis Ferdinand (p. 600)
mobilization (p. 600)
Allied Powers (p. 601)
Central Powers (p. 601)

LOCATE
For locations, see the map on p. 598.

1. militarism, nationalism, and imperialism
2. Austrian annexation of Bosnia and Herzegovina fueled nationalism and led to the assassination of Archduke Francis Ferdinand.
3. formed new alliances to isolate Germany
4. Accounts should include the idea that many soldiers sought glory and wanted to serve their countries.
5. Triple Alliance—p: Germany, Italy, Austria; g: guard against Russian attack; Reinsurance Treaty—p: Germany, Russia; g: German neutrality in Austrian-Russian war; Franco-Russian alliance—p: France, Russia; g: avoid German attack; Anglo-Japanese alliance—p: Great Britain, Japan; g: allow British to concentrate forces in Europe; Triple Entente—p: Russia, Britain, France; g: form closer relationship; overlapping and conflicting alliances increased tension between countries

Theme: War and Diplomacy

At the start of the war, Germany had four holdings in Africa, all of them along different coasts. Togoland was quickly subdued. The Cameroons and German Southwest Africa, which today is Namibia, took longer to conquer. In German East Africa, or Tanganyika, German troops fought Allied troops throughout the war and did not surrender until two weeks after the war ended in Europe.

Critical Thinking Ask students how the fact that Germany's African colonies were located in different parts of the continent made them easier for the Allies to conquer.

ANSWER: Students might answer that the German military forces in Africa would have been widely scattered and unable to coordinate a defense.

SECTION 2
A New Kind of War

FOCUS

- Why was the war from 1914 to 1918 called a "world war"?
- What is a "total war"?
- What effects did the advancement of technology have on the fighting of the war?

World War I was a total war. It differed from all previous wars in both scale and scope, and reflected the impact of the industrial age on warfare. The war effort reached around the world, requiring the full commitment of the warring nations' people and resources. Consequently, the war led many governments to expand and centralize their control over their societies and economies.

Weapons factory in Bethlehem, Pennsylvania, c. 1918

The World at War

World War I affected every major region of the world. Although concentrated in Europe, the fighting spread around the globe. British and German forces fought in West Africa, East Africa, and Southwest Africa. As a result of the Ottoman entry into the war, the Middle East became one of the largest theaters of battle. Naval engagements also occurred worldwide. The North Atlantic, the North Sea, and even the Falkland Islands in the South Atlantic were all sites of important actions.

For the first time the war involved all the world's great powers. The United States entered the war on the side of the Allies in 1917, and Japan, an ally of Britain, declared war on Germany in August 1914. Japanese leaders saw in the war an opportunity to advance Japanese interests in East Asia and in the Pacific. Japanese forces quickly seized the German naval base in China at Qingdao (CHING-dow), gaining control of the valuable Shandong Peninsula. Japan also wanted to control several German-held islands in the Pacific. The Japanese navy escorted Allied shipping in both the Indian Ocean and the Mediterranean.

The Allies also drew their soldiers from many parts of the world. The British Empire contributed 3.5 million men, including 600,000 Canadians; 400,000 Australians; 130,000 South Africans; and 120,000 New Zealanders. Some 1.5 million Indians volunteered for service with British forces; several thousand fought and died in Europe. Many more served in the Middle East, providing the backbone of British forces in the Persian Gulf. Algerians, Moroccans, and Senegalese from French Colonial Africa fought for the Allies on the western front.

World War I involved all the world's major powers and regions.

The Home Fronts

Total war blurred the distinctions between civilian and military life. Everyone, whether at home or in the field, felt the strains of war. Shortages and rationing of supplies affected many. The warring nations had to commit their people and resources fully. France sent some 8 million men into combat—nearly 20 percent of its population. Germany sent 13 million men. Britain eventually fielded almost 6 million men, not including the 3.5 million from the empire.

Economic effects. The war effort also stretched industrial resources to their limits. Labor, like armies, sometimes had to be drafted. Women went to work in factories, replacing men serving in the military. Production soared. French war industry, for example, met orders for 35,000 aircraft and 5,000 tanks. At one point the French produced 300,000 artillery shells a day. In Britain, "The whole island was an arsenal," according to one observer.

In order to field and support such massive armies, governments developed new methods of organization. Great Britain, for example, saw dramatic expansion of governmental power. As the head of Britain's wartime production of munitions described it:

❝ *Nearly all the mines and workshops . . . were in our hands. We controlled and were actually managing all the greatest industries. We regulated the supply of all their raw materials. We organized the whole distribution of their finished products. Nearly five million persons were directly under our orders, and we were interwoven on every side with every other sphere of the national economic life.* ❞

In the United States the war effort also resulted in the centralization of governmental authority.

Wartime propaganda. In order to rally public support for the war effort, governments often used **propaganda**—ideas, facts, or rumors spread deliberately to further a cause. Governments set up agencies to develop propaganda and manage the flow of information about the war. Stories circulated of enemy **atrocities**, acts of great cruelty and brutality. As emotions ran high, propaganda sometimes led to mistreatment of suspected enemy sympathizers, usually first- or second-generation immigrants from enemy countries.

Internal security. Both the Allies and the Central Powers had to deal with espionage and sabotage inside their borders. Governments passed

▲ **Women around the world contributed to their countries' war efforts. Here, English women work in a munitions factory.**

increasingly restrictive security measures. For example, in the United States the government's Committee for Public Information encouraged citizens to watch for German spies.

In the Ottoman Empire security concerns led to tragic consequences. The war strained to the breaking point relations between the Turks and many of their non-Muslim subjects. In eastern Turkey, when leaders of the Christian Armenian population rose in support of their kinspeople across the Russian border, the Turks carried out a brutal campaign of forced relocation. Much of the Armenian population of eastern Turkey was deported and moved west. According to Ottoman records, at least 200,000 people died of starvation or massacre. Armenian sources, however, place the figure as high as 1.5 million. Many people later called this a case of attempted **genocide**, the annihilation of an entire people.

World War I was a total war, involving the mobilization of whole societies and their economies.

Technology and Tactics

The armies and navies of World War I felt the full impact of industrialization. Military planners had to adapt their tactics, or methods of fighting, to the new weapons mass production made possible.

Daily Life
Before the war, textile mills had provided many women with employment, but wages were much higher in the explosives industry. So many women went to work in munitions factories that newspapers published appeals for women not to leave the mills.

Critical Thinking Ask students why they think newspapers believed the shortage of textile workers was a problem.

ANSWER: Students might answer that textile workers were necessary for the war effort and to provide basic supplies for the country.

RESOURCE ACTIVITY

GLOBAL HISTORY RESOURCE CENTER
Reading: *Letters from an American Nurse in World War I*
Reading: *Women and World War I*

Print out and distribute the readings. Have students read about the nurse in France and about wartime industry. Then have them write a letter from a woman working in a munitions factory to her friend working as a nurse in France.

Level 3

Then & Now

Submarines

New technology introduced during World War I changed the nature of warfare. While tanks, planes, and poison gas affected land warfare, the most important innovation at sea was the use of a silent and deadly new weapon—the submarine. Moving underwater, submarines could approach enemy ships on the surface, fire their torpedoes, and silently make their escape, all without being detected. The Germans were the first to utilize submarines effectively. Their *Unterseeboote*, or U-boats, were responsible for most of the Allied ships sunk during World War I.

The idea of underwater boats is an old one. During the European Renaissance, for example, Leonardo da Vinci actually drew up plans for one. In the 1800s Jules Verne, a French writer, popularized submarines in his famous novel, *Twenty Thousand Leagues Under the Sea*.

The submarines of World War I, however, bore little resemblance to Verne's description. They were small, flimsy, and often dangerous to sail. More than 180 German submarines were sunk during World War I, and more than 5,000 crewmen were lost. In those years submarines could travel no faster than 12 knots (nautical miles per hour) and dive only about 200 feet. In fact, they actually spent most of the time on the surface, submerging only to attack.

Today's submarines, however, exceed the expectations of Verne's imagination. American *Ohio* Class submarines, for example, are nearly two football fields long. Nuclear propulsion allows them to remain submerged for weeks at a time, reaching depths reportedly around 2,000 feet. Each *Ohio* Class submarine can carry about 24 ballistic missiles. Each missile can carry multiple nuclear warheads capable of hitting enemy targets thousands of miles away.

Other submarines remain sea hunters, like their World War I predecessors. The U.S. *Los Angeles* Class submarines, for example, are designed to locate and destroy enemy submarines. They can also seek out and destroy enemy shipping. To perform such a mission, each submarine carries special sensors and guided torpedoes.

Modern submarines represent the leading edge of high technology. Submarine captains today must study nuclear engineering and oceanography, as well as naval tactics and navigation. Judging from their history as deadly and effective weapons, submarines are likely to play a leading role in naval operations well into the future.

Modern U.S. nuclear submarine

The technology introduced during the previous several decades had rapidly shifted the advantage in battle from attacking to defending forces. For example, barbed wire and machine guns had already proved a deadly combination in the Russo-Japanese War. Barbed wire strung out along a defensive line slowed advancing troops, exposing them to machine-gun fire. On the western front, this combination effectively limited the advances made by either side. Armies dug elaborate earthworks called **trenches** for protection and to hold the ground they had gained.

Improved artillery was also an important factor in the battles of World War I. Trench warfare on the western front led to an increased reliance on the tactic of bombardment, as each side used its heavy guns to wear down the other. The armies of World War I fielded some of the largest cannons ever developed. Some were so big they had to be mounted on railway cars. In 1918 the Germans introduced the "Paris Gun," which could hit a target 75 miles away.

Air power also seemed a new way to strike at the enemy. Dirigibles—gas-filled airships that carried passengers and bombs—and fixed-wing airplanes increased the ability to strike beyond the range of the largest guns. However, such weapons were still in developmental stages and saw relatively limited use during World War I.

As the war progressed, both sides developed even newer technologies in an effort to overcome and break through the defenses of the enemy. Advances in technology allowed navies to develop submarines, which could travel underwater and attack enemy ships without warning. The armies of World War I became the first to use flame-throwers and poison gas, which made the eyes water, blistered the skin, and clogged the lungs of its victims. The development of wireless radio improved communications. In 1916 the British introduced an armored tractor that carried small artillery and machine guns. Called "tanks,"

▲ Although even the tank was unable to end the stalemate of the western front, the effectiveness of the new weapon improved over the course of the war.

these vehicles worked well at cutting through barbed wire and shielding advancing infantry. A British observer described the first tanks in action:

66 *Instead of going on to the German lines the three tanks assigned to us straddled our front line, stopped and then opened up a murderous machine-gun fire, enfilading [covering] us left and right. There they sat, squat monstrous things, noses stuck up in the air, crushing the sides of our trench out of shape with their machine-guns swiveling around and firing like mad.* 99

Industrial technology transformed the ways in which armies and navies fought.

SECTION 2 REVIEW

IDENTIFY and explain the significance of the following:
propaganda
atrocities
genocide
trenches

1. **Main Idea** What made World War I a "total war"?
2. **Main Idea** Why is it possible to refer to the war

between 1914 and 1918 as a "world war"?

3. **Geography: Human-Environment Interaction** How did soldiers in World War I alter the landscape for defense?
4. **Writing to Describe** Create a diary as if you were a front-line soldier during World War I. Describe how new

weapons and tactics affect you on a daily basis.

5. **Synthesizing** How did World War I change the lives of many people in the warring countries? In your answer consider the following groups: (a) women; (b) young men; (c) factory owners; (d) government officials; (e) ordinary consumers.

WORLD WAR I AND AFTER   **605**

SECTION 2 REVIEW ANSWERS

IDENTIFY
For significance, see the following pages:
propaganda (p. 603)
atrocities (p. 603)
genocide (p. 603)
trenches (p. 604)

1. It involved whole societies and economies.
2. Battles were fought all over the world, and troops from many different parts of the world fought in the war.
3. They built elaborate earthworks and trenches and strung barbed wire in front of their positions.
4. Answers should focus on the ideas that barbed wire slowed advancing troops and exposed them to machine-gun fire, and trenches offered some protection from artillery fire, but increased the hazards of poison gas. Answers should also include the idea that the new weapons changed the nature of warfare forever.
5. (a) replaced men in factories; (b) became soldiers; (c) came under greater government control; (d) centralized authority; (e) experienced rationing

SECTION 3

CORE LESSON PLAN
See pages 593G and
593H for Lesson Plan
22.3.

Theme: War and Diplomacy

The Battle of the Somme began on July 1, 1916, with a barrage of British artillery designed to flatten German barbed wire and kill most of the troops in the German trenches. When the barrage lifted, the British troops passed through spaces cut in their own barbed wire, only to discover that German machine gunners had survived the barrage. British casualties numbered approximately 60,000—the highest number for any single day of the war.

Critical Thinking Ask students why so many British troops were killed in the first day of this battle.

ANSWER: Students should note that the attacking British troops were caught without protection in no-man's-land.

SECTION 3
The Course of the War

- How was the war in the East and the Middle East different from the war in the West?
- What was the importance of the war at sea?
- What effect did U.S. entry have on the war?

World War I lasted more than four years. For over two years, both sides sustained massive casualties without any decisive progress toward victory. In the western theaters—in France, Belgium, and Italy—the fighting quickly turned to stalemate. In the eastern theater—Russia and the Middle East—the fighting proved more fluid but equally costly. The course of the war, however, changed in 1917. Overall German losses, combined with Allied control of the seas, and the boost to Allied morale from American entry into the war, made German defeat inevitable by 1918.

The U.S. secretary of war, blindfolded, draws numbers for the military draft.

The War in the West

Germany's attack on France in 1914 nearly succeeded. In early September German troops reached the Marne (MAHRN) River near Paris. They could see the famous Eiffel Tower from their positions outside the city. On September 5, however, French general Joseph-Jacques-Césaire Joffre ordered his retreating troops to counterattack. The battle raged for five days. At the height of the fighting, the French army rushed reinforcements to the front by rail and even by commandeering many of Paris's taxicabs.

This burst of French resistance on the Marne finally halted the German advance. By mid-September the Schlieffen Plan had completely failed. By the end of 1914, the opposing armies had entrenched themselves along a front stretching from Switzerland to the North Sea. The war in the West became a **war of attrition**—each side trying to wear down and outlast the other.

In February 1916 the German High Command, hoping to drain French resources, concentrated forces on a single strategic point—Verdun. The Germans moved huge cannons in range of the city. The French commander, General Philippe Pétain (PAY-tan), stubbornly refused to yield. "They shall not pass!" he declared. France suffered 400,000 casualties—soldiers killed, wounded, missing in action, or captured—to make his statement true. One French colonel told his men, "You have a mission of sacrifice, . . . it is your duty to fall." For 300 days the French endured relentless bombardment. In December the Germans gave up. They had suffered 350,000 casualties and gained no ground.

In July 1916 the British and French tried a breakthrough. They struck along the Somme (SUHM) River in northeastern France. On the first day alone, the British suffered 60,000 casualties. By the time the battle finally ended in November, the British had suffered over 400,000 casualties. Other Allied forces lost an additional 200,000 men. German casualties numbered around 450,000. One soldier wrote home:

> *We have had dreadful losses again. I shall not get leave I suppose until we have left the Somme, but with our losses what they are, this cannot be long or there will not be a single man left in the regiment.*

The German army never fully recovered from its losses at Verdun and on the Somme.

The Italians fared no better in the Alps than had the Germans at Verdun or the Allies on the Somme. The rugged terrain of Austria's frontier produced one of the war's bloodiest campaigns. Italy lost a million men along the Isonzo (ee-ZAWN-soh) River. The stalemate persisted. "The word 'deadlock,'" a German official later wrote, "was on every lip."

Stalemate between heavily entrenched armies characterized the fighting in the western theaters of the war.

The Western Front, 1914–1918

War of Attrition The Germans never captured the city of Paris.

? Movement Approximately how many miles did the Germans retreat from 1914 to 1918?

The War in the East

Although very costly, the war in the eastern theaters tended to be more fluid than the war of attrition in the West. The terrain was more open, with hilly plains of grassland in eastern Europe and deserts in the Middle East. Mobile forces used these open areas to try to outmaneuver their opponents.

The eastern front. In mid-August 1914 the Russians struck against Germany, sending two armies across the German border into East Prussia. Concentrating their forces first against the Russian army at the city of Tannenberg, the Germans inflicted a crushing defeat and captured some 100,000 men. Then the Germans moved against the other force, which lay farther east around the Masurian Lakes. Once again the Germans quickly defeated the Russians, taking another 30,000 prisoners. The two battles proved decisive. The Russians were never able to invade German territory again during the war.

To the south, Russian forces initially fared better. Austria-Hungary had not expected a full-fledged war and had mobilized only against Serbia. Russia's entry into the conflict caught Austria unprepared. Russian troops were able to overrun Galicia (guh-LISH-ah) and capture some 120,000 Austrians. The arrival of German reinforcements, however, allowed Austria to push the Russians back.

In fact, the overall Russian war effort went badly from the beginning. There were severe shortages of food and war materials. Russian commanders often argued among themselves. The German victory at Tannenberg, for example, was due in part to the failure of quarrelsome Russian commanders to support each other. Such incompetence led to tremendous battlefield losses. By 1915 Russia had suffered about two million casualties.

The Gallipoli campaign. Recognizing Russia's predicament, Allied leaders decided on a daring plan to resupply Russia and possibly introduce

💿 **MULTIMEDIA PRESENTATION STRATEGY**

WORLD HISTORY AND CULTURES VIDEODISCS

Image: *Poison Gas: A Terrifying New Weapon*

Search Frame 975

Image: *French Troops Taken Prisoner in WWI*

Search Frame 978

Show the images as you discuss the fighting in Europe. The captions that accompany each CD-ROM image offer additional details.

All Levels

R **RESOURCE ACTIVITY**

READINGS IN WORLD HISTORY
Reading 22.3
Songs of a Campaign

Have students read the poems by a veteran of the fighting at Gallipoli. Then have them complete the questions.

Level 2

The Allied landing on Gallipoli came after an unsuccessful attempt to move a fleet through the Dardanelles. Allied ships shelled the heavy guns positioned on the Gallipoli Peninsula, but were unable to penetrate the heavy Ottoman fortifications. The Ottoman forces sustained little damage and were able to return fire and repel the Allied ships. Allied difficulties were compounded further by the presence of underwater mines. Although minesweepers were able to eliminate some of the weapons, not all were discovered in time. On March 18, 1915, three Allied ships were sunk and others badly damaged by mines. Unable to avoid the dangers to ships posed by mines, the British decided to take the Gallipoli Peninsula by land.

Critical Thinking Ask students how capturing the Gallipoli Peninsula would have helped Allied ships pass through the Dardanelles.

ANSWER: Students should note that if Allied troops could destroy the Ottoman guns at Gallipoli, then the fleet would have been able to pass through the Dardanelles.

Map Answer

The battle kept Russians from invading Germany during the war.

---

fresh troops into eastern Europe through the Black Sea. Early in 1915 British and French warships tried to force their way through the Dardanelles and into the Sea of Marmara. From there they hoped to bombard Constantinople into submission. The attempt failed, however. Lord Fisher, Britain's senior admiral, declared, "Damn the Dardanelles! They will be our grave."

Next, the British decided to land an army on the Gallipoli Peninsula and take the heights commanding the Straits. On April 25, 1915, an Allied force composed primarily of British troops, supported by ANZAC (Australian and New Zealand Army Corps) and French contingents, landed on the Gallipoli Peninsula. They encountered fierce resistance from Turkish troops and were able to gain only a shallow foothold inland. After eight

The Eastern Front, 1914–1918

Central Powers
Allied Powers
Neutral nation
German victory
Russian victory

Farthest Russian advance, February 1915
Farthest German advance, May 1918
Boundary according to the Treaty of Brest-Litovsk, March 3, 1918
Marsh
National capital

War in Eastern Europe The Central Powers stopped the Russian advance in the East.

? Location Why was the Battle of Tannenberg an important victory for Germany?

---

months of fighting the Allied force abandoned the effort. On the night before their withdrawal, a soldier summed up the failure of the campaign:

   We laughed and yarned and jested, waiting, waiting for God knows what, but for something to break the silence that oppressed that vast empty graveyard, not only the graveyard of thousands of good men, but of England's hope in the Dardanelles. The hills seemed to tower in silent might in the pale, misty moonlight, and the few lights upon them flickered like the ghosts of the army that had gone.

Each side had suffered about 250,000 casualties. Although strategically sound, the Allied invasion of Gallipoli had failed largely because of mismanagement and bad timing.

The War in the Middle East

The Gallipoli campaign was not the first action the Allies fought against the Turks. The main war between the Ottomans and the Allies took place in the Arab lands of the Middle East.

In November 1914 an Anglo-Indian force in Persia captured Basra at the head of the Persian Gulf and began to move north. The terrain was forbidding—deserts, swamps, and insects were numerous. After some initial successes, the campaign ended in disaster. Having pushed too far forward, the Allies were besieged in the town of Kut and forced to surrender in April 1916. The Turks captured some 10,000 men, nearly half of whom later died from mistreatment. In 1917, however, the British re-entered Mesopotamia and retook Kut. This time they advanced steadily. By the war's end Britain had full control of Mesopotamia.

Meanwhile, farther west, Britain's first priority was to safeguard the Suez Canal in Egypt. In February 1915 and again in August 1916, the British repelled Ottoman forces attacking the Suez Canal. In 1915 they also increased their efforts to stir up rebellion among the Ottomans' Arab subjects.

Since before the outbreak of war, the British had been negotiating with Husayn ibn 'Ali, the local ruler of Mecca. Husayn wanted British help to establish an independent Arab state under his own rule as caliph. After lengthy negotiations the British agreed to recognize Arab independence in exchange for an Arab rising against the Ottomans. In June 1916 Husayn and his followers attacked Turkish forces in the Arabian Peninsula.

The British forces had also begun to advance north from Egypt. With the Arabs protecting their flank, in December 1917 British forces commanded by General Sir Edmund Allenby captured Jerusalem. The following year his forces also captured Damascus, and in October 1918 the Ottomans sued for peace. Combined with the Mesopotamian campaign, Allenby's operations left Britain the dominant power in the Middle East.

Unlike the stalemate of the war in the West, the war in the East and the Middle East was a war of movement.

War in the Middle East, 1914–1918

Gallipoli, 1915–1916

The Ottoman Defeat When the Ottomans entered World War I on the side of the Central Powers, their once powerful empire was close to collapse.

Linking Geography and History Which European power controlled key countries in the Persian Gulf?

The War at Sea

Although the bulk of the fighting occurred on land, ultimate victory in World War I depended on the ability to control vital sea lanes to Europe. Across these sea lanes, ships transported the food, raw materials, munitions, and people necessary for the survival of a wartime economy. During the war both Britain and Germany used their navies to set up blockades against the other. The object of the blockades was to starve the other country and ruin its economy. "British sea power, . . ." as Admiral Sir

Herbert Richmond wrote, "was the foundation upon which the eventual victory was built."

Britain relied on surface ships for its blockade. Yet, only one major surface engagement occurred. On May 31, 1916, Britain's Grand Fleet engaged Germany's High Seas Fleet in the North Sea at the Battle of Jutland. The battle proved indecisive, although the British suffered heavier losses. Nonetheless, historians usually consider the Battle of Jutland a British strategic victory because the German fleet remained in port for the rest of the war. Another threat remained, however.

Theme: War and Diplomacy

The *Lusitania* was not the last ship carrying American passengers that Germany sank. In August 1915 the *Arabic* was torpedoed off the southern coast of Ireland. On September 1 Germany officially ended unrestricted warfare against passenger ships. President Wilson had no way to force the Germans to uphold this policy, however, and in March 1916 a U-boat attacked and sank the *Sussex,* injuring several American passengers. It was after this incident that President Wilson threatened to end diplomatic relations with Germany unless attacks on civilian vessels ceased.

Critical Thinking Ask students if they believe Wilson should have declared war on Germany earlier, and why they feel as they do.

ANSWER: Students might feel that Wilson should have declared war earlier since German U-boats had killed American citizens, or they might feel that Wilson was right to avoid heavy American troop losses by staying neutral.

◄ Crew members of a German submarine watch as a torpedo they fired hits an Allied steamer.

The Germans based their blockade on the use of **U-boats,** or submarines. The strategy nearly brought Britain to its knees. A German U-boat officer described an attack on a British ship:

> ❝ *I saw that the bubble-track of the torpedo had been discovered on the bridge of the steamer, as frightened arms pointed towards the water and the captain put his hands in front of his eyes and waited. . . . Then a frightful explosion followed.* ❞

The Royal Navy's surface ships made it possible for the British to board merchant ships, seize any **contraband,** or war material being supplied to its enemy, and release the crew and passengers safely. Germany's submarines, however, had to sink ships thought to be carrying contraband, causing serious loss of life. These submarine attacks soon put Germany at odds with even the powers that remained neutral

▲ On March 1, 1917, a U.S. newspaper printed the Zimmermann Note. The newspaper above, like many others, misspelled Zimmermann's name.

during the first part of the war—particularly the United States.

In May 1915, for example, a German submarine torpedoed and sank the *Lusitania,* a British passenger liner, off the coast of Ireland. More than 100 American citizens died in the attack. Outraged, President Woodrow Wilson warned Germany that the United States would not tolerate another such incident. For the next year and a half, Germany restricted the use of its submarines, hoping to keep the United States out of the war. In 1917 this policy changed.

Ultimate victory in World War I depended on mastery of the sea.

The United States Enters the War

The events of 1917 signaled the beginning of the end of World War I. As the year began, Germany faced critical shortages of food and other vital materials. German leaders concluded that victory had to come soon or not at all. In February they decided to resume unrestricted submarine warfare. They realized that such action would probably bring the United States into the war, but they hoped to defeat the Allies before the United States could mobilize. In the meantime they also planned to keep the United States busy with a diversion.

In January, German foreign minister Arthur Zimmermann cabled the German ambassador in Mexico and ordered him to urge Mexico to enter the war as a German ally. In return, Germany promised to help Mexico regain possession of its lost territory in New Mexico, Texas, and Arizona. However, the Zimmermann Note, as it became known, was intercepted by British intelligence agents and then passed on to the

Wartime Poetry

World War I produced a rich outpouring of literature, particularly poetry. In Great Britain much wartime poetry appeared in books and newspapers—often as a kind of epitaph for authors who had "gone West" (died in battle). Many of the wartime poets on both sides lamented the human costs of war, but, particularly in the early days of the fighting, they also expressed their conviction that they were fighting for a just cause.

1914

War broke: and now the
  Winter of the world
With perishing great
  darkness closes in.
The foul tornado, cen-
  tred at Berlin,
Is over all the width of
  Europe whirled. . . .

For after Spring had bloomed
  in early Greece,
And Summer blazed her glory
  out with Rome,
An Autumn softly fell,
  a harvest home,

A slow grand age, and rich with
  all increase.
But now, for us, wild Winter,
  and the need
Of sowings for new Spring, and
  blood for seed.

1914 (?)
Wilfred Owen

The Barn

Lord, if I'd half *your* brains, I'd
  write a book:
None of your sentimental
  platitudes,[1]
But something real, vital; that
  should strip
The glamour from this outrage
  we call war,
Shewing it naked, hideous,
  stupid, vile— . . .
Men maimed and blinded: men
  against machines—
Flesh versus iron, concrete,
  flame and wire:

Men choking out their souls in
  poison-gas:
Men squelched into the slime
  by trampling feet. . . .

And if posterity should ask
  of me
What high, what base emotions
  keyed weak flesh
To face such torments, I would
  answer: '*You*!
Not for themselves, O daughters, grandsons, sons,
Your tortured forbears wrought
  this miracle;
Not for themselves,
  accomplished utterly
This loathliest task of murderous servitude;
But just because they realized
  that thus,
And only thus, by sacrifice,
  might they
Secure a world worth living in—
  for you.' . . .

October 31, 1917
Gilbert Frankau

Understanding Literature

1. Whom does Owen blame for the war?
2. How does Frankau try to strip the glamor from war? What might the date of the poem have to do with the feelings it expressed?

[1] [commonplace remarks]

WHEN THE WAR IS OVER, MOTHER DEAR (1).
Soldier laddie, somewhere in France,
In the trenches at the close of day,
Writes a letter to someone he loves
In the home town far away;
"Cheer up, mother, you needn't sigh,
There's a good time coming by-and-bye."

Around 1914 a British soldier in France writes a letter home.

Understanding Literature

1. Owen blames the Germans.
2. Frankau describes the violence of war and shows that war is a brutal, dirty undertaking. The poem was written late in the war, so Frankau's feelings may stem from the extended nature of the conflict.

Across the Curriculum: Literature

World War I inspired novelists as well as poets. American author Ernest Hemingway used the war as the basis for some of his most famous books, including *The Sun Also Rises* and *A Farewell to Arms*, both of which depicted the effects of the war on Americans in Europe. In Germany, Erich Maria Remarque wrote *All Quiet on the Western Front*, the story of a young German soldier's experiences in the trenches during World War I.

Critical Thinking Ask students why World War I was such a popular subject for literature.

ANSWER: Students might suggest that the strong emotions of the war provided inspiration to many writers and that so many people had been affected by the war that audiences were very interested in the topic.

United States. Published in the press, it outraged the American people.

From the beginning the United States had tried to stay out of the war. Many Americans saw the war as a European affair in which they had no interest. The country had declared its neutrality when the war began in 1914. President Wilson urged Americans to remain neutral "in thought as well as in action." Yet as the war progressed, many Americans, including the president, had difficulty maintaining this attitude.

The Zimmermann Note, combined with Germany's announcement of unrestricted submarine warfare, brought President Wilson to the end of his patience. At Wilson's request, Congress declared war on April 6, 1917.

THROUGH OTHERS' EYES

The End of the War in Africa

As in Europe, the later years of the war were a time of great turmoil in parts of Africa. Africans in the German colonies were forced to choose whether to remain loyal to Germany, as the Allies pushed the Germans from their territory. After the end of the war, local women in Cameroons composed a song debating the wisdom of some of the people of Cameroons, who had fled with the Germans, and others who had stayed behind to claim discarded possessions:

❝[Chief] Atangana Ntsama, the war is over.
Hé, Atangana Ntsama, the war is over!
The cannon are broken,
Run quickly, why do you languish [wait] there?
All you Ewondo, come and run quickly,
Go tell it to Mindili Ebulu, the son of Ndono Edoa.
How is it that you would like me to leave so
    many goods behind?
Hé! They will surprise you in your greed!
Such riches. I should take some!
You others, move off, what are you doing there?
Friend, there are as many goods as in a market;
Friend, we have marched through all of that
    without taking anything! ❞

Russia Exits the War

Events in Russia had contributed to Wilson's willingness to ask Congress for a declaration of war. The democratically minded president had objected to joining the Allied side so long as it included the autocratic Russian Empire. This obstacle disappeared in mid-March, however, when a revolution forced Czar Nicholas II to abdicate his throne.

Russia's internal situation had grown steadily worse since the failure of the Gallipoli campaign. The Russian people became increasingly depressed by their appalling casualty rates. By early 1917 they had lost all faith in their government and in the czar. Strikes and street demonstrations broke out in Petrograd. By November radical socialists of the Bolshevik Party under Vladimir Lenin had seized control of the government.

The Bolsheviks acted quickly to take Russia out of the war. In December they opened negotiations with the Central Powers at Brest-Litovsk. The Germans demanded a high price for peace, requiring Russia to surrender vast territories, including Poland, the Baltic provinces, the Ukraine, Finland, and Caucasia. On March 3, 1918, the Bolsheviks accepted the terms of the Treaty of Brest-Litovsk, taking Russia out of the war.

The End of the War and the Armistice

The year 1917 was a turning point in the war for other reasons besides the American entry and the Russian exit. Although the Allies gained some initial successes, like the Germans they too experienced a feeling of gloom. In the spring the new French commander in chief, General Robert-Georges Nivelle, launched an offensive that soon failed with enormous casualties. Disillusioned, many French troops mutinied. Although the mutinies were suppressed, they led to a change of command as General Pétain replaced Nivelle. In the summer the British launched a major offensive. The Battle of Passchendaele that followed, however, cost about 250,000 casualties on each side and ended in near stalemate.

In late March 1918 the German army launched its own last great offensive in an effort to end the war before fresh American troops could arrive. Under the command of General Erich Ludendorff, the German armies inflicted heavy casualties on the British and French and gained considerable ground. By June German forces threatened Paris. As the Allies rallied, however, at the end of July Ludendorff had to concede that "the enemy's resistance was beyond our strength." Ludendorff had exhausted the German army by having used up most of its reserves.

Meanwhile, American troops finally began to arrive in significant numbers on the western front. Although the British and French had already practically broken Germany's ability to continue the war, the American arrival ensured a swift and complete Allied victory. In addition to boosting Allied morale, American troops provided the Allied supreme commander, France's Marshal Ferdinand Foch (FAWSH), with the extra military forces necessary to mount an offensive across Germany's borders. In September Foch attacked German positions in France and Belgium in preparation for a final assault against Germany in 1919.

Germany's position had completely crumbled by mid-autumn of 1918. The High Command knew that the war was lost militarily. German allies began to dwindle. Both Bulgaria and the Ottoman Empire sued for peace. In October a revolution toppled the Austrian government. The German government itself faced the prospect of revolution. The new German chancellor, Prince Maximilian of Baden, tried his best to salvage the situation. He approached Woodrow Wilson, who had publicly expressed his hope for a peace that would prevent any one power from having to suffer humiliation. Wilson replied that he would only deal with a government truly representative of the German people. Popular discontent continued to grow in Germany. Finally, the army turned against the monarchy. On November 9, 1918, Kaiser William II abdicated.

On November 11, the leaders of the new German republic agreed to Allied terms for an **armistice**, the ending of hostilities until a formal treaty could be completed. The terms practically amounted to unconditional surrender. In a railway car in the French forest of Compiègne, the representatives of the new German government grimly signed the armistice agreement while the Allies looked on. World War I had ended.

Despite Germany's improved military situation in early 1918, the arrival of American troops ensured Allied victory in World War I.

SECTION 3 REVIEW

IDENTIFY and explain the significance of the following:
war of attrition
Husayn ibn 'Ali
General Sir Edmund Allenby
U-boats
contraband
Woodrow Wilson
General Erich Ludendorff
Marshal Ferdinand Foch
armistice

LOCATE and explain the importance of the following:
Marne River
Verdun
Somme River
Isonzo River
Tannenberg

Gallipoli
Kut

1. **Main Idea** How was the war in the West different from the war in the East and the Middle East?
2. **Main Idea** Why was the war at sea crucial to Allied victory?
3. **Geography: Place** Why were the Bosporus and the Dardanelles of such strategic importance to both sides?
4. **Writing to Persuade** Imagine that you are a member of the U.S. Congress in 1917. Write a letter to

President Wilson explaining why you think the United States should or should not enter the war.
5. **Synthesizing** Make a chart that includes the following battles on the western front: Verdun, the Somme, and Passchendaele. For each battle, list the casualties and the outcome. How does one side win a war of attrition? Judging by your chart, why do you think people often referred to World War I as "the Great War"?

BATTLE	CASUALTIES	OUTCOME
Verdun		

Theme: Social Relations

Wilson's idea of national self-determination relied heavily on the existence of a common language. To many eastern Europeans, however, national identity was defined by a mix of religious beliefs, language, and race. In addition, Wilson believed that people could choose their nationalities, as many immigrants to the United States had done. In eastern Europe, however, religion, language, and race were seen as constants.

Critical Thinking Ask students how these differences might have affected the future of eastern Europe.

ANSWER: Students might suggest that the differences might have set the stage for further conflicts.

SECTION 4

The Peace Settlement

FOCUS

- Why were the Allies unable to agree about the formation of a postwar world order after the armistice?
- What were the results of the peace conference at Versailles?
- What happened to the former territorial possessions of the defeated Central Powers?

After the armistice of November 1918, Allied leaders faced the task of working out the terms of a permanent peace settlement. "Are we making a good peace? Are we? Are we?" worried one diplomat involved in the process. All desired a settlement that would prevent another world war, but disagreement developed over how to achieve lasting peace. Some favored a lenient peace, while others favored a harsh peace designed to punish the Central Powers. The final settlement proved harsh but incorporated many of the ideas proposed by those who favored restraint.

The Past is Behind Us
The Future is Ahead
Let us all strive to
make the future
better and brighter
than the past ever was.

U.S. DEPARTMENT OF LABOR
W.B. WILSON,
Secretary of Labor

This U.S. Department of Labor poster urged a quick recovery from the war.

Visions of a New World Order

The conclusion of World War I signaled to many people the emergence of a new world order. Allied leaders hoped to reshape the international system, making it more stable and peaceful. However, leaders expressed different visions of this new world order.

Wilson's Fourteen Points. In a speech given to Congress in January 1918, President Wilson proposed the **Fourteen Points**, his program designed to lay the foundation of a lasting world peace. Eight of Wilson's points (points 6–13) addressed specific countries and regions, including Russia, Belgium, Alsace-Lorraine, and the Balkans. The remaining six points (points 1–5 and 14) contained plans of a general nature. They called for: (1) no secret treaties; (2) freedom of the seas for all nations; (3) removal of all economic barriers and tariffs; (4) reduction of national armaments; (5) fair adjustment of all colonial claims, considering equally the interests of the colonial powers and the people living under their rule; and (14) establishment of a "general association of nations" to guarantee the security of "great and small states alike."

In his speech President Wilson emphasized two principles in particular. The first principle was **national self-determination**, the right of a people to choose their own government. In theory, the right of national self-determination extended to people sharing such common attributes as language and culture. Wilson specifically hoped to apply the principle in the territories of the Habsburg and Ottoman empires. He did not, however, believe the principle applied universally. Some peoples, he thought, simply lacked the political sophistication required to govern themselves effectively.

Wilson introduced the second, and most important, principle in the last of his Fourteen Points. This was **collective security**—a system in which nations pledge to cooperate in their mutual defense. Wilson hoped to replace the prewar system of opposing alliances with a collective security arrangement including all the world's states. Any state engaging in aggression, he reasoned, would have to face the combined response of the international community. Collective security, Wilson believed, would form the foundation upon which any future peace would rest. He made it his first priority.

Other views. Other Allied leaders, however, disagreed with Wilson over how best to maintain the future peace. Significant opposition to Wilson's plan developed within the United States itself. Perhaps the best-known American opponent was Henry Cabot Lodge, the ranking member of the Senate Foreign Relations Committee and one of Wilson's leading political rivals. Lodge worried that a wholesale commitment to collective security would undermine Congress's constitutional responsibility for declaring war.

British and French visions of the new world order also differed from Wilson's. The differences centered primarily on what to do about Germany. Wilson had spoken earlier of "peace without victory." He hoped for a fair settlement that would restore Germany to the community of nations. Although many of Wilson's proposals enjoyed wide popularity in Britain, many people questioned the wisdom of relying on other nations for Britain's security. Some favored the imposition of a harsh peace designed to prevent the resurgence of a German threat. The French were even firmer in their disapproval of Wilson's plans.

BIOGRAPHY Wilson encountered a staunch and articulate opponent in French premier Georges Clemenceau (kle-mahn-soh). Born in 1841, Clemenceau studied medicine and lived for several years in the United States. After returning to France, he entered politics in 1870, the same year Prussia defeated France in the Franco-Prussian War. Within six years he had been elected to the national Chamber of Deputies. His ruthless and stubborn manner led his fellow legislators to dub him "The Tiger."

During World War I Clemenceau was an outspoken critic of poor leadership in the French army, which he associated with failure and defeat. In November 1917 "The Tiger" became premier of France. Clemenceau's leadership held his country together through

Georges Clemenceau
BIOGRAPHY

Germany's spring offensive of 1918 and saw France through to victory in the fall. For nearly half a century, Clemenceau had lived in the face of a German danger. Now, with his enemies defeated, he saw a chance to destroy the German threat once and for all.

Clemenceau viewed Wilson's proposals as inadequate guarantees of security. "Hopes without certainty," Clemenceau said, "cannot suffice to those who suffered the aggression of 1914." He thought Wilson a noble but naive visionary. Clemenceau had little patience for "peace without victory." He favored an imposed rather than a negotiated peace. Germany, he argued, should be dismembered and its key regions occupied. Only then, he believed, would France and the peace be truly secure.

After the armistice, different Allied leaders expressed different visions of a new order that would shape the nature of the postwar world.

The Versailles Settlement

In January 1919 a conference convened at Versailles, outside of Paris, to work out the terms of a permanent peace. Each of the victorious nations sent delegates. The most important delegates were Woodrow Wilson of the United States, David Lloyd George of Britain, Georges Clemenceau of France, and Vittorio Orlando of Italy. One participant in the proceedings recorded the mood that prevailed at Versailles:

❝ We were preparing not Peace only, but Eternal Peace. There was about us the halo of some divine mission. . . . For we were bent on doing great, permanent and noble things. **❞**

The Allies agreed to make separate peace treaties with each of the Central Powers. The treaty with Germany became known as the **Treaty of Versailles.** Completed in May 1919, the Treaty of Versailles incorporated elements of the different visions expressed by Allied leaders.

BIOGRAPHY

Georges Clemenceau

The Versailles Conference was nearly interrupted by the same kind of action that had sparked World War I. On February 19, 1919, Clemenceau was shot in the back after entering his car. The assailant, Emile Cottin, fired seven shots at Clemenceau from behind the premier's car. Only one bullet struck Clemenceau. During his recovery Clemenceau said, "We have just won the most terrible war in history, yet here is a Frenchman who misses his target six times out of seven at point-blank range. Of course the fellow must be punished for the careless use of a dangerous weapon and for poor marksmanship. I suggest that he be locked up for about eight years, with intensive training in a shooting gallery." Doctors decided not to attempt to remove the bullet, which remained in Clemenceau's chest until he died in 1929.

Critical Thinking
Ask students what Clemenceau's comment suggests about his personality.

ANSWER: Students might answer that Clemenceau's response suggests his sense of humor as well as his courage.

▲ On June 28, 1919, national leaders from around the world gathered in Versailles's Hall of Mirrors to sign the peace treaty.

The League of Nations. The first issue taken up at the Versailles Conference was the idea of collective security. The delegates quickly agreed to Wilson's Fourteenth Point, which called for the formation of a "general association of nations" to settle international disputes peacefully. The delegates at Versailles drafted the covenant for such an organization and included it in the final treaty. The association was called the League of Nations.

According to its covenant, the League of Nations had two main aims: (1) to promote international cooperation; and (2) to maintain peace by settling disputes and by reducing armaments. The League's ultimate goal was to include all independent nations. Three main agencies— an assembly, a council, and a secretariat—would conduct League business. The League, headquartered in Geneva, was to work with a related but independent body, the Permanent Court of International Justice, or World Court, located at The Hague in the Netherlands.

The members of the League of Nations agreed not to resort to war, promising to submit any disputes to the World Court or to specially convened commissions for resolution. In the event that a member nation broke this agreement, the League had the authority to impose penalties, such as breaking diplomatic relations or suspending trade. The League would use military force only as a last resort.

French security. Clemenceau of France hoped that Wilson, having received agreement on the League of Nations, would compromise on other issues. Above all, Clemenceau wanted security against another German attack. This required, he argued, taking over certain German territories. Clemenceau insisted on the return of the former French province of Alsace-Lorraine. In addition, he demanded that the French boundary be extended to include the Rhineland, the territory on the west bank of the Rhine River. He also demanded control of the Saar Valley with its valuable deposits of coal.

In the final settlement Clemenceau received most of what he wanted. The Treaty of Versailles compelled Germany to **demilitarize**, or remove all its troops from, the Rhineland. The treaty provided for the indefinite occupation of the region by Allied troops. The Saar Valley would fall under the administration of the League of Nations for 15 years. During that time all of the coal mined in the area would go to France. After 15 years the people of the region would vote on whether to remain under the League, to join France, or to rejoin Germany.

Reparations and war guilt. Perhaps Wilson's greatest disappointment at Versailles came in the imposition of a punishing peace on Germany. Wilson had hoped to reconcile Germany through a lenient peace. The war, however, had left bitterness, hatred, and a desire for revenge among many people in Allied countries. Ultimately, Germany had to agree to a costly and humiliating settlement. One witness described the scene as the German delegation arrived to sign the treaty:

66 *Through the door . . . come four officers of France, Great Britain, America and Italy. And then, isolated and pitiable, come the two German delegates. . . . The silence is terrifying. Their feet upon a strip of parquet [inlaid wood] between the savonnerie carpets echo hollow and duplicate. They keep their eyes fixed away from those two thousand staring eyes, fixed upon the ceiling. They are deathly pale.* 99

The Treaty of Versailles imposed a heavy financial penalty on Germany. The Germans had to agree to a strict, burdensome schedule of **reparations**—or payment for war damages. Eventually, the Allies fixed the total sum owed by Germany at $32 billion. Germany suffered further humiliation in having to accept the so-called "war guilt clause" of the Treaty of Versailles. This clause attributed to Germany sole responsibility for "all the loss and damage" sustained by the Allies in the war.

The Treaty of Versailles imposed a harsh settlement on Germany and established collective security arrangements to keep the peace.

The Mandate System, 1924

Middle Eastern Mandates

The Geography of Defeat After World War I, the former German colonies in Africa and the Ottoman territory in the Middle East became mandates controlled by other countries.

? **Linking Geography and History** Which African country was assigned to Belgium as a mandate?

The Mandate System

As a result of their defeat in the war, the Central Powers were forced to give up their colonial territories. Germany had to surrender several overseas colonies in Africa and the Pacific. The Ottomans lost control of their empire in the Arab lands of the Middle East.

Under a system developed by the League of Nations, the League would assume responsibility for a colonial area until its inhabitants were judged sufficiently developed for independence. In the meantime, the League would assign the administration of such an area to an "advanced nation," such as Britain or France, as a **mandate**, or responsibility. The administering nation had to pledge to prepare the subject people for self-government and

Theme:
Economic Organization
A great deal of time was spent debating the need for Germany to pay war costs. Two main groups emerged: those who believed Germany should pay all war costs for the Allies, and those who felt that the Germans should pay only for civilian losses. Wilson supported payment for civilian losses, although he believed that the violation of Belgian neutrality entitled that country to full reimbursement. French and British interests prevailed, however, and required huge reparations.

Critical Thinking Ask students if they feel the Allies acted correctly.

ANSWER: Some students may feel that the Allies acted correctly because German aggression had helped start the war, while others may feel that the treaty led to further German discontent.

REVIEW & ASSESSMENT RESOURCES

- Study Guide 22.4
- Daily Quiz 22.4
- Main Idea Activity 22.4

All Levels

For significance, see the following pages:
Fourteen Points (p. 614)
national self-
    determination (p. 614)
collective security
    (p. 614)
Henry Cabot Lodge
    (p. 615)
Georges Clemenceau
    (p. 615)
Treaty of Versailles
    (p. 615)
demilitarize (p. 616)
reparations (p. 617)
mandate (p. 617)

1. collective security, national self-determina-tion, and need for end to German threat
2. group of nations work-ing to ensure interna-tional peace; promote international cooperation and settle disputes
3. Territories were given by the League of Nations to the victorious powers as mandates.
4. Answers will vary but should address the causes of the war as well as the penalties of the treaty.
5. The mandate system was a system of colonial management that divided German and Ottoman colonies between Allied Powers. Each territory was assigned to a man-date class based on how long outside rule was believed to be needed in the area. This system might have led to con-flicts over areas assigned to different powers, as well as tensions with inhabitants of the differ-ent colonies.

▲ Three of the German delegates study the documentation of the Treaty of Versailles before signing the settlement that charged their country with sole responsibility for the war.

to make regular reports on their progress. The League created three different categories of man-dates— class "A," class "B," and class "C."

The former Arab territories of the Ottoman Empire were assigned to Britain and France as class "A" mandates. This meant that their peoples could be prepared for self-government in a relatively short time. France took control of Syria (including Lebanon). Britain assumed responsibility for Iraq, Transjordan, and Palestine. Palestine presented a unique difficulty. In 1917 the British foreign secretary, Arthur Balfour, had issued a state-ment expressing general sympathy with Jewish desires for a "national home" in Palestine. The Balfour Declaration, how-ever, conflicted with other British pledges to protect the interests of the Arab peoples living in the region. Britain tried to balance its conflicting commitments during the period it administered Palestine.

The two other types of mandates were assigned in Africa and the Pacific. Among class "B" man-dates were Germany's for-mer colonies in tropical Africa, which it was assumed could be prepared for self-government over several decades. The League gave these to Britain and France. Class "C" mandates included Germany's former colonies in southwestern Africa and in the Pacific. It was assumed that these areas would have to remain under the rule of more advanced nations indefi-nitely. South Africa assumed the mandate in South-West Africa. Australia, New Zealand, and Japan took over Germany's former Pacific colonies.

As the victorious powers divided up the colonial territories of the defeated powers, they developed a new rationale for colonial rule.

SECTION 4 REVIEW

IDENTIFY and explain the significance of the following:
    Fourteen Points
    national self-determination
    collective security
    Henry Cabot Lodge
    Georges Clemenceau
    Treaty of Versailles
    demilitarize
    reparations
    mandate

1. *Main Idea* What different views went into the creation of the Versailles settlement?
2. *Main Idea* What was the League of Nations, and what were its functions?
3. *Geography: Place* How did the status of the Central Powers' former overseas territories change after the end of the war?

4. *Writing to Persuade* Write a paragraph defending or refuting the following state-ment: *The Treaty of Versailles was a fair and just settlement for Germany.*
5. *Synthesizing* How was the mandate system structured? What problems might have arisen? How might leaders have solved them?

Consequences of the War

Despite the peace settlement, the conclusion of World War I left several questions unresolved. The peace settlement itself created a variety of new problems in international relations. The war also had a tremendous impact on society, changing the way in which many people viewed Western civilization.

World War I veterans gather in protest after the war.

The United States in the Postwar World

Of all the world's nations, the United States emerged from World War I with the greatest potential for power. The country had entered the war a debtor nation and emerged the world's largest creditor. The United States had escaped the war with far less loss of life and property than the nations of Europe. Yet the role that the United States would play in the world remained unclear.

Although President Wilson had been the primary architect of the League of Nations, the United States elected not to join it. The strong and steadfast opposition of isolationist senators and Wilson's refusal to compromise on adjusting the language of the League's covenant prevented U.S. ratification of the Treaty of Versailles. The United States instead negotiated a separate peace settlement with Germany.

After the war the United States remained involved in European affairs, even though the country withdrew its military forces from Europe. American leaders sought to maintain stability in Europe through different diplomatic and economic means. For example, Wilson's successor, President Warren Harding, sought to ease tensions through the reduction of naval armaments. He hosted a conference of the world's major naval powers to discuss a variety of issues. At the **Washington Naval Conference** in 1922 the United States, Britain, Japan, France, and Italy agreed to set limits on the size of their navies.

Two years later, U.S. economic diplomacy played a critical role in resolving a major crisis in Europe. In 1923 Germany defaulted on its war reparations. France and Belgium responded by sending troops to occupy the Ruhr, a vital industrial region in western Germany. In 1924 Charles Dawes, an American diplomat, helped to stabilize the situation by devising a plan to reschedule Germany's reparations payments. His plan also called for Germany to regain complete control over its own economy. The **Dawes Plan** relieved some of the economic pressure on Germany as well as some of the bitterness Germans felt over reparations.

*A*fter World War I the United States chose not to join the League of Nations but remained involved in world affairs.

A New Map of Eastern Europe

The peace settlement changed the world's political geography. The collapse of old empires resulted in the drawing of new boundaries and the emergence of new nations. Nowhere was the map altered so much as in eastern Europe. The demise of the Russian Empire resulted in the emergence of four new states—Finland, Estonia, Latvia, and Lithuania. Russian collapse combined with German defeat enabled the restoration of an independent Poland. The fall of the Habsburg Empire also resulted in the creation of new states, formerly under Austrian control: Hungary became fully independent; Czechoslovakia was formed in Central Europe; and in the Balkans, Serbia joined with areas formerly controlled by Austria to form the nation of Yugoslavia.

These states represented an attempt to apply the principle of national self-determination by

Europe After the Versailles Settlement, 1919–1920

Reshaping Europe After World War I, many new countries were added to the continent of Europe.

? Linking Geography and History Which countries lay between Russia and Germany?

uniting people of each nationality under their own government. Unfortunately, the attempt did not always succeed. For example, a German-speaking population of some 3 million lived in the Sudetenland of Czechoslovakia. In another case, Poland gained access to the Baltic Sea through control of a corridor cutting across an area inhabited by Germans. Some contemporary observers recognized the danger. France's Marshal Foch, for instance, remarked with great foresight that in the **Polish Corridor** lay "the root of the next war."

The peace settlement redrew the map of eastern Europe, creating new boundaries, new nations, and new problems.

Dissatisfied and Outcast Nations

The peace settlement left several nations feeling dissatisfied or outcast. Both Japan and Italy had entered the war on the Allied side, in large part to acquire new territory. Japan sought territory in the Pacific and in China. Early in the war Japanese forces seized German holdings in both areas. Japan wanted to retain control of China's Shandong Peninsula. The United States objected, however, and pressed Japan to restore Shandong to China. This angered many Japanese leaders.

Italy had similar territorial ambitions, and wanted two ports on the Adriatic—Trieste and Fiume—as well as the South Tirol region of the Alps. In the peace settlement Italy gained South Tirol and Trieste, but the other Allies refused to agree to Italian control of Fiume. Italy's failure to secure the territory it wanted in the peace settlement contributed to popular dissatisfaction and political instability in Italy.

Both Russia and Germany emerged from the war as outcasts. The Bolsheviks' commitment to spreading

revolution and Russia's early withdrawal from the war alienated the country from the rest of the international community. Germany's treatment in the peace settlement created a sense of defiance and a desire for revenge among many Germans. "We shall win the final battle," Germany's foreign minister declared upon returning from Versailles.

The peace settlement left some of the major powers dissatisfied, outcast, and angry.

Impact of the War on Society

World War I had a tremendous impact on Western society. Reliable estimates indicate that the war left more than 10 million soldiers dead and over 20 million wounded. According to one estimate, the total cost of the war was over $300 billion—an enormous figure for the time.

The tremendous costs of the war in human lives and property caused many people in the West to adopt a more critical view of Western society. One contemporary observer, considering the losses suffered by his generation in the war, wrote: "This generation has no future, and deserves none. Anyone who belongs to it lives no more." Paul Valéry, a well-known French author, also expressed the disillusionment many people felt after the war:

66 *We are a very unfortunate generation, whose lot has been to see the moment of our passage through life coincide with the arrival of great and terrifying events, the echo of which will resound through all our lives.* 99

World War I also had a devastating impact on the economies of Europe. Allied governments in Europe emerged from the war seriously in debt. They had borrowed heavily during the

▲ In this German postwar political cartoon, Germany protests as European powers and the United States strip it of its possessions.

World War I Battlefield Losses

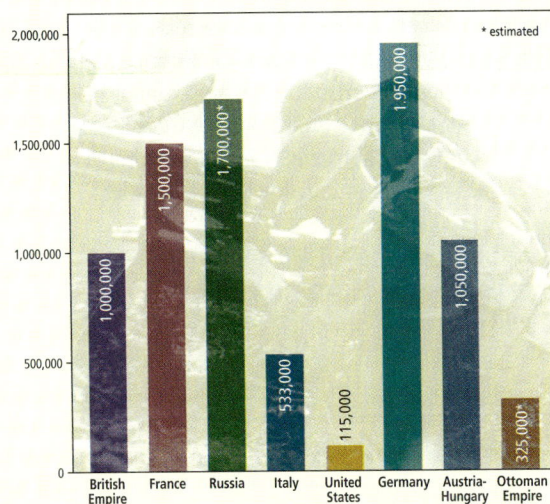

World War I Battlefield dead from World War I, including all the participating nations, numbered about 10 million. In addition, an estimated 20 million people were wounded in the fighting.

❓ **Analyzing** About how many soldiers did the major Allied Powers lose? About how many soldiers did the Central Powers lose? Why were U.S. losses so much lower than those of other nations?

war, mainly from American banks. France's national debt had grown to seven times its prewar level, and Britain's grew by a factor of ten. Germany was saddled with war reparations beyond its ability to pay. The combination of national debts and reparations created a vicious

cycle in the economies of Europe. Britain and France depended on the receipt of reparations to pay off their debts. Consequently, they remained reluctant to relax the financial burden imposed on Germany, whose economic situation only worsened. Moreover, the war had severely disrupted industry and agriculture throughout Europe.

Developments in literature reflected the sense of disillusionment and insecurity that haunted Western society after World War I. Ezra Pound, an American poet, wrote that the war had resulted in "a botched civilization." The writings of the British poet Rudyard Kipling clearly reflected the extent of the catastrophe. Before the war Kipling's work had conveyed the enthusiasm and hope of Western civilization. The war, however, took the life of his only son. Among his "Epitaphs of the War," he wrote bitterly:

> ❝ *If any question why we died,*
> *Tell them, because our fathers lied.* ❞

Popular British novelist John Buchan called World War I "the vastest disorder since the breakdown of the Pax Romana." Indeed, for many people, World War I seemed to mark the beginning of the decline of Western civilization.

World War I transformed Western societies, leaving many people with a sense of disillusionment and insecurity.

SECTION 5 REVIEW

IDENTIFY and explain the significance of the following:
    Washington Naval
        Conference
    Dawes Plan
    Polish Corridor

LOCATE and explain the importance of the following:
    Finland
    Estonia
    Latvia
    Lithuania
    Yugoslavia
    Trieste
    Fiume

1. *Main Idea* How did the United States remain involved in European affairs after the war?
2. *Main Idea* How did the war affect Western societies?
3. *Geography: Location* How did the Versailles settlement change political boundaries in eastern Europe?

4. *Writing to Create* Write a poem, short story, or song about World War I and its consequences.
5. *Hypothesizing* What were some difficulties of Woodrow Wilson's policy of national self-determination? What problems might have arisen in the future because of groups of ethnic minorities, such as the Sudeten Germans, living in the new countries?

Review

On a separate sheet of paper, complete the following exercises:

WRITING A SUMMARY

Using the essential points in the text, write a brief summary of the chapter.

REVIEWING TERMS

From the following list, choose the term that correctly matches the definition.

Dawes Plan   reparations
propaganda   contraband
Central Powers
Allied Powers

1. Britain, France, Russia, and later Italy and the United States during World War I
2. war material supplied to an enemy
3. payments for damages made by a defeated nation to the victors
4. Germany, Austria-Hungary, the Ottoman Empire, and later Bulgaria in World War I
5. rumors, facts, or ideas spread deliberately to further a particular cause or to damage others

REVIEWING CHRONOLOGY

List the following events in their correct chronological order.

1. The British attack at the Battle of the Somme.
2. Russia signs the Treaty of Brest-Litovsk with Germany, taking Russia out of World War I.
3. German troops invade neutral Belgium on their way into France.
4. American diplomat Charles Dawes proposes a plan to relieve some of Germany's economic problems by rescheduling reparations payments.
5. Both sides agree to an armistice, ending hostilities in World War I.

UNDERSTANDING THE MAIN IDEA

1. Why was an alliance between France and Russia a problem for Germany, and how did German leaders try to resolve this situation?
2. How did the Treaty of Versailles affect Germany and the peoples of eastern Europe?
3. What events triggered the outbreak of World War I in 1914?
4. How was the war in the West different from the war in the East?
5. What were the intended functions of the League of Nations?

THINKING CRITICALLY

1. **Analyzing** Why did many Europeans' enthusiasm to enlist and their general conception of war change after 1914?
2. **Synthesizing** Why have many scholars claimed that Europe lost a generation between 1914 and 1918?

Building Your Portfolio

Complete the following activities individually or in groups.

1. **War and Diplomacy** Imagine that you (and your coworkers) are working for a large metropolitan newspaper in one of the nations involved in World War I. You have been asked by your boss to compile a yearbook about a year between 1914 and 1919. You will need to cover the major events of the war or peace settlement for the year you choose. Your yearbook should include articles, which you create, and photos or illustrations of the events you describe. Somewhere in your yearbook, you will need to display a time line.

2. **Daily Life** You have been hired to create a documentary about life on the home front during World War I. You will need to focus on an issue or event that concerned civilians or civilian responses to the war. Use national and local magazines and newspapers from the time to create a script, which should include historical narration and eyewitness reports. Copy images from these sources to create a storyboard to go along with your script. Your script should also describe how your visual and written sources reflect biases of the time.

REVIEWING CHRONOLOGY

3, 1, 2, 5, 4

UNDERSTANDING THE MAIN IDEA

1. An alliance between France and Russia would have put Germany in danger of fighting a war on two fronts. To avoid this, Germany formed the Triple Alliance with Austria and Italy and signed the Reinsurance Treaty with Russia.
2. Germany had to pay massive reparations and accept sole responsibility for the war. In eastern Europe new states such as Lithuania, Latvia, and Estonia were created.
3. War was triggered by the growth of nationalism, imperial rivalries, militarism, and the assassination of Archduke Francis Ferdinand.
4. The war in the West relied on stationary trench warfare, while the war in the East involved a mobile front.
5. The League of Nations was designed to promote international cooperation and to maintain peace by settling disputes and by reducing armaments.

THINKING CRITICALLY

1. Before the war, many Europeans glorified battle and believed that warfare was an appropriate way to demonstrate national pride. The prolonged violence of the war changed these views, and many Europeans became disillusioned.
2. So many soldiers were killed during World War I that Europe essentially lost an entire generation of men.

Chapter 23

Revolution, Depression, and Totalitarianism 1917–1938

Chapter Planning Guide

	TEXTBOOK	CORE RESOURCES	VISUAL RESOURCES	MULTIMEDIA
Introduction	pp. 624–625	Block Scheduling Handbook: Ch. 23		Videodisc Segment 23 and Viewing Guide: *Germany Between the Wars*
Lesson 23.1 The Russian Revolution	pp. 626–630 Map: *Revolutionary Russia,* p. 628 Then and Now: *Two Russian Revolutions,* p. 629	Reading 23.1: *The Storming of the Winter Palace* Geography Activity 23: *The Failure of World Revolution, 1917-1927*		GHRC 23 Reading: *An Eyewitness Account of Famine in Russia* GHRC 23/Videodiscs: Images— *Czar Nicholas II and His Family; Soviet Propaganda Poster*
Lesson 23.2 Postwar Democracies	pp. 631–634 Through Others' Eyes: *German Inflation,* p. 633 Map: *The World: Political,* p. 854–855	Reading 23.2: *Business and Religion* Writing Project 23: *Writing a News Article*		GHRC 23 Reading: *Great Britain's General Strike* GHRC 23/Videodiscs: Images— *Women Move the Mail; Militarism on the Rise in Japan;* Maps—Series of three on *European Democracies*
Lesson 23.3 Society and Culture Between the Wars	pp. 635–640 Literature Through Time: *Berlin Alexanderplatz,* p. 639	Reading 23.3: *Gatsby's Party*	Art and History 23: *Merz 19*	GHRC 23 Reading: *Albert Einstein* GHRC 23/Videodiscs: Image— *French Dadaist Painting;* Audio Clip—*Blues*
Lesson 23.4 The Global Depression	pp. 641–644	Reading 23.4: *The Jarrow Crusade*	Geography and History 23: *Major Currency Blocs, 1930s*	GHRC 23 Reading: *Depression Days in the United States* GHRC 23/Videodiscs: Image— Dismissal: *A Depression Era Painting;* Map—*Unemployment in Europe*
Lesson 23.5 The Rise of Totalitarianism	pp. 645–652	Reading 23.5: *The Trial of Nikolai Bukharin* Skills Activity 23: *Recognizing Stereotypes*	Everyday Life 23: *Nazi Promotional Materials for Sale*	GHRC 23 Readings: *Hitler's Plans; The Reichstag Fire; Kristallnacht* GHRC 23/Videodiscs: Map— *Japan Invades Manchuria;* Video Clip—*Triumph of the Will*
Chapter Investigation and Enrichment	pp. 624–652	Chapter 23 Investigation: *A News Magazine Looks Back* People in World History 23 Explorations in Daily Life 23		GHRC 23/Videodiscs
Review and Assessment	Section 1 Review, p. 630 Section 2 Review, p. 634 Section 3 Review, p. 640 Section 4 Review, p. 644 Section 5 Review, p. 652 Chapter 23 Review, p. 653	Chapter Review Activity 23 Vocabulary Activity 23 Themes Review 23 Section Study Guides 23.1–23.5 Main Idea Activities 23.1–23.5 Daily Quizzes 23.1–23.5 Chapter 23 Test Sheltered English Ch. 23 Test Ch. 23 Test Generator		Audio CDs: Ch. 23 Summary (English and Spanish)

INTRODUCING THE CHAPTER

Textbook pp. 624–625

CHAPTER OVERVIEW

Change and uncertainty marked the postwar years. An authoritarian regime emerged in Russia, and many of the democratic governments that were established after the war faced increasingly difficult times. Even the Western democracies struggled with political and social change as more and more people questioned long-standing traditions. A global depression further shattered Westerners' belief in progress. All these factors gave the old forces of nationalism and militarism a new appeal to many people.

PRESENTING THEMES

On the chalkboard or on an overhead transparency, write the following open-ended theme questions.

- **POLITICS AND LAW** What are some ways in which governments change form?
- **PHILOSOPHY** How might an event such as World War I change people's views about society?
- **ECONOMIC ORGANIZATION** What effects might massive unemployment have on governments and societies?

Have students, either individually or in groups, suggest responses to the questions. For the politics and law question, students might suggest that governments change form after people amend the constitution or participate in a revolution or other political activity. For the philosophy question, students might suggest that people might question a society that started such a war. For the economic organization question, students might suggest that unemployment could make desperate people turn to crime or make them willing to follow any leader promising them jobs. Once students have studied the chapter, you may wish to have them complete the Themes Review, then compare the two sets of answers.

USING THE VIDEO

Segment 23: *Germany Between the Wars*

ENGLISH

Search Chapter 23
Videodisc 2, Side A

SPANISH

Search Chapter 23
Videodisc 2, Side A

Tell students that in this chapter they will apply these theme questions to the Western world in the difficult years after World War I. Then show Segment 23 of the *World History and Cultures Videodiscs*. This segment describes the economic and social stresses that shook Germany and the rest of the world in the 1920s and 1930s. The video also describes the political turmoil that undermined the Weimar Republic and helped to bring about the election of Adolf Hitler. To help the students grasp the significant points of the segment, have them complete Video Viewing Guide 23.

Key to Ability Levels

All strategies and activities are coded to the following ability levels:

LEVEL 1	**Basic** activities suitable for all students
LEVEL 2	**Average** activities suitable for average to above-average students
LEVEL 3	**Challenging** activities suitable for above-average students
SHELTERED ENGLISH	Activities suitable for students with **Limited English Proficiency**

Additional Resources

BOOKS FOR TEACHERS

Gill, Anton. *A Dance Between the Flames: Berlin Between the Wars.* Carroll & Graf, 1993. Emphasizes social and cultural events in Germany.

Pipes, R. *A Concise History of the Russian Revolution.* Alfred A. Knopf, 1995. Argues that Russian beliefs were mixed with Western ideas.

BOOKS FOR STUDENTS

Kruger, H. *A Crack in the Wall: Growing Up Under Hitler.* Fromm, 1982. Recounts a German childhood.

Watkins, T. H. *The Great Depression: America in the 1930s.* Little, Brown and Co., 1993. Tells of the suffering and turmoil that marked the decade.

MULTIMEDIA MATERIALS

The Reckless Years: 1919–1929. Guidance Associates. Video from filmstrips, 39 min. Looks at politics, economics, and lifestyles before the crash.

Ten Days That Shook the World. Granada. Video, 77 min. Looks at the Russian Revolution.

Voices of the 30s. Sunburst. CD-ROM, MAC format. Looks at the depression in the United States.

Textbook pp. 626–630

RESOURCES

Pupil's Edition

Map, p. 628: *Revolutionary Russia, 1917–1921*

Then and Now, p. 629: *Two Russian Revolutions*

Core Resources

Reading 23.1: *The Storming of the Winter Palace*

Geography Activity 23: *The Failure of World Revolution, 1917–1927*

Global History Resource Center

Reading: *An Eyewitness Account of Famine in Russia*

Reading: *New Laws for a New Russia*

Videodiscs or Global History Resource Center

Image: *Czar Nicholas II and His Family*

Image: *Soviet Propaganda Poster*

Search Frame 984

Search Frame 985

LESSON FOCUS

How did Russia become a communist state?

OBJECTIVES

After completing this lesson, students will be able to:

- describe how World War I affected Russia;
- explain what the Russian Revolution accomplished;
- discuss the consequences of Russia's civil war.

HOOK

Discuss the nature of revolution. Ask students if they can think of other examples of revolutions that have occurred in world history. Then ask them to consider some of the reasons why people would want to revolt against their governments. *[Answers could include unfair government practices, such as discriminatory laws; severe social problems; and dissension between various political groups.]*

Conclude by leading a discussion about revolution.
Ask: What conditions might justify a revolution?
   [Answers will vary.]

DEVELOP

Discuss Russia's situation in 1917. Write the following statement on the chalkboard: *In 1914 Russia was the most backward of the major European countries.*

Call on volunteers to offer evidence supporting this statement. Note responses on the chalkboard under the statement. *[Most of Russia's peasantry was mired in poverty; Industrial Revolution came late to Russia; and Czar Nicholas II's rule was very autocratic.]*

Then have students discuss the impact of World War I on the situation in Russia.
Ask: How did World War I affect Russia?
   [A short-lived revolution in 1905 had shown the discontent among Russia's workers, and Czar Nicholas II had responded with some reforms. However, with the outbreak of war, Czar Nicholas became more involved with the war than with domestic affairs in his country. The government mismanaged the war effort, and when the czar took personal command of the troops and left control of the government to his wife, Czarina Alexandra, she mismanaged it. This combination of events resulted in growing discontent among Russians.]

As new points are introduced in the discussion, note them on the chalkboard. Conclude by asking students to use the notes on the chalkboard to create a cause-effect chain of the roots of the Russian Revolution.

PROBE

List the major events of the Russian Revolution during 1917 and 1918. Organize students into several small groups. Have groups draw up a list of the six most important events that took place in Russia during 1917 and 1918. Suggest that students review the text on pages 626–628 to locate events. You might assign Core Resources Reading 23.1 and display the electronic media image of Czar Nicholas II and his family to provide students with additional information. *[Events students might list include bread riots in Petrograd, abdication of the czar, provisional government under Kerensky, Lenin's return to Russia, Bolsheviks' seizure of power in the October Revolution, the Treaty of Brest-Litovsk, and execution of the royal family.]*

Have groups use their lists to create time lines of the Russian Revolution. Encourage students to be creative and provide illustrations to go with the events. Call on group representatives to present their time lines and justify their selection of events.

Link to Today. Refer students to the Then and Now feature on textbook page 629. Then lead a brief discussion on the comparison between the Bolshevik Russian Revolution and the attempted coup in August 1991.

CONCLUDE

Examine the consequences of the civil war in Russia. Direct students to turn to the map on textbook page 628. Call on a volunteer to use the map to describe the course and outcome of the Russian civil war. *[After the Russian withdrawal from World War I, disaffected army officers and their supporters—the Whites—attempted to drive the Bolsheviks from power. Despite help from the Allied Powers, the Whites were unable to defeat the Bolshevik forces—the Red Army.]*

Then have students discuss the impact of the Russian civil war.
Ask: What were some of the consequences of the civil war?
> *[Over 800,000 soldiers were killed; 2 million citizens died from warfare and disease; and the Bolsheviks secured their hold on power in Russia.]*

Next encourage students to examine the steps that the Bolsheviks took to establish their communist government.
Ask: What changes did the Bolsheviks introduce to strengthen their hold on government?

[movement of capital to Moscow; establishment of Council of People's Commissars with Lenin at its head; formation of Congress of Soviets; execution of the royal family; formation of Cheka to suppress dissent; nationalization of industry; collectivization of agriculture; introduction of New Economic Policy; formation of the Union of Soviet Socialist Republics]

To conclude, you may wish to have students complete Geography Activity 23 and then have them read and discuss the Global History Resource Center readings on famine and new laws in Russia. You may also wish to display the electronic media image of the Soviet propaganda poster.

EXTEND
Other Media

Have interested students view the video *Red Empire: Revolutionaries* (Yorkshire Television, color and b/w, 54 min.), which deals with the Bolsheviks' rise to power. Then have students summarize the roles that individual leaders played in the Russian Revolution.

MEET INDIVIDUAL NEEDS
Kinesthetic Learners

Events of the Russian Revolution, such as the abdication of Czar Nicholas II, Lenin's return to Russia, and the storming of the Winter Palace during the October Revolution, lend themselves to role-playing "reenactments." Have small teams of students present re-creations of these events for the rest of the class.

Students Having Difficulty

Encourage students to create a bulletin board display of people and events of the Russian Revolution. To reduce students' confusion over names, groups, and events, refer them to appropriate illustrations on the bulletin board as they read the text.

ASSESS
Review

Have students complete the Section 1 Review. Use answers in the Teacher's Edition, page 630, to assess student mastery of this section.

Lesson 23.2   *Postwar Democracies*

Textbook pp. 631–634

RESOURCES

Pupil's Edition
Through Others' Eyes,
   p. 633: *German Inflation*
Map, pp. 854–855: *The World: Political*

Core Resources
Reading 23.2: *Business and Religion*
Writing Project 23: *Writing a News Article*

Global History Resource Center
Reading: *Great Britain's General Strike of 1926*
Reading: *Lady Astor on Women in Politics*

Videodiscs or Global History Resource Center

Image: *Women Move the Mail: England's General Strike*

Search Frame 986

Maps: Series of three on *European Democracies: 1925, 1933, 1939*

Search Frames 994–996

Image: *Militarism on the Rise In Japan*

Search Frame 993

LESSON FOCUS

How did the democratic nations cope with postwar instabilities?

OBJECTIVES

After completing this lesson, students will be able to:

- describe the economic situation in the major victorious Western democracies after World War I;
- identify problems faced by democracy in Germany after World War I;
- examine how the political situation in eastern Europe and Japan changed after the war.

HOOK

Examine the situation in France after World War I. Tell students that many parts of France were decimated by World War I. To illustrate this point, tell them that one observer, British economist John Maynard Keynes, described northern France as totally devastated, filled with uninhabitable buildings, destroyed fields, shell-holes, and tangled wire.

Point out that France was one of the *victors* in World War I. Then have students consider the problems France might face in the postwar world.
Ask: What postwar challenges confronted France?

[Most students will note that the greatest challenge France faced was to rebuild.]

Conclude by mentioning that all the victorious Western democracies—France, Britain, and the United States—faced challenges in the aftermath of World War I.

DEVELOP

Survey the political and economic situation in Great Britain, France, and the United States in the postwar years. Organize students into three groups. Assign each group one of the following nations: Great Britain, France, or the United States. Encourage group members to work together to brainstorm information about their assigned nations in the post-World War I years. Ask groups to organize their information into a number of periods or phases reflecting the major political or economic developments of the period. Allow groups about 10 minutes to complete this task. Then call on group representatives to report their findings to the class. Note the major points of each report on the chalkboard. Have students use the information on the chalkboard to create three parallel time lines. Suggest that students save their time lines to use for review.

To provide students with further information on the Western democracies in the postwar years, you might assign Core Resources Reading 23.2 and the Global History Resource

Center readings on the strike in Great Britain and on women in politics. In addition, you may wish to display the electronic media image of the general strike in England.

PROBE

Explore the implications of rapid inflation. Direct students' attention to the photograph on page 632. Then have them read the Through Others' Eyes feature on textbook page 633. Call on volunteers to give definitions of the term *inflation*. Focus on definitions that make the following points: 1) inflation is a general increase in prices; 2) money has less buying power.

Next point out that in the early 1920s, Germany experienced *hyperinflation*—annual inflation rates in excess of 500 percent. Mention that in 1923 the Weimar government made inflation worse by printing huge amounts of currency to pay war reparations. Eventually, as the photograph on textbook page 632 shows, paper money had no value at all. Have students consider the impact of rapid inflation on Germany.

Ask: *What were the political repercussions of Weimar Germany's economic problems?*
[The Weimar government's inability to bring hyperinflation under control lost it the support of the German people.]

CONCLUDE

Recognize that the political situation in eastern Europe and Japan changed after the war. Have students turn to the political map of the world on textbook pages 854–855. Have them note the proximity of eastern Europe to Russia. Ask them to consider how this proximity might have affected the political situation in eastern Europe.

Ask: *Why did authoritarian regimes replace democracies in many eastern European countries?*
[Political and social upheaval led to fear that communism might spread from Russia to eastern Europe.]

To illustrate the move away from democracy in Europe, have students view the electronic media maps on European democracies.

Link to Today. You could mention that recently many Eastern European countries have returned to democracy. You might have students pick a country with an authoritarian government after World War I and trace its political development to the present.

Ask students to look at the world map again. Have them note the great distance separating Japan from Europe. Then have them consider how this isolation might have contributed to postwar political change in Japan.

Ask: *Why did militarism and nationalism reemerge in Japan in the postwar years?*
[In the postwar years Japan began to adopt Western ideas. Fearing Western influence, however, some Japanese called for a return to old traditions.]

To conclude, you might display the electronic media image on militarism in Japan. Then ask students how the picture illustrates political change in Japan.

EXTEND

Cross-Curricular Connection: *U.S. History*
Have students research the following topics—the "Red Scare" of 1919-20; the appeal of Harding's call for a "return to normalcy"; support for the Ku Klux Klan in the 1920s; and immigration legislation of the 1920s. Ask students to report on how the events in the United States reflected developments in European nations and Japan.

MEET INDIVIDUAL NEEDS

Auditory Learners
Have students prepare a radio broadcast on international developments in the years after World War I. Suggest that they limit their broadcasts to four news items. You may wish to refer students to Writing Project 23 for guidance on writing a news article.

Gifted Students
Ernest Hemingway's novel *The Sun Also Rises* depicts young American expatriates in Paris in the 1920s. It presents a vivid picture of the psychological effects of war and peace on these members of the "lost generation." Have mature students read the novel. Then have them discuss the novel in relation to this chapter and how if affected their perception of the period.

ASSESS

Review
Have students complete the Section 2 Review. Use answers in the Teacher's Edition, page 634, to assess student mastery of this section.

Lesson 23.3 *Society and Culture Between the Wars*

Textbook pp. 635–640

RESOURCES

Pupil's Edition

Literature Through Time, p. 639: *Berlin Alexanderplatz*

Core Resources

Reading 23.3: *Gatsby's Party*

Visual Resources

Art and History 23: *Merz 19*

Global History Resource Center

Reading: *Albert Einstein's Life and Work*

Reading: *Sherwood Anderson Describes the Assembly Line*

Videodiscs or Global History Resource Center

Image: *French Dadaist Painting*

Search Frame 988

Audio Clip: *Blues by Blind Blake*

Search 6106, Play to 6556
Videodisc 2, Side A
Audio Clip 23

LESSON FOCUS

How did attitudes and culture change between the wars?

OBJECTIVES

After completing this lesson, students will be able to:

- explain why many people adopted new views of society after World War I;
- describe the forms that popular entertainment took during the 1920s and 1930s;
- identify the characteristics of the consumer culture of the 1920s;
- explain why many artists and writers broke with tradition after World War I.

HOOK

Explore new views of society that developed following World War I. Organize students into four groups and assign each group one of the following roles: Albert Einstein, Sigmund Freud, a flapper, and a member of the Temperance Movement. You might want to assign the Global History Resource Center reading on Einstein to the Einstein group. Have group members work together to write a brief speech detailing how their assigned role contributed to or reflected new ways of thinking about society. Have group representatives give their speeches to the class. *[Speeches should note that Einstein's special theory of relativity revolutionized science; Freud analyzed human behavior, arguing that it was dominated by people's attempts to make unconscious desires seem reasonable; flappers represented a rejection of traditional moral values; the Temperance Movement represented an attempt to stop a decline in moral values.]*

Ask: *Why did many people begin to view society differently after World War I?*
[Disillusioned by the war and confused by new scientific ideas, many people adopted new views of society.]

DEVELOP

Describe the types of entertainment that were popular during the 1920s and 1930s. Search public or school library resources to locate tapes of popular radio shows, recordings of jazz musicians, and videos of movies from the 1920s and 1930s. Have students listen to and view selections from these materials. Then ask them to suggest what impact these different forms of entertainment might have had on people's lives. Write their responses on the chalkboard under the headings *Radio, Jazz,* and *Movies*.

Next have students identify sports that were popular during this period in the United States *[baseball]*, Latin America and Europe *[soccer]*, and Japan *[baseball and golf]*. Have students note another sports event that drew large crowds [Olympic Games]. Note responses on the chalkboard under the heading *Sports*.

Conclude by asking students to consider why people showed greater interest in entertainment during this period. *[They had more leisure time and focused more on enjoying themselves than on future plans.]*

Link to Today. Ask students how they imagine popular entertainment has changed from the 1920s to today. *[Answers will vary, but could mention multimillion dollar contracts, and commercialism.]*

PROBE

Define consumer culture and explore its impact on society. Point out to students that the use of the assembly line resulted in increased production and much lower prices for goods. Tell them that a consumer culture is a society in which the key economic issue for manufacturers is how to keep millions of people buying new products.

Ask: How did consumer culture signify an important cultural change?

> *[In the past people were primarily concerned with obtaining goods needed for survival, such as food, clothing, and shelter. The availability of credit enabled them to live for the moment by allowing them to purchase goods easily. Advertising created new attitudes about spending and saving.]*

Conclude by having students read the description of an automobile assembly line by Sherwood Anderson found in the Global History Resource Center.

CONCLUDE

Explore how and why writers and artists broke with tradition after World War I. Have students read the Literature Through Time feature on textbook page 639. Then have them review the reading selection from F. Scott Fitzgerald's *The Great Gatsby*. You might also read an excerpt from *Ulysses*, by James Joyce.

Ask: How are these works different from literature of the past?

> *[Döblin and Joyce rejected old forms and experimented with new methods of expression. Döblin used the montage technique while Joyce experimented with stream of consciousness. Fitzgerald explored new subject areas,*

addressing the changes in society during the 1920s.]

Next display the electronic media image of the dadaist painting and Art and History Transparency 23. Have students view these works as they scan the discussion of dada on textbook page 638. You might also show pictures of the work of architects such as Frank Lloyd Wright and play recordings of Igor Stravinsky's pieces or Brecht and Weill's *Threepenny Opera*.

Ask: How did these works mark a break with the past?

> *[They demonstrated new forms of expression.]*

Ask: Why were postwar artists so ready to part with past traditions?

> *[After the horror of the war years, artists began to express new outlooks on society. Many desired not only to explore new ideas, but also to present these ideas in very different forms.]*

EXTEND

Other Media

Have students further explore art in the 1900s by reviewing the CD-ROM *History Through Art: The Twentieth Century* (Clearvue, Macintosh or Windows format). Ask students how the art of the early 1900s reflected world social and political developments.

MEET INDIVIDUAL NEEDS

Musical-Rhythmic Learners

Have students listen to the Global History Resource Center audio clip and to examples of jazz of the 1920s and then to more formal music from this period, such as George Gershwin's *Rhapsody in Blue* or Aaron Copland's *Piano Concerto*. Then have students discuss how jazz influenced American classical music.

Students Acquiring English

Encourage students not yet fluent in English to respond to the art of this period in nonverbal ways. You might have them make their own drawings or designs to illustrate the artistic styles of this period.

ASSESS

Review

Have students complete the Section 3 Review. Use answers in the Teacher's Edition, page 640, to assess student mastery of this section.

Lesson 23.4 The Global Depression

Textbook pp. 641–644

RESOURCES

Core Resources

Reading 23.4: *The Jarrow Crusade*

Visual Resources

Geography and History 23: *Major Currency Blocs, 1930s*

Global History Resource Center

Reading: *Depression Days in the United States*

Videodiscs or Global History Resource Center

Image: Dismissal: *A Depression Era Painting*

Search Frame 989

Map: *Unemployment in Europe, 1932*

Search Frame 998

Image: *Hunger March in Paris in 1933*

Search Frame 990

LESSON FOCUS

What were the causes and results of the Great Depression?

OBJECTIVES

After completing this lesson, students will be able to:
- identify factors that brought on the Great Depression;
- explain how and why the world economy collapsed;
- describe how the Western democracies responded to the depression.

HOOK: Link to Today

Discuss how economic "bad times" can affect people's lives. Ask students to discuss recent news stories about factory closings, lay-offs of workers, and so on. (You may want to do some research about the subject to help move the discussion along.) Focus the discussion on the impact of these developments on people's lives. Then have students examine the Global History Resource Center selection on the depression and the electronic media image of the depression-era painting. Point out that the Great Depression affected practically every American family. The lucky ones simply had a reduced standard of living. Others were completely impoverished and had to depend on charity just to get by. Emphasize that success and hard work did not protect people from economic disaster. Once-prosperous business owners and hard-working, thrifty people were among those hardest hit by the depression.

DEVELOP

Examine the factors that brought on the Great Depression. Draw on the chalkboard a chart with the following headings: *Condition, Causes, Effects*. In the column headed *Condition*, list the following entries: *increased farm production; easy credit; stock market crash*. Call on volunteers to come to the chalkboard and complete the chart. *[Increased farm production: causes: new industrial equipment, disease-resistant crop strains leading to greater harvests; effects: demand did not match supply, so farm prices fell; Easy credit: causes: desire of American business and government leaders to keep prosperity growing; effects: more buying on credit, buying stock on margin, stock speculation, Great Bull Market; Stock market crash: causes: margin calls, panic selling of stocks; effects: 1929 crash, run on the banks, bank closures, financial ruin for many]*

Encourage students to copy the chart into their notebooks. Suggest that they write a caption for the chart that summarizes the causes of the Great Depression. Then have them use the chart to create a cause-and-effect chain that shows all of the events leading up to the Great Depression.

PROBE

Examine how and why the depression spread across the world. Erase the chart from the chalkboard except for the stock market crash entry. Point out that the 1929 crash triggered economic problems around the world. Ask students to identify the connection between the stock market crash and economic problems in other countries.

Ask: What repercussions did the 1929 crash have in other countries?

[The 1929 crash revealed the weaknesses of the world's agricultural markets, causing commodity prices to tumble. To bolster their finances at home after the crash, many Americans withdrew their investments from Europe, causing bank failures.]

Next write *Tariffs and Trade* on the chalkboard. Have students consider how this factor transformed the depression into a global problem.

Ask: What role did international trade play in the spread of the depression?

[Nations devalued their currencies to make their commodities cheaper in foreign markets. Then Britain and many other nations abandoned the gold standard, making trade difficult. Further, many nations tried to protect their own industries against foreign competition through tariffs and other trade barriers. As a result, the channels of world trade closed.]

To underscore the role of currency devaluation in the spread of the depression, show Geography and History Transparency 23 and assign the accompanying worksheet.

CONCLUDE

Discuss the reactions of Western democracies to the depression. Have students view the electronic media map *Unemployment in Europe, 1932* and the electronic media image *Hunger March in Paris in 1933*. Ask students what these materials show about conditions during the depression. Next assign Reading 23.4 and have students discuss the actions and attitudes of the Jarrow marchers. Then point out that government leaders in the Western democracies feared that unemployment, poverty, and hunger would lead to unrest and revolution.

Ask: How did Western democracies respond to the social and political unrest caused by the depression?

[They increased government intervention in the economy,

offering relief to the most impoverished and introducing various programs to revitalize economies.]

EXTEND

Cross-Curricular Connection: *Journalism*

The rise of photo-journalism in the 1920s and 1930s led to the publication of a large number of memorable photo images of ordinary people during the depression. Have students locate photographs from the depression in books, picture collections, or on one of the CD-ROMs dealing with this era, such as *The Faces of LIFE* (Creative Multimedia, MPC) or *Voices of the 30s* (Sunburst, Macintosh). Encourage students to share their findings with the rest of the class.

Other Media

Have interested students view the movie *Roll of Thunder, Hear My Cry*. Then have them discuss the experiences of African Americans in the southern states during the depression.

MEET INDIVIDUAL NEEDS

Linguistic Learners

Discuss with students the ways in which ordinary people's lives were affected by the depression. Encourage students to imagine they lived during the depression years. Have them write diary entries, poems, or songs describing their experiences. They may need to do further research on the subject. Then have them read aloud or perform their works in front of the class.

Musical-Rhythmic Learners

In the United States, the depression inspired a large number of songs that expressed people's feelings about the times. Have students find recorded examples and share them with the class.

ASSESS

Review

Have students complete the Section 4 Review. Use answers in the Teacher's Edition, page 644, to assess student mastery of this section.

Lesson 23.5 *The Rise of Totalitarianism*

Textbook pp. 645–652

RESOURCES

Core Resources

Reading 23.5: *The Trial of Nikolai Bukharin*

Skills Activity 23: *Recognizing Stereotypes*

Visual Resources

Everyday Life 23: *Nazi Promotional Materials for Sale*

Global History Resource Center

Reading: *Benito Mussolini Explains Fascism*

Reading: *Adolf Hitler's Plans for Germany*

Reading: *The Reichstag Fire of 1933*

Reading: Kristallnacht *and the Plight of German Jews*

Reading: *The League of Nations on Japanese Aggression*

Videodiscs or Global History Resource Center

Maps: Series of three on *European Democracies: 1925, 1933, 1939*

Search Frames 994–996

Map: *Japan Invades Manchuria, 1931*

Search Frame 999

Video Clip: Triumph of the Will

Search 5267, Play to 6104

Videodisc 2, Side A

Video Clip 23

LESSON FOCUS

Why and where did totalitarian regimes arise and what was their impact?

OBJECTIVES

After completing this lesson, students will be able to:

- explain how Mussolini gained power in Italy;
- describe how Hitler transformed German society and government;
- discuss how totalitarianism in the Soviet Union differed from totalitarianism elsewhere;
- analyze why various countries around the world embraced totalitarianism in the 1920s and 1930s.

HOOK: Link to Today

Determine the nature of totalitarianism. Call on students to identify everyday decisions that they, their friends, or relatives might make. Focus on such questions as: Which books shall I read? What movies shall I see? From what source shall I get my news? What religion shall I follow? Where and how shall I express my political opinions?

Ask: **Who makes such decisions in a democratic society?** *[individuals]*

Then point out that totalitarianism creates a different situation. Demonstrate this by asking students to identify their favorite novels, movies, or rock stars. List their responses on the chalkboard. Erase all the choices except one, telling students that this is the only choice available to them because it is the only one that supports the aims of the government.

DEVELOP

Note the steps taken by Mussolini and Hitler to establish totalitarian rule in Italy and Germany. Organize students into several groups. Randomly assign groups to study either Hitler or Mussolini. Have groups develop a list of the steps their assigned leader took to establish totalitarian government, noting the year that each step took place. Suggest that students examine the material on textbook pages 645–649 for information. They might gather additional information from Skills Activity 23, Everyday Life Transparency 23, and the

Global History Resource Center readings on Mussolini's view of facism, Hitler's plans, the Reichstag fire, and *Kristallnacht*. Direct groups studying the same nation to compare their work and draw up a comprehensive list for that nation.

Next attach several sheets of butcher paper to the wall. Draw a horizontal line through the center of the sheets, adding the labels 1920 and 1940 at either end. Then add the title *Progress Toward Totalitarianism*. Have group representatives record Italy's progress at appropriate points above the line and Germany's move toward totalitarianism at appropriate points below the line.

PROBE

Examine the differences between Soviet totalitarianism and totalitarianism elsewhere. Direct students' attention to the wall time line they have just completed. Have them consider what entries they would include if they had to add information on the Soviet Union's progress toward totalitarianism. Then have students compare the Soviet style with Italian and German totalitarianism.

Ask: How was Soviet totalitarianism similar to totalitarianism elsewhere?

[To establish his totalitarian state Stalin used tactics similar to those used by Mussolini and Hitler.]

Ask: How was it different?

[Soviet totalitarianism was based on the communist idea of a collective society ruled by the working class, rather than on the ideas of nationalism and private property.]

To give students an illustration of the tactics employed by Stalin, assign Reading 23.5.

CONCLUDE

Examine why various countries embraced totalitarianism. Mention that the totalitarian approach was quickly adopted by governments across Europe. Have students view the Global History Resource Center maps on European democracies. Ask them to note the number of European countries that had adopted an authoritarian style of government by 1939. Continue by emphasizing that totalitarianism was a global phenomenon. Focus first on Latin America. Discuss reasons why Brazil and Argentina turned to totalitarianism. Next have students investigate the situation in Japan.

Ask: Why did Japan turn to militarism?

[Problems created by the depression exposed the weaknesses of the new democratic government. Some leaders turned from democracy to older ideas of military tradition and discipline. Expansionist policies of militarists were enthusiastically supported by the people.]

To illustrate the role that expansionism played in totalitarian thinking, have students view the electronic media map showing the Japanese invasion of Manchuria. Then have them review the Global History Resource Center reading on Japanese Aggression. Conclude by informing students that in Chapter 25 they will read about the outcome of totalitarian expansionism—World War II.

EXTEND

Cross-Curricular Connection: *Political Science*

Have students write an essay comparing the political ideas of Hitler and Mussolini. Suggest that students pay particular attention to what each leader thought about democracy, socialism, the role of government, national expansion, and the place of the individual in the state. Students might begin their research by reviewing the Global History Resource Center reading on fascism.

MEET INDIVIDUAL NEEDS

Visual-Spatial Learners

Have students view excerpts from Leni Riefenstahl's movie *Triumph of the Will*. Ask students to discuss why they think the images captured by Riefenstahl had such a powerful effect on Germans in the 1930s.

Interpersonal Learners

Have students bring the horror of *Kristallnacht* to life by having some act as American journalists covering the story and others as German Jews being interviewed by the journalists.

ASSESS

Review

Have students complete the Section 5 Review. Use answers in the Teacher's Edition, page 652, to assess student mastery of this section.

In preparation for the chapter test, you may wish to have students complete all or part of the Chapter 23 Review on textbook page 653, the Chapter 23 Review Activity, and the Chapter 23 Themes Review.

Chapter 23

Revolution, Depression, and Totalitarianism

Understanding the Main Idea

Call on a volunteer to read aloud the *Understanding the Main Idea* paragraph. Tell students that societies experienced dramatic change after World War I. Dissatisfaction with tradition led to new standards of behavior. The global nature of the economy meant that one nation's economic turmoil affected the entire world. As people sought to meet their daily needs, many turned to leaders who promised reform in exchange for vast power.

Presenting Themes

See p. 623B for suggestions on introducing themes.

Using the Time Line

Have students list the time line events in their notebooks. After they have read about each event in the chapter, have students write a paragraph explaining its significance.

Chapter 23
Revolution, Depression, and Totalitarianism 1917–1938

Understanding the Main Idea

The years following World War I were a time of uncertainty and change around the world. Even though the 1920s were relatively prosperous, many people believed that Western civilization was in decline. In 1917, revolution swept through Russia. In 1929, the Great Depression threw millions of people out of work. In many countries, dictators soon seized control of national governments.

Themes

- **Politics and Law** What are some ways in which governments change form?

- **Philosophy** How might an event such as World War I change people's views about society?

- **Economic Organization** What effects might massive unemployment have on governments and societies?

In 1933 the National Socialist German Workers Party gained control of the German government under Adolf Hitler. The National Socialists used propaganda, intimidation, and violence to achieve their political goals. Hitler promised to rid Germany of what he considered its racial enemies. But what would make millions of people follow such a leader? Some answers lie in the observations of a schoolteacher from Hamburg, who was present at one of Hitler's speeches in the 1930s:

> *The hours passed, the sun shone, expectations rose. . . . 'The Führer is coming!' A ripple went through the crowds. . . . There stood Hitler in a simple black coat and looked over the crowd, waiting—a forest of swastika pennants swished up, the jubilation of this moment was given vent in a roaring salute. . . . His voice was hoarse after all his speaking during the previous days. When the speech was over, there was roaring enthusiasm and applause. Hitler saluted, gave his thanks. . . . Hitler was helped into his coat. Then he went. How many look up to him with touching faith as their helper, their savior, their deliverer from unbearable distress.*

The rise of Hitler was only one example of the turbulent period of world events after World War I.

1917	1922	1926	1928
October Revolution sweeps across Russia.	Mussolini takes control of Italian government.	National strike takes place in Britain.	Bertolt Brecht and Kurt Weill collaborate on *The Threepenny Opera*.

Civilians in Braunschweig, Germany, watch as rows of Nazi troops march past Hitler's *Sieg Heil!* (victory) salute in 1931.

1929	1930	1933	1938
▲ New York Stock Exchange crashes.	▲ Sigmund Freud publishes *Civilization and Its Discontents.*	▲ Hitler is granted dictatorial power in Germany.	▲ Jewish synagogues and businesses are destroyed during *Kristallnacht* in Germany.

SECTION 1

CORE LESSON PLAN
See pages 623C and 623D for Lesson Plan 23.1.

RESOURCE ACTIVITY

GLOBAL HISTORY RESOURCE CENTER
Image: *Czar Nicholas II and His Family*

Show students the image. Then ask them to write a dialogue between two Russian peasants who have just seen this picture. One peasant supports the old system and one wants reform.

Level 3

SECTION 1

The Russian Revolution

FOCUS

- How did the First World War affect Russia?
- What did the Russian Revolution accomplish?
- What were the consequences of the civil war in Russia?

*F*ew events have had as much influence on modern world history as the Russian Revolution. In 1917 workers in Russia rebelled against the rule of the czar, forcing him to abdicate the throne. Not long after the people overthrew the czar, however, a more radical group of revolutionaries, called the Bolsheviks, seized power and established an authoritarian regime over the nation.

The towers of St. Basil's Cathedral in Red Square, Moscow

The Roots of the Revolution

In 1914 Russia was the most backward of the major European countries. Most of the peasantry still remained in poverty. Despite recent reforms, Czar Nicholas II ruled in a more autocratic fashion than monarchs in other parts of Europe. The Industrial Revolution had arrived late in Russia, and only in the last few decades had the country begun to enter the age of the machine.

In 1905 a short-lived revolution had swept through Russia's major cities, demonstrating the depth of discontent among the Russian people and causing the czar to institute some minor changes. Workers were allowed to form unions and councils, called **soviets**, to express their grievances.

With the outbreak of World War I, however, Nicholas became more concerned with fighting battles than with solving the problems of the people. The government's mismanagement of the war caused even greater discontent. Russian soldiers often went into battle with no weapons and few supplies. By 1917 Russia had suffered over 8 million casualties—soldiers either killed, wounded, or captured.

The Russian people began to lose all faith in their government. When Nicholas decided to take personal command of his troops, he left the government in the hands of his wife, Czarina Alexandra. She chose the eccentric Grigory Rasputin as her advisor because of his ability to stop the bleeding of her son Alexis, who suffered from hemophilia. Soon rumors of misconduct and scandal surrounded the Russian court.

Russia's problems continued to worsen during the first months of 1917. Further defeats on the battlefield, combined with deteriorating supplies of food, provoked mutinies among the soldiers and strikes on the home front.

World War I magnified long-standing grievances in Russia, increasing dissatisfaction with czarist rule.

The February Revolution

The strains increased until March 1917, when the first stage of the Russian Revolution began. This was the **February Revolution**, so called because it was February according to the calendar used at that time in Russia. On March 8, when they were unable to buy bread to feed their hungry families, angry women factory workers in Petrograd (formerly St. Petersburg) staged strikes in protest. They encouraged the soviets and other workers to join them in their protests. By the end of the day, thousands of people demonstrated in the streets of Petrograd. One woman described the scene:

▲ In 1917 Russian women defiantly march down the streets of Petrograd, Russia, to protest high food prices.

66 *The streets were full of people. The trams [streetcars] weren't running, overturned cars lay across the tracks. I did not know then, I did not understand what was happening. I yelled along with everyone, 'Down with the czar!' . . . I yelled again and again. . . . I felt that all of my familiar life was falling apart, and I rejoiced in its destruction.* 99

Troops sent to stop the rebellion instead joined the protest. With no support from either the military or the people, the czar was forced to abdicate.

Russian leaders appointed a group of moderate reformers to set up a provisional government, which was ultimately headed by Alexander Kerensky. From the beginning the government faced overwhelming problems. First, despite calls for peace, Kerensky chose to keep Russia in the war. Second, workers soon became dissatisfied with the provisional government when food prices rose even higher.

The February Revolution toppled the monarchy and replaced it with a moderate provisional government.

The October Revolution

Events were moving beyond Kerensky's control, and he found himself attacked as a defender of the old order. No one attacked Kerensky more successfully than Vladimir Ilich Ulyanov, better known as Lenin.

BIOGRAPHY Lenin had been born in 1870 in the town of Simbirsk. In 1887 Lenin's brother, Alexander, was executed for taking part in a plot to assassinate the czar. From that point on, Lenin devoted his life to promoting revolution against the monarchy. At the university he became a believer in the communist teachings of Karl Marx and was later exiled to Siberia for spreading Marxist materials among workers. In 1900 Lenin left Russia to live abroad.

When the revolution broke out in 1917, Lenin, who was living in Switzerland, desperately wanted to return home. German agents arranged for a special train to carry him across Europe. The train was sealed so that Lenin could not spread revolutionary ideas along the way. Lenin arrived in Petrograd in April 1917.

Lenin
BIOGRAPHY

Upon his return, Lenin assumed leadership of a group of revolutionaries known as the **Bolsheviks**. The Bolsheviks opposed the Mensheviks, who hoped to achieve reform through an elected parliament. The Bolsheviks, who practiced a form of communism, believed that only an elite group of revolutionary leaders should guide the rest of the country. In particular, Lenin reasoned that the masses of peasants wanted strong leadership, an end to the war, and better lives. As soon as he arrived, he began to challenge provisional government, offering the people "Peace, Land, and Bread."

BIOGRAPHY
Lenin
Marxist theory asserted that socialist revolution would be successful only in middle-class capitalist nations. Socialists in pre-industrial countries such as Russia would thus have to support the development of capitalism even as they prepared to destroy it. Lenin disagreed with this view, believing that only a revolution would end czarist rule in Russia.

Critical Thinking Ask students what might have happened if Lenin had agreed with Marx on capitalism and the revolution.

ANSWER: Some students might suggest that the nation's industrial base would have been in place before the revolution. Others might suggest that once capitalism was in place, the Revolution might have been more violent.

Revolutionary Russia, 1917–1921

Legend:
- Bolshevik uprising, 1917
- Area controlled by Bolsheviks, October 1919
- Attacks by foreign forces
- Attacks by the Whites
- Bolshevik counterattacks
- Boundaries, 1921

Czar Nicholas II and his family executed, 1918.

The Fires of Revolution The Bolshevik Red Army faced coordinated opposition from foreign countries as well as from internal opponents.

? Location From which directions did the White armies attack the Bolsheviks?

> *With all my might I urge comrades to realize that everything now hangs by a thread; that we are confronted by problems which are not to be solved by conferences or congresses, . . . but exclusively by peoples, by the masses, by the struggle of the armed people.*

The Bolsheviks had taken over by force. Russia was now under the dictatorial control of Lenin. The Bolsheviks renamed themselves the Communist Party, and in 1918 the Communists concluded the Treaty of Brest-Litovsk with Germany, taking Russia out of the war.

The Bolsheviks instigated the October Revolution, which won them control of the Russian government.

The Civil War

The Treaty of Brest-Litovsk angered many Russians, who considered it a betrayal of the war effort. Former army officers and other groups, such as the Cossacks, formed military units to fight the Bolsheviks. These forces, called the **Whites**, hoped to drive the Bolsheviks from power. Between 1918 and 1920, Russia was torn by a bloody civil war as White forces fought the Bolshevik **Red Army** under Trotsky.

In November 1917 (October by the Russian calendar) the Bolsheviks took power in what became known as the **October Revolution**. Under the skillful leadership of Leon Trotsky, Lenin's right-hand man, Bolshevik military units, including the workers' Red Guards, stormed government offices in Petrograd and Moscow. The provisional government was arrested at its headquarters in the Winter Palace. Lenin addressed the Russian people:

Hoping to keep Russia as an ally and to keep vital war materials from falling into German hands, the Allied Powers sent military supplies and troops to help the White forces in their struggle. Even with this outside help, however, the Whites were unable to fight the Red Army effectively. The Whites were disorganized and could not coordinate their actions. After three years of fighting, the Bolsheviks defeated the White forces, ending the civil war.

Then & NOW

Two Russian Revolutions

In Russia, Communist rule ended as it had begun, with a revolution. The Bolsheviks seized power in November 1917, ushering in the first Russian Revolution and the creation of the Soviet Union. Almost 74 years later, in August 1991, a group of hard-line Communists attempted to take control of the Soviet government. They wanted to halt the reform programs instituted in the previous six years. The failed coup, however, led to the second Russian Revolution—the collapse of Soviet communism.

Swift action was the key to the Bolsheviks' successful power grab. They quickly took control of the provisional government headquarters and arrested all those who might rally opposition. The Bolsheviks also seized telegraph offices and railroad stations and blocked the roads out of Petrograd.

In contrast, inaction and incompetence marked the August 1991 coup. After announcing their seizure of power on August 19, coup leaders were slow to take control of key government buildings in Moscow. They also made little effort to arrest potential opponents. Within hours, opposition forces, rallied by Russian president Boris Yeltsin, had begun to speak out. Yeltsin boldly climbed atop an "enemy" tank to denounce the takeover.

Coup leaders occupied the main television and radio stations and ordered all independent newspapers to stop their presses. However, they failed to recognize that there had been a revolution in communications technology. Reporters armed with cellular telephones kept up a steady flow of information from the opposition headquarters, the Russian parliament building (known as the White House).

Some newspapers also got the story out by fax machine.

This barrage of news from opposition sources severely weakened what little public support there was for the coup. Many people had expressed dissatisfaction with the Soviet government's reforms, but they hardly wanted a return to the old government. "Those fools down there are out of touch," one man said of the coup leaders. "They do not realize that things have changed. . . ." Support among members of the armed services was unreliable. Some of the tanks sent to put down opposition forces at the White House turned their guns away from the building and joined in its defense. Across Moscow, soldiers began laying down their guns. "I could not shoot my fellow citizens," one said. Without the backing of the military, the coup fell apart and was over by August 21.

Boris Yeltsin stands on an enemy tank to show his triumph over the attempted 1991 coup.

Theme: **Politics and Law**

The Cheka relied on terror in its investigations of enemies of the state. One of the organization's missions was to bring "saboteurs and counter-revolutionaries" before revolutionary courts, but members were also to "punish and liquidate" people opposing the revolution. In 1918 Lenin supported the Cheka by removing the organization from the standard judicial system. The Cheka also ran detention camps. In 1922 the Cheka was reorganized as the Political Administration of the State, or GPU.

Critical Thinking Ask students how such an extralegal police force might affect a society.

ANSWER: Students might suggest such a police force would stifle dissent, leaving people afraid to take part in government or speak out at all.

REVIEW & ASSESSMENT RESOURCES

- Study Guide 23.1
- Daily Quiz 23.1
- Main Idea Activity 23.1

All Levels

The civil war resulted in heavy losses for the country. Over 800,000 soldiers had been killed in the fighting, and 2 million civilians had died from warfare and disease. The war had also provided an excuse for the Bolsheviks to form a secret police force, called the Cheka, to suppress dissent.

Russia Under Lenin

As soon as the Communists seized power in 1917, they reorganized Russia's government. They moved the capital from Petrograd to Moscow. Lenin became the head of the cabinet,

▲ At the "Lenin's Way Collective Farm" in Vilshanka, Russia, workers harvesting the fields stop to share a communal lunch.

the Union of Soviet Socialist Republics (USSR). Between 1918 and 1921 the nation followed an economic program known as War Communism, under which all industries were nationalized, or placed under government control. In 1921, however, Lenin announced his New Economic Policy (NEP), which allowed individuals to buy and sell some products and encouraged investment of foreign capital.

In agriculture the government encouraged peasants to form **collective farms**—vast areas of land on which many people shared the work. Most peasants, however, preferred to keep the small plots of land that their families had farmed for centuries.

Although Lenin strongly believed that the NEP would lead the Soviet Union to economic recovery, not all government leaders agreed. When Lenin suffered a debilitating stroke in 1922, and later died in 1924, the future economic prosperity and the leadership of the new nation remained in question.

After the rebels were defeated in the civil war, Lenin's communist government strengthened its hold over the Russian people.

the Council of People's Commissars. Lenin also retained his leadership of the Communist Party. The Communists gave official powers to the Congress of Soviets, a legislative body that the party controlled. To ensure the end of the Romanov monarchy, in 1918 the Communists ordered the execution of the former czar and all of his family.

In 1922 the Communist leaders gave Russia and the territories under its control a new name,

SECTION 1 REVIEW

IDENTIFY and explain the significance of the following:
Nicholas II
soviets
February Revolution
Alexander Kerensky
Lenin
Bolsheviks
October Revolution
Leon Trotsky
Whites
Red Army
collective farms

LOCATE and explain the importance of the following:

Petrograd
Moscow

1. **Main Idea** How did World War I contribute to the Russian Revolution?
2. **Main Idea** How did Russian government change after the February and October Revolutions?
3. **War and Diplomacy** How did the Bolshevik victory in Russia's civil war affect the nation?
4. **Writing to Explain** Imagine that you are a worker in Petrograd in 1917. Write a letter to a friend in another country explaining why the people are rebelling against the czar.
5. **Evaluating** For each of the following political leaders, list some characteristics of his government and the reasons for its success or failure: Nicholas II, Alexander Kerensky, and Lenin. Why were the Bolsheviks more successful than others at maintaining their control of Russia?

Postwar Democracies

- What was the economic situation like in the major victorious Western democracies after World War I?

- What problems did democracy face in Germany after World War I?

- How did the political situation in eastern Europe and Japan change after the war?

For many people around the world, Allied victory in World War I promised a new era for the ideals of liberal democracy. Among the new countries of eastern Europe, democratic constitutions replaced the defeated autocracies. In Japan too the triumph of the Allies led many to believe that democracy was the most efficient form of government for the modern world. In many democratic countries, however, people reacted against the growth of democracy, turning instead to older traditions.

In 1994, a member of the French bomb removal team carefully carries a poison gas shell from a field. More than 29 million unexploded bombs from previous wars have been found in France.

The Western Democracies

The full price of World War I became clear as the economies of the Western democracies began to suffer under the pressures of returning to peacetime production. During the early 1920s all the major Western powers experienced economic hardship and rising unemployment. The United States was the least affected, but even there postwar industrial production began to slow down. With declining production came lower wages and even layoffs. American labor unions called major strikes in heavy industries. France and Britain faced similar problems.

Slow recovery. Of all the victorious allies, France had suffered the most damage from the war. The battlefields of World War I scarred the French landscape, which was covered with burned-out villages and towns and scattered, twisted metal. Land mines and unexploded shells continued to take lives and cause injuries. Vineyards and wheat fields had become barren. Although less physically damaged than France, Britain also had a hard time recovering. After the war, Britain could no longer compete effectively with its wartime allies. As exports declined, unemployment rose. By 1921 some 2 million British people were out of work.

Political and social changes. As they confronted the problems of recovery, the Western democracies experienced considerable internal change. In both Britain and the United States, women gained the right to vote after the war. In 1920 American voters rejected Woodrow Wilson's Democratic Party and elected the Republican presidential candidate, Warren G. Harding, who promised a "return to normalcy," by which he meant the prosperity of the prewar era. In France numerous political parties struggled for power. In Britain too the Conservatives were elected in 1922 on a similar platform of "normalcy."

In the United States many Americans blamed their hard times on "foreign" influences. The Russian Revolution raised fears of a worldwide communist movement. Between 1919 and 1920 a **Red Scare** led to the arrest of thousands of suspected Communists. Organizations such as the

Ku Klux Klan called for "native, white, Protestant supremacy" and violently attacked African Americans, Native Americans, Asians, Catholics, Jews, and labor union supporters.

In Britain hard times led to growing class tensions. In 1924 continuing unemployment led to the election of the first Labour government, under James Ramsay MacDonald. Although the Conservatives returned to power in less than a year under the new leader, Stanley Baldwin, the economic situation did not improve. In 1925 Baldwin stated his own solution to the problem: "All the workers of this country have got to take reductions in wages to help put industry on its feet." Instead, in May 1926, millions of union workers, led by Britain's coal miners, called the first national strike. Refusing to give in, the government called for help from middle-class citizens. As they pitched in, driving milk wagons, running trains, and doing other essential work, the strike collapsed.

New prosperity. Despite these years of hardship and strife, however, by the end of the 1920s all three major Western democracies had experienced some degree of economic recovery. Under Republican probusiness policies, the U.S. economy rebounded and boomed. President Harding died in 1923, but his successor, Vice President Calvin Coolidge, continued this probusiness stance, declaring, "The business of America is business." In 1929 Coolidge's successor, Herbert Hoover, took office as president, expressing the views of many people in his inaugural address:

66 *Ours is a country with rich resources, stimulating in its glorious beauty, filled with millions of happy homes, blessed with comfort and opportunity. . . . I have no fears for the future of our country. It is bright with hope.* 99

Prosperity in the United States flowed over to former wartime allies. With the help of the Dawes Plan, after 1926 the French prospered once more. Even Britain recovered quickly from the national strike, and by the decade's end the nation was once again moderately prosperous.

Despite a period of economic slowdown, the United States boomed after the war, but recovery took longer in Britain and France.

The Weimar Republic

The 1920s were also a time of great turmoil in Germany. A new German republic had been proclaimed on November 9, 1918, just after the kaiser's abdication. The new democracy faced several crises from the start. Almost immediately, Marxist revolutionaries led by Rosa Luxemburg and Karl Liebknecht besieged the provisional government in an effort to establish a communist regime. One participant later recalled:

66 *The People's Representatives [Communists] practically did their work as [if they were] prisoners. Machine-guns rattled day and night in Wilhelmstrasse [and] noisy processions of many thousands, mostly armed to the teeth, were continuously organized by Liebknecht in front of the Chancellery.* 99

Most of the supporters of the new republic, including its first president, Friedrich Ebert (AY-buhrt), were Social Democrats, hoping to work within parliamentary means to form a socialist state. Confronted by revolutionary violence, Ebert desperately appealed to former generals of

▲ By 1924 German currency had lost so much value that it was no longer considered money. Here, children use stacks of money as building blocks.

the German army to save the republic. Secretly, Ebert authorized them to raise volunteer armed bands to crush the communist uprising. The generals accepted the challenge and quickly put down the revolt. Instead of disbanding, however, the generals marched on Berlin and proclaimed their own government. Eventually, the new rebellion collapsed in the face of a general strike called by labor leaders.

Against this background of chaos, German voters elected a national assembly to draw up a new constitution in the city of Weimar. They adopted the new Weimar Constitution in July 1919. Plagued by devastating inflation, at first the future of the new republic looked bleak. After the Dawes Plan went into effect in 1924, however, the German economy gradually recovered. The Weimar government enacted reforms such as women's suffrage and unemployment insurance.

Yet the **Weimar Republic** at best was an artificial creation with little deep-seated support among the German people. In 1923, for example, another rebellion broke out in Munich. Known as the Beer Hall Putsch, or uprising, the revolt was led by the former German general Erich Ludendorff and Adolf Hitler, the leader of a small nationalist party. Although the revolt was easily put down and its leaders jailed, the publicity surrounding their trials only underscored the weakness of the government. One German statesman complained in 1926 that "The weakest spot—and it still exists—is that the people have not yet made it [the Weimar Constitution] a thing of life." They never did.

After the war, Germans established a fragile democracy that was plagued by economic problems and a lack of popular support.

Challenges to Democracy

While the course of democracy was uncertain even in the major countries of western Europe after the war, elsewhere it broke down altogether. The new countries that emerged from the old empires in eastern Europe made efforts to pursue liberal democracy, but these efforts only increased the level of social tensions among the people. Similar problems confronted democracy in Japan.

THROUGH OTHERS' EYES

German Inflation

One of the many problems that confronted the Weimar Republic was the runaway inflation of the early 1920s. By November 1923, it took 4,200 billion German marks to equal one U.S. dollar. American writer Ernest Hemingway, on a trip across the German border from France in 1922, described the problems German shopowners faced in selling their goods because of the declining value of the German mark:

66 Because of the customs regulations, which are very strict on persons returning from Germany, the French cannot come over to Kehl [a town just over the border] and buy up all the cheap goods they would like to. But they can come over and eat. It is a sight every afternoon to see the mob that storms the German pastry shops and tea places. The Germans make very good pastries, wonderful pastries, in fact, that, at the present tumbling mark rate, the French of Strasburg can buy for a less amount apiece than the smallest French coin, the one sou piece. This miracle of exchange makes a swinish spectacle where the youth of the town of Strasburg crowd into the German pastry shop to eat themselves sick and gorge on fluffy, cream-filled slices of German cake at 5 marks the slice. The contents of a pastry shop are swept clear in half an hour. 99

Eastern Europe. In Czechoslovakia, Romania, Bulgaria, and the Baltic countries of Latvia, Lithuania, and Estonia, for example, the new democratic governments angered landowners by breaking apart old aristocratic estates and giving the land to peasants. In the Baltic states and Czechoslovakia, where landowners were mostly German, such policies led to ethnic tensions between German minorities and Czech and Slavic majorities. The new governments also tried to encourage industrialization by raising tariff barriers to protect their industries from foreign competition. These tariffs, however, only added to the disruption of international trade patterns caused by the war. As trade between the new countries began to dry up, so did their prosperity. Landowners and others increasingly feared that communism would spread from Russia to their own countries. Liberal democratic governments began to crumble.

In Hungary, for example, a brief communist revolution led to a reaction from the traditional aristocracy, the middle class, and the peasantry. Banding together, they established a conservative authoritarian regime under Admiral Miklós Horthy, formerly of the Imperial Austro-Hungarian Navy. Landlocked Hungary became known as the "kingdom without a king, ruled by an admiral without a fleet." By 1926 Poland, Yugoslavia, Bulgaria, and Romania had followed the Hungarian example, replacing constitutional governments with either conservative military dictatorships or monarchies. In eastern Europe, only Czechoslovakia remained truly democratic.

Japan. Democracy in Japan also faced challenges after World War I. Along with Japan's industrialization of the late 1800s had come universal education and eventually exposure to new political ideas from the West. These ideas contributed to growing unrest in Japanese society. After the war, as industry experienced a brief depression, trade unionism, socialism, and communism flourished for a time. Nevertheless, most Japanese embraced democracy and wanted it to succeed. In 1925 Japan instituted

▶ **Crowds gather in Tokyo on March 2, 1925, to cheer the passing of universal manhood suffrage. It would be another 21 years, however, before women were allowed to vote.**

universal manhood suffrage in an effort to consolidate its democratic institutions.

Not all Japanese were pleased with these developments. Many worried about the effects of Western influence on the traditional values of Japanese society. Cancellation of the Anglo-Japanese Alliance and continuing restrictions on Japanese trade and emigration by some Western nations convinced many Japanese that westerners would never treat them as equals. As reaction set in, older Japanese traditions of militarism and extreme nationalism began to reemerge. After 1926, when the young emperor Hirohito assumed the imperial throne, a more militaristic faction began to take control of Japanese society.

In eastern Europe and Japan, many people sought security from social and political upheavals in older authoritarian traditions.

SECTION 2 REVIEW

IDENTIFY and explain the significance of the following:
    Red Scare
    Stanley Baldwin
    Friedrich Ebert
    Weimar Republic
    Miklós Horthy
    Hirohito

1. *Main Idea* What economic and social impact did the war have on the victorious Western democracies?
2. *Main Idea* Why could the Weimar Republic be called a "fragile" democracy?
3. *Politics and Law* How did many people in eastern Europe and Japan seek to solve the problems of political instability that followed World War I?
4. *Writing to Create* Create a flyer for a political rally in Germany explaining to people why they should support the Weimar Republic.
5. *Synthesizing* What problems did many nations of Europe have in the post World War I era? How can many of these problems be attributed to the war?

Society and Culture Between the Wars

FOCUS

- Why did many people adopt new views of society after World War I?
- What forms did popular entertainment take during the 1920s and 1930s?
- What characterized the consumer culture of the 1920s?
- Why did many artists and writers break with past traditions after World War I?

World War I changed the way many people thought about themselves and the societies in which they lived. Since the dawn of the industrial age, the future had almost always seemed to promise progress, but the destruction caused by the war made a mockery of that promise. The war caused people to think less about the future and more about the present. This focus on the present shaped the culture that developed during the 1920s and 1930s.

Life magazine advertisement for the 1929 Studebaker

New Views of Society

The Western society that emerged from World War I had changed politically and economically. But the brutality and destruction of the war had also changed society psychologically. Some people saw the time just before the war as a high point in Western civilization—the war and everything following it, they argued, showed decline. In almost every aspect of society, people seemed to be challenging long-standing traditions of Western civilization.

Nowhere was this more true than in the areas of science and psychology. In 1905 Albert Einstein, a German-born physicist, formulated what would become known as the special theory of relativity. By 1916 Einstein had developed his idea that space and time were not absolute, as previously thought, but were relative to particular circumstances. Einstein's theory shattered conceptions of physics that had been in place since the time of Newton. His ideas were to have an enormous impact on the future of science and on people's perceptions of the universe.

Few thinkers in the 1900s have had as much influence on society as the Austrian psychoanalyst Sigmund Freud. Freud argued that human behavior was dominated by people's attempts to make unconscious desires seem reasonable. Freud believed the human personality was composed of the id, or unconscious; the ego, or instinct to survive; and the superego, or conscience. In 1930 Freud published *Civilization and Its Discontents,* in which he applied his ideas about psychology to human civilization. Freud wrote:

❝ *The meaning of the evolution of civilization is no longer obscure to us. It must present the struggle between . . . the instinct of life and the instinct of destruction, as it works itself out in the human species. This struggle is what all life essentially consists of.* ❞

Like many others in the 1920s, Freud was looking for answers to explain the tragedy of war.

New views of society were not restricted to intellectuals, however. Many people in Europe, the United States, and other parts of the world began to reject traditional moral values. In the industrialized nations, many women wore short skirts and short haircuts. These women, known

SECTION 3

CORE LESSON PLAN
See pages 623G and 623H for Lesson Plan 23.3.

Theme: Science

Einstein's theory of relativity is often explained by the "twins paradox." In this illustration one identical twin boards a rocket and travels to a star, and the other twin remains on Earth. For the twin on Earth, several years will pass before the rocket returns. But the twin in the rocket will experience a shorter period of time by traveling near the speed of light. After returning to Earth, the traveling twin will be several years younger than the twin who stayed on Earth.

Critical Thinking Ask students why Einstein's theory might change people's perceptions of the world.

ANSWER: Students should answer that the idea that time was relative led people to question other factors that had seemed certain as well.

as "flappers," frequented parties, movies, and dances. Other groups sought to gain control of society by restoring what they saw as declining morality. In the United States, the Temperance Movement, a movement opposed to the drinking of alcohol, gained a major victory in 1919 with the ratification of the Eighteenth Amendment to the Constitution. The amendment prohibited the sale or consumption of alcohol. Prohibition proved almost impossible to enforce, however, and the amendment was repealed in 1933.

Disillusionment over the war and new ideas in science and psychology caused many people to change the way they viewed society.

Entertainment for the Millions

The present-minded attitude of the decades after the war largely reflected the fact that citizens of the industrialized countries had more free time than before. Twelve-hour and longer work days had been common in industry during the mid-1800s. By the 1890s the ten-hour day was routine, and by the 1920s the eight-hour day became increasingly standard. In order to fill their free time, workers and their families looked to new forms of entertainment and recreation.

Radio. One new form of entertainment was listening to the radio. By the 1920s radio receivers were inexpensive enough that they were common in many ordinary households. In the United Kingdom alone, the number of radios increased from around 2 million in 1926 to around 9 million by the end of the 1930s. Radio listeners tuned in for the latest news, music, and dramatic programs. A radio station in the United States beat the newspapers to the reports that Warren Harding had won the presidential election of 1920.

The Jazz Age. With the help of radio, the 1920s and 1930s witnessed significant developments in popular music. The most innovative style of the era was jazz, which drew on African traditions as filtered through the experience of African Americans in the United States. Jazz blossomed in the American South, particularly in New Orleans. It spread with the many African Americans who left the South for the cities of the North and Midwest, such as Chicago and Kansas City, during and after World War I. Subsequently, jazz caught on in Europe. Radio audiences from New York to Berlin enjoyed the jazz sounds of Louis Armstrong, Bessie Smith, Billie Holiday, and "Jelly Roll" Morton.

Movies. Another innovation, motion pictures, competed with radio for popular attention. Motion pictures had first appeared shortly before the turn of the century. The 1903 picture *The Great Train Robbery* marked the beginning of popular movies. Until the 1920s, movies were silent, but the 1927 film *The Jazz Singer*, starring Al Jolson, brought voices to the silent screen.

Going out to the movies became a ritual in nearly all the industrialized countries. By the late 1930s, for example, some 40 percent of British adults went to the movies once a week; 25 percent went twice a week. For millions of people, the movies offered an inexpensive way to escape the problems of everyday life.

Sports. Organized sports also inspired tremendous enthusiasm during the 1920s and 1930s. In the United States, professional baseball drew millions of fans to ballparks, and the best baseball players rose to the status of national heroes.

Professional sports were equally popular in Europe and large parts of Latin

◀ Recognized as one of the greatest jazz trumpeters, Louis "Satchmo" Armstrong was also a singer and a bandleader.

636

◄ Baseball legend Babe Ruth shows his form as he singles to right field in New York City's Yankee Stadium on May 23, 1931. When asked about the fact that he had earned more money that year than the president of the United States, Ruth reportedly replied, "I had a better year than he did."

America. Heading the list was soccer, also called football. Soccer grew to international status with the establishment of the World Cup tournament in 1930. The Olympic Games were another international athletic event that drew great crowds. Modeled on the ancient Greek contests of the same name, the Olympics attracted the best amateur athletes from all over the world.

The Japanese also latched on to the sports craze. Baseball and golf became increasingly popular in large Japanese cities. Due to the scarcity of land in Japan, "baby," or miniature, golf took the place of the large-scale version.

Radio, movies, and sports were among the most popular forms of entertainment during the 1920s and 1930s.

Consumer Culture

The 1920s not only brought about a revolution in the way people spent their leisure time but also brought new levels of prosperity to some Western nations. In 1913 Henry Ford, an American auto manufacturer, developed the **assembly line** to produce automobiles. Workers stood along a moving belt and attached parts as the cars passed. The result was increased production and lower prices. The price of a Ford Model T went from around $850 in 1908 to around $295 in 1927. Millions of ordinary people could now afford to buy automobiles. One car owner described how the automobile had affected her family:

❝ We'd rather do without clothes than give up the car. We used to go to [my husband's] sister's to visit, but by the time we'd get the children shoed and dressed there wasn't any money left for carfare. Now no matter how they look, we just poke 'em in the car and take 'em along. ❞

Automobiles were not the only things produced using assembly lines. After the war, manufacturers in many industries turned to mass production to make all sorts of consumer goods.

Previously, most people in industrial societies had been concerned primarily with obtaining the goods they needed to survive, such as food and clothing. After the war, however, better wages and lower prices brought many luxury items within reach of millions of workers. The most important economic issue for manufacturers became how to keep the millions of new customers buying products—that is, how to maintain **consumption**.

Manufacturers turned to advertising and the concept of buying on credit to help encourage the new consumer culture. Advertising created wants where only needs had existed before. Advertising executives like Bruce Barton of the United States created glamorous ads for everything from machine tools to dish soap to funeral plots. The new technology of radio gave advertisers the perfect tool to reach millions of potential consumers right in their own homes.

Nothing demonstrated people's emphasis on the present more than the growth of the concept of purchasing items on credit. In the past people had generally saved up all the money they needed

Theme: The Arts

Several different branches of the dada movement appeared during World War I and the 1920s. At the heart of the Zurich dada movement was Hugo Ball, a German conscientious objector who worked to develop an artistic circle at the Cafe Voltaire in Zurich. Although the cafe was open for only a few months, it sparked a series of galleries and exhibitions devoted to dada art. New York dada was heavily influenced by photographer Alfred Stieglitz. He organized gallery showings and published the work of a number of dada artists in the United States. Other circles of dada artists emerged in Paris and Berlin.

Critical Thinking Ask students why dada artists would want to band together and form circles to exhibit their art.

ANSWER: Students might suggest that dada art was strange and ordinary galleries might not want to show it. They might also suggest that by forming circles these artists could learn from and support each other.

---

to buy large items, such as houses and cars. During the 1920s and 1930s, however, companies began extending credit to their customers, allowing people to purchase items and pay for them over time. Buying on credit not only allowed instant purchases of items but also allowed manufacturers to profit from the interest they charged.

The consumer culture was marked by mass production, increased advertising, and purchasing on credit.

The Arts

The enormous changes taking place in society and culture during the 1920s and 1930s were perhaps best symbolized in the arts. In painting, sculpture, literature, architecture, and music, people were expressing new ways of looking at society and breaking away from past traditions.

Painting and sculpture. The Spanish painter and sculptor Pablo Picasso was one of the earliest and best-known experimental artists. He used shapes, especially cubes, to form unusual images in his paintings. As a result, Picasso's style became known as cubism. Another style, known as **expressionism**, began in Germany and other parts of Europe shortly after the turn of the century and continued through the 1930s. Expressionists wanted to create a new type of artistic language, using shapes, lines, and color to communicate complex emotions to their audiences. Wassily Kandinsky, a Russian painter, summed up the expressionists' ideas about color:

❝ *Generally speaking, color is a power that directly influences the soul. Color is the keyboard, the eyes are the hammers, the soul is the piano with many strings. The artist is the hand which plays, touching one key or another, to cause vibrations in the soul.* **❞**

Dada, yet another modern style, was a direct reaction against the human slaughter of World War I. The dadaists saw the war as complete insanity. Even their name *dada* was probably meant as a nonsense word. Dada art often showed objects and ideas with no seeming relationship to one another. Marcel Duchamp, a famous dada artist, was fascinated by random images. In his painting *Tu m'*, Duchamp attached a real bolt to the canvas to "hold" the other objects in place.

In the United States and around the world, artists experimented with new styles. Some American artists traveled to Europe and were influenced by the expressionists and the dada artists. Others, like Georgia O'Keeffe, developed their own distinct styles, but incorporated the ideas of other artists. O'Keeffe wanted to look at nature in a new way. She chose to paint individual objects, such as flowers, in extreme close-up to capture the intricate detail of their forms.

Western influence had an effect on art in China as well. In Shanghai a group of artists followed the experimental style of European painters. The majority of Chinese painters of the 1920s, however, chose to retain traditional Chinese styles. Ch'i Pai-shih, considered the last great traditional Chinese painter, described the perfect painting: "The excellence of a painting lies in its being like, yet unlike. Too much likeness flatters the vulgar taste; too much unlikeness deceives the world."

Literature. Like painting and sculpture, literature in the 1920s also showed a marked departure from past forms. In 1922 the Irish novelist James Joyce published *Ulysses*, the story of the lives of several people in Dublin. In the novel, Joyce perfected a style of writing known as "stream of

▲ In Marcel Duchamp's 1918 painting *Tu m'*, the painted rip in the center of the canvas is held together by real safety pins through the canvas, and the painted squares that seem to be flying off the surface are held back by a real bolt.

Literature THROUGH TIME

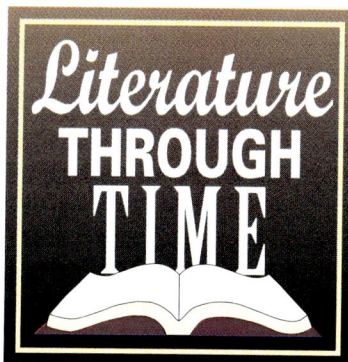

Berlin Alexanderplatz

The 1920s were a time of new experiments in art and literature. Many authors had been influenced by the brutality and destruction of World War I. They felt that the war had proven that civilization in the West was essentially chaotic and ruthless. Some also felt that the growth of large industrial cities was causing life to become impersonal—people no longer knew or cared about their neighbors. In 1929 the German writer Alfred Döblin published the enormously popular novel Berlin Alexanderplatz, *the story of a man just released from prison trying to make a new life for himself in the giant metropolis of Berlin. The novel was soon made into a radio play and a movie. In his novel Döblin experimented with a style called the montage technique, which tries to bring together many different ideas all at once in the text. The result is that readers are often left confused as to who is talking or who is telling the story:*

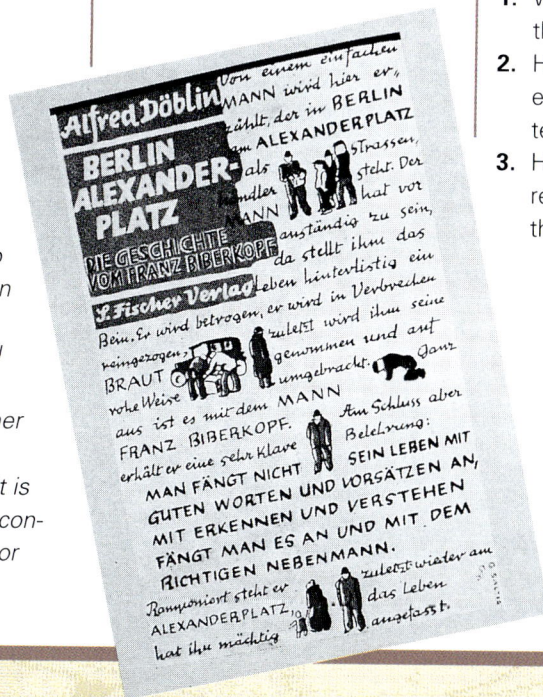

The Rosenthaler Platz is busily active.

Weather changing, more agreeable, a degree below freezing. For Germany, a low-pressure region is extending, which in its entire range has ended the weather prevailing up to now. The few pressure changes now going on indicate a slow extension of the low-pressure area towards the south, so that the weather will remain under its influence. During the day the temperature will probably be lower. Weather forecast for Berlin and surrounding country.

Car No. 68 runs across Rosenthaler Platz, Wittenau, Nordbahnhof, Heilanstalt, Weddingplatz, Stettiner Station, Rosenthaler Platz, Alexanderplatz, Straussberger Platz, Frankfurter Allee Station, Lichtenberg, Herzberge Insane Asylum. The three Berlin transport companies—street-car, elevated and underground, omnibus—form a tariff-union.

Fares for adults are 20 pfennigs, for schoolchildren 10 pfennigs, reduced fares allowed for children up to the age of 14, apprentices and pupils, poor students, war cripples, persons physically unfit for walking as certified by the district charity offices. Get to know about the lines. During the winter months the front entrance shall not be opened for passengers entering or leaving, 39 seating capacity, 5918, to alight from the car, warn the motorman in time, the motorman is forbidden to converse with passengers, getting off or on while the car is in motion may lead to fatal accidents. . . .

Various fruit brandies at wholesale prices, Dr. Bergell, notary and attorney-at-law, Lukutate, the Indian rejuvenation treatment for elephants, Fromms Akt, the best rubber sponge, what's the use of so many rubber sponges, anyway?

Understanding Literature

1. What is being described in the passage?
2. How is the passage an example of the montage technique?
3. How does the passage reflect the German reality of the large, impersonal city?

Alfred Döblin's
Berlin Alexanderplatz,
1929 edition

Understanding Literature

1. weather, transportation, and advertisements
2. The passage moves from one subject to another without transitions and appears to change speakers with each change in subject.
3. The passage does not seem to be addressing any particular reader, but contains information that anyone might encounter during the course of a day.

RESOURCE ACTIVITY

READINGS IN WORLD HISTORY
Reading 23.3
Gatsby's Party

Have students read the excerpt from F. Scott Fitzgerald's novel *The Great Gatsby*. Then have them complete the questions.

Level 2

REVIEW & ASSESSMENT RESOURCES

- Study Guide 23.3
- Daily Quiz 23.3
- Main Idea Activity 23.3

All Levels

◄ Brecht and Weill's *The Threepenny Opera* was a thinly disguised satire of the economic exploitation of the working class.

consciousness," which was an ongoing flow of thoughts and descriptions. Joyce and other novelists of the time made an effort to change conceptions of what a novel should be. The 1920s was also a golden age of drama. Like contemporary novelists, playwrights such as Bertolt Brecht sought to change conceptions of drama. Brecht saw the theater as more of a classroom than a place of performance. Characters would routinely step out of their roles and comment directly to the audience. In 1928 Brecht collaborated with Kurt Weill to produce *The Threepenny Opera*, a highly political work that became a huge international success.

Architecture. Architects in the 1920s hoped to use their creativity to point civilization in a new direction. Walter Gropius, a German architect, founded the Bauhaus school of architecture in Germany. Classes taught at the school emphasized a new style of using simple square shapes in architecture. Gropius commented that the school "would enable the coming generation to achieve the reunion of all forms of creative work and become the architects of a new civilization." One of the greatest architectural innovators of the time was American Frank Lloyd Wright. Wright believed that buildings should conform to their environments. When Wright built the Imperial Hotel in Tokyo, completed in 1922, he built it on a cushion of mud so that it would stand up to Japan's many earthquakes.

Music. Composers after the war used their music to symbolize the contradictions they saw in civilization. Composers such as Igor Stravinsky and Arnold Schoenberg disturbed audiences with their music by directing different instruments to play at the same time in different keys, creating a mixture of unrelated sounds.

In a way, the random tones of these new compositions symbolized the times—various groups adopted new and nontraditional ideas, but like the new music, there was no harmony or stability on which society could be based. It was only a matter of time before the unstable society of the 1920s would come crashing down.

Artists and writers after World War I looked for new means of expression, rejecting past traditions.

SECTION 3 REVIEW

IDENTIFY and explain the significance of the following:
  Albert Einstein
  Sigmund Freud
  Henry Ford
  assembly line
  consumption
  expressionism
  dada

1. **Main Idea** How did the growth of the consumer culture change postwar society?
2. **Main Idea** What did many people do in their leisure time during the 1920s and 1930s?
3. **Philosophy** Why did the 1920s mark a shift in the way many people viewed society?
4. **Writing to Explain** Imagine that you are the owner of a music store, bookstore, or an art gallery during the 1920s.

Write a newspaper review explaining how specific pieces of music, literature, and art attempt to demonstrate principles or ideals from their culture.
5. **Synthesizing** What did forms of mass entertainment have in common with the painting, literature, and architecture of the 1920s and 1930s?

The Global Depression

- What factors brought on the Great Depression?
- How and why did the world economy collapse?
- How did the Western democracies respond to the depression?

While World War I had shaken the confidence of Western civilization, during the 1920s many Westerners believed they could still recover and start again on the path of progress. In 1929 these hopes shattered once more as the global economy crashed into a worldwide depression. As people struggled to find security in the face of economic collapse, many began to look for new forms of economic and political organization. Many governments responded to the crisis by cutting off their markets from foreign trade, hoping to reestablish the prosperity of their own citizens.

Despair in the time of the Great Depression

The Coming of the Great Depression

The fragile state of Western culture after World War I was reflected in the global economy that was dominated by the Western industrial nations. Although on the surface the 1920s seemed to be a boom time with growing economic prosperity, the boom was built on foundations of sand.

Agriculture. The agricultural sector in particular remained extremely weak. During the war much of Europe's farmland had been neglected or turned into battlefields. In Australia, New Zealand, Africa, India, and North and South America, farmers had increased production to take up the slack. New industrial equipment, such as motorized tractors and harvesters, along with the introduction of new disease-resistant plants, led to greater harvests and lowered agricultural prices. Yet demand for many crops, like wheat, coffee, and sugar, did not increase. Supply outstripped demand, and commodity prices fell. With less income from the sale of crops, farmers could not afford to buy manufactured goods.

The Great Bull Market. Despite the slump in agriculture, the introduction of new consumer goods in the 1920s gave Americans a new sense of prosperity. Anxious to encourage this prosperity, the U.S. government and financial leaders deliberately kept the cost of borrowing money low. This allowed Americans to buy more goods on credit, further fueling the economy. Business leaders also encouraged people to join in the prosperity by buying stock in their companies.

Financial firms allowed people to buy stocks **on margin**, which meant purchasers only put up about 10 percent of the value of the stock they bought. As long as a stock's value increased, the investor made a profit. If values fell, however, investors would have to come up with the difference between their down payment and the amount they had borrowed. According to one estimate, 29 to 30 million American families out of a population of about 120 million were eventually involved somehow in the stock market. Competition for stocks sent prices booming upward, launching the **Great Bull Market**. But by the summer of 1929, the American economy had reached its limit of expansion.

CORE LESSON PLAN
See pages 623I and 623J for Lesson Plan 23.4.

Theme: Economic Organization

The last year of the Bull Market was driven almost entirely by speculation. Until 1928 exchange prices reflected the actual performance of the stock—its ability to pay back investors. By 1929, however, some stocks were selling at 50 times what they were worth. For example, the United Founders Corporation, an investment trust that began with an initial investment of only $500, was driven by speculation into a company with a market value of $686,165,000.

Critical Thinking Ask students what might have driven such speculation.

ANSWER: Students might answer that the stock market seemed like an easy way to make money.

The crash. In September 1929 the New York stock market began to fall. By October 21 prices were falling so quickly that stockbrokers began to send out margin calls, demanding that their customers put up the rest of the value of the stocks they had purchased on margin. Desperately, people began selling shares to raise the needed cash. On October 24 the market plunged straight down with no one buying and everyone trying to sell. Large crowds gathered outside the Stock Exchange in shock. On October 29, known forever after as **Black Tuesday**, investors still desperate for cash to pay their margin calls began selling off even the most sound stocks. The entire market collapsed.

Frantically, people began to withdraw their savings to pay their debts. Heavy withdrawals and the need to cover their own unwise investments forced many banks to call in other loans, including those on people's houses and farms. The panic spread, causing a "run" on the banks. Unable to cover all the withdrawals, many banks closed their doors, never to reopen. With them the banks took the life savings of both the prosperous and the frugal, some of whom had never dabbled in the stock market. The **Great Depression** had begun. Gordon Parks, a young African American then working his way through high school, later expressed the bewilderment felt by many:

▲ Crowds gather across the street from the New York Stock Exchange in October 1929. The month would end with many people facing financial ruin.

66 *By the first week of November . . . along with millions of others across the nation, I was without a job. . . . I went to school and cleaned out my locker, knowing it was impossible to stay on. A piercing chill was in the air as I walked back to the rooming house. The hawk had come. I could . . . feel his wings shadowing me.* 99

Low agricultural prices, artificially low interest rates, and stock market speculation were among the factors leading to the Great Depression.

The Spread of the Depression

As the stock market crashed, the weakness of the world's agricultural markets took its toll. Commodity prices collapsed. By 1933, for example, wheat cost less than one fifth of what it had a decade earlier. Cotton prices also collapsed, ruining many small-time planters in Sudan, Egypt, India, and the southern United States. Coffee planters in East Africa and Brazil and cocoa producers in West Africa suffered similar fates.

The stock market crash also caused many Americans to pull investments out of Europe in order to stabilize their finances at home. In addition, new import tariffs closed American markets to European goods. Germany and Austria were especially hard-hit by the loss of American funds. In 1931 the leading Austrian bank, the Credit Anstalt, which had made extensive loans across Europe, declared bankruptcy as its loans defaulted. Credit Anstalt's bankruptcy led to a wave of failures; like a row of dominoes, banks collapsed across Europe. With the failure of major European and American banks, which controlled world credit, the disaster became truly global. In 1931 John Maynard Keynes, a leading British economist, described the impact of the depression:

66 *No country is exempt. The privation [hardship] and . . . anxiety which exists today in millions of homes all over the world is extreme. In the three chief industrial countries . . . Great Britain, Germany and the United States . . . probably 12 million industrial workers stand idle.* 99

First agricultural countries and then industrial nations began to devalue their currencies in hopes of increasing demand for their products overseas. In 1931 Britain, whose currency had been the mainstay of international trade in the 1800s, abandoned the gold standard. As more and more countries followed, international trade became increasingly difficult. Scholars have estimated that between 1929 and 1932 international trade fell by two thirds.

In 1933 representatives from the major world powers met in London at a world economic conference in an effort to resolve the crisis and reopen the channels of world trade. However, none of the leaders were willing to risk their national security to benefit others by lifting newly imposed tariffs or returning to a recognized international gold standard. The conference ended in complete failure. Soon Germany refused to make its reparations payments altogether. In turn, France and Britain defaulted on their debts to the United States. The United States retaliated by denying the defaulting nations the right to raise loans in American markets.

The global economy collapsed as the agricultural market fell, banks closed, and governments refused to cooperate to reestablish trade.

Reactions in the Western Democracies

As the depression deepened, unemployment spread like a plague around the world. Millions lined up in soup kitchens. In the industrial countries alone, around one fourth of the work force was unemployed in 1932. Untold millions of unemployed workers went unreported in the nonindustrial countries of Asia, Africa, and Latin America. In the face of such human misery, social and political tensions rose.

Confronted by growing violence and desperation among farmers and union workers in American cities, President Hoover and his successor, Franklin Roosevelt, recognized the need for

▲ Men share a meal of government-provided bread and soup during the Great Depression. During this time many people relied on soup kitchens and breadlines as their main source of food.

major government intervention in the economy to protect the free-market system from radical revolution. "No president before has ever believed there was a government responsibility in such cases," Hoover wrote; ". . . there we had to pioneer a new field." Fearing that direct relief payments to the destitute might undermine their sense of independence, Hoover instead cut taxes and greatly expanded public works, such as construction of dams, highways, and bridges, to create jobs for the unemployed.

Since tensions remained high and many people began to call for massive social programs, Roosevelt pursued a more extensive intervention policy. Calling his program the New Deal, he instituted immediate relief for the destitute, as well as massive government spending programs to help the economy recover. Finally, Roosevelt enacted major economic reforms, creating permanent government supervision and regulatory powers over much of the economy to prevent such a calamity from ever happening again. Roosevelt conveyed his plan to the American people in "fireside chats," broadcast on radio.

Other leading industrial nations took similar interventionist measures. In Britain, for example, in 1931 Ramsay MacDonald formed a National Coalition government on a platform of protectionism—the charging of high tariffs. With the

INTERNET ACTIVITY

FARM SECURITY ADMINISTRATION PHOTOGRAPHERS
The Farm Security Administration sent photographers out to record the depression.

Activity: Have students search the Web for photographs from the depression. They might want to look at the Library of Congress site. They also might search for information on photographers such as Dorothea Lange or Walker Evans. Ask students to use the photographs they find to write a news story or news headlines on the effects of the depression.

All Levels

RESOURCE ACTIVITY

READINGS IN WORLD HISTORY
Reading 23.4
The Jarrow Crusade

Have students read the selection and complete the questions.

Level 2

REVIEW & ASSESSMENT RESOURCES

- Study Guide 23.4
- Daily Quiz 23.4
- Main Idea Activity 23.4

All Levels

1. The weak agricultural
market, misuse of credit,
and large stock pur-
chases on margin all
made global markets
unstable.
2. Stocks were overval-
ued; when prices started
to fall, brokers had to
issue margin calls; even
sound stocks had to be
sold to pay for invest-
ments on the margin.
3. Britain abandoned the
gold standard, Germany
ended reparations pay-
ments, and Britain and
France defaulted on loans
to the United States. The
United States began mas-
sive public works pro-
grams to help the poor.
4. Letters should discuss
the difficulty of finding
jobs and problems posed
by high levels of debt.
5. In agriculture, mecha-
nization increased supply
to a point far beyond
demand. Germany tried
to save its economy by
ending war reparations
to France and Britain,
who in turn, stopped
payments on debts to
the United States. In
banking, defaults caused
many banks to collapse.
The market crash caused
many Americans to pull
out of European invest-
ments, weakening those
economies as well.

644

▲ In 1933 the U.S. Civilian Conservation Corps was established as part of the New Deal to provide jobs for single young men like these in Virginia. The work involved conserving and developing natural resources.

agreement of the British Dominions overseas, MacDonald also adopted a policy of **imperial preference**, through which the British Empire became a more self-sufficient trading bloc whose members gave preferential treatment to each other. Internally, both MacDonald and his Conservative successor, Stanley Baldwin, pursued an informal alliance of industry, government, and labor unions to deal with the depression's worst effects. Under these policies, by 1937 Britain was producing nearly 20 percent more than in 1929.

In France the depression, which did not hit until 1931, brought upheaval and fears of revolution that led to growing government intervention in the economy. In February 1934, for example, in Paris a huge crowd of right-wing conservatives and antire-publicans openly called for the violent overthrow of the republic. When police charged the crowds, hundreds were injured and several killed. This open threat to the republic brought all center- and left-wing parties into a group known as the Popular Front, under the Socialist premier, Léon Blum. In 1936 Blum passed his own government intervention policy and instituted major social and labor legislation. Soon, however, conservatives regained control of the government, and the Popular Front fell apart.

Western democracies responded to rising social and political tensions of the depression by increasing government intervention in the economy.

SECTION 4 REVIEW

IDENTIFY and explain the significance of the following:
   on margin
   Great Bull Market
   Black Tuesday
   Great Depression
   Franklin Roosevelt
   imperial preference

1. *Main Idea* How did flaws in the global economic system of the 1920s set the stage for the Great Depression?

2. *Main Idea* Why did the stock market crash in 1929?

3. *Economic Organization* How did national governments cope with the crises of the Great Depression?

4. *Writing to Describe* Imagine that you are an industrial worker in 1929. Write a letter to your national leader describing the hardships you and your family are facing.

5. *Synthesizing* How did the interconnected nature of the global economy help spread the Great Depression? In your answer, consider the following: (a) agriculture; (b) war reparations; and (c) bank loans.

The Rise of Totalitarianism

- How did Mussolini gain power in Italy?

- How did Hitler transform German society and government?

- How was totalitarianism in the Soviet Union different from elsewhere?

- Why did various countries around the world embrace totalitarianism in the 1920s and 1930s?

The Great Depression contributed to a growing political crisis around the world. This crisis only reinforced the fear in many people's minds that liberal democracy was perhaps not the most suitable form of government to cope with the modern industrial age. Moreover, the forces of militarism and nationalism that had helped cause World War I once again emerged in the 1920s and 1930s in new forms to disturb the peace of the world.

Symbol of the *fasces* on the cover of a 1925 Italian Fascist Party membership card

The Rise of Fascism in Italy

The first major challenge to liberal democracy in western Europe grew out of Italy's experience during World War I. Many Italians felt cheated by a peace settlement that failed to give them all the territory they wanted around the Adriatic Sea. After the war, parliamentary politics in Italy accomplished little. As Italy began to experience the first effects of economic hard times, the government seemed incapable of handling the challenges. Many Italians began to feel that a stronger hand was needed to govern the troubled nation.

Mussolini. In 1922 a new leader, Benito Mussolini, emerged to claim this position. Mussolini had begun his political career in Italy in the decade before World War I as a left-wing socialist. During the war his experiences at the front led him to become a strong nationalist. Like many Italians, Mussolini was disappointed by Italy's small territorial gains. He became convinced that strength alone could achieve Italy's demands. In 1919, together with other unemployed and disillusioned ex-soldiers, Mussolini formed the Fascist Party. The party was named after the old Roman symbol of the power of the common people, the *fasces*, an ax embedded within a bundle of sticks. The new party was nationalistic, anticommunist, antidemocratic, and expansionist. The party's beliefs became known as **fascism**.

As Italy's economic and social stability deteriorated during the early 1920s, the Fascists saw their chance to gain power. Rising inflation hurt the Italian economy and caused widespread discontent. In the cities, factory workers began to strike, demanding higher wages, better working conditions, and in some cases, complete control of the factories. Radical socialists and members of the Communist Party began to call for revolution.

Plagued by internal factions, the liberal democratic government seemed unable to take strong, decisive action to restore order and confidence in Italy. Under the pretense of restoring order, Mussolini's followers formed vigilante groups to break up workers' meetings and strikes. Before long, however, they were simply beating

CORE LESSON PLAN
See pages 623K and 623L for Lesson Plan 23.5.

Theme: **Politics and Law**

One of the differences between the Fascist Party and the Socialist Party in Europe was that when the Fascist Party came to power, it effectively broke up agricultural strikes. More than 1 million agrarian workers went on strike in 1920, but by 1921 Fascist attacks had reduced the number of striking agricultural workers to only 80,000.

Critical Thinking Ask students why the Fascist Party's willingness to break up strikes might make them more appealing than the Socialist Party.

ANSWER: Students should suggest that by breaking up strikes, Fascists seemed to be imposing order and making sure that people got food.

up and intimidating anyone who disagreed with them. They adopted a paramilitary style of dress and discipline. Because of the color of their uniforms, the Fascists became known as the Black Shirts.

The "march on Rome." By 1922 the Fascists had become a major force in Italian politics. Many government leaders were glad to let the Fascists check the growing power of the radical left. However, when the Fascists openly threatened to march on Rome in October 1922 and to take over the government by force, the Italian cabinet finally realized their danger. Quickly, they begged the Italian king, Victor Emmanuel III, to proclaim martial law. When he refused, the entire cabinet resigned. On the advice of leading conservatives, the king then named Mussolini as his new premier. Mussolini thus gained power without having to carry out the march on Rome.

The Fascists in power. Once installed as premier, Mussolini used his Black Shirts to manipulate parliament through intimidation and also established Fascist control of the electoral process. Under pressure from the Black Shirts, the Italian parliament passed a law that enabled the Fascists to win a majority of parliamentary seats. Early in 1925 Mussolini set into motion his plan of creating a complete dictatorship, declaring, "We wish to make the nation Fascist." He soon outlawed all other political parties. Other decrees imposed press censorship, re-established the death penalty, and led to the arrest of Mussolini's most important rivals. He also created an official secret police and a new Fascist militia. Methodically, the Fascists crushed all opposition and dissent.

Mussolini himself took the title *Il Duce,* "The Leader." Drawing on the romantic and nationalistic ideas of the 1800s and early 1900s, he insisted that Italy was not simply a state, but that it was a living thing:

▲ Benito Mussolini, surrounded by his Black Shirts, raises his fist to illustrate the power of his new Fascist order.

66 *The Fascist State is itself conscious, and has itself a will and a personality. . . . The State is not merely a guardian . . . nor is it an organization with purely material aims. . . . Nor is it a purely political creation. . . . The State . . . is a spiritual and moral fact in itself . . . a manifestation [form] of the spirit.* 99

Mussolini and the Fascists thus tried to give the Italian people a new sense of identity and purpose that would legitimize and support Fascist rule. Mussolini summed up the full extent of the new Fascist doctrine: "Everything within the state, nothing outside the state, nothing against the state . . . the state [is] an absolute in comparison with which all individuals or groups are relative." Mussolini's ideas expressed a form of government known as **totalitarianism.** Totalitarian dictators advocated complete government control of all aspects of society, including politics, the economy, culture, and even the private lives of all citizens.

The "corporatist state." As part of this new view of national identity, Mussolini also tried to create the "corporatist state." All Italian citizens were classified according to their occupation. Eventually all occupations came under the oversight of one of 22 "corporations" established by the government. Directors regulated all businesses and professions within each "corporation"—including work hours, pay scales, and prices. Corporatism was thus a return to a kind of guild structure, but with the state firmly in control.

Fascist imperialism. In addition to his reorganization of the state, Mussolini also preached a new doctrine of imperialism. Adopting ideas like those of the social Darwinists, Mussolini argued that struggle was the nature of the world—those nations that wanted to survive must do so at the expense of weaker nations. Only the strong, he insisted, survived. Fascism thus came to glorify war as a natural part of life.

Mussolini used brute force and appeals to nationalism to gain political power in Italy.

National Socialism in Germany

Germany soon followed the Italian example. There, in 1933 a party of extreme nationalists, under the leadership of Adolf Hitler, gained control of the weak Weimar government.

Hitler was born in Austria, the son of a minor government official and a schoolteacher. As a youth, he tried to pursue a career as an artist in Vienna. When he was rejected by the Art Academy, Hitler blamed his failure on the large and prosperous Jewish population of Vienna. This experience contributed to the young Hitler's violent anti-Semitism. Eventually, he emigrated to Bavaria in southern Germany. After serving in the German Army in World War I, Hitler returned to Bavaria, where he joined an extreme nationalist party, the German Workers Party. Quickly becoming the acknowledged leader of the group, Hitler renamed it the National Socialist German Workers Party—or **Nazi Party**, as it was abbreviated in German.

Imprisoned in 1923 for his participation in the Beer Hall Putsch, Hitler used his time to set out his plans for the future in a book-length statement that he titled *Mein Kampf,* or "my struggle." Although rambling and disjointed, *Mein Kampf* introduced the main elements of his program.

Nazi ideology. Like Mussolini, whom he greatly admired, Hitler was extremely nationalistic, anticommunist, antidemocratic, and expansionist. He also saw the state as represented by the leader, or Führer, whom he believed to be the embodiment of the people. The basis of Hitler's nationalism, however, was actually a kind of pseudoscientific biological racism. Hitler preached the superiority of the Germanic, or "Aryan," race—as he incorrectly called it—and its historical destiny to rule the world. To accomplish this, he called for a program of both racial and cultural "purification" designed to transform the Germans into a "master race." Above all, Hitler identified the Jews as the Germans' greatest racial and cultural enemy.

▲ The cover of the 1936 Olympics special edition of the *Berlin Illustrated Magazine* depicted Hitler's ideal of the superior Aryan race.

Hitler was convinced that Germany had not really lost World War I but had been "stabbed in the back" by a conspiracy of communist Jewish financiers. Communism, which advocated an identity based on worldwide classes, represented a special threat to his racial doctrines.

Like Mussolini, Hitler glorified war and the need for imperial expansion. In *Mein Kampf* he outlined the Nazi plans for eastward expansion into the plains of Poland and Russia. There the Germans would eradicate and enslave the Slavic population to achieve the necessary living space in which to grow.

Hitler's rise to power. Although the Beer Hall Putsch of 1923 ended in failure, Hitler was soon released from jail and continued to organize for the future. The depression finally discredited the weak Weimar government, and by 1932 the Nazi Party had become the largest party in the German Reichstag. Although the violence of Hitler's paramilitary force, the Brown Shirts, worried many Germans, the Nazis' hard line against communism won the support of the more conservative elements in German society.

▲ Members of Hitler's special troops place boycott signs on the window of a Jewish-owned business. This one reads, "Germans! Protect yourselves! Don't buy from Jews!"

In 1933, under pressure from conservatives worried about growing support for socialism, President Paul von Hindenburg invited Hitler to become the new chancellor of Germany in a coalition government. Once in power Hitler soon moved to consolidate National Socialist control over the government. When someone set fire to the German Reichstag building on February 27, 1933, Hitler proclaimed that it was the first step in a communist revolution, and he received sweeping dictatorial powers "as a defensive measure against communist acts of violence." In March 1933 Hitler was granted the power to rule by decree. Opposing political parties were outlawed. Germany was transformed from a federal state into a fully centralized state. One German described Hitler's rise to power:

❝ Now has us the Godhead a savior sent,
Distress its end has passed.
To gladness and joy the land gives vent:
Springtime is here at last. ❞

The Third Reich

With nearly unlimited power, Hitler set about creating what he called the **Third Reich**, or Third German Empire. The first had been the Holy Roman Empire of Charlemagne, and the second the empire created by Bismarck under the Hohenzollerns. Both had failed. But the Third Reich, Hitler promised, would be "the thousand-year Reich." He quickly enacted massive government spending programs that soon stimulated the German economy and helped bring it out of the depression. Although at first he pretended to abide by the restrictions on rearmament included in the Treaty of Versailles, Hitler in fact launched a major rearmament program. He also built an entirely new road system, the German autobahns. Hitler ordered construction of the German Volkswagen, or "people's car," as part of the Nazi scheme to win over ordinary people by promising to provide affordable automobiles for all Germans.

In addition, the Nazis created an organized program of social and cultural education in the principles of National Socialism. Their goal was to transform the German people into a coherent, unified nation under the leadership of the Führer. German youths, for example, were encouraged to join the Hitler Youth and other groups that trained them in Nazi doctrine.

Another method the Nazis used to maintain the allegiance of the German people was propaganda. The Nazis broadcast their political and racial ideas on radio and newsreels. For example, film director Leni Riefenstahl made documentary movies of Nazi Party rallies, complete with music and carefully staged scenes.

BIOGRAPHY Leni Riefenstahl was born in 1902 in Berlin. She worked as a dancer and actress in the booming German entertainment industry of the 1920s. In 1931 she formed the L. R. Studio-Film Incorporated to make films. Because of her talent at capturing images on film, Riefenstahl quickly became the favorite filmmaker of the Nazi Party, and especially Hitler. Possibly her most controversial film was *Triumph of the Will*, a documentary of a 1934 Nazi Party rally in Nuremberg. Filming at night, Riefenstahl captured

Leni Riefenstahl
B I O G R A P H Y

▶ In Berlin, Germany, the morning after *Kristallnacht*, passersby observe the destruction of a Jewish-owned business.

images of thousands of Nazi supporters marching and carrying torches in an eerie scene reminiscent of the Middle Ages. The film was shown all over Germany to millions of people. Riefenstahl's description of the first time she saw Hitler reveals the powerful impression he made on her:

66 *It seemed as if the earth's surface were spreading out in front of me, like a hemisphere that suddenly splits apart in the middle, spewing out an enormous jet of water, so powerful that it touched the sky and shook the earth. I felt quite paralyzed.* 99

One of the most brutal and vicious results of Hitler's Nazi revolution was his program of anti-Semitism. In 1935 the Nazis instituted the so-called Nuremberg Laws against the Jews. Jews were deprived of citizenship and forbidden to marry Aryan Germans. Jews were methodically excluded from the civil service and gradually from all other professions as well. Many Jews, gypsies, and political enemies of the Nazis were sent to new concentration camps, which the Nazis used in place of prisons and which provided the state with what amounted to slave labor.

In November 1938 persecution of Jews erupted in nationwide violence. In one night, over 250 synagogues were set ablaze or destroyed and some 7,500 Jewish storefronts were smashed all over Germany in what became known as the *Kristallnacht*, the "Night of Broken Glass."

*W*hen the Nazis came to power in 1933, Hitler created new government programs and used propaganda and violence to impose his doctrine of racial purity and German unity.

Stalinist Totalitarianism

While Mussolini and Hitler were constructing their nationalist visions of the totalitarian state, in the Soviet Union a similar totalitarianism emerged on a very different foundation. Joseph Stalin, the leader of the Soviet Union after Lenin's death in 1924, adapted Marxist-Leninist theory to fit his own totalitarian regime. Where fascism and National Socialism viewed the state as the most important entity in the nation, Marxism-Leninism maintained that ultimate authority should rest with the worldwide proletariat, led by the Communist Party. To end class differences, the Communists abolished private property rights. Having brought the workers to power, the party hoped to create a worldwide society ruled by the working class, in which the state itself would cease to exist.

However, following Lenin's death, Stalin outmaneuvered his most powerful rival, Leon Trotsky, to take full control of both the Communist Party and the Soviet state. Abandoning the goal of immediate world revolution, Stalin proclaimed instead the doctrine of furthering "revolution in one country." To

▲ On November 25, 1936, Joseph Stalin discusses the draft of the New Soviet Constitution that will make him chairman of the constitutional commission.

> 66 *I am an old Bolshevik. I worked in the underground against the Czar and then I fought in the civil war. Did I do all that in order that I should now surround villages with machine-guns and order my men to fire indiscriminately into crowds of peasants? Oh no, no!* 99

Aware of the resistance to his plans, Stalin created a vast system of state terror to eliminate all dissent. Between 1936 and 1938, he purged both the Communist Party and the Red Army of all potential opponents or rivals. Scholarly estimates of the total number of Stalin's own people who died from his 25-year tyranny range between 20 and 30 million.

Stalin based his brutal totalitarianism on the communist idea of a collective society of the proletariat instead of the ideas of nationalism and private property.

achieve this he tightened the Communist Party's control over every aspect of society.

Instead of decreasing state intervention, after 1927 Stalin increased the level of state control over society by abandoning Lenin's New Economic Policy and forcing the collectivization, or combination, of small, peasant-owned farms into large, state-owned farms. He also established the first of many Five Year Plans, which set quotas for production. When the peasant landowners resisted his collectivization measures, Stalin declared that he would "smash the *kulaks* [wealthy peasant farmers], eliminate them as a class." Many *kulaks* were shot when they resisted or were simply deported to the **gulags**, or forced-labor camps, in Siberia. By the end of 1933 at least 15 million peasants had been forced into collective state farms. By his own estimation, Stalin's collectivization resulted in the deaths of millions of peasants during the famines that this policy produced in the 1930s.

Even within the Communist Party and the Red Army, Stalin established his total control. The collectivization campaign had revealed that not everyone agreed with his ruthless methods. One officer expressed the feelings of many who had to carry out the dictator's orders:

The Spread of Fascist Ideas

As the depression ravaged Europe, many countries, particularly the new eastern European countries, began to follow the Fascist example. Mussolini seemed to many Europeans to have achieved a major miracle in Italy. As was said at the time, "he made the trains run on time," in a country where they were notoriously late. Yugoslavia, Romania, Poland, Hungary, Bulgaria, and Greece all came under authoritarian military regimes. In Portugal the dictator Antonio Salazar instituted a Fascist government in 1932. In 1936 a Spanish general, Francisco Franco, attacked Spain's constitutional government and in 1939, after a bloody civil war, was able to impose his own version of the Fascist state.

Dictatorships in Latin America. Many Latin American countries also faced the same problems as the European nations after World War I. They too often turned to authoritarian regimes for solutions. Conservative authoritarian government had been the rule in Latin America since the early 1800s. In part, these governments were

▲ Getúlio Vargas, surrounded by military leaders, takes office as provisional president of Brazil on November 11, 1930.

designed to keep power in the hands of the descendants of European immigrants, rather than allowing it to pass to Native Americans and mestizos. As the industrial revolution came to Latin America, however, new classes began to emerge.

In the cities of Brazil and Argentina, for example, communities of businesspeople and industrialists developed. New urban working classes followed. Industrialization and the growth of cities soon led to the formation of labor unions demanding better working conditions and higher wages for their members. Anxious for more foreign investment from the great industrial powers like Britain and the United States, the new business class supported strong rulers and governments that would restrict union activities and provide the kind of stability that was required by foreign investors.

In Brazil, Getúlio Vargas seized control of the government in 1930. By 1937 he was powerful enough to dissolve the congress and began to rule as a dictator, suppressing dissent while he modernized Brazil's economy. In Argentina, by 1932, an alliance of conservatives, businessmen, and the military had brought the so-called *Concordancia*, or Concordance, government to power. They too followed a program of restoring order while promising social welfare.

Other Fascist movements. The democracies of western Europe also felt the pull of fascism. In France, for example, a strong pro-Fascist movement developed fairly early. Similarly, in Britain, during the dark days of the 1930s, a well-known politician and aristocrat, Sir Oswald Mosley, established the British Union of Fascists. Despite drawing some support from working people, and at its height claiming some 50,000 members, most people simply disregarded Mosley's Fascist Union. Although such groups remained tiny minorities, the presence of Fascist movements in the Western democracies indicated the extent to which some people had become disillusioned by democracy during the bleak times of the depression.

Militarism in Japan

While Europeans and Latin Americans struggled with the problems of the depression by turning to authoritarian and totalitarian regimes, a similar development was occurring in Japan. Like the other industrial powers of the world, Japan suffered heavily from the effects of the Great Depression. As life became increasingly difficult, the flaws in Japan's relatively new and shallow

WRITING A SUMMARY
See essential points in
the text.

REVIEWING TERMS
1. Nazi Party
2. Great Bull Market
3. totalitarianism
4. consumption
5. soviets

**REVIEWING
CHRONOLOGY**
5, 2, 3, 1, 4

**UNDERSTANDING
THE MAIN IDEA**
1. combination of shaky
agricultural markets,
overextension of credit,
and poor investment
habits
2. focused on rule of
proletariat rather than
on supremacy of state
3. the decades saw gov-
ernment mismanage-
ment of the war effort,
military defeat, inade-
quate food and supplies,
poor social conditions
4. new views of science
and psychology, growing
emphasis on consump-
tion, dissatisfaction with
traditional means of
expression
5. Mussolini formed the
Fascist Party, which used
violence to enforce order
and to gain control of
Italian politics. When
Mussolini threatened to
march on Rome, the king
named him as premier.
Mussolini later pro-
claimed himself dictator.

democratic institutions became apparent. Older ideas of military tradition and discipline began to reemerge in new forms.

Army and navy officers in particular questioned the wisdom of a pro-Western policy. These men had learned different lessons from World War I than those of the triumph of liberal democracy. They had become convinced that future wars would require the complete mobilization of the nation. They also saw expansion in Asia as necessary to Japan's future survival. The situation was particularly dangerous for Japanese democracy, since the civilian government did not control the military; the army and navy reported directly to the emperor. Some officers began to join extreme nationalist organizations, such as the Black Dragon Society. A series of political assassinations targeted civilian politicians, leading industrialists, and even military officers thought to be too timid.

While trying to force changes in Japan itself, in 1931 militarists in the government went even further. In September the Japanese army in

▲ **In 1901 Uchida Ryohei was the president of the ultranationalist association called the Black Dragon Society. The Society's main goal was to drive Russia out of East Asia.**

Manchuria launched an all-out offensive against China, in direct defiance of the Japanese government. When the army quickly completed its conquest of all Manchuria, the enthusiasm of the Japanese public swept away all opposition, and the civilian government fell.

Although civilian politicians remained in the government, the policies of the militarist leaders had prevailed. Eventually, in 1936, a failed coup gave the military an increased role in the government. The new military rulers used propaganda to win supporters and cracked down on their political opponents. Unlike the Fascists, Nazis, or Communists in Europe, the militarists in Japan had accomplished their goals without developing a popular political party. Instead they had relied on age-old Japanese traditions.

Nations around the world turned to authoritarian forms of government to solve the problems caused by the Great Depression.

SECTION 5 REVIEW

IDENTIFY and explain the significance of the following:
- Benito Mussolini
- fascism
- totalitarianism
- Adolf Hitler
- Nazi Party
- Third Reich
- Leni Riefenstahl
- *Kristallnacht*
- Joseph Stalin
- gulags

1. **Main Idea** How were Mussolini and Hitler able to gain power?

2. **Main Idea** How was totalitarianism under Stalin similar to and different from totalitarianism under Mussolini and Hitler?

3. **Economic Organization** What did economics have to do with the spread of totalitarianism in the 1920s and 1930s?

4. **Writing to Explain** Imagine that you are a foreign newspaper reporter in Italy or Germany during the time Mussolini or Hitler has just come to power. Write an article explaining why some people support either dictator.

5. **Comparing** Create a chart like the one below comparing totalitarian regimes in Italy, Germany, the Soviet Union, Brazil, and Japan. What do the examples have in common?

COUNTRY	LEADER(S)/DATE CAME TO POWER	POLITICAL IDEALS	METHODS OF CONTROL
Italy			

Review

On a separate sheet of paper, complete the following exercises:

WRITING A SUMMARY

Using the essential points in the text, write a brief summary of the chapter.

REVIEWING TERMS

From the following list, choose the term that correctly matches the definition.

totalitarianism
Great Bull Market
Nazi Party
consumption
soviets
gulags

1. National Socialist German Workers Party, formed under the leadership of Adolf Hitler
2. period of rising stock prices in the 1920s, resulting in tremendous profits for many investors
3. form of government holding complete control over all aspects of society and government, allowing no opposition
4. the purchase and use of products to satisfy wants
5. councils formed by Russian workers

REVIEWING CHRONOLOGY

List the following events in their correct chronological order.
1. The New York Stock Exchange crashes on Black Tuesday.
2. The Weimar Republic is established in Germany.
3. Mussolini takes control of Italy.
4. Hitler becomes chancellor of Germany.
5. Bolsheviks seize control of the Russian government in the October Revolution.

UNDERSTANDING THE MAIN IDEA

1. Why did the world enter a global depression in 1929?
2. How was totalitarianism in the Soviet Union different from totalitarianism elsewhere?
3. What were the causes of the Russian Revolution of 1917?
4. What cultural changes took place in the postwar societies of the industrialized nations?
5. How did Mussolini come to power in Italy?

THINKING CRITICALLY

1. **Analyzing** What were the long-term effects of World War I on both the victorious and defeated nations?
2. **Synthesizing** What was the effect of economics on politics in the 1920s and 1930s? How does economics continue to play an important role in politics today?
3. **Hypothesizing** How do you think the success of the Bolshevik revolution in Russia affected communist movements in other countries?

Building Your Portfolio

Complete the following activities individually or in groups.

1. **The Russian Revolution** You (and your coworkers) are writers for a news magazine in the 1920s. You have been asked to create an entire issue devoted to the Russian Revolution. You will need to conduct research using multiple sources of evidence to fill your issue with informative articles, maps, time lines, and illustrations that will help American readers understand the key events, major figures, historical background, and political ideas of the revolution. In addition, you should help readers of your article understand the Russian Revolution by comparing it to the French and American Revolutions.
2. **Culture** You (and your coworkers) have been hired by a museum to produce an exhibition on the global influence of jazz in the 1920s. Your exhibition might focus on a few major artists or on a country where jazz became popular. To trace the influence of jazz, your exhibit will need to provide text as well as recordings and visual images that show how jazz was received by international audiences and how it influenced musicians in other cultures and countries.

THINKING CRITICALLY

1. The economic costs of the war were felt by victorious nations as well as defeated nations. Similarly, nearly every nation experienced social and political turmoil.
2. Economic instability caused many nations to lose confidence in democratic government. As jobs became hard to find and money lost value, more and more people turned to strong leaders who promised reform in exchange for totalitarian powers. People continue to support political leaders who promise to meet economic needs.
3. The success of the Bolsheviks inspired other communist groups to continue working toward their goal of revolution.

Propagandist techniques became widely used after modern communications technology allowed information to be easily disseminated to the public. The printing press allowed Thomas Paine to distribute *Common Sense* to a large number of colonists. The invention of radio and television allowed propagandists to reach an even wider audience.

Critical Thinking Ask students if they think radio and television changed the nature of propaganda and why.

ANSWER: Some students might feel that bias is the same in any medium, but other students might feel that radio and television have more power to affect emotions.

RESOURCE ACTIVITY

GLOBAL HISTORY RESOURCE CENTER
Image: "*Our Last Hope*": *Nazi Propaganda Poster*
Image: *Soviet Propaganda Poster*

Show students the images. Have them compare these pieces of propaganda and create a list of the methods each uses. Have students work in groups to create an instruction manual on how to recognize propaganda.

All Levels

HISTORY IN THE Making

Uses and Abuses of History

History is not simply the study of the past. It is also a record by which peoples and societies maintain their connection with the past and their sense of identity as a group. The way in which people view their past often determines the way they view their present and their future. The writing—or rewriting—of history can be a powerful political tool in the hands of people who wish to mold the present and change the course of the future. In some cases, rewriting history results in the production of propaganda.

The word *propaganda* comes from a Latin term meaning "to spread" or "multiply." Today it is used to mean the effort to spread a particular idea or set of ideas—often without regard for the truth. Ideally, historians try to find out and explain, as objectively as possible, what has happened in the past and why. Propagandists, on the other hand, are more interested in using the past—even distorting it if necessary—to gain support for a particular cause. Usually they appeal to people's emotions rather than their reason. As part of this appeal, they try to associate the ideas they oppose with negative images in people's minds and associate their own ideas with positive images.

National Socialist History

Perhaps the most notorious modern use of history as propaganda has occurred in totalitarian states. Both Mussolini's Fascist government and the National Socialist government of Adolf Hitler, for example, rewrote school textbooks to provide support for their own political programs. In Germany this meant adopting the views expressed in Hitler's *Mein Kampf*. Written in the aftermath of World War I, *Mein Kampf* blamed Germany's defeat on a conspiracy between Jewish bankers and Communists—the so-called "stab in the back" theory. Once Hitler came to power, this became the official view of the war taught in Germany's schools.

For the Nazis, the primary actors in history were racial groups. In addition, in the Nazi scheme of history the Jews had played a particularly negative role. Consequently, Nazi propaganda usually portrayed Jews as lowly, dirty, animal-like creatures, while portraying Germans as tall, clean, intelligent human beings. Through such negative and positive images, the Nazis tried to sway people's emotions.

Marxist-Leninist History

A similar revision of the past occurred under communist rule in the Soviet Union. Instead of examining the historical past objectively, for example, and then drawing conclusions about what happened and why, Soviet historians began with the assumption that Marx's and Lenin's interpretations of history were the correct ones. Soviet history was thus made to illustrate the correctness of these ideas. Soviet schools taught that history was an ongoing

▲ Crowds gather in Nazi Germany to watch books being burned. The ritual not only destroyed books but also symbolized the destruction of independent thought.

process of class warfare, which must inevitably be won by the workers of the world, united under the Communist Party.

According to this interpretation, for example, war was caused by imperialism, which Lenin called the "highest stage of capitalism." Only by abandoning or overthrowing the capitalist system, Lenin taught, could people eliminate war from human society once and for all. Thus, Marxist historians sought to associate capitalism with war and destruction while presenting socialism as the key to peace and prosperity.

Methods of Propaganda
To spread their views, totalitarian governments employed the full authority of the state. In addition to rewriting textbooks, for example, in both Nazi Germany and the Soviet Union government authorities removed teachers and scholars who did not support the official line. Books considered controversial by

the Nazi government were often burned in public ceremonies. In their place, the authorities encouraged people to read books favored by the Nazi Party.

In addition to using the educational establishment for propaganda purposes, totalitarian states also used many other means of spreading their message. Art in all its forms including traditional mediums such as painting, sculpture, and architecture, as well as films, radio, and television, was a particularly powerful tool for propaganda. Totalitarian governments attempted to channel art into lines approved by the ruling elites.

In 1937, for example, Joseph Goebbels, the minister for propaganda in Nazi Germany, used an exhibition of modern art, which the Nazis officially titled "The Exhibition of Degenerate Art," to make the case for government control of German art. Goebbels explained:

▶ This portrait of Albert Einstein, painted by Max Liebermann, was part of the Nazis' 1937 "Exhibition of Degenerate Art."

❝How deeply the perverse Jewish spirit had penetrated German cultural life is shown in the frightening and horrifying forms of the 'Exhibition of Degenerate Art' in Munich, arranged as an admonitory [warning] example. . . . Art is a function of the life of the people and the artist its blessed endower [provider] of meaning. And just as the leadership of the state claims for itself the political guidance of other areas of the people's life, likewise does it make the same claim here.❞

The Antidote to Propaganda
While it is often difficult to tell fact from fiction, in the last analysis it is only through careful consideration and examination of any argument that people can distinguish history from potential propaganda. Evidence cited in support of any argument must be tested and weighed. Alternative viewpoints and analyses must be considered. Finally, people must reason logically to avoid the dangers of being swayed by emotion.

Chapter 24

The Beginnings of Colonial Nationalism 1880–1939

Chapter Planning Guide

	TEXTBOOK	CORE RESOURCES	VISUAL RESOURCES	MULTIMEDIA
Introduction	pp. 656–657	Block Scheduling Handbook: Ch. 24		Videodisc Segment 24 and Viewing Guide: *Roads to Independence*
Lesson 24.1 From Empire to Commonwealth	pp. 658–663 Through Others' Eyes: *An Indian Nationalist's View of the West,* p. 661	Reading 24.1: *Indian Home Rule*	Everyday Life 24: *Eviction of Irish Tenants*	GHRC 24 Readings: *The Case for Irish Independence; Gandhi on Passive Resistance* GHRC 24/Videodiscs: Image—*Pray for Ireland's Prisoners;* Map—*Irish Nationalism, 1916–1921; Nationalist Violence in India, 1908–1939*
Lesson 24.2 Nationalism in the Middle East and Africa	pp. 664–670 Map: *New Nations in the Middle East,* p. 665 History Through the Arts: *African Art Influences European Artists,* p. 669	Reading 24.2: *Manifesto of the Second Pan-African Congress* Skills Activity 24: *Analyzing a Primary Source* Writing Project 24: *Writing a Comparison Essay*		GHRC 24 Reading: *Zaghlul Calls for an Independent Egypt* GHRC 24/Videodiscs: Images—*Egyptian Students Riot in Cairo in 1919; Arabs Demonstrate in Jerusalem in 1934*
Lesson 24.3 Nationalism in China and Southeast Asia	pp. 671–675 Map: *Civil War in China, 1925–1935,* p. 673	Reading 24.3: *The Origins of Nationalism*		GHRC 24 Readings: *Chiang's Manifesto to the People of China; Mao Attacks Imperialism in China* GHRC 24/Videodiscs: Image—*Imperialism Comes to Stay in China*
Lesson 24.4 The American Sphere of Influence	pp. 676–680 Map: *U.S. Territories in the Pacific,* p. 677 Teenagers in History: *Princess Kaiulani Pleads for Her Country,* p. 679	Reading 24.4: *A Change in United States Policy Toward Nicaragua* Geography Activity 24: *The Philippine War*	Art and History 24: *Murals for the New School for Social Research* Geography and History 24: *Central America and the Caribbean*	GHRC 24 Readings: *Platform of the Cuban Revolutionary Party; Why the U.S. Should Annex the Philippines* GHRC 24/Videodiscs: Images—*José Martí: Cuban Patriot; U.S. Marines Occupy Nicaragua;* Map—*The United States Expands Its Influence*
Chapter Investigation and Enrichment	pp. 656–680	Chapter 24 Investigation: *Nationalist Manifestos* People in World History 24 Explorations in Daily Life 24		GHRC 24/Videodiscs
Review and Assessment	Section 1 Review, p. 663 Section 2 Review, p. 670 Section 3 Review, p. 675 Section 4 Review, p. 680 Chapter 24 Review, p. 681	Chapter Review Activity 24 Vocabulary Activity 24 Themes Review 24 Section Study Guides 24.1–24.4 Main Idea Activities 24.1–24.4 Daily Quizzes 24.1–24.4 Chapter 24 Test Sheltered English Ch. 24 Test Ch. 24 Test Generator		Audio CDs: Ch. 24 Summary (English and Spanish)

INTRODUCING THE CHAPTER

Textbook pp. 656–657

CHAPTER OVERVIEW

Hoping to maintain its role as a world power, Great Britain allowed some colonies greater self-rule as members of the Commonwealth. As most of the world slowly retreated from imperialism, the United States added to its holdings, acquiring the Philippines in the Spanish-American War.

PRESENTING THEMES

On the chalkboard or on an overhead transparency, write the following open-ended theme questions.

- **CROSS-CULTURAL INTERACTION** How might imperialism contribute to the flow of ideas across cultures?
- **POLITICS AND LAW** How might imperial rule and the rise of nationalism affect the development of new states?
- **SOCIAL RELATIONS** What changes might nationalists demand?

Have students, either individually or in groups, suggest responses to the questions. For the cross-cultural interaction question, students might suggest that imperialists would bring ideas to the colonies and be influenced by the ideas of the people there. For the politics and law question, students might suggest that nationalist responses to foreign rule might foment independence movements that create new states. For the social relations question, students might suggest that nationalists might call for the takeover of foreign-owned industries and an end to foreign rule. Save the responses. Once students have studied the chapter, you may wish to have them complete the Themes Review, then compare the two sets of answers.

USING THE VIDEO

Segment 24: *Roads to Independence*

ENGLISH

Search Chapter 24
Videodisc 2, Side B

SPANISH

Search Chapter 24
Videodisc 2, Side B

Tell students that in this chapter they will examine the imperialist powers and the peoples they ruled in the first decades of the twentieth century. Then show Segment 24 of the *World History and Cultures Videodiscs*. This segment introduces students to Mohandas Gandhi and his use of nonviolent resistance as a means of bringing about social change. To help students grasp the significant points of the video, have them complete Video Viewing Guide 24.

Key to Ability Levels

All strategies and activities are coded to the following ability levels:

LEVEL 1	**Basic** activities suitable for all students
LEVEL 2	**Average** activities suitable for average to above-average students
LEVEL 3	**Challenging** activities suitable for above-average students
SHELTERED ENGLISH	Activities suitable for students with **Limited English Proficiency**

Additional Resources

BOOKS FOR TEACHERS

Fromkin, David. *A Peace to End All Peace: The Fall of the Ottoman Empire and the Creation of the Modern Middle East*. Avon Books, 1989. Discusses the events that shaped the Middle East.

Green, Martin. *Gandhi: Voice of a New Age Revolution*. Continuum, 1993. Presents a thorough biography.

Karnow, Stanley. *In Our Image: America's Empire in the Philippines*. Random House, 1989. Examines the U.S.-Philippines relationship.

BOOKS FOR STUDENTS

Ashton, Stephen. *Indian Independence*. Batsford, 1986. Focuses on the critical years from 1885 to 1945.

Hibbert, Christopher. *The Dragon Wakes: China and the West, 1793–1911*. Penguin, 1989. Examines the changes brought about by contact with the West and the Chinese responses.

Wepman, Denis. *Africa: The Struggle for Independence*. Facts On File, 1993. Details responses to colonial rule.

MULTIMEDIA MATERIALS

India: The Brightest Jewel. Film Incorporated. Video, 20 min. Looks at independence from Britain and the separation from Pakistan.

Roots of a War. Films Incorporated. Video, 60 min. Examines the origins of Vietnamese nationalism.

Twentieth Century Nationalism. Clearvue. CD-ROM, MAC, DOS, MPC formats. Examines Nigeria, Vietnam, Pakistan, and India.

Lesson 24.1   *From Empire to Commonwealth*

Textbook pp. 658–663

RESOURCES

Pupil's Edition
Through Others' Eyes, p. 661: *An Indian Nationalist's View of the West*

Core Resources
Reading 24.1: *Indian Home Rule*

Visual Resources
Everyday Life 24: *Eviction of Irish Tenants*

Global History Resource Center
Reading: *The Case for Irish Independence*
Reading: *Gandhi on Passive Resistance*

Videodiscs or Global History Resource Center

Image: *Pray for Ireland's Prisoners*

Search Frame 1003

Map: *Irish Nationalism, 1916–1921*

Search Frame 1010

Map: *Nationalist Violence in India: 1908–1939*

Search Frame 1011

LESSON FOCUS

Why and how did the British relationship with its colonies change in the early 1900s?

OBJECTIVES

After completing this lesson, students will be able to:

- explain the response of colonial nationalists to British efforts to maintain imperial unity;
- describe how colonial nationalism was dealt with after World War I;
- analyze how Irish nationalism differed from nationalism in other parts of the British Empire;
- explain how Gandhi affected the Indian nationalist movement.

HOOK

Compare nationalist responses to British imperial demands. Ask students how American colonists reacted in the 1700s to Britain's attempts to assert its rights over them. *[They declared their independence and fought a war to gain it.]*

Ask: *In the early 1900s, how did Britain's remaining colonies of settlement view their ties to the empire?*
[Many wanted greater independence.]

Ask: *How did Britain attempt to hold the empire together in the early 1900s?*
[held Imperial Conferences with Dominion leaders to discuss items of mutual concern]

Lead students to see that in the early 1900s, the inhabitants of British possessions wanted more independence.

DEVELOP

Draw a time line to show how problems of colonial nationalism were resolved. Draw a long time line on the chalkboard. Before the starting point of the time line, write the word *Empire*. After the ending point of the time line, write the word *Commonwealth*. Invite students to fill in events that were important during the shift from the British Empire to the British Commonwealth. Encourage students to include as many events as they can about all the colonies of settlement. *[Entries on the time line should include dates and brief information about events such as Britain's declaration of war against Germany in 1914 and the Imperial Conference of 1926.]*

When the time line is completed, have students use it to tell the stories of South Africa, Ireland, and India and to explain how World War I affected Britain's colonial relationships.

PROBE

Consider the unique characteristics of Irish nationalism.

Have students suggest reasons for the intense feelings that surround Irish nationalism. To provide additional background show students Everyday Life Transparency 24 and have them complete the accompanying worksheet. If available, also display the electronic media image *Pray for Ireland's Prisoners* and have students read *The Case for Irish Independence* in the Global History Resource Center. *[Students should recognize that Britain considered Ireland to be an integral part of Great Britain, not a colony or dominion; that opposition to British rule was centuries old.]* Display the electronic media map, *Irish Nationalism, 1916–1921* and have students add events associated with Irish nationalism to the time line. *[1801: Great Britain and Ireland unified; Parliament promised home rule after the end of World War I; 1916: Easter Rising; 1918: Sinn Fein swept the elections and Irish Parliament established; 1921: Ireland partitioned, with the Irish Free State becoming a dominion; 1922: civil war among Irish nationalists; 1937: independent republic proclaimed; many nationalists still seeking independence for Northern Ireland]*

CONCLUDE

Analyze Gandhi's influence on the nationalist movement in India.

Provide students with a point of reference by displaying the electronic media map *Nationalist Violence in India, 1908–1939*. Then have students construct a "spectrum of Indian nationalism" chart on the chalkboard. Write the following individuals and organizations in one column and call on volunteers to identify their approach to nationalism: Indian National Congress, pre–World War I *[loyal but wanted equal opportunity to serve in government]*; Indian National Congress, postwar *[demanded home rule]*; Bal Gangadhar Tilak *[cultural resistance]*; Gandhi *[nonviolent resistance to secure home rule]*; extreme Hindu nationalists *[terrorist campaign against the British]*; Muslim League *[protect rights of Muslims, home rule]*. Be sure students support each identification.

Next have students acquaint themselves with Gandhi's views by reading the Through Others' Eyes feature on page 661, Core Resources Reading 24.1, and the selection on Gandhi in the Global History Resource Center. Then discuss Gandhi's influence. *Ask: How was Gandhi's style of leadership unique?*

[Answers should focus on nonviolent resistance, his

desire to preserve India's spiritual traditions, and his transformation of the Indian National Congress into a mass political movement.]

EXTEND

Cross-Curricular Connection: *Journalism*

Assign pairs of students the following countries: Canada, Australia, South Africa, Ireland, and India. Invite students to write newspaper articles about a change in the relationship between Britain and their assigned country, such as a shift from dominion to commonwealth. One student in each pair should write from the point of view of a British paper. The other student should write from the point of view of a paper in their assigned country. Encourage pairs of students to read their articles and explain why they contain different perspectives. Then have the class discuss the unique relationship each country had with Britain.

Other Media

You might wish to show and discuss the video *Gandhi* (Beacon Films, black and white, 36 min.), which examines Gandhi's character and his commitment to nonviolence.

MEET INDIVIDUAL NEEDS

Logical-Mathematical Learners

Have students devise crossword puzzles to review information in this section. They should use the leaders, countries, events, and terms used in the section in their puzzles. Blank versions of the puzzles could be photocopied and distributed for the class to solve.

Students Acquiring English

Have students use a dictionary to find the definitions and roots of the various terms used to describe lands in this section, such as *colony, dominion, empire, commonwealth,* and *republic*.

ASSESS

Review

Have students complete the Section 1 Review. Use the answers in the Teacher's Edition, page 663, to assess student mastery of this section.

Lesson 24.2   *Nationalism in the Middle East and Africa*

Textbook pp. 664–670

RESOURCES

Pupil's Edition

Map, p. 665: *New Nations in the Middle East, 1922–1939*

History Through the Arts, p. 669: *African Art Influences European Artists*

Core Resources

Reading 24.2: *Manifesto of the Second Pan-African Congress*

Skills Activity 24: *Analyzing a Primary Source*

Global History Resource Center

Reading: *Zaghlul Calls for an Independent Egypt*

Reading: *Britain Promises Jews a National Homeland*

Reading: *Arabs Object to Britain's Balfour Declaration*

Videodiscs or Global History Resource Center

Image: *Egyptian Students Riot in Cairo in 1919*

Image: *Arabs Demonstrate in Jerusalem in 1934*

Search Frame 1004

Search Frame 1005

LESSON FOCUS

What forms did nationalist movements take in Southwest Asia and Africa?

OBJECTIVES

After completing this lesson, students will be able to:

- explain the goals of nationalists in Egypt and the Arab mandates after World War I;
- analyze how British imperialism affected the development of nationalism in Palestine;
- describe how Atatürk's policies affected Turkey;
- describe how urbanization influenced nationalism in Africa.

HOOK

Compare the goals of nationalists in Egypt and the Arab mandates. Display the electronic media image of the 1919 riot in Cairo and read aloud Zaghlul's call for independence in the Global History Resource Center. Then have students draw a time line of Egypt's nationalist movement. The time line could start with the British occupation in 1882 and end with the Anglo-Egyptian Treaty.

Ask: What was the goal of Egyptian nationalists?

[full independence]

Ask: What factors made Britain particularly hesitant to grant Egypt full independence?

[the outbreak of World War I, Britain's strategic need to retain military control of the Suez Canal and the Sudan, and the Italian invasion of nearby Ethiopia]

DEVELOP

Compare the goals of nationalists in Egypt with those of nationalists in the Arab mandates and in Arabia. To provide a point of reference, have students refer to the map *New Nations in the Middle East, 1922–1939* on textbook page 665. Help students understand that many Arabs had expected independence after World War I and felt betrayed when it was not granted. While nationalists in the Arab mandates and in Arabia wanted an end to French and British control, they lacked a sense of belonging to a territorial state. Pan-Arabism and Pan-Islamism movements also hindered the development of territorial nationalism.

Ask: Why did France and Britain want to hold on to the mandates?

[They considered the Middle East strategically important. The French held on in Syria despite revolts. Britain granted Iraq and Jordan independence after they agreed to a military alliance.]

Ask: What kind of state emerged in Arabia?
[The Sa'ud family established an Islamic state through conquest.]

Discuss the effects of British imperialism on nationalism in Palestine. Before discussing nationalist movements in Palestine, have students complete the readings on Britain's promise of a Jewish homeland and the Arab response in the Global History Resource Center, and have them complete the Skills Activity. Next display the electronic media image of the Arab demonstration in 1934.

Ask: Why did the rise of anti-Semitism in Europe lead to conflict in Palestine?
[Motivated by anti-Semitism in Europe, Zionists tried to establish a "national home" in the British mandate of Palestine; Palestinian Arabs reacted with an armed revolt; conflicting promises from Britain led to clashes with the two opposed nationalist movements in Palestine.]

Examine the importance of Atatürk's policies. Next have students examine the very different case of Turkey. Ask volunteers to name Atatürk's reforms and write their responses on the chalkboard. [replaced the caliphate with a constitutional, secular republic; instituted surnames; replaced Islamic law with secular laws, replaced Turkish alphabet with Latin alphabet]

Ask: Why did Atatürk adopt these policies?
[to create a modern state on a Western model]

PROBE

Analyze the ways in which increasing urbanization spurred nationalist movements in Africa. Have students complete Reading 24.2 and the accompanying questions. Then have students form small groups to investigate the effects of urbanization on the growth of nationalist movements in Africa. Have the groups report their findings to the class. List their findings on the chalkboard and have students record the results in their notebooks. [Urbanization facilitated growth of labor unions and workers' associations, which were also used to voice political complaints; urbanization also exposed Africans to racial prejudice and mistreatment; urban population supported new leaders, who, following Gandhi's example, organized strikes, demonstrations, and boycotts; new leaders were also influenced by Pan-Africanism.]

CONCLUDE

Prepare a nationalist speech. Have students write and read aloud a brief speech for a press interview if they were a nationalist leader in the Middle East or Africa. Students should identify their country. Speeches might be: a protest against Britain or France; a statement of their goals and methods; a philosophical talk about why it is time to become a nation.

EXTEND

Cross-Curricular Connection: *Government*
Link to Today. Have students use an almanac to determine what kind of government exists today in the former Middle Eastern and African mandates and colonies of Britain (a constitutional monarchy) and of France (a republic). Students might speculate about why each government is similar to or different from that of its former ruler.

MEET INDIVIDUAL NEEDS

Visual-Spatial Learners
Have students read the History Through the Arts feature on African art. Then have interested students create an exhibit of African art. The exhibit captions should explain how different styles influenced European artists. Alternatively, students might investigate the influence of African art on particular European artists and report their finding to the class.

Intrapersonal Learners
Invite students to imagine that they live in Turkey during the time Atatürk introduced his cultural reforms. Have them write a letter to a friend bemoaning or supporting the new Western ways.

ASSESS

Review
Have students complete the Section 2 Review. Use the answers in the Teacher's Edition, page 670, to assess student mastery of this section.

Lesson 24.3   Nationalism in China and Southeast Asia

Textbook pp. 671–675

RESOURCES

Pupil's Edition

Map, p. 673: *Civil War in China, 1925–1935*

Core Resources

Reading 24.3: *The Origins of Nationalism*

Global History Resource Center

Reading: *Chiang's Manifesto to the People of China*

Reading: *Mao Attacks Imperialism in China*

Videodiscs or Global History Resource Center

Image: *Imperialism Comes to Stay in China*

Search Frame 1006

LESSON FOCUS

Why and how did nationalist movements develop in China and Southeast Asia?

OBJECTIVES

After completing this lesson, students will be able to:

- describe the kinds of changes Chinese intellectuals and nationalists sought;
- analyze why China was unable to achieve unity after the fall of the Qing Empire;
- explain what inspired colonial nationalists in Southeast Asia to fight against Dutch and French repression.

HOOK: Link to Today

Describe the changes intellectuals and nationalists made in China. Ask students if any of them plan to continue their education at a university overseas. Briefly discuss the ready availability of excellent colleges and universities throughout the United States. Then have students explain why in the early 1900s thousands of young Chinese left their country to pursue an education abroad, and have students describe the effect of this phenomenon on China. *[Shunning the traditional Confucian classics, young Chinese sought a modern, Western-style education, which contributed to the start of a new cultural movement in China, modeled on Western ways.]*

Then have students discuss how the new cultural movement broadened into a political movement.

Ask: How did Dr. Hu Shih break with the past, and what effect did his new approach to the Chinese language have on other fields?

[He encouraged writers to replace classical Chinese with the ordinary language of the people. Inspired, other intellectuals called for similar reforms in their own fields. Scholars called for major Western-style social reforms.]

Next display the cartoon of imperialism in China.

Ask: How did the cultural movement affect politics?

[The cultural movement's energy combined with Chinese nationalism to create a powerful force for political change. Some Chinese—such as those in the May Fourth Movement—saw adopting Western ideas as the only way to restore China's independence.]

DEVELOP

Analyze how the struggle between Nationalists and Communists prevented China from achieving unity. Have students complete Core Resources Reading 24.3. Discuss how it applies to Sun Yixian's efforts to unify China.

Ask: What was Sun's goal, and how did he hope to achieve it?

[To unify the country militarily and revive it along

Western lines; he believed that the Chinese had to develop a sense of national spirit to survive as a people.]

Graphically illustrate Sun Yixian's attempt to unify China by drawing a large "vee" on the chalkboard. Write *Nationalists (Guomindang)* above one arm of the "vee." Write *Communists* above the other. Circle the point at which the arms intersect, and label it *unity*. Ask students whether this diagram fully represents the facts. *[No. Sun forged an alliance with the Communists; but after his death the Nationalists, led by Chiang Kaishek, turned on the Communists.]*

Have students read the Global History Resource Center selection by Chiang, in which he states reasons to support the Guomindang rather than the Communists. Then have students read Mao's analysis of China's situation in the Global History Resource Center. Next have students study the map on textbook page 673, and discuss the shifts toward or away from unity in the relationship between Nationalists and Communists over time. *[The two groups moved toward unity during Sun's time; away from unity during the 10 years of Chiang's suppression of the Communists; and toward unity again during the war against Japan.]*

Ask: *What did Mao hope to gain from a truce with the Nationalists during the Sino-Japanese conflict?*
[the opportunity for expansion]

PROBE

Analyze the characteristics of successful nationalist leaders in Southeast Asia. Have students determine the sources of inspiration for nationalist leaders in Indonesia and Vietnam. *[Students should recognize that they drew inspiration from Western political philosophies, including Marxism.]*

Next list *Sun Yixian, Chiang Kaishek, Mao Zedong, Sukarno,* and *Ho Chi Minh* on the chalkboard. Have students provide examples of actions these nationalists took that showed leadership. Then ask students to develop a general description of what makes an effective nationalist leader. You might start them off with the words "*A nationalist leader must . . .*" Have students share their descriptions with the class.

CONCLUDE

Write an editorial concerning nationalist movements. Have students imagine they lived during the early 1900s, either in China or in Southeast Asia. Have them write a newspaper editorial supporting or opposing one of the nationalist movements that occurred during the 1900s as outlined in the section. Each editorial should include details about the movement that reinforce the writer's opinion. Nationalist movements to choose from include those associated with Sun Yixian, Chiang Kaishek, Mao Zedong, Sukarno, and Ho Chi Minh.

EXTEND

Cross-Curricular Connection: *Language Arts*
Invite students to read biographies of one of the leaders discussed in the section. Have them choose one interesting or important event from that leader's early life and explain the effect of that event on the leader's later actions.

MEET INDIVIDUAL NEEDS

Visual-Spatial Learners
Invite students to draw caricatures of the nationalist leaders profiled in this section. Below their drawings, students should write an explanation of what characteristics they were trying to reveal through their caricatures.

Gifted Students
Have students write an essay exploring the connection between communism and nationalism. They might examine how the ideals of revolutionaries in Russia compared with nationalist ideals. They might also talk about why the Soviet Union supported Mao and the Chinese Communists as well as other budding communist/nationalist groups.

ASSESS

Review
Have students complete the Section 3 Review. Use the answers in the Teacher's Edition, page 675, to assess student mastery of this section.

Lesson 24.4   *The American Sphere of Influence*

Textbook pp. 676–680

RESOURCES

Pupil's Edition
Teenagers in History, p. 679: *Princess Kaiulani Pleads for Her Country*

Core Resources
Reading 24.4: *A Change in United States Policy Toward Nicaragua*

Global History Resource Center
Reading: *Platform of the Cuban Revolutionary Party*
Reading: *Why the U.S. Should Annex the Philippines*

Videodiscs or Global History Resource Center

Image: *José Martí: Cuban Patriot*

Search Frame 1007

Map: *The United States Expands Its Influence*

Search Frame 1012

Image: *U.S. Marines Occupy Nicaragua*

Search Frame 1008

LESSON FOCUS
Why and how did nationalism arise in the American sphere of influence?

OBJECTIVES
After completing this lesson, students will be able to:
- explain how the Spanish-American War affected the United States;
- identify the consequence of American intervention in Latin America;
- identify the result of the revival of Hawaiian nationalism in the 1880s and 1890s;
- explain how Filipino resistance to U.S. imperialism affected American colonial policy.

HOOK
Examine the effect of the Spanish-American War on American overseas policy. Have students explain how an "all-you-can-eat buffet" works. Then ask them whether they think people are inclined to eat more or less under these circumstances, and why. [*Most students will say that the temptation is to eat more, for at least two reasons: food consumed beyond a normal portion is thought of as free; and everyone else is doing it.*] Next make the following assertion:

To the United States, the Spanish American War was like an all-you-can-eat buffet. Begin testing the assertion by reviewing the Cuban nationalist movement and U.S. intervention in Cuba. To aid in this review, display the electronic media image of Martí and have students read the platform of the Cuban Revolutionary Party in the Global History Resource Center. Then display the electronic media map of the U.S. sphere of influence.

Ask: What price did the United States pay for victory?
    [*Possible answers: Many soldiers died and much money was spent.*]

Ask: What temptations did victory bring? Why did the United States give in to temptation and change its overseas policy?
[*The temptation was to grab all the available territory. Cuba, Puerto Rico, Guam, and the Philippines were available—"free"—and besides, every other major world power was establishing an empire.*]

DEVELOP
Chart the consequences of American imperialism. Create a three-column chart on the chalkboard to organize the facts from this section. Column headings might be *Historical Event*, *Details*, and *Consequences*. List these major historical events: (1) Spanish-American War, (2) U.S. intervention in Latin

America, (3) Nationalism in Hawaii, and (4) Conflict in the Philippines. Then call on student volunteers to provide both the main details and the consequences of each event. *[Sample results: (1) Cuba becomes American protectorate; Congress annexes Puerto Rico, Guam, and the Philippines; (2) resentment of U.S. intervention in Latin America surfaces as anti-American nationalism; United States has continuing economic influence; (3) nationalist resistance to American influence in Hawaii leads to annexation by United States; (4) huge loss of life; self-government for Filipinos; promise of independence]* Students should copy the finished chart into their notebooks.

PROBE

Analyze motives for imperialism. Have students read the Teenagers in History feature on page 679. Then display the electronic media image of U.S. Marines in Nicaragua while students complete Core Resources Reading 24.4. Also have students read Senator Albert J. Beveridge's speech in the Global History Resource Center. Discuss these readings with students, and ask them what conclusions they can draw about American foreign policy in the late 1800s and early 1900s, using U.S. imperialism in Hawaii, Nicaragua, and the Philippines as examples. *[The needs of business often outweighed other concerns.]*

CONCLUDE

Contrast nationalist and imperialist points of view. Have students write a dialogue that might have taken place in one of the countries in the American sphere of influence. Participants in the dialogue are a nationalist leader and an official representing the U.S. government. Tell students that the nationalist wants independence, or at least self-government, for his or her country. The U.S. official wants to keep the two countries' relationship as it is. Both persons should use persuasive argument to make their case. Encourage students to read their completed dialogues to the class.

EXTEND

Cross-Curricular Connection: *Language Arts*
Link to Today. Have students read the quotation from Princess Kaiulani in the Teenagers in History feature on textbook page 679. Then have them write a poem in response to her plea from the point of view of an American living in Hawaii today.

MEET INDIVIDUAL NEEDS

Musical-Rhythmic Learners
Have students write lyrics and music for a song for or about one of the nationalist groups discussed in this section. Songs might take the form of an anthem, a call to arms, or a ballad.

Kinesthetic Learners
Have students create a brochure inviting businesses to invest in one of the countries in the American sphere of influence. The brochure should focus on the economic incentives as well as other advantages of investing in the country.

ASSESS

Review
Have students complete the Section 4 Review. Use answers in the Teacher's Edition, page 680, to assess student mastery of this section.

In preparation for the chapter test, you may wish to have students complete all or part of the Chapter 24 Review on page 681 of the textbook, the Chapter 24 Review Activity, and the Chapter 24 Themes Review.

Understanding the Main Idea

Call on a volunteer to read aloud the *Understanding the Main Idea* paragraph. Then tell students that the end of the 1800s was a time of growing dissatisfaction among colonial states. In the Middle East, Africa, and Asia, a growing desire for independence led to a conviction that imperial rule was no longer acceptable. Imperial rulers gradually gave way to national governments.

Presenting Themes

See p. 655B for suggestions on introducing themes.

Using the Time Line

Have students list the time line events in their notebooks. After they have read about each event in the chapter, have students write a paragraph explaining its significance.

Chapter 24
The Beginnings of Colonial Nationalism 1880–1939

Understanding the Main Idea

In the age of imperialism, Western industrial powers carried their institutions, their cultures, and their worldviews around the globe. Western-style education produced new local elites heavily influenced by nationalism, liberalism, democracy, and even socialism. As a result, European colonists and non-European elites alike began to develop their own senses of identity, demanding more rights and privileges.

Themes

- **Cross-cultural Interaction** How might imperialism contribute to the flow of ideas across cultures?

- **Politics and Law** How might imperial rule and the rise of nationalism affect the development of new states?

- **Social Relations** What changes might nationalists demand?

In 1930 Mohandas Gandhi, a small bespectacled man in his sixties, led a group of Indian peasants in a protest march to the sea to gather natural salt. Although a simple act, it was actually one of defiance, for the British raj held a monopoly on salt production. Gandhi was arrested shortly thereafter, but his example inspired others.

In the coastal town of Dharsana, a crowd of 2,500 Indians gathered to continue Gandhi's march to the sea. The marchers proceeded to the salt deposits. Scores of policemen waited for them, clubs in hand. A journalist observed:

> 66 *Suddenly, at a word of command, scores of native police rushed upon the advancing marchers and rained blows on their heads. . . . Not one of the marchers even raised an arm to fend off the blows. . . . Then another column formed. . . . They marched slowly toward the police. Although every one knew that within a few minutes he would be beaten down, perhaps killed, I could detect no signs of wavering or fear.* 99

Despite the beatings, wave after wave of people marched on, convinced that they, like Gandhi, were helping to achieve India's independence.

1885	1898	1912	1917
The Indian National Congress forms in Bombay.	The United States achieves victory in the Spanish-American War.	The Chinese republic is proclaimed.	The Balfour Declaration supports a "national home" in Palestine for Jews.

Mohandas Gandhi and his followers on the Salt March, 1930

1921	1922	1935	1936
▲	▲	▲	▲
The Chinese Communist Party is founded in Shanghai.	The Irish civil war begins.	Britain grants India self-rule at the provincial level.	Britain recognizes Egypt as an independent nation.

Theme: War and Diplomacy

In 1900 the Boer War dwindled to sporadic attacks by Boer forces. In response, British troops burned Boer farms and sent the owners to concentration camps. These camps eventually contained over 100,000 Boers. By the time a peace treaty was signed in 1902, some 28,000 Boers had died in the camps. The conditions of these camps caused a great deal of controversy and resulted in growing doubts about imperialism.

Critical Thinking Ask students why the Boers' experience might have been distressing to non-Europeans under colonial rule.

ANSWER: Students might say that non-Europeans worried that a colonial power would treat them even worse than the Boers.

SECTION 1
From Empire to Commonwealth

FOCUS

- How did colonial nationalists respond to British efforts to maintain strong bonds of imperial unity?
- How was colonial nationalism dealt with after World War I?
- How did Irish nationalism differ from nationalism in other parts of the British Empire?
- What effect did Gandhi have on the Indian nationalist movement?

By the end of the 1800s, new senses of identity were beginning to develop among colonial peoples of the British Empire. As colonists in the so-called White Dominions, such as Canada and Australia, began to develop national identities of their own, they also sought a new relationship with Great Britain. Meanwhile, nationalists in Ireland and India also sought greater freedom from British rule. In an effort to acknowledge the demands of these colonial nationalists, and at the same time maintain the unity of the empire, British leaders began to transform the imperial relationship.

Afrikaner family in the late 1800s

The Question of Dominion Status

As Great Britain extended self-government to its settlement colonies in the 1800s, the shape of the empire began to change. Although still bound to Britain by ties of blood, language, culture, and legal traditions, the colonists were also developing new senses of national identity as they adapted to local conditions. Even with full internal self-government—or "dominion status," as it began to be called in the early 1900s—many colonists felt restricted by imperial ties. For example, Britain controlled colonial defense, and Parliament could pass legislation for the dominions and veto colonial legislation. Authorities in London could also overturn the decisions of dominion courts.

Anxious to hold the empire together, British leaders began to meet periodically with dominion leaders in the late 1800s to discuss matters of mutual concern. Despite this system of **Imperial Conferences**, as the meetings were later known, colonial nationalism gradually outweighed imperial unity. In 1900, for example, Canadian prime minister Sir Wilfrid Laurier declared:

> **"** I claim for Canada this, that in future she shall be at liberty to act, or not to act, to interfere or not to interfere, to do just as she pleases, and that she shall reserve to herself the right to judge whether or not there is cause for her to act. **"**

Perhaps the most striking resistance to a strongly united empire came in 1902 after the Boer War in South Africa. Outraged at the British policy of making South Africa more British, the Boers, or Afrikaners as they had begun to call themselves, began to actively establish a separate sense of national identity. By 1910, under two former Boer generals, Louis Botha and Jan Smuts, moderate Afrikaners united and assumed control of all of South Africa. The British granted the colony dominion status as the Union of South Africa. More radical anti-British Afrikaners, however, hoped to transform the union into an independent republic.

Despite British efforts to maintain imperial unity, most colonial nationalists insisted on greater independence.

World War I and Its Consequences

World War I intensified debate about the nature of dominion status. In 1914 the British declared war on behalf of the entire empire—without first consulting the dominion governments. In general the dominions responded loyally. "England has the Empire solidly behind her," declared the *Auckland Star*, a New Zealand newspaper. Australian prime minister Andrew Fisher pledged support for Britain "to the last man and the last shilling."

Some colonial leaders, however, disliked being plunged into war by Britain without even being consulted. Sir Wilfrid Laurier complained that issues of war and peace should be for "the Canadian people, the Canadian Parliament and the Canadian government alone to decide." In South Africa, strong pro-German and anti-British sentiment even led to the outbreak of rebellion among some Afrikaners.

Questions about the nature of the empire continued during the war. Were the dominions really independent or not? After the war, colonial leaders pressed harder for a clarification of their status. Finally, at the Imperial Conference of 1926, former British prime minister Lord Balfour presented a report defining dominion status. According to Balfour, the dominions were

66 *autonomous [independent] communities within the British Empire, equal in status, in no way subordinate [inferior] one to another in . . . their domestic or external affairs, though united by a common allegiance to the Crown, and freely associated as members of the British Commonwealth of Nations.* 99

Balfour's report also suggested procedures for colonies to progress to dominion status. In 1931 Parliament enacted the provisions of the Balfour Report and formally established the British

Commonwealth of Nations in the **Statute of Westminster**. By doing so, Britain hoped to maintain the unity of the empire.

After World War I, Britain and its settlement colonies began to transform the empire into the British Commonwealth.

Nationalism in Ireland

Even before the Statute of Westminster, however, the ideal of Commonwealth unity had been seriously challenged. The challenge came in Ireland, which the British considered to be an inseparable part of Great Britain itself—not a dominion or colony at all. Irish resistance to British rule dated back centuries. After the unification of Ireland with Great Britain in 1801, Irish nationalists pursued their goal of independence in the British Parliament. Home rule for Ireland became one of the most controversial issues in British politics. On the eve of World War I, it brought Great Britain to the verge of civil war. Parliament promised to grant home rule after the war.

Home rule was not enough for some nationalists, however. In the spring of 1916 a small group intent on full independence revolted in Dublin in what became known as the **Easter Rising**. British troops quickly crushed the revolt and its leaders were executed—making them martyrs in the

▶ These women, supporters of Irish independence, march to a political meeting in Dublin.

cause for Irish independence. In the aftermath of the Easter Rising, the Irish nationalist party, Sinn Fein (SHIN FAYN), swept the elections of 1918.

Instead of taking their seats in London, the newly elected Irish members of Parliament proclaimed themselves the Dáil Éireann (DAWL AY-ruhn), or Irish Parliament. They pledged to establish a republic in Ireland. Britain refused to recognize the government, and violence broke out. For several years bitter fighting raged between the Sinn Fein armed forces, known as the **Irish Republican Army** (IRA), and the Black and Tans, special British antiterrorist units.

In 1921 the British offered a compromise. Six northern counties of the province of Ulster, which had a Protestant majority, would remain part of the United Kingdom. The 26 southern counties, in which Catholics were a majority, would become a British dominion as the Irish Free State. As the British made it clear that all-out war was the alternative, Sinn Fein leaders agreed.

Some Irish nationalists, however, saw both partition and dominion status as a betrayal. Éamon de Valera, president of the Dáil Éireann, rejected the compromise, declaring: "I am not going to connive at setting up in Ireland another government for England." In 1922 a brutal civil war broke out among the Irish nationalists. The Free State triumphed. In the 1930s, however, de Valera was elected prime minister of the Irish Free State. He dismantled all elements of dominion status. Finally, in 1937, the Dáil Éireann proclaimed Ireland to be an independent republic.

For many nationalists, however, Ireland would not be truly free until the northern counties had been reunited with the south.

Unlike many other colonial nationalists, Irish nationalists accepted dominion status only as a step toward full independence from Britain.

Nationalism in India

British leaders were similarly troubled by the future status of India, Britain's most important imperial possession. Lord Curzon, viceroy of India, observed: "As long as we rule India, we are the greatest power in the world. If we lose it, we shall drop straight away to a third-rate power." Many Indians also preferred to keep things as they were. British rule had maintained peace among India's various states and peoples.

Early Indian nationalism. Other Indians, however, hoped that British India would achieve the same self-governing status as the dominions. These early Indian nationalists were members of the Western-educated elite that had been created by earlier imperial reformers. Initially these nationalists had no desire to end British rule. Pherozeshah Mehta, a British-trained lawyer from Bombay, expressed the feelings of many Indians:

> When . . . India was assigned to the care of England, she decided that India was to be governed on the principles of justice, equality, and righteousness without distinctions of colour, caste, or creed.

These early nationalists simply wanted an equal chance with the British to serve in government.

Such appeals to the British sense of justice and fair play struck a chord among some British liberals. In 1885 Allan Octavian Hume, a retired member of the Indian Civil Service, invited Western-educated Indians

◄ A riot between Irish nationalists and their opponents left this Belfast house in ruins in 1920.

from all over the subcontinent to attend the first all-India political conference in Bombay. Calling themselves the **Indian National Congress**, the delegates declared their loyalty to the Queen-Empress Victoria and called for equal opportunity to serve in the government of India.

As the British government resisted even these moderate demands, some Indian nationalists called for a stronger approach. One of these leaders was Bal Gangadhar Tilak (TI-lahk), an influential Indian journalist. Tilak called for cultural resistance to the British through traditional festivals celebrating Hindu gods and heroes. Tilak's actions alarmed both British authorities and Indian Muslims.

▲ In 1914 Bal Gangadhar Tilak helped found the Indian Home Rule League.

The partition of Bengal. In 1905 British authorities partitioned the huge province of Bengal in an effort to improve its administration. This move unintentionally fed the flames of Indian nationalism. Many Bengalis felt that their cultural homeland was being torn apart. Moreover, the partition created a new province with a Muslim majority—a fact that encouraged Muslims but outraged many Hindus. Gopal Gokhale (GOH-kuh-lay), the president of the Indian National Congress, complained:

66 *The scheme of partition . . . will always stand as a complete illustration of the worst features of the present system of bureaucratic rule—its utter contempt [disregard] for public opinion, its arrogant pretensions [exaggerated claims] to superior wisdom, its reckless disregard of the most cherished feelings of the people.* 99

The partition of Bengal sparked the first large-scale resistance movement against the British, organized and led by the Indian National Congress. More-radical nationalists even began a terrorist campaign, attacking British officials and

THROUGH OTHERS' EYES

An Indian Nationalist's View of the West

After World War I, Mohandas Gandhi became the most important nationalist leader in India. Although he wanted to preserve the unity Britain had brought to India, Gandhi's vision of an independent India was not that of a modern Western-style state. Gandhi thought that Western civilization had ruined itself through its growing materialism:

66 This civilization is irreligion [not religious], and it has taken such a hold on the people in Europe that those who are in it appear to be half mad. They lack real physical strength or courage. They keep up their energy by intoxication. They can hardly be happy in solitude. Women, who should be the queens of households, wander in the streets, or they slave away in factories. For the sake of a pittance [small amount], half a million women in England alone are laboring under trying circumstances in factories or similar institutions. This awful fact is one of the causes of the daily growing suffragette movement. This civilization is such that one has only to be patient and it will be self-destroyed. 99

murdering them. In 1906, alarmed by this aggressive Hindu nationalism, Muslim leaders formed the **Muslim League** to "protect and advance the political rights and interests of the Musalmans [Muslims] of India."

The Indian home rule movement. Before World War I the British enacted a series of reforms. They appointed Indians as members of the provincial executive councils, as well as the viceroy's council and the advisory council of the British secretary of state for India in London. Indian nationalists, however, sought self-government along British parliamentary lines. At the end of World War I the Muslim League joined the Indian National Congress in its demands for home rule.

India's loyal support during World War I made such demands difficult for British imperialists to deny. In August 1917 Britain announced a new policy to move India toward dominion status. Yet even as the British began to pursue the new policy, violence weakened their efforts.

The Amritsar Massacre. In response to terrorist actions by radical Indian nationalists, the British imposed strict new security regulations in 1919. Protests against the regulations turned violent in the Punjab, where several Europeans were murdered by a mob in the city of Amritsar. The local British military commander immediately banned all public meetings. Soon thereafter, a large group had gathered in a walled field for a Hindu religious festival. Without warning, the British officer ordered his troops to open fire on them—killing some 400 people and wounding about 1,200 others.

The **Amritsar Massacre** shocked both Indians and British alike. When a formal inquiry faulted the British officer in charge but failed to punish him severely, many nationalists decided that the British must leave India once and for all. Perhaps the most influential of these nationalists was a British-trained Indian lawyer named Mohandas K. Gandhi.

Gandhi. Born in western India in 1869, Mohandas Karamchand Gandhi

▲ After the Amritsar Massacre, people gathered to see the bullet holes in the wall of the field where hundreds of Hindus died.

was the son of the chief minister of a small Hindu state. A member of the merchant class, or Vaisya, Gandhi's parents sent him to study in London, where he became a lawyer. While in London he was heavily influenced by both liberalism and Christianity. After briefly practicing law in India, Gandhi moved to South Africa in 1893.

While living in London, Gandhi had come to think of himself as a citizen of the British Empire. While living in South Africa, however, he confronted the racist attitudes that many white South Africans, both British and Afrikaner, held toward Asians. In 1907 Gandhi began his first campaign of *satyagraha*, which means "holding fast to the truth," a method of non-violent resistance to injustice by the authorities.

In 1914 Gandhi went back to India, where he quickly became a member of the Indian

Mohandas Gandhi

BIOGRAPHY

National Congress. During World War I he supported the British war effort, but the Amritsar Massacre helped convince Gandhi that India must achieve complete independence. Realizing the need for broad popular support, he reminded Congress members of their roots in traditional Indian society. For example, Gandhi publicly appeared not in Western clothing but in the traditional loincloth and homespun shawl of an Indian peasant. As he launched *satyagraha* movements in India, he inspired millions. His followers called him Mahatma, or "Great Soul."

Constitutional developments. While Gandhi was transforming the Indian National Congress into a mass political movement, the British slowly began to enact their plans for Indian constitutional development. In 1919

British leaders instituted a new constitution that transferred some powers in the provincial governments to Indian ministers responsible to elected legislative councils.

Despite this steady movement toward responsible government, under Gandhi's leadership the Congress persistently demanded more. The Congress was particularly opposed to measures that guaranteed special seats in the government for the Muslim minority, complaining that such measures were intended to divide Muslims and Hindus. Complete self-government continued to be the Congress's main goal. Consequently, when Britain enacted a new federal constitution for India in 1935 that granted self-rule at the provincial level, the Congress criticized it for not going far enough. Nevertheless, in the 1937 elections the Congress won majorities in many of the new provincial governments as well as in the central legislature.

Not all Indians accepted Gandhi's leadership or methods, however. Extreme Indian nationalists continued to use violence in an effort to drive the British from India. Some Muslims accused Gandhi of trying to substitute a "Hindu raj" for the British raj. The Muslim League, under the leadership of Muhammad Ali Jinnah, another British-trained lawyer, eventually demanded a separate state for Muslims should India become completely independent.

As the British moved India slowly toward democratic self-government, Gandhi helped convince the Indian National Congress to demand a faster pace.

▲ Marchers in Bombay, India, parade through the streets in 1930 with a stuffed dummy of a British soldier, which they planned to burn in protest.

SECTION 1 REVIEW

IDENTIFY and explain the significance of the following:
Imperial Conferences
Statute of Westminster
Easter Rising
Irish Republican Army
Indian National Congress
Muslim League
Amritsar Massacre
Mohandas Gandhi

1. **Main Idea** How did the British deal with colonial nationalism in the dominions of the empire after the end of World War I?

2. **Main Idea** How was Ireland different from other parts of the British Empire in its nationalist movement?

3. **Politics and Law** How were British efforts to maintain its empire received by colonial nationalists?

4. **Writing to Explain** Imagine that you are a member of the Indian National Congress during the early 1900s. Write a short speech explaining how Gandhi has influenced the nationalist movement in India.

5. **Hypothesizing** Could Britain have maintained the unity of its empire and prevented the rise of nationalism among its subjects? Why or why not?

IDENTIFY
For significance, see the following pages:
Imperial Conferences (p. 658)
Statute of Westminster (p. 659)
Easter Rising (p. 659)
Irish Republican Army (p. 660)
Indian National Congress (p. 661)
Muslim League (p. 661)
Amritsar Massacre (p. 662)
Mohandas Gandhi (p. 662)

1. The Balfour Report declared the dominions autonomous, and Britain tried to maintain the unity of the empire by establishing the British Commonwealth.
2. Britain considered Ireland to be part of the United Kingdom. Ireland did not accept dominion status instead of independence.
3. South Africa—rebellion; Ireland—uprisings and civil war; India—peaceful and violent resistance
4. Speeches should mention Gandhi's call for complete Indian independence and peaceful resistance as well as his role in transforming the Indian National Congress into a mass political movement.
5. yes—by granting more independence, recognizing nationalist demands, withdrawing troops from subject nations, not using force; no—subjects gained Western views from European schooling and developed national identities, then applied those values to their own governments

SECTION 2

Nationalism in the Middle East and Africa

FOCUS

- What was the goal of nationalists in Egypt and the Arab mandates after World War I?
- How did British imperialism affect the development of nationalism in Palestine?
- How did Atatürk's policies affect Turkey?
- How did urbanization influence nationalism in Africa?

As India sought self-government within the British Empire, the first new independent nations to emerge from the Western empires were the former Ottoman states in the Middle East and North Africa. Even then the imperial powers tried to continue their control by granting a limited independence. Meanwhile, in the rest of Africa the first stirrings of nationalism were beginning to be felt, as Western-educated Africans began to seek greater participation in their own governments.

Saad Zaghlul Pasha, 1911

Egyptian Nationalism

The first of the former Ottoman territories outside Europe to obtain official independence after World War I was Egypt. Since the British occupation in 1882, many Egyptians had become increasingly impatient with continued British rule. When war broke out in 1914, however, Britain declared a protectorate over Egypt in order to break Egypt's ties with the Ottoman Empire. At the end of World War I, a new popular nationalist party, the **Wafd** (WAHFT) **Party**, emerged under the leadership of Saad Zaghlul Pasha.

The British had delayed discussion of Egyptian independence until after the war was over. In part because of harsh wartime measures imposed by the British, Zaghlul Pasha and the Wafd led a nationwide revolt in 1919. Although the British forcefully put down the revolt, they decided in 1921 they could no longer withhold independence. But given Egypt's strategic importance, Britain needed to find a way to keep a firm hold on Egypt even after independence.

In 1922 Britain proclaimed Egypt independent—but with major reservations. Britain kept responsibility for the defense of Egypt and the Suez Canal; for administration of the Sudan, which controlled the upper Nile; and for the protection of foreign interests in Egypt. Egyptian nationalists rejected these limitations, but a new government appointed by the Egyptian king, Fuad I, accepted the terms. Nationalists continued to demand full independence.

In 1935 Egyptian leaders were alarmed by the Italian invasion of nearby Ethiopia. After intense negotiations that focused on defense matters, Britain and Egypt finally reached an agreement in the **Anglo-Egyptian Treaty** of 1936. Britain was allowed to maintain military control over the Suez Canal for the next 20 years and would defend Egypt in case of war. In addition, Britain agreed to sponsor Egypt for membership in the League of Nations. Still, the continuing presence of British troops in the Nile Valley and Suez left many Egyptians feeling that they were not fully independent.

*A*lthough independent in name, Egyptian nationalists sought to free themselves from Britain's continuing military occupation.

The Arab Mandates and Arabia

At the same time that Egyptians were calling for independence, nationalists in the Arab mandates and Arabia were demanding an end to British and French control. Few Arabs, however, had any sense of belonging to a territorial nation-state as that term was understood in Europe. Under the Ottoman Empire, people had owed their primary loyalty to the Ottoman dynasty and to their particular religious community. Now, Pan-Islamism and Pan-Arabism worked against the growth of strong territorial nationalism.

Many Arabs saw the division of Arab lands between Britain and France after World War I as a betrayal. They believed that Britain had promised to recognize the independence of all the Arabs under Britain's wartime ally, Husayn ibn 'Ali of Mecca. In the aftermath of the Arab Revolt during World War I and the successful British campaign against the Turks, Husayn's son Faisal had even established himself as king of Syria. Nevertheless, both Britain and France refused to give up their claims in the strategic region.

In 1919 Arab nationalists in Syria outlined their own preferences:

66 We ask absolutely complete political independence for Syria. . . . We ask that the Government of this Syrian country should be a democratic civil constitutional Monarchy . . . and that the King be the Emir Faisal. . . . We do not acknowledge any right claimed by the French Government in any part whatever of our Syrian country. 99

In response to these requests, French troops forcefully deposed Faisal and established a colonial administration. The French prime minister declared that France would continue to hold Syria, "the whole of it, and forever."

Over the next 15 years, Syrian nationalists opposed French rule. In 1925 the Druse, a tightly knit religious group with its own strong sense of identity, also revolted. For a time the French even lost control of Damascus. Although the French put down these revolts, continuing nationalist opposition, including general strikes and ongoing fighting, eventually led the French to accept a nationalist government in 1936. The refusal of the French Chamber of Deputies to ratify Syrian independence, however, left the country still under French authority.

New Nations in the Middle East, 1922–1939

BLACK SEA
SOVIET UNION
CASPIAN SEA
Istanbul
Ankara
TURKEY (1923)
CYPRUS
LEBANON
Beirut
Damascus
SYRIA
Euphrates River
Tigris River
Tehran
AFGHANISTAN
IRAN
MEDITERRANEAN SEA
PALESTINE
Jerusalem
Amman
Baghdad
IRAQ (under British mandate until 1930)
TRANSJORDAN
Cairo
Suez
Suez Canal
Sinai Peninsula
EGYPT (1922)
NEUTRAL ZONE
KUWAIT
Persian Gulf
BAHRAIN
Gulf
QATAR
To Oman
Strait of Hormuz
Gulf of Oman
RED SEA
Nile River
SAUDI ARABIA
Mecca (Makkah)
TRUCIAL STATES
MUSCAT AND OMAN
ANGLO-EGYPTIAN SUDAN

1926 Date of independence
British rule or control
French territory

ERITREA
YEMEN
ADEN
SOCOTRA
ETHIOPIA
Aden
Gulf of Aden
ARABIAN SEA
FRENCH SOMALILAND
BRITISH SOMALILAND

N S E W

0   200   400 Miles
0   200   400 Kilometers
Lambert Conformal Conic Projection

A New Tide of Nationalism In the 1920s and 1930s, a renewed feeling of nationalism swept over many countries in the Middle East. But few managed to throw off the yoke of European rule.

❖ Linking Geography and History Which Middle Eastern countries won their independence in this period?

▲ Ibn Sa'ud meets with President Roosevelt. In the 1930s Ibn Sa'ud allowed American companies to drill for oil in Saudi Arabia.

Meanwhile, in 1926 France had carved out a new mandate from its Syrian territory. Based on the old region known as Lebanon, the new mandate included surrounding lands as well. Although Christians had been a large majority in the old Lebanon, in the new mandate state of Lebanon they were a much smaller majority. Lebanese nationalism was complicated by the presence of large Sunni and Shi'ah Islamic communities, as well as Pan-Arabic and Pan-Islamic movements.

Nationalists in Britain's mandates were generally less violent, but just as insistent on self-government and independence. By 1930 Iraq had achieved independence as a constitutional monarchy under King Faisal, who had been deposed by the French in Syria. The British eventually established Abdullah, another of Husayn's sons, as king of Transjordan (later renamed Jordan), which the British had separated from the Palestine mandate in 1921. The British agreed to grant independence to these countries only after they had agreed to sign treaties of military alliance.

While the mandates became Western-style states, a new Muslim state developed in Arabia. During the 1920s the Wahhabis, a conservative sect of Sunni Islam under the command of the Sa'ud family, began to conquer

territory in Arabia. Eventually, under Ibn Sa'ud, the Wahhabis took control of Mecca, forcing Husayn to flee. By 1932 Ibn Sa'ud had established himself as king of the new conservative Muslim state of Saudi Arabia.

Nationalists in the Arab-mandated territories called for independence, but some hoped to replace British and French rule with a Pan-Arab state.

Nationalism and Conflict in Palestine

Palestine proved to be the most troubled mandate in the Middle East because of conflict between Arabs and Jews. Jewish settlement had been known in Palestine since ancient times. In the late 1800s, however, a new movement began as Jews from Europe settled in Palestine. These new immigrants supported a movement begun in the 1890s by Theodor Herzl (HERT-suhl) to create a Jewish state—a movement known as **Zionism**.

Theodor Herzl was born in Hungary in 1860. As a young man he became a journalist in Vienna. In 1891 he was assigned to Paris, where he covered the Dreyfus case (see Chapter 20). Herzl witnessed firsthand the anti-Semitism the case unleashed. Alarmed by the growing levels of anti-Semitism, he came to believe that the root of the problem was the fact that the Jews did not have a state of their own. In his 1896 pamphlet "The Jewish State," Herzl called for the foundation of a Jewish state in Palestine, the ancient home of the Jews.

To accomplish his goal, in 1897 Herzl organized the first Zionist World Congress, which brought representatives from Jewish communities around the world together in Basel, Switzerland. He also helped found and became the first president of the World Zionist Organization. By the time of his death in 1904,

Theodor Herzl
BIOGRAPHY

the organization had taken root in every country that had a Jewish population of significant size. Soon, a small number of Jewish settlements had sprung up in Palestine, and Herzl's dream continued to inspire a growing Zionist movement.

Zionism continued to grow throughout World War I. In 1917 the British cabinet, anxious to obtain all the support they could for the war effort, authorized Lord Balfour, who at the time was serving as the foreign secretary, to write to Lord Rothschild, a leading British Zionist: "His Majesty's Government view with favour the establishment in Palestine of a national home for the Jewish people, . . . it being clearly understood that nothing shall be done which may prejudice the civil and religious rights of existing non-Jewish communities in Palestine. . . . " This **Balfour Declaration** was incorporated in 1922 into the terms of the British mandate for Palestine.

▲ These British soldiers stop a Palestinian Arab to search for hidden weapons. British security forces were constantly on guard against armed resistance.

As Jewish immigration continued into the 1930s, driven by growing Nazi persecution, Palestinian Arabs began to fear that they were losing control over their homeland. Internal disagreements among Palestinian leaders, however, prevented a united front against either the British or the Zionists. While the influential Nashashibi family sought to work within the British mandate structure to further Palestinian Arab interests and limit Jewish immigration, their enemies, the Husayni family, protested both British rule and Zionist immigration.

Hoping to obtain support even from the Husaynis, during the 1920s the British appointed Haj Amin al-Husayni as the leading Islamic religious official of Jerusalem. Instead of cooperating, however, Haj Amin simply used his new position to oppose both British rule and Zionism more forcefully than ever. In the late 1920s Arab protests against Zionist land purchases often resulted in riots and other forms of violence. Eventually, in 1936 an armed Arab revolt broke

out, resulting in the deaths of more than 300 Arabs, Jews, and British personnel. The British put down the revolt, but only with great difficulty. Parliament also sent a royal commission under Lord Peel to investigate the disturbances.

The Peel Commission recommended that the mandate be partitioned into a Jewish state and an Arab state. With war looming in Europe, however, the British government needed the support of the strategically important Arab states. In 1939, therefore, Britain declared its intention to limit further Jewish immigration and eventually to establish Palestine as a single state, with safeguards for the Jews.

The Zionists declared that they had been betrayed. Some extremists even formed terrorist groups, like the Stern Gang and the Irgun, to drive the British out of Palestine.

British rule in Palestine fostered conflicting nationalist movements among Arabs and Zionists.

667

The Turkish Exception

While the Arab countries struggled for a sense of national identity, Turkish leaders decided to create a modern state on a Western model. After the Ottomans' defeat in World War I, a new leader appeared in Turkey—Mustafa Kemal, a general of the army and a war hero. Kemal came to believe that the war had demonstrated the superiority of Western technology as well as the Western idea of nationalism. Declaring "we must teach our people to be free," he instituted radical new reforms.

Kemal saw Islam as the primary stumbling block on the road to modernization. Consequently, he soon abolished the caliphate—the supreme spiritual office of Islam—and established a constitutionally secular Turkish republic. As part of his westernization plans Kemal decreed that all Turks take surnames. He took the name Atatürk, meaning "father of the Turks." He prohibited the wearing of religious clothing outside places of worship. He also established secular schools and colleges, and instituted secular laws in place of what he considered to be outdated Islamic law. He even substituted the Latin alphabet for the Arabic-based Turkish alphabet. Although the shock of the change was enormous for the Turkish people, Turkey became independent and prosperous.

Rejecting the Ottoman past, Atatürk forged a new identity for Turkey as a modernizing, secular nation.

▲ Mustafa Kemal was unanimously elected president of Turkey for four consecutive terms.

North Africa

The spread of nationalism in the Middle East had its counterpart in North Africa. In Tunisia, for example, nationalists aimed for ultimate independence from France—but by a gradual, evolutionary process rather than violent revolt. In Morocco, which France had taken only in the decade before World War I, armed resistance by traditional leaders continued until about 1930—with periodic fighting long after that.

In Algeria, which had long been considered by the French to be a part of France, the presence of a large number of French and other European settlers seriously complicated the development of nationalism. The settlers identified themselves as French, not Algerian. Some Western-educated Algerian Arabs wanted to remain part of France, though they resented domination by the European settlers.

Practicing Muslims, however, could not become French citizens and remained only subjects, unable to vote. Consequently, most Algerian Arabs wanted independence from France. In 1924 an Algerian nationalist named Messali Hajd founded the Star of North Africa movement, which later became the leading nationalist party in the struggle for Algerian independence.

Sub-Saharan Africa

In the rest of Africa, nationalism was driven by a growing realization of the differences between the ideals taught in Western schools and the realities of colonial rule. Many Africans resented such practices as forced labor and low wages, as well as the efforts of colonial governments to destroy traditional African ways of living. European attitudes of racial superiority and acts of political repression also sparked calls for reform and independence.

World War I and the depression. World War I particularly contributed to the growth of a new African nationalism. As thousands of Africans fought on both European and African battlefields, they gained a wider experience of the world. When they returned home they carried with them new ideas of democracy and nationalism. They also expected to find greater opportunities. With newly acquired skills learned in the army, some did

History THROUGH THE ARTS

African Art Influences European Artists

At the beginning of the 1900s, few people in Europe knew much about the art of sub-Saharan Africa. Those who did, one critic charged, looked on such art with distaste. Not everyone shared this view, however. Around 1905 Maurice de Vlaminck and André Derain, two artists living in Paris, began collecting African artwork. Their collection, which Vlaminck said both pleased and troubled them, included a number of West African statuettes and masks. Pablo Picasso, who had recently arrived in Paris, saw one of the masks and was astounded. He too started to collect African artwork. He also began to incorporate elements of African art into his paintings.

Picasso's painting *Les Demoiselles d'Avignon* (1906–07), with its large head and striking facial features, appeared to have been inspired by African masks.

In fact, much of the work that Picasso did in the early 1900s shows the influence of African styles.

Picasso was not the only Paris-based artist who sought inspiration in African art. Vlaminck also incorporated African styles into his paintings. Also through the work of Henri Matisse and Georges Braque, African art began to gain a wider audience throughout Europe.

Thinking About Art
How did African art influence some Europeans in the early 1900s?

Carved wooden mask from Côte d'Ivoire

Thinking About Art
Europeans collected African art; traditional African masks influenced the style of some of Picasso's work.

Theme: The Arts

Until the 1960s African art was essentially a community product. The artist did not produce a work that expressed his or her personal feelings. Instead, the art was produced in order to fulfill a community need. Only in the past few decades have many artists begun to experiment with individual expression in their work.

Critical Thinking Ask students why they think more African artists are expressing their individual feelings in their work.

ANSWER: Students might suggest that Africans felt less of a tie to their communities as more people moved to the cities.

---

get better jobs. Most, however, found that colonial authorities expected them to return to old patterns of colonial life.

When the Great Depression struck in the 1930s, many Africans were laid off or had their wages reduced. Increasingly, they expressed discontent with colonial rule through labor unions and workers' associations. The groups grew in strength as more Africans moved from the countryside into the cities in search of work. Urban life, however, often led to a weakening of the family ties and sense of identity that Africans had known in their traditional communities.

Colonial responses. As urban Africans organized labor protests in the 1920s, they also used these associations as forums for political complaints. In response, most colonial governments tried to reinforce the position of traditional African authorities—government-recognized chiefs and religious leaders. At the same time, however, colonial authorities also realized that they would have to make some reforms to satisfy Africans' grievances.

In places like Kenya and Northern and Southern Rhodesia, conflicts between Africans and colonial governments were complicated by the growing demands of white settlers, who wanted self-government on the same lines as South Africa. In 1923 Rhodesia achieved dominion status. After 1929, however, Britain refused to grant the same to other white settlers.

By the late 1930s, however, even major reforms were not enough to satisfy many Africans. As people increasingly migrated from the countryside to Africa's growing cities in search of work, they began to find more reasons to object to colonialism. Racial prejudice and physical mistreatment remained large parts of the problem.

A new generation of leaders. Perhaps the most dramatic turning point in the emergence of African nationalism in the 1930s, however, was the Italian invasion and conquest of Ethiopia. Both the conquest and the lack of a strong response by the League of Nations angered many Africans.

Drawing support from the growing African urban populations, a new generation of African leaders began to call for independence. The loudest demands for change came from young, Western-educated leaders like Jomo Kenyatta of Kenya, Nnamdi Azikiwe (ah-ZEEK-wah) of Nigeria, and Leopold Senghor of Senegal. Following Gandhi's example, they began to organize strikes, demonstrations, and boycotts against the colonial administrations.

Pan-Africanism. These new leaders drew inspiration from Gandhi, but also from Africans in the Caribbean and the United States who

Marcus Garvey (left) and W. E. B. Du Bois (below) were both important leaders of Pan-Africanism.

preached a message of **Pan-Africanism**. Pan-Africanism promoted the unity and further development of African peoples, the complete elimination of racism in the Americas, an end to colonialism in Africa, and resistance to the humiliation of black people wherever they lived throughout the world. The movement had become particularly popular first outside Africa, under the leadership of Jamaican American Marcus Garvey and the African American educator W. E. B. Du Bois.

Garvey's demand of "Africa for the Africans!" was a powerful message for many Western-educated Africans. By the end of the 1930s, a growing Pan-Africanist movement dedicated to ending colonial rule had developed among the still small number of Western-educated elites in many African colonies.

*A*s more Africans moved to the cities, they grew increasingly angry over the inequalities of colonial rule.

SECTION 2 REVIEW

IDENTIFY and explain the significance of the following:
Wafd Party
Anglo-Egyptian Treaty
Theodor Herzl
Zionism
Balfour Declaration
Mustafa Kemal
Pan-Africanism
Marcus Garvey

1. **Main Idea** What did Egyptian and Arab nationalists hope to accomplish?
2. **Main Idea** How and why did Atatürk promote reforms in Turkey?
3. **Geography: Movement** What did migration to the cities have to do with African nationalism?

4. **Writing to Describe** Imagine that you are a British reporter in Palestine in the 1920s. Write an article describing the situation there.
5. **Comparing and Contrasting** What did nationalists in the Middle East and Africa have in common? How were they different?

Nationalism in China and Southeast Asia

- What kinds of changes did Chinese intellectuals and nationalists seek?

- Why was China unable to achieve unity after the fall of the Qing Empire?

- What inspired colonial nationalists in Southeast Asia to fight against French and Dutch repression?

During the age of imperialism, Western industrial nations extended not only their military power but also their methods of economic and political organization. Exposure to Western civilization led many Asians to challenge their traditional senses of identity. Many Asian peoples began to develop new national identities in an effort to cope with modern industrial society. Some adopted Western-style nationalism and called for reforms along liberal democratic lines. Others turned to Marxism, which denounced imperialism as simply another stage in capitalist expansion.

Japanese forces in China, 1938

Nationalism and Communism in China

The fall of the Qing dynasty in 1911 plunged China into a period of chaos and instability. In 1912 Chinese nationalists declared China a republic, with its capital at Nanjing and Sun Yixian as the provisional president. Sun soon resigned in favor of an imperial general named Yuan Shikai. After Yuan died in 1916, **warlords**—strongmen with private armies—many of whom were former imperial generals, took control of their own regions and ruled like kings.

Cultural transformations. As had happened earlier in China's history, this period of instability and disunity led some Chinese to look for new ideas on which to rebuild China's unity and sense of security. The old Confucian examination system, plagued by corruption, had finally been abolished. As nationalist leaders called for increased modernization, Western-style education took the place of the old Confucian classics. Thousands of young Chinese people went overseas to universities in the United States, Europe, and Japan. They came back convinced that China should follow the example of the West.

One of the most famous of these new intellectuals was a writer named Hu Shi, a graduate of Columbia University. Hu Shi set out to simplify written Chinese. He encouraged his colleagues to use the ordinary language of the people instead of the old-fashioned classical Chinese that most writers used. Inspired by this practical approach, intellectuals called for reforms in other fields as well. Historians began to examine and reevaluate the myths and legends of ancient Chinese history. Literary scholars began to study Chinese folklore more carefully. Many scholars also began to reject the traditional Chinese family system as equally old-fashioned. In addition, they called for major social reforms—including improvements in the status of women.

In an era of warlordism and instability, many Chinese intellectuals rejected traditional values and customs in favor of Western-style political, cultural, and social reform.

SECTION 3

CORE LESSON PLAN
See pages 655G and 655H for Lesson Plan 24.3.

Daily Life

An important aspect of the cultural movement was the transformation in writing. Both the script and the vocabulary used for classical study had changed little since the 200s B.C., and to know the language well required knowledge of the classical texts. *Wenyan* was the language used for classical writing and civil-service examinations and *baihua* was the everyday language used by most Chinese. Hu Shi advocated the use of *baihua* to prevent the exclusion of the majority from classical studies and scholarship.

Critical Thinking Ask students how the use of *wenyan* for civil-service examinations might have affected society.

ANSWER: Students might answer that most Chinese, who could not read *wenyan*, would have been barred from government jobs.

In January 1924 a report on the state of China was published by the Guomindang. In it, the nationalistic principles of the Guomindang were stated: "Members of the Guomindang must exert utmost effort in the fight to emancipate the Chinese people. In this fight they rely on the intelligentsia, on the farmers, on the merchants for defense and support, because all classes are suffering from imperialist aggression, which the nationalist revolution has set out to destroy. Nationalism is the defense of industry because only release from the economic pressure of foreign powers can make it possible for China to develop as an industrial nation. . . . Only in nationalist China can [the workers] escape . . . [those] on whom they now depend and who squeeze and choke them and grudge them a living."

Critical Thinking Ask students to suggest reasons why the Guomindang's statement stresses that they aid "all classes."

ANSWER: Students might suggest the Guomindang wanted to build up widespread support from the Chinese people.

The May Fourth Movement. As China continued to suffer under the demands of outside imperial powers, the new cultural movement soon merged with Chinese nationalism. During World War I Japan had seized control of the Shandong Peninsula from Germany. With the Versailles settlement, the peacemakers allowed the Japanese to keep the peninsula. When news of the decision reached China, thousands of outraged Chinese students rioted in Beijing on May 4, 1919, in what became known as the **May Fourth Movement**. Led by Chinese intellectuals, the May Fourth Movement soon spread through many other Chinese cities. Across China, students, merchants, and businesspeople protested Japanese imperialism by boycotting Japanese goods and even attacking Japanese citizens. They also argued that the only way to make China strong again was through a complete break with the traditional past.

Sun Yixian and the Guomindang. In order to accomplish this break, Sun Yixian and his revolutionary Chinese Nationalist Party, the **Guomindang**, began to build an army to reunite and revive the country along modern Western lines. Unable to obtain aid from Europe or the United States, Sun Yixian accepted the help of the new Communist government in the Soviet Union in 1923. He also forged an alliance with the new Chinese Communist Party.

Sun believed that only by establishing complete unity among all groups in China could the goals of nationalism be achieved. Despite their numbers, he once wrote, "the Chinese people have only family and clan solidarity, they do not have national spirit." His goal was to create such a spirit out of sheer self-preservation:

66 Today we are the poorest and weakest nation in the world. . . . Other men are the carving knife and serving dish; we are the fish and the meat. . . . If we do not earnestly espouse [support] nationalism and weld together our four hundred million people into a strong nation, there is a danger of China's being lost and our people being destroyed. 99

Sun died in 1925, but under his successor, Chiang Kaishek (chang ky-SHEK), the Nationalist army gradually defeated the warlords and regained control over much of China. In 1928 Chiang set up a new national government with its capital in Nanjing.

Despite these gains, however, China remained weak. The great majority of the people were poor peasants living in the countryside, and the country had only just begun to industrialize. In many areas power remained in the hands of local warlords. Bandit armies flourished in many provinces and attacked even strongly fortified towns. In addition, the unity for which Sun had worked was shattered as the Guomindang split between Communists and non-Communists.

Despite their efforts, Chinese nationalists were only partly successful in reuniting China.

◀ Under Chiang Kaishek, the Nationalist Army slowly unified China.

Communists Versus Nationalists

In their desire to modernize China, some Western-educated Chinese nationalists had come to believe that communism was the best means of achieving their goal. Many of them had studied Marxism and traveled in the Soviet Union. In 1921, aided by Russian advisors, these nationalists had founded the Chinese Communist Party in Shanghai. The majority of the Guomindang, however, under the conservative leadership of Chiang Kaishek, disliked communist ideas. They opposed government control of the economy and preferred a capitalist model for modernizing China.

After establishing his position as Sun Yixian's successor at the head of the Guomindang, Chiang soon turned on the Communists. Jailing and killing many Communists, over the next 10 years Chiang waged almost constant war on them. In 1934 Nationalist forces defeated a Soviet-style republic that the Communist Party had established in the province of Jiangxi under the charismatic leader Mao Zedong (MOW ZUH-DUHNG). Fleeing from Chiang's armies, some 100,000 Communists made the so-called **Long March** to the north of China, where they hoped to avoid Nationalist attacks and reorganize themselves. During the march, the party came into closer contact with China's peasants, and a new, unified Communist leadership emerged for the first time under Mao's firm control.

Maoism. Although Marxist theory insisted that industrial workers in the cities would lead the communist revolution, China was still a land of farmers. Mao trained his party leaders to use the language of Chinese peasants and to promise them what they wanted. He later explained his theory in a speech:

66 Today two big mountains lie like a dead weight on the Chinese people. One is imperialism, the other is feudalism. . . . We must persevere [continue] and work unceasingly, and we, too, will touch God's heart. Our God is none other than the masses of the Chinese people. If they stand up and dig together with us, why can't these two mountains be cleared away? 99

Mao's Chinese version of Marxism became known as **Maoism**.

Nationalist reforms. As the Communists retreated on the Long March, Chiang and the Nationalists slowly tried to modernize China. They adopted a new constitution and a new law code. Modern education flourished, and many new schools and universities were established. The Nationalist government enacted new measures designed to build up Chinese industry,

Civil War in China, 1925–1935

A Decade of Conflict In the cities and countryside, the Chinese people experienced tremendous upheaval as various factions vied for control of China.

? Movement Where did Mao Zedong's Long March start? Where did it end?

as well as to improve transportation networks and irrigation and flood control along China's rivers. Ultimately, the Nationalists managed to abolish foreign control over the economy.

Despite the reforms, Chiang's government never fully controlled more than half of China. Moreover, in many places people suffered as much under government forces as they did from bandits. A petition from the province of Sichuan, for example, described the government's local general as "the leader of the wolves and tigers." His actions had so ruined the region, the petition complained, that "East and West . . . the bark of a dog or the crow of a cock is no longer heard. The people sigh that the sun and moon might perish so that they could perish with them."

The war against Japan. Despite the mutual hatred between the Guomindang and the Communists, in the 1930s both groups confronted a mutual enemy—Japan. Chinese and Japanese forces clashed in 1928, and in 1931 the Japanese occupied Manchuria. In 1936, under pressure from the Soviet Union, the Chinese Communists proposed a truce and an alliance with the Nationalists against the Japanese. Chiang agreed, and in April 1937 the two sides worked out a settlement.

Three months later Chinese and Japanese forces plunged into full-scale war. As Japan invaded China, Chiang's forces did the majority of the fighting. Mao, on the other hand, used the war as a chance to extend Communist influence in the Chinese countryside. After the war, the Communists were in a position to challenge the Nationalists for control of all of China.

In China the struggle for national identity and differing political beliefs led to a split between Communists and Nationalists.

Nationalism in Southeast Asia

The success of nationalist movements in India and China inspired other Asian peoples to demand reform and greater participation in their own governments. Nationalist movements in Indonesia and Indochina resisted the repression of their colonial rulers. As in China, many turned to Marxism or other Western political philosophies for inspiration in their struggle for independence.

The Netherlands East Indies. Although the Dutch instituted some minor reforms during World War I, they had no intention of moving rapidly toward major Indonesian participation in the political process. In 1912 Indonesian Muslims established the **Sarekat Islam**, or Islamic Association, as a mass political party. The demands of the Sarekat Islam went largely unmet, however. After the war two new organizations emerged in Indonesia to challenge the Dutch—the Indonesian Communist Party (PKI) and the Indonesian Nationalist Party, which was founded in 1927 by a popular leader named Sukarno.

Unlike the Communists of the PKI or the Muslims of the Sarekat Islam, Sukarno felt bound by no particular creed or beliefs. Instead, he embraced any movement or idea that might contribute to his goal of complete independence for Indonesia. He later described this flexibility and attributed much of his success as a nationalist to it:

▲ In 1932 Japanese soldiers routinely stopped and searched Chinese civilians on the suspicion that they might have been bandits.

> *From Father came . . . Islamism. From Mother, Hinduism and Buddhism. Sarinah gave me humanism. From Tjokro came Socialism. From his friends came Nationalism. To that I added gleanings of Karl Marxism and Thomas Jeffersonism. I learned economics from Sun Yatsen [Yixian], benevolence [kindness] from Gandhi. . . . What came out has been called—in plain terms—Sukarnoism.*

Sukarno's appeal to feelings of nationalism proved extremely effective in rallying support among the Indonesian people. He became the "great puppet master"—a reference to the sacred shadow theater of the Indonesians, signifying the one who is in control. At the same time, Sukarno represented a serious threat to the Dutch—who imprisoned him twice and finally exiled him from the country.

French Indochina. Like the Dutch, the French also met rising nationalism with force in their Asian colonies. In 1930, for example, the Vietnamese Nationalist Party led a revolt sparked by growing economic problems in Vietnam. The French brutally put down the uprising and practically destroyed the Nationalist Party. Such measures drove other nationalist groups underground. The Communist Party of Indochina, for example, which was organized that same year by the popular leader Ho Chi Minh, continued to thrive and grow while in hiding, stirring up strikes, demonstrations, and peasant uprisings. By 1931 the French had regained control—largely by jailing, executing, and deporting thousands of revolutionaries. Such measures, however, only reinforced the commitment of nationalist leaders like Ho to achieve ultimate independence.

In their struggle for independence, many Asian nationalists turned to Marxism or other Western political philosophies for inspiration.

▲ Denounced by the French as a revolutionary, Ho Chi Minh spent years in exile in the Soviet Union and China.

SECTION 3 REVIEW

IDENTIFY and explain the significance of the following:
Sun Yixian
Yuan Shikai
warlords
May Fourth Movement
Guomindang
Chiang Kaishek
Mao Zedong
Long March
Maoism
Sarekat Islam
Sukarno

1. **Main Idea** What were the goals of many Chinese intellectuals and nationalists?
2. **Main Idea** Why was no single group able to achieve unity in China immediately after the fall of the Qing dynasty?
3. **Cross-cultural Interaction** What role did Western political ideas play in the development of nationalism in Southeast Asia?

4. **Writing to Explain** Imagine that you are a Chinese newspaper reporter. Write a brief article explaining the importance of the Long March to the Chinese Communist Party.
5. **Analyzing** Why do you think Sukarno's brand of nationalism made him a more effective leader than other Indonesian nationalists?

SECTION 3 REVIEW ANSWERS

IDENTIFY
For significance, see the following pages:
Sun Yixian (p. 671)
Yuan Shikai (p. 671)
warlords (p. 671)
May Fourth Movement (p. 672)
Guomindang (p. 672)
Chiang Kaishek (p. 672)
Mao Zedong (p. 673)
Long March (p. 673)
Maoism (p. 673)
Sarekat Islam (p. 674)
Sukarno (p. 674)

1. Their goals were major social reforms based on Western example.
2. Warlords controlled separate regions and ruled like kings.
3. They served as an example for Southeast Asian nationalists to follow.
4. Articles should explain that the result of the Long March was a new, unified Communist Party in China.
5. Sukarno was not bound by any particular beliefs, but instead embraced any movement that would help him attain his goal.

R **RESOURCE ACTIVITY**

GLOBAL HISTORY RESOURCE CENTER

Reading: *Platform of the Cuban Revolutionary Party*

Print out and distribute the reading, and have students read the goals of the Cuban Revolutionary Party. Then have them write a diary entry from the point of view of a Cuban nationalist who has been living in exile, but is about to return to Cuba to join José Martí's forces.

Level 2

SECTION 4
The American Sphere of Influence

FOCUS

- How did the Spanish-American War affect the United States?
- What was the consequence of U.S. intervention in Caribbean and Latin American countries?
- What was the result of the revival of Hawaiian nationalism in the 1880s and 1890s?
- How did Filipino resistance to U.S. imperialism affect American colonial policy?

riven by many of the same motives as other imperial powers, the United States joined the scramble for empire in the late 1800s and the early 1900s. Like other imperial powers, the United States eventually confronted growing demands for independence from peoples within its sphere of influence.

An artist's depiction of the explosion of the *Maine*, 1898

The Spanish-American War

In the late 1880s the United States annexed eastern Samoa to provide the U.S. navy with coaling stations in the Pacific. Although they had obtained some possessions earlier, it was not until the 1890s that Americans really entered the scramble for overseas territories. Even then, most Americans were probably less interested in gaining colonies than in helping the people of Cuba throw off Spanish imperialism.

Cuba's struggle for independence. Since 1868 Cuban nationalists had been seeking to overthrow Spanish rule. Spain put down these efforts with brutality. In the face of Spanish persecution, many nationalists left Cuba for the United States, where they found support as well as money for their struggle. The great Cuban poet José Martí, for example, lived many years in exile in New York City. There he did much to unify other Cuban nationalists living in the United States.

Under Martí's inspiration, Cuban nationalists launched another bid for independence in 1895. Martí himself returned to Cuba to lead the nationalist forces but was killed in a battle with the Spanish. Nevertheless, the revolution continued with great brutality on both sides.

In February 1898 the U.S. battleship *Maine* mysteriously blew up in Havana harbor. This event outraged many people in the United States. In April 1898 the U. S. Congress publicly recognized Cuban independence—an act that quickly led to war with Spain. In the eight-month Spanish-American War that followed, U.S. forces won victories in both the Caribbean and the Pacific. In the peace settlement the United States gained control of Cuba and Puerto Rico in the Caribbean, as well as Guam and the Philippine Islands in the Pacific.

The Platt Amendment. After the war U.S. president William McKinley refused to withdraw U.S. troops until the new Cuban government had incorporated into its constitution the **Platt Amendment** passed by Congress. The Platt Amendment gave the United States "the right to intervene for the preservation of Cuban independence, the maintenance of a government adequate for the protection of life, property, and individual liberty"—as well as rights to maintain naval bases on the island. Thus, with its newly acquired territories in the Caribbean and the Pacific, the United States became an imperial power almost overnight.

Victory in the Spanish-American War led the United States into full-scale imperialism.

Intervention in Latin America

Although many people in the United States opposed imperialism, victory in the Spanish-American War gave imperialists the upper hand. After Theodore Roosevelt became president in 1901, the United States pursued a more active policy of projecting its military power overseas. Under the so-called **Roosevelt Corollary** to the Monroe Doctrine, the new president outlined a policy in 1904 that would lead to increasing overseas intervention:

❝*In the Western Hemisphere the adherence [faithful attachment] of the United States to the Monroe Doctrine may force the United States, however reluctantly, in flagrant [glaring] cases of . . . wrongdoing . . . , to the exercise of an international police power.*❞

Over the next several decades, U.S. leaders would use the Roosevelt Corollary to justify U.S. intervention in several Caribbean and Central American countries.

Nicaragua. In 1909, for example, economic chaos brought the Central American country of Nicaragua to the brink of civil war. The Nicaraguan government sought U.S. help to prevent war and stabilize the economy. The United States responded by sending troops to restore order and by seeking investments from leading New York bankers—who soon dominated Nicaraguan finances. In 1926 the nationalist and reformist leader Augusto César Sandino led a liberal uprising against the growing influence of the United States. His followers began to seize American property, and in 1927 U.S. authorities declared Sandino an outlaw.

Panama. In addition to the policing of the hemisphere, Roosevelt also supported the construction of a canal connecting the Caribbean Sea and the Pacific Ocean. The canal would run across the Isthmus of Panama in what was then Colombia. Such a canal would provide the shortest sea route

U.S. Territories in the Pacific, 1857–1912

A Budding Naval Power With a modern new navy and companies eager for trade, the United States acquired Pacific islands in the 1800s.

❓ **Location** Which islands claimed by the United States lie well to the south of the equator?

Theme:
Technology

The construction of the Panama Canal suffered many setbacks. The initial challenge was gaining access to the Isthmus of Panama. Both the United States and Britain became interested in a route across Nicaragua, but in 1881 a French company began to build the canal in Panama. By 1889, however, that company had gone bankrupt. In 1903 the United States gained rights to the Panama Canal and began to build the canal the following year.

Critical Thinking Ask students why Latin Americans might not have allowed the building of a canal in Panama.

ANSWER: Students might suggest that the government did not want foreign powers to have control over their land.

R **RESOURCE ACTIVITY**

READINGS IN WORLD HISTORY
Reading 24.4
A Change in United States Policy Toward Nicaragua

Have students read the selection and complete the questions.

Level 2

Map Answer
American Samoa

Theme: War and Diplomacy

After being forced to turn over rule of Hawaii to a provisional government, Liliuokalani signed this document: "I . . . protest against any and all acts done to . . . the constitutional government. . . . Now, to avoid any collision of armed forces and perhaps the loss of life, I do, under this protest, and impelled by said forces, yield my authority until such time as the government of the United States shall . . . undo the action of its representatives and reinstate me."

Critical Thinking Ask students whether they think Liliuokalani held real hopes of getting control of Hawaii back.

ANSWER: Students' answers will vary.

678

---

between the East and West coasts of the United States. When the Colombian government refused to cooperate, the United States first encouraged a local revolt in the isthmus, then forced Colombia to acknowledge the independence of the region. Thus was born the new Republic of Panama. In the process the United States gained control of the projected 10-mile-wide Canal Zone. The **Panama Canal**, which opened in 1914, became a vital U.S. interest.

The Good Neighbor policy. In 1933 U.S. president Franklin Roosevelt declared an end to the previous policy of intervention. In its place he proposed the so-called **Good Neighbor policy**. That same year Roosevelt withdrew the last American marines from Nicaragua. Sandino was granted amnesty, or excused, for his actions. Nevertheless, the next year Nicaraguan government agents killed Sandino. Such violence on the part of conservative authoritarian governments supported by the United States, as well as stepped-up U.S. investment in the region, inflamed Latin Americans' fears of American imperialism. Nationalism in Latin America quickly took on anti-American overtones.

American policies of intervention fueled anti-American nationalism in many Caribbean and Latin American countries.

Nationalism and Imperialism in Hawaii

As the United States became increasingly aggressive in its expansionist policies in the Pacific, it experienced the rise of local nationalist movements. Unlike other imperial powers, however, in most cases the United States was not the immediate cause of local nationalism. In the Hawaiian Islands, for example, the process of building a Hawaiian national identity had begun in the late 1790s under King Kamehameha (kah-MAY-hah-MAY-hah) I, who united the islands under his rule.

In the 1800s missionaries, businesspeople, and planters from the United States and Europe became major landholders in the Hawaiian Islands. Their influence began to transform the nature of traditional Hawaiian society, and Hawaiian nationalism declined.

After a period of liberal reforms under King Kamehameha III, however, old Hawaiian customs began to resurface. Hawaiian kings tried to limit foreign influences, particularly American. In reaction some 400 of the leading Western traders, planters, and missionaries formed the secret **Hawaiian League**. In 1887 these westerners forced King Kalakaua to accept a new constitution that largely stripped him of power and in effect put the government in the hands of foreigners. Their real goal was the annexation of Hawaii by the United States.

Kalakaua died in 1891 and was succeeded by his strong-willed sister Liliuokalani (li-lee-uh-woh-kuh-LAHN-ee). Like her brother, she was determined to restore full Hawaiian control over the kingdom and to reduce American influence. In 1893, when Liliuokalani announced plans for a new constitution, however, members of the Hawaiian League carried out a bloodless revolution. They declared an end to the monarchy, and with the help of the American minister to Hawaii, who ordered marines ashore to "protect" U.S. interests, they set up a provisional government. After several years as an independent republic, Hawaii was finally annexed by the United States in 1898.

A revival of Hawaiian nationalism led to annexation of Hawaii by the United States.

Queen Liliuokalani (above) and her brother Kalakaua were the last Hawaiian monarchs.

Teenagers IN HISTORY

Princess Kaiulani Pleads for Her Country

Princess Kaiulani, the niece of King Kalakaua, was trained from an early age to assume the role of queen of Hawaii. As part of this training, Kaiulani was sent to school in Great Britain when she was 14 years old. Although half a world away from Hawaii, she managed to keep up with events in her homeland through letters from friends and family. These letters increasingly focused on troubles with the haoles (HOU-LEES), or "foreigners." These haoles—mostly politically powerful American business leaders—were talking about annexing Hawaii to the United States. Letters from her uncle had a grim tone. Just before his death he wrote to Kaiulani, warning her to "be on guard against certain enemies I do not feel free to name in writing." Kaiulani did not discover the identity of these "enemies" until 1893, when a group of prominent haoles deposed Queen Liliuokalani and took control of the government.

Kaiulani, then a 17-year-old student, quickly decided to go to the United States to plead her case for her country. When her ship docked in New York in March 1893, Kaiulani read a statement addressed "to the American People." She explained:

66 Today I, a poor, weak girl, with not one of my people near me, and with all these Hawaiian statesmen against me, have strength to stand up for the rights of my people. . . . And I am strong—strong in the faith of God, strong in the knowledge that I am right, strong in the strength of seventy million people, who in this free land will hear my cry, and will refuse to let their flag cover dishonour to mine. 99

This powerful statement gained Kaiulani the admiration and support of many Americans. She won a promise from President Grover Cleveland that Hawaii's concerns would be given a fair hearing. The forces for annexation proved too strong, however, and in 1898 Hawaii was formally transferred to the United States. Kaiulani was Hawaii's last princess.

Princess Kaiulani, 1893

RESOURCE ACTIVITY

GLOBAL HISTORY RESOURCE CENTER
Reading: *Why the U.S. Should Annex the Philippines*
Image: *Filipino Patriot Aguinaldo and His Followers*

Print out and distribute the reading and image. Have students read the argument for annexation. Then have students compose a letter from Aguinaldo to the U.S. Congress, responding to the senator's speech and presenting his own viewpoint.

Level 3

REVIEW & ASSESSMENT RESOURCES

- Study Guide 24.4
- Daily Quiz 24.4
- Main Idea Activity 24.4

All Levels

Nationalism in the Philippines

Nationalism in the Philippines emerged in the late 1800s, when Filipinos revolted against Spanish rule. In 1898, when American commodore George Dewey defeated the Spanish fleet in Manila Bay, he allied himself with the local nationalists led by Emilio Aguinaldo. Unaware of American plans to annex the Philippines, Aguinaldo was glad to have Dewey's help against the Spanish.

As it became clear that the United States was considering taking control of the Philippines, however, Aguinaldo warned that he would fight just as bitterly against American imperialism as he had against the Spanish. If American troops interfered with his newly proclaimed republic, he

680

warned, "upon their heads will be all the blood." Despite Aguinaldo's warning, there were strong pressures in the U.S. Congress to claim the Philippines. As one supporter of annexation put it:

> ❝ *We have a great commerce to take care of. We have to compete with the commercial nations of the world in far-distant markets. Commerce, not politics, is king.* ❞

Most in Congress had no idea how effective Aguinaldo's threat could be—after narrowly voting to take control of the islands, they soon found out.

For three years the Filipinos fought from the hills—over 4,000 American soldiers and at least 200,000 Filipinos died in the bitter conflict. After Aguinaldo was captured by U.S. forces in 1901, he appealed to Filipinos to lay down their arms and accept American rule. The United States bought off the nationalists with promises of rapid progress toward self-government.

Once in charge, American colonial officials began to pursue a policy of development in the Philippines, focusing primarily on education. Hundreds of American teachers arrived, and about half of the government's expenses went for education. By the 1930s about half of all Filipinos could read, twice as many as before the American occupation. In addition, the Americans built new schools, roads, and hospitals.

▲ The influence of U.S. development—trolley, telephone, and electricity—is seen in Manila in the early 1900s.

Meanwhile, the fight for independence had moved rapidly from the hills of the Philippines into the halls of Congress. Although American attitudes toward Filipinos displayed considerable racism, some Filipino nationalists actually complained that U.S. rule was not harsh enough to create serious opposition among many Filipinos. As one Filipino put it, "Damn the Americans! Why don't they tyrannize us more?" The first steps toward self-government came in 1916, and by 1935 the Philippines had achieved full self-government with a promise of total independence in 10 years.

After the end of bitter fighting, the United States moved rapidly to grant Filipino self-government and independence.

SECTION 4 REVIEW

IDENTIFY and explain the significance of the following:
Platt Amendment
Roosevelt Corollary
Augusto César Sandino
Panama Canal
Good Neighbor policy
Hawaiian League
Kalakaua
Liliuokalani
Emilio Aguinaldo

1. *Main Idea* What effect did the Spanish-American War have on U.S. foreign policy?

2. *Main Idea* What resulted from the involvement of the United States in Central American affairs?

3. *War and Diplomacy* What effect did Hawaiian nationalism have on American interests in Hawaii?

4. *Writing to Explain* Write a brief essay explaining what effects the demands of Filipino nationalists had on the colonial policies of the United States.

5. *Comparing and Contrasting* In what ways was the move to build an American empire similar to and different from European imperialism?

Review

On a separate piece of paper, complete the following exercises:

WRITING A SUMMARY

Using the essential points in the text, write a brief summary of the chapter.

REVIEWING TERMS

From the following list, choose the term that correctly matches the definition.

Irish Republican Army
Zionism
Wafd Party
Guomindang
Platt Amendment
Roosevelt Corollary

1. movement begun in the 1890s to create a Jewish state
2. addition to Cuba's constitution giving the United States the right to intervene in Cuban affairs
3. Egyptian nationalist party led by Saad Zaghlul Pasha
4. Chinese Nationalist Party led by Sun Yixian
5. extension of the Monroe Doctrine that proclaimed U.S. "police power" in the Western Hemisphere

REVIEWING CHRONOLOGY

List the following events in their correct chronological order.

1. Indian representatives meet in Bombay to form the Indian National Congress.
2. The United States defeats Spain in the Spanish-American War.
3. Chinese Communists undertake the Long March.
4. British soldiers fire on a crowd of unarmed Hindus at a religious festival in Amritsar.
5. The Druse revolt against French rule in Syria.

UNDERSTANDING THE MAIN IDEA

1. How was the British Empire transformed after World War I?
2. What effect did Mohandas Gandhi's leadership have on the Indian nationalist movement?
3. How did British policies concerning Palestine affect the development of nationalism there?
4. Why were the Chinese unable to achieve unity after the fall of the Qing dynasty?
5. How did the Spanish-American War affect relations between the United States and other countries?

THINKING CRITICALLY

1. **Analyzing** What effect did World War I have on nationalist movements in the British colonies and dominions?
2. **Evaluating** Was the fall of the Qing dynasty and the establishment of a Chinese republic a complete break in the pattern of Chinese history? Why or why not?

Building Your Portfolio

Complete the following activities individually or in groups.

1. **Politics** Conduct research to find out how the British Commonwealth has changed since the 1930s. Explain why certain nations joined the Commonwealth while others left. Prepare a presentation explaining changes in the Commonwealth since its creation. Use maps to show which nations belonged to the Commonwealth in the beginning, and which nations belong to it now. Create an outline of your research and a bibliography of secondary sources to support your presentation.
2. **Cross-cultural Interaction** Imagine that you are living in Palestine in the 1930s. You have observed over the years how the tensions between Arabs and Jews have escalated. You have decided to publish a book of poems and short stories that tells both sides of the story.

   If you are working on this project individually, write one poem or short story from the perspective of a Palestinian Arab, and one from the perspective of a Jewish immigrant. If you are working as a group, have half of your group write from the point of view of Arabs and the other half from the point of view of Jews.

Chapter 25
Growing Aggression and World War II 1922–1945

Chapter Planning Guide

	TEXTBOOK	CORE RESOURCES	VISUAL RESOURCES	MULTIMEDIA
Introduction	pp. 682–683	Block Scheduling Handbook: Ch. 25		Videodisc Segment 25 and Viewing Guide: *The Lessons of World War II*
Lesson 25.1 Aggression and Crisis in the 1930s	pp. 684–689	Reading 25.1: *A Justification of Japanese Expansionism* Geography Activity 25: *Japan's Drive to Expand in Manchuria*	Everyday Life 25: *Russian Tanks in Berlin*	GHRC 25 Reading: *The Spanish Civil War* GHRC 25/Videodiscs: Image—*The Japanese Bombing of Shanghai, China*
Lesson 25.2 The Early Years of the War	pp. 690–696 Map: *German and Italian Expansion*, p. 691 Teenagers in History: *Anti-Hitler Youth*, p. 692	Reading 25.2: *The Evacuation of Dunkirk* Writing Project 25: *Writing a Speech* Skills Activity 25: *Conducting an Interview*		GHRC 25 Readings: *Remembering the Attack on Pearl Harbor; Last Message from U.S. Forces on Corregidor* GHRC 25/Videodiscs: Images—*The Japanese Attack on Pearl Harbor; Soviet Refugees Flee German Invasion;* Maps—*Operation Barbarossa; Attack on Pearl Harbor;* Audio Clip—*"A Date Which Will Live in Infamy"*
Lesson 25.3 The Holocaust and Other Atrocities of War	pp. 697–701 Map: *Concentration Camps,* p. 698 Literature Through Time: *Survival in Auschwitz,* p. 699	Reading 25.3: *The Burma-Siam Railway*	Art and History 25: *Inside an Internment Camp, World War II*	GHRC 25 Reading: *Christmas in the Auschwitz Death Camp* GHRC 25/Videodiscs: Image—*Rounding Up Jews in the Warsaw Ghetto*
Lesson 25.4 Allied Victories	pp. 702–710 Geography and History: *World War II Battles,* pp. 704–705 Chart: *Losses of the Major Wartime Powers in World War II,* p. 710	Reading 25.4: *The Allied Invasion of Normandy*	Geography and History 25: *World War II in the Pacific, 1941–1945*	GHRC 25 Readings: *The German Surrender at Tunisia; German Soldiers Face Death at Stalingrad; Five Fatal Minutes at Midway; The German Occupation of Rome* GHRC 25/Videodiscs: Images—*U.S. Troops Invade North Africa; Hiroshima After the Atomic Bomb;* Map—*Invasion of Normandy*
Chapter Investigation and Enrichment	pp. 682–710	Chapter 25 Investigation: *Mapping a Global War* People in World History 25 Explorations in Daily Life 25		GHRC 25/Videodiscs
Review and Assessment	Section 1 Review, p. 689 Section 2 Review, p. 696 Section 3 Review, p. 701 Section 4 Review, p. 710 Chapter 25 Review, p. 711	Chapter Review Activity 25 Vocabulary Activity 25 Themes Review 25 Section Study Guides 25.1–25.4 Main Idea Activities 25.1–25.4 Daily Quizzes 25.1–25.4 Chapter 25 Test Sheltered English Ch. 25 Test Ch. 25 Test Generator		Audio CDs: Ch. 25 Summary (English and Spanish)

INTRODUCING THE CHAPTER

Textbook pp. 682–683

CHAPTER OVERVIEW

During the 1930s the democracies of the world failed to curb the growing aggression of Germany and Japan. The Japanese invaded China in 1931, while the Germans occupied much of central Europe. War broke out in 1939 after Germany invaded Poland. In 1941 the United States joined the conflict following the Japanese attack on Pearl Harbor. After years of fighting, war atrocities, and millions of deaths, the war ended with an Allied victory in 1945.

PRESENTING THEMES

On the chalkboard or on an overhead transparency, write the following open-ended theme questions.

- **TECHNOLOGY** In what ways can new technologies be both beneficial and harmful?
- **WAR AND DIPLOMACY** How might diplomatic efforts to avoid all-out war sometimes make the situation worse?
- **SOCIAL RELATIONS** How might racial prejudice be used as a political weapon?

Have students, either individually or in groups, suggest responses to the questions. For the technology question, students might suggest that new technologies can have the potential to be both beneficial and destructive. For the war and diplomacy question, students might suggest that prolonged negotiations can give an aggressor time to build a large, well-equipped army. For the social relations question, students might suggest that political leaders can encourage racial prejudice to gain popularity. Save the responses. Once students have studied the chapter, you may wish to have them complete the Themes Review, then compare the two sets of answers.

USING THE VIDEO

Segment 25: *The Lessons of World War II*

ENGLISH

Search Chapter 25
Videodisc 2, Side A

SPANISH

Search Chapter 25
Videodisc 2, Side A

Tell students that in this chapter they will examine how these theme questions apply to peoples and nations who fought in the second global conflict of the twentieth century, World War II. Conclude by showing Segment 25 of the *World History and Cultures Videodiscs*. This segment describes some of the conditions that led to World War II, presents pictures of the horrors of this conflict, and recalls the lessons drawn by those who lived through the war.

Before showing the video, ask students to pay particular attention to the scale of the conflict: the types of weapons, the extent of damage to structures, and especially the number of people involved. To help students grasp the significant concepts of the segment, have them complete Video Viewing Guide 25.

Key to Ability Levels

All strategies and activities are coded to the following ability levels:

LEVEL 1	**Basic** activities suitable for all students
LEVEL 2	**Average** activities suitable for average to above-average students
LEVEL 3	**Challenging** activities suitable for above-average students
SHELTERED ENGLISH	Activities suitable for students with **Limited English Proficiency**

Additional Resources

BOOKS FOR TEACHERS

Ambrose, Stephen. *D-Day, June 6, 1944: The Climactic Battle of World War II.* Touchstone, 1994. Provides an exhaustive account of this major offensive.

Bullock, Alan. *Hitler and Stalin: Parallel Lives.* Vintage Books, 1991. Offers a double biography of the era's dictators.

Crew, David F., ed. *Nazism and German Society, 1933–1945.* Routledge, 1994. Examines the tensions within Nazi Germany.

BOOKS FOR STUDENTS

Holliday, Laurel, ed. *Children in the Holocaust and World War II: Their Secret Diaries.* Simon and Schuster, 1995. Documents emotional responses.

Lang, Sean. *The Second World War.* Cambridge University Press, 1993. Offers an overview.

Morin, Isabel V. *Days of Judgment.* Millbrook, 1995. Looks at war crimes trials.

MULTIMEDIA MATERIALS

Pearl Harbor: Surprise and Remembrance. Direct Cinema Education. Video, 88 min. Uses documentary footage and interviews.

Powers of Persuasion. Fife and Drum. CD-ROM, MAC, MPC formats. Looks at World War II propaganda.

The English, D-Day, and the Holocaust. BBC/Time-Life. Video, 52 min. Looks at attacks on civilians.

Lesson 25.1 Aggression and Crisis in the 1930s

Textbook pp. 684–689

RESOURCES

Core Resources

Reading 25.1: *A Justification of Japanese Expansionism*

Videodiscs or Global History Resource Center

Image: *The Japanese Bombing of Shanghai, China*

[barcode]

Search Frame 1013

Global History Resource Center

Reading: *The Spanish Civil War: Guernica is Destroyed*

LESSON FOCUS

What were the motives for aggression and appeasement in the 1930s?

OBJECTIVES

After completing this lesson, students will be able to:

- discuss the effectiveness of collective security;
- identify how Hitler threatened the peace of Europe in the 1930s;
- explain Western democracies' responses to Hitler's demands in the 1930s.

HOOK: Link to Today

Discuss the idea of collective security. Have students think about bullies they know in school or knew when they were younger. Have them identify general characteristics of how a bully behaves.

Ask: *How do you deal with bullies?*

> [Students should provide alternatives for dealing with bullies, such as give the bully what he/she wants; refuse to comply with the demands; join with others to stop the negative behavior; or request established authority to stop the negative behavior.]

Ask: *What postwar organization was established to provide collective security and protection from aggressors?*
[the League of Nations]

Conclude by pointing out to students that in the 1930s, the system of collective security set up at Versailles in 1919 failed because of threats by aggressors—Japan, Italy, and Germany. In addition, the Spanish Civil War created further division between nations.

DEVELOP

Identify the causes of the failure of collective security.
Before beginning this activity, you may wish to have students view the electronic media image of Shanghai after a Japanese bomb attack and have them complete Geography Activity 25 and read Core Resources Reading 25.1 to provide them with more information on Japan. Then have students write *Japan*, *Italy*, and *Germany* across the top of a sheet of paper. Ask them to list under the appropriate country the motives each nation had to move beyond its borders. Review responses and list them on the board. *[Japan: critical shortages of raw materials; Italy: conquest of Ethiopia would secure Italy's possessions in Eritrea and Somalia, securing Ethiopia could mean threatening approaches to Suez Canal; Germany: Hitler's goals of world power, racial domination, greater living space]*

Ask students to give a quick background of the Spanish Civil War. *[The war essentially became a conflict between fascism and communism, which tempted governments outside of Spain to interfere.]*

Ask: *Why would other nations be interested in intervening in the Spanish Civil War?*

[It was a testing ground for new weapons and tactics; other nations wanted to support one form of government over another.]

Have students read about the destruction of Guernica in the Global History Resource Center. Have them discuss the images of war described in the reading. Then lead students in a discussion about civil war.

Ask: How does the reading express the evils of civil war? What does civil war do to a nation? How did it affect Spain?
[Discussion comments ought to include the inherent bitterness and cruelty of civil wars. Also, the addition of outside interference made the Spanish Civil War a tragic struggle that shocked the world.]

PROBE

Identify particular points in the 1930s when the Western democracies did not stop Hitler's aggression. Next turn the discussion to Germany. Organize the class into small groups to make a list of dates and places during the 1930s when they believe the Western democracies could have reacted to Hitler's advances. *[Lists should include Hitler's withdrawing from League of Nations and world disarmament talks; reinstituting the draft, forming new armored divisions, and strengthening the air force; moving troops into the Rhineland; increasing rearmament; forming the Axis powers; annexing Austria; annexing the Sudetenland.]* Allow students sufficient time to complete their lists, then ask them what action finally caused other nations to react. *[invasion of Poland]*

Ask them to narrow their list to the *best opportunity* nations had to stop Hitler's aggression by considering the following questions for each action:
- What standards of international behavior were being violated by this aggression?
- What force was Hitler able to apply to get what he wanted?
- What sanctions or force might the democracies have used to stop Hitler?
- Would the democracies' sanctions or force have been likely to be successful in this situation?

When the groups have completed their work, lead a class discussion in which you review each group's opinions.

CONCLUDE

Identify reasons why the Western democracies attempted to appease aggressors for so long. Ensure that students understand the concept of appeasement.

Ask: What does it mean to appease someone? Why do people try to appease others?
[Students should be allowed to discuss and give personal examples.]

Ask: Why did Western leaders adopt policies of appeasement?
[distraction of Great Depression; refusal to work with the Soviet Union; fear of another war; lack of military preparedness; wariness of alliances]

Have the students review the information on the Munich Conference of 1938 on textbook pages 688–689 as an excellent example of appeasement. Tell students that nations were unwilling to make sacrifices or to take risks unless their own survival was at stake. They were very reluctant—and not ready—to go to war.

EXTEND

Cross-Curricular Connection: *The Arts*

Have students research artistic works, including literary pieces, about the Spanish Civil War (suggest that they consider works by Ernest Hemingway and Pablo Picasso, for example). Have them write a short piece explaining why artists were interested in the topic.

MEET INDIVIDUAL NEEDS

Interpersonal Learners

Have students act as journalists interviewing other students playing the roles of Mussolini, Hitler, Daladier, and Chamberlain just after the Munich agreement. The journalists need to prepare two to three in-depth questions for the leaders.

Students Having Difficulty/
Students Acquiring English

Have students plan and present short skits in which they act out the parts of nations—or leaders of nations—involved in various crises in the 1930s. Encourage them to give both public speeches—to appeal to world opinion—as well as private "asides" to express their real motives.

ASSESS

Review

Have students complete the Section 1 Review. Use answers in the Teacher's Edition, page 689, to assess student mastery of this section.

Lesson 25.2 *The Early Years of the War*

Textbook pp. 690–696

RESOURCES

Pupil's Edition
Map, p. 691: *German and Italian Expansion, 1935–1941*

Core Resources
Reading 25.2: *The Evacuation of Dunkirk*
Skills Activity 25: *Conducting an Interview*

Global History Resource Center
Reading: *Remembering the Attack on Pearl Harbor*
Reading: *Last Message from U.S. Forces on Corregidor*

Videodiscs or Global History Resource Center

Map: *Operation Barbarossa, 1941*

Search Frame 1023

Image: *The Japanese Attack on Pearl Harbor*

Search Frame 1016

Audio Clip: *"A Date Which Will Live in Infamy"*

Search 6983, Play to 7750
Videodisc 2, Side A
Audio Clip 25

Image: *Soviet Refugees Flee German Invasion*

Search Frame 1015

Map: *Attack on Pearl Harbor, December 7, 1941*

Search Frame 1024

LESSON FOCUS
How did World War II progress in Europe and eventually involve the United States?

OBJECTIVES
After completing this lesson, students will be able to:
- discuss how the war developed in western Europe in 1940 and early 1941;
- describe Hitler's primary goal and how he tried to achieve it in the summer of 1941;
- identify how Japanese policies in Asia widened the war.

HOOK
Discuss the military and psychological impact of German Blitzkrieg attacks. Refer to the teacher's annotation on textbook page 690 that describes new technology and warfare, including the German Blitzkrieg. Read the annotation to students so that they will understand how the Germans used Blitzkrieg to their advantage. You may then wish to discuss with students how they think soldiers who were trained for the trench warfare used in the First World War responded to the Blitzkrieg attacks and how they think civilians felt as their countries were overrun.

DEVELOP
Identify the events that led to the progression of the war in western Europe. Tell students that Germany was able to overrun much of Europe using lightning-fast assault tactics. Have students refer to the map on textbook page 691 to locate the countries involved in the war. Then ask them to work in teams to make a time line of Hitler's progress through Europe. You may wish to have students complete Reading 25.2. Have students share their results. *[invasion of Poland, September 1, 1939; invasion of Denmark and Norway, April 9, 1940; invasion of Luxembourg, the Netherlands, and Belgium, May 1940; fall of France, June 1940; Battle of Britain, summer 1940; Blitz, September 1940–May 1941; invasion of Yugoslavia, early 1941; invasion of Soviet Union, June 22, 1941]*

PROBE

Examine Hitler's reasons and strategy for invading the Soviet Union. Tell students that Hitler's ultimate goal in World War II was the conquest of the Soviet Union. Then display the electronic media map and image of the German invasion of the Soviet Union. Organize the class into two teams—one for Germany and the other for the Soviet Union.

Ask the German team to prepare to discuss the following:
- What were Hitler's motives and strategy for invading Russia?
- What was the progression of events in Operation Barbarossa?
- What happened to Hitler's strategy?

Ask the Russia team to prepare to discuss the following:
- How did Russia defend itself?
- What happened to the German advance?
- How did the Allies help?

Students on the German team should understand that Hitler hoped to conquer the Soviet Union and thus provide more "living space" for Germans, whom he believed to be superior. His strategy was to first secure alliance with Hungary and Romania, then Bulgaria and Yugoslavia. The *Luftwaffe* attacked the Soviet air force on the ground, and then German forces moved deep into Soviet territory, but failed to reach Moscow before winter slowed their advance.

Students on the Soviet team should understand that the Russians followed a "scorched earth" policy, whereby retreating armies left nothing for the enemy. Weather aided the Soviets—heavy rains made moving the forces difficult for the Germans, and harsh winter weather halted their operations. Britain provided supplies and helped the Soviet Union invade and occupy Iran.

CONCLUDE

Outline the Japanese strategy in the Pacific and Southeast Asia. Ask students to identify the Japanese government's primary concern that led to war with the United States. *[Students should understand that Japanese leaders wanted control of strategic materials, particularly oil.]*

Ask: *Why did the Japanese attack Pearl Harbor in Hawaii?*
> *[By attacking the naval base at Pearl Harbor, the Japanese hoped to destroy American naval power in the Pacific and thus have time to build up their defenses before the*

United States could launch a counterattack.]

Show students the electronic media image and map of the attack on Pearl Harbor. Then have them read the recollections of John Garcia, who was a teenager working at Pearl Harbor when the attack took place, in the Global History Resource Center.

Ask: **What impact did the attack have on the United States?**
> *[Japan's attack galvanized the United States into declaring war on Japan. Then Germany and Italy declared war on the United States.]*

Conclude by playing for students the audio clip of President Roosevelt's address to Congress the day after the attack on Pearl Harbor. Ask them for their reactions to Roosevelt's speech.

EXTEND

Cross-Curricular Connection: *Journalism*
Link to Today. Many people today still have vivid memories of the Japanese attack on Pearl Harbor. Have students complete Skills Activity 25 by interviewing a member of their family or of the community about the attack. Then have them write a short article using their interviews and other information they can find on Pearl Harbor.

MEET INDIVIDUAL NEEDS

Logical-Mathematical Learners
Ask students to figure some of the distances from Germany to Soviet battlegrounds or from Japan to some of the places conquered by the Japanese. Ask students to conduct research on how armies were supplied over such long distances.

Linguistic Learners
Assign the Global History Resource Center reading of the last message sent before the Philippines fell to the Japanese. Ask students to use this message as the starting point for a story or part of a film script about Irving Strobing and the fall of the Philippines.

ASSESS

Review
Have students complete the Section 2 Review. Use answers in the Teacher's Edition, page 696, to assess student mastery of this section.

Textbook pp. 697–701

RESOURCES

Pupil's Edition

Map, p. 698: *Concentration Camps, 1933–1945*

Literature Through Time, p. 699: *Survival in Auschwitz*

Global History Resource Center

Reading: *Christmas in the Auschwitz Death Camp*

Videodiscs or Global History Resource Center

Image: *Rounding Up Jews in the Warsaw Ghetto*

Search Frame 1017

LESSON FOCUS

How and why did brutality and genocide occur on a massive scale during World War II?

OBJECTIVES

After completing this lesson, students will be able to:
- identify the results of Hitler's racial policies during the war;
- discuss the results of the Japanese view of conquered enemies;
- talk about why so many atrocities were committed by the Soviet Union during the war.

HOOK

Illustrate how genocide and other atrocities happened during the war. Ask all the students in the room who have blond hair to stand up. Then tell them that new policies in the classroom decree that all students with blond hair are inferior to the other students and must therefore sit in the back of the classroom and not interact with other students. Ask students to indicate how they would feel about such a ruling.

Ask: *What makes some people feel superior to others?*
[Students should indicate that religious, cultural, or racial differences have sometimes led some people to feel superior to others.]

Ask: *What can happen when feelings of superiority go unchecked?*
[Students should recognize that feelings of superiority can lead to grave violations of human rights, or even genocide.]

Link to Today. Ask students to think of more recent situations in which one group has maintained superiority over another. What happened in these places? *[Responses could include South Africa or Bosnia.]*

DEVELOP

Discuss the strategy behind the Holocaust and other atrocities. Have students work together in seven groups, each representing one of the peoples singled out for mistreatment during World War II:
- German Jews
- Polish Jews in the Warsaw Ghetto
- Gypsies
- Yugoslav civilians under German Occupation
- Chinese civilians in Nanjing under Japanese Occupation
- American and Filipino prisoners of war on the Bataan Death March
- Polish intellectuals and landowners under Soviet occupation

Ask students to answer these questions about their assigned group:

- What happened to these people?
- Where did these atrocities happen?
- Who carried out the atrocities?
- What was the reason behind these atrocities?
- What nations, if any, intervened on behalf of the victims?

Conclude by having a representative from each group give a short report answering each of the above questions.

PROBE

Examine the causes of and responsibilities for the Holocaust. Tell students that Hitler's aims to conquer more "living space" and create a "pure" empire led to his desire to destroy the Jews and other peoples he considered inferior.

Ask: *Where did the Nazis finalize their plans for extermination of the Jews?*
[Wannsee Conference]

Ask: *How did they achieve their goals?*
[They transported the Jews to concentration camps, where they executed them or used them for forced labor or cruel experiments.]

Have students read Sophia Litwinska's recollection of Christmas 1941 at Auschwitz and view the electronic media image of Nazis rounding up Jews in the Warsaw Ghetto. You might also ask them to read the Literature Through Time selection and view the map showing the locations of the concentration camps. Then ask students to imagine that they are Jews living in Germany or Poland during the war. Ask them to write a diary entry expressing their concerns for themselves and their families. After they have finished, ask volunteers to read their entries aloud.

CONCLUDE

Identify conditions that breed genocide and atrocity.
Next ask students to consider why people might not act to help those who are being victimized. *[Student answers might include—it is easier to believe the rumors are false; it is safer to assume that victims deserved what they got; it is safer to believe it is not your business; it is easier to believe there is nothing you can do.]*

Ask: *How did many people in Europe react to what was happening to the Jews?*

[Many people quietly ignored what was happening. Some, however, tried to save as many people as possible.]

Direct students to the discussion of heroic acts by people who tried to help the Jews during the Holocaust, asking them to identify these people and their actions. *[Students should mention the efforts of the Danes; Raoul Wallenberg, who used his position as a diplomat to save Jews; and Oskar Schindler, who saved Jews by employing them in his factories.]*

Ask: *What do you think might have happened to people who interfered with the Nazis' policies?*
[They were at risk of suffering the same fates themselves.]

Conclude by leading a discussion based on students' opinions about the following questions:

- What conditions have to exist in a nation for genocide to happen?
- Are atrocities more likely during wartime?

EXTEND

Other Media

If possible, have students view the movie *Schindler's List*, either in class or as a homework assignment. Afterward have students discuss the transition of Schindler from selfish business promoter to unlikely hero. Ask them why they think Schindler risked so much for the Jews in his factory.

MEET INDIVIDUAL NEEDS

Interpersonal Learners

Have students who are good at interacting with others locate a Holocaust or other atrocity survivor and invite that person to speak to your class. If the person is unable to come to the class, ask students to interview him or her instead and give an oral report.

Intrapersonal Learners

Ask students to write two "internal monologues"—one as a victim of one of the atrocities mentioned in the text and another as a perpetrator of one of the atrocities.

ASSESS

Review

Have students complete the Section 3 Review. Use answers in the Teacher's Edition, page 701, to assess student mastery of this section.

Lesson 25.4   *Allied Victories*

Textbook pp. 702–710

RESOURCES

Core Resources

Reading 25.4: *The Allied Invasion of Normandy*

Visual Resources

Geography and History 25: *World War II in the Pacific, 1941–1945*

Global History Resource Center

Reading: *The German Surrender at Tunisia*

Reading: *German Soldiers Face Death at Stalingrad*

Reading: *Five Fatal Minutes at Midway*

Reading: *The German Occupation of Rome*

Videodiscs or Global History Resource Center

Map: *Invasion of Normandy, June 6, 1944*

Search Frame 1025

Image: *U.S. Troops Invade North Africa*

Search Frame 1020

Image: *Hiroshima After the Atomic Bomb*

Search Frame 1022

LESSON FOCUS

What were the major turning points and final strategies of World War II?

OBJECTIVES

After completing this lesson, students will be able to:

- identify how the war developed in Europe between 1943 and 1945;
- describe how the war developed in Asia and the Pacific;
- discuss what finally brought the war against Japan to an end;
- identify the costs of World War II.

HOOK

Discuss the meaning of unconditional surrender.
Remind students that in January 1943 Churchill and Roosevelt met in Casablanca, where they agreed to seek the unconditional surrender of each of the Axis Powers—Germany, Italy, and Japan. Ask students to discuss the idea of unconditional surrender.

Ask: What is an unconditional surrender?

[An unconditional surrender is an absolute, unqualified surrender.]

Ask: Why do you think the Allies demanded unconditional surrender from both Germany and Japan?

[The Allies wanted total submission of the Axis Powers and did not wish to make any concessions.]

Tell students that they will learn about the progress of events in World War II in Europe, Asia, and the Pacific, as well as find out how the Allies were eventually able to achieve unconditional surrender from the Axis Powers.

DEVELOP

Identify and describe the battles that led to the end of the war in Europe. Tell students that turning points in the European war began in mid-1942. Ask students to identify and make a time line of events leading up to German surrender. Under each event, have students write a brief caption explaining its significance. *[Events include forced retreat of Rommel by British and Commonwealth forces; defeat of the Germans at the Battle of El Alamein; German surrender in Tunisia; German surrender in Stalingrad; Soviet victory at Kursk; Allied control of Sicily; Allied troops entering Rome; execution of Mussolini; strategic bombing against Germany; Normandy invasion; Battle of the Bulge; Allied advance into Germany; and Soviet control of Berlin.]*

To complete students' understanding of these major events, you might want to have them read Core Resources Reading 25.4, as well as the Global Resource Center readings on the German surrender in Tunisia, the battle of Stalingrad, and the German occupation of Rome. They might also examine the electronic media map of the Normandy invasion for a better understanding of this turning point in the war, as well as the image of the U.S. invasion of North Africa.

PROBE

Discuss the events and outcome of the war in Asia and the Pacific. Display the Geography and History Transparency on the war in the Pacific, and complete the worksheet together in class. Then, referring to the worksheet and the text, discuss the strategies of the war in the Pacific. Point out Admiral Nimitz' three-part strategy on textbook page 706 to achieve an Allied victory.

Ask: ***What early naval battles led to the Allies making headway in the war of the Pacific against Japan?***
[*Midway, Guadalcanal, Gilbert Islands*]

To provide students with more information on the Battle of Midway, have them read the Global History Resource Center selection on the battle.

Then tell students that meanwhile, on the Asian mainland, the Japanese continued to attack other nations.

Ask: ***What events signified the final push to stop Japan?***
[*the taking of the Marianas, the Battle of Leyte Gulf, the capture of Manila, the battle for Imphal and Kohima, Iwo Jima, Okinawa*]

Tell students that the resistance encountered at Iwo Jima and Okinawa convinced U.S. commanders that the invasion of Japan would be costly in both U.S. and Japanese lives.

Ask: ***Why did the Japanese eventually surrender?***
[*the dropping of the atomic bombs*]

Have students speculate about the factors President Truman had to consider before making his decision to drop the bomb, and show the electronic media image of Hiroshima.

CONCLUDE

Discuss the consequences of World War II. On the chalkboard, write "Winners" on one side and "Losers" on the other. Then ask:
- Who were the winners in World War II? Why?
- Who were the losers? Why?

Lead a discussion in which students consider what the gains and losses of the war were. Some of the discussion should center around the displacement of people from their homes and the enormous destruction of land, urban areas, and factories; the burden to prevent such massive destruction again; and the question of how to recover. On the positive side, students should note the end of the Holocaust and other atrocities, the end of foreign occupation of much of Europe and Asia, and the restoration of freedom to many parts of the world.

EXTEND

Cross-Curricular Connection: *Science*

Ask students to research some of the differences between technology in World War I and World War II. Suggest that they consider such topics as radar, long-range rockets, the atomic bomb, the improved production of penicillin, the wide use of amphibious warfare, etc. Have students report on their findings.

MEET INDIVIDUAL NEEDS

Students Having Difficulty

Have students who are having difficulty remembering the major national leaders write a few biographical sentences about the leaders, including information on their careers and decisions. Have them include a photocopy of a photograph of the leaders, if possible.

Visual-Spatial Learners

Ask students to locate photographs illustrating various events in World War II in books and other sources. Ask them to bring the sources to class or to make photocopies. Ask students to identify in a paragraph the importance of the event shown in the photograph. Display the photographs in the classroom.

ASSESS

Review

Have students complete the Section 4 Review. Use answers in the Teacher's Edition, page 710, to assess student mastery of this section.

In preparation for the chapter test, you may wish to have students complete all or part of the Chapter 25 Review on page 711 of the textbook, the Chapter 25 Review Activity, or the Chapter 25 Themes Review.

Chapter 25
Growing Aggression and World War II 1922–1945

Understanding the Main Idea

Presenting Themes

Using the Time Line

Understanding the Main Idea

In the 1930s the totalitarian powers of Germany, Italy, and Japan began a period of rapid territorial expansion. This expansion ultimately brought all the major powers of the world into the most destructive war in human history. The great powers of the world fought fierce battles in Europe, North Africa, Asia, and on many scattered islands in the Pacific. By the time the war came to an end, millions of people had lost their lives—many as victims of wartime atrocities.

Themes

- **Technology** In what ways can new technologies be both beneficial and harmful?

- **War and Diplomacy** How might diplomatic efforts to avoid all-out war sometimes make the situation worse?

- **Social Relations** How might racial prejudice be used as a political weapon?

In the summer of 1942, the Nazis began the deportation of Jews from the Warsaw Ghetto to the Treblinka death camp. Determined not to give up without a fight, Jewish resistance leaders launched a major uprising against the Germans on April 19, 1943. From attics and rooftops, with bullets, hand grenades, and bombs, the Jews attacked German troops as they tried to enter the ghetto. The Germans retreated, but returned with tanks, artillery, and eventually aerial bombardment. On April 23 a poster appeared on the streets of Warsaw outside the ghetto with a call to arms:

> **❝**For Our and Your Freedom!
> Poles, Citizens, Soldiers of Liberty!
> Amidst the booming of guns with which the Germans bombarded our houses . . . ; amidst the rattle of machine guns . . . ; amidst the smoke and fire and blood of the Warsaw Ghetto we appeal to you. . . . Like you, we are seething with the passionate desire to avenge all the crimes committed by our common enemy. . . . Long live the brotherhood of weapons and blood of fighting Poland! Long live Freedom!**❞**

For nearly a month the Jews held off the Germans. The German commander finally resorted to blowing up the ghetto house by house, and eventually burned the ghetto to the ground. By mid-May the uprising was over. Some 14,000 Jews died in the fighting.

1931	1936	1937	1939
Japan invades Manchuria.	Spanish Civil War erupts.	Japan launches war against China.	Germany invades Poland, beginning World War II.

In 1946 a young Polish girl looks out over the ruins of what was the Warsaw Ghetto. Tens of thousands of Jews, murdered by the Nazis, were buried beneath the rubble.

As the Germans began to deport Jews from the Warsaw Ghetto to the death camps, thousands of Jews went into hiding in rooms and bunkers beneath the ghetto. As they realized that thousands of Jews had disappeared, German authorities determined to find them. Throughout 1943 German troops attempted to enter the ghetto, only to be driven out by Jewish resistance forces. Only after they brought in tanks, field artillery, flamethrowers, heavy machine guns, police dogs, and listening devices were they able to locate and surround resistance headquarters. In the meantime, the German troops had reduced the Warsaw Ghetto to ashes and rubble.

Critical Thinking Ask students why the Warsaw Jews were able to keep the German troops out of the ghetto for so long.

ANSWER: Students might suggest that Jews knew the area better than the troops and were fighting desperately for their lives.

1940	1941	1943	1944	1945
Much of Europe falls to the Nazis.	Germany invades the Soviet Union; Japan bombs Pearl Harbor; the United States enters the war.	The Soviet Union defeats Germany at the Battle of Stalingrad.	D-Day invasion of Normandy begins the liberation of France.	Germany and Japan surrender, ending World War II.

CORE LESSON PLAN
See pages 681C and
681D for Lesson Plan
25.1.

R RESOURCE
ACTIVITY

**READINGS IN
WORLD HISTORY**
Reading 25.1
*A Justification of
Japanese Expansionism*

Have students read the
Japanese official's
defense of Japanese
expansionism. Ask them
to evaluate the source as
they read and keep watch
for biased reasoning or
language. Then have
students complete the
questions.

Level 2

SECTION 1
Aggression and Crisis in the 1930s

FOCUS

- How effective was the League of Nations in ensuring collective security and preventing aggression in the 1930s?

- How did Hitler threaten the peace of Europe during the 1930s?

- How did Western democracies respond to Hitler's demands?

During the 1930s three powers—Japan, Italy, and Germany—grew increasingly aggressive. Each sought to enhance its influence and to expand its territory through the use of military force. Anxious to avoid war, the Western democracies yielded time and again to the aggressors. Eventually, however, nearly a decade of aggression and crisis ended in 1939 with the outbreak of yet another world war.

Victorious Japanese troops
in Manchuria, c. 1931

The Failure of Collective Security

The system of collective security set up at Versailles in 1919 proved powerless to stop international aggression in the 1930s. Aggressors simply ignored international opinion. In the end, no member of the League of Nations was willing to commit its military forces to stop aggression when its own interests were not immediately threatened.

Japanese aggression in East Asia. The first major acts of aggression began in Asia. Many Japanese were worried by Japan's lack of critical raw materials with which to sustain its growing population. Some prominent Japanese began to call for a "Greater East Asia Co-Prosperity Sphere"—in effect an enlarged Japanese empire. Imperialist officers in the army decided to force the issue by seizing Manchuria, where Japan already controlled the railways.

In September 1931 a small group of Japanese army officers staged a fake attack on the railway at Mukden, the capital of southern Manchuria. Blaming the attack on China, Japanese forces in Manchuria seized the whole province. Within a year, Japan proclaimed Manchuria to be independent under the new name of Manchukuo and installed a Japanese-controlled government.

Unable to defeat Japan, China appealed to the League of Nations for help. The League condemned Japan's aggression and demanded that Manchuria be placed under Chinese supervision. Instead, the Japanese simply withdrew from the League of Nations. Because no member was willing to commit military forces on China's behalf, the League could do nothing to restrain Japanese aggression. In July 1937 the Japanese launched a war against China, and by 1939 the Japanese army had occupied nearly one fourth of Chinese territory.

Italy and the Ethiopian crisis. Collective security was equally ineffective in Africa. During the 1920s Benito Mussolini had strengthened Italy's position in Libya. In 1935 he prepared to invade Ethiopia (also known as Abyssinia), Africa's only independent kingdom. Ethiopia's conquest would help secure Italian possessions in neighboring Eritrea and Somalia. With both

Libya and Ethiopia, Italy could threaten the approaches to the Suez Canal.

On October 3, 1935, Italian forces invaded Ethiopia, whose army proved no match for Italy's armored vehicles, aircraft, and poison gas. As a member of the League of Nations, Ethiopia appealed for support. The League voted to condemn the invasion and to impose trade penalties against Italy. Angered, Mussolini simply ignored the League. By May 1936 Ethiopia had fallen, and Haile Selassie (HY-luh suh-lah-SEE), its former ruler, had fled to Britain.

In June, when the League's Council met to reconsider its policy, Haile Selassie warned the delegates of the dangers of backing down:

❝ *It is not merely a question of a settlement in the matter of Italian aggression. It is a question of collective security; of the very existence of the League; of the trust placed by States in international treaties; of the value of promises made to small states that their integrity and their independence shall be respected and assured. It is a choice between the principle of equality of States and the imposition upon small Powers of the bonds of vassalage [servitude].* **❞**

Despite Haile Selassie's plea, Britain and France, the League's leading powers, declined to use force in Ethiopia. In July the League even voted to lift the penalties against Italy.

The Spanish Civil War. While Japanese and Italian aggression made clear the weakness of collective security, the outbreak of civil war in Spain in 1936 demonstrated the growing division between democratic and totalitarian countries in Europe. Spain became a testing ground for new weapons and tactics, as Germany, Italy, and the Soviet Union used the civil war for their own purposes. Many came to see the **Spanish Civil War** as a struggle between the forces of fascism and communism.

European fascists were sympathetic to the Spanish Nationalists, who included the fascist Falange Party along with conservative and Catholic allies. The Nationalists united under General Francisco Franco in rebellion against the new Spanish Republic. Germany, Italy, and Portugal contributed weapons, advisers, and "volunteers" to the Nationalists. Mussolini, for example, sent more than 50,000 troops to Spain to help Franco.

On the other side, the Soviet Union supported the Republican government. Some 70,000 antifascist volunteers from other countries, including Britain, France, and the United States, also fought on behalf of the Republican government. These units became known as the International Brigades.

Western democratic governments were more cautious. The experiences of British writer George Orwell, who went to the antifascist city of Barcelona in 1937, reflected the dilemma the civil war created for democratic Western leaders:

❝ *Barcelona was something startling and overwhelming. . . . Practically every building of any size had been seized by the workers and was draped with red flags . . . ; every wall was scrawled with the hammer and sickle and with the initials of the revolutionary parties; almost every church had been gutted and its images burnt.* **❞**

▶ **Streets in Barcelona, Spain, were often barricaded during the civil war.**

Theme: Politics and Law

In 1931 Spanish voters replaced the monarchy with a constitution, forming a republic. The first elected government implemented a socialist agenda. The leaders suppressed the influence of the Catholic Church and broke up large estates, distributing land among small farmers. Outraged, conservative and pro-Catholic parties called for the return of the monarchy. As these forces gained power, leftist parties became even more radical.

Critical Thinking Ask students how these events may have led to the Spanish Civil War.

ANSWER: Students should suggest that conservatives and socialists were dividing into increasingly hostile camps.

RESOURCE ACTIVITY

GLOBAL HISTORY RESOURCE CENTER
Reading: *The Spanish Civil War: Guernica Is Destroyed*

Print out and distribute the reading. Have students read the selection aloud. Ask students to work in groups to create short "live" newscasts of the bombing. Have students present their newscasts to the class.

Level 1/ Sheltered English

Hitler's plans for German expansion owed much to theories of geopolitics—the relationship between geographic space and foreign policy. In the early 1900s Englishman Sir Halford Mackinder had argued that a nation's power rested on its control of large areas of land. The most important area, Mackinder believed, was the vast connected landmass of Eurasia and Africa—which he called the World Island. Whoever managed to control the central regions of Eurasia that included Germany and Russia—the Heartland, as he called it—could also control the World Island.

Critical Thinking Ask students how Mackinder's ideas about a country's greatness and the World Island may have affected Hitler's plans.

ANSWER: Students might suggest that these theories influenced Hitler's desire to expand Germany so that it could control the World Island.

During the Spanish Civil War the Communists and other radical groups came to control the antifascist forces. Western leaders did not want to see a fascist or a communist government in Spain. In addition, as Orwell pointed out, both sides were guilty of terrible excesses. Franco's ultimate victory reinforced the French and British sense of helplessness in the face of fascism.

Under the League of Nations, collective security failed to prevent or reverse aggression.

▲ **Polish refugee children, whose parents were victims of Nazi persecution, arrive at their new home in Palestine.**

The Revival of German Power

Of all the threats to world peace that arose in the 1930s, the greatest was the revival of German power under the National Socialist (Nazi) government. Adolf Hitler, the Nazi leader, spoke of revenge for the Treaty of Versailles. His larger goal was German domination of Europe and ultimately the world.

Hitler's expansionist aims. In the 1920s, a decade before he became chancellor of Germany, Hitler had outlined his expansionist objectives in his book, *Mein Kampf.* "Germany will either be a world power," he wrote, "or there will be no Germany." Misguided views on race and the belief that the German population needed additional territory to grow dominated Hitler's thinking.

Believing that the Germans were a biologically superior race, destined to dominate supposedly inferior races such as the Slavs, Hitler felt that Germany had an important destiny to fulfill. He also believed that Jews were the enemy of all races, and that they kept Germany from reaching its greatness.

The other issue Hitler focused on was geographic space. Germany's population was growing rapidly, and Hitler believed that "living space" was necessary to accommodate the growth:

❝*An additional 500,000 square kilometers [almost 200,000 square miles] in Europe can provide new homesteads for millions of German peasants, and make available millions of soldiers to the power of the German people for the moment of decision. The only area in Europe that could be considered for such a territorial policy therefore was Russia.*❞

Before beginning a full-scale war against Russia, however, Hitler believed Germany must first secure its western border from France.

German preparations for expansion. Hitler began to act on his plans for German expansion immediately after becoming chancellor in January 1933. In October he withdrew Germany from both the League of Nations and world disarmament talks. In March 1935 he reinstituted the draft, formed new armored divisions, and greatly strengthened the air force. In 1936, while Britain and France were preoccupied with the Ethiopian crisis, Hitler violated the Treaty of Versailles and moved German troops back into the Rhineland.

When France protested, Hitler insisted that he was merely correcting an injustice in the Treaty of Versailles and promised that Germany had "no territorial demands to make in Europe." In mid-1936, however, Hitler stepped up his program of rearmament. "The German army," he declared, "must be fit for operations in four years' time; the German economy must be ready for war in four years' time."

Hitler's successful remilitarization of the Rhineland improved Germany's standing among other totalitarian powers. In the fall of 1936 Italy agreed to cooperate with Germany's aims, and Mussolini used the word *Axis* to describe the relationship between the two countries. In November Germany concluded the Anti-Comintern Pact with Japan, which recorded each government's opposition to communism. Italy joined the pact in November 1937. With the agreement, the three major aggressors of the 1930s had come together.

The *Anschluss*. Austria occupied a central place in Hitler's plans for German expansion. Not only did he want Austria's resources, he believed that Austria would give Germany "shorter and better frontiers." Most of Austria's population was German-speaking, and Hitler himself had been born in Austria. "Common blood," he said, "belongs in a common Reich [Empire]." On March 11, 1938, the head of the Austrian Nazi Party took over the government in Vienna. The next day he declared the *Anschluss* (AHN-shloohs), or "union," of Austria with Germany, and the German army entered Austria practically unopposed.

The *Anschluss* dramatically altered the strategic situation in Europe. Britain's Winston Churchill warned that the annexation of Austria gave Germany "military and economic control of the whole of the communications of Southeastern Europe, by road, by river, and by rail." Germany was now well positioned for eastward expansion. Nevertheless, Britain and France did not oppose Hitler's moves in Austria.

Despite the objections of Western leaders, Hitler began to revive Germany as an expansionist military power, threatening the peace of Europe.

▶ In the mid-1930's Germany secretly built up its air force and disguised it by using military planes to carry the country's mail.

Appeasement in Europe

Nazi leaders attributed their success in the 1930s largely to the inaction of the Western democracies. In fact, Western leaders had accepted Hitler's demands as part of a deliberate policy of **appeasement**—giving in to an aggressor to preserve the peace.

Reasons for appeasement. The leaders of the Western democracies adopted appeasement for a variety of reasons. For one thing, the Great Depression diverted their attention. In addition, many worried that standing against Fascist Italy and Nazi Germany required working with the Soviet Union. To many people, the totalitarian government of Joseph Stalin appeared no less brutal than those of Mussolini and Hitler.

Perhaps the greatest influence behind appeasement was the impact of World War I in the Western democracies. The enormous cost of the war in both lives and money had led to a widespread belief that all war was ineffective in achieving a nation's goals, as well as unjustifiable. Popular antiwar novels, like Erich Maria Remarque's *All Quiet on the Western Front*, reinforced such ideas.

Not even the rise of Nazism changed many people's attitudes. Soon after Hitler made clear his intention to rearm, for example, the Oxford Union, an elite university debate group in Britain, resolved, "That this House will in no circumstances fight for its King and Country." In

Across the Curriculum: Literature

After World War I, many novelists wrote books exposing the horrors of the war in an effort to encourage people to never let it happen again. *All Quiet on the Western Front* portrayed the experiences of a young German soldier on the western front. Erich Maria Remarque had fought for Germany during the war and had been wounded several times. The pathos with which he described the experience of ordinary soldiers was designed to convince his readers of the futility of war.

Ironically, Remarque's books had their greatest impact not in the Western democracies but in Germany. When the Nazis came to power, they burned Remarque's books. In 1938 they even revoked his German citizenship. After living in Switzerland, in 1939 Remarque moved to the United States, and in 1947 he became an American citizen. He continued to write about the suffering of war in several later novels about the Nazis and World War II.

Critical Thinking Ask students to suggest reasons why Germany reacted so harshly against *All Quiet on the Western Front*.

ANSWER: Students might suggest that pro-war factions in Germany objected to the novel's views.

a 1934 campaign speech, the leader of Britain's Labour Party even promised to "close every recruiting station, disband the Army and disarm the Air Force." A commonly held belief was that, as one influential British magazine put it, "Hitler . . . does not want war. He is susceptible [open] to reason in foreign policy."

The disarmament policies that many nations embraced after World War I also convinced many Western leaders that they had no choice but appeasement. Having ignored the warnings of military experts about the need to maintain and modernize their armed forces, Western leaders found themselves militarily unprepared to deal with aggression. During the Ethiopian crisis of 1935, for example, British prime minister Stanley Baldwin told his foreign minister: "Keep us out of war, we are not ready for it."

Neville Chamberlain, Baldwin's successor, perhaps best displayed the ideas of those who saw appeasement as a legitimate policy. Profoundly affected by World War I, Chamberlain was suspicious of all alliances, blaming them for the disaster of 1914. He was particularly wary of cooperating with France. He also saw the Soviet Union as a potentially greater danger than Nazi Germany. Chamberlain believed that Germany had legitimate grievances, which if resolved would ensure peace. He did not oppose rearming, but insisted that peaceful negotiation was "just as important as rearming."

The Sudetenland and Munich. One of Nazi Germany's primary grievances concerned the Sudetenland (SOO-DAYT-uhn-land), a mountainous region in northwestern Czechoslovakia. Around 3 million Germans lived in the area, which had been part of the Habsburg Empire until World War I. Although the Czech government had taken steps to protect the rights of the Sudeten Germans, Hitler complained about Czech "oppression." He claimed Czechoslovakia was a "dagger pointed at the heart of Germany." In 1938 Hitler demanded that Czechoslovakia turn the Sudetenland over to Germany.

Hitler's demand threatened war. As part of its effort to contain the German threat, France had earlier promised to support Czechoslovakia in case of German aggression. Edouard Daladier (dah-lahd-yay), the new French premier, suspected that Hitler wanted more than the Sudetenland. Daladier observed that, "The ambitions of Napoleon were far inferior to the aims of the present German Reich." However, Daladier also realized that France needed British support to stop Hitler.

Anxious to avoid war, Neville Chamberlain preferred to negotiate. With Mussolini acting as a go-between, British and French leaders met with Hitler in Munich in September 1938. While Czech leaders had to wait outside the council chamber at the **Munich Conference**, Chamberlain and Daladier agreed to German annexation of the Sudetenland, in return for Hitler's promise that this was "the last territorial claim I shall make in Europe."

After the meeting Chamberlain appeared before reporters at the London airport. Waving a copy of the agreement, he claimed to have achieved "peace in our time." A more accurate description was made by Winston Churchill, who observed: "The government had to choose

▲ In 1938 these Sudeten women express strong emotions as they salute German troops in Czechoslovakia.

between shame and war. They have chosen shame and they will get war." Churchill was right—the Munich agreement made war more likely. Hitler now believed that he had little to fear from the Western leaders. "I saw them at Munich," he said. "They are little worms." In fact, Hitler was frustrated by the Munich agreement. He had hoped for a small, glorious war that would prepare the German people for his larger plans yet to come.

Poland and the coming of war. After the Munich agreement, the situation in Europe rapidly worsened. In March 1939 Hitler took over most of the rest of Czechoslovakia and moved to recover territories lost to Germany in the east after World War I. After forcing Lithuania to return the port of Memel, he focused his main attention on Poland.

In 1919 the Treaty of Versailles had established the Baltic port of Danzig as a free city. The treaty had also carved territory from Germany to provide Poland with an outlet to Danzig and the sea. Hitler now demanded the return of both Danzig and the "Polish Corridor." Although he eventually intended to attack the Soviet Union, Hitler first sought Stalin's cooperation in actions against

◄ Neville Chamberlain returns to London with the Munich agreement.

Poland. He secretly negotiated a treaty that would isolate Poland and thereby reinforce Germany's position against Britain and France.

In August 1939 Hitler announced a German-Soviet nonaggression pact. Stalin agreed because he had his own expansionist aims. Germany and the Soviet Union agreed to partition Poland between them, and Germany recognized Soviet "authority" in the Baltic states and parts of the Middle East. Now that Hitler felt no threat from the Soviet Union, the German army invaded Poland on September 1, 1939.

Britain and France, deciding finally that they could no longer tolerate German aggression, issued an ultimatum demanding an immediate German withdrawal from Poland. Hitler ignored their demands, and on September 3, 1939, Britain and France declared war on Germany. World War II had begun.

Unwilling to risk another war like World War I, the Western democracies followed a policy of appeasement toward Hitler's demands.

SECTION 1 REVIEW

IDENTIFY and explain the significance of the following:
Haile Selassie
Spanish Civil War
Francisco Franco
appeasement
Neville Chamberlain
Edouard Daladier
Munich Conference

LOCATE and explain the importance of the following (see the map on p. 691):

Sudetenland
Munich
Polish Corridor

1. **Main Idea** How well did the League of Nations keep peace in the world during the 1930s?
2. **Main Idea** How did Hitler's plans for Germany threaten the peace of Europe?
3. **War and Diplomacy** What was the western European

powers' response to Hitler's aggression?
4. **Writing to Explain** Imagine that you are a Czech citizen of the Sudetenland at the time of the Munich Conference. Write a letter to a friend explaining the current political situation and your personal feelings about it.
5. **Analyzing** What was the significance of the German-Soviet nonaggression pact?

CORE LESSON PLAN
See pages 681E and
681F for Lesson Plan
25.2.

Theme: Technology

World War II saw the complete integration of industrial technology and warfare. In its attack on Poland, Germany unleashed a new concept of mechanized warfare. Blitzkrieg involved several phases. First, dive-bombers destroyed the Polish air force on the ground. Next, tanks and armored vehicles swept across the border, blasting their way into Polish territory. Finally, infantry forces consolidated German control over the conquered territory.

Critical Thinking Ask students why the Germans would destroy the Polish air force first.

ANSWER: Students should answer that removing the danger of air attacks made ground troops safer.

SECTION 2
The Early Years of the War

FOCUS

- How did the war develop in western Europe in 1940 and early 1941?

- What was Hitler's primary goal, and how did he try to accomplish it in the summer of 1941?

- How did Japanese policies in Asia widen the war?

In the three years between 1939 and 1942, a war that had begun in Poland rapidly expanded. By 1942 all of the world's major powers had declared war, forming two great blocs. On one side, Italy and Japan joined with Germany and came to be called the Axis Powers. On the other side, the Soviet Union, the United States, and China joined with Great Britain and France and became known as the Allied Powers.

The Blitzkrieg begins as German tanks enter a Polish village in 1939.

From "Phony War" to the Fall of France

Hitler's attack on Poland was swift and severe. In what became known as **Blitzkrieg**, or "lightning war," German dive-bombers screamed down on the Poles from the skies, while German tanks destroyed all resistance in their path. Unprepared for modern mechanized warfare, the desperate Poles sometimes tried to battle German tanks with mounted cavalry.

In mid-September the Soviet army also invaded Poland, and within weeks the two armies had crushed Polish resistance. Divided up by Germany and the Soviet Union, Poland once again disappeared from the map of Europe. In November 1939 the Soviets attacked Finland. Although the Finns resisted vigorously, they were defeated by March 1940 and were forced to give up some territory to the Soviet Union. Soon thereafter, the Soviets seized Latvia, Lithuania, and Estonia. Confronted with such open aggression, a helpless League of Nations could only expel the Soviet Union from membership.

The "phony war." Despite the declarations of war, things remained so calm in western Europe that newspapers began to write of the "phony war" there. The calm was deceptive, however. Hitler had already begun planning for an offensive against France and Britain, but the coming of winter forced him to delay until the spring of 1940. In the meantime, both France and Britain began preparing for the German attack. The French massed their troops along the Maginot (ma-zhuh-noh) Line, a system of huge steel and concrete fortifications along France's border with Germany and Luxembourg. Meanwhile, Britain sent an army across the English Channel to take up defensive positions in northern France.

Scandinavia and the Low Countries. In April 1940 Hitler's plan finally began to unfold in stages. On April 9 he struck against Denmark and Norway. Both countries quickly fell under German control. Norway was particularly important in Hitler's strategy because it provided air bases from which German forces could attack Allied shipping in the North Atlantic. The long Norwegian coastline also provided good bases for German submarines.

German and Italian Expansion, 1935–1941

Map legend:
- Germany, 1935
- Acquired by Germany, 1935–1939
- German protectorates and Vichy France
- Italy and possessions, 1935
- Acquired by Italy, 1935–1939
- Minor Axis powers, 1941
- → Axis advances
- Controlled by Axis, December 1941
- Controlled by Allies, December 1941
- Area of the Battle of Britain
- Neutral countries
- Farthest Soviet advance, 1940

Ethiopia, 1935–1941

The Fascist Advance The aggressive conquests of Germany and Italy in the late 1930s destroyed the fragile territorial agreements resulting from World War I.

? Location What countries did Italy control in 1935? What additional countries had it invaded by 1939?

Map Answer
Libya, Eritrea, and Italian Somaliland; Albania and Ethiopia

Theme: **War and Diplomacy**
The defensive structure known as the Maginot Line cost the French million of francs. It consisted of a vast series of underground bunkers and fortresses, connected by tunnels and underground railways that could be used to defend the entire frontier against any attack from Germany. However, the Maginot Line proved virtually useless against the German attack in 1940.

Critical Thinking Ask students why the French believed the Maginot Line would be a useful defense.

ANSWER: Students may answer that in building the Maginot Line the French had prepared themselves to defend against the type of trench fighting of World War I.

RESOURCE ACTIVITY

READINGS IN WORLD HISTORY
Reading 25.2
The Evacuation of Dunkirk

Have students read the selection and complete the questions.

| Level 2 |

The following month the German army invaded the Low Countries—Luxembourg, the Netherlands, and Belgium—and by the end of May all three had fallen. Having effectively outflanked the Maginot Line, German tanks drove west toward the English Channel in a successful move that cut off British, Belgian, and French troops in northern France from French forces in the south.

Dunkirk. The Allied forces retreated to Dunkirk, a small French coastal village. The desperate Allies had only one alternative to surrender—retreat by sea. As the British Royal Air Force

struggled to keep the skies free of German planes, every available ship and boat in southern England moved to the French coast to rescue the trapped soldiers. In what seemed a miracle, between May 26 and June 4, some 338,000 soldiers were transported across the Channel to safety in Britain.

The fall of France. After Dunkirk the struggle for France lasted less than a month. Mussolini declared war on the Allies and invaded southern France. Days later the German army entered Paris. Rather than surrender, the entire French cabinet resigned, and a new government was formed by an elderly World War I hero, Marshal

The Vichy regime not only collaborated with the Germans but also sought to institute a conservative authoritarian rule to replace the weak Third Republic. Although some French people continued to struggle, either in the resistance or under the banner of Charles de Gaulle's Free French government in exile, most French people acquiesced to the Vichy regime and the German occupation. Vichy officials became involved in rounding up laborers for the German war effort and Jews for transportation to the death camps. After the war Pétain and other Vichy leaders were tried and condemned to death for their roles. While Pétain's sentence was reduced to imprisonment due to his advanced age, others, including his deputy Pierre Laval, were executed. Even then, collaboration remained a touchy subject in postwar France, as most people tried to forget or deny the extent to which they had cooperated with the Germans.

Critical Thinking Ask students why the French might have wanted to forget or deny collaboration with the Vichy government.

ANSWER: Students might answer that the French did not want to admit that they had willingly helped the Nazis and that they did not want to remember difficult times during the war.

Teenagers IN HISTORY

Anti-Hitler Youth

German teenagers had different reactions to the Third Reich. Most, either by choice or under pressure from adults and peers, became part of the "Hitler Youth," a National Socialist organization that prepared them to become members of the Nazi Party and to serve their country. Some teenagers, however, rejected the racist and militaristic beliefs of the Hitler Youth. Two groups in particular—the Edelweiss Pirates and the Swing Youth—rebelled.

The first Edelweiss Pirates, groups of teens 14 to 18 years old, appeared at the end of the 1930s in several cities in western Germany. In their free time, they often took trips together, on which they could camp, sing popular songs considered inappropriate for the youth of Germany, and taunt the Hitler Youth patrols. Some occasionally attacked and beat up the members of the Hitler Youth. During World War II some went so far as to distribute Allied propaganda and to shelter German army deserters, escaped prisoners of war, and concentration camp prisoners.

The Swing Youth group developed among Germany's upper middle-class youth. These teenagers avoided the "suitable" folk music encouraged by German authorities and instead listened and danced to jazz and swing music, which was condemned by the Nazis. The Swing Youth made their music and dancing into a symbol of a youth culture that rejected the Hitler Youth ideals. Long hair for the boys, English-looking clothes, modern dancing, and an acceptance of Jews into their groups were all ways that this group rejected Nazism. Like the Edelweiss Pirates, however, the Swing Youth generally managed to avoid direct confrontation with the authorities.

Bartholomäus Schink was hanged by the SS on November 10, 1944, for being a member of the Edelweiss Pirates.

Philippe Pétain (pay-tan). On June 22, in the same railway car in which the Germans had signed the armistice in 1918, Pétain signed a surrender agreement dictated by Hitler.

The terms of this agreement were even more severe than those of the armistice of 1918. Germany occupied about three fifths of France, including Paris. Only the southern part of France was left under Pétain's control, with its capital in Vichy (VISH-ee). Thus, the Germans divided the country into occupied France under their own rule and **Vichy France**, which collaborated with the Germans.

In France secret armed groups, known collectively as the **"resistance,"** began to form to fight against the Germans. The French resistance conducted numerous rescue and sabotage operations. Similar resistance movements appeared in most of the other countries occupied by the Nazis, including Germany. Charles de Gaulle (duh GOHL) formed a government in exile in London, calling on French forces worldwide to continue fighting Germany. De Gaulle's "Free French" government organized army and air force units that served with the other Allied forces.

In 1940 Germany launched lightning-fast assaults on Europe, overrunning Scandinavia, the Low Countries, and France.

Britain Alone

The fall of France left Britain standing alone against Germany and Italy. In May 1940 Neville Chamberlain was replaced as prime minister by Winston Churchill.

Britain and Churchill. Churchill was born in 1874, the son of Lord Randolph Churchill, one of Britain's leading statesmen, and Jenny Jerome, an American heiress. As a young man Churchill attended the Royal Military College at Sandhurst and served in the army for four years. After achieving some fame as a war correspondent in Africa, Churchill entered politics in 1900 as a Conservative member of Parliament. He soon switched to the Liberal Party, and in 1911 became first lord of the Admiralty.

After the failure of the Gallipoli campaign during World War I (for which many people blamed him), Churchill resigned from the government and served as an officer with a British regiment on the western front. In 1917 he reentered the cabinet as minister of munitions. After the war Churchill served as colonial secretary and eventually became chancellor of the exchequer. Although he rejoined the Conservative Party, during most of the 1930s Churchill remained isolated even within his own party because of his outspoken opposition to self-government for India. After the rise of Hitler, he also became a strong supporter of rearmament and constantly warned of the growing Nazi danger.

After rejoining the cabinet, in May 1940 Churchill replaced Neville Chamberlain as prime minister. Promising nothing but "blood, toil, sweat, and tears," Churchill nevertheless inspired the British people. Shortly before France fell, he declared his policy:

66 We shall go on to the end, we shall fight in France, we shall fight on the seas and oceans, we shall fight with growing confidence and growing strength in the air, we shall defend our island, whatever the cost may be, we shall fight on the beaches, we shall fight on the landing grounds; we shall fight in the hills and in the streets; we shall never surrender. 99

The Battle of Britain and the Blitz. In the summer of 1940, the German air force, or *Luftwaffe* (LOOFT-vah-fuh), began a series of raids. These raids, along with British efforts to counter them, became known as the **Battle of Britain**. Their purpose was to destroy Britain's air force in preparation for a German invasion. The *Luftwaffe* attacks took a heavy toll on Britain, but British defenses proved so effective that Hitler soon grew impatient. The new British technology of **radar** could detect German airplanes at long ranges. Such early warning of raids gave British fighters time to counterattack.

By September 1940 Hitler decided to indefinitely postpone his plans to invade Britain. Churchill gave credit for the victory to Britain's fighter pilots: "Never in the field of human conflict was so much owed by so many to so few." Hitler then tried to force Britain into submission by bombing its cities. Between September 1940 and May 1941, Britain endured the **Blitz**—regular nighttime air raids against London and other major cities. Britain retaliated with air raids on German cities. The Blitz claimed about 43,000 civilian lives, left thousands homeless, and caused enormous damage, particularly in London. Nevertheless, the British held firm, and in May 1941 the Blitz ended.

▲ **In 1940 British pilots race to their fighter planes during the Battle of Britain.**

Winston Churchill
BIOGRAPHY

As early as September 1939, British authorities, fearing potential air attacks, began preparations for evacuating children from parts of London. Thousands of children were relocated from the great city to temporary homes in the countryside beyond the reach of German bombers. Later, as the Blitz began, many parents sent their children overseas to the United States and Canada. For some children, particularly those from poorer neighborhoods, the relocation gave them their first glimpse of the green fields and countryside that lay beyond London. Although the relocation separated families, it also saved many lives as London underwent the punishment of the Blitz.

Critical Thinking Ask students how World War II might have affected British children.

ANSWER: Students may suggest that by separating children from their families, World War II taught British children to be independent and gave them the opportunity to experience new ways of life.

Britain's lifelines. While war raged in the skies over Britain, the Axis Powers also challenged Britain's overseas communications with its empire. Britain's old dominions of Canada, New Zealand, Australia, and South Africa, as well as India and the other colonies, all made substantial contributions to the war effort. Ensuring communications by sea between these areas, which provided both troops and raw materials for the war, was vital to Britain's survival. Italy's entry into the war threatened Britain's position in Egypt and control of the vital Suez Canal. Italian forces invaded Egypt in September 1940, but a British counterattack quickly repelled them. It was Britain's first major land victory in the war.

In early 1941 British forces invaded Italian-occupied Ethiopia. In May the exiled emperor Haile Selassie returned, and by the end of the year, Britain had driven the Italians out of Ethiopia. In the meantime, however, the situation in Egypt had worsened for Britain. Hitler sent German troops to support Italy's army in North Africa. Led by an inventive officer named Erwin Rommel, Hitler's Afrika Korps began arriving in Libya in February 1941. Rommel's goal was to capture Egypt and the Suez Canal, then ultimately the strategic oil fields of the Middle East.

In addition, Hitler launched a major U-boat offensive in the Atlantic Ocean. German submarines tried to halt the flow of supplies and soldiers into Britain. For Britain, maintaining this overseas lifeline to its empire and to the United States was critical. Churchill realized that an Allied victory would be possible only if the United States joined Britain in war.

Growing American involvement. Barriers existed to U.S. involvement, however. In the 1930s American isolationists had tried to keep the United States out of war by convincing Congress to pass a series of **Neutrality Acts**. These acts prohibited loans and arms sales to warring nations. On the other hand, after the war broke out, many Americans, including President Franklin Roosevelt, sympathized with Britain and the Allies.

Anxious to prevent a Nazi victory, Roosevelt convinced Congress in 1939 to revise the Neutrality Acts to allow weapons to be sold to warring nations. Such measures made the Atlantic sea-lanes even more crucial to Britain.

In September 1940 Roosevelt traded aging American destroyers, which Britain needed to escort its convoys, for six British bases in the Atlantic. The next year he convinced Congress to authorize **Lend-Lease**, which allowed the United States to supply war materials to Britain on credit. By the fall the U.S. Navy and Coast Guard were helping the British escort convoys and detect U-boats.

The growing cooperation between Britain and the United States led to a meeting between Churchill and Roosevelt off the coast of Newfoundland in August 1941. Together they issued a statement of democratic goals in the war, which became known as the **Atlantic Charter**. The charter stated that neither power sought territorial gains and that each believed in the principle of national self-determination.

▲ While much of the East End of London crumbled in the Blitz, Saint Paul's Cathedral remained standing.

After the fall of France in 1940, Britain stood alone against Hitler's forces.

▲ U.S. Coast Guard sailors watch the convoy of British merchant ships that they are escorting.

Operation Barbarossa

Although Britain remained undefeated, in 1941 Hitler turned back toward his primary goal—the conquest of the Soviet Union. To increase his strength he had secured the alliance of Hungary and Romania in 1940, and in early 1941 he convinced Bulgaria to align with the Axis Powers. He also invaded Yugoslavia. Shortly thereafter, Hitler sent German troops to support the Italian forces that had invaded Greece the previous year. By June 1941 Hitler controlled most of Europe.

On June 22 Hitler launched **Operation Barbarossa**—the invasion of the Soviet Union. The German army and air force employed the same Blitzkrieg tactics used in western Europe. The *Luftwaffe* caught the Soviet air force on the ground and claimed to have destroyed nearly 3,000 aircraft in the first 10 days alone. By fall the German army had advanced deep into Soviet territory.

As the Soviet army and civilians retreated, they followed a "scorched earth" policy, carrying away what they could and destroying what remained—buildings, crops, and equipment. In late September and early October, the Soviet Union experienced heavy rains, turning the ground to mud and bogging down Germany's mechanized forces. The German army did not approach Moscow until late fall. By December the bitter cold had further slowed their operations. Only 18 miles from Moscow, the German advance ground to a halt.

Although Stalin had cooperated with Hitler earlier, the Allies decided to support the Soviet Union against Germany, hoping to keep Hitler occupied on the eastern front. British convoys began to make dangerous runs to bring supplies to the Soviet Union, skirting German air and submarine bases in Norway to reach ports in the Soviet north. In August 1941 British and Soviet forces jointly occupied Iran, deposing its ruler, Reza Shah, who was sympathetic to the Germans, in order to establish a secure overland supply route to the Soviet Union. The United States also tried to help by offering Lend-Lease aid to the Soviets.

With most of western Europe under his control, in June 1941 Hitler finally turned toward his ultimate goal—conquering the Soviet Union.

Japan and the United States

Although war did not break out in Europe until 1939, fighting had already begun in East Asia, where Japan had invaded China in 1937. Japan's invasion of China strained its relations with Britain and the United States.

Worried by their dependency on the United States for strategic materials, particularly oil, Japanese leaders longed for sources of supplies that they could control directly. Many eyed the oil-rich British and Dutch colonies in the East Indies. In the fall of 1940, Japanese leaders began to send troops into French Indochina. Prime Minister Konoye hesitated to go farther since seizure of the East Indies would mean war with the Netherlands and Britain—and probably the United States. In October 1941, however, Hideki Tojo, Japan's war minister, replaced Konoye as prime minister and quickly set his country on a course for war.

Japanese plans. The Japanese realized that their most dangerous potential enemy was the United States, which had a large Pacific naval fleet. Convinced that the United States would overwhelm Japan in war, Admiral Isoroku Yamamoto, commander in chief of the Japanese fleet, believed Japan's only real chance for victory was to knock out the U.S. Pacific Fleet quickly. This would give Japan time to build its forces in the central Pacific against a U.S. counterattack. Earlier in 1941 Yamamoto had already devised a plan in which aircraft carriers would launch a surprise air raid on the U.S. fleet based at Pearl Harbor in Hawaii.

R RESOURCE ACTIVITY

GLOBAL HISTORY RESOURCE CENTER
Map: *Operation Barbarossa*

Show students the map as you discuss the German assault on the Soviet Union. As students study the map, ask them to imagine they are German generals who must choose three targets to attack. Have students write a short memo explaining why they have chosen these targets and what they hope to accomplish.

Level 3

R RESOURCE ACTIVITY

GLOBAL HISTORY RESOURCE CENTER
Image: *The Japanese Attack on Pearl Habor*

Display the image to students. After a brief discussion of the photograph, have students write two newspaper headlines that might have appeared after the Pearl Harbor bombing.

Level 1/ Sheltered English

✓ REVIEW & ASSESSMENT RESOURCES

- Study Guide 25.2
- Daily Quiz 25.2
- Main Idea Activity 25.2

All Levels

By late fall of 1941, Japanese-American relations had reached a crisis, largely because of Japan's actions in French Indochina. The Japanese government sent a delegation to the United States, supposedly to resolve the crisis. In fact, Japan had already decided to wage war. In late November Tojo had obtained the consent of the Japanese emperor, Hirohito, to carry out his plans for war.

American entry into World War II. On the morning of December 7, 1941, planes from four Japanese aircraft carriers attacked Pearl Harbor, sinking six of the eight American battleships, damaging the others, and killing more than 2,400 Americans. In spite of the attack's apparent success, Yamamoto cautioned his returning officers not to be overly confident:

“*The real fighting is to come. The success of one surprise attack must not lead to any slackening-off. . . . You are far from having conquered. You have come home only temporarily, to prepare for the next battle.*”

In fact, the attack was not a clear success for the Japanese. It had failed to hit either the U.S. fleet's carriers or its submarines, which would prove vital in the coming Pacific war.

On the same day that Japan's fleet attacked Pearl Harbor, Japanese planes bombed U.S. positions on Guam and Wake Island. The Japanese also launched an attack on British positions in Malaya and Singapore. A few weeks later the Japanese began to land troops in the U.S.-held Philippines. Within six months the islands had fallen. On December 25, 1941, the British colony of Hong Kong also surrendered to Japan. In January 1942 Japan invaded its primary target—the Netherlands East Indies. By March Japan controlled the oil-rich islands.

Meanwhile, Japan's attack on Pearl Harbor pulled the United States into World War II. The day after the attack, President Roosevelt addressed Congress, calling December 7 "a date which will live in infamy" and asking for a declaration of war against Japan. Three days later Germany and Italy declared war on the United States. By the end of 1941 all the world's major powers were engaged in the global conflict.

As part of their plan to dominate East Asia, the Japanese attacked the U.S. Pacific Fleet at Pearl Harbor, thereby bringing the United States into World War II.

◄ A U.S. ship explodes in Pearl Harbor after being hit by a Japanese bomb on December 7, 1941.

SECTION 2 REVIEW

IDENTIFY and explain the significance of the following:
   Blitzkrieg
   Vichy France
   resistance
   Winston Churchill
   Battle of Britain
   radar
   Blitz
   Erwin Rommel
   Neutrality Acts
   Lend-Lease
   Atlantic Charter
   Operation Barbarossa

1. **Main Idea** How did World War II progress in 1940 and early 1941?
2. **Main Idea** What was the Germans' main objective in 1941, and how did they try to achieve it?
3. **War and Diplomacy** What effect did Japanese ambitions in East Asia have on the war?
4. **Writing to Explain** Write a short essay explaining how Britain was able to resist Hitler after most of Europe had fallen.
5. **Hypothesizing** How might the early years of World War II have been different if the United States had refused to help Britain?

The Holocaust and Other Atrocities of War

SECTION 3

CORE LESSON PLAN
See pages 681G and 681H for Lesson Plan 25.3.

FOCUS

- What were the results of Hitler's racial policies during the war?
- What resulted from the Japanese view of conquered enemies?
- Why were so many atrocities committed by the Soviet Union during the war?

World War II witnessed acts of extraordinary brutality. Totalitarian governments used the war as an excuse to eliminate people whom they regarded as enemies of the state. Hitler decided on the extermination of a whole people—the Jews. The dictatorial governments of Japan and the Soviet Union also committed acts of unspeakable inhumanity during the war.

Orphan at the Buchenwald concentration camp

Hitler's Racial Imperialism

Much of the brutality of World War II in Europe was inspired by Nazi racial policies. Hitler's primary goal in launching World War II was to conquer "living space" in eastern Europe and the Soviet Union and to colonize it with Germans. As part of this plan, Hitler anticipated the destruction or enslavement of the Slavic population of eastern Europe and Russia.

The Holocaust. To ensure the "purity" of his new German empire, Hitler planned to eliminate the Jews from Europe in what he called the "Final Solution." Hitler had declared his intentions in *Mein Kampf,* and throughout the 1930s the Nazis had increasingly persecuted German Jews. During the war these policies extended to Jews living in countries occupied by Germany. In 1941 Hitler decided to carry out their final destruction. To the rest of the world, this act of genocide has become known as the **Holocaust**.

The man largely responsible for carrying out Hitler's vision of racial extermination was Heinrich Himmler, head of the *Schutzstaffel,* or **SS**, the military arm of the Nazi Party. In 1941, shortly before the invasion of the Soviet Union, Himmler announced that one aim of the upcoming campaign was "to decimate [decrease drastically] the Slav population by thirty million" to make way for German settlers. Himmler also wrote, "The occupied Eastern territories are to become free of Jews. The execution of this very grave order has been placed on my shoulders by the Führer."

Initially, the SS simply rounded up Jews and shot them on the spot, but they soon developed a more efficient method of extermination—the use of poison gas. In January 1942 senior Nazi officials met in Wannsee (VAHN-zay), a suburb of Berlin. At the **Wannsee Conference** the Nazis finalized their plans for the systematic extermination of the Jews. Over the next three years the SS transported all the European Jews they could find to concentration camps, mainly in eastern Germany and Poland.

The death camps. Jews arrived in the camps by the hundreds of thousands. Once there, SS officers sorted the Jews by age, health, and sex, instantly tearing apart families. The officers

Theme: Politics and Law

The SS began as an armed guard within the *Sturmabteilung* (SA), or Storm Troops, the Nazi private army. Its initial purpose was to provide protection for the Führer and other top leaders. In 1929 the SS came under the command of Heinrich Himmler, a bitter anti-Semite. During the 1930s the SS encouraged Jewish emigration to Palestine. After the war began, however, the SS became the primary instrument for annihilating the Jews of Europe.

Critical Thinking Ask students why the German policy toward Jewish immigration changed.

ANSWER: Students might answer that the war offered an excuse to take an extreme position toward the Jews.

Theme: Technology

At Auschwitz the extermination process itself was run like a business. Private German firms competed for the right to build the "processing unit," whose specifications required a capacity "to dispose of 2,000 bodies every twelve hours." Companies such as I. G. Farben, which made the gas used to murder so many Jews, saw their dividends double between 1942 and 1944.

Critical Thinking Ask students why this businesslike attitude adds to the horror of the Holocaust.

ANSWER: Students might suggest that it represents the ways in which the Nazis devalued certain human beings.

"selected" many for immediate execution and took them off in large groups to gas chambers on the pretext that they were going to take "showers." Those considered healthy enough went to work in camp factories, where regular beatings and slow starvation awaited them. Some found themselves the subjects of cruel medical experiments—including operations conducted without anesthesia. Those not immediately executed had numbers tattooed on their forearms for permanent identification.

Perhaps the most notorious of the camps was **Auschwitz** (OWSH-vits) in southern Poland. Elie Wiesel (vee-ZEL), a survivor of Auschwitz, later described his arrival in the camp at the age of 14:

> An SS noncommissioned officer came to meet us, a truncheon [club] in his hand. He gave the order:
>
> 'Men to the left! Women to the right!'
>
> Eight words spoken quietly, indifferently, without emotion. Eight short, simple words. Yet that was the moment when I parted from my mother. I had not had time to think, but already I felt the pressure of my father's hand: we were alone. For a part of a second I glimpsed my mother and my sisters moving away to the right. Tzipora held Mother's hand. I saw them disappear into the distance; my mother was stroking my sister's fair hair, as though to protect her, while I walked on with my father and the other men. And I did not know that in that place, at that moment, I was parting from my mother and Tzipora forever. 99

Most people sent to the camps were killed. The largest number were Jews, but the Nazis also killed significant numbers of others—Slavs, gypsies, political dissidents, and homosexuals—anyone the Nazis thought stood in the way of their efforts to achieve racial purity.

Initially, the Nazis buried their victims in mass graves, but eventually they resorted to huge ovens in which the dead were cremated. Before the bodies were disposed of, however, the Nazis forced concentration camp prisoners to extract gold fillings from the teeth of the dead and to collect hair, which was to be used for such things as stuffing for the seat cushions of military vehicles.

The exact number of people who died in the Holocaust will never be known, but an estimated 6 million Jews were killed. Half of this number came from Poland and represented 90 percent of that country's Jewish population. The Jews of Germany, Austria, and the Baltic states went to the camps in similar proportions.

Concentration Camps, 1933–1945

The Camps As the German army invaded surrounding countries, Hitler ordered the construction of concentration camps, which became sites of enforced labor and death.

? Location Which European country contained the most death camps? the most labor camps?

Literature THROUGH TIME

Survival in Auschwitz

The horrors of the Nazi death camps have been described in the journals and remembrances of many survivors. Primo Levi, an Italian Jew who was captured and sent to Auschwitz in 1944, recorded in his book Survival in Auschwitz *the terrors that awaited him there. At one point in his account, Levi remembers the terrible "selections" that often took place in Auschwitz, where the SS guards would decide which prisoners would live and which would go to the gas chambers:*

Now we are all in the *Tagesraum* [common room], and . . . there is not even any room in which to be afraid. . . . One has to take care to hold up one's nose so as to breathe, and not to crumple or lose the card in one's hand.

The *Blockältester* [block leader] has closed the connecting-door and has opened the other two which lead from the dormitory and the *Tagesraum* outside. Here, in front of the two doors, stands the arbiter [one who decides] of our fate, an SS subaltern [junior officer]. On his right is the *Blockältester*, on his left, the quartermaster of the hut. Each one of us, as he comes naked out of the *Tagesraum* into the cold October air, has to run the few steps between the two doors, give the card to the SS man and enter the dormitory door. The SS man, in the fraction of a second between two successive crossings, with a glance at one's back and front, judges everyone's fate, and in turn gives the card to the man on his right or his left, and this is the life or death of each of us. . . .

Even before the selection is over, everybody knows that the left was effectively the "*schlechte Seite*," the bad side. There have naturally been some irregularities: René, for example, so young and robust, ended on the left; perhaps it was because he has glasses, perhaps because he walks a little stooped . . . , but more probably because

of a simple mistake: René passed the commission immediately in front of me and there could have been a mistake with our cards. I think about it, discuss it with Alberto, and we agree that the hypothesis is probable; I do not know what I will think tomorrow and later; today I feel no distinct emotion. . . .

There is nothing surprising about these mistakes: the examination is too quick and summary, and in any case, the important thing for the Lager [camp] is not that the most useless prisoners be eliminated, but that free posts be quickly created, according to a certain percentage previously fixed.

Understanding Literature

1. What determines if Levi lives or dies in the selection?
2. How does he feel about the outcome?

Prisoner separation at Auschwitz

Across the Curriculum: Literature

The Diary of Anne Frank is the now-classic account of a young Jewish girl in Amsterdam who hides from the Germans. The family began hiding in the attic of an office building in Amsterdam in 1942. For two years Anne kept a diary of her life. In 1944 the family was betrayed, and Anne Frank died in the Belsen death camp shortly thereafter.

Critical Thinking Ask students why Anne Frank's story is so compelling.

ANSWER: Students might suggest that because of her youth, Frank's sufferings seem undeserved and particularly touching.

Understanding Literature

1. a brief glance from the junior SS officer
2. He feels matter of fact.

RESOURCE ACTIVITY

GLOBAL HISTORY RESOURCE CENTER
Image: *Rounding Up Jews in the Warsaw Ghetto*

Show students the image as you discuss the Warsaw Ghetto. Ask students to create a flyer to be distributed in the United States asking for help for European Jews.

Level 1/ Sheltered English

Resistance to the Holocaust. As the horrifying reality of the Holocaust became clear, some Jews began to resist. The fiercest resistance occurred in the Jewish ghetto of Warsaw, Poland. With few weapons, however, the Jewish fighters were no match for German forces, and eventually

the ghetto was reduced to rubble. The Jewish populations of Europe had long been the targets of anti-Semitism and persecution. However, most were unprepared for Nazi ruthlessness. Although most people in Europe quietly ignored what was happening to the Jews, some did not. In Denmark, for example, the German occupying authorities ordered all Jews to wear the Star of David on their clothing for identification purposes. Some Danes recognized this as a warning for what was to come. The Danes managed to help some 6,500 Danish Jews escape into neutral Sweden to keep them out of Nazi hands.

One remarkable case of heroism occurred in Hungary. Raoul Wallenberg, a Swedish diplomat living in Budapest, used his position to save as many Jews as possible, declaring them to be under the protection of the Swedish Embassy. Wallenberg, however, disappeared after the war, probably imprisoned by Soviet authorities who feared that he would report on their own wartime atrocities.

A similar case occurred in Poland and Czechoslovakia. Oskar Schindler, a German industrialist under contract to the German government, secretly saved as many Jews as he could from the death camps by employing them in his factories. Eventually he went bankrupt in the process. Such acts of heroism, however, were few and far between.

Other atrocities. Hitler's SS was also responsible for a number of atrocities other than the Holocaust. The SS often employed particularly brutal measures to put down resistance in German-occupied countries. In Yugoslavia, for example, the SS carried out reprisals, executing specified numbers of local people in revenge for attacks carried out by resistance fighters hiding in the hills. In many cases the SS wiped out whole villages in reprisal for resistance attacks.

The Nazi SS was also guilty of mistreating Allied prisoners of war. Moreover, during the last major German offensive of the war, SS units under orders to take no prisoners massacred Allied soldiers who had surrendered near the Belgian town of Malmédy. Such cases were rare on the western front, but the eastern front was a different story. Treatment of Soviet prisoners was more brutal, perhaps because of Nazi racial propaganda that branded Slavs as "subhuman."

▶ Japanese soldiers prevented Chinese civilians from receiving British and French supplies in 1939.

In keeping with Hitler's racial theory, the Nazis carried out the genocide of most of Europe's Jews, as well as the elimination of other "undesirables" by special SS units.

Japanese Atrocities

The Nazis were not alone in their cruel treatment. The Japanese army often treated civilian populations in areas it occupied with extraordinary brutality, viewing those who surrendered as being dishonorable. One of the worst cases occurred in December 1937 when Japanese troops occupied the Chinese city of Nanking. For two weeks they looted, burned stores and homes, and conducted mass executions. After the war one Chinese officer testified to Japanese atrocities he had witnessed in Nanking:

66 *I estimate there were above 5,000 who were marched four abreast, and the line was 3/4 of a mile long. When we arrived there [on the bank of the Yangtze River] we were placed in a line near the River. . . . Men were tied five in a group with their wrists tied below their backs, and I saw the first men who were shot by rifles . . . and who were then thrown in the river by the Japanese. . . . We [had] . . . arrived at the bank of the River about seven o'clock, and the binding of the prisoners and shooting kept up until two o'clock in the morning.* 99

During their rampage Japanese troops murdered about 250,000 people in Nanking.

The Japanese army also proved particularly brutal in its treatment of prisoners of war. In the

Philippines, for example, Japanese soldiers subjected about 78,000 starving and exhausted American and Filipino prisoners to a 65-mile forced march up the Bataan Peninsula in 1942. Along the way, Japanese guards beat, bayoneted, shot, and even beheaded many of the prisoners. They killed over 600 Americans and as many as 10,000 Filipinos. The incident became known as the **Bataan Death March**. In other cases, the Japanese army used prisoners for research in chemical and biological warfare and for cruel medical experiments.

Viewing conquered enemies as people without honor, Japanese soldiers treated them with great brutality.

▲ These U.S. prisoners were photographed in 1942, when they were allowed to pause on the Bataan Death March.

Soviet Atrocities

The Axis Powers were not the only totalitarian governments practicing acts of brutality. For nearly two years, between September 1939 and June 1941, the Soviet Union occupied the eastern half of Poland. Soviet policy in Poland bore a striking resemblance to that of the Nazis, but it reflected communist ideas rather than racial theory.

The Soviets did not single out Jews for elimination. Instead, they went after specific classes of the population—landowners, local officials, clergy, teachers, and intellectuals. They urged peasants to murder their landlords. One Soviet pamphlet read: "For Poles, masters and dogs—a dog's death." Soviet officers talked of three types of Poles: "Those who were in prison; those who are in prison; and those who will be in prison."

The **NKVD**, the Soviet equivalent of Hitler's SS, arrived in Poland with the Soviet army. The NKVD subjected thousands of Poles to torture, imprisonment, and execution. They deported about 1.5 million Poles to labor camps in the Soviet Union. Around half of those deported may have died. Sometime in 1940 Soviet forces murdered some 15,000 Polish officers. About 4,000 of them were buried in mass graves near Smolensk. Before retreating in the face of the German invasion of 1941, the NKVD simply began shooting many of the Poles it had imprisoned, probably executing close to 100,000.

The Soviet government also saw the war as an excuse to eliminate people it regarded as enemies of the state.

SECTION 3 REVIEW

IDENTIFY and explain the significance of the following:
  Holocaust
  Heinrich Himmler
  SS
  Wannsee Conference
  Auschwitz
  Raoul Wallenberg
  Bataan Death March
  NKVD

1. **Main Idea** How were Hitler's racial policies put into effect during the war?
2. **Main Idea** How did Japanese soldiers view conquered enemies, and what was the result of this view?
3. **War and Diplomacy** What atrocities did the Soviet Union commit in the war, and why?
4. **Writing to Explain** Write a short essay explaining why you think so many people could have ignored the Holocaust, and how other people fought against it.
5. **Analyzing** How did modern industrial technology help the Nazis in carrying out the "Final Solution"?

SECTION 4
Allied Victories

FOCUS

- How did the war develop in Europe between 1943 and 1945?
- How did the war develop in Asia and the Pacific?
- What finally brought the war against Japan to an end?
- What were the costs of World War II?

*I*n January 1943 Churchill and Roosevelt *met in the Moroccan city of Casablanca. There they agreed to seek unconditional surrender of each of the Axis Powers—Germany, Italy, and Japan. Only two months before the meeting, Allied troops had landed in Morocco, taking control of the country from Vichy France. With that operation, events had begun to turn against the Axis.*

This early color photograph taken in Stalingrad shows a woman preparing a meal in the remains of a stove.

Turning Points in the European War

The turning of the tide against Hitler began in North Africa. By mid-1942 Rommel and his Afrika Korps had advanced nearly 200 miles into Egypt. Short of supplies and overextended, the Germans were forced to retreat in late October by British and Commonwealth forces under General Bernard Montgomery.

Soon Rommel also found himself under attack from the west. A joint Allied force of U.S., British, and Free French troops under U.S. general George S. Patton had taken control of Morocco and Algeria from Vichy forces. The Allies inflicted a major defeat on the Germans at the Battle of El Alamein in October 1942. The trapped Afrika Korps put up a tough defense in Tunisia, but by May 1943 the Allies had full control of North Africa.

Stalingrad and Kursk. By 1943 the Soviets began to make headway against the Germans. In 1942 Hitler had ordered German forces to capture the Soviet oil fields of the Caucasus region. German forces also tried to take the city of Stalingrad on the Volga River. However, the Soviets surrounded Stalingrad and counterattacked. A German officer described the fighting that raged for three months in and around the city:

66*Eighty days and eighty nights of hand-to-hand struggle. . . . Stalingrad is no longer a town. By day it is an enormous cloud of burning, blinding smoke; it is a vast furnace lit by the reflection of the flames. And when night arrives, one of those scorching, howling, bleeding nights, the dogs plunge into the Volga and swim desperately to gain the other bank. The nights of Stalingrad are a terror for them. Animals flee this hell; the hardest storms cannot bear it for long; only men endure.*99

Eventually, Soviet reinforcements surrounded the Germans at Stalingrad. Despite Hitler's orders to fight to the last man, the German commander surrendered in February 1943, having lost some 200,000 men.

Stalingrad marked the turning point against Germany in the Soviet Union. In July 1943 the

Soviets defeated the German forces in history's largest tank battle around the city of Kursk in southern Russia. The Soviet victory at Kursk signaled the failure of Hitler's attempt to conquer the Soviet Union.

Italy. Also in July 1943, British and U.S. forces landed in Sicily. After gaining control of the island, they began landing troops on the Italian mainland in September. Thoroughly demoralized by Allied gains, the Grand Fascist Council deposed Mussolini and placed him under arrest. When the Italian government announced the surrender of Italy, however, German forces rescued Mussolini and took control of the defense of Italy.

The Germans put up stiff resistance as Allied forces advanced north. In January 1944 Allied troops tried to outflank the resistance by landing behind the Axis lines at Anzio. After months of bloody fighting, Allied troops entered Rome in June. The Germans, however, continued to hold positions in northern Italy until the spring of 1945, when members of the Italian resistance finally recaptured and executed Mussolini.

As the Allies began to gather strength in 1943, Italy surrendered, and the war finally turned against Nazi Germany.

The Cross-Channel Invasion

With German forces in retreat and with the Atlantic sea routes finally secure, British and U.S. leaders decided in the spring of 1943 to invade the European continent from Britain the following year. As part of their preparations, they stepped up their campaign of **strategic bombing**, the use of air power to attack an enemy's

▲ In 1944 in Italy, British soldiers load their weapon with shells in preparation for firing into enemy lines.

economic ability to wage war. Strategic bombing proved particularly effective against German oil facilities, as a Nazi report noted:

The enemy has struck us at one of our weakest points. If they persist at it this time, we will soon no longer have any fuel production worth mentioning. Our one hope is that the other side has an Air Force General Staff as scatterbrained as ours!

Allied bombers cut German production of aviation fuel dramatically, helping to cripple the *Luftwaffe*. The bombers also destroyed many German cities.

D-Day. After midnight on June 6, 1944—a day now remembered as **D-Day**—a massive fleet of warships and support ships left British ports bound for Normandy, France. General Dwight D. Eisenhower, commander of the cross-channel invasion, had launched Operation Overlord.

As dawn broke that morning, thousands of landing craft carrying U.S., British, Canadian, Free French, and Polish troops swarmed over the French beaches. Heavy seas made the landings difficult, and the Allies faced fierce resistance from the German defenders. One Allied soldier reported:

We hit two mines going in. . . . They didn't stop us, although our ramp was damaged and an officer standing on it was killed. We grounded on a sandbank. The first man off was a commando sergeant in full kit [carrying all his gear]. He disappeared like a stone in six feet of water. . . . The beach was strewn with wreckage, a blazing tank, bundles of blankets and kit, bodies and bits of bodies.

Text continues on page 706.

Theme: War and Diplomacy

While the major battles against Germany took place on land, in World War II, as in World War I, it was the war at sea that ultimately made victory possible. The Battle for the Atlantic began in earnest with the fall of France in June 1940.

As in World War I, Britain relied on convoys of surface ships to bring supplies from the overseas empire and the United States. German rear admiral Doenitz, meanwhile, organized "wolfpacks" of U-boats to hunt Allied convoys. Some 46 U-boats were ranged around the British Isles. Ultimately, Britain won the Battle of the Atlantic, but only with American help, the use of radar and sonar, and the cracking of the secret German naval code.

Critical Thinking Ask students why naval power was the deciding factor in both World War I and World War II, even though the major battles took place on land.

ANSWER: Students should answer that in both cases the countries at war in Europe depended on supplies from overseas to support their war effort.

Geography AND HISTORY

World War II Battles

During World War II American soldiers in Europe and the Pacific experienced two very different types of war. The following accounts are from two soldiers in World War II, the first fighting the Germans in France, the second fighting the Japanese in New Guinea.

" September 12: *Battle for Brest still rages viciously. We are now into the outskirts of the city, fighting house by house. . . . The city is being utterly destroyed. City burns continuously, but we still haven't reached the inner wall. And the Germans fight though we have taken over 7,000 prisoners already. . . .*

World War II in Europe and North Africa, 1939–1945

Major battles:
- 1 — Britain, July–Oct. 1940
- 2 — Leningrad, Sept. 1941–Jan. 1944
- 3 — El Alamein, Oct. 1942
- 4 — Stalingrad, Sept. 1942–Feb. 1943
- 5 — Kursk, July 1943
- 6 — Anzio, Jan.–Mar. 1944
- 7 — D-Day, June 6, 1944
- 8 — Minsk, July 1944
- 9 — The Bulge, Dec. 1944–Jan. 1945
- 10 — Warsaw, Aug. 1944–Oct. 1944
- 11 — Berlin, Apr.–May 1945

The Relentless War World War II transformed Europe and North Africa into a single huge battlefield.

? Location In which country did the D-Day battle take place?

September 16: *Closing into center of city of Brest now. Troops are massed around the outskirts of the old city wall, which is a real obstacle. Direct fire of 105-millimeter self-propelled guns and 76-millimeter guns is being used against the wall.*

The rainy season was now on in earnest and the daily downpours . . . *turned streams into raging torrents, wiped out bridges, and made the . . . roads impassable. Most of the boys were unshaven, and it was not long before they all became hollow-eyed. They had cold bully beef and biscuits to eat and wet mud for a bed.*

It was difficult to distinguish our own and the Jap[anese] *positions at any time because there was no such thing as a front line. . . . Sometimes the enemy were in foxholes or machine-gun pits only ten yards from us.*

Linking Geography and History

How did geography influence the way the war was fought in the Pacific and in Europe?

World War II in the Pacific, 1941–1945

Island-Hopping To win the islands controlled by the Japanese, Allied soldiers fought intense battles on island after island in the Pacific.

Movement What were the last battles to be fought in the Pacific?

705

▲ **Joyous crowds gather in Paris to celebrate and greet the U.S. troops as they enter the city on August 25, 1944.**

Despite thousands of casualties, the Allies continued their assault. By the end of the day, some 155,000 Allied troops were ashore. By mid-August the Allies had broken through the German lines and had begun the liberation of France. Allied troops also landed in southern France and began to advance northward. On August 25, 1944, Allied troops entered Paris. Other Allied forces began to advance into the Low Countries.

Allied victory in Europe. In December 1944, however, as the main Allied force approached the German border from Belgium, the German army struck back. The Germans had managed to secretly mass a large force of tanks in the Ardennes Forest. Under cover of bad weather, they attacked, catching the Allies by surprise. The following **Battle of the Bulge** cost each side nearly 100,000 casualties before the Allies were finally able to push the Germans back. Nevertheless, the attack only delayed the Allied advance by nearly six weeks. By mid-March 1945 the Allies had crossed the Rhine and were advancing steadily into Germany.

In the meantime, the Soviet army had swept across Poland and entered Germany from the east.

In April the Soviets began their final drive to Berlin. During intense street-to-street fighting, Hitler remained in his bunker under the Reich Chancellery building in the center of the city. On April 30, 1945, Hitler committed suicide rather than face defeat. Days later the Soviet army had control of Berlin, and on May 7 German authorities surrendered unconditionally to the Allies. The war in Europe formally ended on May 8, 1945.

The war in Europe ended as Allied forces advanced into Germany from both the west and the east.

The War in the Pacific

While the war in Europe was fought largely on land, in Asia and the Pacific the war was fought both on land and at sea. Once the United States had declared war against Japan, Roosevelt and Churchill agreed that they would fight to end the war in Europe first, while simply trying to defend their positions in the Pacific. Despite the political decision to tackle Germany first, however, late in 1941 Admiral Chester W. Nimitz was appointed commander in chief of the U.S. Pacific Fleet.

From the very beginning Nimitz directed a complex, three-part naval strategy designed to carry the war to the Japanese home islands and achieve an Allied victory. First, U.S. submarines would attack Japanese shipping to cut off Japan's oil supply in the East Indies. Second, the United States had to establish supremacy on the ocean's surface to secure its primary bases of operation in the Pacific—Hawaii and Australia. Third, U.S. naval and land forces would seize one Pacific island after another, advancing ever closer to Japan. The object of Nimitz's strategy of **island-hopping** was to provide bases close enough to Japan's home islands to subject them to bombing and ultimately to invasion.

In May 1942 U.S. and Australian naval forces engaged the Japanese in the Coral Sea, off Australia. Although neither side won the Battle of the Coral Sea, the Japanese navy had failed in its attempt to control the waters around Australia. In early June the U.S. Navy achieved a decisive victory against Admiral Isoroku Yamamoto's carrier force off the Midway Islands northwest of Hawaii.

◀ During the fierce three-day assault on Tarawa, U.S. marines charge over barricades.

The Battle of Midway removed the immediate Japanese threat to Hawaii, but Japanese aircraft based in the Solomon Islands continued to threaten the sea routes to Australia. Then in August U.S. and Australian forces landed on Guadalcanal in the Solomons. After months of heavy fighting, they finally took control of the island in February 1943. With Hawaii and Australia now secure, the Allies began island-hopping toward Japan in late 1943. Meanwhile, Allied forces under U.S. general Douglas MacArthur were also beginning to make headway against the Japanese in New Guinea.

On November 20 the United States Navy and Marines assaulted the Gilbert Islands, landing on Tarawa. The Japanese had heavily fortified the tiny atoll. The assault resulted in some 3,500 American dead and wounded, plus some 5,000 Japanese casualties. The slow island-by-island advance toward Japan had just begun. Beyond the Gilberts lay the Marshall, Mariana, Volcano, and Bonin Islands.

In the Pacific the Allies began to take away Japanese control of sea routes and island bases.

The War in East Asia

While the war raged in the Pacific, the struggle also continued on the Asian mainland. The war on the Asian mainland played a critical role in the Allied struggle against Japan. In their efforts to conquer China, the Japanese had encountered enormous difficulties. Although Japan controlled most of the coastal areas, China's Nationalist government continued to resist from the interior. Japanese leaders also worried about possible Soviet intervention from the north. Consequently, some 2 million Japanese troops remained pinned down in China throughout the war.

Britain's Indian empire also became a Japanese target. Supplies to China's Nationalist government came primarily from Allied bases located in India and Burma. In addition to halting this flow of supplies, Japan wanted to enhance its own standing and to gain access to new sources of manpower and resources by overthrowing British rule in India. Throughout Asia the Japanese called on all the peoples of the European colonial empires to join Japan's Greater East Asia Co-Prosperity Sphere.

In December 1941 the Japanese army invaded Burma on its way to India, beginning three years of difficult jungle and mountain fighting against stubborn British and Indian resistance. Other Japanese forces invaded Malaya, aiming for the strategic port city of Singapore. On February 15 the British in Singapore surrendered to the Japanese.

As Chinese forces began to collapse in the face of the Japanese advance during 1942, the Chinese Nationalist government of General Chiang Kaishek began to call for more Allied assistance. One of their greatest spokespersons was Madame Chiang, General Chiang's wife.

BIOGRAPHY Born Soong Mei-ling, Madame Chiang was the daughter of a prominent backer of China's revolutionary Nationalist leader, Sun Yixian. She spent her teenage years in the United States, graduating from Wellesley College in 1917. Returning to China, she became active in the local politics of Shanghai and in 1927 married Chiang Kaishek. When war broke out with Japan, Madame Chiang's American experience proved a valuable tool of diplomacy.

In late 1942 Madame Chiang traveled to the United States to

Madame Chiang Kaishek
BIOGRAPHY

Theme:
Cross-cultural Interaction

Encouraging Indian nationalists to free themselves from British imperial rule, the Japanese sponsored the formation of the Indian National Army, or INA. The original idea for the INA came from the extreme Indian nationalist leader Subhas Chandra Bose. In the early 1930s Bose had visited Germany and was impressed by the Nazis. After the outbreak of war, Bose was thrown in jail, but in December 1940 he escaped. He made his way to Berlin, where he formed a government in exile and conceived the idea of a "Free Indian Legion."

Out of some 15,000 Indian troops captured in North Africa, Bose convinced or coerced between 800 and 1,000 to join him. When the Japanese captured more than 65,000 Indians in 1942, Bose went to Japan to organize them into the INA. Through persuasion and intimidation, he recruited some 20,000 Indians. Most refused to join him, however, and many were beaten and tortured as a result.

Critical Thinking Ask students why Indians might remain loyal to Britain.

ANSWER: Students might suggest that although Indians hoped to break free of British rule, they believed that the Nazis posed a bigger threat.

THROUGH OTHERS' EYES

A Turkish View of World War II

During World War II both the Axis and the Allied Powers heavily pressured Turkey to enter the war on their side. Many Turks had mixed feelings about which side they favored—particularly since they regarded the Soviet Union, one of the Allies, as a major threat to Turkey. Falih Rifki Atay, director of a major Turkish newspaper, expressed the difficulty of remaining neutral:

66 We cannot predict whether this nation, who for centuries has never seen a generation be born and die in peace, will be able to survive this war unharmed and unbloodied. . . . But this is our wish. We are after no territorial gain, only an act of force can bring us into the war. But we are not willing to sacrifice any of our honor, our rights or even one hand's breadth of our soil in order to have peace. . . . The war has laid siege to countries such as ours and turned them into fortresses. 99

raise public awareness of the war in China and its importance to an Allied victory. In February 1943 she addressed the U.S. Senate, stressing the similarity of Chinese and American interests:

66 I feel that if the Chinese people could speak to you in your own tongue, or if you could understand our tongue, they would tell you that basically and fundamentally we are fighting for the same cause; that we have identity of ideals; that the 'four freedoms,' which your President proclaimed to the world, resound throughout our vast land as the gong of freedom . . . and the death knell of the aggressors. 99

Madame Chiang received a standing ovation. "I never saw anything like it," said one member of Congress. "Madame Chiang had me on the verge of bursting into tears." Already committed to helping China against Japan, Allied leaders could do little more than they already had. Madame Chiang's visit, however, led to increased public support for the Chinese Nationalist government.

In its war against China, Japan moved forces into India and Burma to cut off supplies to Chinese Nationalist forces.

The Final Push Against Japan

After securing the Gilbert Islands, Nimitz continued his push toward Japan. By August 1944 U.S. naval forces had liberated the Mariana Islands. Taking the Marianas finally provided air bases within range of Japan for the Americans' new long-range B-29 bombers. Late in 1944 American B-29s began flying missions against targets in the Japanese home islands.

Leyte Gulf. Farther south, forces under General MacArthur, supreme commander of Allied forces in the southwest Pacific, began the liberation of the Philippines. Some strategists had argued that Allied forces should bypass the Philippines. However, MacArthur argued that taking the islands would allow the Allies to dominate the South China Sea and cut off Japan's supply line to the East Indies. MacArthur also stressed the moral importance of freeing the U.S. and Filipino prisoners held by the Japanese in the Philippines.

MacArthur's arguments won the debate. He planned to land first at Leyte Gulf in the southern Philippines. Determined to prevent the invasion, Japanese naval forces gathered in the Philippine Sea. In October 1944 U.S. naval forces defeated the Japanese in what proved to be history's largest naval engagement—the Battle of Leyte Gulf. In January 1945 Allied forces began landing on Luzon, the main island in the Philippines. On March 3, they captured Manila.

Imphal and Kohima. Meanwhile, on the Asian mainland the British had by this time reversed the Japanese advance on India. In early 1944 Japanese forces took up positions inside India in the mountainous jungle terrain around Imphal and Kohima. Quickly responding, however, British and Indian troops forced the Japanese to retreat first from Kohima and then from Imphal by July 1944. Supported by American forces, they steadily advanced back into Burma. The battle for Imphal and Kohima marked the failure of Japan's attempt to conquer India.

Iwo Jima and Okinawa. In early 1945 Admiral Nimitz continued his advance up through the central Pacific, seeking bases even closer to Japan. In February 1945 United States Marines assaulted Iwo Jima, one of the Volcano Islands, where they encountered fierce resistance from the Japanese. After weeks of fighting, the Japanese commander recorded his determination to continue even in the face of defeat: "We have not eaten nor drank for five days but our fighting spirit is still running high. We are going to fight bravely until the end." Taking Iwo Jima cost almost 6,000 American lives. Nearly all 21,000 of the Japanese on the island died.

The resistance encountered on Iwo Jima was typical of Japan's final defense. On April 1, 1945, U.S. forces assaulted Okinawa, in the Ryukyu Islands just south of Japan's home islands. In the battle for Okinawa, American ships faced wave after wave of **kamikaze** attacks—suicide runs in which Japanese pilots flew their aircraft directly into American ships. Some 70,000 Japanese troops and around 80,000 Okinawans, mostly civilians, died in the battle. As the end neared, all senior Japanese officers on Okinawa committed ritual suicide, as did many soldiers and civilians.

Having taken Okinawa, U.S. commanders began to plan an invasion of Japan. The resistance encountered on Iwo Jima and Okinawa convinced them that such an operation would prove extremely costly in both U.S. and Japanese lives. However, the development of a powerful new weapon by Allied scientists and engineers made invasion of the Japanese home islands unnecessary.

The atomic bomb. On July 16, 1945, the first **atomic bomb** was successfully tested in the desert near Alamogordo, New Mexico. Its power, which could destroy an entire city, came from the splitting of uranium atoms. Shortly afterward, with the support of the British and the apparent approval of the Soviets, President Harry Truman—who had taken office after Roosevelt's death earlier in the year—ordered the use of atomic bombs against Japan. He hoped to force Japan's immediate surrender.

On August 6, 1945, a lone B-29 bomber called the *Enola Gay* flew toward Hiroshima, an important industrial and military center in southwestern Japan. Reaching the target, the *Enola Gay* released the single atomic weapon it carried. The bomb detonated 2,000 feet above the city, flattening over 4 square miles and killing at least 80,000 people outright. Thousands of others soon died from the radiation released by the bomb.

Japanese authorities, however, did not agree to surrender immediately after the bombing of Hiroshima. Consequently, on August 9 another atomic bomb was dropped on the city of Nagasaki. The same day the Soviet Union finally declared war on Japan and promptly invaded Manchuria.

The next day Japan's emperor Hirohito decreed that his country must surrender. In late August an Allied fleet anchored in Tokyo Bay. There, aboard the U.S. battleship *Missouri*, the Allies received Japan's formal unconditional surrender on September 2, 1945. World War II had ended.

In the face of fierce Japanese resistance, the Allies finally used their ultimate weapon, the atomic bomb, to end World War II.

▶ A kamikaze pilot receives the ritual white scarf in preparation of a mission.

▲ The crew of the *U.S.S. Bunker Hill* fight to put out fires started when two bomb-laden kamikaze planes dove into the ship.

Costs of the War

World War II was the most bloody and destructive war in human history. By 1945 approximately 50 million people, including soldiers and civilians, had died. Millions of others were left homeless. The greatest loss of life occurred in the Soviet Union, where approximately 20 million

For significance, see the following pages:
strategic bombing (p. 703)
Dwight D. Eisenhower
(p. 703)
D-Day (p. 703)
Battle of the Bulge (p. 706)
Chester W. Nimitz (p. 706)
island-hopping (p. 706)
Douglas MacArthur
(p. 707)
Madame Chiang Kaishek
(p. 707)
kamikaze (p. 709)
atomic bomb (p. 709)

LOCATE
For locations, see the maps on pp. 704 and 705.

1. The Allies gained sufficient strength to force Italy to surrender. The Allies then advanced into Germany, and forced the Germans to surrender. World War II lasted from 1939 to 1945.
2. The war in the Pacific was fought on both land and sea, and the Allies eventually took away Japanese control of sea routes and island bases.
3. After successful battles for the islands in the Pacific, the United States dropped the atomic bombs on Japan.
4. Essays should mention the many people killed in battle and through policies of genocide, and the large sections of Europe and Asia that were destroyed by aerial bombing.
5. Students could argue that Japan's surrender was inevitable had the United States waited, or that the bombs were needed to save American lives.

people perished. In addition to the human costs of the war, large areas of Europe and Asia were left in ruins. Aerial bombardment had proven particularly destructive. During the Blitz the Germans had destroyed the ancient British cathedral town of Coventry and much of the centuries-old architecture of London. The Allies also bombed cities, and Hamburg and Tokyo experienced terrible firebombings. One particularly tragic case occurred in early 1945, when Allied air forces destroyed Dresden, a German city renowned for its splendid architecture.

The destructiveness and terror of aerial bombardment reached a new peak with the atomic bomb. Although the blast at Hiroshima actually killed fewer people than conventional air raids on other Japanese and German cities, the psychological impact of a single bomb doing such enormous damage was much greater.

Perhaps the most tragic aspect of the war, however, was the scope it gave to totalitarian dictatorships to wipe out huge numbers of civilians whom they regarded as a threat to their own power. Before the war few people in the West would have believed that a country such as Germany could be the scene of a brutal crime like the Holocaust. After World War II many people became determined to prevent such horror from ever happening again.

World War II was the most destructive war in human history, costing approximately 50 million lives and leaving millions of people homeless.

Losses of the Major Wartime Powers in World War II, 1939–1945

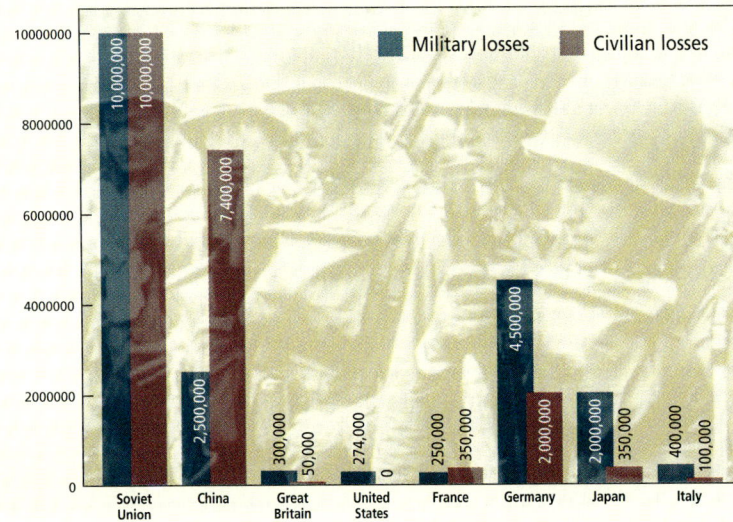

Military losses | **Civilian losses**

Soviet Union: 10,000,000 / 10,000,000
China: 2,500,000 / 7,400,000
Great Britain: 300,000 / 50,000
United States: 274,000 / 0
France: 250,000 / 350,000
Germany: 4,500,000 / 2,000,000
Japan: 2,000,000 / 350,000
Italy: 400,000 / 100,000

The World at War Over 50 million people were killed during World War II. Overall, more civilians were killed than soldiers.

Analyzing What three countries had the highest civilian losses? What factors do you think contributed to these losses?

SECTION 4 REVIEW

IDENTIFY and explain the significance of the following:
strategic bombing
Dwight D. Eisenhower
D-Day
Battle of the Bulge
Chester W. Nimitz
island-hopping
Douglas MacArthur
Madame Chiang Kaishek
kamikaze
atomic bomb

LOCATE and explain the importance of the following:
Stalingrad
Normandy
Iwo Jima
Hiroshima
Nagasaki

1. **Main Idea** How did the Allies win the war in Europe? What years did World War II ultimately cover?

2. **Main Idea** How did the war in the Pacific unfold?

3. **War and Diplomacy** How did the Allies win the war in the Pacific?

4. **Writing to Explain** Write an essay explaining why World War II was so destructive.

5. **Evaluating** Was the United States justified in using the atomic bomb against Japan? Why or why not?

Review

On a separate sheet of paper, complete the following exercises:

WRITING A SUMMARY

Using the essential points in the text, write a brief summary of the chapter.

REVIEWING TERMS

From the following list, choose the term that correctly matches the definition.

appeasement   Blitz
resistance   kamikaze
Battle of the Bulge
Wannsee Conference

1. suicide runs in which Japanese fighter pilots flew their planes directly into enemy warships
2. last German offensive, which delayed the Allied invasion of Europe for only six weeks
3. meeting at which senior Nazi officials planned the extermination of European Jews
4. series of nighttime air raids conducted by Germany against British cities from September 1940 to May 1941
5. Western democracies' policy of giving in to Hitler's demands for territory in order to avoid going to war with Germany

REVIEWING CHRONOLOGY

List the following events in their correct chronological order.

1. Hitler carries out the *Anschluss* of Austria.
2. The United States enters the war.
3. The Germans occupy Denmark, Norway, the Low Countries, and France.
4. The Spanish Civil War begins.
5. The United States drops atomic bombs on Japan to avoid more American casualties.
6. The Soviets defeat the Germans in the Battle of Stalingrad.

UNDERSTANDING THE MAIN IDEA

1. How did Hitler's actions in the 1930s threaten the peace of Europe?
2. How did Japanese activity in Asia eventually draw Japan into war with the United States?
3. What was the significance of the D-Day invasion of Normandy?
4. How did the Allied Powers plan to achieve victory over Japan, and how did they finally accomplish this victory?

THINKING CRITICALLY

1. **Analyzing** Why is the Battle of Stalingrad considered a turning point in the war in Europe?
2. **Synthesizing** How did advanced technology affect the conduct of the war in both Europe and the Pacific?

Building Your Portfolio

Complete the following activities individually or in groups.

1. **Daily Life** Imagine that you are a European, Asian, or Pacific Islander living through World War II. Create a graph that lists the high and low points of the war from your frame of reference. Place at least five dates on your chart and prepare a diary entry to accompany each one. You may make your chart from the perspective of anyone who lived in these regions at the time, including a French resistance member, a German soldier on the front lines, a survivor of the Blitz, a Filipino peasant, or a Japanese civilian living in Tokyo.
2. **Community** How did World War II affect the community that you live in now? Using the resources of your community, such as the local library and community members who lived there during the war, prepare a presentation that shows what life was like during the war. Be creative in the way in which you put together your presentation. You may choose to create a portfolio of sketches, photos, and text that shows what life was like during the war. Create a database about the war's effects by presenting your texts and images in a computerized format.

Unit 7
The World Since 1945
1945–Present

Chapter 26
Postwar Europe and North America
1945–1968

The decades after World War II, although peaceful and prosperous, were marked by the Cold War and its division of the world. How might new weapons influence international affairs?

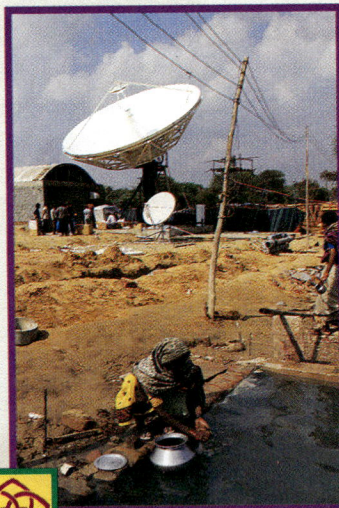

Chapter 27
Independent Asia **1945–Present**

Asia's transformation from colonies to independent nations had varied effects, including internal conflicts, communist revolutions, nationalistic wars, and economic rebuilding. What problems might a nation encounter as it tries to gain its independence from another power?

Chapter 28
Africa and the Middle East After Empire
1945–Present

New states in Africa and the Middle East experienced both the triumphs and the tragedies of independence in the years following World War II. How might religion and culture play a role in people's efforts to cope with modernization?

The decades after World War II greatly changed the world. The Cold War between the United States and the Soviet Union divided the world into two opposing groups behind the superpowers. The world's empires crumbled as colonies gained their independence, which brought both promise and problems to the new nations of Africa and Asia. War exploded in Korea and Vietnam, and many Asian nations experienced internal conflicts. In Latin America, economic development took priority, while political leaders remained deeply divided over how to achieve prosperity. Meanwhile, technological changes provided much of the world with both benefits and problems, and environmental challenges reminded the world's nations that they shared a common planet.

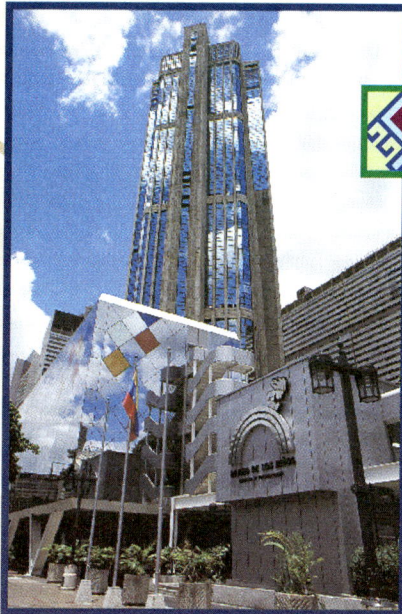

Chapter 29

New Directions in Latin America
1945–Present

Struggling with serious economic and political problems after World War II, Latin Americans remained loyal to their native lands and hopeful for the future. Why might economists emphasize industrial development over agricultural development?

Chapter 30

From the Past to the Future
1945–Present

With the collapse of the Soviet empire in Eastern Europe and the breakup of the Soviet Union, many communist nations began moving toward democracy. Technological advances provided benefits and problems, and the entire planet faced environmental challenges. What common problems confront the nations of the world today, and how might people solve these problems?

Chapter 28

Africa and the Middle East After Empire

Rapid modernization might cause many people to feel insecure about the changes going on around them. They might look to the stabilizing force of tradition to give them a new sense of security.

Chapter 29

New Directions in Latin America

Economists might believe that industrial development is the key to building an entire nation's economy. Industry, and the international trade that might accompany it, could bring in far more money than agricultural development.

Chapter 30

From the Past to the Future

The world faces many problems, including hunger, war, pollution, and disease. Some problems might be solved by nations working together to find solutions.

REVIEW & ASSESSMENT RESOURCES

- Unit Synthesis 7
- Unit Test 7
- Sheltered English Unit Test 7

All Levels

Chapter 26

Postwar Europe and North America 1945–1968

Chapter Planning Guide

	TEXTBOOK	CORE RESOURCES	VISUAL RESOURCES	MULTIMEDIA
Introduction	pp. 714–715	Block Scheduling Handbook: Ch. 26		Videodisc Segment 26 and Viewing Guide: *Television and the Cold War*
Lesson 26.1 From World War to Cold War	pp. 716–721 Biography: *Eleanor Roosevelt*, p. 717 Map: *European Alliances*, p. 720	Reading 26.1: *George Marshall Outlines the Need for a European Rehabilitation Program* Geography Activity 26: *The Berlin Wall* Skills Activity 26: *Interpreting a Diagram*		GHRC 26 Readings: *The Marshall Plan for European Recovery; The Universal Declaration of Human Rights; The Berlin Airlift* GHRC 26/Videodiscs: *Image— The Destruction of Dresden, Germany*
Lesson 26.2 Reconstruction and Renewal in the West	pp. 722–725 Then and Now: *Rising From the Ashes*, p. 723	Reading 26.2: *Charles de Gaulle and Algeria*		GHRC 26 Readings: *Karl Jaspers and German War Guilt; Britain Pioneers the Welfare State; A Progress Report on Europe's Common Market* GHRC 26/Videodiscs: *Image— Germany Rebuilds After the War*
Lesson 26.3 The New Soviet Empire	pp. 726–730	Reading 26.3: *Khrushchev and Hungary*		GHRC 26 Readings: *A Communist Criticizes the Communist System; A Humorous Attack on Soviet Censorship* GHRC 26/Videodiscs: *Map— Communist Europe in 1949*
Lesson 26.4 The Cold War Deepens	pp. 731–734 Map: *North America: Political*, p. 856 Map: *The Nuclear Arms Race*, p. 733	Reading 26.4: *The Path to the Atomic Bomb*	Geography and History 26: *Cold War Defenses*	GHRC 26 Readings: *Nikita Khrushchev on Peaceful Coexistence; John F. Kennedy on Arms and Peace* GHRC 26/Videodiscs: *Images— Testing the Atomic Bomb in 1951; Anti–Arms Race Rally*
Lesson 26.5 Changes in Society and Culture	pp. 735–740 History Through the Arts: *Chapel by Le Corbusier*, p. 739	Reading 26.5: *Growing Up in the Postwar Years* Writing Project 26: *Writing a Diary*	Art and History 26: Return of the Prodigal Son *by Romare Bearden* Everyday Life 26: *Segregation in the United States, 1960*	GHRC 26 Reading: *The Battle of the Sorbonne* GHRC 26/Videodiscs: *Images— Fire Hoses Turned on Civil Rights Protesters; Paris Student Riots*
Chapter Investigation and Enrichment	pp. 714–740	Chapter 26 Investigation: *A Cold War Era Atlas* People in World History 26 Explorations in Daily Life 26		GHRC 26/Videodiscs
Review and Assessment	Section 1 Review, p. 721 Section 2 Review, p. 725 Section 3 Review, p. 730 Section 4 Review, p. 734 Section 5 Review, p. 740 Chapter 26 Review, p. 741	Chapter Review Activity 26 Vocabulary Activity 26 Themes Review 26 Section Study Guides 26.1–26.5 Main Idea Activities 26.1–26.5 Daily Quizzes 26.1–26.5 Chapter 26 Test Sheltered English Ch. 26 Test Ch. 26 Test Generator		Audio CDs: Ch. 26 Summary (English and Spanish)

INTRODUCING THE CHAPTER

Textbook pp. 714–715

CHAPTER OVERVIEW

At the close of World War II the United States and the Soviet Union were the world's most powerful nations. The United States helped rebuild Western Europe, while the Soviet Union dominated Eastern Europe. The Soviet detonation of an atomic weapon in 1949 began an arms race between the two superpowers. As dangerous as the times were, the West enjoyed unprecedented economic growth.

PRESENTING THEMES

On the chalkboard or on an overhead transparency, write the following open-ended theme questions.

- **POLITICS AND LAW** What effects might international affairs have on domestic affairs?
- **WAR AND DIPLOMACY** Why do nations hold diplomatic negotiations?
- **TECHNOLOGY** How might new weapons influence domestic and international affairs?

Have students, either individually or in groups, suggest responses to the questions. For the politics and law question, students might suggest that international affairs might cause a country to go to war or make sacrifices that the people of the country dislike. For the war and diplomacy question, students might suggest that nations conduct diplomatic negotiations to achieve their goals without armed conflict. For the technology question, students might suggest that new weapons might require different defensive strategies and undermine people's sense of security, leading to the formation of new alliances. Save the responses. Once students have studied the chapter, you may wish to have them complete the Themes Review, then compare the two sets of answers.

USING THE VIDEO

Segment 26: *Television and the Cold War*

ENGLISH

Search Chapter 26
Videodisc 2, Side A

SPANISH

Search Chapter 26
Videodisc 2, Side A

Tell students that in this chapter they will apply these theme questions to the troubled and divided world that emerged after World War II. Then show Segment 26 of the *World History and Cultures Videodiscs*. This segment looks at the way in which television brought the issues and fears of the post-war world into the lives of American families.

Before showing the video, ask students to notice the way American television portrayed Soviet people, in particular, and their lives. Have students consider whether the television portrayal of Soviets revealed stereotypes or bias. To help students grasp the significant points of the segment, have them complete Video Viewing Guide 26.

Key to Ability Levels

All strategies and activities are coded to the following ability levels:

LEVEL 1	**Basic** activities suitable for all students
LEVEL 2	**Average** activities suitable for average to above-average students
LEVEL 3	**Challenging** activities suitable for above-average students
SHELTERED ENGLISH	Activities suitable for students with **Limited English Proficiency**

Additional Resources

BOOKS FOR TEACHERS

Blum, John Morton. *Years of Discord. 1961–1974.* Norton, 1991. Discusses the tumultuous 1960s.

Holloway, David. *Stalin and the Bomb.* Yale University Press, 1994. Discusses Stalin's role.

Reeves, Richard. *President Kennedy: Profile of Power.* Touchstone, 1993. A thorough history.

BOOKS FOR STUDENTS

Farber, D. *The Age of Great Dreams: America in the 1960s.* Hill and Wang, 1994. Looks at culture.

Fariello, Griffin. *Red Scare—Memories of the American Inquisition.* Norton, 1995. Collects reminiscences from the McCarthy era.

MULTIMEDIA MATERIALS

The Road to Brown. California Newsreel. Video, 58 min. Looks at the American civil rights movement.

The Cold War. New York Times. Video, 31 min. Covers the Berlin Airlift through Vietnam.

The Cold War. NYT Education Media. 4 videos. Covers the Cold War from 1945–1972.

Lesson 26.1   *From World War to Cold War*

Textbook pp. 716–721

RESOURCES

Pupil's Edition

Biography, p. 717: *Eleanor Roosevelt*

Map, p. 720: *European Alliances, 1955*

Core Resources

Reading 26.1: *George Marshall Outlines the Need for a European Rehabilitation Program*

Global History Resource Center

Reading: *The Marshall Plan for European Recovery*

Reading: *The Universal Declaration of Human Rights*

Reading: *The Berlin Airlift*

Videodiscs or Global History Resource Center

Image: *The Destruction of Dresden, Germany*

Search Frame 1027

LESSON FOCUS

How and why did Allied cooperation dissolve after World War II?

OBJECTIVES

After completing this lesson, students will be able to:

- describe how the Allies dealt with Germany after World War II;
- explain how and why Allied cooperation ended after the war;
- tell how new alliance systems completed the division of Europe.

HOOK

Explore how the Allies dealt with post–World War II Germany. Tell students that the Marshall Plan, designed to provide reconstruction assistance to Europe, sent more than $13 billion to Western Europe—including Germany—between 1948 and 1952. In his explanation of why he promoted the Marshall Plan, President Truman said that it was necessary to be generous, not vindictive, after war, because people were starving, disease was breaking out, and the United States was in a position to help.

Show, if available, the electronic media image *The Destruction of Dresden, Germany.* Then have students discuss whether they agree with Truman's view, asking, Would you have felt "generous" toward Germany? If you had been an Allied leader, what goals would you have had in mind when you were making policy toward Germany? *[Answers will vary, but responses should suggest policies that promote peace rather than provoking future aggression, and so on.]*

DEVELOP

Chart information on Allied actions and alliances directed at dealing with postwar Germany and the postwar world. Create a chart on the board, writing in the left-hand column—*Yalta Conference, Allied Control Council, Elimination of Nazis, United Nations.* At the top of the chart, write *Purpose, Result.* Have students provide information on the purpose and results of each of the items listed. *[Yalta: Churchill, Stalin, and Roosevelt decided to partition Germany temporarily, with U.S., British, French, and Soviet forces each controlling a zone until a postwar peace plan was determined; Allied Control Council: established to oversee a temporary government for Germany, but its members deadlocked on decisions, and each simply governed its own zone; Elimination of Nazis: led to the Nuremberg trials, in which Nazi leaders were prosecuted for war crimes; United Nations: designed to prevent another war, composed of a Security Council, made up of the five major powers, and a General Assembly, in which all nations could be represented]*

At the end of the discussion, you may wish to have the class discuss the biography of Eleanor Roosevelt on textbook page 717. Talk briefly about her involvement with the UN, and ask students to volunteer any additional information they may have about her life.

Next assign Reading 26.1, and have students discuss the Marshall Plan. You may also have students read the Global History Resource Center readings on the Marshall Plan and the Universal Declaration of Human Rights.

Link to Today. You might ask students to think of major world events in which the UN has been involved in the past several years and briefly discuss them. *[Answers could include Bosnia or the Gulf War.]*

PROBE

Describe why Allied cooperation dissolved and how new alliances completed the separation of Germany. Have students debate the different issues confronting the Allies. Divide eight volunteers into two groups—four to participate on a panel representing diplomats from the United States and Britain, and four to be panelists representing the Soviet Union. Moderate the discussion, asking questions of both panels. Students might read the material on the Berlin airlift in the Global History Resource Center in preparation.

Ask groups to discuss the issues mentioned in the section—the countries' different economic and political systems; their views of how the UN should be constructed; their views toward Poland and the Balkans; the Truman Doctrine; the Berlin blockade; the division of Germany; the Marshall Plan; NATO; and the Warsaw Pact.

Encourage students to refer to the map on textbook page 720 as they discuss different areas and nations.

CONCLUDE

Evaluate actions the United States took to counter the expansion of Soviet influence in Europe. Have students complete a Venn diagram illustrating how the United States tried to counter communism by both military and economic means. Draw two overlapping circles on the board, and label the left side *Military Means*, the overlap *Both*, and the right side *Economic Means*. Ask students to work briefly in pairs to place

the terms *North Atlantic Treaty Organization* (NATO), *the Marshall Plan*, and *the Truman Doctrine* into the correct areas. *[NATO is a military alliance; the Marshall Plan provided economic aid to devastated Western Europe; and the Truman Doctrine involved the offer of both military and economic aid to countries resisting communism.]*

Have volunteers display their complete diagrams and ask the class if they think the Soviet Union would have opposed one kind of aid more than another. *[Students should point out that economic aid probably seemed just as threatening to the Soviets as military aid because it served to establish strong anticommunist democracies in much of Europe.]*

EXTEND

Cross-Curricular Connection: *Language Arts*
Have students review President Wilson's plans for peace at the end of World War I. Then ask them to write brief essays commenting on how Wilson might have viewed U.S. foreign policy in the post–World War II period.

MEET INDIVIDUAL NEEDS

Visual Learners
Have students work in small groups to construct collages that illustrate the breakdown of Allied cooperation after World War II. They may copy or use as models photos of the Berlin airlift, the Greek civil war, goods being delivered because of the Marshall Plan, and so on, but the collage as a whole should communicate the tearing apart of the alliance that defeated Germany.

Students Having Difficulty/
Students Acquiring English
Have students having difficulty compile a Cold War glossary as they work through the chapter. Their glossaries should contain and define abbreviations such as the UN and NATO, as well as Cold War terms such as the Marshall Plan. You might also ask students to put their definitions on notecards, and have them work in pairs to test each other on their knowledge of the terms.

ASSESS

Review
Have students complete the Section 1 Review. Use answers in the Teacher's Edition, page 721, to assess student mastery of this section.

713D

Lesson 26.2   *Reconstruction and Renewal in the West*

Textbook pp. 722–725

RESOURCES

Pupil's Edition
Then and Now, p. 723: *Rising From the Ashes*

Core Resources
Reading 26.2: *Charles de Gaulle and Algeria*

Global History Resource Center
Reading: *Karl Jaspers and German War Guilt*

Reading: *Britain Pioneers the Welfare State*

Reading: *A Progress Report on Europe's Common Market*

Videodiscs or Global History Resource Center
Image: *Germany Rebuilds After the War*

Search Frame 1028

LESSON FOCUS
How did the European economy recover after the war?

[Students should mention Truman's argument about being generous after war and not being vindictive. The United States should help get people back on their feet.]

OBJECTIVES
After completing this lesson, students will be able to:
- describe the postwar problems faced by Western European countries;
- explain why the European Economic Community was established;
- examine U.S. and Canadian roles after the war.

HOOK
Examine why it was important to aid Germany economically after the war. Identify the Ruhr region on a classroom map of Europe, pointing out that Allied bombs had ruined much of this industrial area. As one German labor leader from the Ruhr described the situation after the war, the strength of the region had been in the skills and crafts of the people who lived and worked there. Because so much of the region was destroyed, so was its industry. According to the labor leader, severe unemployment of this kind was what led to the support of Hitler, and evil would come again if people were not employed.
Ask: ***How does this viewpoint support Truman's arguments for the Marshall Plan?***

DEVELOP
Explore the social and economic problems faced by Western European nations after World War II. Divide students into three groups, with each group identifying the postwar challenges faced by one of these countries—West Germany, France, and Britain. Ask students to identify the political and economic measures that either helped or hindered postwar reconstruction in the country assigned. Then have a student from each group report findings to the class. *[**West Germany:** problems included the demoralization of its people, displaced persons, and the total destruction of industry and agriculture; it benefited from the Marshall Plan, a free market economy, and the establishment of democratic government; **France:** problems included devastation of towns and cities, split between Nazi collaborators and Free French, strength of the Communist Party, revolts in colonies, particularly Algeria; it benefited from the Marshall Plan, but political fissures caused chaos until de Gaulle and a new constitution brought stability to the nation; **Britain:** problems included near bankruptcy, leading to extension of wartime rationing, and colonial rebellions, particularly Egypt's nationalization of the Suez Canal, which led to unsuccessful intervention and ended Britain's role as an imperial power]*

Have students read more about Britain and Germany after World War II in the Global History Resource Center readings *Karl Jaspers and German War Guilt* and *Britain Pioneers the Welfare State*. Also assign Reading 26.2, asking individual students to report on it to the class. You might want students to read the Then and Now feature on the restoration of the cathedral in Coventry, and show the electronic media image of Germany, to give students an idea of how countries went about rebuilding after the war.

PROBE

Explore economic cooperation among Western European countries after World War II. Tell students that cooperation among Western European nations helped lead them to economic recovery.

Ask: *What was an important incentive that led Western European nations to cooperate?*

[Marshall Plan aid was dependent on the reduction of tariffs and trade quotas.]

Next have students list in order the events that led to the formation of the European Economic Community (EEC).

[The Marshall Plan provided incentive, then the Schuman Plan, which created the European Coal and Steel Community, formed the basis for the EEC.]

Ask: *In what ways might a nation benefit from belonging to the EEC?*

[The benefits of free trade include an increase in the number of markets open to a country's goods, ease in transporting goods, and greater availability of consumer and agricultural products at a lower cost.]

Ask: *What did a nation risk by belonging?*

[The costs include some loss of a nation's ability to make decisions about its economy.]

Have students read and discuss the 1964 progress report on the Common Market in the Global History Resource Center.

CONCLUDE: Link to Today

Explore North American military cooperation and the role of the United States in world affairs.

Ask: *How did the United States and Canada cooperate in defense?*

[The geographic proximity of the two nations caused

them to cooperate in NATO and to build an early warning system of radar stations to detect enemy attack.]

Now ask students how U.S. participation in NATO and the UN represented a break from the past, encouraging the class to contrast these internationalist policies with the isolationist ones followed after World War I. Point out that today there is a great deal of disagreement over what some refer to as the United States's role as "the world's police officer." Have students discuss why the United States assumed this role in the postwar era, and debate whether it should continue to play this role. You may extend the discussion further by exploring U.S. economic aid, pointing out that a majority of the American public favors decreased spending on foreign aid. Ask why the United States became committed to foreign aid after World War II, and have students debate whether there is a need for such aid today.

EXTEND

Cross-Curricular Connection: *Economics*

Have students research and report on one of these current trade organizations or treaties, explaining why it is a subject for controversy—European Common Market, North American Free Trade Association (NAFTA), World Trade Organization.

MEET INDIVIDUAL NEEDS

Kinesthetic Learners

Have students work in small groups to prepare cheers and slogans for one of these political groups—German supporters of Konrad Adenauer, French supporters of de Gaulle, or British Conservatives or Labourites. Before they recite the cheers and slogans for the class, have them list reasons why they support their group.

Interpersonal Learners

Have students read the Global History Resource Center reading on Karl Jaspers. Then have them write a personal letter to Jaspers in Germany in which they respond to his thoughts about German war guilt.

ASSESS

Review

Have students complete the Section 2 Review. Use answers in the Teacher's Edition, page 725, to assess student mastery of this section.

Lesson 26.3 *The New Soviet Empire*

Textbook pp. 726–730

RESOURCES

Core Resources

Reading 26.3: *Khrushchev and Hungary*

Global History Resource Center

Reading: *A Communist Criticizes the Communist System*

Reading: *A Humorous Attack on Soviet Censorship*

Videodiscs or Global History Resource Center

Map: *Communist Europe in 1949*

Search Frame 1036

LESSON FOCUS

How did the Soviet bloc develop and expand after World War II?

OBJECTIVES

After completing this lesson, students will be able to:

- identify postwar changes that took place in the Soviet Union;
- describe the consequences of Soviet rule in Eastern Europe;
- explain how postwar Yugoslavia differed from the rest of Eastern Europe.

HOOK

Identify postwar changes in the Soviet Union. Remind students that in the Soviet Union during World War II, some 20 million people were killed. Then point out that most of these deaths were not caused by fighting with the Germans, but rather were at the hands of the Soviet people's own leader, Joseph Stalin. However, after the war many Soviets remained supportive of Stalin.

Ask: *What overall view of Stalin did Soviet citizens have after World War II?*

[Many Soviets viewed Stalin with admiration because Russia had won the war and its territories expanded enormously. However, Stalin continued to repress Soviet citizens.]

Ask students how Stalin's death affected Soviet policy. *[Khrushchev's policy of de-Stalinization demystified the leader and criticized his brutality and the policy decisions that had led to the Soviet Union's near defeat by Germany. Khrushchev also placed somewhat less emphasis on industrial growth and made greater allowances for people's tastes, especially in the production of food.]* Then direct students' attention to the quotation on page 727, and ask a volunteer to read it aloud.

Ask: *How did the journalist react to Khrushchev's "secret speech?"*

[Students should mention that the journalist expressed the shock that many Soviet people felt at the destruction of their former leader's image.]

DEVELOP

Describe consequences of communist rule in Eastern Europe. Have students explore communist rule in Eastern Europe by looking at the electronic media map of communist Europe. Then ask them to work in pairs or small groups, with one pair or group using butcher paper to make its own version of the map, showing the names of the countries of Eastern Europe. Assign the other groups the following countries—East Germany, Poland, Czechoslovakia, Hungary, Bulgaria, Romania. (You might ask students assigned to Hungary to read Core Resources Reading 26.3 for their information.) Ask them to write brief captions for their assigned countries, describing how the Soviets maintained control. Then have them write the results of their work on the appropriate places on the map prepared by their classmates. [**East Germany**: *the Soviets bled East Germany of resources and in 1953 brutally put down a revolt;* **Poland**: *Stalin eliminated potential Polish leaders by allowing Nazi troops to smash Polish resistance fighters, and Khrushchev allowed the return to power of Gomulka, a canny Polish leader;* **Czechoslovakia**: *the Soviet army backed a coup by pro-Communist forces;* **Hungary**: *Communists executed and harassed a government supported by small landholders; Communists consolidated power and later attempted reforms, which sparked anti-Soviet revolt; Soviets sent tanks to suppress revolt;* **Bulgaria**: *accepted a coalition government, and Communists then purged supporters of the monarchy;* **Romania**: *Soviets intervened by forcing King Michael to hand over power to a leader of a left-wing group; King Michael was forced by Communists to abdicate, and rigged elections led to a communist victory]*

Have pairs read the selection *A Communist Criticizes the Communist System* from the Global History Resource Center. Then ask students to write a brief summary of the reading.

PROBE

Explain how postwar Yugoslavia differed from the rest of Eastern Europe. Ask students to read the information about Yugoslavia on textbook page 730. Then have volunteers role-play the parts of Tito and the U.S. ambassador to Yugoslavia in the 1950s. You, or a volunteer, may interview each, asking Tito about when he gained power, why the Soviet Union expelled his country from the Cominform, and how he responded. Ask the ambassador how the United States reacted to this split within the Communist bloc. *[Students should understand that Tito gained power during the war and retained his base of support even after Soviet forces came to his assistance. When differences between Yugoslavia and the Soviet Union broke out, Stalin expelled Yugoslavia from the Cominform because he did not like an independent communist government so close to the borders of the Soviet Union. Tito then turned to the United States. The United States then sent aid to Yugoslavia.]*

CONCLUDE

Evaluate possible action by NATO or the United States during conflict in Poland, Hungary, East Germany, or any of the Soviet bloc countries in the 1950s. Ask students if they think NATO or the United States should have come to the aid of any of the Eastern European countries that tried to break from the Soviet Union. Tell them they should answer the question from moral, military, and political viewpoints, specifying which countries, if any, should have received U.S. help. Then ask students to speculate on the consequences of NATO or U.S. involvement. Make sure that they understand that the Russians had overwhelming military superiority in the region, that nations sometimes hesitate to become involved in the internal affairs of other nations, and that another war might have ensued—one that American citizens would have been highly unlikely to support.

EXTEND

Cross-Curricular Connection: *U.S. History*
Link to Today. Have students consider the issues of U.S. involvement in Eastern Europe mentioned above. Then have them research some of the areas of the world in which the United States has been involved in the past several years, either militarily or financially. Ask them to list some of the reasons why the United States has chosen to become involved in the affairs of these other regions.

MEET INDIVIDUAL NEEDS

Linguistic Learners
Have students who are interested in writing read the amusing but instructive short story on Soviet-style censorship in the Global History Resource Center. Then ask those students to try writing a story on Soviet repression in Hungary that would be approved by the Soviet censors.

Logical-Mathematical Learners
Remind students that the primary mission of NATO during the Cold War was to protect Western Europe from an attack by the Warsaw Pact nations. Then ask them to put themselves in the place of NATO military planners to determine by what route such an attack was most likely to take place and where NATO troops should be concentrated.

ASSESS

Review
Have students complete the Section 3 Review. Use answers in the Teacher's Edition, page 730, to assess student mastery of this section.

Lesson 26.4   *The Cold War Deepens*

Textbook pp. 731–734

RESOURCES

Pupil's Edition
Map, p. 733: *The Nuclear Arms Race*
Map, p. 856: *North America: Political*

Core Resources
Reading 26.4: *The Path to the Atomic Bomb*

Visual Resources
Geography and History 26: *Cold War Defenses*

Global History Resource Center
Reading: *Nikita Khrushchev on Peaceful Coexistence*
Reading: *John F. Kennedy on Arms and Peace*

Videodiscs or Global History Resource Center
Image: *Testing the Atomic Bomb in 1951*

Search Frame 1031

Image: *Anti–Arms Race Rally*

Search Frame 1032

LESSON FOCUS
How did the development of nuclear weapons affect the Cold War?

OBJECTIVES

After completing this lesson, students will be able to:
- explain some of the consequences of the nuclear arms race;
- tell how the development of nuclear weapons affected international stability;
- detail the effects of the Cuban missile crisis.

HOOK

Explore reactions to the dropping of the atomic bombs on Hiroshima and Nagasaki. Display the image of the bomb testing and ask students to refer to Chapter 25 in their textbook to understand the destructive capabilities of the bombs dropped on Hiroshima and Nagasaki. Also ask them if they have ever seen photos of the destruction from these events. Then have them take turns imagining the reaction to the bombings from the viewpoints of these people—a U.S. Marine fighting in the Pacific, a Japanese soldier, a Japanese newspaper reporter, an American teenager, a Russian scientist, and one of the scientists involved in the Manhattan Project.

DEVELOP

Examine the development of the nuclear arms race and its consequences. Write these events in random order on the board and ask students to put them in sequential order—Special Theory of Relativity, Manhattan Project, bombing of Hiroshima and Nagasaki, fusion bombs, ICBMs (intercontinental ballistic missiles). Then have students explain the significance of each. You might want to have them read Reading 26.4 to give them an understanding of the development of the atomic bomb. *[Einstein's **Special Theory of Relativity** revolutionized thinking about matter and energy. The **Manhattan Project** developed the first atomic bomb. **Hiroshima and Nagasaki** ushered in the nuclear age. **Fusion**, or thermonuclear, bombs combined hydrogen atoms to produce even deadlier weapons. The **ICBMs** built by the superpowers could strike targets from either the United States or the Soviet Union.]*

Now write *arms race* on the board, draw a circle around it, and draw spokes leading in all directions from the circle, with empty circles at the ends of the spokes. Ask students to fill in the empty circles by identifying consequences of the arms race. You might wish to show the electronic media images of the testing of the atomic bomb and of the rally. *[McCarthyism, sparked by fears of communism within the United States; protests, including those focusing on the problem of radioactive fallout from tests;*

increased tensions between the superpowers, heightened by brinkmanship—the act of moving ever closer to nuclear war without actually using nuclear weapons; Soviet efforts to cut Berlin off from the West; the building of the Berlin Wall; the Cuban missile crisis—the Soviet construction of missile sites in Cuba and the subsequent U.S. blockade of the island]

Ask: Why did international disagreements become even more serious after the development of nuclear weapons?
[The development of nuclear weapons meant that disagreements could grow into dangerous crises with devastating results.]

Have students examine the transparency *Cold War Defenses*. Then lead a class discussion in which students give their opinions on how people of different generations from countries around the world might have viewed the Cold War.

PROBE

Analyze how the threat of nuclear war during the Cuban missile crisis forced nations to take a new look at the nuclear arms race. Have students look at the Atlas map *North America: Political* on textbook page 856.

Ask: **Which major American city is closest to Cuba?**
[Miami]
Ask: **How close?**
[less than 250 miles]

Then point out that if missiles had a range of 500 miles, and they were located in Cuba, then the United States could have been in danger.

Ask: **What do you think the United States would have done if it suffered a nuclear attack from Soviet-made missiles in Cuba?**
[perhaps attacked the Soviet Union]

Discuss why this incident was more frightening than other incidents having to do with spy planes over the Soviet Union or with Soviet actions in Berlin. [The United States would not tolerate a nuclear threat so close to home. The Soviets realized this and knew that if missiles were ever launched from Cuba, the Soviet Union itself would become a target.]

If available, have students read the speeches in the Global History Resource Center to compare the views of Soviet premier Nikita Khrushchev and John F. Kennedy on the arms race and prospects for peace.

CONCLUDE

Analyze the effects of nuclear arms on world politics.
Tell students that the Cuban missile crisis and the ongoing threat of nuclear war finally led to efforts by the superpowers to control the arms race. Ask students to identify the treaties that were signed during the 1960s. [Partial Nuclear Test Ban Treaty, Non-Proliferation Treaty]

Link to Today. Then ask students to identify how more recent events have helped ease the fear of an all-out nuclear war. [fall of Soviet Union]

You might wish to engage students in a discussion based on their opinions about the nuclear arms race.
Ask: **Would the world be different if the Soviet Union had not developed nuclear weapons?**
Ask: **What prevented each country from using nuclear weapons after World War II?**
Ask: **Would you ever support the use of nuclear weapons today? If so, in what cases?**

EXTEND

Cross-Curricular Connection: *Science*
Have students work in small groups to research and report on the developments that led to the building of the atomic bomb. You might ask them to read Core Resources Reading 26.4 for more information. Ask them to include in their reports information on the Manhattan Project, Los Alamos, and the scientists who participated in these projects.

MEET INDIVIDUAL NEEDS

Interpersonal Learners
Have students create poems or diary entries from the perspective of a person living at the height of the arms race, or specifically during the Cuban missile crisis.

Linguistic Learners
Have students read the Global History Resource Center selection on what John F. Kennedy had to say about the arms race. Then have them write a newspaper editorial about his message.

ASSESS

Review
Have students complete the Section 4 Review. Use answers in the Teacher's Edition, page 734, to assess student mastery of this section.

Textbook pp. 735–740

RESOURCES

Pupil's Edition

History Through the Arts, p. 739: *Chapel by Le Corbusier*

Core Resources

Reading 26.5: *Growing Up in the Postwar Years*

Visual Resources

Everyday Life 26: *Segregation in the United States, 1960*

Global History Resource Center

Reading: *The Battle of the Sorbonne*

Videodiscs or Global History Resource Center

Image: *Fire Hoses Turned on Civil Rights Protesters*

Search Frame 1035

Image: *Paris Student Riots, 1968*

Search Frame 1034

LESSON FOCUS

How did the people on both sides of the Iron Curtain respond to economic changes and anxiety about the Cold War?

OBJECTIVES

After completing this lesson, students will be able to:

- analyze changes in standards of living in the postwar decades;
- describe the factors that led to the protest movements of the 1960s;
- identify the effects of the protest movements of the 1960s.

HOOK

Explore changes in standards of living in the postwar decades. Tell students that during the 1950s and 1960s the standard of living in much of North America and Western Europe had reached its highest level in history. Economies were strong, and people were able to buy automobiles, televisions, and appliances. Have a volunteer read aloud the quote on textbook page 735 to illustrate these changes.

Ask: **What contributed to boom times in the West?**

[Automobile production and the emergence of television and appliances spurred economic growth in the United States. In Western Europe, first the Marshall Plan and then consumer confidence and government spending helped nations recover from the war.]

Ask: **Why did Eastern Europe fail to take part in the boom times?**

[Communist bloc countries did not participate in the Marshall Plan and they had less industrialized economies before the war. Although Khrushchev implemented some consumer-oriented policies, workers still stood in line for scarce and inferior goods, and housing was poorly built.]

DEVELOP

Discuss social and cultural changes in the post–World War II period. Write these words on the chalkboard—*baby boom, generation gap, affluence.* Ask students to briefly make a cause-and-effect equation with these words in order to explain cultural and social changes in the postwar period. (You might also ask them to read Core Resources Reading 26.5 for more information.) *[Equations should indicate that a postwar baby boom and improved economic conditions led to a large number of young people who were affluent and considered themselves so different from their parents that there was a generation gap.]*

Ask: How did many young people express themselves as a result? *[They wore clothes different from their parents'; listened to different music; and developed a suspicious attitude toward their parents' generation.]*

Next ask students to discuss how social and cultural changes were reflected in the arts. Ask them to read the History Through the Arts feature on textbook page 739 as an example. Students should also mention changes in literature and film.

PROBE

Discuss protest movements in the 1960s and responses to them. Divide the class into three groups, with each group reviewing protest movements in one of these areas—the United States, Western Europe, Communist bloc nations. Then ask students to read the the selection in the Global History Resource Center on the Battle of the Sorbonne. Also have them view the Everyday Life transparency on segregation in the United States and the electronic media images of the civil rights protest and student riots in Paris.

Then have students meet in smaller groups of three, made up of representatives from each of the larger groups. Ask students to share information or to participate in role-playing by assuming the role of someone living in one of the above areas during the postwar decades, and have them comment on protest movements and the reasons for them. Have them also comment on the effects. *[United States: some protested hypocrisy and conformity, others were involved in protest against the Vietnam War, and many struggled for civil rights for African Americans and the struggle for women's equality. Protest resulted in school desegregation, the 1965 Voting Rights Act, and the formation of groups to lobby for equal rights for women; Western Europe: protest developed around many issues—the Vietnam War, university overcrowding, and French educational policy. Violent demonstrations occurred in several countries, and the French protest almost toppled de Gaulle's government; Communist bloc: dissidents spoke out against Stalinist labor camps and other forms of repression. Reforms in Czechoslovakia eventually were crushed by the Soviets.]*

CONCLUDE

Have students imagine they are members of the older, wartime generation viewing protests in their country. Ask them to comment on young people involved in protests

from the viewpoints of a variety of people—a white American veteran or an African American veteran of World War II, an American woman who worked in a shipbuilding plant in World War II, or a Russian survivor of the Battle of Stalingrad.

EXTEND

Cross-Curricular Connection: *Music/Creative Writing*

Ask musically gifted students to write a song about one of the issues discussed in this chapter. Some may want to write both music and lyrics. Others may choose to write lyrics to a popular melody. Have students share their songs with the class.

Cross-Curricular Connection: *Journalism*

Link to Today. Ask students to conduct an interview with someone who lived during the 1960s. To prepare for the assignment, students should write a list of at least 10 questions aimed at finding out about student life and student protest during this era. Then have them write a brief article on their interview.

MEET INDIVIDUAL NEEDS

Students Acquiring English

Ask students acquiring English to perform a similar assignment, interviewing people who lived through the 1950s and 1960s about the unrest and reforms they most remember from that time. Students can then practice their English by sharing what they learned with others in the class.

Linguistic Learners

Have students review the section and pick a topic to debate in front of the class. They might prepare a short speech and then take questions from the audience. You might encourage them to dress for the part they are playing—a young person during the 1960s, an older person during the 1950s, and so on.

ASSESS

Review

Have students complete the Section 5 Review. Use answers in the Teacher's Edition, page 740, to assess student mastery of this section.

In preparation for the chapter test, you may wish to have students complete all or part of the Chapter 26 Review on textbook page 741, the Chapter 26 Review Activity, and the Chapter 26 Themes Review.

713L

Understanding the Main Idea

Call on a volunteer to read aloud the *Understanding the Main Idea* paragraph. Explain to students that one of the most dramatic changes after World War II was the development of two major alliances, one led by the United States and the other by the Soviet Union. The spread of nuclear weapons technology added to the political tensions of the period, and nations throughout the world were affected by the struggle between the two major powers.

Presenting Themes

See p. 713B for suggestions on introducing themes.

Using the Time Line

Have students list the time line events in their notebooks. After they have read about each event in the chapter, have students write a paragraph explaining its significance.

Chapter 26
Postwar Europe and North America 1945–1968

Understanding the Main Idea

The decades after World War II transformed the lives of Europeans and North Americans. The world avoided another major war, and most people in Europe and North America grew wealthier than they had ever been. The postwar years were marked, however, by anxieties over the arms race between the East and the West. By 1950 Europe had divided into two opposing groups behind either the United States or the Soviet Union.

Themes

- *Politics and Law* What effects might international affairs have on domestic affairs?
- *War and Diplomacy* Why do nations hold diplomatic negotiations?
- *Technology* How might new weapons influence domestic and international affairs?

For month after month the planes never stopped flying. They came night and day, in fair weather and foul. The roar of the big American transports never ceased. But the Berliners did not mind. In fact, the sound was reassuring—for it meant that they would have food to eat, clothes to wear, and coal to heat their homes. In June 1948 the Soviet government had blockaded the Western occupation zones of Berlin. At that point the only alternatives facing West Berliners seemed to be war or starvation. But the governments of the Western powers had ordered an airlift to supply the city, surprising the Soviets and the Berliners as well. Through the crisis the people of Berlin never gave in. The mayor of the city encouraged its citizens: "With all the means at our disposal, we shall fight those who want to turn us into slaves. . . . We have lived under such a slavery in the days of Adolf Hitler. We want no return to such times."

American, British, and French pilots landed and took off from West Berlin's airstrips with split-second timing, each day ferrying in thousands of tons of needed provisions. They kept the city of more than 2 million people alive. And at a moment of great danger, the pilots kept the peace. The Berlin blockade, however, was only the first of many crises that would threaten the peace of the world in the years following World War II.

1945	1946	1948	1952	1955
Allies establish Allied Control Council to deal with defeated Germany.	Winston Churchill gives "Iron Curtain" speech in Fulton, Missouri.	Soviets blockade ground transportation routes to Berlin.	First U.S. thermonuclear bomb is detonated.	Soviet Union and nations of Eastern Europe establish the Warsaw Pact.

German children eagerly wait for one of the 272,000 flights that delivered over 2 million tons of supplies to blockaded Berlin between June 1948 and September 1949.

About the Image

In this picture, children watch as an American plane delivers supplies to relieve the Berlin blockade. When the Soviets cut off land and water routes to the city, Berliners were denied food from outlying farms. By some estimates Berlin needed 4,500 tons of food and fuel every day, in addition to medical supplies and other items. Few believed that it would be possible to airlift that much material. However, for 462 days American, British, and French fliers, many of whom had recently been dropping bombs on the city, supplied Berlin's needs. Boys and girls looked forward to the arrival of these pilots, called the chocolate bombers, because they scattered chocolate bars as they landed.

Critical Thinking Ask students to calculate how many tons of food and fuel the pilots delivered.

ANSWER: Students should answer that they delivered around 2,079,000 tons.

1956	1958	1962	1963	1968
Hungarians revolt against Soviet rule.	Charles de Gaulle heads Fifth Republic in France.	Cuban missile crisis occurs.	Martin Luther King, Jr., leads March on Washington.	Mass protest movements sweep Europe.

SECTION 1

CORE LESSON PLAN
See pages 713C and 713D for Lesson Plan 26.1.

Theme: Politics and Law

The principles established in the Nuremberg trials were further developed and later became a part of international law. In 1950 the International Law Commission outlined certain guiding principles and definitions of criminality. War crimes include violations of traditional treatment of civilians and prisoners in time of war. Crimes against peace include plans to begin a war of aggression. Crimes against humanity include extermination, enslavement, deportation, and other persecutions.

Critical Thinking Ask students how war crimes differ from other crimes.

ANSWER: Students should answer that war crimes are committed through governmental policy against large numbers of people.

SECTION 1
From World War to Cold War

FOCUS

- How did the Allies deal with Germany in the years just after World War II?
- Why did Allied cooperation dissolve after the war?
- How did the new alliance systems complete the division of Europe?

After the defeat of the Axis Powers in World War II, most people hoped that victory would bring an era of lasting peace. Disagreements among the Allies over what to do about defeated Germany and how to govern Eastern Europe, however, soon shattered these hopes. Within five years of the war's end, Europe and much of the world had divided into opposing camps behind one of the two superpowers—the United States and the Soviet Union.

Joseph Stalin, Franklin Roosevelt, and Winston Churchill at Yalta

The Occupation of Germany

When World War II ended in Europe on May 8, 1945, the three leading members of the Grand Alliance had not decided what to do about Germany. The problem of Germany had troubled U.S., British, and Soviet leaders for many months, and it would continue to do so for years.

The Yalta Conference. In February 1945 Franklin Roosevelt, Joseph Stalin, and Winston Churchill considered Germany's fate at a meeting at Yalta, a Soviet resort on the Black Sea. At Yalta the three leaders agreed to divide Germany temporarily, for the purpose of supervising the German surrender. British, French, U.S., and Soviet forces would each control one zone. A postwar peace conference would determine the long-term future of Germany.

Germany under Allied control. Following the German surrender in May 1945, the four Allied armies completed the occupation of their respective zones. The U.S., British, and French zones were in the western part of Germany; the Soviet zone was in the east. The German capital of Berlin, though lying entirely in the Soviet zone, was similarly divided into four sectors. At the same time, the Soviet Red Army rolled across Eastern Europe, occupying many nations.

In June 1945 the Allied governments established the Allied Control Council to oversee a temporary government for Germany. All council decisions had to be reached by consensus—any member could exercise a veto. Consequently, the council soon deadlocked over issues of governing the country. Britain and the United States wanted to rebuild the German economy, while the Soviet Union and France hoped to keep Germany weak. Increasingly, the Allies ignored the council and simply imposed their own decisions on their own zones.

The Nuremberg trials. The Allies had no trouble, however, agreeing on what to do with the worst Nazi war criminals. From November 1945 through September 1946, an international panel met at Nuremberg, Germany. At the Nuremberg trials, 22 top Nazis were tried for "crimes against humanity" and other criminal acts—19 were convicted, and 12 of these were sentenced to death. One of the judges at Nuremberg described the Nazis' crimes:

66 *These crimes are unprecedented ones because of the shocking numbers of victims. They are even more shocking and unprecedented because of the large number of persons who united to perpetrate them. . . . [The Nazis] developed a contest in cruelty and a competition in crime.* 99

After the German surrender Allied armies occupied Germany, dividing the country and its capital, Berlin, into four occupation zones.

The United Nations

Germany's fate was part of the larger issue of how to prevent another world war. On this issue, as they had before, the Allies disagreed sharply. Stalin and Churchill called for dividing the world into spheres of influence among the victors. President Roosevelt, however, preferred the internationalist approach that had formed the basis for the League of Nations. Internationalists called for a successor to the League that would keep the peace and punish aggressors.

This clash of views eventually produced a compromise. At a conference held in San Francisco from April to June 1945, 51 countries, including Great Britain, the United States, and the Soviet Union, agreed to establish the United Nations Organization (later simply called the **United Nations**, or UN).

To satisfy those calling for a continuation of the spheres-of-influence approach, the five major powers—the United States, Britain, the Soviet Union, France, and China—became permanent members of the Security Council, which was charged with the task of dealing with large issues of war and peace. Each permanent member could veto any action proposed in the Security Council. The internationalist approach, however, was represented in the composition of the General Assembly. The Assembly was ultimately designed to include all nations that wished to join. All members of the General Assembly would have equal voices and equal votes.

Occupied Germany, 1945–1955

The Allies in Germany Caught in the rivalry between the United States and the Soviet Union, Germany was divided into zones after the war.

? Location In which occupation zone was Berlin located?

Many Americans looked skeptically on the United Nations, with some objecting to its incorporation of internationalist ideas. One person responsible for persuading many of the skeptics to support the new organization was Eleanor Roosevelt, widow of U.S. president Franklin Roosevelt.

BIOGRAPHY Born in New York City in 1884, Eleanor Roosevelt was always interested in social causes. After marrying Franklin and later becoming first lady, she continued to work for civil rights. She maintained that "no one can make you feel inferior without your consent." To set an example, in 1939 Roosevelt

Eleanor Roosevelt
BIOGRAPHY

The Basic Organization of the United Nations

TRUSTEESHIP COUNCIL
Controls territories under UN supervision

GENERAL ASSEMBLY
Debates issues and recommends actions but lacks the power to enforce decisions

SECURITY COUNCIL
Authorizes economic and military action in settling international disputes

INTERNATIONAL COURT OF JUSTICE
Decides questions of international law

ECONOMIC AND SOCIAL COUNCIL
Sponsors trade, education, health, and human rights organizations

SECRETARIAT
Acts as administrator of UN and coordinates work of UN agencies

Many Responsibilities The United Nations is composed of six main bodies, of which the General Assembly and the Security Council are the most important. These six bodies are aided in their many responsibilities by dozens of smaller agencies.

? Analyzing Why do you think the United Nations needs a body like the Secretariat?

resigned from the Daughters of the American Revolution to protest that group's discrimination against African American opera singer Marian Anderson.

In 1945 President Harry Truman appointed Roosevelt as a delegate to the United Nations. In 1946 she was named chairwoman of the UN Commission on Human Rights, where she played a central role in drafting the 1948 Universal Declaration of Human Rights.

The Alliance Dissolves

As demonstrated by the deadlock over Germany, the Great Powers had increasingly contradictory views of what the world after the war should look like. The most striking difference was that the Western nations believed in democracy, while the Soviets supported communism. The Western Allies believed in the principles of a **market economy**—in which private businesses and individuals determined what goods and services should be produced, how they should be produced, and for whom they should be produced.

The Soviets, on the other hand, remained devoted to the principles of a **command economy**, in which the government made all economic decisions. During the period from 1946 to 1948 these disagreements dissolved the Alliance.

Growing suspicions. The Yalta Conference had revealed a basic difference between the United States and the Soviet Union regarding the future of Poland. Stalin insisted that the postwar government of Poland must be friendly to the Soviets. Roosevelt wanted Poland to be democratic. Soon after the war, the Soviet army snuffed out any remaining democratic tendencies in Poland and installed a government that the Soviets could easily control. Many Americans came to believe that Stalin could not be trusted. Suspicions deepened when Stalin publicly announced in February 1946 that the communist struggle for world domination would resume and began to increasingly interfere with democratic elections in Eastern Europe. The following month, in a speech before a gathering in Fulton, Missouri, former British prime minister Winston Churchill voiced what many people feared:

66 *From Stettin in the Baltic to Trieste in the Adriatic, an iron curtain has descended across the Continent. . . . All these famous cities and the populations around them lie in the Soviet sphere and are subject, in one form or another, not only to Soviet influence, but to a very high degree and increasing measure of control from Moscow.* 99

Churchill's "**Iron Curtain**" speech seemed to announce the division of Europe between the democratic West and the communist East.

The Truman Doctrine. Events in the Balkans further deepened the division between the East and the West. In March 1947 President Truman asked Congress for $400 million in military and

The Berlin blockade. Cold War tensions deepened when the Soviets tried to force a decision over the future of Germany. In June 1948 Stalin blockaded Soviet-controlled ground access to the western zones of Berlin. Stalin hoped that by creating a crisis over Berlin he could convince the Western Allies either to place Germany under Soviet control or leave it demilitarized and neutral.

Instead, President Truman ordered that supplies be airlifted to the western zones of Berlin. From June 1948 to September 1949, a steady stream of planes kept the city fed and clothed. Stalin eventually decided that the Berlin blockade was a failure, and in May 1949 he ordered it lifted.

The Truman Doctrine and the Berlin blockade completed the destruction of the Grand Alliance.

▲ In 1947 President Truman speaks to Congress, urging the members to work with him.

economic aid for Greece and Turkey. Turkey had been under pressure from the Soviet Union for some time. In Greece, Communists were waging a bitter civil war against the conservative government. The situation came to a head in February 1947, when the British government told the U.S. government that it would soon be reducing its contributions to Greece because of economic pressures at home.

President Truman decided to take up where Britain had left off. He warned Congress that the situation in Greece was a turning point for democracy in the nation's struggle against communism. The president outlined what came to be called the Truman Doctrine: "It must be the policy of the United States to support free peoples who are resisting attempted subjugation [domination] by armed minorities or by outside pressures." This policy soon became known as "containment"—the United States would contain communism wherever it arose in the world.

Congress approved Truman's request, and the Truman Doctrine became a basic part of U.S. foreign policy. The growing struggle for global power between the United States and the Soviet Union became known as the **Cold War**.

Europe Divides

As the Grand Alliance dissolved, Europe divided in two. In the West were Britain and France and other countries friendly to the United States. In the East were the Soviet Union and the countries occupied by the Red Army.

The Marshall Plan. In June 1947 U.S. secretary of state George Marshall unveiled an American plan for sending reconstruction assistance to Europe. The goals of the Marshall Plan were to ease economic distress in Europe and to help stabilize democratic governments by raising people's standards of living. Western European leaders eagerly sketched a framework for putting the proposed U.S. aid to good use. The Marshall Plan sent more than $13 billion to Western Europe between 1948 and 1952. Originally, the United States had offered Marshall Plan aid to the Soviet Union and the countries of Eastern Europe, but the Soviets rejected it.

The two Germanys. One of the most obvious signs of the divided continent was Germany. The Berlin blockade convinced most people in the West that agreement with the Soviet

Union on the future of Germany would be impossible. Accordingly, the Americans, British, and French supported the creation of the Federal Republic of Germany (West Germany) in May 1949. The new state had its capital at Bonn. Its first chancellor was Konrad Adenauer (AHD-uh-now-uhr), the leader of the Christian Democratic Party, who was elected in September 1949.

Meanwhile, the Soviets created a separate government for East Germany. In October 1949 the German Democratic Republic was formally proclaimed. Its capital was East Berlin, and its leaders were Communists selected and controlled by the Soviet Union.

The creation of two Germanys and the growing division of Europe deepened Cold War tensions.

New Alliances

As Stalin tightened his grip over the countries of Eastern Europe, the Western Allies began to fear what they saw as growing Soviet aggression. In 1949 the Truman administration invited representatives of Great Britain, France, Italy, Belgium, the Netherlands, Luxembourg, Portugal, Denmark, Norway, Iceland, and Canada to

European Alliances, 1955

NATO nations — Neutral nations — • Other cities — Warsaw Pact nations — Iron Curtain — Other Communist nations — ⊛ National capital — The United States and Canada are the North American members of NATO.

Cold War Pacts After the Iron Curtain had descended, disagreements between NATO and the Warsaw Pact reinforced the division of Europe.

Location Where do you think the heaviest concentrations of troops were located? Why might that pattern have developed?

join the United States in a military alliance. The North Atlantic Treaty of April 1949 established **NATO**, the North Atlantic Treaty Organization. This treaty committed the member nations to defend one another in case of attack.

American efforts to fight communism were not restricted to the countries of Europe, however. When communist North Korea invaded South Korea in June 1950, the United States and the United Nations responded by sending troops to Korea to stop the Communists. (See Chapter 27 for a full discussion.)

▲ British diplomat Sir Oliver Franks signs the NATO treaty while other national leaders look on.

The Soviets were also pursuing efforts to ensure their security. Since October 1947, the countries in the Soviet sphere, often called the Communist bloc, had been members of the Communist Information Bureau (Cominform). One of the main goals of the Cominform was to spread communism to Western Europe. The Cominform gave rise in 1949 to the Council for Mutual Economic Assistance (COMECON).

The creation of NATO and particularly the 1955 admission of West Germany into the alliance caused the Soviet Union to form its own military alliance, the **Warsaw Pact**. Established in May 1955, the Warsaw Pact was an agreement of mutual military cooperation among the Soviet Union, Albania, Bulgaria, Hungary, Romania, Czechoslovakia, Poland, and East Germany. The establishment of the two alliance systems marked a division of Europe that would last for decades.

The establishment of NATO and the Warsaw Pact completed the division of Europe by creating two armed camps allied with the two superpowers.

SECTION 1 REVIEW

IDENTIFY and explain the significance of the following:
  United Nations
  Eleanor Roosevelt
  market economy
  command economy
  Iron Curtain
  Cold War
  Konrad Adenauer
  NATO
  Warsaw Pact

LOCATE and explain the importance of the following:

Federal Republic of Germany
Bonn
German Democratic Republic
East Berlin

1. **Main Idea** What issues divided the Allies after World War II?
2. **Main Idea** What was the consequence of the alliance system that arose after the war's end?
3. **War and Diplomacy** What factors led to the establish-

ment of the two German states after the war?
4. **Writing to Explain** Imagine that you are a member of the Allied Control Council. Write an article for a newspaper in your home country explaining how the Allies are dealing with the defeated Germany.
5. **Analyzing** Why do you think the Allies could not agree on what to do with Germany after the war?

SECTION 2

Reconstruction and Renewal in the West

FOCUS

- What problems did Western European countries face after the war?

- Why did some Western European countries form an economic community?

- What roles did the United States and Canada play after the war?

The creation of NATO fostered a feeling of safety in Western Europe against the threat of communist expansion. The revival of the Western economies, including those in North America, and the reestablishment of normal life made this security permanent. At the same time, as the European powers began to grant their overseas colonies independence, they increasingly concentrated on their own domestic affairs and on building up trade relations with other European countries.

Berliners of the Western zones rebuild their city with the help of the Marshall Plan.

The German "Miracle"

Germany had suffered tremendously in the war. In May 1945 a war correspondent surveyed the damage to Germany's capital:

" *Nothing is left in Berlin. There are no homes, no shops, no transportation, no government buildings. . . . Berlin can now be regarded only as a geographical location heaped with mountainous mounds of debris.* **"**

The situation throughout much of the rest of Germany was similar.

After the war's end, millions of displaced persons, including homeless refugees and survivors of the Nazi death camps, roamed Germany, as well as much of the rest of Europe. Factories were in ruins; from those that remained, Allied forces, especially the Soviets, seized equipment and sent it back home. Farms had been overrun and livestock slaughtered or driven off. The Soviets and the French hoped to keep the Germans weak for a long time. However, by the time of the Berlin blockade, Western governments had decided that the Soviets posed a greater threat than a revived Germany.

Like other European countries, Germany benefited enormously from the Marshall Plan. With this renewed economic stability, West Germans began digging out from the destruction left by the war and rebuilding their homes and businesses. West Germany's recovery was spectacularly successful. The country became one of the industrial giants of the world by the mid-1960s. Many people have referred to this amazing recovery as the German "miracle."

Equally essential in Germany's rehabilitation was the establishment of a democratic government. The Christian Democrats provided stability. By the time Konrad Adenauer left the chancellorship in 1963, West Germany had developed into one of Europe's most stable democracies.

New Republics in France

The challenges faced by France after the war were similar in certain respects to those of

Then & Now

Rising From the Ashes

Coventry, a center of Britain's armaments industry, became a prime target for German air raids in the early days of World War II. The deadliest raid took place on the night of November 14, 1940. Shortly after 7:00 P.M., German aircraft began dropping hundreds of bombs, setting the city ablaze.

By morning Coventry lay in ruins. Fully 80 percent of the buildings in the city had sustained heavy damage. About one third of the factories had been severely damaged or destroyed. Public utilities and the public transportation system had been rendered inoperable. The worst damage occurred in the city center, much of which dated from medieval times. At least one third of the buildings there had been destroyed, including the magnificent cathedral, built in the 1300s.

The city council started to plan the reconstruction of Coventry just weeks after the air raid. The actual rebuilding, however, did not begin until the war had ended. The first act came in June 1946, with the unveiling of a huge stone adorned with a phoenix design. City leaders resolved that, just like this mythical bird, Coventry would rise from the ashes. The rebuilding plan called for a new, largely traffic-free, city center. At the heart would be a two-level mall.

The most ambitious project undertaken in Coventry was the construction of the beautiful Coventry cathedral. In an effort

The original Coventry cathedral

to heal the wounds of the past, in 1961 the city leaders of Coventry invited 16 German teenagers to help build a new cathedral that stands next to the bombed one. When the new cathedral opened in 1962, it became a lasting monument to the spirit of renewal in Western Europe after World War II.

Germany. Many French cities and towns as well as much of France's countryside had been ravaged by the fighting in 1940 and 1944. Like Germany, France benefited from U.S. Marshall Plan aid. France's recovery was slower and less spectacular than West Germany's, but, inspired by economist Jean Monnet (MAW-nay), the French economy prospered and grew during the 1950s.

France's political course was rockier, however. The French people remained deeply divided because of the split between those who had collaborated with the Nazis during the war and those who had remained loyal to a free France. In October 1945 French voters overwhelmingly rejected a revival of the prewar Third Republic. Instead, they adopted a new constitution and established the **Fourth Republic** in October 1946.

The new government faced a variety of difficulties. In addition to continuing economic troubles, the active and well-organized French Communist Party posed a major challenge. Perhaps more important were troubles within France's colonial possessions. Nationalist revolt in Indochina led to a bloody war—and ultimately to a French defeat in 1954. The most serious challenge of all, however, came in Algeria when Algerian nationalists revolted against French rule in 1954.

Violent protests broke out in many French cities. The country seemed to be on the verge of civil war. In May 1958 the French assembly turned to General Charles de Gaulle. De Gaulle granted independence to Algeria and, soon thereafter, to the rest of France's colonial possessions. Meanwhile, after voters approved a new constitution in September, de Gaulle became president of the **Fifth Republic**. De Gaulle held the presidency for 11 years, finally bringing political stability to France.

Postwar Britain

Although Britain had not been occupied by enemy troops during the fighting, the war had brought Britain to the brink of bankruptcy. It had also accelerated a trend toward social reforms that had been brewing even before the war. In July 1945 British voters rejected Churchill's Conservatives and installed the Labour Party, with Clement Attlee as prime minister.

Attlee's government took over important parts of Britain's economy. The government quickly nationalized the coal, steel, and transport industries. It established the basic elements

▲ Clement Attlee is surrounded by supporters after the Labour Party wins the 1945 election and Attlee becomes prime minister.

of the **welfare state**—a collection of government institutions that provided social services such as medical care, unemployment insurance, and retirement pensions for all citizens. Although the Conservatives defeated the Labour Party in 1951, the most important aspects of the welfare state survived and became a basic part of postwar British life. Other Western democracies soon followed Britain's lead, adopting many aspects of the welfare state.

Throughout this period, the country continued to face economic hardships. In 1945 the British had to approach the United States for a $3.75 billion loan to avoid complete bankruptcy. Wartime rationing restrictions remained in force in Britain well into the 1950s.

Britain also began to experience turmoil in its colonial empire. The most serious incident occurred in 1956, when the Egyptian government nationalized the Suez Canal. An attempt by Great Britain and France to intervene against Egypt resulted in complete failure—and ended Britain's role as an imperial power.

The Western European nations had to overcome economic hardship and political changes in the postwar era.

Economic Cooperation

Early steps toward European economic integration, such as reduction of barriers to trade and investment, greatly helped Western Europe's recovery. The Marshall Plan provided the first incentive toward economic unity—the U.S. government tied aid to European passage of measures to reduce tariffs and trade quotas. The Schuman Plan, named for French foreign minister Robert Schuman, went into effect in 1952, creating the European Coal and Steel Community. This organization of France, West Germany, and several other Western European countries helped reorganize the coal and steel industries.

The Coal and Steel Community provided the basis for the **European Economic Community** (EEC), or Common Market. Established by the Treaties of Rome in March 1957, the EEC extended the free-trade principles of the Coal and Steel Community to other sectors of the economies of its members. Members included France, West Germany, Italy, Belgium, the

Netherlands, and Luxembourg. Supporters of the EEC reasoned that economic integration would reduce national economic rivalries and thus lessen the possibility of future wars. As the Treaties of Rome explained, the EEC was to encourage

66 *the harmonious growth of economic activity in the [European Economic] Community as a whole, regular and balanced expansion, augmented [increased] stability, a more rapidly rising standard of living, and closer relations between the participating states.* 99

Western European countries hoped to boost their economies and reduce the chance of future wars by forming an economic community.

The United States and Canada

In North America the war had stimulated the U.S. and Canadian economies, ending the Great Depression and restoring a large measure of prosperity. The postwar period also brought other important changes. For the United States, the most important change was a commitment to continued involvement in world affairs.

After the war the United States embarked on a determined policy to ensure free and open trade around the world. The United States took the lead in the postwar reconstruction of the world economy. This included the Marshall Plan, as well as major U.S. financing of the

▲ This radar station on the DEW Line was intended to provide several hours' warning before an enemy attack.

International Monetary Fund (IMF) and of the International Bank for Reconstruction and Development, better known as the World Bank.

Another way in which North America continued its involvement in world affairs was through the NATO alliance. Canadian and U.S. troops, ships, and planes took part in regular military exercises in Europe and the Atlantic. For the United States, Canada served a special purpose in military defense. The United States and Canada jointly constructed the Distant Early Warning (DEW) Line, a string of radar stations across the far northern reaches of North America. The purpose of the DEW Line was to detect attacking Soviet bombers early enough to provide a military shield for North America.

The United States took the lead in promoting international prosperity, and the United States and Canada played an active part in Western military defense.

SECTION 2 REVIEW

IDENTIFY and explain the significance of the following:
Fourth Republic
Fifth Republic
welfare state
European Economic Community

1. **Main Idea** How were the problems faced by

the nations of Western Europe after the war similar? How were they different?

2. **Main Idea** What were the goals of the EEC?

3. **Geography: Location** How did Canada's location make it an important military partner of the United States?

4. **Writing to Describe** Write a short essay describing the new role played by the United States and Canada in world affairs after World War II.

5. **Analyzing** Why did the United States want to rebuild and revitalize Germany after the war? What were the results of this policy?

SECTION 2 REVIEW ANSWERS

IDENTIFY
For significance, see the following pages:
Fourth Republic (p. 723)
Fifth Republic (p. 724)
welfare state (p. 724)
European Economic Community (p. 724)

1. similar—wartime destruction, economic instability; different— Germany: shift to free-market economy; France: split over Nazi collaboration, lost colonial possessions; Britain: near bankruptcy
2. hoped to speed economic recovery and avoid future wars
3. led to joint defenses such as Distant Early Warning Line
4. Essays should describe the effects of Marshall Plan aid and increased military defenses.
5. wanted to avoid international depression, keep Soviets in check; Germany became a major industrial and economic power

Theme:
Economic Organization

The Soviet army's scorched earth policy during World War II had disastrous effects on the national economy as well as on German supply lines. To restore economic strength, Stalin implemented a Five-Year Plan. Within three years the industrial sector had been restored to its prewar level, but agricultural production remained weak.

Critical Thinking Ask students why the agricultural sector did not revive quickly.

ANSWER: Students may say that it took time for fields to return to productivity or that livestock may have been destroyed.

SECTION 3

The New Soviet Empire

FOCUS

- How did the Soviet Union change after the war?
- What was the result of Soviet rule in Eastern Europe?
- How did postwar Yugoslavia differ from the rest of Eastern Europe?

During the two decades after World War II, the Soviet Union expanded its control to include most of Eastern Europe. Though the countries of the Soviet sphere were supposedly independent, the governments there ruled with guidance from the Soviets and were maintained in power by the Red Army. Behind the Iron Curtain, the Soviets ruthlessly put down resistance to their authority. The people of Eastern Europe were in fact subjects of a new Soviet empire.

Soviet tank on parade in Red Square

Changes in the Soviet Union

No other European nation suffered more than the Soviet Union during World War II. The German advance of 1941 had laid waste to much of the western Soviet Union. The Soviet counter-offensive of the following years destroyed much of what the Germans had not.

Some 20 million Soviet citizens were killed during the war, although no precise total can be determined. Most of these casualties were due not to the Germans but to Stalin's brutality against his own people. The fighting also left approximately 25 million homeless. Many of the cities of the western Soviet Union were in ruins; much of the country's best and most productive farmland was left barren. Roughly one quarter of the country's capital stock—productive resources such as industrial machinery and farm equipment—had been destroyed. Hunger and disease were widespread.

Even so, the Soviet Union was among the victors, and victory had its rewards. The Soviet Union in 1945 included nearly 200,000 square miles more territory than it had before 1939. The new territories included the formerly independent Baltic republics of Lithuania, Latvia, and Estonia; a sizable portion of eastern Poland (which Stalin had gained in his 1939 pact with Hitler); East Prussia; territory along the Soviet border with Romania; and the formerly Japanese Kuril Islands.

Moreover, the war had enhanced the reputation of the Stalinist government among many Soviets. Most had no way of knowing that Stalin's incompetence had been largely responsible for the near-defeat by Germany in 1941. During the war Stalin had downplayed communist ideology in favor of traditional themes of Russian patriotism. The dislocation of the war also often hid the ongoing repression of potential rivals. After the war Soviet citizens continued to face arrests, torture, and imprisonment at the hands of the secret police.

De-Stalinization

On March 1, 1953, a bodyguard, worried because Stalin had not been seen since afternoon, broke into a room in Stalin's country home. He found

This **de-Stalinization** extended to economic affairs. Where Stalin had emphasized industrial growth to the exclusion of almost everything else, the new government made greater allowances for consumer tastes. Food production, in particular, was stepped up. "Communism cannot be conceived of as a table with empty places," declared Khrushchev. Nevertheless, the brutal police state that Stalin created continued to be the foundation of the Soviet government's power.

After the war, the Soviet Union reverted to Stalinist repression, which Khrushchev eased somewhat after Stalin's death.

▲ Injured and homeless, Soviet peasants stare at the ruins of their village destroyed by the German army.

the Soviet leader lying on the floor unable to speak; four days later Stalin died. His death led to a power struggle among top Communist officials. Eventually, Nikita Khrushchev (kroosh-CHAWF), former party secretary of the Ukraine, took over as leader of the Soviet Union.

By the beginning of 1956, Khrushchev was sure enough of his leadership position to denounce the excesses of Stalin's policies. In a dramatic "secret speech" given to the Twentieth Congress of the Communist Party in February 1956, Khrushchev condemned Stalin for fostering a "cult of personality," for murdering thousands of loyal and honest Communist officials and party members, for weakening the Red Army to the point of nearly losing the war against Germany, and for various other crimes against the Soviet people.

Khrushchev's attack on Stalin produced a profound shock. As Vladimir Osipov, later an editor of an underground journal, recalled:

❝ *Overthrown was the man who had personified the existing system and ideology to such an extent that the very words 'the Soviet power' and 'Stalin' seemed to have been synonymous [meant the same thing]. . . . Khrushchev's speech and the 20th Congress destroyed our faith, having extracted from it its very core . . . Joseph Stalin.* ❞

East Germany and Poland

To the Soviets' way of thinking, the most important countries of Central and Eastern Europe were East Germany and Poland. Germany had attacked their territory twice through Poland. To prevent another such attack, the Soviets wanted to keep a tight grip on these countries.

East Germany. In contrast to West Germany, no economic "miracle" took place in East Germany. Many of the East German factories not destroyed in the fighting were relocated to the Soviet Union as reparations. Though East Germany became a Soviet ally, ordinary Russians had long looked upon all Germans as the enemy. An East German technician sent to the Soviet Union was astonished at Soviet hostility:

❝ *I spent a whole day arguing with them and telling them that our part of Germany was friends with them and that we were building socialism. But it didn't seem to matter. For them, Germans were Germans and they hated us all.* ❞

Through the early 1950s the Soviet government stripped East Germany of resources, leaving the East Germans few means with which to rebuild their devastated country. The harsh treatment provoked a reaction. In June 1953 construction workers in East Berlin dropped their tools and went on strike. It was not long before the strike grew into a full-scale revolt against the communist government. The government, with assistance from Soviet tanks, brutally put down the uprising, killing dozens of people. Over 100 more were executed as traitors in the revolt's aftermath.

Poland. Although relations were tense between the Soviet Union and East Germany, tensions were even greater between the Soviets and Poles. The events surrounding the end of the war only made matters worse. In August 1944 Polish resistance fighters in Warsaw rose up against the German occupation forces. Stalin ordered Red Army troops approaching the city to halt, giving the Nazis time to smash the Polish forces and eliminate any potential competitors to Stalin's handpicked Polish communist government.

Poles briefly gained hope from the interest Roosevelt and Churchill expressed in Poland's future at Yalta, but as it became clear that neither the United States nor Britain was willing to risk war with the Soviet Union over Poland, the Soviets crushed all opposition. However, opposition gradually revived. In 1956, following Khrushchev's anti-Stalin speech, Polish protesters began insisting on greater rights for the Polish people. Polish workers carried signs demanding "Bread and Freedom."

This time the Soviets did not respond with overwhelming force. They allowed the return to power of Wladyslaw Gomulka (goh-MOOHL-kuh), a former Polish leader deposed by Stalin for wanting to take Poland in a more independent direction. Gomulka proved to be one of the shrewdest and most durable of the Eastern European Communist rulers. He remained in power for 14 years, walking a fine line between what the Polish people demanded and what Moscow would tolerate.

Czechoslovakia and Hungary

Unlike most other countries in Central Europe, Czechoslovakia had been a functioning democracy between the wars. This helped the nation resist Soviet domination longer than its neighbors. In April 1945, with Stalin's support, prewar president Edvard Benes (BEN-esh) reassumed office and appointed a national coalition. Parliamentary elections in May 1946 gave the largest share of the votes to the Communist Party, which then formed another government with several other parties.

In February 1948, however, the Czech Communists staged a coup. Having staffed the key positions in the important ministries with party loyalists and enjoying the backing of the Soviet army, the Communists were able to seize complete power with relative ease. One of the last of the democratic leaders, Foreign Minister Jan Masaryk (MAH-sah-rik), was found dead outside his office building, the result of a fall from his upper-story window. The Communists maintained that he jumped, but many in Czechoslovakia believed he was pushed.

▲ With no other weapons, two young men throw rocks at a Soviet tank that was sent to East Berlin to put down the revolt against communist rule.

► In October 1956 Hungarian protesters deface a toppled statue of Stalin.

In Hungary the opposition to Soviet control came from small landholders. In the November 1945 elections, the anticommunist Smallholders Party won a majority and formed a new government. This victory surprised the Hungarian Communists, who then plotted to destroy the government. In February 1947 the Communists seized the secretary general of the Smallholders Party, eventually executing him on charges of treason. Harassment of the government continued, finally resulting in the forced resignation of the premier in May 1947.

During the course of the next several years the Communists consolidated their control over Hungary, but in 1956 the strong de-Stalinization movement in the Soviet Union encouraged Hungarians to attempt something similar. Premier Imre Nagy (NAJ) announced that Hungary must find a way to adapt socialism to fit Hungarian circumstances—"to cut our coat according to our cloth." He eased police repression and suspended collectivization.

The reform movement soon turned into an anti-Soviet revolution. In October, spurred on by the demonstrations in Poland, Hungarian protesters took to the streets of Budapest by the hundreds of thousands, chanting, "We shall never again be slaves!" Police fired on the crowd, converting the demonstration into a riot. Rioters destroyed Soviet flags and toppled statues of Stalin. An observer recalled the scene:

66 *I saw young students, who had known nothing but a life under Communist and Russian control, die for a freedom about which they had only heard from others or from their own hearts. . . . I saw a girl of fourteen blow up a Russian tank, and grandmothers walk up to Russian cannons.* 99

Amid the excitement, Nagy promised free elections and Hungary's withdrawal from the Warsaw Pact. On October 30 the Soviets had pulled their troops out of Budapest. After it became obvious that the Western powers were not going to come to Hungary's aid, however, the Soviet leadership decided to crush the revolt. On November 4 a huge armored force, including some 2,500 tanks entered Hungary. Thousands of Hungarians died in the fighting; hundreds of thousands fled the country for the West.

Soviet rule in Eastern Europe sparked rebellions in several countries.

The Balkans

Soviet power flowed into the Balkans along with the Red Army at the war's end. The Soviet Union had the easiest time taking over Bulgaria. For a long time Bulgaria has been relatively pro-Russian. It also was the only country under the wartime domination of Germany to successfully resist Berlin's demands to contribute troops to the invasion of the Soviet Union. In September 1944 Bulgaria submitted to Soviet armistice demands and accepted a coalition government with Communists in key posts.

During the course of the next several months the Communists pushed their coalition partners aside and directed a bloody purge of supporters of the monarchy. By November 1945 the Communists in Bulgaria had come to dominate

730

the governing coalition. Thereafter, Communist control was never seriously challenged.

The Red Army invaded Romania about the same time it entered Bulgaria. The Soviets took a more direct role in Romanian politics, however, partly because of traditional Romanian hostility to Russian imperialism and partly because of Romania's position on the Soviet Union's border. In March 1945 Stalin forced King Michael to hand over government authority to the leader of the left-wing Plowmen's Front. In December 1947 Communists forced King Michael to abdicate. The following March the Communist People's Democratic Front won more than 90 percent of the vote in a rigged election.

The story of communism had both a different beginning and a different ending in Yugoslavia than elsewhere in the Balkans. Communism emerged as a powerful force in Yugoslavia through the wartime efforts of Josip Broz, commonly called Tito, and his anti-German partisan comrades. Although Soviet forces came to Tito's assistance in 1944, effective power in the country resided with Tito's Communist National Front.

For three years after the war, Yugoslavia aligned itself with the Soviet Union, but never very closely. In 1948 strong differences of opinion between the Soviets and Tito came to a head. Stalin refused to accept the idea of an independent communist government so close to the borders of the Soviet Union and abruptly recalled Soviet advisors from Yugoslavia. In June 1948 he expelled Yugoslavia from the Cominform.

▲ **Marshall Tito of Yugoslavia speaks to a joint session of the National Assembly in 1952.**

As Tito became an outcast among his fellow Communists, he pursued closer relations with the West, particularly the United States, which was happy to help a European communist power break free from the Soviets. American economic and military aid began flowing to Yugoslavia.

The Soviet Union remained firmly in command of Bulgaria and Romania, but Yugoslavia reasserted its independence.

SECTION 3 REVIEW

IDENTIFY and explain the significance of the following:
  Nikita Khrushchev
  de-Stalinization
  Wladyslaw Gomulka
  Edvard Benes
  Imre Nagy
  Tito

1. **Main Idea** What fueled the process of de-Stalinization in the Soviet Union? How did the Soviet government change after Stalin's death?

2. **Main Idea** How did Soviet domination affect the nations of Eastern Europe?

3. **Politics and Law** How was Yugoslavia an exception to the rule of Soviet control of Eastern Europe?

4. **Writing to Describe** Imagine that you are a student in Budapest at the time of the Hungarian Revolution. Write a letter to your friends in the West describing what is happening and why the nation is in revolt.

5. **Comparing** How did various Eastern European nations resist Soviet domination? Why did most of these movements fail? What were the results of their failure?

SECTION 4
The Cold War Deepens

FOCUS

- What were some of the consequences of the nuclear arms race?
- How did the development of nuclear weapons affect international stability?
- What were the effects of the Cuban missile crisis?

The division of Europe into East and West helped trigger a race between the United States and the Soviet Union to build more powerful and destructive weapons. The arms race in turn intensified the suspicions the superpowers felt toward each other, and more than once pushed the world to the brink of war.

This nuclear bomb called "Fat Man" was the type of bomb dropped on Nagasaki, Japan.

The Arms Race

What made the Cold War different from other eras of great-power competition was the existence of nuclear weapons. These new weapons were enormously more destructive than any previous weapons, and they threatened the world with mass devastation.

Albert Einstein's theory of relativity had brought about a complete revolution in the way scientists thought about matter and energy. Between 1910 and 1939 scientists across Europe performed experiments to discover the mysteries of the atom. Eventually these scientists became interested in a process known as **fission**—the splitting of the nucleus of an atom in order to release great amounts of energy.

In 1942 the United States formally organized a program, known as the Manhattan Project, to develop an atomic bomb. The military gathered many top nuclear scientists at the remote site of Los Alamos, New Mexico, under the direction of J. Robert Oppenheimer, to work on the project. The military director of the Manhattan Project, General Leslie Groves, described the first atomic blast, which took place on July 16, 1945:

66 For a brief period there was a lightning effect within a radius of twenty miles equal to several suns at midday; a huge ball of fire was formed which lasted for several seconds. This ball mushroomed and rose to a height of over 10,000 feet before it dimmed. . . . All seemed to feel that they had been present at the birth of a new age. 99

On August 6 the United States dropped an atomic bomb on Hiroshima and three days later another on Nagasaki to end the war with Japan.

For four years the United States possessed a monopoly over atomic weapons. During that time Soviet scientists worked frantically on a Soviet atomic bomb. Spies who had actually worked on the Manhattan Project and had access to U.S. and British atomic secrets helped the Soviet scientists. In 1949 the Soviet Union exploded its first atomic device.

The successful Soviet atomic test contributed to growing American fears of communism. U.S. senator Joseph McCarthy and others began a campaign to uncover suspected Communists. Without

SECTION 4

CORE LESSON PLAN
See pages 713I and 713J for Lesson Plan 26.4.

R **RESOURCE ACTIVITY**

READINGS IN WORLD HISTORY
Reading 26.4
The Path to the Atomic Bomb

Have students read the selection about the development of the atomic bomb. Then have them complete the questions.

Level 2

Theme: Politics and Law

Joseph McCarthy played an important role in the Cold War. He came to prominence in 1950, when he announced that he had a list of 205 Communists who were employed by the State Department. In the Senate, McCarthy gained control of investigatory committees and proceeded to expose university professors and minor government officials as Communists. McCarthy eventually even attacked the army, which led to an investigation known as the Army-McCarthy hearings. The hearings were televised, allowing the general public to see McCarthy's tactics firsthand. In the wake of the hearings, McCarthy was censured by the Senate.

Critical Thinking Ask students why televising the hearings changed Americans' attitudes toward McCarthy.

ANSWER: Students might suggest that Americans could see for themselves how mean-spirited and vicious McCarthy's attacks were.

any real evidence, McCarthy accused many people of communist activities, ruining their careers and destroying their reputations. Nevertheless, a special Congressional investigative organization, known as the House Un-American Activities Committee, did in fact uncover several Soviet spies.

The Soviet acquisition of the bomb also caused American leaders to press ahead and create more powerful weapons. The Soviets did the same. While earlier bombs produced their energy from fission, another process—**fusion**—promised to yield bombs immensely more destructive. Fusion bombs (also called thermonuclear bombs) derived their energy from combining hydrogen atoms in the same kind of reaction that fuels the sun.

The first U.S. hydrogen blast took place in November 1952. The first Soviet detonation of a hydrogen bomb followed in August 1953. During the 1950s both superpowers also began developing long-range missiles, including intercontinental ballistic missiles (**ICBMs**) that could strike enemy targets from either the United States or the Soviet Union.

Antinuclear Efforts

The nuclear arms race provoked protests by many people who feared that the new weapons would produce a war far more destructive than even World War II. During the early years of the nuclear era, the protests were essentially confined to the United States and Western Europe. A 1946 U.S. proposal would have made atomic energy an international venture after

a transition period, but Stalin rejected the plan.

During the 1950s many antinuclear protests focused on the problem of **fallout**—radioactive dust and other particles from nuclear blasts that are potentially harmful to living things. By the late 1950s scientists could detect radioactive material almost everywhere—in livestock, in crops, in drinking water, in the bones of children. Medical scientists predicted sharp increases in rates of cancer, birth defects, and miscarriages. People everywhere demanded that the superpowers cease testing.

At the end of the 1950s, the superpowers began making plans for talks on nuclear arms control. In 1959 Khrushchev visited the United States, and together he and U.S. president Dwight Eisenhower planned a summit that would be held the following year in Paris. In May 1960, however, Khrushchev announced that an American U-2 spy plane had been shot down over the Soviet Union. Eisenhower refused to apologize for the incident, maintaining that keeping tabs on developments in the Soviet Union was vital to U.S. security. Outraged, Khrushchev refused to meet with Eisenhower.

The arms race produced enormously powerful weapons, as well as fears and protests about the dangers these weapons posed.

To the Brink

The arms race elevated the level of tension between the superpowers. Both countries hoped to gain political advantage by raising the possibility of military action—action that might result in the use of nuclear weapons. This practice became known as **brinkmanship**—the act of moving to the brink of nuclear war without going over.

The Berlin Wall. One of the most dangerous acts of brinkmanship involved Berlin. In

The Nuclear Arms Race, 1945–1970

Soviet Nuclear Strength

✈ 145	▮ 4	⬤ 0
✈ 195	▯ 1220	⬤ 41

CHINA (1964)

SOVIET UNION (1949) • Sverdlovsk

Legend:
- Nuclear nation
- 1945 Year successfully tested bomb
- ✈ Intercontinental bomber, 1960
- ✈ Intercontinental bomber, 1970
- ▮ ICBMs, 1960
- ▯ ICBMs, 1970
- ⬤ Submarine-launched ballistic missiles, (SLBMs), 1960
- ⬤ SLBMs, 1970

Potential ICBM and SLBM trajectories:
- U.S.
- Soviet

May 1960: Soviets shoot down American U-2 spy plane.

August 1961: Soviets resume atmospheric nuclear testing.

1962: Soviets install world's first anti-ballistic missiles (ABMs).

Moscow
Leningrad
EUROPE

AFRICA

August 1961: Berlin Wall heightens tensions between U.S. and U.S.S.R.

ALGERIA (French)

WEST GERMANY
FRANCE (1960)
UNITED KINGDOM (1952)

February 1960: France detonates its first atomic bomb. May 1962: France conducts underground nuclear test.

North Pole

PACIFIC OCEAN

ATLANTIC OCEAN

U.S. Nuclear Strength

✈ 1735	▮ 42	⬤ 32
✈ 501	▯ 1054	⬤ 616

NORTH AMERICA

Washington, D.C.
UNITED STATES (1945)

October 1962: After Soviets send nuclear missiles to Cuba, Kennedy readies ICBMs and demands that missiles be removed. Khrushchev finally complies.

September 1961: Americans resume underground nuclear testing; atmospheric testing resumes 1962.

Los Alamos

July 1945: First atomic-bomb test.

MEXICO   CUBA

0 — 750 — 1,500 Miles
0 — 750 — 1,500 Kilometers
Azimuthal Equidistant Projection

Fears of Nuclear War   Throughout the 1960s the United States and the Soviet Union engaged in an escalating struggle for nuclear superiority.

❓ Linking Geography and History   Which nation tested nuclear weapons in Africa?

November 1958 Khrushchev demanded negotiations on the future of Berlin. He threatened to conclude a separate peace treaty with East Germany—implying that Western access to Berlin might be cut off. The United States, Britain, and France denounced Khrushchev's threats, but they did agree to meet. The discussions, however, led nowhere.

Complicating the Berlin situation was the matter of refugees. Every month, thousands of mostly young East Germans were fleeing their country for the West, often using West Berlin as an exit. Worried by the mass migration, in August 1961 the Soviets and East Germans erected a wall separating East Berlin from West

Berlin. Almost overnight, a wall of concrete and barbed wire, reinforced by guard towers and land mines, went up through the middle of the city.

The Cuban missile crisis. Even more nerve-wracking than the Berlin affair was the Cuban missile crisis of October 1962. The crisis began during the summer of 1962, when the Soviet Union secretly began constructing launch sites for intermediate-range nuclear missiles in Cuba, less than 100 miles from U.S. shores. By the time U.S. spy planes discovered the sites in October, they were nearly operational.

On October 22 U.S. president John F. Kennedy publicly demanded that Khrushchev

---

R RESOURCE ACTIVITY

GLOBAL HISTORY RESOURCE CENTER
Reading: *Nikita Khrushchev on Peaceful Coexistence*
Reading: *John F. Kennedy on Arms and Peace*

Print out and distribute the readings. Have students read both statements. Then ask students to imagine that they are going to interview these two leaders on television. Have students write a list of questions and possible answers.

Level 3

INTERNET ACTIVITY

CUBAN MISSILE CRISIS
The Cuban missile crisis brought the United States and the Soviet Union closer to nuclear war than at any time before or since.

Activity: Have students search the Internet for more information on the Cuban missile crisis. Have students construct a detailed timeline of the events of October 1962. Students may want to illustrate their timeline with maps and photos found on the Internet.

All Levels

SECTION 4 REVIEW ANSWERS

IDENTIFY
For significance, see the following pages:
fission (p. 731)
J. Robert Oppenheimer (p. 731)
fusion (p. 732)
ICBMs (p. 732)
fallout (p. 732)
brinkmanship (p. 732)
John F. Kennedy (p. 733)
domino theory (p. 734)

1. People feared nuclear war and fallout. Several people joined protests and urged governments to limit the testing of nuclear weapons.
2. It emphasized the dangers of possession of nuclear weapons.
3. It increased the threat of worldwide destruction.
4. Paragraphs should address the fear of nuclear war and the economic and political rivalry between the United States and the Soviet Union.
5. Answers should address the consequences of nuclear weapons testing, such as the dangers posed to living things.

withdraw the missiles from Cuba. He announced an American blockade of the island to prevent additional missiles or parts from arriving. He also warned Khrushchev to halt construction:

❝ It shall be the policy of this nation to regard any nuclear missile launched from Cuba against any nation in the Western Hemisphere as an attack by the Soviet Union on the United States, requiring a full retaliatory response upon the Soviet Union.❞

For five days the world held its breath, wondering whether Khrushchev would yield to Kennedy's demand. Finally Khrushchev did, agreeing to pull the Soviet missiles out of Cuba in exchange for a U.S. pledge not to invade Cuba and a confidential promise by Kennedy to withdraw U.S. missiles from Turkey.

The threat of nuclear war meant that international disagreements could grow into dangerous crises.

New directions. Although the Cuban missile crisis did not lead to war, it shook some nations' confidence in the leadership of the superpowers. Within a few years, for example, Charles de Gaulle announced that France was withdrawing its military obligations to NATO. France remained part of the Western alliance, but the French pursued an independent foreign policy.

Most importantly, the Cuban missile crisis finally led to efforts by the superpowers to control the arms race. In August 1963 the United States, the Soviet Union, and Britain signed the Limited Nuclear Test Ban Treaty. This treaty forbade nuclear testing in the atmosphere, the oceans, and outer space. The nuclear powers, however, continued to test underground. A broader arms-control treaty—the Non-Proliferation Treaty—followed five years later. The treaty committed the United States, the Soviet Union, Britain, and eventually more than 100 other countries to refrain from acquiring or spreading nuclear weapons.

Even though the Cuban missile crisis helped slow the nuclear arms race, it did not stop the Cold War. Since the communist victory in China in 1949 and the outbreak of the Korean War, the United States had been concerned with the spread of communism in Asia. In 1954 President Eisenhower warned of the consequences of one nation falling to communism by likening countries to dominoes: "You have a row of dominoes, and you knock over the first one, and what will happen to the last one is the certainty that it will go over very quickly." This idea came to be known as the "**domino theory**." During the 1950s and early 1960s, efforts to halt communist expansion led the United States to send military advisors to South Vietnam. By 1965 U.S. involvement had escalated into a full-scale war in Southeast Asia. (See Chapter 27.)

The Cuban missile crisis caused great fear of a nuclear confrontation, but also led to negotiations to limit nuclear arms and testing.

SECTION 4 REVIEW

IDENTIFY and explain the significance of the following:
fission
J. Robert Oppenheimer
fusion
ICBMs
fallout
brinkmanship
John F. Kennedy
domino theory

1. Main Idea Why were many people frightened of the arms race, and what did some people do in response to these fears?

2. Main Idea Why was the Cuban missile crisis important in East-West relations?

3. Technology How did new weapons technology affect international stability?

4. Writing to Persuade Write a paragraph defending or refuting the following statement: *In 1962 the United States pursued the best course of action by demanding that Soviet missiles be withdrawn from Cuba and by blockading the island.*

5. Hypothesizing Why do you think both superpowers agreed to control the further development and testing of nuclear weapons?

Changes in Society and Culture

SECTION 5

CORE LESSON PLAN
See pages 713K and 713L for Lesson Plan 26.5.

FOCUS

- How did standards of living change in the postwar decades?
- What factors contributed to protest movements in the 1960s?
- What effects did the protests of the 1960s have?

The two decades after 1945 were a time of both prosperity and anxiety. The prosperity resulted from widespread economic growth in the West; the anxiety from the ever-present and growing danger of nuclear destruction. By the mid-1960s many people, particularly the younger generation, began to question the society and values of the previous generation. The result was growing unrest in many Western countries.

The French Citroen 2CV

The Age of Affluence

During the 1950s and 1960s, the standard of living in most of North America and Western Europe reached its highest level in history. The countries of the Soviet bloc lagged behind, but the post-Stalin emphasis on consumer goods demonstrated a new attention to the lives of ordinary individuals.

Boom times in the West. Throughout most of the 1950s and 1960s, the economies of the West experienced strong and steady growth, providing jobs and steady incomes to growing populations. The United States led the way. Economic growth in the United States was in part spurred by two factors: (1) the expansion of automobile production, which fostered the enormous growth of suburbs, and (2) the emergence of new technologies, such as television and dozens of new household appliances. In Western Europe, Marshall Plan funds helped get the national economies of the war-torn countries back on their feet. Consumer confidence and carefully considered government policy helped keep the recovery going through the 1950s and 1960s.

The result of booming economies was the full blossoming in much of Western Europe of the consumer culture that had begun to emerge during the 1920s. In Britain, for example, consumer credit (loans tied to the purchase of consumer goods) tripled between 1957 and 1965. In 1965 British viewers purchased 13 million television sets, nearly 1,000 times the number purchased in 1947. In France the Citroen 2CV automobile became a French counterpart of the Ford Model T. By the early 1970s some 70 percent of French adults owned an automobile. Household appliances such as refrigerators and washing machines came to be seen as necessities. One French woman described the changes these consumer goods brought to European women in the 1970s:

> ❝Charter trips and organized travel; in my day that didn't even enter into your wildest dreams. . . . Blue jeans and the T-shirts, instant mashed potatoes, the transistor radio you can buy for next to nothing, the boyfriend who has a Citroen 2CV he bought second-hand, and off you go to the country.❞

Daily Life
The suburban housing developments that sprang up in the United States after the war emphasized the important place children held in American life at that time. Houses in the suburbs included features that simplified child supervision: kitchens were placed in the front of the house, and living rooms contained large picture windows. Additionally, these houses were only one story high, eliminating the dangers of stairs for small children.

Critical Thinking Ask students to summarize the importance of architecture in the suburbs and list other reasons why people may have moved to the suburbs.

ANSWER: Students might suggest that cars and highways made commuting possible, and that the suburbs seemed clean and safe.

Tougher times in the East. The people of Eastern Europe and the Soviet Union did not enjoy the same prosperity as westerners. Lacking U.S. reconstruction assistance, the Communist bloc recovered more slowly from the war. In addition, the Eastern European countries had generally not been nearly as developed as the West even before the war. Many areas had not industrialized.

Nevertheless, consumer-oriented economic policies under Khrushchev had some effect. A burst of housing construction, starting in 1956, contributed to the sense that things were getting better. So did increases in wages, lengthened maternity leaves, higher pensions and disability benefits, and shorter workweeks. But even these reforms left many problems untouched. New housing was poorly constructed, and workers still had to stand in long lines for scarce and inferior goods. About the only thing that kept the people of the Communist bloc from complaining more than they did was a lack of knowledge about the prosperity of the West.

▲ **This young man displays his rebellion through his clothing and hairstyle.**

The postwar years witnessed widespread prosperity in the West and improved, but still lagging, living standards in the East.

The Generation Gap

The most obvious characteristic of the postwar generation in the West was its great size. Because of economic depression and war, during the 1930s and 1940s millions of couples had put off starting families. By the end of the war, there existed an extraordinarily large group of people ready to have children. (The situation was different in the Soviet Union because of the much greater number of wartime deaths.) The result was the large generation born between the late 1940s and the early 1960s—the generation of the **baby boom**.

Many of the younger people identified themselves quite differently from their parents' generation. The older generation, having experienced material hardship, appreciated what they now had; the younger generation, knowing only prosperity, often took it for granted. The older generation found it easy to focus on what was finally right in their lives, while the younger generation tended to concentrate on what was wrong. In the West these differences came to be called the **generation gap**.

A distinctive culture developed among the young, generally emphasizing youthful tastes in fashion, music, and styles of living. Many young people chose clothing that set them off from their parents—starting with blue jeans and moving on to mini-skirts, tie-dyed T-shirts, and love beads. They listened to different music—from Elvis Presley to the Beatles, the Rolling Stones, and Jimi Hendrix. Many developed an attitude of suspicion toward their parents' generation. A commonly heard warning was "Don't trust anyone over thirty."

The prosperity of the period made the youth culture possible. More than ever before, young people had money to spend on clothes, music, and other forms of entertainment. The chance to attend college also enabled many young people to postpone their entry into the world of work.

The Culture of Protest

In his 1961 inaugural address, President Kennedy urged young Americans to take an active role in their government, saying: "The torch has been passed to a new generation of Americans. . . ." But this invitation was short-lived—for many people, it ended with the assassination of the president in 1963. Disillusioned with politics, young people contributed to the growth of a broad culture of protest. They protested against the unjust and violent policies of governments and what they saw as the conformity of their parents' generation, and for more equality in society.

The antiwar movement. A pressing issue for many young people, both in the United States and other countries, was the Vietnam War. As

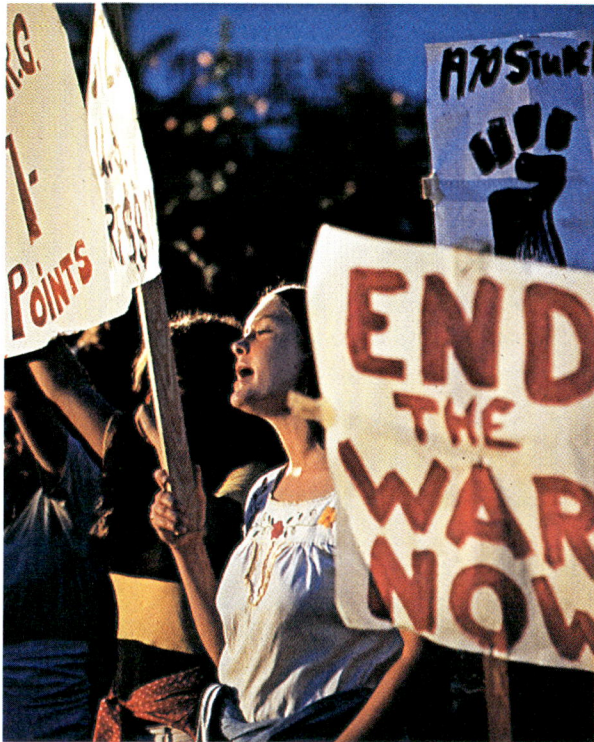

▲ Young citizens gather in Washington, D.C., to call for an end to the Vietnam War.

the U.S. role in the fighting escalated during the mid-1960s, opposition to the war, particularly among college students, escalated as well. Students marched and held rallies, condemning the war as cruel and unjust. Protesters besieged the White House during the presidency of Lyndon Baines Johnson, chanting: "Hey, hey, LBJ, how many kids did you kill today?"

Equal rights. Broader and longer lasting than the antiwar movement was the struggle for equal rights. In the United States after World War II the struggle first focused on civil rights for African Americans. In December 1955 in Montgomery, Alabama, an African American woman named Rosa Parks refused to obey a segregation law that required her to give up her seat on a city bus to a white person. Parks's defiance led Montgomery's African American community to boycott the city buses.

During the early 1960s many people staged sit-ins and other forms of demonstrations against legalized inequality. One of the largest protests was the August 1963 March on Washington. Civil rights leaders, such as the Reverend Martin Luther King, Jr., stirred the consciences of millions. Before a crowd of over 200,000 people, King proclaimed:

66 *I have a dream that one day . . . all of God's children, black men and white men, Jews and Gentiles, Protestants and Catholics, will be able to join hands and sing in the words of the old Negro spiritual, 'Free at last! Free at last! Thank God Almighty, we are free at last!'* 99

Revolt in Western Europe. The dissatisfaction of some Europeans spanned a spectrum of issues, and it produced a series of political explosions. For example, university students throughout Western Europe protested the war in Southeast Asia, as well as university overcrowding. During the spring of 1968, a wave of violent demonstrations swept France, West Germany, and Italy.

The center of the demonstrations was Paris, where a German exchange student, Daniel Cohn-Bendit (nicknamed Danny the Red), led fellow students out of the classroom to protest French educational policy. The protest spread after police resorted to violence to break up the demonstration. Within days industrial workers joined the protest, bringing their own complaints, such as demands for higher wages. Before long, millions of people were on strike across the country.

The May Events, as the uprising was called, nearly toppled the de Gaulle government in France. Although de Gaulle managed to hold on to power for a while longer, the unrest in France, combined with the protests in the other Western European countries, demonstrated the degree to which many people had become alienated from mainstream society.

Literature and film. While most of the protests took place in the political arena, books, movies, and television also served as vehicles for airing grievances and calling for change. A recurrent theme was the danger of nuclear war. Nevil Shute's best-selling book *On the Beach* depicted life in the aftermath of a nuclear war; Eugene Burdick and Harvey Wheeler's novel *Fail-Safe* presented a frightening account of how a nuclear war might start by accident.

Of films dealing with nuclear war, probably the most influential and one of the most hilarious was Stanley Kubrick's dark comedy, *Dr. Strangelove, or How I Learned to Stop Worrying and Love the Bomb*. The film reaches a high point

Theme: Social Relations

Although women's organizations had been forming in France for several years, scholars argue that the first display of women's rights activism there took place in 1970. During a Paris demonstration at the Tomb of the Unknown Soldier, a group of women presented a wreath dedicated "to one more unknown than the soldier, his wife." While some French groups, such as the Féministes Revolutionnaires, worked for the "total destruction of the patriarchal order," others concentrated on the issues of sexism and violence against women.

Critical Thinking Ask students why protest organizations sometimes splinter.

ANSWER: Students might answer that individuals within an organization may disagree on issues and methods.

RESOURCE ACTIVITY

WRITING PROJECTS
Writing Project 26
Writing a Diary

After you have discussed the culture of protest, have students complete the steps for writing a diary.

Level 3

▶ Emergency in a nuclear plant; scene from the film based on Nevil Shute's book *On the Beach*

◀ Actor Slim Pickens poses for an advertisement for the film *Dr. Strangelove.*

with the image of an American cowboy-pilot riding a hydrogen bomb down to its Russian target, waving his hat and yelling at the top of his lungs.

Dissent in the East. Protest was not confined to the West. However, behind the Iron Curtain, protest was more difficult and dangerous. Nonetheless, in the communist countries brave people known as **dissidents** spoke out against their governments. Russian poet Yevgeny Yevtushenko (yef-tuh-SHENG-koh) thought de-Stalinization was less than it seemed. His "Heirs of Stalin" saw the old system waiting to make a comeback:

> *Some of his heirs*
> *tend roses in retirement,*
> *but secretly consider*
> *their retirement temporary.*
> *Others,*
> *from platforms rail against Stalin,*
> *but,*
> *at night,*
> *yearn for the good old days.*

One of the most outspoken of all the Soviet dissidents was Aleksandr Solzhenitsyn (sohl-zhuh-NEET-suhn). *One Day in the Life of Ivan Denisovich,* Solzhenitsyn's novel of life in the Stalinist labor camps, created a sensation in the Soviet Union and elsewhere. Dissidents such as Solzhenitsyn and the Nobel Prize-winning physicist, Andrei Sakharov (SAH-kuh-rawf), were imprisoned or exiled for their protests.

The generation gap, demands for equality, and dissatisfaction with society produced protests in the 1960s.

Reform and Reaction

The civil rights protests of the 1950s and 1960s produced important changes in U.S. race relations. In 1954 the U.S. Supreme Court in *Brown* v. *The Board of Education of Topeka* outlawed segregation in schools. The 1964 Civil Rights Act banned racial discrimination in most business activities. The 1965 Voting Rights Act guaranteed African Americans and other minorities the right to vote. These measures and others like them ended the practice of racial discrimination in government activities and went far toward doing the same in public matters in general.

The civil rights movement also encouraged demands for an end to other forms of inequality, particularly against women. In Europe, for example, Simone de Beauvoir, a leading French socialist writer, compared the position of women in male-dominated European society to that of the colonial peoples in the European overseas empires. Her influential book, *The Second Sex,* first published in 1949, rejected the traditional notion of women as biologically inferior to men. "What particularly signalizes the situation of woman," she wrote, "is that she—a free autonomous [independent] being like all human creatures—nevertheless finds herself in a world where men compel her to assume the status of Other."

In 1963 the American feminist author Betty Friedan's book, *The Feminine Mystique,* summarized the frustration some women felt with society's expectations of them, calling the modern household a "comfortable concentration camp." Friedan was instrumental in the establishment of the National Organization for

History THROUGH THE ARTS

Chapel by Le Corbusier

During the 1950s and 1960s, many writers, artists, and architects used their work to express new conceptions of what society should be like. One such person was the Swiss architect Le Corbusier (luh kor-boos-yay). Le Corbusier was hired to build a chapel in the countryside near Ronchamp, France, to replace a building that had been destroyed in the war. The chapel Le Corbusier designed, Notre Dame du Haut, was a combination of architecture and sculpture. Although it appears large, the chapel is quite small, only able to hold about 200 people. The walls of the building were made by spraying metal mesh with concrete and then painting the mesh white. The roof is also concrete, but it was left unpainted so that it would change color over the years as it weathered. Le Corbusier may have gotten the idea for the unusual design of the chapel from an image of praying hands or the wings of an angel.

Le Corbusier is most famous for his ideas of interior spaces and for his plans for the ideal city. He believed that inside spaces should above all be functional. Le Corbusier's buildings are distinctive for their wide, open interiors, with few walls breaking up the space. Le Corbusier expressed his ideas about what a city should be by saying: "Great cities are the spiritual workshops in which the work of the world is done." His plans for cities emphasized the creation of an environment with specific living space, working space, and recreational space, allowing every interior space in the cities to serve a specific function. Just as Le Corbusier hoped that his cities would provide an inspirational place to work, he hoped that his chapel would provide people with an inspirational place to worship.

Le Corbusier's chapel, Notre Dame du Haut

Women (NOW) in 1966. NOW and other women's groups lobbied on behalf of equal pay for women, greater political representation, improved childcare, reproductive rights, and other measures of special interest to women.

BIOGRAPHY Reformers fared less well in the Communist bloc. In Czechoslovakia demands for reform sparked a violent reaction. The leader of the Czechoslovakian reformers was Alexander Dubcek (DOOB-chek). Born in 1921, Dubcek became a member of the Slovak resistance during the war and also of the outlawed Czechoslovak Communist Party. Dubcek remained a loyal Communist through the 1940s and 1950s, even taking a graduate degree at the Higher Party School in Moscow.

Yet, when Dubcek became the first secretary (leader) of the Czechoslovak Communist Party in January 1968, he decided to back away from the harsh repression that still characterized Czechoslovakia's policies. He eased censorship, allowing greater freedom of speech and political participation, and he laid plans for a new constitution for the country. Dubcek summarized his aims in a party statement in April, at the beginning of what was being called the Prague Spring.

SECTION 5
REVIEW ANSWERS

IDENTIFY

For significance, see the following pages:
baby boom (p. 736)
generation gap (p. 736)
Rosa Parks (p. 737)
Martin Luther King, Jr. (p. 737)
dissidents (p. 738)
Aleksandr Solzhenitsyn (p. 738)
Simone de Beauvoir (p. 738)
Betty Friedan (p. 738)
Alexander Dubcek (p. 739)
Brezhnev Doctrine (p. 740)

1. much higher in the West than in the East
2. hoped for civil rights, equal status of men and women, end to Vietnam War, educational reform
3. United States—led to reforms and policy changes; Czechoslovakia—led to limited reforms followed by harsh repression
4. Articles should explain that both groups hoped to end the legal and eco- momic barriers to com- plete equality.
5. Answers should include examples from the 1960s, as well as con- temporary examples.

CHAPTER 26
REVIEW ANSWERS
(p. 741)

WRITING A SUMMARY

See essential points in the text.

"We engage ourselves in the construction of a new model of socialist society, profoundly democratic, and adapted to Czechoslovak conditions."

Bearing in mind the example of Hungary in 1956, Dubcek was more cautious in challenging the authority of the Soviet Union. He explained that the Czechoslovakian gov- ernment merely wanted to demonstrate that it was "capable of exercising political direction by means other than bureaucratic and police meth- ods." However, other voices were less cautious than Dubcek's. The lifting of censorship brought demands for full democracy and calls to defend Czechoslovakia from the Warsaw Pact.

This was more than the Soviets could tolerate. In August 1968 Soviet Party Secretary Leonid Brezhnev sent in the Red Army. Soviet tanks and other Warsaw Pact units crushed the reform move- ment. This armed reaction established what came to be called the **Brezhnev Doctrine**: the Soviet Union would use force when necessary to ensure the survival of communism in Eastern Europe.

The protests of the 1960s brought reform in the West and armed reaction in the East.

Alexander Dubcek
BIOGRAPHY

THROUGH OTHERS' EYES

An Indian Woman Speaks Out

The women's rights movement that swept Europe and North America in the 1950s and 1960s was not purely a Western phenomenon. In nations around the world, some women began to speak out against discrimination that had been a part of their societies for centuries. In India, for example, even though the practice of giving dowries (gifts from the bride's family to the groom upon marriage) had been outlawed in 1961, many families continued the custom. In an anonymous newspaper editorial, one Indian woman expressed her outrage at the situation:

❝We as women have too long been silent spec- tators, often willing participants in the degrading drama of matrimony—when girls are advertised, displayed, bargained over, and disposed of with the pious injunction: 'Daughter, we are sending you to your husband's home. You are not to leave it till your corpse emerges from its doors.' . . .

Why is it that gifts have to be given with the daughter? Hindu scriptures proclaim that the girl herself is the most precious of gifts 'presented' by her father to her husband.❞

SECTION 5 REVIEW

IDENTIFY and explain the significance of the following:
baby boom
generation gap
Rosa Parks
Martin Luther King, Jr.
dissidents
Aleksandr Solzhenitsyn
Simone de Beauvoir
Betty Friedan
Alexander Dubcek
Brezhnev Doctrine

1. *Main Idea* How did stan- dards of living in the West in the 1950s and 1960s com- pare to those in the East?

2. *Main Idea* Why did many people in Europe and North America take to the streets in protest during the 1960s?

3. *Politics and Law* What were some results of protest movements both in the West and in the East?

4. *Writing to Explain* Imagine that you are a news- paper reporter at a civil rights demonstration or an equal rights demonstration for women during the 1950s or 1960s. Write an article explaining the goals of either of the movements.

5. *Synthesizing* In what ways were the mass media (film, television, print) used as a means for political expres- sion in the 1960s? What similar examples can you think of today? What are the advantages and disad- vantages of using mass media to express political views?

Review

On a separate sheet of paper, complete the following exercises:

WRITING A SUMMARY

Using the essential points in the text, write a brief summary of the chapter.

REVIEWING TERMS

From the following list, choose the term that correctly matches the definition.

dissidents   Cold War
de-Stalinization   fusion
domino theory
generation gap

1. idea that if one country in a region fell to communism, the others would follow
2. period of global struggle between the superpowers and their allies following World War II
3. people who speak out against their government
4. process of combining atoms
5. term used to describe the difference of opinion and outlooks between young people and their parents

REVIEWING CHRONOLOGY

List the following events in their correct chronological order.

1. The United States demands that the Soviet Union remove its nuclear missiles from Cuba.
2. Demonstrators in Czechoslovakia protest Soviet control.
3. The Federal Republic of Germany is established.
4. Revolution breaks out in Hungary.
5. Nazi war criminals are tried and sentenced in Nuremberg.

UNDERSTANDING THE MAIN IDEA

1. How did the Allies deal with Germany after the end of the war?
2. What did people protest in Europe and North America in the 1960s?
3. How would you characterize the recovery of Western Europe and Eastern Europe after the war?
4. What changes took place in the Soviet Union following the end of the war?
5. What were the consequences of the nuclear arms race between the East and the West?

THINKING CRITICALLY

1. **Evaluating** After the war's end the Soviet Union exported many factories and raw materials from the part of Germany under its control. Do you think the Soviets were justified? Why or why not?
2. **Assessing Consequences** What do you think were some of the long-term economic consequences for the United States and the Soviet Union as a result of the Cold War and particularly the arms race?

Building Your Portfolio

Complete the following activities individually or in groups.

1. **Postwar Europe** You (and your coworkers) are cartographers (mapmakers) and have been hired to create a map of Europe during the Cold War. Indicate which countries belonged to NATO, which ones belonged to the Warsaw Pact, and which ones were not attached to either alliance. Choose at least three countries from the East and three from the West and find some picture or symbol that represents an important event in that country's postwar history or culture. For each of the countries you select, also write a paragraph explaining the significance of the image you chose.
2. **Popular Protests** The popular protests of the 1950s and 1960s continue to affect domestic and foreign policy. Choose one protest movement, such as the civil rights movement, the equal rights movement for women, or the movement for human rights in Eastern Europe. Research your movement, making sure to look at both written and visual material, and create a timeline of the major events in the movement and major changes that this movement generated. Illustrate your timeline.

REVIEWING TERMS
1. domino theory
2. Cold War
3. dissidents
4. fusion
5. generation gap

REVIEWING CHRONOLOGY
5, 3, 4, 1, 2

UNDERSTANDING THE MAIN IDEA
1. divided Germany between France, Britain, United States, and Soviet Union
2. civil inequality, gender inequality, Vietnam War, educational policy
3. Western Europe recovered quickly and thoroughly to become a leading economic power. Eastern European countries developed command economies that emphasized industrial production and paid little attention to consumer needs.
4. Khrushchev began the process of de-Stalinization, condemning many of Stalin's activities and allowing consumer demands to play more of a role in the economy.
5. Nuclear weapons spread around the globe, and political and economic tensions heightened between the East and the West.

THINKING CRITICALLY
1. Answers should focus on the idea of reparations for war damages and on economic recovery for East Germany.
2. Answers should examine the enormous expense of developing and maintaining new weapons, and what that meant for domestic programs.

Chapter 27

Independent Asia 1945–Present

Chapter Planning Guide

	TEXTBOOK	CORE RESOURCES	VISUAL RESOURCES	MULTIMEDIA
Introduction	pp. 742–743	Block Scheduling Handbook: Ch. 27		Videodisc Segment 27 and Viewing Guide: *Planning Japan's Future*
Lesson 27.1 Nationalism and Decolonization in South Asia	pp. 744–749 Map: *Religious Divisions and the Partition of India*, p. 745 Through Others' Eyes: *The Partition of the Indian Army*, p. 746 Biography: *Indira Gandhi*, p. 748	Reading 27.1: *Nehru and Nonalignment*		GHRC 27 Reading: *The Survival of India's Caste System* GHRC 27/Videodiscs: Image—*Street Yoga in Calcutta, India*
Lesson 27.2 Revolutionary China	pp. 750–754 Map: *Revolution in China*, p. 751 Teenagers in History: *Teenage Red Guards*, p. 753	Reading 27.2: *The Cultural Revolution in China* Geography Activity 27: *Agriculture in China*	Geography and History 27: *The Economy of South Asia*	GHRC 27 Readings: *Women Defend Mao's New China; The Cultural Revolution* GHRC 27/Videodiscs: Image—*Mao's "Thinking Propaganda Team" on the March;* Map—*China's Urban Centers*
Lesson 27.3 The Reemergence of Japan	pp. 755–758 Biography: *Yoshida Shigeru*, p. 757 Graph: *Growth of Major Market Economies*, p. 758 History Through the Arts: *Japanese Woodblock Art*, p. 757	Reading 27.3: *The Occupation of Japan* Writing Project 27: *Developing a Thesis Statement*	Art and History 27: *Two Bridges for Peace Park*	GHRC 27 Readings: *Rich Country, Poor People; The Japanese Passion for Comics* GHRC 27/Videodiscs: Image—*Japan's Recovery*
Lesson 27.4 War in Korea and Southeast Asia	pp. 759–763 Map: *Korean War*, p. 760 Map: *War in Southeast Asia*, p. 761	Reading 27.4: *Tour of Duty*		GHRC 27 Reading: *Vietnam's Declaration of Independence* GHRC 27/Videodiscs: Image—*Cambodia's Holocaust*
Lesson 27.5 The Asian Road to Development	pp. 764–768	Reading 27.5: *The Goddess of Democracy and Freedom* Skills Activity 27: *Drawing Conclusions*	Everyday Life 27: *A Factory in Hong Kong*	GHRC 27 Readings: *Filipinos Celebrate the Fall of Marcos; A Bangladesh Bank* GHRC 27/Videodiscs: Images—*Election Rally in Pakistan; The Olympics Come to South Korea in 1988;* Video Clip—*Tiananmen Demonstrator*
Chapter Investigation and Enrichment	pp. 742–768	Chapter 27 *Investigation: A Picture Gallery of Postwar Asia* People in World History 27 Explorations in Daily Life 27		GHRC 27/Videodiscs
Review and Assessment	Section 1 Review, p. 749 Section 2 Review, p. 754 Section 3 Review, p. 758 Section 4 Review, p. 763 Section 5 Review, p. 768 Chapter 27 Review, p. 769	Chapter Review Activity 27 Vocabulary Activity 27 Themes Review 27 Section Study Guides 27.1–27.5 Main Idea Activities 27.1–27.5 Daily Quizzes 27.1–27.5 Chapter 27 Test Sheltered English Ch. 27 Test Ch. 27 Test Generator		Audio CDs: Ch. 27 Summary (English and Spanish)

INTRODUCING THE CHAPTER

Textbook pp. 742–743

CHAPTER OVERVIEW

The postwar period saw dramatic change as Asian nations moved toward independence. The British ended colonial rule in India in 1947. The civil war in China ended with a communist victory. Japan went from a defeated nation in 1945 to an economic giant in the 1980s. Vietnam and Korea both suffered wars over what form of government to adopt. Most Asian countries, however, focused on economic growth as the key to the future.

PRESENTING THEMES

On the chalkboard or on an overhead transparency, write the following open-ended theme questions.

- **POLITICS AND LAW** What problems might a nation face as it makes the transition from colonial possession to independent state?
- **WAR AND DIPLOMACY** Why might governments get involved in disputes between other nations?
- **ECONOMIC ORGANIZATION** How might a nation rebuild its economy after a devastating war?

Have students, either individually or in groups, suggest responses to the questions. For the politics and law question, students might suggest that problems encountered can include disagreements over who should lead the nation and over ownership of resources. For the war and diplomacy question, students might suggest that governments could become involved in the affairs of other nations to protect their own interests. For the economic organization question, students might suggest that rebuilding a ruined economy could require financial assistance. Save the responses. Once students have studied the chapter, you may wish to have them complete the Themes Review, then compare the two sets of answers.

USING THE VIDEO

Segment 27: *Planning Japan's Future*

ENGLISH

Search Chapter 27
Videodisc 2, Side B

SPANISH

Search Chapter 27
Videodisc 2, Side B

Tell students that in this chapter they will apply these theme questions to the emergence of independent nations in Asia after World War II. Then show Segment 27 of the *World History and Cultures Videodiscs*. This segment describes the effects of cooperation between government and industry in the rebuilding of the Japanese economy after World War II. The video also highlights some traditional Japanese values at work within the new industrial state.

Before showing the segment, remind students that at the end of the war, Japan was a defeated, demoralized, and physically devastated nation. To help students grasp the significant points of the segment, have them complete Video Viewing Guide 27.

Key to Ability Levels

All strategies and activities are coded to the following ability levels:

LEVEL 1	**Basic** activities suitable for all students
LEVEL 2	**Average** activities suitable for average to above-average students
LEVEL 3	**Challenging** activities suitable for above-average students
SHELTERED ENGLISH	Activities suitable for students with **Limited English Proficiency**

Additional Resources

BOOKS FOR TEACHERS

Black, George and Robin Munro. *Black Hands of Beijing.* John Wiley and Sons, 1993. Tells about pro-democracy advocates.

Fallows, James. *Looking at the Sun.* Vintage Books, 1994. Focuses on Japan's remarkable economic growth.

Jamieson, N. L. *Understanding Vietnam.* University of California Press, 1993. Emphasizes culture.

BOOKS FOR STUDENTS

Butterfield, Fox. *China: Alive in the Bitter Sea.* Times Books, 1990. Portrays the Chinese people.

Dalai Lama. *Freedom in Exile.* HarperCollins, 1990. Presents an autobiography of the Tibetan leader.

Dudley, William. *Japan: Opposing Viewpoints.* Greenhaven Press, 1989. Presents various views.

MULTIMEDIA MATERIALS

Assignment: India. Christian Science Monitor Video. Video, 60 min. Focuses on cultural contrasts.

China and the Forbidden City. NBC. Video, 60 min. Looks at the life of a modern Chinese family.

Japan: A Unit of Study. United Learning. Video, 80 min. Examines culture, politics, and economics.

RESOURCES

Pupil's Edition

Map, p. 745: *Religious Divisions and the Partition of India, 1947*

Through Others' Eyes, p. 746: *A British Officer Describes the Partition of the Indian Army*

Biography, p. 748: *Indira Gandhi*

Core Resources

Reading 27.1: *Nehru and Nonalignment*

Global History Resource Center

Reading: *The Survival of India's Caste System*

Videodiscs or Global History Resource Center

Image: *Street Yoga in Calcutta, India*

Search Frame 1038

LESSON FOCUS

How did nationalism affect India's progress after World War II?

OBJECTIVES

After completing this lesson, students will be able to:

- describe the consequences of decolonization in India;
- discuss how and why Bangladesh became independent;
- identify the position that India took during the Cold War.

HOOK

Put the partition of India into historical perspective.
Discuss with students why neighbors sometimes hold grudges against each other. *[Students might suggest a feud over property boundaries, noise disturbances, personality differences, and so on.]*

Then review with students the historical animosity between Hindus and Muslims in India. *[Muslims and Hindus, whose religious beliefs are at odds, have a history of violent clashes.]* Ask them to consider how centuries of conflict can establish hard-to-change attitudes. *[Prejudice can build up over generations.]*

With this background in mind, have students describe how India and Pakistan gained independence. Have them refer to the map on textbook page 745, and draw their attention to the Through Others' Eyes feature. *[Pressured by the Indian National Congress, Britain prepared to grant independence; the Muslim League demanded a separate state; violence led to partition; predominantly Muslim areas became Pakistan.]*

To conclude, remind students that partition led to further violence, as Muslims and Hindus scrambled to relocate and the two countries fought over territory.

DEVELOP

Chart the controversies that divided South Asia. Have students construct a flowchart to illustrate how South Asia was divided as the result of nationalist movements. Tell them to begin the chart by writing British India in a box. The finished flowchart should reflect the political division of British India into India and Pakistan, the division of Pakistan into West and East Pakistan, and the conversion of East Pakistan into Bangladesh. Ask a volunteer to copy his or her flowchart onto the chalkboard.

Next have students summarize, in an appropriate space on their flowchart, the divisive nationalism that led to the independence of India and Pakistan (as discussed in the Hook activity). When they have completed this summary, ask them to describe in another summary the birth of Bangladesh. *[Answers should reflect the idea that West and East Pakistan suffered from enormous differences and political problems. A nationalist movement emerged in East Pakistan and declared independence after West Pakistan refused to accept the results of an election.]* Have students save the completed flowchart in their notebooks.

PROBE

Analyze India's position in the Cold War. Explain to students that while problems of authoritarian government plagued Pakistan, India established a democratic government, with a consitution, a president, and a prime minister. India's first prime minister, Jawaharlal Nehru, instituted many social reforms and economic policies designed to strengthen his country.

Ask: ***What position did Nehru take in the Cold War? Why?*** *[Believing that India and other poor countries needed help from both capitalist and socialist nations for economic development, Nehru called for a policy of nonalignment. Nonalignment meant that India was neutral and could maintain relations with and seek aid from both sides.]*

You might want to assign Reading 27.1 on Nehru's Cold War policy at this time.

Tell students that although Nehru's policies led to a general increase in prosperity and solved some international problems, they did not address all of India's problems. Have students read the biography on Indira Gandhi. Then have them make a list of Gandhi's actions that made her unpopular during her first term in office. *[Lists should mention that she called for drastic measures to control India's population, devalued the currency, and abolished the privileges of the Indian princes. She was accused of rigging the elections and then declared a state of emergency instead of resigning. She suspended the constitution, ordered the arrest of opposition leaders, suspended all civil rights, censored the press, and pushed through unpopular laws.]*

Point out that political disagreements led to her reelection in 1980. However, she was assassinated in 1984. Although her successor, her son Rajiv, made improvements during his term in office, he was also assassinated in 1991.

CONCLUDE

Summarize the effects of independence on South Asia.

Have students reexamine the effects of independence on India and Pakistan. To begin, ask them to consider the following question: Did independence for India and Pakistan put an end to the hostility that had marked the nationalist movement?

To answer the question, have students roughly sketch an outline map of South Asia. Refer them to the textbook map on page 745 for assistance. Have them identify instances of continuing friction, both within India and Pakistan and between the two countries, using symbols for different events, such as troop movements or battle sites. Each incident should have a date if available in the text. *[examples: widespread violence after partition (1947); tensions in Kashmir (1940s, 1950s, 1960s, 1990s); separatist activities in the Punjab (1980s)]* Have students share and discuss their maps.

EXTEND
Other Media

To give students more information on daily life in India after independence, show and discuss the video *India After Independence* (Films for the Humanities & Sciences, 30 min.). Or have students read and discuss the Global History Resource Center article on the caste system and view the electronic media image of the man performing street yoga.

MEET INDIVIDUAL NEEDS
Students Acquiring English

Write the word *divisive* on the chalkboard. Have students suggest the shorter word on which this word is based. *[divide]* Have students summarize the section, using the word *divide* and other related words (such as *division*) as often as they can to describe the history of South Asia after independence.

Gifted Students

Ask students to think about the various divisions within South Asian society, including ethnic rivalries, castes, rural versus urban, and poor versus rich. Invite students to research and report on one of these aspects of South Asian society.

ASSESS
Review

Have students complete the Section 1 Review. Use answers in the Teacher's Edition, page 749, to assess student mastery of this section.

Lesson 27.2   *Revolution in China*

Textbook pp. 750–754

RESOURCES

Pupil's Edition

Map, p. 751: *Revolution in China, 1945–1949*

Teenagers in History, p. 753: *Teenage Red Guards*

Core Resources

Reading 27.2: *The Cultural Revolution in China*

Global History Resource Center

Reading: *Women Defend Mao's New China*

Reading: *The Great Proletarian Cultural Revolution*

Videodiscs or Global History Resource Center

Image: *Mao's "Thinking Propaganda Team" on the March*

Search Frame 1040

Map: *China's Urban Centers*

Search Frame 1051

Chart: *Population and Projections for Asia*

Search Frame 1048

LESSON FOCUS

What revolutionary changes have swept through China since 1945?

OBJECTIVES

After completing this lesson, students will be able to:

- identify how the People's Republic of China was established;
- describe the consequences of the Great Leap Forward;
- explain how the Cultural Revolution affected China.

HOOK

Identify the outcome of the Chinese civil war. Have students examine the map on textbook page 751. Have them locate Taiwan, and point out that Taiwan is extremely close to the coast of China. Tell students that it is 1949, and the civil war in China has been raging between the Nationalists and the Communists. Have them describe the decisive event in this battle. *[the final Communist offensive, leading to the flight of the Nationalists to Taiwan and a Communist victory]*

Ask: **What was the result of this victory?**
[The Chinese Communists under Mao established the People's Republic of China.]

Ask: **How did Mao maintain control after his takeover of the government?**

[He purged the country of all Nationalists, landlords, and other supporters of the old government, killing around 1 million people.]

Conclude by telling students that despite the violence, the Communist government made several beneficial changes, but it also established totalitarian control over the people. In addition, the new Communist republic sought support from the Soviet Union when it did not receive recognition from the United States, adding to the tensions of the new Cold War.

DEVELOP

Examine the effects of Chinese economic development. Tell students that the Chinese Communist government organized early economic development along Soviet lines.

Ask: **What was called for in the first Five-Year Plan?**
[The first Five-Year Plan called for sweeping land reform, in which the peasantry attacked the landlords and seized their property, and millions of acres were redistributed; and increased industrialization, in which the government invested heavily.]

Next tell students that China's relationship with the Soviets changed drastically after the government launched the first Five-Year Plan. Have students explain this occurrence. *[Mao was unhappy with the Soviets' more open relations with the*

West and relatively liberal policies. Relations worsened, leading to a withdrawal of Soviet technicians from China and border skirmishes.]

Ask: *What was the purpose of the Great Leap Forward?*
[The purpose of the Great Leap Forward was to modernize China overnight and to strengthen China and its leadership position among developing countries.]

Ask: *How did the Great Leap Forward attempt to achieve these goals?*
[reorganized most of China's farmland into people's communes, in an attempt to apply the principles of mass production to agriculture; established an accelerated program of industrialization, in which peasants were taught to use and build blast furnaces to produce steel; attempted to reform social and cultural values to replace loyalties to family with loyalties to party and state]

Conclude by having students write a summary paragraph in which they analyze the disastrous results of the Great Leap Forward. Have a volunteer read his or her paragraph aloud to the class.

PROBE

Explore how the Cultural Revolution affected Chinese society. Point out to students that Mao had to resign as head of the government after the failure of the Great Leap Forward. Then ask students to explain what the slogan "Bombard the Headquarters" meant. *[Mao's proclamation inciting a revolution against what he believed to be the growing bureaucratization of government and the Communist Party]*
Ask: *What was the result of this proclamation?*
[the Cultural Revolution and Mao's return to power]

Next ask students to read the Teenagers in History feature and the Core Resources Reading 27.2. You may also wish to show the electronic media image of Mao's "Thinking Propaganda Team." For two different views on China under Mao, have students read the selections in the Global History Resource Center on the Cultural Revolution and on the new China.

To conclude, have students imagine that they are living in China during the Cultural Revolution. Have them write a journal entry from the perspective of a Red Guard, an intellectual, or a party leader. Have volunteers share their entries with the class.

CONCLUDE

Compare the effects of the Great Leap Forward with those of the Cultural Revolution. Tell students that critics once said that one of Mao's policies caused the biggest setback for the Communist Party, the country, and the Chinese people since the founding of the People's Republic of China. Ask students whether they think this criticism was aimed at the Great Leap Forward or the Cultural Revolution. Lead a discussion in which students support their answers with details from the textbook. *[Either could be argued, though the criticism was actually aimed at the Cultural Revolution.]*

Invite students to take the role of Mao Zedong and write an excerpt from a fictional memoir explaining why he launched the Cultural Revolution. *[Students should focus on the catastrophe of the Great Leap Forward, as well as Mao Zedong's desire to regain control of China.]*

EXTEND

Cross-Curricular Connection: *Geography*
Have students refer to an almanac to compare the population, area, and population density of China and the United States. Then show the electronic media map and chart. Have students discuss how population might affect the quality of life in China.

MEET INDIVIDUAL NEEDS

Visual-Spatial Learners
Have students devise a slogan and poster to promote the Great Leap Forward or the Cultural Revolution. Give them the following examples: *Walk on Two Legs; Don't Crawl Behind Others at a Snail's Pace;* and *Strike While the Iron Is Hot.* Have them present and explain their slogans and posters to the class.

Intrapersonal Learners
To express the conflicting feelings that some Chinese had about government policies, invite students to write an interior monologue for one of the following: a peasant in the Great Leap Forward or a teacher in the Cultural Revolution.

ASSESS

Review
Have students complete the Section 2 Review. Use answers in the Teacher's Edition, page 754, to assess student mastery of this section.

RESOURCES

Pupil's Edition

Biography, p. 757: *Yoshida Shigeru*

Graph, p. 758: *Growth of Major Market Economies, 1980–1994*

Core Resources

Reading 27.3: *The Occupation of Japan*

Visual Resources

Art and History 27: *Two Bridges for Peace Park*

Global History Resource Center

Reading: *Rich Country, Poor People: Postwar Japan*

Reading: *The Japanese Passion for Comics*

Videodiscs or Global History Resource Center

Image: *Japan's Recovery: Making Cars for the U.S.*

Search Frame 1043

LESSON FOCUS

How did Japan remake itself in the years following World War II?

OBJECTIVES

After completing this lesson, students will be able to:

- explain how the American occupation changed the direction of Japanese life;
- outline how the Japanese economy changed during the postwar period;
- determine how Japan found political stability.

HOOK

Discuss how the American occupation affected Japan.
Remind students of conditions in Japan directly after the war—cities in ruin, families shattered, occupying forces everywhere. Have students suggest some words that describe how the Japanese must have felt about their country in ruin. *[possible answers: powerless, depressed, angry, demoralized, hopeless, grieving]* Ask them how they would feel if the United States were in this condition.

Then tell students that the American occupying forces under General Douglas MacArthur, known as SCAP, set about trying to rebuild and reshape Japanese society. In 1945 one of

President Truman's advisors in Japan reported that in his assessment, the Japanese people were more resentful of their own government and officials than they were of the Americans occupying Japan. In addition, he said that people were ready for reform and change.

Ask students how the Americans took advantage of that mood to change the direction of Japanese life. *[purged those responsible for war; had Japan draft a new democratic constitution under U.S. direction; instituted economic reforms]*

To conclude, have students read Core Resources Reading 27.3 on the American occupation of Japan.

DEVELOP

Outline the economic changes in postwar Japan. Refer students to the graph on textbook page 758. Point out that by the 1980s, Japan's economy was the world's second largest market economy. Write the term *Economic Revival* on the chalkboard and draw a circle around it. Then draw spokes out from the circle, and have students list the ways in which the Japanese people or government contributed to Japan's economic revival. Write each contribution at the end of a spoke. *[Contributions should include the selection of promising export industries for special treatment by MITI; the long hours worked for low wages (which kept production costs down); household* savings, contributing to investment in new technologies and facilities; and the acceptance of low profit margins to gain more markets overseas.] Students should copy the information into their notebooks for review purposes.

To give students an idea of industry in Japan, show them the electronic media image of the Japanese automobile factory.

PROBE

Discuss political stability in postwar Japan. Point out that Japan was starting from scratch with its political leaders after the war. For this reason, some conflict occurred as a result of new influences on society and government, including communist influence in some areas of society. Have students read the biography of Yoshida Shigeru on textbook page 757 to discover how conservatives reestablished control over the government.

Ask: *What happened after Yoshida Shigeru resigned that led to Japanese political stability?*
[The Democratic Party and the Liberal Party reunited as the Liberal Democratic Party and became the most powerful party in the country.]

Ask: *Why did people continue to vote for the LDP until 1993?*
[The prosperity of Japan continued to increase and people's lives improved, and they were therefore unwilling to vote the party out of office.]

Conclude by pointing out to students that political stability assisted Japan on its road to recovery.

CONCLUDE

Determine the key factor in Japan's postwar revival. Organize the class into three groups—the Government group, the Economy group, and the Society group. Have students, working individually, find details from the section to support one of the following hypotheses—The key to the reemergence of postwar Japan was 1) its government, 2) its economy, or 3) its society.

Write the three categories on the chalkboard, and have students list all the different details they found. Then have students vote for the hypothesis they favor. *[Answers may vary. Most will probably favor the economy as the key.]* You might let them debate the issue if answers differ.

Then tell students that while Japan is a major economic power, many of its citizens live in less than ideal conditions. According to one Japanese citizen, Japan was economically powerful, but working people did not always feel the success, because they lived in tiny homes, referred to as rabbit hutches; worked extremely hard all year; and worried about life in old age. Have students discuss how Japan's focus on economic recovery might have adversely affected society. For further information, have students read *Rich Country, Poor People: Postwar Japan* in the Global History Resource Center.

EXTEND

Cross-Curricular Connection: *Art*
Have students examine Art and History Transparency 27, *Two Bridges for Peace Park,* and complete the accompanying worksheet. Lead a discussion on the significance of the bridges.

Other Media
To give students more information on the Japanese economy, you might wish to show and discuss the video *Japan: Economic World Power* (Britannica, color, 16 min.), which includes a discussion of the Japanese work ethic.

MEET INDIVIDUAL NEEDS

Visual-Spatial Learners
Have students interested in art and design read the article on Japan's passion for comics in the Global History Resource Center. Then have students draw their own simple comics, in which they depict an event or idea from the section.

Students Having Difficulty
Students having difficulty might benefit from making an outline of the chapter, using the heading of each subsection as a main point in the outline. After they have completed their outlines, have them share their outlines with another student to ensure they have included the appropriate information. Have them save their outlines for review purposes.

ASSESS

Review
Have students complete the Section 3 Review. Use answers in the Teacher's Edition, page 758, to assess student mastery of this section.

741H

Lesson 27.4 War in Korea and Southeast Asia

Textbook pp. 759–763

RESOURCES

Pupil's Edition

Map, p. 760: *Korean War, 1950–1953*

Map, p. 761: *War in Southeast Asia*

Core Resources

Reading 27.4: *Tour of Duty*

Global History Resource Center

Reading: *Vietnam's Declaration of Independence*

Videodiscs or Global History Resource Center

Image: *Cambodia's Holocaust: A Deadly Harvest*

Search Frame 1042

Audio Clip: *Vietnam War Protest Chant*

Search 4408, Play to 4692

Videodisc 2, Side B

Audio Clip 27

LESSON FOCUS

What changes resulted from the warfare that engulfed Korea and Southeast Asia?

OBJECTIVES

After completing this lesson, students will be able to:

• examine the causes and consequences of the Korean War;

• describe why the French left Indochina;

• outline the effects of the war in Southeast Asia.

HOOK

Discuss the Korean War. Have students examine the map on textbook page 760. Point out the division between North and South Korea. Then tell students that before the end of World War II, Korea was under Japanese rule. Remind them that the United States and the Soviet Union decided to divide Korea after the war until Korea's independence could be arranged.

Ask: What was the result of this division?

[*The result was that Cold War rivalries caused greater division within the country, with pro-U.S. and pro-Soviet leaders from each side threatening to reunite the country under their rule. Eventually, war broke out.*]

Next have students make a list of important events of the Korean War, from June 1950 to the cease-fire in 1953. Have a volunteer share his or her list with the class, and write the information on the chalkboard.

Ask: How did the Korean War end?

[*The two sides finally signed a cease-fire, but Korea remained divided.*]

DEVELOP

Describe the end of French control in Southeast Asia. Ask students to describe the situation that Vietnamese nationalists faced after World War II. [*They wanted independence from France, but France wanted to retain its colonies there.*] Then tell students that France tried to restore its rule in Indochina.

Ask: Who were the Viet Minh, and how did they win the Indochina War?

[*The Viet Minh were a nationalist and Marxist group led by Ho Chi Minh. They owed their victory to tenacity and effective guerrilla tactics.*]

Next have students examine the work of the Geneva Conference that ended the war. Write the term *Geneva Conference* on the chalkboard with a circle around it. Ask students what the conference did. [*ended Indochina War, temporarily divided Vietnam, ended French imperialism in the region*] Draw spokes from the circle, with responses at the end of each spoke.

Conclude by discussing the regimes that formed north and south of the dividing line. Explore the consequences of the division. [*ultimately led to another war*] For more information, have students read and discuss the selection on Vietnam's Declaration of Independence in the Global History Resource Center.

PROBE

Describe the reasons for the Vietnam War. Have students discuss how the situation in Vietnam was similar to the situation in Korea. [*Vietnam was divided in two, with a U.S.–backed anticommunist government in the south, and a Chinese– and Soviet Union–backed communist government in the north.*]

Ask: What was the Viet Cong?
[*a group of Vietnamese Communists who were members of the National Liberation Front and who waged guerrilla war in the South Vietnamese countryside*]

Ask: Why did the United States ultimately become involved in the war?
[*American leaders who subscribed to the domino theory believed that if the Communists won in South Vietnam, then other countries might become communist.*]

Conclude by pointing out to students that the United States became increasingly involved in the conflict, and that by 1968 there were around 500,000 U.S. soldiers in Vietnam. You might wish to have students view Reading 27.4 at this time.

CONCLUDE

Describe the results of the war in Southeast Asia.
Remind students that the turning point in the war came early in 1968.

Ask: What was the Tet Offensive, and what was the result?
[*The Viet Cong and North Vietnamese struck South Vietnamese towns and cities on January 30. The Tet Offensive showed that a victory was not imminent, and Americans openly began to oppose the war.*]

Have students listen to the audio clip from the Global History Resource Center at this time. Then have them describe the outcome of the Vietnam War. [*ultimate defeat for the U.S.–backed government and reunification of Vietnam under the Communists; around 58,000 Americans and an estimated 1.3 million Vietnamese civilians and soldiers lost their lives*] Next write *Laos* and *Cambodia* on the chalkboard. Point out that these countries were on the Ho Chi Minh trail—the main supply trail for the Communists—and that they suffered

bombing raids and invasions as a result. Ask students to describe the effects of the Vietnam War on these countries. [**Laos:** *destabilized Laotian government and rekindled the revolt by the Communist–led Pathet Lao, which seized control of the country in 1975;* **Cambodia:** *neutral government led by Prince Norodom Sihanouk was toppled by U.S.–backed Lon Nol, who was then overthrown by the Khmer Rouge*]

Ask: What did the Khmer Rouge attempt to do in Cambodia, and how did its leaders try to achieve their goals?
[*They tried to apply the methods and lessons of China's Cultural Revolution to Cambodia. They ordered the evacuation of all Cambodian cities and executed entire classes of people suspected of supporting the old order.*]

You might wish to show the electronic media image of the effects of the Khmer Rouge at this time.

EXTEND

Cross-Curricular Connection: *Journalism*
Have students research the Tet Offensive and its effects. Then have them write an article for a newspaper in which they describe, in their own words, the mood in the United States at this point during the war. If possible, have them interview someone they know who remembers this period; use the interview to help write the article.

MEET INDIVIDUAL NEEDS

Students Having Difficulty
Have students who are having difficulty remembering the people, places, and events of the wars in Korea and Southeast Asia reread the chapter and make a glossary of significant terms to be used for review purposes.

Linguistic Learners
Invite students to imagine they are Vietnamese students commemorating the twenty-fifth anniversary of the end of the Vietnam War. Have them write a poem for the occasion.

ASSESS

Review
Have students complete the Section 4 Review. Use answers in the Teacher's Edition, page 763, to assess student mastery of this section.

Lesson 27.5   The Asian Road to Development

Textbook pp. 764–768

LESSON FOCUS

How have Asian countries fared in recent years?

OBJECTIVES

After completing this lesson, students will be able to:

- describe the political and economic developments in China in the late 1980s and early 1990s;
- discuss the factors that helped sustain Japan's economic growth;
- identify the Four Tigers and the reason for their nickname;
- discuss what happened to many independent Asian states as they searched for stability and prosperity.

HOOK

Describe the changes that have taken place in modern China after Mao. Read to students the annotation on page 764 of the Teacher's Edition. Then ask them to describe how Deng Xiaoping's policy was different from Mao's Great Leap Forward. *[Students should remember that during the Great Leap Forward almost all of China's farmland was organized into communes in which most of China's rural population lived. The government controlled nearly all aspects of people's lives, including their economic activities.]*

Ask: How did Deng Xiaoping's new policies affect the Chinese economy?

[China's economy grew faster than that of any major country.]

Then ask students to discuss what social effects the new policies had. Then discuss the Chinese government's response to demands for political reform. *[repression]* To illustrate this point, have students read Core Resources Reading 27.5. You might also have them view the video clip of demonstrators in Tiananmen Square in the Global History Resource Center.

DEVELOP

Analyze Japan's economic success. Have students name familiar Japanese products. Then ask them how Japan managed to enter the United States and other foreign markets so successfully. *[They began producing more products for export.]*
Ask: *What policy helped Japanese industries?*
[limiting imports, which created a trade surplus]

Discuss steps taken by the Japanese government and industry to preserve traditional cultural values. *[**government:** recognized traditional artisans and artists as "Living National Treasures"; **industry:** asked workers to transfer loyalties previously felt toward family or feudal lord to business; in return, businesses took care of their workers]*

PROBE

Identify the success of the Four Tigers. Ask students how Japan's success affected other parts of East Asia. *[It spurred economic growth throughout much of the area.]*
Ask: *Which countries were the Four Tigers? Why?*
[South Korea, Taiwan, Hong Kong, and Singapore; because of their aggressive economic policies]

Have students make a chart in which they list the keys to the economic success of the Four Tigers. *[**South Korea:** government put down opposition, encouraged development and investment, kept wages low by restricting labor unions; **Taiwan:** authoritarian government concentrated on economic growth and became one of the most active traders in the world; **Hong Kong:** flourished as a result of its textiles, ships, iron, and steel; **Singapore:** authoritarian government under Lee Kuan Yew supported free enterprise]*

Conclude by having students view Everyday Life Transparency 27 and answer the accompanying questions. You might also have them read the article on South Korea in the Global History Resource Center and view the electronic media images featuring South Korea and Taiwan and the electronic media chart on Asian economies.

CONCLUDE

Discuss Asian countries' search for stability and prosperity. Tell students that several Asian nations' development was thwarted by continued unrest. Have students make a list of the countries mentioned in the section. Then have them create a chart in which they describe the political situation in each country.
Ask: *Why do you think many Asian nations have resorted to authoritarian rule?*
[Students might suggest that such things as wars and social discontent have led nations' leaders to keep an iron grip on their countries.]

Have students pick one country that they think might overcome its problems within the next 30 years. Then have them write a fictional newspaper article, dated 30 years from now, in which they discuss their chosen country's new situation. For more information, you might have them read the selections from the Global History Resource Center on the Philippines, Bangladesh, and democracy in Asia and view the electronic media images of a rally in Pakistan.

EXTEND
Other Media
Show students the video titled *Pacific Horizons: Economic Change and Challenge*, Part I (Close Up Publishing, color, 14 min.).

MEET INDIVIDUAL NEEDS
Linguistic Learners
Have students pick a country and research current information on its economic and political situation. Have them report on their research, accompanying the report with appropriate visuals.

Gifted Students
Ask students interested in foreign affairs to research and report on the postwar relationship between China and the United States and Taiwan. Have them begin by reading the article on China's diplomacy in the Global History Resource Center.

ASSESS
Review
Have students complete the Section 5 Review. Use answers in the Teacher's Edition, pages 767–768, to assess student mastery of this section.

In preparation for the chapter test, you may wish to have students complete all or part of the Chapter 27 Review on textbook page 769, the Chapter 27 Review Activity, and the Chapter 27 Themes Review.

Chapter 27
Independent Asia

Understanding the Main Idea

Call on a volunteer to read aloud the *Understanding the Main Idea* paragraph. Then tell students that the countries of Asia followed different paths to independence. In India, Pakistan, and Bangladesh, for example, removal of imperial controls led to the revival of ethnic and religious conflicts. Elsewhere, as in China, Korea, and Vietnam, the emergence of new fully independent states was complicated by the Cold War. Perhaps the greatest success story was Japan, which, with American help, rebuilt itself into an economic superpower.

Presenting Themes

See p. 741B for suggestions on introducing themes.

Using the Time Line

Have students list the time line events in their notebooks. After they have read about each event in the chapter, have students write a paragraph explaining its significance.

Chapter 27
Independent Asia
1945–Present

Understanding the Main Idea

The process of moving from colonial possessions to independent, developing nations led to many challenges in Asia. While India, Pakistan, and Bangladesh experienced a revival of internal conflicts, China underwent numerous upheavals as the Communists tried to reshape the nation according to their own social views. While Korea and Vietnam exploded into war, Japan rebuilt itself into an economic superpower.

Themes

- **Politics and Law** What problems might a nation face as it makes the transition from colonial possession to independent state?

- **War and Diplomacy** Why might governments get involved in disputes between other nations?

- **Economic Organization** How might a nation rebuild its economy after a devastating war?

On August 15, 1947, Jawaharlal Nehru welcomed the birth of Indian independence in words that echoed for other peoples seeking freedom from colonial rule:

66 *At the stroke of the midnight hour, when the world sleeps, India will awake to life and freedom. A moment comes, which comes but rarely in history, when we step out from the old to the new, when an age ends, and when the soul of the nation, long suppressed [restrained], finds utterance. . . .*

At the dawn of history India started on her unending quest, and trackless centuries are filled with her striving and the grandeur of her successes and her failures. Through good and ill fortune alike she has never lost sight of that quest or forgotten the ideals which gave her strength. We end today a period of ill fortune and India discovers herself again. The achievement we celebrate today is but a step, an opening of opportunity, to the greater triumphs and achievements that await us. **99**

India's achievement of independence was one of the first acts in a political drama that reshaped the face of Asia in the years after World War II. In 1945 most of the countries of Asia were still controlled by foreign powers, but within a generation nearly all governed their own destinies.

1947	1949	1950	1952	1954
The partition of India results in the independent states of India and Pakistan.	Mao Zedong proclaims the People's Republic of China.	North Korean forces invade South Korea.	American occupation forces return control of Japan to the Japanese.	The French lose the battle of Dien Bien Phu and withdraw from Indochina.

In New Delhi, India, modern technology and traditional lifestyles exist side by side.

India presents sharp contrasts between the traditions of the past and the high technology of the present and future. India's population, which grows by more than 16 million each year, resides on slightly more than 2 percent of the earth's total land surface. With so many people in such a small area, modern technology often exists alongside poor peasants. Despite the continuing problems presented by this population growth, life for some has improved as the country modernizes. India now produces enough steel and food grains to take care of its needs. It has made great strides in education, producing some of the best-trained scientific and technical graduates in the world.

Critical Thinking Ask students to name ways in which India might alleviate poverty.

ANSWER: Students might suggest developing goods for export, providing poor people with government assistance, and improving basic education.

1966	1968	1975	1989	1997
Mao sets the Cultural Revolution in motion.	North Vietnamese forces launch the Tet Offensive.	The North Vietnamese take Saigon, and Vietnam reunites.	Prodemocracy demonstrations in Beijing result in the Tiananmen Square Massacre.	Hong Kong reverts to Chinese control.

SECTION 1

CORE LESSON PLAN
See pages 741C and
741D for Lesson Plan
27.1.

Theme: Politics and Law

In early 1947 Clement Attlee, the British prime minister, announced that the British raj in India would come to an end no later than June 1948. Lord Mountbatten, the new viceroy, decided that independence must occur no later than August 1947. On August 15 India established a precedent by becoming a republic, while at the same time remaining within the British Commonwealth.

Critical Thinking Ask students why India became a republic but remained in the Commonwealth.

ANSWER: Students might suggest that it would allow India to be independent and still receive trading privileges with nations in the Commonwealth.

SECTION 1
Nationalism and Decolonization in South Asia

FOCUS

- What were the consequences of decolonization in India?
- How and why did Bangladesh become independent?
- What position did India take in the Cold War?

For centuries the peoples of Asia and Africa were overshadowed by European economic and political systems. In the years following World War II, these peoples rapidly began to regain their independence and to reassert their own sense of identity. One of the first and most important examples of the move from colonial rule to independence was in South Asia. Five new states—India, Burma, Sri Lanka, Pakistan, and eventually Bangladesh—emerged from what had been Britain's Indian empire. These countries became a model of independence for other nations around the world.

Muhammad 'Ali Jinnah, leader of the Muslim League, 1947

The End of Empire in South Asia

In South Asia the road to **decolonization**—the transition from colonial possession to independent statehood—was not easy. Even though the nations of India and Pakistan gained their independence from British rule, religious violence continued to plague the region in the years after World War II.

India during World War II. As in World War I, India contributed considerable resources to the British war effort in World War II. Many Indian soldiers—all volunteers—fought in the British imperial armies. While many Indian nationalists had supported Britain in World War I, few did so during World War II. Since 1937 the Indian National Congress had participated in the new provincial governments established under the Indian constitution of 1935. The Congress ministers were angered when Britain declared war on India's behalf without consulting them and resigned in October 1939, demanding immediate self-government.

Tensions heightened, particularly after the fall of Singapore and Burma to the Japanese. In 1942 the British government sent a cabinet-level mission under Sir Stafford Cripps to negotiate terms for Indian independence after the war. The Cripps mission failed, primarily because of serious disagreements between Muslims and Hindus. Nevertheless, the proposals made during Cripps's visit laid the groundwork for negotiations after the end of the war.

Leaders of the Indian National Congress had once assured the British that it did "not seek [India's] independence out of Britain's ruin" and that "England's difficulty was not India's opportunity." However, in late 1942 Mahatma Gandhi launched a new campaign of nonviolent resistance. He demanded that the British "Quit India." Frustrated by such tactics at a time when the Japanese threatened India's borders, the British viceroy of India ordered the arrest of Gandhi and some 60,000 Congress supporters.

While the Congress used World War II as an opportunity to oppose Britain, the Muslim League and other Indians not associated with the Congress generally supported the British war effort. After World War II the British Labour government of Clement Attlee hoped to grant Indian independence as quickly as possible.

Demands for Pakistan. Both the British and the Indian National Congress hoped that India would become a single independent state. The Muslim League under Muhammad 'Ali Jinnah, however, had come to believe that only the existence of a separate Muslim state, Pakistan, would protect Muslims against domination by a Hindu majority. When Gandhi called on the British to "Quit India," Jinnah and the Muslim League insisted that the British must "Divide and Quit." In 1944 Jinnah told his followers:

66 *We are nearer realization of our goal of Pakistan and the achievement of our freedom than ever before. . . . Muslim India will not rest content until we have realized our goal. . . . For us Pakistan means our defense, our deliverance, and our destiny.* 99

In 1946 Britain proposed that India should become independent under a federal form of government in which Muslims would control the provinces where they were in the majority. The Muslim League, however, proved unable to come to terms with the Indian National Congress over

Religious Divisions and the Partition of India, 1947

India and West Pakistan fought for control of this area.

In 1971 East Pakistan became the independent nation of Bangladesh.

Major religious areas:
- Over 90% Muslim
- 70%–90% Muslim
- Over 90% Hindu
- 60%–90% Hindu
- 30%–40% Sikhs
- 80%–100% Buddhist
- Over 30% Christian
- National boundary
- Disputed border
- Cease-fire line
- ⊛ National capital

Clash of Religions The predominantly Muslim states of West Pakistan and East Pakistan split off from mainly Hindu India in 1947.

❖ **Region** What region had a large population of Sikhs?

INDEPENDENT ASIA **745**

THROUGH OTHERS' EYES

A British Officer Describes the Partition of the Indian Army

In the nearly 200 years of the British raj in India, the primary institution unifying the subcontinent was the Indian army. In 1947, as throughout British rule, the Indian army included not only British officers but also Hindu, Sikh, and Muslim soldiers—all united by nearly two centuries of tradition and a strong sense of brotherhood as comrades-in-arms. Most, particularly the British, disliked the idea of partition. Field Marshal Sir Claude Auchinleck, the last British commander in chief, later described its consequences for the army:

❝All Indian Army officers hated the idea but we did as we were told. They had to be split and then all equipment had to be split with everything else. What it meant was that regiments like my own, half Hindu and half Muslim, were just torn in half—and they wept on each other's shoulders when it happened. It was moving for me and I think it was moving for them. The older officers like myself undoubtedly felt a sense of loss. You felt your life's work would be finished when what you had been working at all along was just torn in two pieces.❞

the powers that would be assigned to the central government in such a federation.

The partition of the Indian subcontinent. Soon, violence broke out between Muslims and Hindus. As the bloodshed increased, the last British viceroy, Lord Louis Mountbatten, decided to partition, or divide, India. On August 15, 1947, the independent states of India and Pakistan were born.

After partition Pakistan consisted of two separate regions—West Pakistan, consisting of the provinces of Sind, the Northwest frontier, and part of the Punjab; and East Pakistan, carved out of Bengal. The two regions were separated by nearly 1,000 miles of India.

When the new borders were announced, chaos engulfed northern India. Millions of Muslims and Hindus clashed as they scrambled to resettle. As many as 1 million people died in the struggle. Gandhi was particularly upset by the violence. "What is there to celebrate?" he asked bitterly. "I see nothing but rivers of blood."

The turmoil did not end with independence. The princely states also sought guarantees that they would have a say in their own future. In the end, however, their demands were ignored, and each was absorbed by either India or Pakistan.

Under Jawaharlal Nehru, India's first prime minister, India invaded and annexed the princely state of Hyderabad, claiming that law and order had broken down and needed to be restored. Although the ruler of Hyderabad was Muslim, its population was mostly Hindu, so few people objected.

In the northern state of Kashmir, on the other hand, a Hindu prince ruled over a largely Muslim population. Despite demands from both local Muslims and Pakistan, Nehru, himself a Kashmiri, refused even to allow a popular referendum to decide the fate of Kashmir. Instead, he used Indian troops to support the Hindu prince against a local Muslim uprising—and to keep Kashmir in India.

Fighting between Muslims and Hindus in Kashmir soon led to clashes between the Indian and Pakistani armies. By the time a cease-fire silenced the guns at the beginning of 1949, Kashmir had been effectively partitioned between India and Pakistan. Ongoing tension over Kashmir, however, led to further conflict in both the 1950s and 1960s. Even as recently as the mid-1990s, Kashmiri Muslims attacked tourists in the region to call attention to their demands for independence from India.

Decolonization in India led to the partition of the subcontinent into separate states for Muslims and Hindus.

Pakistan and Bangladesh

Although the Muslim League succeeded in achieving a state for Muslims, it proved unable to hold the new Pakistan together. The differences between West Pakistan and East Pakistan were enormous. They were separated by language, ethnic background, culture, and geography. After independence the two regions drifted farther apart. Political instability added to their problems. Jinnah died in 1948, and Pakistan's first prime minister, Liaquat Ali Khan, was assassinated in 1951. In 1958 Pakistan fell prey to an authoritarian government in which the military frequently intervened. West Pakistan dominated the army and, consequently, the political leadership of the country—even though the majority of Pakistanis lived in East Pakistan.

As this domination continued, a growing nationalist movement emerged in Bengal, led by Mujibur Rahman, head of the **Awami League**—a political organization that demanded self-government for East Pakistan. In the election of 1970, the Awami League won most of the East Pakistani seats, giving it a majority in Pakistan's National Assembly. West Pakistani leaders, however, refused to accept the election results. Consequently, in early 1971 the Awami League proclaimed East Pakistan independent under the new name of Bangladesh. As troops arrived from West Pakistan to put down this challenge, civil war broke out. Tens of thousands of people were killed, and millions fled as refugees. Arrested by the army, Mujibur Rahman nevertheless called on his supporters to fight on:

66 You should not be misled by the false propaganda of the military rulers. Our struggle is most rewarding. Certain is our victory. Allah is with us. The world public opinion is with us. Victory to Bengal! 99

◀ **Muslim women stand in line to vote in a 1947 election in the new country of Pakistan.**

As some 10 million East Pakistanis streamed into India, the Indian government decided to intervene in the struggle. The Indian army invaded East Pakistan, crushed the Pakistani army, and thus ensured the survival of Bangladesh.

After Pakistan fell under the control of an authoritarian government, civil war led to the creation of Bangladesh.

Independent India

While Pakistan fell under the sway of an authoritarian government, India grew into a strong democracy. In 1950 India adopted a new constitution that established a federal republic with an elected president and a parliament. Although the president was the head of state, real power rested in the hands of the prime minister.

Politics and social reform. Nehru confronted the difficult task of creating a new sense of Indian national identity. India remained a country of vast diversity, particularly in language and religion. The new constitution made the practice of untouchability illegal, although specific penalties for discriminating against the former untouchables were not enforced until the mid-1950s. To help former untouchables gain employment and education, the government set quotas for government jobs and university scholarships.

The new constitution also improved the status of Hindu women by giving them the right to vote and to hold office. Later, a series of laws gave Hindu women the right to divorce their husbands, to inherit property, and to adopt children. By the late 1950s many Hindu women were voting and being elected to city, state, and national offices. Many of the new

INDEPENDENT ASIA **747**

Like Indira Gandhi, Mother Teresa was an important figure in Indian life. She began her career as a nun in India in 1928 and 20 years later founded the Order of the Missionaries of Charity, which served the most destitute of India's poor. Although she was European, she took Indian citizenship and Indianized her order, encouraging nuns to wear a sari as their habit. She won the Nobel Peace Prize in 1979 for her work with India's poor. When she died in 1997, India honored her with a state funeral.

Critical Thinking Ask students why Mother Teresa was an important figure in India.

ANSWER: Students might suggest that through her efforts to help the poor, she improved problems that many Indians felt were intractable.

REVIEW & ASSESSMENT RESOURCES

- Study Guide 27.1
- Daily Quiz 27.1
- Main Idea Activity 27.1

All Levels

▲ Under Jawaharlal Nehru's Five-Year Plans, small businesses, like this brass worker's shop, flourished in India.

laws did not apply to Muslim women, however. The new Indian government accepted the demand of Muslims that they be allowed to retain their own religious laws—governing such matters as divorce and inheritance, for example. Religious affiliation continued to be perhaps the most important element in many Indians' sense of identity.

Economic policies. India's greatest concern was economic development. Heavily influenced by Marxism and the socialist model, Nehru and his colleagues adopted what they called "democratic socialism" in an effort to industrialize as rapidly as possible. Important sectors of the economy, particularly heavy industry, were brought under government ownership, and the government instituted a series of Five-Year Plans for economic development. Indian farmers were free, though, to own their own land, and private entrepreneurs flourished in many businesses. Despite a general increase in prosperity, however, poverty remained widespread—partly due to an explosion in population growth.

Nonalignment. In addition to industrializing and developing India economically, Nehru also sought to establish a sense of unity among the former colonial peoples of the world. For Nehru and others the world seemed to have been divided into three parts: the First World of the Western capitalist nations; the Second World of the socialist nations; and the Third World made up of all the rest.

Nehru believed that India and other poor countries would need help from both capitalist and socialist nations if they were to develop economically. Consequently, Nehru called for a policy of political **nonalignment**—meaning that India would remain neutral in the Cold War, while maintaining friendly relations with and seeking aid from both sides. Many other leaders in the developing world soon adopted this policy of nonalignment.

Nehru's nonaligned policy did not solve all of India's international problems, however. In 1962, for example, India and China waged a brief war over a border dispute. Troubles with Pakistan also continued. When Nehru died in 1964, India still faced many problems.

BIOGRAPHY **Indira Gandhi.** For nearly 20 years after the death of Nehru, his daughter Indira Gandhi dominated Indian politics. She was born in 1917 into her father's Brahmin family in Allahabad. After attending university in India and at Oxford, she married Feroze Gandhi (no relation to Mohandas Gandhi) in 1942. For her nationalist activities, she spent over a year in jail during World War II.

After India gained independence, Indira Gandhi became one of her father's closest advisors, and in 1966 she became prime minister. Her policies soon generated enormous controversy. For example, she called for drastic measures to control India's growing population. She devalued India's currency, the rupee, and abolished the special privileges of the Indian princes who had been deposed at the time of independence.

As her list of opponents grew, in 1971 Gandhi was accused of rigging the elections that had kept her party in power. In 1975 the Indian courts convicted her of voting fraud. Instead of resigning, she declared a state of emergency and suspended the constitution. She ordered the arrest of opposition leaders, suspended all civil rights, and heavily censored the press. She also used her emergency powers to push through numerous unpopular laws—including a forced sterilization program designed to bring India's

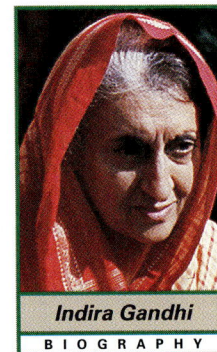

Indira Gandhi

BIOGRAPHY

population growth under control. Although some of her policies stimulated economic growth, Gandhi's authoritarian policies made her increasingly unpopular.

In 1977 Gandhi called off the state of emergency and held new elections. She was promptly defeated by angry voters. Over the next several years, however, opposition parties were unable to agree on how to rule the country. In 1980 the people once again elected Indira Gandhi as prime minister.

In the 1980s Gandhi faced a new challenge. Numerous separatist movements began to demand their own independent states. The Sikhs of the Punjab were particularly vocal. In 1984 they demanded independence for the Punjab, and a group of radical Sikhs began a terrorist campaign, killing hundreds of moderate Sikhs and Hindus. Refusing to accept separatism of any kind, Gandhi ordered an attack on the Sikhs' sacred Golden Shrine in Amritsar, which the separatist leaders had established as their base. Thousands died in the fighting, and the sacred library of Sikh scriptures was destroyed. Several months later Indira Gandhi's Sikh bodyguards assassinated her in revenge.

India after Indira Gandhi. Gandhi was succeeded as prime minister by her son, Rajiv. Rajiv Gandhi was very popular and easily won the December 1984 national election. He improved relations with the United States and strengthened the ties with the Soviet Union that Nehru had

▲ The Golden Shrine was the Punjab Sikhs' central fortress during their 1984 uprising and demand for independence.

established. Rajiv's party lost the national election of 1989, and while campaigning in 1991 he was assassinated in Madras. After Rajiv's assassination, a more militant Hindu nationalism gained ground.

While instituting internal reforms, India followed a policy of nonalignment in the Cold War.

SECTION 1 REVIEW

IDENTIFY and explain the significance of the following:
  decolonization
  Jawaharlal Nehru
  Mujibur Rahman
  Awami League
  nonalignment
  Indira Gandhi
  Rajiv Gandhi

LOCATE and explain the importance of the following:
  West Pakistan
  East Pakistan
  Kashmir

1. **Main Idea** What effects did decolonization have on the Indian subcontinent?
2. **Main Idea** What events led to the independence of Bangladesh?
3. **War and Diplomacy** How would you describe India's foreign policy during the Cold War?

4. **Writing to Persuade** Imagine that you are a foreign diplomat in India in 1947. Write a memo to your supervisor explaining why India should or should not be divided into two separate countries.
5. **Hypothesizing** Why might Rajiv Gandhi have benefited from being from the same family as Jawaharlal Nehru and Indira Gandhi?

IDENTIFY
For significance, see the following pages:
decolonization (p. 744)
Jawaharlal Nehru (p. 746)
Mujibur Rahman (p. 747)
Awami League (p. 747)
nonalignment (p. 748)
Indira Gandhi (p. 748)
Rajiv Gandhi (p. 749)

LOCATE
For locations, see the map on p. 745.

1. It led to the partition of the Indian subcontinent into separate states for Muslims and Hindus.
2. An authoritarian government took control of Pakistan, and then civil war led to the creation of Bangladesh.
3. India followed a policy of nonalignment during the Cold War—remaining neutral while maintaining friendly relations with and seeking aid from both sides.
4. should—Muslims require a separate state to prevent being dominated by the Hindu majority; conflict between Hindus and Muslims; should not—division would lead to intensified conflict between Muslims and Hindus; partition might weaken the region economically
5. They were a powerful and aristocratic family, and Nehru in particular had been a popular and successful leader.

SECTION 2
Revolutionary China

FOCUS

- How was the People's Republic of China established?
- What were the consequences of the Great Leap Forward?
- How did the Cultural Revolution affect China?

*D*ecolonization throughout Asia both influenced and was shaped by developments in China. Although China had never been formally colonized, it had long been dominated by foreign powers. The period of foreign domination came to an end after 1945, as ongoing revolution and civil war swept the nation. From the struggle a new Communist China emerged under the leadership of Mao Zedong.

Workers in China

The People's Republic of China

After World War II civil war resumed between the Chinese Nationalists and the Chinese Communists. In 1949 the Communists launched a final offensive, which drove Chiang Kaishek and the Nationalists off the Chinese mainland to the island of Taiwan.

On October 1, 1949, Mao proclaimed the People's Republic of China (PRC). In one sense this was a victory for Chinese nationalism—China once again ran its own affairs. At the same time, it was also a victory for Chinese communism. Mao and his comrades began to create a communist state. They purged Nationalists, local landlords, and other supporters of the old government. This purge brought waves of violence and terror to the Chinese people. Justifying the violence, Mao quoted part of a famous 1927 report he had made on conditions in Hunan province:

❝ *[One military officer] was personally responsible for killing almost 1,000 poverty-stricken peasants, which he . . . described as 'executing bandits.' . . . Such was the cruelty in former days . . . , and now that the peasants have risen and shot a few and created just a little terror in suppressing [putting down] the counterrevolutionaries, is there any reason for saying they should not do so?* ❞

In fact, after the Communist victory in China, about 1 million people were killed as the Communists purged the country of their enemies.

Despite the violence, in the early years of the PRC, many people hoped that the Communists would bring progress to China. The government "cleaned up" the streets of China's cities, removing beggars and criminals. It controlled inflation, promoted literacy, and stamped out many forms of corruption. In addition, the new Communist government made women equal to men before the law. It soon became clear, however, that the government wanted to establish totalitarian control over the people.

Even though most of their enemies had been silenced by the purge, the Communists still feared the possibility of a counterrevolution. The Nationalists remained in place on Taiwan,

Revolution in China, 1945–1949

Areas occupied by Communists:
- By 1945
- 1945–June 1946
- July 1946–June 1948
- July 1948–June 1949
- July–Sept. 1949
- After October 1949

- National boundary
- ⊙ Communist capital until 1949
- ✪ National capital since 1949
- ★ Nationalist capitals
- • Other city

The People's Republic of China is proclaimed on October 1, 1949.

In late 1949 Chiang Kaishek's Nationalist government flees to Taiwan, where it re-establishes the Republic of China.

Robinson Projection

The Communist Takeover From their stronghold around Yenan, the Chinese Communists conquered all of China by 1949.

◆ **Movement** Which cities were established as Nationalist capitals at various times from 1938 to 1949?

and the United States refused to recognize the new People's Republic of China as the legitimate Chinese state. In the early stages of the Cold War, the republic sought support from the Soviet Union.

After World War II Chinese Communists, led by Mao Zedong, defeated Chiang Kaishek's Nationalist forces in a bloody civil war and established the People's Republic of China.

The Great Leap Forward

The Chinese Communists also looked to the Soviet Union for inspiration in economic development. In 1953, for example, they unveiled a Five-Year Plan, patterned after similar Soviet plans. The plan called for sweeping land reform. The Communist Party organized the peasantry to attack landlords and seize their property. During this reign of terror, millions of people were killed.

In addition, millions of acres were seized and redistributed to former tenants and laborers.

The government was also determined to increase industrialization. With Soviet assistance, the Chinese invested heavily in basic industries such as coal and steel. In many ways, the first Five-Year Plan appeared to be a success. The production of iron, coal, and steel exceeded the plan's goals. In other respects, however, Mao was disappointed at the slow pace of development.

The Sino-Soviet split. After Stalin's death in 1953, Mao became increasingly unhappy with Stalin's successors in Moscow as they pursued more open relations with the West and a more liberal line at home. Sino-Soviet relations worsened over the years. In 1960 the Soviets withdrew all the technicians who had been assisting the Chinese with industrialization. As relations with the Soviet Union continued to decline, Mao began to see the Soviets as China's greatest enemy. During the 1960s and 1970s, the two Communist giants became increasingly hostile and even fought one another in border skirmishes.

Growing tension between Mao and the Soviet leaders also affected China's economic development plans. As early as 1957, for example, Mao criticized China's unquestioning imitation of the Soviet model:

> 66 *I couldn't have eggs or chicken soup for three years because an article appeared in the Soviet Union which said that one shouldn't eat them. Later they said one could eat them. It didn't matter whether the article was correct or not; the Chinese listened all the same and respectfully obeyed.* 99

The second Five-Year Plan. By 1958 Mao was ready to unveil his own development schemes in China's second Five-Year Plan. He called it the **Great Leap Forward**. The new plan was a design for modernizing China overnight—accelerating changes that had taken generations to accomplish in the West. The Great Leap would supposedly strengthen China and establish China's leadership position among the developing countries, particularly those in Asia.

The Great Leap created large collective farms called **people's communes**. China's farmland was reorganized into about 26,000 communes, in which nearly all of China's rural population lived. Each of these huge farms grouped together an average of 25,000 people. Chinese leaders hoped that through these farms they could apply the principles of mass production and efficiency to agriculture.

The second major aspect of the Great Leap was an accelerated program of industrialization. The government sent industrial experts into the countryside to teach peasants to build small blast furnaces to produce steel. Within four months in 1958, 1 million backyard blast furnaces had been set up across China.

Social and cultural reforms. The Great Leap Forward was also a massive effort to transform traditional Chinese society and cultural values. Mao and his colleagues rejected the idea of individualism. The party controlled nearly all aspects of people's lives on the communes—including economic activities, education, medical care, and entertainment. In cities Communist Party block organizations served the same function as the communes of the countryside.

Through both communes and urban block organizations, the Communists tried to destroy the traditionally strong bonds of the Chinese family, replacing them with loyalty to the Communist Party and the state. Children were often raised not by their parents but in communally run nurseries.

Failure of the Great Leap Forward. The Great Leap Forward turned out to be a terrible failure. After having waited for decades for land

▲ In 1958 peasants across China ignored their usual work to build and maintain local blast furnaces like this one.

Teenagers IN HISTORY

Teenage Red Guards

Gao Yuan was 14 years old when Mao launched the Cultural Revolution in 1966 (see p. 754). His father, a Communist Party official, was denounced during the uprising. Even so, Gao Yuan became an enthusiastic Red Guard. Like many other students, Gao Yuan's first major revolutionary act was to take part in "struggle meetings" attacking his teachers. Gao described the abuse of two teachers, Li and Shen, by students from his class:

66 The activists took up ink bottles, brush pens, paper, and paste buckets and trooped off to the Teachers' Building. Little Mihu carried two dunce caps made of white paper. . . . Little Bawang had two wooden boards. The rest of us followed and watched as Li and Shen were dragged out of their offices and onto the porch. . . . The two were capped, and the boards were hung around their necks. . . .

Li and Shen stood on the porch with their heads lowered. Caolan led the crowd in shouting slogans: 'Leniency to those who confess, severity to those who refuse!' 'Li, make a clean breast of your crimes!' . . . 'Long live the Great Socialist Cultural Revolution!'

'Speak!' Little Bawang yelled at Li. 'How many people did you kill before Liberation?' . . .

'I killed no one,' Li said. . . .

'Li is not honest,' Little Bawang cut in. 'Li is playing tricks with us. Don't be taken in by this cunning fox.'

'Down with Li!' Caolan shouted, holding both fists high. 'Down with Li!' voices chorused up and down the porch and through the crowd.

Suddenly, with a plopping sound, the paste bucket was upside down on Li's head. The sticky brown mixture of sweet potato flour and water, still warm, oozed down Li's shoulders and over his back and chest. Little Bawang picked up a broom and began knocking on the bucket. . . . The students on the porch then ordered both teachers to start marching. They paraded Li and Shen around the campus, shoving and pushing the two teachers with almost every step. 99

A Red Guard shouting revolutionary slogans

RESOURCE ACTIVITY

READINGS IN WORLD HISTORY
Reading 27.2
The Cultural Revolution in China

Have students read the Chinese boy's memories of the Cultural Revolution. Then have them complete the questions.

Level 2

RESOURCE ACTIVITY

GLOBAL HISTORY RESOURCE CENTER
Image: *Mao's "Thinking Propaganda Team" on the March*

Show students the image as you discuss the Red Guards. Ask students to write slogans that might have appeared on the Red Guards' banners as they marched in the Cultural Revolution.

Level 1/ Sheltered English

of their own, peasants bitterly resented having to give it up to faceless communes. They also resented having their children taken from them and placed in separate state-run dormitories. Problems in the industrial sector were just as great. China could buy foreign machinery, but lacked the technicians to run it or make repairs. The backyard blast furnaces also proved a disaster, mostly producing lumps of congealed ore unrecognizable as steel and practically useless.

The most tragic result of the Great Leap Forward, however, was one of the worst famines in human history. Agricultural production plunged. Millions starved—perhaps more than 20 million between 1958 and 1960. Millions more were so weakened that they died of disease.

China's Great Leap Forward resulted in widespread discontent, weakened industry, and mass starvation.

The Cultural Revolution

The catastrophe of the Great Leap Forward caused a crisis of confidence in the leadership of the Communist Party, and Mao resigned as head of the government. As others challenged his leadership, however, Mao became determined to fight back. In 1965 he decided to attack what he believed to be a growing bureaucratization within both the Communist Party and the government. In August 1966 he published a proclamation entitled "Bombard the Headquarters," which invited students to do just that.

Thus began the **Cultural Revolution**. Radical students, calling themselves **Red Guards**, staged demonstrations and parades denouncing such figures as Liu Shaoqi, Mao's successor as head of state. They invaded the offices of party leaders accused of "taking the capitalist road" and forced them to confess their crimes against the Chinese people. They also seized university classrooms and buildings.

Meanwhile, Mao was glorified. Many of his quotes were collected into a little red book called *Quotations from Chairman Mao*. This book became the ultimate authority—the sacred scripture of the ongoing revolution. For example, Mao spoke out against intellectuals:

> 66 The . . . intellectuals who are hostile to our state . . . will stir up trouble and attempt to overthrow the Communist Party and restore the old China. . . . Such people are to be found in political circles and in industrial and commercial, cultural and educational, scientific and technological and religious circles, and they are extremely reactionary. 99

▲ At a 1966 rally, thousands of Red Guards read Mao Zedong's little red book.

In response to attacks like this, thousands of intellectuals were forced to leave the cities and universities. Most ended up working in the countryside as laborers and farmers.

For several years the Cultural Revolution swept over China, throwing Chinese society into chaos. Even Mao was unable to control the revolution completely. By the fall of 1968, however, the turbulence had begun to die down. Gradually, Mao reasserted his control over China, making it clear that the time for "bombarding the headquarters" was over.

The Cultural Revolution created a crisis in Chinese politics, society, and culture before giving way once again to the stability of authoritarian Communist rule.

SECTION 2 REVIEW

IDENTIFY and explain the significance of the following:
Great Leap Forward
people's communes
Cultural Revolution
Red Guards

1. **Main Idea** What events took place in China immediately after the end of World War II?
2. **Main Idea** How did the Cultural Revolution affect Chinese society and government?
3. **Economic Organization** How did the Great Leap Forward affect China?
4. **Writing to Explain** In a short essay, evaluate Mao's quote on page 750. Make sure to consider the author and the language of the quote.
5. **Analyzing** Why were the Soviet Union and China unable to maintain strong, friendly ties?

The Reemergence of Japan

- In what ways did the American occupation change the direction of Japanese life?
- How did the Japanese economy change during the postwar period?
- How did Japan find political stability?

World War II left Japan demoralized and ruined—an outcast among nations. At first Japan's future appeared bleak. To the astonishment of many, however, the decades after 1945 became one of the brightest and most successful eras in Japanese history. Japan eventually emerged as one of the world's leading economic powers.

In 1946 a Japanese worker opens crates of supplies provided by the United States.

The American Occupation

In 1945 Emperor Hirohito announced the end of World War II to his people:

&&Despite the best that has been done by everyone, . . . the war situation has developed not necessarily to Japan's advantage. . . . [Japan must] endure the unendurable and suffer what is insufferable.??

During the war 2.3 million Japanese—one fifth of them civilians—had died. Nearly all of Japan's major urban areas were destroyed, and much of its urban population had been killed or scattered. In addition, industrial and agricultural production was paralyzed.

After the surrender, Allied troops, mostly American, occupied Japan. In charge of the occupation was General Douglas MacArthur, the **Supreme Commander for the Allied Powers**, or SCAP, as his whole administration became known.

Under MacArthur SCAP set out to rebuild and reshape Japanese society. One of the first things the occupation forces did was feed the Japanese people. A bad rice harvest, the destruction of much of the fishing industry, and the loss during the war of overseas territory as a food source had led to widespread famine. At the same time, SCAP also set out to remove people who had held influential positions in Japan's war machine. Several top war leaders were executed; another 200,000 former military officers, civilian officials, and private individuals were barred from positions in government or business.

Under U.S. direction Japan enacted a new constitution in May 1947. This constitution created three basic changes in Japan's government. First, it established a system of parliamentary democracy with a bill of rights. Second, it made clear that the emperor was not divine, but merely "the symbol of the State . . . deriving [drawing] his position from the will of the people with whom resides the sovereign power." Third, it included a clause saying that "the Japanese people forever renounce [give up] war as a sovereign right of the nation." In addition, the new constitution also gave women the right to vote, to own property, and to divorce.

***Theme:* Politics and Law**

The 1947 Japanese constitution balanced the powers of the executive and legislative branches, and outlined the separate powers allotted to both the central government and local governments. It established an independent judiciary and a supreme court modeled after the U.S. Supreme Court. Thus, the Japanese constitution enshrined the impersonal rule of law in place of the personal rule of the emperor.

Critical Thinking Ask students how a constitution based on rule of law changed Japanese society.

ANSWER: Students might answer that the rule of law made all Japanese citizens equal and opened opportunity to everyone rather than only to members of the nobility or upper classes.

Along with these political reforms, the Americans hoped to break the powerful alliance between Japanese industry and the military. Between 1945 and 1948, the zaibatsu—industrial conglomerates controlled by powerful families that had dominated Japanese industry since the Meiji Restoration—were broken up. Although some zaibatsu names—like Mitsui and Mitsubishi—survived the breakup, their postwar power was less than it had been. Agricultural reforms also eventually brought some 90 percent of Japan's land into the hands of small farmers.

As the Cold War began to develop, U.S. officials viewed Japan less as the enemy from the last war and more as an ally in the next. The outbreak of war in Korea in 1950 reinforced this view, as Japan served as a staging area for U.S. operations in Korea. The fighting in Korea, and the demands it placed on American military forces, encouraged U.S. leaders to end the occupation of Japan. Under a peace treaty signed in San Francisco, the occupation forces returned control of Japan to the Japanese in 1952.

The American occupation gave Japan a new government and restructured the economy.

Economic Revival

Reviving the Japanese economy after the war took longer than refashioning the government. In addition to widespread food shortages, inflation weakened the value of the Japanese currency—the yen—and threatened people's ability to save and invest. During the next few years, however, conditions gradually improved. The yen was stabilized in 1949, lessening problems of inflation. American aid similar to the Marshall Plan in Europe stimulated business activity.

Most importantly, the Japanese people applied themselves with dedication and intelligence to the task of rebuilding their economy. Rather than embracing the principles of laissez-faire capitalism, the Japanese adopted an approach that emphasized cooperation between government and business. The **Ministry for International Trade and Industry** (MITI) selected promising export industries and provided them with special treatment in terms of taxes, interest rates, and exemption from certain regulations.

▲ Japanese women in the electronics industry contributed to their country's economic revival after World War II.

The Japanese people worked long hours at relatively low wages, and Japanese households saved a large part of their incomes. These savings provided Japanese industry with a large pool of capital to invest in new technologies and facilities, while low wages kept production costs down. Japanese exporters took advantage of their low production costs by accepting small profit margins to gain more markets overseas.

The results were astounding. Japanese exports outsold the competition in one field after another, from textiles to cameras, automobiles, and consumer electronics. Japan's national income soared. Between 1950 and 1973, the country's **gross domestic product**—the value of all goods produced in a country in one year—grew at an average rate of more than 10 percent per year, faster than any other industrialized nation. By the 1970s Japan was wealthier than Britain and France combined; by the 1980s Japan's economy was the second largest market economy in the world.

The postwar decades witnessed an astonishing revival of the Japanese economy.

The Search for Stability

Japanese political life in the postwar period was characterized by a search for stability. By discrediting Japan's former leaders, the war opened the

History THROUGH THE ARTS

The Rebirth of Japanese Woodblock Art

When industrialization began in Japan with the Meiji Restoration of 1868, Japanese artists turned to Western art forms, such as oil painting, for inspiration. This marked the decline of the traditional Japanese art form, known as *ukiyoe*, or woodblock print art. In the 1900s, particularly following World War II, Japanese artists have shown a new interest in reviving this proud artistic tradition.

Woodblock prints are made by carving a design in a block of wood, covering it with ink, and then printing the image on paper. Woodblock prints were produced by the collaboration of several artisans. One person drew the design, one carved the wood to produce a mirror image of the design, another person printed copies of the image, and still another person published the prints.

Modern woodblock artists, however, have adapted the traditional technique of producing prints to fit their own conceptions of art. Whereas earlier art was done on woodblocks in order to make many prints, today the making of the woodblock has become the art form in itself. Modern woodblock artists carve their own blocks, instead of having them made by artisans.

The rebirth of Japanese woodblock print art is actually a combination of traditional techniques and new influences from Western ideas. For example, contemporary artists have depicted such scenes as an American Indian village and Western-style buildings. Each artist has developed his or her own distinctive style, adding to the variety of the art.

One of the most famous groups of modern Japanese print artists is the Yoshida family, which has been producing woodblock art for four generations. The first member of this family to create woodblocks was Kosaburo Yoshida, who began studying art in the 1870s. His daughter Fujio did not carve her first design until she was 67. One of her favorite themes is the simple beauty of flowers. Her *Myoga* is typical of her style, which uses smoothly flowing lines to create wavy images. About her newly found career, Fujio Yoshida said:

"It's an exciting and challenging field, and I like it."

Lady with Umbrella, **woodblock print by Ito Shinsui**

Thinking About Art

What does the revival of woodblock print art reveal about Japanese art and artists?

---

government up to new people and new influences. For a time a wave of radicalism threatened to overturn what was left of a stable society after the war. Communists won positions of influence in labor unions and among students, while Socialists made gains in the Diet, Japan's national assembly. At various times during the late 1940s and 1950s, leftists staged demonstrations that disrupted Japanese life. However, conservatives succeeded in reestablishing their grip on the government. This was largely because of the leadership of the postwar prime minister, Yoshida Shigeru.

BIOGRAPHY Born in 1878, Yoshida Shigeru grew up in Japan under the modernizing effects of the Meiji Restoration. After receiving a law degree from Tokyo Imperial University in 1906, he began a long career as a diplomat. In 1928 Yoshida became Japan's ambassador to

Growth of Major Market Economies, 1980–1994

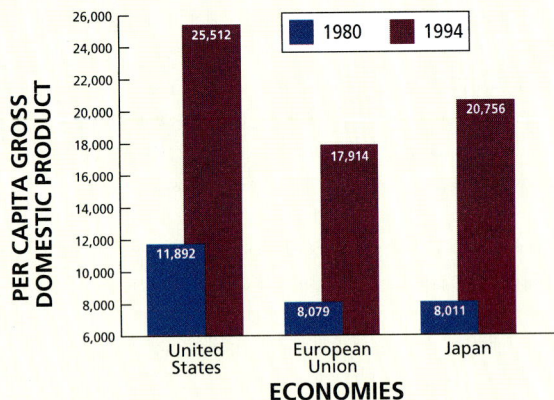

Growing Prosperity The graph shows the growth of three major market economies. The figures represent each region's total gross domestic product divided by the number of people in the country. Economists use these figures as one measure of economic growth.

Analyzing How much did the Japanese economy grow between 1980 and 1994? What are some possible explanations for this increase?

Figures are measured in 1996 U.S. dollars.

Sweden, Norway, and Denmark. Between 1931 and 1935 he was ambassador to Italy. Although he generally opposed the rise of militarism, in 1936 he was appointed ambassador to Great Britain, a post he held until 1939.

As defeat drew nearer for Japan in 1945, Yoshida made peace proposals to the Allies, but was imprisoned. Freed when the war ended, he became Japan's foreign minister. In 1946, as the Allies tried to reconstruct a system of multiparty democracy in Japan, Yoshida became the head of the Liberal Party. In May he was appointed prime minister. An observer described him as "like a veteran bonsai [miniature tree], of some antiquity [age], on whose gnarled branches white blossoms flower year by year."

Yoshida Shigeru
B I O G R A P H Y

In 1953, however, Yoshida was challenged for the leadership of the Liberal Party. The party split when the more conservative elements joined with other right-wing groups in the Japanese Diet to establish the Democratic Party. In 1954 Yoshida resigned as prime minister. After his resignation the Democratic Party and the Liberal Party eventually reunited as the Liberal Democratic Party (LDP), which became the most powerful party in Japan. By the time he died in 1967, Yoshida had lived to see Japan achieve a miraculous recovery from defeat.

Meanwhile, under Yoshida's successors, the LDP kept the Communists, Socialists, and other challengers at bay. As the lives of ordinary Japanese continually improved, few voters wished to tamper with an obviously winning formula. Year after year, Japanese voters returned the LDP to power. Eventually, however, in 1993 charges of corruption led to the defeat of the LDP and the triumph of opposition parties for the first time since the war.

Japan found political stability under the leadership of the Liberal Democratic Party.

SECTION 3 REVIEW

IDENTIFY and explain the significance of the following:
Supreme Commander for the Allied Powers
Ministry for International Trade and Industry
gross domestic product
Yoshida Shigeru

1. **Main Idea** How did the American occupation affect the Japanese government and economy?

2. **Main Idea** How did the Japanese economy change after the war?

3. **Politics and Law** How did Japan become a politically stable nation?

4. **Writing to Explain** Imagine that you are a member of SCAP. Write a brief account explaining how and why SCAP is changing Japan.

5. **Comparing** What role did the Japanese government play in the remarkable economic recovery after the war? How is the relationship between government and business in Japan different from the situation in the United States?

War in Korea and Southeast Asia

After World War II, Asian nationalist movements were often affected by the larger problems of the Cold War. Within this context, Korean and Vietnamese nationalism erupted into open warfare. The Korean War raged in the Korean Peninsula for three years, leaving the country divided. Similarly, the Indochina War devastated Southeast Asia and divided Vietnam. The end of the Vietnam War reunited Vietnam, but at the cost of enormous loss of life and material destruction.

A Korean family flees their home in April 1951.

The Korean War

The defeat of Japan in 1945 ended four decades of Japanese rule in Korea, but did not bring immediate independence. Instead, the United States and the Soviet Union agreed on a temporary division of Korea. American troops took control of the peninsula south of the 38th parallel (north latitude), while Soviet troops occupied the territory north of this line. The future of Korea was to be determined in a subsequent peace conference.

The proposed peace conference never took place, however. Like Germany, Korea remained divided as the Cold War unfolded. In the North a pro-Soviet government of Korean Communists took power, led by the dictator Kim Il Sung. In the South a pro-U.S. government gained power under the heavy-handed rule of Syngman Rhee. Neither Kim nor Rhee accepted the division of Korea. Each threatened to unite the country under his own authority.

The outbreak of war. In June 1950 Kim decided to make good his threat. He ordered North Korean troops across the 38th parallel into South Korea. The attack caught the South Koreans unprepared. Within several days the Communists had captured Seoul (SOHL), the South Korean capital, and were driving the South Korean army down the Korean Peninsula.

Believing that the Communist invasion of South Korea was part of a broader Communist offensive against the free world, U.S. president Harry Truman ordered American ships, planes, and soldiers to Korea. The United States also persuaded the United Nations Security Council to condemn the North Korean attack and to commit UN forces to help repel it.

Chinese intervention. After U.S. forces landed at Inch'ŏn behind North Korean lines, the North Koreans began a rapid retreat. When U.S. and South Korean troops approached the Chinese-Korean border, however, China warned the Americans to stay back. In November 1950 the Chinese sent thousands of troops across the border to attack U.S. and South Korean forces in the frozen mountains of North Korea.

The Chinese assault threw the Americans and South Koreans into confusion and sent them on a hasty retreat. Militant anticommunist leaders in

Korean War, 1950–1953

The Divided Peninsula Cold War tensions exploded on the Korean peninsula when Communist North Korea invaded South Korea in 1950.

❓ **Location** What cities remained outside North Korean control by September 1950?

the United States demanded that Truman order U.S. forces directly against China—even calling for the use of atomic weapons if necessary. Determined not to widen the war, however, Truman strongly opposed the plan. In the early months of 1951, U.S. and South Korean forces managed to halt the North Korean-Chinese advance. By summer the front had stabilized, close to the original division of the Koreas at the 38th parallel. Bitter and bloody fighting dragged on for two more years before the two sides finally signed a cease-fire in July 1953. Korea remained divided.

The Korean War was caused by Kim Il Sung's attempt to reunify Korea by force and resulted in a lasting division of Korea.

🌸 The Indochina War

The end of World War II also brought hopes of independence to French Indochina—the countries of Vietnam, Laos, and Cambodia. Since the late 1800s, when France had colonized the region, nationalist groups had struggled for independence. By 1940 the most important nationalist leader was Nguyen That Thanh, who eventually adopted the name Ho Chi Minh.

As a young man Ho had traveled widely and learned both French and English. Like many other colonial subjects, Ho became both a nationalist and a Marxist while in Europe.

After the Japanese invasion of Vietnam in 1940, Ho returned home to organize a resistance movement to fight both the Japanese and the French Vichy colonial government. He called his movement the League for the Independence of Vietnam, or **Viet Minh**. As the defeated Japanese withdrew from Vietnam in 1945, Ho proclaimed Vietnam independent. The following year, however, French troops returned to reclaim France's colonies in Indochina. Ho appealed to the Vietnamese people to fight the French:

❝ *Those who have rifles will use their rifles; those who have swords will use their swords; those who have no swords will use spades, hoes or sticks. . . . Long live an independent and unified Vietnam! Long live the victorious Resistance!* ❞

In the Indochina War from 1946 to 1954, nationalists fought French efforts to restore colonial rule in Indochina. The most intense fighting took place in Vietnam, where the French, with some support from the United States and pro-French Vietnamese, confronted Ho and the Viet Minh. The Viet Minh waged a guerrilla war, using hit-and-run operations, ambushes, and sabotage. In a climactic battle at Dien Bien Phu (dyen byen FOO) in 1954, the Viet Minh captured some 13,000 French troops. After this disastrous defeat, France agreed to negotiate.

The Geneva Conference in the summer of 1954 ended the Indochina War. The French agreed to withdraw their forces. The conference divided Vietnam temporarily at the 17th parallel and called for elections to be held in 1956 to choose a government for the whole country.

Defeated by local nationalists, the French withdrew from Indochina.

The Vietnam War

Like the division of Korea, the division of Vietnam lasted longer than planned. As in Korea, the Soviet Union and China backed the Communist leaders of the North, while the United States supported the strong anticommunist South Vietnamese government of Ngo Dinh Diem (NGOH DIN dee-em). Mutual suspicions prevented the planned 1956 elections.

Growing hostility. By the late 1950s a rebellion in the South led by the mostly Communist National Liberation Front, or NLF, threatened to topple Diem's government. As Diem cracked down on his opponents, even the influential Buddhist clergy openly opposed his rule. South Vietnam seemed to be sliding into civil war. Fearing a Communist takeover of South Vietnam, the United States began sending aid to help prop up Diem's government.

Supported by the North Vietnamese, the **Viet Cong**, or Vietnamese Communists who were members of the NLF, waged a guerrilla war in the South Vietnamese countryside. As one Viet Cong member later put it: "Our long-range objective was to liberate South Vietnam. First, however, we had to liberate the nearest hamlet [small village]." American leaders, who subscribed to the so-called domino theory, believed that a Communist victory in South Vietnam would lead to further Communist victories throughout Southeast Asia and beyond. To prevent such an outcome, under President John F. Kennedy the United States became increasingly involved in the anticommunist war effort, sending many more military advisors and supplies to South Vietnam.

Deeper U.S. involvement. Meanwhile, Diem's internal policies continued to alienate many

War in Southeast Asia, 1954–1975

A Bitter Conflict Like Korea, Vietnam became engulfed in a war between the Communist-held north and the democratic south. However, the long Vietnam conflict ended with a Communist victory.

Movement What countries did the Ho Chi Minh Trail go through?

South Vietnamese. He ruled autocratically and refused to enact reforms or eliminate corruption from his government. With the approval—though probably not the direct participation—of the United States, a group of South Vietnamese army officers decided in November 1963 to overthrow Diem. In the coup, however, Diem himself was murdered—a move that angered U.S. advisers.

As the struggle in Vietnam continued, the United States soon decided to intervene directly. In 1965 U.S. president Lyndon Johnson ordered a bombing campaign against North Vietnam, which by now was openly supporting the Viet Cong. Despite its intensity, the bombing was not very successful. A British journalist in North Vietnam explained why:

> 66 *Through the daylight hours nothing moves on the roads of North Vietnam, not a car nor a truck. It must look from the air as though the country had no wheeled transport at all. . . . At dusk the roads become alive. The engines are started and the convoys grind away through the darkness.* 99

American efforts on the ground in South Vietnam were not much more successful. Johnson increased the number of U.S. troops by hundreds of thousands, and by 1968 there were around 500,000 U.S. soldiers in Vietnam.

The Tet Offensive. A turning point of the war came early in 1968. On the night of January 30, the Viet Cong and North Vietnamese launched the **Tet Offensive**, named for the Vietnamese lunar New Year on which it began. They struck at cities and towns across South Vietnam, inflicting sharp blows against the Americans and South Vietnamese. Reacting quickly, U.S. and South Vietnamese units drove the Communists back, inflicting heavy casualties.

The importance of the Tet Offensive, however, lay in its psychological effect on Americans. Many Americans had been confident that victory in Vietnam was in sight, but the Tet Offensive showed that such optimism was uncalled-for. Many Americans began to openly oppose involvement in the war.

▲ In 1965 a U.S. helicopter rescues wounded soldiers during the Vietnam War.

Ending the war. In response to the Tet Offensive and growing American opposition to the war, President Johnson announced a halt to the bombing in October 1968, and peace talks began in May. Johnson's successor, Richard Nixon, continued the war effort while seeking an honorable way out for the United States. He established a policy of **Vietnamization**, withdrawing American ground troops while continuing to provide air support, weapons, and training to the South Vietnamese army. Finally, in January 1973 peace talks in Paris yielded a cease-fire.

Violations of the cease-fire occurred until the beginning of 1975, when the North Vietnamese launched their final offensive. The South Vietnamese army, now full of corruption and desertions, melted away before the Communist advance. In April 1975 Communist troops entered Saigon. Within days the capital fell to the invaders. The South Vietnamese government surrendered, and the war ended in a Communist victory. Divided since 1954, Vietnam was reunited 21 years later as an independent nation. Approximately 58,000 Americans and an estimated 1.3 million Vietnamese soldiers and civilians had lost their lives in the fighting.

The Vietnam War resulted in defeat for the U.S.–backed South Vietnamese government and reunification of Vietnam under Communist control.

Laos and Cambodia

The war in Vietnam also had serious consequences for Laos and Cambodia. The **Ho Chi Minh Trail**, the main Communist supply route from North to South Vietnam, ran through Laos. In an effort to stop the flow of enemy supplies, in the mid-1960s the United States ordered bombing raids on the trail. These raids were followed in 1971 by a U.S.-backed South Vietnamese invasion of Laos. This destabilized the Laotian government and rekindled an earlier revolt by the Communist-led independence movement, the **Pathet Lao**. In 1975 the Pathet Lao seized control of Laos.

An even grimmer fate awaited Cambodia. Until the late 1960s Cambodia remained neutral in the Vietnam War, but like Laos, Cambodia suffered the misfortune of lying along the Ho Chi Minh Trail and of providing sanctuaries for North Vietnamese forces. In 1969 President Nixon ordered secret bombing raids in Cambodia to interrupt traffic on the trail, and the next year he sent U.S. troops into Cambodia.

As in Laos, the Cambodian government was destabilized. The neutral government of Prince Norodom Sihanouk was toppled by the pro-U.S. Lon Nol. In 1975, however, a radical Cambodian Communist group called the **Khmer Rouge** seized control of the country with Vietnamese support.

The Khmer Rouge turned out to be the most ruthless rebels in all of Southeast Asia. The secretive group was led by eight people—seven men and one woman—all of whom had studied in Paris, where they had absorbed the lessons of Marxism-Leninism. The Khmer Rouge was determined to apply the methods and lessons of China's Cultural Revolution to Kampuchea (kam-poo-CHEE-uh), as they now called Cambodia. As one Western observer described their program, it was a deliberate plan to:

> **“**psychologically reconstruct individual members of society . . . stripping away, through terror and other means, the traditional bases, structures and forces which have shaped and guided an individual's life . . . rebuilding him according to party doctrines.**”**

▲ In 1975 soldiers of the Khmer Rouge guard a border post on the northern Cambodian border.

The Khmer Rouge ordered a total evacuation of all Cambodian cities, sending city-dwellers to do manual labor in the countryside. The group also executed entire classes of people suspected of supporting the old order, including army officers, civil servants, teachers, and intellectuals. Between 1975 and 1977, according to some estimates, through murder or starvation the Khmer Rouge was responsible for the deaths of about 1.2 million people—nearly a fifth of Cambodia's entire population.

The Vietnam War also inspired Communist victories in Laos and Cambodia and the murder of millions of Cambodians by the Khmer Rouge.

SECTION 4 REVIEW

IDENTIFY and explain the significance of the following:
Kim Il Sung
Syngman Rhee
Ho Chi Minh
Viet Minh
Ngo Dinh Diem
Viet Cong
Tet Offensive
Vietnamization
Ho Chi Minh Trail
Pathet Lao
Khmer Rouge

LOCATE and explain the importance of the following:
38th parallel
Seoul
Dien Bien Phu
17th parallel
Saigon

1. **Main Idea** Why did war break out in Korea? What was the outcome of the conflict?
2. **Main Idea** What caused the French to abandon their colonial possessions in Southeast Asia?
3. **War and Diplomacy** What were the internal consequences in Vietnam of the Vietnam War?
4. **Writing to Explain** Write a short essay explaining how the Vietnam War affected Laos and Cambodia.
5. **Analyzing** What effect did the Cold War have on events in Korea and Vietnam?

✓ **REVIEW & ASSESSMENT RESOURCES**

- Study Guide 27.4
- Daily Quiz 27.4
- Main Idea Activity 27.4

All Levels

SECTION 4 REVIEW ANSWERS

IDENTIFY
For significance, see the following pages:
Kim Il Sung (p. 759)
Syngman Rhee (p. 759)
Ho Chi Minh (p. 760)
Viet Minh (p. 760)
Ngo Dinh Diem (p. 761)
Viet Cong (p. 761)
Tet Offensive (p. 762)
Vietnamization (p. 762)
Ho Chi Minh Trail (p. 762)
Pathet Lao (p. 762)
Khmer Rouge (p. 763)

LOCATE
For locations, see the maps on pp. 760 and 761.

1. Kim Il Sung tried to reunify Korea by force. The war resulted in the division of Korea.
2. war and military defeat
3. South Vietnamese government defeated; Vietnam reunited under Communist control
4. Essays should mention Ho Chi Minh Trail, great destruction and loss of life, destabilization of governments, Pathet Lao, and Khmer Rouge.
5. led to U.S. support of South Korea and South Vietnam and to Soviet support of North Korea and Viet Cong, involvement of superpowers increased destructiveness of wars

Daily Life

Under the more relaxed market policies of Deng Xiaoping, many Chinese returned to traditional methods of business. In the countryside farmers grew their own vegetables for market. Gradually, the new wealth began to transform the face of rural China. An air of excitement and prosperity overtook many parts of China.

Critical Thinking Ask students how the new prosperity may affect the attitude of the Chinese toward their government.

ANSWER: Some students might suggest that prosperous people are not inclined to complain about politics. Others might suggest that as people gain economic control, they also want political control.

SECTION 5
The Asian Road to Development

FOCUS

- What political and economic developments occurred in China in the late 1980s and early 1990s?

- What factors helped sustain Japan's economic growth?

- Who were the Four Tigers, and what was the reason for their nickname?

- What happened to many independent states in Asia as they searched for stability and prosperity?

The end of the Vietnam War occurred at a time of rapid economic growth in several Asian countries. This growth took place under tighter political control than had accompanied the industrialization of the West. This burst of economic activity caused many people to speak of an "Asian way" of development.

The Chinese Gang of Four

China After Mao

In 1976 Mao Zedong died. His death led to a struggle among his potential successors. On one side were those who wanted to continue the Cultural Revolution, led by the **Gang of Four**, a group that included Mao's widow, Jiang Qing (jee-AHNG CHING). On the other side were those who wished to restore order and economic growth, led by Deng Xiaoping (DUHNG SHOW-PING). By the late 1970s Deng had established himself as the victor. The Gang of Four were arrested, imprisoned, and later tried and convicted.

Economic reforms. Criticizing the excesses of the Cultural Revolution, Deng and the new leadership began a complete reform of China's economy through what they called the **Four Modernizations**—improving agriculture, industry, science and technology, and national defense. Rejecting the communist model of centralized state planning, they began to switch to a market economy.

The government also actively invited foreign investment—even from large multinational corporations, which had long been denounced as symbols of Western capitalism. Explaining this remarkable reversal, Hu Yaobang, the new Communist Party secretary, observed: "Multinational companies operate all over the world and they do not injure the independence of any country." As a result of the new direction, in the 1980s and early 1990s China's economy grew faster than that of any other major country.

Calls for political change. Economic reforms also led to demands for political liberties. As early as 1978 a young electrician named Wei Jingsheng printed a poster calling for a "fifth modernization"—democracy. As he explained, "When people ask for democracy they are only asking for what is theirs by right. . . . Are they not justified in seizing power from overlords?" Despite their economic reforms, however, Deng and other Communist leaders were not prepared to give up their own power. They met demands for more political freedom with repression.

The Communists' refusal to yield only led to more pressure for democratic reforms. In the spring of 1989, hundreds of thousands of pro-democracy demonstrators gathered in Beijing's massive Tiananmen Square. They demanded an end to corruption in the Communist Party, a greater say in the selection of their leaders, and better conditions in the universities. As a symbol of their desire for democracy, some art students created a statue of the "Goddess of Democracy and Freedom," styled after the Statue of Liberty.

Thousands of students went on a hunger strike, and Chinese officials tried in vain to convince them to stop. Eventually, the government declared martial law and attempted to clear the square, but by early June their efforts had failed. In June 1989 government leaders ordered tanks and armed troops to evict the unarmed protesters in what became known as the **Tiananmen Square Massacre**. Hundreds of protesters were killed and thousands more injured. Even after the crackdown, however, many people hoped that democracy would eventually triumph in China.

Economic reforms and growth, accompanied by continuing political repression, marked Chinese life during the 1980s and 1990s.

▲ In 1989 Chinese art students raise their statue of the "Goddess of Democracy and Freedom" as a symbol of the democracy they desire.

Japan as an Economic Superpower

Like China, Japan adapted to the changing world economy. In the 1970s, for example, as rising oil prices threatened Japanese prosperity, Japanese automakers rose to the challenge by developing more fuel-efficient cars. Prosperity in the auto industry was matched in other areas as well. By the 1980s the Japanese were making more televisions than the Americans, more watches than the Swiss, and more cameras than the Germans.

In the 1980s Japan overtook American and European companies in the production of high-technology products—computers, machine tools, calculators, and telecommunications equipment. Meanwhile, the Japanese limited the growth of imports—a policy that many competing nations denounced as a restrictive trade practice. Nonetheless, Japan's trade policies have resulted in a growing Japanese trade surplus with other nations.

Still, Japan's prosperity allowed the Japanese to buy more goods from all over the world. As they did so, the Japanese were increasingly influenced by other cultures, particularly American

culture. American music and films, for example, became enormously popular in Japan. However, the Japanese also continued to preserve their own culture. Fearful of losing many traditional arts and crafts, for example, as early as 1950 the Japanese government had begun to recognize leading traditional artisans and artists as "Living National Treasures."

Even in industry, the Japanese harnessed their traditional values to improve efficiency and productivity. Factory workers were encouraged to transfer the loyalty they had once felt for their families and feudal lords to their companies. Companies in turn took care of their employees. Such cooperation helped give Japan a strong advantage in the world marketplace.

Restrictive trade practices and cooperation between employers and employees helped Japan become an economic superpower.

The Four Tigers

Japan's strong economy encouraged dynamic economic growth throughout much of East Asia. South Korea, Hong Kong, Taiwan, and Singapore—

Map Answer
about 1,400 miles

**History and
Current Events**

(p. 767)
Even the smallest
offenses, such as spitting
in public, are punishable
by severe penalties in
Singapore. In the early
1990s a young American
living in Singapore was
convicted of vandalism.
He was sentenced not
only to a jail term but
also to a beating. Such
forms of discipline out-
raged many westerners—
though some wondered
whether such measures
might reduce crime in
their own countries.

Critical Thinking Ask
students if they think
harsh punishments
would reduce crime in
the United States.

ANSWER: Students'
answers will vary.

together known as the **Four Tigers** for their aggressive economic policies—successfully followed the
Japanese model, with local variations.

South Korea. In 1953 South Korea was one of
the poorest countries in the world. Its government,
while strongly anticommunist, was almost equally
antidemocratic. From 1948 until the late 1980s,
the government in Seoul vigorously put down
opposition. At the same time, it actively promoted
development and encouraged investment in such
basic industries as steel and textiles. It kept wages
low by rigidly restricting labor unions. Exports
boomed, and the economy grew rapidly.

As in China, economic growth was accompanied by demands for political reforms. Although
South Korea was technically a republic, most
political power was concentrated in the hands of
the ruling military elite. In 1987 antigovernment
protests in Seoul resulted in some reforms, including the election of the president by direct popular
vote. Gradually the government began to relax
press censorship and lift restrictions on opposition
political parties.

Independent Nations in Southeast Asia, 1945–1984

Economic Giants The spirit of nationalism unleashed after World War II spread
through Southeast Asia and gave birth to new countries with dynamic economies.

? Location About how far is Bangkok from Manila?

Hong Kong. Perhaps the most successful of the Four Tigers was Hong Kong, which absorbed about 1 million refugees from mainland China after the establishment of the PRC. A British colony since 1842, Hong Kong's economy flourished with its production of textiles, ships, iron, and steel.

In 1984 China and Britain agreed that Hong Kong would revert back to Chinese control in 1997, with the provision that it would keep its capitalist system for at least 50 years after the transition. Chinese leader Deng Xioaping's plan for Hong Kong claimed that the Chinese would treat the new territory according to a "one country, two systems" plan. Nonetheless, shortly after regaining the colony, the Chinese government replaced Hong Kong's democratically elected legislature with pro-Chinese officials.

Taiwan. When the People's Republic of China was proclaimed in 1949, millions of Chinese Nationalists had fled the mainland and established a government under Chiang Kaishek on the island of Taiwan. For years Nationalist rule in Taiwan was authoritarian, and the island remained under martial law until 1987.

As in South Korea, the government concentrated on economic growth. Taiwan became one of the world's most active traders. However, economic growth eventually brought pressure for political reform. The Nationalists gradually eased restrictions on political opposition and allowed free elections. China has threatened to use military force to regain control of the island, and after the transfer of Hong Kong, China has renewed its efforts to gain control of Taiwan.

Singapore. From 1965 until 1990, the government of Singapore was led by Lee Kuan Yew. He became a devoted supporter of a market economy. As Lee explained:

66 *The question was how to make a living . . . a matter of life and death for two million people. . . . How this was to be achieved, by socialism or free enterprise, was a secondary matter. The answer turned out to be free enterprise, tempered with [modified by] the socialist philosophy of equal opportunities for education, jobs, health and housing.* **99**

Lee's argument was hard to ignore. Singapore became one of the wealthiest nations in

▲ Singapore, one of the world's greatest commercial centers, has the world's highest literacy rate and the highest standard of living in Asia.

Southeast Asia. Foreigners sometimes criticized the harsh politics of Lee and his successors, but the people of Singapore tended not to—partly because they enjoyed the benefits of economic growth, and partly to avoid arrest.

South Korea, Hong Kong, Taiwan, and Singapore were called the Four Tigers for their rapidly expanding, export-oriented economies.

Other Paths to the Future

Despite the successes of the Four Tigers, not all countries in Asia seemed to have learned the secret to prosperity or peace. In India, for example, although democracy remained strong, separatist violence continued. Pakistan, too, remained in political turmoil. In 1977 the army under General Mohammed Zia ul-Haq once again intervened in the government and arrested Prime Minister Zulfikar Ali Bhutto, who was executed two years later. Zia ruled with an iron hand through most of the 1980s, but finally gave in to demands for elections in late 1988. Bhutto's daughter, Benazir Bhutto, won the elections and became the first woman to serve as the head of government of a Muslim state. Discontent among the generals and charges of corruption led the army to remove her from office in 1990. Fighting back, however, she won re-election in 1993.

Meanwhile, Bangladesh followed a steady path of decline in the face of a series of natural

GLOBAL HISTORY RESOURCE CENTER
Image: *Pro-Democracy Parade in Taiwan*
Image: *Election Rally in Pakistan*
Image: *Filipino Students Welcome Democracy*

Have students compare these three photographs as you discuss democratic efforts in Asian nations. Have students write a caption that will accompany each picture describing positive and negative things about this country's move toward democracy. If possible, have students relate their description to the picture.

Level 1/ Sheltered English

✔ **REVIEW & ASSESSMENT RESOURCES**

- Study Guide 27.5
- Daily Quiz 27.5
- Main Idea Activity 27.5

All Levels

SECTION 5 REVIEW ANSWERS (p. 768)

IDENTIFY
For significance, see the following pages:
Gang of Four (p. 764)
Deng Xiaoping (p. 764)
Four Modernizations (p. 764)
Tiananmen Square Massacre (p. 765)

1. Economic reform and industrial growth were accompanied by continued political repression in China in the 1980s and early 1990s.
2. The Japanese sustained their expanding economy with restrictive trade practices and cooperation between employers and employees.
3. The Four Tigers were South Korea, Hong Kong, Taiwan, and Singapore. They were called the Four Tigers because of their aggressive economic policies.
4. Letters should mention that although economic reforms are successful, people are unhappy with the government and lack of individual rights, and that demands for political reforms are made everywhere.
5. The United States imports many products from Asia, such as electronics and clothing.

CHAPTER 27 REVIEW ANSWERS
(p. 769)

WRITING A SUMMARY
See essential points in the text.

REVIEWING TERMS
1. Awami League
2. Great Leap Forward
3. Khmer Rouge
4. Viet Minh
5. Four Tigers

REVIEWING CHRONOLOGY
1, 3, 4, 2, 5

disasters—floods, hurricanes, tornadoes, and other tragic occurrences. The democratic government, chosen after independence, was toppled in the mid-1970s in a military coup. Beginning in 1982 General Hussain Muhammad Ershad governed harshly. The severity of his rule caused such public resentment that in 1990 he resigned. In elections held the following year, Khaleda Zia became the country's first female prime minister.

Problems also continued to plague Southeast Asia. Reunified Vietnam watched thousands of its citizens—the "boat people"—flee by sea to other countries. Under the communist government's socialist economic policies, the economy stagnated. Consequently, in the late 1980s and particularly in the 1990s, Vietnamese leaders began to move toward free-market policies.

The neighboring state of Cambodia never fully recovered from the Khmer Rouge atrocities. In 1978 Vietnam invaded Cambodia, but in the face of stiff resistance, withdrew in 1989. A 1990 peace agreement brought democratic elections and an uneasy peace. In 1997, as Khmer Rouge leaders fought amongst themselves, violence broke out among elected leaders, and Cambodia returned to autocratic rule.

Burma's government also remained autocratic, having fallen under the control of the military in

▲ **Aung San Suu Kyi was released from house arrest in Burma in 1995.**

the 1960s. Brave dissidents challenged the generals, who resorted to force to put down all opposition. Military assaults on demonstrators killed thousands during the late 1980s. One dissident, Aung San Suu Kyi, won the 1991 Nobel Peace Prize for her democratizing efforts, even though she was under house arrest.

Indonesia's one-party government was less heavy-handed than Burma's and also much more successful in promoting economic growth. General Suharto came to power following a 1965 military coup that overthrew longtime leader President Sukarno. Suharto stifled dissent and practically wiped out the Indonesian Communist Party, while at the same time promoting investment and economic development. By the 1990s many observers saw Indonesia as a potential fifth Tiger.

The Philippines, after gaining independence from the United States in 1946, had the most democratic government in Southeast Asia until the 1970s, when President Ferdinand Marcos declared martial law. Democracy returned only in 1986, following the peaceful "People's Power" revolution of Corazon Aquino, the widow of a murdered opposition leader.

As they struggled for stability and prosperity, some Asian states fell to authoritarian rule.

SECTION 5 REVIEW

IDENTIFY and explain the significance of the following:
  Gang of Four
  Deng Xiaoping
  Four Modernizations
  Tiananmen Square Massacre
  Four Tigers
  Lee Kuan Yew
  Benazir Bhutto
  Khaleda Zia
  Aung San Suu Kyi

1. **Main Idea** How did China's politics and economy develop in the 1980s and early 1990s?
2. **Main Idea** What factors helped the Japanese sustain their expanding economy?
3. **Economic Organization** Which nations or colonies were called the Four Tigers, and how did they get the nickname?

4. **Writing to Explain** Imagine that you are living in Southeast Asia during the 1980s. Write a letter to a friend explaining the problems the region is experiencing.
5. **Analyzing** How does trade with the growing economic powers of Asia affect the United States?

Review

On a separate sheet of paper, complete the following exercises:

WRITING A SUMMARY

Using the essential points in the text, write a brief summary of the chapter.

REVIEWING TERMS

From the following list, choose the term that correctly matches the definition.

Awami League
Cultural Revolution
Four Tigers
Great Leap Forward
Khmer Rouge
Viet Minh

1. nationalist organization that called for the independence of East Pakistan
2. plan initiated by Mao in 1958 to accelerate the growth of the Chinese economy
3. radical Communist group that seized control of Cambodia and ruthlessly slaughtered more than 1 million people
4. Vietnamese nationalist movement led by Ho Chi Minh
5. several small nations or colonies in Asia that experienced tremendous economic growth

REVIEWING CHRONOLOGY

List the following events in their correct chronological order.

1. Mao proclaims the People's Republic of China.
2. Prodemocracy demonstrations in Beijing result in the Tiananmen Square Massacre.
3. The French lose the battle of Dien Bien Phu and withdraw from Indochina.
4. The Khmer Rouge seizes control of Cambodia.
5. Rajiv Gandhi is assassinated in India.

UNDERSTANDING THE MAIN IDEA

1. What were the consequences of decolonization in India?
2. What was the purpose of the Cultural Revolution, and what did it accomplish?
3. How did the U.S. occupation of Japan after World War II affect the Japanese economy and political system?
4. What were the causes and consequences of the Vietnam War?
5. What happened to China's political and economic structure after the death of Mao?

THINKING CRITICALLY

1. **Taking a Stand** Was the United States justified in entering the Vietnam War? Why or why not?
2. **Assessing Consequences** How did the Sino-Soviet split change the direction of Chinese communism?

Building Your Portfolio

Complete the following activities individually or in groups.

1. **Democracy Protests**
   Imagine that you were an American exchange student (or that you and your friends are a group of exchange students) in Beijing at the time of the protests in Tiananmen Square. You were there as the students gathered in the square, and you participated in their debates about democracy and reform in China. Now you have been asked to make a presentation in the United States about these experiences. You may choose to show some of the big posters criticizing Chinese leaders and calling for specific reforms that students put up. You may create a replica of the statue of the "Goddess of Democracy and Freedom" or other mementos of your experience.
2. **Economic Development**
   Imagine that you (and your friends) are citizens of Japan in your late sixties. You have vivid memories of the end of World War II and Japan's great transformation. Your grandchildren want to know what Japan was like after the war. Using different sources of evidence, put together a scrapbook for them, including photos or illustrations, poems, or other items.

UNDERSTANDING THE MAIN IDEA

1. The subcontinent was divided into separate states for Hindus and Muslims.
2. purpose—to attack the growing bureaucracy in the Communist Party and Chinese government and to renew support for Mao; accomplishments—Chinese society was thrown into chaos, but Communist rule was firmly re-established
3. It gave Japan a new government and a successfully restructured economy.
4. causes—conflict between communist and anticommunist forces in Vietnam and the support by the superpowers; consequences—physical destruction of the country, reunification of the country under Communist rule
5. politics—communist regime refused political reforms and demands for democracy; economy—centralized state planning was rejected in favor of a market economy

THINKING CRITICALLY

1. yes—fear of the spread of communism justified preventing Communist takeover in less powerful countries; no—U.S. concern about the spread of communism could not justify the loss of life and the destruction in Vietnam since the United States was not threatened
2. Before the split China had unquestioningly followed the Soviet model of communism. After the split China developed more independently and developed and followed the second Five-Year Plan and other social and cultural reforms.

Chapter 28
Africa and the Middle East After Empire 1945–Present

Chapter Planning Guide

	TEXTBOOK	CORE RESOURCES	VISUAL RESOURCES	MULTIMEDIA
Introduction	pp. 770–771	Block Scheduling Handbook: Ch. 28		Videodisc Segment 28 and Viewing Guide: *On Common Ground*
Lesson 28.1 Decolonization and Nationalism	pp. 772–778 Map: *African Independence, 1946–1993*, p. 773 Through Others' Eyes: *An African American Considers Postwar Colonialism*, p. 774	Reading 28.1: *Decolonization in Africa* Skills Activity 28: *Identifying Sources of Evidence*		GHRC 28 Readings: *Nkrumah Calls for Independence for Ghana; Taking the Mau Mau Oath in Kenya* GHRC 28/Videodiscs: Image—*Kwame Nkrumah Celebrates Ghana's Independence*
Lesson 28.2 The Arab-Israeli Dilemma	pp. 779–782 Map: *Israel, 1947–1994*, p. 780	Reading 28.2: *The Politics of Terror* Writing Project 28: *Determining Relevance*		GHRC 28 Readings: *Israel's Proclamation of Independence* GHRC 28/Videodiscs: Image—*The Search for Peace in Israel;* Video Clip—*Old Enemies Shake Hands at the White House*
Lesson 28.3 Economics and Social Change	pp. 783–786 Map: *Oil Deposits in the Middle East and Africa, 1990*, p. 785	Reading 28.3: *The White Revolution*		GHRC 28 Readings: *The Shah of Iran Loses Touch with Reality; A Traditional Marriage in Egypt* GHRC 28/Videodiscs: Image—*Dawn Prayer in Modern Cairo*
Lesson 28.4 The Resurgence of Islam	pp. 787–790 Literature Through Time: *Arabian Nights and Days*, p. 789	Reading 28.4: *U.S. Hostages in Iran*		GHRC 28 Readings: *Iran Ten Years After Khomeini's Revolution* GHRC 28/Videodiscs: Map—*Iran-Iraq War, 1980–1988*
Lesson 28.5 Independent Africa	pp. 791–796 Then & Now: *Balancing Human and Wildlife Needs in Africa*, p. 795	Reading 28.5: *Politics and Religion in South Africa* Geography Activity 28: *Population in Modern Africa*	Everyday Life 28: *A Literacy Class in Africa* Geography and History 28: *The Economy of Africa* Art and History 28: *Kumasi Market*	GHRC 28 Reading: *Ghana Begins Economic Development* GHRC 28/Videodiscs: Image—*Modern Sculpture from Ghana*
Chapter Investigation and Enrichment	pp. 770–796	Chapter 28 Investigation: *Family History* People in World History 28 Explorations in Daily Life 28		GHRC 28/Videodiscs
Review and Assessment	Section 1 Review, p. 778 Section 2 Review, p. 782 Section 3 Review, p. 786 Section 4 Review, p. 790 Section 5 Review, p. 796 Chapter 28 Review, p. 797	Chapter Review Activity 28 Vocabulary Activity 28 Themes Review 28 Section Study Guides 28.1–28.5 Main Idea Activities 28.1–28.5 Daily Quizzes 28.1–28.5 Chapter 28 Test Sheltered English Ch. 28 Test Ch. 28 Test Generator		Audio CDs: Ch. 28 Summary (English and Spanish)

INTRODUCING THE CHAPTER

Textbook pp. 770–771

CHAPTER OVERVIEW

The postwar era saw nationalism triumph in the Middle East and Africa. The creation of Israel in 1948 led to violent conflict with the Arab states. Middle Eastern nations found that their oil reserves gave them new economic and political power. An Islamic resurgence also occurred as people tried to cope with modernization. In Africa, the leaders of new nations struggled to create a sense of national identity.

PRESENTING THEMES

On the chalkboard or on an overhead transparency, write the following open-ended theme questions.

- **RELIGION AND THE ARTS** What role might religion and cultural revival play in people's efforts to cope with modernization?
- **WAR AND DIPLOMACY** How might ongoing local and international wars contribute to political and social instability in a region?
- **GEOGRAPHY** In what ways might the presence or lack of raw materials affect a country's development?

Have students, either individually or in groups, suggest responses to the questions. List the responses on the chalkboard or the transparency. For the religion and the arts question, students might suggest that traditional practices can comfort people facing disorienting change caused by modernization. For the war and diplomacy question, students might suggest that wars monopolize the resources needed for daily life. For the geography question, students might suggest that a wealth of raw materials can lead to industrial growth and trade, while a lack of resources can hurt development. Save the responses. Once students have studied the chapter, you may wish to have them complete the Themes Review, then compare the two sets of answers.

Tell students that in this chapter they will examine how these questions apply to post-war Africa and the Middle East. Conclude by reading, or having a student read, the chapter introduction on textbook pages 770–771 aloud to the class.

USING THE VIDEO

Segment 28: *On Common Ground*

ENGLISH

Search Chapter 28
Videodisc 2, Side B

SPANISH

Search Chapter 28
Videodisc 2, Side B

Tell students that in this chapter they will examine how these theme questions apply to the nations of Africa and the Middle East in their search for stability and economic development. Conclude by showing Segment 28 of the *World History and Cultures Videodiscs*. This segment describes the efforts of Israeli and Palestinian educators to help their students overcome a divisive legacy of mutual hostility.

Before showing the video, ask students if they know the roots of the word "prejudice" [Pre-judgment]. Ask students to watch for visible signs of mistrust and fear in the scenes they will see. To help students grasp the significant points of the video, have them complete Video Viewing Guide 28.

Key to Ability Levels

All strategies and activities are coded to the following ability levels:

LEVEL 1	**Basic** activities suitable for all students
LEVEL 2	**Average** activities suitable for average to above-average students
LEVEL 3	**Challenging** activities suitable for above-average students
SHELTERED ENGLISH	Activities suitable for students with **Limited English Proficiency**

Additional Resources

BOOKS FOR TEACHERS

Davidson, Basil. *The Search for Africa: History, Culture, Politics.* Curry, 1994. Places African history in a global context.

Fielding, Michael. *Inside the Arab World.* Harvard, 1995. Includes a discussion of the Gulf War.

Friedman, Thomas L. *From Beirut to Jerusalem.* Anchor Books, 1995. Offers a journalist's view.

BOOKS FOR STUDENTS

Abodcher, David J. *Youth in the Middle East: Voices of Despair.* Watts, 1990. Looks at the effects of war on children and adolescents.

Fargues, Philippe and Rafic Boustani. *Atlas of the Arab World.* Facts On File, 1991. Offers a variety of resources.

Hiro, Dilip. *The Longest War: The Iran-Iraq Military Conflict.* Routledge, 1991. Examines the conflict.

MULTIMEDIA MATERIALS

Africa: Tribalism to Independence. New York Times. Video, 27 min. Focuses on Nigeria.

Jerusalem: Within These Walls. National Geographic Society. Video, 59 min. Focuses on the religious aspects of life in Jerusalem.

Middle East in Transition. SCIS. Video, 46 min. Focuses on changes in the 1980s.

Decolonization and Nationalism

Textbook pp. 772–778

RESOURCES

Pupil's Edition

Biography, p. 772: *Kwame Nkrumah*

Core Resources

Skills Activity: *Identifying Sources of Evidence*

Reading 28.1: *Decolonization in Africa*

Global History Resource Center

Reading: *Nkrumah Calls for Independence for Ghana*

Reading: *Taking the Mau Mau Oath in Kenya*

Videodiscs or Global History Resource Center

Map: *Colonialism in Africa, 1945*

Search Frame 1063

Image: *Kwame Nkrumah Celebrates Ghana's Independence*

Search Frame 1053

Image: *Kenya's Oldest Kikuyu Chief*

Search Frame 1055

LESSON FOCUS

How did decolonization and nationalism affect Africa and the Middle East after World War II?

OBJECTIVES

After completing this lesson, students will be able to:

- describe the path to independence followed by most British colonies in Africa;
- explain how French efforts to maintain a unified African empire affected decolonization;
- identify what the struggle for independence was like in Belgian and Portuguese African colonies;
- explain how wartime actions by colonial powers affected decolonization in many Middle Eastern countries.

HOOK: Link to Today

Explore why colonial peoples wanted independence. Ask students to imagine how they would feel if the United States were ruled by people who lived thousands of miles away and had a different cultural tradition than their own. Ask them to discuss how they might feel about independence for their nation. Then display the electronic media map and have students identify the parts of Africa controlled by the colonial powers in 1945.

Next have students read the biography of Kwame Nkrumah on textbook page 772.

Ask: How did Nkrumah lead the way to independence for the Gold Coast?

[He established the Convention People's Party and eventually pressured the British to agree to grant a self-governing constitution, elections, and independence.]

Conclude by telling students that the Gold Coast became the independent state of Ghana. To give students more information on Ghana, you might wish to assign the Global History Resource Center selection on Nkrumah, as well as show the electronic media image of Nkrumah celebrating Ghana's independence.

DEVELOP

Discuss how other British African colonies gained their independence. Tell students that while Ghana was the model for other British African colonies' independence, the process was difficult in some areas.

Ask: What conflict in Kenya led to a major uprising in the 1950s? What was the result?

[The Kikuyu people and the European settlers conflicted over land, especially the Kenyan highlands. Many Kikuyu joined the Mau Mau movement and terrorized the highlands, murdering those in opposition to them, especially other Africans.]

Conclude by telling students that the British eventually put down the Mau Mau, but became convinced that they needed to decolonize in Africa. As a result, the British handed over the power to nationalists, and Kenya and other colonies became independent. To illustrate this point, show students the electronic media image of the Kikuyu chief, and have them read the Global History Resource Center selection on the Mau Mau oath.

PROBE

Compare the different paths toward independence taken by British, French, Portuguese, and Belgian colonies in Africa. Have students form groups to represent the British African colonies, the French African colonies, the Portuguese African colonies, and the Belgian Congo. Write the names of each of the groups on separate sections of the chalkboard. Have groups meet to gather information about the following: (1) the power's attitude toward independence; (2) steps taken in moving toward independence; (4) when and how the colony or colonies became independent.

After the groups have finished gathering their information, have representatives from each group come to the board and summarize the information in the appropriate section of the chalkboard. Give the representatives about 10 minutes to complete their notes. Once the notes have been written on the chalkboard, have another person from each group briefly summarize the group's information for the rest of the class.

Conclude by having students read Core Resources Reading 28.1 and the Through Others' Eyes feature on page 774 of their textbook to give them more information about decolonization in Africa. Then have them imagine that they are members of an African nationalist group fighting for independence. Have them write a short paragraph in which they define and defend their arguments for independence of their particular nation. Have volunteers read their paragraphs aloud to the class.

CONCLUDE

Describe the effects of the colonial powers' wartime actions on Middle Eastern countries after 1945. Write *Iran*, *Egypt*, *Syria*, and *Lebanon* as headings on the chalkboard. Ask students the following questions for each nation and list responses under each nation's name.

- What Allied power intervened in the nation's affairs during World War II?
- What action did the power take?
- What was the result of the intervention on the nation?

Once the chart has been completed, have students compare answers to the questions for each of the countries.

Ask: *How was interference from outside nations during World War II similar in each of these countries?*
[Students should understand that, in general, the Allied powers occupied the nations for their own purposes in the war effort. Once the war was over, the Allies relinquished control slowly, which brought on nationalist reactions.]

EXTEND

Cross-Curricular Connection: *Language Arts*

Have students work in pairs, with one acting as a newspaper reporter and the other acting as a citizen of an African or Middle Eastern nation during the 1950s. Have them prepare a set of questions and answers in an interview format in which they discuss how life has changed since World War II. Have pairs share their interviews with the class.

MEET INDIVIDUAL NEEDS

Gifted Students

Have students read and report on a biography or autobiography of one of the leaders mentioned in this section—Kwame Nkrumah, Jomo Kenyatta, Felix Eboué, Sékou Touré, Felix Houphouet-Boigny, Patrice Lumumba, Joseph Kasavubu, Joseph Mobutu, Muhammad Mosaddeq, or Gamal Abdel Nasser.

Students Having Difficulty

You might wish to have students who are having difficulty practice their skills in identifying sources of evidence by assigning the Skills Activity 28, about the Mau Mau movement in Kenya. Have students discuss their answers in class.

ASSESS

Review

Have students complete the Section 1 Review. Use answers in the Teacher's Edition, pages 777–78, to assess student mastery of this section.

Lesson 28.2 *The Arab-Israeli Dilemma*

Textbook pp. 779–782

RESOURCES

Pupil's Edition
Map, p. 780: *Israel, 1947–1994*

Core Resources
Reading 28.2: *The Politics of Terror*

Visual Resources
Geography and History 35: *Southwest Asia*

Global History Resource Center
Reading: *Israel's Proclamation of Independence*

Reading: *Abba Eban on Israel's Six-Day War*

Reading: *An Egyptian President Seeks Peace in Israel*

Videodiscs or Global History Resource Center

Image: *Refugees Arrive in the New Israel*

Search Frame 1056

Image: *The Search for Peace in Israel*

Search Frame 1057

Video Clip: *Old Enemies Shake Hands at the White House*

Search 4694, Play to 5035
Videodisc 2, Side B
Video Clip 28

Audio Clip: *Israeli Ethno-Pop Music*

Search 5037, Play to 5405
Videodisc 2, Side B
Audio Clip 28

LESSON FOCUS
What conflicts and attempts at peace have taken place between the Arabs and the Israelis since World War II?

OBJECTIVES
After completing this lesson, students will be able to:
- describe events in Palestine after the departure of the British;
- explain what led to the Suez Crisis;
- describe the peace process between Arabs and Israelis.

HOOK
Discuss the early events in Palestine after the departure of the British. Display Geography and History Transparency 35 and have students locate Israel and the surrounding Arab states. Then ask students what roles Britain and the United Nations played in Israel's creation. *[Britain gave up the mandate for Palestine; the UN partitioned it into a Jewish and an Arab state.]*

Ask: Why, despite invading Israel in what the head of the Arab League called a war of extermination, did the Arabs fail to destroy the new Israeli state? *[The Arabs were disunited and did not coordinate their attacks.]*

Ask: How did the Irgun seek to protect the new Israeli state? *[The Irgun attacked the Arab village of Deir Yassin, killing men, women, and children, and released statements designed to heighten Arab fears. Thousands of Arabs fled the country.]*

Conclude by telling students that the Israelis managed to maintain their new state, set up a democracy, and guarantee citizenship to arriving Jewish refugees. To give students more information about the formation of Israel, have them read *Israel's Proclamation of Independence* in the Global History Resource Center and view the electronic media image of the refugees arriving in Israel.

DEVELOP
Discuss the Suez Crisis. Have students examine the map on textbook page 780 and locate the Suez Canal. Help them

recognize the importance of its location.

Ask: Why were other nations so concerned about Egypt's nationalization of the Suez Canal?
[Much of the world's shipping passed through it.]

Ask: How could conflict over the Suez Canal affect world trade?
[Loss of access to the canal would make the cost of transporting goods from Europe to Asia far more expensive and would therefore dampen trade between those areas.]

Next ask students to write summaries of the events of the Suez Crisis, answering the following questions.

- What part did the Aswan High Dam play in precipitating the crisis? [The United States and Britain agreed to help fund the dam, but withdrew financial assistance when Egypt accepted Soviet military aid. Nasser nationalized the Suez Canal partly in retaliation.]
- How did France, Britain, and Israel become involved in the crisis? [They conspired to invade Egypt, retake the canal, and get rid of Nasser.]
- What part did the United States play in the crisis? [The United States threatened to cut off aid to Britain unless the invasion ended; the campaign then collapsed.]

Conclude by asking students to describe the after-effect of the Suez Crisis in the Arab world. [The effect was that Nasser became a hero in the Arab world; European imperialism was discredited; the pace of decolonization picked up.]

PROBE

Discuss later Arab-Israeli conflicts and attempts at peace. Have students create a time line of important events in Arab-Israeli relations from 1967 through 1994, taking time to *discuss the importance of each event.* [sample time line: Six-Day War (1967); terrorists kill Israeli Olympic athletes (1972); Yom Kippur War (1973); Sadat flies to Israel (1977); Camp David Accords (1978); Israel invades Lebanon (1982); beginning of the intifada (1987); Palestinian self-rule established (1993–1994); Rabin assassinated (1995)]

To provide students with more information on Arab-Israeli relations, assign and discuss Reading 28.2. You may also wish to assign the Global History Resource Center readings on the Six-Day War and on Sadat's visit to Israel, and view the electronic media image of the Israeli-Arab peace march and the electronic media video clip of the meeting at the White House.

CONCLUDE

Analyze the Israeli and Arab points of view about Israel.
Write the words *Israeli Point of View* and *Arab Point of View* as headings on the chalkboard. Ask students to imagine themselves first as Israelis, then as Arabs, and to explain why they believe they have a right to claim Israel for themselves. List student ideas on the chalkboard.

Conclude by asking students their opinions on what would help to end the Arab–Israeli conflict. Lead a discussion in which students share their opinions with the class.

EXTEND

Cross-Curricular Connection: *Journalism*
Have the class produce a short newscast of the Suez Crisis. Have one member of the class act as a newscaster to summarize main events and then ask representatives from Great Britain, France, Israel, Egypt, and the United States for opinions. Students can consult the *Readers' Guide to Periodical Literature* for articles written at the time to provide them with more information on the crisis.

MEET INDIVIDUAL NEEDS

Gifted Students
Have students investigate the history of Jerusalem and the city's role in the histories of the Jews, Muslims, and Christians. Students can share their findings in reports to the class.

Musical-Rhythmic Learners
Have students listen to the audio clip of the Israeli ethno-pop music. Ask them for their opinions on the music, and then have them compare it to other forms of popular music. Then have them look for other examples of Middle Eastern music to share with the class. Encourage students to find out what instruments are used and, if possible, bring in pictures of the instruments.

ASSESS

Review
Have students complete the Section 2 Review. Use answers in the Teacher's Edition, page 782, to assess student mastery of this section.

Textbook pp. 783–786

RESOURCES

Pupil's Edition

Map, p. 785: *Oil Deposits in the Middle East and Africa, 1990*

Core Resources

Reading 28.3: *The White Revolution*

Global History Resource Center

Reading: *The Shah of Iran Loses Touch with Reality*

Reading: *A Traditional Marriage in Egypt*

Videodiscs or Global History Resource Center

Image: *The Scouts Get a Boost from the Shah of Iran*

Search Frame 1058

Image: *Dawn Prayer in Modern Cairo*

Search Frame 1060

Image: *Iranian Woman Learns to Shoot a Colt .45*

Search Frame 1061

LESSON FOCUS

How did oil and other economic developments affect life in the Middle East?

OBJECTIVES

After completing this lesson, students will be able to:

- explain why the Middle East became important to the rest of the world;
- identify how many Middle Eastern countries used their oil wealth and what the consequences of these actions were;
- explain how economic development and modernization affected Middle Eastern societies.

HOOK: Link to Today

Discuss the Middle East as a "hot zone" in today's world. Point out to students that many people feel that the Middle East is a "hot zone"—a place of intense interest to other nations of the world. Have students speculate on why this might be so. *[Students should recognize that nations throughout the world had an interest in the Middle East because it is the most important source of energy for industrial society. This makes the area a "hot zone."]*

Point out that many nations have been involved in the conflicts, including the United States (in the recent Gulf War, for example).

Ask: If you were the leader of a world power, how would you feel about getting involved in disputes in the Middle East? *[Answers will vary. Some students might say that becoming involved militarily could spark a major war, while others might say that it would be necessary to preserve U.S. interests in the region.]*

DEVELOP

Discuss how the presence of oil affected the Middle East. Remind students that the discovery of vast oil reserves in the Middle East around the time of World War II led the oil-producing nations to seek greater control over these resources. An important result of this desire for greater control was the formation of OPEC. Ask students to identify on the map on textbook page 785 the Middle Eastern nations that formed OPEC. *[Iran, Iraq, Kuwait, Saudi Arabia]* (Remind them that Venezuela also helped form OPEC.)

Ask: How has OPEC used oil as a weapon in times of peace, as well as during war?

[It tried to control the global oil industry by setting prices and production levels; it also declared an oil embargo against countries supporting Israel during the Yom Kippur War.]

Write the following on the chalkboard: *Mosaddeq; Muhammad Reza Shah; superpower alliances.* Tell students to use the words on the chalkboard to help them answer the question that follows.

Ask: *What impact did Middle Eastern oil have on Cold War rivalries?* *[Students should recall that the United States engineered a coup against the communist-leaning Mosaddeq and replaced him with Muhammad Reza Shah, and that both the Soviet Union and the United States formed strong alliances with different Middle Eastern countries, fueling Cold War rivalries.]*

To conclude, provide students with more information about the Shah's rule by having them view the electronic media image of the Shah and complete Core Resources Reading 28.3 and the Global History Resource Center selection on the Shah.

PROBE

Discuss the impact of modernization on Middle Eastern societies. Tell students that the revenue brought in by oil led many Middle Eastern countries to develop their economies and to modernize. Ask students to discuss some of the development and modernization schemes that occurred in the region. *[Students should mention the White Revolution in Iran; money poured into development schemes by Saudi Arabia; the purchase and use of modern farming techniques and equipment; and the building of hydroelectric and irrigation projects.]*

Then tell students that such economic changes, along with independence, had major effects on Middle Eastern societies. Draw a web diagram on the chalkboard. In the center circle, write *Social and Cultural Changes*. On circles surrounding the center circle, write *Arab Socialism*, *The Urban Landscape*, *Life in the Countryside*, and *Changing Roles for Women and Families*. Ask students for details about the effects of modernization in each of these areas. List details on the web as students suggest them. Have students copy the web into their notebooks and save it for review purposes.

To give students further insight into changes in the Middle East, you might also have them view the electronic media images of modern Cairo and of the Iranian woman shooting the gun. Then ask them to contrast this modernity with the reading on traditional marriages in Egypt.

CONCLUDE

Ask students to imagine that they were born in a Middle Eastern country around 1945 and grew up there. Orally or in writing, have them create "life stories," building on scenarios

such as the following:

- Perhaps they were born in the countryside and moved to the city. What adjustments did they have to make? How was life different for them in each place?
- Perhaps they remained in the countryside, but had relatives who moved to the city and sent money to them. How did they feel about remaining in the countryside? How did they use the money?
- Perhaps they grew up in farm families and became farmers themselves. What impact did modernization have on their farming methods?
- Perhaps they lived in Egypt and worked in a bank that was nationalized. How did they feel about this development? How did it affect their lives?
- Perhaps they lived in Iran and experienced the overthrow of Mosaddeq and then the Shah's White Revolution. What changes occurred in their daily lives?

EXTEND

Cross-Curricular Connection: *Journalism*

Ask students to bring in articles from newspapers and news magazines on current events in the Middle East. Then have students use the articles as the basis for a class discussion on the problems that the region currently faces.

MEET INDIVIDUAL NEEDS

Visual-Spatial Learners

Have a group of students prepare a chart showing the distribution of oil resources in the Middle East and throughout the world. Display the chart for the rest of the class, and ask students to draw conclusions based on the chart. Sources that students might check include *World Almanac*, *Facts on File*, and the *Readers' Guide to Periodical Literature*.

Interpersonal Learners

Have students read the description of a marriage in Egypt in the Global History Resource Center. Then have them discuss this method of choosing a marriage partner.

ASSESS

Review

Have students complete the Section 3 Review. Use answers in the Teacher's Edition, page 786, to assess student mastery of this section.

Lesson 28.4 *The Resurgence of Islam*

Textbook pp. 787–790

RESOURCES

Pupil's Edition

Literature Through Time, p.789: *Arabian Nights and Days*

Core Resources

Reading 28.4: *U.S. Hostages in Iran*

Global History Resource Center

Reading: *The Shah of Iran Loses Touch with Reality*

Reading: *Iran Ten Years After Khomeini's Revolution*

Videodiscs or Global History Resource Center

Map: *Iran-Iraq War, 1980–1988*

Search Frame 1064

LESSON FOCUS

What has been the impact of the resurgence of Islam in the Arab world?

OBJECTIVES

After completing this lesson, students will be able to:

• describe how some Muslims have reacted to the changes brought on by the modern world;

• identify what led to the Iranian Revolution in 1979;

• explain how many women in the Islamic world responded to the resurgence of Islam.

HOOK: Link to Today

Discuss how people demonstrate values through dress. Ask students to think about how the way people dress helps others recognize what they do or what their values are. Ask them if they can identitfy business people or members of a club or team by their dress. Then ask what other ways of dressing help them identify people's roles or values.

Next tell students that the way in which people, especially women, dressed became a source of conflict in some Middle Eastern countries. Conclude by having them discuss this conflict and the reasons for it. *[Students should mention that westernized dress style became a source of conflict, as many Middle Easterners hoped for the return of traditional values.]*

DEVELOP

Discuss the reactions of some Muslims to the changes in their societies after World War II. Have students identify ways in which Western life and traditional Muslim life differ. *[Students may suggest dress; women's roles; and religious influence.]* Then tell students that many of the social, economic, and political changes that occurred after World War II in the Middle East caused an Islamic resurgence—a renewed interest in Islam and the traditions of the past.

Ask: *How did Egypt's Muslim Brotherhood try to counteract Western influences?*

[The Muslim Brotherhood opposed the adoption of Western values that were not rooted in the teachings of the Qur'an and sought Islamic control over all aspects of society.]

Ask: *How did Qaddafi, Hezbollah, and the Mujahideen use Islam as a basis for their actions?*

[Qaddafi used a revolutionary interpretation of Islam to support his authority. Terrorist groups like Hezbollah justified their actions by insisting they were fighting for the faith. The Mujahideen also saw their fight against the Soviets in Afghanistan as a religious war, or jihad.]

(Then tell students that the greatest stimulus to the Islamic resurgence occurred with the Iranian Revolution. Ask students to describe the situation in Iran in 1979.) *[The Shah's policies of modernization, along with his oppressive government and connection to the United States, were unpopular.]*

Ask: What changes did Ayatollah Ruhollah Khomeini bring to Iran?

[Khomeini rejected Western values and customs and reinstated the strict Shi'ah customs, including the wearing of the chador for women. He also imprisoned and executed his opponents and imposed censorship throughout Iran.]

To conclude, have students make a list of the important events in Iran from 1979 through 1989. *[Lists should include: **January 1979**: departure of Shah, return of Khomeini; **November 1979**: Khomeini approves takeover of the U.S. embassy; **1980**: invasion by Iraq; **1988**: cease-fire with Iraq; **1989**: death of Khomeini.]* Have students save the lists for review purposes.

For more information on events in Iran, have students read and discuss the Global History Resource Center selections. Use the electronic media map of the Iran-Iraq War to help students understand that conflict.

PROBE

Discuss women's differing responses to the resurgence of Islam in the Muslim world. As a class, discuss the consequences for women of the Islamic resurgence.

Ask: What changes had occurred in women's lives as a result of modernization after World War II?

[More girls went to school and many got advanced degrees; women had professional careers in law, medicine, and government; women adopted Western-style clothing; and women's rights movements began to emerge.]

Encourage students to consider the points of view of both women who were in favor of their changed roles and those who were not. Ask them why women felt differently about this issue. *[Students should point out that many women enjoyed increased freedom and rejected the return of laws that seemed a step backward. Women who supported the Islamic resurgence believed that westernization had not brought stability or prosperity, and that Islam provided this needed stability.]*

CONCLUDE

Discuss the future of life in Iran. Explain that under Khomeini's rule life became very restricted, although this changed somewhat after his death. In discussing the effects of repressive rule, you may wish to note the Literature Through Time feature on textbook page 789. Then have students write about what they think may be in store for Iran, caught between those who favor tradition and those who look toward the West. In their paragraphs, have them consider:

- If you were Iranian, would you favor tradition or modernization? Why? Which would benefit your country more? Why do you think so?
- If you favored modernization, what would a person who favored tradition argue? What things in Western society might he or she criticize?

Conclude by leading a discussion in which students share their opinions with the class.

EXTEND

Cross-Curricular Connection: *Political Science*
Assign Core Resources Reading 28.4. Then have students discuss the crisis's effect on U.S.-Iranian relations; how the Iranians justified the taking of hostages; and how the United States handled the situation.

MEET INDIVIDUAL NEEDS

Gifted Students
Invite students to read Robin Wright's account of the Khomeini decade, *In the Name of God* (New York: Simon & Schuster, 1989), and then share their impressions of the book.

Students Having Difficulty/
Students Acquiring English
Have pairs of students make and use flash cards to help each other remember key events and terms from this section. Students can write key phrases on one side of the card, with identifying explanations on the other. Examples of events or terms students might use are *Islamic resurgence, Mujahideen, Hezbollah*, etc.

ASSESS

Review
Have students complete the Section 4 Review. Use answers in the Teacher's Edition, page 790, to assess student mastery of this section.

Lesson 28.5 *Independent Africa*

Textbook pp. 791–796

RESOURCES

Pupil's Edition

Then and Now, p. 795: *Balancing Human and Wildlife Needs in Africa*

Core Resources

Geography Activity 28: *Population in Modern Africa*

Reading 28.5: *Politics and Religion in South Africa*

Visual Resources

Everyday Life 28: *A Literacy Class in Africa*

Geography and History 28: *The Economy of Africa*

Art and History 28: *Kumasi Market*

Global History Resource Center

Reading: *Ghana Begins Economic Development*

Reading: *Growing Trees and Democracy in Kenya*

Reading: *Modern Masai in Kenya*

Videodiscs or Global History Resource Center

Image: *Street Scene in Modern Nairobi, Kenya*

Search Frame 1054

Image: *Kenya's Oldest Kikuyu Chief*

Search Frame 1055

Image: *Modern Sculpture from Ghana*

Search Frame 1062

LESSON FOCUS

What problems has Africa faced since independence?

OBJECTIVES

After completing this lesson, students will be able to:

- identify problems faced by African states after independence;
- describe the path of politics in many African states after independence;
- describe ways in which African writers and artists expressed their sense of identity as they confronted the problems of independence.

HOOK

Discuss problems in African states after independence.
Ask students to imagine that they live in an area that has been ruled as a colony by another nation for many years. They have worked for many years to achieve independence for their nation. Finally their hopes have been realized, and their country has become an independent state.

Ask: *What hopes do you have for the future of your country? How do you expect things to improve?*

Have students write down their expectations and share them with the class. Then point out that many Africans finally achieved freedom, but that along with freedom came serious problems that many had difficulty solving.

DEVELOP

Discuss problems of African independence. Write the following headings on the chalkboard: *Economy; Population; Environment; Disease.* Have students create a chart listing the problems for each heading. Then ask them to discuss their entries, and write the entries on the board. You might wish to display Everyday Life 28 and Geography and History 28 and assign the accompanying worksheets before students begin.
[*economy*: *dependence on one or two exports, lack of industrialization, debt for projects that suffered from either poor planning or corruption;* **population: *rising due to better healthcare;* **environment:** *poor farming techniques, deforestation, desertification, drought;* **disease:** *AIDS, ebola, other viruses]*

Students may be interested in reading the Then and Now feature on textbook page 795 for more information on environmental issues.

PROBE

Discuss the political situation in many new African nations. Tell students that one of the most serious problems that many nations faced was political instability, and many ended up with dictators. Have them discuss Kwame Nkrumah's transition from popular leader to dictator in Ghana.

Then tell students that one of the major reasons for political instability in Africa was ethnic conflict. Remind them that as a result of European-drawn boundaries, the people of many African nations had not developed a sense of national identity.

Ask: *How did conflict among ethnic groups contribute to political instability?*
[As rival groups competed for control of the new states, civil wars broke out.]

Ask students to discuss the civil wars in Nigeria, Burundi, and Rwanda to provide examples of ethnic conflict and instability.

Next tell students that while political instability threatened several African nations, some moved toward democracy.

Ask: *Which two nations achieved greater political equality during the 1980s and 1990s?*
[Rhodesia and South Africa]

Conclude with a discussion on the events leading up to the political changes in these two countries. (You might wish to have students read Core Resources Reading 28.5 on South Africa at this time.) Tell students that by the mid-1990s many countries had established democracies.

CONCLUDE

Explore the revival of African culture. Have a student read aloud the excerpt of the work by Ousmane Sembene on textbook pages 794 and 796. Have students explain how this quote shows the trends in African literature of the 1950s and 1960s. *[It attacks the evils of colonial racism.]*

Point out that African literature and art experienced a cultural revival in the years following independence.

Ask: *How did Africans retain their own sense of identity during the colonial years and afterward?*
[Africans preserved and celebrated African arts as a way of protesting colonial rule. For example, East Africans continued to study Swahili and used it in poetry, plays, and novels. Later authors, such as Sembene, protested

the evils of colonialism or the problems of independence. Traditional arts also expressed African identity.]

Ask: *How have many African artists expressed their cultural identity?*
[They have combined both new and old techniques, materials, and ideas, leading to a new vitality and creativity. Often, they have used their work to confront the issues that are plaguing their societies.]

To give students an example of modern African art, show the electronic media image of the modern sculpture from Ghana and Art and History Transparency 28.

EXTEND

Cross-Curricular Connection: *Literature*

Have students read a novel by an African novelist, such as Ousmane Sembene. Have them share with the class the author's feelings about life in African society.

MEET INDIVIDUAL NEEDS

Gifted Students

Have students research traditional art forms from different parts of Africa and pick one on which to do an in-depth report. If possible, have students bring in photographs of different examples.

Intrapersonal Learners

Have students read the story in the Global History Resource Center about the Masai herder who broke with tradition to become an airline pilot. Then ask students to write a journal entry in which they explore the tensions that might be felt by Africans caught between traditional and modern life.

ASSESS

Review

Have students complete the Section 5 Review. Use answers in the Teacher's Edition, page 795–796, to assess student mastery of this section.

In preparation for the chapter test, you may wish to have students complete all or part of the Chapter 28 Review on textbook page 796, the Chapter 28 Review Activity, and the Chapter 28 Themes Review.

Understanding the Main Idea

Call on a volunteer to read aloud the *Understanding the Main Idea* paragraph. Then tell students that during the era of decolonization many people in Africa and the Middle East had high hopes for greater freedom and prosperity. After independence, however, they faced challenges brought on by economic, political, and social change. Many struggled to find a new sense of identity as modern ways of living clashed with traditional ones.

Presenting Themes

See p. 769B for suggestions on introducing themes.

Using the Time Line

Have students list the time line events in their notebooks. After they have read about each event in the chapter, have students write a paragraph explaining its significance.

Chapter 28
Africa and the Middle East After Empire 1945–Present

Understanding the Main Idea

After World War II, newly independent states in Africa and the Middle East experienced both the promise and the problems of independence while they faced grave economic, political, and social challenges. As they confronted these challenges, many people struggled for a new sense of security and self-identity.

Themes

- **Religion and the Arts** What role might religion and cultural revival play in people's efforts to cope with modernization?

- **War and Diplomacy** How might ongoing local and international wars contribute to political and social instability in a region?

- **Geography** In what ways might the presence or lack of raw materials affect a country's development?

On February 14, 1953, a brief ceremony was held in front of the government secretariat buildings in Khartoum, capital of the Anglo-Egyptian Sudan. Huge crowds of Sudanese had gathered, overflowing the porches, stairs, balconies, and even the roofs of the buildings. Under the stony gaze of Lord Kitchener's statue, Governor-General Sir Robert Howe, other leading administration officials, and the Sudanese members of the legislative assembly gathered to celebrate the signing of an agreement between Britain and Egypt. This agreement established the procedures and timetable for Sudanese self-government—in effect, for independence.

In 1956 the Sudanese National Unionist Party proclaimed Sudan's independence ahead of schedule—largely in order to stop an ongoing Egyptian propaganda campaign aimed at unifying the Sudan and Egypt. Both Britain and Egypt accepted the declaration of independence. On January 1, 1956, the new republic of the Sudan became one of the first African territories to achieve independence after World War II. Within three years, however, the Sudan also became one of the first of many independent African countries to experience a military coup. As was the case in the Sudan, the path of independence throughout the continent was to be a rocky one.

1948	1956	1960	1969
The state of Israel is proclaimed and is plunged into war with neighboring Arab states.	The Suez Crisis erupts in Egypt.	OPEC is formed.	Golda Meir becomes Israel's first female prime minister.

The flag of the independent Sudan is raised as the British and Egyptian flags are lowered in 1956.

The Anglo-Egyptian Sudan was a condominium, or jointly controlled area, ruled by Britain and Egypt as equal powers. In practice, however, the territory was ruled by a series of British governors-general, who were nominated by the British foreign secretary and appointed by the Egyptian monarch, who governed through the largely British Sudan Political Service. Nevertheless, because of its condominium status, both the British Union Jack and the Egyptian Star and Crescent flew together over the Sudan until 1956, when both were replaced by the new flag of the independent republic of Sudan.

Critical Thinking Ask students if they think Britain or Egypt held actual power in the Sudan.

ANSWER: Students should suggest that Britain actually controlled the Sudan, since the governors-general and most of the administrators were British.

1979	1980	1994	1995
The Shah of Iran is overthrown.	Zimbabwe proclaims its independence.	The first multiracial national elections are held in South Africa; Nelson Mandela is elected president.	Israeli prime minister Yitzhak Rabin is assassinated.

SECTION 1

CORE LESSON PLAN
See pages 769C and
769D for Lesson Plan
28.1.

Kwame Nkrumah
In 1947 Nkrumah took the
position of secretary of
the recently established
UGCC. After riots in 1948
Nkrumah became increas-
ingly unhappy with the
moderate stance of the
UGCC leaders—who
were in turn alarmed by
Nkrumah's radicalism.
Over the next several
years Nkrumah started his
own paper, founded
Ghana National College,
and established the
Committee on Youth
Organization. These mea-
sures led to his break with
the UGCC and the cre-
ation of the CPP.

Critical Thinking Ask
students why moderates
might have objected to
Nkrumah's more radical
approach.

ANSWER: Students might
suggest that moderates
wanted to share power
with the British or
wanted to avoid violent
confrontation.

SECTION 1
Decolonization and Nationalism

FOCUS

- What path did most British colonies in Africa follow to independence?

- How did French efforts to maintain a unified African empire affect decolonization?

- What was the struggle for independence like in Belgian and Portuguese African colonies?

- How did wartime actions of the colonial powers affect decolonization in many Middle Eastern countries?

As it was in other regions of the world, World War II was a great turning point in Africa and the Middle East. The colonial powers emerged from the war exhausted and bankrupt. During the war the Allies had implied an end to colonialism as part of the postwar settlement. After the war, new nationalist leaders in many African and Middle Eastern countries demanded independence. Eventually, most European colonial powers agreed to these demands with little resistance.

Congolese troops in World War II

Decolonization in British Africa

World War II changed the history of imperial-ism. For many colonial peoples, the Atlantic Charter seemed to promise self-determination after the war. After 1945 the United States also pressured the European colonial powers to accept decolonization—the withdrawal of the colonial powers from their colonies and spheres of influence. The British led the way, and in the late 1940s they started to acknowledge the inevitability of decolonization.

The British government envisioned a lengthy process of preparation, in which they would gradually grant the colonial territories more and more political power. It was hoped that this would ensure stable, democratic, pro-Western governments when the colonies became independent.

Ghana. The first of Britain's formal colonies to achieve independence after World War II was the Gold Coast in West Africa. Nationalism in this area had begun to stir even before the war. Members of the colony's westernized African elite had established the **United Gold Coast Convention**, or UGCC, to demand greater participation in government.

Instead of fighting the British, these African leaders had preferred to cooperate and gain influ-ence as peacefully as possible. In 1947, however, a young African named Kwame Nkrumah (en-KROO-muh) became secretary of the UGCC. He soon became the leader of the Gold Coast nationalist movement.

Born in 1909, Nkrumah was educated in the United States and was heavily influenced by Pan-Africanism. In 1945 he attended the Pan-African conference in Great Britain. When Nkrumah returned to the Gold Coast in 1947, he was determined to trans-form the UGCC into a mass party with popular support from the colony's entire African population.

In 1949 Nkrumah estab-lished the **Convention People's Party**, or CPP.

Kwame Nkrumah
BIOGRAPHY

African Independence, 1946–1993

EUROPE

Cape Verde Islands (inset map)
MAURITANIA
CAPE VERDE 1975
Praia
GAMBIA
SENEGAL
GUINEA-BISSAU
GUINEA
10°N
20°W
Azimuthal Equal-Area Projection

Legend:
- Independent before 1946
- Independence granted 1946–1960
- Independence granted since 1960
- Dependency
- 1980 Date of independence
- National boundary
- Disputed boundary
- National capital
- Other city

A New Spirit Independence movements swept across Africa in the 1950s and the early 1960s.

Location Which African country was the latest to win its independence?

Nkrumah led strikes and demonstrations. The British responded by jailing him. Through his persistence, however, Nkrumah transformed the CPP into a major political party with considerable popular support. Faced with this kind of pressure, the British eventually agreed to grant a new self-governing constitution and allow national elections in 1951. The CPP swept the elections.

The fiery young nationalist leader continued to press for independence, and Britain eventually granted the Gold Coast full self-government in 1957. Nkrumah became the first prime minister of

Theme: **Politics and Law**
Ghana faced immense diversity. The traditional leaders preferred a system of government that recognized the differences among the various ethnic and cultural communities. Nkrumah, however, refused to accept anything less than a united national government. Eventually, this led him to establish one-party rule.

Critical Thinking Ask students how well they think a multiparty system would have worked in Ghana.

ANSWER: Students might suggest that regional and ethnic groups would have formed into separate political parties anyway.

R RESOURCE ACTIVITY

GLOBAL HISTORY RESOURCE CENTER
Image: *Kwame Nkrumah Celebrates Ghana's Independence*

Print out and distribute the image and caption. Have students pick two people in the image—Nkrumah and a tribal leader—and insert "thought bubbles" to describe what each might have been thinking on the occasion.

Level 1/ Sheltered English

the newly proclaimed state of Ghana. The path that Ghana took toward self-government and independence became the model for the rest of Britain's African colonies to follow. The process did not go smoothly everywhere, however, particularly where there were large numbers of white settlers.

Kenya. In Kenya the struggle over land between the Kikuyu people and European settlers led to a major uprising in the 1950s. The Kikuyu were particularly angry that growing white settlement had kept them from the Kenyan highlands, which they considered part of their ancestral homeland. Jomo Kenyatta, a Kikuyu who studied at the London School of Economics before becoming the leader

THROUGH OTHERS' EYES

An African American Considers Postwar Colonialism

The process of decolonization in Africa and Asia attracted considerable attention from African Americans. For example, in 1945, W. E. B. Du Bois called for a new postwar colonial policy to be overseen by the United Nations. In his book *Color and Democracy: Colonies and Peace,* Du Bois, who had been recently appointed as director of special research for the National Association for the Advancement of Colored People, or NAACP, explained:

66A new Mandates Commission should immediately be organized to . . . lay down new procedures for the treatment of all colonial peoples. . . . There should be consultation among colonial peoples . . . asking for the following steps: One, representation of the colonial peoples alongside the master peoples in the Assembly. Two, the organization of a Mandates Commission . . . with definite power to investigate complaints and conditions in colonies. . . . Three, a clear statement of the intentions of each imperial power to take, gradually but definitely, all measures designed to raise the peoples of colonies to a condition of complete political and economic equality with the peoples of the master nations.99

of the nationalist movement in Kenya, once described the importance of land for his people:

66*It is the key to the people's life; it secures them that peaceful tillage [cultivation] of the soil which supplies their material needs and enables them to perform their magic and traditional ceremonies in undisturbed serenity.*99

As the white settlers continued to deny the Kikuyu access to the highlands, many Kikuyu joined a movement in the 1950s that came to be called the **Mau Mau.** Drawing on Kikuyu ceremonies and traditions, members of the movement bound themselves with blood oaths to fight for their land against all who resisted them. For about four years, they terrorized the central highlands of Kenya, murdering many of those who opposed them—mostly other Africans who continued to cooperate with the Europeans.

Winds of change. The British eventually regained control of the colony and put down the Mau Mau movement, but by the late 1950s the British had become convinced that they must make concessions to African nationalists and accept rapid decolonization. In 1961 the British colonial secretary acknowledged that the "winds of change" were sweeping away colonialism. The British began to actively plan for a rapid transfer of power to nationalists within their colonies. In 1963 Kenya became an independent state, with Jomo Kenyatta as the first prime minister.

British colonies in Africa generally followed Ghana's example of constitutional development and eventual self-government.

French Africa

While the British colonies followed a fairly straight path of constitutional development, France's African colonies followed a different pattern. During World War II the Free French forces of General Charles de Gaulle had obtained much support from the African colonies. One of de Gaulle's strongest supporters was Félix Eboué (ayb-way), France's first black colonial governor.

After France fell to the Germans in World War II, Eboué publicly declared his support for Free France. Shortly thereafter, the rest of the colonial governors in French Equatorial Africa followed his lead.

Toward decolonization. Eboué's support for Free France reflected his commitment to the traditional direction of French colonial policy. Unlike the British, the French had always insisted that their goal was to incorporate the African colonies into France itself. After the war, de Gaulle tried to resume this policy, while at the same time responding to calls for greater African participation in colonial government.

France's African colonies were joined together in a federation, from which African representatives were elected to the French National Assembly in Paris. Although many Africans gained political experience in this way, they also continued to feel that their interests were second to those of France. Soon, popular political parties resembling Ghana's CPP began to emerge in the French colonies.

In Senegal, for example, Leopold Senghor, who had lived in France during the 1930s and even considered himself a monarchist, returned to establish a party dedicated to self-government. Felix Houphouet-Boigny (OO-FWAY BWAH-nyuh) of the Côte d'Ivoire and Sékou Touré (TOO-RAY) of Guinea also established nationalist parties and worked for greater self-government. Meanwhile, events in France's North African territories soon transformed the entire colonial situation.

Algeria and North Africa. With roughly 1 million European settlers, Algeria had long been a department, or province, of France itself. After World War II France was reluctant to let go of Algeria, not only because of the Europeans living there but also because of the oil that was discovered there in the early 1950s. France's determination to hang on to Algeria, combined with the attitudes of racial superiority that the European settlers held toward their Arab neighbors, led to the emergence of a strong Arab nationalist movement.

Supported by other Arab countries, such as Egypt and Syria, the **Algerian National Liberation Front** (known by its French initials FLN) launched a guerrilla war in 1954 to obtain independence as an Arab state. The war grew increasingly brutal, and eventually de Gaulle stepped in to resolve the conflict. Instead of crushing the Arab rebels, as many expected him to, de Gaulle negotiated with them. As a result, in 1962 Algeria became independent.

Meanwhile, Arab nationalists in Morocco and Tunisia, both French protectorates, also demanded independence. In the name of Sultan Muhammad V, Moroccan nationalists attacked French troops and waged a general campaign of noncooperation against all French nationals in the country. With French resources already being drained by the Algerian war, as well as the ongoing colonial war in French Indochina, France recognized the independence of both Morocco and Tunisia in 1956.

The French Community. As African leaders struggled for control over their own affairs, de Gaulle offered them a simple choice in 1958. They could either remain associated with France in a new organization known as the **French Community**, they could become actual departments of France, or they could become independent immediately. If they joined the Community, they would have internal self-government, but France would retain control of their foreign relations. These nations would also continue to receive money from France for economic development. If they chose independence, however, they would be cut off from France completely—including French development funds.

Only Guinea, under Sékou Touré, opted for complete independence. Touré told de Gaulle:

> 66 We have to tell you bluntly, Mr. President, what the demands of the people are. . . . We have one prime and essential need: our dignity. . . . But there is no dignity without freedom. . . . We prefer freedom in poverty to opulence [great wealth] in slavery. 99

▶ After Sékou Touré became president of Guinea in 1958, he sought support for his nation from both Western countries and the Communist bloc.

Theme: Cross-cultural Interaction

In the early 1950s, Angola benefited from the growth and prosperity of the world coffee market. Such prosperity encouraged many new immigrants, mostly from Portugal and Cape Verde. By 1970 as many as 300,000 immigrants had settled on the land or established themselves as minor officials, artisans, and retail traders in Angola's towns. Similar immigration occurred in Mozambique in the 1960s. As Africans and white settlers competed for land and jobs, many Africans became increasingly bitter toward Portuguese rule. Rebellion broke out in Angola in 1961 and in northern Mozambique in 1964. As Portugal tried to suppress the rebellions, African leaders accepted support not only from the Soviet Union but also from Communist China.

Critical Thinking Ask students why the Soviet Union and China were willing to give resources to anticolonial rebellions in Africa.

ANSWER: Students might suggest that the Soviet Union and China were trying to weaken the countries of Western Europe, spread communism, and win future allies in Africa.

Upon becoming independent, Guinea was immediately shunned by the other nations of the French Community. With little alternative, Touré turned to the Soviet Union for help. Alarmed by this appeal to the Soviets, de Gaulle eventually reversed his previous policy, and the rest of France's colonies were allowed to obtain complete independence without being cut off from continuing French assistance.

Although France tried to maintain the unity of its African empire, local nationalist movements triumphed, but most former colonies retained ties with France.

▲ Thousands of spectators gathered to celebrate the independence of Guinea-Bissau (formerly Portuguese Guinea).

Belgian and Portuguese Africa

While Britain and France made accommodations for their African colonies to achieve self-government or independence, other colonial powers were reluctant to do so. Portugal, the first European power to establish colonies in Africa, was also the last to give them up. As Portugal continued to hold on, African leaders emerged in the Portuguese colonies of Angola, Portuguese Guinea, and Mozambique to organize "liberation armies." Many drew support from the Soviet Union and its allies. As a result, long years of bloody warfare marked the last decades of Portuguese rule in Africa.

As colonial wars continued to drain Portugal's economy, a military coup in Lisbon overthrew the Portuguese government in 1974. The new military government immediately arranged to withdraw from the colonies and allow them to become independent at last. However, the colonies had not had time to build a firm foundation for either their economies or their administrations.

A similar problem confronted Africans in the Belgian Congo. Like the Portuguese, the Belgians had never really considered preparing Africans in the huge Congo for self-government, much less for independence. The Congo had a vast number of ethnic groups, speaking many languages and living in an enormously diverse country. Although the Belgians had encouraged education at the elementary-school level and the Congo had a relatively high literacy rate at the time of independence, there were almost no Congolese with any higher education. Industrialization had proceeded rapidly in the last decades of Belgian rule, but it was almost exclusively in the hands of Europeans.

As a Congolese nationalist movement emerged after World War II, however, the Belgian government agreed that it should prepare the colony for self-government. Believing that the Congolese had not developed the institutions or acquired the experience needed to manage a modern state, Belgians supported a 30-year timetable to prepare them for eventual independence. Distrusting the Belgians, African nationalists demanded immediate self-government. Consequently, in 1960 Belgium suddenly announced that it would withdraw completely within a year.

With little preparation, many political parties representing different ethnic groups, geographical regions, and political beliefs participated in the first elections ever held in the new Democratic Republic of the Congo. Former postal clerk Patrice Lumumba (luh-MUHM-buh) became prime minister, while his rival and political enemy Joseph Kasavubu (kah-sah-VOO-boo) became president. Lumumba remained opposed to European influence. Angered by his stance, Belgian technicians and experts left the Congo in droves. This proved a major blow to the new country's economy.

Soon, the army mutinied and the copper-rich province of Katanga seceded. The country was plunged into a crisis. An assassin killed Lumumba in 1961, and Kasavubu assumed full power. The chaos and violence continued.

Intervention by the United Nations brought Katanga back into the Congo republic, but order was not restored until 1965, when General Joseph Mobutu seized power from Kasavubu and established a strong and ruthless military dictatorship. Mobutu's military coup echoed events in many other African countries after independence.

Decolonization in Portuguese and Belgian colonies was marked by bloodshed and civil war.

The Middle East

The wave of nationalism that overtook Africa in the 1950s was also accompanied by growing anti-Western sentiments in the Middle East. During World War II the Allies had reimposed control over some Middle Eastern countries that had been independent. The Allies' actions during the war and their relative slowness at giving up power afterward soon brought on a renewed nationalist reaction.

Iran. During World War II Britain and the Soviet Union had occupied Iran to ensure a secure line of supply and communications for the Soviet war effort. Britain had deposed the Iranian leader, Reza Shah, and placed his young son, Muhammad Reza Shah, on the throne. After the war Soviet agents refused to leave northern Iran and actually helped set up a short-lived Soviet republic. Under U.S. and British pressure, however, the Soviets finally withdrew. Meanwhile, British influence remained strong throughout the rest of the country.

After World War II Iranian nationalists, led by Prime Minister Mohammad Mosaddeq (MOHS-ad-dek), became determined to regain full control of the country from the Western powers. In a move that captured the attention of the world and outraged many people, in 1951 Mosaddeq nationalized Iran's oil industry, which was dominated by the British-owned Anglo-Iranian Oil Company. With the Cold War just getting under

way, such actions set the stage for major trouble between Iran and the Western powers.

Egypt. The British had intervened in Egypt during World War II to ensure that they would have an Egyptian cabinet that was not actively hostile to their war effort. In 1942, for example, the British ambassador, Lord Killearn, had surrounded the royal palace with tanks and delivered an ultimatum to King Farouk (fah-ROOK) to change the government or be deposed.

After the war, continued British military occupation of Egypt and the Sudan led many Egyptians to raise their nationalist demands of "Evacuation" of British troops and "Unity of the Nile Valley" once again. The British refused to recognize the Sudan as a part of Egypt, and this resistance only heightened tensions between the Egyptian nationalists and the British. King Farouk proved unable to free Egypt from British domination, and in 1952 a group of army officers staged a coup and overthrew the monarchy. Eventually, Colonel Gamal Abdel Nasser became the president of the new Egyptian republic. In 1954 he negotiated a complete British withdrawal from Egypt after some 70 years of military occupation.

▲ Iranians cheer as their flag is raised over an oil company nationalized by the Iranian government in 1951.

RESOURCE ACTIVITY

READINGS IN WORLD HISTORY Reading 28.1
Decolonization in Africa

Have students read the description of African societies after decolonization. Then have them complete the questions.

Level 2

REVIEW & ASSESSMENT RESOURCES

- Study Guide 28.1
- Daily Quiz 28.1
- Main Idea Activity 28.1

All Levels

SECTION 1 REVIEW ANSWERS (p. 778)

IDENTIFY
For significance, see the following pages:
United Gold Coast Convention (p. 772)
Kwame Nkrumah (p. 772)
Convention People's Party (p. 772)
Mau Mau (p. 774)
Algerian National Liberation Front (p. 775)
French Community (p. 775)
Arab League (p. 778)

LOCATE
For locations, see the map on p. 773.

1. They followed Ghana's example of constitutional development, eventually becoming self-governing.
2. France offered the colonies membership in the French Community. The African states obtained independence and maintained economic and cultural ties to France.
3. While decolonization of French colonies was relatively peaceful, Belgian and Portuguese colonies experienced bloodshed and civil war.
4. Essays should mention that Allies reimposed control over some Middle Eastern countries that had become independent, that Britain and the Soviet Union occupied Iran during the war, and that Iran's oil industry was nationalized.
5. similar—African leaders in Ghana and the French colonies wanted to achieve independence by peaceful means and maintain friendly ties after independence was gained; different—nationalist leaders in Belgian and Portuguese colonies were distrustful of the imperial governments and wanted immediate self-government, for which they fought fiercely

Syria and Lebanon. Several years earlier, the French had also finally withdrawn from Syria and Lebanon. In 1941 British and Free French forces had moved into Vichy-held Syria and Lebanon to stop the Germans from using them as bases. While Syrian nationalists demanded freedom, the Vichy French made promises of self-government, yet refused to leave. Finally, France gave up control in 1946, and Syria became an independent republic.

Meanwhile, French officials had promised independence to Lebanon. A new constitution established a government in which each major religion would be represented according to its proportion of the Lebanese population. This left Christians with a slight majority. By informal agreement the various offices of state were divided among the religious communities. Once they had enacted the new constitution, the French recognized Lebanon's independence, and not long after, the last French troops left the country.

The Arab League. As these newly independent Arab states began to emerge, seven of them—Iraq, Lebanon, Yemen, Jordan, Egypt, Saudi Arabia, and Syria—joined together to form the **Arab League** in 1945. Later, many other countries that identified themselves as Arab also joined the League, including Morocco, Tunisia, Kuwait, Algeria, Sudan, and Libya. In part, the League was a recognition of the still strong influence of Pan-Arabism in the region. It also provided a common front against one of the last holdouts of Western colonialism in the Middle East, the British mandate in Palestine. In particular, the League opposed any and all efforts to establish a Jewish state in Palestine.

Wartime intervention by the colonial powers in many Middle Eastern countries led to growing demands for full independence after the war.

▲ In 1940 infantrymen of the Free French force march past an inspecting officer and his staff at a desert outpost in Syria.

SECTION 1 REVIEW

IDENTIFY and explain the significance of the following:
 United Gold Coast
  Convention
 Kwame Nkrumah
 Convention People's Party
 Mau Mau
 Algerian National
  Liberation Front
 French Community
 Arab League

LOCATE and explain the importance of the following:
 Ghana

 Kenya
 Algeria
 Egypt

1. **Main Idea** How did most British colonies in Africa gain their independence?
2. **Main Idea** How did the French maintain the unity of their empire? What effect did these efforts have on emerging African states?
3. **War and Diplomacy** How did decolonization in the Belgian and Portuguese

colonies differ from that in the British and French colonies?
4. **Writing to Explain** Write a short essay explaining how the actions of the colonial powers during and after World War II affected decolonization in the Middle East.
5. **Comparing and Contrasting** How were the goals of some African nationalist leaders similar? How were they different?

Map A

SECTION 2

The Arab-Israeli Dilemma

FOCUS

FOCUS

- What happened after the British left Palestine?
- What events led to the Suez Crisis?
- What was the process for peace between the Arabs and the Israelis?

Perhaps the most difficult problem confronted by both the colonial powers and the newly developing states of the Middle East was the status of Palestine. In 1948, as frustrated British leaders abandoned the mandate for Palestine, Zionist leaders proclaimed the new state of Israel. War between the Jews and the Arab states broke out immediately. Although Israel survived this and other wars, for many years the history of bitterness between Jews and Arabs cast a shadow of violence and uncertainty over the region.

Jewish refugees arrive in Palestine in 1947.

The Creation of Israel

As the extent and horror of the Holocaust became public knowledge after World War II, Zionist demands for a Jewish state in Palestine increased. Massive numbers of Jews immigrated to Palestine illegally, while some extremist groups such as the Irgun waged a terrorist war against the British. In 1947 Britain announced that it was giving up the mandate. In 1948 the United Nations voted to partition Palestine into two states—one Jewish, the other Arab—and an internationally administered territory around Jerusalem. As the British withdrew, David Ben-Gurion, a leading Zionist, proclaimed the state of Israel on May 14, 1948.

Immediately, the new Israeli state had to defend itself against invading Arab armies. "This will be a war of extermination and a momentous [extraordinary] massacre," declared Azzam Pasha, the secretary general of the Arab League. The Arabs, however, failed to coordinate their attacks. When the war ended in 1949, Israel had more territory than the partition plan had called for, and over half a million Arab refugees had fled the country.

Many Arabs fled as a result of the terror inspired by an Irgun assault on the Arab village of Deir Yassin, where men, women, and children were massacred. Such actions frightened other Arabs into flight. The Irgun released statements intended to heighten Arab fears:

66 We intend to attack, conquer and keep [territory] until we have the whole of Palestine . . . in a greater Jewish state. . . . We hope to improve our methods in future and make it possible to spare women and children. **99**

The ploy worked, but the fleeing Palestinians created another major refugee problem.

Victory in the 1948 war secured Israel's immediate existence. One of the first things the new Jewish government did was to proclaim the **Law of Return**, according to which every Jew who settled in Israel was automatically guaranteed citizenship in the new state. Between 1949 and 1952, roughly 600,000 Jews, mostly refugees from Eastern Europe and the Arab states, made their homes in Israel.

S

COR
See pa
769F for L
28.2.

R **RESOURCE ACTIVITY**

GLOBAL HISTORY RESOURCE CENTER
Reading: *Israel's Proclamation of Independence*

Print out and distribute the reading. Have students take turns reading aloud the proclamation that announced the establishment of Israel. Discuss the reading with students, going over the historical details. Then have students create an illustrated flyer that announces the emergence of the state of Israel.

Level 1/ Sheltered English

780

Theme:
Geography

The Aswan High Dam was built to improve Egypt's economic situation. The dam captures the flow of the yearly Nile flood and allows that water to be used for irrigation. Over a million acres have been converted to farmland since the dam's construction. The storage capacity of the dam, 164 billion cubic meters of water, provides a tremendous reservoir for use in periods of drought. Turbines in the dam also supply part of Egypt's electricity needs.

The dam has caused problems, however. The absence of the yearly flood means that farmland in the Nile Valley is not fertilized by silt. This forces farmers to use chemical fertilizers. Also, the reduced supply of water-borne nutrients has led to a decline in the Nile fishing industry. Silt is constantly building up in the lake above the dam, although the lake is so large that this is not seen as a major problem.

Critical Thinking Ask students if they think the benefits of the Aswan High Dam outweigh the costs.

ANSWER: Students' answers will vary.

Israel, 1947–1994

Jewish state under 1947 UN partition plan for Palestine

Acquired by Israel in 1948 War of Independence

Israeli conquests in the Six-Day War of 1967

Israeli conquests returned to Egypt, 1967–1982

Areas partially under Palestinian self-rule, 1994

National boundary

National capital

Other city

Conflicts in Israel Jews and Arabs warred for more than 40 years for control of the former lands of Palestine.

Location What areas did the Palestinian Arabs begin to rule in 1994?

The Israelis also established a democracy, in which the prime minister and the cabinet were responsible to the **Knesset**, or parliament. All adult citizens, including Arabs, could vote. Israel's firm commitment to Western-style government distinguished it from the Arab states of the region.

As the British withdrew from Palestine, the Zionists proclaimed the state of Israel and successfully defended it against invading Arab armies.

The Suez Crisis

Defeat by Israel shook the self-confidence of many in the Arab states. In Egypt it contributed to the revolution that overthrew the monarchy. Radical Arab leaders soon turned to the Soviet Union for aid. They also looked for ways in which to assert their independence, such as joining the Non-Aligned Movement with other newly independent Asian and African nations.

The new Egyptian president Gamal Abdel Nasser became one of the leaders of the Non-Aligned Movement. After negotiating Britain's withdrawal from Egypt in 1954, he also applied for U.S. and British financial support to finance the construction of the Aswan High Dam, which would provide more water for agriculture and a valuable new source of hydroelectric power to help Egypt industrialize. At the same time, however, Nasser also accepted Soviet military aid in an effort to strengthen and modernize the Egyptian army.

Worried by Nasser's relations with the Soviet Union, the United States and Britain withdrew their financial support in 1956. Nasser then moved abruptly to nationalize the Suez Canal, through which much of the world's shipping flowed. Revenues from the canal would help to finance Egypt's development plans.

In response, France, Britain, and Israel conspired to invade Egypt, retake the canal, and overthrow Nasser. When the invasion began in October, however, it caused a major international uproar. The situation became known as the **Suez Crisis**. When the United States threatened to cut off certain types of aid to Britain, the British government decided to back down and the invasion collapsed. Afterward, Nasser became a hero to the Arab world and European imperialism was thoroughly and finally discredited. The Suez Crisis thus contributed to the rapid pace of decolonization in the late 1950s and early 1960s. Meanwhile, the UN sent troops to Egypt to patrol a cease-fire line as Britain, France, and Israel withdrew their military forces.

Combined with Western support of Israel, superpower rivalries fueled Arab nationalism under Nasser and led to the Suez Crisis.

Renewed Conflict with Israel

Over the next two decades Arab-Israeli relations remained tense. In 1967, fearful of another attack, the Israelis launched a strike of their own. In the **Six-Day War**, Israeli forces overran the Sinai Peninsula, the Golan Heights on the Syrian border, and East Jerusalem, which they promptly annexed. Proclaiming the reunited Jerusalem as their eternal capital (West Jerusalem had been proclaimed the capital in 1948), they defied the 1947 United Nations resolution that the city should be international.

The Six-Day War radicalized the Arab-Israeli struggle. Soon two brutal Arab dictators came to power—Saddam Hussein in Iraq and Hafiz Asad in Syria. In addition, the **Palestine Liberation Organization** (PLO), an umbrella organization for a variety of Palestinian nationalist groups, turned to terrorism to strike back at Israel. In 1972, for example, Palestinian terrorists killed members of the Israeli Olympic team in Munich.

In 1973 Nasser's successor, Anwar Sadat, allied with Syria, launched another war against Israel. Attacking on the Jewish holy day of Yom Kippur, the Egyptians caught Israeli prime minister Golda Meir (may-IR) and her military experts off-guard. Although at first Israel's troops were pushed back, Meir rallied the Israelis to defend their still-young state. With American support, the Israelis once again defeated the Arabs.

BIOGRAPHY Meir herself had been one of the leaders of the Zionist movement since the 1920s. Born in Kiev, Russia, in 1898 as Goldie Mabovitch, she experienced the anti-Semitism of czarist Russia. In 1906 she and her family immigrated to the United States, where they settled in Milwaukee, Wisconsin. There Goldie Mabovitch grew up to become a teacher.

In 1917 she married Morris Meyerson, and four years later they immigrated to Palestine to join the new Zionist settlements. Goldie threw herself into the Zionist movement and labor politics. By 1946 she had established herself as one of the leaders of the Jewish Agency, which oversaw the affairs of the Jewish community in Palestine. In 1956 she became Israel's foreign minister. At the same time she adopted a Hebrew-sounding name—Golda Meir. In 1969 Golda Meir was elected as Israel's first female prime minister, a post she held until her retirement in 1974. When she died in 1978, Israelis mourned her as if she had been the mother of the new nation.

Golda Meir
BIOGRAPHY

The Movement Toward Peace

The Yom Kippur War finally convinced many Egyptians and Israelis of the need to make peace. Even as both sides began to consider ways of working out their differences, however, many people in the Middle East were determined to disrupt the fragile peace process.

Camp David Accords. As the level of terrorist violence seemed to rise around the world, American leaders did their best to bring the two sides to the negotiating table. After secret diplomatic talks in Morocco and elsewhere, in 1977 Egyptian president Anwar Sadat astonished the world by flying to Israel with an offer to open a dialogue with the Israelis. In a speech to the Knesset he explained that the battle for a permanent peace in the Middle East must be won by all:

❝ It is not my battle alone. Nor is it the battle of the leadership in Israel alone. It is the battle of all and every citizen in all our

▲ In 1977 Menachem Begin watches as Anwar Sadat addresses the Knesset about the need to achieve peace.

INTERNET ACTIVITY

ISRAELI AND PALESTINIAN POINTS OF VIEW
One obstacle to the Israeli-Palestinian peace process has been—and continues to be—the two sides' long-held suspicion of each other. This may lead Israelis and Palestinians to interpret events in very different ways.

Activity: Have students search the Internet for information on recent developments in the Israeli-Palestinian peace process. Have them find two sources of information on the same event, one giving an Israeli point of view, the other giving a Palestinian point of view (two useful sites might be the online edition of the *Jerusalem Post* and the website of the Palestinian National Authority). Then have students evaluate the sources and write their own objective report on the event. Students' reports should include their opinions of the outcome of the peace process, based on the different variables they have studied.

All Levels

REVIEW & ASSESSMENT RESOURCES

- Study Guide 28.2
- Daily Quiz 28.2
- Main Idea Activity 28.2

All Levels

territories, whose right it is to live in peace. It is the commitment of conscience and responsibility in the hearts of millions. **"**

In the summer of 1978 Sadat, Israeli prime minister Menachem Begin (BAY-guhn) and U.S. president Jimmy Carter met at Camp David, the U.S. presidential retreat in Maryland. There they hammered out an agreement for achieving peace between Egypt and Israel that became known as the **Camp David Accords**. The following year Egypt and Israel signed a formal peace treaty.

The *intifada*. As Egypt made peace, however, other Arab states and the PLO became more hardline than ever. In Lebanon, PLO activity contributed to the outbreak of a vicious civil war, and in 1982 Israel invaded Lebanon in an effort to drive out or destroy the PLO. Then, in 1987, Palestinians living in the West Bank and other Israeli-occupied territories began an uprising, known as the ***intifada***, or "shaking." Despite Israeli efforts to put down the rebellion, day after day young Palestinians threw rocks, bottles, and anything else they could lay their hands on at Israeli soldiers patrolling the areas.

Palestinian self-government. Both the *intifada* and a growing Israeli peace movement placed enormous pressure on the Israeli government to reach some sort of agreement with the Palestinians. After secret negotiations in 1993 and 1994, PLO chief Yasir Arafat and Israeli leaders Shimon Peres and Yitzhak Rabin finally met and agreed on terms for Palestinian self-rule. For their

efforts, the three were awarded the 1994 Nobel Peace Prize.

Even as self-rule began to take effect, however, the Israeli government resumed its policy of allowing Jewish settlement in Arab territories. This policy rocked the peace process. Nevertheless, in September 1995 a further accord arranged for the withdrawal of the Israeli military occupation force. Even as the troops prepared to withdraw, however, a radical Israeli opponent of the peace process assassinated Rabin in November 1995. Under the more conservative government of Benjamin Netanyahu, elected in 1996, the fate of the peace process remained uncertain.

After decades of war, Egypt and Israel agreed to negotiate for peace. This peace process eventually brought the PLO and Israel to seek an accord of their own.

▲ Peres, Rabin, and Arafat accept the Nobel Peace Prize.

SECTION 2 REVIEW

IDENTIFY and explain the significance of the following:
Law of Return
Knesset
Gamal Abdel Nasser
Suez Crisis
Six-Day War
Palestine Liberation Organization
Anwar Sadat
Golda Meir

Camp David Accords
intifada
Yasir Arafat

1. ***Main Idea*** What happened immediately after the British withdrew from Palestine?
2. ***Main Idea*** What brought about the Suez Crisis?
3. ***War and Diplomacy*** How did Arab and Israeli leaders

work toward peace?

4. ***Writing to Explain*** Write a short essay explaining the challenges Israel faced in its earliest days as a nation.
5. ***Hypothesizing*** In your opinion, what political choices could Middle Eastern leaders make to ensure peace? Consider the choices they have made in the past.

Economics and Social Change

As the Arab-Israeli conflict continued to plague the region, the Middle East and North Africa became even more strategically important because of their vast oil reserves. Some of the new states became enormously wealthy from their underground oil supplies. As these countries used their wealth to fund modernization programs, society and culture throughout the region began to undergo tremendous change.

Gas lines during the oil embargo

Oil and the Cold War

By the end of World War II, oil had become the most important energy source for industrial society. In the Middle East, U.S. oil companies increasingly competed against Anglo-Iranian and other British and Dutch companies for rights to drill for the precious commodity. Soon, Middle Eastern countries began to take control of their own oil resources.

The power of OPEC. In 1960 Iran, Iraq, Kuwait, Saudi Arabia, and Venezuela formed the **Organization of Petroleum Exporting Countries** (OPEC). Other oil producers such as Nigeria joined later. OPEC tried to control the entire global oil industry, particularly by setting production levels and controlling world prices. **Petro-dollars**—oil profits—became an important source of capital in world markets.

The power of OPEC reached its height in 1973. During the Yom Kippur War, Arab members of OPEC tried to use their oil as a weapon by declaring an **oil embargo**, or stoppage of oil shipments, against countries supporting Israel. By cutting back their oil production, they created a shortage of oil and drove up prices for Western consumers, particularly in the United States. Consumers had to wait in long lines and pay much higher prices for gasoline.

Eventually, however, the pressures of the world market and the OPEC countries' own need for revenue broke the power of OPEC to control world oil prices. By the 1980s increased production had resulted in an oil surplus and prices began to fall again.

Cold War problems. The growing dependence of many nations on oil as an energy source increased the strategic importance of the Middle East and contributed to Cold War rivalries between the superpowers for influence in the region. In the early 1950s, for example, U.S. leaders became alarmed not only by the nationalization of Iran's oil industry but also by Iranian prime minister Mosaddeq's acceptance of political support from Iranian Communists. The U.S. Central Intelligence Agency engineered a coup that toppled Mosaddeq from power and restored Muhammad Reza Shah as absolute ruler. The United States also established strong ties with

U.S. Imports of Petroleum from OPEC, 1987–1993

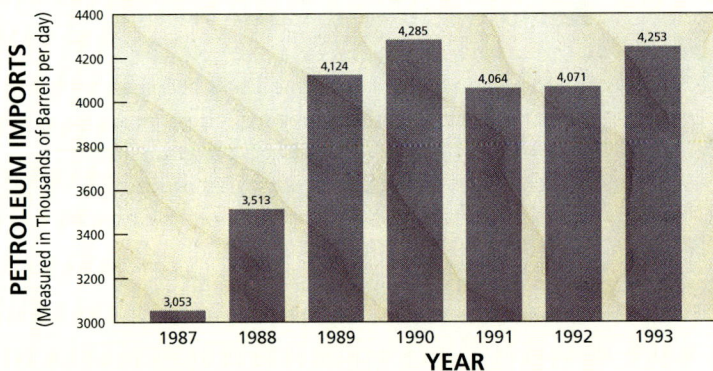

The Need for Oil Like many Western countries, the United States requires a great deal of petroleum to use in the production of many products, such as gasoline. Much of this oil is supplied by the nations of OPEC.

? Analyzing What can you say about the imports of petroleum from OPEC between 1989 and 1992? What factors might have contributed to this trend?

Throughout the Middle East and Africa, oil-producing countries like Saudi Arabia also pumped billions of dollars into development schemes. As they did so, the pace of change in the region intensified. After World War II, for example, tractors and other machines, chemical fertilizers, and improved seeds began to be used more widely in Iraq, Syria, Jordan, and Morocco. At the same time, a declining death rate throughout the region led to a rapid increase in population.

Rapid urbanization led to demands for even greater food production and more economic development. Modern farming techniques and the use of oil revenues to build new hydroelectric and irrigation projects also led more people to abandon herding in favor of agriculture. Farmers began to produce more food for the export market.

Despite these advances, however, the benefits of development remained unevenly distributed. Countries without oil accumulated large debts to fund their development plans. Even Israel depended heavily on support from the United States to maintain its economy.

Saudi Arabia and other conservative anti-communist Arab states, while the Soviet Union supported socialist dictatorships like Iraq and Syria, and for a time Egypt.

The world's demand for oil contributed to the strategic importance of the Middle East and led to U.S. intervention in Iran.

Economic Development

Oil wealth provided the states of the region with the money to modernize. In Iran, for example, the Shah used his increasing oil wealth to fund what he called the **White Revolution**, which began in 1963. Like the Tanzimat reforms of the Ottoman Empire and the Meiji reforms of Japan, the White Revolution was to be a "revolution from the top," as the Shah put it. Among its key elements were a redistribution of land and voting rights for women. The Shah was proud of the massive changes he had set in motion. The White Revolution, he declared, combined:

❝the principles of capitalism . . . with socialism or even communism. . . . There's never been so much change in three thousand years. The whole structure is [being turned] upside down.❞

With oil revenues, many Middle Eastern countries pursued important development and modernization schemes that changed the face of their economies.

Social and Cultural Changes

Both independence and economic development led to rapid social change. In Egypt, Syria, and Iraq, for example, radical leaders came to power determined to modernize. Following Egypt's lead, they adopted what Nasser called "Arab socialism." Egyptian nationalists preached revolution as the means to development:

❝Revolution is the way in which the Arab nation can free itself of its shackles, and rid

Oil Deposits in the Middle East and Africa, 1990

The Oil Region   The desert sands of the Middle East and parts of Africa yield rich and easily attainable supplies of oil. These regions contain the majority of the world's oil reserves.

❓ **Location**   Why has access to the Strait of Hormuz been so important for oil-producing nations?

R   RESOURCE ACTIVITY

GLOBAL HISTORY RESOURCE CENTER
Image: *Egypt Welcomes Soviet Premier Khrushchev*
Image: *Dawn Prayer in Modern Cairo*
Reading: *A Traditional Marriage in Egypt*

Print out and distribute the images and the reading. Have students imagine they work for the Cairo Chamber of Commerce. Have students work in small groups to prepare pamphlets describing different aspects of Cairo.

Level 3

✓ **REVIEW & ASSESSMENT RESOURCES**

• Study Guide 28.3
• Daily Quiz 28.3
• Main Idea Activity 28.3

All Levels

itself of the dark heritage which has burdened it. . . . [It] is the only way . . . to face the challenge awaiting the Arab and other underdeveloped nations: the challenge offered by the astounding scientific discoveries which help to widen the gap between the advanced and backward countries. . . . Socialism has become both a means and an end: sufficiency and justice. ❞

Under Nasser, the Egyptian government took control of most industry and businesses. It also proclaimed laws that limited the hours of work, established a minimum wage, and created other social services. Education was extended even further, and the government tried to improve the status of women. Socialist governments in other countries in the region adopted similar policies. The price for such measures, however, was high—socialist leaders limited or crushed opposing voices. In Egypt itself, Nasser largely focused national attention on himself, much as Stalin had done in the Soviet Union, and as Mao was doing in China.

A changing urban landscape. As more people flocked to the cities of the Middle East, some people's standards of living—and expectations—rose. The new Arab middle classes began to move into those parts of the cities formerly inhabited by foreigners, while migrants from the countryside moved into the sections vacated by the middle classes. Many middle-class Arabs began to adopt European styles of clothing and entertainment. People of all religious faiths moved more freely together, where once they had each been confined to their own quarters of the cities. As the new governments increased state education, Arab children also went to the same secular schools.

Rapid urbanization, however, also led to the kinds of problems that had plagued European cities in the early days of industrialization. High unemployment often resulted in the development of slums. Many people looking for work in

SECTION 3 REVIEW ANSWERS

IDENTIFY

For significance, see the following pages:
Organization of
   Petroleum Exporting
   Countries (p. 783)
petro-dollars (p. 783)
oil embargo (p. 783)
Muhammad Reza Shah
   (p. 783)
White Revolution (p. 784)

1. Many nations' growing dependence on oil increased the importance of the Middle East and contributed to the Cold War rivalries between superpowers.
2. Oil revenues in the Middle East brought higher standards of living, changes in family relations, and changing roles for women.
3. With oil revenues, Middle Eastern countries were able to pursue economic development and modernization schemes.
4. Articles should include education for women and increased responsibilities and job opportunities.
5. benefit—raised standard of living, increased modernization, increased opportunities for women; drawbacks—benefits unevenly distributed, heavy-handed leaders, invited interference by other nations

the overcrowded cities had to leave their families behind in their villages—a practice that often weakened traditional family ties. The importance of the extended family gave way to a growing emphasis on the nuclear family of just parents and their children.

Life in the countryside. Many people who moved to the cities sent money home to their families in the countryside. This helped rural residents improve their standard of living. In addition, people from poorer countries, like Egypt and Jordan, went to work in the oil-rich countries like Saudi Arabia and the Persian Gulf states. Land reforms undertaken in the late 1950s and 1960s in countries like Egypt, Syria, and Iraq also began to change people's lives.

Electricity spread beyond the cities into the countryside as governments funded nationwide modernization. One of the most important factors in change was the rapid spread in the late 1950s and the 1960s of transistor radios and televisions, which soon connected even remote villages to news from the rest of the world.

Changing roles for women. The strains of increasing urbanization and modernization were perhaps most clearly seen in the changing roles and status of women. Education particularly contributed to these changes. Even in poor countries in the Middle East, girls attended school, and more women learned to read and write. In modern cities they could find work in shops and offices, or even in factories when there was a shortage of male laborers. Some women were becoming professionals—doctors, lawyers, social workers, and teachers. In some countries, women even served at high levels in the government.

In the villages where the men had gone to look for work in the cities, women also gained greater responsibilities. Many women had to decide when and what to plant and often had to take responsibility for getting their crops to market.

Nevertheless, for most women the traditions of the past continued—traditions that emphasized the primary position of men and the importance of women remaining faithful and obedient to them. Particularly in the villages, women's lives continued to revolve around traditional Islamic ideals and the holy law—as the Egyptian writer Alifa Rifaat described through the main character of one of her stories:

> **❝** She . . . raised her hand to her lips, kissing it back and front in thanks for His [God's] generosity. . . . During Ahmed's lifetime she would stand behind him as he performed the prayers, . . . listening reverently to the words he recited and knowing that he who stands behind the man leading the prayers and following his movements has himself performed the prayers . . . with his death she had given up performing the regular prayers. **❞**

Economic development and modernization in the Middle East led to higher standards of living, changes in family relations, and changing roles for women.

SECTION 3 REVIEW

IDENTIFY and explain the significance of the following:
   Organization of Petroleum
      Exporting Countries
   petro-dollars
   oil embargo
   Muhammad Reza Shah
   White Revolution

1. *Main Idea* Why was the Middle East an important area in the Cold War?

2. *Main Idea* How did Middle Eastern societies change as a result of economic development and modernization?

3. *Economic Organization* What economic benefits did oil bring to the Middle East?

4. *Writing to Explain* Imagine that you are a reporter for a Western newspaper.

Write a brief article explaining how the roles of women were affected by the growth of urbanization in the Middle East.

5. *Evaluating* Was the presence of large quantities of oil a greater benefit or a greater drawback to Middle Eastern societies? Give examples and explain your answer.

The Resurgence of Islam

As Middle Eastern nations confronted the modern world, many Muslims reacted to the challenge of westernization by embracing their traditional religion and culture. For some this meant rejecting the materialism of the modern world. For others, it meant reclaiming traditional Islamic values without rejecting the benefits of modern technology. The most important case of this resurgence occurred in Iran.

Colonel Muammar al-Qaddati

Islam and the Modern World

The peoples of the Middle East and Africa experienced enormous economic, political, and social changes after World War II. To cope with these upheavals, many people began to reassert traditional values and familiar forms of identity. In the Muslim world, these efforts to cope with change brought on an **Islamic resurgence**, or a renewed interest in Islam. Religious revival allowed people to reconnect with their traditional past and achieve a sense of continuity while also rejecting Western cultural influences.

One of the most influential of the new Islamic revival movements was the **Muslim Brotherhood**, which had formed in Egypt between the two world wars. The Muslim Brotherhood opposed the adoption of Western values that were not rooted in the teachings of the Qur'an and sought Islamic control over all aspects of society.

Others involved in the Islamic resurgence opted for a less literal interpretation of their religion. In 1969 Colonel Muammar al-Qaddafi (al-kah-DAH-fee) overthrew the Libyan monarchy, using an appeal to Islam for his authority. Qaddafi's interpretation of Islam was truly revolutionary:

> As the Muslims have strayed far from Islam, a review is demanded. The [Libyan revolution] is a revolution rectifying [correcting] Islam, presenting Islam correctly, purifying Islam of the reactionary practices which dressed it in . . . clothing not its own. Because Islam is progressive, it is a universalist revolution at the height of the left. The Islamic revolution . . . is neo-scientific socialism.

Qaddafi was only one of many Islamic revolutionaries. Some terrorist groups, like Hezbollah in Lebanon, also justified their methods by insisting that they were fighting for the Muslim faith. In Afghanistan, the Mujahidin (moo-ja-hi-DEEN)—the freedom fighters who fought against the Soviet invasion of Afghanistan in the 1980s—saw themselves as religious warriors and called their fight a jihad, or holy war.

The return to Islam was particularly strong among young people, even those with a Western

Despite his rejection of Western values and his call for a return to strict Shi'ah customs, Khomeini did not oppose the use of modern Western technology. While in exile in Paris, he discovered the advantages of modern technology, particularly telecommunications. Through a telephone link between Tehran and his residence in France, Khomeini transmitted daily messages denouncing the Shah and calling for revolution. In Tehran Khomeini's daily telephone pronouncements were taped, transcribed, and photocopied by the hundreds of thousands.

Critical Thinking Ask students to suggest how events in Iran might have unfolded differently if Khomeini had not had access to modern telecommunications.

ANSWER: Students might suggest that the Shah might have been able to hold onto power.

R **RESOURCE ACTIVITY**

READINGS IN WORLD HISTORY
Reading 28.4
U.S. Hostages in Iran

Have students read the selection. Then have them complete the questions.

Level 1

education. For many the values of modern Western society seemed too secular, materialistic, and even self-centered. Islam provided a secure sense of belonging to a community. For many in the Western world, on the other hand, the resurgence of Islam often seemed a frightening or threatening movement. Perhaps nowhere did it seem to display both its power and its potential destructiveness to westerners more than in the Iranian Revolution.

Many Muslims tried to cope with the uncertainties of the modern world by emphasizing traditional Islamic values.

The Iranian Revolution

The greatest stimulus to the growing resurgence of Islam came in 1979, when Islamic leaders led the revolution against the Shah of Iran. As elsewhere, opposition to both modernization and westernization provided the motivation for revolution.

Since 1963 the Shah had fought to modernize Iran even though many Iranians were opposed. The Shi'ah clergy resented the Shah's strong ties with the United States, which supported not only the Shah and his hated reforms

▲ Ayatollah Ruhollah Khomeini makes his triumphant return to Tehran in 1979.

but also Israel. Many Western-educated Iranians hated the oppressive system of government that depended on the dreaded secret police to maintain power. Eventually, the Shah alienated most levels of society. In the late 1970s mass riots and demonstrations against the Shah erupted. In 1979 the Shah fled into exile and revolutionaries overthrew the government.

The Islamic Republic. The leader of the movement against the Shah was the prominent Shi'ah religious scholar, Ayatollah Ruhollah Khomeini (koh-MAY-nee). Khomeini rejected Western values and ways of living, yet he did not reject modern technology. Returning from years of exile in France, Khomeini came to Tehran in triumph after the Shah left Iran in January 1979. The new Islamic Republic was proclaimed, and Khomeini was declared its supreme religious guide, or *faqih*, a post he retained until his death in June 1989.

Banning Western customs that the Shah had introduced, Khomeini and his supporters returned to strict Shi'ah customs. In public, women once again had to wear the chador (CHUH-duhr), a large cloth that covered the body from head to toe. Khomeini's supporters also imprisoned and executed many of their opponents, and they imposed strict censorship throughout Iran.

The hostage crisis. Khomeini and his colleagues preached against the United States, Britain, and the Soviet Union, calling them the "Great Satans." In November 1979 Khomeini also approved of the takeover of the American Embassy in Tehran by militant anti-Western students. Protesting the U.S. decision to allow the ailing Shah to seek medical treatment in the United States, these anti-Western students took 66 U.S. embassy workers as hostages. Despite worldwide disapproval of their actions, they held 50 of these hostages captive until January 1981.

The Iran-Iraq War. When Iraq launched an attack against Iran in 1980, hoping to gain territory in the confusion of the revolution, Ayatollah Khomeini rallied Iran to resist. As the war dragged on, he called on Iranian men, women, and children to support the war in the name of Islam and, if necessary, to die as martyrs to their faith. Finally,

Literature THROUGH TIME

Arabian Nights and Days

The author Naguib Mahfouz is recognized as one of the leading Arabic novelists of modern times. Long celebrated in his native Egypt and other Arab countries, Mahfouz became well known in the Western world only after winning the Nobel Prize for literature in 1988.

Most of Mahfouz's work deals with contemporary Egyptian life, but he has also explored other subjects and different time periods. For example, Arabian Nights and Days is set in medieval times. In the following excerpt the traveler Sindbad tells the harsh and cruel Sultan Shahriyar some of what he learned on his voyages.

"I also learned, Your Majesty, that freedom is the life of the spirit and that Paradise itself is of no avail [help] to a man if he has lost his freedom. Our ship met with a storm which destroyed it, not one of its men escaping apart from myself. The waves hurled me onto a fragrant island, rich with fruits and streams and with a moderate climate. I quenched my hunger and thirst and washed, then went off into the interior to seek out what I could find. I came across an old man lying under a tree utterly at the end of his resources.

"'I am decrepit [feeble], as you see, so will you carry me to my hut?' he said, pointing with his chin. I did not hesitate about picking him up. I raised him onto my shoulders and took him to where he had pointed. Finding no trace of his hut, I said, 'Where's your dwelling, uncle?'

"In a strong voice, unlike that with which he had first addressed me, he said, 'This island is my dwelling, my island, but I need someone to carry me.'

"I wanted to lower him from my shoulders, but I couldn't tear his legs away from my neck and ribs; they were like a building held in place by iron.

"'Let me go,' I pleaded, 'and you will find that I am at your service when you need me.'

Many of Mahfouz's works have been translated into Hebrew, French, and English.

"He laughed mockingly at me, ignoring my pleas. He thus condemned me to live as his slave so that neither waking nor sleeping was enjoyable, and I took pleasure in neither food nor drink, until an idea occurred to me. I began to squeeze some grapes into a hollow and left the juice to ferment. Then I gave it to him to drink until he became intoxicated and his steel-like muscles relaxed and I threw him from my shoulders. I took up a stone and smashed in his head, thus saving the world from his evil."

Understanding Literature

What lesson do you think Shahriyar might have learned from Sindbad's story?

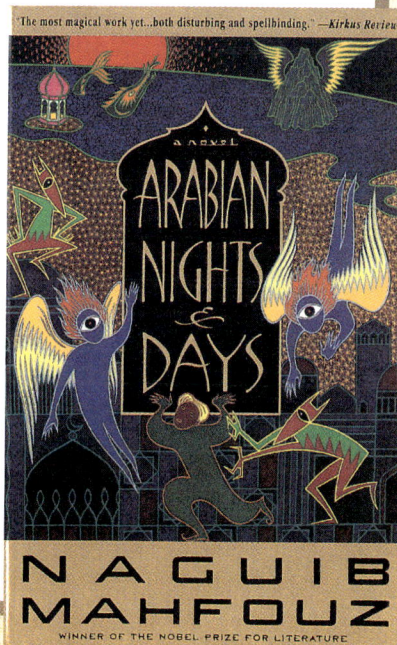

'The most magical work yet...both disturbing and spellbinding.' —*Kirkus Reviews*

A NOVEL
ARABIAN NIGHTS & DAYS
NAGUIB MAHFOUZ
WINNER OF THE NOBEL PRIZE FOR LITERATURE

Khomeini agreed to a cease-fire in 1988. Meanwhile, he also sponsored many groups, such as Hezbollah in Lebanon, that continued the struggle against Israel.

The Islamic resurgence in Iran represented a reaction against the Shah's modernizing and westernizing reforms and led to the Iranian Revolution.

Women and the Islamic Resurgence

For many people the most controversial aspect of the Islamic resurgence was its consequences for women. Since the end of World War I, many women's lives had changed as Muslim countries underwent swift modernization. Girls attended school in increasing numbers, and many went on to college and earned advanced degrees. In some Muslim nations, women built professional careers in law, medicine, and government. Some women adopted Western clothing, abandoning the veil in favor of modern fashion.

Even women's rights movements had begun to emerge in some Middle Eastern countries as many women felt frustrated by the limitations placed on them by traditional Islamic values. Forugh Farrokhzad, one of Iran's leading modern poets, expressed the frustration in a poem:

▲ Muslim women wearing traditional Islamic clothing read the Qur'an inside the Dome of the Rock, Jerusalem.

> 66 My sister, take your rights
> from those who keep you weak,
> from those who through a thousand ploys
> keep you seated in a house. . . .
>
> Rise, uproot oppression,
> revive the heart drenched in blood.
> Struggle, struggle to transform laws
> for the sake of your own freedom. 99

With the Islamic resurgence, however, women were often forced to accept a return to the traditions of the past. In Iran, for example, the Shah had abolished polygamy, child marriage, and death by stoning for adultery. The Islamic Republic of Iran restored all three. For westernized women, in particular, such requirements seemed a step backward.

While some women opposed these seemingly antimodern changes, others embraced them. Many of these women believed that modernization and westernization had brought neither prosperity nor stability. Islam, on the other hand, provided them with a stable foundation, with a set of customs and beliefs that had stood the test of time in their culture. In unsettling times the return to traditional ways gave many women a sense of security and stability. In Iran and elsewhere, many women voluntarily resumed wearing the chador that had been discouraged by modernizing rulers like the Shah. Such customs became a symbol of their pride in their Islamic heritage and their rejection of Western values.

Many women moved by the Islamic resurgence began to take more pride in their Islamic identity.

SECTION 4 REVIEW

IDENTIFY and explain the significance of the following:
    Islamic resurgence
    Muslim Brotherhood
    Colonel Muammar al-Qaddafi
    Ayatollah Ruhollah Khomeini
    faqih

1. *Main Idea* What effect did the changes of the modern world have on Islamic nations?

2. *Main Idea* What factors led to the Iranian Revolution of 1979?

3. *Religion* How has the resurgence of Islam affected many Middle Eastern women?

4. *Writing to Persuade* Given the traditions of the Middle East, write a short essay explaining why women should or should not be required to wear the chador in public.

5. *Evaluating* Should the Shah of Iran have embarked upon a campaign of modernizing along Western lines? Why or why not?

Independent Africa

- What kinds of problems did African states face after independence?
- What path did politics take in many African states after independence?
- How did African writers and artists express their sense of cultural identity as they confronted the problems of independence?

*H*aving achieved independence, African nations soon confronted the problems and the promise that came with their new status. Although most had achieved independence through a relatively peaceful process, their success at maintaining peace afterward varied. Western-educated nationalist leaders faced the task of trying to create for their peoples a true sense of national identity in place of their traditional ethnic and cultural loyalties.

Worker at a copper refinery, Zambia

Problems of Independence

Achieving independence was only the beginning for African nations. For many the end of colonial rule brought not only freedom but also certain problems, such as declining standards of living, environmental concerns, and oppression by heavy-handed leaders.

Economic problems. African economies were fragile because they frequently depended on only one or two exports. With the exception of South Africa, most African countries had not industrialized, and therefore depended on agriculture or the mining of raw materials. Ghana, for example, depended on cocoa. Copper supported Zambia and Zaire, while Nigeria's great asset was oil.

In order to build their national economies, most African states sought development loans from organizations such as the World Bank. Even with loans, however, bad planning and widespread corruption often left the new states with huge national debts and little development to show for it.

Overpopulation and the environment. The new African states also faced overpopulation and environmental problems. Improvements in health care meant that people lived longer and that more infants survived into adulthood. As African farmers tried to expand food production to feed this growing population, however, poor farming techniques led to erosion of the topsoil in many areas. In addition, people needed more trees for firewood, which led to massive deforestation in some areas. In the Sahel, the region south of the Sahara, these practices contributed to **desertification**—the steady advance of the desert. Soon, some African countries could no longer feed their people.

In the late 1960s Africans experienced the first of a series of devastating droughts that would lead to mass starvation in the Sudan, Ethiopia, and Somalia. Civil war and looting often made relief efforts in such cases difficult, if not impossible.

Somalia in particular became a place of human misery as civil war and drought led to enormous suffering. During the 1992 drought, for example, hundreds of thousands of people died as warring

CORE LESSON PLAN
See pages 769K and 769L for Lesson Plan 28.5.

Theme:
Economic Organization
Perhaps the greatest problems accompanying African independence were economic. As elsewhere in the developing world, many African socialist leaders came to believe that the path to prosperity lay in rapid industrialization. Consequently, many of the new states neglected agricultural development in favor of expensive, large-scale industrial development projects that were rarely successful.

Critical Thinking Ask students why many African governments might have favored industrial projects over agricultural development.

ANSWER: Students might suggest that industrial projects carried greater prestige value than agricultural efforts or that governments wanted to diversify their economies.

▲ Slash-and-burn techniques, used by farmers to clear the land, often resulted in serious erosion problems.

groups stole the food provided for the starving by international agencies. The tragedy eventually led to an unsuccessful intervention by the United States and the United Nations. Viewing the misery, one relief worker observed, "I've become sick and tired of seeing kids dying when I know thieves are taking their food."

New diseases. In the 1980s health officials in Africa also had to confront new diseases. Some people believed that as more and more loggers and farmers move into the African rain forests, they may have become exposed to unknown viruses present in animal populations. One new disease, **acquired immune deficiency syndrome**, or AIDS, spread rapidly through parts of Africa. The disease weakens the body's immune system, ultimately resulting in death. In 1995 an outbreak of the deadly ebola virus in Zaire led the government to close its borders in an effort to prevent the spread of the disease.

After independence, African states confronted major problems in economic development, ecological destruction, and disease.

▶ Kwame Nkrumah reviews an honor guard in 1961.

Political Challenges

Perhaps the most challenging problem the newly independent African nations faced was increasing political instability. The new African leaders discovered what the colonial officials had known: that their diverse and varied peoples had not yet developed a real sense of national identity. To rule them, many leaders resorted to the same kind of autocratic methods used by earlier colonial rulers.

The case of Ghana. Perhaps the best example of this pattern was Kwame Nkrumah of Ghana. Although he began as a popular leader, his popularity began to slip, in part because prosperity declined with a drop in cocoa prices. Nkrumah responded to criticism by tightening his control over Ghana. "All Africans know that I represent Africa," he once said, "and that I speak in her name. Therefore no African can have an opinion that differs from mine." Nkrumah also believed that political unity in Africa was the key to future success:

66 *African unity is above all a political kingdom, which can only be gained by political means. The social and economic development of Africa will come only within the political kingdom, not the other way around.* 99

Such sentiments led to the creation of the **Organization of African Unity**, or OAU. In 1966, however, Nkrumah's harsh policies cost him the support of the people, and he was overthrown by a military coup. After Nkrumah was forced out of office, Ghana was ruled by a succession of short-lived military and civilian governments.

Ethnic conflict. Nkrumah's fall discouraged many African leaders in their efforts to achieve Pan-African unity. In fact, unity became next to impossible as many African countries experienced the same sort of instability as Ghana.

A major part of the problem was ongoing ethnic conflict as rival groups competed for control of the new states. Such conflicts often led to destructive civil wars. In 1967 in Nigeria the Ibo-speaking people of the east seceded from the Nigerian federation and proclaimed their own independent state of Biafra. The result was a bloody civil war in which as many people died of starvation as from actual fighting. After almost four years of war and some 2 million deaths, Biafra collapsed, and the territory was incorporated back into Nigeria.

During the 1990s tensions in Rwanda and Burundi between two major groups, the Tutsi and the Hutu, erupted in massive violence. In late 1993 Tutsi soldiers and civilians massacred about 150,000 Hutu. Marie Kaboinja, a Hutu survivor of the massacres, told of the violence her family had endured:

66 *Tutsis charged us with spears and pangas [machetes]. Then came the soldiers. . . . We ran away with my family. But many of us were killed, including my grandfather, father, mother, aunt and my three children.* 99

The violence escalated in 1994, but this time it was the Hutu slaughtering the Tutsi. By October the Hutu had killed half a million Tutsi, and an additional 2 million Tutsi fled Rwanda. In refugee camps in neighboring Zaire, Burundi, and Tanzania, thousands of refugees died of disease, hunger, and thirst in the makeshift camps. Meanwhile, in Rwanda, ongoing civil war continued to take its toll.

Movements toward democracy. While massive violence kept some African nations unstable, other nations moved toward greater democracy. In the 1980s and 1990s, minority white governments in Rhodesia and South Africa finally began to share control with the black majorities, ending many years of white rule.

In 1961 a new constitution in the Federation of Rhodesia and Nyasaland, a British colony with internal self-government, had officially restricted voting in order to keep whites in power. In the face of continuing African opposition, the Federation dissolved in 1963. The following year the minority white government in Southern Rhodesia proclaimed the independent state of Rhodesia. Britain, however, considered the declaration of independence illegal. A new constitution in 1969 once more prevented full black representation in Rhodesia's parliament. Throughout the latter 1970s negotiations between the Rhodesian government and black nationalist groups continued, and in 1979 the first universal suffrage election brought a black majority to parliament. In 1980 Britain recognized the independence of Rhodesia, which became the state of Zimbabwe.

In the 1980s South Africa also increased its slow pace toward racial equality. In the 1940s, while still a member of the British Commonwealth, South Africa had instituted a policy of **apartheid**, which called for separate development and residential areas for white

▲ As South Africa made plans to dismantle apartheid, President F. W. de Klerk attended a peace rally.

R RESOURCE ACTIVITY

READINGS IN WORLD HISTORY
Reading 28.5
Politics and Religion in South Africa

Have students read the passage by Bishop Desmond Tutu. Then have them complete the questions.

Level 2

Theme: Religion and the Arts

As a church leader in South Africa, Anglican Archbishop Desmond Tutu stressed nonviolent resistance to the system of apartheid and won the Nobel Peace Prize in 1984. His experience resisting apartheid led him to develop a theology that incorporated an African concept of community, *Ubuntu*. Through *Ubuntu*, Tutu sought to find common humanity and reconciliation between both oppressor and oppressed. He continued his work as the head of the Truth and Reconciliation Commission, a body appointed by the government of Nelson Mandela to consider political crimes.

Critical Thinking Ask students why Tutu might be appointed head of this commission.

ANSWER: Students should suggest that he was a respected figure and appealed to both whites and blacks.

Afrikaners, black Bantu, Asians, and people of mixed race.

Under this system, only whites could vote or hold political office. Blacks, who made up nearly 75 percent of the population, were restricted to certain occupations and were paid very little for their work. The South African government created separate black territories, called **homelands**, for each ethnic group, then gave all blacks citizenship in the homeland of their ethnic group, regardless of whether or not they lived there. Eventually, the government denied South African citizenship to blacks living outside their homeland.

These restrictive laws led to major protests. Antigovernment violence erupted in many black townships, while black nationalist groups, such as the outlawed African National Congress (ANC), fought to end apartheid. Much of the international community responded to South African apartheid by imposing **trade sanctions**, or restrictions, on South Africa in an attempt to force the nation to abandon apartheid.

Finally, under President F. W. de Klerk, South Africa legalized the ANC in 1990 and began negotiations to enact a new constitution that would end apartheid. In 1994 the homelands were abolished, and the first multiracial elections were held. The ANC swept the elections, and black nationalist Nelson Mandela, leader of the ANC, was elected president.

Other countries in Africa also began to move toward democracy in the 1990s. By mid-1993, some 26 countries had established democracies, and the rulers of 15 others had publicly agreed to hold free elections.

Although some of African politics was marked by ethnic rivalry and violence, some nations enjoyed an expansion of democracy.

Cultural Revival

In the years following independence, many Africans began to reassert their sense of identity through a revival of African culture. During the colonial period much local African culture had been overshadowed by Western culture. Many westerners did not understand the nature of

▲ Nelson Mandela became politically active during his twenties. Together with a partner, he established the first black law partnership in South Africa. The apartheid regime discouraged such efforts, and arrested and tried Mandela.

African art. The oral literature of traditional African societies also meant little to most Europeans—or to many Africans who adopted European views of cultural development.

Literature. African culture may have been overshadowed during colonial rule, but it did not disappear. In fact, it became a means of expressing dissatisfaction with colonial rule. Consequently, many African arts were preserved and celebrated. In East Africa, for example, many Africans continued to study Swahili, which had been a written language since the 1600s and remained a vibrant literary language. As one of the national languages of Kenya and Tanzania after independence, Swahili maintained a strong tradition of poetry, plays, and novels.

By the 1950s a new literature aimed at exposing and ridiculing the evils of colonialism had begun to emerge from African writers. In 1960, for example, Ousmane Sembene of Senegal published *God's Bits of Wood*, a fictionalized account of the struggle of Senegalese workers against colonial authorities in the late 1940s. Sembene directly attacked the problem of colonial racism through his characters. In one passage, an African railway worker expresses his anger:

66 *From the hall Tiémoko interrupted him. 'We're the ones who do the work,' he roared, 'the same work the white men do. Why then should they be paid more? Because they are*

Then & NOW

Balancing Human and Wildlife Needs in Africa

In the late 1800s hunting was still an important part of life in many African societies. Some Africans lived as hunter-gatherers. Others hunted animals for ivory or skins, trading these goods to merchants from foreign lands. Settled farmers hunted to supplement their diet and to protect their livestock and crops from wildlife.

Many Africans were avid hunters, enjoying the adventure and excitement of the kill. Yet some of their attitudes toward wildlife helped to conserve the very animals they hunted. In some societies the hunting of such animals as elephants and hippopotamuses was limited to a privileged few. Other groups looked upon some animals as sacred. Still others considered it taboo to kill or eat certain animals. Many Africans also controlled their hunting practices for practical reasons. Without wildlife to provide them with food and clothing, they would not survive.

This balance between humans and wildlife began to change with the European colonization of Africa in the late 1800s. Most European colonists considered African hunting methods cruel and wasteful. The colonists charged that, if left unchecked, African hunters would soon destroy the continent's wildlife. At the colonists' insistence, the colonial powers established new laws on hunting. The killing of certain animals was banned. Some areas were set aside as wildlife reserves where hunting was not allowed. In addition, hunters had to obtain a license to practice their trade.

These new rules did little to protect wildlife, however. Africans, who now were largely prohibited from hunting, turned to poaching, or hunting illegally. A far greater threat to wildlife came from the safaris conducted by European and American big-game hunters. On one such safari in 1909, President Theodore Roosevelt and his son, Kermit, shot 512 animals, including 17 lions, 12 elephants, and 20 rhinos. The hunting safari—and the killing of African wildlife—reached its peak in the 1920s and 1930s. As a result, the future existence of certain species of animals appeared uncertain.

Efforts to protect and conserve African wildlife were renewed in the years after World War II. These efforts were similar to those of earlier years—protecting certain animals and establishing game reserves. Like those earlier efforts, the new steps took little note of the needs of native peoples.

After independence, many African countries continued these conservation practices. Some went a step further. Kenya, for example, instituted a complete ban on hunting in 1977. In recent years, however, some conservationists have proposed a new approach. Called sustainable development, the new approach considers not only the conservation of wildlife but also the needs of the human population. Under this approach, farmers would be able to use whatever means necessary—even hunting—to protect their crops and livestock from wild animals. Sport hunting would also be allowed to control the animal population and to generate income. Only with such an approach, many conservationists argue, can the needs of wildlife and the human population be balanced.

Theodore Roosevelt (below) and his son Kermit (right) hunting in Africa

SECTION 5 REVIEW ANSWERS
(p. 796)

IDENTIFY
For significance, see the following pages:
desertification (p. 791)
acquired immune deficiency syndrome (p. 792)
Organization of African Unity (p. 793)
apartheid (p. 793)
homelands (p. 794)
trade sanctions (p. 794)
F. W. de Klerk (p. 794)
Nelson Mandela (p. 794)
Ousmane Sembene (p. 794)

white? And when they are sick, why should they be taken care of while we and our families are left to starve? Because we are black? In what way is a white child better than a black child? In what way is a white worker better than a black worker? They tell us we have the same rights, but it is a lie, nothing but a lie! Only the engines we run tell the truth—and they don't know the difference between a white man and a black.' 99

By the 1980s and 1990s, however, many of these earlier authors had taken up new themes. After nearly 30 years of independence, many were disillusioned by Africa's experience of freedom. As writers faced censorship and harassment by the African governments they ridiculed, many found it easier to live and write outside their countries. Similar problems of government interference and censorship laws led many South African writers, both black and white, to live in exile while writing of the evils of apartheid.

Art. While literature was becoming a new means of expressing African identity, so were more traditional arts such as sculpture and music. In workshops in Nigeria, Zimbabwe, and many other countries, African artists began to produce traditional pieces—ceremonial masks, magnificently decorated weapons, traditional African musical instruments, statues carved from wood or cast in bronze, and many other kinds of art—for a growing world market. In many places African artists combined age-old techniques with new materials from beyond their borders. Their willingness to incorporate new ideas and materials into their work gave the revival of African art forms a new vitality and creativity that appealed to many people from other parts of the world.

▲ This Kenyan harpist is one of many musicians and artists keeping the traditional arts of Africa alive.

Confronting the problems of colonialism and independence, many Africans expressed their sense of cultural identity by blending traditional and modern art forms.

SECTION 5 REVIEW

IDENTIFY and explain the significance of the following:
desertification
acquired immune deficiency syndrome
Organization of African Unity
apartheid
homelands
trade sanctions
F. W. de Klerk
Nelson Mandela
Ousmane Sembene

1. **Main Idea** Why was gaining independence only the beginning of a long struggle for many African nations?
2. **Main Idea** Why did many African states experience political violence after independence?
3. **The Arts** How have many modern African writers and artists expressed a new sense of identity?

4. **Writing to Explain** Imagine that you are an African artist. Explain why it is important to you to create works of art in the traditional style for the world market.
5. **Hypothesizing** How might the ethnic violence that plagued some African nations after independence have been avoided?

Review

On a separate sheet of paper, complete the following exercises:

WRITING A SUMMARY

Using the essential points in the text, write a brief summary of the chapter.

REVIEWING TERMS

From the following list, choose the term that correctly matches the definition:

Suez Crisis
apartheid
Camp David Accords
desertification
Knesset
Organization of Petroleum
    Exporting Countries

1. 1978 agreement for achieving peace between Israel and Egypt
2. Israeli parliament, to which the prime minister and cabinet were responsible
3. organization founded in 1960 by many oil-producing countries to control world oil prices
4. policy of legalized racial segregation instituted by South Africa in the 1940s
5. the steady advance of the desert

REVIEWING CHRONOLOGY

List the following events in their correct chronological order.

1. Gamal Abdel Nasser nationalizes the Suez Canal.
2. Iranian students seize the American Embassy in Tehran and hold embassy workers hostage.
3. The state of Israel is proclaimed.
4. The first multiracial elections are held in South Africa, and Nelson Mandela is elected president.
5. OPEC is formed to regulate the production and prices of oil.

UNDERSTANDING THE MAIN IDEA

1. How did most British colonies in Africa achieve independence?
2. What brought about the Suez Crisis?
3. What effect did economic development and modernization have in the Middle East?
4. What factors led to the Iranian Revolution of 1979?
5. How did African writers and artists express their sense of cultural identity?

THINKING CRITICALLY

1. **Synthesizing** How has religious conflict contributed to increased tensions and violence in the Middle East? Why has this fact made a lasting peace in the Middle East more difficult?
2. **Evaluating** Could the colonial powers have done anything to help create more stability in Africa after independence? Explain your answer.

Building Your Portfolio

Complete the following activities individually or in groups.

1. **War** Imagine that you (and your coworkers) are reporters for an international news agency assigned to produce a television documentary on the conflict in the Middle East. Prepare a script for your documentary explaining the long history of conflict. You may also wish to include mock interviews with Israelis and Arabs which express their points of view. It might also be helpful to produce some visual support for your documentary, such as charts, graphs, maps, or illustrations. Be sure that your documentary is unbiased, or balanced.
2. **Politics** You (and your coworkers) have been employed by an international company planning to locate in a nation in Africa. They need information about the country. Choose an African country and research statistical information that might be important to your business, such as trade patterns, natural resources, population growth, major religions, and ethnic populations. Use software to turn your findings into a report with charts, graphs, and visuals, which will help your company prepare for its new location.

UNDERSTANDING THE MAIN IDEA

1. Their leaders chose to cooperate and gain influence as peacefully as possible, although at times they found it necessary to lead strikes and demonstrations.
2. Superpower rivalries inflamed Arab nationalism under Nasser and, combined with Western support of Israel, led to the Suez Crisis.
3. It led to higher standards of living, changes in family relations, and changing roles for women.
4. The Islamic resurgence in Iran represented a reaction against the Shah's modernizing and westernizing reforms and led to the Iranian Revolution.
5. Many African artists expressed their sense of cultural identity by blending traditional and modern art forms.

THINKING CRITICALLY

1. Economic and political problems that might be solved peacefully are intensified and made worse by religious conflicts. Because people tend to feel very strongly about their religious beliefs, religious conflicts cause national and international turmoil that is difficult to overcome.
2. Answers could mention that colonial powers could have offered guidance and peaceful intervention to provide stability in Africa.

In the 1920s Arabs in Palestine had already become distressed by the growing Jewish population. According to a British report at the time, Arabs feared the economic and political consequences of the continued purchase of land by Jewish immigrants.

While immigration was slow during the 1920s, it escalated during the 1930s. In 1932, for example, there were some 5,000 authorized Jewish immigrants, while in 1935 this number jumped to 62,000. This significant increase led to Arab strikes and boycotts in 1936, as well as to the formation of guerrilla forces. As a result of this uprising, a British commission recommended the partition of Palestine in 1937.

Critical Thinking Ask students what factor caused an increase in the number of Jewish people leaving Europe in the 1930s.

ANSWER: Students should note the Nazi rise to power in Germany in the 1930s.

HISTORY IN THE Making

The Arab-Israeli Dilemma: A British Perspective

Few subjects in modern history have raised as much controversy as the struggle between Jews and Arabs for control of Palestine. For many years, scholars and supporters on both sides of the issue argued over which side's claims to Palestine carried greater weight—and each side accused the British of having favored the other. Many historians seemed more concerned with assigning blame than with understanding what had happened and why. In part this was caused by the enormous passion each side felt about the creation of the state of Israel.

As the years have gone by, however, most people have accepted the creation of Israel. Although feelings still run high on the issue, many historians have begun to examine the Arab-Israeli dilemma more objectively. In addition, they have been able to examine new documents. Documents concerning the end of the Palestine mandate began to become available in 1978 from the British Public Record Office in London. These documents—unpublished reports, internal memos, and private minutes, or personal comments, by British officials—have shed new light on how and why the British developed their policies in the mandate of Palestine.

Britain's Dilemma in Palestine

From the documents, it is now clear that British leaders themselves were divided on the question. At the heart of the problem was the fact that they had made conflicting promises to both Arabs and Zionists. At the same time, Palestine became an important link in Britain's own chain of imperial defense, providing air bases and an important oil pipeline and refinery at Haifa on the Mediterranean coast.

Officially, the British Colonial Office was responsible for the administration of the mandate. As a result, the Colonial Office tried to reconcile the conflicting claims of Arabs and Jews resulting from the Balfour Declaration and the mandate for Palestine.

▲ At the 1939 Palestine Conference in London the British government hoped to reach a peaceful agreement for the Arabs and Jews. The Arab delegation is pictured here.

Gradually, Foreign Office interference in the mandate caused a split within the British government between the Colonial Office and the Foreign Office over policy in Palestine. Anxious to fulfill Britain's pledges to both Arabs and Jews, the Colonial Office came to believe that the only solution was to partition the mandate into Jewish and Arab states, or self-governing provinces. The Foreign Office, on the other hand, favored the establishment of Palestine as an independent Arab state with treaty relations with Great Britain, and with adequate constitutional safeguards for the rights of the Jewish minority.

Eventually, following the Arab revolt in 1936–37, and with war looming in Europe, the Foreign Office won the internal debate over policy in Palestine. The British government adopted a new policy in the White Paper of 1939. This new policy tried to resolve the dilemma by limiting immigration to another 75,000 Jews over the next five years. Any further immigration would be subject to both Arab and Zionist agreement. Meanwhile, progress was to be made toward establishing a single, democratic Palestinian state, with adequate safeguards for the Jewish minority.

World War and Cold War

World War II, however, transformed the Palestine situation. Under Winston Churchill, a supporter of the Zionist cause, the British government once again divided over its Palestine policy. The most effective blow to the White Paper policy came at the end of the war, as the true extent of the Holocaust became clear.

Nevertheless, as the Cold War began, the Foreign Office continued to worry about maintaining good relations with the strategically important Arab states. Labour Foreign Secretary Ernest Bevin became convinced that partition was both a dangerous policy for Britain's own interests and an immoral policy that would displace the Palestinian Arabs from their homeland. At the same time, Britain had to get along with the United States. Despite Bevin's efforts to convince him otherwise, President Truman refused to endorse an end to Jewish immigration into the mandate and the establishment of Palestine as an Arab state.

Unable to obtain American help, and facing increasing Jewish attacks against the British in Palestine, both Bevin and the British public finally became disillusioned. Unable to achieve an agreement acceptable to both Jews and Arabs, on May 15, 1948, for the first time in the history of the empire, Great Britain abandoned a colonial responsibility without making any arrangements for a transfer of power.

Political History and Sources

The controversies involved in the creation of Israel will certainly continue. Thus, the role of the political historian remains of central importance in understanding the roots of the problem. The actions of decision makers often shape the world in which ordinary people live. The story of the Arab-Israeli dilemma demonstrates how new documents can improve historians' understanding of the past. Although documents themselves must be carefully weighed and tested before they can be accepted as valid historical evidence, they remain one of our most valuable resources for discovering the actions and motives of decision makers.

◀ This picture of the Jewish delegation was taken at the 1939 Palestine Conference in London. The Jews hoped to win support for the establishment of a Jewish state.

Chapter 29

New Directions in Latin America 1945–Present

Chapter Planning Guide

	TEXTBOOK	CORE RESOURCES	VISUAL RESOURCES	MULTIMEDIA
Introduction	pp. 800–801	Block Scheduling Handbook: Ch. 29		Videodisc Segment 29 and Viewing Guide: *Brazil's Changing Horizon*
Lesson 29.1 Challenges of Economic Development	pp. 802–806	Reading 29. 1: *Daily Life in a Mexican Shantytown* Geography Activity 29: *New Directions in Latin America*	Geography and History 29: *The Economy of Latin America* Everyday Life 29: *Urban Slum in Rio de Janeiro*	GHRC 29 Readings: *Curitiba; Chief Paiakan Fights for the Rain Forest; Latin America's Informal Economy; Mexico City* GHRC 29/Videodiscs: Images— *Unemployed Brazilians Scrounge to Survive; The Informal Economy at Work in Ecuador;* Charts—*Foreign Debts; Latin American Economic Growth*
Lesson 29.2 Revolution, Reaction, and Reform	pp. 807–813 Map: *Democratic Transition in South America,* p. 810 Through Others' Eyes: *A North American Views the Falklands War,* p. 812	Reading 29.2: *Guerrilla Priest* Skills Activity 29: *Linking Economics to History*		GHRC 29 Reading: *Grass Roots Activism Grows in Latin America; Curitiba* GHRC 29/Videodiscs: Image— *Fighting for Indigenous People's Rights;* Map—*Latin American Governments*
Lesson 29.3 Revolution and Democracy in Latin America	pp. 814–819 Map: *Central America and the Caribbean,* p. 815	Reading 29.3: *Conflict in Nicaragua* Writing Project 29: *Writing an Outline*		GHRC 29/Videodiscs: Images— *The Face of War in El Salvador; Democratic Elections in Panama; Aztec Dancers Support the Zapatistas*
Lesson 29.4 Problems of Culture and Society	pp. 820–824 Literature Through Time: *Magic Realism,* p. 821 History Through the Arts: *Modern Latin American Painting,* p. 823	Reading 29.4: *Political Prisoners and Human Rights*	Art and History 29: *Mosaic at the University of Mexico*	GHRC 29 Readings: *The Assassination of Archbishop Romero; Fernando Botero on "Latin American" Art; Mexico's Mother of Dance Folklorico* GHRC 29/Videodiscs: Images— *Human Rights Protest in Argentina; Fernando Botero's Presidential Family;* Audio Clip—*Mariachi Music from Mexico;* Video Clip—*Carnival in Brazil*
Chapter Investigation and Enrichment	pp. 800–824	Chapter 29 Investigation: *Eye on Latin America: A TV News Series* People in World History 29 Explorations in Daily Life 29		GHRC 29/Videodiscs
Review and Assessment	Section 1 Review, p. 806 Section 2 Review, p. 813 Section 3 Review, p. 819 Section 4 Review, p. 824 Chapter 29 Review, p. 825	Chapter Review Activity 29 Vocabulary Activity 29 Themes Review 29 Section Study Guides 29.1–29.4 Main Idea Activities 29.1–29.4 Daily Quizzes 29.1–29.4 Chapter 29 Test Sheltered English Ch. 29 Test Ch. 29 Test Generator		Audio CDs: Ch. 29 Summary (English and Spanish)

INTRODUCING THE CHAPTER

Textbook pp. 800–801

CHAPTER OVERVIEW

Latin America experienced numerous problems in the postwar era. Burgeoning populations strained the economic resources of many nations, and attempts to modernize resulted in urban poverty and environmental devastation. Disagreements over solutions resulted in political factionalism and violence, and the United States often became involved in an effort to protect its interests. Political conflict also resulted in human rights violations.

PRESENTING THEMES

On the chalkboard or on an overhead transparency, write the following open-ended theme questions.

- **GEOGRAPHY** How might rapid population growth affect a region?
- **ECONOMIC ORGANIZATION** Why might economists emphasize industrial development over agricultural development?
- **POLITICS AND LAW** How might national political divisions affect ordinary people?

Have students, either individually or in groups, suggest responses to the questions. For the geography question, students might suggest that rapid population growth can stretch the resources of a developing nation. For the economic organization question, students might suggest that industry can employ more people and generate greater profits than agriculture. For the politics and law question, students might suggest that political divisions can cause conflicts that lead to human rights violations and destroy lives and property. Once students have studied the chapter, you may wish to have them complete the Themes Review, then compare the two sets of answers.

USING THE VIDEO

Segment 29: *Brazil's Changing Horizon*

ENGLISH

Search Chapter 29
Videodisc 2, Side B

SPANISH

Search Chapter 29
Videodisc 2, Side B

Tell students that in this chapter they will apply these theme questions to the nations of Latin America in the decades that followed World War II. Conclude by showing Segment 29 of the *World History and Cultures Videodisc*. This segment illustrates some of the problems and issues that affected Brazil's economic and political development in the years after World War II.

Before showing the video, ask students to pay particular attention to the choices Brazil's leaders made about investments in their country's future. To help students grasp the significant points of the segment, have them complete Video Viewing Guide 29.

Key to Ability Levels

All strategies and activities are coded to the following ability levels:

LEVEL 1	**Basic** activities suitable for all students
LEVEL 2	**Average** activities suitable for average to above-average students
LEVEL 3	**Challenging** activities suitable for above-average students
SHELTERED ENGLISH	Activities suitable for students with **Limited English Proficiency**

Additional Resources

BOOKS FOR TEACHERS

Gilbert, Alan. *The Latin American City.* Monthly Review Press, 1994. Examines urban growth.

Inter-American Development Bank. *Women in the Americas.* Johns Hopkins, 1995. Discusses changing economic roles.

Lowenthal, A. F. and G. F. Treverton. *Latin America in a New World.* Westview Press, 1994. Examines the impact of the Cold War's end.

BOOKS FOR STUDENTS

McIntyre, Loren. *Exploring South America.* Crown, 1990. Offers a photographic survey of the continent.

Page, Joseph A. *Perón: A Biography.* Random House, 1983. Discusses Perón's personal and public life.

Slatta, Richard W. *Cowboys of the Americas.* Yale University Press, 1990. Compares cowboys of North and South America.

MULTIMEDIA MATERIALS

Latin American Lifestyles. Video Knowledge. 5 videos, 50 min. each. Details culture and everyday life.

Let's Visit Mexico. Queue. CD-ROM, MAC, WIN, DOS formats. Offers detailed information in English and Spanish.

South America Series. Encyclopaedia Britannica. 3 videos, 21 min. each. Presents regional views.

Lesson 29.1 *Challenges of Economic Development*

Textbook pp. 802–806

RESOURCES

Core Resources

Reading 29.1: *Daily Life in a Mexican Shantytown*

Geography Activity 29: *New Directions in Latin America*

Visual Resources

Geography and History 29: *The Economy of Latin America*

Everyday Life 29: *Urban Slum in Rio de Janeiro*

Global History Resource Center

Reading: *Curitiba: Brazil's City of Hope*

Reading: *Chief Paiakan Fights for the Rain Forest*

Reading: *Latin America's Informal Economy*

Reading: *Chile's Leftists Turn to Capitalism*

Reading: *Mexico City: World's Largest Urban Center*

Videodiscs or Global History Resource Center

Chart: *Foreign Debts in Latin America, 1986, 1989*

Search Frame 1077

Map: *Urban Population of Latin America*

Search Frame 1075

Image: *Unemployed Brazilians Scrounge to Survive*

Search Frame 1065

Image: *The Informal Economy at Work in Equador*

Search Frame 1066

Chart: *Latin American Economic Growth, 1980–1989*

Search Frame 1076

LESSON FOCUS

How have Latin American countries tried to develop their economies in the modern era, and what have been the results?

OBJECTIVES

After completing this lesson, students will be able to:

- describe the consequences of Latin American efforts to escape the limitations of monoculture;
- explain the Latin American debt crisis;
- identify the environmental consequences of industrialization and urbanization in much of Latin America.

HOOK

Discuss monoculture. Call on a volunteer to define the term monoculture. [the reliance of an entire region or country on a single crop for export] Then read, or have a student read, the passage on textbook page 802 about a family's life on the *finca*. Ask students how this passage confirms what they have just read about monoculture. [Guatemala's crop was coffee, and Menchú's entire family worked the coffee plantation for low wages.]

Have students discuss in small groups how monoculture affected a country and its people.

Ask: Why was monoculture a poor foundation for a national economy?
[It was unstable and only the plantation owners and managers profited from monoculture—small farmers and agricultural workers often lived in poverty.]

DEVELOP

Identify economic policies and consequences. Have students form small groups to discuss the following questions:

- **What did Latin American countries do to address the problem of monoculture?**
  [Countries diversified their exports and promoted industrial growth through import substitution—restricting foreign imports and replacing them with domestically produced goods. Some governments helped developing businesses.]

- **What were the consequences of Latin American efforts to end monoculture?**
  [Countries industrialized and experienced urbanization and population growth.]

Call on different groups to share their discussions with the class. Then create on the board a chart titled "Consequences of Economic Modernization in Latin America." Write the headings "Urbanization" and "Population Growth" on the chart and have groups fill in details about each. Show the electronic media map of population growth as students work.

Distribute Reading 29.1 and display the Everyday Life Transparency. Have students discuss the conditions depicted in these sources and how they underscore the problem of urban growth in Latin America. Then display the electronic media image of unemployed Brazilians and assign the reading on Curitiba. Ask how these reflect economic problems in Brazil and how some hope to solve them.

PROBE

Examine debt and environmental issues. Add two additional headings to the chart on the board—"Debt Crisis" and "Environmental Problems." Point out that both issues arose in Latin America in part as a result of efforts to develop local economies. Have students describe the problems and then add details to the appropriate columns on the board. You might want to have students examine the electronic media chart on foreign debt.

When students have finished filling out this portion of the chart, have them answer the following questions:
- **What were the reasons for the debt crisis?**
- **What environmental problems have resulted from industrialization and urbanization?**
  [**Debt crisis**: the oil crisis of the 1970s caused Latin American countries to borrow money to buy oil. Banks offered only short-term, high-interest loans as Latin American debt grew. Many banks began to restrict

lending and Latin America was in financial crisis. **Environmental problems**: these problems include pollution, deforestation, and soil erosion.]

Distribute Geography Activity 29. When students have completed it, assign the selection on the rain forest in the Global History Resource Center.

CONCLUDE

Analyze economic development. Point out that despite improvements in many Latin American economies, many citizens still suffered from poverty. Then ask students what criteria—economic, social, and environmental—they would use to identify a country as developed. Write their ideas on the board and come up with a consensus definition of economic development. You might also show the electronic media image of Equador's economy and assign the articles about the informal economy and Chile's leftists.

EXTEND

Cross-Curricular Connection: *Geography*
Display the Geography and History Transparency. Have students choose a country and list the major economic activities for that country. Then ask the class questions, such as: Where are the mining areas? Where is commercial farming extensive? Plantation farming?

MEET INDIVIDUAL NEEDS

Logical-Mathematical Learners
Have students examine the electronic media charts on debt and economic growth, then write a paragraph analyzing correlations between debt and growth.

Linguistic Learners
Have students read the article on Mexico City, then discuss the quality of life in Mexico City and why Mexicans still flock to their overcrowded capital.

ASSESS

Review
Have students complete the Section 1 Review. Use answers in the Teacher's Edition, page 806, to assess student mastery of this section.

Lesson 29.2   *Revolution, Reaction, and Reform*

Textbook pp. 807–813

RESOURCES

Pupil's Edition

Map, p. 810: *Democratic Transition in South America*

Through Others' Eyes, p. 812: *A North American Views the Falklands War*

Core Resources

Reading 29.2: *Guerilla Priest*

Skills Activity 29: *Linking Economics to History*

Global History Resource Center

Reading: *Grass Roots Activism Grows in Latin America*

Reading: *Curitiba: Brazil's City of Hope*

Videodiscs or Global History Resource Center

Map: *Latin American Governments*

Search Frame 1078

Image: *Fighting for Indigenous People's Rights*

Search Frame 1069

LESSON FOCUS

What kinds of political changes have taken place in Latin America in the past 50 years?

OBJECTIVES

After completing this lesson, students will be able to:

- identify the policies followed by Brazil and Mexico after World War II;
- explain the consequences of the Cuban Revolution;
- describe political developments in most Latin American countries by the 1990s.

HOOK

Discuss economic and industrial development in Brazil and Mexico. Read to students the teacher's annotation on textbook page 807. Then have them discuss the creation of Brazil's new capital, Brasília. Ask students what symbolism the creation of a new capital might have for a nation.

Ask: *Why did Kubitschek build the new capital of Brasília?*
> [In addition to fostering a sense of nationalism and pride, Kubitschek hoped to open up the interior of Brazil to further economic development.]

Ask: *What began this policy of development and economic nationalism in Brazil?*

> [Getúlio Vargas instituted an ambitious program of industrialization and modernization, created official government unions, supported wage increases, and enacted new social legislation for workers. His successors continued many of these policies of modernization and development.]

Then have students discuss how Mexico's efforts to achieve economic independence were similar to Brazil's. *[The government backed private businesspeople and helped finance factories to produce the goods Mexico needed to be independent. Government also supported labor and backed other development schemes.]*

DEVELOP

Discuss the Cuban Revolution. Remind students of their discussion of the development policies of Mexico and Brazil. *[Both followed policies of economic nationalism and moderate social reform.]* Then point out that this pattern of national development was followed in many Latin American countries.

Ask: *How was Cuba different?*
> [Cuba, under the leadership of Fidel Castro, pursued the path of revolution rather than reform.]

Have students describe the circumstances that brought Fidel Castro to power.

Ask: *What were the consequences of the Cuban Revolution in Cuba ?*

[Students should note that many Cubans fled the island and that Cuba eventually became a communist dictatorship. In turn, other countries in the Americas tried to isolate Cuba and crack down on revolutionary sentiments at home.]

PROBE

Examine the shift away from democracy and reform.
Distribute the Skills Activity and have students complete it. Then ask students to work in small groups to explore why the revolutionary ideas expressed by Fidel Castro might be alarming to other governments or leaders in the hemisphere. *[These ideas and the threat of armed revolution represented a danger to the power of ruling elites.]*

Ask: *How did the Cuban Revolution contribute to the rise of authoritarian government in Latin America?*

[The threat of Marxist revolution prompted the anticommunist military in countries like Brazil and Argentina to overthrow the government and establish authoritarian rule. In Chile, Allende's socialist policies, along with the oil crisis, caused an economic crisis and led to the overthrow of his government by the military leader Pinochet.]

On the board, create a simple chart with the headings "Brazil," "Argentina," and "Chile" at the top. Have groups describe the establishment of authoritarian governments in those countries in the 1960s and 1970s, and list those points on the chart.

CONCLUDE

Analyze the return to democracy. Pointing to the chart on the board, ask how political conditions had changed in those countries, and in much of Latin America, by the 1990s. Have the groups discuss this and report their findings to the class. *[By the 1990s democracies had been established in many countries.]* Display the electronic media map *Latin American Governments* and have students discuss what it shows about the restoration of democracy in Latin America. Ask groups to explain why countries such as Argentina, Brazil, and Chile restored democratic rule, supporting their reasoning with information from the chapter.

Then point out to students that these democracies often remained fragile, and ask students what kinds of political challenges these countries might face. *[Problems include such*

things as the continued strength of the military, lingering economic and financial troubles (such as debt), social problems (stemming from widespread poverty), and lack of experience with democratic practices and institutions.]

Next have students read the two articles on political change and recent political success stories in Latin America in the Global History Resource Center, and look at the electronic media image of Amazonian Indians visiting Brazil's Congress. Ask students why the emergence of political activism at the local level is a sign of health for any democratic society.

EXTEND

Cross-Curricular Connection: *Journalism*

Have students read the Through Others' Eyes feature and think about why George Will opposed Argentina's invasion of the Falklands. Then have them imagine that they are journalists from Argentina who support the Argentine government's actions. Ask them to write a short editorial that supports reclaiming the Falklands.

MEET INDIVIDUAL NEEDS

Visual-Spatial Learners

Have students summarize what they have learned from this section by creating a general time line of political events in Latin America since the 1930s, beginning with the policies of economic nationalism in Brazil and Mexico and ending with the return to democracy in various countries.

Students Having Difficulty/
Students Acquiring English

If students have difficulty grasping the significance of the Cuban Revolution, you might have them make a web showing events and consequences. The web might have a circle labeled "Causes of the Revolution," another labeled "Results in Cuba," and a third labeled "Impact on the Americas." Have students brainstorm topics to fill in the web. Then students can use that information to assess the revolution's importance.

ASSESS

Review

Have students complete the Section 2 Review. Use answers in the Teacher's Edition, page 813, to assess student mastery of this section.

Lesson 29.3   *Revolution and Democracy in Latin America*

Textbook pp. 814–819

RESOURCES

Pupil's Edition

Map, p. 815: *Central America and the Caribbean, 1980s*

Core Resources

Reading 29.3: *Conflict in Nicaragua*

Global History Resource Center

Reading: *Mexico City: World's Largest Urban Center*

Videodiscs or Global History Resource Center

Image: *The Face of War in El Salvador*

Search Frame 1071

Image: *Democratic Elections in Panama*

Search Frame 1067

Image: *Aztec Dancers Support the Zapatistas*

Search Frame 1072

LESSON FOCUS

How and why has the political stability of Central America and Mexico been threatened in recent decades?

OBJECTIVES

After completing this lesson, students will be able to:

- explain why the United States often supported opposition movements in Central America;
- describe the political situation throughout most of Central America by the early 1990s;
- identify problems Mexico continued to face after World War II.

HOOK

Discuss results of the Cold War in Latin America. Have students look at the textbook map of Mexico, Central America, and the Caribbean. Have students identify the countries in which the United States has had a military presence or intervention.

Ask: *In what ways has this region been politically unstable in the past few decades?*

[Students should note that various revolutions, rebellions, and invasions have taken place in the region in the recent past; they should mention Cuba, Nicaragua, and Panama specifically.]

Ask: *Why would instability in this region be of concern to the*

United States?

[because of the proximity of the region and U.S. fears of communism]

Conclude by telling students that Cold War concerns about communist expansion caused the United States to back conservative movements in the region that promised stability and anticommunist rule.

DEVELOP

Describe key events in the region. Ask students to work in small groups to discuss how events in Cuba in the 1960s raised American concerns in Central America. *[The nationalization of American property and the increasing radicalization of Cuba, including its support for revolution in other countries, fanned American fears of communism and led to the Bay of Pigs invasion. After the failure of the Bay of Pigs invasion and the subsequent Cuban missile crisis, the United States promised not to invade Cuba but also attempted to isolate Cuba from the rest of the Americas.]*

Next draw a simple chart on the board with headings for Nicaragua and Panama. Have groups cite major events affecting these countries over the past several decades and put them in the chart. *[**Nicaragua:** Sandinista revolution, U.S. embargo and attempted destabilization of government, contras, 1990 election; **Panama:** canal treaty, U.S. invasion and capture of Noriega, democratic government]* Point out to students that El

Salvador and Honduras also experienced political problems during this period.

To conclude, have students read Core Resources Reading 29.3 and view the electronic media image *The Face of War in El Salvador* to illustrate some of the problems confronting Central America during this period.

PROBE

Analyze the political developments in Central America by the early 1990s. Remind students that in Central America the years after 1945 were often characterized by violence.

Ask: *How did some Latin American nations try to end conflict in the region?*
[Responses should mention the Contadora Principles— the agreement between the leaders of Venezuela, Panama, Colombia, and Mexico to help restore peace to the region—and the conference in Guatemala City, during which Oscar Arias emphasized the importance of democracy for the region.]

Ask: *What was the political situation of several Central American countries by the early 1990s?*
[The fall of the Soviet Union left revolutionaries without support. As a result, some Central American countries— Nicaragua, El Salvador, and Panama—seemed on their way to democracy and peace.]

To illustrate this point you might have students view the electronic media image of the elections in Panama.

CONCLUDE

Examine the causes of instability in Mexico. Have students make a general time line in which they chronicle events in Mexican political history after World War II. Have them begin with the political unrest of the 1960s and 1970s and the government's reaction to it. *[uprisings in 1968—students demanded political openness, and demonstrations led to violence and bloodshed; 1971—a guerrilla group tried to destroy the government, leading to the government's killing or imprisoning the rebels]*

Next ask students to place on their time lines the events affecting the economy in Mexico during the 1980s. *[oil prices fell; 1985—earthquake in Mexico City; 1987—annual inflation rate rose to 132 percent; 1990s—foreign debt had reached near $100 billion, North American Free Trade Agreement signed, devaluation of the Mexican peso, increase of illegal immigrants into the United States]*

Conclude by asking students how the problems of the 1980s and 1990s affected the political situation in Mexico. *[Many people opposed the PRI and supported opposition candidates. Opposition leaders accused the PRI of fraud in the 1988 election. In 1994 the PRI's candidate was assassinated, and conservative elements in the PRI were accused. However, the PRI won the election. Also in 1994 the Zapatista National Liberation Army threatened government control in Chiapas.]*

To give students more information about recent events in Mexico, show the electronic media image of the Aztec dancers, and have students read about the growth of Mexico City.

EXTEND

Cross-Curricular Connection: *Political Science/Economics*
Have small groups of students research current political and economic conditions in Cuba and present short reports to the rest of the class on Cuba's situation and prospects for the future.

MEET INDIVIDUAL NEEDS

Linguistic Learners
Have students examine the electronic media images *Democratic Elections in Panama* and *The Face of War in El Salvador* and consider how each represents a different strategy for change in Latin America. Have students compare and contrast these differing strategies.

Intrapersonal Learners
Have students imagine that they lived in one of the countries mentioned in the section during a period of political instability or violence. Ask them to write a diary entry in which they take on the role of a person involved in the conflict—a politician, a guerrilla, and so on.

ASSESS

Review
Have students complete the Section 3 Review. Use answers in the Teacher's Edition, page 819, to assess student mastery of this section.

Lesson 29.4   *Problems of Culture and Society*

Textbook pp. 820–824

RESOURCES

Pupil's Edition
Literature Through Time, p. 821: *Magic Realism*

History Through the Arts: *Modern Latin American Painting*

Visual Resources
Art and History 29: *Mosaic at the University of Mexico*

Core Resources
Reading 29.4: *Political Prisoners and Human Rights*

Global History Resource Center
Reading: *The Assassination of Archbishop Romero*

Reading: *Fernando Botero on "Latin American" Art*

Reading: *Mexico's Mother of Dance Folklorico*

Reading: *"La Violencia" and Human Rights in Guatemala*

Videodiscs or Global History Resource Center

Image: *Human Rights Protest in Argentina*

Search Frame 1070

Image: *Fernando Botero's* Presidential Family

Search Frame 1073

Image: *Folk Art from Costa Rica*

Search Frame 1074

Video Clip: *Carnival in Brazil*

Search 5407, Play to 5728
Videodisc 2, Side B
Video Clip 29

Audio Clip: *Mariachi Music from Mexico*

Search 5730, Play to 6240
Videodisc 2, Side B
Audio Clip 29

LESSON FOCUS

How have Latin American countries violated human rights and how have their citizens coped with these problems?

OBJECTIVES

After completing this lesson, students will be able to:
- explain how some Latin American countries have violated their citizens' human rights;
- identify what has been done to end human rights violations in some Latin American countries;
- identify themes that inspire Latin American artists and writers.

HOOK

Consider human rights. Ask students to consider how they would react if five uniformed officials broke through the front door one night and forcibly removed their mother or father and an older sibling.

Open this scenario for discussion. Remind students that during the infamous "dirty war" in Argentina, thousands of people "disappeared"—taken away by the military government and killed for alleged political crimes. Have a student read the excerpt from the poem on textbook page 822. Ask students what this passage reveals about the impact of human rights violations on society. Display the electronic media image of the human rights protest in Argentina.

DEVELOP

Discuss the issue of human rights violations and efforts to stop them. Have students define some of the basic human rights, and list these on the board. *[Students should note freedom of expression, freedom of association, due process of* law, equality before the law, and the right to humane treatment.]

Next make a chart on the board with rows labeled "Guatemala," "Cuba," "Argentina," and "El Salvador," and columns labeled "Violations" and "Causes/Circumstances." Have students fill out the chart with information from the textbook. Assign the selection on the assassination of Archbishop Romero and discuss problems in El Salvador.

Next lead a discussion on how some people have worked to end these human rights violations.

Ask: Who were the Mothers of the Plaza de Mayo?
[women who had family among the "disappeared" and worked to launch the human rights campaign in Argentina]

Ask: How have others worked to stop human rights abuses in Latin America?
[Some countries, such as the United States, have imposed sanctions. Human rights groups within Latin America, with the support of international groups, have led the call for a return to democratic rule.]

Also assign students a free writing assignment exploring their personal opinions and values regarding human rights.

PROBE

Examine the social role of art and literature. Remind students that many Latin American writers have used their work to draw attention to the human rights issue. Have students work briefly in small groups to identify the general themes that have inspired Latin American artists and writers. [Artists and writers often explore societal problems; speak out for peace and justice; and affirm Latin American cultural values.] Before students begin, assign the Core Resources Reading 29.4, the textbook feature on magic realism, the Global History Resource Center selections on art and dance, and the electronic media images of Botero's work and of folk art from Costa Rica.

Ask: Why do you think that Latin American artists and writers play a prominent social and political role?
[Artists are sensitive to their nations' problems and feel the need to make a difference and their creative and intellectual abilities allow them to focus attention on critical issues.]

CONCLUDE

Examine issues of peace and justice. Tell students that

Guatemala has a rich tradition of folk art, which includes beautiful textiles woven by Mayan Indians. Have students read the selection about how human rights have been violated in the Mayan community. Discuss the factors that have led to these abuses.

Ask: How might these problems be addressed? Is there a viable solution to the human rights problem in Guatemala and in Latin America?

Divide students into groups to answer these questions. Then discuss students' conclusions. Also have them consider cultural values that have helped Latin Americans cope with social and political problems.

EXTEND

Cross-Curricular Connection: *Art*

Display the Art and History Transparency 29 and ask students to define the term *mosaic*. Explain that the mosaic at the University of Mexico is the largest external mosaic in the world. Have students complete the worksheet and create a small mosaic.

MEET INDIVIDUAL NEEDS

Kinesthetic Learners

Have students read the selection *Mexico's Mother of Dance Folklorico*. Then ask them to learn and demonstrate a dance from Latin America, such as the tango, samba, mambo, and bossa nova, that has spread to the United States.

Musical Learners

Play the audio clip of Mexican mariachi music for students and have them describe their impressions. Have groups research the dance and music of other Latin American countries. If possible, have students bring samples of this music to class.

ASSESS

Review

Have students complete the Section 4 Review. Use answers in the Teacher's Edition, pages 823–824, to assess student mastery of this section.

In preparation for the chapter test, you may wish to have students complete all or part of the Chapter 29 Review on page 825 of the textbook, the Chapter 29 Review Activity, and the Chapter 29 Themes Review.

Understanding the Main Idea

Call on a volunteer to read aloud the *Understanding the Main Idea* paragraph. Then tell students that the postwar years proved difficult for many Latin American countries, which saw increased urbanization and industrialization, as well as widespread poverty. Development schemes created environmental problems and led to debt. Meanwhile, democracy gave way in many places to dictatorship. Still, many Latin Americans continued to work for a better future.

Presenting Themes

See p. 799B for suggestions on introducing themes.

Using the Time Line

Have students list the time line events in their notebooks. After they have read about each event in the chapter, have students write a paragraph explaining its significance.

Chapter 29
New Directions in Latin America 1945–Present

Understanding the Main Idea

Latin America struggled through difficult decades following World War II. A rapidly growing population and the need for economic development greatly challenged Latin American nations. The Cold War cast a shadow over Latin America and affected politics. Many Latin Americans lost their political and civil rights during this time. But in spite of these problems, most Latin Americans remained hopeful about the future.

Themes

- **Geography** How might rapid population growth affect a region?
- **Economic Organization** Why might economists emphasize industrial development over agricultural development?
- **Politics and Law** How might national political divisions affect ordinary people?

At the end of World War II, an optimistic mood settled on Latin America. Almost all Latin American nations had opposed the Axis Powers during World War II. This placed Latin America with the victors, and Latin Americans rightly felt proud of the Allied triumph. Mexico and Brazil were also justifiably proud of their soldiers who had fought in the war. They returned home heroes to cities in celebration. One historian described the scene as a troopship steamed into the harbor of Rio de Janeiro:

66*The cannons of the old fortresses fired salute upon salute; hundreds of boats escorted the troopship toward its moorings [dock] while the great bells of Rio's many churches pealed and crowds gathered in the streets.*99

After the war, large Latin American countries such as Mexico, Brazil, and Argentina thought themselves to be on the verge of a period of growth that would lead to greater prosperity. Argentina was already one of the richest Latin American countries. When Evita Perón, wife of dictator Juan Perón, toured war-ravaged Europe, her elaborate and elegant gowns starkly contrasted with the bombed-out European cities. Europe seemed defeated and finished; Argentina wealthy and victorious. Yet this proved to be an illusion. The four decades after the war were difficult ones in Latin America.

1948	1959	1961	1968
The Organization of American States is founded.	Fidel Castro leads a successful revolution in Cuba.	Cuban exile forces are defeated at the Bay of Pigs.	Student protesters clash with police in Mexico.

The modern architecture of the Children's Museum, Caracas, Venezuela

1970	1982	1987	1990
Salvador Allende is elected president of Chile.	Great Britain and Argentina go to war over the Falkland Islands.	Representatives from across Central America meet at a regional peace conference.	Violeta Chamorro is elected president of Nicaragua.

SECTION 1

CORE LESSON PLAN
See pages 799C and
799D for Lesson Plan
29.1.

Daily Life

Life on the *fazendas* and *haciendas* was harsh and traditional. The farm workers rose before dawn to perform the estate's daily tasks, which changed with the seasons. In addition to raising crops, workers might also be blacksmiths, herders, and storekeepers. Some helped keep the roads of the estate in repair. Most estates remained much like the feudal manors of the Middle Ages in Europe—self-contained and self-sufficient, with a fairly strict set of hierarchical social relationships.

Critical Thinking Ask students how they think ending monoculture might change this system.

ANSWER: Students may answer that as these large plantations diversify, the landowners will no longer be as self-contained and new social structures will have to develop.

SECTION 1
Challenges of Economic Development

FOCUS

- What were the consequences of Latin American efforts to escape the limitations of monoculture?

- How and why did Latin America experience a debt crisis?

- What were the environmental consequences of industrialization and urbanization in much of Latin America?

Like the new nations emerging in Asia and Africa after World War II, Latin American countries also faced new challenges. Latin American nations hoped to modernize and establish their independence from the more developed economies of the Western industrial powers. On the road to modernization, they had to deal with the environmental and social costs of independence.

Workers harvest coffee beans in Guatemala.

The Consequences of Monoculture

Before 1945 most Latin American countries were rural, agricultural countries. Their exports centered on one or two cash crops that were grown for export to European and U.S. markets. Brazil, Colombia, El Salvador, and Guatemala grew coffee; Argentina and Uruguay exported beef; Cuba, Mexico, Brazil, and Peru sent sugar abroad; and Chile, Bolivia, and Mexico exported minerals. This reliance of an entire region, or even an entire country, on a single crop is known as **monoculture**. In good years monoculture brought in high earnings. When world prices were low, however, countries suffered.

Latin American monocultures favored crops grown on large plantations, known as *fazendas* in Brazil, *fincas* in Central America, and *haciendas* in Mexico. Many of the workers on these plantations were families who came to the plantations only at harvest time. Rigoberta Menchú, winner of the 1992 Nobel Peace Prize, described her family's experience as workers on the *fincas*:

“*When I turned eight, I started to earn money on the* finca. *I set myself the task of picking 35 pounds of coffee a day. In those days, I was paid 20* centavos *for that amount. . . . I now felt that I was part of the life my parents lived. It was very hard on me. I remember very well never wasting a single moment, mainly out of love for my parents and so that they could save a little of their money, although they couldn't really save any because they had to tighten their belts so much anyway.*”

In such countries as Mexico, Colombia, or Brazil, small farmers did grow food crops, including corn, beans, vegetables, and coffee. But most of the small farmers owned so little land that they could barely support their families.

Owners and managers of the large plantations often profited enormously from the export of cash crops. But because the wages paid to the agricultural workers were very low, many people in the countryside lived in extreme poverty. In some countries, such as Mexico before 1910, many plantation workers had never received any money for their labor—their wages were used to pay off debts to plantation owners.

The Push for Industrialization

As early as the Great Depression of the 1930s, Latin American leaders realized the importance of economic **diversification**—expansion into more than one market. When the price of sugar, coffee, and other Latin American exports dropped, Latin Americans were unable to buy needed manufactured goods from overseas. Consequently, most Latin American countries adopted policies of economic nationalism after 1930. Many raised high tariff barriers against overseas goods and used government grants or even government investment in businesses and industries to encourage national production and self-sufficiency.

The interruption of global trade that occurred during World War II helped spur diversification. Mexico and Brazil, for example, diversified their exports and developed new markets for their manufactured goods. After the war many Latin American leaders believed the path to prosperity lay in industrialization. Mexico City, Caracas, Buenos Aires, and São Paulo were among the Latin American cities that grew rapidly as they became centers of industry.

Many Latin American countries protected their new industries by limiting the importation of foreign products or by imposing heavy tariffs on these products. At the same time, Latin American governments encouraged their own local industries to produce goods previously imported from overseas. This policy is known as **import substitution**. Soon Colombia, Chile, Mexico, Brazil, and Venezuela had national industries that produced manufactured goods for sale in their respective countries.

Many Latin American governments also became directly involved in developing businesses. In Mexico, for example, the government ran the national petroleum company, PEMEX. In Brazil the government owned and ran the first steel mill, as well as the national oil company, the major electric utility company, and the national airlines. In Argentina the telephone company was owned by the government, as were many other companies. Governments justified their entrance into the economies on the grounds that some industries were too important to be left in the hands of foreign owners.

▲ **This worker in the state of Bahia in eastern Brazil makes fine crystal for export.**

Urbanization and Population Growth

As industrialization increased, individuals from the rural areas moved to the cities looking for work. Young men and women, and sometimes entire families, left the villages where their families had lived for centuries. Some were American Indians who left behind the rich culture of their ancestors. Some were the descendants of African slaves who believed that the cities held better opportunities. Other migrants were the grandchildren of European immigrants who had come to Latin America before World War I. All came to the cities hoping for a better life.

In the cities migrants settled wherever they could. Few had much money or education. They built their neighborhoods out of wood, tin, and cardboard scraps. They lacked running water, electricity, and even sewers. Such neighborhoods became known as *favelas* in Brazil, *barriadas* in Peru, and *colonias* in Mexico. The middle- and upper-class residents of the cities looked

RESOURCE ACTIVITY

READINGS IN WORLD HISTORY
Reading 29.1
Daily Life in a Mexican Shantytown

Have students read the anthropologist's description of life in the Cerrada del Condor shantytown. Then have students complete the questions.

Level 2

Population Growth in Selected Latin American Countries, 1900–2025

Argentina **Mexico**
Brazil **Peru**
Chile

250,000,000
225,000,000
200,000,000
275,000,000
150,000,000
125,000,000
100,000,000
75,000,000
50,000,000
25,000,000
0
1900   1950   1988 2000*   2025*

Rapid Growth The benefits of industrialization have helped produce a tremendous growth in the populations of many Latin American countries. Researchers project that this growth will continue in the future.

? Analyzing Which two countries are expected to have the highest levels of population in 2025? What problems might this cause?

*Projected figures

Family size grew among Latin American urban migrants as these countries industrialized because of what demographers—experts who study population trends—call a **demographic transition**. Preindustrial societies, these scholars point out, typically have high birth rates and also high death rates. Industrialization decreases death rates by increasing standards of living and improving diets and health care. As death rates decline, women eventually choose to have fewer children because they know that their babies will survive. Meanwhile, however, there is a period of demographic transition when birth rates are higher than death rates. Population explodes during this period as large generations of children have children of their own. Thus, even as Latin American countries made great strides in improving overall living conditions, they also contributed to the population boom.

Efforts to escape the consequences of monoculture led to industrial development, urbanization, and a population explosion in many Latin American countries.

down on these slums that lined the roads into the city centers.

Carolina Maria de Jesus, a slum-dweller in Brazil, supported herself and her three children by recycling trash and reselling things from the dumps. In her diary she wrote of her daily struggle to feed her children:

> **❝** I kept thinking that I had to buy bread, soap, and milk for Vera Eunice [her daughter]. The 13 cruzeiros [1.7 cents] wouldn't make it. I returned home, or rather to my shack, nervous and exhausted. I thought of the worrisome life that I led. Carrying paper, washing clothes for the children, staying in the street all day long. Yet I'm always lacking things, Vera doesn't have shoes and she doesn't like to go barefoot. **❞**

The population in the slums grew because of the arrival of new migrants, who generally had large families.

International Debt

With increasing numbers of people to feed, Latin American countries faced serious challenges after World War II. More people meant that more jobs were needed. Rural areas had to produce more

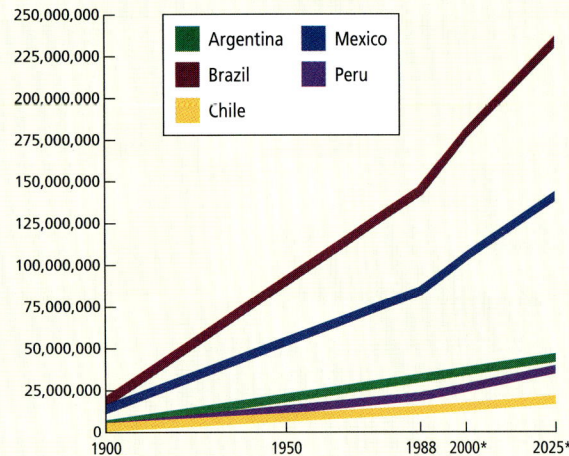

▲ Street vendors in Rio de Janeiro, Brazil, are part of the informal economy that has arisen in response to high taxes and low wages.

food. Schools had more children to educate, and clinics and hospitals had to care for more patients. The only way to keep up with these demands was for countries to develop their economies as rapidly as possible.

By the 1970s many Latin American governments were deeply involved in large-scale economic development projects. In Mexico the government invested heavily in steel plants, oil production facilities, mines, and agricultural schemes for rural areas. In Brazil the military government made plans to develop the Amazon. The government mapped out a vast Trans-Amazon Highway system that would make it possible for Brazilian settlers and Brazilian companies to tap the riches of the rain forest. Argentina and Brazil planned to build huge dams to generate power for their industries.

As a result of the oil crisis of the 1970s, however, many Latin American countries had to borrow more and more money from overseas banks to buy the oil necessary to keep their economies going. As their indebtedness grew, most international banks began to offer Latin American governments only short-term loans at sometimes high interest rates.

By the 1980s the heavy borrowing by Latin American governments began to generate concern in Europe and the United States. Some U.S. banks had lent huge sums to Mexico, Argentina, and Brazil. The banks began to fear that Latin American countries would not be able to pay the interest they owed on the loans. If Latin American countries missed their interest payments, then banks in the United States and Europe might collapse. Experts began to refer to the problem as the **international debt crisis**. Many banks began to refuse further Latin American loan requests.

As the crisis deepened, many Latin American countries continued to print money to pay for government programs they could not afford. The result was rapid inflation. In an effort to end the financial crisis, they sought help from the United States and international agencies. These agencies agreed to lend more money, but only on certain conditions. They required the Latin American governments to cut back on their spending, sell their factories, and lower inflation.

In order to cut spending, governments fired workers and stopped supporting food programs, transportation, and fuel costs. Payment of Latin

▲ The Trans-Amazon Highway promoted settlement and the development of ranches, which led to deforestation.

American debt transferred over $100 billion out of the region. The lack of money for investment in local businesses resulted in widespread unemployment.

Despite these growing problems, however, industrialization generally brought considerable benefits to Latin America. It created and supported the growth of a middle class. It improved sanitation and health in most countries. It also provided expanded educational opportunities, as governments established schools and universities to develop a more educated workforce. In addition, industrialization helped many countries escape the problems of monoculture by diversifying their economies.

As they struggled to feed their people and develop their internal economies, many Latin American countries went deeply into debt, causing a global financial crisis.

Environmental Issues

To solve the problems of excess population growth and debt, Latin American planners emphasized rapid industrialization, the utilization of natural resources, and the settlement of previously remote frontier regions. The settlement of frontiers would relieve overcrowded cities. These strategies carried high environmental costs, however. Developing industries created new jobs, but also gave rise to new problems—particularly pollution.

NEW DIRECTIONS IN LATIN AMERICA   **805**

In Mexico pollution became a serious environmental and health issue. The most severely polluted areas included Mexico City, which, with 15 million inhabitants, was one of the largest cities in the world. Other affected areas included the northern border with the United States and the oil-rich regions of the Gulf of Mexico.

Deforestation in Mexico eventually claimed more than a million acres of forest each year. Trees were cut for lumber, to clear land for farms and ranches, to drill for oil, or to build roads. In the region near PEMEX facilities, beaches were stained with raw sewage and industrial waste. Regular oil spills killed fish and polluted waterways. Once known for its beautiful "transparent" air, Mexico City has instead become noted for its **smog**—air highly contaminated from automobile emissions and factory smoke.

In Brazil government officials saw development of the vast ecologically sensitive Amazon rain forests as the potential solution to both the nation's population growth and its international debt. Development of this area began with the building of the Trans-Amazon Highway in the 1960s to encourage settlers to move into the Amazon frontier. This construction required cutting down hundreds of thousands of acres of virgin forest land. Once the forest canopy had been destroyed, heavy rains washed away the thin topsoil. The tropical heat then baked the soil until

▲ Smog caused by automobiles produces a constant health hazard for the residents of Mexico City.

it was as hard as dry clay, making simple agriculture almost impossible.

Since the Amazon holds rich mineral deposits, the Brazilian government drafted an ambitious program to develop gold, iron, and bauxite mines. They hoped to pay off Brazil's debt with income from the mines. Along the Carajás railway in the northeastern Amazon, the government developed an industrial province organized around mining and steel production. All this development increased the rate of deforestation and pollution in the area. It also created enormous tension between those trying to develop the region and the local Indian inhabitants.

In their rush to industrialize, many Latin American countries experienced pollution and other environmental problems. These, in turn, led to social problems.

SECTION 1 REVIEW

IDENTIFY and explain the significance of the following:
monoculture
diversification
import substitution
demographic transition
international debt crisis
smog

1. *Main Idea* How did Latin American countries attempt to end their dependence on a single crop? What were the results of these efforts?

2. *Main Idea* What problems arose in many Latin American countries as a result of industrialization and urbanization?

3. *Economic Organization* What factors led to many Latin American countries' debt crisis?

4. *Writing to Describe* Imagine that you are a teenager living in a slum outside a large Latin American city. In several journal entries describe your life, role, and hopes for the future.

5. *Evaluating* Do you think plans for rapid industrialization in Latin America are justified? Explain your answer.

Revolution, Reaction, and Reform

- What policies did Brazil and Mexico pursue after World War II?

- What were the consequences of the Cuban Revolution?

- What kind of political developments had most Latin American countries experienced by the 1990s?

he postwar struggle for economic development and independence led to political instability in many Latin American countries. Three major trends emerged, as liberal reformers, radical Marxist revolutionaries, and authoritarian conservatives struggled for power.

Stark modern architecture in Brasília, Brazil

Brazil and Mexico

In the decade following World War II, the two strongest and most prosperous Latin American countries—Mexico and Brazil—were also the most populous. With the two largest populations of any Latin America nations, Mexico and Brazil led the way in postwar development. At the same time, both countries also did their best to enact needed social reforms and to maintain at least a limited form of democracy.

Brazil. Like other Latin American countries, during the Great Depression Brazil had turned to a conservative dictatorship to provide stable government in troubled times. In 1930, as the economic crisis worsened, Getúlio Vargas had led a military coup and had taken control of Brazil's federal government. Appealing to Brazilians' nationalist sentiments, Vargas managed to prevent any serious opposition from developing until 1945. In fact, he became a highly popular dictator.

Pursuing a policy of economic nationalism, Vargas instituted an ambitious program of industrialization and modernization. Although his plan to create official government unions favored business, he tried to appeal to labor leaders and workers by supporting wage increases. He also enacted new social legislation to guarantee workers health benefits, pensions, and paid vacations.

Vargas's successors, particularly President Juscelino Kubitschek (KOO-buh-chek), continued many of these policies of modernization and industrial development. In the late 1950s Kubitschek borrowed heavily from foreign banks to fund further economic growth and to build a splendid new capital called Brasília. Kubitschek also continued Vargas's efforts to shift power from state governments and centralize it in the federal government.

Mexico. Like Brazil, Mexico emerged from World War II determined to establish its economic independence. Unlike Brazil, however, Mexico had undergone a complete political and social revolution before the war. In 1910 a variety of reformers and revolutionaries had banded together against the elitist rule of the authoritarian dictator Porfirio Diaz. In 1917 the revolution had resulted in a new constitution, but fighting continued among the various groups that had

SECTION 2

CORE LESSON PLAN
See pages 799E and 799F for Lesson Plan 29.2.

Theme:
The Arts
Under Kubitschek the Brazilian government fostered a new sense of national pride through architecture. He ordered the building of a new capital city in the interior of Brazil. Brasília was opened in 1960. Kubitschek hoped that the new capital would open up Brazil's interior to further economic development. The city was a model of modern architecture, with gleaming futuristic buildings that inspired admiration and enthusiasm outside Brazil.

Critical Thinking Ask students how this new city would foster a sense of national pride in Brazil.

ANSWER: Students should reply that the progressive look of the capital would give Brazilians a sense of pride in their progress.

deposed Diaz. Nevertheless, the constitution was a major achievement. In addition to providing for universal suffrage, it also mandated major land reforms, established public education, guaranteed benefits for workers, and created rules that strictly controlled and limited foreign capital investment in Mexico.

The constitution was not fully enacted, however, until Lázaro Cárdenas, a revolutionary general and the son of poor parents, was elected president in 1934. Cárdenas launched a program of massive land redistribution, industrial development, and road construction. He also limited the power of the Catholic Church in an effort to prevent conservative bishops and priests from interfering in politics. In politics Cárdenas reorganized the ruling party, known then as the Party of the Mexican Revolution but later renamed the **Institutional Revolutionary Party**, or PRI.

As in Brazil, the Mexican government backed many private businesspeople and helped finance factories to produce the manufactured goods Mexico needed to become economically self-sufficient. Also like Brazil, this pro-business policy in Mexico went hand in hand with efforts to support labor. In 1938, for example, when Mexican unions were engaged in a bitter labor dispute with foreign oil companies, Cárdenas promptly nationalized the foreign-owned oil industry.

Cárdenas's successors pursued similar policies of economic and industrial development, though with less emphasis on social programs. These leaders also threw the weight of the government behind national development schemes. They invested heavily in state-run enterprises and private business development. With such policies

▲ Lázaro Cárdenas carried out promises of reform and ensured Mexico's stability.

the Mexican economy grew at a substantial rate in the 1950s and 1960s. During the period from 1940 to 1970, the percentage of the Mexican population living in cities more than doubled. Since Mexico's growing wealth remained largely in the hands of the upper classes, most of Mexico's growing population continued to suffer from widespread poverty.

After World War II both Brazil and Mexico pursued policies of economic nationalism and moderate social reform.

The Radicals and Cuba

Although other countries, such as Argentina and Chile, tried to follow the example of Mexico and Brazil, the outbreak of revolution in Cuba in the late 1950s transformed Latin American politics. Cuba was the first country where radicals succeeded in gaining full control of the government.

The seeds of revolution. A beautiful Caribbean island, Cuba was a land of contrasts before 1959. In rural areas enormous sugar plantations produced several million tons of sugar each year. Smaller tobacco farms grew the best tobacco in the world. Havana, the glittering capital, looked out over the clear blue waters of the Gulf of Mexico. Havana was also one of the most developed cities of Latin America. Literacy rates, life expectancy, and the ratio of doctors per thousand individuals, for example, were higher in Havana than in nearly any other Latin American city.

Yet before 1959 Cuba was also home to millions of poor people. In the countryside they were the cane cutters, who had reliable work only three months of the year when they cut the sugar crop. In the cities they lived in filthy slums. They also lived under a dictatorship, which had overthrown democracy in Cuba. As middle-class reformers and university students sought a return to democracy, and peasants began to demand better working and living conditions, radicals began to call for revolution.

One of the loudest of these radicals was the bearded revolutionary, Fidel Castro. Castro was an unlikely revolutionary, however. Born in 1926, he was the son of a wealthy landowner. His father, an immigrant from Spain, had made his own fortune by building a sugar estate with some 500 workers. Educated by the Jesuits, Castro later studied law at the University of Havana. Like many other lawyers, he planned to enter politics. In 1952 Castro presented himself as a candidate of the Orthodox Party for the Cuban Congress. His Congressional ambitions were soon destroyed, however, when the Cuban dictator, Fulgencio Batista, returned to power.

In 1933 Batista had led a coup within the Cuban military. He then became an important political figure and was elected president in 1940. In 1944, when Batista's candidate for president was defeated in the elections, Batista retired from politics and left Cuba. It was not long before he returned, however. Three months before the 1952 elections, a military coup restored Batista to power, and he postponed the elections.

Castro committed himself to the resistance that soon sprang up against the dictator. In late 1956 he initiated guerrilla warfare against the Batista government—carrying out hit-and-run raids and bombing attacks and burning sugar fields. Batista responded with brutal measures that only fueled opposition to his government. Eventually, as his support evaporated, Batista once again fled the country in 1959. A schoolgirl described the scene as the victorious Castro led the guerrillas into Havana:

66 Out in the street all the cars were flying pennants, people sang and whistled, strangers embraced each other, and everybody was shouting, 'Viva Cuba libre!' [Long live free Cuba!]. . . . On the day of Fidel's triumphal entry into Havana, I finally saw the barbudos, the bearded, long-haired fighters of the Sierra Maestra I had so longed to see. To me . . . the revolutionaries seemed like legendary heroes. 99

Cuba under Castro. After Batista's fall Castro and his fellow guerrillas quickly took control of the country. In 1959 and early 1960, Castro addressed mass rallies in order to gain popular support for his policies. Instead of calling for new elections as everyone expected, however, the

▲ Huge crowds welcome Fidel Castro upon his arrival in the town of Cienfuegos, Cuba.

Fidel Castro
BIOGRAPHY

new revolutionary elite became more radical. In 1960 Castro seized all properties in Cuba owned by U.S. companies or U.S. citizens. During that year he also seized all major Cuban-owned businesses and millions of acres of land.

Alarmed by these developments, many Cubans made plans to leave the country. Some had already fled—the first wave had gone with Batista, followed shortly thereafter by many wealthy Cubans. But when members of Cuba's upper-middle class also began to abandon the island, thousands of other people followed. Doctors, lawyers, small businessowners, farmers, teachers—even some who had originally supported the revolution—joined the Cuban exile community in Florida. By 1962 some 200,000 Cubans left the island.

In December 1961 Castro finally declared what many already knew: he was a Communist. Castro proclaimed that Cuba's future would be linked to the Soviet Union. Cuba joined the Soviet bloc and became part of the Soviet sphere of influence. Soon Castro turned Cuba into a base for launching other Marxist revolutions in Latin America.

The success of the Cuban Revolution led to the establishment of a communist dictatorship that encouraged revolution throughout Latin America.

BIOGRAPHY
Fidel Castro
It was not until after he graduated from the University of Havana that Castro's commitment to communism became apparent. A turning point in his life occurred in 1948 in Bogotá, Colombia, when a popular leftist politician, Jorge Eliecer Gaitan, was assassinated. For two days, the entire city rioted in reaction. Eventually, as the mobs took over the city, the authorities fled.

In 1953 Castro and his brother Raul led a small band of idealistic youths in an assault on an army barracks in Santiago, Cuba. The attack failed, and the Castros were subsequently imprisoned. Freed after 11 months, Fidel fled Cuba for Mexico, where he began to organize a revolutionary force. In 1956 Fidel and his brother, together with another Marxist revolutionary, "Che" Guevara, returned to Cuba. From a remote mountain base, the young guerrillas organized resistance against Batista—eventually forcing the dictator to flee.

Critical Thinking Ask students why the assassination and riots in Colombia might have been a turning point for Castro.

ANSWER: Students may answer that the riots showed Castro the power that large groups of people had to affect the government.

Revolution and Reaction

The fall of Cuba to Communist revolutionaries sent shock waves throughout Latin America and the United States. In an effort to isolate Cuba's Communist government, the United States convinced members of the **Organization of American States** (OAS) to refuse to recognize the new Cuban government. The OAS is a body that was founded in 1948 to promote cooperation among the various countries of the Western Hemisphere. Only Mexico, in an effort to demonstrate its independence from U.S. influence, maintained ties with the new Cuban dictatorship.

The Cuban threat. Isolated by surrounding countries, Castro quickly came to rely on the Soviet Union for economic and military aid. He also adopted the basic elements of a Soviet-style economy, including collectivized farms, state-owned factories and industry, and political principles designed to create a new "Socialist personality" among Cubans. Castro's government also began to spread its message of violent revolution throughout the Caribbean region and into South America.

Alarmed by the threat of Communist revolution, throughout Latin America conservative governments reacted by cracking down on anything even remotely revolutionary. After nearly 20 years of economic progress and steady movement toward greater democracy, a new period of authoritarian rule descended over most of Latin America.

The conservatives and Brazil. In 1964, for example, the Brazilian military deposed the elected president of Brazil, João Goulart. The military distrusted Goulart because they believed he was sympathetic to left-wing causes. Other groups in Brazil also distrusted him and were not entirely sorry to see him go. Many Brazilians, however, expected the military to act as it had on previous occasions—to serve as a caretaker during the remainder of Goulart's term and then to hold new presidential elections. Instead, the generals created a military dictatorship. They suspended all democratic institutions and ruled the country by decree.

Marcio Moreira Alves, a Brazilian citizen, later described

Democratic Transition in South America, 1975-1995

Elected civilian government, 1975

Date of transition from military to civilian rule:
- 1976–1980
- 1981–1985
- 1986–1990
- 1991–1995

⊛ National capital

CARIBBEAN SEA
Caracas
VENEZUELA
GUYANA
Georgetown
Paramaribo
Cayenne
SURINAME
FRENCH GUIANA (Fr.)
Bogotá
COLOMBIA
ATLANTIC OCEAN
0° Equator
Quito
ECUADOR
Amazon River
PERU
Lima
BRAZIL
La Paz
BOLIVIA
Brasília
Sucre
20°S
PARAGUAY
Asunción
PACIFIC OCEAN
ARGENTINA
URUGUAY
Santiago
Montevideo
CHILE
Buenos Aires
Río de la Plata
40°S
0   400   800 Miles
0   400   800 Kilometers
Modified Chamberlin Trimetric Projection
100°W   80°W   60°W   40°W   20°W
N W E S
FALKLAND IS. (Br.)

From Military to Civilian Rule During the postwar period, South American countries witnessed social upheavals and a series of military coups. By the 1990s, however, elected civilian governments dominated the continent.

◆ Linking Geography and History Which South American nations most recently elected civilian governments?

▲ After the coup that ousted him in 1964, the former Brazilian president João Goulart arrived in Uruguay.

his reaction to the earliest of the new decrees, known as the first Institutional Act. "My liberal sympathies and legal training were shocked," he wrote, "by what I then considered the most arbitrary law ever enacted in the history of Brazil." A second Institutional Act abolished all existing political parties and the direct election of the Brazilian president. It was the fifth Institutional Act, signed in 1968, however, that clearly revealed the transformation of Brazil from a democratic state into a dictatorship. Once again, Alves was shocked at the news:

66 Crowded around the radio in the kitchen of a suburban home in São Paulo, we listened to the Minister of Justice. It was close to midnight, December 13, 1968, a Friday. His high-pitched voice, heralded by the trumpet blasts that the propagandists of the Brazilian military dictatorship so favor, was putting an end to an awkward political period. . . . One by one the rules were spelled out. On our silent faces . . . fell the juridical [legal] jargon, killing what guarantees of political and human rights still existed in Brazil. Congress was shut down. Habeas corpus for political prisoners was rescinded [taken away]. The military could rule by decree, arrest whom they pleased, abolish political rights and electoral posts. Their acts could not be examined by the courts. 99

With criticism silenced and democratic institutions disbanded, the military believed it had protected Brazil from communism.

Argentina. Other countries soon followed the Brazilian pattern. In Argentina the military rulers had already removed the populist leader General Juan Perón. Always suspicious of his appeal to the labor unions and urban workers, in 1955 a successful military coup forced Perón into exile. Although the military soon restored civilian government and regular elections, 11 years later the army intervened once again. This time military rule lasted much longer. After a brief restoration of civilian rule in the 1970s, the army once again took control of the country in 1976. With each round of intervention, the level of repression increased until Argentina finally emerged in the early 1980s as a full-scale military dictatorship.

Chile. Perhaps the best example of how far conservatives would go to fight the threat of communism occurred in Chile. Like other Latin American countries, Chile pursued nationalist economic policies in the years following World War II. Throughout the 1950s and 1960s, the country remained relatively democratic and pursued not only economic development and modernization but also moderate social reforms. Chile's primary problem was inflation caused by government overspending and excessive printing of money.

In 1970, however, Salvador Allende, a self-proclaimed Marxist leading a group of left-wing parties, was elected president of Chile in open elections. The various antisocialist candidates received more than 60 percent of the votes combined, while Allende had gained about 36 percent of the vote. However, with the largest single percentage of votes, Allende was the winner.

Despite the fact that his victory clearly did not reflect the desires of the majority, under pressure from his more revolutionary followers Allende lost little time in enacting a Marxist

THROUGH OTHERS' EYES

A North American Views the Falklands War

In the spring of 1982, Argentina seized the Falkland Islands, a group of islands about 300 miles off the Argentinean coast in the South Atlantic. Great Britain had held the islands, which Argentina claimed under the name of Islas Malvinas, since before Argentinean independence from Spain. The islands' inhabitants, descendants of the original British colonists of the 1800s, called for help from Britain. In response, British prime minister Margaret Thatcher ordered a British fleet to retake the Falklands. World opinion divided over the crisis. In the United States, conservative commentator George Will wrote:

6 6 Little crises have ways of growing, faster than you can say 'Sarajevo.'. . . And what a stimulating lot of disputes there can be if Argentina's 'repossession' principle becomes an infectious precedent [previous example]. . . . Argentina has declared, in effect, that there is no statute of limitations on historical grievances, or at least none on grievances that are only 149 years old. So dust off a 19th-century globe and let's reopen every dispute, from Schleswig-Holstein through . . . well, Heads Up, Texas. Manifest Destiny had its messy aspects. **9 9**

platform. He nationalized industries and forced the breakup of many large estates. His more radical supporters went even further and began to set up workers' committees to take control of factories and peasant councils to seize land in the countryside. The Socialist Party, one of the groups on Allende's side, proclaimed its intentions openly: "The task of the moment is to destroy parliament." Such sentiments angered and frightened many Chileans.

Allende was unable to control the more extreme radicals that had come to power with him. They began to arm themselves, raising the threat of a full-scale bloody revolution. Meanwhile, Allende's socialist policies, combined with the oil crisis of the 1970s, plunged the economy into turmoil. Within a year of taking office, he had to stop payments on the national debt. Inflation soared from about 23 percent when he took office in January 1971 to about 190 percent by the summer of 1973—the highest in the world at the time. As violence and economic disaster loomed, one of Allende's own military appointments, General Augusto Pinochet, led the armed forces in a bloody coup against the government. As many as 15,000 people died, including Allende.

Pinochet established a full military dictatorship, brutally crushing all opposition. He then set out to restore Chile's economic prosperity by reinstituting a free-market, capitalist economy. His plans benefited from the end of the oil crisis. So effective was his program that by 1980 a World Bank report noted:

6 6 Under extra-ordinarily unfavorable circumstances, the Chilean authorities have engineered an economic turnaround without precedent [previous example] in the history of Chile. **9 9**

Although for a time Pinochet's dictatorship was almost popular, as prosperity continued to grow in the 1980s people became more anxious for a restoration of democracy.

Movements Toward Democracy

The Chileans were not alone. By the 1980s people throughout Latin America had grown tired of both Marxist revolution and conservative authoritarianism. Bolivia, Peru, and Ecuador re-established democratic governments after years of military control. Brazil restored civilian rule in 1985. In Chile free elections were held at the end of 1989. When the opposition candidate, Patricio Aylwin, was elected president, General Pinochet stepped down—though he remained in command of the army.

In Argentina military rule led to radical resistance in the late 1960s as a Marxist guerrilla movement emerged. Juan Perón briefly returned to power in the early 1970s, but died before he could put his intended economic and social reforms into practice or deal effectively with the rebels. The army once again assumed power, this time determined to put an end to the guerrilla war once and for all. In what the military called a "holy war," but others called the "dirty war," thousands of citizens were arrested and imprisoned for expressing antigovernment views. Many were tortured. As many as 20,000—known as the *desaparecidos*, or "disappeared"—simply vanished, never again to be seen alive.

Although the revolutionaries were put down, the brutality weakened public support for the **junta**, or ruling military government. To regain support, in 1982 the junta launched an invasion of the British-held Falkland Islands in the South Atlantic. Argentina had claimed the islands since 1820. Much to the generals' surprise, the British chose to fight for the Falklands, all of whose inhabitants were British. After a short campaign, a small but well-trained British force soundly defeated the Argentines and recaptured the islands. Discredited by this failure, in 1983 the junta allowed free elections.

Few of those responsible for the torture and murder of civilians during the military junta were ever brought to trial. Plagued by continuing economic problems, the new civilian governments that followed the junta preferred not to

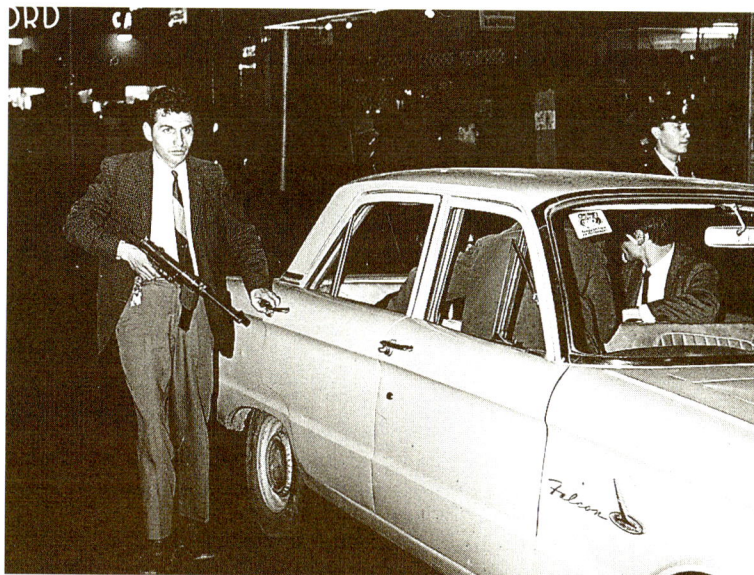

▲ The Argentine secret police carry out an assignment in the streets of Buenos Aires in 1972.

risk yet another military coup. In 1989 Carlos Menem, the Parónista Party candidate, was elected president. Eventually, he pardoned all but a few of those found guilty of crimes during military rule. Many resented this action, however, particularly the relatives of the *desaparecidos*, who still hoped for justice for the victims of the junta.

After years of authoritarian government and military dictatorship, by the 1990s many countries in Latin America had established fragile democracies.

SECTION 2 REVIEW

IDENTIFY and explain the significance of the following:
  Juscelino Kubitschek
  Lázaro Cárdenas
  Institutional Revolutionary Party
  Fidel Castro
  Fulgencio Batista
  Organization of American States
  Salvador Allende
  Augusto Pinochet
  junta

1. *Main Idea* How did Brazilian and Mexican leaders try to solve their nations' problems after World War II?
2. *Main Idea* What effects did the Cuban Revolution of 1959 have on Cuba and other Latin American countries?
3. *Politics and Law* What political developments had Latin American nations made by the 1990s?

4. *Writing to Describe* Imagine that you are a newspaper reporter in Havana in 1959. Write an article describing the revolution and the goals of the revolutionaries.
5. *Analyzing* Why do you think so many people left Cuba during the revolution of 1959? What might have happened to these people if they had remained?

SECTION 3

CORE LESSON PLAN
See pages 799G and
799H for Lesson Plan
29.3.

Theme:
Economic Organization

During the 1960s more than 1 million Cuban refugees fled for the United States. In part the flight was fueled by Castro's economic policies—which soon destroyed the Cuban economy. According to some estimates, by 1981 the Cuban economy under Castro had experienced an annual per capita growth rate of negative 1.2 percent, even as it became the second-largest military power in Latin America.

Critical Thinking Ask students how Cuba's military buildup may have hurt the economy.

ANSWER: Students should reply that money spent on the military might have been spent on developing new industries.

SECTION 3
Revolution and Democracy in Latin America

FOCUS

- Why did the United States often support opposition movements in Central America?

- What was the political situation throughout most of Central America by the early 1990s?

- What problems did Mexico continue to face after 1945?

*L*atin American radicals, reformers, and conservatives did not debate the future alone. Before World War II, U.S. businesses had expanded throughout Latin America. As part of its Good Neighbor policy, the U.S. government had provided economic aid and had helped Latin American countries develop their militaries. After the war the U.S. government became deeply involved in Latin American politics in an effort to protect American investments, prevent the spread of communism, and encourage democratic reforms.

Cuban forces repel the Bay of Pigs invasion force.

The Cold War and Latin America

After World War II the foremost foreign policy goal of the United States was to rebuild Western Europe in order to counterbalance the growing power of the Soviet Union. Cold War concerns also affected U.S. relations with Latin America. Worried that the Soviets would encourage revolutions in Latin America in order to spread communism, the United States grew to distrust Latin American reformers. In the eyes of many Americans, many of these reformers seemed "soft" on communism.

Cuba. As the Cuban Revolution became more radical in 1960 and 1961, relations between the United States and Cuba worsened rapidly. The U.S. government protested the nationalization of American-owned property in Cuba. The growing power of Communists in the revolutionary government led both President Dwight D. Eisenhower and his successor, President John F. Kennedy, to authorize a **covert**, or secret, operation against Fidel Castro. In Miami, the U.S. Central Intelligence Agency had no trouble recruiting Cuban exiles to join an invasion force. However, because the Cuban people did not rally support for the force and President Kennedy was unwilling to back the rebels, Castro defeated the invasion force at the so-called **Bay of Pigs** in April 1961.

American embarrassment over the Bay of Pigs was soon overshadowed by the more dangerous Cuban missile crisis. As part of the compromise that ended the crisis, President Kennedy promised that the United States would not invade Cuba. This promise did not stop Kennedy and later U.S. presidents, however, from attempting to isolate Cuba from the rest of the Americas through an economic boycott. The boycott prevented any U.S. company or individual from engaging in business ventures with Cuba. Through the Organization of American States, the United States asked other Latin American nations to boycott Cuba as well.

Nicaragua. Despite the boycott, American fears that Cuba would inspire and support revolution throughout the region were soon justified. Perhaps the most successful revolutionary movement in the Caribbean region outside Cuba occurred in

Nicaragua. By 1979 a coalition of groups ranging from moderate reformers to radical revolutionaries known as the **Sandinistas** had risen in revolt against the corrupt and oppressive dictator Anastasio Somoza. As Somoza fled with his family, the Sandinistas took control of the government.

The Sandinistas, under the leadership of Daniel Ortega, were unable to enact policies that would please the widely varied anti-Somoza coalition. Instead, Ortega and his colleagues established close ties with Cuba and moved Nicaragua more toward communism, angering many coalition members. The United States also opposed the Marxist Sandinistas, seeing them as friendly to both the Soviet Union and Cuba. Under President Ronald Reagan the United States imposed an embargo on Nicaragua and did its best to destabilize the Sandinista government.

Eventually, Eden Pastora, a former Sandinista leader, organized a new guerrilla group—the **contras**—to overthrow the Sandinistas. The United States supported the group with arms and money. Even after the U.S. Congress cut off funds for the contras in 1984, hidden aid continued to flow from sources within the Reagan administration.

Like Cuba under Castro, the Sandinistas supported revolutions occurring in neighboring countries. For example, the Sandinistas aided radical guerrilla groups that were challenging the conservative government in neighboring El Salvador. Soon Honduras was also affected by the unrest in Nicaragua. The United States responded by providing massive military and financial aid to transform Honduras into a base for contra activities.

Central America and the Caribbean, 1980s

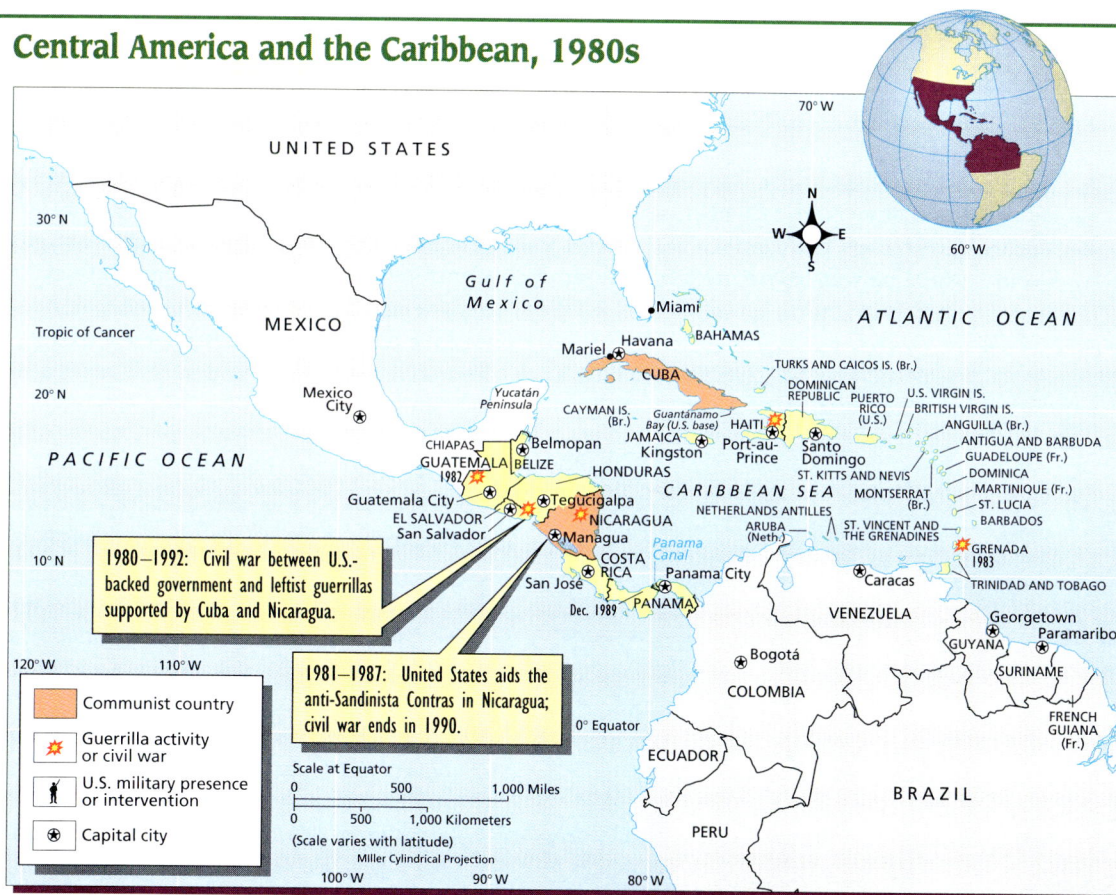

1980–1992: Civil war between U.S.-backed government and leftist guerrillas supported by Cuba and Nicaragua.

1981–1987: United States aids the anti-Sandinista Contras in Nicaragua; civil war ends in 1990.

Scale at Equator
0   500   1,000 Miles
0   500   1,000 Kilometers
(Scale varies with latitude)
Miller Cylindrical Projection

- Communist country
- Guerrilla activity or civil war
- U.S. military presence or intervention
- Capital city

A New Wave of Conflict   Political instability and Cold War tensions brought civil war and military interventions to Central America and the Caribbean in the 1980s.

? Location   Which countries did the United States invade or send troops to during the 1980s?

Map Answer

Honduras, Panama, and Grenada

RESOURCE ACTIVITY

READINGS IN WORLD HISTORY
Reading 29.3
Conflict in Nicaragua

Have students read the description of the activities of the contras. Then have students complete the questions.

Level 2

RESOURCE ACTIVITY

GLOBAL HISTORY RESOURCE CENTER
Image: *The Face of War in El Salvador*

Show students the image as you discuss the spread of revolution from Nicaragua to El Salvador. Ask students to use this picture as a basis for a newspaper headline and picture caption that will describe how they think Latin American governments should respond to the violence.

Level 1/ Sheltered English

Panama. Growing political unrest also affected nearby Panama. After 1945 Panama experienced the same pattern of economic growth and political turmoil as its neighbors. The most burning question in Panamanian politics, however, concerned Panamanian demands for full control over the Panama Canal. Both the canal and the 10-mile-wide Canal Zone surrounding it remained in the hands of the United States. Despite strong opposition from many in the United States, the U.S. Senate ratified a treaty in 1978 that called for the gradual transfer of the canal to the Panamanians by 1999.

During the late 1980s, another dispute between the United States and Panama had arisen. Many U.S. officials accused the Panamanian dictator, General Manuel Noriega, of helping Colombian drug lords smuggle their narcotics into the United States. President Reagan tried to pressure Noriega into resigning. When this failed, the United States cut off all aid, both military and economic, to Panama. When Panamanian soldiers killed one American soldier and detained and beat another in 1989, President George Bush ordered U.S. troops to invade Panama and capture Noriega. The invasion was a success, and Noriega was captured and taken to Florida, where he was later convicted and sentenced to 40 years in prison for drug trafficking.

▲ Federal agents arrested Manuel Noriega on charges of drug trafficking and took him to Florida to stand trial.

Fearful of Cuba's spreading influence, the United States supported anticommunist movements in Central America.

The Contadora Principles

As violence continued to rock Central America, the larger nations of the region began to search for some means of restoring peace. In 1983 the leaders of Venezuela, Panama, Colombia, and Mexico met on the island of Contadora and negotiated a peace for their region without the intervention of the United States. The principles they agreed upon, known as the **Contadora Principles**, called for an immediate freeze on arms sales and general military reductions throughout the region. In addition, the agreement called for negotiations rather than violence to settle all regional disputes.

Calls for peace and democracy. In 1987 representatives from all the Central American countries met in Guatemala City for a regional peace conference. During the conference, Oscar Arias, president of Costa Rica—one of the few economically and politically stable nations in Central America—presented a comprehensive plan designed to bring peace to the region.

Like other reformers, Arias saw a strong connection between peace and the growth of democracy. In addition to calling for negotiated peace settlements to end all fighting in the region, he proposed an end to all foreign aid for rebel groups. Arias also called for substantial democratic reforms in all countries fighting against rebel groups:

66 *The democracy in which many American nations live today cannot be consolidated without economic development and social justice. Before any political or economic conditions can be imposed on the democracies of the Americas, there must be a commitment from the Western world to strengthen democracy in all our nations. In the Americas, peace must be democratic, pluralistic, tolerant, and free. While dogmatism [stubborn opinions] and intransigence [stubbornness] persist and there is no dialogue, peace will be impossible. Working together for democracy, freedom, and development is working together for peace.* 99

▲ In December 1987 Costa Rican president Oscar Arias accepted the Nobel Peace Prize in Sweden.

Costa Rica, El Salvador, Honduras, Guatemala, and the United States supported Arias's proposals. In 1987 Arias received the Nobel Peace Prize for his efforts. Not until the early 1990s, however, did peace seem at hand in Central America.

New leadership. Because of great internal changes in the Soviet Union, Cubans and other revolutionaries could no longer depend on the Soviets for economic support. This meant that the level of violence in the region finally decreased. In 1990 Daniel Ortega agreed to new elections and the return of democratic rule to Nicaragua. Ortega peacefully gave up power when the people elected Violeta Chamorro as president.

Violeta Barrios de Chamorro was born in 1929 into a wealthy ranching family in the Nicaraguan town of Rivas. In 1950 she married Pedro Chamorro, a member of one of Nicaragua's leading families. As editor of *La Prensa*, his family's newspaper, Pedro Chamorro was an outspoken critic of the Somoza dictatorship. Often imprisoned and sometimes even exiled for his anti-Somoza views, he was assassinated in 1978, probably by government agents. Chamorro's

Violeta Barrios de Chamorro
BIOGRAPHY

murder sparked the revolution that brought down Somoza.

As Pedro Chamorro's widow, Violeta Chamorro took a leading role in the struggle against Somoza. She initially supported the Sandinistas. After Somoza's flight in 1979, for example, she was one of the five members of the ruling government that took power. As the Sandinistas turned more toward communism, however, Chamorro became disillusioned with the movement. Eventually, she resigned from the government and took over the editorship of *La Prensa*.

Although members of her own family, including some of her children, remained Sandinista supporters, by 1989 Chamorro had emerged as the leading opposition candidate to Daniel Ortega. In 1990 she won the election, becoming Nicaragua's first female president and a symbol of the triumph of democracy. Despite continuing tensions between the Sandinistas and the new government, democracy finally seemed to have arrived in Nicaragua.

In El Salvador the government and the radical guerrilla group FMLN—under pressure from the United States, Russia, and Mexico—also came to tentative agreement on constitutional reforms. Even Panama began the new decade under a democratic government made up of anti-Noriega parties. Although the new government did not last long, Panamanians seemed committed at last to maintaining democracy rather than returning to the path of military dictatorship.

In the early 1990s, after years of political instability and violence, many Central American countries moved toward democracy and peace.

Mexico

Even Mexico, the largest and most stable country in Latin America, could not escape some unrest. In 1968, for example, numerous confrontations occurred between radical student protesters and the police. The students hoped to bring about greater openness in the political system. The largest of these demonstrations ended in bloodshed when Mexican troops fired into a crowd that refused to disband in the plaza of Tlatelolco in Mexico City. Hundreds of students died in the hail of bullets. The government carried out similar hard-line tactics against a radical guerrilla campaign begun in 1971 to destroy Mexico's democracy. The government hunted down and killed or imprisoned the rebels, and by the end of the decade the threat of revolution had practically disappeared.

Economic problems. Despite its relative political stability, Mexico, like other Latin American countries, suffered economic problems after World War II. The discovery of huge oil reserves in the 1970s made the future seem considerably brighter, however. The nation's earnings from oil skyrocketed from about $500 million in 1976 to some $13 billion in 1981. The government used these revenues to raise large development loans. When oil prices slumped in the 1980s, however, economic disaster loomed. Compounding Mexico's problems, a devastating earthquake in 1985 leveled parts of Mexico City, leaving tens of thousands of people homeless. The costs of rebuilding expanded the national debt. In 1987 Mexico's annual inflation rate rose to 132 percent, and by 1990 its foreign debt was near $100 billion.

In the face of these economic challenges, the Mexican government began to loosen many of the controls it had placed on the national economy. Under President Carlos Salinas de Gortari, who took office in 1988, the government began to negotiate free-trade agreements with Mexico's major trading partners. Salinas also began to permit foreign ownership of Mexican businesses and to sell off the government's own extensive business holdings in an effort to encourage investment in the country. Salinas pushed hard for ratification of the **North American Free Trade Agreement**, or NAFTA, which established a free-trade zone with the United States and Canada. Nevertheless, by the mid-1990s economic pressures forced the Mexican government to devalue the peso, the Mexican currency, further weakening confidence in the Mexican economy.

Crossing the border. As Mexico's economy faltered and jobs became more scarce, many Mexicans, like Latin Americans from farther south, looked for jobs in the United States. Thousands began to cross the border into the United States—some legally, but many more illegally—in search of work.

As tensions rose between the United States and Mexico over the illegal immigration issue, in 1986 the U.S. Congress passed the Immigration Reform and Control Act. The act gave legal status to immigrants who had entered the United States illegally before January 1, 1982. The act also tried to restrict further illegal immigration by requiring U.S. employers to check all job applicants for their residency status. Meanwhile, both the Mexican government and the U.S. government hoped that efforts to improve Mexico's own economy would reduce the flow of illegal immigrants into the United States.

◀ Oil, Mexico's greatest natural resource, is found in deposits along the coast of the Gulf of Mexico from Tampico to Campeche.

▲ In Tijuana, Mexico, a group of would-be immigrants waits for nightfall to cross the fence into the United States.

Signs of the PRI's weakened position came in the elections of 1988. Many opposition leaders claimed that the PRI had resorted to fraud to win the election. In 1994 the country was shocked when the PRI's initial candidate for the presidency, Luís Donaldo Colosio Murrieta, a reform-minded politician, was assassinated. Even more shocking was the suggestion that hard-line conservative elements in the PRI were responsible for the murder. Nevertheless, the PRI's second-choice candidate, Ernesto Zedillo Ponce de León, was elected president with just over 50 percent of the vote.

The position of the PRI was also challenged by events in the southeastern state of Chiapas. There, a new revolutionary guerrilla group calling itself the Zapatista National Liberation Army emerged in early 1994 to challenge government control of the region. The rebels claimed to represent the interests of the local Maya population. After some fighting, eventually the government agreed to talks with the rebels. The rebels demanded economic reforms to improve conditions in Chiapas and greater protection and self-rule for the Maya population of the region. They also demanded greater democracy, not only in Chiapas but for all of Mexico.

Echoes of political instability. The problems of the 1980s and early 1990s had political consequences for the PRI. Increasing numbers of people became displeased by the corruption in the PRI. Many people began to join opposition parties, demanding truly democratic elections and an end to one-party rule.

Although Mexico remained relatively stable after World War II, the country faced many economic and social problems.

SECTION 3 REVIEW

IDENTIFY and explain the significance of the following:
  covert
  Bay of Pigs
  Sandinistas
  contras
  Contadora Principles
  Violeta Chamorro
  North American Free Trade
    Agreement

1. **Main Idea** How had the political situation changed in much of Central America by the 1990s?
2. **Main Idea** What were some of the problems that faced Mexico after World War II?
3. **War and Diplomacy** What political movements did the United States support in Central America? Why did the United States offer its support to these movements?
4. **Writing to Persuade** In a short essay explain why the United States has or has not been justified in its involvement in Central America since 1945.
5. **Synthesizing** What are some of the political problems Latin American nations have faced since 1945? Give some specific examples to support your answer.

SECTION 4

CORE LESSON PLAN
See pages 799I and 799J for Lesson Plan 29.4.

INTERNET ACTIVITY

HUMAN RIGHTS ORGANIZATIONS

Throughout the world human rights organizations have provided information about human rights violations and have organized protests.

Activity: Ask students to search the Web for information about different human rights organizations. [**Note:** some sites may contain graphic material.] Have each student compare the goals, methods, and successes of at least two different human rights organizations. Ask students to report back to the class on what they found and lead the class in a discussion of how best to protect human rights around the world.

All Levels

Problems of Culture and Society

FOCUS

- How have some Latin American countries violated their citizens' human rights?

- What has been done to end human rights violations in some Latin American countries?

- What themes inspire Latin American artists and writers?

The Cold War set the political Left and Right against each other within Latin America, leaving little room for compromise. As a result, violations of basic human rights increased in many Latin American countries after World War II. In light of these problems, Latin American writers and artists have increasingly used their work to address the basic problems their countries face. In addressing such local issues, these artists have created new styles that have influenced cultures around the world.

Struggle of the Classes, mural painted by Diego Rivera in Mexico City

The Struggle for Human Rights

Perhaps the most immediate social challenge Latin Americans faced since World War II has been the lack of basic human rights in many of their countries. Such basic rights include freedom of expression, freedom of association, due process of law in legal matters, and equality before the law. In the Universal Declaration of Human Rights accepted by the United Nations in 1948, member nations committed themselves to respecting such human rights. Similar documents have also been adopted by regional associations.

In Latin America, for example, the Organization of American States adopted the American Convention on Human Rights in 1969. The convention guaranteed 26 basic political and civil rights and freedoms, including the right to humane treatment, a fair trial, participation in government, freedom of conscience, freedom of thought, and freedom of association. The convention also created the Inter-American Commission on Human Rights to monitor violations of human rights in the countries that signed the treaty. Nevertheless, violations of human rights have remained widespread in many Latin American nations into the 1990s.

Guatemala. One of the worst human rights records in Latin America belongs to Guatemala. **Amnesty International**, an agency that monitors human rights violations, has estimated that between 1966 and 1974 there were 20,000 victims of political violence in Guatemala. In the 1980s, when radical guerrilla groups took refuge among the Indians in remote mountains, the military sent soldiers to occupy Indian villages. Indian men, women, and children began to disappear and later turned up dead in mass graves. Tens of thousands of Guatemalan Indians fled to Mexico looking for safety. The situation had improved somewhat by the late 1980s. The Inter-American Commission on Human Rights of the OAS, however, concluded in 1989: "In order for human rights to be adequately protected in Guatemala the military and police must be subordinated to [under the control of] the judicial authorities."

Cuba. Despite its talk of equality and concern for the plight of the poor, following the revolution

Literature THROUGH TIME

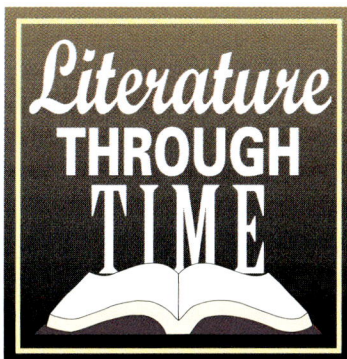

Magic Realism

In recent decades Latin American literature has enchanted readers with a style known as magic realism. According to the Latin American writer Gabriel García Márquez, magic realism allows his readers to view reality in new ways: "Every single line . . . in all my books, has a starting point in reality. I provide a magnifying glass so readers can understand reality better." Magical scenes in García Márquez's writings are not meant to be taken literally. García Márquez explains:

> ❝ I have the character Ulises make glass change color every time he touches it. Now, that can't be true. But so much has already been said about love that I had to find a new way of saying that this boy is in love. So I have the colors of the glass change, and I have his mother say, 'Those things happen only because of love. . . . Who is it?' Mine is just another way of saying the same thing that has always been said about love: how it upsets life, how it upsets everything. ❞

Magic realism has influenced other Latin American writers, such as Isabel Allende. In her book *The House of the Spirits*, Allende uses magic realism to explore the effects of political conflict on the members of a family. Dead ancestors continue to haunt their family's house and grant their children the power to alter reality.

In addition, ideas from magic realism have influenced writers around the world. Congolese writer Sony Labou Tansi mixes magical and realistic elements to create complicated fables about African politics and life. In *Kangaroo Notebook*, Japanese writer Abe Kobo has radish sprouts grow out of a character's body. Russian author Andrey Donatovich Sinyavsky creates a character in his novel *The Makepeace Experiment*

who uses magic to hoodwink Russian villagers. North American writers too have been influenced by magic realism. In her book *Beloved*, Nobel Prize–winning author Toni Morrison combines a realistic story of the horrors of slavery with a fantastic ghost story.

Understanding Literature

1. What is magic realism?
2. Why do authors around the world use magic realism in their writing?

BESTSELLER INTERNACIONAL

ISABEL ALLENDE

LA CASA DE LOS ESPIRITUS

...nífico . . . imaginativo e imponente. . . . Un mundo verdaderamente sorprendente, donde la esperanza jamás se pierde." —Detroit News

NOVELA

Isabel Allende's *The House of the Spirits* has been made into a feature film.

Gabriel García Márquez
One Hundred Years of Solitude

The novel *One Hundred Years of Solitude* is popular around the world.

the Castro government censored the press, punished critics, and prevented Cubans from traveling abroad freely. The revolution took from those who opposed it and gave to those who supported it. New schools taught Marxist theory and stressed the creation of a "new" revolutionary people. No one dared complain, however, for fear of persecution.

In its 1994 report, the OAS human rights commission observed:

> 66 *The Cuban government has continued to demonstrate its inflexibility and control over the population by the imposition of harsh sentences placed on people it considers 'dangerous' under the current Penal Code. Such people include those opposed to the regime [government], who are accused of attempting to destroy the political system, spreading propaganda against the state and favoring foreign interests.* 99

The report listed the number of political prisoners in Cuba in 1993 as 602.

Argentina. Civil rights have been particularly vulnerable in times of civil war and revolution. In Argentina, for example, the war carried out by the military junta against Marxist guerrillas became an excuse for mass repression, torture, and murder. According to some estimates, the war's casualties ran between 10,000 and 30,000 Argentines. The terror these events created in Argentina is reflected in the poem "In My Country" by Etelvina Astrada:

> 66 *My country*
> *is Death,*
> *a gigantic assassin, omnipotent*
> *[all controlling] with power, . . .*
> *a death with dead*
> *but lacking corpses.* 99

El Salvador. The country of El Salvador has also experienced widespread human rights violations. In the civil war between the military and the FMLN, violence reached every corner of El Salvador. Teachers, priests, church workers, union officials, and students who criticized the military faced serious danger. The archbishop of San Salvador, Oscar Romero, a vocal critic of the military, was shot to death while saying mass in

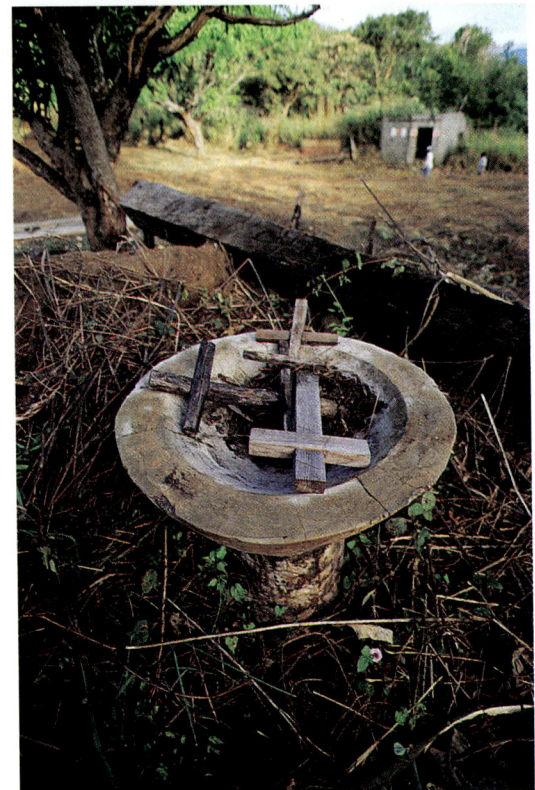

▲ Wooden crosses were placed here to commemorate the tenth anniversary of the El Mozote massacre.

1980. Later that year, four American churchwomen were murdered in rural El Salvador.

The year 1982 began with the grisly news that the entire town of El Mozote had been massacred. In October 1982, then-U.S. Ambassador Deane Hinton told an audience: "Since 1979 perhaps as many as 30,000 Salvadorans have been MURDERED, not killed in battle, MURDERED." Most observers believed that secret military death squads were responsible for the majority of these killings.

In several Latin American countries, people opposed to the government have faced censorship, imprisonment, and murder.

Human Rights Organizations

Individuals and groups throughout Latin America have responded to human rights violations with calls for reform. In Argentina, for example, as the

History THROUGH THE ARTS

Modern Latin American Painting

Many modern Latin American artists have developed their own unique styles by combining the styles of other Western painters with traditional Latin American themes and forms. Fernando Botero of Colombia, for example, combined a careful study of Western art history with the creation of disproportionate images and stereotypical ideas from Latin American art to produce his humorous paintings.

Typical of his paintings is *La Familia Presidencial* (The *Presidential Family*). Botero modeled the painting on a similar work from 1800, *Family of Charles IV*, by the Spanish painter Francisco Goya. *La Familia Presidencial* also reveals common images from Latin American life, such as the fox stole around the neck of the wife, symbolizing the family's new wealth. The humor of the painting is enhanced by Botero's unique depiction of figures and objects, using balloon-like shapes. The smoothness of the shapes means that there is little contrast between people's faces and other images, such as the surrounding mountains, and that images appear out of proportion with one another. When asked about his style, Botero explained: "When I inflate things, I enter a subconscious world rich in folk images." Some critics see an element of social commentary in the painting—suggesting that the puffed up figures make fun of the self-important attitudes of the elite.

La Familia Presidencial by Fernando Botero

The Museum of Modern Art, New York. Acquired through the Lillie P. Bliss Bequest. Photograph copyright 1995 The Museum of Modern Art, New York.

Thinking About Art

Why does Botero use the balloonlike figures?

casualties mounted, 14 middle-aged women who had husbands, sons, or daughters among the "disappeared" formed the **Mothers of the Plaza de Mayo**. The group's efforts on behalf of the victims of military violence helped launch the campaign for human rights in Argentina.

Some countries have also played important roles in trying to enforce human rights in Latin America. During his presidency Jimmy Carter, for example, sought to limit aid to governments that did not respect human rights. The increased violence in El Salvador in the late 1970s and early 1980s also led U.S. government leaders to insist on human rights reform in El Salvador as a condition for future aid.

Within Latin America, human rights groups have become important voices calling for the return of democratic rule. With the strong support of international human rights organizations, national groups have made respect for human rights an issue in their countries. Not surprisingly, greater respect for human rights has accompanied the restoration of democratic governments in Argentina, Chile, Brazil, and El Salvador.

Many people have called for an end to human rights violations, and human rights has become an important issue for new democratic governments in some Latin American countries.

◈ Literature and Art

The difficult and uncertain path of Latin American history since World War II has been reflected in the work of many Latin American writers and artists. Some of the strongest criticisms of human rights abuses in Latin America, for example, are found not only in the reports of human rights agencies but also in the novels and poems of writers from Argentina, Chile, and El Salvador. Female authors in particular have expressed the turmoil and violence they experience living in societies where human rights are abused.

Along with their criticisms, Latin American writers also offer voices of hope. The words of a young refugee from El Salvador perhaps best sum up the hopes and dreams of many Latin Americans:

❝So many things to address
in our new society
we want to see progress
living in fraternity.❞

The experiences and hopes of Latin Americans have also been expressed through the rich tradition of **folk art**. Unlike traditional art forms, folk art is art created by local artists for ordinary use in daily life. Folk art includes toys made from wood, clay, cloth, or tin, as well as the songs handed down from one

generation to the next. Much folk art—such as altars made for the home, statues of saints, or offerings painted to express personal faith—centers on religious beliefs.

Regardless of the kind of art they create, writers and artists have a central place in Latin American life. In literature, song, and art, they express the emotional bonds that tie them to their land and their families. As one Brazilian folk singer put it:

❝I still like to sing for those farmers who will walk five miles in the rain to hear you. They don't have the money to buy bread, and somehow they still find a few coins for the poet because poetry is almost the most important thing in the world for them.❞

Through art, literature, and music, Latin Americans express not only their desires for peace and justice, but also their love of country and family.

◀ **This richly painted giraffe and serpent was created in a traditional style.**

SECTION 4 REVIEW

IDENTIFY and explain the significance of the following:
  Amnesty International
  Mothers of the Plaza de Mayo
  folk art

1. **Main Idea** In what ways have human rights been violated in some Latin American countries?

2. **Main Idea** How have people inside and outside Latin America tried to end human rights violations?

3. **The Arts** What are some common themes of modern Latin American writers, musicians, and artists?

4. **Writing to Create** Imagine that you are a human rights worker in one of the Latin

American countries with a bad human rights record. Create a flyer to be used in the United States that will draw attention to the human rights problems you have seen.

5. **Evaluating** Why might art and literature be powerful means of expressing political and social criticism?

Review

On a separate sheet of paper, complete the following exercises:

WRITING A SUMMARY

Using the essential points in the text, write a brief summary of the chapter.

REVIEWING TERMS

From the following list, choose the term that correctly matches the definition.

Amnesty International
covert
monoculture
Institutional
    Revolutionary Party
smog
junta

1. secret, hidden
2. ruling military government
3. organization that monitors violations of human rights
4. ruling political party in Mexico after 1945
5. air contaminated with factory smoke and automobile emissions

REVIEWING CHRONOLOGY

List the following events in their correct chronological order.

1. Fidel Castro seizes control of Cuba.
2. The Falklands War breaks out.
3. The Brazilian military deposes President Goulart and takes control of the government.
4. U.S. Senate ratifies a treaty agreeing to place the Panama Canal under Panamanian control.
5. Violeta Chamorro is elected president of Nicaragua.

UNDERSTANDING THE MAIN IDEA

1. How have some Latin American countries violated human rights, and how have people responded?
2. What is monoculture? How did many countries in Latin America attempt to overcome dependence on monoculture?
3. Why did many Latin American countries experience a debt crisis after World War II?
4. What are some common concerns of Latin American writers and artists?

THINKING CRITICALLY

1. **Synthesizing** Why were there so many left-wing revolutionary movements in Latin America after World War II? Why has this situation changed in recent years?
2. **Analyzing** How have industrialization and modernization been both helpful and harmful to the countries of Latin America? What might Latin Americans do in the future to solve some of the problems caused by industrialization and modernization?

Building Your Portfolio

Complete the following activities individually or in groups.

1. **Documentary** You (and your coworkers) are on the staff of a television station. Your assignment is to create a documentary focusing on a conflict in Latin America during the Cold War. Write a script for your documentary that tells the conflict's history using evidence from both sides of the conflict. You may want to use this evidence to write imaginary interviews from leaders on both sides and from ordinary people. Attempt to present an unbiased report by using reliable sources to verify the claims of both sides.
2. **International Relations** Imagine that you (and your coworkers) are employees of the U.S. State Department. You are creating a wall chart to illustrate the history of U.S.–Latin American relations since 1945. Your chart should contain the most important conflicts and areas of cooperation between the United States and Latin American countries. Include illustrations or photos, as well as a short paragraph describing each event. You may also want to include maps, statistics, and graphs to help illustrate the events you present on your wall chart.

3. Population growth forced governments to try to develop their economies quickly, using state funds. As a result, many went into debt to buy oil and keep their economies afloat, causing a major financial crisis.
4. Latin American authors, musicians, and artists have used their work to criticize their societies, as well as to express hope for the future and their love for country and family.

THINKING CRITICALLY

1. Radical groups, often influenced by communism, were unhappy with elite control of society and the poor conditions of the masses. Early revolutionary groups could obtain support from the Soviet Union and later Cuba, but after the fall of the Soviet Union, left-wing groups could no longer get the support they needed.
2. helpful—countries no longer rely on just one or two exports, and the growing population could no longer be supported by an agricultural economy; harmful—pollution, slums, and the debt crisis, which have led to political unrest; less government spending on industry (greater privatization), as well as regulations limiting development and regulating pollution, might help some of the problems

Chapter 30

From the Past to the Future 1945–Present

Chapter Planning Guide

	TEXTBOOK	CORE RESOURCES	VISUAL RESOURCES	MULTIMEDIA
Introduction	pp. 826–827	Block Scheduling Handbook: Ch. 30		Videodisc Segment 30 and Viewing Guide: *A New Era*
Lesson 30.1 From Cold War to "New World Order"	pp. 828–833 Map: *The Breakup of the Soviet Sphere,* p. 830 Through Others' Eyes: *The End of a Dictatorship,* p. 831	Reading 30.1: *The Opening of the Berlin Wall* Skills Activity 30: *Analyzing Viewpoints*		GHRC 30 Readings: *The Return of Tribalism; Pollution Threatens Russia's Future* GHRC 30/Videodiscs: Images— *Young Victims of Ethnic Conflict in Sarajevo; Romance Novels Reach Russia;* Video Clip—*Wreckage Left by the Gulf War*
Lesson 30.2 A New Revolution in Technology	pp. 834–839 Literature Through Time: *Science Fiction,* p. 837	Reading 30.2: *Books, Gadgets, and Freedom*	Everyday Life 30: *The AIDS Quilt Project*	GHRC 30 Readings: *Cyberwar: America's Gift to Warfare?; The Brave New Biotech World; Virtual Realities; Hello, Technocracy* GHRC 30/Videodiscs: Images— *Virtual Fishing; Computers Without Keyboards*
Lesson 30.3 Environmental Changes	pp. 840–843 Geography and History: *The Vanishing Forests,* p. 842	Reading 30.3: *Antarctica: A New View* Geography Activity 30: *The Expanding Sahara* Writing Project 30: *Writing an Editorial*	Geography and History 30: *The Global Environment*	GHRC 30 Readings: *Global Warming Alarm Sounded; Pollution Threatens Russia's Future; Rainforest's Revenge* GHRC 30/Videodiscs: Images— *Severe Air Pollution in Eastern Europe; Brazillian Indians Fight for the Rainforest;* Map—*The Global Problem of Acid Rain*
Lesson 30.4 Democracy and Free Trade	pp. 844–848 Map: *Trade Organizations and Alliances,* 1994, p. 847	Reading 30.4: *Looking Toward the Future*	Art and History 30: *Freeway Mural in Los Angeles*	GHRC 30 Readings: *South Africa's First All-Race Elections; Filipinos Celebrate the Fall of Marcos* GHRC 30/Videodiscs: Images— *World's Largest McDonald's Opens in Beijing; Philippine Students Welcome Democracy*
Chapter Investigation and Enrichment	pp. 826–848	Chapter 30 Investigation: *A Look at the Future: the Movie* People in World History 30 Explorations in Daily Life 30		GHRC 30/Videodiscs
Review and Assessment	Section 1 Review, p. 833 Section 2 Review, p. 839 Section 3 Review, p. 843 Section 4 Review, p. 848 Chapter 30 Review, p. 849	Chapter Review Activity 30 Vocabulary Activity 30 Themes Review 30 Section Study Guides 30.1–30.4 Main Idea Activities 30.1–30.4 Daily Quizzes 30.1–30.4 Chapter 30 Test Sheltered English Ch. 30 Test Ch. 30 Test Generator		Audio CDs: Ch. 30 Summary (English and Spanish)

INTRODUCING THE CHAPTER

Textbook pp. 826–827

CHAPTER OVERVIEW

In the late 1980s the Cold War came to an end with the collapse of the Soviet sphere. Just as revolutionary were the technological advances, such as the computer and new medical techniques, that promised to improve lives. Many people hoped that the collapse of communism would lead to an era of greater political and economic freedom.

PRESENTING THEMES

On the chalkboard or on an overhead transparency, write the following open-ended theme questions.

- **POLITICS AND LAW** How might changes at the center of an empire affect regions on the empire's fringes?
- **TECHNOLOGY** How might technological advances be both beneficial and harmful?
- **GEOGRAPHY** What environmental issues face the world today?

Have students, either individually or in groups, suggest responses to the questions. List the responses on the chalkboard or the transparency. For the politics and law question, students might suggest that changes caused by an economic crisis or a power struggle within the government might weaken the empire's hold over outer regions. For the technology question, students might suggest that new technologies can produce goods that benefit society but also have negative effects, such as destroying resources or releasing pollutants. For the geography question, students might suggest that deforestation, acid rain, and global warming are among the world's environmental issues. Save the responses. Once students have studied the chapter, you may wish to have them complete the Themes Review, then compare the two sets of answers.

USING THE VIDEO

Segment 30: *A New Era*

ENGLISH

Search Chapter 30
Videodisc 2, Side B

SPANISH

Search Chapter 30
Videodisc 2, Side B

Tell students that in this chapter they will examine how these theme questions apply to our world today as the divisions of the Cold War fade and our global interdependence increases. Conclude by showing Segment 30 of the *World History and Cultures Videodiscs*. This segment presents scenes of Russia after the decline of the Communist government, focusing on Russians' attitudes about the transition from communism to a democratic society.

Before showing the video, ask students to look for signs that life in Russia has changed since the collapse of the Communist government and the breakup of the Soviet Union in 1991. To help students grasp the signifigant points of the video, have them complete Video Viewing Guide 30.

Key to Ability Levels

All strategies and activities are coded to the following ability levels:

LEVEL 1	**Basic** activities suitable for all students
LEVEL 2	**Average** activities suitable for average to above-average students
LEVEL 3	**Challenging** activities suitable for above-average students
SHELTERED ENGLISH	Activities suitable for students with **Limited English Proficiency**

Additional Resources

BOOKS FOR TEACHERS

Gaddis, John Lewis. *The United States and the End of the Cold War.* Oxford University Press, 1992. Examines the U.S. role in ending the Cold War.

Halberstam, David. *The Next Century.* Avon, 1991. Looks ahead to the twenty-first century.

Lebow, Richard Ned and Janice Gross Stein. *We All Lost the Cold War.* Princeton University Press, 1994. Looks at lost opportunities.

BOOKS FOR STUDENTS

Bulloch, John and Harvey Morris. *The Gulf War: Its Origins, History and Consequences.* Trafalgar Square, 1991. Offers a British perspective.

Kort, Michael. *Mikhail Gorbachev.* Watts, 1990. Looks at his contributions.

Toffler, Alvin. *Powershift: Knowledge, Wealth and Violence at the Edge of the 21st Century.* Bantam, 1990. Looks at the possibilities and perils of the coming century.

MULTIMEDIA MATERIALS

Amnesty Interactive. Amnesty International. CD-ROM, MAC format. Discusses human rights.

The Environment-New Global Concerns. New York Times. Video, 60 min. Discusses a number of environmental concerns.

The Fall of the Berlin Wall. Studio Hamburg/WDR. Video, 50 min. Includes interviews and archival footage.

Lesson 30.1 *From Cold War to "New World Order"*

Textbook pp. 828–833

RESOURCES

Pupil's Edition

Map, p. 830: *The Breakup of the Soviet Sphere, 1989–1991*

Map, pp. 854–855: *The World: Political*

Core Resources

Reading 30.1: *The Opening of the Berlin Wall*

Global History Resource Center

Reading: *The Return of Tribalism*

Reading: *Pollution Threatens Russia's Future*

Videodiscs or Global History Resource Center

Video Clip: *Wreckage Left by the Gulf War*

Search 6242, Play to 6791,
Videodisc 2, Side B
Video Clip 30

Image: *Young Victims of Ethnic Conflict in Sarajevo*

Search Frame 1080

Image: *Romance Novels Reach Russia*

Search Frame 1079

LESSON FOCUS

How and why did the Cold War end?

OBJECTIVES

After completing this lesson, students will be able to:

- explain the purpose of détente and how it affected the United States and the Soviet Union;
- identify the goals of perestroika and glasnost;
- describe how Eastern Europe and the republics of the Soviet Union regained their independence;
- analyze the prospects for a "new world order" after the end of the Cold War.

HOOK: Link to Today

Discuss the effect of détente on relations between the United States and the Soviet Union. Have students discuss gang violence and how it destroys lives. Then have them imagine a scenario in which rival gangs decide to call a truce.

Ask: **What should the truce say in order to be effective?**

[The truce needs to detail its terms, the actions that both sides will interpret as violations of the truce, and the consequences of violation.]

Ask: **What are the benefits and risks of signing a truce?**

[Benefits include the end of violence; risks include the possibility that one side or the other will not abide by the truce.]

Have students relate the idea of a truce to the policy of détente. Ask students to explain what détente was and why it appealed to both the United States and the Soviet Union by the late 1960s. *[Détente was a policy of coexistence and cooperation, which included trade agreements, joint scientific experiments, and agreements on nuclear arms. It appealed to the superpowers because each country was having problems elsewhere, was concerned about China, and had a desire to slow the arms race.]*

Ask: **How did détente change relations between the United States and the Soviet Union?**

[Tensions eased for a number of years, but détente ended because the Soviets became more aggressive in their foreign policy.]

DEVELOP

Examine the end of the Cold War. Have students look at the map on pages 854–855 in their textbook Atlas and ask them to locate the trouble spots of the late 1970s and 1980s that caused a return to the Cold War. *[Students should locate and discuss events in Angola, Nicaragua, Iran, Afghanistan, Grenada, Poland.]*

Next have students discuss the people and events that led to the end of the Cold War.

Ask: What were the aims of Mikhail Gorbachev's glasnost and perestroika?
[Glasnost was a call to Soviet citizens to discuss the Soviet system. Perestroika was an attempt to make the Soviet Union more efficient politically and economically.]

Conclude by pointing out to students that relations improved between the United States and the Soviet Union after glasnost and perestroika. Improved relations led to the 1987 Intermediate Nuclear Forces Treaty and the 1991 Strategic Arms Reduction Talks.

PROBE

Examine how Eastern Europe and the Soviet republics became independent. Tell students that the new measure of reform in the Soviet Union eventually led to independence in Eastern Europe and the Soviet republics.

Ask: How did East Germany, Poland, Czechoslovakia, and Romania break free from Soviet domination?
[Popular demands and protests led to the collapse of the Communist Party in East Germany, Czechoslovakia, and Poland. In Romania, army units seized Romania's dictator and his wife and executed them.]

For more information on the fall of the Berlin Wall in Germany, you might want to have students complete Reading 30.1.

Ask: How did the former Soviet republics become independent?
[Republics pushed for independence. Then hard-liners staged a coup against Gorbachev, but it failed because of popular opposition. After the coup, Gorbachev was unable to hold the nation together.]

For more information, have students examine the map of the Soviet sphere on textbook page 830.

CONCLUDE

Discuss the impact of developments in international affairs since the Cold War. Have students look at a classroom map and ask them to identify the places where conflicts have flared since the end of the Cold War. *[Kuwait, Croatia, Bosnia, Chechnya, Northern Ireland]*

Ask: How have the world powers responded to these conflicts?
[Students should point out the Gulf War, UN peacekeepers' efforts in Bosnia, and the Russian troops' occupation of Chechnya.]

Ask: Why were some people skeptical of the "new world order"?
[The situation in the former Yugoslavia indicated that nations would not be as quick to react if their interests were not threatened.]

Lead a discussion in which students discuss the outcomes of the above-mentioned conflicts. Then ask students to write a few paragraphs that predict the future of the "new world order." You also might want to have students view the electronic media images of the Gulf War and the victim of conflict in Sarajevo and read the selection on the new tribalism in the Global History Resource Center.

EXTEND

Cross-Curricular Connection: *Health*

Assign the selection on pollution in Russia, then ask: Why are Russian public health officials worried? What could be causing the public health problems? How important are health concerns in economic planning in the former Soviet Union?

MEET INDIVIDUAL NEEDS

Visual-Spatial Learners

Display the electronic media image on romance novels. Have students consider what it would be like to be unable to read whatever they liked. Discuss how they think increased access to books will affect Russian society.

Linguistic Learners

Many communities today are home to recent immigrants from Eastern Europe and the former Soviet Union. Invite an immigrant to speak to the class about his or her experiences as a result of glasnost and perestroika.

ASSESS

Review

Have students complete the Section 1 Review. Use answers in the Teacher's Edition, page 833, to assess student mastery of this section.

Lesson 30.2 *A New Revolution in Technology*

Textbook pp. 834–839

LESSON FOCUS

How have changes in technology affected people's lives?

OBJECTIVES

After completing this lesson, students will be able to:

- explain the results of the growing alliance between science and technology after World War II;
- discuss the roles of the United States and the Soviet Union in space exploration;
- examine the effects of television and computers on the world;
- explain the consequences of new developments in biology and medicine after World War II.

HOOK: Link to Today

Discuss the links between science and technology after World War II. Point out to students that some of the innovations in science and technology developed during and after World War II have changed the world forever. To make an example, ask students to raise their hands if they watch over one hour of television every week. Then point out that less than 1 percent of American homes had a TV in 1945, while by 1975 nearly every home had one. (You might want to show the electronic media image *Television on a Pair of Sunglasses* at this time.) Then ask them to imagine how their lives would be different if there were no TV, computers, or antibiotics to treat illnesses.

Conclude by telling students that these things became available with the advances in technology made during and after World War II. Point out that such advances gave people increasing power over their world.

DEVELOP

Discuss the space race in relation to the technology boom. Point out to students that a significant outgrowth of the Cold War came with the development of technology for space exploration. Beginning in the 1950s, the race to gain command of space led to increasing competition between the United States and the Soviet Union.

Ask: **Which country achieved the goal of having the first person in space?**
[the Soviet Union]

Ask: **What was the United States's response?**
[President Kennedy vowed to have a man on the moon by the end of the decade, which was achieved by Presidents Johnson and Nixon through the nation's manned space program.]

Conclude by telling students that the space race led to increasing space exploration. Discuss the space developments that occurred during the 1980s and 1990s. *[space shuttle and space station]*

PROBE

Discuss the Information Revolution and advances in medical technology. Tell students that new developments in communications and medical technology changed people's lives. On the chalkboard, create a chart with the headings *Information Revolution* and *Medical Advances*. Then, at the top of the chart, put the words *Developments* and *Benefits*. Fill in the chart as they answer the following questions.

Ask: *What were the new developments of the Information Revolution?*

[the transistor, the television, miniaturization, lasers, and computerization]

Then ask students to list the benefits of these new technologies. *[**transistor, television**: easy access to news and entertainment, advertisers had new media for their products; **miniaturization**: electronic equipment became cheaper, new products were developed; **lasers**: cut metals and other materials with precision, revolutionized communications and surgery; **computerization**: computers could be used to run new machines, guide space-craft, and diagnose problems in car engines; they also served to revolutionize communications by connecting offices and homes through the Internet]*

Then ask students to identify and discuss medical advances and their benefits made during and after World War II. *[Answers should include vaccinations, which prevented the spread of diseases such as smallpox; antibiotics, which became more available after World War II and enabled doctors to treat infections; and genetic research, which led scientists to the discovery of DNA.]* Put students' answers on the chalkboard. After students have completed the chart, have them copy it and save it for a later exercise.

Point out that one of these advances, genetic research, has raised some ethical questions.

Ask: *Why are people concerned about some genetic research?*

[They fear that people might gain too much control over life's natural processes, such as the creation of humans.]

To give students more information about modern technology, you may wish to have them read the Global History Resource

Center readings and view the electronic media images.

Conclude by having students read and discuss the Core Resources Reading 30.2, which discusses technology.

CONCLUDE

Explain which technological innovations have had the greatest impact on people's lives. Have students refer to their charts to assess the technological achievements discussed in this section. Ask them to rank these innovations in order of importance. Have them write a paragraph explaining the reasons for their rankings. When they are ready, have them share their views with the class. Then discuss whether any of them would change their rankings as a result of hearing the arguments of their classmates.

EXTEND

Cross-Curricular Connection: *Science*

Have students research virtual reality and give a short report on it to the class. You might want them to start their research by having them read the Global History Resource Center reading *Artificial Worlds and Virtual Realities* and view the electronic media image *Virtual Fishing*.

MEET INDIVIDUAL NEEDS

Students Having Difficulty

Tell students to locate each subsection heading and create a question using the words in the heading. For example, "How has medical science successfully combatted diseases?" or "What is the Information Age?" Then have students locate and write down the answers to the questions.

Logical-Mathematical Learners

Have students read the article on cyberwar, or "information warfare," in the Global History Resource Center. Ask them to consider the following question—Is cyberwar more or less moral than other forms of warfare?

ASSESS

Review

Have students complete the Section 2 Review. Use answers in the Teacher's Edition, page 839, to assess student mastery of this section.

Lesson 30.3 Environmental Changes

Textbook pp. 840–843

RESOURCES

Pupil's Edition
Biography, p. 841: *Rachel Carson*

Geography and History, p. 842: *The Vanishing Forests*

Core Resources
Reading 30.3: *Antarctica: A New View*

Visual Resources
Geography and History 30: *The Global Environment*

Global History Resource Center
Reading: *Global Warming Alarm Sounded*

Reading: *The Rainforest's Revenge: Hot Viruses*

Reading: *Pollution Threatens Russia's Future*

Videodiscs or Global History Resource Center

Image: *Severe Air Pollution in Eastern Europe*

Search Frame 1085

Image: *Brazilian Indians Fight for the Rainforest*

Search Frame 1087

Image: *Saving India's Endangered Wildlife*

Search Frame 1086

Map: *The Global Problem of Acid Rain*

Search Frame 1091

LESSON FOCUS
How have urbanization and industrialization threatened the earth's environment?

OBJECTIVES
After completing this lesson, students will be able to:
- explain why many people have worried about continuing industrialization;
- identify how environmentalists have fought to protect the environment;
- discuss concerns over the loss of biodiversity.

HOOK
Discuss why people are worried about continued industrialization. Tell students that by the 1990s, pollution and urbanization had affected the environment. Have students take turns reading aloud from the Core Resources Reading 30.3.

Ask: **What is ozone depletion?**
[the destruction of the stratospheric layer of ozone—a form of oxygen that protects the earth from the sun's harmful ultraviolet radiation]

Ask: **What is the greenhouse effect, and why do some scientists think it is a threat?**
[Excess carbon dioxide from the burning of fuels traps heat near the earth. Some scientists believe it is causing global temperatures to rise, destroying the natural ecological balance.]

Conclude by telling students that many scientists fear that pollution, ozone depletion, global warming, and acid rain are causing serious damage to the earth's environment. For more information, assign the Global History Resource Center readings on pollution in Russia and global warming, and view the electronic media image of pollution in Eastern Europe and the electronic media map on acid rain.

DEVELOP

Identify how some people have worked to help save the environment. Tell students that as the world's environmental problems seemed to mount, many people began to take action, hoping to reverse or stop some of the damage. Have students read the biography of Rachel Carson. Then have them quickly make a simple cause-effect chain that illustrates Carson's work on DDT. *[Chains should show the use of DDT to kill the beetles, the absorption of the DDT by the trees, the falling of the trees' leaves, the eating of the leaves by the worms, the eating of the worms by the robins, and the death of the robins.]*

Conclude by pointing out that while the cause-effect chains are a simplified version of Carson's work, her research explained the interdependence of living things and increased understanding of how the use of chemicals destroyed this balance.

PROBE

Discuss what biodiversity means and why scientists are worried about its preservation. Point out to students that as Rachel Carson's work on DDT proved, nature is locked in a delicate balance.

Ask: What does biodiversity mean?
   [the natural variety of plants and animals in the environment]

Then ask students to discuss why biodiversity is important. *[The loss of biodiversity could threaten the ecological balance of life on Earth. If one part of the ecosphere—the interlocking system of life on Earth—was damaged it might affect other parts of the ecosphere. In addition, some people feel that it is morally wrong to destroy species and their environments.]*

Have students read the textbook feature Geography and History for more information on the destruction of forests, as well as the selection on the emergence of hot viruses from the rain forests in the Global History Resource Center. Then lead a discussion in which students summarize the points that have been made in the section.

CONCLUDE: Link to Today

Explain why nations are at odds over efforts to reduce pollution and stem the loss of biodiversity. Tell students that global involvement in the enforcement of environmental protection has sometimes been a controversial issue. Lead students in an opinion discussion about why this might be so. *[Discussion might focus on the right of one nation to dictate what another nation should do with the land within its boundaries.]*

Ask: Why might responses be different from nation to nation about environmental issues?
   [Wealthier nations can better afford to pay for efforts to curtail pollution. Some say that controlling pollution harms business, costs jobs, and slows economic development.]

Show students the electronic media image of the Brazilian rain forest. Then have them make predictions about the environment in the future. Ask them to write a paragraph on what they think the world should do about environmental problems. Have students share their ideas and suggestions with the class.

EXTEND

Other Media
Have students view the electronic media image of endangered animals in India. Then ask students to look for more information on the World Wide Web about efforts around the world to protect endangered wildlife. Have them report on their discoveries.

MEET INDIVIDUAL NEEDS

Students Acquiring English
Pair new speakers of English with fluent speakers to help them learn unfamiliar vocabulary that might be used in a conversation about environmental problems, such as *pollution, combustion, exhaust, stratosphere, refrigerant, photosynthesis, extinction, species.*

Interpersonal Learners
Have interested students assume the roles of environmentalists at a conference such as the United Nations environmental conference held in 1992. Have them prepare statements on various issues and give a presentation to the class. They might want to accompany their statements with visuals, such as maps, photos, or charts.

ASSESS

Review
Have students complete the Section 3 Review. Use answers in the Teacher's Edition, page 843, to assess student mastery of this section.

Lesson 30.4 *Democracy and Free Trade*

Textbook pp. 844–848

RESOURCES

Pupil's Edition

Map, p. 847: *Trade Organizations and Alliances, 1994*

Core Resources

Reading 30.4: *Looking Toward the Future*

Global History Resource Center

Reading: *South Africa's First All-Race Elections*

Reading: *Filipinos Celebrate the Fall of Marcos*

Videodiscs or Global History Resource Center

Image: *World's Largest McDonald's Opens in Beijing*

Search Frame 1088

Image: *Philippine Students Welcome Democracy*

Search Frame 1047

LESSON FOCUS

How and why did many nations abandon communism and socialism during the 1980s and 1990s?

OBJECTIVES

After completing this lesson, students will be able to:

- explain what happened to communism during the late 1980s and 1990s;
- identify how democracy spread during the 1980s and 1990s;
- describe how international trade developed during this period;
- discuss what prevented the trend toward democracy from occurring worldwide.

HOOK

Discuss the reasons why many communist nations abandoned communism during the 1980s and 1990s. Have students review the idea of the domino theory. *[Eisenhower's theory was that if one country became communist, others would fall in rapid succession.]* Then ask them why by the mid-1990s the domino theory seemed to have worked in reverse.

Ask: **What happened in many communist countries during the** late 1980s and 1990s?

[Most communist governments in Eastern Europe had fallen.]

Ask: **What other political trend occurred during this period?** *[Many formerly authoritarian governments turned to democracy.]*

DEVELOP

Identify where democracy and democratic reforms were adopted in Asia, Africa, and Latin America. On a large classroom map, have students point out the nations mentioned in the text that have become democratic or implemented some democratic reforms in the past 10 years. *[Students should locate South Korea, Taiwan, the Philippines, and South Africa.]* As students are pointing out the countries on the map, have them describe the political developments that have occurred.

Point out to students that one major event in the democratic trend was the election of Nelson Mandela as president of South Africa. Have students read the Global History Resource Center reading on South Africa. Ask students why there was resistance to democratic reform in South Africa. *[Students should understand that the system of apartheid and beliefs of racial inequality kept South Africa from being a democratic nation.]*

Ask: What made South Africa do away with apartheid?

[Students should note that ongoing world boycotts of South African goods eventually led the government to reconsider its apartheid policies.]

PROBE

Explain what the nations of the world have done to promote free trade. Point out to students that the global trend toward democracy led to greater freedom of world trade. List the following trade alliances, organizations, and agreements on the chalkboard—GATT, EU, WTO, NAFTA, AL, OAU, APEC, MERCOSUR, NAFTA. Ask students to identify which are global and which are regional. In addition to the text, have students examine the map on textbook page 847 for more information.

Ask: How have these alliances, organizations, and agreements promoted free trade?

[In general, students should understand that they have reduced and in some cases eliminated barriers to trade and they have created new entities with the authority to resolve trade disputes.]

CONCLUDE

Examine why some nations have resisted implementing democratic reforms. Have students use the large classroom map to name the nations mentioned in the text that have resisted democracy. Ask them to briefly discuss the government situation in each. [**China:** *economic liberalization still limited under Communists;* **Cuba:** *Castro still clung to power, but showed signs of loosening economic controls;* **North and South Korea:** *communist rule continued despite death of Kim Il Sung;* **Iran:** *Muslim government denied democracy to people based on rules of the Qur'an;* **Indonesia:** *Suharto put economics before political rights;* **Saudi Arabia:** *royal family ruled autocratically;* **Iraq, Syria, Burma:** *rulers kept control of power by force*]

Ask: What conditions, if any, might lead these nations to adopt democratic governments?

[Responses might include economic problems, demands of people becoming too powerful, pressure from other nations.]

To conclude, have students read Reading 30.4, in which the author talks about what global and national issues still need to be resolved. Ask students for their opinions on what problems they think need to be resolved and how this can be accomplished.

EXTEND

Cross-Curricular Connection: *Economics*

Have students view the electronic media image of the McDonald's in China in the 1990s. What does this image tell us about economic changes taking place in the largest communist country in the world? How are American companies taking advantage of these changes? If possible, have students briefly research the economic changes that have taken place in China during the 1990s prior to the discussion.

MEET INDIVIDUAL NEEDS

Gifted Students

Have students read the Global History Resource Center selection about the fall of Marcos in the Philippines and view the electronic media image. Ask them to compare the feelings and reactions of the Filipino people with those of the East German woman described on textbook pages 845–846. You might also want students to refer back to the information on the fall of the Berlin Wall in Section 1 of this chapter.

Linguistic Learners

Ask students to imagine that they are news reporters in the year 2015. Tell them they have been assigned to write a news article updating readers on the status of world democracy and trade. Suggest to students that they tell their readers what has happened in China, Cuba, Eastern Europe, the former republics of the Soviet Union, South Africa, and Mexico. In their articles, students should also provide an update on trade organizations such as the European Union.

ASSESS

Review

Have students complete the Section 4 Review. Use answers in the Teacher's Edition, pages 847–848, to assess student mastery of this section.

In preparation for the chapter test, you may wish to have students complete all or part of the Chapter 30 Review on textbook page 849, the Chapter 30 Review Activity, and the Chapter 30 Themes Review.

Chapter 30

From the Past to the Future

Understanding the Main Idea

Call on a volunteer to read aloud the *Understanding the Main Idea* paragraph. Then tell students that the years after 1945 were filled with great political and technological change. After many years of tensions between the super-powers, the Cold War finally ended with the downfall of the Eastern European communist governments and the breakup of the Soviet Union. New technologies in space, medicine, and communications brought both benefits and problems, and environmental issues became more important than ever before.

Presenting Themes

See p. 825B for suggestions on introducing themes.

Using the Time Line

Have students list the time line events in their notebooks. After they have read about each event in the chapter, have students write a paragraph explaining its significance.

Chapter 30
From the Past to the Future
1945–Present

Understanding the Main Idea

After periods of relaxation and renewed struggle, the Cold War ended with the collapse of the Soviet Empire and the breakup of the Soviet Union itself. Many communist nations began moving toward democracy and capitalism. Technological changes provided much of the world with both benefits and problems, and environmental challenges reminded the world's nations that they shared a common, and increasingly smaller, planet.

Themes

- **Politics and Law** How might changes at the center of an empire affect regions on the empire's fringes?

- **Technology** How might technological advances be both beneficial and harmful?

- **Geography** What environmental issues face the world today?

In 1989 the unimaginable happened. The Berlin Wall came down. For 28 years the wall had stood as the very symbol of the Cold War, dividing East from West. For many Berliners the wall had been an ugly scar across their city, a daily reminder of the separation of families and friends.

On November 9 an East German official announced that at midnight East Germans would be able to leave the country at any point along the nation's borders, including the crossing points through the Berlin Wall. Word spread like wildfire, and hours before midnight huge crowds had gathered on both sides of the wall, chanting, *"Tor auf!"* (Open the gate!)

At the stroke of midnight, the gates opened, and thousands of East Berliners streamed into the West, into a part of the city that many had never seen. "I just can't believe it!" cried Angelika Wache, the first to enter West Berlin through Checkpoint Charlie, the famous crossing point. A young man, Torsten Ryl, remarked that "finally, we can really visit other states instead of just seeing them on television or hearing about them."

Throughout the night, joyous Berliners celebrated. Later, Germany would face many problems as it reunited, but for this one evening, there was nothing but unimaginable joy. As the headline read in a major Berlin newspaper the next day, "Berlin is Berlin again."

1946	1962	1969	1972
Researchers develop the ENIAC computer.	Rachel Carson publishes *Silent Spring*.	Neil Armstrong becomes the first person to walk on the moon.	Leaders of the United States and the Soviet Union begin a period of détente.

Crowds gather to celebrate the midnight opening of the Berlin Wall on November 9, 1989.

♻ **About the Image**

This photograph shows the crowds that gathered to celebrate the fall of the Berlin Wall. During the 28 years that the wall stood, many East Germans had been shot at the barrier as they tried to escape the oppression of East Germany. But on November 9, 1989, East Germans stood on top of the wall, dancing and celebrating.

The revelers continued their celebration for two days. During the 48 hours following the opening, almost 2 million East Germans crossed the border to West Germany. At one spot at the border, a 30-mile-long line of cars waited to cross.

Critical Thinking Ask students why so many East Germans wanted to enter West Germany in that first 48 hours.

ANSWER: Students might suggest that many East Germans might have wanted to visit friends or relatives, see West Germany, or simply exercise their new freedom.

1986	1989	1990	1991	1995
▲	▲	▲	▲	▲
The world's worst nuclear power disaster occurs at Chernobyl in the Soviet Union.	Communism collapses in Eastern Europe.	Germany reunites.	The Soviet Union dissolves.	The U.S. space shuttle *Atlantis* docks with the Russian space station *Mir*.

SECTION 1

CORE LESSON PLAN
See pages 825C and 825D for Lesson Plan 30.1.

🔄 *Theme:* **War and Diplomacy**

By the 1970s it became clear that the United States and the Soviet Union both had enough nuclear weapons to destroy each other. Both nations wanted to take steps to ease the tensions. This led to Nixon's historic visit to Moscow in 1972—the first time an American president had visited since the Cold War began. This trip was followed by an exchange of visits, known as the SALT talks, with Leonid Brezhnev.

Critical Thinking Ask students how a series of visits between leaders of rival nations might benefit both countries.

ANSWER: Students might suggest that the visits might lead to good will and better negotiations.

SECTION 1

From Cold War to "New World Order"

FOCUS

- What was the aim of détente between the United States and the Soviet Union, and what was the result?

- What were the goals of perestroika and glasnost?

- How did the Eastern European states and the Soviet republics regain their independence?

- What were the prospects for a "new world order" after the end of the Cold War?

By the late 1960s the division of Europe into superpower spheres—the U.S. sphere in the West, the Soviet in the East—seemed to be a permanent situation. This situation gave rise to a relaxation in tensions between the United States and the Soviet Union. But the appearance of permanence was deceiving, for the 1980s and early 1990s brought a complete breakdown of the Soviet sphere. With the collapse a new set of challenges confronted world leaders.

President Richard Nixon visiting China

🔄 Détente

By the end of the 1960s both the United States and the Soviet Union wanted a break from the Cold War. Many in the United States were focused on the Vietnam War, while many in the Soviet Union wanted to avoid another crisis like the Prague Spring in Czechoslovakia. Leaders in both Moscow and Washington also wanted to slow the arms race, which they saw as dangerous and increasingly expensive. In addition, both superpowers had their eyes on China.

Relations between China and the Soviet Union had grown worse since the 1950s, with the Chinese challenging the Soviets for leadership of the world communist movement. In 1969 fighting actually broke out briefly along the Sino-Soviet border. Hoping to take advantage of this split, in 1972 U.S. president Richard Nixon reopened diplomatic relations between the United States and China for the first time since 1949. The idea of this friendship worried Soviet leaders.

That same year Nixon and Soviet leader Leonid Brezhnev agreed to ease diplomatic and military tensions between their countries through a policy that became known as **détente** (day-TAHNT). Détente included trade agreements, joint scientific experiments, and agreements on nuclear arms. The most significant U.S.-Soviet agreement was the 1972 Strategic Arms Limitation Treaty (SALT), which banned most antimissile systems and limited the construction of offensive missiles.

In a spirit of détente, the superpowers agreed to relax tensions and work to reduce nuclear weapons.

🔄 The Last Gasp of the Cold War

Although détente lasted several years, global competition between the superpowers continued. In Angola civil war broke out between Soviet-sponsored and U.S.-backed opponents. Revolutions in Nicaragua and Iran in the late 1970s replaced pro-American governments with governments hostile to the United States. The end of détente came in 1979, when the Soviet army invaded Afghanistan.

President Jimmy Carter feared further invasions. Growing Soviet influence around the Persian Gulf, a major source of the world's oil, particularly worried Carter. Consequently, he proclaimed what became known as the **Carter Doctrine**:

> 66 *An attempt by any outside force to gain control of the Persian Gulf region will be regarded as an assault on the vital interests of the United States of America, and such an assault will be repelled by any means necessary, including military force.* 99

Carter also called for economic and cultural sanctions against the Soviet Union, including a boycott of the 1980 Olympics held in Moscow.

Confronted by such opposition, the Soviet Union started to take an even harder line against the West. In 1981 Soviet leaders ordered Polish Communists to crack down on **Solidarity**, Poland's independent trade union led by Lech Walesa (LEK vah-LEN-suh). In 1983 a Soviet fighter plane shot down a South Korean airliner that had strayed across the border into Soviet airspace, killing everyone on board, including many U.S. citizens.

Meanwhile, President Ronald Reagan, who had succeeded Carter in 1981, proved even more determined in his opposition to Soviet aggression. Reagan called the Soviet Union "the focus of evil in the modern world" and "an evil empire." Reagan opposed the Soviets by restoring and increasing U.S. defense spending that had been cut in the years of détente. He also approved plans for research into space-based weapons designed to knock down enemy missiles before they could strike the United States—a program officially called the Strategic Defense Initiative, but popularly known as "Star Wars."

Reagan ordered covert, or secret, operations against pro-Soviet governments in Angola, Nicaragua, and Afghanistan. When a Marxist government took power in the small Caribbean island of Grenada in 1983, Reagan ordered an invasion. The Cold War had resumed.

*D*étente ended in the 1980s, as the Soviets became more aggressive in their foreign policy.

▲ After the successful invasion of the island, U.S. soldiers prepare to depart from Point Salines, Grenada.

♻ Reshaping the Soviet System

In 1985 Mikhail Gorbachev became the leader of the Soviet Union. Gorbachev immediately launched sweeping reforms that he called **perestroika** (per-uh-STROY-kuh)—restructuring—and **glasnost** (GLAZ-nohst)—openness. Perestroika, a plan for reforming the Soviet political and economic system, would reduce the role of the state in Soviet life and would introduce elements of the democratic and capitalist systems of the West. Glasnost was a call to Soviet citizens to speak their minds about the failings of the Soviet system.

Gorbachev's reforms caused drastic changes in Soviet life. Most people enjoyed the freedom to speak their minds and to read what they chose. But many were discouraged by the economic hardships that resulted from perestroika. People no longer had guaranteed lifetime employment and a secure income. Although many Soviet citizens embraced the changes, others fondly remembered the old days.

Realizing that the Soviet Union could not afford both reform and a continued arms race, Gorbachev sought arms-control agreements with the United States. In 1987 the Intermediate Nuclear Forces Treaty committed the United States and the Soviet Union to the elimination of intermediate-range missiles stationed in Europe. The 1991 Strategic Arms Reduction Talks specified a substantial reduction in long-range weapons.

*P*erestroika called for restructuring the Soviet system, while glasnost called for openness and self-criticism in Soviet affairs.

Under the new policies of glasnost, much more information was available to the people of the Soviet Union about the true state of the country. By 1989 it was clear that the Soviet economy was in severe decay. Outside observers began to talk about the potential for rebellion among the peoples of the Baltics and Central Asia, groups who had never given up their distinct cultures. There were also signs of discontent among conservatives within the Soviet bureaucracy and the military, who felt the government should crack down on dissent. Amid these difficulties, Gorbachev tried to press on with political and economic reforms.

Critical Thinking Ask students if they think Gorbachev was right to continue with reforms instead of trying to reimpose autocratic power.

ANSWER: Students' answers will vary. Some students may think that Gorbachev did the right thing in trying to continue reforms, but others may think he should have stopped all reforms and concentrated on holding the country together.

Map Answer

Latvia, Lithuania, and Estonia

♻ Eastern Europe Breaks Free

With Soviet citizens enjoying greater rights than ever, the peoples of Eastern Europe soon began to call for similar reforms. The Communist leaders of Eastern Europe, fearful of their own futures, at first resisted reform and looked to the Soviet Union for help. Whereas before the Soviet Union had backed up its communist allies, this time the Soviets announced that the Eastern Europeans were on their own.

The effects of this announcement were dramatic. In East Germany thousands of people demonstrated, and then rioted, to protest the harsh practices of Communist dictator Erich Honecker and particularly of the brutal secret police force. The Communists in Poland tried to meet the demands of the opposition Solidarity movement by offering to hold elections for a minority of seats in the national parliament.

The revolution of 1989. In 1989 revolution broke out across Eastern Europe. Led by Lech Walesa, the Solidarity union in Poland expanded its position in government and soon pushed the Communists aside. In Czechoslovakia change also came relatively peacefully when Vaclav Havel, a dissident-playwright, assumed the presidency. In Romania, however, Communist president Nicolae Ceausescu (chow-SHES-koo) tried to resist the popular tide. Army units soon joined the opposition to the hated government and

The Breakup of the Soviet Sphere

The Empire Unravels The Soviets had kept a firm lid on nationalist movements before 1989. But the collapse of the empire soon unleashed bitter ethnic and religious conflicts.

❓ **Linking Geography and History** Which former Soviet republics were not part of the Commonwealth of Independent States?

seized the dictator and his wife, who were executed on Christmas Day.

Fall of the Berlin Wall. Perhaps the greatest transition occurred in East Germany, where thousands gathered to demand reform, including the right to travel without governmental permission. In November 1989 the East German government threw open the gates in the Berlin Wall. East and West Berliners climbed atop the wall that had divided their city for 28 years as the world watched on television. Two British journalists reported:

66 *Berlin was itself a city reborn. The party clogged the streets as the barriers that divided Germany melted like the ice of the Cold War.* 99

The opening of the Berlin Wall symbolized the end of the old Soviet-dominated order in Eastern Europe. Communism was swept aside as democratic elections installed new governments in the former Soviet satellites. The fall of the Berlin Wall was followed by the reunification of Germany in October 1990.

♻ The Soviet Union Dissolves

The fall of communism in Eastern Europe encouraged independence movements in many of the Soviet republics. The Baltic republics of Lithuania, Latvia, and Estonia led the call for independence. Yet for all his commitment to reform, Gorbachev had no desire to see the Soviet Union disintegrate. Neither did conservatives in the Soviet army and government, who resented Gorbachev's reforms. In January 1991 Soviet troops put down uprisings in Lithuania and Latvia.

Hard-line conservative Communists remained suspicious of Gorbachev. In August 1991 they tried to take over the government. The coup fell apart when it encountered strong popular opposition led by Boris Yeltsin, the president of the Russian republic. Nevertheless, the failed coup signaled the beginning of the end of the Soviet Union. The Baltic republics became independent within days. At this time Ukraine also declared its independence. By December 1991 the Soviet

THROUGH OTHERS' EYES

The End of a Dictatorship

In 1989 the Romanian Communist dictator Nicolae Ceausescu and his wife, Elena, were executed. In December 1989 Simon Haydon, a British correspondent, visited Romania and wrote this description of the dictator's former home:

66 Nicolae Ceausescu lived in a dream house dripping with gold and silver and packed with art treasures, while his nation starved. . . . The sprawling two-story villa with forty rooms stands at the center of a compound of a dozen houses for Ceausescu's ministers, generals, and friends in northern Bucharest. . . . The visitors to the villa were met in an entry hall decorated with precious vases, topped by a golden dome. . . . All the rooms were crammed with paintings, valuable ornaments and gilded [gold-overlaid] furniture. . . . Warm water flowed from gold-plated taps in the Italian-tiled bathrooms. On the balcony downstairs, where exquisite fountains once splashed, a soldier had left his dirty boots, exchanged for a pair of Ceausescu's. 99

Union had dissolved. In its place were 15 independent states, 12 of which later formed a loose confederation called the Commonwealth of Independent States.

The republics of the Soviet Union began to break away from a weakening central government, and the Soviet Union dissolved.

♻ A "New World Order"?

The breakup of the Soviet Union effectively ended the Cold War. For 45 years the United States and the Soviet Union had dominated international affairs. Now the Soviet Union no longer existed. Some observers predicted an era of peace after the Cold War. Others feared a time of increased international instability.

The Persian Gulf War. Even before the breakup of the Soviet Union, the world faced war in the Middle East. In August 1990 Saddam Hussein, the ruler of Iraq, seized the small, oil-rich country of Kuwait and proclaimed it to be part of Iraq. This move gave him control of a sizable portion of the world's oil supply and put him in a good position to threaten neighboring Saudi Arabia, the world's largest oil producer. The outcry around the world was immediate. The United Nations voted to impose economic sanctions on Iraq. Even the Soviet Union, one of Saddam Hussein's strongest allies, voted in the United Nations Security Council for intervention against Iraq.

With UN approval an international coalition, led by the United States under President George Bush, went to war against Iraq in January 1991 to restore Kuwait's independence. After more than a month of bombing raids, coalition forces launched a ground assault that liberated Kuwait within days. The Iraqis suffered heavy casualties—perhaps 100,000 died. Coalition casualties were very light. On February 27 President Bush called off the attack and the war ended—although sanctions continued against Iraq.

War in the former Yugoslavia. During the Gulf crisis, Bush had spoken of a "new world order," in which strong countries like the United States would defend weak countries like Kuwait against aggressors. Skeptics, however, wondered whether the international community would move so swiftly to the defense of small countries that lacked valuable commodities like oil. The skeptics' case was supported by the experience of Yugoslavia.

As communist governments fell, Yugoslavia also began to dissolve. Slovenia and Croatia seceded in 1991, followed in 1992 by the province of Bosnia and Herzegovina (usually called Bosnia). The secession sparked violence among different ethnic groups in Yugoslavia. Fighting erupted in Croatia and also in Bosnia, where the worst of the fighting was between Serbs and Muslims. Bosnian Serbs received help from Serbia (part of the former Yugoslavia). The world watched with horror as the Serbs engaged in so-called **ethnic cleansing**—a campaign of terror designed to drive Muslims out of the parts of Bosnia the Serbs claimed for themselves.

In an effort to end the fighting, the United Nations imposed an arms embargo against both sides—an act that particularly hurt the Muslim-controlled Bosnian government forces, which were not as well armed as the Serbs. NATO airplanes occasionally bombed Serb positions, but not heavily enough to do serious damage. UN peacekeepers also entered Bosnia to monitor periodic cease-fires. As Serbian attacks against the Muslim population continued, the United Nations declared certain areas as "safe havens" under UN protection. Investigations of Serbian atrocities against civilians led the United Nations to charge top Serbian leaders with war crimes and crimes against humanity.

Instead of complying with UN demands that they stop their aggression, Serb forces began to take UN peacekeepers as hostages against further air strikes. In the summer of 1995 the Serbs even attacked and overran several of the UN safe havens. Eventually, NATO forces under U.S. leadership began to attack Serbian positions in Bosnia with an extended bombing campaign. By the fall of 1995, representatives from all warring sides met in the United States and agreed to a peace settlement. NATO countries, including the United States, sent troops to Bosnia to enforce the peace.

Chechnya. As in Bosnia, fighting periodically broke out throughout the former territories of the old Soviet Union as various groups struggled for power in the postcommunist era. Perhaps the most serious case developed in the region of southern Russia known as Chechnya. The Chechens had a long history of conflict with Russia.

In 1991 Chechnya declared its independence. By late 1994, however, Boris Yeltsin, the Russian president, made it clear that he would not allow Chechnya to break away. Fearing that other parts of Russia might follow suit, and unwilling to lose

▲ **Russian UN soldiers are enthusiastically welcomed upon their arrival in Bosnia in 1994.**

Chechnya's rich oil resources, Yeltsin ordered troops into Chechnya to end the rebellion. The Russians suffered heavy casualties in the fighting that followed. Although the Russians captured the Chechen capital, Grozny, after bitter combat, the rebels continued the struggle from the mountains. Finally, in 1997, Russia signed a peace treaty with Chechnya giving the region a high degree of independence.

Despite hopes for a "new world order," events after the Cold War suggested a new era of international instability.

♻ Resurgent Nationalism and Separatism

As events in Bosnia and Chechnya demonstrated, a resurgence of nationalism based on ethnic and cultural identities posed a major threat to unity and peace. Western Europe and North America also saw the rise of separatist movements.

Northern Ireland. Bloodshed and unrest wracked Northern Ireland throughout the 1970s and 1980s as Protestants and Catholics clashed over the mostly Catholic Irish Republican Army's decades-old campaign to free Northern Ireland from British control. Hopes of an end to the bombings and assassinations surfaced in 1993, when the prime ministers of Great Britain

▲ The IRA claimed responsibility for this bus bombing, which took place in the heart of London.

and Ireland jointly endorsed the principles of self-determination in Northern Ireland. The IRA declared a cease-fire but refused to disarm before joining negotiations. Violence soon resurfaced. Only after the Labour Party's victory in the British elections of 1997 did prospects for a settlement improve.

Quebec. Separatism also plagued Canada, where a movement for independence sprang up among French-speaking Canadians in the province of Quebec. In 1976 the separatist Quebec Party won control of the provincial government. The party, however, could not convince voters to support independence for Quebec. In 1980, and again in 1995, voters defeated referendums calling for independence. The second defeat was by a slim margin, however. The question of Canadian unity remains in doubt.

Violence based on religious and cultural differences continued to haunt nations.

SECTION 1 REVIEW

IDENTIFY and explain the significance of the following:
    détente
    Carter Doctrine
    Solidarity
    Lech Walesa
    Mikhail Gorbachev
    perestroika
    glasnost
    ethnic cleansing

LOCATE and explain the importance of the following:

Croatia
Bosnia
Chechnya

1. **Main Idea** What was the purpose of détente, and what was its outcome?
2. **Main Idea** What did Gorbachev hope glasnost and perestroika would achieve?
3. **Politics and Law** How did the weakness of the central

Soviet government affect the independence movements in Eastern Europe and the Soviet republics?
4. **Writing to Persuade** In a brief essay explain why you think the end of the Cold War has or has not led to a "new world order."
5. **Hypothesizing** Was the breakup of the Soviet Union inevitable? Why or why not?

SECTION 1 REVIEW ANSWERS

IDENTIFY
For significance, see the following pages:
détente (p. 828)
Carter Doctrine (p. 829)
Solidarity (p. 829)
Lech Walesa (p. 829)
Mikhail Gorbachev (p. 829)
perestroika (p. 829)
glasnost (p. 829)
ethnic cleansing (p. 832)

LOCATE
For locations, see the map on p. 830.

1. The purpose of détente was to ease tensions between the superpowers. Results included trade and nuclear arms agreements.
2. Gorbachev hoped to reform Soviet political and economic systems and create a new policy of openness.
3. The Soviet Union did not back the Communist leaders of Eastern Europe. Governments were forced to reform. Soviet republics broke away from the Soviet Union, causing its collapse.
4. has—the Soviet Union dissolved; many former communist countries held democratic elections; has not—events like the Gulf War and fighting in the former Yugoslavia suggest a new era of instability
5. yes—only force held it together; no—perhaps it could have been held together by democracy

SECTION 2

CORE LESSON PLAN
See pages 825E and 825F for Lesson Plan 30.2.

SECTION 2
A New Revolution in Technology

FOCUS

- What resulted from the growing alliance between science and technology after World War II?

- How did the United States and the Soviet Union lead the way in space exploration?

- How did television and computers affect the world?

- What were the consequences of new developments in biology and medicine after World War II?

After World War II, new discoveries in medicine saved millions of lives, while developments in agriculture contributed to accelerated population growth. Meanwhile, inventions in transportation and communications technology tied the peoples of the planet together more closely than ever before. Science and technology became more and more closely linked. This alliance solved many problems, but new challenges also arose.

Nuclear power plant

War, Science, and Technology

World War II and its aftermath dramatically demonstrated the power that could be produced by combining science and technology. In physics, for example, the research of atomic and subatomic particles by scientists such as Albert Einstein and James Franck in the early 1900s led to a new understanding of the physical universe. During and after the war, governments sponsored programs that combined these theories with modern engineering techniques to give human beings the ability to change the world around them more than ever before.

Nuclear power. Science and technology came together to produce new sources of power—atomic and then nuclear energy. Although the first use of the new source of power came in war, with the dropping of atomic bombs on Hiroshima and Nagasaki, after the war many scientists and political leaders hoped that atomic and nuclear energy might be used for peaceful purposes. Initially nuclear energy promised to produce low-cost electricity without significant air pollution. In the 1950s several nations, including the United States, Great Britain, France, and the Soviet Union, began to build nuclear power plants. By 1971 about 70 nuclear power plants were in operation around the world.

Even the peaceful use of nuclear power, however, worried many people who feared that the problems it raised outweighed its benefits. In addition to releasing heat, atomic and nuclear reactions released high levels of radiation. If uncontrolled, radiation is destructive to all organisms, including human beings. Nuclear reactors produced radioactive waste materials that were difficult and expensive to get rid of.

Fears of nuclear power increased after serious accidents. At the Three Mile Island power plant in Pennsylvania, a nuclear reactor failed in 1979, nearly causing a meltdown. Even more serious was an explosion in 1986 at the nuclear plant in Chernobyl in the Soviet Union. Within two weeks of the accident, 30 people died from radiation sickness. Scientists estimated that death tolls around Chernobyl caused by radiation sickness, cancer, and birth defects would reach into the thousands. While the area around Chernobyl itself became uninhabitable, much of the radiation was also blown across other countries in Europe. The disaster at Chernobyl led to heightened anxiety about nuclear energy, and by the 1990s some countries had begun to scale back their nuclear power programs.

A new revolution in transportation. Developments during World War II also contributed to ongoing advances in transportation. In Germany, for example, the desire for improved weapons led to the development of jet airplanes and rockets. After the war, advanced airplane designs were adapted for civilian use, and air travel increased around the world. In the 1960s and 1970s jets replaced smaller propeller-driven planes. Flying more than 400 miles per hour, jets allowed people to travel almost anywhere in the world in a matter of hours. Jet planes could also carry more passengers, which helped make air travel more affordable. In the late 1960s France and Britain jointly developed the Concorde, a supersonic jet that eventually reached speeds of more than 1,000 miles per hour.

Similar scientific developments also revolutionized transportation on the ground. Incorporating new aerodynamic designs, high-speed trains in Japan and Europe rocketed along at speeds well above 150 miles per hour. Meanwhile, the abundance of cheap gasoline and the development of smaller, more affordable cars contributed to a global increase in the use of automobiles. In 1950 there was one car for every 46 people in the world, but by 1990 there was one car for every 12 people.

The growing alliance between science and technology after World War II gave people greater power than ever before to transform the world around them.

♻ The Space Race

Perhaps the most exciting combination of science and technology came in space exploration. As the Cold War developed, the implications of combining nuclear weapons with the conquest of the air set the United States and the Soviet Union on a race to gain strategic command of space. In 1957 the Soviets put the first satellite, called *Sputnik*, into orbit. Not wanting the United States to fall behind, Congress established the **National Aeronautics and Space Administration** (NASA) to expand American space technology. In 1958 the United States launched its first satellite, *Explorer I*, and the space race was on.

In 1961 Soviet cosmonaut Yuri Gagarin became the first man in space, and in 1963 his comrade Valentina Tereshkova became the first woman in space. Determined to surpass the Soviets, President John F. Kennedy committed the United States to putting a man on the moon by the end of the decade. Presidents Lyndon Johnson and Richard Nixon fulfilled the pledge, channeling the nation's resources into NASA's manned space program. On July 21, 1969, the *Apollo 11* mission achieved the goal.

Across the globe, millions of people gathered around their television sets to watch the first live transmission from the moon. *Apollo 11* astronaut Neil Armstrong spoke to NASA's mission control from the lunar surface:

❝I'm at the foot of the ladder. . . . The surface [of the moon] appears to be very, very fine-grained. . . . I'm going to step off the LM [lunar module] now. That's one small step for man, one giant leap for mankind.❞

▲ In April 1971 two U.S. Apollo astronauts collected soil and rocks on the surface of the moon.

After the late 1960s, it was the Soviets who hoped to catch up to U.S. missions into outer space. The Apollo moon program was followed by more space flights, as both the United States and the Soviet Union began to explore the solar system with unmanned space probes. Over the coming years many other countries launched satellites for military and scientific purposes.

The 1980s brought continued advances in space. In 1981 the United States launched the first reusable manned spacecraft, the space shuttle *Columbia*. Astronauts carried out dozens of successful shuttle missions over the next several years, despite a horrifying explosion in January 1986 that destroyed the shuttle *Challenger* and killed everyone on board, including Christa McAuliffe, a social studies teacher who would have been the first civilian space passenger.

The end of the Cold War led to American and Russian cooperation in space. In 1995 the U.S. space shuttle *Atlantis* docked with the Russian space station *Mir* for five days, while plans were laid to build a larger space station for joint use.

In 1997 an unmanned NASA probe named *Pathfinder* landed on Mars and collected data from the Martian surface. Many scientists began to discuss the possibility of a human colony on the red planet.

Through a coordination of science and technology, the United States and the Soviet Union led the way in space exploration.

▲ Crew members of the U.S. space shuttle *Atlantis* before their mission to dock with the Russian space station *Mir*

♻ The Information Age

The search for smaller, lighter parts for spacecraft led to many other technological breakthroughs, particularly in the field of communications. The new communications technology allowed ideas to spread so rapidly that some hailed these advances as the **Information Revolution**.

Radio and television. The tiny, lightweight transistor, invented in 1948, replaced much bulkier and heavier vacuum tubes in electronic components. The transistor thus revolutionized communications around the world. Transistor radios became almost universal in the late 1950s and 1960s—only to be surpassed in popularity by the television. Although television had been invented earlier, it was not until after World War II that technological improvements made it inexpensive enough for many people to own. For example, fewer than 1 percent of American homes had a television set in 1945, but by 1975 nearly every home had at least one TV.

Radio and television not only provided people with entertainment and news but also gave businesses new media to advertise their products. Through radio and television many modern consumer products became popular around the world. The results were sometimes dramatic—as President Sukarno of Indonesia once complained:

❝ *You may not think of a refrigerator as a revolutionary weapon, but if a peasant woman sees one on the TV in her village square and realizes what it could do for her and her family, the germ of revolt is planted.* ❞

By the 1990s television was available in every country in the world.

Miniaturization. The growing popularity of radio and television was mainly because of miniaturization—the replacement of bulky, expensive electrical equipment with smaller,

Literature THROUGH TIME

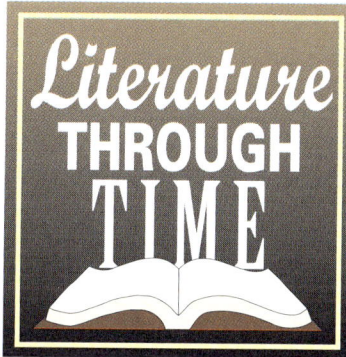

Science Fiction

Although its roots lie in the 1800s, since the end of World War II science fiction has become one of the most popular forms of literature. An important theme of science fiction has been the human dream of spaceflight, and no one has written more eloquently about this human yearning to break through Earth's gravitational field than Ray Bradbury. The following excerpt, from his short story "The End of the Beginning," tells of a couple awaiting with anticipation the first space launch.

His wife, her head back, studied the stars immediately above her and murmured, "Why?" She closed her eyes. "Why the rockets, why tonight? Why all this? I'd like to know."

He examined her face, pale in the vast powdering light of the Milky Way. He felt the stirring of an answer. . . .

"All I know is it's really the end of the beginning. The Stone Age, Bronze Age, Iron Age; from now on we'll lump all those together under one big name for when we walked on Earth and heard the birds at morning and cried with envy. Maybe we'll call it the Earth Age, or maybe the Age of Gravity. Millions of years we fought gravity. When we were amoebas and fish we struggled to get out of the sea without gravity crushing us. Once safe on shore we fought to stand upright without gravity breaking our new invention, the spine, tried to walk without stumbling, run without falling. A billion years Gravity kept us home, mocked us with wind and clouds, cabbage moths and locusts. That's what's so God-awful big about tonight . . . it's the end of old man Gravity and the age we'll remember him by, for once and all. I don't know where they'll divide the ages, at the Persians, who dreamt of flying carpets, or the Chinese, who, all unknowing celebrated birthdays and New Years with strung ladyfingers and high skyrockets, or some minute, some incredible second in the next hour. But we're in at the end of a billion years trying, the end of something long and to us humans, anyway, honorable."

Ray Bradbury

Understanding Literature

1. How does Bradbury view space flight?
2. How does his vision of the future affect his view of the past?

cheaper electronic equipment. Miniaturization made possible dozens of other new products—pocket calculators, digital watches, compact tape recorders, and many other consumer items.

Engineers used miniaturization techniques to develop **lasers**, which concentrate light and release it in bursts of high intensity. Lasers could be used in industry to cut metal and other materials with great precision. They also revolutionized communications, since they could relay signals at the speed of light. In medicine, lasers made possible new, safer, and more efficient types of surgery.

Computerization. Perhaps the most important and remarkable product of the new technological age was the computer. Modern computers evolved from the "analytical engine," a mechanical calculating machine developed in the 1830s by a British inventor named Charles Babbage. Refinements improved the performance of mechanical calculators during the next hundred years, but the major breakthroughs occurred in the mid-1900s. Researchers discovered that electrons could replace the levers and wheels of Babbage's machine. Smaller and much more efficient than mechanical parts, electronic switches made computers faster and more powerful than mechanical calculators.

The first generation of modern computing began with the 1946 development of ENIAC (Electronic Numerical Integrator and Calculator) at the University of Pennsylvania. Using large numbers of vacuum tubes to produce the necessary electronic switches, ENIAC was so large that it occupied an entire room. By the mid-1950s, however, ENIAC was obsolete—replaced by less bulky machines using the new transistors. Further miniaturization in the 1950s gave rise to **integrated circuits**, which contained hundreds and then thousands of transistors on a single silicon chip.

As computers were made smaller and more powerful, they also became standard components in other machines. For example, computers could run new medical machines such as the CAT scanner that helped doctors diagnose illnesses more quickly and accurately. Computers could also guide and track spacecraft and airplanes as well as diagnose problems in car engines. By the 1980s home and office computers could be interconnected through the **Internet**, a global network tying together millions of computers. By 1994 about 40 million people worldwide used the Internet regularly.

The introduction of television and computers allowed people to share information worldwide more easily and rapidly than ever before.

Combatting Disease

In addition to the advances made possible by developments in physics and electronics, equally revolutionary breakthroughs were made in the biological sciences. One of the most important developments was the introduction of **antibiotics**—drugs like penicillin and streptomycin that destroy or limit bacterial infection. Although penicillin was first discovered by Sir Alexander Fleming, a Scottish scientist, in the 1920s, antibiotics did not become widely available until after World War II. Equally important was the widespread use of vaccination against disease. Worldwide campaigns against diseases like polio and smallpox were extremely successful. By the 1980s smallpox had been virtually wiped out.

◄ In February 1946 ENIAC was formally started up. The computer contained 18,000 tubes, and its power source was half as large as the machine itself.

New diseases. At the same time, the appearance of new diseases threatened human life. In the 1980s world health experts were alarmed by the rapid spread of Acquired Immune Deficiency Syndrome, or AIDS. This deadly disease, for which no cure was known, was caused by HIV, or the human immunodeficiency virus. The United Nations estimated in 1996 that about 21.8 million people had developed AIDS or had been infected with HIV.

Genetic research. Perhaps the most promising—and disturbing—medical breakthroughs occurred in genetic research. In 1962 the Nobel Prize for medicine went to three scientists— James D. Watson from the United States and Francis Crick and Maurice Wilkins from Great Britain—for their 1953 discovery of the structure of DNA, or deoxyribonucleic acid. DNA proved to be a basic part of all **genes**, the small units of chromosomes that determine an individual's physical characteristics, such as eye and hair color.

By the 1980s biological researchers had begun to use genetic engineering to alter genes in laboratories to produce new forms of plants and even animals. Many medical professionals saw genetic research as a potential solution to human genetic disorders as well as some diseases. Genetic engineers learned how to produce

▲ A scientist displays genetically engineered vegetables. The process can produce vegetables that resist disease and decay.

specific proteins to treat diabetes and heart disease. Genetic research also raised the controversial prospect of producing "designer babies," whereby parents could determine all the physical characteristics of their children. Many people debated the ethics of humanity's growing control over the processes of life.

After World War II developments in biology and medicine contributed to improved health, but also raised ethical questions about genetics.

SECTION 2 REVIEW

IDENTIFY and explain the significance of the following:
National Aeronautics and
Space Administration
Neil Armstrong
Information Revolution
lasers
integrated circuits
Internet
antibiotics
Sir Alexander Fleming
genes

1. **Main Idea** What were the results of the growing alliance between science and technology after World War II?
2. **Main Idea** What have the United States and Russia accomplished in space exploration?
3. **Technology** How have television and computers changed the world?

4. **Writing to Explain** Imagine that you are a biological researcher. Write a short article for a scientific journal explaining the consequences of biological and medical research since World War II.
5. **Evaluating** Do the risks involved in producing nuclear energy outweigh the benefits? Why or why not?

SECTION 2 REVIEW ANSWERS

IDENTIFY
For significance, see the following pages:
National Aeronautics and Space Administration (p. 835)
Neil Armstrong (p. 835)
Information Revolution (p. 836)
lasers (p. 837)
integrated circuits (p. 838)
Internet (p. 838)
antibiotics (p. 838)
Sir Alexander Fleming (p. 838)
genes (p. 839)

1. The alliance allowed people greater control of the world around them and promoted the development of new sources of power and transportation.
2. The two countries have led the way in space exploration, with such developments as the first moon landing, unmanned space probes, shuttle missions, and a space station.
3. They revolutionized communication around the world, providing people with entertainment, news, and a new market for consumer goods.
4. Articles should discuss the development of antibiotics and vaccinations for the effective treatment and prevention of diseases, as well as the controversial use of genetic engineering to change the natural development of living things.
5. yes—nuclear power can provide low-cost energy with less air pollution; no—possible accidents could be disastrous and disposal of nuclear waste is costly and difficult

SECTION 3
Environmental Challenges

FOCUS

- Why have many people worried about continuing industrialization?
- How have environmentalists fought to protect the environment?
- Why are many scientists concerned about the loss of biodiversity?

A long with the many benefits of new technology and modernization came enormous problems. As the earth's population continued to grow, technological developments and industrialization led to greater changes in the environment. Scientists and environmentalists warned of the potentially harmful effects of continued pollution and loss of biodiversity.

This image shows ozone in the Southern Hemisphere in 1994; the ozone hole is in the center, within the blue boundary.

Pollution

As the world population continued to grow, and as industrialization and urbanization continued to spread after World War II, people became more aware of the impact such growth had on the environment. By the 1990s perhaps the worst cases of pollution were found in the former Soviet Union, where decades of unregulated industrial pollution had left an environmental disaster. Similar problems confronted peoples around the world.

Acid rain. Besides fallout from nuclear accidents like Chernobyl, possibly the most serious new pollution was **acid rain**. Acid rain is a toxic mixture produced when rain or snow falls through air polluted by common products of combustion, such as sulfur dioxide and nitrogen oxide. During the decades after World War II, acid rain ravaged the Black Forest of southern Germany, as well as other forests in Europe. Acid rain also wiped out fish populations in many lakes. Ancient buildings, such as the Parthenon in Greece, have suffered erosion from acid rain.

Ozone depletion. Some scientists also attributed the apparent depletion of the **ozone layer** of the stratosphere to the effects of pollution. Ozone, a form of oxygen with three atoms rather than two, protects the earth from the sun's harmful ultraviolet radiation. Most organisms, including humans, can naturally deal with normal amounts of ultraviolet radiation. Overexposure to ultraviolet radiation is known to cause skin cancers among humans and has led to the destruction of many plant and animal species.

During the 1980s and 1990s, atmospheric scientists noticed that a large "hole" developed seasonally in the ozone layer over Antarctica. Many feared that the hole would spread to other parts of the globe. Some scientists argued that the major cause of ozone depletion was the release of **chlorofluorocarbons** (CFCs)—carbon-based combinations of chlorine and fluorine used in such things as aerosol spray cans, refrigerants, and the manufacture of plastics and electronic components. Some scientists speculated that CFCs released into the atmosphere drifted upward to the stratosphere, where they broke down the ozone. Though not all scientists agreed with this analysis, during the 1980s and 1990s the major

Ozone Depletion, 1991

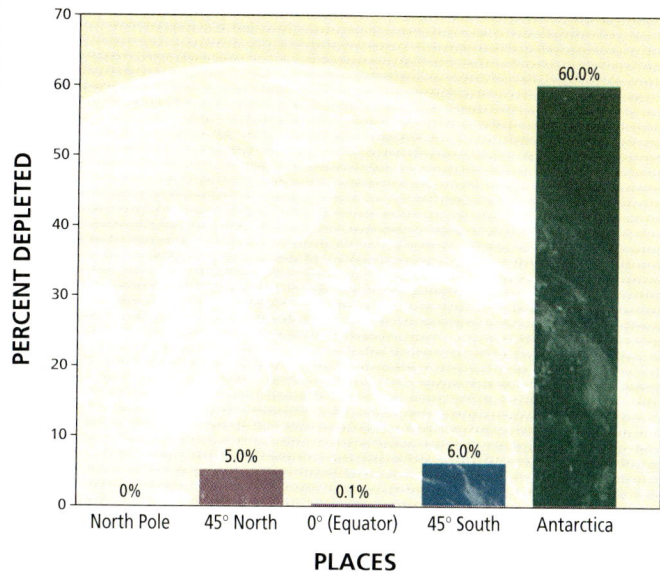

Chart: PERCENT DEPLETED vs. PLACES

- North Pole: 0%
- 45° North: 5.0%
- 0° (Equator): 0.1%
- 45° South: 6.0%
- Antarctica: 60.0%

Environmental Controversy Many scientists believe that ozone depletion in the atmospere has been caused by pollution.

? Analyzing How might a person use these same statistics to argue that ozone depletion is or is not caused by industrialization? *(Hint: Notice where most of the world's major cities are located.)*

industrial countries took steps to cut back on the use of CFCs. In 1994 Germany banned CFC production, while the United States and Canada decided to phase out CFCs by 1996.

Global warming. In the 1980s some scientists also expressed concern about global warming. The burning of fuels, such as gasoline or coal, releases large amounts of carbon dioxide into the atmosphere. This excess carbon dioxide traps more heat near the earth, a process which is called the **greenhouse effect**. Some scientists warned that since the Industrial Revolution, human beings had increased the output of carbon dioxide so much that it threatened to raise global temperatures. They believed that this could have great effects on the delicate ecological balance of the natural environment. Not everyone agreed, however.

Other scientists noted that data on global warming trends was very limited—records do not go back before the 1800s. In addition, geologists and geographers pointed out that the earth had experienced many periods of warming and cooling during the time of its existence. They argued that there was little way to know whether the current trend was caused by industrialization. As the controversy continued, Patrick Michaels, a well-known and respected geographer, warned:

66 *The true legacy of [the] global warming [notion], which the data argue is much more benign [harmless] than it is perceived to be, will be the destruction of the public's faith in science. Tragically, it will be noted by historians in the 21st century, that even by the mid-1980s, the data had indicated that the then-popular vision of climate catastrophe was a failure.* 99

Many scientists warned that the effects of industrialization were harming the earth's environment, but others disagreed.

♻ The Problem of Pesticides

Not all pollution was a matter of industrial waste. By the late 1800s scientific researchers had begun to produce new chemicals, including fertilizers and pesticides, to help increase food production and to eliminate insects harmful to crops. By the 1950s perhaps the most widely used of the new chemicals was the so-called miracle pesticide DDT.

BIOGRAPHY Some scientists, such as American biologist Rachel Carson, opposed the new chemicals. Born in 1907 in Springdale, Pennsylvania, Carson eventually became a biologist. Dedicated to conservation issues, Carson soon began to worry about the effects of synthetic chemicals on the natural environment. In 1962 she published a highly controversial work, *Silent Spring*, warning that overuse of the new pesticides, especially DDT, was killing wildlife and polluting the entire environment.

Graph Answer
There is a significant amount of depletion in the areas where most of the cities are located, but the highest level is in Antarctica, an area which does not have large cities.

R RESOURCE ACTIVITY

GLOBAL HISTORY RESOURCE CENTER
Reading: *Pollution Threatens Russia's Future*
Image: *Severe Air Pollution in Eastern Europe*

Print out and distribute the image and the reading. Have students read about the health crisis in Russia. Then have students create five-point plans that countries of Eastern Europe and the Commonwealth of Independent States could follow to reduce pollution and improve environmental quality.

Level 3

R RESOURCE ACTIVITY

GLOBAL HISTORY RESOURCE CENTER
Reading: *Global Warming Alarm Sounded*

Print out and distribute the reading. Have students read about the potential effects of global warming. Tell students to imagine they are newspaper reporters whose assignment is to write an article explaining both sides of the issue.

Level 3

Geography AND HISTORY

The Vanishing Forests

Imagine that the earth has been filmed for the last 10,000 years and that an audience is now viewing this film on fast-foward, so that each 1,000 years is just one minute of real time.

For the first 7 minutes of the 10-minute film, almost nothing happens. The earth appears mostly blue and green, with forest covering 34 percent of its landmass. Nine minutes into the film, the audience begins to see bare spots across Europe, Central America, China, and India. Within a few seconds, Europe and China have great bald patches. Six seconds later, eastern North America loses much of its forests.

In the last three seconds, which represent the time since 1950, huge amounts of green disappear from Japan, the Philippines, Southeast Asia, Central America, Africa, and parts of North and South America. As the film ends, Siberia and northern Canada lose forest faster than the eye can record what it sees. Only 12 percent of the earth's surface retains its original forest area intact.

Deforestation has become a global concern, particularly in the tropical rain forests. Numerous environmental and governmental agencies have tried with limited success to solve the problem. However, efforts to restrict timber harvest, to recycle, and to provide alternates for wood products are increasing. For example, coal, oil, and natural gas have replaced wood in many industrial countries, and many products traditionally made from trees, such as furniture, are now being made from metals or plastics.

Linking Geography and History

1. During what time period has the greatest amount of deforestation occurred?
2. What can people do to prevent deforestation?

Deforestation Around the World, c. 1940–1995

Losing the Rain Forest In recent decades, the majestic trees of the world's tropical rain forests have been destroyed at an alarming rate.

? Region What country has the world's largest remaining area of rain forest?

Although Carson died in 1964, her efforts inspired major investigations into DDT's effects. In 1972 the U.S. Environmental Protection Agency banned the use of DDT—though other countries continued to use it heavily. In the meantime, *Silent Spring* encouraged a new movement of environmental activism that soon spread from the United States to Europe and other parts of the world.

Rachel Carson
B I O G R A P H Y

Environmentalists have fought against the production and use of certain chemicals that may be harmful to living things.

♻ Biodiversity

In addition to other problems, the growth of population in many countries also led to the conversion of forests, prairies, and wetlands to urban areas. Such destruction of these natural habitats led to the endangerment or extinction of many plant and animal species.

Some scientists and others warned that a reduction of **biodiversity**—the natural variety of plants and animals in the environment—might threaten human health and prosperity. They noted that the global **ecosphere**, or the interlocking system of life on the planet, was intricate beyond present human understanding. What damaged one part of the ecosphere, they argued, might damage other parts, including those that affect humans.

Despite such arguments, efforts to preserve the earth's biodiversity had only mixed success. For example, even after years of environmentalists' warnings about the dangers of destroying the world's rain forests, developing countries in Africa and Latin America continued to follow practices that harmed their natural environments, such as burning forest to clear areas for planting and ranching. Chico Mendes, an environmental activist in Brazil, described the process in his own country—shortly before he was killed by ranchers who disliked his interference in their livelihoods:

❝ In the last half century Amazônia has never seen so many fires as in 1988. They are burning everything. Our airports were closed one week in 1987 because of the smoke. This year they were closed one month for the same reason. When you look down from the airplane, Amazônia is nothing but smoke. How it hurts! ❞

Efforts to protect the environment continued, however. In 1992 environmentalists convinced more than 150 nations attending a United Nations environmental conference in Brazil to sign a Convention on Biological Diversity. But the terms of the treaty were vague, and enforcement appeared difficult, if not impossible.

Many scientists fear that the loss of biodiversity will endanger Earth's ecological balance and destroy plant and animal species useful to humans.

SECTION 3 REVIEW

IDENTIFY and explain the significance of the following:
  acid rain
  ozone layer
  chlorofluorocarbons
  greenhouse effect
  Rachel Carson
  biodiversity
  ecosphere

1. *Main Idea* How has industrialization affected the environment?
2. *Main Idea* What are the possible consequences of the loss of biodiversity?
3. *Politics and Law* What efforts have environmentalists made to protect nature?

4. *Writing to Persuade* Write a short essay explaining why countries should or should not have the right to do what they like with their natural resources, such as rain forests.
5. *Synthesizing* Why are some people concerned about the "health" of the planet?

SECTION 3 REVIEW ANSWERS

IDENTIFY
For significance, see the following pages:
acid rain (p. 840)
ozone layer (p. 840)
chlorofluorocarbons (p. 840)
greenhouse effect (p. 841)
Rachel Carson (p. 841)
biodiversity (p. 843)
ecosphere (p. 843)

1. pollution, acid rain, ozone depletion, and global warming
2. Human health and prosperity may be threatened because of the loss of medicine sources and changes in the ecosphere.
3. fought to get laws passed eliminating the use of pesticides and other possibly harmful chemicals
4. should—more powerful nations should not determine what other countries do with their resources; should not—countries should not be allowed to destroy resources that might impact the entire world
5. They feel that the health of human beings could be directly tied to the health of the planet. Some might also argue that destruction of the planet's species is morally wrong.

SECTION 4

CORE LESSON PLAN
See pages 825I and
825J for Lesson Plan
30.4.

Theme: Social Relations

Nelson Mandela spent 26 years as a political prisoner. During his time in prison, he became a living legend for many people. Africans from all over the country celebrated his release. Thousands of South Africans, as well as many foreign journalists, were on hand for his first speech after his release.

Critical Thinking Ask students why so many black South Africans were interested in Nelson Mandela.

ANSWER: Students might suggest that he was a symbol of triumph over the system of apartheid.

SECTION 4
Democracy and Free Trade

FOCUS

- How did democratic government fare from the 1970s to the 1990s?

- How and why did many governments try to restructure the welfare state in the 1980s and 1990s?

- How did international trade evolve during this period?

The end of the Cold War and the demise of the Soviet Union seemed to foreshadow an end to the ideological struggle that had embroiled much of the world for much of the 1900s. Communism as a political system was dead or dying, vanquished by democracy. Socialism as an economic system was giving way to free market capitalism.

Russians examine sports shoes newly available in Moscow after communism gave way to a free market.

The Rising Tide of Democracy

The most striking feature of the events that surrounded the end of the Cold War was the speed with which the Soviet Union and its Eastern European neighbors abandoned the ideology of communism. Yet the abandonment of communism was part of a larger trend in world political affairs that had actually begun in the mid-1970s as authoritarian regimes in general began to lose legitimacy and democracy made substantial gains. After decades of dictatorship in Portugal a constitutional government finally began in 1976. In 1975, on the death of dictator Francisco Franco, Spain too returned to democracy under the restored constitutional monarch, King Juan Carlos I. This democratizing trend continued in the 1980s and especially in the 1990s after the fall of communism in the Soviet Union and Eastern Europe.

Democracy made particularly important gains in Asia. South Korea and Taiwan both allowed increased popular participation in politics. Democracy returned to the Philippines after nearly 15 years of autocratic rule by Ferdinand Marcos. In Pakistan and Bangladesh, military rulers stepped aside, if not very far and not always for very long. Latin America likewise witnessed a democratizing trend, as Nicaragua, Chile, Brazil, Argentina, Peru, and Mexico moved from various levels of dictatorship and authoritarian rule to more democratic systems of government. In South Africa, the formerly dispossessed black majority elected a government headed by Nelson Mandela.

During the 1980s and 1990s, many countries abandoned communism. The number of democratic or partly democratic countries increased.

Holdouts on Democracy

Despite the advance of democracy, some governments continued to rule in an authoritarian way. Perhaps the most important holdout on democracy was the People's Republic of China, where hard-line communists cracked down on a growing pro-democracy movement even as the country sought to institute free-market reforms.

In Cuba Fidel Castro continued to hold on to power, although the collapse of Soviet support for the Cuban economy caused living standards to drop dramatically. As a consequence, in the early 1990s some 30,000 Cubans tried to flee Cuba for Florida in boats or homemade rafts.

Communist rule also continued in North Korea, despite the death of longtime dictator Kim Il Sung in 1994. There, too, the failure of communist economic policies led to considerable hardship. In the mid-1990s North Korea stood on the verge of mass starvation and had to seek assistance from the international community.

Communists were not the only ones who resisted the trend toward democracy. Muslim revolutionaries limited democratic participation to varying degrees in Iran and Sudan, for example, while older revolutionary dictatorships continued in Syria and Iraq. Saudi Arabia remained under the autocratic rule of the Saudi royal family, with only an appointed council to advise the king. A military junta continued to repress democracy in Burma, which it renamed Myanmar. In Indonesia, President Suharto, who had come to power in a military coup, continued to place economic development ahead of political rights. The world was becoming more democratic as the year 2000 approached, but it still had a way to go.

China, Cuba, and other countries resisted the global trend toward democracy.

♻ The Retreat of the Welfare State

To a considerable extent, the movement toward democracy around the world went hand in hand with a general recognition of the failure of socialist economic models and the success of free-market principles. In many countries in Western Europe and North America, for example, people voiced concern over the effects of the expansion of social welfare programs and increased government intervention in the economy. They charged that such policies and programs hurt the economy and burdened average

citizens by raising taxes and increasing the cost of doing business. In the United States, concern became even greater in the 1970s, after the Arab oil embargo of 1973 dramatically drove up energy costs.

Stagflation. Tax increases and increases in wages led to **inflation**, a general rise in the cost of goods throughout most of Western Europe and North America. By the 1970s, a combination of high unemployment and high inflation called **stagflation** led to a general period of economic hardship. In 1979, the election of Margaret Thatcher as the first woman prime minister of Great Britain signaled the beginning of a general backlash in the Western world against the costs of maintaining the welfare state.

📖 BIOGRAPHY Born in 1925, Margaret Thatcher was raised in the small town of Grantham, England. Always interested in politics, in 1959 Thatcher was elected to Parliament as a Conservative. In 1970 she became the only woman in the Cabinet of Prime Minister Edward Heath. In 1975, shortly after a Labour Party victory, she challenged Heath for the leadership of the Conservative Party and won, becoming the first woman to lead a major political party in Europe. As the new leader of the opposition, Thatcher began to preach her own free-market philosophy as the solution to Britain's problems.

Margaret Thatcher
BIOGRAPHY

In 1979, frustrated by the Labour Government's inability to improve the economy, and especially to control the growing power of Britain's more radical labor unions, the British public elected the Conservatives to power and Margaret Thatcher became the first woman prime minister in the Western world. Thatcher soon put her program of tax cuts and free-market economic principles into practice. During a bitter, year-long strike by coalminers in 1984–85, Thatcher essentially broke the unions' hold over British economic and political life. Over the next several years, she also worked hard to reduce the participation of the government in Britain's economy. In particular, she privatized many major industries, such as British Steel, British Airways, British Gas, and others.

By the late 1980s many in Britain began to feel that Thatcher had remained in power too long. Her popularity gradually declined. Both her opposition to closer political ties between Britain and the European Community and her efforts to impose an unpopular reform of local government led opponents within her own party to challenge her leadership in 1990. Realizing that she was unlikely to win, Thatcher resigned as prime minister and was succeeded by her hand-picked successor, John Major. She had been the longest-serving prime minister since the early 1800s, winning a record three general elections.

Despite the decline in Thatcher's personal popularity, her policies had transformed the basic character of British politics. Apart from a greater commitment to Great Britain's participation in European integration, Prime Minister John Major maintained most of Thatcher's policies during his own premiership. Even when the British people turned many Conservatives out of office in 1997, giving the Labour Party control of the prime ministership, government policies did not change dramatically. Labour Party leader Tony Blair, the new prime minister, accepted many of Thatcher's ideas and generally abandoned his party's traditional socialist policies. Elsewhere in the Western world, other countries also followed Thatcher's lead in restructuring welfare policy.

▲ Many Americans approved of President Reagan's conservative, anticommunist approach.

The United States. Thatcher's ideas were largely shared by President Ronald Reagan. Like Thatcher, Reagan was a devoted free-market capitalist. Reagan's own landslide election in 1980 marked a shift in the United States toward a more conservative approach to government.

Although Reagan wanted to roll back the tide of "Big Government," he especially wanted to win the Cold War. Consequently, he struck a compromise with the Democrats who controlled Congress. He agreed not to press his calls for cuts in social programs in exchange for increased military funding. He was willing to do this because he believed that the money for all of the programs could be raised through a tax cut designed to stimulate the economy. When the tax cut did not generate enough new wealth to cover all of the money that was being spent on the military and social programs, the national debt began to climb.

Despite concerns over the size of the national debt, many Americans continued to desire lower taxes and reforms in the welfare state. Reagan's vice-president, George Bush, was elected president in 1988 at least partly because of his dramatic public pledge: "Read my lips! No new taxes!" When Bush compromised with the Democratic leaders of Congress and accepted a rise in taxes, many voters were outraged. At least partly in consequence, in the elections of 1992, many refused to support Bush, and Democrat Bill Clinton was elected president with less than 50 percent of the vote. Clinton's support was partly due to his pledge that he was a "new Democrat"—meaning that he did not favor "Big Government" as the answer to people's problems. Even so, in the elections of 1994 the American people elected a majority of Republican candidates to both the House of Representatives and the Senate.

Despite the complaints of critics about the social costs of their programs, the general successes of Thatcher and Reagan in stimulating economic growth convinced many other countries of the benefits of allowing market forces to replace government economic intervention as much as possible. Gradually, with a few exceptions, the countries of Western Europe began to modify their welfare states along more market-oriented lines and to draw back from the welfare state policies of the past.

France. Perhaps the most notable exception to the trend was France, where in 1981 French voters elected their first socialist president, François Mitterrand. Mitterrand increased social welfare spending and nationalized major industries. To pay for his programs, he also increased taxes. The result was a considerable increase in inflation and major budgetary problems. Within a short time, Mitterrand had to cancel the bulk of his plans and to cut government spending. Nevertheless, he remained committed to preserving, and when possible expanding, the French welfare state. Not until 1993 did French voters finally tire of the costs of his policies and vote in a conservative majority in parliamentary elections.

In 1995 the French people elected a conservative president, Jacques Chirac, the former mayor of Paris. When Chirac tried to move away from the welfare state policies of his predecessor, however, large segments of the population bitterly opposed him. He found that once extended, the benefits of the welfare state can sometimes prove difficult to take back.

*S*luggish economic growth and the costs of the welfare state led many western governments to reduce their role in the economy and to encourage free-market forces.*

Trade Organizations and Alliances, 1994

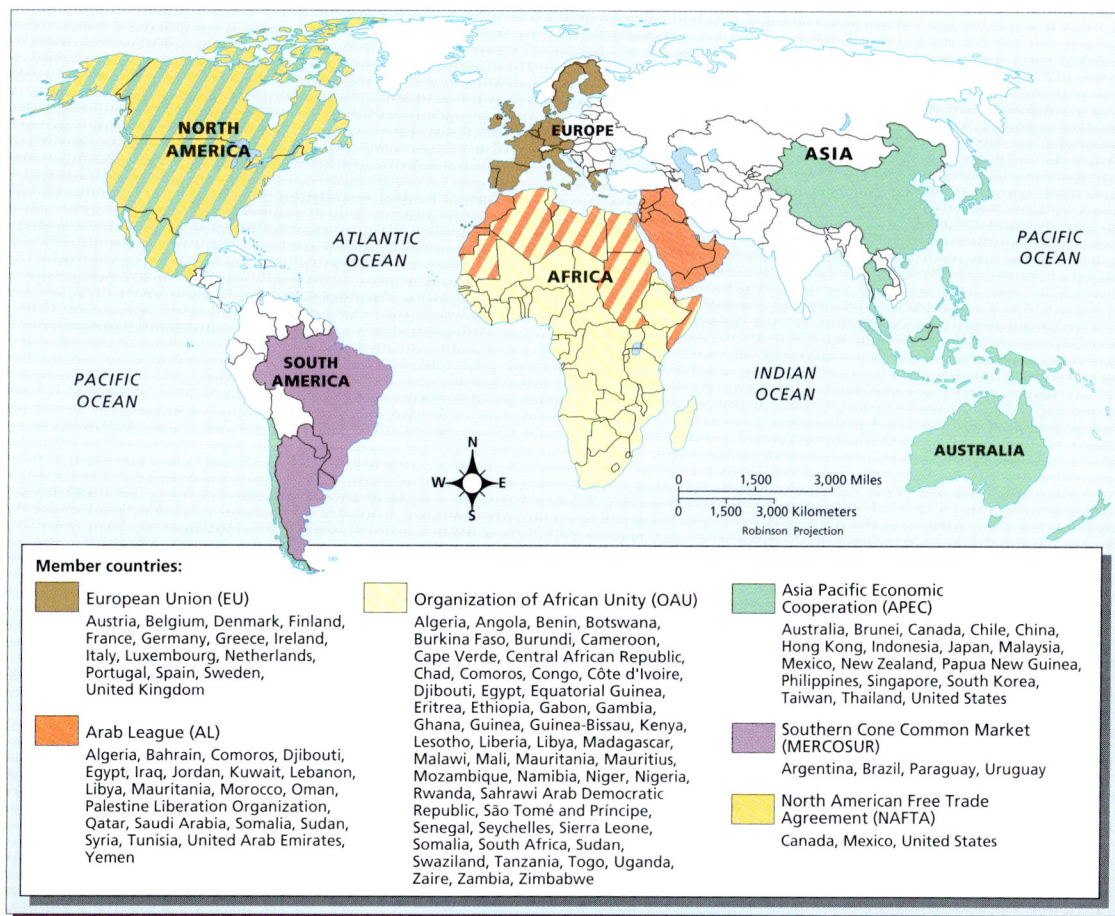

Member countries:

European Union (EU)
Austria, Belgium, Denmark, Finland, France, Germany, Greece, Ireland, Italy, Luxembourg, Netherlands, Portugal, Spain, Sweden, United Kingdom

Arab League (AL)
Algeria, Bahrain, Comoros, Djibouti, Egypt, Iraq, Jordan, Kuwait, Lebanon, Libya, Mauritania, Morocco, Oman, Palestine Liberation Organization, Qatar, Saudi Arabia, Somalia, Sudan, Syria, Tunisia, United Arab Emirates, Yemen

Organization of African Unity (OAU)
Algeria, Angola, Benin, Botswana, Burkina Faso, Burundi, Cameroon, Cape Verde, Central African Republic, Chad, Comoros, Congo, Côte d'Ivoire, Djibouti, Egypt, Equatorial Guinea, Eritrea, Ethiopia, Gabon, Gambia, Ghana, Guinea, Guinea-Bissau, Kenya, Lesotho, Liberia, Libya, Madagascar, Malawi, Mali, Mauritania, Mauritius, Mozambique, Namibia, Niger, Nigeria, Rwanda, Sahrawi Arab Democratic Republic, São Tomé and Príncipe, Senegal, Seychelles, Sierra Leone, Somalia, South Africa, Sudan, Swaziland, Tanzania, Togo, Uganda, Zaire, Zambia, Zimbabwe

Asia Pacific Economic Cooperation (APEC)
Australia, Brunei, Canada, Chile, China, Hong Kong, Indonesia, Japan, Malaysia, Mexico, New Zealand, Papua New Guinea, Philippines, Singapore, South Korea, Taiwan, Thailand, United States

Southern Cone Common Market (MERCOSUR)
Argentina, Brazil, Paraguay, Uruguay

North American Free Trade Agreement (NAFTA)
Canada, Mexico, United States

Free Trade and Cooperation Though conflicts remain, many regions of the world have become more integrated through free-trade agreements and diplomatic alliances

? **Region** Which alliance links some of the countries of Africa with the Middle East? Which links Asia with the Americas?

Map Answer
Arab League, Asia Pacific Economic Cooperation

SECTION 4 REVIEW ANSWERS
(p. 848)

IDENTIFY
For significance, see the following pages:
General Agreement on Tariffs and Trade (p. 848)
World Trade Organization (p. 848)
European Union (p. 848)
1. Many countries returned to democracy or instituted democratic governments.
2. Countries such as China, Cuba, and North Korea resisted democracy for a variety of reasons, and their rulers often maintained control by force.

3. high costs and the desire to move to free-market policies

4. Letters should reflect excitement about the possibility of voting for future leaders and about freedoms that can be enjoyed under new democratic governments.

5. Answers could mention how some of the new trade agreements might affect the economies and strength of the participating members, as well as how some of the holdouts against democracy might eventually be forced to change as they could face being left behind by the new economic agreements.

CHAPTER 30 REVIEW ANSWERS
(p. 849)

WRITING A SUMMARY
See essential points in the text.

REVIEWING TERMS
1. détente
2. perestroika
3. lasers
4. Carter Doctrine
5. greenhouse effect

REVIEWING CHRONOLOGY
4, 2, 3, 5, 1

UNDERSTANDING THE MAIN IDEA
1. The purpose of détente was to relax diplomatic and military tensions between the superpowers.

♻ Freeing Trade

The success of democracy and free-market economics at the domestic level in many countries during the 1980s and 1990s was matched internationally by the advance of free-trade principles. The scope of the 1947 **General Agreement on Tariffs and Trade** (GATT) was repeatedly enlarged in an ongoing series of negotiations among the major trading powers. In 1993 a seven-year round of GATT negotiations known as the Uruguay Round substantially lowered tariffs and protected ownership rights, such as patents, trademarks, and copyrights. It also led to the creation of the **World Trade Organization** (WTO), which had the power to resolve disputes between trading partners.

In addition to such global organizations, regional free-trade associations also began to emerge. In Europe efforts to allow greater freedom of trade led to closer political ties among European countries. In 1993 all 12 members of the European Community ratified the Treaty on European Union at the city of Maastricht, in the Netherlands. The Maastricht Treaty turned the EC into the **European Union** (EU), with a definite plan for further coordinating and integrating the social and economic policies of member states. Under the Maastricht Treaty, nations agreed to drop almost all trade barriers among themselves and to work toward a common currency. The EU also developed political powers to complement its economic powers, though some

▲ French farmers reacted to cuts in agricultural subsidies by dumping potatoes across a busy highway.

nations, notably Britain, remained hesitant about closer political unity. After the Soviet collapse, many of the newly independent countries of Eastern Europe hoped to join the Union.

In 1994 the three largest countries of North America—the United States, Canada, and Mexico—also negotiated a free-trade pact called the North American Free Trade Agreement (NAFTA). Disputes over free trade continued, however. Japan's practices of limiting access to Japanese markets for certain American products, for example, caused increasing tension between the two countries.

*G*lobal and regional trade agreements reduced barriers to international trade and sometimes led to closer political ties among nations.

SECTION 4 REVIEW

IDENTIFY and explain the significance of the following:
General Agreement on Tariffs and Trade
World Trade Organization
European Union

1. **Main Idea** How did democracy fare from the 1970s to the 1990s?
2. **Main Idea** How did such countries as China, Cuba, and North Korea react to the global trend toward democracy?
3. **Main Idea** Why have some governments moved away from the welfare state?
4. **Writing to Explain** Imagine that you are a teenager living in Eastern Europe several years after the fall of the Berlin Wall. Write a letter to a friend in the United States explaining what the growth of democracy in your region and in the world has meant to you.
5. **Hypothesizing** Given the remarkable political and economic changes that have taken place in the last two decades, what changes do you foresee in the next 20 years? Describe the variables that could result in different outcomes.

Review

On a separate sheet of paper, complete the following exercises:

WRITING A SUMMARY
Using the essential points in the text, write a brief summary of the chapter.

REVIEWING TERMS
From the following list, choose the term that correctly matches the definition.

Carter Doctrine
détente
lasers
greenhouse effect
ozone layer
perestroika

1. period of relaxation in the Cold War
2. plan for reforming the political and economic system of the Soviet Union
3. concentrated beams of light released in bursts of high energy
4. policy of the United States to protect the oil supplies of the Persian Gulf from hostile control
5. warming of the earth's surface thought to be caused by the buildup of carbon dioxide

REVIEWING CHRONOLOGY
List the following events in their correct chronological order.

1. The French elect Jacques Chirac.
2. Neil Armstrong becomes the first person to walk on the moon.
3. U.S. president Richard Nixon reopens diplomatic relations with China.
4. Rachel Carson publishes *Silent Spring*.
5. Margaret Thatcher becomes Prime Minister of Great Britain.

UNDERSTANDING THE MAIN IDEA
1. What was the purpose of détente between the United States and the Soviet Union?
2. How and why did the Soviet Union disintegrate?
3. What resulted from the alliance of science and technology in the decades after World War II?
4. Why have many scientists worried about the effects of continued industrialization?
5. What happened to communism and democracy in the 1980s and 1990s?

THINKING CRITICALLY
1. *Evaluating* Which was more significant in breaking apart the Soviet Union: Cold War opposition by the United States, or forces and events within the Soviet Union? Explain your answer.
2. *Hypothesizing* Why do you think that China clung to communism after most other communist nations abandoned it?

Building Your Portfolio

Complete the following activities individually or in groups.

1. **Pollution** Imagine that you (and your coworkers) have been asked to design an antipollution campaign for your city or state. Using multiple sources of evidence at your school or local library, find out what pollution problems exist locally, what is causing the pollution, and what measures have been taken to clean it up. Devise a plan for an antipollution campaign. Create a campaign kit to present to city or state officials. Your campaign kit should include a letter written to your target audience. Your kit should also contain some sort of publicity item, such as a poster, flyer, or script for a television ad.
2. **Science Fair** Choose one of the great scientific inventions or technological advances—such as the computer, jet plane, or the discovery of DNA—that has been developed since World War II. Prepare a display on that topic for an upcoming science fair. Your display should include a written report on how the particular development has changed people's lives, as well as photos or illustrations about your topic. You may also wish to construct a model of some aspect of the development you are presenting.

2. People were demanding change and freedom. Following the Eastern European countries' leads in abolishing communism, Soviet republics broke away from the Soviet Union, causing its collapse.
3. The alliance between science and technology allowed people greater control of the world around them and led to the development of new power and transportation sources.
4. Many scientists were afraid that industrialization was leading to a destruction of the earth's environment from acid rain, global warming, and ozone depletion. They also feared a destruction of the ecosphere.
5. Many communist countries traded communism for democratic principles.

THINKING CRITICALLY
1. Some may argue that economic decline and citizens' demands for freedom caused the Soviet Union to break apart, while others may say that the Soviet Union collapsed because it could not afford to keep up with the United States's increased defense spending under Reagan.
2. Historically, the Chinese government has not been open to change, and it relied on communist principles to provide for and control the country's large population.

WORLD HISTORY
CONTINUITY & CHANGE

Reference Section

The World: Physical

ARCTIC OCEAN
80°N

BEAUFORT SEA
BERING STRAIT
Victoria Island
Baffin Island
Baffin Bay
Greenland
DAVIS STRAIT
DENMARK STRAIT
Iceland
Arc

Yukon River
Great Bear Lake
Great Slave Lake
60°N
BERING SEA
GULF OF ALASKA
HUDSON BAY

Aleutian Islands
Vancouver Island
Lake Winnipeg
Great Lakes
Lawrence River
B BIS

ROCKY MOUNTAINS
40°N
NORTH AMERICA
Missouri River
APPALACHIAN MTS.
ATLANTIC OCEAN
STRAIT OF GIBRALTAR
ATI

Colorado River
Mississippi
Rio Grande
SIERRA MADRE

Tropic of Cancer
20°N
Hawaiian Islands
GULF OF MEXICO
Bahamas
Greater Antilles
CARIBBEAN SEA
Lesser Antilles
Niger

PACIFIC OCEAN
Isthmus of Panama
ANDES MOUNTAINS
GUIANA HIGHLANDS

0° Equator
Amazon River
SOUTH AMERICA
N
W E
S

BRAZILIAN HIGHLANDS

20°S
Tropic of Capricorn
ANDES MOUNTAINS
ATLANTIC OCEAN

Paraná

40°S

STRAIT OF MAGELLAN
Falkland Islands
Tierra del Fuego
Cape Horn

60°S
160°W 140°W 120°W 100°W 80°W 60°W 40°W 20°W
Antarctic Circle
WEDDELL SEA

ELEVATION

Feet		Meters
13,120		4,000
6,560		2,000
1,640		500
656		200
(Sea level) 0		0 (Sea level)
Below sea level		Below sea level

Ice cap

SCALE: at Equator

0   500   1,000   1,500   2,000 Miles

0   1,000   2,000 Kilometers

Projection: Mollweide

ARCTIC 80°N OCEAN

North Cape
BARENTS SEA
KARA SEA
LAPTEV SEA
EAST SIBERIAN SEA

EUROPE
ALPS
BALTIC SEA
BLACK SEA
MEDITERRANEAN SEA

URAL MOUNTAINS
Volga River
Ob River
Yenisey River
Lena River
Kolyma River
60°N
KAMCHATKA PENINSULA
SEA OF OKHOTSK
Sakhalin Island
Lake Baykal
Amur
ALTAI SHAN
Balqash Lake
ARAL SEA
CASPIAN SEA

ASIA
GOBI
He (Yellow R.)
Huang
40°N
Hokkaido
SEA OF JAPAN
Honshu
Shikoku
Kyushu
EAST CHINA SEA

HIMALAYAS
THAR DESERT
Ganges River
Jiang (Yangzi R.)
Euphrates River
PERSIAN GULF
Tigris
ARABIAN PENINSULA
RED SEA
Nile River

SAHARA
AFRICA

Taiwan
Tropic of Cancer
20°N

ARABIAN SEA
BAY OF BENGAL

PACIFIC OCEAN

Sri Lanka
STRAIT OF MALACCA
MALAY PENINSULA

SOUTH CHINA SEA
Philippine Islands

Borneo
Sumatra
Java
Celebes
New Guinea
Solomon Islands

Equator 0°

INDIAN OCEAN

Lake Victoria
Lake Tanganyika
River

Madagascar
MOZAMBIQUE CHANNEL

CORAL SEA
Fiji Islands
Vanuatu

GREAT SANDY DESERT
GREAT DIVIDING RANGE
New Caledonia
20°S
Tropic of Capricorn

AUSTRALIA
GREAT VICTORIA DESERT
Darling River

KALAHARI DESERT

Cape of Good Hope

TASMAN SEA
NEW ZEALAND
North Island
South Island

Tasmania

20°E 40°E 60°E 80°E 100°E 120°E 140°E 160°E 60°S

ANTARCTICA

Europe

North Cape
10°E 20°E 30°E 40°E
KARA SEA
BARENTS SEA

DENMARK STRAIT
Iceland
URAL MOUNTAINS

N
W E
S
60°N
NORTH SEA
KJØLEN MTS.

SCALE
0 250 500 750 Miles
0 250 500 750 Kilometers
Projection: Mollweide

British Isles
BALTIC SEA
Volga River

50°N
Rhine
ATLANTIC OCEAN
BAY OF BISCAY
ALPS

40°N
BLACK SEA

STRAIT OF GIBRALTAR
MEDITERRANEAN SEA
Crete

The World: Political

ARCTIC OCEAN

GREENLAND

ICELAND

ALASKA (US)
Yellowknife
80°N
Whitehorse
CANADA
Godthab
Edmonton
Aleutian Islands
Winnipeg
Vancouver
Quebec
Victoria
Regina
NORTH
Ottawa Fredericton
St. John's
AMERICA
Montreal Halifax
Charlottetown
Chicago
Toronto
ATLANTIC
40°N
UNITED
New York
STATES
Washington, D.C.
OCEAN
Los Angeles
Houston
BERMUDA
(UK)
Rabat
Casablanca
MOROCCO
MEXICO
BAHAMAS
WESTERN
SAHARA
(Sovereignty
Tropic of Cancer
disputed)
Havana CUBA
DOMINICAN
REPUBLIC
20°N
HAWAII (US)
PUERTO RICO (US)
Nouakchott
MAURITANIA
Mexico
City
JAMAICA
HAITI
ST. KITTS AND NEVIS
CAPE VERDE
SENEGAL
GUATEMALA
BELIZE
ANTIGUA AND BARBUDA
Dakar
Bamako
HONDURAS
VIRGIN ISLANDS
GAMBIA
Guatemala
(US, UK)
DOMINICA
GUINEA-BISSAU
GUINEA
City
ST. LUCIA
EL SALVADOR
NICARAGUA
GRENADA
ST. VINCENT AND
SIERRA
CÔTE
Managua
THE GRENADINES
LEONE
D'IVOI
COSTA RICA
PANAMA
TRINIDAD AND
N
LIBERIA
TOBAGO
Caracas
GUYANA
VENEZUELA
Georgetown
SURINAME
W   E
Bogotá
Paramaribo
FRENCH GUIANA
COLOMBIA
(France)
S
0°   Equator
Galápagos
Quito
KIRIBATI
Islands
ECUADOR
(Ecuador)
PACIFIC
PERU
SOUTH
AMERICA
OCEAN
BRAZIL
Lima
WESTERN
AMERICAN
BOLIVIA
SAMOA
SAMOA
La Paz
Brasília
Sucre
20°S
TONGA
PARAGUAY
Rio de Janeiro
Tropic of Capricorn
Asunción
São Paulo
CHILE
ARGENTINA
URUGUAY
Santiago
Montevideo
Buenos
Aires
40°S
FALKLAND
SOUTH GEORGIA
ISLANDS
(UK)
(UK)
SOUTH SANDWICH
ISLANDS (UK)
60°S
160°W
140°W
120°W
100°W
80°W
60°
40°W
20°W
Antarctic   Circle

ATLANTIC

OCEAN

⊛ National capitals
•   Other cities

SCALE: at Equator
0   500   1,000 1,500 2,000 Miles
0   1,000   2,000 Kilometers
Projection: Mollweide

COUNTRY	CAPITAL
1 Czech Republic	Prague
2 Slovakia	Bratislava
3 Slovenia	Ljubljana
4 Croatia	Zagreb
5 Bosnia and Herzegovina	Sarajevo
6 Macedonia	Skopje
7 Yugoslavia (Serbia and Montenegro)	Belgrade
8 Lithuania	Vilnius
9 Latvia	Riga
10 Estonia	Tallinn

North America: Political

ASIA EUROPE

+ NORTH POLE

ARCTIC OCEAN

St. Lawrence Island

BERING SEA

BERING STRAIT

180°

170°E

170°W

Nunivak Island

ALASKA (US)

Yukon River

Anchorage

Kodiak Island

GULF OF ALASKA

Alexander Archipelago

Juneau

Queen Charlotte Islands

PACIFIC OCEAN

Cape Mendocino

160°W

150°W

140°W

130°W

120°W

110°W

100°W

Queen Elizabeth Islands

Banks Island

BEAUFORT SEA

Victoria Island

Great Bear Lake

Mackenzie River

Great Slave Lake

Ellesmere Island

Baffin Island

BAFFIN BAY

GREENLAND (Denmark)

DENMARK STRAIT

ICELAND

Arctic Circle

Cape Farewell

DAVIS STRAIT

LABRADOR SEA

Southampton Island

Coats Island

Mansel Island

HUDSON STRAIT

HUDSON BAY

Peace River

Lake Winnipeg

CANADA

Edmonton

Calgary

Vancouver Island

Vancouver

Seattle

Portland

Columbia River

Snake River

Winnipeg

Minneapolis

Milwaukee

Chicago

Great Salt Lake

Salt Lake City

Denver

Colorado River

Platte River

Kansas City

St. Louis

Missouri River

Lake Superior

Lake Michigan

Detroit

Toronto

Lake Huron

Lake Ontario

Cleveland

Columbus

Indianapolis

Ottawa

Montreal

Quebec

St. Lawrence R.

Anticosti Island

GULF OF ST. LAWRENCE

Newfoundland

Prince Edward Island

Cape Breton Island

ST. PIERRE AND MIQUELON (Fr)

Boston

Cape Cod

New York City

Philadelphia

Baltimore

Washington, D.C.

Norfolk

ATLANTIC OCEAN

Cape Hatteras

BERMUDA (UK)

UNITED STATES

San Francisco

San Jose

Los Angeles

San Diego

Tijuana

Phoenix

Memphis

Atlanta

Birmingham

Red River

Dallas

Austin

San Antonio

Houston

New Orleans

Mississippi River

Jacksonville

Cape Canaveral

Miami

Florida Keys

STRAITS OF FLORIDA

GULF OF MEXICO

Rio Grande

GULF OF CALIFORNIA

Monterrey

MEXICO

Guadalajara

Balsas R.

Mexico City

Puebla

Mérida

BAHAMAS

Nassau

Havana

CUBA

CAYMAN ISLANDS (UK)

Kingston

JAMAICA

TURKS AND CAICOS ISLANDS (UK)

PUERTO RICO (US)

San Juan

DOMINICAN REPUBLIC

HAITI

Port-au-Prince

Santo Domingo

VIRGIN IS. (US, UK)

ST. KITTS AND NEVIS

ANTIGUA AND BARBUDA

GUADELOUPE (Fr)

MARTINIQUE (Fr)

DOMINICA

ST. LUCIA

ST. VINCENT AND THE GRENADINES

NETHERLANDS ANTILLES

BARBADOS

GRENADA

ARUBA (Neth)

TRINIDAD AND TOBAGO

Tropic of Cancer

CARIBBEAN SEA

BELIZE

Belmopan

GUATEMALA

Guatemala City

San Salvador

EL SALVADOR

HONDURAS

Tegucigalpa

NICARAGUA

Managua

COSTA RICA

San José

Panama Canal

PANAMA

Panama City

SOUTH AMERICA

Equator

Legend

⊛ National capitals

• Other cities

SCALE

0   250   500   750   1,000 Miles

0   250   500   750   1,000 Kilometers

Projection: Azimuthal Equal Area

South America: Political

CENTRAL AMERICA

CARIBBEAN SEA

Barranquilla
Cartagena
Lake Maracaibo

⊛ Caracas

VENEZUELA

Orinoco River

Georgetown
Paramaribo

GUYANA

⊛

Medellín

SURINAME

Cayenne

FRENCH GUIANA (Fr)

Cali
⊛ Bogotá
COLOMBIA

Malpelo Island (Colombia)

Río Negro

Amazon River

ATLANTIC OCEAN

Galápagos Islands (Ecuador)

⊛ Quito
ECUADOR

0° Equator

Equator 0°

Amazon River

Belém

Guayaquil

Trujillo

PERU

Ucayali River

Recife

São Francisco River

Callao ⊛ Lima

BRAZIL

Lake Titicaca

BOLIVIA

Salvador

Arequipa

La Paz
Lake Poopó

⊛ Brasília

Sucre

Belo Horizonte

PARAGUAY

Paraguay River

Campinas

São Paulo

PACIFIC OCEAN

Asunción

Curitiba

Rio de Janeiro

Tropic of Capricorn

San Ambrosio Island (Chile)

Tropic of Capricorn

Paraná River

San Félix Island (Chile)

N

W E

S

Pôrto Alegre

Uruguay River

Córdoba

Juan Fernández Islands (Chile)

Rosario

URUGUAY

ATLANTIC OCEAN

Valparaíso
Santiago ⊛

Buenos Aires
Morón
San Justo
Lomas de Zamora

⊛ Montevideo

RÍO DE LA PLATA

CHILE

ARGENTINA

Legend
- ⊛ National capitals
- • Other cities

FALKLAND ISLANDS (UK)

SCALE
```
0    250    500    750    1,000 Miles
0  250  500  750  1,000 Kilometers
```
Projection: Azimuthal Equal Area

STRAIT OF MAGELLAN

Tierra del Fuego

SOUTH GEORGIA ISLAND (UK)

Europe: Political

ASIA

URAL MOUNTAINS

RUSSIA

Nizhniy Novgorod

Moscow

CASPIAN SEA

SOUTHWEST ASIA

National capitals
Other cities

BARENTS SEA

WHITE SEA

BLACK SEA

Ural River
Volga River
Don River

St. Petersburg

Kyiv (Kiev)
UKRAINE
Dnipro
Odesa

MOLDOVA
Chişinău

Bucharest
ROMANIA

BULGARIA
Sofia

Danube River

GREECE
Athens

AEGEAN SEA

Rhodes
Crete

North Cape

FINLAND
Helsinki
Gulf of Finland

Tallinn
ESTONIA
Riga
LATVIA
LITHUANIA
Vilnius

BELARUS
Minsk

Warsaw
POLAND
Łódź
Kraków

SLOVAKIA
Bratislava
HUNGARY
Budapest

Belgrade
SERBIA
YUGOSLAVIA
MONTENEGRO
Skopje
MACEDONIA
Tiranë
ALBANIA
Salonika

ARCTIC OCEAN

SWEDEN
Stockholm
Göteborg

GULF OF BOTHNIA

BALTIC SEA

RUSSIA

Dresden
CZECH REPUBLIC
Prague

Vienna
AUSTRIA
LIECHTENSTEIN
SLOVENIA
Ljubljana
Zagreb
CROATIA
BOSNIA AND HERZEGOVINA
Sarajevo
SAN MARINO

ADRIATIC SEA

NORWAY
Oslo

DENMARK
Copenhagen

Hamburg
Berlin
GERMANY
Leipzig

Munich

Bonn
Cologne

MEDITERRANEAN SEA

Bergen

NORTH SEA

Amsterdam
THE NETHERLANDS
The Hague
Rotterdam
Antwerp
BELGIUM
Brussels
LUXEMBOURG
Luxembourg

SWITZERLAND
Bern
Vaduz
Lake Geneva

Milan
Turin
MONACO
Monaco

Rome
VATICAN CITY
ITALY
Naples

Palermo
Sicily

MALTA
Valletta

Shetland Islands

FAEROE ISLANDS
(Denmark)

SCOTLAND
Edinburgh
Glasgow
UNITED KINGDOM
Belfast
NORTHERN IRELAND
IRELAND
Dublin
Manchester
Leeds
Sheffield
Liverpool
Birmingham
WALES
ENGLAND
London

British Isles

ENGLISH CHANNEL
Channel Islands (UK)

FRANCE
Paris
Seine River
Loire River
Lyons
Rhône River
Marseilles

Corsica (France)
Sardinia (Italy)

AFRICA

Arctic Circle

ICELAND
Reykjavík

BAY OF BISCAY

PYRENEES
ANDORRA
Andorra la Vella
Barcelona
Balearic Islands (Spain)

SPAIN
Madrid
Valencia
Seville

PORTUGAL
Lisbon
Tagus River

Gibraltar (UK)
STRAIT OF GIBRALTAR

ATLANTIC OCEAN

SCALE
250   500 Miles
250   500 Kilometers
Projection: Azimuthal Equal Area

N E W S

50°E
40°E
30°E
20°E
10°E
0°
10°W
20°W
30°W
40°W

80°N
70°N
60°N
50°N
40°N
30°N

Asia: Political

Legend:
⊛ National capitals
• Other cities

SCALE
1,000 Miles
1,000 Kilometers
Projection: Modified Oblique Conic

Labels and place names

Oceans and Seas:
PACIFIC OCEAN, INDIAN OCEAN, ARCTIC, BERING SEA, SEA OF OKHOTSK, SEA OF JAPAN, EAST CHINA SEA, SOUTH CHINA SEA, YELLOW SEA, SEA OF KOREA, PHILIPPINE SEA, CELEBES SEA, JAVA SEA, ARAFURA SEA, ANDAMAN SEA, BAY OF BENGAL, ARABIAN SEA, RED SEA, GULF OF ADEN, PERSIAN GULF, CASPIAN SEA, BLACK SEA, BARENTS SEA, KARA SEA, LAPTEV SEA, ARAL SEA, Lake Baykal, Balqash Lake, GULF OF THAILAND

Countries:
RUSSIA, MONGOLIA, CHINA, JAPAN, NORTH KOREA, SOUTH KOREA, TAIWAN, VIETNAM, LAOS, THAILAND, CAMBODIA, BURMA, MALAYSIA, BRUNEI, INDONESIA, PHILIPPINES, INDIA, NEPAL, BHUTAN, BANGLADESH, SRI LANKA, MALDIVES, PAKISTAN, AFGHANISTAN, KAZAKHSTAN, UZBEKISTAN, TURKMENISTAN, KYRGYZSTAN, TAJIKISTAN, IRAN, IRAQ, SAUDI ARABIA, YEMEN, OMAN, UNITED ARAB EMIRATES, QATAR, BAHRAIN, KUWAIT, JORDAN, ISRAEL, LEBANON, SYRIA, TURKEY, CYPRUS, GEORGIA, ARMENIA, AZERBAIJAN, EUROPE, AFRICA, AUSTRALIA, IRIAN JAYA, MADAGASCAR

Cities:
Moscow, Yekaterinburg, Chelyabinsk, Omsk, Novosibirsk, Irkutsk, Yakutsk, Ulaanbaatar, Harbin, Changchun, Shenyang, Anshan, Fushun, Beijing (Peking), Tianjin, Taiyuan, Jinan, Qingdao, Dalian, Lanzhou, Xi'an, Chengdu, Chongqing, Wuhan, Nanjing, Shanghai, Hong Kong, Guangzhou (Canton), Macao (Port.), Pyongyang, Seoul, Inch'on, Pusan, Taegu, Tokyo, Yokohama, Nagoya, Kyoto, Osaka, Kobe, Hiroshima, Fukuoka, Nagasaki, Sendai, Sapporo, Niigata, Taipei, Hanoi, Vientiane, Bangkok, Phnom Penh, Ho Chi Minh City, Rangoon (Yangon), Mandalay, Kuala Lumpur, Singapore, Bandar Seri Begawan, Jakarta, Bandung, Surabaya, Semarang, Medan, Ujung Pandang, Manila, Colombo, Male, New Delhi, Delhi, Jaipur, Kanpur, Calcutta, Dhaka, Chittagong, Kathmandu, Thimphu, Nagpur, Bhopal, Ahmadabad, Bombay, Pune, Hyderabad, Bangalore, Madras, Karachi, Lahore, Faisalabad, Islamabad, Kabul, Dushanbe, Tashkent, Bishkek, Almaty, Akmola, Ashgabat, Mashhad, Tehran, Isfahan, Shiraz, Muscat, Abu Dhabi, Dubai, Doha, Manama, Riyadh, Kuwait City, Basra, Baghdad, Mosul, Yerevan, Baku, Tbilisi, Ankara, Istanbul, Izmir, Nicosia, Beirut, Damascus, Jerusalem, Tel Aviv, Amman, Aleppo, Sanaa, Mecca, Jidda

Rivers and features:
Lena River, Yenisei River, Ob River, Irtysh River, Angara River, Amur River, Huang He (Yellow R.), Chang River (Yangtze), Mekong River, Brahmaputra River, Ganges River, Indus River, Nu River, Tigris River, Euphrates River, GREAT WALL, Tropic of Cancer, Arctic Circle, Equator, Aleutian Islands, Kuril Islands, Sakhalin Island, Ryukyu Islands, SOCOTRA (Yemen), Lakshadweep Islands (India), MALAYSIA Strait of Malacca, LUZON STRAIT

859

Africa: Political

EUROPE

CENTRAL ASIA

SOUTHWEST ASIA

MEDITERRANEAN SEA

AZORES (Port)

MADEIRA ISLANDS (Port)

⊛ Algiers
Oran •
Tūnis •
TUNISIA
Tripoli •

SUEZ CANAL

Casablanca •
Fez ⊛
⊛ Rabat
Marrakech •
MOROCCO

Benghazi •

Alexandria •
Giza •
⊛ Cairo

RED SEA

CANARY ISLANDS (Sp)

ALGERIA

LIBYA

EGYPT

Lake Nasser

Tropic of Cancer

El Aaiún •
WESTERN SAHARA (Sovereignty disputed)

⊛ Nouakchott
MAURITANIA

MALI

NIGER

CHAD

ERITREA
⊛ Asmará

DJIBOUTI
⊛ Djibouti
GULF OF ADEN

CAPE VERDE
⊛ Praia

Niger River

Omdurman •
Khartoum ⊛

Blue Nile
White Nile

SENEGAL
Dakar ⊛
Banjul ⊛ GAMBIA
Bamako ⊛
Niamey •
Lake Chad
N'Djamena •
SUDAN

Nile River

ETHIOPIA
Addis Ababa •

Bissau ⊛
GUINEA-BISSAU
GUINEA
Conakry ⊛
Freetown ⊛
SIERRA LEONE
Monrovia ⊛
LIBERIA

BURKINA FASO
Ouagadougou ⊛
BENIN
Kano •
NIGERIA
⊛ Abuja
Ogbomosho •
Ibadan •
Lagos •

SOMALIA

CÔTE D'IVOIRE
Yamoussoukro ⊛
GHANA
Lomé ⊛ TOGO
Accra ⊛
Abidjan •
Porto-Novo ⊛

CENTRAL AFRICAN REPUBLIC
Bangui ⊛

⊛ Mogadishu

CAMEROON
Yaoundé ⊛

GULF OF GUINEA
Malabo ⊛
EQUATORIAL GUINEA

UGANDA
Kampala ⊛

KENYA
Nairobi ⊛

SÃO TOMÉ AND PRÍNCIPE
São Tomé •

Libreville ⊛
REPUBLIC OF CONGO
Kisangani •

Zaire River
RWANDA
⊛ Kigali
Lake Victoria

GABON

DEMOCRATIC REPUBLIC OF CONGO

Bujumbura ⊛
BURUNDI

Mombasa •

Equator

N
W E
S

Brazzaville ⊛
⊛ Kinshasa

TANZANIA
Dodoma ⊛
Zanzibar •
Dar es Salaam ⊛

INDIAN OCEAN

Victoria ⊛
SEYCHELLES

CABINDA (Angola)

Lake Tanganyika

ATLANTIC OCEAN

Luanda ⊛

Lubumbashi •

Lake Malawi (Nyasa)

COMOROS
⊛ Moroni

ST. HELENA ISLAND (UK)

ANGOLA

ZAMBIA
Lusaka ⊛

MALAWI
Lilongwe ⊛

MOZAMBIQUE

Zambezi River

Harare ⊛
ZIMBABWE
Bulawayo •

Antananarivo ⊛
MAURITIUS
Port Louis ⊛
RÉUNION (Fr)

MADAGASCAR

NAMIBIA
Windhoek ⊛

BOTSWANA

Tropic of Capricorn

Gaborone ⊛
Johannesburg •
Soweto •

Pretoria ⊛
Mbabane ⊛
SWAZILAND
Maputo ⊛

LESOTHO
Maseru ⊛

SOUTH AFRICA

Orange River

Cape Town ⊛
Port Elizabeth •

⊛ National capitals
• Other cities

SCALE
0   500   1,000 Miles
0   500   1,000 Kilometers
Projection: Azimuthal Equal Area

Pacific Islands: Political

NORTH AMERICA

NORTH AMERICA

ASIA

AUSTRALIA

NEW ZEALAND

NORTH PACIFIC OCEAN

SOUTH PACIFIC OCEAN

INDIAN OCEAN

SOUTH CHINA SEA

PHILIPPINE SEA

TIMOR SEA

ARAFURA SEA

CORAL SEA

TASMAN SEA

Equator

Tropic of Cancer

Tropic of Capricorn

International Date Line

MICRONESIA

MELANESIA

POLYNESIA

SCALE: At Equator
Projection: Mercator
0   500   1,000 Miles
0   500   1,000 Kilometers

N
E
S
W

National capitals
Other cities

BONIN ISLANDS (Japan)

VOLCANO ISLANDS (Japan)

NORTHERN MARIANAS (US)

GUAM (US)
Agana

PALAU
Koror

FEDERATED STATES OF MICRONESIA
Palikir
Truk Is.

Eniwetok I.
Kwajalein Island
MARSHALL ISLANDS
Majuro

WAKE ISLAND (US)

MIDWAY ISLANDS (US)

JOHNSTON ATOLL (US)

Hawaiian Islands
HAWAII (US)

KINGMAN REEF (US)
PALMYRA ATOLL (US)
Teraina   Tabuaeran

HOWLAND ISLAND (US)
BAKER ISLAND (US)
Phoenix Islands
McKean I.
Gardner I.

Starbuck Island

Manihiki Island

KIRIBATI

Gilbert Islands
NAURU
Yaren District
Tarawa

TUVALU
Funafuti

SOLOMON ISLANDS
Honiara
Guadalcanal Island

Bismarck Archipelago
New Guinea
PAPUA NEW GUINEA
Port Moresby

Espiritu Santo I.
Malekula I.
VANUATU
Port-Vila

NEW CALEDONIA (Fr)
Noumea
Loyalty Islands (Fr)

NORFOLK ISLAND (Aust)

TOKELAU (NZ)
WESTERN SAMOA
Apia
AMERICAN SAMOA
Pago Pago
WALLIS AND FUTUNA (Fr)

FIJI
Suva

NIUE (NZ)

TONGA
Nuku'alofa

COOK ISLANDS
Rarotonga Island

Society Islands (Fr)
FRENCH POLYNESIA
Papeete
Tahiti (Fr)
Tubuai Islands (Fr)

Marquesas Islands (Fr)

Tuamotu Archipelago (Fr)
Rapa Island (Fr)

PITCAIRN (UK)
Pitcairn Island
Ducie Island

Easter Island (Chile)

Kermadec Islands (NZ)

Chatham Islands (NZ)

Bounty Islands (NZ)

Auckland Islands (NZ)

GAZETTEER

A

Adulis seaport in Aksum; formerly a leading ivory market in northeastern Africa *m182*

Aegean (i-JEE-uhn) **Sea** sea between Greece and Turkey *m858*

Afghanistan landlocked country between Iran, Pakistan, and the Central Asian republics; conquered by the Mongols in the 1200s *m859*

Africa world's second largest continent; surrounded by the Atlantic Ocean, the Indian Ocean, and the Mediterranean Sea *m852–853, 860*

Aksum ancient kingdom in what is now Ethiopia *m182*

Alexandria, Egypt (31°N 30°E) historic city in north central Egypt; important Christian center around A.D. 100 *m860*

Alps mountain system of south central Europe; crossed by Hannibal and a force of elephants in 218 B.C. *m110, 852–853*

Alsace-Lorraine region in western France taken by the German Empire in 1871, restored to France in 1919 by the Treaty of Versailles, taken again by Germany in World War II, and returned to France at the end of the war *m620*

Amazonia region, mainly rain forests, in northern South America; fed by the Amazon River *m205*

Amazon River major river in South America *m857*

Amsterdam, Netherlands (52°N 5°E) old port city and official capital of the Netherlands *m858*

Andes Mountains great mountain range of South America *m205, 852–853*

Antioch (36°N 36°E) ancient city in present-day Turkey captured by crusaders in 1098 *m101, 291*

Apennines mountain range that runs the length of the Italian peninsula *m238*

Appalachian Mountains mountain system of eastern North America *m467, 852–853*

Aquitaine historical region of southwest France, ruled by Eleanor of Aquitaine in the early 1100s *m287*

Arabian Peninsula region of southwestern Asia occupied mostly by Saudi Arabia *m10, 852–853*

Arctic Circle line of latitude located at 66 1/2° north of the equator; the parallel beyond which no sunlight shines on the December solstice (first day of winter in the Northern Hemisphere) *m852–853*

Arctic Ocean ocean north of the Arctic Circle *m852–853*

Argentina second largest country in South America *m857*

Armenia independent country of the Caucasus region of Asia; former Soviet republic *m859*

Asia world's largest continent; located between Europe and the Pacific Ocean *m852–853, 859*

Asia Minor peninsula in western Asia bounded by the Black Sea and the Mediterranean Sea *m71*

Assyria great ancient empire in western Asia, became part of Persia and later, of the Roman Empire *m50*

Athens, Greece (38°N 24°E) capital and largest city in Greece; ancient polis *m77*

Atlantic Ocean body of water between the continents of North and South America and the continents of Europe and Africa; about half the size of the Pacific Ocean *m852–853*

Auschwitz, Poland (50°N 19°E) village in Poland near major Nazi concentration camp *m698*

Austerlitz (49°N 17°E) formerly in Austria, now Slavkov in the Czech Republic; site of great military victory for Napoleon *m476*

Australia only country occupying an entire continent (also called Australia); located between the Indian Ocean and the Pacific Ocean *m852–853*

Austria country in west central Europe south of Germany, center of former Habsburg Empire *m858*

Avignon, France (44°N 5°E) city in southern France, seat of the Roman church in 1300s *m276*

Azerbaijan (ahz-uhr-bie-JAHN) country west of the Caspian Sea in the Caucasus region of Asia; former Soviet republic *m859*

B

Babylon (32°N 45°E) ancient capital of Babylonia, now ruins near Hilla, Iraq *m50*

Babylonia ancient country in the lower Euphrates River valley *m50*

Bactria ancient country in southwest Asia; became part of the Persian Empire in 550 B.C., conquered by Alexander the Great, then ruled by the Seleucids, and later seceded from Seleucid Empire *m101*

Baghdad, Iraq (33°N 44°E) capital of Iraq; at one time the richest city of Southwest Asia; imperial capital of the Abbasids; sacked in 1258 by the Mongols *m325*

Bahamas independent country consisting of a chain of islands in the Atlantic Ocean southeast of Florida *m856*

Balkans countries occupying the Balkan Peninsula—Albania, Bulgaria, Greece, Romania, the former Yugoslavia, and northwestern Turkey; ruled by the Ottomans in the 1300s

Baltic Sea body of water east of the North Sea and Scandinavia *m858*

Bangladesh South Asian country surrounded by India on north, west, and east; formed from East Pakistan in 1971 *m859*

Basra, Iraq (30°N 48°E) city on the Shatt al Arab; birthplace of Rabi'a al-'Adawiyya; taken by Allied forces in World War I *m251*

Batavia (7°S 107°E) now Djakarta, Indonesia; city on the northwest coast of the island of Java; first colony of the Dutch in Asia *m422*

Bay of Bengal body of water between India and the western coasts of Burma and the Malay Peninsula *m859*

Beijing (BAY-JING), **China** (40°N 116°E) historic city in China, made the capital in 1421 *m859*

Belgium   Benelux country between France and Germany in west central Europe *m858*

Benelux countries   the west central European countries of Belgium, Luxembourg, and the Netherlands *m858*

Bengal   former British province; divided in 1947 into West Bengal, India, and the country of Bangladesh *m580*

Berlin, Germany (53°N 13°E)   capital of united Germany; formerly capital of East Germany, divided into four zones after World War II *m717, 858*

Bethlehem (32°N 35°W)   city in Israeli-occupied West Bank; birthplace of Jesus *m133*

Birmingham, England (52°N 2°W)   major manufacturing center of south central Great Britain *m489*

Bolivia   landlocked western South American country; area of ancient cultures; conquered by the Spanish in 1538; gained independence in 1825 *m857*

Bombay, India (19°N 73°E)   India's largest city, located on the western coast; important trading post established by the British East India Company in the 1600s *m859*

Bonn, Germany (51°N 7°E)   city in western Germany; capital of the former West Germany, replaced by Berlin as the national capital of the reunified country *m858*

Bosnia and Herzegovina   mountainous former Yugoslav republic located between Serbia and Croatia in eastern Europe; seceded from Yugoslavia in 1992 *m830*

Bosporus   the northernmost of two narrow straits that separate the Asian and European parts of Turkey *m609*

Brazil   largest country in South America *m857*

Brest-Litovsk, Russia (52°N 22°E)   city on the Bug River on the border with Poland; site of treaty between Russia and Germany in 1918 *m608*

Britain   island of Great Britain; part of the United Kingdom in northern Europe *m858*

British Columbia   province on the Pacific coast of Canada *m519*

British Isles   island group consisting of Great Britain and Ireland *m858*

Buenos Aires (bway-nuh-SAHR-eez)**, Argentina** (34°S 59°W)   capital and province of Argentina; historical colony of Spain founded in 1536 *m857*

Bulgaria   country occupying part of the eastern side of the Balkan Peninsula in eastern Europe; invaded by the Soviet Union in 1944, regained independence in 1946 *m858*

Burma (Myanmar)   mainland Southeast Asian country between India, China, and Thailand *m859*

Byzantium (41°N 29°E)   ancient city at the site of present-day Istanbul, Turkey; later named Constantinople; capital of the Byzantine Empire *m77*

C

Calcutta, India (23°N 88°E)   giant industrial and seaport city in eastern India; important trade post established by the British East India Company in the 1600s *m859*

Calicut, India (11°N 76°E)   present-day Kozhikode; city along the Malabar (western) coast of India where the fabric calico originated; Vasco da Gama landed there in 1498 after discovering a sea route to the East *m422*

Cambodia   country west of southern Vietnam in mainland Southeast Asia; formerly a French colony *m859*

Cameroon (kam-uh-ROON)   formerly Cameroons; country in central Africa southeast of Nigeria *m860*

Canaan   historical name for the region in present-day Israel near the coast of the Mediterranean *m47*

Canada   country occupying most of northern North America *m856*

Cape of Good Hope   point of land at the tip of southern Africa *m422*

Cape Verde   island country in the Atlantic Ocean off the coast of Senegal in West Africa *m860*

Caracas (kuh-RAHK-uhs)**, Venezuela** (11°N 67°W)   capital of Venezuela *m857*

Caribbean Sea   arm of the Atlantic Ocean between North America and South America *m852–853*

Carthage (37°N 10°E)   city on the northeastern coast of present-day Tunisia; powerful Mediterranean empire in the 300s and 400s B.C.; led by Hannibal in battles against Rome during the late 200s B.C. *m110*

Caucasia   region between the Black and Caspian Seas, now the countries of Georgia, Azerbaijan, and Armenia

Caucasus Mountains   mountain range between the Black Sea and the Caspian Sea in the southern part of the former Soviet Union *m50*

Cawnpore, India (27°N 80°E)   city in northern India where the Indian Mutiny led to a brutal attack on British residents in 1857 *m580*

Central America   narrow southern portion of the North American continent *m856*

Chaco Canyon   canyon in the basin of the San Juan River in northwestern New Mexico; site of Anasazi community *m211*

Chan Chan (8°S 79°W)   ancient Chimú city in central Peru *m205*

Chang Jiang (Yangzi River)   major river in China that flows from the Kunlun Shan across China to the East China Sea *m167*

Changan, China (34°N 108°E)   in 200s B.C. the capital of the first emperor, beginning of the Silk Road *m167, 859*

Chavín de Huantar (10°S 77°W)   ancient ceremonial center in the foothills of the Andes Mountains *m24*

Chechnya   Russian republic in the Caucasus region; declared independence in 1991 but was invaded by Russian troops in an effort to keep it from gaining independence *m830*

Chichén Itzá (chuh-CHEN uht-SAH) (21°N 89°W)   site of extensive ancient Mayan ruins in Yucatán, Mexico *m199*

Chile   country in western South America; liberated from Spanish rule in 1818 *m857*

China   country of East Asia; world's most populous country *m859*

Cochin   region in southwest India; Portuguese outpost, later settled by British in 1635, then captured by the Dutch in 1663 under whom the city (10°N 76°E) became an important trade center *m422*

Cochin China   formerly the southern half of Vietnam, a colony of France *m580*

Colombia   country in northern South America *m857*

Concord, Massachusetts (42°N 71°W)   with Lexington, city where the first fighting of the Revolutionary War began *m467*

Congo River   river that forms the southern boundary of the Democratic Republic of Congo, flows to the Atlantic Ocean; one of the largest rivers in the world *m578*

Constantinople (42°N 28°E) ancient city in the European part of Turkey, once the capital of the Byzantine Empire; sacked by Christians in 1204; now known as Istanbul *m291*

Córdoba, Spain (38°N 5°W) city in southern Spain; capital of Umayyad Empire in the 900s *m251*

Corsica Mediterranean island of France; ruled by Carthage in the 200s B.C., then seized by Rome; purchased by France 1768; birthplace of Napoleon *m858*

Costa Rica country in Central America *m856*

Côte d'Ivoire (kote deev-WAHR) formerly Ivory Coast, Atlantic coast country of West Africa; gained independence from France in 1960 *m860*

Crete Greek Mediterranean island south of the mainland; home of the ancient Minoan civilization *m858*

Crimea small peninsula of Ukraine that juts southward into the Black Sea *m830*

Croatia Eastern European country and former Yugoslav republic; occupies the northern part of the Dinaric Alps and a long coastal region along the Adriatic Sea; seceded from Yugoslavia in 1991 *m830*

Cuba country and largest island of the Greater Antilles in the Caribbean *m856*

Cuzco (KOO-skoh) (14°S 72°W) city southeast of present-day Lima, Peru; ancient capital of the Inca Empire *m205*

Cyprus island in the eastern Mediterranean Sea *m598*

Czechoslovakia (chehk-uh-sloh-VAHK-ee-uh) eastern European country formed after World War I; communist rule ended in 1989; now divided into the Czech Republic and Slovakia *m720, 858*

D

Dahomey (duh-HOE-mee) former French colony, now known as Benin, in West Africa *m575*

Danube River major river in Central Europe that flows into the Black Sea in Romania *m858*

Danzig, Poland (54°N 18°E) now Gdansk, important Baltic port city *m691*

Dardanelles the southernmost of two narrow straits that separate Asian and European Turkey *m609*

Delhi, India (29°N 77°E) city north of New Delhi, India; sacked by Persia in 1739, ending the power of the Mughal Empire *m859*

Delphi (DEL-fi) (38°N 22°E) sacred Greek site *m77*

Democratic Republic of Congo largest and most populous country in central Africa; formerly Zaire; gained independence from Belgium in 1960 *m860*

Denmark Nordic country of northern Europe occupied by Germany during World War II *m858*

Dien Bien Phu, Vietnam (21°N 102°E) town in northwestern Vietnam where French troops were defeated by Viet Minh troops in 1954, leading to the end of French involvement in Indochina *m761*

Dnieper (NEE-puhr) **River** major river in Ukraine; now known as the Dnipro River *m238*

Dublin, Ireland (53°N 6°W) capital of the republic of Ireland *m858*

Dunkirk, France (51°N 2°E) city on the English Channel to which the Allied forces retreated in 1940, leaving France to fall to the Germans *m704*

E

East Berlin (53°N 13°E) the eastern half of Berlin, separated at the end of World War II and made capital of East Germany *m717*

Eastern Hemisphere the part of the world east of longitude 0° (the prime meridian) and west of longitude 180°

East Germany (German Democratic Republic) former nation in north central Europe; formed in 1949 of Russian zone of the former Germany; reunified with West Germany in 1990 *m717*

East Indies region including India, Indochina, and the Malay Archipelago *m414–415*

East Pakistan *See* Bangladesh.

East Prussia region once part of Prussia, separated in 1919, divided between the Soviet Union and Poland in 1945 *m456*

Ecuador country in western South America on the equator *m857*

Edessa (37°N 39°E) ancient city in present-day Turkey captured by crusaders in 1098 and recaptured from the crusaders by the Muslims in 1144 *m101, 291*

Edirne, Turkey (42°N 28°E) formerly Adrianople; important Byzantine city captured by the Ottomans in 1361 *m333*

Egypt country of North Africa east of Libya; gained independence from Great Britain in 1922 *m860*

Elba island off the northwest coast of Italy where Napoleon was exiled in 1814 *m476*

Elbe River major river in Germany *m858*

El Salvador small country of volcanoes and plains on the Pacific side of Central America *m856*

England southern part of Great Britain and part of the United Kingdom in northern Europe *m858*

English Channel channel separating Great Britain from the European continent *m858*

Estonia small Baltic country; became territory of the Soviet Union in 1940; gained independence in 1991 *m830, 858*

Ethiopia East African country in the Horn of Africa *m860*

Euphrates River major river primarily in Iraq in southwestern Asia; Mesopotamian civilization grew up between the Euphrates and Tigris Rivers *m10, 859*

Europe continent between the Ural Mountains and the Atlantic Ocean *m852–853, 858*

F

Falkland Islands islands in the South Atlantic Ocean belonging to the United Kingdom but claimed by Argentina *m857*

Fashoda, Sudan (10°N 33°E) now Kodok, town in southern Sudan seized by the French in 1898, almost causing war between Britain and France *m577*

Ferrara, Italy (45°N 12°E) city in northern Italy; former city-state ruled by the Este family *m370*

Fertile Crescent wide arc of productive land that runs from the eastern shore of the Mediterranean Sea, through the plains along the Tigris and Euphrates Rivers, to the Persian Gulf *m10, 20–21*

Finland country of northern Europe between Sweden,

Norway, and Russia *m858*

Florence, Italy (44°N 11°E) important art and cultural city on the Arno River in central Italy; historic home of the ruling Medici family *m370*

France country in west central Europe northeast of the Iberian Peninsula *m858*

G

Gallipoli Peninsula narrow peninsula extending southwest from the southern coast of Turkey; site of battles during World War I *m609*

Ganges (GAN-jeez) **River** major river in India flowing from the Himalayas southeastward to the Bay of Bengal; center of Indian civilization by the 600s B.C. *m859*

Gaul ancient country covering parts of present-day France and Belgium; attacked in the mid 400s by Attila *m140*

Gaza Strip southwest Asian area formerly part of the British protectorate of Palestine; occupied by Israel from 1967 to 1994; under Palestinian self-rule in 1994 *m780*

Geneva (juh-NEE-vuh)**, Switzerland** (46°N 6°E) diplomatic city in southwestern Switzerland; center of Calvinism in the 1500s *m385*

Germany country in west central Europe between Poland and the Benelux countries; created in 1871 out of Prussia and surrounding states; member of the Central Powers in World War I; fascist aggressor nation in World War II; divided into East and West Germany after World War II; reunified in 1990 *m858*

Gibraltar (36°N 5°W) small territory of the United Kingdom situated at the entrance to the Mediterranean Sea from the Atlantic Ocean *m858*

Gilbert Islands South Pacific island group that makes up part of the country of Kiribati; controlled by Japan in World War II until the Allies took control in late 1943 *m705, 861*

Giza, Egypt suburb of Cairo, across the Nile River; site of famous pyramids *m38, 860*

Gobi Desert desert that makes up part of the Mongolian plateau in East Asia *m325, 852–853*

Gold Coast colonial name for Ghana in West Africa *m442*

Granada, Spain (37°N 4°W) Moorish city in southern Spain *m291*

Gran Colombia state formed in 1819 by Bolívar of present-day Venezuela, Colombia, Panama, and Ecuador; broke apart in 1830 *m530*

Grand Duchy of Warsaw (Congress Poland) kingdom formed at the Congress of Vienna; now Poland *m537*

Great Britain the largest island of the British Isles comprising Britain, Scotland, and Wales; major island of the United Kingdom *m858*

Great Lakes largest freshwater lake system in the world comprising Lakes Erie, Huron, Ontario, Michigan, and Superior; located in North America *m856*

Great Plains plains region in the middle of the United States between the Interior Plains to the east and the Rocky Mountains to the west *m211*

Great Rift Valley geological fault line in eastern Africa that includes the Dead Sea and the Red Sea *m177*

Greece country in southern Europe located at the southern end of the Balkan Peninsula *m858*

Greenland self-governing province of Denmark that lies between the North Atlantic and Arctic Oceans *m856*

Grenada Caribbean island country; invaded by the United States in 1983 *m815, 856*

Guadalcanal South Pacific island that is part of the Solomon Islands; controlled by the Japanese during World War II until 1943 when the Allied Forces took control *m815*

Guam (14°N 143°E) South Pacific island and U.S. territory in Micronesia; became U.S. territory in 1898; occupied by the Japanese in World War II *m705, 861*

Guanahani island in the Bahamas named San Salvador by Columbus; where Columbus first landed *m414*

Guatemala most populous country in Central America, area of ancient Maya culture *m856*

Guatemala City, Guatemala (15°N 91°W) capital of Guatemala; site of 1987 peace conference of representatives from Central American countries *m856*

H

Haiti country occupying western third of the Caribbean island of Hispaniola; gained independence from France in 1804 *m856*

Hangzhou, China (30°N 120°E) city in eastern China; the capital of the Song Dynasty and one of the world's largest cities in the 1100s *m306*

Hanoi (ha-NOI)**, Vietnam** (21°N 106°E) capital of Vietnam *m859*

Harappa (31°N 73°E) ancient city in the Indus River valley, seat of the Harappan civilization *m18*

Havana, Cuba (23°N 82°W) capital of Cuba, located just across the Straits of Florida; in the harbor of Havana the U.S. battleship *Maine* was blown up, leading to the Spanish-American War *m856*

Hawaii U.S. Pacific state consisting of a chain of eight major islands and more than 100 smaller islands; discovered by Captain James Cook in 1778; united by King Kamehameha in 1790s; annexed to the United States in 1898; became a U.S. state in 1959 *m861*

Heian (HAY-ahn)**, Japan** former capital of Japan. *See* Kyoto.

Himalayas mountain system in South Asia; site of world's highest mountains *m345, 852–853*

Hindu Kush high mountain range that cuts across northern Afghanistan in Asia *m167*

Hiroshima (34°N 132°E) city on Honshu island in Japan; site of first atomic bombing during World War II *m705, 859*

Hispaniola (his-pun-YOH-luh) large Caribbean island divided into the countries of Haiti and Dominican Republic *m414–415*

Ho Chi Minh City (formerly Saigon), Vietnam (11°N 107°E) major city in southern Vietnam; capital of the former country of South Vietnam *m859*

Holland *See* Netherlands.

Holy Land Palestine (*see m133*), referred to in Bible as Holy Land; birthplace of Christianity and Judaism *m291*

Honduras country south of Belize in Central America *m856*

Hong Kong (22°N 115°E) prosperous British colony in southeast China; transferred to the control of China in 1997 *m859*

Hormuz, Strait of strait connecting the Persian Gulf and the Arabian Sea; important route for oil tankers *m785*

Huang He (Yellow River) one of the world's longest rivers, located in northern China; site of early civilizations m19, 859

Hudson Bay inland sea almost surrounded by Canada m519

Hungary country in eastern Europe between Romania and Austria; settled by the Magyars in the 800s; became independent nation in 1919 m858

I

Iberian Peninsula peninsula in southwestern Europe comprising Spain and Portugal m414–415

India country of South Asia and second-most populous country in the world; under British rule from 1765 until 1947 m859

Indochina the southeast peninsula of Asia, including the countries of Burma, Thailand, Laos, Cambodia, North Vietnam, South Vietnam, and West Malaysia m580

Indonesia largest island country in Southeast Asia; comprises 13,660 islands in the Indian and Pacific Oceans m859

Indus River major river in Pakistan; site of earliest civilizations m18, 859

Iran (i-RAHN) oil-rich country of southwestern Asia north of the Persian Gulf; formerly Persia m859

Iraq (i-RAHK) oil-rich country between Iran and Saudi Arabia in southwestern Asia m859

Ireland country west of Great Britain on the British Isles of northern Europe; unified with the United Kingdom in 1801, after civil war the country was divided into the Irish Free State and Northern Ireland in 1922 m858

Isfahan (is-fuh-HAHN), **Iran** (33°N 52°E) historic and religious city in central Iran; made capital of Safavid Persia in 1599 m340, 859

Islas Malvinas (EES-luhs mahl-VEE-nuhs) Argentina's name for the Falkland Islands m530

Israel (IZ-ree-uhl) eastern Mediterranean country of southwestern Asia; made a state by UN partition of Palestine in 1948 m859

Istanbul, Turkey (41°N 29°E) largest city and leading seaport in Turkey (m859) See Constantinople.

Italy country comprising a boot-shaped peninsula stretching southward from Europe into the Mediterranean Sea and the major islands of Sicily and Sardinia m858

Iwo Jima (EE-woh JEE-muh) one of the Volcano Islands; captured by the United States in World War II after heavy fighting with the Japanese m705

J

Japan prosperous East Asian country consisting of four large "home" islands and more than 3,000 smaller islands in the western Pacific Ocean m859

Jerusalem (32°N 35°E) capital of present-day Israel; captured by crusaders in 1099, recaptured by Muslims in 1187 m291, 859

Jordan southwest Asian country stretching east from the Dead Sea and the Jordan River into the Arabian Desert m859

K

Kadesh (34°N 37°E) ancient city, site of battle between Hittites and Egyptians in about 1288 B.C.; now Hims, Syria m38

Kadisiya (kahd-uh-SEE-uh) (32°N 45°E) ancient city in present-day Iraq; site of Arab defeat of Persian forces in 637 m251

Kaifeng (KIE-FUHNG), **China** (35°N 114°E) city in northeast China; capital of the Song Dynasty; captured in 1126 by the Jin Empire m306

Kampuchea name given to Cambodia by the Khmer Rouge See Cambodia.

Karakorum (kahr-uh-KOHR-uhm) (43°N 103°E) ancient city, now ruins, in present-day Mongolia; made a capital city by Genghis Khan m325

Karbala, Iraq (33°N 44°E) city in southern Iraq where the Islamic martyr Husayn was killed m251

Kashmir mountainous Muslim region of northern India and Pakistan m745

Kazakhstan large, independent Central Asian country and former Soviet republic m830

Khartoum, Sudan (16°N 33°E) capital of Sudan m860

Kiev, Ukraine (50°N 30°E) old city on the Dnieper River; birthplace of Golda Meir m238

Kish (33°N 45°E) ancient city in Sumer whose ruins can be seen today m10

Korea peninsula on east coast of Asia divided between the countries of North Korea and South Korea; made a vassal state of China in 1600s m859

Kursk, Russia (52°N 36°E) rail center and manufacturing city in western Russia; site of the world's largest tank battle, in 1943 m704

Kush African kingdom (about 800 B.C.–A.D. 350) in present-day Sudan m182

Kuwait small, oil-rich country on the northwest coast of the Persian Gulf in southwestern Asia; seized in 1990 by Iraq, leading to Persian Gulf War m859

Kyoto (kee-OHT-oh), **Japan** (35°N 136°E) formerly Heian, the ancient capital of Japan; present-day manufacturing city on the island of Honshu m859

L

Laos landlocked and mountainous country of mainland Southeast Asia; formed as a French protectorate in 1890s; became independent in 1954 m859

Latin America in general, the Spanish- and Portuguese-speaking countries of Middle and South America

Latvia small Baltic country; became a territory of the Soviet Union in 1940; gained independence in 1991 m858

La Venta (18°N 94°W) ancient Olmec archaeological site in present-day Veracruz, Mexico m24

Lebanon (LEHB-uh-nuhn) country lying between Israel and Syria on the Mediterranean coast; gained independence from France in 1943 m859

Leipzig, Germany (51°N 12°E) city in eastern Germany, where Napoleon was defeated by Russian, Prussian, Austrian, and Swedish armies in 1813 m858

Leningrad, Russia *See* St. Petersburg, Russia.

Lexington, Massachusetts (42°N 71°W)   with Concord, city where the fighting of the American Revolutionary War began *m467*

Leyte (LAYT-ee) **Gulf** (11°N 125°E)   gulf in southern Philippines; site of the largest naval engagement in history, in October 1944, between Japan and the Allies *m705*

Liberia (lie-BIR-ee-uh)   country in southern West Africa; founded in 1822 for the resettlement of freed African-American slaves *m860*

Lima (LEE-muh)**, Peru** (12°S 77°W)   capital of Peru *m857*

Lithuania   Baltic country made a territory of the Soviet Union in 1940; gained independence in 1991 *m858*

London, England (52°N 0°W)   capital of the United Kingdom *m858*

Los Alamos, New Mexico (36°N 197°W)   city in northern New Mexico where the atomic bomb was developed *m733*

Lothal   city 400 miles southeast of Mohenjo-Daro where ancient graves have been found *m18*

Luxembourg   small Benelux country bordered by France, Germany, and Belgium *m858*

Lydia   ancient country in present-day Turkey; conquered by Cyrus in 546 B.C. *m47*

M

Macao (muh-KOW) (22°N 113°E)   Portuguese territory near Hong Kong; trading station established by the Portuguese in 1557; transfers to China in 1999 *m859*

Macedonia   independent Balkan country; former Yugoslav republic; powerful empire led by Alexander the Great; fell to Rome in 168 B.C. *m858*

Machu Picchu (13°S 73°W)   ancient Incan city, now in ruins, high in the Andes Mountains of Peru *m205*

Madras, India (13°N 80°E)   city on the southeast coast of India; established as an important trading post by the British East India Company *m422, 859*

Magdeburg, Germany (52°N 12°E)   city in northern Germany; brutally sacked in Thirty Years' War *m385*

Malacca (muh-LAK-uh)**, Malaysia** (2°N 102°E)   city on the west coast of the Malay Peninsula; historic center of spice trade, captured by Portugal in 1511 *m422*

Malay Archipelago (ahr-kuh-PEHL-uh-goh)   large island group off the coast of Asia that includes New Guinea, Malaysia, Indonesia, and the Philippines *m852–853*

Malay Peninsula   peninsula in southeast Asia comprising western Malaysia and the southwestern part of Thailand *m852–853*

Mali   country of West Africa along the Niger River; area where the Mali Empire flourished *m860*

Malmédy (mahl-may-dee)**, Belgium** (51°N 6°E)   city in eastern Belgium where German troops massacred surrendered Allied troops *m698*

Manchester, England (53°N 2°W)   major commercial city of west central Great Britain *m489*

Manchukuo   name given by the Japanese to Manchuria, 1932–1945 *m673*

Manchuria   former name for a region of northeastern China bordering the Korean Peninsula; invaded by Japan in 1931 *m673*

Manila Bay   bay in the Philippines where the Americans defeated the Spanish in 1898, beginning the Spanish-American War *m677*

Mantua (MANCH-uh-wuh)**, Italy**   city-state in northern Italy ruled by Isabella d'Este *m370*

Marathon   plain northeast of Athens and ancient city on that plain; site of legendary battle between Athens and Persia in 490 B.C. *m77*

Mariana Islands   South Pacific island country; site of fighting in World War II between Japan and the Allies *m705*

Marne River (MAHRN)   river in northeastern France, site of early battle, near Paris, of World War I *m607*

Marshall Islands   South Pacific island country; site of fighting in World War II between Japan and the Allies *m705*

Masurian Lakes   lakes in northeast Poland; site of World War I battles *m608*

Mecca (Makkah), Saudi Arabia (21°N 40°E)   important Islamic city in western Saudi Arabia; birthplace of Muhammad *m859*

Medina (Al-Madīnah), Saudi Arabia (24°N 40°E)   holy Islamic city in western Saudi Arabia *m251*

Mediterranean Sea   sea surrounded by Europe, Asia, and Africa *m858*

Meroe (MEHR-uh-wee)   ancient capital of Kush in present-day Sudan *m177*

Mesopotamia   ancient name for plains along the Tigris and Euphrates Rivers; area known as the location of one of the world's first civilizations *m10*

Mexico   country of southern North America; site of Aztec and Maya civilizations *m856*

Mexico City, Mexico (19°N 99°W)   capital of Mexico, once the center of the Aztec Empire (*m856*) *See* Tenochtitlán.

Miami, Florida (26°N 80°W)   major center for transportation at the southern tip of Florida *m856*

Midway Island   U.S. island territory in the North Pacific Ocean; site of decisive battle for the United States in World War II *m705, 861*

Mississippi River   major river in the central United States *m856*

Mohenjo-Daro (27°N 68°E)   ancient city in the Indus Valley *m18*

Moluccas   group of islands in eastern Indonesia *See* Spice Islands.

Mongolia   large landlocked nation of East Asia surrounded by China and Russia *m859*

Monte Albán (MOHN-tay ahl-BAHN) (17°N 97°W)   ancient site of the Zapotec in southern Mexico *m199*

Montreal, Canada (46°N 74°W)   financial and industrial center of Quebec, Canada; second largest French-speaking city in the world *m856*

Morocco   Islamic kingdom on the Mediterranean and Atlantic coasts of Africa; gained independence from France in 1956 *m860*

Moscow, Russia (56°N 38°E)   capital of Russia; site of major defeat of Napoleon's army in 1812 *m859*

Mount Olympus (38°N 24°E)   mountain (9,570 ft.; 2,917 m) in northeastern Greece, believed to be the home of the Greek gods *m43*

Munich (MYOO-nik)**, Germany** (48°N 12°E)   major city and manufacturing center of southern Germany; site of the Munich Conference in 1938 *m858*

Myanmar   *See* Burma.

N

Nagasaki (nahg-uh-SAHK-ee)**, Japan** (33°N 130°E) port city on southernmost island of Kyushu; trading post established by the Dutch in 1600s; site of second atomic bombing in World War II *m705, 859*

Nanjing, China (32°N 119°E) industrial city along the upper Chang River; occupied by the Japanese during World War II *m859*

Naples, Italy (41°N 14°E) major seaport in southern Italy; scene of nationalist movement in 1820 *m858*

Nara, Japan (35°N 136°E) city on the island of Honshu; former capital of Japan *m310*

Nazareth (31°N 35°E) ancient city in present-day Israel; where Jesus grew up *m133*

Netherlands flat, low-lying Benelux country in west central Europe *m858*

Netherlands East Indies former name of Indonesia *m705*

Neustria political region in northwest France ruled by the Franks beginning in 511; became Normandy, France, in 912 *m276*

New France former possessions of France from the St. Lawrence River to the Mississippi River in present-day Canada *m432*

New Spain former viceroyalty of Spain that stretched from the present-day southwestern United States to Panama *m455*

New York Middle Atlantic state in the northeastern United States *m468*

New York City, New York (41°N 74°W) largest city in the United States and a major commercial, financial, and cultural center; birthplace of Eleanor Roosevelt *m856*

New Zealand island nation southeast of Australia *m852–853*

Nicaragua country in Central America *m856*

Nile River world's longest river (4,187 miles; 6,737 km); flows into the Mediterranean Sea in Egypt *m14, 860*

Normandy, France region of northwestern France; 60-mile stretch of beaches west of Caen, France, where Allied forces landed and began the final battles of World War II in Europe *m704*

North America continent including Canada, the United States, Mexico, Central America, and the Caribbean islands *m852–853, 856*

Northern Ireland the six northern counties of Ireland that remain part of the United Kingdom; also called Ulster *m858*

North Korea Communist country on the northern part of the Korean Peninsula in East Asia *m859*

North Sea major sea between Great Britain, Denmark, and the Scandinavian Peninsula *m858*

North Vietnam Communist nation in southeast Asia established in 1954; began invading South Vietnam in 1964 and took over South Vietnam in 1975 *m761*

Norway Europe's northernmost nation; located on the western side of the Scandinavian Peninsula *m858*

Novgorod, Russia (58°N 32°E) important trade center that provided a link between northern Europe and Asia; one of the oldest cities in Russia *m238*

Nuremberg, Germany (49°N 11°E) city in southern Germany where Nazi war criminals were tried after World War II *m717*

O

Oder River river in Poland forming part of the border with Germany *m704*

Okinawa (26°N 128°E) largest of the Ryukyu Islands; captured by U.S. forces in World War II after heavy losses *m705*

Olympia, Greece (38°N 22°E) site of original Olympic Games *m77*

P

Pacific Ocean Earth's largest ocean; located between North and South America and Asia and Australia *m852–853*

Pakistan large, mainly Muslim country northwest of India in South Asia; gained independence in 1947 by act of British parliament; became Islamic republic in 1956 *m859*

Palenque (pah-LEHN-kay) (17°N 92°W) ancient Mayan city near the Yucatán Peninsula *m199*

Palestine region in southwest Asia at the eastern end of the Mediterranean Sea now occupied primarily by Israel *m665*

Panama country in Central America; invaded by the United States in 1989 in order to capture Manuel Noriega, the dictator involved in drug-trafficking *m856*

Panama Canal canal allowing transport between the Pacific Ocean and the Caribbean Sea, located in central Panama; opened in 1914 *m856*

Paris, France (49°N 2°E) capital of France *m858*

Passchendaele (PAHSH-en-dehl-uh)**, Belgium** small town in northwest Belgium; site of heavy fighting in World War I *m607*

Pearl Harbor (21°N 158°W) port in the Hawaiian Islands where the U.S. Pacific Fleet was destroyed by a Japanese surprise attack in 1941 *m705*

Persian Gulf body of water between Iran and the Arabian Peninsula *m859*

Peru country in northwestern South America; area of ancient cultures, including the Inca; much of the country liberated from Spanish rule in 1821 *m857*

Petrograd, Russia *See* St. Petersburg, Russia.

Philippines (FIL-uh-peenz) country of islands in Southeast Asia lying north of Indonesia and across the South China Sea from mainland Southeast Asia; became territory of the United States in 1898, gained independence in 1946 *m859*

Phoenicia (fi-NISH-uh) ancient country in western Syria famed for its commerce *m187*

Plymouth, Massachusetts (42°N 71°W) town in southeastern Massachusetts; settled by Pilgrims in 1620 *m432*

Poland Eastern Europe's largest and most populous country; invaded by Germany at the beginning of World War II; under communist rule until 1989 *m858*

Polynesia island region of the South Pacific Ocean that includes the Hawaiian and Line island groups, Samoa, French Polynesia, and Easter Island *m861*

Pondicherry (pahn-duh-CHER-ee)**, India** (12°N 80°E) city on the southeast coast of India; established as a trading post by the French East India Company in the 1600s *m422*

Portugal country of southern Europe just west of Spain on the Iberian Peninsula *m858*

Prague (PRAHG), **Czech Republic** (50°N 14°E) capital of the Czech Republic; Thirty Years' War began here in 1618 *m858*

Prussia former German state *m476*

Puerto Rico island commonwealth of the United States in the Greater Antilles in the Caribbean Sea; became a commonwealth in 1952 *m856*

Punjab Province former province of British India currently divided between Pakistan and India *m580*

Pyrenees (PIR-uh-neez) mountain range along the border of France and Spain; crossed by Hannibal and a force of elephants in 218 B.C. *m110*

Q

Qazvin (kaz-VEEN), **Iran** (37°N 50°E) historic city in Iran, capital of Safavid Persia *m340*

Qingdao (CHING-DOW), **China** (36°N 121°E) port city in eastern China; German naval base seized by Japan during World War I *m859*

Quebec, Canada mainly French-speaking province in eastern Canada; permanent French settlement established here in 1608 *m519*

R

Red Sea inland sea between the Arabian Peninsula and northeastern Africa *m860*

Rhine River major river in Western Europe that flows through Germany into the North Sea in the Netherlands *m858*

Romania country in Eastern Europe between Ukraine and Bulgaria; invaded by the Soviet Union in 1944, regained independence in 1947; under communist rule until 1989 *m858*

Rome, Italy (42°N 13°E) capital of Italy, center of the Roman Empire *m858*

Russia giant nation stretching from the center of Europe and the Baltic Sea to the eastern tip of Asia and the coast of the Bering Sea; gained its independence from Mongols in 1480 *m859*

S

Sahara immense desert region in northern Africa *m852–853*

Saigon (sie-GAHN), **Vietnam** (11°N 107°E) city in southern Vietnam; seized by the French in 1859 *(m580) See* Ho Chi Minh City.

St. Lawrence River major river linking the Great Lakes with the Gulf of St. Lawrence and the Atlantic Ocean in southeastern Canada; explored by Jacques Cartier in 1535 *m519*

St. Petersburg, Russia (60°N 30°E) formerly Leningrad; called Petrograd 1914 to 1924; Russia's second largest city and former capital; located on the Gulf of Finland in northwestern Russia *m858*

Samoa group of South Pacific islands divided between American Samoa, which was annexed by the United States in the 1880s, and the independent country of Western Samoa *m861*

San Lorenzo (18°N 95°W) ancient Olmec archaeological site in the state of present-day Veracruz, Mexico *m199*

São Paulo, Brazil (24°S 47°W) Brazil's largest city and the heart of South America's largest and wealthiest industrial area; located in southeastern Brazil *m857*

Sarajevo (SAIR-uh-yay-voe), **Bosnia and Herzegovina** (44°N 18°E) capital of Bosnia and Herzegovina in Eastern Europe; where Archduke Ferdinand was murdered, setting off World War I *m858*

Saratoga, New York (43°N 74°W) site of Revolutionary War battle in 1777 won by American colonists *m467*

Sardinia large Italian island in the Mediterranean Sea west of Italy, ruled by Carthage in 200s B.C.; later seized by Rome *m858*

Saudi Arabia country occupying much of the Arabian Peninsula in southwestern Asia *m859*

Savoy region of southeast France and northwest Italy *m393*

Scandinavia region including Denmark, Norway, Sweden, and sometimes Finland and Iceland

Scotland northern part of the island of Great Britain *m858*

Seoul (SOLE), **South Korea** (38°N 127°E) capital of South Korea *m859*

Serbia republic in Eastern Europe, part of what was Yugoslavia *m830*

Shenyang, China (43°N 123°E) formerly Mukden; city in Manchuria, in northeast China, where the Japanese staged a fake railway attack, blamed it on China, and then seized the province, renaming it Manchukuo *m859*

Siam (sie-AM) *See* Thailand.

Siberia vast region of Russia extending from the Ural Mountains to the Pacific Ocean; known as place of exile for Russian political opponents *m830*

Sicily large Mediterranean island of southern Italy *m858*

Silesia region in east central Europe; seized by Prussia from Austria in 1742, divided and given to Poland and Czechoslovakia after World Wars I and II *m456*

Silk Road ancient Asian trade route from China through Central Asia to the Mediterranean coast of southwestern Asia *m167*

Sinai (SIE-nie) **Peninsula** peninsula of northeastern Egypt in southwestern Asia *m10*

Singapore tiny but prosperous island-country situated at the tip of the Malay Peninsula of Southeast Asia *m859*

Slovenia independent country in Eastern Europe and a former Yugoslav republic; gained independence in 1991 *m858*

Solomon Islands South Pacific island country of Melanesia *m861*

Somme (SUHM) **River** river in northern France; site of great battle of World War I *m607*

South Africa country in southern Africa, ruled by the system of apartheid until the 1990s *m860*

South America world's fourth largest continent; extends from Colombia to Cape Horn *m852–853, 857*

South China Sea body of water between Vietnam and the Philippines *m859*

Southern Hemisphere the part of the world south of the equator

South Korea country occupying the southern half of the Korean Peninsula *m859*

South Vietnam former nation in southeast Asia; invaded by North Vietnam in 1964; fell to North Vietnam in 1975 *m761*

Soviet Union former giant northern Eurasian country of the Union of Soviet Socialist Republics (USSR) comprising 15 republics, including Russia *m830*

Spain country of southern Europe occupying most of the Iberian Peninsula *m858*

Spanish Netherlands historic region in the southern part of the Netherlands that became Belgium; was part of the Spanish Habsburg Empire until the Spanish War of Succession *m385*

Sparta ancient Greek militaristic city-state *m77*

Spice Islands former name of the Moluccas; once famed producers of spices, captured by Portugal in 1511, then by the Dutch in the early 1600s *m414–415*

Sri Lanka formerly Ceylon; island country south of India; settled by the Portuguese in the early 1500s *m859*

Stalingrad, Soviet Union (49°N 42°E) former name of Volgograd, Russia *m704*

Strait of Hormuz strait between the Persian Gulf and the Arabian Sea *m665*

Strait of Malacca channel between the Malay Peninsula and the Indonesian island of Sumatra that links the Indian Ocean with the South China Sea *m859*

Strait of Messina narrow strait separating Sicily from the southern tip of Italy *m110*

Sudan East African country; largest country in Africa; gained independence from Britain in 1956 *m860*

Sudetenland (soo-DAYT-en-land) region in northern Czechoslovakia with large German-speaking population; seized by Germans in 1938, returned to Czechoslovakia in 1945 *m691*

Suez Canal canal linking the Red Sea to the Mediterranean Sea in northeastern Egypt *m860*

Sumer ancient kingdom in Mesopotamia *m10*

Susa (32°N 48°E) ancient capital of Persia, now ruins *m64*

Sweden largest Scandinavian country of northern Europe *m858*

Syracuse ancient Greek city-state on Sicily *m110*

Syr Darya (sir DAHR-yuh) (**Jaxartes**) river draining the Pamirs in Central Asia and forming the northeastern border of the Persian Empire *m20–21*

Syria southwest Asian country between the Mediterranean Sea and Iraq; gained independence from France in 1946 *m859*

Syrian Desert desert region covering parts of Syria, Jordan, Iraq, and northern Saudi Arabia *m33*

T

Tabriz (tuh-BREEZ), **Iran** (38°N 46°E) historic commercial city in northwestern Iran, occupied in 1501 by the Safavids who made it their capital *m340*

Tahiti French South Pacific island in Polynesia; discovered by Captain James Cook *m861*

Taiwan (TIE-WAHN) prosperous, industrialized island country off the southeastern coast of China; Chiang Kaishek and the Chinese Nationalists fled here in 1949 *m859*

Tannenberg, Poland (54°N 20°E) city in northern Poland; part of Germany prior to 1945; site of World War I battle *m608*

Tanzania (tan-zuh-NEE-uh) country along the southern border of Kenya in East Africa; German colony from 1891 until World War I, when it became a British mandate; gained independence in 1961 *m860*

Tarawa, Kiribati capital of Kiribati in the South Pacific *m861*

Tarsus (37°N 35°E) city in present-day southern Turkey where the Christian apostle Paul was born *m133*

Tasmania island state of Australia, formerly Van Diemen's Land; British colony founded in 1823 *m852–853*

Tell al'Amârna, Egypt (28°N 31°E) ancient capital city, now ruins, on the banks of the Nile River *m38*

Tenochtitlán (tay-nawch-tee-TLAHN) (19°N 99°W) center, founded in about 1325, of the Aztec Empire on the site of present-day Mexico City, Mexico *m199*

Teotihuacán (tay-uh-tee-wah-KAHN) (20°N 99°W) ancient Toltec city north of Mexico City *m199*

Thailand (TIE-land) country of mainland Southeast Asia between Burma, Laos, and Cambodia *m859*

Thanesar former state of northern India *m319*

Thebes (38°N 23°E) Ancient Greek city northwest of Athens *m77*

Thermopylae (thehr-MOP-uh-lee) narrow mountain pass in eastern Greece, site of battle between Sparta and Persia in 480 B.C. *m77*

Thrace ancient country surrounded by Aegean Sea, Black Sea, and Sea of Marmara *m77*

Tiber River river that flows through Rome in central Italy *m370*

Tierra del Fuego (tee-EHR-uh del foo-AY-goe) group of islands at the southern tip of South America *m857*

Tigris River major river in southwestern Asia, flowing from Turkey through Iraq toward the Persian Gulf, forming, with the Euphrates River, Mesopotamia *m10, 859*

Tikal (tee-KAHL) (17°N 89°W) ancient Mayan city in northern Guatemala *m199*

Timbuktu, Mali (17°N 3°W) city in Mali and an ancient trading center in West Africa *m354*

Tlacopán (tlak-oh-PAHN) ancient city on Lake Texcoco, formed Triple Alliance with the Aztec *m199*

Togo (TOE-goe) small country situated between Ghana and Benin in West Africa; gained independence from France in 1960 *m860*

Togoland former German colony, divided in 1914 and eventually part of the colony joined Ghana and part became the country of Togo *m578*

Tokyo, Japan (36°N 140°E) Japan's national capital and the heart of a giant urban area *m587*

Tombouctou See Timbuktu.

Torun' (TOHR-oon) in present-day Poland; site of fortified base for the Teutonic Knights *m291*

Tours, France (47°N 1°E) city on the Loire River where Muslims were stopped in 732 *m251*

Trafalgar (36°N 6°W) cape off the southern coast of Spain near which Admiral Nelson sank half of Napoleon's navy *m476*

Transjordan former Turkish territory; came under British protection after World War I; became independent country of Jordan in 1946 *m665*

Trent, Italy (46°N 11°E) city in northern Italy, site of the Council of Trent between 1545 and 1563 *m370*

Trieste (tree-EST), **Italy** (45°N 14°E) port city on the Adriatic Sea; ruled by Austria, then ceded to Italy in 1919 *m620*

Tsushima (tsoo-SHE-muh) **Strait** strait in southwest Japan that connects the Sea of Japan and the East China Sea; site of battle in 1905 in which Japan defeated Russia *m587*

Tula (20°N 99°W) ancient Toltec city northwest of present-day Mexico City *m199*

Turkey country of the eastern Mediterranean occupying Anatolia and a corner of southeastern Europe *m859*

Turkistan region in central Asia, conquered by the Mongols in the 1200s *m325*

Tyre, Lebanon (33°N 35°E) today called Sur; renowned commercial city, once the capital of Phoenicia *m97*

U

Ukraine independent Eastern European country and the second most populous of the republics of the former Soviet Union; gained independence in 1991 *m858*

Ulundi, South Africa (28°S 31°E) city in southeast South Africa where, in 1879, the British fought the Zulu Empire, bringing that empire to an end *m576*

Union of Soviet Socialist Republics (USSR) *See* Soviet Union.

United Kingdom country occupying most of the British Isles of northern Europe; Great Britain and Northern Ireland *m858*

United States North American country between Canada and Mexico *m856*

Uruguay (UHR-uh-gway) country on the northern side of the Río de la Plata between Brazil and Argentina in eastern South America *m857*

V

Valley of Mexico valley in south central Mexico where Mexico City is located; site of ancient civilizations *m199*

Valley of Oaxaca (wuh-HAHK-uh) valley in southern Mexico, area of Zapotec culture *m199*

Venezuela country in northern South America; liberated from Spanish rule in 1811 *m857*

Venice, Italy (45°N 12°E) city of islands and canals in northeastern Italy; commercial center in the Middle Ages *m370*

Verdun, France (49°N 5°E) city in northeastern France; site of great battle of World War I *m607*

Versailles (vehr-SY), **France** (49°N 2°E) city west of Paris; royal palace built in the 1700s by Louis XIV; treaty ending World War I signed here *m393*

Vienna, Austria (48°N 16°E) capital of Austria; center of the Habsburg Empire *m858*

Vientiane (vyen-TYAHN), **Laos** (18°N 103°E) capital of Laos *m859*

Vietnam long, narrow country that occupies the eastern portion of the Indochina Peninsula in mainland Southeast Asia; called Annam in ancient times; former French colony; divided into North and South Vietnam in 1954, then rejoined in 1975 after North Vietnam had invaded the south *m859*

Vistula River river flowing through Warsaw, Poland, to the Baltic Sea *m608*

Volcano Islands South Pacific island country; site of fighting in World War II between Japan and the Allies *m705*

Volga River Europe's longest river; located in west central Russia *m548*

W

Wake Island (19°N 167°E) U.S. North Pacific island territory north of the Marshall Islands; occupied by Japan in World War II *m861*

Wales a country of the United Kingdom occupying a western portion of Great Britain *m858*

Wannsee, Germany (53°N 13°E) a suburb of Berlin where the Nazis met in 1942 to finalize plans for the extermination of the Jews *m698*

Warsaw, Poland (52°N 21°E) capital of Poland; where the fiercest resistance to the Holocaust occurred *m698*

Waterloo, Belgium (51°N 4°E) town in central Belgium and site of Napoleon's final defeat in 1815 *m476*

Western Hemisphere the part of the world west of longitude 0° (the prime meridian) and east of longitude 180° *m716*

West Germany (Federal Republic of Germany) former nation in west central Europe; formed in 1949 of American, British, and French zones of the former Germany; reunified with East Germany in 1990 *m717*

West Indies Caribbean islands lying between North and South America *m432*

West Pakistan what was the western half of Pakistan until the eastern half, Bangladesh, became independent in 1971 *m745*

Westphalia former province of Prussia, site of treaty ending the Thirty Years' War *m476*

Wittenberg (VIT-uhn-behrg), **Germany** city in northeast Germany where Luther posted his 95 theses *m385*

Y

Yangzi River *See* Chang Jiang.

Yorktown, Virginia (38°N 76°W) site of decisive battle in the American Revolutionary War *m467*

Yucatán Peninsula peninsula in southeastern Mexico *m199*

Yugoslavia Eastern European country formed of six republics after World War I; now claimed by Serbia and Montenegro *m620*

Yukon Territory, Canada northern Canadian territory bordering Alaska *m519*

GLOSSARY

This Glossary contains terms you need to understand as you study world history. After each term there is a brief definition or explanation of the meaning of the term as it is used in *World History: Continuity and Change*. The page number refers to the page on which the term is introduced in the textbook.

Phonetic Respelling and Pronunciation Guide

Many of the key terms in this textbook have been respelled to help you pronounce them. The letter combinations used in the respellings throughout the narrative are explained in the following phonetic respelling and pronunciation guide. The guide is adapted from *Webster's Ninth New Collegiate Dictionary*, *Webster's New Geographical Dictionary*, and *Webster's New Biographical Dictionary*.

MARK	AS IN	RESPELLING	EXAMPLE
a	alphabet	a	*AL-fuh-bet
ā	Asia	ay	AY-zhuh
ä	cart, top	ah	KAHRT, TAHP
e	let, ten	e	LET, TEN
ē	even, leaf	ee	EE-vuhn, LEEF
i	it, tip, British	i	IT, TIP, BRIT-ish
ī	site, buy, Ohio,	y	SYT, BY, oh-HY-oh
k	card	k	KARD
ō	over, rainbow,	oh	oh-vuhr, RAYN-boh
ù	book, wood	ooh	BOOHK, WOOHD
ò	all, orchid	aw	AWL, AWR-kid
òi	foil, coin	oy	FOYL, KOYN
aù	out	ow	OWT
ə	cup, butter	uh	KUHP, BUHT-uhr
ü	rule, food	oo	ROOL, FOOD
yü	few	yoo	FYOO
zh	vision	zh	VIZH-uhn

*A syllable printed in small capital letters receives heavier emphasis than the other syllable(s) in a word.

A

abacus Chinese device for doing mathematical calculations by moving beads along rods. **308**

abolition movement Movement led by Britain to end the slave trade and eventually slavery throughout the world. **510**

absolutism Political philosophy focusing on the centralization of political authority in the hands of a national monarch. **390**

Achaemenid dynasty Established in Persia by Cyrus II in 550 B.C. after he overthrew the Median king, whose dynasty eventually included Lydia, Asia Minor, Babylon, and Egypt. **65**

acid rain Toxic mixture produced when rain or snow falls through polluted air. **840**

acquired immune deficiency syndrome (AIDS) Disease that weakens the body's immune system and ultimately results in death. **792**

acropolis Defensible fortification in a Greek polis. **69**

acupuncture Chinese method for treating illness in which needles are inserted into certain points on the body. **168**

African diaspora Forced migration of millions of Africans to the Americas through the slave trade. **446**

Afrikaans Language spoken by the Boers in Britain's African Cape Colony that was a combination of Dutch, French, German, English, and African languages. **570**

agora   Marketplace and center of early Greek life in the polis where food supplies were bought and sold in exchange for artisans' or outside traders' goods. **70**

Agricultural Revolution   Shift from food gathering to food producing. **7** Introduction of new farming methods in Britain in the early 1700s. **485**

ahimsa   Jainist belief in nonviolence. **149**

Algerian National Liberation Front   Movement in Algeria that launched a guerrilla war in 1954 to obtain the colony's independence as an Arab state. **775**

Allied Powers   World War I alliance including Triple Entente countries. **601**

American Anti-Slavery Society   Group of prominent abolitionists formed in 1833. **523**

Amnesty International   Agency that monitors human rights violations. **820**

Amritsar Massacre (1919)   Massacre of Indians by the British at a Hindu religious festival, which came after Indian national protests against strict British security regulations and Britain's subsequent ban of all public meetings. **662**

Angkor Wat   Khmer temple built in the 1100s. **319**

Anglo-Egyptian Treaty (1936)   Agreement between Britain and Egypt allowing Britain to maintain military control over the Suez Canal and calling for British defense and League of Nations sponsorship of Egypt. **664**

animism   Belief that all things in nature have a spirit. **54**

Anti–Corn Law League   Members of middle- and working-class British society who protested the Corn Laws imposed by wealthy landowners in 1815 that limited the importation of cheap foreign grain and thus kept food prices high. **513**

antibiotics   Drugs that destroy or limit bacterial infection. **838**

apartheid   South African policy that called for separate areas for white Afrikaners, black Bantu, Asians, and people of mixed race and allowed only whites to vote or hold political office. **793**

apostolic succession   The granting of Christ's authority to priests by his disciples. **137**

appeasement   Giving in to an aggressor to preserve the peace. **687**

aqueducts   Channels used to bring water to cities of the Roman Empire. **129**

Arab League   Group of seven newly independent Arab states, formed in 1945, that recognized the influence of Pan-Arabism in the region and opposed a Jewish state in Palestine. **778**

archaeologists   Scientists who study past cultures by analyzing human remains and artifacts. **4**

armistice   Ending of hostilities until a formal treaty can be completed. **613**

artifacts   Objects made or altered by human beings. **4**

assembly line   Manufacturing technique in which a product is passed along a line of workers and assembled in stages. **637**

astrolabe   Greek instrument rediscovered by Muslim scientists that allowed observers to chart the positions of the stars and thereby calculate their own position on Earth. **259**

Atlantic Charter (1941)   Joint U.S. and British statement of goals for World War II that said neither power sought territorial gains and that each believed in the principle of national self-determination. **694**

Atlantic slave trade   European importing of people from Africa to work on plantations in the Americas. **441**

atomic bomb   Bomb powered by splitting uranium atoms that can destroy an entire city. **709**

atrocities   Acts of great cruelty and brutality. **603**

Auschwitz   Most notorious of the Nazi concentration camps, located in southern Poland. **698**

autocracy   Political system in which a ruler holds total power. **163**

Avesta   Sassanid Persian collection of the oldest and most basic scriptures of Zoroastrianism. **226**

Awami League   Political organization that demanded self-government for East Pakistan. **747**

B

baby boom   Generation born between the mid-1940s and the early 1960s. **736**

Babylonian Captivity   Chaldean deportation of Judah's population to Babylon in 587 B.C. **51** Period of nearly 70 years, beginning in 1309, during which French kings controlled the papacy. **366**

balance of power   System of equalizing alliances established to prevent one country from attacking others. **371**

Balfour Declaration (1917)   Lord Balfour's statement of British support for Palestine as a national home for the Jewish people. **667**

Bantu languages   Niger-Kordofianian group of languages spoken throughout most of southern Africa. **178**

Bataan Death March (1942)   Forced march of Allied prisoners up the Bataan Peninsula during which Japanese guards killed more than 600 Americans and up to 10,000 Filipinos. **701**

Battle of 'Ayn Jalut (1260)   Mamluks' defeat of the Mongols. **324**

Battle of Britain (1940)   German air force raids and British efforts to counter them during World War II. **693**

Battle of Lepanto (1571)   Combined Spanish and Italian defeat of the Ottomans in the Mediterranean Sea. **420**

Battle of the Bulge (1944)   World War II battle in which Allied troops forced the Germans to retreat. **706**

Bay of Pigs (1961)   Covert operation against Fidel Castro in which exiled Cubans came ashore in an attempt to retake the country. **814**

bedouins   Arab herders who lived in tents and moved from place to place with their animals. **244**

Benedictine Rule   Set of rules that governed monastic life and became a fundamental pattern for Catholic monasteries. **275**

Berlin Conference (1884–85)   Meeting of great European powers to establish ground rules for partitioning imperial possessions in Africa. **572**

bhakti   Complete love and devotion to god as stressed in the *Bhagavad Gita*. **147**

Bill of Rights (1791)   First 10 amendments to the U.S. Constitution, guaranteeing the basic rights of every U.S. citizen. **468**

biodiversity   Natural variety of plants and animals in the environment. **843**

bishop Christian official who supervises church affairs in cities and who has authority over other priests in the region. **137**

Black Death Bubonic plague that arrived in Europe from Asia in 1347, killing between 25 to 50 percent of Europe's population. **362**

Black Tuesday October 29, 1929; day the U.S. stock market crashed. **642**

Blitz Nighttime air raids against major cities in Britain during World War II between September 1940 and May 1941. **693**

Blitzkrieg "Lightning war," descriptive of Hitler's swift and severe attack on Poland. **690**

Bolsheviks Group of Russians who in 1917 believed that the revolution must be led by a small, elite group of reformers who would guide the rest of the country. **627**

Boston Tea Party (1773) Event that occurred when angry colonists threw a shipment of tea into Boston Harbor to protest Britain's granting the British East India Company a monopoly over the tea trade in the British colonies. **465**

Boxers Westerners' name for members of the secret Chinese "Society of the Harmonious Fists" that revolted in 1900 against Western influence in China. **588**

Brezhnev Doctrine (1968) Soviet Union's use of force when necessary to ensure the survival of communism in Eastern Europe. **740**

brinkmanship Act of moving close to the brink of nuclear war without going over. **732**

bureaucracy Complex governmental structure in which civil servants carry out many specialized tasks. **15**

Bushido Strict set of rules governing samurai behavior. **313**

C

caliphs Leaders of the Muslim community who ruled according to the Qur'an and Muhammad's example. **250**

calligraphy Writing that became a beautiful art form in early Chinese society. **55**

Calvinists Protestant religious followers of John Calvin. **382**

Camp David Accords (1978) Peace agreement between Anwar Sadat of Egypt and Menachem Begin of Israel. **782**

cantons Swiss states that secured liberal reforms by peaceful means in the early 1800s. **559**

capital Money or property as a source of income and means to produce money with which to buy other things. **368**

capitalism Use of private money or goods to produce a profit of more money or goods. **485**

capitulations Tax exemptions and other special trade privileges granted to France by Süleyman I of the Ottoman Empire. **420**

captaincies Huge tracts of colonial land in Brazil granted to donataries by John III of Portugal. **431**

caravels Portuguese-developed ships in the 1400s equipped with lateen sails and stern-post rudders that were smaller and more maneuverable than cargo ships. **411**

Carbonari Secret Italian nationalist society that plotted to overthrow the Austrians in the early 1830s. **541**

Carlsbad Decrees Product of Klemens von Metternich's assembly of German Confederation leaders in 1819 that prohibited political reforms conflicting with absolute monarchy, established censorship of newspapers, and formed a secret police force to detect revolutionary activity. **539**

Carolingian renaissance Revival of learning during Charlemagne's rule. **277**

Carter Doctrine (1979) Proclamation by U.S. president Jimmy Carter that the United States would use force, if necessary, to safeguard U.S. interests in the Persian Gulf region. **829**

Catholic Reformation Movement between 1545 and 1563 redefining the doctrines of the Catholic faith. **383**

censors Roman magistrates who recorded the wealth and residence of the population and appointed Senate candidates. **117**

Central Powers World War I alliance of Germany, Austria-Hungary, the Ottoman Empire, and later Bulgaria. **601**

charter of incorporation Royal charter that allowed merchants to govern a town under the king's protection. **295**

Chartists Followers of William Lovett in Britain who in 1836 called for universal manhood suffrage and equal representation for everyone in the country. **513**

chinampas Raised Aztec gardens. **202**

chivalry Code of conduct that required a knight to be brave, fight fairly, and protect women, children, and the clergy. **295**

chlorofluorocarbons (CFCs) Carbon-based combinations of chlorine and fluorine that many scientists believe break down the earth's ozone layer. **840**

Chosŏn First strong Korean kingdom that emerged in the northern part of the country and exerted some control over much of the Korean Peninsula by the early 100s B.C. **309**

Christian humanism Application of humanist principles and the lessons of the classics to religion. **376**

chronometer Accurate timekeeping instrument that helped sailors pinpoint their exact position on the globe. **517**

circumnavigate Sail a full circle around the globe. **416**

citadel City's strong central fortress. **18**

city-states Independent cities with their own governments, orchards, and fields. **10**

civic humanism Form of humanism emphasizing the idea that individual achievement and education is fully expressed only if people use their abilities to serve their cities. **371**

civilization Complex society that has several basic elements: production of surplus food, large towns or cities, and divisions of labor. **7**

civil service Governmental service system in which officials are usually appointed through an examination system. **163**

classical education Education based on rhetoric, grammar, poetry, history, Latin, and Greek. **369**

Classic Maya Period of greatest achievement of the Maya civilization, from about 300 A.D. to 900 A.D. **199**

Cold War Struggle for global power between the United States and the Soviet Union following World War II. **719**

collective farms Farms on which many people share the work. **630**

collective security System in which nations pledge to cooperate in their mutual defense. **614**

College of Cardinals Body of bishops responsible for electing popes. **289**

colonus Tenant farmer during the Pax Romana who replaced slaves on large estates. **127**

colossal style Hellenistic architecture, larger and more spectacular than earlier Greek architecture, whose name derives from the famous Colossus, a gigantic statue in the harbor of Rhodes. **103**

command economy Economic system in which the government makes all economic decisions. **718**

Commercial Revolution Economic development in Europe in the 1400s that led to improvements in business methods and practices. **367**

common law Began as Henry II of England's uniform system of justice in which traveling judges enforced his law throughout the kingdom. **285**

Commune Revolutionary French government proclaimed by Parisians as they continued to fight against the Prussians in January 1871. **555**

communism Economic system established through a dictatorship that abolishes private property and takes over the means of production. **504**

compass Navigational tool with a magnetized needle that points north-south. **411**

compound bows Wooden bows reinforced with pieces of bone for added power. **35**

Concert of Europe (1815) Quadruple Alliance's system of diplomatic cooperation. **538**

Concordat (1801) Agreement by which Napoleon acknowledged Catholicism as the religion of most French citizens and the church gave up claims to its property in France. **475**

Concordat of Worms (1122) Compromise between Emperor Henry V and the church by which the pope would invest the bishops of Germany with their spiritual authority and Henry would retain the right to grant them their symbols of earthly power. **289**

confederation Loose association. **518**

Congress of Vienna Peace conference that met from September 1814 to June 1815 to negotiate a full and definite settlement of European peace following the Napoleonic Wars. **536**

conquistador Spanish conqueror. **428**

constitution Political structure by which the Romans governed the Republic in the late 500s B.C. **117**

constitutional monarchy Political system in which the powers of a ruler are limited by a constitution. **397**

Consulate French government established by Napoleon Bonaparte in 1799. **474**

consuls Two chief executives of the Roman state, each elected for one year. **117**

consumption Purchase of products by consumers. **637**

Contadora Principles (1983) Agreements made during a meeting of Venezuelan, Panamanian, Colombian, and Mexican leaders that called for an immediate freeze on arms sales, general military reductions, and negotiations to settle regional disputes. **816**

Continental System Napoleon's blockade of the British Isles in the early 1800s. **475**

contraband War material supplied to a country's enemy. **610**

Contras Guerrilla group in Nicaragua that was organized to overthrow the Sandinistas and received arms and money from the U.S. government. **815**

Convention People's Party (CPP) Political party in Ghana established by Kwame Nkrumah that pressured Britain into agreeing to grant a new self-governing constitution and allow national elections in 1951. **773**

Coptic Church Christian church that arose in Egypt and eventually split from the Roman Catholic Church. **189**

corporations Business organizations in which large numbers of people purchase shares of stocks, or certificates of partial ownership. **499**

Corpus juris civilis Body of civil law in the Byzantine Empire. **232**

cotton gin Invention of American Eli Whitney in 1793 that separated seeds from cotton more quickly and efficiently than hand separation. **491**

Council of Trent Meeting of Catholic leaders in the Italian city of Trent between 1545 and 1563 to redefine the doctrines of the church. **383**

courtly love Tradition that glorified noble women and praised knights' heroic and gentle virtues. **297**

covenant Solemn agreement. **47**

covert Secret. **814**

crop rotation Method of alternating different kinds of crops to preserve soil fertility. **486**

crusaders Christians who joined the movement against the Muslim world during the Middle Ages. **290**

Cultural Revolution (1966–68) Period of turbulence in China begun by former government head Mao Zedong in which he encouraged demonstrations against the existing government, many party leaders, and most intellectuals. **754**

culture Collective characteristics such as art, literature, and sense of identity that set one people apart from others. **6**

cuneiform Simplified pictographs or script used to represent sounds instead of objects. **12**

curriculum Course of studies. **298**

D

D-Day (June 6, 1944) Day on which Allied soldiers landed on Normandy beaches during World War II to begin the invasion of France. **703**

dada Artistic style in the early 1900s that often featured objects and ideas with no seeming relationship to one another. **638**

daric Gold currency of the Persian Empire. **67**

Dark Age Era in Greece following disappearance of the Mycenaean civilization. **45**

Dawes Plan (1924) American diplomat Charles Dawes's plan to reschedule Germany's World War I reparations payments. **619**

de-Stalinization Soviet leader Nikita Khrushchev's condemnation of Stalin's governmental and economic policies in Russia in the mid-1950s. **727**

Declaration of Independence (July 4, 1776) Second Continental Congress proclamation that the United States of America is an independent nation. **466**

decolonization Transition from colonial possession to independent statehood. **744**

Delhi sultanate Muslim government founded in 1206 that became a center of Muslim culture. **318**

Delian League Greek alliance of more than 140 cities, formed for mutual defense against the Persians. **78**

demagogues People who use their skills of oratory, or speechmaking, to sway crowds. **92**

demilitarize Remove all troops from a location. **616**

demographic transition Period between preindustrial societies and industrialized societies when birth rates are higher than death rates, causing population explosions. **804**

dependent colonies Colonies in which a few foreign officials ruled over the local population. **566**

desertification Steady advance of the desert, resulting from deforestation and topsoil erosion. **791**

détente (1972) Easing of diplomatic and military tensions between the United States and the Soviet Union that included trade agreements, joint scientific experiments, and nuclear arms agreements. **828**

devshirme Tribute levied every few years on the Ottoman sultan's Christian subjects. **336**

dharma In Hinduism, moral duty people must fulfill during each cycle of reincarnation. **147**

Diaspora "Scattering"; period in Hebrew history around 722 B.C. in which Assyrians deported Israelites to Samaria, where they became known as the Ten Lost Tribes of Israel. **50**

dihqans Sassanid Persian soldier-peasants in charge of a village who served as the backbone of the army and the main line of defense in frontier areas. **224**

direct democracy Political system in which legislative and electoral power remains with the popular assembly of all voting citizens. **74**

disciples Followers of Jesus of Nazareth. **132**

dissidents People who speak out against their governments. **738**

divan Ottoman imperial council. **336**

diversification Expansion of a country's economy into more than one market. **803**

Divine Faith Creed established by Akbar of the Mughal dynasty that blended ideas and practices from Islam, Hinduism, Jainism, Christianity, Sufism, and other religions. **346**

divine right of kings Idea that the supreme political authority of national monarchs came directly from God. **391**

domain Portion of the manorial land kept by the lord. **282**

Domesday Book Also called the Day of Judgment Book, Duke William of Normandy's survey of the entire English territory that reported who owned what and what it was worth. **285**

domestication Purposeful adaptation of plants and animals for the benefit of humans. **7**

domestic system System of cloth production in which people worked on the cleaning, spinning, and weaving of wool in their homes. **486**

dominion Self-governing colony. **519**

domino theory President Dwight Eisenhower's warning that one nation's falling to communism would lead to communism in all neighboring nations. **734**

donataries Individuals who agreed to finance Portuguese colonization in Brazil in exchange for political and economic control of their new territory. **431**

Donation of Pepin (c. 756) Pepin's donation to the pope of land in central Italy that created the Papal States and made the papacy a secular as well as a spiritual power. **277**

Dual Monarchy Government of Austria-Hungary established in 1867 after Austria's defeat in the Seven Weeks' War with Prussia. **546**

Dutch West India Company Company for which Henry Hudson sailed in 1609 that established the colony of New Netherland in the Hudson River valley and New Amsterdam, which became New York City. **436**

dynamo Electric generator. **498**

dynasty Family of rulers in which the right to rule passes on within the family, usually from father to son or daughter. **14**

E

Easter Rising (1916) Irish nationalist revolt in Dublin for home rule. **659**

ecosphere Interlocking system of life on Earth. **843**

Edict of Milan (313) Constantine's declaration making Christianity legal within the Roman Empire. **137**

Edict of Nantes (1598) Truce between Roman Catholics and Protestants in France. **385**

egalitarianism Removal of inequalities among people. **223**

Elizabethan Age Renaissance in England, named after Queen Elizabeth I. **376**

Emancipation Proclamation (1863) President Abraham Lincoln's declaration during the Civil War that freed all slaves in those parts of the South still at war with the United States. **524**

enclosures Fenced-in European lands, including those lands that had once been considered common for local farmers and villagers. **398**

encomienda System in the Americas in which colonists were granted land and the labor of a certain number of American Indians who worked on the land in return for lessons in Christianity. **428**

English Bill of Rights (1689) Guarantee of certain fundamental freedoms, such as not being subjected to cruel and unusual punishments for a crime. **397**

enlightened despotism System of government in which absolute monarchs ruled according to Enlightenment principles in order to bring society, politics, and the economy in line with natural law. **462**

entrepreneurs People who risk their wealth by investing in new technology or new business ventures. **484**

Era of a Hundred Schools Period of philosophical development in China at the beginning of the 400s B.C. in which many different approaches to philosophy arose, all based on the idea that everything in the world results from a balancing of yin and yang. **159**

Era of Warring States Several hundred years in China beginning in 403 B.C. during which powerful states destroyed or absorbed weaker ones and the number of states in China declined sharply. **158**

Estates General Representative body established between 1285 and 1314 by Philip the Fair and drawn from the three great classes, or estates (clergy, nobility, and commoners), of French society. **287** Louis XVI's convention of representatives from all three French Estates at Versailles in May 1789. **470**

ethnic cleansing Campaign of terror launched in the 1990s by Bosnian Serbs, designed to drive Muslims out of the areas that Serbs claimed for themselves. **832**

eunuchs Special male servants to the Chinese emperor's personal household. **350**

European Economic Community European common market established by the Treaties of Rome in March 1957 that extended the free-trade principles of the Coal and Steel Community to other sectors of the members' economies. **724**

European Union   Western European trading bloc that evolved from the European Economic Community in 1993. **848**

evangelical movement   Religious revival that occurred in Britain in the late 1700s when people began to see their faith as a deeply personal experience and emphasized the importance of moral conduct in their lives. **510**

Exodus   Flight of the Hebrews in the mid-1200s B.C. out of Egypt and into the desert of the Sinai Peninsula in search of the "promised land." **47**

expressionism   Artistic style of the 1920s and 1930s using shapes, lines, and color to communicate emotions. **638**

extraterritoriality   Aspect of trade treaties between Western nations and other countries that gave westerners the right to be tried only in Western courts under Western law. **586**

F

fallout   Radioactive dust and other particles from nuclear blasts that are potentially harmful to living things. **732**

faqih   Supreme religious guide of Iran. **788**

fascism   Political philosophy that places the nation above the individual and favors nationalistic, anticommunist, antidemocratic, and expansionist beliefs. **645**

Fashoda Crisis   (1898)   Imperial conflict between Britain and France over control of the African town of Fashoda. **573**

February Revolution   (1917)   First stage of the Russian Revolution started by female factory workers in Petrograd who protested their inability to buy bread for their families. **627**

federal system   System of government set forth in the U.S. Constitution that divides powers between the central government and the state governments. **468**

feudalism   Political system created by the Zhou in the early-1100s B.C. in which the king owned all of the land and distributed it to his kinsmen. **55** Practice of lords granting land or fiefs to vassals in return for a pledge of military service. **280**

fief   In feudalism, land granted by a lord to a vassal. **280**

Fifth Republic   French government established with the election of Charles de Gaulle to the presidency in 1958 that brought political stability to France. **724**

financiers   Businesspeople who buy companies as investments. **499**

fission   Splitting an atom's nucleus to release great amounts of energy. **731**

Five Classics   Collection of Confucian works, including the *Book of Poetry, Book of History, Book of Divination, Spring and Autumn Annals*, and *Book of Rites*, which were believed to offer great insights into the art of government. **164**

Five Pillars of Islam   The most important duties expected of Muslims, as laid down by Muhammad in the Qur'an. **256**

flagellants   People who adopted forms of self-abuse as punishment for their supposed sins. **363**

Flemish School   Renaissance painters noted for the exquisite detail of their work and for their dark, cold landscapes. **379**

folk art   Art created by local artists for ordinary use. **824**

Forbidden City   Imperial Palace built in the center of Beijing during the Ming dynasty. **351**

formal logic   Philosophical basis that all assertions must be based on reasoned proof. **82**

Forum   Central market in Rome. **108**

Four Modernizations   Deng Xiaoping's post-Cultural Revolution economic reform policies for improving China's agriculture, industry, science and technology, and national defense. **764**

Four Noble Truths   Buddhist beliefs that (1) all human life contains suffering and sorrow; (2) desire causes suffering; (3) by rejecting desire, people can attain nirvana; and (4) following the Eightfold Path leads to rejection of desire and attainment of nirvana. **150**

Four Tigers   South Korea, Taiwan, Hong Kong, and Singapore, all of which followed aggressive economic policies based on the Japanese model. **766**

Fourteen Points   President Woodrow Wilson's plan, outlined in a speech he gave before Congress in January 1918, designed to lay the foundation of a lasting world peace. **614**

Fourth Republic   French government established by voters in October 1946. **723**

free enterprise   Economic system in which every person is free to go into any business and to operate it for maximum profit. **460**

freemen   Former Germanic warriors (or nobles) who could own land and had some political rights. **273**

French and Indian War   North American eruption of the Seven Years' War around 1754 in which the French and the British made alliances with American Indians. **454**

French Community   African colonies that remained associated with France, and in return for giving France control of their foreign relations, were guaranteed internal self-government and money for economic development. **775**

frescoes   Paintings made on plaster walls. **42**

fusion   Combining hydrogen atoms in the same kind of reaction that fuels the sun. **732**

G

Gang of Four   Group in China following the death of Mao Zedong in 1976 that wanted to continue the Cultural Revolution. **764**

General Agreement on Tariffs and Trade   (GATT) Agreement signed in 1947 by the major economic nations to promote economic growth and development throughout the world. **848**

generation gap   Phrase that refers to differences between generations, with the older generation focused on what was right in their lives and the younger generation focused on what was wrong. **736**

genes   Small units of chromosomes that determine an individual's physical characteristics, such as eye and hair color. **839**

genocide   Annihilation of an entire people. **603**

Gentiles   Non-Jews. **133**

geocentric   Aristotle's Earth-centered model of the universe. **402**

geoglyphs   Complex Nazca system of interlocking lines drawn on the desert floor. **205**

ghazis   Turkish soldiers who saw themselves as "warriors for the [Islamic] faith." **266**

glasnost   Established in 1985 by Soviet leader Mikhail Gorbachev when he called on citizens to speak their minds about the failings of the Soviet system. **829**

Glorious Revolution (1688)   Revolution in which a group of nobles and parliamentary leaders deposed James II of England. **397**

glyphs   Series of symbols that formed the basis of the Maya writing system. **199**

Golden Bull (1356)   Decree by which Charles IV of Germany tried to rebuild his authority by removing the popes from the process of electing the emperor. **365**

Good Emperors   Five emperors in the Roman dynasty established in A.D. 96 including Nerva, Trajan, Hadrian, Antoninus Pius, and Marcus Aurelius. **125**

Good Neighbor policy (1933)   President Franklin Roosevelt's declaration that ended the previous U.S. governmental policy of overseas intervention in Latin America. **678**

Grand Canal   Series of rivers and canals, 1,000 miles long, that connected northern and southern China. **302**

Great Bull Market   Period of economic expansion, reaching its height in 1929, in which American stock prices boomed upward. **641**

Great Chain of Being   Belief held by most medieval Europeans that all things and all people were assigned places in the universe. **398**

Great Depression   Economic downturn that began in 1929, sparked by low agricultural prices, artificially low interest rates, and stock market speculation. **642**

Great Leap Forward   Mao Zedong's second Five-Year Plan unveiled in 1958 for modernizing China overnight. **752**

Great Migration (1630)   Flight of some 60,000 English Puritans from the "corrupt" society of Charles I. **438**

Great Schism (1378–1417) Period in which Latin Christendom was divided between a French and an Italian pope. **366**

Great Trek (1835)   Mass Boer migration from Cape Colony to the African interior. **571**

greenhouse effect   Process caused by the burning of fuels by which excess carbon dioxide traps more heat near the earth and, according to many scientists, results in global warming. **841**

griots   Oral historians of West Africa. **180**

gross domestic product   Value of all goods produced in a country in one year. **756**

guilds   Trade associations for artisans that set standards, restricted competition, and regulated the training of new artisans. **295**

gulags   Forced Russian labor camps in the late 1920s and 1930s. **650**

Guomindang   Chinese Nationalist Party led by Sun Yixian. **672**

gynaeceum   Women's apartments in the Byzantine royal palace. **233**

H

hajj   Islamic followers' pilgrimage to Mecca. **256**

Hanseatic League   Cities of northern Germany under the protection of the Teutonic Knights that controlled most of the trade between Europe, the Baltic, and Russia in the 1500s. **293**

Harappan civilization   Early life in the Indus Valley that developed from about 2300 to 1750 B.C. **17**

Hawaiian League   Secret society formed by leading Western traders, planters, and missionaries in Hawaii in the late 1880s whose goal was U.S. annexation of Hawaii. **678**

heliocentric   Sun-centered description of the universe. **107, 404**

Hellenistic   "Greeklike" culture. **99**

hierarchy   Graded social order. **10**

hieroglyphics   System of writing used as early as 3000 B.C. in the Nile Valley that had more than 600 signs, pictures, or symbols to indicate words or sounds. **13**

hijrah   Muhammad's journey with his followers from Mecca to Yathrib. **247**

Ho Chi Minh Trail   Main Communist supply route from North to South Vietnam. **762**

Holocaust   Act of genocide by the Nazis during World War II in which European Jews were slaughtered. **697**

Holy Alliance (1815)   Alliance of European rulers gathered by Alexander of Russia to keep international peace and commit European rulers to help one another put down internal rebellion and revolution. **538**

homelands   Separate black territories created by the South African government for each ethnic group. **794**

Homo sapiens   "Thinking man," modern humans who began to appear in Africa by about 200,000 B.C. **5**

hoplites   Heavily armed Greek infantry who fought in phalanx formation. **72**

hubris   Idea of pride as portrayed in the plays of the ancient Greeks. **85**

Huguenots   French Protestants. **385**

humanism   Movement that began in Italy during the 1300s focusing on the study of the classics and emphasizing the importance of human beings. **369**

Hundred Days   Napoleon's final effort to restore his empire after escaping from exile in Elba in March 1815. **478**

Hundred Years' War (1337–1453)   Series of conflicts between England and France. **364**

I

ICBMs   (intercontinental ballistic missiles)   Missiles developed during the mid-1950s to strike long-range targets from either the United States or the Soviet Union. **732**

Ice Age   Era between 50,000 and 14,000 years ago when ice covered much of the earth's surface. **23**

iconoclast movement   Reaction against the use of Christian icons. **234**

imams   Ali's successors as leaders in the Shi'ah branch of Islam. **252**

Imperial Conferences   Meetings of British leaders with colonial dominion leaders in the late 1800s to discuss matters of mutual concern. **658**

imperial preference   Policy in the 1930s through which the British Empire became a largely self-sufficient trading block whose members gave preferential treatment to each other. **644**

import substitution   Policy of Latin American governments to encourage their own local industries to produce goods previously imported from overseas. **803**

indentured servitude   System established by the London Company in which people were offered free passage to the American colonies in exchange for a set number of years of work. **437**

Indian Mutiny (1857)   Uprising in India during the rule of the British East India Company. **582**

Indian National Congress (1885)   Political conference of Western-educated Indians in Bombay at which delegates declared their loyalty to Britain and called for equal opportunity to serve in the Indian government. **661**

indulgences   Pardons issued by the pope that people could buy supposedly to reduce their time in purgatory. **380**

Industrial Revolution   Intense phase of technological development that began in Britain during the 1700s. **484**

inflation   Dramatic rise in prices. **131**

Information Revolution   Technological breakthroughs, particularly in the field of communications, that allowed ideas to spread rapidly. **836**

Inquisition   Official department of the Catholic Church created in the 1200s to investigate and prosecute charges of heresy. **293**

Institutional Revolutionary Party (PRI)   Mexican president Lázaro Cárdenas's reorganization of the Party of the Mexican Revolution in 1934. **808**

integrated circuits   Arrangement of thousands of transistors on a single silicon chip. **838**

intendancy   System created in the mid-1700s by Charles II to help re-establish Spanish control in the colonies, which provided for the appointment of governors who would be loyal to the king and not the viceroy. **530**

internal combustion engine   Gasoline-burning device invented in 1876 by German Nikolaus August Otto and used in the first automobile. **498**

international debt crisis   Fear that failure of Latin American countries to pay interest on loan payments would result in collapse of banks in the United States and Europe. **805**

Internet   Global network that ties together millions of computers. **838**

intifada (1987)   Palestinian uprising in the Middle East. **782**

Irish Republican Army (IRA)   Armed forces of the Irish nationalist Sinn Finn Party. **660**

Iron Curtain   Former dividing line in Europe between the democratic West and the communist East. **718**

Iroquois League   Council of 50 representatives from different Iroquois tribes that brought an end to hostilities among the Iroquois in the 1500s. **214**

Islamic resurgence   Renewed interest in Islam. **787**

island-hopping   Allied military tactic during World War II in which strategic Japanese-held islands in the Pacific were seized, allowing the Allies to advance closer to Japan. **706**

J

Janissaries   Trained elite force of slave soldiers in the Ottoman army. **332**

jati   Subgroups of the varna, or social classes of the Indo-Aryans. **146**

Jesuits   Society of Jesus, a religious order founded by Ignatius de Loyola in 1534. **383**

jihad   Holy war or constant inner struggle for faith. **256**

joint-stock companies   Enterprises in which people bought shares of stock in exchange for an equal share of the profits. **368**

Junkers   Aristocratic Prussian landowners in the 1800s. **543**

junta   Ruling military government. **813**

K

Ka'bah   Arab shrine in Mecca to which many people journeyed each year. **246**

kaiser   German emperor. **545**

kamikaze   "Divine wind," Japanese method of attack during World War II in which suicide pilots flew their aircraft directly into American ships. **709**

karma   In Hinduism, moral consequences of actions people take during their lifetimes that determine the next cycle of reincarnation. **147**

kayaks   Canoes used by the Inuit and Aleut tribes to pursue game. **210**

Khmer Rouge   Radical Cambodian communist group that seized control of the country in 1975. **763**

kiva   Round, sacred ceremonial room for extended families of the Anasazi people. **215**

kizilbash   Loyal Safavid Turkoman tribal followers. **339**

Knesset   Israeli parliament. **780**

knights   Mounted warriors. **280**

Kristallnacht   (November 9, 1938) "Night of broken glass" during which persecution of the Jews in Germany erupted in nationwide violence. **649**

Kulturkampf (1872)   Anti-Catholic movement in Germany. **556**

L

La Noche Triste (1520)   "The Night of Sorrows" on which Cortés and his men were driven away from Tenochtitlán by the Aztec. **429**

laissez-faire   Belief that the world economy was self-regulating and should be allowed to function with little interference. **461**

lasers   Concentrations of light released in bursts of high intensity. **837**

lateen sail   Large, triangular sails rigged to the mast that could be trimmed or adjusted to take advantage of the wind, no matter what its direction, giving ships greater maneuverability. **411**

Latin Christendom New civilization in the 600s produced through the interaction of Roman and Christian traditions and institutions with Germanic culture. **276**

Law of Return (1948) Proclamation of the new Jewish government stating that every Jew who settled in Israel was automatically guaranteed citizenship. **779**

legion Divisions of the Roman army commanded by officers called centurions. **109**

legitimacy Prince Klemens von Metternich's principle during the Congress of Vienna of restoring the governments that had ruled Europe before Napoleon and the French Revolution. **536**

Lend-Lease (1941) U.S. program to supply war materials to Britain on credit during World War II. **694**

leveling Han dynasty policy that helped peasant farmers by stabilizing the price of farm products. **168**

liberal arts Collective name for courses in Latin grammar, rhetoric, logic, geometry, arithmetic, astronomy, and music. **298**

liberalism Political philosophy that emphasizes the importance of individual liberty in all areas and the belief that government should ensure equal treatment under the law for all people. **495**

linear A Early Minoan written language. **42**

linear B Written language that came into use after Minoan culture combined with that of Indo-European-speaking groups migrating into the Greek Peninsula. **42**

lobola Payment of cattle a man offered to obtain a wife in many Bantu societies. **194**

locomotive Steam-powered engine that pulled a train of connected cars on iron rails, invented by George Stephenson in 1829. **497**

loess Rich soil formed from yellow dust in the North China Plain. **19**

Long Count System of timekeeping that allowed the Maya to record more than 5,000 years of history. **200**

Long March (1934) Flight of some 100,000 Chinese Communists from the province of Jiangxi to the north of China under Mao Zedong's leadership. **673**

lord In feudalism, noble who granted land to a vassal. **280**

lyric poetry Greek literature that focused on personal feelings and emotions with which everyone could identify. **72**

M

Magna Carta (1215) Great Charter signed by King John of England that made it clear that even the king must observe the law. **286**

maize Corn; most important domesticated crop in Mesoamerica; may have been grown as early as 6600 B.C. **23**

mamluks Turkish military slaves who served in Abbasid armies. **264**

mandarins Officials who controlled government bureaucracy during the Han dynasty. **164**

mandate League of Nations assignment to "advanced" member nations to establish responsible government in former German colonies or other conquered territories after World War I. **617**

Mandate of Heaven Zhou belief that the gods determined who should rule China. **55**

maniples Roman military formations designed to be used in rough terrain. **109**

manorial system Primary economic system during the Middle Ages. **282**

mansabdari **system** Hierarchy of salaried imperial military officials in the Mughal Empire. **345**

Maoism Chinese version of Marxism. **673**

market economy Economic system in which private businesses and individuals determine what goods and services should be produced, how they should be produced, and for whom they should be produced. **718**

martyrs People who voluntarily die for the sake of their faith, thus inspiring others to believe. **133**

Mau Mau Movement in Kenya in the 1950s by Kikuyu people to regain access to the highlands from white settlers. **774**

May Fourth Movement May 4, 1919; riots by outraged Chinese students in Beijing protesting the Versailles settlement, which permitted Japan to keep the Shandong Peninsula. **672**

means of production Capital and equipment needed to make and exchange goods. **495**

Meiji Restoration (1860s) Western-style reforms in Japan that abolished feudalism and adopted a constitution based on the autocratic Prussian model. **589**

memsahibs European women in India in the early 1800s. **581**

mercantilism Dominant economic policy of Europe between 1500 and 1800 rooted in the belief that a country's power depended on its wealth in gold and silver. **434**

meritocracy Government system in which people advanced in government service based upon their merit and abilities, not on wealth or heredity. **475**

microscope Invention in the late 1500s that permitted people to see tiny forms of life never before observed. **406**

middle class Socio-economic class of people between wealthy and poor. **399**

Middle Passage Enslaved Africans' brutal journey across the Atlantic Ocean to the Americas. **445**

militarism Glorification of military power. **596**

millet One of four religious communities in the Ottoman Empire including Islamic, Orthodox Christian, Armenian Christian, and Jewish. **337**

Ministry for International Trade and Industry (MITI) Japanese ministry that emphasized cooperation between government and business. **756**

Missouri Compromise (1820) Congressional compromise that allowed slavery only in the southern part of the Louisiana Purchase. **522**

mobilization Preparation of armed forces for war. **600**

monasticism Humble existence of monks who live solitary lives of religious devotion and self-denial. **139**

monoculture Reliance of a region or country on a single crop. **802**

monopoly Control of the production of goods and services, allowing the domination of a particular market. **499**

monotheism Belief in only one God. **47**

Monroe Doctrine (1823) Policy stating that the United States will not tolerate European military intervention in the Western Hemisphere. **532**

monsoons Seasonal rain-bearing winds. **17**

mosaics Pictures or designs formed by inlaid pieces of stone or other materials. **233**

Mothers of the Plaza de Mayo Human rights group in Argentina formed on behalf of the victims of military violence. **823**

mummification Process developed by ancient Egyptians that involved treating the body with chemicals so that it would dry and remain preserved for centuries. **16**

Munich Conference (1938) Meeting of British and French leaders with Hitler at which agreement to German annexation of the Sudentenland was given in return for Adolf Hitler's promise that it was his last territorial claim. **688**

murshid Heads of Safavid families recognized as "perfect spiritual guides" of the Sufi order. **339**

Muslim Brotherhood Post-World War II Islamic revival movement that opposed the adoption of Western values and sought Islamic control over society. **787**

Muslim League (1906) Group of Muslim leaders in India formed to protect and advance the political rights and interests of Indian Muslims. **661**

Mwene Mutapa Title of "master soldier" first earned by King Mutota and used by later kings of Great Zimbabwe. **354**

Mystery religions Hellenistic cults that introduced worshippers to secret teachings or mysteries that had to do with the secrets of life after death and immortality. **105**

N

Nahuatl Language of the Aztec. **202**

Napoleonic Code Revised and reorganized system of French law that centralized the administration of France and gave Napoleon unlimited power. **474**

National Aeronautics and Space Administration (NASA) Federal agency established in 1958 to direct development of American space technology. **835**

National Assembly Delegates of the French Third Estate who vowed to write a constitution for France during the Estates General in May 1789. **470**

national self-determination Principle emphasized in President Woodrow Wilson's Fourteen Points that set forth the right of a people to choose their own government. **614**

nationalism Recognition of shared common language, culture, and history. **476**

natural law Universal laws rooted in the discoveries of scientific investigators like Newton. **457**

NATO (North Atlantic Treaty Organization) Group established in April 1949, whose members were committed to defend one another in case of attack. **721**

natural selection Darwin's notion that life-forms are in a perpetual struggle for survival and those better adapted to their environment survive long enough to reproduce and pass along those adaptations to their offspring. **502**

Navigation Acts British legislation requiring all goods imported or exported from the colonies to pass through British ports, in British ships, to guarantee British collection of tariffs on the colonies' overseas trade. **452**

Nazi Party (National Socialist German Workers Party) Party led by Adolf Hitler, whose ideology was nationalistic, anticommunist, antidemocratic, and expansionist. **647**

Neutrality Acts U.S. legislation in the 1930s prohibiting loans and arms sales to warring nations. **694**

"new" imperialism Empire-building around the globe between 1870 and 1914 by many of the world's industrialized countries. **566**

New Kingdom Egyptian empire beginning in the mid-1500s B.C. characterized by imperial expansion and a rich culture. **38**

nihilists Russian intellectuals of the late 1860s who believed that traditional social and economic institutions had to be destroyed in order to build a new Russia. **550**

nirvana Buddhist attainment of perfect peace, which frees the soul from reincarnation. **150**

NKVD Soviet equivalent of Hitler's SS during World War II. **701**

nobles Warriors who received land that was distributed by kings as a reward for loyal service. **273**

nomads People who moved constantly in search of food and water. **5**

nonalignment Prime minister Jawaharlal Nehru's policy of maintaining Indian neutrality in the Cold War. **748**

nonconformists Protestants who did not belong to the Church of England. **510**

Norman Conquest (1066) Duke William of Normandy's invasion of England and claim of the English throne. **285**

North American Free Trade Agreement (NAFTA) Treaty that established a free-trade zone for the United States, Mexico, and Canada. **818**

Northwest Passage Waterway sought by France and England around or through North America. **435**

Nubian dynasty Kushite domination of Egypt around 730 B.C. that reunited the country for the first time since the fall of the New Kingdom and lasted for some 50 years. **41**

O

oases Areas of vegetation in the desert where water filtered up from underground. **63**

October Manifesto (1905) Czar Nicholas II's proclamation creating a constitutional monarchy. **550**

October Revolution (1917) Radical phase of the Russian Revolution in which Bolshevik military units seized power by storming government offices. **628**

oil embargo Stoppage of oil shipments from oil-producing countries. **783**

Old Regime French political system before 1789. **469**

oligarchy Rule of a few powerful individuals. **92**

on margin Buying stocks by putting up only about 10 percent of the value. **641**

open-field farming System in which land was divided into strips and worked by villagers who left about one third of it unplanted so that the soil could be replenished with nutrients. **485**

Operation Barbarossa (1941) Adolf Hitler's invasion of the Soviet Union during World War II. **695**

Opium War (1839) Conflict between Britain and China over trade relations. **586**

oracle bones Cattle bones or tortoise shells on which Shang dynasty priests made incisions and then heated over a fire, using the pattern of cracks that formed to interpret divine messages. **54**

oral traditions Stories, songs, poems, and proverbs that maintained a sense of identity and continuity with the past in most early African societies. **180**

Organization of African Unity (OAU) Group of oil-producing countries formed in Ghana that believed political unity in Africa was the key to future success. **793**

Organization of American States (OAS) Body formed in 1948 to promote cooperation among the various countries of the Western Hemisphere. **810**

Organization of Petroleum Exporting Countries (OPEC) Group that tried to control the global oil industry by setting production levels and prices. **783**

ozone layer Protection of the earth from the sun's harmful ultraviolet radiation by ozone—a form of oxygen that has three atoms rather than two. **840**

P

padishah Ottoman emperor who guaranteed prosperity by establishing justice according to Islamic law. **336**

Palestine Liberation Organization Umbrella organization for a variety of Palestinian nationalist groups opposed to the existence of Israel. **781**

Pan-Africanism Promotion in the 1930s of unity and further development of African peoples, elimination of racism in the Americas, an end to African colonialism, and resistance to the humiliation of black people throughout the world. **670**

Pan-Arabism The unity of all peoples sharing a common Arab cultural heritage, supported in Syria and Lebanon by many Christian Arab intellectuals. **551**

Pan-Hellenism Political idea that called for the Greeks to band together against Persia. **91**

Pan-Slavism Nationalist movement by Slavic populations in the Ottoman and Austro-Hungarian empires who looked to the Russian czar for leadership. **598**

Panama Canal Waterway in the Republic of Panama that opened in 1914 and became a vital American interest. **678**

papyrus Paperlike material made from the papyrus plant and used for writing. **13**

Parlement of Paris The supreme court for the entire territory of France through which Philip the Fair tried to gain royal control over the legal system. **287**

Parliament Representative assembly in England in the mid-1200s that gradually evolved over the next several centuries into a two-chamber body, the House of Lords and the House of Commons. **286**

pastoralism Dependency on animals for milk and meat as a primary food source. **7**

paterfamilias Head of the Roman family who was the oldest living male and had extensive powers over other family members. **118**

Pathet Lao Communist-led independence movement in Laos. **762**

patriarchal Society in which fathers exercise strong control over their families. **35**

patriarchs Heads of the oldest and largest Christian congregations in Rome, Jerusalem, Antioch, Alexandria, and Constantinople. **137**

patricians Members of the Roman aristocracy. **109**

Pax Romana The period of Roman Peace lasting from 27 B.C. until A.D. 180. **126**

Peace of Augsburg (1555) Treaty signed by the Catholic emperor Charles V of Germany and the Protestant princes that gave each prince the power to choose the religion of his territory. **384**

pentarchy Five leaders of the Orthodox Church. **233**

people's communes Large collective farms in China created by the Great Leap Forward. **752**

perestroika Sweeping reforms in the Soviet Union launched by Soviet leader Mikhail Gorbachev in 1985, including a plan for reforming the Soviet political and economic system by incorporating elements of democracy and capitalism. **829**

petro-dollars Oil profits. **783**

phalanx Large body of closely packed and heavily armed Greek infantry, each extending a long spear outward. **72**

pharaoh Egyptian king believed to be divine. **14**

philosophes Great thinkers of the European Enlightenment in the 1700s. **456**

pictographs Small pictures on clay tablets used to convey messages. **12**

Platt Amendment (1901) U.S. legislation adopted by Cuba that gave the United States the right to intervene in Cuba and to maintain naval bases on the island. **676**

plebeians The common people of ancient Rome. **109**

pogroms Official massacres organized by Russian czars designed to frighten all Jews out of Russia. **550**

polis Greeks' primary form of political and social organization. **69**

Polish Corridor Strip of land by which Poland gained access to the Baltic Sea. **621**

polytheistic Worship of many gods and goddesses. **11**

pope Bishop of Rome. **138**

popular sovereignty Idea that a government should be created by and subject to the will of the people. **460**

praetors Roman judges who could also act for consuls when they were away. **117**

predestination Idea that God knows who will be saved even before people are born, and therefore guides the lives of those destined for salvation. **382**

prefects Four governors in Diocletian's Roman empire who ruled groupings of small provinces. **136**

proletariat New working class naturally created by industrial capitalism, which Karl Marx believed capitalists took advantage of to make profits. **503**

propaganda Ideas, facts, or rumors spread deliberately to further a cause. **603**

protectionism Practice of newly industrializing nations closing off their markets and sources of supply to protect their developing industries in the 1880s. **567**

Protestant Reformation Protest against the Catholic Church begun by Martin Luther in 1517 that split Christendom into many different groups. **380**

Proto-Bantu "Parent" of all Bantu languages developed in a region near modern-day Cameroon and Nigeria. **193**

pueblos Above-ground adobe villages built by the Mogollon people. **215**

Q

qanats   Long, sloping underground canals in the Plateau of Iran. **63**

Quadruple Alliance (1815)   Alliance of Austria, Britain, Russia, and Prussia that agreed to meet regularly to maintain peace and discuss common interests. **538**

Quechua   Official language of the Inca Empire. **207**

quipu   Series of knots on parallel strings used by the Inca to record important numerical information such as records of harvests, population, and dates. **208**

Qur'an   Holy Book of Islam containing revelations received by Muhammad from God. **247**

quriltai   Great gathering of the people of Mongolia first summoned by Genghis Khan in 1204. **321**

R

rabbis   Jewish scholars who specialized in interpreting the Scriptures and were learned in religious law. **131**

radar   Technology that can track faraway objects using the reflection of radio waves. **693**

radiocarbon dating   Process used to determine the approximate age of artifacts made of materials such as wood or animal bone. **4**

raj   British East India Company's power over India. **579**

raja   Indian ruler. **53**

rationalism   Belief that truth could be arrived at solely by the application of reason, or logical thought, to observation. **457**

realism   Movement of artists and writers in the last half of the 1800s against romanticism, in which they recorded the daily lives of ordinary people. **505**

Realpolitik   "Realistic politics" practiced by Otto von Bismarck that pursued policies based on Prussian interests rather than liberal ideals. **544**

Red Army   Bolshevik forces during the civil war in Russia, which lasted from 1918 to 1920. **628**

Red Guards   Radical Chinese students during the Cultural Revolution. **754**

Red Scare   Fear of a worldwide communist movement in the United States in the early 1920s that led to the arrest of thousands of suspected Communists. **631**

Reign of Terror (1793)   Brutal program initiated by the French National Convention's Committee of Public Safety to silence critics of the republic. **472**

reincarnation   Hindu belief that when people die their souls are reborn in new bodies. **147**

Renaissance   "Rebirth" of European art and learning beginning in the 1300s, marked by an interest in Greek and Latin literature and art, individualism, and intellectual and scientific activity. **369**

reparations   Payment for war damages. **617**

republic   Political system in which elected officials govern the state. **109**

resistance   Secret armed groups in France who continued to fight Germany in World War II after the fall of France. **692**

responsible government   Colonists' desire for a government that was fully responsible to the voters. **518**

rhetoric   Persuasion through the use of public speeches. **91**

Rig-Veda   Collection of more than 1,000 ancient hymns used in Indo-Aryan rituals and sacrifices compiled by 1000 B.C. but not written down until about A.D. 1300. **52**

risorgimento   "resurgence," Italian nationalistic movement in the early 1800s. **541**

romanticism   Movement of artists and writers beginning in the late 1700s that emphasized the importance of emotions and feelings over intellect and reason. **505**

Roosevelt Corollary   President Theodore Roosevelt's addition to the Monroe Doctrine that led to increasing U.S. intervention in Latin America. **677**

Russification   Czar Nicholas's program in the 1830s designed to force the empire's diverse subjects to use the Russian language, accept the Orthodox religion, and adopt Russian customs. **548**

S

sacraments   Ceremonies in the Roman Catholic Church believed to lead to the achievement of salvation. **284**

salon   Gathering of the social, political, and cultural elites for the exchange of ideas during the Enlightenment. **458**

samurai   Feudal Japanese warriors. **313**

Sandinistas   Radical revolutionaries in Nicaragua in the 1970s. **815**

Sanskrit   Oldest version of an Indo-European language remaining today. **52**

Sarekat Islam   Islamic Association established by Indonesian Muslims in 1912 as a mass political party. **674**

Sassanid dynasty   Empire founded by Ardashir that ruled Persia for more than 400 years. **222**

savannas   Vast African grasslands dotted with trees, into which the desert advances yearly. **176**

schism (1054)   Break of the Orthodox Church from the Roman Catholic Church. **235**

Schlieffen Plan (1905)   Strategy by German Field Marshal von Schlieffen that called for Germany to deliver a knock-out blow to France before taking the offensive against Russia. **598**

Scholasticism   Thomas Aquinas's approach that tried to demonstrate that the teachings of Christian revelation were also knowable and provable through the use of logic and reason. **297**

scientific method   Means of investigation based on the combination of logical deductive reasoning (from self-evident principles) and inductive reasoning (from collecting and observing data through repeatable experiments). **408**

Scientific Revolution   Revolution in scientific thought in the early 1500s that questioned and ultimately destroyed the basic explanations past authorities had provided about how the world worked. **404**

Second French Republic   Government of Napoleon III adopted in France in 1848 that had a new liberal constitution guaranteeing universal manhood suffrage. **554**

sectionalism   Loyalty to a particular part of a country. **519**

sects   Small religious groups. **382**

seed drill   Device introduced by Jethro Tull in 1701 that allowed more efficient use of seeds by planting them in regular rows and at the proper depth. **486**

Senate   Supreme governing body of the Roman Republic whose members acted as advisors, controlled public finances, and handled all foreign relations. **117**

Seneca Falls Convention (1848)   First women's rights convention in the United States. **525**

separate spheres   Idea that men belonged in the public world of business and government while women ran the household. **501**

sepoys   Indian soldiers serving under British officers in the Indian army. **579**

serfs   Manorial peasants during the Middle Ages who were tied to their lord's land. **282**

settlement colonies   Colonies in which settlers from the imperialist nations occupied the land. **566**

settlement houses   Community service centers designed to encourage the interaction of poor working-class and middle-class people. **516**

Seven Years' War   First global war that began in 1756 as a result of intensified European rivalries following the War of the Austrian Succession, with Britain supporting Prussia, and France and Russia supporting Austria. **454**

shari'ah   Islamic legal system developed by the *ulama*. **257**

sheikh   Leader of an Arab tribe. **245**

shekel   Silver currency of the Persian Empire. **67**

shi'ah   One of the two main branches of Islam; followers of 'Ali rather than Mu'awiya. **252**

Shinto   Japanese religion that revolves around nature spirits. **311**

shoen   Feudal Japanese estate made up of scattered farmland that was governed as a single unit. **314**

shogun   Japanese general. **314**

Silk Road   Trade routes during the Han dynasty over much of Central Asia. **168**

silt   Deposits of mud and sand that enrich the soil. **8**

Six-Day War (1967)   Israeli annexation of the Sinai Peninsula, Golan Heights, and East Jerusalem. **781**

Slave Coast   Western coast of Africa from which about 20,000 slaves a year were sold to European colonists in America between 1680 and 1730. **442**

smog   Air highly contaminated from automobile emissions and factory smoke. **806**

social Darwinism   Application of Darwin's theories, which portrayed individuals and nations as part of the same struggle for survival as the species. **503**

socialism   Social philosophy that individual interests must give way to the interests of society as a whole and that political equality is meaningless without economic equality. **495**

Socratic method   Way of teaching developed by Socrates that involved asking questions that forced people to think deeply about a particular problem. **92**

Solidarity   Poland's independent trade union led by Lech Walesa in the early 1980s. **829**

Sophists   Philosophers in the 400s B.C. who reflected the growing belief in Greek society that there was no absolute truth to be discovered. **91**

sovereign power   King's claim of sole authority. **364**

sovereignty   Supreme power of national monarchs. **390**

soviets   Russian unions and councils through which workers expressed grievances. **626**

Spanish Civil War (1936)   Struggle in Spain between the forces of fascism and communism. **685**

spheres of influence   Territories in which the interests of a single outside nation are dominant. **566**

spinning jenny   Muscle-powered wooden machine that could spin eight cotton threads at a time, invented by James Hargreaves in England in the 1760s. **487**

Spring and Autumn period   Period in China that began around 722 B.C. in which independent states competed against each other for territory. **158**

SS   *Schutzstaffeln*, or military arm of the Nazi Party. **697**

Stamp Act (1765)   British legislation that required colonists to pay a tax, in the form of special stamps, on many paper goods. **465**

standard of living   Average level of goods, services, and luxuries available in a society. **367**

Statute of Westminster (1931)   British Parliament's enactment of the Balfour Report provisions that formally established the British Commonwealth of Nations. **659**

stela   Carved stone pillar. **181**

strategic bombing   Use of air power to attack an enemy's economic ability to wage war. **703**

stratigraphy   Branch of geology based on the idea that artifacts found in deeper layers of the earth are usually older than those above them. **4**

strike   General walkout of all workers in a union, used to obtain demands, such as higher wages or better working conditions. **496**

Suez Crisis (1956)   Conspiracy of France, Britain, and Israel to invade Egypt and retake the Suez Canal that resulted in failure and the discrediting of European imperialism. **780**

Sufism   Islamic movement that stresses loving devotion to God and a simplistic life. **258**

sultan   Turkish ruler who ruled by the power of the sword. **266**

Sunnis   One of the two main branches of Islam; followers of Mu'awiya rather than 'Ali. **252**

Supreme Commander for the Allied Powers (SCAP)   General Douglas MacArthur's administration during the occupation of Japan following World War II. **755**

suttee   Indian practice in which a wife commits suicide after the death of her husband by throwing herself on his cremation fire. **157**

Swahili   African society that emerged in the late 1100s along the East African coast and combined elements of African, Asian, and Islamic cultures. **353**

T

Taika reforms   Plan designed to transplant the centralizing ideas of the Tang government to Japan. **312**

Taiping Rebellion (1850)   Revolt in China against the Qing emperor by Hong Xiuquan and his followers that weakened China's position against the Europeans. **586**

Taj Mahal   Temple in Agra, India, built by Mughal emperor Shah Jahan for his wife, Mumtaz Mahal, after her death in 1631. **347**

Tanzimat   Long era of reforms in the Ottoman Empire that began in 1839, including a more efficient tax system and fair system of military service. **551**

telescope   Device for observing faraway objects invented by a Dutch lens maker in the 1500s. **404**

Ten Commandments   Moral laws Moses claimed to have received from the Hebrew god Yahweh on Mount Sinai. **47**

Tennis Court Oath (1789)   Pledge of Third Estate delegates to the Estates General that they would not disband until they had written a constitution for France. **470**

tepees   Shelters made of animal skins stretched over poles tied together. **214**

Tet Offensive (1968)   Viet Cong and North Vietnamese attack of cities and towns in South Vietnam that prompted quick response from U.S. and South Vietnamese forces. **762**

theme system   System of administration and defense perfected by Byzantine king Leo III that organized the empire into provinces, each under the command of a military governor. **231**

theology   Formulation of knowledge about the nature of God, God's laws, and God's requirements of human beings. **135**

theory of Forms   Plato's theory that every thing and concept had a perfect Form, which could not be seen. **94**

Third Reich   Third German Empire created by Adolf Hitler in the early 1930s. **648**

Third Republic   French government established by the French Assembly following the overthrow of Napoleon III. **555**

three-field system   System of farming developed in Europe in which farmers planted two thirds of their land, leaving a different third unplanted each season. **294**

Tiananmen Square Massacre (1989)   Injury and slaughter by the Chinese government of hundreds of pro-democracy demonstrators in Beijing demanding an end to corruption in the Communist Party, a greater say in the selection of leaders, and better conditions in the universities. **765**

Tongzhi Restoration   Major reform program in China in the mid-1800s that included lowering farm taxes and undertaking water-control projects. **587**

Torah   The first five books of the Hebrew Bible containing religious scriptures and laws of the early Hebrews. **48**

totalitarianism   Form of government headed by a dictator with complete control of all aspects of society, including politics, the economy, culture, and the private lives of citizens. **646**

trade sanctions   Restrictions on trade. **794**

trade unions   Organization of industrial workers according to their trades. **496**

trans-Saharan trade   Trade routes that connected North and West Africa for which Berbers in the Atlas Mountains and the northern Sahara served as intermediaries to carry goods across the desert. **186**

Treaty of Karlowitz (1699)   Treaty following the Ottoman defeat at Vienna in which the Turks lost control over much of their European territory. **421**

Treaty of Paris (1783)   Treaty ending the War of Independence between Britain and its colonists in America. **467**

Treaty of Utrecht (1713)   Treaty ending the War of the Spanish Succession. **393**

Treaty of Versailles (1919)   Allies' treaty with Germany following World War I. **615**

Treaty of Westphalia (1648)   Treaty ending the Thirty Years' War in Europe. **386**

trenches   Elaborate earthworks dug by armies for protection and for holding ground they had gained. **604**

tribunes   Officials elected by the plebians in the Roman Empire. **116**

Triple Alliance   Secret Aztec alliance with Texcoco and Tlacopán. **202**

Triple Alliance (1882)   Alliance of Austria, Germany, and Italy arranged by Otto von Bismarck as a safeguard against French aggression. **597**

Triple Entente (1907)   Agreement among Russia, Britain, and France in which they agree to define and respect their spheres of influence in Asia. **599**

trusts   Combinations of similar businesses under the direction of a single group. **499**

tsetse fly   Carrier of sleeping sickness. **178**

Twelve Tribes of Israel   Descendants of Abraham and his grandson Jacob who migrated from Palestine to Egypt, and according to Biblical accounts, eventually became slaves of the pharaohs. **47**

tyrant   Ruler who held sole political power in violation of established law but with support of the people. **73**

U

U-boats   German submarines. **610**

ulama   Islamic religious scholars who specialized in studying and interpreting the Qur'an and the sayings and deeds of Muhammad. **257**

Unam Sanctam (1294)   Decree by which Pope Boniface VIII reasserted the pope's authority over all earthly kings. **365**

United Gold Coast Convention (UGCC)   Group established by members of colonial Ghana's westernized African elite to demand greater participation in government. **772**

United Nations (UN)   Successor to the League of Nations established in 1945 for keeping world peace and punishing aggressors, made up of a permanent Security Council and a General Assembly. **717**

universal manhood suffrage   Right of all adult men to vote. **472**

Upanishads   Series of written philosophical dialogues that expressed ideas of the Vedanta, which taught that the world and all things in it, including human beings, are part of a single universal being. **146**

urbanization   Growth of cities. **492**

utilitarianism   Social philosophy stating that institutions and laws should be judged according to their capability to bring "the greatest happiness of the greatest number." **495**

utopian socialism   Concept of creating ideal communities where people could live and work together in perfect harmony. **495**

V

varnas   Three great Indo-Aryan social classes including the Kshatriyas, or warrior nobles; the Brahmins, or priests who performed sacred rituals; and the Vaisyas, or merchants, traders, and farmers. **52**

vassal   In feudalism, former knight who received land from a lord. **280**

Vedas   Indo-Aryan religious texts or hymns to the gods, which expressed ideal conceptions of religion and society, originally as oral tradition. **52**

viceroy   Governor appointed by a Spanish king who oversaw a large colonial province in Central or South America. **432**

Vichy France   Part of France in World War II that collaborated with the Germans. **692**

Viet Cong   Vietnamese Communists who were members of the National Liberation Front and who waged a guerrilla war in the South Vietnamese countryside. **761**

Viet Minh   League for the Independence of Vietnam led by Ho Chi Minh. **760**

Vietnamization   President Richard Nixon's policy to withdraw American ground troops from Vietnam but continue to provide air support, weapons, and training to the South Vietnamese army. **762**

vizier   Heads of specialized government departments in the Abbasid caliphate who oversaw important affairs of government. **255**

W

Wafd Party   Pre–World War I nationalist party in Egypt that emerged under the leadership of Saad Zaghlul Pasha. **664**

Wannsee Conference (1942)   Meeting of senior Nazi officials in suburban Berlin at which plans for the systematic extermination of the Jews were finalized. **697**

war chariot   Two-wheeled cart adapted for battle by Indo-Europeans and pulled more effectively and more rapidly by horses. **35**

warlords   Strongmen with private armies who ruled in China following the death of Chinese nationalist ruler Yuan Shikai in 1916. **671**

war of attrition   Fighting in which each side in a war tries to wear down and outlast the other. **606**

War of the Roses (1455–85)   Civil war between two English noble houses competing for the throne of England. **364**

Warsaw Pact   Military alliance established in May 1955 of mutual military cooperation among countries of the Communist bloc. **721**

Washington Naval Conference (1922)   Meeting of the world's major naval powers at which the United States, Britain, Japan, France, and Italy agreed to set limits on the size of their navies. **619**

water frame   Large water-powered spinning machine invented by Richard Arkwright in 1768. **487**

Weimar Republic   German national assembly that drew up and adopted a new constitution in the city of Weimar in July 1919. **633**

welfare state   Collection of government institutions that provide social services, such as medical care, unemployment insurance, and retirement pensions for all citizens. **724**

westernization   Copying of Western methods and culture. **394**

White Revolution   Shah of Iran's reform program beginning in 1963, including redistribution of land and granting of voting rights to women. **784**

Whites   Former army officers and other groups in Russia, including the Cossacks, who formed military units between 1918 and 1920 to fight the Bolshevik Red Army in the Russian civil war. **628**

World Trade Organization   Union created by the Uruguay Round of the General Agreement of Tariffs and Trade in 1993 to resolve disputes between trading partners. **848**

wuwei   Daoist principle of nonaction. **160**

Y

yasa   Laws laid down by Genghis Khan in 1204. **321**

yin and yang   Chinese idea of balancing forces of darkness, weakness, and inactivity with brightness, strength, and activity. **159**

Young Italy movement   Secret Italian nationalist society launched in 1831 by writer Giuseppe Mazzini. **541**

Young Turks   Movement of educated and westernized army officers devoted to restoring the Ottoman constitution in the early 1900s. **551**

Z

zaibatsu   Enormous industrial and financial organizations in Japan in the late 1800s that dominated the economy and concentrated economic power in the hands of a few families. **590**

zemstvos   Local Russian councils elected in the mid-1860s to oversee matters such as education, public health, and relief for the poor. **550**

ziggurats   Great temples that served as religious and administrative centers for the Sumerians. **10**

Zionism   Movement to create a Jewish state in Palestine begun by Theodor Herzl in the 1890s and supported by Jewish communities around the world. **666**

Zollverein   German customs union set up in 1818 that inspired businesspeople to support German unification. **543**

INDEX

A

abacus, 308
'Abbas: Muhammad's uncle, 254
'Abbas the Great, 341–43
Abbasid caliphate, 254–55; decline of, 264; as dynamic civilization, 256–61, 262–63, f268; killing of last caliph in, 266, 324
'Abd al-Rahman III, 261
'Abduh, Muhammad, 551
Abdülhamid II, 551–52
Abdülmecid I (of Ottoman Empire), 551
abolition movement: American, 523; British, 510–11
Aborigines, 520
Abraham, 47, 247
absolutism: defined, 390; English challenge to, 395–97; in France, 391–93; in Germany and central Europe, 395; in Russia, 393–95
Abu Bakr, 250–51
Abu Talib, 246
Academy: Plato's, 94
Achaemenid dynasty, 65, 222
acid rain, 840
acquired immune deficiency syndrome (AIDS), 792, 839
Acropolis, 69; Erechtheion on, p61
Actium: battle of, 114–115, p115, 122
acupuncture, 168, f169
Adam and Eve, 134, 172
Addams, Jane, 526
Adena, m211, 212
Adenauer, Konrad, 720
Adowa: battle of, 576
Adriatic Sea, 370; Ancient Greece and, m71
Aegean islands: in Delian League, 78; Macedonia's threat to trade in, 96; Minoan trading posts in, 43–44
Aegean Sea, m77, 229; early Egyptian ships on, 15; kingdoms near, 42–45, m43; Persian army crossing, 76–78
Aeneas, 124
Aeneid (Virgil), 124
Aeschylus, 83, 85, 369
Afghanistan, 345; Ghaznavid control of, 265; Mujahideen in, 787; Soviet invasion of, 829
AFL. See American Federation of Labor
Afonso I (of Kongo Empire), 443
Africa: adaptation by peoples to environment of, 178; ancient, m177; arts in, f355; balancing human and wildlife needs in, f795; central and southern, 193–94; change of map as result of Berlin Conference, f574, m574; coast of east, 191–92; cultural revival in, 794; decolonization of Belgian and Portuguese, 776–77; decolonization of British, 772–74; decolonization of French, 774–76; diaspora from, 446; early civilizations in, 174–95; early European settlement in, 570–71; economic and social change in, 783–86; enslavement of people from, See slave trade; European artists influenced by arts of, f669; European empires in, m422; European scramble for, 572–75, m578; family, religion, and oral traditions in, 178–80; geography and people of, 176–80, f177; imperialism in, 570–78; independent, 791–96, m773; invasion and empire in early, 37–41; Iron Age developments in sub-Saharan, 190–94; kingdoms during Iron Age in, m192; language groups of, 178; nationalism in, 668–70; oil deposits in Middle East and, m785; oral traditions in f179, 180; partition of, 572–73; political challenges in, 792–94; resistance movements in, 575–76, 578, m576; state-building in, 353–56; as theater of battle in World War I, 602; trade and empire in, 441–46
African Americans: civil rights for, 737; jazz and, 636; Ku Klux Klan persecution of, 632
African National Congress (ANC), fight to end apartheid by, 794
Afrikaans language, 570
Afrika Korps, 694
Afrikaners, 658, 794. See also Boers
Age of Pericles, the, 79–80
Agni, p155
agora, 70
Agra, 345, 347, 48
Agricultural Revolution, 7 (Later Stone Age), 485 (1700s)
Aguinaldo, Emilio, 679–80
Ahaggar mountain chain, f186
ahimsa, 149
Ahmad, Muhammed, 573
Ahmed III (of Ottoman Empire), 418, p419
Ahmose, 38
Ahriman, 63–64
Ahura Mazda, 63–64, 65, 225; 227
AIDS. See acquired immune deficiency syndrome
Ajatasatru, 152

Akan, 442
Akbar, 330, 345–46
Akhenaton (Amenhotep IV), 39
Akkad, (Agade), 32–33
Akkadian Empire, 32–34, m33
Akkadian language, 32
Aksum: kingdom of, 183–84, m182; stonemasons of, f183
al-'Adawiyya, Rabi'a, 258
al-Afghani, Jamal ad-Din, 551
Alamgir, 348
al-Andalus, 261
Alaric, 140
Alaska: ancient civilizations in southern, 215; Inuits and Aleuts in, 210; land bridge between Siberia and, 23; U.S. purchase of, m523
al-Bakri, 191
Albania: Ottoman conquer of, 334; in Warsaw Pact, 721
Albert (Prince of Saxe-Coburg-Gotha), 501
Albigensians, 292–93
Albuquerque, Afonso de, 421
alchemists, 403
al-Din, Safi, 339
al-Din, Salah, f292
Aleut people, 210
Alexander I (of Russia): 538; at Congress of Vienna, 536, 538; death of, 548; and Holy Alliance, 538
Alexander II (of Russia); assassination of, 550; reforms of, 549
Alexander III (of Russia), 550
Alexander VI (Pope), 416
Alexander the Great, 88, p89, 97–99, p99; Aristotle and, 95; Bucephalus and, f98; conquest of Persia, 98; empire of, 88, m97, 99; invasion of India by, 152; in Shah-nameh, f342
Alexandra (of Russia), 626
Alexandria: and Coptic Church, 189; founding of, 98; as great commercial center in Roman Empire, 128; Persian taking of, 228
Al-Fazari, 190
Alfonso XII (of Spain), 557
al-Fustat (Cairo), f260
algebra, 259
Algeria: in Arab League, 778; decolonialization of, 775; revolt in, 723–24
Algerian National Liberation Front, 775
al-Ghazali, Muhammad, 267
Algiers: French occupation of, 570
Algonquian, m211, 213
al-Hajj, 'Umar, 571
al-Husayni, Haj Amin, 667

cultures in, *m310*; religions in, *m319*; road to development in, 764–68; World War II in, 707–09

Asia Minor: battle of Granicus in northern, 98; Cyrus's conquest of Lydia in, 76; Hittite kingdom in southwest, 35; Indo-Europeans' migration to, 34–35; islands in Delian League, 78; Saljuqs of Rum in, 265; under control of Cyrus, 65

Askia the Great, 356

Asoka, 153

assembly line, 637

Assur, 49

Assyrian Empire, 49–50, *m50*; conquest of Israel by, 50; Median kings' conquering of, 64

Astrada, Etelvina, 822

astrolabe, 259, *p259*

astrology: in Europe, 403; Ottoman study of, 338

astronomy: Muslim scientists' advances in, 259; Ottoman study of, 338

Asunción: Spanish colony of, 431

Aswan High Dam, 780

Atahualpa, 209, 430, *p431*

Atatürk (Mustafa Kemal), 668, *p668*

Ataulf, 140

Athabascan tribes, 210

Athena, *c82*; Athens as city of, 81; Erechtheion as temple to, *p61*; Parthenon as temple to, *p79*

Athens: assistance of Ionian Greeks' revolt against Darius I, 76; democracy in, 78–79; effect of Delian League on, 78; as Greek city-state, 69; in Peloponnesian War, 79–80; Spartan siege of, *p80*

Atlantic Charter, 694

Atlantic Ocean: Hitler's U-boat offensive in, 694; as theater of battle in World War I, 609–10; trade across, *m442*

Atlantis (U.S. space shuttle), 836

Atlas Mountains, 176, 186

atomic bomb, 709, 731

Aton, 39

Atreus, Treasury of, *p44*

atrocities: wartime, 603, Holocaust and other during World War II, 697–701; of Khmer Rouge, 768

Attica, 73

Attila: attack on Rome, 142

Attlee, Clement, 724, *p724*, 745

Auckland, Lord, 583

audiencia, 432

augurs, 119

Augustan Age, 124

Augustine, Saint (Aurelius Augustinus), 138, 189, *p138*, *f173*

Augustus, 123–25, *c125. See also* Octavian

Augustus, Philip (of France), 291–92

Augustus, Romulus, 142

Aung San Suu Kyi, 768, *p768*

Aurangzeb, 348, 424

Auschwitz concentration camp, 698, *f699*

Australia: British colonization of, 518; European discovery of, 517; political reform in, 520

Australian and New Zealand Army Corps (ANZAC), 608

Australopithecus, 4

Austria: French Legislative Assembly's declaration of war on in 1792, 472; Habsburgs in, 365, 395; Joseph II of, 462; as member of Quadruple Alliance, 538; role in third coalition against France, 475; in Seven Years' War, 454–55; in Triple Alliance, 597; in War of the Austrian Succession, 454

Austria-Hungary: empire of, 546–47; ethnic groups in, *m547*; involvement in the Balkans, 599–600

autocracy, 163

Avars: defeat by Charlemagne, 277; invasion of Balkans by, 230

Avesta, 226, *f227*

Avignon: papacy moves from Rome to, 366

A Vindication of the Rights of Woman (Wollstonecraft), 461

Awami League, 747

Axis Powers: challenge of Britain's overseas empire, 694; formation of, 687

Aylwin, Patricio, 812

'Ayn Jalut, Battle of, 324

"Azania," 191–92

Azikiwe, Nnamdi, 670

Azores: Portugal's settling of islands of, 412

Aztec, 202–203; ceremony of, *f203*; religion of, 202–03; Spanish conquest of, 428–30; Spanish explorers' first impressions of, *f429*; tax record of, *p202*; Xipe Totec as god of, *p198*

B

B-29 bombers, 708

Babur, 344

baby boom, 736

Babylon: establishment of, 34; Hanging Gardens of, *p51*

Babylonian Captivity, (500s B.C.) 51, (A.D. 1300s) 366

Babylonian Empire, Old, 34

Bacon, Roger, 298

Bacon, Sir Francis, 407, *p407*

Bactria, 100, *m101*, 222

Baghdad, 261, 262; Buyids seize control of, 264; founding of, 255; as major trade center, 262; Mongol siege of, *m325*, *p326*; nomads' capture of, 266; Saljuq control of, 265

Bahamas: Columbus lands in, 413

balance of power, 371

Balboa, Vasco Núñez de, 416

Baldwin, Stanley, 632, 644, 688

Balfour Declaration, 618, 667, 798

Balfour, Arthur, 618, 659

Balkans: importance to great powers, *f552*; Ottoman rule over, 332; post-World War I, 620, *m620*; post-World War II, 729–30; pre-World War I conflict in, 599

"Ballad of East and West, The," (Kipling), *f568*

Baltic republics: independence from Soviet Union, 831; as territories of Soviet Union, 726

Baltic Sea: English search for northeastern route through, 435; role in Commercial Revolution in Italy, 367; trade routes in, 295

Bangladesh, 746–47, 767–68, 844

Bank of Amsterdam, 423

Bantu languages, 178, 193

Bantu-speakers, 193–94, 353

Ban Zhao, 168

Bar Kokhba, Simon, 131

Barbarossa, Frederick, 291

Barbarossa. *See* Khayr ad-Din

barriadas, 803

Barton, Bruce, 637

Basil, Saint, 139

Bastet, *p16*

Bastille: storming of, 470

Bataan Death March, 701

Batavia: first Dutch Asian colony in, 423

Batista, Fulgencio, 809

Bauhaus school of architecture, 640

Beagle, 502

Beatles, 736

Beccaria, Cesare, 459, *p459*; Catherine the Great's reading the works of, 462

Becket, Thomas, 286

Becquerel, Antoine-Henri, 502

bedouins, 244–45

Beer Hall Putsch, 633

Begin, Menachem, *p781*, 782

Beijing: British and French troops occupation of, 586; as capital of Ming Empire, 351; as capital of Yuan dynasty, 324

Belgian Congo, 564, 573, *m578*, 776

Belgium: after Congress of Vienna, 537; decolonization of African holdings of, 776–77; in EEC, 724; independence of, 559; industrialization in, 500; in NATO, 720–21

Bell, Alexander Graham, 498

Belloc, Hilaire, 567

Benedictine Rule, 275

Benes, Edvard, 728

Benezet, Anthony, 510

Bengal: partition of, 661

Ben-Gurion, David, 779

Benin: art from the kingdom of, *f355*

Bentham, Jeremy, 495

Benz, Carl, 498

Berbers, 186, 187; French war against Muslim, 570; and Umayyads, 254

Berger, Peter L., 328

Berlin, Congress of, 553

Berlin Alexanderplatz (Döblin), f639

Berlin blockade, 714, p715, 719

Berlin Conference, 572, 574, m574

Berlin Wall: building of, 732–33; fall of, 826, p827, 831

Bessemer process, 498

Bhagavad Gita, 147, f148, p148

bhakti, 147

Bhutto, Benazir, 767

Bhutto, Zulfikar Ali, 767

Biafra: declares independence from Nigeria, 793

Bible, 133, 402; Gutenberg, p375; Hebrew, f49; Hebrew writings as foundation for, 47

Bill of Rights: English, 397; U.S., 468

Bimbisara, 152

biodiversity, 843

bishop, 137

Bismarck, Otto von, 544–45; p544, f574; approval of German colonization in Africa, 573; at Congress of Berlin, 553; as German reformer, 556–57

Black Death, 362–63; spread of, m363

Black Dragon Society, 652

Black Forest: destruction of by acid rain, 840

Black Sea: Greek trade and, m71; islands in Delian League, 78; Russian control of after Seven Years' War, 456

Black Shirts, 646

Black Tuesday, 642

Blair, Tony, 846

Blitz, 693

Blitzkrieg, 690

Bloody Sunday, 550

Blue Mosque, p419

Blum, Léon, 644

Bodhisattvas, 154

Bodin, Jean, 390

Boer War, 575, p575, 658

Boers, 570–71, 575, 658

Bohemia: Habsburgs in, 365, 395

Boleyn, Anne, 382, 396

Bolívar, Simón, 530–31, p531

Bolivia, 432; monoculture in, 802; re-establishment of democratic government in, 812

Bolshevik Party, 612, 627–29, f629

Bombay: m422; British trading posts in, 424

Bon Marché, 501

Bonaparte, Louis Napoleon, 554–555. *See also* Napoleon III

Bonaparte I, Napoleon, 473, 474–78, p474. *See also* Napoleon I

Boniface VIII (Pope), 365–66

Bonn: as capital of West Germany, 720

Book of Divination. See Five Classics

Book of History. See Five Classics

Book of Kells, p275

Book of Kings. See Shah-nameh

Book of Poetry. See Five Classics

Book of Rites. See Five Classics

Book of the Image of the Earth (Ibn Hawqal), 260

Book of the Sea (Reis), 338

Borobudur: Buddhist complex in, 319

Bosnia: annexation by Austria, 599; Ottoman conquest of, 334; secession from Soviet Union, 832; war in, 832–833

Bosporus Strait, 137, 229, m231

Bossuet, Jacques-Bénigne, 391

Boston Massacre, 465

Boston Tea Party, 465

Botero, Fernando, f823

Botha, Louis, 658

Boudicca, f120

Bourbon dynasty: beginning of, 385; absolutism of, 391–93; restoration of by Charles-Maurice de Talleyrand, 478

Boxers, 588

Bradbury, Ray, f837, p837

Brady, Mathew, f504

Brahe, Tycho, 404

Brahma, Society of. *See* Brahmo Samaj

Brahmins, 52, 146

Brahmo Samaj, 581

Braque, Georges, f669

Braunschweig (Germany), Nazi troops march in, p625

Brazil: African slaves harvesting sugar cane in, p433; as a colony, 431–32; development and modernization in, 806, 807; dictatorship in, 651, 810–811; independence of, 531, m530; monoculture in, 802; post-World War I industrialization in, 651; re-establishment of civilian government in, 812, 844

Brecht, Bertolt, 640

Brest-Litovsk, Treaty of, 612, 628

Brezhnev, Leonid, 740, 828

Brezhnev Doctrine, 740

brinkmanship, 732

Britain. *See* Great Britain

British Airways, 845

British Commonwealth of Nations, 659

British Dominions: colonization in Australia, Canada, and New Zealand, 517–21

British East India Company, 423–24, 453, 579; British attempt to save from bankruptcy, 465

British Gas, 846

British Royal Air Force, 691

British Steel, 846

British Union of Fascists, 651

Britons: Forging the Nation, 1707–1837 (Colley), 563

Bronze Age: in Crete, 42; transition from Neolithic Age to, 7

Brown v. *The Board of Education of Topeka,* 738

Broz, Josip. *See* Tito

Brueghel, Pieter, 379

Bruni, Leonardo, 369

Brussels: 1830 revolution against Dutch in, 539

bubonic plague, 362. *See also* Black Death

Buchan, John, 622

Buchenwald concentration camp, p697

Buckingham Palace: suffragettes protesting outside, p514

Buddha, 149–50, p149, 226

Buddhism: 153, 318, f329; changes in, 154; development of, 149–51; in Japan, 312; as percentage of world religions, c257; sacred writings of, f305; under Tang in China, 303; Vietnam and, 316

Buenos Aires: Spanish colony of, 431

Bukhara, 264, p265

Bulgaria: 650; post-World War I democratic government in, 633; in Warsaw Pact, 721

Bulgars, 230–31, 238

Bundesrat, 556

Buonarroti, Michelangelo, 374, p374, f378, p378

Burdick, Eugene, 737

bureaucracy, 15

Burial at Ornans, p505

Burma, 153, 315, 744, 845; government of, 768

Burundi: political tensions in, 793

Busbecq, Ogier Ghiselin de, 335

Bush, George, 816, 832, 846

Bushido, 313

Buyids, 264

Byron, Lord, p539

Byzantine Empire: 229–36, m231; Black Death in, 363; Christianity in, 233–35; influences on Umayyad dynasty, 254; law in, 232; Ottoman advance against, 368; reign of Macedonian dynasty in, 235; and Russia, 238–39

Cabot, John, 435

Cabral, Pedro, 431

Caesar, Julius, 122

Cahokia, m211, 212

Cairo: 260, m354, 355; as Fatimid capital, 264

calculus: development of, 409

Calcutta, m422, 424

California: ancient civilizations in, 216

Caligula, 125

caliphs, 250; Abbasid, 255; Ottoman rulers assume title of, 335;

Umayyad, 254

calligraphy, 55; Muslim artists and, 259, *p259*

Calvert, Cecilius, 438

Calvin, John, 382

Calvinists, 382; in Africa, 570; and the Netherlands, 423; in Spain, 384

Cambodia: consequences of Vietnam War for, 762–63; as part of French Indochina, 583

Cambyses II (of Persia), 65; death of, 65–76

camels: for crossing Sahara Desert, *f186, p186*; introduction to North Africa of, 185–86

Camp David Accords, 781–82

Canaan: Philistine settlement in, 46

Canada, 841; Athabascan tribes in, 210; British colonialism in, 518–19; British control of after Seven Years' War, 455; constructs Distant Early Warning Line with United States, 725; dominion status of, 519; French claims in, 435; growth of, *m519*; NAFTA and, 818, 848; in NATO, 720–21; seperatism in, 833

Canarsee tribes: Peter Minuit's purchase of Manhattan Island from, 436

Cannae, Battle of, 111

cannons: in the Hundred Years' War, 365

cantons, 559

Cape Colony, 518, 570

Cape of Good Hope: Bartholomeu Dias sails around, 412, *m414*; Dutch settlers at, 423, 444, 570

Capet, Hugh, 286

Capetian dynasty, 286, *m287,* 364

capital, 368

capitalism, 485

capitulations, 420

captaincies, 431

Caracalla, 130

caravels, 411

carbon 14 dating technique, *f29. See also* radiocarbon dating

Carbonari, 541

Cárdenas, Lázaro, 808, *p808*

Caribbean region, *m815*; Africans in, 446; Anglo-French rivalry for, 452; battle for independence, *m531*; Spanish in, 428

Caribbean Sea: Spanish-American War in, 676

Carloman, 277

Carlsbad Decrees, 539

Carnegie, Andrew, 527

Carolingian dynasty, 277–78; invasions into empire of, 278–79; renaissance of, 277

Carolus Magnus. *See* Charlemagne

Carpini, Giovanni da Pian del, 321

Carson, Rachel, 841, 843, *p843*

Carter Doctrine, 829

Carter, Howard, 30

Carter, Jimmy, 782, 829

Carthage, 46, 110–12, *m187,* 187–89

Cartier, Jacques, 435

cartoons: political, *f527*

Cartwright, Edmund, 487

Castiglione, Baldassare, 371–72

Castillo, *f200*

Castlereagh, Viscount, 537, 538

Castro, Fidel, 808–09, *p809,* 814, 845

Catal Hüyuk, 7

Catalonia: fight for independence from Spain, 557

Cathars. *See* Albigensians

Cathedral of Saint Sophia, 239

Catherine of Aragon, 382

Catherine the Great (of Russia), 395, 455–56, 462, *p462*

Catholic Church. *See* Roman Catholic Church

Catholic Metropolitan Cathedral, *p430*

Catullus, 124

Caucasus Mountains: 62, *m340,* 341, 547

cavalry: Muslim introduction into West Africa, 441

Cave Monastery, 239

Cavour, Camillo Benso di, 542

Cayuga, *f213,* 214

Ceausescu, Nicolae, 830–31

censors, 117

Central America, 814–816, *m815*; battle for independence, *m531*; as site of Mesoamerican civilization, 23–25, 198–203

Central Intelligence Agency: role in Bay of Pigs invasion, 814; role in coup against Mosaddeq in Iran, 783

Central Powers, 601

Cervantes, Miguel de, *f405*

Ceylon, 147, *m422*; Dutch capture of, 423; Portuguese trade and settlement in, 421

CFCs. *See* chlorofluorocarbons

Ch'i Pai-shih, 638

Chadwick, Sir Edwin, 515

Chaeronea, battle of, 97, *m97*

Chaldeans, 51, 64; destruction of Nineveh by Medes and, 50

Chaldiran, battle of, 334

Challenger (space shuttle), 836

Chalukya, 317

Chamberlain, Neville, 688, *p689,* 693,

Chamberlain, Joseph, 575

Chamorro, Violeta Barrios de, 817, *p817*

Champa, 316

Champagne, 295

Champlain, Samuel de, 436, 439

Champollion, Jean François, 13

Chan-Chan, 206, *p206*

Chandra Gupta I and II, 155

Chang Jiang (Yangzi River): Jin Empire reaches to, 306, *m306*; kingdoms along, 170

Changan, 162, 303

Charlemagne, *p271,* 277, *p277*

Charles I (of England), 396, *p396,* 438

Charles II (of England), 396–97

Charles III (of Spain), 530

Charles IV (Holy Roman emperor), 365

Charles V (Holy Roman emperor), 381, 384

Charles V (king of Spain, Holy Roman emperor), 371

Charles VII (of France), 364

Charles VIII (of France), 371

Charles X (of France), 539

charter of incorporation, 295

Chartism, 513

Chartres, Fulcher of, 290

Chavín de Huantar, 26

Chechnya, 833

Checkpoint Charlie, 826

Cheka, 629

Cheops, 15

Chernobyl, 840; nuclear accident at, 834–35

Chiang, Madame, 707–08, *p707*

Chiang Kaishek, 672, 707, 750, 767

Chichén Itzá, *f200,* 201; astronomical observatory at, *p200*

child labor, *f512*; laws regulating, 511

Children's Crusade of 1212, 292

Children's Museum (Venezuela), *p801*

Chile, 430, 432; José de San Martín's liberation of, 530; Marxist government in, 811; military dictatorship in, 812; re-establishment of democratic government in, 812, 844; Spanish conquest of, 431

Chimú, 206, *p206*

China: Black Death outbreak in, 362; communism in, 845; communist victory in, 734; early civilization in, *m19,* 19–22; early imperial rule of, 162–70; at end of Zhou dynasty, 158–59; and Europeans (1600s and 1700s), 424–25; after fall of Qing dynasty, 671–74; historical tradition of, *f173*; intervention in Korean War, 759; Japan and, 590, 602, 674, 695; Ming dynasty in, 349–52, 424–25; nationalism and communism in, 671–74; in Opium War with Britain, 586; political and economic developments of (1980s–90s), 764–65; post–World War II civil war in, 750–51, *m751*; Qing dynasty in, 424–25; Tang and Song dynasties in, 302–08; Shang and Zhou dynasties in, 54–56, *m55*; Yuan dynasty in, 323–24; Yangshao and Longshan cultures in, 22

chinampas, 202

Chinese Communist Party, 672–74

Chirac, Jacques, 847–48

chivalry, 295, *f296, p296*; 297

chlorofluorocarbons (CFCs), 840

Chola dynasty, 317

Chosŏn, 309

554–60

Consulate, 474
consuls, 117
consumption, 637
containment policy: Truman's, 719
Continental Congress. *See* Second Continental Congress
Continental System, 475
contraband, 610
Contadora Principles, 816
Contras, 815
Convention on Biological Diversity, 843
Convention People's Party, 772
Cook, James, 517, *p518*
Coolidge, Calvin, 632
Copernicus, Nicolaus: 404; system of universe, *p404*
Coptic Church, 189
Coral Sea: U.S. engagement of Japan in, 706
Córdoba: as capital of Umayyad Spain, 261; mosque in, *p243*
Corinth: as Greek city-state, 80; League of, 97
Cornwallis, Charles, 466
corporations, 499
corporatist state, 646
Corpus juris civilis, 232–33
Corsica: Carthaginian control of western, 110, *m110*
Cort, Henry, 490
Cortés, Hernán, 428–29
Cossacks, 628
Costa Rica, *m815,* 816
Costilla, Miguel Hidalgo y, 531
Cotton, John, 438
cotton gin, 490
Council for Mutual Economic Assistance (COMECON), 721
Council of Five Hundred, 79
Council of Nicaea, 138
Council of Orthodoxy, 235
Council of People's Commissars, 630
Council of Trent, 383
Council Tree, The, *f213*
Counter-Reformation. *See* Reformation, Catholic
County of Edessa, 291, *m291*
County of Tripoli, 291, *m291*
Courbet, Gustave, *p505,* 505–06
Courtier, The (Castiglione), 371
courtly love, 297
covenant: Hebrew, 47
Coventry: during World War II, *f723*
covert, 814
Coya, Mama Anavarque, *p209*
CPP. *See* Convention People's Party
Crassus, Licinius, 122
Crécy: battle of, 365
Credit-Anstalt, 642
creoles, 529–30
Crete: 370; Minoan civilization in, 42–43, *m43*
Crick, Francis, 839
Crimean Peninsula: Black Death

reaching ports of, 362; Russian control of, 456
Crimean War, 552
Cripps, Stafford, 744
Cro-Magnon, 5
Croatia: fighting in, 832
Croat people, 230
Croesus (of Lydia), 65
Cromwell, Oliver, 396
crop rotation, 486
crops: exchanges of, *f448–49*
Crusades: against heresy, 292–93; Children's, 292; early, 290–92; and Constantinople, *p293;* Islamic view of, *f292;* later, 292; major, *m291;* in north, 293
crystalline spheres, 402
Ctesiphon, 222
Cuba: and Bay of Pigs, 814; communism in, 845; as authoritarian holdout, 845; human rights in, 820–22; and independence, 676; Marxist revolutions in, 809; monoculture in, 802; radicals and, 808–09; reliance on Soviet aid, 810
Cuban missile crisis, 733–34
Cudjoe, 446
Cultural Revolution: Chinese, *f753,* 754
culture: early development of, 6
Cunaxa: battle of, 90
cuneiform, 12
Curie, Marie, 502–03, *p502*
Curie, Pierre, 502
curriculum, 298
Curzon, Lord, 660
Cuzco: 206–08; Manco Inca in, 431; Pizarro in, 430
cynicism, 103
Cyprus: British control of, 553; role in Persian naval warfare, *m64,* 66
Cyril, 239
Cyrillic script, 239
Cyrus, *f227*
Cyrus II (of Persia), 64. *See also* Cyrus the Great
Cyrus the Great: Mausoleum of, *p76*
czar: defined, 393
Czechoslovakia: Prague Spring in, 828; post–World War I, 620, 633; post–World War II, 728; and Soviet Union, 830, *m830;* and the Sudetenland, 688; in Warsaw Pact, 721

D

D-Day, 703
da Gama, Vasco, 412, 421
da Vinci, Leonardo, 373–74
Daboya: king of, 575
Dacia, 126
dada, 638

da Gama, Vasco, 412, *m414–415*
Daguerre, Louis-Jacques-Mandé, *f504*
Dahomey, 442, *m442*
Dáil Éireann, 660
Daimler, Gottlieb, 498, *p498*
Daladier, Edouard, 688
Dalton, John, 502
Damascus, 133, *m133,* 251, 254
Danelaw, *m278,* 279
Danny the Red, 737
Dante, 541
Danton, Georges-Jacques, 473
Danube River: 123, 272, 335; Magyar tribes crossing, *m278,* 279; Ottoman acceptance of Russian access to, 552; Russian control of, 238
Danubian Bulgars, 238
Dao Da Jing, 160, *f305, p305*
Daoism: 160–61, *f173;* as religion of East Asia, *f305*
Darby, Abraham, 490
Dardanelles, 608
daric, 67
Darius I (of Persia): 65; in Europe, 76; power over Gandhara, 152; against Greeks, 76–77; mention in "Book of Kings," *f342;* Palace of, *p66;* tomb of, *p65*
Darius II (of Persia). *See* Xerxes
Darius III (of Persia), 98
Dark Age: in Greece, 45; Greek art after, 86; Greek city-states after, 70
Darwin, Charles, 502, *p502*
Darwinism, 502. *See also* social Darwinism
Dasht-e-Kavīr Desert, 62
Dasht-e-Lūt Desert, 62
dating techniques: carbon, *f28–29*
Daughters of the American Revolution, 718
dauphin, 364
David (of Israel): 48; Kingdom of, 131
Dawes, Charles, 619
Dawes Plan, 619, 632
Day of Judgment, *f172*
DDT, 841, 843
de Beauvoir, Simone, 738
de Gaulle, Charles: 724, 774; announcement of France's withdrawal from NATO, 734; during World War II, 692
de Klerk, F. W., *p793,* 794
de-Stalinization, 726–27
Dead Souls (Gogol), *f549*
death camps: during World War II, 697–99; *m698*
Deccan, The: Aurangzeb's wars in, 424; dynasty in, 317; Mughal territories in, *m345;* terrain of, *p53*
Declaration of Independence (1776), 466; influence on French National Assembly, 471
Declaration of Sentiments, 525
Declaration of the Rights of Man and Citizen (1790), 471; all free men obtained right to vote under,

E

L

labor unions, 528
Labour Party, 724, 833, 845–46
Lac, 315
La Familia Presidencial, f823
Lagash, 10
laissez-faire, 461
Lake Chad, 441, 571
Lake Huron, 439
Lake Ontario, 439
Lake Texcoco, 202
Lake Titicaca, 206
Lakhmid dynasty, 223, 228
Lalibela (of Ethiopia), 193
Lamu, 192
Lancashire: Arkwright's mill in, 487
La Noche Triste, 429
Laos: consequences of Vietnam War for, 762; early civilization in, 315; in French Indochina, 583
Laozi, 160, 402
La Plata, 432, 530
La Salle, René-Robert de, 436
Las Casas, Bartolomé de, 433
lasers, 837
lateen sail, 411
Latin America: challenges of economic development in, 802; Cold War and, 814–16; destruction of rain forests in, 844; environmental issues in, 805–06; foreign reactions to independence in, 532; independence in, 529–32; international debt of, 804–05; literature and art in, 824; modern painting in, f823; movements toward democracy in, 812, 844; new directions in, 800–25; population growth in, c804; post–World War I depression in, 643, 650–51; problems of culture and society in, 820–24; push for industrialization in, 803; revolution and democracy in, 814–19; revolution and reaction in, 810–12; struggle for human rights in, 820; urbanization and population growth in, 803–04; U.S. intervention in, 677–78
Latin Christendom, 274–76
Latvia: break from Soviet Union, 831; post–World War I democratic governments in, 633; post–World War I emergence as new state, 620; in Soviet Union, 726
Laurier, Wilfrid, 658–59
La Venta, 24
Law Code of Manu, 155
Law of Return, 779
Law of Suspects, 472
Law of the Twelve Tables, 117
Le Corbusier: chapel by, f739
League of Corinth, 97
League of Nations, 670; British sponsorship of Egypt in, 664; China's appeal for help with Japanese aggression, 684; establishment of, 616; Ethiopia's appeal for help, 685; Hitler's withdrawal of Germany from, 686; replaced by United Nations, 717

Leakey, Mary, 4
Lebanon: in Arab League, 778; French control following World War I, 618; Hezbollah in, 789; independence of, 778; mandate state of, 666; Phoenicians in, 46; Shi'ah Muslims in, f253
Leeds: air pollution in, p494
Lee Kuan Yew, 767
Legalism, 161
Legalists of China, 391
legion, 109
legitimacy, 536
Leibniz, Gottfried, 409
Leizu, f166
Lend-Lease, 694
Lenin, Vladimir, 612, 627 p627; interpretation of history by, 654–55; Russia under, 629–30
Leo I (Pope), 142
Leo III (Pope), 230–31, 270, 277; and Charlemagne, p271
Leo X (Pope), 380–81
Leon, Ernesto Zedillo Ponce de, 819
Leonidas (of Sparta), 77
Leopardi, Giacomo, 541, p541
Leopold II (of Belgium), 564, 573
Lepanto, Battle of, 420
Lepidus, 122
Les Demoiselles d'Avignon, 669
Lesbos, 72
Lessons for Women, 168
Letter of Tansar, 225
Letter to the Romans (Paul), f134
Levant, The, 46–51, m47
leveling, 168
Levi, Primo, f699
Lexington: colonist gun store in, 465
Leyte Gulf: Battle of, 708
Liao Empire, 304
Li Bai, 308
Libby, Willard F., 29
liberal arts, 298
Liberal Democratic Party (LDP), 758
liberalism, 495: in Austria-Hungary, 546–47; in Germany, 543–44, 556; in Italy, 558; in Russia, 549–50; in Spain and Portugal, 557–58; in Western Europe, 559–60
Liberia: as colony for freed slaves, 523
Libya: in Arab League, 778; Hitler's Afrika Korps in, 694; and independent kingdoms, 41; Mussolini's strengthening of Italy's position in, 684

Li dynasty, 316
Liebknecht, Karl, 632
Liliuokalani (of Hawaii), 678, p678
Limited Nuclear Test Ban Treaty, 734
Lincoln, Abraham, 524
linear A and B, 42

"linear view" of history, 172
Lin Zexu, 586
Li Si, 163
Lithuania: break from Soviet Union, 831; Ivan IV's attack of, 394; post–World War, 620, 633; in Soviet Union, 726
Liu Bang, 163
Liu Shaoqi, 754
Livingstone, David, 569
Livy, 124
lobola, 194
Locke, John, 397, 458–59, 466
locomotive, 497
Lodge, Henry Cabot, 615
Lodi, Ibrahim, 344
loess, 19
Logos, 105
Lombards: sacking of Italy by, 230, 277
Lombardy: Austria and, 541, 546
London Company, 437
Long Count, 200
Long March, 673
Longshan culture, 22
Loos, Adolph, 547
Lord Baltimore, 438
Lorraine: French loss of, 545; German annexation of Alsace and, 567. *See also* Alsace-Lorraine
Los Alamos, 731
Louis IX (of France), 323
Louis the Pious, 277
Louis VII (of France), 297
Louis XIII (of France), 391
Louis XIV (of France), p392; wars of, 393
Louis XV (of France), 470
Louis XVI (of France), 470–72; execution of, p451
Louis XVIII (of France), 478
Louis Philippe (of France), 539–40
Louisiana: La Salle's naming of, 436
Louisiana Purchase, 522–23
Lovett, William, 513
Loyalists, 466
Loyola, Ignatius de, 383
Lucy: discovering, 4, 6
Ludendorff, Erich, 613, 633
Luftwaffe, 695, 703
Lumumba, Patrice, 776
Lusitania, 610
Luther, Martin, 380–81, p381
Luxembourg: in EEC, 725; in NATO, 720–21
Luxemburg, Rosa, 632
Lydia, 65; Cyrus's conquest of, 76
lyric poetry, 72
Lysippus, f104

M

Maastricht Treaty, 848
MacAdam, John, 497

N

NAACP. *See* National Association for the Advancement of Colored People

NAFTA. *See* North American Free Trade Agreement

Nagasaki: atomic bomb dropped on, 709, 731; Dutch and, 423, 427

Nagy, Imre, 729

Nahuatl, 202

Nalanda, 156

Nam Viet, 315

Namib Desert, 176, *m177*

Namibia, 573, *m773*

Nanjing, 349, *m350*, 351, 671

Nanna, 11

Nantes, Edict of, 385

Naples: during Italian Renaissance, 370, 371; Italian unification and, 542, *m542*

Napoleon I (of France), 474–78; Continental System of, 475; downfall of, 476–78; empire of, *m476*; escape from exile in Elba, 478; Ferdinand VII of Spain and, 530; Haitian slave revolution and, 529; Hundred Days and, 478; Josephine and, *p474*; and Portugal, defeat of, 531. *See also* Bonaparte, Napoleon

Napoleon III, 554–55

Napoleonic Code, *f141*, 474

Napoleonic Wars, 475

NASA. *See* National Aeronautics and Space Administration (NASA)

Nasser, Gamal Abdel, 777, 780, 781, 784; Suez Crisis and, 780

Nast, Thomas, *f527*

Nataraja, *f150*, *p150*

National Aeronautics and Space Administration (NASA), 835

National American Woman Suffrage Association, 525

National Assembly: French, 470, 471, 554, 555; Prussian, 544

National Association for the Advancement of Colored People (NAACP), 774

National Coalition (British), 643

National Convention (French), 472, 473

National Liberals (German), 556

National Organization of Women (NOW), 738–39

national self-determination, 614

National Socialist German Workers Party, 624, 647, *f654*. *See also* Nazis

National Woman's Party, 525

nationalism, 476; beginnings of colonial, 656–80; in Africa, 664, 668–670, 772–777, *m773*; in Arab Mandates and Arabia, 665–66; in Austria-Hungary, 546–47; in China, 671–74; in Cuba, 676–77; decolonization and, 772–778; dominion status as response to, 658–59; effects of World War I on, 659; in Egypt, 664; in German states, 543–45, *m544*; in Hawaii, 678, *f679*; in India, 660–663, 744–46; in Ireland, 659–60; and Israel, creation of, 666–67; in Italy, 541–43, *m542*; in Latin America, 529–32, *m530*, *m531*, 678; in Middle East, 664–68, 777–778, 779, 782, *f798–99*; in North Africa, 668; in Pakistan, 746–47; in Palestine, 666–67, 782; in Philippines, 679–80; revolutions of 1848 and, 540; in South Asia, 744–49; in Southeast Asia, 674–75, 760–61; in Sub-Saharan Africa, 668–670; in Turkey, 668

Native Americans. *See* American Indians

NATO. *See* North Atlantic Treaty Organization

Natufian culture, 6

natural law, 457, 458

natural selection, 502

Navigation Acts (British), 452, 464

Nazca, 205

Nazis, 647–49, *p688*; book burning by, *p655*; Nuremberg trials and, 716–17; persecution of Jews and, 682, 697–700; role in revival of German power, 686–87; SS of, 697–700. *See also* National Socialist German Workers Party

Ndebele, 578

Neanderthals, 5

Nebuchadnezzar, 51

Nebuchadnezzar II, 110

Nehru, Jawaharlal, 742, 746, 748, 749

Nelson, Horatio, 474, 475, *p475*

Neolithic Age, 5–7; in China, 19–22; farming communities during, 43

Neoplatonists, 403–04

NEP. *See* New Economic Policy

Nero, 125, *c125*, 135

Nerva, 125

Nestorian Christianity, 323

Netherlands, The: Congress of Vienna and, 537; democratic reforms in, 559; dike construction in, 485, *p485*; in EEC, 725; in NATO, 720–21, *m720*; open-field farming in, 485; Renaissance art in, 379; and Spain, 384, 423; trade and colonization, 423, 436, 570, 584, 674–75; universities in, 375; World War II and, 691. *See also* Dutch

Netherlands East Indies, 674–75; Japanese control of, 696

Neustria, 277

Neutrality Acts (U. S.), 694

New Amsterdam. *See* New York City

New Brunswick, 519

New Castile, 432

Newcomen, Thomas, 490

New Deal, 643

New Economic Policy (NEP): in Soviet Union, 630

New England: English colonization of, 437–38, *p438*

Newfoundland: Cabot and, 435

New France, 435

New Granada, 432

New Guinea: World War II and, *f704–05*, 707

New Harmony, Indiana, utopian community in, 495–96

"new" imperialism, 566

New Kingdom (of Egypt), 14, 38–39, *m38*

New Orleans: jazz in, 636

New South Wales, 520

New Spain, 432

New Stone Age, 5–6

New Testament, 132, 133, *f134*; Luther's translation of, 381

Newton, Sir Isaac, 408–09, *p409*, 457

New World, Columbian exchange and, *f448–49*; Columbus "discovery" of, *p416*

"new world order," 832–33

New York City: beginnings as New Amsterdam, 436; corruption in government of, 526, *f527*

New York Stock Exchange: October 1929 crash and, 642, *p642*

New Zealand: 517, 520–21; agriculture after World War I, 641; World War II and, 694

Ngo Dinh Diem, 761

Ngo Quyen, 315

Nguyen dynasty, 583

Nguyen That Thanh. *See* Ho Chi Minh

Niani, 354, *m354*

Nibelungenlied, *f296*

Nicaragua: democracy in, 844; Sandinista revolution in, 814–15, 828; U.S. intervention in, 677, 815, *m815*

Nicator, Seleucus, 153

Nicholas I (of Russia): and revolt of Hungarian Magyars, 546; repression under, 548–49

Nicholas II (of Russia), 550, 626

Nicola Turk, *f471*

Nigeria, 190, 670, *m773*; art in, *f355*, *p794*, 796; independence of Biafra from, 793; economic problems of, 791

Niger-Kordofanian: language group, 178

Niger River, 176, 190, 354; and trade during Songhay Empire, 356

Nightingale, Florence, 552–53, *p553*

nihilists, 550

Nika Revolt, 230

Nile Delta: *m14*; ancient civilization in, 13–16; Egyptian retreat to, 41; Hyksos settlement in, 37

Nile River, *m14*, 176; rise of civilization around, 2–3, 13–16; trade and, 182

imperial administration of, 65–66; imperial army of, 66; imperial economy in, 67; imperial society and culture in, 68; Indo-Iranians of, 62–63; Mongol conquest of, 323; noble children of, f67; and Persian wars, 76–78, m77, 91; rise of empire, 64–65; and Roman Empire, 130; Safavid dynasty, 339–43, m340; Sassanid dynasty, 222, m224. *See also* Iran

Persian Gulf, 8, 33, m64, 154, 191, 192, 244, 411, 421, 829

Persian Gulf War, 832

Peru: Chimú culture in, 206; Inca culture in, 206; democracy in, 812, 844; monoculture in, 802; Nazca culture in, 205; in viceroyalty of New Castile, 432, m432; prehistoric civilization in, 25–26; San Martín's liberation of, 530

Pétain, Philippe, 606, 612, 691–92

Peter (the Apostle), 138

Peter I (of Russia), 394–95

Peter the Great. *See* Peter I

Petrarch, Francesco, 369, p369, 371

Petrine theory, 138

petro-dollars, 783

Petrograd: worker strikes in, 627

petroleum: c784, m785; Cold War and, 783–84, 829; embargo on, 783; Nigeria and, 791; Persian Gulf War and, 832; production of, 498. *See also* Organization of Petroleum Exporting Countries

phalanx formation, 72

Phan Thanh Gian, 583

pharaohs, 14–16, 37–41

Philadelphia: and U.S. Constitution, 468

Philip II (of Macedonia), 96; Aristotle and, 94

Philip II (of Spain), 384

Philip IV (of France), 365

Philip of Anjou, 393

Philip the Fair, 287

Philip V (of Macedonia), 112

Philippines: nationalism in, 679; democracy and, 844; Spanish-American War and, 676, 679; Srivijaya Empire and, 320; United States and, 676, m677, 679–80; World War II and, 696, 701, p701, m705, 708

Philistines, 46–47

philosophes, 457

Phoenicia, 46–47; Alexander the Great and, 98; Carthage and, 110, 187; and North African trading colonies, 187; and trade with Philistines, 47

Phoenician script, 46

photography: development of, f504

pi (π), 156

Piankhi, 181–82

Picasso, Pablo, 638, f669

pictographs, 12, p12

Pigafetta, Antonio, f414; sketch by, p416

Pilgrims, 437

Pindar, 83

Pinochet, Augusto, 812

Piraeus, 80

Pitt, William (the Elder), 455

Pizarro, Francisco, 430

Plateau of Iran: agriculture in, 62–63; early culture and society in, 63; geography of, 62; Indo-European-speaking peoples of, 51; Indo-Iranians and, 62; nomads from, 52

Plato, 93–94, 95; and Renaissance, 369, 403; Muslim scholars and, 257; on Sappho, 72

Platt Amendment, 676–77

plebeians, 109; and "Plebeian Council," 116

Plutarch, 114

plow: heavy-wheeled, 294

Plowman's Front (Romania), 730

Plymouth, 437

pogroms, 550

Poitiers, battle of, 365

Poland: and attack by Ivan IV, 394; and Congress of Vienna, m537, 538; nationalist uprisings in, 540; Nazi plans for expansion into, 647; partitions of, m456; Russian Empire and, 548; Seven Years' War and, 455, m456; Solidarity trade union in, 829, 830; Soviet Union and, 718, 721, 726, 829, 830, m830; post-World War I, 650; World War II and, 682, p683, p686, 689, 690, m691, 697–99, m698, f699, 701, m704; post-World War II, 718, m720, 721

polis: 69–70, 90

Polish corridor, 621; Hitler's demand for return of, 689

political cartoons, f527

political reforms: in Great Britain, 511–15; in United States, 524–26

Politics Drawn from Holy Scripture (Bossuet), 391

pollution, 840–41

Polo, Marco, f324, 410

Polovtsians, 240

Polybius, f173

polytheism, 11; Muhammad's rejection of, 247

Pompeii: during Roman Empire, p119

Pompey, Gnaeus, 122

Pontifex Maximus, 119

Poor Law, 515

pope, 138

Popular Front (France), 644

Populist (Russia), 550

portolano, p411

Portrait of a Merchant (Gossaert), 423

portrait sculpture: Roman, f124

Portugal: and Asian trade, 421–22, 427; and Atlantic slave trade, 441; and China during Qing dynasty, 424; civil war in, 557–58; colonies in the Americas, 431–34, m432, m530, 531; colonization and trade in Africa, 441, 443–444, 570; and Congress of Vienna, 537; as constitutional monarchy, 539; and decolonization in Africa, 776–77; democracy in, 844; empire in Brazil, 431–34, 531; and exploration, 412, m414–15, 441; Fascist government in, 650; and Kongo Empire, 443; in NATO, 720–21; navigation and shipbuilding and; 411–12; revolution in, 539

Portuguese Guinea, 776

Poseidon, c82

Pound, Ezra, 622

praetors, 117

Prague, and Thirty Years' War, 386

Prague Spring, 739–740, 828

Praise of Folly, The (Erasmus), 376

Pratihara dynasty, 317

Praxiteles, 102, f104

PRC. *See* People's Republic of China

predestination, 382

prefects, 136

Presbyterianism, 396

Presley, Elvis, 736

Prester John, 410

Préveza: battle of, 335

PRI. See Institutional Revolutionary Party

Prince, The (Machiavelli), 372

princeps, 123

Princip, Gavrilo, 600

printing press, p376

prokypsis, 231–32

proletariat, 503–04, 649

propaganda, 603, f654–55

Protagoras, 91–92

protectionism, 567

Protestantism: antislavery sentiments in, 510; spread of, 382–83. *See also* Reformation

Proto-Bantu, 193

Prussia: army of, 453; and Bismarck, 544–45; and Concert of Europe, 538; and Congress of Vienna, 536–38, m537; and Enlightenment, 462; and Habsburgs, 395; Junkers in, 543; and Quadruple Alliance, 538; rise of, 453–54; and Seven Years' War, 454, 455; and Teutonic Knights, 293

Psellus, Michael Constantine, 236

Ptolemy (Greek astronomer), 129, 402

Ptolemy I (Hellenistic ruler), 100

Ptolemy II (of Egypt), 102

pueblos, 215

Puerto Rico: United States and, 676, m677

Pugachev's Rebellion, 462

Punic Wars: 110–12

Punjab, 424; Arya Samaj in, 581

Puranas, 154–55

Sea Peoples, 41
Second Coalition, 475
Second Continental Congress
 (U.S.): adoption of Declaration of
 Independence by, 466; Articles of
 Confederation by, 467
Second Estate, 469
Second French Republic, 554
Second Industrial Revolution,
 498–99
Second Punic War, 111–12
Second Sex, The (Beauvoir), 738
Second Triumvirate, 122
Secret History of the Mongols,
 f322
sectionalism, 519
sects, 382
Security Council: United Nations,
 717
seed drill, 486
Sei Shonagon, 313
Sekander. *See* Alexander the Great
Selassie, Haile, 685, 694
Seleucids, 100
Seleucus I (of Hellenistic Asia),
 p100, f154
Selim I (of Ottoman Empire), 334
Selim II (of Ottoman Empire), 420
Sembene, Ousmane, 794
Semitic languages, 32; Phoenicians
 and, 46
Seneca Falls Convention, 525
Seneca people, f213, 214
Senegal, 670; self-government of, 775
Senegal River, 190
Senghor, Leopold, 670, 775
Seoul: Communist capture of, 759
separate spheres, 501
separatism: in Northern Ireland, 833;
 in Quebec, 833
sepoys, 579
Serbia: independence of, 553;
 Ottoman acceptance of self-rule for,
 552; Ottoman conquer of, 334;
 post-World War I, 620
Serbs, 230; Bosnian, 832
serfs: European, 282–83; Russian,
 549–50
Sermon on the Mount, 132
settlement houses, 516, 526
Seven Weeks' War, 545
Seven Years' War: 454–55; aftermath
 in Europe of, 455–56, m455, m456;
 British control of Bengal after, 579;
 effect on British government, 464;
 French role in, 470
Severus, Septimius, 130
Seward, William H., 523
Seymour, Jane, 383
Sforza, Francesco, p371
Shafi'i school, 258
Shah, Muhammad Reza, 777, 783
Shah, Nadir, p424
Shah, Reza, 777
shah-an-shah eran, 222
shah-in-shah, 65

Shah-nameh, 226, 267, f342
Shah's Mosque, p343
Shaka, 571, f572
Shakespeare, William, 376–77
Shang Empire, 54, m55
Shapur I, 225–26, p223
shari'ah, 257–58, 348
Shatt al Arab: Mesopotamia as, 8
sheikh, 245
shekel, 67
Shi Huangdi, 162
Shi 'ism: 252, f253, 266, 339, 344,
 788; shift of Safavids to, 339; as
 threat to Abbasids, 264
Shikoku, 311
Shinto, 311
shoen, 314
shogun, 314
shogunate: Ashikaga, 314; Kamakura,
 314
Shona people, 353, 578
Shotoku, Prince, 312
Shute, Nevil, 737
Siam. *See* Thailand
Siberia: gulags in, 650; land bridge
 between Alaska and, 23; Lenin's
 exile to, 627
Sicily: Black Death carried to, 362;
 Carthaginian control of, 110; king-
 dom of Two Sicilies, 541–42, m542;
 Norman conquest of, 282; politics
 during Italian Renaissance, 370;
 Roman intervention in, 110
Sick Man of Europe: Ottoman
 Empire as, 552
Sieyès, Abbé, 470
Signac, Paul, 506
Sikhs, 347, 424
Silent Spring (Carson), 841
Silesia: Frederick II seizing of, 454
Silk Road, f166, m167, 168; Samanid
 family and, 264; Tang dynasty
 expansion increases trade on, 306
Silla, 309, m310
silt, 8
Simbirsk, 627
Simeon Stylites, Saint, 139
Simson, Solomon Bar, 290
Sinai Peninsula: during Roman
 Empire, 126; Israeli forces overrun-
 ning of, 781
Sinan, 338
Sinbad the Sailor, 259
Sind region, 318
Singapore: and British, 583; fall to
 Japan in World War II, 744; as Four
 Tiger, 765–67
Sinn Fein, 660
Sino-Japanese War, 590
Sino-Soviet split, 752
Sistine Chapel, 374, p374
Siva, 147, p147, f150, p150, 154
Six Books on the Commonwealth, 390
Skanda Gupta, 156
Six-Day War, 781
skepticism, 103

Slav people: invasion of Balkans by,
 230
Slave Coast, m442
slave ship, p445
slave trade (Atlantic): 441–46, m442,
 p445, 508; abolishment of foreign,
 522; consequences of, 446; Middle
 Passage 444–45
slavery: export from Africa to Arab
 world, 192; in American colonies,
 433, p433, 437, 529; in Greek city-
 states, 70; movements to abolish,
 508, 510–11, 522–23; revolts in
 Roman Empire, 120; revolution in
 Haiti, 529; Trollope's view of
 American slavery, f524; U.S. conflict over, 522–23, m523, 524
Slavic tribes, 237, 279
Slavs: in Nazi concentration camps,
 698
"Sleep, Darling" (Sappho), 72–73
Slovenia: secession from Yugoslavia,
 832
Smallholders Party, 729
Smith, Adam, 460, 495
Smith, Bessie, 636
Smith, John, 437
smog, 806
Smuts, Jan, 658
Snaketown, 215
Sobieski, John, 421
soccer, 637
Social Contract, The (Rousseau), 460
social criticism: during
 Enlightenment, 458–59
social Darwinism: 503; Kipling and,
 f568
Social Democrats, 632; Bismarck
 and, 556
social history, f562–63
socialism, 495; scientific, 503
social reforms: British, 515–16; U. S.,
 525
social sciences: emergence of, 503
Social War, 121
Society of Brahma, 581
Society of the Harmonious Fists,
 588
Society of Jesus, 383. *See also* Jesuits
Socrates, 92–93, p92
Socratic method, 92
Sofala: Swahili trade in, 353
Solidarity, union/movement (Poland),
 829, 830
Solomon (of Israel), 48
Solomon's Temple, 105, 261
Solon, 73, p73
Solzhenitsyn, Alexander, 738
Somalia: as Italian possession, 684;
 mass starvation in, 791
Somme River, 606
Somoza, Anastasio, 815
Song dynasty, 304, m306; economy
 and society of, 306; Kublai Kan's
 final assault on, 323; literature and
 arts in, 308

T

QUOTED MATERIAL

For permission to reprint copyrighted material, grateful acknowledgment is made to the following sources:

Africa World Press: From "Ghana in 1067" by Al Bekri from "Al-Masalik wa 'l-Mamalik," translated into French by MacGuckin de Slane and from "Al Mas'udi: The Country of the Zanj" from *African Civilization Revisited: From Antiquity to Modern Times* by Basil Davidson. Copyright © 1991 by Basil Davidson. All rights reserved.

American Oriental Society: From DNa lines 31–36 and DBI lines 20–24 from *Old Persian: Grammar, Texts, Lexicon*, Second Edition, by Roland G. Kent. Copyright 1953 by American Oriental Society.

Anchor Books, a division of Bantam Doubleday Dell Publishing Group, Inc.: From "Underground" and from "The End of Goulart" from *A Grain of Mustard Seed* by Márcio Moreira Alves. Copyright © 1973 by Márcio Moreira Alves.

Neil Armstrong: Quote by Neil Armstrong upon lunar landing of Apollo 11, July 20, 1969.

BasicBooks, a division of HarperCollins Publishers: From "The Election and the End of the Revolution" from *After the Wall: East Meets West in the New Berlin* by John Borneman. Copyright © 1991 by BasicBooks, Inc., a division of HarperCollins Publishers.

Berhman House, Inc., 235 Watchung Ave., W. Orange, NJ 07052: From "Glückel's Adventures in Childbirth" from *The Memoirs of Glückel of Hameln*, translated by Marvin Lowenthal. Copyright 1932 by HarperCollins Publishers.

Columbia University Press: From "Basic Doctrines of Theravada Buddhism" from *Sources of Indian Tradition*, Volume I, edited by William Theodore de Bary. Copyright © 1958 by Columbia University Press. From "Book Four" from *Odo of Deuil: De profectione Ludovici VII in orientem*, edited and translated by Virginia Gingerick Berry. Copyright 1948 by Columbia University Press. From *The Bhagavad Gita: Krishna's Counsel in Time of War*, translated by Barbara Stoler Miller. English translation copyright © 1986 by Barbara Stoler Miller.

Don Congdon Associates, Inc.: From "The End of the Beginning" from *The Stories of Ray Bradbury*. Copyright 1943, 1944, 1945, 1946, 1947, 1948, 1949, 1950, 1951, 1952, 1953, 1954, © 1956, 1957, 1958, 1959, 1960, 1961, 1962, 1963, 1969, 1971, 1972, 1973, 1976, 1978, 1979, 1980 and renewed © 1970, 1971, 1972, 1973, 1974, 1975, 1976, 1977, 1978, 1979, 1980 by Ray Bradbury.

Doubleday, a division of Bantam Doubleday Dell Publishing Group, Inc.: From "Letter to the Grand Duchess Christina" and from "The Starry Messenger" from *Discoveries and Opinions of Galileo*, translated by Stillman Drake. Copyright © 1957 by Stillman Drake. From "Sinbad" from *Arabian Nights and Days* by Naguib Mahfouz, translated by Denys Johnson-Davies. Copyright © 1979 by Naguib Mahfouz; English translation copyright © 1995 by The American University in Cairo Press.

Dumbarton Oaks Research Library and Collection, Washington, D.C.: From *De administrando imperio* by Constantine Porphyrogenitus, edited by Gy. Moravcsik, translated by R.J.H. Jenkins. English translation copyright © 1967 by R.J.H. Jenkins.

Elizabeth Warnock Fernea and University of Texas Press: From untitled poem from *Wall* by Forough Farrokhzad from "Conformity and Confrontation: A Comparison of Two Iranian Women Poets" by Farzanch Milani from *Women and the Family in the Middle East: New Voices of Change*, edited by Elizabeth Warnock Fernea. Copyright © 1985 by the University of Texas Press.

The Free Press, a division of Simon & Schuster: From "The Attractions of Farming," translated by Clara Yu from *Chinese Civilization and Society: A Sourcebook* by Patrician Buckley Ebrey. Copyright © 1981 by The Free Press.

Grove Press, Inc.: From "Hsiao Ya" from *The Books of Songs*, translated by Arthur Waley. Copyright © 1987 by Grove Press, Inc.

Hakluyt Society: From *The Overall Survey of the Ocean's Shores* by Ma Huan, translated by J.V.G. Mills. English translation copyright © 1970 by J.V.G. Mills.

Harcourt Brace & Company: From translation of "Cette nuit-là" by Victor Hugo from *Europe: 1815–1914*, Third Edition, edited by Gordon A. Craig. Copyright © 1961, 1966, 1971 by Holt, Rinehart and Winston, Inc.; copyright © 1972 by The Dryden Press Inc.

HarperCollins Publishers: From "Everyone Knows" from *The Essential Tao: An Initiation into the Heart of Taoism Through the Authentic Tao Te Ching and the Inner Teachings of Chuang-tzu*, translated by Thomas Cleary. Copyright © 1991 by Thomas Cleary.

Heinemann Educational: From *Distant View of a Minaret* by A. Rifaat, translated by Denys Johnson-Davies. Translation copyright © 1983 by Denys Johnson-Davies.

David Higham Associates Ltd.: From "The Vietnam War: A Reporter with the Vietcong, near Hanoi, 10 December 1965" from *What a Way to Run the Tribe* by James Cameron. Published in 1968 by Macmillan & Co. Ltd.

Hill and Wang, a division of Farrar, Straus & Giroux, Inc.: From *Night* by Elie Wiesel. Copyright © 1958 by Les Editions de Minuit; English translation copyright © 1960 by MacGibbon & Kee.

Henry Holt and Company, Inc.: From "The Heirs of Stalin," translated by George Reavey from *The Collected Poems: 1952–1990*, edited by Albert C. Todd, with Yevgeny Yevtushenko and James Ragan. Copyright © 1991 by Henry Holt and Company, Inc.

Hutchinson, an imprint of Century Hutchinson Ltd.: From "Crimean Summer, Stalingrad Winter" and from "The War in the West 1943–1945" from *The Second World War* by John Keegan. Copyright © 1989 by John Keegan.

Indiana University Press: From "To Italy," translated by Ruth Yorck and Kenward Elmslie from *Leopardi: Poems and Prose*, edited by Angel Flores. Copyright © 1966 by Indiana University Press

The Heirs to the Estate of Martin Luther King, Jr., c/o Joan Daves Agency as agent for the proprietor: From "I Have a Dream" by Martin Luther King, Jr. Copyright © 1963 by Martin Luther King, Jr; copyright renewed © 1991 by Coretta Scott King.

Le Caire: From *Chronique d'Égypte* by Nicola Turk, edited and translated by Gaston Wiet. Copyright 1950 by Le Caire.

Le Livre Contemporaire: From *God's Bits of Wood* by Ousmane Sembene, translated by Francis Price. Copyright © 1962, 1970 by Le Livre Contemporaire.

Maclean's Magazine, Maclean Hunter Publishing Ltd.: Quotes by Ivan Lernikov and Nikolai Amelin from "Red Is Dead" by Malcolm Gray from *Maclean's*, September 2, 1991, vol. 104, no. 35, p. 28. Copyright © 1991 by Maclean Hunter Publishing Ltd.

National Council of the Churches of Christ in the United States of America, Division of Christian Education: From "The Letters of St. Paul" from *Revised Standard Version of the Bible, New Testament.* Copyright 1946 by the Division of Christian Education of the National Council of the Churches of Christ in the United States of America.

Jawaharlal Nehru Memorial Fund: From "A Tryst with Destiny" from *Jawaharlal Nehru: An Anthology*, edited by Sarvepalli Gopal. Copyright © 1980 by Indira Gandhi.

New Directions Publishing Corporation: From "1914" from *Collected Poems of Wilfred Owen*. Copyright © 1963 by New Directions Publishing Corporation.

W. W. Norton: Quote by Haile Selassie, June 30, 1936 from *Between Two Fires: Europe's Path in the 1930s* by David Clay Large. Copyright © 1990 by David Clay Large.

Northwestern University Press: From "Antonio Pigafetta" from *Magellan's Voyage Around the World: Three Contemporary Accounts*, edited by Charles E. Nowell. Copyright © 1962 by Northwestern University Press.

Georg Olms Verlagsbuchhandlung, Hildesheim: "The Light Verse" and "The Throne Verse" from *A Short History of Classical Arabic Literature* by Ignace Goldziher, translated by Joseph Desomogyi. Copyright © 1966 by Georg Olms.

Pantheon Books, a division of Random House, Inc.: "The Star-Money" from *Grimm's Fairy Tales*, translated by Margaret Hunt, revised by James Stern. Copyright 1944 by Pantheon Books; copyright renewed © 1972 by Random House, Inc.

Alicia Partnoy: From "Construction" by Pastora, translated by Andrea Vincent and from "In My Country" by Etelvina Astrada, translated by Zoë Anglesey from *You Can't Drown the Fire: Latin American Women Writing in Exile*, edited by Alicia Partnoy. Copyright © 1988 by Alicia Partnoy.

Penguin Books Ltd.: From *The Book of the Courtier* by Baldesar Castiglione, translated by George Bull. Translation copyright © 1967 by George Bull. Published by Penguin Classics, 1967. From speech by Queen Boudica from *Annals* by P. Cornelius Tacitus, translated by Michael Grant. Translation copyright © 1956 by Michael Grant. Published by Penguin Classics, 1956. From *The Nibelungenlied*, translated by A. T. Hatto. Translation copyright © 1965, 1969 by A. T. Hatto. Published by Penguin Classics, 1965, revised edition, 1969. From "The Search for Everlasting Life" from *The Epic of Gilgamesh*, translated by N. K. Sandars. Translation copyright © 1960 by N. K. Sandars. Published by Penguin Classics, 1960. From "Isocrates: Panegyricus" and from "Isocrates: Philip" from *Greek Political Oratory*, selected and translated by A.N.W. Saunders. Translation copyright © 1970 by A.N.W. Saunders. Published by Penguin Classics, 1970. From *The Age of Alexander* by Plutarch, translated by Ian Scott-Kilvert. Translation copyright © 1973 by Ian Scott-Kilvert. Published by Penguin Classics, 1973. From *The Rise and Fall of Athens* by Plutarch, translated by Ian Scott-Kilvert. Translation copyright © 1960 by Ian Scott-Kilvert. Published by Penguin Classics, 1960. From Books One, Two, Four, Five, Six, and Seven from *Herodotus: The Histories*, translated by Aubrey de Sélincourt, revised by A. R. Burn. Translation copyright 1954 by the Estate of Aubrey de Sélincourt; revision copyright © 1972 by A. R. Burn. Published by Penguin Classics, 1954, revised edition, 1972. From *A History of the English Church and People* by Bede, translated by Leo Sherley-Price, revised by R. E. Latham. Translation copyright © 1955, 1968 by Leo Sherley-Price. Published by Penguin Classics, 1955; Second revised edition, 1968. From "Book One: Introduction," from "Book Two: Pericles' Funeral Oration," and from "Book Three: The Mytilenian Debate" from *History of the Peloponnesian War* by Thucydides, translation by Rex Warner. English translation copyright 1954 by Rex Warner. Published by Penguin Classics, 1954. From *The Jewish War* by Josephus, translated by G. A. Williamson, revised by E. Mary Smallwood. Translation copyright © 1959, 1969 by G. A. Williamson; Introduction and editorial matter copyright © 1981 by E. Mary Smallwood. Published by Penguin Classics, revised edition, 1981.

Peters Fraser & Dunlop: From notes of Louise Solmitz from *Documents on Nazism*, edited by Jeremy Noakes and Geoffrey Pridham. Copyright © 1974 by Oxford University Press.

Pietermaritzburg: From *The Diary of Henry Francis Fynn*, compiled and edited by James Stuart and D. McK. Malcolm. Copyright 1950 by Pietermaritzburg.

Playboy: From "Playboy Interview: Gabriel García Márquez" by Claudia Dreifus from *Playboy*, February 1983. Copyright © 1983 by Playboy Magazine.

Pocket Books, a division of Simon & Schuster: From *Dead Souls* by Nikolai Gogol, translated by Helen Michailoff. Copyright © 1964 by Washington Square Press.

Princeton University Press: Adapted from *Ancient Near Eastern Texts Relating to the Old Testament*, edited by James B. Pritchard. Copyright © 1955 by Princeton University Press.

Frederick Quinn: Lyrics from untitled song from *Changes in Beti Society, 1887–1960* by Frederick Quinn.

Random House, Inc.: From "Jungle Warfare" from *The Fight for New Guinea* by Pat Robinson. Copyright 1943 by Pat Robinson.

Reuters News Service: From "The Museum of Madness: A Tour of Ceausescu's Palace, Bucharest" by Simon Haydon from *The Sunday Correspondent*, December 1989. Copyright © 1989 by Reuters News Service.

Rutgers University Press: Quotes by Piano Carpini, Genghis Khan, and Mongka from *The Empire of the Steppes: A History of Central Asia* by René Grousset, translated by Naomi Walford. Copyright © 1970 by Rugers University, The State University of New Jersey.

Scribner, a Division of Simon & Schuster Inc.: From *The World Crisis* by the Rt. Hon. Winston S. Churchill, C.H. Copyright 1923, 1927, 1929, 1931 by Charles Scribner's Sons; copyright renewed 1951 by Winston S. Churchill. From "German Inflation, 19 September 1922" from *By-line: Ernest Hemingway*, edited by William White. Copyright © 1967 by Charles Scribner's Sons. Translation of a quotation from *A History of China* by

---

For permission to reprint copyrighted material in the Teacher's Edition, grateful acknowledgment is made to the following sources:

Africa World Press: From "Al Omari: Travelling through Cairo" (translated from "Masalik al Absar fi Mamalik al Amsar" by Ibn Fadl Allah al Omari) from *African Civilization Revisited: From Antiquity to Modern Times* by Basil Davidson. Copyright © 1991 by Basil Davidson. All rights reserved.

Arbor House, a division of William Morrow & Company, Inc.: From "The Watergate Era: Richard M. Nixon" from *Inside the Cold War: An Oral History* by John Sharnik. Copyright © 1987 by John Sharnik.

Dutton Signet, a division of Penguin Books USA Inc.: From "We Are Tired of . . . Believing: Letter to the editor of *Tiesa*, March 8, 1989" by Terese Staponiene, Virginija Sadauskiene, Galina Cirvinskiene, Janina Joksiene, Dalia Stoniene, and Stefa Mikalauskiene from *The Glasnost Reader*, compiled and edited by Jonathan Eisen. Copyright © 1990 by Jonathan Eisen.

Greenwood Publishing Group Inc.: From "Lightning Attack on the Luting Bridge" by Yang Chengwu from *We the Chinese, Voices from China* by Deirdre and Neale Hunter. Copyright © 1971 by Praeger Publishers.

Harvard University Press and the Loeb Classical Library: From *Dio Cassius*, LXIII (*Epitome*), 17-18 from *Dio's Roman History*, Volume IX, translated by Earnest Cary. Copyright © 1969 by Earnest Cary. Published by Harvard University Press, Cambridge, Mass.

Librairie Orientaliste Paul Geuthner S.A.: From *Masalik al Absar fi Mamalik al Amsar* by Al Omari, translated by Jean Gaudefroy-Démombynes. Copyright 1927 by Librairie Orientaliste Paul Geuthner S.A.

Little, Brown and Company: Excerpt from article by Crown Prince Rudolf from the *Wiener Tagblatt* from *A Nervous Splendor: Vienna: 1888-1889* by Frederic Morton. Copyright © 1979 by Frederic Morton.

National Geographic Society: Quote by Alexander Ishkov from "Lethal Legacy" by Mike Edwards from *National Geographic*, August 1994. Copyright © 1994 by National Geographic Society.

The New York Times Company: From "Where's Page 2 in TV News?" (op-ed) by David Halberstam from *The New York Times*, February 22, 1991. Copyright © 1991 by The New York Times Company.

Oxford Blackwell: From "Dinner with Attila the Hun, c. AD 450" by Priscus from *Eyewitness to History*, edited by John Carey. Copyright © 1988 by John Carey. Published by Harvard University Press, Cambridge, Mass.

Penguin Books Ltd.: From *The Annals of Imperial Rome* by Tacitus, translated by Michael Grant. Copyright © 1956, 1959, 1971, 1973, 1975, 1977, 1989 by Michael Grant Publications Ltd. Published by Penguin Classics, revised edition, 1989. From *The Later Roman Empire (A.D. 354-37)* by Ammianus Marcellinus, translated by Walter Hamilton. Translation copyright © 1986 by Walter Hamilton. Published by Penguin Classics, 1986. From "Demosthenes: Philippic I" from *Greek Political Oratory*, selected and translated by A.N.W. Saunders. Copyright © 1970 by A.N.W. Saunders. Published by Penguin Books, 1970. From *The Life of Alexander the Great* by Arrian, translated by Aubrey de Sélincourt. Copyright © 1958 by the Estate of Aubrey de Sélincourt. Published by Penguin Classics, 1958. From *The Alexiad of Anna Comnena*, translated by F.R.A. Sewter. Copyright © 1969 by F.R.A. Sewter. Published by Penguin Classics, 1969.

Stanford University Press: From *An Introduction to Japanese Court Poetry* by Earl Miner. Copyright © 1968 by Stanford University Press.

Time Inc.: From "Kissing Hands, Shaking Babies" by John Kohan from *Time*, June 10, 1991. Copyright © 1991 by Time Inc.

Time-Life Books, a division of Time Life Inc.: "Wen Wang is placed above—" from *Ancient China* by Edward H. Schafer and The Editors of Time Life Books. Copyright © 1967 by Time Inc.

Vedanta Press, a subsidiary of The Vedanta Society of Southern California: From "O Brahman Supreme!" from *The Upanishads: Breath of the Eternal* by Swami Prabhavananda and Frederick Manchester. Copyright © 1948, 1957 by The Vedanta Society of Southern California.

Yale University Press: From *Hernan Cortes: Letters from Mexico*, translated and edited by Anthony Pagden. Copyright © 1971 by Anthony Pagden; copyright © 1986 by Yale University.

References: Teacher's Edition

Quote by the rector of the University of Göttingen from "The First Student Revolt, Germany, 1815: 1. A New Spirit Among the Students" from *Bombs, Beards, and Barricades: 150 Years of Youth in Revolt* by Anthony Esler. Published by Stein and Day, 1971.

Quote by Muhammad after his encounter with the Angel Gabriel from *The Life and Times of Muhammad* by John Bagot Glubb (Glubb Pasha). Published by Stein and Day, 1970.

Quote about Ghana burials by al-Bakri from *Ancient Ghana and Mali* by Nehemia Levtzion. Published by Methuen, 1973.

Excerpt from speech by Nelson Mandela from "My People Are Waiting for Me" from *Chained Together: Mandela, De Klerk, and the Struggle to Remake South Africa* by David Ottaway. Copyright © 1993 by David Ottaway.

From "Report on the State of the Nation" from *The Political History of China, 1840–1928*, translated by Ssu-yü Teng and Jeremy Ingalls. Published by D. Van Nostrand Co., 1956.

Description of Feng Meng-lung's stories from *An Introduction to Chinese Literature* by Liu Wu-chi. Published by Indiana University Press, 1966.

Chou Ku-Ch'eng, from *The Ageless Chinese: A History* by Dun J. Li. Copyright © 1965 by Charles Scribner's Sons.

Martin Secker & Warburg Ltd.: From "Preface" from *Facing Mount Kenya: The Tribal Life of the Gikuyu* by Jomo Kenyatta. Copyright 1938 by Martin Secker & Warburg Ltd.

Shuter & Shooter: From *The Diary of Henry Francis Fynn*, compiled and edited by James Stuart and D. McK. Malcolm. Copyright 1950 by Pietermaritzburg.

Simon & Schuster Inc.: From *Sukarno: An Autobiography*, as told to Cindy Adams. Copyright © 1965 by Cindy Adams. From "The Blood-Clot," "The Opening," and "Power" from *The Koran Interpreted*, translated by Arthur J. Arberry. Copyright © 1955 by George Allen & Unwin Ltd. From "The Grail" from *Perceval or The Story of the Grail* by Chrétien de Troyes, translated by Ruth Harwood Cline. Copyright © 1983 by Ruth Harwood Cline.

Stanford University Press: From "Ox Ghosts and Snake Spirits" from *Born Red: A Chronicle of the Cultural Revolution* by Gao Yuan. Copyright © 1987 by the Board of Trustees of the Leland Stanford Junior University.

State University of New York Press: From *Islam in Practice: Religious Beliefs in a Persian Village* by Reinhold Loeffler. Copyright © 1988 by State University of New York.

Stonehenge Press Inc.: From *The Pillow Book* by Sei Shonagon from *Treasures of the World: The Lords of Japan* by Harry Wiencek. Copyright © 1982 by Stonehenge Press Inc.

Time-Life Books Inc.: From *Great Ages of Man: Ancient Egypt* by Lionel Casson and the Editors of Time-Life Books. Copyright © 1965 by Time-Life Books Inc. Adapted from *Ancient Near Eastern Texts Relating to the Old Testament*, edited by James B. Pritchard. Published by Princeton University Press, 1955.

Frederick Ungar, a division of Continuum Publishing Co.: From *Alexanderplatz Berlin: The Story of Franz Biberkopf* by Alfred Döblin, translated by Eugene Jolas. Copyright 1929 by S. Fischer Verlag, A. G. Berlin; copyright 1931 by The Viking Press, Inc.

The University of California Press: From "Sleep, darling" from *Sappho: A New Translation* by Mary Barnard. Copyright © 1958 by The Regents of the University of California; copyright renewed © 1984 by Mary Barnard. From interview with Aniceto Pereira de Lima (Sinésio Pereira), February 28, 1978 from *Stories on a String: The Brazilian Literatura de Cordel* by Candace Slater. Copyright © 1982 by The Regents of the University of California.

The University of Chicago Press: From "Working-Class and Peasant Women in the Russian Revolution, 1917–1923" by Barbara Evans Clements from *Signs*, vol. 8, no. 2, 1982, p. 226. Copyright © 1982 by The University of Chicago Press. From "Oration on the Dignity of Man" by Giovanni Pico della Mirandola, translated by Elizabeth L. Forbes from *The Renaissance Philosophy of Man*, edited by Ernst Cassirer, Paul Oskar Kristeller, and John H. Randall, Jr. Copyright © 1948 by The University of Chicago Press.

University of Minnesota Press: "Yasna 30.3–6" from *An Introduction to Ancient Iranian Religion: Readings from the Avesta and Achaemenid Inscriptions*, translated and edited by William W. Malandra. Copyright © 1983 by the University of Minnesota.

University of Oklahoma Press: From *Crónica Mexicana* by Hernando Alvarado Tezózomac from *The Aztecs: A History* by Nigel Davies. Copyright © 1973 by Nigel Davies.

The University of Pennsylvania Press: From "The First Case of 'Apple-Polishing'" from *History Begins at Sumer: Thirty-Nine Firsts in Man's Recorded History* by Samuel Noah Kramer. Copyright © 1956 by Samuel Noah Kramer; copyright © 1981 by The University of Pennsylvania Press.

Verso: From *I, Rigoberta Menchú: An Indian Woman in Guatemala*, edited and introduced by Elisabeth Burgos-Debray, translated by Ann Wright. Copyright © 1983 by Editions Gallimard and Elisabeth Burgos; translation copyright © 1984 by Verso.

Viking Penguin, a division of Penguin Books USA Inc.: From "October 1944" from *If This Is Man (Survival in Auschwitz)* by Primo Levi, translated by Stuart Woolf. Copyright © 1958 by Giulio Einaudi editore S.p.A.; translation copyright © 1959 by The Orion Press.

Villard Books, a division of Random House, Inc.: From "The Ape That Stood Up: *Australopithecus afarensis*" from *Ancestors: In Search of Human Origins* by Donald Johanson, Lenora Johanson, and Blake Edgar. Copyright © 1994 by Donald Johanson, Lenora Johanson, and Blake Edgar.

Vintage Books, a division of Random House, Inc.: From "Galileo in China" from *The Discoverers* by Daniel J. Boorstin. Copyright © 1983 by Daniel J. Boorstin. From "Book Nine: New Coasts and Poseidon's Son" from *The Odyssey* by Homer, translated by Robert Fitzgerald. Copyright © 1961, 1963 by Robert Fitzgerald; copyright renewed © 1989 by Benedict R.C. Fitzgerald.

A. P. Watt Ltd. on behalf of The Trustees of the Robert Graves Copyright Trust: From *The Twelve Caesars* by Suetonius, translated by Robert Graves. Translation and notes copyright © 1957 by Robert Graves; Foreward, editorial matter, and revisions to the translation copyright © 1979 by Michael Grant Publications Limited.

Yale University Press: From *In Praise of Folly* by Desiderius Erasmus, translated by Clarence H. Miller. Copyright © 1979 by Yale University Press.

Ehsan Yarshater: From "The Shah-Nama" from *The Epic of the Kings: Shah-Nama, the National Epic of Persia* by Ferdowsi, translated by Reuben Levy. Copyright © 1967 by The Royal Institute of Publication of Teheran.

Zed Books Ltd.: From an anonymous editorial from *In Search of Answers: Indian Voices from Manusha*, edited by Madhu Kishwar and Ruth Vanita. Copyright © 1984 by Zed Books Ltd.

REFERENCES

From "I Peter" from *The Jerusalem Bible, Reader's Edition*. Published by Doubleday, 1968.

Quote by General Kuribayashi from "The Americans Will Surely Come" by Colonel Joseph H. Alexander from *Naval History*, January/February 1995. Published by the United States Naval Institute, 1995.

From "We Will Never Surrender" and quotes by Gandhi and Jawaharlal from "You Cannot Break Us" from *Quaid-E-Azam Jinnah: The Story of a Nation* by Gulam Ali Allana. Published by Ferozsons Ltd., 1967.

Quote by Field Marshal Sir Claude Auchinleck from *Plain Tales from the Raj*, edited by Charles Allen. Published by Henry Holt and Company, Inc., 1985.

Description of Pachacutec's transformation from *The Florentine Codex*, edited by Arthur Anderson and Charles Dibble. Published by University of Utah Press.

Quote by Faith Rifki Atay from *Ulus*, January 3, 1942.

From speech by Jules Ferry before the French National Assembly, July 28, 1883 from *Modern Imperialism: Western Overseas Expansion and Its Aftermath 1776–1965*, edited by Ralph A. Austen. Published by D. C. Heath and Company, 1969.

From "The First Radio Signal across the Atlantic, 12 December 1901" by Guglielmo

Marconi from *Scrapbook 1900–1914* by Leslie Bailey. Published by Frederick Muller, 1957.

From *Three Principles of the People* by Sun Yat-sen from *Sources of Chinese Tradition*, edited by William Theodore de Bary, Wing-tsit Chang, and Burton Watson. Published by Columbia University Press, 1964.

Quotes by Asoka about his conversion and about other religions from *Sources of Indian Tradition*, edited by William Theodore de Bary et al. Published by Columbia University Press, 1990.

Quote by Napoleon Bonaparte from "Revolution and Retreat: Upper-Class French Women After 1789" by Barbara Corrado Pope from *Women, War, and Revolution*, edited by Carol R. Berkin and Clara M. Lovett. Published by Holmes and Meier, 1980.

Quote by an Israeli spokesman from Colonial Office transcript (CO 733 477) from *The Palestine Triangle: The Struggle Between the British, the Jews and the Arabs 1935–1948* by Nicholas Bethell. Published by A. Deutsch, 1979.

Quotes by Emperor Menelik and Empress Taytu from *General History of Africa*, Volume 7, UNESCO History, edited by A. Adu Boahen. Published by Heineman, 1985.

From *The Letter of Tansar*, translated by M. Boyce. Published by the Istituto Italiano per id Medio ed Estremo Oriente, 1968.

From "Middle-Class Women" from *Silent Sisterhood: Middle-Class Women in the Victorian Home* by Patricia Branca. Published by Carnegie-Mellon University Press, 1975.

From *The Abyssinians* by D. R. Buxton. Published by Thames & Hudson, London, 1970.

From "Dunkirk" from *Blood, Sweat, and Tears* by the Rt. Hon. Winston S. Churchill. Published by G. P. Putnam's Sons, 1941.

"They are advancing. . . ." from *My Early Life* by Winston S. Churchill. Published by Heinemann, 1930.

From *Confessions* from *Augustine of Hippo: Selected Writings*, translated by Mary T. Clark. Published by Paulist Press, 1984.

Quote by Legalist Han Fei Tzu and from the *Lao Tzu* from *Chinese Thought: From Confucius to Mao Tso-Tung* by H. G. Creel. Published by The University of Chicago Press, 1953.

Wei account of Japan from *The Pageant of Japanese History* by Marion May Dilts. Published by Longmans, Green and Co., 1961.

From "Byzantine-Kievan Relations" from *Medieval Russia: A Source Book 850–1700*, edited by Basil Dmytryshyn. Published by Holt, Rinehart and Winston, Inc., 1991.

From "Qaddafi's Islam" by Lisa Anderson from *Voices of Resurgent Islam*, edited by John L. Esposito. Published by Oxford University Press, 1983.

From a Maidu creation myth from "The Big-Game Vanishes" from *Kingdoms of Gold, Kingdoms of Jade: The Americas Before Columbus* by Brian M. Fagan. Published by Thames & Hudson, 1991.

Quote by Cixi from *China: A New History* by John King Fairbank. Published by Harvard University Press, 1992.

From description of Ch'ang An from *China: A Short Cultural History* by C. P. Fitzgerald. Published by The Cresset Press Ltd., 1935.

Quote by Azzam Pasha from *A Political Study of the Arab-Jewish Conflict* by Rony E. Gabbay, Geneva, 1959.

From "Travels in Mali" from *Ibn Battuta: Travels in Asia and Africa* by H.A.R. Gibb. Published by Cambridge University Press, 1929.

Quote by Hayashi Razan from *Razan sensei bunshu* from *The Cambridge History of Japan, Volume 4, Early Modern Japan*, edited by John Whitney Hall. Published by Cambridge University Press, 1991.

From National Charter, *Mashru' al-mithaq* (Department of Information, Cairo, 1962), from *Arab Socialism*, translated by S. Hanna and G. H. Gardner. Published by E. J. Brill, 1969.

Quotes by Rabi'a Al-Adawiya from *Encyclopaedia of Islam: A Dictionary of the Geography, Ethnography and Biography of the Muhammadan Peoples*, edited by M. Th. Houtsma, A. J. Wensinck, H.A.R. Gibb, W. Heffening, and E. Levi Provencal. Published by Leyden, 1936.

From "The German Hitler Springtime" by W. Beuth from *The 'Hitler Myth': Image and Reality in the Third Reich* by Ian Kershaw. Published by Oxford University Press, 1987.

Quote by relief worker Rick Grant from "Aid Workers Plan New Attack on Famine" by Scott Kraft and Mark Fineman from *Los Angeles Times*, December 11, 1992. Published by The Times Mirror Company, 1992.

From writing on an ancient clay tablet from *The Sumerians* by Samuel Noah Kramer. Published by The University of Chicago Press, 1963.

From "Mónica: Rebellion and Triumph" from *Four Women: Living the Revolution, an Oral History of Contemporary Cuba* by Oscar Lewis, Ruth M. Lewis, and Susan M. Rigdon. Published by the University of Illinois Press, 1977.

Quote by Pedro de Cieza from *Royal Commentaries of the Incas and General History of Peru*, Part I, by Garcilasco de la Vega, translated by Harold V. Livermore. Published by the University of Texas Press, 1966.

Quote by King of Koryo from "Korea" from *The Growth of Civilization in East Asia* by Peter Lum. Published by S. G. Phillips, 1969.

From "Through Perilous Mountain Regions" from *The Silk Road* by Sven Hedin, translated by F. H. Lyon. Published by Dutton, 1938.

Quotes by Kwame Nkrumah from *Democracy on Trial: Reflections on Arab and African Politics* by Mohammed Ahmed Mahgoub. Published by A. Deutsch, 1974.

Quote by Pherozesha Mehta from *History of the Freedom Movement* by R. C. Majumdar. Published by Firma K. L. Mukhopadhyay (Calcutta), 1962.

From poster printed by the Jewish Fighting Organization from *The Uprising in the Warsaw Ghetto* by Bernard Mark. Published by Schocken, 1975.

Description of the Meigs passing Sugar Loaf Mountain from *The Brazilian-American Alliance 1937–1945* by Frank D. McCann, Jr. Published by Princeton University Press, 1973.

From granite inscription from *An Introduction to the Economic History of Ethiopia from Early Times to 1800* by R. Pankhurst. Published by Lalibela House, 1961.

From "The Words of the Griot Mamadou Kouyaté" from *Sundiata: An Epic of Old Mali* by D. T. Niane, translated by G. D. Pickett. Published by Présence Africaine, 1960.

From *Memoirs of the Emperor Jahangueir Written by Himself*, translated by David Price. Published by the Oriental Translation Committee, 1928.

Excerpt from the *Primary Chronicle* from *A History of Russia*, Fourth Edition, by Nicholas V. Riasanovsky. Published by Oxford University Press, 1984.

From "The End of Sumer" from *Sumer to Jerusalem* by John Sassoon. Published by Intellect Books, 1993.

From the *Bhagavad-Gita* and from description of attack by Mahmud of Ghazni from *Historic India* by Lucille Schulberg and The Editors of Time-Life Books. Published by Time-Life Books, 1968.

From "Zoe and Theodora 1042, Constantine IX 1042–55" from *Fourteen Byzantine Rulers: The Chronographia of Michael Psellus*, translated by E.R.A. Sewter. Published by Penguin Books Ltd., 1966.

Quote by David Hume from "The View from England" by Katharine M. Rogers from *French Women and the Age of Enlightenment*, edited by Samia I. Spencer. Published by Indiana University Press, 1984.

Quote by Richard Storry describing Yoshida Shigeru from *The Times Literary Supplement*, September 5, 1980. Published by The London Times, 1980.

From "Last Message to His Administrators, 8 July 1867" by Phan Thanh Gian from *We the Vietnamese* by François Sully and Donald Kirk. Published by Henry Holt and Company, 1971.

From "Lessons for Women" from *Pan Chao: Foremost Woman Scholar of China*, translated by Nancy Lee Swan. Published by Century, 1932.

Quote by Lin Tse-hsü and from "Doc. 48, Proclamations of the Boxers" from *China's Response to the West: A Documentary Survey 1839–1923* by Ssu-yü Teng and John K. Fairbank. Published by Harvard University Press, 1954.

From "The Last 19th-Century War?" from *The Morning After: American Successes and Excesses 1981–1986* by George F. Will. Copyright © 1986 by The Washington Post Company. Published by The Free Press, a Division of Macmillan, Inc., 1986.

From *Chinese Art* by William Willetts. Published by Penguin Books Ltd., 1958.

Quote by Mujibur Rahman from *Roots of Confrontation in South Asia: Afghanistan, Pakistan, India and the Superpowers* by Stanley Wolpert. Published by Oxford University Press, Inc., 1982.

From *Caste Today* by Taya Zinkin. Published by Thames & Hudson, 1966.

PHOTO CREDITS

Abbreviations used: (t) top, (c) center, (b) bottom, (l) left, (r) right, (bckgd) background, (bdr) border.

Front Matter, Page: ii(bckgd), Boston Athenaeum; ii, NASA; iv(bckgd), Boston Athenaeum; iv, Minamikawa/Sipa Press; v, HRW Photo by Sam Dudgeon; vi, HRW Photo by Sam Dudgeon; vi(bckgd), Boston Athenaeum; vii, HRW Photo by Sam Dudgeon; vii(bckgd), Boston Athenaeum; viii(bckgd), Boston Athenaeum; ix(bckgd), Boston Athenaeum; x(t), Reynard Nicolas/Gamma-Liaison; x(b), J. Pierpoint Morgan Library, New York; x(bckgd), Boston Athenaeum; xi, xiii, xiv (bckgd), Boston Athenaeum; xv, Victoria & Albert Museum, London/Art Resource; xvi, Michael Holford.

Table of Contents, Page: xvii, xviii(l), xviii(r), Michael Holford; xix, Jerry Jacka/Courtesy Dennis Lyon Collection; xx, Ronald Sheridan/Ancient Art & Architecture Collection; xxii(t), Brown Brothers; xxii(b), Culver Pictures; xxiv, Scala/Art Resource; xxv(t), Ronald Sheridan/Ancient Art & Architecture Collection; xxv(b), NASA; xxvi, Nick Saunders/Barbara Heller Photo Library/Art Resource; xxvii(t), Ricki Rosen/SABA; xxvii(b), Marc & Evelyn Bernheim/Woodfin Camp & Associates.

Handbook, Page: xxxi(t), Erich Lessing/Art Resource; xxxi(b), Archive Photos; xxxii, Erich Lessing/Art Resource; xxxiii(t), Sonia Halliday Photographs; xxxiii(b), Brown Brothers; xxxiv(t) Boltin Picture Library; xxxiv(b), Scala/Art Resource; xxxv, David Portnoy/Black Star; xxxvii, ©Trustees of the Imperial War Museum; xxxviii, Yale University Art Gallery, Gift from the Estate of Katherine S. Dreier; xl, J (bckgd) AKG London; xl, (b), (bckgd) Hulton Deutsch Collection Ltd./Woodfin Camp & Associates; xlii(t), The Center for American History, the University of Texas at Austin; xlii(b), Harper Libros, a Division of HarperCollins; xlv, Giraudon/Art Resource; xlvi, The Bettmann Archive; xlvii, Southern Oregon Historical Society; li, Michael Holford.

Unit One, Page: 0–1 (bckgd), Arxiu Mas; 0, Gamma–Liaison/Ministere de la Culture et de la Francophone; 1, Erich Lessing/Art Resource; 2–3, Gamma-Liaison, Ministere de la Culture et de la Francophone; 4, Gerald Cubitt; 5, Hinterleitner/Gamma-Liaison; 7, Robert Frerck/The Stock Market; 8, Giraudon/Art Resource; 9, 11, 12, Michael Holford; 13, C. Seghers/Photo Researchers; 15(t), Michael Holford;15(b), Ronald Sheridan/Ancient Art & Architecture Collection; 16, Michael Holford; 17, Nawrocki Stock Photo; 18, Ronald Sheridan/Ancient Art & Architecture Collection; 19, Ancient Art & Architecture Collection for Kadokawa; 20–21(bckgd), Adina Amsel Tovy/Nawrocki Stock Photo; 21, 22, Nawrocki Stock Photo; 23, Nathaniel Tarn/Photo Researchers; 25(t), Richard Stirling/Ancient Art & Architecture Collection; 25(b), Kenneth Garrett; 26, Ronald Sheridan/Ancient Art & Architecture Collection; 28–29(bckgd), British Museum; 28, Michael Holford; 29, James King-Holmes/Science Photo Library/Photo Researchers; 31, 32, Erich Lessing/Art Resource; 33, 34, 35, Ronald Sheridan/Ancient Art & Architecture Collection; 36, Erich Lessing / Art Resource; 37, Michael Holford; 38, Erich Lessing/Art Resource; 39, Ronald Sheridan/Ancient Art & Architecture Collection; 40, Boltin Picture Library; 42, 44, Michael Holford; 45, Ronald Sheridan/Ancient Art & Architecture Collection; 46, Michael Holford; 48, Sonia Halliday Photographs; 49, Boltin Picture Library; 51, Ronald Sheridan/Ancient Art & Architecture Collection; 52, Robert Harding Picture Library; 53, Johnathan Smith/Sylvia Cordaiy Photo Library; 54, Erich Lessing/Art Resource; 56, Library of Congress.

Unit Two, Page 58–59, *Pictorial Ancient History of the World,* John Frost, © 1846; 58(tl), Michael Holford; 58(tr), AKG London; 58(b), Nawrocki Stock Photo; 59(tl), Hugh Sitton/Tony Stone Images; 59(tr), Marcus Rose/Panos Pictures; 59(b), Michael Holford; 60–61, AKG London; 62, Boltin Picture Library; 63, 65, SEF/Art Resource; 66, Michael Holford; 67, 68, Erich Lessing/Art Resource; 69, Boltin Picture Library; 70, Corel Corporation; 71, Ronald Sheridan/Ancient Art & Architecture Collection; 72, Hulton Deutsch Collection /Woodfin Camp & Associates; 73(t), Scala/Art Resource; 74(l), Ronald Sheridan/Ancient Art & Architecture Collection; 74(r), Sonia Halliday Photographs; 75, Robert Harding Picture Library; 76, SEF/Art Resource; 78, F.H.C. Birch/Sonia Halliday Photographs; 79, Michael Holford; 80, Ronald Sheridan/Ancient Art & Architecture Collection; 81, Joan Iaconetti/Bruce Coleman, Inc.; 82(bckgd), Ronald Sheridan/Ancient Art & Architecture Collection; 83(l), Erich Lessing/Art Resource; 83(r), Boltin Picture Library; 84, Ronald Sheridan/Ancient Art & Architecture Collection; 85(l), 85(r), Erich Lessing/Art Resource; 86, Scala/Art Resource; 89, Michael Holford; 90, 91, Ronald Sheridan/Ancient Art & Architecture Collection; 92(t), Erich Lessing/Art Resource; 92(b), Ronald Sheridan/Ancient Art & Architecture Collection; 93, Photo © 1995 The Metropolitan Museum of Art; 94, Image Select; 95, AKG London; 96, Robert

Frerck/Odyssey Productions; 98, R. Guillemot/Image Select; 99, Poseidon Pictures; 100, Ronald Sheridan/Ancient Art & Architecture Collection; 102(t), (b), Michael Holford; 103, AKG London; 104(t), Ronald Sheridan/Ancient Art & Architecture Collection; 104(b), Scala/Art Resource; 105, Hulton Deutsch Collection /Woodfin Camp & Associates; 106, Image Select/ Ann Ronan; 107, 108, AKG London; 109, Pierre Boulat/COS/Woodfin Camp & Associates; 111, Ronald Sheridan/Ancient Art & Architecture Collection; 114–115, Nawrocki Stock Photo; 116, E.T. Archive; 117, Ronald Sheridan/Ancient Art & Architecture Collection; 118, Michael Holford; 119, Alinari/Art Resource; 121, Hulton Deutsch Colllection /Woodfin Camp & Associates; 122, AKG London; 123, Robert Frerck/Odyssey Productions; 124, Erich Lessing/Art Resource; 126, Michael Holford; 128, Werner Forman/Art Resource; 129, Ron Goor/Bruce Coleman, Inc.; 130, Michael Holford; 131, Erich Lessing/Art Resource; 132(l), Scala/Art Resource; 132(r), Andre Held/Sonia Halliday Photographs; 134(t), Scala/Art Resource; 134(b), Reproduced by kind permission of the Trustees of the Chester Beatty Library, Dublin; 136, Scala/Art Resource; 137, Bibliothèque Nationale de France; 138, Scala/Art Resource; 139, Andre Held/Sonia Halliday Photographs; 140, Scala/Art Resource; 141 (bckgd), Victoria & Albert Museum; 141, Michael Holford; 142, Erich Lessing/Art Resource; 145, Hugh Sitton/Tony Stone Images; 146, Ronald Sheridan/Ancient Art & Architecture Collection; 147, The Bettmann Archive; 148, John P. Stevens/Ancient Art & Architecture Collection; 149(t), Christine Osborne Pictures; 149(b), Ronald Sheridan/Ancient Art & Architecture Collection; 150, Michael Holford; 151, Daniel Beltra/Gamma-Liaison; 152, Allan Eaton/Ancient Art & Architecture Collection; 155(t), Stock Montage, Inc.; 155(b), Ronald Sheridan/Ancient Art & Architecture Collection; 157, 158, Nawrocki Stock Photo; 159(t), ChinaStock; 159(b), Nawrocki Stock Photo; 160(t), Alain Evrard/Gamma-Liaison; 160(b), Ronald Sheridan/Ancient Art & Architecture Collection; 161, Wan-go Weng Archives; 162, Dennis Cox/ChinaStock; 163, C & J Walker/Gamma-Liaison; 165, Wan-go Weng/National Palace Museum, Taipei; 166–167(bckgd), Adina Amsel Tovy/Nawrocki Stock Photo; 166(t), Fred Ward/Black Star; 166(b), Giraudon/Art Resource; 168, Nawrocki Stock Photo; 169(t), Ronald Sheridan/Ancient Art & Architecture Collection; 169(b), Christopher Liu/ChinaStock; 169(bckgd), Victoria & Albert Museum; 170, Dennis Cox/ChinaStock; 172–173(bckgd), British Museum; 172, Scala/Art Resource; 173, Christopher Liu/ChinaStock; 174–175, Marcus Rose/Panos Pictures; 176, Marcus Rosshagen/Panos Pictures; 177(bckgd), Adina Amsel Tovy/Nawrocki Stock Photo; 178, Stefano Amantini/Bruce Coleman, Ltd.; 179, Marc & Evelyn Bernheim/Woodfin Camp & Associates; 180, Michael Holford; 181, Mike Yamashita/Woodfin Camp & Associates; 182, Werner Forman/Art Resource; 183, SEF/Art Resource; 184, Marc & Evelyn Bernheim/Woodfin Camp & Associates; 185, Werner Forman/Art Resource; 186, M. Ascani/Gamma-Liaison; 186(bckgd), Victoria & Albert Museum; 189, Michael Holford; 190, Marc & Evelyne Bernheim/Woodfin Camp & Associates; 191(t), Werner Forman/Art Resource; 191(b), Marc & Evelyne Bernheim/Woodfin Camp & Associates; 193, Gerald Cubitt; 194(t), Bruce Coleman, Ltd.; 194(b), Robin White/Fotolex Associates; 197, Michael Holford; 198, Werner Forman/Art Resource; 200, Mireille Vautier/Woodfin Camp & Associates; 201(t), British Museum; 201(b), Merle Greene Robertson; 202(t), Bodleian Library, Oxford; 202(b), Kenneth Garrett; 204, Michael Holford; 205, Boltin Picture Library; 206, Mireille Vautier/Woodfin Camp & Associates; 207(t), Nick Saunders/Barbara Heller Photo Library/Art Resource; 207(b), Courtesy of Nettie Lee Benson Latin American Collection, University of Texas at Austin, HRW photo by Sam Dudgeon; 208, Loren McIntyre/Woodfin Camp & Associates; 209, Courtesy of Nettie Lee Benson Latin American Collection, University of Texas at Austin, HRW photo by Sam Dudgeon; 210, HRW Photo by Sam Dudgeon; 212, Superstock; 213, The Brooklyn Museum of Art, gift of A. & P. Peralta-Romas (Carleback, Rogers) Collection/56. 6. 24.; 214, Jim Brandenburg/Minden Pictures; 215, Jerry Jacka Photography/Courtesy Dennis Lyon collection; 216, Jerry Jacka.

Unit Three, Page 218–219 (bckgd), *An Account of an Embassy to the Kingdom of Ava,* © 1800; 218(t), Ancient Art & Architecture Collection; 218(b), R & S Michaud/Woodfin Camp & Associates; 219–3, Giraudon / Art Resource; 219(bl),Nawrocki Stock Photo; 219(br), Bridgeman / Art Resource; 221, Ancient Art & Architecture Collection; 222, Robert Harding Picture Library; 223, Ancient Art & Architecture Collection; 224, Erich Lessing/Art Resource; 225(t), Courtesy of ©1995 Dumbarton Oaks, Trustees of Harvard University, Washington, D.C.; 225(b), Robert Harding Picture Library; 226, Michael Holford; 227, The Bettmann Archive; 228, Ronald Sheridan/Ancient Art & Architecture Collection; 229, Library of Congress; 232, Ancient Art & Architecture Collection; 233, Ronald Sheridan/Ancient Art & Architecture Collection; 234, Robert Frerck/Odyssey Productions; 235, Photo © 1984 The Metropolitan Museum of Art; 236, E.T. Archive; 237, Arxiu Mas; 239, Library of Congress; 242–243, R. & S. Michaud/Woodfin Camp & Associates; 244, Boltin Picture Library; 245, William Karel/Sygma; 246 (t), Robert Azzi/Woodfin Camp & Associates; 246(b), Ronald Sheridan/Ancient Art & Architecture; 247, Elkoussy/Sygma; 248, Ronald Sheridan/Ancient Art & Architecture Collection; 249, Nitsan Shorer/Black Star; 250, Ronald Sheridan/Ancient Art & Architecture Collection; 252, Staatliche Museen, Berlin; 253, Gilbert Uzan/Gamma-Liaison; 253(bckgd), Victoria & Albert Museum; 254, Hutchison Library; 256, Ronald Sheridan/Ancient Art & Architecture Collection; 258, Bodleian Library, Oxford; 259(l), R. & S. Michaud/ Woodfin Camp & Associates; 259(r), Jean-Leo Dugast/Panos Pictures; 260, R & S Michaud/Woodfin Camp & Associates; 260(bckgd), Adina Amsel Tovy/Nawrocki Stock Photo; 261(t), Ted Horowitz/The Stock Market; 261(b), Erica Lansner/Black Star; 262, Edinburgh University Library; 263, Sonia Halliday Photographs; 264, Michael Holford; 265, Hutchison Library; 266(t), Sonia Halliday Photographs; 266(b), Chris Hellier/ Ancient Art & Architecture Collection; 267, Reza Degnati/Sygma; 268, Bridgeman/Art Resource; 271, Giraudon/Art Resource; 272, University Museum of National Antiquities, Oslo, Norway. Photo by Eirik Irgens Johnsen; 273, British Museum; 274, Bibliothèque Municipale, Dijon; 275, The Board of Trinity College, Dublin; 277, Erich Lessing/Art Resource; 279, University Museum of National Antiquities,Oslo, Norway. Photo by Eirik Irgens Johnsen ; 280, Photo R.M.N.,Musée du Louvre ; 281, Bibliothèque Royale Albert 1er, Bruxelles; 282, Giraudon/Musée Conde, Chantilly ; 283, Governing Body of Christ Church, Oxford; 286, Domesday E31/2 folio 132/Public Record Office, Kew,Richmond, Surrey ; 288(t), Catherine Karnow/Woodfin Camp & Associates; 288(b), Steve Vidler/Nawrocki Stock Photo; 290, Bibliothèque Nationale de France; 293, Bodleian Library, Oxford; 294, The British Library; 295, Giraudon/Art Resource; 296, Universitätsbibliothek, Heidelberg; 297, Mansell Collection; 298, Tom Craig; 300–301, Nawrocki Stock Photo; 302, Dennis Cox/ChinaStock; 303, Wan-go Weng; 304, Nawrocki Stock Photo; 305, 307(t), 307(b), 308, Wan-go Weng; 309, Boltin Picture Library; 311, Ronald Sheridan/Ancient Art & Architecture Collection; 312,

Nicholas DeVore/Tony Stone Images; 313, Michael Holford; 314, Laurie Platt Winfrey/Woodfin Camp & Associates; 315, David Portnoy/Black Star; 316, J.L. Dugast/Gamma-Liaison; 317, Richard Falco/Black Star; 318,320, Orion Press; 321(l), Laurie Platt Winfrey/Woodfin Camp & Associates; 321(r), 322, AKG London; 323, Michael Holford; 325(bckgd), Adina Amsel Tovy/Nawrocki Stock Photo; 326, Sonia Halliday Photographs; 328–329(bckgd), British Museum; 328, Werner Forman Archive/Art Resource; 329, Scala/Art Resource; 331, Bridgeman/Art Resource; 332, E.T. Archive; 334, AKG London; 335(l), Poseidon Pictures; 335(r), Sonia Halliday Photographs; 336, Ronald Sheridan/Ancient Art & Architecture Collection; 338, Sonia Halliday Photographs; 339, Christine Osborne Pictures; 341, Ronald Sheridan/Ancient Art & Architecture Collection; 342, Robert Harding Picture Library; 343, Giraudon/Art Resource; 344(l), Michael Holford; 344(r), Ronald Sheridan/Ancient Art & Architecture Collection; 346, G. Hellier/Robert Harding Picture Library; 347(t), Michael Holford; 347(b), Allan Eaton/Ancient Art & Architecture Collection; 349, Robert Harding Picture Library; 352, Victoria & Albert Museum/Art Resource; 353, Robert Aberman/Barbara Heller Photo Library/Art Resource; 355, Hutchison Library.

Unit Four, Page 358–359(bckgd), Library of the Boston Athenaeum; 358 (t),Scala/Art Resource; 358(b),Bibliothèque Nationale De France; 359(t), IFA/Bruce Coleman,Inc.; 359(b), The Bettmann Archive; 360–361, Scala/Art Resource; 362, Giraudon/Musée Conde, Chantilly; 364, Mansell Collection; 365, British Library; 366, Osterreichische Nationalbibliothek, Vienna; 367, Scala/Art Resource; 368, British Library; 369, National Trust Photographic Library/Art Resource; 372, Art Resource; 373(l), 373(r), 374, Scala/Art Resource; 375, Harry Ransom Humanities Research Center, University of Texas at Austin; 376, Erich Lessing/Art Resource; 377, Nawrocki Stock Photo; 378(t), Scala/Art Resource; 378(bl), Bayerische Staatsbibliothek,Munich; 378(br), Scala /Art Resource; 379(t), Erich Lessing/Art Resource; 379(b), Giraudon/Art Resource; 380, Giraudon/Art Resource; 381(t), Scala / Art Resource; 381(b), Öffentliche Kunstsammlung Basel, Kunstmuseum. Photo by Martin Bühler, 382, British Museum; 383(l), Scala/Art Resource; 383(r), National Portrait Gallery, London; 386, Mansell Collection; 388–389, Bibliothèque Nationale De France; 390(l), 390(r), Bridgeman/Art Resource; 391, NYPL, Rare Books and Manuscripts Division; 392(l), Lauros-Giraudon/Art Resource; 392(r), Giraudon/Art Resource; 394, Nawrocki Stock Photo; 395, Superstock; 396, Mansell Collection; 398, 399, 400(bckgd), 401, © BBC Hulton Picture Library/Tony Stone Images; 402, 403, Library of Congress; 404, Image Select; 405, Bridgeman/Art Resource; 406, Scala /Art Resource; 407 (t),(b), Archive Photos; 409, Michael Holford; 410, Nawrocki Stock Photo; 411, Michael Holford; 412, Scala/Art Resource; 413(l), Superstock; 413(r), Mansell Collection;414–415(bckgd), Adina Amsel Tovy/Nawrocki Stock Photo; 416, Michael Holford; 419, IFA/Bruce Coleman, Inc.; 420, Boltin Picture Library; 421, The Bettmann Archive; 423, "Portrait of a Merchant." Ailsa Mellon Bruce Fund, ©1995 Board of Trustees, National Gallery of Art, Washington, c. 1530, oil on panel, .636x.475 (25 x 18 3/4); 424, SEF/Art Resource; 425 (l),(r), The Bettmann Archive; 426, Reuters/Bettmann; 428, The Bettmann Archive; 430, Murray Greenberg/Monkmeyer Press Photos; 431, Nawrocki Stock Photo; 433, The Bettmann Archive; 435, J. Pierpont Morgan Library, New York; 436, Provincial Publicity Bureau; 437, 438(t), 438(b), 439, The Bettmann Archive; 440, The New York Public Library, Rare Books and Manuscripts Division; 441, Michael Holford; 443, New York Public Library; 444, British Museum; 445, Hulton Deutsch Collection /Woodfin Camp & Associates; 446, National Archives; 448–449(bckgd), British Museum; 448, Martin Rogers/Woodfin Camp & Associates; 449, Courtesy of Nettie Lee Benson Latin American Collection, University of Texas at Austin, HRW photo by Sam Dudgeon; 450–451, The Bettmann Archive; 452, E.R.L./Sipa Press; 453, © BBC Hulton Picture Library/Tony Stone Images; 454, Sipa Press; 457, Art Resource; 458(l), Giraudon/Art Resource; 458(r), 459, The Bettmann Archive; 460, 461(l), Hulton Deutsch Collection /Woodfin Camp & Associates; 461(r), Tate Gallery, London/Art Resource; 462, Erich Lessing/Art Resource; 463, Culver Pictures; 464, The Bettmann Archive; 465(l), Hulton Deutsch Collection /Woodfin Camp & Associates; 465(r), The Bettmann Archive; 466, Hulton Deutsch Collection /Woodfin Camp & Associates; 469, 470, Giraudon/Art Resource; 472, AKG London; 473, The Bettmann Archive; 474(l), AKG London; 474(r), E.R.L./Sipa Press; 475, AKG London; 477, The Bettmann Archive; 478, AKG London.

Unit Five, Page 480–481(bckgd), *Life in the World's Wonderland,* Theodore Gerrish, © 1886 ; 480(t), SEF/Art Resource; 480(b), Oregon Historical Society, Negative #OrHi 36793; 481(t), AKG London; 481(b)Hulton Deutsch Collection/Woodfin Camp & Associates; 483, SEF/Art Resource; 484, Image Select; 485, Adam Woolfitt/Woodfin Camp & Associates; 486, Mansell Collection; 487(t), The Science Museum, London; 487(b), Bridgeman /Art Resource; 488(t), North Wind Picture Archives; 488(b), Ann Ronan Picture Library; 488–489(bckgd), Adina Amsel Tovy/Nawrocki Stock Photo; 490, The Bettmann Archive; 491, Culver Pictures; 492, E.T. Archive; 494, Hulton Deutsch Collection/Woodfin Camp & Associates; 495, The Bettmann Archive; 497, Superstock; 498, The Bettmann Archive; 500(bckgd), Ann Ronan Picture Library; 501, Snark/Art Resource; 502(t), Bridgeman /Art Resource; 502(b), 503(t), 503(b), AKG London; 504, Art Resource; 505, Nawrocki Stock Photo; 506, Art Resource; 508–509, Oregon Historical Society, Negative # OrHi 36793; 510, Poseidon Pictures; 511, Hulton Deutsch Collection/Woodfin Camp & Associates; 512, The Bettmann Archive; 513, 514(t), Mansell Collection; 514(b), The Bettmann Archive; 515, 516, Mansell Collection; 518, National Maritime Museum, London; 520, The Bettmann Archive; 521, Mansell Collection; 525,Lewis W. Hines/George Eastman House; 526, Southern Oregon Historical Society; 527, Poseidon Pictures; 528, Photo by Byron, Byron Collection, Museum of the City of New York; 529, © Stock Montage; 531, Hulton Deutsch Collection /Woodfin Camp & Associates; 535, 536, 538, AKG London; 539, Mansell Collection; 541, The Bettmann Archive; 543, AKG London; 544, Archive Photos; 546, Erich Lessing/Art Resource; 549, Sovfoto; 550, NYPL Picture Collection; 551, The Bettmann Archive; 553, NYPL Picture Collection; 554, Giraudon/Art Resource; 555(t), AKG London; 555(b), Ann Ronan/Image Select; 556, AKG London; 557, The Bettmann Archive; 558, HRW photo by Sam Dudgeon; 559, Image Select; 560, Comite International de la Croix-Rouge, Geneva ; 562–563(bckgd), British Museum; 562, Giraudon/Art Resource; 563, Erich Lessing/Art Resource; 564–565, Hulton Deutsch Collection /Woodfin Camp & Associates; 566, North Wind Picture Archives; 567, AKG London; 568, *Plain Tales from the Hills,* vol. 1, © 1897; 569, Robert Harding Picture Library; 570, HRW photo by Sam Dudgeon/*Punch,* December 2, 1892; 571, Nawrocki Stock Photo; 573, Robert Harding Picture Library; 574(bckgd), Adina Amsel Tovy/Nawrocki Stock Photo; 575(l), (r), E.T. Archive; 577, © 1995 Jason Laurè;

577(bckgd), Victoria & Albert Museum; 579, Hulton Deutsch Collection /Woodfin Camp & Associates; 581, Topham Picture Source/The Image Works; 582, 583, AKG London; 584, Robert Harding Picture Library; 585, AKG London; 586, The Granger Collection, New York; 588(t), (b), AKG London; 589, E.T. Archive; 590, © BBC Hulton Picture Library/Tony Stone Images.

Unit Six, Page 592–593(bckgd), *Illustrated London News,* July, 1891; 592(t), The Trustees of the Imperial War Museum, London; 592(b), Nawrocki Stock Photo; 593(t), Brown Brothers; 593(b), UPI/Bettmann; 595, The Trustees of the Imperial War Museum, London; 596, 597(t), AKG London; 597(b), The Bettmann Archive; 599, Nawrocki Stock Photo; 600, The Burns Collection; 602, The National Archives; 603, Archive Photos; 604, U.S. Naval Institute; 604(bckgd), Victoria & Albert Museum; 605, The Bettmann Archive; 606, HRW photo by Sam Dudgeon; 610(t), The Trustees of the Imperial War Museum, London; 610(b), The Center for American History, The University of Texas at Austin. HRW photo by Sam Dudgeon; 611, Nawrocki Stock Photo; 614, The National Archives; 615, AKG London; 616, The Trustees of the Imperial War Museum, London; 618, UPI/Bettmann; 619, Archive Photos; 621, HRW photo by Sam Dudgeon; 622(bckgd), National Archives; 625, Nawrocki Stock Photo; 626, Steve Vidler/Nawrocki Stock Photo; 627(t), The Bettmann Archive; 627(b), AKG London; 629, Sovfoto/Eastfoto; 629(bckgd), Victoria & Albert Museum; 630, UPI/Bettmann; 631, Antonin Kratochvil/SABA; 632, AKG London; 634, Kyodo News Service; 635, 636, Culver Pictures; 637, The Bettmann Archive; 638, Yale University Art Gallery, Gift from the Estate of Katherine S. Dreier; 639, Nawrocki Stock Photo; 640, Culver Pictures; 641, Library of Congress; 642, AP/Wide World Photos; 643, The Bettmann Archive; 644, UPI/Bettmann; 645, Poseidon Pictures; 646, Culver Pictures; 647, AKG London; 648(t), Eastfoto; 648(b), AKG London; 649, UPI/Bettmann; 650, Sovfoto; 651, UPI/Bettmann; 652, Library of Congress; 654–655(bckgd), British Museum; 655(t), Brown Brothers; 655(b), Hulton Deutsch Collection / Woodfin Camp & Associates; 657, 658, 659, 660, Brown Brothers; 661, Camera Press/Retna; 662(t), Brown Brothers; 662(b), Sygma; 663, UPI/Bettmann; 664, PA News; 666(t), (b), Brown Brothers; 667, UPI/Bettmann; 668, Brown Brothers; 669, Marc & Evelyn Bernheim/Woodfin Camp & Associates; 670(t), (b), Brown Brothers; 671, FPG; 672, Archive Photos; 674, FPG; 675, AP/Wide World Photos; 676, Nawrocki Stock Photo; 678(l), (r), 679, Brown Brothers; 680, Corbis Media; 683, UPI/Bettmann; 684, Nawrocki Stock Photo; 685, Brown Brothers; 686, UPI/Bettmann; 687, Archive Photos; 688, UPI/Bettmann; 689, Nawrocki Stock Photo; 690, Archive Photos; 692, Bilderdienst Suddeutscher Verlag; 693(l), Popperfoto / Archive Photos; 693(r), Nawrocki Stock Photo; 694, Brown Brothers; 695, UPI/Bettmann; 696, Brown Brothers; 697, Corbis Media; 699, Nawrocki Stock Photo; 700, Brown Brothers; 701, Nawrocki Stock Photo; 702, AKG London; 703, Brown Brothers; 704–705(bckgd), Adina Amsel Tovy/Nawrocki Stock Photo; 706, Brown Brothers; 707(t), Archive Photos; 707(b), Brown Brothers; 709(t), Archive Photos; 709(b), Archive Photos; 710(bckgd), AKG London.

Unit Seven, Page 712–713 (Bckgd), NASA; 712(t), The Bettmann Archive; 712(c), Dilip Mehta/Contact Press Images; 712(b), AP/Wide World Photos; 713(t), D. Donne Bryant; 713(b), Alfred/Sipa Press; 715, The Bettmann Archive; 716, Hulton Deutsch Collection/ Woodfin Camp & Associates; 717, Culver Pictures; 719, 721, 722, UPI/Bettmann; 723, Geoffrey Taunton/Sylvia Cordaiy Photo Library; 723(bckgd), Victoria & Albert Museum; 724, UPI/Bettmann; 725, Archive Photos; 726, 727, Itar-Tass /Sovfoto; 728, AP/Wide World Photos; 729, UPI/Bettmann; 730, Culver Pictures; 731, The Bettmann Archive; 732, UPI/Bettmann; 735, HRW photo by Russell Dian; 736, Jeff Foxx/Black Star; 737, Charles Harbutt/Actuality; 738(l), AP/Wide World Photos; 738(r), Photofest; 739, Mangin/Photo Researchers; 740, AP/Wide World Photos; 743, Dilip Mehta/Contact Press Images; 744, Brown Brothers; 747, AP/Wide World Photos; 748(t), T.W.A.; 748(b), AP/Wide World Photos; 749, P. Bartholomew/Gamma-Liaison; 750, Liu Heung Shing/Contact Press Images; 752, New China Pictures/Eastfoto; 753, Corbis Media; 754, Nawrocki Stock Photo; 755, UPI/Bettmann; 756, Consulate General of Japan, NY; 757, Corbis Media; 758, AP/Wide World Photos; 759, 762, Brown Brothers; 763, 764, AP/Wide World Photos; 765,Alon Reininger/Contact Press Images; 767, Greg Girard/Contact Press Images; 768, Robin Moyer/Gamma-Liaison; 771,772(l), AP/Wide World Photos;772(r), Black Star; 775, Edo Konig/Black Star; 776, Alain DeJean/Sygma; 777, Graebli/Black Star; 778, AP/Wide World Photos; 779, Sygma; 781(t), Dennis Brack/Black Star; 781(b), Shlomo Arad/Woodfin Camp & Associates; 782, Norsk Press Service/Gamma-Liaison; 783, Tony Korody/Sygma; 784, Corel Corporation; 787, Hulton Deutsch Collection /Woodfin Camp & Associates; 788, Olivier Rebbot/Woodfin Camp & Associates; 789, From ARABIAN NIGHTS AND DAYS by Naguib Mahfouz, translated by Denys Johnson-Davies, Translation © 1994 The American University in Cairo Press. Used by permission of Doubleday, a division of Bantam Doubleday Dell Publishing Group, Inc.; 790, Ricki Rosen/SABA; 791, Ron Giling/Panos Pictures; 792(t), Trygve Bolstad/Panos Pictures; 792(b), Black Star; 793, Joao Silva/Black Star; 794, Southlight/Gamma-Liason; 795(l),(r), Brown Brothers; 795(bckgd), Victoria & Albert Museum; 796, Marc & Evelyn Bernheim/Woodfin Camp & Associates; 798–799(bckgd), British Museum; 798, 799, UPI/Bettmann; 801, 802, D. Donne Bryant; 803, Hetty Cooper/Black Star; 804, AP/Wide World Photos; 805, David Burnett/Contact Press Images; 806, Stephanie Maze/Woodfin Camp & Associates; 807, Bernard Boutrit/Woodfin Camp & Associates; 808, Kal Muller/Woodfin Camp & Associates; 809(t), Archive Photos; 809(b), R. Gaillarde/Gamma-Liaison; 811, Archive Photos/AFP; 813, Archive Photos; 814, AP/Wide World Photos; 816, DOD/Black Star; 817(t), AP/Wide World Photos; 817(b), J.B. Diederich/Contact Press Images; 818, 819, Alon Reininger/Contact Press Images; 820, Robert Frerck/ Woodfin Camp & Associates; 821(l), Nawrocki Stock Photo; 821(r), Harper Libros, a division of Harper Collins; 822, Jeremy Bigwood/Gamma-Liaison; 824, Reynard Nicolas/Gamma-Liaison; 826–827, Alfred/Sipa Press; 828, Gamma-Liaison; 829, © 1989 Maciej Macierzynski/Reuters/Corbis-Bettman; 832, Tom Haley/Sipa Press; 833, Mathieu Polak/Sygma; 834, Michael J. Howell/Gamma-Liaison; 835, NASA; 836, Gamma-Liaison; 837, Yousuf Karsh/Woodfin Camp & Associates; 838, UPI/Bettmann; 839, James D. Wilson/Gamma-Liaison; 840, NASA; 841, Corel Corporation; 842(bckgd), Adina Amsel Tovy/Nawrocki Stock Photo; 843, UPI/Bettman; 844, B. Swersey/Gamma-Liaison; 845, Sygma; 846, J.L. Atlan/Sygma; 848, Raymond Roig/Gamma-Liason.

Reference Section, Page 850–851 (bckgd), Boston Athenaeum; 850(t), Michael Holford; 850(b), Mangin/Photo Researchers; 851(t), Giraudon/Art Resource; 851(bl) Poseidon Pictures; 851(br), British Museum.